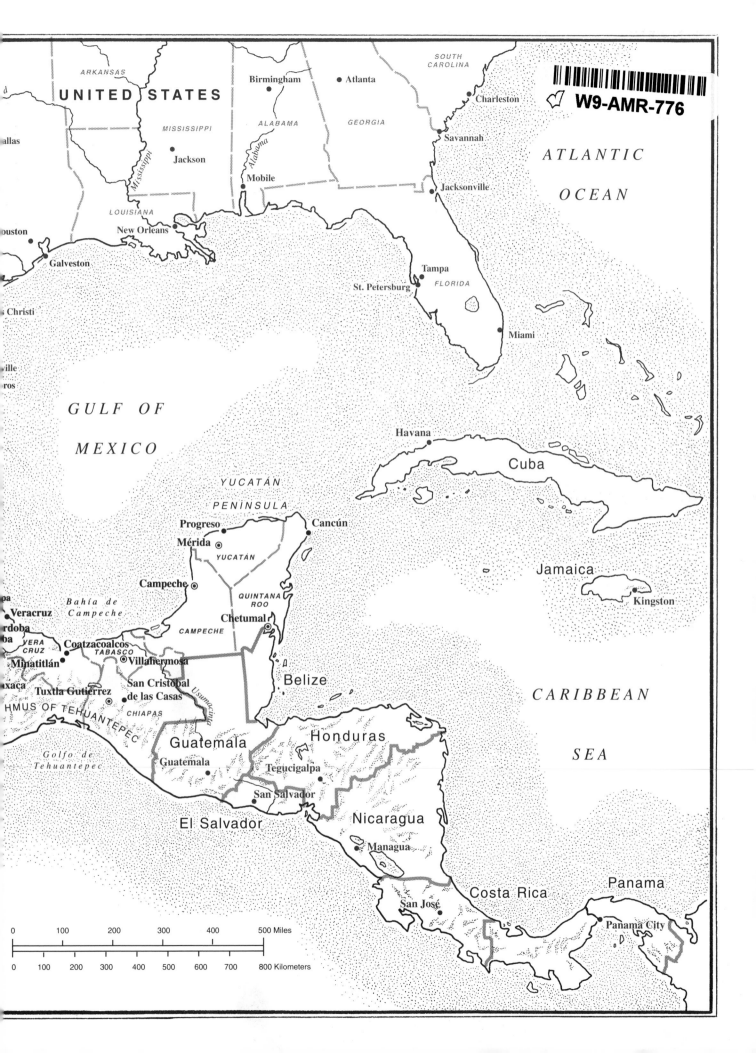

ENCYCLOPEDIA OF
MEXICO

History, Society & Culture

EDITORIAL ADVISORY COMMITTEE

ENCYCLOPEDIA OF
MEXICO

History, Society & Culture

VOLUME I
A – L

EDITOR
MICHAEL S. WERNER

Cartographer
TOM WILLCOCKSON, MAPCRAFT
Woodstock, Illinois

Indexer
AEIOU, INC.
Pleasantville, New York

Commissioning Editor
ROBERT M. SALKIN

FITZROY DEARBORN PUBLISHERS
CHICAGO • LONDON

FITZROY DEARBORN PUBLISHERS
70 East Walton Street
Chicago, Illinois 60611
USA

or

11 Rathbone Place
London W1P 1DE
England

British Cataloguing in Publication Data
Encyclopedia of Mexico: history, society, and culture
    1.Mexico — History — Encyclopedias 2.Mexico — Civilization
    — Encyclopedias
    I.Werner, Michael
    972'.003

ISBN 1-884964-31-1

Library of Congress Cataloging in Publication Data is available

First published in the USA and UK 1997
Typeset by City Desktop Productions Inc., Racine, Wisconsin
Printed by Braun-Brumfield Inc., Ann Arbor, Michigan

Cover illustration: *Pero la fe domina la destrucción, y la tierra alberga la esperanza* (1992; *But Faith Overcomes Destruction, and the Earth Harbors Hope*) by Eusebio Díaz Alejandro. India ink on amate, 22 3/4 x 15 1/4 inches. The original artwork bears the caption "El monstro lanzando en persecución de la mujer y vomita detrás de ella como río de agua para que la abastrara [*sic*], pero la tierra vino en socorro de la mujer abrió la boca y se tragó el río" (loosely, "Flying in pursuit of the woman, the monster vomits behind her like a river of water to sweep her away, but the earth comes to the woman's rescue, opens its mouth, and swallows the vomit"). Private collection. Reproduced from *La tradición del amate: Innovación y protesta en el arte mexicano/The Amate Tradition: Innovation and Dissent in Mexican Art,* edited by Jonathan D. Amith, Chicago: Mexican Fine Arts Center Museum, and Mexico City: La Casa de las Imágenes, 1995.

Cover design: Peter Aristedes, Chicago Advertising and Design, Chicago, Illinois

Frontispiece and endpaper map: Tom Willcockson, Mapcraft, Woodstock, Illinois

CONTENTS

EDITOR'S NOTE

The *Encyclopedia of Mexico* is a collaborative project involving more than three hundred scholars in seven countries. Nurturing scholarly dialogue across disciplinary and national boundaries, the *Encyclopedia* seeks to encourage new approaches to the study of Mexican history, society, and culture. The *Encyclopedia* also seeks to provide students, policy makers, and the general public with convenient access to basic bibliographic and factual data on historical figures, events, and processes, and it is designed to be a useful component for courses on Mexico in the social sciences and humanities.

Although the authors working on this project include many of the top scholars in the field, articles have been selected, written, and edited with a nonspecialist readership in mind. Similarly, it was decided that a straight alphabetical format would be most useful for making basic information accessible to nonspecialist readers. Although the primary focus is on longer synthetic articles, the *Encyclopedia* also includes supplementary articles on specific historical events, figures, and institutions that, in the judgment of the editorial committee, played a particularly important role in Mexican history and were not (or could not be) discussed adequately in the broader synthetic essays.

Key discussions, debates, and themes have been highlighted in a number of ways. First, all topical articles have been extensively cross-referenced, although in the interest of space cross-references generally are confined to topical essays dealing with subjects specifically addressed in the original essay; readers also are encouraged to consult the general synthetic essays and biographical articles. The *Encyclopedia* also includes a detailed thematic outline that traces some of the more complex relationships among article topics. Finally, bibliographies have been organized around works that I believe are most useful to nonspecialist readers. This often was a difficult decision to make, whether I faced a paucity of material or an embarrassment of riches. Where possible, priority was given to English-language sources accessible to nonspecialist readers. Although I have consulted with authors in compiling bibliographies, the final decision rested with the staff at Fitzroy Dearborn and myself.

The *Encyclopedia of Mexico* is primarily historical in scope, emphasizing the development of broad themes, structures, and processes over time. Not only does this focus allow a more richly contextual understanding of specific events, institutions, and figures in Mexican history, it also helps foster a deeper understanding of contemporary Mexico. The *Encyclopedia* includes topics that have been hotly debated for decades or even centuries, as in the case of Guadalupanismo, as well as topics that have emerged from more recent revisionist tendencies in Mexican studies. Indeed, many of the long sections on such topics as urbanism, population, and gender may represent the first real attempt at this sort of historical synthesis. Many articles on more specific topics draw on years of primary research to break new ground.

Like any pedagogical enterprise, however, the *Encyclopedia of Mexico* seeks to raise questions as much as provide information. Article topics were selected in consultation with members of the editorial committee, with additional input from authors and the broader scholarly community. There seemed to be a consensus that long synthetic essays focusing on broad historical questions would allow authors greater latitude to develop their ideas and challenge readers. We felt that an intellectually honest reference work simply could not cultivate an anonymous authoritative voice, and that it would need to highlight key disagreements and debates rather than eliding them.

This strategy—together with the *Encyclopedia*'s multinational, multidisciplinary authorship—allows the *Encyclopedia of Mexico* to mitigate, if never entirely avoid, some of the key hazards of the encyclopedic project. The very idea of the encyclopedic compendium of knowledge was a key part of the ideological project of the European Enlightenment and the second wave of European colonialism, as the early *enciclopedistes* of the eighteenth and nineteenth centuries sought to map categories of division and hierarchy that they understood to be European, modern, and white onto "dark" continents, "dark" races, "dark" classes, "dark" ages in history—even the dark interior spaces of the body. Indeed, it was against this backdrop that the *enciclopedistes* helped constitute individuals, nations, and the continent of Europe itself as historical subjects. In quite different ways, latter-day encyclopedias also have at once responded to and helped define the ideological projects of metropolitan elites. The *Encyclopedia of Mexico*'s emphasis on synthetic historiographic essays allows authors greater freedom to question the very categories that inform the organization of this project. Nonetheless, many of the most difficult and important questions will have to be asked by the readers themselves.

—Michael S. Werner
Chicago, Illinois
August 1997

ACKNOWLEDGMENTS

Coordinating the *Encyclopedia of Mexico* was among the most demanding projects I have ever undertaken. Without the help and support of countless friends and colleagues here in Chicago and throughout the world this project simply would not have been possible. To fully acknowledge the help of each and every person who contributed to this project would be impossible. I hope that for the unnamed, unsung contributors to this project this general statement of gratitude will suffice, even if I know that it cannot.

Thanks certainly will seem superfluous for the staff at the Chicago office of Fitzroy Dearborn Publishers, since they alone know the kinds of sacrifices they have made for this project. I owe a particular debt of gratitude to my commissioning editor Robert M. Salkin, and I hope that the time, energy, and editorial insight that he has put into this project is reflected in the final product.

The editorial advisory committee of this project comprised a community of scholars in the best sense of the term. Its members' editorial and moral support—as well as their sometimes astringent commentary—helped give this project its sense of vision and critical edge. I owe a special debt of gratitude to William O. Autry, Elizabeth Bakewell, Thomas Cummins, Guillermo de la Peña, Ben Fallaw, Gil Joseph, Alan Knight, Claudio Lomnitz, Roger Rouse, Susan Schroeder, Patricia Seed, Emily Socolov, Eric Van Young, Mary Kay Vaughan, and Richard Warren. Going far beyond what was required of them in this project, they became mentors and friends.

This project also drew on a "kitchen cabinet" of informal editorial advisers—authors, translators, and friends who provided invaluable editorial advice and support. Aside from myself and the staff at Fitzroy Dearborn, Jessica Johnson and Lorena Scott Fox probably have seen more of this project than any other people. They were far more than extraordinary translators. Putting in long hours for minimal reward, they also provided detailed, incisive editorial comments, helped me find other authors and translators, and provided much-needed moral support. During the early stages of this project, I also received invaluable translation assistance from Cinna Lomnitz and Stacy Hoult, both of whom helped me line up other authors and translators.

Among hundreds of authors working on this project, I received particularly valuable help from Christon I. Archer, Clara Bargellini, William H. Beezley, Frances F. Berdan, Stanley Brandes, Jane Bussey, Barry Carr, Sarah L. Cline, Linda A. Curcio, Sandra M. Cypess, Seth Fein, María Fernández, Jonathan Fox, Alejandra García Quintanilla, Pilar Gonzalbo Aizpuru, Inés

Herrera, Frances Karttunen, Cecelia F. Klein, Laura A. Lewis, Linda Manzanilla, Robert McCaa, Simon Miller, Rubén Osorio, Alma Parra, Stafford Poole, Vania Salles, William Schell Jr., John F. Schwaller, Enrique Semo, Leslie Sklair, Paul Sullivan, Angela T. Thompson, John Tutino, Jesús Vargas Valdez, and especially Jürgen Buchenau. Arthur James Outram Anderson, who wrote the biographical articles on Alonso de Molina and Bernardino de Sahagún for the *Encyclopedia,* did not live to see this project brought to completion. His scholarly insight and generous spirit will be sorely missed.

I owe a particular debt of gratitude to my colleagues here in Chicago who participated in this project, particularly Thomas Cummins, Friedrich Katz, Claudio Lomnitz, María Elena Martínez, Donald McVicker, Susan Schroeder, Alexandra Stern, David Eduardo Tavárez, and Mary Kay Vaughan, whose advice, friendship, and faith in this project helped me maintain my moral and intellectual center during these difficult three years. Ruby Bugarín, Kelly Gallagher, Lisa Guare, and Beatriz Riefkohl at the Center for Latin American Studies and Tonja Hopkins at the Latin American history office at the University of Chicago provided invaluable logistical and moral support. Mary Janzen and the rest of the staff at the Newberry Library and the staff of the Joseph Regenstein Library at the University of Chicago also provided important research assistance and moral support. The administrators and moderators of the Latin Americanist and Mexicanist electronic discussion groups HLATAM and HMEX provided a vital forum for scholarly interchange and dialogue. I should not fail to mention the staff of the Academic Computing Services at the University of Chicago, whose valiant assistance during my many computer crises quite possibly saved this project. Cecilia Gutiérrez Arriola at the Fototeca of the Instituto de Investigaciones Estéticas at the Universidad Nacional Autónoma de México provided invaluable assistance with illustrations. Even though he was not a part of this project in any formal way, Jonathan D. Amith at Yale University quite generously shared his time and editorial expertise with me over a period of several months. Rosa Rodríguez of the Casa de las Imágenes in Mexico City quite graciously permitted us to use the magnificent image found of the covers of both volumes. I particularly want to thank the artist himself, Eusebio Díaz Alejandro of the community of Ameyaltepec, Guerrero, whose beautiful, frightening images continue to haunt my waking hours and dreams in the closing days of this project.

I do not know where to begin in acknowledging the unflagging support of my parents and grandparents, and of the many friends who have stood by me over these seemingly impossible three years. I particularly want to thank Noah Berlatsky, Katie Brooks, Emiliano Corral, Mark Day, Alyssa Dinega, Rebecca Feldman, Lisa Hernández, Simon Kashama, Christine Longcore, Andrew Tripp, and Arnold Jacob Wolf. Jenny and Richard often saw the worst of me as I worked on this project, and I hope that they can find it in their hearts to understand and forgive. Finally, I owe special thanks to the many teachers who have helped spark and develop my engagement with history, particularly John Brierley, John H. Coatsworth, Paul Gootenberg, Friedrich Katz, James Kloppenberg, Claudio Lomnitz, David Scobey, and Hernán Villafañe.

The *Encyclopedia of Mexico* often seems to be largely a creature of serendipity. In large part this reflects the challenges of coordinating a project of this size and scope, but it also reflects something much deeper. The three-year process of putting together the *Encyclopedia* has done far more for me than raise questions about Mexico. It also has raised fundamental questions about my work as a writer, scholar, and student of Mexican history. I expect that I will be struggling to find answers for the rest of my life.

—Michael S. Werner
Chicago, Illinois
August 1997

ADVISERS

William O. Autry
Elizabeth Bakewell
John H. Coatsworth
Thomas Cummins
Guillermo de la Peña
Ben Fallaw
Jean Franco
Peter F. Guardino
Gil Joseph
Friedrich Katz
Alan Knight

Claudio Lomnitz
Daniel Nugent
Roger Rouse
Susan Schroeder
Patricia Seed
Emily Socolov
Eric Van Young
Mary Kay Vaughan
Brígida von Mentz de Boege
Richard Warren

CONTRIBUTORS

Mariclaire Acosta
Rolena Adorno
Marcos Tonatiuh Águila Medina
Javier Aguilar García
Maureen Ahern
Ignacio Almada
Ida Altman
Salvador Alvarez
Gastón A. Alzate
Arthur James Outram Anderson
Rodney D. Anderson
Dudley Ankerson
Kirsten Appendini
Christon I. Archer
Electa Arenal
Shirley L. Arora
Angélica Arreola Medina
Israel Arroyo García
Emmy Avilés Bretón
Maricela Ayala Falcón
Shannon L. Baker
Elizabeth Bakewell
Adrian A. Bantjes
Clara Bargellini
David Barkin
Eli Bartra
Jean-Pierre Bastian
William H. Beezley
Brian C. Belanger
Thomas Benjamin
John M. Bennett
Frances F. Berdan
Suzanne Bilello
Maurice Biriotti

Yael Bitrán Goren
Jeffrey L. Bortz
Josie Bortz
Viviane Brachet-Márquez
Stanley Brandes
Keith Brewster
Brenda Jo Bright
John A. Britton
Jonathan C. Brown
Kathleen Bruhn
Samuel Brunk
Jürgen Buchenau
Steven B. Bunker
Jane Bussey
Kitty Calavita
Ernesto Camou Healy
Melchor Campos García
Gabriela Cano
Enrique Cárdenas
Barry Carr
Inés Castro Apreza
Mario Cerutti
Fernando Cervantes
John Charlot
Francie R. Chassen-López
John F. Chuchiak IV
Sarah L. Cline
Bruce Colcleugh
George A. Collier
José Mario Contreras Valdéz
Elizabeth Corral Peña
John F. Crossen
Linda A. Curcio
Robert E. Curley

Margarita Vera Cuspinera
Sandra M. Cypess
Diane E. Davis
Alexander S. Dawson
Susan Deans-Smith
Danièle Dehouve
Sophie de la Calle
Víctor de la Cruz
Luz María de la Mora
Guillermo de la Peña
Jesús F. de la Teja
Blanca de Lizaur
Aurelio de los Reyes
Adriana de Teresa Ochoa
Kelly Donahue-Wallace
Peter G. Earle
Ingrid Elliott
Pablo Escalante
Paloma Escalante Gonzalbo
Antonio Escobar Ohmstede
Matthew D. Esposito
Romana Falcón Vega
Ben Fallaw
Seth Fein
María Fernández
Irma Isabel Fernández Arias
Carlos Fernández Dittmann
Martin V. Fleming
Merlin H. Forster
Heather Fowler-Salamini
Jonathan Fox
Lorena Scott Fox
José Z. García
José Manuel García-García
Alejandra García Quintanilla
Paul Garner
Richard L. Garner
Luis Javier Garrido
James A. Garza
Marilyn Gates
Courtney Gilbert
Adolfo Gilly
Julia C. Girouard
Alicia Gojman de Backal
Pilar Gonzalbo Aizpuru
Stella María González Cicero
Manuel González Oropeza
María del Rocio González Serrano
Yólotl González Torres
Gary Isaac Gordon
Felipe Gorostiza Arroyo
Cecilia Greaves Lainé
Virginia Guedea
Matthew C. Gutmann
Paul Lawrence Haber
Diana Hadley
Richard L. Haiman
Nora Hamilton
Brian R. Hamnett
Christopher Harris
John Mason Hart

Neil Harvey
Ross Hassig
Joy Elizabeth Hayes
J. León Helguera
Peter V. N. Henderson
Timothy J. Henderson
Raymond Hernández-Durán
Lawrence A. Herzog
Carol A. Hess
Doris Heyden
Josiah McC. Heyman
Evelyn Hu-DeHart
Antonio Ibarra
Harry B. Iceland
María Elena Victoria Jardón
Jan Jarrell
Errol D. Jones
Frances Karttunen
Benjamin Keen
John E. Kicza
Norma Klahn
Cecelia F. Klein
Alan Knight
John Koegel
Emilio H. Kourí
Sandra Kuntz Ficker
Chris Kyle
David G. LaFrance
Luis Fernando Lara
Luis Leal
John Lear
Thomas Legler
Daniel C. Levy
Laura A. Lewis
Stephen E. Lewis
Sonya Lipsett-Rivera
Bernardita Llanos
Soledad Loaeza
Robert J. Loescher
Cinna Lomnitz
Claudio Lomnitz
Felicia Hardison Londré
Lorenzo C. Lopez
José Borjón López Coterrilla
Rosalva Loreto López
David E. Lorey
Esteban E. Loustaunau
Sarah M. Lowe
Aurora Loyo Brambila
Engracia Loyo Bravo
Matilde Luna
Nora Lustig
Robert McCaa
Emily McClung de Tapia
John Holmes McDowell
Carlos Macías Richard
Corynne McSherry
Donald McVicker
Mary Frech McVicker
Nicholas Maher
Aaron P. Mahr Yáñez

Linda Manzanilla
Carl Henry Marcoux
María Elena Martínez
Carlos Martínez Assad
Rodolfo Mata
José Antonio Matesanz
Álvaro Matute
Teresa A. Meade
Elinor G. K. Melville
Jean Meyer
Simon Miller
Virginia E. Miller
Carl J. Mora
Ron Morgan
John Mraz
Victor Gabriel Muro
David Navarrete G.
Victoria Novelo
Harley D. Oberhelman
Marcial E. Ocasio-Melendez
Enrique C. Ochoa
Patrice E. Olsen
Lisa Collins Orman
Monica I. Orozco
Isabel Ortega Ridaura
José Ortiz Monasterio
Rubén Osorio Zuñiga
María Rosa Palazón Mayoral
Erika Pani
Helen Rand Parish
Max Parra
J. Agustín Pastén B.
Héctor Perea
Armando Pereira
Pedro Pérez Herrero
Michael D. Phillips
Charmaine Picard
Jeffrey M. Pilcher
Stafford Poole, C.M.
Susie S. Porter
Cristina Puga
Jennie Purnell
Eloise Quiñones Keber
Isabel Quiñónez
Vicente Quirarte
Karen Racine
Laura Randall
Kay A. Read
Luis Rebaza-Soraluz
Matthew Restall
Douglas W. Richmond
Edward A. Riedinger
G. Micheal Riley
Arístides Rivera Navarro
Martha Eugenia Rodríguez
Dan Rogers
Eugenia Roldán Vera
Anthony G. Rominske
Ricardo Romo
Charles E. Ronan, S.J.
Kathleen Ross

Anne Rubenstein
Jeffrey W. Rubin
Patricia Rubio
Carlos Rubio Pacho
Jorge Ruedas de la Serna
Jorge Ruffinelli
Terry Rugeley
Craig H. Russell
Antonio Saborit
Delia Salazar Anaya
Vania Salles
Fernando I. Salmerón Castro
Ricardo J. Salvador
Richard Salvucci
Alvaro Sánchez-Crispín
James A. Sandos
Kathleen Mullen Sands
Pedro Santoni
Alex M. Saragoza
William Schell Jr.
Louisa Schell Hoberman
Arthur Schmidt
Samuel Schmidt
Michael Schreffler
Susan Schroeder
Frans J. Schryer
Friedrich E. Schuler
John F. Schwaller
Enrique Semo
Ilán Semo
Juan Antonio Serna
Mónica Serrano
Elisa Servín
Stanley F. Shadle
Thomas E. Sheridan
John W. Sherman
Harold Dana Sims
Leslie Sklair
Emily Socolov
Francisca R. Sorensen
Lois Stanford
Lynn Stephen
Alexandra Stern
Claire T. Stracke
J. Richard Stracke
Clara Elena Suárez Argüello
Paul Sullivan
María Socorro Tabuenca C.
David Eduardo Tavárez
Eva Zorrilla Tessler
Angela T. Thompson
Guy P. C. Thomson
María Celia Toro
Valentina Torres Septién
Yolia Tortolero Cervantes
Rodolfo Tuirán
Esperanza Tuñón Pablos
Julia Tuñón Pablos
John Tutino
Martín Valadez
Paul J. Vanderwood

Eric Van Young
Elisa Vargaslugo
Jesús Vargas Valdez
Mary Kay Vaughan
Patricia Vega
Bryan E. Vizzini
J. Benedict Warren
Mark Wasserman
Mary A. Watrous
Charles A. Weeks
Allen Wells
James W. Wessman

Stacie G. Widdifield
Brian Wilson
Andrew Grant Wood
George Woodyard
Pablo Yankelevich
Elliott Young
Francisco Zapata
José Eduardo Zárate Hernández
Guillermo Zermeño Padilla
Heidi Zogbaum
Eric Zolov

TRANSLATORS

Pilar Maria Bezanilla
Janis Breckinridge
Dennis Brehme
Gilberto Conde Zambada
Louise A. Detwiler
Vanessa Maria Duncan
Lorena Scott Fox
Stacy Hoult
Patricia James

Jessica Johnson
Cinna Lomnitz
Mary McHugh
Patricia Montilla
RoseAnna Mueller
Lynn Osheroff
Ella Schmitt Rich
Laura F. Woford
Ann Wright

ALPHABETICAL LIST OF ENTRIES

Volume 1

Volume 2

THEMATIC OUTLINE OF ENTRIES

This outline is divided into the following four sections:

Culture
Economy
Geography and Demography
Politics

Each of these sections is further divided into numerous subsections. Entries may appear in more than one category.

I. CULTURE

EDUCATION

(TOPICAL ENTRIES)

Ateneo de la Juventud
Casa de España
Contemporáneos Group
Counterculture
Education: Colonial
Education: 1821–89
Education: 1889–1940
Education: 1940–96
Generación de 1915
Generación de 1968 and Generación Fin del Siglo
Historiography
University System

(EDUCATORS)

Aguirre Beltrán, Gonzalo
Altamirano, Ignacio Manuel
Bassols, Narciso
Carrillo Puerto, Felipe
Caso, Antonio
Cosío Villegas, Daniel
Gamio, Manuel
Guillén Sánchez, Palma
Sáenz, Moises
Sierra, Justo
Vasconcelos, José

LANGUAGE

Anthropology
Codices
Gender and Mexican Spanish
Indigenismo and Ethnic Movements
Indigenous Philologies
Mesoamerica: Introduction
Mesoamerica: Maya
Mesoamerica: Monte Albán

Mesoamerica: Olmec
Mesoamerica: Calendrics
Mesoamerica: Writing
Mexican Spanish
Popular Narrative and Poetics

LITERATURE

(TOPICAL ENTRIES)

Anthropology
Ateneo de la Juventud
Autos
Border Literatures
Casa de España
Codices
Conquest: Conquest Narratives
Contemporáneos Group
Corridos
Counterculture
Criollos and *Criollismo*
Generación del Medio Siglo
Generación de 1915
Generación de 1968 and Generación Fin del Siglo
Historietas
Historiography
Indigenous Philologies
Journalistic Novel
Malinche and *Malinchismo*
Modernism
Narrative and National Identity, 1910–96
Popular Narrative and Poetics

(WRITERS)

Alamán, Lucas
Altamirano, Ignacio Manuel
Arreola, Juan José
Azuela, Mariano
Balbuena, Bernardo de
Bustamante, Carlos María de
Calderón de la Barca, Fanny

Campobello, Nellie
Carballido, Emilio
Castellanos, Rosario
Chimalpahin
Clavigero, Francisco Javier
Cosío Villegas, Daniel
Cruz, Sor Juana Inés de la
Cuesta, Jorge
del Paso, Fernando
del Río, Eduardo (Rius)
Díaz del Castillo, Bernal
Erauso, Catalina de (La Monja Alférez)
Feige, Hermann Albert Otto Maximilian (B. Traven)
Fernández de Lizardi, José Joaquín
Fuentes, Carlos
Garro, Elena
Gómez Marín, Manuel
Gómez-Peña, Guillermo
González Martínez, Enrique
Gorostiza, José
Guzmán Franco, Martín Luis
Hernández, Luisa Josefina
Huerta, Efraín
Leñero, Vicente
López Velarde, Ramón
Monsiváis, Carlos
Nervo, Amado
Novo, Salvador
Owen, Gilberto
Pacheco, José Emilio
Payno, Manuel
Paz, Octavio
Pellicer Cámara, Carlos
Poniatowska, Elena
Prieto, Guillermo
Puga, María Luisa
Rabasa, Emilio
Ramírez, Ignacio
Ramos, Samuel
Reyes Ochoa, Alfonso

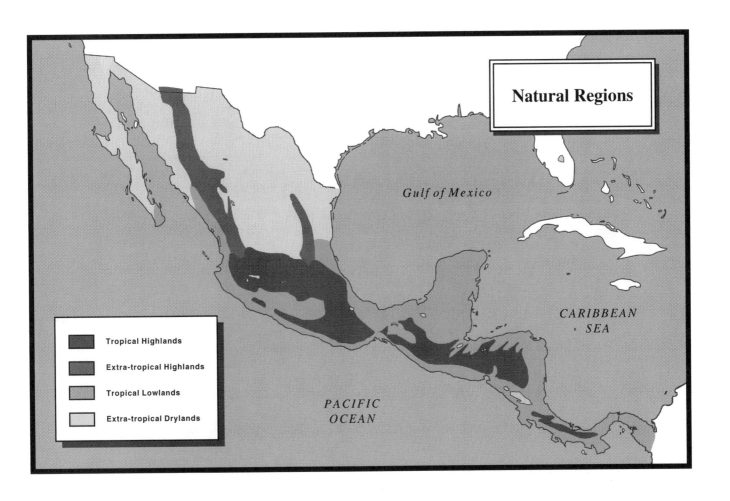

Natural Regions

- Tropical Highlands
- Extra-tropical Highlands
- Tropical Lowlands
- Extra-tropical Drylands

Gulf of Mexico

CARIBBEAN SEA

PACIFIC OCEAN

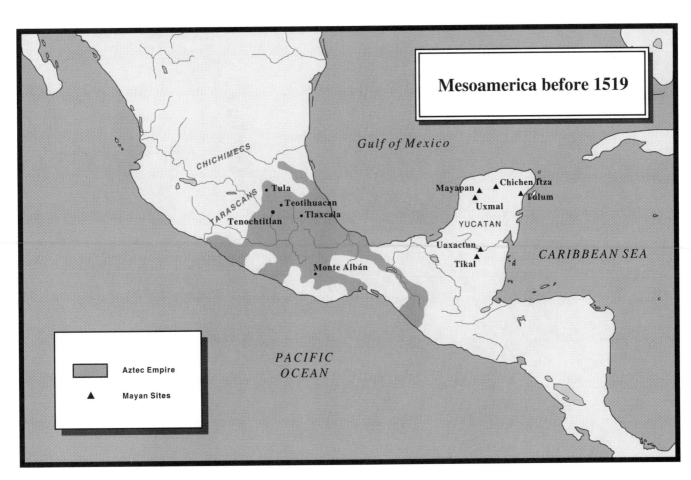

Mesoamerica before 1519

Gulf of Mexico

CHICHIMECS

TARASCANS

- Tula
- Teotihuacan
- Tlaxcala
- Tenochtitlan
- Monte Albán

Mayapan ▲   ▲ Chichen Itza
▲ Uxmal   ▲ Tulum

YUCATAN

Uaxactun ▲
Tikal ▲

CARIBBEAN SEA

PACIFIC OCEAN

- Aztec Empire
- ▲ Mayan Sites

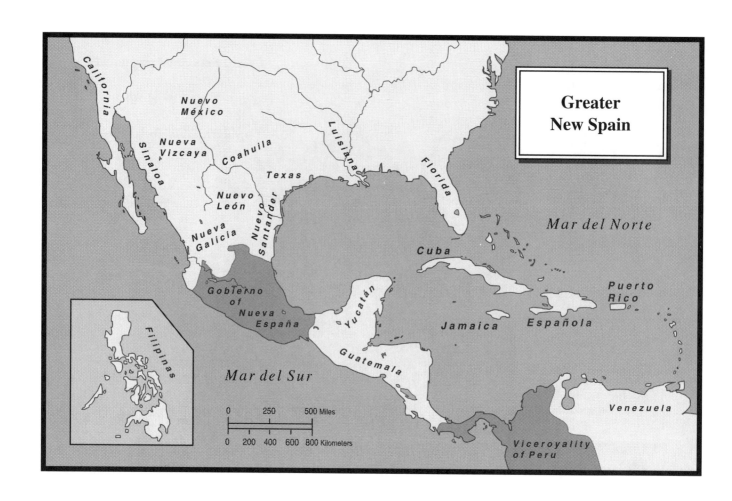

Greater New Spain

California

Nuevo México

Sinaloa

Nueva Vizcaya

Coahuila

Texas

Luisiana

Florida

Nuevo León

Nuevo Santander

Nueva Galicia

Gobierno of Nueva España

Yucatán

Guatemala

Mar del Norte

Cuba

Puerto Rico

Jamaica

Española

Mar del Sur

Filipinas

Venezuela

Viceroyality of Peru

0   250   500 Miles

0   200 400 600 800 Kilometers

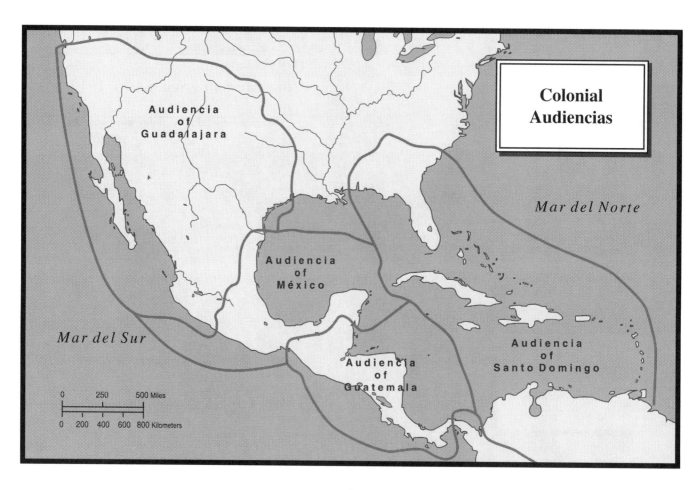

Colonial Audiencias

Audiencia of Guadalajara

Audiencia of México

Audiencia of Guatemala

Audiencia of Santo Domingo

Mar del Norte

Mar del Sur

0   250   500 Miles

0   200 400 600 800 Kilometers

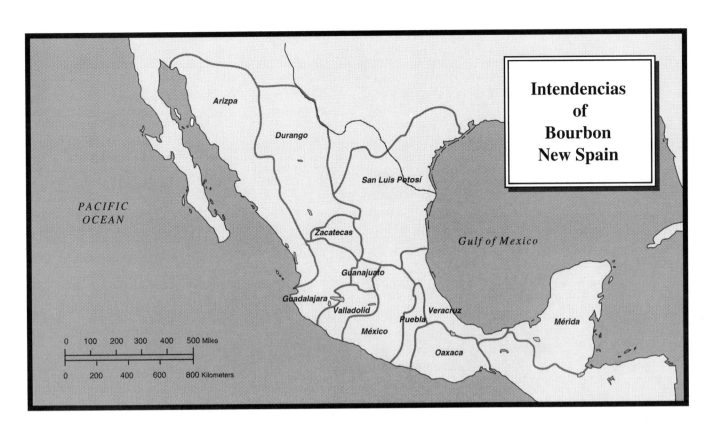

Intendencias of Bourbon New Spain

Arizpa

Durango

San Luis Potosí

PACIFIC OCEAN

Zacatecas

Gulf of Mexico

Guanajuato

Guadalajara

Valladolid

Veracruz

Puebla

México

Mérida

Oaxaca

0 100 200 300 400 500 Miles

0 200 400 600 800 Kilometers

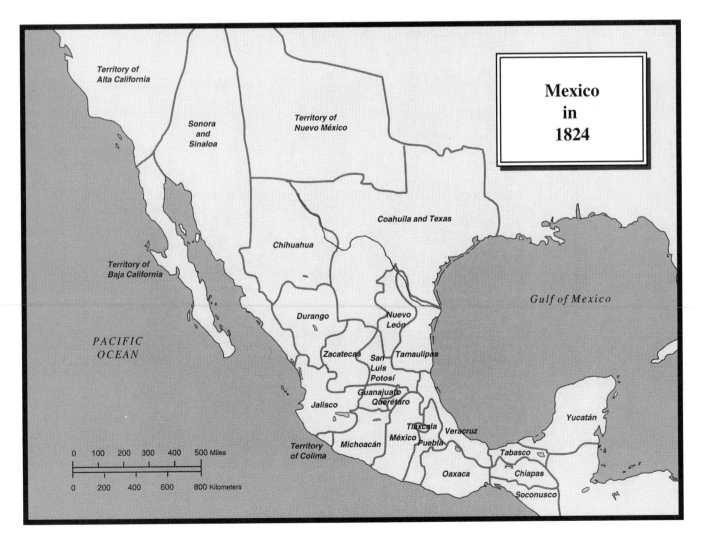

Mexico in 1824

Territory of Alta California

Sonora and Sinaloa

Territory of Nuevo México

Territory of Baja California

Coahuila and Texas

Chihuahua

Gulf of Mexico

Durango

Nuevo León

PACIFIC OCEAN

Zacatecas

Tamaulipas

San Luis Potosí

Guanajuato

Querétaro

Jalisco

Yucatán

Tlaxcala

Veracruz

México

Puebla

Territory of Colima

Michoacán

Tabasco

Oaxaca

Chiapas

Soconusco

0 100 200 300 400 500 Miles

0 200 400 600 800 Kilometers

A

ABASCAL, SALVADOR
1910– • Writer and Catholic Activist

One of the most charismatic leaders of the Sinarquist movement, otherwise known as the Unión Nacional Sinarquista (UNS), Salvador Abascal was an important Catholic activist during 1930s and 1940s. His militancy was impressive, and his abilities as a strategist put him on an equal level with Anacleto González Flores. Abascal arrived a little late on the scene to participate in the Cristero Rebellion of 1926 to 1929. The church by this stage had decided to fall in with the Holy See's recommendations to accept the conditions imposed by the Mexican government and take a course guided by a strategy of conciliation and collaboration.

Abascal retired from the Sinarquist movement after his hazardous attempt to found the colony María Auxiliadora in Baja California. He nevertheless promoted the cause with equal intensity as a writer, producing *La reconquista espiritual de Tabasco* (1942), *Memorias* (1980), *La revolución antimexicana* (1978), *El Papa nunca ha sido ni será hereje* (1979), and *Tomás Garrido Canabal: Sin Dios, sin curas, sin iglesias* (1987).

Abascal was born in the State of Guanajuato in 1910, one of 12 brothers and sisters. His father was a member of the "U," or Unión Popular (Popular Union), a secret organization founded in 1918 by the then rector of the seminary and canon of the cathedral in Morelia, Luís María Martínez. This group would recruit cadres of individuals who would later lead the Cristero movement.

Abascal, like Luis María Martínez before him, entered a seminary at the age of nine; he remained there from November 1919 to December 1925. He left to take up law studies at the Escuela Libre de Derecho in Mexico City, the only school that recognized his seminary studies. On completion of his legal training he worked in various towns in Guerrero as a judge with general responsibilities for initial proceedings in the appellate court. In August 1935 he made contact in Morelia with what remained of the Liga Defensora de la Libertad Religiosa (League for the Defense of Religious Freedom) which by that time had metamorphosed into the Legiones (Legions), a secret organization trying to reorganize the Catholic militants in the wake of the papal agreement of 1929. As a legionary in May 1938 he initiated the "spiritual reconquest," the reopening of the churches in Tabasco, which was controlled by the anticlerical socialist Tomás Garrido Canabal.

Already a member, he was named national leader of the UNS on August 26, 1940; he held the post until December 11 of the following year. Sinarquism was in its heyday during this period, but Abascal's belligerence and aggressive methods led Archbishop Luis María Martínez to force Abascal to hand the reigns of the organization to Manuel Torres Bueno.

A week later Abascal, at the head of 350 people from some 70 families, set out to found the María Auxiliadora Colony in Baja California. The intention of this adventurous enterprise was to prove the effectiveness of Catholicism in a world he considered had abandoned the faith. But once again, he was obliged in March 1944 by Archbishop Luis María Martínez to abandon his post at the head of this initiative.

Abascal went on to work for Jus, a publishing company, where he stayed until 1973, later founding his own publishing house, Tradición. This company edited the monthly bulletin, *Hoja de Combate,* under Celerino Salmeron, head of the Mexican Traditional Falangists.

Select Bibliography

Blancarte, Roberto, *Historia de la iglesia católica en México 1939–1987*. Mexico City: Fondo de Cultura Económica, 1992.

—GUILLERMO ZERMEÑO PADILLA

AFRICAN MEXICANS

Scholars generally agree that the first person of African descent to come to the Americas arrived with Columbus on his second voyage in 1493. He was free. Yet African slave labor, which already was established in a limited way in Spain, quickly spread to the Americas, where indigenous peoples, many also enslaved by Spanish colonists, were being decimated by the mistreatment and diseases brought by Spaniards. As these people were felled and the pressure for labor from settlers grew, so did the demand for enslaved Africans. Between 1501, when the Atlantic slave trade to the Americas began, and 1518, the year prior to Fernando (Hernán) Cortés's arrival off the coast of Veracruz, the Spanish Crown permitted Africans who had been "Hispanicized" in Spain to be brought as slaves to the first Spanish colonies. By 1518, however, pressure from the colonies had forced the Crown to begin permitting direct importations from Africa of enslaved Africans.

At least one free "black" (as they were known), a man named Juan Garrido, apparently accompanied the first conquistadors to Mexico, who also brought with them several slaves. Arriving in 1519 or 1520, Garrido might have taken part in the conquest of Tenochtitlan. He most definitely was involved in post-Conquest expeditions organized by Cortés to control outlying lands, and later became the first person to farm wheat in Mexico. As a free man, Garrido was the exception rather than the rule, however. Most blacks came to Mexico already enslaved. Between 1519 and 1580, the earliest period of the slave trade, about 36,500 such persons were brought to Mexico. Mortality rates were high on board slave ships and in the Americas. Moreover, since two-thirds of the slaves were men, many of whom were destined for hard physical labor, sex ratios generally were imbalanced. Therefore, the replenishment of the slave population depended more on the transatlantic trade than on domestic reproduction.

During most of the colonial period, the trade to the Spanish colonies was regulated by the Crown, which granted licenses to individual traders. These traders depended for supplies principally on the Portuguese, who controlled access to the African coast. Between 1580 and 1640, the heyday of the slave trade to Mexico and a period of union between the Spanish and Portuguese Crowns, Portugal dominated the trade. At various points during the late seventeenth and late eighteenth centuries Holland, France, and England also were involved in supplying slaves to the Spanish colonies, both legally and as contraband. Over the course of this later period, however, Mexico's slave importations slowed dramatically.

By the mid-to-late sixteenth century the enslavement of most indigenous peoples had been made illegal. Through the first decades of the seventeenth century, as Mexico's indigenous population followed that of the Caribbean to a precipitous decline and settlers' demands for imported labor accelerated, Mexico's African and African-descended population grew to be the largest in the Americas. In fact, until importations reached their peak in 1640, Mexico was receiving on average two-thirds of all Africans brought legally to Spanish America and many who were brought illegally. Estimates place the African-descended population of Mexico at about 140,000 in 1650, a figure that included men and women, free persons and slaves, African-born slaves known as *bozales* (a word that scholar Gonzalbo Aguirre Beltrán translates as "brutes" or "savages"), Hispanicized slaves known as *ladinos,* and the mulatto offspring of blacks and Spaniards or blacks and Indians (the latter sometimes called *zambos* or *zambaigos*). Since the status of children followed their mother, mulattoes with slave mothers were also subject to enslavement.

Although requests for enslaved blacks continued beyond the seventeenth century, the slave trade to Mexico steadily declined over the rest of the colonial period as the indigenous population recovered and the "mixed" population of mestizos and mulattoes grew. By the end of the eighteenth century slave importations were occurring mostly in sparsely inhabited districts of the Yucatán, and the Mexican population included only about 9,000 enslaved blacks and mulattoes. In 1817 the slave trade was halted, and in 1821 fewer than 3,000 people were still enslaved in Mexico. When slavery was legally abolished with Independence, it had all but ended. Nevertheless, over the 300-year course of the colonial period, approximately 200,000 slaves had been brought to Mexico.

African slaves first came principally from West Africa, specifically from Guinea-Bissau, Senegal, Gambia, and the coast of Sierra Leone. Later the source shifted to Angola and to the Congo in Central Africa. An internal domestic trade flourished alongside the international trade. With the exception of the northern zones (where Chichimec Indians still were sometimes enslaved), black slaves were concentrated in areas of Spanish settlement. Most were in Mexico City and the surrounding Valley of Mexico. But large slave populations also could be found in the eastern Veracruz-Pánuco coastal region, the Bajío silver mining regions and ranches to the north and west of Mexico City, and the sugar plantations, ranches, and mines that followed the southwestern belt running from the city of Puebla to the Pacific.

The decline in the indigenous population, legislation that protected indigenous peoples from certain arduous occupations, and the widespread Spanish belief that Africans were superior workers were all factors leading to the intensive use of enslaved Africans in New Spain's sugar industry, textile workshops, silver mines, and pearl fisheries. In many situations, however, Indians remained the dominant labor force despite laws of protection, and black slaves filled positions as specialized workers. Household slaves also were quite common; slaveholders often hired slaves out for a daily wage *(jornal)*, most of which was to be paid to the slaveholder. Slave ownership extended to a few Indians of high rank and to some aspiring free blacks.

As property, slaves had few rights. They were bought and sold with other property and given names that marked them as their masters' possessions or by their place of origin. Branding was used at ports of entry to identify slaves. It also could be employed as a form of punishment along with other physical tortures, such as the amputation of arms, hands, or ears; the use of leg irons; and a practice known as *pringar,* which consisted of hot pork fat, candle wax, or pitch dripped onto the skin.

Slaves were routinely, if nominally, converted to Christianity through baptism and indoctrination upon capture or during their passage to the Americas. Religious education for both African-born and American-born slaves was expected to continue throughout their lives. Yet religious freedoms granted to blacks, such as the right to form mutual aid societies *(cofradías),* were sometimes curtailed as fear of organized rebellion grew. In addition, the clergy focused most of its efforts on indigenous peoples. Ultimately, while the Catholic Church played a prominent role in protecting Indians and challenging Spaniards' rights to enslave them, debates over the fate of blacks were few and far between.

Nevertheless, to a certain extent both church and state protected slaves. Laws guaranteed them the right to marry and freedom from excessive punishment. The medieval Spanish legal code, the Siete Partidas, also provided several routes to manumission (freedom). Slaveholders could free their slaves, slaves could purchase themselves for an agreed upon price (which they sometimes paid in installments), and third parties could purchase slaves and free them. Slaveholders could not be forced to give up slaves against their will, however. In addition, even legal statutes meant to give slaves certain rights did not necessarily translate into social practice, since the slaveholders' interests usually came first. Some provisions of the Siete Partidas also were changed to fit conditions in the Americas. For instance, since sexual imbalances in the black and Spanish populations made marriages between black men and Indian women common, and those between black women and Spanish men a possibility, as early as the 1520s Crown and local officials disallowed legislation permitting slaves who married free persons to be freed. Status continued to follow the mother, however, so children born of free women were also free.

Slaves had some access to the courts, where their limited rights to decent care, to a family and, under certain circumstances, to freedom, were recognized and sometimes even enforced. The Inquisition, in particular, oversaw slaveholders' obligations to see to the "Christian" treatment of their charges. But it also persecuted free and enslaved blacks for blasphemy, witchcraft, and other anti-Catholic acts. Other courts oversaw their punishment for secular crimes.

Although slave revolts never produced a substantial change in slave conditions or in the fact of slavery itself, they occurred with frequency throughout the colonial period and were brutally put down. Runaway slaves *(cimarrones)* also were punished severely when caught, often with mutilation and even, occasionally in the case of male slaves, with castration. Fugitive slaves who were not caught often banded together and sometimes established independent communities. Most of these were overrun quickly by colonists, but several groups of *cimarrones* won the legal right to autonomy during the seventeenth and eighteenth centuries. The most famous and successful of these groups was centered in the Orizaba region of Veracruz and led by an African named Yanga. After years of conflicts with settlers and officials, it was granted a charter as a free settlement in 1612. Over a century later in the same general vicinity slave uprisings in sugar mills produced new *cimarrón* activity. Through negotiations with colonial authorities these *cimarrones* came to aid Spaniards in their mid-eighteenth-century war against Great Britain, and were granted autonomy at the war's conclusion. On the Pacific coast during the same period slaves escaped the ports of Acapulco and Huatulco, setting up their own communities in Guerrero and Oaxaca. While in general blacks' freedom was restricted by legislation that persecuted any hint of independence, it is possible that in the relatively autonomous *cimarrón* communities aspects of ancestral cultures could be maintained successfully.

Mexico's free African-descended population grew substantially as the colonial period progressed. Much of that population consisted of women and children, which probably reflected Spanish slaveholders' favorable treatment of their slave mistresses and mulatto offspring. Freed slaves often were no better off than slaves themselves, since discriminatory laws worked to keep them from improving their social and economic status. For instance, all blacks and mulattoes were forbidden from dressing like Spaniards or Indians, unless they were married to them, from bearing arms, gathering in groups, joining certain craft guilds, and even from living without Spanish supervision. Most blacks and mulattoes remained in the lower echelons of the socioeconomic scale, where they toiled as domestic workers, laborers, shoemakers, itinerant traders, and ranch hands. Some, however, held positions as skilled workers (as did many slaves), and despite restrictions on guild membership, guilds became one of the principal ways in which black men advanced as labor shortages eventually forced their integration. Other blacks, such as a woman named Adriana de Cabrera, who was a native and resident of Veracruz in the middle of the seventeenth century, owned their own businesses (in this case, a boarding house) as well as their own slaves.

As populations intermixed over the course of the colonial period, "caste" boundaries became increasingly obscured. By the late eighteenth century an elaborate caste nomenclature had expanded to include dozens of categories of persons classified by fine "racial" distinctions. At the same time, the Crown attempted to forestall "unequal" marriages through the Pragmatic Sanction, which stipulated parental control over marriage partners. In Mexico the determination of marriages as socially unequal rested on genealogy, with black ancestry the principal determinant of low status.

The abolition of slavery was part of the Independence movement of the early nineteenth century. Leaders such as Miguel Hidalgo and José María Morelos, both insurgent priests, challenged the elite by calling for slave emancipation and the dismantling of the caste system as it was written into law. Nonwhites were drawn to the insurgent movement led by these two men, and later by Vicente Guerrero, one of the new nation's first presidents. Guerrero, who was apparently of partial African ancestry, was frequently indicted by the elite during his political ascent for goading nonwhites to insurgence.

Independence brought significant changes at the level of national and local politics as slavery and the caste system were legally abolished and all but Spaniards were permitted to vote and hold public office. Yet whites gained control of the Independence movement and continued to monopolize economic and political power. Nonwhites, therefore, still possessed a lower social status as whites "held the color line" and in many ways even modeled the new government on the colonial one.

Caste classifications were no longer a standard part of Mexican census data following Independence. As the legal and administrative codes based on caste ceased identifying people by ancestry, blacks disappeared from the official record. Between the late colonial period and the post-Revolutionary period in the twentieth century, the mestizo—the biological and cultural product of Spaniard and Indian—became the Mexican national emblem. Although blacks were a substantial presence during the colonial period and beyond, they were excluded consciously from mestizo ideology by nationalist thinkers. For example, the exiled late colonial Jesuit Francisco Javier Clavigero carefully established the place of the ancient Mexicans, ancestors of the exalted mestizo, in Mexican national ideology, but eliminated black slaves and their descendants from his idea of the Mexican nation, declaring that blacks had "damaged blood and a disorderly physical constitution." "What could be more contrary to the idea we have of beauty and human bodily perfection," he asked, "than a pestilent man, whose skin is dark like ink, head and face covered with black wool in place of hair, eyes yellow or the color of blood, thick, blackish lips and flattened nose?"

Such commentaries speak to eighteenth- and nineteenth-century racism, which was crystallizing around the alleged cultural, biological, and even aesthetic inferiority of blacks. Throughout the late nineteenth and early twentieth centuries African-descended immigrants were discouraged from settling in Mexico, as well as in other parts of Latin America, while European immigrants were courted. During this period veneration of the Mexican mestizo culminated in the Revolutionary-era writings of José Vasconcelos, who explicated the "constructive miscegenation" of *mestizaje* based on a "spiritual eugenics," while promoting the idea that the "Negro race" would vanish on its own as "beautiful and

healthy" specimens of the Indian and white "races" spawned the new mestizo. "The inferior types of the species," wrote Vasconcelos, "will be absorbed by the superior type," and blacks soon would become "extinct" as the "ugliest races" made way for the "most beautiful."

The intentional exclusion of blacks from Mexican national ideology during this period perhaps prompted their wider exclusion from the historical and anthropological scholarship on Mexico, as well as from the national consciousness. With few exceptions, little research on Mexico's African-descended population was done until the 1940s and 1950s, when Gonzalo Aguirre Beltrán, the foremost scholar of Mexico's African-descended population, produced two full-length historical and ethnographic works. More recently, several major historical studies have focused on Mexican blacks, for example the works of Colin Palmer and Patrick Carroll.

But in general, blacks have been neglected in Mexican studies. This neglect cannot be attributed to their small numbers. Although those numbers never reached the levels of later Spanish and Anglo-American colonies, and estimates placed Mexico's African-descended population in the latter half of the twentieth century at less than 1 percent, there were even fewer Spaniards than blacks in colonial society. Nevertheless, many works of scholarship focus on Spaniards, as well as on the indigenous majority.

Aguirre Beltrán offers a partial explanation for the disappearance of blacks from national and scholarly discourse. He suggests that they were "integrated" into the wider society through processes of biological and cultural "mixing" dating from the colonial period and continuing through the present. In his estimation, the exceptions to this assimilating process were blacks from the Pacific Coast region known as the Costa Chica. Indeed, while there are self-identified "blacks" in other parts of Mexico, principally in the gulf coast state of Veracruz, the Costa Chica today is widely considered to be the "blackest" part of the country. Costa Chican *negros* or *morenos,* as they are identified by their mestizo and indigenous neighbors, are probably descendants of slaves brought to the coast to work on sugar plantations as well as of runaway slaves from the shipping ports of Acapulco and Huatulco. Mostly peasant cultivators, they tend to occupy a socioeconomic niche between those locally identified as "white" or "Indian." Today, scholars are coming to understand the complex cultural, socioeconomic, and historical ties between these three groups.

Recently the Mexican government also has expressed a new interest in Mexico's African-descended population through support of the project known as Nuestra Tercera Raíz (Our Third Root), which was inaugurated in 1991 to uncover and disseminate knowledge about the African presence in Mexico. In the 1980s and 1990s, research by Mexican, U.S., and European scholars, in conjunction with and independently of this project, has resulted in historical and anthropological studies focused on the presence of African and African-descended peoples on the Mexican landscape.

Currently, anthropologists, historians, linguists, ethnomusicologists, and others continue to explore African Mexican culture and history, and knowledge about African-descended peoples in Mexico is therefore increasing.

Select Bibliography

Aguirre Beltrán, Gonzalo, "The Integration of the Negro into the National Society of Mexico." In *Race and Class in Latin America,* edited by Magnus Mörner. New York: Columbia University Press, 1970.

_____, *La población negra de México.* 2nd edition, Mexico City: Fondo de Cultura Económica, 1972.

_____, "Introducción." In *Fracisco Xavier Clavigero, Antología.* Mexico City: Secretaría de Educación Pública, 1976.

_____, *Cuijla: Esobozo etnográfico de un pueblo negro.* Mexico City: Secretaria de Educación Pública, 1985.

_____, *El negro esclavo en Nueva España.* Mexico City: Fondo de Cultura Económica, 1994.

Bowser, Frederick, "Colonial Spanish America." In *Neither Slave nor Free: The Freedmen of African Descent in the Slave Societies of the New World,* edited by David Cohen and Jack P. Greene. Baltimore: Johns Hopkins University Press, 1972.

Carroll, Patrick, "Mandinga: The Evolution of a Mexican Runaway Slave Community, 1735–1827." *Comparative Studies in Society and History* 19:4 (1977).

_____, *Blacks in Colonial Veracruz: Race, Ethnicity and Regional Development.* Austin: University of Texas Press, 1991.

Cervantes Delgado, Roberto, "La costa chica. Indios, negros y mestizos." In *Estratificación étnica y relaciones interétnicas,* edited by Margarita Nolasco. Mexico City: INAH, 1984.

Davidson, David, "Negro Slave Control and Resistance in Colonial Mexico, 1519–1650." In *Maroon Societies,* edited by Richard Price. Baltimore: Johns Hopkins University Press, 1979.

Gerhard, Peter, "A Black Conquistador in Mexico," *Hispanic American Historical Review* 58:3 (August 1978).

Graham, Richard, editor, *The Idea of Race in Latin America: 1870–1940.* Austin: University of Texas Press, 1990.

Lewis, Laura, "Blackness, Femaleness and Self-Representation: Constructing Persons in a Colonial Mexican Court." *PoLAR: Political and Legal Anthropology Review* 18:2 (November 1995).

Martínez Montiel, Luz María, editor, *Presencia africana en México.* Mexico City: Consejo Nacional para la Cultura y las Artes, 1994.

Palmer, Colin, *Slaves of the White God: Blacks in Mexico, 1519–1650.* Cambridge, Massachusetts: Harvard University Press, 1976.

Rout, Leslie B., Jr., *The African Experience in Spanish America.* Cambridge: Cambridge University Press, 1977.

Seed, Patricia, *To Love, Honor and Obey in Colonial Mexico.* Stanford, California: Stanford University Press, 1988.

—LAURA A. LEWIS

AGIOTAJE

Agiotaje refers to the purchase of high-yield short-term securities issued by the central government in Mexico between 1827 and 1856. The purchasers of these securities are known as *agiotistas* or *prestamistas*. Their number never included more than two or three dozen. Many were peninsular Spaniards or other foreigners, but some, such as Manuel Escandón, born in Orizaba, Veracruz, were native Mexicans. The historical reputation of the *agiotistas* essentially was defined by Juan José de Corral, a treasury official who famously wrote in 1834 that the *agiotistas* were "vampires of the Treasury who work only to advance their own interests"—an evocative phrase later repeated by finance minister Guillermo Prieto as well. This view also is shared by many contemporary scholars, and even those scholars who do not completely accept this damning picture of the *agiotistas* still see them in a critical light.

As the historian Barbara Tenenbaum concludes, *agiotaje* was rooted less in political instability than in an inadequate system of public finance. As early as March 1824, prior to the establishment of the first federal republic, the Mexico City merchant house of Hartley, Green and Ruperti had lent the transitional government 30,000 pesos to be secured by a bond on the Mexico City customs house, as well as by the loan concluded only a month before with the London merchant bank of B. A. Goldschmidt and Company. Later loans were typically secured on the customs revenue of the port of Veracruz, but these were not necessarily liquid, since duties could be discharged in a variety of government notes that circulated at deep discounts.

Events in the 1830s conspired to increase fiscal pressures. 1835 was a watershed. By November 1835, the rebellious province of Texas was at war with Mexico. In late November, the Mexican government authorized a loan of 500,000 pesos for the Texas campaign. The defeat in Texas in May 1836 left the treasury exhausted. A forced loan of up to 2 million pesos was authorized in mid-June 1836 as a result. By 1837, the public debt, according to the Liberal scholar José María Luis Mora, was over 80 million pesos. In 1848, after the ruinous war with the United States, finance minister Mariano Riva Palacio estimated the whole of the public debt at more than 90 million pesos. By 1850, the national government was on the verge of open bankruptcy, and a rescheduling of the public debt was attempted but proved impracticable. Barbara Tenenbaum has found that it was the Reform Laws that ultimately paved the way for a fiscal rehabilitation of the Mexican state.

The impact of *agiotaje* on the early nineteenth-century economy has been the subject of much dispute. For Tenenbaum, *agiotaje* was a source of accumulation that found its way into estate agriculture and mining by the 1840s. The scholar David W. Walker, however, contends that *agiotaje* drained capital into unproductive speculation. In an environment of slow economic growth, the returns on speculative investments exceeded those available in industry, mining, or commerce. In modern terms, Tenenbaum believes that there was little effect on investment, while Walker regards the displacement of productive activities as nearly complete. Walker's view echoes the opinion of the day, which held that financial speculation robbed agriculture and mining of capital. Tenebaum's view more nearly coincides with recent historiography, which finds some reactivation of Mexican mining and agriculture around 1840.

In practice, however, there was a third alternative. Capital flowed abroad as well. Rosa María Meyer has found that around 1850, the *agiotista* Juan Antonio Béistegui had more than 4 million pesos invested in Spanish and French stocks and securities, railroads, banks, as well as public debt instruments. *Agiotaje* may well have depressed economic growth in Mexico, but less speculation in Mexican government paper would not necessarily have directed more capital into productive investments in Mexico.

The diplomatic and political consequences of *agiotaje* are clearer. Foreign lenders, principally British, but also Spanish and French, were deeply involved in schemes to finance, convert, or otherwise fund the internal public debt. Moratoria on payments inevitably brought diplomatic pressures and threats of foreign intervention to bear. Foreign creditors did not hesitate to use the resources of their governments to obtain better terms than those available to their Mexican counterparts. The Mexican government (or, during the Reform Wars, the Liberal and Conservative factions) signed agreements, termed "Conventions," with Great Britain in 1842, 1843, 1849, 1851, 1858, and 1859 to fund interest payments on the public debt out of customs revenues. There were agreements with France and Spain as well. Suspended interest payments on the so-called "Jecker Bonds," issued in 1858 to fund a loan to the conservatives under General Félix Zuloaga, served as one pretext for the French intervention in Mexico in 1862. Moreover, the deep involvement of Mexican *agiotistas* in the operations of the national government, including control of the Finance Ministry on more than one occasion, served to blur the line between private interest and public responsibility. This "patrimonial" notion of the state weakened one of its core institutions, the public treasury. *Agiotaje* and *agiotistas* thus compromised both national sovereignty and the existence of an autonomous Mexican state.

Select Bibliography

Formación y desarrollo de la burguesía en México, siglo xix. Mexico City: Siglo XXI, 1981.
Tenenbaum, Barbara, *The Politics of Penury: Debt and Taxes in Mexico, 1821–1856.* Albuquerque: University of New Mexico Press, 1986.
Walker, David W., *Kinship, Business, and Politics: The Martínez del Río Family in Mexico, 1823–1867.* Austin: University of Texas Press, 1986.

—RICHARD SALVUCCI

AGRARIAN POLICY

This entry includes four articles that discuss state policies in the twentieth century (and their antecedents in the nineteenth century) designed to promote more equitable access to land, water, credit, technology, and markets, and to encourage more efficient farming methods to raise the income of the small- and medium-sized farmer:

Agrarian Policy: 1821–76
Agrarian Policy: 1876–1910
Agrarian Policy: 1910–40
Agrarian Policy: 1940–96

See also Agrarismo; Agribusiness and Agroindustry; Cattle Ranching; Cochineal; Coffee; Hacienda; Henequen; Maguey; Maize; Public Works; Rancheros; Rural Economy and Society; Rural Resistance and Rebellion; Sugar

AGRARIAN POLICY: 1821–76

During the formative decades of the Mexican nation, there was no explicit concept of agrarian policy—that ideological notion developed slowly during a century of agrarian conflicts. Yet as the nation emerged from colonialism, it faced basic questions with agrarian implications: Who should own and use land? Should institutions control property? Should land support the church and community religious activities? Or should land be held only as personal property, freely subject to market forces?

Issues of state, land, and society came to the fore in the conflicts that led to Mexican Independence. During the early national decades, debates consolidated into opposition between two conflicting visions. A traditional view, rooted in colonial practices, allowed that land might be held by persons or by families, by church institutions and peasant communities, and that land use might be oriented to profit—and to the sustenance of church, community, or family. An emerging Liberal challenge demanded that property belong only to individuals, that land be a freely marketable commodity, and that the production for profit was the proper goal of land use. By the 1870s, the Liberal vision was entrenched in Mexican law. Variants of tradition, however, remained strong within Mexican culture—especially in many peasant communities. Agrarian conflicts fueled by conflicting visions of property would persist, exploding into agrarian revolution 1910.

Colonial Traditions

At the end of the colonial era, three basic types of landed property predominated in Mexico: family property, institutional property, and community property. All were debated in the politics of the early nation. All would change. Most would survive—in custom and culture, if not in law.

Rooted in Spanish law, family property developed in Mexico in the late sixteenth and early seventeenth centuries. In a context of consolidated conquest and disease-driven depopulation, the colonial regime awarded land grants, *mercedes,* to favored Spaniards. It later consolidated those awards and other irregular holdings through *composiciones,* regional inspections which, for a fee, granted titles to lands effectively occupied by colonials. Title was legally vested in persons. Inheritance was partible, with male and female heirs each gaining shares upon the death of the holder. Such holdings were family legacies, divided and reassembled in each generation. In most cases, a male patriarch combined his own properties with those of his wife—and perhaps those of other dependent relatives—and operated them as a unit, sustaining family unity while consolidating patriarchal rule. Patriarchal family property dominated among landed elites, as well as among the modest holders known as rancheros.

For a few powerful clans, family property was legally enforced through entail. Awarded by the Spanish Crown (and sometimes replicated via complex endowments sanctioned by the Catholic Church), entails made landed estates inalienable and impartible, passing to a chosen (usually male) heir in each generation. The stated aim was to preserve a family noted for service to the Crown. The reality was to consolidate landed elites, and to offer institutional sanction for patriarchal family property.

Institutional church property had no distinct legal basis during the colonial era. The regime granted some lands directly to clerical institutions. Others came as legacies from pious donors. Still others were purchased. Convents, schools, and hospitals bought and sold lands as interests and resources dictated. What distinguished institutional property was that convents, schools, and hospitals lived on; their lands did not pass periodically through inheritance and division.

Community property emerged from a colonial fusion of Mexican and Spanish traditions. Medieval Spanish towns controlled *ejidos,* pastures and woodlands available for common use. Mexican communities held all lands in common, some allocated to support state and religious functions, some serving as common woodlands, most distributed among families for cultivation. The colonial congregations of the late sixteenth and early seventeenth centuries gave Spanish legal form to Mexican traditions. Land ultimately belonged to communities, with some allocated to support local government and religious observances, some serving as common woodlands, and most held as *tierras de repartimiento* to sustain cultivation by peasant families.

The late colonial era of Boubon reform and wartime pressure affected all types of colonial landholding. Patriarchal family property was reinforced as the Crown awarded numerous titles of nobility with attached entails to create inalienable properties for those who contributed most to economic prosperity, tax receipts, and wartime funding. Church property came under attack. The state expelled the Jesuits in 1767 and took their properties, the most extensive and valuable of all church holdings. Most lands were sold to elite families, reinforcing patriarchal family property among colonial elites. The Romero de Terreros family used mining wealth to obtain the most valuable formerly Jesuit estates and consolidate three entails attached to three noble titles, the most important being that of Conde de Regla.

Community property was debated during the final colonial decades, but little changed. Enlightenment thinking challenged community property, a perspective brought to the center of Spanish discussions by Gaspar Melchor de Jovellanos' *Informe de Ley Agraria.* Wartime financial needs, beginning in the 1790s, led the colonial regime to claim cash proceeds of community lands held in village treasuries. But neither enlightenment proposals nor wartime pressures brought an assault on community landholding prior to 1810. That was one reason the colonial order faced few challenges from the indigenous peasant majority.

Early Postcolonial Policies

The Wars for Independence brought new conflicts to the issues of landed property in Mexico. The Hidalgo Revolt began the decade of insurgency in September 1810. It recruited thousands of rural insurgents, many driven by agrarian grievances in the Jalisco and the Bajío region of north-central Mexico. Yet that first mass uprising did not develop an agrarian program during its brief explosive assault on the colonial order. When insurgency re-emerged as a guerrilla movement led by José María Morelos y Pavón in the southern low country, a key demand was to end rentals of community lands to outsiders. Responding to villagers' anger that rentals denied them use of lands rightly theirs, Morelos confirmed villagers' rights to community properties. In contrast, in 1812, the Spanish liberal Constitution of Cádiz called for the abolition of separate Indian communities and the privatization of community lands. Much debate but little change came to Mexico before the abrogation of the charter in 1814. Nevertheless, a key conflict of Mexican national history had begun: villagers demanded community lands and the right to use them to sustain families and communities, while liberal intellectuals and many elites argued that all lands should become marketable private properties.

When Agustín de Iturbide led Mexicans to Independence in 1821, the Cádiz Constitution of 1812 was again in effect. Again, the consolidation of Indian communities into single municipalities led to innumerable local conflicts over control of village lands. Indigenous peasants pressed for the persistence of colonial custom, while Hispanic townsmen demanded access to newly municipal properties. Conflicts persisted without general resolution. The Spanish liberal constitution also abolished noble titles and entails. In 1812 Mexican elites had opposed that assault on their power and privilege. In 1823, with many landlords in financial crisis, the elites backing Iturbide accepted the abolition of entail. They could sell some lands to gain resources to revive the operation of others. The wealthiest of landed Mexicans lost a legal guarantee of family property. Yet customs of patriarchal rule persisted in most landed families.

The Debate over Communal Property

With the Federal Constitution of 1824, issues of municipal organization and property rights reverted to the particular states. Most maintained the end of distinct Indian communities and consolidated singular municipalities, provoking persistent local contests over the control and distribution of community lands. Most state constitutional conventions debated the abolition of all community landholding. In the state of Mexico, the most central and populous state of the federation, debates accepted that privatization would bring economic efficiency, yet the delegates decided not to act,

acknowledging threats of resistance by villagers. The state of Jalisco, pivotal in the northwest, did enact privatization, and implementation began in many municipalities during the decades that followed, although not without resistance. Many other states enacted abolition, either in constitutions or by subsequent legislation. Implementation often was blocked by villagers' resistance and the limits of state powers in times of political conflict and revenue shortages.

Institutional church property reemerged as an issue in the early Liberal regime of Valentín Gómez Farías in 1833. From that time on, Liberals increasingly attacked ecclesiastical property. Conservatives defended the church, yet demanded that the institution fund the opposition to Liberal programs. Both foes and friends of the church—which was already weakened by the expulsion of the Jesuits, Spanish usurpations of funds during the Napoleonic wars, and the disruptions of insurgency—assaulted its wealth and properties in the intensifying political conflicts of the 1830s, 1840s, and 1850s.

In the aftermath of the war against the United States in the 1840s—a decisive national defeat leading to massive loss of territory—many Mexican leaders again challenged community landholding. Few indigenous villagers had joined in defense of the nation, while massive uprisings in Yucatán, the Sierra Gorda, and the Isthmus of Tehuantepec indicated that many saw the war as an opportunity to address local grievances. National elites facing the crisis of defeat understood that many—perhaps most—peasant villagers identified little with the nation. The landed community was the economic, political, and cultural world for many. Several key states—including Mexico and Puebla—again abolished community lands. Once more, legislation announced elite goals, while resource shortages and political divisions prevented implementation. Conflict over community lands escalated without resolution.

National debates over church and community property came to a head with the Liberal reforms of the 1850s. Juan Álvarez led the 1855 Revolt of Ayutla that brought the Liberals to power. The deeply federalist leader of the state of Guerrero, who regularly responded to agrarian demands in his home region, mobilized mass support for his national political agenda. Once in Mexico City, however, the movement was captured by ideological Liberals deeply distrustful of Álvarez's popular base and agenda. By 1856 the most powerful advocate of popular rights was ousted from the Liberal regime.

With Álvarez removed, in 1856 the Liberal regime promulgated the Ley Lerdo, which abolished all corporate property, explicitly ending church and peasant community landholding. Ecclesiastical lands would be sold, with the proceeds going to the former institutional owner. Community lands devoted to governmental or religious support would be auctioned, with proceeds going to the community. The *tierras de repartimiento* held by village families would become their properties after payment of the costs of surveys and titles. The Ley Lerdo did not expropriate corporate landowners. Church institutions and community governments would receive cash for their lost properties. Peasant families would own the lands they had long cultivated under community title.

Yet the Ley Lerdo provoked deep opposition. For church institutions and community governments, it forced the sale of lands that guaranteed long-term support in exchange for a one-time payment that would be spent, sooner or later. For peasant villagers, it required payment for lands they already held, and left those lands subject to sale or seizure for debt. During 1856 and 1857, there was limited implementation of the Ley Lerdo. Some church holdings were claimed, while Conservative forces mobilized to oppose the law and the Liberal regime that imposed it. A few indigenous communities privatized their holdings, usually in the environs of major cities. Most villagers balked and blocked implementation. In October 1856, the Liberal regime responded to villagers' opposition. Believing that cost was the only reason for opposition, the regime declared peasants' subsistence plots private properties, without fee and without survey and title. The Liberals simply proclaimed *tierras de repartimiento* to be private; peasants were left with lands and no titles—a very insecure position. Nothing was resolved.

When Liberals met in constitutional convention late in 1856, they again debated agrarian issues. The privatization of church property was confirmed with little question. It made lands available to supporters while weakening key opponents of the Liberal program and regime. Community landholding provoked more discussion. Recognizing the role of popular forces in bringing them to power, and fearing mass resistance, many delegates called for some guarantee of peasant land rights. Most insisted that the Liberal goal was a Mexico of propertied small holders. Yet in the end, the Ley Lerdo, including the privatization of community lands, was incorporated into the liberal Constitution of 1857 by a solid majority vote. All property would be private, held only by individuals, and subject to market forces. If widespread modest holdings were the goal, nothing was done to limit land concentrations, or to alter already-existing large holdings. The Liberal program enabled the market to determine landholding. Competition would begin with elites holding large estates, rancheros retaining modest holdings, and peasant villagers struggling to retain small plots without clear title.

The consolidation of that program in the Constitution of 1857 provoked staunch Conservative and ecclesiastical opposition. Intense civil war followed, from 1858 to 1861. Amid that conflict, Liberal president Benito Juárez decreed the nationalization of church properties in 1859. Holdings not already privatized were claimed by the Liberal state and auctioned to the highest bidder, the proceeds supporting the war effort. Liberal victory in 1860 led to the effective end of church landholding in Mexico.

During the War of Reform from 1858 to 1861 and the fight against French occupation from 1862 to 1867, Liberal leaders backed away from alienating village lands. They could not afford to provoke peasant resistance that would cripple the war effort. In the strategic Sierra Norte de Puebla, the Liberals cultivated peasant allies, forces that proved essential to slowing and later defeating the French occupation.

The regime of Emperor Maximilian von Hapsburg, imposed by the French, further polarized agrarian debates in Mexico. Ideologically liberal, Maximilian and his French backers confirmed the alienation of church lands. Later, struggling for survival, Maximilian proclaimed his support for the persistence of peasant community lands. Yet he found no means to bring his program to rural areas.

With the expulsion of the French and the execution of Maximilian in 1867, Liberals ruled the national state unchallenged. They quickly completed the alienation of church lands, and they pressed the privatization of community lands—auctioning communal pastures, woodlands, and the holdings devoted to sustaining local governments and religious festivals, and declaring peasant family lands private properties. The Liberals alienated many peasant allies in the Sierra de Puebla and provoked insurrectionary opposition in rural regions ranging from the outskirts of Mexico City to distant provinces. The uprisings eventually were defeated, and Liberals learned that even with national victory they had to be cautious in forcing the privatization of community lands.

When Porfirio Díaz took power in 1876, Liberals had consolidated a legal regime of individual private property. They had privatized church holdings, transferring most large estates intact to supporters of the Liberal regime. Other former church properties were purchased by pious Conservatives, who aimed to maintain the lands' traditional function. Nevertheless, the issue of community lands, if decided in law, remained open to dispute and periodic conflict in reality. There would be continuing attempts at implementation under Díaz, along with persistent resistance. Peasant villagers' demands for community lands would drive the movement led by Emiliano Zapata beginning in 1910, and the uprising of Zapatistas in Chiapas in the 1990s.

See also Bourbon Reforms; Reform Laws; Water Rights in New Spain

Select Bibliography

Bazant, Jan, *The Alienation of Church Wealth in Mexico.* Cambridge and New York: Cambridge University Press, 1971.

González Navarro, Moíses, *Anatomía del poder en México, 1848–1853.* Mexico City: El Colegio de México, 1977.

Guardino, Peter, *Peasants, Politics, and the Formation of Mexico's National State: Guerrero, 1800–1857.* Stanford, California: Stanford University Press, 1996.

Hale, Charles, *Mexican Liberalism in the Age of Mora, 1821–1853.* New Haven: Connecticut, Yale University Press, 1968.

Ladd, Doris, *The Mexican Nobility at Independence, 1780–1826.* Austin: Institute of Latin American Studies, University of Texas at Austin, 1976.

Lira, Andrés, *Comunidades indígenas frente a la Ciudad de México.* Zamora: El Colegio de Michoacán, 1983.

Meyer, Jean, *La tierra de Manuel Lozada.* Mexico City: Centre d'Etudes Mexcaines et Centraméricaines, 1989.

Mejía Fernández, Miguel, *Política agraria en México en el siglo XIX*. Mexico City: Siglo XXI, 1979.

Powell, T. G., *El liberalismo y el campesinado en el centro de México, 1850–1876*. Mexico City: Secretaría de Educación Pública, 1974.

Tutino, John, *From Insurrection to Revolution in Mexico*. Princeton, New Jersey: Princeton University Press, 1986.

—JOHN TUTINO

AGRARIAN POLICY: 1876–1910

Porfirio Díaz's agrarian policy must be seen within the overall context of his times and the legacies he inherited from the past. When he seized office in 1876, prospects for development hardly could have been more daunting. The nation's integrity and survival still hung in the balance, threatened from the outside by powerful states (United States, France, and Great Britain) withholding diplomatic recognition and pursuing financial claims, and jeopardized from within by endemic disorder and centrifugal tensions between church and state, and between centralized government and federalism—with memories of the unilateral secessions of Texas and Yucatán (and the subsequent Caste War) still painfully fresh.

To compound these problems, the new president also inherited an empty treasury, a severe balance of payments deficit, a precariously weak fiscal constituency, and a prohibitive zero credit-rating abroad. Such ominous circumstances left no room for elaborate policy blueprints. Instead, the political imperatives were simple, exacting, and threefold: to secure domestic stability and national territorial integrity; which, in turn, would restore business confidence and render Mexico attractive to foreign capital; and which, commensurably, would give the Mexican presidency the scope to establish sovereignty in the face of U.S. predatory proximity with the counterweight of European investment.

Díaz was also encumbered by the Liberal tradition in Mexico and its fundamental article of faith (enshrined by Alexander von Humboldt) that the country was a cornucopia of abundant potential, frustratingly confined and concealed by archaic institutions. Liberated from the sterile grip of corporate privilege (such as held by the Catholic Church and the Indian pueblo), these Mexican resources, above all land and labor, would respond to the stimuli of individualism, self-interest, and the free market in a flourishing Jeffersonian renaissance of social harmony and economic prosperity.

Mexico's struggle for independence from Spain coincided with the spread of such Liberal ideas, and visionary faith was invested in the role of private property, especially in the ideal of the owning-occupying smallholder or homesteader. Manuel Abad y Queipo, bishop-elect of Michoacán in 1810 who was heavily influenced by the writings of both Adam Smith and Gaspar Melchor de Jovellanos, provided the fundamentals of the Liberal platform for much of the nineteenth century. The focus of his critique of New Spain was concentrated on two interconnected areas: the state of the

Indians ("groan[ing] under the weight of indigence, ignorance and abjection") and the inefficiency of the colony's hacienda agriculture in competing with the U.S. in the Cuban wheat market.

At the root of these problems lay the question of land. On the one hand Indians remained outside civil society as juridical minors and permanently trapped as individuals by the system of communal tenure bequeathed by the Laws of the Indies. On the other, land had been concentrated in the hands of an elite of criollo (Spanish-descended, Mexican-born) hacienda owners, thereby presumably providing for both the backwardness of Mexican agriculture and the perilously antagonistic divisions between rich and poor. A Liberal model of uniform civic equality founded on the broad distribution of landownership thus was perceived as capable of killing three birds with one stone: a flourishing and modern Mexican agriculture would emerge to make the most of Humboldt's cornucopia; the Indian majority would be liberated from the tyrannical shell of separation, inequality, and communal tenure; and the endemic threat of conflict and social disorder would be eclipsed by the integration of an inclusive property-holding civil society.

However, Liberal ideological limitations on the legitimate scope of state power (the state was to function only as "night-watchman") restricted legislation in the Reforma (period of Liberal rule, 1856–76) to the realm of church and village corporate ownership, leaving the great estate (already privately titled) untouched. It was assumed that unfettered forces in the new marketplace would without state assistance bring about the desired metamorphosis of the traditional, quasi-feudal hacienda. As it turned out this development was slow to take effect, and by the end of the Porfiriato the issue of the gulf between rich and poor in the countryside remained unresolved, thereby contributing to the outbreak of revolution in 1910.

The wider Liberal option had, however, accommodated an alternative measure designed to promote the emergence of a small-holding stratum in the image of the U.S. yeoman homesteader and the French rural bourgeoisie: the colonization of unclaimed state lands. This policy had its forerunners in the colonial period, when efforts were made to secure remote frontiers with loyal settlement, leading paradoxically to the crumbling of the northern territories with the loss of Texas and the U.S.-Mexican War of 1846 to 1848. Despite such setbacks, however, Liberal faith in colonization remained undaunted, and the policy was relaunched as a decree "on the occupation and alienation of unclaimed lands *(terrenos baldíos)*" by the Juárez government in 1863 while it retreated from French intervention.

Thus enacted in the midst of civil war and foreign invasion, however, this two-pronged assault on the agrarian problem had limited impact until the Porfiriato, when the unprecedented extension of state control and stability facilitated its implementation. The first main phase of agrarian policy under Díaz therefore concentrated on this general Liberal strategy of turning land into a commodity and (as elsewhere in the Americas) the mainspring for capitalist development. To this extent it is impossible to detach the agrarian policy from other related Porfirian projects similarly designed to get the engine of Mexican growth moving; increased production from the land and the subsoil to meet growing export demand for tropical crops and minerals thus was interwoven inextricably with the attraction of foreign investment and the extension and improvement of transport networks, shipping as well as railroads, international as well as national. The development model was thus all of a piece, starting and ending with land—at the outset, as a factor brought into the market as private property, precisely demarcated and legally endorsed (and thereafter traversed by the railroad), and at the conclusion, as the source of products with a value in either the domestic market or overseas.

This transfer of ownership in land from public, unchartered, and communal to private title thus has come to dominate the record of the Porfiriato. Laws passed in 1875, 1883, and 1894 to promote the titling of land and its colonization essentially were extensions of the 1863 Juárez decree, but in the context of political stability and commensurate foreign investment they had an impact far beyond the statute book and left a profound impression on the structure of Mexican land tenure and land use. Close to 39 million hectares (96 million acres) of untitled land *(terrenos baldíos)* were brought into private ownership via Porfirian contracts with surveying companies (which received in lieu of payment on the deal a third of the territory chartered). In the hope of integrating village Mexicans into the wider civil society, the process of privatizing communal land was accelerated under pressure from the central government. How far this latter attempt adhered to the Porfirian objective of rooting villagers in private property is as yet unknown, but there were clear instances of abuse leading to the transfer of communal land into elite ownership either within or outside the village.

Agrarian policy during the Porfiriato thus has been depicted largely in terms of its presumed social impact: the devastation of the Indian community and of the struggling smallholder. Viewed from the most respected accounts of the Mexican Revolution, this is the pervasive and residual impression. According to the scholar Alan Knight,

> with the coming of the Pax Porfiriana, the railways and enticing market opportunities, the attack on communal property was renewed *a outrance*. Por-

firian legislators pandered to the new territorial gluttony . . . [and] the 1880s and 1890s thus witnessed a land-grab of unprecedented proportions as "the gates were thrown open for land speculation on a huge scale." . . . The consequent agrarian problem lay at the heart of the popular revolution.

The effect of this historiography has been to subordinate the Porfiriato to the status of a prelude to revolution, and to reduce the significance of the period's growth and transformation by representing the changes as cynical pandering to the interests of the Porfirian elite and its foreign allies.

Much of this picture is the result of limited use of Porfirian sources and dependence on early, less astute studies. A vivid illustration of the patchiness of research on the Porfiriato as a crucial stage in Mexican development is that we still do not have a detailed account of the Ministerio de Fomento (the Ministry of Development), the state apparatus that presided over this project of dynamic change and set up the concessions needed for railroad construction, land surveying, and colonization.

Certain conclusions are nonetheless possible. The policy of colonizing vacant lands with European immigrants, a long-standing Liberal panacea for the problems of agricultural backwardness and civil instability, was a failure. Despite the much-vaunted appeal of Humboldt's cornucopia, Mexican attractions paled beside those of the United States, Argentina, and Brazil, and less than 5,000 foreigners were induced to settle. The original 1883 law had limited individual claims to areas of 2,500 hectares (6,000 acres) and had obliged the recipients of vacant lands to colonize them, but these requirements were removed by the revised law of 1894 in recognition of the failure of previous policies. High-profile agents of foreign interests like Percy Martin (1907) also could be found offering cautious advice against entering into such ventures, as for instance Tehuantepec land for what turned out to be largely unprofitable rubber production, while at the same time pointing up one of the key problems for the Porfirian project: access and transportation. Martin advised, "I may say that the conditions [for colonization] were exceptionally favourable . . . [but] all the free land offered was, and still is, situated many miles from any railway communication" (quoted in Hale, 1989).

The high Porfirian hopes of combining railroad development and land colonization with an infusion of European blood thus foundered on the harsh realities of the Mexican frontiers, both arid and tropical. The conduct of the regime in this attempt does, however, illuminate important aspects of its agrarian policy. In the first place it is clear that the strategy was no subterfuge for a state give-away. Innovative research by R. H. Holden shows that the Ministry of Fomento concessions were concentrated in the years before the 1894 legal amendment, and that the conditions of the contracts were adhered to strictly: only about 40 percent of companies contracted ever received lands in compensation, and where surveyors encountered local opposition or protest, Fomento typically sided with the latter rather than the surveying company, even when the conflict involved a village community.

It is also clear that the Díaz government designed the policy to raise much-needed government revenue, and that Fomento fixed the prices of vacant lands accordingly. No exceptions were made to this rule, as demonstrated by a refusal by Díaz to countenance a request from no less an ally than Evaristo Madero for a reduction in the price of state land in Coahuila and Nuevo León at the end of 1885. His letter of rejection came with the telling justification that "land prices have risen considerably and the government must take great care not to depreciate them since they amount to the only resource we have to get through these difficult times—other sources of revenue are blocked; our credit is nonexistent; commitments mount up—what else could the Government do to avoid going under?" With such pressing financial needs, compounded by the rising budgetary assignments to Fomento itself for railroads, telegraph, and mining as well as colonization projects, it is hardly surprising that Díaz took such a serious view of the sale of state lands, or that it was in this period in the mid-1880s that concessions for surveying reached their peak.

And thus, although the policy failed as a measure to foster immigration and the proliferation of a smallholding class, Díaz's strategy did yield other crucial results. The peripheral regions, for so long remote and barely part of the nation, were developed rapidly and drawn into a more integrated national market via the combined agencies of the railroads and private titling of subsoil and land. The hub of the national economy (and with it, population) shifted away from center toward the peripheries. Capitalist ranching and export agriculture boomed in Chihuahua and the northwest, even promoting important industrial investments in product processing, while at the southern extreme other export crops such as henequen, coffee, and rubber provided the basis, albeit under very different relations of production, for significant capital accumulation; in both areas the advances were conducive to infrastructural development in the prospering urban centers, such as Mérida and Ciudad Chihuahua. The policy thus made a critical contribution to the project of bringing Mexico together economically, and at the same time helped to secure the country's territorial integrity, so urgent a task, especially on the U.S. frontier.

The policy also played its part (as demonstrated in the Díaz letter above) in the government's efforts to establish a degree of much-needed fiscal stability. Increased revenue gave the regime the opportunity to finance public projects requiring major investment (such as ports, telegraph, and railroads) through Fomento and to ease the pressure on Mexican credit abroad by reducing the national debt. Important development milestones thus were passed during the Porfiriato, such as the budgetary trend to shift resources from the army to public works (reflecting in turn Díaz's determination to free Mexico from the entrenched curse of a militarized society and treasury) and the balancing of the budget for the first time in 1896.

The Porfiriato thus presided over an important and necessary agrarian transformation with export products especially to the fore. Even output for the domestic market—staple grains, beans, and chile—was boosted by demographic growth, market integration, and some limited attempts by the state to introduce new methods through government circulars and the promotion of the School of Agriculture. Here it should be noted that stereotypical accounts of the arable hacienda as archaic and traditional, unable and unwilling to meet the challenge of rising domestic demand, have perversely withstood the tide of mounting evidence that food supplies generally matched rising demand and that the source of such increases was the capitalist great estate rather than the marginalized village. It was, however, some time before the inherited, axiomatic discourse of "Humboldt's cornucopia" and the projected panaceas of railroads and colonization were exposed as inadequate prescriptions for Mexico's ills.

Manifestations of such dawning realism appeared in the mid-1890s along with the curtailment of the colonization programs. The agrarian policy thereafter emphasized other routes to agricultural modernization, such as feeder-road connections to the railways, easier credit, and a system of irrigation to compensate for the Mexican climate, but the considerable resources required to confront these problems were not available to the state until after the Revolution. Huge public investments then were made in the 1920s and 1930s to these ends, while at the same time the state intervention previously excluded by Liberalism was brought to bear on the rural inequalities in the shape of the Agrarian Reform. It is a measure of the success of Porfirian agrarian policy that it was only after these massive public investments (above all, in large-dam irrigation) had begun to bear fruit in the 1940s that the levels of national agricultural output achieved before the Revolution were restored and finally superseded.

The imperatives of Díaz's times set severe limits on his policy options: the strategy of economic development ("Order and Progress") before social integration may well have neglected the central issue of rural inequality and in turn led to the Revolution, but the important successes of the period were nonetheless significant and are all-too-easily overlooked and under-researched.

Select Bibliography

Benjamin, Thomas, and William McNellie, editors, *Other Mexicos: Essays on Rgeional Mexican History 1876–1911*. Albuquerque: University of New Mexico Press, 1984.

Hale, Charles A., *The Transformation of Liberalism in Late Nineteenth-Century Mexico*. Princeton, New Jersey: Princeton University Press, 1989.

Holden, R. H., *Mexico and the Survey of Public Lands: The Management of Modernization 1876–1911*. De Kalb: Northern Illinois University Press, 1993.

Katz, Friedrich, "Mexico: Restored Republic and Porfiriato, 1867–1910." In *The Cambridge History of Latin America*, vol. 5, edited by Leslie Bethell. Cambridge and New York: Cambridge University Press, 1986.

Knight, Alan, *The Mexican Revolution*. 2 vols., Cambridge and New York: Cambridge University Press, 1986.

Kroeber, Clifton B., *Man, Land and Water: Mexico's Farmlands Irrigation Policies 1885–1911*. Berkeley: University of California Press, 1983.

Miller, Simon, *Landlords and Haciendas in Modernizing Mexico*. Amsterdam: CEDLA, 1995.

Stevens, D.F., "Agrarian Policy and Instability in Porfirian Mexico." *The Americas* 39:2 (1982).

Wasserman, Mark, *Capitalists, Caciques, and Revolution: The Native Elite and Foreign Enterprise in Chihuahua, Mexico 1854–1911*. Chapel Hill: University of North Carolina Press, 1984.

—SIMON MILLER

AGRARIAN POLICY: 1910–40

Policies for reforming the Mexican agrarian system probably had greater potential for success between 1910 and 1940 than at any other time in Mexican history. The fall of the regime of Porfirio Díaz and the subsequent collapse of the central government between 1910 and 1913, the ensuing civil war between Revolutionary factions, and the subsequent post-Revolutionary period in which the triumphant northerners sought to reconstitute central authority provided the milieu for greater peasant participation in agrarian politics and more responsive behavior on the part of emerging elites.

When the wealthy landowner Francisco I. Madero issued his Plan of San Luis Potosí in October 1910 calling for an armed rebellion against the dictator Porfirio Díaz, he acknowledged that the question of illegal seizures of lands had to be addressed. His pledge to rectify past political policies and practices was quite nebulous, but he recognized that to legitimize himself as a Revolutionary leader and win the support of the peasantry, he had to develop policies aimed at lessening the inequities of the land tenure system. When Madero assumed the presidency in November 1911 after successfully forcing the resignation of Díaz, the peasant armies of Emiliano Zapata and Francisco Villa were still in arms in Morelos and Chihuahua anticipating the rectification of the land question. Unfortunately, Madero was unwilling and incapable of fully addressing their demands for land and better working conditions in a rural landscape where 90 percent of the peasantry had become landless. As a member of a large and highly successful northern landowning clan, Madero's approach to the agrarian problem was decidedly evolutionary and focused on rectifying past abuses rather than restructuring the existing land tenure system. He emphatically remarked, "I have always advocated the creation of small property, but that does not mean that any landowner should be despoiled of his properties." The disappearance of the small- to medium-sized landholding unit, the *rancho*, concerned him more than the elimination of the two types of communal landholding referred to as *ejidos*: town lands on the outskirts of urban settlements originally used for communal purposes and communal lands owned by Indian communities. His inability to grasp the urgency of the land question despite the continued demands of agrarian insurgents stemmed from his obsession with the notion that the democratization of Mexico would solve all other problems.

His newly created National Agrarian Commission did propose a two-pronged solution to the agrarian problem: augmentation of agricultural production and limited redistribution of land. To provide small property owners with access to land, the Department of Development promoted the sale of private land to the government, colonization projects on federal lands, and rectification of *ejido* boundaries so as to facilitate their division into individual plots. These policies failed primarily because they offered too little too late. Agrarian rebellion against the regime, which had commenced in Morelos under Zapata, now spread from the central states to the north and even down to the southern states of Campeche and the Yucatán. Peasants destroyed properties, imprisoned their landowners, and seized lands. By the end of 1912, some administration officials and legislators began to challenge the ineffectiveness of Madero's agrarian policies. From the floor of the Congress in the waning days of the administration, Luis Cabrera recommended a much bolder restructuring of the land tenure system: the insertion of the state into the agrarian reform process with powers to expropriate private lands and to reconstitute the *ejido* as a land tenure unit.

From the onset of the insurgency against Díaz, agrarian populists had demanded a much more radical approach to the solution of the agrarian problem, a solution in which the restoration of the *ejido* to the despoiled peasants was paramount. In his Plan of Ayala of November 1911, Emiliano Zapata called for the rejection of Madero's legal, evolutionary approach to solving the land problem. His plan called for the restoration of *ejido* lands, which had been illegally usurped, through the expropriation of one-third of private rural estates. It did not call for the elimination of the planter class altogether, but envisaged the coexistence of *ejido* and large estate. If the *latifundistas* (owners of large estates) were able to resist these measures, however, the Plan of Ayala called for all their lands to be expropriated. Many scholars have called the Zapatista plan fundamentally nostalgic and reactionary in its desire to recreate a traditional peasant society of a bygone era. There is no question that it set out to resurrect a traditional communal institution. Originally Zapatismo wanted to stay within the law, for the plan called for compensation to the hacienda owners. However, Zapatismo evolved into a self-supporting counter-hegemonic force challenging the administrations of Madero, Victoriano Huerta, and finally Venustiano Carranza. It came to represent an agrarian movement bent on destroying anti-agrarian regimes and creating something to take their place. Where the state had been the agent for carrying out agrarian policies in the past, Zapatismo under the 1914 Convention government returned sovereignty to the villagers, who could carry out land reform themselves by force or by legal procedures. The Agrarian Commission of the South created the formal mechanism to legitimize the restitution of *ejido* lands. In the face of landowner resistance, war was declared on the planter, as Zapatista armies occupied their estates. Some large sugar plantations and grain haciendas were turned over to army units to be run as collectives. Although Zapata did not offer a complete plan of action, his grassroots, violent approach to redressing social injustice represented one of the most powerful influences on agrarian policies long after his death.

While Zapata was an agrarian revolutionary, scholar Friedrich Katz has called the famous northern fighter, Francisco "Pancho" Villa, a mixture between social revolutionary and nineteenth-century caudillo. On the Chihuahuan frontier where military colonists had lived in constant danger of Apache attacks, the agrarian society upheld the traditions of the owners of small landholdings; the traditions included fierce independence and the desire for municipal autonomy. Villa identified with this ranchero world and its mentality, where small private property was sacrosanct and the concept of communal property was practically unknown. His agrarian decree of December 1913 had two purposes: to attack the *latifundistas* as a symbol of injustice, and to provide an immediate source of funds for his army. He immediately expropriated without compensation large holdings of the Mexican oligarchy and many Spanish immigrants. These lands were not immediately distributed as in the Zapatista-controlled regions. Two-thirds of the expropriated lands were placed under the Chihuahuan state government and one-third under individual Villista generals to provide them with revenues to sustain their armies. The law stipulated that once the Revolution triumphed, the lands would be distributed in three ways: to veterans or to their widows and orphans in the form of pensions, to villages whose lands had been seized by the *latifundistas*, and to the state government to compensate for the taxes *latifundistas* had failed to submit. Villa limited agrarian beneficiaries to two groups, his own fighters and their surviving relatives, and peasants whose land had been expropriated. Unlike the Zapatista plan, Villa's scheme did not call for immediate restoration of communal village landholdings; rather Villa saw the future to be dependent on the creation of small private property units. When land distribution took place, it was limited in scope and did not benefit all the landless peasantry. Despite these peculiar features, the promise of land made by their charismatic leader compelled thousands of peasants to join the Villista Revolutionary army. Since Villa's armies were unable to dominate the north completely, the generals of the Division of the North and state administrators never relinquished control over the expropriated estates.

The third major Revolutionary faction, the Constitutionalists headed by Venustiano Carranza, did not include agrarian reform in their plan to restore constitutional government until they had been pushed from Mexico City and forced to take refuge in the port of Veracruz in the late fall of 1914. Individual Constitutionalist generals, particularly in the Gulf states, on their own initiative had promulgated agrarian decrees during 1914 to woo popular support away from the Conventionists (Zapatistas and Villistas), but Carranza had looked askance at these measures. Under increasing military and political pressure, Carranza relented by issuing his famous Law of January 6, 1915, which contained the kernels of the most progressive agrarian policy to counter the Zapatista plan. With the stroke of a pen it declared null all alienations of lands since 1876, and it gave to peasant communities the right to petition for either the restoration or the granting of *ejido* lands. National and local agrarian commissions would process applications made by peasants living in free villages through the expropriation of adjacent lands. Since the Constitutionalists only controlled a small portion of Mexico in 1915, the law also gave military commanders and governors the right to divide (provisionally) estates and give lands to villages. Unlike the Plan of Ayala, Carranza's law viewed the re-creation of the *ejido* as a temporary, stop-gap measure to take place in conjunction with the redistribution of private plots in a time of emergency. His primary concern was the creation of a class of small property owners and the elimination of the worst abuses of large hacienda owners. Although the National Agrarian Commission did not begin functioning until 1916, the forceful expropriation of hacienda lands and the restoration and donation of *ejido* lands by local military generals in the strategic states of Yucatán, Veracruz, Tlaxcala, Sonora, and Puebla was one factor in turning the countryside away from the Conventionists and toward the Constitutionalists.

In 1917 the Constitutional Convention rewrote Carranza's weak draft of Article 27, giving the state additional authority to uphold private property but also to be the agent for implementing a legal land reform process. The maximum size of private property was now for the first time to be limited by each state government, although the sanctity of private property was upheld. Article 27 codified the Revolutionary principle that property had a social function and that the state had the right to distribute land by expropriation for the purpose of creating small properties or communal holdings. For the first time the creation of inalienable *ejidos* from expropriated land was legally recognized. The nation reasserted its dominion over subsoil rights and declared that only Mexicans had the right to own property. If foreigners wished to own properties, they could do so only by agreeing to abide by Mexican law and registering their properties. Landowners did have a legal recourse through the *amparo* (judicial staying order) to protect their properties, which suspended the expropriation process.

Once the land was expropriated, previous owners would receive compensation based on the declared tax value of the estate. Reluctantly, Carranza accepted these revisions to Article 27 in order to curry much needed rural support for his presidential bid. Once in office he elicited little interest in the National Agrarian Commission's efforts to expropriate and distribute land. For the Constitutionalist years 1916 to 1920, only 260 positive presidential resolutions were handed down to 59,848 beneficiaries for 540,000 acres. Most of these lands were located in the Federal District and Tlaxcala, where Carranza was intent on wooing peasants away from the Zapatistas. To remain on good terms with his fellow landowners, Carranza ordered the return of many haciendas taken by his generals during the civil war. Carranza was much more aggressive in his efforts to control and tax the landholdings of foreign oil companies than native *latifundistas* under Article 27. Implementing its controversial provisions on subsoil rights, his administration forced the oil companies to pay higher taxes to replenish the coffers of his financially strapped government.

When General Álvaro Obregón assumed the presidency late in 1920, the agrarian insurgents were in retreat; Zapata had been assassinated and Villa's forces had been so weakened that he did not dare leave his Chihuahuan mountain retreat. Yet agrarian revolutionaries still had high hopes that Obregón would become an active agrarian reformer. Hadn't he distributed lands to his Yaqui and Mayo troops in Sonora to keep them loyal to Constitutionalism? Didn't he establish agrarian commissions and give military possessions of *ejidos* during his campaign of 1915 against Pancho Villa? Yet after his split with Carranza, he had returned to Sonora, where he had built himself a fortune selling agricultural exports and dealing in lucrative land transactions along the border. When Obregón launched his presidential campaign, he promised not to destroy *latifundismo* but rather to create a class of small property owners to coexist alongside the hacienda owners. Obregón favored "social harmony" between the classes; class conflict was to be replaced by cooperation in his quest to pacify the countryside and to build a strong modern state.

Obregón cleverly co-opted the Zapatista leadership by appointing them to positions in his government and negotiating the disarmament of Villa's forces before his assassination in 1923. In the 1922 Agrarian Regulation, the Obregón administration established the guidelines for the implementation of Article 27. The *rancho* was favored over the *ejido,* for the former was preserved as a property as large as 360 irrigated acres or its equivalent in unirrigated lands. An *ejido* parcel could only be 7.2 to 12 irrigated acres in size. Although *ejido* land was inalienable, this land tenure unit was designed as a subsistence agrarian institution, capable of sustaining a peasant family but not able to significantly increase its farm income. Obregón's agrarian law articulated the organization and governmental structure of the *ejido,* which was placed under the supervision of the Department of Agriculture's National Agrarian Commission. Each *ejido* was to elect democratically a governing board composed of three individuals; this board, the Ejido Administrative Committee, supervised the administration of the four parts of the *ejido:* the *fundo legal* (the area the village occupies), the agricultural lands, the pastureland, and the school plot.

Land distribution proceeded excruciatingly slowly, in part because of the complexity of the legal process. Each village had to take the initiative to fill out a petition that required the collection of specific demographic and geographical data. The agrarian procedures were made more difficult because landowners conspired with many military regional commanders to disrupt the legal process through the *amparo* as well as through the use of armed force. To counter some of these roadblocks, the Department of Agriculture actively sponsored the formation of state peasant leagues to serve as pressure groups to speed land reform. Obregón's other objective in sponsoring the groups was to challenge the expanding power of the Regional Mexican Confederation of Labor (CROM), which also was organizing in the countryside. Many of these peasant leagues sponsored by Obregón created armed militias to support his administration in the rebellion of 1923. By the end of 1924, Obregón had signed 738 positive presidential resolutions that gave 4 million acres to 158,204 persons. Most land distribution occurred in the east-central states where the Zapatista movement had been most powerful.

The agrarian policies of President Plutarco Elías Calles (1924–28) favored the private over the *ejido* sector even more than Obregón's had done. His integrated approach to agrarian reform emphasized production efficiency rather than land distribution and trumpeted the advantages of agrarian capitalism over subsistence agriculture. The government encouraged private agriculture through colonization, credit, and irrigation projects. The National Agricultural Credit Bank founded to provide credit for small-scale agriculture through credit societies in fact generously doled large sums to many Callista cronies, including former president Álvaro Obregón, for large-scale commercial agricultural ventures. Expensive state-funded irrigation projects likewise advanced the fortunes of the large farmers of the northwest over the subsistence farmers of the center and south.

Calles and his administration tended to view the *ejido* as a transitional institution or training ground to prepare the *campesino* (peasant) for private ownership. The Law of Ejido Patrimony made division of *ejido* farmland into individual parcels mandatory, although *ejido* lands remained inalienable. It also curtailed the power of village agrarian officials, placing more authority in the hands of the state. Other legislation delayed the amplification process for 10 years after the original grant, while it increased landowner participation in the application process, thereby giving them additional means to block the expropriation of their lands. Although twice as much land was distributed under Calles than under

Obregón, the quality of distributed land deteriorated; it could now be either cropland or arid land. Whereas the land distributed between 1916 and 1924 was good, the land affected between 1925 and 1933 was below-average to inferior. Land distribution patterns also were linked to political criteria; most beneficiaries lived in the old Zapatista strongholds of Hidalgo, Mexico, Puebla, and the state of Mexico. By 1933, according to Eyler Simpson, 50 percent of the 4,060 *ejidos* and 59 percent of the *ejidatarios* were located in the central states.

As the Great Depression wrought havoc on the Mexican agricultural economy, Calles became increasingly convinced that the *ejido* was an anachronism to capitalist development. His enthusiasm for the French smallholding unit grew, and he came to see it as the best model for Mexico. During the Maximato (1928–34), Calles's disenchantment with the *ejido* as an efficient agricultural unit became so pronounced that he began to scale back land distribution. The year 1929 was an exception to this trend, but it seems to be primarily attributable to the seriousness of the March military revolt and the ongoing three-year Cristero Rebellion, which revealed a high level of rural dissatisfaction. Provisional president Emilio Portes Gil therefore thought it wise to increase the amount of land affected; over 4 million acres were distributed in just one year. His replacement, Pascual Ortiz Rubio, however, on instructions from the *jefe máximo* (Calles), significantly slowed land distribution, issuing stop laws to suspend the states' provisional decisions in 12 states and postponing the signing of new permanent presidential resolutions. In defiance of Calles's policies, certain reformist governors including Lázaro Cárdenas and Adalberto Tejeda quickened their granting of provisional land divisions, daring to distribute some lands without federal approval.

By 1933 widespread unemployment, the slowing of land distribution, and the heavy-handed efforts by the Callistas to disarm rural state militias and divide peasant leagues were backfiring; rural unrest and political disenchantment mounted. The reformist wing of the official National Revolutionary Party (PNR) saw the need to address the agrarian problem in its new Six Year Plan and to support a presidential candidate who had impeccable *agrarista* credentials: Cárdenas. The issuing of the Agrarian Code of 1934 was one signal of the shift in agrarian policy, for it permitted another group of peasants, the resident peons, to be eligible to petition for land for the first time, and it dropped the landowners' right to the *amparo*. On the other hand the code further bureaucratized the agrarian reform process by delegating responsibility for organization and supervision of *ejido* agrarian committees to two different state agencies: the Agrarian Department (for land issues) and the National Bank of Agricultural Credit (for economic issues).

Lázaro Cárdenas and his associates brought to the presidency in late 1934 new perspectives on the basic agrarian dilemma: how to promote the more equitable distribution of land while modernizing the agricultural sector. He adopted a different, more positive vision of the role of the *ejido*. He saw the *ejido* as a permanent economic institution that would play a key role in increased agricultural production, modernization of rural life, uplifting of the peasantry, and the future development of Mexico. The *ejido* would also serve as the training ground for the creation of an educated, pro-Cardenista, politically active peasant sector. Two new ingredients were added to the *ejido* institution by the Cárdenas administration. The concept of a collective *ejido* was introduced, which facilitated the wholesale expropriation of large capitalist estates and the grouping of *ejidos* into credit societies, or cooperatives, to run these farms as economies of scale. These collective *ejidos* would be operated by democratically elected committees that would share their land, labor, credit, and technical resources to produce for the market economy. Second, the Cardenista state provided massive financial, technical, educational, and political support for the *ejido* sector, allowing it to compete economically with the private sector. The newly created Ejido Bank supplied the credit and technical assistance to the reformed sector and supervised the credit cooperatives. These programs were complemented by those of the departments of education, communication, health, and agriculture, which funded rural schools, road construction, clinics, and agricultural extension programs to modernize the *ejido* sector.

The Cardenista agrarian policy should not been seen as a rupture with the more conservative Callista one. It evolved out of changing local and external conditions and the adaptation of radical regional agrarian ideologies experimented with in the 1920s. The depression of the 1930s had left large segments of the peasantry unemployed in La Laguna, Yucatán, and Sonora, where export agriculture had been booming. The unemployed agricultural workers wishing to improve their working conditions and to gain access to the land began to organize themselves with the assistance of Vicente Lombardo Toledano's Mexican Labor Confederation (CTM). Rural labor unrest first came to a head in May 1936 in the cotton-producing region of La Laguna, where most of the irrigated land was owned by foreign companies. The CTM-organized rural unions called a general strike when their demands were snubbed. The president felt it was necessary to intervene so as to prevent violence from erupting. Within six weeks he expropriated three-quarters of the irrigated land and one-quarter of the unirrigated land and distributed it to 30,000 *campesinos* in 226 *ejidos* and 185 credit societies. This was the first time commercial estates had been turned over almost in their entirety to agricultural workers rather than villagers. This form of expropriation also was carried out in the Yucatán and Michoacán, where serious *campesino* unrest had existed. To resolve long-standing land disputes, the administration proceeded on a more modest scale to expropriate tens of thousands of acres from large estates in Sonora, Sinaloa, and Chiapas lands.

The impact of these policies can be told through the statistics, but also by the way the peasantry became empowered with their new access to economic resources and avenues of political expression. By the end of 1940 Cárdenas had distributed more than 50 million acres to 800,000 beneficiaries. This sum represented twice as much land as had been distributed between 1917 to 1934. The land also was of better quality, and it was distributed in larger parcels or, in some instances, as an entire estate. Cárdenas's agrarian programs shifted dramatically the percentage of *ejido* landholdings. In 1930s the *ejido* sector had controlled 13.4. percent of the agricultural land, but by 1940 it controlled 47.4 percent.

The president also earmarked abundant resources for the 300 collective *ejidos* in the form of credit and technological resources so they could compete on an equal scale with small- and medium-sized private farms. In fact, collective *ejidos* proved to be just as efficient as the private sector as long as they had access to comparable resources. In 1935 the Laguna credit cooperatives received 36 of the 46 million pesos lent by the National Ejido Credit Bank. As might have been expected, these aggressive state interventions to alter land tenure patterns led landowners to organize against the Cárdenas government and to organize their own rural militias to counter the rising militancy of the farm workers. In response Cárdenas openly encouraged the organizing of rural militias, which had been disarmed during the Maximato. Approximately 60,000 *agraristas* were armed to confront farmer organizations throughout the republic.

Alongside these massive land expropriations, the Cardenistas made concerted efforts to integrate *campesino* beneficiaries, farm workers, and rancheros into a peasant branch of the official party. The formation of the National Peasant Confederation (CNC) in 1938 was the culmination of five years of political groundwork to merge the state peasant leagues into a Cardenista-controlled national peasant organization to serve as a counterweight to the CTM. The integralist Cardenista policies also recognized the need to assimilate the Indian *campesino* into a modernizing rural society and created the National Indian Institute to facilitate this endeavor.

Despite the euphoric rhetoric of pro-Cardenista sympathizer Eyler Simpson, who described the *ejido* as Mexico's "way out," there were limits to the effectiveness of Cárdenas's programs, which in many respects were the culmination of almost 30 years of agrarian policies. Yet the rapidity with which the expropriations occurred and the credit cooperatives were formed, primarily over an 18-month period in 1936 and 1937, created bureaucratic nightmares for a still-developing state ill-prepared to administer such ambitious programs. Because many landowners still retained the best lands in the unaffected parts of their estates, the success of

the Cardenista "experiment" remained contingent on the continued financial and political support of the state. A further problem was that many new landowners in the reformed sector passed from being dependents of the large landowners to dependents of the Ejido Bank. Finally, the rising resistance of landowners, urban dwellers, and foreign landowners to these agrarian policies cannot be underestimated. Coupled with these pressures were the financial and diplomatic constraints placed on Cárdenas by the nationalization of the oil industry in 1938. These political and economic factors forced the president to moderate his agrarian policies in the final two years of his administration. Land distribution remained high through 1940, but the president could no longer prioritize the land question, and no large-scale expropriations occurred after 1937. When Manuel Avila Camacho came to power in 1940, financial support to the *ejido* sector was severely curtailed, foreshadowing the demise of the collective *ejido*.

See also Confederación Nacional Campesina (CNC); Confederación Regional Obrera Mexicana (CROM); Constitution of 1917; Ejido

Select Bibliography
Aguilar Camin, Hector, and Lorenzo Meyer, *In the Shadow of the Mexican Revolution: Contemporary Mexican History 1910–1989.* Austin: University of Texas Press, 1993.

Cumberland, Charles C., *Mexican Revolution.* 2 vols., Austin: University of Texas Press, 1952–72.

González y González, Luis, *Los días del presidente Cárdenas.* Mexico City: Colegio de México, 1981.

Katz, Friedrich, *The Secret War in Mexico: Europe, the United States, and the Mexican Revolution.* Chicago: University of Chicago Press, 1981.

Knight, Alan, "The Rise and Fall of Cardenismo." In *Mexico Since Independence,* edited by Leslie Bethell. Cambridge and New York: Cambridge University Press, 1991.

Markiewicz, Dana, *The Mexican Revolution and the Limits of Agrarian Reform.* Boulder, Colorado, and London: Lynne Rienner, 1993.

Sanderson, Susan Walsh, *Land Reform in Mexico, 1910–1980.* Orlando, Florida: Academic Press, 1984.

Silva Herzog, Jesús, *El agrarismo mexicano y la reforma agraria: exposición y crítica.* Mexico City: Fondo de Cultura Económica, 1959; 2nd edition, 1964.

Simpson, Eyler Newton, *The Ejido: Mexico's Way Out.* Chapel Hill: University of North Carolina Press, 1937.

—HEATHER FOWLER-SALAMINI

AGRARIAN POLICY: 1940–96

In the period after 1940 Mexican governments sought to modernize the agricultural sector along capitalist lines while simultaneously attempting to secure political legitimacy among the peasantry. This dual strategy created a series of policy conflicts that in turn generated political struggles within the state and rural society. Since the regime owed its legitimacy to the Mexican Revolution and had consolidated itself through massive land reform in the 1930s, successive governments inevitably were forced to address agrarian demands, although their economic strategy emphasized productivity. With some exceptions, the commitment to capital accumulation clearly took primacy over that of land reform in the period between 1940 and 1988. The administration of President Carlos Salinas de Gortari (1988–94) was more explicit in this regard and carried out a series of legal and institutional reforms that reduced the state's role in the agricultural sector. The Chiapas uprising in 1994 drew attention to the social costs of these reforms and, once again in Mexico's history, demonstrated the centrality of the rural sector for the country's political and economic stability.

The post-Revolutionary land reform program of the Cárdenas administration (1934–40) laid the basis for greater integration of the rural masses into national development. This integration was led by the state, so that independent peasant organizations remained weak and unable to shape policy. The official Confederación Nacional Campesina (CNC, or National Peasant Confederation), formed in 1938, was an important pillar of support for the corporatist state until the 1980s. As a result of the state-peasant alliance in the 1930s, Cárdenas had been able to order the redistribution of over 50 million acres of land as *ejidos* (communal landholdings), equivalent to over twice as much land as had been distributed since 1917.

While many peasants benefited from land reform, the end of the Cárdenas period signaled a definitive policy shift toward capitalist modernization. Agriculture became an adjunct to the state's overriding goal of industrialization. During the 1940s and 1950s policies were designed to increase output of basic grains in order to meet growing domestic demand in urban centers, and to promote export-oriented commercial crops to generate foreign exchange for the industrialization effort. The incorporation of more land through colonization and agrarian reform also allowed the government to pursue growth-oriented policies.

The dependence of the CNC on the state became increasingly apparent after 1940, when it proved unable to limit policies favoring the private sector. In 1942 President Manuel Avila Camacho introduced an amendment to the Agrarian Code that further extended the right of private cattle ranchers to legally protect their holdings from expropriation. This was followed by another amendment in 1947 (by President Miguel Alemán) that gave all private owners the right to file an injunction against possible expropriation. Alemán also increased the size of private holdings considered to be small properties in accordance with criteria of location, soil quality, and irrigation. The shift in policy emphasis led to splits within the CNC and the formation of more independent organizations that, although unable to change national policies, did provide the basis for stronger regional representation and peasant activism. The CNC was particularly criticized for its inability to maintain official commitment to land redistribution. Most of the land that was given to peasants during the 1950s and 1960s was of poor quality and came without sufficient technical and financial support to make it profitable. The CNC functioned as a transmission belt for government policy rather than as an independent pressure group. Its local and regional leaders constituted a network of political brokers between the state and the peasantry, impeding the formation of alternative organizations by fostering patron-client relations in the provision of resources and inputs such as agricultural chemicals, technology, and credit. This role gave the CNC a degree of institutional legitimacy that allowed it to command support in spite of its evident inability to influence agrarian policy.

The political subordination of the CNC was related to the state's macroeconomic strategies. During the 1950s agriculture became a decisive component of national economic development. In this decade food output grew by 5.7 percent per year, a rate that surpassed that of all other Latin American countries. Modern agribusiness emerged, particularly in wheat and cotton, which disproportionately benefited the northwestern region and private producers. Most land reform beneficiaries *(ejidatarios)* soon found themselves unable to sustain profitability due to poor soils and unaffordable inputs and instead sought off-farm sources of income in the cities or the United States. The government invested heavily in irrigation systems, farm mechanization, improved seeds and chemical insecticides and fertilizers. These inputs tended to form a "technological package" that only a small proportion of farmers could fully use. This led to marked regional and social imbalances. Although the total land area under irrigation in Mexico grew by 21.6 percent between 1950 and 1960, the growth in the northwestern region of Sonora, Sinaloa, and Baja California was 63.3 percent. The percentage of irrigated land in private hands in these states grew from 57 percent in 1950 to 68.4 percent in 1960. Even the relatively small proportion of *ejidatarios* whose land received irrigation were unable to directly benefit because they lacked control of other components of the package, particularly finance. For example, by the end of the 1950s, approximately one-third of the irrigated *ejido* land in the Yaqui Valley of Sonora and in the Laguna region of Coahuila was rented to private entrepreneurs.

The application of Green Revolution technology similarly favored private farmers in the northern and northwestern states. New high yield strains were developed in two commercial crops, wheat and cotton, which proved successful in boosting output in irrigated areas. In contrast, the development of new varieties of maize was less successful because most maize-producing areas were located in rain-fed areas with poorer soils. The introduction of chemical inputs and modern farm machinery also discriminated against poorer farmers and southern states.

The relative neglect of small producers combined with the rapid growth of the urban population led to the loss of Mexico's food self-sufficiency in the second half of the 1960s. Output could no longer keep pace with demand, and the government turned to imports from the United States to meet the shortfall. This strategy negatively affected the trade balance at a time when Mexico's agricultural export sector also was facing protectionist barriers and depressed world commodity prices. The government of Luis Echeverría Álvarez (1970–76) attempted to stem the crisis through greater state intervention in food production and distribution. Echeverría also revived the land reform program and encouraged the organization of productive units among adjacent *ejidos* as a means of improving output and efficiency. Guaranteed prices for corn more than doubled as official policy sought to regain self-sufficiency. At the same time, several state agencies were expanded and new ones created to promote smaller farmers in the production of cash crops such as coffee and tobacco. These reforms were unsuccessful in reversing the rural crisis. The main beneficiaries of higher guaranteed prices were large private owners with irrigated land rather than small producers. Mismanagement and corruption within the new agrarian bureaucracy, particularly the Rural Credit Bank, also limited the potentially positive impact for the majority of farmers.

The administration of José López Portillo (1976–82) only turned its attention to the rural crisis after 1979, when it became apparent that the private sector would not respond to his exhortations to invest in agriculture. Mexico's food import bill grew by 150 percent in 1979–80, and nationalists in the government pointed to the dangers of allowing the United States to use food as a weapon of foreign policy. With abundant foreign exchange from the rapid increase in oil exports and private loans, the government then implemented the Sistema Alimentario Mexicana (SAM, or Mexican Food System), an ambitious plan to regain self-sufficiency in basic grains. The SAM was partly influenced by proponents of a peasant-based development strategy known as *campesinistas,* who had been critical of the urban- and export-oriented bias of previous policies. The main features of this program included guaranteed prices, preferential bank credit, and subsidies on consumption of basic food items. During 1980 the program was blessed with good rainfall and obtained a record harvest of almost 24 million tons of basic grains. Corn production increased from 8.5

million tons in 1979 to 12.4 million in 1980. However, the achievements of the SAM came to an abrupt end with the onset of Mexico's foreign debt crisis in 1982. SAM also was limited to quantitative rather than qualitative changes. The policies of López Portillo did not challenge the existing structures of economic power in the rural sector; rather, they proved a way of avoiding such confrontations. Support for rain-fed agriculture could therefore coexist with the continued concentration of productive assets by the private sector. Nevertheless, in some of the poorest marginal areas of southern Mexico, reformists within the SAM bureaucracy played an important role in opening political spaces for independent, grassroots associations of rural producers. These organizations came to challenge the traditional control exercised by the CNC, leading to varying degrees of political reform in different regions.

Under the administration of Miguel de la Madrid (1982–88), government subsidies to agriculture declined on average by 13 percent annually, after having increased by 12.5 percent per year during the 1970s. Corn producers faced higher input costs owing to devaluation of the peso. They also found that scarce credit was being increasingly directed toward animal feed crops such as sorghum or cash crops. This situation deteriorated after the signing of an anti-inflation pact in December 1987, which froze prices paid to corn producers but increased prices of farm inputs. As a result, the proportion of corn producers operating at a loss jumped from 43 percent in 1987 to 65 percent in 1988. Under de la Madrid, private landowners were also protected against redistributive policies. More certificates of nonaffectability (which exclude land from expropriation for the purpose of agrarian reform) were issued from 1982 to 1988 than in the entire period since 1934. It was clear that land reform was being wound down, although constitutional reforms would be required to officially declare its end.

The administration of Carlos Salinas de Gortari (1988–94) accelerated the neoliberal trend with a series of institutional reforms beginning in 1989. These changes were tied closely to the World Bank's prescriptions for Mexican agriculture. The World Bank conditioned the disbursement of new structural adjustment loans to a radical overhaul of the agricultural sector, recommending the privatization of state-owned enterprises and the gradual elimination of price supports and other input subsidies. The transition to the free market in rural Mexico was governed by macroeconomic decision making and the immediate objective of reducing inflation via wage and price controls and trade liberalization.

After 1989 only corn and beans continued to receive a guaranteed price. For other grains, such as sorghum, soy beans, and rice, a new pricing policy was introduced whereby prices were fixed through negotiations between government, producers, and buyers. However, the new scheme was implemented at the same time that import licenses were removed. This had catastrophic effects for many small producers. In 1990 thousands of soy bean and sorghum producers were unable to sell their crops owing to the sudden inflow of cheaper grains from the United States. Farmers in Sonora, Guanajuato, and Tamaulipas protested by seizing government warehouses and blocking highways. The lack of transitional compensation mechanisms provoked widespread criticism of the model of market integration that the Salinas government was pursuing. More independent organizations called for the creation of European-style development funds to ease the process of trade liberalization. However, as one leader remarked, "the government still treats the majority of peasants as if they were simply painted onto the landscape and can be removed at the stroke of the technocrat's brush."

Ultimately, the relative protection of corn and beans production also was subordinated to the imperatives of free trade. Despite opposition from all national peasant organizations, the two crops were included in the negotiations leading to the North American Free Trade Agreement (NAFTA). However, recognizing corn and beans as "sensitive crops" in the new free trade area, NAFTA provided for a 15-year phase-out of tariffs and import quotas. The Salinas administration justified NAFTA on the grounds that each country and region should produce those goods and services in which they have comparative advantages. This meant that over 2 million small producers in Mexico could not continue to survive as corn producers. At the beginning of the 1990s, average yields in Mexico were 1.7 tons per hectare, compared to 6.9 tons in the United States. Disparities in terms of technological development, subsidies, infrastructure, and climatological factors placed Mexican producers of basic grains at a great disadvantage. Nevertheless, the government argued that Mexico did have significant comparative advantages in the production of vegetables and fruits (particularly in the winter season) and implemented policies designed to promote the most viable and competitive sectors. In order to maintain political stability and limit the expected outmigration from more marginal areas, in 1993 the government announced a direct subsidy program (PROCAMPO). The program was designed to ameliorate the effects of bringing domestic corn prices into line with international prices and, like the NAFTA provisions, was to be phased out over a 15-year period.

In the agro-export sector comparative advantages were almost entirely based on climatic conditions and the availability of cheap labor. The other factors of production faced serious limitations. Under the Salinas administration irrigation costs rose as subsidies were removed. Less sophisticated packing techniques and poorer communications infrastructure also limited the potentially positive impact of free trade. Instead, the liberalization of trade in winter vegetables increased competition among exporters for cheap labor. Some leaders of the large producer associations pushed for reforms in the Federal Labor Law to allow them an even freer hand in the hiring of temporary workers and greater flexibility in the use of labor.

Salinas's most controversial measures concerned several major reforms to Article 27 of the Mexican Constitution of 1917, the legislation governing land tenure. The reforms,

which were passed by Congress and incorporated into a new Agrarian Law in February 1992, gave *ejidatarios* the legal right to purchase, sell, rent, or use as collateral the individual plots and communal lands that make up the *ejido*. Private companies also were allowed to purchase *ejido* land in line with the legal limits ascribed to different crops. At a maximum, a company with at least 25 individual share-holders could purchase holdings of up to 25 times the size of the individually permitted limit. The reforms also allowed for new associations between capitalists and *ejidatarios*. Finally, agrarian reform officially was ended by the deletion of those sections of Article 27 that had allowed peasants to petition the government for land redistribution. Salinas argued that there was simply no more land to distribute, and that the real challenge was to raise productivity by promoting private investment and by giving *ejidatarios* greater individual choice in their farm activities.

The reforms to Article 27 raised concerns that the sale of *ejido* land could lead to a reconcentration of property in private hands. Although the new law explicitly forbids large estates *(latifundios),* it nevertheless potentially allowed for private companies of 25 individuals to own farms of up to 2,500 hectares (6,177 acres) of irrigated land, 5,000 hectares (12,355 acres) of rain-fed land, 10,000 hectares (24,710 acres) of good quality pasture land, or 20,000 hectares (49,420 acres) of forested land.

The early results of the new legislation were neither greater private investment nor massive sales of *ejido* land. The official titling program (PROCEDE) was established in 1993 with the ambitious goal of identifying and demarcating the individual plots of all 2.5 million *ejidatarios* in the country. The program proceeded slowly owing to the multiple boundary disputes and irregularities in earlier titling procedures, which were now brought into the open. In some states the program was actively resisted by peasant organizations and communities fearful that it would lead eventually to dispossession. The armed uprising of Zapatista rebels in Chiapas in 1994 was partly detonated by the reforms to Article 27, in particular by the large backlog of land claims that the authorities had failed to implement. The Chiapas rebellion also drew attention to the social costs of the neoliberal reforms for Mexico's indigenous peoples.

The debate about Mexican rural development was rekindled by the Salinas reforms and the projected impact of NAFTA on rural livelihoods. However, the changes to Article 27 did not provoke widespread peasant opposition. The leadership of the CNC and most other organizations endorsed the reforms while calling for clearer government policies to revitalize the rural economy. In many cases this led to internal divisions as regional leaders tried to distance themselves from the Salinista reforms. In 1992 a broad array of mainly economic organizations of small producers formed a loose coalition called the New Peasant Movement. Reformist currents within the CNC and the Ministry of Agriculture and Water Resources expressed many of the same concerns as the independent organizations. However, the economic crisis in the countryside continued to deepen, and solutions to urgent financial problems were delayed. The political subordination of the CNC to the ruling party reaffirmed itself, and the reformist initiative was aborted. As a result, exasperated regional leaders complained of an ever-widening gulf between daily realities and high-level political alliances. In its race against time, the New Peasant Movement failed to consolidate, not only weakening the reformists' hand within the state but also complicating the search for unity within the fragmented peasant movement. Agrarian policy, as in the 1940s and 1950s, was subordinated to the promotion of export-oriented growth and manufacturing industry. The lack of affordable credit compounded the lack of reliable markets, plunging thousands of small- and medium-sized producers deeper into debt. The rural crisis was exacerbated by the collapse of an overvalued peso in late 1994 and the tight monetary policy adopted by the government of Ernesto Zedillo Ponce de León in 1995. During its first year the Zedillo administration continued to adopt the policies of the previous government in the face of mounting rural protests throughout the country.

See also Confederación Nacional Campesina (CNC); Ejido; Food Production, Consumption, and Policy; Zapatista Rebellion in Chiapas

Select Bibliography

Barry, Tom, *Zapata's Revenge: Free Trade and the Farm Crisis in Mexico.* Boston: South End Press, 1995.

Bartra, Roger, *Agrarian Structure and Political Power in Mexico.* Baltimore: Johns Hopkins University Press, 1993.

Fox, Jonathan, *The Politics of Food in Mexico: State Power and Social Mobilization.* Ithaca, New York: Cornell University Press, 1992.

Gates, Marilyn, *In Default: Peasants, the Debt Crisis and the Agricultural Challenge in Mexico.* Boulder, Colorado: Westview Press, 1993.

Grindle, Merilee S., *Bureaucrats, Peasants and Politicians in Mexico: A Case Study in Public Policy.* Berkeley: University of California Press, 1977.

Hewitt de Alcántara, Cynthia, *Modernizing Mexican Agriculture: Socioeconomic Implications of Technological Change 1940–70.* Geneva: United Nations Research Institute for Social Development, 1976.

_____, editor, *Economic Restructuring and Rural Subsistence in Rural Mexico: Corn and the Crisis of the 1980s.* La Jolla: Center for U.S.-Mexican Studies, University of California, San Diego, 1994.

Sanderson, Steven E., *The Transformation of Mexican Agriculture: International Structure and the Politics of Rural Change.* Princeton, New Jersey: Princeton University Press, 1986.

—Neil Harvey

AGRARISMO

Agrarismo is a concept that first was popularized during the Mexican Revolution. It was used to refer to the combative attitude of peasants struggling for land and autonomy, a reformist doctrine, and agrarian political action. Even if the name is recent, however, the phenomenon of *agrarismo* has been present in Mexican history for more than 150 years, adopting many different forms both in the countryside and the city. *Agrarismo* is one of the great currents of the social and political life of the nation.

Agrarismo is not so much a well-defined political theory as a vast, heterogeneous, and almost always radical movement whose organizing principles are the economic and social emancipation of the peasant and ranchero (independent small farmer), as well as the revalorization of their way of life. Insofar as it considers reform of agrarian structures to be a precondition for national economic and social development, *agrarismo* is a plan for national transformation. When *agrarismo* becomes part of peasant culture it becomes a seedbed for millenarianism, peasant utopias, and legends that nourish and reproduce resistance to oppression. During the Mexican Revolution, the 1920s, and the 1930s, *agrarismo* spread throughout Mexico, profoundly changing ideas about nation and nationalism. The exponents of *agrarismo* ranged from intellectuals to rural schoolteachers to middle-class politicians to Revolutionary leaders. However, the most important personalities in the development of *agrarismo* came from every segment of the Mexican peasantry—communal farmers, peons, small farmers, and tenant farmers. As *agrarismo* came to occupy a place of honor in rural Mexico, peasants, Indians, and mestizos helped popularize it in murals, literature, and later film.

Mexican history is full of plans for agrarian reform, but not all of these belong to *agrarismo*. Until the mid–twentieth century *agrarismo* included only agrarian thought that proposes the expropriation or reduction of large estates, the liquidation or the reform of the hacienda as a system, the distribution of land among rural workers, support for the peasant economy, and defense of the Indian. *Agrarismo* does not include the agrarian reforms that defended the property rights of the owners of large estates, seeking to elevate rural productivity through investment, improved agricultural techniques and technology, and the more rational use of land. Declaring themselves partisans of small property, conservative thinkers refused to countenance measures that would affect largeholdings; proposing to "elevate the Indian," they refused to acknowledge the Indian community (let alone consider that it might be an agent of change); desiring to improve work conditions on haciendas, they neglected to call for the abolition of such practices as peonage; and until the outbreak of the Mexican Revolution, conservative thinkers continued to declare themselves partisans of the modernization of the countryside while opposing peasant revolutionary movements.

Not all peasant agrarian movements were specifically *agrarista* either. Mexican history is full of great social movements in which peasants played an instrumental role, but not all of them responded to such *agrarista* ideals as Emiliano Zapata's famous call for "Land and Liberty." Moreover, there have been countless sporadic local movements that cannot entirely be associated with *agrarismo*.

Early *Agrarista* Thought

Mexican *agrarismo* has antecedents in the Spanish Enlightenment. Claiming that agricultural systems based on free small property are more productive than those based on servitude, in 1743 José del Campillo y Cossío proposed that Indians be given lands, although he believed that Indian landholdings should take the form of small property or lifetime rental rather than their traditional communal holdings. Joseph del Campillo added that *visitadores*—Crown inspectors in the Spain's colonies—should give priority to the rights of Indians. Six decades later, Manuel Abad y Queipo denounced the usurpation of village commons, the concentration of lands in Spanish hands, the precarious situation of tenant farmers on haciendas, and the extreme inequality in the countryside. He proposed that tribute and other discriminatory laws and practices be abolished, unoccupied lands be distributed free of charge among Indians and *castas* (people of mixed ancestry), and that villages be given permission to cultivate fallow lands on large estates.

The Mexican Independence leaders Miguel Hidalgo y Costilla and José María Morelos y Pavón belonged to this same current in *agrarista* thought without going much farther. Their importance in the history of *agrarismo* comes more from their having led the first great social rebellion in which peasants played a central role, paving the way for similar movements in the nineteenth century. Hidalgo advocated a ban on the rental of village commons to private parties and that the funds in community chests be restored to their original donors; Morelos advocated that the expansion of large estates be limited to two leagues (a far more radical program that attacked large properties is attributed to Morelos, but its authenticity is open to question). Although the ideas of Hidalgo and Morelos were far from *agrarista,* they opened the way for an agrarian reform more favorable to the more prosperous sectors of the peasantry.

The first thinker to develop a proto-*agrarista* ideology in independent Mexico was Severo Maldonado, a liberal priest from the state of Jalisco. Maldonado believed that the entailment of rural property should be abolished with "slow and deliberate" measures. He held that the fall of the republics of Greece and Rome was the result of excessive concentration of landed property and that democracy is possible only if based on a nation of small farmers. To reach this objective in Mexico he proposed the abolition of all laws restricting the free buying and selling of lands and the division of all lands into parcels of one-eighth of a league each. Peasants would be guaranteed a lifetime lease on the lands as long as they could get the backing of at least two other people and could pay the rent. If the peasant wanted to leave the parcel, the government would pay him for all improvements he had made on the property. Maldonado also proposed the privatization of Indian communal lands, although the lands should remain in the hands of individual members of the community.

In 1831 the Liberal ideologue José María Luis Mora proposed an important strategy, the mandatory sale of the considerable landholdings of the Catholic Church. This would dissolve a considerable fraction of Mexico's large estates without endangering the large estate as an institution. It also would abolish *diezmo,* the tithe on all agricultural production. As frequently happens, however, Mora's radical analysis did not bear fruit in a program of reforms. In 1842 a more moderate politician, Mariano Otero, claimed that the history of humanity is, in the final analysis, the history of property, and that only by reforming property could social and political life be changed. In Mexico Otero's ideas were implemented in the Liberal program of agrarian reform, a pincher strategy that sought to restrict largeholdings, dissolve peasant communities, and distribute state-held lands. The newly freed lands would be used to create a nation of small property holders. Many figures in Mexican government helped legislate and implement Otero's ideas from 1853 to 1867, among them Sebastián Lerdo de Tejada, Ponciano Arriaga, and Ignacio Vallarta. Their program tended to benefit rancheros and tenant farmers, harm communal villagers, and leave the condition of peons basically unchanged. Ecclesiastic largeholdings were dissolved, but private estates were left basically intact.

The first exhaustive study of the origins and development of landed property in Mexico was Winstano Luis Orozco's *Legislación y jurisprudencia sobre terrenos baldíos,* published in 1895. Orozco echoed the ideas of the earlier Liberal reformers, but his analysis also contained one of the earliest condemnations of private largeholdings and the policies of the government of President Porfirio Díaz. Orozco claimed that Díaz's policies represented a counterreform, abandoning the idea of small property in favor of large property (a position very much in vogue at the time) without renouncing the Liberals' project of dissolving Indian communities. In 1906 the opposition Partido Liberal Mexicano (PLM, or Mexican Liberal Party) adopted Orozco's ideas and made them part of its political program.

The most influential work in the development of *agrarismo,* however, was *Los grandes problemas nacionales* (1909) by the lawyer Andrés Molina Enríquez. Insisting that the hacienda "is not a business," Molina held that largeholdings were harmful both to the peasantry and small farmers. Molina criticized the Liberal land reforms of the mid–nineteenth century as much as Porfirio Díaz's agrarian policies, and he championed the peasant community as a stepping stone to small property. Shortly after, on the eve of the Mexican Revolution, Molina claimed that the only form of abolishing the hacienda would be a "bloody and implacable" revolution.

Early *Agrarista* Rebellions

Molina's insistence that peasant communities—and the peasantry in general—could be agents of social transformation would become a touchstone of the more populist twentieth-century *agrarismo.* However, his ideas had antecedents in the work and struggles of peasant communities in the nineteenth century. In 1849 a revolt in the Sierra Gorda (in the border region between the states of San Luis Potosí and Querétaro) demanded the conversion of haciendas with more than 1,500 inhabitants into communal villages. It also called for the abolition of sharecropping, the reduction of rents of tenant farmers, and payment in cash rather than in kind or scrip to peons. Twenty years later, a rebellion led by Manuel Orozco in Tezontepec declared that it was useless for peasants to try to regain usurped lands through legal means. Peasants should reclaim their lands forcibly.

A quite different socialist version of *agrarismo* also made an early appearance in Mexico. Perhaps the first project along these lines was proposed by Esteban Avila, the young governor of Aguascalientes, who in 1861 proposed a tax law whose consequence would have been the expropriation of all large properties—much to the consternation of hacendados, who mobilized against Avila. If Avila's plan set out in minute detail the means that would be used to expropriate large landholdings, however, it did not try to clarify the type of society it hoped to establish. This lacuna was filled in a manifesto signed eight years later by Julio López, the leader of a peasant rebellion in Chalco, a village southeast of Mexico City. López articulated a socialist peasant utopia based on the free association of egalitarian communities and the abolition of "exploitation and tyranny." Nonetheless, it was Ricardo Flores Magón, the leader of the Partido Liberal Mexicano, who first declared his opposition to the Liberal vision of a society of small farmers. Flores Magón insisted on the necessity of "uniting all land and working it in common, without bosses and without the government."

Early *agrarista* radicalism was nourished by countless other nineteenth-century peasant rebellions, ranging from the extreme north to the Yucatán Peninsula, from uprisings of single villages to rebellions that engulfed entire regions, from sporadic riots to decades-long movements that seriously questioned the legitimacy of the central state. Many of these rebellions were interwoven with the endemic battles between Liberals and Conservatives, or with the struggles between invading foreign armies and the national forces that defined the first half-century of the history of independent Mexico. Eventually the most lucid members of the governing elites began to realize that it was not possible to construct a modern, progressive, and democratic country without resolving the problem of land and the distribution of agricultural wealth. When the Mexican Revolution broke out in 1910, the central ideas of the *agrarista* movements of the next three decades already had been articulated.

Agrarismo and the Mexican Revolution

The Mexican Revolution of 1910 put *agrarismo* in the national spotlight. From its first moments it was a social revolution in which the masses articulated their own demands. The countryside was the main arena of the Revolution, and its energy came from the millions of peasants who were inspired by the idea of agrarian reform. As the author Mariano Azuela describes in his novels, agrarian reformers from the cities linked up with peasants to give *agrarismo* a profundity and a strength that it never before possessed.

The epitome of *agrarista* movements was the movement directed by Emiliano Zapata in Morelos and the surrounding states. Calling for the restitution of village lands and the distribution of a fraction of hacienda lands, the Zapatista program was not particularly radical or original. What made Zapatismo unique was the intransigence with which it defended the ideals of agrarian reform and political autonomy during its nine years of struggle. Zapata formed alliances with forces and individuals whose ideas were quite different from his own, but he never compromised his *agrarista* principles. In its land redistributions, in the organization of its armies based in peasant communities, in its defensive guerrilla tactics, and its economic measures, Zapatismo articulated and confirmed the potentialities and limits of the Mexican peasant movement, articulating a national program in which peasant communities and small farmers would play a central role. Zapata's faithfulness to his agrarian principles—quite rare among the leaders of the Mexican Revolution—would make him an inspiration for Mexican *agraristas* and revolutionaries throughout the twentieth century.

Zapatismo was not the only *agrarista* movement during the Mexican Revolution. Even if they were less persistent, successful, and important, similar uprisings occurred throughout the country. Far from being a unitary movement, the Mexican Revolution was an aggregation of hundreds of rebellions and local movements. Over the course of these movements, peasants lay siege to haciendas, occupied and worked the lands of large estates, and obligated estate owners and political bosses of the ancien régime to emigrate. Peons fled their estates to join Revolutionary armies, and tenants stopped paying their rent. Armed peasants and their leaders formed cooperatives and ran their own mills and other agricultural businesses. From the exhaustion of the old regime and the experience of armed struggle emerged a complex agrarian movement that defined the subsequent 20 years of Mexican history.

Nonetheless, not all peasant Revolutionary movements were *agrarista*. In the north, peasants sometimes became professional soldiers. In other areas Revolutionary caudillos (local strongmen) manipulated their troops to their own ends. Corruption among Revolutionary generals was quite common, and many leaders who emerged from the people quickly acquired the characteristics of the hacendados and political bosses they had supplanted—illegitimate enrichment, conspicuous consumption, authoritarianism. Many other leaders proved all too willing to form alliances with hacendados and local politicians at the cost of the peasants who had put them in power. To this we should add the innumerable criminal gangs who sowed terror without altering the agrarian structures of the ancien régime.

Spurred by the struggle of the rural masses, many moderate intellectuals ended up accepting the inevitability of an agrarian reform in the terms demanded by the peasantry. As early as December 1912 Luis Cabrera called for the liberation of villages from the political and economic pressure of haciendas, improved conditions for rural workers, and the protection of small property as a condition for the reestablishment of peace in Mexico. Given the urgency and volatility of the issue, Cabrera insisted that the government should simply expropriate large estates if need be. Many other Revolutionary leaders were compelled to accept *agrarista* demands even if they did not coincide with their own ideals. This tendency found its culmination in Article 27 of the Constitution of 1917, which declared that landed property devolved upon the nation, and that the government could expropriate land and compensate its owners where there was a clear public interest. It also proposed the necessity of equitable distribution of public wealth, the division of largeholdings, the development of small property, and the creation of new population centers with their own lands. As had happened with other plans, however, an enormous distance separated the legislation and its implementation, substantially reducing its efficacy.

The Second Generation of Revolutionary *Agrarismo*

As order was reestablished in the 1920s, it became clear that *agrarismo* had not been strong enough to bring about the triumph of its ideals. The majority of the large haciendas survived, many communities who had lost their lands had not been able to reclaim them, and peasants who had claimed land plots had not been able to obtain them. Nonetheless, nothing was the same. The balance of forces in the countryside had changed fundamentally, and none of the post-Revolutionary governors could afford to ignore peasant demands. In many areas peasants retained their arms and organization, preparing for a new round of struggles.

Instead of dissipating, the *agrarista* movement grew and generalized during the following two decades. The number of peasants willing to fight for their demands grew and a new generation of urban, middle-class leaders joined the movement, leading labor unions, peasant leagues, and local governments that favored agrarian reform. Unlike the Revolutionaries who had preceded them, this second generation of leaders was defined by its civilian orientation, its willingness to work within the administrative channels set up by the Revolutionary governments, and its efforts to institutionalize the movements they led.

The forms of *agrarista* struggle became more diverse and complex, and their influence on the national government grew. On the regional level, their development followed many different paths. If in some states *agrarismo* constituted a force that converged with local governments, in other cases it was repressed, co-opted, or destroyed. The basic unit of *agrarista* organization was the peasant community, a nucleus of peasants united by ethnic identity, kinship, and common social and religious practice. When communities were organized around land struggles, they became agrarian communities. The procedure was to form a committee that would petition the state agrarian commission for restitution or increase of their common lands, or for outright land grants.

On a regional level these communities formed "leagues of agrarian communities," where peasant representatives worked with a more or less permanent body of rural schoolteachers, minor functionaries, and technicians. These leagues quickly became the principal instrument for agrarian negotiation even as they became an arena for the various national factions that sought to control the peasant movement. In almost every part of the country, *agrarista* political parties also began to emerge, although they never formed a national peasant party (as was happening in many countries of central and eastern Europe during this period). Unions of rural workers grew more slowly, only gaining importance in specific crops such as cotton and sugar or regions such as Puebla and la Laguna.

Between 1920 and 1934 Revolutionary governments adopted an agrarian policy that was geared toward consolidating the power of the Mexican state and pacifying the countryside. Where the relation of forces demanded, they were willing to make concessions as long as they were recognized as legitimate. Nonetheless, these governments often used every resource available to divide, co-opt, and make use of *agrarista* movements. They did promulgate agrarian laws and create institutions and banks to support development in the countryside and in the most militant regions; at the same time, however, the *agrarista* movement was used to suffocate movements that questioned the legitimacy of the national state, most notably the de la Huerta Rebellion and the Cristero Rebellion. In many cases local caciques managed to use agrarian organizations to consolidate their own authoritarian power. In sum, during this period peasants received many promises, some land, and a small amount of credit and education in exchange for the autonomy they had won during the Revolution.

In the early 1920s the Partido Nacional Agrarista (PNA, or National Agrarista Party) was founded by such leading Zapatista intellectuals as Antonio Díaz Soto y Gama,

Aurelio Manrique, Gildardo Magaña, and Rafael Ramos Pedrueza. Through its affiliates in individual states, the PNA helped spur peasant demands, converting them into important local forces. In 1923 the PNA organized the first national agrarian conference, which adopted several important resolutions for the development of the *agrarista* movement: the preservation of peasant militias, amnesty for imprisoned *agrarista* militants, punishment for military officers who impeded land redistribution and harassed peasants. The congress declared that it was in favor of the implementation of agrarian legislation, the defense of peasants' right to vote, and peasant representation in elected bodies. The PNA allied itself with the government of President Álvaro Obregón but clashed with President Plutarco Elías Calles. By the end of the decade internal divisions and corruption had decreased the PNA's influence.

In the mid-1920s the Liga Nacional Campesina (National Peasant League) was formed with the support of Calles. The Liga led struggles for land grants, fought against armed groups allied with large landowners, and defended the *ejido* (village commons) as an economic and social institution. Its leaders included important members of the Communist Party, including Ursulo Galván, Guadalupe Rodríguez, and Rodolfo Fuentes López. Its program included a demand for the socialization of land and all other means of production, and its tactics included negotiation, land occupations, strikes, and sometimes armed self-defense against the army and "white guards" in the service of landowners and local officials. A multitude of local and regional peasant leagues also emerged in every part of Mexico, independent of the large national organizations.

Many of the most important agrarian struggles happened on a local or state level, as occurred in the states on Michoacán and Yucatán. In Michoacán the appointment of Francisco Múgica as governor in 1920 permitted such organizers as Primo Tapia, a former migrant who had been radicalized in the United States, and Isaac Arriaga, a rural schoolteacher, to form *agrarista* organizations. For his part Múgica distributed land, applied agrarian reform legislation, and threw his support behind the formation of *agrarista* leagues, peasant militias, and unions. He was forced to resign in 1922 after a conflict with military commanders in the state, but the Michoacán peasantry continued organizing and fighting. By the end of the 1920s Michoacán *agraristas* had founded the Federación de Obreros y Campesinos (Federation of Workers and Peasants) and the Liga de Comunidades y Sindicatos Agraristas (League of Agrarista Communities and Unions). Nonetheless, Primo Tapia was assassinated and the *agrarista* organizations of Michoacán proved unable to withstand state repression. During the Cristero Rebellion the peasants of Michoacán were divided, and the Calles government was able to mobilize the *agraristas* against the *cristeros*.

In Yucatán, Felipe Carrillo Puerto was appointed governor in 1923. One of the principal leaders of the pro-*agrarista* Partido Socialista del Sureste (PSS, or Socialist Party of the Southeast), Carrillo Puerto promulgated a num-

ber of laws in 1923 allowing the government to expropriate large estates at the request of peasant organizations. He encouraged the development of the peasant movement and land distribution, but he also tolerated corruption and abuse of power by the local caciques (political bosses) who supported him. When the de la Huerta Rebellion broke out in 1923, local hacendados allied themselves with the rebels, and Carrillo Puerto was assassinated together with several members of his family and his closest allies. In the following years the *agrarista* movement in Yucatán was repressed and the hacendados regained control of the state. A vast web of intrigues, corruption, and assassinations ended up nullifying the reforms advanced during Carrillo Puerto's government.

Apotheosis and Aftermath

From 1934 to 1940, the Mexican countryside was the scene of profound and accelerated changes. Millions of hectares were distributed among the peasantry, and new collective forms of organizing production were instituted. This was only possible thanks to the confluence of peasant struggles and the presidency of Lázaro Cárdenas, who led the process of agrarian reform with his peculiar combination of competence and audacity. During the first three years of his administration 22 million acres (9 million hectares) were redistributed, benefiting more than 800,000 peasant families. Large groups of agricultural day laborers were transformed into *ejidatarios,* members of communal agrarian villages.

At the same time that Cárdenas accelerated the distribution of land, he also promoted the unification of peasant organizations. In 1935 the Comité de Organización de la Unificación Campesina (Committee of Organizations of Peasant Unification) was formed. In many states, agrarian leagues were formed at the initiative of the president. Despite the resistance of many of the more radical sectors of the peasantry, who feared a loss of autonomy, this process of unification culminated in 1938 with the formation of the Confederación Nacional Campesina (CNC, or National Peasant Confederation). Integrated with the ruling party from the first, the CNC facilitated the subordination of the peasantry to the state.

Another Cardenista break with previous administrations was his marked support for *ejidos.* While Cárdenas's predecessors had followed the Liberal model of favoring small farmers, Cárdenas saw collective farms as a real alternative for elevating the living conditions of peasants and for increasing productivity in certain crops. In the lands expropriated in the Mexicali Valley, the Laguna region, the Yaqui Valley in Sonora, Nueva Italia in Michoacán, and the henequen region of Yucatán, *ejidos* were organized and performed well as long as they could count on support from the government. In *ejidos* buildings, machinery, credit, irrigation, and even production were organized collectively. Although *ejidos* always were in the minority among landholdings, they had an important effect on the overall environment of agrarian reform.

Cárdenas's reforms changed the very terms of the agrarian question. The peasant base of the regime grew.

Income was redistributed and agricultural production grew steadily over the next two decades. Nonetheless, not all agrarian questions were resolved, and in some parts of the country conditions remained for a new wave of *agrarista* radicalism. Moreover, between 1940 and 1952 the agrarian policy of the Mexican government did an about face. Land redistribution was considerably reduced, support to the peasant sector of the economy contracted, and state control of peasant organizations became more rigid. The following four decades demonstrated that although the conditions for mass *agrarismo* had disappeared, there still were causes for outbreaks of local radical *agrarismo*.

An important example was the Unión General de Obreros y Campesinos de México (UGOCM, or General Union of Workers and Peasants of Mexico), which was founded in 1949. Directed by the veteran labor leaders Jacinto López and Vicente Lombardo Toledano, the UGOCM was centered in the state of Sonora. Its land struggles focused on the U.S.-owned Greene Cattle Ranch, which extended on both sides of the border and contained more than 2.4 million acres (1 million hectares), in violation of the Mexican constitution. After mobilizing approximately 30,000 peasants to claim land on the Greene property, the UGOCM entered into negotiations with the agrarian department and led occupations of part of the Greene lands. On February 5, 1958, approximately 20,000 *agraristas* occupied the ranch. After more than 10 years of struggle and state repression, in 1959 part of the Greene estate was distributed, but members of the UGOCM were excluded from the settlement. The UGOCM also entered the electoral arena. In 1949 Jacinto López ran for the governorship of Sonora. Although he won the elections, the ruling party imposed its own candidate and repressed López's followers. In 1952 the UGOCM supported Lombardo Toledano's bid for the presidency. Lombardo

Toledano's subsequent rapprochement with the Mexican government led to a decline in the UGOCM.

This history repeated itself during the final three decades of the twentieth century in many other parts of Mexico. *Agrarismo* continued to use every form of struggle ranging from petitions to land occupations and strikes to armed struggle, only to be repressed or co-opted. Nonetheless, independent peasant organizations continued to exist, and in many regions they remained an important presence. The Indian uprising of January 1994 in the highlands of Chiapas demonstrated that the history of Mexican *agrarismo* has not yet ended.

See also Anarchism; Coalición Obrera Campesina Estudiantil del Istmo (COCEI); Communism; Confederación Nacional Campesina (CNC); Liberation Theology; Mexican Revolution; Partido Socialista del Sureste (PSS); Social Catholicism; Zapatista Rebellion in Chiapas

Select Bibliography

Harvey, Neil, *Rebellion in Chiapas: Rural Reforms, Campesino Radicalism and the Limits of Salinismo.* La Jolla: University of California at San Diego, 1994.
Herzog, Jesus Silva, *El agrarismo mexicano y la reforma agraria: Exposición y crítica.* Mexico City: Fondo de Cultura Económica, 1959.
Historia de la cuestión agraria mexicana. 9 vols. Mexico City: Siglo XXI, 1988.
Katz, Friederich, editor, *Riot, Rebellion and Revolution: Rural Conflict in Mexico.* Princeton, New Jersey: Princeton University Press, 1988.
Tutino, John, *From Insurrection to Revolution in Mexico: Social Bases of Agrarian Violence, 1750–1940.* Princeton, New Jersey: Princeton University Press, 1986.

—ENRIQUE SEMO

AGRIBUSINESS AND AGROINDUSTRY

To speak of agriculture in Mexico is to venture, however equivocally, into an embattled web of public and private discourse and associated domains of social and political conflict, occasionally violent, that have characterized Mexico throughout its history. Any topic that inspires political and intellectual passions has agricultural referents. The discourse on agriculture is fraught simultaneously with familiar images and sound bites of rural poverty and land hunger and the less familiar compulsions of a not merely international but globalizing economy. As Gustavo Esteva has written, drawing inspiration from the great Mexican novelist Juan Rulfo, "The protagonists of rural Mexico . . . live in a very special way:

they are never what they seem to be. . . . They are very rarely what they think they are."

Terminological Considerations

Each of the terms that comprise the discourse on agriculture reveals something of the forces and constraints that impinge upon the cultivation of foods and fibers on Mexican soil. "Agribusiness," for example, for which the Spanish equivalent *agronegocio* is used infrequently, is less a term of this discourse than it is one employed in external appraisals of efficiency and investment opportunities, as well as in studies of the factors that attract Mexican rural laborers to the United States.

Agribusiness is glossed in Spanish as *agricultura comercial* or *agricultura comercializada,* but this translation does not connote the sense of novelty and entrepreneurial spirit that agribusiness has in English. "Agroindustry" *(agroindustria),* in contrast, is recognized by all participants in the national debate. Neither term, interestingly, is mentioned in the corresponding documentation of the North American Free Trade Agreement (NAFTA).

From the perspective of agribusiness, agricultural producers are but one link in a chain, receiving inputs from distributors and yielding their products to processors and handlers, on the products' paths to global consumers. Accordingly, all links are subject to the same environmental factors, system inputs, and system controls. The very concept of agribusiness includes a tacit acceptance of the doctrine of comparative advantages, by which participants in a global economy confine themselves to that which they do best while they purchase their inputs and sell their products wherever they can obtain the best deal, all under the guiding hand of the market. These products, of course, must be acceptable in the global market. Those who speak of agribusiness often focus on the role of finance capital, especially in Mexico, where credit for cultivation has been so problematic.

The concept of agroindustry, in contrast, places emphasis upon forms of organization and transformation in the domain of production, in which humans and animals are substituted by machinery. It is not difficult to comprehend why *agroindustria* is the preferred term in the discourse on Mexican agriculture, inasmuch as it is in the transformation of agricultural products that value is added and from which foreign exchange is obtained. Agroindustry is conceptualized as a series of stages of elaboration, each of which reveals particular relations between labor and machine, even though the tendency is to focus on the final stages in the elaboration of processed foods. This focus has had tremendous consequences in Mexico, where price controls have been concentrated at the level of cultivators and producers, not that of processed foods: corn and tortilla prices have been under state regulation, but not canned goods made from corn; similarly, milk prices have been regulated, but not bottled water.

While agroindustry generally suffers during economic recessions, agribusiness actually may prosper, benefiting both from the sale of exports and the resale of imports. The price increases early in 1996 in Mexico, affecting corn, tortillas, milk, sugar, and bread (among other goods), make the proposed distinction between agribusiness and agroindustry more salient. The economic agenda of the presidential administrations in the late 1980s and 1990s can only aggravate this situation, favoring as it does finance over industry.

Both agribusiness and agroindustry, of course, are euphemisms for capitalist agriculture. The scholar Steven E. Sanderson is correct in pointing out how difficult it is in Mexico, where social and private property exist alongside each other and where the state has taken such an active role in the economy, to adequately distinguish between peasant agriculture and agribusiness. At times it seems that the topic of discussion is state policy rather than specific forms of economic organization.

This discussion of terminology leads one to a series of debating points intended to clarify the complexities of Mexican agriculture. The essential assertion behind these points is that the concepts used to resolve some ambiguities actually create others. This is particularly the case in treatments of contemporary agriculture.

One must comprehend the character of capitalist agriculture in the Mexican context. The central issue is the distinction between "capitalist" and "noncapitalist" agriculture, which in contemporary scholarship tends to be confused or conflated with the distinction between "modern" and "premodern." Agriculture and rural toilers appear as historically inert, in contrast to dynamic urban industry and laborers; only after the development of urban factories does agriculture appear to be slowly and unevenly drawn into the capitalist regime. This scenario amounts to an urban, industrial bias that obscures rather than clarifies the character of capitalist agriculture, in Mexico and elsewhere.

"Efficiency" is a particularly poor measure for capitalist agriculture, because efficiency is historically and culturally relative. What is seen as efficient today—such as the intensive use of energy derived from petroleum—may be recognized as tragically wasteful tomorrow. More than anything else, ideas about efficiency reflect particular configurations of wealth and prestige—including the enormous power of transnational agribusiness firms.

A huge discrepancy exists between the ways scholars from the United States and Mexico talk about Mexican agriculture. U.S. scholars emphasize efficiency and scale of production, with vague notions of modernity, so that only large-scale, energy-intensive, "modern" agriculture is capitalist. In contrast, Mexican scholars take capitalist configurations of wealth and prestige as their point of departure. In their view, agriculture is capitalist only if dominated by capitalist social relations of production. This is one example, among many, in which U.S. scholars miss the point about Mexico.

A corollary is that capitalist agriculture may incorporate forms of production that are not specifically capitalist. At the same time, agroindustry is capitalist only in that specifically capitalist forms of control and domination—relations of production—are exercised by transnational enterprises. In some cases, this control involves total vertical integration, but in others it involves "indirect but no less efficacious management, exercised by means of the control of certain key stages in the production process" (Rama and Vigorito, 1979). Of course, these forms of control are specific to particular crops, regions, and time periods. Some of these differences are discussed below.

Historical Background

Even during the colonial era, what we today call "agroindustry" existed, in that crops such as corn and wheat had to be processed for markets in which consumers did not grind their own meal and flour. These were not export crops; they were destined for the domestic market, not the international market and certainly not a global market. Later, other agricultural products were more easily comprehended in terms of agroindustry, such as the henequen industry of the Yucatán, which involved the International Harvester Company, and the sugar industry. And Mexico has long had its own bottling industry. But the cultivation of staple crops stubbornly resisted this kind of scholarly analysis until well into the twentieth century. The historical myopia with which agriculture is viewed, together with the notion of culture as emanating inertly from the past, has obscured intriguing evidence of earlier agribusiness operations, such as the attempt by the Ford Motor Company in the 1920s to market its automobiles as farm equipment.

Consequently, few observers talk of agribusiness, agroindustry, or agrarian capitalism before the 1940s, except in some significant research on colonial haciendas. Throughout the twentieth century, since the Revolution of 1910, the modifier "social" has had considerable salience: the *ejido* (communal village landholding) represents *social* property, in contrast to *private* property; the social sector *(sector social),* refers to mutual aid organizations in contrast to those that operate for profit; the government is conceptualized as a *social* state, implying its responsibilities to workers and consumers. Consequently, government priorities are referred to as *social* policies *(política social)* and the type of equity it promotes is *social* justice *(justicia social).*

Beginning with the presidential administration of Lázaro Cárdenas (1934–40), Mexico has embarked upon a series of programs in which the state has manipulated the supply and distribution of basic foods, particularly grains. Cárdenas established a program of public warehouses for grains, which began to be privatized 60 years later. The most important program has been CONASUPO, or the Compañía Nacional de Subsistencias Populares, inaugurated in 1961, which has attempted to balance relations between agriculture and industry by being simultaneously the buyer of grains from growers and the seller of grains to agroindustries, absorbing all costs of commercialization. Initially, CONASUPO handled only the following crops: corn, wheat, beans, rice and sorghum. Later, however, it expanded its scope. In other words, in CONASUPO the Mexican state plays agribusinessman.

How CONASUPO has fulfilled its role has evolved, depending largely upon conditions external to its operations. Initially, CONASUPO served to maintain the floundering peasant economy and to encourage agroindustrialization. When Mexico failed to feed itself in the 1970s, CONASUPO became an importer of grains. What earlier could be justified as an investment in support of both social and private sectors of the economy came to be viewed by later political administrations as a costly and unfortunate drain on finite government resources. In the mid-1990s, it seemed that CONASUPO would surrender to private enterprise its role as primary buyer and seller of Mexico's agricultural commodities.

It is worth noting that even President Lázaro Cárdenas, renowned for breathing life into the agrarian reform provisions of Mexico's Constitution of 1917, turned away from land redistribution and toward priorities of productivity in the final years of his administration. Furthermore, his immediate successors, particularly Miguel Alemán Valdés (1946–52), favored industry over agriculture and, within agriculture, individualized *ejido* plots over collective cultivation. Credit for *ejidatarios* shifted from Cárdenas's Banco Ejidal to private credit institutions.

During World War II, which fell during the presidency of Manuel Avila Camacho, the preconditions for agroindustry were established, as Mexico responded to wartime shortages by embarking upon a program of import-substitution, in which revenues from agriculture were extracted for purposes of industrialization. Private property owners sought and received *certificados de inafectabilidad,* which guaranteed that their properties would not be appropriated by the land reform.

During two decades starting in the 1950s, Mexico experienced a technical revolution in agriculture that has come to be known as the "Green Revolution." Through the development of improved varieties of traditional crops and the application of inputs such as fertilizers, herbicides, and pesticides derived from petroleum, production greatly increased in five agricultural commodities: corn, wheat, beans, sorghum, and soybeans. Green Revolution programs focused on those regions and crops that were amenable to large-scale irrigation, exacerbating regional differences, as the north emerged as the center of agribusiness and agroindustry. Sorghum, which was not a traditional Mexican crop, experienced immense increases in acreage and production. The market for this crop came from processors of animal feeds, reflecting the growth of the Mexican middle class and its demand for meat. The increasing domestic market for wheat also illustrated changes in Mexico's population, as more consumers preferred wheat-based breads and other products over the traditional tortilla made from corn. Although corn production also increased, the new varieties involved changes in taste and texture that were not readily accepted by consumers.

Although the results were astounding in terms of the yields achieved, the legacy of this technical revolution was the changed role of the Mexican state in agriculture. Owing to increased technical sophistication necessary to take full advantage of these changes, the state asserted a firmer hand in defining planting times and other inputs for the peasants who received governmental support. Agribusiness in the guise of distributors of seeds and other inputs, foreign and domestic, assumed a permanent position in Mexico's economy.

The Green Revolution coincided with renewed pressures to fulfill the agrarian demands of the Mexican Revolution, and three successive presidents—Adolfo López Mateos (1958–64), Gustavo Díaz Ordaz (1964–70), and Luis Echeverría Álvarez (1970–76)—formally distributed over 40 million hectares of land to *ejidos;* during the three previous administrations—those of Avila Camacho (1940–46), Alemán (1946–52), and Adolfo Ruiz Cortines (1952–58)—only about one-fourth as much land was redistributed. In the 1970s, much of the land that was "affected" by the agrarian reform was on the so-called "agricultural frontier," or new lands not previously under cultivation owing to poor quality, isolation, or lack of resources such as water. By the end of the 1970s, *ejido* land came to constitute about one-half of the nation's total agricultural land, reconstituting a peasant economy that the scholar Roger Bartra has conceptualized in terms of simple reproduction, from which capitalist agriculture has extracted surplus that has contributed significantly to the development (and underdevelopment) of modern Mexico.

For most contemporary discussions of Mexican agriculture, the presidency of José López Portillo (1976–83) was a watershed that inaugurated an unbroken succession of technocrats committed to the macroeconomic policies known in Mexico as "neoliberalism," based upon strict monetarist policies and the promotion of agricultural and other exports. Although some disagreement exists about the character of neoliberalism, what seems clear is that "neo" refers to the adulation of modern technology. Earlier presidencies had their technocratic features, but not based on neoliberalism, particularly not the later adherence to macroeconomic indicators at the expense of microeconomic dynamics. The presidency of Luis Echeverría, for example, witnessed numerous large-scale projects, some never completed, organized by newly established public trusts *(fideicomisos)*, with accompanying laws, regulations, and taxes, packaged in often incomprehensible technocratic jargon. The later neoliberal agenda, in contrast, contemplated a significant reduction in the state's involvement in the economy and a general withdrawal of governmental control over agricultural decision making.

In March 1980, President López Portillo introduced the Sistema Alimentario Mexicano (SAM, or Mexican Food System), which put the immense financial resources of Mexico's burgeoning petroleum industry behind a policy of food self-sufficiency. Mexico, which historically had been a net exporter of agricultural commodities, had become, especially in the 1970s, a net importer of food, particularly from the United States, trading its finite petroleum patrimony for the food it formerly grew for itself. The decision of U.S. president Jimmy Carter not to sell wheat to the Soviet Union, following the invasion of Afghanistan in 1979, revealed to Mexico how vulnerable it was in relying upon food imports from the U.S., which were given new status as political weapons, or "food power."

At the same time, López Portillo unveiled the Ley de Fomento Agropecuario (LFA, or Law of Agricultural and Livestock Promotion), which in effect introduced a new layer to Mexican agrarian structure by promoting production units comprised of private and social (i.e., *ejido*) lands and other resources. Although the SAM and the LFA seemed contradictory—one sought to support consumers, while the other sought to support producers—their combined message was that greatly increased production had to occur, in whatever units could get the job done.

The first year of the SAM yielded impressive results, but the oil glut of 1982 and the consequent devaluation of the peso meant the demise of notions of food security and the inexorable slide toward an emphasis upon food exports such as high-value fruits and vegetables to gain foreign exchange to purchase staples such as corn and beans no longer produced in Mexico in sufficient quantity. While the SAM captured most Mexicans' imagination in 1980, it was the LFA that had the greater long-term impact. Mexico, which had spurned GATT (General Agreement on Tariffs and Trade) in 1980, eagerly joined in 1986, and in 1994 implemented NAFTA, which President López Portillo had dismissed in 1981 when proposed in concept by incoming U.S. president Ronald Reagan.

After 1982, Mexican agriculture evolved in ways that scarcely were imaginable in the 1960s and 1970s. President Miguel de la Madrid attempted to revive the principles behind the SAM with his Programa Nacional de Alimentación (PRONAL, or National Food Program), but the country's weakened economy so soon after the devastation of 1982 did not permit significant resources to be dedicated to "food sovereignty." Coinciding with much of the period of the Reagan administration in the United States, the de la Madrid regime further undermined the legal status of the *ejido* and paved the way for unabashed support for capitalist agriculture in the presidency of Carlos Salinas de Gortari, by which time food security had been abandoned.

In 1988, Salinas introduced the Programa Nacional de Solidaridad (PRONASOL, or National Program of Solidarity). Over the course of Salinas's administration, this was its biggest program, dedicating immense public resources for purposes of infrastructure and services. The strategy was to increase the efficiency of the rural economy, rather than subsidize production that was then subjected to the accustomed conditions of poor roads, inadequate storage facilities, and so on. Critics saw PRONASOL as another form of state-party patronage that would be self-defeating in terms of expressed goals.

The most dramatic change was in 1992, when President Salinas proposed changes to Article 27 of Mexico's Constitution of 1917, which defined the *ejido* and called for the dismantling of the great haciendas. No other initiative in Mexican state policy has taken such a hold on the literature on Mexican agriculture since López Portillo's SAM over a decade earlier. The revised Article 27 and the new Agrarian Law now permitted commercial stock companies to own rural land and foreign investment in *ejido* operations. In a measure reminiscent of the "production units" of the earlier Law of Agricultural and Livestock Promotion, private interests were allowed to establish long-term contracts regarding *ejido* lands. One of the most abrupt changes was the alienability of *ejido* plots, previously illegal although practiced.

With these legislative changes, the end of the *ejido* could be foretold, as clearly as the abolition of the institution of slavery could be predicted by the demise of the slave trade.

Another of President Salinas's innovations was the Programa de Apoyos Directos al Campo (PROCAMPO, or Program of Direct Support for the Countryside), which he established in 1993. The intent of this program, projected to last 15 years, was support of farm income based on area planted, rather than commodities cultivated, to wean farmers from government intervention so that they would make their planting decisions based on their—and not the government's—assessment of market conditions. The seven basic commodities covered by PROCAMPO were corn, sorghum, wheat, soybeans, cotton, rice, barley, safflower, and beans. (Five of these were the same commodities featured in the Green Revolution of the 1950s through 1970s.)

In Mexico, what in the United States is called NAFTA is known as the Tratado de Libre Comercio (TLC, or Treaty for Free Trade,). The approval of this treaty required all the muscle the ruling Partido Revolucionario Institucional (PRI, or Institutional Revolutionary Party) could muster. Business leaders generally supported NAFTA/TLC, but some agribusiness sectors expressed concern about Mexico's competitiveness. Mexican corn, for example, is only about one-fourth as productive as U.S. corn on a per-acre basis. It did not take a clairvoyant to foresee the continued hemorrhage of Mexico's food security.

In the first years of NAFTA/TLC, the United States exported (among other goods) feed grains; oilseeds; processed food; high quality beef; animal genetics; dairy products; selected fruits, nuts, and vegetables; wood products; selected skins; semiprocessed leather items; livestock and poultry feeds; and wine, beer, and other alcoholic beverages. In turn, Mexico exported these agricultural products: fresh and processed tomato products, frozen broccoli and cauliflower, asparagus, melons, citrus fruits, strawberries, and fresh-cut flowers. The distinction is not perfect, but agriculture north of the Tropic of Cancer seems to have benefited most from NAFTA/TLC, while south of this line the consequences have been negative.

The inauguration of NAFTA/TLC occurred while Carlos Salinas de Gortari was president of Mexico, but it fell to President Ernesto Zedillo Ponce de León to carry out the elaborate provisions of the treaty. His response to the economic calamity of 1995 was to reinforce the policies of his predecessor, without instituting notable innovations, in spite of the growing clamor against his administration's neoliberal agenda. The *estado social* of earlier regimes gave way to *estado de derecho* (state of law) and the components of *justicia social* became *costos sociales* (social costs). Zedillo referred to the distribution of land as the "first stage" of Mexico's agrarian reform, and what he planned for subsequent stages had little if anything to do with the *agrarista* struggles of the first part of the century. Sporting his technocratic colors, Zedillo's response to the country's shortage of basic grains in 1996

included the programmed hiring of 10,000 agronomists for extension work in Mexico's countryside.

It is too early to predict the long-term consequences of NAFTA/TLC. Mexico ran a deficit in its food and fiber trade with the United States in 1994, but a surplus in 1995. A common opinion among Mexican producers is that Mexico opened itself to U.S. exports too fast and too soon. As of the mid-1990s, discord continued over exports of Mexican tomatoes, avocados, and other products.

Contemporary Issues

It may be helpful to take yet another cut through the subject matter, concentrating on the issues dominating the discourse on agribusiness and agroindustry in the mid-1990s. How these issues are dealt with will define the course of this domain of Mexican life in the remaining years to come.

Although the tendency is to think of agribusiness in terms of export crops, Mexican state policy has created a number of scenarios that have all the trappings of modern agribusiness. One intriguing scenario concerns government tortilla subsidies. President Salinas put into effect several programs, beginning in 1989, that subsidized tortillas, a mainstay of the Mexican diet, estimated at 11 tortillas per person daily. In 1995, over three billion pesos a year went toward the tortilla subsidies, with more than half going to the agroindustries (*harineras*) that reconstitute tortilla dough from corn flour (*harina*) and less than half going to traditional mills and tortilla makers that create dough (*masa*)—known as the *industria mixtamalera*—benefiting 14 million consumers, or one in six Mexicans. The government places low-cost corn at the disposition of these enterprises, which in turn provide an inexpensive product to consumers at roughly half its market value.

The controversy that emerged derives from the question of how much the *harineras* actually benefit from this subsidy. Maseca, one of the *harineras*, which operates 19 of the 26 plants in Mexico and is owned in part by the Illinois-based firm Archer Daniels Midland, denied that it or its competitors—Minsa, Agroinsa, and Hamasa—benefit from this arrangement. The *harineras* claim that their operations produce a cheaper and more abundant product and that the subsidies paid their traditional competitors retard the technical advance of the industry. They astutely avoid the role of these low-risk resources in financing their own technical advancement and in making their other products competitive in the domestic market.

The corn-flour-dough-tortilla chain has additional features that make it even more complex. Because the subsidies are generalized, not targeted to specific groups, only one-third of the funds subsidizing tortilla production reach the poor, with the other two-thirds underwriting the consumption of other social classes, or going to food industries, restaurants, or even profiteers (*coyotes*) who buy corn from CONASUPO in the Federal District and sell it elsewhere in the countryside where the retail price is higher. This phenomenon, in which agricultural commodities are purchased from state agencies such as CONASUPO and moved around to take advantage of price differentials, is referred to as "carousels" *(carruseles)*.

It is tempting to refer to the entrepreneurs who function as speculators or *acaparadores* or who overload trucks with grains to resell outside the Federal District as "agribusinessmen." The difference between traditional intermediaries, who buy local produce cheaply and manipulate supply to drive up prices, and modern intermediaries, who occupy specific links in the agribusiness chain, is a matter of technique and social definition. Both drive up consumer prices by exercising their powers. Does it make any difference to cultivators or consumers that today the intermediaries wear suits?

One response to this situation has been the proposal of an "intelligent" credit card for the poor, with which they could obtain necessary staples. This proposal, called, with tongue-in-cheek, the *pobremático* (a play on *problemática*, referring to the problem of poverty in Mexico), demonstrates the government's technocratic bent, according to which the best solution is the most efficient one, regardless of the difficulties in demarcating that part of the population eligible for this support.

Mexico has acquired a certain fame for the corporativist nature of its political system; corporativism is no less evident in the organization of agriculture. The study of agribusiness and agroindustry involves confronting a bewildering array of private and public organizations under such headings as "alliances," "chambers," "coalitions," "commissions," "councils," "confederations," "funds," "foundations," and "trusts" (respectively, *alianzas, cámaras, coaliciones, comisiones, consejos, confederaciones, fondos, fundaciones,* and *fideicomisos),* each with its distinctive acronym. A very short list of such organizations follows:

Alianza de Industriales Productores de Tortilla de
    Masa y Harina de Maíz
Alianza para la Recuperación Económica
Cámara Nacional de las Industrias Azucarera y
    Alcóholica
Coalición de Productores de Masa y Tortilla
Comisión Nacional de Zonas Aridas
Comisión Nacional de Agua
Consejo Nacional de la Pequeña Propiedad
Consejo Nacional Agropecuario
Consejo Mexicano del Café
Confederación Nacional de Productores Rurales
Fideicomiso del Mercado de Azúcar
Fideicomiso Institucionalizada con Relación a la
    Agricultura
Fondo de Desarrollo Comercial
Fundación Mexicana para el Desarrollo Rural

Although a given organization originates in either the public or private sector, it articulates with other organizations in a frankly clientelist fashion, so that sectoral plans are elaborated in negotiations between pertinent state agencies and other private and public organisms. The recombinant logic of these negotiations often makes it difficult to distinguish the forest from the trees.

A contemporary organization that is having significant impact in Mexico because it has rejected corporativist strategies is called El Barzón (referring to members' enforced idleness), which originated among ranchers and agriculturalists in northern Mexico and took as its logo the tractor. Now representing debtors from all regions and social sectors, El Barzón has engaged in civil disobedience and legal maneuvering that have forced changes in the execution of government policies. El Barzón has proposed the "acuerdo nacional para la reactivación económica, el rescate de la planta productiva y el empleo" (national accord for economic reactivization, rescue of productive works, and employment) to counter the overwhelming power differential of Mexico's recently reprivatized banking industry, especially in the wake of the devaluation of the *peso* in December 1995 and the consequent inability on the part of debtors to service their loans. The Mexican government, prioritizing monetary stability over the plight of credit-holders, has pumped billions of *pesos* into the banking industry, in support of its monetarist policies, concerned that continuing high rates of inflation will undermine any prospect of economic recovery, rather than assisting those whose collective debt is known as *la cartera vencida* (overdue portfolio).

This problem of internal debt is extremely complex and resists simplistic solutions. The debtors from 1995 and before are unable to obtain new credit because of problems in their payment records, which makes it even more difficult for them to generate surpluses for the purpose of bringing their accounts up to date. This problem is particularly acute for agriculturalists, who face the loss of their lands, because their production schedules are tied to the seasons. The banks, for their part, face problems of liquidity.

Problems of debt and the inability to acquire new credit is not the only problem facing Mexico's agriculturalists, large and small. Northern Mexico has suffered the worst drought in 55 years, resulting in loss of crops, fields left unplanted, the death of livestock, and environmental damage. Many peasants who had ventured into greater commercial exposure have reverted to subsistence agriculture, providing merely for their own consumption. As often has been said in Mexico, the drought is a natural phenomenon, but the way in which it is dealt with is eminently political.

Horizons and Perspectives

The scholar Juan Martínez-Alier has observed that the "secret" of contemporary agriculture consists in transforming petroleum into food. In most countries, this "secret" involves refurbishing depleted soils with fertilizers and combating weeds and insects with herbicides and pesticides, all derived from petroleum. Since 1980s, Mexico has played its own variation on this theme, exchanging its bountiful but finite petroleum for the food resources it once produced for itself. Under NAFTA and other international treaties, Mexico embarked upon a new path, eschewing the agrarian goals of its Revolutionary past and embracing a neoliberal agenda. In an attempt to create the impression of continuity with Mexico's Revolutionary past, President Zedillo even called his approach "social liberalism" *(liberalismo social).* Critics have pronounced the demise of the agrarian reform and struggle with new terms and rules that suggest their political elite's allegiance to international class interests rather than to a national agenda.

Arturo Warman, secretary of the agrarian reform under Presidents Salinas and Zedillo, called agroindustry *neo-latifundismo,* a term that has had currency since the 1940s, referring to the backlash against the agrarian reforms of the Cárdenas era. This parallel, between Mexico's pre-Revolutionary, post-Revolutionary, and contemporary agrarian institutions, suggests essential continuity in a domain in which policy makers and entrepreneurs tend to stress discontinuity and progress.

The full implications of this difference in perspective merit greater attention than they can be given here, but if one appreciates the continuity between the latifundia (great landed estates) of the nineteenth century and agribusiness in the late twentieth century, it seems logical to ask about possible parallels between the Científicos (technocratic policy advisers of President Porfirio Díaz) and the technocrats of a century later. This inquiry is particularly pertinent because Díaz's rule witnessed the wholesale transfer of communal lands to private hands, rending the social fabric and igniting the Revolution of 1910. In this perspective, the neo-Zapatista movement in Chiapas in the 1990s chose its name very well. In the compressed historical perspective of the mid-1990s, it may well be that the imposition of NAFTA/TLC was the last unilateral move of the Mexican executive and the PRI, given that 1994 also witnessed the eruption of the neo-Zapatista movement in Chiapas, which garnered remarkable support across Mexico and the world, specifically opposed to the neoliberal agenda of Mexico's technocratic state and the agribusiness and agroindustrial interests that threaten agricultural lands and forests in Chiapas.

While there is a marked tendency in the academic literature to assess Mexican agriculture in terms that can be described only as grim, these external evaluations should not obscure the remarkable discourse that characterizes these discussions within Mexico. As Mexicans have learned, each reported demise offers previously unrevealed opportunities for rebirth.

See also Banking and Finance; Ejido; Food Production, Consumption, and Policy; General Agreement on Tariffs and Trade (GATT); North American Free Trade Agreement (NAFTA); Neoliberalism; Rural Economy and Society; Trade and Markets

Select Bibliography

"The Agrarian Question in Mexico: A Review Essay." *Latin American Research Review* 19 (1984).

Barkin, David, and Blanca Suárez, *El complejo de granos en México.* Mexico City: Centro de Ecodesarrollo, Instituto Latinoamericano de Estudios Transnacionales, 1979.

_____, *El fin de la Autosuficiencia Alimentaria.* Mexico City: Centro de Ecodesarollo and Editorial Océano, 1985.

Bartra, Roger, *Estructura agraria y poder político en México.* Mexico City: Era, 1974; as *Agrarian Structure and Political Power in Mexico,* Baltimore, Maryland, and London: Johns Hopkins University Press, 1992.

Burbach, Roger, and Peter Rosset, *Chiapas and the Crisis of Mexican Agriculture.* Oakland, California: Institute for Food and Development Policy, 1994.

Esteva, Gustavo, *La batalla en el México rural.* 2nd edition, Mexico City: Siglo XXI, 1981; as *The Struggle for Rural Mexico,* South Hadley, Massachusetts: Bergin and Garvey, 1983.

Jáuregui, Jesús, Murilo Huschick, Hilario Itriago, and Ana Isabel García Torres, *Tabamex: Un caso de integración vertical de la agricultura.* Mexico City: Centro de Investigaciones del Desarrollo Rural and Editorial Nueva Imagen, 1980.

Martínez-Alier, Juan, "Hombres Sin Tierra." *Bicicleta* 27 (1980).

Rama, Ruth, and Raúl Vigorito, *Tradicionales en América Latina: El complejo de frutas y legumbres en México.* Mexico City: Nueva Imagen, 1979.

Sanderson, Steven E., *The Transformation of Mexican Agriculture: International Structure and the Politics of Rural Change.* Princeton, New Jersey: Princeton University Press, 1986.

Semo, Enrique, *Historia del capitalismo en México: Los orígenes, 1521–1763.* 14th edition, Mexico City: Era, 1986; as *The History of Capitalism in Mexico: Its Origins 1521–1763,* Austin: University of Texas Press, 1993.

Warman, Arturo, "El neolatifundismo Mexicano." *Comercio Exterior* 25 (1975).

Wells, Allen, *Yucatán's Gilded Age: Haciendas, Henequen, and International Harvester, 1860–1915.* Albuquerque: University of New Mexico Press, 1985.

Wessman, James W., *Peasants, Capitalists and the State: Mexico's Changing Agricultural Policies and the "Hungarian Project."* Albuquerque: Latin American Institute, The University of New Mexico, 1982.

—JAMES W. WESSMAN

AGUIRRE, LAURO

1855–1925 • Politician and Writer

Lauro Aguirre was born in Batosegachi, Chihuahua, in 1855 and died in El Paso, Texas, on January 9, 1925. After studying engineering in Mexico City, the Mexico-Guatemala International Boundaries Commission sent him to Tapachula, Chiapas, to work as an engineer. From there he moved to Jalapa, Veracruz, as a member of the Geographical Surveying Commission. Later the Development Ministry sent him to Sonora. On December 30, 1889, he married Tomasa Flores in the port of Guaymas. By then they already had five children: Eduardo, Enrique, Lauro, Juan, and Gabriel. Laura Elena, the youngest, was born after the wedding. In June 1891 Aguirre marked off the municipal territorial limits between Hermosillo and Ures. In 1892 he published *El Independiente* newspaper in El Paso, Texas.

On February 5, 1896, he published "El Plan Restaurador de la Constitución y Reformista," in which he called on the Mexican people to rebel against the regime of President Porfirio Díaz. He symbolically signed the plan in the town of Tomochic (site of a religious uprising against Porfirio Díaz in the early 1890s). The publishing of this text led to his arrest, along with that of Manual Flores Chapa the following month. In July a revolutionary movement, later to be known as the Tomochic War, broke out along the Mexico-U.S. border. On July 12, armed groups attacked the customs office at Nogales, Sonora, and staged a similar raid on August 3 in Ojinaga. And on September 14, a group of 40 revolutionaries assaulted the customs office in Palomas. Several people died in these raids, and some revolutionaries later were apprehended and identified as members of the Santa Teresa Revolutionary Party, known as the Teresistas, named after Teresa Urrea, the so-called Saint of Cabora, a popular religious and military leader.

Mexican Foreign Service documents from 1896 and 1897 link Lauro Aguirre to Teresa Urrea and other revolutionaries and journalists active along the Mexico-U.S. border, such as Manuel Guerra, Inés Ruiz, Cecilio Salinas, Rafael Ramírez, Francisco Benavides, Pomposo Ramos, and Paulino Martínez. Some of these figures were identified as spiritualists.

Aguirre settled in El Paso, Texas, early in 1896, working full-time as a journalist for *El Progresista*. From El Paso he and Teresa Urrea organized the aforementioned raids against customs offices. In March 1897, Pomposo Ramos was arrested and declared that the chief leaders of the revolutionary movement were Aguirre, Teresa Urrea, Tomás Urrea, and Ricardo Johnson.

As a consequence of political persecution, Teresa Urrea left El Paso. Aguirre, however, remained behind for several months, later resuming his propaganda activities through *El Progresista*. Years later, in 1901, he recounted the Tomochic events in *El Progresista*, under the title "Tomochic y ¡Redención!: Revoluciones recientes y futuras de México. Papel y participación en ellas de la Santa de Cabora, la Juana de Arco mexicana" (Tomochic and Redemption!: Recent and Future Revolutions of Mexico. The Role of the Saint of Cabora, the Mexican Joan of Arc). In this text he explains how several future participants in the Tomochic War also played a role in another movement led by Teresa Urrea in 1893, along with residents of Temósachic and Santo Tomás. Presumably, Lauro Aguirre also took part in this movement.

In 1906, revolutionaries led by the Flores Magón brothers organized the first attempt at a nation-wide insurrection from El Paso. At that time, Aguirre was well known in Mexico for his anti-reelectionist activities as president of the "Santiago de la Hoz" club. Chihuahua governor Enrique C. Creel kept a close watch on Aguirre and tried to have him extradited on several occasions. Finally, Creel framed Aguirre on murder charges in a small Chihuahua town, and state officials presented forged documents as evidence to U.S. authorities. Aguirre was put in a county jail for 40 days, but later was released after demonstrating that he had lived in the United States for many years.

Together with such other veteran activists as Santa Anna Pérez, Aguirre worked closely with the Magonistas and now is recognized as one of the precursors of the Mexican Revolution. On June 25, 1908, Mexican officials arrested political activist Prisciliano Silva who was found to be carrying a letter from Enrique Flores Magón to his brother Ricardo, which included several lines describing Aguirre, then a 53-year-old man:

> Lauro Aguirre is the most good-hearted person I've ever met. He's good as Christ . . . as an old, innocent Christ. . . . He's incorruptible . . . he has a pure, just and candid spirit. Don Lauro gives all of what he has. . . . He has the soul of a dove. And those who lack the patience to stand his dotage get angry at him and even become his fierce enemies. . . . Don Lauro is a good sort.

During the years of the Mexican Revolution, Aguirre kept the Mexican community in El Paso informed about the most outstanding events in the conflict between Orozquistas and Maderistas through the newspaper *El Precursor*. In 1913, he retired from political life, dedicating himself to his home and his memories. Perhaps his main accomplishments were as a journalist and a writer. His chief works were his account of the Tomochic War and a long treatise on spiritualism.

The newspaper *La Patria* of El Paso reported on January 9, 1925, the death of Lauro Aguirre in a long article under the following headline: "The old revolutionary journalist, Lauro Aguirre, died today at three o'clock. His work preceded the revolutionary movement that shed Mexican blood during 14 years. A man of virtue, he lived and died as a just man."

The account of his burial at Evergreen cemetery mentioned the presence of a great number of people, chiefly women. W. Tovar y Bueno, editor of *La Patria,* delivered a eulogy at the gravesite. He stressed Aguirre's qualities as a man who dedicated the best of his life to the struggle for liberty and democracy in Mexico during the Porfirio Díaz dictatorship.

Select Bibliography

Valadés, José C., *Porfirio Díaz contra el gran poder de Dios: La rebelión de Tomochic y Temósachic.* Mexico City: Leega-Jucar, 1985.

Vargas Valdes, Jesús, *Tomochic, la revolución adelantada.* Chihuahua: Universidad Autónoma de Ciudad Juárez, 1994.

—JESÚS VARGAS VALDEZ

AGUIRRE BELTRÁN, GONZALO

c. 1918–95 • Physician, Anthropologist, and *Indigenista*

Born in Veracruz in the waning years of the Mexican Revolution, subsequently trained in medicine at the University of Mexico, Gonzalo Aguirre Beltrán was one of the most influential Mexican ethnohistorians and anthropologists of his time. His first ethnohistorical studies of precolonial and colonial Indian society, *El señorío de Cuauhtochco* (1940) and *Luchas agrarias en México durante el Virrenato* (1940), were researched while Aguirre held a public health post in his native state, while his next major historical project, a still-classic study of Africans and their descendants in Mexico titled *La población negra de México* (1946), firmly established Aguirre's reputation as a major twentieth-century Mexican scholar. Though he continued ethnohistorical research until the moment of his death, thereafter Aguirre's career turned sharply toward the theory and practice of aiding Indian communities to integrate themselves fully in the economic, social, and political life of modern nations. Continuing a commitment toward his indigenous countrymen expressed in his previous scholarly work, inspired by his experiences in extending public health services in rural areas, and influenced by his association with the monumental figure of twentieth-century Mexican *indigenismo,* Manuel Gamio, Beltrán turned toward developing a new Indian policy of far-reaching implications.

That policy was articulated in such works by Aguirre as *Teoría y práctica de la educación indígena* (1953), *Programas de salud en la situación intercultural* (1955), and *El proceso de aculturación* (1957), and elsewhere. The most influential exposition of that policy, however, came with Aguirre's 1967 work, *Regiones de refugio.* In that internationally disseminated work translated into English as *Regions of Refuge* in 1979, Aguirre argued that in many Third World nations, Mexico included, in outlying regions with significant indigenous populations, colonial relations of political, social, and economic domination continued long after those relations had been abolished at the national level. Indigenous access to the fruits of technological progress and government programs aimed at improving the lot of indigenous populations were

both obstructed, in Aguirre's view, by the persistence of colonial-like structures at the regional level. Benevolent government action would necessarily direct itself at changing economic, political, and social relations at the regional level, the objects of such action being not only rural Indians but also the non-Indian elites of provincial centers. Only with the transformation of such regional-level colonial structures would the path be open for Indians as citizens of modern nation-states to fully enjoy the benefits of economic progress and social justice that the twentieth century had to offer.

As director of Mexico's Instituto Nacional Indigenista (INI, or National Indian Institute), Aguirre implemented his strategy through regional coordinating centers, sub-units of the institute that would, in accordance with the particular ecological, economic, cultural, and political realities, seek appropriate ways to undermine archaic, anachronistic inequalities through programs of education, public health, road construction, agricultural development, and more.

Aguirre's policies came under sharp attack in the late 1960s from a younger, Marxist-inspired generation of anthropologists, while political and budgetary crises in subsequent decades also severely strained the implementation of Aguirre's indigenist program. The new, initially radical, generation of anthropologists denounced the indigenist policies of Aguirre and others as but a veiled means of continuing the colonial domination of Mexico's Indians, while some further attacked Aguirre and his colleagues for what they called ethnocide implicit in the goal of Aguirre and others to acculturate Mexico's minorities. In such works as his 1973 *Lenguas Vernáculas: Su uso y desuso en la enseñanza* and his 1976 collection of essays, *Aguirre Beltrán: Obra polémica,* Aguirre responded forcefully yet thoughtfully to such often-undeserved attacks upon his work and the collective labor of *indigenismo,* maintaining to the end that the romantic notion that Mexico's Indians could endure as cultural and linguistic (and thereby economic and political) isolates within the Mexican nation was inimical to the welfare of both Mexican Indians and to the future of a democratic, prosperous, and just Mexican nation. While many of his principal critics rose to positions of power within the bureaucracies they once attacked, and as indigenous peoples themselves more forcefully challenged the premises of indigenist policy managed by his successors, Aguirre returned to his first passion, continuing ethnohistorical research in his native Veracruz until the moment of his death in 1995.

Select Bibliography

Aguirre Beltrán, Gonzalo, *Regions of Refuge.* Washington, D.C.: Society for Applied Anthropology, 1979.

Palerm, Angel, *Aguirre Beltrán: Obra polémica.* Mexico City: Centro de Investigaciones Superiores, Instituto Nacional de Antropología e Historia, 1976.

—PAUL SULLIVAN

AGUSTÍN I (EMPEROR OF MEXICO)

See Iturbide, Agustín de

ALAMÁN, LUCAS

1792–1853 • Politician and Historian

Lucas Alamán was born on October 18, 1792, in the province of Guanajuato. While growing up Alamán became a close friend of the mayor of the city of Guanajuato, Juan Antonio de Riaño. A broad circle of physicists, mathematicians, architects, and humanists would gather in Riaño's house. Alamán took classes in French with Riaño's wife, and through Riaño he also made the acquaintance of the priest Antonio Lavarrete, who put his library at his disposal. In Lavarrete's library Alamán was able to read books in English on world history. In the house of his cousins Septien he met two of the most important leaders of the Mexican Independence movement, Miguel Hidalgo y Costilla and the bishop Manuel Abad y Queipo. Alamán later witnessed the sack of Guanajuato by insurgent forces, which would have a lasting impact on him. As the Wars of Independence wracked Guanajuato, Alamán moved to Mexico City, and in 1812 he entered the Royal Seminary of Mining, where he studied mining and chemistry. In the same year his house was raided by the Holy Inquisition, which confiscated several of his books.

Shortly after the restoration of Fernando VII, who had been deposed by the Napoléon, Alamán left for Spain, later traveling to several other countries in Europe. While in Europe Alamán made the acquaintance of such luminaries as Servando Teresa de Mier, José María White, Benjamin Constant, Fouché, Chateaubriand, and Madame Stäel. In February 1820 Alamán returned New Spain—and to his study of classical authors such as Homer and Euripides; Spanish American authors such as Bartolomé de Las Casas, Solis, Francisco Javier Clavigero, Lorenzo Zavala, and Carlos María Bustamante; and European authors such as Shakespeare, Bossuet, Pascal, Voltaire, Montesquieu, and Rousseau.

Alamán entered public life shortly following the restoration of the liberal Spanish Constitution of Cádiz in 1820. In August the viceroy Juan Ruiz de Apodaca appointed him secretary of the Superior Health Council, although he did not have the opportunity to accomplish much in this post. Between October 1820 and February 1821 Alamán served as the representative for the province of Guanajuato in the Cortes of Cádiz, the parliamentary council of Spain and its overseas possessions mandated by the new constitution. Alamán was part of the American faction in Cádiz, which believed that the relationship between Spain and its American possessions should be one of *asociación política*—that is, Spain's overseas possessions and the various regions of Spain should have equal representation in the Cortes, and Spanish Americans should be recognized as full citizens of the Spanish Empire. Although Alamán had important disagreements with much of the American faction, he participated in the final drafting of the American position and was later nominated to be secretary of the Cortes.

The promulgation of General Agustín Iturbide's Plan of Iguala, which called for an independent Mexican empire ruled by a European monarch, and the subsequent capitulation of the Spanish viceroy Juan O'Donojú in the Treaties of Córdoba divided New Spain's representatives at the Cortes. Alamán returned to Mexico just as Iturbide entered Mexico City and proclaimed the independence of Mexico. In April 1822 Alamán was named secretary of state, although he was able to remain in the post for only two years. Nonetheless, he was named secretary of state once again in May 1824 and continued to serve intermittently until 1831. The instability of Mexican government in the first decades following Independence prevented Alamán from ever serving as secretary of state for more than a few months at a time. Nonetheless, his ideas regarding Mexican foreign policy (at least until Mexico's humiliating defeat by the United States in 1847) were marked by a certain political idealism. Between May and July 1823 he gave instructions to Guadalupe Victoria to negotiate an end to military hostilities with Spanish authorities but never to cede on the question of Independence. During the secession crisis in Texas in August 1823 his instructions were similar, as he hoped to return to the treaty signed between the United States and New Spain in 1919. The capstone of his first term as secretary of state was the signing of a treaty between Mexico and Colombia establishing a confederation between the two countries; Mexico also sought similar ties with other Spanish American countries, hoping that this new confederation, like the confederation of American states formed by England's former colonies in North America, would make each country more secure against foreign invasion. In March 1825 Alamán was able to obtain recognition from England, and in 1829–30 he traveled to Europe for a series of extremely delicate negotiations with Spain. Alamán was able to open Mexican territory to Spanish citizens in 1830 and also attempted to reestablish trade with Spain.

Despite his political idealism, Alamán is remembered most for his role in the foundation of the Conservative Party following Mexico's loss of half its national territory to the United States in 1847. The Conservative Party sought to transform Mexico into a constitutional monarchy with a European prince. Nonetheless, Alamán's monarchism was more an attempt to achieve some degree of equilibrium between Mexico and the United States than a negation of the Mexican political system. Moreover, Alamán's conservatism needs to be taken in historical perspective. Alamán participated in the federalist liberal governments of Guadalupe Victoria and Anastasio Bustamante as well as the centralist governments. His role in the drafting of the centralist Constitution of 1835–36 is quite relevant in this regard. On the one hand, Alamán played a key role in the drafting of the constitution as a member of the Conservative Council; on the other, Alamán continued to draft legislation protecting civil rights in the liberal sense of the term.

Although there were clear conservative tendencies in Alamán's thought in the 1820s and 1830s, they did not crystallize until the 1840s with the foundation of the conservative newspaper *El Tiempo* and his completion of the magisterial *Historia de México*. In the *Historia de México* Alamán combined his long-standing advocacy of centralism with a more radical conservatism. Calling for a sort of "historical constitutionalism," Alamán argued that the foundations of the Mexican nation could be found in the institutions of New Spain. He also called for a Mexican monarchy ruled by a European prince to unify Mexico against further U.S. expansionism.

Like many liberals of his time, Alamán never wanted to be a democrat. His preference for corporate political organizations and the preservation of corporate privileges were a centerpiece of his political thought. Nonetheless, his pragmatism would never allow him completely to reject representative democracy. As a young man Alamán was an enthusiastic supporter of the Constitution of Cádiz. In the 1830s Alamán rejected his earlier liberalism and advocated a more restricted franchise based on property and merit. Even in the 1850s Alamán did not reject representative government but only sought to impose further restrictions—a constitutional monarchy with a unicameral legislature with one representative per state.

As an economic theorist, the creator of economic institutions, and businessman Alamán also played a key role in the economic life of Mexico. Alamán's economic ideas tended to parallel his economic thought. He believed that the creation of a strong nation-state rested on an effective national treasury and the development of the country's national wealth. In his brief participation in the government of Guadalupe Victoria in 1823, Alamán was able to obtain a loan from the Casa Staples to alleviate the government's financial difficulties; he also unsuccessfully sought a loan from English banking houses. He also sought to separate the mining industry from the state (the mining industry had been subject to tight state control as a corporate body), but this initiative was rejected by congress. In January 1824 Alamán was named the delegate for the mining industry of Guanajuato before the Tribunal General del Cuerpo de Minería (General Tribunal of the Corporation of Mining). Later that year he organized a mining company with Mexican and English investment.

The 1830s marked an important rupture in Alamán's economic thought, as his mercantilist vision of the Mexican economy based largely on mining changed to an industrialist vision based largely on manufacturing. This new vision would continue until Alamán's death. Between August and October of 1830 Alamán dedicated himself to the creation of the Banco de Avío (Loan Bank) to promote manufacturing and agricultural production. Funds came from the government (as direct loans) and from taxes on imported cotton cloth. The bank was managed by a committee named by the government and chaired by the secretary of foreign relations—at that moment in the hands of Alamán. Alamán organized the Compañía Industrial de Celaya (Industrial Company of Celaya) to promote the cotton textile industry. When the Banco de Avío shut its doors in 1840 Alamán helped organize the Junta de Fomento Industrial (Industrial Promotion Committee) to group together Mexican entrepreneurs independently from government authorities. Within a short period of time approximately 56 committee were formed in the interior of Mexico and a Seminario de la Industria Nacional (Seminar of National Industry) to promote a "modern" vision of Mexican business and publicize the latest advances of Mexican industrialists. Alamán also unsuccessfully sought to establish vocational schools for workers and promoted trade and tariff policy that would protect vulnerable industries while lowering trade barriers for areas that needed imported machinery and raw materials.

Between November and December of 1842 Alamán drafted a law at the behest of President Nicolás Bravo regulating the Dirección General de la Industria Nacional (General Office of National Industry). Alamán based the law on the old colonial mining ordinances, although he did mandate the independence of the mining industry from the state. In the same year Alamán also was named director of the administrative committee of the department of the Federal District. President Mariano Paredes y Arriallga later asked him to create the superior council of the treasury, which would organize and safeguard state income. Nonetheless, he soon resigned that post to take up other responsibilities—congressional representative for the state of Guanajuato, director of industry for the Federal District, and director of the treasury commission. Alamán later returned to his hacienda to begin work on the *Historia de México*. He would not occupy another economic post until 1853, when he founded the ministry of public works, colonization, industry, and commerce.

Alamán also distinguished himself as a historian, and his journalistic writings in *El Universal* and *El Tiempo,* the three volumes of his *Disertaciones sobre la historia mejicana* ("Dissertations on Mexican History"; 1844–46), and the five volumes of his *Historia de México* (1846–52) are considered key in the development of Mexican historiography. The eight volumes of the *Disertaciones* and the *Historia de México* are the work of a consciousness shattered by the bloody Wars of Independence and later by the loss of half of Mexico's national territory in 1847. However, they also are a sort of epic screenplay on "the conservation and continuity of the Nation." The *Disertaciones* and *Historia de México* include Alamán's reflections on politics, social mores, forms of government, and the institutions of New Spain. However, they also are works of narrative history, including descriptions of landscapes and heroic figures in Mexican history.

In the *Disertaciones* and *Historia de México* the politician and historian are fused. For Alamán history was a way to provide an ideological foundation for the Conservative Party and formulate his political project of nation-building. Indeed, the *Historia de México* was written as a counterpoint to the *Cuadro Histórico* of Carlos María de Bustamante. If Bustamante founded his vision of Mexico in pre-Hispanic myth and the insurgent Independence movement, Alamán saw the Mexican nation as emerging from its Hispanic heritage and the harsh realities following 1847. Lucas Alamán died in Mexico City on June 2, 1853.

Select Bibliography

Ferrer de Río, Antonio, *Lucas Alamán: Su vida y escritos.* Mexico City: Jus, 1942.

González Navarro, Moisés, *El pensamiento político de Lucas Alamán.* Mexico City: El Colegio de México, 1952.

Noriega, Alfonso, *El pensamiento conservador y el conservadurismo mexicano.* Mexico City: UNAM, 1972.

Ota Mishima, María Elena, *Alamán ilustrado.* Mexico City: UNAM, 1963.

Quintanilla, Lourdes, *El nacionalismo de Lucas Alamán.* Guanajuato: Gobierno del Estado de Guanajuato, 1991.

Valadés, José C., *Alamán Estadista e Historiador.* Mexico City: Antigua Librería Robledo, José Porrúa e Hijos, 1938.

Velázquez, María del Carmen, "Lucas Alamán Historiador de México." In *Estudios de Historiografía Americana.* Mexico City: El Colegio de México, 1948.

—ISRAEL ARROYO GARCÍA

ALEMÁN VALDÉS, MIGUEL

1900–83 • President

Born on September 29, 1900, in Sayula, Veracruz, Miguel Alemán was unable to attend the schools in his hometown because of the politics of his father, a storekeeper who would eventually become a general in the Mexican Revolution. After graduating from the National School of Law in 1928, Miguel Alemán was drawn to politics. He served as the legal adviser to the Secretariat of Agriculture and Livestock (1928–30), as a justice of the Higher Tribunal of Justice of the Federal District (1930–35), as senator from the state of Veracruz (1934–36), and as governor of Veracruz (1936–39).

He was head of the presidential campaign of Manuel Avila Camacho, who, once elected, named him secretary of government (i.e., security) from 1940 to 1945.

Miguel Alemán is noted primarily for his contributions as president of the Mexican Republic (1946–52), during which time he strengthened the presidency to the point of omnipotence within the state's political structure. An unidentified writer cited by historian Howard F. Cline complained that Alemán made the executive so powerful in an unbalanced way that "from the President of the Republic alone we expect all our political norms, as well as our economic and religious ones, even to the point of settling our conjugal difficulties." At the same time Alemán is credited with diminishing the military's influence in the government as well as reducing its budget by 7 percent of government expenditures, a trend begun by previous administrations. Prior to assuming the presidency he helped reformulate the government party in 1946 into the present Partido Revolucionario Institucional (PRI, or Institutional Revolutionary Party). Membership in the party was now open to more people. The Confederación Nacional de Organizaciones Populares (CNOP, or Nacional Confederation of Popular Organizations), the old popular sector reorganized in 1943 and now composed of the growing middle class, came to dominate the PRI at the expense of labor and *campesinos* (peasants). Working through the reorganized party, middle-class and business organizations exercised increasing influence over the presidency. As a graduate of the national school of law, President Alemán shifted recruitment for the official party away from the army and the bureaucracy to graduates from the Universidad Nacional Autónoma de México (UNAM, or the National Autonomous University of Mexico). Eighty-five percent of his administration's recruits came from the universities.

Although World War II drew Mexico and the United States closer together, Alemán is credited (or castigated, depending on the observer's point of view) with building an even stronger relationship with Washington. In the presidential elections of 1946, Alemán's opponent Ezequiél Padilla, the war-time foreign minister who had worked arduously to cement firm relations with the United States, was suspiciously regarded by most Mexicans as an American "lackey." Candidate Alemán, for his part, quietly sought approval from the U.S. embassy and assured its officials that communists would find no place in his government, nor would the allies of the Marxist labor leader Vicente Lombardo Toledano. Despite nationalist rhetoric and deep distrust of the "northern colossus," Alemán turned for advice and consent to U.S. business leaders and bankers. Accepting the rhetoric for what it was, North American corporations circumvented Mexico's high tariffs by establishing subsidiaries on the other side of the border. Under Alemán, foreign capitalists found Mexico a congenial and highly profitable atmosphere in which to operate. Although not the first Mexican president to promote developmentalist programs, Alemán emphasized industry and large-scale agriculture projects.

Eager to maintain close and cordial relations with his northern neighbors, Alemán accepted U.S. president Harry Truman's invitation to visit Washington; Alemán thus became the first Mexican president to do so. In turn, Truman went to Mexico City and laid a wreath on the monument to the young cadets who had died fighting invading U.S. troops in the U.S.-Mexican War 100 years earlier. Alemán's eagerness to use the military to break strikes, purge the unions of communists, and support the United States in its cold war with the Soviets, earned his country rewards in the form of export-import bank loans and U.S. confidence in its neighbor to the south.

Although his government signed the Inter-American Treaty of Reciprocal Assistance at Rio de Janeiro in 1947 (by which treaty an attack against one American state would be regarded as an attack against all), Alemán refused U.S. military assistance during the Korean War, which would have obligated Mexico to help defend so-called democratic institutions. Alemán already faced a storm of criticism from those who feared that his invitation of foreign capitalists back into Mexico would lead to outside economic domination; to be obligated to intervene militarily in neighboring states because the United States feared "democratic institutions" were in danger would have been a betrayal of Mexico's traditional principle of nonintervention. In his dealings with the United States, Alemán succeeded in extending the Bracero Program, by which landless Mexicans legally could migrate to the United States in search of work, taking pressure off the Mexican government to find them land and remitting dollars to shore up the sagging peso. The United States also spent $20 million to eradicate hoof and mouth disease and agreed to buy Mexican pesos to further strengthen the currency.

Handsome, robustly built, energetic, and smooth, Alemán was Mexico's first civilian president since the overthrow and assassination of Francisco I. Madero in 1913. Alemán represented a break with the past and symbolized a new dynamic and profitable future, especially for the Mexican bourgeoisie and their foreign partners. While expounding Revolutionary rhetoric, the former disciple of Lázaro Cárdenas and labor lawyer purged from public office reformers, radicals, and communists. Turning his back on the rural poor, Alemán poured his energies into public works that would benefit the middle and upper classes. Blessed with a dollar-enriched treasury filled with war-time credits from the United States, Alemán embarked upon construction projects designed to meet the needs of the new industrialists. Huge hydroelectric projects harnessed rivers for electricity, flood control, and irrigation. By 1952 the country's electrical output capacity had tripled, and hundreds of thousands of acres of land had been brought under cultivation in the arid northwest. The government modernized the railway system, built thousands of miles of new all-weather roads, improved the communications network, and avidly catered to the expanding tourist industry. Over 400,000 U.S. tourists visited Mexico in 1952 alone, leaving behind hundreds of millions of dollars. If attracting tourists to Mexico was a high priority for Alemán, he was, nevertheless, most proud of the new campus for UNAM that he constructed on the outskirts of the capital city. A remarkable architectural landmark, UNAM's buildings were adorned with stunning murals and marvelous mosaics by Mexico's most gifted artists. Complaints about the scarcity of books, lack of equipment for labs, or niggardly salaries for professors fell to subsequent administrations to address.

While postwar Mexico boomed and the middle and upper class prospered, the working class faced forced austerity, and rural communal subsistence farmers *(ejiditarios)* were sacrificed to the growth of individual and family farms producing for export. The administration kept taxes low or nonexistent for those with money to invest. High rates of profit, subsidized electricity, and an expanding infrastructure attracted Mexican and foreign capital to invest even greater sums in the industrial sector of the economy. Novelist Carlos Fuentes's fictional Artemio Cruz appears to be the quintessential representative of the powerful Mexican businessmen who came to dominate this era, and Miguel Alemán was their leader.

Despite the expanding capitalist economy, it was clear to most that the boom was lopsided and left the Mexican masses behind. This was not an economy that regarded the working class as a potential market, rather as a cheap source of exploitable labor. Added to this fact was the outrageous corruption that came to be a hallmark of Alemanismo. Historian Ramón Ruiz noted that by the time he left office, Alemán had become a millionaire, owned a great deal of real estate, and "hobnobbed with the international jet set." During his administration "public and private corruption had sundry opportunities, cabinet officers, in cahoots with businessmen, made millions." Together with Raúl Azcárraga of the powerful Monterrey clans, Alemán established Televisa, a private television network linked to the government that in its broadcasts was "hostile to strikes, leftist opinion, Cuba and the Soviet Union, socialist and Communist 'ideas' and friendly to Washington's version of the universe."

Allegations of corruption damaged Alemán's personal reputation and prompted party leaders to select someone with impeccable credentials of honesty as his successor: Adolfo Ruiz Cortines. In an attempt to clean up the scandals, the new president seized over 10,000 acres of farmland near Tampico from his predecessor's cronies as well as a major oil distribution monopoly controlled by Alemán's close industrialist friend Jorge Pasquel. Unfortunately, the Alemán legacy of corruption and lopsided economic development would continue to plague Mexico into the last years of the twentieth century.

After his term ended in 1952, Alemán became the leader of the right wing of the PRI. Starting in 1958 he served as director general of the National Tourism Board, a position he held at the time of his death in Mexico City on May 14, 1983.

Select Bibliography

Camp, Rodric A., "Education and Political Recruitment in Mexico: The Alemán Generation." *Journal of InterAmerican Studies and World Affairs* 18:3 (August 1976).

Medin, Tzvi, *El Sexenio Alemanista.* Mexico City: Era, 1990.

—Errol D. Jones

ALLENDE Y UNZAGA, IGNACIO MARÍA DE

1769–1811 • Soldier and Leader in the Wars of Independence

A major participant in Mexico's initial revolution for independence, Ignacio Allende was born in San Miguel el Grande (now San Miguel de Allende, Guanajuato) on January 21, 1769. Both his father and maternal grandfather were Basque immigrants from Spain. The early death of his mother (about 1771) and his father (1787) left the six Allende siblings (Ignacio was fifth born) in reduced circumstances. Thus, the Allende brothers had of necessity to work hard to recover some semblance of the family's fortune. As a member of the landed gentry class, Allende early on developed into a locally famed horseman, admired for his courage and dash.

Attracted to military service, Allende won appointment as an ensign in the newly formed Dragones de la Reina regiment (October 9, 1795), received a permanent commission as a lieutenant on February 19, 1796. The next decade would see him mainly occupied in garrison duties in or near his hometown. In 1806, he saw service in Jalapa, San Luis Potosí, and Mexico City. Probably because he had no combat experience, his promotion to captain occurred only in 1809. By then, his family fortune was further buffeted by the Spanish Crown's amortization of ecclesiastical funds, and his friend and patron Viceroy José de Iturrigaray's removal (September 1808) by *peninsulares* (Spanish-born Mexicans) hostile to the aspirations of criollos (persons of Spanish descent born in the Americas). These factors combined to push Allende toward opposition to continued Spanish rule. He became, from late 1808 to September 1810, a participant and leader in a network of like minds that stretched from the viceregal capital far into the center, west, and north of the colony. Initially criollo discussion groups, these became conspiratorial cells aimed at creating some sort of criollo-led government.

Allende, a member of the Querétaro–San Miguel network, proposed recruiting from the large number of pilgrims who would assemble at the San Juan de los Lagos fair in December 1810 to raise the standard of rebellion against the colonial authorities. It was expected that other cities and towns would then join the movement. The conspiracy was, however, discovered, and Allende, together with a few others of like intentions, fled to the parish house of Father Miguel Hidalgo y Costilla at Dolores, Guanajuato. On September 15 and 16, 1810, Hidalgo called upon his parishioners for support for the revolution. From Dolores, Allende, Hidalgo, and their burgeoning forces moved to San Miguel on September 16, took peninsular Spaniards as hostages, and proceeded to Celaya, their "army" ever increasing in numbers and violence. The large force, nominally led by Hidalgo, could not be disciplined, despite Allende's strenuous efforts. Looting and the lynching of Spaniards (and unlucky criollos) accompanied the movement's lumbering march on Guanajuato, the rich silver city. The city was taken, with some losses, and still more American and European-born Spaniards were massacred on September 28. Although he had been named lieutenant general on September 21, Allende found little satisfaction in the title, for the horde that he and Hidalgo ostensibly led, grown to 60,000 by mid-October, was unmanageable. Meanwhile, on September 27, Viceroy Francisco Xavier de Venegas had declared Allende and Hidalgo to be outlaws and offered 10,000 pesos for the head of each. Indecisive, Hidalgo, within sight of Mexico City, ordered a retreat (to Allende's chagrin) and moved his force westward. At Aculco on November 6, 5,200 disciplined royalist troops routed Hidalgo's 40,000 men and took much booty, arms, and cash. Allende, disenchanted with Hidalgo, left for Guanajuato, seeking new resources, but had to abandon the city on November 24 and moved (as Hidalgo had done earlier) to Guadalajara on December 9. There he found a large force (80,000 men), a large war chest (500,000 pesos), but few muskets. Allende sought over the next six weeks to create some semblance of an army out of this mass. He failed, and at the Battle of Puente Calderón (January 17, 1811), disaster struck. The Spanish commander, Félix Calleja, routed the

insurgents. Allende and Hidalgo both fled northward, where some support for independence existed. The two leaders, whose relations by no means cordial, met at El Pabellón, a hacienda north of Aguascalientes, on January 19. Allende and his followers secretly deposed Hidalgo from command, and Allende assumed the top office. Encumbered by 2,000 refugees, but bolstered by a treasury of about 200,000 pesos, Allende (with Hidalgo under escort) set off for Zacatecas in late January. The *generalísimo* named agents who were to seek U.S. materiél and manpower to assist the cause in early February. He and his company then moved further north to Saltillo, Coahuila, which they reached on February 28, 1811. Two weeks later, on March 16, Allende decided to retreat to Texas, and from there, to the United States. Riding within a train of 14 carriages, the Allende party left Saltillo. In a brief but effective firefight, the convoy was captured on March 21 at El Baján, south of Monclova. Allende and Hidalgo found themselves prisoners and were taken to the city of Chihuahua. Allende was tried by a drum-head court martial from May 10 to 17 and June 8, 10, and 14, during which he assumed full responsibility as leader of the revolution. On June 26, the death sentence (shooting in the back) was carried out.

Allende's head, with that of Hidalgo and other colleagues, was brought to Guanajuato for public exhibition. Their final resting place is now the Independence Column in Mexico City.

Select Bibliography

Aguilar, Rosalía, *Perfil de una villa criolla: San Miguel el Grande, 1555–1810.* Mexico City: Instituto Nacional de Antropología e Historia, 1986.

Hamill, Hugh M., *The Hidalgo Revolt.* Gainesville: University of Florida Press, 1966.

María y Campos, Armando de, *Allende, Primer Soldado de la Nación.* Mexico City: Jus, 1964.

—J. León Helguera

ALMAZÁN, JUAN ANDREU

1891–1968 • General and Politician

Juan Andreu Almazán was born in 1891 in Olinalá, Guerrero. His formal education commenced in 1907 in Puebla, where he entered medical school. Almazán was quickly caught up in the political activism of the university, supporting Francisco I. Madero's presidential campaign in 1910. Almazán wrote antigovernment articles in the local newspapers and met Maderista organizer Aquiles Serdán.

Almazán took part in preparations for the Maderista revolution, and among his responsibilities was taking over the penitentiary of Puebla. With the government's discovery of revolutionary plans in mid-November, Almazán joined in the defense of Aquiles Serdán on November 18. Later, he helped raise money for Serdán's coffin and funeral.

In late 1910, Almazán returned to his native Olinalá to raise a revolutionary army in Guerrero. Arms were lacking, however, and state authorities had orders to apprehend Almazán. Almazán fled to San Antonio, Texas, with the intention of getting arms from the Junta Revolucionaria (Revolutionary Junta) and then invading Guerrero by boat. In Texas, he found that the Junta Revolucionaria lacked funds to sponsor him. Instead, he was sent on an expedition as chief of medical services for Venustiano Carranza to drive south with the object of taking Mexico City.

Almazán and Carranza had a falling out; Almazán left Carranza and returned to San Antonio. The Junta Revolucionaria sent him out again, this time to the Morelos-Guerrero area south of Mexico City. Here Almazán's mission was to organize the southern Revolutionary groups behind Madero. Almazán met Emiliano Zapata and declared him the Maderista chief of Morelos.

When Zapata was declared an outlaw by the provisional government of Francisco León de la Barra, Almazán remained loyal to Zapata, becoming an anti-Maderista and writing articles defending Zapata. Unsuccessful in his attempts to convince the new government to support Zapata, Almazán returned to Olinalá in August 1911. There he was joined by Zapata, who had escaped a federal ambush in Chinameca; Almazán received Zapatistas fleeing federal troops.

With Zapata's retreat into Guerrero, federal general Victoriano Huerta considered the pacification of Morelos concluded. But Zapata and Almazán rallied their followers and encouraged revolt among the people of Puebla, Guerrero, Morelos, and Oaxaca. When Zapata tried to arrange an agreement with the de la Barra government, Almazán was sent to negotiate. But a formal petition of September 26, 1911, stating the demands of the Zapatistas, and a 15-day truce beginning October 8 ended without accord.

As an ex-Maderista, Almazán found himself in a precarious position in Mexico City. He tried to convince federal general Pascual Orozco Jr. to join the Zapatista cause against Madero. Apparently, once Almazán was in Mexico City, Madero offered him 100,000 pesos and 500 men to fight against the Zapatistas for six months, after which he would be sent to Europe with a pension. Almazán refused the post and was jailed a few days after Madero's inauguration as president on November 6. There Almazán remained until July 1912.

Zapata learned of Madero's offer of an army to Almazán, came to believe that Almazán was a traitor to his cause, and ordered his men to shoot Almazán on sight. When Almazán was released from jail, he set out immediately for Guerrero. Although apprehended by Zapatista troops, Almazán was saved by friends among the soldiers. Once Almazán was back in Guerrero with his own men, he wrote to Zapata, placing himself at his command. Zapata placed Almazán and Guerrero under Julio Gómez, of whom Almazán had a very low opinion. Almazán apparently felt that this act was an attempt by Zapata to humiliate him.

After receiving news of the Huerta coup of February 19, 1913, Almazán headed a negotiating commission to Mexico City. In the capital, Almazán switched sides, entering the ranks of the Huertistas with the title of general. He was sent north under the command of General José Refugio Velasco and remained allied with the Huerta regime through 1913 and 1914. Many reasons for this switch of loyalties may have existed. Almazán had been fighting the Maderistas alongside the Zapatistas, but without the wholehearted support of Zapata. The resignation of Madero meant the end of Maderismo, which Almazán had considered to be his principal enemy. In addition, joining Huerta provided an opportunity to fight against his old enemy Carranza.

With the defeat of the Huerta regime, Almazán again approached Zapata, writing on September 19, 1914, to Zapata, asking to be readmitted to the ranks of the Zapatistas and explaining his views of earlier misunderstandings. Zapata replied by naming Almazán a division general of the Liberating Army of the South.

As the Zapatistas were progressively isolated, Almazán gravitated toward Félix Díaz, supporting Díaz's Plan de Tierra Colorada, proclaimed in February 1916. In July 1916, Almazán joined other followers of Félix Díaz in an unsuccessful attack on the city of Oaxaca. Driven back by Carrancista forces, Almazán was forced to flee into the mountains of Chiapas. After the attack on Oaxaca, Almazán's alliance with Díaz was rather nominal. Until 1919, although operating under the Felicista banner most of the time, Almazán fought relatively independently against Carranza.

After Carranza's death in 1920, Álvaro Obregón named Almazán chief of military operations in the Laguna region. In the years between 1920 and 1940 Almazán held several important positions in the Mexican Army, including general of the division in Nuevo León and Veracruz. In 1929, Almazán played a decisive role in the defeat of the Escobar Rebellion. In 1930, he was named secretary of communications and public works in the cabinet of President Pascual Ortiz Rubio. After the resignation of Ortiz Rubio, Almazán returned to Nuevo León, where Monterrey became his power base.

Almazán accumulated immense wealth through government road and railroad construction contracts in the 1920s and 1930s. His Companía Anahuac undertook construction projects in many parts of the country. Almazán developed the first major tourist hotel in Acapulco.

His considerable power, prestige, and wealth led Almazán to seek the presidency as the principal opposition candidate in 1940. The elections were violent and irregular; it was widely believed that Almazán was victorious in the Federal District. Crying fraud, Almazán left Mexico hoping to build support for a final insurrection. When it became clear that little support for him existed in Mexico or the United States, Almazán gave up a violent resolution of his frustrated presidential bid. Instead he returned to attend the inauguration of Manuel Avila Camacho.

Almazán's well-known 1952 article "En Legítima Defensa" was published in response to accusations of cowardice after the 1940 elections. Almazán claimed that he, not Avila Camacho, should be proclaimed as the unifier of Mexico, as he had sacrificed his own career for the safety of Mexico, saving thousands of lives. Almazán remained out of the public eye after 1952. Rarely venturing thereafter out of the sixth floor of his Acapulco hotel, he died in 1968.

—David E. Lorey

ALTAMIRANO, IGNACIO MANUEL

1834–93 • Politician, Soldier, Intellectual, and Writer

In 1934, 100 years after his birth, Altamirano's ashes were transferred to the Rotunda of Illustrious Men. On February 13, 1993, and in commemoration of the centennial of his death, a purple curtain was drawn at the National Palace revealing the name of Ignacio Manuel Altamirano engraved in gold. Until then, Altamirano had never been recognized officially as one of Mexico's heroes, although he had been nominated for that honor previously. These two twentieth-century acts have assured Altamirano's status as one of the nation's most influential men, a born leader whose unaltering vision would help to redirect the course of the nation's history and literary culture. Altamirano, indeed, dedicated his entire life to the construction and consolidation of a national project that would transform Mexico into a culturally and politically independent and modern republic. A fundamental figure for the nineteenth century, his political vision, educational philosophy, and literary output contributed significantly to the forging of a national project still in the making. Altamirano did this through his double vocation of intellectual and statesman, picking up pen and sword: his energies and determination pushed him to the battlefield, the podium, the classroom, the newsroom, and the literary salon. His life and work, revisited at the end of this century, continues to raise unanswered and fundamental questions of nation building and literary canon formations.

Altamirano was born 14 years after Mexico had won its independence from Spain, during a period of enormous instability, a time when the foundations of a nation were under tense debate. It was also a great moment for beginnings, for the opportunity to construct anew. He did not hesitate to engage in this struggle, articulating a liberal project of political and literary decolonization. Influenced in his early education by Ignacio Ramírez, "El Nigromante," known for his radical liberalism, Altamirano, albeit more moderate, remained faithful to the liberal spirit of the times. He fought in the Revolution of Ayutla against the dictator Santa Anna, in the Wars of Reform against the Conservatives, against Juárez's call for amnesty in 1861, against the French occupation in the Wars of the Intervention, and finally he dedicated himself to reconciliation and reconstruction after 1867.

Born of indigenous parents, Altamirano was able to leave his hometown with a grant given to talented indigenous students. It was at the Instituto Científico y Literario de Toluca that he studied with Ignacio Ramírez, who became his most influential mentor. During this period, he perfected his Spanish, learned Latin and French, studied philosophy, read voraciously, and acquired an extensive education that formally culminated in a law degree. As soldier, statesman, orator, lawyer, judge, attorney general, and consul general in Europe he would be recognized as one of the heroes of the Republic; as novelist, short story writer, poet, literary critic, and feature writer he would become, in the words of the modernist poet Manuel Gutiérrez Nájera, "President of the Republic of Mexican letters," the godfather of all aspiring writers between 1867 and 1887. As educator, he supported a public, secular, and obligatory elementary school, founded the Escuela Nacional de Maestros, taught French and Latin to public school students, and taught world and natural history, the history and politics of Mexico, and philosophy and eloquence to university students. He is known as "el Maestro de la Juventud," the master, teacher, and guide of the young.

Altamirano's progressive politics, based on the creation of an independent liberal democracy, advocated a strict separation of state and church, a program for the consolidation of the nation that fought for an inclusionary politics that would permit the indigenous and mestizo population equality under the law and a voice in the creation of a new society, which would, in fact, recognize the indigenous make-up of the country. His project sought the real integration of the Indian, distancing itself from the Vasconcelista project of the post-Revolutionary period, an *indigenista* discourse that idealized the past and ignored the actual Indian population in praise of a *raza cosmica,* a cosmic race that in fact praised hybridity at the expense of the non-Westernized living Indians. A humanist throughout his life, he was ultimately not able to embrace the positivist creed that his disciple Justo Sierra and his generation promulgated. In fact, Altamirano's diplomatic work abroad at the end of his life is seen by some as conscious distancing from the increasingly changing cultural climate of the Porfirian government, where the sciences had replaced the arts. His historical writings, political articles, and discourses were until the end unrelentingly critical of class and race divisions. In Paris, shortly before his death, he mentored Francisco I. Madero, establishing a link to the struggles of the twentieth century.

Throughout his life, Altamirano absorbed a selective Western humanist culture; appropriating the liberal discourses of Europe, he transplanted literary, political, and philosophical concepts to Mexican territory, ever conscious that the paradigms from across the Atlantic, given the differences in the geographies, histories, politics, and populations of the New World, could serve mainly as points of departure in the construction of a new society. His "Americanist" project sought to liberate Mexico from Spain both politically and intellectually. For this reason, he refused to belong to the Mexican branch of the Spanish Academy, defending instead a transformed Spanish language that had, in fact, already responded to its distinct reality and accepted the modifications brought about by its contact with the native languages. Engaged in the formation of a national literature, he sought literary independence from Europe and praised the writers of the United States and South America for their creation of a New World literature. Above all, he admired Andrés Bello, José Mármol, and Esteban Echeverría, acknowledging them as compatriots with whom he shared a common homeland, Spanish America.

Following the ousting of the French, Altamirano set down his arms and picked up his pen, believing that the construction of the independent nation state he envisioned could best be achieved through cultural venues. He published his manifesto for a literary nationalism in 1868, strongly encouraging a literature that would no longer be subservient to European models. He urged writers to use Mexico as source, its history from pre-Columbian times to the present, its landscapes, customs, aspirations, and idioms to speak for the country and correct the distorted and exoticized representations of Mexico by outsiders that abounded. Of all genres, he considered the novel best suited for his project, deeming it the great genre of the nineteenth century, a protean and universal form with mass appeal and the power to entertain and enlighten, to mold the reader intellectually and morally. His examples were Voltaire, Rousseau, Scott, Stowe, Dickens, Balzac, and Hugo for their use of the novel as a vehicle to popularize philosophical ideas, represent the history and society of a country, or denounce injustices. He admired Scott, Balzac, and Hugo for their historical accuracy, and verisimilar representation of characters and customs. The Mexican novel would teach the readers their history, instill a liberal politics, and guide their taste, language, and conduct in the process of becoming model citizens of the republic. He gave Mexican nationalism a literary program that guided several generations. Altamirano paved the way to the definitive literary and linguistic emancipation from Spain brought about by the Modernists.

Given his project as an intellectual and the severe ideological crisis the nation was undergoing after the Wars of Reform and French Intervention, and following a cen-

tury of upheavals, it is not surprising that his own efforts to narrativize the nation produced two novels and a series of novellas and short stories that served as examples of literary nationalism. An eclectic who did not follow any one movement or school, he produced novels and stories that are classic in form, romantic in themes, and realist in execution. He paid special attention to the formal elements of the text seeking balance and conciseness, rejecting emotional excess and literary affectation. Very conscious of the participant reader, he sought a language that would be accessible and exemplary. Preoccupied with the accurate depiction of Mexican history and society, he is seen as a precursor to the writers of the realist tradition, His self-conscious authoritative fictions, however, made evident their didactic intentions resulting in obvious morality tales such as *Navidad en las montañas (1870)* and *Maestro de escuela (1871)*. In his two novels *Clemencia* (1869) and *El Zarco* (finished in 1888, published posthumously in 1901), the double is used as the organizing principle to critique class and ethnic prejudices. His personal politics inform the racialized discourse in the novels that make of the unattractive dark Indian character the hero, as an unmasking takes place that reveals the winsome and seductive protagonist as the villain. Condemning a society bent on misreading appearances, his novels directed at a feminine audience posit new images of women who are essential partners in the construction of the nation. The ideal passive women of the romantic period are replaced by passionate (at times foolishly so) Bovarist characters who are duly condemned, and strong-minded women whose agency is clearly rewarded. His didactic tales set during the civil wars and Restored Republic both construct an image of the new liberal nation and critique the prejudices, politics, and institutions that prevent its full development at the time of his writing. His elaborate depictions of Mexican landscapes, town life, and customs are skillfully integrated into his national plots. He cultivated *costumbrismo* (literature founded in Mexican national traditions and customs) as a genre on its own, publishing many articles on the subject, as well as *Landscapes and Legends, Traditions and Customs in Mexico* (1884). His poetry, written mainly between 1854 and 1864, constituted odes to his country's natural settings. In 1887 at a literary soiree *(velada literaria)* he read "El Atoyac" (The Atoyac River), which is recognized as the first important public appearance of a Mexican theme in poetry.

As the principal promoter of literary nationalism, his professional activities were multiple. His book reviews and literary societies became the necessary models. The founding of the literary journal *El Renacimiento* (52 issues), however, marked a unique event and caused a veritable literary Renaissance. Begun in 1869 after the defeat of the French, the journal served as a conciliatory cultural space, publishing the writings of opposing ideologies. In the interest of the nation, writers from varied sectors agreed to participate in this literary cultural project, which bridged political as well as generational and disciplinary divisions, creating the necessary climate for Mexico to grow. Many believe that without Altamirano's leadership it would never have materialized. It is said that 35 literary publications came into existence throughout Mexico during the following decade. Opposed to patronage and a long-time believer that writers should be paid for their contributions, his was the first journal to begin the practice. This short-lived publication was followed by others: *The Federalist* (1871), *The Tribune* (1875) and *The Republic* (1880).

Ethnically Indian and culturally mestizo, he condemned the Conquest and the treatment of the Indian without engaging in false idealizations of the past. Born in a time of intense conflict that divided liberals from conservatives, republicans from monarchists, and those who supported the criollo elites from those who fought for the equality of the Indian and mestizo masses, his politics and poetics make evident his positioning. Interestingly it is Altamirano himself both in life and as literary character who represents the new citizen of the utopian nation-state he envisioned.

Select Bibliography

Azuela, Mariano, *Cien años de novela mexicana*. Mexico City: Botas, 1947.

Batis, Huberto, *Estudio preliminar de índices de el renacimiento: Semanario literario mexicano (1869)*. Mexico City: UNAM, Centro de Estudios Literarios, 1963.

Brushwood, John S., *The Romantic Novel in Mexico*. Columbia: University of Missouri Press, 1954.

Díaz y de Ovando, Clementina, "La visión histórica de Ignacio Manuel Altamirano." *Anales del Instituto de Investigaciones Estéticas* 22 (1954).

Homenaje a Ignacio M. Altamirano: Conferencias, estudios y bibliografía. Mexico City: UNAM, 1935.

Martínez, José Luis, "El Maestro Altamirano." In *La expresión nacional*. Mexico City: Imprenta Universitaria, 1955.

Monsiváis, Carlos, *El Zarco* [see especially prologue]. Mexico City: Oceano, 1986.

Nacci, Chris N., *Ignacio Manuel Altamirano*. New York: Twayne, 1970.

Ochoa Campos, Moisés, *Ignacio Manuel Altamirano: El soplo de genio*. Mexico City: SEP, 1966.

Read, John Lloyd, *The Mexican Historical Novel*. New York: Instituto de las Españas en America, 1939.

Sommer, Doris, *Foundational Fictions: The National Romances of Latin America*. Berkeley: University of California Press, 1991.

Warner, Ralph E., *Bibliografía de Ignacio Manuel Altamirano*. Mexico City: Imprenta Universitaria, 1955.

—NORMA KLAHN

ALVARADO, PEDRO DE

c. 1485–1541 • Conquistador

Fernando (Hernán) Cortés's principal captain in the Conquest of Mexico, and leader of many subsequent successful expeditions against the indigenous peoples of Mesoamerica and the Andes, Pedro de Alvarado was a man of striking contrasts. His contemporaries and later historians found in him a fearless and skilled warrior, and a handsome and charming companion in the small community of invaders. Both found in him as well an impulse to destroy, and unbounded cruelty toward Indians, and an avarice for gold and adventure excessive even for the times of great excess that were the Wars of Conquest. Those qualities were to be found in Cortés, as well, although in such proportion and combined with talents for building anew upon the ruins of conquest, that permitted Cortés to cut a more complex and lasting figure in history. Alvarado represented, on the other hand, the starkest and least redeemable aspect of the invasion of the Americas.

Alvarado was born in Extremadura around 1485 and traveled to the New World, to Hispañola (modern-day Haiti and the Dominican Republic), as early as 1510. It was there that he probably met Cortés; both men soon participated in the conquest of Cuba. Although he arrived in this hemisphere with little in the way of personal wealth, the parceling out of Cuban lands and labor made Alvarado a rich landowner. Tending wealthy estates, however, was not to be his life work. He accompanied Juan de Grijalva on an 1518 exploration of the coast of Mexico, and eagerly joined Cortés's expedition to conquer that land, he and his four brothers financing a ship with a complement of sailors, soldiers, and horses. Some historians suggest that it was, indeed, Alvarado, who encouraged and convinced Cortés to undertake not just another exploration of western lands, but a full-fledged conquest of the fabled rich kingdom of the Mexican highlands. Alvarado's eagerness for conquest and spoil were displayed again and again in subsequent years, in his campaign to pacify Tututepeque in Oaxaca (1522), his conquest of the Quiché (1524) and other kingdoms of highland Guatemala and El Salvador, his expedition to the Andes (1534), and Honduras (1535), and again to central Mexico (1540–41).

Alvarado's expeditions provided ample evidence of the cruelty with which contemporaries and historians credited him, although no incident contributed more to that image than his massacre of the Mexica nobles in May 1520. Cortés and his captains already had occupied Tenochtitlan and taken Moteuczoma prisoner without a fight, and it was evidently Cortés's intention to continue the subjugation of the Mexica through some combination of force, guile, courting, and the puppetry of the captive emperor. While Cortés was away briefly on the coast subduing Spanish rivals, however, Alvarado changed all that. Evidently suspecting that the Mexica were about to attack him and the small contingent of Spaniards left in Tenochtitlan, Alvarado struck first, massacring larger numbers of unarmed Mexica celebrants and spectators. From that instant it was war without quarter or surrender between the Spaniards and the ill-fated Mexica.

Alvarado's critics could point as well to the burning of the Quiché capital of Utatlán, his seemingly senseless destruction of countless other Indian settlements, his torture and execution of Indian lords, and his relentless exploitation of pacified Indians in labor on works that Alvarado designated. There was surely some logic to Alvarado's harshness. In the lands that he conquered, Alvarado came not to rule, build, or colonize, but to enrich himself. The effort and expense of peaceful administration detracted from the single-minded devotion of resources toward each next expedition. So Alvarado killed Indian lords who might later organize resistance against him, and used terror liberally in order to secure indigenous compliance. He coerced Indian labor to extremes to build the ships, or to provide the cash to buy the soldiers that his next planned expedition would require. He took Indian women when needed to keep his sailors and soldiers content while they prepared to do his bidding. (On the other hand, he maintained a long union with the daughter of one of the principal lords of Tlaxcala, a woman later known as Luisa Xicoténcatl, by whom he had a daughter; mother and daughter accompanied Alvarado even on his campaigns in the Andes.)

For all his energy and single-mindedness of purpose, when he died on campaign near Guadalajara in 1541, perhaps no conqueror had won more victories and accomplished so little as Alvarado. His failure to invest in lasting administration of productive settlements and hinterlands is one reason. Also, after the initial glory days of the conquest of Tenochtitlan, the freedom of action of subsequent conquerors became very circumscribed, and even opportunities for unchecked plunder vanished. Alvarado's campaign against the Inca was blocked by other conquerors already on the scene, and Alvarado could do nothing but sell his army and navy to Pizarro and return to Guatemala. Conquests in the lowlands of central America brought Alvarado into protracted jurisdictional conflict with Francisco de Montejo and his son, who were then engaged in the systematic pacification of the Yucatán Peninsula. Alvarado's final campaign in the Mixtón Wars was conducted in coordination with and under the superior authority of the viceroy of New Spain. Ironic and oddly fitting it was, perhaps, that when Alvarado was finally slain it was not by the darts or lances of Indians against whom he had so doggedly fought most of his adult life, who called Alvarado Tonatiuh (the Day-time Sun); Alvarado was crushed by the tumbling horse of a fellow Spaniard who rode ahead of him.

Select Bibliography

Recinos, Adrián, *Pedro de Alvarado: Conquistador de México y Guatemala.* Mexico City: Fondo de Cultura Económica, 1952.

Thomas, Hugh, *Conquest: Montezuma, Cortés, and the Fall of Old Mexico.* New York: Simon and Schuster, 1995.

—Paul Sullivan

ALVARADO, SALVADOR

1820–1924 • General and Politician

A few years after his birth in Culicán in 1880, Salvador Alvarado's family moved to Potam, in the Yaquí Valley in Sonora, where his father opened a store. Alvarado received an adequate basic education before working as a pharmacist's assistant in Guaymas. Thereafter, he traveled widely in the region, opening his own store, first in Potam and then in Cananea. An avid reader, Alvarado acquired a philosophy that was a blend of reformist socialism, anticlericalism, and a firm belief in the virtues of self-help. He was offended by the harsh treatment accorded to the Yaquí Indians by authorities and resentful of the exclusive and restrictive officialdom that characterized the later years of Porfirio Díaz's rule. Not surprisingly

he became active in anti-reelectionist politics and joined the Maderista revolt in 1911. Following Francisco I. Madero's victory he helped to install the new administration in Cananea. Alvarado was given command of a local militia unit and led it with other state forces against Orozquista rebels.

Following Madero's overthrow by Victoriano Huerta in 1913, the administration in Sonora refused to recognize the legitimacy of the new federal government. The commanders of the state militia, such as Alvarado, Plutarco Elías Calles, Álvaro Obregón, and Benjamin Hill, confronted the federal army. The Sonorans quickly asserted control over the state except for Guaymas, to which Alvarado laid siege, trapping the large garrison of Huertistas until they surrendered in July 1914. Promoted general, Alvarado was jailed in August by the state governor, José María Maytorena, after vainly attempting to mediate in a political dispute between Maytorena and Calles. Alvarado was released in October, and the following February Venustiano Carranza, the new "first chief," sent him to Yucatán as governor and military commander at the head of 6,000 men to restore Constitutionalist rule there.

Following a swift military victory, Alvarado occupied the state capital on March 19, 1915. He arrived at an opportune moment. Prices for Yucatán's major export, henequen fiber, were rising as a result of World War I. He revitalized the ineffective Henequen Regulating Commission through a decree obliging landowners to sell their produce. By centralizing and controlling marketing of the product, he greatly increased the state's revenues—at a considerable cost to the International Harvester Company, which undertook an unsuccessful legal action in the U.S. courts under antimonopoly legislation. Alvarado used the funds generated by henequen sales to boost the Constitutionalist treasury and finance his local reform program.

Alvarado regarded Yucatán as socially and politically backward, in need of modernization and closer national integration. Like other members of the Sonoran revolutionary elite, he believed private enterprise should be encouraged, but that the state should ensure the resulting wealth produced tangible benefits for the population, rather than enriching a small elite and their foreign partners, which he felt had happened under Díaz. Taking advantage of his position, Alvarado sought to transform the social and economic life of the state in accordance with his ideas.

Almost upon arrival Alvarado sent propaganda teams to inform rural communities of a recent decree abolishing debt peonage and establishing the free movement of rural labor. In addition, between assuming power and leaving office on February 1, 1918, he promulgated 784 decrees affecting almost every aspect of daily life. He passed legislation promoting education, particularly in rural areas, protecting workers' rights, establishing arbitration boards for labor disputes, benefiting rent payers, revising all guardianship agreements (which had been abused to exact unpaid domestic service), banning the sale of alcohol, prohibiting foreigners from acquiring real estate in Yucatán, controlling the activities of the Catholic Church, authorizing divorce, encouraging immigration, and reforming the judiciary. He also established a regional economic development board and sponsored the creation of a political party, the Partido Socialista de Yucatán.

Alvarado's approach to land reform was less radical. He recognized the importance of land redistribution in giving the Indian population a stake in the regime and established a Local Agrarian Commission. In 1915 the commission redistributed over 30,000 hectares (74,129 acres) of land. Thereafter, however, Alvarado limited such redistributions. Much of Yucatán's agricultural land was devoted to henequen production, and

Alvarado did not wish to risk disrupting cash exports of the crop. Furthermore, Alvarado believed land reform should serve to create a prosperous class of rancheros (indepedent small farmers) rather than to reestablish any collectivist system consistent with Mayan tradition, which he considered anachronistic. He therefore emphasized improvements in rural education and living conditions rather than further land redistribution.

Not all of Alvarado's reforms had a lasting effect, but he enjoyed considerable local popularity, not least because he did not abuse his privileged position for self-enrichment. He left in February 1918 to conduct a destructive campaign against the rebels in neighboring Chiapas before eventually returning to Sonora. Along with Calles and Adolfo de la Huerta, he was a prime instigator of the movement of Agua Prieta, which overthrew Carranza in 1920. As provisional president (June to November 1920), de la Huerta appointed Alvarado finance minister, but after two months Alvarado departed for New York to assist in defending the court case against the Henequen Regulatory Commission.

Relations between Alvarado and Obregón, both strong personalities, were never easy, and Obregón did not give Alvarado a post in his administration (1920–24). Back in the army, Alvarado joined the de la Huerta Revolt in 1923. Defeated by Obregón at Ocotlán—according to Obregón, his hardest-won victory—Alvarado fled to the United States. In March 1924 he accepted de la Huerta's appointment as supreme commander of rebel forces and traveled back to southern Mexico. It proved to be a fatal decision. He returned to a lost cause, and on June 10 he was betrayed and murdered by a subordinate.

Alvarado's social origins and political outlook were characteristic of many of Madero's early and more active supporters and common among the restless young men who emerged as leaders of the Mexican Revolution in Sonora. Not surprisingly, his administration of Yucatán foreshadowed in many ways the national governments of the 1920s. An able man and a sincere reformer, his decision to join the rebels in 1923 was a loss to the emerging post-Revolutionary regime.

Select Bibliography

Diccionario Histórico y Bibliográfico de la Revolución Mexicana. 2nd edition, 8 vols., Mexico City: Instituto Nacional de Estudios Históricos de la Revolución Mexicana, 1992.

Dulles, John W. F., *Yesterday in Mexico: A Chronicle of the Revolution, 1919–1936.* Austin: University of Texas Press, 1961.

Joseph, Gilbert M., *Revolution from Without: Yucatán, Mexico, and the United States.* Cambridge and New York: Cambridge University Press, 1982.

Knight, Alan, *The Mexican Revolution.* 2 vols, Cambridge and New York: Cambridge University Press, 1986.

Magdaleno, Mauricio, *Hombres e Ideas de La Revolución.* Mexico City: Instituto Nacional de Estudios Históricos de la Revolución Mexicana, 1980.

—DUDLEY ANKERSON

ALZATE Y RAMÍREZ, JOSÉ ANTONIO

1737–99 • Scientist, Writer, and Publisher

José Antonio Alzate y Ramírez came of age during the Bourbon era of renovation and change. His self-appointed mission was to educate the Mexican public on matters of science and natural history. Throughout his life, Alzate did not waver from this purpose. He published four newspapers from 1768 through 1795 (*Diario Literario de México, Asuntos Varios Sobre Ciencias y Artes, Observaciones sobre la Física, Historia Natural y Artes útiles,* and *Gacetas de Literatura de México)* in addition to assorted other pamphlets and studies. For Alzate, modern science was opposed to scholasticism. Hence, he rejected the notion of revealed knowledge and unquestioning acceptance of traditional authorities, and instead advocated observation, experimentation, and reason as the tools of scientific knowledge. Above all Alzate's science was utilitarian; he aimed to "plant useful ideas" in the Mexican people. Four main topics recur throughout Alzate's publications: medical treatments and prescriptions, mining technology, agricultural practices, and descriptions of the Mexican natural world and antiquities. He included notices, summaries, and critiques of European works as well as articles on local solutions to scientific or medical problems, including reports on his own experiments.

Little is known about Alzate's early life. He was born in Ozumba (in the present-day state of Mexico) to a middle-class family. His father was a Spaniard and his mother was a criolla (a woman of Spanish ancestry born in the Americas), a descendant of the seventeenth-century philosopher and poet, Sor Juana Inés de la Cruz. Alzate entered the Colegio de Ildefonso in 1747 and received a bachelor of arts degree in 1753 and a bachelor of theology in 1956. Shortly thereafter he was ordained as a priest, owing at least in part to his father's establishment of a chantry. Alzate's priestly duties in the chantry were limited to 15 masses per year, leaving him plenty of time to devote to his true calling: science. By the mid-1760s Alzate had established himself as a writer and publisher in Mexico City, where he continued to work until his death.

In large part, Alzate's science reflected his position as a Mexican intellectual in the latter part of the eighteenth century. The Spanish Enlightenment was distinguished by eclecticism and utilitarianism, both evident in Alzate's work. Moreover, Alzate formed part of an international scientific community; he was named correspondent to the French Academy of Sciences and member of the Botanical Garden of Madrid. Yet, Alzate, like many Mexican intellectuals of the period, reacted against colonial and European authorities, at least in subtle ways. He frequently became embroiled in disputes about what constituted legitimate scientific practice. One of the most famous controversies was Alzate's rejection of Carolus Linneaus's botanical classification system.

Spanish authorities had adopted the Linnean system, as had most of Europe, but Alzate found the nomenclature artificial and incomplete. In his view, each plant should be described individually with special reference to its medicinal and practical uses. Alzate's fierce rebuke of Linnean classification is in part an expression of his incipient nationalist sentiment. In an issue of the *Gacetas de Literatura de México,* he posed a question to his readers: if you were to get sick, "would you rely on an herb whose appearance, but not effects, were known? Wouldn't you prefer to wait for a country person or healer to come and advise you on the usefulness and dangers of the plant?"

Increasingly, Mexican intellectuals such as Alzate, Francisco Javier Clavigero, and José Ignacio Bartolache had begun to speak of their native land in terms of *"patria"* (fatherland), "nation," and "our America." Although they were not republicans in a political sense, they expressed a cultural loyalty and pride in the Mexican landscape, and they have come to be seen by modern historians as intellectual precursors to the Independence movement. Furthermore, Alzate's abhorrence of scholasticism and other authoritarian manifestations has been interpreted by some historians as a veiled criticism of Spanish rule. His appreciation of ancient Mexico (Aztec) cultural achievements and indigenous medicinal and agricultural practices confirm his nationalist sentiment. Alzate's principle contribution to neo-Aztecism was a supplement he published to the *Gacetas de Literatura de México* entitled *Descripción de las antigüedades de Xochicalco.* In the dedication to the work, he stated his purpose unequivocally: "How happy I shall be if this short and poorly composed memorandum serves to dissipate the false impressions that have been generated among learned men by the vile information that foreign authors generally provide in their works of the ancient Mexican Indians!" His strong stance flew in the face of European natural philosophy propagated primarily by the Comte du Buffon, which held that "New World" peoples, animals, and environments were inferior to "Old World" varieties.

The adjective most often used to describe Alzate is "encyclopedic." Throughout his nearly 30 years of journalistic publishing, Alzate sought to inform the Mexican public of the latest scientific and technological developments while at the same time inspiring them with an appreciation of specifically Mexican contributions. The late eighteenth century was a transitional moment in Mexican history. Tradition was giving way to modernity, colony to nation. These tensions are visible in the life and work of Alzate. Although ordained as a priest, nearly all of his energies were channeled toward the sciences. He did not consider himself to be a "professional" scientist in his training; yet, he was responsible for much of the dissemination of scientific information within New Spain. His self-training, along with his emphasis on useful knowledge, has prompted comparisons with Benjamin Franklin, whom Alzate admired as a great American scientist. Finally, Alzate's use of the vernacular language in his newspapers suggests that he was targeting a wide audience. It seems that even his combative and sarcastic style served to arouse interest in scientific concerns. It is this unique combination of practitioner and populizer that makes Alzate one of the most influential intellectuals of eighteenth-century Mexico.

Select Bibliography

Moreno, Rafael, "La concepción de la ciencia en Alzate." In *Historia de la Ciencia y la Technología*. Mexico City: Colegio de México, 1991.

Saladino García, *Alberto, Dos Científicos de la Ilustración Hispanoamericana: J.A. Alzate y F.J. Caldas*. Mexico City: UNAM, 1990.

Temple, William E., "José Antonio Alzate y Ramírez and the Gacetas de Literatura de México: 1768–1795." Ph.D. diss., Tulane Unversity, 1986.

—JAN JARRELL

ANARCHISM AND ANARCHIST MOVEMENTS

Anarchism played a crucial role in the formation and history of working-class movements in Mexico during the nineteenth century and in political unrest in Mexico between the 1860s and 1920s. Born of self-regulating working-class practices and experience in artisan shops and rural agriculture before the onset of capitalism, anarchism constituted a political defense of rural and urban working-class culture in the face of the relatively sudden reorganization of power and wealth that took place in the late nineteenth and early twentieth centuries. It was strongest in Latin Europe and Latin America, where peasant and artisan culture still flourished at the onset of the capitalist transformation.

The practice of mutual aid among peasants and artisans and the experience they gained from participation in local polity gave them the ability to organize along anarchist lines. Mutual aid and self-regulation prevailed in the agricultural communities and industrial workshops of the Native American peoples of Mexico before the European invasions of the sixteenth century. The Spaniards, in turn, brought their own clearly defined rural communalist and artisan mutual aid practices with them. Missionaries applied those concepts to the rural populace during the chaos, demographic collapse, and reorganization of the 1500s. From the 1540s onward the Spanish Crown assisted in the process by incorporating Native American pueblos that featured *fondos legales,* or civically owned lands dedicated to town life and agriculture. As 95 percent of the populace died following contact with Europeans, the survivors offered refuge to the disabled, orphans, widows, and stragglers. Later, Spanish artisans and farmers merged their past experience with communal practices in Spain with those of Mesoamerica. As a result of these events a syncretic mestizo working-class culture emerged. Throughout the remainder of the colonial era, and then into the nineteenth and early twentieth centuries,

workers' self-management was a real force in the cultivation of *ejido* (village) properties and in the artisan workshops.

But change was coming. During the eighteenth century foreign trade opportunities helped overcome the lack of a large domestic marketplace for Mexican raw materials such as metal ores, cotton, sugar, henequen, and livestock. The beginnings of the reorganization of agriculture preceded the workplace and meant a drawn out struggle for control of production between communalists in agriculture and those seeking profits through economies of scale and increased commercial intercourse. While industrial unrest influenced by anarchists did not come until the second half of the nineteenth century, communal agriculturalists reflecting a generic anarchism surfaced much earlier.

The rise of anarchist-like agricultural conflict began among the peasantry in and around the sugar plantations south of Puebla at Izúcar. There, in 1780, the rebels complained of outsiders overriding the authority of pueblo and town councils and of their interference in the control of the land and working conditions. The rebels called for the restoration of local autonomy, self-governance, lost landholdings, and the assertion of their political rights by the expulsion of the Spaniards from America. The tension in rural society continued during the multilayered disputes of the Wars of Independence. In many places the peasants rolled back commercial holdings and occupied hacienda properties while artisans and urban workers remained relatively quiescent. But the victory in the countryside was short-lived. Beginning in the late 1820s, the state and national governments began issuing a series of edicts enabling privatization. Several of these innovations provoked unrest among the communalists in the pueblos. The most notable were the uprisings of 1832 and the 1840s that convulsed southwestern Mexico, and the privatization of Catholic Church mission properties, which revolutionized landholding in parts of San Luis Potosí, Querétaro, and California.

In 1856 the victorious Liberals promulgated the Ley Lerdo, which declared the privatization of all rural corporate properties, clerical and pueblo. The crisis deepened. Between 1856 and 1910 the nation underwent a prolonged privatization process in which collective peasant holdings of arable lands fell from 25 percent to only 2 percent of the total. Despite a significant increase in middle-sized holdings, the owners of large commercial estates gained control of the vast majority of arable and nonarable properties. The rural working class experienced a remarkable decline in their access to arable land during this period and resorted to legal and extralegal means of defense. Their resistance became desperate and in many cases merged with urban and industrial anarchism, creating new programs and forms of resistance. The direct contact of artisan and urban anarchists with the peasantry synthesized the confrontation of the working classes and the emergent capitalist elites.

Plotino Rhodakanaty, a political missionary from the European revolutions of 1848 familiar with the left-wing ideologies of Paris and Barcelona, arrived in Mexico in the early 1860s. He became a teacher at the Colegio de San Ildefonso in Mexico City. Teaching the need for universal brotherhood, equal wages, mutual aid, cooperatives, and political federalism between the pueblos, cities, and states, he encouraged the students to form a "Bakuninist Group." They called it "La Social." The membership included a number of industrial workers.

Santiago Villanueva and Francisco Zalacosta, the sons of artisans, assumed leadership roles in these groups. Basing his operations in the La Social and its successors the Círculo Proletario and the Gran Círculo de Obreros de México as workers centrals, Villanueva coordinated the unionization effort in the Valley of Mexico. They created a movement that merged mutualist self-help and management with labor actions in search of collective bargaining agreements that provided higher wages and better working conditions. In 1865 they succeeded in recruiting the memberships of the mutualist societies at the La Colmena and Tlalnepantla textile factories. Strikes ensued at the two plants, followed immediately by another at La Fama Montanesa. However, at the textile plant at Tepeji del Río, Emperor Maximilian's Imperial Guards broke up the massed workers and arrested those on the picket lines.

In the meantime the organizers broadened their efforts to include the artisans. By 1868, when the Liberal government of Benito Juárez had been restored to power, the typesetters, candle makers, and cloth makers had joined the textile factory workers in a new movement. The anarchist leadership had successfully brought together workers practicing mutualist self-help and artisans using collective management strategies through their cooperatives into an organization that supported strikes and political propaganda. In 1869, they created the first workers council in Mexico, the Círculo Prole-

tario, in charge of coordinating the organization of the industrial and agricultural laborers of the central plateau.

By the early 1870s the unification of workers' organizations had progressed to the point of including more than 20 groups. Each unit sent a delegate to the Gran Círculo de México, which met at the Church of Saint Peter and Saint Paul in the colonial section of downtown. The anarchists' objectives were clear. Rhodakanaty declared: "Down with all governments." Although he was not a leader within the Círculo, his influence pervaded the group. Ricardo Velatti, a Círculo spokesman, described their economic adversary: "Capital, here we have the terrible enemy of the worker. . . . [They] act like petty kings in order to fill their coffers from the sweat of those who have to work. . . ." But the workers did not seek to only oppose the new capitalists. They sought utopia: "No more rich and poor, masters and servants, governments and governed, capitalists and workers! All men share the just and dignified task before them!" In other areas of the nation similar unionization undertakings by labor radicals were underway. At this point we know little about them except for their appearances at the Congreso General Obrero de la República Mexicana, which convened in Mexico City in 1876. In those meetings they displayed the same commitment to the politicizing of mutualist and cooperative working-class groups as their metropolitan counterparts. Their balance of anarchist ideals and more generic unionist beliefs paralleled those of the Mexico City delegates. They were a mix of anarchists, radicals, and activists, temporized by their weakness vis-à-vis the government.

By 1878 some 50,000 workers in the textile industry and artisan crafts had joined groups affiliated with the Congress of Workers. The anarchists continued to influence ideology and practical decision making. They reported some 62 anarchist societies in Mexico. The Congreso affiliates adopted the *rojinegra*, the red and black flag of anarchism, as their emblem, and Mexican labor unions continued to use it into the late twentieth century. In 1880 the Congreso split into two groups, one favoring electoral participation in opposition to the national government and the other favoring only local and state participation in the context of a decentralized federalism that emphasized local self-government. The factions never reconciled. In 1881 the anarchist group, which was the largest, endorsed Nathan Ganz, the American publisher of the *Anarchist Socialist Revolutionary Review* of Boston, to represent them at the International Workingmen's meeting in Europe. While no record of his fulfilling that function exists, the Mexicans' willingness to endorse him speaks for itself. In 1882 the government suppressed the labor movement while recruiting the foreign capital needed for its industrialization program. The anarchists continued to operate, but they were out of the limelight for 10 years.

In the agrarian sector Zalacosta undertook organizing the disgruntled ranchers and workers at Chalco, southeast of Mexico City. During the late 1860s he and Julio Chávez López, probably a disgruntled local ranchero who had operated a small olive orchard, organized a large peasants' uprising there. Mexico City land developer Inigo Noriega had provoked the citizenry by privatizing the property and draining Lake Chalco with government permission. In response, Chávez López and Zalacosta issued a manifesto to all the "oppressed of Mexico and the universe" calling for the restoration of the communal lands and municipal autonomy. The Mexican army executed Chávez López, who actually led the 1,500 rebels into battle at Chalco. In the late 1870s Zalacosta organized a communalist agrarian movement. In 1878 the representatives of 80 pueblos and rural communities convened in a congress arranged by Zalacosta at La Barranca. They demanded the restoration of their peasant lands and municipal autonomies. Rebuffed, several armed bands seized properties in the northern parts of the states of Michoacán and Mexico and points in Querétaro and San Luis Potosí. In 1880 the army captured Zalacosta and executed him at Querétaro. The fighting continued from 1878 to 1884 and spread to Tamaulipas, Hidalgo, and Veracruz. In the northern sector of the fighting, the leaders of the peasant forces, Juan Santiago and Padre Zavala, had been in direct contact with the "communists" from Mexico City.

Meanwhile, other radical agrarian programs revealed the deep interconnectedness between anarchist thought and peasant community aspirations. In 1878 Colonel Alberto Santa Fe, once described as "half-Bakuninist, half-Marxist," published his "Ley del Pueblo" in Puebla. Reflecting strong anarchist influences, he called for the distribution of land parcels to all families resident in the pueblos on the basis of their numbers of male offspring. He wanted to end urban ownership of rural land, level income and wealth, abolish wages, and create self-governing *falanges* (or communities, not to be confused with the *falanges* of Spanish fascism). Santa Fe's program anticipated that of the Plan de Ayala of the Zapatistas during the 1910 Revolution. Otilio Montaño, who wrote the Plan de Ayala after becoming an aide to Emiliano Zapata, attended classes at a small public school in Ajusco while Rhodakanaty taught there during the 1880s.

During the 1890s two forms of anarchist activity prevailed. Among the workers, *sociedades de resistencia,* such as the one formed by the textile workers at Río Blanco, Veracruz, survived as long as they escaped the scrutiny of the army and *rurales* (rural police). The other appeared as a student challenge at the National University School of Law to the political dictatorship of President Porfirio Díaz. Led by Ricardo, Enrique, and Jesús Flores Magón, the movement quickly radicalized and fought with the police during demonstrations. Ricardo and Enrique soon became anarchists, espousing the rural communalism found among the indigenous peoples of their native state of Oaxaca, while Jesús remained more moderate, favoring federalism and democracy. By 1900 Ricardo and Enrique Flores Magón had become anarchist revolutionaries.

They then fled to the United States and Canada to escape apprehension by the Mexican authorities. In the United States they established the Partido Liberal Mexicano (PLM, or Mexican Liberal Party), a political party that served as a tranquil front for violent resistance to the Díaz regime. They established a political headquarters in exile at Los Angeles, where they published *Regeneración*, a newspaper of "resistance," and distributed it surreptitiously in Mexico. Their efforts found considerable support. At the large Río Blanco textile mill the *sociedad de resistencia* became a PLM affiliate, while other PLM groups formed along the border in Chihuahua, Coahuila, and Sonora, and as far south as Puebla and Veracruz. The two groups at Cananea became involved in the famous 1906 strike and gun battle that ensued. Although the Magonistas did not instigate the uprising, their propaganda helped delegitimize the authorities. At Río Blanco the Magonistas were a presence in the workers' uprising of 1907. In Veracruz, PLM member Santana Rodríguez, known as "Santanón," led 300 rebels in a four year guerrilla campaign that included an attack on the Orizaba textile complex where Río Blanco was situated before the outbreak of the Revolution in late 1910.

Between 1907 and 1910 the PLM took part in locally supported insurgencies in the north centered at Casas Grandes and Janos in Chihuahua, and at Las Vacas, Coahuila. The authorities, however, compromised the PLM leadership. American agents repeatedly arrested avowed anarchist Ricardo Flores Magón and various members of his junta in Los Angeles. Meanwhile Prisciliano Silva and Praxedis Guerrero, the two anarchist leaders in the north, were also silenced. Mexican soldiers killed Guerrero during an armed battle at Casas Grandes, and American agents seized a cache of arms at the Silva home in El Paso. Like the conflict in Veracruz, however, the PLM-influenced fighting in northeastern Chihuahua continued unabated at the outbreak of the Revolution.

With Ricardo Flores Magón in the territorial prison at Yuma, Arizona, the angry PLM leaders took a prominent role in northwestern Mexico during the first years of the Revolution. In northwestern Chihuahua PLM leaders José de la Luz Blanco and José Inez Salazar controlled the area between Columbus, New Mexico, and William Randolph Hearst's Babicora Ranch almost 200 miles to the south. Commanding some 1,500 men, Salazar ordered the approximately 2,000 Americans in the area to get out. Prominent American settler Junius Romney declared

> that all guarantees, for the safety of life and property of American citizens, were withdrawn, and then by command of said General, large forces of his soldiers proceeded to Colonia Dublan, Colonia Díaz, and other towns where Americans resided, and by acts of violence and atrocities made serious threats, against the families of Americans.

In Mexico City and the other urban and industrial centers, anarchists took the lead in mobilizing the working class. When Francisco I. Madero became president in 1911, he authorized the creation of a government-supported union with which he hoped to control a popular base of support for his regime. However, the anarchists were ahead of him. Amadeo Ferres, a Catalan exile, had formed the Grupo Luz among the typesetters and printing industry workers of Mexico City in 1910. Declaring "The Mexican government and all governments now in existence fail to provide just and equal administration of the law to the working class," Ferres and the *tipogafos* created a *sociedad de resistencia* in order to reorganized the working class. Later they formed the Grupo Luz, published a *Manifiesto Anarquista,* and supported the Magonistas.

In 1912 they created the anarcho-syndicalist Casa del Obrero. Syndicalism refers to anarchism's adaptation to the large-scale production facilities of modern capitalism. The workers would rule the means of production through syndicates involving the thousands of workers in specific industries or found at certain locales. The syndicates replaced the mutualist societies and small craft groupings of the nineteenth century. In 1914, when the Casa had become a nationwide organization, its members added the word "Mundial" to its name. At its peak strength in 1916 the Casa counted some 150,000 members. In 1914 it contributed several thousand members to the revolutionary Red Battalions of General Álvaro Obregón Salido, who in return promised to allow the Casa to organize the workers of the nation without government interference.

The Casa leaders chose to support Obregón's Constitutionalist faction of the Revolution because of Obregón's advocacy of "workers' revolution," his promises of untrammeled working-class organizing, Casa participation in industrial and labor decisions, and agrarian reform, which mollified those who saw the need to satisfy peasant aspirations. Following the defeat of the main military components of the Villistas and Zapatistas, which were led primarily by individuals of peasant and rural working-class backgrounds and therefore culturally and socially distant from the Casa leadership, the urban and industrial working-class leaders of the Casa organized their power and began to challenge the new government. The Casa leadership group known as Lucha and its syndicates had branch organizations in virtually all of the principal cities of the nation, including Monterrey and Guadalajara. These groups comprised more than just unions—they included militiamen and were equipped with armories.

In 1916, the anarchist leadership of the Casa came into direct confrontation with the government of Venustiano Carranza and General Obregón. The anarchist leaders used strikes, marches, and large crowds to protest urgent problems, including food shortages caused by distributors withholding their products for higher prices, the use of scrip moneys by employers, inflation, and the failure of the authorities to support hard-won concessions obtained earlier from the owners of businesses in order to settle strikes. In May and August 1916 the Casa held general strikes that paralyzed Mexico City. In the strike in May the workers shut down transportation and electrical power and marched in several columns to the center of the city, where they convened en

masse at the Alameda. The government immediately agreed to their demands. Surprised, the Casa leaders accepted the concessions. However, they went unfulfilled.

In August the Casa strike committee attempted the same strategy. The effort ended in disaster. Carranza ordered the strike leaders arrested. Obregón refused the appeals of the leaders of Lucha and suggested that the Casa disband. Finally, threatened with immediate death at the hands of a soldier, a Casa striker helped restore electrical power to the city. The government broke the strike by restoring transportation, communications, and lighting services. It broke the Casa by using the army to raid their offices and forcing its leaders into hiding. The army raided the offices of the Casa throughout the nation, disarming the workers in the process. The organization fell apart.

Demoralized, anarchist union leaders made several attempts to reorganize. By the end of the decade their greatest successes centered on the petroleum center of Tampico. Some sixteen syndicates constituted the Casa of Tampico and used it as their organizing center. During these years Germinal, the principal anarchist group at Tampico, and the Casa attempted to convene a nationwide labor congress in order to maintain a working-class movement that was not controlled by the government. However, despite the support of the American Industrial Workers of the World (IWW) and its petroleum workers syndicate, the government and its supporters won a narrow victory. In a series of meetings held in 1917 and 1918, the adherents to the government's drive to create a large labor confederation affiliated with it won out. In 1918 they succeeded in creating the Confederación Regional Obrera Mexicana (CROM, or Regional Confederation of Mexican Workers).

The demoralized anarchists took until 1921 to respond to the CROM by creating the Confederación General de Trabajadores (CGT, or General Confederation of Workers). Virtually all of the radical unions of the anarchist past joined the CGT, giving it a special vitality and color. Yet, the CGT was more than a grouping of anarchists and their generic, but less political, brethren from the mutualist and cooperative movements. The CGT adhered to "libertarian communism" and, like the Casa, was led by a control group, the Centro Sindicalista Libertario. Paralleling the Congreso of the 1870s and the Casa, the libertarians accepted dissent as a part of their polity. Despite anarcho-syndicalist leadership, the CGT included socialists, communists and a variety of radicals. It even flirted with the Moscow-led International and welcomed the Communist Party to a brief participation.

During the 1920s the independent and ideologically driven CGT activists fought with government-supported CROM adherents in Mexico City, Veracruz, Tampico, and other industrial centers. Wildcat strikes and conflict with the CROM at the San Ildefonso textile mills at San Angel, the railroad yards at Nonoalco, and a 1923 Mexico City transit workers strike resulted in rioting by CGT members. During the 1923 transit strike transportation was paralyzed in much of Mexico City. The transit workers and their supporters set up barricades in the downtown section. The army dislodged them taking 100 prisoners, but the strikers shot and killed five riot policemen, two soldiers, and a CROM strikebreaker. Minister of War Plutarco Elías Calles declared martial law in order to end the strike. That year the CGT joined the anarcho-syndicalist International Workingmen's Association.

In the aftermath of the Casa's demise, local members formed some 23 anarchist groups throughout central Mexico and as far north as Nuevo Laredo. The most successful among these efforts was the organization of the renters' strike in Veracruz and the formation of the oil workers' syndicate at Tampico in alliance with the IWW. In the early 1920s anarchist Heron Proal led the Veracruz tenants' union, while former PLM leader Librado Rivera played a prominent role in Tampico publishing a newspaper. In 1922 Proal and a group of CGT anarchists convened a series of public meetings to protest rent increases in the port city. They formed the Sindicato de Inquilinos Revolucionarios, which challenged food and clothing prices as well as rents. A boycott ensued, punctuated by riots. In 1924 the authorities arrested Proal and sent him into exile.

By the late 1920s the impoverished CGT was given a fatal jolt. The government ended its sponsorship of Luis Morones, leader of the CROM, and many of the largest unions in Mexico switched their allegiance to the CGT. That move probably tripled the membership from no more than 80,000 to perhaps 250,000, but it brought people into the organization who already had learned to cooperate with the government. The state on its part continued to consolidate its power. In 1931 the government announced that organized labor and representatives of private capital had accepted the Ley del Trabajo, with its provisions for mandatory arbitration and prior state approval of strikes. The leaders of almost all of the CGT's larger syndicates accepted the accord, and formally organized anarchism in Mexico quietly expired.

In the years that followed, however, an underground appeared. During the 1930s anarchist operatives brought about an uprising at the U.S.-owned Atencingo sugar processing center in Puebla. In the 1940s and 1950s Rubén Jaramillo led an agrarian uprising in Morelos that under-scored the need for village autonomy and a more far-reaching agrarian reform plan with less government interference. On January 1, 1994, the Zapatista Army of National Liberation seized San Cristóbal de las Casas, the second-largest city in the state of Chiapas. Wearing red-and-black emblems and carrying black flags with a red star emblazoned on them, the Zapatistas called for political autonomy in those areas predominantly inhabited by Native Americans. The modern-day Zapatistas reflect many influences from the modern left, but some of their crucial demands are incompatible with Leninism. They seek local self-government and total equality among those in the areas achieving autonomy. In those respects they hearken back to the workers' self-management programs of Rhodakanaty, Alberto Santa Fe and his Ley del Pueblo, Otilio Montaño and the Plan de Ayala, Ricardo Flores Magón and the communal life of rural Oaxaca that he tried to preserve, and the Casa del Obrero Mundial.

See also Casa del Obrero Mundial; Partido Liberal Mexicano (PLM); Zapatista Rebellion in Chiapas

Select Bibliography

Caulfield, Norman E., "The Industrial Workers of the World and Mexican Labor." Ph.D. diss., University of Houston, 1987.

Cockcroft, James D., *Intellectual Precursors of the Mexican Revolution.* Austin: University of Texas Press, 1968.

Gómez Quinones, Juan, *Sembradores: Ricardo Flores Magón y El Partido Liberal Mexicano: A Eulogy and Critique.* Los Angeles: Atzlan Publications, 1973.

Hart, John Mason, *Anarchism and the Mexican Working Class.* Austin: University of Texas Press, 1978.

_____, *Revolutionary Mexico: The Coming and Process of the Mexican Revolution.* Berkeley: University of California Press, 1987.

_____, "Revolutionary Syndicalism in Mexico." In *Revolutionary Syndicalism: An International Perspective,* edited by Marcel van der Linden and Wayne Thorpe. Aldershot, England: Scolar Press, and Brookfield, Vermont: Gower, 1990.

Hodges, Donald C., *Mexican Anarchism after the Revolution.* Austin: University of Texas Press, 1995.

—JOHN MASON HART

ÁNGELES, FELIPE

1868–1919 • General

Felipe Ángeles was born on June 13, 1868, in Zacuatipán, Hidalgo. He died on November 26, 1919, in the city of Chihuahua. Educated at the primary level in Molango, Hidalgo, he went on to study in the Instituto Literario in Pachuca, subsequently entering the Colegio Militar, in Mexico City in 1883, where he obtained the title of lieutenant engineer in 1890. Concentrating on education, he took on various lectureships in the Colegio Militar, the Escuela Nacional Preparatoria and the Escuela de Tiro. In 1896 he was captain of artillery, and by 1901 he had obtained the rank of a major. Three years later he became a lieutenant colonel, becoming a full colonel in 1908, the year he both was appointed director of the Escuela de Tiro and left for France to continue his studies in artillery. He had visited France previously in 1901 to study the artillery materiel manufactured by Schneider Canet.

Ángeles was in Paris when the Revolution broke out in 1910. He requested official permission to return to Mexico, but his suit was rejected. In May of the following year he was awarded the order of Knight of the Légion d'Honneur by the French government. That December General Bernardo Reyes took up arms against the new president, Francisco I. Madero, but Reyes's plot failed and he was imprisoned. Ángeles was back in Mexico on January 1, 1912, and the following day was appointed by Madero director of the Colegio Militar. In June he attained the rank of brigadier general.

The democratic regime of Madero at that time was under attack from all sides, and the president was obliged to send Ángeles to Morelos to take charge of the seventh military zone. In October of the same year Félix Díaz, the old dictator Porfirio Díaz's nephew, was taken prisoner in Veracruz for conspiracy against the government and brought to Mexico City.

On February 9, 1913, a coup d'état was initiated. A faction of the military freed Reyes and Díaz and attacked the National Palace. Reyes died in the attempt and the conspirators barricaded themselves within the Ciudadela, an army barracks. Madero, having appointed General Victoriano Huerta as head of the loyal troops, traveled to Cuernavaca to return with Ángeles. However Madero was not able to put the latter in charge of military operations because of objections by Huerta. After ten days of fighting Huerta openly joined the conspirators (he apparently had used the initial fighting to thin out the ranks loyal to Madero while keeping those forces loyal to him alone safe from the fray). Ultimately, Huerta had Madero, his vice president José María Pino Suárez, and Ángeles arrested. But while Madero and Pino Suárez were forced to resign and subsequently assassinated, Ángeles was accused of murdering a young man, taken to court, freed, and sent into exile to the Mexican Embassy in Paris.

Ángeles did not remain long in Europe. He left for Mexico in October 1913 and joined the Constitutionalist Army in Sonora under Venustiano Carranza. Appointed secretary of war and the navy by Carranza, Ángeles was very quickly treated with hostility by the Sonoran military, especially Álvaro Obregón, who was not keen to see an ex-Porfirista general in the Revolutionary army.

When Ángeles accompanied Carranza on his visit to Chihuahua in January 1914, he convinced Pancho Villa to ask Carranza to put him in charge of artillery for the Division of the North which was preparing for a long and arduous campaign. Carranza agreed and in March Ángeles had joined the Division of the North. He was to participate as chief of artillery in the great military triumphs of 1914: the capture of Torréon, the Battles of San Pedro de las Colonias

and Paredón in April, and the capture of Zacatecas in May. A little before the attack on Zacatecas, Ángeles participated in the so-called disobedience of the generals of the Division of the North, countermanding Carranza's orders to halt their advance on Mexico City. The generals' "disobedience" ensured the defeat of Huerta's army, but it also increased the influence of Villa, Carranza's most important ally in the Revolutionary movement. Ángeles justified his stance in a tough letter to Carranza that he later published under the title "Justificación de la desobediencia de los generales de la División del Norte."

At the end of 1914 Ángeles attended the Convention of Aguascalientes as Villa's representative. After the break between Villa and Carranza, he acted as chief of Artillery for the Convention in the battles that took place in the Bajío region of north-central Mexico in 1915. With the overthrow of the Northern Division, Ángeles left Villa, who had decided to carry on fighting, and went into exile in the United States. In 1916, shortly after Villa's attack on Columbus, New Mexico, Ángeles traveled to New York, where he decided to remain.

At the end of the World War I he worked to prevent the American military invasion of Mexico and tried to appease factional conflicts. In 1918 he participated in the creation of the Alianza Liberal Mexicana (Liberal Mexican Alliance), which brought together exiles of various ideological persuasions linked by the common aim to stop the war in Mexico and form a coalition government representative of all the factions involved in the struggle. He entered Chihuahua clandestinely on December 11 and joined up with Villa, who by then was being pursued by both the Mexican and U.S. governments. Nevertheless, Ángeles, a conciliator, pacifist, and philanthropic socialist who wanted peace at all costs and who showed great admiration for the Americans, was incapable of convincing Villa, who viewed his plans as illusory and lacking any sense. The Revolutionary chief was implacable, intransigent, and decidedly anti-American. Villa did not believe in peace and he did not want to make one with the enemy.

After Villa's attack on Ciudad Juárez in June 1919 (in which Ángeles did not participate), Ángeles was convinced that there was no solution to the bloody war in Mexico and that the United States never would accept Villa. Tired, ill, and very disillusioned, he had no desire to go on living and did not accompany Villa on a raid on Múzquiz, Coahuila. Betrayed by his guards, Ángeles was arrested in the municipality of Rosario, Chihuahua, handed over to the Federal Army, and made to undergo a celebrated court martial. Although the process was illegal and he knew well enough that Carranza never would pardon him, Ángeles made a brilliant defense in response to his enemies' case for the prosecution. The court martial condemned him to death, and on the November 26, while Villa was riding near Coahuila, Ángeles was shot in Chihuahua in the quarters of the Twenty-first Cavalry regiment. He was buried initially Chihuahua, but in 1941 his remains were removed to Pachuca.

Select Bibliography

Guilpain Peuliard, Odile, *Felipe Ángeles y los destinos de la Revolución mexicana.* Mexico City: Fondo de Cultura Económica, 1991.

Katz, Friedrich, *The Secret War in Mexico.* Chicago: University of Chicago Press, 1980.

Mena Brito, Bernardino, *Felipe Ángeles Federal.* Mexico City: Herrerías, 1956.

Obregón, Álvaro, *Ocho mil kilómetros en campaña.* Mexico City: Fondo de Cultura Económica, 1959.

—RUBÉN OSORIO ZUÑIGA

ANTHROPOLOGY

From its beginnings as a professional discipline, Mexican anthropology has been conceived by both anthropologists and representatives of the Mexican state as a key instrument in the forging of a national identity. First, anthropologists have been given the task of rescuing and maintaining of the archaeological wealth of Mexico, discursively constructed as the "cultural patrimony of the nation." Second, anthropology has been expected to provide a profound knowledge of contemporary indigenous cultures, which have made powerful and distinctive contributions to contemporary Mexican culture. Finally, anthropologists have been expected to find a way to "Mexicanize" the indigenous population, incorporating it into national processes. These three tasks have been interpreted in many different ways, in both ideological and practical terms, at times resulting in contradictions or even open conflicts.

From the National Museum to the Revolution

The seminal institution of Mexican anthropology was the National Museum. Founded in the dawn of the Republic in 1825, the Museum reached a peak in during the Porfiriato, the rule of Porfirio Díaz (1876–1910). In 1886 the first issue of the *Anales del Museo Nacional* appeared, and the journal would continue to enjoy great prestige for decades to come. In 1896 and 1897 the first laws were promulgated protecting monuments, declaring that the nation was the sole owner of archaeological properties. To ensure better fulfillment of the law, the museum was put in charge of drafting an archaeological survey of Mexico. In 1906, under the auspices of Justo Sierra, minister of public instruction and fine arts, the museum reorganized its departments of archaeology, ethnography, and ethnohistory to train professionals who could rescue and classify archives and collections as well as protecting and restoring archaeological monuments. Also in 1906 Leopoldo Bartres, the official archaeologist of Porfirismo, began the excavations that eventually would uncover the majestic Pyramid of the Sun in Teotihuacan. During the centennial celebration in 1910, the Great Pyramid would be used as an official symbol of the nation and the regime.

Following an agreement signed among the governments of Mexico, the United States, and Prussia in 1911, Harvard,

Columbia, and the University of Pennsylvania founded the International School of Archaeology and American Ethnography within the National Museum. Many Mexican researchers participated in the program, as well as such international luminaries as Franz Boas and Eduard Seler. The school sought to establish permanent research projects under the guidance of experienced professionals; doctoral students from other countries also would participate in the program. These projects were first directed by Seler, Boas, and such international scientists as Alfred Tozzer, Paul Radin, and Georges Engerrand; they were joined by scholars from Mexico (Isabel Ramírez Castañeda and Manuel Gamio) and other countries (Richard Hay, Hans Mechling, Leopold Wagner, and J. Alden Mason). A student of Boas at Columbia University, Gamio played a key role in a particularly important achievement, directing the first stratigraphic excavation in Mexico. Gamio worked under the supervision of Seler and following a hypothesis of Boas about the sequence of civilizations in the Valley of Anáhuac in central and southern Mexico. Since then, the idea of a single cultural province or area (which later has come to be called Mesoamerica) has been predominant in anthropological studies in Mexico, particularly in archaeology.

The work of the Escuela Internacional continued even after the fall of Díaz, but after 1914 the generalization of the armed conflict and the lack of funds made its work almost impossible. Nonetheless, Gamio found a way to link anthropological study with the emerging Revolutionary governments. From the Inspección de Monumentos Arqueológicos (Inspection of Archaeological Monuments), Gamio proposed a new vision of anthropology as a science that would not only rescue the past but construct the future, helping to resolve the social and economic problems of population and "forge" a national identity. In 1917 Gamio founded within the Secretariat of Agriculture and Development the Dirección de Estudios Arqueológicos y Etnográficos (Directorate of Archaeological and Ethnographic Studies), which later would be renamed the Dirección de Antropología. Gamio used the Directorate to embark on an ambitious interdisciplinary program of regional studies, which would combine the exploration of archaeological zones, the systematization of archives, the foundation of local museums, and the diagnosis of the contemporary situation of the indigenous population. All of these projects would serve as a basis for economic and cultural development, helping to foster the national unity. The first of these projects was in the valley of Teotihuacan, and its results were published in 1922; the far-reaching theoretical and methodological introduction was successfully defended by Gamio as a doctoral thesis at Columbia with the backing of Boas, although Boas gave his support more for Gamio's historicism and cultural relativism than for his faith in "Revolutionary progress," which Boas did not share. Nonetheless, Gamio continued to express this faith in numerous articles in the journal *Ethnos,* the mouthpiece of the anthropologists of the new regime, which Gamio founded and directed.

In 1924 the Dirección de Antropología was transferred to the Secretaría de Educación Pública (SEP, or Secretariat of Public Education), which had been radically reorganized by José Vasconcelos. This reorganization sought to mobilize all the cultural and educational resources of the country to establish the bases of a national culture that, although clearly modern, would find its roots in the fusion of pre-Hispanic and European traditions. Gamio was named subsecretary, although political problems soon forced him to resign and move to the United States, where he wrote pioneering studies on Mexican migrants. Gamio's successor as subsecretary, Moisés Sáenz, also had been a disciple of Boas at Columbia, but he was particularly interested in putting into practice the ideas of his principal mentor, the educator John Dewey. Sáenz's work focused on the foundation and development of rural schools. The Dirección de Antropología became the Departamento de Escuelas Rurales e Incorporación Cultural Indígena (Department of Rural Schools and Indigenous Cultural Incorporation). Sáenz hoped to repeat Gamio's experience of multidisciplinary regional research—albeit on a somewhat more modest scale—in the Purépecha (Tarascan) area known as La Cañada de los Once Pueblos. The hostility of local caciques (political bosses) stymied Sáenz's ambitions, but the experience enabled Sáenz to spread the idea of "social anthropology," in which the scientist also became an agent of *indigenista* policies of national integration.

The archaeological and ethnological research of the Museo Nacional meanwhile continued under the direction of Nicolás León (until his death in 1929). In 1930 the Museo Nacional, along with many other museums and historical buildings, fell under the authority of the Departamento de Monumentos Artísticos, Arqueológicos e Históricos. In the Museo Nacional, the dominant orientation always was German cultural historicism, now driven by Hermann Beyer, a disciple of Seler living in Mexico; in 1919 Beyer had founded a journal with long-lasting influence, *El México Antiguo.* The most important figure in Maya studies until the 1940s, the U.S. anthropologist Sylvanus Morley tended to draw on a similar theoretical orientation, supported by the Smithsonian Institution and the Carnegie Foundation. The incipient Social Anthropology, on the other hand, increasingly was influenced by Anglo-Saxon structuralism following the work of anthropologist Robert Redfield of the University of Chicago in Tepoztlán, Morelos (1928), and in Yucatán (1930–35). The Mexican anthropologist Alfonso Villa Rojas also was influenced by social anthropology, later becoming one of the pillars of official *indigenismo.* The Carnegie Foundation sponsored both the social anthropological research of Redfield and Villa Rojas and archaeological research in Yucatán under the direction of Sylvanus Morley. Tulane University in New Orleans also would sponsor research on Maya archaeology, ethnology, and physical anthropology under the direction of Franz Blom and the Mexican anthropologist Carlos Basauri.

From Revolutionary Nationalism to State Anthropology

The presidential administration of Lázaro Cárdenas (1934–40) brought a new radicalism to the Revolutionary programs of agrarian reform, popular mobilization, and state control over strategic resources and industries. National and anti-imperialist discourse also was radicalized, and the state renewed its interest in anthropology as useful instrument for the incorporation of indigenous peoples. For their part, many anthropologists had embraced leftist ideologies and saw the Cárdenas government as an advance towards socialism.

In 1936, following an idea of Moisés Sáenz, Cárdenas created the Departamento de Asuntos Indígenas (DAI, or Department of Indian Affairs), an autonomous institution dedicated to research and improving the lives of aboriginal groups. One example of the research sponsored by the DAI was the integral study of the Yaqui "tribe" in the state of Sonora in 1938 under the direction of Alfonso Fabila, who sought to provide some foundation for the educational and agrarian policies of the Cárdenas administration. The DAI also sponsored the creation of the Comisión del Valle del Mezquital, which brought together several government institutions responsible for the social welfare of the Otomí people of the region. The Comisión del Valle del Mezquital also served to channel demands and legitimate the government. Another key project of the DAI was the Tarascan Project (1939–40), a pilot program that sought to establish the foundations of literacy programs in indigenous languages. Several Mexican linguists and anthropologists participated in this program, as well as a number of U.S. scholars. In 1935 the Instituto Lingüístico de Verano (ILV, or Summer Linguistic Institute) was created at the recommendation of Sáenz and the sponsorship of Cárdenas. The ILV was directed by the U.S. Protestant minister William Cameron Townsend, who in Guatemala had conducted successful experiments in literacy and in the translation of biblical texts into the Cakchikel language. In Mexico the ILV was put in charge of producing literacy booklets in all indigenous languages.

The teaching of anthropology received an additional impetus from the Universidad Obrera (Workers' University) and the Instituto Politécnico Nacional (IPN, or National Polytechnic Institute). The Universidad Obrera was founded by a group of left-wing intellectuals, among them the anthropologist Miguel Othón de Mendizábal, and sought to promote discussion and research on the working population in the city and countryside, including the indigenous population. The IPN also sought to promote high-level technical education and, at the initiative of Mendizábal, included a department of anthropology in the school of biological sciences, in which courses were given on physical anthropology, archaeology, ethnology, and linguistics. At the same time, ties were developed with the Museo Nacional, the Universidad Nacional, and the Departamento de Asuntos Indígenas, particularly the Proyecto Tarasco. The Universidad Nacional maintained professorships in prehistory and archaeology in the school of philosophy and letters, which were filled by specialists trained in the old Museo Nacional. The jurist Lucio Mendieta y Nuñez founded the Instituto de Investigaciones Sociales (Institute of Social Research) in the Universidad Nacional, which included ethnographic research and interdisciplinary regional studies such as Mendieta's work in the Tarascan region. In 1937 the Sociedad Mexicana de Antropología began to bring anthropologists from a variety of institutions and specialties together in round tables (which continue through the present day) and in the journal *Revista Mexicana de Estudios Antropológicos*.

On February 3, 1939, a law was passed creating the Instituto Nacional de Antropología e Historia (INAH, or National Institute of Anthropology and History). The INAH replaced the Departamento de Monumentos Históricos, Arqueológicos y Artísticos and was separated from the Secretaría de Educación Pública. Several new museums were opened, and the INAH also absorbed the Escuela de Antropología of the IPN, which was rebaptized the Escuela Nacional de Antropología e Historia (ENAH). Research in all branches of academic anthropology was reorganized (leaving applied research to the social anthropologists of the DAI). The first director of the INAH, the lawyer and anthropologist Alfonso Caso, remained in his post for eight years and left his personal imprint on the structure of the institute. A long-standing disciple of Hermann Beyer—and therefore a follower of cultural historicism—Caso had distinguished himself for his spectacular discoveries and reconstructions at Monte Albán, Oaxaca, and at Tzintzuntzan and Ihuatzio in the state of Michoacán. As director of the INAH Caso was the driving force behind the exploration and restoration of several archaeological sites under the close supervision of the Mexican state; the 1939 law had constituted the INAH as the only organ authorized to do archaeological research in Mexico. The INAH's management of archaeological sites would contribute to a more profound knowledge of Mexico's pre-Hispanic past, as well as nationalist pride and the development of the tourist industry. In a related effort to rescue Mexico's artistic and cultural heritage (and to promote tourism), the INAH also took charge of colonial convents and monasteries, churches, and other buildings, forming the Dirección de Monumentos Coloniales

(Directorate of Colonial Monuments). At the same time, research in physical anthropology, ethnography, archaeology, ethnohistory, and linguistics fell to the faculty of the ENAH. Among the first members of the faculty were Martínez del Río, Mendizábal, and Daniel Rubín de la Borbolla (its first director), as well as linguists and ethnologists from the Proyecto Tarasco. The faculty also was joined by five Europeans fleeing fascism, the Spanish Republicans Juan Comas and Pedro Bosch Gimpera, Paul Kirchoff, Ada Daloja, and Robert Weitlaner.

In April 1940 the first Congreso Indigenista Interamericano (Interamerican Indigenist Congress) opened in Pátzcuaro, Michoacán. This conference had been agreed upon at the third and fourth Interamerican Conferences given the clear need for governmental representatives to create scientifically founded common strategies to define and resolve the so-called "Indian problem" of the Americas. The Congreso Indigenista included anthropologists, representatives from indigenous groups, jurists, doctors, and government functionaries from almost every country in the western hemisphere. There were approximately 150 presentations, although only a very small number of the presentations were by indigenous authors. The congress was coordinated by the DAI, and among the officially adopted resolutions were a series of recommendations inspired by work done by Mexican *indigenistas* and anthropologists: the creation of government agencies for *indigenista* research and welfare, which would be staffed in part by anthropologists; literacy training in indigenous languages; and land redistribution to indigenous communities. Nonetheless, there were clear contradictions between representatives who called for unconditional respect for indigenous cultures and those who emphasized the need to subordinate ethnic diversity to the creation of modern, homogeneous national cultures. Resolution 30, for example, opposed the disappearance of indigenous cultures, but the inaugural address of President Cárdenas proclaimed that the goal of the congress was *no indianizar a México sino mexicanizar al indio*—not to "Indianize" Mexico but rather to "Mexicanize" the Indian; many other delegates thought along similar lines. Still other delegates, familiar with the nationalities policy of the Soviet Union, were sympathetic to the idea of American countries defining themselves as multiethnic or even multinational. In the end, however, the vision of the "Indian problem" that predominated was in terms of the need to make Indians participate efficiently in Western progress.

An important result of the congress was the creation of the Instituto Indigenista Interamericano, which was headquartered in Mexico City and directed by Manuel Gamio. After the end of the Cárdenas presidency in December 1940, however, *indigenista* fervor markedly diminished. For the new president, Manuel Avila Camacho, the priority was national unity—particularly with Mexico's imminent entry into World War II—and unity required putting a brake on peasant and indigenous mobilizations. The DAI once again was folded into the SEP, and its energies were focused on teaching Spanish to indigenous peoples. The linguists of the Proyecto Tarasco were dismissed, accused of fomented cultural divisions and imitating the Soviet Union, but the work of the ILV was allowed to continue. Anthropology fell back to the INAH and the ENAH, although it acquired renewed importance in research done in collaboration with U.S. institutions: in the Maya region with the Carnegie Institute and the University of Chicago; in the Tarascan region (where Ralph Beals and George Foster would distinguish themselves) with the University of California and the Smithsonian Institute; in the Totonac region, with the Smithsonian and the leadership of Isabel Kelly; and in the Valley of Oaxaca, where, in addition to archaeological exploration sponsored by the Carnegie Institute and the Panamerican Institute of Anthropology and History, the most famous anthropologist of the day, Bronislaw Malinowski, would do a study of the regional market system under the auspices of Yale University. Many young Mexican anthropologists participated in these studies, later becoming leading figures in their field: Julio de la Fuente (with Malinowski), Pedro Carrasco (with Beals), and Angel Palerm (with Kelly). Carrasco and Palerm were part of the Spanish exile community, but unlike Pedro Bosch Gimpera and Juan Comas, they arrived in Mexico at student age and were educated in the ENAH.

The rise of the various specialties of anthropology gave the ENAH in the 1940s and 1950s a solid international reputation. Physical anthropology specialized in osteological research, working closely with paleontological and archaeological studies. In this field the anthropologists Javier Romero, Eusebio Dávalos, and Santiago Genovés particularly distinguished themselves. Osteologists and paleontologists gained world-wide recognition for their exploration of the fossils of Tepexpan (1945–47), which culminated in the discovery of the oldest human remains in the continent. However, important anthropometric research also was done by Carlos and Manuel Basauri, José Gómez Robleda, and Genovés to understand nutrition and adaptation to the physical environment by indigenous and mestizo groups. In archaeology, in addition to the monumental reconstruction led by Alfonso Caso, Eduardo Noguera, and José García Payón, researchers began working on the systematic study of population centers, looking at the development of agriculture, irrigation, division of labor, and political institutions. This intellectual current, inspired by Marxist concepts and the writings of Gordon Childe and Karl Wittfogel, would be represented brilliantly by Pedro Armillas, Angel Palerm, Pedro Carrasco, and José Luis Lorenzo; however, it did not have the blessing of Caso and was excluded from official versions of the Mexican past. Linguistic research outside of the ILV was dominated by the figure of Morris Swadesch, who had returned to the United States after the dismantling of the DAI. In the United States, however, Swadesch's leftist ideas made him into a target for McCarthyism, and he returned to Mexico in the early 1950s. From his chair in the ENAH, Swadesch once again insisted on the need to educate people

in their mother tongues and, together with a close-knit group of disciples, began a series of studies in the area of historical anthropology and grammatical and phonetic analysis. Ethnological research tended to be confined to historical ethnography (or ethnohistory) under the leadership of Paul Kirchoff. Kirchoff was interested in establishing—always within the canons of cultural historicism—a scientific strategy for approaching primary sources, defining a geographic distribution of cultural features that would be correlated with archaeological information and field observation. Several students of Kirchoff used this focus in their research in Oaxaca: Barbro Dahlgren in the Sierra Mixteca, Johanna Faulhaber in the Chanantla region, and Arturo Monzón in the Triqui region. Kirchoff also published his book *Mesoamerica,* in which he synthesized the information thus far accumulated about the cultural area of central and southern Mexico and northern Central America, advancing definitive hypotheses about its evolution, boundaries, and regional variations. To discuss the concept of Mesoamerica and examine the ties between past and present in terms of cultural change and continuity (or degrees of "acculturation"), the Viking Foundation organized in New York a symposium coordinated by the sociologist Sol Tax, which later would give rise to the book *Heritage of Conquest.*

Ethnohistorical research also took place under the auspices of the Instituto de Historia in the Universidad Nacional, which had been founded by Pablo Martínez del Río and Rafael García Granados in 1947. The Instituto sponsored permanent seminars on Maya and Nahua cultures, developing an important program to rescue pre-Hispanic and colonial Nahua texts under the leadership of Angel María Garibay and his student Manuel León-Portilla. In a different area, the national archives had been reorganized by Manuel Gamio and Gonzalo Aguirre Beltrán, a young doctor interested in social history and trained in cultural anthropology by Melville Herskovits at Northwestern University in Evanston, Illinois. Aguirre Beltrán's documentary research on colonial labor and Inquisition trials resulted in two seminal books, *La población negra de México* and *Medicina y magia,* in which he posited the existence of a colonial caste structure whose consequences continued to be felt even after Independence and the Revolution.

Social anthropology returned to its earlier prominence when in 1948 President Miguel Alemán Valdés created the Instituto Nacional Indigenista (INI) in compliance with the recommendations of the Congress of Pátzcuaro. The Alemán administration was characterized by state policies geared toward economic modernization and capitalist development, seeking a national industrialization oriented toward the internal market. In this context *indigenismo* had the mission of preparing a trained workforce and a rural population capable of consuming Mexican products. The first director of the INI was Alfonso Caso, who later would be rector of the Universidad Nacional and minister of national resources. In addition to putting in place a complex centralized administration,

Caso proposed a "definition of the Indian" in terms of his or her membership in a community. *Indigenista* action thus would be focused on the transformation of communities, which would have to be studied carefully. Caso also brought together a magnificent team of scholars—Gonzalo Aguirre Beltrán, Julio de la Fuente, Calixta Guiteras-Holmes, Alejandro Marroquín, Ricardo Pozas, Alfonso Villa Rojas, and Robert Weitlaner, among others—who insisted on the necessity of drawing on the far-ranging studies of Redfield and Malinowski and in situating the analysis of indigenous communities in a regional context. In 1949 the INI participated in two regional studies linked to federal development projects in the Papaloapan and Tepalcaltepec River basins (inspired by the Tennessee Valley Authority in the United States). Based on these studies, important books were written on the Mazatecos (Villa Rojas), the Popolucas (Guiteras-Holmes), the Chinantecos (Weitlaner), and the Tarascans (Aguirre Beltrán). In all of these studies the indigenous groups, far from being conceived as isolate "tribes," were considered as peasant communities dependent on cities and markets, which in turn were articulated on a nation-wide scale. Similar studies were written by Pozas on Chamula (in the Tzotzil region of Chiapas), de la Fuente on Yalalag (in the Sierra Zapoteca of Oaxaca), and Marroquín on Tlaxiaco (the market town of Oaxaca's Sierra Mixteca).

The theory of "intercultural regions" that guided these studies was formulated by Aguirre Beltrán in his books *Formas de gobierno indígena, El proceso de aculturación,* and *Regiones de refugio.* According to this theory, indigenous communities are meaningful as parts of a regional system of domination. In this system a mestizo (mixed-race) or ladino (white) elite living in the regional capital monopolizes strategic resources and uses the workforce of indigenous communities to its favor, while excluding these communities from the benefits of the national society. To break this power structure, the *indigenista* policies of the Mexican state promoted agrarian reform, training in agronomy, literacy and Spanish language, health campaigns, and municipal political organization, opening the way for acculturation and equality of all citizens. The concept of acculturation, which implied reciprocal interaction, was proposed in place of the concept of incorporation that Gamio had used. The strategy of the INI consisted in founding Centros Coordinadores de la Acción Indigenista (Coordinating Centers of Indigenista Action) in regional centers to break intercultural power. In 1954 there already were ten coordinating centers. The first of these, in San Cristóbal de las Casas, Chiapas, was directed by Aguirre Beltrán himself. This center worked with two new U.S. projects in the Chiapas highlands, the University of Chicago project directed by Norman McQuown and Julian Pitt-Rivers, and the Harvard Project directed by Evon Z. Vogt. The INI also absorbed rural planning and development agencies that had been created in early periods, such as the Patrimonio Indígena del Valle del Mezquital and institutions to promote bilingual education.

During the 1960s 20 anthropologists collaborated with their U.S. colleagues on the *Handbook of Middle American Indians,* a masterful multivolume work that synthesized contemporary Mesoamericanist research and culminated the golden age of anthropological research in Mexico.

Crisis and Diversification of Mexican Anthropology

In 1964 President Adolfo López Mateos inaugurated the new National Museum of Anthropology and History, a sumptuous building that displayed the archaeological and ethnographic richness of Mexico in a dazzling museographic arrangement. The museum building also housed the ENAH, which was still dominated by the old guard of the INAH and some of its disciples: the archaeologists Ignacio Bernal, Alberto Ruz, and Román Piña Chan; the linguists Leonardo Manrique, Roberto Escalante, Yolanda Lastra, Alfredo Barrera, and Silvia Rendón; the ethnologists Fernando Cámara; and the physical anthropologist Arturo Romano. However, a new generation of dissident anthropologists had begun to emerge, denouncing the academic and political monopolies that Mexican anthropology was subject to, as well as the discipline's excessive ties to U.S. institutions and ideas. The strongest criticism came from ethnologists and social anthropologists, who were interested in breaking the domination of *indigenismo* and returning to the discipline's critical engagement with the problems of poverty, hunger, and the cultural and political domination fomented by the Mexican state. In 1968 many students of the ENAH, supported by a group of professors, participated in the student movement that was brutally repressed by the government of President Gustavo Díaz Ordaz. In 1970 a leftist publishing house brought out *De eso que llaman antropología mexicana* (That which they call Mexican anthropology), signed by five of the activists of 1968: Guillermo Bonfil, Margarita Nolasco, Mercedes Olivera, Enrique Valencia, and Arturo Warman. The book was greeted with enthusiasm by many youths and with ire by the anthropological establishment. It attacked almost all the practices that ruled the discipline, from monumental archaeology for tourists to *indigenista* paternalism. The *indigenista* bureaucracy was accused of being inefficient and corrupt.

One consequence of this shake-up was the strengthening of new institutions for anthropological research and teaching. The University of Xalapa and the University of Yucatán already had schools of anthropology independent of the INAH. A third independent department of social anthropology emerged at the Universidad Iberoamericana, a Jesuit university in Mexico City. Opening its doors to such dissidents from the INAH as Angel Palerm and Arturo Warman, the Iberoamericana gained prominence in the 1970s and 1980s. The Instituto de Estudios Antropológicos at the UNAM consolidated, with anthropologists from the Instituto de Estudios Históricos and exiles from the INAH and ENAH joining the faculty.

In 1970 the new president of Mexico, Luis Echeverría Álvarez, proposed a reconciliation with intellectuals and a return to nationalist discourse. Gonzalo Aguirre Beltrán, who had directed the Instituto Indigenista Interamericano during the 1960s, was named director of the INI by Echeverría (replacing Caso, who had directed the INI for 22 years); he simultaneously was named subsecretary of education. From these posts Aguirre Beltrán worked to strengthen Mexican *indigenismo*—the number of coordinating centers of the INI rose to almost 100—and anthropological research. He managed to get Guillermo Bonfil, one of the dissidents from 1968, appointed director of the INAH, and together with Bonfil he created the Centro de Investigaciones Superiores of the INAH (CIS-INAH, or Center for Advanced Studies at the INAH), which was placed under the directorship of Angel Palerm. Other prominent emerging institutions included the Centro de Estudios Sociológicos at the Colegio de México (which included various social anthropologists, among them Rodolfo Stavenhagen), the Centro de Investigación e Integración Social de Oaxaca, the department of social anthropology at the Universidad Autónoma Metropolitana, the Centro de Estudios Antropológicos at the Colegio de Michoacán, the school of anthropology at the Universidad de las Américas in Cholula, Puebla, and the anthropology department at the Universidad Autónoma de Guadalajara.

Many researchers in the 1970s were influenced by Marxism. Under the leadership of Palerm and Carrasco, ethnohistorians explored the analytical possibilities of Marx's model of the Asiatic mode of production to elucidate the formation of the state and social classes in Mesoamerica; some of the most important scholars working in this field included Brigitte Boehm, Johanna Broda, José Lameiras, Mercedes Olivera, and Teresa Rojas Rabiela. Rojas Rabiela later became the driving force behind a dialogue among archaeologists, ethnohistorians, and agronomists on the history of agricultural technology, systems of cultivation, and irrigation. In social anthropology Palerm stimulated a resurgence in regional and peasant studies, combining ethnohistory, ecology, and political economy. Drawing on this resurgence, a series of important studies were written on Acolhuacán (Marisol Pérez Lizaur), Morelos (Arturo Warman, Roberto Varela, and Guillermo de la Peña), the Altos de Jalisco (Andrés Fábregas, Tomás Martínez, and Leticia Gándara), the Sierra Tarasca (Jaime Espín and Fernando I. Salmerón), and the lowlands of Chiapas (Virginia Molina and Mario Ruz). Influenced by Marxist theory and the work of French anthropologists such as Georges Balandier, Pierre Philippe Rey, and Maurice Godelier, anthropologists working on the Mexican peasantry (Rodolfo Stavenhagen, Roger Bartra, and Héctor Díaz-Polanco) produced a series of studies that emphasized the peasantry's subordination to capitalism and its accelerated proletarianization.

The 1970s also were a period of opening for anthropological studies of the city. Larissa Adler Lomnitz used the methodological tool of "social networks" to write a detailed study of survival strategies in a marginal neighborhood in Mexico City. Lourdes Arizpe looked at the migration of Mazahua Indians, demonstrating that intense rural-urban interchange did not destroy the peasant economy or imply a loss of ethnic identity for peasants who established themselves in the city. Jorge Alonso assembled a team that documented the struggle and culture of resistance of inhabitants of urban squatters' colonies.

In 1980 the concept of ethnicity became the focus of many discussions among anthropologists. From the directorship of the CIS-INAH (which later would change its name to the Centro de Investigaciones y Estudios Superiores en Antropología Social, or CIESAS), Guillermo Bonfil put together a seminar that analyzed the multiple demands of the new Indian movements sweeping Latin America; these new movements accused traditional *indigenismo* of promoting ethnocide or, at best, maintaining Indians as perpetual minors and keeping them from managing their own affairs. Under the directorship of Salomón Nahmad, the INI itself gave space to indigenous leaders who demanded respect for their cultures and organization of their ethnic groups. Bonfil and Nahmad also organized a program in ethnolinguistics, providing a space for indigenous students to know and defend their cultures. Some anthropologists, such as Héctor Díaz-Polanco, defended the Soviet model of nationalities as a way to reorganize the ethnic variety in Mexico; other, such as Luis Vázquez, distrusted the corporativist stamp of these new programs. In any case, both *indigenismo* and anthropology had to listen to a new group of organizations that rejected Revolutionary nationalism's pretensions of creating a homogeneous national culture and demanded cultural autonomy. At the same time, the old *indigenismo* and programs of acculturation had lost considerable strength, in large part because the endemic economic crisis had undermined the Mexican state's capacity to sponsor social welfare programs.

At the end of the twentieth century, Mexican anthropology once again had entered a period of transition, but it also continued to flourish. Monumental archaeology continued to be strongly criticized. It continued to be an emblem of Mexico's roots, however, and produced such impressive reconstructions as that of the Templo Mayor in Mexico City, directed by Eduardo Matos Moctezuma. Nonetheless, there also was a new archaeology (particularly in the UNAM) more preoccupied with theory, methodological innovation, and comparative analysis, represented by such figures as Carlos Navarrete, Jaime Litvak, and Linda Manzanilla. Physical anthropology began to free itself from its ancillary role and opened new routes of inquiry in genetics and ecology. Ethnohistorians such as Alfredo López Austin become the avantgarde of anthropological theory, focusing on *mentalite* (roughly, ideology or consciousness) and symbol. Linguistics gained new strength from semiological studies and the discussion of ethnic identities. Ethnography and social anthropology gained a broad range of academic interests, including labor markets, political movements, multiculturalism, deconstructionism, gender, and the creation of border cultures. The debate on *indigenismo* acquired international dimensions, linking itself to broader struggles for human rights—this time led by the indigenous peoples themselves.

See also Indigenismo and Ethnic Movements; Indigenous Philologies; Mesoamerica

Select Bibliography

Arizpe, Lourdes, editor, *Antropología Breve de México.* Mexico City: Academia de la Investigación Científica–UNAM, 1993.

Bernal, Ignacio, *A History of Mexican Archeology: The Vanished Civilizations of Middle America.* London: Thames and Hudson, 1980.

Bonfil Batalla, Guillermo, et al., *De eso que llaman antropología mexicana.* Mexico City: Nuestro Tiempo, 1970.

Caso, Alfonso, et al. *Métodos y resultados de la política indigenista en México.* Mexico City: INI, 1954.

Comas, Juan, editor, *La antropología social aplicada en México.* Mexico City: Instituto Indigenista Interamericano, 1964.

De la Peña, Guillermo, "Los estudios regionales y la antropología social en México." *Relaciones: Estudios de Historia y Sociedad* 2:8 (1981).

_____, "Nacionales y extranjeros en la historia de la antropología mexicana." In *La historia de la antrolopogía en México: Fuentes y transmisión,* edited by Mechthild Rutsch. Mexico City: Universidad Iberoamericana/Instituto Nacional Indigenista/Plaza y Valdez, 1996.

Drucker-Brown, Susan, editor, *Malinowski in Mexico.* London: Routledge, 1982.

Foster, George, "The Institute of Social Anthropology," in *The Uses of Anthropology.* Washington, D.C.: American Anthropological Association, Special Publications 11, 1967.

García Mora, Carlos, et al., editors, *La antropología en México: Panorama histórico.* 15 vols., Mexico City : Instituto Nacional de Antropología e Historia, 1987-88.

Olivé Negrete, Julio César, and Augusto Urteaga, editors, *INAH, una historia.* Mexico City: Instituto Nacional de Antropología e Historia, 1988.

Sullivan, Paul, *Unfinished Conversations: Mayas and Foreigners between Two Wars.* New York: Knopf, 1989.

Vázquez León, Luis, *El Leviatán Arqueológico: Antropología de una tradición científica en México.* Leiden: Leiden University Press, 1996.

—Guillermo de la Peña

ANTICLERICALISM

Anticlericalism is a complex of ideas that holds a key to understanding Mexican history. The modern Mexican state has at its foundation not just the separation of church and state but a basic hostility toward the Catholic Church itself. As it pertains to Mexico, the word "anticlericalism" implies the criticism of ecclesiastical institutions and their representatives to the point of attacking religion itself. Mexico has known periods of intolerance as well as persecution caused by the spread of anticlerical ideas. An understanding of anticlericalism's role in Mexican history is essential in order to apprehend the bases of social organization today.

Anticlericalism was inspired partially by the French Revolution, which also coined the word "Jacobin," the name given to radicals who fought for the separation of church and state. The Mexican version emerged largely from the opposition between the reigning Hapsburg and Bourbon Dynasties in Spain and the latter's support of the abolition of ecclesiastical immunities in 1812.

The monarchical reform of the Enlightenment that brought the separation between the clergy and the Crown benefited the criollos (those of Spanish descent born in the Americas) who were educated in an ecclesiastical environment and prevented from participating in the political and social organization of the colony. Thus, incipient anticlericalism helped open the way for New Spain to achieve independence.

On the proclamation of the Republic in 1824, the Liberals were keen to limit the influence of the church and ensure its subordination to the civil power, as was happening in Spain. The reformist measures of the government convinced the regular clergy (i.e., those belonging to religious orders such as the Benedictines) that the privileges of the upper ranks of the hierarchy were linked to the survival of absolutism.

Various Catholic priests were in agreement with the need for separation between church and state. Among them were José María Luis Mora and Servando Teresa de Mier, who nevertheless avoided falling into an anti-religious stance. But anticlericalism advanced and the Constitutional Law of 1836, drawn up by the centralists, stripped those who had taken religious orders of their civil rights.

The conflict between Liberals and Conservatives came to a climax with the Laws of the Reform of the mid–nineteenth century. The basis of the reformist program tried to abolish the privileges of the Catholic Church, which had accumulated wealth in cities and in extensive rural holdings during the colonial period. At the same time it tried to eradicate the influence the church exercised over the faithful and diminish its control, hence the condemnation of monastic life, the establishment of marriage as a civil contract, and the elimination of church control over the cemeteries.

The participation of the clergy in civil life was reduced, individual liberties were expanded, and the separation between church and state was established formally on July 12, 1859. The conflicts that subsequently manifested were resolved generally in favor of the government, whose leaders had increasingly more influence and acceptance by society. The secularization of daily life began to become rooted in society even while Mexicans maintained tight links with a religious ideology that was implicit in their conception of the world.

The development of Freemasonry contributed to the formation of new liberal societies that followed the principles of creating a "new man" without prejudices and free from the burden of religious dogma. Freemasonry shared the credit with the spread of Protestantism in the creation of "free thinkers." Anarchism also contributed to the anticlerical lack of respect for religious festivals and adoration of the saints.

The Catholic Church in Mexico adapted to its new situation, although it existed under a situation of permanent pressure owing to state vigilance that ensured that it did not transgress the limits within which it was confined. From the Reform onward, public life would be standardized only by the institutions that had arisen from the civil power, thereby confining the church to the sphere of private life, even though in practice this division was not easily applicable in an eminently Catholic country.

Even though the clergy was forbidden to give any form of teaching in schools, it did not abandon education. Religious teaching continued under camouflage in the convents and colleges, children were prepared in the catechism, and housewives were influenced by homilies and sermons. Thus the church maintained a presence within the family circle.

The keystone of Liberal ideology was the constitution of the individual citizen as the fundamental unit of political life. Thus, even as the traditional privileges and immunities of the Catholic Church were attacked and ecclesiastical bodies dissolved, the Liberals sought to guarantee such individual liberties as free instruction in the schools and the recognition of all Mexicans as citizens regardless of their ethnic origins. The Reform Laws also affected other corporate bodies besides the church, however; lacking recourse to the law, Indian villages often lost their communal lands and forests. The Reform Laws also had a negative impact on Mexico's cultural patrimony. Centuries-old monasteries were destroyed or converted into barracks or hotels, although some were made into libraries or schools.

The new vogue of positivist ideology in the nineteenth century gave the anticlerical drive of Mexican Liberals a scientific veneer. The progress of Mexican society was believed to be tied inextricably to the progress of science and rational thought; to modernize, Mexico had to break the chains of tradition and religious superstition. The influence of positivist ideas was particularly felt in education. The Reform Laws had dealt a crushing blow to religious schools and religious instruction in general. Mora himself insisted on destroying what he considered to be the monopoly of the Catholic Church over public education. Nonetheless, there was considerable debate among Liberals regarding how far the anticlerical thrust in education should go. If some believed that it was enough to maintain a strict neutrality, respecting religious beliefs in the educational process, others insisted that teaching should be anti-religious to wipe out any religious "taint" from students' consciousness.

Anticlericalism became one of the pillars of the Mexican state. On occasions there was coexistence with the church, as during the long reign of the dictator Porfirio Díaz, who nevertheless ensured that the state maintained its essential liberalism. On the whole, however, the relation between state and church was characterized by conflict, which increased with the post-Revolutionary governments.

In this context of increasing gains by the anticlericalists, Venustiano Carranza announced in 1915 his intention to strengthen anticlerical legislation. A wide-ranging congress was convoked that counted on a broad spectrum of thinkers who shared many of the principles that would be included in the Constitution of 1917. The ideologues of anticlericalism were more radical than those who promulgated the Constitution of 1857, and even though it was said that Carranza hoped for a more moderate position, he was convinced that religious corporations should not hold property, participate in politics, nor interfere in the educational system. One of the main instigators of this radical approach was the general from Michoacán, Francisco J. Múgica. A member of the Jacobin group within the Constitutional Congress of Querétaro, Múgica influenced the drawing up of Article 130, which laid down the rules for church-state relations from that moment.

Article 130 gave a juridical basis for the anticlericalism later taken up by successive post-Revolutionary governments. It established that "The federal powers will be exercised over matters of religion," "Marriage is a civil contract," and "The Law does not recognize any particular character in the religious groups known as churches." In a particularly decisive statement for the spread of anticlericalism throughout the country, Article 130 declared that "state legislatures . . . have the authority to decide, according to local needs, the maximum number of ministers in matters of worship," but only Mexican-born religious could be recognized as such and be able to practice their faith as a profession.

Political organizations also were forbidden to use any word or sign that would identify them with a religious profession. No political meetings could be held in churches, political commentary was disallowed in religious publications, and the opening of places of worship could be authorized only by the Department of the Interior. Anticlericalism went to such an extreme that the names of saints were removed from streets and towns and replaced with those of heroes from the Independence and Reform movements.

General Álvaro Obregón encouraged the anticlerical demonstrations that swept the country and was strongly censured by the Catholic Church hierarchy for doing so. Many bishops were exiled during these years as a result of their open opposition to the Constitution of 1917. Anecdotes are numerous; there was not a Revolutionary leader who did not take one anticlerical measure or another for the sake of fashion or to be on the winning side. For example, the Casa del Obrero Mundial (House of the World Worker) was established in the former convent of St. Brigida in Mexico City, General Eulalio Gutiérrez confiscated the splendid palace of the bishop of San Luis Potosí, and all the local authorities limited the number of priests who could carry out their ministry on the state level.

Tomás Garrido Canabal was even more radical, instituting that in Tabasco only married priests could exercise their profession, which was obviously impossible without going against the principles of Catholic doctrine. The clergy, of course, reacted angrily to such a patently anti-religious policy promulgated by presidents and governors alike. President Plutarco Elías Calles (1924–28) backed the creation of a Catholic Church separate from Rome, thereby adopting a proposal that had been taking shape throughout the nineteenth century. The project was unsuccessful, however, since the faithful did not regard it as a serious proposition.

Thus in June 1926 the Catholic hierarchy decided to close the churches in protest against the radical measures that the state was taking against them, and it again criticized the Constitution of 1917, demanding changes. Uprisings in different parts of the country took place to fight these anticlerical measures, extending rapidly through the Bajío region of north-central Mexico, which included mainly the states of Jalisco, Guanajuato, Michoacán, and Colima. The number of deaths, both of self-styled *cristeros* rebels and government soldiers, was high until 1929, when the provisional government of President Emilio Portes Gil took power after Obregón's assassination. Agreements then were signed between church and state to put an end to the hostilities.

In the three years during which the churches remained closed, Catholics managed to attend clandestine services. According to the writer Graham Greene, President Calles had initiated the most savage religious persecution that had been seen anywhere since the reign of England's Queen Elizabeth I. The execution of various Catholic priests remained engraved in the memory of the faithful, as in the case of Miguel Agustín Pro Juárez, who was accused of the attempted assassination of President-elect Obregón.

It was difficult to arrive at a status quo between church and state because some churches remained closed until 1938. By the end of the decade the two sides managed a similar brand of coexistence as had been achieved at the height of the Porfiriato. President Manuel Avila Camacho (1940–46)

declared himself a Catholic and reformed Article 3, which President Lázaro Cárdenas before him had changed to recast lay education into a socialist framework.

Little by little the Catholic Church began to made its presence felt, establishing various colleges giving religious education, while religious manifestations returned to the public arena. The tradition of going on pilgrimages reappeared while society itself was growing more secular, in tandem with Mexico's development. Rural culture was being replaced by urban culture, which was strongly influenced by the cinema and television. Nevertheless, the state maintained its lay status and its independence from the church, whose existence was overseen by the Secretariat for Internal Affairs.

Between 1917 and 1985 the political constitution of the Mexican Republic was modified in various details, but Article 130 remained untouched. It was only during the presidential term of Carlos Salinas de Gortari (1988–94) that this article was subject to considerable reform to accept the reality of the Catholic Church's participation in Mexican society.

The reformed Article 130 recognized the legal position of the churches but continued to limit the public life of religious ministers, who received the vote but were barred from holding office themselves. In essence their position continued to be restricted as regards political life, although in practice channels were opened allowing for a greater participation. The principle of secular education was continued, ensuring its separation from all religious doctrine. As the text of the revised constitution declares, education "will be based on the results of scientific progress, it will fight against ignorance and its consequences, slavery, fanaticism and prejudice."

The separation between church and state continues to be maintained. The latter conserves its lay status, but with the march of time and, paradoxically, the broad process of social secularization, it has lost its anticlerical character.

See also Bourbon Reforms; Church and State; Cristero Rebellion; Education; Fueros; Liberalism; Positivism; Reform Laws

Select Bibliography

Martínez Assad, Carlos, *El laboratorio de la Revolución: El Tabasco garridista.* Mexico City: Siglo XXI, 1979.
Meyer, Jean, *La Cristiada.* 3 vols., Mexico City: Siglo XXI, 1995.
_____, "El anticlerical revolucionario, 1910–1940." In *Un ensayo de empatía histórica: Las formas y las políticas del dominio agrario. Homenaje a Francisco Chevalier.* Guadalajara: University of Guadalajara, 1992.

—CARLOS MARTÍNEZ ASSAD

ANTI-REELECTIONISM

Whether abused or respected, anti-reelectionism has been an element in Mexican political life since the restoration of the Republic in 1867. Along with effective suffrage it was the campaign platform of Francisco I. Madero when he overthrew the dictatorship of Porfirio Díaz in 1910–11. Since 1917 it has been one of the guiding principles of post-Revolutionary governments.

Throughout the fist half of the nineteenth century, Mexico suffered from arbitrary central government. Those who framed the Constitution of 1857 hoped to restrain such abuse by inserting in it support for state sovereignty, universal suffrage, and free elections. Regrettably, these measures did not guarantee immunity from abuse of presidential power or manipulation of elections by local authorities. When first Benito Juárez in 1871 and then Sebastián Lerdo de Tejada in 1876 sought reelection to the presidency, the restriction of the president to a single term in office came to be seen as a needed change to protect constitutional liberties. Díaz invoked the principle of non-reelection in his successful rebellion against Lerdo de Tejada in 1876, and he even found it prudent to adhere to the principle initially. He introduced legislation prohibiting immediate reelection to the presidency and stepped down in 1880 in favor of a pliant successor, Manuel González, who ensured Díaz's return to office in 1884.

Thereafter, however, Díaz became the most notorious practitioner of reelectionism in Mexican history. He forged a highly centralized political system revolving around his continuing tenure as president. Initially his repeated reelection and that of many state governors and other senior officials caused little resentment within the country's elites and burgeoning middles classes. The system provided welcome political stability and marked economic growth. By the early twentieth century, however, Díaz's insistence upon continuing reelection evoked increasing criticism. Apart from the government's ideological opponents such as leaders of the Partido Liberal Mexicano, many middle-class elements became frustrated with what they considered the regime's increasing exclusivity and decrepitude, both products of the repeated reelection of officials. Even prominent members of the regime became concerned at Díaz's refusal to make arrangements for succession and pressed Díaz to nominate a vice president who could preside over the transition, such as Bernardo Reyes, the populist governor of Nuevo León. Díaz dashed their hopes by naming as his vice presidential running mate in 1904 Ramón Corral, the notoriously corrupt governor of Sonora, who doubtless found it convenient to forget he had entered politics 40 years previously as an anti-reelectionist.

In 1908 Díaz informed an American journalist he would not seek reelection in 1910. This, combined with his advancing age, reopened the debate over succession. In 1909 a wealthy landowner, Francisco I. Madero, published *La Sucesión Presidencial en 1910,* in which he argued for free elections and the replacement of Corral by a vice president committed to open government. During 1909 Madero and other respectable upper- and middle-class figures formed political clubs in support of such aims. They did not seek to challenge Díaz directly, but focused upon the vice presidency, with Reyes their preferred candidate in most cases. These clubs attracted considerable support from the middle classes and industrial workers, may of whose political, social, or economic aspirations had been frustrated by the authoritarian and closed Porfirian system, in which they saw the same officials imposed for years and decades with consequent corruption and abuse. Increasingly they adopted anti-reelectionism as their predominant theme.

Díaz remained unmoved, indicating that he would both seek reelection himself and also retain Corral as his running mate. Reyes capitulated and accepted a mission to Europe. In contrast, Madero, who already had helped found a Centro Anti-Reeleccionista de México in May 1909, campaigned ever more actively throughout the country. In the face of Díaz's intransigence, anti-reelectionism passed from being a movement of reform aimed at ensuring the election of an enlightened vice president to become a challenge to the entire Porfirian system, including Díaz's own position as president.

In April 1910 the various strands of opposition to Díaz came together in an anti-reelectionist convention in Mexico City. The delegates elected Madero and Francisco Vázquez Gómez as their candidates for the presidency and vice presidency, respectively. Their program called for respect of the Constitution of 1857, a prohibition on the reelection of public officials, and electoral reform. Their campaign slogan was "Effective Suffrage and No Reelection." Díaz faced opponents whose battle cry was the one he had adopted 34 years previously.

Following fraudulent elections Madero eventually came to power through an armed revolt in the winter and spring of 1910–11, only to be overthrown and murdered in a coup 15 months later. However, the cause he espoused was not forgotten. Anti-reelectionism was enshrined in the Constitution of 1917 and has remained a guiding principal of all Mexican governments since. Official documents in Mexico continue to be stamped with the words "Effective Suffrage and No Reelection" to this day. And however much subsequent elections have made a mockery of Madero's defense of effective suffrage, the second pillar of his platform has been respected. Álvaro Obregón, the only Mexican president to seek reelection since

1910—and then not in successive terms—was assassinated in 1928 before he could assume office. In recent years some observers have made the point that prohibiting reelection weakens continuity of policy and tempts presidents and state governors to engage in graft toward the end of what might be their only term in office. For these reasons former president Carlos Salinas de Gortari was reported at one point to be contemplating the proposition of a change in this aspect of the constitution. However, the idea proved unpopular. Most Mexicans continue to regard anti-reelectionism as a worthy defense against abuse of power.

Select Bibliography

Cumberland, Charles Curtis, *Mexican Revolution: Genesis under Madero.* Austin: University of Texas Press, 1952.

Knight, Alan, *The Mexican Revolution.* 2 vols., Cambridge and New York: Cambridge University Press, 1986.

Madero, Francisco, *La Sucesión Presidencial en 1910.* Facsimile, Mexico City: Instituto Nacional de Estudios Historicas de la Revolución, 1986.

Perry, Laurens Ballard, *Juárez and Díaz: Machine Politics in Mexico.* DeKalb: Northern Illinois University Press, 1978.

—DUDLEY ANKERSON

ANTUÑANO, ESTÉBAN DE

1792–1847 • Industrialist

The scion of a wealthy Spanish family, Antuñano was born in Veracruz and educated in Spain and England. A cotton broker and import merchant, Antuñano had diversified into financing cotton and woolen weaving by the time of Independence. An industrialist, Antuñano pioneered modern cotton spinning in Puebla and founded Mexico's first water-driven cotton mill, La Constancia Mexicana, in 1835. As a capitalist, Antuñano in 1838 invested in La Biscaina, a foundry located in Puebla that eventually supplied iron castings and looms to the cotton industry he helped establish. A pamphleteer and propagandist, Antuñano wrote energetically on subjects ranging from agriculture and industrialization to Mexican commercial policy and the monetary system.

Antuñano is best remembered as an advocate of the industrialization of the Mexican cotton textile industry. While his thinking on industrialization may reflect the influence of the French social philosopher and reformer, Claude-Henri de Rouvroy, Comte de Saint-Simon (1760–1825), it was also firmly grounded in a specific appraisal of the Mexican economy in the early nineteenth century. Antuñano rejected the notion that land and its products constitute the only real wealth. With no export markets to speak of, and with domestic markets circumscribed by high transportation costs, the cereals of Antuñano's Puebla region were barely profitable to produce. The countryside, in his view, was poor, not rich. Even land reform could offer scant prospect for improvement, since agricultural supplies would grow as the distribution of land improved. Prices would inevitably fall even more. Antuñano did not share Lucas Alamán's belief in the importance of silver mining. The expansion of the economy would enlarge the demand for imports, but Mexico could offer only specie and bullion in payment. Efforts to rehabilitate the silver mines would be defeated effectively by a deterioration in the balance of payments. For this reason, Antuñano regarded the widely disliked seigniorage policies of the national governments in the 1830s with unusual approval. The depreciation of copper currency drove down the cost of labor, and, in this view, made Mexico a more attractive candidate for industrial investment.

Clearly, then, Antuñano assigned decisive social and economic importance to industrialization. His outlook reflected both moral and economic concerns. Agriculture, in Antuñano's view, was a solitary occupation that offered little scope for social improvement. Industry, on the other hand, was a collective activity that brought people together and had a broader impact on economic activity. For example, Antuñano initially believed that the production of raw cotton would increase in Mexico as a result of industrialization, even though he eventually abandoned this view. For Antuñano, the spread of the cotton textile industry in Mexico was a prerequisite to the reestablishment of social order and political stability, which had collapsed in the wake of Spain's colonial reforms at the end of the eighteenth century. As a beneficiary of industrialization, the Mexican state was then obliged to support domestic industry. Antuñano therefore advocated the imposition of restrictive commercial policy, for cotton textiles from Great Britain and the United States hampered efforts at Mexican industrialization. Yet the state's role went well beyond limiting foreign trade. Antuñano argued for the use of public funds to finance private industrial undertakings. He himself borrowed substantial sums from the nascent Banco de Avío (1830–42), repaying the loans by 1838. In all things, Antuñano was a pragmatist rather than an ideologue, an actor more than a coherent thinker.

Antuñano's influence has been considerable. He was a major industrialist in Puebla. His intriguing, if eclectic brand of political economy has shaped the views of modern historians. Antuñano's advocacy of industrialization was, of course, to be echoed by later generations of Mexican statesmen, economists, and entrepreneurs.

—RICHARD SALVUCCI

APARICIO, SEBASTIÁN DE

1502–1600 • Beatified Lay Brother

Patron of teamsters and farmers, Sebastián de Aparicio was beatified by Pope Pius VI in 1789. The rise of this illiterate man of peasant origins to a position of such spiritual prestige in a very status-conscious society illustrates the power of popular religion in the period. Numerous biographers, basing their work on the sworn testimonies of his contemporaries, previous hagiographic works, and diocesan and papal inquests, contributed through the course of the seventeenth and eighteenth centuries to a rich hagiographic tradition concerning Aparicio. His story highlights the rich spiritual tradition of the Franciscans in New Spain, as well as the influence that the Franciscan order and other religious institutions exerted in colonial Puebla.

Sebastián de Aparicio was born in 1502 to parents of humble means, Juan de Aparicio and Teresa del Prado, in the Spanish village of Gudiña (province of Orense). Having migrated south to San Lúcar de Barrameda, he rose to the position of mayordomo for a wealthy landowner of the region and eventually emigrated to New Spain in 1533. Aparicio settled in the newly founded city of Puebla de los Angeles, where he worked as a farmer, a handler of oxen, a cart-maker, and teamster. Aparicio's success as a teamster enabled him to move his residence to Mexico City and begin transportation services between the viceregal capital and the silver mines of Zacatecas. At the pinnacle of his success, Aparicio purchased an estate near Mexico City and a cattle hacienda in Chapultepec in 1552, both of which prospered.

Sebastián avoided marriage until beyond the age of 60, when he finally consented to two successive marriages to young—perhaps adolescent—women of low socioeconomic status. Following the death of his second wife and a near-death experience of his own, Aparicio donated his estate to the convent of Santa Clara de México (1573), requested acceptance into the convent of San Francisco de Puebla (1574), and made his profession as lay brother (1575). He spent the rest of his long life as *limosnero* (alms-collector) for his religious community.

The death of Sebastián in 1600 was followed almost immediately by popular claims of miracles through his intercession. Crucial to his saintly reputation were the numerous testimonies that his physical body, rather than experience normal decay, was miraculously preserved as a sign of divine favor. A local cult developed very quickly, prompting Bishop Diego Romero to carry out a diocesan inquiry from 1600 to 1604. In 1628, Pope Urban VIII opened the first of several papal inquests regarding Aparicio, and in 1789 Pope Pius VI beatified him, permitting the observance of his cult within the Franciscan order, as well as in the dioceses of Puebla, Mexico, and Guatemala in the New World, and Orense and Astorga in Spain. His body, preserved in an incorruptible state, remains on display in a glass case above the altar of the chapel dedicated to his memory in the church of St. Francis of Puebla. His feast day is February 25.

The hagiographic sources on Sebastián de Aparicio, particularly the "Vida y milagros" of the criollo layman Bartolomé Sánchez Parejo, reveal two important features of the writing of saints' lives in colonial Spanish America. First, standard hagiographic European motifs took on new forms and expressions in the New World. For example, the ability to convert people or beasts from evil to good by the moral force of words is a traditional Franciscan notion, but Sebastián's use of this gift to convince a female cotton-mill owner to free her imprisoned Indian laborers makes this a New World motif. Other Mexican variations on European hagiographic motifs include Sebastián's breaking his fasts with tortillas and chilies, and visits by supernatural beings appearing as natives in indigenous dress.

A second related fact that the hagiographic sources reveal is how the unique social setting of New Spain made possible new perceptions regarding saintly virtue itself. In each of his various entrepreneurial undertakings, Aparicio established a reputation for charity. As a transporter of goods to the northern mining centers, he became known for his aid to the needy, as well as for his amicable relations with the usually intractable Chichimecs. Although he employed indigenous laborers on his haciendas, he was said to have worked alongside them, much in contrast to the usual absentee profit-making of hacienda owners of his day. Once he had acquired considerable wealth and social status, as well as influence among his *hacendado* peers, Sebastián loaned tools and funds without interest, gave seed and food to needy neighbors, and provided aid to poor Indians, blacks, and *castas* (those of mixed ancestry). He also intervened on behalf of oppressed *obraje* workers and paid the debts of those who faced imprisonment. His most famous—and most problematic—acts of charity were his marriages to the two young women whose parents were unable to provide them with dowries. Sebastián de Aparicio's holy dissipation of his own wealth stood in marked contrast to the society in which he lived: debtors were jailed, Indians were overworked, and competing neighbors engaged in constant litigation. Wealthy hacendados not only failed to aid owners of smaller landholdings but even attempted to usurp their lands. The daughters of humble white families were forced into prostitution while wealthy profligates wasted their fortunes in their lavish lifestyles.

The hagiographic literature also illustrates the tension that exited between the popular and official hagiographic traditions. According to the testimony of Sebastián himself, he maintained his lifelong chastity throughout both of his short-lived marriages. Although his biographers interpreted the virginal marriages as a sign of his heroic virtue, papal investigators proceeded with caution. It appears that during Aparicio's lifetime the parents of at least one of the wives voiced disapproval of the fact that he apparently despised their daughter and failed to provide them any progeny. The propriety of his domestic life, in fact, seems to have been a major stumbling block for his beatification, and it was only after university theologians at Salamanca, the Sorbonne, and Padua cleared his name that Sebastián de Aparicio was beatified in 1789.

Select Bibliography

Cuevas, Mariano, *Historia de la Iglesia en México.* 3rd edition, vol. 2, Mexico City: Libro Tercero, 1928.

Espinosa, Conrado, *Fray Sebastián de Aparicio, primer caminero mexicano.* Mexico City: Jus, 1959.

Royer, Fanchón, *The Franciscans Came First.* Paterson, New Jersey: St. Anthony Guild Press, 1951.

Sánchez Parejo, Bartolomé, *Vida y milagros del glorioso confesor de Cristo, el padre fray Sebastián de Aparicio, fraile lego de la orden de San Francisco de la regular observancia, par Bartolomé Sánchez Parejo.* Mexico City: Junipero Serra, 1965.

—Ron Morgan

ARCHITECTURE

This entry contains three articles that discuss the development of Mexican architecure from the colonial era through the twentieth century:

Architecture: Colonial
Architecture: Nineteenth Century
Architecture: Twentieth Century

For a discussion of pre-Conquest architecture in Mesoamerica, see Mesoamerica; Visual Arts: Mesoamerica. *See also* Urbanism and Urbanization

ARCHITECTURE: COLONIAL

Monumental architecture is an art that develops out of and around institutions. In New Spain the two fundamental institutions capable of commissioning substantial building projects were the monarchy and the Catholic Church. The Spanish monarchy was present through its viceroy and the various instances of secular government. The church went further still in dominating life in New Spain. The mendicant friars were fundamental for the evangelization efforts of the sixteenth century, as well as later in frontier areas. They also established themselves in the colonial cities. Other religious orders were equally active in New Spain, while the bishops and secular clergy (those who did not belong to a regular order such as the Franciscans), working out of cathedrals and parish churches, ministered throughout the viceroyalty and prevailed over the regular orders in the seventeenth and eighteenth centuries. Although private patrons built large residences throughout the viceregal period, it was only in the eighteenth century that they commissioned palaces on a truly grand scale.

The religious institutions active in New Spain built a complex web of institutions—and their buildings—that covered all of what is today modern Mexico, as well as the other territories that were then governed from Mexico City and now extend into the United States and Central America. The variety and wealth of religious architecture largely is the result of the fact that, unlike the government institutions whose buildings were erected out of bureaucratic or utilitarian needs, the church was involved in many different areas of social culture and action and enjoyed the support not only of the Spanish Crown, but also of countless individuals and groups for whom religious projects represented solace and pride in this world and guaranteed salvation in the next.

Of course, this process must be seen within its spatial and chronological dimensions to be better understood. Not all the institutions arrived or established themselves at the same time, nor developed at the same rhythm or in the same place. They often competed, sometimes cooperated, and always had to accommodate to one another as the Spanish and Indian societies that initially made up New Spain evolved and developed ways of mixing and coexisting with each other and with other groups, notably black slaves from Africa.

In architectural terms, it can be said that the Spanish monarchy, in the sixteenth century, established the conditions for all the building, both secular and religious, that was to come thereafter. The coasts and frontiers were fortified and schemes were developed for the layout of new settlements of various types. In other words, there was a program to keep out invaders and control rebellions on the margins, while at the same time, within the viceroyalty, new building was regulated with a view to permanent and continued successful settlement.

As far as fortifications were concerned, the ports of New Spain, like others from Florida to Argentina, were protected by bastioned walls against external invaders, generally in the guise of pirates who could also be agents of foreign powers. Italian military engineering tradition was behind such coastal projects as the fortresses of San Juan de Ullúa in Veracruz, of San Diego in Acapulco, and the walls of Campeche, as well as many others throughout Spanish America. These fortifications, fully established by the early seventeenth century, were constantly renovated and amplified. In the eighteenth century, when New Spain underwent a process of militarization, partly in response to the threat of English naval power, they were complemented by fortifications in the interior, such as the fort at Perote, inland from Veracruz.

Defense at the inland limits of New Spain, the northern frontier, was a more flexible and less monumental affair. Boundaries moved and changed as Indian groups rebelled and were repressed. The "presidios" of the north could be wooden palisades, as we know from written and visual documents, or they could be more permanent structures. Little survives of this architecture, and what does has been rebuilt or integrated into later buildings and is thus difficult to assess without archaeological work. Also, the word "presidio" indicates as much a function as a particular building type, a function that could be fulfilled by almost any kind of enclosure.

Another area of architectural activity for which directives emanated from Spain for all of its dominions was that of town planning. The orthogonal grid plan, of ancient and Renaissance traditions, was applied to all new settlements throughout Spanish America. Although formal ordinances were not promulgated until the reign of Felipe II, in 1573, the practices it codified were in use from the earliest period of the Conquest. In New Spain, orthogonal town planning found a parallel native tradition that had associations with time and ritual cycles. In Mexico City-Tenochtitlan itself, the European scheme was superimposed on the previously existing Indian city. The central square or *plaza mayor,* surrounded by the cathedral and the houses of the principal Spaniards, replaced the ceremonial and government center of the former Indian city. The Indians were relegated to barrios at the margins.

Of course, the European grid scheme was followed most closely in Spanish towns, such as Puebla, founded in 1531, which were not superimposed on pre-Columbian urban sites. The grid plan continued to be the founding scheme into the eighteenth century, as new settlements were established in outlying areas. Only in the case of mining towns, which typically grew quickly and without initial planning, was the orthogonal scheme weakened, generally in favor of development along a river or stream, since water was necessary for the processing of mineral ores. However, even there the heart of the grid pattern eventually would come to dominate the whole, when the mines were rich enough to warrant permanent residence; that is, the central square, bounded by a parish church and the houses of government *(casas reales)* and of the principal citizens, almost invariably constituted the easily identifiable core of any town in the viceroyalty.

Smaller towns at previously established Indian sites in central New Spain also were superimposed on existing settlements in the sixteenth century, with the church and monastery of the mendicant friars taking the dominant place on the central square and the Indian inhabitants distributed in barrios within the orthogonal overall plan. More research needs to be done to understand these Christian Indian towns and their relationships to spatial and social organizations of the period immediately preceding the Spanish Conquest as well as their development during the first decades of Spanish rule. The historiography has tended to telescope all of sixteenth-century monastery architecture and treat it as a single post-Conquest phenomenon. The situation was much more complex, and important changes must have taken place between the initial monastic establishments of the 1520s and 1530s and the buildings we see today that date from the middle to the late century. This has recently been proven to be the case at Huejotzingo, one of the first Franciscan establishments, where archaeology has uncovered the buildings that preceded the surviving structures.

Issues of siting and basic distribution seem to follow certain general principles in the great sixteenth-century monastic complexes that rightly have been considered one of the major architectural achievements of Spanish rule in New Spain. Again, it was the Crown that established the conditions that made the monasteries possible by giving first the

Franciscan Convent, Huejotzingo, Puebla
Photo courtesy of Archivo Fotográfico, Instituto de Investigaciones Estéticas de la UNAM

Franciscans, and then the Dominicans and Augustinians, authority in matters of evangelization and the settlements of newly converted Indians. The friars often chose to replace the ceremonial sites of the pre-Columbian religions with their churches and monasteries, thus making an absolutely clear statement about the substitution of the new religion for the old cults. This is easily seen at the Franciscan complex of Izamal, Yucatán, just to cite one obvious example.

A monastery complex in a Christian Indian sixteenth-century town almost invariably included an ample, four-sided, walled open space, called an atrium ("patio" in the sixteenth century), with a large cross at the center and small *posa* chapels at the corners, where processions around the atrium might make pauses. The atrium generally had a main entrance and at least one side entrance. Opposite the main entrance rose the principal buildings of the complex: the open chapel, the church, and the monastery. The element that has attracted the most attention is the open chapel or the *capilla de indios.* This is a covered space, open toward the atrium, which fundamentally served the function of an apse where mass could be said before enormous congregations of

Indians who occupied the chapel itself and the open space before it. The fact that there are so many variations for this part of the monastic complexes is proof that, despite possible European precedents, the open chapel was an American invention, built to fulfill a particular need unique to the New World situation. The situation was that of huge Christian congregations who themselves or whose pre-Hispanic parents and grandparents had been accustomed to worshipping in the open in a benign climate. At the beginning, open chapels were simple grass- or branch-covered spaces *(enramadas),* but the ones which survive took many forms. There are basilica (Cuilapan, Oaxaca) and many aisled plans (Cholula, Puebla), as well as numerous variations on rectangular and polygonal schemes. They could be barrel vaulted (Actopan, Hidalgo) or covered with complex Gothic vaulting (Teposcolula, Oaxaca). They were usually at ground level, but examples of chapels open to the atrium from the upper story of the monastery also exist (Huaquechula, Puebla).

The church buildings were either basilical or, more frequently, rectangular in plan with wooden or vaulted roofs. In the latter case, the vault of the bay in front of the apse was

Catedral de México y Sagrario, Mexico City, by Cristóbal de Medina Vargas, c.1680
Photo courtesy of Archivo Fotográfico, Instituto de Investigaciones Estéticas de la UNAM

generally somewhat raised and more richly decorated. It is interesting that the earliest church at Huejotzingo was basilical in plan, suggesting the possibility of references to early Christian architecture, since the friars were explicitly conscious of their role as new apostles in a pagan world. However, most surviving buildings are massive rectangular structures with decorated portals and details, such as merlons, that remind one of fortress construction. Indeed, much of the historiography refers to these buildings as "fortress churches". However, recent scholarship tends to consider the defensive elements as symbolic of the heavenly Jerusalem and as allusive to the utopian and apocalyptic ideas of the friars. Interior decoration consisted of sculpted architectural details, wall paintings, and in important churches, at least one monumental gilded altarpiece or retablo, with paintings and sculptures. Exterior decoration was sculptural, particularly around the main entrance portal.

The monasteries themselves, where the friars lived, were generally of two stories around a cloister. In the lower story were spaces for communal life (refectory, chapter hall), as well as a monumental entryway (portería) from the atrium,

since public access to the lower cloister, though regulated, was permitted. The upper level was restricted to the friars. On comparing these cloisters to those of European monasteries, their reduced size becomes obvious; there were rarely more than four to six friars at any one monastery in New Spain, and they spent much of their time traveling to nearby towns to attend to congregations at smaller churches (visitas). Accessory buildings associated with agricultural work, animals, and storage completed the monasteries.

The vocabulary of the decoration of churches and other buildings might be Gothic (Yecapixtla, Morelos), classicizing—that is, in a Renaissance mode, be it Plateresque (Acolman, State of Mexico) or Mannerist (Tecali, Puebla)—and include Mudejar elements (Tlaxcala, Tlaxcala). Another term, *tequitqui,* defines sculpture executed in a style that recalls the planarity of pre-Columbian treatment of stone (the *posa* chapels of Huejotzingo and Calpan, and the portal at Tepoztlán). Most of this work, the construction as well as the decoration, painting as well as sculpture, was done by the Indians, who quickly became adept at European techniques, under the supervision of the friars and some European masters. European architectural treatises, particularly *Tutte l'opere d'architettura* (1537–75) by the Italian Sebastiano Serlio, and prints often served as models, especially for ornamental elements.

The initial evangelization process, whose ultimate outcome in architecture were the Christian Indian towns with their great monastery complexes, was over before the end of the sixteenth century. As disease decimated the Indian population and the utopian spirit gave way to the moralizing concerns that emanated from the Council of Trent, and the friars lost their ecclesiastical primacy to the bishops and secular clergy.

The architectural accomplishments of the secular clergy and their congregations can first be seen in the cathedrals built in the principal cities of the viceroyalty beginning in the sixteenth century. As seats of bishops who had extensive territories under their jurisdiction, the cathedrals were the most important buildings of their cities. No other single architectural project attracted the same quality and scale of attention. It helps to understand the colonial cathedrals of New Spain, as well as of the rest of Spanish America, to real-

ize that they were begun a short time after the Reconquest of Spain itself. This makes them almost contemporary to the cathedrals of Andalusía and explains their formal characteristics. As one would expect in the late sixteenth century, the projects are Renaissance in character with strong Gothic reminiscences. All of these Spanish cathedrals are rectangular in plan with an inscribed cross, evident in the nave and transept elevations. Side aisles and side chapels accompany the central nave. Usually there are three portals on the facade and a portal on each side of the building. Two towers generally frame the facade.

The central role of cathedrals made these buildings paradigms of monumental church architecture and the sites of innovations in both structure and ornament, which then passed on to parish and other churches. Furthermore, cathedral projects enjoyed direct financial support from the Spanish Crown and had an architect, known as the *maestro mayor,* assigned to them. Although this post has been studied in depth only for Mexico City (by Martha Fernández), it is clear that these individuals were generally the most renowned architects of their time and were

Basilica of Guadalupe, Mexico City, by Pedro de Arrieta, 1695–1709
Photo courtesy of Archivo Fotográfico, Instituto de Investigaciones Estéticas de la UNAM

responsible for other projects as well. One of the most important structural innovations established at a cathedral was the dome on a drum at the crossing. The model, set at the cathedral of Puebla, which was dedicated in 1649, was repeated in many variations in countless churches throughout the viceroyalty in the seventeenth and in the eighteenth centuries. Because of the strong accent of light that the dome provided in the interior, it became a basic component of Mexican Baroque architecture.

In portal design, also, cathedral architects played an important role. At the cathedral of Mexico City the twisted "Solomonic" column was used by Cristóbal de Medina Vargas in permanent stone on the lateral portals around 1680. It quickly became an almost universal feature in the Baroque architectural ornament of the entire viceroyalty. Another element of the vocabulary of Mexican Baroque architecture also began at the cathedral of Mexico City: the *estípite* column. This support, in the shape of an inverted obelisk, narrower at the base than at the top, and crowned by a cube and a series of capitals, was first seen in monumental form in Jerónimo de Balbás's *Retablo of the Kings* in the apse of the cathedral, begun in 1718. In the 1740s it was used by the architect Lorenzo Rodríguez on the facade of the Sagrario (the church adjacent to the cathedral where parish functions are carried out) and became an identifying element of Mexican Estípite Baroque. This is the phase that in the past often was called Ultrabaroque and sometimes still is known as Churrigueresque.

The religious architecture of the seventeenth and early eighteenth century in New Spain, after the principal cathedrals were practically finished, included the codification of a few specialized church types and their regionalization. These buildings are either parish churches or the work of different religious orders within cities and towns. Other sites for monumental religious architecture were developed around sanctuaries, generally on the outskirts of important urban areas. As in the sixteenth century monasteries and also in the cathedrals, one often can detect the impact of illustrations in European treatises, especially in the portals of these buildings. It also has been shown that architects continued to plan according to medieval geometric traditions well into the eighteenth century.

By far the most widespread type of church preserved from this period is the cruciform vaulted building with a dome over the crossing and a choir loft inside, above the entrance bay. This is the type most often used for parishes and by all male religious orders, with the frequent exception of the Jesuits and sometimes the Dominicans. It is by no means clear, however, precisely how or when the diffusion of this scheme occurred. The type is so common that it has been taken totally for granted. It is also usually repeated that all these churches are alike, differentiated only by their ornament. Although it is true that these buildings were conceived as fairly simple shells to be complemented by elaborate interior decoration in the form of great gilded retablos, they are, in fact, not all alike. There are important and

interesting variations in the proportions of buildings, in the relationships among the nave, the crossing and lateral chapels and in the handling of fenestration and, of course, in the manipulation of the vaults and dome. All these buildings generally have a tower at one side of the facade that permits access to the choir loft and provides a place for the bells that mark the time.

In Mexico City the architect Pedro de Arrieta (active 1691 to 1738) or someone very familiar with his work was responsible for at least one building of the type just described: the parish of San Miguel. However, Arrieta was also the architect of churches with a central nave and side aisles, akin to the plans of the earlier cathedral projects. One of these was the sanctuary church of the Virgin of Guadalupe (built 1695–1709), north of Mexico City, and the other was the Jesuit church of the Profesa (1714–20). In the first of these buildings, Arrieta combines a central plan, appropriate for housing the miraculous painting of the Virgin of Guadalupe, with a longitudinal scheme. On the exterior, he made effective use of narratives in relief over the portals of the building. Two towers frame the facade, as is often the case in sanctuary churches.

The cathedral tradition was taken up as well in a few, important parish churches elsewhere in the viceroyalty. This is the case of the parish of San José in Puebla, and of a group of parish churches in the northern towns of San Luis Potosí (1701–30), whose architect Nicolás Sánchez Pacheco (active 1678–1717) certainly knew Arrieta's work in Mexico City, Zacatecas, and Chihuahua. These three buildings, in turn, became the inspiration for attempts later in the eighteenth century to enlarge existing parishes in other northern towns.

The convent church also became an established type in New Spain in the second half of the seventeenth century. This was a simple, single nave building set longitudinally next to the street. Two contiguous portals permitted access to the public on this street side, while the convent extended to the other side of the church. The entire end of the church opposite the altar, where normally one would expect the entrance to be located, was set aside for the nuns who participated in the liturgy from behind screens. Convents were concentrated exclusively in the cities, with almost none north of San Luis Potosí; the only exception being a single convent in Durango. In general, convent churches, although often richly ornamented inside, were not particularly conspicuous buildings. A famous exception is the church of Santa Rosa de Viterbo in Querétaro (finished in 1752), with its two freestanding buttresses on the street side, possibly the work of Ignacio Mariano de las Casas (c. 1719–c. 1785).

Throughout this period a process of regionalization in architecture was taking place. Fundamentally, this meant that the basic schemes were adapted by local masters using local materials. A few of these masters began their careers in Mexico City, but, with time, more and more masters were working in their places of origin.

Important regional variations include the Mexico City area where *tezontle,* a dark reddish pumice, very light in

Church of La Soledad, Oaxaca
Photo courtesy of Colección Luis Márquez, Archivo Fotográfico, Instituto de Investigaciones Estéticas de la UNAM

weight, was combined with gray limestone, which defined lines and was appropriate for carved details. In the Puebla-Tlaxcala region, builders made frequent use of brick and glazed tiles, as well as exterior and interior plaster work. Glazed tiles on domes spread to other parts of the viceroyalty; they often were used on the exteriors of domes. Plaster work was used extensively, especially to the south, into Central America. These materials made it possible to include bright colors in architecture. Early-twentieth-century historiography was fascinated by this trait and transformed it into a "national" characteristic. Colonial architecture in Oaxaca and to the west and north of Mexico City was able to take advantage of abundant local limestones. This resulted in rich sculptural decoration both on the exteriors and, in the north, in the interiors of buildings as well. Of course, all these limestones were of different colors, thus tinting Oaxaca in greenish-yellow tones, Zacatecas in rose and ochre, Guadalajara in beige and tan, and so on. Other local variations are related to seismic conditions. Thus, churches in the north could be built with tall towers, whereas in Oaxaca, for example, they have squat towers and very thick walls, and their domes are encased in buttressing. Finally, in small towns everywhere, but especially in the northern reaches of the viceroyalty, adobe was used extensively for church architecture. This architecture has been studied seriously only in New Mexico, where adobe construction achieved monumental proportions.

An important development of this time is the retablo facade. Mention already has been made of how elements first used extensively in retablos, namely the Solomonic and *estípite* supports, began to be used in church portals. However, the retablo facade also implied movement in plan at the entrance of the building. Thus, some portals were developed within niches, such as at San Juan de Dios in Mexico City (1729), the work of Miguel Custodio Durán, while others combined recession and protrusion, as in the facade of Arrieta's Basilica of Guadalupe. Given the close relationships between wood retablos and facade design, it should be no surprise that retablo makers were directly involved in architectural projects. This is the case of Jerónimo de Balbás, who came from Spain to construct the *Retablo of the Kings* in Mexico City cathedral and defined himself as an architect.

Prior to the middle of the eighteenth century it is clear, from documents and extant buildings, that considerable discussion and tensions must have existed around the problem of architectural design and its relationship to ornament, as well as around the role of the architect. For one thing, new ordinances for the Architects' Guild, which insisted on the gentlemanly status of architects, were promulgated in 1736. At the same time, in their buildings, architects seem to have been debating about facades based on the classicizing designs derived from treatises and designs derived from Solomonic and *estípite* retablos. An important case in point is the facade of the Jesuit church in Zacatecas (1746–49), relatively severe in its decorative elements, yet

Church of Santo Domingo, Zacatecas
Photo courtesy of Archivo Fotográfico, Instituto de Investigaciones
Estéticas de la UNAM

movemented in plan. Only a block away is the contemporary parish church with its elaborate Solomonic flat screen portal. At Taxco, Cayetano de Sigüenza, who also may have been the creator of the Zacatecas Jesuit facade, took into account the breakdown of classicizing restrictions that *estípite* designs permitted, but insisted nevertheless on using columns in the facade of the parish of Santa Prisca (1748–58). A treatise identified by Ignacio González Polo as probably having been written by Lorenzo Rodríguez, indicates that some architects favored leaving facade design to painters or sculptors altogether and insisted on mathematics and planning as the proper domains of their profession.

The emphasis on planning and project supervision is borne out by a good number of buildings erected in the eighteenth century. For one thing, the designs of facades and the internal decoration of some major buildings was thoroughly integrated both in iconographic as well as in formal terms, as can be seen, for example, at Zacatecas and Tepotzotlán (finished around 1762). Especially as regards the details of iconography, the desires of patrons, especially clerical patrons, must certainly have played an important role. However, architects were taking iconographic needs into account by varying the contours of nave walls, probably to accommodate retablos that were becoming more voluminous, as at the Carmelite church in Querétaro, the work of Juan Manuel Villagómez, finished in 1759.

Cathedral of Zacatecas
Photo courtesy of Archivo Fotográfico, Instituto de Investigaciones Estéticas de la UNAM

Chapel of the Pocito, Mexico City, by Francisco Guerrero y Torres, 1771–91
Photo courtesy of Colección Luis Márquez, Archivo Fotográfico, Instituto de Investigaciones Estéticas de la UNAM

Palacio de Minería, Mexico City
Photo courtesy of Colección Luis Márquez, Archivo Fotográfico, Instituto de Investigaciones Estéticas de la UNAM

More radical experimentation with plans was not frequent, and it is significant that an important early example was the work of a military engineer, that is, of someone with mathematical training. The elliptical convent church of Santa Brígida in Mexico City, irresponsibly destroyed in 1933, was built from 1740 to 1744 by the Spanish engineer Luis Díez Navarro, who later went to Guatemala. Among architects of New Spain, Francisco Guerrero y Torres (1727–92) was the one who most experimented with plans, while never using the *estípite* in portals. Although as yet no document has been found that relates him directly to the building of the church of the convent of the Enseñanza (1772–78) in Mexico City, there can be little doubt that he designed the unique elongated polygonal plan, crowned by a central dome. He also was responsible for the Chapel of the Pocito (1771–91) near the Basilica of Guadalupe. He based this work, which was his personal donation to the Virgin, on a Roman temple plan, published by Serlio, to create a principal centralized space, entered via a smaller centralized narthex that is matched by a similarly shaped sacristy on the opposite side of the building. The exterior presents a compact and colorful form of red *tezontle* walls

with gray limestone detailing, crowned by a large dome and two smaller ones, all three covered by blue and white tile decoration in a zigzag pattern. The building is unified by the blue and white tiles which spill over onto the drums of the domes and by the motif of star-shaped windows that punctuate both the drums of the domes and the *tezontle* walls below. The preciousness of the whole is appropriate for the chapel's commemorative function at the site of a sacred well.

The insistence by important Mexico City architects of the eighteenth century on a relatively sober classicizing ornamental vocabulary is a complex phenomenon. As mentioned above, its roots are in the treatise tradition of architecture in New Spain. However, it also can be related to the Neoclassical movements of eighteenth-century art, against the background of the Enlightenment. Mixed as it is with elements of Mexican Baroque and even of Rococo vocabulary, the language of architects like Guerrero y Torres represents a uniquely New Spanish strain of Baroque Neoclassicism, for which Jorge Alberto Manrique coined the term "Neóstilo," in reference to the renewed use of columnar supports that the *estípite* phase of Mexican Baroque had largely eliminated.

The Neóstilo is not merely an ornamental style, because it corresponds on the interiors to taller proportions and to the use of greater and more diffuse lighting.

The growth of Mexico City and other urban areas and the trends toward secularization in society in the eighteenth century created an expanding need for secular buildings. The plans of grand, civil architecture hardly varied throughout the entire colonial period and recall European Renaissance schemes. Early examples have survived especially in Puebla. Palaces usually were constructed around four-sided central courtyards, with ancillary blocks, also around courtyards, added as need might dictate. The ceremonial quarters were on the first floor, the piano nobile of Renaissance tradition, and the principal entrance was generally on the central axis of the main courtyard. The exception in New Spain is the corner facade of Pedro de Arrieta's Palace of the Inquisition (1733–37) in Mexico City, with its hanging keystone arches at the corners of the inner courtyard. This type was adopted in a number of other civil buildings in New Spain. The hanging keystone proliferated in convents and monasteries as well. In Mexico City, in the later eighteenth century, several truly monumental palaces were built by Francisco Guerrero y Torres. The most interesting is that of the Condes de San Mateo de Valparaíso, with its central courtyard enframed by four great, lowered arches and its double spiral interior staircase.

The official establishment in 1785 of the Royal Academy of San Carlos in Mexico City closes the architectural history of New Spain. The Neoclassicism of the Spanish teachers who staffed the new academy was much more orthodox and closer to Roman precedents than the indigenous Neóstilo. As a consequence, Guerrero y Torres himself had projects rejected by Academy architects and important commissions began to go to the recently arrived Spaniards. The irony was that the artists of New Spain had long wished for an academy, so as to improve themselves and their professional standing. Criollo patrons also were supportive of the establishment of the academy, because it promised to place New Spain on an equal footing with European nations in matters of art and taste. Of course, such matters were related directly to the production of the artisans of New Spain and thus to economic concerns. For the Crown, art academies were also a way to weaken the guild system and exercise control over guild and even over church revenues; all proposed construction projects now had to be approved by the academy.

The major building projects of New Spain around 1800 were taken over by academy architects, especially by Manuel Tolsá of Valencia, who, although trained principally as a sculptor, was responsible for the most impressive Academic Neoclassical buildings raised in New Spain. The most famous of these is the Palace of the School of Mines. Built on the traditional courtyard scheme, its classical vocabulary is sober and free of almost all ornamentation. Column shafts are smooth, pure forms, and pediments are unbroken. Among Tolsá's clients were important criollo families, such as the wealthy Fagoagas, for whom he designed a palace in Mexico City, known as the Casa del Apartado from their title. It is a further irony of history that the Fagoagas were among the principal promoters of the movement for political independence from Spain, which was to result in the war that ended the existence of New Spain and of many of its institutions, including the Royal Academy.

Select Bibliography

Angulo Iñiguez, Diego, et al., *Historia del arte hispanoamericano.* 2nd edition, 3 vols., Mexico City: Instituto de Estudios y Documentos Historicos, 1982.

Atl, Dr., et al., *Iglesias de México.* 6 vols., Mexico City: Secretaría de Hacienda, 1924–27.

Baird, Joseph Armstrong, *The Churches of Mexico, 1530–1810.* Berkeley: University of California Press, 1962.

Bargellini, Clara, *La catedral de Chihuahua.* Mexico City: UNAM, 1984.

_____, "Arquitectura religosa barroca en Querétaro." In *Querétaro ciudad barroca.* Querétaro: Gobierno del Estado, 1988.

_____, *La arquitectura de la plata: Iglesias monumentales del centro-norte de México, 1640–1750.* Mexico City: UNAM, and Madrid: Turner, 1991.

Córdova Tello, Mario, *El convento de San Miguel de Huejotzingo, Puebla.* Mexico City: INAH, 1992.

Díaz, Marco, *La arquitectura de los jesuitas en Nueva España.* Mexico City: UNAM, 1982.

Early, James, *The Colonial Architecture of Mexico.* Albuquerque: University of New Mexico Press, 1994.

Fernández, Martha, *Arquitectura y gobierno virreinal: Los maestros mayores de la ciudad de México, siglo XVII.* Mexico City: UNAM, 1985.

Gutiérrez, Ramón, *Arquitectura y urbanismo en Iberoamérica.* Madrid: Catedra, 1983.

Kubler, George, *Mexican Architecture of the Sixteenth Century.* 2 vols., New Haven, Connecticut: Yale University Press, 1948.

_____, and Martin Sebastian Soria, *Art and Architecture in Spain and Portugal and their American Dominions, 1500–1800.* Baltimore and London: Penguin, 1959.

_____, *The Religious Architecture of New Mexico in the Colonial Period and Since the American Occupation.* 5th edition, Albuquerque: University of New Mexico Press, 1990.

Manrique, Jorge Alberto, "El 'Neóstilo': La última carta del barroco mexicano." *Historia Mexicana* 20 (1970–71).

McAndrew, John, *The Open-Air Churches of Sixteenth Century Mexico: Atrios, Posas, Open Chapels and Other Studies.* Cambridge, Massachusetts: Harvard University Press, 1965.

Schuetz, Mardith, editor, *Architectural Practice in Mexico City: A Manual for Journeyman Architects of the Eighteenth Century.* Tucson: University of Arizona Press, 1987.

Toussaint, Manuel, *La catedral de México y el sagrario metropolitano.* 3rd edition, Mexico City: Porrúa, 1992.

Vargas Lugo, Elisa, *La iglesia de Santa Prisca de Taxco.* Mexico City: UNAM, 1974.

—CLARA BARGELLINI

ARCHITECTURE: NINETEENTH CENTURY

Much has been written about the search for national identity in Mexican architecture, but few scholars explain what is meant by either nation or identity, the terms that presumably define the discourse. Part of the difficulty in clarifying these terms is that they are elusive and constantly changing, since both "nation" and "national identity" are cultural and historical constructs. As early as 1928, José Carlos Mariategui, a Peruvian writer and activist remarked: "The nation . . . is an abstraction, an allegory, a myth that does not correspond to a reality that can be scientifically defined." In a now classic book, Benedict Anderson defined the nation as "an imagined political community—and imagined as both limited and sovereign." The notion of identity is equally problematic because it assumes authenticity and continuity despite multiple ruptures in history. Because of their sociohistorical determination, both nation and identity must be defined as always shifting and never completed. National identity has the dual function of achieving internal cohesion and separating the nation from the outside. Nationalism and national identity are closely related, for the formulation of national identity is a prerequisite for nationalism, and nationalism is the performance or the activation of national identity.

The construction of national identity is based on historical narratives that support the interests of specific groups. This presupposes that multiple versions of national identity can compete and coexist. With the formation of nation states in the nineteenth century, officially sanctioned versions of the nation were created. Although these versions change through history, there is, at any one time in any one place, a dominant version of the nation. This version is the one disseminated through state and state-affiliated institutions such as schools and the mainstream media. It is, in fact, the one that most citizens learn as young children. Alternative versions of the nation offer the potential of challenging, altering, and replacing the official versions.

Architecture takes part in the construction of national identity insofar as it creates or reinforces specific images and narratives of the nation. Because traditionally the history of architecture focuses on monuments commissioned by states and wealthy patrons, it affirms identities constructed by dominant groups. Studies of the representation of identity in architecture are important because they reveal power relations and strategies essential to the construction of nationhood as well as contradictions that the dominant representations of the nation obscure.

The representation of national identity in architecture has been a subject of debate for Mexican architects since the late nineteenth century. Although scholars tend to equate the representation of identity with indigenous building traditions, international styles of architecture have also been used to represent aspects of Mexican identity. By international styles we mean those that had origins in Western Europe and in the United States and subsequently were exported or adopted elsewhere. In fact, if there is one constant in the history of Mexican architecture it is the confluence of indigenous and imported elements.

International styles in architecture are defined by politically or economically influential nations. Thus, the presence of these styles in Mexican architecture indicates an ongoing power relation between the nation and influential outsiders. The representation of locality is frequently achieved through a reinterpretation of construction methods, design, and decorative elements from historical or regional architecture. As most professional architects in Mexico fully partake of contemporary international culture, the representation of national identity in architecture often involves the appropriation of traditions from cultures far removed from the direct experience of the designers. In Mexico, ancient historic architecture was built by indigenous civilizations whose descendants were marginalized and dispossessed. Often, these descendants were also the "anonymous builders" of regional architecture. The incorporation of historical and regional architecture into an ideal construct of the nation frequently functions as a strategy to conceal the state's and the elites' abusive and often violent treatment of marginalized citizens in the nation.

The writing of the history of nineteenth century Mexican architecture is still in its formative stages. Although several scholars have documented and classified numerous buildings from that era, much needed sociohistorical and interpretative work is still wanting. The work of Israel Katzman is the only extensive study, as he photographed and documented over 5,000 buildings and researched the biographies of significant architects of this period. Without his efforts subsequent studies would not have been possible. Other scholars have examined specific stylistic tendencies or focused on the development of specific parts of Mexico City.

Traditional methods of art historical analysis prove unhelpful in the study of nineteenth-century Mexican architecture. Eclecticism is the rule of the period. Yet, despite evidence of a myriad of styles, often practiced by the same architect, sometimes in the same building, scholars have attempted to classify the architecture of the period into discreet categories, such as Classical, Gothic, Romanesque, and Islamic revival. As a result, many buildings fit into more than one category, and specialists are constantly pressured to create additional denominations for buildings that elude classification, such as *ecléctica integrada,* or simplified traditionalism. This situation is not unlike the one created by the classification of colonial Mexican architecture using European stylistic frameworks. European architecture of various periods is similarly eclectic. Perhaps it is time to realize that the notion of style begs for serious revisions, as the purity of style may be a myth, not unrelated to notions of racial purity and stable identities. In the words of Demitri Porphyrios, classifying a building according to style means to focus on the features it shares with others, cleansing it of all impurities. The historian thus elevates the consistencies of the building to the status of principles while silencing or neglecting the building's contradictions. This process resembles the construction of national identity, which favors specific aspects of the nation while excluding others.

For most of the nineteenth century there were no efforts to define a Mexican architecture. Architects and patrons, including the Mexican state, imported European and U.S. architecture to Mexico in an attempt for the country to rival the great world capitals. In other words, international building styles were used to demonstrate the country's participation in modernity. The question of what form a Mexican architecture should take was not even asked for the first half of the century. It was not until the 1860s and most notably in the 1880s and 1890s that the creation of a Mexican architecture employing local architectural traditions as a basis entered architectural debates. Even then, the architects concerned with such questions were few.

During the nineteenth century, Mexico demonstrated no preference for the stylistic currents of one country over another. While various regimes proved fond of Classical styles, which filtered through the Academia de San Fernando in Madrid during the early years of the century and through the Beaux Arts Academy in Paris during the Porfiriato—the era of Porfirio Díaz (president 1876–80, 1884–1911)—stylistic currents from all the developed nations were adopted. This eclecticism parallels the economic policies of the late Porfiriato, when lenders and investors were chosen from various nations in order to prevent dominance of any one country over Mexico.

The history of nineteenth-century Mexico reveals that Mexican elites sought to transform Mexico into a modern nation capable of competing with industrialized European nations and the United States. During this period a series of foreign interventions menaced Mexico's autonomy. By the last third of the century, statesmen and intellectuals were actively searching for forms of indigenous expressions that would symbolically unify the nation and differentiate it from the outside.

One of the few attempts to represent the local took place in the form of pre-Columbian revival buildings inspired by ancient Mexican art and architecture. Although proposals and commissions of works in this tendency were few, these projects signaled Mexico's individuality and resistance to assimilation by another nation and the first attempts by the Mexican state to construct a national identity through architecture.

The City in Nineteenth-Century Mexico

For the first two-thirds of the nineteenth century, Mexico was ravaged first by the Wars of Independence and later by civil wars and foreign interventions such as the U.S.-Mexican War (1846–48) and the Wars of Reform (1858–61).

From 1821 to 1876, Mexico had a variety of governments including two empires: one ruled by a criollo (native-born American of Spanish descent), Emperor Agustín de Iturbide I (1822–23), and another one established under French protection with Maximilian von Hapsburg as emperor (1864–67). This climate of unrest was not propitious for large urban projects or for architecture. Little building took place between 1810 and 1887, despite a few short periods of peace. In addition to the restrictions placed by the political climate, the appropriation of church properties during La Reforma (the period of Liberal rule and influence, 1856–76) put an end to sumptuous commissions by the church that had enriched the urban environments of the colonial period. The most important work of architecture during the rule of Maximilian was the renovation of the castle of Chapultepec by the architect Vicente Manero, who transformed the old colonial building into a veritable palace.

The most stable period for politics, economics, and architecture was the government of Porfirio Díaz. Don Porfirio's regime was characterized by an open door policy to foreign investments and industrialization. Díaz surrounded himself with a group of advisers who became known as the Científicos, technocrats who based their policies on the positivist philosophies of Auguste Comte and Herbert Spencer, equating industrialization with progress. The Porfirian administration introduced to Mexico technological innovations such as electric lighting, telephones, automobiles, movies, and water utility systems. Between 1876 and 1910 railroad tracks increased from 400 to 15,000 miles. In order to make these developments possible, the government confiscated thousands of acres of lands owned by indigenous communities and granted them to powerful landowners and industrial companies. Mexico's stability also was achieved through powerful mechanisms of repression, which included the army and a rural police force who became known as the Rurales.

Because of the introduction of new technologies and the positivist emphasis on hygiene, the physical appearance of cities changed during the nineteenth century, and especially during the Porfiriato. Between 1790 and 1910 the population of Mexico tripled and the population of Mexico City quadrupled. Projects of public hygiene, such as the Obras de Aprovisionamiento de Agua Potable and the Ensanche del Desagüe del Valle de México, were inaugurated in 1907. Cities were reorganized; streets and avenues were paved and widened, efforts were taken to clean the city of garbage and to facilitate the circulation of air. Aqueducts gradually were replaced by lead pipes, and the first electric streetcars cruised the city in 1899. By 1890 numerous states including Aguascalientes, Orizaba, Guadalajara, Hermosillo, Puebla, and San Luis Potosí had adopted electric lighting for plazas and streets. Between 1891 and 1900, 1,570,000 square feet (146,000 square meters) of streets were paved with asphalt in Mexico City. The latter year, two U.S. companies were contracted to pave the streets with concrete and asphalt.

In 1864 Maximilian ordered the Calzada del Emperador, later named Paseo de la Reforma, to be built from the Castle of Chapultepec to the Monument of Carlos IV. Juan and Ramón Agea were responsible for the design. The avenue was 180 feet (55 meters) wide, the widest street in Mexico at that point. The Paseo de la Reforma was later widened under the presidency of Sebastián Lerdo de Tejada, and once more during Díaz's administration.

During the Porfiriato, wealthy districts concentrated on the west and southwest of the historic center of the city. Luxurious *colonias* such as the Colonia del Paseo and the Colonia Juárez developed along the Paseo de la Reforma. Poorer neighborhoods were concentrated on the east and southeast, where the ground was lower, wetter, and more unstable than in the west. This division seems to have been planned by the Porfirian administration. It is not coincidental that new jails inaugurated during the celebration of the centennial of Mexican independence in 1910 were located in the poor neighborhoods.

International Tendencies and the Academy

During most of the Porfiriato upper-class Mexicans wore French and English clothes, danced the minuet, listened to French and Italian operas, and even preferred English to Mexican food. Exclusive neighborhoods with sumptuous Neoclassical homes resembled sections of Paris and Brussels. The owners of these houses often purchased architectural designs in Europe and had them executed in Mexico. Since its founding in 1783, Mexico's Academia de San Carlos de Nueva España (later named Escuela de Bellas Artes) hired mostly European and European-educated instructors. The first director of the section of architecture at the academy was Antonio González Velázquez, a Spanish exponent of Neoclassicism who arrived in Mexico in 1778.

The academy was closed between 1821 and 1824 because of economic difficulties brought about by the Wars of Independence. After 1824, it was of decreasing significance. During this period many of the academy's former students transferred to engineering. The institution reopened in 1843 under orders of President Antonio López de Santa Anna. During his regime, several Mexican architects, including the brothers Juan and Ramón Agea, were sent to study in Europe. On their return to Mexico from Rome in 1846, the Ageas practiced architecture in a Renaissance style; Juan, in particular, introduced to Mexico the theories of Eugéne-Emmanuel Viollet-le-Duc.

In 1856, the academy unified the disciplines of civil engineering and architecture under the directorship of the Italian architect Javier Cavallari, an internationally renowned academic, historian, archaeologist, and former director of the Imperial and Royal Academy of Milan. The study plan was of eight years, including *preparatoria*, or high school. During his stay in Mexico, Cavallari republished a translation of a book he previously had written, with the title *Apuntamientos sobre la historia de la arquitectura* (1860), and he remodeled the building for the Academy of San Carlos. He taught several notable architects, including Eusebio and Ignacio de la Hidalga, Eleuterio Méndez, Manuel F. Álvarez, Antonio Torres Torija, and Manuel Téllez Pizarro. Cavallari returned to Italy in 1864 and Eleuterio Méndez took over the directorship at the academy.

In 1867 the administration of President Benito Juárez mandated the separation of the careers of architect and engineer. The Special School for Engineers was established at the former College of Mining; the career of architect remained confined to the former Academy of San Carlos, renamed the National School of Fine Arts. Despite various attempts to separate architecture and engineering, the two disciplines remained intimately related until the end of the century. For instance, in 1869 the section of architecture at the National School of Fine Arts closed owing to economic difficulties, but the degree of Engineer and Architect continued to be granted at the School of Mines. Persons working for such title had to learn artistic subjects with sculptors and painters at the National School of Fine Arts and technical subjects with civil engineers.

In the beginning of the twentieth century, the faculty of the school of architecture included Maxime Roisin (French), Adamo Boari (Italian), Antonio Rivas Mercado (a Mexican who had studied in England and at the Ècole des Beaux Arts in Paris), Carlos M. Lazo, Carlos Ituarte, Emilio Dondé, and the brothers Federico and Nicolas Mariscal. Rivas Mercado became director of the National School of Fine Arts in 1903. The French architect Émile Bénard, who came to Mexico to work on the Legislative Palace in 1903, founded an architectural studio where he took Mexican students, including Jesús Acevedo and Eduardo Macedo y Arbeau.

Taking into consideration Mexico's welcoming of imported talent, it is not surprising that the most important architectural commissions of the Porfiriato were given to foreigners. Adamo Boari (an Italian) designed the Post Office built by Gonzalo Garita (1902–07) and the National Theater (1904); Silvio Contri (another Italian) was responsible for the Secretariat of Communications and Public Works (1902–11); Émile Bénard and Maxime Roisin, both French, designed the Legislative Palace in 1905. This building was never completed because of the outbreak of the Revolution in 1910, but the importance of the Legislative Palace for the Porfirian regime is evident in the ceremonial laying of the first stone of the building during the celebrations of the centenary of Independence in 1910, although work on the building had begun a few years earlier.

Stylistic Tendencies

As in Spain, academic education in Mexico was based on the model of the Ècole des Beaux Arts in Paris, an institution that traditionally favored architecture based on Classical traditions. Neoclassicism became firmly established in Mexico at the end of the eighteenth century, some decades after it had become an international style. The statutes enacted by Carlos III to the Academy in 1784 prohibited any tribunal to

Central Post Office Building, Mexico City, by Adamo Boari, 1902–07
Photo courtesy of Archivo Fotográfico, Instituto de Investigaciones Estéticas de la UNAM

employ anyone who was not an academician to measure or direct architectural projects.

Neoclassicism

In nineteenth-century Mexico, Neoclassicism must be understood as a tendency to base the features of buildings on the architecture of Classical antiquity or on later buildings derived from that tradition. This implies neither a desire to be archaeologically correct on the part of architects nor exclusive use of these sources in the architecture. The architectural styles represented in nineteenth-century Mexican architecture refer more to decoration than to spatial characteristics, so much so, that to consider a work as Neoclassical it is sufficient that it has Classical columns. During the first half of the nineteenth century the dominant stylistic tendencies of the school of architecture continued to be Classical. Other tendencies became increasingly important during the period of Cavallari's directorship and thereafter.

Most of the influential academic designers during the first half of the century were Spanish. Miguel Constansó, a military engineer born in Barcelona in 1741, went to Mexico

in 1764. Antonio González Velázquez was director of the section of architecture at the Academy of San Carlos until 1794. Manuel Tolsá initially went to Mexico as director of the section of sculpture in the Academy of San Carlos and was appointed director of the section of architecture in 1810. Lorenzo de la Hidalga, born in Álava, Spain, worked in Paris in 1836 under the direction of Henri Labrouste and Viollet-le-Duc and went to Mexico in 1838.

Francisco Tresguerras was one of few active Mexican designers of this period. Born in Celaya, Guanajuato, he was self-educated. In 1794 Tresguerras requested from the academy the degree of Arquitecto de Mérito, a title intended for persons who already had experience in architecture; it is unknown if he received it. Tresguerras exemplifies the confluence of local and international tendencies during the early nineteenth century. Although he regarded himself as a Classicist, many of his works, including his own tomb, align him with the Baroque decorative tradition dominant in colonial Mexican architecture. Because of his eclectic, idiosyncratic style, later scholars variously judged Tresguerras as either a genius or a fraud.

In the West, powerful nations adopted Neoclassical architecture for official buildings in various historical periods. Because Neoclassicism is based on the art of ancient civilizations, its use in later periods is part of a process of validation. Neoclassical styles are ritualistic gestures of empowerment, for they suggest an identification of the nation that commissions them with the great civilizations of Western antiquity. The significance of Neoclassicism in Mexico was double-edged. On one hand, its arrival through Spain signaled a colonial relation; on the other, it was an attempt to legitimize Mexico's independent regimes and to define Mexico as a member of the modern nations. The status of Neoclassicism as an international style during the nineteenth century further problematizes this reading, since the emulation of international tendencies in Mexican architecture suggested Mexico's postcolonial relation of subalternity to Europe and the United States. A chronological listing of notable works in Neoclassical architecture from the nineteenth century includes the Royal Cigar Factory in Mexico City by Antonio González Velázquez and Miguel Constansó (1792–1807); the College of Mining by Manuel Tolsá (1797–1813); the Palace of Government of San Luis Potosí designed by Miguel Constansó (1798–1827); the Church of El Carmen, Celaya, by Francisco Tresguerras (1802–07); the Church of the Teresitas in Querétaro by Manuel Tolsá, Pedro Ortíz, and Francisco Tresguerras (1803–07); the interior of the Cámara de Diputados in the National Palace in Mexico City by Agustín Paz (1824–29); the National Theater, or Santa Ana Theater, in Mexico City by Lorenzo de la Hidalga (1841–44); the Degollado Theater by José Galvéz in Guadalajara (1856–80); the Academy of San Carlos renovations by Javier Cavallari (1863); the Juárez Theater in Guanajuato by José Noriega and Antonio Rivas Mercado (1873–1903); the Palace of Government in Monterrey (1895–1908); the Project for the Legislative Palace by Émile Bénard (1905); and the Monument to Benito Juárez in Mexico City by Guillermo de Heredia (1909–10).

In his book *Arquitectura del Siglo XIX en Mexico,* Israel Katzman discusses five tendencies related to Neoclassicism: integrated eclecticism, semiclassic eclecticism, Baroque, very simplified traditionalist style, and the French style. As mentioned earlier, these categories overlap and are sometimes indistinguishable from one another. According to Katzman, since in nineteenth-century Mexico there is no pure architectural style, the assignation of buildings to specific stylistic categories is a matter of "degrees of kinship." The usefulness of this classification is debatable, but an alternative is yet to be developed.

In Katzman's view, integrated eclecticism is a current that incorporates traces of classical architecture but includes Baroque and eclectic architectural elements. There is no intention on the part of the architect to return to a specific architectural style. Buildings in this tendency include the Neptune Fountain in Querétaro by Francisco Tresguerras (1797); the Arbeau Theater in Mexico City by José Téllez de Girón (1874–75); the Hospital Concepción Beístegui in Mexico City (1886); and details such as column capitals in the interior of the Juárez Theater in Guanajuato by José Noriega and Antonio Rivas Mercado (1873–1903).

Semiclassic eclecticism is one in which a building's classical elements have greater weight than elements deriving from other styles. Buildings such as the Juárez Theater in Guanajuato, the Palace of Government in Chihuahua (1882–92), and the Palace of Government by Luis Long in Guanajuato (1897–1900) are included in this tendency.

"Very simplified traditionalism" refers to buildings of various stylistic tendencies with a minimal amount of ornamentation. Examples include the Hercules Spinning Mill and Textile Factory in Querétaro (1836–64); the Bella Unión Hotel in Mexico City (1840), designed by José Besozzi, a military architect; a project for a penitentiary in Mexico City by Lorenzo de la Hidalga (1848); the Iturbide Theater, later the Cámara de Diputados (1851–56) by Manuel Méndez; the San Francisco Market in Morelia, Michoacán (1872–1910); the Maternity Hospital by Eduardo Tamaríz in Puebla (1879–85); and the Agriculture School in the Hacienda de San Antonio Chautla, Puebla, built at the turn of the century. While the first four buildings are based in the classical tradition, a series of gabled roofs placed at various levels give the halls of the San Francisco Market an orientalized aspect. The last two buildings were inspired by Romanesque architecture. The light, open structures of the Buen Tono Factory in Mexico City (1896–97) by Miguel A. de Quevedo and Ernesto Canseco, both engineers, and the building of the Universal Factories in Mexico City by Miguel A. de Quevedo (finished in 1909) prefigure modern architecture.

Baroque and the French Style

Although in Mexico the Baroque is presumed to have ended in the late eighteenth century, Baroque buildings continued to be built in the nineteenth century. For many Mexicans, after the Wars of Independence, the Baroque came to symbolize Mexico's colonial past. Buildings in this tendency completed in the nineteenth century include the Oratory of San Felipe Neri in Guadalajara, Jalisco (finished in 1812); the Naples Chapel in the Villa de Guadaloupe, Zacatecas (1845–66), designed by Fray Diego de la Concepción Palomar and redecorated by the *maestro de obras,* Refugio Reyes; the tower of the parish church in Lagos de Moreno, Jalisco (finished in 1871); and the Spanish Casino in Mexico City by Emilio González del Campo (1901–03). As in Mexican colonial Baroque, the majority of these buildings exhibit rich surface decoration but lack structural dynamism. In various buildings the placement of columnated porticoes and engaged columns projecting from the facade produce the impression of movement. This technique is used instead of complex geometries in plan and elevation to produce the same effect. Katzman attributes this trait to turn-of-the-century French Classicism. Yet, this characteristic is found in earlier French and other architecture.

The French "style" is recognized by the presence of mansard roofs and dormer windows in addition to elements of Classical architecture and profuse sculptural decoration of surfaces, including busts, caryatids, angels, and vegetation in vertical arrangements. According to Katzman, the taste for heavy surface decoration is of French Classical origin; but similar characteristics and decorative elements can be found in Mexico since the beginning of the colonial period. An important example of the French tendency is the House of the Braniff family in Reforma Avenue, built by Carlos Hall in 1888.

Gothic, Romanesque, and Islamic Revivals

In addition to variants of Classicism, numerous styles were represented in nineteenth-century Mexican architecture, including Gothic, Romanesque, and Islamic revivals, Art Nouveau, and Neoindigenista (or pre-Hispanic revival). None of these currents existed in isolation but often were mixed with other tendencies. The presence of this variety of styles has been explained as a result of Mexico's search for identity. In his book, *Arte del Siglo XIX en México,* Justino Fernández suggests that Mexico's eclecticism meant not only that Mexico admired foreign styles in architecture but that it was involved in a search for its own authentic and unique expression. Although Fernández's interpretation is correct, it does not explain the presence of eclecticism in Europe and the United States during the same time period, nor does he discuss the implications of this search for "authentic and unique expression." The use of foreign models to represent the Mexican nation suggests an implicit acceptance on the part of Mexicans of the cultural superiority of outsiders, an acceptance typical of many postcolonial nations.

The Gothic revival, practiced primarily by *maestros de obras* in the provinces, included works such as the Portico of Medellín in Colima, by Lucio Uribe (1860); the facade of the Church of San Miguel de Allende in Guanajuato by Ceferino Gutiérrez (1880); the Guadaloupe Sanctuary in Zacatecas begun by Refugio Reyes in 1891 (a combination of a Gothic and Classical facade); the chapel of the French Cemetery in Mexico City by E. Desormes (1891–92); the Episcopal Church of Christ, in Mexico City (1895–98); and the Central Post office Building in Mexico City by Adamo Boari (1902–06). This last building has been identified as representing various styles owing to the presence of Romanesque, Byzantine, Isabelline, and Renaissance elements in the facade.

Romanesque revival buildings include the Chapel of the Spanish Cemetery in Mexico City by Ignacio and Eusebio de la Hidalga (c.1880); the Church of San Felipe de Jesús in Madero Street in Mexico City by Émile Dondé (1886–97); the Church of the Sagrada Familia in Mexico City by Manuel Gorozpe (1910–12); and the Church of Santa Ana in Toluca, Mexico.

Sumptuous houses modeled after foreign catalogs of country houses combined the above mentioned styles with elements from medieval English architecture. Katzman calls this tendency *campestre romántica.* Examples include the House of the Braniff family in Chapala (c.1905); the House

Church of San Miguel de Allende, Guanajuato,
by Ceferino Gutiérrez, 1880
Photo courtesy of Archivo Fotográfico, Instituto de Investigaciones
Estéticas de la UNAM

of Alberto Terrazas in the Calzada del Nombre de Dios, Chihuahua (c.1906); and the House in the Paseo de la Reforma 365, Mexico City (1911–12).

Islamic architecture had active representatives in Puebla. Between 1880 and 1884 Eduardo Tamaríz executed several works in this tendency, including the reconstruction of the San Francisco Mill or "El Marqués de Monserrat" (c.1880) and a Kiosk in the Plaza Constitución (1882–83). Several interiors decorated by the Arpa Brothers in the same city exhibit elements characteristic of Islamic architecture such as pointed, horseshoe, and polylobed arches as well as intricate abstract patterns as decoration. The best-known examples of Islamic architecture in nineteenth-century Mexico, however, are the Mexico Pavilion designed by José Ramón Ibarrola for the New Orleans Exposition of 1884–85 and the interior of the Juárez Theater in Guanajuato by José Noriega and Antonio Rivas Mercado (1873–1903). The history of the design by Ibarrola illustrates the eclecticism of the epoch, as the architect submitted two projects to the competition for the building: one inspired by English wooden architecture, and the other, the Islamic pavilion.

Pavilion of Mexico, Universal Exposition of 1889, Paris, by Antonio Peñafiel and Antonio M. Anza
Photo courtesy of Archivo Fotográfico, Instituto de Investigaciones Estéticas de la UNAM

Art Nouveau

Most of the Art Nouveau architecture built in Mexico has been destroyed. Yet, Mexico achieved extraordinary buildings in this style, including Porfirio Díaz's arms' room on Mexico City's Cadena Street, decorated by Antonio Fabrés (before 1905); the staircase of the Mercantile Center, later the Great Hotel, of Mexico City (destroyed); and various rooms and furniture in the spectacular house of don Luis Requena in Santa Veracruz no. 43, designed by the Catalan artist Ramón Cantó (1901–12). A member of a cosmopolitan Mexican aristocracy, Requena informed his requests for the design of this house on examples of architecture he saw in his frequent travels to Europe. In addition to Art Nouveau music room, dining room, bedroom, and children's room, the house included a Mozarabic patio, a Louis XV living room, and Renaissance and Pompeiian rooms.

There has been controversy regarding the designation of the National Theater, also known as Palacio de Bellas Artes (1904), by Adamo Boari as an example of either Art Nouveau or Neoclassicism. This controversy has emerged because scholars have attempted to fit it into a single stylistic category, when in fact it is a hybrid that includes both. This building is important not only because it fuses various currents but because it exemplifies both the Porfiriato's preference for imports and an attempt by Mexican elites at self-representation. Don Porfirio's administration gave the commission for the building design to Adamo Boari. The Italian artists Leonardo Bistolfi, A. Boni, and Gianetti Fiorenzo, the Hungarian sculptor Geza Marotti, and Agustín Querol, a Catalan sculptor, were responsible for the sculptural decorations. Iron works for the exterior were the creation of the Italian artist Alessandro Mazzucotelli. The great stage curtain was designed by Dr. Atl (whose real name was Gerardo Murillo, a well-to-do Mexican painter who was later instrumental in the development of Mexican muralism). Two German firms, the Vereignitemaschinenfabrik and the Maschinenbaugesellshaft, received the commission for its steel structure. This structure would be covered by crystal plates made by Tiffany Studios in New York. The company Milliken Brothers from Chicago was in charge of the buildings's foundations and W. H. Birkmire form New York was to direct most of the construction. The edifice was designed to have a steel structure covered with concrete, in turn covered with marble. Marble architectural details such as columns and pilasters, as well as the reproductions of models for marble and copper sculptures were made abroad by the companies Walton Goody and Triscornia and Hereaux. Machinery, including elevators for the upper and lower stages of the theater, were made by the two German houses mentioned above; the Allgemeine Elektricitats Gesellshaft from Berlin was in charge of the electrical infrastructure for the entire theater.

Despite the predominance of foreign artists and consultants, the National Theater integrated indigenous themes and decoration into a building of international character. Among the sculptural decorations for the facade, Boari included eagle warriors and feathered serpents based on Aztec prototypes; the stage curtain designed by Dr. Atl depicted the Mexican volcanoes Popocatépetl and Iztaccíhuatl. The government's approval of Boari's design indicates an interest on the part of the Porfirian administration to claim a place for Mexican culture next to the cultural heritage of Europe. Similar attitudes clearly were expressed by contemporary architects such as Luis Salazar, Nicolás Mariscal, and Jesús Acevedo, who searched for solutions to create a modern architecture with a national character. While Salazar advocated a Mexican architecture based on ancient indigenous building traditions, Mariscal and Acevedo proposed a national architecture based on colonial buildings.

The image of Mexico represented in the Palace of Fine Arts was primarily one of wealth and sophistication. The state-of-the-art construction techniques, building materials, and infrastructure implied economic power; the international character of the related artworks suggested cultural refinement. Only the references to the landscape and local

Palacio de Bellas Artes, Mexico City, by Adamo Boari, 1904
Photo courtesy of Archivo Fotográfico, Instituto de Investigaciones Estéticas de la UNAM

antiquity identified the building as Mexican. This image of the nation was representative of a very small section of the population: the cosmopolitan upper class. The references to local antiquity recognized Mexico's ancient past as the national heritage, but no reference was made to contemporary indigenes who comprised a significant part of the population. The construction of the National Theater was interrupted from 1917 to 1929 by the Mexican Revolution. Work on the theater finally was resumed in 1930 and completed in 1934 under the direction of Federico Mariscal.

Neoindigenismo

The nineteenth century witnessed the development of pre-Hispanic revival, or Neoindigenista, buildings, a new genre in Mexican architecture. Although it is tempting to regard this tendency as one more example of eclecticism and taste for exotic tendencies that dominated the period, such a judgment is simplistic. In Mexico, pre-Hispanic subject matter had been linked strongly with representations of the local since the colonial period.

The first monument to represent pre-Hispanic themes in a public building was a triumphal arch designed by Carlos de Sigüenza y Góngora for the welcoming reception of a new viceroy to Mexico City in 1680. Built in a traditional style, the paintings of the arch featured the Mexica god Huitzilopochtli and 11 Mexica rulers as the protagonists in allegorical paintings illustrating the virtues of good government. The arch represented a Mexican criollo nation built upon the appropriation of indigenous antiquity by a privileged group. No buildings celebrating indigenous antiquity were constructed in the eighteenth century, although writings such as *Due antichi monumenti di architettura messicana* by Padre Pedro José Marquéz (Rome, 1804) exalted the cultural value of pre-Hispanic monuments.

In the nineteenth century, Neoindigenista architecture played an active part in the representation of national identity as constructed by the Porfirian regime. As wealthy criollos had done in the colonial period, Porfirian elites created an image of the nation embracing ancient indigenous civilizations as the common heritage of all Mexicans. This was a problematic proposition in view of the nation's colonial history and the influx of immigrants to Mexico during the nineteenth century. More importantly, the references to Mexican antiquity without any acknowledgment of contemporary indigenous peoples suggested the extinction of Mexican natives, since archaeological cultures implied a past long gone. In Neoindigenista buildings, Mexican natives represented in paintings and sculptures often appeared as mestizos, suggesting the sacrifice of specific ethnic identities to an ideal image of the nation.

These visual constructs of the nation had roots in attempts to unify the Mexican population. Because of Mexico's growing industrialization during the second half of the nineteenth century, Mexican elites thought of the indigenes as a national "problem." Attempts to deal with this problem ranged from outright annihilation of Native Mexicans—as in the "pacification" campaigns in the north of the country—to proposals for integration of the indigenous population to the nation through education and intermarriage. These proposals had in common the cultural negation and extermination of the natives.

Like buildings in other "neo" styles, no Neoindigenista building was faithful to ancient prototypes, but rather unified various stylistic tendencies. Official commissions of these buildings were few but significant. The first building based on ancient Mexican motifs built in the nineteenth century was the Monument to Cuauhtemoc executed by the engineer Francisco Jiménez and the sculptor Miguel Noreña (1878–87). The monument consisted of a sculpture of Cuauhtemoc resting on a tall pedestal. This pedestal incorporated elements from various pre-Hispanic buildings and sculpture. Cuauhtemoc, the last Mexica ruler, was famous for his resistance to Spanish colonization and later became a symbol of resistance to foreign intervention in general. The placement of this monument in the Avenida de la Reforma, an artery connecting luxurious neighborhoods housing most of Mexico's foreigners, implied Mexico's opposition to foreign intervention. This was a powerful statement given that in the nineteenth century, Mexico suffered substantial territorial losses during the U.S.-Mexican War and later confronted the French Intervention of 1862 to 1867.

The next important Neoindigenista commission was the Pavilion of Mexico in the 1889 Paris World Exhibition designed by Antonio M. Anza and Antonio Peñafiel. Like Boari's National Theater, this building manifested the dual goal of integrating Mexico into modernity and exalting local traditions. The pavilion's plan was based on the Beaux Arts tradition of design, emphasizing regularity and symmetry; but the decorations celebrated Mexico's ancient past. The main entrance was based on various Classic and Postclassic central Mexican buildings, particularly the Temple of Xochicalco. Relief sculptures on the front facade of the building represented mythological figures and Mexica rulers. Although these figures were based on the *Florentine Codex*, the final products took on the classical features and dramatic gestures of French academic sculpture. Constructed with an iron structure and glass, marble, cement, iron, and zinc decorations, the pavilion united two different images: a preindustrial past and a technologically sophisticated present. The use of industrial materials suggested that Mexico was as capable of building as the most powerful lands; the indigenous decorations pointed to Mexico's distinctiveness, implying its resistance to assimilation by another nation.

The choice of ancient Mexican architecture to represent the Mexican nation was influenced at least in part by the great interest that Europeans—particularly the French—demonstrated for Mexican archaeology. In 1864, along with the French intervention, Napoleón III sent an archaeological commission to study Mexican ruins. For the Paris World Exhibition of 1867, the French exhibited a model of the Temple of Xochicalco. During the late Porfiriato, the Mexican government aggressively sought French investment in Mexico with the hope of counterbalancing U.S. influence. The final design for the 1889 pavilion of Mexico was chosen with the help of French critics at the request of a Mexican delegate to the exposition. Thus, in addition to nationalistic concerns, Mexico's representation of itself in architecture was intimately linked with its goals in international politics.

In addition to exemplifying pre-Hispanic revival architecture during the Porfiriato, the Pavilion of Mexico in the 1889 Paris World Exhibition was important because of the theory it generated. At the beginning of the twentieth century, Luis Salazar, an architect and engineer who participated in the government-sponsored competition for the building's design, enthusiastically encouraged architects to create a national style of architecture based on the study of pre-Hispanic ruins (Salazar 1898). His writings would be influential for the nationalistic tendencies in Mexican architecture which developed during the second and third decade of the twentieth century. Other nineteenth-century buildings incorporating pre-Hispanic decorative motifs include the Monument to Benito Juárez in Paseo Juárez, Oaxaca (1899), and a triumphal arch commissioned by the state of Yucatán for the visit of Porfirio Díaz to Merida in 1906.

New Materials

During the second half of the nineteenth century, new building materials including glass, iron, and reinforced concrete were introduced to Mexican architecture. Metallic architecture included buildings in various stylistic tendencies. Iron and reinforced concrete structures frequently were covered with other materials and made to look like buildings in traditional styles.

Students of architecture in Mexico first became familiar with the use of iron as a structural material during Cavallari's term as director of the academy. Initially, iron was used only for discrete parts of the building such as the roof, decorative elements, and outdoor furniture. Iron details often imitated the forms of architectural elements in traditional styles. During the Porfiriato, iron was employed for the whole structure of buildings. At first, this was more common in undecorated utilitarian structures, which in Mexico as in the rest of the world provided important precedents for modern architecture. These utilitarian buildings include the railway station Mexico-Veracruz in Buena Vista, Mexico City (1878); the Metepec-Atlixco Factory in Puebla (c.1889–99); the Slaughterhouse San Lucas in Mexico City by Antonio Torres Torija (1893–95); the glass workshop and warehouse at the factory of Pellandini and Son in Mexico City (begun 1898); and the Mexican Cigarette Factory in Mexico City (1900). Buildings of various stylistic tendencies with iron structures include the Legislative Palace (1905); the National Theater (Palacio de Bellas Artes, 1904); the Central Post Office Building (1902–07);

Church of the Sagrada Familia, Mexico City, by Manuel Gorozpe and Miguel Rebolledo, 1910–12
Photo courtesy of Archivo Fotográfico, Instituto de Investigaciones Estéticas de la UNAM

the Secretariat of Communications (1902–11); La Esmeralda Jewelry Store by Eleuterio Méndez (1890–92); the Mercantile Center (1896–97); and the Casa Boker (1898) and La Mutua (1900), both designed by the American firm De Lemos y Cordes. It shall be noted that the iron used for most of these buildings was imported. This meant that in order to be able to construct a cosmopolitan image of itself, Mexico made itself dependent on other countries, reduplicating the colonial relation.

Reinforced concrete was introduced to Mexico by an association formed by the engineers Miguel Rebolledo, Fernando González, and Angel Ortiz Monasterio, a brigadier who previously had worked with Hennebique in Paris. The first constructions with these materials took place in 1903, but commissions were few because the system was thought to be inappropriate to Mexico's elevation. Later buildings in reinforced concrete include the Church of the Sagrada Familia by Manuel Gorozpe and Miguel Rebolledo (1910–12) and the Monument to Benito Juárez by

Guillermo de Heredia (1910), both in Mexico City. The Juárez Monument exemplifies the tendency to cover iron and reinforced concrete structures with other materials, as marble was used to cover the concrete.

Conclusion

The history of nineteenth-century Mexican architecture is in need of serious revision. So far, investigators have focused on the Porfiriato, when building was most abundant. Although these studies have been basic to the discipline, architecture from the first two-thirds of the century, the period of instability, might illuminate the processes through which buildings are allowed to come into existence. More attention needs to be given to the social and institutional context of the production of specific buildings, as stylistic classification is of little value in the context of eclecticism.

During the Porfiriato, patrons and practitioners of architecture manifested two impulses: to create an architecture that would indicate Mexico's participation in modernity and to emphasize Mexico's difference from other countries through the incorporation of local characteristics into the architecture. The first goal took precedence over the second during most of the nineteenth century.

A brief examination of the Palace of Fine Arts and the Pavilion of Mexico in the 1889 Paris World Exhibition revealed that the Porfirian regime chose to represent Mexico as an independent, wealthy, and powerful country. This representation obscured painful realities of the nation, since despite growing modernization, Mexico was economically dependent on the industrialized nations, and most of the Mexican population lived in poverty.

The representation of the local in Mexican architecture was achieved mainly though themes and decorative motifs inspired by pre-Hispanic antiquity. These representations were essential to the construction of a common heritage by which the nation might be unified. This emphasis on the ancient past distracted the public's attention from the elites' and the government's contemporary mistreatment of indigenous peoples.

Attempts during the nineteenth century to represent national identity through architecture laid a groundwork for further experimentation. After the Mexican Revolution, successive Mexican regimes would use the pre-Hispanic past to represent the nation. Later architects also took inspiration from the architecture of the colonial period and regional architecture as the creation of a genuinely Mexican architecture became a pressing issue during the twentieth century.

Select Bibliography

Alvarez, Manuel Francisco, *El doctor Cavallari y la carrera de ingeniero civil en Mexico.* Mexico City: A. Carranza y Cía, 1906.
_____, "Algunos escritos." *Cuadernos de arquitectura y conservación del patrimonio artístico* 18–19 (January–February 1982).
Anderson, Benedict, *Imagined Communities.* London: Verso, 1983.

Báez Macías, Eduardo, *Evaluación e historia de la Academia de San Carlos.* Mexico City: Talleres Gráficos de la Nación, 1974.
_____, "La Academia de San Carlos en la Nueva España como instrumento de cambio." In *Las academias de arte.* Mexico City: UNAM, 1985.
Bonet Correa, Antonio, and Francisco de la Maza, *La arquitectura de la época porfiriana en México.* Murcia: Publicaciones de la Universidad de Murcia, 1966.
_____, "La Arquitectura de la época porfiriana." *Cuadernos de arquitectura y conservación del patrimonio artístico* 7 (January 1980).
Burns, Bradford, *The Poverty of Progress.* Berkeley: University of California Press, 1980.
Cavallari, Javier, *Apuntamientos sobre la historia de la arquitectura,* translated by Joaquín Velázquez de León. Mexico City: 1860.
Fernández, Justino, *El Arte del Siglo XIX en México.* Mexico City: UNAM, Instituto de Investigaciones Estéticas, 1967.
Fernández, Maria, *In the Image of the Other: A Call for Re-evaluation of National Identity.* Austin: Center for the Study of American Architecture, School of Architecture, University of Texas, 1992.
_____, "The representation of National Identity in Mexican Architecture: Two Case Studies (1680 and 1889)." Ph.D. diss., Columbia University, New York, 1993.
Galindo y Villa, Jesús, *Historia Sumaria de la Ciudad de México.* Mexico City: Editorial Cultura, 1925.
García Cubas, Antonio, *México de mis recuerdos.* Mexico City: Editorial Patria, 1950.
González Gortázar, Fernando, *La Arquitectura del Siglo XX.* Mexico City: Consejo Nacional para la Cultura y las Artes, 1994.
Hall, Stuart, "Old and New Identities, Old and New Ethnicities." In *Culture, Globalization, and The World System,* edited by Anthony King. Binghamton: State University of New York at Binghamton, 1991.
Instituto Nacional de Bellas Artes, editor. *La construcción del Palacio de Bellas Artes: Documentos para la Historia de la arquitectura en México.* Mexico City: Instituto Nacional de Bellas Artes, 1984.
Katzman, Israel, *Arquitectura contemporanea mexicana.* Mexico City: Instituto Nacional de Antropología e Historia, 1964.
_____, *Arquitectura del Siglo XIX en México.* 2nd edition, Mexico City: Editorial Trillas, 1993.
Mariategui, Carlos, *Seven Interpretative Essays on Peruvian Reality.* Austin: University of Texas Press, 1971.
Martín Hernández, Vicente, *Arquitectura doméstica de la Ciudad de México, 1890–1925.* Mexico City: UNAM, 1981.
_____, "Arquitectura porfiriana. Análisis comparativo de la colonia Juárez 1910–1980." In *Apuntes para la historia y crítica de la arquitectura mexicana del siglo XX 1900–1980: Cuadernos de arquitectura y conservación del patrimonio artístico* 20–21 (1982).
Maza, Francisco de la, "Sobre arquitectura art nouveau." *Anales del Instituto de Investigaciones Estéticas* 7:26 (1957).
_____, *Del Neoclásico al art-nouveau y primer viaje a Europa.* Mexico City: Secretaría de Educación Pública, 1974.
Neuvillate, Alfonso, "El Art Nouveau en México." *Cuadernos de arquitectura y conservación del patrimonio artístico* 12 (November 1980).
Porphyrios, Demitri, "Notes on a Method." *On the Methodology of Architectural History. Architectural Design Profile* 96–104 (1981).

Reese, Thomas F., and Carol McMichael Reese, *Revolutionary Urban Legacies: Porfirio Díaz's Celebrations of the Centennial of Mexican Independence in 1910.* Mexico City: UNAM, 1994.

Rodríguez Prampolini, Ida, *La críitica del arte en el siglo XIX.* Mexico City: UNAM, 1964.

Salazar, Luis, *La arquitectura y la arqueología Memoria presentada por el ingeniero Luis Salazar al Congreso de Americanistas en su sesión verificada en México en 1895.* Mexico City: Oficina de la Tipografía de Fomento, 1898.

Schávelzon, Daniel, editor, *La polémica del arte nacional en México, 1850–1910.* Mexico City: Fondo de Cultura Económico, 1988.

Segurajáuregui, Elena, *Arquitectura porfirista: La colonia Juárez.* Mexico City: Universidad Autónoma Metyropolitana Azcapotzalco, 1990.

Tibol, Raquel, *Historia general del arte mexicano.* Vol 3. *Epoca moderna y contemporanea.* Mexico City: Editorial Hermes, 1964.

Vargas Lugo, Elisa, *Francisco de la Maza, Obras Escogidas.* Mexico City: UNAM, 1992.

Vargas Salguero, Ramón, *Historia de la teoría de la arquitectura El porfirismo.* Mexico City: UNAM, 1989.

—MARÍA FERNÁNDEZ

ARCHITECTURE: TWENTIETH CENTURY

During the first three decades of the twentieth century, Mexican architects became preoccupied with the creation of a national architecture expressive of the new society brought about by the Revolution. Some of the stylistic tendencies explored as solutions were revivals of local historic building traditions. It was soon discovered that these did not meet the needs of contemporary life, however, and modern architecture became the preferred idiom. The dialectic between the local and the international already present in nineteenth-century Mexican architecture continued. The tensions and interactions between local and international currents would be at the forefront of architectural debates and practice during the entire century.

Throughout the century, the Mexican state played a crucial role in the development and representation of Mexican national identity in architecture. Successive governments encouraged architects to create nationalist buildings and commissioned grandiose projects that functioned as symbols of the nation. In the beginning of the century various administrations favored the colonial revival style; later, with the exception of a brief period of functionalism, a synthesis of pre-Hispanic decorative traditions and modern architecture was preferred. By the 1950s these developments resulted in a synthesis of international and local styles that earned Mexican architecture international acclaim. During the last four decades of the century, private capital increasingly participated in the construction of Mexican national identity, as individuals and corporations commissioned important buildings.

In contrast to the study of architecture of the previous century, the study of twentieth-century Mexican architecture is less concerned with the classification of buildings than with the role of specific architects in the development of a national architecture. This approach originates in the history of Western architecture, where the architect is traditionally cast in the heroic role of genius. Such rendering contrasts with the presumed anonymity of builders in regional and pre-Hispanic architecture.

Despite a wealth of scholarship on twentieth-century Mexican architecture, various writers agree on the necessity for a more critical approach to the field. As in other parts of the world, in Mexico the job of the architectural historian is often conceived as documenting the works of great architects, or in a revisionist historian mode, giving deserved recognition to figures excluded from the canon. Critical discussion of the work is often unwelcome to both architects and critics.

A critical approach should be concerned not only with the evaluation of aesthetics and the architectural function of buildings but also with the relation of architecture to Mexico's social, political, and economic structures. The writing of such a history is a difficult project for various reasons. Contemporary scholars writing about the latter part of the century often lack the historical and critical distance to identify the relation between architecture and relevant contexts. A contextual analysis of a building is usually more time consuming than a formal analysis, as the former is dependent on archival information that is not always readily available. In addition, it is risky for scholars to write critically about both living architects and those who occupy iconic positions in the history of Mexican architecture. The following essay should be seen not as an example of such a history, but as an outline of significant movements in twentieth-century Mexican architecture that raises questions basic to future criticism.

The history of twentieth-century Mexican architecture exemplifies the construction and affirmation of national identity and nationalism. Various scholars have written about the quest for identity during this period, but many of these studies are limited to identifying the elements and forms that make the buildings "quintessentially Mexican." In addition to recognizing visual constructs of nationhood, a critical history must investigate how these images fit with the everyday reality of the nation. To begin a critical appraisal of nationalist architecture one may ask: Are the images representative of the diversity within the nation? Which groups do the buildings represent? What aspects of the nation are emphasized? What aspects are consistently excluded? To what end? What institutions and individuals benefit from these representations? At what and whose expense are these symbols of nationhood constructed?

Although it is important for historians to recognize the accomplishments of individual architects, the writing of history in a contextual mode entails the possibility that architects and intellectuals contribute to agendas other than their own, knowingly or unknowingly. In any historical period, social and cultural imperatives are achieved through the collaboration of individuals and institutions (governmental, educational, commercial). Individuals work for the advancement of private and institutional objectives but ultimately they may contribute to further more complex projects, often the goals of the state, and more recently, of international corporations.

Various cultural theorists have noted that nationalism is primarily a masculinist project. The existing history of nineteenth- and twentieth-century Mexican architecture supports this idea since it has been almost exclusively a history of men. Recent publications on Mexican architecture credit women collaborators in a few buildings, but the examples are scarce. Photographic illustrations in books on Mexican architecture attest to the education of women in the profession. Women appear among the men in architecture classes and meetings at various institutions, but little is known about the practice of these women as professionals. The erasure of women is characteristic of other regions and periods of architecture history and is indicative of the discipline's focus on elites, usually white and male. To correct this omission, historians might have to engage in a study of struggle, modest achievements, and perhaps even failure, a far cry from documenting the development of genius in the dominant tradition of architecture history.

Revivals

Between 1911 and 1934 Mexico experienced several revolts and seven changes of government, but the promise of the Revolution, the determination to forge a new society, persisted. Influential intellectuals of the period believed that the development of a new Mexican nation and consequently of a national character or identity, depended at least in part upon the creation of a homogeneous culture. The homogenization of the population was thought to be important not only in matters of art. Influential politicians and intellectuals including Manuel Gamio, Andrés Molina Enríquez, and José Vasconcelos proposed *mestizaje,* the mixture of Native Americans and European, as the mark of a new society, a new nation, and ultimately, a superior race. In architecture, the nationalism of this era was manifested as revivals of pre-Hispanic and colonial traditions. Although mixture of these two tendencies occurred infrequently, many architects designed buildings in each current simultaneously.

Neocolonial architecture was established and supported by various post-Revolutionary regimes. Venustiano Carranza (1917–20) decreed the exemption of federal tax to all citizens who constructed their houses in neocolonial style. Álvaro Obregón (1920–24) and Plutarco Elías Calles (1924–28) also commissioned buildings in this style.

One of the most influential theoreticians in the formulation of a Mexican architecture was Federico Mariscal. In his book *La patria y la arquitectura nacional* (1915), Mariscal proclaimed the colonial home as the most truthful expression of "the Mexican character." He justified this choice on the basis of *mestizaje.* Since the majority of the Mexican population was a mixture of Spanish and indigene, national architecture should be the one developed during colonial period, the era where the mestizo, "the true Mexican," originated. As professor of architecture at the National University, Mariscal influenced many architects during the second and third decades of the century.

Carlos Obregón Santacilia worked in both the colonial and pre-Hispanic revivals for a short period of time. The Pavilion of Mexico in the International exposition for the Centenary of the Independence of Brazil, designed by Obregón Santacilia in collaboration with Carlos Tarditi, included a number of colonial motifs including a profusely decorated central retablo around the main entrance. As a complement for the pavilion, the same architects designed a monument to Cuauhtemoc (the last Mexica/Aztec ruler) in which they incorporated pre-Hispanic sculptural motifs such as plumed serpents into the sculpture's pedestal. Favorably impressed with the pavilion, José Vasconcelos commissioned Obregón Santacilia to design the Benito Juárez Primary School (1923–25) in neocolonial style. As secretary of public education, Vasconcelos was instrumental in introducing neocolonial architecture in official buildings. Later buildings in this style include the Renovation of the National Palace by Augusto Petriccioli (1926) and the Departamento del Distrito Federal by Federico Mariscal and Fernando Beltrán y Puga (1934).

In the Secretaría de la Salubridad (1925–27), Obregón Santacilia utilized the figure of an eagle above the entrance, arcades fashioned after colonial buildings, and local materials such as gray stone from Xaltocan. The eagle was a symbol of the sun for late Postclassic central Mexican cultures. Geometrically defined volumes and the scarcity of applied decoration align this building with early modernism. The architecture does not emulate any historically accurate style; it is clear that the architect was more interested in suggesting his sources for ideological reasons than copying or making exact reproductions of traditional architecture.

In 1926, the Mexican government sponsored a contest for the pavilion of Mexico in the Iberoamerican Exposition in Seville. Both neocolonial and pre-Hispanic revival projects were submitted. The winner of the first contest was Ignacio Marquina, but owing to complaints by the other participants, two additional competitions were held. The commission was finally given to Manuel Amabilis. In both Marquina's and

Amabilis's projects, ancient Mexican and specifically Maya decorative elements were used to cover structures derived from Western European architecture. As in the Secretaría de la Salubridad, neither building exemplifies any known style of ancient Mexican architecture. The unification of Western and ancient Mexican architecture was more important than archaeological correctness. In Amabilis's building the references to modernity and pre-Hispanic antiquity are striking even in relatively minor aspects, such as two reliefs set before the entrance: one representing physical labor and the other intellectual work. Partially derived from Maya dynastic stelae, the sculptures depict traditionally attired Maya lords among industrial elements such as cogs and pulleys. The images suggest Mexico's roots in a civilized antiquity and its power as an industrial nation in the present.

In the Yucatán, pre-Hispanic revival buildings were constructed at various times during the nineteenth and twentieth centuries. In the late nineteenth century, pre-Hispanic motifs were used to suggest the independence of Yucatán from Mexico by making reference to a glorious local past. This was primarily in the interest of local merchant elites eager to evade state control. After the Revolution, references to local antiquity were used to express socialist ideals and solidarity with the new Mexican state. Pre-Hispanic revival buildings of this period in Mérida include the Sanatorium Rendón Peniche (1919) attributed to Manuel Amabilis, La Casa del Pueblo by Angel Bachini (1928), the Building of the Diario del Sureste by Manuel and Max Amabilis in collaboration with the sculptor Rómulo Rozo (1946), the Parque de las Américas by Manuel and Max Amabilis (1945), and the Monumento a la Patria designed by Manuel Amabilis in collaboration with Rómulo Rozo (1945–56).

Colonial and pre-Hispanic revival buildings have in common the construction and affirmation of a normative "Mexicanness" based on a celebration of the past and the erasure of the contemporary indigene from the nation. Pre-Hispanic revivals proclaim ancient Mexican civilizations, primarily the Mexica and the Maya, as archetypal Mexicans. Pre-Hispanic architecture and decoration usually establish no links between ancient civilizations and contemporary indigenous peoples, although references to mestizos are present in various buildings. Colonial revivals uphold the mestizo as the quintessential Mexican. Indirectly, this establishes the middle-class individual as a model citizen. As in other areas of Latin America, in Mexico people of European heritage are traditionally associated with the upper class, mestizos with the middle class, and indigenes with the lower class. Gamio was explicit in this respect, since in his opinion the economic improvement of the Indian was a precondition for the ethnic unity of the population. Furthermore he regarded the middle-class individual, not the indigene, as the agent of change.

Modern Architecture

Modern architecture first became known in Mexico through foreign publications introduced by progressive practitioners. Around 1915, Eduardo Macedo y Arbeau educated his stu-

dents in the architecture of Otto Wagner through the magazine *Moderne Bauformen*. During the 1920s, contemporary European and American architecture was known in Mexico through foreign magazines such as *Moderne Bauformen, L'Architecte, Architecture Vivant,* and *Architectural Record.* Soon, Mexican publications began to feature the new architecture. In 1924, *Excélsior* newspaper began a modern architecture section under the direction of Juan Galindo Pimentel and Bernardo Calderón. In 1925, the Tolteca Cement Company began publishing *Cemento,* a magazine that illustrated works by modern architects including Willem Marinus Dudok, Mallet Stevens, Erich Mendelsohn, Joseph Hoffmann, and Le Corbusier. In addition to illustrating works of modern architecture, the magazines featured adds for new materials and modern appliances such as vacuum cleaners and washing machines. *Cemento* was distributed in massive numbers, and hence was influential in educating the public in the properties of cement and in creating desire for electric devices. Between 1929 and 1932, 30,000 copies of the magazine were issued and circulated.

The hybridity exalted as the key to Mexico's new identity, *mestizaje,* was also evident in the architecture of the period. Perhaps as a result of architects learning mainly from architectural magazines, the first modern buildings in Mexico exhibited a mixture of styles and local variations of established design ideas. In these respects, the buildings were comparable to Spanish colonial buildings in New Spain, which often were conceived from the study of European pattern books. Manuel Monasterio's house in Reforma (1922) and the National Treasury designed by Ortíz Monasterio in collaboration with Vicente Mendiola (1926) exemplify these tendencies. The house is basically a chalet from which ornamentation has been stripped in order to modernize it. The habit of eliminating the external ornaments of a building, regardless of style, was a common interpretation of modern architecture at this time. In the National Treasury, dark lines painted on each architectural member indicate corresponding parts of the building's iron skeleton as a sign of architectural honesty.

During the third decade of the century, José Villagrán García emerged as an influential theorist and practitioner. In 1925 he began teaching at the Escuela de Bellas Artes, later Escuela Nacional de Arquitectura, where his most acclaimed course was the theory of architecture (1926–76). Like the French theorist Julien Guadet, he emphasized the architectural program as the determining element of a composition. In Villagrán's view this prevented the architect from falling into the dangers of formalism, since a building resulted directly from an analysis of its functions. He stressed honesty and integrity in the use of architectural elements and materials as well as the idea that architecture should serve a social function. In the context of post-Revolutionary Mexico this meant that buildings should meet the necessities of the working classes. Despite his functionalist agenda, Villagrán also recognized the importance of spiritual or emotional aspects of architecture.

Starting with Villagrán García's Health Center (begun in 1926), and the Sanatorium at Huipilco, also by Villagrán (1929–36), buildings by Mexican architects manifested more sober interpretations of modern architecture. Nonetheless, it was an eclectic modernism that looked for source material in both turn-of-the-century European architecture, especially Austrian and German, and contemporary work. In the Sanatorium at Huipilco, Villagrán employed pilotis, a flat roof, and no applied decorations, but contrary to the international style the building's surface was broken by a weighty structure and sunshades. The use of rough concrete for the walls added to the building's impression of heaviness.

Modern architecture became established during the early 1930s when, with the support of the minister of education, Narciso Bassols, several young architects occupied state positions and were given important commissions. Villagrán worked as architect of the Department of Public Health from 1924 to 1935, Juan O'Gorman served as director of Construction for the Public Education Department from 1932 to 1935, and Juan Legarreta worked in the Section of Construction for the Department of Communications and Public Works. Between 1934 and 1940, Villagrán completed the Health Center, the Sanatorium at Huipilco, and the National Institute of Cardiology. Juan O'Gorman executed a great number of public schools, and Juan Legarreta designed low-cost housing projects. Best-known among these works are the developments at Balbuena (1932), La Vaquita (1934), and San Jacinto (1934). The two latter complexes were built after Legarreta's death but according to his plans.

The rise of modern architecture in Mexico coincided with the populist, progressive administration of President Lázaro Cárdenas (1934–40), which brought the first period of stability in Mexican politics since the rule of dictator Porfirio Díaz. During this period, O'Gorman, Legarreta, Álvaro Aburto, Enrique Yáñez, Augusto Pérez Palacios, and Carlos Tarditi, among others, adopted and radicalized Villagrán's teachings, giving more emphasis to the social function of buildings than to aesthetics. These architects were instrumental in establishing functionalism as the official expression of the Mexican state. The Cárdenas period was typified by attempts to bolster domestic production and curb the importation of foreign goods; nevertheless, in this case European imports—modern architecture and the philosophy of functionalism—were appropriated and transformed in the service of Mexican nationalism.

The success of the rhetoric of functionalism in Mexico was linked to economic limitations. In the opinion of Narciso Bassols, in functionalist architecture "not even a meter of land is wasted, nor the value of one peso nor a ray of sunshine." Functionalist buildings from this period exhibit unfinished materials, uncovered structural elements, and few luxury materials such as glass and aluminum.

Despite state support, many Mexican architects rejected the new architecture, favoring instead European and U.S. currents of art deco. In 1933, Alfonso Pallares, president of the Society of Mexican Architects (SAM), invited his colleagues to a debate with the purpose of determining the position that Mexico should take in respect to modern architecture. The participants were invited to consider the nature and relevance of functionalism, the role of the architect, and the importance of beauty in architecture. Progressive architects, including Legarreta, O'Gorman, and their colleague Álvaro Aburto, argued for a scientifically driven, technical architecture designed to meet Mexico's social needs. In their view, aesthetic considerations were superfluous in the design of buildings. Legarreta voiced the most radical opinion: "A people who live in *jacales* (shacks) and round rooms cannot SPEAK architecture. We will build the houses of the people. Estheticians and rhetoricians, I hope they all die! They will later have their discussions."

Silvano Palafox disagreed with the idea that meeting the needs of the poor should be the primary function of architecture: "There is no doubt that in Mexico there are poor people, there are many poor people, but there are not only poor people. We have other social classes which are worthy of our attention . . . and we have no right to disregard them and much less to ostracize them only because . . . they do not have the misfortune of belonging to the destitute." In addition, the opposition criticized modern architecture for imposing foreign habits on Mexican people and "sterilizing" the personality of the user since formal simplification of the architecture was only a pretext for lack of imagination. The work of Federico Mariscal, Antonio G. Muñoz, and Silvano Palafox exemplify the design attitudes of established professionals during this period.

Functionalism in Mexico began as a socialist, utopian, and humanistic movement. It had as its main goal the solution of urgent housing needs of the majority of the Mexican population. It had as its basis the belief that every person, regardless of class or race, had the right to shelter and to a decent living. Yet, based on European theories, specially the early writings of Le Corbusier, it was oblivious to the legitimacy of indigenous building traditions.

Despite his claim that he designed architecture only according to technical and social considerations, O'Gorman produced some of the most aesthetically minded houses of the period, including the house/studio for Diego Rivera and the house for Frances Toor, both realized between 1929 and 1934. These works were characterized by small spaces, exposed structures, lack of external decoration, and emphasis on the sculptural values of specific elements such as staircases. In subsequent decades, particularly during the 1960s, functionalism in Mexico was to become academic and formalist, devoid of the humanitarian ideals that first inspired its development.

The populist philosophies of O'Gorman, Legarreta, and Villagrán were tremendously influential in Mexican architecture of the 1940s and 1950s, as functionalism became state policy. In 1938 a group of architects including Alberto Arai, Enrique Guerrero, and Raul Cacho founded the Union of Socialist Architects. In 1939 Hannes Meyer, director of the Bauhaus from 1928 to 1930, went to reside in Mexico at the invitation of the Secretariat of Education to create an Institute of Planning and Urbanism. Although his residence in Mexico was marked by problems caused by professional rivalries, Meyer's contribution to the development of functionalism in Mexico has been underestimated. He held influential positions including secretary of the Commissión de Planeación de Hospitales (1944), technical director in the Secretariat of Labor and Social Security (1942), coordinator of the Administrative Committee of the Federal Program for the Construction of Schools (1945–47). Enrique Yáñez, Raul Cacho, and José Luis Cuevas count among his followers.

Integración Plástica

The integration of art—especially mural painting—into architecture became established during José Vasconcelos's term as minister of education. This tradition continued to be important and became known as the "movement for plastic integration" during the 1950s. Some scholars believe that this movement was as short-lived as the architecture of the Mexican Revolution, but others hold that it continued to thrive in succeeding decades and still characterized much of Mexican architecture in the 1990s, particularly state commissions.

During the 1940s, Mexican architects employed the international style for popular and private housing, institutional, commercial, and religious buildings. As in previous Mexican architecture, functionalism was modified to meet national imperatives. Two important state commissions of popular housing were the Centro Urbano Presidente Alemán designed by Mario Pani and Salvador Ortega Flores (1947–49), and the Centro Urbano Presidente Juárez designed in 1950 by the same architects. These projects initiated many proposals for family apartment buildings (multifamiliares) sponsored by the state throughout Mexico. In these buildings, along with the Hospital de la Raza no. 1 (1945) and the Centro Médico Nacional (1954–58), both designed by Enrique Yáñez, the severity of functionalist architecture was modified to include mural paintings and sculptures. Carlos Mérida designed murals and sculptural elements for the Multifamiliar Juárez; David Alfaro Siqueiros and Diego Rivera painted murals for the Hospital de la Raza; and José and Tomás Chávez Morado, Siqueiros, and Francisco Zúñiga, among others, contributed art works for the Centro Médico Nacional.

In the next decade, some Mexican architects designed fine buildings in the so-called international style, whereas others renewed their interest in the country's native architectural traditions. Regardless of style, however, most buildings employed modern building materials. Mexico's airport designed by Augusto Álvarez, Enrique Carral, and others (1953); the Secretariat of Labor and Social Prevention by Pedro Ramírez Vázquez and Rafael Mijárez (1953); Juan Sordo Madaleno's Calle Lieja Office Building (1956); as well as the Torre de Seguros Latinoamericana by Manuel de la Colina, Augusto Álvarez, and Adolfo Zeevaert (1950) exemplify transparent, seemingly weightless edifices achieved through the use of glass, steel, aluminum, and technical devices such as elevators and mechanisms to slide windows. The Torre Latinoamericana, a skyscraper of 40 floors, was the tallest building in Mexico at the time. During this period, tall office buildings became a sign of prosperity and proclaimed the triumph of capitalism in Mexico.

A few Mexican artists and architects denounced the International Style as a colonialist strategy and built works inspired by local traditions. The Anacahualli Museum (1943–57) designed by Diego Rivera, and Juan O'Gorman's house (1958, now destroyed) resulted from these attitudes. The Anacahualli Museum is a massive building reminiscent of the monumentality of pre-Hispanic architecture. It incorporates a variety of pre-Hispanic decorative and architectural motifs, including mural painting, but like previous pre-Hispanic revival buildings it is archaeologically faithful to no particular tradition. O'Gorman's house was planned around a natural cave, like the Pyramid of the Sun at Teotihuacan, and covered with stone mosaic. O'Gorman turned against modern architecture during the late 1930s because he came to regard it as a capitalist movement. Along with Rivera, he advocated a national modern architecture that incorporated pre-Hispanic building traditions and decorative elements including mural painting and polychrome sculpture as well as respect for the natural environment. Consequently, in buildings of this period he brought together modern architectural elements such as pilotis and flat roofs with nativistic motifs. The combination of styles in his buildings followed

Torre de Seguros Latinoamericana, Mexico City, by Manuel de la Colina, Augusto Álvarez, and Adolfo Zeevaert, 1950
Photo courtesy of Archivo Fotográfico, Instituto de Investigaciones Estéticas de la UNAM

his belief that, for Mexico's survival as a culturally and economically independent nation, it was necessary to preserve cultural values while meeting modern needs.

The preceding discussion makes apparent that in Mexican architecture of the modernist period, the differentiation of international from nationalist and regionalist currents is not straightforward. The search for a national architecture that first flourished during the second and third decade of the century continued during the 1940s and 1950s. Like the nationalistic architecture built in the 1920s, these attempts to create a Mexican architecture often incorporated elements from colonial and pre-Hispanic art and architecture. The unification of art and architecture into a total work of art characterized these latter searches. While the tendency known as *integración plástica* had antecedents in architecture of the Porfiriato and of the 1920s, it became an acknowledged movement when a collaboration of architects and artists took the magazine *Espacios* as their forum in the 1950s.

Integración plástica was not restricted to a single period of Mexican architecture; rather, it is the hallmark of twentieth-century Mexican architecture. In addition to the Multifamiliar Juárez and the projects directed by Enrique Yáñez mentioned above, innumerable buildings successfully integrate art and architecture. Masterpieces built prior to 1960 include the Capilla de la Purísima in Monterrey by Enrique de la Mora (1948), the Capilla de la Medalla Milagrosa by Félix Candela (1954) , El Museo del Eco by Mathías Goeritz (1953), and Ciudad Universitaria (1950–56).

The ambitious Ciudad Universitaria (University City) project, made possible by postwar prosperity and liberal market economies, presents an image of the country simultaneously nationalistic and modern. Directed by Mario Pani and Enrique del Moral, University City was the work of many architects, and consolidated the movement of *integración plástica*. Some critics regard it as the culmination of 20 years of modern architecture in Mexico. It was indeed a project of tremendous importance because it unified diverse tendencies such as functionalism, nationalism, as well as intermediate and unique positions. In the same way that the notion of *mestizaje* foreshadowed by a century the postmodern celebration of hybridity, so the eclecticism and proclivities towards historicism and appropriation apparent in University City predate postmodernism in architecture.

Built on a site covered by volcanic lava 1,500 hundred years ago, University City presented an image of the national through the use of local materials including volcanic stones from the site and from other regions of Mexico; the incorporation and integration of pre-Hispanic architectural and decorative motifs; and the integration of artworks representative of Mexican Revolutionary art, such as mural paintings. While international style buildings embodied the image of prosperity that Mexican rulers were interested in projecting, references to local building traditions and the use of local materials aligned these buildings with nationalistic and Revolutionary ideals.

The Central Library at University City, designed by Juan O'Gorman, Gustavo Saavedra, and Juan Martínez de Velasco, became the best-known edifice in the complex. Like O'Gorman's house, the exterior is covered with stone mosaics. At the library these mosaics illustrate the history of Mexico. The images are arranged in a narrative plan reminiscent of some of the great murals of the post-Revolutionary period. Pre-Hispanic cosmogony is represented on the building's north side, Western cosmogony on south, and the Mexican Revolution and the modern world on the lateral facades.

The front facade of University City's stadium is ovoid, with a giant *talud* built of earth and volcanic stone. A *talud* is a sloping element that in Mesoamerican pyramidal structures usually supports an overhanging element. In the stadium, the *talud* displays a mosaic by Diego Rivera. The building was designed by Augusto Pérez Palacios in collaboration with Raul Salinas Moro and Jorge Bravo Jiménez.

In the *frontones* (ball courts) by Alberto T. Arai, modern materials wear traditional dress. Designed as pyramidal forms, the structures are made of concrete covered with volcanic stone to suggest the solidity of pre-Hispanic buildings and to integrate the buildings to the local landscape.

The Pabellón de Rayos Cósmicos, by Félix Candela, represents an idiosyncratic tendency in Mexican architecture: the architecture of shells or *cascarones* for which Candela is best known. A disciple of the Catalan engineer Eduardo Torroja, Candela frequently relied on hyperbolic paraboloids to achieve organic forms in his structures. Candela's architecture is the physical realization of mathematical logic, as he seldom drew a building before its construction but simply described it with an equation. During the 1950s Candela designed shell-shaped, reinforced concrete covers for various marketplaces in Mexico City. The Pabellón de Rayos Cósmicos is conceived as a membrane; its hyperbolic vault is both wall and roof.

Ironically, buildings with nativistic motifs such as the Central Library served both as tourist attractions and as a propaganda tool for the government. Since the buildings were unique to the country, they were likely to attract foreigners. Indeed, it was foreigners who wrote the most about this architecture, particularly about O'Gorman's work. Thus O'Gorman may have helped the Mexican state to achieve an end that was opposite to his own intentions. After 1950 tourism became Mexico's greatest source of income, as well as the county's most important area of dependence on the United States.

During the administrations of Manuel Avila Camacho (1940–46), Miguel Alemán Valdés (1946–52), and the first two years of Adolfo Ruiz Cortines's term (1952–54), economic recovery was facilitated both by petroleum revenues and by the regimes' renewed interest in foreign investments. In addition, the aftermath of World War II favored the demand of Mexican products abroad and the reduction of foreign competition in the domestic market.

The great building projects, including University City, were constructed to signal Mexico's affluence. Yet Mexico's

Central Library, Ciudad Universitaria, Mexico City, by Juan O'Gorman, Gustavo Saavedra, and Juan Martínez de Velazco, 1950–56
Photo courtesy of Archivo Fotográfico, Instituto de Investigaciones Estéticas de la UNAM

development was compromised. Despite various administrations' attempts to substitute Mexican-made products for imports, the value of imports continued to surpass the value of exports. Ironically, the high quality of modern architecture built in Mexico during these years depended upon relaxed restrictions on imported construction materials. Only under such conditions could Mexicans obtain the materials required for the new building styles. Despite the claims that University City was economical owing to its utilization of local materials and workforce, its architects relied heavily on expensive imports.

The construction of University City was not a celebratory occasion for all Mexicans, as 65 million square feet (6 million square meters) of communal lands were expropriated for the project with the stipulation that the owners be given

new homes. Of this land, 22 million square feet (2 million square meters) were used for the construction. Previous Mexican governments had taken similar measures. The Porfirio Díaz administration expropriated communal lands to renovate archaeological sites that later became tourist attractions. As late as 1922, some of the owners of these lands had not been remunerated. This suggests that the representation of national identity in Mexican architecture has an underside not frequently discussed in architectural history: the dispossession of common citizens for the construction of the spectacle of nationhood.

The integration of pre-Columbian forms and qualities into contemporary architectural idioms typified by the Central Library of O'Gorman, Saavedra, and de Velasco continued through the century, particularly in state commissions.

In the Museo de Antropología by Pedro Ramírez Vázquez and others (1963), the wall around the patio is finished with a band or abstract ornament that is a translation of the so-called "Chac noses" found in Maya Puuc architecture to an abstract form. The Heróico Colegio Militar (1975) designed by Agustín Hernández and Manuel González Rul resembles pre-Hispanic ceremonial centers in the placement of buildings in large open spaces connected with avenues and in the monumentality of the edifices. Independent buildings within the complex are inspired by pre-Hispanic architecture and decoration. The armory and the covered swimming pool are pyramidal structures, the Edificio de Govierno forms a large, abstracted Chac mask. In Hernández's Hospital San Gerónimo (1975), each floor was designed to resemble a pyramid profile from Monte Albán. Other architects, including Abraham Zabludowsky, Teodoro González de León, Alejandro Zohn, Francisco Serrano, and Augusto Quijano Axle have incorporated characteristics of pre-Hispanic architecture such as monumentality, durability, solidity, and the preference for enclosed spaces. These architects have received numerous and important governmental and institutional commissions. Zabludowsky and González de León are responsible for Infonavit (1973), the Museo Rufino Tamayo (1975), El Colegio de Mexico (1975), the Universidad Pedagógica Nacional (1979), and the Central Edifice and financial centers for Banamex; Juan Francisco Serrano, Rafael Mijares, and Pedro Ramírez Vázquez were responsible for the Universidad Iberoamericana (1981–87).

Alejandro Zohn designed the Archives of the State of Jalisco and the Unidad Deportiva y Parque 14 de Febrero in Guadalajara, Jalisco (both in 1992). Teodoro González de León, Francisco Serrano, and Carlos Tejeda were responsible for the Palacio de Justicia Federal in Mexico City (1992) . Such works indicate that monumental buildings that allude to the pre-Hispanic past still form the official image of Mexico. In addition, there is a tendency among contemporary architects to incorporate the landscape into architectural design. This tendency is related, although indirectly, to ancient Mexican cultures, as respect for the natural environment characterized pre-Hispanic architecture. The landscape architect Mario Schjetnan, whose most representative work is the Parque Tezozomoc in Azcapotzalco designed in collaboration with J. L. Perez and Jorge Calvillo, exemplifies this tendency.

Regionalism

An imprecise differentiation often is made between nationalist and regionalist architecture. In the opinion of Fernando González Gortázar, the difference between these two categories in one of scale and pretension: where nationalist architecture imitates monumental architecture from the past, often without the intention of reestablishing the original culture, regionalist architecture is closer to vernacular, anonymous architecture. Regionalist architecture seeks to master the local climate and use local materials and construction methods. Still, a hard distinction between nationalist and regionalist architecture is difficult to maintain. In the nationalist project

of University City, local materials and construction methods were incorporated. On the other hand, Luis Barragán and Ricardo Legorreta, masters of regionalist architecture, occasionally have engaged in design projects involving the translation of pre-Hispanic traditions into modern forms.

Born in 1908, Barragán studied civil engineering at the Escuela Libre de Ingenieros in Guadalajara and undertook additional studies to qualify as an architect. In a trip to Europe from 1924 to 1925, he visited the Alhambra in Seville and became acquainted with Ferdinand Bac's books Les Jardins Enchantés and Les Colombieres. These works were to have a profound influence on his ouvre. Barragán's early works—two houses for Robles Castillo (1927–28), Enrique Aguilar's house (1928–31), and especially the house for Efraín González Luna (1928)—synthesize lessons learned from Hispano-Morisque architecture. Barragán was not alone in his interests. During the second and third decades of the century, Guadalajara-based architects including Ignacio Díaz Morales, Pedro Castellanos, and Rafael Urzúa designed buildings incorporating Spanish colonial and Mediterranean traditions. This was part of a larger movement of Spanish revival and Mediterranean architecture in Mexico and in the Western United States.

In 1936 Barragán moved to Mexico City and from that year to 1940 he worked on about 20 buildings in a stark rationalist style. Again, Barragán was working in harmony with the dominant movement of his time. Although little of it remains, Barragán's work from this period is important because it provided the basis for the stark simplicity of his later buildings. Barragán's mature works are characterized by minimalism and a masterful synthesis of multiple architectural and artistic traditions. This synthetic eclecticism makes his architecture both regional and at the same time "universal," or to use a more precise term, modern.

Barragán's buildings differ markedly from international style architecture because—along with the influences of Ferdinand Bac, Mies van der Rohe, Le Corbusier, the Bauhaus, De Stijl, Frederik Kiessler, and Richard Neutra—he combines ancient Mexican, Mexican vernacular and monastic architecture, Mediterranean traditions, Japanese and Islamic gardens, and the work of his friend and contemporary, the painter Chucho Reyes. Barragán's best-known works include the Jardines del Pedregal (1945–50); Antonio Galvéz's house in San Angel (1955); his own house in Francisco Ramírez street (1947); the Chapel for the Capuchinas Sacramentarias del Purisimo Corazón de Maria (1952–55); Satellite City Towers, designed in collaboration with Mathías Goeritz (1957); Las Arboledas residential subdivision (1958–61); Los Clubes Residential subdivision (1963–64); the San Cristóbal Stables and the Folke Egerstrom House at Los Clubes (1967–68); and Francisco Gilardi's house in Mexico City (1976).

In the Jardines del Pedregal, Barragán designed an elite residential area on a landscape of volcanic rock interspersed with small green valleys. The complex is reminiscent of pre-Hispanic ceremonial centers in the respect for the natural landscape, the use of solid stone walls as defining elements, and the interconnection of plazas, causeways, and buildings. The arrangement of rocks, native plants, water, and fountains echoes pre-Hispanic, Mediterranean, Islamic, and Japanese gardens, while the orthogonality of the buildings affirms the presence of modern architecture. It is difficult however, to attribute any one architectural element to a single tradition.

His own house brings together the simplicity, placidity, and privacy of Spanish colonial monasteries with powerful color harmonies and tensions, and constructivist geometries. Also present are surrealistic details such as the sculpture of a white galloping horse inside an otherwise empty courtyard. This motif is reminiscent of the paintings of Giorgio De Chirico and Leonora Carrington.

The Chapel for the Capuchinas Sacramentarias, considered to be his masterpiece, is a succession of severe, unadorned spaces that seem to emanate light. This effect is achieved through the use of stained glass panels and lattices. Colored and filtered by the glass, light is the principal design element. While stained glass was commonly used in Gothic cathedrals, latticework is an element of Islamic and Hispano-Morisque architecture.

At Los Clubes, a residential estate developed and designed by Barragán for horse riding enthusiasts, water becomes a primary element of the design. The Lover's Fountain within the complex serves a practical function—a drinking trough for horses and riders—but at the same time it is a mirror and part of an elaborate stage set through which the riders can parade.

With exception of his brief involvement in the design of the gardens of University City, Barragán was not offered any state commissions. Most of his buildings were small-scale, low-tech, and designed for specific individuals. This fact does not exclude a strong nationalist component in his architecture, however, since to a large extent his work was inspired by vernacular traditions. Profound love for the architecture and artistic traditions of his native land are evident throughout.

When Barragán received the Pritzker Architecture Prize in 1980, he described the guiding lights of his architecture: religion, beauty, silence, solitude, serenity, joy, death, gardens, fountains, architecture (including the architecture of Mexican villages and provincial towns and Mexican monasteries), the art of seeing, and nostalgia. He stated, "Underlying all that I have achieved—such as it is—are the memories of my father's ranch, where I spent my childhood and adolescence. In my work I have always striven to adapt the magic of those remote nostalgic years to the needs of modern living."

Illustrated in catalogs or observed in isolation within their specific settings, Barragán's buildings offer a quaint, tranquil, romantic and colorful image of Mexico. Viewed within the context of Mexico City after 1940—the accelerated population growth, the deterioration of the city's center, the stratification of the population in *fraccionamientos* or *colonias* according to economic and racial affiliations, the

confinement of the working classes and the poor to ever sprawling *villas miseria* (shantytowns), and the flight of the rich to fortress homes in the suburbs—Barragán's architecture takes on a different character. The "architecture of silence" that he lovingly designed were havens for the privileged, eager to leave the increasing pollution, traffic problems, overcrowding, and noise of the decaying city. George Bataille thought of the slaughterhouse as the necessary complement of the museum. In the history of twentieth-century Mexican architecture, Mexico's shanties are the repressed, the ghostly other of Barragán's exquisite work and others like it.

On the other hand, many Mexican architects continued to spend at least part of their careers designing low-cost popular housing, although this work is infrequently included in the history of Mexican architecture. Since the Revolution, the government has sponsored numerous projects for low-income housing. These steadily decreased during the last three decades of the century as a result of budget cuts in social services. In their place, self-made shelters proliferated in urban areas. It is estimated that in 1990 20 million Mexicans lived in self-made houses. By the year 2000, this number is expected to increase to 25 million.

Barragán was not alone in his attempts to incorporate local vernacular tradition into modern architecture. During the 1940s and 1950s in Mexico City, a number of architects including as Enrique del Moral, Juan Sordo Madaleno, and Max Cetto welded functionalist architecture with a sensibility for local building materials and landscape. Since its foundation in 1948, the School of Architecture at the University of Guadalajara has encouraged an architecture based on the functionalist precepts of Villagrán, but with attention to the local climate, materials, and craft traditions. Like the work of Barragán, this architecture makes ample use of patios, plazas, terraces, solid walls and lattice windows. Architects from this school, known as the Escuela Tapatía, include its founder, Ignacio Díaz Morales, Fernando González Gortázar, Gabriel Chávez de la Mora, and Andrés Casillas.

Ricardo Legorreta learned his basic vocabulary from Barragán but went on to elaborate it and to apply it in a new form. While Barragán preferred small-scale residential projects, often in a wild landscape or in a rural context, Legorreta has favored elaborate monumental projects inserted into urban contexts. It is not accidental that his most successful projects are factory complexes and hotels.

Organized around patios and plazas, Legorreta's monumental buildings suggest the placidity of Mexican monastic architecture. Like Barragán, he employs color, light, and water as structural elements and translates elements of various architectural and artistic traditions into a modern idiom. In the Centro Banamex in Monterrey spaces are arranged around patios and plazas. Light penetrates the building through small windows reminiscent of North African architecture. The design of Solana, Westlake/Southlake, Texas (1986)—a complex of office buildings, village center, hotel, and recreation facilities developed by IBM in partnership with Maguire Thomas—consists of a series of compounds defined by walls. The scheme is inspired by Mexican haciendas and by the Convent of the Desierto de los Leones near Mexico City. Legorreta designed the complex in collaboration Peter Walker, Barton Myers, and Romualdo Giurgola. For Legorreta the wall is the ultimate expression of Mexican culture: "We live and see Mexico in the walls, tragedy, strength, joy, romance, peace, light, and color . . . the day the wall dies, Mexico will die."

In Legorreta's Casa de Rancho, California (1987), water runs all though the house, serving different functions: lap pool, swimming pool, jacuzzi, and fountain. A similar concept is discernible in Barragán's Francisco Gilardi House (1976), where the pool is placed next to the living-dining area without any divisions between the two spaces.

Faithful to the tradition of *integración plástica,* Legorreta views a building as a total work of art. His first important work, the Hotel Camino Real in Mexico City (1968) incorporates murals, numerous sculptures, fountains, and graphic design. The inclusion of these artworks in the design delayed the completion of the building by many months but added significantly to its visual appeal.

Legorreta differs most markedly from Barragán in the inclusion of humorous elements in his architecture. In addition to adding a personal touch, these motifs fit within a tradition in Mexican culture of delight in the unexpected and the absurd. At the pool of the Hotel Camino Real in Cancún (1975), for instance, the bartenders operate in an area literally submerged within the water, and clients order drinks sitting on underwater stools.

Like other Mexican architects, Legorreta demonstrates interest in integrating architecture to its natural surroundings. In the Hacienda Cabo San Lucas in Baja California (1972) and the Hotel Camino Real at Ixtapa (1981), the buildings are arranged tightly in the terrain and painted in colors similar to the natural colors of the earth. The buildings are literally buried in the sandy landscapes. In the Hacienda Cabo San Lucas, access to the building is gained by stairs to interior patios as in Native American kivas. Reference to vernacular architecture is also evident in the Chrysler Factory in Automex, Toluca (1964), designed in collaboration with Mathías Goeritz. The complex is inspired by a series of granaries near Santa Mónica, Zacatecas.

In Barragán's architecture references to the vernacular stimulate memory; in Legorreta's hotels, vernacular allusions give the user, especially tourists, a taste of the local within safe boundaries. In vacation resorts, cultured versions of regional architecture may be the visitors' only experience of Mexican architecture. Legorreta's commissions abroad indicate the increasing internationalization of Mexican architecture. The architect's works in the United States suggest the increasing cooperation between Mexican and U.S. elites and business interests, which made possible the North American Free Trade Agreement.

Various critics have noted that Mexican regionalism became formulaic as many architects follow lessons from Barragán and Legorreta without paying attention to regional and climatic differences. Toward the end of the century, a tropical architecture developed, primarily in private residences in the coastal areas of the country. This architecture is characterized by open spaces, local materials, and architectural elements including thatched roofs, and tree trunks in their natural state used as support members. Although these elements have been described as belonging to colonial architecture, they form part of long-standing indigenous traditions in various areas of Mexico. Marco Aldaco and Diego Villaseñor are the two most important exponents of the tropical tendency.

Postmodernism

For many years Mexican architects were unenthusiastic about postmodernism. In the opinion of González Gortázar, Mexican architects owe a debt to Barragán for giving them the tools to fight this tendency: "He proved unnecessary the systematic and sterilizing exhumation of prestigious cadavers, the misnamed 'historical references,' so enthusiastically and unsuccessfully undertaken in other places. Only those who do not have parents look for their parents or invent them." Subsequently, various Mexican architects including Juan Palomar, Carlos Petersen, Ricardo Padilla, Jorge Estévez, Juan Carlos Name and Associates, Antonio Attolini Lack, and the firm of Gustavo Eichelmann Nava and Gonzalo Gómez Palacio y Campos have built work in a postmodern vein.

During the late 1980s and early 1990s, Mexico became increasingly integrated into transnational capitalism, with the reduction of nationalized industry, intensified foreign investments, and the proliferation of foreign-owned assembly plants in the north part of the country. At the same time, postmodernism arrived as a theory and a style. This is a suitable match, since like multinational capitalism, Postmodernism appropriates elements from diverse traditions. Multinational capital has not been wholly beneficial for Mexican architecture. Seeking to receive optimum return for their land investments, foreign investors have sometimes disregarded the seismic conditions of Mexico City and proposed huge projects more appropriate to other regions. In the 1990s, as a response to developers' and investors' pressure, the Mexican authorities relaxed building controls in the center of Mexico City, a seismically fragile zone. The tendency toward monumentality in Mexican architecture of the 1990s ignores the destructive regularity of earthquakes in Mexico City, the most recent of which took place in 1985.

Since the late 1950s, the representation of identity in Mexican architecture has been increasingly defined by private capital. But the Mexican state still plays a part in the representation of national identity. During the regime of President Carlos Salinas de Gortari (1988–94), for instance, Mexican elites dreamed of the integration of Mexico into the First World by virtue of the North American Free Trade Agreement. To some, this integration implied a need for greater technical quality in Mexican architecture, since it meant that Mexican buildings would have to compete with the architecture of the developed countries.

This sentiment coincided with the construction in Mexico of a number of buildings that favored international currents and technologically sophisticated materials. Practitioners who built work in this vein between 1989 and 1995 include Luis Vicente Flores; TEN Arquitectos: Enrique Norten y Bernardo Gómez-Pimineta; and the partnerships Óscar Bulnes Valero and Bernardo Lira López; Agustín Landa Verléz and Jorge Alesio Robles; Francisco López Guerra and A. López-Guerra; and Aurelio Nuño and Associates.

One of the most impressive commissions of the Salinas de Gortari government was the Centro Nacional de las Artes, an extensive complex in which each building was assigned to a prestigious Mexican architect. Legorreta was entrusted the Escuela Nacional de Artes Plásticas, the Edificio Central, and the Torre de Investigación Artística. As usual, he drew from a variety of traditions. The Escuela Nacional de Artes Plásticas includes a round building that recalls the Caracol at Chichen Itza and a multidomed structure reminiscent of both the Monastery of San Francisco at Cholula and the Great Mosque at Córdoba. Legorreta previously employed multiple domes in the Cathedral of Managua, Nicaragua (1993).

The Conservatorio de Música by Teodoro González de León and Ernesto Betancourt takes a surprising postmodern character. Groups of inclined pilasters supporting a frieze in the building's courtyard give the building the appearance of imbalance. This feigned instability recalls aspects of Bernard Tschumi's Parc de la Villete in Paris.

The Teatro de las Artes by Grupo LBC (by Alfonso López Baz and Xavier Calleja) includes references to Classical architecture and a moving Baroque facade. The Escuela Nacional de Danza by Luis Vicente Flores and Associates, and the Escuela Nacional de Arte Teatral by TEN Arquitectos: Enrique Norten y Bernardo Gómez- Pimienta, both exhibit sophisticated steel structures and glass membranes.

The Centro Nacional de las Artes is more than a collection of masterful buildings. The architecture houses advanced teaching, research, and production facilities. On site is the national cultural television channel, Estudios Churubusco, the largest film studio in Mexico, and the Centro Nacional Multimedia, a research center for artists that is the best equipped facility of its kind in the Americas. It includes, among other things, computer, video, sound, virtual reality, and robotic studios as well as exhibition spaces. The center's educational projects include documentation of Mexico's museums on CD ROM and virtual reality simulations of archaeological sites such as Tenochtitlan and Monte Albán.

The architecture of the Centro Nacional de las Artes evidences two concerns that have been at the heart of the representation of national identity since the nineteenth century: the representation of the local and the expression of Mexico's international character. In contrast to nineteenth-century pavilion builders, an architect such as Legorreta does not have to choose between international architecture and historic regionalism, as his work incorporates both tendencies. As in the era of Porfirio Díaz, at the end of the twentieth century Mexico defines its identity in terms of its

Escuela Nacional de Artes Plásticas, Centro Nacional de las Artes, Mexico City, by Ricardo Legorreta, 1994
Photo courtesy of Archivo Fotográfico, Instituto de Investigaciones Estéticas de la UNAM

culturally rich past and its capacity to achieve economic and technical development at the same level as the United States and Western Europe.

Conclusions

For all but a brief period during the 1930s, the representation of national identity in Mexican architecture during the last two centuries supports a narrative or glorious antecedents, unproblematic *mestizaje,* modernity, and affluence. Where pre-Hispanic revival architecture and its elaborations affirm the foundations of the country's greatness in the pre-Hispanic past, architecture based on the colonial period celebrates the hybridity resulting from colonization. During the first two decades of the twentieth century, colonial revival architecture upheld the mestizo as the ideal representative of the Mexican nation. International currents of architecture have been employed to indicate Mexico's participation in modernity and international commerce. These constructions of Mexican national identity have been created by Mexican urban and intellectual elites and have been supported and appropriated by the state and, more recently, by private capital.

That there is some validity in these representations is undeniable. Pre-Hispanic cultures including the Maya and the Mexica were indeed complex civilizations that flourished in Mexican soil and whose significant contributions to world heritage continue to be revealed. Just as the mixture of Spanish and Native Mexican gave rise to the mestizo, the Spanish Conquest of Mexico resulted in new types of architecture. Simultaneously, by virtue of its colonization, Mexico became integrated into the culture of the Western European world and has partaken in western intellectual and architectural currents since the sixteenth century.

During the 1930s Mexico felt the international wave of socialism. In the next two decades, aided by postwar prosperity, the Mexican state invested in impressive social service projects including housing, and public health and educational facilities. Since the colonial period, Mexico has had its share of wealthy families. During the early 1990s Mexico boasted to have at least quadrupled its number of resident millionaires. This wealth, combined with national aspirations to industrialization, resulted in a continuous but partial "modernization" parallel with that of Europe and the United States.

Because the nation is rooted in history, no representation of national identity is ever complete. The pre-Hispanic and colonial past, affluence, and modernity are aspects of the Mexican nation that are constantly reinterpreted and reconstituted. Representations of the nation in architecture omit allusions to conflict and contradiction. Consistently mining from the architecture and from its documentation are narratives or at least indications of alternative ways of experiencing the nation.

Inconsistencies in the traditional narratives of nationhood are exposed not through individual buildings but through fissures that open between the monuments to the viewer traveling the city. Pollution, poverty, destitution, and desperation are evident everywhere. The state offers little help and has no answers. Elites benefit from the traditional representations of the nation precisely because they cover up what is important to repress. The state supports homogeneous and harmonic representations of nationhood since to admit dissonance is threatening to the social order and to state control. In some cases, accepting contradictions is tantamount to admitting responsibility for the marginalization and dispossession of a large part of the Mexican population.

Architects in various countries have shown that it is indeed possible to represent inconsistencies. The problem is to obtain commissions to materialize such projects, since more often than not architects depend on the state and affluent patrons for commissions. More appropriate than a proposal on how best to represent the nation is to question the appropriateness and the relevance of representing the nation in architecture today. In recent years, in many parts of the world, private interest represented by transnational corporations take precedence over public interest, and the traditional roles of the state, particularly those of the welfare state, become the province of private enterprise.

In Mexico, as in other Latin American countries, individuals' alliances to the nation are increasingly replaced by identification with ethnic and class-based consumer identities as well as with smaller communities and interest groups. Consumer identities transcend national boundaries, as does the economic order in global capitalism.

It has been argued that in the late twentieth century it has become problematic to identify culture, nation, and ethnicity because traditional signifiers of these constructs now floated in an undefined geographical space. One can find McDonald's, Guatemalan textiles, Navajo and Persian rugs in any corner of the globe. It is difficult to define the nation geographically as migration and nomadism increasingly characterize contemporary human experience. It is more difficult to maintain the distinction between First and Third World as we find Third World enclaves in First World settings, and vice versa.

In view of these developments, the representation of national identity in architecture is fatally compromised. Now more than ever, it is crucial for architects and critics to invent critical practices to subvert and reconfigure the idea of nation. As Gyan Prakash said in another context, "the urge to fashion a strategic response to the prevailing configuration of knowledge and power requires that we think along differentiated, interpolated, mobile, and unsettling lines."

Select Bibliography

Aja, Marisol, "Juan O'Gorman." In *Apuntes para la historia y crítica de la arquitectura mexicana del siglo XX 1900–1980,* vol. 2, *Cuadernos de arquitectura y conservación del patrimonio artístic.* Mexico City: Secretaría de Educación Pública/Instituto Nacional de Bellas Artes, 1982.

Born, Esther, *The New Architecture in Mexico.* New York: The Architectural Record, 1937.

González Gortázar, Fernando, editor, *La arquitectura mexicana del siglo XX.* Mexico City: Consejo Nacional para la Cultura y las Artes, 1994.

González Lobo, Carlos, "Arquitectura en Mexico durante la cuarta década: El maximato, el cardenismo." In *Apuntes para la historia y crítica de la arquitectura mexicana del siglo XX 1900–1980,* vol. 2, *Cuadernos de arquitectura y conservacion del patrimonio artistico.* Mexico City: Secretaría de Educación Pública/Instituto Nacional de Bellas Artes, 1982.

Katzman, Israel, *La arquitectura contemporanea mexicana.* Mexico City: INAH, 1963.

López Rangel, Rafael, *Diego Rivera y la arquitectura mexicana.* Mexico City: Consejo Nacional de Fomento Educativo, 1986.

Manrique, Jorge Alberto, "El futuro radiante: La ciudad universitaria." In *La arquitectura mexicana del siglo XX,* edited by Fernando González Gortázar. Mexico City: Consejo Nacional para la Cultura y las Artes, 1994.

McClintock, Anne, *Imperial Leather.* London: Routledge, 1995.

Melgar Adalid, Mario, and José Rogelio Alvarez Noguera, editors, *6 años de arquitectura en Mexico 1988–1994.* Mexico City: UNAM, 1994.

Obregón Santacilia, Carlos, *50 años de arquitectura mexicana (1900–1950).* Mexico City: Patria, 1952.

Pinoncelli, Salvador, "La arquitectura en México 1940–1960." In *Apuntes para la historia y crítica de la arquitectura mexicana del siglo XX 1900–1980,* vol. 2, *Cuadernos de arquitectura y conservacion del patrimonio artistico.* Mexico City: Secretaría de Educación Pública/Instituto Nacional de Bellas Artes, 1982.

Ricalde, Humberto, and Gustavo López, "Arquitectura en Mexico 1960–1980." In *Apuntes para la historia y crítica de la arquitectura mexicana del siglo XX 1900–1980,* vol. 2, *Cuadernos de arquitectura y conservacion del patrimonio artistico.* Mexico City: Secretaría de Educación Pública/Instituto Nacional de Bellas Artes, 1982.

Rivadeneyra, Patricia, "Hannes Meyer en Mexico (1938–1949)." In *Apuntes para la historia y crítica de la arquitectura mexicana del siglo XX 1900–1980,* vol. 1, *Cuadernos de arquitectura y conservación del patrimonio artístico.* Mexico City: Secretaría de Educación Pública/Instituto Nacional de Bellas Artes, 1982.

Rivera, Diego, " La huella de la historia y la geografía en la arquitectura mexicana." In *Cuadernos de Arquitectura* 14 (September 1964).

Rispa, Raul, editor, *Barragán: The Complete Works.* Princeton, New Jersey: Princeton Architectural Press, 1996.

Ruíz Barbarín, Antonio, "Rationalist Stage." In *Barragán: The Complete Works,* edited by Raul Rispa. Princeton, New Jersey: Princeton Architectural Press, 1996.

Siller, Juan Antonio, "Precencia prehispánica en la arquitectura neo-Maya de Yucatán." In *Cuadernos de arquitectura mesoamericana* 9 (January 1987).

Toca Fernández, Antonio, "Evolución crítica de la arquitectura en Mexico 1900–1990." In *La arquitectura mexicana del siglo XX,* edited by Fernando González Gortázar. Mexico City: Consejo Nacional para la Cultura y las Artes, 1994.

Vargas Salguero, Ramon, "El Imperio de la Razón." In *La arquitectura mexicana del siglo XX,* edited by Fernando González Gortázar. Mexico City: Consejo Nacional para la Cultura y las Artes, 1994.

Villagrán García, José, *Teoría de la Arquitectura,* edited by Ramón Vargas Salguero. Mexico City: UNAM, 1989.

—MARÍA FERNÁNDEZ

ARMENDÁRIZ, PEDRO

1912–63 • Actor

No actor more than Pedro Armendáriz exemplified the official nationalism of the so-called Golden Age of Mexican Cinema that climaxed in the 1940s. The favored star of the *indígena* genre associated with the work of director Emilio "El Indio" Fernández and cinematographer Gabriel Figueroa, Armendáriz became the face of Mexico for foreign film audiences. By the end of his career, he had appeared in more than 40 Mexican films and almost 30 foreign productions, including important Hollywood features. Despite his nationalist roles, his career exemplified the transnational foundation of Golden Age Mexican Cinema.

Born May 9, 1912, in Churubusco, Mexico City, Armendáriz was reared as an adolescent in San Antonio, Texas, and later attended the California Polytechnic Institute. As a young man he worked on the Mexican railroad and as a Mexico City guide to foreign tourists before entering acting. After a brief career on the stage, the future matinee idol made his screen debut in 1935 in *Rosario,* just as sound production was advancing in Mexico City studios. His rise to stardom, however, took place in the following decade, when Mexican film expanded internationally. Armendáriz's most notable work, undertaken during the mid-1940s, involved romantic, often historical, films set in provincial Mexico. Frequently his roles were representations of Indians and mestizos.

Armendáriz's connections to the United States were complex, especially considering the nationalist label frequently applied to his Mexican work. This complexity reflected the Mexican industry's overall relationship with Hollywood and the U.S. government as it developed during World War II. One of his early wartime roles, as the patriotic mestizo bandit Lupe in *Soy puro mexicano* (1942), directed by Fernández, demonstrates this pattern. To support Mexico's unpopular wartime alliance with the United States, the movie refashioned Mexican nationalism as antifascism, as part of the nation's struggle for sovereignty rather than collaboration with a historically imperialist aggressor. The film's representation of *mestizaje* as the ethnic symbol of the state set a pattern for postwar film-making through which Armendáriz became the leading male filmic personification of the nation. (The production itself was born from the Mexican film industry's collaboration with the U.S. government, which, through the intervention of Nelson Rockefeller's Office of the Coordinator of Inter-American Affairs, accelerated and shaped the Golden Age of Mexican cinema's industrial and ideological development.)

In his numerous works with Fernández and Figueroa, Armendáriz offered often passionate performances that personified official rhetoric in mass entertainment. Postwar films that centered on Mexican history and indigenous culture sought to strengthen the state's ideological project, producing nationalist cultural emblems that masked the ever-more conservative political and socioeconomic project fostered by the state. Figueroa's use of dramatically angled close-ups of the Mexican star accentuated the actor's physical features to craft an image congruent with official versions of nationalist ideology.

His association with this cinematic nationalism of Fernández and Figueroa included many features focused on, or at least set in, Mexican history. In *Enamorada* (1946), Fernández and Figueroa's adaptation of Shakespeare's *Taming of the Shrew,* Armendáriz played a Revolutionary general who wins the heart of an independent-minded provincial beauty (María Félix) by forcing her to yield to his patriarchal control. In many of these wartime films he played opposite Dolores del Río. In *Flor Silvestre* (1943), as José Luis Castro, he defies his conservative, hacendado father by marrying a local commoner, Esperanza (del Río), and joining the forces of revolutionary change, only to die tragically at the hands of bandits after the war is won. *Bugambilia* relates a similarly tragic love story, starring del Río, set in nineteenth-century Guanajuato. In *Las Abandonadas* (1944), Armendáriz plays a Revolutionary-era general who falls in love with a virtuous woman (del Río) forced into prostitution by circumstance. Again, the hero's untimely murder cuts short the love affair, but del Río's character perseveres and triumphs through their son's success as an attorney. Armendáriz also portrayed other urban types in socially significant dramas. In 1943, for instance, he starred in the politically provocative *Distinto Amanecer* as Octavio, a union operative, who with the help of his lover Julieta (Andrea Palma), successfully escapes assassination by a corrupt governor (who has already murdered an honest labor leader) to fight for workers' rights.

The themes of his most enduring Fernández-Figueroa films, however, combined romantic visual representations of indigenous race and rural landscape with messages stressing social justice, condemning exploitation. In the iconographic *María Candelaria* (1943), for example, an over-sexed, corrupt mestizo merchant victimizes Armendáriz's character (Lorenzo Rafael), who unsuccessfully defends the honor of del Río before she is stoned to death over a false rumor of a romantic transgression with a white outsider. In *La Perla,* based on John Steinbeck's original script, he played Quino, member of an indigenous fishing village whose discovery of a gigantic pearl brings tragedy instead of happiness at the hands of local white elites. The Mexican industry's first internationally distributed bilingual production, the movie was released in the United States as *The Pearl* in 1948. The Mexican company FAMA co-produced the feature with RKO at Estudios Churubusco, the modern production site the U.S. studio built in partnership with Mexican media magnate Emilio Azcárraga during World War II. Directed by Fernández and photographed by Figueroa, the film launched Armendáriz's crossover to Hollywood films.

John Ford cast him in a leading role alongside his frequent Mexican film partner, del Río, and Henry Fonda in *The Fugitive* (1947), based on Graham Greene's anti-anticlerical Mexican tale, *The Power and the Glory* (1940). Distributed by RKO, the film was shot entirely in Mexico, on location and at Estudios Churubusco, by Figueroa. (Fernández served as Ford's assistant on the project.) The following year, the U.S. director cast Armendáriz as a Mexican-American in two films starring John Wayne, as a Spanish-speaking U.S. army sergeant in *Fort Apache* and as an ultimately redeemed outlaw in *Three Godfathers*. In *Tulsa* (1949), starring Susan Hayward, he played an Oklahoma Native American involved in an oil controversy. *The Torch* (1950), another Fernández-Figueroa collaboration, was an English-language remake of *Enamorada;* Paulette Goddard played María Félix's part. Although generally cast in Hollywood as Latin American, Mexican American, or Native American, Armendáriz's English-language roles traversed a wide spectrum. In 1955, he even starred in a Mexican-made, juvenile Disney farce, *The Littlest Outlaw*. And perhaps the actor is best known internationally as James Bond's Turkish ally in *From Russia with Love* (1963).

Armendáriz's international career was not unprecedented, but it reversed the dominant migration pattern of many Mexican movie stars, such as his perpetual screen companion Dolores del Río, who repatriated, bringing Hollywood-obtained skills to the Mexican industry as it expanded in the 1940s. Instead, as the Golden Age of Mexican Cinema waned in the postwar period, Armendáriz transferred his Mexican movie-acting experience (and Latin American box-office popularity) to Hollywood. But even as he played in international films, he continued to make Mexican movies. Notable of his later national work is his portrayal of Pancho Villa in the episodic historical trilogy directed by Ismael Rodríguez: *Así era Pancho Villa* (*Cuentos de Pancho Villa;* 1957), *Pancho Villa y la Valentina* (1958), and *Cuando ¡Viva Villa! es la muerte* (1958). Armendáriz committed suicide in 1963, after learning that he had terminal cancer. His son, Pedro Jr., has had a notable, although less successful, career as a film and television actor.

—SETH FEIN

ARREOLA, JUAN JOSÉ

1918– • Writer

Juan José Arreola was born in Zapotlán, el Grande (now Ciudad Guzmán), Jalisco, on September 21, 1918. He was self-educated; from the age of 12, he undertook a variety of work, from employment as a counter clerk to a door-to-door salesman. He belonged to the generation of Juan Rulfo and Antonio Alatorre, and it was thanks to them, in the 1940s, that he began to contribute to two Guadalajara magazines: *Eos* and *Pan*.

At the end of 1936 he moved to Mexico City, where he met writers who were to be crucial to his literary development: Rodolfo Usigli and Xavier Villaurrutia, on the one hand, and Fernando Wagner, on the other, who introduced him to the theater and performing arts. He also joined the poets and narrators who worked together on the journals *Taller* and *Tierra Nueva:* Alberto Quintero, Octavio Paz, José Luis Martínez, and Alí Chumacero. At that time (1939–40), and under the reviving influence of Mexico City, he wrote three short one-act plays: *La Sombra de la Sombra, Rojo y Negro* (inspired by Stendhal's novel), and *Tierras de Dios.*

In 1940, defeated, in a way, by the big city and facing economic ruin, he returned to his hometown and survived by giving lessons as a secondary school teacher. Nevertheless, he continued to write. His first story, *Sueño de Navidad,* influenced by Russian writers of the nineteenth century, was published at Christmas that same year in the Zapotlán local newspaper, *El Vigía.* From then on, his stories continued to appear in the Magazines *Eos* and *Pan*. He later collected those first stories in *Varia Invención* (1949).

Through Louis Jouvet, whom he met in Guadalajara in 1945, he obtained a scholarship from the Instituto Francés de América Latina (French Institute of Latin America) to study stagecraft in Paris. There he came into contact with the Comedia Francesa and some writers, such as Julien Benda, who were instrumental in consolidating his vocation as a writer. On his return to Mexico in 1946, and thanks to the philanthropic influence of Antonio Alatorre, he obtained scholarships to study at the Colegio de México and began work as a proofreader at the Fondo de Cultura Económica.

From the 1950s, he directed several cultural institutions. He was a member of the literary board Consejo Literario del Centro Mexicano de Escritores and founder and manager of the Casa del Lago. Together with Héctor Mendoza, in 1956 he advised on and directed some of the programs of the Poesía en Voz Alta (spoken poetry) movement. He founded and directed literary collections such as *Los Presentes, Cuadernos y Libros de Unicornio,* and the journal *Mester.* He was a professor at the Facultad de Filosofía y Letras of the national university, Universidad Nacional Autónoma de México (UNAM), and he contributed to various cultural programs on radio and television.

Together with that of Juan Rulfo and José Revueltas, Arreola's narrative work was to open new routes in Mexican literature. His intention had always been to transcend apparent reality in order to show the essence of man. In his prose, certain traits stand out and these, in time, became the backbone of his writing: irony, parody, love as an impossibility, woman as an enigma to be deciphered, the human lack of communication, the vicissitudes of old age and physical decline, the radical solitude of man, and—according to Emmanuel Carballo—an undeniable ethical dimension. All of this was fashioned by a formal search in which brevity and conciseness, sobriety and rigor constitute its principal themes. Arreola himself pointed out, "I prefer the germs of ideas to lengthy developments, exhausted by excess of their own verbiage."

Those "germs" would give way to two books essential to Mexican literature: *Confabulario* (1925) and *Bestiario* (1959). The latter is developed on the same lines as the fables of Aesop, La Fontaine, and the *Bestiario Espiritual* of Claudel, and in it, as in its predecessors, Arreola tries to highlight satirically some of the traits of human behavior by means of their analogy to animal behavior. Arreola wrote, "We appear caricatured in the animals, and caricature is one of the best artistic ways of helping us to know ourselves. In it we are horrified to see some of our physical or spiritual traits accentuated."

In 1964 Arreola published his only novel: *La Feria,* in which he recounts the history of his hometown from colonial days to the present time. The story does not follow a linear and chronological order, but is broken into innumerable fragments, like the pieces of a jigsaw puzzle, which it is up to the reader to put together. The main character of the story is the town itself, although represented by each of its inhabitants. In spite of relating the history of a remote town, the novel cannot be placed within a regionalist trend or one of local customs and manners. The problems touched upon—without in any way detracting from local color—are universal ones that affect people everywhere.

It has to be emphasized that in this novel all Arreola's previous work is summarized, both thematically and stylistically. Many of the fragments work as stories in themselves, or as small samples of poetic prose, containing the nucleus of plots that had run through the whole of Arreola's writing, from his very first texts.

As to what La Feria represents in the entirety of his work, the author has indicated that he wrote it to comply with certain voices within me that would not be silenced, and also, to reveal what I am beneath the apparent literary figure: the simple man from Jalisco, the child I was, who spent life in the country watching the development of agricultural work and listening to the sayings and songs of the local people, in short, the boy distressed by the drama of conscience and the eroticism it awakens.

Arreola's work has received many prizes and honors. These stand out among them: the Premio de Literatura Jalisco (1953), the Premio Xavier Villaurritia (1963), the Premio Azteca de Oro (1975), the Premio Nacional de Periodismo (1977), and the Premio Nacional de Letras (1979).

Select Bibliography

Carballo, Emmanuel, *El cuento mexicano del siglo XX.* Mexico City: Empresas Editoriales, 1964.
_____, *Protagonistas de la literatura mexicana.* Mexico City: Secretaría de Educación Pública, 1986.
Glantz, Margo, *Repetitiones:Ensayos sobre literatura mexicana.* Mexico City: Universidad Veracruzana, 1979.
Hensinkveld, Paula R., "Juan José Arreola. Allegorist in an Age of Uncertainty." *Chasqui* 2–3 (1984).
Juan José Arreola: Imágenes y obra escogida. Mexico City: UNAM, 1984.

—Armando Pereira

ARRIAGA, PONCIANO

1811–63 • Politician

Ponciano Arriaga was born in the city of San Luis Potosí in 1811. He is remembered for having written a major part of the 1857 Constitution and passionately defending it in the Constituent Assembly. He was elected president of the assembly almost unanimously on February 18, 1856, after an impeccable career as a lawyer, politician, and patriot.

In 1833, he joined the National Guard to fight with Antonio López de Santa Anna. After holding various important posts in San Luis Potosí (alderman in the *ayuntamiento* and town clerk), he became a deputy in the national parliament in 1843 and 1846. He was minister of justice, religious affairs, and education in President Arista's government from December 13, 1852, to January 5, 1853. However, when Santa Anna took over the presidency, Arriaga was exiled for his liberal ideas. In New Orleans he contacted other liberals, notably Melchor Ocampo and Benito Juárez, and they actively supported the war to overthrow Santa Anna (the Revolution of Ayutla) from exile. When the revolution triumphed, Arriaga returned to Mexico and was elected a deputy in the Constituent Assembly (1856–57) representing the regions of San Luis Potosí, Guerrero, Jalisco, Mexico, Michoacán, Puebla, Zacatecas, and the Federal District.

While Arriaga was not against private property, he advocated a more equitable distribution of land among all members of society. He was conscious of the enormous gap that had always existed between ideas, proposals, projects and theories, and what is put into practice. Arriaga emphasized the sterility of proclaiming rights and promoting education when "the material side of society has remained the same: land in a very few hands, capital accumulated, its circulation monopolized." It was not until one-half century later, when the Revolution of 1910 erupted, that Arriaga's agrarian reforms were put forward again by a movement with broader aims but equally concerned with the unjust distribution of land and the social problems inherent in it.

Arriaga's speech on becoming first president of the Constituent Assembly reflected the aims that guided him in performing such a delicate mission. "Having examined all systems of government, you have seen all their advantages and vices, and, better than the legislators who have preceded you, you can draw up a constitution which, perfectly adapted to the Mexican nation, will erect on democratic principles an edifice in which liberty and order reign forever." This legislator and reformer from San Luis Potosí made his position very clear: eradicate the evils and injustices of previous administrations and with sincerity and honesty create a charter suited to the real needs of the nation.

Arriaga's later speeches to the assembly were equally memorable: on military matters he proposed abolishing the administrative units known as *comandancias generales,* and on political matters he insisted on the need for democratic elections. Most notably, he spoke on the problem of private land ownership; in this last he was ahead of his time. He believed that the enormous tracts of land, in the main unexploited, in the hands of a few large landowners damaged the economy, stymied real development, and condemned a large part of the population to poverty. They were, in his opinion, among the biggest problems facing the country and the greatest obstacle to its achieving true democracy. Ponciano Arriaga died in San Luis Potosí in 1863.

Vicente Quirarte

ARTISANS AND ARTISANAL PRODUCTION

Most history books date the beginning of Mexican industrialization and the first labor associations to around 1867, the so-called Restored Republic, when decades of endemic warfare came to a close. Nonetheless, the first attempts to establish factories in Mexico began somewhat earlier. As early as the 1820s artisans were uniting to oppose attempts to establish textile mills in Mexico, fearing that factories would displace artisans and artisanal production in Mexico. The labor historian Luis Chávez Orozco dates the decline of the artisanal class in Mexico even earlier. In the years preceding Independence, he argues, artisans had to struggle for survival as they slowly were edged out by new forms of production and—starting in 1815—their traditional corporate rights were abolished. Nonetheless, artisans and artisanal production did not simply disappear. Early attempts to establish manufacturing in Mexico starting in the 1830s foundered for want of capital, which remained concentrated in the hands of speculators and the Catholic Church. Attempts to attract foreign capital and establish a bank to finance industrial production also were unsuccessful. Artisans could survive until the final decades of the nineteenth century, although little could halt their progressive decline. In the words of Chávez Orozco, for the artisanal class the nineteenth century was a "slow agony."

Trades

Guild membership gave artisans social and political recognition, as well as a stable and hierarchical organization. During the final years of the colonial period, trades and guilds were organized along ethnic lines. The silversmiths', tinsmiths', blacksmiths', embroiderers', painters', and tailors' guilds were composed mainly of Spanish artisans and produced luxury goods that were sold primarily to the upper classes of New Spain. On the second level were the carpenters and weavers, with a mixed composition of Spaniards, Indians, and mestizos. These trades produced goods for a broader segment of the population. At the bottom were the shoemakers, spinners, and tanners, who were mainly Indians and mestizos. In such trades as cotton and silk weaving, smelting, and pottery guild legislation allowed Indians and mestizos (although not Africans and their descendants) to join guilds, work freely, and even reach the rank of master.

Artisanal production was segmented spatially as well as by ethnicity. In late colonial Mexico City half of the 1,520 artisanal shops were downtown and the rest in the southern part of the city. Tailors, gunsmiths, watchmakers, saddlers, coach builders, painters, sculptors, chandlers, and confectioners were concentrated in the city center, for the most part serving Mexico City's wealth circles. In the southern outskirts of the city were workshops that did not produce finished goods (milling, tanning, construction materials) as well as weavers, dyers, and others tradesmen who depended on commercial capital and were unable to afford workshops with direct access to consumers.

Artisans traditionally worked in workshops run by a master craftsman who worked to order, assisted by skilled craftsmen and apprentices. This system began to decline, however, as guilds were abolished in the early nineteenth century; indeed, this decline might have begun even earlier with the appearance of commercial capital, which introduced cheap imported goods that competed favorably with domestically produced artisanal products. By the mid–nineteenth century most artisans were day laborers who lacked the resources to start their own workshops.

Nonetheless, certain traditions remained. Long after many guilds had lost power and prestige, their religious counterpart, the *cofradías* (confraternities) continued to link members of each trade to a patron saint and act a sort of social insurance, providing medical benefits, burial, and dowries for orphans of guild members. The tailors' *cofradía* lasted at least until 1860. It still was necessary to join a shop as an apprentice to learn a trade. There was a considerable degree of internal stratification within trades—rich and poor apprentices, journeymen, and prestigious master craftsmen. If business did not go well, apprentices could be dismissed. If they managed to finish their apprenticeship, they could open their own shops, work as *rinconeros* (unauthorized craftsmen available on demand), or work at street corners or at home for merchants, other shops, or the occasional consumer.

According to the historian Frederick J. Shaw, in 1849 artisans represented 38 percent of Mexico City's population, which at the time totaled 200,000 people. Around 2,000 workshops existed in the city, each employing approximately five journeymen. Most craftsmen earned barely enough to survive. The most highly paid and prestigious tradesmen were tailors and carpenters. Weavers were among the least prosperous. Artisans produced a wide range of commodities. In 1854 approximately 69 trades were represented in Mexico City that still were based largely in artisanal workshops. However, workshops also had to coexist and compete with manufacturing plants, which had begun to gain ground in both rural and urban areas. By 1837 4 spinning mills had been established in Puebla, and by 1846 52 spinning and cotton textile mills as well as 5 wool mills had been established throughout the country. Moreover, in the countryside, many Indian households produced many crafts within the family rather than relying on mestizo-owned workshops, following colonial and pre-Hispanic traditions of work and aesthetics.

Transformation of Artisanal Production and Organization

The artisanal environment began to change with the establishment of the first factories in Mexico. These new industries depended on the import of foreign equipment, parts, and know-how as much as on the skilled labor of craftsmen who had been forced to become wage workers and the less skilled labor of other impoverished sectors of the population, particularly the peasantry. The decline of the artisanal sector accelerated, since compared to the new factories artisans spent an enormous amount of time in production. Nonetheless, artisans continued to play an important role in peasant communities and wherever there was demand for goods that the manufacturing industry could not satisfy.

Artisans also played an important ideological role. For many years the first labor unions were led by people brought up in traditions of artisanal production. Artisans initially confronted foreign-owned industries in response to the increasing erosion of working conditions both of independent craftsmen and skilled workers; later artisans confronted domestic industries as well.

In 1841 the owners of the largest artisanal workshops in Mexico City formed the Junta de Fomento de Artesanos (Artisans Promotion Association), seeking to protect producers and their wares from the massive inflow of imported goods. In 1853 a group of hatters, later joined by tailors, formed the Sociedad Particular de Socorros Mutuos (Mutual Aid Society). Like other mutual aid societies, the Sociedad Particular acted principally as a benevolent society, setting up a bank to protect the poor, running a shelter for beggars and disabled workers, lobbying for improved working conditions in workshops and factories, and providing assistance for sick members and families of deceased members. Growing against a backdrop of civil war and foreign intervention, the Sociedad Particular called on all members not to participate in political conflict and to work for the restoration of peace in Mexico.

After the fall of the French-supported regime of the Emperor Maximilian in 1867, interest in labor unions took off among workers and artisans. Two general tendencies developed in Mexican labor organization, although there was considerable overlap: mutual aid organizations and organizations that defined themselves as socialist. Mutual aid organization tended to be more influential and demanded respect for artisanal production. Although they were more politicized, the socialist organization also formed mutual aid societies, but they also organized salaried workers. Combining proletarian ideology and artisan values, the socialist organizations ended up defending both underpaid workers and craftsmen still carrying on their trade.

Labor organizations in the late nineteenth and early twentieth centuries tended to be urban in character. The urban working class was still quite fragmentary, and early labor unions found themselves defending a broad range of often-divergent interests. Urban artisans, owners of small workshops, and wage earners all experienced the onset of industrial capitalism in distinct ways. The advent of industrial capitalism had a quite different impact on rural artisans, particularly Indian artisans, who carried on their work in quite different units of production (much as they do today). As rule they were not transformed into wage-earning factory workers; however, they were subordinated to the new industrial capitalist regime through commerce, both of raw materials and finished products.

Artisans and Industry

Industrial capitalism forced many artisanal goods out of the market as society came to perceive them as useless, and as artisans were unable to compete with industry. Nonetheless, artisanal production continues in Mexico to this day, although it has shrunk to rather small proportions. Industrial production has been unable to make certain goods that play a symbolic role in the habits and rituals of popular sectors of Mexican society. Moreover, some artisanal wares sell for less than industrial goods. Finally, enlightened strata of society value manual labor and the high quality of artisanal products compared with mass-produced industrial goods. We can categorize present-day artisanal production according to a variety of criteria: type of work and workers, labor relations, division of labor, use and ownership of tools, and labor and productivity cycles.

Family Artisanal Production

Artisanal production organized around the family survives particularly in rural areas, often alongside agricultural production. Work in family units usually is done with the most undeveloped technology, involving individual work and very few tools. The division of labor is very primitive, along gender and age lines. Trades are taught within or between families, and the family often works on all stages of the production process, from raw materials to finished goods. In some cases, however, raw materials are industrially produced and sold in small quantities and inflated prices to local artisans. The quality of artisanal products produced by families can vary greatly; fine products are differentiated from everyday products particularly in terms of finish and decoration.

Family artisanal production is widespread in many regions of Mexico, producing many basic goods sold in local, regional, and national markets, as well as goods for the immediate family and community. Usually professional merchants buy the family's goods, often lending money or raw materials. Commercial capital tends to prefer family production for certain kind of products, such as textiles and clothing; pottery, baskets, embroidery, fireworks, *papel amate* (bark paper) painting, and other goods also are produced by family units. Merchants distribute raw materials among thousands of domestic units, which in turn carry out specific parts in the production process. The standard of living of such artisans is generally quite low.

Individual Shops

Individual shops exist in cities as well as rural areas and are quite similar to colonial-era workshops. Producers own their tools. They usually are masters in their trades and carry on the entire production process, sometimes assisted by children or apprentices. As a rule jewelers, silversmiths, cabinet makers, saddlers, blacksmiths, and wood engravers have their own shops and produce to order. Each product is produced individually. Shop production usually is restricted to a rather small market.

Workshops with Workers

This form of artisanal production organizes several workers on a regular or temporary basis. Work is organized by the workshop owner, who takes part in manual labor himself. Even though the investment in tools is larger, there is no division of labor. Each individual artisan in the shop makes products from beginning to end; he knows the trade and eventually can use his boss's workshop to make goods ordered directly from them. Trades organized in this way include carpentry and shawl and shoe making.

Manufactories

The manufactory developed out of the artisan workshop and preceded the mechanized factory. Its main feature is the cooperation of workers through the division of labor. Work is organized into different manual operations, and artisanal trade remains the basis of production. The owner of the manufactory is a manager who does not participate in manual labor, although he is involved in product design and marketing. Production techniques are largely manual, but some tools are used to ease work. As in mechanized factories, workers follow a rhythm imposed by the work itself and often are organized in assembly lines. Sometimes manufactories outsource parts of the production process to producers working out of their homes. Blown glass, ceramic, garment, and shoe production organized in manufactories are capable of competing with mechanized production on the open market. Their greater capital enables them to buy raw materials wholesale, plan ahead, and stock production. Management is skilled in marketing techniques, financing possibilities, and business administration.

The forms of production that generally are regarded as the least developed—family and individual shop production—are the most widespread in Mexico today. This only goes to show the unevenness of Mexico's economic development and its integration into the capitalist system. These forms of production permit the subsistence of many families. Regardless of how small their earnings may be, artisanal production turns these families into consumers of industrial commodities, not only of basic staples but also of raw materials required for production. Family production is still largely centered in rural areas; as long as they have a trade, rural families can work in their home communities and avoid migrating to cities.

Artisanal production allows poor sectors of society to have access to many goods that otherwise would be out reach; for the most part, artisanal production can be described as the poor producing for the poor. Low income, difficult access to raw materials, exploitation by commercial capital, total lack of social benefits, and the absence of organizations of family artisanal producers make life difficult for most artisanal producers. Old artisans complain that their descendants prefer to take other jobs and that their trades are dying out. (Larger artisanal establishments, particularly manufactories, tend to be immune to these problems, although their workers also lack organizations to defend them.)

The economic and political crisis that affected Mexico in the 1980s and 1990s seriously damaged the well-being of Mexico's workers, spurring artisans to organize. Throughout Mexico artisans—particularly the so-called *artisanos populares* (popular artisans)—began to demand consistency in the government's plans to promote artisanal production. As practitioners of skilled trades that are part of Mexico's cultural patrimony, artisans deserve job security and the other basic rights of other workers. Promotion of artisanal production can no longer be limited to technical assistance. It should substantially improve the standards of living of artisanal producers, dignify trades and promote professional recognition, facilitate the production of quality artisanal goods, and foster the teaching of this tradition, which remains a vibrant part of Mexican life.

See also Cofradías; Handicrafts

Select Bibliography

Chávez Orozco, Luis, Prologue to *Del artesando al socialismo,* by José María González. Mexico City: Sepsetentas, 1974.

Cook, Scott, "Price and Output Variability in a Peasant-Artisan Stoneworking Industry in Oaxaca, Mexico: An Analytical Essay in Economic Anthropology." In *American Anthropologist* 72:4 (1970).

Littlefield, Alice, *La industria de las hamacas en Yucatán.* Mexico City: SEP-INI, 1976.

Novelo, Victoria, *Artesanías y capitalismo en México.* Mexico City: SEP-INAH, 1976.

—VICTORIA NOVELO

ATENEO DE LA JUVENTUD

Mexican cultural life in the first half of the twentieth century was defined by the presence of intellectuals who, at the end of 1909, had formed the Ateneo de la Juventud. The founders of the Ateneo sought to formulate an alternative to the "medieval rigidity," positivist orthodoxy, and francophile affectation which had defined *fin-de-siècle* intellectual life in Mexico. The very name of the group, the "youth athenaeum," established a counterpoint to the gerontocracy of Porfirio Díaz; products of the Porfirian educational system, most of the founders were between 20 and 28 years old. Without breaking with French culture, the members of the Ateneo returned Mexican culture to its indigenous and Spanish roots and strengthened Mexico's ties with other Latin American countries. Promoting a philosophical and moral renovation, the Ateneo helped fundamentally reorient educational policy in Mexico, particularly in institutions of higher learning.

The immediate antecedents of the Ateneo were the journal *Savia Moderna* and the Society of Conferences. The staff of *Savia Moderna* only managed to publish five issues, the first in March 1906 and the last in July of the same year. The journal opened its doors to young artists and scholars who had been shut out of official venues. Such future members of the Ateneo as Antonio Caso, Alfonso Reyes, Carlos González Peña, and the Dominican Pedro Henríquez Ureña published their early work in *Savia,* and the journal also reproduced artwork by Diego Rivera and Jorge Enciso.

Savia folded when its director and sponsor Alfonso Cravioto departed for Europe, but a nucleus of authors and editors from the journal continued to meet in the workshop of Jesús T. Acevedo, reading and discussing works not recognized in official institutions. The group originally planned organize a series of conferences on Greece. Although they never were able to complete this project, Greek culture continued to be the most important passion of the group and gave it its characteristic humanistic profile. Caso and Henríquez Ureña began to read Bergson, Boutroux, and James, discovering new ways to oppose positivism and renew Mexican philosophy. Their readings later extended to such thinkers as Plato, Kant, Hegel, Descartes, Schopenhauer, Nietzsche, Cros, Poincaré, and Buddha. At Acevedo's initiative the participants in the meetings organized the Society of Conferences to provide a public forum for contemporary ideas. The society organized two cycles of conferences, the first from late May through August 1907, and the second in March and April of 1908. Organized by Caso, the first conference discussed the work of Nietzsche and the second the work of Max Stirner. The dissertation of Pedro Henríquez Ureña on the Castillian poet José María Gabriel y Galán and Isidro Fabela's work on the novelist José María de Pereda marked a return to Spanish language and culture. Jesús

Acevedo's work on architecture in New Spain was a profound reevaluation of the colonial period in Mexico, which the positivist orthodoxy had rejected.

After the conferences on Nietzche and Stirner the Society of Conferences dissolved, although its members individually continued the work begun by the group and helped organize the Ateneo. The Ateneo was founded on October 28, 1909. Its early members included such luminaries as Jesús Acevedo, Antonio Caso, José Vasconcelos, Alfonso Reyes, Pedro Henríquez Ureña, Julio Torri, Martín Luis Guzmán, and Diego Rivera. They were encouraged by the current minister of public instruction and fine arts, Justo Sierra, who exercised a decisive influence on the group.

The Ateneo's influence on Mexican arts and letters was felt almost immediately. In 1909 Antonio Caso organized a series on conferences in the elite Escuela Nacional Preparatoria on the history of positivism, sparking a return to philosophy and metaphysics to institutions of higher learning. A second series of conferences was organized in 1910 to commemorate the centenary of the Mexican independence (the founders of the Ateneo came to be known as the "Generation of the Centenary"). In the 1910 conferences the members of the Ateneo developed the general contours of their ideology: opposition to positivism, reevaluation of key figures and currents in the history of Mexican letters, and the group's connection with Latin American idealist philosophy.

Under the presidency of José Vasconcelos, who was involved in the cause of the leader of the Mexican Revolution, Francisco I. Madero, in 1912 the Ateneo ceased to be a coterie of lovers of culture and became a circle of friends dedicated to political action. Nonetheless, the Ateneo as such never played a direct political role, although many of its members had joined the various factions opposed to the Díaz regime. The Ateneo did not want to promote a social revolution, nor was it in a position to do so. It effected a profound cultural transformation in Mexico, but it cannot be considered an antecedent of the Revolution. Its members would play a marginal role at best in the Revolutionary movement and the formulation of the principles of the Revolution. Indeed, the Revolution impeded the Ateneo from continuing its work "in favor of intellectual and artistic culture" (in the words of the group's charter). In December 1912 the members of the Ateneo founded the Universidad Popular to bring higher learning to the workplace, and from November 1913 to January 1914 they organized another series of conferences. In 1914, however, the group was forced to dissolve.

If the Revolution scattered the members of the Ateneo, they would continue to exercise a decisive influence on national life. Members of the Ateneo would be the first professors of humanities in the School of Advanced Studies (today the Faculty of Philosophy and Letters) in the National University, rectors of the National University, secretaries of education, foreign relations, and the treasury, a candidate for president of Mexico, members of the Mexican legislature and diplomatic corps, high officials in several government agencies, founders of educational institutions, distinguished members of the Academy of Mexican Language, and journalists. They also would become poets, novelists, essayists, philosophers, painters, and musicians who would exercise an incalculable influence on contemporary Mexican culture.

Select Bibliography

Henríquez Ureña, Pedro, "Horas de estudio," "La influencia de la Revolución en la vida intelectual de México," and "La cultura de las humanidades." In *Obra critica,* Mexico City: Fondo de Cultura Económica, 1981.

Hernández Luna, Juan, editor, *Conferencias del Ateneo de la Juventud.* Mexico City: UNAM, 1962.

Ramos, Samuel, "El perfil del hombre y la cultura en México." In *Obras completas,* vol. 1, Mexico City: UNAM, 1975.

_____, "Historia de la filosofía en México." In *Obras completas,* vol. 2, Mexico City: UNAM, 1976.

Reyes, Alfonso, *Universidad, política y pueblo.* Mexico City, UNAM, 1985.

Rojas Garcidueñas, José, *El Ateneo de la Juventud y la Revolución Mexicana.* Mexico City: Biblioteca del Instituto Nacional de Estudios Históricos de la Revolución Mexicana, 1979.

Vansconcelos, José, "El movimiento intelectual contemporáneo de México" and "Don Gabino Barreda y las ideas contemporáneas." In *Obras completas,* vol. 1, Mexico City: Libreros Mexicanos Unidos, 1957.

—MARGARITA VERA CUSPINERA

AUDIENCIAS

"Our monarchs have earned the enduring gratitude of all for the blessings they have bequeathed upon the Indies by the establishment of the royal *audiencias;* . . . for they are the rock and defense of those kingdoms, where justice is done, where the poor are defended from the oppression of the mighty, . . . and where everyone can claim their due in truth and in law."

Thus wrote Juan de Solórzano Pereira, the most distinguished authority on Spanish American law, in his *Política Indiana* (1642). It is true that Solórzano's statement, as one coming from a former *oidor* (local Crown representative), should be read with caution; but it nonetheless conveys something of the outstanding significance that the *audiencias* —which can be defined most loosely as judicial courts—had in the social and political evolution of Spanish America. Not only were they the center of the administrative system, they also provided the most effective curb against illegality and oppression, and they gave the government of the Indies a strong basis of permanence and continuity. For while viceroys came and went, the *audiencias* remained; and although the appointment of peninsular (European-born) Spaniards as *oidores* was common practice, it is no less clear that a large proportion of them ended their days in America and intermarried with important *criollo* families (those of Spanish descent born in the Americas). All this allowed the *audiencias* to take root in the new continent and to become closely identified with local life and interests, a process that was reflected in the acquisition of a strong line of corporate identity and tradition.

Like many other institutions in the Spanish Indies, the *audiencias* were a good reflection of similar institutions on the Iberian Peninsula; namely, the chancelleries or *audiencias* of Valladolid, Ciudad Real (later Granada), and Galicia. These peninsular institutions had developed in large measure as a response to the growing centralization of the legal system, which had been of utmost importance in the unification of Spain. The process cannot be separated from the gradual superimposition of Roman law upon the ancient and customary laws from the thirteenth century onward, culminating with the promulgation of the Laws of Toro in 1505. Yet the advance of Roman law (in both its manifestations of civil and canon law) by no means meant the abandonment of the ancient and customary laws of the peninsula. In fact, the effect of Roman law was to emend rather than to supersede earlier legal practice. The famous thirteenth-century compilation known as the Siete Partidas, for example, was unmistakably influenced by Roman law; yet it drew heavily upon the local traditions of *fueros* (special immunities and privileges) that the privileged classes and municipalities were at pains to defend.

Sixteenth-century Spain would witness the relentless erosion of these local traditions by the growth of a powerful judiciary composed of a large class of professional lawyers with a solid grounding in Roman law, at whose head stood the king. Such a process was not one that the Spanish conquistadors and settlers would tend to favor. Although they would readily accept the notion of the king as the fountainhead of justice, their understanding of this notion was often diametrically opposed to the growth of a centralizing bureaucracy. To give but the most obvious example, Fernando (Hernán) Cortés's decision to found the town of Villa Rica de la Vera Cruz with its own legal structure and town council in 1519 was taken in the full knowledge that, according to Spanish legal tradition, the new town could function as a political entity directly under the authority of the king. Far from being a sign of subordination, however, this appeal to royal power harked back to the medieval practice of appealing to the king in order to defend local interests against the alleged injustices of royal officials. Once the town council—which had been appointed by Cortés himself—had elected him as captain general, Cortés could legally claim to be free of the restraints placed upon him by the instructions given him by the governor of Cuba, and to be acting in the best interests of the community and in the service of God and the king.

It was not long before this interpretation of the function of royal power, prevalent among the conquistadors and early settlers, began to awaken the concern of the Council of the Indies. For although the notion was a clear asset to the enterprise of conquest and settlement, the way in which the conquistadors and their followers used it to distribute land and Indians among themselves in the form of *encomiendas* (native settlements "commended" to the care of a Spaniard—an *encomendero*—who had the duty to protect the Indians, maintain missionaries in the villages, and contribute to the military defense of the region), constituted a clear obstacle in the way of legal centralization by threatening to set up precisely the kind of aristocratic class in the Americas that the Spanish monarchs were attempting to curtail in Spain.

These fears were confirmed after the government of New Spain was entrusted, in 1528, to Beltrán Nuño de Guzmán and four *oidores* (two of whom died en route), who interpreted their instructions as an implicit mandate to despoil Cortés and his followers and enrich themselves and the members of the so-called Velásquez faction. The initiative was a shameful episode (known somewhat misleadingly as the First Audiencia), that provoked the stern opposition of Archbishop Juan de Zumárraga and convinced the Council of the Indies about the evils of the *encomienda* system and of the need to establish a viceroyal system of government, using Naples as a precedent.

It was in this difficult context that the so-called Second Audiencia was established in 1531, with the specific assignment of achieving stability before the arrival of the first viceroy. Its very composition is a good indication of how seriously the Council of the Indies had come to regard the issue. The president was to be the bishop of Santo Domingo, Sebastián Ramríez de Fuenleal, a man with a long experience in the Antilles and whose virtues and integrity were beyond dispute. The four *oidores* appointed to assist him—Vasco de Quiroga, Alonso de Maldonado, Francisco Ceynos, and Juan de Salmerón—were all jurists of standing, and they were entrusted with the delicate task of suppressing all the *encomiendas* granted by Nuño de Guzmán and to place them under the Crown in a centralized system of Indian government known as the *corregimiento*. This was clearly part of a long-term plan to establish a centralized system of Indian

government under royal officials. Yet, as early as 1532 the *encomenderos* had managed to persuade the *oidores* that too frontal an attack on the *encomienda* system might prove counterproductive. To offend the *encomenderos* would inevitably cause deep rifts in the Spanish community and might even lead to the cessation of work in ranches and mines. On the other hand, if the abuses associated with the *encomienda* were allowed to continue unchecked, there was the opposite risk of encouraging discontent and rebellion among the Indians. In these circumstances, the *audiencia* was forced to maintain a delicate balance between the vested interests of *encomenderos,* on the one hand, and, on the other, the direct control of Indian government that the new paternalistic policies of the Crown demanded.

These peculiar circumstances gave the *audiencias* in the Indies a markedly different character from the chancelleries of the peninsula. The latter were exclusively judicial institutions, whereas the American *audiencias* performed a number of special functions reserved in Spain for the royal councils. According to Solórzano, for instance, the *audiencias* were empowered to review *residencias* (routine inquiries into the conduct of retiring *corregidores* and other judges), and they could appoint *jueces pesquisidores* (special commissioners) if additional investigations were deemed necessary. They were the official guardians of the royal prerogative, patronage, and revenue, and they were in charge of investigating any usurpation of royal authority. They could assess (and enforce the assessment of) all legal fees, including Indian tribute payments and fees charged by ecclesiastics for the administration of sacraments. They had the duty to maintain jurisdictional boundaries and were empowered to issue writs of *recurso de fuerza* in restraint of illegal extensions of ecclesiastical jurisdiction. They were instructed to sit regularly in *acuerdo* (a plenary meeting) to analyze and propose initiatives on the administrative matters of their respective territories, and in *acuerdo de hacienda,* jointly with treasury officials, whenever financial matters needed urgent attention. Finally, and this was the most delicate and difficult task confronting the *audiencias,* they were entrusted with the supervision of Indian affairs.

It is true that all these special powers attributed by Solórzano to the *audiencias* were on the border of judicial authority. Indeed, the *audiencias* were always considered primarily as judicial institutions. Nevertheless, they managed to retain a large degree of discretionary authority, particularly in the sixteenth century, when the danger of rebellion was a constant preoccupation. Especially instructive in this context is the case of the *audiencia* of New Galicia, which comprised the modern states of Jailsco, Nayarit, Colima, and Aguascalientes, and parts of Sinaloa, Zacatecas, Durango, Guanajuato, Quertétaro, and San Luis Potosí. As the scholar J. H. Parry explains, the *audiencia* in this area often exercised independent powers of legislation: it occasionally interfered in military and executive activities; it provided for defense and exploration; it created new offices to meet particular needs; and it made nominations to vacant offices that already existed.

Although a comparable study has not been undertaken for the other *audiencias* of New Spain, the case of New Galicia is likely to be characteristic. The steady acquisition of executive power allowed the institution to become the supreme representatives of royal authority within their area of jurisdiction, as well as the principal check upon the arbitrary exercise of power by viceroys and other officials. As a court of law it clearly maintained unquestioned supremacy, saving only the right of appeal to the king or the Council of the Indies. But even in the area of executive affairs and administration, where in theory the *audiencia* should have submitted to the decisions of the viceroy, it still retained a large measure of discretionary power. If viceroys were weak or indecisive, the *audiencia* inevitably would dominate. More forceful and energetic viceroys tended to impose their authority; but even then, they often found themselves in conflict with acrimonious or punctilious judges.

As in the rest of Spanish America, therefore, the *audiencias* were of central importance to the government of New Spain. But they are also of outstanding interest and importance to historians, for they played a crucial role in the development of social and political institutions by giving the cities in which they resided an undisputed political, economic, cultural, and military preeminence, thereby creating a network of common interests and sentiments between them and the surrounding areas. Far from encouraging a narrow particularism, however, the *audiencias* always remained, first and foremost, the representatives of royal authority. As such, they were responsible for the promotion and dissemination of a form of political legitimacy that was directly dependent on the Spanish monarchy while managing to retain a deep sensitivity to local issues and interests. To a large extent, therefore, the function and development of the *audiencia* helps to explain the long and somewhat paradoxical survival of an effective Spanish presence in America, especially during the two centuries after the reign of Felipe II (reigned 1556–98) still commonly regarded as an era of relentless decline and growing weakness.

Select Bibliography

Haring, C. H., *The Spanish Empire in America.* New York: Oxford University Press, 1952.

Merriman, R. B., *The Rise of the Spanish Empire in the Old World and the New.* 4 vols., New York: Cooper Square, 1962.

Ots Capdequí, J. M., *El Estado Español en las Indias.* Mexico City: Fondo de Cultura Económica, 1986.

Parry, J. H., *The Spanish Theory of Empire in the Sixteenth Century.* Cambridge: Cambridge University Press, 1940.

_____, *The Audiencia of New Galicia in the Sixteenth Century. A Study in Spanish Colonial Government.* Cambridge: Cambridge University Press, 1948.

_____, *The Spanish Seaborne Empire.* London: Hutchinson, 1966.

Schäfer, E., *El Consejo Real y Supremo de las Indias.* 2 vols., Seville: M. Carmona, 1935–47.

Simpson, L. B., *The Encomienda in New Spain: The Beginning of Spanish Mexico.* Berkeley and Los Angeles: University of California Press, 1950.

Solórzano y Pereira, Juan de, *Política Indiana.* 2 vols., Mexico City: Secretaria de Programacion y Presupuesto, 1979.

Zavala, S., *Las instituciones jurídicas en la conquista de América.* 3rd edition, Mexico City: Porrua, 1935.

—FERNANDO CERVANTES

AUTOMOBILE INDUSTRY

The Mexican automobile industry has developed in four phases: (1) the assembly phase from the 1920s to the late 1950s, (2) import substitution industrialization (ISI) from 1962 to 1969, (3) the export promotion phase from 1969 to 1981, and (4) the automobile industry's ongoing integration into the emerging global economy. The latter three periods were marked by major shifts in economic policy, as the Mexican government issued decrees to regulate the automobile industry's participation in the overall development of the country. These decrees initially were the result of negotiation with the automobile assembly industry, which was mostly in the hands of multinational corporations. Following the first decree in 1962, however, they have also been the result of negotiation with a domestic auto parts industry. Thus, contemporary development of the Mexican auto industry has resulted from the interaction among the Mexican state, the management of the auto assembly industry, and the Mexican owners of auto parts companies.

Assembly Operation: 1920s to Late 1960s

The Mexican auto industry was established on the basis of assembly plants dating from the 1920s. Mexican subsidiaries of Ford and General Motors assembled and sold cars starting in 1926 and 1937, respectively. In 1938, Auto-Mex did the same under license from Chrysler Corporation. Other Mexican-owned firms also participated in the market under arrangements with other multinational companies. The main motivation behind these initiatives lay in the high tariffs that protected the Mexican market from direct imports.

Import substitution industrialization (ISI) regulated the economic development of Mexico. A fundamental characteristic of this strategy was protection of the internal market. If auto companies wanted to sell cars in Mexico, they had to find a way to assemble the cars domestically, as they could not import them from their foreign locations. This was the starting point of the phase of assembly operations. In the 1920s through the 1940s, internal demand was not very high, so cars assembled in Mexico were quite expensive. Also, plants were small and had little machinery. Most of the parts were brought from outside, and locally produced auto parts were rare. Only after the end of World War II did demand for vehicles rise as a result of the first achievements of ISI, which created a small managerial, bureaucratic, and professional middle class with a degree of buying power. Thus, the volume of assembly operations and the number of companies increased. The auto industry began to play an important role in manufacturing production owing to interactions with the steel, electrical, and other industries. By 1961, 12 firms produced cars, and approximately 60,000 vehicles a year were assembled in that period.

ISI Manufacturing: 1962–69

Domestic automobile manufacturing began in Mexico in 1962 as a result of the government's policy of supporting the vertical integration of the industry. This support was part of a new phase in the government's strategy of import substitution industrialization, which sought to broaden the range of local production to include durables and intermediate goods as well as promote domestic manufacturing of automobiles.

This ISI strategy was based on ideas that enjoyed considerable currency in the economic literature of the time. According to these theories, domestic manufacturing of automobiles and other durable goods would encourage the development of a broader infrastructure to supply the auto industry with power, transport, raw materials, and parts, and would help form a critical mass of technology, capital, and know-how. This broad strategy of economic development would benefit employment, local industry, and regional development, as well as contributing to the national balance of payments through foreign exchange savings. In retrospect, however, this shift in policy can be seen as a much narrower response to the dangerous inroads vehicle and parts imports were making into Mexico's balance of trade. Vehicles and parts accounted for 11 percent of Mexico's total imports. Something had to be done about this imbalance, and domestic manufacturing was seen as the answer.

In August 1962, following a series of negotiations with multinational corporations and domestic companies, the Mexican government issued a decree that, as of September 1, 1964, the level of local content in automobiles manufactured in Mexico had to be 60 percent of the direct costs of pro-

duction. In addition, the decree prohibited the import of assembled vehicles and restricted the use of foreign raw materials by subjecting them to import permits. The decree also established a quota system for each firm. Foreign car makers with manufacturing operations in Mexico would be forced to buy many of their parts from Mexican suppliers, forcing the development of a domestic parts industry. The 1962 decree also limited the possibilities of vertical integration by the foreign-owned auto assembly industry, opening new opportunities for Mexican capital to participate in the auto sector. This conciliation between the auto assembly and the auto parts industry was typical of the way the Mexican state was operating in relation to foreign investment.

The multinational corporations in charge of the auto assembly industry saw the 1962 decree as a threat to their position. They had been favorable to opening auto assembly operations in Mexico, but the actual manufacturing of parts in the country was an altogether different proposition, one implying new investment in a much smaller market than their home country's; economies of scale simply could not operate within this restricted market. Nonetheless the multinational corporations finally accepted the decree, planning for the installation of new auto assembly facilities and arranging for the creation of auto parts factories that could satisfy the demand they were going to develop. This process took some time: increases in production levels were not observed before 1965, when production was 87 percent higher than it had been in 1960. By 1969, production was nearly 200 percent higher that it had been in 1960, proving that the 1962 decree was achieving success. Mexico produced 54,742 cars in 1950 and 163,596 in 1969.

The other objective of the 1962 decree also met with qualified success. Employment levels in automobile production increased by 215 percent between 1960 and 1969. Investment levels, value of production, and value of wages and salaries also increased during that decade. The importance of automobile production rose substantially in the manufacturing sector.

This evolution did not occur without problems, however. The relatively small and highly fragmented market did not generate sufficient demand. Car production was modest by international standards, and cars were expensive. The excessive number of firms in the small domestic market forced many companies out of business. Only those companies that could tap the multinational corporations' capital, technology, and know-how could survive. The single exception to this was Auto-Mex, which lost its independence only in 1971. The auto parts industry was nationally owned by law, however, and remained Mexican.

Despite its successes, the 1962 decree failed to achieve its most important goals. Not only did multinational corporations become the sole owners of the auto assembly industry in Mexico, but the trade deficit in the automotive sector actually worsened. The automobile industry's imports exceeded its exports as a result of increases in the volume of production.

Export Promotion Manufacturing: 1969–81

As a result of the continuing difficulties with the trade balance, in 1969 the Mexican government issued a new decree shifting the automobile industry's central objective from import substitution to export promotion. The government believed that it was no longer possible to continue draining hard currency, and that the earnings from exports could be used to finance the expansion of the internal market. This shift was consistent with the broader development strategy of the time, which emphasized the export of manufactured products.

According to scholars Douglas Bennett and Kenneth Sharpe, the 1969 decree was enacted only after considerably debate within the Mexican government. Discussion centered on two different policy alternatives: the merger plan and the export plan. The merger plan sought to rationalize the market by reducing the number of firms and reversing the expansion of foreign ownership in the industry. A majority of Mexican-owned firms would be created and would control one-half of the auto market. The export plan, on the other hand, sought to improve the balance of payments by generating foreign exchange through exports that could help in the expansion of the internal market.

In the end the export plan won out, but only equivocally. The 1969 decree sought to expand the internal market, but exports were considered only as a way of solving the balance of trade in the automobile sector. Moreover, this new emphasis on automobile exports could not be implemented overnight. The export of finished vehicles began to be relatively significant only in 1973, when US$40.4 million worth of cars were sent outside Mexico, specially to the United States. The jump from 1972 to 1973 is particularly impressive: in that period exports surged from a mere 2,212 cars in 1972 to 20,141 cars in 1973. This jump was not followed by steady increases in volume, however. On the contrary, the figure reached in 1973 is higher than the average for the period between 1973 and 1983, when only 16,382 cars were exported a year. The proportion of finished vehicle exports in the total of all exports was over one-third between 1973 and 1974, but in later years it decreased to an average of 19.6 percent. Moreover, the trade balance in the automobile sector continued to be negative during the whole of the period 1972 to 1982. Only in 1983 was the balance positive. In some years the trade deficit of the automobile sector represented almost one-half of the total trade deficit of Mexico, making it imperative to change the rules according to which the sector was operating.

Multinational corporations were quite amenable to the 1969 decree, in marked contrast to their response to the 1962 decree. The international economic climate for multinational corporations had changed greatly. The decrease in the growth of sales in the United States and the rapid increase in competition among auto makers worldwide made U.S. auto manufacturers quite conscious of their need to strengthen their position outside the United States, and made European and Japanese manufacturers conscious of their need to strengthen

their positions within the United States. This struggle became far more dramatic when the 1973 oil crisis gave non-American auto makers, with their compact, fuel-efficient cars, a decided edge in the U.S. market. As competition among auto makers intensified in North America, multinational corporations tried to reduce production costs by moving manufacturing facilities to developing countries.

The 1969 decree was implemented at precisely the right time. The rules favoring exports from Mexico to the United States meant that U.S. auto makers, with their long-standing presence in Mexico, could gain a competitive edge against their Japanese and European challengers. Multinational corporations located in Mexico could maintain their position in Mexico while exporting to their home countries and elsewhere. It is important to underline that the automobile assembly industry continued to be subject to the 60 percent local content rule of the 1962 decree, and that it had to buy these components from the Mexican auto parts companies. The multinational corporations could not import components for the vehicles they would export. They had to strengthen their links with the national auto parts industry.

New arrangements within the structure of the Mexican automobile industry took place as a result of the 1969 decree. Denationalization, which had started in 1962, was consolidated with Chrysler's takeover of Auto-Mex in 1971; in 1977, Renault acquired equity in Diesel Nacional, a government-owned firm. The market share of majority foreign-owned companies increased from 51.2 percent in 1962 to 96.1 percent in 1984. Many local firms simply could not achieve the export requirements established in the 1969 decree. Local firms were limited to the domestic market, while multinational corporations could tap their contacts both within their home markets and abroad. In addition, multinational corporations could import parts from their home factories to fill out the 40 percent of components not bound by the local contest rule, thereby lowering their manufacturing costs.

As the balance of trade continued to deteriorate, the government intervened again in 1977. It issued a new decree requiring auto makers in Mexico to increase their exports if they wished to remain in the country. Moreover, 50 percent of parts of all cars made in Mexico had to be made by the auto maker, and the other half had to be produced by the domestic auto parts industry. The decree also mandated that auto parts companies had to have 60 percent Mexican capital in their equity. Exceptions were made only for Mexican-owned companies, who were experiencing difficulties opening export markets. No exceptions were made for the multinational corporations, and they were required to increase their local content. Indeed, the 1977 decree went well beyond previous regulations, mandating that local content was to be measured on the basis of the cost of the parts and not on the basis of the cost of production. The only concession made by the decree concerned prices, which were liberated to permit more competition among the companies.

One concrete result of the 1977 decree were plans made by the big five auto makers—Nissan, Volkswagen, General Motors, Ford, and Chrysler—to invest in new facilities, especially in engine factories. Nissan was the first, putting into operation its Toluca engine factory in 1978. Next came Volkswagen, which expanded its Puebla facility to produce 300,000 engines a year for export. In 1981 both General Motors and Chrysler built their Ramos Arizpe (in the state of Coahuila) factories, and General Motors also built an assembly plant at the same location. GM's capacity was 400,000 engines a year, while Chrysler's reached 270,000. Finally, in 1983 Ford began producing engines at its Chihuahua plant with a capacity of 400,000 units per year. As a result of these investments, Mexico reached a capacity of 1,370,000 engines a year in 1983, a considerable jump from the status of the industry only five years before.

Integration into the Global Economy: 1982–96

The gains made by the auto industry could do little to forestall a general crisis in the Mexican economy in 1982, characterized by a precipitous drop in world oil prices, two devaluations of the Mexican peso, and seemingly uncontrollable inflation. Until 1982 the Mexican government had tried to maintain the basic elements of the economic strategy it had pursued for the past 40 years, reasoning that short-term emergency measures were a sufficient response to economic crises. From February to August 1982, however, the Mexican government had to rethink its fundamental vision of the Mexican economy. When President Miguel de la Madrid took office in December 1982, his advisers dealt with the crisis in radical terms. For at least two years (1982–84) the government implemented recessionary measures, plunging Mexico into a serious depression.

Among the measures taken by the de la Madrid administration was a 1982 decree directed at the auto industry. The oil boom of 1979 to 1981 had expanded internal demand for cars and consequently the volume of imports necessary to build them; more than one-half of the total commercial trade deficit originated in the auto industry. The 1982 decree sought to weaken this trend by increasing the local content of vehicles assembled in Mexico. Car makers began to invest in auto parts, and they tried to locate parts manufacture near their assembly facilities. Many companies started new operations between 1984 and 1987.

In this respect the 1982 measures were a continuation of the 1977 decree, which had seen a similar response in the relationship between the auto parts and the auto assembly industries. Increasing local production (to 55 percent by 1986 and to 60 percent by 1987) was only a small part of the 1982 decree, however. The auto industry also had to rationalize its mode of operation. The 1982 decree demanded that the industry decrease the number of makes and models, standardizing production and increasing efficiency. The industry was to be streamlined to 3 makes and 7 models in 1984, 2 makes and 5 models in 1985, and 1 make and 5 models in 1986. Unlike the 1977 decree, the 1982 measures sought to increase savings of hard currency rather than increase earnings of hard currency through export. In controlling the production structure of the auto industry, the Mexican government sought self-sufficiency in foreign exchange and rationalization of supply.

The effort that started in 1978 with the initiation of production at the Nissan Toluca engine factory continued in the 1980s. In fact, Nissan built another engine factory at Aguascalientes in 1984, together with a casting factory at the same location. Renault then opened its Gómez Palacio engine factory with a capacity of 350,000 engines a year. In 1985 Chrysler started production at its Toluca assembly plant, and in 1986 Ford inaugurated its Hermosillo facility, where 140,000 cars were to be assembled entirely for the foreign market. It has been estimated that the auto industry grew at a rate of 14.5 percent a year between 1980 and 1985. Investments by Ford, General Motors, and Chrysler totaled more than US$1.2 billion in that period. This level of investment has permitted the industry to achieve a rank in the exporting industries of the country only second to PEMEX, the national oil company.

Conclusions

Since 1978 the Mexican automobile industry has undergone a number of profound transformations. First, the national auto parts industry has grown as a result of investments made by the auto assembly industry. Second, an export orientation has appeared that did not exist before 1978; if this export orientation had not been promoted successfully, Mexico today would be in a much weaker position internationally. Although export orientation did not produce all the expected results (the industry continued to show a negative trade balance through 1982), it provided an opportunity for the auto industry to build and diversify its productive base. Finally, the construction of new facilities in northern Mexico close to the U.S. border displaced the industry concentrated in central Mexico, promoting the government's policy of economic decentralization.

In the light of previous considerations, one notes several interesting findings. First, the decrees issued by the Mexican government from 1962 to 1983 consolidated a denationalized auto assembly industry centered on the five multinational corporations located in the country, Ford, General Motors, Chrysler, Volkswagen, and Nissan. The domination of the auto assembly industry by the multinational corporations tends to favor both exports to foreign markets through the multinational corporations' global networks and intra-corporation imports of parts. Exports by Mexican subsidiaries can undercut multinational corporations' home country operations, however. The fact that the Mexican auto industry is centered on multinational corporations makes it dependent on the global strategy of the parent multinational corporations.

Second, the great variety of makes and models had made the Mexican auto industry inefficient, owing to the inability to achieve economies of scale. Mexican cars are expensive and not competitive in international terms, and production lines have been short. Only Volkswagen and Nissan have been able to produce relatively high volumes of cars to be sold in the domestic market. The auto assembly industry often has not been able to acquire quality parts from local auto parts companies, making them incapable of exports. Only recently has this tendency been countered, and some auto parts companies have entered the international market.

Third, in spite of having issued relatively strict guidelines for the development of the auto industry, the Mexican state has not been able to control the operation of the auto sector or the decisions of the multinational corporations. Indeed, during the period 1969 to 1983, when the industry theoretically had to balance its trade, the imbalances actually deepened, making it very difficult to continue operating according to the established rules. The chronic deficit in the balance of payments weakened the government position in Mexico and, at the same time, did not favor the expansion of the local auto parts factories, which had to import some of its raw materials to fulfill the demands of the auto assembly industry.

Fourth, until very recently, the cost of labor in Mexican auto factories was higher than it was in other countries such as South Korea, where productivity was higher at lower salary levels. Only in recent contractual agreements have some multinational corporations, such as Ford, been able to radically revise salary levels, especially in the new factories that manufacture engines in the northern part of the country.

The logic of the multinational corporations' participation in the Mexican economy has been different in each of the four phases of the Mexican automobile industry. Initially the multinational corporations' activity was geared toward the internal domestic market. Multinational corporations tried to benefit from the protected character of the Mexican economy and the new strength of the status-seeking middle class. In the years following the 1973 oil crisis, however, American multinational corporations tried to preserve their U.S. market share by relocating manufacturing facilities to obtain lower costs. This trend dovetailed with the 1969 decree, which not actually implemented until 1973.

The future of the Mexican automobile industry is difficult to predict. The present structure of the automobile sector shows that exports are increasing rapidly. The auto parts companies, which remain in the hands of Mexicans, must adapt to the new conditions and try to satisfy the demand of the auto assembly industry even as they try to cultivate new markets outside Mexico. Despite important interventions by the Mexican state, the Mexican automobile industry ultimately has been dependent on the economic strategies of the multinational corporations, and today this is more true than ever. If the multinational corporations continue to favor investment in Mexico, the industry will continue to thrive. But if the multinational corporations evaluate their Mexican operations in a global context, the industry's future could be bleak indeed.

See also North American Free Trade Agreement (NAFTA)

Select Bibliography

Bennett, Douglas, and Kenneth Evan Sharpe, *Transnational Corporations Versus the State: The Political Economy of the Mexican Auto Industry.* Princeton, New Jersey: Princeton University Press, 1985.

Bennett, Mark, *Public Policy and Industrial Development: The Case of the Mexican Auto-Parts Industry.* Boulder, Colorado: Westview, 1986.

Jenkins, Rhys Owen, *Dependent Industrialization in Latin America: The Automotive Industry in Argentina, Chile, and Mexico.* New York: Praeger, 1977.

Lifschitz, Edgardo, *El complejo automotor en México y en América Latina.* Mexico City: Universidad Autónoma Metropolitana-Azcapotzalco, 1985.

Moreno Brid, Juan Carlos, *Mexico's Motor Vehicle Industry in the 1980s.* Geneva: International Labor Office, 1988.

Shaiken, Harley, *Automation and Global Production: Automobile Engine Production in Mexico, the United States and Canada.* La Jolla, California: Center for U.S.-Mexican Studies, 1987.

—Francisco Zapata

AUTOS

Auto is the generic name for a brief theatrical piece with allegorical characters and a moralizing purpose. The term is chiefly associated with the work of the great Spanish dramatist Pedro Calderón de la Barca, whose *autos sacramentales* are incomparably the most exquisite and sophisticated examples of the genre; but the tradition was emphatically popular and by no means a monopoly of educated circles. It made a very early appearance in New Spain, and its central elements can be detected in the first known sermons that were preached to the Indians, both lay and ecclesiastic, where the preachers sought to provide syntheses of Christian doctrine, emphasizing the theme of liberation from sin and portraying the Spaniards as the bearers of the light of Christ. A number of reports show that *autos* were being written and performed in Nahuatl as early as the 1530s. Chapter 15 of Fray Toribio de Benavente's (Motolinía's) *Historia de los Indios de la Nueva España,* for example, is devoted to the description of the feasts of Corpus Christi and St. John in 1538, and Easter in 1539, celebrated in Tlaxcala with performances of several *autos* in Nahuatl dealing with biblical themes such as Zecharias's vision, the Annunciation, the Visitation, and the birth of John the Baptist; or with allegorical themes such as the fall of Adam and Eve, and the fall of Jerusalem. The characters, the message, the dramatic conventions, and the plot are all unmistakably Spanish, and few scholars doubt that they were composed either by Fray Toribio himself or under his careful supervision. The same early Franciscan influence can be found in the large number of extant Nahuatl *autos,* with their rather puzzling disregard of the cult of the saints—which was quickly becoming of central importance to the formation of a Christian identity among Indian communities—and with their strong emphasis on individual morality, specific aspects of Christian doctrine, and biblical stories centering on Jesus and Mary.

Given that Spanish friars relied greatly on Indian help to produce Nahuatl texts, however, a strong case can equally be made in favor of a conscious indigenous participation in the composition of the *autos,* involving some degree of appropriation, reinterpretation, and even independent composition. There are numerous instances of characters in the *autos* taking on Nahua ranks and operating within Nahua social conventions. So too, there is evidence of a number of misspellings of Spanish loan words corresponding to common Nahua substitutions, of some doctrinal irregularities that the friars could not have committed, and even of complete manuscripts in indigenous handwriting, such as the brief *auto* for Holy Wednesday that was interleaved into an unknown Franciscan's book of sermons at the end of the sixteenth century (now at Princeton's Firestone Library).

All this points to the persistence of a tradition among indigenous communities that looked back to the type of Christianity that was preached by the early mendicant orders in New Spain, and which goes a long way toward explaining the otherwise paradoxical fact that most of the *autos* that are known to us are not originals, but copies made by Indians, sometimes as late as the nineteenth century. The genre is an enormously wealthy, and glaringly under-exploited, source for understanding the process of conversion and acculturation of indigenous communities in the sixteenth and seventeenth centuries.

Select Bibliography

Burkhart, L.M., *The Slippery Earth: Nahua-Christian Moral Dialogue in Sixteenth Century Mexico.* Tucson: University of Arizona Press, 1989.

Horcasitas, Fernando, *El Teatro Náhuatl.* Mexico City: UNAM, 1974.

Lockhart, James, *The Nahuas after the Conquest.* Stanford, California: Stanford University Press, 1992.

Ravicz, M.E., *Early Colonial Religious Drama in Mexico.* Washington, D.C.: Catholic University of America Press, 1970.

Trexler, R.C., "We Think They Act: Clerical Reading of Missionary Theatre in Sixteenth-Century New Spain." In *Understanding Popular Culture,* edited by Steven L. Kaplan. Berlin and New York: Mouton, 1984.

—FERNANDO CERVANTES

AVILA CAMACHO, MANUEL

1897–1955 • Soldier and President

Avila Camacho was born April 24, 1897, into a family of middle-class ranchers in Teziutlán, Puebla. His brothers, Maximino (1891–1945) and Rafael (1905–75), served as governors of the state. He attended school in his hometown and then at the National Preparatory School in Mexico City. In 1914 he joined Venustiano Carranza's faction in the Revolution as a second lieutenant, eventually rising to brigadier general (1929) and zone commander of Tabasco (1932–33). In the intervening years he served in a number of capacities including chief of staff of the state of Michoacán (1920), head of military operations in the Isthmus of Tehuantepec (1920), commander of the 38th Cavalry Regiment (1924), and zone commander in Colima (1929). He also fought against Yaqui Indians in Sonora (1920), the de la Huerta Rebellion (1924), the Cristero Rebellion (1926–29), and the Escobar Rebellion (1929).

Avila Camacho first entered the Secretariat of War and Navy in 1933 as official mayor under the watch of the secretary, Lázaro Cárdenas, whom Avila Camacho earlier had served under and befriended. Once Cárdenas assumed the presidency, Avila Camacho rose to subsecretary (1935) and then secretary (1937), remaining in the post until 1939, when he resigned to run, himself, for the top executive office.

Avila Camacho's chief rival for the presidential nomination of the Partido de la Revolución Mexicana (PRM) was General Francisco Múgica, the secretary of communications and public works. Many observers thought Cárdenas favored Múgica because of his more radical Revolutionary credentials. Nevertheless, in order to pacify the rising conservative backlash to his reform program, Cárdenas chose the moderate Avila Camacho.

In the election, Avila Camacho faced General Juan Andreu Almazán, zone commander in the state of Nuevo León and candidate of the conservative Partido Revolucionario de Unificación Nacional (PRUN). As the official candidate, Avila Camacho easily won in a vote marred by violence and fraud. Almazán threatened rebellion, but then reconsidered and went into exile. Avila Camacho assumed the presidency on December 1, 1940.

As a relatively unknown compromise choice for the presidency, Avila Camacho faced the difficult challenge of uniting a very divided country just as World War II appeared on the horizon to threaten the economy and exacerbate internal ideological cleavages. In the domestic sphere, conservative, Catholic, and free market–oriented groups, many of them belonging to the Callista (named after former president Plutarco Elías Calles) wing of the official party competed with the liberal (even socialist), anticlerical, state economy–oriented elements represented by Cardenistas (named after former president Lázaro Cárdenas).

Avila Camacho, following his cautious instincts and the need for stability, arbitrated between these two groups, generally favoring the former. Indeed, even before the election, he had used the term "soy creyente" (I am a believer), thereby revealing his Catholicism and indicating his policy of downplaying enforcement of the anticlerical provisions of the Revolutionary Constitution of 1917. The president also reduced land distribution to peasants, handing out only some 12 million acres during his term in office compared to Cárdenas' more than 49 million acres. In addition, Avila Camacho ended his predecessor's socialist education program, substituting for it an emphasis on basic literacy via private initiative. On the labor front, he replaced the Marxist head of the powerful Confederación de Trabajadores Mexicanos (CTM), Vicente Lombardo Toledano, with the conservative Fidel Velázquez. As a sop to organized workers, who suffered from sharply rising prices and the outlawing of strikes during the war years, Avila Camacho established a government-run health system, the Instituto Mexicano de Seguro Social (IMSS), in 1943.

Spurred by shortages of manufactured goods and the accumulation of capital from raw material exports to the United States during World War II, the Avila Camacho administration embarked on an industrialization program favoring business. This project shifted the socialist-oriented redistributive emphasis of the Cárdenas policies of the 1930s to one that focused on capitalistic production and growth. To this end, the administration created the Nacional Financiera, a government-owned bank designed to stimulate investment, as well as promoting tax incentives, tariff protection, and cheap labor. Newly favored industrialists formed the powerful Cámara Nacional de la Industria de Transformación. These steps marked the implementation of a policy of import substitution industrialization and set the country's economic policy for the next four decades.

The war years also witnessed Mexico under Avila Camacho significantly improve relations with the United States, despite the country's long-time distrust of its northern neighbor. Mexico broke diplomatic relations with Germany in August 1941 and for the remainder of the conflict cooperated closely with Washington. Mexico shut down fascist operations and German and Italian businesses within its territory, modernized its army with Lend-Lease funds, sent an air force squadron to fight in the Pacific theater, sold strategic war materials to the United States at guaranteed prices, and sent laborers (braceros) to work on farms and in factories north of the border. This cooperation with Washington greatly modified the nationalistic, even xenophobic, foreign policy of the Revolutionary years toward the United States and established a new one that, too, would last for decades.

In 1946, Miguel Alemán succeeded Avila Camacho as president. The former chief executive retired to private life, dedicating himself to running his ranch, La Soledad, located near Martínez de la Torre, Veracruz. He died October 13, 1955, in Mexico City.

Select Bibliography

Medina, Luis, *Historia de la Revolución Mexicana, periodo 1940–1952: Del cardenismo al avilacamachismo.* Mexico City: Colegio de México, 1978.

Meyer, Michael C., and William L. Sherman, *The Course of Mexico History.* 5th edition, New York: Oxford University Press, 1995.

—DAVID G. LAFRANCE

AVILA CAMACHO, MAXIMINO

1891–1945 • General and Politician

Avila Camacho was born in Teziutlán, Puebla, August 23, 1891, of middle-class ranchers. One brother, Manuel Avila Camacho (1897–1955), served as president of Mexico (1940–46), while another, Rafael Avila Camacho (1905–75), served as governor of the state (1951–57).

Avila Camacho attended primary school in Teziutlán and then studied at the National Military College in Mexico City. In 1914 he joined the Carrancista faction in the Revolution, eventually rising to the rank brigadier general in 1929 and divisionary general in 1940. During his military career he held the posts of head of the 51st Cavalry; chief of military operations in Aguascalientes, Oaxaca, Puebla, and Querétaro; and assistant and then acting inspector general of the army. He also fought against the Cristero Rebels in Colima and Jalisco. In addition, Avila Camacho worked at different times as a post office employee, Singer sewing machine salesman, cowboy, bullfighter, horse breeder, cattleman, and rancher. Upon his death in 1945, he was estimated to be worth at least two to three million pesos, owning properties and livestock in Acapulco, Mexico City, Puebla, Tehuacán, Teziutlán, and elsewhere.

Avila Camacho began his political career when in 1925 he headed the political police of the secretariat of government. Then, a decade later, when named zone commander of Puebla during his brother Manuel's term as sub-secretary of war, Maximino began establishing the power base that would catapult him into the governorship and beyond.

As chief executive of Puebla he stabilized the politically factious state and consolidated power in a ruling clique linked to the official party that would dominate Puebla into the 1970s. This group included brother and future governor Rafael; U.S. entrepreneur William O. Jenkins; labor leader, politician, and then president (1964–70), Gustavo Díaz Ordaz; businessmen Rómulo O'Farril and his son, Rómulo Jr.; newspaperman José García Valseca; and banker Manuel Espinosa Yglesias. Noted for his arrogance, ruthlessness, and conservative outlook, he used hired gunmen to eliminate opponents and repress and control dissident elements including workers, *campesinos* (peasants), teachers, students, and the press. At the same time he curried warm relations with the Catholic Church, opposed the implementation of socialistic educational programs, and promoted business and industry, to his own personal enrichment. President Lázaro Cárdenas, commonly portrayed as champion of the masses, tolerated Avila Camacho, indicating Cárdenas's greater concern for regime consolidation than socioeconomic justice.

Upon leaving the governorship in 1941, Avila Camacho entered the cabinet of his brother, Manuel, as secretary of communications and public works. He used the position not only for personal gain, but also to wield a great deal of political power at the national level, operating as the informal leader of the right wing of the official party. He aspired to follow Manuel as president, but the onus of charges of nepotism blocked his ambition. Nevertheless, Avila Camacho still tried to play kingmaker, adamantly opposing the nomination of Miguel Alemán, with whom he had a long-standing dispute from the time when the two served as governors, Alemán in Veracruz, which borders Puebla. In the midst of his campaign against Alemán, Avila Camacho suddenly fell ill while on a trip to Atlixco, Puebla, dying a few hours later in Puebla City on February 17, 1945. Speculation arose that Alemán had something to do with the death; nothing concrete was ever proved, and Alemán became the official candidate and then president in 1946.

Select Bibliography

Pansters, Wil, *Politics and Power in Puebla: The Political History of a Mexican State, 1937–1987.* Amsterdam: CEDLA, 1990.
Medin, Tzvi, *El sexenio alemanista: Ideología y praxis política de Miguel Alemán.* Mexico City: Ediciones Era, 1990.

—David G. LaFrance

AYUTLA, REVOLUTION OF

The Revolution of Ayutla is, in scholar Edmundo O'Gorman's words, a "paradox" for the historian. It has been hailed as the starting point of the Reforma, allegedly one of the most profound transformations in the nineteenth century, which supposedly finally broke with the "old régime" and ushered "modernity" into Mexico. Nevertheless, its origin, and what has given the movement its name, is the Plan of Ayutla, proclaimed on March 1, 1854, in a small town in the state of Guerrero, by an obscure colonel, Florencio Villarreal, whom the scholar Felipe Tena Ramírez describes as the typical praetorian with no convictions. The plan's vague content was far from innovative: it demanded the impeachment of the current government, in this case, Antonio López de Santa Anna's dictatorial regime, which had held power since April 1853; the convocation of a national congress, which would constitute the nation as a "popular, representative republic" (Article 5); the lowering of commercial tariffs (Article 6); and the protection of the army, as the "mainstay of order and social guarantees" (article 6). Thus, the plan placed itself in a long list of vaguely liberal military *pronunciamientos* that riddled the first half of the nineteenth century in Mexico. Also in typical fashion, the plan offered the leadership of the armed movement to men of privilege and political and military clout, in this case, Juan Álvarez and Nicolas Bravo, both of whom had fought in the War of Independence. Álvarez would soon become the movement's supreme commander, even though it would be recently retired colonel Ignacio Comonfort, Álvarez's protégé, who would direct most military operations outside Guerrero.

The plan would be reformed by Comonfort a few days later (March 11, 1854) in Acapulco. The term "departments," which implied a centralist system, replaced that of "states." The reformed plan stated that only "liberal"—instead of "republican"—institutions were convenient to the country, but added that the Republic had to be preserved from becoming a "ridiculous monarchy . . . contrary to our character and customs." These modifications reflected both Comonfort's legalistic convictions—the country was in fact divided into departments at the time—and his desire to attract the more moderate elements among both Liberals and Conservatives. His stated objective was to avoid imposing any single system of government on the "national will," which would be known only when expressed through the constituent congress. But by ruling out monarchy as a possibility, and thereby imposing limitations on the national will, Comonfort's reforms in fact reflected the real fear of many political men at the time that a monarchical system could be spawned legally, by a popularly elected congress.

Thus, the Plan of Ayutla, in both its original and reformed versions, was hardly an earth-shattering document.

It reflected, as noted by the scholar Edmundo O'Gorman, not a rebellion against a system, but against the person of the dictator. Although "liberal" and republican in broad terms, it did not in fact propose a "modern" state project: it aimed to protect the privileges of one of the state's constituent groups—the army—that challenged the authority of the embryonic nation-state, and it did not touch on the issue of church-state relations, which was to preoccupy subsequent reforms. Nevertheless, it sparked a series of nation-wide armed movements, which culminated with the fall of the dictatorial government. Santa Anna, who during the first half of the century had been hailed regularly by different political groups as the country's only possible savior, was never to return to power again. Adding to the paradox, the Ayutla Revolution has become a historiographical watershed because it seemingly inaugurated the Reforma, a period that traditional historiography has exalted as one of three "key" moments—with Independence and Revolution—in Mexico's national history. The official state rhetoric that aims to describe Mexican history as a shining, unbroken struggle between the unequivocally good, progressive Liberals and the unequivocally bad, reactionary Conservatives has enthroned Ayutla as a heroic, radically "liberal" movement, on par with the actions of José María Morelos, Miguel Hidalgo y Cotilla, Emiliano Zapata, and Venustiano Carranza, and the ideological wellspring for the political and socially activity of the post-Revolutionary Partido Revolucionario Institucional (PRI, or Institutional Revolutionary Party).

Even though seldom as exaggerated and blatantly adulatory as the preceding, such traditional presentations cloud our understanding of the very complex, multifaceted movement that was the Ayutla Revolution. Despite the vagueness of the principles under which the struggle against the dictatorship was fought, and despite the disunity of the movement itself, Ayutla does seem to usher in a new era in nineteenth-century Mexican politics. The pervasive presence of Santa Anna was permanently exorcised. Ayutla also brought to the forefront of public life a group of men who have been called a "generation of giants": military leaders such as Ignacio Comonfort, Santos Degollado, Santiago Vidaurri, Epitacio Huerta, and Manuel García Pueblita; and radical intellectuals such as Melchor Ocampo, Ponciano Arriaga, Guillermo Prieto, and Benito Juárez. Under the auspices of the government born of the Ayutla movement, Congress promulgated the 1857 Constitution, which would become, under the fire of the Reforma and Intervention Wars, not only the banner of the Liberal Party, but that of the nation. From 1867 to 1910, the 1857 Constitution—the "most liberal code on earth," according to Prieto—was to provide the practically unquestioned formal legal framework of Mexican political life.

What, then, was "the Ayutla Revolution"? If we were to be less romantic and more accurate, we would describe the events as the Ayutla rebellions. For while it is true that the arbitrary, spendthrift government of Santa Anna had managed to alienate the large majority of the political class, while high taxes—compounded by bad weather and crop failures—had ignited popular resentment against the dictator, the image of the nation rising as one against tyranny, its sights set on a definite goal, is exaggerated. By early 1854, the Santa Anna dictatorship, rejected outright by the more radical Liberals and especially by the logically federalist regional strongmen, also had disappointed many Conservatives and even some moderate Liberals—men such as Teodosio Lares and Antonio de Haro y Tamariz, and some of the writers for *El Siglo XIX,* who had hoped a strong, centralized government finally would be able to provide Mexico with a rational, efficient administrative machinery to ensure "regular order" in the state's actions. Initially, the Plan de Ayutla was probably just the localized, angry reaction of Juan Álvarez and his men to the unwanted military intrusion of Santa Anna, who had sent troops into Guerrero under the excuse of helping Álvarez against a possible attack by the French adventurer Rassouet de Boulbon. Nevertheless, the plan was seen as the first open challenge to the dictatorship, and we can say that the nation was perceptive to it: the movement spread to all of Guerrero and Michoacán, while similar movements were started in the northeast, by the young lawyer Juan José de la Garza in Tamaulipas and by Santiago Vidaurri in Nuevo León and Coahuila. In the words of observer and Comonfort apologist Anselmo de la Portilla, the plan "produced a magical effect" throughout the nation.

Nevertheless, it would take over a year for the movement to acquire national dimensions and a pretense of unity. The Ejército Libertador (Liberating Army) of the south was mainly made up of *pintos,* poor peasants from Guerrero, loyal to Álvarez. These men formed guerrilla bands that were successful in disrupting order and, eventually, destabilizing the regime, but were consistently beaten by Santa Anna's army (in the Battles of Coquillo and el Peregrino, for instance). They abandoned the revolution for three to four months in order to harvest their crops. Furthermore, this rag-tag army and the perceived radicalism of Juan Álvarez struck fear in the hearts of all but the most radical of political men. Manuel Doblado, governor of Guanajuato; Generals Leonardo Márquez and José López Uraga; and Antonio de Haro y Tamariz, Santa Anna's old minister of finance, all refused to accept the Plan de Ayutla, even though all opposed Santa Anna. Others, like Santiago Vidaurri, were not willing to submit to anyone's authority but their own.

With the fall of Santa Anna's government in August 1855, the divisions within the revolutionary forces became painfully obvious. As the dictatorship crumbled and Santa Anna fled the country, Haro y Tamariz raised the Conservative flag against Ayutla in San Luis Potosí, while in Piedra

Gorda and Monterrey, Doblado and Vidaurri fostered their own counterrevolutions. In Mexico City, Rómulo Díaz de la Vega, commander of the city's garrison, was astounded by the popular support shown for the Plan of Ayutla; a throng of people had gathered at the Alameda and had spent six hours signing a document demanding the city's adherence to the plan. In accordance with Article 1 of the plan, he formed a junta of departmental representatives in order to elect an interim president, who would in turn issue the convocation for a constituent congress. The junta, made up mostly of moderate Liberals such as Mariano Riva Palacio and Miguel Buenrostro, elected General Martín Carrera, thus angering Ayutla supporters who felt the presidency should go to Álvarez. Valentín Gómez Farías, president of the *ayuntamiento* (city council), resigned in protest. The situation was at an impasse: amid such disturbances, Carrera resigned. The nation would be without government between September 12 and October 4.

The issue of the presidency finally resolved thanks to the careful negotiations of Ignacio Comonfort. On September 16, 1855, Comonfort, Haro y Tamariz, and Doblado signed the Lagos Convention, recognizing Álvarez as the general in chief of the revolution. Vidaurri accepted the situation but refused to sign and did not officially recognize the Álvarez government until early November. Álvarez became president, elected by the Cuernavaca Convention, whose members he named himself, on October 4. His cabinet was to include the biggest names among the radical Liberals: Ocampo as minister of foreign relations; Juárez as minister of justice, Prieto as minister of finance; Degollado as minister of public works; Arriaga as minister of the interior. Comonfort was named minister of war. The new, "legitimate" government notwithstanding, the country was hardly at peace. Disagreements within the cabinet made it impossible for it to issue a program of government. After Arriaga's resignation, no on wanted to accept the post of minister of the interior. In the Sierra Gorda, Tomás Mejía and José López Uraga headed a rebellion that aimed at protecting religion and property, and destroying Álvarez's "rude despotism." After two months of ingovernability, Álvarez—well into his sixties and this point—decided to retire, naming Comonfort substitute president. Álvarez's decree would be ratified by Congress in February 1865. The real engineer of the Ayutla triumph was finally sitting in the presidential chair.

What, then, can one conclude about the historical significance of the Ayutla movements? As we have mentioned, they provided the arena into which came forth a new generation of public men, whose influence on the second half of the Mexican nineteenth century would be decisive. It set the stage for the reforms of the 1857 Constitution. But we consider that the nature of the movement itself is perhaps as meaningful as it accomplishments: the "triumph" of Ayutla was possible only because the movement's principles were watered down; because regional leaders such as Doblado and Vidaurri were cajoled into cooperating; and because moderates from both political tendencies were frightened by the presence of the masses (whose involvement in the Ayutla movements was felt acutely, at least in Mexico City) and by the more extreme political possibilities of monarchy on the one side and demagoguery on the other. Ayutla paints a vivid picture of Mexico's "state-building" process in the middle of the nineteenth century, highlighting the obstacles to the birth of a modern nation-state: the nonexistence of a consensual model of government, the tensions between geographic center and periphery and the autonomy of the different regions, and the dilemma between the political class's wariness of the "people" at its avowed republicanism and respect for the "national will." These were issues that would not be resolved until the advent of the Restored Republic, or even the rule of dictator Porfirio Díaz. More than the harbinger of modernity, the Revolution of Ayutla is a showcase of the heterogeneous ideological and political elements that would have to be dealt with before modern Mexico could be consolidated.

Select Bibliography

de la Portilla, Anselmo, *Historia de la revolución de México contra la dictadura del General Santa Anna: 1853–1855.* Facsimile of 1856 Mexican edition, Mexico City: Biblioteca de México, Fundación Miguel Alemán, 1993.

García, Genaro, *El General Paredes y Arrillaga.* 2nd edition, Mexico City: Porrúa, 1974.

O'Gorman, Edmundo, "Antecedentes y sentido de la revolución de Ayutla." In *Plan de Ayutla. Conmemoración de su primer centenario.* Mexico City: UNAM, 1954.

Juárez, José Roberto, "La lucha por el poder a la caída de Santa Anna." *Historia Mexicana* 10:1 (1960).

—ERIKA PANI

AZCÁRATE Y LEZAMA, JUAN FRANCISCO DE

1767–1851 • Jurist

Juan Francisco de Azcárate y Lezama was a distinguished lawyer who also made an outstanding contribution to Mexican political life. He is considered one of the forerunners of Mexican Independence. He was born on July 11, 1767, in Mexico City. He studied Latin, philosophy, and law in the Colegio de San Ildefonso, one of the viceroyalty's most important centers of learning, and graduated in jurisprudence. He went on to study at the Colegio de Santa María de Todos los Santos and in 1790 was received into the legal profession at the Real Audiencia de México (High Court). As well as practicing law, he taught canon law at the University of Mexico. He was a member of the Academy of Jurisprudence, becoming its vice president, and of the Royal College of Advocates. From 1803 he sat in the Ayuntamiento of Mexico City (City Council), and in 1804 he was made its official receiver.

In the Ayuntamiento, his expert knowledge of Spanish law and his faith in the cause of autonomy gave him a vital role during the imperial crisis of 1808. The crisis was caused by Napoléon Bonaparte's invasion of Spain and King Carlos IV's abdication of the Crown of Spain and the Indies. The problems posed by the absence of a legitimate monarch, the basis of the political system in the colonies, needed an immediate response. This provided New Spaniards (Mexicans) with an unprecedented opportunity to criticize the way they were governed.

At the time the Ayuntamiento consisted of a majority of criollos (Spaniards born and brought up in Mexico), who wanted greater say in decision making. They decided to support autonomy and, by extension, equal rights with Spain. Azcárate composed a document, which was presented to Viceroy José de Iturrigaray on July 19, 1808, in which the Ayuntamiento in Mexico City, being the capital of New Spain and thereby representing it (using valid but lapsed laws), declared it would not recognize any authority that did not stem directly from the legitimacy of the throne. It therefore proposed that the viceroy and other figures of authority continue in their posts after renewing their oath. The Ayuntamiento also proposed that a governing junta meet while other towns and cities in New Spain, and the church and lay organizations, were consulted. This junta would defend New Spain from the French threat, and more important, fill the vacuum that existed between the authorities in New Spain and the sovereign power now that there was no monarch. These proposals made the Ayuntamiento the mouthpiece for those sectors of criollo society whose interests were not tightly linked with the mother country.

If the measures that the Ayuntamiento proposed were accepted, that body would constitute a legitimate, representative, and autonomous government. The Audiencia (the Spanish Crown's judicial/executive council) therefore rejected the Ayuntamiento's claim to speak for the whole of New Spain and insisted there be no change in the colony's government. The Audiencia opposed the creation of a junta that would alter the existing balance of power, a stance that was upheld by those sectors, nearly of them Spanish, whose interests were closely linked with the mother country and whose positions of privilege might suffer if any change took place.

Azcárate took an active part in the meetings called by the viceroy during August and the beginning of September to discuss the possibility of forming a junta. He clearly and forcefully argued the case for autonomy and voted against recognizing directives from Spain. He was imprisoned with Viceroy José de Iturrigaray and the other main criollo leaders during the coup carried out by the Spanish trader Gabriel de Yermo, with the support of the Audiencia, on September 15, 1808. The coup was successful in the short term. The peninsular Spaniards (those born in Europe) succeeded in maintaining the status quo, and with it their positions of privilege, when they cut off the legal routes for criollo demands. However, it caused problems in the long run by raising serious and well-founded doubts among the criollos about the legitimacy of subsequent governments. It also radicalized the position of the Ayuntamiento and its supporters, on the one hand, and the Audiencia and its supporters, on the other.

The coup also made both autonomists and generically disgruntled elements realize the risks they were running by acting openly, and that they could achieve their objectives by resorting to force, a route the peninsular Spaniards had already gone down with considerable success. Miguel Hidalgo's insurrection of 1810 took place on the night of September 15, two years to the day after Gabriel de Yermo's coup. Hidalgo's insurrection marked the open and declared break with the colonial regime by a group of urban criollos who, by enlisting the support of the poorer sectors of the population, turned the autonomist movement into revolution. Although the 1808 coup had succeeded in preventing the creation of a junta, autonomists had not abandoned their ideas; establishing a governing body remained one of their goals. When Hidalgo's insurrection broke out, Azcárate wrote a paper condemning it, a stance he shared with many autonomists and opposition elements because of the violence of the insurgent movement in its early stages.

Freed in 1811, Azcárate took his seat on the Ayuntamiento again in 1814. His autonomist views found a home in the Independence movement that coalesced around Agustín de Iturbide in 1821, and he became a member of the Junta Provisional Gubernativa (provisional governing body) of New Spain during its transition to an independent nation. He held several diplomatic posts in Iturbide's government, among them one dealing with borders and pacification programs of the Comanche Indians, and establishing the border with the United States. He also was appointed minister plenipotentiary to Great Britain, a post he did not assume before the collapse of Iturbide's empire. In 1827, he was a member of the Public Education Board, and in 1828 he was appointed legal adviser to the War and Navy Tribunal. He died in Mexico City on December 31, 1851.

Among the several books Azcárate wrote were *Prospecto para las ordenanzas del hospicio de pobres* (Prospectus Governing Rules for the Poorhouse; 1806) and *Proyecto de reforma de estatutos de la Real Academia de Jurisprudencia teórico-práctica* (Prospectus for the Theoretical-Practical Reform of Statues of the Royal Academy of Jurisprudence; 1812). He left others in manuscript form: *Ensayo panegírico e histórico en elogio de los principales sujetos, así naturales como eurpoeso, que han sobresalido en el reino* (Panegyric and Historical Essay on the Primary Materials Found in the Kingdom, both Natural and Metallurgic). He also wrote poetry and a work, now lost, entitled *Breves apuntamientos para la historia de la literatura de Nueva España* (Short Notes on the Literary History of New Spain).

Select Bibliography

Alamán, Lucas, *Historia de Méjico desde los primeros movimientos que prepararon su independencia en el año de 1808 hasta la época independiente*. 2nd edition, 5 vols., Mexico City: Jus, 1968.

Guedea, Virginia, "El golpe de estado de 1808." *Universidad de México revista de la Universidad Nacional Autónoma de México* 488 (September 1991).

Lafuente Ferrari, Enrique, *El virrey Iturrigaray y los orígenes de la independencia de México*. Madrid: Consejo Superior de Investigaciones Científicas, Instituto Gonzalo Fernández de Oviedo, 1940.

Mier, Servando Teresa de, *Historia de la revolución de Nueva España, antiguamente Anáhuac, o verdadero origen y causas de ella con relación de sus procesos hasta el presente año de 1813*. Paris: Publications de la Sorbonne, 1990.

Miquel y Vergés, José María, *Diccionario de insurgentes*. Mexico City: Porrúa, 1969.

Miranda, José, *Las ideas y las instituciones políticas mexicanas. Primera parte 1521–1820*. 2nd edition, Mexico City: Instituto de Investigaciones Jurídicas UNAM, 1978.

Villoro, Luis, *El proceso ideológico de la revolución de independencia*. 3rd edition, Mexico City: Coordinación de Humanidades UNAM, 1981.

—Virginia Guedea

AZTECS

See Mesoamerica: Mexica

AZUELA, MARIANO

1873–1952 • Physician, Soldier, and Writer

Mariano Azuela's name is inseparable from what has become known as the novel of the Mexican Revolution, the narrative trend largely responsible for modernizing national literature in the first half of the twentieth century. He wrote over twenty novels, dozens of short stories and sketches, and several plays and biographies, covering a wide spectrum of topics on Mexican society and history.

Born to a petty bourgeois family in the state of Jalisco, Azuela studied medicine in the city of Guadalajara and returned to establish a practice in his native Lagos de Moreno in 1900. While practicing medicine, Azuela's literary inclinations, evident since his early school years, led him to join a local group of bohemian literati, among them Francisco González León, José Becerra, Antonio Moreno y Oviedo, and Bernardo Reina. Some of Azuela's writings appeared in the group's collected volumes of *Ocios literarios* (1906, 1908).

A keen observer of Mexico's social life, Azuela followed the steps of José Joaquín Fernández de Lizardi, Luis G. Inclán, and José T. Cuéllar, recorders of popular life in the *costumbrista* tradition, and of the novelist *par excellence* of turn-of-the-century small town life, Rafael Delgado. His literary models, however, were the French and Spanish masters of nineteenth-century romanticism and realism, albeit a *modernista* quality is at times also perceptible in his prose. His positivist medical education made him receptive to the influence of Emilé Zola and naturalism, and the penchant to portray characters in terms of physiological and moral decay.

Azuela's prolific literary production underwent several phases. His early novels, of which *Mala yerba* is perhaps the most accomplished, revealed a socially concerned writer that used realistic techniques to portray social types. His most celebrated works were written during the Revolutionary period, when he took as his subjects the politics of self-interest during the war and the popular upheaval itself. *Andrés Perez, maderista* (1912) is a diatribe against political opportunism in the early phase of the Revolution. In *Los caciques* (written in 1914 and published three years later), Azuela denounces wealthy caciques' (local strongmen's) abuses and attacks on middle-class merchants and intellectuals, which ultimately lead to the Revolutionary uprising. Both novels can be seen as research for the author's most serious undertaking: the war itself. Determined to experience and record the everyday life of "genuine Revolutionaries," Azuela joined a faction of the Villista army in late 1914 and stayed with them for several months. Based on this military venture, a year later he published *Los de abajo,* a novel he began writing on the campaign trail and hastily finished in the border town of El Paso, Texas, after the devastating defeats in the Bajío region of north-central Mexico forced the Villista army to flee north.

An amnesty in 1917 allowed the novelist to move to Mexico City, where he would live the rest of his life, and open a consultant office. Two years later, he published three novels about the revolution: *Las moscas,* a series of sketches that canvasses, in a parodic way, social types during the Revolution; *Domitilo quiere ser diputado,* a political satire against unprincipled politicians and government corruption during the Revolution; and *Las tribulaciones de una familia decente,* a novel about the social dislocation of a provincial middle-class family.

By the early 1920s Mariano Azuela had published eight novels and several short stories and sketches, but he was still virtually unknown. Despaired by his literary anonymity, he turned to the avant-garde narrative trend of the day in hope of gaining critical and readership acceptance. Three novels would come out of this experimental phase: *La malhora* (1923), *El desquite* (1925), and *La luciérnaga* (1927). The latter, one of his most accomplished novels, combines interior monologue and an omniscient narrator to produce a vivid and gruesome description of slum life in Mexico City, a theme that would reappear in *Nueva burguesía* (1941).

It was not his experimental novels, ironically, but those of the previous period, that caught the eye of the critics in the mid-1920s. A debate on the existence or non-existence of a Revolutionary literature lead to the "discovery" of *Los de abajo* by Mexico City's cultural elite. The novel recounts the deeds of the small-time regional *"cabecilla"* Demetrio Macias, a "pure blooded" Indian, and his men who join the Villista army and bravely participate in the crucial battle of Zacatecas, in which the federal army was defeated. Unrestrained and intoxicated by their unopposed military power, the troop falls into a state of primitivism in which plunder, earthly pleasures, and abuse against the civilian population reign. When they finally return to their home region amid dwindling support from their own people, they are surprised and killed in an ambush. Although Azuela claims peasants were the true Revolutionaries, he implies that their lack of clear political objectives and overwhelming ignorance prevented them from being able to bring to a satisfactory end the armed conflict.

Azuela's formal accomplishments in this novel were considerable. Through an innovative combination of direct style, spatial and story shifts, fast tempo, vigorous descriptions, and brilliant recreation of popular speech, he was able to capture the popular, epic dimension of the Revolution. The novelist, however, never relinquished the positivistic belief that social unrest was the result of moral deviation. Ultimately, he could only frame a peasant revolution that went far beyond the liberal principles he stood for (i.e., the inviolability of private property) in terms of the moral degeneration of the masses. This vision notwithstanding, from this point on he was labeled the "true" purveyor of Mexico's Revolutionary spirit, and his vision of peasant defeat provided the master narrative for interpreting popular rebellion in Mexico's literary discourse.

Selected Bibliography

Blanco, José Joaquín, "Lecturas de *Los de abajo*," in *La paja en el ojo*. Puebla: Universidad de Puebla, 1980.

Díaz Arciniega, Víctor, "Mariano Azuela y *Los de abajo:* Entre ser y parecer." *Investigación Humanística (UAM)* 3 (Fall 1987).

Leal, Luis, *Mariano Azuela.* New York: Twayne, 1971.

Rama, Angel, "Mariano Azuela: Ambición y frustración de las clases medias." In *Literatura y clase social.* Mexico City: Folios, 1983.

Robe, Stanley, *Azuela and the Mexican Underdogs.* Berkeley: University of California Press, 1979.

Ruffinelli, Jorge, *Literatura e ideología. El primer Mariano Azuela (1896–1918).* Mexico City: Premiá, 1975.

_____, editor, *Los de abajo,* by Mariano Azuela. Madrid: Archivos, 1988.

—MAX PARRA

B

BALBUENA, BERNARDO DE

1562–1627 • Writer

The poet and man of letters Bernardo de Balbuena (sometimes spelled Valbuena) was born in Valdepeñas, Spain, on the November 20, 1562, and was brought to Nueva Galicia (the province formed by the present states of Jalisco and Nayarit) at a very early age. In 1585 he went to Mexico City to study theology at the university, where he took part in several poetic contests, having won several prizes. In 1590, ordained as a priest, he was sent to Guadalajara, and from there to San Pedro Lagunillas in Nayarit. Wishing to participate in the life of a more intellectual community, he went back to Mexico City in 1602, and there he published in 1604 his best known poem, *La grandeza mexicana*. Two years later he went to Spain to study for a doctorate in theology, which he received from the University of Sigüenza in 1607. He remained in Spain until the following year, when he was appointed abbot of Jamaica, a position he held from 1610 to 1622. In 1619 he had been named Bishop of Puerto Rico, but he did not go there until 1623. Two years later, Dutch pirates burned the city of San Juan and destroyed his library. Balbuena died in that city two years later, on October 11.

Besides *La grandeza mexicana*—an epistolary poem in hendecasyllabic tercets written with the purpose of telling one doña Isabel de Tovar y Guzmán (who lived in Culiacán) about the greatness of the capital—he published, in 1608, in the style of the popular *Arcadia* by Jacopo Sannazaro, a pastoral novel in verse and prose entitled *Siglo de oro en las selvas de Erífile.* It was not until 1624 that his next important poem appeared, the long epic (40,000 verses in hendecasyllabic octaves), *El Bernardo o victoria de Roncesvalles,* in which he glorified the deeds of the medieval Spanish hero Bernardo del Carpio.

Balbuena can be considered as a poet of transition between the Renaissance and the Baroque. In his principal works he uses Renaissance subjects, motifs, and themes, although Baroque images are frequent. The novel *Siglo de oro* and the epic *El Bernardo* belong to the literature of the Renaissance. In the first, a collection of twelve bucolic poems, the mixture of prose and verse as well as the Renaissance forms (*églogas,* sonnets, dialogues) predominate. The themes are those typical of the sixteenth century: the Golden Age, artificial idylls among shepherds, the intervention of gods and goddesses in the affairs of humans, etc. Yet, a few tercets appear, a stanza form seldom used by Renaissance poets.

For his epic poem, *El Bernardo,* Balbuena selected a Spanish medieval subject, the epic deeds of Bernardo del Carpio. However, he transcends the epic mode. In the poem's 24 books there are geographical descriptions, legends, acts of magic, historical references, allegorical fables, and marvelous adventures. In order to integrate the great variety of materials, he had to create a fictitious character, Wizard Malgesí, who, among other fantastic deeds, travels through the air over the American continent, stopping over the capital of New Spain to describe its greatness. In the following self-conscious verses he describes the volcano Xola:

> El gran volcán Xola, monstruo horrible
> del mundo, y sus asombros el más vivo,
> que ahora con su roja luz visible
> de clara antorcha sirve a lo que escribo.
> (The great Xola volcano, horrible monster
> of the world, with its bright wonders
> now with its visible red light
> serves as a clear torch for my writing.)

Fantastic descriptions abound in the *El Bernardo,* the most spectacular being those of the fairies Morgana (book 1) and Galiana (book 5). In spite of this lack of unity (a Baroque characteristic), the poem is of interest because of its vivid descriptions and the variety of imaginative adventures that it contains.

El Bernardo has not attained the popularity of *La grandeza mexicana,* Balbuena's most inspired composition. In this descriptive poem in tercets the author glosses an initial octave in which a synthesis of the contents of the total poem is provided.

> De la famosa México el asiento,
> origen y grandeza de edificios,
> caballos, calles, trato, cumplimiento,
> letras, virtudes, variedad de oficios,
> regalos, ocasiones de contento,
> primavera inmortal y sus indicios,
> gobierno islustre, religión, estado,
> todo en este discurso está cifrado.
> (Of famous Mexico the seat,
> Origin and greatness of its buildings,
> Horses, streets, manners, courtesy,
> Letters, virtues, variety of occupations,
> Gifts, moments of merriment,
> Immortal spring and its designs,
> Illustrious government, religion, state,
> Everything in this discourse is summarized.)

Since the poem is just a description of the city as it was in 1604, all historical and archaeological information about Mexico is omitted. Balbuena describes what he sees, presenting everything idealized and using a hyperbolic style. For *La grandeza mexicana,* as well as the rest of his poetry, Balbuena is remembered as a poet of superior imagination and great descriptive ability and fluency.

Select Bibliography

Rojas Garcidueñas, José, *Bernardo de Balbuena, la vida y la obra.* Mexico City: Instituto de Investigaciones Estéticas, 1958.

Van Horne, John, *Bernardo de Balbuena, biografía y crítica.* Guadalajara: Librería Font, 1940.

—Luis Leal

BANDITRY

Throughout the history of Mexico, the epithet or complement "bandit" has been applied to a variety of individuals, groups, and movements. In the eyes of merchants, hacienda owners, rancheros (small farmers), mine owners, soldiers and police officials, bureaucrats from distant capitals, foreign investors, travelers, muleteers, train engineers, and anyone who opposed robberies and violence by groups of rural *campesinos* (peasants), those who committed crimes against constituted authorities and broke the law by stealing were common criminals. On the other side, those individuals with special grievances against abusive land owners, tax collectors, resource developers, and others who sought to challenge or change traditional situations perceived banditry in quite different terms. In their view, people who took up arms were avengers who addressed wrongs, fighters for justice, and heroic protectors of community against outside interference that they considered illegal according to their own interpretation of traditional laws and practices. Of course, it is clear that some Mexican bandits possessed no social consciousness whatsoever and engaged in banditry as robbers interested solely in profit. From the sixteenth century and probably even before the Spanish Conquest, brigands lurked at mountain passes, lay in wait along empty roads for weary travelers, or formed gangs to prey upon the livestock and resources of peaceful communities.

Whether they were outright criminals, Robin Hood–like figures called social bandits, or complex figures spurred by a mix of social, political, and economic motives, Mexican bandits are extraordinary both for their fame and their range of activities. Mexico was a rugged country divided by mountain ranges, impenetrable forests, deep *barrancas* (canyons), and deserts; the distances between settled regions were often great. Even today, small bands of brigands, rebels, or guerrillas—depending upon the point of view of the observer—can simply disappear into mountainous terrain of many Mexican states. Sometimes they avoid detection for lengthy periods even with the use of modern techniques of detection and rapid responses by heavily armed helicopter-borne police or military forces. In the past, slower communications, weak police forces, and strong identification by the people with province, region, and district prevented central government authorities from exerting full control. The diverse population included traditional indigenous agricultural communities, mixed mestizo villages and towns, and larger urban centers with their elites and different social classes. The constant competition for land, water, and other resources and the ongoing struggle to protect traditional property, rights, and privileges set the scene for attacks by local people against outside interlopers. Gangs of men and sometimes women robbed livestock, attacked isolated buildings, intercepted commerce, murdered hacienda managers, and appeared to act like insurgents almost as much as bandits. During major crises provoked by uprisings, revolutions, and even invasions, these fighters for popular local or district causes sometimes attached their own struggles to broader conflicts.

The breadth of typologies and loose usage of terms such as *bandolero* make banditry a confusing as well as a compelling topic. Well before the twentieth century, Mexican writers grappled with different sorts of brigandage and recognized that some notorious bandits enjoyed remarkable popularity in their home regions. In recent decades, the study of banditry has become popularized by the provocative ideas of Eric Hobsbawm on the nature of the social bandit. Hobsbawm pointed out that bandits regarded as criminal outlaws by the state and other authorities often appeared to others as local or regional heroes, champions, and sometimes liberators. Among the factors Hobsbawm noted as key for the rise of banditry were inaccessibility of a region, the existence of an oppressed peasant class, and periodic famine. He also pointed to occasions when bandits joined peasant armies as soldiers of revolution. Although Hobsbawm did not focus upon Mexico, he described the movement of Francisco "Pancho" Villa during the Mexican Revolution as typically bandit-based and that of Emiliano Zapata as "unbandit-like agrarian agitation." Hobsbawm repeated the well-known story about Villa's outlaw origins:

Villa entered the struggle by avenging the honor of his sister who had been raped, then continued his involvement as he distributed captured loot to the poor, and finally culminated his Revolutionary career as a general.

Subsequently, other historians have viewed Mexico as one of the most promising sites for additional research on banditry. Rootless vagabonds and idle elements appeared in the population as early as the sixteenth century following the Spanish Conquest; brigands sometimes disturbed the colonial calm of the seventeenth century; and during the epoch of the eighteenth-century Bourbon Reforms, outright bandits preyed upon the narrow trails that passed as roads, raided hacienda livestock, and engaged in robberies. Sometimes they encroached into cities such as Guadalajara, Guanajuato, Zacatecas, and San Miguel. During the Wars of Independence, revolution and the fragmentation of New Spain produced a complex war of insurgency and counterinsurgency, with guerrilla bands fighting against soldiers of the *divisiones volantes* (flying divisions). The era led to the militarization of Mexican society and was a seed ground for banditry. Following Independence and until the third quarter the nineteenth century, wars, revolutions, and foreign invasions often permitted centrifugal forces to hold the upper hand. When General Porfirio Díaz grabbed control of the country in 1876, former bandits often became the policemen of the Rurales, a colorful force that developed its own mystique and characteristic showy uniform that was similar to the outfits worn by infamous brigands. In their new guise, the Rurales kept alive many other characteristics of their violent past.

During the Mexican Revolution, the nation once again fragmented to permit anarchic elements and local caciques (bosses) to regain their autonomy. In his authoritative two-volume study, Alan Knight examined the different sorts of banditry and identified social bandits who combined criminal, social, and political elements. After some historians had criticized and downgraded Hobsbawm's ideas, Knight found that the general theoretical precepts actually fit Mexico quite well. After 1910, ubiquitous bandits assaulted haciendas, factories, trains, mines, smelters, and towns. From north to south, upland to lowland, Mexico was "infested" by bandits who preyed upon landlords, shippers, foreigners, and others like primitive parasites that lived off but did not kill their hosts. In a complex landscape populated by multitudes of bandits, Pancho Villa was simply the most famous. The Revolution opened new possibilities for former brigands who could become powerful local caciques or even regional or national caudillos (strongmen). In this guise, some former bandits survived their years of combat into the 1920s and 1930s. The Revolutionary bandits of different variations left behind a variety of archetypes for their successors. In their struggle for land and rights, rural people sometimes returned to violence and to brigandage. Their opponents in government circles, urban centers, and industry hurled the old epithet of criminal bandit against those who occupied lands, poached logs, or otherwise resisted progress as defined by outside forces.

The Colonial Era

In many respects, Mexican banditry must be placed into the context of a long period beginning in the eighteenth century and including the Wars of Independence, the chaotic nineteenth century, and the Mexican Revolution. During the 1780s, banditry emerged in Nueva Galicia following a period of sustained famine and epidemics. Near Guadalajara, gangs of brigands infested surrounding towns and villages, sometimes encroaching upon the city to rob, assault, and to commit murder. In 1789, some of these gangs became so brazen that they pillaged the offices of the royal tobacco monopoly, the Colegio de San Diego, and the homes of some members of the *audiencia* (high court). The same year, a gang led by a well-known criminal, José Madera, assaulted the Acordada Jail at Puebla in a bid to free a prisoner. Shocked by the audacity of the bandits, Viceroy Juan Vicente de Güemes Pacheco y Padilla, dispatched a dragoon regiment and some infantry companies to restore order.

Notwithstanding police and militia activity backed by harsh sentences imposed by Acordada officers, the increase in rural banditry and attacks by highwaymen became notable. In 1795, bandit gangs operated in the Intendancies of Guadalajara, Valladolid (Michoacán), Guanajuato, and Puebla. One band at Huautla, Puebla, stole 1,700 pesos from a government office. During an attack against a merchant mule train near the mining town of Zimapán, a bandit gang grabbed 11,000 pesos in mixed goods. Viceroy Miguel de la Grúa Talamanca y Branciforte feared that the pattern he observed of increased bandit activities might be a prelude to general sedition based upon an unknown revolutionary ideology. While Acordada officials discounted the existence of organized communications between the bandits, they became concerned when army deserters turned up among more than 200 brigands arrested in the Intendancies of Guadalajara and Valladolid. At Guanajuato, night patrols by mobilized militia picket forces dispersed gangs that coalesced for criminal purposes and tracked them down in the nearby mountains. Everywhere, muleteers and agricultural workers carried weapons such as machetes or lances and related stories about numerous assaults and robberies. In 1799, during an invasion of the home of Doña Rosalia Marín del Valle, a prominent Guadalajara resident, a gang with painted faces brutally stabbed to death a servant. These brigands tied up the other servants, looted furniture, and left behind an atmosphere of fear among the elite families of the city. In response, Viceroy Miguel José de Azanza demanded exemplary punishments including public executions and the exhibition of cadavers as "a healthful example" for any other would-be bandits.

Prior to 1810, the level of bandit activity reflected economic and social factors in the regions. Loosely organized and fluid in membership, the small criminal gangs attracted unemployed miners, muleteers, hacienda workers, and itinerant day workers. At Querétaro for example, over 3,000 transient laborers worked at the tobacco factory and in the *obrajes* (textile manufactories) of the city. There were so many idle vagabonds present that in 1809 the army stationed four teams of recruiters in the city to conscript jailed delinquents, gamblers, and unemployed petty criminals. Throughout 1809 and 1810 a subsistence crisis occurred in the Bajío region of north-central Mexico, caused by late frosts and summer drought conditions that reduced the maize crop and drove up prices on all staple foods. As the numbers of beggars, delinquents, and unemployed workers increased, some men formed bandit gangs for survival. At Querétaro, troops had to be deployed in rural districts to protect maize destined for city granaries. The subsistence crisis compounded existing problems so that by March 1810, the town markets of Taxco either lacked food, or vendors sold at inflated prices. At Guanajuato, Intendant Juan Antonio de Riaño, threatened to mobilize the militias to collect maize for his city. Poor harvests and shortages accentuated smoldering anti-urban attitudes of village people and made many men and some women take to the side of the outlaw *bandoleros*.

The Wars of Independence

The Hidalgo Revolt that erupted on September 16, 1810, was a defining moment in the history of Mexican banditry as well as that of the nation. First, the regions of New Spain most affected by bandit activities from 1790 to 1810 became prime centers of rebellion under Miguel Hidalgo y Costilla. Earlier, some bandits condemned by the regime as pure criminals exhibited "social" and "political" characteristics. Linked closely to villages, clans, and families, these bandits sustained their people through rustling livestock, robbing travelers, assaulting communities and isolated haciendas, and raiding merchant mule trains. With the existence of wide-scale insurrection and the activities of Hidalgo's agents who spread the revolutionary message, banditry took on a quite different complexion. For those who were true believers in Hidalgo and others who attached themselves to the rebellion as its parasites, chaos provided a license to transform bandit gangs or land-based pirates into quasi-legal guerrilla bands fighting as a sort of insurgent privateers. Through his deputies, Hidalgo granted military commissions and titles that were the equivalent of issuing letters of marque to sea captains to engage in legal raiding. Banditry continued to be a lucrative business, but after 1810 both the criminal and the "sociopolitical" aspects could be joined to the revolutionary platform of Hidalgo or his successors.

All over the Bajío provinces and in some other regions, small guerrilla or insurgent bands emerged that survived beyond Hidalgo, José María Morelos y Pavón, and other transient chiefs during the decade of war. These forces raided royalist mule trains, plundered haciendas, attacked towns, robbed travelers, and in the eyes of their royalist enemies were nothing more than criminal *bandoleros*. Upon closer scrutiny, many of the bandit *cabecillas* (ringleaders) were men who prior to 1810 had engaged in contraband, tax evasion, robberies, and other crimes. With the collapse of law and order, they claimed to be guerrilla or insurgent chiefs and plundered with impunity. At the same time, some *cabecillas*

shifted part of their attention away from pure pillaging and attempted within their spheres of control to restore agriculture, commerce, and good governance. They defined their revolutionary legitimacy and within their own spheres of influence acted much like Hobsbawm's social bandits.

Although it is difficult to characterize this blend of bandit, criminal, rebel, insurgent, and guerrilla who populated the Bajío (especially Guanajuato), Valladolid, Nueva Galicia, Veracruz, and the great stretch of rugged country from Mexico City to the Acapulco coast including today's Guerrero State (then called la Dirección del Sur), the insurgents may be described as people of mixed motivations. They were "guerrilla-bandits" or "insurgent-bandits." Many were pure opportunists who capitalized upon the war to achieve their own agendas. They raided, pillaged, sought revenge, and bullied their populations while they also claimed to uphold the political program of the revolution and the cause of Independence. Post-Independence guerrilla-bandits through the nineteenth century and in the Mexican Revolution followed a surprisingly similar pattern and drew comparable responses. Since guerrilla-bandits looked like other provincial *vaqueros* (cowboys), laborers, or *campesinos* when they were not actually engaged in their marauding, police response or counterinsurgency was difficult and tended to be extremely oppressive.

Beginning in 1810, royalist officers such as Brigadier José de la Cruz, who arrived from Spain with knowledge of the techniques used by the French against Spanish guerrillas, organized highly mobile *divisiones volantes*. These units fell upon districts and ravaged the strongholds of the guerrilla-bandits, punishing the entire population and demanding abject obedience. However, the royalists and their later Mexican army successors in the business of counterinsurgency soon discovered that amnesties were much cheaper than outright suppression. Even better, those who accepted government pardons could be turned almost instantly against their erstwhile comrades. In the Independence Wars, guerrilla-bandits one day became royalists the next and often drifted from one side to the other depending upon the fortunes of the war. In the process, as later would happen under Antonio López de Santa Ana, Benito Juárez, and Porfirio Díaz, former bandits could be used as merciless pursuers of their former comrades. Recidivism among the amnestied population was very high, and some men changed sides as many as eight or nine times before they were caught red-handed in some robbery or with stolen goods and executed by hanging or firing squad. With each successive breakdown of order during rebellions, revolutions or invasions, guerrilla-bandits appeared and multiplied. By the latter stages of the war, royalist troops often lost the stomach for combat and simply abandoned the countryside to guerrilla-bandits who traded, regulated agriculture and stock raising, issued permissions for transit, and also preyed upon their enemies. In Veracruz province, they resettled villages, interdicted communications, and raided right up to the walls of the port city.

Comparing the revolutions commencing in 1810 and 1910, one is struck by the parallels in which literally hundreds of guerrilla-bandit chiefs replaced the bureaucrats of the central and outlying regimes. In 1810 for example, the districts bordering upon the main arterial road from Mexico City to Querétaro became a bandit's paradise. From towns such as Tula, Huichapan, Calpulalpan, Jilotepec, Matanza, and Nopala, gangs of 500 to 600 bandits plundered commerce and raided neighboring haciendas. The royalists responded with convoys guarded by detachments of soldiers, but this measure failed to prevent shipments of munitions, equipment, provisions, and merchandise from being directed to the bandit town of Huichapan. Within these towns, a complex network of clans, family connections, and other working relationships linked people who for a long time operated at or beyond the margins of the law. Long before the war, many muleteer families engaged in contraband trading, rustling, and petty brigandage. Through district networks, clan members worked as hacienda managers, ranchers, muleteers, livestock dealers, inn-keepers, minor government officials, renters, and served as the employees of absentee land owners. Some joined local militia companies where they learned something about firearms and how to organize a group of men. Local clergymen cooperated with leading families, expressed similar views, and probably made profits through dubious business deals. Through their illicit activities as well as their legitimate contacts, clan members and their leaders dealt with and influenced the leadership and populations of more isolated Indian villages that later joined the general insurgency under chiefs they knew and trusted.

Two major clans, the Anayas and the Villagráns supported by subsidiary families controlled many of the bandit gangs operating between Mexico City and Querétaro. The leader, Julián Villagrán of Huichapan, a former militia captain, was said to have been involved for years in many unsavory enterprises. The royalists believed that he joined the rebellion in 1810 to free his son José María Villagrán, known as El Chito, from a charge of murder. The Anayas formed an even larger clan, experienced in criminal activities from contraband to assassination. Naming themselves insurgent generals and field marshals, these clan leaders carved out bandit empires that extended from Tula and Huichapan toward Zimapán and the Huasteca. They dealt in stolen property, moved livestock, and pillaged haciendas owned by royalists. In their relations with their own people, they were social bandits—distributing booty, acting as veritable philanthropists, and settling accounts with old opponents. Even in 1813 when the royalist army chased down and executed clan leaders such as Julián Villagrán and El Chito, other clan members replaced them as regional and district bandit chiefs. Royalists who refused to cooperate with the clans perceived these guerrilla-bandits as common criminals and brutal terrorists. To maintain control, these bandits often committed exemplary atrocities, sometimes cutting to ribbons the bodies of their enemies and sowing the fields outside of non-complying towns with mutilated corpses.

The Nineteenth Century

The development of stalemate in the war after 1816 made permanent the existence of many guerrilla-bandit satrapies that transcended Independence in 1821 to perpetuate endemic violence in many regions. Scholar Paul J. Vanderwood has illustrated how bandits played their roles in keeping Mexico in turmoil during political, social, and economic struggles—sometimes serving the armies of politicians, robbing convoys, or kidnapping important people for ransom. Since there was no effective policing in most regions, wealthy merchants and hacendados had little alternative other than to deal with brigands. Bandits flourished during the U.S.-Mexican War (1846–48), the War of the Reform (1858–61), and the French Intervention (1862–67). Brigands who served the Liberal side during the 1850s interdicted roads and diverted the revenues of their Conservative enemies.

With the French Intervention during the 1860s, the existence of guerrilla-bandits provoked the reintroduction of counterinsurgency policies reminiscent of the Independence Wars. Bandits infested the roads, making travel difficult and causing many travelers to arrive at their destinations without their valuables and sometimes even without their clothing. The well-dressed *plateado* (silver-plated) bandits of Morelos cut fine figures in *charro* (cowboy) outfits with suede jackets and tight trousers trimmed with silver. By 1861, *plateado* bandits formed large gangs that nearly paralyzed commerce in Morelos, and they controlled mountain passes leading in and out of the Valley of Mexico. Many of the *plateados* accepted amnesties and fought tenaciously against the French invaders. President Benito Juárez followed the traditional practice of transforming bandits into peace-makers when he organized the Rural Police Force (the Rurales). Dressing his men in *charro* outfits much like the *plateados,* the Rurales were sometimes policemen and often part bandits.

Banditry flourished through the 1870s and into the era of Porfirio Díaz, who struggled to tame old brigand traditions. With railroads, telegraph systems, and foreign investments to plunder, bandits adjusted to new conditions and did not disappear. Outlaws such as Heraclio Bernal, the Thunderbolt of Sinaloa, and other brigand chiefs became almost heroic figures who attracted widespread pubic sympathy. Raiding Sinaloa and Durango, Bernal was the subject of many popular songs, poems, and much later the inspiration for a television character. In fact, most bandits of the period were common rustlers, robbers, kidnappers, and often murderers, but in terms of popular culture their reputations contained real or imagined elements of the Robin Hood image of the social bandit.

The Mexican Revolution and Its Aftermath

Although banditry never died out during the Porfiriato, after 1910 the Mexican Revolution once again unleashed the guerrilla-bandits. Entire regions such as the Bajío were overrun by large bands of brigands, sometimes numbering thousands of men who described themselves as rebels with political agendas and acted more like outright criminals than social bandits. Some fitted Hobsbawm's model in that they directed their anger against oppressive hacendados, mine owners, merchants, railways, and foreign enterprises, and they distributed stolen goods to the common people. Sometimes bandits executed train crews, and foreigners caught up in raids were killed either on purpose or simply as victims of the general violence. Reminiscent of the Independence era, by 1912 guerrilla-bandit gangs coalesced in sufficient numbers to raid large towns and even provincial cities such as Silao. In the state of Veracruz, agrarian violence produced numerous uprisings and bandits who raided close to the port city, where federal troops feared to leave the protection of their fortifications. Endemic banditry produced strange relationships as landowners had little alternative than to make deals and forge relationships with the brigand chiefs. Still, opponents, such as those who preferred the central government or some other party, employed the term bandit to describe almost any rebel.

In the north, Pancho Villa emerged from obscurity to become the most famous bandit and a man who for a time some Americans referred to as "Our pet bandit." Although some of Villa's methods transcended regional banditry and he formed large armies, his men often behaved like brigands as they terrorized those who were not their loyal supporters. The agrarian rebels who supported Emiliano Zapata in Morelos included many different sorts of bandits—including some considered by the Zapatistas themselves to be obnoxious criminal brigands. Pressures by rebel forces upon civilian communities for food, lodging, labor, and livestock appeared to the victims as acts of outright confiscation and criminal banditry. Gradual loss of popular support for rebel or guerrillas-bandit groups caused by excessive demands produced the use of increased force and additional violence. As order crumbled, some states became inundated by brigand gangs that assumed the guise of social bandits in one district and outright terrorists elsewhere. Similar to the era of Independence, during the Revolution the distinguishing elements between social banditry and insurgent guerrilla operations were difficult to separate. As revolutionaries, rural bandits attacked haciendas, captured trains, pillaged anything of value, and sometimes assaulted the more wealthy people. In the late 1910s, the regime of Venustiano Carranza confronted a plague of predatory bandits produced by years of upheaval and dislocation who were the ultimate detritus of revolution. In some regions, these bandits continued to cooperate with local village people, and elsewhere they preyed on the villagers for provisions, sustenance, and recruits. Against them, government troops practiced the brutal counterinsurgency, robberies, and indiscriminate violence reminiscent of the turbulent nineteenth century.

By the 1920s, government forces gradually exterminated most bandit gangs and returned relative peace to the regions. Pancho Villa, who had graduated from bandit-generalissimo to national leader and back to bandit, found the inhabitants of Chihuahua towns in 1916 no longer willing to put up with the depredations of his men. Repeating earlier experiences in the nineteenth century, when Mexican bandits ran amok as criminal predators, villagers formed local militia forces and built fortifications strong enough to resist attacks by lightly armed horsemen. By 1920, Villa faced the reality of defeat and made a deal with the government to retire on an estate in Durango in return for keeping the peace. As a hacendado himself, Villa complained about rustlers who stole his livestock. In 1923, he perished in a hail of bullets fired by assassins when he returned home in his car after having spent the night with a mistress. Even after the passing of Villa and other bandit leaders of his generation, Mexico continued to produce some criminal types who practiced banditry in more isolated districts and those who used political disturbances connected with revolution and reform to justify their predatory ways. In the 1970s, small radical political groups used terrorist tactics to attack trains, kidnap wealthy politicians and industrialists for ransoms, and to commit other crimes that the press and government described as criminal banditry. In Guerrero, a former school teacher, Lucio Cabañas, recruited a guerrilla band, attacked army posts, and kidnapped a candidate for governor of the state. Although the term guerrilla-bandit was not used, Cabañas exhibited some of the social and political elements that had motivated his predecessors. In the 1990s, the modern Zapatistas of Chiapas who struggled against ranchers and outside concepts of progress appeared to many urban Mexicans as dangerous brigands and reactionaries. Like other rural populations confronting poverty and change, these new Zapatistas illustrated for modern television audiences the complex mix of motivations that made them obnoxious criminals to some and avengers, reformers, and protectors to others. Beyond folkloric images and popular songs that recall the exploits of Pancho Villa and regional *bandolero* chiefs with Robin Hood reputations, rural Mexicans—without access to land, jobs, or adequate assistance—may once again renew their old traditions of banditry for survival, revenge, and community protection.

See also Mexican Revolution; Rural Economy and Society; Rurales

Select Bibliography

Archer, Christon I., "Banditry and Revolution in New Spain, 1790–1821." *Bibliotheca Americana* 1:2 (November 1982).

Brunk, Samuel, "The Sad Situation of Civilians and Soldiers: The Banditry of Zapatismo in the Mexican Revolution." *American Historical Review* 101:2 (April 1997).

Florescano, Enrique, *Precios del maz y crisis agrícolas en México (1708–1810)*. Mexico City: El Colegio de México, 1969.

Hamnett, Brian R., *Roots of Insurgency: Mexican Regions, 1750–1824*. Cambridge: Cambridge University Press, 1986.

Joseph, Gil, "On the Trail of Latin American Bandits: A Reexamination of Peasant Resistance." *Latin American Research Review* 25:3 (1990).

Hobsbawm, Eric, *Bandits*. New York: Pantheon Books, 1981.

Knight, Alan, *The Mexican Revolution*. 2 vols., Cambridge: Cambridge University Press, 1986.

Martin, Norman F., *Los vagabundos en la Nueva España*. Mexico City: Jus, 1957.

Slatta, Richard, Bandidos: *The Varieties of Latin American Banditry*. New York: Greenwood Press, 1987.

Taylor, William B., "Bandit Gangs in Late Colonial Times: Rural Jalisco, Mexico, 1794–1821." *Bibliotheca Americana* 1:2 (November 1982).

Taylor, William B., "Banditry and Insurrection: Rural Unrest in Central Jalisco, 1790–1816." In *Riot, Rebellion and Revolution: Rural Social Conflict in Mexico,* edited by Friedrich Katz. Princeton, New Jersey: Princeton University Press, 1988.

Vanderwood, Paul J., *Disorder and Progress: Bandits, Police and Mexican Development*. Lincoln: University of Nebraska Press, 1981.

—CHRISTON I. ARCHER

BANKING AND FINANCE

This entry includes three articles that discuss banking and finance, both public and private:

Banking and Finance: 1821–1910
Banking and Finance: 1910–40
Banking and Finance: 1940–96

See also Industry and Industrialization; Trade and Markets

BANKING AND FINANCE: 1821–1910

During the National Period and Porfiriato, finance emerged as a distinct sector within the Mexican economy, marking the transition of this economy to a form of tributary capitalism in which foreigners were integral. At Independence, colonial structures and cultural patterns still persisted. Local elites dominated agriculture, urban real estate, and (for a time) mining. Foreigners dominated commerce, infant industry, and eventually mining; banking and credit operations were incidental to their business. There were no banks per se, although small loans were made by Monte de Piedad, a pawnshop dating from 1775. By the eve of the Mexican Revolution of 1910, however, banking and credit operations had become the touchstone of the foreign investment that drove the Porfirian economic recovery. Yet these developments also made México increasingly vulnerable to the fluctuations of the international economy.

Banking first made its appearance in connection with government borrowing, as politicians looked abroad for alternatives to local merchant moneylenders known collectively as *agiotistas* (loan sharks). In 1824, federalists floated a £3,200,000 issue of 5 percent bonds taken up by the London banking house of B. A. Goldschmidt and Company at 58 percent of face value; the republic received £2,000,000. The next year, Barclay, Herring, Richardson and Company of London handled a second government loan and, more important, opened permanent offices allow-

ing Mexicans to buy and sell foreign exchange for the first time. War with the United States and rounds of civil war exacerbated patterns of desperate borrowing. Thus, a victorious, but bankrupt, Benito Juárez suspended debt payments in 1861, which led to the seizure of Veracruz and the joint administration of its customhouse by England, Spain, and France, and to the French Intervention in 1862. In 1864, a branch of the Banco de Londres y Sud America opened, later protocolized as the Banco de Londres y México under the 1865 Commercial Code. Banco de Londres issued Mexico's first paper money, accepted for private debt but not public.

Government-chartered private banking weathered the sort of political disorder that largely caused the failure of government-capitalized banks such as the Banco de Avío. Established in 1830 to promote industrial (textile) development, the Banco de Avío was capitalized by earmarking 20 percent of the tariff revenue on raw cotton imports. When this proved insufficient, a 100,000-peso loan was negotiated, but the bank failed after the Texas war erupted and tariff revenues were withdrawn. Efforts to create a national bank from the revenues of confiscated Catholic Church properties also came to grief when the government forced a 50 percent devaluation of the bank's copper coinage.

With relative political stability after the French Intervention, foreign-led private banking sprouted. In 1875, two banks opened in the state of Chihuahua; both were founded by Americans, both issued banks notes. A year later, the Tuxtepec Rebellion installed Porfirio Díaz. Díaz explored the possibilities of central banking and in 1879 chartered Monte de Piedad to issue notes that the government would accept in payment of taxes and fees. Like the other government banks, Monte de Piedad did not do well and eventually resumed its role as the national pawn shop.

The real boom in banking and finance began during the interregnum administration of Manuel González (1880–84) with the entry foreign capital. González granted three 30-year bank concessions. The Franco-Egyptian Bank organized the Banco Nacional Mexicano in 1881, which absorbed the independent Banco Mercantil to become the Banco Nacional de México (Banco Nacional) in 1884. Its concession authorized it to issue bank notes to three times its cash reserves and, like Monte de Piedad, its notes were accepted in payment of public debts. A standing account with Banco Nacional was created for the Ministry of Hacienda (Treasury), making banking an integral part of state finance for the first time. Almost immediately, Banco Nacional was weakened by government overdrafts on its account.

French capitalists founded two banks the next year. The Banco Mercantil, Agricola e Hipotecario was authorized to issue bonds as well as notes. The Banco Hipotecario Mexicano issued cash bonds, made mortgages and loans on property in the Federal District and Baja California, and bought and sold agricultural machinery on credit. Later reorganized as the Banco Internacional e Hipotecario, it was permitted to do business throughout Mexico and to issue certificates of deposit payable on sight in Mexico and abroad, de facto bank notes. In 1882, Enrique C. Creel, son of an American father and a niece of Chihuahua's then governor Luis Terrazas, opened the Banco Minero. Creel would found 11 more banks and become the most prominent banker in Mexico, president of the Mexican Banker's Association, ambassador to Washington, and governor of his state.

Toward the end of his term, beset by financial woes, González recognized British debt claims, a necessary but unpopular decision. A slowdown in foreign investment triggered a recession and runs on Banco Nacional and Monte de Piedad. The Banco de Londres and the government saved them by accepting their notes without discount. Even González's well intentioned measure to end the shortage of small change by issuing 4 million pesos in nickel coin backfired. The nickel was easily counterfeited and heavily discounted by merchants, leading to social unrest known as the Nickel Riots.

Upon his return to office, Díaz appointed as Hacienda minister Manuel Dublan, who began the process of rationalizing banking regulation. Dublan implemented the Code of Commerce of 1884, which established the rules of incorporation for banks, set minimum capital requirements, standardized the one-to-three ratio of reserves to banknotes, forbid banks to own real estate, required the publication of monthly statements in *Diario Oficial,* and ordered protocol-

ization under Mexican law of banks incorporated abroad. Existing banks were recognized, but the right to grant new concessions was vested exclusively in the federal government, and it prohibited the issue of notes without a concession. Banco de Londres y México, Banco Minero, and other concessionless banks then issuing notes protested vigorously. After lengthy court actions, a modus vivendi was reached in 1886 enabling them to acquire concessions by such means as absorbing smaller chartered banks. Dublan also regularized the national debt. In 1886, after running yearly deficits of about 6,000,000 pesos the Díaz government defaulted. Dublan consolidated the debt in 1888 with a £10,500,000 bond issue purchased by German bankers at 70 percent of face value. Mexico received £7,350,000 while paying 6 percent on the full debt. Deficits continued, however, and government overdrafts threatened to bankrupt Banco Nacional.

Dublan bought time but solutions to the deeper, systemic problems awaited the arrival of the positivist technocrat par excellence, José Yves Limantour. In 1892, Matías Romero replaced Dublan at Hacienda and brought Limantour as subsecretary. In 1893, Limantour secured a European loan through Banco Nacional. In fiscal year 1895–96, he gave Mexico its first balanced budget with a 1,000,000-peso surplus that grew to more than 5,000,000 pesos the following year; only in fiscal year 1897–98 would the surplus be less than 4,000,000 pesos. Subsequently, Limantour was able to float unsecured bond issues at increasingly lower interest rates and use a greater percentage of the capital raised.

In 1897, Limantour annulled unfulfilled speculative banking concessions and oversaw the drafting of a new banking law that formalized the three existing classes of banks. First were issue (*emision*) banks, which issued notes of fixed denominations not to exceed twice metallic reserves or three times capital, and made loans of not more than nine months duration. Second were mortgage (*hipotecario*) banks, which made loans secured by real estate or dividend-paying stock, issued interest-bearing bonds of short and long term up to 40 years, and were allowed to purchase their own bonds. Finally there were auxiliary development (*refaccionario*) banks, which offered credit for mining, industry, and agriculture through mortgages, collateral loans, and two-year bonds (*bonos de caja*) of up to twice their active capital. The 1897 law required a minimum capital of 200,000 pesos with 50 percent active for the auxiliary banks, and 500,000 pesos for the other two classes of banks, with all three setting aside 10 percent of net profits for a reserve equal to one-third of capital.

To redeem state bank notes at par in the Federal District, a de facto central bank, the Banco Refaccionario Mexicano, was capitalized at 1,000,000 pesos. In 1899, it was reorganized as the Banco Central Mexicano, and its authorized capital increased to 6,000,000 pesos supplied through a syndicate of the Deutsche Bank, Bleichroeder and Company, and J. P. Morgan and Company. State banks held Banco Central stock worth 5 percent of their active capital as corresponding banks and Banco Central stabilized banks with liquidity problems, as in its 1907 bailout and reorganization of failed Yucatecan banks. In 1897, Mexico had only nine chartered banks with a combined capital of just 35,350,000 pesos; by 1902 there were 25 with a combined capital of 83,300,000 pesos. In that same period loans doubled to 44,000,000 pesos and assets increased from 176,193,000 to 270,141,624 pesos. By the end of 1910, Mexico's 32 chartered banks reported assets in excess of 1,117,000,000 pesos.

The maturation of the Mexican financial sector, reflected in the growth of its chartered banks, was also evident with the rise of commercial banking corporations in the wake of the rapid expansion of American investment after 1896. In that year, American investment totaled about US$225 million, increasing to 500 million by 1901, 600 million by 1905, and over 1 billion by 1910—this accounted for 50 percent of all U.S. foreign investment. The diversification of investment, from rails and mines into commerce, industry, land speculation, and tropical plantations, required banking services not provided by chartered banks. American-owned commercial banks, joint stock companies with corresponding banks in the United States, mushroomed: the Trust, Loan and Agency Company; the Monterey Building and Loan; the American Banking Company of Parker H. Sercombe (who later founded the Mexican Trust Company, which became the International Banking and Trust Company); the United States Banking Company (USBC) of George I. Ham; the Building and Loan Company of Mexico; the U.S.-Mexican Trust Company of A. E. Stilwell; the Banco de Chiapas; the International Mortgage Bank of Mexico—all were open for business by 1902. When the Mercantile Banking Company opened its doors in 1905, the four major American banks alone had 18,000,000 pesos in combined deposits and 8,000,000 pesos in capital. In 1906, a group of private, commercial, and chartered banks, most within the Federal District, established a clearinghouse with monthly transactions fluctuating at 50 to 70 million pesos. A 1911 consul general's report estimated the combined assets of American-owned banks, trusts, and insurance companies at 61,100,000.

In Mexico City, Tampico, Jalisco, Veracruz, the Tehuantepec Isthmus, and elsewhere, American commercial banks financed industrial and urban development, port, and public works projects by purchasing and marketing bond issues; they also backed speculative ventures, particularly tropical plantations. Limantour, wary of undue American influence, stopped states from floating bond issues with American banks and vetoed direct ownership of chartered banks by Americans. The only American-owned chartered bank, Banco de Chiapas, authorized under the Pan-American Railway concession, was eventually purchased by Creel. But a numbers of American banks had interlocking directorates, shared stock, and made reciprocal deposits with state banks of issue. George Ham, unable to secure a charter for his U.S. Banking Company, acquired a controlling interest in Banco de Estado de México, increasing its capital fourfold to 3 million pesos. USBC financed the Mexican Packing Company (POPO), but in 1910 POPO's demands for substantial unsecured loans, irresistible given the number Porfirian notables

among its directors, brought down USBC. A local financial crisis was averted only by the entry of the Bank of Montreal (USBC's corresponding bank). Another Canadian institution, the Canadian Bank of Commerce, entered Mexico by financing the operations of F. S. Pearson's Mexican Power and Light Company.

Limantour did make use of American banking houses to finance the creation of Mexico's national rail system. Lorenzo B. Speyer represented the New York house of James J. Speyer, which had bankrolled C. P. Huntington's Mexican projects. In 1901, Speyer bought control of the Mexican National Railroad and later, in partnership with Pierce-Waters Oil, the Mexican Central Railroad. From 1903 to 1909, Speyer and the Deutsche Bank of Berlin anchored Limantour's various banking groups as he acquired railroad after railroad. This included the 1904 issue of US$40 million in 50-year bonds at 4.49 percent interest, the first not secured by customs revenues and the first to sell at almost face value (98 percent). In 1906, Speyer and the Deutsches Bank formed the Banco Mexicano de Comercio e Industria with active capital of 10 million pesos. Among its directors was Hugo Scherer Jr. of Scherer and Company, a prestigious private German bank with close links to Wall Street.

The maturation of Mexico's financial sector also was evident in the growth of a national insurance industry. Until 1903, New York Mutual Life dominated that industry. In that year New York passed a law strictly limiting the amount of foreign business its insurance companies could conduct. With this, Mexican-based companies came into their own. Oscar and Thomas Braniff, Guillermo de Landa y Escandon, Hugo Scherer Jr., Julio Limantour, and others created La Compañía Latino-Americano Mutualista, capitalized at 2 million pesos. American and Mexican capital created the Mexican Title Insurance Company (MTIC), which insured real estate titles, issued mortgage insurance, managed property for absentee owners and, significantly, made real estate loans. MTIC had ties to La Compañía Latino-Americano Mutualista, to USBC, and to the National Property Company, which issued bonds based on downtown Mexico City real estate equity. The booming urban real estate market led to the 1907 merger of the American Bank and the Condesa and Nueva del Paseo Extension Company, which together formed Cia Bancaria de Fomento y Bienes Raices de México, capitalized at 10 million pesos and headed by Fernando Pimentel y Fagoaga, president of Banco Central.

Of Limantour's accomplishments—the abolition of the *alcabalas* (internal tariffs), rationalization of national finances, renegotiation of Mexico's foreign debt to 4 percent unsecured bonds by 1911, regulation of banking, creation of a national railway system—it was his 1905 conversion of Mexico to the gold standard that made his reputation. That shift to the gold standard produced very mixed results, however. One of these, a prolonged shortage of peso and fractional coin, had corrosive effects on commerce and society as a whole, contributing to the destabilization of the regime before 1910.

Prior to the conversion to gold, the peso commodity market was the keystone of Mexico's free-silver economy and monetary system. Of the estimated 4 billion pesos coined by 1905, less than 100 million circulated in Mexico itself. The remainder circulated in Asia, where the peso had been the primary trade coin since colonial times. Regional economic conditions and differential movement in peso and silver prices drove the peso market. Peso exports increased when the price gap widened between coin and bullion. Under free coinage, Mexico's money supply increased in response to economic expansion, while economic downturns increased peso exports because more of year's coin production was excess, lowering peso prices relative to bar silver.

Some looked favorably upon what was, until 1891, a gradual decline in silver prices punctuated by periods of recovery. A natural protective tariff, it encouraged industrial import replacement, stimulated export agriculture, returned hard currency profits, and generated high interest rates attracting investors discouraged by low rates in their own countries. Economic downturns in the United States created surges of American investment in Mexico, an inverse relationship that persisted until the 1905 shift to the gold standard, which synchronized Mexican and U.S. economic cycles and reversed the conjunction of increased peso exports with economic slowdown.

Those with hard currency obligations, however—importers, merchants, and bankers for whom bonds were more important than the peso trade—stood to benefit from a gold standard. Foremost among these was the Mexican government. In 1900, silver began a two-year slide to a historic low. Limantour pursued a two-track policy. He attempted a coalition with China, Japan, and India to support the silver standard and formed an exchange and currency commission to study the option of shifting to the gold standard. When diplomacy failed, the commission engineered the conversion to gold, assisted by America's first "money doctors," Jeremiah W. Jenks (professor of political economy at Cornell) and Charles A. Conant (prominent financial correspondent and partner in the Morton Trust Company), the chief theoreticians of Dollar Diplomacy.

Limantour's establishment of the gold standard ended free coinage of silver and the use of bullion (gold and silver) as bank reserves, permitting only the use of coin. The 1905 law pegged the peso at 49 U.S. cents, its average exchange rate prior to 1900, but the law of supply and demand placed it at as high as 56 cents in 1907 and as low as 44 cents in 1909. Significantly, commission members Creel and Casasus, both prominent bankers, disagreed with the decision to suspend free coinage, predicting it would decrease business by 30 to 50 percent of the currency reduction. They recommended establishing a gold reserve from Mexican mines to support the peso, but were overruled. The coincidental rise in silver prices, usually interpreted as aiding Limantour's reform, in fact worsened economic conditions. Arbitrage became profitable and was facilitated by Limantour, who took advantage of the price to build gold stocks. Pesos drained from the country; chartered and commercial banks exported over 50 million pesos to Asia in 1906 alone, while only 5 million were coined.

The period from 1904 to 1907 saw a paradox: currency contraction and coin shortages on the one hand, and economic expansion and inflation on the other. Early in 1904, interest rose sharply from 5 percent to 9 percent, owing to the capital demands of a growing economy and the extension of loans to favored borrowers, such as 7 million pesos for the troubled Mexican Sugar Trust. Conservative Mexican bankers did issue more notes against diminished cash reserves but never approached the legal limits. Their banknote issues barely exceeded their specie holdings, a tendency reinforced by Limantour's obsession with maintaining maximum liquidity, particularly after 1907 as the foreign financial markets dried up. Bankers removed coin from circulation to build their reserves, tying up more than two-thirds of the newly minted gold coin and about one-half of the new silver pesos. The symbiotic dynamic of economic growth and the peso commodity market no longer governed the money supply. Deprived of currency elasticity, Mexico, more dependent on foreign capital markets, found its economic cycles synchronizing with those of the United States, thereby transmitting the 1907 Wall Street Panic to Mexico by early 1908.

The gold standard did not increase the rate of foreign investment as promised. From 1905 to 1908, investment increased at its slowest rate since 1893. Mexico's financial community responded by attempting to systematize delivery of foreign capital. In 1905, Porfirian heavy-hitters Sebastian Camacho, Martínez del Río, Jaoquin Casasus, and Pablo and Miguel Macedo formed the Asociacion Financiera Internacional as a conduit for U.S. investment. In 1906, Banco Germanico de la America del Sur opened with capital of DM20 million. In 1907, J. M. Neeland, Pan-American Railroad Company vice president, became a USBC director and, with Ham, bought the Bank of Southern California in Los Angeles to revive flagging American investment in Mexico. The dramatic investment increase starting in 1909 can be seen as a response to the more efficient links between foreign and Mexican banks.

In 1908, Limantour again undertook banking reform. The Hacienda Ministry imposed standard accounting practices and federal inspection and issued gold reserve certificates allowing banks to release their coin reserves into circulation, but worsened the credit crunch by increasing capital requirements and further restricting maximum duration of loans. To offset these problems, Limantour arranged over 11 million pesos in loans for selected companies. He also reintroduced government capitalized banks. He created a "rediscount bank," the Caja de Prestamos para Obras de Irrigación capitalized at 50 million pesos, by marketing bonds in New York priced in the 80s (when most Mexican bonds sold at over 90 percent) and by the sale of 10 million pesos of stock in Mexico. The bank became a feeding trough for the 96 elite hacendado clans, who consumed 53,540,000 of the 55,237,405 pesos that the bank loaned in 1908.

In February 1908 when the Mexican public read Díaz's interview with James Creelman, in which the president expressed a wish to retire, the economy was stagnant for the first time in 14 years. By January 1909, the price of bar silver hit a low of 51 U.S. cents. All but the richest and most efficient mines were driven to the wall; thousands of miners were put out of work. Lacking consumers, textile mills closed. Unemployment rippled through northern Mexico, which just was beginning to recover from the collapse of copper prices in late 1907. Merchants who, encouraged by the promised benefits of a "fixed" currency, had bought excessive stocks of imported goods now found themselves with few customers and large, unpaid-for inventories.

Mexican silver miners, a desperate group that some observers felt had revolutionary potential, began to agitate for a return to free coinage. The fall in silver prices, they said, had been artificially created by international bankers to force the adoption of gold despite the fact that silver was intrinsically a better standard for small business and the humble classes. *El Tiempo,* a conservative, Catholic, ultra-nationalistic, anti-American journal, carried a letter signed by a group of miners criticizing the regime's foreign-led program of economic development as one that exported profits and left only wages behind. They proposed a program of development by Mexican capital explicitly linked to a return to free silver. Limantour ignored their criticism, and currency shortages continued to unravel the economic fabric, bankrupt silver miners, and foment unrest.

As the Porfirian regime began to crack, Limantour focused on the national debt to the exclusion of all else. In August 1910, he traveled to New York for talks with J. P. Morgan in New York and sailed on the *Lusitania* for Europe. By February 1911, with Francisco Madero's revolution gaining steam, he completed conversion of Mexico's 1899 debt to 4 percent unsecured bonds with S. Bleichroeder and a consortium of other German, French, and English banks. Díaz resigned on May 25; Limantour stayed a week to put the Hacienda Ministry books in order. His final budget projected a surplus of more than 10 million pesos and cash holdings of over 64 million pesos.

Initially, Mexico's financial sector proved remarkably resilient in the face of revolution, in part because Madero was so much a part of the system. In 1911, his family owed Mexican banks over 8 million pesos, including a loan of 210,000 pesos arranged by Limantour through Banco de Londres y México shortly before the "Apostle of Democracy" declared against Díaz. From 1911 to 1912 there was little change in bank balance sheets, perhaps because Madero was able to get 40 million pesos in two loans from Limantour's old reliable, Speyer and Company. By 1915, however, all but one of Mexico's banks were in ruins.

See also Agiotaje; Científicos

Select Bibliography

Conant, Charles A., *The Banking System of Mexico.* Washington, D.C.: Government Printing Office, 1910.

Díaz Dufoo, Carlos, *Limantour.* Mexico City: Victoria, 1922.

Haber, Stephen H., *Industry and Under Development: The Industrialization of Mexico, 1890–1940.* Stanford, California: Stanford University Press, 1989.

Instituto Nacional de Estadística, Geografiae Informatica, *Estadisticas Historicas de México.* 2 vols., Mexico City: Secretaria de Programacion y Presupuesto, 1986.

Martin, Percy F., *Mexico of the Twentieth Century.* 2 vols., New York: Dodd, Mead, 1908.

McCaleb, Walter F., *Present and Past Banking in Mexico.* New York: Harper, 1920.

_____, *The Public Finances of Mexico.* New York: Harper, 1921.

Potash, Robert A., *Mexican Goverment and Industrial Development: The Banco de Avío.* Amherst: University of Massachusetts Press, 1983.

Schell, William Jr., "Money as Commodity: Mexico's Conversion to the Gold Standard, 1905." In *Mexican Studies/Estudios Mexicanos* 12:1 (1996).

Wasserman, Mark, *Capitalists, Caciques and Revolution: The Native Elite and Foreign Enterprise in Chihuahua, 1854–1911.* Chapel Hill: University of North Carolina Press, 1984.

—William Schell Jr.

BANKING AND FINANCE: 1910–40

On the eve of the Mexican Revolution, the Mexican banking sector, like many other sectors of the economy, was controlled by foreigners. The most important national banks, the Banco Nacional de México and the Banco de Londres y México, linked foreign merchants and investors with major Mexican and immigrant commercial, mining, and industrial interests. Several government officials were also shareholders in the major banks as well as other firms, and government regulation was arbitrary and discriminatory, tending to favor those banks with close ties to the government. Credit was generally restricted to a narrow circle of domestic and foreign investors, in turn an important element in industrial and commercial concentration during the Porfiriato (the rule of dictator Porfirio Díaz).

Private banks issued their own banknotes, but only those of the Banco Nacional de México and the Banco de Londres y México were accepted at the national level, and only those of the Banco Nacional could be used for tax payments. The Banco Nacional also enjoyed a special position as intermediary between the state and foreign financial interests and in effect operated as the bank of the state.

The armed conflict of 1910 to 1917 had a devastating effect on Mexico's monetary and financial system, with various Revolutionary factions and generals issuing their own banknotes which quickly became worthless. This resulted in a generalized distrust of paper money, which lasted throughout the 1920s. In the context of the political and economic instability of this period, the development of a modern banking system was an important component of economic reconstruction and the centralization of political authority in a powerful national state.

The new system would differ from that of the pre-Revolutionary period in several important respects, notably in the official role of the state in the regulation and control of the banking system and in the definition of financial policy, as well as the establishment of a banking system independent of foreign capital. At the same time, the functioning of the banking system would come to resemble that of the Porfiriato for several reasons. First, the Porfirian-era bankers soon succeeded in reestablishing a close association with the post-Revolutionary governments; this association would be reinforced over the succeeding decades. Second, the banks were to have an important role within the emerging economic groups that eventually would concentrate much of the wealth accruing from Mexico's dramatic economic growth between 1940 and the early 1980s.

Nationalist opposition to foreign economic dominance and resentment of the privileges enjoyed by the Porfirian elite shaped the initial formulation of the banking project. Venustiano Carranza, first president of post-Revolutionary Mexico (1917–20), called for a single, state-controlled bank with monopoly over currency issue, formed with domestic capital to avoid dependence on foreign capital, and for state control of the banking sector through the Ministry of Finance. The establishment of a government bank controlling the issue of currency was incorporated in Article 28 of the 1917 Constitution, although it was several years before this goal could be realized given the critical financial situation of the government.

In the meantime, Mexico's foreign debt and international concern regarding the nationalist thrust of the Revolution resulted in the formation of an International Bankers Committee (IBC) in 1918, led by Thomas Lamont of Morgan Guaranty Trust, which took charge of debt negotiations with Mexico on behalf of U.S. and European creditors. The committee was a manifestation of the emergence of the United States from World War I as a major economic power and creditor, and of the increasingly significant international role of the New York banks. In 1920, an International Finance Commission held in Brussels under the auspices of the League of Nations advocated the formation of central banks that would respond to concerns of U.S. and European financial groups for a mechanism to collect debts in Latin America and other countries. Subsequently a U.S. commission, the Kemmerer Mission, supervised the establishment of central banks in Chile, Bolivia, Ecuador, and Peru.

The governments of Álvaro Obregón (1920–24) and Plutarco Elías Calles (1924–28) sought a new accommodation with both foreign creditors and the Porfirian bankers. The Obregón government reached agreement with the International Bankers Committee in 1922 regarding the repayment of the debt, including the commitment of taxes on railroads and on petroleum exports to interest payment. Nevertheless, government efforts to obtain international loans for capital for a new central bank were rejected by the Bankers Commission despite its general support for the idea of a central bank, in part owing to concern that funds earmarked for debt service would be used instead for the bank.

The Porfirian bankers differed with the government leadership regarding the ownership of the new issue bank, which they believed should be private. However, the government saw the establishment of a state-controlled issue bank as essential for financial sovereignty. In the context of growing social pressures and military revolts against the central government during the 1920s, it was also important to be able to secure the resources necessary to respond to demands from organized groups and to meet military expenditures, without depending on loans from private domestic or foreign interests.

The Calles government therefore was determined to establish the new bank despite the inability to obtain foreign loans. To obtain sufficient domestic resources, Finance Secretary Alberto Pani initiated an austerity program limiting government expenditures and instituted new sources of revenue, including an income tax. The government also suspended debt payments, to the chagrin of the IBC, and channeled these funds to capital for the new bank.

Despite resistance to the concept of a government-controlled central bank on the part of many of the Porfirian bankers, and distrust of the bankers by some groups within the state, the government needed their expertise in the development of new banking legislation. In 1924, the first National Banking Convention brought government and private bankers together to discuss the establishment of the new banking system. In January 1925 the General Law of Credit Institutions was passed, which reinforced the concept of the state as director of the banking system with monopoly over the issue of currency, required banks to pay taxes (from which they had previously been exempted), established that the Finance Ministry would oversee the banking system, and prohibited banks from owning shares in other banks.

A commission was formed of government financial experts and Porfirian bankers to draft legislation for the new, lone issue bank, and in August 1925 the Banco de México was established. The bank would be controlled by the government, which was to hold 51 percent of the shares; the remaining 49 percent would be offered for sale to private banks and individuals (although only a small number were bought). The functions of the new bank, in addition to its monopoly over note issue, would include regulation of money circulation, exchange rates, and interest rates, and supervision of private banks in conjunction with the National Banking Commission of the Ministry of Finance. The bank was also the treasurer of the government, with loans to the government limited to 10 percent of capital.

However, the composition of the administrative board of the bank included several private bankers as well as leading industrialists, thus ensuring that private financial interests would have a role in the management of the new bank. In fact, the pattern of collaboration between government and private bankers would be reinforced in succeeding years through joint membership on the boards of private and government banks and the career patterns of bankers who moved between the public and private sector.

Subsequent legislation in 1932 required that all banks, national and foreign, associate with the Banco de México and use their resources for investment within Mexico, a measure that led foreign banks to withdraw from the country and created space for the formation of domestic banks. Over the next decade a significant number of new banks were established, some of which, such as the Banco de Comercio, subsequently became quite powerful, rivaling the Banco Nacional de México and the Banco de Londres y México, which also grew during this period. The new legislation also called for the establishment of investment banks, or *financieras,* and during the following years several were formed, frequently with government support. Many of the new banks were incorporated into existing or emerging economic groups, which included industrial firms, commercial houses, and other institutions and well as banks, linked by common ownership, generally by a small group of investors and in some cases a single family. The financial institutions had an integral function within these groups, with much of their financing going to firms within their particular economic group.

During the 1920s and 1930s the government also established several government banks to provide credit for specific development projects or for groups that would not otherwise have access to credit. These included the Public Works Bank (Banco Nacional Hipotecario Urbano y de Obras Públicas) to finance infrastructure, especially road construction and irrigation systems; the Agricultural Credit Bank (Banco Nacional de Crédito Agrícola) to provide loans to small farmers who received land under the agrarian reform; the Foreign Trade Bank (Banco Nacional de Comercio Exterior), for the purpose of promoting agricultural exports; and the Ejidal Bank (Banco Nacional de Crédito Ejidal), which provided loans to *ejidos* (communal landholdings) created under the agrarian reform of Lázaro Cárdenas in the 1930s. The most significant of these was Nacional Financiera (NAFINSA), the national development bank, which would have an important role in financing both government and private sector projects in the subsequent decades.

The collaboration between the official financial sector and private bankers continued during the Cárdenas administration (1934–40) despite the antagonism of many within the private sector toward the pro-agrarian, pro-labor, and nationalist policies of the Cárdenas government. Within the financial sector, government efforts to promote development through increased government spending, and in some cases deficit financing, was opposed by many of the bankers. However, Mexico's rapid recovery from the Great Depression, the impetus given to the economy through government initiatives, particularly road construction and the establishment of irrigation systems, and the restoration of relative political stability after two decades of conflict and anarchy, led to increased investment during the 1930s.

The government continued to provide equity support for the establishment of new *financieras,* and the recently created Nacional Financiera provided loans to private as well as government projects. A new insurance law passed in 1935 over the objections of foreign insurance agents also eliminated some of the restrictions on the investment of insurance reserves, at the same time confining such investment to Mexican securities. The new law, and the subsequent departure of foreign insurance firms, were factors in the establishment and growth of Mexican insurance firms during this period.

Despite the encouragement given by the Cárdenas government to labor organization, the government supported the bankers when some of the bank employees attempted to unionize. Legislation to prevent the formation of unions by bank employees was engineered by Luis Montes de Oca, Director of the Banco de México (and later founder and president of a private bank, Banco Internacional), in collaboration with the Mexican Bankers Association, and was justified on the basis that a work stoppage would negatively affect public confidence in the credit system and thus pose a threat to the national economy. The bank employee regulation, passed in November 1937, provided benefits to bank employees but constrained their ability to organize by prohibiting strikes, requiring that employee contracts be individual, and stipulating that employer-employee disputes be resolved by the Finance Ministry or Federal Labor Board.

In summary, the new banking system, initially conceived as a means to strengthen financial sovereignty, to channel financial resources to economic development, and to limit the concentration of wealth by a small elite, has a mixed legacy. On the one hand, it ensured a government role in the banking system and made it possible to direct financial resources to economic goals through the establishment of a state-controlled issue bank, a regulatory mechanism for government oversight of private banks, and a series of government banks to promote development projects and provide credit for specific groups. On the other, it was the product of a close association between the Porfirian bankers and government financial officials, which has been reinforced in subsequent decades. And it has been a factor in the growing concentration of resources in a few major banks and economic groups that has accompanied Mexico's subsequent development. The reconstruction of Mexico's banking system thus can be interpreted within the framework of the ongoing debate regarding the Mexican Revolution and the extent to which it signaled a break with the past or simply interrupted (or reinforced) an already established trajectory.

See also Great Depression

Select Bibliography

Cárdenas, Enrique, *La hacienda pública y la politica económica: 1929–1958.* Mexico City: Fondo de Cultura Económica and Colegio de México, 1994.

Haber, Stephen, *Industry and Underdevelopment: The Industrialization of Mexico, 1890–1940.* Stanford, California: Stanford University Press, 1989.

Hamilton, Nora, *The Limits of State Autonomy: Post-Revolutionary Mexico.* Princeton, New Jersey: Princeton University Press, 1982.

Maxfield, Sylvia, *Governing Capital: International Finance and Mexican Politics.* Ithaca, New York: Cornell University Press, 1990.

Moore, O. Ernesto, *Evolución de las instituciones financieras en Mexico.* Mexico City: Centro de Estudios Monetarios Latinoamericanos, 1963.

Sánchez Mártinez, Hilda, "La politica bancaria de los primeros gobiernos constitucionales, antecedentes inmediatos para la fundación del Banco de Mexico." In *Banca y Poder en México, 1800–1925,* edited by Leonor Ludlow and Carlos Marichal. Mexico City: Grijalbo, 1986.

Smith, Robert Freeman, "The Formation and Development of the International Bankers Committee in Mexico." *Journal of Economic History* 23 (December 1963).

Zebadúa, Emilio, *Banqueros y revolucionarios: La soberanía financiera de México.* Mexico City: Fondo de Cultura Económica and Colegio de México, 1994.

—Nora Hamilton

BANKING AND FINANCE: 1940–96

From the 1940s, Mexican banking and financial experts crafted policies designed to fulfill short-term solutions to problems of growth and stability. Designed to promote industry and trade, these post–World War II changes led to repeated crises and long-term paradoxes beginning late in the 1960s.

Following the intent of the Constitution of 1917 and the leadership of Revolutionary leaders, postwar governments continued to privatize industries and to create a paragovernmental sector for industrial development within the political control of the national party, the Partido Revolucionario Institucional (PRI, or Institutional Revolutionary Party). Repeatedly, monetary reformers allowed the peso to float on the international exchange market, using a combination of price and salary regulations to stop resulting inflation. Mexican officials utilized extensive foreign borrowing to finance a trade policy that continued to rely heavily upon extractive products, such as oil, silver, and gold, as well as to develop an import-substitution industrial base (import substitution industrialization refers to a set of policies implemented by an activist, interventionist state designed to encourage the domestic production of previously imported manufactured goods). Depending upon the world's demand for these materials and for cheap labor, Mexico's government administrators encouraged direct foreign investment into privatized, Mexican-owned industries and swung between extremes of monetary management as they faced cycles of abundance and deficiencies. Between 1945 and 1968, Mexican officials obtained loans from the new international monetary institutions, the International Monetary Fund (IMF) and World Bank (WB), which they spent on modernization and expansion of the nation's industrial base. Simultaneously, they ignored and subordinated the needs of agriculture and their promises to laborers.

A social and political crisis in 1968 led to union strikes, assassinations, and other products of social unrest and signaled the beginning of acute international and domestic problems. On the surface, the complaints of laborers faded relative to the favorable significance of rising oil prices that led entrepreneurs and officials into a false sense of security. Maintenance of payments on those foreign loans, however, set the stage for catastrophe when international oil prices stagnated beginning in 1978. The reality of an acute financial crisis stimulated protective strategies by Mexican businesses and further aggravated banks' liquidity until President José López Portillo devalued the peso early in 1982. In mid-summer, he emotionally announced that Mexico would not be able to meet its foreign debt obligations. During the next decade, Mexicans experienced some of the most severe financial dislocations since the Revolution of 1910. Stabilization and reform programs concentrated upon the traditional remedies to control the peso, trade, and industry; however, such short-term remedies produced even more severe economic and social disparities in the 1990s. Paradoxically, the remedies for the problems of the 1980s and 1990s led Mexico to closer financial dependency upon its traditional antagonist, the United States.

World War II to 1968

Mexico emerged from the World War II era with an economy perched on the edge of enormous success. Banco de México and the Financiera Nación had over two decades of experience in solving the problems of depression and wartime inflation. The nation had benefited from the good will of the European allies and the United States in the refinancing and dismissing of most of its long-term debt during 1946 negotiations. Experts agreed that Mexico stood to benefit mightily from the results of the 1944 Bretton Woods Conference agreements and the World Bank/International Monetary Fund, created to facilitate trade, to organize interest rates and industrial development, and to coordinate monetary exchanges.

Mexico's presidents focused upon development of a modern industrial base at all costs. The growth rate in Mexico's industrial sector between 1940 and 1945 averaged 10.2 percent, while it maintained a 7.3 percent per year growth rate during the last half of the decade. Inflation accompanied this growth and threatened stability, but officials turned to a monetary policy that devalued the peso in 1948 and allowed it to float at between 5.85 pesos per U.S. dollar and 6.80 pesos per U.S. dollar on the international exchange. Continuing inflation, owing in large part to the increased demand for raw materials during the Korean War, however, necessitated a subsequent devaluation in April 1954. Strong political pressure on the Mexican labor movement and upon industrial elites enabled the Mexican government to stabilize exchange rates and wholesale prices while the gross domestic product (GDP), which rose from around 7 billion pesos in 1940 to over 154 billion pesos in 1960, continued to ascend at 5 percent to over 7.5 percent per year throughout the 1960s. Growing imbalances in social status, typical of developing nations' growth, appeared when average family incomes of 4.2 percent to 3.8 percent between 1950 and 1963 fell to only 2.2 percent during the next decade—while GDP rose by almost 8 percent per year.

The continued expansion of the international market for Mexican commodities during the 1960s led the government to continue its policies, particularly using the readily available services of the IMF and WB to finance industrial expansion of the private sector. While the government's income from all sources rose from 577 million pesos in 1940 to 19.458 billion pesos in 1960, the value of the peso relative to the U.S. dollar receded from 4.85 per U.S. dollar to 12.50 per U.S. dollar owing largely to inflation. What seemed to be the true miracle of total development for Mexico, and the abundance of investment funds, stimulated the Banco de México to relax its reserve requirements and expand lending guidelines for member banks. Slowly, government officials began to exhibit a new openness toward foreign investments, and new trade and manufacturing regulations opened a zone along the U.S.-Mexican border for the operation of assembly and manufacturing plants, *maquiladoras,* for combined U.S.-Mexican operation (primarily U.S. companies employing Mexican labor). These operations and the substantial

demand for Mexican oil, reflected in its strong price rises, produced a harmony between political elites and economic elites not seen since the age of Porfirio Díaz (1876–1910). Furthermore, the growing middle class, 17 percent of the population, saw this alliance as entirely appropriate and necessary to their continued well-being and their becoming members of the elite class themselves.

1968–82

Seen in retrospect, the social and political crisis of 1968 initiated the end of the "Mexican Miracle" and the beginning of a new series of crises. The demonstrations of college students and workers from July through October, while seemingly in reaction to excesses of government spending on the upcoming Olympic games, in truth represented the anger of the poor, who were becoming poorer, and signaled the end of Mexico's brief flirtation with a promising future. Sons and daughters of the elite and middle classes led the rebels, who saw the fallacy of Mexico's growth in the sharply decreasing standard of living for all levels of workers; the ending of social services, necessitated by the Olympic preparations, represented the weakness of the entire industrial growth. Although embarrassing Mexico before the international community, this demonstration and the subsequent massacre of hundreds of young people did not end the praise government officials and economic experts lavished on their fabulous successes. Everyone from President Gustavo Díaz Ordaz to Banco de México director general Miguel Mancera Aguayo dismissed these episodes as necessary readjustments to realign the economy for new growth in the early 1970s. Indeed, at the end of the 1960s, all financial indicators in Mexico recorded stable growth; especially the often-cited statistic that Banco de México assets had risen from 1 billion pesos in 1940 to almost 35 billion pesos in 1968.

During the presidency of Luis Echeverría Álvarez (1970–76), however, Mexico's agricultural, industrial, and financial growth began to suffer growing and complicated instabilities. Large industries continued to expand production and to record increasing profits, and experts continued to believe that disruptions within various sectors signaled only normal readjustments to a rapidly growing economy. Echeverría promised not to expand fiscal reforms past the tax increases of 1971 and assured financiers and industrialists that neither banks nor industries would be nationalized, regardless of the economic stresses and worker demonstrations. As subsequent investigations have revealed, Mexico's adherence to a fixed exchange rate of 12.50 pesos per U.S. dollar, established in 1955, aggravated Mexico's level of inflation in a manner similar to that being experienced by other American nations during the early 1970s. Unfortunately, growing social unrest and demands by workers required attention in 1973, when the patriarch of the Monterrey industrialists' group, Eugenio Garza Sada, was assassinated by a guerrilla organization, the 23rd of September League. Continuing threats of similar retaliation by workers, who resented their loss of wage with an inflated peso, forced the Banco de México to adopt a floating exchange rate in 1977. During 1976, the bank advocated a devalued rate of 15.69 pesos per U.S. dollar; however, this strategy did not protect Mexico from the continuing effects of inflation. The international community, as a whole, suffered from an inflationary spiral that, added to the failure of the Bretton Wood system in 1973 and the escalation of war in Southeast Asia, upset most financial balances.

The dislocations that had threatened since 1972 became realities after 1977. As the value of oil exports grew in response to U.S. demands relative to its commitment in Vietnam, the government liberalized restrictions on imports to placate the middle class and elites, who desired foreign products, as well as U.S. industrialists, who wanted admittance to Mexican markets. This combination of events increased the inflation that harassed laborers as well as small and medium-sized Mexican-owned industries, and led to even further worker demonstrations. Liberalization policies continued, however, as officials and experts believed that the continuing increase in the oil boom eventually would compensate for these minor disalignments. Heavy dollarization of financial transactions posited another element of the short-run monetary instability within Mexico's financial situation in the late 1970s, as the Banco de México freely allowed deposits of overvalued U.S. dollars against floating peso accounts. The fluctuation of demand balance between foreign and domestic currency accentuated the negative effects of capital flight, particularly after 1976. When the oil market began to suffer demand and price declines between 1979 and mid-1981, however, these various instabilities within the Mexican financial system converged to create the severest of crises. Initially, officials responded to falling prices by cutting the price of Mexican crude oil to meet international market competition. By early 1982, these trade conditions, dollarization, and other inequities combined with the ensuing capital flight (which may have totaled as much as US$36 billion from 1978 to 1982) and speculation on the peso to lead to complete collapse. Afraid of the political repercussions to the PRI, outgoing President José López Portillo did not attempt to rescue the severely overvalued peso. Instead, he refused to approve an end to the liberalization of imports late in 1981 and sanctioned rapidly rising foreign interest rates, thereby adding to the already heavy foreign debt payment. Consequently, when the Banco de México froze all external credit transactions out of a fear of bank failure, Mexico became insolvent. Although the nation muddled through with patriotic rhetoric until that summer, by February 1982, the nation faced an enormous deficit in its balance of payments without funds to begin to meet the obligation.

1982–96

The greatest set-back to Mexican financial stability since the Revolution of 1910, the problems faced during 1982 resulted from continuation of strategies for industrial growth begun in the post–World War II and Korean War eras and not significantly adjusted in response to Mexico's changes relative to other nations, particularly the United States. The IMF and WB had supported Mexico's development with few questions, fewer restrictions, and had repeatedly refinanced and expanded its debt load during the 1960s and 1970s. Phenomenal industrial expansion that depended upon Mexico's only renewable resource, cheap labor, and the desire of the United States to promote a ready trade in crude oil, particularly outside the Middle East, masked the need for revision of long-term economic strategies. Mexico's situation in 1982 did not differ significantly from that of other oil-producing nations in the Americas, but Mexico's crisis rapidly became the most severe.

The fading miracle led Mexico back to historical conflicts. Abundant national resources, greatly desired by many, and a growing labor force should have led to growth and prosperity, but continuation of that prosperity was contingent upon the support and advocacy of an ancient adversary that intended to keep Mexico a dependent supplier of labor and resources. An examination of the crisis of 1982 revealed that immediate and early assistance might have prevented complete collapse because many "depression characteristics" existed in the severe cash flow shortage. As such, the immediate remedy could have been easily forthcoming, except the WB officials hesitated to provide necessary liquidity without U.S. approval. The U.S. Federal Reserve Bank and the largest New York City banks could have underwritten the Mexico peso at the first signs of trouble, but they chose not to do so. The hate/love combination of the U.S. citizens' prejudices against Mexican laborers and the U.S. business community's desire for free access to Mexican resources produced a dilemma for publicity-conscious President Ronald Reagan. Mexico's assistance to Nicaragua and other problematic Central American nations, as well as its trade with Cuba, angered Reagan and led him to oppose aid for the Mexican bankers. He quietly became convinced by the U.S. business community to change his position after they received Mexico's assurances that restrictions against foreign investment and land ownership would soon be eased. Consequently, in August 1982, when Mexico officially announced its inability to meet its foreign debt payments in a timely manner, the Federal Reserve and Treasury Department, along with 11 large international banks, extended an emergency loan of US$1.85 billion, bringing Mexico's total external debt to over US$85 billion. However, it would exceed US$100 billion by 1985, as interest escalated, but oil prices did not. The loan required dedication of oil production to the United States to be sold at a guaranteed low price, a measure that further limited Mexico's financial alternatives. The crisis of 1982 was both a severe personal assault upon Mexico's status as a developing nation and a signal of the necessity to return to closer economic ties with the United States.

The ghosts of 1982 continued to haunt Mexico as banking and economic officials began the long process of correction and attempted to structure a new development plan. The severe devaluation of the peso by more than 70 percent, accompanied by the setting of its value at a freely floating exchange rate based upon the dollar, plus a new system of exchange controls to stop the outflow of money, led to the beginning of nationalization of the private banking system. During 1982, these measures did little to repair the damage, but they reflected a deeper change in financial philosophies and the beginning of slow but steady changes in economic and political structures.

Mexico's economy did not grow during the next six years, and the costs of restructuring rested firmly on the working and middle classes, while the wealthy reaped multiple rewards. The government slashed social and public services to the bone at a time when the number of people living on less than the government-established minimum wage (reduced by 40 percent during the crisis) increased from 40 percent to 60 percent of the population. Simultaneously, fewer Mexicans had access to any wage labor as small and medium-sized businesses closed and the work force rose by an average of 1 million people per year. The consequences of this condition appeared most strongly in the rising rate of nonviolent crimes, burglary, and larceny, and upon drug trafficking. Administration officials of the Miguel de la Madrid presidency (1982–88) dismantled outdated protectionist policies, but political friction between the United States and Mexico continued owing to Mexico's continuing support to governments in Central America that were out of favor with the United States. However, the United States supported Mexico's subsequent requests to the IMF for loans, which brought the outstanding foreign debt to over US$100 billion during 1985. The unfortunate consequences of this debt load, including the reduction of investments in the infrastructure and public services, continued to retard Mexico's recovery and to hamper the nation's ability to cope with monetary and political instability in the 1990s. Although refinancing the debt in 1988–89 brought some relief, dependence upon the availability of foreign capital and accompanying annual servicing at almost 20 percent of national exports, meant that true financial strength remained a dream for the future.

Mexico's financial problems continued into the 1990s, particularly with the peso crash in December 1994, and continuing monetary softness, mixed with new international agreements and expectations for perennial reforms. Expansion of *maquiladora* industries in the late 1980s, Mexico's inclusion in the unified North American Free Trade Agreement (NAFTA), and the return to privatized industries all produced stronger connections with U.S.

industry. Fiscal announcements by President Ernesto Zedillo Ponce de León of an economic pact for 1997 between business and labor leaders set goals for 15 percent inflation, accompanied by salary increases of 8 to 10 percent and continuation of the floating monetary exchange. Mexico now planned for "moderate" inflation in the expectation of foreign exchange gains under NAFTA and a healthy rise in tourism income. Simultaneously, PRI efforts to liberalize the political establishment in Mexico to make it more resemble the U.S. model, rather than to make it more responsive to the Mexican people, often met the roadblock of the old conservative versus liberal arguments. In 1994, the political assassination of PRI-designated presidential candidate, Luis Donaldo Colosio, and the organized rebellion in Chiapas reflected the chaos caused by the continuing economic transformation in Mexico.

See also General Agreement on Tariffs and Trade (GATT); Neoliberalism; North American Free Trade Agreement (NAFTA); Peso Crisis of 1994

Select Bibliography

Aguilar Camín, Héctor, and Lorenzo Meyer, *In the Shadow of the Mexican Revolution: Contemporary Mexican History, 1910–1989,* translated by Luis Alberto Fierro. Austin: University of Texas Press, 1993.

Davis, Charles L., and Kenneth M. Coleman, "Neoliberal Economic Policies and the Potential for Electoral Change in Mexico." *Mexican Studies/Estudios Mexicanos* 10:2 (Summer 1994).

Edwards, Sebastian, "Introduction" and "Exchange Rates, Inflation and Disinflation: Latin American Experiences." In *Capital Controls, Exchange Rates, and Monetary Policy in the World Economy.* Cambridge: Cambridge University Press, 1995.

Ize, Alain, "Resource Mobilization and Investment Promotion: Current Growth Perspectives for Mexico." In *The Dynamics of North American Trade and Investment,* edited by Clark W. Reynolds, Leonard Waverman, and Gerardo Bueno. Stanford: Stanford University Press, 1991.

Ortiz, Guillermo, "Dollarization in Mexico: Causes and Consequences." In *Financial Policies and the World Capital Market: The Problem of Latin American Countries,* edited by Pedro Aspe Armella, Rudiger Dornbusch, and Maurice Obstfeld. Chicago: University of Chicago Press, 1983.

Sachs, Jeffrey D., *Developing Country Debt and Economic Performance: The International Financial System.* Chicago: University of Chicago Press, 1989.

Schott, Jeffrey J., "Global Implications of the Canada-U.S. Free Trade Agreement." In *The Dynamics of North American Trade and Investment,* edited by Clark W. Reynolds, Leonard Waverman, and Gerardo Bueno. Stanford: Stanford University Press, 1991.

—MARY A. WATROUS

BASES ORGÁNICAS

On December 23, 1842, President Nicolás Bravo, a former participant in the War of Independence, designated 80 notables to form the Junta Nacional Legislativa (National Legislative Junta), which eventually replaced the Congress. The goal was to draw the guidelines for Mexico's future Constitution. From the offset, January 6, 1843, the notables made it clear that their role was to adopt a new—centralist—Constitution, and not simply draft some basic guidelines that they would pass along for discussion by a new legislative body to be designated later. The draft Constitution was presented for discussion April 8. However, all its parts were unanimously adopted with no discussion whatsoever, the first time such a thing had happened in Mexican history. The resulting document was called the Bases de organizacíon política de la República Mexicana (Bases for the Political Organization of the Republic of Mexico), otherwise known simply as las Bases Orgánicas.

The Junta included several outstanding members, such as Manuel de la Peña y Peña, future head of the Supreme Court and interim president of Mexico; Sebastián Camacho, former governor of Yucatán; and General Gabriel Valencia. José Fernando Ramírez deserves special mention among the Junta's members because he already had prepared a well-known draft constitution (presented on November 3, 1842) together with Mariano Otero, Octaviano Muñoz Ledo, and other noteworthy jurists. Ramírez's failed efforts to attenuate all-out centralism in the National Legislative Junta made him resign. During the approval of the Constitution, all supporters of federalism were persecuted and isolated for 44 days. Conflict within the country's political class deepened extremely, setting the scene for the future U.S. invasion.

The Bases Orgánicas divided the Mexican territory into provinces, called *departamentos.* Each province had a Provincial Assembly, or Asamblea Departamental. The Californias and New Mexico were subject to a "closer subordination" to the general government, as a result of U.S. claims over these territories.

The section concerning human rights is outstanding. Freedom was guaranteed to all inhabitants, including members of Indian communities. It forbade slavery even for those who entered Mexico who had been slaves abroad. This provision foresaw a situation that later took place in the United States with the *Dred Scott v. Sanford* case in 1857. Foreigners explicitly enjoyed all rights mentioned in the fourteen sections of Article 9, in addition to rights deriving from other laws and international treaties.

Mexican citizenship was accorded to those born in Mexican territory, regardless of parental citizenship, to the children of Mexican parents, even if born abroad, to foreigners living in Mexico since 1821, and to foreigners lawfully naturalized as Mexicans. To become a naturalized Mexican it was enough to marry a Mexican, work at Mexico's service, or work for a Mexican establishment. However, Article 15 already endowed preference to Mexicans over any foreigner for work. Citizenship was given at 18 years of age, but was conditioned to annual income, the minimum of which varied according to the *departamento.*

Public administration included four ministries, or *secretarías.* Secretaries could be required by the president or the chambers to attend Congress sessions and deliver reports. They were accountable for all presidential actions endorsed by them, and held responsible if such actions were later determined to be unlawful or unconstitutional. The Bases Orgánicas included the existence of a Governing Council inherited from the 1824 Constitution. The Council was a consulting body for the executive power. Its functions included proposing regulations and public policies. It was formed by 17 members, whose tasks were distributed according to *secretaría* needs.

The Bases Orgánicas required naming one representative to the lower Chamber of Deputies, a *diputado,* for every 70,000 inhabitants, and all *departamentos* had at least one *diputado* representing them. Eligibility requirements included a minimum age of 30 years, birth in the represented *departamento* or residence there for at least 3 years, and an annual income of 1,200 pesos. Half the members of the Chamber of Deputies were changed every two years.

The Senate was composed of a fixed number of members—63. Two-thirds of the senators were designated by the Asambleas Departamentales, and their candidates could be farmers, miners, proprietors or merchants, and manufacturers. The other third of the Senate was jointly nominated by the president, the Chamber of Deputies, and the Supreme Court. These candidacies were studied by the Senate, which had the last word. Requirements included Mexican citizenship, a minimum age of 35 years, and an annual income of 2,000 pesos.

The president, *diputados,* and Asambleas Departamentales were allowed to move bills concerning any topic. The Chamber of Deputies was the first to examine any given bill. The Senate had to revise them, and the president had to publish the adopted laws. To veto a bill, the president required approval by the Governing Council within 30 days of its submission. Otherwise, the new law or decree had to be published with no delay.

The Supreme Court was meant to serve as a last instance court for all kinds of cases and to pass judgment over the accountabilities of public servants. However, in line with the liberal thought of the epoch, the Bases Orgánicas defined the function of Supreme Court judges and established an ad hoc accountability court to supervise its actions.

The Bases Orgánicas was innovative in its introduction of electoral power. The population elected primary voters, which in turn elected secondary voters.

The judicial system included arbiter judges, who mediated in civil and even penal cases whenever the offense concerned purely personal conflicts. This shows the inclusion of conciliatory and arbitrating measures within judicial activities.

The Bases Orgánicas were adopted by President Antonio López de Santa Anna on June 12, 1843. Soon after, however, Santa Anna was forced to resign in the face of a rebellion led by General Marino Paredes y Arrillaga in Guadalajara. He was replaced by Interim President Valentín Canalizo and later by the head of the Governing Council, José Joaquín Herrera. Herrera governed one year under the Bases Orgánicas, from December 1844 to December 1845. The only amendment, which concerned the Senate, ever made to this constitution was introduced on December 25, 1845.

General Paredes rebelled again in San Luis Potosí, and Herrera was removed from office. In January 1846 the new president called for a National Assembly to change the constitution and the laws, and committed "not to block its sovereign decisions." The assembly began meeting on June 9, but its existence came to a halt only two months later. General Paredes acted with the support of the leading Conservative Lucas Alamán. By then the Conservatives already had shown an inclination for the reestablishment of monarchy in Mexico. However, in August 1846 a rebellion headed by Mariano Salas at Plaza de la Ciudadela in Mexico City canceled the validity of the Bases Orgánicas.

Select Bibliography

Costeloe, Michael P., *The Central Republic in Mexico, 1836–1846: Hombres de Bien in the Age of Santa Anna.* Cambridge and New York: Cambridge University Press, 1993.

Tena Ramírez, Felipe, *Leyes Fundamentales de Mexico 1808–1971.* Mexico City: Porrúa, 1971.

—MANUEL GONZÁLEZ OROPEZA

BASSOLS, NARCISO

1897–1959 • Jurist, Educator, and Politician

Narciso Bassols was born in Tenango del Valle, Mexico State, on October 22, 1897. In 1907 he began his studies in the San José School in Mexico City. In 1911 he enrolled in the National Preparatory School, and he concluded his studies in 1915. From 1916 to 1919 he studied in the College of Law, where he was president of the student association and author of its bylaws. One of his teachers, Antonio Caso, considered Bassols to be his most distinguished disciple. In 1919 he passed the bar exam and established a law firm along with Joaquín Álvarez Icaza. In that same year he also began to teach a class on logic at the National Preparatory School. Between 1921 and 1931 he taught classes in rights, protection under the law, and constitutional law. At the same time, he gave speeches urging young law students to rescue the cultural values of the country and to "intervene in life in the making of history." In 1925 he was named a consultant to the Department of Health and later to the Secretary General of the Mexican government. In 1927, at the behest of the secretary of agriculture and development, he wrote the law of water endowments and restitution, which fell under Article 27 of the Constitution. He also wrote the Ley Agraria (Agrarian Law), which removed the restrictions in the Agricultural Regulation of 1922 that had been contrary to Article 27; under Bassols' Ley Agraria, all population centers in which there were peasants without land had a constitutional right to community lands.

In 1929, for a brief period, he was the director of the College of Law and Social Sciences at the National Autonomous University of Mexico (UNAM). He supplemented the curriculum with three elective subjects and a class on agrarian law because he felt that the question of land and agrarian reform were Mexico's largest problems. The College of Law had become a conservative stronghold, however, and so he departed from the university. Bassols was a Marxist, and he believed that new laws should contribute to creating a new society and not to conserving the old way of doing things. During 1930 and 1931 he participated in the writing of the law on the liquidation of the old credit banks, and he presided over the liquidating committee. He assisted with the writing of the Agriculture Credit Law of 1931, the Organic Law of the University in 1933, the Agrarian Code in 1934, and in the reform of Article 3 of the Constitution in 1934.

As secretary of education during the presidencies of Pascual Ortiz Rubio (1930–32) and Abelardo L. Rodríguez (1932–34), Bassols carried out an important study and evaluation of the educational system. He strengthened agricultural teaching and also regional development based on the in-depth study of each area, and he created new rural educational institutions, such as the Regional Rural

Schools. His fundamental concerns were to raise peasant productivity and combine educational advances with agrarian reform. He reorganized the Department of Technical Education within the Bureau of Public Education (SEP), and he presented the bill for the Organic Law of the University to the Congress. He later resigned the office of secretary because of the opposition awakened by his measures, among them the removal of religion from private education and the project, never carried out, to establish sex education within the schools.

In 1934 he was secretary of the interior and later secretary of the treasury during the government of Lázaro Cárdenas (1934–40), at a stage when the country was recovering from the effects of the 1929 economic crisis. Surrounded by efficient aides, he performed an important function. His most significant action was substituting the traditional monetary system based on the circulation of metallic coins "for a more rational system—economically effective, cheaper and more flexible—that of paper money backed by a strong metals reserve."

Cárdenas gave Bassols the unenviable task of asking former president Plutarco Elías Calles to leave the country. Although Bassols was a Cárdenist, loyalty to Calles made Bassols feel obligated to resign from his position as treasury secretary, where his management looked truly promising. Bassols never again occupied a high office within the government. In the second half of the 1930s he was a minister in England, the Mexican representative in the League of Nations—where he defended Ethiopia as a victim of Italian fascism—and minister in France. At the end of 1936 he gave up his diplomatic charges, but he visited Spain as a demonstration of solidarity. In Mexico, in 1937, he organized the publishing house Editorial Revolucionario and wrote in the journal *Hoy y Futuro* against the dangers of fascism. His fight against fascism and his solidarity with other peoples was the principal occupation of the last years of Bassols' life. In 1944 he was named ambassador to the Soviet Union. Upon his return to Mexico in 1947, he contributed to the creation of the Popular Party (PP), of which he was vice president until October 1949. In 1949 he represented Cárdenas at the meeting that created the World Peace Council. He was an advisor to Adolfo Ruis Cortinez (1952–58) until the devaluation of the Mexican peso in 1954. From that point on he dedicated himself to promoting Mexican participation in international congresses for peace and cooperation among nations, and he supported the struggles of workers. Another of Bassols's contributions in these years was his participation in the compulsory law of Article 27 of the Constitution about petroleum, which attempted to quantify the extent of the nationalization of the petroleum industry. He wrote numerous texts, articles, and essays, and translated several works, among them an anthology of essays by the economist John Maynard Keynes. He also created the weekly *Combate*. He died in an accident on July 24, 1959. During all of his life he gave proof of honesty, integrity, and dedication to just causes.

Select Bibliography

Bassols, Narciso, *Obras*. Mexico City: Fondo de Cultura Económica, 1964.

—ENGRACIA LOYO BRAVO

BENAVENTE, TORIBIO DE (MOTOLINÍA)

c.1490–1569 • Missionary and Chronicler

One of the twelve Franciscans in the first formal expedition of religious to arrive in New Spain in 1524, Toribio de Benavente adopted the name Motolinía after hearing the Nahuatl word, which means "poor or stricken one," being used by the indigenous people to describe him. He is best know today through his writings, which embody three important facets of Mexican history. First, his histories of New Spain reflect the Franciscan "open arms" policy of evangelization, influenced by the reforms within the mendicant orders in Europe as well as millenarian views of some members of the Franciscan order. Motolinía's work also represents the "golden age" of the early colonial period, in which the mendicant orders were, to the exclusion of the secular clergy (i.e., those not belonging to a particular order), charged with the evangelization of the indigenous population of New Spain. During this period, the friars exhibited great optimism and zeal. Finally, Motolinía's defense of the Franciscans and the *encomenderos* (trustees of landholdings and accompanying Indian labor) in response to Bartolomé de Las Casas's criticisms signals the transition from early to mature colonial society. In this phase the Spanish Crown renewed its interest in New Spain; it effected this desire to exert royal authority by undermining the *encomendero* class and replacing the mendicants with secular clergy.

The Franciscan order's philosophy was influenced by the Christian humanism of Desiderius Erasmus (1469–1536) and to some degree by the millenarian beliefs of Joachim de Fiore (c. 1130–1201). These influences manifested themselves in an emphasis on learning about the customs and history of the indigenous peoples of the Americas as well as their major languages. In addition, the millenarian view that the Christianization of the population of New Spain would help usher in a new spiritual age lent a sense of urgency to the evangelical efforts. The Franciscans practiced an "open arms" policy in which baptism was performed as soon as the convert demonstrated a basic understanding of Christianity. This approach contrasted with that of the Dominicans, who stressed an extensive education and fairly thorough understanding of Christian doctrine before baptism.

Memoriales o Libro de las Cosas de la Nueva España y de los naturales de ella and *Historia de los Indios de la Nueva España,* written between 1536 and 1543, are records of indigenous history and religious practices, as well as the Christianization of the Indians in central Mexico by the Franciscans. In these works Motolinía seeks to establish a historical context for the friars' work. He also describes the methods of evangelization and the criteria for administering the Sacraments. In support of the Franciscan open arms policy of baptism, Motolinía cites the devotion and the urgency of the Indians who came to him and other friars, pleading to receive the Sacrament of baptism. He describes in several passages how in some cases thousands of converts were baptized in a single day. Finally, the friar describes the dedication of the Franciscans despite the hardships and the difficulty of their mission in central Mexico and other parts of the Spanish Empire.

The Franciscan order's experience working among the Indians was a key argument in a letter Motolinía wrote to Carlos I in 1555 answering the Dominican friar Bartolomé de Las Casas's criticism of the Spanish presence in the Americas. In particular, Motolinía cites Las Casas's failure to learn Nahuatl and his refusal to baptize Indians seeking the Sacrament. These criticisms of the Dominicans, and the defense of the existing system illustrate the rivalry and fundamental differences between the two orders. Motolinía's letter to the emperor was written in a time in which Las Casas's views were better suited for the long-term goals of the Spanish Crown. By midcentury the Crown had realized the increased potential for extracting wealth from New Spain and Peru, and set about to weaken the *encomenderos* and their monopoly on indigenous labor. The Crown also sought to put in place civil and ecclesiastical personnel loyal to it. The mendicant orders were considered too independent from royal authority. As a result, by the mid–sixteenth century, the role of the mendicant orders continued to decline rapidly in all except frontier regions.

Motolinía returned to the convent of San Francisco in Mexico City in 1569 and died shortly after. He was the last of the original twelve Franciscan missionaries to New Spain. With his death ended the golden age of the "Spiritual Conquest" of New Spain. By the late sixteenth century, the initial optimism and zeal of the early friars had dissipated. The severe decline of the indigenous population owing to disease, the growth of the Spanish population, and the influx of secular clergy signaled a shift in colonial society away from early policies and institutions to those that would enhance royal authority.

Select Bibliography

Motolinía, Fray Toribio, *Memoriales o Libro de las cosas de la Nueva España y de los Naturales de Ella,* edited by Edmundo O'Gorman. Mexico City: UNAM, 1971.

_____, *Historia de los Indios de la Nueva España,* edited by Edmundo O'Gorman. Mexico City: Porrúa, 1969.

O'Gorman, Edmundo, *La incognita de la llamada "Historia de los Indios de la Nueva España" atribuida a Fray Toribio Motolinía.* Mexico City: Fondo de Cultura Económica, 1982.

Perez Fernandez, Isacio, *Fray Toribio Motolinía, O.F. M. frente a Fray Bartolomé de Las Casas, O. P.* Salamanca: Editorial San Esteban, 1989.

Phelan, John Leddy, *The Millenial Kingdom of the Franciscans in the New World.* Berkeley: University of California Press, 1970.

Ricard, Robert, *The Spiritual Conquest of Mexico,* translated by Lesley Byrd Simpson. Berkeley: University of California Press, 1984.

Weckman, Luis, *The Medieval Heritage of Mexico,* translated by Francis M López-Morillas. New York: Fordham University Press, 1992.

—MONICA I. OROZCO

BERNAL, HERACLIO

1855–88 • Bandit and Rebel

Known as the Thunderbolt of Sinaloa, the bandit Heraclio Bernal terrorized officialdom and titillated the public during the latter part of the nineteenth century. He was born on a Sinaloan *rancho* (small farm) in 1855 at a time when civil war and soon after foreign intervention convulsed the country. Political rivals contested claims to power at all levels, and the Bernal family was in the midst of the local struggles. In 1879 Heraclio joined a rebellion against President Porfirio Díaz, lost the political fight, but escaped into banditry (always tinged with political aims). In this way he resembled many nineteenth-century brigands. Persistent unrest normally spawns brigands who vie for spoils of turmoil. Many of the bandits are also political losers who seek revenge on a rival or hope for eventual incorporation into the new regime. Mexican political winners frequently incorporated their adversaries into their ranks during this epoch.

By the early 1880s Bernal headed a band of brigands which fluctuated into the hundreds. Their main targets were mule trains heavily laden with silver from mines in neighboring Durango as well as in his home state. Merchants who supplied the mines also felt his sting, so frequently in fact that the brigand's ties to competing merchants became obvious. Naturally he robbed people with money and property—the rich—and so won the reputation as a sort of Robin Hood, who robbed the wealthy to serve the poor. Although Bernal's reputed largess toward the weak and humble is difficult to substantiate, his badgering of officialdom is not, which assured him popularity among all those who decried authority, especially the arbitrary and overbearing sort so common in Mexico.

Heraclio loved to thumb his nose at the governor. On one occasion, for example, the governor organized a sumptuous dinner for a visiting dignitary in the state capital. Bernal taunted him by arranging an even more lavish banquet for the bandit's friends at a nearby pueblo. Once Bernal invited the governor to a dance he sponsored for his compatriots. As might be expected, the governor sent troops in his stead, but by the time they arrived, Heraclio and his band were nestled in the safety of surrounding hills. "Here comes Heraclio Bernal" became a haughty slogan which symbolized justice and jest, terror and respect, and reverberated throughout the countryside and beyond. Other Mexican bandits of the period—such as Chucho el Roto and Santanón—enjoyed the same sort of ambivalent notoriety.

Displaying the ambivalence toward their chosen pursuits so common among these sorts of brigands, Bernal made a bid to enter government service in 1885 (indeed some bandits had been incorporated into Mexico's famous Rural Police Force, the Rurales). In exchange for his return to the law and personal loyalty to the regime, the Thunderbolt asked President Díaz to appoint him a *jefe político* (a regional political boss) in Sinaloa. He also demanded 30,000 pesos to support a public security unit in the zone, plus the release of his imprisoned gang members, including his brother. Had Díaz been less in control of his government, he might have made a deal with Bernal—as his presidential predecessor did—but Díaz could afford to scoff at such presumptuousness. Nonetheless, the president indicated that he might pardon Bernal if he surrendered to federal authority, a deal the brigand defiantly refused (probably because he feared that summary justice, or the *ley fuga,* awaited him).

If Díaz would not allow the bandit into his government, Bernal determined to overthrow it. He joined revolts against the regime, and in 1887 issued his own proclamation in which he called for fulfillment of the nation's constitution, particularly those provisions which limited presidents to one four-year term and prescribed fair elections. But this challenge to Porfirian authority raised little public enthusiasm, and the Porfirian army squelched such outbursts of armed resistance, even if some smoldered into the next century.

In the latter part of the 1880s the army's relentless wars against the intractable Yaqui Indians to the north simmered down, and troops could be spared for the pursuit of Bernal. The governors of Sinaloa and Durango offered a 10,000-peso reward for the head of the Thunderbolt. As frequently (practically predictably) happens in these circumstances, two members of Bernal's gang took the bait and betrayed their leader to authorities. On January 5, 1888, the turncoats helped to set up the ambush in which Bernal died on January 5, 1888. His gang split up and some were said to have joined up with another notorious bandit, Ignacio Parra, who purportedly tutored Pancho Villa.

However, as is well known, the bullets of soldiers cannot kill revered and feared bandits, and notices of Bernal's escapades far outdistanced his lifetime. Today he is celebrated in no less than thirteen lusty *corridos* (uniquely Mexican folk songs), four poems, and four motion pictures, some of them periodically replayed on television. Mexicans cherish this bandit's memory, especially for his antigovernment exploits. Some even hunger for his return.

Select Bibliography

Giron, Nicole, *Heraclio Bernal: ¿Bandolero, cacique o precursor de la Revolución?* Mexico City: Instituto Nacional de Antropología e Historia, 1976.

Vanderwood, Paul J., *Disorder and Progress: Bandits, Police, and Mexican Development.* Wilmington, Delaware: Scholarly Resources, 1992.

—PAUL J. VANDERWOOD

BLANCO, LUCIO

1879–1922 • General

Lucio Blanco is remembered in the annals of the Mexican Revolution for having achieved the first triumph—the taking of Matamoros in 1913—against the government of Victoriano Huerta; for having been the first to distribute hacienda lands to peons; and for his tragic death near Laredo, Texas. He was born in the village of Nadadores, Coahuila, on July 21, 1879, the son of Bernardo Blanco and María Fuentes. During his youth he went to live in Múzquiz, Coahuila, but returned to his father's ranch to manage his properties. Inspired by the ideas of his godfather, Atilano Barrera, Blanco took up arms against the dictatorship of Porfirio Díaz as early as 1906; with some *vaqueros* (cowboys) from his ranch, he tried to take the border town of Las Vacas (today Ciudad Acuña). Like Don Quixote during his first sally, he was defeated and went back to his ranch.

As a result of the events that took place in Puebla in 1910 (the assassination of Revolutionary leader Aquiles Serdán), he joined the Maderista movement. After the *coup* by Victoriano Huerta, Blanco joined Venustiano Carranza and signed the Plan de Guadalupe, which did not recognize Huerta's government but named Venustiano Carranza as the first chief of the army. Blanco, with the rank of lieutenant colonel, was given the command of the first regiment of the Libres del Norte to operate in the states of Nuevo León and Tamaulipas. His first and most important early triumph was the taking of the border city of Matamoros on June 4, 1913. There his soldiers committed atrocities for which Blanco was blamed.

Carranza promoted him to the rank of brigadier general for having taken the city, but this early and unexpected glory was short lived. On August 30, 1913, Blanco distributed the lands of the hacienda Los Borregos, the first agrarian reform in the history of the Revolution. Carranza, disappointed with Blanco's action, accused him of having gone too far, beyond what was stipulated in the Plan de Guadalupe, which makes no mention of agrarian reform. As punishment, Blanco was recalled and sent to Sonora to serve under the orders of General Álvaro Obregón. He placed his own regiment under the command of the inept general Pablo González. Although Blanco obtained great power later, this early action by Carranza prevented him from becoming a national hero, alongside Francisco Villa and Emiliano Zapata. Blanco is hardly known today by the general public.

As stated by several persons who knew him personally—for instance, Martín Luis Guzmán—Lucio Blanco had a noble and elegant figure, a friendly and humane disposition, and a very friendly manner. In *The Eagle and the Serpent* (1928) Guzmán remembers him as being all gallantry and nobility; "he was so noble that he disliked glory—that was his weakness; he was so human, that the horror of killing paralyzed his actions after the first revolutionary fury."

Under Obregón, Blanco was commissioned to organize a cavalry division in Sinaloa, to be part of the Army of the Northwest. His principal accomplishments were the taking of the cities of Tepic and Guadalajara, the last one considered to be his greatest triumph after Matamoros. Alongside Carranza and Obregón, Blanco arrived in Mexico City in August 1914. The Zapatista armies also were marching toward the capital. Blanco, being sympathetic to Zapata's land reform program, gave orders for his army to receive them cordially. He personally greeted the Zapatista leaders when they arrived.

During the last months of 1914, Lucio Blanco was one of the most powerful generals in Mexico City. Both Carranza and Obregón, however, began to suspect that he wanted to defect with his army and join Villa. This moment marks the beginning of Blanco's downfall. Soon Carranza considered him, without having any evidence, as a traitor, and Blanco's disagreements with Obregón escalated, especially as a result of his having played a prominent part in the Aguascalientes Convention of October 1914 (in which the armies of Zapata and Villa broke with Carranza), and having been named secretary of the interior during the temporary government of Eulalio Gutiérrez. Obregón suspected that Blanco had abandoned his faction, the Constitutionalists, and detained him. Although he wanted to have Blanco court-martialed, Carranza promised to safeguard his life.

In 1916 Blanco was tried for treason, found guilty of insubordination, and condemned to five years in prison. After Obregón resigned as secretary of war, Carranza was able to reduce Blanco's sentence and give him his liberty. Fearful of Obregón, Blanco decided to take refuge in Laredo, Texas. In June 1922, Mexican government agents led Blanco to believe that some officers in Nuevo Laredo were eager to have him lead them in a revolution against the central government. He agreed and they took him across the river about 7 P.M. in a boat, accompanied by Ramón García and Colonel Aurelio Martínez. When they reached the Mexican shore of the river, at a place called Paso del Indio, about five miles from Nuevo Laredo, García tried to imprison both Blanco and Martínez, and in the struggle the three fell into the river. Waiting for them was a group of about 20 soldiers of the 20th Regiment led by Anaya Terán; the soldiers killed Martínez and García while the men were still in the water. Blanco, they claimed, was not killed, but had drowned.

Who gave the orders to kill Lucio Blanco? It is known that the attorney general of the Laredo, Texas, district, John Wales, gave orders to detain Plutarco Elías Calles in case he came to the city. On the other hand, the Revolutionary general Francisco Murguía, who also was in exile in Texas during the same period, blamed Obregón, president at that time. As in many of the crimes committed during the Revolution, the death of Lucio Blanco was the result of quarrels among the principal chieftains. Regardless of who is to blame for Blanco's death, he will be remembered as one the few honest leaders of the Mexican Revolution.

Select Bibliography

María y Campos, Armando de, *Vida del General Lucio Blanco.* Mexico City: Instituto Nacional de Estudios Históricos, 1963.

—LUIS LEAL

BORDER LITERATURES

Since the 1980s the concept of "the border" has become quite important in many academic disciplines. In the United States, "border studies" have sought to "dismantle the patriarchal and Anglocentric limits of the word 'American,' especially in the context of 'Mexican literature'" (Anderson, 1995). In Mexico, border studies have made manifest the disarticulation of Mexican literature, giving new visibility to the cultural production of border regions (Anderson, 1995).

Today literary and cultural criticism seems to resist fixed taxonomies, but it has not managed to escape the ancient art of cataloging. Nevertheless, the trend now is to utilize tropes that allow the object and subject of study to maintain a certain dynamism and largely avoid being pigeonholed. The metaphor of the "border" or the "borderland" has become one of the most popular rhetorical tropes in literary theory. In the United States terms such as "border literature," "borderland or border literature" and "criticism on the border" have been mainly linked to work largely produced by Chicano writers and critics since the mid-1980s. This new Chicano writing and criticism around the border has permitted a broader understanding of Chicano culture, but it also has helped make the literature from the Mexican side of the border invisible.

Chicano border criticism and the Mexican border literature movement emerged at roughly the same time. Both sought to define "border literatures" that were independent of their respective "national" literatures. The marginality of U.S. and Mexican border literatures has made them somewhat contentious, and both contain a series of discourses of oppression and accepted representations that they seek to break down. Despite these similarities, however, the asymmetry between the United States and Mexico has pushed U.S. and Mexican border literatures in quite different directions. The literature of the U.S. border is dominant and that of Mexico dominated. This is owing mostly to the politics and cultural practices of each country, including the possibility of publication, distribution, and finding or creating spaces in the world of academe. In the United States Chicano literature has won space thanks to the work of critics and writers and an institutionalized system that demands equal opportunities, regardless of ethnicity, race, and class. It is not difficult to find in U.S. universities programs or complete departments dedicated to Chicano, African American, indigenous American, or ethnic studies that fund research work and publications on these cultures within and outside the United States.

In Mexico, however, it is almost impossible to find individual chairs in regional literature, let alone whole programs dedicated to the study of cultures of individual states. The Universidad Nacional Autónoma de México (UNAM) does have a Center for Chicano Studies and a Research Center on the United States—but no center for regional studies within Mexico. From this one can infer that the transnationalization of literature coming from the United States arrived in the Mexican capital before the emergence of regional literature; or that the new cultural and literary expressions of regions such as the northern frontier of Mexico were not part of the national scheme.

It has been very difficult for the work of writers and critics of border literature to be recognized at a national level; occasionally, it is not even recognized within their own region. On one hand, hegemonic cultural politics has represented Mexican literature as emerging from the central area of the country or from the so-called cultural centers (Jalapa, Guadalajara, Monterrey); on the other, the same official version has inculcated a negative attitude toward the border area. This view has qualified the inhabitants of the region as barbarians and lacking a national identity and their main urban centers, Tijuana and Ciudad Juárez, as cities of perdition.

The perspective of the center and the region itself on the northern border has been conforming increasingly with its social reality. From the 1980s onward Mexico's interest in the border has increased with analyses focusing on economic themes, migration, the *maquiladora* (assembly plant) industry, environment, public health, and Mexican-U.S. relations. This focus is not exclusively based on analyses undertaken within academic institutions in the border zones. Since the 1970s several important publications have sought to encourage attempts to formulate a theoretical critique of the border area. Several national publications on the border region have been created, most notably *Cultura Norte* and *Cultura Sur* (today merged into a single journal, *Fronteras*), created by the Consejo Nacional para la Cultura y las Artes (National Council for Culture and the Arts), and the collection *Letras de la república*. Other journals have emerged from the border region itself, including *Hojas, El oficio, Esquina Baja, Travesía, Trazadura*, the *"inventario"* of *Diario 29 El Nacional, Lavidaloca, Papel, Palabras sin Arrugas, Nod, Azar*, and *Puentelibre*. These journals have encouraged the articulation of a new conceptualization of the border that is less totalizing and oppressive, and more grounded in everyday life on the border.

Since 1986, the theoretical bases of Mexican and U.S. border criticism also have diverged. Mexican criticism has been characterized by descriptions of literature from the northern border and observations of the sociocultural phenomena that brought this literature to light. U.S. border criticism analyzes Chicano culture from the theoretical discourse of postmodernism and other critical stances with the prefix "post" (postcolonialism, postfeminism, etc.) or from the viewpoint of cultural studies. Apart from proposing the reassessment of "American Literature" within the United States, Chicano theory has led critics to take particular interest in the recognition of the literary and cultural heritage of Mexico and Latin-America.

It is worth remembering, however, that the rearticulation and popularization of Chicano literature as "border literature" was based on the theoretical and critical work of Chicano scholars during the mid-1980s—and not the numerous creative works that have dealt with the real border between Mexico and the United States. In this critical discourse the border seen from the United States was a textual border, more theoretical than geographic. Scholars and writers such as José David Saldívar and Emily Hicks used the metaphor of the border to open a multicultural space in the country and erase its geographic limits, drawing on diverse literary Latin American and Chicano texts; Guillermo Gómez-Peña used performance to challenge cultural, geographic, and textual borders. Other texts, such as those anthologized by Héctor Calderón and José Saldívar, sought to translate Chicano identity and literature from the imaginary space of Aztlan—the mythical northern homeland of the Mexica (Aztecs), which became a locus of Chicano identity during the 1960s and 1970s—toward "the border," playing out the numerous geographic, cultural, ideological, and linguistic borders that Chicanos have crossed. Gloria Anzaldúa and Harry Polkinhorn used the actual border to construct an alternative Chicano discourse and denounce the centralist hegemony of the United States and Mexico. In Anzaldúa's words, the U.S.-Mexican border is an "open wound," but it is also a place to search for roots. The viewpoint of Roland Romero includes as much the textual as the geographical border to explain the series of discourses that have created social realities in this territory. In contrast to

the rest, Juan Bruce-Novoa defines the border as an area that will continue to produce numerous and interesting permutations in its discourses as long as it exists, without being either paradise or hell. In all of these theoretical approaches "the border" is neither a specific place nor an everyday space. It is a place where reading or writing manifests through memory. "The Borderlands" for the majority of Chicanos is the promised land, the return to the Mexican or Latin-American tradition: it is the seat of a desired identity.

In Mexican territory the emergence of the so-called border literature and criticism in the north of Mexico and analysis of the same was the result of different factors. Francisco Luna, Rosina Conde, and Minerva Margarita Villarreal, among others, agree that the interest in borderland culture and literature was emphasized in the mid-1980s by a concern from the center of the country to "reinforce the romantic package of national identity" (Luna, 1994), or give work to friends in what was then the Programa Cultural de las Fronteras (Borders Cultural Program). Official policy promoted programs to place a "chastity belt on nationality," seeking to oblige those living on the borders to "assume a role in making a decision based on false prejudice, that they do not accept . . . [that in the north] *huitlacoche* [an edible fungus used in Mexican cuisine] does not exist and *flor de calabaza* [squash flower] is not eaten" (Conde, 1992). However, in the 1980s and 1990s other social causes allowed for a greater development of literature in the area than in previous years.

In his book *Obstáculos y problemas* (1994) Francisco Amparán contends that one of the causes of this development has been the fact that many writers active before 1968 that were born outside the Mexican capital studied in their particular region rather than Mexico City or other cultural centers and developed their art in locally based literary workshops. In *Mi generación* (1994) Gabriel Trujillo Muñoz goes further, stating that the workshops helped poets to be more conscious of their task and to take on a more critical attitude. Humberto Félix Berumen and Sergio Gómez Montero mention other factors that opened the way to a rapid development in literature in the borderland northern states. These include the expansion of the middle classes prior to 1982 and their demands for more and better educational services; the fact that the writers decided to do creative work from their own regional areas and promote their work from there; the increase in publications on culture and literature at a local and regional level; easy access to national and international information; and finally, the increased relevance of many border cities on a national level. In other words, the dynamic and significant growth of the frontier states during the previous decade tended to favor regional literature.

These viewpoints reflect two currents, one a rejection of the centralized administration and the other an affirmation of regionality. Both of these viewpoints are somewhat paradoxical. On the one hand, these discourses rearticulate and recreate local paradigms that distance them as much from the center as from official polices that try to "domesticate the northern barbarians." On the other, these same writers and critics to a certain degree have made their *presence* possible through literary forums *of* the northern frontier, promoted by official projects. It would be naive to think that in a country like Mexico, with so little autonomy on a state level, that one could promote an artistic and cultural movement without having, at least in the beginning, the blessing of the Mexican state. In other words, one can hardly talk about the visibility of cultural production of the borderland zones without the patronage of writers in the Mexico City bureaucracy. These reflections require us to question the Mexican point of view regarding border literature; indeed, some writers from the border have even questioned whether a literature *of* the border exists at all.

Authors such as Rosina Conde who were born in the border region or whose work has been produced there, refuse to be categorized as "border writers," rejecting the Programa Cultural de las Fronteras and the Border Arts Workshop/Taller de Arte Fronterizo (BAW/TAF) headed by the performance artist Guillermo Gómez-Peña. Rosina Conde considers that to accept the category of "border writer" is to accept the stereotype that tries to institutionalize the official program. She believes that the BAW/TAF wants Mexicans to accept its borderlands projects as the only ones, to accept fashionable icons as if they were intrinsic to Mexican culture. The writers José Javier and Minerva Margarita Villareal declare that the label "border writers" precludes the possibility of their work becoming part of "Mexican literature." Rosario Sanmiguel also considers that to recognize herself as a border writer is to accept her marginal position in Mexican national literature. The day that a well-known publisher prints her work and distributes it like that of nationally known writers such as Federico Campbell or Jesús García, Sanmiguel insists, it will cease to be "border." For her the border and the borderlands signifies being distant from power.

Nonetheless, many writers in the border region of northern Mexico conceive border literature as a something personal. Writers such as Francisco Amparán, Guadalupe Aldaco, Humberto Félix Berumen, Sergio Gómez Montero, Francisco Luna, Inés Martínez de Castro, Leobardo Saravia, and Gabriel Trujillo do not see such labeling as an imposition because they were writing, publishing, and researching from the border region prior to the arrival of support from the central government. This classification does not imply being outside "Mexican literature." Rather, it has allowed border writers to strengthen their regional ties and recognize their local context with greater clarity. In the words of Francisco Luna, "the narrative of the northern frontier has given more authenticity and legitimacy to our northern identity than any other icon. It has delineated our geography, our space and has given us history, time and a sense of place" (Luna, 1994).

Each writer thus has his or her particular opinions regarding the "pigeon-holing" of the literature produced in the north, but during the mid-1980s they all were concerned in one way or another with the question of defining *lo fronterizo,* the "borderland." Moreover, writers' individual negotia-

tion of *lo fronterizo* has become more collective as writers and scholars regularly meet under the auspices of the Programa Cultural de las Fronteras to exchange writing and ideas. Writers and researchers undertake creative work, research, and the work of dissemination as never before. Distancing themselves from the hegemony represented by the literature of the center, they made it possible to create an emergent discourse—that of an alternative "national" literature.

In general terms, literary expression on the northern border of Mexico, like its geography, does not exist as a totality. The border region includes a variety of topographies, natural resources, and climates, and even urban development varies greatly from state to state. Thus literature appears as a manifestation activated by distinct cultural factors produced along the borderland. Scholars such as Humberto Félix Berumen, Sergio Gómez Montero, Francisco Luna, and Gabriel Muñoz Trujillo see border literature as emerging and consolidating during the 1970s, principally in the most important border cities or the capitals of border states. Narrative and poetry are the most common genres, with geography (mountain, sea, desert, border cities) being particularly important. The colloquial and vernacular nature of their language allows these writers to represent urban space and create a linguistic reality that is particular to the region without falling into the provincialism of the past.

Nonetheless, not all border writers only write on regional themes. Many of them distance themselves from matters of daily relevance and the sociological conflicts that afflict that area of the country. For example, some prefer fantasy, science fiction, and crime novels, while others favor a more intimate approach and focus on the transcendent role of love. Since the first writers' and essayists' workshops met in the border region, writers and scholars have attempted to formulate a possible definition or "identifying features" for border literatures, and the question continues to be debated. The multiplicity of expressions goes beyond any attempt impose an overall description of the work.

One of the difficulties in attempting to find a unifying principle in Mexican border literatures is the lack of academics studying its varied genres. To date there has been more research on narrative, even though poetry is the most popular genre. Research on theater is practically nonexistent, despite the presence of playwrights and critics. This lacuna is largely owing to the lack of seminars specializing in literary criticism of regional literature, although there are important centers of higher education in the border region. Except for the Universidad de Sonora (University of Sonora), the Instituto Sonorense de Cultura (Sonora Cultural Institute), and the Universidad Autónoma de Baja California (Autonomous University of Baja California), which have promoted literary studies in their respective regions, there is no permanent seminar or course that includes contemporary regional literature in any of the border areas.

Another difficulty is the definition of the territorial limit implied by the term "northern border." In his work on narrative, Berumen includes writers that live and work in the urban centers on the border as well as those that live 700 kilometers from the Mexico-U.S. frontier. One of the arguments that he uses in his selection is that in literary terms one cannot delimit an area according to its "administrative aspects" but rather for its sociocultural characteristics. This is the less convincing point of Berumen's argument since there exist more differences than similarities in the area he defines. Beyond thinking of growth and development in the cities and in the idiosyncrasies and regionalism of its inhabitants, one must be aware of the discourses current over the 1980s and 1990s on the border and which continue to be valid for many inhabitants, writers included.

This debate on the delimitation of the border region is commented on by the critic Luis Leal in his description of literature from the northern states. Leal argues that it is difficult to define geographical space, as the geographers themselves have not been in agreement on the limits of the region. One could easily speak about border states, but in fact this border has existed for relatively little time, only since the 1848 Treaty of Guadalupe Hidalgo and the 1853 Gadsden Purchase. Leal's conception of border literatures is interesting, but he overlooks the quite real importance of political borders. Although—as Leal himself points out—"the literature of northern Mexico originated in precisely those states that Mexico lost to the United States," the literatures on either side of the U.S.-Mexican border have developed in quite different directions. Failing to taken into account the political boundary between the United States and Mexico, Leal falls back on an arbitrary definition of the border region. Luis Leal includes the state of Baja California Sur in his discussion of border literature even though it is not contiguous to the U.S.-Mexican border.

Another debate regarding border literature is the position of border writers working in such important cultural centers as Monterrey and the city of Chihuahua. On one side literature in Monterrey and Chihuahua cannot be considered borderland—that is to say, peripheral—since both cities have received considerable support from federal cultural programs, in marked contrast to cultural promotion in the cities on the border itself until the 1980s. The peculiarities of the relationship between Mexico City and northern economic and cultural centers, particularly Monterrey, reflects the tensions between the center and the northern region as a whole more than the border region. Other scholars have contended that the distance between cultural centers such as Monterrey and Chihuahua and the border means that they cannot faithfully convey the viewpoint of the border. The border, they insist, cannot be represented by someone who does not live there on a daily basis.

Both of these positions are quite problematic, assuming that cultural and political regions are fixed and possess a single essence. The first position downplays the almost exclusive support northern institutions give to centers of power such as Monterrey and Chihuahua, overlooking the quite real antagonism between those who work in the cultural centers in these cities and those who live and work on the border itself. The second positions, however, essentializes the border itself, insisting that border writers stick to a sort of documentary realism that reflects *lo fronterizo* and illogically suggests that border authors write exclusively about regional issues.

Another important debate concerns the very terms by which "border literature" is classified. Should one speak of borderland literature or border literature, literature *of* the border, or literature *about, in,* or *from* the border? If, as the scholar Danny Anderson states, the approach of border authors constitutes a historical accumulation of representations that highlights originality and often the polemical weight of the cultural production that is proliferating on the frontier and the borderland states, we also can describe such nationally prominent writers as Laura Esquivel, Carlos Fuentes, Ethel Krauze, and Paco Ignacio Taibo II—all of whom have set much of their work on the northern border but write and are published from Mexico City—as border writers and take their work as representative *of* the border; however, this would only make the work of those writing *from* the border less visible. In this context it is important to point out the difference between literature about the border and literature produced in the region. Hegemonic practices continue on a local, national, and international level, but writers *of* the northern border fight back from their geographical area.

Like the border itself, the literary movement of the northern border in Mexico is in constant development. As with the Chicano literature in the United States, the border literature in Mexico that has emerged since the 1970s articulates a textual border in which the border region becomes a locus of identity—but not in relation to the United States or even the rest of Mexico and Latin America. Part and parcel of the decentralization of Mexico, the border region has become a "third space" between the hegemonic cultures of the United States and central Mexico. If in Chicano literature the border region is an "original paradise," an inexhaustible topic, in Mexican border literature it has become almost routine, often not represented or even mentioned.

Select Bibliography

Amparán, José Francisco, "Obstáculos y problemas de una generación perdida: Los escritores norteños pre-68." In *Literatura fronteriza de acá y de allá: Memoria del Encuentro Binacional "Ensayo sobre la literatura de las fronteras,"* edited by Guadalupe Beatriz Aldaco. Hermosillo, Sonora: Instituto Sonorense de Cultura, and Mexico City: CONACULTA, 1994.

Anzaldúa, Gloria, *Borderlands/La Frontera: The New Mestiza.* San Francisco: Aunt Lute, 1987.

Bruce-Novoa, Juan, "The US-Mexican Border in Chicano Testimonial Writing: A Topological Approach to Four Hundred and Fifty Years of Writing the Border." *Discourse: Theoretical Studies in Media and Culture* 18:1–2 (Fall 1995–Winter 1996).

Calderón, Héctor, and José David Saldívar, *Criticism in the Borderlands: Studies un Chicano Literature, Culture, and Ideology.* Durham, North Carolina: Duke University Press, 1991.

Conde, Rosina, "¿Dónde es la frontera?" *El acordeón. Revista de Cultura* 7 (1992).

Hicks, Emily, "Deterritorialization and Border Writing." In *Literatura de Frontera México/Estados Unidos—Mexican/American Border Writing: Memoria del primer encuentro de escritores de las Californias—Proceedings of the First Conference of Writers from the Californias,* edited by José Manuel Di-Bella, Sergio Gómez Montero, and Harry Polkinhorn. Mexicali: Dirección de Asuntos Culturales, and San Diego: Institute for Regional Studies of the Californias, University of California, San Diego, 1987.

_____, *Border Writing: The Multidimensional Text.* Minneapolis: University of Minnesota Press, 1991.

Leal, Luis, "Mexico's Centrifugal Culture." *Discourse: Theoretical Studies in Media and Culture* 18:1–2 (Fall 1995–Winter 1996).

Luna, Francisco, "Visiones fronterizas." In *Literatura fronteriza de acá y de allá: Memoria del Encuentro Binacional "Ensayo sobre la literatura de las fronteras,"* edited by Guadalupe Beatriz Aldaco. Hermosillo, Sonora: Instituto Sonorense de Cultura, and Mexico City: CONACULTA, 1994.

Polkinhorn, Harry, "Alambrada: hacia una teoría de la escritura fronteriza." In *La línea: Ensayos sobre literatura fronteriza México-norteamericana,* vol. 1, edited by Harry Polkinhorn, Gabriel Trujillo, and Rogelio Reyes. Mexicali: UABC, and San Diego: University of California, San Diego, 1988.

Romero, Rolando, "Border of Fear, Border of Desire." *Borderlines: Studies in American Culture* 1:1 (September 1993).

_____, "Postdeconstructive Spaces." *Siglo XX/20th Century* 11 (1993).

Saldívar, José David, *The Dialectics of Our America: Genealogy, Cultural Critique and Literary History.* Durham, North Carolina, and London: Duke University Press, 1991.

Trujillo Muñoz, Gabriel, "Mi generación: Poetas bajacalifornianos nacidos entre 1954–1964." In *Literatura fronteriza de acá y de allá. Memoria del Encuentro Binacional "Ensayo sobre la literatura de las fronteras,"* edited by Guadalupe Beatriz Aldaco. Hermosillo, Sonora: Instituto Sonorense de Cultura, and Mexico City: CONACULTA, 1994.

—MARÍA SOCORRO TABUENCA C.

BORDERS

See Border Literatures; Foreign Policy; Migration; Politics and Government; Regions and Regionalism; Trade and Markets; Transport and Communications; Southern Border; U.S.-Mexican Border

BOURBON REFORMS

Impressed by Louis XIV's France and its achievements, the Bourbon Dynasty in the eighteenth century sought to revive Spain's faltering economy. To secure the revenues required to finance military expansion and reclaim its position in Europe, it implemented a series of measures known as the Bourbon Reforms. They represent a heady blend of "-isms": mercantilism, Gallicanism, Jansenism, Neoclassicism, and to a lesser degree economic liberalism. Characterized more by pragmatism and haphazard application that varied in pace and intensity throughout the eighteenth century, the Bourbon Reforms resulted in short-term fiscal gains but also contributed significantly to the erosion of the imperial relationship between Spain and America.

Spain's political and economic problems proved fertile ground for Spanish *arbitristas,* theorists who sought to provide enlightened solutions. Most notably among these *arbitristas* were Benito Gerónimo Feijóo y Montenegro, Baltasar Melchor Gaspar María de Jovellanos, José del Campillo y Cossío, Pedro Rodríguez de Campomanes, and Gerónimo de Ustáriz. If reform was the focus, however, it was reform from above with the objective of functional improvement rather than fundamental change in economic and social structures; the point was not to radically alter the existing social order but to make it function more effectively in the Spanish Crown's interests. Recommended reforms emphasized the importance of state intervention in the economy to stimulate industry, improve agriculture and transportation, and initiate fiscal reform. Since Spain possessed few industries, the majority of its exports were agricultural products, and much of its American silver was used to pay for imports of manufactured goods from the rest of Europe. Spain effectively acted as a conduit for commerce between its colonies and the rest of Europe. Not surprisingly, particular emphasis in the reforms was placed on foreign trade and the need to improve the economic management of Spain's American colonies. Furthermore the type of military, political, and economic expansion that Spain sought could not be achieved without the improvement of the individual Crown subject. The strong state that the Bourbons wished to forge also demanded efficient urban planning, secular control over sanitation, hospitals and education, and development of productive public employment.

In combination with the development of a standing army and a professional bureaucracy, the new Bourbon regime laid the foundations of an absolutist state, its crucial reform instrument. The agents of the absolutist state regarded provincial and corporate privileges with deep suspicion and demanded centralization and uniformity. Under Felipe V (1700–24, 1724–46), duke of Anjou, grandson of Louis XIV, and the first Bourbon to sit on the Spanish throne, attempts were made to strengthen the state apparatus by centralizing power in the monarch's hands. To do that, the Hapsburg method of conciliar government was replaced, although never completely, by ministerial government. Instead of a horizontal structure of committees dominated by a conservative Spanish aristocracy, a vertical structure was introduced. At the top were the ministries: the Secretariats of State, Exchequer, Justice, War, Navy, and the Indies. Beneath these were the intendants in charge of economic reform and renovation at the regional levels, and at the base lay a professional corps of salaried bureaucrats. Increasingly, the state relied on career officials, military and civilian, who were subject to assessment and promotion. Their appointments were based on merit not background, and they received fixed salaries as opposed to fees of office.

In addition to its domestic concerns, Spain faced political as well as economic problems in its overseas empire. Almost two centuries of lax rule under the Hapsburgs, combined with distance, resulted in the creation of semi-autonomous oligarchies (primarily lawyers, large landowners, and clergy from the criollo elite—i.e., those of Spanish descent born in New Spain) formally subject to the government in Madrid, but able to privilege their own vested interests over those of the Crown. Sale of office was prevalent, and collection of state revenues depended upon a system of farming out to merchants. The clergy occupied a central role as the intellectual and spiritual mediators in colonial society. Reforms in America accelerated under Carlos III (1759–88) after the temporary capture of Havana and Manila by the English demonstrated Spain's inability to protect its overseas dominions.

As the largest and richest of all of Spain's American possessions, Mexico became a major focus of the reformist ambitions of the Bourbon state. Such ambitions were made painfully manifest with the arrival of José de Gálvez in 1765 as visitor general in Mexico to assess its current situation and recommend reforms that eventually reorganized colonial government but that proved harmful to the interests of the Mexican population.

The single most important corporation that came under attack was the Catholic Church. Such attacks were aimed not at doctrine but at the privilege and power of the church in both Spain and America. It was protected by *fueros* (special immunity from civil jurisdiction), and its wealth made it the largest source of investment capital in Spanish America. Such attacks were justified by a reemphasis on the Divine Right of Kings and assertion of the rights and autonomy of the national church in the face of papal monarchy (Gallicanism). The state's ambitions found support among the party in the Catholic Church known as the Jansenists.

The Jesuits bore the brunt of Bourbon political ambition when a decree ordered their expulsion from Spain and all Spanish territories in 1767. Notorious for their independence of episcopal authority, refusal to pay ecclesiastical tithes, devotion to the papacy, and widespread influence, their expulsion demonstrated that the Crown would brook no opposition. About 680 Jesuits were expelled from Mexico, 450 of whom were criollos. Perhaps the most perversely spectacular of Bourbon attacks on the church, the Jesuit expulsion was not the only one; other policies, most of them unsuccessful, were implemented at different times to erode the church's power. The regular clergy (i.e., those belonging to a particular order, such as the Benedictines) were replaced by secular priests (who did not belong to such an order) in rural parishes in the 1750s. In 1771 a church council was summoned in Mexico to tighten church discipline; general inspections of the religious were called for, as was the imposition of the common life, although little came of this activity. The Mexican bishops collaborated with the Crown in its attack on the regular orders, only to find themselves in the 1780s subject to attacks on their own jurisdiction and income, which included the transfer of tithe collection to committees controlled by royal officials (canceled due to an outraged clergy). In 1795 ecclesiastical immunity was suspended. The imposition of small taxes on the clergy pales, however, in comparison, to the controversial Consolidación de Vales Reales (December 26, 1804), which ordered the sequestration of charitable funds in America and their remission to Spain. Mexico was affected particularly adversely by the decree, and the Bourbons may have collected as much as 10 million pesos before it was repealed in 1808. The moneys collected not only resulted in a reduction of capital available for economic transactions but also drained away badly needed specie since most of what the government "borrowed" was exported to Spain in cash. In addition, because much of the capital of religious institutions was invested in loans granted to landowners, the consolidation decree threatened them with loss of property and bankruptcy. The major outcome was alienation and embitterment of both the colonial elites and the priesthood. Indeed, the ranks of the latter would supply many of the insurgent officers and guerrilla leaders in the Mexican insurgency of 1810.

Bourbon attacks on the church affected the population at large in a variety of ways. The Jesuits had exercised a formidable influence in colonial society. They educated the sons of the criollo elite in the most important cities and towns, and they also managed mission stations in Sonora in the far northern frontier. The Jesuits' life-long exile caused resentment not only among themselves but also among their families and friends who lost sons, brothers, and teachers in the expulsion. Even though some wealthy families purchased lucrative Jesuit properties expropriated in 1767, many criollos regarded the expulsion as a despotic act. The Jansenizing spirit made itself felt at the popular level. Confraternities were criticized not only in an attempt to end corporate privilege but to reform popular religious fiestas and devotions. Bourbon reformers increasingly viewed Baroque piety as ridiculous and unacceptable. Even the exuberance of Baroque church architecture and ornamentation was denounced as offensive to Christian piety and as lacking the good taste that Neoclassicism, the official style of the Bourbons, possessed.

The Bourbon attack on corporations was not consistent. As it sought to limit the power of the church it deliberately created a new source of power and privilege, the military. In the absence of a standing army in America, Spain relied on colonial militias, strengthened by a few peninsular units. From 1760 a new military force was created. Protection against foreign external aggression and domestic unrest increasingly rested on colonial economies and personnel. Mexico eventually had an army of almost 10,000 men (four regiments of infantry and two of dragoons); a large proportion of the officers from captain down were criollos. Alongside recruitment of permanent colonial regiments occurred the organization of numerous militia units. In Mexico an estimated 22,277 troops were reasonably well-armed and disciplined. The military buildup enabled Spain to defend its imperial frontiers in America; in Mexico expeditions were mounted to secure effective possession of the northern provinces of Sonora, Texas, and California. The military became a new professional opportunity for criollo sons complete with titles and legal privileges (the military *fuero*) and was seen as a way to attract the loyalty of the criollo elite. Such titles and privileges, however, proved to be a poor substitute for any real share of power, as criollos realized that access to high-ranking positions in the military were just as difficult to acquire as they were in the Bourbon colonial bureaucracy.

Underlying the sweeping administrative reforms implemented in Mexico was a deeply rooted suspicion of criollos and entrenched local interests. Such suspicion resulted in the displacement of criollos from high-ranking positions and their replacement by *peninsulares* (those born in Spain). The impact of the new policies is illustrated in the changing composition of the *audiencias,* the high courts of justice. Gálvez broke the criollos' traditional domination of the courts by increasing the *audiencia* membership and implementing a deliberate policy of transfer, promotion, and retirement such that peninsular appointments outweighed those of criollos. In the 1770s the ratios were approximately 8 criollos to 3 *peninsulares;* within 10 years, the ratios had shifted to 10 *peninsulares* to 4 criollos.

The introduction of the intendancy system was designed to introduce state presence at the regional level (in the most important provincial cities), to improve the administration of local government, and to reduce the power of the

viceroys. Although Gálvez recommended the introduction of intendants in 1768, it was not until 1786 that 12 intendancies finally were established in Mexico. The majority of intendants were recruited from peninsular military and fiscal officials. Intendants were responsible for public administration, promotion of economic growth and revenue collection, administration of justice and military affairs within their provinces, and improvement of local government, especially of indigenous communities. The intendancy system proved more efficient at the provincial level, developing the infrastructure (building bridges and roads, improved sanitation and water supply) than it did in correcting the deficiencies of local government.

A central problem that occupied Bourbon ministers was the corrupt nature of local government and the practice of the *repartimiento de comercio* (forced distribution of goods). The attack on *repartimientos* was justified on the grounds that commercial monopolies reduced the volume of trade and that their abolition would expand commerce, enable indigenous villagers to enter the market freely, and generally benefit smaller merchants and traders. This practice brought together in a highly unequal and exploitative relationship indigenous villagers, *corregidores de indios* (Crown officials who administered indigenous communities) and *alcaldes mayores* (chief magistrates, or mayors), and local merchants. Its rationale lay partly in the fact that *alcaldes mayores* did not receive a fixed salary, only a small percentage of tributes and fees from conducting local judicial business. Participation in local commerce provided them with additional sources of revenue. On both counts—improved local government at the hands of the new officials, the *subdelegados,* and the abolition of the *repartimientos*—the reforms proved to be a dismal failure. For the most part *subdelegados* at the district level replaced *alcaldes mayores* in name only. No fixed salaries were introduced, unlike those received by high-ranking Bourbon bureaucrats, and the source of income for the Crown officials remained unchanged. (The new Ordinance of Intendants of 1803 provided for a salary and prohibited the *repartimiento,* but costs and continued opposition prevented it from going into effect.) As a result, these positions remained unattractive to talented officials. The abolition of the *repartimiento* in 1786 did not result in market expansion as predicted. The practice of *repartimientos* reappeared in Mexico as *subdelegados* sought to increase their income, as landowners sought to continue to control labor, and as merchants tried to reestablish former consumer markets.

Urban areas and their populations did not escape the sweep of the reforms either. Emphasis was placed upon campaigns to eliminate popular vices and to inculcate in the popular masses the virtues of hard work, sobriety, and public propriety. Such a campaign was spearheaded, ultimately unsuccessfully, by the establishment in 1782 of the *alcaldes de barrio,* a neighborhood police force that attempted to reform Spain's colonial vassals and to make them—and by extension the colonial economies—more rational and productive. For the body politic to be strong, the individual needed to prosper as well; public health and sanitation, hospitals and workhouses, schemes of public employment and education, and the establishment of law and order thrust the colonial state into the lives of its servants—albeit temporarily—in unprecedented ways. Economic reforms had significant social and cultural ramifications for existing structures of gender and class as the guilds' powers were attacked and lower-class women were encouraged to enter the workforce. Such measures, for the most part unrealized, provided the basis of the Bourbon reformers' vision of late colonial industry: freedom from guild restrictions (the bête noir of Spanish industry according to Bourbon reformers), appropriate work for women, and a salaried, trained workforce. Even the physical face of Mexico began to change as the new "official" style—Neoclassicism—made Bourbon ambitions manifest in late colonial architecture (the College of Mines, for example) and redesign of public space (the Alameda, the Plaza Mayor) implemented by a cadre of artists and architects trained in the new Royal Academy of San Carlos (established 1783). All of this came at the expense of Baroque architecture, which had dominated the towns and churches of Spanish America since the late sixteenth century.

Economic policy focused on two major objectives: to liberalize where possible (and thereby stimulate economic growth) and to create a salaried fiscal bureaucracy to ensure efficient collection of taxes and fees. Mercantilism remained the foundation of Bourbon commercial policy, as it had been for the Hapsburgs; the main difference lay in an emphasis on developing a more rational imperial economy and maximizing Crown revenues.

The existing and inefficient system of tax farming was replaced by direct revenue collection to reduce fraud and to standardize the assessment and collection of taxes by a fiscal bureaucracy. In 1754 the *alcabalas* (internal tariffs) of Mexico City were entrusted to salaried officials, and in 1776 the same system of direct administration was applied throughout the colony. Few other treasury functions had as broad an impact because most commercial transactions (including sales of commodities, properties, and slaves) were subject to taxation. This impact was particularly relevant in the case of agriculture, which was not a prime target of the Bourbon reformers in Mexico; rather, it was indirectly affected by its linkages with other sectors of the colonial economy that were directly targeted by the Bourbons. The agricultural sector was, nevertheless, subject to a variety of taxes on marketing animals, much to the ranchers' irritation; growers and producers of sugar and spirits also complained of high duties. Consumers in general complained about taxes on goods in daily use—by 1790, residents of Mexico paid 84 separate taxes—that created a climate of resentment and a desire for local autonomy free from Bourbon prohibitions. Despite complaints, corruption, and co-optation, increased revenues suggests that the system worked well enough to justify its continued enforcement, which did not change significantly prior to 1810.

Another major fiscal innovation was implemented in 1765 with the establishment of the state tobacco monopoly in Mexico. Tobacco planting was restricted to a specific zone in the state of Veracruz. All planters contracted to sell their crops to the monopoly, which produced cigars and cigarettes in its manufactories and distributed them throughout the colony through licensed stores. Fiscally successful, the monopoly employed more than 17,000 people and at its peak produced profits to the Crown of nearly 4 million pesos. Royal monopolies in addition to the one on tobacco were established for a range of goods such as salt, cockfights, ice, mercury (critical in silver ore processing), playing cards, and gunpowder.

After 1776 the colonial state played an important role in the renovation of the silver mining industry. It favored its interests in the form of subsidized prices for gunpowder and mercury, reduction of production costs, the establishment of a College of Mines, and exemption of mining equipment and raw materials from *alcabalas*. The industry made a significant recovery from its mid–seventeenth century depression; during the eighteenth century the Mexican industry accounted for 67 percent of all American output of silver. At the same time the mining sectors of Mexico paid substantial sums in the royal fifth, war taxes on silver, duties on refining and coining, fees on state-controlled supplies of mercury and gunpowder, war loans, and other types of extraordinary contributions. Thus, although it generated the badly needed revenues for the Crown, the silver miners increasingly viewed the conditions under which the industry operated as obstructive and counter-productive to increased profits.

Transaltlantic commerce expanded as the *comercio libre* (free trade) decree of 1778 opened new ports in Spain that could trade legally with Spanish America and finally abolished the Cádiz staple and the fleet system. Trade between the chief ports of the empire and the Iberian Peninsula was conducted by individual merchant vessels. The few restrictions that applied in Mexico were removed in 1789. Customs duties at Cádiz were lowered and preference given to Spanish manufacturers. Between 1778 to 1796 registered exports from Spain to America quadrupled. The result in the short term was a commercial crisis as prices fell throughout the empire and profits declined as imports saturated colonial markets. Many merchants went bankrupt and others cut their losses by withdrawing from transatlantic trade and investing instead in agriculture and mining. Bullion drained out of circulation as huge sums were shipped abroad to pay for increasing quantities of European imports. Merchant protest was rejected as viceroys argued that the expansion in trade was beneficial to both colonial consumers and Spanish industrialists. Opposition by the Mexico City merchant guild to the establishment of two new merchant guilds in Veracruz and Guadalajara also was ignored. Unfortunately for the Crown, these reforms produced results contrary to Bourbon objectives. Although Spain's share in exports increased, primary goods accounted for the bulk of exports, as opposed to Spanish domestic manufactured goods; the hoped-for transformation of Spanish domestic industry remained unrealized.

Historian David Brading has argued that it is in the performance of state revenues that the "true significance of the changes in colonial government is to be found" (Brading, 1984). Commercial reform, reorganization of the tax structure, expansion in mining, and economic activity, all underwritten by population growth, resulted in the revenue increases that the Bourbons so desperately needed. Revenues in Spain increased from 5 million pesos in 1700 to 36 million pesos by 1790. Mexico proved to be the most profitable colony, with treasury receipts increasing throughout the eighteenth century from 3 to 20 million pesos. While some of the new revenues remained in Mexico to finance the newly created Bourbon bureaucracy, the majority were converted to specie and shipped to Spain, often depriving local economies of an adequate money supply. Such fiscal success did not, however, result in any radical transformation of the Spanish economy or the development of its manufacturing sector. A greater price of the reforms and revenues and one that distinguished the Spanish absolutist state from its European contemporaries was its failure to form any alliance with the leading sectors of colonial society. The long-term consequence was the alienation of the criollo elite and ultimately the loss of empire.

Although some sectors of the colonial population may have benefited from some of the reforms, responses to the Bourbon measures ranged from ambivalence to simmering resentment and hostility. For many criollos, any economic prosperity or new opportunities offered in mining, commercial agriculture, and transatlantic commerce could not compensate for their exclusion from public office; loyalties were strained even further by the attempted reforms of the Mexican church. Popular uprisings occurred in 1766–67 in protest against the establishment of the tobacco monopoly, formation of the militia, and expulsion of the Jesuits. Only the presence of regiments from Spain allowed Gálvez to suppress the movements, which he did with ferocity. The impact of the reforms on the indigenous populations has yet to be fully researched and analyzed. Many indigenous communities, for example, were deprived of a source of income when tobacco growing was restricted to Veracruz. Scholar Nancy Farris makes a compelling argument that the reforms and the economic changes associated with them represented a "second Conquest" for the Maya communities in Yucatán, as radical in their impact as the sixteenth-century Conquest.

Scholars continue to debate the achievements of the Bourbon reforms and their consequences for the imperial relationship, and for colonial society and economy. Studies of Bourbon Spain agree that the transition from a state based on compromise and consensus to an absolutist state was incomplete. Recent studies of the Bourbon reform measures in colonial Mexico suggest a similar consensus. Scholars agree that a "revolution in government" was achieved in the upper ranks of the imperial bureaucracy but that this was counteracted by failures in local government and a gradual slide from authority in the 1760s to compromise or outright failure of reform measures by the beginning of the

nineteenth century. Despite continued controversy over the problems of quantifying Crown revenues, scholars seem to agree on the increased capacity of the state to exploit its colonies and increase its fiscal revenues. Interpretations vary as to the significance of this capacity. Some view it as "justified costs" of a stable society, while others argue that the impact of the treasury on the development of the Mexican colonial economy in particular could have reached "a substantial if not a destructive scale by the end of the colonial period" (Garner, 1994).

Recently, scholars have turned their attention to a reassessment of the nature of the Bourbon state and its impact on colonial society. While some, such as John Coatsworth, see the colonial state as largely irrelevant outside of urban areas and economic affairs, others, such as William Taylor and Susan Deans-Smith, conceptualize it as a more pervasive influence in colonial society. This reassessment also has resulted in the acknowledgment that while we may have a sense of the general content, achievements, and limitations of the Bourbon reform measures in Mexico, we know much less about their implementation on a regional basis and their impact on different sectors of the colonial population. Only now are scholars beginning to look carefully at what has been termed the "grass roots" responses to Bourbon reform and reorganization where, in the words of Stanley Stein, "the origin and implications of change and of opposition to change can be most clearly discerned." Significantly, many of the interventionist ambitions of the Bourbon state, however incomplete in their implementation, affected gender, ethnic, and class relationships to varying degrees. We need to know more about the responses of the colonial population and how those responses aided, ignored, distorted, or deflected the intentions of the Bourbon reformers. The impact on society at all levels of changing church-state relations, of the policies to modernize Mexico's towns and cities and its populace, and the cultural dimensions of the reform measures—essentially, the struggle between tradition and modernity—have yet to be examined systematically.

See also Architecture: Colonial; Church and State: Bourbon New Spain; Fueros; Military: Bourbon New Spain; Mining: Colonial; Religious in New Spain; Trade and Markets: Bourbon New Spain

Select Bibliography

Archer, Christon I., *The Army in Bourbon Mexico, 1760–1810.* Albuquerque: University of New Mexico Press, 1977.
Arnold, Linda, *Bureaucracy and Bureaucrats in Mexico City, 1742–1835.* Tucson: University of Arizona Press, 1988.
Brading, D. A., *Miners and Merchants in Bourbon Mexico, 1763–1810.* Cambridge: Cambridge University Press, 1971.
———, "Bourbon Spain and Its American Empire." In *The Cambridge History of Latin America,* vol. 1, edited by Leslie Bethell. Cambridge: Cambridge University Press, 1984.
———, *Church and State in Bourbon Mexico: The Diocese of Michoacán 1749–1810.* Cambridge and New York: Cambridge University Press, 1994.

Coatsworth, John H., "The Limits of Colonial Absolutism: The State in Eighteenth Century Mexico." In *Essays in the Political, Economic and Social History of Colonial Latin America,* edited by Karen Spalding. Newark, Delaware: University of Delaware Press, 1982.

Deans-Smith, Susan, *Bureaucrats, Planters, and Workers: The Making of the Tobacco Monopoly in Bourbon Mexico.* Austin: University of Texas Press, 1992.

Farriss, Nancy M., *Maya Society under Colonial Rule: The Collective Enterprise of Survival.* Princeton, New Jersey: Princeton University Press, 1984.

Garner, Richard L., and Spiro E. Stefanou, *Economic Growth and Change in Bourbon Mexico.* Gainesville: University Press of Florida, 1993.

Lynch, John, *Bourbon Spain 1700–1808.* Oxford and Cambridge, Massachusetts: Blackwell, 1989.

Pietschmann, Horst, "Consideraciones en torno el protoliberalismo, reformas borbónicas y revolución: La Nueva España en el último tercio del siglo XVIII." In *La revolución de Independencia,* edited by Virginia Guedea. Mexico City: Colegio de México, 1995.

Stein, Stanley J., "Bureaucracy and Business in the Spanish Empire, 1759–1804: Failure of a Bourbon Reform in Mexico and Peru." *Hispanic American Historical Review* 61:1 (1981).

Taylor, William B., "Between Local Process and Global Knowledge: An Inquiry into Early Latin American Social History, 1500–1900." In *Reliving the Past: The Worlds of Social History,* edited by Olivier Zunz and David William Cohen. Chapel Hill: University of North Carolina Press, 1985.

Viqueira Albán, Juan Pedro, *¿Relajados o reprimidos? Diversiones públicas y vida social en la cuidad de México durante el Siglo de las Luces.* Mexico City: Fondo de Cultura Económica, 1987.

Voekel, Pamela, "Peeing on the Palace: Bodily Resistance to Bourbon Reforms in Mexico City." *Journal of Historical Sociology* 5:2 (1992).

—SUSAN DEANS-SMITH

BRACERO PROGRAM

On September 29, 1942, 500 Mexican farm workers arrived in Stockton, California. Transported by the U.S. government, these Mexican workers were the first installment of a program designed to fill the wartime labor shortage in U.S. agriculture. Over the next 22 years, in what proved to be the largest foreign worker program in U.S. history, 5 million *"bracero"* contracts were made with growers and ranchers in 24 states. The term *"bracero"* comes from *"brazo,"* the Spanish word for arm, and can be translated loosely "farm hand." Its literal meaning, "arm-man," hints at the function these *braceros* were to play in the agricultural economy, supplying a pair of arms and imposing few obligations on the host society.

Mexico was considered an ideal labor source for U.S. employers owing to its proximity to the United States (compared to the other major sources of immigrant workers, Asia and Europe) and its ability to expand and contract its labor supply at a moment's notice. The Bracero Program institutionalized that flexibility and injected an element of control over both the worker's entrance and, at least theoretically, departure. Furthermore, the *bracero* was a contract laborer, a status that placed him outside the free labor market.

The Bracero Program was in fact a series of programs that for the purposes of discussion can be separated into three periods: 1942 to 1947; 1947 to 1951, and 1951 to the program's termination in 1964. While the basic contours of the program—and its substantial advantages for U.S. agriculture—remained the same throughout, these periods were distinct with regard to the specifics of the recruitment process and wage determinations, and the relative roles of the Mexican and U.S. governments.

1942–47

In April 1942, Mexico and the United States signed the first bilateral agreement upon which the wartime Bracero Program was based. Essentially a labor contract between Mexican officials (as the workers' representative) and the U.S. Department of State (as the growers' representative), the compromise served as a blueprint for all subsequent agreements. It established that *braceros* were not to be paid less than domestic workers doing similar work and specified that piece rates allowed the average *bracero* to earn at least the minimum hourly wage of 30 cents. Mexican negotiators insisted that a subsistence wage be paid to *braceros* who were unemployed for more than 25 percent of the contract period, and that *braceros* be permitted to elect representatives to bring complaints to their employers, as long as these complaints did not involve attempts to upgrade the terms of the contract, which were non-negotiable. Finally, Texas was excluded from the program, as Mexican negotiators cited a history of discrimination and abuse of Mexican workers in that state.

A contract was initiated by requests from agricultural employers in the United States for a given number of Mexican workers for a specified period of time. After a "shortage of labor" at "prevailing wages" had been certified, an order was placed with officials in Mexico City. Mexican officials selected *bracero* candidates from regions around the country (although the vast majority came from the least developed and most remote regions of Mexico) and transferred them to recruitment centers in the interior. Representatives from both countries made selections from this pool and processed the workers for distribution to agricultural employers in the United States.

In practice, the program often deviated from its formal specifications. It was not uncommon for wages to be set by growers who met at the beginning of each season, determined what they were willing to pay, and then informed state officials of the "prevailing wage." Employers sometimes simply ignored contract provisions they found inconvenient. For example, wages did not always meet the minimum 30 cents per hours, hours worked were not consistently recorded, payments were delayed, and housing and food frequently failed to meet the minimum standards required by the contract. Finally, the U.S. Immigration and Naturalization Service (INS) often used its discretion to circumvent the bilateral nature of recruitment and the exclusion of Texas from the program. Although short-lived, an early interpretation by the INS allowed employers to recruit Mexican workers directly at the border, bypassing the Mexican recruitment process altogether. Besides permitting growers to select their own workers and reducing the time consumed in government processing and transportation, direct border recruitment had the effect of opening up the program to Texas employers. In May 1943, the INS admitted over 2,000 *braceros* who were contracted at the border to employers in El Paso, Texas, with 1,500 entering in one day.

Altogether, more than 219,500 Mexican *braceros* came to the United States during World War II. Although this constituted only 2.7 percent of the wage labor force in U.S. agriculture, *braceros* were an integral component of agricultural production in some states and for some crops. During 1945—the peak year of the wartime program—California growers employed 63 percent of the total *bracero* workforce. *Braceros* were concentrated in cotton, sugar beets, fruits, and vegetables, and in some areas comprised the bulk of the manual labor for these crops.

When the war ended, the wartime labor program was extended. Increasingly, however, an informal INS legalization system replaced the formal Bracero Program. In this circumvention of bilateral agreements, the INS legalized on the spot undocumented Mexican farm workers and contracted them to their employers as *braceros*. During the summer of 1947, when only 31,331 *braceros* were imported or recontracted, the INS legalized 55,000 undocumented workers in Texas alone, once again effectively sidestepping the exclusion of Texas from the formal program. This legalization of undocumented Mexican farm workers by the INS continued for the next several years to be an integral part of the Bracero Program—sometimes sanctioned by international agreement, at other times used as an administrative bypass of the conditions imposed by the agreements.

1947–51

Beginning in 1947, the government-to-government contracts that Mexico had demanded during the war were replaced by direct grower-*bracero* work agreements. Now that growers contracted directly with *braceros* at recruitment centers and were responsible for the cost of transportation to places of employment, the growers intensified their long-standing demand that recruitment centers be set up at the border intensified. The placement of recruitment centers had always been one of the most hotly disputed and enduring issues for negotiation, and one on which Mexican officials rarely were willing to compromise. Policy makers in Mexico were convinced that border recruitment contributed to illegal immigration, as workers who congregated at the border and were not selected as *braceros* often immigrated illegally. Such a mass exodus from the northern border depleted that rich agricultural region of seasonal farm labor. When Mexican negotiators continued to insist on reception centers in the Mexican interior, growers increasingly rejected the Bracero Program and turned to illegal labor.

Acting on the belief that it would decrease the number of illegal immigrants in the United States and thus reduce employer abuses of vulnerable undocumented workers, Mexican negotiators agreed to a provision in the 1949 bilateral accord that illegal immigrants already in the United States be given preference for *bracero* status over newly imported *braceros*. Although legalization—the INS slang for which was "drying out the wetbacks"—clearly made recruitment easier for growers, Mexico's hopes that it would reduce the number of illegal immigrants in the United States proved to be misplaced. Instead, it increased illegal immigration; word spread among would-be workers that the way to get a *bracero* contract was to cross the border illegally. Between 1947 and 1949, only 74,600 *braceros* were contracted from Mexico, while 142,200 undocumented workers were legalized and contracted directly to growers. In 1950, fewer than 20,000 *braceros* were imported, and over 96,000 illegal immigrants were paroled to local employers.

The "drying out" of illegal immigrants and the preference given them for *bracero* employment gave aspiring *braceros* little incentive to remain in Mexico until they were contracted legally. The program triggered illegal immigration in other ways as well, as returning *braceros* spread word of employment opportunities in the United States. Since there were more *bracero* candidates than there were official slots for them, and because it was quicker and cheaper to bypass the contract system, many Mexican workers took matters into their own hands, crossing the border illegally.

Those who did enter into *bracero* contracts in this period found that contract provisions often were violated with impunity. Mexican negotiators had insisted on government-to-government contracts in the earlier stages of the program because they had anticipated—correctly, it turns out—that enforcement would be perfunctory if the U.S. government was not held directly accountable. Indeed, the period from 1947 to 1951 has been called the "laissez-faire era" because the wage and working conditions specified in *bracero* contracts rarely were enforced, and a hands-off policy generally prevailed.

1951–64

In 1951, with the outbreak of the Korean War, the U.S. Congress moved to restore order to the chaotic Bracero Program with Public Law 78. With only minor changes, PL 78 and the Migrant Labor Agreement between Mexico and the United States set the official parameters for the program until its termination in 1964. The agreement stipulated that the U.S. government, not the individual employer, was the guarantor of *bracero* contracts. It provided for recruitment centers in the interior of Mexico as before, but supplemented them with border "reception centers" where *braceros* were distributed to U.S. employers. Contracting illegal workers already in the United States was no longer permitted, at the insistence of Mexican negotiators who were now convinced that it had encouraged illegal immigration. *Braceros* were to be paid the prevailing wage for given crops in specific regions or a piece-rate equivalent. As in the past, if *braceros* were unemployed for more than 25 percent of the contract period (which varied from a minimum of 6 weeks to a maximum of 18 months), the grower was to provide them with a subsistence wage. Housing and meals for a nominal price also were to be provided. Finally, no state was to be blacklisted or barred from importing *bracero* labor.

Despite these efforts to stabilize the labor system, illegal immigration continued to increase and drew the attention of the U.S. media, the public, and policy makers. In response, on June 9, 1954, the U.S. attorney general initiated the ill-fated enforcement drive code-named "Operation Wetback." The U.S. Border Patrol set up road blocks, boarded trains, and cordoned off neighborhoods detaining Mexican immigrants. Police were instructed to arrest suspects on vagrancy charges and turn them over to Border Patrol agents. The INS launched a buslift to return apprehended immigrants to the interior of Mexico, hoping to make reentry more difficult and to encourage Mexicans to depart on their own.

The INS declared Operation Wetback an unqualified success and boasted of having deported close to 1 million Mexican workers and their families. But there were widespread allegations of INS abuses. So vivid were the reports of Mexicans and U.S. citizens of Mexican descent being beaten, harassed, and deported, that "Operation Wetback" came to be synonymous in the public mind with human rights violations in the name of immigration control.

Operation Wetback reduced undocumented immigration from Mexico in the short term, and *bracero* contracts quickly increased, going from little more than 200,000 in 1953 to a peak of 445,197 in 1956, and exceeding 400,000 a year for the rest of the decade. The average number of *braceros* entering annually between 1951 and 1959 was 10 times higher than the number admitted during the wartime program of 1942 to 1947, when a labor emergency had been declared. In 1959, nearly 50,000 farms employed *braceros*, with the vast majority concentrated in Texas, California, Arkansas, Arizona, and New Mexico.

The program in this period operated in the following way. Once the U.S. Department of Labor had certified a need for labor, Mexican officials were notified how many workers would be required. Aspiring *braceros* had to obtain a permit from municipal Mexican officials, and were then sent to central recruiting centers, where there were sometimes 10 applicants for each *bracero* position. After security screening and medical examinations, the selected *braceros* were dispatched to border reception centers where they signed contracts (countersigned by the two governments) with employers' representatives. Workers technically had some freedom of choice in this process, but those who turned down their first offer of employment often were blacklisted by subsequent employers and sent home empty-handed.

Lax enforcement of the contract provisions continued to be the norm, and by the end of the decade the Bracero Program was under increasing attack. Not only was there evidence of continued violations of the terms of the contracts and revelations of substandard working conditions, but there were repeated charges that the program depressed wages and contributed to unemployment among U.S. farmworkers. The moral position of the program's opponents in the United States was buttressed in late 1960 by the widely acclaimed CBS television documentary, *Harvest of Shame,* which graphically depicted the poverty and despair of migrant farmworkers in the United States, and precipitated a deluge of mail to CBS and to the U.S. Congress from an outraged and conscience-stricken public.

At the same time, increasing mechanization of certain crops meant that U.S. growers were less dependent on the Bracero Program, which by law prohibited using *braceros* on power-driven machinery. By 1964, the number of *braceros* was lower than at any time since 1951. Facing increasing attacks from organized labor in the United States as well as the liberal administration of U.S. president John F. Kennedy, and now confined to the relatively few crops that had eluded mechanization, the controversial Bracero Program was allowed to die in December 1964.

By the end of the program, a relationship of symbiosis between Mexican workers and U.S. growers had become thoroughly entrenched, fostered by formal and informal U.S. policies. Almost 5 million workers had been brought to the United States as *braceros;* approximately 5 million undocumented workers were apprehended during the same period. Not surprisingly, undocumented immigrations increased significantly with the demise of the formal program, each year exceeding the previous year's record. Although INS apprehensions of course are not a precise measure of the increase in illegal immigration, there is little dispute over the fact of the increase or the role of the Bracero Program in fueling the movement.

In 1986, 20 years after the last *braceros* left the fields, apprehensions of undocumented immigrants reached over 1.5 million. Nor did the Immigration Reform and Control Act of 1986 (IRCA)—touted by its proponents as the solution to illegal immigration—have any significant effect on the flow. In the mid-1990s, the U.S. Congress, apparently ignorant of the historical role of the Bracero Program in fostering increased immigration, has revisited the possibility of a *bracero*-like program in a last-ditch effort at immigration control.

Select Bibliography

Calavita, Kitty, *Inside the State: The Bracero Program, Immigration, and the I.N.S.* New York: Routledge, 1992.

Galarza, Ernesto, *Strangers in Our Fields.* Washington, D.C.: Joint U.S.-Mexico Trade Union Committee, 1956.

_____, *Merchants of Labor: The Mexican Bracero Story.* Santa Barbara, California: McNally and Loftin, 1964.

Gamboa, Erasmo, *Mexican Labor and World War II: Braceros in the Pacific Northwest, 1942–1947.* Austin: University of Texas Press, 1990.

García, Juan Ramon, *Operation Wetback: The Mass Deportation of Mexican Undocumented Workers in 1954.* Westport, Connecticut: Greenwood, 1980.

García y Griego, Manuel, "The Importation of Mexican Contract Laborers to the U.S., 1942–1964: Antecedents, Operation, and Legacy." In *The Border that Joins: Mexican Migrants and U.S. Responsibility*, edited by Peter G. Brown and Henry Shue. Totowa, New Jersey: Rowman and Littlefield, 1983.

Kirstein, Peter Neil, *Anglo Over Bracero: A History of the Mexican Worker in the United States from Roosevelt to Nixon.* San Francisco: R. and E. Research Associates, 1977.

Kiser, George C., and Martha Woody Kiser, editors, *Mexican Workers in the United States: Historical and Political Perspectives.* Albuquerque: University of New Mexico Press, 1979.

Moore, Truman, *The Slaves We Rent.* New York: Random House, 1965.

Morgan, Patricia, *Shame of a Nation: A Documented Story of Police-State Terror against Mexican-Americans in the U.S.A.* Los Angeles: Committee for the Protection of Foreign Born, 1954.

President's Commission on Migratory Labor, *Migratory Labor in American Agriculture.* Washington, D.C.: Government Printing Office, 1951.

Scruggs, Otey, *Braceros, "Wetbacks," and the Farm Labor Problem: Mexican Agricultural Labor in the United States, 1942–1954.* New York: Garland, 1988.

—Kitty Calavita

BRANIFF FAMILY

Thomas H. Braniff, born in 1829 on Staten Island of well-off Irish immigrant parents, built a business empire in Porfirian Mexico. A founder of both the Jockey and American Clubs, a key member of Porfirio Díaz's central *camarilla* (Círculo Nacional Porfirista) who from 1896 organized foreign business interests behind Díaz's reelections, Braniff was perhaps the most important of those foreign entrepreneurs whose presence was integral to the operation of the Porfirian system. He and his well-born French-Canadian wife, Lorenza, were intimate enough with Díaz to visit his home informally. When Braniff died in the arms of his son, Tomás, on January 22, 1905, his last wish was to see his friend Porfirio. Díaz and doña Carmen, his wife, entrusted their business affairs to Braniff's management through Banco de Londres y México. Don Porfirio and doña Carmen attended both the marriage of Braniff's eldest son, Oscar, to Guadalupe Canovas y Portillo, and of son George to Concepción Lascuráin y Landa, daughter of Roman S. Lascurain, vice president of the Banco Hipotecario on whose board Braniff served. Braniff's daughter, Lorenza, was educated with others of the Porfirian elite at England's Sacred Heart Convent School. Oscar stood as *padrino* for General Gerónimo Trevino's grandchild. In short, the progress of Braniff and his family was of gradual assimilation into the Mexican nation.

As a young man, Braniff took a "stake" from his father and joined thousands of others in the gold rush to California, where, like most prospectors, he failed to find gold. Instead he found employment with Henry Meiggs, a British engineer, and followed him to Peru, where he learned practical construction and engineering building railroads. He came to Mexico in the early 1850s with his brother, John (later killed by payroll bandits), as superintendent of construction for the Mexico City–Veracruz Railway and remained as general manager and, eventually, director. Braniff began his fortune by using the duty-free terms of the Mexican Railway concession to smuggle contraband. He bought and upgraded factories along his railroad's route, most notably the San Lorenzo textile mill in Orizaba, Veracruz.

Braniff had close relations with a group of prominent expatriate French financiers that included Henri Tron, Leon Signoret, and Eugenio Roux, who, in 1884, reorganized the Banco de Londres y México as a Mexican corporation and unanimously elected Braniff president. In 1889, he sold the San Lorenzo mill to the French group for shares in its textile conglomerate, Compañía Industrial de Orizaba, S.A.

(CIDOSA). By the 1890, Braniff was "Mexico's Midas," said to have invested in every modern commercial enterprise in the country. His diversified interests included holdings in 3 railroads, 6 manufacturing companies, 15 mining companies, 7 haciendas (along with urban real estate), several commercial and investment banks, and 2 utility companies—an estate estimated at 4 million dollars.

Unlike French and Spanish merchants, whose sons rarely followed them in business, four of Braniff's five Mexican-born sons (George, Oscar, Tomás, and Arthur—Albert was too young) were entrepreneurs who catalyzed Mexican capital investment in industry and finance. George and Oscar owned and operated Braniff and Company, selling agricultural machinery and Westinghouse electrical equipment, a line of business opened by their father to supply heavy machinery for the *desagüe* (drainage of the Valley of Mexico). Their company contributed significantly the electrification of the country after 1900, especially in mining, and supplied huge motors for the water pumping stations and electrical generators for the city of León and for F. S. Pearson's hydroelectric projects. Oscar and brother Tomás were partners in a steel beam construction company whose modern buildings raised Mexico City's skyline from 1900.

Although the Braniffs invested in haciendas partly for prestige, they modernized their agricultural and ranching operations. Oscar invested in a milling operation for his Federal District wheat hacienda to integrate growing, processing, and marketing. They innovated in even the most traditional arenas. George, a bullfight enthusiast, used scientific breeding at his hacienda, San Juan del Rancho Viejo, to raise fighting bulls that brother Arthur, an amateur *torero*, occasionally fought in Mexico City's Plaza de Toros de la Colonia de la Condesa, a modern concrete and steel municipal bullring, built by Oscar's and Tomás's construction company. In addition to updating traditional amusements, George and Oscar helped introduce modern sports such as baseball and bicycles. George's passion for automobiles also fueled an automotive craze among the elite that led to a road building program in Mexico State. Arthur was Mexico's pioneer aviator and survived a number of well-publicized crack-ups while learning to fly his French aircraft.

The Braniffs were pillars of Mexican banking and were associated with Treasury Minister José Yves Limantour's camarilla. Oscar was one of the Mexican directors of the Banco Mexicano de Comercio e Industria that brought together the interests of Speyer and Company of New York and London, the Deutches Bank of Berlin, and the Scherer

banking house in which Limantour was a partner. In addition to the usual Porfirian notables, the directors included Henry Clay Pierce of Waters-Pierce (Standard) Oil Company; Franz Boker (Boker y Cia.); J. B. Body, who represented Sir Weetman Pearson's (Lord Cowdray) interests; and E. N. Brown, the director of the Mexican National Railway.

Although the family's considerable political influence was largely informal and personal, some Braniffs sought office. In the halcyon Porfiriato, George served on Mexico City's *ayuntamiento* (town council), where he reformed and standardized the city's hack service, requiring cabbies and, later, streetcar drivers to wear uniforms with a picture badge *(milagro)*. In the final days before his resignation in 1911, Díaz turned to Oscar to represent him at secret New York meetings with the family of the leading revolutionary, Francisco I. Madero. During the brief Madero democracy, Tomás ran for governor of Veracruz but was smeared as a "gringo" and lost. The Braniffs were able to gain a measure of influence, however, when Francisco I. Madero replaced Foreign Minister Manuel Calero with George's brother-in-law, Pedro Lascuráin. In 1912, however, Oscar threw his support to Pascual Orozco's revolt, as did Enrique C. Creel and other wealthy Mexicans. It was Oscar who assured U.S. ambassador Henry Lane Wilson that Orozco's movement was pro-American.

By the time Huerta's government fell in 1914, the Braniff family had relocated to Oklahoma, where, despite the loss of Mexican assets, they continued to prosper under the leadership of Tomás, who erected the Braniff building in Oklahoma City, then the tallest in the state and, in 1927, founded Braniff Airlines which became one of the Americas' largest airlines.

Select Bibliography

Haber, Stephen H., *Industry and Underdevelopment: The Industrialization of Mexico, 1890–1940.* Stanford, California: Stanford University Press, 1989.

Hanrahan, Gene, *The Bad Yankee.* Chapel Hill, North Carolina: Documentary Publications, 1985.

Icaza, Alfonso de, *Así era aquello: Sesenta anos de vida metropolitana.* Mexico City: Botas, 1957.

Martin, Percy F., *Mexico of the Twentieth Century.* New York: Dodd Mead, 1908.

Prida, Ramon, *De la dictadura a la anarquía.* Mexico City: Botas, 1958.

—WILLIAM SCHELL JR.

BRAVO, NICOLÁS

1786–1854 • General, Politician, and Interim President

A pivotal figure of the early national period, Nicolás Bravo was both a determined centralist leader and a staunch advocate of Mexican Independence. A defender of Mexico's inherited institutions and their corporate privileges (such as ecclesiasticas and military *fueros,* which gave the church and the military far-reaching powers of self-government), Bravo nevertheless was a moderate and not prone to revolutionary activities, as were some of his more ambitious peers.

Born September 10, 1786, in Chilpancingo (today Chilpancingo de los Bravos, Guerrero), Nicolás Bravo was the first son of Leonardo Bravo, a wealthy and influential hacienda owner. Receiving only an elementary education, Nicolás was raised with the expectation that one day he would assume full responsibility and control over his family's extensive land holdings and would lead a comfortable, relatively tranquil life. The coming War for Independence, however, was to change all this. By 1810 the Bravo family, like other criollo leaders in the region, had become disenchanted with Spanish colonial rule. When the insurgent forces of José María Morelos y Pavón advanced into the region in 1811, the entire Bravo family (including Nicolás's uncles Máximo, Miguel, and Victor) declared its unequivocal support for the revolution.

Despite Bravo's lack of formal military training, the young caudillo (then only 26) immediately evinced both daring and a natural proficiency in strategic and tactical maneuvers against the royalist forces. Enlisting under the command of Hermenegildo Galeana, Bravo was quickly promoted through the ranks. He attracted Morelos's attention in 1812 when he designed the formidable fortifications in the southern town of Cuautla. Largely responsible for the city's defenses, Bravo's breastworks withstood the bloody siege of a large royalist force for more than two months and won an important psychological victory for the insurgent side.

Having established both his valor and his instinctive military acumen, Bravo received both praise and promotion from Morelos. Entrusted with the military command of Veracruz, Bravo successfully directed, over the next six years, numerous guerrilla and regular field operations against some of the royalist army's most capable and celebrated military commanders. Particularly noteworthy were his victories over the esteemed Spanish commander Juan Labaqui, at San Agustín del Palmar (August 19, 1812), and his successful capture and defense of the strategic town of San Juan de Coscomatepec (July 13, 1813). The six-week siege of his 450 insurgent fighters inside that town, against the vigorous attacks of more than 2,000 royalist regulars, won him both the ire of New Spain's last viceregal governors and the nervous respect of the king's military officials.

Following Independence, Bravo was recognized for his services to the nation and was awarded the title of Benemérito de la Patria (November 23, 1822). Promoted by the recently crowned emperor Agustín de Iturbide to the rank of brigadier general, he was now responsible for both the Seventh Division (Veracruz) and the Operational Division of the South. Bravo's military renown and patriotism also helped launch his post-Independence, political career. Indeed, his military service during the Independence War was never forgotten by any of his later political adversaries.

Losing a bid for the presidency in 1824 to Guadalupe Victoria, Bravo was chosen instead as Victoria's vice president. A leading centralist and grand master of the Scottish Rite Masons, Bravo soon clashed with Victoria, who increasingly demonstrated his own orientation by appointing radical York Rite Masons, who tended to be staunch federalists, to the most powerful cabinet positions. When the new Yorkino (York Rite) Congress passed (in 1827) the first of a series Spanish Expulsion laws, Bravo joined with other Scottish Rite Masons to lead an ultimately unsuccessful coup d'état. The failed revolt was put down by the federalist, Yorkino general, Vicente Guerrero. Exiled to Ecuador, Bravo did not return to Mexico again until he was granted amnesty in 1829. That same year the government of now-president Vicente Guerrero fell victim to a centralist-supported coup led by another vice president, Anastasio Bustamante (Guerrero also had come to power through force).

Federalist-centralist wrangles continued after the fall of Guerrero, and except for the short-lived reform government of Valentín Gómez Farías (1833–34), centralists maintained control of the Congress and the National Palace throughout the 1830s and much of the 1840s. In this proclerical, promilitary environment, Bravo's career once again prospered. Resuming his old military command in the south, Bravo was soon given command of the Northern Army (1833), commanding a region where Anglo-Texan settlers were preparing for secession. When President Antonio López de Santa Anna himself took control of the northern campaign against the Anglo-Texan rebels (1835–36), embarking on an odyssey that ended in fiasco, Bravo resigned in disgust. Retiring to his hacienda near Chilpancingo, Bravo emerged periodically over the next 10 years to take up one official charge or another. These included two brief periods as interim president (1839 and 1843) and a term as a congressional deputy for the state of Mexico (elected 1841).

Following another brief interlude of Liberal-federalist rule in the 1840s (a federalist coup brought José Joaquín de Herrera to power in December 1844), Conservative-centralists once again returned to power in early 1846. Throughout the autumn of 1845, rumors circulated in the capital that Herrera's Liberal government had been negotiating with the United States for the sale of Texas, New Mexico, and the Californias. The Conservative press denounced such a move as treasonous and unconstitutional. Having ignored Mexico's sternest warnings, the United States had recently formalized their annexation of Texas. Many Mexicans now felt that the Anglos were in need of a pointed lesson from the Mexican army; anything less would be an insult to Mexico's national honor and would further excite the U.S. appetite for more Mexican territory.

Capitalizing on the public outrage in December, General Mariano Paredes y Arrillaga declared himself in open rebellion against the government. The main justification proffered for the revolution was the Herrera regime's failure to effect the recapture of Texas. Perceiving a dire threat to the nation's sovereignty, Bravo declared his adherence to Paredes's Plan, which promised swift action in Texas. Marching into the capital on January 1, 1846, Paredes was soon anointed president with Bravo named vice president. Nonetheless, theirs was an extremely short-lived government. Within seven months, Mexico and the United States had declared war on each other, Mexico's large Northern Division had been humiliated in the opening battles of the conflict, and the Paredes government had fallen to a new federalist coup.

Temporarily out of grace with the government in Mexico City, Bravo received absolution the following year when his military services once again were needed. Recalled to duty to help prepare for the defense of the capital, Bravo himself directed the defense of Chapultepec Castle when the U.S. assault finally came. In one of the hardest-fought battles of the war, the Mexican defenders inflicted heavy losses on their American attackers. The castle fell on September 13, 1847, and Bravo was taken prisoner.

Nicolás Bravo was a figure of major military and political significance from the Independence era through the first 30 years of national sovereignty. A powerful centralist leader and an adept military commander, Bravo's influence stretched from the Morelos insurgency through the American invasion of 1846 to 1847. Throughout he defended Mexican independence and intervened in the democratic process only when he felt the nation was imperiled from without or within. Nicolás Bravo died in his native Chilpancingo in 1854.

Select Bibliography

Arce, General Fracisco O., *Album literario dedicado al eminente General Nicolás Bravo en el centenario de su nacimiento*. Mexico City: Oficina de la Secretaría de Fomento, 1886.

Carréno, Alberto María, *Jefes del Ejército Mexicano en 1847: Biografías de Generales de División y de Brigada y de Coroneles del Ejército Mexicano por fines del año de 1847*. Mexico City: Secretaría de Fomento, 1914.

Costeloe, Michael P., *La Primera República Federal de Mexico, 1824–1835*. Mexico City: Fondo de Cultura Económica, 1975.

_____, *The Central Republic in Mexico, 1835–1846: Hombres de Bien in the Age of Santa Anna*. Cambridge and New York: Cambridge University Press, 1993.

Green, Stanley C., *The Mexican Republic: The First Decade, 1823–1832*. Pittsburgh, Pennsylvania: University of Pittsburgh Press, 1987.

Parrish, Leonard, "The Life of Nicolás Bravo, Mexican Patriot (1786–1854)." Ph.D. diss., University of Texas at Austin, 1951.

—BRUCE COLCLEUGH

BUCARELI Y URSÚA, ANTONIO MARÍA

1717–79 • Captain General of Cuba and Viceroy of New Spain

Scion of a leading aristocratic family of Seville, Spain, that sent many sons to serve the army, the royal bureaucracy, or the Catholic Church, Antonio María Bucareli y Ursúa was born January 24, 1717, and commenced his military career as an army cadet at age 15. He quickly won recognition for his intelligence and zeal in many sieges and battles in Naples and northern Italy during Felipe V's campaigns to recover lost territories. Bucareli was promoted to captain in 1740, colonel in 1744, and returned to Spain in 1746 to become inspector general of cavalry and dragoons as well as inspector of coastal fortifications of Granada and Murcia during threats of invasion or raids. Promoted to lieutenant general, he served in the campaign against Portugal and as a commissioner to negotiate an end to hostilities. In 1766, King Carlos III appointed Bucareli governor and captain general of Cuba, a post he held with distinction for almost five and one-half years. Bucareli gained recognition as an efficient, honest, and effective administrator, a builder of defensive fortifications, and the organizer of the 1769 expeditionary force dispatched to capture New Orleans under Alejandro O'Reilly. Although the climate of Havana weakened Bucareli's health and made him anxious to return to Spain, in 1771 he received the appointment as viceroy of New Spain.

Bucareli assumed command of New Spain on 22 September, 1771, and spent the ensuing months studying how to deal with the heavy responsibilities of governing such an enormous country and organizing the chaotic, unindexed files in government offices. Before he left New Spain, Visitador General José de Gálvez briefed Bucareli about his blueprint for administrative and economic reforms designed to produce greater revenues. Bucareli expanded the viceregal secretariat to encompass these various issues. Notwithstanding pressures from the imperial government, Bucareli was critical of Gálvez's major project to implement a new administrative system based upon a system of provincial intendants and district subdelegates. The viceroy believed that the economies of most provinces in sparsely populated New Spain could not afford larger and more expensive bureaucracies. At Mexico City and in other cities and towns, Bucareli reported that there were too many unemployed people and naked vagabonds. He concluded that the existing administrative structure of the *alcaldes mayores* and other officials could be made to work efficiently. Indeed, increased mineral production during the 1770s initiated a period of expansion and prosperity as new silver mines opened and old veins were returned to productivity. During his tenure in Mexico, Bucareli was active in developing mine production, but he opposed the creation of the privileged Cuerpo de Minería, the mining guild.

Bucareli's defense programs for New Spain reflected his conservative approaches and his dedication to a policy of fiscal constraints. He oversaw projects to improve fortresses such San Juan Ulúa at Veracruz and the construction of the inland fort at Perote. Although New Spain was at peace for the first years of his viceregency, Bucareli worked with Field Marshal Pascual de Cisneros to recruit disciplined provincial militia regiments. In the north, chronic warfare against the Apaches, Comanches, and other tribes led to the introduction of a string of fortified presidios and the implementation of Gálvez's recommendation for the creation of the Comandancia General de las Provincias Internas under the command of Brigadier Teodoro de Croix. The fact that the northern provinces required stronger garrisons and additional funds led to strained relations and acrimony between the two leaders. Concerning defense questions, Bucareli remarked that to be captain general of New Spain in wartime must be the greatest misfortune that an officer could experience.

Also to the north and west of New Spain, Bucareli received information that Russian explorers had opened commerce with the natives on the North American coast north of the newly explored and thinly settled province of Alta California. The Spanish minister of state, Marqués de Grimaldi, ordered Bucareli to dispatch an expedition to verify the extent of encroachment and to detain any foreigners found in Spanish territories. Based upon his reading of reports from Monterey about the backwardness of native societies, Bucareli did not believe that the coastal Indians would be much use as Russian allies. After delays needed to locate a suitable ship, Bucareli commissioned a senior pilot, Juan Pérez, to conduct the reconnaissance mission. Carrying

detailed instructions from the viceroy, Pérez sailed north with a single vessel to the Queen Charlotte Islands (about 55 degrees latitude) and returned after a short offshore stop at Nootka Sound on Vancouver Island that became famous in 1778 following the visit of Captain James Cook. Pérez's exploration was not completely successful since he did not land a party to take possession of the coast. His reports of high native cultures and possible resources impressed Bucareli, who dispatched a second expedition in 1775 commanded by Ignacio Arteaga and Juan Francisco de la Bodega y Quadra that reached Alaska waters. A third expedition in 1779 stopped at Bucareli Sound, Prince of Wales Island, and investigated Alaskan waters westward to Cook Inlet without locating any Russians. Other land expeditions authorized by Bucareli under the command of Captain Juan Bautista de Anza, Francisco Garcés, and Friars Silvestre Vélez de Escalante and Francisco Atanasio Domínguez, explored California and reached into what are today the states of Colorado and Utah.

A sincerely religious man who served as knight commander of the Order of Malta, Bucareli's administration in New Spain was moderate, careful, and even conservative. Although many viceroys served mainly as bureaucrats without significantly altering the system or the country, Bucareli adopted strong positions on administrative reform pressed by Gálvez, delayed the introductions of the provincial intendancies, and advanced New Spain's Pacific and northern frontier expansion. Bucareli's activity in every area can be noted by his voluminous official correspondence and reports that are found in Mexican and Spanish archives. After five years in the demanding job as viceroy, in 1776 Bucareli requested permission to return to Spain. Although he withdrew this petition when it appeared likely that Spain would soon be at war with Britain, Bucareli's already delicate health suffered further from the long hours he spent daily in his viceregal duties. He fell ill on March 31, 1779, with an illness diagnosed by his doctors as pleurisy, and he died shortly thereafter.

Select Bibliography

Bobb, Bernard E., "Bucareli and the Interior Provinces." *Hispanic American Historical Review* 34:1 (February 1954).

_____, *The Viceregency of Antonio María Bucareli in New Spain, 1771–1779.* Austin: University of Texas Press, 1962.

Brading, David A., *Miners and Merchants in Bourbon Mexico, 1763–1810.* Cambridge: Cambridge University Press, 1971.

Calderón Quijano, José Antonio, *Fortificaciones en Nueva España.* Seville: Escuela de Estudios Hispano-Americanos, 1953.

_____, editor, *Los virreyes de Nueva España en el reinado de Carlos III.* Vol. 1, Seville: Escuela de Estudios Hispano-Americanos de Sevilla, 1967.

Cook, Warren L., *Flood Tide of Empire: Spain and the Pacific Northwest, 1543–1819.* New Haven, Connecticut: Yale University Press, 1973.

Priestley, Herbert I., *José de Gálvez: Visitor-General of New Spain, 1765–1771.* Berkeley: University of California Press, 1916.

Velasco Ceballos, Rómulo, editor, *La administración de D. Frey Antonio María de Bucareli y Ursúa, cuadragésimo sexto virrey de México.* 2 vols., Mexico City: Talleres Gráficos de la Nación, 1936.

Weber, David J., *The Spanish Frontier in North America.* New Haven: Yale University Press, 1992.

—Christon I. Archer

BULLFIGHTING

The practice of bullfighting in Mexico was imported from Spain immediately after the Spanish Conquest. The first official bullfight, or *corrida,* took place on August 13, 1529, celebrating the feast of St. Hippolito, on whose saint's day Tenochtitlan (site of present-day Mexico City) was conquered by Fernando (Hernán) Cortés. Two of seven selected bulls were killed and the meat was distributed to "monasteries and hospitals." An infrastructure supporting local *corridas* was laid when Juan Gutierrez Altamirano, cousin of Cortés, imported fighting bulls and cows from Navarra, Spain, in 1552, an event that caused a group of Indians two years later to petition the viceroy to intervene on their behalf, since the bulls were damaging their crops and menacing farmers. The Atenco ranch founded by Gutierrez Altamirano still sells fighting bulls today.

Until the eighteenth century bullfighting in Spain and Mexico was a chaotic affair. Several bulls were penned into an enclosed area; men on horseback, usually nobles, would incite them, try to outrun or sidestep them, and eventually kill them with lances. Enthusiastic audiences watched. In Mexico these spectacles were held on the feast of St. Hippolito and to celebrate the arrival of a new viceroy, the signing of peace treaties affecting Spain, the canonization of a saint, or the birth or marriage of a member of the royal family of Spain. On such occasions the Plaza Mayor in Mexico City would be fenced in and box seats would be constructed for dignitaries.

When Felipe V, grandson of Louis XIV, acceded to the Spanish throne in 1700, his antipathy for bullfights caused much of the Spanish nobility to shun *corridas* altogether. It continued among the lower classes, but its form changed from an exercise primarily on horseback—the prerogative of nobles—to one by men on foot. This development gave rise to the advent of professional *toreadores,* and to the evolution of cape work to control the bull's charge. While horsemanship continued in bullfights, action on the ground predominated. Joaquin Rodríguez, known as Costillares, a Spaniard, revolutionized the killing of the bull in the late eighteenth century with a technique known as the *volapie* (flying feet), in which the matador charges the bull head-on, thrusting a sword deeply between the shoulder blades, severing the aorta and producing a rapid death. This technique can be executed with relative safety only when the bull's neck is lowered, and after Costillares the use of lances *(pics)* thrust from horseback into the bull's neck muscles to produce the desired lowering became widespread.

With these innovations, bullfighting became a popular and lucrative activity, resulting in the construction of the first single-purpose bullrings in Spain, Mexico, and other parts of Latin America, and in standardization of the spectacle. In 1769 in Mexico City, for example, the bullfight season, under control of the viceroy, lasted for two weeks in November and December, with 12 distinct *corridas,* bringing in 35,000 pesos in total ticket sales (for an audience of about 2,000) and profits to the state of 25,000 pesos after expenses. The most expensive matador, a Spaniard named Tomás Vanegas "El Gachupin Toreador," was paid 240 pesos for his participation in eight *corridas.* Two hundred and ten bulls were purchased at a cost of 10 pesos each and were fought by *cuadrillas* (teams) of bullfighters including two matadors, six *banderilleros,* and seven horsemen. The first permanent bullring in Mexico was constructed in Mexico City in 1788 and the *corrida* spread rapidly throughout Mexico. By 1790, to celebrate the accession of Carlos IV to the Spanish throne, *corridas* were held in Mexico City, Durango, Paplantla, Veracruz, Pátzcuaro, Guanajuato, Tehuantepec, Aguascalientes, Tabasco, Valladolid, Real del Catorce, Chilapa, Zamora, and San Luis de la Paz.

After Independence bullfighting in Mexico declined. But the spectacle was invigorated in 1829 when the Mexican national government began sponsoring *corridas* and again in 1835 when Bernardo Gavino Rueda, a Spanish bullfighter not fully accredited at home, traveled to Mexico to become "director of *corridas* and teacher of bullfighters." He established a bullfighting school that incorporated the Spanish tradition, although he did not teach the *volapie* technique. Jesús Villegas "Catrin," his student, fought in Spain in 1857, probably the first Mexican to do so. Bullfighting was forbidden during the presidency of Benito Juárez, beginning in 1867, initiating another period of decline that lasted until the prohibition was rescinded in 1887. Bullfighting resumed in all states except Oaxaca, where it still is forbidden today. In 1889 one of the best Mexican bullfighters, Ponciano Díaz, traveled to Spain, where modern styles were evolving rapidly, and he fought for a season with the finest matadors there, including Frascuelo and Guerrita, from whom he learned techniques he carried back to Mexico. For some time thereafter bullfighting in Mexico flourished as native and Spanish matadors fought side by side in the largest bullrings of both countries. Rodolfo Gaona became the first Mexican matador to achieve first-ranking status shortly after his arrival in Spain in 1908, where he remained for much of his career until his retirement in 1925. One of the passes he invented, the *gaonera,* in which the matador holds one end of the cape behind his back while the other hand guides the cape, has become part of the standard vocabulary of passes.

The Mexican Revolution decimated the cattle industry in Mexico, from which the breeding of fighting bulls did not recover until the early 1920s. In 1916 President Venustiano Carranza forbade bullfighting in Mexico, a prohibition that coincided with part of Gaona's bullfighting career and lasted until May 1920. In 1927 Fermín Espinosa "Armillita" replaced Gaona as the top Mexican matador when he traveled to Spain at the age of 17, quickly becoming one of the most popular bullfighters there until his retirement in 1949. He, in turn, was replaced by Carlos Arruza, who fought frequently in Spain from the time of his first arrival in 1944 until his retirement in 1953. His career in Spain, like Armillita's before him, coincided with another decline in Mexican bullfighting, this time caused by a severe loss in the stock of fighting bulls, product of an epidemic of hoof-and-mouth disease lasting from 1946 to 1952. After Arruza, no Mexican matador has reached top ranking in Spain, a status still considered the pinnacle of achievement.

The relationship between Mexican and Spanish bullfighting during most of the twentieth century has been complex. During the first decades Mexican *corridas* prospered from the introduction of new styles from Spain. The period between the high point of Joselito's career and the retirement of Juan Belmonte (top Spaniards who fought during the 1920s and 1930s), known as the "golden age" of bullfighting, was one in which bullfighting changed from a relatively static, more "heroic" event for the matador, who waited head-on for the bull to charge, to a more fluid and dynamic event. Belmonte proved that a matador could stand much closer to the bull, from an oblique angle requiring a good deal more movement with the arms to guide the bull's charge. This permitted the linking of one pass to another in a series of fluid motions usually capped off by a *pase de pecho,* in which the matador reverses the direction of the pass across his body, stopping the action. This style favors a smaller, more predictable bull and as it became popular in Spain, breeders began providing smaller bulls. Matadors in Mexico, already accustomed to the smaller, more agile bull bred there, quickly adapted to the new style, and by the mid-1930s more than 300 contracts per year were being issued to Mexican bullfighters in Spain, 50 of these to Armillita alone. But in 1936 the Spanish government, lobbied by an association of native matadors, prohibited the entry of Mexican bullfighters to Spain except under difficult conditions. Mexico recipro-

cated, and the mutual boycott lasted until 1944 and then was renewed from 1947 to 1951. It has been invoked intermittently since then. By the time Mexicans matadors could return to Spain in 1944, the Spanish Civil War had ruined herds there, and relatively small bulls were fought for a number of years, further enhancing the Spanish careers of Mexican matadors. There is little cross-breeding between the herds of the two countries, owing in great part to stringent veterinary health regulations in each country.

Since the end of the Spanish Civil War, interchange of matadors between Mexico and Spain has been influenced by disparities in fees paid to matadors. During the 1940s, 1950s, and 1960s top-flight matadors in Spain were paid lower fees than they could command in Mexico or other Latin American countries where bullfighting is practiced (Peru, Ecuador, Colombia, and Venezuela). This encouraged Spanish matadors to contract in those countries. From the 1970s to the present, however, the relationship has reversed, and bullfighters can command fees two, three, or more times higher in Spain (sometimes above $50,000 per fight) than they can in comparable bullrings in Mexico. In contrast a Mexican matador near the low end of the top 20 rankings will typically earn about $3,000 to $5,000 per *corrida,* fight 20 to 30 times per year, and must pay travel costs and share his earnings with his *cuadrilla* of four. By the mid-1990s only two or three among the top bullfighters from one country fought in the other in any given year, and the administrative agreement governing exchanges of matadors between Mexico and Spain remained problematic.

Thus, with the bulls of each country bred separately, and with only intermittent and infrequent interaction among matadors, Mexican bullfighting has developed a personality of its own, despite nearly identical regulatory statutes. Mexican bulls continue to be slightly smaller than Spanish bulls, but they are faster and they tend to have more stamina, enabling a matador to extract more passes from them during the last part of the bullfight. They are said to be highly tenacious and fierce but also more "collaborative," in that their charges tend to be more smoothly articulated and more predictable. While this latter quality makes the bull less dangerous, and hence less exciting, it permits a matador, when facing an excellent bull, to execute a rich variety of lively, close passes, complete with flourishes and "adornos," such as posing (briefly) in front of a standing bull with an elbow on its nose. In comparative terms, the Mexican bullfight tends toward something of a cross between the flashy, elegant Sevillian style in which the bull is dazzled by the matador, and the more "classic," slow-moving tempo of the Ronda style, in which the tragic character of the bull is emphasized.

Bullfighting in Cultural Context

The *corrida,* an asymmetrical encounter between humans and a dangerous bull, takes place within a rigorously structured set of norms leading to the death of the bull. Since the bull is a major protagonist, the *corrida* can be viewed as a tragic metaphor, not unlike the Greek conception of tragedy, in which it is precisely the bull's nobility that leads to its death; indeed, one of the major qualities hoped for in a fighting bull is *nobleza*. Certain bullfighting styles, such as the "classic" style of Ronda, lend themselves to this bull-oriented interpretation. Emphasis on the matador as protagonist, on the other hand, suggests the triumph of intelligence, skill, and human organization over brute force, and is readily apparent in certain bullfighting styles, such as the intensely athletic manner of Carlos Arruza. Since *corridas* evolved in societies with highly developed concepts of authority, the bullfight also can be seen as an illumination of two distinct conceptions: the animalistic, physical authority posed by the raw brute power of the bull versus the more subtle authority of the matador, whose skill ultimately places him in a lethally dominant position. The sexual symbolism of the bull as a masculine figure is nearly universal, and some observers have seen in the modern *corrida* an intricate interplay of masculine and feminine qualities in the actions of the matador with the bull. Bullfighting clearly has its origins in ritual sacrifice, an element that distinguishes it from contemporary sports events or theater, linking it to ancient practices such as those found in the Old Testament or in Mesoamerican civilizations, and on the Iberian Peninsula. Fascination with wild bulls in the Mediterranean region is ancient—the caves of Altamirano in Spain, estimated to be 20,000 years old, contain vivid images of bulls.

Although it has roots in the Spanish and Mexican colonial aristocracies, modern bullfighting in both Spain and Mexico is an urban entrepreneurial activity that developed simultaneously in large, industrializing cities, appealing to large sectors of the middle classes while still remaining popular among the upper classes. The development of nationalistic feelings, cutting across highly unequal class structures in Spain and Mexico during the first half of the twentieth century, may in fact have been assisted by the popularity of the *corrida*, one of the few public spaces outside of politics available simultaneously to various social classes. Little, however, has been written on the subject. Likewise, few studies exist on the social contexts in which bullfighting takes place in the smaller bullrings in Spain or Mexico. The statistics of bullrings in Mexico, however, are suggestive. There are about 200 bullrings throughout Mexico, but only in 37 of these are there at least 4 bullfights per year. By far most bullfights take place in small towns with only one *corrida* per year, and it is unclear whether the phenomenon is different in these settings: whether ethnic and social correlates surrounding bullfights differ in largely indigenous communities, for example, or whether the element of ritual or religious symbolism accompanying *corridas* is stronger in these communities. It is also possible that, as is the case in Spain, informal *corridas* may be held in small communities, with local villagers acting as impromptu bullfighters to demonstrate their courage.

Although bullfighting has prospered in Mexico more than in any other Latin American country, it is still not relatively as important as it is in Spain, where one bull is killed (in novice or regular bullfights) for approximately every 5,000 inhabitants. In Mexico the figure is roughly one per 19,000. Mexico, with more than double the population of Spain, had only about 750 bullfights in 1996, compared to about 1,450 in Spain. And while the number of novices and fully accredited matadors in each country is roughly the same (419 in Spain and 455 in Mexico in 1996), Spanish matadors have far more engagements, a factor particularly important to young matadors trying to hone an individual style through "live" practice.

Women and Bullfighting

From the time it was institutionalized in Mexico until the present women have participated as bullfighters, although far less frequently than men. In November 1779, for example, a *cuadrilla* of four women fought bulls in Mexico City, and the next day six women fought. In December 1791 María García fought with two male matadors, each earning 50 pesos per fight. A royal decree issued in Spain in 1908 expressly forbade women from bullfighting; the decree was enforced until the death of General Francisco Franco. A Peruvian woman, Conchita Cintron, was well known as a *rejoneadora* (fighter of bulls on horseback) throughout the bullfighting world during the 1950s. During the 1980s one Spanish woman, Maribel Atienzar, known as La Espanolita, and Raquel Martínez, a Mexican, fought bulls. As of 1996 the only accredited female bullfighter from Spain was Cristina Sánchez, and the only female bullfighter from Mexico was the novice Monica Hernández.

The Bullfight Described

All aspects of the bullfight—minimum weights of bulls and horses; sizes of the *pic* and *banderillas* (spears about 30 inches—75 centimeters—long, with small, sharp, harpoon-like points), the provision of clinics at bullrings, maximum time limits to kill the bull—are regulated by detailed government statutes, and each bullring has a designated judge empowered to enforce them. Normally six bulls are killed by three matadors who alternate in highly structured three-part performances for each bull. In the first *tercio* the bull enters the ring, charging one or more bullfighters fending with large capes; then two horses with protective covering and ridden by *picadores* enter the ring and incite the bull to charge. While the bull is engaged with the horse the *picador* shoves the point of a lance about two inches (five centimeters) into the back of the bull's muscular neck. Bulls that continue to charge while feeling the *pic* are admired for their bravery. The *pic* may be repeated up to three times until the bull is deemed by the judge to be sufficiently punished for it to be fought and killed but still strong enough to provide spirited challenge to the matador. The horses leave the arena, beginning the second *tercio* in which a bullfighter holds two short *banderillas* with raised arms and, using one of several standard techniques, drops them sharply onto the muscular part of the bull's back as it passes by. This may be repeated up to three times, after which the final *tercio* begins. The matador, holding a red cape (*muleta*) incites the bull to charge at close range, guiding the bull as gracefully as possible through a series of linked passes. After a few minutes—in Mexico the bull must be killed within 16 minutes of the beginning of this *tercio;* otherwise its life will be spared—the matador profiles directly in front of the bull, aims his sword in his right hand while trying to divert the bull's charge with the *muleta* in his left hand, and charges, attempting to insert the sword between the shoulder blades while going over the bull's horns. If he succeeds the first time, and the crowd has been pleased by the capework, the matador may be awarded with one or both ears, and, for an extraordinary performance, the tail, taken from the dead bull. During moments of well-executed action a band will play music, usually in the *pasodoble* form associated with bullfighting. The great Mexican popular songwriter Agustín Lara (author of "Grandada") composed a number of highly popular *pasodobles,* some still played today.

Although each bullfight is structured identically, the quality varies considerably, and *aficionados* often have reasons to be less than fully satisfied. The bull can be overly punished by a *picador,* rendering it too weak to charge gamely; or under-punished, making it too dangerous for close passes or the kill. Occasionally the bull refuses to charge at all, or hooks too dangerously to handle at close range. The *banderillas* may be placed badly, causing much pain. The matador

may have difficulty executing close passes or the kill. These defects are frequent, and audiences are likely to protest loudly at perceived abuses to the bull or other incompetent behavior. Although unusual, sometimes all six bulls are killed without the granting of a single ear to a matador, and rarely are more than two or three ears granted in an afternoon. However, when the bull exhibits tenacity, vigor, and stamina; when it has been handled skillfully by *picadors* and *banderilleros;* and when the matador has executed close, linked passes with sculptural grace, audiences are sometimes moved to tears at the moment of a bull's death.

Select Bibliography

Anuario Taurino de Mexico, 1995–1996. Naucalpan: BIT, 1996.
De Cossio, J.M., *Los Toros.* 2 vols., Madrid: Espasa-Calpe, 1995.
Marvin, Garry, *Bullfight.* Oxford and New York: Blackwell, 1988.
Rangel, Nicolas, *Historia del Toreo en Mexico, epoca colonia (1529–1821).* Mexico City: M.L. Sanchez, 1924.
Rivero, Sergio, *Tauromaquia Mexicana: Imagen y pensamiento.* Mexico City: Fernandez Cueto, 1994.
Vinyes, Fernando, *Mexico: Diez veces llanto.* Madrid: Espasa-Calpe, 1991.

—JOSÉ Z. GARCÍA

BULNES, FRANCISCO

1847–1924 • Statesman and Writer

Educated in civil engineering at the National Mining School, Francisco Bulnes joined the National Preparatory School as a professor of mathematics; he later taught hydrology, calculus, political economy, and meteorology at the Engineering School. He was also a member of the Society of Geography and Statistics and went to Japan in 1874 on a scientific mission to study Venus. With this type of technological background, it should not be surprising that Francisco Bulnes became one of the main figures in Mexico's liberal-positivist school, collectively known as the Científicos. Bulnes shared with that group an admiration for the power and wealth of the Anglo-Saxon world and a belief that economic progress held the keys to national social development; in language reminiscent of European positivists Herbert Spencer and Hippolyte Taine, Bulnes compared the nation to a human body and noted that if one did not meet the material conditions for life first, there could be no intellectual or moral development.

Bulnes began his career as a political liberal under Lerdo de Tejada and served as engineer on the Veracruz Railway line. From this influential commission, Bulnes quickly

moved into national politics. He knew and worked with Porfirio Díaz, although never as closely as his detractors charged, and he certainly shared that president's goal of material progress for Mexico. In fact, Bulnes as a Científico helped provide the intellectual justification for the Díaz regime when he wrote admiringly of the United States and Great Britain and attacked the power of the Catholic Church in Mexican national life. Bulnes believed that the institutionalized Catholic religion represented nothing but lies and actually worked against the well-being of the Mexican working class by recommending passivity and suffering where hard work and application were preferable. By stressing rewards in the afterlife, the Catholic Church discouraged industry and denied the possibility of personal advancement through one's efforts; Bulnes suggested that Protestantism was perhaps more suited to modern cultures.

Bulnes judged history in similar terms. He viewed the first 70 years of independent Mexico's national life, from Miguel Hidalgo y Costilla's revolt to Benito Juárez's Reforma as the era of demolition; in contrast, he presented the Díaz years as ones of reconstruction, characterized by the reestablishment of order and material progress. Bulnes followed Lucas Alamán in suggesting that short-lived emperor Agustín de Iturbide should be restored to a proper place of respect in Mexican history; after all, he was not an opponent of Independence itself but of the destructive radical insurgents. Bulnes consistently opposed popular suffrage and instead looked toward England where government was "of the people by the best of the people." In contrast to the United States, where popular participation often meant the elevation of some questionable characters, government in Britain was by a cultivated and concerned working aristocracy with a monarch who could dissolve Parliament should it become too anarchic or corrupt; for Bulnes, this was the best practical combination for government.

Bulnes spent 30 years as a senator and deputy in the Congress; he drafted the first Bank Law and the Mining Code of 1880 and its revisions in 1892, and he consistently fought for the establishment of an independent judiciary and tried to limit presidential power and terms in office. Bulnes occupied a tenuous middle ground between conservatives who were angered when he attacked the church and traditional ways, and the liberals who called him a reactionary when he criticized their great heroes and events just as harshly. Because of his long association with the Díaz regime, Bulnes faced sometimes threatening attacks during the 1910s. He left Mexico for New Orleans and Havana for five years, returning in 1921. His most influential published works are *El porvenir de las naciones latinoamericanas ante las recientes conquistas de Europa y norteamérica* (1899), *El verdadera Juárez* (1902), *Las grandes mentires de nuestra historia* (1904), *Juárez y las revoluciones de Ayutla y de Reforma* (1905); *El verdadera Díaz y la Revolución* (1920).

Select Bibliography

Cockcroft, James, *Intellectual Precursors of the Mexican Revolution.* Austin: University of Texas Press, 1968.

Cosmes, Francisco, *El verdadero Bulnes y su falso Juárez.* Mexico City: Talleres de Tipografía, 1904.

Gómez Quiñones, Juan, *Porfirio Díaz, los intelectuales y la Revolución.* Mexico City: El Caballito, 1981.

Lemus, George, *Francisco Bulnes, su vida y sus obras.* Mexico City: Ediciones de Andrea, 1965.

Romanell, Patrick, *The Making of the Mexican Mind.* Freeport, New York: Books for Libraries Press, 1969.

—Karen Racine

BUSTAMANTE, ANASTASIO

1780–1853 • Soldier and President

An affluent politician and military leader best remembered for his key role in Mexico's experiment with centralized rule (1835–44), Anastasio Bustamante followed a path to power that was remarkably similar to those of other Mexican leaders in the first half of the nineteenth century. Born in Jiquilpan, Michoacán, to Spanish parents, Bustamante attended school in Guadalajara and Mexico City before settling in San Luis Potosí to practice medicine. The Wars of Independence subsequently provided Bustamante with an avenue of both military and political advancement. Following the Hidalgo Revolt in Guanajuato, Bustamante joined Félix María Calleja de Rey's royalist forces in subduing the insurgents in Aculco, Guanajuato, Puente de Calderón, and Cuautla. Bustamante rose to the rank of general when he abandoned the royalist cause in 1821, seized the cities of Guanajuato and Celaya, and proclaimed his support for Agustín de Iturbide and the Plan de Iguala. Iturbide, upon ascending the Mexican throne, presented Bustamante with a captaincy general. At the same time, Bustamante took advantage of the fame and recognition that accompanied his military successes to secure himself a political post on the Junta Provisional Gubernativa (Provisional Government).

Bustamante's upbringing, along with his credentials as both an Iturbidista and a well-known military hero, appealed strongly to conservative political factions in the decades following Iturbide's fall from power. First, his Spanish heritage and traditional education established him in the eyes of the clergy and affluent classes as an *hombre de bién*—an individual who was both cultured and well-to-do, like themselves, and who would preserve the existing social hierarchy. Second, Bustamante's identification with the Iturbide monarchy appealed to advocates of a centralized form of government. Finally, conservatives were quick to realize that any viable candidate for political office (and especially the presidency) needed the support of the military, which wielded enormous power after Independence.

Without a stable base of support, Bustamante's hold on power would remain tenuous. Unlike Mexican caudillos Juan Álvarez and Antonio López de Santa Anna, whose power and influence stemmed from networks of local supporters in their home states, Bustamante's supporters represented a regionally diverse and frequently changing coalition of members and interests. In short, his popularity depended largely upon his maintaining a state of political, economic, and social stability, in which the conservatives could thrive. The bitter bipartisan struggle between liberals and conservatives, as well as the country's worsening economic crisis, made Bustamante's task increasingly difficult.

Bustamante's ascent to the presidency began in 1829 when he was elected vice president in the Vicente Guerrero administration. Bustamante served as a counterweight to Guerrero, whose mixed ancestry and efforts to politically mobilize the Mexican masses terrified many *hombres de bién*. Guerrero's reluctance to relinquish the extraordinary powers granted him during the Spanish invasion in the fall of 1829 led Bustamante to revolt against the president. Shortly thereafter, Bustamante assumed the presidency and ruled from 1830 until 1832. During this period, he strengthened his ties to the conservative factions by filling his cabinet posts with well-known conservatives like Lucas Alamán and enacting legislation that increasingly centralized power in the national government. At the same time, Bustamante directed the government forces fighting to suppress Guerrero and his followers in the so-called War of the South. The capture and execution of Guerrero in 1831 proved to be simultaneously the crowning glory and the death blow to Bustamante's administration.

Although conservatives lauded Bustamante's centralization policies and his administration's decision to execute a seemingly dangerous demagogue, Mexican liberals, who had begun to regain their popularity owing to Bustamante's inability to resolve either the country's foreign debt crisis or the general state of economic stagnation, portrayed the president as a would-be monarch and the murderer of a national hero. In 1832 liberals backed Santa Anna's rebellion against the Bustamante government. Shortly thereafter, Bustamante resigned the presidency and went into exile.

Within five years, the same forces that swept Bustamante from office would return him to the presidency. Continuing economic problems, along with the growing threat of war with the United States over Texas, had undermined the liberals' support and breathed new life into the conservatives' cause. *Hombres de bién* of all political persuasions came to believe that Mexico's only salvation lay in a strong centralized government. Anastasio Bustamante returned from exile and was elected president of the newly created Central Republic in 1837.

Bustamante subsequently attempted to bring stability to Mexico's political system by adopting a neutral stance and co-opting conservatives and liberals alike into the new government. Events in the late 1830s almost immediately began to undermine Bustamante's efforts, however. First, the French blockade and siege of Veracruz in the 1838 Pastry War, despite proving unsuccessful, demonstrated that a centralized government was no more immune to external threats than its predecessor. In addition, as the states of Yucatán, Tabasco, and Chiapas followed Texas in seceding from the nation, and as Mexico's economic situation went from bad to worse, Bustamante attracted the growing criticisms of both political camps. Conservatives looked upon his socializing with well-known liberals as evidence of his defection from the conservative cause, while liberals feared that his increasing need to assume extraordinary powers in times of crisis would lead ultimately to a monarchy. Disillusioned with their country's unending economic and political crises, Mexicans of all political convictions began to call for extreme measures. Bustamante's efforts to avoid measures that might alienate one faction or the other led to his being caricatured as apathetic and unable to follow a single course of action. The disintegration of his political base left the beleaguered president poorly equipped to handle the series of revolts that began in 1840 and ended with the dramatic siege of Mexico City in 1841, when Bustamante was forced from office and into exile. Although he returned to the Mexican political scene in the late 1840s, age and health led him into retirement in San Miguel de Allende, where he died in 1853, just five years after leading government forces one final time against a rebellion led by General Manuel Paredes y Arrillaga.

Select Bibliography

Bustamante, Carlos María de, *El gabinete Mexicano durante el segundo periodo del presidente D. Anastasio Bustamante*. Mexico City: J.M. Lara, 1842.

Costeloe, Michael P., *La primera república federal de México, 1824–1835*. Mexico City: Fondo de Cultura Económica, 1975.

⸻, *The Central Republic in Mexico, 1835–1846*. Cambridge and New York: Cambridge University Press, 1993.

—BRYAN E. VIZZINI

BUSTAMANTE, CARLOS MARÍA DE

1774–1848 • Journalist, Writer, and Politician

Carlos María de Bustamante played a major role in the emancipation process of New Spain and the initial years of Independent Mexico. His work as a historian is particularly important, forming the foundation on which official Mexican historiography is based.

Born in Antequera de Oaxaca on November 4, 1774, Bustamante started a career in law in Mexico City in 1794, obtaining the title of lawyer in the Guadalajara High Court of Justice in 1801, the same year he was appointed court reporter. In Mexico City he worked as defense counsel in the Royal Halls of Criminal Justice, Mexico City, and shortly afterwards began work in the office of Licenciado Francisco Primo de Verdad y Ramos.

Captivated by journalism, Bustamante contributed to the *Diario de México,* becoming editor in 1805 under the directorship of Jacobo de Villaurrutia, a distinguished criollo (Mexican of Spanish descent) based in the capital who was known for his libertarian ideas. Bustamante manifested the same tendencies quite openly in 1808, when the City Council called for greater criollo participation in the decision-making processes of New Spain after the Spanish renunciation of the Crown in favor of Napoléon Bonaparte. The coup d'état of September 15 of the same year and the suspicious death of City Council councilman Primo de Verdad in prison sharpened his libertarian predilections. Bustamante sympathized, although not openly, with the rebel movement initiated by Miguel Hidalgo y Costilla in September 1810; he had met the priest in Guanajuato with the doctor Antonio Labarrieta, a friend of Hidalgo and protector of Bustamante.

The establishment of the Constitution of Cádiz in September 1812 allowed Bustamante to take advantage of the freedom of the press provided therein to publish *El Juguetillo,* a newspaper that covered important political questions of the day and criticized the colonial regime. Bustamante also took part in the electoral process initiated on November 29, 1812, to designate ballot holders for the constitutional City Council of the capital. Those chosen were entirely libertarian criollos unhappy with colonial rule, some of whom were even rebel partisans. Bustamante exercised the vote for the parish of San Miguel with José Manuel Sartorio, who was a convinced libertarian and connected with the Guadalupes, a secret society that was helping the rebels while promoting the interests of those fighting for freedom within the colonial system.

Bustamante never managed to use his vote since the viceroy Francisco Xavier Venegas suspended both the electoral process and the freedom of the press, and ordered his arrest. Bustamante decided to join with José María Morelos in Oaxaca, managing to flee the city with the help of the Guadalupes and arriving in Zacatlán. He took charge of the administration and government for the Apan Plains area and the Puebla Highlands, an area known as the Department of the North, which was controlled by the rebel José Francisco Osorno; there Bustamante established a secretariat and also organized troops, cast artillery, and made gunpowder. He kept in contact with the main rebel leaders such as Ignacio López Rayón and Morelos, ensuring sworn obedience to the Suprema Junta Nacional Americana (National American Supreme Council), the main administrative organ of the rebel government. He handled the finances and the religious administration, as well as writing to the viceroy in an attempt to draw the focus of the war toward attending to the rights of the people. The viceroy offered Bustamante amnesty, but when the proposal was rejected, he ordered the arrest of Bustamante's wife, Manuela García Villaseñor. She also fled the capital for Zacatlán.

In May 1813 Bustamante went to Antequera de Oaxaca, where he organized the rebel troops, took charge of the newspaper *Correo Americano del Sur,* and helped appoint the fifth member of the Supreme Council; at the same time, he proposed to Morelos the organization of a new rebel publication. Bustamante went on to represent the Province of Mexico in the Supremo Congreso Nacional Americano (National American Supreme Congress), established in Chilpancingo in September 1813, dictating and signing the Act of Independence issued on November 6.

At the beginning of 1814 he left the Congress to join up with Ignacio López Rayón, with whom he took refuge once again in Zacatlán. He took over both the administration and government of the Department of the North while also writing to the colonial authorities to open up negotiations and to the Papal Nuncio in the United States on questions relative to religious administration.

When Zacatlán fell into royalist hands in September 1814, he and his wife managed to escape together. After a long trek during which he was subject to attack by rebels as much as by royalists and made an unsuccessful attempt to enter the United States, he returned to Zacatlán and stayed there until the middle of 1815, when he rejoined the Congress.

Tired of royalist persecution, Congress decided to move to Tehuacán to be closer to the coast and thereby facilitate possible foreign aid, but it was dissolved in December of that year by Manuel Mier y Terán. While in Tehuacán, Bustamante met the American businessman William Davis Robinson, who was selling arms to the rebels (in 1820 he published a history of the rebel movement largely based on Bustamante's notes). Foiled once again in his attempt to cross the border into the United States, Bustamante was granted amnesty in 1817 only to be imprisoned in San Juan de Ulúa, Veracruz, where he met up with Robinson again. After two years of imprisonment, he was kept under civic arrest in the city of Veracruz. Freed on the restoration of constitutional order in 1820, Bustamante joined Antonio López de Santa Anna and became his secretary. By 1821 he had enrolled in the Independence movement of Agustín de Iturbide. Once Independence was achieved, he continued with his journalistic activities as editor of *La Abispa de Chilpancingo,* in which he recalled the glorious deeds of the rebels. He acted as deputy for Oaxaca in the first Constitutional Congress, making an effective contribution as provisional president. His opposition to the new emperor, Iturbide, and his participation in a republican conspiracy led him to prison in 1822.

In 1823, after Iturbide's overthrow, he was deputy to the new Congress, this time as the representative for Mexico City. His centralist ideas isolated him from political activity in the presidency of Guadalupe Victoria, but later he took up the reins again, making notable contributions as member of various congresses. In 1827 he was named legal adviser to the army, and two years later he returned as deputy, this time for Oaxaca, a responsibility he left in 1833 until he took it up again under a centralist regime in 1835. He formed part of the conservative government of 1837 to 1841 and later was appointed deputy to the congress of 1844 to 1845, once again representing Oaxaca. He died in Mexico City on September 21, 1848, deeply disturbed by the U.S. invasion of Mexico the previous year. A prolific writer, his entire *oeuvre* would occupy many pages. Among

his works are: *Cuadro historico de la revolución de la América mexicana* (first edition, 1821–27; second edition, 1843–46); *Continuación al cuadro* (1832); *El gabinete mexicano durante el segundo periodo de la administración del Exmo. Señor presidente D. Anastasio Bustamente* (1842); and *El nuevo Bernal Díaz del Castillo* (1847), an account of the U.S. invasion. He also edited several classics of Mexican historiography, such as the works of Bernardino de Sahagún and Andrés Cavo. He also wrote the very interesting *Diario histórico de México,* which has largely remained unexamined.

Select Bibliography

Bustamante, Carlos María de, *Cuadro histórico de la revolución mexicana, comenzada por el ciudadano Miguel Hidalgo y Costilla, cura del pueblo de los Dolores, en el obispado de Michoacán.* 2nd edition, 5 vols., Mexico City: José Mariano Lara, 1843–46.

Leomoine, Ernesto, editor, *Carlos María de Bustamante y su apologética historia de la revolución de 1810.* Mexico City: UNAM, 1984.

O'Gorman, Edmundo, editor, *Guía bibliográfica de Carlos María Bustamante.* Mexico City: Condumex, 1967.

Ortega y Medina, José Antonio, "El historiador Carlos María de Bustamante ante la consciencia histórica mexicana." In *Anuario de historia,* Year 3, Mexico City: UNAM, 1963.

—Virginia Guedea

BUSTOS, HERMENEGILDO

1832–1907 • Painter

Hermenegildo Bustos was born on April 13, 1832, in Purísima del Rincón, a village in the state of Guanajuato, which it seems he never left. Having no more than a primary education, he gathered frost to make ices and worked as a tinsmith, goldsmith, tailor, carpenter, musician, and painter, among several other odd jobs that have been attributed to him as a poor man of dogged character and versatile disposition. Years after his death in 1907 (possibly from ingesting a left-over bucket of lemon sorbet) he became known as a great painter, one of the most puzzling and dissonant in the Mexican pantheon. As Octavio Paz admits at the beginning of his essay on Bustos: "How to explain it?"

Among the little that is known about Bustos, myth is hard to divorce from reality in the wake of the rapturous imaginations of early biographers such as Pascual Aceves Barajas. There are many contradictions in our glimpses of Bustos: married in 1854 to Joaquina Ríos, with whom he had no children, he was a womanizing and even abusive husband. Yet when she died a year before him (and was buried in one of

the two home-made coffins that stood in a corner of his tiny bedroom-studio for 20 years) no mourners, contrary to social tradition, were allowed at the wake, which he held alone. Fiercely Catholic, he single-handedly provided the costumes, props, and martial choreography of the yearly passion play; he also wore an Oriental conical hat of unknown provenance and designed for himself a bizarre outfit of ecclesiastico-military appearance, with his name embroidered on the collar. Vanity and humility are hard to distinguish in a man who regularly signed his works "I, Hermenegildo Bustos, amateur painter, an Indian from this village. . . ."

His surviving opus falls into three categories: religious murals in the village parish church, ex-votos, and portraits. The first two are predictably unoriginal, the murals being largely expressionless copies of colonial or vaguely Italianate models, the small ex-votos on metal full of the charming naiveté of the genre. It is in the 90-odd portraits (some of disputed attribution), weak in all but the faces blazing with immediacy, intimacy, and realism, that Bustos transcends his education and milieu. The desperate hypothesis that he might have gleaned his technique from some months' training at the academy of Juan N. Herrera in the nearby city of León stems from Bustos's discoverer, the poet Francisco Orozco Muñoz; it has been discredited for lack of evidence. Bustos distilled his colors from plants, nutshells, and ants in the utmost secrecy, and we must assume that his skill with squirrel-tail brushes was an equally personal achievement. Ignorant of academic, theoretical, or art-historical contexts, he strove simply to represent what he saw in the faces of local peasants, priests, tradesmen, squires, dowagers, and children, with Balzacian severity and vividness.

On blank, usually dark backgrounds, typically framed in an oval like the daguerreotypes that only reached Purísima at the end of Bustos's life, these portraits possess a spirit unusual for Mexican art in that they display neither the colorful, imaginative stylization of popular works, nor the rhetoric of the marvelous that characterizes the high tradition. Bustos cannot be hijacked for the history of myth and magic: the fervent Christian is a stern materialist where this life is concerned, nourished by a positivism all his own. The man who measured his sitters' features before drawing them also made a rudimentary telescope and a water clock. He is said to have ducked under the table when confronted by a phonograph, to see who was playing, and he certainly kept a laconic diary of the weather and its effect upon the populace and his sorbet sales. Two paintings of cosmic phenomena, accompanied by precise dates and descriptions, mark his interest in the major points of nature, while two still-lifes of fruits and vegetables are an attempt to understand the minor ones: arranged in sensible but formally balanced rows, without ostentation or symbolism, the sensuously exact objects would put a seventeenth-century Dutchman to shame. Bustos had a scientific, taxonomic mind and an urge to measure his skill against that of nature as if to appropriate it for human capability (claiming to have attempted the self-portrait "to see if I was able"). Nothing therefore stands between the objectivity of this artist and the personalities grimly etched on his sitters' faces, as are the scars on their skins and the ambition, pride, or disappointment in their eyes.

The unique and involuntary experiment in realism represented by Bustos found references in the 1920s, in accordance with the post-Revolutionary fascination for untutored Mexican genius pursued by intellectuals such as Dr. Atl (Gerado Murillo). His first solo exhibition was held in Bellas Artes in 1951. He has won no disciples, nor lost his eccentric's popularity, since that date.

Select Bibliography

Aceves Barajas, Pascual, *Hermenegildo Bustos, su vida y su obra.* Guanajuato: Imprenta Universitaria, 1956.

Hermenegildo Bustos, 1832–1907, catalogue essay by Gutierre Aceves Piña. Monterrey: MARCO Museum of Contemporary Art, 1993.

Paz, Octavio, "I, a Painter, an Indian from This Village." In *Essays on Mexican Art,* New York: Harcourt Brace, 1993.

Tibol, Raquel, *Hermenegildo Bustos, pintor de pueblo.* 2nd edition, Mexico City: Era, 1992.

—LORENA SCOTT FOX

C

CABAÑAS, LUCIO

1938–74 • Guerrilla Leader

The life of Lucio Cabañas is closely bound up with the history of armed struggle in the post–World War II period. Unlike many of its southern neighbors, Mexico did not experience the wave of guerrilla movements which swept through Latin America in the aftermath of the Cuban Revolution, and armed struggle has not been a significant element in the repertoire of the Mexican left. However, during the late 1960s and early 1970s, armed movements did emerge in several areas of Mexico, particularly in the state of Guerrero, a region with a long history of violent encounters between caciques (local strongmen) and peasant cultivators. Two movements, led by Lucio Cabañas and Genaro Vázquez surfaced within a year of each other. The Partido de los Pobres (PP, or Party of the Poor), Cabañas's movement, was the more successful, surviving well into the 1970s, long after the disappearance of Vázquez's Asociación Cívica Nacional Revolucionaria (ACNR, or National Revolutionary Civic Association), which never recovered from Vázquez's death in a 1972 automobile accident.

A graduate of the "red" rural teaching training college (Escuela Normal Rural) of Ayotzinapa, Cabañas's political career was shaped by his experience as a rural schoolteacher, a familiar theme in the history of agrarian radicalism in Mexico. Like the *maestros rurales* (rural teachers) of the 1920s and 1930s and Cabaña's fellow graduates of Ayotzinapa (including Genaro Vázquez), Cabañas fought battles over land rights, municipal autonomy, educational resources, and curriculum content. His political engagement while a teacher in the Federal School of Atoyac led to a period of internal exile in the north-central state of Durango 1965. His early political career began with a period as member of the Partido Comunista Mexicano (PCM, or Mexican Communist Party) from 1963 to 1966. Based in Atoyac, Cabañas worked with the party, organizing branches of the leftist Frente Electoral del Pueblo (People's Electoral Front) and building local units of a new peasant group, the Central Campesina Independiente (Independent Peasant Central), which challenged the hegemony of the peasant mass organizations affiliated with the ruling party, the Partido Revolucionario Institucional (PRI, or Institutional Revolutionary Party).

Cabañas took up arms in May 1967 after state police and soldiers massacred seven people in Atoyac, including Cabañas's brother. The *matanza* was the culmination of several weeks of struggle in which parents had forced the Guerrero state education system to replace an unpopular school administrator. Wounded in the assault, Cabañas managed to escape into the nearby hills, where he formed the PP as an armed self-defense group.

The party drew support and recruits from the peasantry of the Costa Grande of Guerrero, in particular the four municipalities of Atoyac de Álvarez, Tecpan, San Jerónimo, and Coyuca de Benítez. This region, which runs from south of the Pacific resort of Acapulco to the border of Oaxaca, is a desperately poor area of an impoverished state and has a long history of rural unrest, punctuated by tension between resource-starved *ejidatarios* (communal farmers) and private farmers and merchants who monopolize scarce water resources and the purchase and distribution of the region's main cash crops—coffee, coconuts, marijuana, timber, and sesame. The Costa Grande is also a region with a high rate of violence, illiteracy, and poor health. The stranglehold enjoyed by rural bosses, or *caciques,* at the municipal level and the political monopoly over the state government exercised by a few wealthy families has generated a series of civic action movements directed against unpopular state governors.

The Partido de los Pobres financed its activities through bank robberies and kidnappings of wealthy individuals, especially between 1971 and 1973. The most spectacular of the kidnappings involved a 74-year-old PRI senator and candidate for the governorship of Guerrero, the millionaire businessman Rubén Figueroa, who was held by the PP for over three months before being ransomed for 25 million pesos. The organization's *brigadas campesinas de ajusticiamento* (peasant execution brigades) also killed a number of ranchers, hostile journalists, and other alleged "exploiters." The actions of the Partido de los Pobres and of Genaro Vázquez led the Mexican army to deploy thousands of troops in search operations in Guerrero. Nevertheless, armed encounters between the guerrillas and the army were infrequent. Most of them occurred in 1972, five years after Cabañas's flight into the hills, when the PP twice ambushed army patrols.

The PP's ideological affiliation was populist and socialist. Although its core base was in Guerrero, it found allies and supporters in Sonora, Tamaulipas, Aguascalientes, and the Federal District and among students, Christians, and intellectuals who had been radicalized by the student popular movement of 1968 and the repression unleashed by the government of President Gustavo Díaz Ordaz. While he was not formally allied to any national political party, Cabañas maintained contact with elements of the PCM. This was facilitated by the Communist Party's sharp turn to the left after the events of 1968 when many communists, especially in the youth wing, abandoned the party to launch armed struggle movements in the city and countryside. Some light was thrown on this still obscure relationship during the kidnapping of the PCM's general secretary, Arnoldo Martínez Verdugo, in 1985 by survivors of the PP who alleged that the PP had entrusted funds obtained from kidnappings and bank robberies to the care of the Communist Party.

Cabañas's death in December 1974 at the age of 36 in an engagement with army troops and the elimination the following year of urban guerrilla groups such as the Liga 23 de septiembre (23rd of September League) ended the left's attempt to confront the state by force. State repression, including torture and the "disappearance" of suspects, contributed to the destruction of the armed movements of the late 1960s and early 1970s. The armed left's almost total isolation from the legal political and mass movements also denied it the protection and mass constituency that might have sustained it for a while.

Select Bibliography

Suárez, Luis, *Lucio Cabañas: El guerillero sin esperanza*. Mexico City: ROCA, 1976.
Carr, Barry, *Marxism and Communism in Twentieth Century Mexico*. Lincoln: University of Nebraska Press, 1992.

—Barry Carr

CABRERA LOBATO, LUIS

1876–1954 • Writer, Jurist, and Politician

Luis Cabrera was born in Zacatlán, Puebla, on July 17, 1876. His father, Cesáreo Cabrera, was a baker. An uncle, journalist Daniel Cabrera Rivera (1858–1914), directed *El Hijo de Ahuizote,* an influential anti–Porfirio Díaz publication. A brother, Alfonso Cabrera Lobato (1884–1959), served as governor of Puebla (1917–20). Luis Cabrera married Elena Cosío, and one of Luis's sons, Enrique, cofounded the National Liberation Movement of the 1960s.

Cabrera attended primary school in Zacatlán before going to Mexico City to study in the National Preparatory School (1889–93) and then the National School of Law, from which he received a degree in 1901. In the two decades before 1913 he also practiced journalism (often using the pseudonym "Lic. Blas Urrea," under which he criticized the Porfirio Díaz regime), worked as a school teacher in the state of Tlaxcala, practiced and taught law, and served as dean of the National School of Law.

In 1908, Cabrera first backed the pro–Bernardo Reyes political movement in the maneuvering for the 1910 presidential election. Reyes's son, Rodolfo, had been a fellow law student and then law partner of Cabrera. When Reyes refused to challenge long-time president Díaz, Cabrera joined the group supporting Francisco I. Madero for president and helped to form the Partido Antirreeleccionista. Cabrera worked in the law firm of Madero's cousin, Rafael Hernández. In 1911, interim President Francisco León de la Barra offered Cabrera the post of subsecretary of government, but Cabrera refused in order to run for federal deputy. The next year Madero's advisors vetoed him as too liberal for the post

of secretary of development. In 1912–13 Cabrera served as deputy from the Federal District, where he formed part of the progressive Bloque Renovador.

Following Madero's overthrow and murder in 1913, Cabrera joined the Revolutionary faction of Venustiano Carranza. He served as one of the "First Chief's" principal aides, often credited for being the intellectual behind and theorist of Carrancismo. His duties under Carranza were many, including special agent to the United States (1913), secretary of the treasury (1914–17, 1919–20), president of the United States–Mexico Mixed Claims Commission (1916–17), federal deputy from Puebla (1917–18), and envoy to South America (1918). In May 1920 Cabrera accompanied Carranza from Mexico City to Tlaxcalantongo, Puebla, where the president died at the hands of his political enemies.

Cabrera played a key role in the governing of the country between 1914 and 1920. He is best remembered for his authorship of the agrarian reform law of January 6, 1915, and his handling of the difficult financial situation during these turbulent Revolutionary years. However, as a moderate, middle-class civilian with no military experience and who championed liberal, reformist, capitalistic policies, Cabrera came under attack from more radical elements and the army, which especially resented his orthodox economic policies and distaste for soldier politicians. Indeed, to a large degree, Cabrera served Carranza as a lightening rod, deflecting much criticism from the president.

Following Carranza's death, Cabrera fell into official disgrace for many years and thereafter played mostly an indirect role in the political life of the country. He spent his time practicing law and writing about economics, politics, and sociology. His criticism of the Revolution and the governments it produced clearly placed him in the conservative camp during the next three decades. Cabrera especially condemned the leftist-leaning Lázaro Cárdenas (1934–40) government. In 1931 President Pascual Ortiz Rubio briefly deported him to Guatemala for his public statements made in a speech in the National Library. Twice opposition groups offered Cabrera their nomination for president, the Partido Antirreeleccionista in 1933 and the Partido de Acción Nacional in 1946, but on both occasions he declined. However, during World War II he served the Manuel Avila Camacho government (1940–46) as president of the Junta de Intervention de los Bienes del Enemigo and later as an adviser to President Adolfo Ruiz Cortines (1952–58). Cabrera died in Mexico City on April 12, 1954.

Select Bibliography

de Beer, Gabriella, *Luis Cabrera: Un intelectual en la Revolución mexicana.* Mexico City: Fondo de Cultura Económica, 1984.
Meyer, Eugenia, *Luis Cabrera: Teórico y crítico de la Revolución.* Mexico City: SEP 80, 1982.

—DAVID G. LaFRANCE

CACIQUISMO

In general speech, the term *cacique* is applied to any individual who exercises power over others in a despotic and arbitrary fashion. *Caciquismo* indicates the dominion established by this type of leader—the exercise of a real power through illegal coercion and the appointment and manipulation of formal authorities. Such control is carried out in an extralegal fashion, based on the control of the most important strategic resources (political, economic, and cultural) and through frequent recourse to physical force.

English-speaking authors have debated the specificity of the term *cacique* and the usefulness of employing it to indicate something more than a *jefe político local* (local political boss). Even though some authors have used both terms without making a distinction, the prevailing opinion has been that *caciquismo* refers to a specific type of political activity.

The detailed treatment of *caciquismo* in sociological literature has emphasized its most important characteristics. Pablo González Casanova has insisted that this form of authoritarianism implies total control over wealth, honor, public office, and political power. Moreover, the *cacique* is both owner and master of his territory and the life and destiny of its inhabitants. He has more power in his region than any other more formally established political organization. In a similar fashion, Paul Friedrich defined the *cacique* as "a strong and autocratic leader in regional and local politics whose power to command, characteristically informal, individualist and frequently arbitrary, is backed up by a nucleus of family members, 'fighters' and dependents, and is particularly characterized by the use of threats and the exercise of violence." To these characteristics Antonio Ugalde has added political control over a geographical area and the potential use of violence, the recognition and legitimacy established on the axis between accord with his authority and the support of external political leaders. Luisa Paré gave the term *caciquismo* to a form of political control in rural areas typical of a period when capitalism is penetrating noncapitalist modes of production. According to Paré, during such a time traditional authority based on a representation of collective interests within a community tends to disappear in favor of an individual or group of individuals who act as the main agents for capitalist penetration in a given community. Recent literature on local politics and *caciquismo* has insisted on its role as a form of political intermediation which has enormous relevance in the process of the creation of the Mexican state.

The History of *Caciquismo*

The term *cacique* is derived from "kassicuan," a word in Arawak (the language of an indigenous Caribbean people) meaning "to have or keep a house." The first recorded use of the term comes from the diary of Christopher Columbus, who heard it after his disembarking in Hispaniola, when it was used to describe the chief or lord of the indigenous Taínos people with whom he dealt. The Spanish conquistadors employed the term *cacique* to indigenous leaders and *cacicazgo* to aboriginal chieftainships.

During the colonial period, *cacicazgo* consisted in the Spanish Crown's recognition of certain indigenous titles and privileges as well as particular rights and obligations that were assigned to those Indian leaders who were identified as belonging to the aboriginal nobility. This investiture was rather more formal than actual, eventually becoming an institution of indirect government, a means of mediating between conquerors and conquered.

In Spain, the term *cacicazgo,* apart from referring to the chieftainship of an indigenous village or people, is also applied to the excessive use of influence in public affairs. In this sense it becomes a label for extralegal means of control of electoral results based on influence and pressure exercised by strongmen backed by state administrative apparatuses at the local level. This political institution predominated in rural Spain during the first third of the nineteenth century and the first third of the twentieth century in relation to living conditions in the country.

In Independent Mexico, which sought to foster a direct, unmediated relationship between the citizen and the state, colonial *cacicazgo* was destroyed by liberal anti-corporatism, which sought to foster a direct, unmediated relationship between the citizen and the state. The term survived nevertheless, but identified with the exercise of a personal, autocratic leadership that was locally powerful but held a monopoly on links with the outside world, particularly with regard to public authority.

During the last third of the nineteenth century, both the erosion of local government and the institution of political bosses during the Porfiriato led to order on a local level depending on authorities nominated from Mexico City who seemed tyrannical, despotic, and arbitrary to the local inhabitants. The terms *cacique, cacicazgo,* and *caciquismo* all reappeared in this context. Thus a large percentage of the local rebellions that led to the Revolution of 1910 originated to combat the tyranny of the *caciques*. During the Revolution, bandits and rebels first obtained local political control. In the process they too became regional *caciques,* thereby freeing themselves from the control of the central authorities.

Caciquismo in Modern Mexican History

The role of the regional *caciques* that emerged from the Revolution was decisive in the formation of the post-Revolutionary Mexican state. The way in which the activities of these regional leaders linked with the process of state consolidation has been a constant theme in the studies on Mexican history and politics. The most important regional leaders included individuals such as Dámasco Cárdenas, Primo Tapia, and Francisco Múgica in Michoacán; Adalberto Tejeda and Cándido Aguilar in Veracruz; Tomás Garrido Canabal in Tabasco; Saturnino Cedillo and Gonzalo Santos in San Luis Potosí; Felipe Carillo Puerto in the Yucatán; the Figueroa clan in Guerrero; and José Guadalupe Zuno in Jalisco.

Many of these leaders came to power in regions that had no large or spontaneous *campesino* (peasant) revolts during the Revolutionary conflict. The *campesino* mobilization in favor of agrarian distribution benefited from an important ingredient: external organization that needed the formation of nuclei of intermediaries with extra-regional contacts. Here the role of the local *caciques* proved decisive. Minor local *caciques* developed in direct relation with regional leaders, basing their local political control on their ties to hierarchical systems of patronage. The best documented case is that of Carrillo Puerto in the Yucatán. However, studies on *caciquismo* and regional power in Michoacán also clearly illustrate this phenomenon. Cases such as that of the Prado family in La Cañada de los Once Pueblos, the Ruiz brothers in Taretan, Martínez and Zavala Cisneros in the north-central area, or Dámaso Cárdenas in La Ciénaga de Chapala are relevant.

The participation of these local strongmen was decisive in the initial stages of the construction of the post-Revolutionary Mexican state. Even though rural areas were the privileged locus of action, their role in the cities also has been relevant. The later growth of the state political and administrative apparatus led to conflict with and, to a large extent, the dissolution of these *cacicazgos*. The centralist political organization severely limited the autonomous bases of the regional *caciques* to the point that it destroyed their sources of independent power, the availability of armed forces, and their privileged access to state resources. At the same time their guarantees of security and the satisfaction of material necessities mediated by the *caciques* became tied to the control and dependency of their clientele in relation to the state. Although in many cases the process made the presence of the *cacique* unnecessary, it institutionalized mediation as a means to exchange support for guarantees and benefits that favored the state. In this sense the *caciques* were a fundamental element in the establishment of the client-based character of the Mexican political system.

Caciquismo and Political Intermediation

The role of *caciquismo* as a means of intermediation has been emphasized from various analytical points of view. Luisa Paré sees *caciquismo* as a phenomenon of intermediation apparent where there are situations in which links are to be made between different means of production. In this context it is the requisite mechanism for the implanting of capitalism in a non-capitalist environment. Historically this process occurred with multiple regional variations. Nevertheless in general it is presented as a structuring process for local power whereby popular leaders personally benefit from the strong support of their followers by mediating their demands. Through this process they become *caciques*. The centralist political apparatus favored this transition, once the pressures of the system had largely been eased by the co-option and corruption of the local leaders, before attending to the demands of the group these *caciques* represented. This co-optation favored the economic aspect of the mediation. The *cacique* generally made a profit from the introduction of "progress" and "modernity," along with goods and services introduced into his areas of control. At the same time he appropriated resources removed by diverse means from the people under his rule. These activities included the direct exploitation of *campesinos* and *jornaleros,* various forms of usury, illegitimate use of community possessions, the exploitation of labor on a community and cooperative basis, as well as speculation and corruption. These activities required political control to bring to fruition. Thus, though the interest of the *cacique* was the maintenance of control outside the economic field, political interests came first on many occasions. From this perspective, the *cacique* as intermediary in a process of control mixes in the political advantages that he needs to obtain economic benefits. Hence the *cacique's* intermediary position is of equal relevance in both political and economic spheres.

The *cacique* is thus placed in two distinct realities and takes advantage of his skills and structural position to make connections. In Eric Wolf's terminology, a *cacique* in his role as political intermediary protects the links or points of communication that connect the local system with a wider society. The economic role of the institution is less relevant in this case. Most important is that the intermediary acts as a connecting link between different levels of contact. If these levels are defined in terms of power differences, one must analyze how they are exercised. The intermediary is looking for power on two levels; he manipulates the control he has on one to strengthen his position with regard to the other. Thus the control he holds in each sphere depends on the success with which he maintains control over the other.

Following this line of argument, Guillermo de la Peña has proposed that *caciquismo* should be understood within the context of the relationship between the dual process of the creation of the state and the creation of the nation. He states that given that the project of consolidation on a state level demands the disappearance of alternative powers within its territory, the state makes use of political intermediaries to generate or increase the dependency of individuals who manifest a degree of independence. On the other hand, the process of national consolidation brings with it the establishment of a symbolic universe of connections that are generally accepted and shared by all members of the nation. This implies an important transculturation of those segments of the population that have to unify the nation, which frequently forces a redefinition and reorganization of these connecting levels. The intermediaries create the points of connection between their base sector and the rest of society, aiming to assure a specific behavior pattern from the population in particular areas, in exchange for expected benefits. *Caciques* play an important part in this process since they maintain their own activities and obtain personal benefits through obligatory monopolies on certain channels of access.

See also Caudillismo

Select Bibliography

Bartra, Roger, et al., *Caciquismo y poder político en el México Rural.* 8th edition, Mexico City: Siglo XXI, 1986.

Brading, David, editor, *Caudillo and Peasant in the Mexican Revolution.* Cambridge and New York: Cambridge University Press, 1980.

de la Peña, Guillermo, "Poder local, poder regional: perspectivas socio-antropológicas." In *Poder local, poder regional,* edited by Jorge Padua and Alain Vanneph. Mexico City: Colegio de México-CEMCA, 1986.

Friedrich, Paul, "The Legitimacy of a Cacique." In *Local-Level Politics: Social and Cultural Perspectives,* edited by Marc J. Swartz. Chicago: Aldine, 1968.

Kern, Robert, editor, *The Caciques: Oligarchical Politics and the System of Caciquismo in the Luso-Hispanic World.* Albuquerque: University of New Mexico Press, 1973.

Martinez Assad, Carlos, editor, *Estadistas, caciques y caudillos.* Mexico City: UNAM-IIS, 1988.

Salmerón Castro, Fernando I., "Caciques: Una revisión teórica sobre el control político local." *Revista Mexicana de Ciencias Políticas y Sociales* 30 (1984).

—FERNANDO I. SALMERÓN CASTRO

CAJEME, JOSÉ MARÍA LEYVA

c.1837–1887 • Leader of the Yaqui Indians

The Yaqui Indians of northwestern New Spain, a region that later became the states of Sonora in Mexico and Arizona in the United States, are well known to history as a people particularly intent, successful, and creative in resisting domination by outside groups and cultures. Such resistance over the course of 500 years has taken various forms, depending on how the Yaquis perceived the larger political and economic environment and the relationship they developed with external forces. During the early years of Porfirio Díaz's regime, Yaqui resistance took a new turn under a leader popularly known simply as Cajeme.

José María Leyva Cajeme had spent his adolescence outside the Yaqui communities and served with distinction in the Sonoran strongman Ignacio Pesqueira's Liberal army. He returned to the Yaqui River when Pesqueira rewarded him with an appointment as Yaqui *alcalde mayor* in 1873, confident no doubt that Cajeme would tame the rebellious Yaqui spirit. No sooner had he returned to his people, however, than Cajeme stunned the Mexicans and probably the Yaquis as well by organizing new rebellions.

Under Cajeme, Yaqui society underwent significant changes, as most Yaquis who had gone into exile began to drift back to their old pueblos. Using a combination of Yaqui traditions and strategies he had learned from the Mexicans, Cajeme guided his people to rely on their own resources, initiatives, and leadership, rather than working for, pillaging from, or allying with outsiders. His goal was not to extend Yaqui hegemony beyond the confines of Yaqui territory, but to strengthen and preserve the autonomy that they always had claimed. To achieve economic self-sufficiency and produce revenues, Cajeme revived the old Jesuit practice of community plots, which each pueblo cultivated by rotations of workers. Trade also was revived to enhance revenues, which enabled Cajeme to accumulate a sizable stockpile of weapons. In the political arena, he renewed the importance of traditional village leaders (gobernadores) by designating them his chief administrative assistants, but he subordinated them to the captains for war. Also revitalized were the traditional sacristans (temastianes), put in charge of organizing fiestas and ceremonies. Finally, Cajeme reactivated the Yaqui councils. Although indisputably the supreme leader, Cajeme clearly intended for a revitalized tribal government to form part of his larger plan to strengthen the bases of Yaqui culture and identity, creating what Mexicans came to recognize belatedly and with great alarm as a state within a state.

Not surprisingly, such a political anomaly was totally unacceptable to the Mexican government. Unable to trust the state government to deal decisively with the problem, the federal government of Porfirio Díaz launched in 1879 a two-pronged attack on Cajeme's Yaqui "republic": a large-scale military campaign to crush Cajeme's regime combined with large-scale economic development of Yaqui land. This two-pronged strategy dovetailed with broader trends in northwestern Mexico; in the 1880s the Apaches were finally pacified and the first Sonoran railroads were built, while new mining laws and relaxed restrictions brought a mining boom to the state.

After several intense, brutal campaigns, the Mexican army finally crushed Cajeme in 1887. His strategy of a defensive war based on a series of fortifications distributed throughout Yaqui territory ultimately failed because the Yaquis were unable to resist the larger and much better equipped federal army. On April 21, 1887, a captured Cajeme began a march through all eight Yaqui pueblos, chiding the guard who assured him that nothing was going to happen to him: "Do not waste your jokes on a man who is about to die." Arriving at the village of Cocorit on April 25, he was executed by firing squad. His people then solemnly buried him in a quiet ceremony.

Among Mexicans who met and wrote about Cajeme was Sonoran Ramón Corral, a prominent spokesman for progress who later became Díaz's vice president. At Cajeme's death, he wrote these wishful words: "The sacrifice of Cajeme was very painful, but it would give the effect of securing peace in the [Yaqui and neighboring Mayo] rivers, the basis and beginning of a period of civilization for the tribes." He could not have been more wrong, because in a matter of months after Cajeme's execution, the Yaquis had chosen new leaders and reactivated their armed struggle for sovereignty, this time against a government more powerful, more determined, and more experienced than any previous regime to dispossess and integrate them.

Select Bibliography

Hu-DeHart, Evelyn, *Yaqui Resistance and Survival: The Struggle for Land and Autonomy 1821–1910.* Madison: University of Wisconsin Press, 1984.

_____, "Peasant Revolts in Mexico: The Yaquis of Sonora, 16th to 20th Centuries." In *Riot, Rebellion, and Revolt: Rural Social Conflict in Mexico,* edited by Friedrich Katz. Princeton, New Jersey: Princeton University Press, 1988.

—EVELYN HU-DEHART

CALDERÓN DE LA BARCA, FANNY

1804–82 • Writer

Fanny Calderón de la Barca was the author of *Life in Mexico during a Residence of Two Years in That Country.* The book recounts her experiences in Mexico from 1839 to 1841, when her husband, Angel Calderón de la Barca, was Spain's first envoy to Mexico.

Frances Erskine Inglis, who was always called Fanny, was born in Scotland on December 23, 1804, the fifth of ten children. Her father was moderately prosperous, and the children were well educated. When Fanny was 23 her father was forced into bankruptcy. This destroyed his health, and he moved to Normandy with his wife and several of his children. Two years later he died. In 1831 Fanny, her mother, three sisters, and four nieces emigrated to Boston to open a school. The school began well but soon incurred problems.

The family split up; Fanny and her mother stayed in Boston while the others moved to Pittsburgh to teach. In 1837 Fanny and her mother moved to Staten Island.

When and where Calderón met Fanny is not clear, but they courted while she was in New York. Calderón seems to have been a man of wide interests. Calderón, like Fanny, had a scholarly aptitude and was very personable. Fanny was perhaps the more open and less conservative of the two. Fanny and Calderón were married on September 24, 1838.

Life in Mexico begins October 1839 onboard the ship sailing to Havana en route to Mexico. The book is based on Fanny's extensive journal-like letters to her family, supplemented by Fanny's private journal. Fanny's letters had been shared with relatives and friends, including the historian

William Prescott. Prescott urged Fanny to publish the letters, and he wrote the preface to the book. Prescott later utilized Fanny's descriptions in his *Conquest of Mexico* (1843). The first edition of *Life in Mexico* has a publication date of 1843, although it was published by December 1842. The reviews in the United States were favorable; reviews were less enthusiastic in Mexico. Prescott also assisted in arrangements for a British edition. Reviews in the British press were largely favorable.

Fanny was a critical observer, but less judgmental than many travel writers. She was curious and welcomed opportunities for new places or new experiences. Her tone is sometimes ironic. She is not always complimentary, but neither is she spiteful or mean-spirited. Fanny did not spare her acquaintances or the society they moved in, which may account for the unfavorable reception her book received in Mexico.

After returning to the United States, Calderón and Fanny spent a year in Madrid. Calderón was then reappointed Spanish minister to the United States, and they lived in Washington for nine years. In 1853 they returned to Madrid; when the government fell they fled to France. Fanny began writing again, first a translation from Italian of Father Daniel Bartoli's book on the life of St. Ignatius Loyola, then, anonymously, *The Attaché in Madrid*, recounting their recent turbulent experiences in Spain.

Fanny and Calderón returned to Spain in 1856, where Calderón died of a fever five years later. Shortly after, Fanny was asked to become teacher to the Infanta Isabel. She stayed with the royal family for most of the remainder of her life. In 1876 she was named Marquesa de Calderón de la Barca. She died after a short illness in 1882, at age 77.

Today, the most complete edition of *Life in Mexico* is the one edited and annotated by Howard T. Fisher and Marion Hall Fisher, published in 1966. The editors restored material that had been deleted in earlier editions, replaced the customary initials and dashes with full names, and supplemented the material with information from Fanny's journals. *Life in Mexico* is still lively and entertaining to read, surprisingly undated in style. Fanny's careful descriptions capture the place and time for the reader. Her book remains an invaluable source of information about life in and around Mexico City at that period.

Select Bibliography
Fisher, Howard T., and Marion Hall Fisher, editors, *Life in Mexico: The Letters of Fanny Calderón de la Barca.* New York: Doubleday, 1966.

—MARY FRECH MCVICKER

CALLES, PLUTARCO ELÍAS
1877–1945 • President

Plutarco Elías Calles was born in 1877 into one of the oldest farming and cattle ranching families in northern Sonora. His parents were Plutarco Elías Lucero and María Jesús Campuzano. Orphaned at the age of three, he went to live with his father's sister, Josefa Campuzano, and her husband, Juan Bautista Calles. In gratitude for his adoption, Plutarco took the last name Calles.

Although his birth was registered in Guaymas, he spent his formative years in Hermosillo. In the years leading up to the Mexican Revolution, Calles was particularly interested in teaching, agriculture, and business. He was among the first teachers at the prestigious Colegio Sonora, and he occasionally published articles on the educational shortcomings of the time. In Guaymas he published a short-lived monthly review, *La Revista Escolar*, and he published a few love poems in *El Correo de Sonora*, one of the most influential publications in Guaymas. He later resigned his teaching duties because—as he confessed years later—he found the profession too "conformist."

It was not until his adulthood that Plutarco met the family of his biological father. He adopted the family's name, Elías—although he did not renounce the name of his adoptive family, Calles—and inherited some of his father's land. From 1898 to 1909 Calles devoted himself to farming, with disappointing results, on the family estate of Santa Rosa near the U.S. border, and then to managing the Excélsior mill near the town of Fronteras. As sympathy for Francisco I. Madero waxed in Sonora, Calles returned to Guaymas, where he made contact with Madero's supporters and attended several meetings called by José María Maytorena, one of the most important figures in the Sonoran opposition to the dictatorship of Porfirio Díaz.

Like many other Sonorans, Calles became deeply involved in politics only after Madero came to power. He was mayor of the border town of Agua Prieta until Madero was ousted from the presidency, and he then led the resistance to the military dictatorship of Victoriano Huerta in northeast Sonora. Together with other figures who later would become important in the region—Manuel M. Diéguez, Pedro Bracamonte, and Estéban Baca Calderón—Calles published the Manifesto of Nacozari, in which he urged Sonorans to fight by all means possible the "criminal" Huerta and his accomplices.

During the anti-Huerta campaign in Sonora Calles proved to be better suited for politics than military battles. Nonetheless, Calles remained connected with the upper echelons of the Revolutionary military forces. When long-simmering rivalries among the various Revolutionary factions finally erupted, Calles became the head of the forces loyal to Venustiano Carranza. In the second half of 1915 he defeated the forces of Maytorena, who had allied with Pancho Villa. As interim and later constitutional governor of Sonora, Calles implemented an ambitious program of social reform. Like his friend Salvador Alvarado in Yucatán, Calles introduced a minimum wage. He also introduced a number of educational reforms, founding the state teachers' training college and establishing a technical school for children who had been orphaned during the Revolution. Many of his reforms were controversial, however, particularly his decision to expel Catholic priests (whom he considered bastions of conservative thought) from Sonora and his excessive punishment of those who produced, distributed, and consumed alcoholic beverages. He even directed his ire at the interim governor Cesáreo Soriano, whom he expelled from his post, accusing him of covering up alcohol sales in Navojoa. Calles also directed a war without quarter against the Yaqui Indians of Sonora.

In period leading up to the presidential campaign of 1920 Calles rejected at least two offers of cabinet posts from President Carranza before accepting the position of minister of industry, trade, and labor in 1919. Carranza clearly hoped to neutralize a conspicuous ally of the Sonoran presidential candidate Álvaro Obregón. However, Calles left the ministry only a short time later, distancing himself from the Carranza administration and openly supporting Obregón.

The final break between Carranza and the Sonorans came in April 1920 when Calles published the Plan de Agua Prieta, calling for the overthrow of Carranza. Even once the Sonorans seized power, however, Calles continued to jockey for political advantage. His political influence was briefly contained when he was appointed minister of war during Adolfo de la Huerta's presidency, but during his three-year tenure as minister of the interior under Obregón, Calles began forming political alliances with such political and labor leaders as Felipe Carrillo Puerto, Saturnino Cedillo, Aarón Sáenz, and Luis N. Morones, paving the way for his own bid for the presidency. He eventually clashed with his old friend de la Huerta over the presidential candidacy, obtaining the support of Obregón. When de la Huerta formed a broad coalition of army officers opposed to his presidency, Calles himself led an efficient military campaign against them in the states of San Luis Potosí and Coahuila. Calles was elected president in 1924.

During his campaign and presidency, Calles sought to explain the fundamental ideas girding the reconstructive phase of the Mexican Revolution. Between 1923 and 1925 elements in Mexico and the United States accused Calles of being a radical or even a Bolshevik. Nonetheless, Calles's vague (if emphatic) laborism contrasted, particularly during the early years of his presidency, with his norteño vision of the Mexican countryside, which saw the small farmer—and not the *ejido* (communal village) or collective farm—as the key to economic prosperity. In this sense he insisted on developing the countryside in a "nondestructive" way, assisting small landowners with irrigation, seeds, practical education, and credit. With the advice of seasoned politicians such as Manuel Gómez Morín, Luis L. León, José Manuel Puig Casauranc, and Luis Cabrera, Calles set up commissions for irrigation and road works, an agricultural bank, and technical schools. Assisted by politicians in the treasury who had benefited from the defeat of de la Huerta, Calles organized a modern banking system, most notably the Bank of Mexico, and reorganized the federal treasury.

Calles also sought to implement the secularist and anticlerical provisions of the 1917 Mexican Constitution (Articles 3, 5, 27, and 130), campaigning against the Catholic clergy with the same energy he had earlier directed against them as governor of Sonora. Calles managed to alienate not only the Catholic hierarchy, but also broad sectors of Mexican society, which exploded in the Cristero Rebellion that wracked western and central Mexico from 1926 to 1929. Backed by a large number of Obregón's supporters in Congress, Calles rewrote Articles 13 and 82 of the constitution, allowing presidents to be reelected. The assassination of President Elect Obregón in 1928 prevented these amendment from being put in to practice.

Faced by one of the most grave political crises of twentieth-century Mexico and almost at the end of his presidential term, Calles decided to renounce the power conferred upon him by his leadership and abolish the old-style model of government, which he called "a one-man nation." Faced with a vacuum in the political system caused by Obregón's death and the imminent collapse of the fragile Revolutionary coalition, Calles promoted the formation of the Partido Nacional Revolucionario (PNR, or National Revolutionary Party), the antecedent of the current ruling party, the Partido Revolucionario Institucional (PRI, or Institutional Revolutionary Party).

During the period from 1929 to 1935 politicians and the press referred to Calles as the *"jefe máximo* (commander-in-chief) of the Revolution." On the one hand, despite Calles's stated intention to hold Mexico to the straight and narrow of laws and institutions, the absence of mature political institutions lead to the growth of political structures centered on Calles, and hence the weakening of the presidency; this was particularly clear during the administration of Pascual Ortiz Rubio (1930–32), probably due largely to his lack of political experience and support from any particular social group. On the other hand, Calles clearly used his skill as a power broker and his wide range of alliance with groups in Congress and the armed forces as well as cabinet members in successive administrations to increase his influence and to control policy.

In 1934 Calles supported the presidential candidacy of General Lázaro Cárdenas, who had been one of his officers during the 1915–18 military campaign against the Villistas. However, his relationship with President Cárdenas deteriorated after Calles made statements to the press in June 1935 criticizing the president's excessive sympathy for labor mobilizations and the "inconvenient" formation of a left wing in Congress. Calles's huge influence on Mexican politics declined when Cárdenas removed his supporters from key military and government posts. Street demonstrations against Calles, particularly by the emerging labor organizations, played an important part as Cárdenas dismantled the Calles machine. Calles himself was deported in April 1936, when he was accused (among other things) of setting up an independent political party. He spent his exile in San Diego, maintaining a regular correspondence with prominent opponents of the Cárdenas administration. He returned to Mexico at the invitation of President Manuel Avila Camacho in 1944 and took part in official meetings to solidify national unity during the final days of World War II. He died in Mexico City on October 19, 1945.

See also Calles Administration and Maximato: Interpretations

Select Bibliography

Córdova, Arnaldo, *La Revolución en crisis: La aventura del maximato.* Mexico City: Cal y Arena, 1995.

Chaverri Matamoros, Amado, and Clodoveo Valenzuela, *El verdaero Calles.* Mexico City: Patria, 1929.

Krauze, Enrique, Jean Meyer, and Cayetano Reyes, *Historia de la Revolución Mexicana, 1924–1928,* vol. 10, *La reconstrucción económica.* Mexico City: El Colegio de México, 1977.

Krauze, Enrique, *Reformar desde el origen: Plutarco E. Calles.* Mexico City: Fondo de Cultura Económica, 1987.

Kubli, Luciano, *Calles: El hombre y su gobierno.* Mexico City: L.J. Miranda, 1930.

Macías, Carlos, editor, *Plutarco Elías Calles: Correspondencia personal (1920–1935),* vols 1 and 2. Mexico City: Instituto Sonorense de Cultura, 1991, 1993.

Medin, Tzvi, *El minimato presidencial: Historia política del maximato, 1928–1935.* Mexico City: Era, 1982.

Zevada, Ricardo, *Calles, el presidente.* Mexico City: Nuestro Tiempo, 1971.

—CARLOS MACÍAS RICHARD

CALLES ADMINISTRATION AND *MAXIMATO*: INTERPRETATIONS

Historians consider the period from 1924 to 1935 to be decisive in the formation of the contemporary Mexican state. Political conditions blended in such a way to make possible the birth of lasting national institutions, the creation of infrastructure (communications, finance, education, irrigation), the redefinition of constructive links with the United States, and, above all, the progressive subordination of *caudillo* (regional strongman) interests and the creation of new apparatuses of legitimate representation (the official party and its organizations).

The presidency of General Plutarco Elías Calles (1924–28) and its "extension," the period known as the *maximato,* during which Calles was given the title *"jefe máximo de la Revolución"* (Supreme Chief of the Revolution) and continued to control events behind the scenes, was framed by the continued presence of the group of individuals from the state of Sonora who had ruled the country since 1920 (Adolfo de la Huerta, álvaro Obregón, and Plutarco Elías Calles).

The books written on the Calles administration and the *maximato,* as well as the political figure cut by the man himself, have long been a subject for debate. This is not strange, given that this administration promoted several controversial policies. These included attacking the religious practices of an important sector of the population with rigor and in cold blood, establishing alliances and cooperative relations with labor leaders of doubtful antecedents, and above all undermining the constitutional bases of authority of three Mexican presidents between 1929 and 1935, through the discretional use of influence and power.

As in other post-Revolutionary periods, a great number of the texts written on Callismo were eyewitness accounts written by former politicians. Generally these works were written as genre pieces, either in chronicle form or as autobiographies. Both those giving an official point of view (Chaverri Matamoros, 1929; Kubli, 1930) as well as those that take a more or less critical stance (Alessio Robles, 1936; Portes Gil, 1954; Guzmán Esparza, 1957), adopt a partisan focus that is understandably subjective. But they also have the peculiar characteristic of focusing on the most controversial aspects of Callismo and not on the *maximato* as a whole. Ramón Puente's work (1933; second edition, 1994) is a notable exception to this rule; even when the author was in exile he attempted to present a balanced work—even though it took the form of a biographical essay—on the career, thought, and actions of President Calles.

The most outstanding U.S. analysts of the period to make a deep study of the Mexican situation were Ernest H. Gruening (1928), Frank Tannenbaum (1929), and Carleton Beals (1931). Adopting rather different approaches, their texts and liberal perspective, grounded in what in time would be defined as the popular or *populista* interpretation of the Mexican Revolution, had common ground in their reevaluation of the national culture, *mestizaje* (ideologies of race mixture), *indigenismo,* and the transitional organization of the rural population. The focus of their work was unique in part because it differed from that of contemporary U.S. public opinion of Mexico. Ambassador James Sheffield and the wealthy newspaper magnate William R. Hearst opined that the post-Revolutionary government of Mexico was inspired by "resentment of Indian nationalism" and "Bolshevik tendencies."

Gruening wrote a broadly based and well documented work that aimed to underline the modernizing, constructive qualities of the Calles administration while censuring (as had the Spanish writer Vicente Blasco Ibáñez in 1920) what seemed to be a chronic disease of the Mexican politics, notably militarism. Tannenbaum specialized in the study of rural Mexico, documenting its antecedents and providing a valuable contrast for later historiography on the productive units of the Mexican countryside while advocating further agrarian distribution.

Initially Beals praised and publicized in various U.S. media (the *Nation* and the *New Republic,* in particular) the "anti-aristocratic" laborist tendency that kept Callism in power, but later he was to criticize particularly the performance of the *jefe máximo* and the presidents of the *maximato.* According to Beals, the most negative aspects of the *jefatura máxima* consisted in having renounced agrarian reform and *indigenismo* on the altar of European economic doctrines. The Partido Nacional Revolucionario (PNR, or National Revolutionary Party), rather than representing the opportunity to minimize personal quarrels and avoid protest demonstrations, represented for Beals a backward step in terms of the original proposals of the Revolution, given that military personnel still predominated over social leaders.

Academic analyses of the Calles administration and the *maximato* proliferated in the last 30 years of the twentieth century. Mexican, U.S., and European researchers published numerous works on movements, political links, and specific and regional tensions that are enormously relevant for the understanding of the nation's political system, economy, and post-Revolutionary social life in general. Among these themes are the Cristero Rebellion, labor and *campesino* (peasant) organizations, relations with the United States, the administration of public finance, the electoral process and political transition, control and reorganization of the army, and the construction of the PNR.

Among the works that have tackled the Calles period with overall vision and depth, those of Jean Meyer and Enrique Krauze deserve particular mention. Desiring to emphasize what they consider as major chapters of Calles's four-year term, these authors deal with the reorganization of the military, the essential conflicts of the state with society and the Catholic Church (a theme that Meyer has analyzed in great depth), as well as problems of public finance (debt and the bankers' front) and the governmental measures that established the basic infrastructure of the country. Their exhaustive researches clearly present one of the major peculiarities of Calles's period, notably the conscious amplification and support of the economic role of the state, "sole interpreter of public interest . . . [that] began to define itself in those years as a *sui generis* institution with direct and wide-ranging economic responsibilities" (Meyer et al., 1977). These influential studies find a happy complement in Krauze's biography of Calles (1987), which gives a balanced interpretation on the origins and expression of Callist ideology.

Ricardo Zevada's book (1977), with its focus on Revolutionary nationalism, pays attention to the constructive proposals of the regime. The former politician defines the Calles program as "revolutionary, Mexican style," accenting the pragmatism that, according to him, was shown by the Mexican leaders of the 1920s in their attempt to renovate the social structure without taking on the socialist formulas that were being tried in Europe at the time. The author restates, in particular, the tangible repercussions of the educational policy of the time (the establishment of farming schools and the cultural missions) and lasting fiscal reform (foundation of the Mexican system) but warns that one of the difficulties of Callist agrarian policy was the attempt to stimulate and consolidate three social strata: those of the *ejidatarios* (workers of communal village lands, called *ejidos*), smallholders, and large-scale landowners. Zevada, faithful to his ideas, considered that the program of infrastructural development would have produced the best results with the suppression of private property in the countryside and the strengthening of the *ejido* system.

Another work worthy of mention that presents an overall view of the period was written by John W. F. Dulles (1961). Backed by a wide range of sources, this investigation is extremely useful for understanding the country's development during the years it was governed by the so-called Sonoran triangle (Álvaro Obregón, Adolfo de la Huerta, and Calles). Nonetheless, Dulles's work is more narrative than analysis.

The documentary anthologies prepared by Carlos Macías (1991 and 1993) based on Calles as a political figure shed light on more than one dozen governors, party leaders, and military bosses of other federal entities who are contextualized as essential links in the network of Callist regional alliances. These personal connections (to such men as Raymundo Enríquez, Genaro V. Vázquez, Carlos Real, Manlio Fabio Altamirano, and Saturnino Cedillo) were vital not only in the moment of promoting the government program and confronting social resistance and political opposition, but also when the mechanism of the *jefatura máxima* was established and imposed.

The interpretations on the regularities or points in common between the Calles administration and the *maximato* are of a different order. Some works written at the end of the 1930s (notably that of José Manuel Puig Casauranc, 1938) whose impressions have been preserved to this day in a large number of studies, insisted that General Calles changed in his wide-ranging plan from a radical ideological opinion to one that was notoriously conservative. The main argument in favor of this was the permanence of Calles as strongman in national politics, regardless of his promise, expressed in 1928, to retire into private life, as well as his systematic opposition to the labor policies of President Lázaro Cárdenas (1934–40). It is worth pointing out that this opinion, although incontrovertible in essence, found a recognizable echo during the 1970s in the opinions of his contemporaries, by this stage respected former government officials characterized by their liberal vision and administrative experience, men such as Manual Gómez Morín and the previously mentioned progressive former official Ricardo Zevada (1977). The first of them, for example, pointed out that the veteran general Calles in reality was "more revolutionary than conservative," since he had a broad and workable national program with a vision of the national economy supported by realistic and attainable criteria (Wilkie and Monzón, 1969).

The fact that the essential characteristic of the period known as the *maximato* was the enormous discretionary power concentrated in the hands of former president Calles, to the evident impediment of presidential authority, has led diverse authors over the decades to designate this stage as being one of patent retrogression or, at the very least, of stagnation in the post-Revolutionary process. Tzvi Medin (1982) argues that the *maximato* implied the end of presidentialism since it subordinated a president's decision making capacity. The author insists on the reality of the "total destruction" of the *maximato* "as regards the political mechanism that could maintain the dominion of Calles" to explain the moment in which Lázaro Cárdenas "recovered" presidential authority.

The work of Medin is unique in his synthesis of the old interpretation of the *maximato* as a circumstantial period in national life stamped almost exclusively by personal struggles, by factional disputes, and by intrigues between politicians and military men that ended up diminishing not just the institution of president but also the credibility and authority of Congress. This interpretation, apart from now seeming imprecise or erroneous, is a partial vision of the complex process of political rearrangement that was occasioned by the assassination of the president-elect in 1928. His approach is enriched by a collection of testimonies left by some of the protagonists. These include work written by long-standing enemies of the *jefe máximo* (Amaya, 1947; Vasonccelos, 1968), as well as politicians considered to be of Calles's persuasion (Alamada, 1936; León, 1987). Other sources include those who maintained a relative independence of opinion such as Emilio Portes Gil (1954), Abelardo Rodríguez (in Gaxiola, 1938), Pascual Ortíz Rubio (1981), Francisco Díaz Babio (1939), and José Manuel Puig Casauranc (1938). All these wrote their accounts from a subjective viewpoint, emphasizing the play of individual interests and the fickle shifts of factions. Such a viewpoint is seen even in more recent works, such as that of Holland Dempsey Watkins (1968) and Luis L. León's own delayed publication (1987).

Seen thus, the *maximato* does not seem to have taken immediate effect on certain central and transcendent aspects of the Mexican political system, such as the progressive subordination of the army and the institutionalization of the struggle for power. This interpretation of the *maximato* could not represent a historical moment of social or economic restructuring but focuses instead on an episode that revolved "fundamentally around the political intrigues in which the principal participants of the dominant political oligarchy are measured" (Medin, 1982).

A distinct line of interpretation has emerged from studies such as those published by Lorenzo Meyer (1977; 1978, co-authored with Rafael Segovia and Alejandra Lajous). The authors suggest, among other proposals, that the *jefatura máxima* contributed to resolving political tensions generated by the power vacuum of 1928. In their opinion it seems worthwhile to restate the fact that the *maximato*—independent of the political actors that Calles created, promoted, and confronted—also could have sown the conditions and instances for a new and decisive concentration of power. They have restored the idea that the *maximato* could have made the dominant party "its lasting legacy."

The previous perspective seems to be backed, curiously, by the texts of authors, such as Arnoldo Córdova, whose research has been initially centered on the regime of Lázaro Cárdenas and later periods. In his study on the *maximato* (1995), analyzed as a product of political structure, Córdova conceptualizes his theme as a "kind of forge" from which Cardenismo was created. "Without the *maximato,*" he emphasizes, "Cardenismo could not have happened or even been conceived." The premise of his work is his conviction of the essential role of the *jefatura máxima* in the concentration of power in the corporativization of the party. "Cardenismo," he argues, "culminated rather than replaced the work of the *maximato,* as has always been imagined previously. In many aspects they are not opposite poles, but one and the same thing."

Select Bibliography

Alessio Robles, Vito, *Desfile sangriento.* Mexico City: A. del Bosque, 1936.

Almada, Pedro J., *Con mi cobija al hombro: Autobiografía.* Mexico City: Alrededor de América, 1936.

Amaya, Juan Gualberto, *Los gobiernos de Obregón: Calles y regímenes "peleles" derivados del callismo, tercera etapa, 1920 a 1935.* Mexico City: n.p., 1947.

Beals, Carleton, *Mexican Maze.* Philadelphia and London: Lippincott, 1931.

Blasco Ibáñez, Vicente, *El militarismo mejicano: Estudios publicados en los principales diarios de los Estados Unidos.* Valencia: Sociedad Editorial Prometeo, 1920.

Brading, David, *Caudillo and Peasant in the Mexican Revolution.* Cambridge and New York: Cambridge University Press, 1980.

Britton, John A., *Carleton Beals: A Radical Journalist in Latin America.* Albuquerque: University of New Mexico Press, 1987.

Calles, Plutarco Elías, *Plutarco Elías Calles: Correspondencia personal (1920–1935),* edited by Carlos Macías. 2 vols., Mexico City: Instituto Sonorense de Cultura, 1991–93.

Chaverri Matamoros, Amado, *El verdadero Calles.* Mexico City: Patria, 1929.

Córdova, Arnaldo, *La Revolución en crisis: La aventura del maximato.* Mexico City: Cal y arena, 1995.

Díaz Babio, Francisco, *Un drama nacional: La crisis de la Revolución; Declinación y eliminación del general Calles. Primera etapa, 1928–1932.* Mexico City: León Sánchez, 1939.

Dulles, John W. F., *Yesterday in Mexico: A Chronicle of the Revolution, 1919–1936.* Austin: University of Texas Press, 1961.

Gaxiola, Francisco Javier, Jr., *El presidente Rodríguez, 1932–1934.* Mexico City: Cultura, 1938.

Gruening, Ernest H., *Mexico and Its Heritage.* New York: Century, and London: Stanley Paul, 1928.

Guzmán Esparza, Roberto, *Memorias de don Adolfo de la Huerta, según su propio dictado.* Mexico City: Guzmán, 1957.

Krauze, Enrique, *Plutarco E. Calles: Reformar desde el origen.* Mexico City: Fondo de Cultura Económica, 1987.

_____, Jean Meyer, and Cayetano Reyes Garcia, vol. 10 of *Historia de la Revolución Mexicana, 1924–1928: La reconstrucción económica.* Mexico City: El Colegio de México, 1977.

Kubli, Luciano, *Calles, el hombre y su gobierno: Monografía histórica.* Mexico City: L. J. Miranda, 1930.

León, Luis L., *Crónica del poder: En los recuerdos de un político en el México revolucionario.* Mexico City: Fondo de Cultura Económica, 1987.

Medin, Tzvi, *El minimato presidencial: Historia política del maximato, 1928–1935.* Mexico City: Era, 1982.

Meyer, Jean, Enrique Krauze, and Cayetano Reyes Garcia, vol. 11 of *Historia de la Revolución Mexicana, 1924–1928: Estado y sociedad con Calles.* Mexico City: El Colegio de México, 1977.

Meyer, Lorenzo, "La etapa formativa del Estado Mexicano contemporáneo, 1928–1940." *Foro Internacional* 17 (April–June 1977).

_____, Rafael Segovia, and Alejandra Lajous, vol. 12 of *Historia de la Revolución Mexicana, 1928–1934: Los inicios de la institucionalización.* Mexico City: El Colegio de México, 1978.

Ortiz Rubio, Pascual, *Memorias.* Morelia: Universidad Michoacana, 1981.

Portes Gil, Emilio, *Quince años de política mexicana.* 3rd edition, Mexico City: Botas, 1954.

Puente, Ramón, *Hombres de la Revolución: Calles.* 2nd edition, Mexico City: Fondo de Cultura Económica, 1994.

Puig Casauranc, José Manuel, *Galatea rebelde a varios pigmaliones.* Mexico City: Impresores Unidos, 1938.

Tannenbaum, Frank, *The Mexican Agrarian Revolution.* New York: Macmillan, 1929.

Vasconcelos, José, *El proconsulado.* 5th edition, Mexico City: Jus, 1968.

Watkins, Holland Dempsey, "Plutarco Elías Calles: El Jefe Máximo of Mexico." Ph.D. diss., Texas Technological College, 1968.

Wilkie, James W., and Edna Monzón, *México visto en el siglo XX: Entrevistas de historia oral.* Mexico City: Instituto Mexicano de Investigaciones Económicas, 1969.

Zevada, Ricardo, *Calles, el presidente.* 2nd edition, Mexico City: Nuestro tiempo, 1977.

—CARLOS MACÍAS RICHARD

CAMPOBELLO, NELLIE

1900– • Dancer and Writer

Nellie Campobello, registered at birth as María Francisca Moya Luna, was born in Villa Ocampo, a small town in Durango, which her ancestors helped to settle in the seventeenth century. Her father, Jesús Felipe Moya, a supporter of Francisco I. Madero and a Villista general, died in the Battle of Ojinaga in 1914, leaving her mother Rafaela Luna to care for the family. The widow remarried Stephen Campbell, a doctor from Boston whose last name Nellie assumed and altered to Campobello. Never marrying and preferring "freedom to love," Campobello engaged actively in the nationalist cultural renaissance of the post-Revolutionary period as writer and ballerina. Seen as a precursor of Mexican modern dancing, and called the Isadora Duncan of Latin America, she established her reputation as ballerina, choreographer, and teacher of dance. She founded and directed the National School of Dance (1932–53), the Folkloric Ballet of Mexico (1937), and the Ballet of Mexico City (1943). Recognized as an authority on indigenous and folk dance, she coauthored *Ritmos Indígenas de México* (Indigenous Rhythms of Mexico) with her sister Gloria Campobello. They studied and recorded the dances of the first Mexicans as illustrated in codices and sculptures, integrating them to contemporary movements.

Campobello's contribution in the field of dance was recognized early on. Her status as writer, however, has taken longer to establish and is still growing. A contemporary of Frida Kahlo, Leonora Carrington, Remedios Varo, Nahui Olin, and María Izquierdo, her work has received increasing critical attention from feminists and literary revisionists. Nellie's first book, *Yo*, a collection of 15 coming of age poems, was published in 1929 under the name of Francisca. Some of these poems were translated by Langston Hughes, whom she met in Cuba, and they appeared later in Dudley Pitts's *Anthology of Contemporary Latin American Poetry* (1942). Although Campobello did not publish more verse, a poetic sensibility marks her two novels, *Cartucho: Relatos de la lucha en el norte de México* (1931) and *Las manos de mamá* (1937).

The publication of *Cartucho*, in particular, situates Campobello generationally with Mariano Azuela, Martín Luis Guzmán, and José Ruben Romero, among others, who experienced, witnessed, and wrote about the armed phase of the Mexican Revolution. Her original and innovative nonfiction novel was the only female vision and version of the Revolution to appear amid the many memoirs and testimonial novels published at the time. It anticipated and is now studied in dialogue with other women's rendering of the Revolutionary period, such as Elena Garro's *Los recuerdo del porvenir* (1963) and Elena Poniatowska's testimonial novel *Hasta no verte, Jesús mio* (1972), whose historically real protagonist disagrees with Campobello on Francisco "Pancho" Villa's image.

Campobello was a staunch Villa supporter and anti-Carrancista when the official discourse was erasing or maligning Villa's participation. Seen as ideologically out of line, Nellie spoke against the promotion of a nationalist and centralizing discourse as historically inaccurate or as depoliticized folklore. In interviews she declared that she wrote to counteract the obliteration of the Northern Revolution, its territory and peoples, with whom she strongly identified. Structured as a series of short narrative portraits, soldiers such as Cartucho, the prototype of the revolutionary, are immortalized as their heroic deaths are recorded. Written as epitaphs or eulogies, the narratives, as remembered by the child or collected by the adult from popular memory, ballads, and legends, pay tribute to the everyday struggles of towns in the north, and the men and women who sacrificed their lives for a cause. The romantic nostalgia for a time of heroes and heroism is readily displaced by the violence depicted. Seen from the female sphere, the horrors of war elude glorification. The chaos disrupting the domestic and private abode of family life is exacerbated as this smaller and injured unit becomes the microcosm of the nation. *Cartucho*'s epic quality has not diminished as it renders homage, not to the Revolution being institutionalized, but to the northern popular movement and the men who died fighting for their beliefs.

The positive and extensive critique of *Cartucho* from her life-long friend and supporter Martín Luis Guzmán, who had published his novel on Villa, *El aguila y la serpiente*, in 1928, was not a surprise since both believed that the Revolution had been betrayed by those who came to power after the fighting ended. In 1940 and from a more objective stance, Nellie herself took up the theme in *Apuntes sobre la vida militar de Francisco Villa* (Notes on the Military Life of Francisco Villa), a researched account of the military campaigns of the "Centauro del Norte." Guzmán followed it with *Las memorias de Pancho Villa* (1951), for which Nellie provided documents and information she held from Villa's private archives. Villa's place in history, still debated today, was officially recognized in 1966 when the government erected a monument in his honor in the Glorieta de Riviera in Mexico City.

Las manos de mamá (1937) is a poetic tribute to her other lifetime model, her mother, who mitigated the brutal world surrounding the child. In this fictionalized testimony the mother is representative of the valor Campobello attributes to the women from the north, who transcended their traditional roles as their familiar world collapsed. It is also a tribute to the northern terrain and the Raramuni (Tarahumaras), its original settlers. Her admiration for this indigenous group persuaded André Bretón to visit their territory during his visit to Mexico in 1937. A second edition of *Las manos de mamá* appeared in 1949, illustrated by José Clemente Orozco, a friend of the family.

In 1960, a compendium of all her works was published with the title *Mis libros*. A long introduction provides an excellent glimpse into her life and era. Campobello disappeared from the literary scene, but was still Director of the National School of Dance in 1983 when she was honored by a special performance at a celebration of the School's fiftieth anniversary. In 1988, a translation into English of her two works *Cartucho* and *Las manos de mamá* appeared in one volume with an introduction by Elena Poniatowska. She confirms that Campobello, who never received the necessary recognition to stimulate her vocation as a writer, still lived isolated in Tlaxcala at the age of 87.

Select Bibliography

Cázares, Laura, "El narrador en las novelas de Nellie Campobello: *Cartucho y Las Manos de Mamá*." In *Mujer y Literatura Mexicana y Chicana: Culturas en Contacto,* edited by Aralia López-González, Amelia Malagamba, and Elena Urrutia. Tijuana: COLEF, 1988.

_____, "Nellie Campobello: Novelista de la Revolución." *Casa de las Américas* 183 (1991).

Campobello, Nellie, "Prólogo." In *Mis libros*. Mexico City: SepSetentas, 1973.

D'Acosta, Helia, "Nellie Campobello." In *Veinte Mujeres.* Mexico City: Editories Asociados, 1971.

De Beer, Gabriella, "Nellie Campobello, escritora de la revolución de mexicana." *Cuadernos Americanos* 223 (1979).

_____, "Nellie Campobello's Vision of the Mexican Revolution." *The American Hispanist* 4:34–35 (1979).

Emmanuel, Carballo, "Nellie Campobello." In *19 protagonistas de la literatura mexicana del siglo XX.* Mexico City: Empresas, 1965.

Meyer, Doris, "Divided against Herself: The Early Poetry of Nellie Campobello." *Revista de Estudios Hispánicos* 20:2 (May 1986).

_____, "Nellie Campobello's *Las manos de mamá:* A Rereading." *Hispania* 68:4 (December 1985).

Parle, Dennis J., "Narrative Style and Technique in Nellie Campobello's *Cartucho." Romance Quarterly* 32:2 (1985).

Poniatowska, Elena, "Introduction." In *Cartucho and My Mother's Hands,* by Nellie Campobello, translated by Doris Meyer and Irene Matthews. Austin: University of Texas Press, 1988.

Robles, Martha, "Nellie Campobello." In *La Sombra Fugitiva: Escritoras en la Cultura Nacional.* Vol. 1, Mexico City: Diana, 1989.

Verlinger, Dale E., "Nellie Campobello: Romantic Revolutionary and Mexican Realist." In *Latin American Women Writers: Yesterday and Today,* edited by Yvette E. Miller and Charles M. Tatum. Pittsburgh: Latin American Literary Review, 1977.

—NORMA KLAHN

CANTINFLAS

See Moreno Reyes, Mario (Cantinflas)

CARBALLIDO, EMILIO

1925– • Playwright

Emilio Carballido's prominent place in Mexican and international theater was recognized at various events in 1995, celebrating such milestones as his 70th birthday, the 45th anniversary of the stage production that launched his playwriting career, and the 25th anniversary of *Tramoya,* the theater periodical he founded. Among those who paid homage to the author of over 100 plays were a few of the many playwrights whose careers he had nurtured. His influence has extended to his contemporaries Luisa Josefina Hernández and Sergio Magaña as well as to the next generation of dramatists: Sabina Berman, Felipe Galván, Oscar Villegas, Alejandro Licona, and others. His concern for the young people of his country is evident not only in his plays like *Yo también hablo de la rosa (I Too Speak of the Rose,* 1966), but also in his stories for children and in the several anthologies of plays for youth that he has edited. Carballido has been called "a god in the Mexican theater."

Emilio Carballido was born on May 22, 1925, in Córdoba, Veracruz, Mexico. He attended the Universidad Nacional Autónoma de Mexico from 1945 to 1949. The following year saw the premieres of three of his plays in different theaters. It was *Rosalba y los Llaveros (Rosalba and the Llaveros Family),* which opened at the Palacio de Bellas Artes on March 11, 1950, that signaled an exciting new voice in the Mexican theater. The psychological comedy of a city girl who comes to live with a provincial family and creates emotional havoc did not challenge the realistic mode that had dominated the theater of the 1940s, but it captivated audiences with its humor and sympathetic awareness of a variety of social concerns.

La hebra de oro (The Golden Thread, 1954) marks a turning point in Carballido's writing, at which he first succeeded with a technique that has become characteristic of his best work: the injection of a vein of fantasy into his fundamental realism, or perhaps more precisely, bringing together multiple realities. This "dance of death in three acts" with its interactions on physical and spiritual planes helped to redirect the course of Mexican theater toward greater experimentation. *La hebra de oro* also has been cited as one of a number of his plays that show the influence of Sor Juana Inés de la Cruz in its borrowing of elements of the *auto sacramental* (a medieval form of short religious play) combined with Mexican symbology. Carballido's poetic sensibility consists in seeing the miracle in the ordinary, in heightening what is real by bringing it into contact with the unreal.

According to Carballido himself, his other most important plays are *El relojero de Córdoba (The Clockmaker from Córdoba,* 1960) for its craftsmanship and *Yo también hablo de la rosa,* which he has called his "clearest personal statement." The high-stakes drama of the clockmaker has a fairy tale quality with its strong narrative, overlapping stories, and happy ending. The one-act *Yo también hablo de la rosa* (the title is taken from a sonnet by Sor Juana) again presents multiple realities, this time in viewing a disastrous youthful prank from a variety of perspectives. The skillful integration of theatrical metaphor, poetic vision, and social concerns achieves extraordinary evocative and allegorical power.

Carballido's other major plays include two reinterpretations of Greek myth, *Medusa* (1960) and *Teseo (Theseus,* 1962). *El día que se soltaron los leones (The Day They Let the*

Lions Loose, 1959) is a farce with political subtext, in which humans and animals interact. Women are the focus of many plays, including the two-woman drama *Una rosa, con otro nombre* (*A Rose, by Any Other Name,* 1972) and the popular allegorical comedy *Orinoco* (1979), in which two showgirls drift on a crewless boat on the Orinoco River. *Fotografía en la playa* (1977) is a Chekhovian piece in which members of an extended family come together without really communicating; the photograph finally unites them at least on a visual level for a fleeting moment that is hauntingly juxtaposed with accounts of the deaths of the principal characters.

In addition to his plays and literary criticism, Carballido has written opera and ballet librettos, five novels, and children's stories. Carballido at 70, according to Jacqueline Bixler in 1995, was still young in spirit, still the "enfant terrible" of the Mexican theater, and still writing new plays that add to his stature in national and world theater.

Select Bibliography

Bixler, Jacqueline Eyring, "A Theater of Contradictions: The Recent Works of Emilio Carballido." *Latin American Theater Review* 18 (Spring 1995).

Carballido, Emilio, *Tne Golden Thread and Other Plays,* translated by Margaret Sayers Peden. Austin: University of Texas Press, 1970.

Peden, Margaret Sayers, *Emilio Carballido.* Boston: G.K. Hall, 1980.

Skinner, Eugene R., "The Theater of Emilio Carballido: Spinning a Web." In *Dramatists in Revolt: The New Latin American Theater,* edited by Leon F. Lyday and George W. Woodyard. Austin: University of Texas Press, 1976.

—FELICIA HARDISON LONDRÉ

CÁRDENAS, CUAUHTÉMOC

1934– • Governor and Presidential Candidate

Born in Mexico City on May 1, 1934, Cuauhtémoc Cárdenas lived his first years in the presidential residence as the only son of one of Mexico's greatest and most revolutionary presidents, General Lázaro Cárdenas. He spent much of his adult life in his father's enormous shadow. However, at the age of 54, Cuauhtémoc Cárdenas made his own mark, ironically by leaving the Partido Revolucionario Institucional (PRI, or Institutional Revolutionary Party), which his father had helped create, and running the most successful opposition presidential campaign in Mexican history. After the election, Cárdenas played a leading role in the foundation of a new leftist party that unified many of the diverse groups that had supported his 1988 candidacy. He became the first president of the Partido de la Revolución Democrática (PRD, or Party of the Democratic Revolution) and guided it for the first four years of its existence before resigning to participate as the PRD's candidate in the 1994 presidential election. He remains one of the most influential figures on the modern Mexican left.

The political career of Cuauhtémoc Cárdenas began almost before he could walk. As Lázaro Cárdenas's only son, Cuauhtémoc acted as his father's aide de camp in many political ventures. He knew or met virtually every important figure in the Mexican elite and on the independent left at that time through his father. From his early experiences, he absorbed much of his father's political style, thought, and objectives.

At the age of 17, he participated in the early stages of the presidential campaign of General Miguel Henríquez Guzmán. Lázaro Cárdenas had encouraged his fellow leftist, close ally, and friend to run as an independent candidate in order to put pressure on President Miguel Alemán Valdés (1946–52) to select a less conservative successor at the end of his term. Henríquez and Lázaro Cárdenas asked that the PRI accept more open participation within the party in the designation of the next presidential candidate. While Alemán refused to democratize candidate selection, he did choose a candidate more acceptable to Cárdenas, and Cárdenas abandoned Henríquez Guzmán. This was the first serious attempt by the Cárdenas family to move the PRI towards the left by demanding internal democratization of the PRI and threatening an elite split.

In 1961, Lázaro Cárdenas sponsored a second such effort, in the Movimiento de Libración Nacional (MLN, or Movement for National Liberation). At 27, Cuauhtémoc Cárdenas represented his father on the first National Committee of the MLN. This political experience reinforced many of the political themes that would characterize his presidential campaign in 1988. The MLN grew out of an international movement to support Cuba against the United States, but quickly turned to domestic issues of national sovereignty and economic independence in Mexico. Specific goals included independence from the International Monetary Fund, internal democratization in the PRI and its affiliated unions, municipal autonomy, decentralization, and support for agrarian reform.

In the MLN, Cuauhtémoc Cárdenas also built or strengthened personal relationships that would prove useful in 1988, with such leftist intellectuals and Communist Party activists as Gilberto Rincón Gallardo, Arnoldo Martínez Verdugo, Ricardo Valero, and Heberto Castillo. Castillo also had been his instructor in the engineering department at the Universidad Nacional Autónoma de México (UNAM, or the National Autonomous University of Mexico), where Cárdenas received his degree. In 1988, Castillo would resign as the presidential candidate of the Mexican Socialist Party in order to support the candidacy of his former student. He remained a strong ally—and critic—of Cárdenas within the PRD.

The MLN eventually split over whether or not to participate in elections. Lázaro Cárdenas felt that electoral involvement would weaken the MLN's ability to influence policy. When communist activists in the MLN formed a Frente Electoral del Pueblo (FEP, or People's Electoral Front) to run candidates in the 1964 presidential election, the MLN split. Lázaro Cárdenas withdrew, and Cuauhtémoc Cárdenas began to distance himself. By early 1967, Cuauhtémoc had joined the PRI.

In the PRI, Cuauhtémoc Cárdenas participated in a newly created Technical Advisory Council, part of the Confederación Nacional Campesina (CNC, or National Peasant Confederation), to study agrarian problems. Other participants included economist Ifigenia Martínez, his childhood friend Janitzio Múgica, and a former university acquaintance, Leonel Durán. All of these PRIistas later participated with Cárdenas in the internal dissident group he helped create in 1986, the Democratic Current. Other future Democratic Current members worked together with him at different times on a commission studying development projects in the Las Balsas River basin from 1963 to 1974.

Lázaro Cárdenas died in 1970. From him, Cuauhtémoc Cárdenas had learned to value popular mobilization as a tool. Mobilization made oil expropriation possible. It tried to pull the PRI toward the left during the 1952 Henríquez campaign, and in the MLN period. Coalitions with leftist parties and social activists were constructed in both cases. And in both cases, democratization of the PRI became a central demand. Cuauhtémoc Cárdenas also learned much of his political philosophy from his father, and from the movements in which they both participated. Across more than 60 years, this philosophy stressed national sovereignty, economic independence, and the state's role as an ally in popular struggles. Cuauhtémoc's personal style often reflected his father's, including Lázaro's emphasis on indefatigable small-town campaigning. Perhaps most important, Cuauhtémoc Cárdenas inherited from his father a deep reservoir of popularity and public goodwill that helped him in 1988. Without the Cárdenas name, his candidacy might never have materialized, and it certainly would have attracted far less electoral support.

After his father's death, Cárdenas broke PRI ranks for the first time as an independent agent when he publicly sought the PRI's nomination for governor of Michoacán in 1974. When the PRI ignored him, Cárdenas withdrew, accusing the PRI of forcing members to surrender them-

selves unconditionally to the party leaders. Yet for the next 12 years, his career followed a fairly typical PRI pattern. In 1976, he became a federal senator, but only served three months. He resigned to become subsecretary of forestry and fauna in the Ministry of Agriculture. In 1979 he finally was tapped by the PRI to run for governor of Michoacán. Apart from some minor clashes, Cárdenas was relatively uncontroversial and even popular for most of his term, from 1980 to 1986.

However, as his term came to an end, Cárdenas embarked on a course of action that led to his leaving the party he had served for 20 years. As Mexico's economic crisis dragged on, President Miguel de la Madrid turned to policies that many on the left in the PRI found unacceptable. These critics argued that the government should not put debt payments ahead of social welfare, because the debt had resulted from the irresponsible behavior of creditors as well as the Mexican government. They objected to deepening budget cuts, accelerating privatization, and dismantling Mexico's traditional model of protectionist import substitution. They expressed concern that the government's apparent indifference to suffering caused by the crisis would lead voters to reject the PRI. And finally, they had fewer and fewer options for influencing policy within the system, owing to their gradual exclusion from policy-making posts.

Within Michoacán, Governor Cárdenas began to sponsor discussion groups to consider ways of putting pressure on the government to change its direction, and he began to make public statements criticizing federal policy. These statements marked him as someone willing to oppose the PRI publicly. By the spring of 1986, his contacts extended to Rodolfo González Guevara, Mexico's ambassador in Spain, and Porfirio Muñoz Ledo, a former PRI president who recently had been relieved as United Nations representative. González Guevara suggested that to influence economic policy, they might copy the example of the "Critical Current" in the ruling Spanish Socialist Workers' Party (PSOE), which opposed certain policies of the PSOE from within the party. However, attempts to influence policy increasingly focused on the presidential succession. According to tradition, Mexican presidents chose their own successors. Left to himself, de la Madrid probably would choose someone with similar policy preferences, prolonging the isolation of leftist PRIistas. Cárdenas and Muñoz Ledo called for potential PRI presidential candidates to declare their interest in running for president and engage in public debates.

They also began to organize the "Critical Current" that González Guevara had proposed. González Guevara proposed nominating Cárdenas as a "precandidate of sacrifice" in the PRI, in the hope that his participation would force public debate over economic policy and the nomination of a more socially oriented candidate, although probably not Cárdenas himself. In the midst of these early discussions, a press leak revealed the group's existence in August 1986 and dubbed it the Corriente Democrática (Democratic Current). For more than a year Democratic Current members used public pressure and negotiation to influence the PRI nomination process from within the party. During this period, the role of Cárdenas became increasingly significant. He became a de facto "candidate," conducting "campaign tours" to raise the issues that concerned the Democratic Current. Only Cárdenas had the public recognition to attract the curious to rallies, as well as an extensive organizational network from his term as governor. It was also Cárdenas who took the first steps toward a split when he sent a public letter to newspapers after the PRI's March 1987 National Assembly, accusing the party's leaders of antidemocratic, intolerant, and un-Revolutionary behavior that prevented any respectful collaboration. His refusal to accept party "discipline" deepened the confrontation between the Democratic Current and the PRI.

Ultimately, the Democratic Current had to recognize complete defeat when de la Madrid named Carlos Salinas de Gortari—architect of most of the detested neoliberal economic program—as the PRI's presidential candidate. Within days, Cárdenas accepted the nomination of the first of four parties that would support his candidacy for president. In January, three of these parties and an assortment of popular movements and unregistered parties formed the Frente Democratico Nacional (FDN, or National Democratic Front), to support his candidacy.

By the spring of 1988, several surprisingly well attended rallies had converted Cárdenas into the candidate of those who sought to punish the PRI for the economic crisis. He attracted support from protest voters in developed areas such as Mexico City and rural states such as Morelos and Michoacán. His relationship to Lázaro Cárdenas was a significant campaign advantage, because it reminded people of a time when they felt the PRI served social interests. Personally, Cuauhtémoc Cárdenas was known as a singularly uncharismatic speaker. However, he also was seen as honest, and he focused on issues that targeted the major complaints of many Mexicans. The combination of these factors led him to receive, on July 6, 1988, the largest official vote for any opposition presidential candidate: 31 percent.

Nevertheless, considerable evidence suggests that the 1988 elections were marred by electoral fraud, including suspiciously high PRI votes in rural states such as Chiapas, where the opposition had few poll-watchers, and stacks of partially burned ballots marked in favor of the FDN. Most believe Cárdenas did much better than 31 percent, and Cárdenas himself claimed victory. Neither the Partido de Acción Nacional (PAN, or National Action Party) nor the FDN supported the confirmation of Salinas in the Electoral College.

At the same time, Cárdenas refused to call for aggressive mobilization or acts of civil disobedience (like the seizure of public buildings) to defend his claim. He did not want to take responsibility for behavior that had a high probability of ending in violent repression. He did not think that the FDN had sufficient organization to communicate directions effectively to local supporters, and he did not want to risk uncontrolled escalation. Meanwhile, he hoped that public opinion would force Salinas to resign. Others in the FDN argued in

favor of much more aggressive action. The refusal of Cárdenas to support such policies therefore played an important role in the decision of the FDN not to go in that direction. Salinas succeeded in winning confirmation and took office in December 1988.

Still, the confrontation over electoral results set the tone for relations between the government and the PRD, the party founded by Cárdenas after the 1988 election. Dominated by his conviction that Salinas had stolen the election, Cárdenas encouraged his party to reject any cooperation with the government that might strengthen the political position of Salinas. This resulted in policies that effectively punished PRD-allied movements or politicians who negotiated with the state in order to meet constituent demands. Later, the party became more willing to support such negotiations, but throughout the Salinas administration, Cárdenas himself refused to meet with Salinas or engage in negotiations without a specific agenda. Only with perfect transparency, he argued, could people be assured that he had not sold out their votes for his own benefit.

The personal influence of Cárdenas had a complex and contradictory effect on the party. On the one hand, his position on negotiation tended to pull the party toward confrontation, mobilization, and intransigent defense of principles, often frightening swing voters. Moreover, his overwhelming presence often circumvented party procedures and encouraged rebellion against decisions made by committee, inhibiting party institutionalization. On the other hand, the PRD might never have been created without the unifying consensus among former PRIistas and socialists that his unique authority provided. He was elected the PRD's first president without opposition and had considerable influence over the composition of its first Executive Board. He remained the key arbiter of conflicts during his term as president, and in some ways continued this function afterward. The party might well have fallen apart without the legitimacy that his approval brought party decisions, the electoral help that his campaign presence provided, and the constant expectation that Cárdenas would again run for president in 1994.

Not until after the 1994 election, when he failed to attract more than 17 percent of the popular vote, did his influence begin to decline. Under the leadership of his old PRI colleague Porfirio Muñoz Ledo, the PRD sought full participation in negotiations with the PRI and PAN on institutional reform, culminating in a 1996 agreement.

Nevertheless, many in the party remained unsatisfied with the results of negotiation. In the 1996 internal election to pick Muñoz Ledo's successor, the winning candidate was Manuel López Obrador, a close ally of Cárdenas who shared many of his tactical and political preferences. Both supported a political alliance with the Zapatista rebels in Chiapas, favored the use of mobilization as a prenegotiation tactic, and saw the PRD's mission as much in terms of support for "popular struggles" as in electoral terms. Cárdenas pressured López Obrador to run for the party presidency and actively campaigned on his behalf. López Obrador's election therefore marked a resurgent influence of Cárdenas within the PRD. In 1997, Cárdenas himself was elected as mayor of Mexico City. As much as any man in the late twentieth century, Cuauhtémoc Cárdenas shaped the modern Mexican left.

Select Bibliography

Aguilar Zínser, Adolfo, ¡Vamos a ganar!: La pugna de Cuauhtémoc Cárdenas por el poder. Mexico City: Editorial Oceano, 1995.

Bruhn, Kathleen, Taking on Goliath: The Emergence of a New Left Party and the Struggle for Democracy in Mexico. University Park: Pennsylvania State University Press, 1997.

Carr, Barry, and Steve Ellner, editors, The Left in Latin America: From the Fall of Allende to Perestroika. Boulder, Colorado: Westview Press, 1993.

Castañeda, Jorge, Utopia Unarmed: The Latin American Left after the Cold War. New York: Knopf, 1993.

Gilly, Adolfo, editor, Cartas a Cuauhtémoc Cárdenas. Mexico City: Era, 1989.

Taibo, Paco Ignacio, II, Cárdenas de cerca: Una entrevista biográfica. Mexico City: Grupo Editorial Planeta, 1994.

—KATHLEEN BRUHN

CÁRDENAS, LÁZARO

1895–1970 • General and President

Lázaro Cárdenas was president of Mexico from 1934 to 1940, a period distinguished by a high level of peasant and labor mobilization, an extensive agrarian reform, the expropriation and nationalization of the foreign-owned petroleum companies, and the creation of an enduring government party structure incorporating labor, peasant, and popular sectors. The Cárdenas administration has also been subject to extensive debate regarding its long-term impact and the original intentions of Cárdenas himself.

Cárdenas was born on May 21, 1895, in Jiquilpan de Juárez, Michoacán. His trajectory to the presidency began in 1913 when he joined the Constitutional Army, serving under both Álvaro Obregón and Plutarco Elías Calles. He advanced to the rank of division general by 1928 and held several positions in the new post-Revolutionary government during the 1920s and early 1930s, including secretary of government, secretary of national defense, and governor of his home state of Michoacán, as well as president of the new Partido Nacional Revolucionario (PNR, or National Revolutionary Party). His experience in those tumultuous years of military revolts, attempted coups, and religious rebellion undoubtedly shaped his belief in the importance of a strong, centralized state that could maintain some control over the heterogeneous forces unleashed by the Revolution. He thus shared the state-building orientation of the post-Revolutionary leadership.

In other respects, however, his principles diverged from those of many of these leaders, including his mentor and former commander Calles, who was becoming increasingly conservative during this period. As governor of Michoacán, Cárdenas antagonized traditional landowners by carrying out an agrarian reform, even arming the peasants when they were threatened with retaliation by armed guards of the landlords. Cárdenas became a leader of a radical agrarista faction that opposed the efforts of the more conservative faction within the government, led by Calles himself, to end agrarian reform in order to reassure commercial landowners and increase agricultural investment and production. The agrarista faction nevertheless gained control of the 1934 PNR nominating convention, approving a radical six-year plan for the next government and nominating Cárdenas as presidential candidate.

When he assumed the presidency in 1934, Cárdenas began to assert his independence by supporting labor in a series of labor disputes, resulting in an open break with Calles. He encouraged labor organization, including the formation of industrial unions and federations that could bargain collectively with employers in a given industry, and the establishment of a national labor confederation, the Confederación de Trabajadores de México (CTM, or Confederation of Mexican Workers). His continued support for labor, including tolerance and indeed encouragement of strikes, antagonized many business groups who were concerned not only about his radical stance but also the growing power of the mobilized workers. Labor conflicts were to have a prominent role in the two most significant initiatives of the Cárdenas period, the agrarian reform and the expropriation of the foreign-owned petroleum companies.

The most important phase of the agrarian reform began with a labor dispute on the cotton estates of the Laguna region in the states of Coahuila and Durango. Prior to the Cárdenas administration, the agrarista goal of land distribution had been regarded as incompatible with developmental goals of increasing agricultural production and productivity; the distribution that did occur targeted only traditional haciendas. Large commercial estates such as those of the Laguna region, regarded as the most productive form of agricultural holding, generally were exempt from expropriation.

The decision of the Cárdenas government to resolve the Laguna conflict through the expropriation of the estates therefore established a precedent that subsequently was followed, with variations, on the henequen plantations in Yucatán, wheat and rice estates in the Yaqui Valley of Sonora, rice and cattle haciendas in Michoacán, and several large sugar estates in the state of Puebla. Drawing on the experience of several state governments during the 1920s, which in turn drew from communal traditions of the precolonial period and influences from the Soviet Union, especially the Soviet *kolkhoz,* the government distributed the estates as collective *ejidos,* or village cooperatives, that would be farmed by the new owners as a unit, thus maintaining the economies of scale thought to be necessary for high levels of productivity.

The expropriation of commercial estates, their conversion to collectives, and the level of mobilization of peasants and rural workers evoked considerable opposition. In the traditional agricultural areas of west-central and southern Mexico, opposition to land reform was combined with resistance to Cárdenas's promotion of "socialist" education, designed to undermine the control traditionally exercised by the Catholic Church by emphasizing secular and Revolutionary values. Attacks in the press condemned the "communist" policies of the government; in some areas the landowners took up arms or hired mercenaries to attack the new *ejidatarios.* As was the case with attacks on the church in the previous decade, Cárdenas's promotion of socialist education was opposed by many peasants as well, some of whom joined the Sinarquista Rebellion in many of the same areas where the pro-Catholic, peasant-based Cristero Rebellion had erupted a decade before.

Less violent and more indirect efforts to undermine agrarian reform may have been more successful in the long run. In several cases, commercial landowners were able to retain much of the infrastructure of the previous estates, including processing facilities. In Puebla, for example, some landowners retained control of the sugar refineries that peasant owners and *ejidatarios* were obliged to use. The landowners often had allies among officials at the local and state levels who were able to delay or undermine the process of implementation. Although the Cárdenas government created the Ejidal Bank to provide loans to the *ejidatarios,* funds were insufficient to meet the need even during the Cárdenas administration, and subsequent administrations provided little support for the bank or more generally for the agrarian reform sector.

Nevertheless, the achievements of the agrarian reform were significant. The Cárdenas government distributed more land to more peasants than all of his predecessors: 4.5 million acres (18 million hectares) were given to 800,000 peasants during his administration. The proportion of agricultural land in *ejidos* increased from 15 percent of the total cultivated land to nearly 50 percent between 1930 and 1940; and traditional "feudal" relations of production in the countryside were reduced greatly. Despite their problems, some of the collective *ejidos* achieved relatively high levels of productivity, comparable to those of the private sector. Over the next 30 years the agricultural sector was able to satisfy the food demand of the growing urban sector and to support industrialization through exports of agricultural products.

The labor dispute that culminated with the expropriation of the U.S.- and British-owned petroleum companies began with a demand by petroleum workers for a collective contract and for increased wages and benefits. The owners protested that they were unable to meet the wage and benefit requests, and following extensive negotiations as well as a temporary strike the dispute was referred to the Federal Labor Board. The decision by the board in favor of the workers was contested by the owners, who took the issue to the Mexican Supreme Court. When the companies refused to abide by the Supreme Court ruling upholding the decision of the Federal Labor Board, Cárdenas, after consultation with his cabinet, decreed their expropriation.

The decision had both immediate and long-term repercussions. Within Mexico, where the oil companies were regarded as representative of foreign economic imperialism at its worst, the expropriation resulted in a massive outpouring of support for Cárdenas. The oil companies pressured their respective governments to take measures against Mexico: Britain broke diplomatic relations, and the U.S. State Department insisted on immediate indemnification, boycotted Mexican petroleum exports to the United States, and established an embargo on the exports of petroleum equipment to Mexico. The expropriation was also a factor in substantial capital flight, which, in the context of decreased export earnings, led to a devaluation of the peso and severe constraints on government expenditures in the remaining years of the Cárdenas presidency.

In the longer term, the expropriation, and the shifting of the Mexican petroleum companies from foreign to state ownership and management, definitively established the role of the state as a major economic actor and validated its claim as guarantor of national interests in relation to foreign powers. Subsequently the government would gain control of other key industries under foreign control, including electric power, mining, and communications.

Despite frequent conflicts with business and landowning sectors, the Cárdenas government promoted economic development, including support for both national and foreign business interests. Government investments in infrastructure, particularly roads and highways, and in agricultural irrigation (which benefited the large private estates as well as new collective *ejidos* in the north) increased substantially during this period; government banks provided loans to private industries and financial institutions; tariffs and tax exemptions were implemented to protect and encourage "new and necessary" industries; foreign investment in manufacturing (as opposed to extractive industries) was encouraged. Government support for agrarian reform and for higher wages in the urban sector increased the market, another factor in business growth, and thousands of new manufacturing firms and dozens of new financial institutions were established during the Cárdenas administration.

Nevertheless, the last years of the Cárdenas administration were marked by increased concern regarding the tenor of reforms and the growing strength of the labor movement, not only on the part of business groups but also more conservative groups within the government and the governing party. To this was added the uncertainty of the international situation given the outbreak of war in Europe and pending U.S. involvement in war in both Europe and Japan. In the last years of the administration, the reforms were checked, and Cárdenas attempted to consolidate his support through restructuring the government party to incorporate various constituencies.

The party was restructured on a corporatist basis, with four sectors incorporating labor, the peasantry, popular groups, and the military. Apart from the military (which subsequently was dropped), the sectors were comprised of organized groups: the CTM and other confederations and independent unions in the case of labor; the major peasant organizations, which would be grouped in the Confederación Nacional Campesina (CNC, or National Peasant Confederation) established later in the year; and, in the popular sector, organizations of government workers, as well as women, youth, and other groups excluded from the labor and peasant sectors. The sectoral structure allegedly would enable each constituency to have greater input in the new party, which was now called the Partido de la Revolución Mexicana (PRM, or Party of the Mexican Revolution).

The limited input of the respective sectors in party decisions became quickly evident, however, with the nomination of the PRM candidate for the 1940 presidential elections. Progressive groups within the government and party supported General Francisco Múgica, the secretary of communications under Cárdenas, who could be expected to continue the reforms of the Cárdenas administration. However, in an effort to appease conservative groups within the party—and reflecting his own concerns regarding the polarizing effects of a continuation and perhaps expansion of reforms on conditions of internal instability and international uncertainty—Cárdenas chose General Manuel Avila Camacho, a more conservative and certainly less controversial candidate. Although the various sectors within the party were supposed to nominate the candidate, the candidacy of Avila Camacho was in effect imposed on them, and the respective nominating conventions simply ratified the decision.

The Avila Camacho candidacy succeeded in uniting the leadership and most of the rank and file of the party (excepting some of the labor and peasant organizations that supported Múgica and walked out of their respective conventions). However the PRM would face serious opposition in the form of another conservative general, Juan Andreu Almazán, who was supported by a heterogeneous mix of business groups and labor and peasant dissidents who had favored Múgica, as well as the Partido de Acción Nacional (PAN, or National Action Party), formed in 1939 by a group of conservative businessmen and Catholic intellectu-

als opposed to Cardenista reforms and particularly to socialist education.

Official and highly suspect election returns gave Avila Camacho a resounding victory, reinforcing a pattern of government party control of the electoral process that would continue to ensure the dominance of the PRM (and that of its successor, the Partido Revolucionario Institucional, or PRI—Institutional Revolutionary Party) within the Mexican political system in succeeding decades. The conservatizing trend that began during the last years of the Cárdenas administration was reinforced by the subsequent administration of Avila Camacho and particularly by his successor, Miguel Alemán Valdés.

Cárdenas subsequently held several positions within the government, including secretary of defense (1942–45), executive director of the Tecalpatepec Commission in Michoacán for the Secretariat of Hydraulic Resources (1947–58), executive director of the Río Balsas Commission of the Secretariat of Hydraulic Resources (1969–70), and president of the board of the Las Truchas Steel complex (1969–70). He became unofficial leader of the left or progressive wing of the PRM/PRI and continued to oppose U.S. intervention in the hemisphere, condemning the U.S.-supported invasion of Guatemala in 1954 and the 1961 invasion of Cuba. His efforts on behalf of nonintervention and peace included participation in the Latin American Conference for National Sovereignty, Economic Emancipation, and Peace, held in Mexico in 1961; in the International Tribunal against War Crimes in Vietnam (Russia Tribunal) in 1966; and in efforts to bring about an understanding between the Soviet Union and China on behalf of the people of Vietnam. Cárdenas died on October 19, 1970.

In retrospect, many of those groups that had most strongly opposed the Cárdenas reforms ultimately benefited from them. The expansion of the domestic market through wage hikes and agrarian reform served the interests of industrial capitalists, as did Mexico's ability to support imports of industrial inputs through agricultural exports; businesses also were subsidized through reduced prices for inputs from nationalized firms formerly under foreign control. Perhaps most important, Cárdenas had in effect "resolved" the problem of popular mobilization through an extensive agrarian reform that brought "social peace" to the countryside and the construction of a party system facilitating control over urban and rural labor and the peasantry.

Given this outcome, some revisionist interpretations have taken a cynical view of the Cárdenas era, suggesting that Cárdenas deliberately manipulated workers and peasants in order to bring them under the control of the state. In this sense, he allegedly shared the goals of his predecessors but was much more astute in recognizing the need to organize the workers and peasants and even encourage their mobilization in order to control them more effectively, whether to serve the interests of capitalist development or to reinforce the hegemony of a monolithic state.

Other studies have recognized the distinction between initial intentions, implementation, and long-term effects. The development of regional historical studies has revealed the complexity in the implementation of post-Revolutionary reforms at the local and state levels. Among other aspects, they have demonstrated the resistance by local officials who often identified with the landlords or business interests and who supported reforms only for reasons of political expediency. Regional studies also have provided a new understanding of the role of the would-be beneficiaries or victims of reforms (peasants, indigenous populations) in supporting, resisting, or negotiating different elements of the Cárdenas program (e.g., accepting land reforms but opposing "socialist" education). In short, the actual implementation of the Cárdenas program involved the interaction and negotiation among a plethora of federal government bureaucrats, landowners, state governors, local strongmen, business interests, peasants, workers, and other interests, leading to varying results across different regions and localities.

Among the Cardenistas themselves, policy goals and strategies were formulated in a highly charged context in which both national and international events and intellectual perspectives gave primacy to the state in promoting economic development—whether capitalist or socialist—and in protecting the interests of labor and other popular sectors. Cárdenas and his associates could claim to be determined state builders and dedicated *agraristas* without apparent contradiction. They also could see the state as a vehicle for economic development, a means to control the excesses of capital, and a benevolent, if paternalistic, instrument to secure the rights of peasants and workers.

Finally, the achievements of the Cárdenas government should not be minimized. Hundreds of thousands of peasants received land under the agrarian reform, and the nationalization of petroleum represented a turning point in economic relations with foreign interests, not only for Mexico but other countries of the hemisphere. While controversy undoubtedly will continue to characterize interpretations of the Cárdenas administration, Cárdenas and his associates seized the opportunities provided in that chaotic period to carry reforms further than any of their predecessors in Mexico or their counterparts in other Latin American countries.

See also Cardenismo: Interpretations

Select Bibliography
Anguiano, Arturo, *El Estado y la política obrera del cardenismo.* Mexico City: Era, 1975.

Becker, Marjorie, *Setting the Virgin on Fire: Lázaro Cárdenas, Michoacán Peasants and the Redemption of the Mexican Revolution.* Berkeley: University of California Press, 1995.

Córdova, Arnaldo, *La política de masas del cardenismo.* Mexico City: Era, 1974.

Gilly, Adolfo, *El cardenismo, una utopía mexicana.* Mexico City: Cal y Arena, 1994.

González, Luis, *Los Artífices del Cardenism: Historia de la Revolución Mexicana,* vol. 14. Mexico City: Colegio de México, 1979.

Hamilton, Nora, *The Limits of State Autonomy: Post-Revolutionary Mexico.* Princeton, New Jersey: Princeton University Press, 1982.

Hernández Chávez, Alicia, *La mecanica cardenista: Historia de la Revolución Mexicana,* vol. 16. Mexico City: Colegio de México, 1979.

Joseph, Gilbert M., and Daniel Nugent, editors, *Everyday Forms of State Formation: Revolution and the Negotiation of Rule in Modern Mexico.* Durham, North Carolina: Duke University Press, 1994.

Knight, Alan, "Cardenismo: Juggernaut or Jalopy?" *Journal of Latin American Studies* 26 (1994).

—NORA HAMILTON

CARDENISMO: INTERPRETATIONS

No current of the Mexican Revolution has developed such a powerful mystique as Cardenismo. The image of Lázaro Cárdenas, president of Mexico from 1934 to 1940, has, indeed, become a Revolutionary symbol, imbued with a near messianic quality. However, the persistence of Cardenista utopianism makes it extremely difficult for historians to break through the Cardenista myth and reconstruct the contours of Mexican history during the crucial period of the 1930s.

The phenomenon of Cardenismo has been interpreted from a variety of contradictory perspectives that mirror the diverse utopian hopes of sympathizers and reflect the process by which its history has been symbolically appropriated or demonized by an array of political movements. Thus confusion reigns: historians have alternately characterized the Cárdenas administration as communist, socialist, social-democratic, liberal, Bonapartist, national reformist, corporatist, authoritarian, and populist. Cárdenas has been hailed as a "Mexican democrat" and viciously attacked, in the words of Arnoldo Córdova, as the creator of "that enormous concentration camp that Mexico was becoming."

The Official PRI Version and Contemporary Foreign Interpretations

Contemporary government rhetoric, popular perceptions, and the work of sympathetic historians coalesced to form an "official" Partido Revolucionario Institucional (PRI, or Institutional Revolutionary Party) interpretation that portrayed Cardenismo as the culmination of the Revolutionary process, the most authentic expression of the Revolution. Cárdenas's son Cuauhtémoc, while a leading PRI member, described his father as "the incarnation of the Mexican Revolution," and one influential U.S. observer, Frank Tannenbaum, conflating the legendary leader and the Mexican people, marveled at the "almost complete merging of the President of the country with the common folk. . . . In some ways the people are part of him. . ." (Townsend, 1952). According to this version, which predominated until 1968, it was Cárdenas who finally addressed the deep-rooted popular grievances that sparked the Revolution of 1910. He created a powerful alliance with organized labor and the peasantry, which was solidified by the formation of the Confederación de Trabajadores de México (CTM, or Confederation of Mexican Workers) in 1936 and the Confederación Nacional Campesina (CNC, or National Peasant Confederation) in 1938. The *campesinos* (peasants) benefited from the largest agrarian reform program in Mexican history, which destroyed the Porfirian hacienda and redistributed 4.5 million acres (18 million hectares) to some 800,000 landless peasants. A newly galvanized labor movement finally saw the labor stipulations of the Constitution of 1917 implemented: real wages increased, working conditions improved, and labor, now unionized on a massive scale, gained an enhanced bargaining position vis-à-vis capital. Cárdenas served the Revolutionary cause of economic nationalism by triumphantly expropriating the foreign-owned petroleum sector in 1938, forming a national state monopoly, Petróleos Mexicanos (PEMEX). He created Mexico's unique, remarkably stable, corporatist political system by founding, in 1938, the official Partido de la Revolución Mexicana (PRM, or Party of the Mexican Revolution) in an effort to institutionalize the political participation of the Cardenista masses and to safeguard the achievements of reform for the future.

This official interpretation is closely linked to post-Revolutionary politics. Since 1940 the ruling party and government of Mexico have discursively appropriated Cardenismo in a self-serving attempt to maintain political legitimacy, based, in the eyes of workers and peasants, on an ongoing concern for Revolutionary goals such as agrarian reform, laborism, and economic nationalism. This has contributed to the hegemony of the Mexican political elite into the 1960s and beyond.

That Cárdenas presided over such a series of remarkable reforms cannot be denied, but one should not overstate the unique nature of Cardenista reform. Instead, Cardenismo must be placed within the broader context of the Mexican Revolution. Cárdenas followed in the footsteps of earlier reformers, in particular regional Revolutionary strongmen,

who, in their "laboratories of the Revolution," already had experimented with social and political reform for more than a decade. Thus Cardenismo should be seen as the culmination of a historical process dating back to the early years of the Revolution or even to the nineteenth-century liberal reform movement. Also, many of his policies developed in an ad hoc, reactive fashion, and were hardly part of an overarching master plan. Cardenista land and labor reform was, to a significant extent, the result of popular pressure from below.

Foreign treatments of Cardenismo also have colored our perceptions of Mexican history. During the 1930s foreign observers sympathetic to the Mexican Revolution and, in some cases, to socialism, such as Nathaniel and Sylvia Weyl, William Cameron Townsend, and Frank Tannenbaum, echoed official rhetoric, portraying Cardenismo as a genuinely popular, social reformist, democratic movement similar to Franklin D. Roosevelt's New Deal, an ally in the struggle against fascism and big business. They characterized Cárdenas as an honest, idealistic, "Mexican Democrat" and often projected their wider concerns with global issues such as world socialism, Pan-Americanism, and the geopolitical position of the United States during World War II, onto their analysis of Mexican affairs. But they did play a crucial role in defining foreign attitudes towards the Cárdenas regime at a precarious historical moment, promoting Cárdenas's political survival despite increasing criticism from foreign governments and business interests in the wake of the 1938 petroleum expropriation.

Marxist Interpretations

In opposition to this official version of Cardenismo, left-wing critics of the PRI, disappointed by the conservatism of Mexico's post-Revolutionary elite, as well as foreign Marxist analysts, began to portray the Mexican Revolution and Cardenismo as a lost opportunity, a failed socialist movement. Anatoli Shulgovski, for example, depicted Cardenismo as a step on the path toward socialism and an integral part of the world socialist Revolution. Marxist interpretations concentrated on Cárdenas's attempts to socialize the means of production, his alliance with Mexico's proletariat, and his staunch anti-imperialism. More recently, Adolfo Gilly, moving away from a purely structuralist approach, described Cardenismo as an "imaginary" (a utopian project), which utilized socialist theory to delineate the contours of a future Mexican society.

However, Marxist historians generally acknowledged that Cardenismo was a failed attempt at implanting socialism, owing to flawed policies, bureaucratization, divisions between workers and peasants, pressure from the national bourgeoisie and foreign interests, and even the negative influence of Stalinism. Prominent leaders of the international socialist movement failed to see Cárdenas as a socialist. Leon Trotsky, for example, considered him an anti-imperialist liberal, a bourgeois national reformist.

From the 1930s on the notion that Cárdenas was a socialist, or even a communist, was echoed by Mexico's right-wing opposition, which strongly opposed his socializing policies. Conservatives with liberal or Catholic backgrounds as diverse as Luis Cabrera, Salvador Abascal, José Vasconcelos, and José Valadés lambasted Cárdenas as an anti-Mexican, communist traitor, a dangerous Marxist radical who negated the ideals of the Revolution and imported exotic ideologies with the purpose of destroying liberty, private property, family, and religion. These attacks foreshadowed the end of Revolutionary reform and the rise of a conservative post-Revolutionary political system after 1940.

Some Mexican analysts such as Roberto Blanco Moheno, uncomfortable with the socialist appropriation of Cardenismo and eager to prove its Mexican-ness or Latin American–ness, represented Cardenismo as a hybrid type of socialism *a la mexicana,* strongly influenced by indigenous practices and nineteenth-century liberalism. Gilly regarded Cardenismo as part of a broader, specifically Latin American socialist movement represented by Mariátegui, Sandino, and Martí. Some even argued that Cárdenas never really understood the subtleties of socialist theory. These qualifications are valid. Although influenced by the Bolshevik Revolution and desirous to abandon the tenets of classic liberalism, Cárdenas certainly did not seek the implantation of a Soviet-style system in Mexico, and openly denounced communism. Instead he envisaged a society in which a strong state would act to balance the interests of capital and a working class strengthened through unionization and cooperativism. Marxist interpretations of Cardenismo are more reflective of the prevalence of Marxist theory in Latin American academia and left-wing politics, especially after the Cuban Revolution of 1959, than of Mexico's reality during the 1930s.

Post-Revolutionary Revisionism

Interpretations of Cardenismo underwent a sea change in the wake of the 1968 Tlatelolco Massacre, perpetrated against hundreds of peacefully demonstrating students and workers by what seemed an authoritarian regime backed by a ruthless military. The official myth of the Revolution as an ongoing project of social justice and democracy was finally shattered. Tlatelolco invited a thorough reexamination of the official version of the Revolution, including Cardenismo. The slaughter finally convinced many intellectuals that Mexico was just another Latin American authoritarian regime, despite its Revolutionary legacy. Among the Mexican intelligentsia a new pessimism about the Revolution emerged that stressed the might of the Leviathan State and the capitalist nature of the Mexican economy. Cardenismo was no longer considered the culmination of the Revolutionary process, but seen as the very foundation of a Mexican version of bureaucratic-authoritarianism, or, at least, classic populism.

Revisionists have analyzed Cardenista state-labor relations in detail. Arturo Anguiano and Jorge Basurto, for example, argued that under Cárdenas the working class had been manipulated through economic concessions (enhanced wages and working conditions, the right to unionize and strike, collective bargaining), co-opted through socializing

rhetoric, and depoliticized and subordinated by the state's corporatist party system, thus consolidating a paternalistic state apparatus. Workers and peasants were kept divided by the creation of separate labor federations, the CTM and the CNC, and separate sectors within the PRM. Accidentally or intentionally, this process benefited a nascent national bourgeoisie and, stressed Octavio Ianni, capitalist development, in particular the creation of a national market, capital accumulation, and industrialization. Economic historians agree that the twentieth-century launch of Mexican industry commenced during the 1930s, boosted by government spending and economic policies.

Revisionists also emphasized the power of the post-Revolutionary state. Arnaldo Córdova considered the emergence of an authoritarian, monolithic state and a strong presidentialist political system as the direct fruits of Cardenismo. Historians like Alicia Hernández Chávez increasingly viewed Cárdenas as a Machiavellian master politician who manipulated political factions, the military, and popular organizations to create a powerful "Cardenista machine." Recent regional studies stress the use of caciquismo (boss rule), corruption, and violence in maintaining Cardenista control at the local and state level.

A second wave of revisionism during the 1980s and 1990s moved beyond politics and the economy to focus on the cultural authoritarianism of the Cardenista state. Based on research on Cárdenas's home state, Michoacán, these historians argued that Cárdenas—ignorant, condescending and disdainful toward *campesino* culture, and trampling on indigenous traditions of democracy, religiosity, and economic justice—embarked on a brutal attack on popular cultures. Revisionist historians of Cardenista agrarian reform emphasized the imposition of an inappropriate collectivism on an unwilling rural population. They linked the issue of cultural revolution to older themes such as the consolidation of state power and the harnessing of the lower classes to the project of capitalist development. However, although these studies may explain why some Mexicans rejected the Cardenista project, they fail to account for its widespread support and persisting appeal. Mexico's popular classes resisted Cardenista cultural policies, often with violence, in particular the anti-clerical "defanaticization" campaigns, socialist education, moral reform, and collectivist agriculture. But they did embrace certain aspects of the cultural project, in particular a new nationalist civil religion. Support for Cardenismo is still strong in certain regions of contemporary Mexico. Thus one must ask the question: Why does Michoacán remain loyal to the Cardenista myth in the 1990s, even though this has meant losing government patronage and becoming a pariah within the official political system?

Neo-Populist Approaches

Defying such revisionism are what might be labeled "neo-populist" analysts such as Nora Hamilton, Alan Knight, and Tzvi Medin; these scholars assert that Cardenismo was a genuinely radical and popular political movement, which created a progressive alliance between the Cardenista government and workers and peasants and thus temporarily attained, in the words of Hamilton, a state of "relative autonomy," experimented with quasi-socialist policies, destroyed the landowning class, challenged industrialists and foreign investors alike, and advocated a progressive foreign policy. Cardenismo allowed for substantial "bottom-up" political representation, albeit not in a liberal, democratic fashion.

Cardenismo was, however, a pragmatic and realistic movement, hemmed in by domestic and international political and economic constraints. The Mexican government remained dramatically dependent on revenues from the taxation of (foreign-owned) minerals production, especially as Mexico entered a severe financial crisis in 1937. It was opposed not only by a coalition of national and foreign business interests, but also by powerful Revolutionary factions that objected to Cárdenas's radical policies and, by the late 1930s, by broad sectors of the middle and lower classes, especially those hurt by inflation and bypassed by reform. These constraints precluded the implementation of further radical policies. These neo-populist analysts deem the ultimate results of Cardenismo limited. The rollback of Cardenista reform after the election of Manuel Avila Camacho in 1940, and in particular during the presidency of Miguel Alemán Valdés (1946–52), was rapid and successful. The Mexican bourgeoisie recovered, foreign capital remained powerful, socialist education was phased out, and the agrarian reform project was, from a long-term perspective, a failure.

Neo-Cardenismo

The image of Cárdenas, more than that of any other Mexican political leader of the twentieth century, today functions as a powerful symbol of the unfulfilled ideals of the Mexican Revolution, such as nationalism, popular democracy, and social justice. The utopian project of Cardenismo was appropriated by a powerful opposition movement to PRI hegemony in 1988, when Cárdenas's son Cuauhtémoc split from the PRI and formed the Frente Democratico Nacional (FDN, or National Democratic Front), which participated in the presidential elections, gaining an unprecedented 31 percent of the vote, despite alleged electoral fraud by the PRI. The movement's rapid growth and popularity with the lower classes can in part be explained by popular loyalty to the image of President Cárdenas and to the "real" Revolution, that is, to the ideals of democracy, laborism, agrarian reform, and economic nationalism. Neo-Cardenistas portrayed themselves as the heirs of the Cardenismo of the 1930s. They reorganized their party into the Partido de la Revolución Democrática (PRD, or Party of the Democratic Revolution) and participated in the 1994 presidential elections. Although their popularity declined somewhat, the economic and political crisis starting in 1994 created conditions for a possible PRD resurgence. In response to neo-Cardenista opposition, official state discourse de-emphasized the centrality of Cardenismo, which now carried a potentially subversive message.

Future Research Trends

Many of the key components of earlier interpretations of Cardenismo are now being reviewed by a new generation of postrevisionist historians, who, through detailed research in new sources, question many of the widely held assumptions about Cardenismo, for example the primacy of presidentialism in fields like labor politics and foreign affairs or the notion of rising real wages. Approaches borrowed from the "new cultural history" and postmodern theory have been particularly fruitful, allowing historians to examine the cultural forms used by the Cardenista state in its efforts to foster political hegemony. Historians have begun to explore the cultural ramifications of the "developmentalist" ideology of the Revolutionary elite, which included moral reform, anticlericalism, productivism, hygiene, and nationalism. They have studied the cultural or discursive tools employed in this modernizing "cultural revolution," such as socialist education, civic ritual, iconoclasm, popular art, and indigenism. Marjorie Becker's work (1995) offers a balanced evaluation of Cardenismo that explores both official and popular cultures. She argues that Cardenismo in Michoacán, although initially oblivious to peasant values, was a malleable movement. The interaction of the Cardenista project with *campesino* culture resulted in the emergence of a new, hegemonic political culture, which allowed for a modicum of peasant participation. These scholars also note that Cardenismo clearly was gendered. While male peasants received land and new political space from the Revolutionary government, women were relegated to the traditional realms of childrearing, religion, and the household.

Further research will need to balance populist and revisionist theses and flesh out the multiple and "everyday" ways in which local/popular/subaltern cultures interacted with official Cardenista culture to create a new political hegemony in post-Revolutionary Mexico. In addition, many neglected aspects of Cardenismo, especially economic and gender issues, need to be explored in greater detail.

One can conclude, however, that Cardenismo had and has a variety of meanings. It was not a monolithic ideology and movement, but a site of symbolic, political—at times armed—struggle, a process in which diverse political cultures clashed violently. During this conflictive phase of Mexican history there were not only "many Mexicos," but "many Cardenismos" as well.

Select Bibliography

Anguiano, Arturo, *El Estado y la política obrera del cardenismo*. Mexico City: Era, 1975; 7th edition, 1983.

Bantjes, Adrian A., "Politics, Class and Culture in Post-Revolutionary Mexico: Cardenismo and Sonora, 1929–1940." Ph.D. diss., University of Texas, Austin, 1991.

Basurto, Jorge, *Cárdenas y el poder sindical*. Mexico City: Era, 1983.

Becker, Marjorie, *Setting the Virgin on Fire: Lázaro Cárdenas, Michoacán Peasants, and the Redemption of the Mexican Revolution*. Berkeley: University of California Press, 1995.

Córdova, Arnaldo, *La política de masas del cardenismo*. Mexico City: Era, 1974.

Gilly, Adolfo, *El cardenismo, una utopía mexicana*. Mexico City: Cal y Arena, 1994.

Gledhill, John, *Casi Nada: A Study of Agrarian Reform in the Homeland of Cardenismo*. Albany: Institute for Mesoamerican Studies, State University of New York Press, 1991.

González y González, Luis, *Los días del presidente Cárdenas*. Mexico City: Colegio de México, 1981.

Hamilton, Nora, *The Limits of State Autonomy: Post-Revolutionary Mexico*. Princeton, New Jersey: Princeton University Press, 1982.

Hernández Chávez, Alicia, *La mecánica cardenista*. Mexico City: Colegio de México, 1979.

Ianni, Octavio, *El Estado capitalista en la época de Cárdenas*. Mexico City: Era, 1977.

Krauze, Enrique, *Lázaro Cárdenas, General misionero*. Mexico City: Fondo de Cultura Económica, 1987.

Medin, Tzvi, *Ideología y praxis política de Lázaro Cárdenas*. Mexico City: Siglo XXI, 1972; 13th edition, 1986.

Schuler, Friedrich E., "Cardenismo Revisited: The International Dimensions of the Post-Reform Cárdenas Era, 1937–1940." Ph.D. diss., University of Chicago, 1990.

Shulgovski, Anatoli, *México en la encrucijada de su historia*. Mexico City: Fondo de Cultura Popular, 1968.

Townsend, William Cameron, *Lazaro Cardenas, Mexican Democrat*. Ann Arbor, Michigan: George Wahr, 1952.

Weyl, Nathaniel, and Sylvia Weyl, *The Reconquest of Mexico: The Years of Lázaro Cárdenas*. London and New York: Oxford University Press, 1939.

—ADRIAN A. BANTJES

CARRANZA, VENUSTIANO

1859–1920 • General and President

Carranza rose to power by means of social and economic reforms that attracted significant popular support and allowed him to dominate Mexico during the turbulent years of the Revolution and the early post-Revolutionary era. A statesman who articulated nationalism in order to define his international policy, Carranza failed when he lost sight of his original goals and promises.

Carranza's nationalistic convictions merged with his early ambitions. Born in 1859 to Colonel Jesús Carranza in Cuatro Ciénegas, Coahuila, Venustiano Carranza received a good education in Mexico City before returning to Coahuila, where he excelled at farming and ranching. An avid reader, Carranza was interested in Latin American rather than European history. Elected as *presidente municipal* of Cuatro Ciénegas, Carranza earned popularity for his educational improvements. He also defied the Porfirio Díaz–appointed governor and in 1893 led a successful revolt, forcing Díaz to allow Carranza and his brothers to exercise considerable influence throughout Coahuila. As a senator in the national Congress, Carranza inserted new provisions into laws to regulate foreign investors. Although Carranza disapproved of the Científicos (influential intellectuals and policy advisers), he supported the nationalistic tendencies of the late Porfiriato. Nevertheless, Carranza yearned for substantial change. Initially, he backed Bernardo Reyes and then Francisco I. Madero when the 1910 presidential campaign began. Carranza also participated in Madero's revolt against Díaz; in return, Madero permitted Carranza to control Coahuila.

As governor of Coahuila from 1911 to 1913, Carranza pursued reform with a zeal that won him the loyalties of most of the northern state's inhabitants. Carranza introduced firm regulation of economic concessions, progressive taxation, improved working conditions, and dramatic educational reforms, and he encouraged unionization and insisted upon improved health facilities. Taken as a whole, these actions positioned Carranza not as a liberal but as a populist who became a nationalist.

A new phase of the Mexican Revolution began when Carranza assumed leadership of the forces that fought Victoriano Huerta's dictatorship, which had been established after Madero's assassination in February 1913. Within weeks, Carranza received support from northerners willing to preserve reforms by siding with Carranza's national insurrection. At this time, Carranza urged caution because he felt that this movement could be snuffed out easily by larger federal forces. His Plan de Guadalupe avoided appeals to social revolution; it merely outlined the procedure for toppling Huerta and united temporarily Carranza's supporters. Now the "First Chief," however, Carranza began responding to popular grievances. The Carrancistas' ability to feed hungry people by means of bringing in food to hard-hit areas became a particularly popular policy. Carranza's officers forced merchants to sell their goods at low prices, which they listed on the doors of these mercantile establishments.

Carranza's land policies had a direct bearing upon his early success. Those who opposed him often had their lands seized for being "enemies of the people." Seized land remained usually in the hands of loyal supporters, who administered it for the Carranza movement. Hence the term *carrancear*, which means "to swindle." Yet the masses received modest numbers of provisional land titles after they occupied properties or received awards from sympathetic army officers.

Most of the famous women *soldaderas* (female soldiers and/or camp followers) were Carrancistas. What encouraged women to support Carranza? Carranza attracted females because he decreed divorce legal, encouraged feminist groups to organize, and subsidized their publications and speaking tours. In a country long dominated by traditional relations between sexes, this represented a risky political venture. But it was a legitimate social demand that Carranza did not deny.

Pressured by the forces of Carranza, Francisco "Pancho" Villa, Emiliano Zapata, and invading U.S. troops who captured Veracruz, Huerta finally resigned and left the country on July 15, 1914. Carrancista forces under General Álvaro Obregón entered Mexico City on August 15, and Carranza himself entered the capital on August 20. Under the Treaties of Teoloyucan, the various Revolutionary factions were to form a National Junta. On October 10, in the town of Aguascalientes in neutral territory, leaders from the civil war gathered for the Sovereign Revolutionary Convention. The convention's early calls for unity soon gave way to an irreconcilable split between the Carrancista (whose spokesman there was Obregón) and the more radical factions of Villa and Zapata. Ultimately, the Carrancistas lost control of the proceedings, and Eulalio Gutiérrez was chosen as provisional president, an office Carranza himself assumed he would possess.

When news of the events reached him, Carranza withdrew his forces from Mexico City and set up a separate Constitutional government in Veracruz, with himself as president; Villa, meanwhile, installed Gutiérrez as president of the Conventionalist government in Mexico City. Even these political divisions soon became more complex, as Gutiérrez abandoned Mexico City for Nuevo León, the Zapatistas threw their support behind Roque González Garza as president, and Villa governed independently from Chihuahua. The new phase of the Mexican Revolution soon devolved into anarchy, with independent civil wars ranging in various states. Eventually, however, the Constitutionalists began to gain the upper hand, in large part because of the military victories of General Obregón.

But Carranza's political and economic policies were a major contributor to his ultimate triumph as well. Carranza regulated the banks tightly and stopped inflation by the end of 1916. As a nationalist, Carranza increased governmental authority over foreign investments; he forced foreign investors to renounce formal diplomatic protection and consider themselves Mexican citizens. To the delight of many, taxes on oil companies increased seven-fold from 1917 to 1920. Taxes on the Guggenheim mining interests were eight times higher than the Villista taxes on the same firm. Carranza also seized the railroads, telegraphs, and telephones; moreover, the regime's administration of communications became surprisingly efficient. To encourage local entrepreneurs, Carranza raised tariff protection. Despite such restrictions on foreign trade, exports doubled from 1916 to 1920.

Land and labor reforms clinched Carranza's victory. His January 6, 1915, decree gave land taken from peasants by Liberals and Porfirians back to villages and petitioners. It also authorized temporary land seizures by the government. Carranza reduced foreign land ownership considerably. Eventually, a decline in food production, common to nations engaged in land reform, forced the regime to curtail land distribution. Yet Carranza also supported the working class. Carrancistas outlawed debt peonage and the *tienda del raya* company store. The eight-hour day and minimum wages became the norm in areas controlled by Carrancistas. Carranza also allied with the Casa del Obrero Mundial in February 1915. These anarchosyndicalists furnished Carranza six "red" battalions in return for permission to strike and unionize. Carrancistas placed the Casa del Obrero Mundial headquarters in the elite Jockey Club; they backed Carranza until a 1916 general strike led to a parting of the ways. But Carranza allowed laborers to form a moderate labor confederation, the Confederación Regional Obrera Mexicana (CROM, or Regional Confederation of Mexican Workers) in 1918. In general, Carranza did not interfere with the general growth of working-class organizations.

As president, Carranza soon became the precursor of the strong executives that were to characterize twentieth-century Mexico. Carranza interpreted his authoritarian approach as a form of democracy in which he enjoyed the support of the majority in defining public policy. Embracing egalitarianism meant that upper-class political traditions declined after 1915. The Carrancistas clamored consistently for industrialization, economic growth, education, land reform, and an expanded role for Mexico in world affairs. Self-made leaders now controlled regional and local governments. Military *caudillos* (strongmen) also enjoyed political legitimacy, particularly when they championed themselves as reformers. Eager for status and material gain, many of the new leaders worked to reestablish friendly ties with older elites. But political parties struggled with little success to compete with Carranza and his cohorts because the legislature played a minor role in reforming the country after 1913. A new form of personalistic populism tended to define the political tempo.

Carranza was not a classic dictator. Carranza was a patrician, but this did not prevent him from walking casually through Mexico City's Merced Market. Citizens looked up to Carranza because he exuded idealism and toughness. His personal charisma had limits, but Carranza's quest for greatness was a mixture of humility and grandeur that remains an unmistakable part of the civil war years. Carranza's error was his attempt to convince Mexicans that class demands were sectarian and that his new order would balance the interests of all within the context of a well-run political machine that usually carried out the president's wishes.

Carranza's relations with governors meant that his decisions had to be respected. Carranza encouraged his subordinates to overhaul judicial, tax, electoral, and public service policies so that they came in line with Carranza's usually progressive views on civil reform. It became a fact of life that by late 1914, governors had to check with Carranza before carrying out important proposals. Despite their subordination to Carranza, the governors played a significant role in solidifying a regime constantly under attack. Governors such as Gustavo Espinosa Mireles in Coahuila, Cándido Aguilar in Veracruz, and Salvador Alvarado in Yucatán became instrumental in aiding the national government. In general, those states ravaged by warfare were usually ones in which local reforms were at a minimum. A fair amount of democracy existed, but Carranza failed to establish a ruling political party.

Wishing to give his regime greater political legitimacy, Carranza called for a constitutional convention to be held in Querétaro in November 1916. Although Carranza viewed the document produced by this convention—the Constitution of 1917—as too radical, he ultimately accepted it. Under the authority of this constitution he was officially elected president in special elections held in March 1917, and on May 1 he took the oath of office.

The 1917 Constitution continues to be the Mexican Revolution's repository of goals. Three items represent the most well-known provisions: Article 3 proclaimed that education was secular and free and that the Catholic Church could no longer teach in secondary and primary schools. In general, Carranza protested such extreme anticlerical measures as outdated relics from the Liberal past. But he supported Article 27, which contained his land reform decree and maintained that land always must have a social function. Resting its legitimacy on this concept of public utility, Article 27 further states that the state can nationalize land to benefit the people and promote economic development. Finally, Article 27 insists that Mexico's subsoil wealth belongs to the state, not private concessionaires. Article 123 provides labor with an eight-hour day, minimum wages, and the rights to strike and to organize for collective bargaining.

Education yielded promising but eventually disappointing results under Carranza. Although he sincerely desired educational progress, Carranza's plans were undermined by his conviction that local governments should control school policies; he believed that all would benefit by casting off the tightly centralized Porfirian system. Carranza based his plans upon the success that decentralized municipal education enjoyed in Coahuila. But state governments often found it difficult to spend the necessary amounts to improve education; as a result, the illiteracy rate changed little. Still, other achievements took place. Schools for the deaf, blind, and retarded appeared, as well as a string of industrial and technical schools. New textbooks drilled students with Carranza's nationalism by emphasizing racial unity, mestizo contributions, and an appreciation for Mexico's indigenous heritage. Beginning in 1917, the government carried out large-scale excavations of the Mexican ruins at Teotihuacan under the direction of Manuel Gamio.

The most consistently nationalistic feature of the Carranza regime was its strident diplomacy. Carranza asserted Mexican sovereignty to an unusual degree, partially because his diplomacy endeavored to protect domestic reforms. An outstanding diplomat, Carranza usually got what he wanted.

Diplomatic relations with the United States ranged from tense to violent. Carranza and his advisers discovered early that Woodrow Wilson was determined to protect U.S. interests in nearly every phase of the U.S. State Department's dealings with Mexico. Because Wilson would not extend de facto recognition to Carranza's regime in 1915, Carranza decided to support a Mexican-American uprising in Texas known as the Plan de San Diego Revolt. Hundreds of troops disguised as *tejanos* crossed the Río Bravo (Rio Grande) to fuel the fighting until Wilson gave in and recognized Carranza in October 1915.

The following year, the Pershing expedition sparked renewed conflict along the border. Launched shortly after Villa's surprise attack upon Columbus, New Mexico, in March 1916, the arrival of U.S. troops into Chihuahua surprised and infuriated Carranza, who ordered that U.S. troops not advance further. After Carranza ordered his forces to fire on advancing U.S. troops, a battle resulted in a Mexican victory at Carrizal in June 1916. Carranza's resistance provided mass support for about two years. A U.S.-Mexican conference in Atlantic City centered upon Wilsonian attempts to force Carranza to curtail his reforms. But Carranza resisted stoutly; weary U.S. negotiators gave up and Pershing's forces withdrew from Mexico empty-handed on the day that Carranza proclaimed the 1917 Constitution.

Neutrality during World War I represents a defiance of Wilson that also appealed to national pride. Carranza's courting of the Germans resulted in the infamous Zimmermann telegram, an offer of territory lost in 1848 as well as financial aid in return for a military alliance with the kaiser. Carranza's public silence on the matter added to Wilson's apprehension about Mexican aims. Yet the shrewd Carranza resisted overtures from Germany because Berlin hoped merely to distract the U.S. government rather than aid Mexico significantly.

Carranza's relations with other nations yielded tangible dividends. Germany, Spain, and other European nations sent Mexico war matériel secretly. Japan supported Carranza actively, particularly when the Japanese constructed a munitions factory in Mexico City. Carranza's overtures to Latin America focused upon pleas for stronger unity to oppose economic imperialism and dollar diplomacy. Carranza's diplomacy was quite successful in central America, where he secured a strong alliance with El Salvador that kept Guatemala from intervening into Chiapas.

Carranza's decline resulted in part from a slackening of social reforms by 1919. The sympathetic but legalistic land reform bureaucrats could do little when land awards came to a virtual end. Eager to find political allies and increase food production, Carranza returned properties to large landowners such as the Terrazas family. While Carranza himself prospered and his estate expanded to 125,000 acres (50,000 hectares), the 1919 restrictions on the distribution of communal village lands stated that *campesinos* (peasants) had to pay taxes on and indemnify the government for land awards.

A fall in rural wages also angered the rural population; in a further setback to their cause, the *campesinos* of south-central Mexico lost their most powerful leader when Carranza laid a trap for Zapata, leading to his assassination on April 10, 1919. Meanwhile, falling wages also affected urban workers, who proceeded to strike in large numbers. The educational system also became a source of discontent when cutbacks began in 1918. A shortage of competent teachers exacerbated the problem of educational frustration.

On the international level, the end of World War I meant that Carranza could not resist the United States and count upon substantial European aid. Oil companies began fomenting dissident groups to attack Carranza on the northern border or deep within Mexico itself. Nationalists protested Carranza's last-minute courting of U.S. investors.

Yet the spark that set off the successful revolt that toppled him was Carranza's disastrous decision to impose a colorless successor during the 1920 elections. Many generals attempted to persuade the stubborn president to allow them to elect one of their own. General Álvaro Obregón decided to oppose Carranza. Obregón expected the presidency; he had never been defeated in battle and enjoyed popularity. When Sonora revolted in April 1920, most of the army joined Obregón. Carranza attempted to flee to Veracruz but instead died at the hands of an assassin on May 21, 1920.

Carranza's vision was not revolutionary, but his all-embracing nationalist ideology changed Mexico significantly. By 1920, however, political mobilization had reached the point at which concern over the threatened loss of political rights overrode the success of Carranza's earlier nationalist triumphs. Mexico did not acknowledge Carranza's legacy until the Cárdenas regime revived Carranza's image in the 1930s. Amid tremendous ceremony, Carranza's remains were deposited in the crypt of the Monument to the Revolution in 1942, when Mexico entered World War II. Although U.S. historians of Mexico are usually more critical of Carranza than Mexican scholars, there is no doubt that the Carranza regime represents a major transition in Mexican history.

Select Bibliography

Katz, Friedrich, *The Secret War in Mexico: Europe, the United States and the Mexican Revolution.* Chicago and London: University of Chicago Press, 1981.
Knight, Alan, *The Mexican Revolution.* Lincoln and London: University of Nebraska Press, 1986.
Richmond, Douglas W., *Venustiano Carranza's Nationalist Struggle, 1893–1920.* Lincoln and London: University of Nebraska Press, 1983.

—Douglas W. Richmond

CARRILLO PUERTO, ELVIA

c.1880–1965 • Politician and Feminist

Elvia Carrillo Puerto's public career owed much to her brother Felipe Carrillo Puerto, governor of Yucatán from 1922 to 1924, who played a decisive role in his younger sister's ideological education. Fervently anticlerical and staunch liberals, convinced of the need for social reforms to raise the living standards of the peasants, Elvia and Felipe shared many views on agrarian reform, rational education, women's suffrage, free love, contraception, and divorce.

Soon after she turned 20, Elvia's husband Vicente Pérez Mendiburo, whom she had married when she was barely 13, died. She had one son, Vicente Pérez Carrillo. A school-teacher specializing in domestic science, Elvia entered politics as a clandestine messenger for the forces opposing dictator Porfirio Díaz's government. After the Revolution that brought Francisco I. Madero to power, her political work in her home town of Motul consisted mainly of setting up peasant women's organizations.

Elvia's political rise mirrored that of her brother Felipe in the Partido Socialista Yucateco (PSY, or Yucatán Socialist Party). He was leader of the party from 1918 to 1921 and became state governor in 1922. While Felipe was leader of the PSY, Elvia founded the Liga Feminista Rita Gutiérrez de Cetina (Rita Gutiérrez de Cetina Feminist League), an organization that coordinated the work of feminist leagues in various parts of the state.

The high point of Elvia Carrillo Puerto's career was her election as deputy to Congress. At the end of 1923, the teacher from Motul took her seat in Congress with two other women, Raquel Dzib and Beatriz Peniche. As candidates for the PSY, they were the first women in Mexico ever to win seats in a legislative body. Women had gained the vote in Yucatán the previous year, and another woman, Rosa Torres, became president of Mérida council. These pioneering women deputies did not keep their seats long, however; they lost them a month later after Felipe Carrillo Puerto's government fell when he was assassinated by political enemies on January 3, 1924. When the PSY regained power later that same year, the women deputies were not reinstated. Elvia Carrillo Puerto then left the Yucatán Peninsula to live in San Luis Potosí.

As head of the Liga Feminista Rita Gutiérrez de Cetina, Elvia started educational programs for women, which included literacy, domestic science, hygiene, and child care. The Liga also organized campaigns to combat alcoholism, prostitution, and drugs. The activities of the Mérida Feminist League provoked strong reaction in conservative quarters. A particularly large scandal erupted when they distributed a pamphlet giving information about contraception, "Guide in the Home" by Margaret Sanger, and set up pre-natal clinics.

Free love and divorce were other controversial aspects of Elvia Carrillo Puerto's radicalism. Like her brother Felipe, she defended free love, in the sense of a voluntary union between man and woman, a spontaneous bond rather than a civil or religious contract, which could be dissolved quickly on the request of either party. This idea was included in the Divorce Law passed in Yucatán in March 1923.

In May of that same year, Elvia spoke in favor of free love, divorce, contraception, and sex education at the First Pan-American Feminist Congress in Mexico City. She also proposed organizing a countrywide network of feminist resistance leagues. Her radicalism and combative attitudes (she accused the women at the congress of being bourgeois, reactionary, and ignorant of peasant women's poverty) attracted the attention of the press in Mexico City, but she had little influence on the resolutions passed at the end of the congress. Nevertheless, she managed to get the congress to officially support birth control, and although they were not in favor of free love, they recommended that the insincerity and theatricality of weddings be avoided in order to dignify marriage.

The death of Felipe Carrillo Puerto began a new stage of Elvia's political career. After moving to San Luis Potosí, she became a candidate for state office in 1925. Women had gained the vote two years earlier, but it was restricted to literate women who did not belong to religious associations. Elvia endeavored to ensure that her *suplente* candidate (the person who would take her place if she was no longer able to hold office) was also a woman. She took no notice of local politicians who told her there was not a single woman in the whole of San Luis Potosí who was neither Catholic nor reactionary, and willing to be a candidate. Indignant, she publicly criticized those men whose limited liberalism had prevented them from sharing with their wives, daughters, and sisters their progressive and anticlerical views. Finally, after a thorough search, she found Hermila Zamarrón, who agreed to be her *suplente.*

Elvia Carrillo Puerto's campaign had the political and financial support of General Adalberto Tejeda, the secretary of the interior, but it was opposed by the governor of San Luis Potosí, Abel Cano, a declared enemy of women's suffrage. In the weeks leading up to the election, Elvia began even to fear for her life. She was the victim of an unsuccessful attack in the village of Guadalcazar by henchmen of the opposition candidate, who was the governor's choice.

The San Luis Potosí authorities recognized that Elvia Carrillo Puerto had won the largest number of votes in the election, but she never occupied the seat she had won. The Electoral College of the House of Deputies denied her victory by applying the 1918 Electoral Law, which said that being of the male sex was a prerequisite to enjoying full citizens' rights.

Elvia Carrillo Puerto retired from public life in 1938. She lived in Ribera de San Cosme, Mexico City, until her death on April 18, 1965. The death of the "Red Nun," as the newspapers called her during her most radical days, went almost unnoticed by the Mexico City press.

Select Bibliography

Bolio Ontevereiros, Edmundo, *De la Cuña al Parredon: Anecdotario Historico de la vida, muerte y gloria de Felipe Carrillo Puerto.* 2nd edition, Mérida, Yucatán: ZAMNA, 1973.

Macías, Ana, "Felipe Carrillo Puerto and Women's Liberation in Mexico." In *Latin America Women,* edited by Asución Lavrin. Westport, Connecticut: Greenwood Press, 1978.

—Gabriela Cano

CARRILLO PUERTO, FELIPE

1874–1924 • Governor

Felipe Carrillo Puerto was born in 1874 to a middle-class, mestizo family in the provincial Yucatecan city of Motul. Like Lázaro Cárdenas, Carrillo Puerto's father owned a pool hall, a center of male sociability that often was a seedbed of popular liberalism. Like most provincial *catrines* (Yucatecans of mainly European descent who followed Western cultural ways), Felipe learned Maya language and folkways as a child. Unlike most members of the Yucatecan bourgeoisie, he sympathized with the Maya peons on the henequen haciendas and openly challenged the political and economic dominance of the Yucatecan planter elite. As a young farmer and muleteer, Carrillo Puerto was jailed and at one point whipped for defending Maya peasants and peons. His attempts to organize a meat-selling cooperative to help fellow peddlers also led to legal conflicts with the local elite.

Between 1897 and 1914, he collaborated on a number of opposition campaigns waged by dissident members of the plantocracy. During one campaign, he was jailed for murder in self-defense during an assassination attempt, leading him to flee to Morelos and join the Zapatista army in 1914. There he earned the rank of colonel and acted as an agrarian engineer.

In 1915, Carrillo Puerto returned to Yucatán after a short stint as a stevedore in New Orleans. Upon returning home, he was briefly jailed by the Constitutionalist military governor Salvador Alvarado. But soon he was freed in order to organize peasants for Alvarado's party (Partido Socialista Obrero, or PSO) and to help peasants petition for land in his hometown of Motul. In March 1917, he became president of the party Alvarado founded, now known as the Partido Socialista Yucateco or PSY.

Carrillo Puerto's political star rose rapidly after the departure of Alvarado. In 1918, he served as president of the state legislature and interim governor for a month, passing a radical labor code and consolidating his hold over the PSY.

By 1919 he was the leading political figure in the state. His support for the presidential aspirations of Álvaro Obregón caused President Carranza to order federal forces to dismantle his party. Forced into exile in Mexico City for much of 1919 and early 1920, Carrillo Puerto forged connections with Plutarco Elías Calles and Luis Napoléon Morones, and served briefly in the ephemeral Latin American bureau of the Communist International. With the defeat of Carranza and with the backing of the Sonoran dynasty (Obregón and Calles), Carrillo Puerto returned home and rebuilt his political base, now known as the Partido Socialista del Sureste, or PSS. With the backing of the PSS, Carrillo Puerto won election first to the federal legislature from 1920 to 1922, and then to the governorship from 1922 to 1926.

As governor, Felipe Carrillo Puerto presided over one of the largest land reforms in Mexico, which returned non-henequen land seized from villages during the Porfiriato and as well as granting some federal land to about 34,000 peasants. Shortly before his death, Carrillo Puerto proposed an even more radical agrarian program that would have turned over abandoned henequen land to peasants. He also turned control of henequen export over to a state cooperative, thus preventing the largest producers and U.S. speculators from manipulating the sisal market.

While the Carrillista agrarian reform excluded peons, his administration improved their access to labor arbitration. Urban workers, on the other hand, clashed frequently with Carrillo Puerto over wage demands and his attempts to incorporate their independent urban unions into his Socialist Party.

Some of Carrillo Puerto's most radical initiatives came in the fields of social and cultural policy. He liberalized divorce law, though in the process he stripped women of some legal protection and never granted them equality before the law. An advocate of feminism, he supported the participation of women in the PSS and ran three women on the PSS congressional slate of 18 candidates.

Despite his radical reputation, Carrillo Puerto quietly ignored anticlerical legislation passed by Alvarado, instead emphasizing a Yucatecan *indigenismo* (Mayanism) and fabricating secular rites of socialism such as red baptism. To spread appreciation of the Maya past, his administration supported the restoration of the ruins at Uxmal and Chichen Itza, published pre-Columbian and colonial Maya documents, and opened the state archaeological museum.

Like Alvarado, Carrillo Puerto shared a zeal for education. He promoted rural schools for the children of peasants and peons, supported night schools for adults, and opened the state's first university.

While Carrillo Puerto hoped to transform Yucatán, he was economically hamstrung by the collapse of the henequen economy after World War I.

His administration and life was cut tragically short by the failed Adolfo de la Huerta coup against Obregón and Calles in December 1923. Mutinous federal troops stationed in the state jailed and court-martialed Carrillo Puerto. His execution on January 3, 1924, has been blamed on the intervention of Yucatecan landowners.

Carrillo Puerto's political ideology has been the subject of much argument by his contemporaries and by modern scholars alike. Because Carrillo Puerto never put down much of his ideology in writing, debate over it has centered on his political formation in his youth, his actions as governor, and his (relatively limited) correspondence. While Carrillo Puerto's ideology was a pastiche of various leftist and radical sources (including Benito Juárez's liberalism, anarchism, Zapatismo, and the ideas of the Rumanian-American socialist Roberto Haberman), his overriding goal was social justice and equality for poor, Maya-speaking peasants. Indeed, the scholar Gilbert Joseph argues convincingly that the lack of an ideological canon never limited don Felipe's popular appeal, and in fact allowed his party to communicate effectively its radical program to a largely illiterate, previously marginalized peasantry.

After his death, Carrillo Puerto was venerated in a secular cult sponsored by the Partido Socialista Sureste. President Calles blamed his "martyrdom" on the tools of capitalism and elevated him into the national Revolutionary pantheon.

Carrillo Puerto's short but influential political career has been gilded in Revolutionary hagiography and tarred by past and present Yucatecan conservatives. Few would deny, however, that Carrillo Puerto's regime completed the destruction of the Porfirian regime in Yucatán begun by Salvador Alvarado, politically mobilized large segments of the peasantry, and influenced later national state formation projects.

Select Bibliography

Bolio Ontevereiros, Edmundo, *De la Cuña al Parredon: Anecdotario Historico de la vida, muerte y gloria de Felipe Carrillo Puerto.* 2nd edition, Mérida, Yucatan: ZAMNA, 1973.

Joseph, Gilbert M., *Revolution from Without.* 2nd edition, Durham, North Carolina: Duke University Press, 1987.

Macías, Ana, "Felipe Carrillo Puerto and Women's Liberation in Mexico." In *Latin America Women,* edited by Asución Lavrin. Westport, Connecticut: Greenwood Press, 1978.

Paoli, Francisco J., and Enrique Montalvo, *El socialismo olvidado de Yucatán.* Mexico City: Siglo XXI, 1977.

Spenser, Daniela, "La Politica Economica del Socialismo en la Frontera Sur, 1918–1923." In *Sociedad, Estructura Agraria y Estado en Yucatan,* edited by Othón Baños Ramírez. Mérida: Ediciones de la Universidad Autónoma de Yucatán, 1990.

_____, "Workers Against Socialism? Reassessing the Role of Urban Labor in Yucatecan Revolutionary Politics." In *Land, Labor and Capital in Modern Yucatan: Essays in Regional History and Political Economy.* Tuscaloosa: University of Alabama Press, 1991.

—BEN FALLAW

CASA DE ESPAÑA

The Casa de España was founded on August 20, 1932, to provide a place for intellectuals and artists fleeing the Spanish Civil War to work and study. The establishment of the Casa de España was part of a more general policy of solidarity with the beleaguered Republican government in Spain. Virtually alone among the governments of the world, the government of Lázaro Cárdenas stood by the Spanish Republic in its struggle against the fascist forces of General Francisco Franco, selling arms to the Republican army, underwriting arms purchases from third parties, supporting the Republic in the League of Nations, providing food, shelter, and education for children orphaned during the Spanish Civil War, and providing asylum for Spanish refugees.

The Casa de España was the initiative of a group of Mexican intellectuals and politicians—among them Daniel Cosío Villegas, Alfonso Reyes, Narciso Bassols, and Lázaro Cárdenas himself—who admired the new currents in literature, philosophy, and social thought that had emerged in early-twentieth-century Spain. Indeed, the Casa was modeled on the Junta para Ampliación de Estudios e Investigaciones Científicas (Committee for the Extension of Scientific Research and Study) and its adjunct Centro de Estudios Históricos (Center for Historical Studies) in Madrid, which had helped foster the intellectual renaissance in the years preceding the Civil War. The first sponsors of the Casa included the Ministry of Hacienda (Treasury), the Ministry of Public Education, and the National Autonomous University of Mexico.

The first guests of the Casa de España were the jurist and philosopher Luis Recaséns Siches, the poet León Felipe Camino, and the poet, painter, and art historian José Moreno Villa, who were already in Mexico when the Casa was established; other Spanish scientists, artists, and intellectuals came throughout 1938 and 1939. Although the primary purpose of the Casa was to provide support for Spanish exiles, Mexicans also joined the Casa, including the writer Alfonso Reyes—who at one point had been exiled in Spain—the poet Enrique González Martínez, and the philosopher Antonio Caso. In 1939 Reyes was named president of the Casa de España.

Although the Mexican public by and large welcomed the exiles, there were key elements in Mexican society who were less than sanguine about the Cárdenas administration's policy of supporting the Republic. These conservative elements, including Franco supporters, Catholics, and enemies of Cárdenas, regarded the Spanish Republicans as anti-Catholic and Communist. Nonetheless, the exiles soon won over most Mexicans, organizing seminars in provincial cities, teaching courses in Mexican universities, and writing for the Fondo de Cultura Económica, the new publisher of high-quality, mass-market books founded by Daniel Cosío Villegas. Not all exiles arriving in Mexico were members of the intellectual and political elite, but the work of the Spanish artists, intellectuals, and professionals made it far easier for the Mexican public to accept the far larger numbers of Spanish refugees who were to arrive in the coming years.

The defeat of the Spanish Republic on April 1, 1939, brought a new flood of refugees to Mexico and new challenges for the Casa de España. The Casa simply did not have the funds to support all of the refugees, nor did their talents precisely match the Casa's mission. The Casa worked as a clearinghouse for Spanish exiles, working with the Spanish Cultural Council, which originally had been created by the Republican government, and the Institute for Intellectual Cooperation in Paris to recruit Spanish intellectuals exiled in France, particularly physicians, for academic posts in Mexico city and provincial universities; the Casa also supported the establishment of a chemistry laboratory at the National University. The largest number of refugees started arriving in June 1939, when 1,800 exiles disembarked from the ship *Sinaia*. Overwhelmed by the flood of new applicants, the Casa directed many of them to the National University, the Polytechnic Institute, hospitals, private corporations, and other institutions. Although conflicts among Republican leaders and the outbreak of World War II slowed the influx of Spanish refugees, they continued arriving until 1942. Between 20,000 and 40,000 Spanish exiles found refuge in Mexico.

As the Cárdenas administration came to a close, the leaders of the Casa de España sought new ways to ensure future financial and institutional support. On October 8, 1940, the Casa de España became the Colegio de México, opening doors to Mexican students and intellectuals and eventually becoming one of the leading universities in Latin America. Supported by the Ministry of Treasury, the National University, the Fondo de Cultura Económica, and the Bank of Mexico, the Colegio was able ensure both its intellectual continuity and its continued participation in the intellectual life of Mexico.

The Casa de España helped promote a new ethos of intellectual rigor and respect for creative work in Mexico. Reevaluating the historical roots of Mexico and Spain, the Casa helped foster a new awareness of Latin American and pan-Hispanic unity. The transformation of the Casa de España into the Colegio de México parallels the integration of the Spanish exile community into Mexican society. As Mexicans grew to accept the exiles and as the exiles were forced to abandon the dream of a triumphant return to a liberated Spain, the exile community played an increasingly important part in all parts of Mexican society. Even as the exile community became more Mexican, it helped reconcile Mexico to its Spanish roots and promote a new cosmopolitan vision of Mexico's place in the world.

Select Bibliography

Cincuenta años del exilio español en la UNAM. Mexico City: UNAM, 1991.

El exilio republicano español en México, 1939–1982. Mexico City: Salvat, 1982.

González y González, Luis, *Los dias del Presidente Cardenas.* Mexico City: Colegio de México, 1981.

Jackson, Gabriel, *La república españole y la guerra civil, 1931–1939.* Barcelona: Orbis, 1985.

Lida, Clara E., and José Antonio Matesanz, *La Casa de España en México.* Mexico City: Colegio de México, 1988.

_____, *El Colegio de México: una hazaña cultural, 1940–1962.* Mexico City: Colegio de México, 1990.

Martínez, Carlos, *Crónica de una emigración: La de los republicanos españoles.* Mexico City: Libro-Mex, 1959.

Medin, Tzvi, *Ideologia y praxis del cardenismo.* Mexico City: Siglo XXI, 1976.

Pla, Dolores, *Los niños de Morelia: Un estudio sobre los primeros refugiados españoles en México.* Mexico City: INAH, 1985.

—José Antonio Matesanz

CASA DEL OBRERO MUNDIAL

The Casa del Obrero Mundial, or House of the World Worker, emerged in Mexico City and became the most significant regional locus of worker organization during the military phase of the Mexican Revolution. Its origins and development were rooted in such factors as the lingering tradition of anarchism among rural and urban workers; the transformation of work and community in Mexico City in the three decades preceding the Revolution; and the material conditions, ideological effervescence, and political events of the Revolution itself.

The Casa del Obrero epitomized the tentative break with mutualism (the doctrine that individual and collective well-being is attainable only by mutual dependence) and government control of worker organizations that started with worker support for opposition presidential candidate Francisco Madero in 1910 and accelerated with the fall of Porfirio Díaz in 1911. Attempts by the government of President Madero after 1911 to consolidate and control support among workers through the creation of a department of labor and an officially sponsored labor organization, the Gran Liga Obrera, proved insufficient to capture the loyalty of the increasingly independent and articulate working-class leaders and organizations that had emerged by 1912.

The leadership and cultural orientation for much of worker organization and the definitive move away from mutualism began with the Graphic Arts Confederation, formed in 1911, and soon passed to the anarchist-inspired Casa del Obrero, formed in September 1912 as a "center of doctrinaire dissemination of advanced ideas." Founding and early members were made up of two groups. The most important was a variety of skilled trade workers and their "mutualist" or "resistance" societies, including the associations of stonecutters, tailors, and coach drivers. Among their leaders were the tailor Luis Méndez and the mechanic and metal worker Jacinto Huitrón, both of whom had passed briefly through the Socialist Workers' Party. Although a number of Spanish anarchist workers were important organizational catalysts and frequent speakers at Casa del Obrero cultural events, they were neither as numerous nor as important in the leadership of the Casa del Obrero as its critics at the time and some later historians have claimed. Far from being a foreign transplant, anarchism had deep roots in the Mexican countryside, craft shops, and factories.

The second group of early members of the Casa del Obrero Mundial was a handful of middle-class radicals and intellectuals, including the journalist Rafael Pérez Taylor, the congressional deputies Heriberto Jara and Serápio Rendón, and Antonio Díaz Soto y Gama. Many of these individuals had passed briefly through the Mexican Liberal Party of the Flores Magón brothers as well as the more moderate Liberal

Party before growing disillusioned with Maderista politics. While lacking in any clear union base, these intellectuals were readily incorporated and central to public activities and cultural events of the Casa del Obrero. Their significant intellectual influence was reinforced by the financial difficulties of the component unions (with the exceptions of the printers and electricians' unions), which often made it necessary for middle-class members such as Díaz Soto y Gama, or sympathetic members of Congress such as Heriberto Jara, to help sustain the Casa del Obrero with personal funds.

It is worth noting that the considerable influence of these intellectuals depended very much on their daily participation in the workings of the Casa del Obrero. Even a radical intellectual of the stature of Díaz Soto y Gama maintained little influence in the Casa del Obrero after he joined the Zapatistas in Morelos in early 1914. Similarly, in spite of the respect many Casa members felt for the anarchist Flores Magón brothers, their revolutionary rhetoric from distant Los Angeles or U.S. jails was resented by the working-class leadership of the Casa del Obrero and had little effect on decisions within the organization and its component unions.

The Casa del Obrero as a whole had a dual role. The first was as a cultural organization, instituting night classes to develop vocational skills and self-improvement, holding plays and poetry readings, and giving general exhortations to sobriety and discipline in work and family life. They fulfilled the pragmatic desire of workers to improve their skills as well as their intellect. For example, in June 1913, the Casa del Obrero offered classes in cloth cutting, line drawing and calligraphy, clay modeling, geometry, grammar, bookbinding, geography, mechanics, physics, and the French and English languages. Drawing on the teachings of the Catalan anarchist educator Ferrari Guardia, founders of the Casa del Obrero also sought to develop a working-class consciousness and educate members in ways that identified working-class traditions and interests as unique and central to the organization of society. The texts they chose were primarily the writings of radical European thinkers and the histories of other working-class movements such as the 1870 Paris Commune. At the same time, the Casa del Obrero appealed to Mexican nationalism by celebrating new Mexican working-class heroes and symbols ("the martyrs of Rio Blanco") and denouncing the hold of foreign capital and foremen in the urban economy.

The other role of the Casa del Obrero was as a catalyst for the formation of unions and the implementation of direct action, generally through strikes, as well as a series of public demonstrations and protests that turned the traditional social hierarchy of public space in the capital city upside down during the years of the Revolution. Within a year of its founding, the Casa del Obrero moved away from emphasis on education and moral regeneration to criticize more directly the terms of labor and the political sources of inequality. Through both roles, the Casa del Obrero played a fundamental role in nursing the transition from mutualism to syndicalism, while maintaining links across work and community.

The Casa del Obrero's efforts were bolstered by the ambivalence of the Madero government toward labor reforms and even more so by the farce of electoral democracy under Madero's successor, the dictator Victoriano Huerta. The transition from mutualism to resistance also was aided by the material conditions brought on by the military fighting of the Revolution as well as its ideological currents. The fiscal policies of Huerta, and after his defeat in August 1914, the multiple currencies and disruption of the economy brought by each successive occupation of Mexico City during the Revolution, brought an inflationary cycle that decimated the funds of mutual aid societies for the compensation of unemployment, sickness, and death at the very time members lost their jobs, or faced sickness or death from the hunger and disease that frequented the city from 1914 to 1918. These conditions encouraged a shift in strategy for many organizations toward formal union structures and more open confrontation with employers or direct demands on the government, often under the leadership of the Casa del Obrero.

Within two years of its founding, many of the principal workers' groups in the city—teachers, carpenters, shoemakers, printers, bricklayers, boilermakers, and others—had joined the Casa del Obrero, with the Casa del Obrero leadership continually attempting to bring less skilled workers into its ranks. The terms of "resistance" were debated continually within workers' organizations and the Casa del Obrero itself. Workers within a particular sector might organize in a number of ways: retreating toward mutualism, organizing industrial unions, or forming elite trade unions that protected the strategic position of the most skilled workers. All three types of organizations coexisted to some extent within the Casa del Obrero, in spite of the clear radical leanings of the leadership. Perhaps emblematic if not typical was an affiliated local textile workers' union that reorganized in September 1914, allowing half of the weekly dues of 20 centavos to go for "the class struggle" and the other half to a mutual aid fund.

Two divergent strike strategies within the Casa del Obrero emerged, one a social strategy that sought to press demands against employers, free of the intervention of government or military officials, and another, political strategy that relied on appeals to government authorities to support their demands and strikes. Whereas the unions of more skilled trades and workers in the most strategic sectors of the economy such as printers and electricians were most likely to follow the social strategy, most unions and the Casa del Obrero as a whole wavered between direct confrontations with employers and political appeals to authorities, depending on the type of demand, the course of a particular conflict, and the relative sympathy of particular government and military officials.

An important moment of consolidation for the leadership role of the Casa del Obrero among the working class of the city was its organization in 1913 of the capital's first public May Day, celebrated in defiance of the orders of General Huerta, who had recently deposed Francisco Madero. On May 1, work in the city practically stopped, as around 20,000 workers marched through the city center behind red and black flags and a huge banner declaring, "The Casa del Obrero Mundial Demands the Eight-Hour Day and Sundays Off." Among the marchers were most of the key workers groups in the capital, and both resistance societies and a wide array of mutualist societies marched side by side. In the months after the Casa del Obrero celebrated the first May Day in Mexico City, the majority of the affiliated workers' groups took on the name and many of the functions of syndicalist unions, commonly invoking "the class struggle and direct action," and the Casa del Obrero itself added the adjective *mundial* (of the world) to its name. A year later, on May 1, 1914, the Casa del Obrero organized a formal federation, the General Federation of Workers, just weeks before General Huerta moved to close down their organization.

After Huerta's defeat in August 1914, a new group of Revolutionary military leaders from the Constitutionalist army briefly held power in Mexico City, and the Casa del Obrero reopened and resumed its attempt to organize the city's workers across gender and skill lines. In the space of months, unions for streetcar workers, seamstresses, female cigarette workers, electrical workers, and many others were formed, achieving a reported membership of 52,000 by the time of the Convention-Constitutionalist split at the end of 1914. This latest phase of organization included the creation of industrial unions such as those of the streetcar workers and the electricians, based primarily in the Anglo-Canadian electrical company. These powerful unions would play an ever greater role in leading strikes and asserting themselves within the Casa del Obrero.

Working-class unity soon dissolved, however. The presence of powerful industrial unions in many ways challenged the recent consolidation of the *obreros cultos* (skilled labor), particularly the printers, in the leadership of the Casa del Obrero. Another problematic division occurred over the intimacy of relations between some Casa del Obrero members and unions and the leaders of the occupying Constitutionalist army, in particular charismatic and reforming figures like former Casa-member Heriberto Jara, the painter Dr. Atl (Gerardo Murillo), and General Álvaro Obregón. These Constitutionalists shared with workers an apparent hostility to foreign capital and management prominent in many industries in the city and were often willing to impose reforms against the worst employer abuses and work conditions.

As unemployment and material conditions in the city worsened in the first months of 1915, and after a brief interlude of rather ineffectual control of the city by the Convention forces of Francisco "Pancho" Villa and Emiliano Zapata, the Casa del Obrero split in February 1915 over their professed neutrality in the national military struggle between the two Revolutionary factions. In what remains one of the most controversial and least understood events in modern Mexican working-class history, the majority of the leadership of the Casa del Obrero agreed to join the Constitutionalist forces in their stronghold in Veracruz, organizing approximately 5,000 employed and unemployed workers into the historic Red Battalions to fight against the Convention troops of Villa and Zapata. A minority of the Casa del Obrero leadership opposed the pact, and a majority of its former members remained in Mexico City. Under the guidance of the electricians and restaurant workers, remaining unions continued an intense cycle of strikes and maintained fairly good relations with the Convention government that occupied Mexico City through July 1915.

Participation in the Red Battalions, as provided in the terms of the pact, gave the Casa del Obrero opportunities to organize workers in provincial cities and gained it for the first time a truly national extension; at the same time, its organizers almost immediately came into conflict with the Constitutionalists, especially First Chief Venustiano Carranza, over their determination to organize workers in provincial cities such as Veracruz, Orizaba, and Tampico, and lead them in strikes to improve the terms of work. By contrast, Carranza and his department of labor were determined to mediate directly between workers and employers, preventing disruptive strikes and what they increasingly referred to as "the tyranny of the laboring classes."

The tension between these fundamentally different ideas about the role of unions were to burst into open conflict as the period of worst fighting came to a close during the summer of 1915, and the Red Battalions were demobilized and returned to Mexico City. The returning Casa members soon reconciled with those unions that had remained in Mexico City, and the creation of a new formal federation, the Federation of Unions of the Federal District (FSODF), acknowledged the power and prestige of the Electricians' Union and further strengthened the union movement in the city. Within months the uneasy alliance between the Casa del Obrero and the Constitutionalist leadership was all but broken, as the unions of the Casa del Obrero and the FSODF expanded their membership (to a claimed total of 90,000) and dominance over other working-class organizations, repeatedly organized public demonstrations for affordable food and housing, and went on strike to demand union recognition and wage increases in keeping with an inflation driven by food scarcity and multiple paper currencies. The period from August 1915 to August 1916 witnessed the greatest unity, militancy, and independence for the working-class movement in Mexico City and other areas of Mexico during the decade of the Revolution. In May 1916, the Casa del Obrero and the FSODF called a general strike that closed down the city for a few hours before the municipal military commander brought all parties to negotiate what would prove to be a short-lived solution. In July, as the value of the latest Constitutionalist paper currency dwindled, various unions again made a series of demands to employers, and indirectly to military officials, including payment of all wages in gold. On July 29, after neither business nor the provisional authorities had responded, the Casa del Obrero and FSODF called a second, surprise general strike, which brought the city to a standstill for three days. First Chief Carranza responded by jailing the strike committee, declaring martial law, and permanently dissolving the Casa del Obrero Mundial in the name of the public good. Carranza's repression not only extended the life of his nearly worthless currency and imposed a harsh social peace, but also assured that members of the most important labor organization to emerge during the Revolution would play no role in drafting labor rights provisions at the Constitutional Convention that convened in late 1916.

Although the Casa del Obrero was shut down, the chastened FSODF survived, and many of its leaders and constituent unions eventually formed the core of the powerful government-supported federation of the 1920s, the Regional Confederation of Mexican Workers. The independent unionism that had distinguished the Casa del Obrero throughout most of its existence became, if not a thing of the past, at least an important minority current in the Mexican labor movement of the 1920s, continued by a few national and Mexico City unions such as that of the railway workers and electricians, and others regrouped in the anarchist General Federation of Workers (CGT).

Select Bibliography

Araiza, Luis, *Historia del movimiento obrero mexicano*. 2nd edition, 4 vols., Mexico City: Ediciones de la Casa Mundial, 1975.

Carr, Barry, *El movimiento obrero y la política en México, 1910–1929*. 2 vols., Mexico City: Era, 1976.

_____, "The Casa del Obrero Mundial, Constitutionalism and the Pact of February 1915." In *El Trabajo y los trabajadores en la historia de México,* edited by Elsa Frost. Mexico City: Colegio de México, and Tucson: University of Arizona Press, 1979.

Hart, John M., *Anarchism and the Mexican Working Class, 1860–1931*. Austin: University of Texas Press, 1978.

_____, "The Urban Working Class and the Mexican Revolution: The Case of the Casa del Obrero Mundial." *Hispanic American Historical Review* 58 (1978).

Huitrón, Jacinto, *Orígenes e historia del movimiento obrero en México*. 3rd edition, Mexico City: Editores Mexicanos Unidos, 1984.

Salazar, Rosendo, and José Escobedo, *Las Pugnas de la Gleba*. Mexico City: Editorial Avante, 1922.

—JOHN LEAR

CASO, ANTONIO

1883–1946 • Educator and Intellectual

A gifted student at the positivist-dominated Escuela Preparatoria Nacional, Antonio Caso studied under the famous intellectuals Ezekiel Chávez and Justo Sierra. Collectively known as the Científicos, this earlier generation of liberal-positivists stressed political order and economic progress as the formula for Mexico's future success; they drew upon theories of August Comte and Herbert Spencer to construct the intellectual support for Porfirio Díaz's long tenure in office. Antonio Caso and others of his generation rejected positivism along with the Porfiriato, however, and urged greater national control over the economy and cultural life of Mexico. With José Vasconcelos, Pedro Henríquez Ureña, and Alfonso Reyes, Caso founded the Ateneo de Juventud, a discussion and study group dedicated to the propagation of the new generation's ideals. The members of the Ateneo opposed positivism as an imported ideology that appealed to man's basest instincts and discounted his generous, human impulses. In place of a scientific materialist society, Caso and the Ateneo suggested that each nation had its own unique identity that deserved cultivation and respect. For them, Mexicans were capable of a creative, dynamic, and heroic national life based upon selflessness and Christian charity.

Antonio Caso, as a historian and social philosopher, quite naturally took a great interest in the education of Mexican youth. After the tumult of the Mexican Revolution, as others of his generation and intellectual inclination assumed power, Caso took a leading role in the country's educational system. He held concurrent professorships in philosophy at Universidad Nacional Autónoma de México and at the law school, and was rector at the Universidad Nacional. He always viewed education as an art, as an active and engaging search for truth rather than a dull accumulation of facts simply to be memorized. In the 1930s, Caso lost his job when he spoke out against the presidential decree that mandated schools to teach socialism; Caso was a great proponent of academic freedom and opposed all grand theoretical systems equally, whether political (Marxism), religious (Catholicism), or philosophical (positivism). Caso wanted Mexicans to be free to think for themselves, to make their own choices in thought and action according to the twin goals of moral progress and individual self-perfection. His trust in Mexicans' inherent preference for goodness and in the national maturity must have made Caso a popular professor indeed; his dismissal prompted such an outcry from the students and faculty that Caso won reinstatement.

As a philosopher of national identity, Caso incorporated the work of his younger brother, noted anthropologist Alfonso Caso, to reconcile Mexico's many pasts. He urged Mexicans to move beyond resentments based on class, race, political affiliation, and social caste in order to forge a "cosmic race"; through the comingling of criollos, mestizos, and Indians, Mexico had a unique opportunity to create a vibrant, creative culture that allowed each member to progress toward self-perfection. Society was a "moral union of men," and the state existed to protect the rights of its citizens in their quest.

Besides his educational projects, Antonio Caso also held several diplomatic posts during an ambassadorial career that took him to Brazil, Argentina, Chile, Peru, and Uruguay. He participated in several spirited debates in Mexico's popular press, most notably over freedom of speech in the 1930s. His work is characterized by three main goals: a defense of academic freedom, a rejection of the extremes of both Marxism and materialism, and the focus on Christian humanism as an alternative path to human development.

Among the major works of Antonio Caso are *La existencia como economía y como caridad* (1916), *La existencia como economía, como disinterés y como caridad* (1919), *El concepto universal y la filosofía de los valores* (1933), *La persona humana y el estado totalitario* (1941), and *El peligro del hombre* (1942).

Select Bibliography

Garrido, Luís, *Antonio Caso, una vida profunda*. Mexico City: Universidad Nacional Autónoma de México, 1961.

Haddox, John Herbert, *Antonio Caso, Philosopher of Mexico*. Austin: University of Texas Press, 1971.

Krauze de Kolteniuk, Rosa, *La filosofía de Antonio Caso*. Mexico City: UNAM, 1961.

Sutton, Delia L., *Antonio Caso y su impacto cultural en el intelectomexicano*. Mexico City: Secretaria de Hacienda y Crédito Público, 1971.

—KAREN RACINE

CASTAÑEDA, ALFREDO

1938– • Painter

Related to a continuing Latin American interest in Surrealism, the meticulously painted and often autobiographical images of Alfredo Castañeda stand alone in their relationship to the mainstream of Mexican art in the last quarter of the twentieth century.

Alfredo Castañeda was born in Mexico City, February 18, 1938. When only 12 he began to study drawing and painting seriously with his maternal uncle, the painter J. Ignacio Iturbide. Deciding, however, to become an architect, he entered the Universidad Nacional Autónoma de México in 1956. While he visited France, Spain, and Portugal in 1959, his interest in painting was rekindled, and when he returned to Mexico, his time was divided between painting and architecture. Although he finished his architecture degree in 1964, he increasingly focused on painting after marrying Hortensia de la Barrera in 1967. Castañeda's first one-person exhibition was in 1969 at the prestigious Galería de Arte Mexicano in Mexico City. Images such as *La madre de la mariposas* (Mother of the Butterflies, 1969) relate his early works to the poetic metaphors typically found in the magic realist works of Latin American authors Carlos Fuentes of Mexico and Gabriel García Márquez of Colombia. *Bipartición de un sabio pensador* (Bipartition of a Wise Thinker, 1969) and *Proceso de autoconocimiento* (Process of Self-Knowledge, 1970) reflect his continuing conflict between being an architect or a painter. In 1971 Castañeda finally decided to devote himself entirely to painting and was asked to be one of the Mexican painters in the Spirit of Surrealism exhibition held in Cologne, Germany. A 1972 showing of recent works at the Museo de Arte Moderno in Mexico City established his importance as one the leading Mexican artists of the 1970s. In 1981 Castañeda moved to Cuernevaca, where he continues to produce contextually provocative images widely exhibited throughout the Americas and Europe.

Castañeda frequently includes personal memorabilia in his work, and he occasionally employs Mexican ethnic icons such as a heart *milagro*. He is not, however, a part of the Neo-Mexicanist movement of the 1980s. His non-expressionistic imagery has a cerebral coolness found in the works of René-François-Ghislain Magritte and Remedios Varo—technique, color, space, forms, and content are all precisely controlled. He shares with other Hispanic artists a preference for irony, paradox, and dualism. Titles such as *A veces compredemos algo* (At Times We Understand Something,1986) are as suggestive as the images themselves. Using enigmatic contradictions and fragmented imagery, Castañeda, like the Argentinian writer Jorge Luis Borges, addresses the relativity of meaning and disjunctures in the time-space continuum. The unsettling layered meanings of painted autobiographical dreams and reveries are inquisitive rather than declarative.

Castañeda's multiple and often fragmented self-images observe the spectator, thereby implicating artist and viewer in the collective unconscious.

—ROBERT J. LOESCHER

CASTELLANOS, ROSARIO
1925–1974 • Writer

"It isn't enough to discover who we are. We have to invent ourselves," a character shouted in a radical play written by Rosario Castellanos in 1973. The novels, short stories, poems, essays, and plays that Castellanos wrote between 1948 and 1974 respond to her lifelong inquiry into women's place in creativity and culture in Mexico. Today we continue to read her as a writer and thinker who was decades ahead of her time, not only in terms of pioneering the discussion of relationships among gender, race, and class in her writing by and about women in Mexico, but particularly in terms of her keen insights into the conflicts between indigenous peoples and landholding families in her native region of Chiapas.

Castellanos was born on May 25, 1925, and grew up on her family's ranch in Comitán, Chiapas, near the border with Guatemala. She was educated in Mexico City, where she graduated from the National Autonomous University with a master's degree in Philosophy in 1955. There she became part of the group of young Mexican and Central American writers known as the Generation of 1950. From 1951 to 1957 Castellanos worked in cultural programs for the National Indigenist Institute in San Cristóbal de las Casas, Chiapas, and traveled throughout the region. Those experiences are reflected in her writing, which explores two areas of experience long overlooked in Mexican letters: the critique of racial and cultural oppression of indigenous peoples in Chiapas and the status of women in provincial and urban Mexico. Her fiction focuses on women's struggles to assert their authentic selves during the period of rapid change that followed the land reforms of the Lázaro Cárdenas administration in 1941 and the rapid industrialization and urbanization of Mexico.

Her first novel, *Balún Canán* (1957), winner of the Mexican Critics' Prize for best novel in 1957 and the Chiapas Prize in 1958, drew on her memories of Tzotzil world and myth as seen through the eyes of a solitary child. The short stories in *Ciudad Real* (1960) examine conflicts between Indians, mestizos, and landholders in terms of power relationships between the conquerors and the colonized. Her second novel, *Oficio de tinieblas* (1962), which used the

historical events of a Chamula Indian uprising in San Cristóbal in 1867 to recast the struggle of a woman leader against modern colonialism, is still considered to be one of the very best examples of neoindigenist writing in Latin America, marking a break with lurid representations of indigenist cultures as exotic worlds populated by poetic victims. The stories in *Los convidados de agosto* (1964) focused on women's relationships with each other within the patriarchal society of provincial Chiapas. *Album de familia* (1971) shifted its attention to the alienation of women in modern Mexico City who struggle to develop professional vocations. For example, "Lección de Cocina" uses the metaphor of a cookbook and a cooking lesson to satirize middle-class marriage in Mexico. In her play *El eterno femenino: farsa,* published posthumously in 1975 and staged in 1976, ironic humor demolished the myths and stereotypes that have oppressed women in Mexico for centuries.

From 1960 to 1974, Castellanos wrote hundreds of short chronicles for *Excelsior, Novedades, ¡Siempre!* and other Mexican periodicals, which have been partly collected in *Juicios sumarios* (1966), *Mujer que sabe latín* (1973), *El uso de la palabra* (1974), and *El mar y sus pescaditos* (1975). Her reading of Simone de Beauvoir, Simone Weil, and Virginia Woolf inspired her to explore the cultural myths of la Malinche, the Virgin of Guadalupe, and Sor Juana. These archetypal figures provided Castellanos with a rich cluster of metaphors to explore gender, sexuality, and inequality in Mexico throughout all her writing.

Poesía no eres tú (1972) collected the twelve books of poetry that Castellanos had written since 1948. In *Mujer que sabe latín* she describes "the cardinal points" of her verse as "humor, solemn meditation and contact with my carnal and historical roots." "I am a wide patio, a great open house: a memory," shouts the female speaker of "Toma de Conciencia." Yet her concept of otherness transcends gender, becoming the passage to creativity itself. In "Poesía no eres tú" she writes, "The other. With the other, humanity, dialogue, poetry, begin." "Hablando de Gabriel" considered pregnancy in terms of a changing relationship between body, self and other. Many poems and essays examined how language or silence shut women out of power structures, a decade before U.S. and French feminists began discussing these issues. "We have to find another language, we have to find another starting point," she wrote in 1973 in her essay on "El lenguaje como instrumento de dominación." After contemplating female characters and writers whose existence led to suicide, silence, and self-denial, her poem, "Meditación en el umbral" searched for "another way" of living and writing for women that was beyond madness, muteness, or penance. "Another way to be human and free. Another way to be." In 1995 her letters to her former husband, Ricardo Guerra, were published in *Cartas a Ricardo,* an intimate chronicle of that anguished relationship.

From 1960 to 1970 Castellanos was press and information director for the National University of Mexico, where she also held a chair of Comparative Literature. In 1971 President Luis Echeverría Álvarez named her Mexican ambassador to Israel, where she became a popular diplomat and occasionally taught at Hebrew University in Jerusalem. On August 7, 1974, at age 49, she was electrocuted in her home in Tel Aviv, leaving an only son, Gabriel Guerra Castellanos. Mexico paid tribute to her at a state funeral in Mexico City, where she is buried.

Select Bibliography

Ahern, Maureen, editor and translator, *A Rosario Castellanos Reader.* Austin: University of Texas Press, 1988.

_____, and Mary Seale Vásquez, *Homenaje a Rosario Castellanos.* Valencia: Albatros-Hispanófila, 1980.

O'Connell, Joanna, *Prospero's Daughter: The Prose of Rosario Castellanos.* Austin: University of Texas Press, 1995.

Schwartz, Perla, *Rosario Castellanos: Mujer que supo latín.* Mexico City: Katún, 1984.

—MAUREEN AHERN

CASTE WAR OF YUCATÁN

Few episodes in Mexican history were as dramatic as Yucatán's Caste War. The largest and most successful rural rebellion in nineteenth-century Mexico, the Caste War began in July 1847, when Maya peasants rose up against local authorities. Rebels conquered over half the Yucatán Peninsula by the following May, only to be pushed back to the eastern rain forests. The rebellion decimated Yucatecan society. The provincial criollo (Spanish-descended, American-born) elites withdrew to the north and west, where they dedicated themselves to the lucrative henequen industry. Maya rebels carved out an independent state in eastern Yucatán and constructed a new religion based on the worship of a speaking cross. Hostilities between the two worlds flared for decades. More than any other event, the Caste War defined southeast Mexico.

Origins

The lurid mythology surrounding the Caste War of Yucatán obscures its real origins. Far from being the loin-cloth clad *huits* who populate much of the historical literature, the Yucatecan Maya had played an active role in the peninsula's economy and political struggles in the decades preceding the Caste War. Although subsistence farming remained the bedrock of the peasant economy, Mayas gradually had entered the market economy as wage earners and petty entrepreneurs, and actively defended their interests through lawsuits and other forms of resistance. Maya peasants depended on patronage ties outside of the immediate community. Prominent Mayas shared the ambitions of local criollos,

while certain marginal criollos and mestizos understood the customs, language, and ambitions of rural Mayas. Intra-elite conflicts mobilized the Maya peasantry in what amounted to dress rehearsals for the Caste War itself.

Isolated from central Mexico, Yucatán had remained a backwater throughout the colonial period. Even as a boom in the region's agricultural economy in the mid–eighteenth century brought new prosperity to the region's criollo elite, Yucatecans maintained a sense of isolation from Mexico. After Mexico achieved independence in 1821, Yucatecans continued to govern their own affairs, and in 1839 the caudillo (local strongman) Santiago Imán launched a revolt that formally separated Yucatán from Mexico. Although Imán mobilized peasants around the issue of tax abolition, his revolt ignited almost millenarian expectations among the Maya peasantry. Moreover, Imán's triumph sparked a cycle of internecine violence as everyone from wealthy Mérida planters to village peasants and mestizos struggled for power. By 1847 Maya peasants from throughout the peninsula had taken part in two wars against pro-Mexican centralists, as well as innumerable local revolts.

Even as many Maya entered into cross-ethnic alliances, however, other factors had heightened interethnic tensions. Mayas chaffed under forced military conscription, heavy tax burdens, and excessive moral scrutiny by the Catholic church. Although some Maya entrepreneurs were able to benefit, a boom in the agricultural economy of Yucatán had a devastating effect on many communities. In the two decades preceding the outbreak of the Caste War in 1847, conflicts over land and other resources had become desperate: the Maya population had been growing steadily for over a century, non-Mayas were flooding the countryside, and criollo elites privatized large amounts of national land previously available to peasant cultivators.

The region's network of social mediators also had begun to break down. Although Maya communities still governed themselves through the *pueblos de indios* instituted during the colonial period, they scarcely existed in isolation. Maya elites were bound to their communities by language, culture, and kinship, but they were also part of a complex system of middlemen and cultural brokers who negotiated Yucatán's rural tranquillity. During the early national period privileged Mayas, particularly the *batabs* (village headmen or caciques), were active in local politics and often became relatively affluent; by the 1830 and 1840s, however, their situation had become increasingly untenable. By disrupting the rural tax system, criollo caudillos disrupted an important key to the batabs' livelihood, and resignations became ever more frequent. Moreover, criollos often dragged Maya elites into their own political quarrels, exposing them to a level of political violence that they had not experienced since the Conquest. The crisis of the Maya elites went beyond their local communities. It disrupted the entire social fabric of rural Yucatán.

Far from being isolated primitives, then, Maya peasants were part of a complex series of social, political, and economic networks. Indeed, the villages of eastern Yucatán that formed the backbone of the Caste War were bound together by a commercial network linked to the British colony of Belize, trading local commodities for sugar, staple foods, distilled alcohol, and contraband (including arms). As the people of these communities came to know each other, they developed a regional identity that set them apart from the other subregions of the peninsula dominated by Mérida and Campeche. Most of the Caste War's soldiers and virtually all of its leaders came from a single 30-mile (50-kilometer) string of villages, and the early stages of the rebellion drew in a number of whites, mestizos, and other non-Mayas from this region as well.

The War to 1863

The Caste War erupted in the early morning hours of July 30, 1847. Some days earlier, criollos had gotten wind of a conspiracy among the village leaders in the aforementioned string of communities. They executed one of these—Manuel Antonio Ay—and immediately began a roundup of purported accomplices. Chief among these were Jacinto Pat and Cecilio Chi, the *batabs* of villages along the contraband trade lines. But would-be insurgents were now ready. Chi raided his home village of Tepich, killing the non-Mayas and thus sparking the war. Thereafter, Chi's forces dominated in the north, while Pat, a prosperous landowner and distiller, dominated southern insurgents and maintained access to the Belizean arms merchants. By March 1848 they controlled approximately half of the peninsula.

Complex forces conditioned the fortunes of the war. On one hand, the rebels suffered all the weaknesses of peasant revolts. Perhaps the most important of these were the rebels' ill-defined aims. Despite their public rhetoric of exterminating *"españoles,"* the leaders had far more limited and specific goals. From the beginning, a series of abortive peace negotiations focused on tax relief, with land, debt, and the curtailment of administrative abuses as related issues. Rebels also demanded that the execution of criollo caudillos who apparently had betrayed their trust. By spring 1848 it became clear that the rebels could not achieve these goals under the current political arrangement, and their goals shifted toward complete political independence.

Also problematic were the rebels' inadequate arms and supplies, poorly trained forces, and general lack of cohesion. Although the rebels obtained some materials from Belizean merchants, they often had to make do with improvised munitions. In place of lead bullets, many used small, sharpened sticks known as *palenquetas;* others relied on the trusty machete. Rebels repeatedly had access to sophisticated weapons such as cannon and mortars, but for various reasons failed to take advantage of them. There was no single Maya army, but rather a loose confederation of bands under the command of their own caudillos, each profoundly jealous of the others. Discipline remained scant. These factors ultimately caused the revolt to break down into feuds and intrigues, particularly when the rebellion's momentum stalled and Maya peasants returned home to complete their spring plantings.

On the other hand, the criollo elites suffered their own problems. The rebellion initially panicked them into a retreat that left the field open to rebel advances. But the situation was never as dire as accounts have suggested. The rebels had overextended themselves long before reaching the apogee of their conquests. Campeche in particular was impregnable, and throughout early 1848 arms and supplies continued to pour into the Yucatecan ports from Havana. In mid-1848 the army took the offensive. At the same time Yucatecans rejoined the Mexican Republic, which sent General Manuel Micheltorena to organize a massive counterinsurgency; his campaign proved effective but highly expensive, and in May 1851 he ceded command to General Rómulo Díaz de la Vega, who operated by more flexible methods. By 1853 the Yucatecan government had retaken the bulk of its lost territory.

The rebels were now desperate. They suffered crippling shortages of arms, salt, meat, and even simple clothing. Ambitious subordinates assassinated the original caudillos and assumed command. Disappointed by reality, the caste warriors retreated to the supernatural, rallying around the commands of a Speaking Cross, a device that, although patently controlled by the generals, nonetheless addressed deep-seated concerns and symbols of the rural folk. Rebels now became *cruzob* (cross people) who obeyed their oracle's call for a war without compromise. The remote settlement of Chan Santa Cruz (Little Holy Cross) became their capital.

Fortune smiled on the *cruzob*. In 1853 Yucatán's criollo elite embarked on a decade of coups, revolts, and civil wars as various factions—partly political, partly military—vied for supremacy. Campeche split off as a separate state in 1858. Yucatán's bloody factionalism owed partly to the region's poverty (much of the struggle revolved around control of two scant commodities: customs receipts and political patronage). In part it stemmed from the political instability of Mexico itself in the 1850s; and in part it reflected tensions and havoc generated by the war itself. These internecine conflicts erupted just as rebel fortunes had reached their nadir, and they gave new authority to the Speaking Cross. The *cruzob* now regrouped under a previously unknown leader, Venancio Puc, an iron-willed revolutionary consolidator in the mold of Joseph Stalin. Ruling in concert with a junta of generals, Puc imposed severe discipline on the rebels. He maximized the cult of the Speaking Cross, centralized the partition of spoils, declared his own monopoly on distilling alcohol, expanded trade with Belize, and established rents on farming and logging within *cruzob* territory. In 1857 Puc launched a renewed offensive that culminated in the capture of Bacalar in February of the following year. The Cross now controlled the entire east coast from Tulum to the Belize border. A related policy of intermittent raids helped to intimidate and fragment the Yucatecans. Puc's creation was a harsh militarized society, but it was strong enough to survive into the twentieth century.

Aftermath and Reorganization

The war wrought economic havoc on Yucatán. Whole regions of commercial agriculture collapsed for years. The peninsula's sugar industry recuperated, only to perish under competition from the increasingly mechanized sugar giant, Cuba. Until the henequen boom of the 1870s, Yucatecan estate owners had to content themselves with supplying grain and cattle products to Havana. Moreover, estate owners were profoundly ambivalent toward the war itself. Eager for an army victory, they also used all means in their power to avoid furnishing men and resources for the effort. Prominent locals resented the intrusion of the politically powerful military officers, and the struggle between war polity and municipal society remained a defining feature of the 1850s and 1860s.

Another consequence of the Caste War was the relocation of peoples. From a prewar high of 500,000 to 600,000, the population declined to some 300,000 by 1850. An undetermined number perished, less from battle than from the scarcities and disease that came in its wake. In 1853, for example, a cholera epidemic tore through towns and *ranchos* alike. But if many died, the majority simply changed address. Refugees of all races fled outward to Tabasco, to northern Guatemala, and to the sparsely populated islands of Yucatán's eastern coast. The most important exile community took shape in northern Belize. Here, the survivors from Yucatán's sugar belt reconstructed their old lives as property owners, cultivators, and merchants of alcohol. Still others became internal refugees. Countless Mayas fled into the Yucatecan forests to eke out subsistence. In the process of reconquest the army routinely swept the backlands, capturing and relocating these people whom its officers called "presenters" on the pretext that they had "presented" themselves for removal to the pacified zone.

Not every Maya became a caste warrior; in fact, it is doubtful that more than a minority actually revolted. Peasants of the north and the west had less connection with the socioeconomic lines that had spawned the revolt. They had little exposure to the people and issues outside of their territory, and the aims of the eastern rebels made little sense to them. For this nonradicalized majority the Caste War was a terrifying event. More joined the rebellion than is commonly realized; but most found themselves caught between insurgent armies and a rabid criollo paranoia. Many fled. Other peasants were dragooned into the army as porters and road-clearers, military corveé laborers that the Yucatecans called *hidalgos* after an old colonial term for privileged Mayas who had aided in the conquest. In the pacified zones the peasants, faced with starvation, violence, or conscription, accepted onerous labor contracts that bound them to the land for periods as long as 15 years. Most evidence suggests that the average peasant lived in mortal terror of the *cruzob*, who made periodic violent raids throughout the 1850s and 1860s, and who were known for killing peaceful Mayas or abducting them as slave labor.

Beginning in 1851 certain rebel communities—the so-called *pacíficos* of the deep south—made peace. These were rag-tag collections of Mayas, deserted soldiers, Belizean blacks, and refugees from Central America's ongoing wars. The *pacíficos* signed treaties with the Mérida governments in which they promised to aid the war effort in exchange for amnesty, tax exemption, and the right to keep their arms. They supplemented a subsistence economy by trade with Belize and Campeche. The arrangement amounted to a near-total political autonomy. The *pacíficos* had no interest in serving the Yucatecan state, only in being left alone. Social structures were anarchic; titular leaders had little real control over their "followers." The *pacíficos* simply ignored political obligations such as extradition. Moreover, while they reveled in small skirmishes with the *cruzob*, they shunned systematic and extended military mobilization. The many criollo plans for some united crusade against the Speaking Cross were thus fantasies.

One of the most sordid features of the war was the return of human slavery. Criollo politicians and military officers, finding themselves with minimal resources and innumerable prisoners, sold *cruzob* prisoners as slaves to the insatiable Cuban sugar estates. Given the psychosis of war, it was inevitable that these same traders, finding captured rebels in short supply, began to enslave peaceful Mayas and mestizos as well. The trade became integral to Yucatán's political instability, as exile groups living in Havana financed their own invasions on the returns from this nefarious enterprise.

The French Empire in Yucatán

The years of the French empire in Yucatán (1863–67) formed a brief but important period of peninsular history. The imperialists momentarily quieted Yucatán's revolts. They also presided over a short-lived cotton boom, a byproduct of the U.S. Civil War. But the empire also escalated hostilities again with Chan Santa Cruz and in so doing provoked the last true episode of caste warfare.

A combination of forces led to this turn. Renewed warfare against the *cruzob* was partly an attempt to strike a nationalist posture. The imperialists hoped that a crusade of reconquest would earn them the support of Yucatán's notoriously quarrelsome elite. But the *cruzob* helped provoke the decision, since the months surrounding the arrival of imperial power were a time of energetic rebel sorties into the pacified zones. By 1864, then, the empire committed itself to a war almost as large as the one it was waging against Benito Juárez and his Liberal government.

The new masters of Yucatán soon stumbled over the realities of a bitterly conflicted peninsula. Imperial commissar José Salazar Ilarregui tried to imitate Spanish colonial methods by moderating the draconian 1847 labor code and appointing a full-time legal defender for the Mayas. But these mild checks on the prerogatives of the landed class merely provoked outrage. At the same time, Yucatecans were more reluctant than ever to mobilize for war. Desertion was endemic, and the populations of the *pacífico* communities swelled with runaway soldiers. Ironically, the imperial war also reinvigorated Chan Santa Cruz, which in 1864 was bordering on fragmentation (a coup eliminated Venancio Puc in January, and although military hard-liners managed to regain control, the threat of internal divisions was clear). In October 1866 the imperial-led army narrowly escaped annihilation at the hands of the *cruzob*. Subsequent army mutinies, combined with a strong nationalist resistance pressing in from Tabasco, doomed the empire in Yucatán.

Peninsular affairs eventually stabilized. With the empire out of the way, the *cruzob* ravaged their hated enemies, the *pacíficos*. The last *pacífico* to challenge seriously the *cruzob*'s southern trade routes was the bellicose Marcos Canul, who died in an abortive raid on Orange Walk, Belize, on September 1, 1872. The Cross at last enjoyed uncontested control of the southeast. Yucatecans, meanwhile, had fought themselves into exhaustion. They contented themselves with the burgeoning profits from henequen, a maguey plant whose fiber provided twine for mechanized wheat-binders. Tightly interlinked with U.S. monopoly capital via secret purchasing agreements, the criollo elites now assumed their role as Yucatán's infamous *casta divina*, an oligarchy that worked its Maya peons like so many slaves and built homes of marble opulence along the grand avenues of Mérida. The only lingering symptoms of warfare were occasional raids, along with a general aura of fear and taboo surrounding the southeastern forests.

The Reconquest of the Southeast

Between 1880 and 1930 the Mexican nation-state reclaimed its control over the storied kingdom of the Cross. Mexican president Porfirio Díaz initially abided the peninsular situation, since it provided a check on the fractious Yucatecans. Over time, however, an economic reconquest swept through the southeast. Mexican fortune-hunters entered the rain forest, lured by resources such as chicle and precious woods. The *cruzob* chiefs alternately resisted and joined forces with the new entrepreneurs, at times even providing their own soldiers as labor gangs.

Eventually the forces of economic and political modernity overwhelmed the *cruzob*. As Mexico's Revolutionary government consolidated itself after 1920, the People of the Cross found it hard to resist the incursions of anthropologists, archaeologists, political agents, and rain forest entrepreneurs. The last of these holdout villages accepted government land titles in the 1920s, hence placing themselves within national political authority. The southeast territory, now renamed Quintana Roo, remained relatively underdeveloped until the 1970s; statehood arrived in 1974, along with a boom in tourism. The effects of this last influence were mixed. Confined largely to the coast, tourism caused little direct incursion into the interior villages. But it raised local prices, and as Mexico's agricultural economy declined throughout the petroleum years following 1976, many villagers migrated to Cancún or Cozumel for construction work. The cult of the Speaking Cross outlived its war-torn origins, but after 1899 it permanently fragmented into rival communities, each with its own Cross.

Mayas of the henequen region also experienced a problematic evolution. The 1910 Revolution abolished debt peonage and ultimately brought agrarian reform. It also helped legitimate Maya culture and bring peasants into politics at the local and state level. But over time residents of the rural *ejidos* (collective farms) became reconstituted peons to an agrarian bureaucracy. To compound problems, the world markets for henequen slid into uninterrupted decline after World War II. By the 1990s the industry was dead. Rural Yucatecans now struggled with subsistence farming, migrated to the cities in search of jobs, and continued to search for viable nontraditional exports. Life in the countryside was difficult indeed. However, in all parts of the peninsula the memory of the Caste War remained a source of pride, the historical emblem of a people's search for dignity and self-determination.

Select Bibliography

Angel, Barbara, "The Reconstruction of Rural Society in the Aftermath of the Mayan Rebellion of 1847." *Journal of the Canadian Historical Association* 4 (1993).

Baqueiro, Serapio, *Ensayo histórico sobre las revoluciones de Yucatán desde el ano de 1840 hasta 1864.* 3 vols., Mérida: Manuel Heredia Arguelles, 1879.

Dumond, Don E., "The Talking Crosses of Yucatán: A New Look at Their History." *Ethnohistory* 32 (1985).

Farriss, Nancy M., *Maya Society under Colonial Rule: The Collective Enterprise of Survival.* Princeton, New Jersey: Princeton University Press, 1984.

Gonzalez Navarro, Moises, *Raza y tierra: La guerra de castas y el henequen.* Mexico City: El Colegio de México, 1970.

Konrad, Herman W., "Capitalism on the Tropical-Forest Frontier: Quintana Roo, 1880s to 1930." In *Land, Labor, and Capital in Modern Yucatán: Essays in Regional History and Political Economy,* edited by Jeffery T. Brannon and Gilbert M. Joseph. Tuscaloosa: University of Alabama Press, 1991.

Patch, Robert W., "Decolonization, the Agrarian Problem, and the Origins of the Caste War, 1812–1847." In *Land, Labor, and Capital in Modern Yucatán: Essays in Regional History and Political Economy,* edited by Jeffery T. Brannon and Gilbert M. Joseph. Tuscaloosa: University of Alabama Press, 1991.

Reed, Nelson, *The Caste War of Yucatán.* Stanford, California: Stanford University Press, 1964.

Reina, Letitia, *Las rebeliones campesinos en México (1819–1906).* Mexico City: Siglo Veintiuno, 1980.

Rugeley, Terry, *Yucatán's Maya Peasantry and the Origins of the Caste War.* Austin: University of Texas Press, 1996.

Sullivan, Paul, *Unfinished Conversations: Mayas and Foreigners Between Two Wars.* New York: Knopf, 1989.

Villa Rojas, Alfonso, *The Maya of East Central Quintana Roo.* Washington, D.C.: Carnegie Institute, 1943.

Wells, Alan, *Yucatán's Gilded Age: Haciendas, Henequen, and International Harvester, 1860–1915.* Albuquerque: University of New Mexico Press, 1985.

—TERRY RUGELEY

CATHOLIC CHURCH

This entry includes two articles that discuss the structure, divisions, and hierarchy of the Catholic Church:

Catholic Church: New Spain
Catholic Church: Mexico

See also Church and State; Cofradías; Festival Cycle; Ritual, Religious and Civic; Virgin of Guadalupe and Guadalupanismo; Virgin of los Remedios

CATHOLIC CHURCH: NEW SPAIN

The hierarchical structure of the Catholic Church in New Spain was the result of one and one-half millennia of development. This article will consider the finished product of this evolution as it was found in Spain and New Spain, beginning in the fifteenth century and reaching its completed form in the sixteenth.

Holy Orders

The structure of the Catholic Church was based on the various levels of ministry globally known as Holy Orders, of which the most important were priesthood and episcopate.

The first step taken by an aspirant to the clerical state was known as tonsure, a ceremony whereby part of his hair was cut to symbolize renunciation of the world and entrance into the status of cleric (*clérigo*) or of the clergy (*clerecía*), terms derived from the Greek *kleros,* meaning "lot," that is, one who has cast his lot with the Lord. In its widest sense *clérigo* meant any person who had entered the clerical state via tonsure. In the sixteenth century it also was synonymous with the diocesan priest—that is, a priest who served as a member of a diocese under a bishop rather than in a religious order. As a sign of their state, clerics in that century wore a small shaven area on the back of the head, which in English is called a tonsure (in Spanish *corona*).

After this the aspirant passed through eight orders or stages. Four were called minor orders: porter (doorkeeper), lector (reader), exorcist (one who cast out demons), and acolyte (assistant at liturgical ceremonies). The other four were called major orders and were subdiaconate, diaconate, priesthood, and episcopacy. Each of these steps conferred more responsibility than the preceding one. The first of the major orders, the subdiaconate, carried with it the obligation of celibacy and the daily recitation of the canonical hours, also called the divine office or the breviary. The four minor orders and subdiaconate were not considered sacraments.

The order of deacon carried with it the obligation and right to preach, perform solemn baptisms, and conduct funerals. After this came the priesthood and episcopate, the latter in the sixteenth century being considered the fullness of the priesthood because it carried with it the power to impart orders to others.

Territorial Administration

The lowest geographical division of ecclesiastical administration was the parish (*parroquia*), which was under the direction of a priest called a pastor (*párroco*). The term *cura* was also used, although it had the more generic meaning of any priest carrying out a parochial ministry. Above the parish was the large grouping called the diocese (diócesis, obispado) ruled by a bishop (obispo), who had genuine legislative, executive, and judicial power. The bishop's immediate assistant was his vicar general (gran vicario) or his chief ecclesiastical judge (provisor), who sometimes ruled the diocese in the absence of the bishop and were his delegates for all kinds of business, especially that involving ecclesiastical trials. Sometimes a bishop's successor would be appointed in the lifetime of the incumbent and would be called coadjutor with the right of succession (coadjutor cum iure successionis). The practice of having auxiliary or assistant bishops was unknown in New Spain during the colonial period.

The administration of a diocese was shared by the cathedral chapter (cabildo eclesiástico or, in archdioceses, metropolitano). It had a twofold function: first, to act as a board of consultants and advisers to the bishop, and, second, to recite the canonical hours in public in the cathedral. This latter function was carried out with varying degrees of liturgical ceremony. The chapter usually ruled the diocese in the interim between bishops (sede vacante), often through an elected representative called the vicar capitular. In some dioceses the cabildo had the right to nominate the new bishop, but this was not done in the Spanish dependencies.

The cabildo had four ranks: five dignitaries (dignidades), ten canons (canónigos), six racioneros; and six medio-racioneros. The five dignidades had other functions in addition to the two mentioned above and enjoyed the honorific title of don. The dean (deán), usually the senior member of the cabildo, was its president and presided over its meetings in the absence of the bishop. He was in charge of all ceremonies and divine worship and acted more or less as the pastor of the cathedral church. The archdeacon (arcediano) originally was the head of the deacons who participated in the cathedral ceremonies. By the sixteenth century he was examiner of those who presented themselves for ordination. He sometimes acted as administrator of the diocese in the bishop's absence and was ordinarily expected to have at least a bachelor's degree in canon law. In the sixteenth century this was the most powerful position on the cathedral chapter of Mexico. The schoolmaster (maestrescuelas) was in charge of the cathedral school. He was required to offer Latin classes to all clerics and aspirants who asked for them, and he was ordinarily required to have a bachelor's degree in canon law or philosophy. The choirmaster (chantre) was in charge of the cathedral choir and had to do some of the singing personally. The treasurer (tesorero) was in charge of the administration of the physical plant and the revenues from the patrimony, or foundation, of the cabildo. These included the fábrica, or income for the upkeep and maintenance of buildings, and the superávit, or surplus funds, at the end of each year. The canónigos, racioneros, and medio-racioneros had descending levels of importance and income.

Any ecclesiastical office to which a salary (frutos) was attached, such as pastor or administrator of a hospital, was called a benefice (beneficio). Consequently a beneficiado was any cleric who lived by an income attached to an ecclesiastical office. Benefice is a wider term than prebend (prebenda), which meant the right to receive a share of the income (mesa) from the cathedral. All prebendados were beneficiados, but not all beneficiados were prebendados. The matter of cleric's having an income or means to live was very important in the sixteenth century, and even until recent times no one could be ordained to the subdiaconate who did not have a guaranteed means of sustenance (título).

Dioceses were grouped into larger territorial units called provinces (provincias eclesiáticas, not to be confused with the provinces of religious orders to be mentioned below), of which the chief bishop, whose diocese was called the archdiocese (arquidiócesis), had the title of archbishop (arzobispo) or metropolitan (metropolitano). There was only one archdiocese in a province, the others being called suffragans (sufragáneos). The metropolitan had no jurisdiction over the internal administration of his suffragans, although in some cases his courts could hear appeals from theirs.

The terms patriarch and primate are honorary, although ordinarily the primatial diocese or see (sede, meaning seat) was the oldest one in a particular country. There is no indication of the term being used in Mexico before or after Independence. The term Patriarch of the Indies was, however, secured for some bishops by the Spanish Crown. The title had a confused history, having been used by the Crown as a means of augmenting its control over the church in the Indies and by the papacy in an attempt to restrict that same control. The title, however, was totally honorary and carried with it no jurisdiction or authority.

A meeting of the bishop of a diocese with his priests to resolve problems and enact legislation was called a synod (sínodo). A meeting of all the bishops of an ecclesiastical province was called a provincial council (concilio provincial).

Religious Orders

A religious order (religión or orden) was one whose members took public vows and lived together in community under a rule (for which reasons they are also sometimes called regulares). A monastery (monasterio) was a religious house in which the members were monks (monjes) who lived all their lives in the monastery, which was an autonomous or semiautonomous unit. The best-known of the monastic orders are the Benedictines. It should be noted that in the sixteenth century the term monastery had come to be used loosely for any religious house of men or women. Similarly a convent (convento) could be a religious house of either men or women.

The friars (frailes), on the other hand, did not commit themselves to life in an individual house but belonged to international groupings with a different form of administration. Some of these orders had originated in the Middle Ages and were called mendicants (mendicantes) because they originally had lived by begging. The best-known of these orders were the Franciscans (Order of Friars Minor), the Dominicans (Order of Preachers), the Augustinians, and the Mercedarians (Orden de la Merced Redención de Cautivos). The Jesuits were neither monks nor friars but were originally clerks regular. However, after 1583 they were canonically religious, while remaining distinct from the mendicants.

Mendicant administration existed side be side with that of the bishops and frequently in competition with it. By a privilege called exemption, most male religious orders composed predominantly of clerics were free of the bishop's jurisdiction in regard to their internal affairs while working in a diocese. Geographically, the orders were divided into provinces (not to be confused with the ecclesiastical provinces mentioned above) ruled by a provincial superior (*provincial*), assisted by a council (whose members sometimes were called *definidores*). Individual houses of religious were ruled by superiors or priors, who among the Franciscans were called guardians. The parallel administrations of bishop and religious caused dissension and controversy throughout the sixteenth century. In these struggles the religious relied heavily on the various privileges and exemptions granted them by the papacy, of which the most important was the papal bull *Exponi nobis*, known as the *Omnímoda*, of 1522. In the process of evangelization, the mendicants made use of the mission/presidio system, that is, mission stations protected by a sufficient number of Spanish soldiers. Eventually the mission would become stabilized and become a *doctrina*, a quasi-parish of newly converted Indians. Throughout the sixteenth and a good part of the seventeenth centuries, the *doctrinas* were a bone of contention between bishops and friars.

The term ordinary (*ordinario*) was applied to any office or officeholder with true jurisdiction exercised in his own name and not in that of another. It is the opposite of vicar or vicarious. Although in strict canonical terminology it could be applied to the provincials of a religious order, in everyday speech it more often indicated a bishop, especially in the phrase local ordinary. Anyone who held ordinary power, whether bishop or religious provincial, was called a prelate (*prelado*), though the term was ordinarily used for bishops alone.

Church Structure in New Spain

The Catholic Church in New Spain has been called a "church of friars" because the first missionary work was carried on by the mendicants, prior to the arrival of any bishop. The first diocese was that of Tlaxcala, with the Dominican Julián Garcés as bishop. Mexico City was made a diocese in 1530, with the Franciscan Juan de Zumárraga as the first bishop. Until 1547 it was suffragan to the archdiocese of Seville, but in that year an independent ecclesiastical province of Mexico was established. Even after that, however, diocesan structure and practice in New Spain tended to follow the model of Seville.

The church in New Spain was entirely supported by the Crown through a system of tithes (*diezmos*). Theoretically the tithe was a 10 percent tax on agricultural production, although in practice the percentage fluctuated. In the sixteenth century there was a strong debate on whether the Indians should count as part of the tithe. Eventually they paid a tithe on wheat and cattle. They also contributed to church support through labor, often of a forced nature. A royal *cédula* of 1501 defined which items were subject to tithing and the amounts for each. Although church authorities collected the tithe, the money went to the Crown, which redistributed it to the church according to a complex formula. In addition the church received donations and bequests and eventually became a major source of money, land, and financing for capitalist ventures in the colony.

Two important institutions in New Spain did not belong to the hierarchical structure of the church: confraternities (*cofradías*) and convents of nuns. Bishops rather consistently attempted to extend their control over the former, not always successfully. Orders of nuns did not enjoy the privilege of exemption, and so the internal or disciplinary life of a convent was subject to the jurisdiction of the local bishop.

The Patronato Real

Relations between church and state in New Spain under the Hapsburgs were governed by a complex series of laws and privileges collectively called the *patronato real*. It was codified in 1574 in the *Ordenanza de patronazgo*, which sharply restricted the rights of both mendicants and bishops. No church or monastery could be founded without royal permission The king had the right to found all ecclesiastical offices and to draw the boundary lines of dioceses. Archbishops and bishops were nominated by the king, who presented their names to the pope, while he had the right of immediate appointment for many lower offices.

At the conclusion of the War of the Spanish Succession, the Bourbon Dynasty was established as the ruling house of Spain. Under the monarchs of the Enlightenment, especially Carlos III (1759–88), state control of the church became virtually absolute. Royal policy took on overtones of anticlericalism and even a certain hostility toward traditional religious practices that it had not had before. This hostility reached its climax in the expulsion of the Jesuits from Spanish dominions (1767). The Crown also extended its control over ecclesiastical finances.

Church structure in New Spain followed that of the mother country very closely, with relatively few adaptations, such as the *doctrinas*. This structure was characterized by an intrinsic tension between the diocesan and mendicant elements and by an encroaching state control that eventually made the church a virtual department of state. The difficulties caused by this state control carried over into the national period.

See also Bourbon Reforms; Cofradías; Convents in New Spain; Fueros; Inquisition; Missions and Reductions; Religious in New Spain

Select Bibliography

Mazín, Oscar, *Entre dos majestades*. Zamora: Colegio de Michoacán, 1987.

Montúfar, Alonso de, *Ordenanzas para el coro de la catedral Mexicana 1570*, edited by Ernest J. Burrus. Madrid: J. Porrúa Turanzas, 1964.

Padden, Robert, "The *Ordenanza del Patronazgo*: An Interpretive Essay." *The Americas* 12 (April 1956).

Poole, Stafford, *Pedro Moya de Contreras: Catholic Reform and Royal Power in New Spain, 1571–1591*. Berkeley: University of California Press, 1987.

Ricard, Robert, *The Spiritual Conquest of Mexico*, translated by Lesley Byrd Simpson. Berkeley: University of California Press, 1966.

Schwaller, John Frederick, "The Cathedral Chapter of Mexico in the Sixteenth Century." *Hispanic American Historical Review* 61:4 (November 1981).

_____, "The *Ordenazgo del Patronazgo* in New Spain, 1574–1600." *The Americas* 42 (January 1986).

_____, *Origins of Church Wealth in Mexico: Ecclesiastical Revenues and Church Finances, 1523–1600*. Albuquerque: University of New Mexico Press, 1985.

—STAFFORD POOLE

CATHOLIC CHURCH: MEXICO

In the Independence period the Catholic Church's economic, political, and social influence was noticeably diminished, but this was not the reason for its ceasing to have the primacy it had enjoyed during the colonial years. Even during the latter colonial era, Bourbon regalist politics had severely affected the interests and the status of the clergy. The expulsion of the Jesuits in 1767, the confiscation of an enormous quantity of church property and capital, as well as the Napoleonic intervention in Spain, not only affected the church's social and religious role but also exacerbated the anti-Spanish feeling of native-born ecclesiastics and provoked a polarization between upper and lower ranks of the clergy.

This explains why two priests, Miguel Hidalgo y Costilla and José María Morelos y Pavón, would lead the Independence movement in its initial stage (1810 to 1814), and why approximately 400 of the clergy would participate outright in the movement and four-fifths would help it directly or indirectly.

Between 1821 and 1856 the Catholic Church was made up of 10 dioceses, more than 1,000 parishes, and almost 300 convents and monasteries, administered by around 7,000 priests, of which 3,000 members belonged to the secular clergy (i.e., those not belonging to a particular order such as the Franciscans) and the remainder to the regular clergy (those who did belong to a particular order).

Once Independence was achieved with the signing of the Treaties of Córdoba on August 24, 1821, by Viceroy Juan O'Donojú and the former royalist Agustín de Iturbide, there arose the problem of whether or not the royal *patronato* (by which the Spanish king controlled clerical appointments) would continue even though the church still maintained supremacy as the only accepted religious institution. The new state demanded that the *patronato* exercised by the Spanish monarchs should be handed over, using the argument that it was the transmission of sovereignty from one state to another. In contrast, the church was of the opinion that this right had been conceded by the kings of Castile and was not operative in emancipated territory. It was concluded in the Diocesan Council, held from March to November 1821, that if the new government wished to enjoy this privilege, then it should be requested from the Holy See itself. Under pressure from Spain, the pontificate of Leo XII was hostile to the new American governments, and the *patronato* was not reestablished.

Catholicism was recognized as the only accepted religious faith in the Constitution of 1824. Nevertheless, a marked sympathy for liberal ideas had arisen among middle-class intellectuals and politicians, many of them former clergy (the most renowned were José María Luis Mora and Servando Teresa de Mier). In essence this tendency pointed out the necessity to strip power from the church in order to impose a new social economic policy. From this point forward, this argument provoked an ideological and violent confrontation between two great parties, the Liberals and the Conservatives, whose beginning can be traced clearly to 1833. This was the year, during the first presidential term of Antonio López de Santa Anna, when Vice President Valentín Gómez Farías promulgated various laws that attempted to diminish the power and influence of the military and the church. Secularization was the means to achieve this. This legislation tried to confiscate church properties, suspend ecclesiastical exemptions, and secularize all missions. The Universidad Pontifico de México was closed, regular clergy were allowed to renounce their vows, and the obligatory payment of tithes was suspended. Nevertheless, the strong reaction of the church and the Conservatives motivated Santa Anna to suspend these measures and remove Gómez Farías from office. From then until 1854, there was a continuous and alternate sharing in power between the Conservatives and the Liberals.

The more the Liberals increased in political power, the more they persisted in attacking the church. The balance of power was finally altered, however, by the war against the United States. The grave financial crisis this provoked motivated Gómez Farías's Liberal government to propose a forced loan from the church. Some Catholic groups responded by inciting the rebellion of the Polkos, one further handicap for the Mexican army, whose numbers were thereby reduced to deal with the U.S. troops. Santa Anna negotiated again with the church for the resignation of Gómez Farías in return for financial support. This led the Liberals to take up more decisive action against the Conservatives.

The Plan de Ayutla (1854) heralded the final defeat of Santa Anna; after they forced him from power, the Liberals were able to impose their program. The new legislation attacked clergy directly. The Ley Juárez (Juárez Law, 1855) did away with the ecclesiastical immunities, and Ley Lerdo (Lerdo Law, 1856) confiscated their property. In May 1855 the Estatuto Organico Provisional (The Institutional Provisional Law) denied the clergy citizens' rights. In June the Constituent Congress expelled the Jesuits. The Constitution of 1857 incorporated these laws and moreover excluded the church from the realm of education, excluded the clergy from election to the presidency or Congress, and allowed the state to have authority in matters of worship. The reaction of the pope and the Mexican bishops to the Constitution helped foment a bloody civil war that lasted three years (1858–61).

During this War of the Reform, Benito Juárez, the Liberal leader, promulgated the Reform Laws. These included the separation between church and state, the confiscation of church property, setting up the civil register, the secularization of cemeteries, the prohibition of government members to attend acts of worship, and the dissolution of monastic orders. When the Liberals won the war and entered Mexico City in triumph on January 1, 1861, almost all the bishops were in exile.

On the other hand the Conservatives, backed by the church, organized for the installation of Maximilian von Hapsburg as emperor of Mexico to block the Liberal reforms. Although the emperor (who took power in 1864 with the backing of European troops) sought to maintain Catholicism as the state religion, he was sympathetic to religious toleration, the creation of a clerical body financed by the state, and the establishment of a hereditary *patronato*. These proposals diminished his support from the clergy and the Conservatives.

On the execution of Maximilian in 1867 by the Liberal army, Juárez reestablished the Republic and reassumed the presidency without concerning himself with the religious issue. His successor, Sebastián Lerdo de Tejada (1872–76), incorporated the Reform Laws into the Constitution in 1873, thereby reviving the religious conflict. The uprising of the *religioneros* in the Bajío region of north-central Mexico was ended by General Porfirio Díaz's defeat of Lerdo de Tejada.

During the Porfiriato (1876–1910) the Reform Laws were not applied, and the conflict vanished. Díaz's tolerance of the church allowed the latter to recover some of its privileges. Structurally it was strengthened by the creation of 11 dioceses and 5 ecclesiastical provinces, the creation of many religious orders for men and women, and the arrival of others from abroad. Church councils were held and universities and seminaries headed by the clergy were reopened. This fresh impetus was promoted further by the development of *catolicismo social* (social Catholicism), the result of the application of Pope Leo XIII's encyclical *Rerum Novarum* (1891). Four

congresses were organized between 1903 and 1909 (in Puebla, Morelia, Guadalajara, and Oaxaca) in which were discussed strategies to achieve a better distribution of wealth, collaboration between social classes, and the improvement of conditions for workers, *campesinos*, and indigenous people. Catholic Unionism emerged in this period with the Círculos Obreros of Guadalajara. In 1909 the Operarios Guadalupanos appeared, disseminating socialist-Catholic views in their periodicals.

The end of the Díaz dictatorship seemed to mark the beginning of a major new development of the church; Catholic Unionism was given even further impetus with the Confederación Católica Obrera. This latter attempted to establish mutual societies, workers' schools, and conferences on civic and religious themes. The Partido Católico Nacional was created on May 3, 1911, with a very wide program. This accepted the separation between church and state; sought to maintain freedom of schooling, of association, and of conscience; and accepted the adoption of laws in accordance with the teachings of social catholicism to resolve major social problems. Their motto was *Dios, Patria y Libertad* (God, Country, and Freedom). When Francisco I. Madero won the presidential elections in this same year, the Catholic Party was widely accepted, gaining 4 seats in the Senate, 31 deputyships, and 4 governorships.

The *coup d'état* of Victoriano Huerta in 1913 had fatal repercussions for the church, not only because it provoked the uprising *en masse* of the *campesinos* (peasants) and thereby interrupted its dynamic growth, but also because it was unjustifiably accused by the opposition led by Venustiano Carranza of having taken part in Madero's overthrow, given that there was clear sympathy for Huerta on the part of some well-known Catholics. This was the argument used by the followers of Carranza to antagonize the church during the conflict and to include various anticlerical articles in the new Constitution of 1917. It was clear that Carranza was attempting to neutralize the church's recently renewed power. For this reason the Constitution of 1917 was more radical than that of 1857, not only in that it established the separation of church and state, but also that this was not recognized on a legal basis. The church simply remained subject to the state as the following articles in the Constitution show: Article 3 excluded the church from primary and private education; Article 5 prohibited vows for monks and religious orders; Article 27 denied the church's right to possess, acquire, or administer properties or to direct charity institutions, and their effects became property of the nation; Article 130 established that the clergy could not participate in politics, that only individual state legislatures could determine the number of ministers in each church and that only a Mexican by birth could take up a religious ministry.

The church officially protested, and many Catholics rebelled. In response, Carranza tried to reform Articles 3 and 130 but was prevented by powerful opposition in the Congress. Although President Álvaro Obregón (1920–24) did not demand rigorous adherence to the Constitution, he did not stop being hostile to the church. For example, he ordered the expulsion of the apostolic delegate, Ernesto Filippi, for having attended the laying of the first stone of the national monument to Christ the King on the Cerro de Cubilete. Nevertheless, in 1923 the government invited the Catholic Church freely to develop their activities but without interfering in areas that were the responsibility of public administration.

In contrast Obregón's successor, Plutarco Elías Calles (1924–28), unleashed a radically anti-Catholic policy. On the one hand Calles tried to instigate a schism by setting up the Mexican Catholic Apostolic Church headed by the patriarch Pérez, which did not work out satisfactorily; on the other hand he violently attacked the church. In February 1926 after the declaration by Archbishop José Mora y del Rio, published in a newspaper, that the bishops' indignation against the Constitution of 1917 would remain firm, Calles began to apply the law strictly. Foreign priests began to be exiled; private schools and colleges, as well as asylums and hospitals supported by religious organizations, were closed down; the press was censured; and private worship was forbidden. Church property was nationalized and in each state of the Republic the number of priests was limited. On July 31, 1926, the bishops, in protest, ordered all the churches to be closed to pressure the government.

Calles's actions provoked the Cristero Rebellion, a peasant-led pro-Catholic uprising that sought to defend religion and fight the government. Meanwhile, the Liga Nacional Defensora de la Libertad Religiosa (National League for the Defense of Religious Freedom), an organization with an urban background created to fight on a patriotic basis against the measures adopted by the Calles regime, organized a boycott on tax payments and luxury spending. When this group did not succeed in its objectives, it supported and tried to direct the armed movement in the countryside, provoking much friction between the two fronts.

The exiled bishops justified Catholic resistance even as they tried to negotiate with the government for church autonomy. The war developed principally in the Bajío region of the country over a period of three years. The *cristeros* not only successfully resisted but also extended their movement when the struggle was suspended. In June 1929 President Emilio Portes Gil and Bishops Leopold Ruiz y Flores and Pascual Díaz, after two years of negotiation mediated by U.S. ambassador Dwight Morrow, signed the peace accord ("the arrangements" as they were called) against the will of the combatants. This agreement was considered by many to be a betrayal since it only revealed flexibility on the part of the government and did not modify the anti-religious legislation.

Although the regime of Lázaro Cárdenas (1934–40) had an anticlerical posture, above all in establishing socialist education, it was far more tolerant in the application of the law and made significant steps to end the religious conflict. This was in good measure owing to the conciliatory attitude of the new Mexican archbishop, Luis María Martínez, who urged Mexican Catholics to cooperate with the government in its socialist program. During the same period the National Sinarquist Union was founded in 1937 and the Partido de Acción Nacional (National Action Party) in 1939, both strongly linked to the church, to act on a political basis against the Revolutionary and anti-Catholic stance of the regime.

Manuel Avila Camacho's assumption of the presidency in 1940 initiated good relations with the church. Once again the church concentrated on reorganization and expansion. Seminaries were reopened and created, new dioceses founded, and priests and those belonging to religious orders arrived in Mexico from abroad. Acción Católica (Catholic Action), founded in 1929, became the principal organization to prepare lay cadres to play a role in varied social areas. Associations were formed of youth, women, workers, professionals, students, and businessmen of a militant character that were linked to the Catholic hierarchy.

By the 1950s the church had made substantial inroads in society. More than 4,000 priests, a vast editorial production, and the approximately 500,000 members of Catholic Action indicated a dynamic growth. On a parallel basis, the Secretariado Social Mexicano (Mexican Social Secretariat), led by Father Pedro Valázquez, a central figure in ecclesiastical social life, was an important negotiator for cooperativism, social promotion, centers of technical training, and independent unionism.

The reformist atmosphere of Vatican Council II (1962–65) led to notable changes, as much in the composition of ecclesiastical organizations as interinstitutional relations. At the same time various institutions changed and others arose with proposals for the internal renewal of the Catholic Church, such as the Unión de Mutual Ayuda Episcopal (Episcopal Union for Mutual Aid) and the Confederación de Organizaciones Nacionales (Confederation of National Organizations). However, tensions arose between these and the episcopacy, which showed itself to be conservative when confronted by the fresh impetus of these new church organizations. The bishop of Cuernavaca, Sergio Méndez Arceo, notable for his progressive social and theological tendencies, became the leader of this innovative current. From 1968 to 1974 the arch-episcopacy, not without conflict, eliminated or removed from the main structure of the church all those ecclesiastical institutions that demanded radical changes in pastoral areas. Nevertheless, in some dioceses many of the proposals of these institutions were adopted.

During the 1970s the relations between church and state remained stable, but they were not free from tensions, mostly because of the protests of ecclesiastical organizations against governmental policy on birth control and the inclusion of sexual education in the government-sponsored free textbooks as well as declarations on clergy on political topics. These latter tensions increased after the first visit of Pope John Paul II to Mexico in 1979 to attend the III Conferencia del Episcopado Latinamericano (Third Latin American Episcopal Conference) held in Puebla.

Starting in the 1980s two trends revealed a change in the church's presence within society: the growth of very influential institutions within the middle classes, such as the Movimiento de Renovación en el Espiritu Santo (Movement for the Renewal in the Holy Spirit), Opus Dei, the Legionarios de Cristo (the Legionaries of Christ), and an open civil activism on the part of the bishops. The most notable case of the latter trend was the intervention of prelates of the Southern Pacific Pastoral Region (especially that of Samuel Ruiz, bishop of San Cristóbal de Las Casas, Chiapas) and Chihuahua, in the social and political processes that took place in these areas.

The growing pressure of the church, including the second visit of the pope to Mexico in 1990, and the weakening of anticlericism at the state level led in December 1991 to the reform of those constitutional articles that restricted the activity of the church in the social and political spheres. Thereafter the bishops in general criticized the government and its policies, provoked by the assassination of Cardinal Juan Jesús Posadas in 1993, the severe economic crisis of the 1990s, and corruption in the country. With 12 archdioceses, more than 60 dioceses, vicariates and prelacies, and a team of around 110 bishops, 12,000 priests, and 25,000 monks and nuns, the church in the mid-1990s influenced the daily life and political development of around 90 percent of the population, who were self-described Catholics.

See also Cristero Rebellion; Liberation Theology; Social Catholicism; Unión Nacional Sinarquista (UNS)

Select Bibliography

Gutierrez Casillas, José, *Historia de la Iglesia en México*. Mexico City: Porrúa, 1974.

Historia general de la Iglesia en América Latina, vol. 4. Salamanca: Sigueme, 1984.

Meyer, Jean, *La cristiada*. 9th edition, 3 vols., Mexico City: Siglo XXI, 1985.

Muro, Victor Gabriel, *Iglesia y movimientos sociales en México, 1972–1987*. Mexico City: Colegio de Michoacán, 1994.

Negrete, Martaelena, *Relaciones entre la Iglesia y el Estado en México.* Mexico City: Colegio de México–Universidad Iberoamericana, 1988.

Puente Lutteroth, Maria Alicia, editor, *Hacia una historia mínima de la Iglesia en México.* Mexico City: Jus/Cehila, 1994.

—Víctor Gabriel Muro

CATTLE RANCHING

One can date the arrival of cattle in Mexico from the Spanish landing in Veracruz in 1519 and increasingly so from the Conquest of Tenochtitlan in 1521. Imports were such that in 1523 Caribbean ranchers prohibited the sale of cattle to the new continent under pain of death, with the intention of establishing a monopoly. Protest from New Spain succeeded, making the Spanish Crown abolish this prohibition in 1525 with the result that the number of cattle rose enormously over the following decades. An indication of this increase is revealed by the fact that in 1532 a pound of beef cost 17.5 *maravedis;* six years later the same amount was a quarter of the price.

Ranchers quickly organized themselves to solve complaints and defend their interests. In 1537 the first *mesta* (association and guild of cattle breeders) was set up in Mexico City; its statutes were confirmed by the viceroy in 1537 and by the king three years later. Over the next decade *mestas* were established in Puebla, Oaxaca, and Michoacán.

From 1526 a conflict between ranchers and agriculturists arose, a struggle essentially between the Spanish and the Indian populations owing to cattle consistently invading arable lands. The problem was rooted in the fact that the old Castilian tradition considered pasture as a gift of nature; thus, vacant and fallow land was open to being taken over as pasturing by the ranchers. These cattlemen wanted to fence off land for their animals to the detriment of the Indians and the poorest members of the population. In 1532 King Carlos I (Emperor Charles V) decreed that royal territory should be for common use, *but after the harvest.* This practice continued during the first half of the sixteenth century, since there was almost no royal document that granted pasture land to anyone, and the gifts of land and labor specified the obligation of common pasture after the harvest.

Herds continued to expand to the extent that by 1542 a pound of meat cost under 1 *maravedi.* This increase meant that the price of young bulls dropped radically, making ranching only remunerative when carried out on a large scale. It therefore became an occupation for the wealthy.

In the second half of the sixteenth century beef was one of the most important foods for the Spanish and indigenous populations alike. But the increasing demand for slaughtered beef led to an increase in the price of meat and a reduction in the number of animals. For example, in 1576 the total number of cattle in Guadalajara was 33,746; by 1602 this had dropped to 25,123. The decrease in herds was not only the result of meat consumption. The sale of fat for soap and candles and the call for leather, much in demand by the Spanish army and by the silver mines for carrying minerals and drying out pits and galleries, also accounted for this drop in quantity. At the beginning of the seventeenth century those prospecting for precious metals had brought cattle to Zacatecas, Pánuco, Lagos, and Aguascalientes. There were also ranches along the Pacific coast as far north as Villa de Culiacán.

During the eighteenth and nineteenth centuries cattle ranching became an activity for criollos (those of Spanish descent born in Mexico) and affluent Mexicans. Throughout the country there were extensive territorial developments that derived the larger part of their earnings from land rents. Nevertheless, in many areas there was also a parallel increase in small-scale cattle ranching by *campesinos* (peasants) and the indigenous population, orientated toward dairy production and the breeding of draft animals. Cattle, fed on the leftovers from the harvest, pulled ploughs and carts, and in the case of an emergency or festivity were sold for cash.

In the mid–nineteenth century the Ley de Desamortización de Fincas Rústicas y Urbanas Propiedad de las Corporaciones Civiles y Religiosas (Law on the Disentailment of Country Farms and Urban Property Belonging to Civil and Religious Corporations; 1856) was passed, forcing indigenous communities and religious orders to sell the land that they owned under collective title. This law initiated a process of privatization in the Mexican countryside and established conditions for the consolidation of large haciendas and cattle ranching properties in various regions of the country.

In the northern states cattle ranches were created that in some cases were as large as 250,000 acres (100,000 hectares). The central and tropical regions also boasted haciendas of enormous proportions. In some zones, such as the Bajío region of the north-center and the western regions, the most common tendency was for smallholdings that employed the domestic labor force to manage and take care of the cattle and the maize crops. Thus a strata of small- and medium-sized ranch owners lived scattered throughout various zones, at a distance from urban centers and proud of their economic independence and self-sufficiency. They gradually established a culture of rancheros—private proprietors, farmers, and cattle owners who tapped minimal labor sources outside the family circle and prized their ability to live off their own produce. They were usually deeply religious, adhering to the Mexican version of Catholicism that involved veneration of the Virgin of Guadalupe, and maintaining a conservative and individualist outlook.

During the era of Porfirio Díaz (1876–1910), cattle ranching started to be modernized. During the 1880s around 800,000 head of cattle were butchered every year. This annual slaughter was around 1 million animals that yielded a dressed carcass of approximately 330 pounds (150 kilograms). Beef started to be exported to the United States during this period; by the beginning of the twentieth century such exports were averaging around 141,000 head of cattle per year.

During the Mexican Revolution the large cattle ranches suffered constant depredations of their herds. It was common practice for the various armies to confiscate cattle to feed their soldiers. Pancho Villa in the north expropriated live-stock from the large haciendas to sustain his troops and to sell in the southern states of the United States to finance his cause as well as purchase provisions, arms, and munitions. In the mid-1920s the national herd was vastly diminished as a result of 15 years of conflict. The entire country had to reorganize its political, social, and economic system, and cattle ranching was no exception. The Constitution of 1917 protected the agrarian rights of small-scale *campesino* and indigenous holdings and put limits on the extent of cattle ranching properties. This measure aimed to regulate the old conflict on land use between agriculturists and cattle ranchers. The former were given the right to ask for and receive land in usufruct (the right to enjoy the fruits of another's property) to sustain their families. The ranchers' properties were limited in terms of size, although they were allowed to seek judicial injunctions *(amparo)* against agrarian resolutions pending appeal.

Nevertheless, the successive Revolutionary governments avoided giving the *campesino* and indigenous communities pasture land, constituting an effective protection against the development of cattle ranches. The Mexican state seemed to have accepted the notion that while agriculture could be taken on by anyone from the smallest farmer to the largest business enterprise, cattle breeding was an activity reserved only for the great landowners. For various decades agrarian distribution only consisted of land suitable for agricultural use; pasture land was ignored. During the government of Lázaro Cárdenas (1934–40), large-scale cattle ranchers were given just under a total of 1,000 certificates of immunity to protect them from demands for land in their regions. Thus for 5 years between 15 and 22 acres (6 and 9 million hectares) were abstracted from the land pool available for distribution, almost all in the north of the country.

This security of tenure had a negative effect, since the large majority of the beneficiaries had no incentive to modernize their properties, preferring to continue large-scale exploitation of their territories. With very few exceptions, these ranchers chose to maintain their ranches and haciendas as vast areas of natural pasture grazed by criollo cattle, descendants of the animals that the conquistadors brought in the sixteenth century, just as they had since the beginning of the century. Most of the profits came from the use of this rural land, on which cattle pastured freely, that was neither improved nor given the benefit of capital investment. Thus economic success depended on the extent of landholdings and not on investment and modern technology.

Cárdenas passed the Ley de Asociaciones Ganaderas (Law on Cattle Ranching Associations; 1936), which was meant to protect the development of large-scale ranching businesses and became a powerful obstacle to agrarian distribution. The justification for leaving ranching in private hands and blocking pasture distribution to the *ejidos* (communal village properties) was the fact that the state had no resources to finance efficient cattle ranching at this level and considered it better to leave such activities in private hands. Under this law the state therefore recognized cattle ranching associations as the exclusive representatives of those dedicated to breeding livestock. The Confederación Nacional Ganadera (National Livestock Association) was set up with various smaller subgroups on the state and municipal levels. Since its beginnings, the association has been controlled by private properties, the big cattle ranchers in particular, and it has defended their interests at the expense of the needs of smaller scale *campesino* and indigenous smallholders.

Thus activity became polarized, the small nucleus of large- and medium-scale ranchers, owners of enormous tracts of lands and the majority of the herds, on one side and on the other a multitude of small cattle breeders with herds no larger than 20 animals. The majority of the latter were *ejidatarios, campesinos,* and indigenous people who regarded ranching as one more economic alternative for their family members. This represented an efficient way of using *ejido* lands without the need to invest too much labor in pasturing and with the hope of selling an animal in case of an illness, accident, or fiesta.

In 1946 permission was granted to import 327 head of Zebu cattle from Brazil. These were initially quarantined for several weeks to check that they were not infected by apthous fever or foot-and-mouth disease before they were unloaded and pastured on Veracruzan fields. Nevertheless, by the end of October the municipality of Veracruz was infected with aphthous fever with 300 head of cattle reported as suffering from the illness. By December 26 of the same year the epidemic was recognized officially, and the Untied States closed their frontier to Mexican cattle and meat products. One month later the infected area included 17 neighboring states and threatened 15 million head of beef, lamb, goat, and pig. By January 1947 the total had risen to 35,000 infected animals. A commission was formed to eradicate the disease, and drastic measures were thought up to fight it. Ranchers from the United States put pressure on their government to help Mexico, since the disease was a serious threat to their own industry. One March 1, 1947, U.S. president Harry Truman signed a law to initiate a cooperative program between the two countries to fight the infection, co-directed by a Mexican and a U.S. citizen.

On April 1, 1947, the Comisión México-Americana para la Erradicación de la Fiebre Aftosa (CMAPEFA, or Mexican-American Commission for the Eradication of Apthous Fever), set to work. Areas were labeled "clean" or "infected," and buffer zones were established. From the beginning the commission adopted the strategy of sacrificing sick or potentially sick animals, a policy that became known as the "hygienic bullet." This initiative was strongly resisted by the Mexican *campesinos,* while the majority of the ranchers did not clearly understand the disease and its risks. Mexican and U.S. scientists and army personnel participated in the campaign, and the support of governors, municipal presidents, and the clergy in the affected areas was sought.

Financial compensation was offered for each animal killed, but in some regions corruption made work more difficult, putting the scientists' lives as risk. Indeed Mexican and

U.S. workers died as a result of various incidents. Moreover the closing of the frontier put cattle in the north of the country under interdict. The states of Sonora, Chihuahua, and Coahuila were forced to stop sending around 300,000 head a year, with a total value of 30 million pesos, to the United States. In the central area of the country, the loss of small herds owned by *campesinos* reduced the supply of meat and dairy products, leading to scarcity. The slaughter of draft animals hindered agricultural work, causing a considerable drop in the amount of land seeded with maize, since this was done almost entirely using animal traction.

The pressure from *campesinos* and private ranchers was so strong that the commission was forced to change its strategy. Instead of total destruction it opted for selective slaughter and vaccination programs. This change was carried out despite the opposition of officials in the United States, who considered that vaccination had been insufficiently tested and might prove less effective. By 1948 sufficient vaccine had been produced to fulfill the needs of the program, and in 1949 its manufacture had reached 2 million doses a month.

The impossibility of selling their animals in the United States led the northern states to create a series of canning factories to export cooked meat that had no risk of infection. In 1948 the United States Department of Agriculture bought 73 million pounds weight of tinned meat at prices that averaged half the market price for live animals. By 1951 the United States had acquired 218 million pounds of tinned meat. This somewhat reduced the pressure created by the closing of the frontier.

The vaccination and selective slaughter campaign began to show results during the beginning of the 1950s, and by May 1954 Mexico was declared free of the disease. Pastures throughout the country were repopulated with animals of better quality than their predecessors. From colonial times the criollo cattle had been practically the only breed grazing in Mexico from the tropical forest lands to the northern deserts. At the beginning of the twentieth century Herefords and Aberdeen Anguses were introduced into the north of the country and Zebu or Brahman cattle in the tropical zones. During the mid-1950s a program of artificial insemination was introduced to improve the Mexican stock, and the northern plains began to be populated by animals imported from the southern United States. The objective was to adapt Mexican breeds to the requirements of the international markets.

During the presidency of Miguel Alemán Valdés (1946–52), Article 27 of the Constitution was amended to define small ranching properties on the basis of varying extents of territory according to an index of pasture land. There was a limit of 300 head of mature cattle that could graze on a "smallholding" but no limit to the landholding itself, since it was supposed that it would have different foraging capacity depending on the region.

In the mid-1950s cattle began to be exported on the hoof to the United States. In 1960 almost 400,000 mainly young animals not exceeding 550 pounds (250 kilograms)

crossed the frontier. Ten years later 933,500 were exported, 84 percent of them bull calves weighing less than 330 pounds (150 kilograms). Thus the northern region began specializing in the production of yearlings to be fattened for slaughter in the southeastern United States. The U.S. demand imposed conditions on the genetic composition of the northern herds. As U.S. purchasers preferred animals with characteristics that satisfied consumer taste, they began to pay different prices according to the type of animals. Criollo cattle received a lower price than those crossbred with U.S. or European breeds. This obliged the northern ranchers to change breeds and create an animal less tough than the criollo, requiring more attention but yielding greater marketability.

At the beginning of the 1960s statistics indicated that ranching was almost exclusively in private hands. In 1960 a total of 93.7 percent of the nation's ranching properties and 79.4 percent of cattle were in private ownership, while *ejidos* and communities made up the remainder.

During the 1960s ranching was increased in the humid tropical areas of the country. Up to the middle of the century there were large tracts of tropical forest in Veracruz, Tabasco, Campeche, and Chiapas. This land was used mostly by the indigenous population, and to a lesser extent the *campesinos,* to plant maize using the slash and burn technique. This method was based on the existence of large areas of available forest, however, in which the farmer could make a clearing for his maize, beans, squash, and other products for one or two years and then leave the land fallow for up to 20 years to allow the development of secondary forest. Under this scheme a family needed to have two and one-half acres (one hectare) under cultivation and up to 47 acres (19 hectares) lying fallow to ensure the continued existence of arable land.

During the second half of the twentieth century tropical areas witnessed a change in land use from farming to ranching through the creation of pasture on cleared land. The private sector was responsible for destroying forest areas to establish meadows of tropical grasses such as Pangola or Estrella de Africa using the sharecropping system. The owner of the land would "lend" a *campesino* family a piece of forest to clear a *milpa* (field). The second year, instead of leaving the land fallow, he sowed grass, thereby converting the land into pasture. The agricultural cycle repeated itself with the same *campesino* being given another tract of land to clear, plant, and again lay down for pasture, At the end of one or two decades, the original *milpas* had been converted into cattle pasture.

Also during the 1960s the northern states of the country began a transformation that constituted a technological change in cattle ranching. Breeding animals were introduced from the United States and Europe that gradually began to substitute the criollo herds that had adapted to climate and the area since colonial times. Herefords, Aberdeen Anguses, Saint Gertrudes, Charolais, and crossbreeds of these with Zebu cattle appeared.

The new animals did not adjust well to the semidesert pastures of the north. Private ranchers improved their properties to facilitate the adaptation process. In Sonora, Buffel grass of African origin was introduced that quintupled the pasture in the region, adapting well to the climate and the coastal plains of the area. However, it did not improve the capacity of the ranches. Ditches, fences, and pasture land were created to prevent the new breeds from wandering great distances to drink or graze. It was soon clear that to survive the hostile climate of the desert the Aberdeen Angus and Charolais required vaccinations, support, and care, attentions that the criollo had never needed. This meant that ranching in the north had to be transformed through additional investment in infrastructure and improved technology.

In the 1960s the consequences of the agricultural policy followed since the administration of Miguel Alemán Valdés began to be felt. The government of Luis Echeverría Álvarez (1970–76) was obliged to respond to the *campesinos,* who were pressuring the government by invading ranching latifundia. The president promised a revision of land ownership to free up what was left to distribute. Thus the first technical studies were made to discover the indices of pasture land that had remained undistributed since the Alemán administration. The 25 years of immunity granted by Cárdenas's certificates had now passed. Echeverría handed over approximately 200 to private proprietors, almost all of whom were in the north of the country.

The pressure from the *campesinos* was considerable, obliging the government to deal with their demands through formal channels. The state thus officially recognized the land grabs and declared itself in favor of continuing land distribution and against the immunity of the ranchers and the agrarian *amparo.* Some latifundia were affected by this recognition of *campesino* demands; nevertheless, a substantial amount of ranching properties in the country survived. Some were reduced in Tlaxcala, Zacatecas, and San Luis Potosí, and those affected were compensated with substantial sums.

From the 1960s the northern region devised an initiative to increase the value of a sector of beef production. Even though the animals were bred mainly for export, corrals for fattening livestock began to be constructed in various cities in the northern states. Animals were confined there from two to four months and fed to achieve a determined quality of meat to supply the well-to-do end of the national market (with an eye to future exports to Europe and Asia).

This experiment had a certain amount of success until the end of the 1980s, when Mexico signed the General Agreement on Tariffs and Trade (GATT) accords and later the North American Free Trade Agreement (NAFTA; 1994). These permitted the introduction of U.S. beef onto the Mexican market but prevented the import of certain grains, maize in particular, that were used as fodder for fattening the herds. These measures forced the closure of a large number of corrals and placed the rest in a tight economic situation. In the years since the GATT accords this sector of the industry has witnessed a decline.

During the second half of the twentieth century, a regional specialization has begun to emerge. The northern states turn over virtually 100 percent of their production to the U.S. market, having adapted their herds and pastures to supply corrals on the other side of the border. Hereford, Aberdeen Angus, and Charolais predominate in the north, along with other breeds that square with the demands of the U.S. market. In the tropical areas from the Gulf of Mexico to Chiapas, Zebu or Brahman cattle predominate; these cattle acclimate easily to the tropical humidity and are destined for consumption in the central region of the country, the capital in particular.

Cattle are bred in the central states that are later sent to fatten in the Huasteca region and sold to those who supply the Federal District in particular. The dairy industry predominates in the central *meseta,* relying on specialty dairy cows such as Swiss and Holstein.

Ranching has expanded since the middle of the twentieth century. In 1960 there were a total of approximately 16 million cattle in the country, a quantity that almost had doubled by 1979 to 31,632,000. In 1994, 15 years later the total was 30,649,000. Nevertheless, in overall terms, traditional land usage predominates, characterized by lack of substantial investment and free grazing only on unimproved meadowland. This approach is largely that of private proprietors who tend to expand by increasing the extent of their pastures rather than investing capital in new methods. For this reason the expansion of cattle ranching has been at the expense of the jungle in the tropical areas and the devastation of the semidesert regions in the north of the country.

See also Bullfighting

Select Bibliography

Camou Healy, Ernesto, editor, *Potreros, Vegas y Mahuechis: Sociedad y ganadería en la Sierra Sonorense.* Hermosillo: Gobierno del Estado de Sonora, 1991.

Chevalier, Francois, *Land and Society in Colonial Mexico: The Great Hacienda.* Berkeley: University of California Press, 1966.

_____, *La formación de los latifundios en México.* Mexico City: Fondo de Cultura Económica, 1976.

Esparza Sanchez, Cuauhtémoc, "Historia de la Ganadería en Zacatecas 1531–1911." In *Zacatecas, Anuario de Historia.* Zacetecas: Universidad Autónoma de Zacatecas, 1978.

Feder, Ernest, "Vacas Flacas Ganaderos Gordos: las ramificaciones internacionales de la industria del ganado vacuno en México." In *El Desarrollo Agroindustrial y la ganadería en México.* Mexico City: S.A.R.H., 1982.

Fernandez Ortiz, Luis María, and María Tarrio García, *La especialización ganadera y la soya: desperdicio de recursos y dependencia tecnológica y alimentaria.* Mexico City: Universidad Autónoma Metropolitana, 1986.

_____, *La crisis agrícola en México: algunos planteamientos y algunos desacuerdos.* Mexico City: Universidad Autonóma Metropolitana, 1986.

Machado, Manuel, *The North Mexican Cattle Industry, 1910–1975: Ideology, Conflict, and Change.* College Station: Texas A&M University Press, 1981.

Perez Lopez, Emma Paulina, *Ganadería y Campesinado en sonora. Los Poquiteros de la Sierra Norte.* Mexico City: Consejo Nacional para la Cultura y las Artes, 1993.

Reig, Nicolas, "El Sistema Ganadero-Industrial: su estructura y desarrollo." In *El Deserrollo Agroindustrial y la ganadería en México.* Mexico City: S.A.R.H., 1982.

Rutsch, Mechthild, *La ganadería Capitalista en México.* Mexico City: Editorial Linea, 1984.

—Ernesto Camou Healy

CAUDILLISMO

A generic Spanish term for leader, *caudillo* often is associated with authoritarian and personalistic governments in Spanish America. The term incorporates a multitude of modifiers to explain the legitimacy of the leadership, the means of taking power and of holding on to it. There are, according to scholar Hugh M. Hamill, certain characteristics common to most caudillos: personalistic leadership, charisma, machismo, access to economic and political power, and reciprocal arrangements between themselves and their followers that are advantageous to both.

The term *caudillo* derives from the Latin word *capitellum,* the diminutive form of *caput* (head). Its roots lie in civilizations where, according to historian François Chevalier, written contracts meant little, and security and leadership were based on personal bonds and blood ties such as the *gens* and *clientes* of the Roman Empire which encompassed and left its mark on the Iberian Peninsula.

In medieval Spain family or friends became the retainers or *criados* of the great estate owners, their relationship based on honor and reward. Scholar Glen Cudill Dealy echoes Chevalier's theory of reciprocity, noting that leadership in Catholic societies often was based of the support of family members and *compadrazgo* (godfather relationships) with friends who became a "loyal" extended family. He asserts that the amount of wealth actually held was not as important as the number of friends and supporters these men commanded.

During the Conquest, Spaniards used the term *caudillo* loosely to denote any local leader, although they attached no legitimacy to the term within the Spanish political system. It may have been used synonymously with the term *cacique,* an Arawak word, which the Spaniards used in both Mexico and Peru to describe hereditary chiefs. Spanish colonial officials often used *caudillo* as a pejorative term to denote a rebel leader in a troublesome province.

Under Fernando (Hernán) Cortés the term *caudillo* began to embody its current political meaning. As a *criado* of Diego Velázquez, the governor of Santo Domingo, Cortés received the reward of an *encomienda* (a native settlement "commended" to the care of a Spaniard—an *encomendero*—who, in return for the Indians' labor, had the duty to protect the Indians, maintain missionaries in the villages, and contribute to the military defense of the region). Accompanying Velázquez to Cuba as a clerk of the treasurer, Cortés demonstrated both military ability and resourcefulness and was awarded another *encomienda.* Using these rewards as an economic base Cortés raised livestock and became a merchant. Now a business man, a landowner, and a government employee he had created the proper social backing to become a leader.

Ambitious, Cortés sacrificed his relationship with Velázquez to create a personal empire. He completed the process by offering his followers the riches and glory of conquest in the Yucatán—his inability to "pay" his retainers was of no consequence. Cortés became then, the patron of a *clientela,* a band of armed men who could keep him in power and create an ever-widening circle of retainers. All that was left was to establish legitimacy with the Spanish Crown.

Acting in the "name of the king" he founded a municipality, appointed a governing body, and resigned leadership, allowing the "citizens" to establish his legitimacy through the electoral process. Unable to pay the men in his army, Cortés chose to reward them with the supplies and equipment he had purchased for the expedition. Many of his "soldiers" became "client caudillos" establishing their own estates and power bases. Military leader, great landowner, charismatic leader, and patron, Cortés embodied the basic characteristics of the caudillo. Spain's government was quick to establish colonial agents to counteract his power in New Spain.

Wealth through *encomienda* and conquest created a group of caudillistic leaders who used their armies of explorers to maintain political authority through feudal reward. *Encomienda* established a social hierarchy linked vertically through the patron-client or landlord-peasant relationship, which stymied more horizontal class associations. Patrons in search of greater resources or power became the "clients" of stronger men, creating an impenetrable society based on personal loyalty and "spiritual" kinship that often skirted or flagrantly broke Spanish law.

The regionality of Mexico's geography and the judicial and spiritual nature of Spanish government further compartmentalized colonial society, including its clerics. The hacienda or *estancia* owner as landlord, godfather, patron, and leader of his own private army supported the Crown through initiative and strength. Loyalty was placed in the traditional and spiritual legitimacy of the throne, not necessarily in its representatives. John Lynch has described it as an atmosphere of "dominance and dependence" that marked later Mexican history as well.

Although Mexican officials were economically and politically stronger then those in Peru and the Río de la Plata, the great expanse of territory under their jurisdiction often fell prey to another form of *caudillismo* under bandit chiefs. A sparse population was often at the mercy of bandits or thieves, who like other caudillos organized bands of supporters whose loyalty rested on reward. It was difficult at best for the Tribunal of the Acordad, assigned to maintain the peace or to keep pace with such organized crime in rural areas. The government frequently allowed the hacendado to dispense his own "personal" justice to peons and slaves. John Lynch notes that hacienda jails were often as common as hacienda chapels. In this environment the hacendado became the protector of the populace, building greater power in the name of stability.

As Mexico's population grew, the pressure on local resources often meant oppression of the local workforce or even the smaller land owners. In central and southern Mexico oppressed groups simmered, waiting for a local caudillo or cacique to arise and lead them against their oppressors. Yet, until the twentieth century, the bandit caudillo more often stood for survival and escape than for a greater ideology of peasant equality.

Toward the end of the colonial period the term *caudillo* had come into common usage in Mexico. The colony held various rural caudillos whose interconnected power served to create order in the times of oppression and held tacit government approval. It is not surprising then that many of these men would lend their private armies and initiative to the drive for Independence in the nineteenth century.

If the Wars of Independence demolished the institutions of Spanish government to build Mexican ones, they also created a power vacuum that strengthened the might and authority of the caudillo and spawned new varieties of these leaders. The leaders of Mexico's armies of liberation fought with professional soldiers and guerrilla forces and struggled with each other for power, politicizing their constituency in the process. Guerrilla leaders were often given titles and status within the army with great pomp and ceremony. During the ritual the rural caudillo often obtained both social mobility and legitimacy.

As they had in the colonial period, the spiritual leadership of the clergy legitimized their political power in the minds of Indians and peasants in their flock. Miguel Hidalgo's priesthood, then, never interfered with his machismo or his enlightened political beliefs. Indeed his priestly authority allowed Hidalgo to become the *curadillo* (a play on words combining *cura*—priest—and caudillo) of an army of the poor and oppressed. His army has been likened to a religious crusade, but the *curadillo's* power was limited to an ideal, and his rebels expected rewards that they extracted from the local populace.

The wars also spawned local caudillos whose banditry and power struggles advanced their own desires, not those of the revolution. Intimidation and violence frequently became a hallmark of these caudillos, who carried that behavior beyond the war. Caudillo Manuel Lozada, for instance, dominated the area around Nayarit (north of Guerrero) through terrorism until his death in 1873.

The first half of the nineteenth century is frequently referred to as the Age of Caudillos. Liberal or Conservative, the Mexican people struggled to create legitimate government in the aftermath of Independence. Scholar Max Weber divided political legitimacy into three "ideal types": traditional, legal, and charismatic. In Mexico, traditional authority represented the authority of the Spanish monarchy sanctified by religion and "time honored" tradition. In contrast, legal governments were legitimized by rational ideas of law and power distribution and were associated with constitutional government. The sanctity of the charismatic leader, however, rested on the exceptional character and heroism of the leader himself, which commanded the obedience of his followers. Failure to do so meant ultimate failure of leadership; in Mexico, this failure was experienced by revolutionary president, emperor, and caudillo Agustín de Iturbide, who failed to transform his charisma into moral authority. One of the greatest necessities of the caudillos of the early nineteenth century, then, was the personality cults they established.

Within Mexican history Antonio López de Santa Anna is an exceptional example of the personality cult. Santa Anna's personal drive for honorific titles and power led him to overthrow the government and lead the country to war in the name of Mexican nationalism. As an elected president his self-aggrandizement knew no limits. The Mexican treasury was depleted by constant war and his need to build a personal fortune. His exploits led intellectuals like José María Luis Mora to call Santa Anna the "Attila of Mexican civilization."

It was Santa Anna's ability to convince the public of his belief in Mexican nationalism and his ability to create order that maintained his following. He came to power through personalism and the cultivation of a powerful following that elected him legitimately, thereby granting moral authority. Once in power, as a true caudillo Santa Anna sought to "stabilize" Mexico through authoritarian government, often suspending constitutions and dissolving Congress in order to "restore law and order." It was not until the final loss of Mexican territory in the Gadsden Purchase that the Conservative elite forced him to abdicate power. Santa Anna exhibits the classic behavior of the caudillo: a regional power base, a personality cult founded on both patronage and interest groups, and a desire for personal dictatorship obtained through *golpe* and *pronunciamiento* (uprising). He adds the marks of the nineteenth-century caudillo, the idea of a nationalistic leader who creates order through strength.

Lyle McAllister describes Mexico in the first half of the nineteenth century as a "praetorian state" characterized by *golpe* and military revolution. Santa Anna's machinations fit that description. The midcentury Reforma (the era of Liberal rule) established a republican president and instituted a regime of social and political reform, but it did not stabilize Mexico; Benito Juárez and other Liberal presidents exercised authoritarian tactics, including the establishment of a rural police force to "impose" unity and order in Mexico. Those tactics were not lost on one of Mexico's greatest caudillos—Porfirio Díaz.

The reign of Porfirio Díaz, or the Porfiriato (1876–80; 1884–1911), has been variously labeled as dictatorship, modernization, neocolonialism, and the reestablishment of the patronage system. Díaz's enemies called it tyranny, while his friends labeled it a patriarchy. It was, perhaps, both; Díaz rose to power in the name of Liberalism and despite plebiscites retained power through authoritarian means reminiscent of Santa Anna. Yet Díaz was more than a revolutionary dictator, and he established his power base on both native and foreign support. Far from the leader who isolates his country, Díaz envisioned a modern Mexico. He dragged Mexico into the world market and opened its doors to European investment. European money, ideas, and art flowed into his country, although he employed the specifically Latin American version of positivism: order and then progress. To accomplish order Díaz employed the idea of *pan o palo* (bread or stick): politicians had to accept offers on his terms or suffer the outcome at the hands of his enforcers. As president he used the Rurales (rural police) as a sort of mercenary army to create what Lyle McAllister has described as a "Gendarmist State." He swerved from Liberalism again where the Church was concerned, rationalizing that the clergy could educate the countryside and teach the rural population to be subservient to both God and Díaz.

Díaz also fits the model of personalistic leadership. Luis González has likened him to a "golden calf" worshipped by elite society. That same society, however, allowed him to sell Mexican soil and business to foreigners and sat idly by as Díaz let agriculture decline. The effect of his economic policies, like those of previous caudillos, alienated both the poor and middle class.

The dictatorship of Porfirio Díaz based its power on republican ideal and authoritarian tactics. A champion of laissez-faire economics and modernity, Díaz stands apart from the traditionally conservative *caudillismo* of Santa Anna, although as a personalistic leader Díaz's power reigns supreme in the history Independent Mexico. Díaz's nationalism was not feigned, and like Juárez he strove for national unity and created a strong political machine to "institutionalize" his ideas of government. Still, by the first decade of the twentieth century the Porfiriato had not unified Mexico. Regionalism continued, and regional caudillos arose to defend the downtrodden in Mexico from the Rurales and indifferent government. Caudillos also developed out of a new intellectual class determined to overthrow dictatorship and *caudillismo* in Mexico.

The caudillos of the Mexican Revolution showed as much variety as the nineteenth-century version. Men such as Emiliano Zapata came from the lower classes and sought agrarian reform. Francisco I. Madero arose from an upper class of small estate owners determined to institute constitutionalism, while Francisco "Pancho" Villa represented the regional hacendado. Still others, such as Victoriano Huerta, represented military interests.

The conspiracy to overthrow Díaz's dictatorship was strongly based on regional needs held together only by a belief in the charismatic leadership of Madero. Madero stands, then, as a traditional caudillo, coming to power through *golpe,* surrounded by his clients and the army in the name of Mexican nationalism, unity, and constitutionalism. After his death regionality, opposing views of the Revolution, and personal differences threw Mexico into instability. Even worse, it began a practice of eradicating the competition through execution and murder rather than the abdication and exile common to the nineteenth century.

All the Revolutionary leaders depended on a circle of armed men, whether it was the Mexican Army under Huerta or rural bandits under Pancho Villa. Personalism and machismo were favored. General Álvaro Obregón declared himself a candidate for the presidency as a soldier of the Revolution who knew how to ensure the well-being of his people. Military domination, however, did not seem to aid the longevity of a twentieth-century caudillo's time in office.

The real change was that the caudillos of the twentieth century also went armed with the banner of constitutionalism: their ultimate goal was to create a civilian state. Gradually, then, the *golpe* disappeared, and the army was decommissioned and reduced. If machismo seemed to fade, charisma and personalism rose to the forefront as presidents "appointed" their successors and based their power on reciprocal agreements with various professional organizations.

By the 1940s the caudillo seemed to disappear in Mexican politics as the ideals of the revolution were engulfed by a new political party, the Partido Revolucionario Institucional (PRI, or Institutional Revolutionary Party). Perhaps, the traits of the caudillo also were institutionalized as Mexico's political caciques retained many of their characteristics. The power of government still rested in the power of its army. Personalistic leadership and patronage were incorporated into a political machine designed to elect handpicked PRI candidates from its own circle of family and friends. Election was gained through a distribution of rewards rather than on clear policies or ideals. Nationalism, prior to the presidency of Carlos Salinas de Gortari (1988–94), had returned to nineteenth-century caudillistic policies of isolation and statism, while the need for stability and unity suppressed indigenous revolts, such as that in Chiapas, and intellectual outbursts, such as the student protests at Tlatelolco.

See also Banditry; Caciquismo; Presidencialismo

Select Bibliography

Brading, D. A., editor, *Caudillo and Peasant in the Mexican Revolution.* Cambridge: Cambridge University Press, 1980.

Dealy, Glenn Cudill, *The Public Man: An Interpretation of Latin American and Other Catholic Countries.* Amherst: University of Massachusetts Press, 1977.

Ditella, Torcuato S., *Latin American Politics: A Theoretical Framework.* Austin: University of Texas Press, 1990.

Taylor, William B., "Bandit Gangs in Late Colonial Times: Rural Jalisco, Mexico, 1794–1821." *Biblioteca Americana,* 1:2 (1982).

Hamill, Hugh M., editor, *Caudillos: Dictators in Spanish America.* Norman: University of Oklahoma Press, 1992.

Johnson, John J., "Foreign Factors in Dictatorship in Latin America." *The Pacific Historical Review* 20 (1951).

Katz, Friedrich, editor, *Riot, Rebellion, and Revolution: Rural Social Conflict in Mexico.* Princeton, New Jersey: Princeton University Press, 1988.

Lynch, John, *Caudillos in Spanish America 1800–1850.* Oxford: Oxford University Press, 1992.

—Julia C. Girouard

CEDILLO, SATURNINO

1890–1939 • Guerrilla Leader, Soldier, and Governor

Saturnino Cedillo was born in 1890 in the small farm community of Las Palomas, located in the Valle del Maíz, a region in the southeast of the state of San Luis Potosí, which has a long tradition of agrarian conflicts. In June 1912, while the state was the scene of considerable social unrest, Alberto Carrera Torres emerged as a central leader of the agrarian movement. Apparently influenced by the Plan de Ayala issued by the followers of Emiliano Zapata in the state of Morelos, this educated advocate of the region's farmers formulated a radical program that called for the return of expropriated lands to the traditional and collectively managed farm communities called *ejidos,* and for the distribution of land to landless *campesinos* (peasants).

A small rebel band emerged that was closely allied to Carrera and led by a poor but well-known family in the region: the Cedillo brothers—Cleofas, Magdaleno, and Saturnino—who worked a goat farm that also produced *ixtle* (a tough vegetable fiber). Their parents owned a modest plot of land and operated a small general store while their closest relatives were mule drivers. The family had begun having major conflicts with the owners of neighboring haciendas since 1909. By the summer of 1912 the Cedillo brothers were leading an armed rebellion by a group of *campesinos* who had been brutally repressed by the local authorities, and in November they took over the town of Ciudad del Maíz and read the Plan of Ayala to the local population.

In the following years of armed conflict they tended to put forward demands reflecting the interests of the poorest *campesinos* of the state, whose support they enjoyed. As a result, they not only were obliged to fight those who identified with the old power structures from the dictatorship of Porfirio Díaz, but also against those hacienda owners who became leading figures in the Mexican Revolution, including the Barragán family. Both the Carrera and Cedillo families fought against the dictatorship of Victoriano Huerta that overthrew the government of Francisco I. Madero, but by no means were close to opposition leader Venustiano Carranza, opting instead to ally themselves with the most radical factions who were eventually defeated during the Revolution. In 1914 and 1915 they openly broke with Carranza by supporting the Convention of Aguascalientes, and later allied with the forces led by Francisco "Pancho" Villa. While they exercised control over the southeast region of San Luis Potosí, their regime was marked by radical and free-wheeling policies focused on class struggle. They intervened in a number of landed estates and frequently reacted violently against hostile landowners and administrators, including the execution of one of the region's most affluent and powerful hacienda owners, Javier Espinosa y Cuevas.

Following the defeat of Pancho Villa's forces by Carranza's troops, the Carrera and Cedillo families and their followers returned to their humble existence while continuing to sustain small-scale guerrilla war in the inhospitable and sparsely populated Valle del Maíz. Suffering a series of defeats, desertions, and betrayals, they were also subject to deteriorating living conditions marked by extreme hunger and disease. During this period Cleofas and Magdaleno Cedillo lost their lives, as did Alberto Carrera Torres. The last of the guerrilla band was on the verge of starvation and living in caves when their luck took a dramatic turn for the better in 1920: their old nemesis Carranza was defeated by the forces led by Álvaro Obregón, who recognized their authority over the Valle del Maíz. The federal government allowed them to form what were designated as Military Agrarian Colonies and to remain armed, taking their orders from Saturnino Cedillo rather than from the federal army. This allowed Cedillo officially to reaffirm his credentials as a champion of agrarian reform, guarantee the peaceful well-being of his followers, establish a working relationship with the new leaders of the federal government, and shore up his own personal power. His guerrilla band, converted into a semi-official militia, would be the key element in Cedillo's personal power structure for the rest of his life.

The generals and regional commanders who emerged out of the Revolution played a key role in allowing federal officials to consolidate the political life of the country. In this, Cedillo proved to be paradigmatic figure. He was able to keep the territories under his command in relative peace by playing a mediating role between the federal authorities and the various social forces and regional interests in San Luis Potosí, while combating those who tried to rebel against the new system. Later given the official post of chief of military operations in San Luis Potosí, Cedillo successfully defeated the local supporters of a series of uprisings throughout the 1920s, beginning with the rebellion led by Adolfo de la Huerta in 1923. When the Cristero movement took up arms from 1926 to 1929 in the central states of Mexico, Cedillo captured and executed one of the movement's main leaders and cut off his forces from the regions where they enjoyed support among the population. He was similarly successful in combating the local supporters of José Gonzalo Escobar, who rose in 1929.

These military successes allowed Cedillo to strengthen his ties with the federal government and parlay that relationship into a greater degree of autonomy in exercising control over the state. He consolidated his iron grip on the state beginning in 1925, when he defeated his former ally, the radical agrarian reformer Governor Aurelio Manrique, and by 1927 he had established his own position as governor of the state. While he served only one term (1927–32), he continued to exercise control by placing a series of loyal followers in the governorship during the succeeding years.

However, it was his native Valle del Maíz that remained the focus of his personal and political attention. The Palomas ranch, where he was born, became his private fiefdom and the heart of his political operation. Acting virtually as a feudal lord, his home was open night and day, providing food and shelter to all who asked for help and, when possible, monetary assistance and jobs. In exchange for the military and political support of the people of the region—who also were asked to render other services to Cedillo, his family, and closest circle of aides, and followers—he made sure their basic needs were met. Those who had taken up arms under his command during the Revolution, and the widows and orphans of those who had fallen in battle, were provided with land, water, schools, loans, jobs, and protection. The resulting paternalistic ties survived the passing of years and the effects of modernization that dramatically changed the social and political life of many other regions of Mexico. It was as if time had come to a halt in the Valle del Maíz, and the personal authority of Saturnino Cedillo proved so powerful that many years after his death he continued to be a major reference point in the region, regarded with a mix of gratitude and admiration.

Outside of the region, however, his intense forms of personal control gradually waned. His initial success in extending his patronage-based system of control over the rest of the state was entirely dependent on the aid he received from the federal government, and on his ability to offer material compensations to his supporters and to punish those who questioned his authority. His relationship with unionized workers in the state and elsewhere in the country always proved conflictive.

Although he was not primarily interested in national policies, he did manage to play a role in the political life of the country. He twice served as minister of agriculture, once under the brief presidency of Pascual Ortiz Rubio (September–October 1931) and later under Lázaro Cárdenas after supporting Cárdenas in his fight against former president Plutarco Elías Calles. However, Cedillo later abandoned his cabinet post when he developed serious ideological, political, and personal differences with Cárdenas.

Cedillo's particular brand of *cacicazgo,* or patronage-based political machine, had many features in common with many other post-Revolutionary fiefdoms that emerged throughout the country. Real legal and administrative power was exercised by Cedillo's relatives and most loyal followers rather than by those who formally held office. Key issues such as fiscal policies and agrarian reform were implemented based on the personal criteria of Cedillo and his closest associates rather than in line with the letter of the law. This system, which was based on the loyalty of Cedillo's traditional followers, his agrarian militias, and the peasantry of the region, proved more resilient than other *cacicazgos* to efforts by federal authorities to dismantle such regional power structures. To a certain extent, it was a prototype of the *cacicazgos* that played a central role in the political life of the country in the 1920s and 1930s.

However, the days of semi-autonomous and armed *cacicazgos* were drawing to a close. As federal officials consolidated a national state structure and pacified the country, the agrarian militias in San Luis Potosí began to outlive their usefulness and be seen as a hindrance and affront to the new regime. The state was busy building a professional army, establishing civilian channels for resolving differences between the Revolutionary generals and caudillos (strongmen) who comprised the ruling elite, and developing corporatist labor and peasant unions as a means of assuring the control by the presidency and the ruling party over the political and social life of the country. This latter development led to the establishment of sectoral power structures that replaced the regional structures key to the existence of *cacicazgos* like that of Cedillo.

This objective conflict between cacique-based and sectoral structures combined with a growing ideological conflict between Cedillo and the federal government. Cárdenas proved much more radical than Cedillo, who maintained a more moderate attitude toward the Catholic Church and who had come to oppose the system of collectively managed *ejidos,* which was not only the centerpiece of the agrarian revolution but Cárdenas's preferred vehicle for modernizing Mexican agriculture and achieving social justice in the countryside.

By 1937 tensions between Cárdenas and Cedillo reached their limit as the latter increasingly emerged as a major figure in the conservative opposition to the president. After Cedillo was dismissed as minister of agriculture, the federal government began to suspend the agrarian funding that was key to the cacique's support from the *campesinos* in the Valle del Maíz. Cárdenas drew on the new muscle of the official labor and peasant unions to establish loyal state and municipal officials and finally undercut Cedillo's military

might by deposing his old ally Francisco Carrera Torres as the head of military operations in the region.

Owing to his ideological conflict with Cárdenas, Cedillo was approached by many right-wing groups, including the fascist organization known as the "gold shirts." However, such links have been exaggerated by official and left-wing versions of the Cedillo rebellion, who have tried to portray him as an ally of the foreign oil companies whose Mexican holdings were expropriated during the zenith of Cárdenas's Revolutionary nationalist measures in March 1938. While the oil companies undoubtedly were pleased by any efforts to overthrow Cárdenas, the aging, increasingly ill, and militarily weak Cedillo never enjoyed any concrete support from Washington, the oil companies, or even the fascist governments in Europe, who saw little to be gained from such an adventure.

Cedillo's rebellion was virtually stillborn. The federal government had made certain that it possessed all the necessary elements to defeat the caudillo from Palomas before forcing Cedillo to rebel by demanding that he leave his base in the Valle del Maíz. When he was forced to take up arms in 1938, it was basically a suicidal gesture in defense of his personal honor and a refusal to recognize that his days as the caudillo of San Luis Potosí and his local project in the Valle del Maíz were a thing of the past. In a display of the depth of the personal loyalty Cedillo enjoyed, the doomed rebellion had the support of former guerrilla fighters and *campesinos,* particularly in the agrarian colonies concentrated in the same region from which he had operated since 1912. Since he viewed the rebellion as a personal conflict with Cárdenas, however, Cedillo declined the offer of support by many groups of armed *campesinos* and instead opted to take to the hills along with a small band of relatives and close supporters. Their participation in the rebellion was not based on any illusion of success but on the deep gratitude and affection they felt for Cedillo and the fact that their way of life depended on the system he had built in the region.

The old caudillo repeatedly declined various amnesty proposals from the government, which included an offer to send him abroad for medical treatment. Despite Cárdenas's apparent wish that Cedillo not be killed, many of his closest relatives, including his sister Higinia, were tortured and murdered. Saturnino and his son Suyo were killed by federal troops on January 11, 1939, after associates reported where they were hiding. Nevertheless, many followers remained loyal to his cause, and the last Cedillo rebel did not put down his arms until 25 years later.

Saturnino Cedillo was the last of the great military caciques of the Mexican Revolution who maintained his own quasi-private army. He preferred to die rather than see his legend and honor tarnished before the eyes of those who had served under him during decades of fighting and in the construction of his *campesino* fiefdom.

—ROMANA FALCÓN VEGA

CENSUS

Although it is likely that population has been counted in Mexico since the rise of the first Mesoamerican states, the only pre-Columbian census of which we have a clear record and interpretation is found in the *Matrícula de Tributos,* the *Codex Mendoza,* and the *Información sobre los tributos que los indios pagaban a Moctezuma.* Scholars believe that all three of these early post-Conquest documents derive from a lost, possibly pre-Hispanic, prototype. The documents list the tribute due the Triple Alliance (Tenochtitlan-Tetzcoco-Tlacopan) by each of their subjected *altepetl* (jurisdictions). The amount of tribute set for each such jurisdiction was meant to reflect the population size in each settlement. It is in part thanks to these documents that scholars have been able to estimate the population of Mexico at the eve of Conquest.

After the Spanish invasions, the amount of tribute that individuals paid, the forms of tribute payment (including a shift toward payment in money and the extensive use of forced labor), and changes in the forms and areas of settlement occurred without a major transformation in the system of counting people. In other words, during the first decades of colonization Spaniards relied on the traditional amounts that the various *altepetls* paid to the Aztecs. This situation contributed to the demographic collapse that occurred after Conquest, because the population decline was not successfully factored into the traditional tribute requirements, thereby causing periodic famine in villages that were left short-handed for their own labor requirements.

The combination of concern over the extent of population loss, the growing scarcity of indigenous labor—and hence the competition for that labor between powerful Spaniards—and the Spanish Crown's desire to know and administer the new territories generated new mechanisms for counting and mapping the population. Thus, a number of *padrones* (registries) and *matrículas* (registers) of tributaries were carried out in the decades following the Conquest, including copies of the Aztec system of tribute, and lists of tributaries and of tribute due from specific towns and regions. Some of the latter documents were generated for litigation between *encomenderos* (trustees of land grants—*encomiendas*—who also held the labor of Indians on the land) or between *encomenderos* and Indian villages. Numbers of tributaries were both important and disputed in these early decades after the Conquest, when Indians in *encomienda* were changing hands frequently; religious orders had intense labor requirements for the construction of churches, convents, and plantations; and the labor prerogatives of the indigenous nobility were still in dispute.

These various listings of inhabitants in Indian towns and Spanish cities were not carried out systematically, however, a situation that changed with the royal ordinance of September 24, 1571, when King Felipe II created the post of Royal Cosmographer and Chronicler. The role of the Royal Cosmographer was to systematize and synthesize data com-

piled in the Indies. The first systematic, kingdom-wide census was carried out through the famous *relaciones geográficas* of approximately 1580. These *relaciones* include information on crops, location of villages, population, natural resources, languages spoken, political and religious jurisdiction, transportation, and other outstanding features, and they were commissioned by the king and carried out by regional Spanish authorities *(corregidores* and *alcaldes mayores),* who in turn relied heavily on Indian governors and, especially, on parish priests for information on each locality. The *relaciones geográficas* of 1580 provided a full dictionary of peoples and places in the viceroyalty of New Spain for the Crown's own use. They are the most systematic census on the population, resources, and geography of New Spain to have been carried out under the Hapsburgs. Interestingly, the questionnaire that was developed for this census of the Indies was soon applied in Spain itself; thus the desire for systematic information on the overseas kingdoms affected the production of state knowledge on Iberia itself.

There were three other significant efforts to generate systematic, kingdom-wide statistical information under the Hapsburgs: these were the *relaciones geográficas* of 1608 to 1612, those of 1648, and the census of 1679 to 1683. All of these efforts produced incomplete data that generally lacked the detail and wealth produced by the efforts of the 1570s and 1580s. It is arguably the case that the lax attitude in the production of systematic census materials in the seventeenth century is itself a reflection of the decadence of the Hapsburg Empire.

The Crown was not the only generator of statistical information, for along with the various *visitas* that were carried out on orders of the royal bureaucracy (which sometimes involved gathering census materials), the various religious provinces also had their *visitas,* for instance for confirmation, in which bishops or archbishops gathered information on numbers of inhabitants in the various towns of their province. Moreover, in the case of the 1679 to 1683 census, it was the bishops, not the civil authorities, who were charged with compiling all information.

The church was critical in the production of knowledge on the population because parish records were the only legally enforced register of births, deaths, and marriages. Other forms of counting, including economic censuses, relied strongly on the existence of royal monopolies for their existence. For instance, silver production in New Spain was monitored closely by officials thanks to the Crown's monopoly on the production of mercury, a product that was indispensable for silver mining; the numbers of Spaniards in the territory were monitored through the royal monopoly on Transatlantic shipping; the slave trade also depended in theory on royal franchises controlling numbers of Africans being brought into the Americas; indigenous population was counted thanks to the royal monopoly over the dispensation of tribute and forced labor as well as to the church's rights to tithes. Finally, the fact that commerce was organized through a monopolistic structure that had the Casa de Contratación of Seville, with its merchant *consulado* at the apex and the *corregidores* of indigenous provinces at the bottom, also meant that accounts were kept on trade in the polity as a whole.

Three aspects of the colonial system of census and record production are significant. The first is that reliance on Crown monopolies over trade, mercury, tobacco, and the like produced highly useful but also necessarily incomplete information. For instance, the Crown knew how much silver was produced in Mexico but had no reliable information on gold production because gold mining was not easily controlled through royal monopoly. Contraband was a perennial problem for the Crown in the colonies, and this made for systematic underestimates in the registers not only of trade, but also of numbers of Spaniards and slaves in Mexico.

The second feature of the colonial system of census production is the close interdependence between church and Crown officials. The church's responsibility over the life-cycle of individuals and the presence of priests in indigenous parishes made the clergy into experts on local affairs and local accounting.

The third major characteristic is that censuses and statistics were gathered on the orders of specific officials, and census taking reflected direct relations of governmentality between the state and specific constituencies (villages, cities, haciendas, mines) or administrative provinces either of the Crown or of the church. Accordingly, statistics were not a matter of "public" debate except in the relation of a specific constituency and its corresponding statistic. On the contrary, statistics on the population, productivity, or resources of the kingdom was information that was privy to the Crown, a state secret that was jealously guarded from the eyes of European competitors. For example, in his instruction for the compilation of *relaciones geográficas,* King Felipe II warned that the information generated by this exercise would be useful to Spain's enemies and should therefore be kept under lock and key. The royal cosmographer and chronicler was thus understood to be a counselor of the king, and not a public intellectual in the modern sense. Published maps and censuses from Mexico of this period tend to be printed by enemies of Spain: England, Holland, France, and Germany.

During the so-called Bourbon Reforms of the eighteenth century, the colonial system began to move away from its reliance on the church as principal statesman and the ad hoc quality of statistics. The Bourbon Reforms can be seen both as an administrative reform and as a symptom of profound cultural changes. If Spain's Bourbon monarchs believed that they needed to revamp the system of state revenues, the influence of Enlightenment thought in Spain gave new authority to liberal theories of wealth as a product of human labor and trade between nations, and it also created new respect for science as a practical art whose utility was related to the public good. Both of these factors contributed to deep changes in the production of social statistics.

This shift had two significant aspects. First, the production of a wealth of information was necessary for various administrative and urban reforms: the maximization of state revenue, and the rationalization of production and of urban life all required a reliable basis of information. Second, eighteenth-century conceptions of public utility tended to make censuses and statistics into matters of public concern and, therefore, into part of the ideological arsenal for the thriving nationalist sentiment of the period. It is perhaps no accident that two of the major scientific figures of New Spain in the latter half of the eighteenth century, father José Antonio Alzate and Francisco Javier Clavigero, were both passionate nationalists whose science was seen as part of a public service.

One example of the connection between public administration and census production under the Bourbons is the 1753 census of Mexico City, which is a detailed and meticulous survey of the city's population, infrastructure, and wealth that was in part carried out as a response to urban insecurity. The city was perceived as housing vagabonds and a rabble that had to be located, counted, and subsequently treated as a public problem. The census would ideally serve, among other things, to guarantee that Indians continue to live in their segregated communities and not in the city.

The connection that was made between enlightenment and public utility eventually split into attitudes regarding the publicity due to censuses and statistics. This process was crowned with the royal approval that was granted to Baron Alexander von Humboldt's scientific expedition, the first such permit that ever was granted to a foreigner by the Spanish Crown. Humboldt's published statistics on Mexico's population and wealth was a momentous achievement, for even as late as 1791 the Inquisition had barred Viceroy Juan Vicente Güemez Pacheco y Padilla from publishing the results of the population census that he had ordered. Although Humboldt merely aggregated and published data that was furnished to him by local administrators, these census materials had been part of the state's secret arsenal of information. So, when Simón Bolívar claimed that Humboldt's books had done more for American independence than any other writing it was because his work was the consummation of an idea of public information that allowed for an aggregated view of the Americas as political communities.

Humboldt's publication inaugurated a new era in the politics of censuses, an era that had its first serious political debut for the organization of political representation (*diputados provinciales*) for the Cortes at Cádiz in 1812, but whose issues were repeated in the constitutional debates that lead to the 1824 Constitution and in all subsequent debates regarding political representation, including debates on the shape and form of electoral districts in the 1990s. Correspondingly, in 1822 the *diputados provinciales* were ordered to make censuses of their provinces, though only the census for Michoacán was ever published. The Constitution of 1824 made the census mandatory as a mechanism to determine the number of deputies that each state could send to Congress.

The idea that the state could function as an administrator of public utility through science became a key dogma of nineteenth-century nationalists, as can be appraised in the following quotation from an official report by the government of the state of Mexico in 1849:

> Society, like men, has it obligations, and if a father deserves the spite and hatred of the public in addition to the sanctions of a judge if he abandons his children and watches them grow in the mud of immorality and misfortune without remedying the situation or attempting to direct their actions . . . in the same way society deserves the spite of the enlightened man and of all of the peoples that observe it when it watches the unfortunate lives of its disgraced orphans, when it witnesses steps descending towards corruption and misfortune . . . and has never once thought of remedying the situation. . . . (cited in Mayer, 1995.)

Independence gave a new dimension to population statistics because these statistics were connected not only with the national imaginary, but also with the power struggles between regions. In fact the new uses of statistics in the national period eventually undermined the three major characteristics of colonial censuses: they tended no longer to rely as heavily on the church (eventually they gained independence from the church altogether), they tended to be in the public domain, and they were usually less reliable than colonial statistics because they did not have the backing of state commercial monopolies and because of the politicization of state bureaucracy that followed Independence. On the other hand, there was a great profusion of statistics and of public concern over both the realities that they were meant to reflect and over the images that could be conjured through them.

In 1833 the Instituto Nacional de Geografía y Estadística was founded, and its first *Boletín* was published in 1839 and has been published more or less continuously ever since. The activities of mapping and counting the population, the resources, and the wealth of the nation was claimed as a matter of national interest, but the decline of the central bureaucratic apparatus that followed Independence meant that only the army and state governors had the needed resources for more systematic counting. It is no coincidence that the three major figures in early Mexican social statistics were military men (J.J. Gómez de la Cortina, J.N. Almonte, and J. Vázquez de León).

The statistics that were generated in the decades following Independence were imagined as contributions to a map of the nation's resources and human characteristics. More subtly, these statistics, which usually pertained to one region or another and were not simultaneous national endeavors, furthered the political claims of the governors and regionalists that fostered them. The endeavor of fashioning a useful and reliable base of information for statecraft that was imagined by eighteenth-century scientists such as Alzate was not realized after Independence; this was the result, on the one hand, of the lobbying and competition between states, a situation that was exacerbated by the decline of a centralized bureaucracy, and on the other of the war with the United States.

One significant innovation of social statistics in the years after Independence were studies of deviations from the norm: the proportion of prostitutes, of criminals, illiterates, or physically malformed individuals in relation to the population as a whole. These studies, which often were based on statistics gathered in Mexico City (which soon became the capital of Mexican public opinion), were deployed to show that the Mexican people were good raw material for nationhood. Deviations from the norm were shown alongside comparable statistics from Paris to show the superiority of Mexicans. It is noteworthy that France, and not Spain or the United States, was the standard point of comparison for these statistics of the 1830s and 1840s.

Although statisticians of the post-Independence period were often military men, population figures still depended largely on parish records, while information on agricultural production and the like was captured by municipal presidents, *jefes políticos,* and heads of military zones. With the Wars of Reform and the Constitution of 1857, Liberals ended the monopoly of the Catholic Church over state interference in social reproduction: lay education was promoted along with freedom of religion. As a result, birth, death, and marriage no longer needed to be registered by the Catholic Church, and a civil registry was created in which all citizens by law had to register their newly born, their marriages, and their dead. Thus, although conditions for generating censuses were poor from 1850 to 1870, the mechanisms for generating such statistics were placed squarely in the hands of the state.

After the Mexican-American War, statisticians were forced to face the fact that the knowledge of the Republic that they had produced was not sufficient or sufficiently precise. The efforts that had been lavished in the 1830s and 1840s on showing that as a people Mexicans were every bit as good as the French may have been useful in consolidating a utopian nationalism that displayed much vitality throughout the nineteenth and twentieth centuries, but it was not useful for the real situations that confronted the Mexican state. As that state consolidated its hold over the national territory after the Mexican-American War, statisticians concerned themselves more explicitly with the question of acquiring steady and reliable information. Thus, in 1853 the Ministerio de Fomento (Ministry of Finance) was formed and charged with the compilation of statistics, and in 1867 a special section in the Ministry of Hacienda (Treasury) was created to forge the statistics that were required for the stabilization of taxation.

The regime of Porfirio Díaz (1876–80; 1884–1911) had the pretense of fashioning itself on the principles of public utility spearheaded by a positive science. This idea evidently buttressed the production of statistics, a tendency that was also materially possible thanks to the political consolidation of a centralized state and to the creation of a national economy linked internally by rail. The Dirección General de Estadística was formed under Díaz in 1882, and this institution and its successors have been in charge of carrying out censuses on a regular basis, and the *Boletín Anual de Estadística* (later called the *Anuario Estadístico de la República Mexicana*) was published beginning in 1893. The first nationwide census was carried out in 1895 as a trial run, and starting in 1900 it has been applied regularly every ten years.

The birth of the Dirección General de Estadística reflected both a significant transformation in methods of state vigilance and a critical articulation of an international system for monitoring "progress" and for shaping an image of the nation. The call for regular standardized national census taking was made at the first International Congress of Statistics, held in Brussels in 1853, and it was repeated in the twentieth century by institutions such as the United Nations and the Organization of American States. The regular production of these standardized statistics under Díaz helped consolidate Mexico's position as an emerging independent nation.

The creation of an institutional home for statisticians also reshaped the techniques of state vigilance. For instance, in his inaugural speech as Academician of the Sociedad Mexicana de Geografía y Estadística, Salvador Echagaray explained that "[t]he cause of the alteration of data is the personal interest of those that provide it: changes in age or in marriage status are relatively secondary, but when it comes to the information provided by agriculturists or miners on their own production, the amounts tend invariably to be reduced for fear of their serving as a basis for taxation." As a result, Echagaray asserted the need to develop methods of control and vigilance: "[k]nowing the interests, customs, worries, in a word, the psychology of the group on which one is to operate is indispensable for a director of statistical research," and he advocated using the internal consistencies and inconsistencies between statistics to exert pressure on data gatherers. The experience of the first few censuses was thus part of a process wherein statistics ceased being primarily manipulated by state governors and became the purview of the national government, whose agents attempted to utilize statistical regularity and irregularity as a secret weapon to induce data gatherers to get the truth from people. In this sense, one can argue that a panopticon-like technique of state power comes to be associated with the Mexican census only as late as the turn of the twentieth century. To quote again from Echagaray:

> It is evident that data-collecting agents shall not give information lightly and that they shall take care to register the truth when they feel a continuous and methodical vigilance [based on statistical irregularities], and that they shall seek to avoid being shamed by the Dirección General de Estadística which, through the conduit of the Governor of their State, shall demonstrate their lack of attentiveness.

Nevertheless, it would be wrong to imagine that this moment sealed the fate of centralized state control over population and social statistics. The Mexican Revolution interrupted the work of statisticians in at least two ways: first, the country was not safe for census-taking in 1921, and that census suffered correspondingly; second, the laws of agrarian reform tied land grants to population, and provided for an intense politics of counting and recounting in the countryside, particularly during the 1930s. Nevertheless, the decentralization of state power produced by the Revolution proved to be short-lived, and the connection between the central state and statistics was consistently fortified after the 1920s. In 1939 the first industrial, commercial, and land-value census was undertaken. In 1940 it was the first census of *ejido* (communal village landholdings) and agricultural production. Economic censuses have been produced regularly in five-year intervals since 1931. The combination of factors reviewed here, including the existence of the Civil Registry and the consolidation of a national bureaucracy, has allowed for an ever more refined and regular production of official statistics.

One final shift in the production of statistics began roughly in the 1970s. This shift was the partial result of two factors: the development of marketing research on one hand, and the rise of polls as an aid against traditional methods of electoral control by the reigning party, on the other. The history of marketing research in Mexico has not been studied as of yet, but the story of private polling is more recent and public, and therefore easier to sketch out.

The 1988 presidential elections in Mexico were the first seriously contested elections in decades. Several newspapers and nongovernmental organizations carried out surveys before, during, and after the elections as a method of control. This experiment in constituting an idea regarding the nature of public opinion that was not controlled directly by the government was not isolated. A few private foundations, such as the Fundación Banamex, had financed surveys intended to construct up-to-date profiles of opinions, culture, and habits of Mexicans in previous years. These surveys have been utilized to construct a representation of public opinion that purports to be scientific, and it tends to substitute earlier forms of manifesting public opinion, such as political rallies and journalistic interpretations of popular sentiment.

Since the late 1980s, polls have been utilized as the basis for representing popular sentiment by various political actors, including government agencies, nongovernmental associations, political parties, and news agencies. These alternative representations of public opinion based on statistical research purport to end the governmental monopoly on the representation of the Mexican public opinion. More subtly, perhaps, the methods also centralize the means to represent public opinion, veering away from earlier constructions of public opinion through mass demonstrations and journalism, and towards a mechanism of opinion-gathering that is controlled by adequately funded corporations.

The census has not only transformed mechanisms of state planning and vigilance, it also has shaped a national imaginary by transforming public opinion from a phenomenon that is forged in public (through newspapers, in rallies and demonstrations, etc.) to the aggregate of opinions expressed in the privacy of one's home. Thus the most recent stage in census gathering allows for competition between state and private agencies in the representation of the Mexican people, while it collapses forms of popular self-representation that involve public action into a sum of private opinions whose veracity is monitored by ever more refined methods for detecting statistical inconsistencies.

See also Migration; Population; Relaciones Geográficas

Select Bibliography

Echagaray, Salvador, "El método estadístico y algunas de sus aplicaciones." *Boletín de la Sociedad Mexicana de Geografía y Estadística* 6 (1913).

Gerhard, Peter, "Un censo de la diócesis de Puebla en 1681." *Historia Mexicana* 30:4 (1981).

Humboldt, Alexander von, *Ensayo político sobre el reino de la Nueva España.* Mexico City: Porrúa, 1984.

Mayer Celis, Laura Leticia, *Estadística y comunidad científica en México, 1826–1848.* Ph.D. diss., Centro de Estudios Históricos, El Colegio de México, 1995.

Moreno, Rafael, "La ciencia y la formación de la mentalidad nacional en Alzate." *Quipú* 6:1 (1989).

Rouaix, Pastor, "Algunas rectificaciones al Censo del Estado de Durango, practiado en el año de 1921." *Boletín de la Sociedad Mexicana de Geografía y Estadística* 37 (1928).

Secretaría de Programación y Presupuesto, *El censo de población de Nueva España 1790, primer censo de México.* Mexico City: SPP, 1988.

Vázquez Valle, Irene, *Los habitantes de la Ciudad de México vistos a través del censo de 1753.* Master's thesis, Centro de Estudios Históricos, El Colegio de México, 1975.

—Claudio Lomnitz

CENTRAL AMERICA

See under Foreign Policy

CHARLOT, JEAN

1898–1979 • Artist and Writer

Charlot was born in Paris and died in Honolulu. He worked in France, Mexico, the continental United States, and the Pacific. In each place, he was inspired by the local culture and contributed to it in the visual arts, literature, and scholarship.

Charlot's maternal French forebears migrated to Mexico in the early nineteenth century and intermarried with Mexican, Jewish, and Nahua families. Charlot's great-uncle Eugène Goupil donated the Boturini-Aubin collection of codices to the Bibliothèque Nationale in Paris as a memorial to his Nahua mother. The Goupils—along with Désiré Charnay, Auguste Génin, and Eugène Boban—were part of a movement to revalorize Mexica (Aztec/Nahua) culture through scholarship and the arts. Charlot grew up in Paris surrounded by Mexican art and folklore, studying Mexica literature and art, and conversing in Spanish with family and friends visiting from Mexico.

A prolific artist and writer from his youth, Charlot belonged to a group of social-minded Roman Catholic liturgical artists who wanted to create public art that was both authentically modern and as legible and moving as the medieval cathedrals. In World War I, however, he was drafted from school into the horse artillery, saw combat, and participated in the occupation of the Rhineland. In his saddlebags he carried the wood blocks of his first great work, the *Way of the Cross,* into which he poured all the feeling inspired by the war. Demobilized in 1920, he was forced to liquidate his deceased father's business and was frustrated by the rejection of his mural project for a parish church. He and his mother decided to join their Mexican family in 1921.

Charlot was overwhelmed by Mexico: its light, its peoples, and its cultures. He soon met artists and writers who became important cultural figures. In their memoirs, they describe Charlot informing them of the latest European movements and sharing his vast technical and historical knowledge. He introduced Mexican poets to the French Symbolists and illustrated books by the Estridentistas Manuel Maples Arce and Germán List Arzubide.

Charlot's friends record also that he opened their eyes to many aspects of their own world with visits to the new museum of archaeology and his studies of colonial and popular culture, especially his discovery of the print-maker José Guadalupe Posada. Charlot was filling the role of the cultural catalyst, the insider-outsider, the participant-observer. As an up-to-date Parisian, he could reassure his colleagues that the national art they were developing together was more valuable than the imitations of Europe promoted by others.

Charlot's role as a visual artist in the Mexican Mural Renaissance has been the subject of controversy, but is increasingly recognized as central to the development of style, themes, techniques, and ideology. In Charlot's judgment, Mexican subjects previously had been treated with borrowed and thus inadequate styles. Artists had created new views, but not a new vision. Using his *Way of the Cross* as a base, Charlot and others produced a series of woodcuts that were aggressively different: Indian faces pushed up through the wood in dark masses and rough, conflicting lines. In their raw strength, the sheets could have been pulled from the street; in their expressiveness, they made visible the frightening energy still seething from the Revolution.

Just as the Greeks had based their art on the body, Charlot studied the Indian body to develop a new aesthetic, using his knowledge of Cubism and the French appreciation of geometric forms. Charlot chose Luz Jiménez, later a major Nahuatl writer and anthropological-linguistic informant, as the model of Aztec beauty, which he analyzed in line drawings and prismatic paintings. He then synthesized the powerful and memorable image that can be traced from codices and followed throughout the Mexican Renaissance.

Charlot deepened the received themes of Mexican art by opening them to symbolic interpretation. The *Cargador* (Burden Bearer) was not depicted as a colorful detail of a street scene, but was *Crucified to the Stone,* Christ seen in the poor. The kneeling mother grinds corn on the *metate* while the infant strapped to her back is rocked to sleep by her motion: *Rest and Work,* the heroism of everyday life. The *Volador* intones a classic chant before diving from the high pillar to twirl tethered by his feet to the ground. The viewer recognizes the laborer of the day in the poet of the night, a peer in the universal quest of experience and art.

Charlot created three monumental expressions of such themes in his 1923 frescoes in the Secretariat of Education. His earlier *Massacre in the Main Temple* in the Preparatory School was the first completed true fresco of the Mexican Renaissance and the first monumental depiction of a theme that would become standard: the Conquest as the tragic crucible of modern Mexico. The classic and dynamic geometry of Charlot's compositions demonstrated that the new movement could use and extend the highest achievements of the past.

Throughout his stay in Mexico, Charlot was conscious of the historic importance of the period. He collected information, gathered documents, and wrote articles and books that are valuable both for their data and for his interpretation; most prominently, *The Mexican Mural Renaissance, 1920–1925* (1963). He extended his studies to Nahuatl, writing a puppet play in that language in 1946. From 1926 to 1928, he worked as an artist and archaeologist on the Carnegie expedition, coauthoring the official report, *The Temple of the Warriors at Chichén Itzá, Yucatán* (1931), and supervising its publication.

In the United States and the Pacific, he continued the pattern he had begun in France and perfected in Mexico: he studied the people and the local culture in order to develop an aesthetic that could express them powerfully. Young Hawaiian artists now recall his images, and his iconic still-life of Fiji was installed in the parliament of that newly independent nation. In 1968 and 1994, the Mexican government recognized Charlot's contribution with major retrospectives.

Select Bibliography

Brenner, Anita, *Idols Behind Altars: The Story of the Mexican Spirit.* Boston: Beacon Press, 1970.

Charlot, Jean, *The Mexican Mural Renaissance: 1920–1925.* New Haven and London: Yale University Press, 1963.

_____, *An Artist on Art: Collected Essays of Jean Charlot.* 2 vols., Honolulu: University Press of Hawaii, 1972.

Klobe, Thomas, editor, *Jean Charlot: A Retrospective.* Honolulu: University of Hawaii Art Gallery, 1990.

Koprivitza, Milena, and Blanca Garduño Pulido, *México en la obra de Jean Charlot.* Mexico City: Consejo Nacional para la Cultura y las Artes, 1994.

Moore, Ethel, "Jean Charlot, Paintings, Drawings, and Prints." *Georgia Museum of Art Bulletin* 2:2 (Fall 1976).

Morse, Peter, *Jean Charlot's Prints: A Catalouge Raisonné.* Honolulu: University Press of Hawaii and the Jean Charlot Foundation, 1976; supplement, 1983

—JOHN CHARLOT

CHARRERÍA

Charrería is a complex social, aesthetic, and athletic tradition that dates to seventeenth-century New Spain and finds its sources in medieval Spanish and Arabian horsemanship. It incorporates folk arts in elaborate costuming and horse trappings, and it upholds Mexican norms of patriotism, mastery of precision equestrian and roping skills, family and community cooperation, and the value of work in rural ranching society.

The athletic and aesthetic elements of *charreada,* the primary public manifestation of *charrería* tradition, originate from roundup fiestas on haciendas established in the seventeenth century. Today *charreadas,* sponsored by family and community *charro* associations in cities and towns across Mexico, celebrate Mexican history and identity.

For those who perform in and attend *charrería* events, the *charro* is gentleman rider, patriot, inheritor and performer of the New World's oldest equestrian tradition. His horse, his equestrian skill, his mastery of aristocratic social protocols, and his historical role in the forging of Mexican national identity link him to the conquest and development of Mexico.

Though the *charro* is a uniquely North American figure, his identity, and the broader tradition of *charrería* of which he is the dominant symbol, has been forged from materials, practices, and attitudes adapted from Moorish, Spanish, and Native American cultures. From the Spanish Riding School and the agile *jinete* riding style of North African Moors, the *charro* inherited a mixed equestrian style adaptable to the rugged landscape and livestock industry of the Americas. The shaping of this tradition began with the landing of 20 horses of mixed European and Moorish Barb stock on the Mexican mainland April 21, 1519, the onset of Fernando (Hernán) Cortés's conquest of Mexico.

The rich valley surrounding what is now Mexico City provided an ideal environment for propagating horses. Adapting to this new environment, horses became stockier and hardier. Their agility and endurance suited them to expeditions to expand the frontiers of New Spain and especially to the emerging cattle industry. When, in 1549, Viceroy Luis de Velasco ordered ranching moved to the arid regions of the north, the hacienda system that generated the social and occupational bases for *charrería* began.

Working wild longhorn cattle on mountainous and arid landscapes required lighter gear than the iron-treed saddles and heavy tack (harness) used by the conquistadors. Despite laws banning indigenous people from riding horses, the introduction of livestock by missionaries soon necessitated exemption for Indian herders, who contributed a light-weight wooden saddle tree and ropes woven from fiber of the maguey cactus. These long ropes replaced barbed spears used in Europe for controlling docile cattle. Natives also used a style of gradually gentling horses that survives today in the *charro* method of schooling young horses for performance. While the horse, saddle form, and neck-reining techniques of the conquistadors contributed basic elements for *charro*-style horsemanship, Native innovations shaped the *charro*'s method of taming, riding, and controlling stock and contributed directly to the unique emphasis in *charreada* on skill in handling and flourishing lengthy maguey fiber ropes.

Charros are most directly the cultural descendants of the hacendados and rancheros who practiced the new riding style and controlled the rural economy and much of the social structure of Mexico until the early twentieth century. As landowners, these prototypes of the contemporary *charro* were intensely involved in the day-to-day activities of their operations.

Bi-annual roundups offered an opportunity for rancheros to invite their neighbors to share work and enjoy celebrations that included equestrian games, lavish feasts, music and dancing, courtship, and religious rituals. The work and play of the roundup established the events of the *charreada.*

During roundup, catching wild horses required riders to throw *piales,* underhand casts of the loop to catch galloping horses' back legs and bring them to a slow halt by playing out a long rope dallied around the plate-shaped saddle horn. *Ternas,* catching the head and heels of bulls and stretching them out for branding, offered each rider a chance to display skills at flourishing the rope. *Colas,* tailing bulls, allowed riders to cull animals from the herd and throw them to the ground by twisting the tail. This task took on a competitive edge when riders chased bulls along a wall and competed for prizes for making the quickest catch. Throwing *manganas,* ropes to catch a galloping horse's front feet and shoulder-roll it to the ground, either while on foot or from horseback, was the most demanding demonstration of roping. For the sake of competitive panache, *charros* sometimes ran one noose around their own necks and flung the other end over the horses' forelegs, throwing themselves backwards to jerk horses to the ground, a dangerous feat that still brings great admiration from spectators.

Selecting certain wild horses for use as mounts allowed owners and workers alike to demonstrate their staying power as they attempted to ride out the broncs' leaps and bucks and dismount a quieted horse ready for training. Bull riding was pure bravado, an opportunity for the daring to pit themselves against the power and cunning of enraged bulls. Games also provided displays of horsemanship. In one such game, *rayar,* a line was drawn and the rider galloped toward it from the opposite end of a runway, pulling the horse to a sliding stop calculated to come to the line but not cross it. Now performed as a competitive reining event, this demonstration of control also includes spins and backing the horse into the alley of the *lienzo,* the key-hole shaped modern day site of *charrería* competition.

Charreadas commemorate the work and competitions of the hacienda and *ranchería* not only in their nine events but in the costumes of participants. The *charro* costume and tack make this gentleman rider distinctive throughout the world. Each outfit is unique, though it must fall within rules of dress for competition and varying degrees of formal social activities. In the *charreada* arena, the performer wears the working outfit with leather chaps and simply adorned high crowned, broad brimmed hat. Suede jacket, a collarless shirt with butterfly tie, and tailored pants complete the outfit. For very formal occasions, the *charro* may wear a black suit and *sombrero* adorned in pure gold or silver filigree and a sidearm equally lavishly embossed. In competition his saddle carries a braided quirt, a sheathed sword, and a *sarape,* all reminders of the origins of the tradition on vast ranches that required riders to carry their comforts with them. For *congresos,* championship competitions, or formal social events like association's queen's balls or elegant *charro* weddings, the saddle and bridle are richly tooled with silver and intricate maguey fiber stitching. The designation *charro* is as much a recognition of a distinctive mode of dress as it is of horsemanship, though without a horse, a *charro* might be mistaken for a *mariachi* musician. Those *mariachi* costumes are not individually designed; they are a corruption of the *charro* semi-formal outfit. *Charros* resent being identified with entertainers, for the *charrería* tradition requires not only equestrian skills and performance but adherence to a strict code of social conduct and a commitment to patriotic service that they see as distinguishing them from members of leisure or occupational groups. Because of a history of military service, today's *charros* still serve as a reserve army and wear pistols as part of their costumes.

The connection between *charrería* and patriotism originates in *charro* participation and leadership in both Mexico's War of Independence and the 1910 Revolution. The ranchero rose to national prominence in the 1810 war to overthrow colonial rule, though the identification of the *charro* with independent Mexico began well before the actual war. In the eighteenth century in many rural areas, dissatisfaction with restrictions imposed by the Spanish Crown fed dissension. Because independent ranchers and hacendados were self-sufficient and passionately attached to the land, and they commanded the loyalty of *vaqueros* (cowboys), they became military leaders. They commanded the rugged and cunning local horsemen in successful battles against the army of the Crown and made the their distinctive costume—short jacket, blue pants, red sash and bandanna, braid-adorned sombrero—and horsemanship a symbol of free Mexico. Though the term *charro* in Spain once designated a crude peasant, their patriotism in Mexico elevated it to a term of honor.

At the same time, rural women all across Mexico, even the wives of hacendados, donned the traditional village costume of peasant blouse and embroidered skirt and shawl to show their support of the War for Independence. Today, the *china poblana* costume is worn by *charras* for social occasions and is embellished richly to meet the formality of the *charro's gran gala* costume. Like the *charro,* the *charra* is featured frequently in media, arts, tourism, and patriotic representations of Mexico.

Independence did not guarantee self-rule for Mexico; in 1861, Europe forced the new Mexican Empire to accept Maximilian von Hapsburg as emperor. He soon elevated *charrería* to new heights of elegance by introducing the black *traje* (suit). He brought *charro* attire to an urban setting, foreshadowing the migration of *charreada* from hacienda and rural village to city arena during the subsequent four decades under the dictatorship of Porfirio Díaz.

During his regime, hacendados several generations removed from their hardy frontiersmen ancestors became conservative and isolated from the rural populations, leaving their ranches in the hands of administrators and moving to the capital to enjoy rounds of lavish social events. For them, the working traditions of *charrería* became pastimes; they developed urban competitions and exhibitions to meet their nostalgia for rural life and to pass gentlemanly equestrian traditions to their sons. Because of urban performance of *charro* events and skills, the last quarter of the nineteenth century was a golden age for *charrería,* with professional *charros* touring Europe, South American, the United States, and cities throughout Mexico, which laid the foundation for regulated *charreada* competition after the Revolution. In the twentieth century, upper-class urban *charros* would be remembered as the *guardia vieja* (old guard), preservers of the *charrería* tradition despite their connection to a period of political corruption.

When the abuses of the Porfiriato became unbearable, rancheros mobilized the rural population in a massive upheaval of civil war. Epitomizing the patriotism, horsemanship, and honor of the *charro* during this period is Emiliano Zapata. He was a natural horseman, a famous horse trainer and *charreada* competitor, and something of a village dandy in his *charro* costumes even before he gained fame as a revolutionary. As a result of his reputation as a military leader, he became and still is the most revered figure of *charrería.*

The role of women in the Revolution expanded the symbolic role of the *china* into an active performance role for women in contemporary *charrería,* first as association royalty and exhibition performers. Then in the 1950s, women became *charreada* performers, and in the 1990s competitors, in an event called *escaramuza.* This term, which means skirmish, connects *charras* to the Revolution, as does the Adelita costume: a nineteenth-century style full-skirted, high-necked, long-sleeved, colorful costume said to have been worn by a heroine of the civil war. It is now worn by young women who ride side-saddle to perform intricate drill patterns and mounted slides at a full gallop. This colorful element of *charreada* displays traditional feminine qualities of modesty and elegance, yet requires extraordinary equestrian skill and athletic strength. It imposes a genteel iconography on dangerous and arduous equitation. Like the *charro,* the *charra* is an ambiguous icon of Mexican identity, a symbol of the aristocratic social and ranching traditions of the colonial period but also of the patriotism of two bloody revolutions against privilege and tyranny.

The 1910 Revolution broke the hacienda system. The great herds of cattle and horses were severely diminished, the old guard cast aside, and skilled saddle and tack makers either dead or dispossessed. *Charrería* was in danger of extinction. Yet for many, particularly for the *vaqueros,* rancheros, and hacendados who survived, the possibility of losing the horsemanship skills that linked them to the land and its history prompted a resurgence of public performance that was congruent with the post-Revolutionary resurgence of concern for a distinctly national culture. This concern created a fertile environment for the propagation of *charrería* as a reminder of the glory of Mexico's past and as a symbol of the merging of Native American and Spanish cultures into a uniquely Mexican identity.

City *charros* revived the *colas, piales, ternas, manganas,* and other competition events that had been part of hacienda fiestas. Detached from the work of the countryside, *charreada* became primarily a sport, though it has remained strongly enmeshed in a context of social events and traditions and still has ties to working ranch culture. Because of the arts associated with the tradition, *charreada* became a refined combination of athletic skills and artistic style and costuming. In 1919, the first *charro* association was formed in Guadalajara, and in 1921, the National Association of Charros began in Mexico City and established formalized competition and costume regulations. Today hundreds of family and community *charro* teams are governed by the Federacíon de Charros with headquarters and *charrería* museum in Mexico City, though the National Association of Charros still survives as a separate and more conservative and exclusive organization in the capital.

By codifying rules and simplifying the context for performance, the newly formed organizations transformed *charrería* from a land-based tradition to a highly symbolic competition and dramatic reenactment of an idealized national history in which the tension between its aristocratic practices and Revolutionary identification are resolved at least for the two-hour period of performance. Today, approximately 700,000 *charros* in Mexico and the United States participate in Federacíon de Charros sanctioned competitions, exhibitions, and calendared events such as the Charro Espectacular held each February in Mexico City. Thus, hundreds of thousands of Mexican citizens annually witness military, social, and economic history of their culture as it is played out in the parades, national anthems, and salutes that open the *charreada*; in patriotic commemorations; and in the social events that display the costumes, horsemanship, and aristocratic behaviors of *charros* and *charras.* At the numerous *charreadas* held every weekend across Mexico and at the *congresos* that mark championship competitions, the *lienzo* becomes a symbolic map of Mexico, and the *charreada* reenacts a pageant of Mexican identity that bends the linear flow of time into a circle of repetition and celebration of the continuity of equestrian folk community in an age of horseless carriages, ahistoricism, and alienation.

While contemporary *charros* and *charras* look to the past for coherence and meaning, they also project a vision of a viable, dynamic future for their tradition. Perpetuating *charrería* is not only a matter of initiating their children and newcomers into its practices, values, and history but of adapting to new social and environmental circumstances. *Charrería* migrated northward with 1910 Revolution refugees and continues to gain support and participants from contemporary immigrants to the United States. In both Mexico and the United States it instills ethnic pride and expresses allegiance to an idealized cultural past.

The viability of *charrería* as an enduring tradition is symbolized by the annual celebration of Charro Day, September 14, just one day before Mexican Independence Day. In their gentility and their association with the horse, *charros* and *charras* may seem anachronistic, but popular films and public monuments, museum exhibits, a well-established school of fine art, tourism, and high attendance figures at *charreadas* all attest to the importance of the traditions and performances of *charrería* to Mexican national identity.

See also Rancheros

Select Bibliography

Alvarez del Villar, José, *La charrería mexicana.* Mexico City: Panorama Editorial, 1987.

LeCompte, Mary Lou, "The Hispanic Influence on the History of Rodeo, 1823–1922." *Journal of Sport History* (Spring 1985).

Norman, James, *Charro: Mexican Horseman.* New York: Putnam, 1969.

Rincon Gallardo, Carlos, *El libro del charro mexicano.* 6th edition, Mexico City: Porrúa, 1983.

Sands, Kathleen M., *Charrería Mexicana: An Equestrian Folk Tradition.* Tucson: University of Arizona Press, 1993.

_____, "Performance and Dynamics of an Equestrian Folk Tradition in Mexico and the United States." *Studies in Latin American Popular Culture* 13 (Fall 1994).

Slatta, Richard, *Cowboys of the Americas.* New Haven, Connecticut: Yale University Press, 1990.

Valero Silva, José, *El libro de la charrería.* Mexico City: Gacela, 1987.

—Kathleen Mullen Sands

CHÁVEZ MENDOZA, CRUZ

1858–92 • Popular Leader and Revolutionary

Cruz Chávez was born in the town of Tomochic, in the Guerrero district of the sierra of western Chihuahua, the son of Teresa Mendoza and Jesús José Chávez; in 1850 his father had been among the first mestizos (mixed-race) to settle in Tomochic. Cruz was the third of five children. Unlike most of the other children in the town, the children of the Chávez family learned to read and write. Cruz also was a musician and came to take quite seriously the ideas of law, respect among individuals, honor, and dignity. By his 20s he had become a leader in the community. The Chihuahuense historian Francisco R. Almada described him as "a tall thin man of robust complexion, clear eyes, of little hair, and beardless."

In his youth Chávez held the characteristic jobs of most men of rural Mexico, working as a laborer, cowboy, mule driver, and farmhand. Although he informally acted as representative for Tomochic on various occasions, there is no record in the archives of the Guerrero district of him ever having held political office. However, the archives do give some indication of his early career as a popular tribune. One letter dated August 24, 1882, directed to the *jefe político* (local official appointed directly by the state government) of the Guerrero district, denounces one Reyes Domínguez for having baselessly accused him of sedition. Over the next few years Chávez wrote several more letters to local authorities denouncing Reyes Domínguez, linking him to Joaquín Chávez, an important cacique (political boss).

Cruz Chávez's difficulties with Reyes Domínguez were part of a larger accumulation of grievances among the townspeople of Tomochic. During the dictatorship of Porfirio Díaz they had suffered loss of their lands, religious problems, and the worst excesses of boss rule. On December 7, 1891, approximately 30 townspeople clashed with a contingent of soldiers that had been sent to apprehend them. Eight days earlier the *jefe político* of the Guerrero district had been informed that Cruz Chávez and his followers had declared themselves to be in rebellion, not recognizing any political or religious authority. After this first clash the partisans of Tomochic fled toward Sonora, hoping to meet the charismatic eighteen-year-old Teresa Urrea, whom they revered as Santa Teresita. During the first half of 1892, however, political activity in Chihuahua centered on elections. Until August the townspeople of Tomochic gradually returned home to tend their crops, adopting a new political organization under the leadership of Cruz Chávez.

On February 3, 1892, Cruz Chávez received the congressman Tomás Dozal y Hermosillo, who had been dispatched by the state government of Chihuahua to attempt a peaceful resolution of the conflict. Dozal y Hermosillo proposed that the people of Tomochic request a pardon from the governor, and he also submitted an amnesty law to the state legislature, which was rejected. Although he met with Cruz Chávez several times, Dozal y Hermosillo was unable reach an agreement, and on September 2 a column of approximately 500 troops was sent against the rebels in Tomochic. The federal troops were defeated, and their commander almost was captured when he was cut off from his army.

On October 20 a final offensive was launched against Tomochic, mobilizing 1,500 troops from throughout Mexico (including part of the crack ninth infantry battalion from Mexico City). 100 defenders withstood the federal siege for nine days without food or water. On October 29 the last remaining defenders were defeated. Cruz Chávez and six of his companions, all gravely wounded, were dragged from the adobe hut where they had been holding out. Cruz was able to move only one arm, in which he brandished an empty carbine. He still was able to shout to the soldiers that he did not surrender. The soldiers propped him against a wall and, after allowing him a final cigarette, shot him together with his companions. After burning the few houses in the town, the soldiers left for Ciudad Guerrero, taking 53 women and 71 children, the widows and orphans of the defenders of Tomochic.

News of the heroic defense of Tomochic spread like wildfire among the towns of the sierra from Chihuahua to Sonora, and until the Revolution of 1910 the name of Tomochic was present in the proclamations and revolutionary movements against the Porfirian dictatorship. The names of Cruz Chávez and his brother Manuel are preserved to this day in the popular memory of the region as symbols of heroism and bravery.

Select Bibliography

Almada, Francisco R., *La Rebelión de Tomochic.* Chihuahua: Sociedad Chihuahuense de Estudios Históricos, 1938.

Chávez, José Carlos, *Peleando en Tomochi.* 3rd edition, Chihuahua: Centro Librero la Prensa, 1979.

Vargas Valdez, Jesús, *Tomochic, la revolución adelantada.* Chihuahua: Universidad Autónoma de Ciudad Juárez, 1994.

—Jesús Vargas Valdez

CHÁVEZ Y RAMÍREZ, CARLOS ANTONIO DE PADUA

1899–1978 • Composer and Conductor

Chávez was born June 13, 1899, at Calzada de Tacuba, and as a small child studied piano with Pedro Luis Ogazón. In 1911, against the backdrop of the Revolution, Chávez began lessons with Manuel Ponce, the dean of twentieth-century Mexican music. Although Ponce's style tended toward the conservative (he has been labeled a "Porfirian-epoch" composer), he advocated the study of new music for his students. Chávez absorbed this spirit early on: at age 13 he performed in an all-Debussy program that Ponce organized, helping to acquaint the Mexican public with a repertory many Europeans still considered radical.

At age 20 Chávez began publishing his earliest songs and piano pieces; these show a marked French influence. After the installation of Álvaro Obregón as president in 1921, Chávez gained access to high circles in Mexican cultural politics and assisted in the official effort to bring culture (especially indigenous culture) to the masses. This involvement is reflected in his ballet *El fuego nuevo* (1921), commissioned by the Secretariat of Public Education. With an Aztec legend as its subject matter, the ballet is Chávez's first important work.

Shortly after *El fuego nuevo*'s completion Chávez traveled in France, Austria, and Germany, where he became acquainted with the most recent developments in music. Upon his return to Mexico he gave concerts of Stravinsky, Schoenberg, Satie, Milhaud, and others. In 1923 Chávez visited New York for the first time, where he found an audience receptive to his works. He also met American composers such as Aaron Copland, Henry Cowell, and Roger Sessions, whose music he would champion in Mexico. In 1924, back in Mexico City, he began working as music critic with the newspaper *El Universal,* establishing his reputation in Mexico as a supporter of ultramodern music.

In 1925 Chávez composed another ballet on an Aztec theme, *Los cuatro soles,* and the following year he traveled to New York for the staging of his *Danza de los hombres y las máquinas* by the International Composers' Guild. In 1928 he was appointed Director of the National Conservatory in Mexico City, a post he held until 1934. It was during this period that Chávez founded the Orquesta Sinfónica de Mexico, an ensemble still in existence today (in 1948 it was renamed the Orquesta Sinfónica Nacional); he would serve as its director until 1949. Although the original personnel consisted mainly of jazz and theater musicians, Chávez had them perform complex symphonic works of the European and North American avant-garde, such as Honegger's *Pacific 231* and Copland's *Short Symphony.* (The latter was performed in Mexico even before receiving its U.S. premier.) Chávez's daring programming is all the more remarkable given the general lack of education in art music for much of the Mexican

audience. Perhaps most important was Chávez's commissioning of works from many of his compatriots (among them Silvestre Revueltas). In all, he gave 82 performances of new Mexican works.

On March 31, 1932, Chávez's *Caballos de vapor* premiered in Philadelphia, where it attracted the notice of conductor Leopold Stowkowski. Diego Rivera's sets and costumes complemented the score, which drew upon numerous popular elements, including the *zandunga, huapango,* Mexican folk songs, and several non-Mexican sources such as the Argentine tango. The presence of the well-known U.S. tune *Sidewalks of New York* (juxtaposed with the Latin American popular material) has been said to represent tensions between the regimented, industrialized North and the more sensual South.

In 1933 Chávez was named chief of the Department of Fine Arts, a post he resigned abruptly in 1934 because of political frictions. The *Sinfonía proletaria (Llamadas)* for chorus and orchestra of the same year is one of his more overtly political works, however. Its political allusions emerge through the composer's quotation of revolutionary songs and texts, among them several *corridos.* Other overtly political works are *El Sol* (1934) for chorus and orchestra and *Chapultepec* of 1935 (also known as *Obertura Republicana*).

Chávez's next major work is by many accounts his finest. While visiting New York in 1935 he began the *Sinfonía India,* a compendium of the Mexican musical heritage. In addition to incorporating authentic Aztec melodies, Chávez calls for native instruments to enhance the symphonic texture: a two-keyed xylophone, or *teponaztli,* several types of drums (the Yaqui drum, the *tlapanhuehuetl,* and others), and numerous percussion instruments, including the water gourd, the rattle, the rasp, and the *tenabari* (a string of butterfly cocoons). The *Sinfonía India*'s mixed meters, driving rhythms, repeated motives, and melodies of narrow range have caused the work to be described as Chávez's most "primitivist"; the image of an "Indianist" composer was one Chávez did much to cultivate in the United States. The work's premier took place January 23, 1936, with the composer conducting the Columbia Broadcasting Symphony Orchestra.

Chávez served the administration of President Miguel Alemán Valdés by designing a National Institute of Fine Arts, an agency he directed himself from 1946 to 1952. Throughout the last decades of his life he continued to visit the United States. During 1958–59, following in Stravinsky's footsteps, Chávez was appointed Charles Eliot Norton Lecturer at Harvard. The lectures he presented were published in 1960 under the title *Musical Thought*; a previous book, *Towards a New Music,* had been published in 1937. The expatriate Spanish composer Rodolfo Halffter compiled a detailed catalog of Chávez's works (published in 1971). An orchestral work (*Mañanas mexicanas*, 1974), a trombone concerto (1975–76), and some piano pieces (*Caprichos*, 1975–76) occupied his last years. He died in Mexico City on August 2, 1978.

Chávez was more than just a prolific composer. He rejuvenated musical life in Mexico through the founding of the Orquesta Sinfónica Nacional and raised the level of musical culture in Mexico through his newspaper articles and bold programming. He encouraged the establishment of a uniquely Mexican school of composition, both through his own works and the commissions and encouragement he extended to his compatriots. Throughout his career he emphasized the importance of indigenous culture. An energetic administrator, he did not shy away from political expression in music, and, as an international figure, he did much to foster musical dialogue between North and Central America.

Select Bibliography

Béhague, Gerard, *Music in Latin America: An Introduction.* Englewood Cliffs, New Jersey: Prentice-Hall, 1979.

Chávez, Carlos, *Musical Thought.* Cambridge, Massachusetts: Harvard University Press, 1961.

García Morillo, Roberto, *Carlos Chávez: vida y obra.* Mexico City: Fondo de Cultura Económica, 1960.

Parker, Robert L., *Carlos Chávez: Mexico's Modern-day Orpheus.* Boston: Twayne, 1983.

Rosenfeld, Paul, *Discoveries of a Music Critic.* New York: Harcourt, Brace, and World, 1936.

Stevenson, Robert M., *Music in Mexico: A Historical Survey.* New York: Crowell, 1952.

Weinstock, Herbert, Mexican Music: *Notes by Herbert Weinstock for Concerts Arranged by Carlos Chávez.* New York: William E. Rudge's Sons, 1940.

—CAROL A. HESS

CHIAPAS ZAPATISTA REBELLION

See Zapatista Rebellion in Chiapas

CHIMALPAHIN

1579–c.1660 • Indigenous Chronicler

Unique among the chronicles and histories of indigenous peoples in New Spain are the Nahuatl annals by Chimalpahin. Written 100 years after the Conquest of Mexico, from approximately 1610 to 1630, his accounts represent the most comprehensive extant writings by a known Nahua in his own hand and language.

Born in Amecameca in 1579 and baptized Domingo Francisco, a sure sign of his humble beginning, he moved at the age of fourteen to Mexico City, where he found employment at the tiny church of San Antonio Abad in Xolloco, located just over one mile (two kilometers) due south of the cathedral. Little is known of his boyhood in Amecameca, although he does identify his parents as well as relatives and other acquaintances from whom he gathered oral and written histories about his hometown. His schooling was likely at the hands of the Dominicans, whose province included the large church, Santa María Asunción, in the center of Amecameca. Chimalpahin once in his writings made reference to a father-in-law, but he never named his wife nor spoke of having children. However, from his accounts it is evident that he traveled between Amecameca and Mexico City, and worked on his histories in both locales.

In Xolloco Chimalpahin was on the fringe of the capital's social and political establishment, yet he knew of and wrote about much of the goings on in the city. Often he included an eyewitness version, adding *"huel oniquittac"* (truly I saw it). Thus we know something of the Nahua perspective of the grand processions through the capital, the floods, disease, and death, as well as his personal reflections from time to time on such issues as *mestizaje* (racial mixture) and how it affected indigenous roles and status. Just who provided him with the expensive paper, ink, and leisure to write an Indian history of Mexico is not certain, but surely he enjoyed the patronage of the priest at San Antón, Agustín del Espíritu Santo, whom he described as *"totlaçotatzin"* (our precious father). Chimalpahin worked at the church probably until 1624, when fray Agustín died suddenly and unexpectedly of a stomach ailment, and the church was closed.

What happened to Chimalpahin—a man of great intelligence and talent, and still in his prime—is not known. His last dated entry in his texts is 1631, and elsewhere there is an unsubstantiated reference to his death in 1660. It is possible that he went to work for the Jesuits as a copyist at the Colegio de San Gregorio, their Mexico City secondary school for Indians. San Gregorio was located close to the cathedral, and certainly it was a mecca for Indians and Nahuatl-language ecclesiastical studies and services. One of Chimalpahin's manuscripts, the *Diario,* was kept in San Gregorio's library until the expulsion of the Jesuits in 1767.

Chimalpahin knew Juan de Tovar, the famous Jesuit Nahuatl-speaking orator, priest, and rector at San Gregorio, who held services at San Antón on occasion and assisted some of Chimalpahin's contemporaries from Amecameca in their religious training. It may be that Father Tovar was also instrumental in Chimalpahin's scholarly production.

Chimalpahin is best known for his *Relaciones* and *Diario,* two collections of manuscripts located for the last century at the Bibliothèque Nationale, Paris. In the 1980s a heretofore unknown cache of his Nahuatl (and some Spanish) texts was discovered in the British and Foreign Bible Society library, now housed at Cambridge University in England. Chimalpahin also produced a copy, but with his own emendations, of Francisco López de Gómara's *Conquista de México,* as well as a Nahuatl and Latin theological treatise, the *Exercicio quotidiano,* the original version of which is ascribed to the great Franciscan ethnographer, Bernardino de Sahagún.

While in large part it was Chimalpahin's intention to emulate the respective micropatriotic accounts written by mestizo colleagues Hernando de Alva Ixtlilxochitl and Hernando Alvarado Tezozomoc and write a history in glorification of his own Amecameca, he in fact brought together an account of epic proportion that treats numerous indigenous peoples and places and spans close to 1,000 years, 670 to 1631. Writing for a Nahua readership, he recorded optimistically that he wanted the generations of the future to know their extraordinary past. Moreover, his methodology as a historian was quite exceptional: his sources included his transliterations to Roman alphabetic script of a great variety of pictorial manuscripts; he collected oral histories and personal interviews of individuals in Mexico City and beyond; and he read and borrowed from both Nahuatl- and Spanish-language manuscripts and published books. He always preferred to use the most ancient records, and he corroborated the information with other sources whenever possible. Some time in the course of writing those accounts he began to fancy himself as someone of noble birth and high status, thereafter signing himself in his writings "don Domingo de San Antón Muñón Chimalpahin Quautlehuanitzin." It is doubtful that he was either known or called by such an appellation, however.

How Chimalpahin came to have access to such an impressive array of sources, including López de Gómara's forbidden book on the Conquest, is not known. Perhaps they were in the library at the Colegio de San Gregorio. Certainly, he was known by Indians and Spaniards alike and participated in, or at least attended, key events in the capital. Yet, to date, there is no mention of Chimalpahin by his contemporaries, only an obscure note in one of his Nahuatl manuscripts by criollo intellectual Carlos de Sigüenza y Góngora (1645–1700), who surely consulted it for his own histories.

Chimalpahin's contributions to Nahua history are nearly immeasurable. By keeping to the indigenous tradition and using the annals form, he furnished the closest equivalent possible to ancient practices for documenting events. That indigenous annals were still current in the seventeenth century is strong attestation to Nahua cultural continuity even in a colonial milieu. The content of his annals is rich and complex and provides many centuries' worth of information about the formation and developments of the many ethnic states in central Mexico, the roles and activities of both women and men in society and politics, their cosmologies, and the seemingly little difference the presence of the Spaniards had on the traditions of most Nahuas. Indeed, Chimalpahin's annals move right past the Conquest and into the seventeenth century, the most obvious difference being greater detail (as a first-hand observer) and the addition of the time of day (by the ringing of church bells) to his Nahua-Gregorian calendric system.

Chimalpahin's Nahuatl language is eloquent and difficult, which accounts for his histories being little studied or translated. Comprehensive and precious because they furnish an authentic indigenous perspective, Chimalpahin's histories are a fine complement to Sahagún's twelve-volume Nahuatl-Spanish *Florentine Codex: General History of the Things of New Spain.*

Select Bibliography

Rendón, Silvia, *Relaciones originales de Chalco Amaquemecan: Escritas por Don Francisco de San Antón Muñón Chimalpahin Cuauhtlehuanitzin.* Mexico City: Fondo de Cultura Económica, 1965.

Romero Galván, José Rubén, *Octava relación: Obra histórica de Domingo Francisco de San Antón Muñón Chimalpahin Cuauhtlehuanitzin.* Mexico City: UNAM, 1983.

Durand-Forest, Jacqueline de, *L'histoire de la Vallée de Mexico selon Chimalpahin Quauhtlehuanitzin.* Paris: L'Hartmattan, 1987.

————, *Troisième Relation et Autres Documents Originaux de Chimalpahin Quauhtlehuanitzin.* Paris: L'Hartmattan, 1987.

Schroeder, Susan, *Chimalpahin and the Kingdoms of Chalco.* Tucson: University of Arizona Press, 1991.

—SUSAN SCHROEDER

CHINESE

In 1513, Spanish explorer Vasco Núñez de Balboa's sighting of the Mar del Sur, the first European name for the Pacific Ocean, set in motion Spain's "discovery" and exploration of the Pacific coast of Spanish America. By the end of the century, the Spanish finally learned to accomplish what Columbus had failed to achieve—finding a way to the Orient by sailing westward. Spain established the Manila Galleon trade, which lasted some three centuries and linked China and Japan via the Philippines to Europe in an exchange of Mexican silver for Oriental luxury goods.

Not long after the Manila trade was established, the first Asian colony in the Americas appeared. In 1635, Spanish barbers in Mexico City submitted a complaint to the viceroy, decrying the presence of Chinese barbers in their midst. They specifically requested the removal of these excessively competitive "Chinos de Manila" from the city center to special quarters at the outskirt of town and therefore out of competitive range. Although this early settlement of Asians did not continue as a permanent colony during the colonial period, it left legacies now firmly entrenched in Mexican folklore, notably the embroidered blouse known as the *china poblana* worn by women in central Mexico.

It was not until the mid–nineteenth century that organized, large-scale Asian immigration to Latin America and the Caribbean took place, consisting almost exclusively of Chinese, Japanese, and East Indians. Most of the Chinese went to Cuba, Peru, Mexico, and parts of Central America; the Japanese settled largely in Peru and Brazil, with smaller numbers going to Bolivia and Mexico; and the East Indians were sent almost exclusively to the British West Indies upon the termination of slavery in the 1830s.

A quarter million Chinese, mostly men, arrived in Peru and Cuba between 1847 and 1875, part of the nineteenth-century international labor migration that accompanied the worldwide development of capitalism and imperialism. After a period of laboring under harsh agricultural conditions on large estates and plantations, most of the surviving Chinese made the transition to independent farming, shopkeeping, or other commercial activities.

Chinese immigrants began arriving on the west coast of Mexico in 1876, after the period of coolie labor migration. This movement accelerated after 1882, when the United States passed its first anti-Chinese Exclusion Act. Entering through the Pacific coast ports of Mazatlán and Guaymas, the Chinese spread throughout Mexico, but primarily to the northern border states, no doubt attracted by their proximity to the United States. However, an initial tendency to cross illicitly into the United States abated, as the Chinese moved swiftly into a widening economic space in the rapidly developing frontier region, where the bulk of U.S. investment was concentrated.

Unlike the Chinese in the western United States, those in northern Mexico did not take up laboring jobs, which were filled by Mexicans, but rather, entered commerce as small independent entrepreneurs, and occasionally in partnership with U.S. mine and railroad owners in the company towns. It was quickly established that Chinese shopkeepers followed the trail of Yankee capital.

Nowhere was this pattern clearer than in the northwestern state of Sonora, which bordered the then-Mexican territory of Arizona. Astutely avoiding competition with established European and Mexican merchants in old towns such as Guaymas and Hermosillo (the state capital), the Chinese ventured into some remote villages of the interior, but mostly to new working-class settlements that sprang up along railroad and mining sites, and later, to modern agricultural colonies. These were the new towns that grew in the wake of foreign, mainly U.S., investment in northern Mexico during the last quarter of the nineteenth century. The Chinese were often the first *comerciantes* to reach these new localities, thus the first shopkeepers to cater to the needs of the workers.

Within two generations, they had succeeded in monopolizing the small commercial sector of the state's economy. Far from being a hindrance, the Mexican Revolution actually furthered their commercial growth in several ways. First, with most Mexicans engaged in the civil conflicts, the Revolution retarded the emergence of Mexican small businesses to compete with the Chinese. Second, even during these turbulent times, towns—including mining and railroad centers that continued to operate—needed to be supplied with goods and services. Third, the various Revolutionary armies needed to be provisioned. As aliens, the Chinese remained officially "neutral" and willing to do business with all Revolutionary factions. Although some of the sales were on "forced loan" bases, whereby Chinese merchants were given a credit slip for future payment by Revolutionary generals who commandeered goods and supplies, the Chinese figured these inconveniences to be part of the cost of doing business in the midst of chaos. Fourth, further solidifying the Chinese position in Sonoran commerce was the weakening of traditional commercial links between Mexico and Europe during World War I, which coincided in time with the Mexican Revolution. Some of the departed German, French, and Spanish commercial houses were replaced by Chinese firms, which turned to U.S. suppliers, thereby forging new Mexican-U.S. commercial ties. These ties in turn strengthened the existing symbiotic relationship between Chinese merchants and U.S. interests in Sonora, and explains the actions frequently taken by U.S. consuls to protect Chinese persons and businesses when they came under violent attacks by Mexicans.

Most of the Chinese immigrants were young males who arrived in Mexico near penniless, armed with only a willingness to work long and hard. However, a small number of Chinese capitalists also went early to Mexico to set up merchant houses in Guaymas and Hermosillo, with branches in important new towns such as Magdalena along the Sonoran Railroad, and Cananea of the Greene Consolidated Copper Company. In some cases, they added factories next to the stores to manufacture cheap shoes and clothing. These large merchants hired almost exclusively fellow Chinese in the stores and factories. They also, significantly, extended goods on credit to enterprising but poor compatriots to peddle their wares in small, remote mining towns, and to set up new stores throughout the state. By the twentieth century, they controlled the trade in groceries, dry goods, and general merchandise. Some Chinese truck-farmed on land they leased, then carted the fruits and vegetables to local markets, which often were dominated by Chinese-owned stalls. Other Chinese worked as artisans and small-scale manufacturers, producing shoes, clothing, brooms, *masa* (dough for tortillas), pasta, and sweets. In these multiple ways, the Chinese succeeded in creating a production, purchasing, supply, and distribution network among themselves, a closed system with some clear characteristics of "vertical integration" that, in effect, became the state's first commercial infrastructure. This remarkable system endured until the early 1930s, when most of the Chinese were expelled from Sonora and their businesses nationalized.

In 1910, the Chinese population in Sonora had reached 4,486, in a total population of 265,383, making them the largest foreign colony in the state, surpassing the 3,164 U.S. presence by over 1,000, and well above the 259 Spaniards and 183 Germans. In 1910, according to Mexico's official census, there were 13,203 Chinese in all Mexico, to be found in every state except Tlaxcala.

The Chinese colony in Sonora and all Mexico was almost exclusively male, Even as late as 1930, the census noted only 412 women among the 3,471 Chinese recorded for Sonora. Not even all these 400 or so women were necessarily Chinese, for Sonoran law had begun to strip Mexican women married to Chinese men of their citizenship and nationality, while consigning them to their husband's ethnic group.

The highest number of Chinese in Sonora was recorded in 1919, when the Chinese colony itself supplied the count of 6,078. The sharp drop to the 3,571 noted for 1930 can be explained in a number of ways, aside from unreliable statistics. It reflected declining new immigration into the state at a time when Sonora had begun expulsion proceedings against established residents, many of whom were nationalized Mexican citizens. During the 1920s, as anti-Chinese campaigns mounted in intensity and frequency, many Chinese fled the state—back to China, illegally across the border to the United States, south to Sinaloa, and, it appears, especially across the gulf to Baja California, which recorded 5,889 Chinese in 1927 compared to 3,785 for Sonora.

When the Chinese first began arriving in Sonora in the last quarter of the nineteenth century, they congregated in Guaymas, the port of entry, and in the capital of Hermosillo. Then they moved to newer towns, notably the railroad hub

of Magdalena north of Hermosillo, and to the state's leading mining town of Cananea on the northeast corner of the state close to the U.S. border. By 1904, Chinese could be found in all nine districts of the state, although unevenly distributed. While still prominent in Guaymas, Hermosillo, and Magdalena, by far the largest number had gone to Arizpe district, which included Cananea as well as a number of smaller mining camps and border towns. Eight hundred of Arizpe's 1,106 Chinese resided in Cananea. By contrast, the districts of Altar, Sahuaripa, and Ures, which had no significant mining or railroad activities, had only a few Chinese residents each. The informative 1919 census, whose data was provided by the Chinese Fraternal Union to the federal government's Department of Labor, noted 6,078 Chinese distributed across all nine districts and in 58 of the state's 62 municipalities. Only 4 very small towns in Sahuaripa and Ures districts had no Chinese at all.

The 1919 community was composed overwhelmingly of young to middle-aged men, that is, men of working age. Eighty-four percent were between 21 and 45, the percentage increasing to an astonishing 91 percent if the upper limit were raised to 50. Only 331 individuals, or 5.4 percent, were under 20, and only 170, or 2.8 percent, were older than 51. In terms of years of residency in Mexico, as of 1919, 41 percent had been in Mexico for 10 to 15 years, and another 37 percent for 5 to 10 years. Thus the vast majority, almost 80 percent, had at least 5 years' experience in Mexico. The data also suggest that a significant number, 1,459 or 24 percent, had entered Mexico during the active Revolutionary years, 1912 to 1915.

The first year for which there is good commercial data on the Chinese was 1913, published by the International Chinese Business Directory. For Sonora, 279 Chinese businesses were noted, most of them in general merchandise or groceries, located in 26 towns. There were also 40 restaurants, 16 laundries, 4 hotels, 2 dry goods, 2 clothing factories, 1 shoe factory, and 2 pharmacies (probably Chinese herbal goods).

In 1919, of the 6,078 Chinese residents in Sonora, 70 percent of them (4,258) were noted occupationally as *comerciantes,* which probably included stores owners, partners, and clerks. Common or day laborers, *jornaleros,* were a distant second, at 12.8 percent. There were very few cooks or laundrymen. Artisans and craftsmen of various kinds—tailors, shoemakers, jewelers, carpenters, bakers, tanners—constituted another 2 percent.

By 1925, although the Chinese population had declined sharply, as noted above, they maintained a solid hold on local small businesses throughout the state. Only a handful of traditional communities in Ures, Altar, and Sahuaripa districts had no Chinese presence. What is important is that these towns had probably no stores whatever. In other remote communities, such as Atil, Tubutama, and San Pedro de Cueva, with only one or a few commercial outlets, they were all Chinese-owned and operated. Even more significant, the commerce of certain mining towns, such as Nacozari de García near Cananea, was also exclusively in Chinese hands. The same was true for rapidly developing commercial agricultural towns in the southern part of the state, such as Cocorit in the Yaqui Valley, with 42 Chinese merchants, and Etchojoa and Huatabampo in the Mayo Valley.

The widespread distribution of Chinese businesses must also be noted in the context of their capitalization. In 1913, only 15 Chinese businesses were capitalized at 20,000 pesos or above, for a total of 731,830 pesos, compared to 238 non-Chinese businesses, with a total of 18 million pesos. The average Chinese in this group had capital of 48,789 pesos, compared to 75,630 pesos among the others. Only three of the Chinese firms had over 50,000 pesos; by contrast, 98 non-Chinese firms were capitalized at over 50,000 pesos. If this group can be characterized as Sonora's "grande bourgeoisie," then the Chinese were only an insignificant part of it. Chinese participation at this level of economic activity did not grow with time. From 1917 to 1920, Chinese entrepreneurs formed some 80 "mercantile societies," or companies. The vast majority of the 80 were capitalized under 5,000 pesos. Mexican, European, and U.S. companies, by contrast, were typically capitalized at 25,000, 50,000, in the hundreds of thousands, and up to one or two billion pesos for the big mining, railroad, land, and agricultural enterprises.

The detailed report prepared by the Mexican Labor Department on capital invested in the Sonoran economy in 1919 further confirms the low Chinese presence among the large enterprises and the fundamentally petit bourgeois nature of the Chinese business community. Total Chinese-owned capital did not lag far behind all other capital combined, 2,186,935 pesos compared to 2,813,540 pesos. However, there were almost twice as many Chinese establishments as all others combined—U.S., German, French, Arab, Japanese, and other foreigners, and Mexican. The average Chinese business capital was 2,644 pesos, compared to 6,482 pesos for others. Of the 827 Chinese businesses distributed over 60 communities, 740 were capitalized under 5,000 pesos.

Finally, in 1925, in the midst of a vigorous anti-Chinese campaign that called for their expulsion from Sonora, the state government once again took stock of the Chinese business profile, this time comparing it to Mexican industrial and commercial holdings. By this time, it should be noted, a Mexican industrial and large commercial bourgeoisie had firmly established itself in Sonora, home to President Plutarco Elías Calles and former president álvaro Obregón as well as many other Revolutionary leaders who all laid claim to land and other properties in the state except for what the Chinese still held. Mexican-owned enterprises can be characterized as falling within the medium to large range: 27 capitalized at 5,000 to 10,900 pesos; 28 at 11,000 to 99,000 pesos; and 5 over 100,000 pesos. Among the Chinese, a considerable number, 41, fell between 5,000 and 10,900 pesos, but only 4 between 11,000 and 99,000 pesos, and only 1 above 100,000 pesos. The vast majority of Chinese businesses were capitalized under 5,000 pesos, with most of them actually worth between 1,200 and 2,500 pesos. There was only one Mexican-owned business in this modest category. Moreover, the 517 Chinese businesses were spread over 65 of the state's 70 municipalities; the 61 Mexican businesses were to be found in only 14 towns.

In short, this commercial/industrial survey conducted by the state government conclusively demonstrated the Chinese monopoly of the small commercial sector, to the practical exclusion of Mexicans. The situation was not particularly alarming to the large Mexican capitalists who in turn controlled the large commercial/industrial sector of the economy, but it would provide fodder for the average Mexican who could, and did, aspire to the small commercial sector that was firmly in Chinese hands. The ubiquitous nature of these Chinese comerciantes, while providing a necessary service to all Sonorans, also became a thorn in the side of working- and middle-class Mexicans. Modest in fact, but prosperous in comparison to ordinary Sonorans still struggling to improve their lives well after the Revolution that many of them fought in the name of social justice, the Chinese also reminded Sonorans just how much foreigners had historically controlled their destiny, and how much farther they would have to go to reclaim Mexico for the Mexicans. Mexican workers, landless peasants, and their families formed the backbone of the various campaigns to remove the Chinese from their midst.

Sonorans launched their final and successful campaign against the Chinese in 1929 during the Great Depression. In Governor Francisco Elías, the anti-Chinese forces in Sonora found their most zealous supporter in the government. Equally significant in finally unifying local and national solidarity behind the movement was the Sonoran former president Plutarco Elías Calles, the jefe máximo who remained the most powerful politician in Mexico even after he left office. A series of discriminatory work, health, and marriage codes, designed specifically to harass the Chinese, were rigorously applied. Local ligas antichinas organized massive and loud demonstrations; vigilante groups surfaced to terrorize Chinese storekeepers. In the face of international criticism and even some from Mexico City, Governor Elías and his successor, Rudolfo Elías Calles (son of the jefe máximo) defended the campaign as entirely legal, moral, and in the highest national interest.

Unable to comply with the work and sanitary laws, intimidated by the ban on interracial marriages, harassed by Mexican immigration officials, unsuccessful in their solicitation of U.S. support at a time when the United States launched its own Good Neighbor Policy of nonintervention in Latin American affairs, the Chinese who had survived previous persecutions in Mexico admitted defeat in 1931. In August they announced plans to abandon the state as soon as they could sell their goods, lands, and properties, which they had to liquidate in a hurry and at a tremendous loss. By October 1931, with most of the Chinese out of the state, Governor Calles triumphantly declared the campaign successfully concluded. Although Sonoran and federal authorities denied that they expelled the Chinese, in leaving them no choice but to abandon the state, the mass exodus was characterized internationally as tantamount to expulsion.

Where did the expelled Chinese go? It is hard to trace all their steps. Many tried to enter the United States, where they still were barred by U.S. law; those caught were deported at U.S. expense back to China, some with their Mexican wives (who had lost their Mexican citizenship) and their mixed-blood children. Others made their way to slightly more hospitable parts of Mexico, such as Mexico City, Sinaloa, Chihuahua, and Baja California Norte, where Chinese laborers had been instrumental during the previous two decades in opening land for large-scale cotton cultivation. Throughout Mexico wherever they fled during these turbulent years, they also faced persecution, although nowhere comparable to the degree and consequences as experienced in Sonora.

The history of the Chinese in Sonora constitutes the core of the history of the Chinese in Mexico. In that northwestern state bordering the United States, for half a century straddling the rule of Porfirio Díaz, the Revolution, and the first decade of the post-Revolutionary era, the populous Chinese community formed the first comprehensive petit bourgeois class of a frontier society and practically monopolized local retail commerce. That very success, however, also doomed them to eventual persecution by Mexicans grappling with their own growing nationalism at once stoked by the flames of the Mexican Revolution and threatened by the looming world depression. Almost exactly one century after the expulsion of the Spaniards in the immediate post-Independence period, the Chinese in Sonora suffered a similar fate, their properties confiscated and their commercial infrastructure nationalized. If the decade of the 1930s—widely recognized as Mexico's most nationalistic—concluded with President Lázaro Cárdenas's unanimously applauded expropriation of the powerful foreign oil companies, it was foreshadowed by a similarly nationalistic action against the powerless and vulnerable Chinese in Sonora.

Select Bibliography

Cumberland, Charles, "The Sonoran Chinese and the Mexican Revolution." *Hispanic American Historical Review* 40 (1960).

Dubs, H. H., "The Chinese in Mexico City in 1635." *Far Eastern Quarterly* 1 (1942).

Hu-DeHart, Evelyn, "Immigrants to a Developing Society: The Chinese in Northern Mexico, 1932–1975." *Journal of Arizona History* 21 (Autumn 1980).

_____, "Racisim and Anti-Chinese Persecution in Mexico." *Amerasia Journal* 9:2 (1982).

_____, "The Chinese of Baja California Norte, 1910–1934." In *Baja California and the North Mexican Frontier.* San Diego: San Diego State University Press, 1986.

Jacques, Leo, "The Chinese Massacre in Torreon (Coahuila) in 1911." *Arizona and the West* 16 (Autumn 1974).

—EVELYN HU-DEHART

CHURCH AND STATE

This entry contains four articles that discuss the relationship between the Catholic Church and the state in both New Spain and Mexico:

Church and State: Hapsburg New Spain
Church and State: Bourbon New Spain
Church and State: 1821–1910
Church and State: 1910–96

See also Anticlericalism; Catholic Church; Cofradías; Education; Popular Catholicism; Ritual, Religious and Civic; Virgin of Guadalupe and Guadalupismo; Virgin of los Remedios

CHURCH AND STATE: HAPSBURG NEW SPAIN

In the colonial period, church and state were deeply intertwined institutions, both headed by the Spanish monarch. With the bull Inter Caetera (1493), Pope Alexander VI granted the Spanish Crown title to lands 100 leagues west of the Azores, essentially dividing spheres of control between the Spanish and Portuguese in their overseas activities. The motivation for the Spanish Crown to petition the pope on this matter was to prevent the Portuguese from infringing on territories Spain was claiming. However, Queen Isabel's wish to extend Christian faith to new lands doubtless was also a powerful reason to pursue the matter with the papacy. With this papal bull, the Spanish monarchs became "apostolic vicars" over the New World, since they exclusively were entrusted with its evangelization. In a separate bull (Eximae

Devotionis), Alexander VI granted the Spanish Crown the "right of presentation"—the right to present the names of candidates for ecclesiastical posts to the pope for final appointment. In effect it was the power of patronage.

A third major papal concession was made in 1501, by granting the Crown the use of tithes. Tithes were theoretically a 10 percent tax on agriculture and mining for support of the Catholic Church. By granting the tithe income to the Crown, the papacy provided a means to compensate it for the expenses of conquest and evangelization. The power granted the Crown for its overseas holdings exceeded that on the Iberian Peninsula, where tithes went directly to the church rather than first into Crown coffers for later allocation to the church.

The absolute right of *patronato real* (royal patronage) for church affairs in the New World was granted to the Spanish Crown by Pope Julius II in 1508, with the bull Universalis Ecclesiae. Construction of churches, demarcation of dioceses, power of appointment, and the tithe revenues were all under Crown control.

Taken together, these papal bulls gave the Spanish Crown absolute control over the Catholic Church in the Indies. Some scholars assert with good cause that this was the most important of the Crown's powers. Although the Spanish monarchs were not granted power to make religious doctrine, a right reserved to the papacy, nevertheless the Crown could speed or delay the proclamation of doctrine in its overseas colonies, or suppress it entirely.

Although the monarch had absolute control over the Catholic Church in New Spain, there was ecclesiastical intrusion in civil and political affairs. Civil law had religious or spiritual justification; in fact, the Crown based its right to rule on the papal bulls naming the Crown as the agent to evangelize the Indians.

In terms of institutional structure, church and state hierarchies were parallel in many ways. The viceroy was the highest local authority of both church and state, being patron of the church and head of state in New Spain. When the office of viceroy was vacant, the archbishop served as interim viceroy, which happened on more than one occasion. Both the viceroy and the archbishop were based in the capital, while secondary cities, such as Guadalajara and Oaxaca were the seats of civil high courts *(audiencias)* and bishoprics. At the local level, civil jurisdictions were headed by *corregidores* (the civil representative of the Crown), with priests overseeing parishes. Because the Crown had the power to determine the boundaries of both civil and ecclesiastical jurisdictions, they usually coincided.

There was cooperation between church and state on fundamental questions: that civil and moral order be maintained, royal authority be respected, and the "True Faith" (i.e., Catholicism) be the only religious belief permitted. In practice, however, there was considerable friction between civil and religious institutions over primacy of authority and jurisdiction. A standard feature of colonial Mexico was rivalry between the archbishop and the viceroy, or between the bishop and the *audiencia*. The Crown was ultimately the arbiter of these disputes, since it had authority over both hierarchies. In the Hapsburg period the Crown did not subordinate one hierarchy to the other, but nonetheless there were tensions between the two.

At times, jurisdictions or functions of the two hierarchies were overlapping, a clear example being the extension of Spanish sovereignty to new realms by the Catholic Church. The regular clergy (those belonging to a religious order)—especially the Franciscans, Dominicans, and Augustinians—divided territory in the central regions during the immediate post-Conquest period, establishing a permanent Spanish presence in existing native polities. Later the regular clergy established missions on the northern frontier. This was done mainly by the Jesuits during the Hapsburg era, but with their expulsion during the Bourbon period (1767), missions were established by the Franciscans. Although the church's primary goal was to convert the native populations to Christianity, its very presence in regions with no other Spaniards meant the establishment of Spanish royal authority.

In the Conquest period in central Mexico, the mendicant orders were a prime agent of Spanish expansion, following closely the military conquest of central Mexico in 1521. Fernando (Hernán) Cortés invited the Franciscans and Dominican orders to the newly conquered lands. These two orders had undergone a reform in Spain in the late fifteenth and early sixteenth centuries, and it was argued that they would be superior to the secular clergy (those not belonging to a religious order) as agents for converting the natives. There was a practical side to Cortés's invitation as well, since the regular clergy were less firmly under the control of the Crown than the secular clergy, and could therefore be potential allies in his own conflicts with the Crown over jurisdiction and authority. In order to fulfill the function of conversion in its fullest manner, the mendicant orders were granted power by Pope Adrian VI in 1522 to act as parish priests, dispensing the sacraments to the laity, a responsibility that previously had been reserved for the secular clergy.

Although the regular clergy served the Crown's purposes well during the early phases of the colony, the Crown moved to install the secular clergy as parish priests, their traditional role. This was formally done in 1574 with the Ordenanza del Patronazgo, which placed the regular clergy exercising powers of the secular clergy under the authority of the bishops. This was in keeping with edicts from the Council of Trent in the mid–sixteenth century, which placed all clergy with parochial powers under the authority of bishops. Implementation of the *ordenanza* was uneven. As with much colonial legislation that had an impact on civil and ecclesiastical institutions, standard regulations were modified to fit local conditions. Thus, through legislation the Crown could set priorities and goals, but how those were met depended on local powers.

The *ordenanza* marks the Crown's assertion of control over the clergy, particularly aiming to replace mendicants with the secular clergy as the primary spiritual ministers to the Indians. In its efforts to assert control over the ministry to the Indians, the Crown set educational standards for secular clerics and ordered that they learn the Indian languages. The requirement that clerics learn indigenous tongues gave an edge to criollo clerics (those born in the Americas). In the late sixteenth century, criollo clerics came to dominate cathedral chapters, as the Crown in this period clearly favored more local control.

Both church and state agreed in the goal of achieving moral behavior in society. The Inquisition in New Spain became a prime tool of regulation in matters of faith and religious practice, and formally was constituted as a separate office in 1571. The Inquisition criticized both secular and regular clergy, and inquisitors often were arrogant in their actions toward clerics not part of the Inquisition. Although the Inquisition had considerable authority to arrest, imprison, and try individuals (both lay and clerical, but not Indians), it did not formally carry out sentences of execution. Those sentenced to die were "relaxed to the secular arm"—that is, were released to civil custody. Autos de fe, the elaborate ceremonies in which the Inquisition's victims were publicly humiliated or executed, were events of high religious content, but were under the jurisdiction of civil authorities.

Since the Crown had been granted the use of tithes by the papacy, it could enjoy considerable income and power. In fact, the Crown gave the bulk of the revenue to religious institutions and officials. Crown officials had the task of collecting the tithes. Where there were shortfalls from tithe income to support the clergy, the remainder was to be supplied from the royal coffers. The tithe income was divided into four parts. One-quarter of each went to the bishop and to the cathedral chapter. The remaining half was divided into nine parts (novenos): two went to the king (this part usually was spent on churches), four to the lower secular clergy (parish priests), one and one-half to hospitals, and one and one-half on "temporalities" (i.e., the material property of the church). Everyone was subject to the tithe, although there was some debate in the early period as to the Indians' obligation. The Jesuits strenuously resisted payment of the tithe, arguing the order was exempt due to pontifical privileges. Jesuit intransigence on this point produced tension between the state and the order (also between the Jesuits and other religious orders, which did pay the tithe), but was not a direct cause of the order's expulsion from the Spanish realm in 1767.

Spanish colonial society was corporate in nature, ensuring special status via *fueros,* rights and privileges granted to specific groups. Clergy were protected by the *fuero eclesiástico.* Separate ecclesiastical courts had jurisdiction over clerics who committed minor criminal offenses or where a cleric was a party in a civil suit. Clerics who committed major crimes were subject to royal courts. In cases of heresy or violation of the sacraments, Inquisition courts had jurisdiction. Such protection for the church as an institution and its personnel lasted through the Hapsburg era, but under the Bourbon monarchs, these privileges came under attack, with the church increasingly subordinated to the state.

During the Hapsburg period, the dual role of the monarch (and by extension, the viceroy) as the head of state and patron of the church gave him power in both the spiritual and temporal spheres. Although tensions existed between the hierarchies of the state and the church, the essential order of colonial rule was not questioned. Some scholars see the Bourbon kings' attempts to subordinate church power to that of the state as a major factor undermining the legitimacy of the Spanish monarch's role, easing the way for overthrow of colonial rule.

See also Convents in New Spain; Fueros; Inquisition; Missions and Reductions; Religious in New Spain

Select Bibliography

Cuevas, Mariano, *Historia de la iglesia mexicana.* 5 vols., Editorial Revista Catolica, 1928.
Gibson, Charles, *Spain in America.* New York: Harper and Row, 1968.
Mecham, Lloyd, *Church and State in Latin America.* Chapel Hill: University of North Carolina Press, 1966.
Ricard, Robert, *The Spiritual Conquest of Mexico.* Berkeley: University of California Press, 1966.
Schwaller, John Frederick, *The Church and Clergy in Sixteenth-Century Mexico.* Albuquerque: University of New Mexico Press, 1987.

—SARAH L. CLINE

CHURCH AND STATE: BOURBON NEW SPAIN

Although the Bourbon monarchs ascended the Spanish throne after victory in the War of the Spanish Succession (1713), there were no substantial changes in church-state relations until approximately 1760. With the accession to the throne of Carlos III in 1759, in the wake of Spain's defeat by England in the Seven Years' War, the Spanish Crown initiated a sweeping program of change, generally known as the Bourbon Reforms. Until the mid–eighteenth century, the relationship between church and state shifted from a generally coequal status to one of primacy of state power.

Since the establishment of Spain's overseas empire in the late fifteenth and early sixteenth centuries, the papacy ceded control over the church affairs in the New World to the Spanish monarch. This included the right of the *patronato real,* giving the monarch power of appointment of all clerics in the Americas; control over collection and disbursement of the tithe; and de facto veto over the promulgation of papal decrees. The viceroy during the Hapsburg period was both head of state and patron of the church. Although there was not perfect cooperation between church and state, their status and powers were equal and complementary.

The Bourbon Crown, under Carlos III, initiated major changes in institutional structures and functions, aimed at expanding regal power and developing economic prosperity. In terms of church-state relations in the Bourbon period, the Crown (1) redefined the *fuero eclesiástico* (ecclesiastical privileges and immunities); (2) undermined the status and function of parish priests; (3) expelled the Jesuits (1767); (4) secularized missions founded by the regular clergy; (5) sought control of church wealth; (6) refocused the duties of the Inquisition, and (7) entered the regulation of marriage. Taken together, these constituted a revolution in church-state relations that increasingly alienated the church hierarchy from support of the Spanish monarchy.

In its move to redefine church-state relations, the Crown undermined the *fuero eclesiástico*. The *fuero* was a legacy of Iberian practice, giving special privileges to the church and individual priests in legal matters. Ecclesiastics and the institutional church were entitled to have legal disputes of all kinds adjudicated before canonical rather than civil courts. These included lawsuits over property, be the church either a plaintiff or defendant, which effectively gave the church enormous leverage in the economic sphere. In addition, clerics who committed criminal offenses were protected from trial before any but canonical courts and were granted immunity from corporal punishment. Such *fueros* were part of the corporate organization of society, giving members of corporations more rights and privileges than those who were not. Ecclesiastics were but one group with such privileges, miners and merchants being other corporations holding them. In undermining the ecclesiastical *fuero,* the Crown was especially targeting church power, for it established at the same period a *fuero* for members of the newly established institution of the military.

With the Crown's limitation on the coverage of the *fuero eclesiástico,* the church's control over its property and personnel was undermined and the status of clerics reduced significantly. For the absolutist monarchy, this accomplished two purposes. First, it gave the Crown economic power at a point when it was attempting to revivify stagnating economies on the peninsula and in the colonies. Second, it undercut churchmen's privileged status, putting religious personnel on an equal footing with commoners in both civil and criminal proceedings. In a status-conscious society, this was a severe blow to the religious. Some scholars have argued that by undermining the institutional church, the Crown was eroding its own power, authority, and legitimacy.

Under the Bourbon Reforms, parish priests' functions were increasingly confined to a solely spiritual sphere. In many remote areas of New Spain, the parish priest was sometimes the only representative of Spanish power. In other cases

the friar and the *corregidor* (the civil representative of the Crown) were the only Europeans among the indigenous population, so that the two officials of Crown and clergy equally represented the Monarch's authority. With the political reorganization of New Spain from *corregimiento* (a system of indirect rule based on purchased offices) to the creation of new jurisdictions known as intendancies, the cooperation that had existed between civil and religious personnel virtually disappeared. The subdelegates (officials in charge of subunits of the intendancy) were to function as the sole representative of Crown power. For parish priests, the special status accorded them as representatives of the Crown was eliminated, placing the priests more on a par with their parishioners and in an adversarial relationship with the subdelegate. Increasingly, parish priests and rural parishioners came to see the Crown not only as despotic, but as an illegitimate power.

One of the most decisive and far-reaching exercises of state power over an ecclesiastical corporation was the expulsion in 1767 of the Jesuits from all Spanish realms. The Jesuits had been under attack by several European monarchies, so their expulsion by the Spanish Crown was not unprecedented. However, more so than in France, Portugal, or their respective colonies, their expulsion from Spain and its empire left a significant vacuum in the spheres of education and missionization of the native peoples. The Crown had intervened in the affairs of the regular clergy (those belonging to particular orders) during the Hapsburg era, and expulsion of individual clerics was within the Crown's power, a tool that could keep ecclesiastics in line. Nothing so sweeping as the Jesuit expulsion had been enacted previously, however.

With the expulsion of the Jesuits on June 25, 1767, the Crown cited its "supreme economic authority" to protect its citizens and the rights of the Crown. Although the expulsion was nominally justified in economic terms, the Crown's motives were more politically charged. There was widespread perception that the Jesuits were less controllable than other religious orders since the Jesuits' organization was not only more centralized but also under the direct influence of the papacy. In the Crown's view, the Jesuits as "soldiers of the pope" could not be depended on to pursue purely Spanish interests.

Their expulsion, however, had unintended consequences for the Crown. Since the Jesuits were the key educators of the sons of the elites as well as the order of choice for elites following a vocation in the regular clergy, criollo (those of Spanish descent born in the Americas) families felt the impact of the order's abrupt expulsion. Many criollo elites were sympathetic to the Jesuits, for the men of the family were educated by them. More directly for elites was the loss of their kin who were Jesuits, for those religious spent the rest of their lives in Italian exile. The Crown's action resulted in alienation by criollo elites toward the increasingly regalist state, making independence from the Spanish monarchy a more possible course for them. Another unintended consequence was the weakening of the Spanish presence on the northern frontiers, since Jesuits had been the successful and virtually sole agents of sovereign expansion. Jesuits in frontier missions obeyed the order of expulsion, which left their mission outposts devoid of personnel. The neophyte native-converts did not linger on the mission sites, awaiting replacement religious personnel.

On the frontier, the Crown continued to rely on the regular clergy, mainly the Franciscans, to extend areas of Spanish presence, mainly Alta California with a string of missions from San Diego north. However, the Crown moved in more central areas to limit the regular clergy's control by placing under the secular (non-order) clergy parishes that previously had been in the hands of the orders. The secular clergy was more directly answerable to the Crown via the episcopal hierarchy than regular clerics organized via their religious orders.

Access to church wealth was a Crown goal. Expulsion of the Jesuits for "economic reasons" meant that the order's rich and extensive estates came into the Crown's hands. More interested in liquidity than real estate, the Crown sold the estates, which had funded the Jesuits' educational institutions and northern missions. The estates generally passed into lay hands, with the purchase price going to the Crown. Another effort to gain control of church wealth was the short-lived attempt to place collection of the tithe, a tax on agricultural production for the support of the church hierarchy, entirely in the hands of royal treasury officials. Vociferous protest by clerics was successful in returning tithe collection to church hands.

Church dominance in the adjudication of testaments was a more successful target of state initiative. Most final wills and testaments included bequests to the church. Because the church had exercised its *fuero* to claim that any dispute to which it was party would be adjudicated in canonical courts, in effect the church had tremendous power to affect the distribution of wealth and enforce its claims. Maintaining that church property was "spiritual" not "temporal," the church had a powerful control of its economic resources. Bourbon legal theorists fundamentally changed the concept of property from a division of spiritual and temporal nature of property to a solely temporal interpretation. Thus, the sovereign monarch in his temporal role had jurisdiction over property, no matter that the church might have an interest in that property. Thus, civil rather than canonical courts gained control over property, virtually eliminating the church's advantage in this sphere. This was an important move by the Crown, since it increasingly viewed the church's hold on the economy as a major stumbling block to economic development.

The state sought to place barriers in the way of further church accumulation of property through elimination of tax exemptions, the levy of 15 percent tax on property passing into mortmain (perpetual church holding), and finally, in 1804, the order abolishing property belonging to *capellanías* (chantries) and *obras pías* (pious works), another form of donation to the church for charity.

These changes, particularly the order to eliminate *capellanías,* had a direct impact on the lower secular clergy. Many lower secular clerics had meager incomes, even if they served as parish priests with an ecclesiastical stipend. A good number of secular clerics received income from *capellanías,* whereby families set aside untaxed income from property to employ a priest to say masses for the soul of the founder of the *capellanía.* In fact, this was a standard way for families to keep a portion of their wealth for their kin. Quite often one of their own relatives held the post of *capellán.*

The funds for pious works and chantries not only supported many secular clerics, but they also were used for the charitable work of the church and a source of capital for mortgages. Thus the Act of Consolidation of 1804, which was designed to take money away from the church and place it in Crown control, had the effect of destroying credit for criollo elites. The church was required to call in all its debts, which meant that long-term loans to criollo elites came due immediately, ruining many financially. What was intended as an attack on the economic power of the church by the state had the effect of dispossessing criollo elites.

The Holy Office of the Inquisition became active in the Bourbon period in a new sphere, that of persecuting political dissent against the Crown and the monarch himself. Statements questioning the right of the monarch could result in their authors being brought before the Inquisition. Thus, that institution was drawn into the political sphere as an instrument of state power rather than dealing exclusively with the moral and doctrinal lapses of the non-Indian population of New Spain.

Another sphere in which the state began to assert itself was in the regulation of marriage, traditionally in the hands of the church. Concerned about the obvious evidence of racial mixing and perceived lowering barriers between white elites and the mainly darker lower classes, the state forbade unions between unequal partners. Although the canonical courts continued to have formal jurisdiction over regulation of marriage, these new state-mandated policies were enforced by canonical courts. The state strengthened the control of parents over their children's marriage choices, with parents instigating suits before canonical courts to block unions to which the parents objected. The traditional position of the church was that marriage was by the consent of the couple wishing to marry, if there were no canonical impediments to the union. The church sanctified the union in a ceremony that could be secret if some outside party sought to prevent the union. However, the new state-mandated marital policies asserted the state's interest as a fundamental aspect of social organization. Evidence is that the church continued to enable couples to sanctify their unions, but that parents attempted to exercise new rights over their children, empowered by the state.

The Bourbon period was one of fundamental change in church-state relations. Scholars have argued that the leading role of the lower secular clergy in the first phase of the Wars of Independence, such as Miguel Hidalgo and José María Morelos, directly followed from their alienation from the Crown because of its actions. The Crown was no longer able to draw on the spiritual loyalties of its colonists, having spent half a century implementing policies that weakened the church as an institution and distanced the monarch as the spiritual head of the church. Thus, when the government of Spain was set to implement the liberal, anticlerical elements of the Constitution of 1812, the clerics in Mexico saw political independence from Spain as New Spain's best course to preserve and expand the power of the church. Mexico's independence from Spain in 1821 had strong support from the episcopal hierarchy, for Agustín de Iturbide's Plan of Iguala had guaranteed that Catholicism would be the only religion tolerated in the independent country and that the clergy would retain their rights and privileges. Parish priests preached support of the plan and its political arm, the Army of the Three Guarantees. The church had much to gain in asserting itself in the new order, emerging from the struggles for independence as a much stronger power than the state.

See also Bourbon Reforms; Convents in New Spain; Fueros; Inquisition; Missions and Reductions; Religious in New Spain

Select Bibliography

Cuevas, Mariano, *Historia de la iglesia mexicana.* 6th edition, 5 vols., Mexico City: Porrúa, 1992.

Farriss, Nancy M, *Crown and Clergy in Colonial Mexico, 1759–1821: The Crisis of Ecclesiastical Privilege.* London: Athlone Press, 1968.

Mecham, Lloyd, *Church and State in Latin America: A History of Politicoecclesiastical Relations.* Revised edition, Chapel Hill: University of North Carolina Press, 1966.

—SARAH L. CLINE

CHURCH AND STATE: 1821–1910

In the last years of the Spanish American empire, serious church-state conflicts arose from the Bourbon monarchy's attempts to limit the religious orders, eliminate the ecclesiastical *fuero* (or immunity from civil prosecution), and appropriate the debts owed to charitable funds in America. Nevertheless, the Wars of Independence were by no means anticlerical or anti-religious. Indeed, the extent and contradictory character of clerical participation in the wars, and the pervasiveness of Christian symbolism, are indicative of the intricate ways in which religion and the Catholic Church were involved at every level of Mexican politics, economics, and society.

At the heart of the nineteenth century church-state conflict was the Catholic Church's special relationship with the poor and the dispossessed of Mexico, that is, the Indians and *castas* (those of mixed blood) who accounted for as much as 90 percent of the population. For these people, the local parish priest often seemed the only bulwark protecting them from the exploitative powers of the state and of local elites. Parish priests interceded not only between the people and the divine, but they were vital brokers to the temporal world of Mexico as well. They would tend to the sick, help communities plead cases in court, and defend community interests against rapacious outsiders. Moreover, the lives of the poor—urban and rural alike—centered on the Catholic Church. For such communities, church ceremonies and fiestas provided practically the only relief from an otherwise grim and monotonous existence, while church *cofradías* (lay brotherhoods) provided for a measure of welfare and mediated social life in general.

The parish priest, then, became a figure of some controversy. Liberal purists were suspicious of his exaggerated power and authority among the poor, supposing that he used his position to inculcate superstition and possibly subversion. Others—liberals and conservatives alike—argued that the parish priest typically received few rewards beyond the gratitude and veneration of his flock. His salary was invariably miserable, even while royal policies often prevented him from engaging in lucrative commercial enterprises. The only tangible benefit he received from the state was his exemption from civil prosecution, a key element of his authority with the masses. Apologists for the Catholic Church argued that only the parish priest stood between Mexico's tiny, white-skinned elite and a general explosion of popular wrath. Their worst fears were confirmed when Father Miguel Hidalgo, the parish priest of the small town of Dolores (Guanajuato), rallied his Indian and mestizo parishioners in the name of religion and independence, setting off what scholar Nancy Fariss called a "spark . . . that ignited the whole kingdom."

The degree of popular devotion to church and clergy was a decisive factor not only in the course of the Wars of Independence, but it placed definite limits on policy making in the post-Independence era. Liberals who dreamed of transforming Mexico into a progressive, egalitarian nation by breaking up latifundia (great landed estates), ending corporate privilege, promoting private enterprise, and enhancing the power of the central government, would have to negotiate a minefield of clerical special interests. Despite the yawning gulf in income and standards of living between the parish priests and the church notables, there was to be no class struggle within in the Catholic Church in independent Mexico: nearly all clerics and their allies formed a ready pool ripe for political mobilization by the hierarchy. And the hierarchy, early on in Mexico's national life, formed a staunch alliance with conservatives who felt that church wealth and clerical privilege were simply necessary to restrain the base and unruly impulses of the masses. Liberals, for their part, tended to be suspicious of Catholic Church, seeing in it a potential alien power in their midst that inevitably would obstruct the successful consolidation of a modern nation-state. They also resented the Catholic Church's wealth and blamed its lending policies for the continued existence of the great latifundia, which they identified as a key obstacle to the modernization of agriculture.

Although independence was achieved by conservatives who guaranteed clerical privilege and official protection for Roman Catholicism, conflict was not long in coming. An early focus of conflict was the *patronato real*, or extensive political control of the American church that the papacy had granted to the Spanish monarchy in 1508. Most of Mexico's new rulers believed that such political control over the church was necessary to the smooth functioning—and perhaps to the very survival—of the state, and they argued that the right of patronage was inherent in sovereignty. They explicitly claimed that right in the Constitution of 1824. The papacy, meanwhile, was unwilling to offend Spain by recognizing Mexico's new government and granting it patronage over the church. It argued that the right of patronage was abrogated when imperial ties were severed. Although the papacy recognized Mexico's independence in 1836, following the death of Fernando VII, the dispute never was definitively resolved.

The patronage issue had a major impact on the Catholic Church's fortunes. Given the sweeping nature of the patronage, the colonial Mexican church had tended to depend more upon Madrid than upon Rome, and the end of the empire had set off a crisis of legitimacy and a scramble for power that mirrored developments in the civil realm. The struggle eventually favored radically intransigent fringe elements within the church. While the patronage dispute dragged on many church benefices went unfilled. Indeed, with the death of the bishop of Puebla in 1829, not a single resident bishop remained in Mexico, and the archbishopric would remain vacant until 1840. Lacking bishops to perform ordinations and confirmation, the number of priests and faithful fell dramatically, irrevocably damaging church authority and weakening its hold on the masses.

The early governments of the republic generally upheld clerical privilege and were at least circumspect in their attacks on the wealth of the Mexican Catholic Church. The government of Anastasio Bustamante (1830–32) renounced the right of patronage, even while unleashing intemperate repression against liberal rivals. That, in turn, provoked a liberal reaction in 1833 under the leadership of the powerful caudillo Antonio López de Santa Anna, who upon his election to the presidency retired to his Veracruz estate. The government thereupon fell into the hands of Santa Anna's ultraliberal vice president, Valentín Gómez Farías. Gómez Farías, backed by a zealously liberal congress, passed a series of sweeping anticlerical measures, including the confiscation of the resources of the wealthy Catholic missions, secularization of the entire educational system, an end to government support for the collection of tithes, resumption of the right of patronage, and a declaration that monastic vows no longer were to be considered binding. The liberals of 1833 erred in supposing that profound reform could be accomplished by government fiat. Not only was society at large unprepared for such sweeping reform, but the government hardly was strong enough to step into the void left by the sudden dispossession of the Catholic Church. The reaction of late 1834, taking up the durable battle-cry of *"religión y fueros,"* was swift, decisive, and headed by none other than President Santa Anna himself. The new dictator dissolved Congress and decreed most of the anticlerical laws invalid.

The liberal experiment of 1833 showed that Santa Anna, heretofore a reputed liberal, in fact was possessed of shallow as well as endlessly flexible political principles, and considerable deftness in turning popular sentiment to his advantage. The episode also demonstrated just how polarized the church-state issue had become. In particular, the first decades of independence led to such a hardening of clerical intransigence that even the archconservative, proclerical Anastasio Bustamante—restored to the presidency in 1837—was subject to clerical reprisals when he sought a loan from church coffers. Not even conservatives, in those days of severe government penury, could fail to take notice of the apparent opulence of the Catholic Church This opulence was simply too tempting for anyone governing in an age of chronic deterioration in the national economy and treasury, and it blinded statesmen to the fact that such sumptuousness was not an accurate reflection of the Catholic Church's actual holdings, which never were as endless as generally rumored.

The attack on church wealth and property was more often a practical than an ideological matter. It was the one area where liberals and conservatives coincided, if not with respect to means then certainly with respect to ends. The need for the government to appropriate a share of church wealth became especially imperative when the government of Santa Anna and Gómez Farías (restored to power in 1846) needed funds to prosecute the war with the United States. After heated debate, they passed a bill in Congress authorizing the government to demand a loan of 15 million pesos from the Catholic Church, which would be secured by a mortgage on church property. Since this amounted to the de facto nationalization of nearly a tenth of all church wealth, the hierarchy responded with predictable vehemence, threatening with excommunication any who dared to enforce the law. Santa Anna eventually rescinded the law in exchange for a large cash payment from the clergy—in effect, a bribe to restrain him from further attacks on church property. This marked the start of yet another period of ascendancy of church interests in Mexico. Under the auspices of a reconstituted conservative Santa Anna, some anticlerical legislation was repealed and the Catholic Church received some guarantees for its property. But the wily old dictator by now had lost touch with popular sentiment. Under a storm of accusations of absolutism, treason, and corruption, Santa Anna was overthrown for the last time in 1854.

This liberal Revolution of Ayutla marked the ascendance to power of a new generation of dogmatic and doctrinaire liberals, who were fairly quick to undertake the most sweeping and devastating attack on the Catholic Church yet seen in Mexico. These liberals aimed once and for all to liberate the country from clerical and military domination and to create an egalitarian civil society founded upon values of private property, freedom of conscience, the free circulation of capital, secular education, and nationalism. Nearly all of the outstanding figures in the new liberal government were freemasons and staunch anticlericals.

The legislative assault began in November 1855 with the passage of the so-called Ley Juárez (Juárez Law), named for Justice Minister Benito Juárez. This decree stripped the ecclesiastical and military courts of jurisdiction in civil matters. While this was a moderate measure that did not seek to interfere with ecclesiastical jurisdiction in ecclesiastical matters, it aroused a storm of protest. The church and the military, both having been attacked by the same measure, united and revived the old battle cry of *"religión y fueros."* The Ley Juárez was followed shortly (June 25, 1856) by the so-called Ley Lerdo, which barred all civil and ecclesiastical corporations from owning or acquiring real property except that for the immediate purposes of worship. Church land was to be portioned off and sold at prices equal to those currently being charged in rent. The law was formally defended as a purely economic measure, designed to take land out of the "dead hands" of the Catholic Church and of Indian communities—which hitherto had held their lands in mortmain, a system the liberals deemed wasteful and unproductive—and make that property mobile. Specifically, the Catholic Church would benefit from collecting mortgage payments on property sold, the government would benefit from a 5 percent sales tax on all transactions, and Indians and small farmers would benefit from the impetus to improve and make profitable their private holdings. Although not formally stated, the law would bring the residual benefits of weakening the Catholic Church and helping to remove a major obstacle to the liberals' own economic and political ambitions.

The decree had a powerful negative impact not only on the Catholic Church but also on the Indian villages. The village-based *cofradías*, or lay brotherhoods, owned properties that now were slated for disentailment. Moreover, the extensive landholdings of the villages, although theoretically exempted from the initial Ley Lerdo, began to be portioned off and sold. And while the erstwhile property owners or tenants were supposed to get first consideration in the bidding for the new plots, in practice the distribution of the land was uneven and often corrupted by the machinations of the wealthy and powerful. Dispossessed villagers once again became natural allies of the church in a dispute with civil authority. Shared grievance overcame the badly diminished role of the church in popular everyday life, which was most clearly evidenced in the scant numbers of parish priests resident in the republic (barely one per 3,000 souls in the mid–nineteenth century).

Further injury to the Catholic Church came with the Iglesias Law of 1857, which limited the amounts parish priests could collect in fees they charged parishioners for sacraments and other services. The final blow came with the promulgation of the Constitution of 1857, which declared public education to be free, nullified the compulsory observance of religious vows, incorporated the Juárez and Lerdo Laws, barred ecclesiastics from holding high public office, and granted the federal government the right to intervene "in matters of religious worship and outward ecclesiastical forms" in accordance with the laws. The Constitution stopped short of formally separating church and state and declaring religious liberty, but neither did it uphold the traditional relationship of church and state. In fact, it was altogether silent on the subject. For champions of the church, that silence was ominous indeed.

Upon its promulgation on February 12, 1857, the Constitution was greeted with open hostility by the clergy. Mexicans suddenly found themselves caught between civil and religious power; the government demanded that public officials swear allegiance to the document, even while the clergy threatened excommunication and denial of sacraments to any who did so. The liberal legislation was denounced roundly in broadsides, books, and pamphlets, which often urged civil disobedience and rebellion against the government. By December, an alliance of church and army under the leadership of General Félix Zuloaga declared war on the Constitution and called for a full return to the status quo ante, including return of church property, protection and guarantees for church and clergy, religious intolerance, and if possible the establishment of a monarchy.

The ensuing war was, in effect, a civil war fought in the name of religion. Perhaps because both sides viewed it as something of a holy war, the extent of brutality exceeded anything Mexico yet had experienced. Tales were rife of prisoners massacred in cold blood, doctors and nurses slaughtered, churches sacked. The contending sides were roughly equal in numbers and strength, and ironically both found themselves obliged to finance their operations by preying on church property. While the conservatives nominally made good their promise to return church property, they at the same time solicited loans from the church, which normally were paid in bonds guaranteed by church property. These bonds were then sold at a discount to financiers with ready cash, who eventually came into full possession of the properties when the church was unable to redeem the bonds. The liberals, for their part, often financed their efforts through outright confiscation of church property, or by promising handsome amounts of real estate to creditors, which would be delivered in the event of a liberal victory. In this fashion, foreigners and financiers came into large amounts of real estate at bargain prices, and both church and state fared poorly.

The inevitable polarization attending civil war led the liberals to carry their anticlerical legislation to its logical conclusion. Decrees ordered the suppression of the religious orders, the complete separation of church and state, religious tolerance, prohibitions against religious ceremonies and the wearing of clerical garb in public, and nationalization of virtually all ecclesiastical holdings. The liberal victory in December 1860 led to further reprisals against conservative enemies, including the expulsion of the archbishop and four other bishops from the republic and the suppression of all cathedral chapters.

The nationalization of church property, however, was so compromised by the exigencies of wartime financing that its benefits to the national treasury were slight. The government of Benito Juárez defaulted on its foreign debts in 1861, providing the pretext for the French Intervention, an intervention aided and abetted by disgruntled clergy for whom an end to national sovereignty seemed a small price to pay for the return of their traditional privileges and properties. Invading French troops were hailed with Te Deum masses as they marched on Mexico City, but the outcome of the intervention was decidedly disappointing to the clergy. The French emperor, Napoleon III, determined to support those who had bought nationalized church property in good faith. His appointed puppet-emperor, the Austrian archduke Maximilian von Hapsburg, proved to be of a liberal persuasion and not amenable to the importunings of extremist clerics. Pope Pius IX did not, as Maximilian had hoped, support a conciliatory policy. He demanded instead that the emperor nullify all reform laws, decree religious intolerance, restore the religious orders, return education to clerical supervision, and lift all remaining government restrictions on the Catholic Church. Maximilian, alive to the inflammatory potential of such proposals and eager to negotiate, was stunned by the pope's intransigence, which had the effect of driving him further into the liberal camp, at least in religious matters. Far from abrogating the reform laws, Maximilian ratified most of them.

Maximilian's efforts were unproductive; as far as the liberals were concerned, they could not atone for his role in the violation of national sovereignty, even while these moves simultaneously lost him any support he might have desired from the clergy. When Napoleon III withdrew his troops, Maximilian was abandoned by both parties to the conflict, a victim of the century's most intractable conflict. He was executed upon the triumph of the liberals, who immediately set about resurrecting and enforcing their anticlerical legislation.

By the last quarter of the nineteenth century, the Mexican Catholic Church was battered and bitter, possessing only a shadow of its former prestige and grandeur. Pius IX did nothing to help the situation when he intensified his war against liberalism and democracy with the promulgation in 1869 of the famous Syllabus of Errors, which made clear that the Catholic Church would in no way compromise with the modern world. Nor were the liberals disposed to compromise on the issue. The objectionable anticlerical laws, which until now had been largely hypothetical elements in the Constitution, were made more immediate by enabling legislation passed in 1874.

The Catholic Church may have been beleaguered, but it still retained some wealth, primarily in the form of properties held for it by proxies. More importantly, it retained the faith and adherence of the majority of the Mexican people, which made it a force to reckon with and a potential menace to the peace of the republic. The dictator Porfirio Díaz (1876–80; 1884–1911) determined that the church was too formidable to suppress, and that continued government efforts in that direction could only undermine the "order and progress" that were the watchwords of his regime. He proposed, then, to subdue the issue through a policy of conciliation. This meant simply that, while anticlericalism remained the law of the land, for the most part it went unenforced so long as Catholics and clergy recognized Díaz's supreme political authority and tempered their criticism of civil government. The Catholic Church fairly easily accommodated itself to such minor annoyances as civil baptisms and marriages. The hierarchy generally acquiesced, too, in the suppression of the religious orders. Restrictions on religious education were enforced only mildly: private religious schools continued to function, and on occasion religious instruction was offered even in public schools, albeit after hours. Somewhat more conflict was generated by the constitutional restrictions on wearing clerical garb, bell ringing, public religious ceremonies, and other outward manifestations of religiosity. In many cases, such restrictions simply were ignored and the Catholic Church practiced its ceremonial life quite publicly and unimpeded. In other cases, zealous local officials took it upon themselves to uphold the letter of the law, and considerable friction resulted, especially when the occasion was one of great popular resonance such as Holy Week. The most serious source of conflict was the official policy of religious tolerance. Popular hostility toward Protestants and free-thinkers often was abetted by the hierarchy, who feared that religious liberty was the first step in a descent into immorality and atheism. Attacks on Protestants and Protestant missionaries were frequent, and often quite vicious.

Under the conciliation policy, the Catholic Church managed to regain some of its economic power and much of its prestige. Donations from well-to-do Catholics made some parishes quite wealthy. Tithes were sometimes collected surreptitiously and illegally, with collectors going from house to house threatening ostracism for nonpayers. Clergymen once again became moneylenders, landlords, and businessmen. Some, like the ultrawealthy Archbishop Eulogio Gillow y Zavalza, were close personal friends of the dictator and moved in the inner circles of his regime. According to one estimate, the value of church property doubled in the years from 1874 to 1910.

This apparent resolution of the church-state conflict in Mexico was superficial, if not wholly illusory. The Catholic Church depended upon the dictator for the maintenance of its special privileges, and accordingly much of the wrath directed toward Díaz found its way, by association, to the church. Wealthy and conservative clerics were identified easily with the class of oppressors. Zealous liberals, meanwhile, never reconciled themselves to the conciliation policy and became more vocal in their denunciations once the policy became more overt after 1890.

Perhaps the most dangerous development of all was the rise of Social Catholicism following the promulgation by Pope Leo XIII of the encyclical *Rerum Novarum* in 1891. A direct response to the rise of socialism in Europe, *Rerum Novarum* was a fundamentally conservative document in which the Catholic Church gave its attention to the "social question." In place of class conflict, the encyclical urged class harmony, devotion to the commonweal, and corporatism. This new orientation coincided with certain renovations in the Mexican Catholic Church, notably the replacement of the monarchist archbishop Pelagio Antonio Labastida with the more moderate and nationalistic Próspero María Alarcón. At the same time, Catholic administration was revamped with the creation of seven bishoprics and three archbishoprics. With its new social orientation and more responsive administration, the Catholic Church was shaken out of its old traditionalism and passivity and became more activist and enterprising, offering its flock something more than promises of celestial rewards. The hierarchy began urging the faithful to involve themselves directly in their communities through the media of press, schools, theater, political parties, and labor organizations. This movement struck a nerve with the popular classes, who had borne the brunt of certain Porfirian trends such as the dramatic population increase and consequent surplus labor force, the fall in real wages, the expansion of haciendas, the increasing proletarianization of the peasantry, and the decline of artisanry with the massive introduction of imported manufactures. In accordance with the postulates of *Rerum Novarum*, Catholic labor unions were formed to push for shorter hours, an end to child labor, improvements in the status of women, improved and more extensive education and medical care, and better pay—all, presumably, to be achieved without recourse to open class warfare. Catholic organizations and press also mounted a major moralization campaign, denouncing alcoholism, concubinage, and other vices. In 1908, under the energetic leadership of Father José M. Troncoso, numerous "Catholic workers circles" united to form the Catholic Workers Union. By 1911, this organization, under the name National Confederation of Catholic Workers' Circles, claimed a national membership of 14,366.

The church had thus become a serious competitor in the political arena, a circumstance that was violently resented by its rivals. As the virulent anticlericalism of the revolutionary years proves, the church-state conflict had undergone only a relatively brief hiatus during the Porfiriato. It had by no means been resolved.

See also Conservatism; Constitution of 1824; Constitution of 1857; Liberalism; Positivism; Reform Laws; Wars of Independence; Wars of Reform

Select Bibliography

Bazant, Jan, *Alienation of Church Wealth in Mexico: Social and Economic Aspects of the Liberal Revolution, 1856–1875*. Cambridge: Cambridge University Press, 1971.

Ceballos Ramírez, Manuel, "La Encíclica Rerum Novarum y los trabajadores católicos en la Ciudad de México, 1891–1913." *Historia Mexicana* 33:1 (July–September 1983).

Fariss, Nancy, *Crown and Clergy in Colonial Mexico, 1759–1821: The Crisis of Ecclesiastical Privilege*. London: Athlone, 1968.

Fernando Iturribarría, Jorge, "La política de conciliación del General Díaz y el Arzobispo Gillow." *Historia Mexicana* 14:1 (July–September 1964)

Mecham, J. Lloyd, *Church and State in Latin America*. Chapel Hill: University of North Carolina Press, 1934.

Schmitt, Karl M., "The Díaz Conciliation Policy on State and Local Levels, 1876–1911." *HAHR* 40:4 (November 1960).

—TIMOTHY J. HENDERSON

CHURCH AND STATE: 1910–96

After the struggles for Independence and the civil wars of the nineteenth century, the Liberal state tried to use the Catholic Church, which maintained control at a social rather than a political level, in its program of national construction. Although the state occasionally expressed a desire to destroy the church, it was decided to take control of the institution in order to control and unify civil society. This variant of republican regalism lasted until 1990. The Revolutionary state (1914–40) rejected the church as a social institution and aimed to take it apart with the help of Freemasonry, Protestants, and the "reds." It was not a process of secularization, whereby the autonomy of secular society was affirmed in the context of the church as representative of religious society and sacramental power, but rather a process whereby one group achieved political hegemony over society in general. The church was treated as an obstacle in the way of progress, science, and modernization. Those in power became both antipopular and anticlerical, as revealed during the "rational" and "socialist" education campaign that affected the popular sector during the 1930s.

The Catholic Church reacted to this state of affairs in three ways. In terms of historical continuity, it defended its traditional rights, gambling on education and the family, the development of pedagogical institutions, the Catholic press, and devout practices. The church also attempted to win over the elites and also keep control over the masses, in the hope of taking over the state at some future date. Finally, the church obtained considerable help from Rome as well as French, Spanish, German, and Belgian churches.

Between 1880 and 1914 the polemic between Liberals and Conservatives, church and state, and positivism (loosely, empiricism and scientific inquiry) and clericalism, disguised deep problems within society. Social Catholicism and the workers' movement emerged discretely, almost without being noticed. Posivitism as the dominant ideology stimulated a reaction that was nationalist and Catholic, socialist and cultural (through such movements as modernism and idealism); this reaction to positivism appeared in Mexico earlier than in other countries. This dynamic period witnessed for the first time the emergence of important Protestant groups that would play a role in the Mexican Revolution. Although under Liberal rule from 1859 to 1910, the Catholic Church also had carried out a second evangelization that evolved through civic and social action movements in the spirit of Leo XIII's encyclical *Rerum Novarum*. The church was thus in a highly expansive period when the Revolution broke out. The initial three years favored the church as well as the ephemeral Partido Católica Nacional (PCN, or National Catholic Party, 1910–13).

The fall of the democratic president Francisco I. Madero in February 1913 renewed the revolutionary violence, and the triumphant faction turned against the Catholic Church. The victors were men from the north of the country, white men stamped by the U.S. frontier and imbued with the values of Anglo-Saxon Protestantism and capitalism, unknown in the old Mestizo, Indian, and Catholic Mexico. For these individuals the church was the incarnation of all they opposed. The Constitution of 1917 gave the state the right to legislate over the "clerical profession," whose power it detested and against whom it frequently clashed, particularly in the areas of education and the union movement. While a moderate president such as Álvaro Obregón (1920–24, reelected in 1928 but immediately assassinated) was in power, none of the numerous small incidents that occurred unleashed a crisis. But scarcely had his successor, General Plutarco Elías Calles, taken sides with some violence when events started a downward spiral. Calles was the representative of a group of politicians in Mexico, Spain, and other countries who believed that Catholicism was incompatible with the state and that a Catholic cannot be a good citizen if his first loyalty is to Rome. Having tried unsuccessfully to create a schismatic (i.e., non–Roman Catholic) church, the government elaborated legislation that considered infractions in matters of worship as violations of common law, obliging the priests to register with the Ministry of Internal Affairs for the right to practice their profession. The law took advantage of the potential for limiting the number of priests. The church responded on July 31, 1926, by suspending the per-

formance of public worship. When the bishops attempted to seek an agreement with the government on August 21, Calles informed them that they could choose between submitting to the force of law or taking up arms.

The church did not choose war, since the Vatican never considered Calles as a Nero—even if it did, it also never forgot that he was also Caesar, and it was more advisable to negotiate. Talks extended over three long years during which certain foreign diplomats and U.S. and Mexican bankers took on the role of intermediaries, and the peasantry took up arms in a pro-Catholic uprising known as the Cristero Rebellion. The conflict, not expected by either church or state, was a pleasant surprise for certain young Catholic militants who dreamed of taking power by force of arms.

Immediately after the tentative schism of 1925, the militants of Acción Católica (Catholic Action), in particular those of the Associación Católica de la Juventud Mexicana (ACJM, or Catholic Association of Mexican Youth), had started up a great political organization, La Liga (the League) and realized an intense campaign of civil resistance and legal action. The first revolts had occurred spontaneously in the moment of the suspension of church services. In August 1926 these events convinced the organizers of La Liga that the conflict would end in rapid victory owing to the unpopularity of the government and the predominant Catholicism of the people. The war lasted for three years, mobilizing 40,000 rebels known as *cristeros.* Dwight Morrow, U.S. ambassador to Mexico, noted on May 3, 1929, that all possibilities of returning to normality were extremely slight if the government did not arrive at an agreement with the church that allowed the resumption of worship.

When the Cristero Rebellion was at its height, the state decided to come to an understanding with the church. Matters were quickly settled in June 1929, just prior to the presidential elections, to avoid a possible alliance between the urban political forces, the revolutionary factions of the opposition, and the *cristeros,* who could have assumed the role of armed support. According to the "Arrangements," as the agreements became known, the law was not changed but its application was suspended. Amnesty was guaranteed between the combatants, as was the restitution of the churches and the priests.

The Peruvian scholar José Mariategui commented in 1928 that in the Latin American countries, the extreme development of liberalism during the nineteenth century led to the approval of Protestantism and the national church as logical necessities for the modern state. This logic never went beyond speculation except in Mexico, where it took concrete form between 1926 and 1938. The policies of President Calles between 1926 and 1934 and of President Lázaro Cárdenas until at least 1938 aimed at integrating the Catholic Church into the state machine. Catholics who traditionally had been kept outside the political camp until 1910 now had become dangerous rivals; the attack on the church was thus a measure of its influence. The incomplete nature of the nation (prior to the Revolution the state was still in the process of creation) pushed the Revolutionary president-generals toward control, centralism, and constriction.

Mexican bishops, insecure as to which path to follow and divided over whether or not to encourage Catholic unionism (at its height 1920–26) and political participation, in the majority accepted with a certain relief their return to the line traditionally dictated by Rome for Mexico: the restriction of the lay members within tightly controlled Acción Católica groups. The encyclical *Paterna Solicitudo Sano* of February 2, 1926, clearly specified this but could not avoid the imminent collision between church and state that resulted in the Cristero Rebellion. The encyclical's application was strictly enforced after June 1929, and the rebellious Catholic organizations were dissolved, beginning with the ACJM. Thus, 40 years prior to emergence of the Latin American left (of both Catholic and non-Catholic persuasion), Mexican Catholics experienced the problem of choosing between an armed or peaceful road to power. The political Catholics of the PCN, Acción Católica, Catholic unionism, and La Liga prefigured the Christian Democracy of the 1960s in other Latin American countries.

Later, Catholics were able to locate their interests in a stable political party—the Partido de Acción Nacional (PAN, or National Action Party)—and in a movement—the Union Nacional Sinarquista (National Sinarquist Union, also known as *sinarquismo*). Both were founded at the end of the 1930s at a moment when the modus vivendi signed in 1929 was about to become a reality. Both party (of urban character, drawing followers from the Catholic middle classes) and movement (which attracted a mass following of mostly rural and provincial origin) were linked to the Catholic Church, although the latter always took care not to give an official seal of approval. Both were opposed and indeed hostile to the state that emerged from the Revolution, but both had learned that the time for revolutions had come to an end in Mexico and that rebellion was no longer a political solution.

The Cristero Rebellion left a deep scar on the country and the Mexican Catholic Church. It explains many differences between Mexico and other Latin American countries. Mexico's church became more cautious than those elsewhere in Latin America, but at the same time it became far more national, practically without a foreign priesthood and backed by numerous members of religious orders. Institutionally, the Mexican Church was the first to create its own episcopal conference, in 1925–26. It also became a church linked to the papacy, symbol of the faith during the uprising; the *cristeros'* battle cry had been "Long Live the Pope!"

State-church cooperation after the 1920s consisted largely of the latter's acceptance that the social field was the exclusive monopoly of the state in Mexico. This modus vivendi continued until the beginning of the 1950s. The abandonment of control over social movements to the state in the wake of the Cristero Rebellion, the permanent renunciation of Catholic unionism, and the freezing of Catholic "political" activities led the church, without realizing it, to destroy the integral vision of Catholicism. In exchange, the church's victory was that Catholicism came to be seen as one of the essential elements of Mexican nationality. Later there were other moments in which the church appeared to approve the social policy of the state, especially between 1963 and 1965, and 1970 and 1976. In both cases the church seemed to have inclined toward support of government policies that coincided with its own reformist project for society. Such support was neither unconditional nor absolute, since important differences existed over issues such as birth control and education. It was a conditional cooperation. The church played no part in the state's "apparatus of ideological domination." It is not possible to describe the relationship between church and state as "mistaken complicity." The absence of open conflict should not be confused with the existence of an agreement or complicity.

After 1940, three developments marked the Catholic Church in Mexico: an expansion of activities in social and economic affairs, the increasing role of the laity, and the positive, immediate, and generalized response to Rome's directives regarding the material condition of man. Thus was posed the problem of knowing what role the church could and wished to play in the economic and political development of the country. Regardless of events in Mexico, the spectacular commitment of the church and its lay congregation in worldly affairs undoubtedly would have been stimulated and accelerated by the Vatican Council II of 1962 to 1965 and the general evolution of the Roman Church, among the most important events of the twentieth century. This evolution implied renewed confrontation both inside and outside the church as well as the resumption of the old conflict between church and state on different terms, since both powers had changed radically in the meantime.

The scholar Roberto Blancarte has stated that throughout the second half of the twentieth century, two social and political currents were present within the church: the "integral/intransigent" and the "conciliatory/pragmatic." At least two further currents can be added, which became more defined after Vatican Council II: the "integrist" and the "neo-intransigent." These latter were in large measure offshoots of the first two. The "integral/intransigent" current included all those opposed to a commitment to the state and who fought against the imposition of the social model of the Mexican Revolution. The "conciliatory/pragmatic" tendency opted for cooperation with the Mexican state without reneging on the doctrine or principles of the Catholic Church; members of this group also have displayed a burning desire for justice. The "integrist" current was a product of the "integral/intransigent" tendency and has developed to the degree that the latter lost ground to the other currents; this current was made up of the most stubborn elements, resistant to any change or adaptation of the church to the modern world. Finally the "neo-intransigent" tendency, risen from the rank and file of the "intransigent" as much as the "conciliatory" groups, has defended theses of accommodation that aim to modernize the Catholic Church in order to spread their social program more effectively in the contemporary world.

Since the first visit of the pope to Mexico in 1979, the church has manifested its dislike of being confined to the sacristy and has increasingly entered the public arena, solidifying its role as one of the key institutions of civil society at a time when society had become more secularized than ever. As such, the church has exercised a role of counterweight to state authoritarianism. This attitude was accompanied by a radical change on the part of the government, presided over by Carlos Salinas de Gortari. From the start of his mandate at the end of 1988, Salinas showed his willingness to put an end to a modus vivendi that had been current for 50 years but that no longer corresponded with reality. In May 1990 Pope John Paul II made a second tour of Mexico, and the president pointed out that even the Soviet Union had reestablished diplomatic relations with the Vatican. Nevertheless, the old anticlerical lobby continued to resist these moves toward reconciliation. In July 1991 Salinas visited the pope, and in November of the same year in his State of the Union Address declared that the time had arrived to put an end to a situation, to "reconcile the clear secularization of our society with effective freedom of belief . . . whereby making a further step toward internal concord within the framework of modernization." In December the Congress received an initiative for constitutional reforms that were quickly approved. The new Article 3 allowed religious instruction in private schools; the revised Article 5 authorized the existence of religious orders; Article 24 permitted cultural demonstrations outside the churches; Article 27 allowed religious associations to own property; and Article 130 recognized the legal existence of religious associations and gave religious ministers the right to vote (although not to be elected). Nevertheless, the Constitution maintained important restrictions, and the regulations attached to Article 130 in 1992 allowed for an interpretation that has angered the churches. In fact, its uneven application has drawn criticism, provoking for example in 1996 a serious confrontation between the secretary for internal affairs and the Catholic Church, supported by Protestant churches, on the topic of ecclesiastical participation in the political life of the nation. In September 1992 diplomatic relations were established between Mexico and the Vatican. In August 1993 the pope visited Mexico for the third time, but for the first time in an official capacity. Thus after 150 years the Catholic Church and the Mexican state achieved "the separation of the two kingdoms" in a positive way.

See also Constitution of 1917; Cristero Rebellion; Liberation Theology; Partido de Acción Nacional (PAN); Protestantism; Social Catholicism; Unión Nacional Sinarquista (UNS)

Select Bibliography

Barranco, Bernardo, and Raquel Pastor, *Jerarquía católica y modernización política en México.* Mexico City: Palabra, 1989.
Blancarte, Roberto, *Historia de la iglesia católica en México 1939–1987.* Mexico City: Fondo de Cultura Económica, 1992.
Gakt Corona, Guillermo, *Ley y religión en México.* Guadalajara: Iteso, 1995.
Levine, Daniel, editor, *Churches and Politics in Latin America.* Thousand Oaks, California: Sage, 1980.
Meyer, Jean, *La Cristiada.* 3 vols., Mexico City: Siglo XXI, 1995.
Pike, Frederick, *Church and State in Mid-century Latin America.* New York: n.p., 1965.
Schmitt, Karl, *The Roman Catholic Church in Modern Latin America.* New York: n.p., 1972.

—Jean Meyer

CIENTÍFICOS

With reason, Mexican historian Daniel Cosío Villegas included a chapter entitled "El Misterio Científico" (the Científico Mystery) in his monumental work about politics in the Porfirio Díaz era. Indeed, the Científicos, an influential group of intellectuals and policy advisers, defy easy description and analysis. Not only do historians differ as to the membership of the Científico camarilla (a clientelist network of amity and interest), but issues such as the ideological orientation of the group and its influence on Díaz have provoked widespread debate. A review of the historical literature leads to an interesting conclusion: while the Científicos advocated the adoption of European political and social models, they ultimately played the game of camarilla politics that characterized much of Spanish America in the nineteenth century.

In discussing the Científicos, scholars must distinguish between myth and reality. During the last years of the Porfiriato, many of Díaz's opponents conflated the Científicos and their own political and social grievances and thus used the term "Científicos" as an epithet summarizing their opposition to the Díaz regime. The Científicos, many Mexicans thought, monopolized national as well as state politics, abused their power by means of an unprecedented venality, and slavishly served foreign interests. Therefore, when the revolutionaries of 1910 and 1911 shouted "death to the Científicos," they meant the entire Díaz regime. Foreign critics of Porfirian Mexico have further ensconced the myth of the omnipresent, corrupt, and pro-foreign Científicos. Writing in 1932, Carleton Beals called the group "completely Creole-minded, completely reactionary;" their true program, he stated, was "scientific stealing."

In fact, however, the Científicos, a very small camarilla, contended for power with other factions and represented a wide spectrum of opinion. Although most of them held influential posts in the Porfirian cabinet, the group numbered no more than a dozen people even at the height of its power during Díaz's last full term (1904–10). Other members of the governing elite either belonged to a rival camarilla or had no factional affiliation whatsoever. Among those who opposed the Científicos, we find not only General Bernardo Reyes, the head of a rival faction, but also Foreign Secretary Ignacio Mariscal, most of the leading army officers, and many of the governors. Politically, Treasury Secretary José Yves Limantour found little common ground with Sub-Secretary of Public Instruction Justo Sierra, and perhaps even less with Senator Francisco Bulnes, although Auguste Comte's positivist doctrines and Herbert Spencer's social Darwinism influenced all three of these elite intellectuals.

To understand the Científico mystery, we must first discuss the influence of Gabino Barreda, the intellectual grandfather of the group. As President Benito Juárez's secretary of justice and the founder of the Escuela Nacional Preparatoria (ENP), Barreda propagated Comtean positivism in Mexico. In his famous "Oración cívica" of 1867, he juxtaposed the "positive" character of Juárez's Reforma government with the "negative" nature of the deposed emperor Maximilian's French-supported regime. In Barreda's opinion, the positive forces of progress had defeated the negative forces of reaction, and Mexico had emerged ready to advance toward a new age. This new era, he thought, would bring the "mental emancipation" of the Mexican people, an emancipation that would ultimately fuse all political platforms, doctrines, and social sciences into a "scientific" approach to government. Barreda concluded that a time of "liberty, order, and progress" had come to Mexico, as liberty of expression accompanied by enforced social order would facilitate material progress.

Barreda's views encapsulated the "doctrine of scientific politics," the notion that technocrats, rather than politicians, should shape a country's destiny. Current in France, Spain, and the rest of Latin America and closely related to Conservative Liberalism, this doctrine seemed particularly appropriate to Mexican metropolitan elites. These elites resented the fact that the democratically elected Congress carried on in endless procedural debates while a series of rural revolts threatened the social order. Moreover, as both Barreda's supporters and detractors among the elites agreed, most Mexicans remained marginalized from the political process and hence in need of tutelage and direction from above. As

Juárez's successor, Sebastián Lerdo de Tejada, put it, Mexico needed "menos política, más administración"—less politics and more administration. Scientific politics, in the words of historian Charles A. Hale, implied "an attack on doctrinaire liberalism . . . an apology for strong government to counter endemic revolutions and anarchy, and a call for constitutional reform" to guarantee freedom of expression. Therefore, the "Oración cívica" constituted a summons for a technocratic governing elite.

During the next ten years, Barreda helped create that elite in his capacity as rector of the ENP. Through a positivist curriculum that favored arithmetic, sciences, and logic over the arts and humanities, the ENP passed the torch of scientific politics to a new generation that included many of the most brilliant minds of the Mexican elites. By the end of the Restored Republic, teachers and students of this elite academy had come to see themselves as exactly those technocrats for whom their mentor had called. The social background of these young intellectuals proved a good match for Barreda's views. Most of them came from the middle bourgeoisie, almost all of them had spent part of their formative years in Mexico City, a majority of them were mestizos, and many of them studied law only to go on to other professions such as banking and commerce.

During Díaz's first administration (1876–80), some of Barreda's followers began to influence the national political scene by advocating a brand of scientific politics in the pages of La Libertad, a new Mexico City newspaper. Led by Justo Sierra, a history professor at the ENP and former orthodox liberal, the editorialists of La Libertad provided posterior justification for Díaz's Tuxtepec coup against the democratically elected Lerdo de Tejada. La Libertad fused Comtean positivism and social Darwinism to argue that Mexico needed a strong hand, and not the "anarchy" of formal democracy, to guide its political and social evolution. Only the "most fit" (i.e., the educated criollo and mestizo elites) could provide the necessary guidance in that endeavor. In a series of notable editorials, Sierra advocated the formation of a "new Liberal" ruling party, a party that he believed would find no rival in Mexican society. This party, he wrote, would merge the conservative value of order with the liberal emphasis on free political institutions such as the press and the judiciary. To protect the president as a symbol of unity, Sierra also advocated that cabinet members, and not the president, be accountable to the Mexican Congress for government failures. Sierra thus became the architect of an important aspect of Porfirian camarilla politics. While Díaz's ministers took the heat for failed policies, the president himself remained above the fray.

Sierra and his friends, however, had to wait more than a decade to reach the pinnacle of national power. Most of them had been affiliated with the cause of José María Iglesias, who as chief justice of the Supreme Court had challenged the legality of both Lerdo's 1876 reelection and Díaz's coup. Since the veterans of Tuxtepec and some of Lerdo's adherents dominated Díaz's first cabinet as well as the government of President Manuel González (1880–84), the future Científicos remained at the margins of the Mexican political system. Díaz and González, whose governments remained besieged by instability and the threat of coups d'état, gave lip service to the 1857 Constitution, the very document that *La Libertad* attacked for its orthodox liberalism.

Despite the limited political influence of the Sierra group, the Díaz regime and *La Libertad* soon began to cooperate as they shared common ground in seeking what Hale has called a "principle of authority in the wake of upheaval." The publication received a government subsidy, and in return, Sierra and his colleagues "forgave" Díaz for leading a revolution against an established government. Thus, later in the 1880s, when Díaz prepared the way for his successive reelections and the consolidation of dictatorial rule, Sierra and his cohorts came closer to joining the national governing elite.

It was Díaz's father-in-law, Manuel Romero Rubio, who helped Barreda's disciples onto the national political stage. As part of his attempt to orchestrate his son-in-law's return to the presidency after the González interregnum, he began to meet with Sierra, Limantour, and six other lawyers (Joaquín Casasús, Fernando Duret, José María Gamboa, Roberto Núñez, Emilio Pimentel, and Rosendo Pineda) in his law offices. This new discussion group shared a basic political consensus: Sierra and his allies agreed with Romero Rubio on the need to reconcile the old Liberal Party's faith in material progress and the freedom of the press with the Conservatives' authoritarian and proclerical values. The group desired to create a ruling party that would represent the culmination of Díaz's policy of national reconciliation. The final result of these discussions was the Unión Liberal Nacional (ULN), a group formed in 1892 with the official purpose of promoting don Porfirio's reelection.

The program of the ULN largely followed Sierra's political ideas expressed in *La Libertad,* but with a new twist. According to its manifesto adopted in 1892, the ULN intended to promote a "scientific orientation" in Mexican politics, and, specifically, "a strong president within a progressively strengthened constitutional structure." In its manifesto, key elements of which were submitted to the Mexican Congress a year later, the group called for Díaz's reelection, the creation of the office of vice president, an independent judiciary steered by irremovable federal judges, the freedom of the press, and the formation of a national party that would transcend Mexico's traditional reliance on clientelist networks.

This program reflected the monumental transformation of Mexican politics between 1878 and 1893. *La Libertad* had responded to a widespread elite fear of continued social unrest. Hence, Sierra had advocated a type of democratic Caesarism, the notion that the executive power needed to be strengthened and protected from criticism. The Científicos of 1893 lived in an established dictatorship that had quelled these threats to the social and political order. In fact, the for-

mation of the ULN signaled the arrival of a national ruling class that soon overpowered the regional strongmen that had supported Díaz's first three administrations. As a result, the same Justo Sierra—the group's leading thinker even while Romero Rubio remained the unofficial head—emerged as a constitutionalist who sought to guarantee liberty of expression within a framework of authoritarian rule. In Sierra's words, if "effective peace has been acquired by the strengthening of authority, definitive peace will be acquired by its assimilation with liberty."

In the ensuing constitutional debate of 1893, carried out both in the press and in the Mexican Congress, the ULN found itself at the center of a complex argument. On one side, orthodox positivists and old Porfiristas, with the journal *El Siglo XIX* as their mouthpiece, agreed with the strengthening of the office of the president but opposed the irremovability of federal judges, a step that would have greatly enhanced the independence of the judiciary. On the other side, orthodox liberals writing in *El Monitor Republicano* desired a free press and an independent judiciary but opposed any changes that increased the powers of the president; they believed that the irremovability of judges would strengthen, and not weaken, executive authority. In the course of this debate, Sierra broke with his orthodox positivist colleagues from the days of *La Libertad,* some of whom joined *El Siglo XIX.* It was the most lasting legacy of the debate that *El Siglo XIX* coined the term "Científicos" as a derisive moniker. A publication subsidized by the Díaz regime, *El Siglo XIX* joined many old Porfiristas who did not believe that Mexico was ready for constitutional reform in opposing the reforms as outlandish importations thought up by egghead intellectuals. Don Porfirio agreed; hence, the Científicos' attempt to limit the powers of the executive failed.

The Científicos, however, soon reconciled themselves with the rules of the national political game. Thus, they emerged as a camarilla to end all camarillas, an inherently paradoxical proposition. On the one hand, they advocated measures that would have lessened the strong vestiges of *caudillismo* (rule by regional and military strongmen) and *personalismo* (personalist rule) in Porfirian Mexico. On the other hand, the Científicos favored Díaz's reelection and accepted the political terms for his tutelage of the faction.

By the turn of the century, what might have become a genuine opposition party had evolved into a camarilla within the national ruling class. Bolstered by the addition of several new members (Francisco Bulnes, Enrique Creel, Miguel S. and Pablo Macedo, Olegario Molina, and Rafael Reyes Spíndola), the Científico faction shared defining characteristics with other Porfirian camarillas. Their extremely small membership was limited to the national governing elite, their leader served as one of Díaz's most important retainers and jockeyed to succeed the aging dictator, and their ideology reflected their economic and political interests within the Porfirian system rather than a genuine commitment to reform. However, in contrast to their rivals—the camarilla of

General Bernardo Reyes as well as some minor cliques—the Científicos enjoyed the support of Mexico's first mass-produced newspaper, *El Imparcial,* a publication owned by Reyes Spíndola and subsidized by the Díaz regime.

Beginning in the early 1900s, the Científicos boasted privileged access to Díaz. Concerned about a possible challenge to his rule from the Mexican army, a challenge personified by Defense Secretary Bernardo Reyes, Díaz decided to give more power to a group that had criticized him. Between 1900 and 1903, a shakeup of the Porfirian cabinet gave the Científicos a number of key cabinet positions: José Y. Limantour became treasury secretary, Roberto Núñez his subsecretary, Sierra was appointed subsecretary of public instruction, and the pro-Científico Ramón Corral headed the powerful Secretaría de Gobernación (Ministry of the Interior). The favored relationship with the dictator (which never amounted to a monopoly of power) helped the group's members amass wealth and enter profitable business relationships with foreign investors. Some of the Científicos such as Sierra and Bulnes did not enrich themselves much in the process, but others such as Enrique Creel and Olegario Molina freely accepted bribes from investors in order to use their influence with Mexican courts, governors, and *jefes políticos* (political bosses).

In the process of integrating themselves into the Porfirian governing elite, most of the Científicos embraced the interests of the metropolitan bourgeoisie and foreign investors. They advocated French cultural models and Anglo-Saxon economic precepts, but jealously sought to safeguard Mexican political sovereignty. In their view, the growth of foreign investment (which many Mexicans feared as the so-called Peaceful Conquest) was the best way to bring economic development to Mexico, and the only way to prevent aggressive forms of U.S. and European imperialism. "Laissez-faire" economic liberalism, they thought, should not lead to Mexican dependency on the United States.

To the contrary, the Científicos, as demonstrated in the awarding of a sweeping oil concession to British citizen Weetman Pearson, favored a balance of foreign investments and opposed any special treatment for U.S. capitalists. A strong European economic presence, they argued, would serve as a deterrent against U.S. aggression. Some of the Científicos, including Limantour, had quite personal reasons for seeking a balance of investments. They enjoyed close ties with European financiers, and they engaged in joint ventures with less well-established European capitalists, who proved more willing than their entrenched U.S. counterparts to work with a Mexican business partner.

The Científicos agreed that the plight of Mexico's indigenous population constituted a major obstacle to Mexican development, and they shared a paternalistic attitude toward the lower classes. They also concurred with the social Darwinist notion that natural elites, in which they included themselves, needed to direct the destinies of nations. They disagreed, however, on how to confront the problem: while Bulnes advocated European immigration and blamed the problem on poor nutrition, Sierra favored education.

The ascendancy of Limantour accompanied the transformation of the Científico faction. After Romero Rubio's death in 1895, Limantour became the unofficial spokesperson for the Científicos, a position cemented by his appointment to manage the Mexican treasury. Limantour gained much prestige both within and without Mexico for his handling of public finance. Even though later events would reveal profound flaws in his policies, he gained a reputation as a financial wizard who helped Mexico attain a rock-solid image with foreign investors. In 1898, the death of Matías Romero, Díaz's main foreign investment adviser due to his long tenure as Mexican ambassador to the United States, allowed Limantour to further his political ambitions. By the early 1900s, he had become don Porfirio's most indispensable retainer, the man behind Mexico's economic success.

As Limantour's influence waxed, that of Sierra waned. Sierra found his main goals of constitutional reform and the creation of a nationwide system of primary public education impossible to attain in his role as a cabinet member of lesser importance. Disappointed, he encouraged Díaz to step down after the conclusion of his presidential term, arguing that only the peaceful transfer of power to an elected successor would prove the worth of Mexico's progress during the Porfiriato. Henceforth, Sierra dedicated himself to two tasks: the creation of a national university, and a synthetic study of Mexican history that pointed out the greatness of the country's indigenous and Spanish past. A disciple of his era's faith in social evolution, Sierra spoke optimistically about the future but warned of the dangers of U.S. expansion. The work provided a nationalist argument for the education of women and the indigenous population that the regimes of the Revolution would advance again later.

These changes within the Científico camarilla corresponded to a polarization of Mexican national politics that ultimately contributed to the crisis and demise of the Porfiriato. Before the turn of the century, Díaz had skillfully maintained a balance among several elite interests in his cabinet; the Científicos had represented only one of these interests. After 1903, however, Bernardo Reyes's camarilla and landowners such as Francisco I. Madero left the fold of the Díaz regime. The grievances of the Reyistas went beyond Díaz's preference for the Científicos. Following Limantour's advice, the old dictator refused to reform the Mexican army as Reyes had demanded, a refusal that would cost him dearly at the onset of the Revolution. Moreover, in 1903, Díaz forced the popular Reyes to resign his post as defense secretary and to retreat to Nuevo León, where he remained a force to be reckoned with. The opposition of Madero and Venustiano Carranza stemmed from Díaz's and the Científicos' interference in state politics: in Coahuila, Díaz used heavy-handed tactics to impose the gubernatorial candidate of his choice, and in Chihuahua, the Científico Creel became governor. These alienated northern elites hated the

Científicos, but this hatred, coupled with Reyes' potential as a presidential candidate, only served to reinforce the Díaz-Científico alliance.

Limantour's ongoing rivalry with Reyes served as the background of the second national convention of the ULN in 1903. This sequel to 1893 took up the issues of the creation of political parties and a separate vice presidential position in addition to the customary nomination of Díaz to yet another presidential term. The political changes in Mexico permeated the entire convention: Senator Bulnes was the only Científico of note to attend, and the delegates made acerbic speeches that criticized orthodox liberals as well as the Reyistas. Bulnes reminded those in attendance that only the "anarchy" that had existed during the Restored Republic had justified Díaz's dictatorship; now, he argued, it was time to form both a Liberal and a Conservative party. This call for parties must be understood as a critique of regional strongmen such as Reyes. Dominated by metropolitan elites, a party system would have entrenched scientific politics (and, hence the rule of a widened Científico circle) while reducing the influence of the army and regional *caudillos.*

The Reyes-Limantour rivalry also permeated the discussion of the issue of the office of vice president. Díaz's brief illness in 1901 had revived calls to solve the problem of succession; the president was already 73 years old, and he had not groomed an heir apparent. By law, the foreign secretary succeeded the president, but Ignacio Mariscal was the same age as his boss. With Limantour and Reyes both in the cabinet (Reyes had not yet left his post as defense secretary at the time of the convention), a major conflict loomed in the event of Díaz's death, a conflict that could prove detrimental to the political stability of Mexico. This argument finally swayed Díaz: while he did not consent to the establishment of political parties, he agreed to create the position of vice president. Don Porfirio's choice of Ramón Corral for the 1904 presidential election revealed his attitude toward the Científico camarilla. He wished to appoint a Científico, but was afraid of giving Limantour too much personal power.

The last chapters of the history of the Científicos are intimately tied to the crisis and fall of the Porfiriato. The economic crisis of 1907 demonstrated deficiencies in Limantour's financial management, and it revealed the downside of the export-led economic development advocated by the Científicos. In the following four years, the Porfirian regime began to unravel as a result of a multitude of factors, including Díaz's increasingly inflexible and tyrannical rule, a number of political blunders, the rapidly worsening conditions in much of the Mexican countryside, the effects of the economic crisis, the growing discontent among the northern landed elites, and the rise of economic nationalism. The Científicos contributed to this process through the corrupt dealings of some of their members, their close association with Díaz, their arrogant behavior in public, their support of unpopular candidates in state politics, and their apparent contempt for the popular classes. To add insult to injury, Limantour shifted the burden of the economic crisis to the middle classes by means of a tax increase. In the face of these problems, the Científicos' attempt to pay homage to nationalism by imposing legal limitations on foreign economic activity and by opposing imperialist U.S. designs in the Caribbean could not erase their unfavorable image. By 1910, the Científicos formed part of what was widely regarded as a decrepit gerontocracy. Hence, claiming that most of the Científicos bore a notable physical resemblance to walking mummies, Mexicans invented a new nickname for them: the *cien tísicos,* or the Hundred Tuberculosis Sufferers.

Even though the Científicos steadfastly contended that they had kept only the best interests of the Mexican nation in mind, Madero's revolutionaries identified them with the malaise of their country. As we know today, some of that criticism missed the mark, since there was enough blame to go around to cover Díaz himself, his innumerable retainers (whether Científico or non-Científico), hacendados, governors, *jefes políticos,* avaricious foreign investors, diplomats, bankers, and world economic conditions, to mention just a small number. Nevertheless, the Científicos served as the highly visible tip of the iceberg that represented the problems of the late Porfiriato, and they deservedly took the fall along with Díaz.

The history of the Científicos did not end with Díaz. Madero's proposed reforms contained a number of Científico solutions to Mexico's problems: his constitutionalism recalled Sierra's views, and he shared the group's faith in export-led development. Citing the Maderistas' ties to Científico business partners and banks, historian John Womack has argued that the Revolution initially led to the establishment a Madero-Científico government. By early 1912, however, the Científicos fought the Madero regime tooth and nail. By then, the president had proven incapable of repressing social unrest, and a group of his advisers had concocted a scheme to free his government from its financial dependence on the Científicos. Through their control of *El Imparcial* and a small number of congressional delegates, the Científicos assailed the Madero regime for its failure to restore "order" in Mexico. Through the medium of don Porfirio's nephew, Félix Díaz, the Científicos finally reconciled themselves with Bernardo Reyes and helped him forge the Pact of the Embassy that brought Victoriano Huerta to power. Only Huerta's defeat in August 1914 brought the era of the Científicos to an end.

Some of the ideas of the Científicos survived much longer than the men who conceived of them. For example, the *indigenismo* of the Revolution owed much to the thought of Justo Sierra. Most recently, the faith of the regimes of the post-Revolutionary period (and, in particular, the Carlos Salinas de Gortari administration of 1988 to 1994) in economic and technocratic solutions to Mexico's social and political problems have led some observers to speak of a "neo-Científico" resurgence. While this comparison between the Científicos and the Salinas administration may be overdrawn, it illustrates the larger problems facing intellectuals within the Mexican government: their alienation from the socioeconomic and cultural reality of most Mexicans, and the difficulty of effecting change without being co-opted and corrupted by the system.

Therefore, the story of the Científicos is one of all-too-human failings. As young intellectuals, they sought to transform their country into a politically stable and authoritarian, yet economically progressive country in which liberty of expression and the independence of the judiciary (but not of Congress!) remained respected. In that manner, they desired to make Mexico a "modern" nation in the European image and to eliminate the instability caused by the incessant scheming of ambitious regional and military strongmen. No sooner had Díaz weakened *caudillismo* in Mexico, however, than the Científicos were absorbed into a camarilla system that functioned by the same rules that the group had attacked so bitterly. As a result, the more idealistic and constitutionalist Sierra lost ground to the more corrupt and pragmatic Limantour, and the Científicos became a faction that ended up reaping maximum political and material benefits from the Díaz regime. It is easy for us today to judge the group in teleological fashion, from the vantage point of the coming of the Revolution. It is only when we consider the entire history of the Científicos that both the political complexity and the ultimate tragedy of Porfirian Mexico come into full view.

See also Positivism; Social Darwinism

Select Bibliography

Beals, Carleton, *Porfirio Díaz: Dictator of Mexico*. Philadelphia and London: Lippincott, 1932.

Brenner, Anita, and George R. Leighton, *The Wind that Swept Mexico: The History of the Mexican Revolution, 1910–1942*. 2nd edition, Austin: University of Texas Press, 1971.

Córdova, Arnaldo, *La ideología de la Revolución Mexicana: la formación del nuevo régimen*. Mexico City: Era, 1973; 12th edition, Mexico City: UNAM, 1992.

Cosío Villegas, Daniel, *Historia moderna de México: El porfiriato: Vida política interior: Segunda parte*. Mexico City: Hermes, 1972.

Gómez-Quiñones, Juan, *Porfirio Díaz, los intelectuales y la Revolución*. Mexico City: El Caballito, 1981.

Hale, Charles A., *The Transformation of Liberalism in Late Nineteenth-Century Mexico*. Princeton, New Jersey: Princeton University Press, 1989.

Katz, Friedrich, *The Secret War in Mexico: Europe, the United States, and the Mexican Revolution*. Chicago: University of Chicago Press, 1981.

_____, "The Liberal Republic and the Porfiriato, 1867–1910." In *Mexico Since Independence*, edited by Leslie Bethell. Cambridge and New York: Cambridge University Press, 1991.

Limantour, José Yves, *Apuntes sobre mi vida pública*. Mexico City: Porrúa, 1965.

MacLachlan, Colin M., and William H. Beezley, *El Gran Pueblo: A History of Greater Mexico*. Englewood Cliffs, New Jersey: Prentice Hall, 1994.

Raat, W. Dirk, "Ideas and Society in Don Porfirio's Mexico." *The Americas* 30:1 (July 1973).

_____, *El positivismo durante el porfiriato*. Mexico City: Colegio de México, 1975.

Womack, John, "The Mexican Revolution, 1910–1920." In *Mexico Since Independence*, edited by Leslie Bethell. Cambridge and New York: Cambridge University Press, 1991.

—JÜRGEN BUCHENAU

CLAVIGERO, FRANCISCO JAVIER

1731–87 • Priest and Intellectual

Clavigero is noted as an innovator in the teaching of philosophy in Mexico, a respected historian of ancient Mexico and of Baja California, and a staunch advocate for the accomplishments of criollo (Spanish-descended American) intellectuals. While he lived in Mexico, Clavigero's forum for teaching was the Jesuit *colegios* in Morelia and Guadalajara (Clavigero was a member of the Jesuit order). He is hailed for his role there in introducing modern philosophy to Mexico, a modified Aristotelian philosophical cosmology that was strongly influenced by the eighteenth-century sciences and empirically based critical analysis

In 1767, Carlos III expelled the Jesuits from the Spanish Empire and exiled them to the papal states. Taking up permanent residence in Bologna after the suppression of the order by papal decree in 1773, Clavigero turned to the writing of Mexican history. Clavigero's historical study stemmed not only from love of his homeland but also from his desire to dispel the ignorance about the New World that he found among his Italian hosts. Clavigero especially hoped to refute the insulting theory of American degeneration that was being spread throughout Europe by a group of noted writers, especially the Prussian Corneille de Pauw. These writers argued that the western hemisphere, just emerging from flood waters that had covered it for centuries, was like one enormous swamp and cursed with a malignant climate. Not only were the native inhabitants, such as the Mexica (Aztecs), who were considered just a step above the orangutan, affected adversely by these conditions, but even Europeans who settled in the

New World deteriorated, as did their criollo offspring, as evidenced by their stunted intellectual development.

Clavigero bristled at these unfounded charges, and his indignation resulted in the four-volume *Storia antica del Messico* (Ancient History of Mexico; 1780–81). Pointing out that these defamers of the Americas were nothing but badly misinformed armchair critics of the New World who had never set a foot in that hemisphere, he demolished their arguments by citing unimpeachable witnesses regarding the healthy climate of the Americas and the accomplishments of criollo culture. Clavigero argued forcefully that the scorned civilization of ancient Mexico was not only superior to the civilization of Europe's ancient tribes but was the New World counterpart of classical Greece and Rome. Well received by the public, the *Storia antica* was hailed for its able refutation of adversaries, its enlightened treatment of Mexica history, its defense of criollo culture, its pleasant literary style, and its critical sense, all essential features in the eyes of an eighteenth-century European readership that looked upon history as a species of literature rather than a science. Also praiseworthy was the fact that it was the first complete history of ancient Mexico brought together under one cover.

The first three volumes of the *Storia antica del Messico* comprise the history of the Mexica down to the arrival of Fernando (Hernán) Cortés in 1521, while the fourth volume contains nine dissertations on controversial points that the author preferred to discuss separately. Although heavily quarried from Torquemada's *Monarquía indiana,* the *Storia antica* is a great improvement over Torquemada's turgid baroque history. Translated into English, German, and Spanish, the *Storia antica* played no small part in dissipating Europe's ignorance about the Americas and about criollo intellectual accomplishments, defining European public opinion regarding pre-Hispanic Mexico for many decades until more scientifically written histories on the subject replaced it. It also engendered a spirit of "neo-Aztecism" among Clavigero's compatriots and an increased feeling of regionalism, all of which blended into a sort of Mexican prenationalism. The *Storia antica* is still the object of study today.

Also of consequence was Clavigero's posthumously published *Storia della California* (History of California; 1789), the first complete history of Jesuit activity in Baja California, from the missionaries' entrance in 1697 until their expulsion from the Spanish Empire in 1767. Its purpose was threefold: first, to acquaint the public with the true nature of the peninsula and its primitive inhabitants; second, to record the activities of the Jesuit missionaries who labored there; and third, to refute the false charges of writers such as De Pauw regarding the entire enterprise. As a historical document, it has held up better than the *Storia antica* but it never attained the popularity or prestige of the earlier work. Written in a polished literary style, it is a creditable history, however, that has measured up to the accepted canons of historical literature and is still cited by scholars today.

Mexico's esteem for Clavigero is seen in the ceremonious repatriation of his remains from Bologna in 1970, during the presidency of Gustavo Díaz Ordaz (1964–70), and their entombment in the Rotunda of Illustrious Men in the Panteón Civil de Dolores, Mexico's Westminster Abbey. Hailed as one of the republic's favorite sons, he had returned to his homeland after two centuries in exile to be buried in the soil he loved.

Select Bibliography

Ronan, Charles E., S.J., *Francisco Javier Clavigero, S.J. (1731–1787), Figure of the Mexican Enlightenment: His Life and Works.* Rome: Institutum Historicum, and Chicago: Loyola University Press, 1977.

—CHARLES E. RONAN

CNC

See Confederación Nacional Campesina (CNC)

CNOP

See Confederación Nacional de Organizaciones Populares (CNOP)

COALICIÓN OBRERA CAMPESINA ESTUDIANTIL DEL ISTMO (COCEI)

In Juchitán, Oaxaca, a poor people's movement challenged the local and national authorities of the Mexican government, withstood violent repression and military occupation, and succeeded in winning municipal elections and becoming a permanent leftist force in regional politics. This movement, the Coalition of Workers, Peasants, and Students of the Isthmus (COCEI), has been one of the strongest grassroots movements in Mexico since its formation in the early 1970s, and its successes have demonstrated that radical mobilization can bring about substantive political change in Mexican politics.

The origins of the COCEI's exceptional mobilizational ability lie in the dynamic nature of Zapotec culture. In the nineteenth and early twentieth centuries, to be Zapotec in Juchitán meant to be part of a multiclass pueblo struggling against outside encroachments through nonviolent resistance and armed rebellion, including prominent activity by women. After 1934, Juchiteco general Heliodoro Charis succeeded in garnering Zapotec support for the new national state precisely because it left the isthmus alone, permitting Juchitecos the sort of autonomy for which the rebellions had been fought. During this time, the ruling Partido Revolucionario Institucional (PRI, or Institutional Revolutionary Party) hardly existed in the Isthmus. Zapotec ethnicity, which continued to be a multiclass phenomenon, now coexisted with *cacique* politics and with a national government that claimed Indian identity as part of its new nationalist project. In this context, Zapotec women forged innovative forms of autonomy in Juchitán, and Zapotec practices were maintained and elaborated with relatively little outside intrusion.

By the end of General Charis's rule, national economic development plans had stimulated a process of agricultural change and urbanization, with conflicts over development projects and political office coming to a head in the 1960s and early 1970s. At this time, Juchiteco elites sought to make use of one of the legacies of the past—the unity of the multiclass pueblo against the outside—to maintain cultural and political leadership and to establish new guarantees for private property and clean government. In mobilizing peasants and workers behind these goals, however, elites began a process of politicization that COCEI built upon in its class-based mobilizations.

COCEI itself formed in 1973, during President Luis Echeverría Álvarez's administration's *apertura democrática* (democratic opening). Using direct-action organizing tactics, the movement won widespread popular support for strikes, marches, occupations of government offices, negotiations with government officials, and Zapotec cultural and artistic activities. Women played prominent roles in political mobilization, and through their efforts helped keep Zapotec culture, which undergirded the movement, alive and adaptive;

images of militant women were central to COCEI's public image. At the same time, however, and illustrative of COCEI's complex internal characteristics, women did not hold positions of leadership in COCEI, and public representations of the movement's past were created exclusively by male artists and intellectuals.

Through its militant campaigns, COCEI secured gains in living and working conditions for peasants and workers in Juchitán and surrounding towns. COCEI successfully claimed Zapotec cultural leadership as well. Political authorities and local elites responded with considerable violent repression, including the killing of more than 20 supporters in the 1970s. Despite this violence, COCEI secured an official place in elections by allying with the newly legalized Mexican Communist Party in 1980, during the period of electoral opening fostered by Mexico's electoral reform. COCEI then succeeded in pressuring the regime to recognize its victory in municipal elections, making Juchitán the first and only city in the country with a leftist government.

Through political meetings, public gatherings, street theater, and a COCEI radio station, the COCEI government changed the panorama of municipal life. In response, local PRI politicians and businesspeople formed new groups to fight the radical movement on the local level and pressure state and national authorities to act against it. By 1983, these pressures coincided with regime efforts to limit opposition electoral activity, and COCEI was thrown out of office by the state legislature and the army.

Despite these actions, COCEI maintained its capacity to mobilize. Together with the enduring strength of local political bosses and ongoing factionalism within the local PRI, COCEI's strength placed limits on the government's plans to defuse radicalism through reform of the official party and investment in infrastructure. While the army stood guard on the balconies of Juchitán's city hall, COCEI resumed its organizing and electoral campaigning. Following 1986 municipal elections, COCEI joined a coalition municipal government, headed by a PRIísta, in an arrangement overseen by the new governor of Oaxaca, himself a reformist within the PRI. In 1989, and again in 1992, COCEI was declared the winner in municipal elections. During these administrations, COCEI took the controversial step of signing accords of *concertación social* with the administration of President Carlos Salinas de Gortari, bringing extensive funds as well as official political recognition. Subsequently, the COCEI government of 1989 to 1992 was praised from across the political spectrum for its efficient administration of public works projects, an unprecedented phenomenon in Juchitán.

Today's democracy in Juchitán is complex and conflictual. COCEI faces difficult choices concerning cooperation with the central government, conciliation with local middle-class and business groups, and representation of poor Juchite-cos during a period of regional economic decline. In addition, COCEI is experiencing internal conflict over hier-archical decision-making procedures, as well as over the con-tinuing predominance of the movement's original leaders. Along with these conflictual characteristics of democratic politics, significant political and cultural rights have been secured in Juchitán, and a framework for formal democratic practices and negotiation over economic issues established.

Democratization in Juchitán was facilitated by COCEI's repeated exercise of limited political sovereignty. However, democratization can be said to have occurred in Juchitán not simply because of elections and the transfer of municipal office, but because poor Juchitecos in the 1980s had more voice, and could hold those in power more accountable, in more arenas of their lives, than they could in the 1960s and 1970s. Juchitecos exercised such voice and demanded such accountability in their relatively unproblem-atic assertion of their cultural identity, their capacity to pres-sure agrarian agencies and labor courts for fair treatment, their freedom to bring their own language to official offices, their access to complex networks of information, and their influence in municipal government.

COCEI's successes in Juchitán are virtually without precedent among indigenous and leftist movements and have changed the landscape of Mexican politics. The Mexican government recognizes COCEI's legitimacy and autonomy, respects the results of democratic elections in Juchitán, invests in municipal services, and curbs human rights abuses. Such an outcome indicates that spaces for democracy and autonomy can be carved out within the existing system through militant and threatening opposition, and that such spaces change the system in the process.

—JEFFREY W. RUBIN

COCEI

See Coalición Obrera Campesina Estudiantil del Istmo (COCEI)

COCHINEAL

The name cochineal refers to the insect *Dactylopius coccus* and the red dye derived from it. The female of the species, which produces the dye, clings to the fleshy leaves of the nopal cac-tus *(Opuntia ficus)*, preferably the "castilla" nopal, which has fewer thorns. At harvest time they are whisked off the cactus with a short, thick brush and laid out on mats to dry. They are then ground and boiled to obtain the red dye. The main months of harvest are August, September, and October.

The harvest of cochineal dates from well before the Conquest. Cochineal's name in Nahuatl is *nocheztli,* "blood of the nopal fruit" (from *noch-tli,* "nopal fruit," and *ez-tli,* "blood"). It was used throughout Mesoamerica to dye cloth and was part of the tribute paid to Moteuczoma. Nonethe-less, production peaked after the Spanish Conquest, when Spaniards expanded cochineal cultivation, principally in Tlaxcala and Oaxaca; cochineal production also was brought to Guatemala, Peru, and the Canary Islands, where it contin-ues to this day. According to the *cronista* Bernardino de Sahagún, in the sixteenth century the dye was exported as far as China and Turkey.

During the seventeenth and eighteenth centuries demand for cochineal increased in the European textile industries, par-ticularly in England, and it became the second largest export from New Spain. Prices fluctuated. The best decade was from 1770 to 1780, when the price rose from 15 pesos to more than 30 pesos a pound. After 1782 the price dropped dramatically and never recovered.

Although there were a number of nopal haciendas that produced cochineal, production remained largely in the hands of the indigenous population. Until the end of the six-teenth century Indians sold cochineal to the Spaniards to raise cash for tribute payments to the Spanish Crown. From the beginning of the seventeenth century, royal officials knows as *alcaldes mayores* began cornering the market through the *repartimiento* system. Under this system, *alcaldes* linked to Spanish merchants required indigenous communi-ties to purchase cattle or cash on credit, which in turn could only be repaid in cochineal. Their official posts provided the *alcaldes* with a monopoly, and they forced the Indians to sell cochineal at lower than market price. Although in principle forbidden by law, this practice eventually became commonplace and was finally officially recognized in 1718, when the Bourbon monarchs stopped paying salaries to its officials, and the *alcaldes* were obliged to engage in the cochineal trade in order to live. In 1751 the Crown formally granted the *alcaldes* permission to obtain cochineal through the *repartimiento* system.

Indigenous communities found many ways to resist the *repartimiento* exactions. There were many ways of mixing cochineal with other ingredients such as onion seeds or "false cochineal" that had no color. In the most important center of cochineal production, the diocese of Oaxaca, a registry office was set up in 1756 to monitor the quality of cochineal. Communities also sought to lower *repartimiento* requirements through armed struggle. In 1660 the diocese of Oaxaca was the scene of nearly 20 uprisings by indigenous communities, and in Tehuantepec Indians killed the *alcalde mayor* and his servants. Similar revolts broke out in the central region of Tlaxcala and Michoacán.

José de Galvéz, inspector general for New Spain from 1765 to 1771 and minister of the Indies from 1776 to 1787, penned a series of reforms in the trade and government of New Spain. He banned the *repartimiento* system and replaced the *alcalde mayores* with salaried officials knows as intendants. Nonetheless, in Oaxaca the cochineal *repartimiento* continued in the face of increasing indigenous resistance. By the end of the century production had dropped off and prices had begun to rise. In 1858, however, the discovery of aniline (a chemical dye) in England effectively ended cochineal export. It is still cultivated today in some indigenous communities for domestic or regional use in textiles and in the kitchen.

Select Bibliography

Alzate, Joseph Antonio de, and Jose Antonio de Ramirez, *Gacetas de Literatura de México.* Puebla, Reimpresa en la Oficina del Hospital de San Pedro, 1831.

Cordry, Donald Bush, and Dorothy M. Cordry, *Mexican Indian Costumes.* Austin and London: University of Texas Press, 1978.

Dahlgren de Jordán, Barbro, *La Mixteca, su cultura e historia prehispánicas.* Mexico City: Imprenta Universitaria, 1954.

_____, *Nocheztli, Economía de una región: La grana cochinilla.* Mexico City: Nueva Biblioteca Mexicana de Obras Históricas, 1963.

Gómez de Cervantes, Gonzalo, *La vida económica y social de Nueva España.* Mexico City: Antigua Librería Robredo de José Porrúa e Hijos, 1944.

Hamnett, Brian R., *Politics and Trade in Southern Mexico, 1750–1821.* Cambridge: Cambridge University Press, 1971.

—DANIÈLE DEHOUVE

COCHISE

c. 1812–74 • Apache Leader

During the mid–nineteenth century, Cochise evolved into the most powerful chief of the Chiricahua Apache tribe in recorded times. A war chief of the Chokonen, or central, Chiricahua band, he attained unprecedented authority and influence among the highly fragmented and scattered Chiricahua groups on Mexico's northwestern frontier. From their traditional homelands in the mountain ranges of what is today southeastern Arizona, Cochise's nomadic Chokonens ranged over a large area that extended into modern-day southwest New Mexico, northeast Sonora, and northwest Chihuahua. During a time of unprecedented social disruption and violent subjugation of the Apache tribe, Cochise's defiance of Mexican and U.S. authority, his devotion to Chiricahua autonomy, and his personal bravery and war skills gained him respect among all the Chiricahua. Among non-Indians on either side of the international border, his name became synonymous with violent Apache raiding and warfare.

Little is known of the chief's early years. Possibly the son of a noteworthy Chokonen chief, Cochise was trained as a boy in the art of warfare and raiding. He reached adulthood shortly before Apache rebellion became general across the frontier in the early 1830s. In the ensuing years of cyclical violence, he found countless opportunities to perfect his trademark style of audacious raids against the ranches and towns on the frontier.

His rise to prominence was slow. Throughout the 1830s and 1840s his name appeared on several temporary truces made between the different Chiricahua groups and the Mexicans, principally at the Presidios of Janos and Fronteras. His name usually was associated with one of several senior Chiricahua chiefs, most notably Pisago Cabezón, Yrigollen, Miguel Narbona, and the Chihenne Chiricahua chief Mangas Coloradas. Although it remains unclear whether Cochise was present at the massacres of Chokonens and other Chiricahua by the bounty hunters Jack Johnson in 1837 and James Kirker in 1846, the events instilled in him, as they did in all Chiricahua, a deep sense of outrage and need for revenge. His contempt deepened in 1848 after he was captured near Fronteras and probably tortured before escaping.

The partition of the Chiricahua's ranging area after the Mexican-U.S. War and the entry of the U.S. Army into New Mexico and Arizona impacted irreversibly on Chiricahua culture. For years, American traders had provided a ready market for the Chiricahua's raiding booty, but after 1848 they came in increasing numbers. Evidence suggests Cochise first sought to ally with the newcomers against the Mexicans, but as that proved unfeasible tensions between the Chiricahua and the United States heightened. A string of violent encounters in Mexico, included massacres of Chokonens at Fronteras and Janos in 1858 and an attempt by the Chihuahua government to poison rations at Janos in 1858, fueled Cochise's defiance.

Whatever mutual tolerance had been achieved between Chokonens and Americans was broken in 1861 after an encounter between Cochise's band and a detachment of U.S. soldiers under Lieutenant George Bascom at Apache Pass in southern Arizona led to the deaths of several members of Cochise's family, including his brother Coyuntura. For the next 10 years, Cochise waged war against both the United States and Mexico, leading his band across the international border at will to raid, elude pursuit, trade booty for supplies and whiskey, or gain temporary respites by forcing brief truces on Mexico's poorly defended frontier towns. Cochise's War, as it became known, spread rapidly in the early 1860s as both the United States and Mexico were preoccupied with internal political and social conflict. But after 1865, the U.S. policy of concentrating all Apaches on a handful of reservations gained new vigor, and the triumph of the republican forces in Mexico refocused the frontier states' attentions toward combating the Apache raiders. As a result, Cochise's War became more defensive, and pressure to submit to the reservation program intensified. He acquiesced in 1869, agreeing to join the Chihenne chiefs Loco and Victorio at Cañada Alamosa, New Mexico. When rations proved unreliable and rumors spread that the army planned to move the Chiricahua to a Mescalero Apache reservation, Cochise bolted to the mountains of Sonora and Chihuahua. He conducted several raids against the northern villages until Sonoran forces chased him across the border and into the Dragoon mountains.

In 1871 Cochise agreed to return to the reservation and settled at Cuchillo Negro, near Cañada Alamosa, until rumors of removal caused him to flee with his greatly diminished band of 300 men, women, and children. Late the next year, facing unbearable pressure but still maintaining the deference of nearly all Chiricahua chiefs in the region, Cochise came to an agreement with General Otis Howard, the new U.S. Indian agent, that established a reservation, chosen by Cochise, in the Chiricahua mountains along the Sonora-Arizona border. It sought to permit Cochise, now well into his sixties, to live the remainder of his life without white interference.

The newly created reservation immediately incited protests from both sides of the border. The U.S. Army disdained its lack of jurisdiction over the Chiricahua. More important was the outrage felt in Sonora. Placing the reservation on the international border gave Cochise an open door to raid into Sonora, with which he was still at war. Indeed, many of Cochise's junior chiefs led raids into Sonora while living under the protection of the Chiricahua reservation. Worsening matters, other Chiricahua, including Juh's Nednhis and Chihennes under Victorio and Loco, sought refuge on the reservation. As a result of rising international tensions, the United States reconsidered its policy of settling the Chiricahua on the border. Although Cochise cooperated by ordering all raiding into Sonora to stop, by this time his authority and health were slipping. He died of stomach cancer somewhere in the Chiricahua Mountains in 1874, as the United States prepared to move the Chiricahua to reservations in New Mexico. His death caused a vacuum in Chiricahua leadership that further weakened the tribe's resistance to subjugation.

Select Bibliography

Lockwood, Frank C., *The Apache Indians.* New York: Macmillan, 1938.
Sweeney, Edwin R., *Cochise: Chiricahua Apache Chief.* Norman: University of Oklahoma Press, 1991.

—AARON P. MAHR YÁÑEZ

CODICES

The word "codex," from the Latin, was originally used to describe any ancient manuscript. Nevertheless, in both Mexican historiography and common parlance the word is used to describe pictographic manuscripts that were created by the indigenous Mesoamerican people prior to and after the Conquest.

Ancient Mesoamerican codices took the form of a *tira,* or a strip of material that was painted and subsequently interpreted horizontally along its length. The *tira* could be made of deerskin or a paper made from the vegetable fiber of maguey or a certain kind of *ficus* that was called *amatl* (hence the word *amate* when referring to this variety of paper). The material was given a white coating concocted from certain resins and lime. The *tiras* usually were folded like a screen, but they also could be rolled. Even though the *tira* seems to have been the commonest form of codex, large *lienzos,* or coarse cotton cloths, also were used, mostly for recording cartographic information and military strategy. In the colonial period deerskin rarely was employed, while the use of *amate* predominated. Several manuscripts also were composed of European paper.

Every Mesoamerican codex consisted of two basic components: figures, which were used to create scenes, and a system of signs that detailed the information provided by these scenes. For example, a scene could be composed of two people sitting face to face holding between them a partridge and a bunch of bloodied grass. The signs associated with these images, commonly known as glyphs, inform that one of them is called 4 Jaguar (four dots and the head of a feline) and the other 8 Deer (represented by eight dots and a deer's head). The second person has the pseudonym "Jaguar Claw" (shown by placing a claw close to him). The offering of partridge blood occurred on the day 4 Serpent, according to other glyphs located by both individuals. The scenarios that appear immediately afterward inform the reader that the sacrifice took place before both allies started a military campaign.

Writing in the strict sense of the word is not found in Mesoamerican codices, except for those produced by the Maya. It nevertheless has been possible to detect an incipient phoneticism in Nahua codices. For example, the name Mazatlan derives from two roots, *mazatl* (deer) and *tlan* (place). The toponymic glyph for this place is represented by the head of a deer and some teeth. The reason for this is clear since the Nahuatl word for teeth is *tlantli,* and the aim of the exercise was to evoke the sound *"tlan."* This incipient form of phonetic writing had a very limited role, since the majority of the information is derived from the pictographic scenes and the ideographic glyphs.

Evidence in Mesoamerica for the use of codices dates to A.D. 300; two semipetrified examples from the early Classic period (A.D. 200–900) have been found in the Maya area. But it is possible that codices were used far earlier, since the graphic registration of calendric inscriptions and some other signs appear at Monte Albán around 500 B.C. At the same site identical scenes have been found to those appearing in codices, carved in stone and dating from the beginning of the Christian era.

The few surviving pre-Hispanic manuscripts, the numerous examples that were created in the colonial period, and the information written in sixteenth-century sources give an idea of the enormous functional variety of the codices, including the registering of the annual cycle of religious festivals and the divinatory calendar of 260 days (fundamental in the baptism of children, healing, and performing magic), the description of astronomical cycles and their cosmological consequences, the setting down of the characteristics and various stages of specific rituals such as that of matrimony,

the genealogical registration of noble lineage, the historical chronology of the main events of a reign, the geographical description of a territory, the registration of property, the defining of boundaries, the creation of tribute census, the cataloging of belongings and jewels, and the recording of damages for a legal plea.

The pre-Hispanic codices that have been preserved to date come mainly from three areas of Mesoamerica, notably the Maya, the Mixteca, and the Puebla-Tlaxcala zone. The Maya codices differ from the rest in that they utilize a writing with a kind of alphabet that registers independent sounds and syllables. This writing seems to have a more relevant role than the limited pictographic scenes that appear. For this reason these codices are studied by Maya epigraphists. Even so, it must be emphasized that the few scenes depicted in Maya codices have an important relationship with those appearing in other codices; the stereotypical style of representation and form and the postures of the human figures are all similar. The pre-Hispanic Maya examples that have survived are the *Tro-Cortesianus,* the *Dresden,* and the *Pérez* or *Paris Codices.*

Those from the other zones all were painted within the same stylistic and iconographic tradition known as the Mixteca-Puebla. This name derives from their origin, evidence of which is to be found mostly to the south of the modern state of Puebla and the Mixteca area, particularly the mountainous zone. Mural painting, ceramics, and codices belonging to this tradition also have been found in peripheral areas to this central region.

An important group of manuscripts, such as the *Colombino* and *Becker 1 Codices,* were elaborated by Mixtec-speaking peoples from the coastal area of the Mixteca region, while the *Nuttall, Vindobonensis,* and *Bodley Codices* come from the mountainous area of the Mixteca. The *Selden Codex,* an example from the early colonial period, can be added to this group. The content of these Mixtec codices (the *Vindobonensis* to a lesser extent) is fundamentally historical and genealogical. The attitude to these two themes is typically Mesoamerican, with emphasis on place and mythic narrative. The majority of the Mixtec codices refer to the origin of noble Mixtec lineages, their emergence from the tree of Apoala, and the foundation of the dynasties of Tilantongo and Teozacoalco. It also is common to find references to some rulers that are partially historical and partially mythical (in the style of Quetzalcoatl of Tula). The most outstanding examples are the great conqueror 8 Deer, Jaguar Claw, and 9 Wind. Even though sites and specific individuals corresponding with local history are mentioned in each codex, all the Mixtec codices allude to origins, symbols, and mythic individuals that they hold in common.

Other groups of ancient pictographs come from the modern states of Puebla and Tlaxcala. These included the group consisting of the *Borgia, Cospi,* and *Vatican Codices.* It is a common error to believe that the *Laud* and *Fejérváry-Mayer* come from the same area. This mistake is owing to the fact that the last two codices have a calendrical content similar to those of the first three and have been grouped together by virtue of their content under the category of the Borgia Group, which is not organized on a regional basis. The mural paintings and ceramics from Tehuacán, Cholula, Huejotzingo, and Tlaxcala reveal close iconographic and stylistic similarities with the *Borgia, Cospi,* and *Vatican Codices,* leading the majority of researchers to think that the three codices come from the area demarcated by these three sites. The *Laud* and *Fejérváry-Mayer* codices reveal certain iconographic peculiarities that indicate a possible origin in the areas around the Gulf of Mexico, either in the Mixtequilla zone or Tabasco. The similarity between these two manuscripts is so close that they probably originate from the same place at the same time.

As previously mentioned, the three codices from the Puebla-Tlaxcala region and the two of unknown origin (although most probably with a source in the Gulf of Mexico area), have been grouped according to thematic purposes under the name of the Borgia Group. The 260-day calendar (in Nahuatl, *tonalpohualli*) plays an important role in all five of the codices. All seem to have a divinatory function, but some seem to emphasize particular themes. The *Borgia* has abundant information on astrology (the Venus cycle in particular), the *Laud* gives an important role to goddesses such as Tlazolteotl-Ixcuina, and the *Fejérváry-Mayer* emphasizes the bearer gods and those of the merchants.

All these codices considered are generally pre-Hispanic, except for the *Selden,* which has great affinity with other historical Mixtec examples, although it is known to have been painted after the Conquest. It is worth pointing out that the pre-Columbian origin of several examples has been questioned; the *Cospi* is a case in point. Also, some of the manuscripts that have been considered to be of colonial origin, such as the *Tonalamatl de Aubin,* could be pre-Hispanic.

During and after the Conquest, the Spanish destroyed the majority of the Mesoamerican codices. Considerable destruction occurred during the armed conflict that ruined the archives of the principal cities. Moreover, when the friars arrived they saw a link between idolatry and the books and therefore decided to burn them. Many were destroyed in the first attempts at evangelization, in Tlaxcala in particular. Others perished in the punishments that were applied to some indigenous peoples and communities that continued to worship their ancient gods after their supposed conversion. The most celebrated burning of codices took place in Yucatán, under the auspices of the Franciscan Diego de Landa.

The Spaniards also saw the codex tradition as a useful resource, however, and allowed them to be produced, at least when their use was not strictly religious. From the days of the Conquest the Spaniards had seen that the Indians communicated "by figures," and they themselves had taken advantage of the paintings to inform themselves on some aspects of Mexica (Aztec) military strategy and the geography of the Gulf of Mexico.

Once the Conquest was over, the Indians continued to conceal and paint their manuscripts. Those of religious content were kept hidden, as the friars discovered during the course of some lawsuits. Others that recorded genealogies,

territories, histories, and possessions not only were evident but had to be shown to the Spaniards during the litigation process. The use of pictographic manuscripts for juridical ends was extended widely when the Second Audiencia (1531–35) gave an opportunity for the Indians to present complaints and demands. The *Codex of Huejotzingo* was one of the first manuscripts to be admitted as legal evidence. From this time onward the codices of the Indians were a common sight in the tribunals of New Spain.

During the sixteenth century the style of the Mesoamerican codices changed significantly. The common style during the pre-Hispanic epoch, based on the Mixteca-Puebla tradition, was abandoned in the colonial period. Three factors were fundamental for this change in pictographic content during the sixteenth century. First, the discipline and teaching systems of the pre-Hispanic period, which guaranteed unity, had been lost. Second, Indian artists began to receive systematic instruction in the craft schools set up by the monastic friars, and in particular the School of San José de los Naturales founded by Pedro de Gante in Mexico City. Finally, European models had wide circulation through religious cards and engravings that illustrated bibles, confessionals, catechisms, and other books that were consulted by numerous Indians.

For example, the codex known as the *Matrícula de tributos,* which must have been ordered by the authorities of the Second Audiencia or Viceroy Antonio de Mendoza (1535–50), informed the Spanish authorities concerning the tributes paid by different provinces to Moteuczoma II. *The Codex Mendoza* was painted on the orders of Viceroy Mendoza to inform the king of Spain about the economy and traditions of the new territory. Codices such as the *Borbonicus,* the *Tudela,* and the *Magliabechi* seem to have been painted by the Indians at the request of the friars in the context of the ethnographic research undertaken by the latter to understand ancient religious customs. The *Codex Telleriano Remensis* contains calendrical and ritual information that must have been solicited by the friars, but also included some narratives that extend from the Mexica foundation myth to the 1640s. The annals of this codex and those of the so-called *Mexican Codex* seem to have been drawn up in monasteries or by painters with close links to the cloth.

The work of Bernardino de Sahagún, Diego Durán, and the indigenous informants of both, deserves separate mention. Both friars used indigenous paintings for their research prior to writing their treatises. Both utilized codices or fragments thereof, and Sahagún also employed paintings that the Indians made professedly to explain the different themes. Finally, both Sahagún and Durán decided that the final version of their work should carry illustrations; these were provided by indigenous painters. Despite their being distributed throughout the text in the manner of European vignettes, they still contain a good many features that echo the ancient codices.

Among the paintings created for the use of the indigenous people themselves, the most plentiful are those used for legal ends, in the majority loose pages and small paintings, although on occasion they are of substantial size and surprising quality. The *Codex Kingsborough,* painted to denounce abuses by the Spaniards, is one of the masterworks of colonial pictography. Other paintings created for indigenous patrons include catalogs of goods (such as that listing the jewels of Martín Océlotl), maps, histories, and genealogies. The *Tlotzin* (containing genealogical information) and *Quinatzin* (containing historical accounts) *Codices,* and the *Codex Xolotl* (a large map of Mexico with plentiful historical information), are of particular importance. These three were painted during the colonial period for the descendants of the royal house of Texcoco.

During the mid–seventeenth century, when the art of creating codices was deteriorating and on the verge of extinction, a new version of manuscripts arose that was both vigorous and uniform in style. A small group of Indian artists visited the population on the periphery of Mexico City (particularly in what is now the Mexico State), selling their services as manuscript painters. The indigenous communities of the region thus obtained painted books, with some glosses in Nahuatl, in which they asserted their land rights. This group of manuscripts, painted in the last half of the seventeenth century and the beginning of the eighteenth, is called the Techialoyan Group, since the first example to be studied was the *Codex San Antonio Techialoyan.* The phenomenon of the Techialoyan codices is tightly linked to that of the so-called primordial titles, Nahuatl-language municipal histories that sought to give a legal and historical basis to communal landholdings threatened by the growth of great landed estates. This was the last great episode in the history of Mexican codices. In some Mexican villages, and indeed in some barrios of Mexico City, pictographic codices, created during the colonial period, are preserved to this day.

See also Indigenous Philologies; Mesoamerica: Writing

Select Bibliography

Berdan, Frances F., and Patricia Rieff Anawalt, *The Codex Mendoza.* 4 vols., Berkeley: University of California Press, 1992.

Boone, Elizabeth H., *The Codex Magliabechiano and the Lost Prototype of the Magliabechiano Group.* 2 vols., Berkeley: University of California Press, 1983.

Caso, Alfonso, "El mapa de Teozacoalco." *Cuadernos americanos* 8:5 (1949).

_____, *Interpretación del Códice Bodley.* Mexico City: Sociedad Mexicana de Antropología, 1960.

_____, *Interpretación del Códice Selden.* Mexico City: Sociedad Mexicana de Antropología, 1964.

_____, *Reyes y reinos de la Mixteca.* Mexico City: Fondo de Cultura Económica, 1979.

Códice Borbónico. Mexico City: Fondo de Cultura Económica, 1992.

Códice Florentino. 3 vols., Mexico City: Secretaría de Gobernación, Archivo General de la Nación, 1979.

Nicholson, H. B., and Eloise Quiñones Keber, editors, *Mixteca-Puebla: Discoveries and Research in Mesoamerican Art and Archaeology.* Culver City, California: Labyrinthos, 1994.

Robertson, Donald, *Mexican Manuscript Painting of the Early Colonial Period.* New Haven, Connecticut: Yale University Press, 1959.

_____, "The Mixtec Religious Manuscripts." In *Ancient Oaxaca,* edited by John Paddock. Stanford, California: Stanford University Press, 1966.

Wauchope, Robert, Howard Cline, Charles Gibson, and H. B. Nicholson, editors, *Handbook of Middle American Indians,* vol. 14, *Guide to Ethnohistorical Sources.* Austin: University of Texas Press, 1975.

—PABLO ESCALANTE

COFFEE

Coffee is Mexico's most important agricultural export. Owing to the superior quality of its *café de altura* (high-grown coffee, mostly cultivated above 1,000 meters/3,300 feet) of the arabica variety, the nation has become Latin America's third and the world's fifth largest exporter, after Brazil, Colombia, Indonesia, and the Ivory Coast. In 1993–94, Mexico produced 4.2 million bags (of 60 kilograms/132 pounds each) of green beans and projected a harvest of 4.3 million bags for 1994–95. In 1994, Mexico placed second to Brazil as a supplier to the United States, the world's largest market, selling almost 2.6 million bags.

Coffee prospers in tropical mountainous zones that enjoy warm climates and abundant precipitation. Eight states—Veracruz, Chiapas, Oaxaca, Puebla, San Luis Potosí, Guerrero, Nayarit, and Hidalgo—provide over 90 percent of production. Of these, the first three states produce three-fourths of all Mexican coffee. Over 750,000 hectares (1,853,000 acres) of land are cultivated and approximately 2 million Mexicans are involved in coffee production.

The origins of coffee cultivation in Mexico are unclear. Some believe that the first beans were brought from Cuba in the eighteenth century and cultivated in Córdoba, Veracruz, and Uruapan, Michoacán. Another version attributes the first commercial production to Spanish-owned haciendas in the vicinity of Cuernavaca. Whatever the case, by 1802 coffee emerged as a new agricultural export for New Spain, when 272 *quintales* (46 kilograms/100 pounds each) left the port of Veracruz. Nevertheless, the struggle for Independence devastated the crop: in 1826, Mexico exported only 20 *quintales* of coffee.

As the nineteenth century progressed and the industrial revolution spread, demand for coffee spiraled in Europe and the United States. In response to this burgeoning demand and parallel to trends in other Latin American nations, cultivation in Mexico expanded, first in Veracruz, Oaxaca, Chiapas, Tabasco, and Michoacán, and later in Puebla, Hidalgo, Guerrero, and other states.

Coffee emerged as a major cash crop for Mexico during the regime of General Porfirio Díaz (1876–80; 1884–1911), whose economic policies encouraged commercial agriculture. While foreign interests exploited Mexico's mineral wealth during this period, coffee production, like henequen, remained largely in Mexican hands, with the exception of German interests in the coastal areas of Chiapas and Oaxaca. Díaz himself took an active interest in the development of coffee in his native state of Oaxaca. Always well-stocked with Oaxaca's finest coffee, he proudly served it at his home on Cadena Street. in Mexico City. He also owned El Faro, one of Oaxaca's most modern coffee *fincas* (medium to large estates). However, distribution and commercialization on the international market fell increasingly into foreign hands.

The expansion of coffee cultivation transformed patterns of labor and land tenure in various regions of Porfirian Mexico. On one hand, since coffee often opened sparsely populated regions, the scarcity of labor became a serious problem for producers. Some workers were tied permanently to estates through debt peonage, but labor arrangements varied widely. Sharecropping, tenant farming, and wage labor also were common. At harvest time, coffee producers frequently had to import workers to their estates, particularly from the densely populated central states. As Mexican peasants and day laborers learned the particulars of coffee farming, they began to cultivate trees on their own parcels to earn some cash, and the number of small producers increased.

On the other hand, the expansion of coffee intensified the pressure exerted by entrepreneurs and speculators to privatize communal lands held by indigenous villages and to buy out small landowners in the areas suited for cultivation. The dispossession of peasants throughout Mexico provided the land and also the necessary labor, as peasants were forced to work for a wage to survive.

Of all the cash crops that flourished in nineteenth-century Latin America, coffee promoted the most diversity with respect to landholding. It inserted the most isolated regions and small indigenous producers into the international division of labor. Mexico exhibited all the diversity of types of production, from large *fincas* with over 100,000 trees in Chiapas and Veracruz to medium-sized holdings, to small indigenous landowners and communal villages. Nevertheless, coffee subordinated both large and small producers to the vicissitudes of prices on the international market.

Mexican production jumped from 4.6 million kilograms (10.1 million pounds) in 1874 to a high of 50 million kilograms (110.2 million pounds) in 1907. However, with coffee production increasing in Mexico, Brazil, Colombia, Costa Rica, El Salvador, and Guatemala, high prices could not be maintained. Because it takes four or five years for a tree to produce acceptable beans, the expanding supply triggered a crisis in the 1890s. While the price of coffee on the United States market fluctuated between 24 and 17 cents per pound between 1860 and 1895, in the following years prices plummeted to reach 7 cents per pound in 1900. Increasing competition had tempered the boom, and Mexican production dropped to 35.7 million kilograms (78.7 million pounds) by 1910.

Coffee production, during the Porfiriato as well as today, only can be understood by taking into account the gendered division of labor and the family as the unit of economic analysis. Men usually prepare the land for planting, care for the seedlings, and prune the trees as they grow. Women and children as young as 6 years old have been favored for weeding and harvesting—they are believed to possess greater patience in picking only the ripe berries. For the most part, men also have been responsible for cultivating the subsistence crops: beans grown in between the rows of coffee trees, bananas to shade them, and corn and pasture on neighboring parcels. Women also have worked in the coffee processing plants. For example, by 1907, approximately 500 women and 150 men worked in the four processors located in Córdoba, Veracruz. Once again, owners favored female laborers to sort superior and inferior quality beans.

Although the Revolution of 1910 had a negative impact on coffee production, by 1918 production recuperated, and in the late 1920s and early 1930s it hovered around 40 million kilograms (88 million pounds). Between 1921 and 1929, cultivated land increased from 51,000 to 90,515 hectares (126,000 to 223,660 acres). However, the Great Depression represented a setback as international prices fell. In the 1930s, Germany had been second only to the United States as an importer of Mexican coffee, given German investments in this sector. However, during World War II, the government nationalized German-owned estates and processors.

In the 1930s, large producers formed regional associations in Chiapas, Veracruz, and Oaxaca to defend their interests. In September 1949, private coffee producers from all over Mexico banded together to constitute the National Agricultural Union of Coffee Producers (UNAC), which included producers, processors, exporters, and regional associations, the elite of the coffee industry. In line with its interventionist economic policies, the post-Revolutionary Mexican state also took a more active role as the international market revived after the Great Depression. President Miguel Alemán Valdés established the National Coffee Commission on October 17, 1949. Encouraging the use of modern technology, this commission sought to improve cultivation by raising productivity and cutting costs. Under the influence of both of these organizations and growing demand, coffee exports increased 65 percent between 1948 and 1954, hitting 1.8 million bags by 1958.

As its purview expanded and Mexico took part in the international defense of coffee prices, the commission was transformed into the Mexican Coffee Institute (IMC) on December 30, 1958. Created to promote the development of coffee cultivation, processing, and marketing, the IMC greatly expanded the activities of the former organism. For example, it established stations in Garnica, Veracruz, and near Tapachula, Chiapas, to experiment and provide free technical training to producers. It also became involved in processing, storage, and marketing coffee, nationally and internationally.

The IMC also attempted to improve the life of small producers. To this end, promoters were sent out to organize Economic Units of Production and Marketing (UEPCs) in order to facilitate the small producers' dealings, especially to obtain credit, with the IMC. In turn, members of these units had to sell their harvest to the IMC in order to repay loans. This arrangement permitted the IMC to exercise a growing influence over the price of coffee in Mexico. Although many of the reforms of the IMC were initially advantageous, too many UEPCs fell under the domination of local caciques and corruption spread. Nevertheless, the institute successfully oversaw the recuperation of coffee as a major export during the 1970s; production reached 4 million bags by 1976, and cultivated land increased by 229 percent.

Nevertheless, as scholars Margarita Nolasco Armas and Anna María Salazar Peralta have demonstrated, the production of coffee in Mexico today is characterized by a situation of extreme polarization. Over 84 percent of the producers have 1 to 5 hectares (2.5 to 12.3 acres), while 70 percent have 2 hectares (4.9 acres) or less; this sector produces only 30 percent of the national output. Most of these producers are poor indigenous families in isolated mountain regions, who also produce maize and beans for subsistence, with almost no means of transportation and little access to credit. Over 60 percent of these producers live in extreme poverty and are forced to seek supplementary income elsewhere, often working for a wage on neighboring *fincas*. Another 14 percent of coffee farmers, with fincas of 6 to 20 hectares (14.8 to 49.4 acres), produce almost as much coffee as the first group.

In contrast, 2 percent of the producers hold 33 percent of the most productive land, frequently combining coffee with cattle ranching. These major agribusiness producers, in Pluma Hidalgo, Oaxaca, northern Chiapas, and the Córdoba-Jalapa region of Veracruz, furnish 40 percent of Mexican coffee. In all three states, these producers represent a significant economic and political force. They own their own processors, means of transportation, and have access to credit and the latest technology. Even so, overall, Mexico's productivity still lags behind that of Brazil, Costa Rica, and El Salvador. In addition, despite their weight in the national economy, internationally their influence in the commodity markets of New York and London is insignificant. With respect to commercialization, while national companies handle over half of Mexico's exports, they are intimately tied to the most important multinationals: General Foods and Nestlé.

Unfortunately, in the 1980s and 1990s, a number of factors united to generate further problems in this sector of the economy. The collapse of the quota system of the International Coffee Organization in 1989 coincided with the 1980s neoliberal restructuring of the Mexican economy and climactic problems that reduced the 1987–88 harvest. In consonance with his anti-interventionist economic policies and privatization of industries, President Carlos Salinas de Gortari began to dismantle the IMC. Thus, this transition to a free market economy aimed to encourage individual "self-management" by producers.

However, even before the enactment of economic stabilization policies, producers had begun to form independent regional organizations to process, store, and market coffee outside of the bureaucracy of the IMC and control of local caciques. Thus, President Salinas's decision to reduce the functions of the IMC was well-received in many quarters. The IMC began to privatize its storage and processing centers, but no new coherent regulatory policy materialized. Distinct branches of the government, such as the Rural Credit Bank and the Ministry of Agriculture and Water Resources, began to pursue varied and sometimes competitive policies.

Thus, according to scholars Luis Hernández Navarro and Fernando Célis Calleja, the Mexican government's attempt to assemble a new system resulted in a host of problems, particularly for the 259,000 small producers (with less than 5 hectares/12.4 acres). The scarcity of credit, high interest rates, and rising prices for fertilizer and other necessities, coincided with a 60 percent drop in prices, a consequence of the collapse of the international quota system. As a result, some producers were forced to the abandon their *fincas*.

In response, the Salinas administration's antipoverty National Solidarity Program (PRONASOL) targeted small coffee producers, in the spirit of stimulating individual initiatives, grassroots organizations, and more "co-responsibility" between authorities and communities. Working with the National Indigenous Institute (INI), PRONASOL established assistance programs for coffee producers in 12 states, including the organization of 3,000 Solidarity Committees. In effect, PRONASOL replaced the credit functions of the IMC for small producers; funds now were channeled through these committees to individuals (not UEPCs) and had to be reimbursed in cash (but with no interest payments), not in coffee.

Although this cash connection aimed to encourage individual initiative and free the market, indebtedness was enormous and credit funds were sorely insufficient in the mid-1990s to support small producers' subsistence and improvement. The new Fideicomiso para el Café (FIDE-CAFE, or Coffee Trust Fund) failed to fill the gap left by the withdrawal of the IMC. In addition to the need for ample credit, other problems confronting producers in the 1990s were low productivity and the lack of technical assistance. Losses most frequently were transferred onto the producer by exporters and intermediaries in order to maintain their profit margins. To manifest their discontent, coffee producers throughout the nation mobilized and organized demonstrations and sit-ins in 1992.

Producers united to form independent grassroots organizations to defend their interests. For example, they created the Oaxaca State Coffee Producers' Network (CEPCO) despite government opposition. According to scholar Jonathan Fox, "by 1992, CEPCO represented about one-third of small coffee producers in Oaxaca, and both the state government and the CNC [National Peasant Confederation] have had to recognize their capacity for 'interlocution' in other arenas, including the official Oaxaca State Coffee Council and a joint coffee-processing venture between the CNC and CEPCO." Nevertheless, considering the trend of declining coffee prices worldwide (with the exception of a short-lived rise in mid-1994), neither independent grassroots organizations nor Solidarity Committees found a solution to the fundamental problems of Mexican coffee producers.

Thus, in the context of today's globalization, coffee is the product that links impoverished indigenous populations of Mexico to the world of trade and finance. Some commentators have speculated that the North American Free Trade Agreement (NAFTA), inaugurated on January 1, 1994, will have positive repercussions for coffee. However, since neither Canada nor the United States (with the exception of Hawaii) produce coffee, there were no coffee tariffs to be reduced. In addition, consumption in the U.S. has continually declined, from 35.7 gallons in 1970 to 23.4 gallons per capita in 1994, while Mexican production costs have risen, making its coffee less competitive. Increasing investment by multinational firms may result in the elimination of local intermediaries, polarizing conditions further. NAFTA also may encourage another possible danger: triangulation, the rerouting of Guatemalan, Brazilian, or Colombian coffee through Mexico to Canada and the United States. It remains to be seen if Mexican coffee will receive special treatment under NAFTA.

Select Bibliography

El Café en la perspectiva del Tratado Libre de Comercio. Chapingo: Universidad Autónoma de Chapingo, 1991.

Early, Daniel K., *Café, Dependencia y Efectos: Comunidades Nahuas de Zongolica, Ver., en el Mercado de Nueva York.* Mexico City: Instituto Nacional Indigenista, 1982.

Fowler-Salamini, Heather, "Gender, Work, and Coffee in Córdoba, Veracruz, 1850–1910." In *Women of the Mexican Countryside, 1850–1990: Creating Spaces, Shaping Transitions,* edited by Heather Fowler-Salamini and Mary Kay Vaughan. Tucson: University of Arizona Press, 1994.

Fox, Jonathan, "Targeting the Poorest: The Role of the National Indigenous Institute in Mexico's Solidarity Program." In *Transforming State-Society Relations in Mexico: The National Solidarity Strategy,* edited by Wayne A. Cornelius, Ann L. Craig, and Jonathan Fox. La Jolla: Center for U.S.-Mexican Studies, University of California at San Diego, 1994.

Hernández Díaz, Jorge, *El café amargo: Los procesos de diferenciación y cambio social entre los chatinos.* Oaxaca: Instituto de Investigaciones Sociológicas, UABJO, 1987.

Hernández Navarro, Luis, and Fernando Célis Callejas, "Solidarity and the New Campesino Movements: The Case of Coffee Production." In *Transforming State-Society Relations in Mexico: The National Solidarity Strategy,* edited by Wayne A. Cornelius, Ann L. Craig, and Jonathan Fox. La Jolla: Center for U.S.-Mexican Studies, University of California at San Diego, 1994.

Nolasco Armas, Margarita, *Café y sociedad en México.* Mexico City: Centro de Ecodesarrollo, 1985.

Romero, Matías, *El estado de Oaxaca.* Barcelona: Tipo-litografía de España, 1886.

Roseberry, William, Lowell Gudmundson, and Mario Samper Kutschbach, editors, *Coffee, Society, and Power in Latin America.* Baltimore, Maryland: Johns Hopkins University Press, 1995.

Salazar Peralta, Ana María, *La producción cafetalera en México, 1977–1988.* Mexico City: Universidad Nacional Autónoma de México, 1992.

—FRANCIE R. CHASSEN-LÓPEZ

COFRADÍAS

A *cofradía* (confraternity, brotherhood) is one of various types of associations of Roman Catholic faithful, composed usually of lay women and men, who "strive by common effort to promote a more perfect life or to foster public worship or Christian doctrine or to exercise other apostolic works, namely to engage in efforts of evangelization, to exercise works of piety or charity, and to animate the temporal order with the Christian spirit" (Code of Canon Law 298, 1983). Although this definition taken directly from Canon Law is a modern one it nonetheless encompasses the multiple and changing functions and goals *cofradías* have undertaken since the colonial period. The history of the *cofradía* varies widely from region to region, and its nature has shifted significantly since its colonial foundations. Much of the complexity lies in the fact that *cofradías* formed part of the fabric of nearly every church and convent, in rural and urban settings, among rich and poor, Spanish and Indian, directed harmoniously by clergy or antagonistic to church authority. Confraternities have been resilient, surviving attempts by church and state to control, define, and even abolish them. The *cofradía* (and the nearly synonymous *mayordomia* and *hermandad*) continues to exist, rooted in the spiritual and social identity of many Mexican communities.

The structure and organization of the *cofradía* can be traced to European models. Brotherhoods were prevalent in western Europe at the time of the Mexican Conquest. These associations sponsored festivals, but, of equal or perhaps greater importance, they served as mutual aid and charitable societies. Although a small number were established in Mexico in the sixteenth century, the greatest period of expansion began after the first decade of the seventeenth century, with an ever-increasing number established as the century continued. Some authors argue that the *cofradía* is a continuation of pre-Hispanic patterns of religious expression and civic organization. Issues of popular religious practice and syncretism aside, the structure and function of the *cofradía* is more likely linked directly to European precedents.

The one function commonly pointed to as the principal motivation behind any *cofradía* is its sponsorship of a yearly feast in honor of its patron—either a saint, the Virgin Mary, or some other devotion. While this does indeed remain the prime function of the *cofradía* today, its colonial counterpart was in the main a more complex institution.

In addition to the payment made to the priest for masses and payments made for the upkeep of the church building and its decoration, most *cofradías* of the colonial period were founded to provide mutual aid to members in the event of sickness, old age, or destitution. Upon the death of a member, all necessary arrangements were provided by the confraternity. Some *cofradías* founded and staffed hospitals, especially those affiliated with Franciscan houses, and they frequently created endowments to provide dowries for the daughters of members. Other confraternities took charge of catechetical instruction, or brought meals to the imprisoned and the infirm, and some even were dedicated to accompanying condemned prisoners to the gallows. A confraternity in the colonial period, then, supported cult worship through feasts and stipends to the clergy and perhaps through the maintenance of a separate altar in the church, it served as a mutual aid society for its own members in times of need, and it looked outside of its own membership to provide some type of charitable service.

Confraternities were divided along a number of lines, among them race, ethnicity, gender, and wealth. A local cleric, secular or religious, oversaw the penning of statutes and, at least in theory, submitted them to higher church authorities for approval. The majority of statutes were taken from a standard model, and varied only in details such as the devotional focus, the amount of membership dues, and the specific charity to be supported. *Cofradías* were headed by a *mayordomo,* elected each year, and typically a council of

diputados, or councilors, also elected on a yearly basis. Membership might be exclusively reserved for Spanish and those who claimed pure Spanish lineage, or exclusively for the Indian populace. Other *cofradías* were reserved for blacks, mulattos, or for mestizos. Nearly all confraternities allowed membership of both sexes, although men almost always retained positions as officers. The few *cofradías* reserved for women were those affiliated with convents of nuns. Members were required to pay the yearly dues, take their allotted turn in visiting sick members, and participate in some way in the liturgical practices of the group, be it a weekly mass, a processional float during Holy Week, or preparation for the yearly feast.

Certain religious orders retained for themselves exclusive rights over particular devotions, such as the Cofradía del Cordon of the Franciscans or the Cofradía del Rosario of the Dominicans. In these cases a confraternity might assume the title *archicofradía,* or one which had a network of affiliates. Perhaps the most common of these was the Archicofradía of the Blessed Sacrament, a devotion that every parish church was encouraged to foster and that provided the secular clergy with a consistent source of income.

Economically, the *cofradía* during the colonial period held an important position in the community. *Cofradías* very likely owned flocks of sheep, cattle, or goats that they administered directly through hired employees or that they lent out. They purchased lands that were leased for pasturage or agriculture, and held other rental properties such as houses. Such a productive use of corporate moneys provided the *cofradía* with sufficient income to support the cult as well as its charitable projects and church construction and decoration, which became a vital aspect of confraternity identity in the seventeenth and first half of the eighteenth centuries. Lavish spending on festivals, altar vessels, adornments, statues, reliquaries, and the like are recorded in account ledgers throughout this period, during which *cofradías* nonetheless remained solvent.

At times the *cofradía* has been confused with the trade guild, or *gremio,* of the colonial period. This is because each *gremio* had its own brotherhood for the support of the patron of its particular type of artistry or labor, such as Saint Martin for tailors, Saint Ann for sewers, and Saint Crispin for shoemakers.

Beginning in the mid–eighteenth century, and allowing for regional differences, the history of the *cofradía* entered into decline. Shifts in political, economic, and ecclesiastical attitudes conspired against the *cofradía.* The Spanish hierarchy favored simpler liturgical rites in an effort to reduce what they perceived to be anachronistic devotions bordering on superstition. A particular target of the hierarchy was the Indian population, whose religious practices were held with suspicion. Reformist, modernizing bishops of the Bourbon church put forth as the ideal an intellectual religion in which the faithful would understand the truths of the faith and practice the liturgy with decorum, eliminating the excesses of the festivals. In *cofradía* spending these bishops saw a tendency toward waste. As agents of the Bourbon state bent on greater imperial efficiency, they supported drives to control confraternity property and income, with an emphasis on dividing communal Indian lands. Several times in the latter half of the eighteenth century officials of both church and state made general inquiries into *cofradía* affairs, inquiries that invariably resulted in allegations that frivolity was the norm, and that recommended ever stricter control. Discouragement among *cofradía* members and a decline in confraternity activity resulted.

Secularization of the properties of religious orders made the decline all the more rapid. The Bourbon church viewed religious orders with a mistrust on par with popular superstition. From the mid–eighteenth century, religious orders were deprived of their properties in favor of the secular clergy. The majority of *cofradías,* long associated with the religious orders, floundered in their forced transfer to secular parishes. Often the transfer resulted in a loss of *cofradía* devotional items and even lands. Attacks against *cofradías* negatively affected all such associations, urban and rural, Spanish and Indian, wealthy and poor.

It has been argued that these attacks against popular religious organizations contributed in some way to the Independence movement, especially with regard to possible motives behind the discontent of the average parish priest who lost a principal source of income. The Wars of Independence caused serious devastation to already threatened confraternity livestock and property. Herds were killed and lands were divided or sold in the period following 1820. Certainly membership in the brotherhoods declined rapidly, especially in the cities among the elite and Spanish-based associations. Confraternity record keeping practically disappeared during the first decades after Independence. The *cofradía* as it was known during its colonial zenith, as a strong communal mutual aid and charitable corporation with income-producing properties, and which celebrated its existence with a yearly feast, had collapsed.

In the nineteenth century attacks on church property accelerated, affecting even further what remained of the *cofradía* system. Reform Laws at midcentury suppressed brotherhoods, culminating in an 1860 presidential order that required the sale of all income producing properties still in the hands of *cofradías.*

Yet the *cofradía* endured. In the nineteenth century the influence of the clergy was so greatly diminished as to allow the faithful, particularly in rural areas, to recreate the *cofradía* as it chose. The most striking need, as evidenced by what survived, was the yearly feast in honor of a patron saint. The *cofradía* in its nineteenth-century guise undertook sponsorship of the public fiesta as well as serving as a vehicle for individual piety. It was also intimately connected with a sense of place and with civic pride, but no longer controlled communal lands, rental properties, or productive sources of capital. It was also not strictly divided along ethnic and racial lines. Funding for the feast was often made available through what is known as the cargo system, by which wealthy individuals in a type of rotation take their turn in underwriting costs. Charitable functions such as visiting the sick and imprisoned were adopted by larger regional and national organizations such as Catholic leagues and Catholic worker circles inspired by late-nineteenth- and early-twentieth-century Catholic social teaching.

The economic and political power of the *cofradía,* of no consequence by the twentieth century, meant that direct attacks by the Revolutionary government against the structure or properties of brotherhoods was unnecessary. *Cofradías* nonetheless were among the targets of efforts at abolishing public worship (in the 1917 Constitution and the 1926 "Calles Law"). The violent hostility of the faithful toward such laws, indicating a strong attachment to public expression of religious devotion—and the *cofradías* that made these expressions possible—led to the lifting of the bans. Normalization of church-state relations in 1992 had little direct effect on *cofradías* since they had for decades been viewed by the state as neutral, or folkloric at best, expressions of local pride and faith with no real political or economic import. Contemporary fascination on the part of outsiders with *cofradía* activity stems from the attraction of traditional pageantry and the exoticism of folk religion.

Significant shifts in the history of the *cofradía* make its definition a complicated one. In the first place, allowances need to be made for different characteristics in urban and rural settings and among various ethnic groups. Differences from region to region need also be considered, as do affiliation with religious orders or with secular clergy, and matters of wealth. Yet three general, sweeping periods can be outlined. The first consists of the colonial foundation of the *cofradía* as an income-producing corporate body that supported public worship, provided insurance for members, and fulfilled the call to charitable works. The vitality of this structure lasted through the mid–eighteenth century. The second period is one of decline, during which traditional means of income were disrupted and membership dissipated. This period, culminating in the mid–nineteenth century, witnessed not simply the end to colonial brotherhoods but also their resurgence in a new form, especially in rural areas. The third period, from the latter half of the nineteenth century to the present, places the *cofradía* on the level of a localized organization charged with supporting a community celebration centered on a popular cult, and with fostering individual piety.

See also Festival Cycle; Popular Catholicism; Ritual, Religious and Civic: Processions

Select Bibliography

Brooks, Francis, "Parish and *Cofradía* in Eighteenth-Century Mexico." Ph.D. diss., Princeton University, 1976.

Chance, John K., and William B. Taylor, "*Cofradías* and Cargos: An Historical Perspective on the Mesoamerican Civil-Religious Hierarchy." *American Ethnologist* 12 (February 1985).

Cole, Jeffrey, editor, *The Church and Society in Latin America.* New Orleans, Louisiana: Tulane University Press, 1984.

Foster, George, "*Cofradía* and Compadrazgo in Spain and Spanish America." *Southwestern Journal of Anthropology* 9 (1953).

Meyers, A., and D.E. Hopkins, editors, *Manipulating the Saints.* Hamburg: WAYASBAH-Verlag, 1988.

Weckmann Muñoz, Luis, *La herencia medieval de México.* 2 vols., Mexico City: Colegio de México, 1984.

—BRIAN C. BELANGER

COMANDANCIA GENERAL DE PROVINCIAS INTERNAS

See Provincias Internas, Comandancia General de

COMMUNISM AND COMMUNIST PARTIES

Although communism never developed a stable mass base or a consistent electoral presence in Mexico, its influence in social movements, politics, and culture has been considerable. The main protagonist was the Partido Comunista Mexicano (PCM, or Mexican Communist Party), founded in 1919 and, until its dissolution in 1981, Mexico's oldest political party.

Strictly speaking, communism never has been a unitary phenomenon; there have in practice been several Mexican communisms. This is the result of the orgy of expulsions that forced successive waves of "dissidents" out of the PCM over the decades. Small groups of left oppositionists created the first of many Trotskyist formations in the early 1930s: the Liga Comunista Internacionalista. Later, at the end of the 1940s, the "golden age" of sectarianism, hundreds of expelled communists formed the Partido Obrero-Campesino Mexicano (POCM, or Mexican Worker-Peasant Party), which played an important role in several peasant and labor unions in the period from 1950 to 1960.

Moreover, the Communist Party, for all its insistence on doctrinal closedness and discipline, became a de facto cadre training school for a wide range of other political parties and organizations. Both the ruling Partido Revolucionario Institucional (PRI, or Institutional Revolutionary Party) and parastate parties of the left such as the Partido Popular (later Partido Popular Socialista, or PPS) consistently have recruited activists whose skills were forged originally in the world of the communist movement. Mexican communism, then, has helped shape the contours of the nation's global political culture.

The PCM's history can be divided into six main stages. In its earliest years, from 1919 until 1923, the party was ideologically pluralist. The continuing influence of anarcho-syndicalism was reflected in the party's militant anti-electoral stance. In its earliest years, the PCM began to establish a presence within the working class and peasantry; it is in the early 1920s that the party made its first contacts with Ursulo Galván and Primo Tapia, and with tenants' movements in major cities. In its second phase, from early 1923 until 1928, the party pursued a "united front" strategy toward the governments of the Sonoran Dynasty, softening its stance on the reformist line of President Plutarco Elías Calles and committing its peasant and worker forces to the defense of the Álvaro Obregón government during the Adolfo de la Huerta rebellion of 1923 to 1924. The party further strengthened links with peasant leagues, miners, and rail workers.

It was also at this point that the PCM's deep involvement with the cultural life of the Mexican Revolution was consolidated—most clearly signalled by the incorporation into the party of leading painters and Revolutionary muralists such as David Alfaro Siqueiros and Diego Rivera. The "red" muralists contributed prestige, resources and the skills that made the PCM's paper, *El Machete,* one of the most graphically exciting journals in Mexican history.

Beginning in 1928, the PCM entered an ultraleft phase, echoing the left turn within the Comintern (the Communist International). The party broke with its allies in reformist unions and organizations (sacrificing critical links with peasants in Veracruz), established a rival labor and agrarian organization and vigorously contested the state. The resulting government repression forced the party into a semi-clandestine status. Dozens of communists were arrested and exiled to the Islas Marías penal colony from 1929 to 1933, and there were bloody massacres of agrarian activists.

The "golden age" of the party commenced in the second year of the presidency of Lázaro Cárdenas (1934–40). The PCM drastically altered its hostility to the post-revolutionary regimes and, following the new Comintern line, embraced the Cárdenas administration as a Mexican version of the Popular Front (the loose coalition of left and liberal groups aligned against fascism). Hailing the land reforms and other reforms of the Cárdenas government, in which its members played a key role, the PCM adopted a policy of critical support for Revolutionary nationalism (Unity At All Cost). The party's goal was now to push the Mexican Revolution to the left.

The immense labor and peasant mobilizations of this period, including the creation of the Confederación de Trabajadores de México (CTM, or Confederation of Mexican Workers) and the Confederación Nacional Campesina (CNC, or National Peasant Confederation), and the bold experiments in socialist education provided opportunities for the party to create a solid base among key unions—rail workers, miners and teachers—and among the intelligentsia. But there was a cost. The party's uncritical acceptance of the need for "labor unity" led it to support, or at least abstain from serious criticism, of the antidemocratic direction that the CTM and the CNC took in the 1940s. The party leadership also embarked on an endless and fruitless crusade to gain entrance to the official party. Furthermore, the prestige and industrial strength achieved by the PCM during the Cárdenas years encouraged the indiscriminate acceptance into the party of many people who sought to use it as an aid in their search for jobs in the government and trade union bureaucracy.

The fourth and longest phase in the life of the PCM began with the purging of the party's national leadership at the Extraordinary Congress of 1940, at which Valentín Campa and Hernán Laborde were expelled. The party's new general secretary, Dionisio Encina, a man closely tied to the PCM's key base among the reform ejidatarios (workers of communal landholdings, called ejidos) of the Laguna region, ruled the party for the next 20 years.

Despite the formal condemnation in 1940 of the opportunistic interpretation of the Unity At All Cost strategy, the party maintained the basic thrust off this line during the 1940s. It endorsed a policy of class peace during World War II and gave qualified support to the administration of Miguel Alemán (1946–52) during its first two years as part of its "productivist" enthusiasm for the task of industrialization of Mexico.

The policies pursued by the PCM during the war, plus the mass exodus of members removed from the party in two major waves of expulsions in 1943 and 1948, greatly weakened the PCM's strength. This weakening stood in sharp

contrast to the situation in most western European countries, where the communist movement emerged from the war with an increased membership and enhanced prestige. From a peak of 30, 000 at the end of the Cárdenas administration, membership fell to 10, 000 in March 1945, recovering slightly in the late 1940s. In the 1950s membership collapsed, and by 1960 there were only 1,900 members in the party. The formation of the Mexican Worker-Peasant Party (POCM) in 1950 (taking a large number of the PCM's rail worker cadres as well as its popular leader Valentín Campa) and defections to Vicente Lombardo Toledano's Popular Party (to which the PCM had loaned a number of its leading organizers) deepened the party's decline.

The PCM's collapse, especially from 1947 to 1960, cannot be blamed simply on the party's many mistakes. The anticommunist onslaught launched by the Alemán government weakened the left's strengths in the national industrial unions of railroad, petroleum, and mining workers. Meanwhile, the state's encouragement of capitalist agriculture at the expense of the ejido sector (an important base for the PCM), severely eroded the PCM's industrial and agrarian strength. These developments, plus a sharp increase in government repression of the party's membership, led the PCM finally to acknowledge what its members long had suspected. In December 1949 the party denounced the Alemán government as a "government of national betrayal."

The final stage in the PCM's evolution began in the late 1950s. In a bitter internal struggle General Secretary Dionisio Encina was removed at the party's Thirteenth Congress in 1960, and an attempt to "renew" the party's platform, strategy, and tactics commenced. The first plank of the renovation process involved a repudiation of the PCM's adulation of Lombardo Toledano and Lombardismo and the first real attempts at coming to terms with the concrete and novel features of Mexican capitalism. This led the party to abandon the old Comintern-inspired notion of Mexico as a semi-colonial society, and to recognize the tremendous changes brought about in the country's class structure. This shift of vision enabled the PCM to diversify its agrarian base, moving away from its traditional ejidatario constituency and toward the building of organizations among peasant land petitioners and wage-earning rural proletarians. New organizations such as the Independent Peasant Central (CCI) enabled the PCM to mount a modest challenge to the dominance of official and semiofficial peasant federations like the CNC.

The most decisive of the changes introduced into the PCM's theoretical baggage was a rejection of the "ideology of the Mexican Revolution" as bankrupt, and an endorsement of the view that the cycle of bourgeois revolutions in Mexico had been definitively completed. The bloody repression of the student-popular movement in 1968, in which dozens of communist activists were jailed, consolidated this rupture between the party and the state. The brutality exhibited by the police and army in 1968 and in the next three years also caused a sharp although short-lived radicalization of the

PCM's line. The party called for a policy of confrontation with despotic presidentialism, denounced the third-worldist populism of President Luis Echeverría Álvarez, and embraced a campaign of active electoral abstention.

Most remarkably, the PCM argued that the beginnings of a revival of independent labor activism in the 1970s (the *insurgencia obrera*) indicated that a "new" revolution was on the immediate horizon and that armed struggle was a possible option for the left. Some of the PCM's youth members, angered and disillusioned by the events of 1968, joined the armed struggle fronts that proliferated in major cities and in certain areas of the countryside (Chihuahua and Guerrero) from 1968 to 1973.

The collapse of the *guerrilla* by the mid-1970s and the deepening economic crisis and austerity of the second half of the 1970s pushed Mexican communists to jettison their brief flirtation with ultraleftism. The PCM returned to the electoral arena and secured its electoral registration, taking advantage of the electoral reforms under President José López Portillo. It also embraced the idea of creating a "Coalition of the Left" with other socialist forces. This strategy took a number of forms: the launching of the Coalición de Izquierda in 1979, which secured 750,000 votes in the 1979 congressional elections and brought 18 deputies in the lower house, and the forging of electoral alliances with Trotskyist parties (the Partido Revolucionario de los Trabajadores) and parties of the independent left with no history of association with the communists, such as the Partido Mexicano de los Trabajadores (PMT) led by Heberto Castillo.

At the same time, the PCM's embrace of the electoral path was accompanied by a significant change in the social composition of its membership. With the formation of powerful unions of university teachers and administrative workers in the massively expanded tertiary education system, the party acquired a strategic base within the ranks of intellectuals, university teachers, and other educational sectors. The PCM's conquest of the universities occurred on a national scale—at the campuses of the Universidad Nacional Autónoma de México (UNAM, or the National Autonomous University of Mexico) and Universidad Autónoma Metropolitana (UAM, or Autonomous Metropolitan University) in Mexico City and at several provincial universities, most notably the state universities in Puebla, Sinaloa, and Guerrero.

For the last few years of its existence (roughly from 1975 to 1981), the PCM seemed to be moving along a Euro-communist track. The party abandoned the term dictatorship of the proletariat and slowly jettisoned its vanguardist claims to be the sole interpreter and architect of the socialist project in Mexico. Like many communist parties in Europe, the PCM adopted a "war of position" strategy, throwing itself into the battle to win power at the municipal level. Unlike its model, the Italian Communist Party, however, the PCM's success in local politics was extremely modest. Apart from winning the impoverished municipality of Alcozauca in

Guerrero and the city of Juchitán in Oaxaca, the PCM was unable to make much headway. More successful was the attempt to build ties with constituencies previously rejected by the Marxist left. The PCM supported the reestablishment of diplomatic relations between Mexico and the Vatican and called for the abolition of the constitutional prohibition on political and electoral rights for the clergy.

The drive toward cooperation with other sections of the left eventually led to the decision to dissolve the PCM and create a new unified socialist party with a variety of other left parties and formations. In 1981 the oldest political party in Mexico announced its formal dissolution. The new left party carried the name Partido Socialista Unificado Mexicano (PSUM). It was a fusion of the PCM (by far the largest grouping) and four other parties, including two old-fashioned Marxist-Leninist formations and a small but influential group of intellectuals and unionists shaped by the important tradition of Revolutionary nationalism.

The period of introspection following the end of the PCM, and the greater access to archival materials in Mexico and the former Soviet Union, have modified traditional perspectives on the evolution of communism in Mexico. Interpretations that see Mexican communism merely as a tool of the Communist International carry less conviction. The subordination of the PCM to the dictates of the Soviet Union and (until 1943) the Comintern was without doubt a crucial element shaping the party's history. There were numerous conjunctures in which the influence of Moscow (and sometimes of the Communist Party of the United States) were registered. These include the decision to launch the "left turn" (1928); the abandonment of the ultraleft Third Period stance and the adoption of Popular Front in 1935; the anti-Trotsky campaign from 1938 to 1940 and the purging of the party's national leadership in 1940; and the Browderist episode of 1944 to 1945, in which the PCM adopted most, but not all, of the creative Marxism designed by Earl Browder in the Communist Party of the United States.

But Mexican communists also interacted with traditions and experiences outside of the revolutionary socialist tradition on which they drew. The PCM shared a surprisingly large part of the vision articulated by ideologists and politicians of the Mexican Revolution. Thus the party's atheistic and anticlerical stance on religious issues and its strong presence among rural teachers neatly dovetailed with the rationalist, scientist, and radical liberal strains in the statecraft of the Mexican Revolution. The PCM welcomed capitalist industrialization, just as enthusiastically as the governments of Cárdenas, Manuel Avila Camacho, and Miguel Alemán did, and it embraced the centralizing and nationalizing thrust of the post-Cardenista state.

Mexican communism, then, was caught up in an immensely complex and internally contradictory web of tendencies. The PCM criticized capitalist modernization; yet at the same time it supported industrialization and the massification and proletarianization that accompanied it. Communists opposed despotic actions of the state and struggled to build autonomous mass organizations of the working class and peasantry; yet simultaneously, the PCM embraced the statist and nationalist project of the Mexican Revolution, which subordinated the independence of mass organizations to the struggle for cross-class unity and a strong nation. The painters, writers, and intellectuals of the PCM pioneered a combative revolutionary aesthetics but they also, especially muralists such as Rivera and Siqueiros, tended to mimic, and were mimicked by, the official artistic view of the Mexican Revolution. In this way they unwittingly contributed to the deepening of folkloric "Revolutionary" treatments of popular culture and strengthened the hegemonizing and regulating capacity of the state.

Select Bibliography

Campa, Valentín, *Mi testimonio: Memorias de un comunista mexicano.* Mexico City: Ediciones de Cultura Popular, 1980.

Carr, Barry, *Marxism and Communism in Twentieth Century Mexico.* Lincoln: University of Nebraska Press, 1992.

Márquez Fuentes, Manuel, and Octavio Rodríguez Araujo, *El partido comunista mexicano.* Mexico City: El Caballito, 1973.

Martínez Verdugo, Arnoldo, editor, *Historia del Comunismo en México.* Mexico City: Grijalbo, 1985.

Schmitt, Karl M., *Communism in Mexico: A Study in Political Frustration.* Austin: University of Texas Press, 1965.

Taibó, Paco Ignacio II, *Los Bolshevikis: Historia narrativa de los orígenes del comunismo en México 1919–1925.* Mexico City: Joaquín Mortíz, 1986.

—BARRY CARR

COMONFORT, IGNACIO

1812–63 • General and President

Ignacio Comonfort was born on March 12, 1812, in the town of Puebla. The death of his father when he was very young meant he had to abandon studies he had started in the Colegio Carolino and help support his family. His public life began in 1832, when he joined the movement, headed by Antonio López de Santa Anna, trying to overthrow President Anastasio Bustamante. For his role in military engagements like San Agustín del Palmar (September 29) and in the siege of Mexico City itself (January 3, 1833) he was promoted to captain of cavalry.

Comonfort was elected to Congress in 1842 and 1846 but had to leave office both times after Congress was dissolved (first by Santa Anna and then by Mariano Paredes y Arrillaga). During the war with the United States in 1847, he took part in various engagements in defense of the valley and city of Mexico. He entered Congress as a new deputy in 1848 and was then a senator until 1851. In 1853 he took charge of administering the customs post at Acapulco, a post that was arbitrarily removed from him by Santa Anna. This and other abuses of authority committed by Santa Anna in the south led various well known people in this region—most notably Juan Álvarez, the governor and commander general of the state of Guerrero; General Tomás Moreno; and Colonel Florencio Villarreal—to coordinate and proclaim the Plan of Ayutla on March 10, 1854. Comonfort added his support on March 11, at the head of the garrison at Acapulco. This movement proposed three fundamental aims: to take supreme charge of the nation away from Santa Anna; to designate an interim president who could call a Congress; and to give this Congress a constitutional role to provide the country with a fundamental set of laws to serve its needs.

On March 16 Santa Anna set out at the head of an army of 5,000 men to confront the rebels. Comonfort laid in wait for him in the fort of San Diego, Acapulco, in charge of only 500 men. The defense was heroic and Santa Anna had to retreat as a result of a lack of provisions and bad weather. This victory was among the greatest moments in Comonfort's life, giving the insurgent movement a great boost in prestige.

Later Comonfort traveled to the United States in an urgent search for funds to salvage the revolution. After much effort, Gregorio Ajuria finally provided what he needed. Just as the movement was about to collapse, Comonfort returned with the eagerly anticipated funds on December 7. He established a garrison at Michoacán and then transferred to Jalisco and took Zapotlán (Ciudad Guzmán), Colima, and Guadalajara. Similar uprisings were repeated in other states of the Republic, forcing Santa Anna to abandon Mexico City on August 9 and resign as president three days later. By way of a circular sent on August 22, 1855, in Guadalajara, Juan Álvarez was declared the incumbent president of the Republic. The administration of General Álvarez was very short since his health was delicate and he had little stomach for the ensuing struggles between Liberals and Conservatives. Álvarez resigned from his post and Ignacio Comonfort, then secretary of war, was named his replacement.

On December 11, 1855, when Comonfort took office, the country was profoundly divided. The split between Liberals and Conservatives had become irreconcilable since the proclamation of the Ley Juárez (Juárez Law) on November 22, 1855. Drafted by Secretary of Justice Benito Juárez, the Ley Juárez curtailed the *fueros,* or special military and ecclesiastic privileges and legal exemptions.

The Liberal government itself was divided between *puros* (radical Liberals) and *moderados* (moderate Liberals). By nature a compromiser, Comonfort provided weak leadership. He moved the country toward economic prosperity but proved unable to heal the divisions that threatened to plunge the Republic into civil war.

Comonfort's government saw the promulgation of further Reform Laws that antagonized the clergy and the military. Among these laws was the Ley Iglesias, through which the poor were exempt from paying for parish rights and church bonuses; the decree of June 5 by which the Society of Jesus was abolished; and the Ley Lerdo of June 25, which called for the disentailment of church property as part of the abolition of all communal property. Conservative forces erupted into open resistance in Puebla on December 19 with the Rebellion of Zacapoaxtla, which rallied around the cry of *Religion y Fueros*. This rebellion was followed by other uprisings, such as one in San Luis Potosí that the president himself put down. Once overpowered, the rebels leaders and officials were severely punished. Comonfort even confiscated the bishop of Puebla's possessions, since he believed the ecclesiastic authorities had supported the rebels both morally and economically.

Unrest worsened with the drafting of the Constitution of 1857 (which had been called for by the Plan de Ayutla). Conservatives had little voice in the drafting of the document, which task fell mostly to *puros* and *moderados*. Ultimately, the Constitution incorporated many of the earlier Reform Laws, such as the Ley Juárez, the Ley Lerdo, and the Ley Iglesias. On the basis of this document, Comonfort was designated president of the Republic, and Benito Juárez became chief justice of the supreme court (and therefore next in line for the presidency). When Conservatives and their supporters voiced dissent over the Constitution, Comonfort ordered all clergy and government officials to swear allegiance to the document or be dismissed. Such tactics only widened the divisions in the nation and hastened civil war.

Backed by the clergy and the military, General Félix Zuloaga announced the Plan of Tacubaya on December 17,

1858, and staged a coup d'état, dissolving Congress and imprisoning Juárez. Initially Comonfort backed the plan, under the naive hope that this single act could pacify the country and achieve conciliation between Liberals and Conservatives. Ultimately, the coup only exacerbated the antagonisms, and Comonfort's position earned him contempt from both sides. On January 11, 1859, Zuloaga ordered the removal of Comonfort from office. That same day, Comonfort freed Benito Juárez. On January 17, Comonfort left Mexico City and went into exile in the United States. Benito Juárez assumed the constitutional office of the presidency and fought Zuloaga's Conservative forces in the ensuing War of Reform.

Comonfort returned from exile and once more fought for the defense of the Republic during the French Intervention. As chief of the Army of the North, he was defeated by Interventionist forces on May 8, 1863, on the ridge of San Lorenzo near Puebla. Later, when the constitutional government was established in San Luis Potosí, Comonfort was appointed minister of war and general in command of expeditionary forces leaving Mexico. Days later, on November 11, 1863, when Comonfort passed San Miguel de Allende at Celaya with an escort of 100 men, he was ambushed and killed near Chamacuero by a group of 200 men. Later he was buried in the pantheon of San Miguel de Allende.

Select Bibliography

Bazant, Jan, *Alienation of Church Wealth in Mexico: Social and Economic Aspects of the Liberal Revolution, 1856–75,* translated by Michael P. Costeloe. Cambridge: Cambridge University Press, 1971.

Rodríguez O., Jaime E., editor, *The Evolution of the Mexican Political System.* Wilmington, Delaware: Scholarly Resources, 1993.

Scholes, Walter V., *Mexican Politics during the Juárez Regime, 1855–1872.* Columbia: University of Missouri Press, 1957.

Sinkin, Richard N., *The Mexican Reform, 1856–1876: A Study in Liberal Nation-Building.* Austin: University of Texas Press, 1979.

—VICENTE QUIRARTE

CONFEDERACIÓN DE TRABAJADORES DE MÉXICO (CTM)

From its birth through the 1990s, the Confederation of Workers of Mexico has been the most important labor union in the country. Incorporated into the "labor sector" of the ruling Partido Revolucionario Institucional (PRI, or Institutional Revolutionary Party), the CTM—more than any other corporate entity—has come to play a pivotal role in government policy and the economy.

The most important precursor of the CTM was the Comité Nacional de Defensa Proletaria (CNDP, or National Committee of Proletarian Defense), which was organized during the early years of the administration of President Lázaro Cárdenas (1934–40). The CNDP was a response to pressure by Plutarco Elías Calles, the former president and *jefe máximo* (maximum chief) of the ruling Partido Nacional

Revolucionario (PNR, or National Revolutionary Party), against labor militancy and the more populist Cárdenas administration. On June 11, 1935, Calles issued a proclamation denouncing the increased labor mobilization of the past year and a half. Strikes were "unjustified," Calles insisted, and "inflicted greater damage on the government than on capital, since they shut off the sources of prosperity." Calles's declaration was as much an oblique criticism of the more pro-labor stance of the Cárdenas administration as a rejection of labor organization.

Labor's response was not long in coming. On June 12 a group of labor organizations headed by the Mexican electricians' union gathered to formulate a new strategy to counter the Callista threat. After four days of discussion, the unions decided to form the CNDP, signing a "pact of solidarity." The pact called for the unification of worker and peasant movements. All organizations signing the pact would be guaranteed representation in the CNDP, and their autonomy within the organization would be guaranteed. The pact also declared that the CNDP would call a general strike if necessary to defend freedom of association, the freedom to strike, and the freedom to hold public demonstrations.

On February 21, 1936, the CNDP opened a national congress of labor organizations. Delegates at the congress represented more than 500,000 workers. Although the congress was intended to unify the Mexican working class, the congress highlighted the tremendous divisions in Mexican labor. Workers in the national Confederación General de Obreros y Campesinos de México (CGOCM, or General Confederation of Workers and Peasants of Mexico) were divided into the Lombardistas represented by Vicente Lombardo Toledano and Rodolfo Piña Sorio and the Velazquistas represented by Fidel Velázquez, Fernando Amilpa, and Blas Chumacero. A third faction, Communists from the Confederación Sindical Unitaria de México (CSUM, or Sole Syndical Confederation of Mexico), was represented by Valentín Campa and Miguel A. Velasco. In addition to the three main currents, national trade unions also flexed their political muscle.

Moreover, the broader national political context made this a particularly complicated time for the Mexican labor movement. Tensions were high between Cárdenas and Calles. In the city of Puebla the Confederación Regional Obrera Mexicana (CROM, or Regional Confederation of Mexican Workers) and the Federación Regional de Obreros y Campesinos (FROC, or Regional Federation of Workers and Peasants) struggled for control of the local labor movement, and the Monterrey glassworks were shut down in a particularly prolonged and bitter strike. The rise of fascism and the formation of popular front alliances between communist and bourgeois democratic parties in Europe and Latin America also had an important impact on the Mexican labor movement. Finally, the rising tensions forced the Cárdenas administration to intervene in labor disputes.

There was little dispute among the labor representatives at the congress about the overall principles of the new union.

Adopting the slogan "for a classless society," the declaration of principles of the CTM had a strong anticapitalist tone. There also was considerable unity around the choice of Vicente Lombardo Toledano as secretary general of the CTM. The process of electing a secretary, however, threatened to tear the organization apart. The two candidates were Miguel A. Velasco, supported by the national trade unions and the CSUM, and Fidel Velázquez, supported by the CGOCM. In the first round of voting Velasco emerged as the clear victor. When Velázquez's supporters threatened to withdraw from the congress, however, the CSUM withdrew Velasco's candidacy. In the second round of voting Velázquez was elected secretary of organization and Velasco secretary of education. The congress closed with a marked sense of confusion and discontent.

The early years of the CTM were marked by internal struggles, splits, and expulsions. These tensions came to a head during the fourth CTM congress of March 26 to 28, 1947. The months leading up to the fourth congress saw workers divided over who would serve in the new executive committee of the CTM and who would be the new secretary general. The *lobitos* (wolf cubs) headed by Velázquez as well as Toledano and his supporters pushed the candidacy of Fernando Amilpa for secretary general, while the train workers' union, the streetcar workers' union, the union of telephone workers, and 20 other industrial unions pushed the candidacy of the more progressive Luis Gómez Zepeda, who headed the radical railway workers' union, together with the Communist Valentín Campa.

The CTM already had been weakened by several important schisms. The Sindicato de Trabajadores Petroleros de la República Mexicana (STPRM, or Union of Petroleum Workers of the Republic of Mexico) had withdrawn from the Central when the CTM refused to support its economic demands. The miners' and electrical workers' unions also had withdrawn from the CTM. Indeed, the railway workers' union was the only major industrial union still within the CTM fold, which perhaps was why the railway workers' union felt it could push its own candidate for the position CTM secretary general.

During the third CTM congress in January 1947, however, the Lombardistas and Velazquistas had imposed a series of legal restrictions to limit the participation of the railway workers in the CTM. On March 20, 1947, shortly before the fourth congress, Gómez Zepeda broke with the CTM leadership, withdrawing his candidacy and calling for the formation of a new national labor central, the Central Única de Trabajadores (CUT, or Sole Workers' Central). With their only opposition absent, the Lombardistas and Velazquistas were able to impose their own candidates at the fourth congress, and Amilpa was elected secretary general.

In the new union constitution adopted at the fourth congress, the CTM dropped most of its earlier militancy. The anticapitalist principles of the first congress were eliminated in favor of immediate economic goals, and the slogan "for a classless society" was dropped in favor the more bland "for the emancipation of Mexico." Assuming a tactic of national unity, the CTM resolved to "struggle for the economic and social development of Mexico." Moreover, the new CTM leadership resolved to purge the rank and file of democratic, socialist, and communist tendencies.

The person who had contributed most to the new language of the CTM constitution was Vicente Lombardo Toledano, who believe the Velazquistas at the fourth congress supported his project of forming a new political party, the Partido Popular. Once the fourth congress had been saved and Fernando Amilpa installed as secretary general, however, the CTM leadership purged Lombardo Toledano and his supporters from the union. The Velazquistas' *coup de grace* was to pull the CTM out of the Federación Sindical Mundial (World Union Federation) and the Confederación de Trabajadores de América Latina (CTAL, or Confederation of Latin American Workers).

The 1947 congress marked the consolidation of Velazquista control over the CTM, which remained as of the mid-1990s. Under the leadership of Velázquez, the CTM became an important source of support for the administrations of Lázaro Cárdenas, Miguel Avila Camacho, and Miguel Alemán. The year 1952 proved a watershed for the CTM. The government abandoned the model of export-driven development of the 1930s and 1940s in favor of a strategy of substituting imported manufactured goods for internally produced products (import substitution industrialization, or ISI). The Velazquistas were able to eliminate the last remnants of internal dissent. Finally, the new statutes of the PRI gave the CTM a new importance, strengthening labor corporatism in Mexico.

Despite its incorporation into the PRI, the CTM has been far from static, responding to changes in the Mexican economy, state policy, and the labor movement itself. From 1953 to 1970 union corporatism served as a lever for national economic development and political stability. The CTM continued to be the principal organization of the Mexican labor movement, and it was able to maintain consensus internally and in its relations with the Mexican state. The CTM's collaboration with the Mexican state and political system was an important impetus for the government's new ISI policies and the increasing participation of transnational capital in the Mexican economy.

From 1970 to 1982 the state's policy of "stabilizing development" began to erode, and the pax priista of the previous two decades came to an end. The Mexican government faced great problems in continuing its traditional policies of income distribution, particularly with the labor sector. The leadership of the CTM for the first time was put in doubt by the president of Mexico and other representatives of the Mexican state. The CTM also was questioned by a growing insurgent labor movement. The growing social and political unrest spurred the Mexican government in 1970 to propose a political reform, the so-called "call for a democratic open-

ing." Nonetheless, the "democratic opening" was little more than a formalism until 1977. As the Mexican economy collapsed in 1981–82, labor corporatism was subjected to ever more strenuous criticism from the dissident labor movement and the state.

From 1983 to 1995 the CTM faced harsh criticism from the Mexican state, employers, other labor unions, and its own rank and file. No aspect of the CTM—its policies, its structure, its leadership, or its corporatist strategy—was immune from questioning, and the CTM leadership proved incapable of responding to the crisis. Although the CTM formally was allied with the state, the administrations of Miguel de la Madrid, Carlos Salinas de Gortari, and Ernesto Zedillo were determined to marginalize the organization as they sought to impose a new model of economic development based on technological change, liberalization of trade, export of manufactured goods, and fiscal austerity. In this new model there was no place for an entrenched, corporatist labor union like the CTM. It seemed clear that the old corporatism would have to be replaced by a new one, in which the CTM would no longer be the principal labor confederation (much less the only one). The relationship among the CTM, the PRI, and the state would have to be fundamentally transformed. In this new environment the CTM would no longer have the organizational clout to mediate between pressure from above (from the Mexican state) and pressure from below (from workers themselves).

Indeed, during the 1980s and 1990s perhaps the greatest challenge to the CTM's control of the labor movement came from workers, who showed considerable social and political awareness. Working both within and outside official channels, they mobilized around such issues as returning wages and benefits to pre-1980s levels, defending their constitutional rights and the process of collective bargaining, and protesting the skyrocketing unemployment brought about by the government's structural adjustments. Workers increasingly voted against PRI candidates in local and national elections. It was not clear if the political status quo would be maintained, minimally reformed—or if a new phase in the political history of Mexico was about to begin. It was clear, however, that the increasing social and political mobilization of workers meant that the Mexican government would not be able simply to impose a new corporatism on Mexican labor.

Select Bibliography

Aguilar García, Javier, "Los Sindicatos Nacionales." In *El obrero mexicano*, vol. 3, *Organización y sindicalismo*. Mexico City: IISUNAM–Siglo XXI, 1985.

Araiza, Luis, *Historia del movimiento obrero mexicano*. 4 vols., Mexico City: Casa del Obrero Mundial, 1975.

CTM, 50 años de lucha obrera. 11 vols, Mexico City: Instituto de Capacitación Política del PRI, 1986.

CTM, 1936–1941. 2 vols., Mexico City: Instituto de Capacitación Política del PRI, 1981.

González Casanova, Pablo, editor, *La clase obrera en la historia de México.* Vols. 10–14, Mexico City: IISUNAM–Siglo XXI, 1980–88.

Historia de la CTM, 1936–1990, 2 vols., Mexico City: IISUNAM and UNAM, 1990.

Velasco, Miguel A., *Del Magonismo a la fundación de la CTM.* Mexico City: Cultura Popular, 1990.

—Javier Aguilar García

CONFEDERACIÓN NACIONAL CAMPESINA (CNC)

Throughout its history, the Confederación Nacional Campesina (CNC, or National Peasant Confederation) has been linked closely to political developments of Mexico's post-Revolutionary corporatist state in its role as the nationally recognized *campesino* organization. Despite this loose relationship, the government and CNC periodically renegotiated their alliance, reflecting changes in agrarian policy, the CNC's internal struggles, and its search for political legitimacy in the countryside. At various times, dissident *campesino* organizations have questioned the CNC's representation of Mexican *campesinos,* but the CNC historically remained the most powerful and influential peasant union. In the 1980s and 1990s Mexico's restructuring of its national economy, combined with the 1992 reforms to Article 27 of the Constitution (which deals with land issues), presented the CNC with a crisis of legitimacy unlike those experienced in previous periods.

The CNC's historical roots lie in the early independent *campesino* organizations of the immediate post-Revolutionary period. During the 1920s, peasant groups and leaders established the first autonomous association, founding the Liga Nacional Campesina (LNC, or National Peasant League) in 1926 under the direction of Ursulo Galván, leader of the militant agrarian leagues of Veracruz. In 1933, responding to this independent movement, presidential candidate Lázaro Cárdenas proposed to integrate the LNC into the national political party, then the Partido Nacional Revolucionario (PNR, or National Revolutionary Party). Divided over the prospects of government alliance, the LNC split into two factions, one of which, the Confederación Campesina Mexicana (CCM, or Mexican Peasant Coalition), entered the PNR. Recognizing the CCM's limitations as a regional group, President Lázaro Cárdenas advanced the CNC as a national organization to unify *campesinos* throughout Mexico. Constituted in 1938, the CNC initially joined the new national party, the Partido de la Revolución Mexicana (PRM, or Party of the Mexican Revolution), and later represented one of three original sectors that comprised the Partido Revolucionario Institucional (PRI, or Institutional Revolutionary Party) from its inception in 1946.

In establishing the CNC, Cárdenas believed that an organized peasantry would represent a political force capable of confronting the established landholding elite, as well as providing a critical voting block for the new Mexican state. Using a patron-client relationship, the Mexican state institutionalized a state-*campesino* alliance, through which the state targeted financial support to CNC *campesino* groups in return for CNC political support in the state's battle against private industrial and landholding classes. Thus the CNC operated as broker, mediating between the government and *campesinos.* Recognizing the importance of an economic base to contest traditional political structures, Cárdenas channeled land reform, agricultural credit, irrigation, and other rural infrastructural development projects through the CNC. In return, CNC *campesinos,* many armed, actively supported Cárdenas's socialist vision of collective agriculture, as witnessed in the areas of La Laguna, Yucatán, Michoacán, and Sinaloa. As part of their political platform, the CNC battled for collective organization of agriculture and land redistribution to hacienda workers, indigenous peasants, and landless households. The original 1938 statutes did not distinguish forms of land tenancy, incorporating *ejidatarios* (workers on village holdings known as *ejidos*) and small and medium private landholders in the organization's confrontations with large landowners. The CNC focused its efforts on land redistribution, assuming that agrarian reform would resolve the problem of landlessness.

Scholars disagree in their interpretations of Cárdenas's intent and vision of the CNC's future. Some contend that Cárdenas envisioned a relatively autonomous CNC that would serve as an independent and compelling advocate for *campesino* political interests, land tenure rights, and access to rural development projects, while others suggest that the inherent structure of these patron-client relations precluded *campesinos* from developing politically autonomous organizations. The CNC's relative autonomy and capacity to act as an advocate for *campesinos* varied over time and space. Under Cárdenas, the CNC actively exerted political force at the local level, filing legal petitions through local agrarian committees and invading land with CNC support. CNC political action also varied throughout the different organizational levels. Organized in a pyramidal structure, the CNC has been comprised of *ejido* committees at the local level, the leagues of agrarian communities at the regional level, and the national executive committee at the top. Within this structure, political activity and independent activity varied considerably between the local and national levels.

The post-Cardenista administrations differentiated between land tenure in the distribution of credit and institutional support. The government moved to support large agricultural enterprises and divided the *ejido* sector between those with commercial opportunities and those with poorer land. Thus, although the 1938 statute included both *ejidatarios* and private producers as members, the CNC primarily represented the *ejido* sector by the 1940s. New legislation also threatened the gains of earlier agrarian reform, including the halting of land redistribution, reestablishment of landowner's legal rights, and increased allowable size for private landholdings. The post-Cárdenas administrations distributed less land and land of poorer quality; in addition, less financial support was available for the *ejido* sector. Shifts in economic policy targeted credit, investment, and infrastructural development toward commercial agriculture, controlled primarily by private producers.

Lack of government support and shifts in agrarian policy undermined the *ejido,* particularly the "collective" *ejidos*. Most collective *ejidos* were restructured into individual *ejidos,* in which the *edjido* held land communally, but *ejidatarios* individually farmed their plots. Unable to deliver economic services to its constituents, the CNC also faced increasing disputes within the organization over its legitimacy and capacity to defend *campesino* interests. Thus agrarian policy shifts resulted in the emergence of dissident *campesino* organizations. By 1947 nonconformist *ejidatarios* and peasant leaders abandoned the CNC, joining the Alianza de Obreros y Campesinos (AOC, or Workers' and Peasants' Alliance), headed by Vicente Lombardo Toleadano. Joining with another group, the Confederación Única de Trabajadores (CUT, or Sole Confederation of Workers), the AOC then constituted the Unión General de Obreros y Campesinos de México (UGOCM, or General Union of Workers and Peasants of Mexico) in 1949. By 1950 the UGOCM comprised 77 regional federations and 6 state federations, mostly from Sonora, Sinaloa, Chihuahua, and Nayarit. Internal political conflicts over militancy and the organization resulted in the UGOCM's disintegration into three different groups, all claiming the name and authority of UGOCM.

The second major dissident organization, the Central Campesino Independiente (CCI, or Independent Peasant Central) was established in 1963 at a congress of 1,000 delegates representing 500,000 *campesinos*. Lázaro Cárdenas's presence at the CCI congress further questioned the CNC's legitimacy as Mexico's major political *campesino* institution. In 1970, a small group, the Consejo Agrarista Mexicano (CAM, or Mexican Agrarianist Confederation), departed the CCI and incorporated into the PRI. The CCI further split into two divisive factions, one of which allied itself with the Communist Party, and the other joined the PRI. Under the administration of Gustavo Días Ordaz (1964–70), the government reintroduced an official agrarian discourse, respond-ing to the demands and social conflicts in the countryside. The CNC became the institutional channel through which the government channeled agricultural programs targeted at the *ejido* sector. Scholars contend that through this process the CNC ceased to operate as an organization capable of exerting great political pressure on the government, yet the CNC maintained its presence and power in the political arena. Within the dissident organizations internal conflicts and factions often led the groups to self-destruct. As the factions left the autonomous groups, the CNC often assimilated them, reducing the groups' autonomy and effectively eliminating any potential competition.

Under the administration of Luis Echeverría Álvarez (1970–76), the state moved from agrarian discourse to implement new programs. The administration shifted agricultural policy, again directing credit, collective organization, and commercial opportunities to the *ejido* sector, although efforts were primarily concentrated in northwestern Mexico. In efforts to reduce rural conflict and land invasions, the government responded through both political efforts and institutional restructuring. Recognizing the proliferation of new organizations and problems in managing these groups, the government initiated the Congeso Permanente (CONPA, or Permanent Congress) in 1973, affiliating the seven major *campesino* organizations in an effort to control the emerging militarism among Mexican *campesinos* during this period. In 1974, seeing CONPA's inactivity, the government founded the Pacto de Ocampo, in another effort to unify the major dissident *campesino* organizations under the CNC's tutelage and direction. Between 1974 and 1976, *campesino* mobilization and struggles in the Mexican countryside undermined the Pacto de Ocampo, as organizations confronted local problems separately.

In restructuring agrarian institutions, Echeverría was more successful at addressing rural economic problems, although this action undermined the CNC's role in *campesino* affairs. The government created new federal agencies that delivered services previously controlled by the CNC. As a new ministry, the Secretaría de Reforma Agraria (SRA, or Ministry of Agrarian Reform) responded to *campesino* demands for land redistribution, granting the CNC the formal responsibility of delivering the agrarian rights certificates. Government financial support, such as credit and agricultural extension, were channeled through the appropriate government agencies, Banco Nacional de Crédito Rural (BANRURAL, or National Rural Credit Bank) and the Secretaría de Recursos Hidráulicos (SARH, or Ministry of Agricultural and Water Resources), respectively. In supporting the government line, the CNC moved into the role of mediator between the public institutions and those *campesinos* who used these services. This shift further undermined the CNC influence even within the PRI, since the government recognized the CNC's increasing bureaucratization and lack of legitimacy with militant *campesinos*.

Under President José López Portillo (1976–82), the government downplayed agrarian reform, instead offering small producers a rural development program oriented toward raising agricultural productivity, in which *campesino* participation in producer organizations should improve rural incomes. Both the state and the CNC moved to incorporate rural producers and agricultural workers in new forms of organization. First, the state moved to strengthen the *ejido* organizations, through the creation of *ejido* unions and regional unions comprised of local *ejidos*. These groups participated in the CNC political arena but overall were less successful as economic ventures. Second, in 1965 and again in 1972, the CNC revised its statutes to expand membership to associations of professionals and individuals who were not *campesinos*. By 1976 the CNC moved to create alliances between *ejidatarios* and smallholders, referred to as "authentic private producers," within the organizational structure of large unions. In these large producer unions, such as the local agricultural associations and regional agricultural unions, producers were grouped together by economic activity rather than land tenancy. Most important were the producer unions of sugar cane, tobacco, coffee, and wheat. Third, the CNC proposed to address problems of the landless through a new union, thus challenging the autonomous Confederación de Trabajadores de México (CTM, or Confederation of Mexican Workers) in its effort to represent agricultural laborers. The CNC broadened its platform to address concerns of agricultural organization, productivity, and agricultural wages, while downplaying its historical demands for land reform. The CNC responded to internal and external pressures by adopting a strategy of broadening its potential membership. Despite these efforts, *ejidatarios* still constituted the majority of CNC membership.

During this same period, outside the *ejido* structure, *ejidatarios,* private producers, and private investors began to establish autonomous regional organizations. In the late 1970s, different agricultural associations emerged, registered under the jurisdiction of other ministries. These new forms of productive organizations, such as regional associations in collective interest, rural production societies, and societies of social solidarity were organized as economic associations and not restricted by territorial boundaries or *ejidatario* membership. They were also more efficient and less corrupt in delivering credit, input distribution, and commercialization of agricultural products. Despite incorporating different producers and investors, the new organizations conserved a wide range of political ideologies, differences that the members set aside in the interest of building viable productive organizations. Their economic success, as demonstrated by the Unión Nacional de Organizaciones Regionales Campesinas Autónoma (UNORCA, or National Union of Autonomous Regional Peasant Organizations) and the Coordinadora Nacional de Organizaciones Cafeteleras (CNOC, or National Coordinating Body of Coffee-Producer Organizations), supported autonomous efforts to negotiate product and market niches for their producers, in a movement known as the "appropriation of the productive process."

With the 1980 approval of the Ley de Fomento Agropecuario (Law for Agricultural and Livestock Production), the government promoted increased association of private investment and *ejido* associations. Agricultural production policies differentiated between those producers with commercial opportunities and those *ejidatarios* on the poorest land. By the late 1980s government agencies faced financial cutbacks and privatization of their bureaucratic functions. Under privatization, the state reduced major regulations that had protected *campesinos* from the market, reduced agricultural trade protection, and presented reforms to Article 27 of the Mexican Constitution.

Combined with the economic restructuring, new political strategies and alliances now pose challenges for the CNC. Between 1988 and 1990, under the administration of Carlos Salinas de Gortari, the government developed a new rural development strategy of supporting both autonomous and government-affiliated producer organizations. First, funding dissident organizations undermined their potential for political opposition, as well as targeting successful economic ventures, such as UNORCA and the CNOC. Under this program of "social contract," autonomous groups wrestled with the risks of financial support, possible co-optation, and the process of rural democratization. In approaching these new groups the government bargained for rural votes with patronage and projects, recognizing the CNC's inability to deliver under the old, corporatist system. Second, by financing specific producer groups within the CNC, the government supported the confederation's more modern wing and undermined the entrenched old guard. In so doing, the administration exacerbated tensions among the existing factions within the CNC.

By 1991, the government dropped all pretense of mitigating the impacts of economic privatization, and new agricultural policies opened the countryside to market forces. The economic restructuring laid the groundwork for political reforms to the *ejido* sector. During the first phase of land reform, cabinet members and government advisers debated the alternatives in secret, and publicly announced proposed reforms only after government advisers had reached their own consensus. The major *campesino* organizations, including the CNC, were not prepared to respond with coherent alternatives, and within all groups, internal debates resulted in great divisions. In meeting with representative *campesino* leaders, Salinas persuaded almost all national and regional leaders either to support the proposed reforms, or at least, not to oppose them. The autonomous organizations split, with the more militant organizations identifying with the political opposition, and some groups agreeing with the government in an effort to secure some funding. Within the CNC, a similar division emerged, between the more political groups, the traditional authoritarian groups siding with the PRI, and the more moderate producer-oriented subsector, comprised of groups interested in new market opportunities and forms of organization. The linkages between some autonomous groups and more moderate CNC elements was represented clearly in the 1992 power struggle within the CNC. Hugo Araujo, formerly of UNORCA, one of the successful autonomous groups, was elected CNC president and quickly moved to reorient the state and regional CNC organizations. Regretting the CNC's total silence in the debate over the Article 27 reforms, producer groups of both independent and official CNC organizations initiated conferences in 1991 and 1992 under the auspices of the "new peasant movement." After one independent leader directly criticized new policies in Salinas's presence, discussions disbanded. When the production-oriented branches within the CNC were unable to maintain internal political control, the CNC political vanguard returned to the corporatist tenets of the PRI.

As a corporatist union, the CNC has survived historical shifts in agrarian policy by several strategies. The organization alternated between a role of mediating broker and that of an advocate, responding to both government policy and local rural militancy. Facing dissident organizations, the CNC waited out the emergence of internal divisions in the opposing groups, assimilating these factions into the CNC proper. After the late 1980s, however, the state reduced government support to agriculture, withdrawing the economic services by which the CNC maintained its political authority and control. Mexico's restructuring of its economy posed new challenges to the CNC and exacerbated the existing divisions within the organization, between traditional corporatist and moderate market-oriented advocates. Whether or not the CNC survives this shift in agrarian policy will reflect internal factors but also external factors, such as financial investment in agriculture, economic growth, and market conditions, factors over which the CNC no longer exerts much influence.

Select Bibliography

Confederación Nacional Campesino, *Políticas y programas para el campo en la CNC.* Mexico City: CNC, 1994.

Escárcega López, Everardo, and Saúl Escobar Toledo, *Historia de la cuestión agraria mexicana,* vol. 5, *El Cardenismo: un parteaguas histórico en el proceso agrario, 1934–1940.* Mexico City: Siglo XXI–Centro de Estudios Históricos del Agrarismo en México, 1990.

Fox, Jonathan, "Political Change in Mexico's New Peasant Economy." In *The Politics of Economic Restructuring: State-Society Relations and Regime Change in Mexico,* edited by María Lorena Cook, Kevin Middlebrook, and Juan Molinar Horcasitas. La Jolla: Center for U.S.-Mexican Studies, University of California, San Diego, 1994.

González Navarro, Moisés, *La Confederación Nacional Campesina en la reforma agraria mexicana.* Mexico City: El Día, 1985.

Hardy, Clarissa, *El estado y los campesinos: La Confederación Nacional Campesina (CNC).* Mexico City: Centro de Estudios Económicos y Social del Tercer Mundo–Nueva Imagen, 1984.

Hellman, Judith Adler, *Mexico in Crisis.* 2nd edition, New York: Holmes and Meier, 1988.

Hernández, Luis, "La UNORCA: Doce tesis sobre el nuevo liderazgo campesino en México." In *Autonomía y nuevos sujetos sociales en el desarrollo rural,* edited by Julio Moguel, Carlota Botey, and Luis Hernández. Mexico City: Siglo XXI, 1992.

—Lois Stanford

CONFEDERACIÓN NACIONAL DE ORGANIZACIONES POPULARES (CNOP)

Established in March 1943 to bring the so-called popular middle classes into the official party's corporatist structures, the Confederación Nacional de Organizaciones Populares (CNOP, or National Confederation of Popular Organizations) is the least studied of the three sectors of the official party today called the Partido Revolucionario Institucional (PRI, or Institutional Revolutionary Party), although it is the most diverse and organizationally complex. Unlike the party's labor and peasant sectors, the CNOP—or popular sector as it typically is called—comprises a grab-bag of sundry organizations and occupations more than a relatively class-coherent body with a homogenous constituency. This distinctive character has raised many questions about its origins and purpose, even among party leaders, who starting in 1989 introduced a series of party reforms that leave the popular sector's future in question.

Because the CNOP was officially founded during a period of conservative retrenchment after the presidency of Lázaro Cárdenas (1934–40), conventional wisdom is that the CNOP's founding was forcibly imposed by party leaders in order to divide the labor movement and weaken labor's organizational strength within the party. The CNOP, in fact, generally is considered to serve little purpose except to offer a formal mechanism for propelling conservative middle-class delegates into congress. That the Confederación de Trabajadores de México (CTM, or Confederation of Mexican Workers) vehemently opposed the party's plans to create the CNOP lends some credence to these interpretations, as does the fact that one of the country's largest and most powerful organizations of workers, the Federación de Sindicatos de Trabajadores al Servicio del Estado (FSTSE, or Federation of Unions of Civil Servants), was originally positioned in the CTM but ultimately ended up in the CNOP, apart from other powerful labor federations. Some of the most politically centrist members of congress have come from the CNOP, moreover, a state of affairs that also sustains the view that the CNOP's foundation was intended purposefully to realign the balance of class power within the party.

However, the conventional wisdom about the CNOP rests more on post hoc interpretation than serious historical examination. Not only do most prevailing explanations fail to take into account the fact that state workers had been institutionally separated from industrial workers as early as 1938, well before the CNOP's establishment; they also fail to recognize that in the years immediately preceding the CNOP's founding Mexico's political leaders faced extensive middle-class opposition in both urban and rural areas. These and other factors suggest that the CNOP's genesis is as traceable to changing social and political dynamics in the late 1930s and early 1940s, which motivated state actors to respond to the groundswell of political opposition from selected popular and middle classes, as it is to the party/state's willful efforts to demobilize labor. To the extent that the CNOP's foundation successfully preempted debilitatingly widespread political opposition, moreover, at least for several decades, this sector's establishment and subsequent activities must be acknowledged as playing a key role in sustaining one-party rule, primarily by widening the ruling party's sectoral reach to accommodate middle classes and by offering the military an institutional locale for political participation in the party.

The CNOP was officially established on March 1, 1943, during the presidential administration of Manuel Avila Camacho at a constitutive assembly held at the Teatro Degollado in Guadalajara, Jalisco. Attending the convention in an orchestrated show of unity were leaders of the Partido de la Revolución Mexicana (PRM, or Party of the Mexican Revolution, forerunner of the PRI) and its peasant and labor sectors, the Confederación Nacional Campesina (CNC, or National Peasant Confederation) and the CTM, and Lieutenant Colonel Antonio Nava Castillo, who would become CNOP's first secretary general. The CNOP was founded at a moment of crisis for the PRM. The emergence of an opposition Confederación de la Clase Media during the waning years of the Cárdenas administration had signaled increasing middle-class dissatisfaction with the ruling party, as did the provincial middle class's widespread support for *sinarquismo*, a right-wing extremist pro-Catholic movement. Moreover, at the close of his administration Cárdenas had eliminated the PRM's military sector, sparking additional right-wing opposition. In the 1940 election both the middle class and former

military personnel threw their support behind the right-wing opposition candidate, General Juan Andreu Almazán, and the victory of Cárdenas's appointed successor, Manuel Avila Camacho, was tainted by credible allegations of electoral fraud. In the wake of the election the Partido de Acción Nacional (PAN, or National Action Party) enjoyed increasing support with the military and former military personnel, and there were rumblings of a coup d'état by *almacista* elements in the Mexican military.

One particularly vocal and violent source of middle-class opposition had been concentrated in the central highlands of Jalisco and in Guanajuato, where small farmers (rancheros), merchants, and others with strong Catholic sentiments long had struggled against the ruling party. But equally if not more significant was the growing middle-class opposition that emerged in Mexico City, where the political exclusion of middle classes and certain elements of the urban popular class generated extensive social mobilization at the seat of national government. It is well known that during the Cárdenas period there was substantial middle-class opposition in rural areas from landowners of various plot sizes upset with land collectivization, including family farmers, and among traditional middle classes in small towns and provincial capitals, as just noted. But little attention has been paid to the urban opposition and unrest in the capital city during the Cárdenas period, especially among shopkeepers, self-employed artisans, tradesmen, local mothers' clubs, and other urban residents who collectively took to the streets unhappy with service scarcities and infrastructural neglect in Mexico City.

Much of the Mexico City–based political dissatisfaction during this period can be traced to the elimination of democratic institutions in the capital in 1928. Without elections for mayor or local legislative mechanisms for advancing their political concerns, residents of Mexico City were especially dependent on party structures for accommodating their grievances. And when the PRM established corporatist structures for industrial laborers and peasants starting in 1936, and then for bureaucrats in 1938, many of the city's urban popular and middle-class residents resented their exclusion, especially as their concerns moved to the bottom of the party's policymaking agenda. During Cárdenas's administration urban public works received a declining proportion of the national budget, and new social programs mainly benefited organized labor, including extensive investments in health, education, and new housing for constituents of the labor and bureaucratic sectors only. Few resources went to water, drainage, street paving, public lighting, and markets, which had been the principal demands of traditional middle-class residents, especially shopkeepers and small industrialists who relied on these services for their livelihood, and poor residents of *barrios*.

Urban middle classes and much of the urban poor were further mobilized by the deteriorating economic situation of the 1930s. Self-employed street vendors, artisans, and shopkeepers were not covered by minimum wage legislation, unlike industrial and state workers in the PRM, and they suffered accordingly. Moreover, while Cárdenas proved willing to distribute urban and rural lands to workers and peasants, as well as construct housing for bureaucrats and industrial workers in the capital and elsewhere, he generally refused to respond to demands by well-organized and highly mobilized renters *(inquilinarios),* many of them quite poor, and small shopkeepers for legislation on rent control. Perhaps more than any other issue, the renters' movement brought together the urban poor and middle classes in an anti-Cárdenas alliance, and marches and rent strikes became common occurrences in Mexico City in 1938 and 1939.

Starting in 1939, the PRM attempted to repair the damage by making political linkages with existent organizations of artisans, traders, and *colonos* (urban residents) in Mexico City, at first advocating their inclusions in the party's bureaucratic sector, which occasionally was referred to as a popular sector. But these half-hearted efforts did not prevent widespread urban opposition to the PRM and its presidential candidate, Manuel Avila Camacho, who lost Mexico City to General Almazán in the 1940 election. In 1941, shortly after Avila Camacho took office, the PRM initiated a more substantial set of reforms. The first was to create the Confederación de Organizaciones Populares (COP, or Confederation of Popular Organizations), which functioned as a coordinating body for a wide variety of middle-class groups in the capital, including renters, shopkeepers, artisans, and professionals. This Mexico City–based organization served as the prototype and principal organizational base upon which the CNOP was built a little over a year later, once state delegations were sufficiently organized to present themselves at the founding convention.

This new sector's stated purpose was to organize the middle classes and to integrate them into a federation with other popular classes already within the party's grasp. In practice however, the CNOP's organizational scope was not limited to a narrowly defined middle class. According to the party's official records, among the groups slated for inclusion were "artisans, small farmers, small industrialists and shopkeepers, professionals, young workers and students, revolutionary women, schoolteachers, bureaucrats, cooperativists, neighborhood organizations, artists, and other occupations of sizable presence who apparently have been forgotten by the Revolutionary Regime." Accordingly, while the CNOP's so-called middle-class character was an important part of its defining purpose, the CNOP also was conceived as a sector for those groups whose most pressing concerns diverged from those of peasants and industrial laborers, as well as those most involved in opposition activities during the late 1930s and early 1940s. Given the fact that some of the CNOP's members were incorporated on the basis of gender, age, and other nonclass identities, as well as the fact that the new sector targeted those who may have considered themselves as workers and not just middle classes, such as state workers, the sectoral and party leadership generally referred to the CNOP as representing the country's "popular middle classes," in

recognition of the diversity and ambiguous class character of some of its constituency.

Despite the lip service paid to its popular constituents, the CNOP's self-consciously middle-class character counted as an important rhetorical component of its projected identity and the organizational logic of its foundation. With the exception of support for popular housing construction, most of the sector's founding principles were crafted around the material and ideological concerns of the country's middle classes: protection of private property, legal rights for professionals, credit for small rural and urban producers, financial support for small industries, the elimination of "fanaticism" (i.e., leftist ideology) in national education, cooperation with foreign capital, rent control legislation, and national defense. At key moments in Mexico's subsequent political history, moreover, especially during struggles over education policy in the late 1950s and after the 1968 massacres at Tlatelolco, party leaders continued to emphasize the CNOP's middle-class character more than its popular-class constituency, precisely to appeal to the nation's disenfranchised middle sectors and encourage their loyalty and participation in party politics.

Patriotic language also permeated the CNOP's founding documents. The sector was to promote nationalism, defend the fatherland, strengthen the moral and civic education of the people, and cultivate a love of country. Although this language in part might have been an appeal to the conservative middle class and a recognition of the importance of continental solidarity with the United States during World War II, it was also a signal of the military's unstated role in the new organization. In 1941, the active members of the military had been formally excluded from national politics; the PRM's military sector had been eliminated shortly before. Most readings of Mexican demilitarization take these restrictions to mean that the military was excluded from all politics. Although they were never explicitly defined as a key constituency, however, ex-military personnel—many of whom maintained strong links in the military—were an important part of the CNOP, sharing many of the middle class's political sentiments. After the formal dissolution of the military sector and its delegate bloc in Congress in 1941, the majority of the military delegates joined the CNOP. Former military personnel were able to capture the secretary generalship of the CNOP as well as two coveted positions on the organization's executive committee, the secretary of finance and the secretary of political affairs. According to the official PRI history of the organization, through its participation in the "popular middle-class sector" the military "acquired a numerical force that, in any given moment, could shift the balance of voting" in Congress.

In addition to providing the military a covert institutional home in the party, the CNOP also gave the ruling party a new way of organizing and incorporating state workers, or bureaucrats as they frequently were called. State workers' absorption by the CNOP both eliminated their privileged sectoral autonomy (which first was achieved under

Lázaro Cárdenas in 1938, when he created a Bureaucratic Sector in the PRM) and ideologically placed them with middle classes, despite the fact that many saw themselves as sharing much more affinity with workers in the CTM. For both reasons, state workers were among those most opposed to the CNOP's foundation, fearing diminished political power upon being regrouped in this large and heterogeneous sector. Yet the logic of inclusion was both political and juridical. While many state workers did see themselves as working-class and strongly allied with the industrial labor movement, others were educated white-collar workers and employees who saw themselves as middle class and who opposed the Cárdenas government's pro-labor sentiments, ranging from his efforts to include them in the CTM in 1936 to a 1938 juridical statute that gave them the right to strike. A measurable number of state workers, in fact, organized for and supported opposition candidate Almazán during the 1940 presidential election. When in 1941 the government of Avila Camacho invalidated Cárdenas's statutory reform, partially in response to several high-profile groups of state workers' own articulated concerns about being treated like workers with rights to strike rather than employees with civil service privileges, both the juridical and institutional rationale were established for separating state workers from industrial laborers and incorporating them into the popular middle-class sector.

The CNOP's extraordinarily diverse organizational reach helped preempt widespread political opposition to the ruling party from state workers, ex-military personnel, urban popular and middle classes, and even some members of the provincial middle class. But over time, its heterogeneous composition also generated a series of political and administrative problems that eluded the party's other two sectors. For one, the CNOP was charged with balancing the competing concerns of urban as well as rural residents, which frequently diverged. For another, the sector's leadership had to field ideologically diverse demands, since the wide variety of middle classes contained within its midst included some of the nation's most radical (e.g., teachers) and most reactionary (e.g., small farmers, ex-military personnel) elements. Last, the sector leadership had to accommodate an impossibly broad spectrum of social and economic demands. For example, bureaucrats envisioned the CNOP as bargaining for wage and workplace concessions, small farmers expected it would help establish new credit programs or favorable crop and fertilizer prices, urban residents hoped it would provide or regulate and guarantee affordable urban services, and small shopkeepers sought its aid in evicting street vendors and keeping retail taxes low.

Faced with these diverse and frequently contradictory claims, it did not take long for the CNOP to face serious problems of legitimacy. This first was apparent with respect to those original constituents whose numbers or circumscribed political power prevented them from adequately controlling the sector's political agenda. As early as the mid-1950s, for example, the voice and influence of small farmers and other provincial residents paled in comparison to those of state workers on the one hand, who served as the CNOP's largest, most active, and most organizationally coherent constituency, and in comparison to Mexico City–based residents on the other, who from the 1950s onward were growing rapidly in number despite their diverse composition. With the exception of a 1958 controversy over educational policy, in which conservative middle classes—many of them based in the provinces—pitted themselves against a radical faction of teachers in the state worker–affiliated Sindicato Nacional de Trabajadores de la Educación (SNTE, or National Union of Education Workers), by the late 1950s the priorities of state workers, and less so urban residents, generally prevailed over those of the sector's provincial (or nonurban) constituents.

In addition to sheer numbers, however, the diminishing significance of small farmers and provincial middle classes relative to other constituents in the CNOP also was a result of the highly centralized nature of the ruling party (after 1946 labeled PRI) and the Mexican political system in general. The CNOP, like all major party and government institutions, was headquartered in Mexico City. To the extent that most state workers also lived in the capital city and were thus an everyday presence for the CNOP leadership, as were most of the sector's other constituents, who included Mexico City's street vendors, small businesses, and colonos, the sector's leaders were hard-pressed to ignore their demands. This dynamic helped reinforce the salience of state workers and Mexico City–based populations even as it limited the power and visibility of small farmers and other provincial populations.

Owing to the strategic position held by state workers and Mexico City residents within the sector, by the early 1960s the CNOP began to assume a dual function, basically devoting its energies to coordinating urban-specific demands of its broad-based Mexico City constituency while at the same time protecting state workers. The concerns of its rural and provincial constituents, in contrast, fell by the wayside by and large. By the early 1970s, however, even this began to change as Mexico City's population expanded uncontrollably and the number and urgency of urban problems began to demand a greater proportion of the sector leadership's attention. By the 1980s, the CNOP leadership devoted most of its attention to dealing primarily with the political demands of Mexico City residents, a growing number of whom were joining social movements and taking to the streets to make demands on the government.

There were several reasons that the CNOP leadership eventually became so preoccupied with its Mexico City constituents. Starting in the late 1960s, state workers started turning elsewhere to press their demands. As of 1965, the FSTSE was given representative status in the Congreso de Trabajo, an umbrella organization that joined federations of industrial workers from the CTM and the Confederación

Revolucionario de Obreros y Campesinos (CROC, or Revolutionary Confederation of Workers and Peasants) with state workers from the CNOP and that subsequently took on the task of coordinating national labor and wage policy. Once these key constituents had another mechanism for articulating demands, the CNOP was freed to concentrate more directly on its diverse urban constituency. Also, urban problems in Mexico City began to intensify in the late 1960s and throughout the 1970s, as the capital burgeoned out of control and its residents mobilized around demands for land, housing, transport, water, electricity, and other key urban services. Several other political movements in this period, especially the 1968 student movement, also mobilized much of the Mexico City population, including students, university professionals, and other key constituents of the CNOP. With demands from residents in the capital city accelerating, and local democratic structures still absent, the CNOP leadership had little choice but to turn full attention to the mobilized masses in Mexico City.

Once the CNOP began to gear itself primarily to the concerns of these urban populations, however, it faced new problems. First, as the capital city's urban problems accelerated more rapidly than could be accommodated readily, especially in the 1980s when economic crisis severely restricted government revenues, the CNOP soon began to earn its reputation as serving no function for many of its rank-and-file constituents, since it was increasingly difficult to deliver the goods in accordance with accelerating urban demands. This state of affairs slowly chipped away at the CNOP's legitimacy, even among urban populations. Second, the sector itself became hamstrung by internal divisions among its constituents, as the more affluent urban middle classes concerned with the rapidly deteriorating urban environment frequently pitted their policy demands against those of the sector's more humble members. Indeed, one of the most divisive issues of the early 1980s was whether or not to restrict illegal settlement and street vending in more affluent neighborhoods. Efforts later in the decade to privatize urban public services were equally divisive, pitting *transportistas* and less affluent residents who supported subsidized services against car-owning middle classes who preferred a balanced budget.

With growing intrasectoral conflicts debilitating the CNOP, some in the party began to question the sector's existence. When in a highly controversial decision party leaders reformed Mexico City government in 1988 by allowing direct election of delegates to a nonlegislative local governing body (called the Asamblea de Representantes del Distrito Federal) entrusted with servicing and administering the capital city and its populations, many felt the CNOP was left without much of a purpose. Despite the fact that it was founded as a national organization designed to represent all the nation's popular and middle classes, over time the CNOP focused ever more intensively on its Mexico City bases. When these populations could turn to the locally commissioned *asamblea* instead, the nationally constituted CNOP

lost much of its utility. A year later, in 1989, the PRI announced the popular sector's "disappearance," marking the first fundamental change in any of the party's sectoral structures since before the official founding of the PRI in 1946.

But announcements of the "popular" sector's death must be seen as premature. With Mexico City's *asamblea* embued with only consultative power and the mayor still presidentially appointed, residents soon realized that the *asamblea* was not that much more responsive to their demands than the CNOP had been. Meanwhile, party leaders recognized that they could ill afford to abandon the middle class politically, especially given the growing popularity of the PAN and other opposition parties. Within one year after having abolished the CNOP, the PRI scrambled to create a new sectoral federation that could accommodate these key populations. Called UNE, Ciudadanos en Movimiento (Citizens in Movement—the acronym "UNE" in fact stood for nothing at all), the new organization was structured to incorporate many of the same urban social movements, neighborhood constituents, and state workers as the old CNOP, but it also reached out to a growing number of new middle-class environmental and citizen movements. Still, within two years it was clear that even the new logic of social movements was not bringing a sufficiently broad spectrum of popular middle classes to the party's side. In 1992 the PRI tried once again. Another new sectoral organization was created to replace the UNE, called the Frente Nacional de Organizaciones y Ciudadanos (FNOC, or National Front of Organizations and Citizens), and it was structured as a broadly cast front of diverse occupations and organizations similar to the original CNOP in its incoherence. Unlike the old body, however, the FNOC offered more scope for the political participation of nonorganized middle classes by providing a broadly defined territorial rather than occupational or urban basis for political participation. With this change, the PRI also hoped to re-incorporate provincial middle classes into the party, an ever more pressing objective since political decentralization and the revitalization of state and regional politics indicated that it may be precisely these more centrist provincial populations, long neglected by the Mexico City–biased CNOP, that hold the key to the party's future political successes.

Still, change has to be the watchword here. As of mid-1996, the PRI appeared to have decided to reinvigorate a form of the old popular sector once again. Whether this was merely a discursive strategy intended to keep long-standing CNOP loyalists in the fold, or a real institutional change that would make the FNOC obsolete, remained to be seen. But it was clear that the PRI seemed to be intent on appealing to a diverse and heterogeneous collection of popular and middle-class citizens, both in Mexico City and the provinces, just as it did in the late 1930s and early 1940s, trying different strategies and betting that an appropriately inclusive, sectorally drawn party organization could still serve as a key to popular legitimacy and national political success.

Select Bibliography

Confederación Nacional de Organizaciones Populares, *Primer consejo nacional.* Mexico City: n.p., 1944.

Davis, Diane E., *Urban Leviathan: Mexico City in the Twentieth Century.* Philadelphia: Temple University Press, 1994.

_____, "Uncommon Democracy in Mexico: Middle Classes and the Military in the Consolidation of One-party Rule." In *The Social Construction of Democracy, 1880–1990,* edited by Herrick Chapman and George Reid Andrews. London: Macmillan, and New York: New York University Press, 1995.

_____, "New Social Movements, Old Party Structures: Discursive and Organizational Transformations in Mexican and Brazilian Party Politics." In *Social Change and Economic Restructuring in Latin America,* edited by William C. Smith and Roberto P. Korzeniewicz. Boulder, Colorado: Lynne Reinner, 1996.

Garrido, Luis Javier, *El partido de la revolucion institucionalizada: La formacion del nuevo estado en México (1928–1945).* Mexico City: Siglo XXI, 1982.

Instituto Nacional de Estudios Históricos de la Revolución Mexicana, *Historia del Sindicato Nacional de Trabajadores de la Secretaria de Gobernación.* Mexico City: INEHRM, 1986.

Loaeza, Soledad, *Clases medias y política en México.* Mexico City: El Colegio de México, 1988.

Marbán, Miguel Osorio, *El Sector Popular de PRI: La esencia de la nación.* Mexico City: Coordinación Nacional de Estudios Históricos, Políticos, y Sociales, 1994.

Nava Nava, Carmen, *Ideología del partido de la Revolución Mexicana.* Mexico City: Centro de Estudios de la Revolución Mexicana "Lazaro Cardenas," 1984.

Partido Revolucionario Institucional (PRI), *Historia documental de la CNOP.* 3 vols., Mexico City: Edicap, Instituto de Capacitación Política, 1984.

Perlo Cohen, Manuel, *Estado, vivienda, y estructura urbana en el cardenismo.* Mexico City: Instituto de Investigaciones Sociales, UNAM, 1981.

—DIANE E. DAVIS

CONFEDERACIÓN REGIONAL OBRERA MEXICANA (CROM)

The Regional Confederation of Mexican Workers was the most important labor organization in the country between 1918 and 1928. It lays claim to being the first post-Revolutionary workers' organization and its experiences regarding worker-employer and worker-state relations proved pivotal for future developments in those areas.

Antecedents

The struggle of the workers to go beyond mutual benefit societies and consolidate their unions occurred during the Mexican Revolution, especially from 1911 to 1913. The anarchist movement that had dominated labor since the late nineteenth century and that by 1911 had shaped the Casa del Obrero Mundial (COM, or House of the World Worker) signed a political pact with the Venustiano Carranza administration on February 20, 1915, which stated that at the end of the Revolution Carranza's administration would comply with workers' demands regarding future labor conflicts caused by work contracts. Consequently, the activities of the COM focused on the spread of union organization and the support of armed revolt as practiced by the Red Batallions. In 1915 and 1916, other union organizations were created, such as the Federación de Sindicatos Obreras del Distrito Federal (FSODF, or Federation of Workers' Unions of the Federal District), which comprised 14 groups of which 11 belonged to the COM. Owing to Carranza's subsequent repression of the COM and his refusal to enforce Article 123 of the 1917 Constitution, workers of the nation's biggest cities and especially members of the COM began the task of creating a national confederation that would represent them permanently before the businesses and political institutions. Their goals were the abolition of fees, the collectivation of production and consumption facilities, and the strengthening of union powers to obtain improved wages and benefits.

Foundation

After two frustrated attempts to create a national confederation (in Veracruz in 1916 and in Tampico the following year), the governor of Coahuila sponsored the Congreso Obrero (Workers' Congress) in Saltillo in 1918 to prevent the organization of independent workers, seen as a threat by Carranza's administration. Thus, on May 1, 1918, a total of 115 delegates came to the congress, representing 113 organizations and 7,000 workers from 18 states. All agreed to establish the CROM; to determine its political philosophy, organization, and objectives; and to choose its future leaders.

During the Saltillo Congress, which took place from May 1 through May 12, three points of view were heard: first, that of the revolutionary union movement of the International Workers of the World (IWW), representing its branches throughout the country; second, that of the anarchist union movement and its many variants, with members in the COM and some cultural institutions; and finally, that of a heterogeneous reform group seeking to end the supposedly apolitical workers' movement, led by individuals interested in occupying political posts. The latter two collided in their attempts to gain power. The anarchists proposed the principle of *acción directa* (direct action) as the CROM's guiding ideology, meaning the rejection of state intervention in labor conflicts; the opposing reformers (led by Luis Morones, an electrician) proposed *acción multiple* (multiple action) as the best alternative, namely to go beyond economic demands in order to seek active participation in national politics, which implied reaching an agreement with the federal government in the application of Article 123 of the Constitution.

These opposing views were nothing new. The previous two congresses had heard them and nothing had been resolved, but this time the reformers managed to impose their ideology on the incipient CROM with their program of multiple action. The reformers' leader Morones was elected secretary general, Ricardo Treviño became first secretary, and J. M. Tristán the second secretary. Thus, a powerful, disciplined, and well-organized core group formed around Morones and named itself Grupo Acción, known by the others as the Apostolate of the Razor Strap. This group was fully supported by the Sonora group of Revolutionaries: Álvaro Obregón, Adolfo de la Huerta, Benjamín Hill, and Plutarco Elías Calles.

Among the objectives proposed for inclusion in the CROM General Program were the fight for land distribution, the appropriation of industry by the direct producers, the control of the educational system, and the application of Article 123. In short, workers who were members of the CROM decided to organize themselves according to the principles of the Constitution of 1917 and foster conciliation with the state. In the congress it was decided that the core of the new movement would comprise the unions, grouped together as local, regional, and industrial federations, which in turn would form confederations at the national and international level.

Among the 114 groups that signed the founding charter of the CROM were the mining workers, the Labor Chamber of Orizaba, the Mexican Union of Electricians, the United Steel and Iron Guilds of Monterrey, and the Federation of Unions of Puebla. In the course of 1918 one of the most important labor organizations joined the CROM, the FSODF, which became the most important source of recruitment for the CROM's executive central committee. The FSODF also became the pilot organization in which union programs and tactics first would be tried before being implemented in the rest of the confederation. After the Saltillo Congress ended, a new alliance between the CROM and the American Federation of Labor (AFL) began. Later, another international alliance was formed, the Latin American Labor Confederation, presided by Samuel Gompers, who at the same time was president of the AFL.

1919–23

In June 1919, Obregón publicly announced his presidential candidacy, and two months later he made a secret pact (known as the Private Covenant) with Morones, in which the labor leader actively supported Obregón's campaign, and the latter would in turn support the political arm of the labor organization, the Partido Laborista (Labor Party), and also write and apply the Labor Law.

Thus, in December 1919, the CROM founded the Partido Laborista Mexicano (PLM, or Mexican Labor Party) at a time when the triumphant forces of the Revolution needed a solid social base. The creation of a new political party caused a reshuffling of existing parties and the establishment of the social democratic block that confronted the Constitutionalist Party. The block opposed the application of Article 123 and the creation of a Ministry of Labor during Obregón's administration.

Since its founding and until the 1924 Convention, the CROM went through a phase of organization and alliance with de la Huerta, Obregón, and Calles. During de la Huerta's provisional presidency of 1920, many CROM leaders occupied public posts: Morones was given the leadership of the manufacturing and military institutions; Celestino Gasca became the governor of the Federal District; Eduardo Moneda was made head of the Department of Social Provision of Industry, Commerce, and Labor; and finally Ramiro Elourduy was appointed chief of the presidential quarters. Thus, the Grupo Acción saw one of its objectives come true: the dual participation of unions and government, binding labor and state so that a new type of Mexican corporativism emerged. At the same time, the CROM used some resources from *acción directa* to organize the big labor march of September 1920 in Mexico City, where CROM members demanded the application of Articles 123 and 27 of the Constitution, coupled with wage increases and price reductions. Álvaro Obregón became president on December 1, 1920, and began fulfilling the promises he had made to the labor movement by embarking on a nationalist and populist course, giving in to workers' and peasants' demands without going beyond the interests of the state, as stated in the 1917 Constitution. Obregón's proposed amendments to Article 123 met with fierce opposition in the National Congress and national and regional employers' organizations. The Supreme Court did not grant judiciary powers to the president, so he was not able to change labor laws. Another event that pressured the government was the massive forced repatriation of Mexican workers in the United States at the end of World War I.

The unity of the CROM slowly fragmented. On February 15, 1921, several of the CROM-sponsored union groups that had survived the COM, together with the Youth Section of the Mexican Community Party, organized the so-called national Red Convention, from which the Confederación General de Trabajadores (CGT, or General Confederation of Workers) emerged. The COM workers and the communists were unified in their rejection of the alliance between the PLM and the government of Obregón, and in their disapproval of the CROM's international affiliation with the AFL of the United States; in addition, both groups discouraged the search for government posts by the leaders of the CROM. A total of 43 groups composed the CGT, whose main support came from the textile unions of central Mexico, including the Federal District. The CGT began with 15,000 members, as opposed to the CROM's 150,000.

The newly created CGT incorporated and applied the tactics of the *acción directa,* with the result that the administration of Obregón constantly repressed the movement. Nevertheless, strikes increased in number, going from 173 in 1920 to 310 the following year, and most of them were organized by the CGT and other independent organizations, such as the Railway Workers' Union. Whereas the CROM had forged an alliance with the victorious political wing of the Revolution, the CGT tried to organize independently of the permitted channels of political participation as stated in the 1917 Constitution. During Obregón's four years as president, the CROM spread to the countryside, Morones and Gasca continued in their respective posts, and workers occupied even more positions. The PLM was slowly gaining members in the Mexico City municipal government and in the Federal Congress.

The CGT and the CROM differed in the way they handled workers' demands, and after the important strikes organized by the independent unions of the railway workers (1921) and of the streetcar drivers in Mexico City (1923), de la Huerta was perceived as their ally, as well as the CGT's. When de la Huerta rebelled against Obregón, he had the support of some members of the CGT; nevertheless, the CROM-state alliance proved resilient, and the rebellion failed. By 1923, Article 123 of the Constitution was already being applied in 14 states, although not yet at the federal level. In the same year, the CROM already had 800,000 members, a number that increased to 1,200,000 the following year.

1924–28

In the years 1920 to 1924 the basic judiciary guidelines of labor relations had been established, so conditions were ready to proceed to the next stage of the alliance between the workers and the state. In its sixth national convention celebrated in Ciudad Juárez from November 7 to 22, 1924, the CROM decided to support the presidential candidacy of Plutarco Elías Calles, and the Executive National Committee led by Morones was given even more far-reaching powers in order to defend the interests of the Mexican proletariat and the "socialist" government of Calles; the labor-state alliance had been consolidated.

In office, Calles reached the conclusion that, owing to the bad state of the nation's economy, it was necessary to depend on foreign investment to implement his plans for national modernization, and that investors had to be given a high degree of security. In order to achieve this objective, and for the "benefit of the nation," the CROM and the Mexican state would cooperate; in exchange for this cooperation, the workers' demanded from the state full support of their unions and the proclamation of a law that would establish the rights of workers and employers. The state, in turn, would give the workers its full political and economi-

cal support so they could unify all their organizations through the CROM.

The period 1924 to 1928 has been called a "glorious" one for the Confederation. The political participation of the CROM through its affiliate the PLM intensified, and in 1926 Morones was promoted to secretary of state, and many other members were appointed: 2 department heads, 40 representatives, and 11 senators to the National Congress, as well as 2 state governors and numerous other regional and local posts of lesser importance. The CROM's presence in the federal government allowed it to introduce a system of obligations, which amounted to voluntary contributions by federal employees to support the CROM and its affiliate, the PLM. Furthermore, the CROM could now strengthen the power of its unions, thereby broadening its organizational infrastructure. In short, the CROM became the most important workers' organization in Mexico. During the Calles administration, the PLM became the country's strongest party, recruiting its members through the CROM, and its demonstrations had solely electoral aims, namely to oppose the enemies of the Grupo Acción.

In order to foster the project of industrializing the country, the CROM controlled the Ministry of Industry, Commerce, and Labor and the Department of Labor. The head of the former was Reynaldo Cervantes Torres, and the latter was headed by Morones himself. Through these government agencies, the CROM standardized the steps to solve labor conflicts, the technical inspections of the working places, the centers of employment, and the planning of laws to enforce Article 123. The CROM also gave advice to meetings of arbitration, which resulted in the creation of the Federal Arbitration Council on September 17, 1927. The most important labor conflicts of this four-year period were in the sectors of mining, oil, textiles, and railways, and most of the time the council decided in favor of the capitalists.

The country's modernization was not easy. The main obstacle was the economic power wielded by the large hacienda owners, the foreign investors who controlled almost 100 percent of the nation's industry, and, on the ideological-political level, the powerful Catholic Church; all opposed Calles's reforms. As early as 1926, the application of Article 27 of the Constitution met with stiff resistance from the foreign companies operating in the country, and two days later a few paragraphs of the article had to be amended, especially owing to the overproduction of oil, which caused a worldwide drop in prices, but also owing to anti-Communist campaigns that accused Calles of being a "Bolshevik." At the national level, the pro-Catholic, peasant-based Cristero Rebellion propagated a bad image of his administration. The stage was set for the political, social, and economical crisis that would come with the reelection of Álvaro Obregón and his subsequent assassination.

The years 1927 and 1928 were critical, and they started with the amendment of Articles 82 and 83 of the Constitution to grant legitimacy to Obregón's reelection, which resulted in deeper political division. On September 2, 1927, the PLM, in spite of internal differences, decided to support Obregón's candidacy. In the following spring, on April 30, 1928, Morones made an analysis of the activities of the CROM and the PLM and decided to reinstate the tactics of *acción directa;* in essence, war between the CROM and Obregón had been declared. When Obregón was assassinated on July 17, the Partido Nacional Agrarista (National Agrarian Party) and other sectors accused Calles and Morones of being responsible for the murder. The accusations weakened them politically, and four days later Luis Morones, Celestino Gasca, and Eduardo Moneda resigned their public posts.

About one month later, on August 17, 1928, the CROM witnessed a massive desertion. The conflict originated in the lack of agreement on how to establish pacts with the new government and how to occupy public posts. As a consequence the CROM's membership drastically declined in the following years: from 1,172 affiliated organizations in 1928 to only 349 four years later, with dissidents even creating a "cleansed CROM." The weakening and disintegration of the CROM started in 1928, and the strength that had nurtured it for 10 years was drastically reduced when the Confederation's leaders left the stage, and the social and political force it once possessed gradually disappeared. A new political structure now emerged: the era of the new Partido Nacional Revolucionario (PNR, or National Revolutionary Party), created by the strongman Calles.

Select Bibliography

Carr, Barry, *El movimiento obrero y la política en México 1910–1929.* 2 vols., Mexico City: Secretaría de Educación Pública, 1976.

Guadarrama, Rocío, *Los sindicatos y la política en México: La CROM (1918–1928).* Mexico City: Era, 1981.

Leal, Juan Felipe, *Agrupaciones y burocracias sindicales en México 1906/1938.* Mexico City: Terra Nova, 1985.

Reyna Muñoz, Manuel, *La CROM y la CSUM en la industria textil (1928–1932).* Mexico City: Universidad Autónoma Metropolitana, 1988.

Tamayo, Jaime, *La clase obrea a en la historia de México: En el internato de Adolfo de la Huerta y el gobierno de Alvaro Obregón (1920–1924).* Mexico City: Instituto de Investigaciones Sociales de la UNAM, 1987.

Velasco, Miguel A., *Del magonismo a la fundación de la CTM.* Mexico City: Ediciones de Cultura Popular, 1990.

—JAVIER AGUILAR GARCÍA

CONGREGACIÓN

Congregación was the name given to a policy of spatial reorganization that Spanish authorities imposed on the indigenous population in sixteenth-century New Spain. This policy was part of a broader attempt to transform the system of domination over indigenous peoples. It included reforming the tribute system, organizing "indigenous governments," and evangelization. Faced with an indigenous population living largely in isolated mountainous regions, under the control of "natural lords"—descendants of the original, pre-Conquest elite—whose networks of power were complex and difficult to control, the Spaniards sought to create towns which could function as centers of Spanish civil and religious administration. The main goal of the *congregaciones,* also called *juntas* or *reducciones,* was to concentrate dispersed villages into compact towns designed according to a set plan, ideally central plazas and straight roads.

The religious orders and the Crown joined forces in 1550. The Franciscans, Dominicans, and Augustinians, as well as the secular clergy, chose privileged locations for their convents, churches, and chapels, surrounded by cemeteries. Streets and central plazas were laid out on a grid, with specific locations for town halls, private residences, and vegetable gardens. These small towns were settled by people often belonging to specific ethnic groups, who were assigned the patron saints the town was named after.

A *congregación* was a *pueblo,* or town, defined in terms of its specific urban layout, but it also occupied a particular place in the political and administrative structure promulgated by the Crown. This structure was organized around *cabeceras* ("head towns"), which were assigned an indigenous government with a *gobernador* (governor) responsible for collecting royal tribute. Under the *cabeceras* were *pueblos sujetos* (subject towns), and around both the *cabeceras* and *sujetos* were *estancias,* settlements without a formal urban structure which recognized the authority of the *cabeceras.* The formation of the *cabecera-sujeto* system, which continues to the present day, was intimately linked to the first *congregaciones.*

The results of these early reforms can be seen clearly in a 1580 list of congregated towns. They appear to have been established mainly on plains, in mining areas, or along the *caminos reales,* the royal high roads. Mountainous areas remained areas of dispersed habitation controlled from the *cabeceras* by clergy, Crown representatives, and Indian governors. The pandemic and demographic collapse of the late sixteenth century depopulated entire areas. Vacant lands passed into Spanish hands as the few remaining Indians were concentrated in the *congregaciones.* Thus, the *congregaciones* formed part of a general process of spatial reorganization of the indigenous population brought about by the new economic priorities of the colonizers.

The *congregación* program was virtually halted following the death of Viceroy Luis de Velasco, but toward the end of the sixteenth century it was given a new lease on life as a second *congregación* program was instituted by Velasco's successors, Gaspar de Zúñiga and Juan de Mendoza y Luna. A new demographic collapse brought about by the epidemics of 1576–1581 and 1599 provided the opportunity to further concentrate the indigenous population. Nonetheless, the new *congregación* program was not supported by the clergy and was more bureaucratic in nature.

In each district the *congregación* program was implemented by *comisarios* (administrators) and *jueces de congregación* (*congregación* judges), who conducted *visitas,* or tours of inspection, in 1598 and 1599. Thanks to the information they collected we have far more extensive information about this second program. The final phase of the *congregación* program was the concentration of the population in *congregaciones.* Over the space of a few days, each family was assigned a lot where it could build its house. The process was formally concluded a few months later when the *comisario* visited the new houses. Nonetheless, the program was brought to an end in 1604, when a royal decree ordered greater that the policy of *congregación* not be applied so strictly. Demographic recovery permitting, many of the Indians who had been resettled in *congregaciones* returned to their places of origin in the seventeenth century.

Select Bibliography

Dehouve, Danièle, *Quand les banquiers étaient des Saints, 450 ans de l'histoire économique et sociale d'une province indienne du Mexique.* Paris: Centre National de la Recherche Scientifique, 1990.

————, *Entre el caimán y el jaguar: Los pueblos indios de Guerrero.* Mexico City: Centro de Investigaciones y Estudios Superiores en Antropología Social, Instituto Nacional Indigenista, 1994.

García Martínez, Bernardo, *Los pueblos de la sierra, el poder y el espacio entre los indios del norte de Puebla hasta 1700.* Mexico City: Colegio de México, 1987.

Gerhard, Peter, "Congregaciones de indios en la Nueva España antes de 1570." *Historia Mexicana* 26:3 (1977).

Simpson, Lesley B., *Studies in the Administration of the Indians in New Spain.* Berkeley and Los Angeles: University of California Press, 1934.

—Danièle Dehouve

CONQUEST

This entry contains six articles that discuss the Spanish conquest of the territory that eventually would become New Spain:

Conquest: Spanish Background
Conquest: Central Mexico
Conquest: Yucatán
Conquest: Northern Mexico
Conquest: Ecological Impact
Conquest: Conquest Narratives

See also Catholic Church; Congregación; Conquistadors; Criollismo; Encomienda; Family and Kinship: Colonial; Gender and Sexuality: Colonial; Hacienda; Llorona, La; Malinche and Malinchismo; Mesoamerica; Mestizaje; Migration; Politics and Government; Population: Colonial; Region and Regionalism; Rural Economy and Society; Rural Resistance and Rebellion; Trade and Markets; Tribute

CONQUEST: SPANISH BACKGROUND

Spain and Portugal, the two great peninsular kingdoms of the modern age, were notable for their precocious colonizing impulse. Placed at the *finis terrae* of the known world, naval powers by necessity, Christian powers by both conviction and convenience, the peninsular nations flung themselves eagerly into enterprise on the high seas. Tacked to the back of Europe like a watchtower over the Atlantic, first line of fire in the battle against Islam, they aspired to a leadership that had little to do with their position on the geographical sidelines. A long history of colonizations and invasions had branded the peoples of the Iberian Peninsula with a peculiar distrust toward the outside. Moreover, their medieval past had been quite distinct from that of other Europeans, marked by rivalry and war more often than by peace and harmony.

The various ethnic groups long settled in Spain found their differences exacerbated by the geographical characteristics of the terrain they inhabited, as by their contacts, cordial or otherwise, with unfamiliar peoples and cultures. The south and east, opening on the Mediterranean, had assimilated Graeco-Roman cultural patterns centuries before the advent of the Christian age; these regions subsequently maintained trade relations with and even political sway over Italy, Greece, southern France, and northern Africa. The north and west, on the other hand, remained attached to vestigial pagan cults while facing a far more perilous sea. Thus they remained entrenched in isolation until the Lower Middle Ages (eighth through eleventh centuries), when they began to court maritime adventure along Europe's Atlantic seaboard. The central plateau—a land short on natural resources, supporting a people insensible to the finer points of classical civilizations—fought to maintain its independence, making war into a way of life and adopting a readily fanatical, uncompromising brand of religiosity that frequently took the upper hand.

From the Roman presence onward, there were repeated attempts to unify the whole peninsula, each so shaky that it immediately failed. The barbarian groups that conquered the Hispanic provinces after the fall of the Roman Empire were hard-pressed to sustain their own precarious unity under the Wisigoth command, established in the central region, but preceded in Hispania by the Vandals (settled in modern-day Andalusia), the Sweves (in Galicia), and the Alani (in Lusitania, today's Portugal). There were other peoples who had not been Romanized and still others, of Latin language and culture, who only accepted the Teutonic yoke under duress.

The Muslims, goaded by the preaching of a holy war, routed the Wisigoth army in 711 and within seven years spread their dominion over virtually the whole peninsula. However, the disproportion between their moderate numbers and the extensive lands beneath their control prevented this from being a wholesale occupation, especially since armed resistance was immediately launched by rebellious enclaves of Hispano-Romans who had retreated from the Crescent Moon to the highlands of Asturias and the Pyrenees. Thus began the slow wresting back of territory, celebrated as the Reconquista. Until that moment, the ideal of unity always had come hand in hand with invasion; but now, a mystique of national regeneration took hold, built around religious faith inasmuch as Islam and Christianity were the two forces pitted against one another on Iberian soil.

The war between Spanish Christians and African Muslims (who were dubbed Moors, though not all came from Mauritania) lasted almost eight centuries, from 718 (the Battle of Covadonga) until 1492 (the fall of Granada). By the thirteenth century, Spanish kingdoms had obtained papal recognition for their Crusade, with all attendant privileges for those who fought under such a banner.

The movement of reconquest crept from north to south, in campaigns separated by intervals of peace and conducted with varying intensity, according to the strength of the enemy and the level of squabbling among the Christian realms. As a rule, the spells of peaceful coexistence were longer than those of struggle and intolerance. The powerful Caliphate of Cordova splintered into small kingdoms that gave way one by one before the defenders of the Cross. In a series of pacts and treaties, the advancing peninsular rulers partitioned the territories assigned to each, right down to the southern coast. The kingdom of Aragon, linked since the thirteenth century to the county of Barcelona, accomplished its share of the Reconquista in good time and proceeded to pursue its interests in the Mediterranean. This policy led it to dominate parts of France, Italy, and Greece and brought it into conflict with the sultanates of North Africa.

The realms of Castile were joined and parted several times in wills and in wars, until Portugal won its independence and Asturias, Galicia, León, and the original county of Castile were definitively united in the kingdom of that name. Castile completed the expulsion of the Moors from Granada in 1492 and its monarchs were henceforth called Catholic—unlike their predecessors, whose title had been "Of the Three Faiths," since both Muslims and Jews had been their vassals. Shortly afterward, the kingdom of Navarre was united with Castile in the person of Fernando the Catholic, to create the largest, richest, and most populous kingdom in the peninsula.

The marriage of Isabel I of Castile to her cousin Fernando II of Aragon in 1469 amalgamated two very different realms in terms of territorial extension, economic potential, demographic numbers, ethnic composition, political aspirations, and social relations. The Aragonese regarded the power of Castile with understandable misgivings, fearing that such a union might prove counter to their interest. Indeed, under the Hapsburg monarchs in the sixteenth and seventeenth centuries, the court sat either at Toledo, Madrid, or Valladolid, all in Castile; only exceptionally, and for brief periods, did it move to Barcelona, Zaragoza, or Valencia, the most important cities of Aragon.

The experience of war with a religious justification, the experience of living side by side with other religions, and the missionary urge produced by both had become part and parcel of the mental makeup of the Spanish people at the time of the discovery of America. The chronological coincidence between the termination of any Arab presence in Spain and the appearance of new lands over the ocean spurred the religious ardor of the Catholic monarchs and many of their servants, for none could doubt the perpetuation of Castile's destiny as God's instrument for the expansion of the true faith. When Elio Antonio de Nebrija presented Isabel with his *Gramática castellana* at the camp in Santa Fé de Granada, he still assumed that southward expansion would be directed across the straits toward Morocco. His phrase "language has ever been the handmaiden of empire" encapsulated a fundamental aspect of colonial policy. The opening of a New World unexpectedly broadened the possibilities of expansion; now that the whole of Spanish soil was safely under the Cross, the hour had come to carry it into infidel territory.

The memory of a lengthy but triumphant war against Islam was never far away at the moment of elaborating governmental dispositions concerning the New World. The attempts to evangelize the Muslims of Granada, the boarding schools for the sons of Moorish noblemen, the rules of dress and personal adornment, and the tireless vigilance for signs of heresy—all these were the model for subsequent missions to the Americas. Even more useful was the familiarity with Arabic text transcribed into Latin characters, an adaptation that had been current for several hundred years among Mozarabs, or Spanish Christians living under Muslim rule. By the end of the fifteenth century, the conquest and colonization of the Canary islands, a Spanish bridgehead in the Atlantic near the African coast, constituted the immediate precedent for the American undertaking.

Ever since the Turks mopped up the remains of the Byzantine Empire, trade with the Far East had become difficult, expensive, and occasionally impossible. Goods and spices from China and Southeast Asia were highly prized by Europeans, who could no longer do without them. Portugal led the quest for a southern naval route to Asia, and its sailors explored the African coasts, drew maps, defined the most practical itineraries, and embarked on massive slave-trading to pay for it all. This human commerce was to reach its peak with the high demand for labor in American sugar and cotton plantations. Ten years after Columbus landed at Guanahaní, Vasco da Gama reached India, marking the culmination of the Portuguese journeys.

In search of a western approach to the coveted Spice Islands, Christopher Columbus came across lands that were called the Indies from then on, although by 1505 it was clear that this was not Asia but an unknown land mass. From the outset, the conquest of the new continent fell to Castile, and the great majority of explorers, conquistadors, settlers, and officials who traveled to the Indies were natives of that kingdom. They negotiated with Pope Alexander VI the concession of rights over all lands discovered or awaiting discovery. Both the Portuguese and the Spaniards claimed their conquests justified by the barbarity of African and American peoples, and sanctified by the duty to save their souls; both clamored to the Holy See for approval of what they considered to be their rights. In response to these demands, an imaginary line was drawn dividing the world into two hemispheres, the east for Portugal and the west for Castile. On the basis of this ambiguous papal verdict, a discussion of actual borders was conducted in the town of Tordesillas. The meridian traced on that occasion enabled the Portuguese to occupy, as well as their Asian colonies, a portion of the new continent corresponding to modern Brazil. Castile had the Pope's blessing to appropriate the rest of America, and also managed to plant its flag in the Philippine Islands of south-

east Asia. Portuguese and Spanish fleets thus had multiple occasion to cross one other on the high seas, with resulting in frequent showdowns and skirmishes. The first circumnavigation of the globe was completed by a Castilian, with a fleet that began its voyage under Portuguese command.

Early explorations of the West Indian islands and mainland coastlines proved disappointing in terms of profit, for neither jewels nor precious metals were found, neither spices nor artistic treasures such as those described by Marco Polo in his accounts of Cipango and Cathay (Japan and China). The subjugation of Mexico inaugurated a new stage, in which silver became both the motive for conquest and the means of financing costly campaigns and cumbersome bureaucracies; the entire world economy was affected by the plentiful production of this metal and consequent decline in its price, which destabilized the anterior equilibrium. The Spanish empire encompassed a vast territory that it never explored or measured with precision. The riches it yielded promptly vanished into the coffers of the Royal Treasury, to be squandered on interest payments against the king's debts or on all kinds of goods that were no longer manufactured in Castile. Even humble households indulged in bedlinen from Holland, hangings from Rouen, carpets from Turkey, and velvet or silk cushions from Italy, France, or China, as we know from dowry agreements involving quite modest sums of money.

The precarious alliance of the "Spains," as the joined provinces were called in some documents, was almost broken by the death of Queen Isabel la Católica and her husband's new nuptials with Germaine de Foix. But Fernando's second marriage was childless and the kingdom of Aragon remained permanently wedded to Castile with the accession of Queen Juana, whose madness prevented her from ruling. With the premature death of her husband Felipe, Cardinal Ximénez de Cisneros was appointed regent until Carlos should come of age—the young grandson of the Catholic Kings who was brought up in Flanders and years later would fulfill his aspiration to the imperial throne of Germany.

The reign of Carlos I of Spain (also crowned Emperor Charles V of Germany) was distinguished by its involvement in European politics. This activity befitted Carlos not only as German emperor but also as the tireless antagonist of Francis I of France, as the champion of Aragon's territorial ambitions in Italy, the bulwark of papism against Protestantism, and the instigator of the Council of Trent, in which Spanish theologians played a prominent role. During the early years of his reign he had to deal with serious movements of revolt, among the nobility (the so-called Communities of Castile) and among the artisans of Valencia (the "Germanías" of Aragon). These protests found an echo among the many who were angered by the young monarch's moves to curb seigneurial privilege and undermine common law, his imposition of new taxes, his authoritarianism, and those European enterprises that struck many Castilians as ill-advised. The rebels were put down by force, popular discontent found other targets and Spain, like the rest of European countries, stepped into a new historical epoch on the brink of modernity.

Castilian politics were only temporarily and superficially modified by Carlos's imperial adventurism. His marriage to a Portuguese princess favored the interests of Castile, soothing its yearning for an undivided peninsula with the hope that future matches between the heirs of both realms might culminate sooner or later in unification. Such hopes were short-lived. After 1580, Felipe II held on to both crowns through force rather than by any legitimacy of parentage; Felipe III kept them yet more precariously together and Felipe IV was forced to separate them, granting Portugal its independence in 1640.

It was under Carlos I that Fernando (Hernán) Cortés struck out for Mexico and found himself conquering the Mexica Empire. Carlos, busy as ever with wars and treaties, was nonetheless struck by the potential of this new conquest as soon as he laid eyes on samples of the Mexica lords' treasures, including fine pieces of worked gold and silver ingots corresponding to the king's portion, the Royal Fifth. Mines were being discovered in quick succession: first Taxco, Zacualpan, Sultepec, Temascaltepec y Pachuca; soon after, Zacatecas; and in the following century, Guanajuato. Meanwhile, Peruvian gold and the contents of the "silver hill" at Potosí were poured into sustaining the imperial pomp clung to by a permanently debt-ridden and bankrupt metropolis.

Aragon was sufficiently on the margins of Castilian undertakings to devote some energy to its economic development, and maintain steady population growth; this suffered a severe setback at the beginning of the seventeenth century, when political expediency inspired an order to expel all the *moriscos* (converted Moors) from the territories under Spanish rule. The Mediterranean tradition of smallholding agriculture and many crafts and trades were shattered by this measure.

Meanwhile, Castile was being drained of its lifeblood: American emigration was taking its toll on the population, while the lavish unearned income from overseas was not only a disincentive to consolidate what had been a budding but prosperous textile industry; it also was thrown away consistently on the importation of luxury goods.

Although Felipe II could boast that the sun never set over his dominions, Spanish power was already sinking into twilight. Incessant war, state debts, neglect of production, and endemic corruption at every level of government were eroding the foundations of the empire. The ills of the metropolis had repercussions in the farthest outreaches of the colonies, for American silver was financing no more than an artificial prosperity, enough to maintain Spain's ostentatious court and its hitherto invincible regiments, which now began to taste defeat.

Throughout the reigns of the last three Hapsburg kings in the seventeenth century, Spain maintained the appearances of a spurious grandeur: neither the infantry nor the navy, neither financial nor human capital sustained this fiction. At the same time, local elites were gaining strength in the colonies, networks of regional influences were being created, and new, economically powerful groups emerged, ready to defy the representatives of the metropolis.

Select Bibliography

Bennassar, Bartolomé, *La España del siglo de oro.* Barcelona: Crítica Grijalbo, 1983.
_____, *Historia de los españoles.* 2 vols., Barcelona: Editorial Crítica, 1989.
Dominguez Ortiz, Antonio, *Instituciones y sociedad en la España de los Austrias.* Barcelona: Ariel, 1985.
Garcia Sanz, Angel, *Desarrollo y crisis del Antiguo Régimen en Castilla la Vieja.* Madrid: Akal, 1977.
Garrido Aranda, Antonio, *Moriscos e indios. Precedentes hispánicos de la evangelización en México.* Mexico City: UNAM, 1980.
Kamen, Henry, *Una sociedad conflictiva: España, 1469–1714.* Madrid: Alianza Editorial, 1984.

—Pilar Gonzalbo Aizpuru

CONQUEST: CENTRAL MEXICO

On April 21, 1519, a Spanish fleet led by an obscure Spaniard named Fernando (Hernán) Cortés reached San Juan Ulúa on the Veracruz coast of the Gulf of Mexico. The expedition came officially on behalf of the governor of Cuba, Diego Velázquez, who was eager to conquer new lands in his own right, but who was still a mere deputy of Christopher Columbus's heir and admiral of the Indies, Diego Colón. For at least two years now Velázquez had been trying to break free from Colón's jurisdiction: he had sent out the exploring and trading expeditions of Hernández de Córdoba and Juan de Grijalva in 1517 and 1518, and he had dispatched personal agents to Spain to urge the Crown to grant him the title of *adelantado* of Yucatán, with the right to conquer and settle the region. Clearly, Velázquez's initiative to send Cortés in search of Grijalva's fleet and of any Christians held captive in Yucatán was intended to keep his claims alive while he awaited the Crown's decision. What remains somewhat of a mystery is his choice of Cortés to lead the new venture; the future conqueror had no experience, although he might have had the financial means to secure his appointment as captain by contributing substantially to the cost of the expedition.

There is, in fact, enough evidence to suggest that Velázquez himself was having second thoughts about the wisdom of his choice, and that he was becoming apprehensive about Cortés's increasing power and even tried to prevent him from being supplied with provisions. In these circumstances, it is not surprising that when Cortés heard that Grijalva's fleet had returned safely to Cuba, he decided to leave swiftly, before Velázquez had time to prevent him. From this moment he found himself in a delicate and highly dubious position, both in relation to Velázquez and to the Spanish Crown, and it is no great surprise that as soon as he learned about the existence of a powerful ruler called Moteuczoma II, his mind was set firmly on reaching him and somehow persuading him to acknowledge the sovereignty of Queen Juana and her son Carlos, for this was the one sure way to justify and legitimate his original act of rebellion.

The existence of Moteuczoma II was confirmed by a group of Indians sent by Tentil, the Mexica (Aztec) governor of the region, who came to meet Cortés at San Juan Ulúa. On subsequent days the Indians returned loaded with lavish gifts from the Mexica, among which were found objects commonly offered to the gods.

The gesture can be interpreted as an open acknowledgment that the Spaniards were gods, and it is often used in support of the legend that Muteuczoma might have thought that Cortés was Quetzalcoatl, the ancient deity who had left for the east and promised to return. There is, however, no contemporary evidence to support this, and it is almost certainly a later reinterpretation of the events. To insist on it, moreover, obscures the more significant fact that, to Cortés and his followers, the presentation of gifts would have appeared as an admission of conditional subservience and subordination. Through the gifts, in other words, the Mexica were acknowledging Cortés's superior rights; but at the same time they demanded that he not go to the Mexica capital of Tenochtitlan and that he move his camp away from San Juan Ulúa. When, a few days later, five Totonac Indians came to offer their services to Cortés, the reasons why Tentil had expressed concern about the Spanish presence in the area became clearer: Cortés now realized that the Mexica had enemies, and this made the prospect of conquest feasible.

In all these exchanges Cortés had the invaluable help of two interpreters: the Spaniard Jerónimo de Aguilar, who had been shipwrecked in Yucatán around 1511 and had lived among the Maya until he managed to escape and join Cortés's fleet as it passed by on its way to Veracruz in 1519; and doña Marina, one of the 20 Indian women that the people of Coatzacoalcos presented to Cortés in March 1519. She was bilingual in Nahuatl and Maya, and would soon learn Spanish and become Cortés's main interpreter. In the early stages, however, the collaboration of Aguilar was essential: Nahuatl messages were translated by doña Marina into Maya and by Aguilar into Spanish.

Once his mind was made up about conquest, Cortés's priority was to consolidate the support of his followers and to set it firmly upon legal grounds. Given his highly equivocal legal position the issue was especially delicate, but Cortés's solution was masterly. His first step was to found the town of Villa Rica de la Vera Cruz, with its own legal structure and town council. According to Spanish legal tradition, this meant that the new town could function as a political entity directly under the authority of the king. After deciding that the authority granted by Velázquez had lapsed, since the expedition had now fulfilled the governor's mandate, the town council—which had been appointed by Cortés himself—elected their leader as captain. The initiative freed Cortés from the legal restraints placed on him by Velázquez, but it also made it essential for him to succeed in his plan for conquest; for if he failed he would still be liable to the charge of treason against one of the king's governors.

It was in this state of mind that Cortés marched to Cempoala, the nearby town of the Totonacs who had come to the Spanish camp to offer their services. At Cempoala, where he arrived on June 3, Cortés confirmed that the Totonacs were eager to support him against the Mexica, to whom they paid allegiance out of fear rather than loyalty. Cortés would be careful to exploit such political cleavages and grievances among the Mexica tributaries. Accordingly, from now on he adopted a consistent policy of "divide and rule," forging an alliance with the Totonacs and enlisting their much-needed support for the march to Tenochtitlan, while sending persistent signals of friendship to the Mexica.

At this stage, it seemed as if Cortés's plans for conquest would face more opposition from the Spanish than from the Indian side. Upon his return to Veracruz, Cortés learned that King Carlos I (Emperor Charles V) had given Velázquez authority to trade and to found settlements. Cortés responded by sending the king, on July 26, all the gold collected so far, in addition to the royal fifth to which Spanish monarchs legally were entitled. Rumors of Cortés's intention reached Velázquez, who failed to capture the ship and then began preparations for a large fleet under Pánfilo de Narváez to capture Cortés. The situation became especially urgent for Cortés when it was discovered that there were a number of supporters of Velázquez among Cortés's followers, some of whom were conspiring to sail to Cuba. Cortés could afford to take no chances. Swiftly he had the two principal conspirators hanged, the pilot's feet cut off, and the sailors lashed. He then stripped the ten remaining ships of their anchors, sails, and cables and sank them. With no hope of returning to Cuba, Velázquez's potential supporters had no choice but to side with Cortés, who then put Juan de Escalante in charge of Veracruz with about 100 soldiers and, with the vital help of the Totonacs, began the slow march to Tenochtitlan.

Progress was smooth until the Spaniards approached Tlaxcala in early September. The Tlaxcaltecs were well known for their hostility to the Mexica, and Cortés naturally hoped to enlist their support. Yet the fact that the bulk of Indians traveling with Cortés were Mexica tributaries made the Tlaxcaltecs suspicious, and accordingly they attacked the Spaniards with unprecedented ferocity and determination. The Tlaxcaltecs were skilled soldiers who attacked in unison using both shock and projectile weapons with great expertise. They posed a much greater threat to Cortés's forces than he had imagined. In normal circumstances, the most prudent policy from the military point of view would have been to withdraw.

The threat to Cortés, however, was not merely military but, above all, strategic. Withdrawal would inevitably have been seen as a sign of weakness that would have done irreparable damage to the fragile alliance with the Totonacs. Under the circumstances, Cortés was wise to adopt a defensive stance from where he could make use of Spanish crossbows, harquebuses, and rapid-firing artillery to beat back Indian attacks. The tactic was successful; but given the Tlaxcaltec's overwhelming numerical superiority and the rapid dwindling of Spanish provisions and projectiles, it was a precarious and emphatically short-term solution.

Cortés knew that a continuing defensive strategy soon would degenerate into a war of attrition that the Tlaxcaltecs inevitably would win. He therefore wisely combined his defensive strategy with messages of peace, threats, and quick attacks on neighboring villages with the purpose of obtaining provisions and terrorizing the local populations. Gradually, the Tlaxcaltecs began to reconsider their position. Since Tlaxcala was governed jointly by the rulers of four confederated kingdoms, support for the war depended upon reaching a consensus among these rulers. As the war wore on, and as Tlaxcaltec casualties increased, support for the war waned. Once the Spaniards were recognized as a major military force, the Tlaxcaltecs gradually were persuaded by the obvious advantages of seeking an alliance with them. The decision was made in the hope of being able to shift the balance of power against the relentless advance of the Mexica.

The Tlaxcaltec decision to seek an alliance was a momentous triumph for Cortés. He had had enough problems trying to keep the peace in his own camp, where many of his men were near mutiny. Once in Tlaxcala, Cortés learned that the Mexica ruler Moteuczoma II had not been able to conquer his newly acquired allies, despite repeated attempts. This lead him to suppose that the Mexica military power was roughly comparable to the Tlaxcaltec. This impression, he was later to realize, was based on a gross misunderstanding of Mexica military tactics and of their puzzling reluctance to attack the Spaniards, which Cortés at the time interpreted as a sign of weakness. For the moment, however, the misunderstanding meant that the slow march to Tenochtitlan would continue.

The Spaniards stayed in Tlaxcala for two weeks before resuming their march on October 10. For reasons that probably will never be entirely clear, they decided to go via Cholula, a city traditionally allied to Tlaxcala and Huejotzingo but which recently had become an ally of the Mexica. There they were housed and fed for two days. Then Cortés made one of his most puzzling decisions: he ordered a massacre of unarmed Cholultecs, including the king, the cream of the army, and a number of important leaders, whom he had asked to assemble in the main courtyard.

The Spanish accounts are unanimous in their agreement that the massacre was necessary because the Cholultecs were planning to attack them with the help of a Mexica army, but there is no clear evidence to support this. It seems more likely that the attack was suggested by the Tlaxcaltecs, who had a much better understanding of the internal divisions of the Cholultec system, and attempted to exploit the situation in order to open the field for a pro-Tlaxcaltec successor to the massacred king. Although the attack inevitably would put the Spaniards in opposition to Moteuczoma, it also cemented Cortés's friendship with the Tlaxcaltecs and served as a lesson to Cholula for its recent change of allegiances, a lesson that, from Cortés's point of view, might also shake the confidence of other Mexica allies. More importantly, Moteuczoma now was aware that the new king of Cholula had assumed power with Spanish help. So, too, he must have been acutely sensitive to the potentially dissident groups within his own region. Any opposition to Cortés might easily turn these groups against him and endanger his own position. In the circumstances, his choice to welcome the Spaniards into Tenochtitlan, where he greeted them on November 8—a mere six-and-one-half months after they had landed in San Juan Ulúa—was not a sign of weakness or ineptitude, but a carefully considered and logical decision.

Even as they entered Tenochtitlan, the precariousness of their situation must have begun to dawn on the Spaniards. The Mexica capital was a formidable city by any standards, far beyond anything that the Spaniards had encountered before, either in America or in Europe. Its location on an island, moreover, meant that it would not take much effort for the Mexica to trap the Spaniards. It is no surprise that many of Cortés's followers began to suspect that Moteuczoma had allowed them in as part of a dubious strategy to finish them off in the easiest possible way. Soon after their arrival, moreover, news reached Cortés that a Spanish force sent by Escalante to defend the Totonacs against a Mexica attack had been defeated. Fearing that the news would entice other allies to defect, yet unable to leave Tenochtitlan to deal with the situation himself, Cortés again deployed his remarkable instinct for leadership by taking what is perhaps his most memorable and momentous initiative: on November 14, he approached Moteuczoma and seized him.

The ease with which Moteuczoma submitted to Cortés continues to puzzle historians, and understandably so. It often has been seen as yet another sign of indecision and weakness. From Moteuczoma's point of view, however, the situation was rather more delicate. A refusal to cooperate with Cortés would have brought the Mexica political system to a standstill and threatened Moteuczoma's authority against the claims of the many contenders to the throne in the region, especially those who had opposed the Spanish entry into the city. Cortés tried to use Moteuczoma's friendship and willingness to cooperate to the best possible advantage;

but he could not have understood the intricacies of the way in which the Mexica tributaries were integrated into the Mexica state, and of the nature and limits of the king's power. Control of the tributaries, for instance, depended on cooperation rather than on coercion. Such cooperation, moreover, required confidence in the Mexica king's authority and ability to act effectively. Although Cortés controlled Moteuczoma, he often persuaded him to take decisions that were actually contrary to Mexica interests. This led to a marked erosion of support for Moteuczoma among the people and the nobility, and to a consequent rise in the vulnerability of the Spanish position, a situation about which the Spaniards themselves were not fully aware.

Meanwhile, Pánfilo de Narváez's expedition from Cuba had been making slow progress and eventually landed at San Juan Ulúa in late April 1520. As soon as the news reached Cortés, he placed Pedro de Alvarado in charge of Tenochtitlan and marched to the coast. He reached Cempoala in late May, launched a surprise attack after midnight, captured Narváez, had him imprisoned, forced his men to surrender, and persuaded them to join him. He then began the march back to Tenochtitlan with an army of approximately 1,300 men. On their way they were joined by some 2,000 Tlaxcaltec warriors.

The renewed Spanish army entered Tenochtitlan unopposed on June 24. Cortés's confidence was partly the result of precedent. After all, he had entered Tenochtitlan before, and with a much smaller army. Now, however, the situation had changed quite dramatically. During Cortés's absence, Pedro de Alvarado had massacred thousands of Mexica nobles during the May festival of Toxcatl in honor of the god Hitzilopochtli. His motive was that he thought the Mexica were about to attack the Spaniards. The massacre caused disarray and confusion among the Mexica: their forces had been decimated and their very best soldiers had been killed. Although it could be said that in strictly military terms the massacre was a coup for the Spaniards, politically it proved an irreparable mistake. Not only did it turn the tide definitively against them, but it led to the complete withdrawal of support for Moteuczoma. Cortés was aware that the situation had deteriorated, but he was still confident that he could control the situation with Moteuczoma's assistance. His decision to reenter Tenochtitlan thus was taken on the basis of a very inadequate understanding of the mechanisms of Mexica kingship, and it proved to be his most disastrous tactical mistake.

Tenochtitlan had become a trap, and by the time of Cortés's return the Spaniards had been besieged in Moteuczoma's quarters for about three weeks. Their reinforced military power proved useless against the relentlessness of Mexica resistance. Having failed to negotiate a withdrawal, Cortés persuaded Moteuczoma to order the Mexica to stop the attack and brought him out onto the roof, but he was struck down and died. Whether Moteuczoma was killed by the stones thrown by the Mexica, as Spanish accounts aver, or killed by the Spaniards, as Indian testimonies would have us

believe, probably will never be known with certainty. The Spanish version seems the most probable; but the Indian account is plausible, given that the Spaniards by now would have realized that Moteuczoma had become a liability. Besides, the official period of mourning for a dead king would have given them a welcome respite.

However that may be, it was now blatantly clear to Cortés that the only option was to flee. He also must have been painfully aware that such a display of weakness would inevitably affect his political alliances, but now the only alternative was death. So in the middle of a heavy rainstorm, late in the evening on June 30, the Spaniards began their escape. They were attacked and many Spaniards were killed along with most of the Tlaxcaltecs and Huejotzincas and some horses. Many were trapped and forced to return to their quarters where they were later killed. All the cannons were lost.

Cortés finally reached Tacuba. From there, he began the march to the north and round the lakes toward Tlaxcala. Mexica assaults continued, but the fighting was now relatively light by comparison, and the Spaniards resumed their defensive formations to maximize the effectiveness of the weapons they still possessed. More important were the horses, since cavalry charges created gaps that could be exploited easily by troops with swords. By the time they reached Tlaxcala, however, Cortés had lost nearly 900 Spaniards and over 1,000 Tlaxcaltecs, and his remaining 440 Spaniards, 20 horses, 12 crossbowmen, and 7 harquebusiers all were wounded.

Cortés was second to none in his ability to learn from his mistakes. It was now clear to him that Tenochtitlan never could be conquered without first establishing a secure line of communications with the coast, which was his only source of supply for reinforcements. Additionally, he needed to reestablish firm alliances with the Indians, especially Mexica tributaries, in order to secure a steady supply of food. For the purpose, Cortés could take advantage of some recent developments he had been studying with care, foremost among which was Mexica factionalism. Even while under assault from the Mexica, Cortés had noticed that many of their tributaries were only too willing to lend him their support. This suggested that allegiance to the Mexica was effective only insofar as a mutual interest existed. Beyond that, loyalty was entirely dependent on fear of Mexica reprisals. Aware of this, Cortés adopted a policy of gradual, piecemeal conquests of Mexica tributaries, a policy that he was careful to combine with promises of protection against Mexica reprisals to facilitate quick shifts in allegiance. A key moment in this strategy was the conquest of Tepeyacac, where Cortés founded and fortified the town of La Villa de la Segura de la Frontera, which he used as a base for Spanish reinforcements and for retaliation against Mexica allies. From Tepeyacac, too, Cortés engineered a number of regional conquests that gradually secured him control of most major towns from Cholula to Ahuilizapan, where the road descended to Veracruz.

In late December, Cortés felt confident to begin the slow march back to the Valley of Mexico. He had 8 cannons, 550 Spanish soldiers (including 40 horsemen), and 10,000 Tlaxcaltec soldiers. Near the great city of Texcoco, Cortés was approached by a group of nobles who invited the Spaniards into the city. Their motive was to take advantage of Cortés's presence in order to shift the political balance against Tenochtitlan and end years of political divisions and dynastic crises. The new alliance, engineered by Ixtlilxochitl, gave Cortés an ideal base for his attack, and it brought with it the automatic allegiance of some adjacent subordinate towns, such as Otompan, that depended on support from Texcoco.

Gaining the loyalty of other areas proved more difficult. The area around Chalco, for instance, long had been antagonistic to Tenochtitlan, and it was of enormous strategic importance to Cortés, since it lay on the road to the coast. Quick to realize this, the Mexica subjected the area to repeated assaults.

Although the Spaniards were generally successful against Mexica attacks—particularly when they could face the Mexica on open ground—there were so many towns on the eastern side of the lakes that Cortés could not possibly hope to defend them all. Paradoxically, therefore, Spanish expansion only served to compound Cortés's problems. The only solution was to take the offensive and strike directly at Tenochtitlan. Yet, any such action would bring the Spaniards closer to the lakes; and there, the Mexica would use the great mobility of their canoes to force the Spanish back, as they consistently had done. If the conquest was to succeed, therefore, Cortés needed to gain control of the lakes. It was no doubt with this in mind that, early in February, he ordered the construction of 13 brigantines.

The ships were launched on April 28, 1521. Each could hold 12 oarsmen, 12 crossbowmen and harquebusiers, a captain, and artillerymen to control a cannon mounted in the bow. The launching was coordinated with the mainland offensive, which was divided into three armies. The first one was lead by Pedro de Alvarado and went to Tacuba with 30 horsemen, 18 crossbowmen and harquebusiers, 150 Spanish soldiers, and 25,000 Tlaxcaltecs. A second army, lead by Cristóbal de Olid, was sent to Coyoacan with 20 crossbowmen and harquebusiers, 175 Spanish soldiers, and 20,000 Indians. Finally Gonzalo de Sandoval was sent to Ixtapalapa with 24 horsemen, 25 crossbowmen and harquebusiers, and over 30,000 Indians. The choice of these cities was not by chance. Each of them controlled access to a major causeway linking them to Tenochtitlan, and their control allowed Cortés to initiate a calculated strategy of starving out the defenders by cutting off the Mexica capital's supplies of food and water.

Their first mission accomplished, Sandoval and Olid returned to join Alvarado at Tacuba and began the slow march to Tenochtitlan along the causeway. Despite their technological superiority, the sheer mass of Mexica defenders was overwhelming, and the initial assault was forced back

with heavy losses. Meanwhile Cortés had had the chance to prove the superiority of his brigantines against the Mexica canoes in a naval engagement just off the fortified island of Tepepolco. Their effectiveness greatly complicated the Mexica defensive strategy, which hitherto had been concentrated along the narrow fronts where causeways ran. Now the Spaniards could land forces virtually anywhere around the Valley of Mexico and bring artillery into range of many areas of Tenochtitlan that the Mexica had assumed safe.

With this new advantage, the Spaniards began to make more progress along the causeways. The Mexica responded with a number of tactics that still managed to keep the Spaniards off balance. Foremost among these was the astute use of feigned withdrawals and ambushes, whereby the Spaniards would be drawn forward and then cut off and counterattacked. On June 30 the Mexica feigned one such withdrawal against Cortés, who pursued them, neglecting to fill a breach before he crossed. The Mexica then sent their war canoes into the breach and caught the Spaniards between the two forces. Eight horses and many men were killed, and 68 Spaniards were captured alive, taken to the great temple, sacrificed, flayed, and their faces tanned and sent to allied towns as proof of Spanish mortality and as a warning against betraying the alliance.

Mexica attacks continued during the next few days. For a while it must have seemed as if the tide of battle had turned against Cortés, because most of his Indian allies began to defect and to return home. The most notable exception to this trend was Ixtlilxochitl, who remained at Cortés's side, advising him to continue blocking food and water supplies to Tenochtitlan with the brigantines.

Gradually, Indians began to return from allied towns as the Spaniards took the offensive once again. Yet, news of recent Mexica successes and Spanish vulnerability had led some Mexica allies to attack cities that had allied with the Spanish. Aware of the political consequences that such developments could have on the balance of power, Cortés was quick to act. As soon as he heard that troops from Malinalco had started an attack on Cuauhnahuac, he sent a force under Andrés de Tapia to rout them. Two days later, Sandoval was sent to the Valley of Toluca to rout the Matlanzincas, who were planning an attack on the Spaniards. The policy was successful in consolidating the support of Cortés's Indian allies and regaining that of those who were beginning to waver; but it ran the danger of diverting attention from Tenochtitlan at a time when men were being lost and gunpowder almost exhausted. Just then, in mid-July, a fleet of Spanish ships reached Veracruz with fresh supplies of ammunition and reinforcements. The event, which Cortés saw as a clear sign of God's favor, allowed the Spaniards to make their final advance into Tenochtitlan.

As they entered the great Mexica capital the Spaniards were attacked from the buildings lining the streets. In response, Cortés ordered his allies to send their farmers to Tenochtitlan to raze the buildings on both sides of their advance. The rubble then was used to fill the breaches to facilitate the troop's access into the city. The Mexica then retreated north to Tlaltelolco, where the causeways were still intact and the brigantines would be less of a threat. But the Spanish advance continued, and eventually reached the great market of Tlaltelolco in early August. Meanwhile, Ixtlilxochitl had captured his brother, Coanacoch, and forced the Texcocans to shift their loyalty to Cortés. On August 13, at the final land assault, the Mexica surrendered. Then the inhabitants of Tenochtitlan were massacred for four days. Cortés had conquered the Mexica with a surviving force of 900 Spaniards, but the crucial role had been played by his 200,000 Indian allies.

Cortés's achievement was remarkable by any standards, but it should be remembered that it was as much a triumph for European disease as for Spanish military prowess. The part played by epidemics, smallpox in particular, in sapping the Indians' ability and will to resist, especially in densely populated areas like central Mexico, is fundamental for understanding the thoroughness of the Spanish success. So too, the internal weaknesses in the structure of the Mexica political system, particularly the repressive nature of their domination, facilitated a revolt by the subjugated peoples against their overlords without which the Spanish conquest would have been unthinkable. As we have seen, however, Cortés's military tactics and political genius played a fundamental and decisive role at every step.

Even more important in the long run was Cortés's conviction that "without settlement there is no good conquest," as Francisco López de Gómara put it. This was a conviction that derived from Cortés's experience in the Antilles, where the absence of a policy of settlement had lead to massive destruction and exploitation. In his desire to prevent a similar development in Mexico, Cortés repeatedly tried to turn soldiers into citizens by creating new towns wherever possible. The first instance of this practice, as we have seen in the foundation of the town at Veracruz, was a purely legal act; but it nevertheless provided the pattern for a similar process of municipal incorporation, which led to the proliferation of cities and towns intended for Spaniards and based on the model of the Spanish town. In this, Cortés displayed unusual

foresight and common sense, and the initiative set an important precedent for the pattern that Spanish settlement of the New World would take. It is true that in order to attract Spanish settlers Cortés had to favor the introduction of the system of *encomienda,* an idea to which he was initially hostile, having witnessed the destruction that it had occasioned in the Antilles. But Cortés's *encomienda* was to be an improved and reformed institution, which was part of the conqueror's vision of a settled society in which Crown, conqueror, and Indian were linked in a chain of reciprocal obligation sanctioned in practice by the mendicant orders. When, eventually, the New Laws of 1542 attempted to abolish the *encomienda,* even the Dominicans declared themselves in its favor in New Spain. The contrast with other regions of Spanish America is immediately evident, and a large proportion of the credit for the relative stability and prosperity that ensued in central Mexico after the conquest must be given to Cortés.

See also Virgin of Guadalupe and Guadalupanismo; Virgin of los Remedios

Select Bibliography

Cortés, Hernán, *Letters from Mexico,* translated and edited by Anthony Pagden. New Haven, Connecticut, and London: Yale University Press, 1986.

Elliott, John H., "The Mental World of Hernán Cortés." *Transactions of the Royal Historical Society* 17 (1967).

Hassig, Ross, *Mexico and the Spanish Conquest.* London and New York: Longman, 1994.

León Portilla, Miguel, *The Broken Spears: The Aztec Account of the Conquest of Mexico.* Boston: Beacon Press, 1966.

Sahagún, Bernardino de, *Florentine Codex: General History of the Things of New Spain.* Salt Lake City: University of Utah Press, 1981.

Thomas, Hugh, *The Conquest of Mexico.* London: Pimlico, 1994.

Yáñez, Agustín, editor, *Crónicas de la Conquista de México.* Mexico City: UNAM, 1950.

—FERNANDO CERVANTES

CONQUEST: YUCATÁN

In two short years Fernando (Hernán) Cortés toppled the mightiest empire in Mesoamerica and was rewarded with treasure, tribute, and bountiful Indian labor. Francisco de Montejo's conquest of the Yucatán Peninsula was vastly more prolonged and difficult, and much less bountiful in its reward. From Montejo's first invasion of the peninsula in 1527 to the founding of his capital at Mérida in 1542, Spaniards twice had to abandon Maya territory completely. Even with the suppression of the Great Rebellion of 1546 to 1547, Mayas continued periodically to rebel and resist over the next 150 years, greatly limiting the spread of Spanish control across large parts of what are now the Mexican states of Yucatán, Campeche, and Quintana Roo; the Guatemalan department of the Petén; and the nation of

Belize. The last independent Maya redoubt—Tah Itza in the Péten—finally was conquered in 1697, though by then prolonged Maya resistance and the growing intrusion of pirates and a rival European power had ensured that much of the peninsula would remain only lightly administered by the Spanish and little known to outsiders until well into the twentieth century.

When Montejo landed with 300 men on the east coast across from Cozumel Island in 1527, he could not have taken the Maya completely by surprise. Long before his arrival they knew that Spaniards were coming. Columbus probably made contact with Maya during his final New World voyage in 1502; a shipwreck in 1511 or 1512 dumped Spanish survivors on the peninsular coast; Ponce de Léon seems to have touched there while traveling between Cuba and Florida in 1513; and Indian canoes from the mainland reportedly made periodic contact with the suffering indigenous population of Spanish-ruled Cuba. In those early years Maya prophets began to speak of the coming of bearded strangers who would bring a new religion. Some, like the famed Chilam Balam of Mani, exhorted his Maya audiences to accept the strangers and the new life they brought. Most Maya, however, were not ready to do so, as Hernández de Córdova found when bested in bloody battles in 1517. Subsequent Spanish visitors such as Juan de Grijalva (1518) and Cortés (1519) enjoyed peaceable receptions, as long as they made their stays brief and continued their westward voyages. Montejo, however, armed with a royal commission and the soldiers, horses, and firearms that his own capital and that of his colleagues could finance, came to Yucatán to conquer, to settle, and to rule over a Maya people made loyal subjects of the Spanish Crown.

The east coast of the peninsula was a poor place to begin. Naum Pat, the Maya lord of Cozumel Island, was friendly to the Spaniards, and more than once lent valuable aid. But coastal forests were unhealthful for the Spaniards, and New Spain, from which supplies and new recruits would come, was too far away. Having established a nascent settlement called Salamanca there in 1527, Montejo marched the bulk of his force to the north and then west, searching for a better site to make his capital. The rulers of some of the Maya provinces through which he passed received him peaceably, and those who did not were defeated in battle. Spanish horses, arms, and organization proved time and again effective against vastly superior numbers of Maya warriors wearing cotton armor, wielding nonmetal blades, and hurling light projectiles. Still, by the summer of 1528 Montejo's men had suffered severe attrition to wounds and illness, and dreams of quick riches were fading. What is more, Montejo had discovered how decentralized Maya society was. The capture of a single prize or target would not ensure submission of the entire land, as the capture of Tenochtitlan did for the invaders of central Mexico. Rather, the peninsula was divided into at least 16 separate provinces, each one of which would have to be courted or forced into submission, and any one of which, as long as it remained independent, would pro-

vide a refuge and rallying point for the culturally and linguistically homogenous indigenous population of the peninsula. Understanding now the magnitude of the tasks ahead, Montejo returned to New Spain for supplies and soldiers, eventually abandoning altogether the eastern approach to the conquest of Maya lands.

After pausing to pacify Tabasco, which fell (along with parts of modern-day Guatemala and Honduras) within the domain that the Crown had authorized Montejo to conquer and rule, Montejo returned to the peninsular campaign. This time he approached from the west. Moving from their base in Tabasco, Spanish forces received peaceable receptions from the Maya rulers of the western provinces of Couoh, Canpech, and Ah Canul, and Montejo founded a Spanish settlement near the present-day city of Campeche. By 1531 the conquest of the peninsula seemed well progressed, as Maya rulers around Campeche pledged loyalty and supplied Spaniards with food and labor, though it was slowly dawning upon Mayas that such gifts were in fact tribute that they would be expected to provide in perpetuity. To expand his control of the peninsula, Montejo sent soldiers under his trusted lieutenant, Alonso Dávila, back overland to the east coast to subdue and settle in the Maya province of Chetumal. Soon after Dávila's force set out, however, Mayas around Campeche launched a massive assault upon Montejo's diminished army, while on the other side of the peninsula Dávila was locked in what became months of desperate fighting and siege at Chetumal. Dávila was forced into an extraordinary seven-month retreat down the coast to Honduras, but Montejo managed to defeat the Maya around Campeche and to send his son, also named Francisco de Montejo, to extend the conquest deeper into the interior.

Montejo's son, aided by Maya auxiliaries from friendly western provinces, established a second settlement in the hostile territory of the Cupul amid the ancient Maya ruins of Chichen Itza. There, as had happened before and would happen again, the defeat of initial Maya resistance, pledges of future loyalty from local Maya rulers, and the provision of food and labor deluded the Spaniards into thinking their domination of the Maya was firm. As quickly as possible the Montejos christened their soldiers citizens of the new settlements, assigned houselots and estates, and divided the local indigenous population into *encomiendas* (native settlements "commended" to the care of a Spaniard—an *encomendero*—who, in return for the Indians' labor, had the duty to protect the Indians, maintain missionaries in the villages, and contribute to the military defense of the region). However, around Chichen Itza, as earlier around Campeche, months of quiescence and colonial life was shattered when the Maya attacked in astonishing numbers. After many weeks of destructive warfare, Montejo's son was forced to evacuate Chichen Itza, heading first toward the north coast and eventually linking with his father. Before the Montejos could renew their conquest of hostile Maya provinces, however, the progressive disillusionment and desertion of their colleagues and subordinates forced the would-be conquerors to abandon the peninsula once again. After many months of combat, Spaniards really controlled little more than the immediate environs of their encampments. Protestations of loyalty from Maya rulers could change to deadly hostility without warning. Finally, the peninsula offered little immediate treasure to conquerors who had financed their own participation and that of their subordinates, and the sale of numerous Indian captives into slavery in New Spain or the West Indies was blocked by royal edicts. So when news arrived of the fabulous wealth to be had in the conquest of the Incas and opportunities for lucrative adventure elsewhere in Mesoamerica, only the Montejos and their most die-hard supporters would continue to sacrifice in the war against the Maya. For the time being, they were too few.

Montejo's son led the third invasion of the Yucatán Peninsula, greatly aided by his cousin, also Francisco, while his aged father oversaw the enterprise and occupied himself in the pacification and administration of other parts of his vast domain. This younger Montejo returned to the west coast at the end of 1540, joining a smaller Spanish force that had been sent ahead. Circumstances on the peninsula had changed to favor this latest attempt at permanent conquest. Maya around the Spanish foothold at Champoton— their numbers greatly reduced from flight and probably disease, consequences of earlier episodes in the conquest— were offered perpetual release from tribute and service in return for their cooperation with the Spaniards. Thus the Spanish began to solidify Maya cooperation with the conquest. Maya rulers of other western provinces had other reasons for offering more vigorous support of the Spanish cause this time, as conflicts between western and central Maya provinces had grown more bloody and bitter since the last Spanish invasion, partly in consequence of the seeming collaboration of western Maya with the earlier Spanish forays. This internal conflict aided the conquest. Defeats the Montejos had suffered during the earlier invasion also had taught them valuable lessons, such as not to send expeditions to found settlements deep in hostile territory. This time, instead, they would extend their conquest gradually up the coast and then toward the east in more methodical fashion, subduing each Maya province in turn, founding settlements or strong bases, and ensuring adequate means of communication and supply between them before proceeding on their slow march across the peninsula. Spanish arms always would win the day in pitched battle, although Maya resort to guerrilla war and siege could strain Spanish resolve severely. During the earlier invasions, when the Mayas abandoned their indefensible settlements, plugged up wells, destroyed their own food supplies, and fled into the forest, the Spanish would raid, take captives, steal food, but eventually hunger and the attrition of numerous small skirmishes took their toll on the invaders, as happened to Montejo the son at Chichen Itza or to Dávila around Chetumal. On this, their third attempt to conquer the Maya, Spaniards were better poised to endure such prolonged and bitter resistance, having ensured their own supply from friendly stations in the

west. So one by one the Maya provinces fell, Maya returned to their settlements, and tribute of food, cloth, wax, honey, cacao, and more began to flow.

A broad Maya coalition lead by Nachi Cocom failed to drive the Spaniards from their new capital in 1542, and the Maya suffered heavy casualties that crippled their ability to launch subsequent grand assaults. Maya priests and rulers were able to organize one final, massive attempt to expel the Spaniards, attacking them on the night of November 8–9, 1546. A score of Spaniards caught on their estates were killed, along with hundreds of their Maya supporters, although the main Maya attacks on the Spanish settlement of Valladolid failed and the uprising around Mérida never got properly underway. Months of fighting was necessary to suppress the Maya again, and the alleged leaders of the uprising were executed. The Spaniards emerged from the Great Rebellion as secure rulers of a devastated land. During the conquest up to two-thirds of the Maya of the Yucatán Peninsula may have perished in battle, or to starvation and disease. The Spaniards suffered early, too, with only some 160 of the 700 to 800 who fought with the Montejos surviving to enjoy final victory.

The voice of defiant Maya leaders had not been entirely silenced, and much of the southern portion of the Yucatán Peninsula still lay beyond effective Spanish control. Montejo had sent an expedition back to Chetumal province in 1543 under the command of Gaspar Pacheco and his son and nephew, and that expedition succeeded with the usual difficulty in subduing the Maya of that region. The Pachecos were so brutal and destructive (by the judgment even of their peers) that the land along both sides of the present international boundary between Mexico and Belize, once populous and prosperous, was left sparsely populated and tribute poor, and the local Spanish settlement at Bacalar never became more than a remote and precarious colonial backwater. Meanwhile the focus of resistance to further conquest shifted to the Maya center at Tah Itza on a lake in the Péten, and to allied centers in western Belize (Tipu) and what is today southern Quintana Roo (Ixpimienta). Mayas who found Spanish exactions in the north too onerous, or who otherwise saw opportunity in life on the margins of colonial rule, fled south into those areas. Several efforts to court or force the Itza into submission failed. An uprising in 1638 destroyed most of the still-fragile Spanish colonial structure in the south.

Throughout the seventeenth century colonial authorities periodically sent expeditions to round up the fugitive and independent Maya, and Tah Itza was finally subdued in 1697. By that time, however, pirate attacks along the Caribbean coast and increasing British interest in the forests of the Caribbean rim made permanent Spanish presence in that region untenable, and the Spanish colony that the Montejos established remained largely based in the west, north, and central regions of the peninsula conquered in the third invasion led by Montejo's son. A Maya uprising in the mid–nineteenth century again clearly divided the Yucatán

Peninsula along that old colonial line, with much of what is presently the state of Quintana Roo and part of Campeche resorting to independent or semi-independent Maya rule, until British forces could subdue the troublesome Maya of western Belize and a Mexican army at the turn of the twentieth century once again could pacify the Maya of Quintana Roo. While the Maya of the Yucatán Peninsula could not resist forever the force of Europeans wielding superior weapons, their prolonged, dogged, costly, and often religiously inspired resistance to conquest profoundly shaped the society in which they would live alongside the descendants of the bearded men come from the east; as a result, the Yucatán Peninsula to this day is home to one of the most vital indigenous cultures in the Western Hemisphere.

See also Caste War of Yucatán

Select Bibliography

Chamberlain, Robert S., *The Conquest and Colonization of Yucatán, 1517–1550.* Washington, D.C.: The Carnegie Institution, 1948.

Clendinnen, Inga, *Ambivalent Conquests: Maya and Spaniard in Yucatán, 1517–1570.* New York: Cambridge University Press, 1987.

Cogulludo, Fray Diego López, *Historia de Yucatán.* Mexico City: Editorial Academia Literaria, 1957.

Farriss, Nancy, *Maya Society Under Colonial Rule: The Collective Enterprise of Survival.* Princeton, New Jersey: Princeton University Press, 1984.

Jones, Grant, *Maya Resistance to Spanish Rule: Time and History on a Colonial Frontier.* Albuquerque: University of New Mexico Press, 1989.

—PAUL SULLIVAN

CONQUEST: NORTHERN MEXICO

One of the most surprising aspects of the great conquests of the sixteenth century is the enormous mobility of the conquistador armies. The conquest of northern New Spain effectively began in 1524, when Francisco Cortés Buenaventura explored the Pacific coast north of Colima, penetrating as far north as the so-called provinces of Xalisco and Tepique, the present-day states of Jalisco and Nayarit. In 1530, Nuño de Guzmán led a long, bloody campaign of conquest, passing through the provinces of Michoacán, Xalisco, and Tepique and arriving as far north as Culiacán, in the present-day state of Sinaloa. In 1531 a new province, Nueva Galicia, was established in the region with its capital in the town of Compostela.

Nonetheless, these conquests were precarious at best. In 1536 Nuño de Guzmán, who had long had a stormy relationship with Spanish authorities, was taken prisoner and sent into exile. Many of his soldiers fled Nueva Galicia, and the indigenous population plunged under the twin onslaught of disease and European avarice. The weak Spanish towns of Compostela, Chiametla, and other coastal settlements practically disappeared in a very short period of time, and much of the Spanish population retreated to the highlands of the present-day state of Jalisco. After several years of inactivity, however, the exploration of northern New Spain gained a new impetus with the expedition of Francisco Vásquez de Coronado, who pushed up the Pacific coast in an ultimately fruitless quest for the fabled Seven Cities. As the remnants of Coronado's troops retreated south, they met an army personally commanded by Viceroy Antonio de Mendoza, which had been dispatched north in 1541 to quash the indigenous revolt known as the Mixtón War. The combined forces of Coronado and Mendoza helped strengthen the Spanish population of Nueva Galicia, making Guadalajara the new capital of the province.

In 1546 a small group of explorers pushed past Guadalajara toward the mountain pass of the Sierra Madre Occidental, crossing it and discovering what later would be the royal mines of Zacatecas. One of the explorers, Diego de Ibarra, established an encampment on the site. Shortly after several of the most important *encomenderos* of Nueva Galicia joined him in the first Spanish exploitation of the region's rich silver deposits (*encomenderos* were trustees of *encomiendas,* or native settlements the labor of which the *encomendero* was to receive in return for the responsibility of protecting the Indians, maintaining missionaries in the region, and defending the area militarily). The fame of Zacatecas quickly spread as far as Mexico City. Hoping that Zacatecas would become a new version of Potosí, the fabulously rich silver mine in Peru, many of the leading figures in New Spain—among them Martín Cortés, the marquis of the Valley of Oaxaca—arrived in the region, bringing labor and equipment to intensify mining activity. By 1554 approximately 300 Spaniards and 1,500 Indian peons had settled in Zacatecas, making it the most important population center in northern New Spain. In 1586 the mines received the title of *ciudad* (city), giving it added status and important legal privileges.

With the opening of Zacatecas, the exploration and conquest of the north accelerated. Until then, the exploration and settlement of the region had been concentrated almost exclusively in the Pacific coastal region, while the plateau north of Querétaro remained terra incognita. With the opening of a direct road from Mexico City to Zacatecas, however, new, larger groups of migrants headed north, forming new groups of conquistadors.

One of these groups, led by Francisco de Ibarra, nephew of the founder of Zacatecas, explored the territories north of Zacatecas in search of the mythical kingdom of Copala. Although the group never found Copala, it did find silver deposits and sites for agricultural haciendas that later would be settled. During his second campaign, begun in 1562, Francisco de Ibarra received from Viceroy Luis de Velasco the title of governor and captain general of all the lands he discovered north of Zacatecas. That same year he created a new province, Nueva Vizcaya, establishing its capital in the town of Durango. Despite its status as capital of a new province, the Spanish population of Durango grew slowly. Between 1563 and 1564 Francisco de Ibarra resumed his exploration of northern New Spain, eventually settling with many of his people in the region around Chiametla (near the present-day city of Mazatlán, Sinaloa). With the reconquest of the region a large part of the northern Pacific coast, particularly the region that today forms the states of Sinaloa and Sonora, ended up in the territory of Nueva Vizcaya, with only a small enclave around Culiacán remaining under the jurisdiction of Nueva Galicia. For a brief period Chiametla, with its rich silver deposits and abundant supply of Indian labor, had the largest Spanish population and was the greatest producer of silver in all of northern New Spain outside of Zacatecas. In 1563 the mining settlement of Indé was established in the north of the present-day state of Durango, and in 1567 Santa Bárbara was established in the southern part of present-day Chihuahua. Until the end of the sixteenth century Santa Bárbara was the northernmost Spanish settlement in the Americas.

Much as had happened in the case of Nueva Vizcaya, other regions of northern New Spain were settled by expeditions that departed from Zacatecas as well as Nueva Vizcaya itself, generally in search of silver deposits. Among the most important expeditions were those led by Alberto del Canto in the 1570s, which discovered mines in what later would be Monclova, as well as the Valleys of Extremadura (near what later would be the city of Monterrey) and Saltillo. In 1579 Luis de Carvajal received royal authorization to settle the regions explored by del Canto, extending his domain as far as the region of Pánuco. In 1581 the new governor finally established himself in the Valley of Extremadura. In 1587, however, he was denounced by the Inquisition as a crypto-Jew and arrested, spurring an almost total abandonment of the region by Spanish settlers. Many of these settlers fell back to the recently founded town of Saltillo, which remained under the jurisdiction of Nueva Vizcaya. The settlement of Saltillo received an additional boost when a group of Tlaxcalteca colonists settled nearby in 1591, founding the town of San Esteban de la Nueva Tlaxcala. In 1596 the new province of Nuevo León was founded in the region originally settled by del Canto, and a new capital was established in Monterrey.

The Spanish settlements north of Zacatecas during the last third of the sixteenth century suffered for a lack of one basic resource—people. Given the sparse settlement of the region, the new towns in northern New Spain depended on the arrival of new immigrants and only to a far lesser degree internal growth. As the period of great conquests came to an end, what had been a series of rapid territorial advances became a long and sporadic process of colonization. An important case in point is the conquest and foundation of New Mexico. Given the title of *adelantado* in 1598, Juan de Oñate organized a large expedition to conquer the region beyond the Rio Grande. Toward the end of 1598 the army of Oñate had managed to install itself in San Juan de los Caballeros, in the heart of the territory of the Pueblo Indians. After several years of consolidating their presence, the colonists founded the town of Santa Fé, which served as the capital of the new province.

During the following decades New Mexico became an authentic Spanish enclave, with minimal contact with the major population centers of New Spain. Although in 1609 the viceregal authorities instituted triennial caravans of wagons to bring goods to and from New Mexico, the Spaniards of the new province frequently could go six or seven years without receiving news from the rest of New Spain. Nonetheless, other settlements such as Santa Bárbara, Saltillo, and Nuevo León were even more isolated. In 1601 the bishop of Culiacán remarked that the Spanish settlers in the region could be compared with the first children of Adam, "because they do not think or understand that there are other people in the world."

From the 1580s through the eighteenth century, the occupation of northern New Spain became a slow process of colonization. Nonetheless, this did not prevent the newly settled regions from being incorporated into the Spanish Empire. A key zone of colonization was Santa Bárbara. From 1580 until the end of the 1620s the Spanish population of the region took refuge in agricultural haciendas, practically abandoning its mining activities. During this period the indigenous population of the region was pacified and eventually settled in *reducciones* (roughly, reservations or ghettos) administered by Jesuits and Franciscans. By 1620 Santa Bárbara had become one of the principal granaries of the north. By 1631 the workforce had expanded enough to begin exploitation of the mines of El Parral. Parral was the first lasting mine established in the north since Zacatecas. By 1635 approximately 500 Spaniards had settled in the region; by the subsequent decade it had become the capital and most important population center of Nueva Vizcaya, with approximately 10,000 inhabitants.

Under the influence of Parral, a new extension of the main north-south road in New Spain, the Camino Real de Tierra Adentro, was constructed linking Zacatecas and Parral via the Bolsón de Mapimí. Able to handle carts and mule trains, the Camino Real intensified travel and commercial links between the north and central New Spain. However, it did not lead directly to the opening of new territories. Rather, zones already settled by Spaniards saw their populations grow. The Pacific coastal region, including the provinces of Sinaloa and Sonora, was slowly settled until the first decades of the seventeenth century. Aside from tenuous Spanish settlements in Sonora, Culiacán, Chiametla, and the Fuerte River, the only colonial presence in area was the Jesuit mission to the Yaqui and Mayo Indians.

Between the end of the 1630s and the beginning of the 1640s, however, several important transformations took place. In 1636 a captain by the name of Pedro de Perea solicited a charter from the Spanish Crown to settle Spaniards in Sonora, until then terra incognita called Nueva Andalucía. In 1640 the charter was granted, but Perea died soon after. Nonetheless, the charter inspired other colonists to settle the region, establishing such mining and agricultural settlements as San Pedro de los Reyes, San Juan Bautista, Nuestra Señora del Rosario de Nacozari, and shortly after San Ignacio de Ostimuri, which later would be the namesake for the entire Yaqui River basin. This second wave of colonization was linked indirectly to the new prosperity of Parral. Sinaloa and Sonora became the principal source of forced Indian labor in the mines of Parral. Moreover, the only road linking Sonora with the rest of New Spain was a route following the Papagochic River as far as Parral. In 1651 a second road to Sonora from Parral was constructed, which passed through the settlements of Casas Grandes and Janos. Nonetheless, during the rainy season the roads linking the Pacific slope to Parral were virtually impassable, increasing the isolation of the region. By the end of seventeenth century, however, Spanish colonization had pushed as far north as Fronteras, in the north of the present-day state of Sonora, opening the road for the Spanish expansion into the Pimería Alta and Alta Sonora, the present-day state of Arizona.

Other regions that had been terra incognita to Spaniards were settled in the seventeenth century as well. An important landmark in this process of colonization was the establishment of missions, reductions, and agricultural settlements from 1650 to 1680 north of the Río Conchos in the present-day state of Chihuahua. Until the middle of the seventeenth century the Río Conchos had marked the limit of Spanish colonization, increasing the isolation of New Mexico. The growth of the agriculture in the valley of San Bartolomé near Parral, however, sparked new waves of migration that could be channeled toward the pacification and colonization of the Tarahumara region around the Papagochic River; the mines of Cusihuiriachi later were established in the region. A similar series of events occurred around the present-day city of Chihuahua. Thanks to the solid agricultural colonization of the region in the late seventeenth century, by the beginning of the eighteenth century several important grain haciendas had been established. In 1707 the Santa Eulalia mine was established, and in 1709 San Francisco de Cuellar. The Chihuahua region soon displaced Parral as the most important silver-producing region in Nueva Vizcaya. In 1718 on the site of the present-day city of Chihuahua, the town of San Felipe el Real de Chihuahua was established (although local historiography identifies San Felipe el Real with San Francisco de Cuéllar, in reality they are separate towns). One of the most important effects of the settlement of Chihuahua was the establishment of regular trade and travel with New Mexico, breaking much of the isolation of the region.

Chihuahua was the last great town founded in northern New Spain. According to eighteenth-century sources, by 1725 the Chihuahua region had 25,000 inhabitants, making it one of the most important populations of New Spain. There were a few other processes of colonization during the eighteenth century, much of which emerged out of processes of migration to the northern frontier in the seventeenth century. Among these was the province of Texas, settled from the zone of Coahuila. Aware of French efforts to colonize the region, viceregal authorities sent a series of colonizing expeditions to Texas in the 1690s. Nonetheless, these initiatives only bore fruit in the following century. The most notable settlement in Texas was San Antonio de Béjar, founded in 1715. San Antonio later was reinforced by the opening of missions such as Nuestra Señora de Pilar and Nuestra Señora de Loreto. Nonetheless, Spanish settlement in Texas always was tenuous at best.

A similar process occurred in Alta California in the mid–eighteenth century, although the numbers involved were greater. Spurred by the *visitador* José de Gálvez, who had made a tour of inspection in northern New Spain, several advance posts were established in Alta California in 1769, including the ports of San Diego and San Francisco. In the following decades San Diego, San Francisco, and other enclaves were settled largely by people from Sonora, although we cannot speak of well constituted society in Alta California until the nineteenth century. Alta California was the last territory settled from New Spain. Nonetheless, the wave of settlements in the seventeenth century and the last few settlements in the eighteenth century only gave rise to weak local societies.

See also Missions

Select Bibliography

Alvarez, Salvador, "Chiametla: Una provincia olvidada del siglo XVI." *Trace* 22 (1992).

———, "Agricultural Colonization and Mining Colonization: The Area of Chihuahua during the First Half of the Eighteenth Century." In *In Quest of Mineral Wealth: Aboriginal and Colonial Mining and Metallurgy in Spanish America,* edited by Alan Kraig and Robert C. West. Baton Rouge: Department of Geography and Anthropology, Louisiana State University, 1994.

Cramaussel, Chantal, *La provincia de Santa Bárbara en Nueva Vizcaya 1563–1631. Primera pagina de historia colonial chihuahuense.* Ciudad Juárez: Universidad Autónoma de Ciudad Juárez, 1990.

Gerhard, Peter, *The North Frontier of New Spain.* Norman and London: University of Oklahoma Press, 1993.

Hernández Sánchez-Barba, Mario, *La última expansión española en América.* Madrid: Instituto de Estudios Políticos, 1957.

Mecham, John L., *Francisco de Ibarra and Nueva Vizcaya.* New York: Greenwood, 1968.

Mota y Escobar, Alonso de la, *Descripción geográfica de los reinos de la Nueva Galicia Nueva Vizcaya y Nuevo León.* Guadalajara: Instituto Jaliciense de Antropología e Historia, 1966.

Navarro Garcia, Luis, *Don José de Gálvez y la Comandancia General de las Provincias Internas del norte de la Nueva España*. Sevilla: Escuela de Estudios Hispano-Americanos, 1964.

Ortega Noriega, Sergio, and Ignacio Del Rio, editors, *Tres siglos de historia sonorense (1530–1830)*. Mexico City: UNAM, Instituto de Investigaciones Históricas, 1993.

Porras Muñoz, Guillermo, *Iglesia y estado en Nueva Vizcaya (1562–1821)*. Mexico City: UNAM, 1980.

Spicer, Edward H., *The Cycles of Conquest*. Tucson: University of Arizona Press, 1962.

—SALVADOR ALVAREZ

CONQUEST: ECOLOGICAL IMPACT

Mesoamerican ecosystems reflect millennia of interaction between humans and nature. Until the sixteenth century, the relations between humans and American ecologies evolved in virtual isolation from the rest of the world. At this time, indigenous patterns and processes were interrupted by invading Europeans, who introduced exotic animals and plants, new systems of land management, and alien understandings of what a landscape should look like. These European transplants interacted with native species and local processes, and with indigenous land management systems and world views, and set in motion processes that resulted, ultimately, in the formation of the modern Mexican environments.

The following discussion does not pretend to cover all the possible permutations of the environmental changes put in motion by the Conquest process, or the associated social and cultural processes. Rather, it reflects the somewhat limited scope of research on the immediate ecological consequences of the European invasion; and hence, it focuses primarily on the impact of Old World diseases and grazing animals, changing patterns of forest exploitation, and the consequences of the introduction of Spanish systems of land management.

The best-known and best-studied aspect of the European impact on the Mesoamerican environments is the introduction of Eurasian and African disease organisms. Indeed, researchers such as Woodrow Wilson Borah and Sherburne Friend Cook pioneered the new field of environmental history in Latin America in studies that demonstrated the course of the diseases and, most especially, the consequences for human population demographics. They found that the introduction of diseases such as influenza, small pox, bubonic plague, measles, chicken pox, whooping cough, typhus, typhoid fever, cholera, scarlet fever, malaria, yellow fever, and diphtheria resulted in almost universal infection in populations that were without defenses. Because Mesoamerican populations (in common with the rest of the Native American populations) had effectively been isolated from the rest of the world's population for millennia, they had never been infected with these diseases and thus had not acquired immunity to them. The alien diseases swept through the populations in terrible epidemics that were repeated regularly over the first 100 years until the indigenous populations acquired some immunity, a process that appears to have taken from four to six generations. The repetition of several distinct infections with very high mortality rates resulted in the demographic collapse of the indigenous populations. The demographic collapse, in turn, played a major role in shaping colonial land-labor regimes.

Disease organisms enter a population in various ways. Some of the new diseases, small pox and measles for example, depended entirely on human carriers for propagation in the American populations. Others were introduced along with the Old World animal species: plague came with the fleas of the domestic rat, swine flu with pigs, malaria with mosquitoes. Yet other diseases took advantage of circumstances that developed in the course of European invasion to extend their range into the Mesoamerican environment: the yellow fever virus, for example, is carried by a mosquito that prefers to breed in water carried in manufactured containers, and the virus was transmitted along with stores of water on board slave ships sailing to the Americas; malaria spread with the expansion of sugar plantations and the consequent increase in standing water.

The very limited variety of domestic animal species in the Americas meant that the indigenous human populations were not accustomed to sharing their domestic environments with a wide range of animals. This situation contrasted markedly with Eurasia, where human populations lived in close association with an extraordinary array of domestic animals. The introduction of alien animal species, along with all their micro-flora and fauna, transformed American disease environments.

When the Spaniards began to settle in Mesoamerica, they brought the animals necessary to reproduce their world in these new lands. They brought grazing animals such as cattle, sheep, goats, horses, donkeys, mules, and pigs in order to produce familiar foods (e.g., milk and meat), material for manufacture (e.g., wool and hides), and muscle power for carrying and traction (e.g., for plowing and drawing wheeled vehicles). They also brought birds of various types, such as chickens, ducks, and geese for their eggs and meat. They introduced animals that were not crucial for subsistence or manufacture, but that were part of their daily life and culture, such as cats and dogs. And they introduced species they would probably far rather have left behind: pests such as lice and fleas, and all the other parasites and plagues that coexist with humans and their domesticated species. And indeed, the sudden introduction of these alien species into the immediate physical environment of the Mesoamerican communities resulted in an increase in the microbial flora and fauna and the development of gastrointestinal infections; and Indians complained bitterly of the contamination of their water supplies by all these animals. The pollution was increased by the effluent from tanning establishments, slaughter houses, and woolen mills, and possibly caused even more illness.

The introduction of this array of domesticated species also may have increased the virulence of the diseases that accompanied the Europeans and Africans into the Americas by producing a situation in which new diseases could evolve. We already have noted the propensity of disease organisms to take advantage of environmental disruption and to move into human niches. The diversion of animal viruses into humans also can lead to the development of "new" viruses (composed of reshuffled genes of familiar viruses) that demonstrate enhanced virulence when they move into human hosts. Hence, the introduction of alien animals into the Americas, and the environmental disruption associated with the invasion, meant not only the introduction of alien diseases such as the swine flu that struck the Caribbean in 1493, but also the possibility of new strains of increased virulence as they evolved in their new setting.

The number of new species introduced into the Mesoamerican environments by the Spaniards was extraordinary: as well as the animals already mentioned, the Spaniards planted wheat, grape vines, and olive trees in order to have the bread, wine, and olive oil so necessary to the Mediterranean diet; and they planted fruit trees, herbs and flowers, grains such as barley, and all the other plants that were necessary to provide the flavors and foods familiar to them. As in the case of the domestic animals, the plants were associated with "useless" species, such as dandelions and thistles, that thrived in the new environments. The success or failure of the portmanteau biota (scholar Alfred Crosby's term for the totality of the species carried into the Americas) depended on the ability of these Old World species to adapt to New World climates, soils, vegetation, and water resources. The adaptation depended, as well, on the ability of the Spaniards, and those Mesoamericans who added the new species to their cultural repertoire, to develop the systems of land management specific to each species, thereby providing the specialized ecosystems necessary for their survival.

Judging by the unexpected consequences of the introduction of alien species into foreign ecosystems in the present day, and given the implications of unanticipated ecological change for modern human communities, all these additions must have changed the intersection between biological and social process (e.g., deforestation and erosion) in Mesoamerica. On this point there is not much disagreement.

But, given the paucity of research aimed at distinguishing causal relations between human activity and environmental change in the early Conquest era, it is not an easy matter to demonstrate how and to what extent these introductions influenced indigenous biological and social processes. As a preliminary ordering of events and processes, we can state that in some cases the introduction of alien species initiated entirely new biological processes and resulted in the transformation of certain ecosystems. In other cases, processes already in place when the Spaniards arrived were accelerated; in yet others indigenous processes were decelerated. Further, because we find examples of all these changes occurring in the same space, we can state that Spanish landscapes did not simply replace indigenous landscapes, nor that indigenous landscapes persisted unchanged; rather, the processes by which the colonial landscapes evolved were underlain by extremely complex and mutually influencing processes of environmental and social change. All of this may appear obvious, but it is apparently necessary to state clearly, given popular notions of the power of the Europeans to destroy indigenous landscapes and environments.

The complexity of the environmental impact of the Spanish invasion is exemplified by changes in patterns of forest use and the location and causes of erosion. It is difficult to discern a clear pattern either to deforestation or erosion in the sixteenth century, let alone demonstrate a causal link between specific examples of these processes. Shifting patterns in human and animal demographics, and shifting patterns in land use and consumption, were reflected in changing patterns of tree cover and soil structure. But rather then the simple replacement of one pattern by another—the replacement of indigenous patterns by Spanish, for example—we find a far more fluid situation that is not easily predicted by either indigenous or Spanish experience.

Prior to the arrival of the Spaniards, Mesoamerica was a densely populated region with perhaps as many as 25 million inhabitants. Vast areas of land were given over to agriculture to feed this population, and sometime in the past these lands had been cleared, to a greater or lesser extent, of trees, That is to say, deforestation the pre-Hispanic era was associated with high human population densities.

This pattern changed with the arrival of the Spaniards. Land clearance during the Conquest era was no longer carried out to accommodate a huge human population; indeed the indigenous human population declined by around 90 percent over this period, and the immigrant population of Spaniards and Africans was not large enough, nor did it increase sufficiently quickly to fill the space left by the demographic collapse. Land was now cleared for domestic grazing animals, and trees were cut for lumber needed in the silver mines and in the construction of Spanish cities, and for wood used to manufacture lime and charcoal. Such shifts in land use and in the destination of forest products meant that forests and woodlands that had survived the pre-Hispanic clearance, because they were far from the centers of population or because they were protected by pre-Hispanic legal codes, were cut. Deforestation in the Conquest era, therefore, occurred in regions of low population densities and in regions that were not cleared at contact. At the same time, however, the demographic collapse of the indigenous populations was reflected in an increase in fallow lands, and hence the possibility of forest regrowth—and in some places forests did grow back.

Patterns of erosion also shifted with the changing patterns in land use and tree cover. Not too surprisingly, pre-Hispanic patterns of erosion were primarily associated with dense human populations. Erosion in the Conquest era, by contrast, appears to have been associated with accelerated tree cutting for mining and the manufacture of charcoal and lime, with land clearance for grazing, and with overgrazing. That is, erosion in the Conquest era often occurred in areas that were characterized by very low or falling densities of human populations, where cutting, burning, and/or overgrazing put unusual pressure on the soils by removing the vegetative cover and opening the soils to the erosive forces of wind and rain. But the likelihood of erosion also appears to have increased with the spread of plowing. The European plow disturbed the soil far more deeply than the indigenous foot plow, thereby loosening the soil and making it more liable to increased wind erosion. As well, plowing formed rows that channeled rainwater in ways that the mounds made by the indigenous farmers did not, thereby increasing water erosion. That is, erosion also occurred in agricultural regions near population clusters, as it had in the pre-Hispanic era.

The picture of vegetative change is further complicated by the fact that Spanish invasion and settlement not only resulted in changing patterns of tree cover and soil loss, it also had consequences for the structure and composition of the vegetative communities. The introduction of pastoralism, for example, led to quite spectacular shifts in the composition of the vegetative cover as a result of the processes by which ungulates (hard-hooved herbivores) expand into new ecosystems. When ungulates are introduced into a new ecosystem, and are successful in adapting to the local climate and vegetation, they begin a process of rapid population increase that continues until their population density exceeds the carrying capacity of the range; the population crashes from lack of sufficient food, then adjusts to the reduced range. The vegetative cover goes through a reciprocal trajectory of decrease, recovery, and adjustment to the changing herbivoral population. As well, animals selectively browse the vegetation, eating those species they prefer and leaving unpalatable or "armed" (e.g., spined) species of plants alone. By the time an introduced animal population and the native vegetative communities have adapted to each other, the composition of the vegetative cover has been modified—quite drastically so in some places. The most common changes are reduction in the height of the vegetative cover and increase in the spaces between plants, and hence an increase in asolation (drying) of the soils. The development of arid microclimates leads in turn to the invasion by arid-zone species with a high proportion of wood to foliage. As the composition

and structure of the vegetation changes, so do the associated faunal populations. The end result is a transformed biological regime, and a transformed landscape.

Such changes are not necessarily permanent, and if the ungulate population is removed, the original vegetative cover with its complement of fauna will return. When, however, the ungulate population is managed and maintained by humans, the results are often permanent. Because humans manage grazing animals by controlling breeding patterns, birth rates, eating habits, migrations, and death rates, they have the capacity to influence the relationship of the animal populations with the vegetation. When pastoralists hold the animals in very high densities, for example, they amplify the vegetation changes to the point of total loss of vegetation cover, thereby increasing the possibility of the permanent loss of floral and faunal species and soil erosion. Since their goal is to increase the extent of grasses available for forage, pastoralists also practice deforestation to open the land for grazing, and burning to stimulate grasses; both practices reduce the soil cover and hence increase the likelihood of erosion.

The extent of the changes brought about by the Spanish invasion, and conversely, the persistence of indigenous environments, depended on many variables: biological factors such as the climate, soil, and vegetation; political-economic factors such as the distance from the centers of Spanish power, the presence (or absence) of resources attractive to the Spanish, and access to the markets where new products were sold; and cultural factors such as the acceptability of the new cultural items, knowledge of their use, and practice in their application. Many animal species were accepted and became an integral part of the village economies and the Mesoamerican ecosystems, changing the biological regime as they expanded into these ecosystems, and, in turn, being changed by this process. In fact, variants of the original species developed that were highly adapted to the local environments, the so-called criollo breeds. These ecotypes are so important to local economies and ecologies that it is now often necessary to cross-breed the scientifically "improved" breeds with the criollo breeds so that the newcomers are not rejected by the local ecosystems. Plant species were not always and everywhere accepted. Some plant species like fruit trees became part of the cultural and environmental repertoire of the indigenous peoples. Other such as wheat were not accepted so easily, apparently because they did not provide any perceived advantages over indigenous species, such as maize.

The process of adaptation and acceptance was not all one-way, however, and the Spaniards were forced to adapt to American realities, often at quite significant expense and dislocation of settled routines. Wheat growing provides a clear example of the need to adapt, not only to new climates and soils, but also to indigenous systems of production. At first wheat was planted in the mounds typical of indigenous maize agriculture; and it was planted to take advantage of the summer rains. When it became clear that wheat production on a commercial scale competed with Indian work schedules, most especially maize cultivation, and that the best grains for bread could not be grown successfully during the summer rainy season, the Spaniards changed their scheduling: from spring sowing of rain-fed wheat and a fall harvest, to fall sowing of irrigated wheat and spring harvest. The shift to a spring harvest meant that threshing was postponed to the following fall, when traditional methods of threshing with the *trilla*, or with large numbers of mares on a flat area of hardened ground, was not threatened by early rains and did not use animals needed for preparing the ground for maize.

A further example of Spanish adaptation to and use of indigenous infrastructure is the use and adaptation of indigenous water management practices. The Spaniards made extensive use of indigenous irrigation systems, and they expanded and modified canals and dams. It is interesting to note, however, that they left the extremely sophisticated systems of wetland agriculture in the hands of the Mesoamericans, making little or not attempt either to adopt the technology or take over these lands—they might have left them alone because of a lack of understanding of the principles involved in this method of soil-water management.

In other areas of water management, the Spaniards applied technologies developed in Europe, and not always with felicitous results. The technology applied to the Basin of Mexico illustrates the problems faced by the Spaniards in their attempts to develop a familiar landscape in this new world, and the consequences of the application of European technology in alien ecologies. The Basin of Mexico is an inland basin with no natural external drainage, and there were constant problems with floods in the city of Mexico-Tenochtitlan in the sixteenth century. But instead of working with the wetlands as the Mesoamericans did and regulating the water levels with dikes as had been done quite successfully in the pre-Contact era, the Spaniards attempted to resolve the problem of flooding by draining the basin. They began the ill-fated *desagüe* (drainage), a process that has had drastic and long-term consequences for both Mexico City and the extensive wetlands that ringed the lakes. The production of dry lands fit for plow agriculture was an added incentive for the drainage of the basin and reflects the entirely different approaches to soil-water management of the Spaniards and Mesoamericans.

The changes that took place in the Conquest era would seem to imply that each region—perhaps each village—was shaped by different processes, or at least by different groupings and arrangements of similar processes. But perhaps this confusion is a factor of the current state of environmental history, or historical ecology as it is known by anthropologists. Our understanding of the implications of the Spanish invasion, and the strength of indigenous ecosystems to persist, is very much at an early stage. Interest in this topic is such, however, that an increasing number of scholars is studying the mechanics of "ecological imperialism," and we can look forward to clarification of some of the problems posed by this topic in the near future.

See also Population: Colonial; Rural Economy and Society: Colonial; Water Rights in New Spain

Select Bibliography

Borah, Woodrow Wilson, *The Population of Central Mexico in 1548: An Analysis of the Suma de Vistas de Pueblos.* Berkeley: University of California Press, 1960.

_____, *The Aboriginal Population of Central Mexico on the Eve of the Spanish Conquest.* Berkeley: University of California Press, 1963.

Cook, Sherburne Friend, *The Population of Mixtec Alta, 1520–1960.* Berkeley: University of California Press, 1968.

Crosby, Alfred, *Ecological Imperialism: The Biological Expansion of Europe, 900–1900.* Cambridge and New York: Cambridge University Press, 1986.

Bauer, Arnold J., "La cultura Mediterranea en las condiciones del Nuevo Mundo." *Historia* 21 (1986).

Licate, Jack A., *The Creation of a Mexican Landscape: Territorial Organization and Settlement in the Eastern Puebla Basin 1520–1605.* Chicago: University of Chicago Press, 1981.

Melville, Elinor G. K., *A Plague of Sheep: Environmental Consequences of the Conquest of Mexico.* Cambridge and New York: Cambridge University Press, 1994.

Rojas Rabiela, Teresa, *Historia de la agricultura. Epoca prehispánica–siglo XVI.* 2 vols., Mexico City: INAH, 1985.

Simpson, Lesley Byrd, *Exploitation of Land in Sixteenth Century Mexico.* Berkeley and Los Angeles: University of California Press, 1952.

—ELINOR G. K. MELVILLE

CONQUEST: CONQUEST NARRATIVES

Spanish participants in the Conquest of Mexico left important eyewitness accounts of that dramatic event. In the century after the Conquest, Indian, mestizo, and Spanish chroniclers provided new information and viewpoints on the subject. Since they reflect different interests and ideologies, all these accounts are to some degree partisan versions of the events with which they deal. Often they disagree on points of fact. For example, who killed King Moteuczoma II, the

Spaniards or the Indians? Did the Mexica (Aztecs) actually regard Fernando (Hernán) Cortés as the representative of the god Quetzalcoatl or Quetzalcoatl himself? Their disagreements sparked historical debates that continue to this day. Many of the chronicles were written (at least in part) with a self-serving purpose that complicates the problem of authenticating what really happened. For example, one of the best-known sources, the letters of Cortés, grossly skews or omits important events to advance his interests. Other conquistador-chroniclers wrote to convince the Spanish Crown that they had not been rewarded adequately for their great services to God and king. In still other cases, Indian and mestizo chroniclers, descendants of the old native nobility, hoped to legitimate their claims to land and titles by showing that their ancestors had joined and aided the Spanish invaders. Moved by self-interest and tribal loyalties, these native chroniclers magnified or diminished the exploits of one or another ethnic group, suppressed certain episodes, or even fabricated events.

In general, the chronicles of the Conquest fall into three groups. The first consists of the first-hand accounts by conquistadors. Their proximity to the events they describe and their wealth of detail, sometimes providing a day-by-day narrative of campaigns, has gained them a privileged position among sources on the Conquest. The second group comprises tribal histories written in Nahuatl or Spanish by members of the native nobility who had been educated in *colegios* established by the Franciscans and other religious orders. A third group of chronicles consists of histories of ancient Mexico and its civilization written in the second half of the sixteenth century by members of the mendicant orders (chiefly Franciscans and Dominicans). Like the Indian and mestizo histories, these chronicles drew much of their information from native codices or picture writings glossed for them by tribal elders, and the recollections of these elders. As a rule these accounts were ambivalent toward the Conquest, viewing it as a providential event that enabled the missionaries to gather in a harvest of Indian souls, but sharply criticizing its cruelties and other abuses of the Indians.

We should note that few of the chronicles discussed here were published before the nineteenth century or even later. In part this was owing to technical and financial problems, complicated by the need to secure prior official approval of publication. Royal fear of the excessive power of conquistadors and *encomenderos* (trustees of large landholdings worked by Indian labor) led to a ban in 1527 of the circulation of Cortés's first letters, and an order in 1555 for the confiscation of all copies of Francisco López de Gómara's history of the conquest of Mexico, which was considered too eulogistic of Cortés. Under Felipe II, who favored the secular (i.e., non-order) clergy and distrusted the friars, the sharpest critics of the Crown's Indian policy were silenced, and even the study of Indian history was forbidden. In 1577 the viceroy of New Spain was ordered to seize and send to the Council of the Indies all the works of the great friar-ethnologist Bernardino de Sahagún and other writings of the same character.

The Conquistador Chroniclers

Among the eyewitness accounts of conquistadors, the *Cartas de Relación,* the letters sent to King Carlos I of Spain by the conquistador Fernando (Hernán) Cortés, are especially important both because of what they tell and what they omit. Written between battles and difficult marches, or amid political storms, the letters impress the unwary reader by their serene, unhurried flow and wealth of precise observations. Indeed, the scholar Beatriz P. Bodmer has called Cortés's description of Tenochtitlan and Mexica material culture and society "a model of rational classification"; his careful, detailed description of the great market at Tenochtitlan-Tlatelolco could have been written by a modern ethnologist.

When it comes to military and political events, however, Cortés's approach changes. Despite his insistence that he is writing a "true relation," his letters are largely an exercise in fictional justification, intended to free him from restraints that could prove more dangerous to his ambitions than Indian resistance. Cortés technically commanded an expedition on behalf of the governor of Cuba, Diego Velázquez, whose instructions permitted Cortés to explore and trade with the newly discovered lands to the west, but not to conquer or colonize, rights that Velázquez hoped to secure for himself from the Spanish court. By founding the town of the Villa Rica de Vera Cruz on the coast of Mexico, then advancing into the interior to conquer the Mexica Empire, Cortés flouted Velázquez's instructions and could have been charged with rebellion against the royal governor. His problem was how to transform his rebellion into service to the king, himself into a loyal servant bent on winning an empire for his royal master, and Velázquez into a traitor to the king, "moved more by cupidity than any other passion." In the words of scholar John H. Elliott, Cortés's letters display "a masterly capacity for suppression of evidence and ingenious distortion" as he maneuvers to achieve these ends.

An example of Cortés's suppression of evidence and distortion is his treatment of one of the most important episodes of the Conquest, the Mexica uprising in 1520 that forced the Spaniards to flee Tenochtitlan and destroyed Cortés's hopes of an easy conquest of the Mexica Empire. Almost all the native versions of these events attribute the Mexica rebellion to an unprovoked massacre of the celebrants of the feast of Toxcatl, a massacre ordered by Pedro de Alvarado after Cortés had departed from the capital to deal with the expedition of Pánfilo de Narváez, sent by Velázquez against Cortés. In his *Historia verdadera de la conquista de la Nueva España,* Bernal Díaz del Castillo cites this explanation, then complements it with Alvarado's own explanation to Cortés that the massacre was a preemptive strike against a Mexica conspiracy to attack the Spaniards. Díaz quotes an angry Cortés as telling Alvarado he had committed "a bad thing and a great mistake." But in his second letter Cortés makes no mention of the slaughter and its role in the loss of Tenochtitlan. Instead he shifts the entire blame to Narváez and his master Velázquez, who had forced Cortés to leave the capital and incited the Indians to rebel against the Spaniards. This version of events had the added value of providing

Cortés with new ammunition for his campaign to malign and discredit Velázquez.

Cortés's portrayal of his role in the Conquest implicitly ascribed the Spanish victory to his wise leadership and decisions, downplaying or omitting the services of other conquistadors and avoiding reference to his mistakes. This account was accepted without question by Cortés's chaplain, Francisco López de Gómara, in his *La conquista de México* (1552). Despite its derivative character, Gómara's book is still important because of his close links with Cortés and the Cortés family. Don Martín Cortés, son of the conquistador, paid Gómara 500 pesos for his literary services.

From first to last, the book is a celebration of the man whose genius and heroism made it possible for a small band of Spaniards to conquer a vast empire. Following classical models, Gómara assigned to Cortés and other personages long, made-up speeches that modern readers find absurd, but Gómara's racy, trenchant style helps to explain the book's immense popularity. His sources included Cortés's letters and other information given him by Cortés and the conquistador Andrés de Tapia.

Gómara's hero-worshipping book played a part in the formation of the work that is generally regarded as the most complete and informative eyewitness account of the Conquest, Bernal Díaz del Castillo's *Historia verdadera de la conquista de la Nueva España*. After taking part in two preliminary reconnaissances of the coast of Mexico in 1517 and 1518, Díaz aged about 22, joined Cortés's expedition the following year. After the capture of Tenochtitlan, he took part in campaigns led by Gonzalo de Sandoval and Pedro de Alvarado, and from 1524 to 1526 accompanied Cortés on his disastrous expedition to Honduras. In 1541 he settled down in Guatemala as an *encomendero* (a trustee of Indian labor), and—possibly between 1551 and 1557—he began writing his history. It was not published until 1632.

The book undoubtedly has the character of a *relación de méritos y servicios* (a "relation of merits and services"), a formal petition to the Crown for land, offices, or other privileges, written to support Díaz's incessant pleading for grants of more land and Indians by the Crown. In this, observes the Mexican historian Ramón Iglesia, he was "a true representative of that turbulent generation of conquistadors who, when they stop fighting the Indians, spend the rest of their lives bombarding the Crown for favors that will allow them to live without working." For Iglesia this importuning for land and Indians is "the foundation, the very root, of Bernal's *True History*."

Like other conquistadors, Díaz also felt threatened by the campaign to end the *encomienda* system of Indian labor and tribute, a campaign waged in the Spanish court by defenders of the Indians such as Bartolomé de Las Casas. His book offers a heated defense of the conquistadors against the charges of cruelty leveled by Las Casas. Reading his massive, sprawling, untidy book, however, it is difficult to escape the impression that this veteran of more than 100 battles was haunted by his past, that his brain teemed with vivid memories and images, and that—whatever other motives were involved—he felt driven to record for posterity what he and his comrades had done and seen.

Díaz already had written some chapters of his chronicle when he came across Gómara's book. Although Díaz paid tribute to Cortés's bravery and other military virtues, he was angered by Gómara's "great man" view of the Conquest, with its exclusive focus on Cortés that left in oblivion the deeds of other captains and ordinary soldiers like himself. He repeatedly claims that Gómara wrote as he did because "his palm had been greased and he had been paid for it" (which may not have been far from the truth), and suggested Cortés's complicity in the skewing of facts: "In my opinion it is not [Gómara's] fault but that of his informer." Time and time again Díaz calls attention to Gómara's alleged factual errors. Díaz himself can be charged with errors and distortions (for example, he virtually ignores the decisive contribution of Cortés's Indian allies to the Spanish victory), but in balance his account is richer, more complete, and more realistic than Cortés's carefully tailored letters to the king.

A virtue of Díaz's book is that it is written from below, from the viewpoint of the ordinary soldiers of the Conquest. His vivid descriptions of his comrades contribute to the book's sense of realism and immediacy. He remembers Jerónimo Mejía, known as Rapapelo, the Scalper, "because he himself said he was the grandson of a Mejía who was a great thief when don Juan was king"; the Sevillian Tarifa Manos Blancas (White Hands), so called "because he was no good for war or when it came to work, but only to talk about past things"; and Pedro de Solís, Tras la Puerta (Behind the Door), who owed his nickname to his habit "of looking at those who went by in the street without letting himself be seen." We also owe to Díaz, who was one of Moteuczoma II's guards during his captivity, the most detailed and intimate description of the Mexica ruler. Díaz always shows much respect and even affection for the royal prisoner, recalling the gifts he and other guards received from the "great" Moteuczoma.

The basic writings of Cortés and Díaz del Castillo can be supplemented by a number of lesser but useful narratives. One is the *relación* of Andrés de Tapia, who as a youth of 24 sailed with Cortés on the expedition from Cuba to Mexico and became one of his most trusted captains. In general, this brief chronicle closely follows Cortés's version of events. Although it ends abruptly with the 1520 campaign against Panfilo de Narváez and his capture, it describes the major events up to that point and provides certain details not found elsewhere.

The conquistador Alonso de Aguilar also came to Mexico with Cortés and took part in the whole course of the Conquest. In 1529, aged 50, he gave up his allotment of land and Indians and entered the Dominican order. When he was more than 80, his fellow monks persuaded him to write an account of his experiences in the Conquest. The result was his *Relación breve de la conquista de la Nueva España*. The chronicle covers the story of the Conquest from the preliminary voyage of Juan de Grijalva to the final capture of Tenochtitlan in August 1521. Aguilar gives a vivid account of the Mexica siege of the Spanish quarters and the desperate effort of the Spaniards to break out of Tenochtitlan. Although he offers the standard Spanish explanation that Moteuczoma II died as a result of injuries caused by a Mexica hail of stones, he notes that before the flight from the city Cortés ordered all the great lords held with Moteuczoma killed, "leaving not a single one"; this information is not found in other sources.

Pedro de Alvarado, one of Cortés's principal lieutenants, ordered the massacre of Mexica nobles that led to the Mexica revolt and the temporary loss of Tenochtitlan. After the fall of the city in August 1521, he went on to other campaigns, and in 1523 by order of Cortés set out for the conquest of Guatemala. He recorded his devastating march through that Maya region in two letters, or *relaciones*, to Cortés. No less brutal was the conquest of Michoacán by Nuño de Guzmán in 1529–30. The atrocities and other abuses committed against the Indians by Guzmán led to an investigation by the Second Audiencia, or high court, of New Spain that included questioning of one of Guzmán's henchmen, García del Pilar, who had formed part of Cortés's army. In his testimony against Guzmán, observed the scholar Patricia de Fuentes, Pilar "makes himself as shadowy as possible, seemingly intent on appearing as a mere bystander at the scene of Guzmán's crimes."

The Vision of the Vanquished

Indian histories of the Conquest of Mexico reflect the conflicts among the states and ethnic groups making up the ancient Mexican world and their different responses to the arrival of Cortés and his small army on the coast of Mexico. The city-state of Tlaxcala, which controlled the sierra through which Cortés had to pass on the way to Tenochtitlan, was a traditional enemy of the Mexica, but the Spaniards had to defeat the Tlaxcalans in battle before obtaining an alliance with this powerful tribe. Cortés's shrewd policy of playing off one Indian group or faction against another was particularly successful in the case of the Mexica Confederacy (or "Triple Alliance") of Tenochtitlan, Texcoco, and Tlacopan (modern-day Tacuba). Although little Tlacopan remained faithful to Tenochtitlan, the ruling elite of the large and rich Texcocan domain split, one faction supporting Tenochtitlan, another joining the Spaniards. Meanwhile tributary peoples such as the coastal Totonacs and the Chalcans in the Valley of Mexico, long restive under the oppressive Mexica rule, flocked to the Spanish banners. Estimates of the number of Indian allies vary greatly, but Cortés claimed that they brought the size of his total army to 150,000.

Reflecting these divisions and secessions, most Indian and mestizo accounts of the Conquest have an extremely biased character. One of the most tendentious is the *Historia de Tlaxcala,* composed by the mestizo chronicler Diego Muñoz Camargo between 1576 and 1595. As a reward for its services to the Spanish cause in the Conquest, Tlaxcala enjoyed for a time a privileged position among the Indian peoples of New Spain. The desire to defend the privileges of Tlaxcala and its native nobility certainly figured among Muñoz Camargo's motives for writing his book. For his information he relied on Gómara and some manuscripts of the Franciscan Bernardino de Sahagún; he also drew on the memories of native informants.

Muñoz Camargo left no doubt that he considered himself first of all a Spaniard; referring to the Conquest he consistently spoke of the Spaniards as *los nuestros* (our people) and to the Tlaxcalans as *nuestros amigos* (our friends). To the Indians he assigned negative traits in the manner of Gómara. Still, he emphasized that the Indians had some glimmerings of light that enabled them to discern, however darkly, the truths of Christianity. In this manner Muñoz built a bridge between the pagan faith of his Indian ancestors and the Catholic religion.

Muñoz was most tendentious in relating the events of the Conquest itself. He portrayed Tlaxcalans as invoking the Spanish Saint James in the heat of the struggle with the Mexica. He invented other imaginary events. One was the baptism of Moteuczoma; another was an attack by the Cholulans on an embassy sent to them by Cortés, a fiction needed by Muñoz to justify Cortés's massacre at Cholula. Finally, Muñoz distorted the whole course of Spanish-Tlaxcalan relations by wiping from the pages of history the resistance initially offered to the Spaniards by Tlaxcala.

A mestizo descendant of the last king of Texcoco, the seventeenth-century *cronista* (chronicler) Fernando de Alva Ixtlilxochitl left important historical works, most of which remained unpublished until 1891. Although he held various posts under the Spanish colonial administration, he complained pitifully of his poverty and the indignities suffered by himself and other members of the royal house of Texcoco, claiming that they had not only lost their patrimony of land and vassals but were reduced to the condition of tribute-payers. No doubt the hope of securing restitution of land and other favors by proving that his ancestor of the same name had greatly aided the Spaniards encouraged Ixtlilxochitl to write his histories. But an authentic pride in his Indian heritage and in the splendor of Texcoco, the cultural center of the Mexica Empire, also inspired his historical efforts.

Educated in the Franciscan Colegio de Santa Cruz at Tlatelolco, Ixtlilxochitl displayed a mastery of European historical technique (i.e., those of Plutarch, Livy, etc.) and made extensive use of knowledgeable native informants and codices while writing his works. They fall into two parts. One consists of a number of relations that are basically Spanish versions of Nahuatl documents. The other is Ixtlilxochitl's major work, the *Historia Chichimeca,* which offers a Texcocan version of the history of the Valley of Mexico. The work displays an intense anti-Mexica bias, natural enough in view of the strained relations between the two states on the eve of the Conquest. It devotes much space to the life of an ancestor, also named Ixtlilxochitl, who took the side of the Spaniards against his own brother, King Cacama, and who seized and turned him over to the Spaniards. The birth of this prince is accompanied by signs and portents that he would embrace a new faith and ally himself with the enemies of his people, fulfilling another ancient prophecy that new people would come to possess the land. The *Historia* terminates abruptly with the Spanish final assault on Tenochtitlan in June 1521, and contains no criticism of the Conquest or its aftermath.

Ixtlilxochitl's *Relación décimotercera,* on the other hand, overflows with an immense bitterness. The relation includes an account of the expedition Cortés led to Honduras (1525), during which, on suspicion of a conspiracy, he executed Cuauhtemoc, the leader of the last Mexica resistance, and other Mexican princes who accompanied him, among them a brother of Cortés's Indian ally, Ixtlilxochitl. From an indictment of this action the chronicler moves to a general attack on Spanish conduct in the Indies. There is an astounding boldness about his comment on Spanish treatment of the Indians. "So great is their misery that I have read in many books which treat of the tyrannies and cruelties of other nations that neither separately nor all together can those tyrannies compare with the toil and slavery imposed on the Indians."

The same anti-Mexica bias and ambivalence regarding the Conquest mark the historical *relaciones* written in Nahuatl by the Chalcan Francisco de San Antón Muñón Chimalpahin in the first decades of the seventeenth century. He wrote primarily to keep alive the glories of the Chalco confederacy before its conquest by the Mexica and their allies in 1465, a conquest that in Chimalpahin's eyes forced legitimate kings into exile and replaced them with puppets imposed by the Mexica overlords. Naturally, Chimalpahin's brief account of the Conquest displays an extreme pro-Spanish bias; unlike the majority of native sources, he assigns the origin of the Mexica uprising not to Alvarado's massacre of the Mexica nobility but to Cortés's pious zeal in destroying the paste idol of the god Huitzilopochtli. But Chimalpahin also charged Cortés with killing Moteuczoma and other legitimate rulers, condemned his execution of Cuauhtemoc and other Indian princes on the march to Honduras, and blamed him for turning the old political order, governed by ancient noble lineages, upside-down by deposing rightful rulers and installing his favorites in their places.

Of the native accounts that present the Mexica version of the Conquest, the fullest, most authentic, and most revealing of the Mexica mentality is the work of the great Franciscan missionary-scholar Bernardino de Sahagún, obtained from native informants—contemporaries and participants in that struggle—in Tlatelolco (c. 1550–55). This account later became Book 12 of Sahagún's monumental encyclopedia of Mexica civilization, *Historia general de las cosas de Nueva España,* written in Nahuatl, with a Spanish paraphrase. The very notion of obtaining a native account of the Conquest as a foil to what had been written by the Spanish victors suggests the modernity of Sahagún's thought.

The account begins in an atmosphere of mystery, with a series of evil portents that foretell the Mexica doom. Messengers arrive from the gulf coast, bringing news of the approach from the sea of winged towers containing men with white faces and heavy beards. These events, presaging the prophesied return of the god Quetzalcoatl to reclaim his lost kingdom, strike terror into Moteuczoma and his subjects.

Moteuczoma sends rich gifts to Cortés, including the finery of the great gods Tezcatlipoca, Tlaloc, and Quetzalcoatl. The native account stresses that the strangers took great pleasure in the gold objects; "they thirsted mightily for gold; they stuffed themselves with it, and hungered and lusted for it like pigs." But nothing stops their inexorable advance. Then Moteuczoma sends a band of sorcerers to conjure away the mysterious strangers, with no more success. Eventually Moteuczoma welcomes Cortés at the entrance to Tenochtitlan as a rightful ruler returning to his throne or as his representative. The story then moves to its tragic climax. In an atmosphere of growing tension Alvarado orders the massacre of the celebrants of the feast of Toxcatl; the Mexica revolt forces the Spaniards to flee the capital; they return in overwhelming force, reinforced by naval power; and after a siege of four months that last Mexica king, Cuauhtemoc, surrenders amid the laments of his starving people.

Leaving aside its fantastic elements, the description in Sahagún's *Historia general* of the Mexica reaction to the Conquest and the march of events, provided by actors in or observers of those events, is probably more trustworthy than most other native accounts, offers a remarkable insight into the Mexica mentality, and is marked by a striking simplicity and power.

Recently, however, some scholars, notably Susan Gillespie and James Lockhart, have questioned the reliability of the first part of Book 12 of the *Historia general,* dealing with the arrival of the Spaniards on the coast and the initial reactions of Moteuczoma and the Mexica to Cortés and his men. Specifically, these skeptical scholars question whether the Mexica initially viewed the Spaniards as gods and variously suggest that the legend of the return of the god-king Quetzalcoatl is a post-Conquest native rationalization of the Mexica defeat or a combined Spanish-Indian creation, or even a pure invention of Cortés, who twice cites a version of the legend as told by Moteuczoma. Lockhart has suggested that the first part of Book 12 is a "late reconstruction" and observes that the earlier *Anales de Tlatelolco* lacks most of the incidents mentioned in the "suspect portion" of Book 12. We note, however, that the *Anales de Tlatelolco* also speaks of Cortés as a god *(teotl).* In general, the new skepticism strikes supporters of the traditional point of view as ahistorical. History records numerous legends prophesying the return of redeemer-gods or kings. If medieval Germans could believe in the return of Emperor Frederick Barbarossa, if Renaissance Portuguese could believe in the return of King Sebastian, why could not Mexica believe in the return of the god-king Quetzalcoatl?

Chronicles of the Friars

The sixteenth century, especially its second half, saw the writing of numerous Indian chronicles by members of the Mendicant orders, especially Franciscans and Dominicans. These missionaries believed that paganism could not be successfully combated without a thorough study and understanding of the pre-conquest Indian history and way of life. In Mexico there arose a genuine school of ethnography devoted to making an inventory of the rich content of Indian culture. If the primary and avowed motive of this effort was to arm the missionary with the knowledge he needed to discover the concealed presence of pagan rites and practices, intellectual curiosity and delight at the discovery of the material, artistic, and social achievements of the vanished Indian states also played a part. This stance went hand in hand with a protective attitude toward the Indian, whose salvation and very life were threatened by the greed and cruelty of some conquistadors and *encomenderos.*

After Sahagún's great *Historia general,* the most important chronicle of the Mendicant school is the Dominican Diego Durán's *Historia de las Indias de Nueva España,* completed in 1581. Like Sahagún, Durán made extensive use of native picture writings and informants. In particular, he drew on a document written in Nahuatl, perhaps an "official" Mexica history, which he translated. Because of the similarities between Durán's work and a number of other sixteenth-century chronicles, this missing document, regarded as the antecedent of a whole group of works, has been called *Crónica X.*

Like Sahagún, Durán took a providential attitude toward Mexica history and the Conquest. Mexico before the coming of the Spaniards was under the direct sway of Satan; the Conquest was a divine chastisement of their sins. But if the Conquest was of divine inspiration, Durán could not say the same of the methods of the conquistadors. He described Alvarado's massacre of the Indian nobility of Tenochtitlan as "an atrocious, tyrannical cruelty" and implicated Cortés in its planning. He was inclined to accept the Indian assertion that Moteuczoma's death was caused by the Spaniards. Telling of a hermitage erected by the conquistadors in memory of some comrades who had been slain by the Indians, Durán observed wryly that God alone knew if He accepted their martyrdom. "I hold it a fearful thing to preach with sword in hand, taking by force what belongs to another." He even denounced the actions of Cortés's chaplain, Fray Bartolomé de Olmedo. Olmedo should have been suspended and excommunicated, Durán wrote, for "I understand that he washed his hands in innocent blood more often than Pilate washed his hands with water at Christ's death."

In the prevailing political climate at the Spanish court, where the pro-Indian teachings of Bartolomé de Las Casas had fallen into disrepute and the friars were charged with improper meddling in questions of Indian policy, such denunciations of the cruelty of the Conquest could be regarded as little less than subversive. It should come as no surprise that Durán's book, along with the works of Sahagún and other mendicant chroniclers, gathered dust for centuries. Conforming to that new political climate, in 1585 the aged Sahagún prudently revised his Spanish paraphrase of the Indian account of the Conquest in his *Historia general,* giving it a strongly pro-Spanish flavor. In this new version, Sahagún vindicated Alvarado's massacre of the Mexica nobility; he also assigned to Cortés a speech that justified the whole Conquest.

Most of the chronicles of the Conquest published in Spain in the seventeenth century either practiced self-censorship or accepted unquestioningly the official view of the Conquest as wholly just and beneficial. These works include the massive history of the Spanish discoveries and conquests in America, *Historia general de los hechos de los castellanos en las islas y tierra firme del Mar Océano,* by the official chronicler Antonio de Herrera y Tordesillas, published between 1601 and 1615; the account of the Conquest of Mexico in Fray Juan de Torquemada's monumental *Monarquía indiana* (1615); and the *Historia de la conquista de México* (1684) by Antonio de Solís. Solís's book, in particular, is marred by an unwavering partiality for the Spanish side and systematic disparagement of the Indian character and actions. As a result of their "official," apologetic character, these seventeenth-century accounts of the Conquest of Mexico lack much originality and critical spirit. However, we must exempt from this charge Bernal Díaz del Castillo's *Historia verdadera,* not published until 1632, whose homely speech and plebeian fractiousness the aristocratic Solís severely criticized.

See also Codices; Popular Narratives and Poetics

Select Bibliography
Barba, Francisco Esteve, *Historiografía indiana.* Madrid: Gredos, 1964.
Bodmer, Beatriz P., *The Armature of Conquest: Spanish Accounts of the Discovery of America, 1492–1589,* translated by L.L. Hunt. Stanford, California: Stanford University Press, 1992.
Brooks, Francis J., "Moteuczoma Xocoyotl, Hernán Cortes, and Bernal Díaz del Castillo: The Construction of an Arrest." *Hispanic American Historical Review* 75:2 (1995).
Cortés, Hernán, *Letters from Mexico,* translated and edited by A.R. Pagden. New York: Grossman, 1971.
de Fuentes, Patricia, editor and translator, *The Conquistadors: First-Person Accounts of the Conquest of Mexico.* Norman: University of Oklahoma Press, 1993.
Díaz, Bernal, *The Conquest of New Spain,* translated and with an introduction by J.M. Cohen. Baltimore: Penguin, 1963.
Durán, Diego, *The History of the Indies of New Spain,* translated, annotated, and with an introduction by Doris Heyden. Norman: University of Oklahoma Press, 1994.
Iglesia, Ramón, *Columbus, Cortes, and Other Essays,* translated and edited by L.B. Simpson. Berkeley: University of California Press, 1969.
Leon-Portilla, Miguel, editor, *The Broken Spears: The Aztec Account of the Conquest of Mexico.* Boston: Beacon Press, 1962.
Lockhart, James, *We People Here: Nahuatl Accounts of the Conquest of Mexico.* Los Angeles: University of California, Los Angeles Center for Medieval and Renaissance Studies, 1994.

—BENJAMIN KEEN

CONQUISTADORS

The immense body of writings on the Spanish Conquest presents varied images of the conquistador, ranging from the heroic to the villainous. These discordant images reflect the different ideological lenses through which historians and others have viewed the subject. The long dispute over the conquistador's character and conduct forms part of a larger debate over Spain's work in America. Two highly polemical phrases coined in the early twentieth century, "Black Legend" (Leyenda Negra) and "White Legend" (Leyenda Blanca), sum up the issues in the debate. The phrase "Black Legend" implied that critics of Spain's colonial record had defamed it with exaggerated, tendentious, and factually wrong charges of Spanish cruelty and bigotry; the phrase "White Legend" implied that defenders of that record had utterly distorted it by their stress on the relative mildness and benefits of Spanish colonial rule. In recent decades, with the rise of a supposedly more dispassionate, objective scholarship, the fires lit by that debate have died down, but they still smolder, kept alive by the publication of books such as *Dogs of the Conquest* (1983) by J. G. Varner and J. J. Varner, with its evidence that some conquistadors committed cruelties of a "grotesque fiendishness"; and by charges such as historian Joseph P. Sanchez's recent claim that the defamatory "Black Legend sentiment survives within the very backbone of our educational system—the monograph and the textbook."

It would be naive to deny that many conquistadors were hard, ruthless men—hard in dealing with each other and harder still with the Indians. We do not have to rely for proof on defenders of the Indian such as the famous Bartolomé de Las Casas. The evidence comes from official chroniclers such as Gonzalo Fernández de Oviedo and Antonio de Herrera; Oviedo, an ardent imperialist who shared the typical contempt of the colonists for the Indian, wrote that some conquistadors could more accurately be called "depopulators or destroyers of the new lands." Official reports and letters provide a mass of testimony on the subject. A report to Felipe II by Alonso de Zorita, a Spanish judge of great integrity who spent 18 years in New Spain and the Caribbean (1548–66), contains this striking phrase: "When the Spaniards discover a new mine, vultures gather."

Spain's economic backwardness and immense inequalities of wealth, which sharply limited opportunities for advancement or even a decent livelihood for many Spaniards, help explain the desperate valor of the conquistadors as they roamed the New World in quest of golden kingdoms; they also suggest one reason for the conquistadors' harsh, intensely exploitative treatment of the Indians. By no accident, many great captains of the Conquest—Fernando (Hernán) Cortés, Francisco Pizarro, Pedro de Valdivia, Basco Núñez de Balboa—came from Extremadura, Spain's poorest province. We should note, too, the climate of violence that prevailed in contemporary Spain, a legacy of the Reconquest—the long struggle to expel the Moors from Spain—and the social and economic conditions it created.

In the Indies, this propensity for violence found a large new field of action. In the first phase of the Conquest, in the absence of a strong Crown presence, it generated incessant feuding among the early conquistadors, culminating in almost three decades of murderous civil wars in Peru; it also contributed to a barbarous mistreatment of Indians that sometimes assumed the proportions of genocide. The semifeudal values and ideals of the conquistadors, who were determined to *valer más* (rise in the world) and achieve a life of ease by whatever means were necessary, who regarded gold as the prime symbol of wealth, also contributed to the Conquest's predatory character, often abetted by the impotence or complicity of royal officials. After plundering and melting down the available stock of Indian gold and silver objects, the conquistadors turned to other means for extracting wealth from the natives: the imposition of intolerable tribute burdens on the Indians, the destructive, wasteful exploitation of Indian labor in enterprises like mining and pearl-fishing, and in some areas a large-scale traffic in Indian slaves. These practices led to the almost complete extinction of the Indians in the Caribbean islands, the adjacent fringes of South America, and parts of Central America. In heavily populated Mexico and Peru the Indian population suffered a decline of perhaps 90 percent in the sixteenth century. Most recent studies agree that diseases of European origin to which the Indians had no acquired immunity—smallpox, measles, yellow fever, malaria, among others—were the major factor producing this demographic catastrophe. But overwork, malnutrition, social disorganization, and loss of will to live contributed to the terrible mortality associated with the great epidemics and even with epidemic-free years.

Finally, we should note the brutalizing effects of a colonial war waged by Europeans against a people of different race, color, and culture, many of whose traits, especially their religious practices, these Europeans found abhorrent. The encounter bred an intense chauvinism and racism in the invaders, and helped transform some ordinary Spaniards who once may have lived peacefully in their native villages into killers and torturers. The epithet "dogs" *(perros),* commonly applied by the conquistadors to the Indians, served to dehumanize them, contributing to the atmosphere in which the massacres and other well-verified horrors of the Conquest took place.

Not until 1542 did the Crown, fearing the rise of a powerful conquistador feudalism in the Indies and alarmed by the rapid decline of the Indian population, promulgate the reformist New Laws that—although often weakened by the Crown's retreat under pressure from the conquistadors—

put some checks on tribute burdens and the exploitation of Indian labor. The New Laws came too late to save the Indians of the Caribbean, but improved the condition of the Indians of New Spain and Peru enough to prevent a repetition of the demographic disaster that occurred in the islands.

To concede the barbarous, rapacious character of the Spanish Conquest is not to ascribe to the conquistadors a unique capacity for cruelty or deviltry. Every colonial or imperialist power has its own Black Legend that is no legend but a dismal reality. The brutality of the Spanish Conquest is matched by that of the genocidal Indian wars waged by the United States in the nineteenth century. What distinguishes Spain from many other colonial or imperialist powers of history is that it produced a minority of men who denounced in the face of the world the crimes of their own countrymen and did all in their power to stop what Bartolomé de Las Casas called "the destruction of the Indies." Jean-François Marmontel, author of the best-selling novel *Les Incas* (1777), a lachrymose account of the destruction of the Inca Empire that usually is regarded as a source of the Black Legend, paid generous tribute to this Spanish trait. "All nations have had their brigands and their fanatics, their times of barbarism, their fits of fury. The finest peoples are those which accuse themselves of their crimes. The Spaniards have this proud trait, worthy of their character."

That Spanish dissident minority included some conquistadors who were transformed by their experiences, were taught humility and respect for Indian values, or even came to concede the moral superiority of the Indian over the Spaniard. Alvar Núñez Cabeza de Vaca learned that lesson in the course of his immense eight-year trek from the Gulf Coast of Texas to Mexico (1528–36), which he survived thanks to the generosity of the Indians. In his account of his adventures he reverses the roles of the Indians and the Spaniards; the Spaniards are presented as savages and the Indians as humane and civilized. Another conquistador, Pedro Cieza de León, the "prince of chroniclers," criticized the cruelties of the conquest of Peru and clearly sympathized with the ideas of Las Casas. Yet another conquistador, Alonso de Ercilla, author of the finest Spanish epic poem of the sixteenth century, *La Araucana,* dealing with the struggle of the Araucanian Indians of Chile against the Spaniards, reverses the customary roles; he praises and even glorifies the Indians who appear throughout the poem as a heroic people determined to be free, while the victorious Spaniards are often portrayed as cowardly, greedy, and selfish.

Granted that not all thought or acted alike, what sort of men were the conquistadors? The Conquest of America attracted a wide variety of types. There was a sprinkling of professional soldiers, some with backgrounds of service in the Italian wars and some with pasts that they preferred to forget. The old conquistador Gonzalo Fernández de Oviedo had such men in mind when he warned the organizers of expeditions against "fine-feathered birds and great talkers who will either slay you or sell you or forsake you when they find that you promised them more in Spain than you can produce." In one of his *Exemplary Tales,* Cervantes describes the Indies as

"the refuge and shelter of the desperate men of Spain, sanctuary of rebels, safe-conduct of homicides." No doubt men of this type contributed more than their share of the atrocities that stained the Spanish Conquest.

But the background of the conquistadors was extremely varied, running the whole gamut of the Spanish social spectrum. Few, however, came from its extremes: high-ranking, wealthy nobles who did not need to leave and paupers who generally lacked the means to leave. The majority were commoners: artisans, peasants, tradesmen, seamen (who often jumped ship on arrival in an American port), and professionals or semiprofessionals like notaries or apothecaries and barbers (who sometimes doubled as doctors). In this *Historia verdadera de la conquista de la Nueva España,* the conquistador Bernal Díaz del Castillo claims he and most of his comrades were nobles, but modern-day scholar Fernando Benítez observes that "the beings he paints are men who have not yet shed their smell of earth and onions. . . . One can almost see their callused hands and hear their mule bells, their country songs, and their nicknames." We should note, however, that the terms *hidalgo* (a member of the lower nobility) and "peasant" and "artisan" were not mutually exclusive. Earning one's living may have been ideally incompatible with the nobility's values and way of life, but, as the scholar Ida Altman notes in her study of sixteenth-century emigration to the Indies from Extremadura, the region's villages were filled with humble *hidalgo*-farmers "who worked land with a pair or two of oxen," and some *hidalgo*-artisans held honored posts in town councils.

Many conquistadors were marginal *hidalgos* of a different type, poor gentlemen who wished to improve their fortunes; some were *segundones* (second sons), disinherited by a tendency among the Spanish nobility to entail the family estate in the eldest son; others, like the famous conqueror of Peru, Francisco Pizarro, were illegitimate sons of nobles. Of the 168 men who captured the Inca emperor Atahualpa at Cajamarca in 1532, 38 were *hidalgos* and 91 plebeians, with the background of the rest unknown or uncertain. According to James Lockhart, who has studied the men of Cajamarca, 51 members of the group were definitely literate and about 76 "almost certainly functioning literates." The group included 19 artisans, 12 notaries or clerks, and 13 "men of affairs."

Of the Spanish kingdoms, Castile provided by far the largest contingent of emigrants, with natives of Andalusia dominating the first, or Caribbean, phase of the Conquest, and men from Extremadura the largest single group in the second, or mainland, phase. Foreigners were not absent from the Conquest. Oviedo, in an attempt to clear Spain of sole responsibility for the crimes committed in the Indies, assures us that men had come from every part of Christendom: there were Italians, Germans, Scots, Englishmen, Frenchmen, Hungarians, Poles, Greeks, Portuguese, and men from all the other nations of Asia, Africa, and Europe.

An institution inherited from the Spanish Reconquest, the *compañía* (warrior band), whose members shared in the profits of the enterprise according to certain rules, provided a model for the organization of the American expeditions of conquest. At its head stood a military leader who usually possessed a royal *capitulación* (contract), which vested him with the title of *adelantado* (commander) and with governing powers in the territory to be conquered. Some leaders were wealthy in their own right and contributed large sums or incurred immense debts to finance the expedition. Cortés contributed a substantial portion of the financing of the Mexican venture from his own resources, and also went into debt. Much of the capital needed to fit out ships, acquire horses and slaves, and supply arms and food was provided by Italian, German, and Spanish merchant capitalists and royal officials grown wealthy through the slave trade or other means.

In principle the warrior band was a military democracy, with the distribution of spoils carried out by a committee elected from among the entire company. After subtracting the *quinto* (royal fifth) and the common debts, distribution was made in accordance with the individual's rank and contribution to the enterprise. Despite its democratic aspect, the leaders, captains, large investors, and royal officials dominated the enterprise of conquest and took the lion's share for themselves. Describing the distribution of spoils after the fall of Tenochtitlan, Bernal Díaz recalls in his *Historia verdadera* the grumbling of the cavalrymen and foot soldiers who complained how little was left for them after deducting the royal fifth, another fifth for Cortés (29,600 pesos), and shares for each of the captains, priest, and royal officials. The sums received by some 750 common soldiers, ranging between 80 and 50 pesos, at a time when a sword cost 50 pesos and a crossbow 60, were so paltry that some suggested, ironically or in earnest, that the whole should be distributed among their comrades who had lost their limbs, or were lame or paralyzed or had suffered powder burns, or among the families of the dead. Many had contracted large debts for the purchase of arms and other needs, and naturally resented such meager rewards for their hardships and suffering; they vented their anger at Cortés, claiming that he had hidden part of the gold and making other scurrilous remarks; some of the things they said, Díaz writes, were not fit to repeat in his history.

At a later stage of each conquest came the distribution of *encomiendas* (assignments of Indians who were to serve the grantees with tribute and labor). Craftsmen and other plebeians received *encomiendas* after the Conquests of Mexico and Peru; later, however, only the leaders and *hidalgo* members of expeditions were rewarded with such grants. As a rule, the military leaders and captains received much more populous and valuable *encomiendas* than those granted to rank-and-file conquistadors. After the Conquest of Mexico, Cortés reserved for himself the tribute of rich towns in heavily populated areas, forming a huge feudal domain. The *encomienda,* supplemented by a land grant, typically small, became the principal source of wealth or livelihood for the former conquistadors. If gold or silver could not be obtained directly, the *encomenderos* sought to obtain them by sale in local or distant markets of the tribute goods produced by the Indians. In time the *encomienda* became the basis of great

landed estates and their owners a colonial seigneurial class whose power challenged that of the Crown.

The Spanish Conquest was, among other things, a conquest of women. From the time of the Discovery, Indian women were frequently subjected to rape, enslavement, and other brutalities. In Mexico, the fall of Tenochtitlan was followed by the enslavement of both Mexica (Aztec) men and women. A native account, the *Florentine Codex,* tells that "the Spaniards seized and set apart the pretty women, the fair-skinned ones. And some women, when they were robbed, covered their faces with mud and put on old mended shirts and rags for their shifts. . . ." Cortés had ordered that all the slaves taken by the soldiers should be branded so that he could take the royal fifth and his own share of the captives. Bernal Díaz relates that when they returned the next day to take their shares of the remaining slave women they discovered that Cortés and his officers had "hidden and taken away the best looking slaves so that there was not a single pretty one left. The ones we received were old and ugly. There was much grumbling against Cortés on this account. . . ." Much casual sexual intercourse accompanied the Conquest, contributing to the swift rise of a mestizo class. Spanish authorities sometimes required that Indian women be baptized before intercourse. In 1538 the commander of an expedition in present-day Colombia was ordered to see to it that "no soldier slept with any Indian who was not a Christian," but the conquistadors do not seem to have taken such injunctions very seriously. After the Conquest, the *encomienda* provided former conquistadors with a large pool of Indian female servants who often became their concubines.

Bravery, tenacity, and an incredible capacity for enduring hardships were among the conspicuous virtues of the conquistador. The legendary Castilian austerity prepared the conquistador for the difficulties he encountered in the New World. The Spanish common soldier of the War of Granada ate only once a day, fortifying himself with swigs of the thin, sharply bitter wine he carried in a leather bottle. His single meal was a salad of onions, garlic, cucumbers, and peppers chopped very finely and mixed with bread, crumbs, olive oil, vinegar, and water. Soldiers with such traditions were capable of marching a day's journey on a handful of toasted corn.

A fierce nationalism and a religious fanaticism, more often manifested in a brutal contempt for the Indian than in a desire for his or her conversion, were essential elements in the conquistador's psychological make-up. Add to these traits the quality of romanticism. The Reconquest, filled with a thousand combats, raids, and ambushes, had heated the Spanish imagination to an incandescent pitch. Spanish romanticism found expression in a rich literature of romances, popular ballads that celebrated the exploits of the frontier wars against the Moors and that were frequently on the lips of the conquistadors.

The literate soldiers of the Conquest were also influenced by their reading of classic literature, especially of the romances of chivalry with their prodigious line of perfect knights and their mythical islands, Amazons, and giants, which the fantasy of the conquistadors placed in one or another part of the Indies. Some conquistadors were romantically conscious of their historical role. When some of Cortés's soldiers boasted to him that neither the Romans nor Alexander had ever performed deeds equal to theirs Cortés replied that "far more will be said in future history books about our exploits than has ever been said about those of the past."

Of the trinity of motives (God, Gold, and Glory) commonly assigned to the Spanish conquistador, the second was certainly uppermost in the minds of most. "Do not say that you are going to the Indies to serve the king and to employ your time as a brave man and an *hidalgo* should," observed Oviedo in an open letter to would-be conquistadors, "for you know the truth is just the opposite: you are going solely because you want to have a larger fortune than your father and your neighbors." Pizarro put it even more plainly to a priest who urged the need of spreading the faith among the Indians. "I have not come for any such reasons. I have come to take away from them their gold," The chronicler of the Conquest of Mexico, Bernal Díaz del Castillo, ingenuously declared that the conquistadors died "in the service of God and of His Majesty, and to give light to those who sat in darkness—and also to acquire that gold which most men covet." But Díaz wrote with the self-serving end of gaining additional rewards for his "great and notable services to the king," and his book was meant for the eyes of their grave worships, the members of the Royal Council of the Indies.

Most conquistadors dreamed of eventually returning to Spain with enough money to found a family and live in a style that would earn them the respect and admiration of their neighbors. Only a minority, chiefly large merchants and wealthy *encomenderos,* acquired the capital needed to fulfill that ambition, and not all of them returned to Spain. The majority, lacking *encomiendas* or other sources of wealth, remained and often formed ties of dependency with more powerful Spaniards, usually *encomenderos,* whose service they entered as artisans, military retainers, or overseers of the *encomiendas* or other enterprises.

After 1535 more and more would-be conquistadors came to the Indies, opportunities for joining profitable conquests diminished, and disillusioning failures abounded. The problem of a large number of unemployed and turbulent Spaniards, many of whom wandered about, robbing and abusing the Indians, caused serious concern to royal officials and to the Crown itself. One viceroy's proposed solution to rid Peru of the plague of unemployed conquistadors was to send them off on new conquests, "for it is well known that they will not work or dig or plow, and they say that they did not come to these parts to do such things." In 1555 King Carlos I (Emperor Charles I) agreed; permission for new conquests, he wrote, would serve to "rid and cleanse the country of the idle and licentious men who are there at present and who would leave to engage in that business. . . ."

Carlos therefore revoked a decree of 1549, issued at the urging of Las Casas, which prohibited new Indian conquests, and in 1559 the viceroy of Peru authorized an expedition to search for a golden kingdom rumored to exist in the heart of the Amazon. If one aim of the project was to rid Peru of "idle and licentious men," it backfired, for its abject failure produced a mutiny led by a veteran conquistador, Lope de Aguirre. He as been variously described as a forerunner of Latin American independence and a bloodthirsty madman and rebel, but in his own way he typifies the underdogs of the Conquest, the conquistadors who had lost out in the struggle for gold and *encomiendas.* Aguirre devised an audacious plan that called for the conquest of Peru, removal of its present rulers, and rewards for old conquistadors like himself who had "won those Indians with our persons and effort, spilling our blood at our expense, [but] were not rewarded." Accordingly he launched a "cruel war of fire and sword" against King Felipe II of Spain; his revolt caused many deaths, including his own, before it collapsed.

Of the many captains and their followers who rode or marched under the banner of Castile to the Conquest of America, few lived to enjoy in peace and prosperity the fruits of their valor, suffering, and cruelties. "I do not like the title of *adelantado,*" wrote Oviedo, "for actually that honor and title is an evil omen in the Indies, and many who bore it have come to an evil end." Of those who survived the battles and the marches, a few received the lion's share of spoils, land, and Indians; the majority remained in modest or worse circumstances, and frequently in debt. The conflict between the haves and the have-nots among the conquistadors, exemplified by the Aguirre revolt, contributed significantly to the explosive, tension-ridden state of affairs in the Indies in the decades following the great conquests.

See also Conquest; Encomienda; Hacienda; New Laws of 1542; Tribute: Colonial

Select Bibliography

Altman, Ida, *Emigrants and Society: Extremadura and America in the Sixteenth Century.* Berkeley: University of California Press, 1989.

Cerwin, Herbert, *Bernal Díaz: Historian of the Conquest.* Norman: University of Oklahoma Press, 1963.

Himmerich y Valencia, Robert, *The Encomenderos of New Spain, 1521–1555.* Austin: University of Texas Press, 1991.

Kelly, John E., *Pedro de Alvarado, Conqueror.* Princeton, New Jersey: Princeton University Press, 1932.

Lockhart, James, *The Men of Cajamarca: A Social and Biographical Study of the First Conquerors of Peru.* Austin: University of Texas Press, 1972.

Pereyra, Carlos, *Las huellas de los conquistadores.* Mexico City: Porrúa, 1986.

Thomas, Hugh, *Conquest: Montezuma, Cortés, and the Fall of Old Mexico.* New York: Simon and Schuster, 1993.

—BENJAMIN KEEN

CONSERVATISM

Almost at the end of his life Lucas Alamán, the most organized intelligence behind Conservatism in Mexico, said of himself: "I am a dry leaf that the wind of adversity has driven to and fro." Alamán never imagined that these same words he borrowed from the Book of Job would presage the oblivion into which his political work would fall in the long term, as his "party," the Conservatives, became labeled as reactionary. This was a misleading label, however, because in its origin, Conservatism was created in reaction to the destructive and wide-ranging effects of the French Revolution, whose Mexican variant was the War of Independence. Conservatism was not, as is commonly conceived, a negation of the idea of change or progress, nor did it decry political freedom, republicanism, or the bases of elective representation. Conservative thought in Mexico, as in other countries, was just another branch on the flourishing tree of modernity, taking the English version and the writings of Edmund Burke as the best exemplar. The ancien régime (the political system in France before the Revolution) and Conservatism were terms that ended up being linked together, but they never shared the same meaning.

In Mexico a false dichotomy was soon established, with the Liberals as "the party of progress" and the Conservatives as the "reactionary party." Furthermore, a Manichean historiography soon predominated, which saw Liberalism as synonymous with federalism and Conservatism as synonymous with centralism. Nothing could have been further from reality of the Mexican historical process. Both Liberalism and federalism and Conservatism and centralism have very different doctrinal and historical backgrounds. In the post-Revolutionary France of 1789, for example, Liberalism was frequently compatible with centralism. In Mexico at the beginning of the nineteenth century, a definite pragmatism distinguished the leaders of political groups rather than a clear difference between the groups per se. Lucas Alamán was an enthusiastic Liberal in the Cortes de Cádiz (regent parliamentary council of the Spanish Empire) and secretary of foreign and state affairs in the federalist administration of the 1820s. Valentín Goméz Farías, the radical Liberal vice president (1833–34) and president (1846), was one of the 46 deputies who initially encouraged the proclamation of Agustín de Iturbide's First Mexican Empire (July 1822–March 1823). Servando Teresa de Mier was the main leader of the American group of the Constitución de Cádiz and an unimpeachable Liberal and republican in the first independent Mexican Congresses; at the same time he never stopped being either doctrinally or in practice a fierce defender of centralism. Carlos María Bustamante, a zealous defender of the heterogeneous insurgent movement and author of *Cuadro histórico,* was pro-Iturbide and Liberal in the 1820s, but by the next decade had become a partisan of centralist government and member of the Supremo Poder

Conservador (Conservative Supreme Authority) of the centralist republic of 1836.

Francisco Manuel Sánchez de Tagle, who along with José María Luis Mora was one of the founders of *El Observador de la República Mexicana,* had read the works of Jeremy Bentham, the baron of Montesquieu, and Gaspar Melchor de Jovellanos from an early age. Despite this record, he later was the principal coauthor of the centralist Constitution of 1836 and secretary of the Supremo Poder Conservador of the same government. José María Gutíerrez Estrada was a republican and a Liberal in the 1820s; two decades later he had become the most obvious sponsor of a foreign constitutional monarchy. José Joaquín Pesado, author of the novel *Año nuevo* that criticized the Inquisition, a poet and government man, was also cofounder of the federalist Liberal periodical *La Oposición* (1833–34) and keen partisan of the suppression of the monasteries and confiscation of possessions belonging to religious communities in Veracruz (1833–34); nevertheless the same individual was later foreign secretary in the centralist administration of Anastasio Bustamante (1837–39), and during the short-lived "promonarchist" government of Mariano Paredes Arrillaga (1846) he was chief editor of the Catholic journal *La Cruz* (1855–58) and member of the governing council in the Félix Zuloaga–Miguel Miramón administration (1858–60).

The list could be enlarged further, but it is important to point out the lack of a simple dichotomy between federalism-liberalism, on the one hand, and centralism-conservatism, on the other. If this is the case, and if pragmatism or opportunism is evident, then why is there a problem discussing Conservatism in Mexico? Did a Conservative Party really even exist?

The answer in general terms is yes. Nevertheless, the existence of a Conservative philosophy and a Conservative political "protagonist" requires, in the first instance, temporal specificity. Conservatism in Mexico, like Liberalism, did not always remain the same; it was characterized by various protagonists and various specific features that depended on the political circumstances of the time. The study of Conservatism also makes sense in the context of a political "protagonist," rather than a political party, the former made manifest by various generations, plural ways of thinking, and above all the promotion of a national political project different from that of other political "protagonists" in the Mexican historical process. On the other hand, the notion of Conservatism becomes fragile or useless when it is explained as a monolithic and immovable entity.

The First Stage of Centralist Government

Traditional historiography has qualified the centralist republic of 1836 to 1841 as the first stage in Conservative government. The roots of this position can be found both in the automatic association between centralism and Conservatism that was assumed to counter the performance of the previous government, as well as in the political group (the names of Alamán, Sánchez de Tagle, and Gutíerrez Estrada all appear in this context) that encouraged a constitutionalism by the proclamation of the Siete Leyes (Seven Laws). Despite this theory, the events of the time indicated another course of action.

At the end of 1834, Antonio López de Santa Anna made an alliance with the political forces of Anastasio Bustamante. The reaction was basically against the structure of federalist government, but had no intention of annulling republicanism. This reaction is registered in the "Bases" (charter) for the new government of 1835, authored by Lucas Alamán. The new group in power proposed that the previous Congress took on the powers of a constituent assembly. José Ignacio de Anzorena, José María Cuevas, Antonio Pacheco Leal, Francisco Manuel Sánchez de Tagle, and Miguel Valentín were put in charge of the Constituent Commission. Even though it is evident that there was a clear relationship between the "Bases" of Alamán and the Siete Leyes, Sánchez de Tagle is recognized as being mainly responsible for drawing up the latter.

The final result of the new Constitution was not Conservative; instead, it instituted a centralist republic with proportional and Liberal representation. The document opens with the first declaration of the rights and duties of the Mexican and foreign inhabitants of the Independent Republic of Mexico. This is in great contrast with the federalist constitution of 1824, which is more concerned with the kind of government than the preservation of the Rights of Man.

Sánchez de Tagle started from the idea that these rights and obligations emerged from a rational and social pact, in that these concrete rights of man were born in the moment that individuals associated within a collective identity. The essential point was to forge and protect through the Constitution and the relevant guarantees that which is known today as negative freedom, or the "freedom from," given that the rights of man did not need to be named. They were prescriptives, ahistorical, and inherent in man himself.

As the preservation of the rights of the Mexican citizen was the most important concern, the Constituent Commission did not eliminate the division of powers and instead modified the "classical" form. Inspired by the constitutionalist treaties of Bentham, they established a fourth power, that of the Supremo Poder Conservador (Conservative Supreme Authority). This body not only would limit the abuses of the executive and legislative powers, but also provide security and guarantee the citizenry against sudden changes in authority. The Constituent Commission also guaranteed the rights of the Mexican citizen by means of the division of powers and a certain kind of limited right of *amparo* (which loosely can be translated as a writ of habeas corpus from the executive branch).

The most obvious breaks with the Constitution of 1824 were in the projection of a centralist Republic, evidenced by variations in the electoral system and public representation. The first issue in the new Constitution divided the states into political departments with the intention of putting an end to local rule through a delicate accommodation that would follow the natural divisions of the colonial past. In reality the move was not extremist, serving only to further concentrate the administrative functions and create government councils within the political departments. In the second area the change was more radical. The democratic Liberalism adopted by the Constitution of Cádiz since 1813 and adhered to with brief interruptions ever since, was damaged gravely. An electoral system of proportional representation was set up that had not existed in the previous constitution. The number of inhabitants necessary to constitute a municipality was increased from 1,000 to 8,000, and the vote was restricted, although not immediately, to those citizens who could read and write. It was all very clear. Just like the English tradition of the eighteenth century and greater part of the nineteenth century, the constituents of 1835 to 1836 were "liberals" of the Enlightenment, not democrats.

This brings to mind the idea that if there were differences of principle between the protagonists concerning the structure of federalist and centralist government, then there also were elements of similarity between the political groups of the 1820s and 1830s. Among these points of agreement were respect for individual rights, rejection of despotic government, the permanence of a representative system, the division of public power, written constitutionalism, republicanism (as opposed to any derivative of colonial monarchism), and the pragmatism or opportunism of the Mexican political class.

Faced by this constellation of facts, the existence of a Conservative "party" in the 1830s is inconceivable in the strict sense of the word. It is not, however, in doubt that the various members, writers, governors, or assessors of the Constituent Commission of 1836 would become the future founders of the Conservative group. Alamán himself in his *Historia de México* confesses that links existed between the Conservative group of the period and the thinkers and politicians that adhered to the Scottish Masonic Rite of the 1820s and 1830s. Nevertheless, he decreed that they were not the same; these groups had gone through various alterations and changes of thought, and in the Conservative epoch of the 1840s things did not work according to the logic of the old Masonic lodges.

The Alamán Period, Apogee of Conservatism

It must be emphasized that the Conservative political protagonist with a real identity, although it still was not black-and-white, was a phenomenon of the late 1840s. If there were various thinkers of that group who could be characterized for their support of Enlightenment concepts and practical governing ability, none could touch Lucas Alamán. Alamán was the only thinker and statesman that had conceived a political project at the state level in the widest sense of the phrase. In economic matters Alamán placed his confidence in the shift from trade to manufacturing as the new basis of Mexican wealth. Government protectionism and the private industrial enterprise were the main means of generating social progress. Alamán considered that education was a basic condition for the social and political evolution of the Mexican people. His means of achieving this was a "total education system" that would strategically place specialized colleges throughout the country.

He regarded Catholicism as being the only unifying link in the structure of Mexican society. As a result the establishment of the agreement on mutual respect between the state and the church was essential. From Alamán's perspective, this implied the protection of the privileges and economic corporativism of the church hierarchy, the nonintervention of the state in matters connected with *patronato real* (appointment of clerical positions), and the maintenance of freedom of conscience.

Alamán's *Historia de México* does not mention art and culture as a specific responsibility of government. Nevertheless Alamán the statesman was an assiduous promoter of theater groups and scientific magazines, and the founder of museums and national archives.

Alamán was the first creator of a Mexican foreign policy in support of independence and against U.S. expansionism. The line of his political romanticism did not vary: he stood for sovereignty (independent of the type of government), Catholicism, and economic self-sufficiency.

The most delicate issue at stake was the change in government structure. When Alamán wrote the fifth volume of the *Historia de México,* he was a broken man. The loss of Texas and other territories as a result of the war with the United States and the instability of the previous governments could have done no less. The mature Alamán forgot his enthusiasm for democratic Liberalism of the 1820s and the centralist republicanism of the 1830s to return to the history of Mexico and his old teacher, Edmund Burke, and his political vision. From this Alamán adopted and adapted a preference for reforms made with "pious fear and trembling solicitude," indicative of his preference for gradual as opposed to radical change as inherent in the concept of revolution. Political problems were seen in intimate relationship with issues of morality and religion; the defense of social and political differences in the citizenry were contrasted with the liberal uniformity of the French and the universalist democracies; the defense of constitutionalism and proportional representation was set against unlimited monarchism; political romanticism was contrasted with foreign universalist or expansionist concepts, and political pragmatism as opposed to paper governments; variety and pluralism of the historical traditionalism was favored instead of French liberal uniformity and abstractionism; the defense of the "organized freedom" (associated with security of property) was contrasted with "unchained liberalism."

To sum up, the government structure favored by Alamán led him away from his clean federalist republicanism and centralism, and at the same time brought him closer to constitutional monarchy and some of the centralizing emendations of the centralist Constitution of 1836.

Federalism in Alamán's opinion favored local abstentionism and the sacrifice of "the general good for the particular." Nor was it possible to establish a system of general taxation or a national army under the federalist system. For the moment he had to strengthen the executive. As he had announced himself as being very strongly against dictatorship, he proposed first of all to restore the old colonial injunction against the viceroys. Second, even though he again restricted election of public authorities, Alamán did not eliminate political representation. He fought to change the make-up of the Congress by symmetrical and uniform systems in the provinces or political departments. This would have implied the breaking up of the large states and the rearranging of smaller ones to avoid all attempt at separatism or confederatism. At the national level the Congress would have had a single chamber—one deputy for each department—or two chambers if it was considered necessary. Alamán nevertheless allowed elective proportional representation, notably the weakening to a degree of the indirect electoral system by the holding of direct elections for the posts of deputy and president. The task of the Congress would be to legislate, approve the budget, declare war or peace, and regulate tariffs. The other chamber would be smaller than that of the deputies and not participate in the traditional elective system. It would be filled, in brief, by the representatives of governing councils of each department and the ministries of finance and justice to create the "General Council of the Nation." Alamán proposed to install a constituent congress composed of a few members for the reform of the constitution, which would operate the system of commissions and subcommissions with the participation of government agencies according to the theme and branch of business.

The Conservative group had matured by the 1840s and forged its own identity. It was necessary "to accommodate political institutions to events" and not vice versa. Historical constitutionalism supported the remaining characteristics or general principles that had made the Conservatives a political protagonist. It is worth enumerating them briefly. First, they favored gradual rather than revolutionary change. This did not imply the disappearance of the use of violence as a last resort to sustain the existence of the collective and traditions. Second, they favored political pragmatism and realism over uncontrolled abstractionism or idealism. Third, they preferred the provincial interpretation of history as the ultimate explanation of events, as opposed to secular visions. This did not imply the negation of the European Enlightenment; on the contrary there were notable connections with the movement as evidenced in the concept of freedom and property as inseparable entities. Fourth, they had faith in everyday structures instead of uniformity and liberal equality. Fifth, they viewed order and stability as the most important values for collective existence. They exchanged hierarchy for what was most prized by the Liberals: freedom.

The Conservative group participated as an organized political protagonist in the elections for the Mexico City Council in 1849. Alamán was the winning candidate, backed by the newspaper *El Universal.* Changes in government were initiated again in 1853 when Alamán invited the exiled Santa Anna to take up the Presidency once more on the condition that the two would adjust the "Bases" of the administration of the republic that had been drawn up by the Conservative leader. These "Bases" pronounced in favor of a centralist republican government and a reduced legislative council; Conservative principles were reiterated, while distance was established from the dangers of projecting a monarchical regime. Lucas Alamán and José María Tornel y Mendívil died shortly after Santa Anna took possession. Antonio de Haro y Tamariz was deposed from the presidential cabinet. These events gave way to the tyranny of 1853 to 1855 that had no connection with what had been the first exercise in Conservative government, in the strict sense of the word.

The Monarchist Period

Monarchism was without a doubt a further vein of Conservatism in Mexico, but paradoxically not all monarchs had a conservative identity. The political survival of monarchism both preceded and accompanied the creation of the Mexican state. The Spanish Empire, of which New Spain formed a part, lasted three centuries; the Empire of Iturbide only seven months. Prior to the declaration of the federalist Constitution of 1824, there were different promonarchist factions in the various constituent congresses. In January 1827 Father Joaquín Arenas created a chimerical plan to reestablish Spanish dominion over Mexico and restore the old relationship with the Vatican state. The same luck befell the plan of the curates Carlos Tepisteco and Epigmenio de la Piedra (February 1834) to establish a constitutional indigenous monarchy and maintain the Catholic faith.

Even so, the true association between Conservatism and monarchism arose parallel with the political existence of the latter. The most outstanding figure of this Conservative tendency was José María Gutíerrez Estrada. In 1840 he sent an open letter in which he proposed the formation of a new Constituent Congress. In his opinion, republicanism, be it centrist or federalist, had led only to oppression and anarchy. The party struggle had made necessary a third element to balance the forces. From his perspective, liberty and monarchy were not incompatible terms, nor were despotism and monarchy synonymous. For this reason the constitution should not be suppressed, nor the elective office. The monarch tended to act as protector of the people and the chosen electoral system. Gutíerrez Estrada imagined a proportional system like that proposed in the Constitution of 1836. His preference for a foreign sovereign with royal blood was based both on the three-century-old colonial tradition and the defense of Catholicism against Protestantism as well as his prophetic anticipation of territorial expansionism of the United States. He knew, as an avid reader of Montesquieu, that the best way of governing was not the most modern but that which "best accommodated the customs, morality, and particular circumstances of each country." Disheartened, he believed in the 1840s that monarchy would be the best system to preserve Mexican independence. On a rational basis Gutíerrez Estrada adopted the monarchic system but his "heart," as he himself said, "was purely and sincerely republican."

The monarchic possibility annoyed the military partisans, who preferred to conspire in secret. The scandal was so great that Gutíerrez Estrada was exiled and obliged to depart for Europe. Even so, the promonarchists returned to take power in 1846 with the coup d'état of Mariano Paredes y Arrillaga. The participation of the plenipotentiary of Spain, Salvador Bermúdez de Castro, and that of Manuel Sánchez de Tagle and Lucas Alamán in their capacity as journalists for the periodical *El Tiempo* are noteworthy in this case. Both of them publicly declared themselves to be sympathizers of constitutional monarchy. The reasons they gave were not substantially different from those voiced by Gutíerrez Estrada. What they did not count on was that the U. S. intervention would weaken their hopes for a monarchy. When the Constituent Congress reunited in June 1846 no one dared to defend monarchism as a form of government. The Constitution of 1824 was redeclared, and the presidency handed over to Santa Anna. Paredes y Arrillaga was banished, never to make any further substantial contribution to Mexican politics.

The return of the Conservatives would not occur until the Catholic opposition to the Constitution of 1857, the War of the Reform (1858–61), and the French Intervention (1862–67). This was in fact the historical period, the Reform especially, in which the antagonism between Liberals and Conservatives is most clearly seen. Paradoxically, the Conservatism defended in this period lacked a serious program. It explored Catholicism (Clemente de Jesús Munguía, José Joaquín Pesado, and José María Roa Bárcena), militarism (Félix Zuloaga and Miguel Miramón), and monarchism (Gutíerrez Estrada, Father Fancisco Javier Miranda, Emperor Maximilian von Hapsburg, and Miramón) but never proposed a wide-ranging national program as had Lucas Alamán in his time. Moreover, the search for a foreign prince in 1863 ended with a counter-productive measure for the Conservatives. Maximilian was, in many senses, a Liberal. The alliance between the government of the United States and Juárez simply annihilated them. At the end of the Restored Republic (1867–77), the Conservatives tried to make a comeback in the elections of 1877 but were roundly defeated. From then on Conservatism in Mexico transformed into a socioreligious phenomenon or the political stance of isolated individuals that gradually became diluted in the first stage of the Porfirio Díaz's rule.

See also Bases Orgánicas; French Intervention; Liberalism; Monarchism; Wars of Reform

Select Bibliography

Alamán, Lucas, *Historia de México desde los primeros movimientos que prepararon su independencia en el año de 1808 hasta la época presente.* 5 vols., Mexico City: Fondo de Cultura Económica, 1985.

Fuentes Mares, José, *Miramón, el hombre.* Mexico City: Joaquín Mortiz, 1974; 5th edition, Grijalbo, 1986.

Munguía, Clemente de Jesús, *En defensa de la soberanía, derechos y libertades de la iglesia.* 2nd edition, Mexico City: Tradición, 1973.

Noriega, Alfonso, *El pensamiento conservador y el conservadurismo mexicano.* Mexico City: Universidad Nacional Autónoma de México, 1972.

Pascal Gargiulo, Jeanne G., "Lucas Alamán, Mexican Conservatism, and The United States: A History of Attitudes and Policy, 1823–1853." Ph.D. diss., Fordham University, 1992.

Quintanilla Obregon, Lourdes, *El nacionalismo de Lucas Alamán.* Guanajuato: Gobierno del Estado de Guanajuato, 1991.

Roa Bárcena, José María, *Biografía de D. José Joaquín Pesado.* Mexico City: Jus, 1962.

Sierra, Justo, José María Gutiérrez Estrada, and Mariano Otero, editors, *1840–1850: Documentos de la época.* Mexico City: Secretaría de la Reforma Agraria, 1981.

Sordo Sedeño, Reynaldo, *El Congreso en la primera república centralista.* Mexico City: Colegio de México, 1993.

Zoraida Vázquez, Josefina, coordinator, *La fundación del Estado mexicano, 1821–1855.* Mexico City: Nueva Imagen, 1994.

—Israel Arroyo García

CONSTITUTION OF 1824

Through the Constitution of 1824, the Republic and the federal system were established for the first time. This Constitution was not an immediate or necessary consequence of the country's independence, achieved in 1821; rather, it was the result of the conflict between the two factions that rose up in the country. On one hand were the Liberals, who were proponents of the federal system, and on the other hand were the Conservatives, who supported either a constitutional monarchy or a centralist republic. The Conservatives already had managed to introduce a monarchy as the first form of government of the independent country, at whose head was Augustín I, the former royalist colonel Augustín de Iturbide who consummated the independence and was anointed as emperor by the Mexican Constituent Congress in 1822. However, the Liberal and federalist forces from that same Congress began to propose the republican form of government as a result of the provinces' requests for autonomy. The plural Congress had been inaugurated on February 24, 1822, on the site of the Great College of Saints Peter and Paul, pillar of the Jesuit culture in the new world; but when the emperor precipitously ordered the Congress to be cloistered and jailed some of the Liberal delegates on October 31, 1822, a revolution was organized to demand Congress's immediate reinauguration. The revolution, formed around the Plan de Casa Mata of February 1, 1823, forced the imperial authority to reestablish the Congress one month later, on March 7, 1823.

In light of these events, Congress considered Augustín I's titles and decided that it would no longer recognize them in the decree of April 8, 1823. In that same decree, Congress abolished the Empire and named Guadalupe Victoria, Nicolás Bravo, and Pedro Celestino Negrete, persons with distinct political tendencies, as a triumvirate with executive power as of March 30 of that same year. This collective executive power agreed with the proposal, written in the insurgent's Constitution of Apatzingán of October 1814, of not placing all executive power in the hands of one person who could abuse it, as Iturbide had done.

With the object of eliminating the Conservatives from the Constituent Congress, on June 30, 1823, a Second Constituent Congress was summoned to be inaugurated on November 7 of that same year. One of the first acts of the Second Constituent Congress was to approve Article 5 of the Constitutive Act of the Mexican Federation, which established the federal system for the Mexican Republic by 70 votes in favor and 10 against, in the session of December 16, 1823. This act was approved on January 31, 1824, and became the first constitutional document of independent Mexico that defined the republican form and the federal system as norms of Mexican constitutional government and delineated the structure of the federal powers and of the state governments. Antipathy toward the European forms of government was one of the motivations for accepting republicanism; just as the United States of America had distanced itself from the English monarchy, Mexico did the same with regard to the Spanish monarchical government.

In preparing for the creation of the 1824 Constitution, one of the federalists' first tasks was to define the system for their colleagues. So it was that on July 8, 1823, delegate Antonio J. Valdés wrote in *The Federalist* that the federal form of government "is a national body made up of several states, provinces or sections, endowed with a private government under the republican form and a general government composed of the three powers, legislative, executive and judicial, for the Union regime or the confederation of states into the body of a nation." In the same way, delegate Juan de Dios Cañedo defined, in the Second Constituent Congress, that the new sovereignty of the states meant the existence of each state's own government, independent of the federal government, with the ability to determine definitively the matters within its domain and organized according to their trilogy of powers already mentioned.

Federalism had vocal opponents, however; as early as 1823, moderates such as Servando Teresa de Mier prophesied that Mexico did not possess the political maturity as a consolidated nation to attempt, immediately after its status as a colony and then as an empire, the decentralized form of government that federalism implies. Conservatives, of course, made the case even more strongly. They argued that the federal system would be a debacle, that the "invention" of federalism was so foreign to the centralist tendencies of the country that it would only yield disunion and anarchy. This campaign against federalism would not cease until the reestablishment of the Republic in 1867, with intermediate stages where at times the federalist tendencies seemed to be reborn, as happened in 1846. Despite such criticisms, the fundamental structure of the federal system clearly coincided with the aspirations to liberty and independence of the provinces that formed Mexico.

It was evident that the form of government adopted in the Federal Constitution of 1824 had been inspired by the Constitution of the United States of America. One of the delegates of the Constituent Congress who later would figure predominantly in the political history of Texas, Lorenzo de Zavala, harshly criticized the Mexican Constituent Congress for gaining access to the constitutional text from the United States only in a poor translation into Spanish that had been printed in the city of Puebla. (Evidence exists showing a very acceptable translation into Spanish published in 1823 by the press of Mariano Rivera Galván from Mexico City that accompanied a translation of two George Washington speeches, one of which was the Farewell Speech of 1796, that without a doubt, could have been consulted by all of the members of the Constituent Congress.) Yet it is necessary to agree that the problem of federalism was not a semantic one, but one of political and jurisprudential evolution, since the form of government organized in the U.S. Constitution was very schematic, and its subsequent evolution gave much of the form to the current government. Some aspects of U.S. federalism were developed slowly (and long after the adoption of the U.S. Constitution) through the precedents of the Supreme Court, whose recognition in Mexico would have been less probable, such as *McCullock v. Maryland* (1819), which defined the principle of implied powers, or *Gibbons v. Ogden* (1824), which developed the federal control of interstate commerce.

The U.S. Constitution was not the only influence on the Second Constituent Congress. It should be remembered that the principal drafter of the constitutional project of 1824, Miguel Ramos Arizpe, previously had been a delegate to the Cortes of Cádiz where he had taken a significant part in the formulation and promulgation of the Constitution of Cádiz of 1812. In it, the provincial delegations had been established as a reply to the need for autonomy in the Spanish provinces, from which, as scholar Nettie Lee Benson in her work about the provincial delegations correctly asserts,

initiated self-government in the Mexican provinces, and as a consequence, were the beginning of federalism.

The Mexican Constitution of 1824 did not contain a declaration of human rights modeled upon the Bill of Rights in the U.S. Constitution or the Universal Declaration of the Rights of Man and of the Citizen from France. This aspect also confirms the influence of the original U.S. Constitution of 1787, based on a concept of Natural Law that stated that the Constitution and laws did not have to enumerate the rights of man since these existed before the inception of the state.

Two laws enacted subsequent to the promulgation of the 1824 Constitution defined the Federal District or Mexico City and the province of Tlaxcala as federal territories and not as states, which meant that they did not have their own government, but that they were under control of the federal government. Federal territories continued to exist from the date of this Constitution until 1974. In this sense, the same principle as the U.S. federal system was continued, that of creating a federal city free from any interference from the states, by which the government of Mexico State was deprived of its natural capital; Mexico State suffered until finally establishing its capital in the city of Toluca in 1830.

The Constitution of 1824 placed the executive power in one person, as was the case in the U.S. Constitution, but not without first overcoming a very complex debate that discredited the advantages of collective executive power that the 1814 Insurgent Constitution of Apatzingán had adapted from the French Constitutions of 1795 and 1799. There was to be no separate election for vice president; the new vice president was to be the candidate who received the second-largest number of votes in the presidential election, as had been the case in the United States prior to the passage of the Twelfth Amendment to the Constitution. Because of this procedure, the office of the vice presidency was viewed with suspicion in Mexico; it was feared that the vice president would promote rebellions and coups and would conspire against the president. Finally, in 1857, the institution of the vice presidency was stricken from the Mexican Constitution.

The influence of the United States also presented itself in the creation of a second legislative body within the Congress—the Senate—with the intention of representing the federation entities on an equal plane and thus correcting the overrepresentation of the more populous states in the House of Delegates (Cámara de Diputados). In the end, the judicial power also was molded according to U.S. precedent, in this case, the Law of Judicial Organization of 1789 of the United States; Mexico established a Supreme Court with eleven justices to preside over the structure of the juridical apparatus in the country.

One forgotten item in the 1824 Constitution was the lack of a reference to municipalities, that afterwards would be regulated by the first Centralist Constitution of 1835.

The Constitution of 1824 contained a complicated reform system, as it did not permit any reform until six years after its approval, with the object being to discourage changes. Thus, it sought to contain the spirit of reform always present since then in Mexico. The attempt to discourage reforms proved counterproductive, however; by 1830 lawmakers demanded not simply pertinent reforms but the absolute and total change of the Constitution.

The Constitution only had 17 formal alterations of its text, most initiated by the legislatures of the states. The procedure required two sessions of the federal Congress: once the initiative for alteration was received, it was preliminarily discussed and then sent for publication and distribution before a second legislative session of the Congress of the Union could definitively approve or reject it. The sole objective of this procedure was to give thought to the process of constitutional reform, which was to be abused so much during the twentieth century in Mexico.

The general characteristics that were established for the first time in the Constitution of 1824 continue until the present day, despite the many constitutions containing substantial changes that were approved in the nineteenth century. The republican form of government, the federal system, the investiture of executive power in a single person, the bicameral congress, and the structure of judicial power are legacies of the 1824 Constitution to the political organization of Mexico.

Select Bibliography

Alba, Pedro de, and Nicolás Rangel, *Primer Centenario de la Constitución de 1824: Obra commemorativa publicada por la H. Cámara de Senadores de los Estados Unidos Mexicanos.* Mexico City: Talleres Gráficos "Soria," 1924.

Barragán, José, *El juicio de responsabilidad en la Constitución de 1824.* Mexico City: UNAM, 1978.

Melgarejo Vivanco, José Luis, *La Constitución de 1824.* Veracruz: Gobierno del Estado de Veracruz, 1975.

Rabasa, Emilio O., *Historia de las Constituciones Mexicanas.* Mexico City: UNAM, 1994.

Reyes Heroles, Jesús, *El liberalismo mexicano,* vol. 1. Mexico City: Fondo de Cultura Económica, 1976.

Sierra Brabatta, Carlos J., *La Constitución Federal de 1824.* Mexico City: Departamento del Distrito, 1983.

—Manuel González Oropeza

CONSTITUTION OF 1857

The 1857 Constitution has its origins in the Revolution of Ayutla in 1854. For its part the uprising of Ayutla can be regarded as a centripetal force, the convergence of territorial disputes that destroyed the despotic centralism of Antonio López de Santa Anna. Juan Álvarez, the undisputed leader of the movement, became the interim president of the Republic in October 1855. Given the mandate of the Plan of Ayutla (March 1, 1855) and the Reform Plan of Acapulco (March 15, 1855), Álvarez announced elections to form a constituent assembly. The call to elections had as a historical reference the electoral system of 1843, and in general the Constitution of Cádiz (which operated by indirect elections via three stages), which had almost completely dominated the first half of the nineteenth century. The election of the constituents fell to a cultural elite rather than a wealthy elite. Nevertheless, it was also the result of a biased and partisan election—members of the clergy and the Conservative Party were not included.

The Constitution of 1857 can only be understood in the light of the two dominant trends of the era, the *puros* (radical liberals) and the *moderados* (moderates). Despite this, the deputies from each state did not represent uniform political positions; rather, political and ideological loyalties cut across state lines. Constitutional rule could be restored with considerable independence from local and regional concerns.

The idea of independence of the representatives becomes more powerful if a distinction is made between the Plan de Ayutla, the Reform of Acapulco with the Constitution of 1857, and the breakdown of Ignacio Comonfort's government when faced with the political aim of the Constitution. In the first case the Ayutla plan left a large measure of ambiguity about the government structure for a future constitution. A popular, representative republic was discussed, but the proposal to encourage federalism was never made explicit. In fact, the Reform Plan of Acapulco, linked to Comonfort's political aims, meant an explicit vote for Liberal unitarism. The Provisional Statute of Law of his government leaves no room for doubt about this. In the second case, the question is much more transparent; Comonfort ended by disowning the Constitution of 1857 and establishing a loose alliance with the Conservatives. The Constituent Congress was installed in February 1856 and the Constitution was announced on February 5, 1857. The Constitution is made up of 127 articles divided into eight headings; 29 articles refer to the rights of man, 25 to the legislative power, 15 to the executive, and 13 to the judiciary.

In general terms the 1857 Constitution can be said to belong to a classically liberal line of constitutions. Individual liberty and the inviolability of property take precedence over institutions and forms of government. The constitution did maintain the Mexican state's official intolerance of all other religions beside Catholicism and did little to separate church and state; however, in all other respects the Constitution of 1857 was a departure from all previous constitutions in Mexico. A particularly important innovation was the introduction of judicial *amparo* (roughly, right of *habeus corpus*), which remains an important guarantee against abuse of public authority.

Establishing the division of public powers into executive, legislative, and judicial branches underlined the Liberal inheritance of the Constitution. It is clear that no system of power could, in fact or by law, operate in a disconnected way and with total independence among all its elements. However, the eventual design created the problem of favoring Congress over the executive, a reaction to the despotism of Santa Anna. Public posts were subject to elections. The dilemma of the permanent nature of the magistrates of the Supreme Court of Justice was highlighted early by Comonfort himself. Nevertheless, in the Constitution of 1857 the idea held sway of a democracy based on the supremacy of Congress over the executive and of a universal (male) vote to elect any public official of broad standing.

The pact between the *moderados* and *puros* acted in harmony with this form of republican government, representative and popular. But the same was not true of deciding the type of federalism to include: a return to the Constitution of 1824, a U.S.-bicameral style of federalism, or federalism without a Senate. The Constituent Assembly opted for the last option. The creators of this amendment based their arguments on the supposed aristocratic origins of the Senate and a possible future alliance with the executive. The Senate was restored in 1874 after a long and bitter negotiation.

As the historian Daniel Cosío Villegas has affirmed, the prestige and relevance of the 1857 Constitution was born, paradoxically, from neglect and its durability. It was rejected by Comonfort, by the schismatic "Conservative government" opposed to the radical Liberal government during La Reforma (the period of *puro* rule), and by Maximilian's empire. It later was the object of criticism and reform in the Restored Republic. Nevertheless, it served as a flag of the struggle during La Reforma and the French Intervention. Even though Maximilian rejected its substance, he utilized many of its precepts because he was an ideological liberal. During the Restored Republic and the era of Porfirio Díaz, it was reformed and violated many times, but it never stopped being the strong idea of change and an essential model of government. Between 1916 and 1917 many of its fundamental principles were adopted to create the Constitution that today rules Mexico. The Constitution of 1857 and its reforms in 1874 did become, despite the length of time it took, a true Constitution.

Select Bibliography

Cosío Villegas, Daniel, *La constitución de 1857 y sus críticos.* Mexico City: Sep-Setentas 98, 1973.

Guerra, Francois-Xavier, *México: del antiguo régimen a la revolución,* vol. 1. Mexico City: Fondo de Cultura Económica, 1988.

Hale, Charles A., *The Transformation of Liberalism in Late Nineteenth-Century Mexico.* Princeton: Princeton University Press, 1989.

Rabasa, Emilio, *La constitución y la dictadura: Estudio sobre la organización política de México.* Mexico City: Porrúa, 1982.

Reyes Heroles, Jesús, *El liberalismo mexicano,* vol. 3. Mexico City: Fondo de Cultura Económica, 1974.

Ruiz Castañeda, María del Carmen, *La prensa periódica en torno a la Constitución de 1857.* Mexico City: Instituto de Investigaciones Sociales, UNAM, 1959.

—ISRAEL ARROYO GARCÍA

CONSTITUTION OF 1917

The Plan of Guadalupe of December 26, 1913, which laid the foundations of the Constititionalist faction headed by Venustiano Carranza, was the product of the Mexican Revolution and the banishment of Victoriano Huerta. Although established according to the Constitution of 1857, the Additions to the Plan of Guadalupe were to promote substantial reforms to that document. Promulgated in Veracruz on December 12, 1914, they saw the need to legally adopt social measures and to reorganize governmental authority, given the events of the Revolution. Government in its turn was reformed explicitly to summon a constitutional congress on September 14, 1916.

These reforms would comprise what would be known henceforth as the Constitution of 1917. Of course the form or procedure of reforming the text of the 1857 Constitution by means of an ad hoc Constitutional Congress provoked tremendous criticism from the detractors of the Constitutionalists. Among the latter were Jorge Vera Estañol, the minister of justice under Victoriano Huerta, who in exile wrote *Al margen del la Constitución,* published in Los Angeles in 1920. Such men considered that these reforms to the 1857 Constitution were not in agreement with the procedure laid out in that very document. It must be recalled that many constitutional reforms had followed different procedures to those laid down by constitutional law in the political history of Mexico. The Reform Act of 1847 did not stick to the procedure laid down by the Constitution of 1824, and the Constitution of 1857 itself had been passed by an Extraordinary Congress, without following any regular procedure at all. All this proved that in exceptional circumstances, such as the American invasion in the first instance or the Revolt of Ayutla against Antonio López de Santa Anna in the second example, a congress had been convened to make substantial reforms that did not stick to procedures established by the previous constitution.

Once summoned, this new Constitutional Congress differed from preceding ones in various particulars. First, it took place in Querétaro, rather than Mexico City, to avoid any accusation of being centralist. Second, only reform projects would be debated by the Congress, and no other matter, contrary to what had occurred with other Congresses. Finally, the election of the deputies to the Congress was made directly and their election verified on October 22, 1916, in accordance with the convocation of September 19, of the same year.

Membership of the Congress was various, as evidenced in the results of the debates. There were 232 landowning deputies with their respective aides. Chihuahua only had one deputy since the territory was largely occupied by Francisco Villa, at that time in opposition to Carranza, but there was adequate representation for the remaining states. Among the membership were close collaborators of Carranza such as Pastor Rouaix, Gerzayn Ugarte, and Cándido Aguilar. Luis Manuel Rojas, who was also collaborating in the Federal Public Administration, presided over the Congress, while José Natividad Macías was president of the Constitutional Commission.

The process of certifying representatives to the Congress lasted from November 21 to December 1, 1916. Despite some individual cases, the matter was considered to be advanced by December. On December 6, the projected reforms to the Constitution were made known and decisions began to be issued three days later. The commissions within the Congress distributed their decisions by title. The first commission, composed of Francisco J. Múgica, Alberto Román, Luis G. Monzón, Enrique Rocio, and Enrique Colunga, dealt with human rights or individual guarantees. The second commission, dealing with the government, the form it should take and its powers, was composed of Paulino Machorro Narváez, Heriberto Jara, Agustín Garza González, Arturo Méndoza, and Hilario Medina.

The most notable debates were those on education, agrarian reform, and work. There is no doubt that the most dramatic contribution was the inclusion within the Constitution of social guarantees for the protection of industrial and agricultural labor. Such guarantees fell outside the traditional bounds of Constitutional subject matter—primarily the establishment of individual rights and the organization of political power—as had been determined from the eighteenth century with the Declaration of the Rights of Man.

What previously had been considered as belonging to the realm of legal regulations was regarded by the Constitution of Querétaro as mandatory within the new constitutional arrangements. Changes were less spectacular in the area of governmental powers, since the Senate already had been reestablished in a reform of 1874. The presidential succession had been transformed in 1882, and the clause prohibiting reelection had been imposed in the reform of 1911. Nevertheless, aspects such as the strengthening of the presidential system over the parliamentary system (as originally conceived in 1857) and the suppression of political bosses to free up the municipalities were notable changes in the reformed Constitution.

The sessions continued until January 12, 1917. To commemorate the Constitution that they were so substantially altering, the new one was promulgated on February 5, 1917; it was published exactly one week later and became law on May 1.

As a result of the Constitution of 1917, the fifth term of the *Semanario Judicial de la Federación* (Weekly Gazette of the Federal Judiciary), which began on June 1 the same year, presented new constitutional interpretations elaborated by the federal judiciary. Even though the previous four terms, the first of which was initiated in 1871, were decided by the federal courts at top level, they now were consulted and occasionally cited but generally considered as historical anachronisms since they were interpreting the Constitution of 1857; the reforms of 1917 generally were considered to be so substantial as to create a new Constitution entirely.

From July 8, 1921, until mid-1996, there have been 102 decrees that have legally reformed the 136 articles that make up the Constitution of 1917, not including the temporary clauses. Only 38 articles have not suffered a single alteration since 1917. In a long history of modifications, the article that has been altered the most, 34 times to be precise, is number 73, which dealt with the powers wielded by Congress. Given that Mexico has a rigid system of competition between the federal government and the individual states, according to Article 124, which is more appropriate for a confederation than a federation, each time that the federal government wishes to take up an additional responsibility, the Constitution has to be reformed to include the new jurisdiction. This has been the situation since 1883, when for the first time the exclusive power of the federation to legislate on commercial matters appeared. Form this moment the federal government has continued to exclusively take on the regulation of topics of greater consequence.

From the 1970s one can see a tendency towards cooperative federalism, which now operates through education, health, ecology, and urban housing. Areas of competence in these topics, which are expressly discussed within the Constitution, are divided according to congressional law between the federal government, the states, and the municipalities.

The Constitution also imposed a concurrent system on state and federal government, given that the municipalities do not have legislative powers, which provides the federal government with two means of taxation. First, it can impose all those taxes or contributions it judges sufficient to satisfy public expenditure (Article 73, Section 7); second, it can reserve exclusively certain taxes such as those derived from foreign trade and petroleum, thus excluding state government from being concurrent in tax imposition in important materials (Article 73, Section 29).

The Congress of the Union is unique in having a Senate; this mechanism disappeared at the state level at the same time as it originally was eliminated on a federal level in 1857. Although the Senate was restored within federal government in 1874, this did not occur at state level.

The Mexican legislative process has peculiar constitutional characteristics, since a hierarchy of laws has not been totally defined in the country. The presence of exclusive and excluding power for the federal government in tandem with reserve powers for the states means that federal and state laws cannot clash given their separate areas of competence. If some of these laws appear to enter into conflict, it is only necessary to determine their constitutionality to the extent that they have overrun the strict distribution of competence.

According to Article 72 of the Constitution, legal reform must coincide with the procedure followed to make the law in the first place (in other words by the same legislative organ and observing the same process). Thus in the case of an international treaty, which always is ratified by the Senate without the participation of the Chamber of Deputies, the approving decree does not follow the same agenda as a regular law, since treaties and laws cannot modify each other within the Mexican constitutional system.

The federal executive power was strengthened by the Constitution of 1917; it made the president politically not responsible to the Congress of the Union and unable to be prosecuted other than for transgressions against the law, betrayal of his country, and serious crimes. This Constitution suppressed the vice presidency, which had been reestablished in 1904, in a reform to the previous Constitution, stating that in the case of total absence of a vice presidential successor, the Congress of the Union would take over. The six-year presidency was abolished in 1917, only to be reestablished in 1928. From 1824 the executive power was unified and absolutely free to nominate and remove secretaries of state and those responsible for public agencies that participate within the administration. The power held by the president of the United States as regards the military and international relations is very similar to that established for Mexico in the 1917 Constitution.

No reelection has been a principle since 1833, for which reason the president cannot be reelected. Nevertheless the Mexican president is intimately linked to the destiny of the political party that promoted him, and through this position his limited constitutional powers are increased to control the political life of the nation. Mexico differs from the old socialist countries in that the president of the Republic in turn controls the political party when in power and not the reverse.

The power of the federal judiciary has evolved through a ruling of varied nature: the decision of *amparo* (legal protection). From its creation in 1847, this legal ruling protected the people's human rights and individual guarantees from executive or legislative acts as well as decisions of the judiciary at the state level. Nevertheless, the ruling of *amparo* has become a control mechanism of constitutionalism. From 1869 the law of *amparo* could change the sentences of higher courts in every state when these overstepped an individual guarantee, for example when the letter of the law is not applied "exactly," according to Article 14. The organization of the judiciary is very similar to that of the United States, with 11 ministers in the Supreme Court, collegiate and circuit courts (established since 1950), as well as district juries.

In December 1994 the Council of Judicature was created by means of the corresponding constitutional reform that put the administrative functions of the federal judiciary and the appointment of federal judges within the ambit of the Supreme Court.

See also Agrarian Policy: 1910–40; Anticlericalism; Reform Laws

Select Bibliography

Ferrer Mendiolea, Gabriel, *Crónica del Constituyente.* Facsimile, Mexico City: Estado de Querétaro-Instituto Nacional de Estudios Históricos de la Revolución Mexicana, 1987.

Gutiérrez, Sergio Elias, *La Constitución Mexicana al final del siglo XX.* 2nd edition, Mexico City: Las Lineas del Mar, 1995.

Melgarejo Randolf, L., and Fernández Rojas, *El Congreso Constituyente de 1916 y 1917.* Mexico City: Departmento de Talleres Gráficos de la Secretaría de Fomento, 1917.

Romero Flores, Jésus, *Historia del Congreso Constituyente 1916–17.* Mexico City: Estado de Queretaro, 1986.

Sayeg Helú, Jorge, *El Congreso Constituyente de 1916–1917.* Mexico City: Biblioteca del Instituto Nacional de Estudios Históricos de la Revolución Mexicana, 1978.

Tena Ramírez, Felipe, *Derecho Constitucional Mexicano.* 29th edition, Mexico City: Porrúa, 1995.

—MANUEL GONZÁLEZ OROPEZA

CONTADORA GROUP

See under Foreign Policy

CONTEMPORÁNEOS GROUP

This designation refers to a now-distinguished group of Mexican literary figures who as young writers in the 1920s took as a central rallying point a journal they entitled *Contemporáneos,* published in Mexico City from 1928 to 1931. Individual members of the group, together with the journal itself (which carried the subtitle "Revista mexicana de cultura"), played an important role in the intense cultural and literary discussions that followed the Revolution of 1910. In contrast to more nationalistic voices, these writers consistently argued in favor of a cosmopolitan Mexican literature, a literature that was aware of its own roots but at the same time was in touch with the innovative developments visible in Europe and the United States.

The nucleus of the group was established in Mexico City prior to 1920, with the preparatory school friendships of Jaime Torres Bodet, Bernardo Ortiz de Montellano, José Gorostiza, Carlos Pellicer, and Enrique González Rojo. They were joined soon thereafter by Salvador Novo and Xavier Villaurrutia, and then by Jorge Cuesta and Gilberto Owen. During the 1920s these young writers collaborated in a number of literary and editorial projects, among them the journals *La Falange* (1922–23) and *Ulises* (1927–28) and the rather tendentious *Antología de la Poesía mexicana moderna,* for which Cuesta took responsibility in the name of the entire group.

Their most ambitious and most significant group enterprise, however, was the publication of *Contemporáneos,* a broadly ranging monthly publication on literature and culture in the already established European tradition of the French *Nouvelle Revue Franjaise* or the Spanish *Revista de Occidente.* The journal appeared in 11 volumes and 43 numbers, from June of 1928 through December of 1931. Prepared first in the printshops of Cultura and then in those of Mundial, all of the numbers include excellent reproductions of paintings, drawings, etchings, and photographs, and each volume has a useful and complete index. Approximately two-thirds of each number is dedicated to essays, critical studies, and creative writing; the remaining third contains comments and reviews with the title of "Motivos," comparable to the well-known "Notas" in the *Revista de Occidente.* The monthly scheme of *Contemporáneos* was never interrupted, but there were two separate periods in its publication history. The first eight numbers came out under the direction of an editorial board made up of Torres Bodet, Ortiz de Montellano, and González Rojo, together with Bernardo J. Gastélum, director of the Department of Public Health where most of the young writers from the group were employed at that time. With the support of Genera Estrada in the Ministry of Foreign Relations, Ortiz de Montellano took over sole editorship of the journal for the remaining numbers. A year later, in the May 1931 number, Ortiz de Montellano reaffirmed the dual cultural goal of the journal: to be both intensely Mexican and at the same time informed as to things outside that national frame.

The journal provided the young collaborators with an important avenue for the publication of their own creative and critical works, and at the same time expressed their clearly outward-looking view of culture and art. There is evidence, for example, of a notable affinity and level of communication between these young Mexican and other similar groups and writers in the Hispanic world. Indications of that communication are the contributions from the Spaniards Gerardo Diego and Benjamín Jarnés, or the published texts by the Spanish Americans Pablo Neruda, Vicente Huidobro, and Jorge Luis Borges (included with others in two special poetry numbers). In addition, a great many of the critical commentaries and reviews in the "Motivos" section make clear the group's ongoing concern for developments in Spain and Latin America. The journal also reveals an expansive interest in non-Hispanic literature and art. In literature this interest was expressed principally through a variety of translations the goal of which was to present to an educated Mexican reader controversial and significant works written in languages other than Spanish. Especially important examples were the translated texts by such authors as André Gide, Jules Romain, St. John Perse, D. H. Lawrence, Thornton Wilder, T. S. Eliot, and Waldo Frank. Equally evident was an interest in contemporary art and photography, as can be seen in the reproductions of experimental paintings by Miró, Salvador Dalí, and Giorgio De Chirico, and of photographic works by Sergey Eisenstein and Man Ray.

Mexican literature and culture were also amply represented in the journal, to be sure, but with an insistent assertion that *mexicanidad,* or the sense of being Mexican in spirit or substance, can be fully appreciated only when taken in an international context. The representation of this concept took various forms in the pages of the journal. There were essays and articles on nonliterary or nonartistic topics, for example the studies by Bernardo Gastélum and Samuel Ramos on Mexican social and cultural problems as seen from an international perspective. Mexican art, and particularly contemporary art, was the subject for a number of commentaries, and many excellent reproductions are to be found in the pages of the journal. Alfonso Reyes, presented a series of canvases from the sixteenth century, and the studies of García Maroto and Ramos on the work of Diego Rivera and the reproductions of paintings by José Clemente Orozco and Agustín Lazo provide an excellent example of the group's interest in contemporary Mexican art. As might be expected, Mexican literature also occupied a prominent place in the pages of the journal. There are texts by established and recognized authors, such as Enrique González Martínez, and Alfonso Reyes for example. Francisco Monterde published the text of a theatrical piece, *Proteo, fábula en un acto,* which a few months before had been premiered in Julio Bracho's experimental theater. Mariano Azuela's transitional 1923 novel *La malhora* was republished in the journal, and in 1931 a chapter of Azuela's openly experimental *La luciérnaga* appeared for the first time. In the "Motivos" section there were many critical commentaries and reviews on Mexican authors and works. Ortiz de Montellano was a frequent contributor to this section, and beginning with Number 9 he included as an integral part of each issue of *Contemporáneos* a bibliography of works published in and on Mexico.

Beyond the forum created in the pages of the journal, with its insistent national-international duality, the group made significant contributions to the development of the theater and the visual arts of the 1920s and early 1930s in Mexico. Some of the young writers took part, for example, in the experimental theatrical groups Teatro de Ulises (1928) and Teatro de Orientación (1932–34, 1938). Under the leadership of Antonieta Rivas Mercado, Ulises presented four short-run productions, among them Jean Cocteau's *Orphée* and Eugene O'Neill's *Welded,* with Novo, Villaurrutia, and Owen involved as translators, actors, and directors. The productions of Orientación were more extensive, but were in large part also translations of non-Mexican plays, both classic and modern. An occasional Mexican play was produced, however, and as with Ulises several members of the *Contemporáneos* group took part as translators and actors. In both the Ulises and Orientación groups, a number of aspiring young Mexican painters prepared original set designs and scenery; these associations allowed Villaurrutia, Novo, and

others of the group to come to know their work well and to become interested in promoting the work of talented young visual artists. Agustín Lazo, Carlos González, Roberto Montenegro, Julio Castellanos, Carlos Mérida, and Manuel Rodríguez Lozano were some of the lesser-known figures with whom the *Contemporáneos* writers developed close relationships. The best-known single figure was Rufino Tamayo, who was responsible for several theater set designs and for whom some members of the group organized a 1935 exhibition at the Galería de Arte Mexicano.

In the last months of 1931 the journal did not survive the resignation of Estrada in the Ministry of Foreign Relations and the simultaneous illness of Ortiz de Montellano; *Contemporáneos* ceased publication with Number 43, which appeared in December of that year. By that time the "grupo sin grupo," to use Villaurrutia's graphic phrase, was substantially scattered, with both its youthful impetus and its compelling sense of common activity much diminished. With the passing years, however, this group of Mexican writers, together with *Contemporáneos* as its principal project done in concert, would come to be seen as the most distinguished single group in Mexican literature of the twentieth century. Notwithstanding individual contributions of the first order to Mexican poetry, theater, prose fiction, criticism, and journalism, the group's most significant achievement may well have been the passionate defense of a fundamental cultural position: Mexican art and literature can realize their full potential only when they are in fruitful contact with artistic currents beyond their own national borders.

Select Bibliography

Brushwood, John S., "*Contemporáneos* and the Limits of Art." *Romance Notes* 5:2 (1964).

Dauster, Frank, *Ensayos sobre poesía mexicana: Asedio a los "Contemporáneos."* Mexico City: Ediciones de Andrea, 1963.

Durán, Manuel, "'Contemporáneos': ¿Grupo, promoción, generación, conspiración?" *Revista Iberoamericana* 48 (1982).

Forster, Merlin H., *Los Contemporáneos, 1920–1932: Perfil de un experimento vanguardista mexicano.* Mexico City: Ediciones de Andrea, 1964.

Mullen, Edward J., "Critical Reactions to the Review *Contemporáneos.*" *Hispania* 54:1 (1971).

Quirarte, Vicente, *Perderse para reencontrarse: Bitácora de Contemporáneos.* Mexico City: UAM-Azcapotzalco, 1985.

Sheridan, Guillermo, *Los Contemporáneos ayer.* Mexico City: FCE, 1985.

Torres Bodet, Jaime, *Teimpo de arena.* Mexico City: FCE, 1955.

—MERLIN H. FORSTER

CONVENTS IN NEW SPAIN

Toward the middle of the sixteenth century, with the rise in both the criollo and the mestizo populations, the Spanish community felt the need to create environments in which the chastity and "feminine purity" of their descendants might be preserved. Convents and nunneries emerged in order to provide havens for Spanish and criolla women who remained unmarried, whether for reasons of vocation, orphanhood, or poverty.

Convents were established through the charity of men and women of Spanish origin who, concerned for the well-being of criolla and Spanish women, founded trust funds out of donations specifically intended for the building in whole or in part of a convent. (Although the vast majority of convents were supported by Spaniards and criollos, a very small number—for example, the convent of San Juan de la Penitencia in Mexico City—was supported by Indian communities.) These trust funds were backed by local institutions such as city halls and the clergy, and juridically endorsed by public certification before a church notary. The trust would then have to be approved by the canonic and royal authorities. Once all the formalities had been completed, the convent was considered founded, normally remaining dependent upon its order's highest ecclesiastical authority. The only exceptions were the nuns of St. Clare, who answered to the provincial of the masculine Franciscan order.

Convent nuns undertook commitments agreed upon with both trustees and their own relatives: they were to pray on given dates for the souls and ultimate salvation of their benefactors, and reserve places for the founder's descendants.

Some nunneries started out as beguine convents, or places set aside for the seclusion of pious lay women devoted to prayer, who took temporary vows of poverty, chastity, and obedience under the spiritual direction of mendicant friars. In New Spain, a total of 56 nunneries of diverse orders were established, in two main waves. The first began with the foundation of La Concepción in Mexico City, towards 1540, and ended in 1636 with the foundation of the San Bernardo convent. This period was characterized by the great expansion of the Conceptionists and the Dominicans. The second stage fell between 1665, when San Felipe de Jesús, the first Capuchin convent, was founded, and ended in 1853 with the barefoot (discalced) Carmelite convent of Santa Teresa in the city of Durango. This was the heyday of Franciscan, Carmelite, and Marian expansion policies. Table 1 offers a breakdown of the various convents and the order to which they belonged.

With the establishment of the Conceptionists in the viceroyal capital, convent life in New Spain was launched. Between 1540 and 1630, the first eleven foundations of that order in Mexico City were built, followed by one in Puebla and two in Guadalajara. Toward 1596, with Nuestra Señora de la Consolación in Mérida, the geographical boundaries of this order under the colony had been met.

The other congregation that left its cultural mark was the Franciscan, with fourteen houses. With their flexible interpretations of the regulations, they founded establishments for Poor Clares, Capuchins, and Clares of the first order. Poor Clares arrived in New Spain between 1570 and 1610. This rule was distinguished by its active expansion in and beyond New Spain, since in addition to convents in Puebla, Atlixco, and Querétaro they founded further centers in Manila (1621), Havana (approximately 1610), and Guatemala (1699). A similar outreach policy was implemented by the austere Capuchins, who started convents in the Bajío region and Oaxaca. The regular Clares were responsible for the foundation of Corpus Christi in 1724, the first monastery for well-born Indians.

Puebla was the site of the first Dominican nunnery in New Spain. The Dominicans began canvassing for their trust around 1556, and by 1568 St. Catherine of Siena was founded, soon to spawn another eight convents of the same rule. This order initially concentrated its efforts on Puebla (three convents), followed by Guadalajara (two) and Morelia (two, 1590 and 1747). In almost parallel fashion, the Oaxaca foundation (1576) provided the nuns who were to staff the Mexico City branch in 1593.

The first barefoot (discalced) Carmelite convent was built around 1604, in Puebla. It gave rise to seven sister establishments throughout Mexico, reaching as far as Caracas in 1731. The convents of the Company of Mary are particularly interesting, in that they were the first to hold female education as their main objective. The distribution of convents in New Spain is displayed in Table 2.

The convents of Mexico City, Puebla, and Oaxaca were early urban settlements primarily connected to the evangelizing project and the supplying of a colonial market grounded on the trade and export of silver en route to Spain

TABLE 1

Distribution of Conventual Foundations in New Spain and Their Respective Orders

Order	Number of Convents in New Spain
Conceptionist	15
Franciscan	14
Dominican	9
Carmelite	7
Company of Mary	4
Augustinian	3
Jeronimian	3
Saviorist	1

Source: Josefina Muriel de la Torre, *Conventos de monjas en la Nueva España.* Mexico City: Santiago, 1946.

TABLE 2
Number of Nuns' Convents in New Spain, 1540–1780

Mexico City	Puebla	Guadalajara	Oaxaca	Morelia
9 Conceptionist	3 Dominican	2 Franciscan	2 Franciscan	2 Dominican
4 Franciscan	2 Conceptionist	2 Dominican	1 Conceptionist	1 Franciscan
2 Carmelite	2 Franciscan	1 Conceptionist	1 Dominican	
2 Company of Mary	2 Carmelite	1 Augustinian	1 Augustinian	
2 Jeronimian	1 Augustinian	1 Carmelite		
1 Dominican	1 Jeronimian			
1 St. Brigid				
21	11	7	5	3

Note: An additional 9 convents were distributed as follows: in Querétaro, 2 Franciscan and 1 Carmelite; in San Miguel El Grande, 1 Conceptionist; in Mérida, 1 Conceptionist; in Salvatierra, 1 Franciscan; the Company of Mary founded 1 in Irapuato and 1 in Aguascalientes; finally, in Atlixco, there was 1 Franciscan convent.

Source: Josefina Muriel de la Torre, *Conventos de monjas en la Nueva España.* Mexico City: Santiago, 1946.

via Veracruz. The convents in Guadalajara, Morelia, and Aguascalientes responded in large part to the creation of a new urban model thrown up by the displacement of commercial and productive activity, and the self-sufficiency of the mining areas of the north.

The convents were founded with a two-fold aim: on the one hand, the recreation of a contemplative life of prayer, and on the other, the education of women.

The Contemplative Life

A contemplative way of life required ample premises, preferably within the walls of the Spanish city and removed from indigenous communities. Some convents began as conversions of existing houses donated by their patrons, later modifying the architecture in order to make room for the great cloisters and other collective and private spaces. The exterior of these complexes constituted a dominant part of the urban landscape with their domes, buttresses, spires, bell towers, and public fountains.

The contemplative life began with the observances of prayer, performed at set times, and of the vows of poverty, chastity, and obedience as stipulated by the constitutive rules and ordinances of the establishment. Overall, almost all convents were dedicated to contemplation, praying for the church and the salvation of the world. The particular charisma of each convent varied from order to order, along with the canonic timetable and other constitutional variants. The nuns, both *calced* and otherwise, followed their monastic vows first and foremost, but there were differences in the flexibility of interpretation of such precepts. Barefoot *(discalced)* Carmelites were noted for the stringency of their regulations and rigid austerity, in the wake of the Carmelite reform. The Clares and Capuchins lived in accordance with the Franciscan brand of austerity. Recollet nuns were characterized by a way of life that was above all ascetic.

The norms of daily conduct were based upon the repression of sexuality through chastity, the breaking of the will through obedience, and the denial of material and bodily comforts through poverty. The most significant role played by nuns' convents was the safeguarding of individual chastity, guaranteeing the immaculacy of family honor thanks to observance of the three vows.

Obedience was considered to be one of the features of the state of perfection, symbolizing the nun's surrender to God. By this vow, the nuns undertook to maintain the unity of the order and bow to the will of the ecclesiastical hierarchy. Hierarchical stratification within the cloister itself began with obedience to the mother superior, prioress, or abbess. The holder of this post was elected by a voting caucus of professed nuns, with the right to a secret and private ballot once a certain seniority had been reached. The result of the election was then approved by the bishop or his representatives.

The prioress was in charge of the day-to-day running and maintenance of the convent. She appointed her council and sub-prioress or deputy, together representing the highest level in the internal power structure. Next she delegated lesser responsibilities to the "teaching mothers," assigned to postulants, young girls, and servants.

The head nun and her council determined the internal allocation of the duties required of each nun in the offices, administration of assets, the admissions area, or the enforcement of rules. Most decisions were taken in the chapter room. Here, complaints were investigated and personal confessions made, and collective disciplines were imposed as well as individual mortifications.

The vow of individual and collective poverty was understood as a "voluntary renunciation of the realm of all things by means of perfection." By this definition, nuns took the vow in order to free themselves from worldly attachments, and consecrate themselves entirely to spiritual work within the convent walls. The contemplative life and evangelical poverty to which the nuns aspired was only possible thanks to the possession of incomes and assets by which they could be maintained. These goods consisted almost entirely in the yield from their dowries, administered by a financial manager; the manner of their internal distribution, and the level of expenses, was determined by the rules of each establishment. The accumulation of dowries and annuities enabled the convents to concentrate a considerable proportion of urban property.

The vow of poverty was interpreted in a number of ways; the joint and individual poverty prescribed at barefoot (discalced), recollet, and Capuchin institutions was rigorously observed. In calced orders, the vow was followed with relative laxity, for nuns were allowed to own properties that might help maintain them if the convent were unable to provide for all their needs. In such arrangements, handicrafts were important as a source of income for the nuns. Some convents became specialized in the manufacture of particular articles, which managers and servants marketed outside. The observance of voluntary or collective poverty was an attempt to ensure the internal administration of convent property.

Using the example of Christ, chastity was touted as an evangelical prescription. This vow purported to make a clear distinction between the holy love reserved for God, and any other form of earthly affection. The immediate condition for the observance of the vow of chastity was strict seclusion; the penalty for breaking this rule was excommunication.

The cloistering was made watertight by careful supervision of the areas communicating the convent with the outside world: gate lodges, tradesmens' entrances, and visiting rooms, the latter being the supreme site of permitted sociability for the community.

Population

Several types of women animated the conventual world: black-veiled and choir nuns, lay sisters or "white-veiled" nuns, young girls, and servants. All these residents represented a wide range of economic, social, and even ethnic groups. Their heterogeneous composition influenced the various models of communal life developed within each convent. Novices who aspired to taking final vows had to be able to offer a dowry worth between 3,000 and 4,000 pesos (in the seventeenth and eighteenth centuries). Black veil nuns could join convents without dowries if they showed promising qualities such as knowing how to count well or talent in music. Women who could prove that they were descendants of the founders of the monasteries also had their dowries waived and served as chaplains. In addition, the founding deeds of some convents explicitly mentioned that they were intended for impoverished Spanish or indigenous women, who were not required to produce a dowry. Sometimes dowries were pooled for charitable works for orphans.

All convents enforced strict limitations on numbers. Carmelite, recollet, and Capuchin life was conditioned by a predetermined numerical balance of consecrated and lay nuns. This rule was not followed by calced orders, some of which might shelter upward of 80 nuns by the end of the

seventeenth century, most attended by their private maids. On the opposite extreme, in some convents even the community as a whole was prohibited from having servants.

In addition to the dowry, a certificate of blood purity was required, and a copy of the baptism certificate to prove that one was over 15, under 25, and above all a legitimate child. The main occupation of these nuns consisted in reading divine office in the choir. The Catholic Church prescribed communal recitation of the Psalms, which demanded skills of reading, writing, and in some cases the rudiments of Latin.

Lay sisters were often those who had proved unable to fulfill all the requisites for taking final vows; their most common shortcoming was lack of a dowry. There was marked discrimination between them and their black-veiled colleagues, expressed in number of prayers, exclusion from divine office or the meniality of the tasks they were called upon to perform.

Alongside their contemplative lifestyles, convents were an important bastion of education in New Spain. The first establishments formed part of an educational project that countered the original plan for the instruction of indigenous nobles.

The educational progress of young Spanish and criolla girls under the auspices of the convent was important, since the few existing girls' schools were inadequate to service the rapidly growing population. Although the Council of Trent had banned the reception of lay persons within the cloister, it was the custom in Spain and Latin America to admit lay girls and women. Over time, it became common practice to send girls to be raised in certain convents, keeping company with the nuns and following their lives of seclusion and prayer. Although not all that many young women were educated in such convents, their influence was disproportionate in that it advertised a highly desirable educational model. By the eighteenth century, it was estimated that there was approximately one girl for every nun.

Some convents only accepted women who were likely to take the habit as professed nuns. This policy ensured a reliable supply of postulants. There were girls who would never take orders, and others who left the convent to get married. The "ideal of feminine perfection" was thus disseminated outside the cloister.

Between 1765 and 1773, Archbishop Lorenzana of Mexico City and Bishop Francisco Fabian y Fuero of Puebla launched a series of reforms that had direct bearing upon the operation and goals of nuns' convents. These reforms ordered the expulsion of lay nuns, girls, and maids. They also frowned upon the amount of time spent in manual, income-generating activities, and especially the frequency with which nuns received visitors, often encroaching upon the times for collective prayer. The new measures revolutionized the lifestyle of calced nuns in their private cells.

The reforms of 1765 disarticulated individual spaces and broke up close enclaves of coresidents, cemented by affection and habit. This was one of the most controversial points of the reform. After a period of change and tension, the new rules were enforced in a gradual manner; however, there is evidence that the unique lifestyle of *calced* convents managed to survive for some time.

Select Bibliography

Foz y Foz, Pilar, *El convento de la Enseñanza de México: Ambivalencias de una joya colonial.* Bogotá: CELAM, 1990.

Gonzalbo Aizpuro, Pilar, *Las mujeres en la Nueva España.* Mexico City: Colegio de México, 1987.

Lavrin, Asunción, "Los conventos de monjas en la Nueva España." *Cahiers des Amériques Latines* 8 (1973).

Loreta Lopez, Rosalva, "La distribución de la propiedad urbana en la ciudad de Puebla en la década de 1830." In *Investigaciones Universitarias de urbanismo,* Mexico City: DIAU-Universidad Autónoma de Puebla, 1986.

_____, "La sensibilidad y el cuerpo en el imaginario de las monjas poblanas del siglo XVII." In *El monacato Femenino en el Imperio Español: Monasterios, beaterios, recogimientos y colegios,* edited by Manuel Ramos Medina. Mexico City: Condumex, 1995.

Morales, María Dolores, "Estructura Urbana y distribución de la propiedad en la ciudad de México en 1813." In *Ciudad de México, ensayo de construcción de una historia,* Mexico City: INAH, 1978.

Muriel de la Torre, Josefina, *Conventos de monjas en la Nueva España.* Mexico City: Santiago, 1946.

Ramos Medina, Manuel, editor, *El monacato Femenino en el Imperio Español: Monasterios, beaterios, recogimientos y colegios.* Mexico City: Condumex, 1995.

—ROSALVA LORETO LÓPEZ

CONVERSOS

Along with the Spaniards who came to New Spain came the *conversos* of Jewish origin. The term refers to anyone who converts from his or her original religion. The conversion happened for two reasons. Some converted voluntarily, to achieve success and wealth; others were forced. In Spain, forced conversions began in the fourteenth century when the peaceful coexistence among the three groups who had lived on the Iberian Peninsula—the Arabs, Jews, and Christians—came to an end. In 1391, many Jewish communities were destroyed by anti-Jewish riots, and many Jews were forced to convert to Christianity. The free exchange among the three cultures ceased when the state and the church imposed one religion in an effort to unify Spain.

The *aljamas,* or Jewish communities, were forced to integrate into Christian Spanish society. Religion and religious observances became a mark of identity of "Spanishness." The term *converso,* or "new Christian," applied to those who voluntarily converted, and "cryptojew" to those who had been forced to convert and who secretly continued Jewish religious observances. Other terms designated *conversos:* one was *marranos,* or pigs, a reflection on the contempt with which Christians viewed the insincerity of their conversion; another was *anusim,* the Hebrew word for those forced to convert. Those who broke with the Jewish community were condemned to live in a marginalized, transitional society until 1492, when the Jews were expelled from Spain.

With the joining of the kingdoms of Aragon and Castile under the reign of Fernando II and Isabel I, the *converso* issue gained national prominence. To safeguard fidelity to Christianity and to punish the heresy of the recent con-

verts, the "Catholic Monarchs" established the Tribunal of the Holy Inquisition in 1481. Spaniard split in two groups: the traditionalists, who isolated themselves from the "New Christians" and would not accept them into their families nor allow them to hold public office, and those who became related to *conversos* by marriage and came to share their concerns.

At this point, the term "clean blood" appears, related to the search into one's roots for traces of Jewish ancestry. Beginning in the fifteenth century, this became an obsession in Spain and Portugal. The obsession later was brought to America. Christians with Jewish or Moorish ancestry feared that the least indication of being impure would bar them from being admitted to the Catholic Church, government, or the military.

There were four classes of *conversos.* The first consisted of those born during the second half of the fifteenth century, who were brought up in the bosom of a Jewish family and then tried by the Inquisition between 1485 and 1495, or who were "reconciled" to the Catholic Church during the first few years of the sixteenth century. The second group was composed of those born at the end of the fifteenth century and the beginning of the sixteenth who were singled out because their parents had been tried by the Inquisition and punished for being practicing Jews. The third group formed the nucleus of converts born during the first half of the sixteenth century, mostly children. And the last group was composed of those born during the second half of the sixteenth century, who were fully integrated into society; many still clung to a few observances handed down through oral tradition, but others had forgotten even these and were faithful

Catholics, although they continued to suffer the stigma of having "impure blood."

The immigration of *conversos* of Jewish origin to parts of the New World began between 1492 and 1700. There was a marked difference between those who came from Castile and those who came from Aragon, as there was a difference between those who came from Spain or Portugal. Those Jews who had left Spain for Portugal in their attempt to remain Jewish were forcibly converted in Portugal in 1497. Because this conversion was more recent than that in Spain, and because these Jewish families had fled to Portugal precisely to retain their heritage, Portuguese *conversos* were more steeped in Jewish law and traditions than those who remained in Spain and converted. There was also a noticeable difference in Spain between the voluntary converts and the ones who had been coerced.

Hostility and secrecy played an important role in adaptation in the Americas. If the *conversos* gave up their religion, there were no obstacles to colonial life. But a large number kept their religion secret; openly they were Catholics, but privately they were Jews.

It is difficult to obtain a clear picture of the lives of Jews expelled from the Iberian Peninsula who came to the New World under false names and permits, because these went undetected by the church. On the other hand, those who continued to practice and were tried by the Inquisition can be studied through their trials, which provide rich sources of information about their lives, their adaptation, the secrecy in which they practiced their customs, and traditions.

The *conversos* who emigrated to America instead of Turkey or Holland or Italy—where they could continue to be Jews—lived their lives like Spaniards and chose not to renounce their Hispanicity. They considered themselves to be as Spanish as Christians.

It is difficult to arrive at the number of Jews who left Spain, perhaps 200,000, of which 120,000 went to Portugal, since it was the closest country and was easy to enter. The rest went to France, Italy, Navarre (which was still an independent kingdom), the Ottoman Empire, or Palestine. The number of those who remained was important since there were many cases of conversions before they left, given the obstacles; others returned after suffering hardship on their journey. It is possible that 200,000 remained in Spain.

The Holy Inquisition was established in Portugal in 1536, and with it began there the mass persecution trials of the *conversos*. These groups then began leaving Portugal for Spain, and from there to New Spain. When Portugal became part of the Spanish Crown in 1580, the floodgates of direct migration to New Spain were opened for Portuguese *conversos*. A huge wave of Portuguese *conversos* sought refuge from the Inquisition's persecution in the newly conquered lands.

Latin America and especially Mexico became attractive to both cryptojews and genuine converts. The advantage of living in these territories was that they offered a familiar culture and the possibility of contact with the mother country.

For those who wished to live as Catholics, distance from the Peninsula and the sparse population helped them to shed their Jewish pasts; the American continent erased all traces of their previous religion and eased their integration into life in New Spain. Among this group were prominent people such as fray Bartolomé de Las Casas, fray Alonso de la Veracruz, and fray Bernardino de Sahagún, and many others within the Catholic Church, the military, and the government who were more difficult to trace.

Getting to New Spain was not easy. The forging of false permits became a skill, and the punishments imposed only served to drive up the cost of creating them. For the so-called foreigners (among them the Portuguese before 1580) passage to the Indies was banned. But there was always a way to get around the edicts to get permits or a royal certificate of naturalization. The requirements changed with the times. At first, a 10-year residency in Spain and marriage to a local woman was a requirement. But this later changed to a 10-year residency only. On the other hand, one could purchase an "individual permit" in other ways, such as holding a title, or by paying what was called a *composición,* an extension of the permit that allowed legal entry to the Indies.

Even being caught did not deter the immigration of *conversos;* with the help of established *conversos* there were ways to avoid deportation. The first was to contract marriage with a resident woman. This often was performed in jail, while the prisoner awaited deportation to Spain. Such a contract of marriage might facilitate the immigrant's residency or at least obtain him a permit to allow him to remain in the city. The second way was to post bond, which obligated the person to stay in the area until return transport to Spain could be arranged. Usually, however, when the detainee escaped, the bondsman paid, forfeiting the fine, and the case was closed.

The *conversos'* arrival to the New World can be divided into six stages. Between 1492 and 1502 they fled from the Holy Inquisition and were expelled from Spain. This stage began with the voyages of Christopher Columbus, in which the *conversos* played an important role. Eighty-six *conversos* participated in the admiral's four voyages. Some stayed behind in the recently discovered islands and others returned to Spain, where they told of their adventures and encouraged others to travel. *Conversos* financed the expeditions and the conquest and supported Columbus's exploration, including lending him the capital to arm his fleet. The Spanish Crown imposed few restrictions during the first stage.

The second stage began in 1502 with the voyages of Commander Nicolás Ovando to Santo Domingo, and ended in 1519 with the preparation of Fernando (Hernán) Cortés's fleet to discover *terra firme.* During this stage the Spanish Crown imposed a series of restrictions so that those with "unclean blood" could not emigrate to America, nor children of Jews, nor recent converts to Catholicism, nor those who had been tried by the Inquisition. In 1511 these restrictions were lifted temporarily. The colonies needed to be populated with Spaniards, especially those practiced in the trades. The royal treasury was empty and King Fernando granted permits to some merchants to go to the Indies for two years to sell their wares and then to return to Spain. Among these were several *conversos*.

The third period began with the preparations for the Conquest of *terra firme* in 1519 and ended in 1571 with the official establishment of the Holy Office of the Inquisition in New Spain. During this stage, several *conversos* were part of Cortés's conquest of Mexico-Tenochtitlan. We know about them through the 1528 trial of four people: the Morales brothers, Hernando Alonso, and Diego de Ocaña. The latter was the first scribe in New Spain, and during his trial he alleged having obtained this job through "public auction" and claimed his right to continue. Diego de Morales and Hernando Alonso were burned at the stake as Jewish heretics.

There was an influx of *conversos* from Spain, especially from Madrid and Seville during this stage. They came as soldiers, conquerors, and later as colonists. The ports of entry were the same ones used by the conquistadors. By 1536 there was a community of cryptojews in New Spain, and we learn of this through the trial of Francisco Millán, who was suspected of practicing Judaism. He was a tavern keeper who denounced a number of *conversos* who frequented his wineshop to buy wine for the Sabbath and who identified themselves as Jews or as practicing the Law of Moses. At this time there were small nuclei of *conversos* in Mexico City, Tlaxcala, and Mérida.

During the 1560s the number of New Christians arriving from Portugal increased. They had formerly lived in Spain or had moved to Africa, where they engaged in the slave trade. Ten years later another wave of Portuguese migration happened to coincide with the establishment of the Inquisition in New Spain. Mining districts became settlements for *conversos* and cryptojews. One such mining area that sprung up in 1532 was centered in Taxco, Zacualpan, Zumpango del Río, Espíritu Santo, and Tlalpujahua. A second district had been established by the middle of the sixteenth century, made up of the Reales de Monte of Pachuca and Atotomilco. By 1547 Zacatecas was developed, and Guanajuato by 1554.

The fourth period began in 1571 and was a prelude to the great migration from Portugal that ended in 1625. This period can be considered a time of consolidation for the *converso* community. They arrived through the ports of Veracruz, Campeche, Yucatán, and Pánuco. Starting at this point, especially after 1590, there arose a clandestine group in the Reales de Monte of Pachuca. During that time the New Kingdom of León was founded by a *converso*, Luis de Carvajal y de la Cueva, "the Elder," who took part in the conquest and colonization of the northern part of the country and helped in the pacification of the Chichimeca Indians. After reporting his deeds to the Spanish Crown, he was given a territory of 200 square leagues to establish the New King-

dom of León, and he was allowed to bring with him 100 Spanish families to colonize the territory. Of these, around 75 percent were Jewish *conversos*.

The great Portuguese migration began in 1580 and included a great many practicing Jews, descended from those who had been expelled from Spain. It was a secret community, but in 1589 it was discovered that García González Bermejero was one of the spiritual leaders of cryptojews in Mexico. He was tried and burned at the stake.

At the same time groups of *conversos* lived in different parts of Mexico City, and in Guadalajara, Puebla, Querétaro, Pachuca, Oaxaca, Michoacán, Taxco, and Zacatecas. In these cities, *conversos* clustered in specific neighborhoods and lived on specific streets. This was a time of commercial growth and greater participation in cultural and political life. *Conversos* had commercial establishments. For example, Tomás Treviño de Sobremonte owned several shops, one of them in Oaxaca. Tomás de Fonseca, "the Elder," lived in New Spain for 32 years and established the mines in Tlalpujahua, where he engaged in mining and commerce. *Conversos* played an important role during the intense period of trade with Manila and the Philippines.

Conversos began to ascend the social ladder. They married Spanish Christians and their participation in cultural and political life became important. Their children were sent to Spain to complete their studies after having attended the best preparatory schools for *criollos* (persons of Spanish descent born in the Americas) and after their mothers had instructed them in religion at home.

In 1622 a synagogue on Santo Domingo Street in Mexico City was reported. These were years of great economic growth; there were many important trials against *conversos*, and large Autos de Fé (ceremonies accompanying a pronouncement or judgment of the Inquisition) were held in the streets of Mexico City. For example, in the 1590 Auto de Fé many *conversos* from Portugal and from Seville were tried, among them Hernando Rodríguez de Herrera, Tomás de Fonseca Castellanos, and members of the Carvajal family.

In 1596 46 *conversos* were tried, and some of Luis de Carvajal's relatives were burned at the stake, including his nephew who had become one of the spiritual leaders of the Mexican community. In 1601, 45 *conversos* were sentenced, and between 1574 and 1603, 115 people of Jewish ancestry were tried. During these trials, other members of the faith were implicated, which led to the discovery of the clandestine community in Pachuca. Some Indians, who probably had been converted by their masters in an effort to keep from being denounced to the Inquisition, also were accused of being Jews.

The Inquisition trials allow us to study the secret lives of the *conversos*, their jobs, their obligations, their relations, and their active roles in colonial society. Among their occupations were shoemaker, tailor, wool carder, silversmith, blacksmith, barber, physician, carter, painter, musician, lawyer, and solicitor.

The *conversos* fifth period of immigration took place from 1625 until the end of the seventeenth century. During this span of time, the small cryptojewish communities saw their greatest growth and the establishment of small industries, as well as trades. This time shows an increase in persecutions, and the confiscation of their property filled the coffers of the Inquisition. Immigration began to decrease in 1640, when the Kingdom of Portugal achieved independence from Spain, and *conversos* emerged as rebels in the conflict between the two countries. The coming of the Messiah was an idea that emerged in the cryptojewish communities. The arrival was expected in 1648. Women were accused of claiming to be the mother of the Redeemer.

Between 1620 and 1650 the Inquisition accused more than 200 people, and from 1672 to 1676 it accused an additional 100, most of whom were Portuguese. By this time, some held public office, like Domingo Márquez, the governor of Tepeaca, who was accused of being a Jew in 1644. Diego Muñoz de Alvarado was magistrate of Puebla de los Angeles and was a shipowner who traded with Europe and amassed a fortune. Diego was also accused of being an unfaithful Christian and died in the jails of the Inquisition in 1683.

The groups then concentrated in Mexico City, Puebla, Oaxaca, Pachuca, Acapulco, Guadalajara, Campeche, Sombrerete, Orizaba, Veracruz, and Zacatecas. Autos de Fé took place in 1646 against 40 *conversos*, in 1647 against 21, in 1648 against 40 others, and finally on April 11, 1649, 35 were tried, 8 of whom were burned at the stake. From that point on the "reconciled" were deported to Spain, where it would be harder for them to fall back on their old religious practices than it would be in the Indies, where they could evade the watchful eyes of the Inquisition more easily. These deportations decreased the number of *conversos* in New Spain. Among the deported were Tepeaca governor Domingo Márquez and Captain Matias Pereira Lobo, both tried in 1662; Captain Augustín Muñoz de Sandoval, sentenced in 1695; and a Jewish friar, José de San Ignacio, tried in 1706.

The sixth and last period of immigration began in 1700 and ended in 1821. During this time Veracruz was the meeting place of *conversos*, since it was a port for many ships from other countries. In 1701 the commissioner denounced a large number of *conversos* there. From then on, there were no immigrations, and only a small nucleus of *conversos* arrived from the Low Countries and the Caribbean. Groups of *conversos* continued to live in Mexico City, Guadalajara, Puebla, Veracruz, and Acapulco as well as in some parts of the Yucatán. Religious persecution of *conversos* diminished, as persecution efforts were directed at readers of banned books, such as those written by the French encyclopedists.

A few trials were held, such as that of Diego Rodríguez, a resident of Tlaxcala, who owned a butcher shop and was accused in 1723. There is the case of María Felipe de Alcazar, from Oaxaca, suspected of being a Jew and tried in 1739. From then on there is greater assimilation into colonial society, and many Jewish customs and traditions either were lost or were blended into Christian practices.

The survival of cryptojewish communities in New Spain from 1521 to 1821, despite persecution by the Inquisition, was the result of several factors. Their family ties were of utmost importance. This family tie did not extend only to parents and their children, but also to distant relatives, all their friends, and those in their circle who practiced the same religion. No one would divulge their beliefs; if one were jailed by the Inquisition, the entire family was imprisoned with them.

Mothers formed the center of the family, which generally contained at least four or five children. Fathers provided support and protection and were the leaders. While fathers were revered and venerated, mothers were considered the transmitters of Jewish values and identity. Family gatherings, often centered on feasting and fasting, were an important way to preserve their secret religion and strengthen their family ties. Even when younger members of the family emigrated or traveled for any reason, the nucleus of the family remained intact and persisted. Their regimen was geared to the preservation of the group, avoiding fragmentation and assuring the continuity and integrity of the family's legacy and traditions. Endogamy (marriage within the community) was almost sacrosanct among the cryptojews in New Spain, not only to ensure the survival of the *converso* group but also for personal safety. There were marriages between relatives—uncles married nieces, and cousins married each other.

The sense of mutual support was well defined among the *conversos*, so that when anyone arrived in New Spain they knew where to go for help for credit to start up a business, or to be a merchant or a hawker. Although the Jewish part of their lives was practiced in absolute secrecy, *conversos* always knew about each other. Even those who came from distant places could always count on finding food and shelter quickly.

While there was no religious hierarchy, leaders called rabbis emerged. These were charged with the spiritual leadership for local groups. The cryptojews' beliefs were formed around vague ideas and deep convictions concerning salvation through the Law of Moses and especially messianic beliefs. The beliefs in the coming of a Redeemer was hoped for fervently; considering the hardships they had endured, cryptojews felt it to be close at hand. Cryptojews were convinced that the Messiah described by the prophets of the Hebrew Bible had not yet appeared. This formed a part of the teachings of the Cabala (a system of medieval Jewish mystical beliefs) and followed them to New Spain. From 1605 to 1666 cryptojews in New Spain were sure that not only would the Messiah appear, but that he would be born to a *converso* woman.

Among many of the cryptojews who left Portugal after 1580, fervor for their secret Jewish religion increased when they arrived in New Spain. They viewed most *conversos* to be sinners because they had abandoned the Law of Moses and were living false lives as Catholics, performing alien rites and ceremonies, and receiving the Christian sacraments. To atone for the sins of these *conversos,* the cryptojews fasted frequently.

Fasting was an end in itself. Not only was it practiced on Yom Kippur (the Day of Atonement) and other holy days, but fasting was observed on Mondays and Thursdays from sunrise to sunset. Keeping the Sabbath was very important; they did not work on that day. Men might open their shops, but they would not work. Circumcision was another important part of Jewish practice that was performed, but it was quickly detected by doctors in the Inquisitorial prisons. Cryptojews also followed certain dietary restrictions and laws, including slaughtering certain animals with a special knife, after which the flesh had to be drained of blood and soaked for an hour and then placed in salt for an additional hour.

At the beginning of the nineteenth century, many of the *conversos* assimilated into colonial life. The stigma of not having "clean blood" arose only when they had to present their pedigree or Patent of Clean Blood to take public office or to enter the Catholic Church, the university, or the army, an insignificant detail for those who thought themselves to be Mexican. During this century filled with turbulence and political crises, very few arrived claiming to be Jews. Those who came kept their religion secret and came only for short stays.

By the time the *criollos* of New Spain gave thought to independence, many *conversos* took part. When this movement was successful in 1821 and many Spaniards left Mexico because of the economic crisis, the *conversos* who were better off returned to Spain, where they felt more at home. Those who remained integrated into Mexican life, assimilated into Christianity, although they continued to practice certain customs and rituals handed down from generation to generation, the origins of which, in many cases, were unknown to the practitioners.

Conversos became prominent families who helped to shape independent Mexico, forgetting their pasts and the secret life their parents had led. One exception was Francisco Rivas Puiggcerver, a university professor who published a newspaper, *El Sábado Secreto* (The Secret Sabbath). He used this vehicle to write about the Inquisitorial trials against the Jewish *conversos* during colonial times. There is also the example of the communities of Venta Prieta in Pachuca and in Veracruz and of the Vallejo neighborhood in Mexico City, which preserved their Jewish identity until the twentieth century, when they could practice their religion openly.

See also Inquisition; Limpieza de Sangre

Select Bibliography

Amador de los Ríos, José, *Historia social, política y religiosa de los judíos de España y Portugal.* Madrid: Aguilar, 1960.

Beinart, Haim, *Conversos ante la inquisición.* Jerusalem: Hebrew University, 1965.

Capdequi, Ots, J.M., *El Estado Español en las Indias.* Mexico City: Fondo de Cultura Económica, 1965.

Carvajal, Luis de, *Procesos de Luis de Carvajal El Mozo.* Mexico City: Talleres Gráficos de la Nación, 1935.

Cuevas, Mariano, *Historia de la Iglesia en México.* 5 vols., Mexico City: Patria, 1946.

Domínguez Ortíz, Antonio, *El antiguo régimen: Los Reyes Católicos y los Austrias.* Madrid: Alfaguara, 1973.

Greenleaf, Richard, *The Mexican Inquisition of the Sixteenth Century.* Albuquerque: University of New Mexico Press, 1969.

Gojman Goldberg, Alicia, *Los Conversos en la Nueva España.* Mexico City: Enep-Acatlán, UNAM, 1984.

Lafaye, Jacques Mesías, *Cruzadas y Utopías: El judeocristianismo en las sociedades Ibéricas.* Mexico City: Fondo de Cultura Económica, 1984.

Liebman, Seymour, *Los Judíos en México y en América Central.* Mexico City: Siglo XXI, 1971.

Toro, Alfonso, *Los Judíos en la Nueva España: Documentos del siglo XVI correspondientes al Ramo Inquisición.* Mexico City: Archivo General de la Nación, 1982.

—ALICIA GOJMAN DE BACKAL

CÓRDOBA MONTOYA, JOSEPH MARIE

1950– • Presidential Confidante

Joseph Marie Córdoba Montoya played his role as the power behind President Carlos Salinas de Gortari during much of the 1980s with the skill of an Old World adviser. The son of Spanish immigrants to France walked one step behind the Mexican president, toiled long hours over presidential paperwork, answered when addressed, and kept out of the eye of the Mexican public.

More than just presidential chief of staff, his official title, Córdoba was considered the second most powerful man in Mexico during the Salinas administration. Everyone in the higher echelons of government and the ruling Partido Revolucionario Institucional (PRI, or Institutional Revolutionary Party) knew Córdoba and his power. Richelieu, said some; Rasputin, whispered others. The debate surrounding Salinas's chief of staff was hushed.

The controversy centered on the inordinate amount of power Córdoba amassed in just a decade in Mexico, a country where he had no prior connection until he arrived to find his fortune at age 29. His rise to power was even more startling given Mexico's constitutional guards against foreign influence—provoked by foreign intrusions that ranged from Archduke Maximilian's ill-fated attempt at building an empire for France in the New World to American troops in Veracruz in the twentieth century. Until 1994, only third-generation Mexicans were eligible to run for president.

Born in La Ciotat, near Marseilles, on June 1, 1950, Córdoba studied engineering at the Paris Polytechnical School, went to Stanford University in 1974 to pursue an economics degree, and spent a year teaching at the University of Pennsylvania before going to work at Mexico's central bank in 1979. Córdoba had briefly advised the socialists in France, but he was much more successful in Mexico. He quickly fell into the circle of economists surrounding Salinas, starting in 1980 as director of regional planning in the Budget and Planning Ministry. He was the director of social and economic policy at the ministry twice when Salinas was the minister, although he withdrew from the position in 1984 over policy disagreements with others in the ministry. He married a Mexican, Sofía Urrutia, in the late 1980s.

Córdoba's contribution to the Salinas camp was his broad world view, especially when compared to the narrow outlook of Mexican politics and its technocrats. His lasting significance in Mexican politics, according to political analysts, was his central role in convincing Salinas that adopting free trade and deregulation as the wave of the future would make Salinas the rave of Washington and the International Monetary Fund. In this aspect, Córdoba understood long before the rest of Mexico's technocrats what the country's elite would gain from embracing global economic integration. His assessment was correct and the product he shaped—Salinas and Mexico's policies—were a smashing success from Washington to Wall Street.

Córdoba may have been Mexico's first neoliberal, but like most of the technocrats who ran the country, his ideas of dismantling the state only came later in life. The young Córdoba was keenly interested in central planning. This is reflected in the draft of his dissertation, entitled "Prices and Quantities in Planning Procedures," which explored how to make centrally planned government more efficient. Although Córdoba's official biography distributed by the Mexican government reported that he had received a doctorate from Stanford in 1977 and gave the title of his thesis, Córdoba never turned in a final version of his work and never received a degree. The revelation in 1989 that Córdoba called himself a doctor of economics without having the degree was the first time the low-profile official came under close public scrutiny in Mexico. No one stopped addressing him as "Doctor" in the presidential residence of Los Pinos, where he worked, but it was his first brush with uncomfortable publicity.

Córdoba's powerful role in Mexican government was a far cry from Córdoba's shy and studious demeanor during his student years. At Stanford, Córdoba's dedication to study caused his former dissertation adviser Mordecai Kurtz to liken him to a Talmudic scholar. Kurtz's most lasting memory of Córdoba was his devotion to a project on game theory, the analysis of resolving a situation involving conflicting interests.

The range of Córdoba's influence in the Mexican government was broad. Throughout the Salinas presidency, Córdoba became the unofficial liaison with Washington, first secretly negotiating Mexico's offer of a free trade agreement with the administration of President George Bush and then meeting regularly with top security and financial officials in the government of President Bill Clinton.

But his role was much broader. On the night of Salinas's disastrous presidential election, July 6, 1988, with the vote count running against Salinas (the ruling party candidate), Córdoba led a group of Salinas faithful that arrived at the Ministry of Internal Affairs to take charge of the vote count by declaring a system-wide failure. Later, Córdoba called the shots from behind the scenes on renegotiating Mexico's foreign debt with commercial banks, flying to New York to untangle the blocked negotiations. He wrote key electoral legislation, helped select PRI candidates for public office, and negotiated labor disputes. His influence on foreign policy was palpable. Córdoba sat near the president at the National Palace when new foreign ambassadors presented their credentials. According to analysts, it was Córdoba who brought the country's foreign policy more in line with Washington's view, particularly in Central America.

Córdoba's exit from Mexico and his descent into scandal was nearly as quiet as his arrival. The powerful adviser departed unobtrusively following the March 1994 assassination of PRI presidential candidate Luis Donaldo Colosio. Córdoba was particularly close to the stand-in for Colosio, Ernesto Zedillo Ponce de León, who had worked with Córdoba at the Banco de México. But his departure to take up the post as Mexico's representative to the Interamerican Development Bank in Washington—a way of placing him out of the growing controversy over the killing—only generated more scandal.

Allegations surfaced almost immediately that Córdoba and Salinas were involved in the assassination. There is no real evidence beyond the intriguing execution-style deaths on a southern California freeway of two Mexican intelligence agents carrying a letter of introduction signed by Córdoba. But in March 1996, Colosio's father publicly accused Córdoba of involvement in his son's slaying. In the fall of 1996, Córdoba answered questions at the Attorney General's Office about the case and later railed against a panel of opposition legislators, defending himself by threatening to sue them for defamation.

In 1995, the newspaper *Reforma* published transcripts of telephone wiretaps revealing that Córdoba maintained a close and personal relationship with a one-time Mexican television announcer named Marcela Bodenstedt, who was linked by drug enforcement agents to convicted narcotics trafficker Juan García Abrego. "My pirate," Bodenstedt called Córdoba. The questions arising from a relationship between the second most powerful man in Mexico and a woman whose telephone was tapped by anti-narcotics agents were never pursued. But after the stories appeared, Córdoba resigned his position at the development bank and became a consultant to the World Bank.

Córdoba spent the mid-1990s developing his comeback. In 1996 he returned to Mexico to set up a base, attacking his opponents in newspaper articles and defending himself against the taint of the Colosio assassination. He also returned to Stanford and completed his degree. The title of the thesis was the same, but by 1996, the era of centrally planned governments was past, and the final version was significantly different from the original.

—JANE BUSSEY

CORONA, RAMÓN

1837–89 • General and Politician

Ramón Corona was born on October 18, 1837, in the state of Jalisco. He came from a poor family and started work at a very early age as a shop assistant in various stores in the city of Tepic. He eventually rose to be manager of the Motage Mining Company. When the revolution in support of the 1857 Constitution broke out after Ignacio Comonfort's coup d'état, he immediately joined the Constitutionalist cause. Together with José M. Villanueva, he organized an uprising in Acaponeta, in the state of Tepic. The town was controlled by the cacique (local strongman) Manuel Lozada, who while he had previously been just a bandit, now sported the rank of general in the service of the Conservative government. This uprising on November 18, 1858, was the beginning of Ramón Corona's military career. Although he had very few weapons and not many men, his natural intelligence and steady temperament helped him win a series of partial victories in western Mexico. On April 3, 1859, after he and Villanueva had joined Liberal general Ignacio Pesqueira, he took the fort of Mazatlán. This decisive victory in Sinaloa earned him the rank of commander. Subsequently, when Colonel Bonifacio Peña was killed in battle on June 11, 1859, Corona was made commander of the Tepic Battalion. Clashes with Lozada's forces followed, with alternating victories and defeats, but Corona always displayed a great ability to recover from adversity. His military successes spread beyond the borders of his own state. On October 15, 1859, General Ogazón, governor and military chief of Jalisco, rewarded him with the rank of colonel in the National Guard. Ogazón did not, however, send assistance for his troops since he did not have the means to do so.

The following year, despite the fact that victory at the Battle of Calpulalpan had opened the doors of Mexico City to the legitimate government, the war continued on a smaller scale in various parts of Mexico, Tepic among them. In 1862, during the early stages of the French Intervention, Corona asked General Ogazón's permission to march eastward with 1,000 men of the Jalisco Brigade to the aid of the national army. Ogazón agreed, but Corona's plan was frustrated when he learned that Lozada had taken Tepic on June 1. He returned to the city immediately to fight his long-time enemy. On October 19, Corona attacked Tepic with 2,000 men but was beaten back.

In November 1862, he was promoted to the rank of general by General Manuel Doblado, who had taken over as governor of Jalisco and had a high military command in western Mexico. Despite Corona's new rank, the precarious situation of his troops, the Tepic Brigade, did not improve. He had received no help from the state of Sinaloa, so he was forced to join a movement by Colonels Antonio Rosales and Joaquín Sánchez Román ousting the governor, General Jesús García Morales. Colonel Rosales replaced him, taking office in October 1864.

Together with Rosales and Sánchez Román, Corona organized a counter-offensive to prevent the advance of the imperialist forces, now reinforced by Manuel Lozada, in several states in the north of Mexico. They had partial victories but also defeats. These actions, however, brought him recognition from the president, Benito Juárez, since after his active role in ousting Governor García Morales he had been considered persona non grata. He was also made brigade general, a rank already given him by General Manuel Doblado. He was ordered to continue his campaign, first in Durango and then in Sinaloa.

On May 26, 1866, the federal government named him commander of the western forces, with full powers to remove and appoint governors and military commanders in Sinaloa, Jalisco, and Colima, as well as to dispose of federal income in the area under his jurisdiction and raise whatever taxes he considered necessary for his army's needs. With these additional resources, Corona was now in a better position to attack the enemy. He was able to send troops to Sonora, and his campaign was consolidated with the fall of Guaymas to Republican troops on September 15. With French forces concentrated in the port of Mazatlán, Corona surrounded them knowing the Republican army's superior position and that Napoléon III was about to order foreign troops to leave.

On November 13 French troops hurriedly evacuated Mazatlán, and the port was occupied by the Liberal forces.

A few days later, Corona's courage and perseverance earned him promotion to Division General. He then left Mazatlán for the interior to mop up the remnants of the French troops. He entered Guadalajara, captured Colima, and was second in command of the army that besieged Querétaro. He finally went to Mexico City and helped General Porfirio Díaz recapture the capital. Once constitutional rule was reestablished, he achieved his ultimate military victory. As commander of the Fourth Division in the West, he finally defeated Lozada who at the head of 6,000 men attempted to take Guadalajara.

From 1874 to 1885, he was Mexican minister plenipotentiary in Spain. On his return to Mexico in early 1887 he was named governor of Jalisco. On November 10, 1889, he was fatally wounded by a young school teacher (who then committed suicide) and died the following day.

—VICENTE QUIRARTE

CORONELAS

See Soldaderas and Coronelas

CORRAL, RAMÓN

1854–1912 • Vice President

A wealthy landowner from Sonora, Ramón Corral served as vice president under Porfirio Díaz from 1904 to 1911. Weak in political stature, Vice President Corral was more important for what he represented than for what he did. His ties to the Científicos (influential policy advisers and intellectuals) indicated the trust the old dictator placed in that group. Díaz's choice of Corral also revealed that he did not want to encourage the political ambitions of the powerful and popular northern general Bernardo Reyes, an adversary of the Científicos. Corral's role as vice president, on the other hand, scarcely deserves mention, as Díaz did not share any power with his designated successor.

The fact that Díaz selected Corral as his running mate was a testament to the Sonoran's political weakness. Fearing an eventual challenge to his rule, Díaz had not wanted to create the position of vice president, much less choose a capable candidate for that position. Outside pressures, however, finally had forced Díaz to change his mind: as the Mexican president approached old age, both foreign investors and the Científicos wondered who would eventually succeed him. By 1904, don Porfirio already had spent 28 years in power, all without either grooming a successor or encouraging the type of at least nominally representative democracy that could have favored the emergence of an experienced national leader. That 1904 (a year of presidential elections), Díaz followed the advice of the Científicos and agreed to create the office of vice president. From the viewpoint of an aging dictator placing his personal interests above those of the regime on the whole, Corral was the ideal choice. Leaning toward the Científicos, he enjoyed the backing of Finance Minister José Y. Limantour, who in turn enjoyed respect among foreign investors. Better yet, he lacked both Limantour's political connections and Reyes's charismatic appeal; he could never pose a challenge to Díaz.

Even though Reyes never had declared his own candidacy for the post, his allies were furious over what they perceived as a slight of one of Mexico's most popular leaders. Therefore, the 1904 election, which sanctioned Díaz's sixth consecutive term as president and Corral's first as vice president, turned many of the northern landowners against the Porfirian regime. Even though open discontent would not manifest itself until the end of the decade, the 1904 election helped politicize the contests for the post of governor in the northern states, contests that usually ended in a presidential fiat. As a result, Díaz's favored candidates in the states of Chihuahua and Coahuila came to be identified with Corral. By contrast, nonfavored contenders such as the Coahuilans Francisco I. Madero and Venustiano Carranza viewed themselves as sharing the fate of Bernardo Reyes.

Six years later, Díaz failed to take a good opportunity to assuage this growing opposition. During his last candidacy for president in 1910, he again had to choose a running mate. To the disappointment of a field of hopefuls that included many of the disaffected northerners, Díaz elected to stick with Corral. The eternal dark horse Reyes proved loyal to don Porfirio, and he even accepted a diplomatic assignment in Europe that removed him from the Mexican political scene. But opposition figures such as Madero and Carranza saw the decision in Corral's favor as further evidence that Díaz pampered an ossified camarilla that sought to exclude them from power.

By the time of the celebrations commemorating the centennial of Miguel Hidalgo's independence declaration in September 1810, the opposition to Corral had spread beyond these elite figures. Both as governor of Sonora and as vice president, Corral frequently had expressed utter disdain for Mexico's indigenous population and for the plight of the country's numerous landless poor. Now that the Díaz regime came under increasing attack from many different quarters, it was Corral who came to embody much that was wrong with the Porfiriato: the coterie of fawning politicians surrounding Díaz; the venality, arrogance, and decadence of key government leaders; the absence of political opportunity at the state and national level; and the lack of autonomy at the municipal level. While Díaz himself remained relatively popular despite

Madero's stinging indictment of his rule, Corral came to bear the brunt of the widespread criticism that ultimately culminated in the insurrection of November 20, 1910.

One certainly cannot explain the outbreak of the Mexican Revolution by pointing to an intra-elite struggle brought on with Díaz's installation of an inept and unpopular vice president. Nevertheless, it would be fair to say that Corral's legacy consists of his helping to mobilize many Mexicans, rich and poor, against a regime that once had appeared nearly invincible.

Corral fled Mexico in March 1911, although he did not formally resign from office until May. He died in Paris the following year.

Select Bibliography

Cosío Villegas, Daniel, *Historia moderna de México: El porfiriato: Vida política exterior.* 2 vols., Mexico City, Editorial Hermes, 1960–63.
_____, *The United States versus Porfirio Díaz,* translated by Nettie Lee Benson. Austin: University of Texas Press, 1964.

—Jürgen Buchenau

CORRIDOS

The *corrido* is a narrative song genre, a ballad form, that has served as a popular commentary on the events shaping Mexican history over the last hundred years. Related to similar song traditions among Mediterranean peoples and their American off-shoots, the Mexican *corrido* has taken root in the imagination of Mexico as no other member of this cluster has in any other setting, attaining in Mexico something of the prominence of its progenitor, the Spanish *romance*, during its heyday in sixteenth-century Spain. Pervaded by an attitude of indifference towards death, the *corrido* evidently draws as well on a backdrop of indigenous Mexican sentiment, belief, and expression.

The term *corrido* derives from a label applied in Spain to a particular sort of *romance,* the broad term used at first to designate any poem in the vernacular language, and later to encompass the diversified tradition of Spanish narrative poetry and song. A *romance corrido* was a through-sung ballad that became popular at the height of the Spanish exploration and settlement of the colonies. Later, in New Spain and eventually Mexico, the term *romance* was dropped and the off-shoot of the tradition became known simply as the *corrido.*

The European antecedents of this narrative song tradition were brought to the Americas by Spanish soldiers, missionaries, and settlers. The chronicles of the Conquest provide evidence of the importance the ballads held in the

imagination of this first wave of Europeans in the Americas. In several passages the chroniclers call to mind lines and verses from the *romances* as they contemplate events or scenes encountered in New Spain. For example, Bernal Díaz del Castillo, loyal witness of the Conquest of what was to become Nueva Espana and later, Mexico, cites a number of dramatic moments and incidents that brought lines from the "old romances" to the minds of Fernando (Hernán) Cortes and the soldiers in his retinue. The Spanish authority Ramón Menéndez Pidal views these instances as part of a general pattern:

> Surely in the memory of every captain, of every soldier, of every merchant, went along something of the extremely popular Spanish *romancero,* as a reminder of a revered childhood often to sweeten the sentiment of loneliness for the home country, to lessen the boredom of those endless trips or the fear of the adventures awaiting them in the unknown world they set foot on.

Remnants of the old ballads are reported in every niche of Spanish America, from Argentina and Chile to New Mexico, and variants in Portuguese have been found in most regions of Brazil.

But the Mexican *corrido* is not a regional vestige of a European ballad tradition. In Mexico, to a degree unrivaled elsewhere in the Americas, these narrative roots produced what the Mexican-American scholar Américo Paredes calls "a living ballad tradition," a practice of creating and performing narrative song in response to events affecting local communities. In the living ballad tradition, the singers no longer focus on the old stories about the Spanish nobility, of exploits in the Reconquest of the peninsula. They sing instead about the heroes and villains of their own time and place, of contemporary events that leave a mark on the community or the nation. The term *corrido* has been reported elsewhere in Latin America, notably in Colombia, Argentina, Cuba, and Venezuela, and there is evidence of narrative song approximating the *corrido* in these and other areas, but only in Mexico does this narrative potential flourish into a tradition so prevalent as to be almost atmospheric.

The first substantial evidence of *corridos* in Mexico traces to the middle of the nineteenth century. A few ballad-like lines and stanzas are preserved from the early decades of that century, but the earliest texts that exhibit the *corrido* style date to the 1860s and 1870s. Scholars have puzzled over this hiatus, the barren years between the arrival of the *romance* and the emergence of the *corrido*. The dean of Mexican ballad scholars, Vicente T. Mendoza, imagined a continuous line of ballad production in Mexico in forms such as the *décima,* and saw the *corrido* as evolving out of this tradition of narrative song during the second half of the nineteenth century.

If the *corrido* is hard to detect in the historical record until the closing decades of the previous century, it comes squarely into its own as a popular chronicle of the Mexican Revolution and the ethnic conflict along the Texas-Mexican border at the outset of the twentieth century. During the Revolution, *corridos* were produced by those close to the fighting as well as by hacks working from newspaper accounts in Mexico City. They were circulated through performances by wandering troubadors and musicians tied to particular factions in the struggles, and through a broadside ballad industry that manufactured and distributed *ojas sueltas* or "loose sheets" with ballad lyrics and emblematic wood-carvings. The broadsides issued by Antonio Vanegas Arroyo with the collaboration of the artist José Guadalupe Posada, many of them preserved in modern collections, testify to the vitality and reach of this publishing venture. There are numerous accounts of blind singers and other troubadors performing these ballads and selling the broadsides in the squares, markets, and plazas of Mexican cities, towns, and villages. The poetic activity of local composers as well as city interpreters assured a diversified stylistic profile for the genre, in which the local ballads stand out for their simple strength of language.

In the aftermath of the Revolution, the popular *corrido* persisted as a running narrative of conflict and violent confrontation associated with outlaw bands and local strongmen.

At the same time, the newly nationalistic literati discovered in the *corrido* the authentic voice of the Mexican people, and during the 1920s and 1930s the genre inspired pictorial, poetic, and musical treatments by the artistic elite of the nation. Thus the circle surrounding Frida Kahlo and Diego Rivera held *corrido* evenings, and the mural movement associated with Rivera, José Clemente Orozco, and David Alfaro Siqueiros drew its epic sweep in part from the powerful *corrido* narratives. Under the spell of this post-Revolutionary nationalism, the dean of Mexican composers, Carlos Chávez, wrote in 1934 *El Sol,* a Mexican *corrido* for mixed choir and large orchestra.

As the twentieth century reached its midpoint, the *corrido* had evolved into a new phase in its development as the ballad of contemporary Mexico. The second half of this century saw the *corrido* retain considerable importance as a body of national history commemorating the deeds of the heroes, as a resource for political messages from both the government and its opponents, and as a local chronicle of violent encounters in several *corrido* pockets around the country. Most recently, the genre has experienced a revival through popular and commercial renderings of events tied to the trade in illegal drugs. Commercial recording groups such as Los Tigres del Norte routinely include *corridos* of this ilk on their new releases, and even *banda* music, the dance sensation of the early 1990s, includes newly composed *corridos*. This body of commercial releases dispenses with some of the formalities but remains clearly oriented to the *corrido* tradition as it depicts the clash of federal forces with the *traficantes* (drug traffickers), the accumulation of fortunes, and the early deaths of those involved in this business.

Corrido as Expressive Form

The *corrido* can be characterized broadly as a genre of narrative song, but within the confines of the genre there is room for a great deal of diversity in style, form, and content. Perhaps the most typical *corrido* is the *corrido trágico,* often consisting of stanzas of eight-syllable lines exhibiting assonance or rhyme on the even-numbered lines, and telling in third-person narrative discourse of events involving mortal danger or loss of life. These *corridos* normally open with an introductory stanza in which the singer requests the indulgence of the audience:

> Voy a cantar un corrido
> para los que me están oyendo. . . .
> (I will sing a *corrido*
> for those who are listening to me. . . .)
>
> ...
>
> Para cantar un corrido
> pido permiso primero. . . .
> (In order to sing a *corrido*
> I ask permission first. . . .)
>
> ...

Voy a cantar un corrido
sin agravio y sin disgusto. . . .
(I will sing a *corrido*
without malice and without anger. . . .)

These polite opening formulas establish a zone of safe social interaction for the ensuing performance of the song. The *corrido* normally closes with the singer's *despedida,* or farewell, using phrases such as *Ya con esta me despido* (Now with this I take my leave) and *Ya me voy a despedir* (Now I am going to say farewell). Between these framing stanzas, the typical tragic *corrido* sets the scene for the action, often providing the names of protagonists, place names, and dates and times of action, and then moves on to narrate the action, often featuring the exchange of words among protagonists in a state of mortal conflict. In these ballads, the heroes are men of action and of words, and in many instances the *corridos* place primary emphasis on the defiant statements of the protagonists.

But many other kinds of *corridos* are recognized and accepted by the Mexican public as valid members of the genre. One prominent sub-form is the *bola suriana,* cultivated in Morelos and Guerrero, a narrative song consisting in specific combinations of eight- and twelve-syllable lines. *Corridos* need not deal with violent encounters at all; there are first-person narratives of prisoners and drunkards, lyrical songs of love and love lost, tales of memorable horse races, and even humorous *corridos* making fun of pretentious language or telling tales about enormous fleas and other exaggerations. At one extreme, virtually any popular song with a narrative component can be included within the *corrido* genre. In various contexts, people will make finer distinctions, and at the heart of the genre one finds the *corrido trágico,* with its evocation of heroes confronting scenes of mortal danger.

The music of the *corrido* is also open to a range of forms and styles. Some *corrido* tunes are *pasodobles,* set to the lively rhythm of the bullfighting arena; others are in triple rhythms like the waltz or double rhythms similar to those found in many popular *ranchero* or *norteño* tunes. The melodies are in major keys except on the Costa Chica of Guerrero, where minor keys also appear, giving these *corridos* the aura of dirge or lament. There are several families of *corrido* melodies, with new melodies formed by minor alterations of existing melodies, and existing melodies often reused with new *corrido* lyrics. The instrumentation also varies, although the basic requirement is a guitar. From this minimal unit, the singer and guitar accompaniment, instruments can be added in accordance with the regional taste in ensemble playing: in the north, the ubiquitous accordion, often with electric bass and rhythm guitar; in the central mesa, the mariachi orchestra; in the south, the harp. In rural settings *corrido* singers even will hold forth against the raucous background of a brass-band accompaniment.

Corridos are composed by individuals recognized for this ability and are learned and to some degree recomposed by the musicians who perform them. It is interesting to fol-

low the fate of a local *corrido,* composed by someone in the community and performed by this person or passed on to singers known to him. Some local *corridos* perish without achieving further recognition. Others become part of a local repertoire and may persist in a recognizable form through two or more generations of singers. Occasionally a local *corrido* arrives at the national level, as in the case of "Simón Blanco," a ballad about the assassination of a gentleman in a town on the outskirts of Acapulco, Guerrero, probably in the 1930s. A few old-timers recall the original ballad that must have begun to circulate shortly after the event. From this original a standard ballad has emerged, shorn of local names and details and reduced to less than half its size, but preserving the core element of *compadre* murder. Influential in this process has been the release of recorded versions fixing the shortened ballad in people's memories.

The *corrido* today is a major treasure of the Mexican people, recognized throughout the nation as a body of narrative song commemorating the heroes of the Revolutionary past. Ballads about Pancho Villa and Emiliano Zapata and a host of lesser figures enjoy the status of national balladry, performed at local venues, recorded on commercial records, tapes, and disks, and even celebrated in Mexican cinema. Concurrent with this national presence is the persistence of the *corrido*-making tradition in specific pockets of the nation, mostly in rural areas with a *ranchero* background, and in urban areas among working-class males. *Corridos* are heard in cantinas, in public spaces, on the radio, and at private homes. There is a checkered pattern to the distribution of interest in the *corrido*. Some regions, especially those dominated by the presence of indigenous communities, evince little interest in the genre; others display a historical *corrido* tradition that is now largely inactive; and others exhibit a continuous *corrido* trajectory from the Revolutionary period to the present. In active *corrido* areas, some individuals are deeply involved with the genre, while others are indifferent or even hostile to it. Women are less involved than men, although there are female performers of *corridos,* and women are active as audience members during *corrido* performances in homes and in public venues.

Controversies and Issues

The *corrido* has spawned a number of controversies, both among the general population and among scholars of Mexican culture and politics. Perhaps the most dramatic controversy has revolved around the argument that the *corrido* is of indigenous rather than European origins. The highly respected scholar and author, and also composer of *corridos,* Celedonio Serrano Martínez, has forcefully argued against tracing the *corrido* to the Spanish *romance.* Correctly pointing out that the *corrido* cannot be reduced to one of its major prototypes, the *romance*-derived octosyllabic quatrain with assonance on the even lines, Serrano Martínez argues for an origin in the narrative poetry and song of the indigenous cultures of Mexico. There is, of course, ample evidence for narrative song traditions among the Mexica (Aztecs) and other major groups, although the available examples do not closely resemble *corrido* discourse. At the same time, for all the similarity in form and content between *corridos* and *romances,* there is a distinctive flavor to the *corrido,* evident in the defiant attitude of the hero, his indifference toward death, that could derive from indigenous sources. The wisest position to adopt in this crossfire is a probable and difficult to decipher conjoining of Europe and America in the *corrido,* a conclusion that seems reasonable in assessing the origins of most of Mexico's cultural forms.

Another interesting controversy lies in the overall function of the *corrido.* Scholars have tended to view the *corrido* as a kind of oral newspaper, spreading word of catastrophic events in its stanzas about accidents, acts of nature, and violent confrontations. It is likely that at some times and in some places the genre has operated to this effect. But another, deeper role can be discovered through an inspection of the *corrido* in its local settings, that of commemorating significant heroes and episodes affecting the community. In these settings, news of violent confrontations, deadly accidents, or devastating acts of nature, circulates by word of mouth before the *corridos* arrive. The narratives in such *corridos* are often dependent on prior awareness of these core events. The *corridos* enter the scene not to inform but to commemorate, to propose in the artistic guise of poetry set to music an interpretation of events already widely known to the public. This commemorative intent is evident in the sometimes intermittent quality of narrative, presupposing and building upon local knowledge. In this process ordinary events often are assimilated to the heroic archetype of the hero standing firm in the face of mortal danger.

The *corrido trágico* raises interesting issues regarding the association of poetry and violence. The genre flourishes in areas where violence has remained endemic, and it takes this violence as the centerpiece of its narratives. The distinguished Mexican scholar Gonzalo Aguirre Beltrán saw in the *corridos* of Guerrero's Costa Chica the manifestation of an aggressive ethos, and he saw the heroes in these Costa Chica *corridos* as role models for the young men of the region. There is evidence to suggest that some men do attempt to imitate the life of these heroes, a life of fast living and early death. On inspection, however, another editorial posture can be detected, one that seeks to impose on the narrated events a moral consciousness, a sense of destiny based on the consequences of actions taken in a world presided over but not closely managed by a just God. Thus, when Simón Blanco is killed by his *compadre* and the Martínez boys, it is not surprising that in a short time these assassins themselves perish, for to kill a *compadre* is "to offend the Eternal":

A los tres días de muerto
se fallecieron los Martínez,
decían en su novenario
que eso encerraba un misterio,
porque matar a un compadre
es ofender al eterno.

(When he was dead three days
the Martínez boys passed away,
they were saying at their wake
that this thing held a mystery,
for to kill a *compadre*
is to offend the eternal one.)

Likewise, when Nicho Esteven is killed, his own mother has to admit that it was God's will:

Estaría de Dios que pagaras
la muerte de dos criaturas.
(It would be God's will you repay
the death of two little children.)

These interpretive touches offer another dimension to the *corrido*'s handling of violence, one that seeks to understand it, to place it in a larger interpretive framework, rather than simply to promote it.

In areas where *corridos* still are being composed, the attitude of the general public is that the *corrido,* unlike other resources such as newspaper and official accounts, delivers the real truth. One is frequently told to disregard the stories in the newspapers and wait for the true story in the *corridos.* Expressions such as *dice la pura verdad* (it tells the pure truth) and *son verídicos* (they are really true) are used in assessing the truth value of the *corrido.* Thus it is interesting to hear composers explain things rather differently. Composers stress their efforts to secure reliable information from first- or second-hand sources; they read the newspaper accounts and listen in on the public discussion of events in formulating their poetic narratives. But within this commitment to accuracy there is also a recognition that the whole truth can rarely be presented, for fear of offending one party or another, of stirring up additional trouble, even out of concern for one's own security. Specifying in public verse the perpetrators of murder can fan factional disputes, and direct allegations of cowardice or villainy can arouse a desire for vengeance. Moreover, in the politically charged climate of contemporary Mexico, the authorities do not react kindly to *corrido* composers who fashion narratives presenting the government in an unflattering light. *Corrido* composers tread a fine line between two conflicting goals, telling the truth as far as possible while guarding against unwanted complications.

The *corrido* always has gravitated toward expressing the viewpoint of *los de abajo,* the underdogs, the marginalized classes. The *corrido* hero is typically a revolutionary fighting the power of the state, a border hero resisting the onslaught of the *americanos,* a local man standing up against the encroachment of the national or state authorities, a drug runner hoping to make a quick fortune. There are *corridos* written as overt protest song, but their ideological language sets them apart from the typical *corridos* wherein opposition is expressed indirectly and implicitly. The paradigm is the hero of the Revolution, taking up arms against an abusive central government. *Corridos* from the Revolutionary period assimilate their protagonists to the heroic archetype, leaving unstated the often barbaric activities for which they were responsible. The contemporary *corrido* hero acquires something of the luster of these Revolutionary figures owing to a common motif of standing against the government in a context where national and state authorities have yet to establish their legitimacy in the eyes of the general public.

Select Bibliography

Aguirre Beltrán, Gonzalo, *Cuijla: Esbozo etnográfico de un pueblo negro.* Mexico City: Fondo de Cultura Económica, 1958.

Díaz del Castillo, Bernal, *Historia verdadera de la conquista de Nueva España.* Buenos Aires, Argentina: Editorial Universitaria de Buenos Aires, 1964.

Herrera, Hayden, *Frida: A Biography of Frida Kahlo.* New York: Harper and Row, 1983.

McDowell, John, "Folklore as Commemorative Discourse." *Journal of American Folklore* 105 (1992).

Meierovich, Clara, *Vicente T. Mendoza: Artista y primer folclorólogo musical.* Mexico City: UNAM, 1995.

Menéndez Pidal, Ramón, *Los Romances de América y otros estudios.* Madrid: Espasa-Calpe, 1939.

Mendoza, Vicente T., *El romance español y el corrido mexicano: Estudio comparativo.* Mexico City: UNAM, 1939.

Paredes, Américo, "The Ancestry of Mexico's *Corridos*: A Matter of Definitions." *Journal of American Folklore* 76 (1963).

Serrano Martínez, Celedonio, *La Bola Suriana: Un espécimen del corrido mexicano.* Chilpancingo: Gobierno del Estado de Guerrero, 1989.

Simmons, Merle, "The Ancestry of Mexico's *Corridos*." *Journal of American Folklore* 76 (1963).

—JOHN HOLMES MCDOWELL

CORTÉS, FERNANDO (HERNÁN)

(1484 or 1485–1547) • Conquistador

Fernando Cortés (better but erroneously known as Hernán or Hernando Cortez) was a greedy entrepreneur who sought and found personal aggrandizement for himself and his progeny; he was also a faithful, if ruthless, crusader who sought and found greater glory for his God and his monarch. Cortés was born in Medellín in the kingdom of Castile in 1484 or 1485, when Desiderius Erasmus was probably 18 or 19 and Martin Luther was a babe of one or two. He died in Castilleja de la Cuesta in Castile on December 2, 1547, as infamous in his Catholic world as Luther who died the year before, and more famous than Erasmus who died 21 years earlier.

His parents, Martin Cortés de Monroy and Catalina Pizarro Altamirano, were of modest circumstance but of noble and honorable Castillian families. Fernando Cortés himself had four legitimate heirs, the children of his second wife, Juana de Zúñiga: Martín, María, Catalina, and Juana. He also had five illegitimate but recognized heirs: Martín, son of doña Marina (La Malinche), his indigenous American translator; Luís, son of a Spanish woman named Antonia Hermosillo; Leonor, daughter of Techiupo (Isabel Moteuczoma), sister of the Mexica (Aztec) chieftain, Moteuczoma II; Catalina, daughter of a Cuban Indian woman called Leonor Pizarro; and another daughter born of an Indian woman, neither of whose names are known.

Following a childhood of which we know little, Fernando Cortés was sent to Salamanca in Castile when he was thirteen or fourteen to study grammar and law and to live with his aunt, Iñez de Paz, and her husband, Francisco Nuñez de Valera. Although some combination of restless ambition, lack of funds, adolescent amorousness, and reoccurring illness brought him back to Medellín after two years, the education he received in that well-known university town served him very well in later years as a notary, chronicler, governor, and captain general. At age 19 or 20 he set out to seek his fortune, and before him were two enterprises that promised great adventure and fortune.

Outfitting for major expeditions to Naples and to the West Indies ordered by their monarch, Fernando I, were two tried and trusted royal officers, *el gran capitán* Gonzalo Fernández de Córdoba and fray Nicolás de Ovando, newly appointed governor of the Spanish Indies.

Distantly related and well known to the latter and apparently at least known to the former, Cortés joined Ovando's group in Seville but, felled by an amorous adventure, he failed to sail with it. He then set out for Valencia to join the Naples venture, but for unknown reasons did not do so. After traveling in Castile and another sojourn in Medellín, he left again for Seville in 1506 with funds provided by his father to join a merchandise fleet of five ships preparing to sail to the West Indies. This time he sailed to the island of Hispaniola (modern-day Haiti and the Dominican Republic). There his familial relationship to Ovando soon led to participation in several campaigns on the island, directed at subjecting the native Arawak peoples to Spanish colonial authority.

For his services Cortés received an assignment of Indians in *encomienda,* which provided him a labor force to which no wages had to be paid, some land, and an appointment as *escribano,* or notary, for the newly founded town of Azúa. These emoluments provided the basis for his first entrepreneurial activities, which included trade, livestock, and perhaps sugar cane, all of which apparently were profitable. His services also placed him among Ovando's chief lieutenants, such as Diego Velázquez, a former companion of Christopher Columbus and one of Hispaniola's wealthiest citizens.

In 1511, Ovando's replacement as governor of the West Indies, Diego Colón (son of Christopher Columbus), commissioned Velázquez to undertake a punitive expedition to Cuba to bring that island under Spanish control. Cortés accompanied as chief deputy to the royal treasurer for the expedition. During the eight years that followed, Cortés secured additional *encomienda* grants as well as lands including some in the newly established towns of Baracoa and Santiago de Cuba. Using some of his *encomienda* laborers he successfully panned the rivers in eastern Cuba for gold, and he may have established a foundry and developed a sugar plantation. Although he and Velázquez, now governor of Cuba, had differed often, in 1518 they were allies and Cortés was serving as *alcalde,* or chief magistrate, of Santiago. He was married to Catalina Suárez, had an illegitimate but recognized daughter and was a leading citizen of the Spanish Indies. That year Velázquez selected Cortés to lead an expedition to follow those dispatched in 1517 and 1518 under the commands of Hernández de Córdoba and Juan de Grijalva to explore along the Gulf Coast of today's Mexico. Velázquez chose him in part because Cortés had the necessary wealth to finance a major part of the effort and sufficient status in the colonial community to command it.

Using personal and borrowed funds, Velázquez and Cortés, evidently as equal partners, assembled an expeditionary force that ultimately composed 11 ships, 530 men, 16 horses, a large supply of armaments including some cannons, and a larder of foodstuffs. In mid-November 1518 as the expedition prepared to sail, Velázquez, having grown suspicious once again of Cortés's reckless independence and growing popularity, tried to relieve him of its command. Cortés, warned about Velázquez's intentions, stealthily hastened the expedition to sail on November 18, 1518.

The events that took place from 1518 to 1521 demonstrated Cortés's audacious and effective leadership, his military prowess, his superior political skills, and his uncanny luck. Foremost among these events were his acquisition of two interpreters of the primary languages and cultures of the Maya, Mexica, and neighboring Indian states: the Spanish castaway, fray Gerónimo de Aguilar, and the formerly enslaved indigenous noble woman, doña Marina; the astute founding of the town of Veracruz and use of its town council, or *cabildo,* to legitimate his leadership and to communicate directly with his monarch in Spain; the burning of all of his ships save those sent back to Spain to prevent the mutiny and retreat to Cuba threatened by the followers of Velázquez in his expeditionary force; his use of the fragmented character of the Mexica state and the presence around it of peoples who had successfully resisted domination by it to garner

allies who helped force the Mexica to accept domination; his manipulation of the indigenous people's beliefs and traditions; his decisive conversion of the forces sent by Velázquez into allies and much-needed reinforcements, even though Velázquez had dispatched these forces precisely to take control of the Mexican expeditionary effort out of Cortés's hands; and his imaginative besiegement of Tenochtitlan after his forces had been driven from its temples and causeways (Cortés's besiegement techniques included the construction of ships and use of his principal Indian allies, the Tlaxcaltecans, to cut off the city's waterway avenues to supplies and reinforcements).

Emerging from the struggles with the Mexica not only as their master and a hero among his countrymen but as a brutally destructive and greedy conqueror suspected of a disregard for established authority, Cortés set about the establishment of Spanish colonial agencies and sent several of his lieutenants outward from Tenochtitlan–Mexico City to bring other areas of what are today central, northeastern and southern Mexico and Guatemala under his control. He undertook these talks from the fall of 1521 until the tall of 1527, first as a self-anointed governor and captain general and, the, after October 25, 1522, as a formally appointed official with both of those titles. Despite the fact that the Spanish monarch had forbade any further use of the *encomienda* system (by which the indigenous population was forced to labor for European overlords) because the system appeared to have been a major contributor to the decimation of the Indian populations and because the system was vilified as un-Christian by such Spanish missionary clergy as Bartolomé de Las Casas, Cortés began making *encomienda* assignments of Mexica and other subjected peoples of the central Mexican area and using those assignments to reward himself and his followers. As he did so, he used the Mexica and other tribal systems of tribute or taxes in goods and required labor service systems he discovered during the Conquest. His *encomienda* grants, therefore, provided entitlement to both tribute goods (such as cotton textiles, foodstuffs, and some minerals) and labor services from specified numbers of Indians delivered at stipulated intervals. His grants were perceived as indefinite in term and, therefore, transferable.

Cortés also began making grants of lands taken from conquered Indian rulers, nobles, and priests to himself and his followers, and he began to rebuild Tenochtitlan–Mexico City as a Spanish colonial center. He established town governments for it and other Spanish colonial towns he and lieutenants founded, and he formed a provincial government with himself at its head. In his request of his monarch that he be made governor and captain general of the territory that he called New Spain, he asked that missionaries, preferably Franciscans who were not opposed to agencies of colonization such as the *encomienda* (as were many of their counterparts in the Dominican and other orders), be sent to convert and "civilize" the peoples he was conquering. In response, the Spanish Crown in 1524 dispatched the first twelve of what would become hundreds of missionaries. He assisted the first twelve "Mexican apostles" with the establishment of the first of many of missions placed in Indian towns and provinces. As he did so he also created an Indian governance structure comparable to that in Spanish towns and provinces, and he charged Indian officers with functions and powers similar to those of their Spanish counterparts.

In 1524, as he surrendered his royal tax collecting authority to four treasury officials sent to the colony by his monarch, King Carlos I (Emperor Charles V), Cortés made his ill-fated decision to proceed to Guatemala and Honduras to take control of the conquest efforts in those areas, which appeared to be slipping into the hands of ambitious lieutenants such as Cristóbal de Old. Leaving two of the royal treasury officials and two trusted associates to govern New Spain, Cortés set off with several captives, former Mexica and other Indian chieftains whom he felt could not be left behind safely and from whom he sought directions, and a considerable force of Spanish conquistadors and Indian allies. He was to be absent for nearly two years, during which time he was rumored dead, robbed of many of his newly acquired lands and *encomiendas,* and denied the extensive political and military authority he had enjoyed during the preceding five years.

Jealous rivals and unsatisfied former allies, committed clerics who saw his treatment of the Indians as viciously brutal, and Carlos I himself, combined to relieve him of his titles as governor and captain general, to subject him to investigation of his conduct as a royal governor and captain general, and to seize and embargo a substantial share of his properties. From his return to New Spain in 1526 until he sailed for Spain in 1528, Cortés spent much of his time and remaining liquid resources attempting not altogether unsuccessfully to defend himself and to recoup his property losses.

His efforts in Spain were of like character but included the astute use of his still sufficient funds, prestige, and connections among family and allies to obtain rewarding recognition from his king and a marriage with a member of a noble family, doña Juana de Zúñiga. He returned to New Spain in 1530 as a member of the Spanish nobility, marquis of the Valle of Oaxaca, with a formal title to 22 *encomienda* towns and with the restored (and extended) title of captain general of New Spain and the Mar del Sur (the latter was the fruit of his Honduras enterprise and his dispatch of ships from New Spain's Pacific coast to the Malacca Islands). These rewards and restorations, all in the form of royal *cedulas* (orders), included, in addition, the right to entail as an estate his *encomiendas,* his landholdings, and his trading, mining, and milling properties as the Marquesado del Valle de Oaxaca. Restored to him as well were a number of embargoed or seized properties, and released to him was compensation he was due for exploratory and other services. Not restored to him, however, was his title as governor.

For a decade, 1530 to 1540, the conquistador gave his time and energies to developing the Marquesado, founding a legitimate and noble family, and expanding his trading and related investment interest. At the same time, as captain general, he sought with some initial success (but after 1535 with increasingly less success) to command and participate in the continuing extension of Spanish colonial authority into the northern and southern portions of today's Mexico and into Central America. His efforts to the northwest of the central valleys of Mexico led to discovery of the Baja California peninsula, the nearby "sea" that bears his name, and the long gulf it forms. His exploratory and trading enterprises also took his agents south to Panamá and the northern Pacific perimeters of the vast Inca state that his countryman and probably distant relative, Francisco Pizarro, was bringing under Spanish domination, and across the Mar del Sur (the Pacific) to the Philippines and southeast Asia.

These years were increasingly frustrating for the conquistador, however, as his powers and privileges were circumscribed incrementally by royal officials and royal policies directed at reducing the influence of the conquistadors as well as bringing the *encomienda* system to an end and the Indian peoples of the Indies under direct royal supervision and control. Among the new royal officers, the most difficult for Cortés and other conquistadors like him was the first viceroy appointed in the New World, Antonio de Mendoza; among the most difficult of the new royal edicts were the ordinances reducing *encomienda* tribute payments and reducing and regulating the labor services due *encomenderos* from their Indian *encomienda* charges. Equally vexing for Cortés were the continuing legal battles into which he was drawn by competitors, dissatisfied former followers, and envious Crown officials. In 1540, having just been rebuffed again by Viceroy Mendoza as he sought to exercise what he felt were his rights and powers as captain general in advancing Spanish authority far to the north into the land of Cíbola, just reported by Cabeza de Vaca, Cortés decided to return to Spain to again seek relief and more appropriate recognition. He also returned to arrange marriages for his legitimate children and to secure appointments for his sons in the service of Prince Felipe II, Carlos I's heir.

Cortés's experiences in Spain during, as it turned out, the last seven years of his life, were not unlike those of the preceding decade in New Spain: frustrating and unrewarding. Although his wealth increased in these years and his children secured the recognition due them as young members of Spain's nobility and—in the case of his illegitimate children—its upper-class gentry, he was denied the recognition he felt was his due. He felt particularly neglected when he used his own funds to accompany Carlos I and his army into Tangiers in North Africa to regain Spanish domination in that area, and he was not afforded the opportunity he sought to lead Carlos's forces in the same fashion as he had led his conquistadors against Moteuczoma's imperial troops, Finally, ill and preparing for his death in a small town not far from Seville, he prepared a will that sought to right some of the wrongs he felt he had perpetrated against some of his Indian followers, servants, and slaves, and against his God. His will also passed his title, marquis of the Valle of Oaxaca, and his estate, the Marquesado, to his first-born legitimate son, don

Martín Cortés y Zúñiga, and made financial and property provisions for all of his other children, his wife, his servants, and his God.

Founder of the Spanish colonial system on the mainland of the Americas, peerless conquistador, creator for better or worse of the Mexican tradition of "La Malinche," and forerunner of a host of Mexican leaders most of whom were desperately inferior replicas, Cortés was less insensitive and brutal than most of his ilk and was a great deal more effective as a leader and colonizer. He was at the same time very much a man of his times, a crusader who brooked no competition in the advancement of his beliefs and his mercenary interests. Unlike most of his conquistador peers, he was amply rewarded for his services to his Spanish monarch, although not as handsomely as he thought was his due. Unlike many of them he left heirs who for centuries after his time enjoyed a privileged place in Euro-American society. Like many of them, however, he was contrite and disillusioned as he met his end at home again in Spain where in many circles he was, as he is today, both infamous and famous.

For a detailed discussion of Cortés's role in the conquest of central Mexico, see Conquest: Central Mexico

Select Bibliography

Arteaga Garza, Beatriz, and Guadalupe Pérez San Vicente, editors, *Cedulario Cortesiano.* Mexico City: Editorial Jus, 1949.

Cortés, Hernan, *Cartas y Documentos,* edited by Mario Hernandez Sanchez-Barba. Mexico City: Porrua, 1963.

Díaz del Castillo, Bernal, *The Discovery and Conquest of Mexico, 1517–1521.* New York: Farrar, Strauss and Cudahy, 1956.

Gómara, Francisco López de, *Cortés: The Life of the Conqueror by His Secretary Francisco López de Gómara,* translated and edited by Lesley B. Simpson. Berkeley: University of California Press, 1964.

Madariago, Salvador de, *Hernan Cortés.* Madrid: Espasa Calpe, S.A., 1984.

Riley, G. Micheal, *Fernando Cortés and the Marquesado in Morelos, 1522–1547.* Albuquerque: University of New Mexico Press, 1973.

Scholes, France V., "The Spanish Conqueror as a Businessman." *New Mexico Historical Quarterly* 27 (1958).

Thomas, Hugh, *Conquest: Montezuma, Cortés and the Fall of Old Mexico.* New York: Simon and Schuster, 1994.

Wagner, Henry Raup, *The Rise of Fernando Cortés.* Los Angeles: Cortés Society, 1944.

—G. MICHEAL RILEY

COSÍO VILLEGAS, DANIEL

1898–1976 • Intellectual

A key figure in the intellectual history of modern Mexico, Daniel Cosío Villegas was born in 1898. He received his bachelor degree in law in 1925, and continued his studies at Harvard, the University of Wisconsin, Cornell, the London School of Economics, and the Ecole Libre des Sciences Politiques de Paris. Daniel Cosío Villegas was a member the so-called Generation of 1915, the political and cultural nucleus of university students which, without participating in the armed phase of the Mexican Revolution, assumed the role of "critical conscience" of the Revolutionary movement. Entering the civil service, the Generation of 1915 participated actively in the political, economic, and cultural reconstruction initiated during the administration of Álvaro Obregón. The members of the Generation of 1915 were both heirs and disciples of the Ateneo de la Juventud, which had sought to formulate an alternative to the positivist orthodoxy that had predominated in late-nineteenth- and early-twentieth-century Mexico; Cosío Villegas in particular recognized his debt to two members of the Ateneo, Antonio Caso and Pedro Henríquez Ureña. Caso introduced Cosío Villegas to the academic study of Mexico's social realities; while still a student, Cosío Villegas worked as an adjunct professor under Caso in his School of Mexican Sociology. Henríquez Ureña

helped develop Cosío Villegas's capacity for rigorous critical engagement with Mexico's society and history, which would remain a pillar of his life and work.

"One tried to do something for the new Mexico which had begun to be forged even before the gaze of those who had fallen in the civil war had been extinguished," Cosío would later explain his work in the national reconstruction of the 1920s. During the Obregón presidency, Cosío Villegas, then a law student and president of the Federation of University Students, participated in the efforts at educational and cultural reform led by José Vasconcelos. It was Cosío Villegas's graduate studies in economics and agriculture, however, that would have an especially profound impact on his professional life. Cosío Villegas became one of the pioneers in the academic study of fiscal and monetary policy, as well as agricultural development; in 1929 he helped found the school of economics at the National Autonomous University of Mexico, and he also directed the department of economic studies at the Bank of Mexico. During the 1930s Cosío Villegas's concerns extended to Mexico's international relations, not simply as an area for study and reflection, but also for diplomatic service. Particularly important were Cosío Villegas's efforts to rescue and move to Mexico intellectuals and scientists displaced by the Spanish Civil War. Cosío Villegas also helped found the Casa de España, where many of the exiles would apply their talents to teaching and research. With the establishment of the Casa de España, Cosío Villegas emerged as one of Mexico's most important cultural and academic leaders, helping to found the Colegio de México and the publishing house Fondo de Cultura Económica. He also founded some of the most important academic journals in Mexico, including *El Trimestre Económico* (1934–48), *Historia Mexicana* (1951–61), and *Foro Internacional* (1960–63).

In the 1950s Cosío Villegas concentrated his energy in two areas, the history of Mexico and the contemporary political reality. Cosío Villegas's study of Mexican politics, particularly in his devastating analysis of the governments that had emerged from the Mexican Revolution, *La crisis de México* (1947), marks a turning point in his intellectual development. Disentangling the mechanisms of political power in Mexico, Cosío Villegas developed what would be a central preoccupation in his work, the promotion of an order founded in economic and social justice, political democracy, and profound respect for individual liberties. These concerns led him to study Mexican history, particularly its political evolution during the second half of the nineteenth century. Over the course of almost two decades, Cosío Villegas directed a team of historians and economists whose most important work was the monumental *Historia Moderna de México*. The response to the *Historia Moderna*, however, was not entirely positive. Some critics objected to the work's partiality, as journalistic sources were privileged over archival records; others argued that the *Historia Moderna* merely described historical processes without really attempting to interpret them. Nonetheless, seen from a distance the work is a colossal effort to make historical research more scientific and professional, and it has become an indispensable reference tool for specialists. A milestone in the study of Mexican history, the *Historia Moderna de México* is considered a classic in the historiography of nineteenth-century Mexico.

"The historical drama of Mexico has above all a political origin," Cosío Villegas would insist. This sentence condenses not only the principal obstacles Mexico faced in the construction of a democratic society, but also Cosío Villegas's own conflicts with political power in Mexico. In his work as a sociologist, economist, historian, political analyst, journalist, essayist, editor, promoter of culture, diplomat, and internationalist, Cosío Villegas always maintained a sense of professionalism and ethics, privileging the defense of liberty over political deal-making. "The intellectual is a man who turns all answers into questions," Cosío Villegas claimed. Cosío Villegas died in 1976.

Select Bibliography

Cosío Villegas, Daniel, *Memorias*. Mexico City: J. Mortiz, 1976.
Krauze, Enrique, *Daniel Cosío Villegas: Una biografía intelectual*. 2nd edition, Mexico City: J. Mortiz, 1991.
Martínez Báez, Manuel, *Homenaje de el Colegio Nacional a la memoria de Daniel Cosío Villegas*. Mexico City: Colegio Nacional, 1977.
Wilkie, W. James, and Edna Wilkie Monzón, "Daniel Cosío Villegas." In *Frente a la Revolución Mexicana: 17 protagonistas de la etapa constructiva. Entrevistas de historia oral*, vol. 1. Mexico City: Universidad Autónoma Metropolitana, 1995.

—PABLO YANKELEVICH

COTTON TEXTILE INDUSTRY

Cotton was a principal item of clothing in Mesoamerica prior to the Spanish Conquest. When Spaniards conquered Mexico, they imported their cloth from the Old World rather than obtaining it from indigenous producers. Through the long period of colonial rule (1519–1821), the upper classes continued to import cloth and clothes. Nonetheless, there was the development of local cloth production in artisan centers, *obrajes*. Although some *obrajes* were quite large, there was nothing in New Spain to compete with events in England, which in the late eighteenth century created the model for manufacturing that we know as the industrial revolution. The English mechanized the production of cotton cloth, powering the new machines with steam engines. By gathering together raw materials, machines, power sources, and "operatives" into one building, they created the factory system and factory-driven urban centers.

If England's industrial revolution dates from the last third of the eighteenth century, Mexico's began in 1830, although in the same industry, cotton textiles. The three founders of the modern Mexican cotton textile industry were Pedro Sáinz de Baranda, Lucas Alamán, and Esteban de Antuñano. In 1830, Sáinz de Baranda became the *jefe político* (political boss) in Valladolid, where he established Mexico's first mechanized textile factory, La Aurora Yucateca, in 1834. Within ten years, La Aurora employed 117 workers, remaining a modest success until it was destroyed by the Caste War, which wracked the Yucatán Peninsula during the latter half of the nineteenth century. Also in 1830, Lucas Alamán, a preeminent figure of early independent Mexico and a minister in Anastasio Bustamante's government, founded the Banco de Avío. The purpose of this first development bank was to finance industrialization with capital provided by tariffs on cotton textile imports. The bank underwrote the purchase of foreign textile machinery. In July 1830, Esteban de Antuñano entered into an agreement with Gumersindo Saviñón, owner of the San José El Mayorazgo flour mill. With the support of the Banco de Avío, Antuñano built La Constancia Mexicana, which many scholars consider the first modern textile operation in Mexico. Using foreign machines purchased with the help of the Banco, and contracting ten maestros ingleses (English technicians), Antuñano opened the factory near Puebla on January 7, 1835. La Constancia spun crude cotton, selling the yarn to artisans who transformed it into cloth. In 1836 Alamán himself entered into a business agreement with the Legrand brothers to build a textile factory in Cocolapan, near Orizaba in Veracruz. Cocolapan became the country's largest mill in the first half of the century.

The early factories took advantage of new laws in 1829 and 1830, the first of which created protection for an incipient cotton textile industry, the second of which created the Banco de Avío. The bank established a fund of 1 million pesos to finance national industry. Despite political turmoil and civil wars that prevented the bank from functioning optimally, five sets of cotton machines and one of wool eventually were sent to Mexico City, Puebla, Morelia, Celaya, Tlaxcala, and Querétaro.

Although wealthy Mexicans continued to prefer imported cloth and clothes, and despite the persistence of subsistence agriculture and isolated communities that lived mostly outside the market, many poor rural and urban Mexicans could and did buy the cheap cotton cloth, or manta, produced by the factories. The local cloth was cheaper than that of foreign competitors because of the newly established government tariffs and the de facto protection of high transport costs. With a modest local, albeit protected, market, and initially financed by the government-sponsored Banco de Avío, Mexican capitalists bought imported machines, built large factories, and brought foreign technicians to oversee the production process. The creation of a cotton textile industry and a true factory system comprised Mexico's industrial revolution, although one limited to a single industry.

The industry grew rapidly. By 1836 there were eight cotton textile factories in the country. The number of mills continued to increase: 17 in 1840, 47 in 1843, 52 in 1844, and 62 in 1845. Some of the factories were quite large for the period. Gumersindo Saviñón, the former partner of Antuñano, converted El Mayorazgo into a mill with 2,400 spindles. Antuñano's La Constancia Mexicana had 7,680 spindles, and his La Economía Mexicana had another 3,900. The new factories demanded larger and more regular supplies of raw cotton than had the old obrajes, stimulating a shift in the countryside from small ranchos to large haciendas.

During the first half of the nineteenth century many of the factories were located near important population (consumer) centers. Even though Cocolapan, which by now held significant French capital, was the country's largest factory, Mexico City and Puebla led in number of textile factories and amount of cloth produced. While mostly producing cheap manta for local markets, the factories imported all of their machinery. By 1862 45 of the country's 57 factories produced manta while the other 12 fabricated yarn. Yarn production that year totaled 7,853,779 pounds, selling for 1,963,444 pesos; 1,258,963 pieces of manta were produced, selling for 4,581,370 pesos. The total number of spindles now reached 133,122.

Mexico's industrial revolution differed considerably from England's. In Mexico, capitalists imported all of their machinery and technology and often the most skilled workers as well. The technology could be quite up to date but was never truly a function of local conditions; it was simply what foreigners had to offer. As technologies became more capital intensive in England and then in France, Germany, and the United States, Mexico adopted these innovations in labor-saving devices although the country had an abundance of unskilled workers. Productivity in the Mexican industry, however, was barely sufficient to allow Mexican producers to compete in local markets; the country's factories never fully acquired the capacity to compete in foreign markets. Mexico's new manufacturing sector imported technology and exported little. Many of the factories were built in old haciendas, many of which had flour mills. The new establishments acquired some of the characteristics of the haciendas: large, ornate buildings, workers' houses on the premises, and paternalism in running the enterprise. Some of these characteristics would stay with the industry well into the twentieth century.

From Independence until the last quarter of the nineteenth century, the violence, political instability, foreign invasions, and lack of capital and capitalists that plagued the country's overall development also hindered the growth of the cotton textile industry. Despite continued protection, Mexican industrialists suffered from high costs, a lack of native technology, difficulties in financing, poor transport systems, an almost complete inability to export, and an anemic internal market. In light of these difficulties, the success of the early cotton textile factories was quite surprising.

During the long dictatorship of General Porfirio Díaz (1876–80, 1884–1911), the Mexican economy experienced its first period of stable economic growth. The cotton textile industry benefited from Porfirian stability, the revolution in transport costs led by railroad development, and the modest increase in the internal market. From 1876 to 1890, the industry expanded, but during the 1890s the growth rate jumped significantly as companies, factories, and machines became larger and more modern. Instead of a deepening of the country's industrial revolution, however, the result was a crisis in the industry in the years just prior to the outbreak of Revolution in 1910.

The textile expansion of the 1870s and 1880s changed little of the industry's geographic structure and technology. The main textile centers were Puebla, Tlaxcala, Mexico City, Veracruz, Querétaro, and Jalisco. In 1877, the country counted 86 mills, 8,132 looms, 234,386 spindles, and

10,871 workers. During the 1890s the industry grew dramatically, and in 1900 there were 141 mills, 18,553 looms, 600,707 spindles, and 28,192 workers.

According to Scholar Stephen H. Haber, the principal characteristics of Porfirian industrialization were a high degree of horizontal and vertical integration, capital-intensive production, and consolidation of ownership. Concentration of capital, more modern technologies, new companies, and larger factories certainly characterized the Porfirian textile industry. At the height of the textile boom, the country witnessed the emergence of large industrial enterprises such as the Compañía Industrial de Orizaba (CIDOSA). CIDOSA bought the Cerritos and San Lorenzo mills in 1889, opened Río Blanco in 1892, and brought Cocolapan into the fold in 1899. Typical of the new factories, Río Blanco started with 35,000 spindles and 900 looms. Another giant, the Compañía Industrial Veracruzana, opened the Santa Rosa mill near Orizaba in 1898 with 33,000 spindles and 1,400 looms. Before 1890, the average mill had had only 300 spindles, so the clear tendency was toward larger, more modern factories. The new factories were equipped with automatic looms and electric spindles, which increased productivity.

The modernization of the industry also brought some shift in the geographic location of the industry. Although the early mills opened near population centers, later mills were located near rivers in order to take advantage of hydroelectric power. The expansion of the industry in Orizaba reflected that shift, as did the establishment of large factories in Atlixco, a booming mill town south of the city of Puebla. With French capital, the large Metepec plant near Atlixco opened in 1902 with 36,852 spindles and 1,570 looms.

Metepec, Santa Rosa, Río Blanco, and the other large mills employed hydroelectric power to operate the new, automatic machinery. The growing use of electric energy changed the industry. Electric energy increased the use of automatic machinery, which in turn required larger capital investments. This led to an increase in production, productivity, and factory size. Automatic looms and high-speed spindles now characterized the industry. By 1900, 44 percent of Mexico's hydroelectric power was generated by plants installed in textile factories.

Along with electric energy, another new (to Mexico) technology that drove the industry was the railroad, which dramatically reduced transport costs. The price of shipping one ton of cotton from Mexico City to Querétaro dropped from 61 pesos in 1877 to 3 pesos in 1910. Many American and English engineers and technicians participated in the construction of the large factories and the installation of modern machinery and up-to-date hydroelectric plants. Meanwhile, an influx of Spanish (Puebla) and French (Orizaba and Mexico City) industrialists changed ownership groups, just as the country began the development of joint stock companies.

The growth of the cotton textile industry brought workers, labor organizations, and labor strife to the forefront of Mexican society. In 1800, there was no true factory proletariat in Mexico. In 1900, the 141 textile factories employed 30,000 workers, many of them in modern factories with more than 1,000 mill hands each. By 1922, Río Blanco employed 2,592 workers; Santa Rosa, 1,554; Metepec, 1,162; Covadonga in Puebla, 997; La Carolina in Mexico City, 1,048; and El Hercules in Querétaro, 1,115. The labor force was overwhelmingly male; women worked in some factories and in some jobs but almost always were paid less than men, usually significantly less. It was more common to find women workers in associated industries and in the smaller shops, particularly those producing cotton goods and clothing. Most of the industrial workers lived in four places: two textile towns (Atlixco and Orizaba), Puebla, and Mexico City. In the half century between 1860 and 1910, these workers formed labor organizations, led violent and sometimes successful strikes against the owners, and created a working-class culture that resisted management control inside the factories. In the mill towns and industrial cities, they communicated easily with other workers, radicals, and revolutionaries. If life in the factory was better than the often-oppressive conditions in the countryside, it was still a sharply stratified existence in which owners and bosses looked down on skilled and unskilled workers alike.

Although labor conflict in the mills was endemic, modernization, increasing mill size, and more distant ownership were explosive elements when the Porfirian economy turned downward in the last years of the dictatorship. In late 1906 and early 1907 mill hands in Puebla, Tlaxcala, and Veracruz carried out a successful general strike, leading to a massacre of workers in Río Blanco in January 1907. Puebla and Tlaxcala, which contained a large percentage of the country's industrial workers, became places of early and protracted revolutionary conflict.

When Revolution erupted in 1910, none of the participants foresaw the vast slaughter and destruction that would take place in Mexico's countryside during the ensuing decade. Most of the textile industry was located in zones where combatants fought bitterly. Zapatistas operated actively in Mexico City and Atlixco, while other Revolutionary bands fought incessantly in Puebla, Tlaxcala, and Veracruz. Although most of the factories were not damaged

TABLE 1
Regional Production of Cotton Textiles, 1880–1910

State	% of National Production before 1880	% of National Production in 1910
Puebla	23%	32%
Federal District	14%	12%
Veracruz	9%	21%
Tlaxcala	4%	6%
Others	50%	29%

Source: Dawn Keremitsis, *La Industria Textil Mexicana en el Siglo XIX.* Mexico City: Secretaría de Educación Pública, 1973.

severely during the Revolution, the disruption of markets, the physical destruction in towns and haciendas, and the extreme political instability affected the industry. Workers took advantage of the fighting to carry out a successful strike in 1911–12, leading to an industry-wide contract in July of that year, the first of its kind in Mexico and the forerunner of Mexican labor contract law (contrato-ley).

Like the workers, the owners also organized for political battles. When textile workers founded the Gran Círculo de Obreros Libres in Río Blanco in April 1906, the textile owners responded by organizing the Central Industrial Mexicano (CIM), which promptly issued a new set of work rules for the industry. That unilateral decision set in motion the events leading to the massacre in Río Blanco. In the midst of the 1912 conflict, Tomás Reyes Retana helped a group of textile owners establish another industrial group, the Confederación Fábril Nacional Mexicana (CFNM). For the next two decades, the CIM represented Puebla and Tlaxcala industrialists while the CFNM expressed the views of the large companies in Orizaba and Mexico City. While various labor organizations fought each other for control of workers, the two owners' groups battled one another to gain competitive advantage.

After 1920, the industry grew steadily but not spectacularly. The number of factories rose from 120 in 1920 to 193 in 1940, while the number of workers increased from 37,936 to 43,698. The problems of the industry paralleled the problems of the country as a whole: recuperation and modernization. Industrialists wrestled with an industry that was more dependent than ever on high tariffs and that imported virtually all its machinery while mostly unable to export its final products. They tried to control a labor force that was now completely unionized and whose labor organizations maintained strong ties to the state. The union leaders in the mill towns of Atlixco and Orizaba gained virtual control of local politics, where figures such as Antonio Hernández and Martín Torres became legendary, as did the union violence and labor wars that continued unabated through the 1930s. Although there was some return to profitability and productivity growth during the 1930s, there is evidence that it was led by newer and smaller firms rather than the Porfirian giants that still dominated the industry.

A number of post-Revolutionary textile meetings tried to solve the industry's problems; the most important of these were the tripartite conventions of 1925 to 1927 and 1937 to 1939, which formalized the system of contrato-ley. The contrato-ley brought a sort of labor peace to the industry and thereby became a model for other industries. Textile leaders helped the country draft a new labor code in 1931. In later years, other industries would turn to the contrato-ley pioneered in cotton textiles. Although the contrato-ley provided many protections for workers, it imposed a series of constraints on changing work rules and increasing productivity. The owners blamed the unions for stagnating productivity; the unions blamed the owners for their lack of innovation. After World War II, wages stagnated.

TABLE 2
Real Weekly Wages in Cotton Textile Industry, 1939–55
(in 1939 Pesos)

Year	Nominal Wage	Real Wage
1939	27.32	27.32
1940	29.08	28.15
1941	30.56	29.27
1942	31.86	26.33
1943	36.61	23.10
1944	41.48	20.83
1945	45.92	21.51
1946	55.10	20.66
1947	57.50	19.15
1948	60.77	19.06
1949	71.9	21.41
1950	74.78	20.99
1951	80.69	20.10
1952	81.61	17.77
1953	92.46	20.60
1954	97.6	20.60
1955	118.1	21.58

Source: Gabino Islas, *La mano de obra en la industria de hilados y tejidos de algodón.* Mexico City: Banco de México, 1956.

Concerned about economic development, industrialization, and modernization, the Mexican government sponsored a number of conferences and studies during World War II aimed at modernizing and expanding cotton textile production. At these conventions, owners and labor leaders fought over union rules while both sides agreed that protection was necessary. Meanwhile, the general wartime prosperity of Mexican industry mitigated conflict in the textile industry. After the war, however, a new threat arose. Cotton fiber was now a mature industry threatened by the wartime development of artificial fibers. From 1950 to 1956, the production of cotton cloth increased 13.3 percent while the manufacture of artificial fibers jumped 150.2 percent. During this period Mexico developed many new industries, ranging from automobiles to electrical appliances. There had been a period when Mexican industry was synonymous with textiles; that period was now gone forever. Productivity and output in cotton textiles lagged behind Mexico's newer industries, and fell further behind that of international competitors. Not surprisingly, wages declined relative to other industries despite the presence of strong unions. From 1939 to 1955, real wages in cotton textiles fell 21 percent.

Although the Mexican economy did well in the 1960s, in the 1970s it entered into a period of prolonged crisis that continued through the 1990s. Massive peso devaluations (1976, 1982, 1984, 1994) set off periods of extreme inflation, a collapse of the internal market, and great uncertainty for old and new businesses alike. The cotton textile industry was not immune to these changes. Between 1982 and 1993, the industry's gross domestic product (GDP) fell 15.9 percent, while its production as a percent of national manufacturing

TABLE 3
Mexican Cotton Textile Industry, 1845–1954

Year	Factories	Looms	Spindles	Workers	Year	Factories	Looms	Spindles	Workers
1845	56		113,813		1925	124	28,934	780,691	42,359
1854	42	4,393	161,860	10,316	1926	131	29,446	786,144	44,114
1861	50		133,122		1927	132	29,290	777,380	41,008
1877	99	9,214	258,458	12,346	1928	132	29,295	791,333	38,889
1888–89		8,048	249,561	15,063	1929	139	28,825	792,936	38,881
1893–94	103	11,796	392,124	17,578	1930	141	29,229	800,023	38,860
1894	95	11,633	395,254	17,589	1931	142	29,228	799,129	36,883
1895	99	12,333	409,841	18,046	1932	137	27,900	773,579	34,626
1896	103	13,235	438,446	20,128	1933	155	31,438		40,937
1897	107	13,922	463,341	21,288	1934	160	32,605		50,319
1898	112	14,263	474,827	22,018	1935	179	32,861	876,771	40,321
1899	125	15,497	508,876	24,521	1936	207	33,971	875,672	42,716
1900	141	18,553	600,707	28,192	1937	224	35,631	865,356	43,249
1901	134	18,478	593,617	26,709	1938	221	34,987	865,626	43,299
1902	125	29,271	632,601		1939	175			42,603
1903	120	20,506	641,060	27,706	1940	193			43,698
1904	131	22,021	678,058		1941	218			45,999
1905	131	22,774	688,217		1942	225			49,111
1906	129	23,507	693,842		1943				
1907	131	24,997	732,876		1944				
1908	137	25,327	726,278		1945	74			
1909	131	25,921	732,888		1946	74			42,652
1910	127	26,184	723,963		1947	66			40,393
1917	99	20,489	573,092	22,187	1948	66			40,495
1918	104	25,017	689,173	27,680	1949	66			38,064
1919	114	27,020	749,237	33,185	1950	74			40,008
1920	120	27,301	753,837	37,936	1951				40,532
1921	121	28,409	770,945	38,227	1952				44,632
1922	120	27,819	758,624	39,677	1953				44,161
1923	113	27,770	752,255	38,684	1954	69			39,556
1924	109	26,536	721,580	37,080					

Source: INEGI, *Estadísticas Históricas de México.* Mexico City: INEGI, 1994.

production declined by a third, from 6 percent to 4 percent. In 1995, the domestic market for Mexico's textile factories plunged 60 percent. Meanwhile, artificial fibers continued to grow at the expense of the cotton industry, and by 1993 national consumption of artificial fibers was three-fifths that of all soft fibers, including cotton. In the short run, the North American Free Trade Agreement (NAFTA) did little to save the industry.

During the nineteenth century Mexico's industrial revolution was synonymous with cotton textiles. This was the first factory industry in Mexico. It pioneered modern machinery, steam and electric power, new forms of business organization, and ultimately, new methods of labor control. Despite these contributions to Mexican society, the industry could not escape the basic contradictions of Mexican industrial growth: dependence on tariffs and government supports, the need to import technology without a consequent ability to export finished products, and reliance on a government-sponsored labor system that brought stability without pro-ductivity gains. Toward the end of the twentieth century Mexican textiles had become the mature industry that they were in other countries. The industry continued to grow in absolute importance while nonetheless losing forever its preeminent place in Mexican industrialization.

See also Obraje System

Select Bibliography

Anderson, Rodney D., *Outcasts in Their Own Land: Mexican Industrial Workers, 1906–1911.* DeKalb: Northern Illinois University Press, 1976.

Bortz, Jeffrey L., "The Genesis of Mexico's Modern Labor Relations System: Federal Labor Policy and the Textile Industry 1925–1940." *The Americas* 52:1.

Colon Reyes, Linda Ivette, *Los orígenes de la burguesía y el banco de avío.* Mexico City: El Caballito, 1982.

de la Peña, M.T., *La Industria Textil del Algodón: Crisis, salarios, contratacion.* Mexico City: Sindicoto Nacional de Economistas, 1938.

Gamboa Ojeda, Leticia, *Los Empresarios de Ayer: El grupo dominante en la industria textil de Puebla 1906–1929*. Puebla: Universidad Autonoma de Puebla, 1985.

Haber, Stephen H., *Industry and Underdevelopment: The Industrialization of Mexico, 1890–1940*. Stanford, California: Stanford University Press, 1989.

Hart, John M., *Anarchism and the Mexican Working Class, 1860–1931*. Austin: University of Texas Press, 1978.

Keremitsis, Dawn, *La Industria Textil Mexicana en el Siglo XIX*. Mexico City: Secretaría de Educación Pública, 1973.

Levin, Baron F., "Mexico's Textile Industry." *El Mercado de Valores* (March-April 1996).

Quijano, Jesus Rivero, *La Revolución Industrial y La Industria Textil en México*. 2 vols., Mexico City: Porrúa, 1990.

Ramos Escandon, Carmen, "Working Class Formation and the Mexican Textile Industry: 1880–1912." Ph.D. diss., State University of New York at Stony Brook, 1981.

—JEFFREY L. BORTZ

COUNCIL OF THE INDIES

The Council of the Indies, or Real y Supremo Consejo de las Indias, was the most important governing institution for Spanish America during the sixteenth and seventeenth centuries. It owed its separate and legal existence to a decree of King Carlos I (Emperor Charles V), issued in 1524 as part of an attempt to rationalize and improve Spain's administrative machinery at a time when the new state was passing from an age of conquistadors to one of civil servants. The council's foundations, however, can be traced back to 1493, when Queen Isabel entrusted her chaplain, Juan Rodríguez de Fonseca, with all matters pertaining to the newly discovered territories.

Between 1511 and 1519, the Council of the Indies was essentially a standing committee of the Council of Castile. Soon after the accession of Carlos I, however, there gradually emerged a *junta* for Indian affairs, chaired by Fonseca and composed of a few members of the Council of Castile. Then in 1520 a *procurador* (public prosecutor) and a *relator* (council reporter) were added to the *junta,* and in 1521 an *abogado de los pleitos de las Indias* (ombudsman for the Indies). Although this group soon came to be referred to as the Council of the Indies, at this stage all matters of justice were still the responsibility of the Council of Castile, and the Council of the Indies was still primarily an administrative body. It was only after Fernando (Hernán) Cortés's conquest of Mexico that the need was seen to give the Council of the Indies autonomous rank as a "royal and supreme council" with complete administrative and judicial authority.

In its early days both the composition and the place of residence of the council were variable. Like most governmental bodies at this time, it tended to follow the peregrinations of an essentially itinerant Court. The records for the first decade show that salaries were paid to a president, four to six councillors, a secretary, a *fiscal* (same as a *procurador*), a *relator*, and a porter. The president was, as a rule, a prelate. The first president was Fray García de Loaisa, master general of the Dominican order, bishop-elect of Osma, and Carlos I's confessor. The councillors, on the other hand, were drawn primarily from the legal profession. In the sixteenth century the bulk of them were professional lawyers. In the seventeenth, they began to include noblemen and royal favorites with no formal training in the law; but even then, the council remained primarily a legal body. A common practice was to promote councillors from the Chancelleries of Valladolid and Granada, or from among the *alcaldes de corte* (officials of the royal court). A less common practice was to recruit them from among those who had served in the Indies, particularly in the *audiencias* (high courts), with a view to benefiting from their experience. The most distinguished of Spanish colonial jurists, for instance, Juan de Solórzano y Pereira, author of the monumental *Política Indiana,* had been *oidor* (local Crown representative) at Lima before becoming a councillor of the Indies.

In tune with many early modern Spanish institutions, the Council of the Indies was a somewhat amphibious institution, reflecting the uneven and often paradoxical developments of a rapidly changing system of government. When dealing with important cases, it had the function of a supreme court of appeal. Otherwise, it was an advisory council to direct and supervise New World affairs. In most respects the council was completely independent of all the royal councils, including the Council of Castile, and responsible only to the king. The principle here was that, from the legal point of view, the Indies were separate kingdoms (the word "colonies" was never used and it is a gross anachronism), linked to the Spanish realms only through the person of the monarch of Castile. The competence of the council extended to every sphere of government—legislative, judicial, financial, ecclesiastical, commercial, and military—and all other officials were forbidden to interfere in its affairs. The king, in other words, was absolute lord of the Indies, and the council—which resided at Court and whose deliberations were secret—was his mouthpiece.

Nevertheless, a formal body of ordinances for the council was not issued until November 1542, as the first nine chapters of the famous New Laws; and it was followed by a second and more complete corpus of ordinances in September 1571. By this time Felipe II, in his efforts to bring the administration of his world-wide domains more strictly under his control, already had introduced a number of measures that directly curtailed the council's autonomy. Foremost among these was Felipe's decision, in 1556–57, to centralize the administration of all royal revenue and expenditure, including revenue from the Indies, in the Council of Finance. This meant that the Council of the Indies had to secure agreement from the Council of Finance before spending any money in America. All its requisitions for outfitting the fleets or for any general administrative issue had to be approved by a royal order issued by the Council of Finance. Although the new arrangement gave Felipe much more freedom to act, it was also a fruitful cause for dispute, and it set a malign precedent to the frequent conflicts of jurisdiction and long delays that would plague the council's activities in the seventeenth century.

A second initiative of Felipe's that directly affected the council's administrative and judicial autonomy was his decision to place all the activities of the Inquisition in the Indies, after its formal introduction there in 1570, under the direction of the Supreme Council of the Inquisition, the Suprema. This meant, effectively, that the Council of the Indies had absolutely no control over the activities of the Inquisition in the New World. The decision was taken in the wake of an inquiry into the activities of the council, conducted by Juan de Ovando of the Suprema in 1569–70. Ovando made no secret of his dismay about the council's ignorance of American affairs. The sharpness of his criticisms led to his appointment as president of the council in 1571. His term of office witnessed the appointment to the permanent staff of the council of a *cronista mayor* (head chronicler), whose role was to compile a "General Description" of the Indies from the replies to the many questionnaires, signed by the king himself, that had begun to be sent to the viceroys, *audiencias,* and other officials in the New World. Although the "General Description" was never concluded, the *relaciones geográficas* that came into the council in the 1570s and 1580s are an incomparably rich source of information about the Indies at this time, and they form the documentary basis of specialized works such as Antonio de Herrera's *Historia General.*

No less important during Ovando's presidency was a marked improvement in the efficiency and organization of the council's work, especially administrative problems, which were increasingly entrusted to smaller and more specialized committees, in tune with the gradual establishment of Madrid as a permanent administrative capital. Through these committees, the council prepared and dispatched all laws relating to the administration, taxation, and police of the Indies, and no significant scheme could be put into effect by American officials without being submitted to the council for approval. In consultation with the king, the council traced the territorial division of the American territories; it proposed the names of officials to be appointed by the monarch; it corresponded with, and kept watch over, American authorities, both lay and ecclesiastical; it nominated clerics to all important benefices; and it had the power to veto any papal letters or decrees intended for the American church. In its judicial capacity, it sat as a court of last resort in civil suits appealed from the American *audiencias;* it made arrangements for *residencias* of viceroys, governors, judges and other officers; and, if it deemed fit, it sent *visitadores* to carry out very thorough investigations into the life and administration of particular areas of America. Additionally, the council exercised powers of censorship; and, as can be attested from the massive *Recopilación de leyes de las Indias,* finally published in 1681 under the council's auspices, it exercised considerable influence upon legislation.

Despite all this, the council was much more a deliberating than a deciding or commanding institution. It rarely, if ever, initiated action. Ideas on policy usually originated in the Indies themselves, where viceroys and *audiencias* made proposals and then sought royal authority for them through the council. The members of the council were collectively responsible for advising the king; but it was the king who decided. Only then would the council transmit the monarch's decisions to the relevant authorities in America in the form of *cédulas* (bulls).

The council worked smoothly under Felipe II, but the system clearly possessed the defects inherent in conciliarism. Notably, it lacked individual responsibility and it fomented a paralyzing spirit of routine, as well as a tendency to throw greater responsibility back upon the sovereign. If the king lacked energy, decision, or was absent, the result was debate and procrastination. These defects became more evident as the seventeenth century wore on; and by the time of the pitiful reign of Carlos II, the authority and prestige of the Council of the Indies had reached a very low ebb indeed.

It is true that from the point of view of American officials, these developments were not entirely regrettable. Its very weakness soon forced the Crown to take into account the great regional differences that characterized the Americas, and as a result, there developed a surprising degree of regional autonomy, alongside a substantial amount of customary law, which had a recognized legal force if accepted by the Crown and if no written legislation was applicable. In this way, viceroys, captains general, and other Spanish-American officials became accustomed to modifying royal orders freely in order to meet the exigencies of a given local situation.

This coexistence of regional strength and autonomy with a weak center goes a long way toward explaining the long survival, relative efficiency, and general stability of a worldwide system of government commonly seen in terms of decline and bureaucratic inefficiency. Nevertheless, the system was bound to clash with any attempt to increase centralization and fiscal and administrative efficiency. This is what occurred when the Bourbons came to occupy the Spanish throne at the beginning of the eighteenth century and began to replace the conciliar system with a more modern, French-style governmental organization based on cabinet ministers.

As early as 1714, the Bourbon Felipe V appointed a secretary of marine and Indies, to whom were transferred all matters relating to war, finance, navigation, and commerce, as well as the nomination of most ministers, including members of the Council of the Indies. The fact that the secretary himself was frequently president of the Council of the Indies suggests that the Hapsburg theory of the relation between the Crown and its American possessions had begun to be forgotten or ignored. The practice foreshadowed the later reforms implemented during the reign of Carlos III; notably, the decrees of 1773 and 1776, which divided the council into three chambers, two of government and one of justice; the decree of 1787 appointing a second secretary of the Indies, with jurisdiction over justice and patronage, both civil and ecclesiastic; and the decree of 1790, which suppressed the functions of the two ministers and redistributed them among five ministers who presided over the respective departments of government for the peninsula. This was the last, and the clearest, attempt to bring about the unification and coordination of Spain and the American kingdoms in a single organism.

After these reforms, the Council of the Indies continued to serve in an advisory capacity to the king, but its former powers had been curtailed beyond recognition. It is thus no great surprise that, after the Napoleonic invasion of Spain, Spanish Americans found no opposition to their decision to abolish the council at the Cortes of Cádiz in 1812. The council was then reestablished by Fernando VII after his restoration in 1814; but after the loss of the bulk of Spain's American possessions, it was finally abolished by a law in 1834, 310 years after its formal creation by Carlos I.

See also Audiencias; Bourbon Reforms; New Laws of 1542; Relaciones Geográficas

Select Bibliography

Haring, C. H., *The Spanish Empire in America.* New York: Oxford University Press, 1952.
Merriman, R. B., *The Rise of the Spanish Empire in the Old World and the New.* 4 vols., New York: Cooper Square, 1962.
Ots Capdequí, J. M., *El Estado Español en las Indias.* Mexico City: Fondo de Cultura Económica, 1986.
Parry, J. H., *The Spanish Theory of Empire in the Sixteenth Century.* Cambridge: Cambridge University Press, 1940.
_____, *The Spanish Seaborne Empire.* London: Hutchinson, 1966.
Schäfer, E., *El Consejo Real y Supremo de las Indias.* 2 vols., Seville: M. Carmona, 1935-47.
Solórzano y Pereira, Juan de, *Política Indiana.* 2 vols., Mexico City: Secretaria de Programacion y Presupuesto, 1979.
Zavala, S., *Las instituciones jurídicas en la conquista de América.* 3rd edition, Mexico City: Porrua, 1935.

—FERNANDO CERVANTES

COUNTERCULTURE

Generally, the term "counterculture" is used in a limited sense, to refer to the radical confrontation of traditional social and political values by middle- and upper-class youth during the 1960s in the United States, especially, but also in many Western European societies. What is less often considered, however, is that the counterculture of the 1960s was also a global phenomenon. Much of the music, film, fashion, literature, and political values that helped energize countercultural rebellion in the United States and Europe also was introduced into parts of the Third World and, often less overtly, Communist societies as well. Owing to the new rapidity in global communications and aggressive marketing strategies by the large recording companies, the "youth market" was becoming, in a fundamental sense, international. Yet while young people from cities around the world increasingly shared similar cultural sensibilities and styles—or, as some began to argue, became "American-ized"—the local environments continued to remain as distinct as Boston is from Bombay. Thus, with the globalization of the counterculture came an immense variety of local responses, each conditioned to local political, economic, social, and cultural circumstances.

Mexico was especially influenced by this globalization process. Its spectacular post–World War II growth rates greatly increased the size of the middle classes, and in 1960 the balance of the population shifted from rural to urban for the first time in Mexican history. By the late 1950s cities around the country, and especially the capital, were experiencing a breakneck pace of modernization. Along with this modernization came changes in cultural values and tastes, as the folkloric nationalism of the 1930s was replaced by an emergent cosmopolitanism reflected in art (abstraction in place of muralism), film (urban rather than rural themes), fashion (pants instead of dresses), and music (rock and roll rather than *rancheros*), among others. This new "sensibility," especially among the younger generations, transpired, however, in the context of mounting political authoritarianism and social inequalities between the middle classes, urban poor (who flooded the capital looking for jobs), and the impoverished countryside. Thus, for example, whereas in the United States the counterculture railed against the Vietnam War, racism, sexism, and the dehumanization of everyday life, in Mexico growing numbers of young people incorporated countercultural values in their struggle against an official nationalism that masked a closed political system and flagrant class disparities, while sanctioning *machismo*.

The Mexican counterculture, also known as la Onda, has its origins in the awakening of a critical youth consciousness in the mid-1960s, although its full importance was realized only in the wake of the 1968 Massacre of Tlatelolco in Mexico City, in which hundreds of student protesters were gunned down by the Mexican army. Although heavily criticized then (and to a significant extent still today) for merely copying the music, styles, gestures, and even language of countercultural protest then raging in other parts of the industrialized world, la Onda in fact reflected an active appropriation and reformulation of the transnational protest culture by middle- and later by lower-class youth rebelling against their parents' conservatism and against state repression. Centered on native rock musical performance, la Onda by 1971 posed a complex series of challenges for the ruling regime, which, in the wake of the 1968 massacre, desperately needed to reestablish its credibility, especially among the middle classes.

La Onda literally translates as "the wave" and thus connotes the means of modern communications, as in radio waves. When the term first appeared in the early-to-mid-1960s, however, it referred more narrowly to "a plan, a party, an ambience." Around 1967 the term entered the public discourse to refer to an inchoate hippie movement *(jipismo)* then emerging among youth of the middle classes, especially in Mexico City. In the years following the Massacre of Tlatelolco, la Onda came to encompass protest and avant-garde movements in literature, music, art performance, film, and fashion. Grounded in the fusion of foreign and Mexican cultural idioms, the significance of la Onda lay precisely in its capacity to challenge authority by creating a sense of national identity distinct from that imposed by the ruling Partido Revolucionario Institucional (PRI, or Institutional Revolutionary Party). Still, the direct adaptation of foreign youth styles and pursuit of countercultural imports led conservatives and leftist intellectuals alike to criticize efforts by Mexican youth to forge an independent, countercultural identity. The PRI later would use these criticisms as a vehicle for the dual strategy of repression and co-optation.

As the name for a movement in literature, the term la Onda first was applied by the Mexican literary critic Margo Glantz to refer to a new generation of writers, such as José Agustín, Gustavo Sáinz, and Parménides García Saldaña, whose style, language, and choice of subject matter indicated a sharp break with the previous generation. In fact these writers often quoted English-language rock lyrics, particularly in later writings. Usually translated into Spanish, although sometimes left in English, these lyrics established a shared sense of "hipness" with the reader (who certainly would have been aware of the musical groups, if not the particular songs cited) and offered a direct link to the avant-garde of other countries. At the same time, rock-inspired language provided this literature with a sense of organized chaos that framed the new sensibility among youth, challenging traditional boundaries and hierarchies. A second element of la Onda literature was the presence of contemporary youth slang. The emergence of an inventive, insulating jargon among youth both separated them from an older generation and underscored their identification with others in the movement, even across class divisions. A final element of this literary movement was the authors' unorthodox approach to literary structure, coupled with a focus on youth concerns and situations. Particularly in its chaotically hip exploration of middle-class youth identity, the literature of la Onda was, in the phrase of Margo Glantz, a "literature by youth and for youth."

The glue that increasingly held Mexican urban youth together—and eventually bridged the gulf separating the provinces and the capital—and linked their countercultural protest to a "universal" movement was rock music. Rock and roll from the United States had been introduced by multinational and local recording companies in the late 1950s. Almost immediately, carefully tailored Mexican imitations of U.S. bands were recruited actively by television and the record companies. Performing translated versions of imported rock and roll, these bands were embraced by the upper and middle classes for their clear associations with "modernity." After 1963, when the impact of the Beatles and other British bands transformed the listening tastes, fashion styles, and perspectives of middle-class youth, the older, more circumscribed Mexican rock and roll was challenged by a new wave of bands. Although high government tariffs limited their access to imported music, Mexico City youth were among the first to learn of the new music and performance styles through native sources: Mexican musical groups cultivated along the northern border region descended on the capital in search of recording contracts and larger audiences. Accustomed to performing for tourists in border nightclubs and directly influenced by the proximity of the United States, these new bands brought with them an intimate knowledge of the counterculture emerging abroad. English-language covers of imported songs increasingly replaced the Spanish-language covers that had dominated an earlier generation. Singing in English, accompanied by the mimicry of styles and gestures of the foreign youth movement, these bands appealed to restless, middle-class youth, especially in the capital and larger provincial cities, eager to participate in a cosmopolitan culture.

Whatever their ideological sympathies, however, these Mexican rock and roll bands remained largely isolated from the student protest movement that erupted in the summer of 1968 in Mexico City. Record companies still dictated what music groups could record, even forcing bands that performed in English to record in Spanish. Moreover, most bands seemed more concerned with their television and record contracts than jumping into the fray of student politics. Nonetheless, the student movement was influenced broadly by countercultural protest values then in vogue. This influence was reflected particularly in students' mockery of political authority, as well as their public listening to native folk protest music and their private listening to foreign rock. The connections being made in other parts of the world between political protest and cultural revolt were also present in Mexico.

Still, the student protest movement was no love-in. It was marked by extended political debate on campuses, direct engagement with middle- and working-class populations, and carefully orchestrated public statements and marches. These actions often were met with police repression, infiltrators, and a hostile press. Maintaining a respectable, "patriotic" image became essential for student protesters, who feared they might be accused of succumbing to foreign agitators and alien ideas. Following the Massacre of Tlatelolco, however, all avenues for protest were closed (aside from guerrilla organization). Youth began to fill the ranks of the incipient *jipismo* movement, broadening rock music's Mexican audience and propelling countercultural protest to the forefront of youth activity.

Many Mexican intellectuals, while admiring the "authenticity" of the counterculture abroad, were disparaging of Mexico's own hippie movement. Alternately called "hippies," *jipis, jipitecas/xipitecas,* or simply la Onda, middle-class youth were influenced not only by the availability of music and fashion from abroad, but also more directly by youth traveling to Mexico from the United States and Canada. Starting in the mid-1960s and rapidly climbing in numbers thereafter, thousands of foreign hippies made their way to Mexico in search of an escape from war and materialism, often in search of the "indigenous experience" that formed such a vital component of the counterculture's ideology in the industrialized world. Ironically, it was partly through contact with these foreign hippies that a rejuvenated interest in indigenous culture took hold among Mexican youth. Following the example set by foreigners, Mexican youth began to appropriate indigenous clothing and jewelry styles that previously were seen as "backward" or reserved for trinket-seeking tourists. Long hair among men not only challenged strictly drawn gender boundaries, but also suggested a symbolic identification with Mexico's indigenous peoples.

Increasingly, a significant number of Mexican youth, mostly middle-class men, left their homes to traverse the Mexican countryside, following the pattern of foreign hippies. There they directly encountered both the poverty and the cultural practices of indigenous peoples, and learned to view them outside the official versions of Mexico's "indigenous heritage" in order to incorporate that native presence as a direct element of their lives. One place in particular held a magnetic charm for *jipiteca* youth. This was the village of Huautla de Jiménez in the mountains of Oaxaca, where hallucinogenic mushrooms were integral to local religious practice. First "discovered" by the mushroom enthusiast and banker R. Gordon Wasson in the 1950s, by the late 1960s the village had become world famous for its reputation as the "birthplace" of psilocybin, the chemical basis for LSD. Transformed, too, was a local shaywoman, María Sabina, who now found herself a cult personality, pursued by hippies of all stripes.

As scores of Mexican youth appeared to "drop out" of society, conservatives lambasted the decadence of U.S. influence while leftist intellectuals publicly questioned what Mexican youth were dropping out *from*. Still reeling from the repression against the student movement, many on the left showed little understanding or patience with a movement that appeared to reject political action while embracing a cultural critique established by foreigners, and thus "inappropriate" for Mexico's own situation. Bolstered by public outcry against foreign hippie influence, the administration of Gustavo Díaz Ordaz (1964–70) cracked down on the burgeoning *jipiteca* movement by deporting long-haired foreigners, staging armed raids on Huautla de Jiménez and other communal sites, and in general promoting an image of *jipi* youth as a degenerate, subversive menace. These actions led to an officially sanctioned harassment and discrimination against long-haired youth during this period. One sanctuary for avant-garde culture during this period was the business-backed tourist district baptized the Zona Rosa, in the heart of Mexico City, where a gallery and café culture emulating New York's Greenwich Village provided work for avant-garde artists and musicians. Even the Zona Rosa was not immune to drug raids and round-ups of *jipitecas* by the police, however. In its relentless pursuit of *jipi* youth, especially from 1968 to 1969, the regime worked to displace middle-class sympathy for the massacred students of Tlatelolco, and hence fears of the regime, with mounting concerns of youth challenges to traditional family values. President Díaz Ordaz's anti-hippie policies thus became a new yardstick by which the middle classes could measure his efforts to safeguard family and nation.

The transformation of the native rock movement from relative marginalization within the broader context of political and cultural dissent into the vanguard of native countercultural protest occurred toward the end of 1969 and was conditioned by two important factors. First was the support of the entertainment industry, which began to shed its conservative approach toward youth marketing in favor of a bolder strategy that embraced the countercultural market on its own terms (a strategy already adopted by media corporations abroad). One consequence was the switch by record companies from delayed, haphazard releases of foreign rock music (often in compilation albums) to the Mexican pressing of U.S. and British rock and roll albums in their entirety. Although the imported "original" albums were still inaccessible to the majority of listeners because of tariff restrictions, local reproductions with their attention to cover detail and musical arrangement, established the ideological foundation upon which la Onda would flourish. Youths throughout Mexico now had direct access to the music and images igniting their counterparts in other countries. Another important consequence of this change was that record companies began to promote a Mexican rock and roll on its own terms, dropping earlier directives on what contracted groups must record. Mass marketing in turn spurred other parts of the entertainment industry—radio, television, fanzines, concert organizers—toward active promotion of a native rock movement that no longer aped foreign models, but fused native and foreign musical and cultural traditions in new and exciting ways.

This Mexican rock movement came to be called la Onda Chicana. The meaning of "Chicano" in this context was radically different from that in the United States at this time. In Mexico, "Chicano" embodied the aspirations of youths seeking to participate in an Anglo-generated cultural movement, but on local terms. English language and hippie protest values were not repudiated (as generally happened in the Chicano movement in the United States), but were adopted and transformed into something uniquely meaningful for Mexican youths. Through the language, styles, sounds, and gestures of la Onda Chicana, Mexican youths challenged authoritarianism while reimagining symbols of the nation—and its problematic relationship with the United States—in new terms. This transformed nationalism was reflected particularly in the names and images of the numerous bands emerging during this period: la Revolución de Emiliano Zapata, la División del Norte, Peace and Love, Nuevo México. Symbols of the nation and icons of the Mexican Revolution were wrested free from their official status and forged—only now as mass cultural commodities—into symbols of youth power and resistance. At the same time, while la Onda Chicana was clearly influenced by U.S. models, it transformed the question of imperialism into a celebration of the cultural fusion that so profoundly had invigorated Mexican countercultural protest.

The second factor that permitted the explosion of the counterculture was the policy of apertura (political and cultural "opening") of the administration of Luis Echeverría Álvarez (1970–76). Anxious to restore the PRI's credibility among youth and intellectuals, Echeverría briefly created the necessary political conditions for the free development of la Onda. From 1970 to 1971 rock bands and live performance proliferated not only in the capital, but in the provinces as well. Music magazines that had been in the hands of writers from an earlier generation now passed to a younger cadre influenced by the drug culture, feminism, environmentalism,

and especially the scars of 1968. New magazines also emerged, the most celebrated being Piedra Rodante, an unauthorized Spanish-language version of Rolling Stone that features articles in translation, along with local interviews and editorials on the cultural and political changes sweeping Mexico. These magazines became an important outlet of expression for la Onda, bridging provincial, class, gender, and racial boundaries to establish la Onda as a vibrant national awakening.

If the jipiteca movement was composed initially of middle-class men, other constituencies were drawn in as la Onda became a national movement. This growth brought with it problems, however. As women increasingly participated in la Onda, they often found themselves trapped by a double standard of sexual liberation that praised open relationships but condemned female promiscuity. But many women did find an important participatory space in the counterculture nonetheless, and insofar as la Onda directly confronted the limited traditional roles expected of women, it encouraged their independence. Far less equivocal was the new influence on la Onda of the urban poor, who by 1971 constituted an important base for the movement. Ironically, this broadening of support was a result of restricted club spaces. Bands increasingly were forced into marginalized areas where they could perform to larger audiences without harassment by authorities. Often transient in nature, these performance spaces acquired the name hoyos fonquis (funky holes). The working-class youths saw in la Onda Chicana an alternative to the ranchero and tropical dance rhythms of their parents. Thus la Onda had broadened beyond the upper and middle classes to incorporate a mounting segment of the population who served as testimony to the uneven development wrought by the processes of modernization in Mexico. This incorporation began to have a profound impact on the evolution of la Onda just when the movement was targeted by the regime after 1971.

Bridged in many ways by a common youth lexicon, a shared repertoire of rock idols and images, and the breakdown of culturally and economically prescribed dress codes, sharp class differences showed the promise of partial transcendence. Such transcendence represented the ideal of a renewed national community at the heart of la Onda. Although this ideal was rife with gender and class contradictions, it nonetheless served as a unifying cry for a generation of youth rendered cynical, if still defiant, of official nationalism and the political process. Thus it was through the language, fashion, and musical performance of la Onda that a new fusion of cultural and class values was beginning to emerge in which oppressive authority and cultural paternalism was directly challenged by a mass youth movement.

The culminating moment of la Onda was the outdoor music festival held at Avándaro, about 100 miles from Mexico City, in September 1971. With the example of the 1969 Woodstock Festival on the minds of organizers and audiences alike, the Avándaro Festival was regarded by many in the entertainment industry as a pivotal moment in the commercialization of the la Onda Chicana. An important indication of this trend was the omnipresence of Telesistema, the precursor of state television network Televisa, which was on hand to film the more than one dozen native bands who performed. Occurring just months after a deadly attack in the capital by the paramilitary "Halcones" and nearly three years to the day after the October 2 Massacre of Tlatelolco, this enormous youth gathering raised fears for the participants as well as the state. Many feared that the state would orchestrate some sort of provocation, justifying more repression. The state ultimately used far more blunt measures. Fearing that the gathering would turn into a political rally, the Echeverría administration sent hundreds of armed soldiers to police the festival's perimeters; access to stage microphones was restricted by armed guards. Ironically, the police would be criticized afterward not for their repression, but for turning a blind eye to (or, some reports alleged, even participating in) the open consumption of drugs at the festival.

As word of the concert spread, hundreds of thousands of youths—crowd estimates range from 200,000 to 500,000—made the trek from across the country, although most came from Mexico City. Most reports suggest that the majority of those who attended Avándaro were middle-class youths, but others have argued that lower-class youths were an even larger element. In any event, youths of all classes were represented, sharing a common space outside the dictates of the ruling party (soldiers kept their distance). Even more than at Woodstock, the importance of such a huge and diverse gathering of youth superseded the significance of the music itself, which was plagued by rain and faulty equipment. Despite the restrictions on explicit political oratory, Avándaro took on important political significance. Drugs and nudity were flaunted, while national symbols were displayed not as symbols of xenophobic pride, but of political resistance and the cultural fusion at the heart of la Onda. In one case a national flag had the eagle and serpent replaced with a peace sign. The U.S. and British flags were also present, not as hated symbols of imperialism but rather as symbols of the contribution that Anglo culture had made to the emergence of Mexico's own counterculture. If there was any doubt of this, from the stage came a cry: "We've done it! We don't need *gabacho* [U.S.] or European groups. Now we have our own music!"

The hopes for a renewed community and continued commercial sponsorship of native rock were shattered in the days and weeks following the festival. Images and tales of the event were distorted by a government-pliant press; descriptions of nudity, drug use, and the "corruption" of national symbols often reached hyperbolic proportions. Intellectuals joined the attack by condemning the "cultural imperialism" suggested by Mexican youth waving foreign flags and singing in English. (Most Mexican rock at this point was being written and performed in English, although a transition to Spanish-language compositions was under-

way.) When Carlos Monsiváis, a leading critic at the time, claimed that cultural imperialism had rendered Mexican youth "the first generation of foreigners born in Mexico," he was expressing the fears not simply of the Mexican left, but of the right as well.

Riding the public backlash that followed Avándaro, the PRI set out to roll back the native rock movement and co-opt the youth counterculture on terms defined by the regime. The Echeverría administration followed a three-part strategy. First, direct pressures were applied against the radio and recording industry to halt further promotion of native (but not foreign) rock. Second, rock performances were met with police repression or canceled outright. Finally, the Echeverría administration encouraged leftist critique of la Onda as a direct manifestation of cultural imperialism. At the same time, Echeverría openly embraced the politically charged New Song Movement (*nueva canción, nueva trova*) that was identified closely with revolutionary regimes in Cuba, Chile, and Peru. These moves coincided with a broader platform of cultural and economic nationalism that included attacks upon the commercial mass media and support for a folkloric revival in music and the arts. The regime looked to substitute the more politically radical (but more readily co-optable) musical culture of *la nueva canción* for the politically inchoate (but wholly uncontrollable) native rock movement. By redirecting la Onda away from its Chicano fusion and toward a renewed emphasis on Latin American "authenticity," the Echeverría administration was able to bring middle-class youths back into the fold of a rejuvenated official nationalism. Lower-class youths, on the other hands, saw their lives as more connected with urban blues than Andean folklore, and nurtured an underground rock movement that has survived in the *barrios*.

The musical legacy of la Onda has been all but lost as the music industry has yielded to pressure from the Mexican state. Most Mexican youths have heard of Avándaro, but cannot connect it to actual images or music in a shared cultural repertoire. It is perhaps best seen as a "non-memory," ironically recalled more in terms of Woodstock than la Onda. On the other hand, the broader legacy of Mexico's *jipitecas* has been profound. Middle-class youth now identify openly with indigenous culture by adopting the artisanal jewelry popularized during the late 1960s, wearing *huaraches* (sandals) and indigenous dress, growing their hair long, and traveling the Mexican countryside. The literature of la Onda also is widely known, and much of the vocabulary from the period is still in circulation. In sum, the cultural legacy of la Onda, with its emphasis on cultural fusion between "modern" and "traditional" practices, continues to offer Mexican youth an avenue for the ongoing reimagination of national community, fused today with Latin American, Mexican, and Anglo rock and folk culture. The state has tried to repress and co-opt this counterculture ever since its emergence, but dynamism of Mexican youth bears witness to the state's ultimate failure to do so.

See also Generación de 1968; Generación de 1968 and Generación Fin del Siglo; Massacre of Tlatelolco; Rock and Roll

Select Bibliography
Agustín, José, "¿Cuál es la Onda?" *Diálogos* 10:1 (January–February, 1974).

Glantz, Margo, *Onda y escritura en México.* Mexico City: Siglo XXI, 1971.
Marroquín, Enrique, "Dios quiere que llueve para unirnos." *Piedra Rodante* 6 (October 30, 1971).

—ERIC ZOLOV

COVARRUBIAS, MIGUEL

1904–57 • Artist and Scholar

A Mexican by birth, Miguel Covarrubias spent most of his life in the United States, and he produced his most successful work for a public he conquered at a very early age, that of the east coast of the United States. The formal studies of El Chamaco (the Kid), as he was known in Mexico and the United States, were little more than an impetus for his adolescent creativity. Dropping out of school, Covarrubias published his first drawings in small, short-lived Mexico City journals in the 1920s, and shortly after he graduated to such nationally circulated journals as *El Heraldo* and *El Universal Ilustrado.* Within a short time his friends and colleagues (including the journalist and intellectual Daniel Cosío Villegas) saw in his drawings the signs of a considerable artistic talent.

Encouraged by the artists Genaro Estrada and José Juan Tablada, Covarrubias settled in New York City in the latter half of the 1920s. In Manhattan Covarrubias followed in the footsteps of the Mexican painter and caricaturist Marius de Zayas, who had moved on to Paris by the time Covarrubias arrived. Covarrubias published in many of the same magazines that had published de Zayas's caricatures from the world of theater and high fashion alongside the acid commentary of the theater columnist Charles Darnton. In *Vanity Fair,* which began publishing Covarrubias's work in 1924, Covarrubias developed his characteristic style, and many of his graphics from the magazine later were used in his first book, *The Prince of Wales and Other Famous Americans* (1925). Playing a key role in the foundation of *The New Yorker* in 1925, Covarrubias continued working for the magazine for the next two years. He also found the time to exhibit his work in galleries, do book covers and illustrations, and design theater sets. He was an active participant in the intellectual and political ferment in 1920s New York, working with Langston Hughes, Carl van Vechten, and other figures of the Harlem Renaissance. Drawing on this collaboration, Covarrubias produced a second book in 1927, *Negro Drawings.*

In 1930 Covarrubias married the dancer Rosa Cowan Rolando. Their honeymoon was a round-the-world junket, with stops in Japan, China, the Philippines, Java, Sumatra, Singapore, Egypt, and France. The trip also included a nine-month layover on the island of Bali, the point of departure for Covarrubias's later anthropological studies. On returning to the United States, Covarrubias resumed his work with *Vanity Fair* and *The New Yorker,* documenting the worlds of radio and film. In 1934, however, a Guggenheim grant enabled Covarrubias to spend a year in Bali and write a voluminous study, *Island of Bali* (1937), which was illustrated with his own drawings and photographs taken by his wife.

Ethnography began to play an important role in the work of the mature Chamaco, which found its way into his new murals and canvases. In 1937 Covarrubias published a book with six maps of the Pacific basin, *Pageant of the Pacific,* and as the 1930s drew to a close he also planned a second book on the indigenous cultures of the Isthmus of Tehuantepec in southern Mexico. He also curated the exhibit *Twenty Centuries of Mexican Art* for the Museum of Modern Art in New York. In 1946 Covarrubias published his book on Tehuantepec, *Mexico South: The Isthmus of Tehuantepec.* Returning to Mexico, Covarrubias began to play an increasingly important role in Mexican museography, anthropology, and archaeology. In 1943 Covarrubias held the first-ever chair in museography in the Escuela Nacional de Antropología y Historia (ENAH, or National School of Anthropology and History), curating the exhibitions *Mexican Masks* (1944) and *Indian Art of North America* (1945), painting an ethnographic mural of Mexico in 1947, and teaching courses on pre-Hispanic and primitive art at the ENAH.

In 1950 the director of the Instituto Nacional de Bellas Artes (National Institute of Fine Arts), Carlos Chávez, named Covarrubias head of the department of dance. Over the following two years Covarrubias designed the sets and costumes for such ballets as *Cuatro soles, Tonantzintla, Antigone, Redes, Huapango, Tozcatl, Muros verdes, El invisible,* and *Movimientos perpetuos.* All of the members of Chávez's exceptionally talented team at Bellas Artes moved on to create some of their most inspired work, and Covarrubias was no exception. Shortly after leaving Chávez's company, Covarrubias began work on a continent-wide study of indigenous art. The first volume of his study, *The Eagle, the Jaguar, and the Serpent,* was published in 1954. The second volume appeared shortly after Covarrubias's death in 1957. Covarrubias's papers have been archived at the Universidad de las Américas in Cholula, Puebla.

Select Bibliography
Covarrubias, Miguel, "Chiametla: Una provincia olvidada del siglo XVI." *Trace* 22 (1992).

_____, "Mining Colonization and Agricultural Colonization: The Area of Chihuahua during the First Half of the Eighteenth Century." In *Aboriginal and Colonial Mining and Metallurgy in Spanish America,* edited by Alan Kraig and Robert West. Baton Rouge: Louisiana State University Press, 1994.
Covarrubias, Miguel, and Chantal Cramaussel, "El plano de 1722 de la villa de San Felipe El Real de Chihuahua." In *Arte y Coerción.* Mexico City: UNAM, 1993.

—Antonio Saborit

COWDRAY, LORD

See Pearson, Weetman Dickinson (Lord Cowdray)

CREEL, ENRIQUE CLAY

1834–1931 • Banker, Governor, and Ambassador

One of the preeminent bankers during the rule of Porfirio Díaz, Enrique Creel was, perhaps, the most visible symbol of the Díaz regime's commitment to economic development through foreign investment. At the same time, he was at the forefront of a number of consortia of domestic capital centered in northern Mexico in the Laguna region of Durango and Coahuila, Chihuahua, and Monterrey. In addition, as the son-in-law of Chihuahuan political boss Luis Terrazas, Creel stood squarely amid the regional and national politics of the pre-Revolutionary era.

Creel was born in Chihuahua, the son of the U.S. consul there. He married the daughter of General Luis Terrazas and subsequently took charge of the Terrazas family's wide-ranging financial and industrial interests. He was the foremost banker of the Porfiriato, founding and managing the Banco Minero de Chihuahua and several other banks.

The financier was the preeminent dealmaker of the Porfirian era. He was at the center of extensive arrangements between various regional economic interests that created important industrial enterprises, such as the Compañía Industrial Jabonera de la Laguna and the Compañía Nacional Mexicana de Dinamita y Explosiva. Creel also was allied closely with the Monterrey group of entrepreneurs and Científicos (intellectuals and policy advisers to Díaz) based in Mexico City. He instigated the formation of a number of regional and national industrial trusts. The Terrazas-Creel axis virtually monopolized flour milling in

Chihuahua, for example. Creel tried unsuccessfully to build a meatpacking trust.

As a banker, the bilingual Creel was the most important intermediary between Mexican and foreign capital. He served on the boards of a number of foreign companies. He often arranged government subsidies and tax abatements and financial support for foreign firms.

Creel had a long, distinguished political career. He was a member of the Chihuahua state legislature from 1882 to 1885 and 1897 to 1900. He was an alternate federal deputy from Chihuahua from 1892 to 1894 and a deputy from Durango from 1900 to 1902 and from Chihuahua from 1902 to 1906. In 1904 Luis Terrazas resigned as governor of Chihuahua in Creel's favor. Creel won election in his own right in 1907, serving until 1911. While governor, Creel had additional responsibilities nationally as Mexican ambassador to the United States (1907–08) and secretary of foreign relations (1910–11). In the latter post Creel headed the intelligence operations against rebels such as the Flores Magón brothers and the anti-reelectionists.

One of the leading members of the Científicos, Creel became one of the most hated symbols of the Porfirian regime. He was a widely unpopular governor. His efforts to modernize and streamline state government drew protests from local communities that fiercely guarded their autonomy. The favoritism he showed to his own family and associates and to foreigners elicited deep dislike from the state's middle classes.

Creel was also among those who influenced Díaz to sit for an interview with journalist James Creelman, in which Díaz declared that he would not seek another term as president. The interview, published in March 1908, touched off a flurry of political activity, as various leaders jockeyed to replace the aging dictator. Rumors soon circulated that Creel himself was the candidate of choice of U.S. president Theodore Roosevelt. Perhaps because of these rumors, Creel was recalled from his post as ambassador to the United States shortly thereafter.

Creel lived in exile during the violent stage of the Mexican Revolution, suffering enormous financial losses. The revolutionaries expropriated his landholdings and looted his Banco Minero. Creel was active in support of the conservative elements, acting at one point in 1915 to bring together an attempted comeback of Victoriano Huerta and Pascual Orozco Jr. The banker went back to Mexico in the early 1920s and served as an adviser to President Álvaro Obregón Salido.

Select Bibliography

Wasserman, Mark, *Capitalists, Caciques, and Revolution: The Native Elite and Foreign Enterprise in Chihuahua, Mexico.* Chapel Hill: University of North Carolina Press, 1984.
_____, "Enrique C. Creel: Business and Politics in Mexico, 1880–1930." *Business History Review* 59 (Winter 1985).

—MARK WASSERMAN

CRIOLLOS AND *CRIOLLISMO*

The term criollo is probably derived from the Portuguese *crioulo,* a word of uncertain origin which meant an African slave born and raised outside of Africa. It was apparently devised by blacks born in Guinea to differentiate themselves from those born outside of Africa. In New Spain the term first appeared in the Puebla area in the second half of the sixteenth century and had a similar meaning, referring to slaves and livestock that were native born. Very soon, however, it came to signify a person of European blood born in the New World. Hence the only difference between a criollo and a peninsular (one born in the mother country) was the place of birth.

The first persons with European blood born in New Spain were not criollos but mestizos. Because of a lack of European women, this meant a mixture of Spanish men with indigenous women. The proportion of European women who migrated increased after 1550, and as a result so did the number of Europeans born in New Spain. By 1566 the criollos had come to constitute a distinct, if still young and inchoate, force in the colony. The interests of this burgeoning class were closely entwined with the question of the encomienda, the system of tribute and forced labor that was the principal sustenance of many of the conquistadors and their descendants. The question of the inheritance, or perpetuity, of the encomienda was crucial, since the permanence of family fortunes centered on it. Though the criollos' financial situation was comfortable, it was also precarious. The Hapsburg monarchy, which only a few decades before had consolidated its rule in Spain, was concerned about the rise of a new, semi-feudal class that had control of large numbers of natives, and sought to restrict it. The New Laws of 1543 attempted to abolish perpetuity, but the more stringent regulations were soon modified or rescinded. The uncertain situation of the encomienda made it difficult for the criollos to establish family fortunes that could be passed from generation to generation. The Spanish Crown's efforts to undermine the encomienda found support among churchmen and other humanitarians who viewed it as gross exploitation of the native classes. The conquistadors, however, and their criollo descendants viewed these efforts as base ingratitude toward those who had won a great kingdom for the Crown.

Spanish control became more firmly consolidated in 1535 when the first viceroy, Antonio de Mendoza, took up rule in New Spain. The establishment of the viceregal system was in one sense a major setback for the conquistadors and criollos because it centralized authority in an official responsible to the king, not the local elite. The viceroys were almost exclusively peninsulars. Since they were directly responsible to the king, their interests did not coincide, and often conflicted, with those of the criollos. Some viceroys, however, did identify with criollo aspirations, while others found it politically necessary or expedient to ally with them.

Still, the nascent criollo class felt threatened, and their discontent soon found a focus or leader in Martín Cortés, the sole legitimate son of the conqueror of New Spain, Fernando (Hernán) Cortés. In 1563 the younger Cortés returned from Spain, where he had been educated and had enjoyed royal favor. He set himself up in a palace and began to live in semiregal style. Two young brothers, Alonso and Gil González Avila, frequented his palace and together with other young criollos devised a clumsy conspiracy to separate New Spain from Spanish rule and enthrone Martín Cortés as king of Mexico. The plot was discovered and in 1566 the *audiencia,* which ruled the kingdom in the interim following the death of Viceroy Luis de Velasco in 1564, ordered the arrest of the ringleaders. The Avila brothers were tried for treason and beheaded. Cortés was sent back to Spain, and a brutal repression broke whatever will to independence there had been. The criollos remained discontented, but they were henceforward circumspect about expressing it.

The criollos themselves were divided by class distinctions: the nobility, composed of descendants of conquistadors or members of peninsular noble families, and the bulk of ordinary criollos. Yet they were united on a number of issues. For the most part criollos did not expect to hold the highest offices, such as viceroy or archbishop of Mexico. They did, however, seek entrance to the lower level positions, such as judges of the *audiencia,* the combination of law court and viceregal council that held great power in New Spain. The Crown, on the other hand, feared the growth of a native elite with access to positions of strength and so insisted on appointing peninsular judges. Hapsburg policy sought to prevent alliances between royal officials and the local elite. Judges (*oidores*) of the various *audiencias* were forbidden to marry in New Spain without royal approval and could not even attend the weddings and funerals of criollos. In 1637 the city council (*cabildo*) of Mexico asked that half the seats on the *audiencia* be reserved for criollos, and at the end of the colonial period criollos appear to have dominated the city council.

The contrast between criollos and peninsulars became more marked after 1570 and gave rise to a seething hostility between the two classes. The latter developed a number of prejudices against the criollos, some of them based on biological determinism. It was believed that the climate, even the proximity to the sun, had an intrinsically debilitating and enervating effect that showed itself in intellectual torpor, effetism, laziness, and irresponsibility. Many peninsulars believed that the criollos would continue to deteriorate until they would be indistinguishable from the Indians. Any peninsular, no matter how lowly his birth, felt superior to those born in the colony. The criollos in turn resented what they considered to be their second-class status, especially since Hapsburg policy systematically excluded them from the highest positions in church and state. It has been estimated that in the colonial period only 32 of 171 bishops were criollos, while the proportion of viceroys was 3 out of 61. Criollos tended to be sensitive to criticism by outsiders and displayed a latent sense of inferiority.

The antagonisms became particularly acute in the religious orders, especially the Franciscans. Peninsular friars believed that the criollos were incapable of living the religious life properly and that they contributed to its deterioration. The criollos, in turn, resented the peninsular domination. Each group tried to achieve dominance, often by a reckless admission of new members. In 1629 the viceroy nullified the election of a criollo provincial among the Augustinians, replaced him with a peninsular, and forbade the further admission of criollos until the proportion had been equalized. Eventually, the friars worked out a system, the *alternativa,* whereby the two groups alternated in power. The first known instance of it was in 1622, but it must have existed earlier.

Criollo discontent surfaced again in the civil disturbances of 1624. The riots had many causes, including the personal enmity between Archbishop Juan Pérez de la Serna and the viceroy the marqués de Gelves; the antagonism between criollos and peninsulars; and the volatile population of natives, *castas* (mixed bloods), and *léperos* (beggars and vagabonds) that made up the underclass of the capital. The disorders that ensued were complicated by personal and institutional rivalries and a fluid shifting of alliances. The clergy, both diocesan and religious, played a major role. A royal visitor, Martín Carrillo, later accused the clergy of being the organizers and perpetrators of the riots. With prescience, he also noted that "the hatred of the mother country's domination is deeply rooted in all classes of society, especially among the Spaniards [criollos]."

By the seventeenth century the criollos were in the majority in the ranks of the lower clergy and most of the mendicant orders, though in the latter peninsular influence continued to be felt. As a result the archbishop and bishops, themselves overwhelmingly peninsular, found it necessary to come to terms with their criollo clergy. They particularly needed them as allies in their conflicts with the religious orders and viceroys. Some prelates, such as Pedro Moya de Contreras, Juan Pérez de la Serna, Francisco Manso y Zúñiga, and Juan de Palafox y Mendoza, strongly sympathized with the criollos. In general the upper ranks of the secular clergy offered the criollos more opportunities for advancement than did civil administration.

By the early seventeenth century the peninsular prejudice against the criollos became less blatant. The dismal prophecies about their deterioration had not been fulfilled. The numbers and wealth of the criollos made them a force to be reckoned with. The educational work of the Jesuits raised the intellectual and cultural level of the criollos and also forged a bond between them and the Society of Jesus. What criollos sought more than anything else was an equality with the peninsulars. They had no particular sympathy for the native classes or the various *castas.*

In absolute terms the criollos outnumbered all other classes in New Spain except the Indians. In 1570 there were approximately twice as many criollos as peninsulars. By 1793 the proportion was closer to nine to one. The term criollo came to include the racially mixed descendants of the original criollo class, and as with other categories in society, it was possible to buy one's way into it. In the seventeenth century the term came to include Hispanized persons of any race. Because of this and other pejorative connotations, the term criollo fell into disuse in the latter half of the seventeenth century and as replaced by *"americano"* and *"indiano."* The new designations also reflected an enhanced sense of national identity. The Spanish honorific titles Don and Doña were appropriated by local criollos of all classes, a pretension that both amused and irritated peninsulars.

Though often depicted as frivolous and parasitic, many criollos attained a high cultural and intellectual level. Carlos de Sigüenza y Góngora was a polymath who achieved distinction as a historian, poet, archaeologist, linguist, mathematician, and astronomer. His work *Libra astronómica y filosófica* (1690), a record of the disputes that arose from the comet of 1680–81, is supremely important in the history of science in

Mexico. He was also an ardent criollo patriot, as can be seen in his *Teatro de virtudes políticas* (1680) and his Guadalupan poem *Primavera indiana* (1680). The Jesuits Francisco Javier Clavigero and Francisco Javier Alegre were renowned historians, and Clavigero in particular stood out for his attempts to combine traditional learning with the thought of the Enlightenment. There were other notable historians, who were either mestizos or peninsulars who identified with the criollos. Among the former were Fernando de Alva Ixtlilxochitl and the Franciscan Diego de Valadés, who rose to prominence in his order, while among the latter were the Dominican Diego Durán and the Franciscan Juan de Torquemada. Probably the supreme glory of criollo literature was Sor Juana Inés de la Cruz, a Hieronymite nun who was also a great poet, dramatist, and pioneer feminist. Two of her poems, "Hombres necios que acusáis" and *Respuesta a Sor Filotea de la Cruz,* are landmarks in feminist thought in Mexican history.

In other arts Miguel Cabrera was the outstanding painter of the colonial period. In the field of plastic arts, criollo New Spain probably reached its high point in architecture. The cathedrals of Mexico City and Puebla are fine examples of the best, and perhaps most monumental, in colonial architecture. In the eighteenth century an extravagant outgrowth of the baroque, called Churrigueresque, used a proliferation of decoration to express a criollo sense of exuberance and self-confidence.

A major step in the development of criollo consciousness was the story of the apparitions of Our Lady of Guadalupe. In 1648 a criollo priest, Miguel Sánchez, published a book *Imagen de la Virgen Maria,* which for the first time told how the Virgin Mary had appeared to an Indian neophyte, Juan Diego, at the hill of Tepeyac in 1531. According to this story she commanded him to take a message to the bishop-elect of Mexico, Juan de Zumárraga, that he should have a church built on that site. As a sign of the divine nature of his mission, Juan Diego was to collect flowers from the hill, a barren place, at a time when they would not ordinarily grow. He gathered the flowers in his cloak and when he unfolded it in Zumárraga's presence, the Virgin's picture was imprinted on it.

Although the message of Guadalupe was directed primarily to the Indians, it struck an immediate, responsive chord among the criollos. Sánchez gave the story a strongly criollo emphasis, stressing that it was intended for "those born in this land." He believed that the criollos had a special relationship to the Virgin and that her appearance placed Mexico City on a par with all other religious centers in the Catholic world. The criollos found in it an almost messianic sense of divine election for the city of Mexico and ultimately for all of New Spain. The devotion spread rapidly among the criollo population. Preachers from 1660 until the time of independence continually emphasized the unique identity of criollos, depicting them as a new chosen people who were destined to be a source of blessing to all the peoples of the world.

The devotion quickly became popular throughout New Spain. In 1754 the Virgin of Guadalupe was named patron of Mexico City, then of New Spain. The Franciscan missionary college of Our Lady of Guadalupe, founded at Zacatecas by fray Antonio Margil de Jesús, quickly became an entirely criollo institution. A comparable college, Santa Cruz in Querétaro, catered to peninsulars.

In 1713, by the Treaty of Utrecht that ended the War of the Spanish Succession, Felipe V, the grandson of Louis XIV of France, was formally recognized as king of Spain, thus inaugurating the rule of the house of Bourbon. The new dynasty brought a change of policy throughout the Spanish empire, particularly under Carlos III (1759–88). Enlightenment thought became predominant. Colonial government became even more centered in the mother country, and local government was sharply curtailed. Bourbon reforms brought greater efficiency and dispatch to colonial government but did so at a great cost to colonial society. The government's policy was also anti-criollo and sought to remove them from any positions of influence. The Bourbon reforms and attitudes were brought to New Spain by the royal visitor, José de Gálvez, who conducted a general visitation and reform from 1765 to 1770. Gálvez was anti-criollo and consistently worked against their interests. He reorganized government, tax, and accounting systems. He also introduced a standing army and militia and the dreaded *leva,* or conscription.

The Bourbon monarchs sought to bring the church even more under royal control and showed themselves hostile both to religious orders and traditional religious practices, especially the *cofradías,* or confraternities, some of which were quite wealthy. Bourbon policies toward the church were incompatible with criollo religiosity, which was strongly influenced by the reforms of the Council of Trent (1545–63) and the baroque. The process of turning Indian parishes (*doctrinas*) over to the secular clergy was accelerated. Many friars arbitrarily were removed from houses they had held since the sixteenth century. Since by this time the majority of the orders were criollos, this was viewed as a move against them. Enlightenment thought was hostile to religious orders, which were thought to be too numerous, non-productive, and obscurantist. The Crown regulated the number of novices that could be received into any order and the number of new houses that could be founded. Despite that the majority of criollo clergy, both religious and diocesan, favored the use of the native languages in religious activities, a position to which peninsular clergy, who often did not know the languages, and officials, who sought to impose Spanish on the natives, were hostile. Taxes and tributes were increased, and the Crown took over the administration of tithes, something that had previously been in the hands of bishops and cathedral chapters (in Michoacán this was done in 1766).

Bourbon policies toward the criollos and the church coincided and culminated in the expulsion of the Jesuits in 1767, a move that was unpopular among the criollos, many of whom had been educated by the Jesuits. The Jesuits had also identified strongly with the criollos and were sympathetic to them. The expulsion, which was planned and organized in the utmost secrecy, was catastrophic for the church of New Spain. At one blow the educational and missionary work of the Jesuits, which extended throughout the kingdom, was destroyed. The expulsion, which came as a total shock to the unsuspecting criollos, coincided with popular discontent over new taxes.

The *visita* of Gálvez and the imposition of Bourbon changes coincided with a period of fiscal crisis in New Spain. The disturbances that followed on the imposition of new taxes showed a criollo hostility to rule from Spain. Though most of the disturbances were by Indians and *castas,* the criollos shared this hostility. In the valley of San Francisco one priest, Juan García Jove, a former Jesuit, openly preached revolution and independence. He later claimed to have been temporarily insane. In the modern states of San Luis Potosí, Guanajuato, Michoacán, and Colima there were riots against the expulsion, the added taxes, the tobacco monopoly, and the formation of militias. Gálvez blamed disturbances on the Indians and *castas.* Gálvez's repression of the disturbances was brutal and was intended to crush all resistance once and for all. Some bishops, like Pedro Anselmo Sánchez de Tagle of Michoacán, tried to be the voice of reason but the *visita* of Gálvez marked the nadir of episcopal power. From that time on the clergy were more and more anti-Spanish and ripe to be the leaders of a national movement. As D. W. Brading has said, "a powerful ecclesiastical corporation had been brutally destroyed by the simple fiat of the Crown and the populace savagely repressed for their resistance to change." This left a lasting legacy of anti-peninsular feeling.

Bourbon reforms also brought the first standing army to New Spain, an innovation that was financed by additional or increased taxes. Eventually the criollos came to dominate the officer class. In 1764 the Crown made tobacco a royal monopoly and closely supervised its cultivation. The so-called reforms of the Bourbons alienated the criollos and laid the groundwork for the independence movement of the early nineteenth century. Miguel de Hidalgo y Costilla was a young student in Valladolid when these things took place and was strongly influenced by them.

The situation of the criollos improved somewhat and their discontent was alleviated by the enlightened administration of two subsequent viceroys, Antonio María Bucareli (1771–79) and the second count of Revillagigedo (1789–94). The latter in particular was one of the greatest officials of the colonial period, and he succeeded in implementing a number of important reforms without alienating the local population.

The Bourbon assault on local privilege and independence continued. In 1786 the system of intendants, based on a French model, was established in New Spain to replace a confused and inefficient system of some 200 local offices. This was a system imposed from above, however, and of the twelve intendants only one was a criollo. In 1786 the Crown sought to remove the administration of the tithe from the bishops, but this measure failed because of determined resistance. In 1795, however, the government succeeded in curtailing clerical immunity from civil courts in criminal cases. This was part of an overall attempt to reduce or curtail ecclesiastical jurisdiction. The coup de grace for local interests was the Consolidation Decree of 1804. Desperate for funds the Crown decreed that all church capital should be turned over to the local treasury, which would administer it from that time forward. This was a severe blow to the local economy, since in the absence of a banking system the church had functioned as the chief moneylender for ranchers and entrepreneurs in New Spain. The principal on these loans was rarely repaid; rather, the interest payments acted as a guaranteed annuity for the church in supporting its various institutions and activities. The decree compelled the church to call in these loans with devastating effects on the colonial economy. It convinced the criollos that their interests were being sacrificed to those of the mother country.

Though criollos were in general a socially conservative class whose principal ambition was to retain their privileges and advance their interests, their conservatism was directed primarily at retaining the established social order in New Spain. At the same time they were influenced by Enlightenment thought. Despite halfhearted efforts at censorship, the works of Voltaire, Rousseau, Locke, and Jefferson were well known among the educated criollos and were discussed and popularized in various literary societies and discussion clubs. The criollo clergy in particular helped to spread this thought. They had special grievances against peninsular domination of the church and the repressive nature of the Bourbon reforms.

Napoléon's deposition of Carlos IV in 1808 and his appointment of his brother Joseph as king of Spain brought the festering criollo discontent to full term. In an aftermath characterized by divided loyalties and confusion as to the true ruler of the empire, the situation in New Spain became highly charged. In Spain the people revolted against the French presence, and the de facto leadership of the rebels fell to local *cabildos* and eventually to a national *cortes* (parliament). The latter was centered in Seville and then Cádiz. It declared the criollos to be the equals of peninsulars, and there were some criollo delegates to it. The unstable situation encouraged the criollos' thirst for independence and set the stage for revolution.

Criollismo lay behind the move to independence by Father Miguel Hidalgo y Costilla in 1810. The criollos, however, wanted a political revolution, not a social one. Their ambition was to replace the peninsulars as the ruling class in an independent Mexico. When Hidalgo's revolt took on the character of a social movement, with the Indians united against their white oppressors, the criollos turned against it. After the defeats of Hidalgo and his successor José María Morelos, the independence movement languished and seemed headed for final defeat. However, in 1812, the revolutionary junta of Cádiz convoked a *cortes,* or parliament, with elected representatives from all over the empire, including New Spain. The *cortes* enacted a liberal constitution which was abrogated by Fernando VII when he came to power two years later. In 1820 a military revolt led by Colonel Rafael Riego compelled the king to restore the constitution, which contained a number of anticlerical clauses. In alarm over events in the mother country, the conservative criollos of New Spain moved toward independence. This was confirmed by the Treaties of Córdoba in 1821. The coming of independence fulfilled the criollo dream of supplanting the peninsulars as the ruling class.

See also Nationalism

Select Bibliography

Bacigalupo, Marvyn Helen, *A Changing Perspective: Attitudes toward Creole Society in New Spain, 1521–1610.* London: Tamesis, 1981.

Brading, D. W., *The First America: The Spanish Monarchy, Creole Patriots, and the Liberal State, 1492–1867.* Cambridge and New York: Cambridge University Press, 1991.

Israel, J. I., *Race, Class and Politics in Colonial Mexico, 1610–1670.* London: Oxford University Press, 1975.

Mazín, Oscar, *Entre dos majestades.* Zamora: Colegio de Michoacán, 1987.

Miller, Robert Ryal, *Mexico: A History.* Norman: University of Oklahoma Press, 1985.

—Stafford Poole

CRISTERO REBELLION

Between 1926 and 1929, tens of thousands of peasants throughout central-west Mexico rebelled against the new Revolutionary regime in what came to be called the Cristiada or the Cristero Rebellion. The immediate cause of the rebellion was a conflict between church and state over the anticlerical provisions of the Constitution of 1917. When President Plutarco Elías Calles issued the legislation necessary to implement these constitutional measures at the national level, the Mexican Episcopacy responded with a clerical strike, ordering that all churches be closed and public worship suspended as of July 31, 1926. Sporadic uprisings in support of the Catholic Church erupted almost immediately throughout the republic, from Chihuahua in the north to Oaxaca in the south, involving both peasants and urban lay Catholics. After a period of several months, however, large-scale rebellion was sustained only in the central-west states, particularly within the ranchero villages. The great majority of *cristero* rebels were peasants who opposed the anticlericalism of the new regime, as well as the highly politicized application of the Revolutionary agrarian reform program, and the displacement of local religious and political authorities with allies of Revolutionary officials. Neither the federal army nor the thousands of pro-regime peasants organized in *agrarista* militias were able to defeat the *cristeros* militarily. The rebellion ended only when the Mexican Episcopacy reached an agreement with the administration of Emilio Portes Gil in June 1929, and the hierarchy condemned any further rebellion in support of the Catholic Church.

Antecedents

Anticlericalism had become a dominant feature of Revolutionary ideology and practice by 1914, when generals supporting Venustiano Carranza celebrated military victories by confiscating ecclesiastical property, placing restrictions on religious worship, and expelling foreign priests. The vigor with which the Carrancistas attacked the Catholic Church was in part due to the Mexican Episcopacy's support of the regime of Victoriano Huerta. But anticlericalism was much more deeply rooted in the thinking of Revolutionary elites, as it had been in nineteenth-century liberal ideology: even though it had lost much of its landed wealth through the liberal reforms of the 1850s, the Catholic Church still was seen as a central obstacle to Mexico's social and economic development, insofar as it was perceived as encouraging superstition, fanaticism, and the squandering of economic resources on religious practice. Furthermore, the Catholic Church was viewed as an obstacle to the consolidation of the Revolutionary state: promoting its own unions, rural cooperatives, and political associations, the Catholic Church and its affiliated lay organizations were, after the military defeat of the Zapatistas and the Villistas, one of the Carrancistas' main rivals in the construction of the new order. Revolutionary orthodoxy held that the church was monolithically reactionary, but official anticlericalism was at least in part the result of the Revolutionary elites' desire not to compete with a Catholic political opposition capable of drawing considerable popular support.

Carrancista anticlericalism was codified in the Constitution of 1917, which placed strict limits on the social, political, and religious activities of the Catholic Church as an institution, and on the clergy and lay Catholics as individuals. The constitution denied the juridical status of "religious institutions known as churches," thus leaving the Catholic Church without legal standing; required that all primary education, both private and public, be purely secular in nature; denied the clergy the right to vote as well as freedom of speech in political matters; prohibited political parties from adopting names with religious references; and required that all religious practice be confined within church buildings, which were, along with all ecclesiastical real estate, declared to be the property of the nation. One of the most contentious provisions was that granting the state the right to administer the clergy as it would any other "profession," including the right to limit the number of priests and to require their registration with state authorities.

Neither President Venustiano Carranza (1915–20) nor President Álvaro Obregón (1920–24) made much of an attempt to enforce the anticlerical provisions of the Constitution at the national level. Between 1917 and 1924, conflict between anticlerical and Catholic forces was largely the product of efforts by state-level authorities to impose limits on church activities and religious practice. In Michoacán, for example, dozens of people were killed in 1921, when the police opened fire on some 10,000 Catholics protesting the desecration of the Morelia Cathedral by supporters of the anticlerical governor Francisco Múgica. In Jalisco, a boycott of all nonessential goods was declared by lay Catholic organizations in 1918, in response to a decree that limited the number of priests permitted to officiate in the state; in addition, the archbishop of Guadalajara, Francisco Orozco y Jiménez, suspended all public religious worship. The success of organized Catholic resistance in forcing the state government in Jalisco to rescind the anticlerical decrees led Catholics at the national level to adopt a similar strategy when first confronted by the anticlericalism of the administration of Plutarco Elías Calles (1924–28).

In contrast to Carranza and Obregón, Calles was intensely anticlerical; as governor of Sonora, he had imposed strict limits on religious practice. In February 1925, shortly after taking office, Calles directed a memorandum to the state governors, reminding them that it was the responsibility of all state and municipal authorities to oversee church activities and to ensure that they were within the narrow limits allowed by the constitution. That same month, he encouraged the formation of a schismatic movement; churches throughout the republic were seized by members of the Regional Confederation of Mexican Workers (CROM), Calles's main base of political support, in the name of a new Mexican Catholic Church, independent of the authority of the Vatican. Soon after the seizure of the churches, and in response to Calles's memorandum, several states began to place severe restrictions on religious worship. With this intensification of official anticlericalism, urban lay Catholics from the former National Catholic Party (PNC), the Catholic Association of Mexican Youth (ACJM), and other Catholic Action organizations joined in March 1925 to form the National League for the Defense of Religious Liberty (LNDLR). By June, the LNDLR claimed a membership of 36,000, with local chapters in almost all states of the republic.

At the national level, the conflict between church and state came to a head with the publication on July 2, 1926, of what became known as the Calles Law, the legislative package necessary for the implementation of the anticlerical constitutional provisions. Municipal authorities were charged with enforcing the law, and local neighborhood committees were to be appointed to administer all church property. The government declared its right to decide which church buildings might be used for religious practice, and which were to be converted for use by Revolutionary schools, peasant leagues, and unions. The law was to go into effect on July 31, 1926.

Bearing in mind the success of organized Catholic resistance in Jalisco, the Mexican Episcopacy and the LNDLR initially advocated nonviolent opposition to the Calles Law, including the nonpayment of taxes, a boycott of all nonessential goods, and a petition drive to overturn the relevant constitutional provisions. The Vatican, meanwhile, attempted, without success, to negotiate a compromise with the Calles administration. On July 25, shortly after those negotiations collapsed, the episcopacy announced that all priests would withdraw from their churches on July 31, the day that the Calles Law was to go into effect. Thus began the three-year clerical strike that closed Mexico's churches and sparked the popular uprisings that would, after a period of several months, coalesce as the Cristero Rebellion.

The Rebellion of 1926 to 1929

During the second half of 1926, the Cristero Rebellion was characterized by sporadic, disorganized, and short-lived violence, often connected to the seizure of churches by federal troops. The LNDLR had begun to discuss the possibility of rebellion as early as September, but urban lay Catholics directed most of their activities toward the economic boycott declared in response to the Calles Law. Reports of sustained rural uprisings in support of the Catholic Church in Colima and Jalisco began to reach Mexico City, however, and encouraged the LNDLR leadership to contemplate the armed overthrow of the Revolutionary regime. LNDLR leaders met with the episcopacy in November to request official ecclesiastical approval of the rebellion; the hierarchy declined to openly support the LNDLR's plans, but agreed in principle that rebellion against political authorities was, in some cases, justified. The LNDLR proceeded to create a military command structure and, in a manifesto published in both the United States and Mexico in December, called for a mass insurrection on January 1, 1927, to overthrow the Revolutionary regime and establish a new constitution with guarantees of religious freedom.

The LNDLR's attempt to generate and lead a mass rebellion led to a complex and sometimes conflicting alliance between peasant villagers and Catholic elites, both lay and clerical. The Cristero Rebellion entailed far more than the defense of the institutional prerogatives of the Catholic Church by the clergy and organized lay Catholics: at the popular level, it was essentially an antistate movement, rooted in the defense of community institutions and autonomy vis-à-vis a rapidly encroaching central state. The anticlerical policies of the 1920s entailed a fundamental assault on peasant values, culture, and local political autonomy. These policies certainly limited the role of the Catholic Church in education and the clerical duties of the parish priest, but they also outlawed religious festivities and practices that, while they often had very little to do with the institutional Catholic Church, were at the very heart of community economic, social, and political organization. For many communities, this attack on local institutions was reinforced by the Revolutionary agrarian reform program, and the often top-down *agrarista* mobilization of the period: while the agrarian reform might well increase access to land, it also entailed a radically increased role for the state in the peasant community and a subsequent loss of local autonomy in the regulation of community resources and civil-religious authority. In some regions, particularly those in which there were few haciendas, the highly politicized application of the reform actually threatened community access to land, as when *agrarista* minorities, allied with state officials, made claims on either peasant smallholdings or communal property.

The vast majority of *cristero* rebels, therefore, were far more concerned with defending community institutions and practices against the intrusions of the Revolutionary state than they were with the political ambitions of the LNDLR leadership or the institutional concerns of the episcopacy. The tacit approval of the Catholic hierarchy lent legitimacy to the rebellion, and the LNDLR was able to provide the peasant rebels with logistical support and some military leadership. But peasants, unlike urban lay Catholics, did not rebel in direct response to the LNDLR's manifesto, nor did they readily accept the LNDLR's notions of military discipline, much less the often inept military leaders appointed in Mexico City. With a few exceptions, the peasant rebels recognized the authority of local leaders, be they parish priests, village elders, caciques (local strongmen), or fellow peasants. The *cristero* villagers of the center-west generally did ally themselves in some fashion with the Mexico City–based LNDLR, but the timing, evolution, and nature of the rebellion were much more a product of local conditions and organizations than they were of LNDLR decisions and orders.

Until August 1927, *cristero* rebels operated in small and uncoordinated groups, without a centralized leadership or a coherent military strategy; poorly supplied with arms and ammunition, most *cristero* rebels stayed close to home, engaging in sporadic guerrilla warfare rather than larger-scale and strategic attacks on federal garrisons or major towns. Nearly all of the uprisings that occurred in response to the LNDLR's call for mass insurrection were easily repressed or dispersed, particularly when they entailed members of the LNDLR and ACJM acting on their own or in conjunction with small groups of workers or peasants. Even in areas where the LNDLR was particularly well organized, including the Federal District as well as the states of Chihuahua and Puebla, sustained rebellion proved impossible in the absence of widespread popular support and participation. With the easy suppression of these early uprisings, many urban lay Catholics, particular those in the ACJM, quickly defected from the rebel ranks. By mid-1927, the rebellion was sustained only in the central-west states of Jalisco, Michoacán, Guanajuato, Colima, Zacatecas, and Nayarit. In these states, the strength of the rebellion came from high levels of popular support, as well as the organizational density and military effectiveness of two lay Catholic organizations based in Jalisco: the Popular Union (UP), led by Anacleto González Flores until his execution by federal troops in April 1927; and the U, a clandestine organization with cells throughout much of Jalisco and Michoacán.

Beginning in August 1927, two LNDLR-appointed leaders began to reorganize and coordinate the various local and regional groups operating in the center-west. Jesús Degollado y Guízar was appointed chief of operations in southern Jalisco, Colima, Nayarit, and western Michoacán. Enrique Gorostieta was placed in charge of organizing the rebels in central and northeastern Jalisco; his scope of authority gradually increased over the following year, and in August 1928 he was appointed the position of first chief of the Liberation Army. Gorostieta was unusually successful in gaining the respect of the *cristero* rebels, in part because of his military experience as a general in the federal army under Huerta (1913–14). A much more important factor, however, was his recognition of the authority of the local and regional leadership; one of his first steps in taking command of the *cristeros* was to officially recognize what had always been the de facto leadership of the rebellion.

By late 1927, the *cristeros* began carrying out larger-scale attacks that involved rebels from different regions and states. This was in part the result of improved organization and coordination under Gorostieta's leadership. Another important factor, however, was the military rebellion of Generals Arnulfo Gómez and Francisco Serrano, sparked by Obregón's decision to run for the presidency a second time. The Gómez-Serrano Rebellion was short-lived, lasting only a few weeks in October and November, but it did require the withdrawal of federal troops from the center-west, leaving a military opening for the *cristero* rebels. It was at this point that the regime began to rely more heavily on the *agrarista* militias: some 5,000 to 20,000 pro-regime peasants fought alongside of, or instead of, federal forces throughout the course of the rebellion; the numbers fluctuated in accordance with changing military requirements. Many of the *agrarista* peasants came from the neighboring state of San Luis Potosí, where they constituted the military base of the Revolutionary cacique Saturnino Cedillo. Many others, however, came from the region of the center-west itself, and particularly from the state of Michoacán, where popular support for both the *cristero* and the *agrarista* movements was quite strong.

The situation might have remained one of a military stalemate had it not been for two events. First, Gorostieta was killed in an encounter with federal troops on June 1, 1929; Degollado y Guízar took his place as supreme commander of the Liberation Army, but never was able to command the same respect as his predecessor. Second, the episcopacy explicitly condemned the rebellion at the end of month, having reached its own agreement with the regime on June 29, 1929, after two years of negotiations mediated by U.S. ambassador Dwight W. Morrow. The key stumbling block on both sides had been whether or not there would be any actual revisions of the Constitution of 1917: as Morrow carefully pointed out to Calles, the requirement that priests register with the state, and the right of governors to establish limits on the number of priests practicing within their jurisdiction, did, in fact, represent a real threat to the integrity of the Catholic Church as an institution. After considerable effort, Morrow finally produced an agreement acceptable to both the Catholic hierarchy and to Calles. On June 21, 1929, representatives of the episcopacy and the administration of Emilio Portes Gil issued a joint statement to the press, declaring, among other things, that the requirement that priests register with state officials did not mean that the government could recognize members of the clergy not designated as such by ecclesiastical authorities. Once the agreement was reached, the episcopacy explicitly condemned the rebellion, ordered the LNDLR to cease its political and military activities, and commanded all of the *cristero* rebels to surrender themselves and their arms.

The agreement reached between church and state did not, in fact, reform or modify any of the existing anticlerical laws or constitutional provisions. The state gave no guarantees that religious practice would be tolerated even within the narrow confines of the existing body of law, even as the Catholic Church agreed to register priests with the government, the one provision it had declared itself unable to abide three years earlier. The church's explicit condemnation of the rebellion brought the Cristero Rebellion to an end, however; slowly, and often with great bitterness toward the Catholic Church, the rebels surrendered to federal forces throughout the summer of 1929. Sporadic uprisings continued to occur throughout much of the center-west during the 1930s, in what some authors have called La Segunda, or the Second Cristiada. These uprisings lacked the legitimacy of church approval, however, and were, in fact, condemned by the episcopacy. According to a 1932 statement by Archbishop Maximino Ruíz y Flores of Michoacán, the pope explicitly had forbidden armed struggle, and if the episcopacy had said or written anything in favor of rebellion in 1926, such thinking no longer held.

Interpretations of the Cristero Rebellion

The central controversy in the literature on the Cristero Rebellion concerns the relative importance of the episcopacy, urban lay Catholic organizations, and the peasantry in defining the course and the nature of the rebellion; a corollary to this issue concerns the motivations of the center-west peasants who rebelled in the context of the crisis between church and state at the national level.

Early accounts of the Cristero Rebellion tend to treat it as one episode in a much longer conflict between church and state in Mexico: beginning in the late colonial period, with the expulsion of the Jesuits, this conflict came to a head during the liberal reform period of the 1850s and 1860s, subsided temporarily during the era of Porfirio Díaz (1876–1910), broke out again in full force during the Mexican Revolution (1910–20), and then culminated in the Cristero Rebellion of 1926 to 1929. In this view, the rebellion was part of a last-gasp effort by the Catholic Church to assert its institutional and political prerogatives vis-à-vis the Revolutionary state. Once that state was consolidated under President Lázaro Cárdenas (1934–40), secular elites had little to fear from the politically weakened church, and the long-standing conflict all but came to an end, with church and state coexisting in an at times uneasy but essentially durable modus vivendi. Given this basic understanding of the Cristero Rebellion as one episode in a long-standing intra-elite conflict, the orthodox approach has focused almost exclusively on urban elites and national institutions. The issue of peasant partisanship in the rebellion seldom arises in this literature, the rural rebels most often are subsumed under the general category of "Catholics," thus erasing any distinctions between countryside and city, and between elites and popular-sector groups. When peasant participation in the rebellion is recognized, it generally is attributed to religious fanaticism.

Revisionist studies of the Cristero Rebellion, such as the works by scholar Jean Meyer, differentiate between elite and popular interests in Revolutionary Mexico, particularly during the decade of the 1920s, when, in Meyer's view, a new elite consolidated the Revolutionary state in part by running roughshod over peasant values and institutions. In contrast to the orthodox account, Meyer argues that in terms of motivations, leadership, and organization, the *cristiada* was first and foremost a popular rebellion against a tyrannical state bent on destroying and recreating Mexican society according to a new Revolutionary ideology. More recent work continues to treat the *cristiada* as a popular antistate rebellion but is more explicitly concerned with the question of peasant partisanship, and thus focuses on the local and regional characteristics of the rebellion and the divisions within the peasantry with respect to the policies of the new Revolutionary regime, particularly those policies affecting property rights, religious practice, and political authority.

Select Bibliography

Bailey, David C., *¡Viva Cristo Rey!: The Cristero Rebellion and Church-State Conflict in Mexico.* Austin: University of Texas Press, 1974.

Foley, John, "Colima, Mexico and the Cristero Rebellion." Ph.D. diss., University of Chicago, 1979.

González, Luis, *Pueblo en vilo.* Mexico City: Secretaría de Educación Pública, Fondo de Cultura Económica, 1968.

———, *San José de Gracia: Mexican Village in Transition.* Austin: University of Texas Press, 1974.

Jrade, Ramón, "Counter-revolution in Mexico: The Cristero Movement in Sociological and Historical Perspective." Ph.D. diss., Brown University, 1980.

———, "Inquiries into the Cristero Insurrection Against the Mexican Revolution." *Latin American Research Review* 20:2 (1985).

Meyer, Jean, *La Cristiada.* 3 vols., Mexico City: Siglo XXI, 1973–74.

_____, *The Cristero Rebellion: Mexican People between Church and State*. Cambridge: Cambridge University Press, 1976.

Olivera Sedano, Alicia, *Aspectos del conflicto religioso de 1926 a 1929: Sus antecedentes y consecuencias*. Mexico City: Instituto de Antropología e Historia, 1966.

Purnell, Jennie, "The Politics of Identity: Cristeros and Agraristas of Revolutionary Michoacán." Ph.D. diss., Massachusetts Institute of Technology, 1993.

Quirk, Robert E., *The Mexican Revolution and the Catholic Church, 1910–1929*. Bloomington: Indiana University Press, 1973.

Tutino, John, *From Insurrection to Revolution in Mexico: Social Bases of Agrarian Violence*. Princeton, New Jersey: Princeton University Press, 1986.

—JENNIE PURNELL

CROM

See Confederación Regional Obrera Mexicana (CROM)

CRUZ, JOSÉ DE LA

1786–1856 • General

José de la Cruz served for almost exactly a decade (1811–21) as military and political chief of western New Spain from his capital at Guadalajara in the old kingdom of Nueva Galicia (today the state of Jalisco with adjacent parts of other states). Typical in some respects of many of the tough Spanish military men thrust into prominence by the wars to liberate the Iberian Peninsula from the French (1808-1814), Cruz made a brilliant career for himself in Mexico and returned to enter political life in the mother country after Mexico gained its independence in 1821. Remaining fiercely loyal to the monarchy until the end, and engaging in a policy of blood and iron to suppress the stubborn popular insurgency begun by Father Miguel Hidalgo y Costilla in September 1810, Cruz never seems to have appreciated the irony that a guerrilla fighter who had fought for the liberation of his own fatherland was now fighting guerrillas committed to the liberation of their own.

Born in 1786 in the town of Arapiles, in the province of Salamanca, José de la Cruz was a student at the University of Salamanca when the guerrilla war against the French invaders of Spain broke out in 1808. He campaigned against Napoléon's forces with some distinction, remained in the army, and arrived in New Spain, already a brigadier, as subinspector of infantry with newly named Viceroy Francisco Xavier de Venegas in September 1810, the very month of the insurgency's outbreak. Serving under the military command of a Spanish career soldier of long experience in New Spain, Félix María Calleja del Rey, Cruz marched with his forces late in 1810 upon Guadalajara, where Hidalgo's rebel government had taken refuge, recovering along the way the important city of Valladolid (today Morelia) from the insurgents (December 28, 1810), but failing to arrive at Guadalajara until after Calleja's army had defeated Hidalgo's enormous but ill-armed and disorganized force at the Battle of Calderon on January 17, 1811. There followed major actions against the rebels, among them the forces of Julián and José María "El Chito" Villagrán in the Huichapan area. Sent by Calleja to pacify the important coastal zone of Tepic and re-assert royalist control over its port town, San Blas, Cruz took advantage of the fortuitous death of the famous rebel leader Father José María Mercado and a loyalist rising by the Spanish inhabitants of Tepic to capture the town on February 12, 1811, after which he returned to Guadalajara.

As a reward for his military services, Cruz was named president of the Audiencia (High Court) of Guadalajara, governor of Nueva Galicia, and comandante general of western Mexico, posts he was to hold for the next decade while his sometime mentor Calleja, his senior by 30 years, made a military career as chief commander of Spanish forces in the colony, and eventually viceroy. In 1811 José de la Cruz occupied himself chiefly with sending major detachments to combat rebels in the southern parts of his vast military zone, including Sayula, Zacoalco, Jiquilpán, Zamora, and La Barca, while he himself was forced to reside in Guadalajara as loyalist political chief in the west, a role the gruff military man often found chafing. Several stubborn foci of rebel military resistance developed during these early years of the insurgency, chiefly in the south of Nueva Galicia and along the Pacific coastal lowlands, in the Altos region of Jalisco, and around Lake Chapala. Indigenous rebels, mainly from the lakeside villages, fortified themselves on the two small Mezcala Islands in Lake Chapala, holding out for three years (1813–16) against Cruz's efforts to reduce them, including a naval blockade, several amphibious assaults, and ill-fated attempts to mount heavy cannon on barges. This embarrassing episode proved a major thorn in the ambitious military man's side, pinning down major royalist resources, damaging his reputation, and serving to aggravate further the cooling of his relations with Calleja. When Calleja was appointed viceroy in 1813, he deprived Cruz of military jurisdiction over the important regions of Michoacán and Guanajuato. Still, Cruz' career advanced, and he was promoted to field marshal in 1812. Some degree of economic recovery came to Guadalajara with the opening of the port of San Blas and a new mint (1811, but closed 1815), enabling Cruz's government to mount a respectable military effort against the insurgents for a decade, although he frequently complained of the lack of arms and other resources to fulfill his military mission. By 1817 or so, with the reduction of the insurgent redoubts in Lake Chapala and elsewhere in the west, much of the country was, if not pacified, at least under nominal royalist control. In the meantime Cruz himself had married a Mexican woman of good family.

As an anti-insurgent commander and chief political figure in the west, Cruz acted throughout his decade in power with extreme harshness to suppress the insurgency, which in his view enjoyed not a shred of legitimacy. From his entry into Guadalajara in February 1811, he imposed a series of draconian measures, including death penalties for a wide range of civilian and military offenses. He was fond as a matter of military policy of razing rebel villages, offering pardons upon which he later reneged, and decimating groups of captured rebels. In his early dispatches to Viceroy Venegas, he tended to portray himself as more conciliatory than he actually was. He also used the printing presses of Guadalajara to launch a propaganda war against the rebels through newspapers, pamphlets, and a constant stream of public proclamations. One of the most interesting aspects of his career was his complex relationship with the much older Calleja, quite close for a year or so until it soured under the pressures of military and political jealousies, declining into a litany of mutual recrimination and complaint, especially on the part of Cruz. The two men's correspondence, however, still preserved in the Mexican archives, speaks not only to their unforgiving political attitudes toward Mexican aspirations for independence, but also to their astuteness, remarkable education (they dashed their letters with French and literary allusions), and the hard life of constant military campaigning.

As a result of political events in Spain, José de la Cruz was caught up in 1820 and 1821 in the transition of Mexico from colony to nation under conservative criollo auspices. Indecisive in the face of Agustín de Iturbide's attempt to unite Mexican factions against colonial rule under the Plan of Iguala, Cruz was essentially ousted from his post in Guadalajara in June 1821 by a sort of coup led by his talented and long-loyal subordinate and fellow Spaniard, Pedro Celestino Negrete. Cruz fled to Durango, where he surrendered his authority and remaining forces on August 31, 1821. He traveled thence to Mexico City, obtained a guarantee of safe conduct from Iturbide, and left the country. Upon his return to Spain he was named minister of war by a restored King Fernando VII and promoted lieutenant general, though he was shortly thereafter deprived of his post, imprisoned for his moderate political stance, and banished from Spain. He returned from exile and was named an alternate member of the Council of Regency upon Fernando's death in 1833, occupying again briefly the portfolio of war, but was forced into exile a second time, dying in Paris in 1856.

—Eric Van Young

CRUZ, SOR JUANA INÉS DE LA

1651–95 • Nun and Writer

If Shakespeare is synonymous with Renaissance England, Sor Juana Inés de la Cruz is synonymous with Baroque Latin America. She lived and worked at the end of the so-called Siglo de Oro, a nearly two-century golden age marked by extraordinary literary, artistic, and musical brilliance, in the metropolitan and colonial centers of the Spanish-speaking world.

Regardless of sex, class, or age, millions of people in Latin America are familiar with Sor Juana's portrait and a few lines from the poem that begins "You foolish and unreasoning men/who cast all blame on women" (*Hombres necios que acusáis/a la mujer sin razón*). The most often reproduced image of Sor Juana—it appears on Mexican currency—was painted in 1750 by Miguel Cabrera. Its idealized elegance has contributed to her fame as "peerless," *"rara avis"* (rare bird), "Phoenix of Mexico," and "Tenth Muse." The last label was used also for Anne Bradstreet (1612–72), inaugural poet of the Anglo-American colonies, with whom Sor Juana has been compared and contrasted, and for other women poets as far back as Sappho. In the twentieth century, scholar

Dorothy Schons called Sor Juana's *Respuesta a Sor Filotea de la Cruz* (Answer to Sister Filotea de la Cruz, 1691), a women's declaration of intellectual emancipation; in Mexico, in 1974, the poet was ceremoniously awarded the title "First Feminist of the Americas."

The extraordinary sweep of both Sor Juana's literary art and of her consciousness of gender are now being more fully understood and appreciated. Lack of biographical documentation, combined with the "worship" and "envy" stirred by her talent gave rise to a distorting mythography. She was not, for instance, either saintly or a mystic; as a sage she was at once daring and humble, but her expressions of humility were largely conventional and tactical. Although she suffered persecution and outrage, and was pressured or convinced to greatly modify her worldly intellectual life about two years before she died, she was not under direct threat of punishment by the Inquisition; the Catholic Church had a less drastic mechanism for instilling compliance. Nor did she die in an ascetic cell while nursing her sister nuns during an epidemic as has been claimed since publication of the first biography by the Spanish Jesuit Diego Calleja (1700). An inventory of her belongings when she died, made public in 1995, lists books, art works, and other possessions. Review of death records at the convent shows no indication of a plague.

Sor Juana was born almost certainly in Nepantla—not far from the two dormant volcanoes, Popocatéptl and Iztaccíhuatl, mentioned in her verses—in 1651 as noted by Calleja and registered in the convent annals. Her mother Isabel Ramírez, who though unschooled efficaciously managed lands leased from the church, had six children, perhaps with three partners, none of whom she married; Juana Inés, the prodigious second child, was probably the daughter of a Basque, as she states, about whom little is known. (Many people, including Octavio Paz, her most recent and influential biographer, had been convinced that the baptismal record witnessed in 1648 by family members at the church of Chimalhuacán for a natural child, named Inés, was hers.) She rhymed before she could speak in prose, she tells us, and strove uncommonly hard to master Latin in a short time. At 10 she was taken to Mexico City, where she lived with a well-connected aunt and uncle, wrote her first poem, and attracted attention and a job at court.

Sor Juana represented herself as an insatiably curious reader, a solitary, hard-working learner and an innately gifted poet. She wrote that her real vocation was the silent, arduous, and sacred one of the scholar. Her great passion was study. First her grandfather's sizable collection of books, then the viceregal palace's, and finally her own convent library, which held hundreds of volumes, but was not the largest in Mexico (as has been claimed), fed her appetite for knowledge.

After living for approximately five years at the royal court (1664–69) as Juana Inés de Asbaje y Ramírez de Santillana, favorite servant-companion to the vicereine, Leonor Carreto, Marquise de Mancera, she became Madre Juana Inés de la Cruz, nun of the order of St. Jerome. Before leaving the palace, Calleja tells us, she stunned the most knowledgeable men in the realm with her brilliance in a public examination organized by the viceroy (c. 1668). That such events were not unknown is evidenced by the fact that several decades earlier another scholar, Juliana Morel, born in Barcelona, later an abbess and translator of St. Augustine into French, was similarly examined in Lyon and Avignon. Sor Juana depicted an analogous performance in writing of the legendary St. Catherine of Egypt, who along with two other mothers of wisdom, Isis (Mother of the Gods), and the Virgin Mary, was her intellectual and spiritual model. Quintilian, Ovid, and Virgil could head the list of her Latin influences; Luis de Góngora, Pedro Calderón de la Barca, and Baltasar Gracián were first among her Spanish literary mentors. About Egyptology and the natural and physical sciences she learned most in books by the German Jesuit encyclopedist Athanasius Kircher. St. Teresa of Avila and María de Agreda she mentioned and implicitly debated.

At court and in the convent as well, Sor Juana was a professional writer: much of her literary production was commissioned, some paid for, some exchanged for favors and gifts. The two volumes published during her lifetime (in Madrid, 1689, and in Seville, 1692) and the third (with Calleja's biography and many poems of praise, shortly afterward, 1700), were so popular they went through several editions. Yet she had to guard her time for study and writing from the demands of monastic life. Recent research has confirmed that as treasurer of her convent of St. Paula (now a university and museum, dedicated, in part, to promoting studies of the great author's work and her times), Sor Juana was for many years in charge of finances, managing sizable sums of money and making investments beneficial both to the convent and herself.

Sor Juana's privileged intellect evolved in kaleidoscopic New Spain, festively effusive on one hand, ascetically reserved on the other. She absorbed much from books but also from her variegated social milieu. Some of her poems echo popular songs and dances, their images as colorful as market-places, filled with fruit, vegetables, and clothing; others are as elegantly ornate as the cathedrals where her *villancicos* were sung and the aristocratic salons where her plays were performed.

Sor Juana utilized many tonalities and styles of language in her plays, poems, and prose: the accent of non-native speakers of Spanish (Portuguese, Nahua, African, and Basque); the erudite cadences and classical rhetoric of clerics in the Latin church; the tradition of dramatic authors and the poetry "academies" of Madrid and Seville. Her vernacular and cultivated nuances reveal both the elite pages of the enormous number of books she read and the idiomatic turns of phrase she heard from people in every strata of Mexican society (servants, priests, enslaved laborers, aristocrats). Humorous, witty, and ironic, Sor Juana's mature works reflected so richly the viceroyalty's artistic and religious visions, and were so deftly crafted, that their coded critical and revisionary dimensions long escaped many of her readers.

Sor Juana's complete works include 65 sonnets (some 20 of them love sonnets, deemed by many to be among the most beautiful of the seventeenth century); 62 *romances* (similar to ballads); and a profusion of poems in other metrical forms. For dramatic performance, Sor Juana wrote 3 sacramental *autos* (1-act dramas) and 2 comedies (1 a collaboration); 32 *loas* (preludes to plays, sometimes sung and performed separately for religious and viceregal celebrations); 2 *sainetes* (farces) and a *sarao* (celebratory song and dance), performed between the acts of one of the plays; and 15 or 16 sets of *villancicos* (carols—8 or 9 songs on religious themes such as the Nativity, Assumption, Immaculate Conception, and legends of Sts. Joseph, Peter, and Catherine of Alexandria).

The 12 years of Sor Juana's most intense literary labors began in 1680 when she was chosen by the outgoing viceroy, Archbishop Payo de Rivera, patron of the arts and a friend, to design one of two triumphal arches to be set up in Mexico City, culmination point of pomp and ritual-filled ceremonies to welcome the new head of state and his wife. (Don Carlos de Sigüenza y Góngora, entrusted with the other, may have supervised the execution of both). The colorful paintings were addressed to the massive crowd gathered for the occasion in Mexico City's main plaza. The text included the poems performed at the ceremony held in front of the arch, and for the initiated, an erudite explanation and description of the 14 paintings and emblems she had devised, together with the Latin mottoes and the Spanish verses (two in Latin) that framed the top and bottom of each image. Considered modern in its day, it required a familiarity all educated people of the time had with emblematic literature, books of myths, and the iconographies prepared for use by artists. As far as we know Sor Juana is the only woman in history to receive such an assignment. The arch, titled *Neptuno alegórico* (*Allegorical Neptune*, 1680) brought her glory and scandal—such a public presence was considered forbidden for women, let alone nuns.

About two years later Sor Juana dismissed her confessor Antonio Núñez de Miranda in a sharp letter (1681 or 1682) in which she contests his censure of her having undertaken to design the arch, and his decade of public complaint against her "scandalous" literary activity. Although most scholars believe she wrote it, the letter cannot be authenticated definitively because the copy is from the eighteenth century. Until 1980, when it was discovered, biographies stated that she had been dismissed by Núñez, and that he agreed to serve as her confessor again two years before her death.

The 975-verse *Primero sueño* ("First Dream," also known simply as *Sueño*, or "Dream," c. 1685), celebrated as the most important philosophical poem in the Spanish language, is at once Sor Juana's most abstract and personal work. Long read as a poem of intellectual disillusionment, more recent readings comment on its exploration of quests for knowledge, inductive, logical, intuitive; of the anatomy and functioning of the human body; of the geometrical movements of the stars; of mechanics and medicine; of the human (female) spirit's need for unfettered growth. Its autobiographical vision, not unlike Descartes's, fuses poetry and science.

Finally, Sor Juana wrote two prose essays, the unauthorized publication of the first of which, the *Carta atenagórica* (1690), prompted the writing of the second, the already mentioned *Respuesta a Sor Filotea de la Cruz*. The author stated that at the request of the bishop of Puebla, Manuel de Santa Cruz, and for his eyes only, she prepared and sent a manuscript of her spoken critique, a magnificently logical disagreement with a sermon written 40 years earlier by Antonio Vieira, a well-known Portuguese-Brazilian Jesuit. Santa Cruz had it printed as *Carta atenagórica* (Letter Worthy of Athena; it is also known as *Crisis sobre un sermón*—Critique on a Sermon), adding an admonitory prologue in the form of a letter signed "Sor Filotea de la Cruz." Surprised and angered by the attacks against her critique, within three months Sor Juana had penned her most extraordinary prose work, the *Respuesta*, a response to three major churchmen, "Sor Filotea" (Fernández de Santa Cruz), Núñez de Miranda, and Aguiar y Seijas (the ascetic and woman-phobic archbishop of Mexico), and to all those who would silence her and prevent women from learning, teaching, and writing.

The *Respuesta*, often referred to as a spiritual autobiography, mimics nuns' *Lives*, but is actually structured according to classical judicial and epistolary rhetoric, as a legal document. Praising scientific and pluridisciplinary inquiry, Sor Juana's tour de force defends the legacy of women's contributions to culture, and her own life in letters. Priding herself on being "as much daughter of the Company" as the Jesuit Vieira, she produced a self-defense, a wily and witty 33-page essay on silence and speech, religion and history, on language, knowledge, and interpretation.

In 1995 Elias Trabulse made public as Sor Juana's a short verse satire signed by Serafina de Cristo, and also written in 1691, a mocking retort that implicates Núñez de Miranda rather than Vieira as a main target of the theological critique and emphasizes Sor Juana's capacity to jest. *Enigmas* (Riddles), prepared at the request of a group of Portuguese nuns, discovered around 1970, but not published until 1994, echoes Sor Juana's inveterate playfulness and offers proof of contacts, however indirect, with European religious women. Lost are a treatise on music, *El caracol,* and her reputedly voluminous correspondence, which might tell us more about her self-fashioning. Some scholars underline Sor Juana's doubt, conflict, and melancholy, others her mocking confidence in waging the unending struggle to continue writing despite her ambiguous and often embattled position.

Sor Juana's staunch refusal of marriage and the dynamism of her treatment of love relationships in many works, sacred and profane, may in part be attributed to her mother's relative autonomy, as well as to mythological readings and acquaintance with art; unsettled family life and observations of the fickleness of courtly behavior could also have influenced her elaborations on the classical myths of sexual strife between goddesses, gods, and humans. Nothing is known about the poet's own possible human loves, although much has been invented over the centuries—marking the romantic and unfailingly sexist fashions of the moment.

Critics and scholars generally agree that Sor Juana's most vividly ardent love poetry is found in verses directed to the two vicereines most supportive of her genius and to the

Virgin Mary. Drawing upon the wealth and development of reverence for the Virgin of Guadalupe, she made of Mariolatry a foundation that authorized and profoundly inspired her writing. She identified divinity with wisdom and exceptional human beings with godliness.

One of the keenest minds and scintillating pens of an era, Sor Juana helped create Mexican identity, with its intricate linguistic usages. As a Mexican nun of the second half of the seventeenth century, she was famous as an anomaly; as a poet, playwright, and feminist intellectual of the early modern period, Sor Juana forms part of what we now know to have been a formidable tradition of female thinkers and artists in the Western world.

Select Bibliography

Arenal, Electa, and Amanda Powell, editors and translators, *The Answer/La Requesta: Including a Selection of Poems.* New York: The Feminist Press at the City University of New York, 1994.

Bénassy-Berling, Marie-Cécille, *Humanismo y religión en Sor Juana Inés de la Cruz,* translated by Laura López de Belair. Mexico City: UNAM, 1983.

Daniel, Lee A., *The Loa of Sor Juana Inés de la Cruz.* Fredricton, New Brunswick: York Press, 1994.

Flynn, Gerard C., *Sor Juana Inés de la Cruz.* New York: Twayne, 1971.

Merrim, Stephanie, editor, *Feminist Perspectives on Sor Juana Inés de la Cruz.* Detroit: Wayne State University Press, 1991.

Montross, Constance M., *Virtue or Vice?: Sor Juana's Use of Thomistic Thought.* Washington, D.C.: University Press of America, 1981.

Paz, Octavio, *Sor Juana Inés de la Cruz, o las trampas de la fe.* Mexico City: Fondo de Cultura Económica, 1982. As *Sor Juana or the Traps of Faith,* translated by Margaret Sayers Peden. Cambridge, Massachusetts: Bel Knap Press, 1988. Retitled as *Sor Juana: Her Life and World.* London: Faber and Faber, 1988.

Poot Herrara, Sara, editor, *Y diversa de mí misma/entre vuestras plumas ando: Homenaje internacional a Sor Juana Inés de la Cruz.* Mexico City: El Colegio de México, 1994.

Sabat de Rivers, Georgina, "Ejercicios de la Encarnación: Sobre la imagen de María y la decisión final de Sor Juana." In *Estudios de literatura hispanoamericana: Sor Juana Inés de la Cruz y otros poetas barrocos de la Colonia.* Barcelona: PPU, 1992.

———, "Apología de América y del mundo azteca en tres loas de Sor Juana." In *Revista de Estudios Hispánicos: Letras coloniales.* San Juan: Universidad de Puerto Rico, 1992.

Tavard, George H., *Juana Inés de la Cruz and the Theology of Beauty.* Notre Dame, Indiana: Notre Dame University Press, 1991.

Trabulse, Elías, *Sor Juana Inés de la Cruz: Ante la historia.* Mexico City: UNAM, 1980.

—ELECTA ARENAL

CTM

See Confederación de Trabajadores de México (CTM)

CUBA

See under Foreign Policy

CUESTA, JORGE

1903–42 • Writer

One of the most brilliant members of the twentieth-century "Contemporáneos" group, and by all reports the most intense and the most unstable, Cuesta was born in Córdoba, Veracruz, September 21, 1903, and died by his own hand in Mexico City on August 13, 1942. He completed his early education (through the first years of preparatory school) in his native city, and in 1921 went to Mexico City to begin his university training. Cuesta studied chemical sciences for the next several years, and at the same time began to develop friendships with some of the young literati in the capital city (his unusual combination of interests caused some of them to dub him "the Alchemist"). In early 1926 he accepted a position with a sugar company in rural Veracruz, but returned to Mexico City before the end of the year. He became increasingly involved with the young writers who would become known as the Contemporáneos, and fell madly in love with Guadalupe Marín, then the wife of Diego Rivera. In an attempt to change the course of his son's life, Cuesta's father insisted that he travel to Europe in 1928. After only three months in London and Paris, however, he returned once again to Mexico City and married Marín, with whom he maintained a tumultuous relationship until their separation in 1932. During the early 1930s Cuesta held several minor government positions and continued his collaboration in *Contemporáneos* and a number of other literary journals; toward the end of the decade he was appointed to a research position in the National Society for Alcohol Products and from that post became involved in several bizarre scientific experiments. In the early 1940s his long struggle with insanity and certain sexual obsessions became more intense, and in August of 1942 he took his own life while confined to a mental institution.

Cuesta's writings appeared almost entirely as journal contributions, and were never collected during his lifetime. His first literary text, for example, is a short story, "La resurrección de don Francisco," which appeared in the July 1924 issue of *Antena*; his poems and essays were published over a period of some 15 years in the pages of a number of journals, among them *El Libro y el Pueblo, Revista de Revistas, Ulises, Contemporáneos, Letras de México, Taller,* and *Romance.* Some political essays appeared as short separate publications (in 1934, for example, *El plan contra Calles* was printed as a 30-page pamphlet), but in reality the only book-length publication that appeared under his name was the 1928 *Antología de la poesía mexicana moderna,* the controversial Contemporáneos project for which Cuesta took authorship in the name of the whole group. It was not until 1964, with the four-volume *Poemas y ensayos* prepared by Luis Mario Schneider and Miguel Capistrán, that Cuesta's relatively complete work was easily accessible for study and commentary.

In spite of the instability of his life and a relatively late inclusion among the young writers of the Contemporáneos, Cuesta nonetheless made several significant contributions to the group and to Mexican literature in general. The first, as already mentioned, was his coordination during 1927 and 1928 of the preparations for the tendentious Contemporáneos poetry anthology. This volume, which actually appeared during Cuesta's brief 1928 stay in Europe, was roundly criticized for its partisan inclusions and exclusions. As the sole editor listed on the title page, Cuesta's name was much in

evidence in those negative comments. "Es una antología," scoffed its detractors in a derisive pun, "que vale lo que Cuesta" (one could loosely translate this as "it is an anthology that is worth what it costs," "Cuesta" being the third person singular conjugation of the verb, "to cost"). In spite of its mixed reception at the time of its publication, however, the anthology is now seen as a major landmark in the serious study of twentieth-century Mexican poetry.

A second dimension of Cuesta's contribution is to be found in his own intense and carefully crafted poetry, which consisted of some 30 sonnets and *sonetillos* and a longer text published just weeks after his death. Cuesta was probably the best sonneteer of the group, and his compositions in this form explore the complexities of human existence under the stress of fleeting time and an unattainable desire for perfection. His longest poetic text, "Canto a un dios mineral," with 37 balanced sextets of 11- and 7-syllable lines, was a product of his final years. Published posthumously, its brilliant but often hermetic imagery, disposed within a careful external form, expresses the unresolved struggles of a soul in change and torment.

Finally, Cuesta's scientific and cultural background, coupled with a lucid and argumentative style, made him a formidable essayist, again perhaps the best in the Contemporáneos group. His political essays, some 30 in number, range widely over such areas as university and pre-university education, reform of the 1917 Mexican Constitution, socialism, Marxism, and international affairs in general. His more than 60 literary essays show an equally broad range of interests, including general commentaries on international and Mexican art and literature, discussions of such period styles as classicism, romanticism, and vanguardism, and more specific critiques of individual authors, artists, and works. All of Cuesta's essays, both political and literary, are frequently pugnacious in tone and share the same complexities of structure and style. They demand much from a present-day reader, but taken together they represent yet another register of an unusual and often under-appreciated figure in modern Mexican literature.

Select Bibliography

Cuesta, Jorge, *Poemas y ensayos,* edited by Luis Mario Schneider and Miguel Capistrán. 4 vols., Mexico City: UNAM, 1964.
Katz, Adolfo, *Jorge Cuesta o la alegría del guerrero.* Mexico City: FCE, 1989.
León Caicedo, Adolfo, *Soliloquio de la inteligencia: La poética de Jorge Cuesta.* Mexico City: INBA, 1988.
Panabière, Louis, *Itinerario de una disidencia: Jorge Cuesta (1903–1942).* Mexico City: FCE, 1983.
Sylvester, Nigel Grant, *Vida y obra de Jorge Cuesta (1903–1942).* Mexico City: Premiá Editora, 1984.

—MERLIN H. FORSTER

CUEVAS, JOSÉ LUIS

1934– • Artist and Critic

José Luis Cuevas was born in Mexico City in 1934 and rose to fame in the late 1950s and early 1960s with his frontal attacks upon the Mexican art establishment and the intensity of his line drawings, whose subject matter initially came from the underside of the nation's "miracle" of modernization. Renowned for his egomania, Cuevas used his art and polemics as a litmus test for the maturation of Mexican nationalism, which he regarded as provincial and oppressive. While still active as an artist as of the mid-1990s, by that time he was revered more for an earlier impact than for his contemporary work, which had changed little from his trademark style. In fact, while his image remained captured by a caricaturing of his own creation, that of an *efant terrible,* his later art itself proved less relevant to Mexico's more dynamic, postmodern influenced art scene.

Cuevas broke into the Mexican and international art world in the mid-1950s as much through his contorted drawings of characters taken from Mexico's urban underside as his polemical diatribes against the cultural authoritarianism that was the legacy of the Mexican muralist movement. Forming part of a small movement of young artists who became known as neo-figurists *(nueva presencia),* Cuevas became the most outspoken, elevating the group's artistic aims into an ideological assault on the narrowly defined nationalism of the time. Shortly his stature superseded that of the movement itself, as he leveraged his growing international recognition to local advantage. In 1954 he first appeared at a Washington exhibit of the Pan American Union and in 1955 at a gallery in Paris, at which Picasso bought two of his drawings. By the late 1950s his attacks on David Alfaro Siqueiros and the Bellas Artes bureaucracy turned into a raucous confrontation carried out in the press. While acknowledging the significance of the Mexican school of muralism and its direct influence on his own work, Cuevas denounced Siqueiros as the "Trujillo of Tenochtitlán" and attacked the art bureaucracy organized through Bellas Artes as a stifling monopoly of officialdom. His polemic, "The Cactus Curtain," first published in Mexico City in 1956 and reproduced in the *Evergreen Review* in 1959, questioned the strength of a cultural nationalism that had become inbred and conformist.

Upon his success abroad, Cuevas's work shifted to reflect the direct inspiration he received from literature (Doestoevsky, Kafka), other artists (Dürer, Goya, Posada), and even film. His style, however, remained consistent. He rejected realist depiction for allegorical exploration on the themes of death, nightmare, and persecution, reflected in the distorted, often monstrous figures he created. Decrying what he regarded as the "useless nationalisms and provincial attitudes" of Mexico's artist community, Cuevas made a public issue of his professed cosmopolitanism, publishing editorials from his various residences in New York, Paris, and Mexico City. In 1967, already a champion of the young, Cuevas staged an act of performance theater aimed at galvanizing a critical consciousness while further securing media attention for himself. This act involved the creation of an "ephemeral mural" located in the heart of Mexico City's avant-garde enclave, the Zona Rosa. Lasting less than a month, the "mural"—a triptych whose strongest visual element was a self-sketch of the artist signing his name—aimed at mocking the longevity of muralism's influence on cultural circles. Placed in the middle of an electoral campaign, it furthermore was an implicit critique of the monopolization of wall space used for political propaganda by the ruling Partido Revolucionario Institucional (PRI, or Institutional Revolutionary Party). In 1970 Cuevas capped a history of dissent—and self-promotion—by launching an independent candidacy for the national legislature, an effort which failed (probably due to fraud).

Cuevas continued his polemical attacks against the political and cultural authoritarianism of the PRI, but his words lacked the rigor or relevancy of his earlier critique. Indeed, while his work gained a wide reception at galleries and museums throughout the United States, Europe, and Latin America, Cuevas himself failed to move artistically beyond his commitment to ink drawing (often mixed with watercolor backgrounds and overlaid with text). Even his subject matter seemed to stagnate, evidenced by an entire book of collected self-portraits with model. Just at a time when Mexican nationalism indeed was moving beyond its narrow provincialism, a transformation reflected throughout the arts, Cuevas seemed to cling tightly to his reputation as iconoclast.

José Luis Cuevas no longer faced the political or artistic marginalization that once characterized his career in Mexico. Awarded the National Prize for Fine Arts in 1981, he thus reached an important goal that cleared many official barriers to the dissemination of his work through state channels. A seminal figure in contemporary Mexican art, Cuevas also is remembered for his early challenges to the cultural establishment of the PRI. Although his status as an artist is still respected widely, his influence seems to have faded, ironically surpassed by a reputation cultivated from an earlier epoch.

Select Bibliography

Cuevas, José Luis, "The Cactus Curtain," *Evergreen Review* (Winter 1959).

_____, *Cuevas por Cuevas: Notas Autobiograficas.* Mexico City: Era, 1965.

_____, *Cuevario.* Mexico City: Grijalbo, 1973.

_____, *José Luis Cuevas: Self-Portrait with Model.* New York: Rizzoli, 1983.

_____, *Historias del Viajero.* Mexico City: Premiá, 1987.

Goldman, Shifra M., *Contemporary Mexican Painting in a Time of Change.* Austin: University of Texas Press, 1981.

Ponce, José Bernardo, *José Luis Cuevas: ¿Genio o Farsante?* Mexico City: Signos, 1983.

—ERIC ZOLOV

CUISINE

Connections between cuisine and identity—what people eat and who they are—reach deep into Mexican history. The native inhabitants of Mesoamerica worshiped their staple crop maize as a god and even may have equated this plant physically with human flesh. Spanish conquistadors assigned great significance to the Mediterranean staff of life, wheat, the only grain acceptable for Catholic communion according to an eleventh-century papal decree. Within the hierarchical society of New Spain, food served along with clothing and language as a status marker, distinguishing criollo (Spanish-descended) patricians with their crusty wheat bread from Indian and mestizo plebes who ate corn tortillas. Following Independence, Mexican leaders abolished legal distinctions within society, but cultural differences continued to impede their efforts to forge a united nation. Cuisine, in particular, offered a promising space for all Mexicans, not just the leaders, to define their national identity.

Scholars have largely agreed on the modern origins of nationalism, rejecting the nineteenth-century idea that nations possess essential characteristics determined in the distant past. Benedict Anderson described nations as "imagined communities" that emerged in the eighteenth century as a product of the Enlightenment. The standardization of vernacular languages through the spread of print and literature allowed people from different ethnic groups to imagine "national" communities that had not previously existed. Anderson emphasized the role of newspapers and novels in establishing a uniform language, but other forms of literature can perform the same service. Arjun Appadurai has shown that cookbooks in contemporary India opened a medium for middle-class women to communicate with one another, helping to dissolve regional, ethnic, and caste boundaries, and thus to foster Indian nationalism. In Mexico, women relegated to the domestic sphere always had assigned meaning to their lives by feeding their families. Culinary literature therefore offered them a natural language to imagine a national community in the kitchen and to define for themselves *lo mexicano.*

Mexican cuisine developed from two quite separate culinary traditions, the indigenous and the Spanish. Native Americans created a highly sophisticated cuisine based on maize, beans, squash, and chilies. This essentially vegetarian diet arose of necessity, for most large mammals had become extinct in North America 10,000 years ago. Nevertheless, the four staples satisfied human nutritional needs for carbohydrates, protein, minerals, and vitamins. Pre-Columbian cooking techniques maximized the value of these foods; for instance, the method of boiling corn in lime (calcium oxide) multiplied available nutrients, while the complementarity of corn and beans provided a complete amino acid chain, allowing the full utilization of vegetable proteins, although either food alone would be deficient. Indeed, Mesoamerican agriculture may have been productive enough to support 25 million people.

In addition, cuisine held a central place in pre-Columbian society and culture. To demonstrate the grandeur of the Aztec Empire, Mexica rulers such as Moteuczoma (Montezuma) dined on spectacular banquets filled with the finest delicacies including turkey, duck, pheasant, fish, rabbit, and venison. Special foods such as tamales also provided communion with the gods during the many religious and civic festivals in the Mexica calendar. Finally, cuisine provided a way for the Mexica to distinguish themselves from neighboring societies. According to the *Florentine Codex,* the Otomis, a northern tribe considered barbaric by the Mexica, picked their corn before it ripened, while the Toluca, a similarly marginalized group on the western slopes, did not eat chilies. The Purépecha, a people living farther to the west, supposedly cooked with neither skill nor sanitation. These imperial rivals, who regularly defeated Mexica warriors in battle, received the ultimate snub: in a land where fresh tortillas were the height of culinary excellence, the Purépecha ate leftovers. These chauvinistic accounts demonstrated the importance of food as an identifying social trait among the Mexica. People who ate tortillas freshly made of golden corn and spiced with chili peppers could claim the Toltec mantle of civilization; all others still wandered the Chichimec wilderness of savagery.

Meanwhile across the Atlantic, Spanish cuisine developed from a long series of invasions. Three thousand years ago, Iberian people introduced wheat cultivation and sheep herding methods from Syria and Egypt. Over the next millennium, successive Celtic, Phoenician, Greek, and Carthaginian settlers planted grapes, olives, and chickpeas. The Mediterranean staples of wheat bread, olive oil, and vinifera wine thus were established firmly when Roman armies conquered Hispania. This culinary trilogy persisted long after the empire's collapse, for Catholic priests could use only wheat bread and wine for the Holy Eucharist, while olive oil was essential for baptizing children. Nevertheless, fifth-century Visigoth invaders had revived the Iberian pastoral economy and medieval Spaniards consumed a carnivorous diet including sheep, cows, pigs, goats, and chickens. Finally, the Muslim occupation (711–1492) imparted to Spanish cuisine an Asian flavor from spices such as pepper, ginger, cinnamon, clove, cardamom, mace, nutmeg, saffron, and sugar. The Arab's heavy hand with spices later influenced the Mexican creation of *mole poblano,* a fragrant deep brown sauce served with turkey.

This long history of exchanging foods made the introduction of European crops a natural step in the conquest of America, but the natives clung stubbornly to their corn-based cuisine. The *Florentine Codex* recorded their initial reaction to wheat bread as being "like famine food . . . like dried maize stalks." Indians found wheat not only distasteful, but also expensive. The European grain required large capital investments in iron plows, oxen teams, grist mills, and brick ovens, none of which were needed for making corn tortillas. Moreover, wheat yields fell significantly below those of corn. As a result, Indians generally needed to be compelled to grow wheat, except for some entrepreneurial farmers who sold the grain to urban markets. Most rural dwellers ate wheat only at communion or in special loaves purchased for religious festivals at the behest of Spanish priests. Indians living in urban areas consumed more wheat—many were drafted into working as bakers—but their preference for corn tortillas remained strong, if only because wheat prices ran as much as ten times higher than corn. While wheat compared unfavorably to maize, many other Old World plants and animals found ready acceptance among the Native Americans. European livestock such as pigs, sheep, and chickens offered significant gains to their largely vegetarian diet, although cattle met with some disapproval because of the damage caused by grazing in corn fields. Indian gardeners also grew European vegetables including cabbages, cucumbers, onions, garlic, and lettuce.

Spanish cooks meanwhile adapted Old World techniques to New World ingredients, creating a criollo cuisine. Immigrants insisted on eating wheat bread and only the most impoverished subsisted on corn tortillas. Nevertheless, American game such as turkey fit readily into recipes for stewed chickens, and indigenous beans proved superior to Iberian chickpeas. Other culinary changes resulted from the inability to obtain traditional ingredients such as grapes and olives, neither of which grew in New Spain for reasons of both climate and imperial policy. Criollos learned to fry with pork fat instead of olive oil, but found no universally accepted substitute for wine, and drank whatever they could afford: imported sherry, sugarcane brandy, native *pulque,* or sweetened chocolate.

Criollo cuisine acquired its most distinctive tastes from Native American chili peppers. The addition of various red and black chilies transformed fragrant Arabic stews into uniquely Mexican *moles.* Peppers likewise imparted a delicious new piquancy to *chorizo,* an already-spicy smoked sausage from Extremadura, and to Iberian *adobos,* vinegar marinades used to preserve meats. Perhaps the most interesting twist given by criollo cooks to European cuisine was the creation of *chilies en nogada,* a green chili pepper stuffed with minced meat, covered with a pure white walnut sauce, and garnished with bright red pomegranate seeds. The green, white, and red of the Mexican flag have made this a modern national icon, but historical texts demonstrate its roots in Renaissance Italy. Diego Granado in his 1599 *Libro del arte de cocina* (Book of the Art of Cooking) gave a comparable recipe for stuffed cabbage in "a composition called *nogada.*"

The distinctiveness of criollo cuisine became all the more prominent as European cooking styles changed in the eighteenth century. French chefs began this transformation about 1700 by replacing the sugar and spices prominent in medieval foods with the salt and herbs characteristic of modern European cooking. Enlightenment ideals dictated that a cook should reveal rather than distort the true nature of foods. Medical literature meanwhile banished spicy foods as a positive health hazard, leaving Mexican cuisine as a self-conscious anachronism. José Luis Juárez, in a study of eighteenth-century manuscript cookbooks, has shown that criollo chefs responded to this attack with some ambivalence, adopting French names but not their techniques. A typical recipe for *sopa francesa* insisted on French bread, but also included many spices that had disappeared from continental cooking. After Independence, the distinction provided by chilies constituted a central theme in the construction of a national cuisine.

Mexico's first published cookbooks appeared in 1831 as part of a broader instructional literature providing women with standards of proper domestic behavior. These first two works, *El cocinero mexicano* (The Mexican Chef) and the *Novísimo arte de cocina* (New Art of Cooking), were followed by at least a dozen other volumes spaced relatively evenly over the course of the century. Multiple editions bring the number up to nearly 40, with a few thousand copies for each run, for a total of as many as 100,000 cookbooks. Additional recipes printed in domestic manuals, calendars, and newspapers assured that cooking instructors reached a broad audience, at least among the middle and upper classes. The authors of these works generally remained anonymous, but most were probably men. Only one book printed before 1890 claimed a female author, the 1836 *Nuevo y sencillo arte de cocina, repostería y refrescos, dispuesto por una mexicana, y experimentado por personas inteligentes antes de darse a la prensa* (New and Simple Art of Cooking, Baking, and Refreshments, arranged by a Mexican woman, and tested by intelligent people before being sent to the press).

These published cookbooks reinforced the ideals of a patriarchal society and patriotic behavior. Gender roles that evolved over the course of the nineteenth century established an inherently unequal relationship, placing women under the authority of men, yet assigning mothers responsibility for the family's moral order. Jacinto Anduiza elaborated this theme in an 1893 cookbook that attributed many of the worst domestic calamities to failures in the kitchen. He warned that men dissatisfied with their wives' cooking would seek their pleasures in taverns and bordellos. Moreover, cookbooks contained explicitly nationalist language to help ensure that women raised patriotic sons. The Mexican Chef began this insistence on culinary patriotism, praising "truly national" spicy dishes and deriding delicate European palates unaccustomed to chili peppers. His successors likewise differentiated the national cuisine from foreign foods and advertised recipes specifically accommodated to Mexican palates.

While emphasizing national unity, cookbook authors also recognized the regional diversity of Mexican cuisine. Common references appeared to the *moles* of Puebla and Oaxaca, the black beans and seafoods of Veracruz, and the grilled meats of Guadalajara and Monterrey. Yet compared with modern works, nineteenth-century cookbooks included within the national cuisine only a handful of regional traditions, essentially those with heavy Hispanic settlements. The virtual monopoly of criollo kitchens becomes apparent in the comparative treatment of *mole*. Oaxaca is known today as "the land of seven *moles*," but nineteenth-century works ignored the more indigenous versions such as *verde*, a green stew perfumed with the incomparable anis-like fragrance of *hoja santa*. They focused instead on a black version, *negro*, which like Puebla's dish, contained the spices characteristic of medieval stews.

By defining regional cuisines in criollo terms, authors ignored a gastronomic geography dating back to the pre-Columbian times. Native culinary traditions centered around civilizations such as the Maya, Mexica, Zapoteca, Mixteca, and Totonaca—ethnic groups that rarely corresponded to Mexican political boundaries. The Huasteca, for example, split between the states of San Luis Potosí and northern Veracruz, contained only a small Hispanic population with little national significance. Nevertheless, large numbers of native communities thrived in the area and developed an enormously sophisticated cuisine. Modern ethnographers have counted 42 distinct varieties of tamales, including the meter-long *zacahuil*. Other regional dishes such as the Pacific Coast hominy stew *pozole* likewise received little notice because of their indigenous associations.

Elite cooking manuals gave little attention to the lower-class cuisine of corn. Many cookbooks contained no recipes at all for tamales, *gorditas,* or *quesadillas,* and books that did mention them consigned them to a ghetto labeled "light brunches." Of course, a lack of written recipes does not prove that elites never ate popular foods. The servants who did the cooking hardly needed instructions for making enchiladas, and most were illiterate anyway. Nevertheless, cookbooks often contained positive censures against the derogation of serving Indian foods. One volume explained that the wealthy had virtually no use for the popular corn drink *atole*. The *Diccionario de cocina* (Dictionary of Cooking), published in 1845, pointedly questioned the morals of any family that ate tamales, the food of "the lower orders."

By the time of Porfirio Díaz's dictatorship in the late nineteenth century, the nascent national cuisine, already divided along regional and class lines, had split further according to gender. As Científico elites sought to develop Mexican society by emulating all things European, French haute cuisine prepared by male chefs became de rigueur for fashionable Mexicans. To supply this demand, translations appeared of classic French volumes such as a cookbook by the Paris Jockey Club's celebrated chef Jules Gouffé, and Mexican kitchen manuals included recipes for continental entrées including veal blanquette and chicken cardinal. Aspiring gourmets indulged their appetites for continental cuisine in Mexico City restaurants and social clubs such as the Tívoli of San Cosme and Sylvain Daumont. Banquet menus from these establishments testify to the cosmopolitan tastes of the country's leaders. A dinner for 500 held in the National Theater to celebrate President Porfirio Díaz's birthday in 1891 featured French food, wines, and cognac. Only men were seated for this banquet; their wives had to view the proceedings from a balcony, a significant indication of their exclusion from full citizenship in the patriarchal nation. The quest for imported civility reached its pinnacle in 1910 at the centennial of Independence in a series of banquets honoring President Díaz, cabinet members, and foreign dignitaries. Not a single Mexican dish appeared at any of the score of dinners dedicated to this patriotic occasion. Even the Mexican colony in New York commemorated the centennial with French food.

But at the same time, women began to write their own manuscript and community cookbooks in which they defined an alternate vision of the national community and its cuisine based on Hispanic and even pre-Columbian traditions. By the 1880s foreign travelers already had noticed a growing number of women who filled notebooks with recipes, many copied from family and friends. These manuscripts often served as albums recording family traditions, with dishes handed down from mothers and grandmothers. The fact that the older women often were illiterate added further to the value of their daughters' books. The exchange of cooking tips also reached beyond the extended family to become the focus for Catholic charities, which were one of the few legitimate female activities outside the home. A group of matrons in Guadalajara prepared a recipe manual to support the local orphanage, and several community cookbooks from Mexico City were dedicated to works such as cathedrals for Saint Rafael and Saint Vincent DePaul.

In 1896, Vicenta Torres de Rubio extended this community of cooks throughout the Republic in her *Cocina michoacana,* a serialized guide to the cuisine of Michoacán. Printed in the provincial town of Zamora and sold by subscription, it began with local recipes submitted by women within the state. Nevertheless, she soon expanded her audience to reach cooks from all over the country. A woman from Celaya sent her recipe for "Heroic Nopales," from Guadalajara came a green chili lamb stew, a Mexico City matron offered her favorite meat glaze, and a reader in the border town of Nuevo Laredo even presented her "Hens from the Gastronomic Frontier." By printing recipes from throughout Mexico, Torres provided the first genuine forum for a national cuisine. Contributors exchanged recipes with middle-class counterparts they had never met and began to experiment with regional dishes, combining them in new ways that transcended local traditions. Thus women began to imagine their own national community in the familiar terms of the kitchen, rather than as an alien political entity formulated by men and served up to them in didactic literature.

This exchange of recipes in community cookbooks even began to cross established class and ethnic lines. Unlike the usual practice of segregating enchiladas and other corn dishes into a section of "light brunches," the community cookbooks tended to integrate these with other recipes for meats and vegetables. One volume prepared by a charitable women's organization in Mexico City gave more recipes for enchiladas than for any other type of food. Vicenta Torres made a virtue of including recipes of explicitly Indian origin, assuring readers that these "secrets of the indigenous classes" would be appropriate at any party. Along with tamales, she included *gordita* cordials, *pozole* de Quiroga, and *carnero al pastor* (Shepherd's mutton), but out of deference to her Porfirian audience, she set them apart with the label *indigenista.*

Care must be taken in interpreting this acceptance of native food as an indication that ties of gender were breaking down lines of class. Even middle-class women, after all, generally could count on a household servant to do the difficult work of grinding corn and chilies. Moreover, these same women shared with elites an admiration for French haute cuisine. Yet they also embraced a genuinely Mexican national cuisine based on colonial *moles* and even pre-Columbian tamales that were rejected by Eurocentric male elites. Being excluded from power themselves, perhaps women simply had less motivation to maintain the distinctiveness of criollo culture. After all, they based their image of the nation on the Virgin of Guadalupe, a symbol shared with the Indian masses, rather than on the trappings of western industrial society idealized by elite men.

This Porfirian faith in imported progress was replaced in the Revolution of 1910 by *indigenismo,* a somewhat misleadingly named nationalist ideology that revalued the indigenous past yet looked to the mestizo for Mexico's future. The search for modern Mexico's roots in the pre-Columbian past, which inspired the mural renaissance led by Diego Rivera and the restoration of Teotihuacan by Manuel Gamio, also gave new legitimacy to Native American foods.

Liberal intellectual Andrés Molina Enríquez, in his prophetic book *Los grandes problemas nacionales* (1909), stated that maize "represented in an absolutely indubitable manner the national cuisine." Folklorist Virginia Rodríguez Rivera searched the country, interviewing everyone from poor indigenous cooks to wealthy criollo matrons, to record traditional Mexican recipes. Artist Frida Kahlo and her avantgarde friends meanwhile recreated pre-Columbian banquets of tamales garnished with Quetzalcoatl figures as an expression of their national identity.

More conventional middle-class women of the post-Revolutionary era likewise explored domestic representations of *lo mexicano.* Community cookbooks, first produced at the turn of the century, became ever more common. These social gatherings of women sharing family recipes developed into organized cooking classes, and successful teachers in turn provided recipes to women's magazines and published cookbooks of their own. The most prolific of these teachers, Josefina Velázquez de León, traveled throughout the republic, holding cooking classes and collecting regional recipes. Her most important work, *Platillos regionales de la República mexicana* (1946), gathered for the first time in a single volume the distinctive dishes of each state. Upon her death in 1968, she had published more than 150 cookbooks exalting tamales and enchiladas as culinary manifestations of Mexican nationalism. Her audience came from the rapidly growing middle class, the wives of businessmen and professionals who shared her vision of the mestizo nation.

These cookbooks portrayed an image of Mexico quite different from the official ideology of the ruling party. Middle-class female cookbook authors paid little attention to traditional heroes of Mexican history such as Benito Juárez and Emiliano Zapata. Instead, they centered their culinary history on the legendary seventeenth-century nuns credited with inventing *mole poblano,* on Emperor Agustín Iturbide, the conservative Independence leader who reputedly inspired the creation of *chiles en nogada,* and on the ill-fated French-imposed emperor Maximilian and empress Carlota, who supposedly introduced French cooking to Mexico. Conservative, religious figures thus formed the pantheon of domestic, middle-class patriotism. The inclusion of tamales and enchiladas within the national cuisine represented not the radicalism of Frida Kahlo but rather an effort to assert hegemony by appropriating Native American symbols and sanitizing them of their former lower-class associations.

Twentieth-century Mexican authors have imagined cuisine to be a symbol of their national identity, a mestizo blend of Native American and Spanish influences. Virtually every dish in the modern kitchen betrays this mixed heritage, from European sausages and stews infiltrated by American chili peppers to the indigenous beans and tamales now cooked with fat from the conquistadors' pigs. Nevertheless, Mexican elites accepted this blending only with great reluctance, preferring the more fashionable culture of Europe. The creation of Mexico's national cuisine is therefore a story of contributions to society made by subordinate groups, both the wealthy women who handed down recipes for colonial *moles* and the poor ones who preserved the pre-Columbian art of making tamales. These culinary traditions, once scorned by a Eurocentric elite, now provide lasting symbols of *lo mexicano*.

See also Coffee; Food Production, Consumption, and Policy; Maguey; Maize; Sugar

Select Bibliography

Appadurai, Arjun, "How to Make a National Cuisine: Cookbooks in Contemporary India." *Comparative Studies in Society and History* 23 (1988).

Coe, Sophie D., *America's First Cuisines.* Austin: University of Texas Press, 1994.

Corcuera de Mancera, Sonia, *Entre gula y templanza: Un aspecto de la historia mexicana.* 2nd edition, Mexico City: Fondo de Cultura Económica, 1990.

Lomnitz, Larissa Adler, and Marisol Pérez-Lizaur, *A Mexican Elite Family, 1820–1980: Kinship, Class, and Culture.* Princeton, New Jersey: Princeton University Press, 1987.

Novo, Salvador, *Cocina mexicana; o, Historia gastronómica de la Ciudad de México.* Mexico City: Porrúa, 1967; 6th edition, 1993.

Ross, Oliver D., "Wheat Growing in Northern New Spain." *North Dakota Quarterly* 45 (Summer 1977).

Super, John C., *Food, Conquest, and Colonization in Sixteenth-Century Spanish America.* Albuquerque: University of New Mexico Press, 1988.

—Jeffrey M. Pilcher

D

DAY OF THE DEAD

The Day of the Dead has long been one of Mexico's richest, most varied, and famous annual holidays. Foreign visitors flock to Mexico during the last days of October and first days of November to witness a fantastic, original, and creative cultural display. Candies, breads, paper cutouts, and toys fashioned of plastic and clay, all playing humorously on the theme of death, are evident everywhere. Miniature sweets in the form of skulls, skeletons, and caskets give evidence of an almost irreverent confrontation with mortality. During November 1 and 2, Mexicans visit cemeteries to clean and adorn the tombs of deceased relatives. *Ofrendas,* or offerings, consisting of flowers, candles, and food, are arranged artistically on graves in honor of the deceased. In some parts of the country, including celebrated places like Mizquic immediately south of Mexico City and Purépecha villages around Lake Pátzcuaro in the state of Michoacán, family members hold an all-night vigil at the graves of the departed. Throughout the country, people erect home altars, usually made of plain wooden tables elaborately adorned with offerings of candles, flowers, food, and drink, especially comestibles that the deceased was known to enjoy.

Some Mexicans claim that the souls of the departed watch over their living relatives during the Day of the Dead. Negligent family members await punishment, whether on earth or in the afterlife. Throughout Mexico, this belief is invoked to explain the substantial outlay of time, money, and energy invested in the two-day ceremony. At the same time, it is clear that the holiday provides a boost to local economies, through its promotion of tourism and the lucrative sale of sweets, candles, and flowers. Increasingly, Day of the Dead iconography is employed by small businesses and large department stores to augment the sale of industrial, mass-produced products. Lively drawings of animated skulls and skeletons adorn bakeries, candy stores, and supermarkets throughout large Mexican cities. Reproductions of the *catrina*—the famous female dandy, sporting fleshless face, billowy scarf, and wide-brimmed, plumed hat—are used by salespeople everywhere to attract customers from all social classes and ethnic backgrounds. If the Day of the Dead was ever restricted to a particular social class or ethnic group, the holiday is now celebrated in every geographic region and stratum of Mexican society. It has become among the most salient Mexican national symbols.

It is essential to note that, although the Day of the Dead is associated with Mexico and Mexico alone, its celebration coincides with pan–Roman Catholic feast days, specifically All Saints' Day on November 1 and All Souls' Day on November 2. The term *Día de Muertos* is essentially Mexican, although perhaps the earliest use of this term comes from a Catalan document produced on October 15, 1671, by the Barcelona silversmith's guild in which reference is made to the *Diada dels Morts.* Throughout the Spanish-speaking world outside of Mexico, All Saints' Day is generally called *el Día de Todos Santos,* while All Souls' Day is referred to variously as *el Día de Animas* (Souls' Day) or *el Día de los Fieles Difuntos* (the Day of the Faithful Deceased). In the state of Michoacán, the most popular term is *la Noche de Muertos* (the Night of the Dead), which emphasizes the importance of the all-night candlelight vigil on November 1–2 to the celebration of the holiday in this region.

To the Vatican, only one thing counts in the celebration of All Saints' and All Souls' Days: the observance of special masses on November 1 in honor of the saints and on November 2 in honor of the souls in purgatory. Special masses date from medieval times. During the first third of the eighth century, Pope Gregory III set aside November 1 as a sacred occasion for the Christian faithful to commemorate all the saints. All Souls' Day, November 2, is liturgically the more critical day of the two. On this date, the Office for the Dead and Requium Masses are celebrated in sympathy with the deceased in order to help them achieve final purification. The choice of November 2 is generally attributed to St. Odilo (d. 1048), the fifth abbot of Cluny. By the fourteenth century, both these dates had assumed a permanently important place in the liturgical calendar. Nowadays, the Catholic Church requires that parish priests recite one special mass on November 1 and another on November 2, although three masses on November 2 are more common: one in honor of the departed souls, a second in honor of a cause designated each year by the pope, and the third in recognition of a cause designated by the parish priest himself.

These special masses constitute what might be called the official celebration of these two feast days. Most observers of Mexico would agree, however, that masses are not the most salient parts of the celebration. The majority of the activities and artistic displays connected with the Day of the Dead represent a folk elaboration, a deviation from orthodox religious practices. Halloween is the U.S. version of this popular celebration, a version so secularized that only the centrality of sweets, the incorporation of ritualized begging, and the prevalence of skeleton costumes and skull-like Jack-o-Lanterns connects it to the contemporary Mexican event.

Scholars have engaged in an ongoing debate about the origins of the Day of the Dead. Because the Day of the Dead is a flamboyant, colorful holiday of considerable renown, it is often cited as expressing a uniquely Mexican view of death, one that demonstrates, in Octavio Paz's words, that "The Mexican . . . is familiar with death, jokes about it, caresses it, sleeps with it, celebrates it; it is one of his toys and his most steadfast love." The alleged Mexican lightheartedness toward death often is contrasted with U.S. denial of death and Spanish lugubriousness. The Day of the Dead is taken as the epitome of Mexican attitudes toward death and dying. Perhaps for this reason, the Day of the Dead, more than any other Mexican ritual, is often said to be either a basically pre-Conquest Indian concept with a European Catholic veneer or a near-seamless fusion of pre-Conquest and Roman Catholic ceremonial practices. The celebration has become a marker of Mexican identity. Consider for example the opinion of scholars Robert V. Childs and Patricia B. Altman, who claim that

> the beliefs and practices associated with contemporary observances of Día de Muertos, although not a direct and simple survival of pre-Hispanic ritual, have their roots in the ancient religions of Mesoamerica. . . . However successful the Spanish church may have been in the destruction of state cults, it is apparent on close scrutiny that much "Catholicism" of contemporary Indian communities is pre-Hispanic in origin, especially the beliefs and customs related to death and the dead.

True, the ancient Mexica (Aztecs) expressed an inordinate concern with death. They celebrated a number of feast days in honor of the dead, among the most prominent being Miccailhuitontli, or the "Feast of the Little Dead Ones," and Miccailhuitl, or "Feast of the Adult Dead." In contemporary Mexico, in fact, November 1 is generally the day in which people mourn the death of children, while November 2 is the day set aside for mourning those who died in maturity. To this extent, there is a probable correspondence between ancient Mexica practices and those today. Further, the Mexica displayed an elaborate iconography of death. Rows of human skulls lined the four sides of the rectangular *tzompantli,* or skull rack, atop which countless sacrificial victims died. Several Mexica deities, including the death god Mictlantecuhli and the earth goddess Coatlicue, are portrayed with fleshless faces.

Much of the justification for claiming pre-Columbian antecedents derives from such ancient Mesoamerican iconography, with its undeniable plethora of skulls and skeletons, corresponding to the equally plentiful presence of similar motifs during the Day of the Dead today. Then, too, the Mexica, like contemporary Mexicans, incorporated anthropomorphic sweets into their religious ceremonies. Periodically, throughout the ritual year, the Mexica fashioned images out of wood, which they covered with *tzoalli,* or amaranth seed dough, shaped in human form. The images, usually representing deities, were distributed for consumption among certain social classes. It of course has been tempting for scholars to interpret these *tzoalli* as ancient precursors of the special breads known as *pan de muerto* as well as of the skull-shaped sugar candies widely sold during late October and early November in Mexico today.

And yet, it is important to refine our comparisons and recognize critical distinctions between ancient and contemporary skulls and skeletons. For one thing, skulls today tend to be humorously decorated sugar confections that are named after and given as presents to living friends and relatives. No contemporary Mexican death ceremony utilizes a real human skull. By contrast, the Mexica used real skulls as decorative motifs. Although these might be adorned with eyes, noses, or other features made of semi-precious stone, the basis of the statuary was actual bone. Anthropomorphic candies like *tzoalli,* on the other hand, represented full-fleshed supernatural beings, not live humans. Moreover these figures were serious in intent and, insofar as we know, completely devoid of the playfulness that characterizes contemporary Day of the Dead sweets. In fact, there is no evidence that the Mexica cult of death even remotely approximated the humorous tone that characterizes the Day of the Dead as we know it.

For the historical record as well as for defining Mexican national identity, it is important to analyze precisely what, if anything, is unique about the Day of the Dead. To begin, consider several ritual elements that usually are considered traditional in the popular celebration of this holiday. First comes the graveside vigil at cemeteries. Family visits to the graves of the departed are absolutely critical to the Mexican celebration of the Day of the Dead. Visits to the graves occur throughout Spain and parts of Latin America, although they almost always take place during the daytime. Most of Mexico in fact follows this general pattern. However, in specific regions of rural and urban Mexico, the graveside vigil, normally called *la velación* (after the candle lighting), occurs principally at night.

Where nighttime visits to the graves occur, the event has become a major tourist attraction for both foreign tourists and urban Mexicans. Scholar Jesús Angel Ochoa Zazueta, who has studied the impact of tourism on the Day of the Dead in Mixquic, says that visitors are required to pay an entrance fee to observe the cemetery vigil. "The visitors on this day pay for everything," he adds. In Tzintzuntzan, on the shores of Lake Pátzcuaro, the enormous influx of outsiders to the cemetery on the night of November 1–2 has induced some mourners to insist that tourists pay for taking photographs. Without doubt the nighttime vigil is an expression of sincere concern for the ongoing spiritual presence of the departed. Nonetheless, it also assumes a theatrical dimension in which mourners enact what they know to be an exotic performance in exchange for cash. In urban Mexico, an opposite process occurs: mourners actually pay performers, specifically musicians, to sing at the gravesides. At Panteón Dolores, the municipal cemetery in Mexico City, mariachis and other musicians wander among the graves seeking work. Mourners hire these musical groups to sing to the departed.

A second important element in the Mexican celebration of the Day of the Dead is the erection of altars in homes, commercial establishments, and public institutions. Altars in honor of the saints are, of course, an integral feature of homes, stores, hospitals, and schools throughout Spain and Latin America. But altars of extraordinary elaborateness and exuberance erected in honor of the departed are a special feature of the Mexican celebration of All Saints' and All Souls' Days. The simplest home altars consist solely of candles and flowers, almost always the yellow *cempasúchil* (from the Nahuatl *cempoaochitl*). Most include bread and fruit, sugar and *mole;* beer, tequila, and other liquor; and pictures of saints and of the deceased.

The decoration of home altars is increasingly replicated on tombstones and in public urban settings. The grave site of Pedro Infante, at the Panteón Jardín in Mexico City, is replete with head shots and photographs showing the movie idol in his most famous roles. Taped recordings of his singing blare from a loudspeaker resting to one side of his tomb. At the Plaza Río de Janeiro in the Colonia Roma, Mexico City, the gay community erects dozens of altars in honor of AIDS victims. In addition to candles, flowers, photographs, and sugar skulls, these altars display condoms and informational pamphlets. Schoolchildren create altars to decorate school entrances and hallways, and supermarket employees use store products to create elaborate Day of the Dead altars, which greet customers at store entrances.

A third critical element of the Day of the Dead celebration is ritualized bell ringing and begging. Traditionally, both in Spain and Latin America, the night of November 1–2 has been one in which the church bells should *doblar,* that is, toll in lugubrious indication of mourning, precisely in the manner that occurs when an individual in the community dies. In Mexico, religious brotherhoods or male youth typically have been in charge of the bell ringing. It has been characteristic of All Saints' and Souls' Days, too, that charity is dispensed. Hence, in both traditional Spain and Mexico, needy members of the community would walk from grave site to grave site, asking for the right to pray in honor of the deceased; in return they receive bread, fruit, or other foodstuffs from the mourners. In communities of the state of Michoacán, the youth who are in charge of bell tolling traditionally have had the right to go from house to house, begging for food and drink. On the night of November 1–2, they stay up taking turns ringing the church bells, while others built a fire in the churchyard, which they would use to stay warm and cook the food collected on this occasion. Children throughout Mexico have long used the Day of the Dead as an opportunity to beg passersby for *mi muertito* (little dead one)—the term used to refer to any sweet or item of food the targeted adult is willing to donate. Nowadays children walk through grave sites and city streets with small plastic Jack-o-Lanterns, begging for *"mi Halloween,"* which denotes any small coin or candy.

Ritualized begging and bell ringing, graveside vigils, altars with simple or elaborate offerings—all of these elements are associated elsewhere than Mexico with the celebration of All Saints' and All Souls' Days. Nonetheless, it would be difficult to find another country that celebrates this holiday with the color, exuberance, and sheer outlet of money and effort that can be found in Mexico. To this extent, the Mexican Day of the Dead is unique.

There are two additional ways in which the Day of the Dead is unique. First is the prevalence of humor. As befits any extensive mortuary ritual, the Day of the Dead certainly has its serious, mournful side. However, this annual celebration is and has long been used to poke fun not only at death itself but also at political leaders and public figures. The traditional vehicle for ridicule, and one that seems to grow in prominence with every passing year, is the *calavera,* literally, skull. *Calaveras* come in the form of sugar, chocolate, and amaranth seed sculptures molded as skulls. Candy *calaveras* come in all sizes; they are whimsically decorated with multicolored designs and the name of a living person, to whom the item is presented as a gift.

The term *calavera* refers also to satirical poetry composed to highlight the shortcomings of the person to whom it is dedicated. Friends and relatives write *calaveras* for one another, thereby demonstrating a important social tie; the assumption is that poet and recipient are so close that the bond between them can withstand the shock of ridicule. More prominent, however, is the *calavera* in the public domain, mainly newspapers and magazine supplements, in which artistic caricatures of politicians and well-known literary figures, screen stars, singers, and other celebrities are accompanied by often biting, satirical poems. The poetic *calavera* provides a safe, predictable outlet for the expression of hostility against the privileged and wealthy. Just as the sugar *calavera* implicitly communicates the idea that none of us is immune from death, so the poetic *calavera* shows that the wealthy and powerful are no better than the mass of humanity. The *calavera* is a brilliant social leveling mechanism. It, together with the rest of the humor and whimsy that characterize the Day of the Dead, is unique to Mexico.

A related feature unique to the Mexican Day of the Dead is the pervasiveness of sugar skulls, caskets, cadavers, and other mortuary figurines. To be sure, people in different parts of Spain, Italy, and other European countries eat sweets specially fashioned for All Saints' and All Souls' Days; on the island of Mallorca, they sell *panetets de mort* (little dead breads); in Spain *ossos de sant* (saints' bones); and in Portugal, *maminhos do preto* (little dark breasts). All of these utilize sugar but have a base of some other substance, be it nuts or flour. Only in Mexico are the figurines actually fashioned from sugar in a paste known as *alfeñique*. The earliest evidence of this practice comes from the Capuchin friar Francisco de Ajofrín, who in the mid–eighteenth century wrote,

Before the Day of the Dead they sell a thousand figures of little sheep, lambs, etc. of sugar paste, which they call *ofrenda,* and it is a gift which must be given obligatorily to boys and girls of the houses where one has acquaintance. They also sell coffins, tombs, and a thousand figures of the dead, clerics, monks, nuns and all denominations, bishops, horesmen, for which there is a great market.

Sugar figurines have been a unique and central part of the Mexican Day of the Dead for at least the past 250 years.

The Day of the Dead, in the form we know it today, probably dates from colonial times. It shares much with All Saints' and All Souls' Days traditions elsewhere in the West and Latin America, but is sufficiently elaborate and unique to be considered essentially Mexican. There is very little evidence—with the notable exceptions of the iconography of skulls and skeletons and the separation of days devoted to the mourning for youth and adults—that the holiday derives from pre-Conquest ritual practices. More likely, it is a product of colonial circumstances, in which death through disease and warfare was so rampant that conditions were ripe for an elaborate mortuary ritual to take firm hold. It is possible, too, that both the humor and sugar figurines operated in the past as a psychological defense against the heartbreaking reality of extraordinarily high mortality rates.

Nowadays, the Day of the Dead operates principally as a marker of Mexican national identity. Fifty years ago, along the vast northern border of Mexico with the United States, it was uncommon—even exotic—for Mexicans to celebrate the Day of the Dead. The Day of the Dead was associated in the minds of these northerners with central and southern Mexico, while these *norteños* themselves dressed their children in scary costumes and went trick-or-treating in celebration of Halloween. Slowly, from the 1960s on, the Day of the Dead spread throughout the entire Mexican republic, as this holiday became increasingly identified with Mexico. Halloween, by contrast, became associated in Mexican minds with the United States. Especially since the 1980s, however, Halloween has begun to take hold in Mexico, as Sanborns, Superama, Aurora, and other large and powerful commercial chain establishments use sophisticated advertising techniques to sell Halloween masks, costumes, candy, and plastic Jack-o-Lanterns. Many Mexicans, especially the intellectual and artistic elite, express resentment of this incursion of Halloween into central Mexico. They detect in this trend a threat to what they consider to be the survival of pre-Hispanic customs as represented by the Day of the Dead.

And yet, most of the Mexican bourgeoisie and working class seem to have adopted this American holiday with fervor.

At the same time, the Day of the Dead has crossed the border into the United States, where Chicanos and other citizens of Mexican ancestry have made the holiday an expression of national identity. Throughout the southwestern United States, elaborate Day of the Dead altars are erected. Increasingly, too, family members visit and adorn the graves of their departed relatives on November 1 and 2. Schoolchildren in California and states as far away from Mexico as New Jersey learn not only about Halloween but also the Day of the Dead. The Day of the Dead has thus become transnational, a holiday that expresses Mexican identity, to be sure, but also a celebration that increasingly belongs to citizens of both Mexico and the United States.

Select Bibliography

Ajofrín, Francisco de, *Diario del Viaje que por Orden de la Sagrada: Congregación de Propaganda Fide Hizo a la América Septentrional en el Siglo XVIII,* edited by Vicente Castañeda y Alcover. 2 vols., Madrid: Real Academia de la Historia, 1958.

Brandes, Stanley, *Power and Persuasion: Fiestas and Social Control in Rural Mexico.* Philadelphia: University of Pennsylvania Press, 1988.

Brodman, Barbara, *The Mexican Cult of Death in Myth and Literature.* Gainesville: University Presses of Florida, 1976.

Carmichael, Elizabeth, and Chloë Sayer, *The Skeleton at the Feast: The Day of the Dead in Mexico.* London: British Museum, 1991; Austin: University of Texas Press, 1992.

Childs, Robert V., and Patricia B. Altman, *Vive tu Recuerdo: Living Traditions in the Mexican Days of the Dead.* Los Angeles: Museum of Cultural History, 1982.

Curet, Francesc, *Visions Barcelonins, 1760–1860.* Barcelona: Dalmau and Jover, 1953.

Ingham, John M., *Mary, Michael, and Lucifer: Folk Catholicism in Central Mexico.* Austin: University of Texas Press, 1986.

Nutini, Hugo, *Todos Santos in Rural Tlaxcala: A Syncretic, Expressive, and Symbolic Analysis of the Cult of the Dead.* Princeton, New Jersey: Princeton University Press, 1988.

Ochoa Zazueta, Jesús Angel, *La Muerte y los Muertos: Culto, Servicio, Ofrenda y Humor de una Comunidad.* Mexico City: Secretaria de Educacion Publica, 1974.

Paz, Octavio, *El laberinto de la Soledad.* Mexico City: Cuadernos Americanos, 1950; 2nd edition, Mexico City: Fondo de Cultura Económica, 1959; as *The Labyrinth of Solitude: Life and Thought in Mexico,* New York and London: Grove, 1961.

—STANLEY BRANDES

DE FUENTES, FERNANDO

1894–1958 • Director

A recent poll of leading Mexican film critics revealed that they overwhelmingly consider *Vámonos con Pancho Villa* (1935) to be the best movie ever made in Mexico. Its director, Fernando de Fuentes, was the first filmmaker of note in the country, and his unsurpassed interpretations of the Mexican Revolution are as fundamental to the culture as are his contributions to what might be described as the favorite national genres: the ranchera and the "mothers' melodrama." Early sound film production was dominated by foreigners: Russians who accompanied Sergey Eisenstein in the making of *¡Qué viva México!* (1930), Spaniards who had passed through Hollywood, Cubans, and U.S. citizens who somehow ended up there. De Fuentes was one of the first Mexicans given a chance to direct sound films in his country, and the results set standards that have rarely been equalled.

Fernando de Fuentes was born in Veracruz on December 13, 1894. After working in the theater and as manager of the Olympia Cinema, de Fuentes served for several years as editor and assistant director of films. In 1932 he was offered the opportunity to direct by Compañía Nacional Productora de Películas. Almost immediately, de Fuentes began exploring the history of the cataclysmic upheaval whose cultural expression then resounded principally in the extraordinary murals of Diego Rivera, David Alfaro Siqueiros, and José Clemente Orozco. The "Revolutionary Trilogy" of *Prisionero 13* (1933), *El compadre Mendoza* (1933), and *¡Vámonos con Pancho Villa!* (1935) does not in any way glorify the civil war, as had the first sound film made on the subject, *Revolución (La sombra de Pancho Villa)* (1932), and as would be typical of films on this event. Rather, the trilogy is more in the tone of Orozco than of Rivera or Siqueiros: the films emphasize the pain and torment, rather than the transformations; they exude a disenchantment with the Revolution's shortcomings, instead of celebrating its achievements.

Prisionero 13 recounts the story of Colonel Carrasco, an alcoholic officer who serves Porfirio Díaz and then Victoriano Huerta. His wife leaves him during the reign of Díaz, taking their son. The film flashes forward to the Revolution: Carrasco is to execute conspirators against Huerta's usurpation but is bribed by the mother of one to free him. A substitute is needed, and Carrasco's soldiers unknowingly capture his son. Carrasco's ex-wife alerts him to the danger, and he hurries to save him. He would be too late but awakens to discover that it was all a nightmare caused by drinking. The artificial return to the Porfiriato at the film's end was evidently tacked on in a vain effort to mollify the military's objections to its "denigrating" image of the army, but the change apparently did not go far enough; *Prisionero 13* quickly was withdrawn from circulation. Nonetheless, Juan Bustillo Oro, later an important director, contrasted this work to the "servile

imitation" of foreign films typical of the country's cinema. He called for movies with "themes that are flesh of our flesh and the breath of our sweet and equally terrible land"; for him, *Prisionero 13* was "the first Mexican film."

El compadre Mendoza also provoked commentaries about national character, although they were protestations against identifying Mexicans with a "vile traitor." Rosalio Mendoza is an opportunistic hacienda owner who pretends to be friends to all sides, something he demonstrates by wining and dining his visitors under a portrait of the appropriate leader, depending upon whether they are Zapatistas, Huertistas, or Carrancistas. He becomes close friends, and later compadres, with the Zapatista general Nieto. However, as the situation becomes increasingly difficult, he betrays Nieto to the Carrancistas and flees to Mexico City with his family. The film's "cruel and macabre" finale was much criticized, but de Fuentes replied that he was searching for an authentic aesthetic: "Mexican cinema ought to be a faithful reflection of our severe and tragic way of being . . . not a poor imitation of Hollywood."

¡Vámonos con Pancho Villa! demystified one of the great Revolutionary legends. Although the title creates the expectation that Villa would be a key figure, it is part of this film's brilliance to restrict his appearances to a few episodes. The movie's protagonists are six *campesinos* (peasants), "Los Leones de San Pablo," who join the bola largely because of Villa's charisma. However, despite the identification the film initially establishes with Villa and the Revolution, it insistently cuts back against that identification, alienating the viewer from Villa by showing his cruelty and making the Leones' deaths increasingly unheroic. When the first León dies, Villa recognizes his courage, but by the time the third is killed, the leader shrugs it off callously. The deaths of the last three Leones are metaphors for the self-destruction of the Revolution: the first is a victim of "friendly fire," the second dies in a suicidal game, and the third is killed by the only remaining León who, under orders from Villa, shoots his friend who is sick with smallpox, and walks away from the Revolution. The film has an alternative ending that is even harsher: Villa finds the last León, now safe on his ranch with his family. In order to remove any impediments to León rejoining the struggle, Villa kills his wife and daughter.

Immediately after finishing *Vámonos,* de Fuentes directed *Allá en el Rancho Grande* (1935); the progenitor of the *charro* genre, this immensely popular film introduced the Mexican singing cowboy in Latin America. The attraction of such mystified nostalgia for a never-existent Arcadia of song can be seen in the fact that in the year following *Rancho Grande's* release, more than one-half of the Mexican films produced were similar pastoral fantasies. The genre has continued to be a staple of Latin American cinema. Among genre figures, the *charro's* dominion is challenged by the Mexican mother. De Fuentes directed perhaps the most palatable of such movies, *La gallina clueca* (1941) starring Sara García, the character actress who became the national paradigm for the sainted, long-suffering, self-sacrificing mother. However, in de Fuentes's hands, the overworked oedipal melodrama is denied its usual histrionics; for many, this eminently watchable movie is the definitive work of this genre.

De Fuentes's career as a director went from the sublime to the ridiculous. In one year he plummeted from the heights of *¡Vámonos con Pancho Villa!* to the depths of *Allá en el Rancho Grande*. The enormous commercial success of the latter

film sealed de Fuentes's fate; it was popular because he was a talented director, but the rewards came at a high price. After *Vámonos*, de Fuentes settled into mediocre and conventional formula films. One senses that he had much more to offer. He died on July 4, 1958.

Select Bibliography

García Riera, Emilio, *Fernando de Fuentes (1894/1958)*. Mexico City: Cineteca Nacional, 1984.
Mraz, John, "La trilogía revolucionario de Fernando de Fuentes." *Nitrato de plata: Revista de cine* 18 (1994).

—JOHN MRAZ

DE LA BARRA, FRANCISCO LEÓN

1863–1939 • President

Best known as the interim president who bridged the gap between the dictatorship of Porfirio Díaz and the inauguration of Francisco I. Madero in 1911, Francisco León de la Barra was a multitalented diplomat and international lawyer whose career spanned four decades. The son of a Chilean immigrant who became a Liberal general during the War of the Reform and the French Intervention, de la Barra so excelled at his studies at the National Preparatory School that he received an appointment as instructor of mathematics and logic at age 21. Three years later he completed his law degree, writing his thesis on a facet of international law, the first of a series of monographs he produced during his lifetime.

At the same time, de la Barra began consulting for the minister of foreign relations, eventually becoming a career diplomat. Part of the Porfirian meritocracy, a group of highly trained and well qualified professionals who were promoted to significant positions because of their expertise, de la Barra was posted to the Southern Cone nations, the Low Countries, and as Mexico's envoy to the Hague Peace Conferences. He ultimately was appointed ambassador to the United States, the plum assignment in the diplomatic corps. His efforts to convince President William H. Taft to enforce U.S. neutrality laws during the Madero Rebellion of 1910 raised de la Barra's stock even higher with Porfirio Díaz, who elevated de la Barra to minister of foreign relations, second in line for the presidency in the reform cabinet of 1911.

De la Barra's promotion dovetailed with the plans of Francisco Madero and his civilian friends, who had been negotiating a settlement with Porfirio Díaz for months. The nature of the ongoing negotiations, which began in late November 1910 and continued through May 21, 1911, suggest strongly that Madero and his civilian allies wanted to

preserve the basic tenets of the Porfiriato, and not to foist a social revolution on Mexico. What prevented settlement earlier was Porfirio Díaz's reluctance to leave the presidency. Ultimately he capitulated in the Treaty of Ciudad Juárez and resigned, giving the civilian Maderistas control of the governorships and about half of the cabinet positions. Wanting a neutral apolitical figure to supervise new elections, the civilian Maderistas appointed Francisco León de la Barra provisional president.

De la Barra's presidency has always received mixed reviews. For proponents of law, order, and business development, his was the most stable regime of the decade, although far from the halcyon days of the Porfiriato. For the ultimate victors in the decade-long struggle, the de la Barra government was a betrayal of their ideals. A more accurate depiction lies between these two extremes. De la Barra announced in his inaugural address that he had three goals: the restoration of order, the conduct of free and democratic elections, and the continuation of the progressive reforms announced in the dying days of the Porfiriato. He enjoyed only partial success in his first goal, the restoration of order. In many states over the course of the summer of 1911, life nearly returned to normal, with only sporadic disturbances. The initiators of most of these disturbances tended to be former rural Maderista soldiers, and many of the most troublesome of these had joined the revolution only shortly before Díaz's surrender. De la Barra's government reaffirmed its intention to discharge these irregular forces, take their weapons, remove them from the federal payroll, and send them home.

The rural Maderistas often resisted the mustering-out policy, however, preferring their status as soldiers, which provided regular high wages and afforded them the opportunity to settle old scores and revise the social structure in the countryside. Tensions between federal soldiers and the former insurgents culminated in the mid-July clash in downtown Puebla. De la Barra blamed his Maderista minister of the interior, Emilio Vázquez Gómez, for the Puebla fiasco, and discharged him with Madero's consent. Some insurgent generals saw this dismissal as the triumph of the "reaction" and complained bitterly, but most politicians went along with de la Barra.

After Vázquez Gómez's resignation, the quest for pacification enjoyed more success. The only significant exception was in Morelos, where Emiliano Zapata wanted no part of demobilization. Zapata demanded immediate agrarian reform, but both Madero and de la Barra insisted on the slow process of constructing a legal framework for the transfer of land ownership. When Zapata failed to lay down his arms, de la Barra dispatched Victoriano Huerta and the Federal Army to force Zapata to submit, to no avail. Uprisings in Baja California, Oaxaca, and Chiapas were handled more successfully, but all of these episodes showed that the Porfirian stability could not be restored without the government enjoying greater legitimacy.

De la Barra had much more success with the other two goals of his inaugural address, the conduct of free and fair elections and the continuation of reforms; he has seldom received much credit for either, however. The elections of 1911, although fraught with charges of fraud and violations of personal liberties, were basically fair and popular. Civilian Maderista candidates triumphed almost universally in the gubernatorial elections. De la Barra expressed his intent to foster democracy in many public forums and furthered his goal by resisting pressure to run for the presidency. The vice presidential election caused controversy because Madero insisted on dumping his former running mate, Vázquez Gómez, for a nonentity. The presidential election ultimately was not contested, although de la Barra tried to protect the rights of opposition candidate Bernardo Reyes. The atmosphere of calm surrounding the 1911 election should be seen, at least in part, as the result of de la Barra's efforts, but Madero generally receives all the credit.

De la Barra also promoted a social reform package in the fall of 1911. He improved public education by funding more rural schools. He promoted agrarian reform by implementing colonization schemes and federally funded irrigation projects to increase the quantity of productive land. His labor reform package included worker's compensation, the eight-hour day, and the right of the government to intervene in strikes, all progressive ideas for the times. De la Barra's friends at the state level also endorsed the ideas of progressive-era U.S. social reformers, supporting temperance and the abolition of gambling. Although seldom recognized, the reform package that de la Barra and the Porfirian Congress put together in 1911 suggests that few Porfirians wished to return to the status quo of the dictatorship. Rather, the thoughtful, progressive members of the Porfirian meritocracy recognized the need for change along the lines of reforms then being implemented in the United States.

De la Barra's historical importance did not conclude with the end of his presidential term on November 6, 1911. He continued to serve Madero in a diplomatic capacity, and then in the democratic elections of 1912 won a Senate seat and later the governorship of the state of Mexico. But de la Barra made a fatal error when he became involved with the unsavory Victoriano Huerta, who overthrew Madero in February 1913. De la Barra's role began innocuously enough; he and a host of senators encouraged Madero, whom they regarded as irresolute and incompetent, to resign during the coup attempt. De la Barra later accepted the position of foreign minister in Huerta's first cabinet, however and—in the eyes of some Mexicans—shared the responsibility for Madero's execution. De la Barra's legalistic method of dealing with Woodrow Wilson's refusal to extend diplomatic recognition to Huerta, as well as purely political motives, led Huerta to send de la Barra abroad, first as ambassador minister to France and subsequently as a special envoy to Japan. Returning to his ambassadorship in France, de la Barra ended his years of public service in July 1914, when the victorious Constitutionalists eliminated from office anyone who had served the Huerta dictatorship.

De la Barra's 25 years in exile were not time wasted. He became professor of international law at the University of Paris and served as a legal consultant to the Versailles Conference at the end of World War I. He received several appointments to preside over European arbitration tribunals in the 1920s and early 1930s; winning international recognition for his advocacy of arbitration as an alternative method of resolving disputes between nations. De la Barra died in 1939, predicting that arbitration, diplomacy, and reason would prevent the outbreak of war in Europe.

Select Bibliography

Beezley, William H., *Insurgent Governor: Abraham González and the Mexican Revolution in Chihuahua.* Lincoln: University of Nebraska Press, 1973.

Knight, Alan, *The Mexican Revolution.* 2 vols., Cambridge: Cambridge University Press, 1986.

LaFrance, David G., *The Mexican Revolution in Puebla, 1908–1913.* Wilmington, Delaware: Scholarly Resources, 1989.

Meyer, Michael C., *Huerta: A Political Portrait.* Lincoln: University of Nebraska Press, 1972.

Womack, John, Jr., *Zapata and the Mexican Revolution.* New York: Knopf, 1969.

—PETER V. N. HENDERSON

DE LA HUERTA, ADOLFO

1881–1955 • President

A key figure in the Mexican Revolution, Felipe Adolfo de la Huerta Marcor was born in the port city of Guaymas, Sonora, on May 26, 1881. His father was a merchant who had established good relations with the Yaqui Indians of the region, and the family's comfortable middle-class status enabled it to send Adolfo to Mexico City to study. He made good use of his time there, studying bookkeeping as well as singing (he had a very good tenor voice) and the violin. His father's death abruptly ended his studies, and he was forced to return to Guaymas. He found work as an accountant for a local bank and later as an administrator in a tannery, although he also found time to develop his artistic talents.

De la Huerta's political doubts were first awakened by the propaganda of the Jacobin Partido Liberal Mexicano (PLM), and he subscribed to its newspaper, *Regeneración*. De la Huerta was alienated by the PLM's radicalism, however, and in 1909 he supported the failed presidential bid of Bernardo Reyes. He later supported Francisco I. Madero in his campaign to oust the dictatorship of Porfirio Díaz, and he was part of the reception committee that welcomed Madero to Guaymas.

De la Huerta was an active Madero supporter during the Revolution of 1910, presiding over the Revolutionary Party of Sonora, and after Madero's victory he was elected as local representative in the state legislature. As a state representative he supported Plutarco Elías Calles in his bid for commissioner of the border town of Agua Prieta and clinched Álvaro Obregón's bid for the municipal presidency of Huatabampo. He participated in the fight against Orozquista rebels and proposed solutions to the endemic problems with the Yaqui Indians.

De la Huerta happened to be in Mexico City during the coup d'état against the Madero government, and he returned north to organize opposition to the coup's leader, Victoriano Huerta. He made contact with the governor of Coahuila, Venustiano Carranza, and provided a link between him and Revolutionary forces in Sonora. He attended a meeting in Monclava, Coahuila, in which the Revolutionary forces accepted (provisionally at least) Carranza's leadership. Following defeat of Huerta in October 1914, de la Huerta was named chief of staff in the Ministry of the Interior under Carranza, and in August 1915 he was promoted to secretary of the interior. In May 1916 he assumed the post of interim governor of Sonora.

During his tenure as interim governor, de la Huerta implemented a number of important social reforms. He attempted to broker a peace settlement with the Yaqui Indians and, on a somewhat more sour note, issued decrees against Chinese immigrants in Sonora. One of his most important reforms was the establishment of a state "chamber of workers" to represent workers and mediate labor disputes. At the end of his term de la Huerta handed the governorship to General Plutarco Elías Calles and returned to Mexico City as chief of staff in the Ministry of the Interior; he later served as consul general in New York. In 1919 he was nominated as the official governor of Sonora, and the good impression he had made as interim governor helped him win the election handily.

Nonetheless, de la Huerta's relationship with the federal government during his term as constitutionally elected governor would be far less amicable. In June 1919 the Sonoran Álvaro Obregón was named a candidate for the presidency, and Carranza's opposition to his candidacy alienated the people of Sonora. De la Huerta's first direct confrontation with Carranza was over a seemingly minor technical matter. The federal government declared that the Sonora River belonged under its jurisdiction, while the state government insisted that it belonged under local jurisdiction, since it did not flow into the ocean. In fact, the Carranza administration was looking for an excuse to drop de la Huerta and thus decrease the influence of Sonora. General Manuel M. Diéguez was sent to Sonora as a new military commander for the region. As military commander Diéguez posed a grave threat to the constitutional government of Sonora, attempting to provoke a confrontation with the Yaquis and gain control of the state. With his characteristic diplomatic acumen, de la Huerta armed a contingent of volunteers and was able to convince the officers at Diéguez's operations headquarters to ally with him and not obey Diéguez. Realizing that he had lost control of his own army, Diéguez returned to Guadalajara.

Meanwhile, the national political crisis had begun to heat up. In February 1920 Calles resigned as secretary of industry, commerce, and labor to help lead the Obregón campaign. Following his return to Sonora in April, de la Huerta named him state military commander. Tensions between Sonora and the Carranza administration continued to mount, and when Obregón narrowly avoided capture at the hands of federal authorities in Mexico City a rebel plan was drawn up in Sonora. Titled the Plan of Agua Prieta, the plan was published on April 23 and began a broad national movement of not recognizing Carranza or the governors of the states that supported him. In what has been termed a "generals' strike," the majority of officers in the Mexican army refused to support Carranza; Diéguez, one of Carranza's last military supporters, was taken prisoner in Guadalajara. Carranza attempted to move his government to Veracruz as he had done in 1915, but railway lines had been cut and Carranza and his entourage were forced to retreat on horseback into the Sierra of Puebla, where he was attacked and killed on May 21. Congress named de la Huerta interim president of Mexico until presidential elections could be held and a new president sworn into office on November 30, 1920.

De la Huerta traveled from Sonora to Mexico City to assume the presidency on July 1. The major accomplishment of the de la Huerta administration was, after almost a decade of civil war, to achieve the pacification of Mexico. Carranza had clashed with numerous groups: the Revolutionary followers of Emiliano Zapata and Pancho Villa, counterrevolutionaries such as Manuel Peláez and Félix Díaz, states' rights movements in Oaxaca and Chiapas, and many others. Now that Carranza, their old enemy, was dead, de la Huerta was able to convince the rebels to lay down their arms. Some were integrated into the new government; others, such as Pancho Villa, retired to private life. Only Félix Díaz was forced into exile.

In contrast to the harder line taken by his fellow Sonorans Obregón and Calles, de la Huerta developed a more conciliatory style of government. He formed a cabinet that represented a wide range of anti-Carranza groups. He named José Vasconcelos, who had been living in exile, rector of the national university, and he presided over a veritable educational revolution. De la Huerta's six-month term of office saw considerable labor unrest, but he was able to contain the conflicts. De la Huerta's greatest problem was the United States' refusal to recognize his government. All of de la Huerta's overtures failed, and the problem remained unresolved when he handed the reigns of government to Obregón in 1920.

During the Obregón administration de la Huerta was named secretary of the treasury. De la Huerta, Obregón, and Calles—who had been named secretary of the interior—formed the so-called Sonoran Triangle, which was seen as the pinnacle of power in Mexico. De la Huerta was able to regain control of the federal budget, as taxes from Mexico's burgeoning petroleum production helped fill depleted government coffers. He also was able overcome problems with Mexico's external debt, signing an agreement with Thomas Lamont of the International Banking Committee in 1922.

Obregón still needed to obtain recognition from the United States, and in 1923 a bilateral commission composed of two representatives from each country was established to work toward a new trade and friendship treaty. Although Obregón did not name de la Huerta as one of the members of the commission, he did ask him to intervene at particularly tense moment when the U.S. representatives threatened to walk out. Nonetheless, de la Huerta opposed the final agreement, the so-called Bucareli Accords, believing that they reversed many of the achievements of the Revolution.

De la Huerta's opposition to the Bucareli Accords came at a moment when candidates were being named for the next presidential election. Although de la Huerta was considered one of the most viable potential candidates, he threw his support behind Calles. Nonetheless, when the president of the Partido Nacional Cooperatista (National Cooperatist Party) was defeated in his bid for the governorship of San Luis Potosí, he named de la Huerta as the party's candidate for the presidency, and de la Huerta resigned as secretary of the treasury. The Cooperatistas also opposed the Bucareli Accords, and Senator Field Jurado was assassinated in the dispute.

The situation between September and December 1923 was quite tense. Although Calles was supported as the candidate of the Partido Laborista (Labor Party), the Cooperatistas were attacked and persecuted. A number of generals, chiefs of military operations, and other officers allied themselves with de la Huerta, and after receiving the support of General Guadalupe Sánchez of Veracruz in December, de la Huerta led a rebellion against the government. The rebellion extended along two fronts, the eastern front, which comprised the states of Puebla, Veracruz, and Tabasco, and the western front, which was centered in the state of Jalisco. As much as 60 percent of the army supported the rebellion; some generals who had been living in exile, including Salvador Alvarado and de la Huerta's old enemy Diéguez, returned to Mexico to support the uprising. Nonetheless, the rebel forces lacked a unified leadership that could coordinate their activities; the uprising has been dubbed *la rebelión sin cabeza* (the headless revolt). Obregón was able to maintain lines of communication between Mexico City and the U.S. border, preventing the two fronts of the rebel forces from uniting. Fighting continued until the first months of 1924, when the eastern front was defeated in the Battle of Esperanza and the western front at Ocotlán.

Many of the generals who had supported the rebellion were executed, but de la Huerta, Prieto Laurens, and other members of the civilian leadership were able to escape to the United States. De la Huerta spent most of his exile in Los Angeles, where he earned a living as a singing instructor. In 1935 President Lázaro Cárdenas granted him amnesty, naming him inspector general of Mexican consulates in the United States and later director general of civil retirement pensions. He died in Mexico City on July 9, 1955.

Select Bibliography

Dulles, John W. F., *Yesterday in Mexico: A Chronicle of the Revolution, 1919–1936.* Austin: University of Texas Press, 1961.

—ÁLVARO MATUTE

DE LA MADRID, MIGUEL

1934– • President

When he became president of Mexico in 1982, Miguel de la Madrid faced the daunting task of guiding a nation teetering on the brink of economic collapse. His predecessor, José López Portillo, left office in the middle of a fiscal panic in which the value of the Mexican peso to the U.S. dollar slid from 26 to 1 in January 1982 to 80:1 in August. By the time de la Madrid was to leave office in 1988, the ratio would hit an astounding 2300 to 1. Mexico was in a full-scale economic depression.

De la Madrid could hardly have looked forward to governing under such agonizing conditions. Born in December 1934 to an influential family in Colima, he was raised in Mexico City, where he attended private schools until entering law school at the National University (UNAM). He excelled in law studies, graduating near the top of his class while serving as vice president of the Law Student Society. In the mid-1960s he earned an M.A. in Public Administration from Harvard, where he took courses with famed economist John Kenneth Galbraith. Back in Mexico, he authored articles, attended conferences, and taught constitutional law at UNAM before beginning years of work in the Treasury Department.

As minister of budget and planning under López Portillo (1979–82), de la Madrid was well positioned to receive the nod as the official party's certain-to-win presidential candidate. Yet his *destape,* or designation, was greeted with unusual hostility from some sectors of the political establishment—an indication of the emerging rift between old *políticos* and emerging technocrats that was destined to wreak havoc in Mexico during the 1990s. De la Madrid was very much the technocrat: young (only 47 years old when sworn into office), educated in public management, abreast of macroeconomic theories, and willing to experiment with change. He and his advisers criticized the traditional populism of their predecessors and advocated a "moral renovation" of the Mexican body politic.

There was a great gap between de la Madrid's rhetoric and practice, however. Although he exposed the perverse excesses of the López Portillo administration, which led to the imprisonment of the national oil company's (PEMEX) chief, Jorge Díaz Serrano, his own government was by no means immune to graft and bribery. The opportunities for milking the system were far fewer during International Monetary Fund (IMF)–imposed austerity programs. There was no meaningful "moral renovation" in terms of civil liberties, either; with political stability a top priority, de la Madrid increased military spending, even while basic human rights conditions deteriorated.

U.S.-Mexican relations were especially critical during de la Madrid's term, as U.S. influence reached new heights concomitant with Mexico's burgeoning foreign debt. The president attempted to assuage his powerful northern neighbor at first, only taking it to task for its Central American policies—and even that was orchestrated largely for domestic political consumption. By midterm, however, his patience with the United States on a number of sensitive issues began to wane. The administration of President Ronald Reagan not only pursued its headstrong Central America agenda—with little regard for the Mexican-sponsored Contadora peace initiative—but it aggravated tensions with Mexicans by nearly letting the nation default on its debt. Illegal immigration to the United States, soaring as a result of Mexico's economic turmoil, was answered with hot rhetoric and the controversial Immigration Reform and Control (Simpson-Rodino) Act of 1986. The 1985 murder of U.S. Drug Enforcement Agent Enrique Camarena was another low point for U.S.-Mexican relations (aggravated by an irresponsible U.S. news media). By 1987 a frustrated de la Madrid was prepared to chide the United States: "The damaging problem of drug trafficking," he candidly explained, "originates with the market for drugs in the United States."

Tensions with the United States notwithstanding, de la Madrid closely adhered to the economic recipes of the IMF and World Bank. In doing so, he put Mexico on the neoliberal course (characterized by strict monetary policies and the promotion of exports) so aggressively pursued by his successor, Carlos Salinas de Gortari. History will probably view Miguel de la Madrid favorably over the long term—not because what he did was so good, but because what came before and what followed him was so incredibly awful.

Select Bibliography

Purcell, Susan K., *Mexico in Transition: Implications for U.S. Policy.* New York: Council on Foreign Relations, 1988.
Riding, Alan, *Distant Neighbors: A Portrait of the Mexicans.* New York: Vintage, 1986.

—JOHN W. SHERMAN

DE LAS CASAS, BARTOLOMÉ

See Las Casas, Bartolomé de

DEL PASO, FERNANDO

1935– • Writer, Cartoonist, Painter, and Diplomat

Fernando del Paso was born in Mexico City in 1935. He spent more than a decade as an advertising designer. In 1958 he published *Sonetos de lo diario,* his first foray into the literary world. From 1964 to 1965 he received a grant from the Mexican Writers' Center and a year later produced his first novel, *José Trigo,* which was awarded the Xavier Villaurrutia prize in 1966. In 1969 he was guest writer at the International Writing Program Iowa City, and in 1970 he received a grant from the Guggenheim Foundation. He moved to London where he had his first exhibition of drawings (1974), worked for the BBC, and finished his second novel, *Palinuro de México* (1975), for which he received the Mexican Novel Prize (1975), the Rómulo Gallegos International Novel Prize (1982), and the French award for best foreign novel (1986). For a time he served as the Mexican cultural attaché in France and then consul general. In 1987 he published his third novel, *Noticias del imperio,* which won the Mazatlán Literature Prize that same year and made him popular in Mexico.

Del Paso returned to his native land in 1992. Since then he has been director of the Octavio Paz Library in Guadalajara. His book *Memoria y olvido: Vida de Juan José Arreola (1920–1947) contado a Fernando del Paso* was published in 1994. It introduced an exciting new kind of autobiography to Mexico, in which an important writer, del Paso, served as intermediary for another great writer, Juan José Arreola, to recount his memoirs. Del Paso's novel *Linda 67: Historia de un crimen,* published in 1995, was his first attempt at crime fiction.

Del Paso's work stands at the forefront of contemporary Latin American fiction. Three of his books, *José Trigo, Palinuro de México,* and *Noticias del imperio,* create an intricate network of references to writers and works in the history of Western literature. With these three works del Paso joins those Mexican writers who have approached literature in a highly experimental spirit, breaking the barriers of established rules and traditions. He attempts to throw off the constraints of academia and turn language into a free instrument, to be played with in terms of both vocabulary and syntax, in an environment where an all-enveloping imagination prevails. There is an awareness of the imaginary nature of all narrations; they are, above all, colossal verbal constructions. Del Paso's novels make for difficult reading and require active participation by the reader.

Del Paso also includes key moments in Mexican history in his novels. Instead of the antihistorical escapism some critics see in these novels, there is a clear and conscious decision to reject, in the words of the scholar Juan Bruce-Novoa, "simple answers and supposedly objective explanations which disguise monological opinions." Del Paso has chosen juxtaposition to demonstrate the fallacy of a historiography that proposes one sole version of events. This characteristic, already present in *José Trigo,* is most highly developed in *Noticias del imperio,* in which we see del Paso's clear refusal to accept the concept of a definitive history that necessarily would imply the imposition of a partiality masquerading as unquestionable truth. Hence, these novels reflect the author's desire not to evade history and, at the same time, to create poetry. In the words of Juan Bruce-Novoa, del Paso places history "beside invention, allegory, and also beside runaway fantasy."

Select Bibliography

Bruce-Novoa, Juan, "Noticias del imperio: La historia apasionada." *Literatura Mexicana* 2 (1990).

Corral Peña, Elizabeth, "Del Paso: Entre historia y ficción." *Literatura Mexicana* 4 (1993).

Fell, Claude, "Charlotte, 'Baronne du néant, princesse de l'écume, reine de l'oubli.'" In *La construction du personnage historique: Aires hispanique et hispano-américaine,* edited by Jacqueline Covo. Lille: Lille University Press, 1991.

Fiddian, Robin W., "Palinuro de México: A World of Words." *Bulletin of Hispanic Studies* 58:2 (April 1981).

Mansour, Mónica, *Los mundos de Palinuro.* Mexico City: Universidad Veracruzana, 1986.

—Elizabeth Corral Peña

DEL RÍO, DOLORES

1904–83 • Actress

Dolores Asúnsolo López Negrete, better known under the name of Dolores del Río, was born August 3, 1904, in the city of Durango. Dolores was the only child of Antonia Asúnsolo and Jesús López Negrete Jacques. Her parents, part of Mexico's upper classes, were able to raise Dolores in a cradle of luxury.

In 1911, soon after the Mexican Revolution erupted, Jesús migrated to the United States, while Antonia and Dolores fled to Mexico City. Antonia sent her young daughter to a Josephine nuns' boarding school. Dolores remembered herself as a shy young girl, unhappy with her dark complexion, and longing to be blond. Together with her studies, she took dance classes and secretly decided to become a dancer.

In 1921 Dolores married Jaime Martínez del Río, also a man from the upper classes. The couple's social milieu only sharpened Dolores's restlessness. Although Dolores was able to practice Spanish dances at high-society parties, her social position prevented her from fully developing her talent, as the upper classes considered it improper for someone of Dolores's status to dance professionally.

In 1925 U.S. film director Edwin Carewe visited Mexico City for his honeymoon and also to film some images of Mexico. Carewe hoped to penetrate the rebellious and difficult Mexican market, which was hypersensitive to the negative image of Mexicans reflected in the U.S. cinema. Carewe met Dolores at a party where she performed a Spanish dance. Excited by Dolores's talent and charisma, Carewe promised to turn her into a feminine Rudolfo Valentino. The economic difficulties of the Martínez del Río family made Carewe's proposal sound all the more favorable. Jaime traveled to Hollywood to study the offer and soon flew back for Dolores, who then began a brilliant new career.

Dolores's early professional life, from *Joanna* (1925) to *Evangelina* (1929) took place under the shadow of Carewe. Although she played under several directors in these silent films, it was Carewe who managed her career. Despite publicity and a flashy wardrobe, she went almost unnoticed in her first four movies. Her fifth film, *What Price Glory?* (1927), brought her worldwide popularity. *Resurrection* (1927), *The Loves of Carmen* (1927), *Ramona* (1928), and *Revenge* (1928) fulfilled Carewe's prediction by turning Dolores del Río into a female Rudolfo Valentino. Ironically enough, her dark complexion was the key to her success. However, her husband, Jaime, proved unable to cope with Dolores's success. He died in 1928.

In talking movies Dolores's accent shocked movie viewers, even though filmmakers gave her roles as foreigners, hoping to soothe the reaction. She played a French woman in *The Bad One* and a Mexican in *The Girl of Río* (both 1931). In both these pictures Dolores chose scripts and directors, a privilege accorded by her contract with United Artists. At that time she was earning US$9,000 a week while Greta Garbo made US$4,000 and Al Jolson US$15,000. United Artists terminated her contract allegedly because she suffered from ill health.

In 1930 Dolores married Cedric Gibbons, the art director at Metro Goldwin Meyers. Gibbons introduced art deco in cinema and turned Dolores del Río into the art deco beauty. Her audacity to perform nude in *Bird of Paradise* (1932) gave her back her popularity. Renowned photographers such as Cecil Beaton took her picture. They praised the versatility of her face and even said she was more beautiful than Greta Garbo and Marlene Dietrich.

Few of the movies she made during these years are worth mentioning, excepting *Flying Down to Río* (1933), in which Fred Astaire and Ginger Rogers appeared for the first time, and *Wonder Bar* (1934). Her last movie in Hollywood was *Journey into Fear* (1942). Around that time she had a brief and secret love affair with Orson Wells. This caused her divorce with Cedric Gibbons and indirectly her expulsion from Hollywood.

Dolores del Río returned to Mexico at a time when Mexican cinema was acquiring strength and needed a female celebrity. If Hollywood could do without her, Mexico spiritedly hoped for her return. She set her conditions. She only would act directed by Emilio "El Indio" Fernández, with whom she had a romance. El Indio directed her in *Flor Silvestre* (1943), *María Candelaria* (1944), *Las abandonadas* (1944), and *Bugambilia* (1945). *María Candelaria* was awarded the Golden Palm in the first Cannes Film Festival in 1946.

After her relationship with Fernández ended in 1945, Dolores entered a more mature stage, in which she managed her own career. She decided to stop being a star and become an actress, and she succeeded. Her performance in *Doña Perfecta* (1950) and *El niño y la niebla* (1953) won her two Ariel Mexican film awards for best performance by a leading actress. Dolores del Río's movies sold more tickets than those of any other actress in Latin America.

Ever since her career had begun to decline in Hollywood in the 1930s she had talked about the possibility of going into the theater. She used to say the movie camera would tell her when to make the move. In 1956 she made her first appearance on the stage in New England, when she played in Marcelle Maurette's *Anastasia*. But it was not until 1958, with her unfortunate role in *La cucaracha,* that she actually reached a turning point. Now she preferred the theater to the movies. She acted under the guidance of a man she met in 1951 and married in 1959, Lewis Riley. In 10 years she performed in plays such as Oscar Wilde's *Lady Windermere's Fan,* Henrik Johan Ibsen's *Ghosts,* Robert Sherwood's

The Road to Rome, George Bernard Shaw's *My Dear Liar,* and Alexandre Dumas's *La Dame aux camélias.* A backbone illness eventually prevented Dolores from continuing her career. She instead began working in her union, promoting the conservation of Mexico's artistic heritage, and serving social causes.

Dolores del Río never totally left her international film career. She played in *El fugitivo* (1946), *Historia de una mala mujer* (1948), *Flaming Star* (1959), *Cheyenne Autumn* (1964), *La dama del Alba* (1966), *C'era una volta* (1966), and others. Dolores said farewell to Mexican cinema in 1966 with *Casa de mujeres.* She also worked for U.S. television and Cuban radio.

Dolores received several awards worldwide. She served on the jury at the Cannes, Berlin, and San Sebastián film festivals. The Organization of American States (OAS) gave her an acknowledgment; President Jimmy Carter of the United States gave her a diploma. In 1981 the San Francisco festival was dedicated to her.

Her sickness grew worse during 1982, and the following year Dolores died of cancer. Riley was her last husband and outlived her. Dolores del Río lived a successful professional life, which she began by accident, but to which she gave the best of herself. In both Hollywood and Mexico, she experienced the rise of the movie industry's system designed around the film star, a role she played brilliantly.

Select Bibliography

de los Reyes, Aurelio, Davíd Ramón, María Luisa Amador, and Rodolfo Rivera, *80 años de cine en México.* Mexico City: Dirección General de Difusión Cultural, UNAM, 1977.

García Riera, Emilio, *Historia documental del cine mexicano,* 2nd edition, 18 vols., Guadalajara and Mexico City: Universidad de Guadalajara, Gobierno de Jalisco (Secretaría de Cutlura), Consejo Nacional para la Cultura y las Artes, Instituto Mexicano de Cinematografía, 1992–95.

Mora, Carl J., *The Mexican Cinema: Reflections of a Society, 1896–1988.* Berkeley, Los Angeles, and London: University of California Press, 1989.

—AURELIO DE LOS REYES

DEL RÍO, EDUARDO (RIUS)

1934– • Cartoonist

The only Mexican cartoonist to achieve international renown, Eduardo del Río works under the pen name Rius. He has produced two comic books but is best known for his much-imitated *"infolibros,"* the *Para principiantes* series.

Eduardo del Río was born in Zamora, Michoacán, in 1934. His father, a shopkeeper, died shortly after his birth, and his mother moved the family to Mexico City. She enrolled her sons in a Catholic seminary to avoid the "socialist" education of the era; Eduardo del Río's formal education came to an end after seven years of study with the Salesians, only a week before he was to be admitted as a novice monk, because he lacked the proper respect for authority.

Del Río converted this attitude into a career. Upon returning to Mexico City, he took a number of odd jobs (including funeral parlor receptionist) but also began drawing. The humor magazine *Ja-já* first published his work in 1954; del Río drew a series of wordless cartoons for them, adopting the pen name Rius. This work and his subsequent style were influenced by two cartoonists: Romanian American Saul Steinberg and Mexican Abel Quezada. From them he learned to use a strong, clear, simple ink line and to leave as much blank space on the page as possible.

In 1956 Rius became—at Quezada's recommendation—the primary editorial cartoonist for a left-of-center Mexico City newspaper. By then he was contributing regularly to several other periodicals and was able to make a living as a cartoonist. In 1959 he won his first award, the Premio Nacional del Periodismo, and the American State Department invited him to tour the United States. This failed to have the intended effect on Rius, whose politics moved further left. By 1960 he had joined a Marxist study group formed by cartoonist and editor Carlos Vigil; in 1961 he first visited Cuba and entered the Mexican Communist Party (PCM), in which he remained until 1968.

Rius has boasted of being fired by almost every periodical that ever employed him. By the mid-1960s that included almost every Mexico City daily. In search of a steadier income (particularly since he was, in 1965, newly married and supporting an infant daughter), he decided to turn some cartoons that had appeared a few years earlier in the magazine *Política* into a comic book in the style of the popular *El Familia Burrón.*

This project evolved into *Los Supermachos,* set in an imaginary small town in central Mexico, San Garabato de las Tunas, and featuring a naive but rebellious Indian named Juan Calzónzin. Unlike the characters of any other comic book, the caciques, bureaucrats, and policeman who inhabited San Garabato spoke and behaved realistically. The comic book's humor grew out of Juan Calzónzin's puzzled, rational reaction to the quotidian absurdities around him. Although nowhere near the graphic quality of its models, *La Familia Burrón* and *Los Supersabios,* the new comic book found an audience for its quirky political humor, reaching a circulation of about 100,000 by 1967 (in comparison, the most popular comic books of the day sold almost 1 million copies per week).

As the comic book extended its political critique, its publisher—Editorial Meridiano, owned and operated by former journalist Octavio Colmenares—attempted to control its contents, changing words without Rius' permission and on one occasion removing a whole page. In 1967 Rius quit after completing issue 101, only to find that Colmenares had illegally registered the characters of *Los Supermachos,* along with the title, as his own intellectual property. Editorial Meridiano continued publishing the comic, with different artists and writers, and without any very noticeable change in its political stance.

Rius, meanwhile, started another biweekly comic book called *Los Agachados* in 1968. This comic book lacked continuing characters, a fixed locale, or narratives, and never reached the high circulation figures of Rius's earlier comic. But it represented an artistic departure for Rius and for the field of comic books as a whole: the elaboration of a funny, politically informed "educational" comic. Using collage elements (often borrowed from late-nineteenth-century printed sources) and a text-heavy format, Rius renewed his drawing style while tackling such seemingly unfunny subjects as the Mexican Revolution, birth control, student activism, and vegetarianism—in other words, the whole spectrum of topics that comprised la Onda (the Mexican counterculture).

As well as starting this new venture, Rius passed through Czechoslovakia early in 1968—where he was impressed by the Prague Spring—and donated much time and artistic effort to the Mexican student movement. Perhaps owing to these involvements, he was kidnapped, held overnight, and threatened with death by men associated with the military in January 1969. His life may have been saved by the intervention of his mother's cousin, Defense Secretary Marcelino García Barragan.

In 1966, Rius published the first of what would be (by 1995) 85 books, *Cuba para principiantes.* In the same jokey, colloquial voice as *Los Agachados,* but even more text heavy, the book strongly supported the Cuban Revolution. A second book, *La Joven Alemania,* published in 1968, resulted from his connection to the PCM. By 1970 the first book had been published in English translation and by 1995 it had appeared in at least 20 languages (often, Rius has complained, in pirated editions). *Cuba para principiantes* is probably more widely distributed than any other text on the Cuban Revolution. Almost as broadly disseminated is *Marx para principiantes,* probably Rius' masterpiece.

After 1980, Rius concentrated his efforts on writing and drawing these *infolibros.* His other books have covered a broad range of subjects, from the myth of the Virgin of Guadalupe to human sexuality. In *Lastima de Cuba,* he revisited the terrain he covered in his first book, managing to criticize Cuba ferociously without departing from his secular-left perspective. No matter what the topic, Rius always writes in easily accessible language and incorporates witty collage elements into his spare, linear drawings. Though few of his books have had initial print runs of more than five thousand, they have tended to stay in print for years at a time (in contrast to most books published in Mexico). For the popularity and breadth of his work, he should be considered one of the most important voices of the modern Mexican left.

Select Bibliography

Foster, David William, *From Mafalda to Los Supermachos: Latin American Graphic Humor as Popular Culture.* Boulder, Colorado: Lynne Reinner, 1989.

Hinds, Harold, and Charles Tatum, *Not Only for Children: The Mexican Comic Book in the 1960s.* Westport, Connecticut: Greenwood, 1992.

Rius, *La Vida de Cuadritos: Guia incompleta de la historieta.* Mexico City: Grijalbo, 1984.

_____, *Mis Supermachos.* Mexico City: Grijalbo, 1990.

_____, *Rius para principantes.* Mexico City: Grijalbo, 1995.

—ANNE RUBENSTEIN

DÍAZ, FÉLIX

1868–1945 • Politician and Nephew of Porfirio Díaz

Best known to his contemporaries as "the nephew of the uncle" (Mexican dictator Porfirio Díaz), Félix Díaz came to symbolize the Porfirian Party and the values of the fallen dictatorship, rightly or wrongly, during the decade of violence of the Mexican Revolution from 1910 to 1920. As a youth, Félix Díaz resided in Mexico City, benefiting from his uncle Porfirio's patronage. He was educated as an engineer at the Military College. Well connected with the aristocracy both in Mexico City and in Veracruz, where his wife's family held

real estate, Félix Díaz utilized these friendships to accumulate a sizable fortune and numerous properties, not always scrupulously. Part of Porfirio Díaz's enduring legacy, however, was the ability to separate petty corruption from the important business of politics. While willing to allow Félix Díaz's chicanery in business dealings, Porfirio purposefully excluded his nephew, who had his limitations, from politics.

Young Félix served as inspector general of the Mexico City police, and as a deputy in the Porfirian Congress, but never obtained a major political plum such as a governorship. In fact, when his friends brought forward Félix's candidacy during the 1902 Oaxaca gubernatorial campaign, Porfirio Díaz exiled his nephew to Chile as consul for one and one-half years.

Félix Díaz's exclusion from political office, coupled with his dislike of key members of the Porfirian inner circle, known as the Científicos, caused him to side with supporters of Bernardo Reyes and other anti-Científicos as the 1910 vice presidential campaign began. Once Reyes bowed out of the race, a few factional diehards proposed Félix Díaz as his uncle's running mate, but the dictator would not hear of it. The vast majority of political dissidents preferred Francisco Madero. Only in the final month of the regime, when the dictator hoped to forestall Madero's military victory by eliminating the Científicos from the cabinet and governorships did Félix Díaz receive the coveted governorship of Oaxaca. By now reforms were too late, viewed as an admission of weakness on Porfirio's part. The dictatorship collapsed, and the Díaz family, with the exception of Félix, went into exile at the end of May 1911.

During both the interim regime of Francisco León de la Barra and the presidency of Francisco Madero, Félix Díaz became an important symbol as an opposition politician. His gubernatorial campaign in 1911 foundered; his rival Benito Juárez Maza linked forces with the civilian Maderistas to rout him at the polls. After Bernardo Reyes's coup against Madero failed, it was Félix Díaz's turn to lead the Porfirian faction. His revolt of October 1912 was stillborn, however; Díaz's engineering background did not provide him with the military skill necessary to inspire rebellious thoughts and deeds in the Federal Army. Furthermore, although many Mexicans hoped for the restoration of peace and order and blamed Madero for failing to provide stability, Díaz promised little more than a military dictatorship. His revolutionary plan had little to allay civilian fears, and his desultory actions during the rebellion—he never left the barracks during the rebellion except to parlay—did little to inspire the confidence of fellow generals. Díaz's poor preparations for combat allowed the loyal elements of the army to invade Veracruz, capturing him with scarcely a struggle.

Although neither Reyes nor Díaz had succeeded in felling Madero individually, together they hoped they could. From their respective jail cells the two generals and their friends plotted another coup, which toppled Francisco Madero from power in February 1913. Despite the presence of two key generals in the rebel leadership, the military showed remarkable professionalism, with only a few units deserting to Reyes and Díaz. Reyes was killed in the initial skirmish at the Presidential Palace, which forced Díaz and his troops to hole up in the Mexico City arsenal, the Ciudadela. Well supplied with ammunition and gaining civilian recruits daily, Díaz held out for 10 days, bombarding federal targets throughout the city before he and the supposedly pro-government commanding general Victoriano Huerta

negotiated an agreement. Huerta switched sides, and after a deal consummated in the presence of the U.S. ambassador, assumed the provisional presidency while agreeing to back Félix Díaz in the next election. Shortly thereafter, Madero and his vice president were conveniently murdered during a prison transfer, a crime in which Félix Díaz, with his pivotal role in initiating the coup, shares some moral responsibility, even though only circumstantial evidence links him to the actual murders. The February coup would be as close as Félix Díaz would ever come to the presidency.

Although he did not realize it at this time, the fall of Madero marked the beginning of the third portion of Félix Díaz's career, in which he returned to the role of political outsider. Shunted out of the picture by a more forceful Victoriano Huerta, Félix Díaz temporarily had to join his relatives in exile, his presidential ambitions frustrated by Huerta's refusal to call an "early" election in accordance with their agreement. After three fruitless years abroad trying to reach accommodation with virtually every faction in the civil war, Díaz in 1917 launched his own rebellion in Veracruz, where he left an important mark on the Revolution.

Although traditional historiography has decried the Felicista Revolt as reactionary, in fact Félix Díaz's Plan de Tierra Colorado espoused land reform as well as other progressive measures at least as advanced as those proffered by Constitutionalist first chief Venustiano Carranza. Ultimately, the differences between Porfiristas such as Félix Díaz and revolutionaries such as Madero and Carranza are subtler than is often assumed. Nearly all of the Porfirians conceded that Mexico could not turn back the clock to 1910. Félix Díaz also capitalized on local sentiments that resented the intrusion of the national state, personified by Venustiano Carranza, into local affairs in the south. Nevertheless, Félix Díaz's revolt failed like his previous three. The anti-Carranza forces, only occasionally cooperating among themselves, could not match the strength of the new middle-class politicians and generals. When popular general Álvaro Obregón turned against Carranza in April 1920, most of the Felicistas capitulated. Díaz himself made peace in the fall and went into exile in New Orleans. In the late 1930s President Lázaro Cárdenas's reconciliation policy allowed Díaz to return to Veracruz, where he died on July 9, 1945.

Select Bibliography

Brunk, Samuel, *Emiliano Zapata: Revolution and Betrayal in Mexico.* Albuquerque: University of New Mexico Press, 1996.

Henderson, Peter V. N., *Félix Díaz, the Porfirians, and the Mexican Revolution.* Lincoln: University of Nebraska Press, 1981.

Knight, Alan, *The Mexican Revolution.* 2 vols., Cambridge: Cambridge University Press, 1986.

Licéaga, Luis, *Félix Díaz.* Mexico: Jus, 1958.

Meyer, Michael C., *Huerta: A Political Portrait.* Lincoln: University of Nebraska Press, 1972.

—PETER V. N. HENDERSON

DÍAZ, PORFIRIO

1830–1915 • General and President

This entry contains two articles that discuss the life of Porfirio Díaz:

Díaz, Porfirio: Biography
Díaz, Porfirio: Interpretive Discussion

For a general discussion of the era of Díaz's rule, see Porfiriato: Interpretations

DÍAZ, PORFIRIO: BIOGRAPHY

Born in the city of Oaxaca on September 15, 1830, Porfirio Díaz was the son of José de la Cruz Díaz and Petrona Mori. He lost his father at age three and worked odd jobs to help support mother and family while attending private and public school. In 1843 he began attending Conciliar Seminary in Oaxaca, but the U.S. invasion in 1846 interrupted his studies, leading him to drill with a local battalion. Díaz saw little action and returned to the seminary but abandoned it again to pursue legal training at the Institute of Arts and Sciences of Oaxaca in 1849. He studied law until 1854 but did not receive a degree.

Liberal leaders in 1855 appointed Díaz *jefe político* (political boss) of the Ixtlán District because of his support of the Plan de Ayutla, which led to the overthrow of Antonio López de Santa Anna. He joined the Oaxaca National Guard in 1856 and fought on the Liberal side during the Wars of Reform (1858–61), attaining the rank of brigadier general in 1861. After briefly serving as a federal deputy from Oaxaca, Díaz joined the forces of Benito Juárez during the French Intervention and led a successful attack against the French army at Puebla on May 5, 1862, helping achieve the great Mexican victory celebrated annually as Cinco de Mayo. Afterward, he commanded the Army of the East in more than 25 battles, including the liberations of Oaxaca, Puebla, and Mexico City. Díaz retired in 1867 following the victory over the French, but he later accepted command of the second division of Tehuacán, Puebla. He invested in a telegraph line between Oaxaca and Puebla and presided over its inauguration on January 19, 1868.

When Juárez chose to run for a fourth term as president in 1871, Díaz and Sebastián Lerdo de Tejada ran against him. When no clear winner emerged, the constitution threw the election to Congress. Juárez, whose supporters held the most seats, carried the day. Díaz, unlike Lerdo de Tejada, refused to accept the results and declared a rebellion against Juárez, the Plan de la Noria, on November 8, 1871. The revolt failed and Juárez died afterward, leaving Lerdo in the presidency. Díaz retired to Tlacotalpan, Veracruz, to build furniture and plan a new political campaign.

Díaz issued the Plan de Tuxtepec on January 10, 1876, against Lerdo, charging him with violating state sovereignty.

Díaz led a military force against government troops in Tlaxcala, and reinforced by Manuel González, triumphed and took Mexico City on November 21, 1876. After submitting to Congress a no-reelection amendment to the Constitution, Díaz successfully ran for president, assuming office on May 5, 1877. During his first term, various revolts of political and agrarian origin plagued him. The most serious rebellions occurred along the U.S. border, led by supporters of exiled president Lerdo de Tejada. Not only did Díaz put down uprisings such as these with brute force, he often ordered the execution of the participants. One example occurred in Veracruz, when Díaz sent a telegraph containing the order *Mátalos en caliente* (Kill them on the spot) to Governor Luis Mier y Terán concerning various prisoners. Díaz centralized political and economic power, decreasing the power of the regional governors and reorganizing finances. The increased strength of the government led to new debt and border security agreements with the United States.

Díaz chose not to run for reelection in 1880 despite pressure from supporters. Instead, he tapped Manuel González, who easily won the office. Díaz briefly remained in government as head of the Department of Development and later as governor of Oaxaca, serving in the post from December 1881 to October 1883. His wife, Delfina Ortega y Reyes, died in 1880. The following year Díaz married Carmen Romero Rubio, daughter of Manuel Romero Rubio, a cabinet member and prominent Positivist. She was 18 and he 51. In 1884, he successfully ran again for president, ushering in a period of increased development while consolidating his rule. In fact, Díaz was elected for five additional terms between 1888 and 1910. The government, under the guidance of Treasury Minister José Yves Limantour, improved credit and reorganized the banking system. In addition, Díaz presided over the modification of Mexico City's drainage system and the dedication of numerous public buildings, monuments, parks, and statues.

Under Díaz, the philosophy of Positivism permeated the upper echelons of government. The Científicos, as those who advocated the application of the scientific method to government became known, were rarely optimistic in their belief that Mexico could educate the Indian masses. Most

Científicos believed the nation's future lay with the upper classes and advocated a paternalistic attitude toward the indigenous population. Regarding the nation's economy and foreign trade, during the 1880s and 1890s Díaz presided over a government program that lowered or eliminated most import duties and negotiated a series of loans with favorable rates of interest. Most important, Mexico moved from the silver to the gold standard. Although these measures resulted in a positive image abroad, poverty increased among the poor in Mexico.

Díaz advocated increased industrialization, especially railroad expansion. In 1876, 400 miles (650 kilometers) of track existed in all of Mexico. By 1911, 15,000 miles (25,000 kilometers) were in use. Major lines were completed from Mexico City to outlying border regions and ports, including one from the capital city to Laredo, Texas, in 1888. Financed with mostly U.S. and British capital and using foreign technology, the railroads opened the Mexican countryside to development. Agricultural production in outlying areas such as the Laguna region in northern Mexico allowed domestic textile mills to use Mexican cotton instead of imported stock. Sugar planters in Morelos imported technology to modernize their facilities. Overall, the railroads allowed Mexican industry to ship raw materials to factories and move finished goods to domestic markets and port facilities.

The use of force to pacify the countryside made industrial expansion possible. Díaz strengthened the *rurales,* a rural militia, into a powerful force to be used to put down revolts. In the urban sector, Díaz expanded police forces, projecting an image of safety to potential foreign investors. Occasionally the inner reality of police corruption revealed itself, as on September 16, 1897, when Arnulfo Arroyo, a known drunk, assaulted Díaz during a military procession. Díaz was unharmed, but agents, acting under the orders of the inspector general of police, murdered Arroyo in his cell. Perhaps the most ingenious method used by Díaz to maintain regional control involved playing off one powerful group or leader against the other. Díaz appointed judges and replaced provincial leaders who had grown too independent.

As Mexico neared the centennial year of Independence, 1910, Díaz grew confident that the system of control he devised would keep the peace. In a 1908 interview with U.S. journalist James Creelman, Díaz said he would retire in 1910. Encouraged by the news, Francisco I. Madero, a northern industrialist, began to campaign for free elections. Soon, Madero joined the Anti-Reelectionist cause and ran for president when it became apparent Díaz would not step down. Briefly imprisoning Madero, Díaz won the presidency for the eighth time. The regime, however, could not squelch the fires of opposition. On November 20, 1910, the first phase of the Mexican Revolution began with a series of regional revolts that spread throughout the country, culminating in the surrender of Ciudad Juárez in May 1911. Díaz, faced with a successful rebellion, resigned the presidency and left Mexico on May 31, 1911, for exile in Paris. During his last years he received accolades from world leaders and toured other nations. He died on July 2, 1915.

Select Bibliography

Beals, Carleton, *Porfirio Díaz: Dictator of Mexico.* Philadelphia: Lippincott, 1932.

Beezley, William H., and Colin M. MacLachlan, *El Gran Pueblo: A History of Greater Mexico.* Englewood Cliffs, New Jersey: Prentice-Hall, 1994.

Camp, Roderic, *Mexican Political Biographies, 1884–1935.* Austin: University of Texas Press, 1991.

Cosío Villegas, Daniel, *Historia moderna de México: El porfiriato, La vida política interior, segunda parte.* Mexico City: Hermes, 1972.

Meyer, Michael C., and William L. Sherman, *The Course of Mexican History.* 4th edition, Oxford and New York: Oxford University Press, 1991.

Tello Díaz, Carlos, *El Exilio: Un Relato de Familia.* Mexico City: Cal y Arena, 1993.

—JAMES A. GARZA

DÍAZ, PORFIRIO: INTERPRETIVE DISCUSSION

Porfirio Díaz is a vitally important but also a thoroughly controversial figure in the history of modern Mexico. As president for a total of 31 years (1876 to 1880 and 1884 to 1911), he holds the record, and the dubious honor, of being the country's longest-serving constitutional leader during Mexico's often painful evolution as a modern nation-state. His contribution to the construction and evolution of the Mexican nation is often overlooked and frequently has been denigrated in the post-Revolutionary era, since official historiography after 1910 toppled him from his pedestal in the pantheon of Liberal patriots, a position that Díaz himself and his closest associates had attempted to cultivate in his lifetime. As a consequence, Díaz became vilified as a despot, a villain, and traitor to his country by those who sought to legitimize both the Revolution and the political system that emerged from it. Only in recent years has there been an attempt to reevaluate the image of Díaz, first in the light of the growth and sophistication of historical research, especially in Mexico, and second, in accordance with the reformist, cosmopolitan, and neoliberal preoccupations during the presidential administrations of the 1980s and 1990s, especially those of Carlos Salinas de Gortari (1988–94) and Ernesto Zedillo Ponce de León (1994–). These factors, in combination with the political and economic uncertainties unleashed by the North American Free Trade Agreement and *neozapatismo,* have fostered a wave of nostalgia for and revisionism of the Porfirian era (also known as the Porfiriato), most clearly demonstrated by the creation of more than 100 episodes of the historical soap opera (enigmatically titled *El vuelo del águila,* the Eagle's Flight) based on the life of Díaz shown by Televisa, the national television network in 1994.

One of the principal problems in the interpretation of Díaz and his regime is the fact that too much attention has been paid to the final period of presidential office (1906–10), a period in which the regime struggled unsuccessfully to find an adequate response to the economic, social, and political problems engendered by the rapid transformation of the Mexican economy in the 1880s and the 1890s. The years immediately preceding 1910 can be seen, ironically, as a period in which the regime became a victim of its own economic success, since during the Porfiriato Mexico had vastly increased the scale of its mineral and agricultural exports to international markets, attracted ever-increasing levels of foreign investment, and embarked upon an ambitious project of railway construction and public works that transformed the economic and social infrastructure of much (but certainly not all) of the country. This developmentalist economic strategy had made a significant contribution to the consolidation of the regime, but, at the same time, had created a growing number of problems related to the uneven distribution of land and economic resources and the failure to broaden the scope of political participation and democratic legitimacy.

The regime's response to the growing crisis after 1906 was hesitant, inconsistent, internally divided, and, on certain notorious occasions (such as the repression of the mining and textile strikes of 1906 and 1907), highly repressive. It was, in addition, obviously unsuccessful, as demonstrated by the rapid momentum gained by the Madero Revolution after November 1910. In the succinct metaphor of historian Alan Knight, the regime on the eve of the Revolution resembled a creature which could no longer adapt to the changed surroundings of its environment: "like some saurian monster, the regime lacked a political brain commensurate with its swollen economic muscle: hence its extinction."

But to interpret the entire regime largely on the basis of its character and conduct in these last years would be a mistake, since the image clearly would be distorted. All too often the regime has been examined from the perspective of the Revolution and its aftermath: in order to comprehend the regime more fully, it must be seen from the perspective of the nineteenth century.

The political longevity of the Díaz regime was founded upon the construction of a modus vivendi between the three most important components of nineteenth-century Mexican and Latin American politics. First, the traditions of patriar-chal authority and the complex network of patronage represented by *caudillismo* (the exercise of personal, authoritarian, noninstitutional power so common in the Hispanic world); second, the diverse and often contradictory traditions within nineteenth-century Mexican Liberalism (constitutionalism, the supremacy of civil power and the secular state, the effective expression of popular sovereignty and representation, and the conflict between centralism and federalism over the distribution of political power between central and regional government); and third, the emergent conservative ideology of Positivism, with its emphasis on "scientific" politics (organic political harmony, social order, and industrial progress). This is not to suggest, however, that the balance was equal between the component parts of the regime. If we examine each of these in turn, then it is clear that the first two elements were far more significant than the third in the origin, structure, and evolution of the regime.

Most historians of *caudillismo* would acknowledge the difficulties of generalization in describing a phenomenon that affected the whole of the continent of the Americas for much of the nineteenth century (and beyond). Most would agree, however, that the "classic" caudillo who dominated the early post-Independence period in Spanish America was a combination of warrior, patriot, and *patrón,* who rose to political power and prominence from a local or regional base. There can be little doubt that Porfirio Díaz demonstrated all of these attributes to a greater or lesser extent both before and after his ascent to the presidency, although his powers of patronage did not result from personal wealth, landed estates, or business acumen, but rather from the military status and political offices he enjoyed from a relatively early age—by the age of 31 he had become both a brigadier general and a *diputado* (member of the National Congress).

There were very early indications of his future development as both warrior and patriot. At the tender age of 16 (in 1846), the young Porfirio, who was preparing under the guidance of his uncle (and future bishop of Oaxaca), José Agustín Domínguez, for a career in the priesthood, volunteered his services to the Trujano Battalion of the National Guard, formed in his native Oaxaca to defend the country in the wake of the invasion of Mexico by U.S. troops. Even though the battalion never saw active service, Díaz's interest in and affinity for military matters lasted throughout his lifetime, and his personal correspondence shows a long-standing interest in military affairs in general and especially in the latest developments in weaponry and military technology. This does not mean, however, that Porfirio Díaz was another in a long line of authoritarian Spanish American military caudillos who represented the interests of the army in the struggle with civil authority. During his long tenure of office, not only did Díaz demonstrate that he was the only nineteenth-century Mexican president able to control the military, but he was also most successful in removing the threat of the frequent military interventions into politics that had characterized the post-Independence period.

Díaz also must be distinguished clearly from the archetypal caudillo in terms of his Liberal political convictions. Whereas "classic" caudillos were characterized by an absence of personal ideological commitment, or, more frequently, were the agents, allies, or subordinates of Conservative interests, Díaz was an ardent supporter of the Liberal cause. At the age of 18 he gave up his studies at the seminary to study law at the liberal Institute of Arts and Sciences in the city of Oaxaca. In fact, when Díaz did eventually take up arms in December 1854, he did so not in pursuit of a professional military career, but, significantly, in response to the dictates of his Liberal political convictions.

The broader, national context for the launch of Díaz's political and military career in 1854 was the political challenge from dissident liberalism to the regime of Antonio López de Santa Anna, a challenge embodied in the Plan de Ayutla of March 1854. After the initial persecution and arrest of its most prominent Liberal enemies (which in Oaxaca included Benito Juárez, and Díaz's liberal *padrino,* the lawyer Marcos Pérez), the regime called for a national plebiscite in December 1854. In Oaxaca, despite the official claim that the vote was to be a free expression of the popular will, voting took place in public in the central square of the city under the watchful gaze of the governor and the military commander of the state, General Ignacio Martínez y Pinillos. Díaz, following the completion of his studies at the institute, had been appointed as a temporary professor of natural law in that same institution. When it was publicly announced that the staff of the institute unanimously supported the continuation of Santa Anna in office, Díaz asked to register a vote of abstention, but, following a public accusation that he had failed to register his vote out of fear, Díaz responded by openly declaring his support for the leader of the Ayutla Rebellion in the state of Guerrero, General Juan Álvarez. An order was issued for Díaz's arrest, and he was obliged to flee the city and to find refuge with a rebel band in the *sierra.*

The drama of this event—which confirmed the image of Porfirio Díaz as committed Liberal, determined rebel, the resolute and fearless leader who possessed the courage of his convictions—has without doubt been embellished for posterity, especially in the proliferation of biographies of Díaz that appeared during the last years of his presidency, when his cult of personality was at its height. Nevertheless, it is tempting to see in the events of 1854 and 1855 the encapsulation of vital elements that would be central to his rise to presidential power in 1876: the tenacity and self-confidence, the thirst for power, the qualities of leadership, and his patriotic liberalism. These attributes would be demonstrated frequently during his subsequent military career between 1855 and 1867, especially during the Wars of Reform (1858 to 1861) and the French Intervention (1862 to 1867). His military career gave him the status of national hero, associated above all with the liberation of Puebla on April 2, 1867. It also enabled him to broaden his network of contacts, subordinates, allies, and admirers, and to pursue his relentless quest for presidential office, whether by means of election (when he stood unsuccessfully against Benito Juárez in the presidential elections of 1871), or by insurrection (unsuccessfully in the Rebellion of the Noria in 1871, and, successfully, in the Tuxtepec Rebellion of 1876).

In the phase of political consolidation that followed his ascent to the presidency for the first time in 1876, the political base that had been nurtured over the previous two decades was fostered and extended. As a consequence, political power in the Díaz system was exercised through a wide network of formal and informal personal relationships carefully cultivated across a broad social spectrum (from peasants to cabinet ministers), and based upon negotiated rather than enforced exchanges of deference and loyalty to the patriarchal figure of Porfirio Díaz. His personal correspondence shows that Díaz adopted a variety of strategies that were skillfully employed to maintain control over the political life of the nation, ranging from the overt use of flattery, discretion, personal appeals to loyalty, patriotism, and self-sacrifice to the covert, but no less effective use of duplicity, manipulation, and, in the last resort, the threat of force or federal military intervention. This political apparatus also was fueled by the provision of multiple opportunities for profit (and graft) to individuals who acted as agents, partners, or intermediaries in foreign enterprises, which proliferated in the wake of the considerable success the regime enjoyed in attracting foreign investment. In short, the political style was fundamentally pragmatic, emphasizing the practice of realpolitik, not only in the conduct of everyday politics, but also with regard to the key political triumphs and successes of the regime: the manipulation and control of regional elites, the reconciliation between church and state, the professionalization (and political emasculation) of the army, the control of the press, and the restoration and extension of diplomatic relations after very inauspicious beginnings in 1876. Díaz's political skills were much in evidence in each of these areas of policy, all of which were vital to the consolidation and survival of the regime.

In spite of the emphasis placed here on pragmatic politics, and in spite of the clear manipulation of liberal ideology and rhetoric by the regime, the basic tenets of political liberalism never were relinquished (personal and political freedom; a secular, republican state without corporate structures or privileges; a society posited upon economic progress; social mobility; and private property). Díaz's commitment to liberalism, however, remains controversial and ambiguous, despite his repeated declarations of loyalty to its principles (as in, for example, his famous declaration to the U.S. journalist James Creelman in 1908, that "I believe democracy to be the only true, just principle of government," before going on to declare—falsely, of course—that he would retire from office in 1910).

Nevertheless, it is increasingly clear that liberalism, traditionally interpreted as an esoteric ideology espoused by and for the benefit of a minority elite, enjoyed considerable popular support among rural communities throughout Mexico in the nineteenth century. As a consequence, liberalism provided both a popular political base for Porfirismo, especially in its early years, as well as a constitutional and ideological framework around which the regime was constructed.

However, while the regime claimed legitimacy through the adherence to the Constitution of 1857 and to constitutional practices (such as elections), in practice it blocked the creation of institutions (i.e., political parties, institutions of government, or an independent judiciary) that would have restrained presidential or personal authority. As an advocate of pragmatic politics, Díaz himself openly admitted his skepticism of constitutional or ideological purity, if we are to believe an anecdote recounted by one of his biographers (J. F. Iturribarria). In response to a request from a journalist as to how to respond to accusations in the opposition press (made in the newspaper *El Partido Liberal*) that the regime had violated the principles of the 1857 Constitution, Díaz chose to draw an analogy with the practice of religion:

> The answer is simple: Catholics violate the 10 Commandments every day, because it is impossible to comply rigorously with every one of them: it is equally impossible for the government to adhere strictly to the letter of the law as laid down in our Constitution.

Díaz's natural pragmatism and cynicism were given further endorsement by a third component that provided ideological justification for the regime, particularly in its latter years: Positivism. A powerful faction within the ruling elite warmly embraced this fashionable ideology because it provided them with a political theory that advocated economic progress and social planning under the control of a technocratic elite and bolstered by an authoritarian government. Despite his resolute support of pragmatism rather than ideology as the basis for political action, and despite his claims to be a Liberal, Díaz endorsed the Positivist view that the practice of politics should not concentrate, as liberalism demanded, on the protection of individual freedom, the equality of the individual before the law, or on a guarantee of effective suffrage or democratic representation, but on the protection of social order and the promotion of material (or scientific) progress. As he explained to James Creelman in 1908:

> We have preserved the republican and democratic form of government. We have defended the theory and kept it intact. Yet we adopted a patriarchal policy in the actual administration of the nation's affairs, guiding and restraining popular tendencies with full faith that an enforced peace would allow education, industry and commerce to develop elements of stability and unity.

As Díaz himself admitted in the same interview, however, the political situation of 1908 demanded a new form of popular representation. Unfortunately for the regime, the factional divisions within the elite made it impossible to reform the system from within, and no alternative or successor could be agreed upon. The political reforms promised in 1908, which had aroused considerable expectations and political activity throughout the country, failed to materialize.

The indifference with regard to the maintenance of the content as well as the form of Liberal constitutional practice became one of the regime's greatest shortcomings. While the restrictions on the development of political institutions and parties helped to keep opposition to a minimum, it deprived the regime of both institutional forms of succession and of a means of channeling the demand for wider political participation in a society that had undergone a profound transformation by 1910. In addition, the adherence to Positivism, by widening the ideological and factional divisions within the Porfirian elite, narrowed the ideological base as well as the constituency of support for the regime. It was also obvious to many observers that Díaz, as he approached his eightieth birthday in 1910, no longer possessed the capability nor the energy to sustain the necessary degree of control over a personalist system under increasing strain.

As a consequence, the regime's response to the growing political crisis was inadequate, inept, and counter-productive. As the anti-reelectionist movement gained steady momentum after 1908, the regime attempted to repress and erradicate opposition, and, in desperation, persuaded the old caudillo to stand for another term of office in the elections of 1910. Less than a year later, the Maderista Revolution had forced Díaz to relinquish power and go into exile in Paris, where he died in 1915.

For nearly two generations following the death of Porfirio Díaz, his regime was associated in the popular imagination with the worst of excesses of tyranny: the willful violation of Mexican sovereignty, the abuse of constitutional authority, dictatorship, repression, and elitism. In the 1980s and 1990s, however, there have been encouraging signs, however, that official anti-Díaz satanization is increasingly moribund. As the Mexican historian Enrique Krauze stated in a biographical sketch of Díaz in 1987,

> a more generous interpretation—which has always been absent in Mexico—would concede, without distorting the truth, that Porfirio Díaz made a decisive contribution to the material construction and the national consolidation of his country.

Select Bibliography

Cosío Villegas, Daniel, *Historia Moderna de México*. 10 vols., Mexico City: Hermes, 1965–74.

Díaz, C. Tello, *El Exilio: Un Relato de Familia*. Mexico City: Cal y Arena, 1993.

Díaz, Porfirio, *Memorias de Porfirio Díaz*. 2 vols., Mexico City: Consejo Nacional Para la Cultura y las Artes, 1994.

González, L., "La dictadura de Díaz." In *Dictaduras y Dictadores*, edited by J. Labastida Martín del Campo. Mexico City: Siglo XXI, 1986.

Guerra, F.J., *México: Del Antiguo Régimen a la Revolución.* 2 vols., Mexico City: Fondo de Cultura Económica, 1988.

Katz, Friedrich, "Liberal Republic and Porfiriato." In *Mexico Since Independence,* edited by L. Bethell. Cambridge and New York: Cambridge University Press, 1991.

Knight, Alan, *The Mexican Revolution.* 2 vols., Cambridge and New York: Cambridge University Press, 1986.

Krauze, Enrique, *Porfirio Díaz: Místico de la Autoridad.* Mexico City: Fondo de Cultura Económica, 1987.

Taracena, A., *Porfirio Díaz.* Mexico City: Jus, 1960.

Valadés, J., *El Porfirismo: Historia de un Régimen.* 3 vols., Mexico City: Porrúa, 1941–48.

—Paul Garner

DÍAZ DEL CASTILLO, BERNAL

c.1495–1584 • Conquistador and Chronicler

Bernal Díaz del Castillo is acclaimed today as the author of the most popular and comprehensive eyewitness account of the conquest of Mexico. Despite the extravagance of some of his claims and the inaccuracy of some of his data, his *Historia verdadera de la conquista de la Nueva España* (True Account of the Conquest of New Spain) remains the most rich and compelling version available, eclipsing even Fernando (Hernán) Cortés's famous *Cartas de relación* (1519–26).

Born in Medina del Campo in Old Castile, Bernal Díaz declared that he arrived in the New World in 1514 on Pedrarias Dávila's voyage to Tierra Firme (Nombre de Dios in Panama) and that he participated in the first three expeditions to Mexico, which were those of Francisco Hernández de Córdoba (1517), Juan de Grijalva (1518), and Hernán Cortés (1519). Although it is doubtful that he took part in the second of these expeditions, he is widely acknowledged to have participated as a foot-soldier in Cortés's first overland march to the Mexica (Aztec) capital of Tenochtitlan in 1519 as well as the second major offensive that resulted in the fall of that island capital (the site of today's Mexico City) in August 1521 and subsequent events in Mexico up to 1524. He accompanied Cortés on the disastrous expedition to Hibueras (Honduras) in 1524–26 and spent the remainder of his life in New Spain, sustained by titles of trusteeship *(encomienda),* whereby the labor and goods produced by Indians inhabiting the area held in trust were granted to the trustee *(encomendero)* as tribute. With early grants in the 1520s near Coatzacoalcos in Tabasco and in Chiapas (which he lost in the 1530s), Bernal Díaz settled permanently in Guatemala in the 1540s after the first (1539–41) of his two trips to Spain to secure greater reward for his conquest efforts. The second trip, which either awakened or confirmed his worst forebodings about the future prospects of the *encomendero* class, occurred in 1550–51. He died an octogenarian in Santiago de Guatemala on February 3, 1584.

Bernal Díaz began to write his *Historia* around 1550, some 30 years after the fall of the Mexica capital; in 1568 he finished a version of the work, which he sent to Spain in 1575 for publication. In the meantime he continued to work on the manuscript in his possession, adding the last touches close to the time of his death. During his lifetime, other historians of Mexico, such as Alonso de Zorita (1560s) and Diego Muñoz Camargo (1576), mentioned Bernal Díaz's writings in their own; at least one local resident in Santiago de Guatemala, the municipal official Juan Rodríguez del Cabrillo, stated in 1579 that he had read Bernal Díaz's chronicle.

Bernal Díaz's work thus had at least a limited local circulation in manuscript during his lifetime, but the version sent to Spain was not published until 1632, when it suffered the emendations of Fray Alonso de Remón and Fray Gabriel Adarzo y Santander, who sought to highlight the work of their Mercedarian order and the Christian mission in general in the conquest of Mexico. The manuscript that remained in Guatemala was transcribed and published in Mexico by Genaro García in 1904–05 and now is regarded as the authoritative version of the work.

Although Bernal Díaz's *Historia* concentrates on the events of the Mexican conquest from 1519 to 1521 (chapters 19–156), the work covers events in Mexico from 1517 through 1568 (chapters 1–18, 157–212); it includes the discussion of affairs pertinent to the well-being of the viceroyalty of New Spain that occurred at court in Spain as well as in the seats of governance of Hispaniola and Cuba. Broader in scope than the 1519–21 conquest of Mexico that is the heart of the work, Bernal Díaz's objective was to place New Spain in the context of the Spanish Empire at the time and to ensure that the importance of Mexico was not eclipsed by the subsequent discovery of Inca Peru and its spectacular mineral wealth in the South American Andes.

Equally if not more pressing was his desire to claim for the common conquistador (himself and his remaining peers and their heirs) the privileges and prestige that he understood to be their due and to ensure that those rewards would endure in perpetuity. His trips to Spain taught him that the interests of the *encomenderos* were being eroded by a series of royal decrees that had begun with the New Laws of 1542 as well as by competing claims for royal recognition from others, not the least of which was a developing royal bureaucracy dedicated to managing the Crown's resources at home and abroad. Politically, the conquests in America had come under increasingly severe pressure from Fray Bartolomé de Las Casas and his colleagues, who persuaded the emperor, in the name of Christian evangelization and justice, to curtail the prerogatives of private citizens and their access to the native populations of the Indies.

Even the writing of history had dealt the conquistadors a severe blow. Cortés's published letters (1522–26) effectively attributed the victory over the Mexica to his own brilliance as a military strategist and faith in Divine Providence, and Francisco López de Gómara (1552) and other historians likewise emphasized Cortés's role to the detriment of that of his men. Additionally, these authors inadvertently but effectively undermined the conquistadors' interests by complacently assuming the justice of the conquests at the very time they came under political and legislative attack. This attack was vividly realized in Las Casas's tract the *Brevíssima relación de la destrucción de las Indias,* which appeared in print in Seville in 1552 and which was rebutted by Bernal Díaz in his *Historia* with the same or greater vehemence and scorn that he heaped on López de Gómara's work.

Bernal Díaz's *Historia* is thus of great interest today not only for its inimitable account of the conquest of Mexico, written several decades after the fact, but also for its compelling dramatization of how an old conquistador struggled year by year to keep pace with the events that threatened his economic and political well-being. His greatest achievement was his attempt to grant to the soldiers-conquistadors of Mexico the glory he thought ought to be theirs in accordance with the long Castilian tradition of the Christian warrior who fought against pagans and infidels in the name of his Christian faith.

Select Bibliography

Brooks, Francis J., "Moteuczoma Xocoyotl, Hernán Cortes, and Bernal Díaz del Castillo: The Construction of an Arrest." *Hispanic American Historical Review* 75:2 (1995).

Díaz, Bernal, *The Conquest of New Spain,* translated and with an introduction by J. M. Cohen. Baltimore: Penguin, 1963.

Pastor Bodmer, Beatriz, *The Armature of Conquest: Spanish Accounts of the Discovery of America, 1492–1589,* translated by L. L. Hunt. Stanford, California: Stanford University Press, 1992.

—ROLENA ADORNO

DÍAZ ORDAZ, GUSTAVO

1911–79 • President

Gustavo Díaz Ordaz presided over Mexico during the most successful stage of the Import Substitution Industrialization model (which sought to promote industrialization by substituting domestic manufactures for import), but the authoritarian presidentialist system entered into crisis following his violent repression of student and labor demonstrators in 1968.

Díaz Ordaz, born in Ciudad Serdán, Puebla, on March 11, 1911, the son of a government accountant, included in his ancestry the conquistador-chronicler Bernal Díaz del Castillo. He was educated at the universities of Oaxaca and Puebla, graduating in law in 1937. His entire career was spent in public service, first in Puebla's government (1932–43), then in federal government (1943–70). He became a federal deputy (1943–46), then senator (1946–52). Díaz Ordaz next served in the Department of the Interior (1952–58), then became secretary of government under President Adolfo López Mateos, a post that placed him in the customary line of succession for the presidency. In 1964 he won the presidential election with, allegedly, 90 percent of the vote. The new president became the brunt of many a popular pun because of his markedly receding chin.

During Díaz Ordaz's term in office, Mexico's Gross National Product (GNP) expanded from under US$16 billion to over US$23 billion, while per capita GNP grew from US$426 to US$510. Although Díaz Ordaz stressed industrial development and the quest for foreign capital, his administration distributed more than 9 million hectares (22 million acres) of land to *campesinos* (peasants), and under his watch Mexico achieved agricultural self-sufficiency for the first (and last) time in the twentieth century. Inflation remained modest and the peso steady. Schools were built and teachers trained in large numbers; secondary school enrollment increased by 20 percent. He rewarded the loyalty of officially organized labor by implementing profit sharing. But Mexico fell behind Canada to second place in world silver production, while the radio and television industry came increasingly under government control.

His failing was political: Díaz Ordaz opposed the reforms and democratization urged upon him by ruling Partido Revolucionario Institucional (PRI, or Institutional Revolutionary Party) president Carlos A. Madrazo. The consequences were felt as Mexico prepared to host the 1968 Olympics, the first to be staged in a Third World country. Opponents of the single-party state objected to the regime's public distortions of Mexican reality and its uses of the games for propaganda purposes. Massive student-worker demonstrations in the Federal District, Puebla, and other cities called for a broadening of civil liberties and cancellation of the expensive Olympics. A desperate and authoritarian government responded with military violence: hundreds were killed, especially in the Plaza of Tlatelolco on October 1, 1968, and the Olympics took place in a somber atmosphere. The prestige of the all-powerful presidency and the PRI were considerably diminished by this calamity. Díaz Ordaz's economic achievements would forever be obscured by this political miscalculation. His successor would confront a festering credibility problem, especially with intellectuals, more severe than previous PRI administrations.

Díaz Ordaz selected his government minister, Luis Echeverría Álvarez, to succeed him. Echeverría eventually appointed Díaz Ordaz as ambassador to Spain, a post the ex-president was forced to decline due to hostile reaction at home. He then retreated from public view until his death on July 15, 1979.

Select Bibliography

Covarrubias, Ricardo, *Los 67 gobernantes del México independiente.* 3rd edition, Mexico City: PRI, 1968.

Hansen, Roger D., *The Politics of Mexican Development.* Baltimore: Johns Hopkins University Press, 1971.

Hellman, Judith Adler, *Mexico in Crisis.* 2nd edition, New York: Holmes and Meier, 1983.

Zermeño, Sergio, *México, una democracia utópica: El movimiento estudiantil del 68.* 8th edition, Mexico City: Siglo XXI, 1978.

—Harold Dana Sims

DÍAZ SOTO Y GAMA, ANTONIO

1880–1967 • Intellectual and Politician

Many years after the Mexican Revolution, Antonio Díaz Soto y Gama apologized for his "scandalous outbursts that today strike me as unpardonable," though he noted that the blame was not entirely his own. "There is, whether we like it or not, a Revolutionary psychosis, a state of being [that is] characterized by the flood of passions that twist and unbalance the mind and lead it into paradoxes and extraordinary aberrations." To be sure, if overheated rhetoric is a sin, Díaz Soto y Gama had much to atone for: he was among the most impassioned and intransigent intellectuals of the revolutionary years, an urban lawyer who made common cause with peasant rebels and emerged as one of their most vociferous spokesmen.

Díaz Soto y Gama was one of 16 children born to Conrado Díaz Soto and Concepción Gama in the city of San Luis Potosí. His father, a provincial lawyer, instilled in his children both an idealistic adherence to the ideals of nineteenth-century liberalism and a hatred of the regime of Porfirio Díaz. Porfirian San Luis Potosí was a city in ferment, where a burgeoning middle class found itself excluded from power by a rigid class of landlord-industrialists, many with close links to foreign capital. Many ambitious professionals felt themselves stifled politically and downwardly mobile economically. Díaz Soto y Gama earned a law degree in 1901 from the Scientific and Literary Institute, which later became the state university of San Luis Potosí, but he found employment hard to find. By 1909, the best job he could find was as a clerk in a U.S. law firm that served business interests.

While a student, Díaz Soto y Gama immersed himself in the works of European anarchist and socialist theorists and participated in student politics, activities that placed him in close association with other revolutionary precursors such as the Flores Magón brothers, Camilo Arriaga, and Juan Sarabia. He served as vice president of the important Club Liberal "Ponciano Arriaga." His gift for fiery oratory was early apparent, especially in a memorable speech he delivered in Pinos, Zacatecas, in July 1901, in which he denounced the Porfirian oligarchy for its links to foreigners, the Catholic Church for its reactionary opposition to liberal reforms, and the dictator himself for betraying democracy and liberal principle. The speech was sufficiently inflammatory that Díaz ordered the young lawyer arrested and thrown in Mexico City's Belén Prison, where he remained for the remainder of the year. Before, during, and following his imprisonment, he contributed prolifically to various radical periodicals including *El Demófilo, El Hijo de Ahuizote,* and *El Diario del Hogar.*

In addition to his repeated imprisonment, Díaz Soto y Gama was forced into a brief period of exile in the United States in 1903 following his denunciation of Nuevo León governor Bernardo Reyes. He returned to San Luis Potosí in 1904, but his family's economic plight and tensions within the radical movement kept him on the political sidelines until after the end of the Díaz dictatorship in May 1911. He campaigned briefly for the governorship of his home state but soon withdrew from the race in favor of the Maderista candidate. For a time, he moderated his rhetoric, downplaying social reform in order to bolster the unsteady presidency of Francisco I. Madero. By mid-1912, however, he split with Madero over the latter's suppression of freedom of the press and his military repression of the agrarian movement of Emiliano Zapata.

This marked the beginning of Díaz Soto y Gama's virtually single-minded commitment to the principles of *agrarismo*. His position was that the upheaval in the countryside had advanced to such a stage that only a massive and radical seizure and division of the country's bloated haciendas would calm it. Moreover, the dangers of foot-dragging on the issue could, he believed, lead to a truly grievous situation, possibly the introduction of communism, which he deplored. His libertarian tendencies became clear in 1912, when Díaz Soto y Gama, together with Sarabia and Arriaga, helped found a Socialist School that aimed at securing benefits for workers. That school soon metamorphosed into the anarcho-syndicalist Casa del Obrero Mundial, an organization that injected an anarchist note into the Mexican labor movement and that was influential for many years. This orientation led him vehemently to eschew politics in favor of "direct action," a principle he easily applied to the country's desperate agrarian situation. In early 1914, when President Victoriano Huerta closed the Casa del Obrero, he carried his convictions into action by joining the Zapatista rebels of Morelos.

The largely provincial and semiliterate leadership of the Zapatista movement welcomed such sophisticates into their ranks, making them the movement's chief theorists as well as pressing them into service as "secretaries" (spokesmen and brokers with the outside world). Díaz Soto y Gama was among the most famous of the urban intellectuals affiliated with Zapatismo. He did little to smooth relations between the Zapatistas and their enemies; indeed, he was instrumental in counseling the southerners against compromise of any sort. His most famous moment was his speech of October 27, 1914, at the convention of Revolutionary factions held at Aguascalientes. In this notorious oration, he heatedly exhorted his Zapatista comrades to defy both the Carrancistas and the Villistas. At one point, he seized the Mexican flag—which parties to the convention had been signing as a patriotic gesture—and crumpled it in his fist, denouncing it as a pernicious symbol of the clerical reaction headed by the nineteenth-century emperor Agustín de Iturbide and of the repression of the conquered indigenous race. This bold and impetuous gesture was greeted with pandemonium from the audience, complete with shouted death threats and cocked pistols. Only the timely intervention of some of the convention's most respected figures managed to restore order.

Although Díaz Soto y Gama later may have regretted his impetuousness, vitriolic oratory and controversy continued to be a hallmark of his style. After Zapata's death in 1919, he supported the Aguaprieta Rebellion and the presidential campaign of Álvaro Obregón. In 1920, he cofounded (with Aurelio Manrique) the National Agrarian Party and was elected federal deputy from the district of Atlixco, Puebla. He used his position in congress insistently to urge for immediate and massive seizure and redistribution of land.

The turbulent decade of the 1920s turned him against Marxism, which he had embraced early in the decade, and toward an increased commitment to Catholicism. By the early 1930s, he was a vociferous opponent of Plutarco Elías Calles and an advocate of religious teaching in the schools. In 1940, he backed the presidential candidate of the extreme right, Juan Andreu Almazán. In subsequent years, while teaching Mexican history in the National Preparatory School and agrarian law at the National School of Law of the Universidad Nacional Autónoma de México (UNAM), he became a bitter and outspoken critic of communism in general and of Soviet communism in particular. He came to believe that communism was a godless religion presided over by sectarian fanatics bent on subjugating the individual will. He also believed that capitalism was an amoral and heartless system that could be redeemed only by the "humanitarian spirit" and Christian morality imparted by the Roman Catholic Church.

Select Bibliography

Cockcroft, James, *Intellectual Precursors of the Mexican Revolution, 1900–1913.* Austin: University of Texas Press, 1968.

Díaz Soto y Gama, Antonio, *La revolución agraria del sur y Emiliano Zapata su caudillo.* Mexico City: Ediciones "El Caballito," 1976.

_____, *Otro holocausto.* Mexico City: Jus, 1980.

Dulles, John W. F., *Yesterday in Mexico: A Chronicle of the Revolution, 1919–1936.* Austin: University of Texas Press, 1961.

Hart, John M., *Anarchism and the Mexican Working Class, 1860–1931.* Austin: University of Texas Press, 1978.

—TIMOTHY J. HENDERSON

DÍAZ Y BARRETO, PASCUAL

1875–1936 • Archbishop

One of the more controversial members of the Mexican Catholic hierarchy, Díaz y Barreto was a key figure in the defining of church-state relations in the nation. He was born on June 22, 1875, to a humble family in Zapopan, Jalisco, site of an important cult to the Virgin of that name. Like the majority of Catholic children from the provinces, he first studied in the Franciscan Apostolic College, later entering the Guadalajara seminary on October 18, 1887. There he took courses in Latin, philosophy, dogmatic and moral theology, canon law, sacred scripture, and civil rights.

He took minor orders in 1897, being nominated presbyter on September 17, 1899. In 1903, after various attempts, he entered the Jesuit Order. Two years later he took up the novitiate in Oña, Burgos, Spain, returning there years later and traveling on to Enghien, Belgium, where he took his doctorate on June 16, 1913.

While revolution unfolded in Mexico, Father Díaz y Barreto continued his apprenticeship in Champagne, Amsterdam, Liège, and Louvain. He returned to Mexico on August 25, 1913, at a time when there was no possibility of taking up any priestly position. He stayed briefly in the monastery of Tepozotlán until the Jesuit Provincial, Marcelo Renaud, commissioned him to teach in the Mascarones Scientific Institute in Mexico City. A little later it was closed by Revolutionaries under General Alvaro Obregón.

When this first wave of anti-Catholicism calmed down, Father Díaz was put in charge of the Church of the Holy Family, where he first gained a reputation as an excellent preacher. But it was his appointment to the Diocese of Tabasco on December 10, 1922, that was to mark him for life. He was consecrated Bishop of Tabasco on February 2, 1923, in the Basilica of Guadalupe with great pomp and ceremony by the apostolic delegate Leopoldo Ruiz y Flores.

He arrived shortly afterwards in Tabasco, where Governor Tomás Garrido Canabal had begun a ferocious anticlerical movement. Pascual Díaz y Barreto took charge of the Villahermosa Cathedral. Unlike those in other states, the Cathedral precinct in Tabasco consisted of a shabby-looking building and a simple belfry as the facade. The evangelists had not constructed any beautiful baroque buildings there as in other areas, and as a result no religious order had remained for any length of time in this tropical spot.

Although he could count on the support of some families, Díaz y Barreto could not counteract the influence of a governor, whom his critics described as a "devourer of priests." When the rebellion under Adolfo de la Huerta flared up in December 1923, there was no protection for the new bishop, and he was promptly accused of backing the anti-Obregonist insurrection; as a result, in mid-1924 he was obliged to leave his post permanently.

Two years later the pro-Catholic, peasant-based Cristero Rebellion erupted in the Bajío region of north-central Mexico. On July 26, 1926, the Catholic hierarchy decided to close the churches as a means of putting pressure on the state, governed at the time by Plutarco Elías Calles (1924–28), in protest against its anticlerical measures. The government put a stop to the reopening of the churches, and guerrilla groups calling themselves Cristeros took up arms against the government. The struggle lasted for three years and gave rise to the most violent religious persecution in Mexican history.

Pascual Díaz y Barreto, appointed secretary of the Episcopal Committee, which was to meet with the secretary of the interior to resolve the problem, played a key role in the political negotiations. Yet the very day of the first meeting, January 10, 1927, Díaz was expelled from Mexico. He suffered considerable penury in New York before he was able to find adequate rooms. Dedicating himself for nearly a year to the study of English, he was eventually proficient enough to fulfill his intention of holding a number of conferences to broadcast the situation of the Catholic Church and clergy in Mexico.

Pope Pius IX nominated him "Official Intermediary" with regard to all that concerned the Mexican Catholic hierarchy. Meanwhile a change of government and the bullets of a Catholic fanatic ended Obregón's dreams of reelection. Emilio Portes Gil became provisional president and immediately started talks to arrive at "arrangements" with Rome. Díaz y Barreto and Apostolic Delegate Ruiz y Flores were largely instrumental in finding a solution to the conflict.

The bishop of Tabasco's performance merited a reward. On June 21, 1929, he was informed by the pope's representative that he had been nominated archbishop of Mexico. One week later he celebrated his first mass as the head of the Catholic hierarchy in the Old Church of La Profesa, which had been selected as a provisional cathedral, since the actual cathedral remained in the hands of the government.

As archbishop he was responsible for organizing the festivities for the fourth centenary of the Appearance of the Virgin of Guadalupe, celebrated in 1931. Enormous crowds flocked to the basilica, demonstrating Mexico's ardor for the faith that had been restored after years of persecution. Nevertheless a bomb exploded on the altar at the feet of the image of the Guadalupe. It was considered a miracle that the blast did not damage Juan Diego's cloak on which the image of the Virgin appears. Díaz sought redress from President Pascual Ortiz Rubio, but those responsible were never found.

Much criticism had to be dealt with and procedures undertaken to open the churches, which remained closed at the discretion of the authorities. Meanwhile, Díaz y Barreto dedicated a part of his time to encouraging Catholic action groups throughout the republic. After a painful illness, Díaz y Barreto died on June 19, 1936. His funeral rites were the most impressive ever witnessed for a prelate of his rank; thousands accompanied him to his last resting place in Mexico Cathedral.

Select Bibliography

Brush, David Allen, *The De la Huerta Rebellion in Mexico 1923–1924*. Syracuse, New York: Syracuse University Press, 1969.

Martínez Assad, Carlos, editor, *A Dios lo que es de Dios*. Mexico City: Editorial Aguilar, 1995.

Sosa, Francisco, *El Episcopado mexicano: Biografía de los Ilmos. Señores arzobispos de México desde la época colonial hasta nuestros días*. 2 vols., Mexico City: Jus, 1962.

—CARLOS MARTÍNEZ ASSAD

DIÉGUEZ, MANUEL M.

1874–1924 • General and Politician

The son of working-class parents, Manuel Diéguez was born in Guadalajara on March 10, 1874, where he received a basic education. He left home at age 15 and in Mazatlán joined the crew of the warship *Oaxaca,* where he worked as a kitchen hand. In 1904 he was able to find work as assistant paymaster in the Cananea Consolidated Copper Company in northern Sonora. In 1906 he helped found a labor union in the Cananea mine, the Union Liberal Humanidad, forming links with the anarchist Partido Liberal Mexicano (PLM, or Mexican Liberal Party). A leader of a violently suppressed strike at Cananea, Diéguez was imprisoned in the notorious island prison of San Juan de Ulúa in Veracruz and was not released until the triumph of the Revolutionary forces of Francisco I. Madero. Returning to Cananea, he was named municipal president in 1912.

Following general Victoriano Huerta's coup d'état against Madero in 1913, Diéguez raised a volunteer force of 400 men to fight the federal army and was named a colonel in the Constitutionalist forces under Álvaro Obregón. Pushing south through the states of Sonora and Sinaloa, Diéguez was able to defeat the federal forces in the territory of Tepic, opening the way for Constitutionalist forces to take Guadalajara. After Revolutionary forces split in 1915 Diéguez remained loyal to Obregón and Venustiano Carranza. Defeated by Pancho Villa's forces in February 1915 Diéguez was able to regroup and once again advance on Guadalajara, taking the city in April of that year. He participated in the rout of Villista forces at la Trinidad, and on June 14 he was promoted to the rank of division general. Sent to Sonora in pursuit of the remnants of the Villistas, he defeated the Villista ex-governor of Sonora, José María Maytorena, in the Yaqui River valley.

In April 1916 Diéguez was named interim governor and military commander of the state of Jalisco, and his mandate as governor was renewed in state elections the following year. Diéguez's tenure as governor was marked by his radical pro-labor policies and the zeal with which he applied new federal anticlerical legislation. The archbishop of Guadalajara, Francisco Orozco y Jiménez, was expelled from Mexico after protesting against Diéguez's policies, and many churches were closed. Diéguez also served as chief of operations for the military zone comprising the states of Querétaro, Guanajuato, San Luis Potosí, as well as southern Nuevo León and the Huasteca region of Hidalgo and Veracruz. In 1919 he resigned as governor, taking charge of Constitutionalist forces trying to contain Villa's forces in northern Mexico. After resigning as governor Diéguez became a landholder, joining the Cámara Agrícola Nacional Jalisciense (National Agricultural Chamber of Jalisco), which sought to defend landholders against the government's agrarian reform initiatives.

During Venustiano Carranza's conflict with the Sonoran government in 1920, Diéguez was dispatched to Sonora to bring governor Adolfo de la Huerta to heel. De la Huerta was able to convince Diéguez to withdraw to Guadalajara, however, where he was imprisoned by Carranza loyalists. During his advance on Mexico City, de la Huerta, already named interim president, freed Diéguez; however, during the early years of the Obregón administration Diéguez chose to remain in exile in the United States. He returned to Mexico in December 1923 when general Enrique Estrada launched a rebellion in Jalisco in support of the presidential candidacy of de la Huerta against Plutarco Elías Calles, Obregón's anointed successor. After the western front of de la Huerta's forces were defeated, Diéguez fled south as far as the state of Chiapas, where he was captured by general Donato Bravo Izquierdo. After being tried by a council of war, Diéguez was shot on April 21, 1924.

—ÁLVARO MATUTE

DOÑA MARINA

See Malinche and Malinchismo

DRUG TRADE

The illicit production of and commerce in drugs in Mexico is oriented toward exports. Most of the marijuana and heroin produced in Mexico, as well as the cocaine traversing the country, is smuggled to the U.S. market. The use of these drugs has not yet become a significant public health problem in Mexico. The only available national household survey on drug abuse (published by *Encuesta Nacional de Adicciones* in 1989) showed that in 1988, of the total Mexican population between 12 and 65 years of age, living in urban areas, 2.99 percent had used marijuana at least once in their lifetime, 0.33 percent had tried cocaine, and 0.11 percent had experimented with heroin. The prevalence of drug use in Mexico, according to this survey, was less than one-tenth that in the United States in 1990, and among the lowest in Latin America.

More important than users as a determinant of the drug trade in Mexico has been the relationship between the price of drugs in this country and their price in the United States, which is largely the result of antidrug law enforcement in both nations. In this market, the costs of producing and exporting drugs reflect the risks of engaging in these illicit activities, which in turn depend on more or less stringent levels of enforcement. Historically, the Mexican drug market has reacted to changes in U.S. antidrug policy, which has followed an increasingly punitive trend. By and large, U.S. efforts to stop drugs (marijuana, heroin, and cocaine) before they enter U.S. territory have worked against domestic Mexican efforts to fight drug trafficking. Furthermore, largely unsuccessful Mexican attempts to curb this illegal market have, over time, had a severe impact on Mexican society and institutions, as well as on U.S.-Mexican relations.

Origins of the Drug Trade

Drug smuggling became a lucrative activity in Mexico at the beginning of this century when the United States approved laws that prohibited the import of opium and cocaine, which had been legal until then. As a result of restrictions on production and trade in drugs, a large part of the American drug market went underground. The U.S. government decision to limit vice markets, drugs and alcohol in particular, resulted in an overnight increase in the prices of these goods, an increase that had a direct effect on Mexico. The enactment of the Opium Exclusion Act of 1909, outlawing the importation and use of opium, of the Harrison Narcotic Law in 1914, prohibiting over-the-counter sale of opium and cocaine in the United States, and of the 1922 Narcotic Drug Import and Export Act, further restricting the import of crude opium and coca leaves, effectively created a profitable market for narcotics in the United States and provided an incentive for Mexicans (and others) to ship drugs into the United States and take advantage of the high prices.

Mexican exports of opium and heroin for U.S. consumption flourished in the 1910s and 1920s. Something similar happened with Mexican exports of marijuana, as more and more states in the United States regulated its use, production, and sale. The cannabis plant, which had been produced legally in Mexico and exported since the late nineteenth century, if not earlier, mostly for industrial and medicinal purposes, quickly reached the U.S. market in larger quantities in the 1920s and 1930s. Thus, a significant contraband along the U.S.-Mexican border emerged after 1910, basically prompted by prohibition in the United States.

Opium coming from other countries also was introduced into Mexico, apparently in large quantities, to be smuggled later into the United States. As a result, Mexico became not only a more prominent producer and exporter of opium and its derivatives, and of marijuana, but a temporary importer too, since its territory offered an attractive transit point for opium smugglers (and later for those carrying cocaine) on their way to the United States.

As opium, morphine, heroin, cocaine, and marijuana dealers became federal or state offenders in the United States, Mexico also became a safe haven for those engaging in illegal transactions across the border, since transgressors could cross the frontier to escape from U.S. law-enforcement authorities. It was not unusual for U.S. officers to cross the border in "hot pursuit" of Mexican or American criminals.

It should not be surprising then that Mexico's first legislation against drugs, introduced by President Venustiano Carranza in 1916, prohibited the import of opium, the use of which was practically nonexistent in Mexico. By banning opium imports Carranza was trying to counter the impact of American antiopium laws on Mexico, that is, the growth in Mexican opium imports and exports, the flight of drug dealers into Mexican territory, and the ensuing U.S. law enforcement raids across the border.

At the same time, Mexican law enforcers and politicians (such as Esteban Cantú, strongman and local governor of Baja California Norte) offered protection to or became active organizers of opium contraband into the United States. In 1917, only a year after banning the importation of opium, Carranza outlawed opium transactions in Baja California Norte, where Cantú ostensibly was contravening the prohibitory statutes.

In response to the proliferation of opium poppy production, President Álvaro Obregón instructed governors in the northern states to ban cultivation and to destroy existing fields before they could be harvested, and in 1923 he promulgated a new decree prohibiting the importation of opium, cocaine, and heroin, and mandating harsher penalties for drug growers and manufacturers. The federal government had already prohibited the cultivation and sale of marijuana in 1920. By the mid-1920s, most of the drug trade in Mexico was illegal.

Yet efforts to enforce antidrug laws only led to the creation of a persevering smuggling business. To the extent that antidrug laws proved to be unenforceable both in Mexico and the United States, more forceful attempts to prohibit the drug trade led to the creation of an ever more lucrative market, largely organized around the use of violence and corruption. By 1927, when President Plutarco Elías Calles signed yet another decree banning the export of marijuana and heroin, it was clear that Mexico was no longer an important transit point for international drug smugglers, but that drug production and trafficking had become entrenched in certain areas of the country. As the 1930s came to an end, Mexican officials had learned that the drug trade could not be stamped out by decree and that efforts to enforce antidrug laws invariably resulted in the corruption and killing of numerous officials. Marijuana and opium poppies were readily available, and their cultivation had expanded beyond northern Mexico. Although presumably the bulk of the drug contraband still originated in Baja California, Sinaloa (by 1943 opium had become the largest cash crop in the state), Sonora, and Chihuahua, large smuggling operations also were organized, for the first time, in states located farther south, such as San Luis Potosí.

Mexican Drug Trade from 1945 to 1980

In 1948 the Mexican government tried to confront a thriving drug market by organizing La Gran Campaña. This program became the first national crop eradication campaign to cover virtually the whole country; a specialized unit of antinarcotic police and a small number of soldiers (no more than 400, according to official accounts) were assigned to the campaign. Since then, these forces have participated in antidrug programs on a permanent basis.

The end of World War II, as well as the subsequent increase in the use of heroin—notorious in the 1950s and 1960s in the United States—had a negative impact on the Mexican drug market. The scant information available indicates that the traditional heroin routes were disrupted as a result of the war, and as traffic from the Far East and Europe through Central America was interrupted, Mexico became an attractive alternative for international heroin traffickers to reorganize their smuggling of heroin into the United States. Apparently, the Mexican government was able to postpone with U.S. assistance (mostly from agents of the Federal Bureau of Investigation) the relocation of heroin trafficking organizations in Mexican territory. However, after heroin manufacturing in Italy and France was banned in the 1950s and 1960s, and after Turkey enforced a draconian program against the cultivation of opium poppies in the late 1960s, Mexico finally became the primary source country for heroin bound to the U.S. market (according to the President's Commission on Organized Crime, 1986). It is possible that up to 10 tons of heroin were processed every year in Mexico during the mid-1970s, 6.5 tons of which probably were smuggled into the United States.

In the case of marijuana, a considerably larger market in terms of users, Mexican producers and smugglers took perhaps the lead, although often aided by U.S. traffickers, in supplying the heavily expanding demand among the American population in the 1960s. With the exception of a few years, Mexico has been the most important foreign supplier of marijuana for the U.S. market.

Figures on the size of the Mexican drug market can vary considerably, as a result of both political interests and technical difficulties in estimating illegal markets. All sources, however, indicate that by the early 1970s Mexico was supplying more than 80 percent of the heroin and marijuana available in the United States, and was already an important transit point for cocaine (still a small market in those years).

As Mexico emerged as a major producer and exporter of heroin and marijuana, the U.S. government became interested in organizing a joint U.S.-Mexico drug law enforcement program to improve the effectiveness of Mexican policy against the illicit narcotics business. Practically all authors consider U.S. pressure the most important factor explaining the launching, at the end of 1975, of a major antidrug campaign in Mexico—a turning point in Mexico's history against drugs. The typical example of those pressures (and universally considered evidence of the new, more forceful U.S. antidrug policy) is Operation Intercept, which virtually stopped border crossings for a few weeks in September 1969 by meticulously inspecting millions of cars and individuals every day. More important, however, than this exercise in coercive diplomacy was Mexico's evaluation of the risks for Mexican society and institutions of the notorious increase in drug trafficking activities and, equally important, Mexico's perception of the threat that U.S. antidrug policy and agents could represent for the autonomy of its own law enforcement programs.

Drug trafficking organizations had acquired considerable power in traditional drug producing and exporting areas, such as Durango and Sinaloa. The Mexican military, then basically relying on manual destruction of plants, had to fight not only the increase of illegal crops throughout the country but, more significant, a growing number of peasants and smugglers armed and organized for the defense of their illicit activities.

For years, the U.S. government had been fighting for a more stringent enforcement of antidrug laws in Mexico. But by 1973–74, the newly created Drug Enforcement Administration (DEA) was concentrating its efforts on the Mexican case and was ready to fight drug traffickers on its own or through a joint law enforcement program, in which the Mexican government refused to participate, fearful of entering into negotiations with foreign police—technologically and organizationally superior to the Mexican police—for the improved enforcement of its antidrug laws.

Thus, in order to regain control over areas of intense drug trafficking and to maintain antidrug law enforcement as a national affair, the Mexican government opted for a major change. Effective implementation of its new antidrug policy, however, had to rely on U.S. cooperation. The U.S. government offered financial and technical assistance (aerial photographic equipment, telecommunications, helicopters and other aircraft, spare parts, etc.), but most important, police training and support. DEA agents trained a special antinarcotics police unit in Mexico, assisted in the identification of fields, and compiled and shared intelligence with their Mexican counterparts in order to build conspiracy cases against drug traffickers. Three different programs were organized following the DEA's advice: a massive aerial eradication campaign with defoliant chemicals, which seemed adequate under the circumstances (large extensions of land covered with marijuana and opium poppy plants, and powerful, armed traffickers organizing their defense); a program for the interdiction of drugs in transit (including cocaine); and a program oriented toward the dislocation of major drug trafficking organizations. This three-pronged policy remained unaltered for more than 20 years, although resources committed to any one of the programs, as well as targets and tactics, varied over this period.

The results of Operation Condor, the core program, were astonishing. Mexican authorities were able to destroy most of the clandestine production of marijuana and opium poppy in a few years; thousands of hectares were defoliated (between 1975 and 1978, an annual average of 6,000 hectares of marijuana and more than 11,000 of opium poppy). The amount of heroin and marijuana seized reached the highest levels ever, except for 1984. Major drug traffickers were incarcerated (Sicilia Falcón, members of the Herrera family, Jorge Favela Escobar, and others). Mexico's share of U.S. heroin and marijuana imports, usually taken as a proxy for the size of the Mexican drug market, tumbled to around 25 percent or less by 1980, the lowest percentage since the 1940s.

The 1980s Drug Boom and Its Consequences

The "wars on drugs" launched by the Ronald Reagan and George Bush administrations in the 1980s represented a major change in U.S. antidrug policy and diplomacy that had far-reaching effects on the Mexican drug market and on U.S.-Mexican relations regarding the contraband of drugs.

The U.S. government decided to assume a larger responsibility in stopping the traffic of drugs by financing a major domestic interdiction program oriented to halt the illegal import of narcotics at traditional U.S. ports of entry. At the same time, the U.S. government decided to increase its capacity to assert extraterritorially its criminal laws by changing antidrug legislation and heavily expanding federal expenditures to control drugs.

The U.S. interdiction program resulted in an elevation of risks and costs for drug smugglers, and consequently in an unprecedented increase in the price of drugs in the United States. The Mexican government was unable to counter this major change in the relative price of narcotics.

Thus, Mexican drug production and exports effectively boomed in the 1980s. As the smuggling of cocaine, mostly from Colombia and entering the United States via Florida, encountered new obstacles, traffickers reorganized and began sending their merchandise through Mexican territory, even-

tually striking alliances with local drug smugglers. By the mid-1980s Mexico was again the main supplier of both marijuana and heroin for U.S. consumers, and had become the most important transit point for cocaine.

This new generation of drug traffickers, however, was considerably more powerful than those of the 1970s. The wealth amassed by drug trafficking organizations in very short periods of time and the institutional weaknesses of the Mexican police and criminal justice system explain why drug trafficking became such a formidable challenge for state authority in the 1980s and 1990s. Starting in the mid-1980s, the autonomous enforcement of Mexican antidrug laws became increasingly difficult, as DEA agents began to fight drug traffickers in Mexico more and more frequently on their own, that is, without the consent of Mexican authorities, and as Mexican institutions were increasingly unable to counter not only the economic incentives to smuggle drugs into the U.S. market but the deleterious political effects of the booming drug trade.

In 1987 President Miguel de la Madrid declared narcotics trafficking a national security problem and completely reorganized Mexican antidrug policy, a reorganization that, on similar grounds and with even larger funding, was furthered by the Salinas administration. Notwithstanding a considerable growth in financial and human resources (more than 25,000 soldiers engaged year-round in the eradication program, one-third of the nation's defense budget, and over half of the Attorney General's Office's funds), the viability of the new antidrug programs required, again, U.S. support, especially in police training and intelligence sharing.

The refurbished policy obtained historically unprecedented figures regarding the seizure of cocaine—largely the result of the joint U.S.-Mexican Northern Border Response Force, organized for the aerial interdiction of cocaine smuggling at the border. The Mexican eradication program, nevertheless, has showed increasingly diminishing returns over the 1980s and 1990s. The renewed fight against drug trafficking in Mexico also led to the incarceration of major drug lords, such as Rafael Caro Quintero (held responsible for the torture and murder of DEA agent Enrique Camarena in Mexico in 1985, which unleashed a severe U.S.-Mexican diplomatic crisis), Miguel Angel Félix Gallardo, and Ernesto Fonseca Carrillo. Others, such as "El Güero" Palma, "El Chapo" Guzmán, and Humberto and Juan García Abrego, were detained.

By and large, the Mexican government proved unable to control the illegal drug business. To the extent that drug policies raise the price of drugs, and consumers continue to number several million people capable of financing an expensive habit, prohibition results in a permanent incentive to produce and smuggle drugs. Moreover, trying to suppress such a large and lucrative market has taken a heavy toll on the traditionally weak Mexican criminal justice system. The expansion and persistence of this illegal market has damaged Mexican society and institutions in unanticipated and unpredictable ways.

The conspicuous impact of drug trafficking on the Mexican economy and political system is, however, difficult to evaluate. Estimates in 1987 and 1988 of total Mexican drug revenues (i.e., export earnings) oscillated between US$2 billion and US$6 billion a year, not all of which was invested or spent in Mexico. These figures probably had increased by the mid-1990s, but not dramatically. What changed was the amount of drug trafficking money entering the Mexican financial system as the country became a major money laundering center in the early 1990s.

Considering that Mexico's Gross Domestic Product was $288 billion in 1991, one could argue that drug-related income did not modify the Mexican economy at the macroeconomic level. However, after the mid-1980s, it had an important influence on rural areas, small towns, and even large cities such as Guadalajara, where traffickers successfully established their operations. Drug profits were invested in different economic activities: cattle ranching, real estate, restaurants, shopping centers, the stock market, vacation centers, currency exchange houses, small retail businesses, and local banks; much, of course, also was spent on luxury cars and ostentatious homes.

It has been reckoned that by the mid-1990s between 40,000 and 50,000 peasants in Mexico were involved in or made a living from the cultivation of marijuana and opium poppies. The economic incentives are appalling: growers would need to sell one ton of corn in order to earn as much as they make from one kilogram (2.2 pounds) of marijuana. Yet this should not obscure the fact that many people in the countryside are "talked into" illicitly growing the drug plants: traffickers have a considerable capacity not only to pay, but also to coerce and intimidate peasants (and others, including governmental authorities). They offer seeds, fertilizers, money, weapons and, equally important, protection from law enforcers, who may also intimidate peasants and even collude with traffickers.

The number of participants in this illegal market is, of course, much larger than the peasant population mentioned: pilots, drivers, middlemen, gunmen and people hired for protection—in certain cases, small private armies—money launderers, and other professionals offering a variety of legal and financial services. Starting in 1987 and continuing through the mid-1990s, more than 17,000 persons were apprehended every year on drug trafficking charges.

And yet, the economic consequences of the drug trade in Mexico pale compared with the political costs, in particular the extent to which the impossibility of enforcing antidrug laws undermined the rule of law and thus profoundly affected citizens' confidence in the state. Rumors and scandals became the standard means of learning and informing about drug trafficking.

Drug-related corruption affected the police more than any other state agency. The Mexican police, despite continu-

ous professionalization efforts, sooner or later became involved—offering protection or actively participating in the illicit drug business. To a lesser extent, drug money also bought favors from the military, local politicians, prison custodians, pilots participating in eradication programs, and middle-level officers and officials. Many more, including journalists, prosecutors, and judges, were bribed, intimidated, or killed by drug lords.

Corruption and the use of violence—among traffickers; of traffickers against authorities; of traffickers against possible witnesses; and at times, simply to establish or reinvigorate a reputation for the effective use of violent means—unfortunately were the most infamous results of the illegal drug trade and efforts to curb it. Killings among traffickers as well as the assassination of police and other government authorities at the hands of traffickers increased to unprecedented levels in Mexico during the 1980s and 1990s. The private organization of violence by drug traffickers, to deter and even kill both law enforcers or their rivals, represents a major challenge to the monopoly of the state as the ultimate guarantor of law and order. In this sense, drug trafficking has seriously undermined political legitimacy.

Select Bibliography

Craig, Richard, "Human Rights and Mexico's Anti-Drug Campaign." *Social Science Quarterly* 60 (March 1980).

_____, "Operation Intercept: The International Politics of Pressure." *The Review of Politics* 42 (October 1980).

Dirección General de Epidemiología and Instituto Mexicano de Psiquiatría, *Encuesta Nacional de Adicciones.* 3 vols., Mexico City: Secretaría de Salud Pública, 1989.

Lupsha, Peter A., "Drug Trafficking: Mexico and Colombia in Comparative Perspective." *Journal of International Affairs* 35:1 (1981).

Musto, David F., "Patterns in U.S. Drug Abuse and Response." In *Drug Policy in the Americas,* edited by Peter H. Smith. Boulder, Colorado: Westview, 1992.

Nadelmann, Ethan A., *Cops Across Borders: The Internationalization of U.S. Criminal Law Enforcement.* University Park: Pennsylvania State University Press, 1993.

President's Commission on Organized Crime, *America's Habit: Drug Abuse, Drug Trafficking, and Organized Crime.* Washington, D.C.: Government Printing Office, 1986.

Reuter, Peter, and David Ronfeldt, *Quest for Integrity: The Mexican-U.S. Drug Issue in the 1980s.* Santa Monica, California: Rand, 1992.

Toro, María Celia, *Mexico's "War" on Drugs: Causes and Consequences.* Boulder, Colorado: Lynne Rienner, 1995.

Walker, William O., III, *Drug Control in the Americas.* Revised edition, Albuquerque: University of New Mexico Press, 1989.

White Paper on Drug Abuse: A Report to the President from the Domestic Council Drug Abuse Task Force. Washington, D.C.: Government Printing Office, 1975.

—María Celia Toro

DURÁN, DIEGO

c.1537–88 • Missionary and Chronicler

The chronicle of Diego Durán, today regarded as one of the most important ethnographic records of pre-Columbian and early colonial Mexico, brought him little fame in his lifetime and only came to public knowledge three centuries after it was written. Durán was born in Seville, Spain, but came to Mexico (then New Spain) as a small child. He grew up in Tezcoco and, as he wrote in his *Historia de las Indias de Nueva España,* "Although I did not acquire my milk teeth [in that city], I got my second ones there." This comment places the child Diego in Tezcoco, a center of learning in pre-Hispanic times, the home of an extensive library, poets, and pleasure gardens. It was here that Durán learned the Nahuatl language, which he claimed was more polished in Tezcoco than in other parts and which became a valuable aid in communicating with the indigenous peoples of his adopted country.

It has been suggested that Durán's father was a shoemaker, but he must have held a position higher than that; in his writings Diego notes that his family owned servants who had been slaves, which indicates that he grew up in relative prosperity and enjoyed a moderate, if not high, social status. We really know little about Diego Durán as a child and youth except that he entered the Dominican order in the mid-1550s—after the family had moved to Mexico City—and he became a friar in 1556. He was a deacon in the Dominican monastery in that city but in 1561 is said to have been sent to Antequera (now Oaxaca) to the monastery established there by his order. He is not mentioned among the Dominicans in the monastery records there, however, and on one occasion asked a Spaniard who had been in Oaxaca what it was like. He resided and worked in the Marquesado, the present state of Morelos, in the town of Huaxtepec (Oaxtepec), where there still were remains of Moteuczoma's pleasure gardens, and eventually he became vicar in Hueyapan, high on the slopes of the Popocatepetl volcano. This was a Nahuatl-speaking region so Durán must have felt quite at home. While attending his religious duties, he found time to interview in that language people of all stations, thus adding many anecdotes to his rich ethnographic store. Durán was happy in that cold region, yet he was enchanted with the "hot lands" of the Marquesado, where Huaxtepec was located and where its capital, Cuauhnahuac, had become Cuernavaca. He wrote: "This is certainly one of the most beautiful and pleasant lands in the world. . . . There are delightful springs, rivers full of fish, the freshest of woods, and orchards of many kinds of fruits . . . a thousand different fragrant flowers [and] cotton."

Durán consulted many Indian informants, at times going far into the country to find a wise elder or to search for an obscure document, for example a pictorial manuscript at Coatepec that he believed was the life of Topiltzin-Quetzalcoatl (culture hero and religious leader of the Toltec people).

The Dominican was obsessed by the idea that Topiltzin could have been Saint Thomas and the Toltecs and Aztecs of Hebrew origin. In some towns he found codices whose images seemed to reinforce his theory, but these "ancient paintings" were so highly valued that he was not allowed to keep them; they since have been lost forever.

Durán, like friars in other religious orders, was commissioned to write about the beliefs and customs of the people in the New World, in order to form a manual for the conversion of the natives to Christianity. He accomplished this by interviewing people and observing life around him. He seems not to have used a questionnaire as the Franciscan friar Bernardino de Sahagún did, and his informants were mainly people with whom he came in contact in his daily rounds, the *macehualtin* (commoners), not the *pipiltin* (highborn) that Sahagún questioned. For his *Historia,* however, Durán relied on a manuscript written in Nahuatl, an official history of the Aztecs, now called the *Crónica X.*

With all his activities—preaching, searching for a possible Lost Tribe of Israel, studying the Indian ways—Durán still managed to write three books: the *Libro de los dioses y ritos* (Book of the Gods and Rites; 1574–76), *El calendario antiguo* (The Ancient Calendar; 1579), and *Historia de las Indias de Nueva España y Islas de Tierra Firme* (History of the Indies of New Spain; 1581). Perhaps owing to the expropriation of writings by friars at the time of Philip II of Spain, or because of waning interest in the fate of souls of the Indians in the latter part of the sixteenth century, Durán's works found their way to the National Library of Madrid, where they were forgotten until the Mexican scholar José Fernando Ramírez discovered them in the 1850s and had them copied by a scribe. The original manuscript in Madrid is in the Sección de Manuscritos. The Ramírez copy is preserved in the Archivo Histórico of the Biblioteca Nacional de Antropología e Historia in the National Museum of Anthropology in Mexico City. An incomplete edition of the Ramírez copy was published in 1867, the rest in 1880. Some faulty editions of this copy also have been published; the one by Angel María Garibay of 1967 is the most reliable. The 1994 edition is a translation into English of the original Madrid manuscript.

Although Durán's works were little known during his lifetime, the Jesuits Juan de Tovar and Joseph de Acosta drew information from them for their own writings, evidently with Durán's permission. A brother Dominican, Agustín Dávila Padilla, in 1596 wrote that Durán's work on the history and customs of the Mexican Indians was "the finest account ever written in this field," and Garibay states that, among the Spanish chroniclers of Mexico in the sixteenth century, it would be difficult to find one as important as Durán.

Durán did not realize that he was a great ethnographer whose written words would illuminate scholars in the religion, history, and customs of the Aztec-Mexicas of ancient Mexico. Little is known of this Dominican's last years. In 1586 he was in Mexico City, where he served as an interpreter for the Inquisition, owing to his knowledge of Nahuatl; he died there in 1588.

Select Bibliography

Colston, Stephen A., "Fray Diego Durán's 'Historia de las Indias de Nueva España e Islas de Tierra Firme': A Historiographical Analysis." Ph.D. diss., University of California at Los Angeles, 1973.

Dávila Padilla, Agustín, *Historia de la fundación y discurso de la provincia de Santiago de México, de la Orden de Predicadores,* with an introduction by A. Millares Carlo. Mexico City: Academia Literaria, 1955 (facsimile of first edition, 1625).

Durán, Diego, *Códice Durán.* Manuscript in the Biblioteca Nacional de Madrid, Vitrina 26-II, 1581.

_____, *Historia de las Indias de Nueva España y Islas de Tierra Firme,* edited by José F. Ramírez. 2 vols., Mexico City, 1867–80.

_____, *Book of the Gods and Rites and The Ancient Calendar,* translated and edited by Fernando Horcasitas and Doris Heyden. 2nd edition, Norman: University of Oklahoma Press, 1977.

_____, *The History of the Indies of New Spain,* translated and edited by Doris Heyden. Norman: University of Oklahoma Press, 1994.

Sandoval, Fernando B., "La relación de la conquista de México en la 'Historia' de Fray Diego Durán." In *Estudios de la Historiografía de la Nueva España.* Mexico City: Colegio de México, 1945.

—DORIS HEYDEN

E

EARTHQUAKE OF 1985

On the morning of September 19, 1985, an earthquake measuring 8.1 on the Richter Scale struck central Mexico, causing massive loss of life, injury, and destruction of property. Fatality figures range from under 5,000 to over 20,000, with 10,000 emerging as the most commonly cited figure. Fortunately, the quake occurred at 7:19 A.M., before most people were at work, and children had not yet gone to school. If the quake had hit several hours later, the human toll would have been much higher because large public office buildings collapsed at alarming rates.

While a number of localities suffered human and material damages, the downtown area of Mexico City bore the majority of casualties and physical damage. The quake, which lasted 90 seconds, wreaked havoc on a city constructed on unstable landfill in which many buildings, including many buildings owned by the government, did not meet internationally recognized earthquake standards. Another serious earthquake occurred the following evening, measuring 7.3 on the Richter Scale, which complicated rescue efforts, caused additional damage, and added to the level of anxiety and terror that gripped the city.

Mexico City is divided into political jurisdictions known as delegations. The delegations of Venustiano Carranza, Cuauhtémoc, Benito Juárez, and Gustavo A. Madero received 80 percent of the material damage. Among these, Cuauhtémoc, which is located in the heart of the downtown area, received the most damage: 258 buildings completely crumbled, 143 partially collapsed, and 181 were seriously affected. In Venustiano Carranza, the numbers were 83 completely destroyed, 128 partial collapses, and almost 2,000 individual dwellings were damaged. According to official figures, approximately 250,000 people were left homeless as a direct result of the earthquake. Unofficial figures are often much higher.

The earthquake resulted in a host of political difficulties for the ruling Partido Revolucionario Institucional (PRI, or Institutional Revolutionary Party) and a huge political opportunity for independent popular movements. Attention focused primarily on mobilizing and organizing the homeless, or *damnificados*. Three major groups of *damnificados* organized on a territorial basis in immediate response to the earthquake and in resistance to state's emergency response and initial reconstruction plans: 1) residents from Tlatelolco and Colonia Roma, who were mostly middle class; 2) families of *Multifamiliar Juárez*, a public housing project constructed in the 1950s and 1960s that housed retired state bureaucrats and the middle class; and 3) the *colonias* of El Centro, Morelos, Guerrero, Doctores, Obrera, Peralvillo, Asturias, Nicolás, Bravo, and other *colonias* located in the downtown area that housed workers and the urban poor.

On October 24, 1985, over 20 territorially based urban popular movements, along with the Sindicato Nacional de Costureras 19 de Septiembre, which itself had been constituted only four days earlier, joined together to form the Coordinadora Única de Damnificados (CUD). By November 9, when the CUD held its II Foro de Damnificados de la Ciudad de México, 42 organizations were in attendance. For the next year and one-half, the CUD served as the primary coordinating body for earthquake victims and the most dynamic expression of popular urban militancy between 1985 and 1987. The CUD itself built upon and incorporated existing organizations dedicated primarily to housing issues. Of them, perhaps the most important was the Coordinadora Inquilinaria del Valle de México. The leadership of the Coordinadora came from two well-known radical left organizations, the Asociación Cívica Nacional Revolucionaria (ACNR) and Punto Crítico. One of the points of dispute within the literature on the CUD concerns the balance of power within the CUD, with some arguing that power rested essentially with the popular movements and others arguing that the CUD was dominated by middle-class interests.

The drive to mobilize and organize collectively was encouraged by the fact that the government's response to the earthquake was widely criticized by a cross-section of Mexican society, and the fact that recognizing their inability to deal with the crisis through "official channels," government agencies were willing to open up the process to "opposition groups." Certainly the earthquake presented a crisis of such proportion that even governments of more wealthy nations would have had difficulty responding. Nonetheless, the response of the PRI, from the local neighborhood political machine bosses to President Miguel de la Madrid himself aggravated the political implications of the earthquake in ways not directly related to the lack of material resources. For example, de la Madrid's devotion to stabilization policies was so great that he did not take the opportunity to cut debt payments after the quake, despite public outcries to do so and political fallout for failing to explain his reasoning.

The government exacerbated political problems for itself from the outset, by announcing through the Secretariat of Urban Development and Ecology (SEDUE) that there already existed sufficient housing to absorb all those left homeless from the earthquake. Subsequent statements regarding the need to relocate downtown residents to the periphery (which is where the new housing for those left homeless from the earthquake supposedly already existed or would be constructed) was widely perceived by the CUD and large sectors of public opinion (including middle-class opinion) to be a shallow attempt by the government to use the disaster to implement a long-term goal, namely the gentrification of the downtown area.

Popular movement representatives met on September 27, 1985, with the head of SEDUE, Guillermo Carrillo Arena. Movement leaders present at the meeting have described Carrillo Arena as maintaining a very "despotic" attitude, insisting that the movements incorporate themselves into corporatist channels before expecting government concessions. Movement demands that SEDUE not give preference to PRIista demands were met with scorn, as were requests that the director assist the petitioners in their efforts to repel the eviction plans of powerful landlords.

The government began the process of reconstruction with repeated reference to *concertación* (consensus building) as the operative means by which the program could best take place. Critics responded from the outset that *concertación* required coordination between citizen's groups and the state, which was being undermined by the state's preference for working with PRI organizations and the exclusion of popular movements from the decision-making process. The fact that the government was widely perceived to have been both authoritarian *and* incompetent in its immediate response to the emergency (with tensions already running high owing to the economic crisis and governmental austerity measures) provided for the opposition an ability to favorably shape public opinion in a manner and to a degree perhaps not seen since the Revolution. Organizations such as the CUD were populated with radical leaders who had long dreamed of just such an opportunity. They moved swiftly to politicize reconstruction to the greatest degree possible.

On October 2, more than 15,000 people marched in support of demands put forward by one of the first coalitions of *damnificados,* the Comité Popular de Solidaridad y Reconstrucción (COPOSORE). They demanded that the reconstruction be "democratic" (i.e., that it include non-PRIista popular movements), that the military pull out of neighborhoods severely affected by the quake in which popular movements were attempting to take political control despite contrary efforts by PRI organizers and the military, that the rights of tenants be respected, and that the state ensure an end to evictions. De la Madrid granted a seven-minute audience to about one dozen urban popular movement leaders, which turned into a 45-minute meeting in which the president was given a document outlining what were to remain core popular movement demands throughout the reconstruction process: expropriation of all condemned buildings and

the land upon which they were situated, followed up by a "popular" and "democratic" reconstruction project, which would include the active participation of popular movements. On October 11, the president announced the expropriation of 5,500 properties, covering an area of 550 acres in the delegations of Cuauhtémoc, Venustiano Carranza, Gustavo A. Madero, and Benito Juárez. The presidential decree led to a landslide of expropriation demands by other *colonias* and their representatives.

The administration recognized very early that existing organizational arrangements were inadequate for managing both the technical and political dimensions of the crisis. On October 14, a presidential decree was issued that established the Programa de Renovación Habitacional Popular (PRHP), which was to operate under the direction of the Departamento del Distrito Federal (DDF). These new governmental locations thus became the site of many political contests between groups competing for resources and decision-making influence.

Public protest and mass mobilization designed to reform and expand official reconstruction efforts characterized the months following the earthquake. On October 26, the CUD (which had only formed two days earlier) held its first march, attended by 30,000 people. Protesters did not limit their demands to reconstruction: they insisted that the government declare a unilateral debt moratorium and channel the savings into the reconstruction effort, along with the resignation of the head of the department of the Federal District, Ramón Aguirre, and the head of SEDUE, Carrillo Arena. The protesters emphasized the need for "honest and impartial experts" to administer a reconstruction plan based on an expanded expropriation decree. Scholar Sergio Tamayo notes that the first stage of reconstruction was characterized by "political contention" and suggests that the mix of popular resistance and administration of government programs resulted in "political frictions" at the highest levels of the PRI/government over how to best manage the political fallout resulting from the crisis.

The first task of the PRHP was to produce a census, intended to identify *damnificados* and issue authorizations regarding the rights of individuals to be incorporated into the program. Renovation Councils (Consejos de Renovación) were established to facilitate this process. They quickly became locations of political conflict, particularly on those not infrequent occasions in which receiving rights under the renovation program became contingent on joining or previously belonging to the PRI. Parcero López, ex-secretary of the "third leg" of the PRI, the Confederación Nacional de Organizaciones Populares (CNOP, or National Confederation of Popular Organizations) and then federal deputy from a downtown district, was at the center of the stormy controversy regarding the politicization of reconstruction programs. CUD leaders attended these meetings and defended their memberships' right to receive impartial treatment under the program, regardless of political affiliation. While the president consistently emphasized the importance of participation from urban popular movements, officially referred to as "citizen groups," many of those in charge of implementing those programs, particularly during the early stages, made this promise a hollow one, as those not affiliated with the PRI were treated to bureaucratic run-arounds, paper trails, and other obstacles while those more willing to comply with the PRI's wishes were more promptly attended to. According to the scholar Susan Eckstein, this had the effect of encouraging some *vecindad* (neighborhood) associations "to affiliate with the party because they thought their prospects of getting state assistance would thereby be improved."

Tensions ran high between the CUD and government officials during the period of October 1985 to February 1986. It became increasingly apparent to both sides that they needed each other if they were to make any substantial progress in the realization of their respective goals. This reality led to the alliance between state reformers and popular movements that was to follow. Certainly, not all popular movements representing *damnificados* belonged to the CUD, but a majority of the most important did. Owing to the multiclass nature of the CUD, it was impossible for the government to respond only to the CUD's middle-class interests while ignoring the interests of the popular classes, also represented by the CUD. So, while the government was learning that they could not ignore the CUD, or deal with them effectively in traditional clientelistic fashion, the CUD was learning that it would have to bargain with the federal government if it was to gain concessions. Most accounts of earthquake politics agree that the replacement of Carrillo Arena of SEDUE with Manuel Camacho Solís was a decisive turning point in the reconstruction effort.

Carrillo Arena had a number of political liabilities. His ineffectiveness during this period resulted primarily from his unshakable belief in the continued feasibility of clientelistic practices as the sole means of relations between the state and civil society, despite changes in the political context that allowed popular movements to resist such an attitude and participate more on their own terms. Furthermore, Carrillo Arena was a key architect for both the Hospital Juárez and the Multifamiliar Benito Juárez, both of which had collapsed during the earthquake, causing hundreds of deaths. On February 18, the CUD sent a telegram to de la Madrid congratulating him on the sacking of Carrillo Arena.

Immediately upon taking office, Camacho Solís reformed the political atmosphere by announcing what amounted to an open-door policy with the CUD and other popular movement representatives. In March, only weeks after taking office, the Programa de Reconstrucción Democrática de Tlatelolco was announced, thereby defusing one of the most important political hot spots in the city. Camacho recognized Tlatelolco citizen groups as legitimate interlocutors. On March 12, 1986, Camacho announced that only 11 buildings would require demolition, in place of the 27 that Carrillo Arena previously had announced. According to a CUD pamphlet, Camacho also admitted that the previous Carrillo Arena estimate contained "diagnostic errors." By discrediting and distancing himself from "people's enemy" Carrillo Arena, Camacho built on his credibility not only with the CUD but with the media, which had become more of an ally to popular movements following the earthquake than at any other time since the 1968 Massacre of Tlatelolco. While this change in policy content and the way in which policy was designed, announced, and administered did not completely reverse the political liabilities associated with reconstruction, it certainly was an important instance of damage control. The success reformers such as Camacho had in dealing with this political crisis contributed not only to the continued professional mobility of the reformers into the administration of President Carlos Salinas de Gortari but also directly bore on the tack taken by the Salinas administration in dealing with popular movements.

In early March, PRHP distributed 39,000 certificates of housing rights to be administered under the program, a substantial percentage of the total number of units to be constructed. Repairs and reparations, which had been long delayed, began finally to be carried out with increased regularity. On April 1, Parcero López was replaced with Manuel Aguilera Gómez, who immediately upon taking office, guaranteed that the PRHP would implement no program without first consulting the intended beneficiaries.

On May 16, political ace Manuel Camacho Solís met with all the significant groups representing the *damnificados*. In return for what turned out to be a truly extraordinary commitment of government resources to construct 48,000 units in a little over a year, Camacho obligated each of the movements to sign the *Convenio de concertación democrática para la reconstruction de vivienda*. The document committed the PRHP to provide "housing actions" that would benefit 250,000 people. In direct response to popular movement demands, this *convenio de concertación* put in writing that the new housing units would respect the "urban characteristics and cultural identity" of the inhabitants from the city's center. The document also stated that beneficiaries would not be expected to pay back loans at rates beyond their means and recognized the importance of public participation in the design and implementation of the projects. As to credit terms, the document was very specific: the total cost of the loan would be repaid in a period from five to seven years at a monthly interest rate of 16 to 17 percent, which would require beneficiaries to pay between 25 and 30 percent of the minimum salary. Eckstein, in reference to the *convenio,* notes that

> safe provisional housing was to be provided for families during the reconstruction period, close to their original homes, or families were to receive economic assistance, if they found their own temporary accommodations; . . . beneficiaries would only have to repay the direct building costs; and a committee, comprised of representatives of the organizations

participating in the agreement, would evaluate proposed alternative projects in terms of the norms of the agreement and existing building codes.

Not unexpectedly, the meaning and desirability of this highly publicized *convenio de concertación* was widely discussed and debated. There were 106 signatories, including the directors of SEDUE, DDF, and PRHP on behalf of the federal government; and la Federación de Comités de Reconstrucción del PRI, el Directorio de Damnificados del PST, and independent *damnificado* movements (of which CUD was the most important but certainly not the only one). The response of Cuauhtémoc Abarca, a key CUD leader, was representative of most popular movement leaders. He understood the *convenio* to be a concession by the state that the reconstruction could not happen without the independent movements, as well as an acknowledgment (however late in coming) by the government of the contribution these same organizations had been making since the beginning of the earthquake crisis. He emphasized the extent to which the *convenio* included the "immense majority" of CUD demands and saw the *convenio* as a testament to the fact that persistent mobilization and organization is capable of achieving the rights of those without significant resources.

Eckstein offers an interpretation that is quite different from that of Abarca:

> *Damnificados* did not need to belong to a group that signed the *convenio* to get housing, but the principal groups that had actively mobilized for housing all had to sign; in so doing, they agree, in effect, to work with and not against the state. The accord therefore included all relevant groups in the resolution of the political crisis. . . . The state as well as the slum-dwellers benefited from the housing reform. To get housing, defiant groups had to agree to quiescence and to accept the terms of housing imposed by the government. Meanwhile, the government allocated housing in a manner that undermined the social base of the "new social movement" type groups.

The political implications of the *convenio* are not adequately or accurately captured by either Eckstein or Abarca. Abarca misses the fact that the *convenio* is, by definition, a mutual concession on the part of all signers. *Convenios de concertación* of both the de la Madrid and Salinas administrations should be understood as political bargains based on the exchange of valuable concessions on the part of all participants.

A review of CUD activities after the *convenio* signing suggests that the CUD in fact did alter its radical stance, in part because once the implementation of housing programs began, individual movement organizations within the CUD had their hands full overseeing the implementation of programs that were in constant threat of being sidetracked or

more completely derailed by local PRI elites, real estate interests, and state employees who felt their interests threatened by specific housing projects and/or the increased popular movement influence in the political affairs of particular barrios and Mexico City politics more generally.

While Eckstein is correct that both state and popular movements benefited from the agreement, she is wrong to imply that by signing the agreement defiant groups became quiescent. Some did, others did not. In general, although the political tone of at least some popular movement activities was moderated, there is ample evidence to support the CUD's insistence that they remained anything but quiescent. Furthermore, while the government certainly endeavored to allocate housing in a manner that undermined the social base of the new social movements, it did not succeed. Many of these same signers continued to participate openly in acts of collective dissent. In fact, on May 13, 1986, when SEDUE formally submitted the signed *convenio* in a public act, upon taking the microphone, CUD representatives reiterated their insistence that the CUD would need to maintain a critical stance vis-à-vis the implementation of the program so as to ensure that the rightful demands of the *damnificados* were fulfilled to the fullest extent possible. On September 11, the CUD held a mass rally to protest a declaration made the previous day by the president of the Mexico City PRI in which he commended his party's role in the immediate emergency earthquake response and then again in the reconstruction process. The CUD declared that such comments "concealed" the true character of the PRI response, which was an effort to immobilize the *damnificados*. They were specific in their charges by reminding the PRI that their own federal deputies had judged the September 24, 1985, expropriation proposal made by independent representatives of Colonias Guerrero, Morelos, Roma, and Tlatelolco "as adventurous, radical, and an effort to exploit an emergency situation for their own unjust reasons." This, and numerous other similar occasions in which the CUD and other *convenio* signers were to speak out against PRI and government officials, received considerable media attention and contributed in no small way to a growing disenchantment in Mexico City with the PRI, later capitalized on by opposition candidate Cuauhtémoc Cárdenas in the 1988 presidential election.

By July 1986, the Programa Emergente de Vivienda (PEV)-PRHP had assigned, repaired, and constructed nearly 80,000 housing units, to the benefit of 400,000 habitants. This level of commitment to the reconstruction, and the way in which the reconstruction had been implemented, would have been very different if not for the presence and skillful political maneuvering of popular movements. At the same time, the second phase (Fase II) of the PEV was announced with the intent of meeting the needs of the 8,000 eligible people under this program who had not had their rights fulfilled in the first stage of implementation. Fase II, which sought to provide housing to *desdoblados* (persons who live in the homes of others, sharing space and often expenses) and to those who had lost housing that existed on properties exempted from expropriation, is widely perceived to be a direct result of the persistent pressure applied by CUD and other relevant popular movements. While the movements failed to expand the number of expropriated properties, they were insistent in their call that the government was morally obligated to respond to the needs of the remaining *damnificados*. Based on official PRHP figures, Tamayo recorded that only 18 months after expropriation, the PRHP had itself reconstructed 44,500 units. While the CUD had experienced many internal divisions based on both personal and ideological differences as well as struggles for organizational control, it had been successful in presenting a unified front in dealings with the government. As observers of popular movements will appreciate, this was no small feat.

Even as Mexico City's urban popular movements involved in the reconstruction expanded their political agendas to include multiple aspects of a broad-based democratization project, most have not lost sight of the goal of providing basic housing and services to their rank-and-file. There are few periods in Mexican history during which such dramatic public works projects have been implemented with, and to a significant degree because of, independent popular movements.

Select Bibliography

Cuéllar Vazquéz, Angélica, *La noche es de ustedes, el amanecer es nuestro: Asamblea de Barrios y Superbarrio Gomez en la Ciudad de México*. Mexico City: Universidad Nacional Autonoma, 1993.

Da Cruz, José, *Disaster and Society: The 1985 Mexican Earthquakes*. Lund, Sweden: Lund University Press, 1993.

Haber, Paul Lawrence, "Collective Dissent in Mexico: The Politics of Contemporary Urban Popular Movements." Ph.D. diss., Columbia University, 1992.

Presidencia de la Republica, Unidad de la Cronica Presidencial, *Las razones y las obras: Gobierno de Miguel de la Madrid: Cronica del sexenio 1982–1988 (Trecer Año)*. Mexico City: Presidencia de la Republica/Fondo de Cultura Económica, 1986.

—PAUL LAWRENCE HABER

ECHEVERRÍA ÁLVAREZ, LUIS

1922– • President

Luis Echeverría was born in Mexico City on January 17, 1922. He won a scholarship to study in Chile, Argentina, France, and the United States in 1941, and in 1945 he graduated from the law school of the Universidad Nacional Autónoma de México (UNAM, or the National Autonomous University of Mexico). Echeverría was the last president with military connections, serving as private secretary to the president of the national executive committee of the ruling Partido Revolucionario Institucional (PRI, or Institutional Revolutionary Party), General Rodolfo Sánchez Taboada, and marrying the daughter of General José Guadalupe Zuno, former governor of Jalisco. Unlike previous presidents in post-Revolutionary Mexico who had experience in government and close ties to groups that had emerged from the Revolution, Echeverría was selected for his bureaucratic merits. Joining the PRI in 1946, Echeverría became a rising star in the party bureaucracy. As subsecretary of the interior he managed Gustavo Díaz Ordaz's presidential campaign in 1964, and he later was named secretary of the interior in Díaz Ordaz's administration. In 1970 he was named the PRI candidate for the presidency, and on December 1, 1970, he assumed office.

As president Echeverría faced economic deterioration and political crisis. The economic boom of the previous three decades came to an abrupt end as inflation jumped from 3 percent in 1969 to 22 percent in 1976. Echeverría's erratic management of public finances led to economic stagnation, and the public debt increased 553.3 percent during his six-year term, reaching a staggering US$19.6 billion. Equally grave was the breakdown of the corporatist political order that had guaranteed the PRI a monopoly of political power in Mexico. As secretary of the interior, Echeverría widely had been held responsible for the massacre of hundreds of protesters in the Plaza of Tlatelolco on October 2, 1968; on Corpus Christi, June 10, 1971, student protesters again had been massacred, this time by a paramilitary group known as los Falcones, which followed wounded students to hospitals to finish them off.

Following the Tlatelolco and Corpus Christi massacres, 17 guerrilla groups were formed in various parts of Mexico and conducted a number of spectacular actions—most notably the kidnappings of Echeverría's father-in-law and the U.S. consul. As a candidate for the presidency, Echeverría had traveled to the most important zone of conflict, the state of Guerrero, to attempt to broker the disarmament of guerrilla groups. As president, however, he maintained a hard-line policy, sending 15 percent of the Mexican army to Guerrero. The army's counterinsurgency campaign in Guerrero was characterized by widespread human rights violations, including the use of napalm against rural communities.

Despite the widespread repression during his administration, Echeverría also attempted to co-opt popular opposition. At one point during his election campaign he called for a moment of silence to remember the victims of the Massacre of Tlatelolco, offending the army and almost prompting Díaz Ordaz to request his resignation. As president Echeverría traveled throughout Mexico giving populist speeches and distributing government largesse (running up Mexico's federal debt in the process). Attempting to bolster his image as an *agrarista* president, Echeverría responded to a series of massive peasant-led land invasions by authorizing a spectacular redistribution of land in the states of Sonora and Sinaloa (characteristically, the groups that had led the invasions were excluded from the final settlement, and Echeverría's successor, José López Portillo, paid generous indemnities to those who had lost their lands). Echeverría also attempted to remove the secretary general of the PRI labor union, the Confederación de Trabajadores de Mexico (CTM, or Confederation of Mexican Workers), and encouraged the growth of an independent union in Mexico's electric industry. By the end of his term, however, Echeverría was forced to give in to the determined opposition of the CTM. The secretary general of the CTM, Fidel Velázquez, was allowed to remain in office, and the independent union was crushed when Mexican troops occupied electrical facilities in 1975.

Echeverría also attempted to distract attention from the economic and political crisis (and win international support for his government) by maintaining a nationalist and anti-imperialist posture in foreign policy. He strongly supported the socialist president of Chile, Salvador Allende, and after Allende's overthrow in a U.S.-sponsored coup d'état, he opened Mexico's doors to Chilean refugees; he also gave asylum to refugees from other military regimes in Latin America. In an attempt to isolate Mexico's guerrilla movements, Echeverría authorized the Palestinian Liberation Organization to open an office in Mexico City. In the United Nations Echeverría's administration adopted a third-world strategy with a strong anti-U.S. tint. Echeverría promoted a revision of the Law of the Sea, extending patrimonial waters to 200 miles, and he also sponsored changes in Charter of Rights and Obligations for member countries in the U.N. Both of these measures had an important impact on U.S. interests. Mexico also voted for the controversial U.N. resolution equating Zionism with racism. Echeverría considered himself a strong candidate for secretary general of the United Nations, and he lobbied tirelessly to raise Mexico's (and his own) profile in the U.N.

Echeverría's populist posturing did not endear him to Mexico's business community. The powerful Monterrey Group held him responsible for the kidnapping of its CEO,

and business people rebelled against political controls. The business community was able to stymie Echeverría's attempt to revise Mexico's tax code, and in 1975 Mexico's most powerful business organizations united to form the Consejo Coordinador Empresarial (CCE, or Business Coordinating Council), introducing their own platform in opposition to the PRI's. The CCE marked a first step toward ending the PRI's long-standing policy of "godfather capitalism," in which the PRI exerted considerable informal influence over the business community without exerting direct control.

Echeverría also faced dissent from within PRI ranks. His authority within the party was damaged by numerous jokes and rumors, including one particularly ugly story that he was plotting a military coup d'état. The turbulence came to a head when a faction within the PRI attempted to impose Mario Moya Palencia as secretary of the interior. The principal authors of the plot were punished severely, most notably the governor of Sonora, Carlos Armando Biebrich, who was forced to resign and leave political life. The presidential succession was quite tense.

After leaving office Echeverría retired to a semiacademic life. He attempted to create a "University of the Third World," but had to content himself with his appointment as president of the somewhat more modest Centro de Estudios Económicos y Sociales del Tercer Mundo (CEESTM, or Center for Economic and Social Studies of the Third World). There was no love lost between the CEESTM and officials of the López Portillo administration, however, and the institution was allowed to languish until it was finally sold to a multinational corporation. During the 1980s and 1990s Echeverría kept a low profile, although many continued to blame him for ongoing conflicts inside the PRI. In one of his last political interventions, he sided with president Ernesto Zedillo Ponce de León against his predecessor Carlos Salinas de Gortari.

Select Bibliography

Ángeles, Luis, *Crisis y coyuntura en la economía mexicana*. Mexico City: El Caballito, 1979.

Basañez, Miguel, *La lucha por la hegemonía en México*. Mexico City: Siglo XXI, 1985.

Centeno, Miguel Angel, *Democracy within Reason: Technocratic Revolution in Mexico*. University Park: Pennsylvania State University Press 1994.

Newell, Roberto, and Luis Rubio, *Mexico's Dilemma: The Political Origins of Economic Crisis*. Boulder, Colorado: Westview, 1984.

Saldívar, Americo, *Ideología y política del estado mexicano 1970–1976*. Mexico City: Siglo XXI, 1981.

Schmidt, Samuel, *The Deterioration of the Mexican Presidency*. Tucson: University of Arizona Press, 1991.

—SAMUEL SCHMIDT

ECOLOGY

The post–World War II period in Mexican ecological history has been marked by three interrelated but often apparently contradictory currents. First, responding to broad changes in the global political economy, the Mexican government downplayed its economic strategy of replacing imported goods with domestic manufactures ("Import Substitution Industrialization," or ISI) in favor of an export-driven model of economic development. Second, this shift occurred even as Mexico faced an environmental crisis of unprecedented size and scope. Third, the environment increasingly became an arena for state intervention and popular contestation.

Article 27 of the 1917 Mexican Constitution established that all lands and waters are part of the national patrimony subject to control by the state for the public good. Specifically, the state claimed the right, in the words of scholars José Luis Zaragoza and Ruth Macías, "to regulate use of exploitable natural resources in order to make an equitable distribution of public wealth and to care for its conservation." Despite this early assertion of eminent domain, the federal government has been slow to create effective environmental legislation both because of the government's economic development models and its belated recognition of how deeply these models have degraded the environment.

By the mid-1980s, however, the environmental crisis was widely acknowledged. Media attention focused on horror stories about health hazards from border *maquiladoras* (export manufacturing plants), massive oil spills, factory and pipeline explosions, toxic waste dumping, and the asphyxiated capital, Mexico City, arguably the world's most polluted city. Meanwhile, millions of Mexicans have to cope routinely with more mundane irritants such as bad water, tainted food, open sewers, urban congestion, mountains of garbage, and the pollution that is poverty itself. At the same time they are faced both with the ongoing depletion of natural resources—massive destruction of ecosystems, poisoned or eroded soils, contaminated lakes and rivers, desertification, and rapidly vanishing forests—and with increasing pressures internationally from lending agencies and trading partners, and domestically from the government and environmentalists, to arrest this degradation.

Paradoxically, Mexico's environmental crisis has come to a head at a time of impressive achievements with respect to environmental legislation, mitigation, and conservation initiatives. These actions can be seen as part of an ongoing preemptive reform strategy aimed at co-opting the rapidly growing environmental movement and smoothing Mexico's path to a neoliberal economic model (i.e., economic liberalization, diversification, and fiscal austerity). The gap between environmental policy and practice remains vast, however, because of incompatibility with cultural mores, social structural conditions, fiscal austerity, and other political and economic factors at odds with enforcement of and compliance with environmental regulations.

Roots of the Environmental Crisis

The structural roots of Mexico's contemporary environmental crisis lie in the import-substitution strategy adopted after World War II. Until the late 1950s, a rough balance between agricultural and industrial development was maintained, contributing to the "Mexican miracle" of unprecedented growth and diversification. There was a net transfer of value from agriculture to industry, however, through production of cheap food for the new urban areas, where low wages also could be sustained. Mexico City became the national growth pole, as its population doubled between the 1940s and 1960s, while that of the surrounding federal district tripled.

By the late 1960s, critical economic bottlenecks began to emerge as the strategy of rapid industrialization at all costs exacerbated preexisting problems such as rural-urban migration, skewed income distribution, increasing regional disparities, and inefficient, overprotected industries. Agricultural growth rates declined and market forces reshaped production as staple crops increasingly were replaced by export, industrial, and forage crops. From 1970 on, Mexico was forced to import large quantities of basic foods as a consequence of technological modernization, the fruit of the internationalization of the economy.

The consolidation of the shift toward an export-led economy in the 1970s and 1980s reinforced development imbalances and accelerated ecological decline. The increasingly large role of petroleum in the national economy during the late 1970s contributed to the 1982 debt crisis and the transition to free-market policies. Mexico joined the General Agreement on Tariffs and Trade (GATT) in 1986, and the North American Free Trade Agreement (NAFTA) with the United States and Canada was implemented in 1994. Ongoing austerity measures, including social spending cuts and wage and price controls, together with the December 1994 peso crisis followed by soaring interest rates, cumulatively had a severe impact on many sectors of the population and the milieus within which they live and work. The continuing decline in living standards together with frustration over the apparent failure of political reform engendered an unprecedented level of popular protest, including a growing focus on environmental issues. At the same time, the structural adjustment required by the neoliberal transition reduced the resources available for protection of the environment at a time when it was under most pressure because of the imperative of economic competitiveness. Modernization has been achieved at high economic, social, and environmental costs. Yet, the public will to promote economic diversification, foster civil empowerment, and protect resource renewability appears to be on the upsurge.

Environmental Policy

The articulation of formal environmental policy in Mexico was prompted by the widespread international concern (fomented by United Nations initiatives in the late 1960s and early 1970s) over the impact of industrialization on the global resource base. In 1971, the first comprehensive Mexican environmental legislation was enacted, establishing principles for avoiding contamination of air, water, and soil, together with the corresponding penalties. The legislation did not, however, stipulate the norms and standards necessary for implementation, and it lacked effective regulatory authority. Consequently, throughout the 1970s environmental enforcement was negligible.

A more focused environmental law was proclaimed in 1982, prompted by growing public concerns about rising levels of smog in Mexico City, domestic nuclear power development, and the impact of oil exploitation. In 1982, the incoming president Miguel de la Madrid established Mexico's first cabinet-level environmental agency, the Secretaría de Desarrollo Urbano y Ecología (the Ministry of Urban Development and Ecology, SEDUE). In addition, the president encouraged the formation of environmental organizations via an extended national campaign to promote public awareness of the impact of human actions on the natural surroundings. The onset of the debt crisis and ensuing fiscal restraints reduced SEDUE's budget, however, and the ministry was criticized heavily for its failure to confront Mexico City's air pollution, for its response to the 1985 earthquake and other environmental disasters, as well as for generalized corruption and patronage. The de la Madrid government's commitment to environmental protection remained largely symbolic until the end of its term, when a new environmental law with more juridical teeth and greater regulatory capacity was enacted.

The 1988 Ley General del Equilibrio Ecolóligo y el Protección al Ambiente (General Law of Ecological Equilibrium and Environmental Protection) differs from its predecessors in its integral ecological approach to the goal of environmental "preservation, restoration, and improvement." The law underscores the connections between rapid economic modernization, population growth, and environmental deterioration, and the fallacy of presuming that industrialization and urbanization automatically improve quality of life. The law assumes that greater sensitivity to the socioeconomic causes of ecological problems, clarification of institutional responsibilities, decentralization of protection functions, and increased social collaboration will permit environmental amelioration "without interrupting or interfering excessively in productive processes." In other words, the law opts for ecological politics based on the possibility of continuing economic development on an environmentally sustainable basis.

The next president, Carlos Salinas de Gortari (1988–94), emphasized environmental protection early in his term of office, through a widely publicized campaign to address pollution and water supply problems in Mexico City, as well as the identification of several areas of the country as domestic policy priorities, including the U.S.-Mexican border region, several river basins, and southern Mexico. After 1990, however, Salinas's environmental policy focused on concerns related to NAFTA raised by environmental groups and other interested parties in the United States and Canada and by domestic critics. In May 1992, SEDUE was replaced by the Secretaría de Desarrollo Social (the Ministry of Social Development, SEDESOL) in an attempt to improve policy implementation. Factory inspection rates, fines and other penalties, and closures of some of the worst sources of industrial pollution increased, while public relations exercises directed at the appearance of environmental sensitivity proliferated.

Other significant actions by the Salinas regime to improve Mexico's environmental image at home and abroad included the elaboration of the Integrated Border Environmental Plan (IBEP) in collaboration with U.S. agencies, measures to protect endangered species and biodiversity, and the decree of a variety of national parks, wildlife preserves, heritage sites, and biosphere reserves, in part as a result of energetic actions by environmentalists. At the same time, however, land reform legislation was revised and new national forestry and water laws proclaimed in order to open previously protected sectors to private investment. While neoliberals maintained that these reforms would improve management efficiency and economic competitiveness, critics argued the likelihood of accelerating resource depletion under diminished state stewardship.

Overall, these initiatives constituted a substantial conservation and protection package, at least on paper. This strategy seems to have succeeded in reassuring the international financial community that Mexico will respect environmental concerns in the process of opening the country to free trade. The government's role in encouraging the formation of largely urban-based environmental interest groups in the early 1980s also was successful initially in facilitating their political manipulation to legitimize reforms. This strategy may have backfired, however, in that a number of these groups have broken with their original sponsors and have begun to act as independent lobbies for environmental policies, often in direct conflict with government interests. Such independent action has been particularly evident in the recent period of transition to neoliberalism as social, economic, and environmental concerns appear to be coalescing in an unprecedented popular challenge to the Mexican government.

Urban Pollution

Competing with Tokyo for the rank of the world's largest city, Mexico's capital also vies for the dubious honor of being the world's most polluted city. As a result of the acceleration of the rural exodus after 1945, reinforced by the government's policy of concentrating investment, industrial infrastructure, and political power in the metropolis, the population reached 15,048,000 in 1990 (as counted by the Dirección General de Estadística). The ensuing extreme pollution; congestion; shortages of housing, service, and water; and administrative paralysis are a dismal testimony to the repercussions of unchecked industrially based urban growth.

According to the United Nations Environment Program and World Health Organization, more than 30,000 industries and 12,000 service facilities operated in the Valley of Mexico in 1994, and almost 3 million motor vehicles were on the streets engaged in an estimated 30 million journeys daily. Atmospheric emissions from these sources are compounded by Mexico City's location in a high-elevation basin on a former lake bed surrounded by mountains; as a result, air drainage is poor and surface as well as upper-air temperature inversions occur frequently. Urban sprawl and associated energy consumption have caused microclimatic changes, reflected in heat anomalies owing to replacement of natural by artificial surfaces, warmth from combustion, and atmospheric alteration from the emission of gaseous and solid pollutants. As a result of these climatological and topographic factors, pollutant emissions are trapped close to the city. National and international air quality standards for sulfur dioxide, ozone, nitrogen dioxide, carbon monoxide, lead, and total suspended particles regularly are exceeded. Health repercussions include chronic respiratory illnesses, cardiovascular diseases, child development disorders, and gastrointestinal infections and hepatitis transmitted by inhalation of fecal dust consequent on poor sanitation facilities.

Shortly after assuming office, President Salinas announced an agenda for improving environmental conditions in the Federal District, including the regulation of vehicle emissions, the introduction of lead-free gasoline, and a traffic revision system. This announcement was followed in 1989 by an innovative program called *un dia sin auto* (a day without a car), whereby drivers must leave their cars at home one day a week in an effort to curtail commuter traffic. Although this program apparently was well received both by environmentalists and the general public, many affluent commuters have been able to circumvent it by purchasing an extra car, while the government continues to encourage the production and consumption of motor vehicles. Other innovative approaches include debt-for-nature swaps, mobilization of neighborhoods to restore or expand green space, and the proposed construction of a 30,000-foot (9,000-meter) "ecological wall" as part of the Metropolitan Area Preservation Project. More conventional measures include the conversion of power plants and vehicle retrofitting to run on natural gas, the closure of an antiquated petroleum refinery, and the lowering of fuel sulfur content. A contingency plan has been developed to cope with prolonged episodes of high air pollution levels as measured by the automatic monitoring network completed in 1985. This plan includes curtailing the activity of the most polluting industries and closing schools or rescheduling classes in periods of extreme atmospheric contamination.

In 1990 a comprehensive pollution control program was announced, *el Programa Integral Contra la Contaminación Atmosférica de la Zona Metropolitana de la Ciudad de México* (The Integral Program Against Atmospheric Contamination in the Metropolitan Zone of Mexico City, PICCA). PICCA focuses on the following strategic actions: improvement in fuel quality; rationalization and restructuring of urban transport; modernization of production technologies and pollution emission control, including prohibition of new contaminating industries and relocation of industries unable to comply with environmental regulations; rescue, protection, and rehabilitation of sensitive or degraded ecological areas; improved solid waste control and disposal, including extension of the sewer network; and education, communication, and citizen participation.

The last area, citizen participation, was central to the environmental policy of the Salinas administration, placing the ultimate responsibility for environmental improvement on the public at large. Obviously, such a Herculean task as cleaning up Mexico City cannot be achieved without active collaboration between state and society, but even the most comprehensive environmental reforms on paper have little chance of success without an effective implementation and enforcement capacity. During the economic and political restructuring and austerity of the mid-1990s, it seemed unlikely that this would be achieved unless a near-lethal threshold of livability should prompt a radical reallocation of priorities.

Cleaning Up the U.S.-Mexican Border

Perhaps even more intractable than the environmental predicament of Mexico City is that of the U.S.-Mexican border region, which extends some 2,000 miles from Tijuana–Metropolitan San Diego to Matamoros-Brownsville. Much of this area constitutes an environmental disaster zone, where rivers contain raw sewage, industrial discharges, dead animals, and domestic garbage; water tables are mined and contaminated by agrochemicals and other toxins; hazardous wastes are dumped; fish and wildlife species are endangered; air pollution is widespread, and so forth.

Most of these problems relate to the influx of migrants intent on a better life on *el otro lado* ("the other side") in the United States, or attracted by the prospect of better-paid jobs in the new industries established in the border free-trade zone, as well as by the increasing dynamism of the northern Mexican economy overall. Border population on the Mexican side grew from 2.89 million in 1980 to an estimated 3.9 million in 1988 (according to scholars Robert A. Pastor and Jorge G. Castaneda); such growth rates were twice the national average, far exceeding the provision of infrastructure and services. The combined urban population on both sides of the border was 6.5 million in 1980, with growth projected of at least another 43 percent by 2000, up to 9.2 million (Rich, 1992).

Although the *maquiladora* assembly plant program was established in 1965, many environmental problems did not get out of hand until the second-wave boom of urban and industrial growth after 1982, promoted yet unrestrained by national policy. The economic liberalization, diversification, and fiscal austerity required by the International Monetary Fund (IMF) as a condition of debt restructuring created a favorable climate for increased investment in *maquiladoras* by foreign corporations attracted by large, unskilled pools of cheap labor, lax environmental regulations, and low taxes.

The number of *maquiladoras* expanded rapidly from 620 in 1980 to nearly 1,900 in 1990, while the *maquiladora* labor force grew from 100,000 to 450,000 (Gereffi, 1992). Tariff relaxation in preparation for NAFTA facilitated the construction of new, more advanced export operations in Mexico's interior in cities such as Saltillo, Hermosillo, and San Luis Potosí, and even as far away as the Yucatán Peninsula. The border zone remained an investment magnet, however, as NAFTA stimulated the growth of additional *maquiladoras* and new transborder service industries on the Mexican side and a proliferation of low-wage subcontracting plants on the U.S. side.

The environmental impacts of this rapid and uncontrolled urban and industrial expansion on the sensitive ecology of the mainly arid borderlands obviously extend across the international boundary regardless of the points of origin. By the early 1980s, it became evident that the border's twin-city metropolitan regions such as El Paso–Ciudad Juárez and Tijuana–San Diego were verging on environmental crisis.

In 1983, the Mexican and U.S. governments signed the La Paz agreement, the first comprehensive border environmental cooperation accord. This agreement was useful as a means of generating international dialogue, but it focused mainly on pollution associated with *maquiladoras* and did not address other pressing problems such as the region's growing shortage of fresh water, the illegal dumping of toxic and hazardous wastes generated mainly by U.S. companies operating in Mexico, and infrastructural deficiencies. Communities, environmental agencies, and nongovernmental organizations looked to the proposed NAFTA as a possible alternative way to deal with natural resource depletion and environmental degradation in the border zone by integrating these concerns into the free-trade debate. The 1990 joint presidential resolution ensued, resulting in the Integrated Border Environmental Plan (IBEP) produced in collaboration by SEDUE and the U.S. Environmental Protection Agency (EPA) in 1992.

IBEP has been criticized for its lack of specifics on implementation, compounded by the considerable difference between the United States and Mexico in the legal and regulatory framework. The lack of attention to budgetary constraints was also a concern, as estimates of the cost of cleaning up the border ranged from $5 billion to $15 billion. IBEP also has been criticized for the shortcomings of the public participation process on both sides of the border. Nevertheless, the very act of community consultation in planning via public hearings was unprecedented in Mexico, and the plan served to focus the attention of both federal governments on a sorely neglected region and a previously under-acknowledged linkage, that between trade and the environment.

As a result of the NAFTA environmental side agreements, the Border Environmental Cooperation Commission (BECC) was established in 1994. The principal concerns of this joint commission were wastewater, drinking water, and municipal solid waste projects on both sides of the border. The BECC's main function was to certify projects to the North American Development Bank (NADBANK), a binational creation also deriving from the NAFTA side agreements, to provide US$2 billion to US$3 billion in financing for border environmental projects. Together, the BECC and NADBANK were intended to offer a different strategy from conventional development banking, with a bottom-up approach to lending to individuals, cities, corporations, and governments on a binational basis.

In October 1995, Border XXI, the successor to IBEP, was announced. Border XXI, in response to the lessons learned from IBEP, was a more open-ended long-range plan to coordinate federal, state, and local government agencies to deal with sustainable development, public participation, decentralization, and local empowerment. As such, it was intended to constitute a reflexive process emerging from the concerns of border residents rather than a top-down plan. At the time of its creation, its likely priorities included air, water, hazardous and solid waste, energy generation, pollution planning, emergency response, and environmental health.

It remains to be seen whether grassroots input and targeted funding are sufficient to offset the economic forces that continue to concentrate population and industrial growth in fragile borderlands ecosystems. Two years after its inception, it appeared that contrary to the predictions of its proponents, NAFTA has exacerbated environmental degradation in this area. In a context of a weakened Mexican economy, public-sector budget cuts on both sides of the border, and continued enforcement problems, prospects of environmental mitigation look dim.

Agriculture: The "Industry of Disasters"

In many respects, Mexico's current environmental crisis derives from the longer-standing agricultural crisis, which emerged in the late 1960s but was rooted in the post-1945 development strategy privileging industry and urban development over agriculture and rural development. Despite the early emphasis after the Mexican Revolution on land redistribution to peasants in *ejidos*, a unique form of communal land tenure, the subsistence sector was neglected by the government in favor of private investment in large-scale commercial agriculture, propelled by rapid advances in agricultural techniques and technologies worldwide—the so-called Green Revolution. As the internationalization of Mexico's economy prompted the increasing emphasis on export crops in this sector, the onus of basic foods production shifted to the peasantry. After 1970, the government initiated a massive and expensive campaign to modernize agricultural production on *ejidos*. Rather than promoting an efficient, expanded productive base, however, this interventionist approach resulted in the institutionalization of an *industria de siniestros* (industry of disasters) in which crop failure, corruption, and chronic indebtedness have been the norm. The economic, social, and environmental costs of agricultural modernization in both the peasant and the private sectors have been devastating.

In the arid regions of northern Mexico, where the government invested heavily in rural infrastructure to foster private irrigated agriculture, salinization has caused the abandonment of thousands of acres. Mining of groundwater for irrigation and to support increasing settlement is reaching critical levels in some regions, such as Baja California Norte and Sonora. Decades of monoculture (the use of farmland to grow single crops, such as fruits and vegetables for export, or cotton, sugar, and rice for both domestic and foreign consumption) have resulted in soil exhaustion and pesticide-resistant plagues. Meanwhile ever-increasing and often indiscriminate use of agrochemicals, including a number of highly toxic pesticides banned or restricted in the United States, has engendered a wide range of health hazards. Other areas suffer from increasing soil erosion and desertification as a result of over-cultivation or over-grazing of marginal lands.

Perhaps the worst environmental degradation incurred by agricultural modernization has been in the tropical forests of southeastern Mexico. According to scholar Ivan Restrepo, tropical forest acreage overall declined from 170 million in 1975 to 47 million in 1980. The Lacondón region of Chiapas has lost 70 percent of its original forest cover. Twenty-five years ago, almost two-thirds of the state of Campeche was forested. At least 1.5 million acres have been cleared in the interim for frontier colonization and logging, mechanized agriculture, or pasture, often in that sequence with cattle as the end phase in the cycle of destruction now typical of the tropical forests of Central and South America.

Mechanized agriculture has been particularly destructive of diverse and complex tropical ecosystems. One hectare (2.5 acres) of forest may contain as many as 200 different species of trees and innumerable smaller plants, animals, and insects, each adapted to a very specific ecological niche. Once large areas have been cleared for agriculture and settlement and the delicate natural equilibrium has been upset, many of these species are unable to survive and reproduce. In particular, direct transfer of agricultural technologies from temperate zones has caused incalculable damage ecologically and has failed to achieve production goals. Attempts to turn the tropical lowlands into a granary have proven especially destructive in that unnecessary expanses of land have been clear-cut; heavy machinery, fertilizers, and monocultures have destroyed fragile tropical soils; and the introduction of crops unsuited to the climate, soils, and terrains has had disastrous results. The predominant solution for these failed agricultural development projects for peasants has been "cattle-ization" by design or by default, at an incalculable cost in terms of the loss of biodiversity.

The environment is likely to be under increasing stress as a consequence of the opening of agriculture to international competition under NAFTA. Currently, Mexico is competitive only in a handful of agribusiness enclaves while the basic foods sector remains stagnant. In this context, the revitalization of agriculture requires a reversal of traditionally paternalistic and protectionist state policies involving long-standing explicit and implicit subsidies, extensive restructuring of inefficient government agencies, intensification of production, and the development of a climate conducive to the expansion of investment, both foreign and domestic. The amendment of the previously sacrosanct Article 27 of the 1917 Mexican Constitution in 1992 to end land redistribution and permit the legal sale or rental of *ejido* plots seems particularly problematic in terms of potential environmental repercussions, such as another massive rural-urban migration of peasants dispossessed for a pittance. In this scramble for the survival of the fittest farmers, official concerns for conserving resources for the future seem to have been eclipsed by the imperative of free market forces.

Sustainable Development or Developing Sustainability?

The preamble to the 1988 General Law of Ecological Equilibrium and Environmental Protection maintains that the solution to Mexico's environmental problems is not to abandon the pursuit of development, given the country's pressing needs with respect to food, employment, and housing. Rather, the answer lies in continuing but more environmentally aware economic growth following the neoliberal path to prosperity, on the assumption that it is easier for rich nations to be green. Unfortunately, the adjustments required by neoliberal transition has been at odds with this conception of sustainable development. The government's priority of opening the Mexican economy preempts effective environmental legislation, and fiscal austerity reduces resources available for environmental protection.

Another approach to sustainable development calls for a radically different economics, producing much lower rates of growth, if any, to ensure future ecological stability by fully recognizing the processes and limits of the biosphere. This approach, with an additional emphasis on the importance of cultural as well as biological diversity, the right to democracy, and the satisfaction of basic human needs, has been embraced by a number of rural communities, citizen groups, ecological organizations, and segments of the Mexican intelligentsia. In this view, sustainable development becomes more than a core concept in environmentalist rhetoric and a fashionable "buzz term" within the political and economic mainstream. Instead, it constitutes a direct challenge to neoliberalism, voiced by those segments of the population that have been marginalized by the dominant model of development.

It has been suggested that, paradoxically, a key opportunity to promote this type of sustainability may arise from the current crisis in the Mexican countryside, resulting from development policies that have degraded the resource base, promoted inefficient land use, created massive unemployment and underemployment, and prompted ongoing outmigration. These crisis conditions could provide a starting point for sustainable development via small-scale, diversified production to meet basic needs and stimulate local economies in combination with employment of the surplus workforce in environmental reconstruction. An emphasis on the *process* of developing sustainability rather than on the *product* could act as a bridge between the government's commitment to confronting environmental problems and spontaneous, bottom-up initiatives. Such an approach is likely to involve new forms of both policy and practice, with priorities given to community initiative, building knowledge about ecosystems, and holistic planning and management, emphasizing mediation of environmental, economic, and social goals at local and regional levels.

This scenario may not be unrealistic, whether or not free trade promotes significant economic growth and increased employment in Mexico, especially if the hemispheric trading partners see a common interest in breaking the linkages between economic restructuring, environmental degradation, poverty, and social unrest. The January 1994 Chiapas uprising may have provided some incentive in this direction. The financial setbacks Mexico experienced in 1995 underscore the imperative of promoting local environmental solutions rather than relying on government actions in a time of extraordinary economic, political, and social adjustment.

See also Conquest: Ecological Impact; Industry and Industrialization; Mesoamerica: Agriculture and Ecology; Migration; Population; Urbanism and Urbanization

Select Bibliography

Barkin, David, *Distorted Development: Mexico in the World Economy.* Boulder, Colorado: Westview, 1990.

_____, and Blanca Suárez San Roman, *El fin de la autosuficiencia alimentaria.* Mexico City: Centro de Ecodesarrollo and Nueva Imagen, 1982.

Barry, Tom, *Zapata's Revenge: Free Trade and the Farm Crisis in Mexico.* Boston: South End Press, 1995.

Berry, Brian J. L., and Frank E. Horton, *Urban Environmental Management: Planning for Pollution Control.* Englewood Cliffs, New Jersey: Prentice-Hall, 1974.

Carley, Michael, and Ian Christie, *Managing Sustainable Development.* London: Earthscan, 1992; Minneapolis: University of Minnesota Press, 1993.

Davis, Diane E., *Urban Leviathan. Mexico City in the Twentieth Century.* Philadelphia: Temple University Press, 1994.

Dirección General de Estadística, *Censo General de Población.* Mexico City: Dirección General de Estadística, 1990.

Gates, Marilyn, *In Default: Peasants, the Debt Crisis, and the Agricultural Challenge in Mexico.* Boulder, Colorado: Westview, 1993.

Gereffi, Gary, "Mexico's Maquiladora Industries and North American Integration." In *North America Without Borders? Integrating Canada, the United States, and Mexico,* edited by Stephen J. Randall, Herman Konrad, and Sheldon Silvermann. Calgary: University of Calgary Press, 1992.

Lacy, Rodolfo, editor, *La calidad del aire en el Valle de México.* Mexico City: Colegio de México, 1993.

López Portillo y Ramos, Manuel, editor, *El medio ambiente en México: Temas, problemas y alternativas.* Mexico City: Fondo de Cultura Económica, 1982.

M'Gonigle, R. Michael, and Ben Parfitt, *Forestopia: A Practical Guide to the New Forest Economy.* Madeira Park, British Columbia: Harbour, 1994.

Pastor, Robert A., and Jorge G. Castaneda, *Limits to Friendship: The United States and Mexico.* New York: Knopf, 1988.

Rich, Jan Galbreath, *Planning the Border's Future: The Mexican-U.S. Integrated Border Environmental Plan.* Austin: U.S.-Mexican Policy Studies Program, LBJ School of Public Affairs, University of Texas, 1992.

Secretaría de Gobernación, *Ley General de Equilibrio Ecológico y la Protección al Ambiente.* 11th edition, Mexico City: Secretaría de Gobernación, 1995.

—MARILYN GATES

EDUCATION

This entry includes four articles that discuss education and government education policy:

Education: Colonial
Education: 1821–89
Education: 1889–1940
Education: 1940–96

See also Anthropology; Church and State; Escuela Nacional de Medicina; Family and Kinship; Gender; Historiography; Indigenismo and Ethnic Movements; Mesoamerica: Writing; Nationalism; Teachers' Movements; University System

EDUCATION: COLONIAL

There is a widespread belief that the Spanish Crown neglected the education of its colonial subjects in the Americas through three centuries of colonial domination. Modern conceptions of colonization and optimistic notions of education have even led some scholars to maintain that the viceregal authorities actually went out of their way to preserve American ignorance in the belief that the colonial subjects' minimal knowledge guaranteed their submission.

The documentary evidence shows, however, that educating the native population was a crucial justification of the colonizing enterprise, and that criollo (Spanish American) culture was encouraged as a vehicle for integrating the new Americans into the "motherland." Of course, such education did not include literacy; training in mechanical skills was imparted at the same time by the teaching friars. Both clerical and secular educators desired the socialization of emerging generations, the preparation of young people for the tasks that would be theirs when they grew up, and the internalization of those values considered essential by the ruling classes.

The original purpose of Indian evangelization was to introduce the ways and customs of western Christian civilization. As colonial society became more complex, the religious goal gave way to that of social regulation, so that throughout the three centuries of colonization, a system was imposed to inculcate each individual with the belief that his or her place in society was ordained by providence. Although formal schooling was confined to the urban minority, a Christian education, with its accompanying respect for the established order pervaded the consciousness of one and all, regardless of age, gender, or status, ensuring overall acceptance of inequality and the stability of the colonial regime.

Any colonial undertaking that stops short of the extermination or exile of the local population implies a didactic commitment. The invading power, believing itself the depository of a higher culture, is responsible for the dissemination of this culture among the invaded, who are by definition reckoned to inhabit a lower cultural and intellectual sphere. This task furnishes a moral alibi for colonization, as well as corresponding more often than not to a legal framework. This principle was reinforced, in the American case, by the messianic outlook of Spanish Catholicism.

The bulls Inter Caetera, signed by Pope Alexander VI in May 1493, granted Castile dominion over the Indies, with the obligation to spread the Catholic faith. Although not every conquistador was inclined to take such an injunction to heart, the Catholic monarchs tirelessly drummed it into governors, captains, explorers, and viceroys. In New Spain, Fernando (Hernán) Cortés warned that if this obligation were to be neglected, the right to command and exploit the new territories would be forfeited.

It might have been adequate for purposes of legitimation to stage ostentatious scenes of mass baptism, but this would fail to satisfy the evangelical impulse; it would damage material interests and dash hopes of turning the Indians into loyal subjects of the monarchy. Christianity required profound transformation of beliefs and customs, not only the repression of pagan ritual and other external signs of piety; during the early decades at least, missionary fervor imposed profound changes upon Mesoamerican society. The identification of education with evangelization is not, therefore, an academic axiom advanced by contemporary historians but rather the result of ideas prevalent between the sixteenth and eighteenth centuries, which held that proficiency in Christian doctrine was in itself sufficient education. This was not as irrational as it sounds, if we consider that a handful of monks, preaching among the nonbelievers, succeeded in pacifying the territory far more effectively and incomparably more cheaply than any regiment.

Indigenous Education

The conversion of the Indians was a priority for the Spanish Crown, which imposed this responsibility first on the encomenderos (holders of land trusts and the profits of their Indian laborers) and subsequently on the regular religious orders. The first Franciscan mission reached New Spain in 1524, to a solemn welcome from Cortés himself. A few months earlier, three other Franciscan friars had arrived from Flanders without ceremony or fanfare, to prepare the way for their order. Once reunited, they began to plan their strategy, founding four communities each with its respective monastery, the bases for sending out future missionary expeditions. Two other mendicant orders, the Dominicans and the Augustinians, arrived later still but followed their predecessors' methods in large part.

The spacious monastery atriums became outdoor classrooms for the evangelization of men, women, and children, separated by age and gender into the four corners of the patio where they memorized the catechism by the "mutual assistance" method, by singing, and by insistent repetition. Adults attended on feast days, children were summoned daily.

Highborn Indian boys, or "principals," as well as those who distinguished themselves by their merit, were promoted to more advanced levels of instruction, becoming boarders in special quarters built for them inside the monastery. There they absorbed liturgical chant, reading, and writing in their own language, and learned the rudiments of Latin so that they could assist the friars in their religious duties.

The growth of the three mendicant orders through all the territory of New Spain responded to practical and political exigencies. Monasteries proliferated in the most densely populated regions; with overt competitiveness they ousted one another in the areas of early occupation or with powerful overlords; and they partitioned the remaining lands among themselves, delimiting precise areas of influence. All took pains to train their charges in crafts and trades, whether as common monasterial practice or in special schools such as San José de los Naturales, a Franciscan establishment in Mexico City, or Tiripetío in Michoacán, founded by the Augustinians.

Heartening results obtained with the first monastery-educated generations encouraged the Franciscans to design an institute of higher studies, teaching humanities and philosophy. On January 6, 1536, the Santa Cruz college was inaugurated at Santiago de Tlatelolco in the capital, intended for Indians of noble birth. The project was sponsored by both the viceroy and the bishop, with formal endorsement and financial aid from the emperor. Its 70 boarders displayed the utmost keenness and talent in the assimilation of their courses on humanities and philosophy. They acted as the friars' language teachers and provided invaluable data regarding their traditions and ancient history.

It was thanks to the Tlatelolco students that much of the labor of Sahagún and Bautista, among other Franciscan scholars, was able to be accomplished.

A number of circumstances conspired to cancel the project of giving higher education to Indians. The most important was the implantation of a new regime that ignored the category of noble or privileged natives, expecting all to get down to work for the greater economic good of Spain. In a move not unconnected with the above, as of 1555 a series of provincial councils forbade the ordination of indigenous people. Another factor was the alleged disappointment of the Franciscans at the spectacle of their boys, groomed for holy orders, blithely enjoying female companionship. There was also new concern for an orthodoxy shaken by too many trials against stubbornly idolatrous natives, notably the cacique don Carlos, of Tezcoco. Lastly, the college at Tlatelolco lost the support of its major patron, Juan de Zumárraga, and was demoted to the status of an ordinary monastery school teaching no more than the catechism.

Once the first great evangelizing drive had run out of steam, Indian instruction was no longer a priority. The lay churches and the monastery schools continued to run children's catechism classes and to test engaged couples for their knowledge of doctrine, but that was as far as it went. Some towns might offer elementary schooling, but there was little concern for the learning of the masses until the last quarter of the eighteenth century, when an enlightened monarchy urged the religious and civil authorities to set up Spanish language schools.

Criollo Education

The founding of the Royal University, although not directly related to the decline of the college of Santa Cruz, crystallized the policy swerve begun around 1550 and consolidated by the end of the century. Fernando (Hernán) Cortés, the councilors of Mexico City, and the first viceroy Antonio de Mendoza all had appealed for a license from the king and the Council of the Indies to establish a house of General or Royal Studies. In September 1551, Prince Felipe (the future Felipe II) signed the warrants inaugurating the universities of Lima and Mexico City; two years later, classes began in the Mexican institution, with the peculiarity of being totally independent of the regular teaching orders.

The Royal University was created with the aim of being capable both of interpreting reality and justifying the status quo. It was in this persistently medieval spirit that it had been solicited by local authorities, and thus it was understood by its first professors, Fray Alonso de la Veracruz and Fray Pedro de la Peña. In 1553 and 1554, the legitimacy of the titles of Conquest was discussed, alongside the theological issues generated by the conversion of Indians.

The Counter-Reformation mandated a new orthodoxy in Catholic doctrine, administration, and religious practice, altering the course of studies in New Spain. They came under more rigid management, with regulations that stipulated identical topics and textbooks to those followed in the metropolis and in the other Catholic universities affiliated to Rome. Thus from the last third of the sixteenth century, the university devoted itself to the preservation of orthodox knowledge. Such a goal determined the basic shape of higher studies, for to preserve knowledge was to reject innovation, and jealous orthodoxy implied a systematic distrust of all that came from outside.

The university maintained its privileges as a corporation, and throughout the colonial period it was exclusively entitled to bestow academic degrees, despite the appeals of the higher studies establishments run by the regular orders. Its status as "Pontifical," added to the title "Royal," was much appreciated by professors and students, for their degrees were now equivalent to those of the most prestigious European universities. There is no formal evidence of a greater or lesser attendance rate during the sixteenth and seventeenth centuries, so that the frequent and violent oscillations in student numbers came about at arbitrary moments and for arbitrary reasons.

The faculty of theology did not relinquish its lofty position as "Sovereign among Schools" owing to the high regard for these studies, in spite of the fact that not more than 70 to 90 students were ever registered at one time. The faculty of arts and philosophy (functioning as a kind of preparatory school for adolescents fresh from the humanities cycle) was the most popular, as the antechamber to more significant faculties. The number of matriculations depended on demand from the colleges, so that courses for 30 students and courses for 180 could coexist during one and the same decade. Canon law remained steady, with a constant average of 70 to 80; likewise, medicine and law, with 10 and 20 pupils respectively per year. The eighteenth century saw a marked rise in student numbers across the board.

We gather from this that university students were a very rare breed—a fact that did not prevent this institution from being the most influential and respected cultural agent in the life of New Spain.

Since nothing resembling a national education scheme or official control of studies ever existed, the chaotic process of educational regulation in the colony must not surprise us. Whenever a new need arose, the authorities were begged to regulate it; thus, when after the university's establishment the Jesuits introduced their own schools and colleges for the humanities in the late sixteenth century, the Council of the Indies was asked to arbitrate the competition of the two institutions. It was not until the beginning of the following century that the viceroy announced the Ordinances for Masters of the Noble Arts of Reading and Writing, which regulated the elementary instruction of children.

The rivalry between the Jesuits and the university was resolved by banning the former from the granting of academic titles; they were permitted to teach arts, however. Although they did not desist from teaching theology and canon law, especially to novices of the order, their graduates enjoyed no official recognition. Jesuit schools always were free for outside students, charging to seminarists or other interns only what it cost to maintain them. It also cost nothing to attend courses at the Royal University, but the fees for bachelor and doctorate degrees were extremely high.

The Masters' Ordinances enshrined the obligation to teach children the catechism, reading, various types of writing and basic arithmetic. They also warned the *amigas,* lady teachers of girls, against admitting any male pupils whatsoever regardless of age. In practice, however, boys from three to six went to *la miga,* who, as well as catechizing them with monotonous chants, introduced them to the rigors of timetables, silence, and good manners. Masters and *amigas* charged variable amounts, according to the standard of the school and the economic possibilities of parents.

Because not all towns in New Spain could offer private teachers, the Jesuits generally were responsible for the elementary education of the great majority of criollo children, many of mixed race, and even some blacks, "always with the proper segregation," however, as they declared to appease parents who complained of intolerable promiscuity. Smaller groups learned Latin grammar (humanities), and the members of the elite vied to get their offspring into boarding schools, the nursery for the most successful academics. Since the humanities cycle was required to enter the university, the Jesuits guarded the gate to all the faculties.

The Company of Jesus's schools introduced new pedagogical techniques and reduced or eliminated corporal punishment in favor of incentives. Other innovations were peer competition, homework, compulsory recreation periods, the organization of lessons into groups of 10 supervised by *decurions* (monitors elected by the students), the use of Latin in the classroom, and the promotion of literary and pious activities in extracurricular clubs and congregations. The expulsion of the Jesuits in 1767 broke the backbone of criollo education. After the matter was placed in the hands of laypersons and other religious orders lacking a specialty in education, teaching standards took a long time to be restored.

During the last years of the colonial regime, a renovation of the studies scheme began outside the old institutions of the teaching tradition. The Surgeons' College began to pay attention to anatomy and to experimental knowledge—rubrics held in much contempt at the faculty of medicine, with its devotion to Hippocrates. At the San Carlos Fine Arts Academy, which taught drawing and trained future sculptors, painters, and architects, a new aesthetics was creeping in. The Botanical Gardens responded to the increasing interest in nature within a scientific framework by adopting European classificatory taxonomies, pioneered by Carolus Linnaeus. The Mining School was perhaps the institution that best represented the spirit of the Enlightenment in New Spain: it was a center for mathematics and science, as well as researching technologies for the extraction of precious metals.

Women's and Mestizos' Education

Each one of the regular orders established novice training centers, which in some cases, like that of the San Luis General Studies, acted as parallel universities without formal recognition. Conciliar seminaries were operating from the second half of the seventeenth century, providing lay clergy to far-flung dioceses. Most outstanding for the number of its students, the size of its income, the magnificence of its premises, and the dynamism of its founder (Bishop Juan de Palafox) was that of Puebla, divided into various colleges by age and level of knowledge. Representatives of the Royal University of Mexico used to travel to Puebla to examine the students at Palafox's seminary and at the Jesuit college.

Women generally were ignored by educational institutions; they had very few options should they wish to develop an intellectual life, and they were debarred from pursuing their studies at the Royal University. Even an education with the *amigas* was available only for the daughters of urban families. There were a number of orphanage schools in the larger towns and retreats for girls who sought a life of perfection or were committed as a punishment for improper conduct.

Girls' schools were sponsored by confraternities and protected by bishops, who were concerned to shield respectable maidens from the perils of the "world." It was therefore common for a candidate to have to present certificates of legitimacy and "pure" blood. It was easier to gain access to some nuns' convents, where many inmates took in relatives, friends, or servants to share their cells. Judging by the applications alone, it is hard to distinguish among educated girls, prospective novices, and women destined for the service of the nuns who received them. At any rate, neither colleges nor convents made a priority of educating the women who might enter their walls from the age of eight, to remain cloistered for the rest of their lives.

The scarcity of teaching institutions was no obstacle for the women of New Spain, who got by on the slenderest of educations as the times required. It would have benefited them little given their social roles to spout Latin, philosophy, or arithmetic, but it was essential that they should speak, sing, and dance prettily, know their prayers, practice their devotions, and be able to run a household. This was enough for well-born girls and future wives; less fortunate spinsters and widows had to fend for themselves, sending out for sewing or laundry, teaching music, or becoming domestics. The more enterprising among them might set up their own businesses or manage workshops or stores inherited through the family. Knowledge of the catechism or of fancy needlework was of no use in such circumstances.

The early plan to devote special care to the education of children of mixed race was rapidly abandoned, and the colleges founded for this purpose were given over to Spanish children, orphans, or the needy. Mestizos ceased to be a rarity, becoming a substantial group whose integration into society depended upon their economic ease, their family connections, and their profession; in a word, upon what their "quality" might be. Those who were able, hired private tutors, and those who boasted a decorous social and family position had their children admitted into Jesuit schools; the rest were consigned to marginality and the universal school of experience and wits afforded by the city streets. Education was, in short, highly selective as befits a stratified society, and the possibilities of self-realization were a lottery of birth rather than talent.

Select Bibliography

Becerra Lopez, José Luis, *La organización de los estudios en la Nueva España*. Mexico City: Cultura, 1963.

Castañeda Garcia, Carmen, *La educación en Guadalajara durante la Colonia, 1552–1821*. Mexico City: El Colegio de México-El Colegio de Jalisco, 1984.

Gomez Canedo, Lino, *La educación de los marginados durante la época colonial*. Mexico City: Porrúa, 1982.

Gonzalbo Aizpuru, Pilar, *II: La educación de los criollos y la vida urbana*. Mexico City: El Colegio de México, 1990.

Kobayashi, José María, *La educación como conquista*. Mexico City: El Colegio de México, 1974.

Larroyo, Francisco, *Historia comparada de la educación en México*. Mexico City: Porrúa, 1962.

Luque Alcaide, Elisa, *La educación en Nueva España en el siglo XVIII*. Seville: Consejo Superior de Investigaciones Científicas, 1970.

Osorio Romero, Ignacio, *Colegios y profesores jesuitas que enseñaron latín en Nueva España, 1572–1767*. Mexico City: UNAM, 1980.

Seminario de Historia de la Educación en Mexico, *Historia de la lectura en México*. Mexico City: El Colegio de México-El Ermitaño, 1988.

Tanck de Estrada, Dorothy, *La educación ilustrada (1786–1836)*. Mexico City: El Colegio de México, 1977.

Vazquez, Josefina Z., et al., *Ensayos sobre historia de la educación en México*. Mexico City: El Colegio de México, 1981.

—Pilar Gonzalbo Aizpuru

EDUCATION: 1821–89

The surprising continuity of goals and methods in Mexican education from the Bourbon reforms until at least the mid–nineteenth century betrays a society unmoved by political upheavals where educating its children was concerned. This was a period of reflection regarding the most progressive ideas of an era, converting them into banners of the reformist tendency that conceived of improved education as the surest way to achieve a higher standard of living and a stronger state. It was also hoped that improved education might act as a catalyst for the various "races" to converge in the embryonic Mexican nation.

The history of education after 1821 is intimately connected with public health and the government's economic policy. Public figures of the day, whatever their political leanings, agreed on the desirability of extending the availability of *primeras letras* (as ungraded primary schooling was then called) to the whole country. They understood that Mexico could not be modernized without including the people and without updating the humanist culture of the lettered minority who were the only sector capable of taking the reins of this emergent nation-state. Such a consensus led to two important aims: first, to extend elementary education to the masses, and second, to replace the mental structures born of dogma and dispute with a spirit of investigation and doubt, more appropriate to the implementation of modern, pragmatic solutions.

An enlightened citizenry was the shared dream of all political groups. However, they proved unable to alleviate the misery of indigenous peoples or the neglect suffered by the urban poor. Indian education was touted as a kind of "regenerator" that would elevate its beneficiaries to a higher social position, necessary for the juridical equality of all those born on Mexican soil. In practice, however, only urban populations were incorporated into national life by the new rulers; the rural masses were left to their age-old illiteracy. Outside the towns, much of the Indian population was flatly monolingual, despite belated attempts by the Spanish Crown to Hispanicize them toward the end of the colonial period.

With the establishment in 1822 of the first Mexican Empire of Agustín de Iturbide, educational efforts were focused on urban youngsters so that they might learn "proper respect" for the authorities. Thus Iturbide's government favored education as a way of "obtaining order-loving citizens"—that is, subservient men of the new regime.

The first Republic, inheriting the problems that had bedeviled Emperor Agustín, was somewhat more successful in its bid to bring letters and civic awareness to a broader portion of the population, thanks in large part to the system known as "mutual learning." This method was not precisely new, having been applied in Britain's so-called Bethlehemite schools for indigent children since the second half of the eighteenth century as a prolongation of the ecclesiastical societies that flourished in eighteenth-century England with a mission to spread "Christian knowledge" among the people. The Lancastrian System (as it was called after one of its founders) consisted of using some of the older pupils as monitors, who would help to get the teacher's words and questions across to younger students. This was an exceptionally cheap system, whereby a single teacher (rather, a kind of inspector) could rely on a complex web of mechanical exercises to oversee a considerable number of students. The system was introduced into Mexico by Manuel Cordoniu, founder of the newspaper *El Sol*, who arrived in 1821 with the last governor sent to administer New Spain, Juan

O'Donoju. The first Lancastrian school was set up in the old palace of the Inquisition on August 22, 1822, and met with such a good reception that the Finance Ministry, in its annual reports of 1829 and 1830 listed the school in its general expenses records.

During much of the early Independence era, both the government and the thinkers of the day assumed that basic as well as higher education were deserving of society's full attention, implying the official dissemination of a set of overall rules, with a view to a uniform educational system in reality as on paper. The annual reports of the Ministry of External and Internal Relations for 1823, 1825, 1827, and 1830 proposed a "general scheme of instruction" that would encompass all disciplines and impart the knowledge necessary for the "conservation, prosperity, and development" of society. Crucial to this plan was an increase in the number of primary schools, since these would form the cornerstone of public education across the nation. It was along such lines that in 1829 Lorenzo de Zavala, one of the leading federalist ideologues, declared that it was necessary and "fundamental to the society of the United States of Mexico that elementary schools should multiply, and furthermore all the funds that are frittered away elsewhere should be invested in them."

Not everyone agreed with him, however. In 1830, Minister Lucas Alamán split the curriculum into four branches, one of which was to be housed in each of the existing colleges; new subjects were introduced, and theology classes were to be abolished. Alamán's plan was concise and moderate, for as he himself once remarked, the administration of President Anastasio Bustamante invariably would choose reform over any fresh creative endeavor.

The debates concerning the education system were not as civil as one might like to believe, especially once the Catholic Church came under fire for allegedly monopolizing education. In 1833 the government proposed an educational reform that was designed to weaken the power of the church in this area and to produce a new kind of man, able to galvanize society with greater, more progressive vigor. During the short life of the Reform of 1833 (what the liberal theoretician José María Luis Mora preferred to call the Revolution of 1833), Vice President Valentín Gómez Farías decreed the suppression of the national university on October 21, 1833, and the institution of a General Office of Public Instruction for the Federal District and territories, which henceforth was to be the government department in charge of education. Gómez Farías also ordered that all funds belonging to the former education colleges be handed over to the new office. The members of this organ included politicians, former insurgents, and educators, all of whom left their mark on nineteenth-century Mexico; among them was Juan José Espinoza de los Monteros (president), Manuel Eduardo Gorostiza (secretary), Andrés Quintana Roo, José María Luis Mora, Bernardo Couto, and Juan Rodríguez Puebla (rector of the only Indian college of higher education, located in Mexico City). Rodríguez Puebla did not sign the bill of October 19, 1833, for he only began to attend the meetings of the General Office as of January 8, 1834. He repeatedly voiced his misgivings at the closure of the Colegio de San Gregorio, arguing that it had been established by the Jesuits and subsequently supported by post-Independence administrations in order to impart "higher" education to indigenous students. The college reopened after the fall of Gómez Farías; it was ultimately closed in 1853, and its resources delivered to the new School of Agriculture.

On June 2, 1834, the administration issued the General Regulations for Systematizing Public Instruction in the Federal District. Freedom of education was broached for the first time and applied scientifically in the six schools created to replace the former colleges. Each establishment would offer wide-ranging and specialized courses, subject to central control, in contrast to the old system in which most colleges duplicated one another to become what critics termed a parade of "Gothic error." José María Luis Mora and Lorenzo de Zavala wielded their most devastating anticlerical rhetoric to attack the old educational system. For example, Mora dismissed college education as a monkish cloister, smothering all possibility of civil learning.

The public men of the time suspected that a student's life was closer to mystical retreat than to that of any common Christian. In this view, religious festivals, processions, and funerals took up too much of the student's time, for he had no outlook on life other than that indoctrinated by pious literature. Nineteenth-century thinkers sought to create a more positive man with their educational reforms; they aspired to the individualistic model of an industrious, enlightened being conscious of his own interests, a virtuous citizen whose greatest bliss would be deposited in the secular state.

It was not long before the Laws of Reform were rescinded by President Antonio López de Santa Anna, under pressure from the Conservative social sectors that had delivered the presidency to him. It is interesting to note that the plan put forward by Gómez Farías was strikingly similar to that of Lucas Alamán (1830), but unlike the latter, provoked barely a ripple in Mexican society.

On July 31, 1834, the General Office was officially shut down, the six higher studies institutes abolished, and their funds returned to the colleges that had lost them one year before. This measure, compounded by the political disgrace of Gómez Farías and many of his supporters, meant that secularization had to wait for the appearance of Gabino Barreda one generation later. The Reform of 1833 had been overthrown by the forces of restoration, led by Santa Anna.

By the 1840s, once more under the presidency of Santa Anna, the educational affairs of the country were gathered together under a single authority. The pillar of this achievement was Manuel Baranda, a lawyer from Guanajuato, former inspector of public instruction, former governor of his home state, and secretary of public instruction. Baranda's successes seemed unique at a time when the country was undergoing constant changes of government and economic crises. Baranda's annual report of 1844 reckoned that there were 1,310 schools throughout the Republic with a total of 59,744 pupils. Although in another document of the same period he calculated the total as a quarter of a million students, this still seems a dubiously low figure for a country with almost 7 million inhabitants.

With the Liberal rise to power and the elaboration of the 1857 Constitution, education once more became a national preoccupation. The authors of the Constitution of 1857 believed that man's possession of socially useful knowledge was akin to "a common national treasure." In the Congress of 1856–57, Francisco Zarco requested the reinstatement of the Indian College of San Gregorio, claiming that it was important to "maintain houses of learning and contribute to the civilization of the native race."

Political controversies and military armed conflict between Liberals and Conservatives postponed the drafting of any law to define educational policy in Mexico. Once the capital had been taken by Liberal forces and the constitutional order reestablished, it was time to attempt a formulation of the broad lines that were to endow Mexico with a coherent structure. The principal cohesive element had hitherto been provided by Catholicism; Liberal thinkers concluded that the Catholic Church's influence across the fields of society, politics, culture, and economics was an obstacle to the establishment of a powerful Liberal state. The country's future was deemed to depend upon a joint effort, in which education would play the unifying role. Accordingly, on February 11, 1861, President Benito Juárez overhauled the ministries and founded one more by decree, that of Justice and Public Instruction. This body would control every aspect of primary, secondary, and professional schooling in the Federal District and the territories.

Although their political adversaries by no means had been wiped out, and despite imbalances in the public finances, the Liberals published a decree on April 15, 1861, inaugurating the reorganization of education supervised by public authorities and predicated upon the separation of church and state. For the first time in the history of Mexican education, the law Concerning Public Instruction in Establishments Dependent upon the General Government abolished catechism classes in all schools that were not financially independent. Catechism was replaced by "morals," a subject that headed the list of topics to be taught in elementary classrooms. Secondary schooling in the Federal District was covered by one preparatory school and seven specialized centers (jurisprudence, medicine, mining, arts, agriculture, fine arts, and commerce).

Private schools had survived with difficulty during the first half of the nineteenth century. The law of April 1861 required students to be examined in the public establishment of their choice in order to obtain a degree, and obliged some schools to make arrangements with the ministry to supply adult education at night and on Sundays. Juárez and his minister of public instruction, Ignacio Ramírez, legislated for the bulk of the population; they were concerned with the masses rather than with the privileged enclaves that could choose from a wealth of educational opportunities.

Just when it seemed that the Liberal vision of a genuine Mexican nation-state would become a reality, French troops landed in Veracruz as envoys of the London Convention, whose members demanded the settlement of old debts contracted with Spain, France, and England. Undeterred by the somber prospect of war, Juárez issued a circular on March 26, 1863, granting religious freedom to all colleges. In public instruction schools, pupils were to comply with religious duties only by the express order of parents or guardians.

A year after invading European troops forced the Liberal government to abandon Mexico City, the invaders installed Maximilian von Hapsburg as emperor, and the Second Mexican Empire began. As soon as he landed in Veracruz, Maximilian proclaimed a policy of conciliation intended to unify the country; in the north, the Liberal faction maintained a semipassive resistance. Maximilian recognized education as a prime issue around which to build the consensus of the Mexican people. In December 1864, a "prevention" was circulated in order to gather data about the state of primary teaching; this document required each primary teacher to submit a detailed report on his or her school before resuming work in February 1865, including the school's name, date of foundation, subjects taught, and the name of the director and other teachers; however, no evidence survives to confirm that these instructions ever were carried out.

In April 1865, the emperor drafted the Provisional Statute of the Mexican Empire, a body of legislation with marked liberal leanings, directed at the whole territory. Education was carefully considered within the statute. As a result, the Ministry of Public Instruction and Religions was restructured to promote and improve "primary, secondary, and preparatory instruction as well as the higher and professional levels." The ministry elaborated a teaching program that was to be compulsory for all schools maintained by the state.

On December 27, 1865, the Law of Public Instruction was passed, stipulating the four levels of teaching: primary, secondary, higher, and special studies. Article 165 of this law undertook to cancel the posts of chaplains and sacristans as of January 1886, as well as suspending daily mass and prayers in all state-maintained schools. Catholic students were to attend mass on Thursdays, Sundays, and feast days, and be confessed three times a year; these measures were even more liberal than those that had so stunned conservatives and clerics when ordered by Juárez's administration. Other innovations introduced by the law of December 1865 included an identical teaching program for both girls and boys, and the concept of homework. Private schools, ostensibly under strict supervision, were in fact little affected. Sheltered by freedom of worship, they were able to continue with traditional Catholic pedagogy. Over the years, several such schools turned into veritable bulwarks in defense of the faith.

On June 19, 1867, the emperor fell before the firing squad in the city of Querétaro, and the Liberal government returned to power. In the eyes of the victors, the Second Empire represented a violent aggression that had imperiled the nation's sovereignty along with the institutions of republicanism. The grudges of war had intensified this feeling, leading to wholesale rejection of all imperial institutions and any who had supported them. Juárez's return to the capital on July 15, 1867, brought back the notion of education as a single umbrella which would unite the entire nation. There was demand for a uniform studies plan that would endow Mexico with the lineaments of a free nation, at once civilized and conscious of its obligations; thinkers of the second half of the nineteenth century considered the arts and sciences to be the most suitable instrument for this, but the government was unable to achieve such a goal alone, and thus it appealed to parents, students, and teachers to shoulder some of the responsibility in accordance with their respective socioeconomic conditions.

The idea of grounding the country's well-being in the teaching imparted during childhood and youth became more widespread in tandem with the idea of nationhood and the vigorous pride in manifestations of "Mexicanity"—or *mexicanidad*—all as part of an attempt to cast off the ill-repute born of so many years of internal conflict in pursuit of some kind of national feeling. But this incipient nationalism was split, from the outset, into two strands: one Liberal (innovative and with secularizing tendencies), the other Conservative (traditional and preponderantly Catholic). This schism provoked heightened conflicts between laws and customs in the wake of the Organic Law of Public Instruction, promulgated by the Juarista government in December 1867. Under this new law, the branches of primary education were further divided, with the addition of basic physics, arts, chemistry and practical mechanics, line drawing, urban planning, constitutional law, and others. The law also established a directors' board for primary and secondary education in the Federal District, which was to propose a list of textbooks four months before the beginning of each school year.

Until this period (shortly before the rise of Porfirio Díaz and the unleashing of positivism upon the classroom), policy makers aimed at achieving national progress, herding the country into the fold of nineteenth-century modernity. Together with craft, religious, intellectual, and teachers' organizations, policy makers strove to include a greater number of the population into the ranks of the schooled. Yet their task was hindered by countless obstacles: the geography of the terrain, ethnic and linguistic diversity, defense expenses against foreign invasion, and the internal confrontations between the various factions anxious to impose their own hegemony. The efforts of all of these groups contributed, however, to the shaping and consolidation of Mexico, for this was the moment when national consciousness began to evolve among a range of social sectors and to ponder its own significance, both locally and universally.

Select Bibliography

Escobar Ohmstede, Antonio, "La educación para indígenas en la Colonia y en el siglo XIX." In *La Antropología en México: Panorama Histórico*, vol. 3, edited by Carlos García Mora. Mexico City: INAH, 1988.

_____, "El Colegio de San Gregorio: Una institución para la educación de indígenas en la primera mitad del siglo XIX (1821–1857)." In *Indios, peones, hacendados y maestros: Viejos actores para un México nuevo (1821–1943)*, vol. 1, edited by Lucía Martínez. Mexico City: UPN, 1994.

Hale, Charles, *El liberalismo mexicano en la época de Mora, 1821–1853*. Mexico City: Siglo XXI, 1978.

Staples, Anne, "Panorama educativo al comienzo de la vida independiente." In *Ensayos sobre historia de la educación en México*. Mexico City: Colegio de México, 1985.

_____, editor, *Educar: Panacea del México independiente*. Mexico City: SEP–Ediciones El Caballito, 1985.

Vázquez, Josefina Z., *Nacionalismo y educación en México*. Mexico City: Colegio de México, 1975.

Zavala, Lorenzo de, *Ensayo histórico de las últimas revoluciones de México, 1808–1830*. 3 vols., Mexico City: El liberalismo pensamiento y acción, 1949.

—Antonio Escobar Ohmstede

EDUCATION: 1889–1940

Between 1889 and 1940, the Mexican federal government bid to control education to promote development. It did not entirely succeed in centralizing education. However, federal policy emanating from the Revolution of 1910 influenced the democratization of education, the creation of a national culture, and the orientation of technical and higher education toward development goals. At the same time, education policy offended religious sentiments and helped to centralize political power.

The Constitution of 1857 had separated church and state; subsequent legislation made curriculum in public primary schools secular. Because under the dictator Porfirio Díaz (1876–1911) the Secretaría de Justicia y Instrucción Pública and, after 1906, the Secretaría de Instrucción Pública y Bellas Artes controlled education only in the Federal District and territories (Baja California, Quintana Roo, Nayarit, and Tepic), most primary schools were in the hands of municipalities or private individuals and corporations—Catholic, Protestant, and nondenominational. After 1880, state governments assumed greater control of public primary schools. The type of control depended on the state governor's commitment to education and his resources. It could range from the establishment of normal (teachers' training) schools to the creation of incipient inspection systems, from oversight of local educational expenditures to their subsidization. It usually involved the appointment of teachers by the governors' prefects, or *jefes políticos*.

In 1889, the federal government made clear its desire to homogenize and unify primary education. The initiative came from Justice Minister Joaquín Baranda and his undersecretary of instruction, Justo Sierra. Sierra, the towering educational thinker of the late Porfiriato, saw centralization as necessary to national development. He said now that

> our life is linked with iron chains to the industrial and economic life of the world, all that there is of centrifugal force in the heterogeneity of habits, languages, and needs must be transformed into cohesion thanks to the sovereign action of the public school. . . . [The Mexican people need] as a means of their own preservation (a task which becomes more painfully urgent with the gigantic advances of our neighbors) to improve their elements of work to make them more productive; above all, the generating element of the worker himself [sic] . . . instruction must transform him. [quoted in Secretaría de Educación Pública, 1975]

With contempt for both the Indian and Spanish legacies, Sierra wagered the school would defanaticize Mexicans and instill a scientific understanding of the universe. In 1889 and 1891, he unveiled his plans at Congresses of Primary Education attended by representatives of Mexico's states and normal schools. The pedagogy that guided Sierra and normal school social engineers in creating a national curriculum was faculty development education, then in vogue in Europe and the United States. Based on "the objective method of lessons of things" (i.e., empirical observation of the natural world), faculty development pedagogy was a rigid program to discipline the mind, body, and emotions. It emphasized modernization, rather than rights. The law of primary education for the Federal District published in 1908 viewed civics instruction as instilling proper attitudes toward order: obedience, discipline, and patriotism.

Because the Secretaría de Justicia y Instrucción Pública had restricted jurisdiction, faculty development pedagogy was to be introduced to Mexican public primary schools through new state laws and normal school curriculum. By 1900, most Mexican states had normal schools. Pedagogues such as Enrique Conrado Rébsamen visited these schools to introduce the program. How many of them accepted it fully or in part is a question for research. For instance, in Coahuila, the state education director and governor jettisoned the program because he felt that it placed too much emphasis on rote memorization and was too authoritarian; instead, he pursued more open, child-centered pedagogies in vogue in the United States. The chances for diffusing the central state's program through normal schools were slim

because the overwhelming majority of primary school teachers lacked such training. One could anticipate that the faculty development curriculum was most effectively introduced in the Federal District, which had the best trained teaching staff, the most fully developed inspection system, and strong funding. However, even here, program implementation was handicapped by inadequate textbooks and supplies, unhygienic conditions, high rates of student absenteeism, and lack of punctuality.

While the faculty development program may not have permeated deeply, primary education was very much alive in Porfirian Mexico. Scholars have begun to document rich variations in local practice. Some schools remained closely identified with the popular liberalism of the period from 1859 to 1880. Others were staunchly Catholic, antiliberal schools. Many were pragmatically oriented toward imparting literacy and numeracy skills.

During the Porfiriato, according to statistics compiled by Moisés González Navarro, the number of public primary schools more than doubled from roughly 5,000 in 1878 to almost 10,000 in 1907; enrollments more than tripled to nearly 600,000 students. These represented approximately 75 percent of primary school enrollments; 25 percent were enrolled in private schools. Almost 30 percent of children between the ages of six and ten attended school. According to compilations by the Instituto Nacional de Estadística, literacy (then defined as the capacity to read and write in Spanish) increased from 20 percent of the population over six in 1895 to 28 percent of the population over ten in 1910 (32 percent male and 24 percent female). Like enrollment statistics, these figures hid serious regional, sectoral, and gender disparities. The newly settled, market-oriented, and revenue-rich northern states spent the most on primary schooling, had the strongest enrollments, and achieved the highest adult literacy rates: an average of 45 percent, compared with 27 percent in central Mexico and 14 percent in the impoverished south. Moreover, male and female literacy rates were on a par in the northern states, whereas the gender gap grew as one moved south. Overall, literacy was higher in cities and large towns than in small population centers and haciendas.

There were only a few primary superior schools offering the fifth and sixth grades. In 1901, Justo Sierra divided primary superior schools in the capital into vocational and secondary, pre-preparatory schools. The vocational schools were to prepare disciplined and loyal workers. They were a far cry from the dream of artisans for the Escuela de Artes y Oficios when it was founded in 1869. Then, craftsmen had hoped to participate fully in Mexican development. Instead, Porfirio Díaz turned to foreign capital, technology, and know-how. The government did little to prepare Mexican workers, although authorities in the states created Escuelas de Artes y Oficios, offering training in carpentry, iron and wood working, plastering, printing, and other trades; in 1892 training for railroad machinists and electricians was introduced to the capital's trade school. A sizable increase in vocational students in the Porfiriato—from 420 to 2,062—was in large part owing to the entry of women into Escuelas de Artes y Oficios para Mujeres, created in most states and the capital. These schools offered classes in embroidery, sewing, artificial flower making, cooking, domestic economy, and after 1900, commercial and clerical skills. While intended for poor women, these schools helped hard-pressed middle-class families to spare their daughters the misfortune of factory or street work.

Most states had at least one public preparatory school for boys, in addition to Catholic and sometimes Protestant schools. Preparatory enrollments increased by 122 percent from 1878 to 1900, from 3,373 students to 7,506. Preparatory education was an important avenue of mobility for middle-class men. José Vasconcelos, Antonio Caso, and Martín Luis Guzmán were among those privileged to attend the jewel of Porfirian educational policy, the Escuela Nacional Preparatoria, in Mexico City. Based on Auguste Comte's notion of the positive sciences, the EPN curriculum was designed to assist elite young men to overcome their so-called Spanish disdain for entrepreneurship and practical work and their liberal penchant for abstract principles. However, the ENP promoted a reification of science more than its application.

This consequence stemmed in part from the persistently traditional character of higher education. The capital's schools of law and medicine were far more popular than those of architecture and engineering. Most states offered training in law, but eight had medical schools, twelve offered engineering, and eight had some kind of commercial education. Commercial schools like the Escuela Superior de Comercio y Administración in Mexico City and another in Chihuahua expanded rapidly after 1900.

Around 1900, elite intellectuals and policy makers began to worry about the preponderance of foreign capital in Mexico and took corrective steps. The agricultural and engineering schools were modernized and internships were introduced with national and foreign firms. In 1910 as part of Mexico's Centennial celebrations, Minister of Public Instruction Justo Sierra created the National University, which was to commit itself to national development and to research and knowledge on a world scale. The National University was made up of the professional schools, institutes for the study of medicine and disease, major libraries and museums, and the Escuela de Altos Estudios modeled on the Ecole Normal Superieure of France for the training of secondary- and professional-level teachers.

In 1907 in Mexico, professional school enrollments were 1.4 percent of public primary enrollments; over half were in normal schools. These were created in most states. They took scholarship students from all political districts within the states. Unlike other areas of professional education, they were open to women, who made up 1,998 of 2,552 normal students in 1907. Perhaps because normal education was the largest, most democratic, and socially committed area of higher education, it produced many middle-class revolutionaries as well as the substrate for the Revolution's crusade for schools.

Emanating from the Revolution of 1910, Article 3 of the Constitution of 1917 reiterated principles in the Constitution of 1857: public primary education would be lay and free. However, it was explicitly anticlerical: it required inspection of private elementary schools and their adoption of a secular curriculum and prohibited religious corporations or ministers from administering them. Following the Constitutional Convention, President Venustiano Carranza abolished the Secretaría de Instrucción Pública to return education to the "free municipality." In 1921, President Álvaro Obregón reversed direction. He acted upon a proposal drawn up by university rector José Vasconcelos to create the Secretaría de Educación Pública (SEP) with power to establish schools in the states. The creation of the SEP obeyed the logic of state- and nation-creation critical to the fledgling central government as it sought to gain control over the far-flung geographical space of the republic.

Several achievements of the SEP between 1921 and 1940 rank among the finest in twentieth-century cultural history. First, SEP minister José Vasconcelos launched a movement of cultural nationalism in 1921 that produced major art in the murals of Diego Rivera, José Clemente Orozco, and David Alfaro Siqueiros. These murals defied prevailing notions of social Darwinism and white racial superiority to celebrate the nation's Indian roots, the mestizo as the prototypical Mexican, and Mexican history as a popular struggle for social justice against foreign imperialists and the rich. In the 1930s, the SEP popularized mural art as part of its elaboration of a national, multi-ethnic, folkloric culture and a rewriting of Mexican history to stress popular inclusion and agency. This project engaged hundreds of teachers in gathering local music, dance, and aesthetic traditions for their dissemination through the school system and civic festival.

The cornerstone of SEP policy was the rural federal school. According to the government's *Anuarios estadísticos* (Annual Reports), the number of these schools grew to 12,561, with 720,647 students in 1940. In the 1920s, pedagogues Rafael Ramírez, Moisés Saenz, and others took contemporary notions of child-centered, action education and fashioned them into a learning-by-doing curriculum oriented toward community development: the cultivation of new crops; the raising of animals, poultry, and bees; marketable arts and crafts; the introduction of modern hygiene and medicines; the beautification and sanitation of towns; the formation of cooperatives; and the celebration of patriotic festivals. Teachers learned the pedagogy through a new system of rural normal schools, cultural missions, and training seminars run by federal school inspectors.

With the founding of the Partido Nacional Revolucionario (PNR, or National Revolutionary Party) in 1929, rural education became critical to state and party formation and took on new, political dimensions. To enact the federal labor law of 1931 and gain control over employers and workers, the federal government took over or created so-called Article 123 schools in industrial, agricultural, and mining establishments. Educational policy became increasingly anti-religious under SEP Minister Narciso Bassols (1932–34) and culminated in the approval of reformed Constitutional Article 3 in December 1934 mandating socialist education, explicitly defined as anti-religious and understood by its supporters as revindicative of the rights of peasants and workers. So strong was the Catholic protest against this measure in the countryside and city that President Lázaro Cárdenas (1934–40) retreated from the campaign in late 1935 and asked teachers to focus instead on mobilizing peasants for land reform and rural workers for trade union rights. Thus teachers played a major role in the destruction of the hacienda system, the building of labor unions, and the restructuring of power and property in the countryside. They were instrumental in organizing the Confederación Nacional Campesina (CNC, or National Peasant Confederation) and the Confederación de Trabajadores de México (CTM, or Confederation of Mexican Workers), which Cárdenas integrated into the reformed national party, the Partido de la Revolución Mexicano (PRM, or Party of the Mexican Revolution), in 1938. After 1938, the SEP curbed teacher radicalism and reoriented federal schools toward literacy skills, social improvement, and patriotism.

In the 1920s, post-primary education became a priority for the SEP in the Federal District and in cities on the U.S. border. By 1932, there were eight secondary schools in Mexico City and seven in the states, with 6,885 students. Policy makers also promoted technical training. During the Revolution, Félix F. Palavicini, Carranza's educational secretary, had converted the Escuela de Artes y Oficios para Hombres into the Escuela Práctica de Ingenieros Mecánicos y Electristicas. In the 1920s, the SEP created two more schools, one for construction workers and engineers and the Instituto Técnico Industrial; new careers were added in advertising, commercial accounting, auto mechanics, radio and telegraph operation, and engineering. Of 13 vocational schools in the Federal District in 1926, nine were for women. They offered training in domestic-related industries and in clerical work and accounting and were designed to remove women from factory production and return them to the home, petty production, or office where it was imagined they would be more protected from economic and sexual exploitation: it was also part of a state project to restructure, preserve, and moralize the nuclear family for purposes of stability and development.

Between 1907 and 1928, enrollments in technical and vocational schools rose by 312 percent, while those in secondary and preparatory schools rose by 177 percent. By 1930, there were 20 technical and industrial schools in Mexico with 13,000 students. Most were concentrated in the capital and enrolled middle-class children, who could afford them.

In the 1930s, secondary schools became the object of bitter dispute among the SEP, Catholics, and the national university. In 1930, most secondary schools were private and many accepted SEP inspection and curriculum. In 1931, President Pascual Ortiz Rubio signed a decree denying the incorporation of any secondary school operated by a reli-

gious organization, or in which a religious minister taught, or in which religious symbols were used. Implementation of the decree absorbed the energies of SEP minister Narciso Bassols between 1932 and 1934 and anticipated reformed Constitutional Article 3 making anti-religious socialist education obligatory for private and public schools. Throughout Mexico, many schools closed on their own initiative or that of the authorities.

The national university became embroiled in this dispute. The Revolution had dashed Justo Sierra's hopes for a comprehensive university dedicated to national development. By 1914, leadership in higher education had fallen to a generation that had rebelled against the Escuela Nacional Preparatoria's science in favor of humanities and the arts. They tended to keep themselves aloof from the Revolutionary fray. As one of their most brilliant representatives, Antonio Caso, quipped: "No me gustan ni las misas ni las masas, prefiero las mozas y las musas. (I like neither religious masses nor the popular masses; I prefer servant girls and the muses)." When in 1921, university rector José Vasconcelos created the Secretaría de Educación Pública and called upon those associated with the university to leave their ivory towers to "civilize" the masses through teaching, some joined the crusade, but the university as an institution divorced itself from the effort and fought for autonomy. In 1929, the government awarded partial autonomy to the university but suggested that it would receive no significant financial subsidy unless it committed itself to meeting national needs. In October 1933, the dispute between the state and university reached a new level in debates between Antonio Caso and Vicente Lombardo Toledano, head of the Mexican labor movement, over socialist education. This government policy would have imposed a curriculum on the university stressing Marxism, class struggle, and social service. Lombardo Toledano defended it on principles of justice and progress; Caso insisted upon academic freedom. Caso won the debate. Reformed Article 3 of 1934 did not apply to the university. However, the university council, emboldened by the Catholic-controlled students' association, challenged the state's bid to control secondary education. The council voted to extend the two-year curriculum of the university's Escuela Nacional Preparatoria to five years to include secondary education and to accommodate private schools reluctant to submit to state control. Cárdenas responded by placing public and private secondary education under the state. In large part because the state determined the university's budget, it prevailed.

To counter the university's resistance to making a strong commitment to address development needs, Cárdenas created the Instituto Politécnico Nacional in 1937 to prepare technical professionals. The Instituto Técnico Industrial, the Escuela Nacional de Constructores, and the Escuela de Ingenieros Mecánicos y Electricistas formed its core. The IPN offered degrees with 22 areas of study from mechanical engineering to textile technology, architecture, accounting, and statistics.

In the 1930s, the SEP also sought to increase the number of working-class and *campesino* (peasant) children in technical schools. The Cárdenas government inaugurated five new prevocational primaries in the capital and ten in the states, increased the number of scholarships, and created the Departamento de Educación Obrera (Department of Worker Education). In 1938, the department attended 20,714 students. In agricultural education, the SEP in 1932 converted the Escuelas Centrales Agrícolas created under the Departamento de Agricultura in the 1920s into Escuelas Regionales Campesinas to serve the children of *ejidatarios* (workers of communal village holdings), small farmers, and artisans. Their number increased from 10 in 1934 with 900 students to 33 in 1940 with 4,116 students. Combining theory with economic practice and social commitment, the schools were instrumental in assisting communities in obtaining land and credit and improving production and marketing. As most graduates became rural school teachers, the Escuelas Regionales Campesinas contributed to democratizing and skilling the rural teaching corps.

By 1940, 54 percent of national primary school enrollments were in federal, predominantly rural schools. Forty-two percent were enrolled in systems of Mexican states, primarily in large towns and cities. By 1940, state systems adapted to SEP guidelines. Four percent of primary students attended private schools. A good portion of secondary education was private, although subject to state inspection. Public universities enjoyed formal autonomy from federal and state governments but depended upon them for financing. In the 1940s, government financial support gradually increased as the Universidad Nacional Autónoma de México (UNAM, or the National Autonomous University of Mexico) assumed greater national responsibility in the field of education and science.

By 1940, 70 percent of Mexican children between the ages of six and ten were enrolled in school, versus 30 percent in 1910. Male literacy had risen from 32 percent for men over the age of 10 to 50 percent and from 24 to 42 percent for women. Regional disparities persisted between the north (67 percent overall literacy in 1940), center (45 percent), and the southern states of Guerrero, Chiapas, and Oaxaca (23 percent). Literacy in the Federal District was 73 percent. Between 1929 and 1949, UNAM enrollments tripled from 8,154 to 23,527. These changes reflected the growth of an urban middle class. Eighty-two percent of 1949 enrollments were male.

Select Bibliography

Bazant, Milada, *Historia de la educación en el Porfiriato*. Mexico City: Colegio de México, 1993.

Britton, John A., *Educación y radicalismo en México*. 2 vols., Mexico City: SEP-Setentas, 1976.

Estadísticas históricas de México, vol 1. Mexico City: Instituto Nacional de Estadística Geografía e Informática, 1986.

Gónzalez Navarro, Moisés, *Estadísticas sociales del Porfiriato*. Mexico City: Colegio de México, 1956.

Knight, Alan, "Popular Culture and the Revolutionary State in Mexico, 1910–1940." *Hispanic American Historical Review* 74:3 (1994).

Mabry, Donald J., *The Mexican University and the State: Student Conflicts, 1910–1971*. College Station: Texas A & M University Press, 1982.

Meneses Morales, Ernesto, et al., *Tendencias educativas oficiales en México, 1911–1934*. Mexico City: Centro de Estudios Educativos, Universidad Iberoamericana, 1986.

_____, *Tendencias educativas oficiales en México, 1934–1964*. Mexico City: Centro de Estudios Educativos, Universidad Iberoamericana, 1988.

Raby, David L., *Educación y revolución social en México*. Mexico City: SEP-Setentas, 1976.

Ruiz, Ramón Eduardo, *Mexico: The Challenge of Poverty and Illiteracy*. San Marino, California: Huntington Library, 1963.

Secretaría de Educación Pública, *Primer Congreso Nacional de Instrucción, 1889–1890*. Mexico City: SEP, 1975.

Vaughan, Mary Kay, *The State, Educación and Social Class in Mexico, 1880–1928*. DeKalb: Northern Illinois University Press, 1982.

_____, "Primary Education and Literacy in Nineteenth Century Mexico: Research Trends, 1968–1988." *Latin American Research Review* 24:3 (1990).

_____, *Cultural Politics in Revolution: Peasants, Teachers, and Schools in Mexico, 1930–1940*. Tucson: University of Arizona Press, 1997.

Vázquez, Josefina Zoraida, *Nacionalismo y educación en México*. Mexico City: Colegio de México, 1970.

—MARY KAY VAUGHAN

EDUCATION: 1940–96

Most historians agree that the late 1930s and early 1940s were a watershed in Mexican history. External threats, most notably World War II, and internal dissension from both the right and left led President Manuel Avila Camacho to engage in policies that would promote political stability, social harmony, and economic growth. An important factor in these policies was the normalization of relations between the Catholic Church and the Mexican state, which was greatly facilitated when Avila Camacho declared himself a "believer."

The convention of the Partido de la Revolución Mexicana (PRM, or Party of the Mexican Revolution) in 1939 established education as a priority. Considering education to be a prerequisite for national development, the convention proposed to amend Article 3 of the Mexican Constitution, raising educational standards and making education more responsive to a just social regime. There also was discussion of an accelerated campaign against illiteracy; organizing educational campaigns on farming, patriotic themes, and hygiene; and promoting institutions dedicated to workers' education. Convention delegates were particularly concerned about higher education, especially in technical fields, which they believed offered an opportunity for workers and peasants to improve their lot—and for the Mexican state to promote the scientific research and development needed for economic modernization.

Nonetheless, the implementation of these ambitious goals was slow and complex. The leadership of the Secretariat of Education was a revolving door in the early years of the Avila Camacho administration. The first secretary of education, the "recognized Communist" Luis Sánchez Ponton, reorganized the department but was accused of wanting to continue the educational policies of former president Lázaro Cárdenas. Avila Camacho forced Sánchez Ponton to resign and replaced him with Octavio Vejar Vásquez. Turning against Sánchez Ponton's radical populism, Vejar Vásquez promoted what he termed the *escuela de amor* (school of love), an educational agenda that would put an end to ideologies that were alien to the national consciousness and make unity possible. Education, he believed, should be organized in accordance with the "general feeling" of the nation, and he spoke of a spiritual and moral renaissance among Mexican youth. Coeducation was rejected as a mistake from the previous administration, and private schools were encouraged with the support of Mexican businessmen and capitalists. The Organic Law on Education of 1942 was the prelude to the reform of Article 3.

Nonetheless, Vejar Vásquez soon was replace by Jaime Torres Bodet, who tried to give coherence to educational policy and fought for an adequate budget for education. Torres Bodet's accomplishments as secretary of education were numerous. He promoted literacy, organized the first congress on teacher training, began publication of the *Bibliotecas Encyclopedia Popular,* launched a program of school construction, founded Instituto Federal de Capacitación del Magisterio (National Institute of Teacher Training), and oversaw the publication of the textbook series *México y la cultura.* He also fought for ideological neutrality in education, respecting freedom of belief and seeking to create a nationalist and democratic educational program. Hoping to end the disputes that were wracking Mexican educational institutions, Torres Bodet made the reform of Article 3 a top priority.

Torres Bodet saw the dilemma between freedom of education and secular instruction as a question of conscience. He thought that the Constitution of 1857 had decreed freedom of education as a synonym for pure liberalism, but at the same time he believed that the conscience of a child should not be shaped prematurely by teachers subordinate to the interests of a particular creed. The new text of Article 3 proposed the development of all human faculties, patriotic themes, and an awareness of international solidarity; education should be secular, free of any religious doctrine, and based on scientific truths. It also had to act as a bulwark against ignorance and its consequences, such as slavery and fanaticism, while encouraging a personal sense of worth and brotherhood and upholding the equality of all citizens under the law.

Between 1940 and 1950, Mexico experienced high and sustained growth. The economy changed from being basically agricultural to urban and industrial. This focus on industrialization meant that priority was given to technological modernization. At this stage, the idea that the educational level of the population determined the economic development reemerged. Nevertheless, there was no structured project sufficiently planned that could address the issue. Fifteen years of effort of varying intensity and different points of view had produced few results.

President Adolfo López Mateos (1958–64) appointed Jaime Torres Bodet once again as secretary of education. The latter recently had stepped down from the presidency of UNESCO, where he had tried other methods to carry out basic education in Latin American countries. The secretary presented the president with a document stating his opinion on the situation in the educational field and material that would be the basis for what would become the Eleven-Year Plan. The document pointed out the distressing conditions of education in the country. The demand for primary-level education totaled virtually 6 million children, of which only one-half had access to a school. Of these, less than one-fourth finished primary education, and only one in one thousand ended up in a professional career. It was considered that out of every two Mexicans, one could neither read nor write. The lack of schools and teachers was another negative factor.

The situation was such that in December 1958 President López Mateos announced the start of new educational reforms. He sent an initiative to Congress to establish a commission to resolve the educational problem. This commission would elaborate a plan that should continue for at least two further presidential terms to avoid the break at the end of each administration. The Plan Nacional para la Expansión y Mejoramiento de la Educación Primaria (National Plan for the Expansion and Improvement of Primary Education, also called the Eleven-Year Plan) was an initial effort in educational planning to combat the serious educational problem. During this period, educational backwardness was to be overcome and all children of school age were to be given access to a classroom. The training of teachers and the increase in the number of classrooms were thus considered indispensable, taking population growth into account. It was certain that the problem was not only academic but also economic. Nevertheless, the conditions of the country only allowed for the modification of educational arrangements. Moreover, the plan was limited to primary education. The plan decided that it was necessary to create 21,249 new groups, with a capacity of 54 pupils in each, in the five remaining years of López Mateos's administration. Sixty-seven thousand teachers had to be instructed, some 5,600 in the first five years of the plan. It also was indispensable to rehabilitate the teacher training system and create regional teacher training centers. Given the lack of certified teachers, pupils in their third year of secondary education were used as practicing teachers. There were attempts to renew the Instituto Federal de Capacitación del Magisterio (Federal Institute for Teachers Training) to certify the more than 27,000 teachers without such documentation. The plan also included the need to revise plans and programs of study with the object of improving the quality of teaching. This occurred in February 1961.

Within this renewed educational framework was born the idea of editing and distributing textbooks for all children at primary level with the object of making schooling more democratic and, effectively, free. The president intended for these books to be handed out in all the schools in the country, including private colleges. On February 12, 1959, the Comisión Nacional de los Libros de Texto Gratuito (CNLTG, or National Commission for Free Textbooks) was created. The decree pointed out that many children were in no position to acquire textbooks each year, and the government could not allow these texts to be a means of commercial profit for authors and editors; thus, they were distributed at no cost. These textbooks were intended to encourage "national unity" and "educational unification" with the aim of creating a strong national and Mexican identity. On February 9 of the same year, the Secretaría de Educación Pública (SEP, or Secretariat of Public Education) declared that "the use of the free textbook is obligatory in all primary schools whether private or governmental, federal or state schools as well as municipal schools, except for the last two years of primary teaching." Thus, the free textbook became obligatory, and the debate it provoked reached alarming levels.

When Gustavo Díaz Ordáz became president in 1964, he took vigorous action in the educational field following lines established at the international level. The student crisis of 1968, which partly was blamed on the educational system, highlighted the need for reform in this area as a part of wider social reform. These would include the simplification of curricular programs and the adoption of methods of learning and teaching on a practical basis. The extensive use of the communications media as educational tools, television especially, were of particular note during these years.

When Luis Echeverría Álvarez became president in 1970, public education was in a bad state; colossal population growth had outstripped that predicted in the Eleven-Year Plan. It had been impossible to go beyond the barrier of 6 million illiterates during the three previous presidential administrations. The average curriculum did not go beyond fourth grade, resulting in the loss of educational investment. Eight out of every ten children that completed their primary education signed up for secondary school, but of these, one-quarter left before they obtained their diplomas. More than one-third of those leaving basic middle education immediately looked for employment but often were unable to find it for want of training or lack of availability. Such problems affected mostly the states with the fewest resources. In the countryside, only one of every ten children starting primary education actually completed it. Of the total number of children that began primary education, 54 percent in the cities finished their schooling while only 10 percent did so in the rural areas.

The social demand for education grew so quickly that it could not be contained. This demand not only included children or adolescents that never started schooling but, above all, those who gave it up. In 1970, 8.5 percent of all students left school. This cost the country 41 percent of the current federal government expenditures and 4 percent of state government expenditure. The greatest demand for education came from the urban sector, which determined in turn the inequality of redistribution of opportunities.

Without doubt, one of the greatest challenges of education was to incorporate the greatest possible number of Mexicans into productive activities. Adult education became a top priority in an environment where so many citizens had no opportunity to incorporate themselves into the existing economic system. According to the 1970 census, a total of 18,280,000 Mexicans over 15 years of age (70 percent) had not finished primary education. Of these, 8,196,000 (31.6 percent) lacked all form of schooling. The average curriculum lasted 3.32 years. As a result, the level of participation of adults in the economic system was very low, given that the majority were unemployed or underemployed. In his presidential campaign, Echeverría offered "a profound and integrated educational reform on every level with the collaboration of the teachers, students, and the diverse sectors of our society." Once installed in office, he broadened this approach to make educational reform permanent. This was interpreted as a change in the content and methodology of the teaching-learning process, the creation of new institutions, the passing of new legislation, the rewriting of school texts, and even the expansion of the school system. The reform was a "permanent process" to transform educational reality. Government made an effort to assure the people that this reform meant a "democratic opening" that tried to break with the Mexican political past, which in fact was impossible.

The concern was to bring education up to date, a modernization that allowed teachers and students to use the most advanced techniques and tools in the teaching-learning process; an opening up that referred to the capacity to reach all social levels and make possible the popularization of education; and flexibility that allowed education to adapt itself to the needs of society as well as facilitate the horizontal and vertical movement of the students, as well as the diverse varieties and modalities of the system. The bases of educational reform were governed by the Federal Law on Education, which was passed on December 14, 1973. The law defines education as "the fundamental medium to acquire, transmit, and allow culture to grow; this is a permanent process that contributes to the development of the individual and the transformation of society, and is the determining factor in the acquisition of knowledge and the creation of the individual with feelings of social solidarity." Education remained established as a continuous process for the development of the individual and the society that organized the teaching system in the country, disseminated social education, determined the bases of the educational process, and established rights and obligations in this regard. Without doubt, the most important innovation in the law was its stimulation of academic functions and their renewal, which were centered almost exclusively in primary education, with the new concept of teaching-learning and in the creation of "media to realize this task efficiently." The law pointed out the need to link the school with the community within the economic capacity of the state and its decentralized and private institutions, in order to give rewards in conformity with the requisites established by educational curricula. These latter were totally reformed.

The Plan Nacional de Educación para Adultos (National Plan for Adult Education) was very important in this context. This plan was created in consideration of basic problems inherent in the establishment of an infrastructure that would make it possible for adults to have access to education. This law, which was passed in 1975, defined education as the "adequate medium for the acquisition of practical knowledge and values to promote development with justice and integrate those sectors that make up modern society." This definition, much less ambitious than that proposed by the Federal Law on Education, established the basis of what would become adult education in order to promote an integrated development of people and society. The law benefited those over 15 years old who had received no schooling or who had not finished their primary or secondary studies. Thus, adult education was available on an equal basis to all the inhabitants of the country, making it possible for the adult to achieve, at the very least, the level of knowledge equivalent to basic general education, including secondary as well as primary teaching. The flexibility of plans and programs allowed for movement from one modality to another through self-education. In other words, adults acquired knowledge and abilities in basic education through their own efforts and with the support of staff and educational institutions.

On December 1, 1976, José López Portillo became president and nominated Fernando Solana as his secretary of education. The prevailing conditions in the country at the beginning of López Portillo's regime showed no significant signs of change. In 1976, the population of Mexico totaled 60 million people. To deal with the educational problem confronting the country at the time, 97,577 population centers had to be taken into consideration, of which 91,165 were located in rural areas, which presented special problems, particularly, a profound lack of products and services. The remaining 6,412 centers were located in urban areas.

The period was characterized by continued educational deficiencies and extreme marginalization of Mexico not only culturally but also economically, socially, and even politically.

The educational statistics were even more alarming than those registered for the previous presidential term. According to government reports, there were 6 million illiterates as well as 13 million adults with incomplete primary education and 7 million that had not begun or finished secondary education; during 1976–77 scarcely 330,000 of these 26 million adults were served. It was pointed out that the index of illiteracy in 1977 was 18 percent, and that there already existed around 1 million Indian adults who did not speak Spanish.

The National Plan for Adult Education was adopted by the new regime in response to such educational challenges. Two objectives had been taken into consideration: "in the short term that all Mexicans have a minimum education to the ninth grade; in the medium term that this acts as a way to improve and modernize on a permanent basis for each individual, making exhaustive use of modern means of social communication." During his presidential campaign, José López Portillo had been told throughout the country of the need to link education with productivity and work; above all, there existed a demand for training in productive work.

Education reformers began the search for a practical idea that would put the necessities of the country in consonance with the educational demands of society. Nevertheless, the economy did not create employment at the necessary speed to absorb and give work to all those leaving the school system. Only a part of the problem was considered, even though the intention existed to resolve all. The only alternative to the demand for education was seen to be training through open or extracurricular systems. This was not regarded as a complement to education, which would be to "marginalize" the noneducated (the majority of Mexicans), but an opportunity for permanent education as members of the community and as workers. Under the banner of "Education for all," the program for adult education was put into operation in March 1978. The secretariat considered that, in order to be efficacious, the education program should be accompanied by schemes related to other vital necessities such as health, food, and work.

In 1980, the Programa Nacional de Alfabetización (Pronalf, or National Literacy Program) was initiated to reduce the number of nonliterates. This institute operated on eight levels of literacy. The previous lack of such an institution and the inefficiency of existent ones to integrate the activities of numerous federal, state, and private institutes provoked a number of programs that were parallel and occasionally duplicated. This paved the way for the creation of a coordinating institution for adult education founded under the name of the Institute Nacional de Educación para Adultos (INEA, or National Institute for Adult Education) on August 31, 1981, as an institute independent of public administration. Its functions have been and continue to be to promote research into adult education, train necessary staff needed for adult teaching, create teaching materials, credit primary and secondary school curricula, and coordinate its activities with other institutions to extend its services to various sectors of the population.

The administration of Carlos Salinas de Gortari (1988–94) put great emphasis on the economic transformation of the country and saw education as the key to transforming the workforce and making it more productive, as well as promoting higher education. Educational modernization was defined not in terms of a quantitative change but what would serve to "destroy the old practices and inertia to innovate practices at the service of permanent ends; to go beyond a framework of now outdated rationalism and adapt to a dynamic world . . . [which] in the educational field means a new relationship between the governmental requests and civilian society."

Throughout the administration, public education recovered in budgetary terms, but the difficulty of putting the plan into action provoked four changes of secretary in this area: Manual Bartlett, Ernesto Zedillo Ponce de León, Fernando Solana, and Angel Pescador Osuna. In 1989, the Programa para la Modernización Educativa (Program for Educational Modernization) was announced to eliminate geographical and social inequalities, improve the quality of teaching, and integrate the educational process with economic development. This program was boycotted by the director of the Sindicato Nacional de Trabajadores de la Educación (SNTE, or National Union of Educational Workers), who saw the dangers that decentralization meant for the union. Hence there was a long delay in putting the program into action. The Consejo Nacional para la Cultura y las Artes (National Council for Culture and the Arts) was created to diffuse all manifestations of cultural activity in response to intellectual groups that proposed the creation of a secretariat of culture. The council incorporated already existing institutions such as the INBA, INAH, publishing, etc.

In 1992, the Acuerdo Nacional para la Modernización de la Educación Basica (National Agreement for the Modernization of Basic Education) was signed, which proposed the "federalization" of education, thereby giving the states a certain amount of administrative autonomy. It also was agreed to return to the teaching of history, geography, and civics as separate course subjects. A particularly troublesome polemic arose over the edition of new texts on the history of Mexico composed by intellectuals committed to the regime that were severely criticized for justifying Salinist politics. A new edition was produced by means of a competition, but despite being awarded prizes the texts were not published. In their place appeared a small booklet on Mexican history. In 1993,

the Ley General de Educación Pública (General Law on Public Education) was published, which described education as a permanent process to which all Mexicans had a right. Higher education grew markedly, even though the majority of the institutions continue to be located in Mexico City.

Well into the term of Salinas's successor, former secretary of education Ernesto Zedillo Ponce de León, all Mexican education remained a level below the country's needs. Lack of resources, excessive centralization, lack of deep research on the subject, entrenched power bases and economic interests, among other reasons, created a very diffuse panorama. Repeatedly voiced demands echoed those of the 1940s, with its similar problems and solutions that are still viewed as improbable.

See also Massacre of Tlatelolco; Student Movement of 1968

Select Bibliography

Britton, John A., *Educación y radicalismo en México, 1934–1940.* 2 vols., Mexico City: SEP, 1976.

Christlieb Ibarrola, Adolfo, *Monopolio educativo o unidad nacional: Un problema de México.* Mexico City: Jus, 1962.

Gómez Navas, Leonardo, et al., *La educación: Historia, obstáculos y perspectives.* Mexico City: Nuestro Tiempo, 1967.

Latapí, Pablo, *Educación nacional y opinión pública.* Mexico City: CEE, 1965.

_____, "Reformas educativas en los cuatro últimos gobiernos, (1952–1975)." *Revista de Comercio Exterior* (December 1975).

Loaeza, Soledad, *Clases medias y política en México.* Mexico City: El Colegio de México, 1988.

Meneses Morales, Ernesto, *Tendencias educativas oficiales en México, 1934–1964.* Mexico City: Centro de Estudios Educativos, 1988.

Seminario de Historia de Educación de El Colegio de México, *Historia de la alfabetización y de la educación de adultos en México,* vol. 3. Mexico City: Seminario de Historia de la Educación de El Colegio de México, Secretaría de Educación Publica-Instituto Nacional para la educación de los adultos, 1994.

Vázquez, Josefina Z., *Nacionalismo y educación en México.* Mexico City: El Colegio de México, 1979.

Villa Lever de Alba, Lorenza, *Los libros de texto gratuitos.* Guadalajara: Universidad de Guadalajara, 1981.

Villaseñor García, Guillermo, *Estado e Iglesia: El caso de la educación.* Mexico City: Edicol, 1978.

—VALENTINA TORRES SEPTIÉN

EJÉRCITO ZAPATISTA DE LIBERACIÓN NACIONAL

See Zapatista Rebellion in Chiapas

EJIDO

An *ejido* is land granted by the Mexican state to rural population through the agrarian reform. The original concept of the *ejido* comes from the fusion of a pre-Hispanic form of land tenure and the Spanish feudal organizations in which communal lands of the peasant villages were known as *propios* or *ejidos*. The legal foundation of the modern-day *ejido* was the Agrarian Law of 1915, decreed by the Revolutionary government of Venustiano Carranza (1915–20). The *ejido* was given constitutional status in Article 27 of the 1917 Mexican Constitution, which recognized three kinds of property: private property, *ejido* property, and communal property. Article 27 set limits to the extent of rural property in each type.

The right to form an *ejido* was given to rural villages reclaiming lands that had been lost as a result of nineteenth-century legislation abolishing communal property (the Ley de Desamortización of 1856); landless peasants also were granted *ejidos*. Land was granted by means of restitution or distribution of land from rural estates exceeding the limits established for private property. *Ejido* land also were granted on federal lands.

Communal land is land held by villages in common property, which also was legislated by Article 27. This kind of land tenure originates in the tenure rights of Indian villages during the colonial era and is held mainly in regions where indigenous populations predominate.

Under the *ejido* regime, peasants were given usufructuary land rights (i.e., they are allowed to enjoy the fruits or profit of a portion of the communal property), but they had limited property rights of their own. After the reform of agrarian legislation in 1992, property rights were circumscribed to the decisions of the *ejido* village assembly. During the previous 75 years, *ejido* property was restricted to the right of direct usufruct by the entitled peasant and his family, which inherited this right. This right was not transferable by sale, lease, tenancy, or any other arrangements.

An *ejido* includes the land for the site of the village, cropping land, and noncropping land such as pastures, forests, or other uncultivated land. *Ejidos* may be worked collectively or individually. The latter is the most common form of organization on cropping land, while pastures, forests, and other uncultivated land is held as common lands for the *ejido*.

The agrarian reform and the constitution of the *ejido* established a specific form of economic, political, and social organization in the Mexican countryside. The economic function of the *ejido* was predominated by the state, particularly in the case of the *ejidos* with agricultural and livestock activities linked to the market. State agencies provided the bulk of productive resources such as credit, inputs, technical assistance, and often market outlets for basic grains. Certain crop systems actually were controlled by the state through organizations in charge of processing and marketing commodities. Such was the case of the sugar, tobacco, and coffee industries from the 1970s to the early 1990s.

Political life in the *ejido* was articulated into the corporate political system of the dominant party—the Partido Revolucionario Institucional (PRI, or Institutional Revolutionary Party)—and not until the 1980s did a struggle to free the *ejido* from corporate structures begin to take place in certain regions through the attempt to built an autonomous peasant movement.

The mixed land tenure system that characterizes rural Mexico was the outcome of the agrarian struggle in the Mexican Revolution beginning in 1910. The Revolution was fought by peasant soldiers. The best known peasant leader, Emiliano Zapata, gathered the demands of the peasants under the banner of Tierra y Libertad (Land and Freedom). The peasants under Zapata demanded the restitution of communal lands that had been taken from them during the second half of the nineteenth century under the laws of privatization of church and communal property. When the armed Revolution ended, however, the winning faction was the so-called Generals of the North, an entrepreneurial group that represented the emerging bourgeoisie. Although land reform was enshrined in Article 27 of the 1917 Constitution, it was not much in the interest of the leaders of the post-Revolutionary governments, who themselves owned large farms, mainly on the irrigated lands of the northwest. Rather, President Álvaro Obregón (1920–24) and the following president, Plutarco Elías Calles (1924–28), believed rural development should be based on private enterprise following the model of the United States. They supported a modernization policy, building infrastructure—mainly irrigation in the northwest—where private landholdings were thriving in commercial agriculture. As for the peasantry, land distribution was considered a transitory political issue, a means of giving the peasant family a small plot to live on and grow basic subsistence crops as a complement to wages they would earn as farm laborers on the larger, privately owned farms.

During the 1920s and early 1930s, land distribution was very limited, responding to local or regional pressures, as in Morelos, where Zapata had fought for land. The role of the *ejido* in the economic and political development of Mexico changed radically in the late 1930s. Local and regional peasant uprisings again were raising the issue of land, hired land laborers on large estates were organizing and demanding the benefits of labor legislation, and the Great Depression was affecting agriculture, especially export crops. When Lázaro Cárdenas became president of Mexico in 1934, the ground was fertile for change. The new model of development promoted by the government was based on industrialization and strong leadership by the state, which would participate directly in building infrastructure and investing in key economic sectors. This new model also was to revindicate some of the most urgent demands of the rural population: distributing land and incorporating the peasantry in a growing economy.

This model required profound changes in agriculture, restructuring the rent-seeking agriculture of the large estates into a modern profit-seeking agriculture, and freeing the peasantry of its labor ties to the large estates. Land distribution was a means of creating efficient farms both on private and on *ejido* lands. On the *ejido*, viable family farms growing basic crops and collective farms on the large entrepreneurial estates would supply the necessary agricultural surplus for a fast urbanizing and industrializing economy. Starting in 1935, Cárdenas began an intensive land reform program that mainly affected private holdings in excess of those permitted by Article 27. By the end of his administration, over 50 million acres had been distributed, half of the rural land in the country.

Starting in 1940, land distribution slowed, particularly distribution through the expropriation of private estates. Throughout the 1940s and 1950s, land distribution was marginal and consisted mainly of poor and substandard lands. In the 1960s land distribution was increased, but the quality of land remained poor as the agricultural frontier was diminishing and successive governments were not eager to affect private property. Federal land was distributed and nonagricultural activities such as forestry, tourism, and mining were incorporated under the *ejido* regime.

The *ejido* on marginal land increasingly became stressed under population pressure and lack of productive resources. Migration of family members became frequent, as did wage labor; remittances of migrant earnings and wages of family members became part of the necessary income to support peasant families.

In the 1970s under President Luis Echeverría Álvarez (1970–76), an attempt to reactivate the agricultural sector by promoting peasant agriculture gave a last historical attempt to support agrarian reform and the reorganization of the *ejido*. The agrarian legislation was modified to incorporate a wider range of activities within the *ejido*, among them productive programs for *ejido* women. Nineteen million hectares (47 million acres) were distributed.

Land distribution practically stopped during the 1980s, as successive presidents declared that no more land was available for distribution. The future growth of the *ejido* was to be achieved by means of its productive modernization, focusing the development of the *ejido* on productivity rather than land distribution.

According to the agrarian and livestock census in 1991, 31 percent of rural land was under *ejido* and communal land tenure; this comprehended 50 percent of crop land. The 1988 *ejido* census registered 43 percent of total grazing land and 62 percent of forest land under *ejido* tenure. In 1991 there were 29,983 *ejidos* and *comunidades agrarias*

employing 7.3 million people (13 percent of these were women). Family work accounted for 79 percent of labor in the *ejidos* and *comunidades agrarias*.

The main activity of *ejidatarios* is agriculture, and 80 percent of arable land is devoted to basic crops (corn, beans, wheat, rice, sorghum). Seventy-five percent of the land is rain fed, with the remaining 25 percent under irrigation. The average *ejido* plot is 11.7 hectares (28.9 acres), and the average plot for cropping is 5.9 hectares (14.6 acres); however, 59 percent of *ejido* plots average only 2.2 hectares (5.5 acres) of cropping land. The *ejido* remains the basis of agriculture for peasants with limited access to resources.

Ejidos vary greatly from one region to another. *Ejidos* in the center and south of Mexico characteristically are sites of peasant agriculture on rain-fed land, often growing food staples—maize and beans—of which an important part is for self-consumption, and a variety of cash crops in small amounts, depending on the region. Wage income from family members is usually an important source of household income, either from local activities or, more likely, from migrants, mainly those in the cities or the United States. In the irrigated districts or better quality rain-fed lands, such as in the northwest, *ejidatarios* are engaged in commercial agriculture and constitute a class of middle farmers; prior to economic policy reforms in the 1980s, these *ejidatarios* had access to productive resources channeled through public institutions.

Agrarian legislation was reformed in 1992, when Article 27 of the Constitution was modified. This proved a radical change in the agrarian tradition rooted in the Mexican Revolution. The reform aimed at redefining property rights and liberalizing the constraints on rural property by allowing for a more flexible law concerning the *ejido*. The reformers hoped to attract investment and promote the modernization of agriculture within a market economy. The changes occurred in the overall context of economic liberalization and privatization in Mexico starting in the 1980s.

The two main pillars of the new legislation were the decree to end land distribution and to allow for the privatization of *ejido* and communal land. The reform enabled the *ejidos* and *comunidades* to decide the property regime of the village and its land, thus opening the way to privatization of land. It allowed for a range of tenure arrangements that formerly had been prohibited, such as leasing, tenancy arrangements, associations with private capital, using land as a credit collateral, and ultimately opting for the individualization and private property of the *ejido* plots and common lands. Such decisions were to be based on the majority of the *ejido* assembly votes following the regulations established by the *ejido* itself.

Private property was also regulated by Article 27. A new disposition of the reformed law allowed corporate companies to own rural property. In order to define and regulate property rights according to the 1992 agrarian law, a program for land certification and urban parcel titling was established (Programa de Certificacion de Derechos Ejidales y

Titulación de Solares Urbanos—PROCEDE), as well as agrarian courts to resolve conflicts.

By the mid-1990s, changes in land tenure had been slow. The *ejidos* bordering urban localities were most likely to become rapidly privatized, many already had shifted to semi-urban or urban use, and the value of land increased accordingly.

Land markets concerning *ejidos* with agricultural activities will likely develop unevenly depending on such factors as the quality, location, and resources. In the short term it is more likely that the reform of the *ejido* will have an impact on other forms of access and collaboration between the *ejidos* and private capital (for example, leasing arrangements and joint ventures) than on direct privatization of *ejido* plots. The same is true for *ejido* forest lands.

The 1992 reforms also changed the relationship between the state and the *ejido*. First, the state is no longer the main source of land and other productive resources. Second, the forms of organization and representation within the *ejidos* were modified, weakening government intervention in the internal affairs of the *ejido*.

See also Agrarian Policy

Select Bibliography

Appendini, Kirsten, and Vania Salles, "Crecimiento económico y campesinado: Un análisis del ejido en dos décadas." In *El campesinado en México,* edited by Appendini, K., M.L.P. Martínez, V. Salles, and T. Rendón. Mexico City: El Colegio de México, 1983.

Centro de Investigaciones Agrarias, *Estructura Agraria y Desarrollo Agrícola en México.* Mexico City: Fondo de Cultura Económica, 1974.

de Walt, Billie, and Martha N. Rees, *The End of Agrarian Reform: Past Lessons, Future Prospects.* La Jolla: Center for US-Mexican Studies, University of California, San Diego, 1994.

Instituto Nacional de Estadística e Informática, *Estados Unidos Mexicanos. VII Censo-Agrícola Ganadero.* Mexico City: INEGI, 1994.

_____, *Encuesta Nacional Agropecuaria Ejidal, 1988: Resumen General.* Mexico City: INEGI, 1990.

Randall, Laura, editor, *Reforming Mexico's Agrarian Reform.* New York and London: M. E. Sharpe, Armon, 1996.

—KIRSTEN APPENDINI

ELÍAS CALLES, PLUTARCO

See Calles, Plutarco Elías

EL INDIO FERNÁNDEZ

See Fernández Romo, Emilio (El Indio)

EMPLOYER ORGANIZATIONS

Employer organizations have played a pivotal role in the economic and political life of contemporary Mexico. The legal basis of employer organizations was established in Articles 73 and 123 of the Constitution of 1917. Article 73 establishes employers' and workers' right to unite in defense of their respective interests, and Article 123 refers to the balance that should exist among the "factors of production" and the "harmonization" of their rights by the state. The Law on

Chambers of Commerce and Industry (1936) requires businesses to affiliate with the appropriate business associations, which are defined as "public institutions of autonomous character" subject to government regulation. The principal function of these "public institutions" was to serve as consultative organs for the government. The law proscribed partisan political activity by the business associations and their leaders. Although not all employer organizations are subject to this law, it places important limits on political organization by the business sector. During the 1990s the law came under serious question.

Although employer organizations legally are defined as corporate institutions, in practice (until the early 1980s) the equilibrium between management and labor was based on a complex of political and economic factors. Businessmen, whose economic power allows them a degree of political independence, have been excluded from political office—and particularly from the official Partido Revolucionario Institucional (PRI, or Institutional Revolutionary Party). Labor, on the other hand, has been incorporated into the PRI along with other popular sectors. The government's arbitration power has been based as much on its presence in the Mexican economy—its regulatory power, its control of patronage, and its ownership of state enterprises—as on its political power.

Although employer organizations are quite heterogeneous, they are loosely grouped together in a broad umbrella organization, the Consejo Coordinador Empresarial (CCE, or Business Coordinating Council), which was founded in 1975. The CCE has become the most important mouthpiece for the Mexican business community, uniting most of the principal business organizations in Mexico. It has been able to maintain its independence from the government and the PRI, although it has received government recognition. The CCE is composed of eight national organizations: the Confederación de Cámaras Nacionales de Comercio (CONCANACO, or Confederation of National Chambers of Commerce), the Confederación de Cámaras Industriales de los Estados Unidos Mexicanos (CONCAMIN, or Confederation of Industrial Chambers of the United States of Mexico), the Confederación Patronal de la República Mexicana (COPARMEX, or Employer's Confederation of the Republic of Mexico), the Asociación de Banqueros de México (ABM, or Association of Bankers of Mexico), the Asociación Mexicana de Instituciones de Seguros (AMIS, or Mexican Association of Insurance Institutions), the Asociación Mexicana de Intermediarios Bursátiles (AMIB, or Mexicana Association of Stockbrokers), the Consejo Nacional Agropecuario (CNA, or National Farmers' Association), and the Consejo Mexicano de Hombres de Negocios (CMHN, or Mexican Businessmen's Council). Two other organization that deserve mention are the Cámera Nacional de la Industria de la Transformación (CANACINTRA, or National Chamber of Transformation Industry) and the Cámera Nacional de Comercio de la Ciudad de México (CANACO-D.F., or National Chamber of Commerce of Mexico City). Although CANACINTRA and CANACO-D.F. formally are affiliated with CONCAMIN and CONANCO, respectively, they historically have been relatively independent of their parent organizations and have their own representation in the CCE. The CCE also includes four broad lobbying and research centers, the Consejo Empresarial Mexicano para Asuntos Internacionales (CEMAI, or Mexican Business Council for International Affairs), the Centro de Estudio

Económicos del Sector Privado (CEESP, the Center for Economic Studies of the Private Sector), the Centro de Estudios Sociales (CES, or Center for Social Studies), and the Centro de Estudios Fiscales y Legislativos (CEFYL, or Center for Fiscal and Legislative Studies).

The two oldest organizations in the CCE are the CONCANACO and CONCAMIN, which were formed in 1917 and 1918, respectively. Subject to the 1936 Law on Chambers of Commerce and Industry, they both are defined as public autonomous institutions. Because of their relatively nonspecific character—and because the 1936 law requires most businesses to affiliate with one organization or the other—the CONCANACO and CONCOMIN are among the largest employer organizations. The CONCANACO includes commerce, service, and tourism industries and has approximately 500,000 affiliated businesses, and the CONCAMIN includes manufacturing industries and has approximately 125,500 affiliated businesses. Although on the most basic level CONCANACO and CONCAMIN represent businesses, they are structured in quite different ways. CONCANACO is organized regionally, while CONCAMIN is organized by industry—the shoe industry, cement, pharmaceuticals, iron and steel, and so on—and is comprised of 75 industrial chambers that can vote in the organization; however, CONCAMIN also includes 42 industrialists' associations that can affiliate either by industrial sector (e.g., the Asociación Mexicana de la Industria Automotriz—Mexican Automobile Association) or by region (e.g., Asociación Industrial de Tlalnepantla).

Its most important affiliate, CANACINTRA, presents something of a special case. Including 82,000 of the 125,000 members of the CONCAMIN, the CANACINTRA includes those industries that do not belong to industrial sectoral organizations in the CONCAMIN. Founded in 1941, the CANACINTRA has been characterized by its close relationship with the government and its defense of small business. It has a highly complex organization, grouping industries by the types of goods they manufacture or by locality.

Founded in 1929, COPARMEX is an employers' union with approximately 30,000 members. Unlike CONCANACO and CONCAMIN, COPARMEX is not regulated as an autonomous public institution, and membership is voluntary. Regulated by the Federal Labor Law, COPARMEX includes 57 regional employer "centers" and 8 broad federations. Like COPARMEX, the CNA is composed primarily of small- and medium-sized businesses. Founded in 1984, the CNA is the youngest CCE affiliate. It includes approximately 250,000 producers organized by sector or region into 34 associations, unions, and confederations defined as "members" and 59 "associates," organizations of agroindustrial businesses and wholesalers.

Unlike the commercial, service, and tourism sectors, which are grouped into a single organization, the financial sector is represented by three different organizations. All three of these organizations are relatively small—the ABM has approximately 30 members, the AMIS 59, and the AMIB only 25. All three organizations are subject to the civil code rather than the 1936 law, so membership is voluntary. Nonetheless, the three organizations represent almost all potential members in their respective sectors. The economic power of the financial sector and its multiple representation in the CCE has given it a considerable degree of political power. The oldest of the three organizations is the ABM, which was founded in 1928, followed by the AMIS (1946), and the AMIB (1980).

The smallest of the CCE's members, the CMHN, was founded in 1962 and includes approximately 40 presidents or directors of the most important Mexican corporations. Membership is by invitation only.

The organization of the CCE by industrial sector has weakened the influence of regional interests and small businesses while increasing the power of large corporations, which operate in several industrial sectors and hence are represented in several different organizations. The financial sector, which often associated with large corporations, has particularly benefited from the one association–one vote organization of the CCE; the CMHN, whose express purpose is to provide a forum for the heads of large corporations, has further increased the power of big businesses in the CCE at the expense of small businesses.

Employer organizations are not only heterogeneous in the types of economic interests they represent, but also for the distinct political and ideological tendencies that characterize them. The close relationship between employer organizations and the state has fostered two different general tendencies. The moderate wing of the CCE tends more toward negotiation with the government and is represented principally by the CONCAMIN, the organizations of the financial sector, and the CMHN. The radical wing has been particularly active in moments when the state has tried to amplify its powers and is represented especially in the COMPARMEX, CONCANACO, and the CNA. Nonetheless, conflicts with the government have been among the most important factors spurring even moderate business interests to activate or even create employer organizations. The CMHN, for example, was created during a conflict between business interests and the administration of Adolfo López Mateos, and the CCE itself was formed in response to the populist posturing of President Luis Echeverría Álvarez. The nationalization of banks in 1982 led business organizations to rethink their political strategy.

Under the leadership of the radical current of the CCE, between 1982 and 1985 business interests fought for political recognition. Since the 1980s business interests for the first time have become important participants in party politics and the electoral process, calling for important political, economic, and social changes in Mexico. The business organizations have been among the political actors calling for a democratization of the Mexican political system, advocating a bipartisan system with a balance of powers. They also have called for a "social market economy" and have sought to promote the values of individual initiative and family, as well as the social agenda of the Catholic Church.

Between 1985 and the early 1990s, the reform of the Mexican state, the privatization of state enterprises, and the liberalization of markets have given the upper hand to the moderate faction of the CCE. The principal beneficiaries of these changes have been large corporations and the financial sector, which regained much of its power with new gains in the Mexican stock market and the reprivatization of the banking industry. The power of export-oriented industries and the financial sector also increased with the reincorporation of the ABM into the CCE and the creation of the Coordinadora de Organizaciones Empresariales de Comercio Exterior (COECE, or Coordinator of Foreign Trade Business Organizations) for the negotiation of the North American Free Trade Agreement (NAFTA). The COECE formed an organizational base for the CCE to incorporate business organizations related with foreign trade. If the early 1990s brought profound changes in Mexican politics, economy, and society, they also brought important changes to employer organizations. Many business interests openly questioned whether the 1936 Law on Chambers of Commerce and Industry was compatible with the freedom of association mandated in the Mexican constitution.

The increased power of large corporations and the financial sector in the CCE has not gone uncontested. New organizations have emerged representing regional interests and small business. A new political current based in the industrial sector—particularly small and medium businesses—has emerged, publishing its "Proposals of the Private Sector for the 1994–2000 Presidential Term" under the leadership of the COPARMEX, CONCANACO, CANACINTRA, AMIS, and the CNA. The new current's proposals call for an active industrial policy that addresses problems of particular economic sectors as well as problems related to the size, technological capacity, and geographical location of businesses. It also calls for the creation of conditions of real economic competition in Mexico and a closer relationship between macroeconomic and microeconomic policy. Finally, the proposals call for the broad-based, decentralized participation of the totality of business interests in public policy decisions.

Select Bibliography

Arriola, Carlos, *Los empresarios y el Estado 1970–1982.* Mexico City: Miguel Angel Porrúa and UNAM, 1988.

Camp, Roderic Ai, *Los empresarios y la política en México.* Mexico City: Fondo de Cultura Económica, 1996.

Luna, Matilde, *Los empresarios y el cambio política: México 1970–1987.* Era and UNAM, 1992.

——, "Entrepreneurial Interests and Political Action in Mexico: Facing the Demands of Economic Modernization." In *The Challenge of Institutional Reform in Mexico,* edited by Riordan Roett. Boulder, Colorado, and London: Lynne Rienner, 1995.

Luna, Matilde, and Ricardo Tirado, *El Consejo Coordinador Empresarial: Una Radiografía.* Mexico City: UNAM, 1992.

Puga, Cristina, *México: Empresarios y poder.* Mexico City: Miguel Angel Porrúa and UNAM, 1993.

_____, *Organizaciones Empresariales mexicanas: Banco de datos.* Mexico City: UNAM, 1994.

Tirado, Ricardo, editor, *Los empresarios ante la globalización.* Mexico City: UNAM–Instituto do Investigaciones Legislativas, 1994.

Tirado, Ricardo, and Matilde Luna, "El Consejo Coordinador Empresarial de México: De la unidad contra el reformismo a la unidad para el TLC (1975–1993)." *Revista Mexicana de Sociología* 57:4 (1995).

—MATILDE LUNA

ENCOMIENDA

The *Encomienda* is an ancient economic and political system applied with varying degrees of success in the Spanish colonies. *Encomienda* is derived from the Spanish verb *encomendar:* to entrust a mission or an object for someone to fulfill, to care for, or to protect. In this sense, the *encomienda* system, as applied in New Spain, was the mission to care for and protect the indigenous people living on lands temporarily granted to men who had served the Crown. The recipient of the land was called an *encomendero.* He was committed to the indoctrination of his wards into the Christian faith, acculturating them into European standards so that New Spain could participate in the European market and economy. In return for this service the Crown allowed the *encomendero* to collect tributes and receive personal services from his wards. Toward the end of the sixteenth century, the *encomienda,* instead of establishing the expected bureaucratic tributary system, had helped to destroy it by activating a form of capitalism.

Origins and History of *Encomiendas*

Although the *encomienda* became an economic and political term, its origins were religious in nature. The *encomienda,* as defined above, is first found in the fifth-century statutes of the Council of Regla, where the problem of destitute priests was addressed. It was decreed that a bishop who buried another prelate could keep his church and benefit from the parishioners' alms.

A somewhat different version of the *encomienda* developed in Medieval Spain. A knight seeking acceptance into some religious order donated all of his landed property to a church or monastery. In return, he was allowed the usufruct (the right to enjoy the fruits of another's property) of a portion of that land with the understanding that upon his death it would escheat (revert) to the church.

Late in the fifteenth century another version of *encomienda* was instituted. In 1492, having nothing to reward its soldiers for their participation in the destruction of the Kingdom of Granada, the Spanish Crown parceled the conquered land into *encomiendas.* The soldiers who received them were commissioned to Christianize the Islamic Moors on their land.

Nicolás de Ovando, lord commissioner of the Military Order of Calatrava and former governor of conquered Granada, was appointed governor of Hispaniola in 1500. His mission was to repair the damage of the previous misrule. Faced with the need of feeding the population, getting useful work done, Christianizing the Indians, and converting them into loyal subjects, Ovando introduced the *encomienda* system that had been so successful in Granada. However, the indigenous people lacked an agricultural background and were unaccustomed to the harsh working conditions imposed upon them by their new overlords. For the most part, the *encomenderos* in Hispaniola were undisciplined, thoughtless, and greedy individuals who disregarded the precepts of the law behind the *encomienda* that clearly stated that Indians were vassals and not slaves. Complaints from colonizers who felt indignation at the inhuman treatment toward the Indians reached the Court of Spain. The outcome was the proclamation of the 1521 Laws of Indies, which all but abolished the *encomiendas.*

The *Encomienda* in Mexico

The Laws of Indies arrived in New Spain too late, however; Fernando (Hernán) Cortés already had given his men at arms *encomiendas.* They had lived in Hispaniola and considered the *encomienda* a reward due to them for conquering the Mexica (Aztec) Empire. Cortés acceded to their demands because he realized that his men would remain in this land and help protect it for the Crown only if they were given the proper incentives.

Although he granted lands to his followers, Cortés amended the conditions by which the *encomenderos* were to keep their land. Among his 1524 instructions, the *encomenderos* were to receive tribute as well as personal household services from their wards in exchange for food, clothing, technical direction, care, and religious instruction. In an effort to avoid excesses, and in compliance with Mesoamerican social practices, women and boys younger than 12 years of age were exempt from personal service. Furthermore, the *naturales* (as Indians were called) were to serve for periods no longer than 20 days with a minimum 30-day interval between service periods, at which time they could tend to their own fields, produce their own sustenance, and pursue personal activities. Oddly enough these regulations also accorded well with the 1521 Law, which clearly declared Indians to be vassals of the Crown and not subject to induction, fear, or harassment.

The Council of Indies sent a judicial council, the First Audiencia, to govern in the name of the Crown, with instructions to enforce Spanish law and to impart justice. Nuño de Guzmán, an unscrupulous man, was appointed president of the Audiencia. He arrived in New Spain, along with his body of judges and a copy of the Laws of Indies, determined to impart his own brand of justice. A naturally cruel and greedy man, Guzmán proved to be a poor choice. He made enemies among the Spanish when, under pretext of law, he seized as many *encomiendas* as possible, escheating to the Crown those belonging to dead *encomenderos* and keeping for himself and his closest allies the best ones. The Crown could not ignore such arbitrary behavior for long. In 1528, faced with the threat of a rebellion among the *encomenderos*, the Council of Indies removed Guzmán and dissolved and dismissed the First Audiencia.

Bishop Juan de Zumárraga was appointed president of the Second Audiencia. Under his wise leadership the body of judges made some modifications to the *encomienda* system while continuing the Crown's struggle to reduce the feudal *encomenderos'* power. Among the modifications were the reduction of tributes and the abolition of the practice of using Indians as beasts of burden. Those *encomiendas* having imperfect titles (granted by Guzmán) were removed by the Second Audiencia and incorporated to towns by the Crown and ruled by salaried magistrates called *corregidores*.

Once the aggrieved *encomenderos* had been appeased, the Audiencia granted Indian communities the right to self-government and the administration of justice under their own elected officers. Furthermore, they were allowed to continue their old form of government under the supervision of Spanish clergymen and Crown officials of whom Antonio de Mendoza, first viceroy of New Spain and president of the Royal Audiencia, was most important. A practical, just man, Mendoza enforced the laws of the Council of Indies protecting the Indians. He availed himself of Bishop Zumárraga to further the Crown's efforts to reduce the *encomenderos'* power. To accomplish such a purpose, the viceroy enforced the law allowing the Indians to move about the land at will, while forbidding the *encomenderos* to transfer them anywhere against their will.

Acting with keen common sense in handling the complaints of *encomenderos* and natives, the Royal Audiencia won much respect, especially after Mendoza and Zumárraga successfully averted the threat of revolt after the enactment of the New Laws of 1542. The Council of Indies had promulgated the New Laws for two reasons: first, to abolish the *encomiendas* and to escheat them to the Crown upon the holders' deaths, and second, to abolish Indian chattel slavery. Aware that the New Laws were being drafted, Zumárraga and Mendoza sent a lobby to the Council of Indies in Spain in hopes of postponing them. In the meantime they persuaded the *visitador* who arrived in 1544 to postpone their enforcement until further notice. The lobbyists made clear to the Council of Indies the indignation and disappointment of the *encomenderos*. Their argument that escheatment to the Crown would throw their children into immediate poverty and destitution was so effective that in 1546 Felipe II had the New Laws revised to be more realistic and workable. The *encomenderos* were allowed to enjoy their grants and pass the right to the next generation, but they forfeited the privilege of personal service.

Outcome of the *Encomienda* System

Of the three devastating pandemics that struck New Spain during the sixteenth century, only the second (1545) and the third (1575) had any effect on the *encomienda* system. While the court of Spain was modifying the New Laws, extending the number of lifetimes an *encomendero* could enjoy this privilege, a most virulent form of illness struck, killing millions of Indians. By the time the laws were received, large expanses of land had become so depopulated that their *encomenderos* had no wards to protect or exploit. Seeing that no work could be done or tributes received, they were forced to cede the land to the Crown. Others, more fortunate, helped their communities to diversify their communal interests, promoting economic enterprises whose products could be marketed. Finding their economic markets and selling to the best bidders, the Indians were better equipped to pay their tributes in gold currency. The *encomenderos* found this arrangement more agreeable because with the money they could buy property that would not escheat to the Crown. The third pandemic caused the greatest and most dramatic effect upon the *encomienda* system. This last epidemic was so virulent that it nearly wiped out the already severely reduced indigenous population. Many *encomenderos* had no alternative but to release their surviving wards from tributary duties.

Despite the 1546 Laws, the *encomienda* system was allowed to continue. The Crown extended the privilege to various generations of *encomenderos,* escheating only those without heirs or which were irregularly obtained. Only by the middle of the eighteenth century had all *encomiendas* become Crown property and all Indians vassals.

A modified version of the *encomienda* seems to have survived the colonial period in distant regions of Chiapas and Yucatán, while in the arid north, the *encomienda* died almost immediately. Because the Indians in the north were primarily nomadic, it was difficult to recruit a labor force. Because the transfer of people against their will was against the law, the *encomenderos* had to resort to slave labor or to pay salaries.

Although slavery was frequently used at the silver and copper mines during the first half of the sixteenth century, conditions were such that slave mortality rates soared and escapism became the norm. Those slaves who succeeded in escaping joined nomadic Indian tribes who harbored them and waged war against the Spaniards. With the threat of a paralysis in production, the mine managers decided to offer monetary incentives as an attraction to work in their mines. Viceroy Mendoza, usually correct in his evaluation of human behavior, proved wrong when he declared that "it was absurd to think that Indians would work voluntarily for Spaniards, even for pay." The mining industry, he decried, was doomed. Happily for Spain's coffers, he was wrong. Indians and Spaniards alike traveled great distances to work in the mines in such places as Zacatecas, Pachuca, and Potosí.

Paid labor became the norm in most of New Spain during the second half of the century. The *encomenderos* had, by their decision to require the tributes' worth in gold rather than kind, inadvertently propitiated the system's downfall by helping to activate a quasi-capitalistic form of economy.

See also New Laws of 1542; Tribute

Select Bibliography

Gibson, Charles, *Los Aztecas Bajo el Dominio Español (1519–1810)*. Mexico City: Siglo XXI, 1977.

Riva Palacio, Vicente, *Mexico a Través de Los Siglos*, vol. 3. Mexico City: Cumbre S.H., 1984.

Semo, Enrique, *Historia del Capitlalismo en Mexico: Los Origenes 1521–1763*. Mexico City: Era, 1973.

Simpson, Leslie Byrd, *Many Mexicos*. Berkeley and Los Angeles: University of California Press, 1959.

Suarez, Clara Elena, *La Politica Ceralera y La Economia Novohispana: El Caso del Trigo*. Mexico City: Centro de Investigaciones y Estudios Superiores en Antropología Social, 1985.

Zavala, Silvio, *De Encomiendas y Propiedad Territorial en Algunas Regiones de la América Española*. Mexico City: Aurrúa, 1940.

—FRANCISCA R. SORENSEN

ERAUSO, CATALINA DE (LA MONJA ALFÉREZ)

1585?–1650 • Nun and Adventurer

Catalina de Erauso, the soldier nun, was born in San Sebastián de Guipuzcoa, Spain, toward the end of the sixteenth century, probably in 1585. Her baptism certificate was issued in 1592, registering her as the third legitimate daughter among seven siblings. At a young age she entered the convent of San Sebastián el Antiguo, where a maternal aunt governed as prioress. She became a novice when she was 15, but having strong differences with an older, widowed nun, she resolved to escape from the convent. She fled to a chestnut grove and hid there for several days. Then, dressed as a man and with cropped hair, she journeyed to Victoria where she found work with a professor. On discovering that she knew Latin, this man urged her to pursue her studies, but to no avail. For three years she wandered around the country, adopting various lifestyles and settling in a number of places until she reached San Lúcar, whence she set sail for America as a cabin boy.

After fighting an enemy fleet in order to dock at Cartagena de Indias, Catalina traveled much of Spanish South America. She typically sought board and employment among the more affluent emigrants from her own land, the Basque country, and this trail took her to Nombre de Dios, Panama, Puerto de Paita, Trujillo, Lima, Puerto de Concepción, Puerto de Pacaibi, Valdivia, Nacimiento, Valle de Puren, Tucumán, El Potosí, Charcas, Santiago, la Plata, Piscobamba, Cochabamba, Llanos de Mizqui, la Paz, Cuzco, Andahuailas, Huancavelica, Huamanga, Bogotá, Zaragoza, and Tenerife.

She earned her living in these places as clerk, trader, soldier, administrator, muleteer, and at last, as nun; but whatever the hat she wore, she sooner or later picked violent quarrels with her colleagues, who emerged from these conflicts either dead or wounded. Such incidents drove her to take sanctuary in a church or to flee, although she was arrested more than once and narrowly escaped execution. In one such fight she killed her own brother, who had come to America separately and failed to recognize her. As a soldier, she was noted for her courage and promoted to the rank of second lieutenant. She was also a great gambler, with a weakness for women. She was wounded a number of times, none seriously. Having committed many sacrileges, she confessed her adventures at last to the bishop of Huamanga. Once it was confirmed that she was a woman in male attire, the bishop pardoned her and advised her to retire to the convent of Santa Clara. The Bishop of Lima intervened, summoning her to his court, where she was presented to Viceroy Francisco de Borja. Later, she herself chose a convent where she would withdraw, but it emerged that she had not taken final vows in Spain. Permission therefore was granted for her to leave the convent and return to Spain.

Catalina disembarked at Cadiz and proceeded to Seville and Madrid. On her way to Rome for the Holy Jubilee, she was captured at Turin, suspected of being a spy. Released, she failed to reach her destination and returned to Madrid, where she submitted a report to the king relating her services in America. This document was approved by the Council of the Indies, which granted her a life pension of 500 pesos a year, to be deposited in the royal treasuries of either Peru, Manila, or Mexico. Catalina opted for Mexico, then under the rule of the marqués of Cerralvo, to whom she presented the royal warrant that underwrote her pension. She bought a drove of mules and some black slaves, and with these she plied her trade between Mexico City and Veracruz via Jalapa. In 1650, close to Orizaba, she abruptly fell ill and died. She was buried at this spot with lavish ceremony, since she was known and loved by the religious community there.

Catalina de Erauso assumed a variety of names during her lifetime, including Francisco de Loyola, Alonso Díaz Ramírez de Guzmán, and at the end, Antonio de Erauso. She caused considerable commotion in her wake, and accounts of her were published as early as 1618. She became an important figure in colonial mythology, inspiring poems and novels with her turbulent deeds. During the nineteenth century she attracted the attention of several scholars, including Vicente Riva Palacio, whose *México a través de los siglos* dwells on part of her life. In the twentieth century, Nicolás León published a study about her.

Select Bibliography

León, Nicolás, *Aventuras de la Monja Alférez.* Mexico City: Complejo Editorial Mexicano, 1973.

—Clara Elena Suárez Argüello

ESCUELA NACIONAL DE MEDICINA

After the Spanish conquest of Mexico-Tenochtitlan in the sixteenth century, a series of cultural, juridical, and religious institutions were established in the territory that would henceforth be called New Spain. Among these was the Real y Pontifica Universidad de México (Royal and Pontifical University of Mexico), founded in 1553. The first lectures in the university were on sacred theology, canon law, arts, grammar, holy scripture, law, and rhetoric. It was many years before medicine began to be taught there. On December 12, 1576, Dr. Pedro Arteago Mendiola, rector of the university, took the initiative to propose the foundation of a chair of medicine to the Spanish king. The idea was accepted on January 11, 1578, in a document in which the monarch expressed the rationale behind this decision: "Desiring that our vassals enjoy a long life and maintain perfect health, it is Our duty to provide them with Doctors and Teachers to discipline and instruct them as well as cure their illnesses." The establishment of the Faculty of Medicine, as it was named, would ensure the education of physicians according to the western medical tradition, which at that time followed the teachings of Hippocrates and Galen, as opposed to the indigenous medical practices of the Americas.

The first chair of medicine, the *prima de medicina,* supposedly was inaugurated on June 14, 1578, although in fact no classes were given until January 7 of the following year. The professor concerned, Dr. Juan de la Fuente, was the doctor for the Holy Office of the Inquisition and the Royal Hospital of the Indies. According to the statutes, the professor had a four-year tenure. As no suitable candidate was available to succeed him, de la Fuente took on an additional term beginning November 7, 1582.

In the meeting of the university faculty on November 27, 1598, it was suggested there was a need to establish a second chair of medicine, the *vísperas de medicina.* The first professor was Dr. Juan de Placencia, who began teaching classes on January 7, 1599. From this moment the four-year medical training included two areas of study: the first covered the body in health, anatomy, and physiology; the second included pathology and healing techniques.

Many years were to pass before a third chair was integrated into the medical curriculum. In 1621 *método medendi* was created under Dr. Cristóbal Hidalgo y Vendabal. This chair was responsible for lectures on the body in sickness, healing techniques, and certain pharmaceutical studies. On November 29 a further chair in *anatomía y cirugía* was established, also under Dr. Hidalgo's supervision. Anatomy was taught from Galen's books, which were based on animal dissections and were thus the source of many errors. The final branch of the discipline to be included was that of *astrología y matemáticas,* established on February 22, 1637, and taught in Spanish. The remainder of the courses were taught in Latin. The first professor was Father Diego Rodríguez, who taught that in some men there existed certain properties that did not derive solely from the four bodily humors that depended on qualities of cold, heat, moistness, or dryness, but rather on a hidden celestial influence. There was thus an intimate relationship between astrology and medicine.

Medical ideas of the day were derived from the classical works by Hippocrates and Galen and that of the medieval Arab doctors such as Rhazes and Avicenna. The medical system was based on the theory of the four humors (blood, phlegm, black bile, and yellow bile), elemental fluids that, apart from defining the temperament of the patient (choleric, phlegmatic, melancholic, and bilious), caused changes in certain areas and provoked disease if unbalanced within the body. Environment and health were very connected; the season of the year, the place, and the time of day all had a part to play. This system was taught on an official basis in the Faculty of Medicine until the end of the colonial period and only began to be modified at the end of the eighteenth century through the introduction of some additional courses that complemented or enriched the five programs discussed above. These new courses were given in institutions independent of the university, such as the Real Colegio de Cirugía (Royal College of Surgery) and the Jardin Botanico (Botanical Garden). Changes also came from some lecturers influenced by Enlightenment thinking that disagreed with the old ideas. Among these lecturers were José Ignacio Bartolache and Luis José Montaña. The former was the founder of Mexico's first specialist medical publication, the *Mercurio Volante* (1772–73), in which he expressed his concern about the anachronistic system still being taught in the university. In the periodical and in his classes, Bartolache taught that medicine was a science and not an art, its results grounded in observation and experiment. In 1773 he was markedly unsuccessful in demanding that the teaching of medicine should be based on chemistry, physics, anatomy, and botany, as proposed by the Dutch doctor Hermann Boerhaave. The Real Tribunal del Protomedicato, an institute that was in charge of keeping a watch over the exercise of medicine and its instruction, defended the traditional method. Until the mid–eighteenth century, it ordered that Hippocrates, Galen, and Avicenna were required reading.

Luis José Montaña, who entered as a teacher in the Faculty of Medicine in 1804, gave a class on *Clinica medica o medicina práctica* that had been taught in Europe since the mid–eighteenth century. His field of operations was no longer the traditional classroom but the Hospital de San Andrés. This was the first official move toward modernizing the teaching of medicine. Not only were the students no longer condemned to recite the writings of the classical authors, but their professor was the first to reject purely theoretical teaching. Montaña was convinced of the relevance of the connection that existed between chemistry, physiological, and pathological phenomena. Starting in 1797 he organized private courses on clinical observations in the Real de Naturales and San Andrés Hospitals. Unfortunately, his efforts and keenness to give practical classes were interrupted by the events of 1807. He nevertheless managed to foster a spirit of research among his pupils.

The Royal College of Surgery, created in the Real de Naturales Hospital in 1768, although independent of the university, contributed greatly to medical teaching. When its doors opened on April 10, 1770, it marked a new stage in teaching surgery, one very different from the course on anatomy and surgery in the university. The new courses were anatomy, operations in theory and practice, and physiology. Students not only included those who were studying to be surgeons, but also medical students that wanted to study the subject in greater depth.

The Royal Botanical Garden was another institute that contributed to the improvement of medical teaching. Estab-
lished on the initiative of the Aragonese doctor Martín Sessé in 1788, the foundation focused not only on studying Mexican plants but also the very important task of researching the medicinal properties of Mexican herbs for therapeutic purposes. In tandem with the opening of the Botanical Garden, a botanical expedition was organized to explore colonial territory and the chair of *botanica* (Botany) was created, initially occupied by the pharmacist Vicente Cervantes. The course was obligatory for the students of medicine and surgery and those who wanted to become pharmacists. Great emphasis was placed on practical analysis, which took place largely in the Botanical Garden itself, and on other occasions in the country outside the capital. Between them the botanical expedition and the garden managed to amass a considerable plant collection and a large number of drawings, examples of which were sent back to Spain.

The year 1810, the beginning of the War of Independence, was a terrible one for the university and marked the beginning of its decline. The Faculty of Medicine was used as a barracks, and the viceroy ordered the students to present a certificate from doctors of various hospitals as proof that they had worked under them for a set length of time.

The political change produced by Independence in 1821 was followed by economic, social, cultural, and scientific flux, eventually ending colonial organization. When the embargo that had prevented the import of books and instruments to New Spain had been lifted, doctors began to adopt certain techniques derived from European countries, France in particular. Among the works that were introduced and read in the classes was the *Diccionario de ciencias médicas,* published in Paris in 1819. This work included an article on the stethoscope and another on percussion.

In the second decade of the nineteenth century, many professors criticized the stagnation of medical teaching in the university. They proposed to end the diversity of careers (medicine, surgery, botany, or pharmacy) and tried to bring them together in one course to train doctor-surgeons. One who fought on behalf of this reform was Manuel Carpio, a discipline of Montaña. His reformist spirit was evident in his publications and his lectures in which he commented on the texts of Franÿois Magendie, whose work was based on experiment through observation and interpretation. To help his students further, Carpio translated various works from Latin and French into Spanish, such as that previously mentioned on the stethoscope. Finally, in 1824 the texts of Hippocrates and Galen were deemed obsolete and officially substituted by modern texts. For example Xavier Bichat's *Anatomie générale appliquée à la physiologie et à la médicine,* published in 1801, was adopted by the department *prima de medicina.* The other curricula also benefited from updated texts.

After having achieved many reforms, the university was closed—at the time Mexico was manifesting anti-religious tendencies, including the separation of education from the church. In 1833 the government, authorized to make changes in public education, began with the university and its papal seal. On October 23, a decree was passed ordering the institution, along with many others, to close down, substituting for it an establishment of higher education to be called the Establecimiento de Ciencias Médicas (Scientific Medical Establishment). From this moment the changes that the teaching staff had long planned could be realized.

The Establecimiento de Ciencias Médicas was inaugurated on December 4, 1833, under Dr. Casimiro Liceaga, who previously had taught in the university. The teaching staff boasted many individuals of great renown, including Dr. Miguel Jiménez, the first Mexican clinician responsible for introducing percussion and auscultation, and Dr. Francisco Montes de Oca, creator of new operation techniques, including one for leg amputation. The impact of new reforms was felt immediately. The first reform linked medicine and surgery and created a new plan of studies. *Prima de medicina* and *visperas de medicina* were scrapped, while new courses finally were brought up to date in their subject and content. The 1833 study plan contained 11 topics, including general anatomy, physiology, hygiene, internal and external pathology, operations and obstetrics, the theory and practice of pharmacy, legal medicine, and internal and external clinical medicine. The number of areas increased considerably compared with those of the old university, allowing the student to graduate with a broader understanding of medicine.

From 1833 there was a change of paradigm in which the theory of the humors was replaced by the biological model of illness, which defines an illness as a functional alteration in the organs of the human body. Through visual signs and symptoms the problem was to be discovered and a diagnosis made. The new program included knowledge of the body in health, pathology, and finally the study of medical and surgical therapeutic resources. From this moment the study of medicine as a modern science began in Mexico.

All textbooks were imported from abroad. Largely French, they informed both the teaching staff and the students of the Establecimiento de Ciencias Médicas on the advances being made in Europe. These included the famous physiologist Magendie's *Précis élementaire de physiologie* (1833), Chevalier's *Journal de chimie médicale de pharmacie et toxicologie* (1827), and Roche's *Nouveaux éléments de pathologie médico-chirurgicale* (1833). It was only in the last years of the nineteenth century that the study program began to include work by British and German writers.

During the nineteenth century the plan of studies was constantly modified, as were the textbooks. In 1846 two important areas for the understanding of medicine, chemistry and physics, were added to the curriculum. Such increase of topics meant that the program was extended from four years to six. At the same time, the system of internship was introduced into the curriculum of 1912; sixth-year students now had to gain practical experience working in hospitals.

The Establecimiento de Ciencias Médicas did not last long. It was closed in 1834 by President Antonio López de Santa Anna because of political conflicts between Liberals and Conservatives. It was reopened on November 12 of the same year but under another name: Colegio de Medicina

(Medical College). Over the ensuing hundred years its name would be changed to Escuela de Medicina (School of Medicine), the Escuela Nacional de Medicina (National School of Medicine), and finally, in 1914, to the Facultad de Medicina (Faculty of Medicine). During the nineteenth century the school was an official institution dependent on the Secretaría de Instrucción Pública y Bellas Artes (Secretariat of Public Instruction and Fine Arts) and the federal government. Despite the various changes of name, the internal organization was not modified; the subjects of the texts, of courses, were modified according to the necessities of the time.

Other than providing training for career doctor-surgeons, the National School of Medicine provided courses on pharmacy, dental surgery, and midwifery. At the end of the nineteenth century, an independent school for the training of midwives was founded. In 1912 the curriculum of the medical school included a new training course for nurses. The course on pharmacy lasted three years, during which theoretical and practical topics were studied. As well as attending a determined number of courses, the students had practical work experience in the Beneficencia Pública (Public Welfare Office) and in government hospitals. The three-year training in dental surgery took place in the Consultorio Nacional de Enseñanza Dental (National Dental Training Clinic), an annex of the National School of Medicine; graduating exams were taken in the latter building. Courses in obstetrics and midwifery for female students lasted two years. The theoretical aspect of the training was held in the School of Medicine, while practical experience was gained in the Maternity Hospital. Study for the nursing career lasted four years, covering general theory such as anatomy, physiology, and hygiene, with an emphasis on obstetrics. Each trainee was required to work 40 shifts a year in the General Hospital's maternity department before taking her final exam.

Acceptance onto the teaching staff required a candidate to fulfill certain conditions. These included the professional title of doctor, pharmacist, or dental surgeon, Mexican nationality, and a "high standard of morals." Doctors were included on the obstetrics teaching staff. A prospective professor had to enter a public competition and be evaluated by a group composed of up to four professors and three doctors from the Consejo de Salubridad (Council of Health).

Student examinations on each topic took place at the end of each scholastic year and at the end of the course. The final graduate examination consisted of a discourse by the pupil followed by questions from the examiners. In 1869 these discourses were replaced by the writing of theses on medicine and pharmacy. By 1880 an average of 35 professional exams were submitted for the career of medical surgeon, and between five and eight for that of pharmacist. Foreign doctors who wanted to practice in Mexico had to revalidate their title with the school and the Secretaría de Instrucción Pública y Bellas Artes.

The school changed locations several times until 1854, when the teachers combined resources to buy a building that had belonged to the Tribunal of the Holy Office of the

Inquisition. Today the building houses the Department of Medical History of the Universidad Nacional Autónoma de México (UNAM, or the National Autonomous University of Mexico). Once the school had its own building, salons were turned into classrooms and laboratories for the study of physiology, bacteriology, and pharmacy, and an amphitheater was created for dissection purposes.

The influence of Positivism during the rule of Porfirio Díaz led the National School of Medicine to fight for a theoretical-practical form of teaching. Clinical material was taught in the San Andrés Hospital, where a professor, Dr. Rafael Lucio, founded a pathology museum that in 1899 became the Instituto Patológico Nacional (National Pathological Institute). The San Andrés Hospital was replaced in 1905 by the General Hospital, which became the most important of its time, with independent pavilions as well as laboratories where the students could make scientific evaluations of their patients. Dr. Eduardo Liceaga, director of the school, commented in 1903 that he aspired to total objectivity in medical training through the teaching of things as they are, and not from books. In conformity with the curriculum of the time, the students were to set up their own experiments, bacteria cultures, chemical analyses, and learn to compare clinical cases. The director was of the opinion that good professionals were laboratory trained, not library trained.

The official birth of specialized medical fields of study took place in the 1880s. The periodical *La Escuela de Medicina* (Volume I, 1880) pointed out a lack in the curriculum and the need to add certain special subjects to raise the currently low academic level of the graduate students. The 1888 curriculum included five topics that could be considered specialties and postgraduate study material: ophthalmology, gynecology, bacteriology, mental illness (now psychiatry), and topographic anatomy. In 1894 clinical medicine for children (now pediatrics) and histology were added to the list. Attendance of these subjects was permitted after having completed a minimum of three years of medical training. The title of specialist was granted only to a graduate medical surgeon who had studied his subject for two years.

To improve teaching, after 1905, training courses in medicine and pharmacy began to be held in the General Hospital as well as the school and the San Andrés Hospital. At the end of the nineteenth century further institutions were included within the training scheme, such as the Beneficencia Pública (Public Welfare) hospitals, the Consultorio Central de la Beneficencia Pública (Public Welfare Central Office), and the Alamacén Central de la Beneficencia Pública (Public Welfare Central Stores), where the pharmacy students undertook some practical training. Also included was the Instituto Médico Nacional (National Medical Institute), whose function was research into the medical and chemical properties of Mexican flora and fauna; its main links with the school were through the provision of therapeutic train-

ing. The Instituto Patológico Nacional (National Pathological Institute), which studied illnesses prevalent in the republic, specialized in pathological anatomy. Finally, students of the Instituto Bacteriológico Nacional (National Bacteriological Institute) studied bacteriology and the infectious diseases of the country as well as prepared vaccinations and serums. For the first years of the twentieth century, these three institutes formed part of the nucleus of the School of Medicine, thereby reflecting the importance that practical themes and laboratory work were acquiring in medicine. In the twentieth century the school focused as much as possible on practical teaching, while adhering closely to the scientific method.

The student population increased throughout the nineteenth century. In 1833 a total of 93 pupils had entered in courses. By 1880 this number had risen to 225. The first woman to enter the institution was Matilde Montoya in 1883.

President Porfirio Díaz founded the National University by a decree dated May 26, 1910. According to this decree, the university was to include various professional schools and faculties if they ran postgraduate studies. The university depended on the Ministerio de Instrucción Pública (Ministry of Public Education) until 1929, when it was made autonomous. The political disturbances of the Mexican Revolution provoked frequent change of directors, which prevented many plans from being brought to fruition. The National School of Medicine became the Faculty of Medicine in 1914 though it was later renamed "School" and subsequently, "Faculty." During the first half of the twentieth century, the Faculty continued in the old tribunal building. In 1954 the classrooms and research departments moved to the new UNAM university campus, leaving only the Department of History and Philosophy of Medicine behind in the old building.

The social aspect of medicine has played an important role in medical studies, as witnessed by the creation of obligatory social services in 1936 for trainee doctors. A career in medicine continues to demand six years of training with a biological, psychological, and social focus.

Select Bibliography

Flores y Troncoso, Francisco, *Historia de la medicina en México desde la época de los indios hasta la presente (1888)*. 4 vols., Mexico City: Instituto Mexicano del Seguro Social, 1982.

Ocaranza, Fernando, *Historia de la medicina en México*. Mexico City: Laboratorios Midy, 1934.

Plaza y Jaén, Bernardo de la, *Crónica de la Real y Pontificia Universidad de México escrita en el siglo XVIII*. 2 vols., Mexico City: UNAM, 1931.

Rodríguez, Martha Eugenia, "El paso de la teoría humoral de la enfermedad al nacimiento de la clínica moderna en México." *Quipu, Revista Latinoamericana de Historia de las Ciencias y la Tecnología* 9:3 (September–December 1992).

—MARTHA EUGENIA RODRÍGUEZ

ETHNIC MOVEMENTS

See Indigenismo and Ethnic Movements

EUGENICS

Eugenics, a term first used in 1865 by Charles Darwin's cousin, the British statistician and naturalist Sir Francis Galton, fully entered the scientific lexicon in the early twentieth century when eugenics societies emerged across the globe. Largely a western elite response to the societal strife and dislocations induced by large-scale industrialization, shifting demographic patterns, and rapid urbanization, eugenics was a set of theories and policies aimed at controlling and monitoring the reproduction of individuals and social groups. Eugenicists—comprised of a diverse group of anthropologists, sociologists, animal breeders, physicians, and politicians that was at once national and transnational—infused nineteenth-century evolutionary theories (which implicitly and explicitly venerated the "pure," white European "races") with ideas originating within the emerging field of genetics. Through laboratory experiments with plant hybridization, family pedigree studies, intelligence tests, and an obsessive drive to quantify, categorize, and serialize individuals and groups according to moral and biological constructs, eugenicists sought to imbue all social action and stratification with scientific meaning. The significance and aims of eugenics movements varied depending on the national context in each of the more than 30 countries with official organizations by the 1920s.

In some countries, such as the United States and Germany, eugenics was based on the assumption that all human capacities, ranging from hair color to musical talent, were determined solely by heredity and genetic transmission. In others, especially those in Latin America, eugenicists took a somewhat softer approach to the question of inheritance and human value, often asserting that individual and generational ills gradually could be ameliorated and, in a sense, genetically erased, by environmental modifications. The eugenics movement in Mexico stood in the middle of these two extremes. The promotion of eugenics organizations and the use of eugenic language should be seen as one of many facets of the project of modernization and nation-building embarked upon by the post-Revolutionary generation that came to power in the 1920s and 1930s. Furthermore, its broader effects are linked to other important historical processes of the time, such as anticlericalism, Sinophobia, a new educational program that sought to assimilate the "backward" Indian, and generalized attempts to taxonomize and define the Revolutionary citizen.

The official embodiment of eugenics in Mexico was the Sociedad Mexicana de Eugenesia (Mexican Eugenics Society) founded in 1931 by two physicians trained during the turbulent years of the Revolution, Alfredo M. Saavedra and Adrian Correa. The goal of the organization, according to its journal, *Eugenesia,* which was published in two phases (1932–35; 1939–49) was to study "the problems of heredity and promote the betterment of the race." Throughout close to two decades of activity, the Mexican Eugenics Society sponsored conferences and published articles on topics such as prophylaxis of tuberculosis and smallpox, the inheritability and evils of alcoholism, hygiene in industry and the classroom, the necessity of prenuptial exams and marriage certificates, and prospective ways to categorize the Mexican population according to ethnicity, "race," and other putatively biological characteristics. Saavedra, Correa, and other members of the society had institutional links to several dozen civic and governmental agencies (including the Department of Public Health, the National Preparatory School, the Mexican Society of Puericulture, and the National Academy of Medicine), and along with their own journal, disseminated eugenic ideas via radio programs and in periodicals such as *El Heraldo de México* (for which Correa was the medical editor) and *Medicina.* The editors of *Eugenesia* drew from eclectic and frequently contradictory scientific doctrines; sometimes articles propounding hard heredity ran side by side others espousing faith in environmentalist approaches. This adherence to divergent theoretical models was mirrored by the society's alliances, on the one hand, with the premier eugenics society in the United States, the American Eugenics Society, and on the other, the Latin Federation of Eugenics Societies, formed in 1935 in reaction to the imperious and overtly racist posture of the Anglo eugenics movement. This double positioning of the Mexican Eugenics Society was largely owing to the fact that its intellectual and institutional roots, forged by the Porfirian Científicos (influential intellectuals and policy advisers to President Portirio Díaz) who fervently embraced evolutionism, were "Latin," primarily French and Italian, while its consolidation occurred during a period of increasing U.S. economic, cultural, and ideological hemispheric dominance.

The effects of eugenics reached beyond the work of the Mexican Eugenics Society. Eugenics brought the Mexican elite into the fold of a transnational scientific and policy-making community, which in turn recognized the modernizing aims of the post-Revolutionary administration and its principal overseer, Plutarco Elías Calles. Beginning in the early 1920s, members of the post-Revolutionary state began to participate in the international eugenics community. For example, in 1921, J. Joaquin Izquierdo—the head of the influential *Sociedad Científica Mexicana Antonio Alzate* (to which many Mexican eugenicists at some point belonged) presented a paper on his own genealogical history at the Second International Eugenics Congress held in New York. Manuel Gamio—perhaps the most prominent social scientist in Mexico during this period—also represented his country at this conference. The First Pan-American Conference of Eugenics and Homiculture, convened under the direction of Cuban eugenicists, was held in Havana in 1927 and attended by Dr. Rafael Santamarina, a delegate from the Department of Public Education. These patterns were reinforced at the 1928 Third Race Betterment Conference, sponsored by the U.S. eugenicist and health reformer John Harvey Kellogg and held in his home town of Battle Creek, Michigan, where Mexican eugenics and sanitation were discussed by several members of the Mexican medical community. Mexican eugenicists also participated in the Latin Federation of Eugenics Societies, hosting their inaugural meeting in Mexico City in 1935.

The impact of eugenic thought and policies was widespread, albeit uneven, during the decades following the end of the Revolution. In an environment in which a newly emerging secular state was seeking to extirpate the entrenched power of both official and popular Catholicism, the invocation of science became central to legitimizing cultural and social programs. Evolutionary and eugenic notions undergirded the construction of the icon of the state of the 1920s and 1930s, the *mestizo*. A transcendent symbol of nationalism, the mestizo was an individual representation of the intellectual José Vasconcelos's "cosmic race." According to Vasconcelos, a Hispanophile whose journeys through the Americas in the early 1920s had compelled him to invent and coin the term, the "cosmic race" combined the essences of all the region's "races"—European, African, Asian, and Indian—to produce a superior and sacred fusion. Consistently represented as a virile male, the glorified mestizo conformed to the universalism of Revolutionary rhetoric, embodied industriousness, and celebrated instead of disparaged biological and cultural hybridity.

However, proclaiming the modern mestizo as the quintessential Mexican citizen came with an unintended corollary, namely the need to assimilate the Indian into a homogeneous populace. Eugenic notions of racial purity fostered a policy toward indigenous groups in the 1920s and 1930s that simultaneously sought to encase the ancestral, timeless noble savage in the museum and incorporate the liv-

ing, breathing Indian into the nation. The post-Revolutionary centerpiece of Indian assimilation was the educational system molded by Vasconcelos and Gamio, both of whom were influenced by eugenic ideas and examples.

Toward this end, the Department of Public Education created a Department of Pyschopedagogy and Hygiene in 1925. Directed by Dr. Santamarina, the goal of this new branch of the post-Revolutionary government was to test, categorize, and standardize Mexican school children. Modifying I.Q. tests such as the Binet-Simon (first comprehensively deployed in the United States during the World War I draft) and the Ebbinghaus, Santamarina set out to demonstrate that the younger sector of Mexico's population was on par with that of any other nation. Until the department's disappearance in 1941, Santamarina and his numerous underlings mixed, experimented with, and implemented eugenic techniques such as anthropometry, biometrics, intelligence testing, and the gathering of demographic data. The ample funds this department received, twice the amount allocated for the Department of Normal and Primary Education during its second year of operation, reveal its importance to developing ideas of citizenship and national homogenization.

Along a similar vein, eugenics also played a critical role in the unfolding of Sinophobia in Mexico. Anti-Chinese slogans were written with a eugenic, exclusionary vocabulary. Groups with names such as the Comité Pro-Raza and the Union Nacionalista Mexicana "Pro-Raza y Pro-Salud" decried the defilement of the Mexican "race" and placed the blame on the Chinese. These Mexican nationalists claimed that the Chinese were involved in numerous illicit activities such as smuggling and ingesting opium and narcotics. Seeking to protect a nation, which they presented as feminine, with appeals to a nationalism embodied and defended by the manly *mestizo*, these Sinophobes were most outraged by allegations that numerous Chinese-run prostitution rings were dragging chaste Mexican women into the urban underworld. In order to protect their honor, Mexican nationalists—principally in the northern states—sought to pass legislation banning Chinese-Mexican marriages beginning in the 1910s. Such notions of contamination also justified the boycotting of Chinese stores and the institution of segregated neighborhoods. The expulsion of hundreds of Chinese from Sonora in the early 1930s resembles similar Sinophobic reactions in the United States, which were also worded in racialized and medicalized terms of contamination and criminality. Eugenic language and ideas also helped to structure the 1926 Sanitary Code, and two consecutive Migration Laws, passed in 1926 and 1930, all of which prohibited the "dysgenic"—identified as those with contagious diseases such as tuberculosis and leprosy, anarchists, the insane, as well as contingently defined undesirable and unassimilable "races"—from entering and crossing the boundaries of the nation. Such ideas were further consolidated several years later in the General Population Law passed under President Lázaro Cárdenas in

1936. This federal legislation aimed to thoroughly taxonomize the Mexican population, encourage *mestizaje* (the reproduction of the mestizo above any other "race"), and impose marriage restrictions on syphilitics and other individuals deemed diseased or abnormal.

One of the most striking examples of the effects of eugenics, and moreover, of the ways in which the U.S. brand of eugenics left its mark on Mexico, was the passage of a sterilization law in the state of Veracruz in 1932. Backed by the staunchly anticlerical and statist governor, Aldaberto Tejada, the formulation of such a law was undoubtedly affected by the Rockefeller Foundation's intensive campaign to eradicate yellow fever from the port city in the 1920s. The novelty of Tejada's actions rested in his adaptation of a negative and typically Anglo strategy to promote the reproduction of the ideal post-Revolutionary citizen. Along with this law, Tejada decreed the creation of a new service, called the Section of Eugenics and Mental Hygiene, which was to work in conjunction with local and state sanitary agents and realize studies of the role of heredity in transmitting physical and behavioral defects across generations. Although few if any sterilizations were conducted in Veracruz, the fact this law was passed, and moreover, that a copy of it was requested by the Nazi German government in 1937, illustrates that many Mexican post-Revolutionaries promoted eugenics and were recognized for their unique contributions by the transnational eugenics community.

The disappearance of eugenics as a movement is frequently attributed to rising moral outrage over the heinous crimes committed under its banner in Nazi Germany. In Mexico, however, eugenic manifestations lasted into the 1940s. *Eugenesia* continued publication until 1949; Vasconcelos published the short-lived *Timon* in 1940, which praised the organizational and social accomplishments of Hitler, and a spectrum of nationalistic organizations such as the Comité Pro-Raza and the Comité Anti-Chino y Anti-Judio galvanized many supporters during the 1930s and early 1940s. The longevity of the eugenics movement and the seemingly unabashed utilization of eugenic discourse during the emergence of fascist and racial hygiene movements in Europe reflects at least a latent sympathy for proto-fascism in some sectors of Mexican society. It also illustrates the elasticity of eugenics in Mexico; it can be neatly correlated neither with the right or the left, but rather more generally with the advent of modernity and especially interwar nationalism pursued through science and secular objectivity.

Following World War II, eugenics began a process of splintering. For the most part the movement was absorbed by the increasingly solid field of genetics, on the one hand, and sociological quantitative methods, on the other. That Mexico began to merge demography and eugenic methods is evidenced by the preparation of a quantitative survey by the Department of Indigenous Affairs's Section of Ethnology and Eugenics in 1943. Presented at the First Inter-American Demographic Congress, this brief paper used the latest genre of "social mathematics" to echo earlier eugenic recommendations for immigration restriction and state-led forms of internal colonization. When almost all formal eugenics organizations faded in the 1950s, eugenic causes were absorbed and recast by burgeoning international organizations focused on population control, family planning, and the management of global health crises and epidemics.

See also Anthropology; Chinese; Indigenismo and Ethnic Movements; Mestizaje; Nationalism

Select Bibliography

Benítez, Agustín Basave, *México mestizo: Análisis del nacionalismo mexicano en torno a la mestizofilia de Andrés Molina Enríquez.* Mexico City: Fondo de Cultura Económica, 1992.

Cueto, Marcos, editor, *Missionaries of Science: The Rockefeller Foundation and Latin America.* Bloomington: Indiana University Press, 1994.

Izquierdo, José Jorge Gómez, *El Movimiento antichino en México (1871–1934): Problemas del racismo y del nacionalismo durante la Revolución Mexicana.* Mexico City: INAH, 1991.

Kelves, Daniel J., *In the Name of Eugenics: Genetics and the Uses of Human Heredity.* 2nd edition, Cambridge, Massachusetts: Harvard University Press, 1995.

Knight, Alan, "Racism, Revolution, and *Indigenismo*: Mexico, 1910–1940." In *The Idea of Race in Latin America, 1870–1940*, edited by Richard Graham. Austin: University of Texas Press, 1990.

Montfort, Ricardo Pérez, *"Por la Patria y Por la Raza": La Derecha Secular en el Sexenio de Lázaro Cárdenas.* Mexico City: Facultad de Filosofía y Letras, UNAM, 1993.

Stepan, Nancy, *'The Hour of Eugenics': Race, Gender, and Nation in Latin America.* Ithaca, New York: Cornell University Press, 1991.

—ALEXANDRA STERN

EZLN

See Zapatista Rebellion in Chiapas

F

FAMILY AND KINSHIP

This entry includes three articles that discuss household structures and kinship relations, family strategies and life course, and the relations among law, family, and the state:

Family and Kinship: Hapsburg Colonial Period
Family and Kinship: Bourbon Colonial Period and Nineteenth Century
Family and Kinship: Twentieth Century

See also Education; Gender; Women's Status and Occupation

FAMILY AND KINSHIP: HAPSBURG COLONIAL PERIOD

The family was the central feature of colonial Latin American society. It was in the family that the first implications of the new forms of colonial life were manifested. The study of the family gives tremendous insights into every aspect of colonial life. In general one can approach the family from three different perspectives. First are internal considerations: relationships between family members, family strategies, and the life course of individuals in the family. Second are forces from the society at large, which have repercussions on the family: household structure, kinship, and the family as part of a larger social network. Last are the state-imposed normative requirements on the family through law and custom; these norms in turn influenced the internal and external forces on the family.

The essence of the family traditionally has been the couple and their offspring. In both native society and Spanish society, the nuclear family also was merely the starting point for the broader institution of the family, which included the extended family of parents, siblings, offspring, and affines (relatives by marriage). The household and the family largely were considered to begin at the common point of the nuclear family. Both societies then expanded the definition of the household to include nonrelated individuals living with the nuclear family.

Several important early colonial documents give us insights into the nature of the family in the late pre-Columbian period, and as such offer suggestions about changes that occurred in native families with the Conquest. The two most important of these are the *Florentine Codex* and the *Codex Mendoza*. The latter provides fairly detailed information about the life cycle, with observations on moral issues and the rearing of children. The former provides many insights into the pre-Columbian family structures among the Nahua. Nevertheless, for the colonial period we must rely on more tangential sources of evidence. These include census data, wills and testaments, religious tracts, sermons and confessionaries, and various types of lawsuits.

One of the most important changes brought by the Conquest was the imposition of Christianity on the native peoples of Mexico. Christianity brought with it European models, out of the Judeo-Christian tradition, of the family, which were often in conflict with the native traditions. Perhaps in no other realm than marriage choice did the two cultures collide with such force. Christianity had adopted monogamy as the sole and unique acceptable matrimonial form. The native peoples of Mexico recognized several other models, with polygamy being the one most often singled out for attack by the missionaries.

A census of villages in what is today the state of Morelos made in the 1540s shows how ineffective the missionaries had been in imposing the new family order on the natives. Even some two decades after the Conquest, Christian marriage was a relatively rare event in some communities. In others as many as half of the marriages had church sanction. Concubinage and polygyny were still evident as well, especially among households headed by men of power and wealth. Although Christian monogamy was extolled as the norm for the natives, it never seems to have been fully implemented. Throughout the colonial period, preachers inveighed against concubinage. Likewise there are indications that some men openly maintained multiple spouses in spite of church opposition.

While the nuclear family was undoubtedly the core feature of Nahua society following the Conquest, the household was the functional core institution. Each nuclear family, or adult married couple, occupied a single house, but these house structures frequently were built around a common courtyard to form a compound. The residents of this compound were considered the household insofar as they shared many important duties with one another, including food preparation and consumption. The household normally consisted of a nuclear family along with various consanguineous (descended from the same ancestor) and affinal kin. A household consisting exclusively of a nuclear family was not the most common household in those that have been studied. Most common were what are called "joint families." In the joint family more than one nuclear family, with various dependents, share a household compound. Of the joint families, the most common type was for brothers with their wives, children, and dependents to share the household. Families and households among the Nahua remained dynamic and flexible in order to adapt better to rapidly changing circumstances. Even the extreme mortality rates that nearly destroyed native communities were unable to rupture the traditional family units. In fact the Nahua were relatively slow in adopting Spanish terminology for family members, preferring to continue to use the indigenous system and terms well into the late seventeenth century.

The point at which the Spanish and native family systems intersected was in the realm of mixed marriages. These marriages more often were conditioned by colonial demonstrations of power than by equality in family roles. The overwhelming majority of such unions were between Spanish men and native women. The family system brought to bear was uniformly that of the Spanish. Even the presence of offspring, in the form of individuals of mixed ethnic heritage, called mestizos, did not bridge the gap existent in colonial power relationships, but in fact often raised them in high relief. Children of irregular or casual unions normally were raised in the family of the mother and took on her ethnic identity. Children of recognized unions, especially where there was a formal recognition of the colonial power relationship between husband and wife, would be raised in the Spanish household and reflect that ethnic identity. Thus in the early decades following the Conquest, the mestizo population did not threaten the existing dichotomous social order, since the mestizos tended to identify with one or the other of the two ethnic groups. It was only in the late sixteenth and early seventeenth century, when there was a critical mass of mestizos who identified with neither group, that a truly new ethnic entity came into existence.

The acceptance of racially mixed marriages, and the fact of racially mixed children, ran counter to the nominal Spanish policy of dividing society into racially distinct castes. As the racial mixing continued through the colonial period, it was necessary to recognize each mixture officially and to define it legally. By the end of the seventeenth century the system of castes began to break down because of its complexity and owing to the fact that the racial differentiation became a mostly subjective exercise. Evidence has shown a great discrepancy in the racial categorizations made by various colonial officials depending on the ultimate purpose for the information. The same individual would be categorized in one way for a baptismal record and in another for a census.

There was a tendency for the native nobility to marry into Spanish society. While there was a general social stigma attached to Spaniards who married natives, if the native were a member of the elite that stigma was lessened. Such marriages carried with them the economic potential of control over the lands of the ancestral native lords. As a result of these advantageous intermarriages, many of the native lords by the beginning of the seventeenth century were in fact mestizos.

The Spanish family can be seen as consisting of three different groups. The nuclear family constituted the irreducible minimum. Beyond that was the larger household, which, like the native society, contained both consanguineous and affinal kin. In addition there were individuals who did not reside with the family but who were related by ceremonial ties. Principal among these are the baptismal sponsors of children, known as godparents, and sponsors at other religious acts such as confirmation and marriage. The godparents were considered to be legal kin of the family. The biological parents of the child were linked by ceremonial and customary ties to the godparents, each respecting the others as a co-parent or *compadre*. With the passage of time, and the greater incorporation of the native peoples in Christian ritual, *compadrazgo* also took on an important role in native families. Often economic and social considerations went into the selection of godparents. It was not uncommon for humble Spaniards to choose members of the elite to serve as godparents. This assured that the child would have a powerful patron when he or she grew to maturity. Likewise the child's parents then had ties of *compadrazgo* with an influential individual who potentially could benefit them.

There was a wide range of members of an extended household. Among the Spanish elite this might include native servants, slaves, Spanish retainers, and many others. When families immigrated to the Americas, they frequently brought their servants from Spain. Likewise, when establishing households in New Spain they would look to people from their home village or region for their first social ties. In this manner entire villages frequently were reproduced in New Spain. Slaves and Indian servants also were important household members. Many members of the criollo (American-born Spaniard) elite learned native languages at the breast of their wet nurses. Slaves were ubiquitous in Spanish and criollo households.

More humble Spanish residents also maintained complex households in which both affinal and consanguineous kin resided. Mixed family households were also not uncommon; in such a household, two or more families might inhabit the same general residence, mutually supporting one another. A large number of single men in the early colonial period also meant that uniquely male households existed alongside family and complex family households. Even in later periods this would be true of frontier regions and mining districts.

Affinal kin were no less important in the scheme of family and kinship. The role of the church in the family was important. Among the Spanish, residence was patrilocal, with a newly married couple often residing in the house of the groom's family. During the early colonial period it was the church, and not the state, that regulated marriage. Marriage is one of seven sacraments of the Catholic Church. As a sacrament it is believed to have validity only when the parties enter into it through the exercise of free will. A marriage could be declared null if either partner were coerced into it. Consequently, marriage choice was one way in which children could take an active role in determining their own future. The state assisted the church in enforcing decisions over marriage choice. The act of marriage created important ties between the two families. Parents might seek alliances with other families for economic or political reasons. This choice might be at odds with the choice of the young person. In cases of outright conflict, the church normally sided with the young person, although by the early eighteenth century this had changed, and the church began to reflect cultural values rather than theological principles.

Marriage was the linking of two different families. The economic importance of this was recognized in the giving of gifts. At the time of marriage, the father of the bride normally gave money or real property to the groom, a dowry or *dote,* ostensibly to protect the economic position of the bride. Although the dowry was administered by the husband, it was legally the property of the woman. Any decision to sell or alienate the property was subject to the approval of the woman. Likewise, at the time of marriage the groom would often give a gift (*arras*) to the bride. Like the dowry, the *arras* remained the possession of the woman. The basic principle with regard to the administration of these funds was that they would not be lost or diminished, but conserved. The wife also might control her own personal property, especially goods brought into the household at the time of the marriage, aside from those explicitly part of the dowry. Beyond this she also had a claim to wealth generated by her husband during the course of the marriage. This normally would be divided equally between the spouse and any other heirs, such as children.

Inheritance laws played an important role in the colonial Mexican family. Contrary to what one might believe, colonial Hispanic inheritance laws were remarkably egalitarian. Codified in the early sixteenth century, the Laws of Toro governed inheritance. Simply put, children shared equally in the estates of their parents. Parents could designate up to approximately 40 percent of their estate, called an "improved share," to a single heir, often going to the eldest son. Nevertheless, in general, equal distribution was the rule. The rules concerning inheritance placed a tremendous obstacle to the transmittal of concentrated wealth from generation to generation, since the rules tended to break up large estates.

The colonial inheritance system did provide for the creation of entailed estates (*mayorazgos*) formed from the "improved share" of one heir. To create an entailed estate it was necessary also to receive royal permission and pay annual taxes, but once created the estate could not be sold, mortgaged, fragmented, or alienated in any way. The *may-*

orazgo had to pass wholly from generation to generation. It was an effective means of transmitting wealth but exceptionally cumbersome. In times of economic downturn it was extremely difficult to turn the estate into cash. Clearly it was only reasonable to entail large estates in this manner, since the costs involved made the practice unreasonable for smaller holdings.

In order to secure some of the advantages of the entailed estate without so many of the difficulties, many colonial families used chantries (*capellanías*) in a similar fashion. The chantry was an ecclesiastical endowment normally invested in a lien on a piece of real property. The interest paid for the services of a priest, usually to say masses for the benefit of the founder and his family. The lien often would be extended to another family member, while yet another family member was the titular beneficiary, a priest who enjoyed the fruits and performed the masses. The chantry could be used as the basis upon which the priest would be ordained. The operation of the chantry was subject to the scrutiny of the church but otherwise could be administered to maximize benefits for an extended family. Like the *mayorazgo,* the *capellanía* was inalienable, but it usually consisted of a smaller capital investment.

Another means whereby families attempted to avoid the destructive effects of inheritance laws was to practice careful career planning of their children. By limiting the number of children who eventually married, a family could concentrate wealth by jumping a generation. If, for example, of several children, only two married and had offspring, the portion of the parents' estates that would have gone to the others could be inherited by the offspring or the siblings who married, upon the death of the siblings who did not. Part of the inheritance might go the church in the form of dowries for daughters who became nuns, part might go to religious orders to support the male members of the family who became friars, but normally enough would remain to be inherited by the second and third generations to allow for some reconcentration of wealth.

Families were linked in marriage. Wealth could be concentrated in the hands of a few through the judicious use of marriage. Brothers from one family might marry sisters from another, thereby increasing the possibility that the wealth of two families might be held in the second generation by only two households. The Spanish elite also were concerned with nobility. Marriage alliances for the sake of acquiring nobility were not uncommon. Wealthy merchant families frequently married into the ranks of the older landed elite. The landed elite, often with ties to the conquistadors and early settlers, would enhance the nobility of the merchants, while the merchants might improve the wealth of the elite family.

The colonial Mexican *encomienda* was an important institution that determined early marriage and kinship relationships. *Encomiendas* were native settlements "commended" in trust to a Spaniard—the *encomendero*—who, in exchange for receiving the Indians' labor, had the duty of protecting the Indians, maintaining missionaries in the villages, and contributing to the military defense of the areas. Initially one could pass an *encomienda* to an heir. As the Spanish Crown tightened control over the institution, inheritance became limited to three "lives." Yet the definition of "life" included the lives of both the husband and wife. In several instances elderly *encomenderos* married young women to extend the "life" of the *encomienda*. The spouse, upon the eventual death of the older partner, could then remarry, and the *encomienda* would still be considered in the first life. For example, the *encomienda* granted to "la Malinche," doña Marina, passed to her husband, Juan Jaramillo, upon her death. He remarried and the grant then was enjoyed by him and his second wife, doña Beatriz de Andrade. When Jaramillo died the grant was split between Jaramillo's and doña Marina's children and doña Beatriz de Andrade. In this manner a grant that dated from the Conquest continued on until the close of the sixteenth century still in its first "life."

Certain colonial public offices, such as notary public and town councilman, were subject to public sale. By the end of the sixteenth century these offices also were sold with the right to pass the office to one heir, upon the payment of one-third the current value. Subsequent inheritance was not allowed, and upon the death of the heir the office would be resold at public auction. Nevertheless, this became an important means of ensuring family wealth and social status.

The familial naming system used in the colonial period differed from the patterns observed in Mexico today. Parents exercised a much freer reign in the naming of their children. A child might receive the mother's surname rather than the father's or might use a surname of a valued uncle or other affinal relative. Often, in order to inherit a *mayorazgo* or benefit from a chantry, the recipient would need to take the surname of the founder. Consequently, tracing families over time is complicated by the lack of stability in the use of surnames. For example, one of the legitimate sons of the famous conquistador of Mexico, Bernal Díaz del Castillo, was named Bartolomé Becerra.

Among the colonial elite one can see two basic marriage practices. The group tended to marry from within its own ranks. Because of the relatively limited number of suitable spouses, the children of the conquistadors tended to marry children of conquistadors. This developed a rather easily identifiable colonial elite group. Yet new arrivals from Spain provided a secondary source of spouses, especially government officials, merchants, and others with established wealth or social standing. Nearly all of the titled nobles who emerged in Mexico in the seventeenth century could trace their lineage to both the group of conquistadors and early settlers and to more recent immigrants, especially government officials.

Marriage choice for criollos and Spaniards outside of the elite did not differ dramatically. Marriage partners usually came from roughly the same social group. Most marriages used some form of broker, an individual to introduce the two partners. Clearly the likelihood of someone meeting a suitable partner from one's own social group was far more likely than meeting one from a distinct group. While the choice of a marriage partner was reserved to the individual contracting marriage, family and friends could, and did, play an important role. Marriage for love was not an alien concept in early colonial New Spain. Both the Catholic Church and the state accepted the right of the individual to choose a marriage partner, in spite of interference from family members and others.

The elite tended to get married at a slightly older age than did natives or Africans in the society. Research suggests that Spanish women as a whole married at about 25, with criollos marrying slightly younger, nearer to 21. While data are very sketchy on native marriages, the average seems to be much younger, perhaps 16.

The institution of marriage was regulated by both canon and civil law. Yet, most cases dealing with irregularities were heard in either the church courts or by the Holy Office of the Inquisition. In general, church courts dealt with cases of concubinage, incest, and adultery. On the other hand, the Inquisition heard cases of bigamy and clerical solicitation. Concubinage and adultery were similar offenses. Concubinage consisted of unmarried people engaging in sexual relations, or of a married man having sexual relations with an unmarried woman. Two unmarried persons engaging in sexual relations were expected to be married, and could be considered married under most circumstances, if neither had a preexisting obligation to marry another. A woman who engaged in premarital sex was placed in a difficult situation if the male partner did not eventually marry her, since others would not be inclined to do so. According to the norms of the time, adultery was defined only as a married woman engaging in extramarital sexual relations. Adultery was seen as an affront to the woman's husband, and a potential attack on his personal property, since the adulterous union might produce a child who would inherit from the legal, but not biological, father. Incest consisted of sexual relations between those related by blood or marriage within the fourth degree. Consequently, it was illegal for a man to engage in sexual relations either with his sister, or sister-in-law, or blood relatives as near as second cousins, for example. While all of these offenses were serious, each was dealt with by local clerical judges and resulted in minor ecclesiastical and civil punishments. Far more serious offenses were those of bigamy and solicitation. In each instance the guilty party consciously had ruptured the permanence of a holy vow, a vow of marriage or of clerical celibacy. As such these offenses were subject to the scrutiny of the Inquisition. Punishments were far more severe, including long incarceration prior to trial, exile, corporal punishment, heavy fines, and banishment.

The family in colonial New Spain was a complex and multivaried institution. It included blood kin, kin by marriage, kin established during church rituals, and persons affiliated with the household as slaves, servants, retainers, or hangers-on. Native households were equally complex, encompassing the biological family, family networks, and others associated with the household. Natives had an influence on Spanish households, owing to their presence in them as servants. The colonial elite frequently were bilingual and commonly used words from the native tongues in everyday speech. Their foods were prepared by native cooks, using local foodstuffs. Their cloth was woven by native artisans. The native contribution was ubiquitous. The native households frequently were forced to comply with Spanish notions of household and family. In short, while the exchange was far from being an equal one, exchange there was.

Select Bibliography

Boyer, Richard, *The Lives of the Bigamists: Marriage, Family and Community in Colonial Mexico.* Albuquerque: University of New Mexico Press, 1995.

Cline, S. L., editor and translator, *The Book of Tributes: Early Sixteenth Century Nahuatl Censuses from Morelos.* Los Angeles: UCLA Latin American Center, 1993.

Gibson, Charles, *Aztecs under Spanish Rule.* Stanford, California: Stanford University Press, 1964.

Gonzalbo Aizpuru, Pilar, *Las mujeres en la Nueva España.* Mexico: Colegio de México, 1987.

_____, editor, *Familias novohispanas: Siglos XVI al XIX.* Mexico City: Colegio de México, 1991.

Lavrin, Asunción, editor, *Sexuality and Marriage in Colonial Latin America.* Lincoln: University of Nebraska Press, 1989.

Lockhart, James. *The Nahuas after the Conquest.* Stanford, California: Stanford University Press, 1992.

Seed, Patricia. *To Love, Honor, and Obey in Colonial Mexico.* Stanford, California: Stanford University Press, 1988).

—JOHN F. SCHWALLER

FAMILY AND KINSHIP: BOURBON COLONIAL PERIOD AND NINETEENTH CENTURY

From the middle of the eighteenth century until the 1870s, Mexico experienced significant political and economic upheaval resulting in its independence from Spain and in its emergence as a republic. Even as the nation adopted republicanism and tried to move toward the ideal of social equality, the authoritarian ideology rooted in a strong patriarchal family tradition prevailed and worked as a powerful force in shaping the politics and culture of the nation. Despite the persistence of patriarchalism, however, by the 1870s and 1880s the family as a basic social and political unit was being transformed by changing economic conditions and by educational and legal reforms that slowly eroded traditional relations of authority within the family and, in turn, in society.

The eighteenth-century administrative and economic reforms of the Spanish empire, known collectively as the Bourbon reforms, attempted to make Spain's American colonies more economically efficient and productive in a world experiencing rapid demographic growth and accelerated economic and diplomatic activity. Indeed, reforms stimulated changes and kindled crises throughout the colonies, for Spain sought to improve the imperial economy by imposing greater control over all aspects of social, political, and economic life. In New Spain, the Crown's efforts in this regard can be seen in new laws, taxes, monopolies, bureaucratic organization, military conscription, and in the expulsion of the Jesuits. Some of these reforms precipitated swift and violent reaction throughout the colony in the 1760s and ultimately contributed to the political ferment that resulted in Mexico's independence in 1821.

The global demographic and economic processes that propelled the eighteenth-century state to seek greater economic productivity impacted the family because the state aggressively promoted the secularization and reorganization of society through reforms in education and health and in family and property law. After Independence in 1821, reforms in these areas accelerated, and, in concert with economic and demographic change, they affected families in all social and ethnic groups, both positively and negatively.

Family Law and the State

The *patria potestad,* or power of the father, served as a fundamental concept in Spanish family law and practice. Although not in complete agreement about the reach of the *patria potestad* (particularly over marriage of children), secular and ecclesiastical authorities generally recognized and protected paternal prerogatives. Most of the diverse racial, ethnic, and social groups of Spain's American colonies accommodated it in one form or the other. The Catholic Church also insisted upon marital monogamy and the permanence of the marital bond. Legal insistence upon paternal authority, monogamy, and protected inheritance of children favored the predominance of the nuclear family of parents and children, but cultural traditions among all ethnic groups and economic conditions made other kinship ties also important. In New Spain, as Spanish authorities and Catholic fathers assumed control over Indian communities, resulting in their increasing Hispanicization by the eighteenth century, Indian families accepted the basic concept of paternal power, which was similar to their own beliefs in male superiority. The major change for Indian families was the Catholic Church's attempt to prohibit polygamy in Indian communities. This was not entirely successful, since many couples, Indian and non-Indian alike, resorted to a variety of informal relationships that undermined the church's insistence on monogamy and its restrictions against absolute divorce.

Beginning in the 1770s, changes in marriage, divorce, and property laws, and the abolition of slavery impacted the *patria potestad* in various ways; some legal changes strengthened it while other laws undermined it. Additionally, Catholic doctrine toward free will in marriage often had created tensions between parents and children over marriage choice and, over time, in concert with other developments probably helped to undermine the *patria potestad*. In fact, the Spanish monarch Carlos III, realizing that paternal authority had weakened to the point that both the authority of the state and the corporate social order were threatened, determined that the Crown's interests were best served by protecting parental power in conflicts over marriage choice and by reducing the Catholic Church's influence in these matters and thus its influence in society. To this end, the Spanish Crown promulgated the Royal Pragmatic on Marriage (Real Pragmática-Sanción de Matrimonios) on March 23, 1776.

Earlier Spanish canon and civil law codified in the Siete Partidas recognized both church and state interests in marriage, considering it both a sacrament and a contract. Church and state interests did not always coincide, however. Because church doctrine privileged marriage as a sacrament in which the main purpose was to bring a woman and man together to procreate and educate offspring, the church considered its responsibility was to maintain the viability, harmony, and permanence of this union. To maintain a marriage in harmony required that the couple enter into it of their own free will. The canon law of the Siete Partidas governed this aspect of marriage. The Council of Trent confirmed the church's support of free will in marriage and strengthened priests' role in protecting against forced marriage, but in prohibiting clandestine marriage, the council also gave leverage to parents.

For its part, the state tended to privilege the contractual role of marriage in order to preserve the social order and to protect and distribute property to support family members. This concept, also contained in the Siete Partidas and developed further in the Laws of Toro of 1505 and the Recopilación de Leyes de las Indias, was manifest in community property rights of spouses, in equal, partible inheritance rights of legitimate children, and in preserving the communal and collective landholding traditions of Indian communities. These rights could not be abrogated easily, because the family, in both its nucleated and extended form, was recognized as the basic institution of social welfare (even illegitimate children had the right to seek basic support from their families for food, clothing, and shelter, called *alimentos*). The potential contradiction between church and state interests arose when parents attempted to force children into undesirable marriages, in which case the church was obligated to protect the children.

The Royal Pragmatic, promulgated in New Spain in 1778, was intended to cement parents' control over their children's marriages to preserve the social order and protect property by preventing marriage between unequals: "the indecency of children entering into inequal marriages without the counsel or consent of their parents" *(el abuso de contraer matrimonios desiguales los hijos de familia, sin esperar el consejo y consentimiento paterno)*. All children under age 25 were required to have their father's permission to marry or, in his absence, that of their mother, grandparent, relative, guardian, or local judge, in that order; children over 25 also were supposed to seek consent. Parents could disinherit children who married in violation of this law, not easily done previously under Spanish law. The Royal Pragmatic provided some protection for children in that parents or relatives were not supposed to force children into marriages against their will. The ultimate decision in disputes was left to royal judges, not priests or ecclesiastical judges. In this respect the Crown undermined the prerogatives of ecclesiastical courts in handling conflicts over marriage choice: "the royal authority must conform exactly to canonical law" *(la potestad Real debe dispensar al mas exacto cumplimiento de las reglas canónicas)*. A decree that accompanied the Royal Pragmatic charged prelates and ecclesiastical judges to comply with the Pragmatic. Certainly the law intended to privilege the *patria potestad* in these acts, but ambiguities in the Pragmatic opened it up to interpretations that had the potential of undermining parental wishes.

Because the Pragmatic did not precisely define what constituted an unequal marriage *(matrimonio desigual)*, except that it concerned the status, quality, and condition of the two people involved, unequal was interpreted differently in different places within the Spanish empire, especially by the last decades of the eighteenth century, when the basis of social status was increasingly determined by economic condition and individual reputation rather than by condition of birth or association. Although the attempt to preserve the hegemony of white Europeanized elites threatened by a growing Indian and *casta* (mixed-race) population may have been part of the motive for promulgating this law in the colonies, clearly many local officials interpreted the law to mean that as long as a couple could support themselves and both parties were good, reputable people, then a marriage, even between people of different races, was acceptable, although parents or relatives may have strongly objected. Other limits to parental control over marriage were that many children were orphaned before they reached the age of marriage and that a majority of parents had little or no property with which to threaten disinheritance if their children disobeyed. Most parents and guardians, then, had to use other family and community pressures to force compliance on unruly offspring.

The broad and varied interpretations of the Pragmatic in the late-eighteenth- and early-nineteenth-century Mexico not only demonstrated the changing basis of social status but also the decreasing importance of honor as defined by family *limpieza de sangre,* which meant blood or racial purity (determined by the sexual purity of a family's women). By the nineteenth century, especially after Independence in Mexico when racial categories were dropped in all official records, honor and reputation were increasingly dependent upon individual virtue, based upon an individual's decent behavior that could be learned through education and earned through economically productive activity. It no longer depended only or necessarily on birth or association. Illegitimacy continued to be stigmatized, but legitimization (which could only be granted by governmental decree) was more easily obtained. As a result, by the late eighteenth century, people of illegitimate birth could seek positions in the government, church, and military that previously had been denied to them.

Following Independence in 1821, Mexico generally recognized Spanish family law and the concept of *patria potestad* with the 1804 modifications that extended some of the rights of the *patria potestad* to widowed mothers and grandmothers, a recognition of the significant percentage of families with children headed by women. As motherhood became more important in the nineteenth century, married women increasingly were permitted some of the prerogatives of the *patria potestad* over their own children. Also, adult children, especially adult single daughters, were emancipated from parental authority. All of these changes slowly eroded the legal power of fathers and parents over children, but changes in the law often followed social practices that already had changed.

For several decades after Independence, the new Mexican state continued to recognize church control over birth, marriage, death, and ecclesiastical divorce (divorce that only separated the parties and eliminated the marriage obligation but that did not allow remarriage). Until the 1850s, Mexican law also recognized community property, equal, partible inheritance, and communal rights of Indian communities.

The civil conflicts of the 1850s and 1860s had a more profound impact on family law than did Independence. The Reform Laws, the culmination of the process of economic liberalization and secularization of social policy, were passed as a result of these conflicts. Their purpose was to limit church and corporate control over family and community life in order to give impetus to economic renewal by making more property available to individuals and by encouraging the free movement of wealth and capital.

The Ley Lerdo (1856) required towns, church institutions, and other corporate bodies to sell real property holdings not needed to carry out their missions and required Indian communities to sell communal holdings. It also suppressed entailed property. Supposedly meant to increase production by providing more families and individuals with land, over time privatization of landholdings actually facilitated the concentration of land in fewer hands, forcing many families and individuals to become dependent peons or wage laborers on haciendas and in cities. Indian communities were especially hard hit as some of them lost former communal property to non-Indians.

In 1857 state governments were charged with taking control of records of births, marriages, and deaths, and of local cemeteries, breaking the church's monopoly control over these basic family concerns. The Law of Civil Matrimony of July 1859 shifted control over divorce from the church to the state and codified the process of liberalization of divorce under way since the 1820s, especially in regard to simplifying the procedure for seeking divorce. This law did not, however, allow a marriage to be completely dissolved; thus, the parties were not allowed to remarry as long as they both lived. Whereas the 1859 marriage law recognized the equal right of either party to seek divorce if the other committed adultery, the 1870 Civil Code allowed women to seek divorce on this ground only if the husband's adultery was committed in the conjugal home, he had a concubine, his adultery caused public scandal, or his lover abused or insulted the wife. Civil law then legitimized and thus strengthened the sexual double standard that had persisted in the form of cultural practice. (Also, within a few years the national government issued instructions for regulating prostitution, thus legitimating that practice and perpetuating sexual inequalities by race, class, and gender.) The 1870 code did allow a couple to seek divorce by mutual consent, thus codifying another liberalization of divorce. Finally, in 1917, during the Mexican Revolution, Mexican women won the right to absolute divorce and remarriage. Until then, men and women both found ways around the strictures of divorce by cohabitation, concubinage, or by remarrying in another place.

Changes in the divorce laws also brought some changes in the custody of children, for although the rights of fathers and the obedience of wives to husbands remained paramount, the 1870 Civil Code expanded women's authority over their children. But decades before in divorce cases, and probably in cases of informal separation, women often retained custody of children, and for the same reasons that women sought divorce more than men: because of abandonment or abuse. By the middle of the nineteenth century, it is clear that alcohol often was involved in cases of abuse, which spurred organization and publications by women against drinking. Mexican women, like women elsewhere in North America and Europe, used problems of drinking and its relation to family abuse to liberalize divorce laws. It seems that profligate males among the rising middle class precipitated women's temperance activities, for it was from the middle class that the increasingly literate and activist women who organized against alcohol came.

Family property laws departed significantly from previous legal tradition in the 1870 and 1884 Civil Codes by lifting spousal and parental restrictions on designation of their property through community property and equal, partible inheritance (including the suppression of dowries for daughters). After 1870, upon marriage a couple could choose to participate in community property or to maintain their property separately. The 1884 Civil Code ended guaranteed inheritance to children. These changes, made with a clear economic motive of allowing individual choice in the use of one's property in order to encourage free movement of wealth, varied in their impact on individuals and on parental authority. On the one hand, the changes eliminated the legal economic safety-net that community property and dowries provided for married women and that equal, partible inheritance had given to both daughters and sons, just as the earlier Ley Lerdo had diminished the economic safety-net of Indian communities. On the other hand, the laws undermined the authority of husbands by assuring women control over their separate property and income without their husbands' interference, and potentially that of parents over children if children knew that they would not inherit. In most cases, the practice of giving daughters part of their inheritance at marriage through the dowry already had declined. Children, especially sons, could seek independence from parents by taking advantage of expanding educational and economic opportunities that developed in the nineteenth century. Women, however, especially those from propertied families, were left the most vulnerable by changes in inheritance laws. Parents had the option of channeling most of a family's wealth to the potentially most productive members: their male offspring. Unlike sons, daughters had fewer opportunities for education, jobs, and investment, and thus fewer opportunities for seeking economic independence from parents or family. The changes in family property law potentially undermined a fundamental function of the Mexican family: that families had the responsibility of providing for all family members throughout their lives.

Family Strategies and Kinship Relations

Family law provided a framework for family relations in eighteenth- and nineteenth-century Mexico but did not necessarily determine the behavior and experience of individual families or their members. Furthermore, some changes in family law were responses to transformations in society that already had taken place. Families responded to the upheaval in politics and the economy of this period by continuing to rely on consanguineous (blood relative) and affinal (marriage) kinship relations, on surrogate kin, and on ties of patronage, as part of the diverse strategies families relied upon to help them survive difficult times or to take advantage of opportunities as they presented themselves.

Family strategies and the obstacles families faced as they approached and moved through the nineteenth century can be discerned by following the life courses of family members through the family cycle of birth, upbringing, marriage, and death. Family strategies often depended on having offspring to perpetuate the family as a lineage and kin groups, help support family members, preserve or enhance social status and wealth, and carry cultural values and tradition to succeeding generations.

Within a year of marriage, a Mexican couple generally had their first child. Fertility was high and depended on the age at marriage. Indian couples tended to marry for the first time very young, at around 16 for women and 18 for men, and they had during the women's childbearing years seven or eight children, on the average. Those of mixed race and whites married somewhat later and had about five to seven children. Most mothers nursed their own children for about a year, making the interval between births about two years. Military officers and bureaucrats—who tended to be mostly white until the mid–nineteenth century, when the composition of both occupations became more diverse—married much later. By the beginning of the nineteenth century, the age discrepancy between spouses was decreasing substantially, probably leading, at least among some groups, to more companionate marriages. Also, among all groups the age at first marriage rose slightly during the nineteenth century. Infant and child mortality, however, was very high, and thus only about two to four children survived to have children of their own. Child mortality declined some in the nineteenth century because of the implementation of public health measures such as the use of smallpox vaccine and improvements in hygiene in some of Mexico's cities. A decrease in child mortality may have been one factor in the increase in Mexico's population in the nineteenth century.

Children, or *hijos de familia,* were under their father's or their family's authority from infancy to young adulthood, and they relied on parents and family for upbringing, security, sustenance, and affection. Children owed parents respect and obedience, and testimony from a variety of documents indicates that most social and ethnic groups valued this respect for parents. In return parents cared for and taught their children the skills needed to survive as adults, and children often followed in their parents' footsteps, the boys doing what their father did and girls generally taking on the domestic role of their mothers. By their midteens, most youths were shouldering adult responsibilities, even though they did not yet have adult rights. Until public education became widely available, it was parents, then, who were the most important educational agents in the lives of children. Kin, neighbors, and even strangers sometimes stepped in when parents were absent and intervened when they were remiss, but the alternatives did not always fulfill a child's need for sustenance and guidance. The loss of parents often compromised a child's well-being and disrupted the socialization process that was important to the child's future livelihood. Parents also bore the major responsibility for their offspring by tradition and law. Other family members were not always available, and the lack of a developed system of social services left children to depend on parents. Even parents were not always dependable; thus, many needs of the minor population went unanswered. Families were not always supportive institutions. Children suffered abuse, abandonment, incest, rape, and harsh punishments.

Nevertheless, Mexican parents, family, and society in general valued children, although some suffered abuse or exploitation. Mexican parents credit the Virgin of Guadalupe with caring for their dead children on their journey to heaven and nursing them upon arrival there. Furthermore, the legal tradition that Mexico inherited from Spain in both secular and canon law, although in disagreement on specific points, reflected an ideology that valued children and sought to protect them. Neither parents nor others charged with carrying for children were supposed to use harsh punishments.

Because the period from the mid–eighteenth to mid–nineteenth centuries in Mexico, as in the rest of the Americas and Europe, was a period of reform, crisis, and change, children increasingly received attention as the means to change society. In particular, the productivity and well-being of society was seen as a product of the health, well-being, and education of its children. In Mexico, much of the literature of this period promoted improving the education, in the larger sense of upbringing, of children. Mexico's most noted author of the early nineteenth century, José Joaquín Fernández de Lizardi, wrote often about the upbringing of children. Two of his best-known novels, *El Periquillo Sarniento* (1816) and *La Quijotita y su prima* (1818), were meant to show parents the right and wrong way to raise children and the consequences of bad upbringing. Mexican newspapers addressed similar issues, and some didactic periodicals directed toward children and youth appeared as well. Journalist Juan Sánchez de la Barquera advocated that mothers nurse their own children and that women have access to education in order to instill morality into their children in his newspaper *Diario de México*. Barquera also founded the first Mexican periodical for children in 1813, *El Correo de los Niños*. A publication advocating better education for Mexican women written by a young Mexican woman was *Cartas sobre la education del bello sexo* (1824). All of these publications wanted Mexican society to enjoy the progress that could be attained through proper education and upbringing of children.

As a result of this attitude toward children, public policies gave more attention and resources to social, educational, and health services for children, especially school-age children and youths. The purpose, of course, was to organize a more obedient and skilled workforce for a more economically productive society, but improving human potential of society was seen as the means to this end. As a consequence, after Independence, states began to organize public school systems to provide schooling, mostly at the primary level, for both boys and girls. They also established programs to train teachers, for as numbers of schools increased substantially in the nineteenth century, the demand for teachers, both male and female, also increased, contributing to greater opportunities for both men and women. Public schooling reduced dependence on parents for training. Public policy toward children, however, was more effective in urban areas.

Household size and structure in Mexico during this period varied considerably. Elite families, who had the greater access to political and economic resources, tended to have larger households because they could afford more servants and their children tended to live longer. But at any one point in time, the majority of households (50 to 80 percent) of most social and ethnic groups had only about four to six people, and the related family in the household was usually parents, or a parent, and children. If we look at households over time, however, we see constant movement in and out of them as family and kin were born, died, or moved, as others married into the family, were adopted, or were taken in as wards, borders, clerks, apprentices, or servants.

The most common household arrangements involving extended family were those in which a parent lived with a married child or a young unmarried child lived with an older married sibling. In both cases, we see the effect of demographic factors. The parent had been widowed and the child orphaned. In fact, few teenaged children had a grandparent living in the same household with them. Unmarried adult women also tended to live in households with other kin. These included both widowed women and single adult women who had not married. Census records and wills at several points in time throughout this period indicate that as much as 30 to 40 percent of the adult female population was widowed. Widows, especially widows with children, were much less likely to remarry than widowers, and they were also more vulnerable to become impoverished because of more limited economic opportunities for women; thus, these women were forced to live with or depend on relatives more often than men.

Some working families engaged in occupations that required the cooperation and cohabitation of an extended family. The families of the mostly mulatto and mestizo muleteers, for example, lived in extended family compounds that included parents, married children, and unmarried children. The father, the older sons, and often the sons-in-law drove the mule trains and thus were often away from home. Meanwhile, the women and young children kept the home and cared for the extra animals that the family used in its business.

In fact, with the large-scale disruptions from 1760 to 1870 caused by riots, famine, epidemics, war, and economic stagnation that brought death and impoverishment to families, many individuals and families were often on the move trying to escape these problems or looking for a better way to make a living. Frequent migration helps explain why some communities had at least 20 to 30 percent of households headed by women. While women remained to care for the home and children by taking in laundry, sewing, or cooking, by renting rooms to boarders, or by selling food or other items as peddlers or in the markets, men migrated to other areas to find work. Family members, as part of a family's strategy, often worked in a variety of occupations that often required some of the members, usually the adult males and sometimes the young single females, to migrate from place to place. As the United States took control of the northern part of Mexico after 1848 and as Mexico's own population grew during the nineteenth century, migration continued not only within Mexico but also across the border, but the family strategy involved was essentially the same. An important consequence was, and is, that in communities that relied on male migration for income, the women developed a keen sense of autonomy and self-reliance. In some communities, too, legal traditions and family strategies that became cultural practice allowed women significant control over a family's real property. We find nineteenth-century women acquiring real estate specifically for their daughters as a hedge against debt. Other women leased family real property to provide themselves with income.

Families relied on kin beyond the household. Certainly the precarious economic condition of many families that existed from the middle of the eighteenth century made kinship ties important for survival of many members of society, especially women and children. Consanguineous and affinal ties helped families secure and protect social status, jobs, and resources. Bureaucratic, merchant, landowning, and mining families developed extensive family networks for this purpose. Godparentage and co-parentage also cemented or extended ties of kinship. Reliance on kin continued to be an integral part of strategies that Mexican families devised as the country accelerated industrialization and urbanization during the last decades of the nineteenth century.

Select Bibliography

Anderson, Rodney, *Guadalajara a la consumación de la Independencia: Estudio de su población según los padrones de 1821–1822,* translated by Marco Antonio Silva. Guadalajara: Gobierno de Jalisco Secretaría General Unidad, 1983.

Arnold, Linda, *Bureaucracy and Bureaucrats in Mexico City, 1742–1835.* Tucson: University of Arizona Press, 1988.

Arrom, Silvia M., *The Women of Mexico City, 1790–1857.* Stanford, California: Stanford University Press, 1985.

_____, "Changes in Mexico Family Law in the Nineteenth Century." In *Confronting Change, Challenging Tradition: Women in Latin American History,* edited by Gertrude M. Yeager. Wilmington, Delaware: Scholarly Resources, 1994.

Balmori, Diana, Stuart F. Voss, and Miles Wortman, *Notable Family Networks in Latin America.* Chicago: University of Chicago Press, 1984.

Bazant, Jan, *Cinco haciendas mexicanas: Tres siglos de vida rural en San Luis Potosi, 1600–1910.* Mexico City: El Colegio de México, 1975.

Brading, David, *Miners and Merchants in Bourbon Mexico, 1763–1810.* Cambridge: Cambridge University Press, 1971.

_____, *Haciendas and Ranchos in the Mexican Bajío: León, 1700–1860.* Cambridge: Cambridge University Press, 1978.

Calderon de la Barca, Fanny, *Life in Mexico.* Berkeley: University of California Press, 1982.

Carroll, Patrick J., *Blacks in Colonial Veracruz: Race, Ethnicity, and Regional Development.* Austin: University of Texas Press, 1991.

Chance, John K., and William B. Taylor, "Estate and Class in a Colonial City: Oaxaca in 1792." *Comparatives Studies in Society and History* 19 (1977).

Deans-Smith, Susan, *Bureaucrats, Planters, and Workers: The Making of the Tobacco Monopoly in Bourbon Mexico.* Austin: University of Texas Press, 1992.

Gonzalbo Aizpuru, Pilar, *Las mujeres en la Nueva Espana: Educacion y vida cotidiana.* Mexico City: El Colegio de México, 1987.

_____, editor, *Familias novohispanas: Siglos XVI al XIX.* Mexico City: El Colegio de México, 1991.

Gutiérrez, Ramon, *When Jesus Came, the Corn Mothers Went Away: Marriage, Sexuality, and Power in New Mexico, 1500–1846.* Stanford, California: Stanford University Press, 1991.

Harris, Charles H., III, *A Mexican Family Empire: The Latifundio of the Sánchez Navarros, 1765–1867.* Austin: University of Texas Press, 1975.

Kicza, John E., *Colonial Entrepreneurs: Families and Business in Bourbon Mexico City.* Albuquerque: University of New Mexico Press, 1984.

Ladd, Doris M., *The Mexican Nobility at Independence, 1780–1826.* Austin: University of Texas Press, 1976.

Lavrin, Asunción, editor, *Latin American Women: Historical Perspectives.* Westport, Connecticut: Greenwood Press, 1978.

_____, editor, *Sexuality and Marriage in Colonial Latin America.* Lincoln: University of Nebraska Press, 1989.

Lomnitz, Larissa Adler, and Marisol Perez-Lizaur, *A Mexican Elite Family, 1820–1980: Kinship, Class, and Culture,* translated by Cinna Lomnitz. Princeton, New Jersey: Princeton University Press, 1987.

Seed, Patricia, *To Love, Honor and Obey in Colonial Mexico: Conflicts over Marriage Choice, 1574–1821.* Stanford, California: Stanford University Press, 1988.

Smith, Raymond, editor, *Kinship Ideology and Practice in Latin America.* Chapel Hill: University of North Carolina Press, 1984.

Thompson, Angela T., "To Save the Children: Inoculation, Vaccination, and Public Health in Guanajuato, Mexico." *The Americas* 49:4 (April 1993).

_____, "Children and Schooling in Guanajuato, Mexico, 1790–1840." In *Molding the Hearts and Minds: Education, Communications, and Social Change in Latin America,* edited by John A. Britton. Wilmington, Delaware: SR Books, 1994.

Yeager, Gertrude M., editor, *Confronting Change, Challenging Tradition: Women in Latin American History.* Wilmington, Delaware: SR Books, 1994.

—ANGELA T. THOMPSON

FAMILY AND KINSHIP: TWENTIETH CENTURY

During the twentieth century, changes in Mexico's society and economy and their complex interrelationship with demographic change exerted a profound influence on Mexican family life. The accelerated process of urbanization and industrialization, as well as advances in health and education throughout the twentieth century, contributed to the transformation of the family environment. Among the more notable changes affecting family life were changes in the structure of production, which led to the gradual loss in importance of family kinship as the basis of production; the waning of patriarchal power structures and the increasing economic independence of individual members of the family group; and finally, the disappearance of the ideologies and practices that reduced the exercise of human sexuality to the task of reproduction.

The beginning of the twentieth century was characterized by high and fluctuating levels of mortality. Life expectancy averaged 30 years in 1920, increasing to 70 years in 1990. The consequences of this drop in the mortality rate were numerous and tended to have repercussions in different areas of family life. These included the increase in the duration of a marriage before termination by the death of a spouse; the postponement of the experience of widowhood; the proportional reduction in the number of minors having to deal with the death of one or both parents, which has meant a drastic decline in the numbers of orphans; and the increased survival of grandparents during one's childhood and early adolescence, thereby increasing the potential for interaction between various successive family generations.

The drop in the mortality rate eventually was accompanied by a marked decline in fertility. In the last three decades of the twentieth century, the global birthrate declined from an average of 7 to 2.7 offspring per woman. This reduction originated in changes in attitude and behavior toward reproduction, initially adopted by a small group of urban-based women born during the 1930s. The modification observed in the reproductive behavior of spouses led to a decrease in family size, changing norms in the age difference between children, and a marked reduction in the time dedicated to procreation in terms of the time elapsing between the first and last born.

The changes in the levels and patterns of mortality and birth were followed by a greater complexity in the norms respective to the formation and dissolution of marital ties. At the end of the century, a small increase in the number of single people was observed, especially among the male population. Nevertheless, matrimony continued to be practiced by almost all Mexicans prior to reaching 50 years of age. At the same time, there was an increase in sexual relations before marriage among young people, a phenomenon largely provoked by greater sexual freedom and the loss of cultural values attributed to female virginity. Marriage sanctioned by the church and state increased as the most common form of union. By the 1990s, three out of every four women began their married life with a civil or religious wedding. At the same time, there was a slight rise in the age of first marriages among women (from 21.5 in 1930 to 22.2 in 1990), while the male average remained more or less constant (24.8 in 1930 to 24.7 in 1990). These tendencies reduced the age difference between spouses.

Family life was affected by notable changes in the means by which matrimony is dissolved (widowhood, separation, and divorce). With the gradual increase in life expectancy, widowhood gave way to separation and divorce as the predominant means of ending a marriage. Indeed, the annual rate of separation and divorce for unions of less than five years' duration and among women who married prior to

18 years of age proved higher among more recent generations than previous ones. The explanation as to why separation and divorce became more frequent is to be found in numerous factors related to wide social changes, particularly more tolerant social, familial, and personal attitudes, the instilling of more permissive guidelines on the theme of matrimonial breakup, as well as the controversy over double standards with regard to sexual mores.

Demographic changes in the country, interacting with other economic, social, and cultural processes, contributed not only to a significant increase in the number of households but also influenced a reduction in their average size and transformed the composition and internal dynamics of the family structure. Among the numerous examples in Mexico of change and continuity in this regard were (1) the continued existence of households on a low subsistence level and the worsening of the absolute and relative number of families in a state of poverty, a fact of prime relevance in the context of the family; (2) the plurality of lifestyles within the home and family, especially the preponderance of nuclear households, and the continuance of those of large and complex type whose increase in the 1980s and 1990s has been interpreted by some authors as a family response to two decades of crisis and economic adjustments; (3) the decline in the relative importance of children within the family structure, a change associated mainly with the drop in the birthrate; (4) the high percentage of elderly in the home, which reflected increases in life expectancy; (5) the high percentage of households consisting of married spouses without children and the decreasing proportion of homes made up exclusively of a married couple with unmarried children (conjugal nuclear families); (6) the increasingly greater percentage of nuclear households made up of one spouse and his or her children; (7) the increase in reconstituted households, made up of individuals who have separated from their previous partners; (8) the growing relative importance of households headed by women; and (9) the large proportion of households made up of people living alone. Various of these changes were reflected in the evolution of the civil codes that governed family life during the twentieth century.

The Legal Context of Family Relations in the Twentieth Century

Mexican families are channels for numerous influences that have operated since the colonial period. These are basically derived from some indigenous customs, transmitted and adapted principally by mestizo (mixed-race) and criollo (Spanish descended) families. The legacy of the African culture, established in several states of the Mexican Republic through the slave trade, was added to this varied and complex mix of influences. The family developed from this original foundation, under the protection of traditions and rules hallowed by custom, influenced by codes and norms derived from Christian morality, and legitimated by the state.

In the twentieth century diverse changes gradually were introduced into the Mexican civil code governing family life, reformulating the dispositions present in various codes of the nineteenth century. These nineteenth-century codes include that promulgated by Benito Juárez on December 8, 1870, which became law on March 1, 1871; and that of 1884, enacted by Manuel González and which came into operation on June 1 of that year. These two codes included restrictions on women, placing them on an inferior level with respect to the male in various spheres of civil life. Only males were allowed to exercise parental authority over children, and marital separation was not accepted nor adoption recognized.

Fundamental changes in this traditional concept of the family came with the Mexican Revolution. In 1916 Venustiano Carranza declared to the Constituent Congress that he would promulgate laws to establish the family on "more rational and just foundations that would elevate spouses to the lofty mission that society and nature have placed in their care." The following year the Ley de Relaciones Familiares (LRF, or Law on Family Relations) was enacted, on the basis that "modern ideas of equality, widely spread and accepted in almost all social institutions, had not achieved a convenient measure of influence on the family." This law, which postulated bases for equality and reciprocity between spouses, despite its lacking a federal character, was adopted in the Federal and Territorial Districts and in various states of the Republic. The LRF took into consideration that "the woman and especially the Mexican woman . . . has frequently been the victim of exploitation . . . that the state should prevent." It arranged, in contrast to previous legislation, that inheritance should be administered according to mutual agreement, that each spouse should maintain control over the administration and ownership of his or her personal property and the profits thereof, and complete freedom with regard to contracts and obligations. The law made it understood "that both spouses had rights to consider themselves as equals within the home," from which followed several rights for the woman. Nevertheless, a rigid sexual division of labor was assumed in a clause stating that the husband was obligated to support the family even if the woman cooperated in this matter. But is also warned that the work of a married woman should not draw her from the fulfillment of her prime obligation: the direct care for the house and children. Parental authority was understood as a collection of obligations that nature imposed on the marital pair for the benefit of their offspring. This law renewed the requisites for the entrance into matrimony and established adoption as a means whereby a child belonging to neither of the married pair could enter a family, thereby crystallizing the aspirations of those matrimonies that had not succeeded in procreating children. The situation of illegitimate children improved with the suppression of the qualification of bastardy within the codes to facilitate these children's recognition and legitimation and give them the right to bear the surname of the individual by whom they were recognized and to receive nourishment and their hereditary portion under the same conditions as any other child.

One highly novel measure that radically changed the dispositions of 1874 on the durability of matrimony was the establishment of divorce, included in Section 6, Article 75 of the LRF. This stated that "divorce dissolves the marriage link and leaves the couple in a fit state to contract another." Thus it was specified that a marriage could be dissolved during the lifetime of the spouses by mutual and free consent or as the result of grave provocation as established by local laws, thereby freeing both to contracting a new legitimate union.

A new civil code was expedited by Plutarco Elías Calles in 1928, becoming common law on October 1, 1932, for the Federal and Territorial Districts and federal law for the entire Republic. The legislation of March 31, 1884, and the LRF of 1917 were abrogated on the appearance of this latter ruling. The new civil code established the equality of both sexes before the law in clearer terms. The second article specified that "opportunity under the law is equal for men and women; as a result a woman does not remain in a subordinate position for reasons of gender and is not restricted in the acquisition and exercise of her civil rights." From 1917 a legislative tendency in the LRF had been in agreement with this new law. Equality between the sexes had wide-reaching effects: women had authority and legal considerations equal to those of their husbands; they could organize all matters connected with education and the establishment of the sons on the basis of mutual agreement; it was determined that a woman, without requiring marital authorization, could take a job or exercise a profession to the extent that it would not prejudice her attention to her work in or the running of the home. The code established equal rights in the motives for divorce in that these referred to both sexes and confirmed the legality of separation through mutual consent. Additionally, the thesis of the equality of legitimate and illegitimate children before the law was restated. The law also protected the concubine (the mistress of or a woman married only by the church to a single man) and the offspring of the relationship. As a result of this code, a woman did not lose parental authority over the children of previous marriages, even when she married again. Syphilis, tuberculosis, or any chronic or incurable illness, and the excessive and habitual use of alcoholic beverages or debilitating drugs, were established as an impediment to matrimony. The marital couple were obliged to establish community or separation of goods, attempting through this measure to guarantee the woman's interests.

As of the mid-1990s, family life in Mexico was still ruled by the Civil Code of 1932, although with some reforms. It is well known that while family codes frequently have a long duration, family life depends on flexible arrangements and contingencies experienced on a day-to-day basis. The relative short-term effectiveness of the codes in the context of the reality they seek to normalize creates disparities between law and actual practice in family relations. Mexico has experienced profound social change; over time the diverse social movements that have taken place have consolidated, thereby revindicating the extension of human rights and constitutional guarantees. Within this framework the feminist movement has played an important role in its fight for the improvement in the condition of women, questioning the institutional guidelines that have directed and formed family relations. Various changes suggested by Mexican women have been placed in an international context sensitive to feminist aspirations. From the 1970s various reforms were introduced into the Civil Code of 1932. These include those established during the presidential term of Luis Echeverría Álvarez, especially the reforms of 1974 referring to the rights and obligations that arise from matrimony. Article 162 is most important in this context since it established on one side the mutual obligation of assistance by both spouses, and on the other the rights to decide on the number and age difference of the children.

The 1974 reforms established the domestic equality of the spouses, independently of the economic contributions of each one. The husband's previous obligation to support the family had led to his being considered to have greater prerogatives within the marriage. The economic power that the husband still exercises in many Mexican homes where he continues to fulfill the role of sole provider determines relationships and family life. Meanwhile, in December 1974 Article 4 of the Mexican Constitution of 1917 was reformed, establishing that both spouses are equal under the law.

Democratization within the Domestic Sphere

These reforms imply important changes in legislation, but as of 1996 many essential features of the 1932 Civil Code remained operative. As a result, organized actions have been taken up to organize legislation in conformity with new familial realities. The stability and viability of their social functions have increasingly depended on the progressive consolidation of a context that aids the democratization of family relationships between genders and generations and promotes a fairer division of tasks in the domestic sphere.

Codes referring to this theme could help create conditions adequate for families to make the best of their material, human, and cultural resources, moving them toward the crystallization of family relations based on the equal distribution of rights and responsibilities of its members.

Select Bibliography

Aguilar Gutiérrez, Antonio, *Bases para un anteproyecto de Código Civil uniforme para toda la República.* Mexico City: UNAM, 1967.

Beltrán, Ulises, Fernando Castaños, Julia Flores, and Yolanda Meyenberg, *Los mexicanos en los noventa: Encuesta Nacional de Valores.* Mexico City: UNAM, 1996.

Código Civil del Distrito Federal y Territorio de la Baja California. Mexico City: Aguilar, 1885.

Código Civil para el Distrito Federal en Materia Común y para toda la República en Materia Federal, vol. 1. Mexico City: UNAM, 1993.

Código Civil para el Distrito Federal y Territorios Federales (1932). Mexico City: Andrade, 1964.

Ley sobre relaciones familiares. Mexico City: Edición Económica, 1917.

Perez Duarte, Alicia Elena, *Derecho de familia.* Mexico City: Fondo de Cultura Económica, 1995.

Salles, Vania, "La familia, las culturas, las identidades." In *Decline y auge de las identidades,* edited by José Manuel Valenzuela. Tijuana: El Colegio de la Frontera Norte, 1992.

_____, "Nuevas miradas sobre la familia." In *La voluntad de ser,* edited by María Luisa Torrés. Mexico City: El Colegio de México, 1994.

—Vania Salles and Rodolfo Tuirán

FEIGE, HERMANN ALBERT OTTO MAXIMILIAN (B. TRAVEN)

1882–1969 • Writer

The writer who signed his works "B. Traven" became world famous during the 1920s and 1930s for a string of novels that presented a panorama of the Mexican Revolution. He later became arguably even more famous as the twentieth century's greatest literary enigma. During the 1980s and 1990s some light was shed on his life, however, and a biography much more detailed than the author ever wanted revealed can now be assembled.

B. Traven's real name was Hermann Albert Otto Maximilian Feige. He was of humble origins and began a career as a provincial actor and also dabbled in writing. During World War I, under the assumed name of Ret Marut, he began to edit a fiery anarchist and antiwar journal in Munich, which led to his appointment as censor of one of the leading regional dailies during the short-lived Munich Soviet Repub-

lic of April 1919. Sentenced to death by firing squad following the fall of the republic, he managed to escape. Feige finally left Germany in 1923 without papers, his revolutionary dreams in tatters.

In London he apparently made contact with agents of the Industrial Workers of the World (IWW), who helped him enter Mexico illegally in the summer of 1924. His arrival in Tampico coincided with an exciting but brief episode when anarcho-syndacalist trade unions exercised enormous authority in the oil town. His dream of Munich seemed to have come true in Mexico, and he began to produce vivid accounts of what he saw around him in the form of novels that he signed B. Traven. His first work, *The Cottonpickers* (1925), was accepted by the leading German Socialist newspaper *Vorwarts,* where it was spotted by the

Büchergilde Gutenberg, the book club of the German printers' guild, which became Traven's lifelong publisher.

While making his literary debut, B. Traven already began to cultivate a personal image that eventually would become the mainstay of the Traven mystery. He refused to reveal any details about his person, but let it be known that *The Cottonpickers,* the account of an American drifter looking for work in Mexico, was autobiographical. In reality he lived near Tampico in relative comfort on one of the properties of an American farmer who engaged him to teach his young daughter English.

In 1926 B. Traven received an invitation to participate as photographer in an expedition to Chiapas. The lifestyle of the Chamula Indians was a revelation to him; combining his new discoveries with experiences from Tampico and a seriously misunderstood rendition of *indigenismo,* he wrote the travelogue *The Land of Spring* (1928). The book is an ode to the Mexican Revolution, which he believed had given state power to trade unions, and to the government of Plutarco Elías Calles (1924–28), whom he believed to be a true workers' president.

During two subsequent trips to Chiapas, however, B. Traven discovered the horrors of the *monterías,* the mahogany logging camps in the remote and inaccessible Lacandon Forest, where thousands of slave laborers had been worked to death. The last of the large *monterías* had closed only in 1924, and their continued operation well into the era of the Revolutionary government cured Traven of his delusions about the Revolution and President Calles. Traven is one of the first writers who observed the continuities between Porfirian and post-Revolutionary government. In five powerful novels, the so-called Jungle Cycle, Traven analyzed and described debt peonage from the emotional viewpoint of the victims.

Hiding his identity now became a necessity for the author; his novels were populated by thinly disguised real-life characters from Chiapas and Tabasco who, when they heard of the publication of Traven's novels in Germany, let it be known that Traven had better never set foot again in the southern states. At the same time, because the Jungle Cycle was an indictment of the Mexican state and its abandonment of the native population, the books rendered their author liable to prosecution under the Noxious Foreigners Act and extradition to Nazi Germany, where his works had been publicly burned. Traven now retired to his Cashew Farm property near Acapulco, where he was flushed out in 1948 by a Mexican journalist.

The outbreak of World War II in 1939 effectively severed Traven from his trade union audience and his only source of income. After 1940 Traven ceased to create anything of impact. The coming of the Cold War rendered his ideological world irrelevant, and his German had deteriorated badly. He spent his last two decades living in comfort in Mexico City, where he rewrote and tampered with his earlier work. He now concentrated on the promotion of the Traven mystery, which kept him in the public eye but also obscured the historical relevance of his work.

Select Bibliography

Goldwasser, James, "Ret Marut: The Early B. Traven." *Germanic Review* 68:3 (1993).

Guthke, Karl S., *B. Traven: Biographie eines Rätsels.* Frankfurt am Main: Büchergilde Gutenberg, 1988; as *B. Traven: The Life behind the Legends,* translated by Robert C. Sprung, Chicago: Lawrence Hill, 1991.

Schürer, Ernst, and Philip Jenkins, *B. Traven: Life and Work.* University Park: Pennsylvania State University Press, 1987.

Wyatt, Will, *The Man Who Was B. Traven.* London: Cape, 1980; as *The Secret of the Sierra Madre,* Garden City, New York: Doubleday, 1980.

Zogbaum, Heidi, *B. Traven: A Vision of Mexico.* Wilmington, Delaware: Scholarly Resources, 1992.

—Heidi Zogbaum

FELIPE DE JESÚS

1572–97 • Christian Martyr and Saint

Felipe de Jesús, a Franciscan martyred in Japan in 1597, is the only native of Mexico to be beatified and canonized by the Roman papacy. The events of his life tie the history of Mexico to that of the Philippines and Japan. Yet, San Felipe de Jesús remains relatively unknown in Mexico despite attempts by past devotees to identify him as patron saint of Mexico.

Felipe de las Casas Martínez was born to the Spanish merchant Alonso de las Casas and his wife Antonia Martínez on May 1, 1572, in Mexico City. As a boy he studied in the Jesuit Colegio of San Pedro y San Pablo under P. Gutiérrez.

After having entered the Franciscan novitiate in the Colegio of Santa Barbara (Puebla) in 1589, he left for unknown reasons. The reasons for his subsequent move to Manila are equally obscure, but once there he again joined the Franciscans. This time he persisted, taking holy vows in 1594. In 1596, he embarked on a ship for Mexico, where he was to say his first mass in the presence of his parents.

The voyage to Mexico did not go according to plans, for a storm caused the ship to go ashore on the Japanese coast near the city of Miyaco on October 18, 1596. The shipwrecked group, including Felipe, became victims of a political environment distrustful of and increasingly hostile to the Catholic missionaries. On February 5, 1597, Felipe de Jesús was among the six Franciscans, three Jesuits, and approximately twenty Japanese converts who were crucified by order of the shogun Toyotomi Hideyoshi.

Fellow Franciscans who escaped martyrdom removed the body of Felipe de Jesús to Manila, whence relics later were sent to Mexico. Pope Urban VIII beatified the martyrs of Nagasaki on September 14, 1627. Less than two years later, Felipe de Jesús was proclaimed "patron" of Mexico City in festive celebrations attended by his own mother.

Beginning in 1683, Mexican writers concerned with promoting the canonization of Felipe de Jesús eulogized him as a Mexican martyr and criollo (native-born American of Spanish descent) patriot. In response to allegations that the absence of a baptismal record made it impossible to determine the martyr's birthplace, Balthasar de Medina quoted the entire testimony made by Felipe's mother, Antonia Martínez, on January 26, 1629. Calling Felipe a "criollo of this city" and "our compatriot and patron," he further upbraided those responsible for having not provided the saint's mother with an adequate pension in her widowhood.

Panegyrists of Felipe de Jesús have countered the opinion that he was an accidental saint whose life prior to martyrdom had shown no signs of heroic virtue. They seek to identify the suffering and endurance of San Felipe on the cross with the example of Jesus Christ himself, even observing that in his anguish he cried out "Jesus" three times.

Alfonso Mariano del Rio published a sermon in 1715 in which he distinguished Felipe as singular among the 26 "protomartyrs" of Japan for having received three lance thrusts instead of the one or two suffered by the others. In a sermon delivered February 5, 1781, José Martínez de Adame likewise declared that the saintliness of Felipe went beyond simple martyrdom. Observing that the people of Lima had their own saint in Rosa of Lima, he urged the Spanish Crown to favor the people of Mexico by promoting the cause of canonization of Felipe.

In the years prior to and following 1810, there appears to have developed a greater patriotic interest in the figure of Felipe de Jesús. A number of sermons, novenas, and biographies of the martyr were published between 1781 and 1824, including two works by José Fernández de Lizardi and José Maria Montes de Oca's book of engravings on Felipe's life. Felipe de Jesús was canonized by Pius IX on June 8, 1862. Although his devotees were successful in their efforts to gain his canonization by the papacy, however, their promotion of San Felipe de Jesús as a national symbol was less fruitful. He never attained the stature of Our Lady of Guadalupe in Mexico or Rosa de Lima in Peru.

Select Bibliography

Quesada Brandi, Manuel, editor, *San Felipe de Jesus.* Mexico City: Porrúa, 1962.

—RON MORGAN

FÉLIX GÜAREÑA, MARÍA DE LOS ANGELES

1914 or 1915– • Film Actress

María Félix is not only one of Mexico's most famous film stars, but she is also the incarnation of a myth: of the vamp who takes away men's strength, of self-sufficiency, of the power that derives from beauty and money.

María de los Angeles Félix Güareña was born in Alamos, Sonora, on April 8, "in a year that many people would like to know, but I don't want to tell," which could be either 1914 or 1915. She was the daughter of Bernardo Félix and Josefa Güareña. The family moved to Guadalajara, where she led the simple life of a student, although her personality and beauty soon shone through; she was crowned the queen of the Carnival of Guadalajara. Very young she married Enrique Álvarez, a salesman of beauty products and with whom she had a son. They divorced soon after, a scandal in provincial society. The problems created by this situation made her try her fortune in Mexico City, where she began a successful career in the cinema under the tutelage of

the engineer Fernando Palacios. María Félix starred in 47 films, and from the beginning she took starring roles.

Her first film was in 1942, *El peñón de las ánimas,* in which she starred jointly with Jorge Negrete, who was already a film idol. The animosity between them was obvious at the time, although they were married years later. A second film that year, *María Eugenia,* in which she appeared in a scene with a very tight bathing suit, was considered a scandal but created much publicity.

It was *Doña Bárbara,* directed in 1943 by Fernando de Fuentes, that started her image as a man-eater and in which she picked up the nickname of La Doña. This film was based on the novel by the Venezuelan Rómulo Gallegos. It was this film that set her style, which would develop through other films: *La mujer sin alma* (1943), *Amok* (1944), *La devoradora* (1944), *La diosa arrodillada* (1947), *Que Dios me perdone* (1947), and *Doña Diabla* (1948). In these she portrays a strong woman who is not a victim but a villain, the femme fatale of this cinema. It is important to highlight the significance of this role in a film industry such as the Mexican one, full of machismo, in which the female prototype is a submissive and self-denying mother. María Félix filled the screen with her beauty and her forceful presence. Her importance can be understood from the Mexican version of the "star system": she is the star who invoked the phenomenon of fetishism, imitation, and admiration in the masses, the *diva* who was not asked to do a good deed but who represented, one way or another, herself. Her love affairs and marriages, in particular to Agustín Lara and Jorge Negrete, added to her image as a woman who would let nothing hinder her rise to stardom. Emilio "El Indio" Fernández directed her in films that gained a universal audience, such as *Enamorada* (1946), *Río Escondido* (1948), and *Maclovia* (1948). In 1953 she worked with this director again in *El rapto* and *Reportaje*.

Whereas Dolores del Río became famous in Hollywood, María Félix never wanted to film in the United States; instead, she moved to Europe. Between 1948 and 1951 in Spain she filmed *Mare Nostrum, Una mujer cualquiera,* and *La noche del sábado.* In Tétouan, Morocco, in 1951, she made a Spanish production *La corona negra,* from a screenplay by Jean Cocteau. In that same year she filmed in Italy: *Mesalina* and *Icantésimo Trágico,* which in Mexico was called *Hechizo Trágico.* In France, between 1954 and 1955, she made *La bella Otero, French Cancan,* and *Los héroes estan fatigados.* She also worked in Argentina, where she was the star of *La pasión desnuda* in 1952.

After this international phase she returned to Mexico, where she had lead roles in many different types of films, although in all of them she maintained the stereotype of the wild woman. She starred in several films about the Revolution, such as *La cucaracha* (1958), *Juana Gallo* (1960), *La bandida* (1962), *La valentina* (1965), and *La generala* (1966). In 1962 she attempted comic cinema with *Si yo fuera millonario,* and in 1963 she made *Amor y sexo,* the first and only time she appeared nude.

Three projects showed great promise but were never filmed: in 1967 *Zona sagrada,* based on the novel by Carlos Fuentes, which deals with the complex relationship between a famous star and her son, was to have been filmed with María's own son Enrique Álvarez Félix; in 1981 *Toña machetes,* from a text by Margarita López Portillo; and finally *Eterno esplendor,* which would have been directed by Jaime Humberto Hermosillo.

María Félix has declared that the secret of her popularity was "the image of success. My image is health, of someone who feels good in their own skin and is at one with herself. My image is the joy of life." She stated that she represented "the triumphant Mexican, who doesn't get duped by anyone."

Select Bibliography

Poniatowska, Elena, "Las alzadas de ceja de María Félix." *Todo México.* Mexico City: Diana, 1990.

Sánchez García, José María, *María Félix: Mujer y artista.* Mexico City: Netzahualcóyotl, 1949.

Serna, Enrique, editor, *María Félix: Todas mis querras.* Mexico City: Clío, 1993.

Taibo, Paco Ignacio, *María Félix: 47 pasos por el cine.* Mexico City: Joaquín Mortiz-Planeta, 1985.

—JULIA TUÑÓN PABLOS

FEMINISM

The term "feminism" began to be used in Mexico during the last years of the nineteenth century. By the beginning of the twentieth century it had entered common usage among the cultured class of the country's capital. In that period feminism involved fighting for sexual equality (e.g., recognition of women's intellectual capacity and their right to education) while at the same time battling for appreciation of a series of subjective attributes considered characteristic of the feminine sex, including emotional capacity, kindness, and moral superiority. Rooted in liberal thought, feminism saw secular and rational education of women as the means to achieve its main goals: the dignification of the role of wife and mother as well as the increase of female influence in the family and extending the boundaries of women's individual freedom. Focused on these causes, feminism at the end of the nineteenth century and the beginning of the twentieth century put equal rights in second place. Women's political participation was seen as desirable but possible only in the long term.

Before the term feminism entered general use, ideas on female emancipation appeared in various women's periodicals published in Mexico City as early as the 1880s; these periodicals sought to widen the cultural horizons of women and praise the role of wife and mother within the family. Excepting the oldest, *El Correo de las Señoras* (1881–83), these periodicals were organized by editorial teams made up of women. There was no uniformity in the style of these magazines, but there were elements of continuity between them.

Among such elements were articles by the writer Laureana Wright González de Kleinhans, the most brilliant and radical defender of women's emancipation in her time, who conceptualized the relation between the sexes as bonds of ownership entrenched in the realm of thought. From her perspective, the subordination of women was based on their intellectual weakness. Hence, education and moral strengthening were a priority, the only means of achieving personal autonomy and leaving the narrow existence of domestic life within which women's life was conducted. Wright asserted that motherhood was an essential part of a woman's life, but she did not accept that maternity was the only possible human option for the female sex. Among the most outstanding works by Wright were *Educación errónea de la mujer y medios prácticos para corregirla* (1891), *La emancipación de la mujer por medio del estudio* (1892), and the posthumous volume, *Mujeres notables mexicanas* (1910).

The philosophy of Wright coincided in many aspects with that of the jurist and historian Genaro García, author of *La desigualdad de la mujer* (1891) and *La condición de la mujer* (1891). For García the subordination of women in society was imposed by the state through legislation. In his opinion the main stumbling block to individual rights of women occurred within matrimony. A married woman lived a kind of slavery because the Civil Code (1884) left her incapable of acting in civil life alone and without the permission of her husband. Influenced by the English philosopher John Stuart Mill, Genaro García was interested in female education and was a radical defender of equality between the sexes before the law. Precursor of egalitarian feminism in the theoretical field, García was not interested in the practical and organizational aspects of the emancipation of women.

During the first decade of the twentieth century the opposition to the government of Porfirio Díaz favored the inclusion of women in political activity. Among the women writers who attacked the regime were the teacher Dolores Jimenez y Muro and Juana Belén Gutiérrez de Mendoza. Both denounced injustices and called for rebellion in articles published in the clandestine press. Moreover, Gutiérrez de Mendoza for years edited the opposition newspaper *Vesper*. Their work on behalf of women's rights earned the two writers persecution and imprisonment.

Many other women participated in anti-Porfirist organizations. These included liberal clubs, Magonist groups (i.e., those associated with the Flores Magón brothers and their Partido Liberal Mexicano), and from 1908 associations that supported the candidacy of Francisco I. Madero for the presidency of the republic. Women's activity in the liberal and Magonist opposition was full and intense but in general isolated from feminist ideas. Neither women's suffrage nor equal rights interested these agitators in a significant way, focused as they were on organizational duties and propaganda for their cause.

The demand for equal rights seeded itself among the female contingents of the Maderist movement that raised the banner of "Effective Suffrage. No Reelection." Nevertheless, beyond isolated petitions for the vote, feminism did not concern itself in a consistent manner either with the groups of female Maderists nor any sector of the government headed by Francisco I. Madero once he assumed power.

From 1915 the Constitutionalist faction of the Mexican Revolution created political openings that favored the development of some feminist issues. Even though the latter's influence in reforms and Revolutionary legislation was restricted and had a secondary character, Constitutionalism was the only one of the contending factions in the Mexican Revolution that favored egalitarianism both in education and in civil legislation (Law on Family Relations, 1916) and labor (Constitution of 1917, Article 123). The same did not occur for citizens' rights. The Constitutional Congress (1916–17) denied female suffrage. This demand had caught on among some Constitutionalist women on the initiative of Hermila Galindo, confidential collaborator of Venustiano Carranza.

The formulation of the demand for female suffrage and the call for women to exercise their influence in society through political action and not just within the family environment distinguished the feminism that emerged from the Mexican Revolution from that of the Porfiriato. This feminism of the Revolutionary period was voiced in the periodical *La mujer moderna: Semanario ilustrado* (1915–18), founded and edited by Hermila Galindo. Its pages covered cultural themes and domestic economy and included literary texts in prose and verse, just as had the feminist periodicals of the previous epoch. However, the speciality of *La mujer moderna* was that it favored Constitutionalism and was against the Zapatista and Villista factions.

Feminism acquired a political relevance that it had never possessed before during the regime of Salvador Alvarado (1915–18), governor and military commander of the Yucatán, who had been imposed by the Constitutionalist forces. A radical anticlericalist, Alvarado was interested in feminism to the extent that it could help combat the influence of the Catholic Church within society, the major obstacle to progress, according to liberal thought. Thus the government of Salvador Alvarado sought to give secular and rational education to Yucatec women, mainly indigenous *campesinas* (peasants), and promoted the creation of employment that allowed women to exercise their domestic responsibilities as wives and mothers while at the same time earning their own salary. Alvarado's feminist project contemplated the incorporation of women in plans for economic modernization but not their participation as citizens in a political democracy. What was most important was that the women exercised their influence as mothers, wives, and teachers in favor of the secular state and not the clergy.

In January and December of 1916 two feminist congresses were promoted, organized, and bankrolled by Alvarado's government that sought above all to create a consensus in educational and social reform. Even though the themes for discussion and working procedure were previously determined by the organizers, the debates evolved with relative freedom. The first congress was attended by 600 women and the second by 200, almost all of whom in both congresses were primary school teachers. Both touched topics related to women's education and work. Those attending discussed freely and allowed their differences of opinion a public airing. The major point of debate, which ended up being a public scandal, resulted from the contribution of Hermila Galindo, who affirmed that the sexual impulses of women were as powerful as those of men and proposed that female education included information on human biology.

In 1919, after the armed stage of the Mexican Revolution had ended, Elena Torres, Evelyn Roy, and María del Refugio García founded the Consejo Feminista Mexicano. Unlike previous women's organizations, the Consejo Feminista Mexicano focused on an explicitly feminist political agenda. Its program of action covered three points: the economy (equal pay, work security, maternity protection); the social (the creation of libertarian groups, workers' sleeping and dining quarters, the "regeneration" of prostitutes); and the political (equal rights, reform of the Civil Code). This wide political program contained concerns that would interest feminism in the 1920s and 1930s but did not represent concrete actions of the organization, which were restricted to the setting up of public sewing areas and the edition of *La mujer. Revista quincenal. Organo del Consejo Feminista Mexicano* (1921–22), edited by the teacher Julia Nava de Ruisánchez. The importance of the Consejo Feminista was rooted not only in its pioneer political character but also in its incorporation of Marxist and communist concepts to its analysis of the social status of women's conditions while putting greater emphasis on the egalitarian elements of feminism than the social differences between men and women.

The Consejo Feminista maintained an international and pacifist posture, seeking to create links with women's groups in the United States that shared its political sympathies. In 1922, with the support of the Secretariats of Foreign Affairs and Public Education, the Consejo Feminista Mexicano accepted an invitation to attend a Pan-American Women's conference in Baltimore, Maryland, organized by the League of Suffragette Women of the United States. Elena Torres, Eulalia Gúzman, and Luz Vera attended as official delegates of the Secretariat of Public Education, while Julia Nava de Ruisánchez and María Rentería de Meza represented the Consejo Feminista Mexicano itself.

In Baltimore it was agreed to hold the First Pan-American Feminist Congress for the Improvement of Women the following year in Mexico City. This congress was attended by more than 100 delegates, most of whom had come from fewer than 20 states within the republic. Highly egalitarian, the resolutions that were adopted covered very diverse subjects: civil rights, political rights, divorce, sexual mores, prostitution, birth control, economic problems, social protection of women and children, educational problems, the moralization of the press, and community service. Although the congress demanded equality between the sexes, it favored the notion that the spheres of action and the social functions of men and women had to remain clearly differentiated. The work of the First Pan-American Feminist Congress was marked by the political differences between the participants. Few agreed, for example, with the sanctioning of free love proposed by Elvia Carrillo Puerto, delegate from the state of Yucatán. Unity was maintained thanks to the conciliatory efforts of the teacher Elena Torres, president of the congress.

On the other hand, no agreement was reached in the Congreso de Mujeres de la Raza (Congress for Indigenous Women), organized in 1925 by the Liga de Mujeres Ibéricas e Hispanoamericanas (League of Spanish and Spanish-American Women) at the prompting of Sofía Villa de Buentello. Hardly had the congress started when the conflict between Villa de Buentello, on one side, and the more left-leaning María del Refugio García and Elvia Carrillo Puerto, on the other, created a split within the ranks. While the left-wing faction put priority on the economic situation of women and the problems encountered by female workers, Villa de Buentello was more concerned with moral and judicial issues. Author of *La mujer y la ley: Estudio importantísimo para la mujer que desee su emancipación y para el hombre amante del bien and la justicia* (1921), a work that took up the ideas of Genaro García, Sofía Villa de Buentello supported the equality of the political rights of men and women but categorically opposed divorce.

A similar conflict arose in the Congreso contra la Prostitución (Congress against Prostitution). Scarcely had the congress opened when the left-wing group retired to work apart in such a way that by June 1934 two Congresses on Prostitution were having sessions on a parallel basis in Mexico City. The main difference between the conservative and left-wing factions was based on the causes of prostitution. The conservative group emphasized moral and cultural aspects; thus, their proposals to eliminate prostitution included the establishment of a moral egalitarian criteria for both men and women, coeducation, and sexual responsibility of both sexes. The left-wing group, on the other hand, based the reasons for prostitution in poverty and economic inequality between social classes.

Despite such differences and ruptures between feminists, these congresses had a relatively important position in the political scene of the epoch. They generally counted on the presence of governmental representatives and enjoyed wide press coverage. At the same time they managed to draw the attention of the public to feminist issues and became a source of political identification for women, the majority of them teachers, who sought to widen the possibilities of political action in the public sphere and strengthen their personal independence and influence within the family. Many themes of feminist interest during the 1920s were covered by the monthly periodical *Mujer: Periódico independiente para la evaluación intelectual y moral de la mujer* (1923–26), edited by María Ríos Cárdenas, who proposed that domestic work should be salaried. In New York the Mexican Elena Arizmendi wrote on various aspects of Mexican feminism in *Femi-*

nismo internacional, a periodical she edited between 1922 and 1923.

During the 1920s feminism had a certain influence in civil legislation. The Civil Code of 1928 contained elements (some already present in the Law on Family Relations) that had been highlighted by the feminist movement repeatedly since the beginning of the century. These were equality under the law for men and women; the increase of the wife's influence in the education of her children; and the recognition of a woman's right to bequeath her possessions and to be employed or take up a profession, but only with permission of her husband. This code increased the rights of married women, established the obligatory nature of domestic work, and maintained unequal criteria for men and women with regard to divorce.

The 1930s marked an increase in women's political organizations. Paradoxically, in these years the term "feminism" fell into disuse, probably because of the predominance of Marxist political language, which disqualified feminism as an issue that concerned only bourgeois women, and thus was far removed from the interests of the proletariat. Women's activity in this period was orientated to the popular sectors and incorporated demands of workers and *campesinas,* but this shift did not mean a break with the larger feminist demands of earlier times.

The three congresses of workers and *campesinas* held in 1931 and 1933 in Mexico City and in 1934 in Guadalajara laid the foundation for the organizational and ideological bases of the women's movement of that decade. With a large percentage of teachers from basic levels of education from various regions of the country, these congresses prepared the ground for the foundation in 1935 of the Frente Unico Pro Derechos de la Mujer (FUPDM, or Single Front for the Rights of Women) under the political control of communist women headed by María del Refugio García.

Of particular interest was the creation of the minority political interest within the FUPDM dubbed the "Feminine Republic" in which figured, among others, the veteran fighter Juana Belén Gutiérrez de Mendoza and Concha Michel, a *campesina* organizer, militant communist, and popular singer. This faction fought for acceptance of the idea that the antagonism between the sexes had the same social relevance as that between social classes; because the group considered specific conditions occasioned by maternity, they avoided the reductionism of viewing women only in the light of their maternal function and not as members of the workforce. The FUPDM succeeded in bringing together some 800 political organizations and cultural associations of women of varying socioeconomic status, regional origin, and political affiliation. It was a unifying effort that overcame the paralyzing schisms characteristic of feminism of the previous decade.

Despite the breadth of their political program—it included socioeconomic issues, workers' demands, and political declarations against fascism and foreign intervention— from 1937 FUPDM activity was based on women's suffrage.

Its strategy in this regard was to nominate Refugio García and Soledad Orozco as candidates for the post of deputy in the electoral districts of Michoacán and Tabasco, respectively. Both declared that they had obtained a majority at the polls, but their triumph was not recognized.

In the same year President Lázaro Cárdenas sent to Congress an initiative that would establish the civic rights of women by reforming Article 34 of the Constitution. Despite that fact that it was passed by both the Chamber of Deputies and the Senate, the measure was not published in the *Diario Oficial* and thus never became law. At the last moment the opinion of sectors in Congress that considered women's suffrage as favoring conservative and ecclesiastical interests in public affairs won out.

Women's suffrage ceased to be a theme for public debate during the 1940s. In this decade the women's movement grew steadily weaker until it practically disappeared from the political scene. In 1947 the civic rights of women were recognized at municipal but not at the state or federal level. These latter rights were not established until 1953, under the presidency of Adolfo Ruiz Cortines. By then female suffrage had been converted into a symbol of the image of political modernity that the regime was keen to project, and it had ceased to be a political goal sustained by a wide-ranging feminist political mobilization. In this moment the suffragette cause was taken up by the Alianza de Mujeres de México (Mexican Women's Alliance) created in 1952 and presided over by Amalia Castillo Ledón.

Equal civic rights for women were established in 1953 by the reform to Article 34 of the Constitution. For the first time in Mexican history, women participated in the electoral process with the same rights as men in 1955 elections in Baja California Norte and in the 1955 presidential elections.

Feminism was revitalized at the beginning of the 1970s in the search for liberation inspired by the counterculture in university campuses. The women's liberation movement in the United States had decisive influence on this resurgence. Pioneer activists, many of them veterans of the student movement of 1968, were familiar with the latest political and theoretical developments of U.S. feminism. The meeting held in 1970 in San Francisco to celebrate the fiftieth anniversary of the recognition of women's rights in the United States had particular resonance and was widely reported in the Mexican press.

At the beginning of the 1970s the concerns of the women's liberation movement—criticism of inequality in daily life, sexual mores, and domestic work—totally replaced the demands for equal rights that feminism had proposed during the first half of the century. The feminists of the new mold took the limitations of equality under the law as their point of departure. Mexican law formally mandated equality in the area of salaries and political rights, but did not eliminate the flagrant discrimination that women endured in both public and private life. The accusatory declaration "La abnegación, una virtud loca" (Submission, an insane virtue) was developed by the Chiapanecan writer Rosario Castellanos to highlight the social and moral consequences implicit in women's lack of rights. This discourse by the lucid voice of the new feminism was read in 1971 in a government-sponsored public gathering, one of the rare occasions in this period when feminist themes were expressed in such a public and official fashion.

Belittled by the media by means of satire and jokes, feminism at the beginning of the 1970s appealed to only a few. These were largely women from the middle classes, with a university education and linked to political organizations of Marxist leanings, active in left-wing political movements but with weak lines of intercommunication and almost without social influence. Concerned to show the link between the personal and the political, the feminists formed consciousness groups aimed to analyze the social and political dimensions of their personal experiences, especially in the context of sexuality. Day-to-day relations between men and women in both a personal and work setting took central place in the new Mexican feminism. Inequality in the distribution of domestic work did not play a crucial role in the political platform of the new feminism in Mexico as it did in countries with a more modern social structure, however. The diminished role of this issue was the result both of the meager pay given for domestic service in Mexico and also the greater domestic support given to Mexican women by extensive family networks. This support diminished the pressure that fell on women who had the double responsibility of salaried employment and domestic work.

In 1975 the celebration in Mexico City of the World Women's Conference and the declaration of the International Women's Year by the United Nations led the government to dictate a series of legal reforms intended to eliminate the inequality of men and women under the law. Various discriminatory clauses in the Civil Code of 1928 were repealed, including that which demanded the written permission of the husband of a married woman who wanted to take on salaried work. It also established equal rights of men and women to receive gifts of land and women's equal rights as *ejidatarias* (workers of communal village lands, known as *ejidos*).

During the World Women's Conference feminist activists organized a counter-congress to express their differences with the United Nations. They considered that the latter's political position was governmentally influenced, that its analysis of women's conditions was superficial, and that the measures it agreed to were insufficient. The counter-congress had little relevance, given that its work had no impact on the work of the international delegates and had restricted press coverage. It nevertheless had a crucial role in the formation of organizational structures in feminist sectors.

The following year saw the formation of the Women's Coalition, which reunited feminist groups around the political issues that would shape the feminism movement for the following decades: voluntary maternity, the struggle against sexual violence, and the assertion of free sexual expression, including homosexuality. A second effort toward unification on the part of feminist political action came in 1979 with the Frente Nacional por la Liberación y los Derechos de los Mujeres (National Front for the Freedom and Rights of Women), which brought together not only feminist associations but also groups in favor of homosexual liberation and some independent unions of worker's corporations and feminist branches of political parties belonging to the Marxist left.

The legalization of abortion (still cited in 1996 as an offense in the penal code of the Federal District and federal territories and in the majority of the states' criminal legislation) was the imperative that brought together the strongest efforts of the feminists. Considering maternity as voluntary, feminists supported every woman's right to make decisions that affected her body and her sexuality; they insisted on the necessity for sexual education and the responsible use of contraceptives, and they sought to modify legislation on abortion through activism and the diffusion of their arguments in the press. In 1976 feminists presented the Chamber of Deputies with a legal program on voluntary maternity, and in 1979 deputies belonging to the Mexican Communist Party legally recognized the project. No legal reform was enacted in either case, however.

Feminists achieved greater success in their denunciation of sexual violence and their characterization of violation and sexual harassment as abuses of power and not natural manifestations of masculine sexuality. In 1977 the first rape support center was created by a feminist collective. Later, with the help of various feminists and the opposition of others, the Procuradería de Justicia of the Federal District established the first agency specializing in the prosecution of sexual crimes, inspiring various other agencies of the same kind. In 1991 a series of reforms were incorporated into the penal code, facilitating the identification and prosecution of sexual offenses, including sexual harassment.

The years from 1976 to 1982 saw feminism flourish. Recently formulated, their political demands took hold, despite the organizational weakness of the movement. At the same time there was a cultural feminist critique that was expressed through various creative channels. The bulletin *Cihuatl: Organo de la Coalición de Mujeres Feministas* was published, along with the magazine *Revuelta*. The first edition of *Fem: Publicación feminista trimestral* was issued in 1976 on the initiative of Alaíde Foppa and Margarita García Flores. Marta Lamas, Elena Poniatowska, Carmen Lugo, and Elena Urrutia, among others, later joined the editorial board. In its early period, *Fem* played a crucial role in the diffusion of feminist cultural theory and critique and was pioneering in its denunciation of various manifestations of sexism. Despite changes in editorial approach, *Fem* could boast 20 years of uninterrupted publication in 1996, when it was under the editorship of Esperanza Brito. Starting in 1987 *Doblejornada: Suplemento mensual de La Jornada,* coordinated by Sara Lovera and published in Mexico City, performed a similar task. In these years radio also was brought into play to disseminate feminist ideas. The pioneer work in this area was that of Alaíde Foppa, with the program *Foro de la mujer,* transmitted by Radio Universidad.

The social composition of the feminist movement at this time was dominated by middle-class women with a high level of formal education. Feminism did not find an audience with working women; this objective never amounted to more than the worthy intentions that arose from the first activists' Marxist organizational policies. Nevertheless, at the beginning of the 1980s, the struggle initiated by women from the popular sector to obtain urban services (light, drainage, provisions) and better salaries and credits began to acquire feminist elements. Between 1980 and 1987 10 widely based national and sector-based meetings were held of workers, *campesinas,* and neighborhood groups with an average attendance of 500 women, and at least 50 local or regional encounters took place. Known as "popular feminism," this process was characterized by the intent to link feminist demands of the previous decade with the particular needs of women from diverse sectors. The paradigm experience was the Regional de Mujeres del Valle de México (Regional Group of Women from the Valley of Mexico) that was a part of the Coordinadora Nacional de Movimiento Urbano Popular (CONAMUP, or National League of Popular Urban Movements).

Popular feminism was present in the IV Encuentro Feminista Latinamericano y del Caribe (Fourth Latin-American and Caribbean Feminist Convention) held in Taxco, Guerrero, in 1987. Here the social and ideological variations of feminism were made clear. In this international meeting some activists with more senior feminist credentials drew attention to the lack of democratic practices among feminists.

In more general terms, the concern for democracy in Mexico became acute as a result of the electoral process of 1988, which was widely attacked as fraudulent by the growing political opposition to the government regime. Numerous groups of women linked to the opposition sprang up, some of them, like the Coordinadora Benita Galeana (Benita Galeana League) and Mujeres en Lucha por la Democracia (Women's Struggle for Democracy), heirs of 1970s feminism, incorporating a gender perspective to their political platform.

During the 1980s feminists also emerged in the academic field, a process that would increase as the century drew to a close. If in the 1970s there were isolated courses on feminism in university institutions, in the 1990s many more specific courses were dedicated to this issue. Parallel to the increase in academic studies on gender was the rise in specialized publications that sought to disseminate advances in feminist theory and cultural critique. The first of this kind was the biannual magazine *Debate feminist,* first published in 1990 under the editorship of Marta Lamas. It aimed to be a bridge between the political and theoretical aspects of feminism. Focused on gender studies, *La ventana* appeared in 1995, edited by the University of Guadalajara under the editorship of Cristina Palomar.

Throughout the 1980s feminism had won legitimacy in the states of the republic, thanks mainly to the work of communications media that favored the institutionalization of regional feminist organizations working in both the political and academic spheres. During the 1990s feminism gained national coverage, particularly in urban areas.

The influence of feminism can be appreciated in the majority of the country's political organizations. From the moment that the Ejército Zapatista de Liberación Nacional (EZLN, or Zapatista Army of National Liberation) in Chiapas emerged onto the national political scene on January 1, 1994, they demanded a just and egalitarian treatment for the indigenous population. They drew up a women's revolutionary law that recognized the equality of the women revolutionaries and the right for women to decide on the number of children they should bear, choose their own partner, and not be beaten or badly treated.

Starting in the 1980s a good part of the feminist activity in Mexico was performed by nongovernmental organizations (NGOs), many of which obtained resources from abroad. This access to resources stabilized feminism, particularly in the areas of education, popular organization, women's health, and the defense of reproductive rights, even though at the same time it placed conditions on the organizations' autonomy. The importance of Mexican feminist NGOs was recognized in 1995 in the IV Conferencia de la Mujer (Fourth Women's Conference) and the Foro de Organizaciones no Gubermentales (Forum of Nongovernmental Organizations), where these groups played a central part.

At the end of the twentieth century feminism in Mexico had not developed into a defined and visible social movement, and its positions were far from being accepted generally. Nevertheless, its egalitarian ideas, defense of women's freedom, denunciation of sexual violence, and critique of androcentrism as a basis of knowledge represent a focus of opinion with varying grades of influence in the creation of public politics in social organizations, the communications media, academic institutions, and daily life.

See also Family and Kinship; Gender; Gender and Mexican Spanish; Homosexuality; Llorona, La; Malinche and Malinchismo; Soldaderas and Coronelas; Women's Status and Occupation

Select Bibliography

Cano, Gabriela, "Revolución, feminismo y ciudadanía en México (1915–1920)." In *Historia de las mujeres en Occidente,* vol. 5, edited by Georges Duby and Michelle Perrot. Madrid: Taurus, 1991.

_____, "Una ciudadanía igualitaria: El presidente Lázaro Cárdenas y el sufragio femenino." *Desdeldiez Boletin del Centro de Estudios de la Revolución Mexicana Lázaro Cárdenas, A.C.* (December 1995).

Castellanos, Rosario, "La abnegación, una virtud loca." *Debate feminista* 6:3 (September 1992).

Fem: Diez añis de periodismo feminista. Mexico City: Planeta, 1988.

Lamas, Marta, "Algunas características del movimiento feminista en el Ciudad de México." In *Mujeres y participación política: Avances y desafios en América Latina,* edited by Magdalena León. Bogotá: Tercer Mundo, 1994.

Monsiváis, Carlos, "De resistencias y últimos recursos: Notas para una crónica del feminismo en México." *Casa del tiempo* 71:8 (May–June 1987).

Rojas, Rosa, *Chiapas, ¿y las mujeres qué?* Mexico City: Ediciones La Correa Feminista-Centro de Investigación y Capacitación de la Mujer, 1994.

Steinbach, Nancy Saporta, Marysa Navarro-Aranguren, Patricia Churchryk, and Sonia E. Alvarez, "Feminism in Latin America: From Bogotá to San Bernardo." *Signs* 17:2 (1992).

Tuñon Pablos, Esperanza, *Mujeres que se organizan: El Frente Unico Pro-Derechos de la Mujer 1935–1938.* Mexico City: Miguel Angel Porrúa-UNAM, 1992.

—GABRIELA CANO

FERNÁNDEZ, MANUEL FÉLIX

See Victoria, Guadalupe

FERNÁNDEZ DE LIZARDI, JOSÉ JOAQUÍN

1776–1827 • Writer and Journalist

José Joaquín Fernández de Lizardi was born in Mexico City and raised in Tepotzotlán in the present-day state of Mexico. He later moved back to Mexico City, and there studied Latin grammar with a private teacher and began to study for a philosophy baccalaureate in the Colegio de San Ildefonso, although he never finished the degree. He probably worked as a public servant. In 1805 or 1806 he married María Dolores Orendáin, with whom he had a child in 1813.

For some months in 1810 he worked as lieutenant of justice in Taxco, replacing the Spaniard in charge, who had fled fearing an imminent attack by Miguel Hidalgo y Costilla's insurgent troops. After notifying the viceroy of his plans, he gave arms, ammunition, and gunpowder to the rebels. He was taken prisoner by Spanish authorities and sent to Mexico City. However, he was freed after explaining the circumstances that forced him to act in such a way. After that he chiefly lived from his writing. Nonetheless, years later the administration of Guadalupe Victoria allocated him a pension as a retired captain in recognition of his services to the country. In 1825 he also worked as editor for the *Government Gazette.* He was in prison several times during his lifetime, and died of tuberculosis.

Fernández de Lizardi began his literary career in 1809, with the poem "Polaca en honor de nuestro Católico Monarca el Señor don Fernando Séptimo con motivo de su coronación." He wrote poems, fables, 7 plays, 4 novels, 9 journals, 279 pamphlets, and assorted articles in various newspapers in the country.

His *El Periquillo Sarniento* was among the earliest Latin American novels. However, Fernández de Lizardi substantially was a journalist and pamphleteer committed to Mexico's everyday life. He chose to write novels largely because the government suspended freedom of press, and censors kept close watch over his texts.

Convinced of the importance of education, Fernández de Lizardi tried both to teach and delight his audience, and therefore adopted a tone of moral sermon in his novels. Fernández de Lizardi also criticized the domestic and formal education of his time. Like all periodicals and pamphlets of early nineteenth-century Mexico, his works combine dialogues, fables, verses, editorial comments, news, and letters. His most innovative works sought to reproduce the dialects and ironic sense of humor of the different classes in Mexican society.

Very early Fernández de Lizardi openly disapproved of the corruption of the colonial order. In his journal, *El Pensador Mexicano,* after congratulating the viceroy for his birthday, he asked him to render null and void a decree that authorized the military to try rebel priests, which violated legitimate jurisdictions. Owing to this request the viceroy suspended freedom of press and sent Fernández de Lizardi to jail.

Fernández de Lizardi always insisted that the 1810–11 insurrection was poorly improvised owing to Hidalgo's lack of armament and military experience. (Such a case is made in his 1812 poem "Aviso patriótico a los insurgentes de la sordina.") However, he never attacked Hidalgo's ideology, and he praised José María Morelos y Pavón's struggle. He also maintained his allegiance to the federalist and pro-independence views of American representatives to the Cádiz Courts. After the 1812 Constitution was reinstated, he analyzed in detail this political document in his 1820 journal *El Conductor Eléctrico*. In 1821 the Spanish army had defeated all rebel armed movements except the one headed by Vicente Guerrero. This year in his pamphlet *Chamorro y Dominiquín. Diálogo jocoserio sobre la independencia de la América,* Fernández de Lizardi asserted that Spain's political and economic situation had deteriorated to the point that independence would come by itself.

In the struggle for independence, he joined the party of Agustín de Iturbide. From Tepotzotlán he directed the army's portable press. Before Iturbide was crowned emperor, Fernández de Lizardi advocated for a republican system. However, later he accepted the monarchy with a local emperor, arguing that according to the Treaties of Córdoba a Bourbon could rule over Mexico. Nonetheless, he sought to convince Iturbide to organize a constitutional monarchy (as he advocated in his journal *El amigo de la paz y de la patria* and his pamphlet *Segundo sueño,* both from 1822). Finally, he urged Iturbide to abdicate as emperor because, as the Casa Mata Uprising showed, the population preferred the republican system. After the death of the emperor, he excused him in his play *Unipersonal de don Agustín de Iturbide, emperador que fue de México.* In 1823, he minutely dealt with the advantages of a federal republic in *El payaso de los periódicos.*

Therefore, in his 1823 journal *El hermano del perico que cantaba victoria,* Fernández de Lizardi alerted against the possibilities of a new Spanish conquest of Mexico. Until the first years of President Guadalupe Victoria's administration, independence was still incomplete because Spain continued to hold the San Juan Ulúa island, off Veracruz, the main Mexican port of maritime trade. Moreover, from his 1824–25 journal *Conversaciones del payo y el sacristán* until his last writings, Fernández de Lizardi insisted on the danger of

Mexico being conquered by the Holy Alliance. Toward the end of his life he joined an anti-Spanish movement, but later he abandoned it.

Fernández de Lizardi's reformist ideals deserve special attention. Fernández de Lizardi defended several theses. He was for equality before the law, freedom of the press, direct election of legislative representatives, and the importing of foreign technology and labor, forcing capital to remain in Mexico. Although he was a convinced Catholic, he denounced the Inquisition's repressive methods from the beginning. As of 1822 he proposed several measures: that the state expropriate Catholic Church properties and control the tithe, and that priests make chastity vows only after the age of 40. He also asked for the suppression of canonries and the enactment of religious tolerance. In his 1826–27 *Correo semanario de México,* he summarized the history of the Roman Catholic papacy, showing that popes had failed, and that some had been corrupt and tyrannical. In 1822 he published his *Defensa de los Francmasones.* This pamphlet was used as an excuse to excommunicate him. He asked forgiveness, and the Catholic Church pardoned him. Nonetheless, Fernández de Lizardi insistently continued to promote his reformist proposals. When he died, his remains were shown to refute the legend that he was possessed.

Select Bibliography

Fernández de Lizardi, José Joaquín, *Obras,* edited by María Rosa Palazón Mayoral, et al. 13 vols., Mexico City: UNAM, 1963–.

González Obregón, Luis, *Novelistas mexicanos: Don José Joaquín Fernández de Lizardi (El Pensador Mexicano).* Mexico City: Botas, 1938.

Spell, Jefferson Rea, *The Life and Works of José Joaquín Fernández de Lizardi.* Philadelphia: University of Pennsylvania Press, 1931.

—MARÍA ROSA PALAZÓN MAYORAL

FERNÁNDEZ ROMO, EMILIO (EL INDIO FERNÁNDEZ)

1904–86 • Director and Actor

Emilio Fernández Romo, known as El Indio (The Indian) Fernández, was the Mexican film industry's most colorful director. He directed 41 films and was also an actor. His work in the 1940s epitomized the golden era of Mexican cinema.

Fernández was born in the mining area of El Hondo, Coahuila. As a boy he took part in the Mexican Revolution, and in 1923 in the de la Huerta Rebellion, after which he had to emigrate to the United States, where he took various jobs, including work as a film extra. According to his own version of these events, in Hollywood he had the opportu-

nity to see the rushes of *Tormenta sobre México* by Sergey Eisenstein, which impressed him tremendously and focused his ideas on the social function of cinema.

In 1933 he was deported to Mexico and went to the capital to start in the film industry as an actor. One of his starring roles was in *Janitzio* (directed by Carlos Navarro in 1934). In 1937 he played the lead and narrator in *Adios Nicanor* (directed by Rafael Portas). In 1941 he directed his first film, *La isla de la pasión,* and followed this in 1942 with *Soy puro mexicano.* Many of his stylistic obsessions appeared in these two films. In 1942 he teamed up with Agustín Fink, who as head of the production company Films Mundiales was interested in establishing a national cinema. In 1943 Fernández directed *Flor Silvestre*, in which his leading actress was Dolores del Río (who had become a top star in Hollywood), and his leading man was Pedro Armendáriz (who had starred in two of his previous films). Fernández put a first-class team together including the photographer Gabriel Figueroa and the scriptwriter Mauricio Magdaleno. In 1943, also with Dolores del Río and Pedro Armendáriz, he filmed *María Candelaria*, which won prizes at the Cannes Film Festival of 1946 and at Lucerne in 1947. As a result, he acquired an unusual influence in the Mexican film industry and was recognized internationally.

The most important period of his career came during the 1940s, in which he made classics such as *Las abandonadas, Bugambilia, Pepita Jiménez, La perla, Enamorada, El fugitivo* (co-directed with John Ford), *Río Escondido, Maclovia, Salón México, Pueblerina, La malquerida*, and *Duelo en las montañas*. These films were successful at home and abroad, and even today they are presented as prototypes of quality Mexican cinema. His later films tended to repeat his themes and obsessions—the director did not adapt to the new needs of the public, so he remained rather isolated. Among the more notable of these later works were *Víctimas del pecado, La bien amada, El mar y tú, La red*, and *La rosa blanca*.

Fernández undoubtedly stamped his films with his personality. Its essence is nationalist in tone, inspired by the Mexican school of painting, and particularly murals. Fernández wanted to create a Mexican school of cinema that would place images with a social meaning onto celluloid. In this sense he wanted to underline the value of the indigenous population in Mexican culture. He insisted on the symbolic importance of land as the material from which nationhood was nurtured and land as educator, as the *sine qua non* medium of progress.

If much of this approach to cinema was influenced by Eisenstein, the Russian director also influenced Fernández's visual style, for example in his taste for vast plains and pictures of the countryside presented in tangible form. The last point is evident from the frequency that prickly pears and magueys fill the screen, shot from their most aesthetically pleasing angle, and also the slow rhythm of the narrative. For Emilio Fernández, the preoccupation with the beauty of the countryside takes on an element of painting, inasmuch as his images often appear as fixed frame. His admiration for Mexican art led him to show great works of architecture, sculpture, and painting from all periods. The director also recognized the influence of the U.S. cinema, and in particular the director John Ford.

The majority of his films were rural dramas, and the theme of the Mexican Revolution was ever present. Nevertheless, he attempted some urban dramas, and even tried a comedy. His films were shown frequently in Mexico, and won prizes in various international festivals, among them Cannes, Lucerne, Karlovy-Vary, and Venice.

Fernández actively participated in the creation of his public image as "El Indio," which allowed him to play out his cinematic fixations in his own personality. He liked to exaggerate that part of himself (his mother was a Kikapoo), dress in the elaborate *charro* costumes of Mexican *rancheros*, and display a violence that he thought virile, while seemingly inconsistently sensitive at the same time. El Indio portrayed himself as the quintessential macho Mexican. His films attempt to find the essence of what is Mexican in a series of folkloric stereotypes, and he considered himself to be an authentic representative. In this sense, the violence forms a part of his fame, and he was notorious for starting quarrels. In 1976 he killed a peasant in Coahuila, a crime for which he spent six months in jail.

During the last years of his life he felt abandoned and betrayed by those running the Mexican film industry. He died in Mexico City on August 7, 1986.

Select Bibliography

Fernández, Adela, *El Indio Fernández: Vida y mito*. Mexico City: Panorama, 1988.

García Riera, Emilio, *Emilio Fernández:* Guadalajara: Universidad de Guadalajara, CIEC-Cineteca Nacional, 1987.

Mora, Carl J., *Mexican Cinema: Reflections of a Society, 1896–1982*. Berkeley: University of California Press, 1982.

Rozado, Alejandro, *Cine y realidad social en México: Una lectura de la obra de Emilio Fernández*. Guadalajara: CIEC, 1991.

Taibo, Paco Ignacio, *El Indio Fernández: El cine por mis pistolas*. Mexico City: Joaquín Mortiz-Planeta, 1991.

Tuñón, Julia, *En su propio espejo: Entrevista con Emilio "Indio" Fernández*. Mexico City: UAM-Iztapalapa, 1988.

——, "Emilio Fernández: Un regard derrière les grilles." In *Le cinéma mexicain*, edited by Paulo Antonio Paranagua. Paris: Editions du Centre Pompidou, 1992.

—Julia Tuñón Pablos

FESTIVAL CYCLE

The Mexican calendar is punctuated by several overlapping festive systems that map the year's trajectory. While the annual calendar varies from region to region, reflecting differences in local history, settlement patterns, and seasonal activities, a rotating festive cycle with its preferred mechanisms for commemoration and organizational style may be identified as pan-Mexican. While these celebrations are broad based, observed by many members of a large constituency (e.g., all Mexicans, all Catholics, all residents of a particular state or city), individuals often mark personal life passage rituals, in conjunction with mass celebrations linked to the culture's annual celebratory system.

The festive round has changed over time and traces its earliest forerunners to the cycle of calendrical celebrations that characterized precontact Mesoamerican culture. The festival is a complex genre combining a range of performance forms from drama to music, special foods to processions, religious masses to political rallies, fireworks to costumes.

While the majority of commemorated dates in Mexico are religious in nature, a significant number of festivals have a secular focus, commemorating affairs of state of a political nature. The celebration of this network of festivals was initiated in the post-Independence period, when the goals of state formation were served through historical commemorations. Often the litany of festive forms and elements are not strictly distinguishable from those present in purely religious festival, where the patriotic element is seldom absent.

The periodicity of regional markets and the highly interactive patterns of economic exchange suggest that markets and, later, commercial expositions or *ferias* may be understood correctly in relation to the festive cycle. They occur seasonally or periodically on a regional, state, or city-wide basis. Often featuring local specialties, these expositions may be devoted to the products of a single industry or sector. Often, specialized markets take place in conjunction with cultural celebrations, tailoring commercial products to particular festive needs and select symbols.

Mexico has experienced an influx of transculturated celebrations in the secular and religious realm; from Christmas to Halloween, Mother's Day to May Day, these events have been embraced and naturalized to varying degrees. Like canned food and *la semana inglesa* (the westernized workweek), the degree to which these foreign-born celebrations have taken root is an indication of patterns of acculturation and cultural resonance.

The dramatic and attractive qualities of festival have historically been recognized and exploited by the government and tourist-related industry as a tool for promoting Mexican culture to visitors and residents. Here festival functions as a tool for nation building and revenue production. Deductively, philosophers of Mexican national character have seized upon festival as a model for understanding *lo mexicano* (the Mexican), seeking in the metaphor of material excess and masked identity a cultural verity.

On the local economic level, festival often requires an enormous mobilization of resources and necessitates a modification of usual fiscal arrangements: household funds may be shared, collectivized, or redirected from usual channels. As economics are rearranged, so is "business as usual" suspended: mundane work yields to the special work of festival. Mundane time is overshadowed by the intensified quality of festival time; celebrations that reoccur over the calendar cycle mark the unity of human purpose over the years while they underscore the changes that occur in human lives from year to year.

Pre-Columbian Annual Cycle

Among the pre-Columbian Mesoamericans, notions of chronology and of the calendrical cycle were well in place. Both the Mexica (Aztecs) and the Maya calculated that their respective cultures had passed through prior ages that had concluded in apocalypse. The measurement of a greatly extended period is especially evident in the Maya. Their long count, a roughly 5,000-year period, was based on the vigesimal (20-based) count and was itself divided into a range of smaller periods of years and days. These cycles were based in highly evolved astronomical observations.

The reckoning of time and notation of its passage served a range of ends. Charting the succession of natural phenomena—such as the changing seasons and the shifting constellations—was anchored to a set of social rituals contrived to ensure the smooth continuation of that succession. The cyclical pattern of time's recorded passage was evidence of the regenerative potential of time and living things and the importance of seasonal renewal. In addition, fates and fortunes—for individuals, groups, and the culture as a whole—were augured through portents based on calendrical calculations of auspicious or blighted dates.

The dominant cycle in terms of individual human life span is the calendar round of 52 years, observed by Maya and Mexica alike, although probably not synchronously. The calendar round consisted of two simultaneously occurring day counts. One consisted of 260 days, which cycled 73 times in the 52-year period; the other consisted of 365 days, which cycled 52 times in that same number of years. Every day was named in two ways, according to the two calendars, and it would take the 52 rotations of 365 days for the concurrence of the identical pairing of days on the two calendars to repeat. All possible combinations of the two calendars were exhausted after 18,980 days, equaling 52 years.

The 260-day cycle, called Tonalpohualli by Mexica and Tzolkin (according to some sources) by the Maya, pertains to the sacred, ritual, or divinatory year. The cycle consisted of 260 days built into 13 periods of 20 days each. Days were identified by the assignment of 20 day names and 13 numbers, given in succession so each of the 260 days had a unique name and number combination. This was the basic ritual calendar utilized through Mesoamerica. Under the Mexica the Tonalpohualli was the most important cycle, with each of the 13 periods under the patronage of a specific deity or deities. The cycle of rituals were conducted by a priestly class.

The other cycle comprised the solar or agricultural year consisting of 365 days. This was called Haab by the Maya and Xiuitl by the Mexica. Here there were a total of 18 months of 20 days comprising 360 days with an additional period of 5 days called Nemontemi by the Mexica and Wayeb by the Maya; this extra 5-day period was considered very unlucky. A series of 4 day names were given on a rotating basis to the years in this cycle, known as the Year Bearers among the Maya.

Among the Mexica, the beginning of the calendar round was celebrated with the New Fire ritual. An additional ceremony was held every four years when the cycle of four day names had run through. Every eight years were marked by a celebration that commemorated the coincidence of the year with the planet Venus's 584-day period. Ce ueuetiliztli (One Old Age) the longest period in Mexica chronology, represented the completion of two 52-year cycles, the coincidence of the years of the sun and the years of Venus were marked with ritual. The Maya, extremely sophisticated in systems of numeration and the recording of dates, had a similar set of ritual observances. The first month of the new year, Pop (corresponding to July in the Gregorian calendar) was a time for renewal ceremonies.

Post-Conquest

With colonization came the imposition of the Gregorian calendar, a modification of the Roman calendar inherited ultimately from Egypt. This new calendar, complete with notions of a beginning of sacred time and method of time measurement, was based on twelve months, each with a set number of days. An additional day was added every four years. Each of the days had a name that repeated over the seven-day weekly cycle. Movement through mundane time was cyclical through 365 days comprising 52 weeks and 12 months, yet every day was uniquely identified based on the sequence of years. While the calendar marked mundane time, the Catholic Church had other systems for marking sacred time. The year was divided according to the two central festivals and their seasons. Regularity in the Christian calendar may be seen in the repetition of Sunday worship, recitation of the rosary, and confession. Certain holidays were fixed; others were movable, scheduled in relation to each other and the occurrence of Sundays.

Advent (Adviento), which marks the beginning the church year commencing around the end of November, is the period preceding Christmas (Navidad). The Sunday after Christmas celebrates the Epiphany and Adoration of the Three Kings (Epifania/Adoración de los Santos Reyes). A week later is the Sunday that concludes the Christmas season, the Baptism (Bautismo) of Christ.

Following this season is the first period of ordinary time, which ensues through Lent (Cuaresma). Preceded on Tuesday by Mardi Gras (Martes de Carnaval), Lent begins on Ash Wednesday (Miercoles de Ceniza) and comprises the 6 Sundays and 40 weekdays that lead up to Easter (Pascua) and Holy Week (Semana Santa). Following Easter, the second block of ordinary time begins, ultimately ending with the period of Advent. Unlike the earlier period of ordinary time, there are a series of major movable feasts that occur during this period. Among these are these are the Assumption of Christ (Ascención del Señor), Pentecost (Pentecostes), Trinity Sunday (Santisima Trinidad), and Corpus Christi. The feast of Christ the King (Cristo Rey) is the last Sunday of the church year.

Fixed feasts often are associated with commemoration of particular saints and events in the life of Jesus, such as the Birth of Christ (Nacimiento) on December 25 and All Saint's Day (Todos Santos) November 1. Several holy days are associated with the Virgin Mary, including the Immaculate Conception (La Purisima Concepción de Maria Santisima) on December 8, Solemnity of Mary (Solemnidad de la Santisima Virgen Maria Madre de Dios) on January 1, and the Assumption of Mary (La Asunción de la Santisima Virgen) on August 15. Candlemas (Candelaria) on February 2 as well as the Nativity of Mary (El Nacimiento de la Santisima Virgen) on September 8, while no longer holy days of obligation, are still practiced as feasts in Mexico. Virtually every day is assigned to the commemoration of the feast day of one or more biblical or postbiblical saint. Mandatory days for national religious observation for individual saints other than Mary include the feast of Saint Joseph (March 19) and Saints Peter and Paul (June 29).

As with the pre-Conquest traditions, children often were named for the personage on whose special day their birth fell. The other important way in which the round of saints' days is commemorated is through the celebrations that mark the assigned patron of every level of civil organization within Mexico, from the national patron, the highly revered Virgin de Guadalupe (December 12), to the patrons of the cities, towns, and barrios of the republic. The guilds, cofradías (confraternities), religious orders, and other groups also sponsored elaborate festivals for their patrons in colonial Mexico. Special patterns of reverence endure that link festival to a particular saint or a specific manifestation of the saint made immanent through holy image with miraculous powers.

A range of new religious observations were imposed by the Catholic Church with its inventory of festive practices that shared common features with the preexisting indigenous vocabulary of celebration. While the forms and practice of Christianity were imposed, the native perspective on these ritual observances resisted obliteration. A religious *mestizaje* (mixing of indigenous and European) relating to calendar customs prevailed in practices such as the dual naming of the religious pantheon, the integration of indigenous traditions of material culture (use of incenses, botanicals, foods, sacred bundles, paper figures, etc., which ensured that indigenous forms, while eclipsed, have survived). The superficially Christian worship at sites of indigenous importance and aspects of the contemporary structures of festival organization also may hold pre-Conquest traces. Foremost among the genres of festival commemoration with strong indigenous antecedents are the festive dance-drama cycles that have become associated with patronal celebrations as well as those commemorating Christmas, New Year's Day, and, on a national level, the feast day of the Virgin of Guadalupe. Although highly influenced by the festive dramas taught by Spanish friars and other religious as part of the project of catechistic indoctrination after the Conquest, festive performance has reverted to the dominion of the local populace—away from the control of the official church. At least 80 dance or dramatic forms have been listed as comprising a part of local festival celebration. Distinctive among these are dramatic cycles such as the Moors and Christians (Moros y Cristianos) and its many variants. Others include the Apaches, Aztecas, Concheros, Conquista, la Pluma, Malinche, Matachines, Moctezumas, Negros, Pastores, Tecuanes, Tlacololeros, Vaqueros, and Voladores. *Pastorelas* (Nativity scenes) occur during the Christmas season.

Civic Celebrations

Initiated in the post-Independence period, a civic calendar with special national observances was promoted energetically. As the national project was transformed through the Reforma (1856–62), the French Intervention (1862–67), the Restored Republic (1867–76), and the Porfiriato (1876–1910), the goals and content of national pageants changed dramatically. Festival was used to legitimize power arrangements and create social cohesion and a sense of corporate purpose and identity. Although nominally secular, commemorations of a civic nature were well laced with religious overtones. By the close of the Revolutionary period, the catalog of civic holidays observed today had taken form. The key observances marked the trajectory of nation formation, codifying important birth dates, battles, and steps toward autonomy. National holidays in this group include Independence Day, September 16; the anniversary of the Mexican Revolution, November 20; and the anniversary of the Constitutions of 1857 and 1917, February 5. Of a somewhat lesser magnitude are the birth date of Benito Juárez, March 21; Labor Day, May 1; the Battle of Puebla, May 5; and the opening of Congress, September 1. National celebra-

tions where businesses are not mandated to close include Flag Day, February 24; Nationalization of Oil, March 18; Pan American Day, April 14; and Día de la Raza, October 12. Political rallies spontaneous and focused on contemporary concerns, may occur in conjunction with key historical dates, sometimes in locations of key symbolic significance for the nation, often using the rhetoric and form that characterizes the patriotic discourse of commemoration.

As in earlier periods of cultural intervention and interpenetration, transnational secular holidays have been adopted in cosmopolitan centers. Valentine's Day—celebrated in Mexico as a national day commemorating friendship—and Mother's Day and the Day of the Child have fairly permanent calendrical slots. Celebrations such as Fathers' Day and Secretary's Day have had slower acceptance rates. Secularized celebrations such as Halloween have been commercially promoted in competition with the traditional Día de Los Muertos (Day of the Dead), a celebration after Todos Santos with strong indigenous elements. This trend has elicited vocal resistance in many social sectors.

While U.S. calendars have adjusted the timing of many civic holidays to occur on weekends, in Mexico these holidays as well as religiously linked celebrations generally are observed on the actual day on which they fall. Newer, inherited holidays are more mutable.

See also Day of the Dead; Mesoamerica: Calendrics; Posadas; Ritual, Religious and Civic

Select Bibliography

Beezley, William H., Cheryl English Martin, and William E. French, editors, *Rituals of Rule, Rituals of Resistance: Public Celebrations and Popular Culture in Mexico.* Wilmington, Delaware: SR Books, 1994.

Leon, Imelda de, editor, *Calendario de fiestas populares.* 2nd edition, Mexico City: Dirección General de Culturas Populares, 1988.

Paz, Octavio, "Mexican Masks." In *The Labyrinth of Solitude.* New York: Grove Press, 1985.

Sahagún, Bernadino de, "Libro Segundo: Que trata del Calendario: Fiestas y ceremonias, sacrificios y solemnidades que estos naturales de esta Nueva España hacían a honra de sus dioses." In *Historia General de las Cosas de Nueva España.* Mexico City: Porrúa, 1979.

Schele, Linda, and David Freidel, *A Forest of Kings: The Untold Story of the Ancient Maya.* New York: Morrow, 1990.

171° Calendario del más antiguo Galván para el año de 1994. Mexico City: Libreria y Ediciones Murguia, 1996.

Toor, Frances, *A Treasury of Mexican Folkways.* New York: Crown Publishers, 1947.

—EMILY SOCOLOV

FLORES MAGÓN, RICARDO

1873 or 1874–1922 • Intellectual and Politician

Ricardo Flores Magón was born in Oaxaca, the second of three sons of a mestiza mother and an Indian father. While studying law, he began his political life by demonstrating against the dictator Porfirio Díaz's fourth reelection in 1892; Flores Magón earned arrest and imprisonment for his efforts. Initially, his opposition to Díaz took the form of mild criticism, but the newspapers he worked for were shut down and Flores Magón himself arrested. Like many others, Flores Magón became convinced that wholesale reform, even revolution, would be necessary for Mexico. Unlike others, however, Flores Magón concentrated on the disinherited and came to see radical anarchism as the only solution to the problems created by capitalism in Mexico and the world. Thus while beginning with efforts to change the Mexican government, Flores Magón gradually came to oppose any form of government anywhere as merely disguised tyranny. Flores Magón was perceived as a dangerous man by the United States as well as by various Mexican governments. He spent 20 years in the United States continuing his "subversive" activities and died in an American prison at Leavenworth Penitentiary, Kansas. Historical assessments frequently concentrate on his earlier, reform-minded thinking, and slight Flores Magón's commitment to anarchism.

Despite affiliations with other dissident presses, Flores Magón is indissolubly linked to the newspaper he created, edited episodically, and wrote for continuously, *Regeneración*. Flores Magón began *Regeneración* in Mexico City in 1900, as a reformist periodical. He ran afoul of the Díaz regime for printing "critical" articles about the dictator a year later and spent a total of 22 of the subsequent 29 months in darkened cells in Díaz's most notorious prison for various crimes against the regime, all committed by Flores Magón's intellect and voiced in the pages of *Regeneración*.

Frustrated by the ongoing harassment of the Mexican dictatorship, Flores Magón went to the United States in 1904, where he believed freedom of speech would allow him to express publicly the thoughts silenced in his native country. Díaz's agents, however, continued their harassment across the border, causing Flores Magón, his younger brother Enrique, and their associates to spend several long months moving from city to city. At last Flores Magón reestablished *Regeneración* in Los Angeles, where he continued to publish it intermittently, with Enrique's help, until U.S. authorities finally suppressed it.

By 1904, at least, Flores Magón had moved beyond the goal of reforming the Mexican regime and committed himself to radical violence to overthrow it. Drawing upon the conspiratorial theories of Mikhail Bakunin, Flores Magón created *focos*, paramilitary bands capable of invading Mexico from the United States to attack small cities, the winning of which would spark the general uprising that Flores Magón believed would topple the regime. Flores Magón followed this course from 1904 until about 1909.

As Flores Magón pursued anarchist thought, however, he gradually became convinced that he should cease his conspiratorial approach, abandon direct control of the *focos,* and invest his trust in the disinherited poor. To do so, Flores Magón decided to engage the enemy through a propaganda effort massive enough to mobilize the entire Mexican nation. To Flores Magón, toppling the regime was insufficient; the Mexican people had to seize control directly of all the means of production and distribution. The Mexican people should do so as one person, without central direction. Flores Magón would support no leader, nor would he lead a faction or party himself, despite his leadership of the opposition Partido Liberal Mexicano (PLM). Flores Magón instead would serve as watchdog and critic for all. Not until the PLM manifesto of September 23, 1911, however, did Flores Magón fully reveal himself as anarchist, formally disavowing the very reform program (as expressed in a July 1, 1906, manifesto) that had given both the PLM and Flores Magón their greatest popularity.

Irony, contradiction, dedication to the plight of the poor, and personal suffering were the essence of Floresmagonismo. Flores Magón's leaderless *focos* began the violence we now call the Mexican Revolution, yet the wealthy landowner and opposition politician Francisco I. Madero captured the most important of these forces and converted them to his adherents en route to his victory over Díaz. Flores Magón fled to the United States to avoid a return to prison, but he spent nearly half of his 20 years in America jailed or imprisoned and had 15 years remaining on his last sentence when he died of an apparent heart attack. U.S. courts convicted him of violating U.S. neutrality laws, of conspiring to overthrow the U.S. government, and of sending obscene materials through the mail. Most of these charges were based upon articles and editorials he had published in *Regeneración*.

By choosing propaganda by the pen over propaganda by the deed, by choosing anti-politics, Flores Magón made himself progressively more irrelevant to the ongoing political struggle of the Mexican Revolution. Remaining in the United States contributed to his isolation from Mexican affairs. From Los Angeles, Flores Magón denounced Madero, Venustiano Carranza, Francisco "Pancho" Villa, and others as mere personalists and maintained a cautious distance from Emiliano Zapata, fearful that Zapata might succumb to the same failing as the others. Yet Flores Magón's determined commitment to the poor earned him a small but intensely loyal following.

After his death, Flores Magón's body was returned to Mexico for burial by Mexican workers. In eulogizing him before the Mexican Chamber of Deputies, Antonio Díaz Soto y Gama proclaimed Flores Magón "the precursor" of the Mexican Revolution, a well intentioned but superficial assessment that stressed Flores Magón's early reformist strategies while ignoring his anarchism. The Mexican state, seeking to consolidate its power, saw the value of presenting Flores Magón as "precursor" to Madero, and on May Day, 1945, the state reburied Flores Magón in the Rotunda of Illustrious Men to celebrate his role in bringing about the Revolutionary regime. In death and reburial, Flores Magón became what he had denounced in his mature life—a supporter of the state. Still, his trenchant analyses of the unresolved economic and social ills of Mexico and the United States, reprinted regularly since his death, have won Flores Magón new readers on both sides of the border and in every generation succeeding Madero's.

Select Bibliography

Abad de Santillán, Diego, *Ricardo Flores Magón: El ápostol de la revolución social mexicana.* Mexico City: Grupo Cultural "Ricardo Flores Magón," 1925; 3rd edition, Mexico City: Secretaria del Trabajo y Prevision Social, 1986.

Albro, Ward S., *Always a Rebel: Ricardo Flores Magón and the Mexican Revolution.* Fort Worth: Texas Christian University Press, 1992.

Avrich, Paul, *Anarchist Portraits.* Princeton, New Jersey: Princeton University Press, 1988.

Bartra, Armando, editor, *Regeneración, 1900–1918: La corriente más radical de la revolución mexicana de 1910 a través de su periódico de combate.* Mexico City: Era, 1977; 5th edition, 1985.

Ferrua, Piero, *Gli Anarchici nella Rivoluzione Messicana: Praxedis G. Guerrero.* Ragusa: La Fiaccola, 1976.

MacLachlan, Colin M., *Anarchism and the Mexican Revolution: The Political Trials of Ricardo Flores Magón in the United States.* Berkeley: University of California Press, 1991.

Raat, W. Dirk, *Revoltosos: Mexico's Rebels in the United States, 1903–1934.* College Station: Texas A & M University Press, 1981.

Sandos, James A., *Rebellion in the Borderlands: Anarchism and the Plan of San Diego, 1904–1923.* Norman: University of Oklahoma Press, 1992.

—JAMES A. SANDOS

FOOD PRODUCTION, CONSUMPTION, AND POLICY

Since 1940, food consumption has risen dramatically in Mexico, in large measure owing to significant increases in production. These improvements were the result of the accelerated implementation of the agrarian reform and a significant investment in research and infrastructure. This success is also the consequence of an effective institutional effort to subsidize essential foods and distribute a minimum package of goods through a chain of government-affiliated outlets that assured broad coverage for the program. With the implementation of structural adjustment programs to combat recurring crises since 1982, however, public policy was reoriented toward opening the country to greater trade and foreign investment, with critical effects on food production and consumption in Mexico.

In 1920, in the wake of the Revolution, the Mexican countryside was in disarray. Large numbers of people had been killed and huge areas left untilled. Peasants were clamoring for land, but large-scale distribution was not to be implemented until the latter half of the 1930s. As early as the turn of the century, however, it was already obvious to many policy makers that the secret to confronting the growing crisis of food production and the poverty of Mexico's population lay in increasing physical yields in the rain-fed food-producing areas cultivated by peasant communities; the Estación Experimental de San Jacinto (transformed into the Instituto de Investigaciones Agrícolas in the 1940s) initiated a serious research and extension program to provide

small-scale farmers with technical assistance to raise yields and reduce post-harvest losses.

Peasant society was galvanized by the change in land distribution policy. President Lázaro Cárdenas (1934–40) accelerated the difficult task of implementing the agrarian reform, creating a new environment in which peasant agriculture could thrive. As a result of the transfer of vast areas from the landed gentry to peasant communities and the confirmation or extension of the holdings of indigenous communities, small-scale producers were assured the security of tenure they needed to embark on long-term programs to improve soil and water management, raising the quality of their lands and dramatically increasing agricultural output and rural welfare.

The improvements were evident almost immediately. During the following quarter century (1940–65), the cultivated area in Mexico grew at a compound annual rate of 3.74 percent; the area under cultivation increased 250 percent from 5.2 million to almost 14.8 million hectares (14.6 million to 36.6 million acres). Most of this new area was dedicated to basic crops: maize, beans, wheat, and rice; they accounted for more than two-thirds (69 percent) of the increase.

At the same time, important advances were being made in improving yields. The most publicized was the ambitious program of collaboration with U.S. scientific institutions to apply emerging technologies to wheat cultivation, creating what would come to be known as the "green revolution," for which the Nobel Peace Prize would be awarded to Norman Borlaug. Wheat yields increased from 600 kilograms per hectare (535 pounds per acre) in 1940 to more than 2.5 metric tons (2.8 short tons) in 1965 (6.1 percent a year), reflecting two important changes: the shift from dry-land cultivation in the central part of the country to the new irrigation districts in the northwest, controlled by a new rural elite; and the introduction of new varieties of seeds that were resistant to plagues and prevented the problem of lodging, or the bending of the stalk that caused the seed to rot before harvest. Although less spectacular, the sustained increase in maize yields, 2.8 percent compounded annually during 25 years, reflects the impressive efforts of the peasantry to bring to bear their knowledge and hard work to improve productive conditions in the absence of a research program or an effective governmental program to assist poorer farmers in the rain-fed (or dry land) areas of the country. When measured in value terms, and adjusting for the increase in cultivated area, the rise in the productivity of the basic food crops during this period was 2.8 percent per year compounded annually, a remarkably high rate that reflects the combined contribution of the scientific community, government investment, and peasants.

The increase in domestic food output not only permitted an end to food imports but also an improvement in consumption standards. With the exception of 1963, the decade of the 1960s was notable for the achievement of food self-sufficiency; this was so important that in 1962, the president anticipated events, predicting that henceforth, Mexicans would not have to suffer the ignominy of having to make their tortillas from imported grain. The process was all the more remarkable because of the significant rise in caloric intake and the quality of the diet. The physical quantity of food increased by 39 percent from 1940 to 1965, lifting average consumption to more than 2,700 calories per day; this increase was attributed not only to the greater availability of grains, but also to a broader inclusion of animal products and fruits and vegetables in the daily diet. As peasant food output became a major factor in the national supply system, it is not surprising that these national averages also reflect widespread improvements in nutrition that were generally observable.

Even as politicians were celebrating these accomplishments, however, the country gradually was falling back to a pattern of dependency on international trade to feed the people. Two related phenomena were decisive in shaping the future evolution of agriculture, both tied to the way in which Mexico was being integrated into the world economy. The first, amply commented on at the time, was the growing influence of livestock in agricultural production. Between 1965 and 1982 the area dedicated to forage crops and pasture grew at a compound annual rate of 13.5 percent, from less than 500,000 to more than 3.8 million hectares (or from 1.2 million to 9.4 million acres); as a consequence, the area sown with basic food crops declined from 10.8 million to 8.5 million hectares (26.7 million to 21.0 million acres) in the same period.

This dramatic change was the direct result of the intervention of transnational animal feed companies. To create a demand for their genetic stock, animal feed, and other inputs, they promoted new technologies for transforming poultry and hog raising from a backyard sideline into a full-fledged industry. Their most striking innovation was the introduction of sorghum as an animal feed; previously unknown in Mexico, this grain became the crop of choice for privileged farmers who could obtain the seeds and credit, since it could be sown on the same lands as corn but without the onerous restrictions and limited returns created by the government control system for corn production. Thus, in spite of the fact that there were no government research or credit programs to promote this process, Mexico found itself in the midst of a production revolution, initiating a process that would eventually create a profound agricultural crisis, disintegrating peasant communities throughout the country.

A related process was set in motion by the substantial investments by the public sector in infrastructure. A program to harness Mexico's considerable water resources for regional development was initiated in the 1930s, but received its strongest stimulus after World War II. Beginning in the northern part of the country, huge dams were built to irrigate desert-like landscapes and supply hydroelectric power where the terrain permitted. Initially, these projects were wildly successful in increasing output of commercial crops for industrial use as well as for export; the scale of the program was expanded to the larger rivers in the southern tropics. Little importance was attached to the wide sweep of environmental damage and social dislocation these projects occasioned; only later did it become obvious that the promised cornucopia would not be realized. The further extension of cattle raising and planting of food and export crops was so disruptive of social and natural processes that few of these projects have been successful enough to repay the costs.

With livestock development and commercial agriculture crowding out basic food production, the national government assumed the responsibility of guaranteeing adequate supplies of basic foodstuffs throughout the country. After 1970, CONASUPO, the national food supply and regulatory agency, was forced to import large quantities to supply local needs and keep domestic prices from exerting an upward pressure on urban wage rates. Subsidies became increasingly generalized and complex, rising in cost as more food had to be delivered to broader segments of the population below cost or for free.

These programs further weakened rural communities. The support system was designed to assist urban consumers, rather than producers. For lack of access to credit, water, and technical assistance, most farmers had no alternative but to continue planting their traditional crops. Low, stable guarantee prices led to a decline in output for corn, as productivity fell and many farmers left their land idle; continuing productivity gains, subsidized fees for water, and abundant credit counterbalanced the freeze in wheat prices, allowing output to expand in the northern irrigation districts; an ambitious milk delivery program efficiently targeted a needy population, but low market prices discouraged production, and Mexico became the world's largest importer of powdered milk. In an effort to improve the effectiveness of its regulatory mission, CONASUPO created its own network of stores and helped finance consumer and producer cooperatives, especially in the areas with large concentrations of urban poor or peasants.

At the end of the 1970s, the national debate about food self-sufficiency heightened as rural social conditions deteriorated and imports grew. More than 20 million Mexicans lived in conditions of extreme poverty, and an equal number suffered from nutritional deficiencies; imports, often comprised of grain of inferior quality not suited for the Mexican diet, represented more than one-fifth of the total supply. Domestic pressures to attack these problems intensified to the point that in 1980 the executive was obliged to announce its commitment to achieve self-sufficiency in the production of staple foods through a well-funded program, the Sistema Alimentario Mexicano (SAM, or Mexican Food System), of direct subsidies for inputs and attractive producer prices.

The SAM was well financed. It proposed to attack the problems of poverty and imports by stimulating production among peasant producers and broadening subsidies for urban consumers. At first much of the money, however, found its way to wealthier farmers who switched to planting corn in the irrigation districts to take advantage of the subsidies for fertilizers and modern varieties of seeds, as well as the ready availability of low interest rates for credit. Unfortunately, when the intended peasant beneficiaries finally began to participate, the 1982 foreign debt crisis forced its suspension. The experience of the SAM did show, however, that when prices are favorable and resources are available, all social groups in the Mexican countryside are capable of responding rapidly by increasing output and productive efficiency; agricultural production rose an average of 5.2 percent a year during the life of the program from 1980 to 1982. Together with more funds assigned to the tortilla program, the program was able to assure a broader coverage for consumers during these years, underscoring the potential effectiveness of direct delivery systems to attack the problem of hunger, even when poverty remained serious. Finally, the program demonstrated that if productive stimuli are to be efficient, a much better system of targeting must be developed to avoid the extravagant waste that exposed the program to widespread ridicule as part of an attack against the peasantry in the following years, obscuring the important lessons learned about the rural society's potential to contribute to national economic development.

The following years of crisis and adjustment took a heavy toll on economic opportunity and living standards of the majority. Ironically, in the first years of the period of austerity and foreign exchange shortage (1982–87), aside from the wealthy who continued to prosper, the peasantry was one social group whose living standards fell least. Since the government had fewer resources with which to implement its program of social and productive controls, rural communities took advantage of this greater freedom from institutional restraints to increase output significantly, thereby mitigating some of the pressures of the crisis, in both rural and urban areas. CONASUPO's role was more narrowly defined to assuring the delivery of basic products to a shrinking proportion of the population and to import staple products to guarantee adequate supplies to the urban areas.

Following the 1987 crisis, strict implementation of structural adjustment and severe wage controls were imposed. While real wages had been falling since 1977, real living standards fell even more sharply in these years, along with food output. The success of the adjustment program in reducing open inflation attracted large inflows of capital that further heightened internal polarization among social classes and especially in the countryside. Rural development policies were reoriented from supporting producers to stimulating corn production, reinforcing price supports with subsidies for the use of irrigation water, seeds, and fertilizers, and acreage controls in the irrigation districts. As a result, the country's wealthiest farmers uprooted export crops to plant this staple while the peasants were not able to maintain production.

Inevitably, the macroeconomic policies further deepened the production and social crisis. Emigration intensified from the countryside, and real wages fell throughout the country. Poverty and marginal working conditions became more common, while pressures strengthened for women and children to join the labor force in search of even substandard wages from precarious employment in the service sector. For poorly skilled job seekers, only the *maquiladora* industries (generally foreign-owned assembly plants along the northern border) offered any ray of hope; for the well educated, however, opportunities in electronics, financial and information services, and management were expanding rapidly. A new anti-poverty program, Solidarity, directed resources to the areas of greatest political resistance, while imports were used along with increased subsidies for tortillas and milk to restrain food price increases; for the growing numbers of workers who lost their jobs in the formal economy and the millions of peasants being pushed from their lands, these food support programs were only partially effective in slowing the slide of their families into misery.

In late 1991, President Carlos Salinas de Gortari proposed sweeping changes in Article 27 of the Mexican Constitution. These changes ushered in a new era and a new relationship between the state and rural society: the state rapidly withdrew from supporting basic food production and peasant communities. In this new regime, staple food production declined precipitously as lands could not be profitably cultivated without credit, technical assistance, and stable prices. The legislative changes granted individual titles to the communal lands distributed during more than 70 years of the agrarian reform program; it gave peasants and their communities the authority to sell the rights to use the land or even the parcels themselves. A controversial piece of legislation, it was quickly rubber-stamped by the Congress and the state legislatures, provoking the ire of peasant groups throughout the country. The counter-reform, as it has been labeled by many analysts, facilitated the participation of private capital in financing production for those fortunate beneficiaries who have access to well-drained or irrigated lands; it also expedited and legalized the process of transforming agricultural lands on urban peripheries into serviced areas for residential, commercial, and industrial expansion.

By the mid-1990s, Mexico was in the throes of another economic crisis, the most serious in more than one-half century. International economic integration and financial speculation left the country more vulnerable to international market pressures. Staple food production fell further, now that farmers in the irrigation districts once again were producing for export, and peasants were forced to leave much of their land untilled. International pressures to tighten the austerity program left the government unable and unwilling to continue the subsidy programs for basic foods, provoking an unprecedented phenomenon in Mexico: inflationary pressures were greater for the package of basic consumer goods than for the economy as a whole, further accentuating the polarizing effects of economic policy. Food imports rose, and with a rising foreign debt, external pressures simultaneously rose for the continuation of austerity programs. In this setting, there was little prospect of relief for the majority.

Peasant leaders, opposition parties, and urban consumer groups once again began calling for strategies of food self-sufficiency. In the coming years, the country once again would have to find some balance between the demands of the international market and the needs of its people.

See also Agrarian Policy; Agribusiness and Agroindustry; Cattle Ranching; Ejido; Maguey; Maize; Sistema Alimentario Mexicano (SAM). *For a discussion of the cuisine of Mexico, see* Cuisine

Select Bibliography

Appendini, Kirsten, *De la Milpa a los Tortibonos: La restructuracion de la politica alimentaria en México.* Mexico City: Colegio de México, 1992.

Austin, James, and Gustavo Esteva, editors, *Food Policy in Mexico: The Search for Self-Sufficiency.* Ithaca, New York: Cornell University Press, 1987.

Barkin, David, *Distorted Development: Mexico in the World Economy.* Boulder, Colorado: Westview, 1990.

Barkin, David, and Blanca Suárez San Roman, *El fin de la autosuficiencia alimentaria.* Mexico City: Centro de Ecodesarrollo and Nueva Imagen, 1982.

Barkin, David, and Billie R. DeWalt, "Sorghum and the Mexican Food Crisis." *Latin American Research Review* 23:3 (1988).

Fox, Jonathan, *The Political Dynamics of Reform: State Power and Food Policy in Mexico.* Ithaca, New York: Cornell University Press, 1991.

Hewitt de Alcantara, Cynthia, *Modernizing Mexican Agriculture.* Geneva: United Nations Research Institute for Social Development, 1976.

Luiselli, Casio, "The Way to Food Self-Sufficiency in Mexico." In *U.S.-Mexico Relations: Agriculture and Rural Development,* edited by Bruce Johnston, et al. Stanford, California: Stanford University Press, 1987.

Walsh, John, "Mexican Agriculture: Crisis within Crisis." *Science* 219 (1983).

—DAVID BARKIN

FOREIGN POLICY

This entry includes four articles that trace the development of Mexican foreign policy since Independence and four additional articles that discuss Mexico's role as a regional power, particularly in its relation toward the Caribbean and Central America:

Foreign Policy: 1821–76
Foreign Policy: 1876–1910
Foreign Policy: 1910–46
Foreign Policy: 1946–96
Foreign Policy: Cuba
Foreign Policy: Central America, 1821–1930
Foreign Policy: Central America, 1930–96
Foreign Policy: Contadora Group

See also Banking and Finance; Migration; Military; Nationalism; Petroleum; Southern Borders; Trade and Markets; U.S.-Mexican Border

FOREIGN POLICY: 1821–76

Most observers have described Mexican foreign relations in the first half-century after Independence as a never-ending tale of nightmares. Between 1821 and 1876, Mexico endured four major foreign interventions, at least three of which threatened the country's existence as an independent nation. Moreover, Mexico lost half of its territory to the

United States, and the country was constantly in debt to European creditors. Nevertheless, Mexican foreign relations in the so-called National period contributed to the consolidation of the Mexican state. The manifold instances of foreign intervention helped warring factions rally behind national leaders, and Mexican responses to these interventions strengthened a nationalism that had remained weak even by Latin American standards. Ultimately, Mexico's international history of the early and mid–nineteenth century laid the groundwork for the foreign policy during the rule of the dictator Porfirio Díaz and the subsequent Revolutionary regime. While Mexican foreign relations in the National period showed the country's vulnerability to foreign intervention, they also demonstrated the value of a principled policy of nonintervention and respect of international treaties, and they highlighted the nation-building potential of foreign policy.

When Mexico achieved its independence from Spain, its rulers faced a daunting task in their attempt to establish effective central authority. The country paid for the decade of violence that had preceded Independence with a prolonged state of chaos. During the Wars of Independence, rival caudillos had carved out spheres of power. After 1821, their armies upheld their bosses' claims to both regional and national influence, defying the authority of the central government. The only one of these caudillos to remain a national force throughout the next few decades, General Antonio López de Santa Anna, occupied the presidential chair many times but usually returned to his hacienda after a few months in Mexico City. Not surprisingly, the state of the Mexican economy resembled that of the country's political order. The wars had devastated Mexico's granary, the Bajío; the mining industry lay in ruins; the national treasury was empty; and commerce had declined precipitously.

Furthermore, the country's northern frontier remained unsettled and undefended. This region was Mexico's "Wild North," a vast expanse of mostly barren terrain inhabited by some 200,000 people, most of whom belonged to nomadic Indian tribes. To be sure, small towns such as San Antonio and Santa Fe dotted the landscape as tiny islands of Hispanic presence. But on the whole, this region's ties to Mexico were little more than juridical in character—and were threatened by dynamic U.S. expansionism. Much like the fellow Spanish American republic of Gran Colombia, Mexico faced imminent disintegration. Central America's secession in 1823 appeared to prove the point.

As a consequence, Mexican foreign policy after Independence, inasmuch as the government could pursue one, regarded the defense of the country's territory as its paramount goal. To remain master of the vast expanses that it had inherited from the viceroyalty, the Mexican government needed to tackle two difficult tasks: extending central government control into the entire country (and thus preventing secessions), and forestalling the encroachment by U.S. settlers.

In 1823, only two years after independence, Mexico seemed to fall woefully short in achieving the first of these goals, as the new government of Guadalupe Victoria stood idly by while Central America seceded. That year, however, a problem surfaced that demonstrated that in spite of its weakness, Mexico could act to prevent a further loss of territory in the south: the Chiapas question. Using superior political, diplomatic, and military force, Mexico incorporated the former Central American province and even increased its territory at the expense of Guatemala.

Meanwhile, foreign intervention and continued instability repeatedly threatened Mexico's own sovereignty. Spain's attempt at reconquest in 1829 led to the exodus of more than 25,000 Spaniards, among them many of the leading merchants and intellectuals of the former colony. In 1837, Britain and France used military force to obtain payment of overdue debts in the "Pastry War." A few years later, the planter elites in the Mexican state of Yucatán attempted to secede and applied to enter the United States. Even though the U.S. government rejected the overture, notice had been served that further secessions in the Mexican southeast remained a possibility.

Mexico's greatest problem, however, was the proximity of the United States—a country whose settlers pushed ever westward in search of their "manifest destiny." From the beginning, the Mexican leadership expressed concern about U.S. expansion, a concern that grew in proportion to the U.S. territorial acquisitions of the first half of the nineteenth century. In particular, the Mexican government feared the de facto annexation of the region of Texas through an unbridled migration of Anglo-Saxon farmers and fortune seekers. To prevent this scenario, President Victoria invited U.S. farmers of Catholic faith to settle permanently in Texas. As a condition, Victoria made these settlers promise to respect the sovereignty of Mexican law.

This scheme ultimately proved futile. In 1836, the settlers rebelled and succeeded in wresting Texas from Mexico; nine years later, the "Lone Star Republic" joined the United States. But Texas only whetted U.S. appetite for more Mexican territory. In 1846, complications resulting from a dispute over Texas's southwestern boundary led both countries into a war that ended with the U.S. Army in Mexico City and the loss of half of Mexico's territory. A deeply traumatic experience, the war with the United States demonstrated that the country faced either disintegration or further U.S. annexations unless political stability and economic growth could be achieved. Central America, the unity of which had been shattered in the 1830s, served as a lurid example of what could happen to Mexico in the event that further attempts at political centralization were not successful.

The experience of foreign occupation led to a surge in nationalism of both the popular and elite variants, and it contributed to the formation of national political parties. Earlier, so-called Conservatives and Liberals had gathered in the York and Scotch Masonic lodges in Mexico City, respectively. As Santa Anna's own vacillations between factions illustrate, these labels often were covers for personal ambitions. In the wake of the U.S. occupation of Mexico City, however, the influential statesman and historian Lucas

Alamán headed a genuine Conservative Party, while Liberals coalesced around leaders such as Miguel Lerdo, Benito Juárez, and Ignacio Comonfort. Conservatives and Liberals disagreed fundamentally on the lessons that could be drawn from the lost war with the United States.

In Alamán's view, Mexico (mainly criollo—or Spanish-descended—Mexico, of course) represented the best of Catholic Europe: a fear of God and a stable society based on hereditary privilege. The Protestant United States, he thought, threatened this idealized Hispanic Mexico, both by its push for land and by its espousal of liberty and juridical equality. Not only did Alamán deem such ideas inapplicable to Mexico; he also realized that they attacked the existing social order in his home country. To minimize both U.S. political influence and the threat of future annexations, the Conservatives urged the Mexican elites to preserve the country's Hispanic heritage. They also sought to restore the short-lived Mexican monarchy of Agustín de Iturbide by offering the Mexican throne to a Catholic scion of a European dynasty. In addition, Alamán favored the retention of the *fueros,* special immunities enjoyed by the nobility, the Catholic Church, and the army, and he called for the veneration of the Jesuits and conquistador Fernando (Hernán) Cortés as heroes of an Ibero-Mexican tradition.

For their part, Liberals admired the rapid industrial development of Great Britain, Mexico's main trading partner, and opposed protectionist trade barriers and the paternalistic *fueros.* They regarded the United States as a society to be admired, not just to be feared. Mexico, the Liberals maintained, needed to emulate the Anglo-Saxon nations to avoid being swallowed up by the United States. Had the U.S. success in the war, they asked, not been brought about by a superior political and economic system? In the view of the Liberals, Mexico's captivity in tradition and privilege had been its major weakness in the war with the United States. In contrast to the Conservatives, the Liberals feared Spain: as early as the early 1850s, Juárez favored Cuba's independence as a means of removing the principal Spanish "springboard" into the western hemisphere.

Liberalism, however, lacked the cohesiveness of Alamán's Conservatives, as the Liberals remained divided in two camps: the *puros,* or radicals, and the *moderados,* or moderates. While *puros* such as Lerdo were more anticlerical than *moderados* such as Comonfort, the *puros* also distinguished themselves from their rivals in that they favored a radical capitalist transformation as a prerequisite for political reform. Seeking (at least in theory) the complete juridical equality of all Mexicans, the *puros* advocated the primacy of privately over corporately held property and favored unfettered individualism as the engine of economic growth.

Thus, the Mexican elites, apart from a few radical Liberals who flirted with the idea of annexation by the United States, shared a deeply rooted fear of U.S. territorial and political expansion, but they disagreed profoundly on how to prevent further annexations. In short, the Conservatives wanted Mexico to survive by turning to Spain and isolating itself from influences from the north. The Liberals dreamed of borrowing from Anglo-Saxon models to beat the United States at its own game.

During the immediate postwar period, Mexican foreign policy attained a noticeably Conservative touch. Having failed time and again to entice a European prince to occupy the Mexican throne, Alamán sought to enhance relations with the European powers and to increase diplomatic contact with the other Latin American republics. Alamán's ultimate Bolivarian dream—to situate Mexico in an international web of Hispanic culture to safeguard against both the real external threat posed by the United States and the potential internal threat of an uprising against the criollo elites—remained elusive. Naturally, protection of the country's sovereignty remained the primary goal. Many Mexicans still worried that the United States ultimately might annex more or all of their country, and Alamán feared U.S. expansionism into Central America. This fear was justified: many politicians from the southern United States openly advocated further annexations in order to obtain slave territories.

In 1853–54, the very anti-Yankee feelings espoused by Alamán contributed to the downfall of the Conservatives. Santa Anna's sale of a strip of Sonora to the United States in the Gadsden Purchase resulted in widespread outcry over this further loss of territory, and rumors of plans to sell even more of the Mexican north helped end Santa Anna's reign. A year later, the Revolution of Ayutla ousted the Conservatives. The era of chaos had invited U.S. annexation of half of Mexico, and further U.S. territorial gains appeared likely. The task in which Conservatives thus far had failed so dismally—political centralization—had, in the minds of many Mexicans, become a matter inextricably intertwined with the survival of national sovereignty.

It was not surprising, then, that the Reforma of 1855 to 1858 concerned itself with foreign policy as much as with domestic reform. Directed by *puro* Liberals such as Lerdo and Juárez, the Reforma was backed by a large and diverse coalition, including landowners, merchants, army officers, and peasants. This coalition agreed on one fundamental issue: to achieve political stability, Mexico required economic modernization through the promotion of private capital accumulation. In the view of the *puros,* the attraction of foreign immigrants and investment as well as the disentailment of the Catholic Church holdings were necessary steps to that end. Ideally, the Reforma would have created a capitalist yeoman class; the fact that large commercial estates ultimately benefited most from the redistribution mattered little to the program's original appeal.

In matters of foreign policy, the ruling *puros* were friendly to the United States, wary of the European powers, and hostile toward Guatemala. They did not fail to recognize the danger of further U.S. expansionism; nor did Juárez, provisional Liberal president after 1858, want to sell more Mexican territory. But they did believe that a "special economic relationship" with the United States could help Mexico build its infrastructure and attract immigrants, and thus make the country strong enough to prevent further foreign invasions and annexations.

The abortive 1857 Montes-Forsyth Treaties provide a good illustration of this strategy. In these agreements, the Liberal government accorded U.S. investors a dominant position in exchange for a buyout of Mexico's foreign debt. Whether the goal was a U.S. economic protectorate or a milder form of economic hegemony, the Liberals pursued a difficult strategy with these treaties. They intended to give U.S. business interests free rein to develop Mexico "from without" in order to blunt both U.S. territorial expansion and European debt collection *à la* the Pastry War. This Liberal plan, however, had the backing only of U.S. minister John Forsyth, not of his superiors. The administration of President James Buchanan did not demonstrate a great interest in intimate economic ties with Mexico, and the U.S. Senate rejected the Montes-Forsyth treaties.

Despite the enormous U.S. territorial gains of the past decades, Juárez soon found Buchanan to be as aggressive as many of his predecessors. Pressed by southern expansionists, the U.S. president sought territorial concessions from Juárez in exchange for diplomatic recognition and assistance. Yet even when the Mexican Conservatives came close to defeating the Liberals in the civil war known as the War of Reform (1858–61), Juárez would not sell territory. The Liberals proved more flexible on the subject of awarding other strategic advantages, however: at the nadir of their fortunes in the War of Reform, they agreed to give the United States free commercial transit rights across Sonora and the Isthmus of Tehuantepec in exchange for assistance. Fortunately for Mexico (and the patriotic image of the Liberals), the U.S. Senate rejected the proposal known as the McLane-Ocampo Treaty.

Soon after Juárez's victory in the War of Reform, the French Intervention afforded the Liberals a chance to demonstrate their patriotism. In 1862, Emperor Napoleon III, backed by Britain and Spain, sent an invasion force into Mexico. Two years later, the French emperor installed Maximilian von Hapsburg on the throne of a recreated Mexican empire. Helped by the French-Conservative coalition, the Mexican federal army brought Juárez to the brink of disaster. But Maximilian's waffling on key political issues and the departure of the French army in March 1867 gave Juárez an opportunity to seize the momentum. Deserted by its erstwhile allies, Maximilian's regime collapsed. The French Intervention bestowed nationalist credentials upon the Liberals and thus strengthened their rule. The Conservatives, who earlier had criticized the Liberals for the McLane-Ocampo Treaty, now found themselves discredited as collaborators of a foreign power.

Because the futile French takeover further heightened awareness of Mexico's vulnerability to foreign intervention, the country's foreign relations once again influenced the course of domestic politics. If distant France had been able to impose and sustain a monarch in Mexico, how could Mexicans hope to resist another foreign invasion that might sig-

nal the end of their country as an independent nation? Thus, the specter of foreign aggression strengthened Juárez's case for creating a strong presidency in Mexico and helped allow the Mexican president to strengthen government authority in the late 1860s. The Juárez regime created a rural police force, the *rurales;* it smoothed out differences with the Catholic Church; it strengthened a burgeoning executive apparatus at the expense of the legislature; and it began to negotiate with regional caudillos to obtain their allegiance. Ultimately, the construction of the "Restored Republic" entailed the co-optation of many of the Conservatives. Frightened by social unrest and the prospect of foreign intervention, and influenced increasingly by European positivist ideas, many Liberals had begun to embrace the type of authoritarian rule long deemed indispensable by the Conservatives. As a result, "conservative liberalism" became a dominant doctrine in post-1867 Mexico. Under the motto of "order and progress," conservative liberalism embraced both modernization and authoritarian rule. The final result, consummated by the regime of Porfirio Díaz, was the construction of a political "machine" that brokered power at the local, regional, and national levels.

These changes in Mexican politics in turn influenced the formulation of Mexican foreign policy. By the end of the Restored Republic, three different major factions had emerged within the governing elite: the militarists, the reformed *puros,* and the positivists. Together, these groups not only represented different perspectives within a larger "Conservative-Liberal" consensus; they also expressed different ideas about Mexican foreign policy.

The militarists were in essence "reform Conservatives." Many of them had fought against the Liberals and only recently had reconciled themselves with the new order. Free from Alamán's infatuation with Spain, the militarists cast an admiring glance at newly unified Germany and Italy as models for national integration. Both Germany and Italy had been unified by "blood and iron": while the militarists conceded the significance of economic development, they thought that true national integration only could be achieved by military means. Concentrated within the army, and characterized by strong anti-Yankee sentiments, the militarists advocated the building of a strong military to counter threats from abroad. Future president Manuel González, who had fought for the Conservatives in the beginning of the war against the French, numbered among the most influential militarists in the Restored Republic.

The reformed *puros,* by contrast, continued to advocate the adoption of Anglo-Saxon political and economic models. Tempered by political realism and sobered by Buchanan's aggressive diplomacy, reformed *puros* such as Juárez and Porfirio Díaz had given up on the more radical versions of a "special relationship" with the United States. Despite their declining enthusiasm for the United States, however, they were easily the least anti-American of the three factions, and the only one that still entertained the notion that republican democracy was feasible in Mexico.

Dominated by Mexico City elites, the positivist faction emphasized the need for a strong, authoritarian state. Most positivists argued that a type of "democratic Caesarism" was a necessary step in the country's evolution from a backward to a progressive nation. Most of them were more impressed with European than with U.S. models, and some of the positivists even viewed the United States as barbarian and plebeian. Examples of prominent positivists, who later influenced the development of the Científico faction, included Juárez's justice secretary Gabino Barreda.

Led by the reformed puro Juárez, the early Restored Republic enjoyed good relations with the United States. Since the French Intervention had disrupted Mexico's relations with the major European powers, Juárez depended on good relations with the United States. Moreover, U.S. secretary of state William H. Seward reassured Mexican minister Matías Romero that the era of U.S. territorial acquisitions in Mexico was over. Therefore, relations with the United States soon became cordial.

Assured of U.S. goodwill, Juárez refused to negotiate with the European powers on the subject of the exorbitant claims made by their nationals against the Mexican government—a subject on resolution of which the reestablishment of diplomatic ties depended. The clearest manifestation of this stance came during the inauguration of the Mexican Congress in December 1867. Rather than proposing an active agenda for reestablishing diplomatic ties with Britain, France, and Spain, Juárez cast his remarks in distinctly negative tones. He claimed the Europeans had "voluntarily" broken diplomatic relations. Mexico would reestablish relations with these countries only if these powers assumed the initiative. Juárez also demanded that his former enemies forfeit all treaties signed prior to 1862, and that new accords be negotiated on "just and fair" premises. With this principled stance, he gained many admirers in Mexico. Inevitably, however, he thrust his country into the embrace of the United States: the three European powers refused to renew diplomatic relations.

Juárez had reason to believe that this gamble was well worth it. The onset of large-scale industrialization in the United States offered a chance to revive the Liberals' old quest for a "special economic relationship" that would bring "all the fruits of annexation without any of the dangers." Indeed, with the victory of northern industrial over southern agricultural interests in the U.S. Civil War, the goals of U.S. diplomacy had shifted. While plans for further territorial growth remained immobilized, access to Latin American raw materials and an end of European intervention in the hemisphere attained a crucial importance. Mexico, with its proximity to the United States, its hostility to the European powers, and its great diversity in agricultural and mining products, seemed the best Latin American candidate for a close partnership. Even though U.S. capitalists initially had little money to spare, Juárez hoped that the lure of the rich mines in northern and central Mexico eventually would induce them to fund the construction of a railroad system.

Thus, Juárez instructed Romero to promote Mexico as a target for U.S. investments. In particular, he sought the assistance of bankers and railroad magnates to promote the development of Mexico's desert north. Juárez envisioned the construction of railroads linking Mexican mining centers with North American markets. This project represented the old puro strategy of using economic development as a shield against U.S. invasions.

This strategy, however, entailed a pronounced Mexican dependence on its relationship with the United States, accentuated by the scarcity of contacts to the rest of Latin America and the absence of diplomatic relations with Britain, France, and Spain. In the end, such a unilateral dependence only could bring harm to Mexico. For that reason—and because the Juárez regime incorporated a growing number of militarists and positivists nervous about U.S. power—the Mexican government slowly moved away from its exclusive reliance on U.S. goodwill. Juárez's successor, the positivist-leaning Sebastián Lerdo de Tejada, gave a voice to these concerns when he criticized the railroad project with the words "between strength and weakness, [let there be] the desert."

By the time of Lerdo's presidency (1872–76), old problems with the United States had resurfaced. While the U.S. expansionist fever had subsided, two nagging problems led to a deterioration of relations: Apache attacks on the United States from Mexican territory, and a number of (partially frivolous) U.S. claims. Some of these claims antedated the 1848 Treaty of Guadalupe Hidalgo that had expressly relieved the Mexican government from all old claims; others dealt with U.S. damages during the War of Reform and the French Intervention. Even though Lerdo enjoyed full U.S. diplomatic recognition, most potential U.S. investors held off investing in Mexico while a joint commission studied the issue. Having first convened in 1869, this commission did not finish its work until 1877. It did not help Mexico that U.S. president Ulysses S. Grant eschewed the relatively cautious and tactful approach of his two predecessors in favor of a blunt and aggressive policy.

Nevertheless, by 1876 direct European and U.S. aggression appeared a thing of the past. The leaders of postwar Mexico had realized that the United States would henceforth play a dominant role in their country. They had disagreed on how to confront that role: whether to reject it through alliances with European powers or whether to embrace it, in the hope of leading U.S. influence into constructive channels. The faction that had advocated the latter course had won out against the determined resistance of the Conservatives, the Catholic Church, and the European powers, even if much of its program had fallen victim to expediency and compromise.

Mexico's position toward the great powers was well defined. As Porfirian diplomacy would show, the country would seek the economic benefits of its proximity to the northern colossus, but it would not give up its political sovereignty. As long as the United States sought economic gain, its presence was welcome. But if U.S. expansionism should once again threaten Mexico, the U.S. government could count on determined opposition. European political influence, on the other hand, was on the wane, a casualty of the French Intervention.

As this discussion has shown, one cannot separate foreign relations from domestic politics in the National period: the interplay of both presaged future Mexican policies and predicaments. Between 1821 and 1876, the country's political stability was so tenuous, and foreign intervention in Mexican internal affairs so frequent, that Mexico's relationship with foreign powers created realities of domestic politics. The Pastry War, the U.S.-Mexican War, and the French Intervention all highlighted the importance of constructing a central government and ultimately contributed to the creation of a stronger state. These foreign wars stocked an incipient pantheon of Mexican patriotic heroes; Mexicans even today venerate the young cadets who died defending Chapultepec from U.S. troops as Niños Héroes (the Boy Heroes), and the names Ignacio Zaragoza and Benito Juárez stand for the Liberals' patriotic war against the French invaders. The turbulent domestic scene also affected Mexican foreign policy. While some of the political programs and debates of the time may not have reflected significant social or political realities, the debates about Mexico's position in a dangerous world belied the supposedly monolithic nature of Mexican foreign policy. As in the twentieth century, for example, some nineteenth-century Mexican leaders advocated an isolationist policy in order to stave off U.S. aggression, while others favored an attempt to "ride the tiger" so as to extract benefit from the country's vicinity to the United States. Thus, as Mexico struggled for its survival, the country lived through experiences that proved formative for subsequent foreign policy.

See also French Intervention; Guadalupe Hidalgo, Treaty of; Mesilla, La; Texan Secession; U.S.-Mexican War; Wars of Independence

Select Bibliography

Bazant, Jan, "Mexico from Independence to 1867." In *Cambridge History of Latin America,* edited by Leslie Bethell. Cambridge: Cambridge University Press, 1985.

Benson, Nettie Lee, "Territorial Integrity in Mexican Politics, 1821–1833." In *The Independence of Mexico and the Creation of the New Nation,* edited by Jaime E. Rodríguez O. Los Angeles: University of California, Los Angeles, Latin American Center, 1989.

Brack, Gene M., *Mexico Views Manifest Destiny, 1821–1846: An Essay on the Origins of the Mexican War.* Albuquerque: University of New Mexico Press, 1975.

Hale, Charles A., *Mexican Liberalism in the Age of Mora, 1821–1853.* New Haven, Connecticut: Yale University Press, 1968.

_____, *The Transformation of Liberalism in Late Nineteenth-Century Mexico.* Princeton, New Jersey: Princeton University Press, 1989.

Knight, Alan, "El liberalismo mexicano desde la Reforma hasta la Revolución." *Historia Mexicana* 35:1 (July 1985).

_____, "Peasants into Patriots: Thoughts on the Making of the Mexican Nation." *Mexican Studies/Estudios Mexicanos* 10:1 (Winter 1994).

Olliff, Donathon C., *Reforma Mexico and the United States: A Search for Alternatives to Annexation, 1854–1861.* Tuscaloosa: University of Alabama Press, 1981.

Perry, Laurens B., *Juárez and Díaz: Machine Politics in Mexico.* DeKalb: Northern Illinois University Press, 1978.

Pletcher, David M., *The Diplomacy of Annexation: Texas, Oregon and the Mexican War.* Columbia: University of Missouri Press, 1969.

Reed, Nelson, *The Caste War of Yucatan.* Stanford, California: Stanford University Press, 1964.

Scholes, Walter V., *Mexican Politics During the Juárez Regime, 1855–1872.* Colombia: University of Missouri Press, 1957.

Schoonover, Thomas D., *Dollars Over Dominion: The Triumph of Liberalism in Mexican–United States Relations.* Baton Rouge: Louisiana State University Press, 1978.

Valadés, José C., *Lucas Alamán: estadista e historiador.* Mexico City: Porrúa, 1938.

Vázquez, Josefina Z., and Lorenzo Meyer, *The United States and Mexico.* Chicago: University of Chicago Press, 1985.

Zorrilla, Luis, *Historia de las relaciones entre México y los Estados Unidos de América, 1800–1958,* vol. 1. Mexico City: Porrúa, 1965.

—Jürgen Buchenau

FOREIGN POLICY: 1876–1910

The regime of Porfirio Díaz often has been described as one of the most pro-foreign in Mexican history. In particular, historians and contemporaries alike have condemned it for its allegedly single-minded pursuit of foreign investment and its preferential treatment of foreign workers and investors. While conceding that these measures led to great improvements in infrastructure, a balanced budget, and the creation of an incipient middle class, most scholars agree that Mexico's commercial opening gave wealth to only a relatively small group of people, increased the country's dependence on the United States, squandered national resources, and accelerated the process of disentailment of Indian village land. Not for nothing did the famous dictum "México: madre de los extranjeros y madrastra de los mexicanos" (Mexico: mother of foreigners and stepmother of Mexicans) gain currency during the long Díaz dictatorship. Thus, most of the existing scholarship contends that the Porfiriato was a time of cordial relations with the United States and the European countries (as an example, see the work of Josefina Z. Vázquez and Lorenzo Meyer, 1985).

This tale of willing subordination and cordial relations, however, does not contain the entire story. Instead, the historical evidence reveals that Díaz often promoted a nationalist and independent foreign policy. A veteran and decorated hero of the war against the French, Díaz made frequent reference to his own role in the struggle against foreign invaders. His government sought to inculcate an "official nationalism" in its subjects—a nationalist vision fraught with imagery hostile to foreigners, and especially Spanish, British, French, and U.S. citizens. This nationalism did not limit itself to a two-faced rhetoric that would have cloaked the regime's supposed role as a broker for foreign interests. For instance, Díaz refused to pay more than a token compensation for decades-old European claims against Mexico, a stance that delayed British diplomatic recognition until 1884 and cost the Mexican government much-needed credit from its main source of investments at the time. The perennial dictator did not favor the United States with deferential treatment, either. The Díaz government frequently asserted Mexican interests in the face of aggressive U.S. policies toward Mexico and other Latin American countries. Even as regards foreign investment, Díaz and his associates belatedly recognized the limits of laissez-faire individualism: near the end of their rule, they adopted a number of measures aimed at giving the Mexican state a greater degree of control over the country's enormous mineral resources.

The case of Porfirian foreign policy thus presents an apparent paradox. On the one hand, the Porfirians, disciples of the modernizing philosophies of the nineteenth-century West, believed that closer ties to the burgeoning North Atlantic industrial nations would create a strong Mexican state and thus end the political instability and foreign invasions of decades past. Hence, just like many of their Latin American contemporaries, they agreed to hand over significant privileges to propertied foreigners. On the other hand, the Porfirians continued to fear encroachments on Mexico's political sovereignty and consciously acted to oppose it. Therefore, Díaz occasionally played the part of the cranky nationalist dictator that historians have usually reserved for personages such as Venezuela's Cipriano Castro and Nicaragua's José S. Zelaya.

The early years of the Porfiriato (1876–84) provided the Díaz regime with a number of historical lessons that influenced the development of such a seemingly Janus-faced policy. When he came to power in 1876, Díaz faced an immediate standoff with U.S. president Rutherford B. Hayes. Hayes not only loathed the overthrow of Sebastián Lerdo's constitutionally elected government; he also intended to use Díaz's lack of legitimacy as a point of leverage to obtain concessions in a number of border and financial disputes. To make his point, the U.S. president dispatched troops to the Mexican border and threatened military action;

Díaz, on the other hand, ordered General Gerónimo Treviño to resist a possible invasion at all costs. Just when it appeared that this impasse might bring down the Mexican government, Díaz found the help of U.S. railroad and industrial interests. Impatient with the lack of economic opportunities caused by the absence of diplomatic recognition, a number of influential investors and bankers induced the U.S. Congress to appoint a committee to investigate the Mexican situation. In April 1878, Hayes awarded diplomatic recognition with no strings attached and subsequently withdrew U.S. forces from the border. This spat with Hayes had important repercussions for Porfirian foreign policy.

First, the crisis offered Díaz a chance to employ foreign policy as a nationalist cement for his regime. Mid-nineteenth-century Mexican nationalism had centered around a fear of foreign invasion, which gave rise to popular notions of *patria*. Mexico's social and regional divisions made the meaning of the term contested: in some instances, it referred to the *patria chica,* or region; in others, it denoted the *patria grande,* or country. Díaz now launched an effort to promote the *patria grande* in order to strengthen central control and thus crush the *patrias chicas.*

In this effort to foment an official nationalism as an aid in the larger project of state building, Díaz often pointed to his foreign policy. Long after the crisis had passed, he used the conflict with Hayes to show himself as a patriotic leader, an image that built on his earlier heroics facing the French Intervention. The significance of Díaz's principled position vis-à-vis the United States thus had transcended the strictly diplomatic realm. A foreign policy attuned to questions of "national honor," duly applauded by the loyal press, had allowed Díaz to tap into an important well of Mexican nationalism: the fear of foreign invasion.

Díaz made sure that Mexicans would not forget his newfound nationalist credentials: his supporters began to propagate a Liberal patriotic cult that insinuated strong continuities from Benito Juárez's nationalist posture to that of Díaz. With his tribute to Juárez, Díaz not only portrayed himself in Juárez's footsteps; he also extended an olive branch to the old Juaristas, some of whom still resented don Porfirio's seizure of power by force. This effort at constructing an official nationalism became ever more important as Porfirian modernization created a "national ruling class" in Mexico.

How did the Porfirians propagate this official nationalism? They lacked modern means of propaganda, such as radio, television, or even the dissemination of printed information to a large literate public. But the Porfirians did employ important media to spread their agenda outside their small ruling circle: newspapers, anniversary commemorations, schools, and public works projects. History textbooks, street names, plaques, and statues soon reminded Mexicans of the Liberals' nationalist deeds.

It is difficult to measure the actual effect of this official nationalism for the political cohesion of Porfirian Mexico. The radical Liberal opposition venerated its own version of the nationalist Juárez, and many Conservatives still viewed Díaz as a pro-Yankee iconoclast. But despite the Porfirians' predictable failure to monopolize the nationalist discourse in Mexico, they had provided a set of readily identifiable symbols that promoted the "imagining" of a national community and thus strengthened their rule. The Revolutionary governments—and to a greater extent, those of the Partido Revolucionario Institucional—would only refine this strategy.

Second, Díaz came to understand that foreign investors could be better allies of his regime than foreign governments. As diplomatic relations with the United States remained volatile over the next five years, Díaz and his successor, Manuel González, increasingly relied on foreign investors to smooth out differences with the powerful "northern colossus." González in particular counteracted the occasionally hostile policies by promising U.S. businesses generous concessions in Mexico. During his rule (1880–84), the Mexican Congress passed a slew of legislation amending the old colonial-era agricultural and mining codes that considered land and subsoil the property of the Mexican nation. Henceforth, foreign proprietors could operate as owners rather than concessionaires of mining enterprises, and an 1883 law lifted most restrictions on foreign ownership of land. González also began the practice of appointing foreign investors as confidential Mexican government agents in Washington, and he reorganized the Foreign Ministry (Secretaría de Relaciones Exteriores) to reflect this greater emphasis on economic ties. Never a puppet of Díaz, González thus completed the construction of the legal framework of the Porfirian program of externally driven modernization begun during La Reforma (1855–58). In the process, he created the conditions for better relations with the United States.

As Díaz and González moved toward closer ties with the U.S. economy, they also improved diplomatic relations with a group of old enemies: Great Britain, France, and Spain. The Porfirians regarded at least the first two of these nations as important sources of investment capital, and they also sought to forestall the realistic danger of an excessive dependence on U.S. capital. Therefore, Díaz opened negotiations with France and Spain and won the unqualified diplomatic recognition of his government. González, for his part, negotiated a settlement with Great Britain, the most recalcitrant of the old enemies. In both efforts, investors played a key role in persuading their governments to normalize relations with Mexico.

After Díaz's return to power in 1884, Mexican foreign policy sought to balance the desires of foreign investors against those of Mexican nationalists. Two experienced advisers helped Díaz with this balancing act: the secretary of foreign relations, Ignacio Mariscal, and Matías Romero, the chief Mexican diplomatic representative in the United States. Even though both of these two former associates of Benito Juárez hailed from the state of Oaxaca (as did Díaz), they held widely different views of Mexican foreign relations. While the nationalist Mariscal (who remained close to military circles around González) held a profound mistrust of

U.S. intentions and advocated stronger efforts to attract European capital, the pro-business Romero (a former radical Liberal) regarded the United States as the main potential source of the capital needed to build up Mexico's infrastructure. Whereas Mariscal feared that the flow of U.S. investments might one day amount to a "Pacific Conquest" no less dangerous than the U.S.-Mexican War, Romero thought that the existence of strong economic links would make U.S. aggression much less likely. Díaz used the advice of both of these politicians to construct his foreign policy: Mariscal shaped Mexico's inter-American and European diplomacy, and Romero handled most of the negotiations with U.S. investors from his office in Washington, D.C. During the next 14 years, the Oaxacan triumvirate of Díaz, Mariscal, and Romero confronted international issues with a relatively great degree of success.

U.S. diplomacy continued to be capricious and unpredictable: on various occasions, including the famous case of the arrest of newspaper editor Augustus K. Cutting in 1886, the U.S. government assumed an unreasonable position regarding the rights of U.S. citizens in Mexico. Moreover, the government in Washington did not approve a single Mexican extradition request, in the southwestern United States, politicians talked about the possible annexation of Sonora and Baja California, and President Grover Cleveland even warned Díaz to accommodate his government lest he desired to risk losing the flow of U.S. capital. To add to these problems, the two governments haggled over the territory of El Chamizal, a small area near El Paso. Not surprisingly, Mariscal felt vindicated in his opinions about the United States; nevertheless, he asserted Mexico's positions with great prudence.

In terms of hemispheric issues, Central American conflicts and the First Inter-American Conference demanded constant Mexican attention. In March 1885, Guatemalan President Justo Rufino Barrios declared the forcible unification of Central America—a step that threatened Mexico because of consistent Guatemalan desires to recover Chiapas. In keeping with the Mexican tradition of weakening Guatemala, Díaz helped the eventually victorious alliance against Barrios: by sending troops into the border state of Chiapas, he diverted a large part of the Guatemalan army that stood poised to invade El Salvador. Held in Washington, the Inter-American Conference constituted another type of threat: the United States had placed on the table a proposal for a hemispheric customs union that would have seriously jeopardized the ongoing efforts to prevent unilateral dependence on the United States. Fortunately for Díaz, many other Latin American governments were similarly unwilling to concede advantages to U.S. investors over their European rivals, and a majority of Latin American delegations including the Mexican representative defeated the proposal.

One of Díaz's finest hours as a critic of U.S. hegemonic pretensions came in the wake of the formulation of the so-called Olney Corollary to the Monroe Doctrine. In 1894, U.S. secretary of state Richard Olney had intervened in a long-standing dispute concerning the exact boundary between Venezuela and British-held Guyana. Olney had defended the Venezuelan position by arguing that any revision of the boundary in Great Britain's favor would violate the Monroe Doctrine's prohibition of new European colonization. As the British acquiesced without a fight, Díaz had seen no reason to criticize Olney for his remarks. A few months later, however, Olney boasted that the United States was "practically sovereign" in the hemisphere and that its "fiat" was law, and he enjoined all Latin American nations to accept U.S. protection against European imperialist designs. These remarks ultimately prompted Díaz's 1896 speech on the Monroe Doctrine:

> [I am a] partisan of Monroe's principles, if well understood. . . . But we do not think . . . that the responsibility for helping the other republics of the hemisphere against the attacks of Europe . . . should be solely incumbent on the United States. . . . Each one of those republics ought to . . . proclaim . . . that every attack . . . of a foreign power . . . would be considered an attack upon itself (González, 1966).

The Díaz Doctrine—the belief that the Monroe Doctrine should be multilaterally enforced by all countries in the Americas—has since formed an important cornerstone of Mexican foreign policy. On the surface, the doctrine appeared evenhanded in its rejection of both European and U.S. intervention. But the wording and timing of Díaz's address suggest that it was primarily directed against U.S. interventionism. The Díaz Doctrine, in fact, marked the coming of a new era in the history of Mexican foreign policy. With European intervention and problems on Mexico's southern border remote threats, U.S. expansion grew in importance among Mexican foreign policy concerns.

It soon became clear, however, that Díaz commanded a limited radius of action for initiatives designed to slow the U.S. drive for a greater political and military role in the Caribbean. Having attempted to mediate between the United States and Spain, for example, Díaz could only watch idly as the two countries clashed to decide the future of Cuba and Puerto Rico. The resultant U.S. control over Cuba infuriated both Díaz and many Mexican nationalists who wished to see the Mexican government at the vanguard of a Latin American anti-imperialist league. In 1903 and 1904, U.S. interventions in Panama and the Dominican Republic likewise met with widespread criticism in Mexico, but virtually no word of official protest.

This "Cuba Shock" following the Cuban-Spanish-American War helped set in motion a shift in Porfirian diplomacy. After many years of fostering nationalist expectations in the Mexican public, Díaz found himself unable to deliver on these expectations. As successfully as his government had defended Mexican political sovereignty against aggressive U.S. policies, the Porfirian balancing act now teetered on the brink. Díaz's stance became even more difficult owing to the growing perception that foreigners enjoyed a privileged status in Mexico. Anti-Yankee conservatives soon joined liberals on the radical fringe in demanding more opportunities for Mexicans, and a more assertive diplomacy toward the United States.

To add to these developments, Romero's death in 1898 (the same year that ended with U.S. gunboats in Havana) shifted the balance of power within the Porfirian governing elite toward Mariscal's more nationalist position. The man who replaced Romero as a key foreign-policy adviser, Treasury Secretary José Y. Limantour, was no friend of Mariscal's, but he desired to increase European investments in Mexico as a way of lessening the country's dependence on capital from the United States. To be sure, Limantour played his role intelligently, avoiding at all costs the alienation of U.S. investors. Nevertheless, the 1903 signing of Mexico's largest petroleum contract to date with the British entrepreneur Weetman Pearson signaled the growth of Limantour's influence, and that of the Científico camarilla in general. This ascendancy of the Científicos—and the parallel rise of a much more nationalist camarilla around General Bernardo Reyes—made the Díaz regime ever more wary of U.S. intervention in Latin America.

Between 1904 and 1905, Díaz forestalled an effort to drag Mexico into this rising tide of U.S. intervention: on several occasions he rejected U.S. overtures to make Mexico a regional peacemaker by the grace of Uncle Sam. First, U.S. president Theodore Roosevelt offered Mexico a free hand in the annexation of Cuba, Puerto Rico, the Dominican Republic, and the Central American countries (an offer that was no doubt insincere). When Díaz would not be baited, Roosevelt proposed that Mexico assume a police function in the area. The Mexican president, however, saw through this overly transparent scheme as well. The U.S. president desired to lend a veil of legitimacy to his own intervention by joint action with major Latin American countries. Therefore, even though the plan promised to increase Mexico's prestige, Díaz rejected the idea, terming it vague and injurious to the interests of the smaller nations. As his ambassador to the United States commented, "it was not decorous to offer our share to [U.S.] foreign policy." The creation of virtual spheres of secondary imperialism could give Mexico only the vacuous privilege of acting as Roosevelt's enforcer in the Caribbean.

In the years 1906 to 1908, good fortune and a measure of diplomatic skill allowed Díaz to continue his balancing act. Díaz established a good relationship with President Roosevelt and his second secretary of state, Elihu Root. This relationship—buttressed by continued cooperation on matters of foreign investment—allowed Porfirian foreign policy to register some impressive successes. Most significantly, the successful co-mediation of Central American disputes added to Díaz's stature abroad and prevented direct U.S. military intervention. Mexican delegates on the program committee for the Third Inter-American Conference held in Rio de Janeiro in 1906 helped forestall the presentation of U.S. initiatives similar to those of 1889. In 1907, the Díaz regime agreed to renew an old U.S. lease on the coaling station of Bahía de la Magdalena in Baja California, but it limited the new contract to three years. Even though none of these successes derailed the overall growth of U.S. influence in Mexico and the country's neighborhood, Díaz did make full use of the leeway that his international prestige, Mexico's political stability, and a friendly U.S. government accorded his regime.

During Díaz's last years in office, however, all of these conditions for a successful foreign policy evaporated. The global recession of 1907 sent the Mexican economy into a tailspin and highlighted the privileged role of foreigners: while hundreds of thousands of Mexicans lost their jobs, most white-collar foreign employees continued to earn their paychecks. Moreover, the publication of the famous Creelman Interview, an interview in which Díaz announced his intention not to stand for reelection, ended the so-called "pax porfiriana" and woke up Mexico's sleepy political scene. Díaz's subsequent change of heart caused the organization of strong opposition movements that ultimately coalesced around Francisco I. Madero. Finally, the November 1908 elections in the United States brought to power William H. Taft, a president who did not share his predecessor's willingness to accommodate Díaz in matters of foreign policy.

During the following years, the aging Porfirian regime responded with the time-honored method of "bread or the stick" (pan o palo) to the growing outcry of the many Mexicans who felt that their government had failed them. As demonstrated in the brutal suppression of the 1906 miners' strike at Cananea, Sonora, and the 1907 massacre of textile workers in Río Blanco, Veracruz, Díaz used force against the mounting labor protests of the time. But he also ordered the Mexican Congress to reconsider the agricultural and mining legislation of the 1880s and 1890s. Of course, the Díaz regime could not revoke existing concessions to foreign investors without risking serious international repercussions. Nevertheless, the Mexican Congress prepared laws on subsequent concessions that contained many of the provisions of the Revolutionary Constitution of 1917 in nuclear form. For instance, a 1909 law prohibited foreign mining activities close to the border, and the Porfirians created the nationally owned Ferrocarriles Nacionales de México, or National Railroads of Mexico.

As the Porfiriato approached its demise, U.S.-Mexican relations grew more turbulent in several areas. In particular, the activities of anti-Díaz rebels north of the border proved a major irritant in U.S.-Mexican relations. Taft (like Roosevelt) fully cooperated within the scope of his country's neutrality laws, but Mariscal and his successor, Enrique C. Creel, viewed these actions as insufficient. In Porfirian Mexico, authorities arrested and shot troublemakers with nary a hint of due process of law; thus, Mariscal and Creel simply could not understand why U.S. officials spent months and even years fighting legal challenges by Mexican rebels. Moreover, the inception of Dollar Diplomacy damaged U.S.-Mexican relations. As the U.S. State Department increasingly acted as a promotional agency for U.S. investors, Díaz's favoring of Europeans to offset the growing North American economic presence became a political issue. Secretary of State Philander C. Knox regarded U.S. economic ties with Mexico—which by now surpassed those between Great Britain and Mexico—as a security asset. Finally, the cooperation in Central American issues broke down. In April 1909, when Knox attempted to gain Mexican help for bringing down the Nicaraguan regime of José Santos Zelaya—a key ally of Díaz's in Central America, Mariscal declared that Mexico no longer would enforce peacekeeping measures jointly with the United States. Later that same year, Díaz and Knox faced off over Zelaya again. After Zelaya resigned in the face of a revolt supported by the United States in December 1909, the Porfirians gave him asylum and supported his handpicked successor against the continuing rebellion. Ultimately, however, Díaz could not prevent the triumph of the pro-U.S. faction.

All of these problems contributed ultimately to the overthrow of Díaz. To be sure, one cannot accuse the Taft administration of active collusion: his government may have been lukewarm in the application of the neutrality laws to Madero and his followers, but there is little evidence that it desired Díaz's removal. Nevertheless, the existence of the border, and the fact that the Mexican rebels could move relatively freely in the United States, played a great role in facilitating the Madero rebellion. Moreover, with the publication of John K. Turner's *Barbarous Mexico* and other essays critical of Díaz, U.S. public opinion had turned against the Porfirians. Books such as *Barbarous Mexico* gave verbal ammunition to Madero and his followers, and the growing U.S. opposition to Díaz made it impossible for Taft to crack down on Madero the way his predecessor had disposed of the Flores Magón brothers. Many of the Porfirian confidential agents in the United States now deserted the regime and directly or indirectly supported the opposition.

It was no coincidence that Madero made Díaz's foreign policy a key point of attack in his pamphlet *La sucesión presidencial en 1910* (The Presidential Succession in 1910). From Madero's propagandistic vantage point, both aspects of Porfirian foreign policy had failed. On the one hand, Díaz's practice of attracting foreign investments had increased foreign influence in Mexico and brought about the economic crisis of the previous few years. On the other hand, Mexican anti-imperialist measures had failed to stop U.S. encroachments on the sovereignty of Latin American nations.

Modern historians, however, need to guard against the dangers of teleology. Eager to ascribe significance to each one of Díaz's failings in order to explain the coming of the Mexican Revolution, too few historians have undertaken to understand Porfirian foreign policy on its own terms. The fact that the Porfirian balancing act failed in the end should not distract us from the observation that it registered modest successes for many years.

In sum, the Díaz era was hardly one of strident nationalism or unlimited servitude. Instead, the Díaz regime—prodded in different directions by opposing camarillas, foreign investors, and public opinion—remained caught in the same contradictory position that the vicinity of the United States has always imposed on Mexican governments. The modernization of Mexico with the help of foreign capital had allowed the Díaz regime to play a significant international role and to defend Mexico's political sovereignty. In that regard, the Porfirians had successfully followed the national project begun under La Reforma. But the growing economic linkages with the United States and the revival of U.S. hegemonic aspirations in the 1890s and 1900s had made the Porfirian balancing act increasingly difficult, to the point that growing nationalism and xenophobia contributed to the outbreak of the Mexican Revolution. Any analysis of Mexican foreign relations from 1876 to 1911 must thus recognize their essential continuity with those of the regimes preceding and succeeding the rule of Mexico's modernizing nationalist dictator, Porfirio Díaz.

Select Bibliography

Anderson, Benedict, *Imagined Communities: Reflections on the Origins and Spread of Nationalism.* London: Verso, 1983.

Buchenau, Jürgen, *In the Shadow of the Giant: The Making of Mexico's Central America Policy, 1876–1930.* Tuscaloosa: University of Alabama Press, 1996.

Coerver, Don M., *The Porfirian Interregnum: The Presidency of Manuel Gonzalez of Mexico, 1880–1884.* Fort Worth: Texas Christian University Press, 1979.

Cosío Villegas, Daniel, *Historia moderna de México: El porfiriato: Vida política exterior.* 2 vols., Mexico City: Hermes, 1960–63.

————, *The United States versus Porfirio Díaz,* translated by Nettie Lee Benson. Austin: University of Texas Press, 1964.

Deger, Robert J., Jr., "Porfirian Foreign Policy and Mexican Nationalism: A Study of Cooperation and Conflict in Mexican-American Relations, 1884–1904." Ph.D. diss., Indiana University, 1979.

González, Luis, editor *Los Presidentes de México ante la nación.* Mexico City: Cámara de Diputados, 1966.

Katz, Friedrich, "The Liberal Republic and the Porfiriato, 1876–1910." In *Mexico Since Independence,* edited by Leslie Bethell. Cambridge and New York: Cambridge University Press, 1991.

Knight, Alan, "Peasants into Patriots: Thoughts on the Making of the Mexican Nation." *Mexican Studies/Estudios Mexicanos* 10:1 (Winter 1994).

Langley, Lester G., *America and the Americas: The United States in the Western Hemisphere.* Athens: University of Georgia Press, 1989.

Meyer, Lorenzo, *Su majestad británica contra la Revolución mexicana, 1900-1950: El fin de un imperio informal.* Mexico City: Colegio de México, 1991.

Schell, William B., "Integral Outsiders, Mexico City's American Colony, 1876–1911: Society and Political Economy in Porfirian Mexico." Ph.D. diss., University of North Carolina at Chapel Hill, 1992.

Vázquez, Josefina Z., and Lorenzo Meyer, *The United States and Mexico.* Chicago: University of Chicago Press, 1985.

Weeks, Charles, *The Juárez Myth in Mexico.* Tuscaloosa: University of Alabama Press, 1987.

—Jürgen Buchenau

FOREIGN POLICY: 1910–46

At the beginning of 1910 it seemed as if Mexican foreign relations would continue as in previous years of the Porfirio Díaz regime. Díaz's balancing act had deadlocked the interests of various European powers against each other and against those from the United States. In spite of the frustrations that this approach caused, another presidential term for Díaz promised what all foreign powers desired most in Mexico: political continuity and stability for future economic activity.

Thus, when the Revolution of 1910 began, it was perceived by foreign observers as just another normal Latin American uprising. When it continued, U.S. oil interests used the opportunity to weaken the English position in the Mexican petroleum sector by reinforcing Revolutionary leader Francisco I. Madero's reservations toward British business. Suddenly, British and French interests found themselves isolated from Madero, whereas German financial houses enjoyed unexpected access to the newly elected president.

By 1912 diplomatic game playing became more serious. Suddenly, all foreign powers recognized that Mexico stood at the beginning of a new historical period. In the words of scholar Friedrich Katz, all foreign powers agreed that the Madero Revolution had unleashed undesirable social forces that needed to be tamed.

But solutions to the "problem" differed sharply. European powers desired violent repression of social uprisings and, therefore, backed the successful counterrevolution led by Victoriano Huerta and Félix Díaz (nephew of Porfirio). The new U.S. president Woodrow Wilson finally paid more attention to the unauthorized conspiratorial activities of his ambassador Henry Lane Wilson (no relation), who had joined the European efforts to remove Madero from office. While the ambassador favored Félix Díaz as future Mexican president, the idealistic President Wilson wanted to put an end to traditional Great Power politics. Mexico became a testing ground for his new foreign policy ideas. he envisioned Mexico as a parliamentary democracy that later could serve as model for all Latin American countries. Thus, U.S. policy soon supported the Constitutionalists in the Mexican north against the Mexico City regime now led by Huerta alone. In addition, the U.S. Navy occupied Veracruz and imposed an arms embargo on Huerta. The counterrevolutionary had to go.

The outbreak of World War I in 1914 once again changed foreign attitudes about events in Mexico. Suddenly, all sides tried to enlist and exploit Mexican Revolutionary movements to serve their geopolitical global strategies. Previous issues-oriented or regional policies seemed no longer appropriate. Domestic and external forces alike began to exploit each other mutually for the benefits of the changing military situations in Mexico and the battlefields of the world. The immediate need for victory by each Revolutionary faction and its foreign supporter became more important than long-term considerations.

Victoriano Huerta was forced out of office by an interplay of domestic and foreign factors. Historian Alan Knight portrayed changes in Mexico during this period largely as a result of domestic pressures. Friedrich Katz, however, has provided overwhelming evidence of the direct and indirect foreign interventions into Mexican affairs between 1914 and 1917. Each faction of the northern Constitutionalists tried to gain U.S. support for its leader. In turn, the United States tried to gain control over the outcome of the Revolution by arranging a Pan American conference between Argentina, Chile, Brazil, and the Revolutionary factions, hoping to pick a desirable successor for Huerta.

President Wilson's decision to abandon Pancho Villa set off a course of events that helped Venustiano Carranza to gain the presidential chair against the original intent of U.S. players. Villa reacted to his rejection by the Wilson administration with an attack on the small border town of Columbus, New Mexico, on March 9, 1916. His goal was to provoke a U.S. invasion into Mexico that would humiliate Carranza and force him out of office. Indeed, U.S. popular nationalism caused Wilson to dispatch General John Joseph Pershing with 10,000 men deep into Mexican territory with the mission to catch Villa. Ironically, this U.S. invasion evoked a strong Mexican nationalist reaction that bolstered President Carranza's resolve to firmly reject U.S. pressures to install a more pro-U.S. president or to turn Mexico into a protectorate, as had been done with Cuba. In the end Carranza won. President Wilson withdrew the Pershing expedition without any concessions from Carranza. Carranza had avoided being drawn into a war with the United States.

Carranza's opposition to Wilson, however, also cost him access to U.S. government or private funds for the reconstruction of the war-torn Mexican economy. By 1917,

the only way out seemed to be closer economic cooperation with Germany. When Carranza approached the Germans to explore the issue, the Germans responded with their megalomaniac Zimmerman Telegram, which offered Mexico the return of lands lost to the United States in the War of 1846–48 in exchange for a German-Mexican alliance—thus assuming that Germany would not merely defeat its enemies on the battlefields of Europe, but actually would conquer the United States as well. Again, Carranza realized that the German proposal was not to Mexico's advantage. Until the end of World War I he kept the Germans engaged in discussions, thus avoiding an unfriendly rupture of German-Mexican relations. It also protected the Mexican petroleum industry from possible German sabotage, an event that certainly would have caused the next U.S. invasion of Mexican territory. When World War I ended, Carranza could look back to major foreign policy achievements. His skillful tactics had kept Mexico's territory united and free from foreign occupation. In addition, his diplomatic skill had prevented Revolutionary Mexico from becoming a victim of Great Power designs during the war.

In addition, he used a series of speeches and announcements to formulate a distinct post-Revolutionary Mexican foreign policy doctrine, later coined the Carranza doctrine. It demanded the rejection of the U.S. Monroe Doctrine; foreign respect for and obedience of Mexico's law; the elimination of foreign privileges or monopolies in Mexico; Mexican solidarity with other Latin American nations based on mutual respect and absolute nonintervention; and the negotiation of alliances with European and other Latin American countries. Later, in 1930, Mexican foreign minister Genaro (Félix) Estrada added the Estrada Doctrine to Carranza's directives. It demanded recognition for all Latin American government, regardless of whether they had come to power by the ballot or by the bullet.

Carranza's assassination in 1920 once again changed the focus of Mexican foreign relations. From 1920 until 1923, the U.S.-Mexican relationship dominated Mexican foreign relations. During these very frustrating years President Álvaro Obregón defended his government against pressure from U.S. minister of interior Albert B. Fall and the by-now-familiar schemes of U.S. oil companies. In the end, like Carranza, he protected Mexico's economic sovereignty, gained the essential U.S. diplomatic recognition, and refused to put in writing any statement that limited Mexico's future economic development. Ironically, recognition brought not only access to international financial markets but also U.S. military support to defeat the substantial threat of the rebellion led by Adolfo de la Huerta in 1923. For once, proximity to the United States helped the Mexican government.

After U.S. recognition in 1923, European countries followed suit. Newly elected president Plutarco Elías Calles developed a strong foreign policy that was accommodating and compromising with U.S. interests inside Mexico, while at the same time confrontational in Central America and the Pan American Conference system, the predecessor of the

Organization of American States. In addition, Mexicans employed a sophisticated propaganda campaign inside the United States that aimed at protecting the rights of Mexican Americans who were increasingly victimized as a result of resurgent U.S. nativism. When the pro-Catholic Cristero Rebellion tossed Mexico into its next major crisis in 1926, pressure by U.S. Catholics became a new factor in U.S.-Mexican foreign relations.

A critical change in U.S.-Mexican relations occurred with the dispatch of U.S. ambassador Dwight Morrow to the Mexican capital in 1928. From then on, major U.S.-Mexican issues were handled behind the scenes, directly between Mexican presidents and U.S. ambassadors. This relationship continued with U.S. ambassador Josephus Daniels and Mexican president Lázaro Cárdenas (1934–40), as well as with Ambassador George S. Messersmith and President Manuel Avila Camacho (1940–46). The special relationship between U.S. ambassadors and Mexican presidents proved critical to more constructive bilateral relations and the creation of U.S.-Mexican interdependence during the 1930s.

The worldwide economic depression that shook the capitalist system from 1928 on became the critical impulse for the United States to end its interventionist policies in Latin America. U.S. president Herbert Hoover laid the foundation for Franklin Delano Roosevelt's Good Neighbor policy, which was based on nonintervention. From that moment on, Mexican policy makers decided to move from the limited Pan-American Conference system to the League of Nations in Geneva, which still recognized the U.S. Monroe Doctrine. But unlike the Pan American Conference system, the League of Nations was not dominated by the United States, and the most serious threat of foreign intervention was beginning to come from the rise of fascist states in Europe and Asia.

Under Cárdenas, Mexican delegates used the League of Nations as a platform against international war and intervention. Mexican diplomats acted as mediators in the Chaco War between Bolivia and Paraguay, and condemned vehemently the interventions by Italy into Ethiopia, by Germany into the Ruhr area, and by Japan into China. The Cárdenas administration also was the only government besides the Soviet Union to provide military aid to the Republican forces during the Spanish Civil War. While European powers and the United States stood idly by, Cárdenas's convictions led him to try to prevent a victory of fascist forces in Spain, which he feared might spill later into Latin America.

At the same time, behind the scenes in Mexico City, a crucial professionalization of Mexican foreign relations occurred that added another dimension—technocratic foreign policies—to the more traditional diplomatic initiatives of prior administrations. The 1920s had been the decade when the growth of the post-Revolutionary state had revived the institutionalization of foreign relations within the Ministries of Foreign Affairs and Hacienda (Treasury). The aftermath of the Great Depression professionalized the Mexican foreign service from a traditional diplomatic service into a modern intelligence-gathering bureaucracy. After an administrative

reform in 1933, Mexican consuls and diplomats were ordered to act as the government's eyes and ears in the world of continuing international economic depression and growing violence. From 1934 on, these "diplomatic scouts" received the added task of finding markets for Mexico's state-sponsored agricultural modernization and Mexico's petroleum industry after the expropriation in 1938. In addition, the newly founded Ministry of National Economy, the Ministry of War, and the Ministry of Communication and Public Works all pursued contacts with foreign governments and companies, often without oversight from the presidential palace. In the 1930s Mexican foreign policy was diversifying. Some policy areas such as the U.S.-Mexican relationship and the League of Nation policy were supervised by the Mexican president himself; others were developed and executed by bureaucratic technocrats whose central loyalty was to national economic development, not political ideals. The president no longer was the alpha and omega of Mexican foreign relations.

In 1937 the coming together of Cárdenas' fiscal policies, the imperialistic behavior of U.S. and British/Dutch foreign oil companies, the policy of Mexican petroleum syndicates, and a bad harvest triggered an unexpected economic crisis that changed the course of Mexican foreign relations forever. During 1937 the technocrats of the Ministry of Hacienda tried to prevent an economic and political collapse of the Cárdenas administration with the help of diverse and mutually opposing foreign support: the despised British/Dutch oil conglomerate received extensive new drilling rights, a German government agency was used to bring the Tehuantepec oil region into accelerated production, and the U.S. Treasury provided massive support to the fledgling Cárdenas government. When these measures failed, the Cárdenas government expropriated and nationalized the oil industry in 1938 in a desperate attempt to regain governmental control over the national economy and budget and to ensure the survival of the Cardenista agenda.

Initially, the oil expropriation ushered in a foreign policy of survival that focused on circumventing and eliminating the economic boycott of the foreign oil companies and their associated suppliers. But by the time the Mexican state had reestablished some firm ground under its feet, World War II had begun. The new international situation convinced the technocrats in the Mexican ministries to abandon their current developmental policy. Between 1938 and 1940 this policy was replaced with one that used the economic stimuli of the world war as a new engine for Mexico's economic development. Scholar Steven Niblo has demonstrated how a wholesale change in Mexican economic accounting, suggested by U.S. economists, established a new vision of Mexican economic development that was free of any social or political concerns. In 1939 the victory of the Allied powers in World War II was by no means certain. And yet outgoing president Cárdenas, his successor Avila Camacho, and the majority of Mexican technocrats decided that no immediate threat to Mexico existed until Great Britain was defeated. And while these men were using the war to develop their country, they also prepared for a variety of outcomes of the war. Still, Cárdenas allowed the U.S. Federal Bureau of Investigations (FBI) to build a Mexican counterintelligence service that eliminated all dangerous Axis subversive activities by 1941. Under his presidency a very close consultation and cooperation between U.S. and Mexican military forces was initiated that became the official U.S.-Mexican Military Commission at the end of 1941. Cárdenas spent his last months in office defending Mexico against the formation of any unnecessary or hasty military alliance with the United States. A military alliance could open the door to U.S. troops on Mexican soil, which, it was feared, might continue once the war was over. After the end of his presidential term, Cárdenas continued to strengthen Mexico's self-defense capabilities as commander of the Pacific Coast and again later as Avila Camacho's minister of war.

The war added transnational labor issues to the agenda of Mexico's foreign relations. Whereas in the 1930s the Cardenista state had acted to protect Mexican Americans and Mexicans in the United States from nativism, in the 1940s the Avila Camacho administration engaged the Roosevelt administration in the actual management of Mexican labor in the U.S. agricultural and industrial sectors. The outcome was the Bracero Program, through which 300,000 Mexicans obtained permits to work in the United States.

Steven Niblo and Blanca Torres Ramírez examined the economic impact of the war from a social perspective. Indeed, the majority of Mexico's population experienced the war as imposed economic hardship owing to inflation, a lack of available consumer goods, as well as food shortages that caused hunger. Niblo demonstrated how these sacrifices for the policies of the Mexican government and the Allied war effort failed to translate into the expected broad developmental benefits for Mexico's population.

But for the administration, the war proved advantageous. Until November 1941, the Avila Camacho administration maintained some limited channels of communication with Nazi Germany and Hispanistic anti-American groups in Latin America, just in case Mexico would have to trade with a Hitler-dominated Europe after the end of the war. Eventually the defeat of the Germans in Stalingrad and their failure to conquer England gave the pro-U.S. faction within the Avila Camacho government enough strength to conclude their move toward a historically unprecedented close economic, political, and military cooperation with the United States and the Allied powers. The Japanese attack on Pearl Harbor generated enough momentum to justify this cooperation to the Mexican public. Even then, Mexico only ruptured diplomatic relations with Axis powers; it did not yet declare war on them.

This tactic paid off. Mexican negotiators were able to extract from U.S. interests critical concessions that they never would have achieved during peacetime: weeks before Pearl Harbor an agreement with U.S. oil companies in the nationalization dispute had been reached. Thereby Cárdenas's intent to assure national control over Mexico's petroleum sector had

been achieved. Furthermore, the United States agreed to buy all Mexican raw materials for the war period, providing Mexico with a guaranteed market. A Lend-Lease agreement provided the Mexican military with modern equipment and revived the fledgling Mexican Air Force. Later, Minister of Hacienda Eduardo Suárez was able to renegotiate Mexico's foreign debt and reduce it by 90 percent, a dramatic repositioning of Mexico for the international financial markets during the postwar period. The Avila Camacho administration also was able to settle agrarian and water rights issues and gained funds for critical street infrastructure projects. In addition, the U.S. government paid for the complete overhaul of the desolate Mexican railway system. The creation of a special U.S.-Mexican industrial commission gave the Mexican leadership special access to U.S. industrial technology. No other Latin American country enjoyed similar preferences during the war. Finally, U.S. pressure was critical for the renewal of British-Mexican diplomatic relations, thus further weakening the position of expropriated British oil companies vis-à-vis the Mexican government. In short, the policies of the Mexican leadership achieved unprecedented gains for the Mexican state, but it failed to translate them into significant gains for Mexico's citizens.

The nationalists in the Avila Camacho administration regained importance once the U.S. victory at Midway and the German retreat in the Soviet Union proved that the Western Hemisphere would not be invaded militarily by Axis forces. Immediately, Mexico renewed diplomatic and economic relations with the Soviet Union, Great Britain, and the French de Gaulle faction and positioned Mexico as an important Latin American player in the postwar international system, organized by the United Nations.

In the end, the Mexican military also found a way to participate actively in World War II, overcoming strong opposition from U.S. military planners. Mexico sent its air force to fight in the Philippines in 1945. In addition, 250,000 Mexicans served in the U.S. military, 14,000 saw combat as part of the U.S. Army, and 1,000 received the Purple Heart. German submarine attacks on Mexican tankers in 1942 also allowed President Avila Camacho and Foreign Minister Ezequiél Padilla to declare war on the Axis powers on May 22, 1942. This move allowed the Mexican government to confiscate the production sites and patents of the German chemical industry in Mexico, which had enjoyed a monopoly in dyes, pharmaceuticals, and fertilizers. Thus the Mexican government added another critical industrial sector to its petroleum industry without resorting to expropriation. These very selective anti-German acts allowed Mexico to claim after 1945 that, unlike during World War I, it had been a staunch supporter of the Allied cause.

By the time the war ended, Mexico had been engaged in close cooperation with the United States without surrendering its territorial sovereignty or signing agreements that would allow the continued presence of U.S. troops in Mexican territory during the Cold War. Once again, the Mexican leadership had shuttled its nation through a Great Power conflict and exploited its circumstances for domestic gains. Mexico had reinvented itself as proud supporter of the western democracies and the United Nations project. It was uniquely prepared to participate in the reconstruction of the international political and economic system alongside the victors of the war.

See also Bracero Program; Import Substitution Industrialization (ISI); Mexican Revolution: Foreign Intervention; Plan de San Diego

Select Bibliography

Cronon, Edmund David, *Josephus Daniels in Mexico.* Madison: University of Wisconsin Press, 1975.

Herman, Donald L., *The Comintern in Mexico.* Washington, D.C.: Public Affairs Press, 1974.

Katz, Friedrich, *The Secret War in Mexico: Europe, the United States and the Mexican Revolution.* Chicago: University of Chicago Press, 1981.

Knight, Alan, *U.S.-Mexican Relations 1910–1940: An Interpretation.* La Jolla: Center for U.S.-Mexican Studies, University of California, San Diego, 1987.

Meyer, Lorenzo, *Mexico and the United States in the Oil Controversy 1917–1942.* Austin: University of Texas Press, 1977.

Niblo, Stephen, *War, Diplomacy and Development: The United States and Mexico 1938–1954.* Wilmington, Delaware: Scholarly Resources, 1995.

Powell, T.G., *Mexico and the Spanish Civil War.* Albuquerque: University of New Mexico Press, 1981.

Schuler, Friedrich E., *Between Hitler and Roosevelt: Mexican Foreign Policy in the Age of Lazaro Cardenas 1934–1940.* Albuquerque: University of New Mexico Press, 1997.

Smith, Robert Freeman, *The United States and Revolutionary Nationalism in Mexico, 1916–1932.* Chicago: University of Chicago Press, 1972.

Torres Ramirez, Blanca, *Mexico en la Segunda Guerra Mundial.* Mexico City: Colegio de México, 1979.

—FRIEDRICH E. SCHULER

FOREIGN POLICY: 1946–96

A rapidly changing world brought about momentous shifts in Mexican foreign policy between 1946 (the wake of World War II) and 1996 (the first year of the North American Free Trade Agreement). The Cold War, Mexico's growing links with the United States, and the country's urbanization and industrialization all produced important changes in the formulation and implementation of Mexican foreign policy. While the superpower conflict and increasingly intimate relations with the United States imposed significant limits on Mexican foreign policy, urbanization and the growth of a middle class pushed the Mexican government in the opposite direction. Nevertheless, much of the framework of Mexican foreign policy persisted through all these innovations. As it had done since the mid–nineteenth century, the Mexican government attempted with limited success to reap the benefits of U.S. dominance without suffering the drawbacks. At least between 1958 and 1988, it also continued the balancing act between limited possibilities and growing nationalist expectations that had characterized Porfirian, Revolutionary, and post-Revolutionary foreign policies alike.

The transition from President Manuel Avila Camacho to Miguel Alemán Valdés in 1946 marked the adjustment to a postwar economy and society. Mexico had helped the Allied effort primarily through its function as a source of much-needed raw materials. Alemán (Mexico's first civilian president since Madero) faced a United States no longer in dire need of Mexican resources. With the Cold War far from heating up to full intensity, the United States turned its back

on promises to repay the Latin American countries for their wartime collaboration. As had become evident during the Inter-American Conference on War and Peace Problems held in Mexico City in 1945, the administration of Harry S. Truman refused to heed calls for a Latin American version of the Marshall Plan. Meanwhile, U.S. businesses turned away tens of thousands of Mexican workers hired under the Bracero Program in the early 1940s, and the influx of hundreds of thousands of undocumented aliens (dubbed "wetbacks") caused much ill will in the southwestern United States. Moreover, a growing supply of U.S.-made agricultural and mining products amounted to reduced opportunities for Mexican exporters. As a result, Mexican export revenue declined, and inflation and an ever greater gap between the rich and the poor initially belied the expectations of a postwar economic boom.

Faced with this slump, the Mexican government turned to the advice of the Argentine economist Raúl Prebisch, the president of the United Nations' Economic Commission for Latin America. Prebisch had diagnosed the reliance on externally driven development, that is, the export of raw materials to pay for imported industrial goods, as the cause for most of the economic problems of the region. According to Prebisch's analysis, trading raw materials for manufactured products constituted an "unequal exchange," as the prices of raw materials tended to decline in relative terms over a long period of time. To offset this trend that resulted in a continuous flow of capital from "Third World" to industrialized countries, Prebisch proposed government-assisted import substitution industrialization (ISI) programs accompanied by a protectionist trade policy. Picking up on the beginnings of such a program under Avila Camacho, who had fomented import substitution in order to compensate for the wartime shortage of imported industrial goods, Alemán decided to join other Latin American leaders in a strong push toward state-assisted modernization.

In the late 1940s, Mexican foreign policy played a significant role in assisting the industrialization project. Most importantly, the state sheltered the new industries by imposing new protectionist tariffs on imported manufactured goods, and it took advantage of the existing links between the U.S. and Mexican private sectors to assist in the creation of joint industrial ventures. This policy particularly benefited the Monterrey Group, a faction of wealthy northern industrialists. The Monterrey Group had risen to key status in the Avila Camacho years and enjoyed close ties with investors in Texas and other U.S. states. In addition, Alemán's diplomats continued Avila Camacho's policy of friendship with the Truman administration and worked on assuaging U.S. misgivings about their country's industrialization. As Mexican demand for imports, and particularly for expensive capital goods necessary for industrialization, increased, the former U.S. critics of the Mexican government fell silent. Finally, in 1947, Truman and Alemán exchanged visits to each other's capital cities in an unprecedented show of goodwill. During his visit, which roughly coincided with the centennial of the U.S.-Mexican War, Truman paid homage to the *niños héroes,* the cadets who had died defending Chapultepec Castle, and he even returned some of the Mexican banners seized during that war.

Afraid of relying exclusively on U.S. investments, Alemán also moved to normalize relations with Mexico's wartime enemies. In the absence of commercial and diplomatic relations with Germany and Japan until the 1950s, this normalization primarily affected the treatment of confiscated Axis property in Mexico. Having opposed the expropriation of the holdings of Mexican citizens of German, Italian, and Japanese descent as Avila Camacho's secretary of Gobernación (the interior), Alemán returned more than 60 percent of confiscated property to its former owners. In the process, he collected handsome kickbacks from proprietors eager to recover their businesses, farms, or real estate from years of neglect and mismanagement. The appropriately named president especially favored German- and Italian-Mexicans in the resolution of their claims. However, he disappointed many Japanese-Mexicans, most of whose property had been sold by the Avila Camacho administration during the war.

In the 1950s, the so-called Mexican Miracle dominated the direction and formulation of foreign policy. Characterized by rapid industrialization and economic growth, the Mexican Miracle brought new opportunities to educated and propertied Mexicans. The upper and middle classes—in other words, those most interested in foreign policy—benefited disproportionately from these new opportunities. Mexi-

can investors realized enormous profits during these years, and a burgeoning service sector offered relatively high-paying jobs to doctors, lawyers, and teachers. Meanwhile, many workers and peasants saw at best a marginal improvement in their living conditions despite the government's insistence that the *desarrollo estabilizador* (stabilizing development) would improve the lives of all. Many workers continued to subsist on minimal wages, agriculture remained in a state of virtual neglect, and most peasants who moved to the cities found that industrialization had not created as many well-paying jobs as the government had promised. The Mexican Miracle thus served the material interests of the elites and middle classes. Even though Alemán and his successor, Adolfo Ruiz Cortines, continued to claim the heritage of Mexico's epic Revolution, their policies marked a return to the Porfirian program of development from without, with the new twist that foreign capital flowed primarily into industry rather than agriculture or mining. In fact, had the Porfirians lived to see the 1950s, they might well have advocated much more caution in embracing U.S. investments than the helmsmen of the Institutional Revolution.

The diplomacy of the Mexican Miracle distinguished itself in its solid support of the United States in Cold War issues and in its anticommunism. Mexico backed the United States in the United Nations on a variety of matters ranging from Korea to Eastern Europe, and it maintained chilly relations with the Soviet Union. Alemán's and Ruiz Cortines's anticommunism resulted in part from personal conviction, in part from ceaseless U.S. radio and press propaganda in Mexico, and in part from the presidents' desire to accommodate and exploit the shrill tones coming out of Washington. In the fall of 1949, the communist triumph in China had heightened the U.S. fear of a world revolution. By the summer of the next year, the U.S. involvement in the Korean War had led to a complete military mobilization. As mobilization again promised lucrative contracts to Latin American mineral exporters, tough anticommunist talk could help procure these contracts for Mexico. The victory of World War II hero Dwight D. Eisenhower in the November 1952 presidential elections in the United States made an anticommunist diplomacy even more important. As the CIA-assisted coups in nationalist Iran (1953) and revolutionary Guatemala (1954) demonstrated, Eisenhower did not continue Truman's relatively flexible policies toward economic nationalism and socialism in the Third World. In this context, even a more left-leaning Mexican government could not have professed friendship for socialist experiments around the world.

As the case of Guatemala revealed, however, this anticommunist attitude found its limits in the matter of U.S. aggression in Latin America. To avoid U.S. hostility, Mexico—as it often had done in prior instances of U.S. intervention—presented its objections at an international diplomatic forum. At the occasion of the Tenth Inter-American Conference held in Caracas in March 1954, U.S. secretary of state John F. Dulles presented an ambiguously worded resolution against communist subversion. Recognizing this resolution as a cloak for future aggression against Guatemala, the Mexican delegation at the conference introduced a number of motions designed to rephrase and weaken the resolution. When a majority defeated most of these motions in Caracas, Mexico joined Costa Rica and Juan Perón's Argentina in abstaining on the final vote (Guatemala cast the only negative vote). This meek protest, however, was all the Mexican government could do to criticize U.S. aggression. As the CIA mercenaries deposed the democratic government of Jacobo Arbenz, Ruiz Cortines remained silent. This stance constituted a compromise between the demands of business leaders and the nationalist left. While business leaders criticized Ruiz Cortines for his cautious challenge to the Eisenhower administration, the left led by ex-President Lázaro Cárdenas deplored the president's failure to condemn the U.S. intervention.

By the late 1950s, conditions were ripe for a more assertive foreign policy. Most importantly, Mexico's international prestige had grown immensely, and the recovering European and Japanese economies took notice of its potential as an investment target. Furthermore, international issues played an increasingly important role in political discourse. Labor and peasant unrest prompted the Mexican government to display a nationalist foreign policy that recalled the days of Cárdenas in an effort to mask the shortcomings of the Mexican Miracle for a majority of the people. The Cuban Revolution left a great initial impact on Mexican public opinion, and the Mexican government found itself between an anti-Castro business community and largely pro-Castro popular organizations. The mass media had created a sizable foreign-policy constituency (the group of people that cares about foreign policy) among the burgeoning middle classes, a constituency that expected Mexico to play a greater role in world affairs. Lastly, as decolonization reached Africa and as Egyptian president Gamal Nasser led Arab countries onto a more nationalist course, these developments weakened the dominance of NATO and the Warsaw Pact in the United Nations General Assembly in favor of the "Third World."

Presiding over the apex of the Mexican Miracle—a time when Mexico appeared to be on the brink of joining the exclusive club of "developed" nations—Adolfo López Mateos inaugurated a much more assertive diplomacy. The election of this young leader, a self-proclaimed champion of land reform and labor unions, represented the decline of Alemán's camarilla and the ascent of neo-Cardenista politicians. Strikingly, the new diplomacy did not come at the cost of a deterioration in U.S.-Mexican relations. Indeed, López Mateos maintained cordial relations with the U.S. government, and particularly the new president, John F. Kennedy. In 1961, Mexico became one of the signatory members of the Alliance for Progress, a program designed to forestall Castro-type revolutions in Latin America with a U.S.-sponsored array of social and economic reforms. A year later, Kennedy proclaimed during a visit to Mexico City that the goals of the Alliance for Progress were identical with those of the Mexican Revolution. Nevertheless, López Mateos was not content

with limiting his country to an intimate relationship with the United States; instead, he sought to open up new economic and political partnerships in Europe, East Asia, and the Third World. His government gravitated toward the nascent Non-Aligned Movement, and Mexico became one of the founding members of the Latin American Free Trade Association (LAFTA). The new president toured the globe in an effort to attract new foreign investment and to foster his country's prestige, so much so that Mexicans nicknamed him "López Paseos" because of his frequent travels. At the end of his term, López Mateos could point to a few impressive successes: the United States had returned a strip of disputed border territory (the Chamizal) to Mexico, and Mexico City had become the first Latin American city to be chosen as a site for the Olympic Games.

Fidel Castro's revolution in Cuba revealed both the nature and the limits of this more assertive foreign policy. Initially, López Mateos enthusiastically welcomed Castro's triumph. When the United States opposed the nationalist direction of the revolution and Castro proclaimed himself a socialist, however, the Mexican government ceased to praise the Cuban leader. Instead, López Mateos defended Cuba's right to national self-determination and maintained that posture in the face of enormous U.S. pressure after the April 1961 Bay of Pigs invasion. Not even the Cuban Missile Crisis of October 1962 could make a dent in this Mexican opposition to U.S. intervention. While López Mateos joined Kennedy in condemning Castro for requesting Soviet nuclear missiles, he cautioned that his action did not imply an acquiescence in a U.S. invasion of Cuba. Nevertheless, his government would go no further than this time-honored support for the principle of nonintervention, a principle that enjoyed the support of Mexican conservatives and leftists alike. By the end of his administration, what had been a heartfelt friendship between the Mexican and Cuban governments had cooled to a distant relationship, the existence of formal diplomatic ties notwithstanding.

The administration of Gustavo Díaz Ordaz (1964–70) continued the outlines of López Mateos's foreign policy on a smaller scale. Díaz Ordaz became the first Mexican president to visit Central America; he continued his predecessor's efforts at economic integration; and in 1965, he condemned the U.S. intervention in the Dominican Republic. But the new, much more conservative president, a member of Miguel Alemán's clientelist network, did not share López Mateos's interest in global diplomacy. Conscious of the fact that large sectors of the Mexican middle class had opposed López Mateos's brief flirtation with Castro, he sought to reestablish the focus on economic development only. Bilateral problems with the United States took center stage, including immigration, border troubles, and the continuous relative depreciation of Mexican exports. Indeed, issues concerning "Mexamerica" (the area on both sides of the border that has since taken on a distinctly binational identity) steadily grew in importance. To offset the effects of the termination of the second Bracero Agreement—an action that produced widespread unemployment in Mexican border towns and increased undocumented entry into the United States—Díaz Ordaz and U.S. textile, toy, and electronics manufacturers promoted the Border Industrialization Program. As a result, the Mexican north became the area of *la maquiladora,* the assembly plant for U.S. industry.

By the end of Díaz Ordaz's rule, the Mexican government had enough domestic problems on its hands to turn away from activism in international affairs. In particular, middle-class unrest and runaway population growth accompanied a gradual decline of Mexico's economic indicators. In addition, as Mexican-Americans won small victories in their civil rights movement in the United States, their own relative success highlighted the authoritarian nature of the ruling Partido Revolucionario Institucional (PRI, or Institutional Revolutionary Party). In October 1968, the Tlatelolco Massacre, during which authorities killed hundreds of student protesters on the eve of the Olympic Games, revealed the stress of the Mexican political system and the political bankruptcy of the unpopular Díaz Ordaz regime. The bloodshed registered an impact far beyond Mexico's boundaries: it unmasked the hollow myth of the Institutional Revolution to even the most casual observer, and it shook the international credibility of the Mexican government. Luis Echeverría Álvarez, the former secretary of Gobernación and the putative "henchman of Tlatelolco," thus inherited a volatile situation when he became president in 1970.

Echeverría decided to confront the unrest with a two-pronged strategy used since the days of Porfirio Díaz: the carrot and the stick. In the neo-Cardenista mold, he used deficit spending to meet some of the most immediate demands, launching a new land reform program and putting people to work in ambitious public projects. The new president also displayed a strong economic nationalism. He nationalized Mexico's small copper and tobacco industries, he toughened existing requirements that stipulated Mexican co-ownership in many economic sectors, and his government bought the majority of the shares of the national telephone company. He also encouraged greater openness in political debate, less government interference in universities, and the strengthening of opposition parties. But the new president also ruthlessly cracked down on guerrilla movements and protesters, an effort that culminated in the Corpus Christi Massacre of June 1971.

An activist foreign policy, motivated in part by the realization that U.S. demand could never be the main engine for sustained economic growth, played a key role in the "carrot" part of Echeverría's strategy. Echeverría resumed López Mateos's travel diplomacy, traveling to a total of 36 countries during his six years in office. While continuing to nurture the relationship with the United States, he aggressively courted the European Economic Community and Japan as trading and investment partners. Together with Venezuelan leader Andrés Pérez, he created the Latin American Economic System (SELA), a trade bloc that included Cuba while it excluded the United States. In his frequent meetings with

Central American presidents, he inaugurated what came to be known as the "guayabera diplomacy," a diplomacy named after the colorful Mexican peasant shirts that the president gave out at these opportunities. To the chagrin of U.S. president Richard Nixon, with whom he maintained a good working relationship, the Mexican president also improved relations with the communist and socialist nations of the world. Taking advantage of the atmosphere of détente (lessening of tensions) that existed between the superpowers, he visited both the Soviet Union and Cuba. Subsequently, Echeverría negotiated a commercial, scientific, and cultural treaty with COMECON, the economic organization of the Soviet Union and its satellite states. Finally, Echeverría made himself into a champion of the "Third World" and presented the Charter of Economic Rights and Duties of States to the UN General Assembly. Designed to stop the exploitation of "Third World" countries, the measure passed, but the United States and the major countries of Western Europe disregarded it. A highlight of this effort was Echeverría's April 1972 visit with the socialist president of Chile, Salvador Allende Gossens, a visit that culminated in a joint communiqué stressing the right of every country to control its natural resources and determine its own internal structures.

This new foreign policy was a made-for-television publicity show with limited practical results. Photo opportunities with Palestinian leader Yasser Arafat and anti-Israeli votes in the UN General Assembly made for good press coverage and met with applause from many left-leaning intellectuals. Eminent social scientists—scholars who otherwise might well have stood at the forefront of opposition to his government—lauded Echeverría's "new foreign policy" that "opened the country to the outside world." Echeverría's foreign policy, however, did not reduce Mexico's dependence on the United States. Even though the U.S. share of Mexico's foreign trade declined from 66 to 59 percent between 1969 and 1974, U.S. investors still held the same percentage (62 percent) of direct foreign investment that they had owned five years earlier. More Mexican jobs than ever were tied to the U.S. economy. In addition, Echeverría lived on borrowed time: his lavish spending more than quadrupled the debt of the public sector, inflation rose sharply, and the peso lost half of its value in 1976 alone. By the end of his rule in 1976, the IMF (International Monetary Fund) watched the Mexican economy closely and threatened to impose conditions for future lending. As the squalor of many rural dwellings and the growing ring of shantytowns around the capital and other cities attested all too well, neither the social programs nor diplomacy succeeded in narrowing the gap between the upper and middle classes and the average Mexican. As the crisis deepened, Echeverría's activist foreign policy therefore lost credibility both at home and abroad.

Mexico's next president, José López Portillo, began his tenure with a piece of good news that restored the verve of the first four years of his predecessor's administration. In 1976, geologists had discovered vast new oil reserves offshore in the Gulf of Mexico that increased the country's known oil reserves by 1,200 percent. Almost immediately, the news restored much investor confidence in the Mexican economy. As a result, López Portillo, a close associate of Echeverría and the first in a long line of technocrats to ascend to the presidency, presented a refurbished version of his predecessor's populist policies. Of course, the subsequent quadrupling of Mexican oil production could not solve the country's deep social and economic problems. Nevertheless, in a decade of rapidly rising oil prices, Mexico's newfound subsoil wealth rid the López Portillo administration of many of the IMF strictures. The new oil also allowed the government to borrow freely from international lenders giddy about the exorbitant interest rates prevalent during the era; it led to a new phase of corruption and recklessly irresponsible behavior with public finances; and it permitted the financing of more social programs and public works than Mexico could afford.

Relations with the U.S. government initially resulted in further encouragement to the López Portillo administration. During a trip to Washington in February 1977, the Mexican president learned that his U.S. counterpart, Jimmy Carter, intended to accord Mexico a special position in U.S. foreign relations. Carter classified both Mexican oil and the Mexican economy as issues of vital national interest: the former was a key mineral resource, and a breakdown of the latter could have severe implications for the United States in general and the southwestern states in particular. Notwithstanding a series of subsequent spats, López Portillo knew that Carter regarded Mexico as an important strategic partner in Latin America. Carter's own good disposition toward Mexico, however, could not prevent a deterioration of relations in the late 1970s produced by conflicts about a pipeline delivering natural gas to the United States that offended nationalist sensibilities on both sides of the border.

These developments enabled López Portillo to pursue a scaled-down version of Echeverría's global diplomacy. Like his predecessor, the Mexican president acted under pressure from the left, as many Mexicans felt that the export of oil and natural gas would only increase their country's dependency on its northern neighbor. Unlike Echeverría, however, López Portillo concentrated his energy on a few crucial areas. In that respect, no area was more important than Central America, Mexico's southeastern neighbors.

In May 1979, López Portillo started his Central American offensive with a bang when he became the first head of state to break off diplomatic relations with the dictatorial regime of Nicaraguan president Anastasio Somoza Debayle. After the Sandinista triumph in July of that year, the Mexican government became one of the principal supporters of the new, socialist-leaning Nicaragua. López Portillo also attempted to mediate in the civil war between the repressive, right-wing government of El Salvador and two bands of Marxist guerrillas. In August 1981, he and French president François Mitterrand issued the now-famous joint communiqué that recognized the rebels as a representative political force. Finally, when the Sandinistas ran into the rock-solid

resistance of Carter's successor, Ronald Reagan, the Mexican leader offered himself as a mediator between the conservative U.S. administration and the Nicaraguan revolutionaries. The Mexican government gained international prestige with these endeavors, and even the Reagan administration accorded it a grudging respect. López Portillo's assertive Central American initiatives, however, in no way constituted a sharp departure from previous foreign policies. Instead, they followed the twin objectives of encouraging political factions friendly to Mexico and limiting the U.S. political and military influence in Central America that both the Porfirians and the Revolutionary governments had pursued during much of the previous century. Like previous initiatives in Central America, they found their limit in the U.S. resolve to achieve policy ends by military force: the Mexican government backed off from its assistance to the Nicaraguan government when Reagan decided to wage an undeclared war on the Sandinistas by means of the Contra rebels.

As had been the case with Díaz Ordaz and Echeverría, however, economic crisis, scandals, and corruption undid López Portillo's diplomacy. Toward the end of his reign, reports of an economic slowdown and massive graft within the Mexican government resulted in an enormous capital flight from Mexico. During a 12-month period ending in June 1982, more than US$20 billion left the country. Even as López Portillo attempted to prevent further capital flight by nationalizing all major national banks in July of that year, the damage had already been done. At the same time, oil prices fell precipitously, the Mexican economy ran up an enormous balance-of-payments deficit, and foreign debt skyrocketed. Finally, in August 1982, Mexico declared that it no longer could pay the interest on its debt, an announcement that caused a ripple effect throughout Latin America. Thus began a debt crisis that shook the world financial system and ultimately resulted in the imposition of IMF austerity rules on the Mexican government, measures that included price hikes for basic commodities as well as a sweeping devaluation. By May 1983, real wages had plummeted to less than 50 percent of their 1981 level. The country's currency told an ever sadder tale. While a dollar had fetched 25 pesos in 1980, it bought as many as 2,500 only six years later.

By the time Miguel de la Madrid took office in December 1982, Mexico was mired in a deep economic slump that made ambitious diplomatic initiatives unlikely and refocused the country's foreign policy on the United States. As service on the foreign debt consumed almost half of Mexican export revenue, the government had to cut its social expenditures as well as its modest oil-for-credit shipments to the Sandinistas, shipments that already had been curtailed in the face of Reagan's aggressive policies. De la Madrid's first job as president, then, was to placate the IMF and the foreign investment community. He did so by making Mexicans swallow the harsh austerity measures prescribed by the IMF. Protests remained limited, as many Mexicans realized that their government could not oppose the dictates of an international lending organization, however much they justifiably vilified that organization as an instrument of U.S. economic policy. Nevertheless, the crisis had done what U.S. policy had not been able to accomplish: it forced Mexico to adopt neoliberal economic precepts. After all the spending and corruption of the López Portillo years, the Mexican state now found itself unable to influence the country's economy through budget policy. With deficit spending no longer an option and economic policy a captive of IMF advice, the country's leadership increasingly turned to solutions that combined Margaret Thatcher's austere monetarism in Great Britain with Reagan's nod to supply-side economics.

Indeed, the crisis propelled de la Madrid onto a course that must have made his two predecessors cringe. Not only did he patch up relations with the Reagan administration and abandon all populist economic rhetoric; he also initiated steps toward reducing the state's extensive role in the Mexican economy. In particular, he began to decrease tariffs, limit government regulation, and to sell some of the numerous state-owned enterprises. In the process, de la Madrid paved the way for the eventual destruction of the post-Revolutionary model of state-mediated capitalism. These measures accelerated the ever greater integration of the U.S. and Mexican economies. Viewing López Portillo's assertive policies as impractical and detrimental to the vital relationship with the United States, de la Madrid also limited the Mexican role in Central America. In 1983, the foundation of the Contadora Group permitted a graceful withdrawal from what had become a difficult situation for the Mexican government. While de la Madrid discontinued material aid to the Sandinistas, the opportunity to co-mediate the Central American crises with the leaders of Colombia, Panama, and Venezuela offered him an opportunity to participate in an honorable international peacekeeping effort. This attempt rescued him from charges from the left that he was selling out the Sandinistas to the United States, and it also led to some progress in the peace negotiations.

De la Madrid's new, more cautious course proved prudent, as new problems with the United States came to the fore. In particular, undocumented immigration further complicated relations. The immigration issue had long been a sensitive topic in both the United States and Mexico. During the preceding two decades, the number of undocumented Mexicans in the United States had grown exponentially; after 1982, the economic crisis added significantly to these numbers. Reagan, a former governor of California, made "illegal" immigration a focal issue in his administration. As a result, he helped state governors beef up border patrols, and the U.S. Congress debated several versions of an immigration reform bill. The debate pitted the beneficiaries of immigration, which included farmers and other entrepreneurs that employed undocumented workers, against a diverse anti-immigration alliance that included the ultra-conservative Senator Jesse Helms along with the American Federation of Labor–Congress of Industrial Organizations (AFL-CIO) and the United Farm Workers of America. Known as the Immigration Reform and Control Law, the final compromise granted amnesty to all undocumented workers with at least two years of continued residence in the United States, but it imposed harsh penalties on employers hiring new arrivals without immigration papers. Waged with a number of emotionally charged and even racist arguments, the immigration debate upset many Mexicans. As most Mexicans saw it, the undocumented workers put up with conditions that would be unacceptable for virtually all U.S. citizens in order to earn a fraction of the minimum wage. Moreover, immigrants who crossed the border illegally frequently endured human-rights violations and indignities at the hands of border patrols, criminal gangs, and the notorious coyotes, guides that were not always trustworthy in selling their services for border crossings. Thus, de la Madrid was in a difficult position. During the legislative debate, he lobbied for the civil rights of Mexican citizens in "El Norte," but he consistently manifested his respect for the right of the United States to determine its own immigration policy.

The increasing trafficking in illicit drugs constituted another newly explosive issue between the United States and Mexico. In 1985, the assassination of a Drug Enforcement Agency (DEA) official in Mexico and the subsequent Mexican failure to apprehend suspects led to widespread U.S. charges that the de la Madrid administration was, at best, not serious about the so-called war on drugs, and at worst, engaged in drug trafficking of its own. Frustrated, the Reagan administration assumed the arrogant attitude of demanding that U.S. law enforcement agents be permitted to make arrests in Mexico. Predictably, the Mexican government rejected this imposition on national sovereignty. It did not feel that it should shoulder most of the responsibility for the increasing U.S. drug imports. Even though de la Madrid wholeheartedly cooperated with the Reagan administration in intercepting shipments of controlled substances—shipments that led to increased drug use in Mexico and a surge in drug-related violence—he viewed the drug problem as one of demand rather than supply. As Mexican officials argued persuasively, drugs would come into any country as long as consumers were willing and able to pay large amounts of money to purchase them.

In the face of all these difficulties, the next president, Carlos Salinas de Gortari, decided to cast Mexico's lot firmly with the United States. Yet another technocrat at the helm of the Mexican government, Salinas had many reasons to seek a new departure in international relations. As a neoliberal economist trained at Harvard, Salinas shared the faith of the Reagan administration in free trade and reducing the role of the state in the economy. Even more importantly, the highly questionable outcome of the 1988 presidential elections had undermined his political legitimacy even before he took office. Under the leadership of the charismatic Cuauhtémoc Cárdenas (the son of the popular former president), the Echeverría wing of the PRI had joined smaller leftist parties in the Frente Democratico Nacional (FDN, or National Democratic Front). Attracting widespread support in the Mexican south as well as in the capital, the FDN had mounted a strong challenge to Salinas, the official candidate of the PRI. At the same time, the austerity measures and government repression had alienated the middle class, which helped Manuel Clouthier, the candidate of the conservative Partido de Acción Nacional (PAN, or National Action Party), challenge Salinas in northern Mexico. In the end, official results declared Salinas a narrow winner over Cárdenas, with Clouthier finishing a distant third. A three-week delay in posting the results as well as numerous irregularities, however, had given substance to widespread charges that electoral fraud had deprived Cárdenas of victory. In this situation, Salinas desperately needed political allies. By 1989, he had found them in the PAN, the constituency of which favored closer links with the United States and much less government intervention in the Mexican economy.

Salinas made radical and unprecedented moves to improve relations with the new U.S. administration of George Bush, an administration that combined the pursuit of Reagan's objectives with a more pragmatic approach to achieving them. The Mexican president agreed to crack down on drug rings operating in Mexico, he promised to cooperate with U.S. border authorities on the matter of illegal immigration, he sold many state-owned businesses to private investors, and he added Mexico to the list of members of the General Agreement on Tariffs and Trade (GATT). While he continued to pay lip service to Mexican nationalism, Salinas also moved into formerly sacrosanct territory: he began to revise the post-Revolutionary legislation designed to protect Mexico from foreign exploitation. First, he amended the 1973 Law on Foreign Investment to allow for full foreign ownership of property. Then, he even undermined the hallowed Article 27 of the 1917 Constitution, the article that declared land and subsoil the patrimony of the Mexican nation. Thus, in a span of only five years, Salinas had accommodated important U.S. foreign-policy goals that dated to the nineteenth century. Most importantly, he had abridged two important prerogatives of the Mexican state: to steer and manage the flow of capital, and to regulate foreign ownership of strategic resources in Mexico.

The final objective of Salinas's strategy was the negotiation of the North American Free Trade Agreement. The NAFTA negotiations led to acrimonious debate in all three countries. In Mexico, Salinas's supporters portrayed economic integration as both welcome and inevitable, and they reiterated the nineteenth-century argument that the free-trade agreement would bring "all the fruits of annexation without any of its dangers." Salinas hoped that NAFTA would give Mexican exporters unlimited access to U.S. and Canadian markets. Further, he expected that low wages would lure many North American companies to move their assembly plants south of the border and thus create jobs in Mexico. The younger Cárdenas, on the other hand,

denounced the treaty even as it sailed smoothly through the Mexican Congress. As Cárdenas correctly observed, the treaty would make Mexico an economic appendage of the United States, and it would end the right of the Mexican government to protect national sovereignty and the well-being of its citizens. These critiques, however, paled in comparison to the response of a guerrilla group in Chiapas. On January 1, 1994, the day that NAFTA took effect, the Ejército Zapatista de Liberación Nacional (EZLN, or Zapatista Army of National Liberation) began its uprising, in large part to protest the adverse effects that the agreements could bring to the Mexican countryside. In Canada, proponents lauded the potential increase in exports to the United States, while opposition leaders raised the specter of a virtual loss of national independence. In the United States, two strange alliances opposed each other. Led by new president Bill Clinton and ex-president Bush, the NAFTA supporters argued that the treaty would bring new opportunities to U.S. exporters and thus create jobs in the United States. On the other side, labor leaders, self-styled populists, environmentalists, and xenophobic conservatives opposed the treaty. While the former two groups feared that millions of U.S. jobs would be lost to Mexico, the environmentalists warned against the imminent dumping of U.S. hazardous waste in Mexico, a country with lax environmental laws. The conservatives, finally, could not stomach the idea of perpetually granting free-trade privileges to a "Third World" country. This coalition brought together individuals as diverse as presidential candidate Ross Perot (who anticipated a "giant sucking sound of jobs going south"), U.S. House of Representatives majority leader Richard Gephardt, and the fire-breathing Senator Helms. Ultimately, the supporters prevailed in all three countries, and a vast experiment in international economic relations began.

Despite Salinas's move toward integration with the North American economies, he did not forget the rest of the world. In fact, during the early 1990s, Mexico again made its presence felt in Latin America. In 1991—long before the signing of NAFTA—Salinas negotiated a free-trade agreement with Chile. His Central America policy strikingly resembled George Bush's approach to Mexico on a smaller scale. Hoping to make Mexico a nexus between the United States and the Central American countries, he offered to extend free-trade privileges to Mexico's southern neighbors, who reacted warily to the prospect of increased commerce with their own "colossus of the north." Salinas also began a series of bilateral negotiations with the government of Guatemala to tackle his country's own immigration dilemma: that of Guatemalan refugees in Chiapas. Finally, the Mexican president made significant overtures to Japan and the European Community. His hopes of attracting significant new investments, however, were disappointed. With the end of the Iron Curtain, Eastern Europe became a new primary investment target for the industrial powers of Western Europe, and Japan invested heavily in the rest of East and

Southeast Asia. The end of the Cold War, then, had brought no peace dividend to Mexico, and it instead had highlighted the country's dependence on the United States.

While it is too early to assess the effect of Mexico's most recent crisis of 1994 to 1995 on foreign policy, a few observations deserve mention. The economic and political crisis has further eroded the legitimacy of the PRI while undermining international and domestic confidence in the Mexican economy. Salinas's successor, Ernesto Zedillo, has never been able to make Mexicans forget the slain heir-apparent to Salinas, Luis Donaldo Colosio, who had promised to complement NAFTA with a new economic and political arrangement that would benefit all Mexicans instead of a privileged few. At the same time, another devaluation of the Mexican peso, rampant corruption at the highest levels in the last years of the Salinas regime, and yet another round of high inflation have more than eroded the modest gains of the middle class registered in the early 1990s. As a result, Zedillo now faces the same choice that his predecessors faced at the outset of their terms in office: whether to turn toward the United States for support (and a bailout of outstanding loan payments), or whether to embrace populist, nationalist rhetoric to shore up crumbling support at home. Thus far, Zedillo, like the two presidents before him, has made a clear choice for the former option. In the process, he has raised the question of whether the other option remains a viable one in today's world. If it is not, Mexican foreign policy will seek an ever closer approximation with the United States rather than the time-honored compromise between international realities and domestic expectations. The track record of the last 50 years of the twentieth century, however, indicates that more twists and turns may still lie ahead, and that

nationalism has not yet disappeared as an important factor of Mexican foreign policy.

See also Bracero Program; Drug Trade; General Agreement on Tariffs and Trade (GATT); Import Substitution Industrialization (ISI); Maquiladoras; North American Free Trade Agreement (NAFTA); Peso Crisis of 1994

Select Bibliography

Green, Rosario, "México: la política exterior del nuevo régimen." In *Centro de Estudios Internacionales: Continuidad y cambio en la política exterior de México.* Mexico City: Colegio de México, 1977.

Langley, Lester D., *Mexico and the United States: The Fragile Relationship.* Boston: Twayne, 1991.

Niblo, Stephen, *Diplomacy and Development: The United States and Mexico, 1938–1954.* Wilmington, Delaware: Scholarly Resources, 1995.

Ojeda, Mario, *Alcances y límites de la política exterior de México.* Mexico City: Colegio de México, 1976.

Pellicer de Brody, Olga, and Esteban L. Mancilla, *Historia de la Revolución Mexicana, 1952–1960: El entendimiento con los Estados Unidos y la gestación del desarrollo estabilizador.* Mexico City: Colegio de México, 1978.

Rodrigo Jauberth, H., et al., *The Difficult Triangle: Mexico, Central America, and the United States.* Boulder, Colorado: Westview, 1992.

Roett, Riordan, editor, *Mexico's External Relations in the 1990s.* Boulder, Colorado: Lynne Rienner, 1991.

Vernon, Raymond, *The Dilemma of Mexico's Development: The Roles of the Private and Public Sectors.* Cambridge, Massachusetts: Harvard University Press, 1964.

—Jürgen Buchenau

FOREIGN POLICY: CUBA

Ever since the War of 1898, Mexico's relations with Cuba have been an exercise in frustration. The island always has been of crucial importance to Mexico, both in terms of its history and its strategic location at the two main entrances to the Gulf of Mexico. At the same time, the island's proximity to the United States—a mere 90 miles from Key West—has denied the Mexican government the kind of influence it has desired to assume in Cuba. In fact, the presence of the United States (and, earlier, that of Spain) has been so formidable that Mexico has never been able to assert the significant influence in Cuba that it has enjoyed in Central America. Extreme caution on both sides always has marked official Mexican-Cuban relations. Despite initial signs to the

contrary, the Cuban Revolution has made only a slight, but not a definitive, change in this pattern.

At the unofficial level, however, Mexican-Cuban relations have been significant. Mexicans have long followed developments in Cuba with considerable interest, Cubans have always paid keen attention to Mexican affairs, and on occasion, Cuban rebels even used Mexico as a staging ground for their political activities. Mindful of their own country's experience with foreign intervention, Mexicans have sympathized with Cuban struggles against Spanish and U.S. influence. Cubans such as Fidel Castro have attempted to learn from Mexican efforts to achieve social and economic change as well as a greater degree of independence from the United

States. These mutual sympathies influenced the formulation of Mexican foreign policy: for example, instances of Spanish and U.S. aggression in Cuba produced official and popular outbursts of anti-Spanish and anti-Yankee sentiments. Hence, events in Cuba—and, in particular, the struggle for independence in the 1890s and the Cuban Revolution—affected Mexican foreign policy even though direct Mexican influence was never a real possibility.

Mexican frustrations began with the protracted Cuban struggle for independence in the mid–nineteenth century. From the outset, the fragile Mexican government was sympathetic to the cause of "Cuba libre." A Spanish colony until 1898, Cuba had served too often as a springboard of Spanish aggression. After all, Fernando (Hernán) Cortés had invaded Mexico from Cuba, and as recently as 1827, Spain had launched a futile attempt at reconquest from there. Not surprisingly, the Mexican Liberals—unlike Conservatives such as Lucas Alamán, who favored a greater political and cultural approximation to the *madre patria*—desired to see the Spanish colonial presence end. As early as the late 1850s, Benito Juárez favored Cuba's independence as a means of removing the principal Spanish springboard in the western hemisphere. After the end of the French Intervention in 1867, Juárez publicly defended the cause of the Cuban rebels in the Ten Years' War. Juárez's timid protestations, however, could not sway the Spaniards to relinquish their control over the island. The Cuban rebellion failed, and the perceived threat to Mexico's national security remained.

The continued Spanish grip on Cuba helped complicate Spanish-Mexican relations into the late nineteenth century. From the Mexican perspective, the refusal to grant independence to Cuba branded Spain as a country whose leadership had not abandoned its dreams of a worldwide empire. Spanish policy in Cuba dovetailed with the country's involvement in the Triple Alliance, the coalition with France and Great Britain that had sanctioned the French Intervention and the imposition of Maximilian von Hapsburg as "Emperor of Mexico." It was not surprising, then, that Mexican president Porfirio Díaz never lent an ear to Spanish cries for a pan-Hispanic league that could fend off U.S. aggression. For the Díaz government, aggression by Mexico's former colonial master seemed as tangible a threat as U.S. expansion. At that time, many Mexicans agreed: while popular fears of the United States had receded to a minimum after the French Intervention, hatred of the *gachupines* (native-born Spaniards) remained widespread.

Thus, Mexican leaders continued to watch the situation in Cuba with concern and sympathy. Díaz repeatedly expressed his opposition to Spanish colonialism, knowing full well that he could not affect the situation. With official blessing, Mexican newspapers assailed Spanish brutality in repressing the Cuban revolt. On March 7, 1886, the Liberal newspaper *El Diario del Hogar* even stated that the United States might be justified in intervening in Cuba, even though U.S. rule might not be an improvement for the Cuban people.

By the late 1890s, however, more assertive U.S. policies had begun to change this overwhelming Mexican perception of Cuba as a princess in Spanish captivity. Motivated by the growth of an industrial economy, the desire to end European intervention, and dreams of making the United States a great power in its own right, U.S. policy makers began to advance U.S. interests in Latin America much more aggressively. This push for a greater role in Latin America included attempts to force Latin American countries to accept mandatory U.S. arbitration in pending disputes, U.S. intervention in the famous Guyana boundary dispute between Great Britain and Venezuela, and an attempt to gain acceptance of the Monroe Doctrine in all of Latin America. Finally, the U.S. press joined the campaign. By 1897, William R. Hearst's newspapers attacked the abuses of the Spanish colonial regime on a regular basis, and particularly the *reconcentrado* policy of Governor Victoriano Weyler, which consisted of herding the rural population into concentration camps to flush out the rebels. The U.S. press helped produce widespread public support for the intervention. Even though nobody in Mexico agreed with Weyler's methods, the danger of a U.S. military presence in the Caribbean came to outweigh the concerns over Spanish colonialism.

These developments contributed to a surge in anti-U.S. sentiments—not only in the Mexican public but among Mexico's cultural elite as well—that further drove Díaz to oppose U.S. influence in Cuba. Influential Mexicans such as Justo Sierra avidly read the writings of the Cuban José Martí, the Nicaraguan Rubén Darío, and the Uruguayan José Enrique Rodó, who attacked what they viewed as the materialist and self-centered "American way of life." Along with this growing criticism of Yankee imperialism, a critique of Díaz's inability to confront U.S. influence also mounted.

As a result of these changes, the Díaz regime shifted toward a hands-off policy friendly to Spain. While Díaz still supported Cuban independence in principle, he knew that the imposing shadow of U.S. influence would make real independence impossible. In a dispatch to the Mexican consul in Havana, Foreign Secretary Ignacio Mariscal shared his personal belief that U.S. "influence, intervention, and Machiavellianism" marked the Cuban insurrection. In 1896, Díaz prohibited a celebration of the first anniversary of the second Cuban insurrection planned by Cuban exiles. Finally, in October 1896, the Díaz regime intimated to the U.S. press that the Mexican government would be happy to mediate between Spain and the United States. Several months later, however, the interventionist William McKinley assumed the U.S. presidency, and the mediation effort failed.

The reaction of Mexico's heavily censored press highlighted the frustrations within the Díaz government about being forced into such a cautious course of action. Throughout 1896 and 1897, the pro-government daily *El Nacional* waged a vigorous, yet futile campaign for Mexican annexation of Cuba. Such an annexation, *El Nacional* argued, would make Mexico a great power in the Caribbean and constitute an acceptable solution for both Spain and the United States. The semi-official *El Imparcial* took a different tack by praising Spanish plans for limited Cuban autonomy. The Conservative opposition newspapers *El País* and *El Tiempo,* finally, encouraged Díaz to back Spain overtly. Cuba's independence, these papers argued, would be worthless if purchased at the price of Yankee domination of the island. The fact that Díaz allowed free reign to both the subsidized and the opposition press indicates that his own government wished to play a more decisive role in the Cuban conundrum.

The explosion of the U.S.S. *Maine* in February 1898 rendered moot the entire discussion. When war broke out between Spain and the United States, Díaz issued a formal order of neutrality and informed both parties that Mexico regretted the war and wished for a cessation of hostilities. Even though the press of all stripes printed diatribes against Yankee aggression and further intensified their editorials following the imposition of a U.S. protectorate over Cuba after the war, Díaz could not criticize the United States: to do so would have jeopardized more important policy objectives.

The events of 1898 can best be characterized as Mexico's "Cuba shock": a sudden awareness of a new danger of U.S. intervention. This awareness made Díaz's job as president much more difficult. Although the U.S. actions did not threaten Mexican sovereignty, the Conservative and radical Liberal opposition now united in their demands for a nationalist, anti-Yankee foreign policy. These demands first prompted Díaz to assert Mexican national interests elsewhere in the hemisphere; later, they helped cement the Revolutionary alliance against the Porfirian regime. As a consequence, a frustrated policy toward Cuba—Díaz's hand-wringing neutrality—had brought about significant change in Mexican foreign policy.

For 60 years after the war, Mexican policy toward Cuba remained virtually inactive. While the United States repeatedly enforced the Platt Amendment in Cuba in the form of military intervention, the Revolution rendered the Mexican government unable to respond to events on the island. From 1898 to 1956, numerous informal contacts and the membership of both countries in international organizations constituted the only significant bonds between Mexico and Cuba. As far as informal contacts were concerned, student exchanges, visitors, media, and cultural organizations allowed Mexicans to know about Cuba, and Cubans to learn about Mexico. The years 1917 to 1924 constituted the high point of a Mexican effort to strengthen these ties: the governments of Venustiano Carranza and Álvaro Obregón fostered knowledge of Mexican culture everywhere in the hemisphere, including Cuba. As regarded Mexican and Cuban membership in international organizations, their role in the Organization of American States (OAS) and the United Nations highlighted differences rather than similarities. Whereas Mexico pursued relatively independent policies in world affairs, the Cuban representatives almost always voted with those of the United States.

Castro's insurrection offered a brief opportunity for greater Mexican-Cuban friendship. Because he had spent much of his exile there, Fidel Castro knew and admired Mexico: not surprisingly, it was from Mexican soil that he launched his rebellion. After his victory, Castro—who initially expressed nationalist rather than socialist views—referred to the Mexican Revolution as his guide during the struggle against the regime of Fulgencio Batista y Zaldívar. On the Mexican side, the Cuban Revolution struck a chord with many Mexicans. Castro's early policies, which included agrarian reform and the nationalization of foreign property, resembled the initiatives of President Lázaro Cárdenas in the 1930s.

President Adolfo López Mateos, Mexico's most progressive leader since Cárdenas, recognized the power of this political symbolism. As leader of the Partido Revolucionario Institucional (PRI, or Institutional Revolutionary Party), López Mateos knew that support for the Cuban Revolution could help many Mexicans forget that their own glorious upheaval of the 1910s had been in good measure co-opted and asphyxiated. Therefore, when the U.S. government cut the Cuban sugar quota (an action that helped Mexican sugar growers) as a reprisal for the expropriation of U.S.-owned oil refineries, the Mexican president cautiously extolled the Cuban Revolution. In June 1960, on the occasion of Cuban president Osvaldo Dorticós's visit to Mexico, López Mateos declared: "We, who have gone through similar stages, understand and value the Cuban effort at transformation. . . . We hope that the Cuban Revolution might be, like ours has been, another step toward the greatness of America."

These protestations of solidarity quickly vanished under the weight of U.S. hostility. In April 1961, CIA-trained Cuban exile forces landed at the Bay of Pigs in southern Cuba. Castro's troops quickly crushed the invasion, but the incident, officially ignored by the Mexican government, highlighted continuing U.S. efforts to topple "Communist" regimes in the hemisphere.

The Bay of Pigs invasion illustrated the eternal quandary of Mexico's Cuba policy. While U.S. hostility forestalled overt acts of Mexican sympathy for Castro, López Mateos, like Díaz, needed to respond to domestic political pressures. Unlike Díaz, however, López Mateos faced the problem of placating two groups that espoused opposite agendas. On the one hand, leftists and nationalists vainly demanded that López Mateos support and defend Castro. For instance, former president Cárdenas led a demonstration against the U.S. intervention, and he even pondered going to Cuba to help Castro fight such foreign intervention. On the other hand, conservatives and foreign investors—a group much more crucial to the Mexican government than the left—urged the Mexican government to join the United States in its condemnation of the Castro regime. Only in their rejection of U.S. military intervention in Latin America did these two groups find common ground.

Therefore, when Castro announced in December 1961 that his revolution would lead Cuba on a socialist path,

López Mateos began to pursue a difficult balancing act: he ignored the Castro regime but defended the Cuban right to national self-determination in the inter-American system. This balancing act satisfied Mexican leftists, nationalists, and conservatives alike; it did not critically damage U.S.-Mexican relations, and it agreed with the president's own anticommunist, yet nationalist, views. With this policy, López Mateos followed the country's diplomatic tradition, begun under Porfirio Díaz, of invoking Mexico's own bitter experiences with foreign powers as an argument for opposing U.S. intervention in the Caribbean and Central America.

Strongly opposed to the evolving Cuban-Soviet alliance and the radicalization of the revolution, the Mexican president stopped emphasizing the similarities between the historical experience of Mexico and Cuba. It had become obvious that Castro had chosen not to repeat the Mexican experiment in gradual reform. His hurried nationalizations and his ruthless acts of repression revealed that the Cuban leader (unlike, at least in hindsight, the winners of the Mexican Revolution) had decided not to give his opponents a chance to influence revolutionary policy. We do not yet know to what extent Castro's judgment of the Mexican Revolution influenced his commitment to radical reform in Cuba. But from the standpoint of the anticommunist Mexican elites, Castro aspired to be a Marxist dictator who embraced an economic doctrine alien to Latin America instead of pursuing the rightful path of fighting for land and liberty, the path represented by an idealized Mexican Revolution. In January of that year, Foreign Secretary Manuel Tello declared that Marxism-Leninism was incompatible with membership in the Organization of American States.

López Mateos remained firm, however, in his rejection of foreign intervention in Cuba. Later in 1962, when the United States and most of the Latin American states voted to expel Cuba from the OAS, the Mexican government refused to break diplomatic relations with Cuba. The Cuban Missile Crisis in October 1962 is another case in point. To be sure, López Mateos, upon consultation with U.S. president John F. Kennedy, did not hesitate to join the OAS in condemning Castro for requesting the Soviet missiles. However, López Mateos added an important qualification to his support of the motion by stating that Mexico's posture did not imply acquiescence in a U.S. invasion of Cuba. Two years later, the Mexican government refused to heed an OAS resolution that would have cut all diplomatic and travel ties to Cuba. Mexico did not discontinue jet service between the two countries, even though it placed all passengers on a blacklist made available to the U.S. embassy in Mexico City.

The period from 1964 to 1970 tested this policy of reserved toleration of the Cuban Revolution. During this time, Mexico moved to the right under President Gustavo Díaz Ordaz, while Castro made sporadic efforts to encourage Latin Americans to emulate his revolution. Invoking the same arguments that it had used in the defense of the Cuban Revolution against U.S. intervention, the Mexican government opposed Castro's efforts, which were viewed as interference in the internal affairs of other nations. As a result, Mexican-Cuban relations deteriorated. Significantly, however, Castro never aided subversive movements in Mexico: the Cuban leader either spared Mexico because of its principled diplomatic efforts, or he feared U.S. reprisals in case he stirred up trouble in a country that bordered the United States.

Throughout the 1970s, a variety of issues combined to encourage the Mexican government to seek better relations with Cuba. Elected president in 1970, Luis Echeverría Álvarez had strong reasons to display a nationalist, progressive foreign policy. The new president had served as interior secretary in the Díaz Ordaz administration and shouldered much of the blame for the 1968 massacre of peaceful student protesters at the Plaza de las Tres Culturas; as a result, he was eager to play to the Mexican left. From his perspective, the timing for a rapprochement could not be better: superpower relations were improving, and Castro had discontinued his support for subversive movements in Latin America. Therefore, Echeverría became the first Mexican head of state to visit both Cuba and the Soviet Union, and he promoted modifications to the OAS charter that resulted in a partial suspension of the hemispheric embargo against Cuba. Together with Venezuelan president Andrés Pérez, the Mexican president created the Latin American Economic System (SELA), a group that included Cuba. Ultimately, Echeverría had to retreat, as the U.S. government remained staunchly opposed to Castro even in the context of détente with the Soviet Union. By the late 1970s, however, large oil discoveries had revived Mexican optimism about relations with Cuba. In 1979, Mexican president José López Portillo met with Castro on the Mexican island of Cozumel for largely symbolic talks.

More recently, the administrations of Miguel de la Madrid, Carlos Salinas de Gortari, and Ernesto Zedillo have resumed López Mateos's balancing act. Forced to ask for U.S. assistance in the middle of a severe economic crisis, de la Madrid distanced himself from Castro, yet maintained Mexico's old stance in defense of national self-determination. For his part, Salinas could ill afford to improve relations with Cuba as he pursued negotiations with the United States and Canada concerning the North American Free Trade Agreement. Under his leadership, Mexico joined Venezuela and Colombia in forming the Group of Three, a group that has repeatedly criticized Castro for his human rights record. Nevertheless, Salinas steered an independent course within this alliance as well: perhaps in light of the failure of his own promises of democratic reform in Mexico, he refused to call for democracy in Cuba, as his Venezuelan and Colombian colleagues had done. By the time Ernesto Zedillo came to power in December 1994, the Mexican government needed to attend to a new economic and political crisis. Moreover, the Castro regime had begun to disintegrate.

What role, then, has Cuba played in Mexican foreign policy? Whether at the end of the nineteenth or in the middle of the twentieth century, obtaining influence in Cuba has proven an impossible task for any Mexican government. Enough Mexicans knew and cared about the island to make Cuba an important issue in the formulation of Mexican foreign policy. Nevertheless, the influence of the United States—and, more recently, the hostility of Mexican conservatives to the Castro government—always has frustrated Mexican attempts to play a role on this Caribbean island.

Mexico's Cuba policy, then, is more significant for its domestic political than for its geopolitical implications. Backed by popular demands to stop U.S. influence in the Caribbean, Porfirio Díaz made a half-hearted attempt to prevent war between the United States and Spain. The predictable failure of this attempt and the Spanish-American War of 1898 unified both the radical Liberal and the Conservative opposition against Díaz and thus contributed to Díaz's subsequent nationalist gestures and the eventual downfall of the Porfirian regime. Seeking to demonstrate a heartfelt commitment to social and political change in Latin America, López Mateos initially welcomed the Cuban Revolution. After U.S. intervention and the radicalization of the revolution eroded this initial support for Castro, the defense of Cuba's right to self-determination played to Mexico's time-honored nationalist diplomatic tradition. In defending Cuban independence rather than Castro's policies, López Mateos showed both Mexicans and the world that his government always would defend each nation's right to make its own laws. By recalling Mexico's past struggles against foreign intervention, this policy found the support of both progressives and conservatives. Interested in Mexican political stability, the U.S. government gave Mexico "a special dispensation to dissent" in foreign-policy matters; it was a dispensation that Díaz had not enjoyed in his Cuba policy.

This special dispensation, however, required that Mexico not oppose the United States in its attempts to isolate Cuba from the rest of the Americas. Save for a few symbolic acts, Mexican governments since 1962 have complied with this requirement. Therefore, recent events only have highlighted the fact that the Mexican government cannot confront the United States over Cuba. While showing a considerable degree of independence, Mexican gestures on behalf of "Cuba libre" masked the country's extremely limited options in Cuban matters, during Díaz's days as well as today. Only time will tell whether Mexico's relations with post-Castro Cuba will be different.

Select Bibliography

Buchenau, Jürgen, *In the Shadow of the Giant: The Making of Mexico's Central America Policy, 1876–1930.* Tuscaloosa: University of Alabama Press, 1996.

_____, "Mexico as a Middle Power: A Historical Perspective." In *Perspectives on Inter-American Relations in the Twentieth Century,* edited by Thomas M. Leonard. Tuscaloosa: University of Alabama Press, 1997.

Chabat, Jorge, "Mexico: So Close to the United States, So Far from Latin America." *Current History* 92:568 (February 1993).

Cosío Villegas, Daniel, *Historia moderna de México: El Porfiriato: Vida política exterior: Segunda parte.* Mexico City: Hermes, 1963.

Deger, Robert J., Jr., "Porfirian Foreign Policy and Mexican Nationalism: A Study of Cooperation and Conflict in Mexican-American Relations, 1884–1904." Ph.D. diss., Indiana University, 1979.

Gilmore, N. Ray, "Mexico and the Spanish-American War." *Hispanic American Historical Review* 43:4 (November 1963).

Hamnett, Brian, *Juárez.* London and New York: Longman, 1994.

Knight, Alan, *U.S.-Mexican Relations, 1910–1940: An Interpretation.* San Diego: Center for U.S.-Mexican Studies, University of California, San Diego, 1987.

Mares, David, "Mexico's Foreign Policy as a Middle Power: The Nicaragua Connection, 1884–1986." *Latin American Research Review* 18:1 (Fall 1988).

Ojeda, Mario, *Alcances y límites de la política exterior de México.* Mexico City: Colegio de México, 1976.

Padilla Nervo, Luis, "The Presence of Mexico at the United Nations: The Cuban Case." In *Latin American International Politics: Ambitions, Capabilities, and the National Interest of Mexico, Brazil, and Argentina,* edited by Carlos A. Astiz. Notre Dame, Indiana: University of Notre Dame Press, 1969.

Pellicer de Brody, Olga, *México y la revolución cubana.* Mexico City: Colegio de México, 1972.

_____, and Esteban L. Mancilla, *Historia de la Revolución Mexicana, 1952–1960: El entendimiento con los Estados Unidos y la gestación del desarrollo estabilizador.* Mexico City: Colegio de México, 1978.

Riguzzi, Paolo, "México, Estados Unidos y Gran Bretaña: una difícil relación triangular." *Historia Mexicana* 41:3 (January 1992).

Smith, Arthur K., "Mexico and the Cuban Revolution: Foreign Policy-Making in Mexico under President Adolfo López Mateos (1958–1964)." Ph.D. diss., Cornell University, 1970.

Vázquez, Josefina Z., and Lorenzo Meyer, *The United States and Mexico.* Chicago: University of Chicago Press, 1985.

—JÜRGEN BUCHENAU

FOREIGN POLICY: CENTRAL AMERICA, 1821–1930

Because economic ties between Mexico and Central America lacked significance before 1930, Mexican policies toward Central America during this period reflected primarily political and cultural goals. First and foremost, these policies highlighted the Mexican government's desire to limit both foreign (and particularly U.S.) intervention and Guatemalan ambition in the region. Second, these policies showed a consistent desire to expand Mexico's own political and cultural role in the isthmus; not without reason do many Central Americans regard Mexico, and not the United States, as *el coloso del norte* (colossus of the north). Finally, and especially beginning with the dictatorship of Porfirio Díaz (1876–1911), Mexican policy in Central America sought to legitimize the ruling Mexican regime.

Four distinct phases mark Mexico's policies toward Central America from 1821 to 1930: an aggressive phase (1821–c. 1842); a defensive phase (c. 1842–c. 1871); a diplomatic phase (c. 1871–c. 1908); and an anti-interventionist phase (c. 1908–c. 1930). The first and the third phases reflect an active Mexican posture, while the second and the fourth phases mark periods of chiefly reactive policies. The ebb and flow of Mexican initiatives in Central America correspond to conditions in Central America, U.S. policies, the degree of political stability in Mexico, the domestic political agenda of the Mexican governing elite, and the personal interest of the Mexican president.

Mexico's interest in Central America was a product both of history and geography: in colonial times, the Audiencia de Guatemala, which included Central America as well as Chiapas, formed a semi-autonomous portion of New Spain. Mexico City's authority, however, was more hypothetical than real. The viceroy in Mexico City never could assert his rule over a remote area whose elites resented ties to Mexico and waged interminable feuds with one another. Central America's exposed geographic location further weakened central control. By the late eighteenth century, foreign intervention had made a mockery of New Spain's nominal sovereignty over Central America. While filibusters and pirates established strongholds on the region's Atlantic coast, Britain seized control of two coastal enclaves, Belize and La Mosquitia.

Not surprisingly, the Wars of Independence further loosened these nominal ties. Immediately after the achievement of independence in 1821, a Central American revolt erupted against Agustín de Iturbide's Imperio Mexicano. Even though the troops of general Vicente Filísola crushed this revolt, Central America's separation from Mexico was not long in coming. Upon the victory of republican forces over Emperor Iturbide in early 1823, the region that had comprised the Audiencia de Guatemala seceded. The new state soon became a federal republic under the name Provincias Unidas del Centro de América (United Provinces of the Center of America), with Ciudad de Guatemala as its capital city. This secession provided the first serious blow to Mexico City's claim to succeed the old viceroyalty in its entirety. Only 13 short years later, the secession of Texas would create a far more serious problem.

In Chiapas, however, Mexico reclaimed a small portion of Central America. In order to retain at least the westernmost part of Central America, the Mexican government exploited existing sentiments against Guatemala City in one of Chiapas' foremost cities, Ciudad Real (present-day San Cristóbal de Las Casas). The government of Guadalupe Victoria considered the Central American secession on the whole inevitable, and it did everything in its power to assist Ciudad Real in its separation from Central America. In late 1823, the Victoria regime organized a plebiscite in both the highland area around Ciudad Real and the fertile lowlands around that city's more pro-Guatemalan rival, Tuxtla Gutiérrez. Predictably, the pro-Mexico vote prevailed in the highlands, but not in the lowlands. Nevertheless, claiming that the entire area had voted as one, Mexico incorporated it in its totality. This annexation of Chiapas sowed the seeds of a bitter antagonism with Guatemala that would continue into the late nineteenth century.

The term "aggressive phase" thus denotes an interesting anomaly in Mexican foreign policy from 1821 to 1842. While the Mexican government found itself the victim of political instability and foreign intervention, it aggressively asserted its claims over Chiapas. As subsequent events showed, Mexican rulers even expanded the area under their control: in 1842, General Antonio López de Santa Anna's forces rode into the coastal province of Soconusco and incorporated it into Chiapas. In the meantime, the ability of Central American leaders to resist such incursions had diminished greatly. By 1837, the federal republic had dissolved into the new states of Guatemala, El Salvador, Honduras, Nicaragua, and Costa Rica. Left alone and frequently at war with El Salvador, Guatemala could not resist Mexican encroachments.

By 1846, however, the war with the United States had forced Mexico into a defensive posture. Whereas previous difficulties with foreign nations had hampered but not prevented Mexican action in Chiapas, the U.S. Army's occupation of Mexico City ended any dreams of further pecking away at Guatemalan territory. The war with the United States also demonstrated something the Mexican elites had long feared: Mexico's southern border was much more secure than its northern one. As a result of the enormous territorial losses following the U.S.-Mexican War, the shaky Mexican government began to neglect the situation in Chiapas, fearing further U.S. annexations.

The beginning of the period of Liberal rule known as La Reforma in 1854 ushered in a unique era in Mexican–Central American relations, relations that thus far had remained confined to Mexico and Guatemala. During the upheaval of the 1850s and 1860s, the Guatemalan government seriously threatened Mexican control over Chiapas. Guatemalan caudillo Rafael Carrera, nominally a Conservative, did not like the Liberal seizure of power in Mexico. Disentailing Catholic Church wealth and imperiling the time-honored privileges of army, clergy, and nobility, the Mexican reform legislation of 1856–57 directly opposed Carrera's own policy. Moreover, a festering caste war in Chiapas, the War of Reform, and the French Intervention offered the nationalist Carrera a rare chance at revenge. Carrera openly supported Benito Juárez's Conservative rivals and gave assistance to separatist factions in Chiapas. Both of these attempts failed in the end, but they highlight a sudden reversal of fortunes in the Mexican-Guatemalan relationship: now Guatemala acted and Mexico reacted.

In 1871, the relationship changed yet again, this time in Juárez's favor. During the past decades, Guatemalan Liberals who admired the Reforma had gained ground steadily, and they finally made their move to seize power. Still attempting to strengthen his hold on all of Mexico, Juárez could not do much to help Miguel García Granados's Liberal forces. Nevertheless, he gave modest military assistance to the García Granados faction, and he allowed them to use Chiapas as a staging ground. With the Liberal triumph in Guatemala early in 1871, Juárez had reason to believe that relations with Guatemala would change for the better.

The more active policy that marked the "diplomatic phase," however, took more than 10 years to develop, as the Chiapas issue first had to be resolved. Juárez's successor, Sebastián Lerdo de Tejada, took little interest in Central America. A weak ruler beleaguered by factional conflict and growing difficulties with the United States, Lerdo did not pay attention to the Chiapas controversy. The next president, Porfirio Díaz, found himself unable to pursue a permanent settlement during his first term in office for lack of U.S. diplomatic recognition. Meanwhile, the rapid development of coffee plantations in Guatemala (and the potential for coffee growing in Soconusco) made a permanent settlement necessary. Failure to draw a legitimate boundary threatened to frighten both domestic and foreign investors, especially close to the existing, improvised border. Therefore, Mexican president Manuel González and Guatemalan leader Justo Rufino Barrios finally came to an agreement in 1882. In this endeavor, González's move to resolve outstanding boundary issues dovetailed with Barrios's goal to free military resources to consummate the old dream of a Guatemalan-led Central American Union. While not entirely satisfactory to González, the 1882 treaty amounted to a net increase of Mexican territory, and it affirmed Mexico's possession of all of Chiapas.

In the mid-1880s, with the boundary controversy resolved and political stability achieved, the Mexican government could at last consider a policy that would transcend the old focus on the Guatemalan boundary. Instead, Díaz made limiting Guatemalan dominance over the rest of Central America one of the goals of his second administration. Events soon tested this goal: in March 1885, Barrios had the Guatemalan Congress proclaim the unification of Central America by force. The next day, the governments of El Salvador, Nicaragua, and Costa Rica appealed to Mexico in the hopes that Díaz would oppose the use of force in the achievement of the Central American Union.

Díaz did not disappoint the anti-Barrios alliance. While Foreign Secretary Ignacio Mariscal denounced the unification proclamation, Díaz asked his minister to the United States, Matías Romero, to attempt to gain U.S. support for a common policy of opposition. One week later, he also sent Mexican troops to the Guatemalan border. But this was as far as the Porfirians were willing to go. Knowing that

Barrios's forces could reach the border before his own, Díaz did not declare war on Guatemala. Even as the Guatemalan army invaded El Salvador, the Díaz regime joined the U.S. government in a policy of "moral suasion." This stance proved sufficient: Barrios was killed during the invasion of El Salvador, and the idea of a forcibly unified Central America died with him.

The crisis of 1885 presaged the signature strategy of the "diplomatic phase." Conscious of its increasing international prestige as well as its relative military weakness, the Díaz regime would neither condone the use of force in Central America nor itself use military means to achieve its goals. At a time when U.S., British, French, and German gunboats jockeyed for supremacy in the Caribbean, the use of force had become a risky matter. Instead, the Mexican government used diplomacy to extend its influence in Central America.

Although this policy had been conceived with the primary idea of weakening Guatemala, events during the last decade of the nineteenth century forced Díaz to direct his attention to U.S. influence in Central America. The Spanish-American War of 1898 formed the most traumatic experience of those years. To be sure, U.S. military intervention in the Cuban struggle for independence did not directly affect the Central American countries. But Díaz and his advisers feared that Central America—as a probable site for an Atlantic-Pacific canal—might very well be the next victim of U.S. military intervention. The rhetoric coming from Washington did little to allay these fears: as early as 1894, U.S. secretary of state Richard Olney proclaimed that the U.S. "fiat" was law in the Western Hemisphere. In 1903, the U.S.-assisted secession of Panama from Colombia seemed to confirm the worst nightmares. The U.S. government, it appeared, would stop at nothing to dominate the Caribbean region, and U.S. armies one day might encircle Mexico from both the north and the south.

Even though these fears proved exaggerated, they were sufficiently widespread among Mexicans to add a domestic policy dimension to Díaz's posture in Central American affairs. As Mexicans felt increasingly vulnerable to the effects of U.S. economic penetration, the government's image among its retainers and the middle classes came to depend in part on how it fared in confronting U.S. expansion, in Central America and elsewhere in the Western Hemisphere. Therefore, Mexican concerns about Guatemala gradually were displaced by a policy designed to limit U.S. military intervention as well as placate Díaz's nationalist opposition.

As internecine wars devastated Central America during the first years of the twentieth century, however, Díaz's policy remained focused on diplomacy and at least partially responsive to the initiatives of Guatemalan strongman Manuel Estrada Cabrera. As these wars threatened to bring about both Guatemalan hegemony and U.S. intervention to prevent unrest close to the new canal, Díaz decided to use his influence to pacify Central America. After refusing to become U.S. president Theodore Roosevelt's cop on the beat (Roosevelt had suggested in 1904–05 that Mexico assume the role of peacemaker in Central America with U.S. bless-ing), he agreed to co-mediate Central American disputes with the U.S. government. In July 1906, and again in March 1907, Díaz and Roosevelt succeeded in ending short Central American wars at the negotiating table. This endeavor cul-minated in the joint sponsorship of the 1907 Washington Conventions that established an arbitration framework for future conflicts, and it gave don Porfirio much to boast about. Not only could the new mechanism constrain U.S. intervention, but the newly created Court of Central Ameri-can Justice could also rein in Guatemalan schemes for the domination of the isthmus. Best of all, Central American representatives, and not the U.S. government, would adjudi-cate pending disputes.

Ultimately, however, several processes forced Díaz to choose between confronting U.S. influence and withdrawing from Central American affairs. U.S. president William H. Taft proved much less amenable than his predecessor to dia-logue with Mexico, and much more willing to use force in Central America. Soon, aggressive U.S. policies put Díaz at odds with the U.S. State Department. The Taft administra-tion desired the removal of Nicaraguan president José S. Zelaya, whose staunch opposition to both U.S. and Guatemalan influence had made him a key Mexican ally in Central America. Moreover, the intense hatred between Zelaya and Guatemala's Estrada Cabrera made the work of the Court of Central American Justice difficult. Both leaders incessantly conspired against each other: while Zelaya attempted to bring down the pro-Cabrera government of El Salvador, Cabrera sought to oust the pro-Zelaya Honduran president. Finally, events in Mexico also forced Díaz's hand. As his increasingly unpopular regime faced the severe reces-sion of 1907–08, Díaz could not allow his nationalist critics to portray him as being in league with U.S. peacekeeping efforts in Central America.

Thus began the "anti-interventionist phase" of Mexico's Central American policy, a period that many scholars mistak-enly identify with the governments of the Mexican Revolu-tion only. During this stage, the Mexican government sought to limit U.S. intervention as its primary goal, particularly in Nicaragua. Coinciding with the peak of U.S. military inter-vention in the Caribbean, the "anti-interventionist phase" witnessed a number of Mexican efforts to blunt U.S. pene-tration into the region. In these efforts, the extension of Mexico's own influence (and occasional problems with Guatemala) remained important issues.

The new posture became clear as early as 1909. In April of that year, when U.S. secretary of state Philander C. Knox announced plans to eliminate Zelaya, Díaz let it be known that he could no longer cooperate with the United States in maintaining peace in Central America. In November 1909, when the U.S. government began to support a revolt against the Nicaraguan president, the Mexican leadership did everything in its power to keep Zelaya's party in office. Díaz awarded immediate recognition to Zelaya's hand-picked suc-

cessor, José Madriz; he sent an envoy to Washington in the hopes of persuading Taft to end the intervention; he gave asy-lum to Zelaya against the strong objections of the U.S. State Department; and he sent arms and ammunition to the Madriz forces. Ultimately, these measures could not keep Madriz in power, as his opposition soon acquired the support of U.S. gunboats. But Díaz's cautiously anti-imperialist diplomacy did demonstrate his opposition to unilateral U.S. intervention.

The fall of the Porfiriato and the beginning of the Mexican Revolution forced a hiatus in these policies, a break accentuated after 1912 by the presence of U.S. Marines in Nicaragua. With the disintegration of central authority in Mexico, the decade following 1910 in many ways was a throwback to the "defensive phase" of 1842 to 1871. Once again, Mexicans had to defend their country's southeastern boundary: between 1911 and 1917, Guatemalan dictator Manuel Estrada Cabrera aided separatist forces in Chiapas as well as enemies of the respective Mexican governments. In particular, Estrada Cabrera allowed the counterrevolutionary faction of don Porfirio's nephew Félix Díaz to use Guatemalan territory as a sanctuary, and he furnished arms and ammunition to that faction. Thus, the Revolutionary government of Venustiano Carranza could consider itself fortunate that it was able to put an end to the incursions through both force and negotiation with Estrada Cabrera. While Carranza's speeches promised more assertive policies, including bringing the example of the Mexican Revolution to other Latin American nations, the political reality dic-tated a defensive approach that focused mainly on the vague goal of promoting Mexican culture in Central America. With U.S.-Mexican relations souring after the Revolution, the conservative Central American elites dreading revolu-tionary upheavals, and U.S. soldiers occupying Nicaragua, the chances for future Mexican initiatives in Central Amer-ica appeared slim.

Surprisingly, however, Mexico's margin of action increased just as the more pragmatic words of Álvaro Obregón and Plutarco Elías Calles replaced Carranza's revolu-tionary nationalist rhetoric. Estrada Cabrera's ouster in 1920 led to a rare, pro-Mexican government in Guatemala City. Even though this government fell in December 1921, having been unsuccessful in its objective of fomenting a Central American union, the new rulers of Guatemala remained friendly to Mexico. In 1923, Obregón procured U.S. diplo-matic recognition and thus put his government in a position to negotiate with the largely pro-U.S. regimes on the isthmus. Finally, in 1925, the U.S. Marines withdrew from Nicaragua, leaving a fragile nationalist government that sought to emu-late many of the reforms of the Zelaya administration.

Emiliano Chamorro's coup against that government on the heels of the U.S. withdrawal finally brought Mexican policy out of its long dormancy. Knowing that the U.S. gov-ernment had pledged itself in the 1923 Washington agree-ments to help uphold the constitutional order in all of the Central American republics, Mexican president Calles calculated that he could afford to help the beleaguered but legitimate Nicaraguan president, Carlos Solórzano. Through his minister in Managua, Calles offered Solórzano military assistance and the use of a Mexican gunboat. In January 1926, however, the Nicaraguan president decided to resign in favor of Chamorro rather than risk a prolonged military standoff.

But Calles was not out of options altogether. Beginning in June 1926, he supported a faction in rebellion against Chamorro. Calles acted at a seemingly propitious moment. Seeking to extricate itself from its military commitments in Latin America, the U.S. government had withdrawn its legation guard from Nicaragua. In addition, U.S. secretary of state Frank B. Kellogg appeared to sympathize with Mexico's position: he, too, refused to recognize Chamorro as the country's legitimate head of state. Moreover, Liberal leader Juan Bautista Sacasa, as former vice president, could lay some claim to representing the constitutional order. In the end, however, the deployment of U.S. Marines forced Calles to retreat. Kellogg perceived Mexican meddling in Nicaragua as a threat to the U.S. position in the isthmus. He also saw an aggressive policy in Nicaragua as a way of forcing the Mexican government to pay U.S. claims for damages incurred as a result of the Revolution and Mexico's new constitution.

As these events showed, Calles had a much tougher time asserting Mexican interests than Díaz because he did not enjoy the Porfirians' relatively cordial relations with the United States. Rather than ushering in a nationalist diplomacy, the Revolution had complicated Mexico's position in Central America. As a result, efforts to increase Mexican influence in Central America remained sporadic and unsuccessful.

The failure of the Sacasa rebellion thrust Mexican policy back into its previous anti-interventionist pattern. This fact became clear at the next opportunity: in 1929, the Nicaraguan rebel Augusto C. Sandino, who had been fighting the U.S. Marines since 1927, asked for political asylum in Mexico. Mexican president Emilio Portes Gil assented and immediately sought to use Sandino's request as a bargaining chip with the United States. After gaining U.S. approval for granting Sandino asylum in Yucatán, Portes Gil's agents offered Nicaraguan president José M. Moncada a quid pro quo: if Moncada asked the U.S. government for a withdrawal of the Marines, Portes Gil would undertake to prevent Sandino from organizing his rebellion from Mexican soil. Moncada rejected the proposal, however, and nothing came of the idea. Aware that he could extract propagandistic benefit from giving asylum to a widely admired Nicaraguan patriot, Portes Gil decided to honor his offer of asylum. At the same time, he still hoped that the U.S. government would withdraw its troops if he could neutralize Sandino in Mexico; thus, the Mexican president put his "guest" under house arrest in Mérida, Yucatán. Ultimately, Sandino escaped and the Marines remained in Nicaragua, but Portes Gil's actions—the last such initiative for many years—once again had demonstrated Mexico's opposition to U.S. intervention in Central America. After the Sandino episode, the coming of the Good Neighbor Policy and changes in the Revolutionary state ushered in yet another phase in Mexico's Central America policy.

An analysis of Mexican policy toward Central America from 1821 to 1930 suggests both change and continuity. Mexican objectives in Central America varied widely during this period. As Mexico emerged from its tumultuous era of civil war and foreign intervention, the security of its southeastern border emerged as the main issue. During the Porfiriato, Mexico found this security and pushed to play an active role in Central America, not the least because Díaz desired to project a nationalist image in Mexico. Finally, when the U.S. government began to use military force to achieve its goals in Central America, Mexican policy recognized this new danger to the country's national security as its main concern in the region. There also was a degree of continuity to Mexico's policy from 1821 to 1930, however. The means and strategies of policy, circumscribed by Mexico's relative weakness in the international arena, changed little, particularly between 1876 and 1930. Diplomacy remained the country's most important device; after 1842, military action or other forms of coercion rarely played a role. In addition, the Mexican Revolution—so often perceived as the central watershed of Mexican national history—did not bring about fundamental change in the country's Central America policy. In fact, the Revolutionary regimes essentially followed Díaz's initiatives of his last years in power.

This absence of a clear rupture between the policies of the Porfiriato and those of the Revolution suggests two significant points. First, the difference between Porfirian and Revolutionary foreign policies was not as great as often has been assumed. Indeed, Díaz pursued a nationalist foreign policy in Central America; just like its successors, the Porfirian regime recognized all too well the dangers inherent in expanding U.S. power. Second, both the international context and the degree of political stability in Mexico have significantly shaped the country's Central America policy. In that regard, one might note the similarities between Juárez and Carranza on the one hand, and Díaz and Calles on the other hand.

In conclusion, Mexico's Central America policy between 1821 and 1930 was a crucial sideshow to the country's relations with the great powers. Central America was important to Mexican national security, both in terms of relations with Guatemala and because of the danger of U.S. intervention. For Mexican policy makers, a friendly but largely uneventful relationship with the Central American countries appeared a good relationship; better, certainly, than facing either Guatemalan soldiers in Chiapas or U.S. troops on both sides of Mexico's borders.

Select Bibliography

Best, Edward H., "Mexican Foreign Policy and Central America Since the Mexican Rebolution." Ph.D. diss., Oxford University, 1988.

Buchenau, Jürgen, *Calles y el movimiento liberal en Nicaragua*. Mexico City: Fideicomiso Archivos Plutarco Elías Calles y Fernando Torreblanca, 1992.

Campbell, Hugh G., "Mexico and Central America: The Continuity of Policy." In *Central America: Historical Perspectives on the Contemporary Crises,* edited by Ralph L. Woodward. New York: Greenwood, 1988.

Cosía Villegas, Daniel, editor, *Historia moderna de México*. 9 vols., Mexico City: Hermes, 1955–74.

Salisbury, Richard V., *Anti-Imperialism and International Competition in Central America, 1920–1929*. Wilmington, Delaware: Scholarly Resources, 1989.

Villanueva, Carlos, *Sandino en Yucatán, 1929–1930*. Mexico City: Secretaría de Educación Pública, 1988.

Zorrilla, Luis G., *Relaciones de México con la República de Centro América y con Guatemala*. Mexico City: Porrúa, 1984.

—JÜRGEN BUCHENAU

FOREIGN POLICY: CENTRAL AMERICA, 1930–96

Daniel Cosío Villegas, one of Mexico's preeminent historians, has written that Mexican relations with Central America retained "imperial aspirations" until 1927. The uncontested dominance by the United States over both Mexico and Central America following World War I, however, severely limited Mexican goals and strategies in the isthmus. From 1917 to 1925, Mexico's Central American policy emphasized strategies of cultural penetration, promoting Mexican film, literature, and artwork that emphasized a common Mesoamerican cultural and "racial" heritage. A common cultural heritage did not translate into political alignment as easily as the Mexican government hoped, however, as Central Americans' own cultural heritage included a quite real fear of Mexican imperialism. Moreover, Central American elites (and U.S. interests) saw a suspicious resemblance between Mexican cultural policy and Bolshevik propaganda.

After the failure of Mexico's unilateral military and political support for Nicaragua's liberals in 1926–27, Mexican policy retreated from attempts to directly influence the politics and ideology of Central American governments. By 1930, Mexico had abandoned any remaining imperial aspirations and had recognized the limitations of its ability to guide events in the isthmus through direct intervention or cultural courtship. Further, the full realization of U.S. dominance in the region and the destabilizing effects of the Great Depression caused Mexico to seek new ways of securing its interests in Central America. In the years following 1930, Mexican policy toward Central America has been defined by two main features: (1) the neutral defense, through multilateral international forums, of self-determination for all states, and (2) economic initiatives intended to develop regional trade as an alternative to dependency on North Atlantic countries (i.e., the United States, Canada, and western Europe). In both cases Mexican policy was aimed at finding alternatives to unilateral U.S. control over the political and economic fortunes of the region.

The first of these strategies was articulated by Mexico's foreign secretary Genero Estrada in September 1930, in what became known as the Estrada Doctrine. This doctrine asserted that the practice of recognizing new governments implied that the "legal capacity of governments or authorities appears to be dependent upon the opinion of foreigners." Accordingly, Mexico would not presume to determine the legitimacy of other governments through recognition or nonrecognition, but would limit itself to the exchange or withdrawal of diplomatic agents according to bilateral relations, rather than ideological judgments.

In 1930, however, questions of the relative sovereignty of weaker nations were eclipsed by domestic economic problems caused by the Great Depression. The decline in exports and the increased cost of imports forced Mexico to seek both new import sources and foreign markets for Mexican products. Central America seemed to offer a solution. In 1931 Mexico sought to establish a customs union with the Central American republics. The United States was able to dissuade Central American governments from pursuing such arrangements, but Mexico remained convinced that its economic troubles demanded increased trade with the isthmus. In 1932 the Mexican Ministry of Industry, Trade, and Labor determined that Central America, by virtue of its proximity and cultural affinity, was the natural market for Mexican exports. The road to this market was beset with numerous obstacles, however, the most obvious being the fact that the Central American economy was competitive, not complementary, with Mexico's. U.S. economic interests had no intention of allowing Mexico to begin exporting products to a region that previously had been provided by the United States; these U.S. interests were willing to use their economic strength to undersell Mexican competition. Even without these obstacles, the existing transportation and communication infrastructure was not sufficient for increased trade on the scale imagined in Mexican financial circles. More important in the view of the Mexican government was a general indifference to Mexico's advances on the part of Central Americans. Mexico had no relations with occupied Nicaragua; Guatemala, Honduras, and Costa Rica were suspicious of Mexican intentions, preferring to rely on the United States rather than become the focus of U.S.-Mexican competition. Only El Salvador responded enthusiastically, seeking Mexican loans, arms, and advice on the development of a central bank.

These inherent obstacles were not enough to deflate the hopes of Mexican economic experts. Indeed, Mexico sought to make small steps toward economic cooperation that ultimately would promote better political and cultural connections, thereby starting a cycle of improved relations and economic opportunities. The solution to Mexico's economic difficulties was seen to lie in establishing itself as the middleman in the international economy: Central America would provide raw materials, Mexico would provide manufactured goods, and the advanced industrialized nations would provide advanced technological products. The price and variety of Mexican manufactures, however, were not attractive enough to interest Central Americans. The only advantage Mexico had was in its oil industry, but the Central American nations had contracts with U.S. companies that controlled the processing of Mexican oil; the only way Mexico could benefit from its petroleum industry was through taxation, and this made its oil uncompetitive.

By 1933 the U.S. occupying force had left Nicaragua, but the National Guard dominated its politics and Mexican relations did not significantly improve. President Franklin D. Roosevelt's Good Neighbor Policy improved relations with the United States, but the right-wing isthmian regimes of the period were clearly aligned with the United States, and an alternative to U.S. capital resources was not necessarily one of their immediate goals. Nonetheless, the Mexican push for greater economic integration continued, and in 1934 Mexico sent a Special Commercial Mission and established the First Convention of Mexican–Central American Chambers of Commerce, both of which were designed to promote Mexican products and regional economic solidarity. These initiatives met with resistance from Guatemala, where the dictator Jorge Ubico feared that a regional economic bloc of Mexican design would decrease his own regional influence. Ubico therefore sought to promote a Central American economic bloc independent of Mexican leadership. Beyond the traditional Guatemalan suspicion of Mexican imperial intentions, his fears were exacerbated by the presence of Guatemalan exiles in Mexico disseminating anti-Ubico propaganda.

Later that year Mexican goals of forging closer economic ties with Central America were inadvertently jeopardized by private Mexican business interests who invited all of the Central American presidents to join an economic "junta," a regional bloc that accepted Mexican leadership as the "advance sentinel of *la Raza* (the race)" against U.S. imperialism. Despite Honduran president Tiburcio Carias's enthusiasm for the junta, such rhetoric made the other republics uneasy that Mexico was intending to implicate them in radical anti-U.S. statements.

Further attempts at economic relations were derailed when Mexican president Lázaro Cárdenas came out in support of Republican Spain in 1936. Both Ubico and Nicaragua's Anastasio Somoza García found Mexican solidarity with the Spanish left as grounds for concern that Mexico would promote communist agitation in their countries. They feared that the Soviet Union was using Mexico as a headquarters for the penetration of international communism into Latin America. Mexico denied any official sympathy with international communism, but as Mexican arms shipments to Spanish Republicans became known, Central American fears of Mexican military support for leftist rebels increased. Officially, Mexican support was for the "Nationalists" as a democratic alternative to communist dictatorship, but this assertion was undermined when the Mexican minister in Nicaragua announced, at a diplomatic dinner party, that his country had great sympathy for Spain's "Reds," and the specter of bolshevism continued to cloud Mexican–Central American relations.

As Somoza moved to seize power in Nicaragua, President Juan Bautista Sacasa requested Mexican aid, as he had in 1926. But the events a decade earlier had strengthened neither Sacasa's cause nor Mexico's international position. President Cárdenas proposed that the situation be submitted to joint Mexican-U.S. arbitration, but this was rejected by both the United States and Nicaragua. Unwilling to intercede unilaterally and unable to arbitrate, Mexico remained aloof. When Carlos Brenes Jarquín was named president, Mexico was caught between recognizing what it deemed to be a basically unacceptable transfer of power, or betraying its avowed ideals of foreign policy, which asserted that nonrecognition was, indirectly, intervention. Cárdenas initially chose to ride the fence by declaring "diplomatic abstention," and he exchanged diplomatic personnel only after Sacasa himself had apparently accepted the transfer of power.

During the mid-1930s Mexican labor propaganda began to increase in Central America, further heightening fears about Mexico's connections to international communism. Although a few years earlier Nicaragua had been the most responsive to Mexican labor ideologies, this changed under Somoza, who led the regional move to recognize Spanish fascist Francisco Franco. Mexico was appalled that Central American nations supported Franco and had voted to banish Republican Spain from the League of Nations' Council: Mexican newspapers referred to their neighbors on the isthmus as the "Dictators League against Communism." Despite Cárdenas's personal assurances, Ubico accused Mexico of conspiring with Republican Spain and Communist Russia in arming Central American revolutionaries for communist takeovers. Similar accusations were voiced in El Salvador and Nicaragua. In defense against these accusations, the Mexican press ran articles criticizing the conservative dictatorships in Central America; these actions, in turn, led to the criticism that freedom of the press was being used to destabilize foreign governments. Although the articles were designed for domestic circulation, the Mexican government put pressure on its press to avoid publishing pieces that would undermine its general stance of non-intervention in the domestic affairs of weaker nations.

When in 1938 Cárdenas pursued the radical nationalization of the country's resources, he expected the move to be applauded by Central American governments that could benefit by following the precedent. Too large of a rift by now existed between Mexico and the isthmus, however, and Central America saw the oil expropriation as confirmation of Mexico's leftist tendencies. Far from applauding Cárdenas, Central Americans looked to the United States for assurances that they would be defended against Mexican revolutionary activity; President Ubico went so far as to inform the United States that military intervention against the oil expropriation would be supported by Guatemala. The growing conflict in Europe, however, had focused U.S. military attentions elsewhere and functioned as a deterrent to U.S. intervention against Mexican expropriations. Nevertheless, domestic instability resulting from the Cárdenas reforms caused Mexico to quiet its voice in the international realm while it regrouped, and the ultimate U.S. boycott created an urgent need for alternative markets for Mexican oil. To this end Mexico sought to improve relations with the two more powerful Central American governments, curbing the activities of Guatemalan exiles in the country and making it clear that Mexico would not support former Nicaraguan president Emiliano Chamorro Vargas—then in exile in Mexico—in a challenge to Somoza. Both Guatemala and Nicaragua responded to Mexico's gestures with an increase in oil purchases, at least until 1939, when the United States pressured Nicaragua to join the boycott. Far from making Mexico the champion of weaker nations' seeking to extricate themselves from the mechanisms of neocolonialism, the oil expropriation had caused Mexico to seek a much more conservative international appearance in Central America.

Mexico sought to distance itself from associations with communism and its endorsement of class conflict by advertising its domestic system as based on national class unity. As Mexico began to slow labor and agrarian reforms, both the United States and Central America were encouraged by its less radical character. Improved relations, however, did not keep Mexico from criticizing what it saw as a transparent U.S. attempt to buy Central American loyalty with loans, credit, and technical advisers. One Mexican paper concluded that "the Good Neighbor doctrine is transforming itself into a league of 'mestizo' dictators, with the United States destined to guarantee the slavery of Latin American peoples." Yet, ironically, the U.S. boycott caused significant oil exports to Hitler's Germany and Mussolini's Italy (although an increasingly large portion of Mexican oil production remained at home for an expanding domestic market).

U.S.-Mexican tensions over compensation for the expropriated oil properties were resolved quickly as the U.S. State Department refused to back the oil companies' demands for compensation far greater than the sums determined by a U.S.-Mexican joint commission. Mexico was considered strategically important to U.S. national security in the event of an escalation in the global conflict, and President Avila Camacho refused to cooperate fully with hemispheric security plans until the issues raised by the 1938 expropriations had been resolved. After two Mexican tankers were sunk by German U-boats in May 1942, Mexico formally joined the Allied forces. All of the Central American states had responded to the call of the United States and declared war on the Axis powers. The impact of the war on Mexican–Central American relations was most apparent in increased trade. Although the United States conceived of Central America's role in the wartime economy as a source of substitutes for Pacific products, U.S. industry was forced to reduce the production of several manufactured goods, such as textiles, which Central America then exported to Mexico. By the end of the war Central America was, for the first time, a significant source of Mexican imports. Mexico, however, did not offer a consumer base able to absorb significant amounts of luxury commodities, such as coffee, and the impact of Mexican–Central American trade during the war was not lasting. The trade of both was dominated by the United States, and the war ultimately strengthened U.S. economic hegemony in the region.

Of more lasting impact was increased tensions between Mexico and Guatemala over Guatemalan exiles who, by 1943, again were agitating against the Ubico regime from Mexican soil. The motivation for the earlier Mexican promise to curb these activities had passed, and Guatemala renewed its complaints to the United States that Mexico was seeking to spearhead socialist revolutions in Central America. Ubico's accusations did not convince the United States, which determined that the source of agitation was nongovernmental and that Mexico had demonstrated its commitment to democracy by cooperating with Allied strategic defense of the region. Moreover, Central American complaints of Mexican radicalism no longer caused the same alarm in Washington, for Mexico had institutionalized its revolutionary reforms and seemed willing to participate in the new international order as envisioned by the United States. Central Americans, on the other hand, were just beginning to rebel against the social and political injustices and unequal distribution of wealth under the Depression-era dictators; it was now the Mexican elite who began to worry about Central American radicalism and the influence it might have on domestic politics.

In 1944 a popular uprising unseated Ubico and paved the way for the social reforms of Juan José Arévalo Bermejo. Mexican public opinion encouraged President Avila Camacho to be the first to recognize Arévalo, but he chose not to champion the regime, preferring to offer support only in concert with the rest of the hemisphere. Although Mexico hoped to distance itself from a Guatemalan reform movement that cited Mexico as its example, events in El Salvador made that difficult. The reformist government that had replaced President Martínez proved unable to establish power and was forced into exile. The possibility that a reactionary move in El Salvador might undermine the new democracy in

Guatemala led Mexico to announce that it would support the new Guatemalan regime with arms in the event of a rebellion from Salvadoran soil. Mexican-Guatemalan relations did enjoy their greatest solidarity during Arévalo's administration, which withdrew recognition from Franco and declared that it had ceased its anti-Mexico policy. The United States viewed these statements dimly: despite the fact that the Mexican Revolution had stabilized and U.S.-Mexican relations were enjoying a special friendship, it was clear that the Mexican Revolution remained a potent symbol of radical social and economic reform to Central Americans. Indeed, the Mexican experience remained influential, even if no longer promoted officially by Mexico.

Relations with Guatemala during this period included the sale of Mexican war materials and reciprocal scholarships for officer training in military colleges. The militant Mexican socialist labor leader Vicente Lombardo Toledano was invited to give speeches to Guatemalan labor groups. Although he made no contacts with the Mexican Embassy, his visits and the fact that he was named co-president with Arévalo of the Second Annual Labor Congress of Guatemala alarmed those still convinced of Mexico's complicity with international communism. At the very least, Washington was concerned over Arévalo's unabashed admiration for Cárdenas and his frequent claims that Guatemala was undergoing a Mexican-style revolution. President Avila Camacho, however, did not reciprocate the comparisons and pursued an antirevolutionary pan-Americanism while expressing concern over communist agitation emanating from Guatemala. Guatemala's revolutionary identity was at a stage through which Mexico already had passed and to which it did not wish to return.

Mexican international principles nevertheless committed it to oppose the 1954 U.S. proposal of hemispheric defense through collective intervention in the internal politics of supposedly communist states. Mexico suggested that collective action should take place only when there was clear and direct foreign interference, rather than the abstractly defined "presence of international communism"; when this suggestion was rejected, Mexico abstained from voting on the proposal. The abstention was intended to establish that Mexico rejected U.S. interventionism without directly antagonizing the United States.

As the regime of Jacobo Arbenz in Guatemala faced a mounting challenge, it appealed to both Mexico and the Soviet Union for aid, but only the latter responded with offers of support—and this support was minimal and mismanaged. Popular opinion in Mexico supported Arbenz, however, and there was a privately founded Society of Friends of Guatemala that compared the two nations' revolutions and was endorsed by former president Cárdenas. The Mexican left, represented most vocally by Lombardo Toledano, claimed that security interests, as well as ideological ones, necessitated official support for Arbenz, asserting that Mexico did not want to be, again, surrounded by U.S. power. Instead, Mexico supported an investigation by the Inter-American Peace Commission to consider collective action against communism in general, and the Guatemala situation specifically. Arbenz was overthrown before the committee could determine a position on Guatemala, however. Following the U.S.-sponsored coup, Mexico wished to maintain a posture of nonintervention, and it neither condemned nor endorsed the overthrow. The Cold War had, indeed, limited the range of possible Mexican stances; in the eyes of the United States, there was no neutral ground between a pro-U.S. or pro-Soviet stance.

By the end of the decade Mexico had replaced the nationalist class unity of the Cárdenas period with a triple alliance of state, transnational corporations, and local capital. The trade deficit was growing, and the need for foreign investment created what domestic critics saw as a return to strategies of dependent development not seen since the regime of Porfirio Díaz (1876–1911). Indeed, where there had been no foreign capital in Mexican public investment programs in 1940, by 1961 a full 35.4 percent of those programs were financed abroad. In order to reduce its growing dependence on foreign capital, Mexico once again looked to its neighbors.

In the early 1960s Mexico sought greater economic cooperation with Latin America and joined the newly formed Latin American Free Trade Association (LAFTA), through which Mexico was able to increase exports. At this time Central America created the Central American Common Market (CACM), designed to protect the region from competition between the republics. Although Mexico was not a member of the CACM, Mexican industrialization had developed manufactured goods needed in Central America, where industrialization efforts required Mexican raw materials. The CACM was an obstacle to improved trade relations, however, as Central Americans feared anything that might stunt their infant industries. As an economic bloc, the CACM could provide much of what Mexico offered; but Mexico encouraged its southern neighbors to pursue complementary industrialization and thereby avoid a competitive overlap in manufactured goods similar to their competition in raw materials.

To this end, Mexico pursued a number of regional economic projects, including offers of credit to Central America from the Mexican National Foreign Trade Bank (1962), an agreement between the Bank of Mexico and the Central American Clearing House (Cámara de Compensación Centroamericana) for deals up to US$5 million (1963), and a Special Mission to encourage trade links between the CACM and Mexico (1964). Although these initiatives did increase Mexican investments and subsidiaries in Central America, it had little impact on total Mexican foreign trade, 63 percent of which was with the United States in 1963. Foreign trade still accounted for a relatively small portion of the Mexican economy, however, and Mexico sought to ensure that any increase in that portion would come from Latin America.

In 1965 the secretary of trade and industry met with all the economic ministers of Central America in order to build a mutual defense of export prices, suppress tariff barriers, and study the possibilities of improved industrial complementarity. A year later, Mexican president Gustavo Díaz Ordaz toured Central America and announced an increase in both public and private credits to the isthmus and a loan of US$5 million to the Central American Bank of Economic Integration. Over the following two years each of the Central American presidents reciprocated with visits to Mexico City. Díaz Ordaz was aware, however, of traditional suspicions that Mexico was interested in establishing its own neocolonial economic domination, and made numerous assurances to the contrary: Mexico would not expect investment guarantees or seek majority holdings of Central American firms.

Despite Mexican efforts, regional economic cooperation again failed to provide a real alternative to U.S. capital. The LAFTA had failed to reduce tariff barriers and the CACM was unable to develop complementary industry before it was destroyed by regional conflicts. Mexico continued to pursue economic integration with Central America by directly promoting complementarity with each republic. During the early 1970s Mexico attempted to increase its purchase of Central American primary products. Despite the poor response to these initiatives, the success of the Organization of Petroleum Exporting Countries (OPEC) in 1973 convinced Mexico that a multilateral approach was still worth pursuing, and new attempts continued over the next several years: a new Central American loan of US$10 million was announced in 1972, import licenses automatically were granted for all goods that previously had been imported from Central America, and in 1975 Mexico created an economic "frontier zone" in Guatemala, where exports could enter Central America under reduced tariffs. Initiatives continued until the end of the decade, when political events eclipsed economic projects.

Although relations with Central America were limited mainly to the economic sphere, the 1970s saw Mexico turn increasingly away from the United States in its international posture. When, in 1971, President Richard Nixon announced a new 10 percent surcharge on U.S. imports, it became clear that the "special friendship" between Mexico and the United States no longer offered preferential treatment. Partly in response to this, President Luis Echeverría Álvarez became increasingly active in stabilizing relations with nations clearly at odds with U.S. international objectives. Echeverría visited China and Chile (1972), the USSR (1973), and Cuba (1975), and he passionately condemned the overthrow of Chilean Marxist president Salvador Allende Gossens in 1973. In the United Nations he called for economic and political "decolonization" of the global economy, developing what has been called a policy of Third-Worldism. One tangible result of Echeverría's policy was the formation of the Latin American Economic System (SELA), which included Cuba but not the United States.

President José López Portillo continued to pursue increased trade with Central America, and in 1976 Mexico expanded the list of goods that could enter the frontier zone

under lowered tariffs. Mexican domestic policies also indirectly affected Central America when the minimum wage was increased, sending U.S. electronic companies to Central America in search of cheaper labor. Despite the failure to solve the vexing problems of complementarity and U.S. economic domination, the López Portillo administration continued to reach further agreements on economic cooperation and joint enterprises; in order to address the underlying obstacles, Mexico convinced the United Nations Economic Commission for Latin America (ECLA) to study the possibilities of further cooperation between the two regions.

These efforts to increase trade with Latin America in general and Central America in particular were balanced with attempts to improve relations with the United States. The López Portillo administration went so far as to build a pipeline from the Reforma oil fields to the U.S. border, which domestic critics saw as an undermining of Mexican economic independence based on alternative markets for its oil resources. These strengthened ties to the United States only jeopardized Mexican relations with Central America. Despite further reduction of tariffs to the isthmus, Mexican interest in trade with Central America was met with suspicion. Central Americans recognized that increased trade would not in itself achieve the economic goals of either region, so they feared that Mexican motivation was political and that Mexico continued to have regional hegemonic aspirations. They saw the same risks with Mexico as they had with the United States (open trade between unequal partners tended to be exploitative), and they preferred to take those risks with an economy that possessed sufficient resources to benefit them. This hesitancy deepened when the ECLA completed its study and concluded that the only reason for greater cooperation between Mexico and Central America would be political affinity.

As the economy began to recover from the recession of the mid-1970s, however, Mexico renewed its interest in championing third world pluralism and repeated its general support for self-determination and the importance of international law in protecting weaker nations, noting that "the powerful possess other means to defend and impose their interests." This shift was in part a product of López Portillo's attempts to relegitimize the ruling Partido Revolucionario Institucional (PRI, or Institutional Revolutionary Party) by increasing the possibilities for domestic opposition within the Mexican party system. During the 1970s Mexico had practiced virtual isolationism and thereby was permitted by the United States, as scholar Mario Ojeda noted, "to dissent from . . . [U.S.] policy in everything which is fundamental for Mexico, even though important but not fundamental for the United States." Yet relations between Mexico and the United States suffered in 1977 and 1978 as the United States proved unwilling to accept Mexican gas prices, forcing Mexico to choose between adopting a passive and dependent posture or searching for new markets that could not possibly replace the consumer capacity of the United States. Mexico felt pushed to demonstrate that it was not a "pro-imperialist lackey" of its neighbor to the north. One way to demonstrate this was to express solidarity for those countries attempting to throw off dependent relations and enter the global community as fully sovereign members.

After the January 1978 assassination of Nicaraguan president Anastasio Somoza Debayle's principal rival, Pedro Joaquín Chamorro, there was considerable domestic pressure for Mexico to withdraw recognition, but the government used the Estrada Doctrine to defend continued relations. Again, Mexico asserted its posture of nonintervention when it declined the U.S. invitation to participate in a collective mediation of the Nicaraguan conflict. Mexican foreign secretary, Santiago Roel, bluntly stated: "You Americans created a monster, so you get rid of him. We don't want to be involved." By 1979 the López Portillo administration had stabilized, at least partially owing to increases in oil revenues, which promoted greater public spending. The oil boom also encouraged the administration to believe that it had gained some leverage in international influence. In April 1979 Mexico broke relations with Somoza and endorsed his overthrow by supporting the Sandinista National Liberation Front (FSLN). This move helped precipitate international ostracism of Somoza, despite the successful effort by the United States to dissuade the rest of Latin America from following Mexico's lead. Mexico then opposed U.S. proposals in the Organization of American States (OAS) that it use an inter-American peacekeeping force to establish an interim government that included Somocistas; Mexico made counterproposals emphasizing "absolute respect for nonintervention." Minister of Foreign Relations Jorge Castañeda asserted that Nicaragua had the right to rebel against tyranny, just as Mexico had done in 1910. Castañeda's declaration put Mexico squarely at odds with the United States. In July, Mexico recognized the Nicaraguan government of National Reconstruction and was a leader in offering emergency aid. In October, the Permanent Conference of Latin American Political Parties (COPPPAL) was established in Oaxaca and emphasized the solidarity of all nationalist, pluralist, democratic, and anti-imperialist Latin American political parties. At this time, El Salvadoran president Carlos Humberto Romero visited Mexico City in a successful attempt to ensure that Mexico would not break relations with his increasingly troubled country; he was given reassurances that Mexico perceived the Salvadoran rebels as extreme left-wing guerrillas not seeking the same kind of pluralist democracy as the FSLN.

Under the new U.S. administration of President Ronald Reagan, Washington reinvigorated Cold War rhetoric and reintroduced an emphasis on the strategic importance of Central America. Over the next decade several countries in both Latin America and Europe independently proposed diplomatic and economic initiatives in attempts to counter an increasingly aggressive and possessive U.S. posture in the region. Mexico was foremost among these nations. Where the United States and its most loyal allies endorsed the view that Central American conflicts were the product of external conspiracies, Mexico viewed the crises as local. Mexican support for the Nicaraguan government increased between 1979 and 1981; President López Portillo made several visits, donated US$39.5 million in cash and goods (constituting 21 percent of the aid received by the Sandinistas during that period), and gave US$72.9 million in loans and credits (constituting 14 percent of loans to the new government). Mexican support went beyond providing funds as the López Portillo administration became actively involved in the restructuring of Nicaraguan social and economic systems with aid in the form of technical and organizational assistance in the fields of education, commerce, oil explorations, and agriculture. One of the most dramatic displays of support for the Sandinista government came in August 1980, when Mexico and Venezuela established the San José Agreement, which promised to provide Nicaragua 160, 000 barrels of oil daily, 30 percent of which would be delivered on credit. Under this agreement, Nicaragua would not be required to pay for 5 years if the oil was simply consumed, and would have over 20 years if it used the funding to develop its national resources.

On another front, Mexico and other nonaligned countries promoted a human rights resolution in the United Nations, which recognized a need for dialogue with the armed opposition. Mexican defense of nonintervention led López Portillo to meet with President Reagan and argue that U.S. economic aid, known as the Mini–Marshall Plan, should be distributed region-wide without political or ideological strings attached. He insisted that military aid should be entirely separate from development aid in order to ensure that the funds would not be used to bolster regimes from without. Further, he declared that it would be a "gigantic historical error to decide in favor of American intervention in Cuba or Nicaragua." On the occasion of Nicaraguan comandante Daniel Ortega's July 1981 visit to Mexico, however, López Portillo asserted that Mexico would "defend the cause of Nicaragua as its own." The cause was to defend the South against an imperialist North defined by East-West competition.

Early in 1981, as the governing junta in El Salvador lost power to the military, members of the junta fled to Mexico, where they told of repressive paramilitary actions sponsored by U.S. military and economic aid to the regime of José Napoleon Duarte. Mexico viewed Duarte as only a figurehead over what had become a military dictatorship and argued that U.S. aid was prolonging a violent path to the inevitable success of a popular uprising. In August, after its offer to mediate the conflict was rejected, Mexico turned to the United Nations, where, together with France, it cosponsored a proposal to the Security Council that endorsed an internationally negotiated end to the violence and recognition of the legitimacy of both the Democratic Revolutionary Front (FDR) and the Farabundo Martí National Liberation Front (FMLN). The junta did not embrace the Franco-Mexican proposal, believing that U.S. support through a strategy of "elections plus anti-guerrilla warfare" would ensure the junta's continuing rule. Foreign Minister Castañeda claimed that the U.S.-sponsored domino theory—which imagined a Soviet strategy of establishing communist regimes in one Central American country after another until finally Mexican oil resources would become part of the Soviet sphere of influence—was a "stupidity." In contrast, he claimed that Mexico sought nonviolent paths to reconciliation, which could result in the pluralistic democratization of the region.

In Honduras and Costa Rica, Mexican relations reflected these ideals. Mexico preferred the National Liberation Party candidate in Costa Rica over the Conservative president Rodrigo Carazo Odio, but after the Conservative's victory, Mexico supported Costa Rica's right to self-determination and relations remained mutually supportive. In Honduras, Mexico applauded the 1981 decision to hold democratic elections and return to civilian rule. In Guatemala, however, where the growing conflict in many ways seemed similar to that in El Salvador, Mexico refrained from taking a strong position, although the Mexican military was reported to be aiding the conservative government forces against the insurgents. In July, Mexico began deporting Guatemalan refugees who had fled the increasing violence. Both sides of the conflict were critical of Mexican policy: the Conservative government accused Mexico of tolerating and even supporting guerrilla activities in Mexican territory, while the Guatemalan left argued that Mexican support was not forthcoming for its cause as it had been in Nicaragua and El Salvador. They believed that Mexico traditionally had preferred a strong Nicaragua and a weak Guatemala in order to ensure its greatest influence in the region, and that this revealed a hypocrisy in Mexican foreign policy.

Mexican support of the Nicaraguan Revolution was celebrated in February 1982 when López Portillo visited Managua and was decorated with the order of Augusto César Sandino. He applauded the Nicaraguans for refusing to allow their conflict to be defined by the "terrible East-West" dichotomy. The Mexican president also argued that resolutions to the crises in Central America depended on a cessation of Cuban-U.S. tensions and offered to negotiate between them. The United States declined. When Miguel de la Madrid assumed the presidency, he continued Mexican attempts to negotiate settlements to the crises and offered to mediate between the United States and the opposition forces toward mutual arms reductions and regional nonaggression pacts that included the proviso that neither Honduras nor the United States could be used as territory in which combatants were armed and trained. Negotiations were necessary, according to Mexico, because the March elections in Nicaragua were not designed to address the structural problems of the nation. Despite the emphasis on dialogue and an official opposition to violent transitions of power, Foreign Minister Jorge Castañeda supported the right of the rebel forces to resort to violence, stating: "when there is no other path, Revolution is justified."

With the intensification of the U.S.-sponsored Contra War in Nicaragua and the resultant flow of refugees into Honduras and Costa Rica, Mexico looked to include more Latin American nations in multilateral negotiations. In September 1982, Mexico once again cooperated with Venezuela, this time in an initiative to explore ways of deflating the conflicts in Central America, particularly along the vulnerable and controversial Honduran borders. A month later an international group of foreign ministers met in San José to define specific objectives designed to promote political democratization in Central America, but Mexico and Venezuela refused to attend because the United States dominated the group and Nicaragua was excluded on the basis that it was currently nondemocratic. On January 8 and 9, 1983, the foreign ministers of Mexico, Venezuela, Panama, and Colombia met on Contadora Island to form a multilateral group interested in resolving the Central American crisis. The group declared that the crisis had developed from domestic problems outside the context of East-West conflicts; the group also pledged continuing noninterventionist economic aid.

The Contadora Group was the main theater of Mexican involvement in isthmian affairs until 1987, but Mexico continued to emphasize in the United Nations the need for multilateral protection of the sovereignty of weak nations. In 1984–85 Mexico denounced both the U.S. mining of Nicaraguan waters as part of an economic blockade and a U.S. commercial embargo that Mexico claimed had been designed to undermine the sovereign will of Nicaragua, thereby violating UN and OAS resolutions. In 1986 the International Court of Justice ruled against the United States on Nicaragua's claim that U.S. support of the Contras was illegal. The United States used its veto power to avoid abiding by the ruling. Mexico argued that the United States should not be able to vote on a case in which it was involved; and that allowing the United States to do so was tantamount to accepting the fact that international justice would not be applied to U.S. actions in Latin America.

In 1988 the Esquipulas III meeting saw presidents from the isthmus seeking to "Central Americanize" the negotiations and distance themselves from the larger Latin American community. Mexico's new president Carlos Salinas de Gortari weakened ties with Central America, focusing on domestic political and economic problems. Mexican initiatives in Central America declined rapidly at the end of the 1980s as the Contra War declined and the Cold War reached a partial conclusion with the destruction of the Berlin Wall. In 1990, the Nicaragua crisis resolved with the electoral victory of Violeta Chamorro over Sandinista president Daniel Ortega, and in 1991 FMLN rebels reached a UN-mediated peace agreement with the conservative government of President Alfredo Cristiani.

The reduction of tensions in Central America coincided with a growing crisis in the Mexican economy. Both of these factors contributed to increasingly close economic ties between Mexico and the United States, displacing the decade-long ideological conflicts over Central America. Yet the basic structural problems in Central America have not changed. Central American nations continue to be heavily dependent on foreign interests that limit their ability for self-determination and long-term development and take little account of social justice. The increasingly global economy makes Central America increasingly vulnerable. Yet, for a variety of reasons, Mexico is no longer in a position to champion international sensitivity to issues of socioeconomic inequalities. The Central American crises have subsided and opposition groups are not making enough noise to command international attention to the internal problems of the region; furthermore, the East-West dichotomy has faded as a target for Mexican opposition to U.S. hegemony. Domestically, Mexico's economy has faltered and membership in the North American Free Trade Agreement (NAFTA) reflects closer ties with the United States. Finally, the Democratic administration of President Bill Clinton has reduced U.S. involvement in Central America. Where involvement has been maintained, Washington has abandoned its reliance on repressive dictators, preferring instead instruments such as the National Endowment for Democracy, which successfully backed winning candidates in elections in Costa Rica, Honduras, and Nicaragua.

Since 1930 Mexico has repeatedly attempted to increase the breadth and intensity of its economic relations with Central America. At times the interest in closer economic ties was spurred by the search for solutions to domestic economic weaknesses, at times it was the result of weakened economic relations with the United States, and at times it was generated by a desire to capitalize on and increase the successes of Mexican industrialization. The current economic crisis and Mexican membership in NAFTA has caused concern for Central Americans that their economies, which provide little not available in Mexico, will be increasingly exploited by the international division of labor. Yet, so far Mexico has continued to honor the San José Agreement and has pursued further bilateral economic agreements in the interest of increased trade with Central America.

Mexican foreign policy with Central America has been most dramatic in its promotion of international arbitration for regional conflicts. Mexico has helped bring international attention to the unacceptable outcomes of an international order based solely on strict ideological dichotomies, regardless of local conditions. U.S. scholars have suggested that domestic crises in Mexico, whether economic or political, have in the past caused its presidents to seek increased legitimacy from the Mexican left through activism in defense of Central American revolutionary nationalism, but events have not supported this interpretation: political involvement in Central America often has increased when the Mexican economy and political conflicts have stabilized. Although there is often a clear correspondence between internal Mexican developments and activism in Central America, it has not been simple and linear. Likewise, although traditional tensions with Guatemala and its own fluctuating relations with the United States have impacted Mexico's approaches toward Central America since 1930, Mexico consistently has championed the right of small nations to self-determination free from the goals, expectations, and even perspectives of great-power or super-power machinations. As the isthmus shares borders, history, and culture with Mexico, Central America has been seen as a natural ally in the defense of the national sovereignty of weaker states.

Selected Bibliography

Bagley, Bruce M., "Mexico in Central America: The Limits of Regional Power." In *Political Change in Central America: Internal and External Dimensions,* edited by Wolf Grabendorff and Heinrich W. Krumwiede. Boulder, Colorado: Westview, 1984.

Bender, Lynn Darrell, "Contained Nationalism: The Mexican Foreign Policy Example." *Revista/Review Interamericana* 5:1 (Spring 1975).

Cosío Villegas, Daniel, *Historia moderna de México: El porfiriato: Vida política exterior.* 2 vols., Mexico City: Hermes, 1960–63.

Fagen, Richard R., and Olga Pellicer, *The Future of Central America: Policy Choices for the U.S. and Mexico.* Stanford, California: Stanford University Press, 1983.

Heller, Claude, "U.S. and Mexican Policies toward Central America." In *Foreign Policy in U.S.-Mexican Relations,* edited by Rosario Green and Peter H. Smith. La Jolla: Center for U.S.-Mexican Studies, University of California, San Diego, 1989.

Herrera Zúñiga, René, and Mario Ojeda, "Mexican Foreign Policy and Central America." In *Central America: International Dimensions of the Crisis,* edited by Richard Feinberg. New York: Holmes and Meier, 1982.

_____, "La Politica de México en la Region de Centroamérica." *Foro Internacional* 23:4 (April–June 1983).

Jauberth, H. Rodrigo, Gilberto Castañeda, Jesús Hernández, and Pedro Vuskovic, *Difficult Triangle: Mexico, Central America, and the United States.* Boulder, Colorado: Westview, 1992.

Levy, Daniel C., "The Implications of Central American Conflicts for Mexican Politics." In *Mexico's Political Stability: The Next Five Years,* edited by Roderic Camp. Boulder, Colorado: Westview, 1986.

Pellicer, Olga, editor, *La Política Exterior de México: Desafíos en los Ochenta.* Mexico City: CIDE, 1983.

Reynolds, Clark W., and Carlos Tello, *U.S.-Mexico Relations: Economic and Social Aspects.* Stanford, California: Stanford University Press, 1983.

Zorrilla, Luis G., *Relaciones de México con La Republica de Centro América y con Guatemala.* Mexico City: Porrúa, 1984.

—NICHOLAS MAHER

FOREIGN POLICY: CONTADORA GROUP

The Contadora Group (Mexico, Colombia, Panama, and Venezuela) emerged in January 1983 in response to a series of military conflicts in Central America that included the Contra War in Nicaragua as well as civil wars in El Salvador and Guatemala. Named after the island off the coast of Panama where the first meeting of the foreign ministers of the four countries took place, the group worked for the peaceful resolution of these conflicts and opposed foreign intervention in the crises. The Mexican role in Contadora constituted a particularly interesting case study of foreign policy. While the country's participation represented, in the words of scholars René Herrera Zúniga and Manuel Chavarría, a "return march to the traditional limits of its foreign policy," it marked a significant innovation in that the Mexican government agreed, for the first time, to negotiate Central American conflicts in concert with other Latin American countries.

The Mexican government headed by Miguel de la Madrid participated in Contadora with several important motivations in mind. Most significantly, U.S. intervention in Central America, a shift to the right of the ruling Partido Revolucionario Institucional (PRI, or Institutional Revolutionary Party), and a severe economic crisis had combined to foil Mexico's earlier, more assertive efforts on behalf of the Sandinista regime in Nicaragua. In addition, U.S. intervention and the flow of Central American refugees into southeastern Mexico constituted a twin threat to Mexican national security as defined by the de la Madrid administration. Finally, the governments of Venezuela, Colombia, and Panama—all of which had criticized the Mexican government for its friendship with the Sandinistas—had expressed interest in helping to mediate the Central American conflicts.

Any analysis of Mexico's participation in the Contadora Group must begin with a discussion of President José López Portillo's assertive Central America policy in the period from 1979 to 1982 . In July 1979, López Portillo became the first head of state to break relations with the Nicaraguan dictatorship of Anastasio Somoza Debayle. Upon Somoza's ouster in July 1979, Mexican influence in Nicaragua arrived with the Sandinista revolutionary junta, which was flown into Managua aboard a Mexican jet. In the first years of the revolution, López Portillo generously lavished favors on the "new Nicaragua." Not only did the Mexican government award US$39 million in cash and goods to the Sandinistas; it also extended loans worth almost twice that amount and allowed Nicaragua to buy Mexican oil on favorable terms. Then, when the Sandinistas clashed for the first time with U.S. president Ronald Reagan, López Portillo also helped Nicaragua on the diplomatic front. While the U.S. State Department depicted the Nicaraguan revolution as the work of "Cuban-Soviet" subversion and cut off U.S. economic aid, López Portillo sponsored a U.S.-Nicaraguan dialogue in the Mexican port town of Manzanillo. He also took up the subject of Nicaragua in the course of two meetings

with Reagan in January and June 1981. He failed, however, to persuade the U.S. president to assume a more conciliatory posture toward the Sandinistas.

Beginning in 1981, López Portillo also participated in attempts at ending a protracted civil war between a government controlled by right-wing death squads in El Salvador and two left-wing opposition groups. In August 1981, he issued a joint communiqué with French president François Mitterrand. This declaration recognized both opposition groups as "political forces representative of the Salvadoran people."

The civil war in Guatemala, however, was quite a different story. While Mexico supported the Sandinistas and attempted to award a degree of political legitimacy to the Salvadoran rebels, Mexico cooperated with the Guatemalan government against the peasant-based revolt of the Guerrilla Army of the Poor (EPG) and other rebel groups. This seemingly paradoxical attitude followed historical precedents. In this case, Mexico's own security appeared threatened by the existence of large guerrilla bases along the Mexican-Guatemalan border. In addition, the ongoing warfare—and the scorched-earth policies of the Guatemalan military—swelled the ranks of Guatemalan refugees in Mexico. The Mexican government, then, saw little choice but to cooperate with the Guatemalan military, easily the most ruthless and repressive in the Central America of the 1980s.

Mexico's new activism in Central America yielded considerable payoff at home and abroad. Even as the López Portillo administration came under increasing criticism for its domestic policies, its stand in Central America earned it a great degree of support in Mexico. And even though the Reagan administration resented Mexican support for the Sandinistas, it too accorded López Portillo a grudging respect and often negotiated Central American issues bilaterally with the Mexican government.

This active Mexican role in Central America, however, had depended in great part on the personal interest of the Mexican president, the economic and political stability of Mexico, and restraint in U.S. policies toward the isthmus. Unlike his predecessor, who had espoused an ambitious agenda to assume leadership of the so-called Third World, López Portillo had focused his attention on the Central American countries. He had strong incentives to display a nationalist foreign policy. The discovery of new oil deposits had fueled optimism about Mexico's future as an economic power, and many Mexicans had demanded that their president show that power in the international arena. Moreover, López Portillo had been able to use an assertive diplomacy to camouflage shortcomings of his regime as well as Mexico's weakness vis-à-vis the United States, a country that he frequently had berated in his speeches. The international system had also been favorable to López Portillo. The Sandinistas' challenge to Somoza had given him the chance to deal with a friendly political force in Central America. In its fight against

Somoza, the Sandinistas had often invoked the Mexican Revolution as a model and inspiration for their struggle. For his part, Reagan's predecessor, Jimmy Carter, publicly had criticized the dismal human-rights record of the Somoza regime. Both the Mexican and the U.S. governments had disliked the regime in power in Managua, and López Portillo, confident of U.S. sympathy for his actions, had taken the initiative to help change this undesirable state of affairs.

By the time the Contadora Group first met, all of these conditions for an assertive policy had disappeared. The new Mexican president, Miguel de la Madrid, did not share López Portillo's admiration for the Sandinistas. He increasingly criticized the Sandinistas for their "socialist" orientation and for seeking Soviet-Cuban military support. Moreover, de la Madrid needed to face a severe economic crisis brought on by a collapse in oil prices, mounting foreign debt, and the large-scale corruption during the López Portillo regime. By the end of 1982, an acute debt problem and a plummeting peso had increased Mexico's dependency on U.S. goodwill—and the country's support for the Sandinistas had already brought about enough disagreements with the Reagan administration. At the same time, the U.S. government had begun to put its foot down in Nicaragua. Citing "Soviet influence" in the Sandinista junta and alleging Nicaraguan aid to the rebels in El Salvador, the U.S. government trained and armed Nicaraguan exiles in bases in Florida and Honduras. Known as the "Contras" because they proudly referred to themselves as counterrevolutionaries, the rebels had begun to launch forays into Nicaragua.

Therefore, its participation in the Contadora Group constituted a diplomatic retrenchment for the Mexican government. By joining three governments critical of the Sandinistas in calling for a negotiated solution, de la Madrid had in effect conceded the failure of López Portillo's policies. His participation in Contadora revealed the persistence of a pattern established as early as during the regime of Porfirio Díaz. When the U.S. government resorts to military intervention in Central America, the Mexican government cannot pursue its policy goals in the area unless it proposes a mediating role—and even then, its options are extremely limited.

Nevertheless, de la Madrid could count the creation of the Contadora Group as a major success. The governments of Colombia, Panama, and Venezuela not only had expressed hostility to the Sandinista government; until the Contra War, they had supported Reagan in his aggressive Nicaragua policies. U.S. support for the Contras, however, prodded these three governments to distance themselves from Reagan. Public opinion in all three of these countries was heavily critical of Reagan's new policies, and the government of Panama had its own reasons to fear U.S. intervention. Most importantly, all of the Contadora countries including Mexico feared a widening of the war—a reason that figured prominently in the formation of the group. As neighbors of Central America, all four governments viewed a general war, complete with the deployment of U.S. ground forces and a flood of refugees fleeing the area westward as well as eastward, as a nightmare scenario. Therefore, seen from the angle of the

other three participants, Contadora constituted a convergence of formerly opposite foreign-policy objectives and the beginning of multilateral rather than bilateral Mexican foreign policies in Central America.

Signed at the conclusion of their first meeting, the first communiqué of the Contadora Group delineated a Latin American view of the Central American conflicts. According to the communiqué, these conflicts were the product of internal historical circumstances rather than communist subversion from without. Further, the document called for a Central American solution to the conflict and demanded the withdrawal of all "foreign" troops, bases, and military advisers from Central America.

In the course of the next two years, the Contadora Group succeeded in opening a dialogue among the Central American leaders. In September 1983, the Contadora Group and the five Central American governments signed a Document of Objectives that compiled the different viewpoints of all the affected parties as well as the Contadora suggestions. A year later, the nine foreign ministers negotiated a draft of a treaty on peace and cooperation in Central America.

The Contadora Group thus challenged the policies of the Reagan administration. The group insisted that economic backwardness and old structures of power and domination had caused both the Sandinista rebellion and the civil wars in El Salvador and Guatemala. Reagan and his cohorts, however, continued to assert that the Soviet Union, Cuba, and their supposed new ally, Nicaragua, shared the blame for the peasant rebellions in El Salvador and Guatemala. The Contadora Group proposed to treat the Central American crisis as a regional problem with regional solutions. Reagan, on the other hand, viewed the conflicts within the context of East-West superpower relations.

The existence of the Contadora Group forced the Reagan administration to pursue a two-track strategy. On the one hand, Reagan lent rhetorical support to the group, lauding its efforts to bring about peace in general terms. Reagan also backed down from his earlier insistence that the Sandinistas be excluded from all regional peace talks and supported talks between the Central American governments and the Contadora Group. On the other hand, the U.S. president continued to seek the military overthrow of the Sandinista government in Nicaragua. Aside from increasing its assistance to the Contras, the Reagan administration pulled out all the stops short of the deployment of U.S. troops in order to destabilize the Nicaraguan government in a steadily worsening war of attrition. In 1984, the U.S. government even mined a Nicaraguan harbor in a most blatant violation of international law.

To offset the influence of the Contadora Group, Reagan also encouraged Latin American alliances either supportive of his policies or focusing on other hemispheric issues. Among the former groups, the Tegucigalpa Bloc (El Salvador, Honduras, and Costa Rica) remained foremost. Formed in 1981 in opposition to the Sandinistas, the Tegucigalpa Bloc embraced Reagan's notion of communist subversion and helped provide a pretext for U.S. aggression against

Nicaragua. Among the latter groups, the creation of the Contadora Support Group (Argentina, Brazil, Peru, and Uruguay) in 1985 ironically amounted to another challenge to Contadora. Even though this new group ostensibly supported the peace effort in Central America, its focus on other regional issues and the distance of its members from the Central American conflict had the effect of lessening the influence of the Contadora Group.

In the end, the U.S. determination to topple the Sandinistas and Reagan's efforts to undermine Contadora combined to doom the Latin American effort to provide a negotiated settlement to the Central American imbroglio. In late 1984, realizing that it had not paid enough attention to the Contadora Group, the Reagan administration began to pressure the Central American governments not to ratify the peace agreement negotiated under Contadora auspices. By early 1985, Reagan had succeeded, as the strongly anticommunist government of Costa Rica—and, to an extent, those of El Salvador and Honduras—fell in line with the U.S. government in demanding the ouster of the Sandinistas before any peace treaty could be ratified. Shortly after these events, the Lima Group, a second bloc of nonaligned Latin American countries, merged with Contadora to form the Group of Eight (later renamed Group of Rio after the exclusion of Panama). For his part, de la Madrid abandoned his attempts on behalf of peace in Central America and turned his attention to bilateral problems with the United States, including Mexican immigration to the United States, the debt crisis, and steps to create a North American common market.

Even though the Contadora Group had not achieved its goals in its short existence, many of its key objectives became reality in the following years. Most importantly, Central America avoided the general war the Contadora leaders had feared, and foreign military intervention ceased. Controlled by the opposition Democratic Party, the U.S. Congress terminated funding for the Contras and thus forced the Reagan administration to seek a negotiated solution. In addition, the Central American governments picked up where Contadora had left off. Under the leadership of the new Costa Rican president, Oscar Arias, and aided occasionally by the Group of Eight, the Esquipulas negotiations produced the Central American peace agreement that the Contadora Group had worked to achieve. Thanks in part to negotiations facilitated by de la Madrid's successor, Carlos Salinas de Gortari, this peace agreement has helped end the fighting in El Salvador, and it has aided in reducing significantly the level of violence in Guatemala. Finally, events in Nicaragua ended U.S. intervention. The 1990 elections turned the Sandinistas out of power; weary of the protracted war and encouraged by U.S. promises of economic assistance in case of a Sandinista defeat, the Nicaraguan electorate gave a majority to Violeta Chamorro's UNO coalition. Seen from the vantage point of the mid-1990s, both the United States and the Contadora Group ultimately achieved their policy objectives, with the Sandinistas emerging as the main losers.

Mexico's participation in the Contadora Group reflects the country's eternal dilemma as a middle power: too small to carry out an effective role in Central America and the Caribbean, but too large and too close to the area to ignore it. De la Madrid had pooled his resources with three other Latin American governments during a difficult period. While U.S. aggression against Nicaragua minimized the policy options of the Contadora Group, the economic crisis forced all four participating countries to refrain from opposing U.S. policy directly. In the end, Mexico's (and Contadora's) main contribution to the peace process may have consisted in building up an atmosphere of mutual trust among Central American leaders that not even Reagan's divide-and-rule policies could destroy.

Therefore, Contadora represented a new wrinkle in a time-honored Mexican diplomatic strategy: confront force with negotiation, and dictates with persuasion. In contrast to earlier decades, however, the Mexican government will no longer go it alone in confronting U.S. intervention in Central America.

Select Bibliography

Aguilar Zinser, Adolfo, "Mexico and the Guatemalan Crisis." In *The Future of Central America: Policy Choices for the United States and Mexico,* edited by Richard R. Fagen and Olga Pellicer de Brody. Stanford, California: Stanford University Press, 1983.

Bagley, Bruce M., "Mexican Foreign Policy: The Decline of a Regional Power?" *Current History* 82 (December 1983).

Best, Edward H., "Mexican Foreign Policy and Central America Since the Mexican Revolution." Ph.D. diss., Oxford University, 1988.

Buchenau, Jürgen, *In the Shadow of the Giant: The Making of Mexico's Central America Policy, 1876–1930.* Tuscaloosa: University of Alabama Press, 1996.

Campbell, Hugh G., "Mexico and Central America: The Continuity of Policy." In *Central America: Historical Perspectives on the Contemporary Crises,* edited by Ralph L. Woodward. New York: Greenwood Press, 1988.

Chabat, Jorge, "Mexico: So Close to the United States, So Far from Latin America." *Current History* 92 (February 1993).

Herrera Zúniga, René, and Manuel Chavarría, "México en Contadora: Una búsqueda de límites a su compromiso en Centroamérica." *Foro Internacional* 24:4 (April 1984).

Jauberth, H. Rodrigo, Gilberto Castañeda, Jesús Hernández, et al., *The Difficult Triangle: Mexico, Central America, and the United States.* Boulder, Colorado: Westview, 1992.

Ojeda, Mario, editor, *Las relaciones de México con los países de América Central.* Mexico City: Colegio de México, 1985.

Rico, Carlos F., "Mexico and Central America: The Limits of Cooperation." *Current History* 86 (March 1987).

—JÜRGEN BUCHENAU

FRANCO, HERNANDO

1532–1685 • Musician and Composer

Considerable confusion has surrounded the birth of Hernando Franco. Some authors mistakenly have labeled him an indigenous American; more recent research establishes his birthplace near the Portuguese-Spanish border in Garrovillas or in the La Serena village of Galizuela. Regardless of such discrepancies regarding the location of his birth, modern scholars agree that he was born in 1532 and spent his early years (1542–49) at the Segovia Cathedral under the tutelage of Gerónimo de Espinar, the chapel master who later instructed another young talent in the art of composition—Tomás Luis de Victoria. Two other young choirboys, Lázaro del Álamo and his brother Hierónimo, were in Segovia concurrently with Franco, and the three forged a friendship that was to last throughout their lives. They followed their patron Mateo Arévalo Sedeño first to Guatemala, where Franco was appointed chapel master (perhaps as early as 1554). Eventually, all of them accepted opportunities that took them to Mexico City: Lázaro del Álamo rose to the chief post of chapel master at the Mexico City Cathedral, and Sedeño eventually was appointed the rector of the University of Mexico. Lázaro was succeeded by Juan de Vitoria, who then foolishly lost his job through a blatant satire of the viceroy. With the post suddenly left vacant, Franco succeeded Vitoria as the Mexico City Cathedral chapel master on May 25, 1575. Almost immediately he and his musician cousin, Alonso de Trujillo, ran up an astronomical debt of 4,000 pesos; Franco's respectable annual salary of 600 pesos and Trujillo's 200 pesos amounted to a pittance in comparison. Fortunately, the chapter tolerated their indiscretion (probably the result of gambling) and helped bail them out of trouble. Their salaries fluctuated widely in the ensuing years, primarily owing to the financial drain brought about by the ambitious construction project to build the new cathedral: chapter funds were sunk into the building rather than salaries. When Franco and Trujillo learned that their pay was to be reduced, they went on strike and threatened to quit. Although that crisis was averted, salary adjustments continued to be an issue: on more than one occasion Franco was docked pay for his refusal to teach the choirboys. He fell ill in November 1685, died on November 28, and was interred right behind the viceroy's chair in the cathedral.

Over 22 of Franco's sacred works are still extant, with the *Franco Codex* in Mexico City preserving his most ambitious accomplishments. This *Codex* contains pairs of *Magnificat* settings arranged by mode: the first setting of a pair develops the odd-numbered verses, and the second setting uses the even-numbered verses. Initially the manuscript had contained settings in all eight modes; unfortunately, the sheets that contained the *Magnificats* in mode 3 have been sliced from the document. The two Nahuatl hymns previously ascribed to Franco (the "Sancta María yn ilhuicac cihuapille" and "Dios itlaÿonantzine cemicac") are probably by a different composer—an indigenous Native America *cacique* with the same name—since the source for the two hymns identifies their author as "Don Hernando Franco"; the royal prefix "Don" would be appropriate to an Indian convert of noble blood, but not to a European composer with an unimpressive lineage.

In Franco's seven extant *Magnificat* settings, he scrupulously adheres to the chant tune as the basis for the cantus or soprano line; he elongates phrases, however, by brief interpolations that embellish the general outline of the cantus firmus. Stylistically, Franco often preserves a relatively slow harmonic rhythm in block four-part harmony with a preference for reiterations of the same chord several times in a row to complete small snippets of text. Franco instills these repeated chords with invigorating energy through the use of clever, impulsive rhythmic patterns. Frequently, the voices declaim the motive in homorhythmic unity, driving the phrases forward. When Franco delves into counterpoint, he generally shuns rigorous points of imitation; instead, he prefers phrases that gradually unfold in ever-increasing activity, culminating in passages of parallel thirds or sixths. Additionally, there is frequent voice crossing.

Select Bibliography

Barwick, Steven, editor, *The Franco Codex of the Cathedral of Mexico.* Carbondale: Southern Illinois University Press, 1965.

Estrada, Jesús, *Música y músicos de la época virreinal*, edited by Andrés Lira. Mexico City: Secretaría de Educación Pública, 1973.

Saldívar y Silva, Gabriel, and Elisa Osorio Bolio de Saldívar, *Historia de la música en México: Épocas precortesiana y colonial.* Reprint, Mexico City: Ediciones Gernika and Secretaría de Educación Pública, 1987.

Stevenson, Robert, *Music in Mexico: A Historical Survey.* New York: Thomas Y. Crowell, 1952.

_____, "Mexico City Cathedral: The Founding Century." *Inter-American Music Review* 1:2 (Spring–Summer 1979).

_____, "Hernando Franco, el más notable compositor renacentista en México." *Heterofonía* 11 (March–April 1970).

—CRAIG H. RUSSELL

FREEMASONRY

An eighteenth-century merger of Christian fraternalism and corporate labor guilds, Freemasonry has spread throughout the world as a highly organized and ritualistic secret society that stresses good works, community service, and loyalty to the Masonic institutional order itself. Linked to the shadowy world of Rosicrucians, the Knights Templar, and other pseudo-Christian secret societies, Freemasonry does indeed have its own foundation mythology, beliefs, symbols, initiation rites, an ordered hierarchical structure, and sponsored membership; its self-conscious secretiveness has added to Freemasonry's mystique and contributed to the general public's mistrust of the organization's activities. For much of the last two centuries, however, Freemasons have played a large role in the public life of western Europe and the American Continent. In Spanish America, and in Mexico especially, Masonic lodges played a tremendously important role in the Independence and early national periods. Crossing over from London and Cádiz in the early nineteenth centuries, these lodges served as both fraternal and conspiratorial cells through which the rational and scientific thought of the Enlightenment could be disseminated, and as vehicles to recruit and bind new members to the independence movement itself.

Although there are references to Masonic guilds dating as far back as 926 in York, modern Freemasonry dates from the founding of the Great Lodge of London in 1717. At this time, several independent groups joined together and formalized their existence with a constitution and code of behavior that included tolerance, love, knowledge, virtue, study, activity, justice and self-preservation. True to its occupational origins, the Masonic order styled God as "the Architect of the Universe" and cast its members as the most crucial elements of any society: its builders and planners. For this reason, Freemasons placed great value on science, order, rational and free thought, religious toleration, and the applied sciences; not surprisingly then, Freemasonry included some of the eighteenth century's most inquisitive and progressive thinkers. Furthermore, Freemasonry's strict code of secrecy, its advancement based on merit and accomplishment, its democratic and fraternal culture, and elaborate ritual made it attractive to disaffected protonationalists in Spanish America. Although nominally a Christian organization, Popes Clement XII and Benedict XIV issued anti-Masonic bulls and the Spanish Inquisition, too, was determined to root out and execute the members of this secret and therefore undoubtedly subversive sect.

Spanish Masons broke away from their British forebears in 1756 and eventually formed a national Grand Lodge in 1780 under the patronage of Charles III's prime minister, the Conde de Aranda. Beginning in the late 1790s, Spanish Americans in Europe also began to set up their own lodges expressly identified with the nascent independence movement. In London in 1797, Francisco de Miranda established the Masonic lodge Gran Reunión Americana (also known as the Sociedad de los Caballeros Racionales) with himself as grand master. His disciples founded chapters in Paris, Cádiz, and then throughout Spanish America, where they initiated countless leaders of independence movements and future statesmen into the Masonic Order: José Cecilio del Valle, José de San Martín, Simón Bolívar, Bernardo O'Higgins, Carlos Alvear, Manuel Moreno, Vicente Rocafuerte, Fray Servando Teresa de Mier, Antonio Nariño, Antonio José de Sucre, and thousands of others. The Masonic connection is crucial in these years because it bound the independence partisans together with shared signs and rituals, gave the movement a more extensive continental character, diffused practical knowledge, and provided an institutional and organizational backbone through which campaigns could be coordinated. Many of the new American lodges adopted Miranda's original motto, "Union, Firmness and Valor," as their own, and a sampling of lodge names reveals something of Masonry's core values at the time: Regularity, Amity, Union, Contentment and British Union, Three Theological Virtues, Columbus, Fraternity, Prudence, Fraternal Love, Hope, Tolerance, Sons of Life, Reconciliation, America, Cosmopolitan, Rectitude, True Philanthropy.

Masonic activity appeared in New Spain as early as 1791 when a discussion group gathered in Juan Esteban Laloche's home in Mexico City; its participants read Enlightenment authors, debated the progress of the French Revolution, and held ceremonies around Masonic dates such as the solstices. It was not, however, until 1806 that the first formal Mexican Masonic lodge received its letter of patent; the Grand Lodge "Moral Architecture" operated out of the home of Manuel Luyando, the *regidor* of the city's *ayuntamiento* (town council). It met clandestinely until 1810, when Spanish colonial authorities cracked down on unauthorized civic organizations in the wake of the Hidalgo Revolt. There is still some controversy over whether Miguel Hidalgo y Costilla had been a member of the Moral Architecture Lodge; Masonic historians like Ramón Martínez Zaldua who favor Hidalgo's revolt happily claim him as one of their own, while opponents in the Masonic movement including Luís Zalce emphatically deny that Hidalgo had anything to do with Freemasonry.

It is clear, however, that Freemasonry and its practitioners played an important role throughout the independence period and the early years of national state formation. In 1813, occupying Spanish troops facilitated the reintroduction of the Ancient Scottish Rite Masonic Lodge into Mexico, which celebrated a contract of union with the British Grand Lodge in December of that year. Through participation in Masonic lodges, Mexican patriots enjoyed access to current European thought and were indoctrinated into ideals of independence, freedom of belief, press, and religion, and the crucial idea that through personal effort and rational investigation into the scientific laws of nature and society, individuals could perfect both themselves and humanity. It was a profoundly radical concept, one that implied an assault on both privilege and traditional society. Furthermore, it explains the tremendous value that the first statesmen of independent Mexico placed on education and laws; using Masonic imagery, they viewed themselves as the moral architects of a new society and intently focused on designing the best constitutional forms for a progressive society. The problem was, however, that not every one could agree on the best form, and a deep schism soon appeared in the polity.

Mexican Freemasonry had been dominated by the Scottish Rite school (whose adherents became known as Escoceses) until the mid-1820s, when a group of disaffected members, led by parish priest José María Alpuche é Infante of Tabasco, joined with U.S. Ambassador Joel Poinsett and defected to the younger and more progressive York Rite school (whose adherents became known as Yorkinos). It seems Poinsett was alarmed at the pro-British and monarchical character he observed in existing Scottish Rite Mexican lodges and attempted to counterbalance this with a U.S.-sponsored York Rite lodge chartered out of New York. Freemasonry, while declaring itself officially apolitical, therefore became caught up in international diplomatic intrigues. President Guadalupe Victoria himself anticipated Masonic groups as an early form of institutionalized political party structures for Mexico, and there is some justification for his view. Members of the Scottish Rite lodge tended to be Europhiles, monarchists, more favorable to the interests of the Catholic Church and conservative on social issues; York Rite Masons were generally more dogmatically liberal, favored a federal republic, and opposed privilege in its various forms. The two interest groups struggled for control of the government and the legislature in an attempt to advance their respective positions. As an example, the December 20, 1827, Law for the Expulsion of Spaniards generally is viewed as a product of York Rite lobbyists who believed national security required a greater Americanization of Mexican society. Similarly, many Mexican Yorkinos participated in the project of national identity formation through a resurrection of Aztec words and imagery; the York Rite Grand Lodge India Azteca included Vicente Guerrero, Carlos María de Bustamante, and Miguel Ramos Arizpe, and the vehemently liberal administration of Valentín Gómez Farías even sponsored an entirely new Mexican National Rite to aid its assault on church and military privileges.

Freemasonry in Mexico, therefore, became associated with political competition from its earliest days. Rather than functioning as an ideological doctrine in itself, Masonry instead provided a forum in which like-minded persons could gather together and forge social networks for future joint action. Thus persons of opposing political views such as Presidents Benito Juárez and later Porfirio Díaz could both reach the highest Masonic grade, the 33rd degree, yet offer such extremely divergent programs for Mexico's future. Although he himself was a Mason, José María Luís Mora criticized the lodges for the divisive impact of competing camps within the same political system; thus Mexican Freemasonry mirrored the larger struggle taking place within the political life of the country, as statesmen and legislators tried to devise a workable system of governance that could combine both freedom and order.

Throughout the nineteenth century, Freemasonry grew during times of national difficulty. Antonio López de Santa Anna was a Mason, and in 1842 he successfully resurrected the Mexican National Rite Lodge after it had fallen into disuse. Similarly, Mexican Masonry rallied around the national cause during the wars with the United States. Its meetings and presses were harnessed to the war effort and served as powerful influences on public opinion. After Santa Anna's fall from power and the inevitable reaction against his administration and the aftermath of war, Masons retreated into their officially apolitical role. In practice, however, members of the National Mexican Rite lodges tended to form the core of the growing Liberal Party.

New lodges formed, grew, declined, and disappeared throughout the nineteenth century. As the years passed, however, international Masonry became more organized and intertwined, with conventions and congresses being held periodically in Europe and North America. Travel to these events provided Mexican Masonic delegates with important connections to other cultures and ideas and facilitated the import of many scientific and intellectual developments. For example, not long after the First Feminist Masonic Banquet was held in Paris in 1870, satellite lodges in Mexico began to set up mixed-gender meetings and sanctioned the female Grand Lodge Mexican Soul; a youth organization, Grand Lodge Ajef, soon followed. The Masonic institution therefore not only provided social cohesion for male members, but also facilitated the incorporation of other sectors into public life as their potential contribution to society became more widely recognized. Through their presence at international Masonic meetings held in Lausanne (1875), Paris (1881), Chicago (1893), Amberes (1984), and Geneva (1989, 1921), Mexican Masons were able to return home with the latest ideas and inventions of Europe and North America. It should not be surprising that many Masons numbered among the Científicos, liberal-positivist intellectuals and policy advisers of the dictator Porfirio Díaz; they shared an admiration for the material culture of the North Atlantic and welcomed a renewed emphasis on science, order, and progress as the quickest path to happiness and modernity. In fact, recent scholars have tried to link the growth of Masonic orders with the emergence of a capitalist economy in regions traditionally dominated by corporatist social organization.

Not surprisingly, Masonic lodges such as the Grand Lodge Valley of Mexico played a role in the Mexican Revolution as well. Francisco I. Madero was a practicing Mason in good standing, and his opponent Victoriano Huerta attempted to muzzle Maderistas by shutting down their York

Rite lodges. By 1916, full lodge activity was restored and Masons participated fully in the post-Revolution government. President Plutarco Elías Calles was a Mason and advanced a progressive anticlerical platform during his administration, something long urged according to the Masonic belief system. Presidents Emilio Portes Gil and Lázaro Cárdenas were both Masons whose popularity increased Masonic activity among Mexican youth and who tried to establish good works, including hospitals and libraries, as part of their oath to the brotherhood. As late as 1977 there were 19 grand lodges operating in Mexico, each with its regional affiliates.

Freemasonry has played a tremendous role in the public life of independent Mexico. As a Christian-based, voluntary organization that champions rational, free thought, democratic ideals, the values of tolerance, service and patriotism, Freemasonry has attracted many of the nation's most active citizens. Although it is officially neutral and boasts members from across the political spectrum, Freemasonry tends to appeal to liberal republicans who oppose traditional authority and privilege. Thus since the earliest days of Independence, Mexican Masonry has contributed to the complex alliance of forces that rule the country. As a fraternal organization with secret initiation rites, institutional loyalty, and a definite public identity, Masonry has provided a forum in which individuals can gain a sense of belonging, practice their leadership skills, and advance through their own efforts. It is a vehicle for patronage and for making useful contacts both within Mexico and on the international stage. In fact, Masonic membership is a common characteristic among those in the highest political offices, including Presidents Guadalupe Victoria, Valentín Gómez Farías, Benito Juárez, Sebastián Lerdo de Tejada, Porfirio Díaz, Francisco I. Madero, Venustiano Carranza, Plutarco Elías Calles, Lázaro Cárdenas, Emilio Portes Gil, Pascual Ortiz Rubio, Abelardo Rodríguez, and Miguel Alemán.

See also Spiritism and Spirituality

Select Bibliography

Carnicelli, Américo, *La masonería en la independencia de América (1810–1830)*. 2 vols., Bogotá: n.p., 1970.

Corro Viña, J. Manuel, *La Masonería contra el Presidente Lic. Gustavo Díaz Ordaz*. Mexico City: n.p., 1964.

Ferrer Benimeli, José Antonio, *Masonería y inquisición en Latinaoamérica durante el siglo XVIII*. Caracas: Instituto de Investigaciones Históricos, 1973.

Martínes de Codes, Rosa María, "El impacto de la Masonería en la legislación reformista de la primera generación de liberales en México." In *Masonería española y América*, vol. 1. Zaragoza: Centro de Estudios Históricos de la Masonería Española, 1993.

Martínez Zaldúa, Ramón, *Historia de la Masonería en Hispanoamérica*. Mexico City: B. Costa–Amic, 1978.

Smith, Justin Harvey, "Poinsett's Career in Mexico." *Proceedings of the American Philosophical Society* 24 (1914).

Zalce y Rodríguez, Luís J., *Apuntes para la historia de la Masonería en México*. 18th edition, Mexico City: Banca y Comerico, 1983.

—Karen Racine

FRENCH INTERVENTION

The French Intervention or "Second Empire" was one of the most bizarre and tragic episodes in Mexico's history. From 1862 to 1867 French troops occupied the nation in support of the puppet emperor Maximilian. These years brought repression, guerrilla resistance, and countless deaths and abuses. But they also were a watershed. The presence of foreign invaders heightened Mexican nationalism, hardened the resolve of political elites, and ultimately set the stage for the dictatorship of Porfirio Díaz.

Origins

The French invasion had numerous causes. Mexican prelates and Conservatives, unwilling to accept their defeat in the Reform Wars of 1857 to 1861, escaped to France, where they circulated stories of a Mexico pining for the monarchical Catholic rule of colonial times. Mexican president Benito Juárez inadvertently played into their hands when, on July 17, 1861, he declared a two-year moratorium on payment of the Mexican foreign debt. His announcement lent credence to reports that Mexico was suffering under the heel of an immoral and incompetent regime.

In Paris, Emperor Napoléon III dreamed of the profits to be gained in Latin America. In 1846, some years before seizing power, he had written a pamphlet advocating a transoceanic canal for Nicaragua. But in Mexico the overriding economic goal of the imperialists was to revive the nation's fabled mining industry. In the eighteenth century the silver mines of the Bajío had been the greatest in the world; and they would be great again, when vast sums of foreign capital revived them during the reign of Porfirio Díaz. They had fallen into disrepair during the violence of the Wars of Independence and had resisted subsequent attempts to revive them. But their promise remained strong.

At the same time, Napoléon III wanted France to assert itself in Europe's growing competition for global dominion, a sort of colonialism for its own sake. A combination of buffoon and canny dictator, Napoléon III thrived on spectacle and understood the political value of grandiose national undertakings such as foreign wars. France had successfully invaded Algeria in 1830 and Saigon in 1859. Mexico now seemed a vulnerable target. Not only were dissident Mexicans inviting him in, but the area was politically chaotic, and a French empire offered the prestige of containing an expansive U. S. society on behalf of a culture that was monarchical, Iberian, and Catholic. Indeed, the moment seemed right. Seven days after the Mexican moratorium declaration, the first Battle of Bull Run signaled that the United States had embarked on a long civil war, and that the Union, an opponent of European interference in the Americas, would offer only muted protest.

France's government also was susceptible to the influence of bond speculators. Although French lenders held only $2.8 million of Mexico's total $81.5 million foreign debt, these individuals enjoyed special access to Napoléon III. Lacking any direct experience with Mexico, and without the benefit of a British-style foreign service, the French emperor relied upon the speculators as his main source of information. Together with the Mexican exile community, they painted a picture of a nation ready for French-sponsored monarchy.

Only too aware of the international disapproval that would result, Napoléon masked his intervention in an elaborate plot. He prevailed upon Britain and Spain to accompany France in a multinational occupation of the Veracruz customs house as a means of collecting on Mexico's foreign debt. The operation began in December 1861. Within a few months, however, the adventure's real intentions became clear, and the other two nations pulled out. France was now alone in the field.

The first attempt to seize Mexico City met unexpected resistance. On May 5, 1862, Mexican soldiers at Puebla dealt the invaders a stunning defeat. The French attempted an ill-planned uphill attack on the city's fort and were surprised by heavy rains, artillery, cavalry charges, and above all by daring resistance: Miguel Negrete, one of the Mexican commanders, wisely had kept his soldiers behind a high wall until the last minute, so that they would not be intimidated by the sight of French sabers and uniforms. Some 460 French soldiers perished, while Cinco de Mayo became a national holiday and the Mexican commanders—Negrete, Ignacio Zaragoza, and Porfirio Díaz—became national heroes. With General Zaragoza's untimely death from typhus, command passed to Jesús González Ortega, who heavily fortified and garrisoned Puebla. But within a year the French returned in force. On May 17, 1863, Puebla surrendered after a siege of 62 days. A

month later French forces marched directly to Mexico City itself. With the old capital now lost, Juárez relocated his government to San Luis Potosí in order to lead a guerrilla resistance against the invaders. For the next five years, two governments ruled Mexico.

Imperial Mexico

The French soon discovered that circumstances in Mexico differed considerably from those described by the Conservative exiles. The actual amount of Conservative support had been wildly exaggerated; any serious attempt at government would have to include Liberals as well. Moreover, the French generals were disgusted by the presumptions of the Mexican church, which was among the Conservatives' strongest supporters. Three centuries of colonialism had shielded the church from reforms and from the struggles with state power that had characterized European history. For all its purported Catholicism, France was now a secular nation, and its military officers had no intention of sharing power with an almost medieval clergy. The generals refused to restore confiscated clerical properties or to revive the church's lost political rights. Chances for a purely Conservative regime thus perished from the onset.

While the invasion was in progress, Napoléon arranged for a neutral figure to serve as emperor: someone neither French nor Mexican, a man removed from the raging ideological quarrels. The first candidates wisely turned down his offer. But he eventually managed to interest Archduke Ferdinand Maximilian von Hapsburg, brother to the Austro-Hungarian emperor Franz Josef. Maximilian was second-rate royalty who dreamed of power and popular adulation, and he quickly realized that without Mexico he would be destined to a life of idle entertainments and minor ceremonial functions. He arrived in Veracruz on May 28, 1864, with his Belgian wife Charlotte—now to be known as Carlota—and began a three-year reign as emperor of Mexico.

The royal couple immediately embraced their new country. They added Spanish to their already extensive repertoire of languages. In the winter of 1863–64 the French army under the iron fist of General Achilles Bazaine had staged a ruthless pacification campaign throughout Mexico; with these many towns now under occupation, they staged a referendum that naturally supported imperial rule. Thus convinced that the people loved him, Maximilian came to relish *lo mexicano* and was fond of appearing in the ostentatious costumes of rural Mexican dandies. He immediately set about planning an imperial makeover for the clothing, architecture, and social protocol of the Mexico City elite. The emperor himself designed the broad Calzada del Emperador (later renamed the Paseo de la Reforma). Maximilian also imposed the metric system, a lasting contribution. Like the kings of medieval Europe, he delighted in touring his realm, reveling in the exotic sights and sounds and occasionally taking a hand in the sugarcane harvest. Above all, he dreamed of railroads.

In other aspects, the empire remained perched halfway between its Conservative collaborators and its Liberal enemies. Maximilian, like the French generals, had no interest in placating Mexico's anachronistic prelates. He refused to overturn the reforms enacted under Juárez and Sebastián Lerdo de Tejada. Political ambivalence was the hallmark of the Second Empire, and it ultimately antagonized all sectors.

Nowhere was this more true than in Maximilian's attempt to construct a base of peasant support. The indigenous peasantry was the soul of the nation, and it had suffered greatly under the Liberal assault on communal property. The emperor's plan was to establish a body known as the *junta de protectores* to review and redress agrarian grievances. In Yucatán, the system took the form of an itinerant defense attorney known as the *abogado defensor de indios*. In theory the idea was sound; after all, this was how Mexico's Revolutionary government would establish itself one-half century later. But imperial efforts were too brief and too few. As the experiences of those later Revolutionaries revealed, real agrarian reform could come only through years of patient and often dangerous investigation, through peasant mobilization, and through organic links between peasants and the state. Maximilian's empire had none of these. His *juntas* and *defensores*, like his decrees against debt peonage, did little more than antagonize the propertied class.

Alliances with regional strongmen were thus inevitable. The best example came from the Monterrey area, which acquired new economic vitality in the early 1860s. Its growth had less to do with imperial policy than with the U.S. Civil War, which had resulted in a Union blockade of Confederate shipping to Europe. In response, the Confederates began to ship cotton south across the border, stockpiling it in a Matamoros tent city known as Bagdad. From there it was shipped to foreign purchasers. The entire district was under the administration of a purported Liberal, Santiago Vidaurri. But in 1862 Vidaurri changed loyalties to the empire rather than surrender the power and the lucrative profits of his situation. An inadvertent consequence of the empire, then, was to contribute to Monterrey's capital accumulation and subsequent industrialization. The prodigious flow of cotton through Tamaulipas and Nuevo León enriched the Monterrey merchants who, under the leadership of the Garza and Sada families, came to control the nation's largest industrial concerns.

A second important stage for imperial power was the southeast. This was particularly true of Yucatán, where rural rebellion and factional wars had raged for nearly two decades. Desperate to get the upper hand with their rivals, certain Yucatecans welcomed in the invaders. As imperial commissar, Maximilian appointed the capable José Salazar Ilarregui, a former engineer and college professor who had helped survey the U.S.-Mexican border after the treaty of Guadalupe Hidalgo. Carlota herself came here in 1865 and entertained representatives from all sectors of the society, from the landed elite to rural Maya caciques. But practicalities proved more difficult than social protocol. Salazar Ilarregui discovered that the Yucatecan propertied classes

accepted the empire as long as they themselves ruled at home. Reaction was overtly hostile in neighboring Tabasco, where nationalists, mobilizing around the caudillo (strongman) Gregorio Méndez, took advantage of the lively arms business that had grown around Yucatán's separatist territory of Chan Santa Cruz. They purchased guns and ammunition in Belize, then smuggled them across the relatively open territory of northern Guatemala.

The imperial passions and persuasions amused Mexican urbanites. But for all its comedy, the Second Empire was cruel, bloody, and unsparing. French troops killed or executed some 40,000 to 50,000 Mexicans, not to mention countless others who were imprisoned, tortured, or harassed. Under pressure from the imperial army, Juárez relocated his government ever northward, until he reached El Paso del Norte, the border town later renamed in his honor. In October 1865 the French generals, frustrated by the continued resistance, pressured Maximilian into signing what became known as the "Black Decree," an executive order authorizing the army to shoot armed Juaristas within 24 hours of their capture.

The Empire's End

From 1865 onward the tide of events turned against the empire. General Achille Bazaine's army captured the old Liberal stronghold of Oaxaca City on February 9, 1865, capturing its commander Porfirio Díaz (who soon escaped). But it was to be the last imperial victory. Mexican resistance remained tireless and effective. While imperialists occupied key cities, the guerrilla fighters persisted in the countryside. The rural towns, pacified and then abandoned by the invaders, soon returned to Liberal hands. Moreover, the French had difficulty holding Caribbean coastal areas because of Europeans' susceptibility to tropical disease. Tamaulipas and northern Veracruz in particular remained scenes of guerrilla raids.

The resistance government also maintained a viable political posture. Juárez avoided crossing the border for reasons of political prestige: he did not want to take on the shadowy status of government-in-exile. Indeed, the resistance movement endowed the Liberals with a national popularity that they had not previously possessed. In earlier years the Liberal policies had been bitter and divisive, but now Juárez and his generals became the defenders of national sovereignty. Despite rivalries and lean times, they endured and gradually began to reclaim territory.

The end of the U.S. Civil War brought increased foreign pressure. The imperialists initially tried to turn the situation to their advantage by courting Confederate expatriates as a class of loyal settlers. After all, Confederate colonies were springing up throughout Latin America. In Mexico, the most successful colonies formed in mountainous west Veracruz. The colonies boasted such lofty names as "Villa Carlota" and "New Virginia." They included key Confederate figures such as Jubal Early, notorious for his daring raids on Pennsylvania. It would be Confederate engineers who surveyed the land for the railroad line between Mexico City and

Veracruz. Maximilian finessed the slavery issue by allowing the white settlers to keep their black servants in "apprenticeship" for a period of 5 to 10 years.

Eventually, however, the victorious Union government brought full pressure against the interventionists. General Philip Sheridan ended the Confederate exodus by closing the Rio Grande border in 1866. Moreover, Union officers continued to funnel arms and supplies to Juárez's forces in the north. This assistance also acquainted nationalist generals such as Porfirio Díaz with military and economic connections in the United States, a knowledge that later would prove instrumental in constructing Díaz's 35-year dictatorship.

Imperial prospects further deteriorated in 1866, when Napoléon III found himself confronting an expansionist Prussia. In preparation for the coming war, he began to withdraw troops from Mexico in November. Attempts to replace the French legionnaires with Mexicans proved impossible. The Mexican soldiers were poorly trained and even more poorly paid, and unlike the nationalists they had no ideological commitment to their cause. The withdrawal of French troops resulted in bloodbaths of reprisals against collaborators throughout the country. Carlota herself returned to Europe to plead for help from Napoléon and the pope, but her efforts were in vain.

Simultaneously, the empire's southeastern outpost collapsed in the wake of a disastrous campaign against the Maya rebels of Chan Santa Cruz. The effort to mobilize Yucatán in an all-out crusade merely antagonized property holders; soldiers deserted by the hundreds, and the army itself narrowly escaped annihilation by the rebels in October 1866. By this point Tabascan Liberals were pressing from the west. An army rebellion led by Colonial Manuel Cepeda Peraza toppled the regime in June 1867, although the empire's former collaborators—some in exile, others scattered throughout the countryside—continued to cause trouble throughout the year.

For Maximilian the end came swiftly. With the French soldiers now gone, the emperor had only a handful of loyal Conservative generals and a collection of international adventurers. The last imperialists fought on; from April to June they held out in the city of Querétaro. In his spare moments on the battlefield, Maximilian played chess with his officers. After a series of losing battles he was forced to surrender. Pleas of clemency flowed in from Europe, but Juárez knew that he risked an army rebellion if he spared the former emperor. Moreover, he believed that imperialism needed to be graphically repudiated. On June 19, 1867, Maximilian, together with Conservative Mexican generals Miguel Miramón and Tomás Mejía, died before a firing squad at Cerro de Campanas, "Hill of the Bells." His body eventually was returned to Europe and buried in the Hapsburg family crypt.

Many protagonists in the intervention faired poorly thereafter. Napoléon III lost his war with Prussia in 1870 and went into exile, dying shortly thereafter. Salazar Ilarregui escaped to New York City, while Santiago Vidaurri was executed in a barnyard. Another Conservative general named Leonardo Márquez, "the Tiger of Tacubaya," fled to Havana, where he operated a pawn shop for many years; in the 1890s Márquez, who once had executed prisoners without compunction, returned to Mexico to die a forgotten old man. Carlota went completely mad and, until her death in 1927, remained confined to her Belgian family castle. She never again spoke of her Mexican experiences.

For Mexico itself the imperial occupation had enormous political consequences. The restored Juárez administration inherited pure chaos. The war had exhausted the nation's economic resources and left many Mexicans hungry for stability and growth. Moreover, the collapse of imperial power sparked local bloodlettings and a wave of lawlessness as gangs of former soldiers preyed on the countryside. Initially the restored Liberal government exiled, imprisoned, and even executed former collaborators. However, the persecutions soon ended, as the need to fill the political bureaucracy compelled Juárez and later Porfirio Díaz to employ former imperialists. As one minister later put it, "In Mexico there has not been treason, only mistakes."

The imperial war also set the stage for future authoritarianism. The Liberals long had advocated more democratic practices for Mexico, but conditions now forced Juárez to adopt a form of machine politics that segued into the dictatorship of Porfirio Díaz. The general from Oaxaca emerged from the war with strong national credentials and a reputation for honesty. But he also nursed powerful ambitions, and after 1873 entered into his own alliances with foreign capital in order to realize them. Under the hand of don Porfirio, the railroads and powerful state that had been the fascinations of Emperor Maximilian became a reality, and in the process transformed Mexico forever.

Select Bibliography

Arias G., María Eugenia, et al., *Tabasco: Una historia compartida.* Villahermosa: Gobierno del Estado de Tabasco, 1987.

Dabbs, Jack A., *The French Army in Mexico, 1861–1867: A Study in Military Government.* The Hague: Mouton, 1963.

Hanna, Alfred Jackson, and Kathryn Abbey Hanna, *Napoleon III and Mexico: American Triumph over Monarchy.* Chapel Hill: University of North Carolina Press, 1971.

Hart, John M., "Miguel Negrete: La epopeya de un revolucionario." *Historia mexicana* 24:1 (1974).

Perry, Laurens Ballard, *Juárez and Díaz: Machine Politics in Mexico.* DeKalb: Northern Illinois University Press, 1978.

Ridley, Jasper, *Maximilian and Juárez.* New York: Ticknor and Fields, 1992.

Sánchez Novelo, *Faulo, Yucatán durante la intervención francesa (1863–1867).* Mérida: Maldonado Editores, 1983.

Valadéz, José, *Maximiliano y Carlota en México: Historia del Segundo Imperio.* Mexico City: Editorial Diana, 1976.

—TERRY RUGELEY

FUENTES, CARLOS

1928– • Writer

Carlos Fuentes is the son of Rafael Fuentes Boettiger, a career diplomat who as a cadet had fought against the U.S. invasion of Veracruz, and Berta Macías Rivas. Born in Panama City on November 9, 1928, during one of his father's diplomatic assignments, Fuentes spent his childhood in Quito, Montevideo, Rio de Janeiro, and finally Washington, D.C., where he lived from 1934 to 1940.

Fuentes's early life in Washington left a profound mark on him, making him feel at once at home in and alienated from U.S. culture. Attending elementary school in Washington, Fuentes learned English as his first formal language. He was an avid reader, devouring the works of Mark Twain, Robert Louis Stevenson, and Emilio Salgari. He discovered the difficulty of being a Mexican in the United States following the nationalization of the petroleum industry by the administration of Lázaro Cárdenas in 1938, when Mexicans collectively were condemned as Communists. Fuentes's exposure to Mexican culture was through his family, in that imaginary territory created by an embassy trying to replicate the homeland. He also spent summers with his grandparents in Mexico City so that he would not forget the language and history of Mexico. Fuentes's childhood experience of living between cultures, languages, and nations would repeat itself throughout his life, becoming one the key principles that would inform his work.

In 1940 Fuentes's family moved to Santiago de Chile, where it remained until 1944. Fuentes published his first stories in the *Boletín del Instituto Nacional de Chile*. Defined by the radical experience of Chile's Popular Front government and the tensions of World War II, the literary culture of 1940s Chile was characterized by neo-Romanticism and political poetry, particularly the work of Gabriela Mistral and Pablo Neruda. Taking advantage of the relative tolerance of the diplomatic world, Fuentes's literature teachers, Pedro Aguirre Cerda and the Spanish exile Alejandro Tarragó, introduced him to the work of the Argentinian writer Jorge Luis Borges and the authors of the Generation of 1929.

In 1944 Fuentes returned to Mexico, finishing high school. Entering law school at the national university, Fuentes quickly abandoned his formal studies to frequent the bordellos, cabarets, and other haunts of the Mexico City demimonde, which continued to figure prominently in his writing throughout the 1950s and 1960s. The Spanish exile community also had considerable influence on him, and he later studied with the Spanish philosophers Eduardo Nicol and José Gaos. In the *Revista memorias y ideas de México*, Fuentes published a series of short stories and essays that drew on his meticulous reading of the genre that since has come to be called "the novel of the Mexican Revolution." He also sought to formulate a critique of the "philosophy of *lo mexicano*" then in vogue. He also wrote news articles and analyses for the magazines *Hoy, Novedades,* and *Voz*. From the first he was a dissident from official policy and a severe critic of the Cold War and U.S. policy toward Latin America. The house of Fuentes's parents was frequented by the architects of a Mexican foreign policy based on national autonomy and nonintervention, familiarizing him with a vision of the world that married nationalism with a critique of imperial domination.

The 1950s were a defining period for Fuentes. In 1950 he entered the Mexican diplomatic corps, where he served in posts tightly linking him to the world of the arts and literature in Mexico and abroad. He also returned to law school and helped run the journal *Medio Siglo. Medio Siglo* became a nucleus for writers and thinkers of Fuentes's generation, including such figures as Salvador Elizondo, Sergio Pitol, Marco Antonio Montes de Oca, and—in the early stages of their careers—José Emilio Pacheco and Carlos Monsiváis. Fuentes also formed ties with key political players of his generation, including Mario Moya Palencia, Porfirio Muñoz Ledo, and others. However, this period was particularly fertile for Fuentes's own writing. From 1954 to 1962 Fuentes published four books that—together with Octavio Paz's *Labyrinth of Solitude*—would help determine the shape of contemporary Mexican literature.

Los días enmascarados (1954) brings together a series of short stories that seek to represent "the distinct voices of history" coming together in Mexico City during the 1950s, ranging from a Chac Mool—one of the Maya sculptures of reclining figures—to an attorney wavering about whether he should enter politics to advance his career and fortunes. Fuentes established himself as one of the most important writers in Latin America with *La región más transparente* (1958), the saga of a Mexican family in twentieth-century Mexico from the Revolution through 1950s. In both books Fuentes developed what would become a trademark of his narrative, his intimate engagement with the urban space of Mexico City. "Mexico," he wrote, "is a three-story country"—but he also might have been writing of the three stories of the city in his narrative: at the base, the "profound city" of streetwalkers, indigenous peoples, and historical identities; in the middle the "ambiguous city" of *mestizaje,* the search for identity, the deracinated middle class, and folkloric stereotypes; and at the top the invulnerable, totemic city of elites. In *La muerte de Artemio Cruz* (1962) the last 12 hours before a political cacique's death unfold in a narrative of countless voices. Perhaps Fuentes's most accomplished work, *La muerte de Artemio Cruz* develops many of the technical innovations, motifs, and themes that later would become hallmarks of the Latin American "boom" literatures—the dissolution between narrator and narrative, the shredding of the national myth of *mestizaje,* and the use of urban rather than rural speech. *Aura* (1962), *Cantar de ciegos* (1965), *Líneas para Adami* (1966), *Zona sagrada* (1967), and *Cambio de piel* (1967) further refine these innovations.

If most Mexican literature—as well as the social sciences and humanities—had been characterized by an insular concern with Mexican realities or by submission to western models, Fuentes's broader interest in Latin America as a whole made him something of a *rara avis* in Mexican letters. In his essays and lectures Fuentes sought to represent Latin American literature as a coherent literary and cultural movement. After reading *La nueva novela hispanoamericana* (1969), in which Fuentes coined the term "magic realism" to define the new narrative style that had emerged in Latin American literature, Gabriel García Márquez called him the inventor of the "boom." This concern with Latin America also was a touchstone of his political work. Traveling to Havana for the first time to support the Cuban Revolution in 1959, Fuentes frequently returned in subsequent years, developing a close friendship with the Cuban writers Alejo Carpentier, Lezama Lima, and Cintio Vitier. Expelled from the cultural supplement of the daily newsmagazine *Novedades* for their support of the Cuban Revolution, Fuentes and other writers joined the cultural supplement of *Siempre.* In 1962 Fuentes resigned from the diplomatic corps and joined the Movimiento de Liberación Nacional (MLN, or National Liberation Movement), which united the populist former president of Mexico, Lázaro Cárdenas, with various groups on the Mexican left. Supporting the Cuban Revolution, criticizing United States policy toward Latin America, and seeking to democratize Mexico, the MLN eventually was defeated and forced to dissolve. In 1963 and 1964 Fuentes traveled to Europe, beginning his close association with such other writers of the Latin American "boom" as Julio Cortázar, Gabriel García Márquez, and Mario Vargas Llosa.

In 1965 Fuentes broke with the Cuban Revolution when its cultural bureaucracy launched a campaign against Pablo Neruda. He also became increasingly critical of Soviet authoritarianism, although he never shied from his fierce defense of the right to self-determination and his criticism of U.S. Cold War policies. In 1968 he wrote an account of the Paris uprising, *Paris: La revolución de Mayo,* and later that year he traveled to Prague with Cortázar and García Márquez to support the Czechoslovak writers and intellectuals who were protesting the Soviet invasion of their country; they were hosted by Milan Kundera. On his way back to Mexico in 1969, he was refused entry into the United States for "Communist sedition." Norman Mailer and the Pen Club launched a campaign in his defense, which was later taken up by Senator J. William Fulbright. Fuentes continued his political engagement in the 1970s. His first two plays, *El tuerto es rey* (1970) and *Todos los gatos son pardos* (1971), were biting critiques of authoritarian power structures in Mexico. Fuentes established close ties with the administration of Luis Echeverría, and in 1975 he was named ambassador to France.

In one of the most controversial moves of his career, however, he resigned in 1977 to protest the naming of former president Gustavo Díaz Ordaz, who had assumed responsibility for the massacre of hundreds of student protesters in October 1968, as the first Mexican ambassador to Spain since the fall of the Republic.

The Massacre of Tlatelolco and the death of Fuentes's father shortly after sparked a creative crisis that led Fuentes to experiment with new literary models and new ideas. This period of experimentation culminated with the publication of *Terra Nostra* in 1975. Taking Fuentes's concern with the loss of the narrative subject to its greatest extreme, *Terra Nostra* is a history of a people without a history—a people who only can see themselves in alien mirrors. Fuentes seeks to destroy these mirrors, creating characters who are seen in language itself and in their immediate otherness. Fuentes's attempt to construct an epic of Latin America (unsuccessful in the opinion of many critics) won him the Xavier Villaurrutia prize in 1977.

The final years of the 1970s saw a reconciliation between Fuentes and the United States. Teaching and lecturing at several U.S. universities, in 1987 Fuentes was named to the Robert F. Kennedy chair at Harvard University. Fuentes continued to remain a sharp critic of U.S. foreign policy and a defender of Latin American sovereignty, publishing frequently in U.S. newspapers and magazines. Many of these concerns are played out in *Gringo Viejo* (1985), which later was made into a film starring Jane Fonda and Gregory Peck. In *Latin America: At War with the Past* (1985), Fuentes proposes a reinterpretation of the United States' role in Latin America. Fuentes continued to refine his thematic concerns and his experiments with language in *Una familia lejana* (1980), *Agua quemada* (1981), *Cristóbal nonato* (1987), and *La campaña* (1990). He also continued his study of Latin American history, literature, and identity in *Valiente mundo nuevo* (1990), *Geografía de la novela* (1993), and *El naranjo* (1993), "an interiorized history of our language." In 1991 he traveled extensively in Spain, Argentina, Mexico, and California filming *The Buried Mirror,* a cultural history of Spanish-speaking countries prepared for the British Broadcasting Corporation.

In 1994 Fuentes returned to political essay writing in Mexican newspapers and magazines, criticizing neoliberal policies, the administration of Carlos Salinas de Gortari, and a foreign policy that weakened Mexico's political autonomy vis-à-vis the United States. In one of his most telling phrases, he described the 1994 Chiapas uprising as "the first postmodern guerrilla movement" founded "more in the stories of [Mexican writer Carlos] Monsiváis than in the theories of Marx." He continues to participate in the Grupo San Angel, a group of prominent dissident writers and intellectuals that promotes the democratization of Mexico.

Select Bibliography

Brody, Robert, and Charles Rossman, editors, *Carlos Fuentes: A Critical View.* Austin: University of Texas Press, 1982.

Durán, Gloria, *La mágia y las brujas en la obra de Carlos Fuentes.* Translated as *The Archetypes of Carlos Fuentes: From Witch to Androgyne.* Hamden, Connecticutt: Shoestring Press, 1980.

Durán, Victor Manuel, *A Marxist Reading of Fuentes, Vargas Llosa, and Puig.* Lanham, Maryland: University of America Press, 1993.

Faris, Wendy, *Carlos Fuentes.* New York: Ungar, 1983.

Feijoo, Gladys, *Lo fantástico en los relatos de Carlos Fuentes.* New York: Senda Nueva de Ediciones, 1985.

García Gutiérrez, Georgina, *Los disfraces: La obra mestiza de Carlos Fuentes.* Mexico City: Colegio de México, 1981.

García Núñez, Fernando, *Fabulación de la fe: Carlos Fuentes.* Xalapa, Mexico: Universidad Veracruzana, 1989.

Giacoman, Helmy F., editor, *Homenaje a Carlos Fuentes: Variaciones interpretativas en torno a su obra.* New York: Las Américas, 1971.

González, Alfonso, *Carlos Fuentes: Life, Work, and Criticism.* Fredericton, New Brunswick: York Press, 1987.

Ibsen, Kristine, *Author, Text and Reader in the Novels of Carlos Fuentes.* New York: Peter Lang, 1993.

Ordiz, Francisco Javier, *El mito en la obra narrativa de Carlos Fuentes.* León: Universidad de León, 1987.

Velarde, Agustín, *Carlos Fuentes y "Las buenas conciencias."* Mexico City: Buena Prensa, 1962.

—ILÁN SEMO

FUEROS

In Mexican historiography, *fueros* often are described as special privileges, usually of the church and military. More exactly, *fueros* codified unwritten laws of use and custom by which the estates, towns, guilds, and military orders of the Hapsburg Empire governed and regulated themselves. This corporate structure was so entrenched by the eighteenth century that the new Bourbon monarchs could conceive no better way to advance their administrative and economic reforms than by granting new *fueros. Fueros* proved so resilient that, after Mexican Independence, it took multiple civil wars for liberal state-builders to root them out.

For practical purposes, *fueros* may be said to have originated with the conciliation of Visigothic and Roman law culminating in the Fuero Juzgo of 694. Over the centuries, various attempts to codify the mass of conflicting local laws, such as the Siete Partidas of Alfonso X, were resisted by the people. Further, the Spanish Crown encouraged settlement of the Iberian frontier opened to Christians by the Reconquista by granting *fueros* of various sorts modeled on other municipal *fueros* (often of Salamanca or Ávila) adapted to local use. Kings extended their authority by reciprocity; their rule was legitimate because they legitimated local tradition and rule in accordance with it. Carlos I's confirmation as king, first by the Cortes of León-Castile and then by that of Aragon, was contingent upon his promise to respect their ancient liberties. When his grand chancellor Gattinara advised Carlos to put aside local *fueros* in favor of Roman law, the Castilian *comunidades* (self-governing representative assemblies) revolted. When Fernando (Hernán) Cortés suggested in his last letter to Carlos from Mexico that insufficient royal reward might lead his men to form *comunidades,* he was summoned to court to explain himself.

At the end of the *comunidades* revolts, grand chancellor Gattinara spoke of love and respect for the monarch as the glue of empire, not uniform Roman law. From this realization emerged the Hapsburg social contract that confirmed use, custom, and *fuero* as embodied in the phrase uttered so frequently by His Majesty's viceroys in response to unpopular royal laws: *"Se obedece, pero no se cumple"* (I obey but do not comply), meaning that, although the viceroy was the king's obedient servant, he could not enforce a law that contravened local practice and custom and might provoke revolt. This implicit confirmation of revolt as a legitimate means to seek political redress found expression in another well-known formulaic cry: "Long live the king; death to bad government," heard by many a colonial official. Indeed, given Mexico's organic, tradition-encrusted corporatism and the fragmentation of administrative and judicial systems dominated by legally constituted special interests, revolt was the only effective mechanism of check and balance.

The clergy and the nobility, the first two social orders of colonial Mexico, each possessed *fueros* unique to its estate. Clergy were not obligated to pay personal taxes (*pechos*) and could be tried only by church courts in most civil and criminal cases; other *fueros* governed the relationship of the Crown to the many corporate clerical entities, such as religious orders, monasteries, and *cofradías* (lay brotherhoods), which were also tax exempt. Corporate tax exemption created the conditions by which the Catholic Church acquired vast estates and became New Spain's chief source of credit, often in the form of perpetual loans.

Like the clergy, nobles paid no personal taxes. They had no exemption in civil cases but, for most criminal offenses, they could be tried only by their peers. They could not be imprisoned for debt, nor could their property be seized. In Mexico, nobles were of two sorts: *magnates* (the titled nobility), of which there were only about 40 at Independence, and *hidalgos,* a status claimed by every peninsular (those born on the Iberian Peninsula) and many criollos (those of Spanish descent born in the New World). In Spain, mass ennoblement came through the *fueros* of Vizcaya, Navarre, Asturias, León, and Old Castile, which conferred *hidalgo* status on all free men of those kingdoms. In Mexico, *hidalgo* status was claimed by those of European descent on the basis of freedom from tribute payments required of conquered peoples. The Crown was consistent, however, in its opposition to the emergence of an independent colonial nobility, and few Mexicans claiming *hidalgo* status actually held it by royal grant.

There was no single *fuero* for commoners; rather, they enjoyed *fueros* through corporate membership, guilds, municipalities, and, later, the military. Guild *fueros* governed master-apprentice relationships and regulated production, and each guild had its own patron saint, *cofradia,* distinctive clothing, and special place in public processions reflecting its place in society. *Fueros* usually authorized courts and, in some cases, the right to levy taxes *(alcabalas),* thus fragmenting the economy as well as the judicial system. The merchants' guild *(consulado),* for example, enforced commercial law, while universities exercised juridical authority over students and faculty. *Mestas* (cattlemen guilds) regulated all aspects of stock-raising, from the registration of brands to trying rustlers, and generally sought to preserve the ancient institution of village *ejidos* (communal properties), which provided grazing essential to their marketing operations.

Municipalities in New Spain were corporate entities, but few had true *fueros.* Mexican *cabildos* (councils), dominated by local notables, were largely inactive and the *procuradores* (city attorneys or solicitors) were forbidden to meet as *comunidades.* Those municipalities identified as Indian, however, possessed de facto *fueros* arising from the Hapsburg's recognition of the existence of a *república de indios* (Indian republic) possessing an inherent corporate structure similar to that of Spain. The syncretic result was an Indo-Iberian tradition of rural municipal governance centered on regulation of village lands through private "usufructs" (the right to enjoy the fruits of that legally belonging to another party).

The Bourbons approached the issue of *fueros* pragmatically, the absolutist ambition expressed by their dictum "one king, one law" notwithstanding. On one hand, they restricted the *fueros* of overly powerful corporate groups. They whittled away the independence of the Catholic Church in New Spain by replacing regular bishops and prelates (i.e., those belonging to a particular order, such as the Franciscans) with secular clergy (those not belonging to a specific order). Relations with the Jesuits grew so strained that, in 1767, Carlos III expelled the order from New Spain and all his realms. Carlos III also ended clerical immunity from civil and criminal courts. In 1884, the Crown further alienated the Mexican Catholic Church and criollos by the Act of Consolidation, which transferred its charitable funds to Spain, forcing the church to call in its loans, ruining countless hacendados and rancheros, and destroying the credit and informal banking structures dependent on the church's corporate wealth.

In other instances, the Bourbons granted new *fueros* to promote economic reform and growth. To stimulate New Spain's mining industry, for instance, Carlos III created a miner's guild with its own *fueros.* To encourage rational economic behavior by the nobles, he modified the prohibition on their engaging industry and commerce by declaring these pursuits to be noble activities. And, although his declaration of *comercio libre* (free trade) effectively ended the monopoly of the Mexico City *consulado,* it gave rise to new *consulados* in Veracruz and Guadalajara, each with its own *fuero.* In short, the Bourbons sought to rationally manage the Hapsburgian corporate state, not to replace it.

The most far-reaching changes came with Carlos III's extension of the *fuero militar* to the criollo militia, part of an effort to improve colonial defenses following Spain's humiliating defeat by the British in the Seven Years Wars. This opened political space for criollo sons through commissions and gave *castas* (those of mixed race) a chance to improve their social position by militia membership. By Independence, the provincial militia numbered 22,000 and the urban militia, 44,000. The extension of the *fuero militar* provided a juridical basis for the *hidalgo* status claimed by criollos and created an aristocratic military caste, enamored of honors and glory, composed of men like Antonio López de Santa Anna, who considered themselves above the law—the caudillos.

The fate of Miguel Hidalgo after his defeat and capture in January 1811 provides an excellent illustration of the multiple and conflicting jurisdictions created by *fueros.* When he was captured in 1811, Hidalgo was remanded to the Inquisition, which found him guilty of heresy and treason, although the latter charge technically fell outside the scope of clerical courts. Because the Catholic Church could not impose the death penalty, he was (in the terminology of the Inquisition) "relaxed" to secular authorities for execution by firing squad. Seeing the possible implications of Hidalgo's trial, Viceroy Francisco Vengas rushed to assure secular jurisdiction over other rebel priests and issued his "blood and fire" decree authorizing military commanders to try clerics taken under arms. Vengas's abrogation of clerical *fuero* greatly distressed even loyalists, as it sacrificed one of their key principles on the altar of political expediency, and it was rescinded. In 1815, Hidalgo's successor, the priest José María Morelos, also would be tried by Inquisition before being handed over to secular authorities for execution.

Under Morelos the movement became more revolutionary, advocating racial equality, the dismantling of Mexico's corporate structure, the dismantling of Catholic Church estates into small properties, and the abolition of *fueros.* In 1812, as Morelos's movement reached its high-water mark in the south, the Cortes of Cádiz promulgated a liberal constitution abolishing *fueros.* As the Mexican clergy attacked the constitution from the pulpit, New Spain's viceroys dealt with it in the usual way *(Se obedece, pero no se cumple),* refusing to implement its provisions. Liberal politicians around Morelos saw an opportunity to win over independence-minded, fence-sitting liberal criollos and called a congress, proclaimed independence, and produced a constitution not unlike that of the Cádiz Cortes. The criollos did not respond. Military reversals and the execution of Morelos left only localized resistance under Guadalupe Victoria and Vicente Guerrero. Meanwhile, Fernando returned to the throne as a reactionary, putting aside not only the Constitution of 1812 but also some later Bourbon reforms, allowing the Jesuits to return, and restoring noble *fueros.*

In 1820, Rafael Riego's military coup ended Fernando's absolutist foray. That year the Cortes restored the 1812 Constitution and ordered the suppression of monastic orders and the Jesuits. The Cortes forbid the acquisition of additional lands by corporate bodies (civil or religious), annulled clerical and military *fueros,* and also struck at emerging caudillo power bases by ordering the separation of civil and military authority and by placing local militias (now sans *fueros*) under civilian control. This attack on *fueros* and corporate society contributed significantly to the collapse of royalist sentiment. Thus there was widespread support for Agustín de Iturbide's Plan de Iguala and its three guarantees: independence (as a constitutional monarchy, preferably under a Spanish Bourbon), union (national unity expressed as civil rights for all Mexicans regardless of caste), and religion (which necessarily entailed the acceptance of a corporate society ordered by *fueros*). Iturbide's plan temporarily left the laws of the 1820 Cortes in place, yet even the most conservative clergy and criollos supported the Army of the Three Guarantees, assuming correctly that the corporate order and their *fueros* would be restored. Within months of the crowning of Iturbide as Emperor Agustín I in 1822, Antonio López de Santa Anna, the quintessential caudillo, rebelled at Veracruz and was quickly joined by Guerrero, Nicolás Bravo, and Guadalupe Victoria. With appropriate irony, the general sent by Iturbide to quash the revolt joined it and ensured its success.

The Federal Republic established by the Constitution of 1824 left corporatism intact; clerical and military *fueros* again were guaranteed, and the presidency was imbued with monarchical potential by dint of its emergency powers. Not until the presidency of Valentín Gómez Farías did the liberals feel strong enough to abolish all *fueros.* It did not last long and *fueros* were restored under Santa Anna's conservative Constitution of 1836. This began a period of revolving constitutions that ended with the Ayutla Revolution. Their victory won, the liberals immediately passed two laws restricting *fueros.* The Ley Juárez of 1855 did not abolish clerical and military *fueros* but it confined the jurisdiction of their courts to cases involving canon and military law. The Ley Lerdo, which followed in 1856, prohibited corporate ownership of property, which affected both the church and *municipios.* Both laws subsequently entered the Constitution of 1857. Parading under their old banners of *religion y fueros,* the clergy vehemently denounced the document and began the War of the Reform. The liberal victory in 1861 marked the end of *fueros.* Even during the French Intervention, Emperor Maximilian declined to restore them. Without *fueros,* Mexican corporatism assumed economically based

republican forms during the Restored Republic, which continued to evolve through the reign of Porfirio Díaz to the present day. Likewise, the traditions of obedience without compliance and "death to bad government" still survive as a legitimate political option of last resort.

See also Bourbon Reforms; Church and State; Military

Select Bibliography

Anna, Tim, "Spain and the Breakdown of Imperial Ethos: The Problem of Equality." *HAHR* 62 (1982).
Arnold, Linda, *Bureaucracy and Bureaucrats in Mexico City, 1742–1835.* Tucson: University of Arizona Press, 1988.
Babier, Jacques, "The Culmination of the Bourbon Reforms, 1787–1792." *HAHR* 57 (1977).
Bethell, Leslie, editor, *Colonial Spanish America.* Cambridge and New York: Cambridge University Press, 1987.
_____, *The Independence of Latin America.* Cambridge and New York: Cambridge University Press, 1987.
Brading, David, "Government and Elite in Late Colonial Mexico." *HAHR* 53 (1973).
Burkholder, M.A., and Lyman Johnson, editors, *Colonial Latin America.* 2nd edition, New York: Oxford University Press, 1994.
Camp, Roderic Ai, *Politics in Mexico.* New York: Oxford University Press, 1993.
Costeloe, Michael P., *Church Wealth in Mexico, 1800–1856.* Cambridge and New York: Cambridge University Press, 1967.
Farriss, Nancy M., *Crown and Clergy in Colonial Mexico, 1759–1821.* London: Athlone, 1968.
Graham, Richard, *Independence in Latin America: A Comparative Approach.* 2nd edition, New York: McGraw-Hill, 1994.
Hamill, Hugh, "Early Psychological Warfare in the Hidalgo Revolt." *HAHR* 41 (1961).
Headly, John M. "The Hapsburg World Empire and the Revival of Ghibellinism." In *Proceedings of the Southeastern Institute of Medieval and Renaissance Studies,* edited by Siegfried Wenzel. Chapel Hill: University of North Carolina Press, 1978.
Hendrick, Charles D., "Charles V and the Cortes of Castile: Politics in Renaissance Spain." Ph.D. diss., Cornell University, 1976.
Ladd, Doris Maxine, "The Mexican Nobility at Independence, 1780–1826." Ph.D. diss., Stanford University, 1972.
Lear, Floyd S., "The Public Law of the Visigothic Code." *Speculum* 26 (1951).
MacKay, Angus, *Spain in the Middle Ages: From Frontier to Empire.* London: Macmillan and New York: St. Martin's Press, 1977.
McAlister, Lyle N., *Spain and Portugal in the New World, 1492–1700.* Oxford: Oxford University Press, and Minneapolis: University of Minnesota, 1984.
Meyer, Michael C., and William L. Sherman, *The Course of Mexican History.* 5th edition, New York: Oxford University Press, 1995.
Scott, S. P., translator, *Las Siete Partidas.* 3 vols., Chicago: Commerce Clearing House, 1931.
Wiarda, Howard, editor, *Politics and Social Change in Latin America: Still a Distinct Tradition?* 3rd edition, Boulder, Colorado: Westview Press, 1992.

—WILLIAM SCHELL JR.

G

GADSDEN PURCHASE

See Mesilla, La

GALINDO ACOSTA DE TOPETE, HERMILA

1886–1954 • Feminist, Writer, and Politician

Hermila Galindo was born in Ciudad Lerdo, Durango, on May 29, 1886, to Rosario Galindo and Hermila Acosta de Galindo. Hermila's mother died when she was a few days old, and she was brought up by her father's sister. She went to primary school in the city of Durango and secondary school at the Girls' Technical College in Chihuahua. When her father died young, her knowledge of English, shorthand, typing, and bookkeeping enabled her to give private lessons.

Hermila Galindo's first incursion into political activity was in Torreón, Durango, on March 21, 1909, during a celebration commemorating the birth of Benito Juárez. She was a fervent admirer of Juárez and took down in shorthand the speech made that day by Francisco Martínez Ortiz, a lawyer who opposed longtime dictator Porfirio Díaz. This shorthand version meant the speech survived, despite attempts by the local authorities to suppress it. Months later, a group of Partido Democrático (Democratic Party) members (Benito Juárez Maza, Diódoro Batalla, and Heriberto Barrón) heard of her exploit and asked her to join the political struggle.

When Francisco I. Madero's Revolution triumphed in 1911, Galindo was living in Mexico City, where she was active in politics and taught shorthand in state schools. Her brief political career began in August 1914, when she gave a speech on behalf of the political club "Abraham González" welcoming the Constitutionalists to Mexico City. Her oratorical skill in drawing parallels between Benito Juárez and the Constitutionalist Venustiano Carranza, and her staunch defense of the Reform Laws, earned her an invitation to work directly for Carranza.

Galindo moved to Veracruz at the end of 1914 when, squeezed by the rival Conventionalist armies, Carranza's government established itself there. She worked tirelessly in the press and at political meetings in support of the Constitutionalist revolution, and her defense of equal rights for women also made her the best-known suffragette of the Mexican Revolution.

In response to a request from the Constitutionalist government, Galindo went on a political tour of the states of Tabasco, Campeche, and Yucatán in the latter half of 1915. Her work in Yucatán inspired the First Yucatán Women's Congress (January 13 to 16, 1916), convened by Salvador Alvarado, a Constitutionalist general who was governor and military commander of the state from 1915 to 1918.

Although Galindo did not actually attend the First Women's Congress personally, her speech "La mujer del porvenir" (The Woman of the Future), which closed the congress, had an enormous impact. Quoting various European thinkers, Galindo expounded a rational education for women to include intellectual activity, physical exercise, and knowledge of human anatomy. She shocked the congress by stating that the female sexual urge was as strong as the male. She said that infanticide and abortion were social problems stemming from the prevailing sexual double standard, which applauded male sexual conquests yet condemned the female victims of male seduction to social opprobrium. Despite being deemed immoral, the speech was included in the official papers of the Women's Congress because Galindo had the political support of Governor Alvarado.

In response to these accusations of immorality, Galindo wrote "Estudios de la Señorita Hermila Galindo con motivo de los temas que han de absolverse en el Segundo Congreso Feminista de Yucatán" ("A Paper by Miss Hermila Galindo Outlining Matters to Be Discussed in the Second Yucatán Women's Congress," which was held from November 23 to December 6, 1916). Published as a pamphlet, this document, Galindo's most radical, took the ideas set out in "The Woman of the Future" even further. She took the classic liberal stance of demanding the right of women to take part in the lawmaking process and share equal voting rights with men. She also proposed modifying the Civil Code to recognize equal rights for women in marriage.

For four years starting September 15, 1915, Galindo edited *La mujer moderna: Semanario ilustrado* (Modern Woman: An Illustrated Weekly). Under her own name, or under the pseudonyms Justa Paliza (Just Beating) or Victoria Segura (Certain Victory), she demanded political and civil rights for women and at the same time supported the Constitutionalist cause against its enemies, the Zapatistas and Villistas. In this sense Galindo was unusual; she gave the same importance to her feminism as her political support for Constitutionalism.

La Mujer moderna did not defend equal rights for women in a vacuum but saw female emancipation as inextricably linked to the country's political development. Hence, Galindo demanded the immediate inclusion of women in public life and saw women's suffrage as a prerequisite to this.

In 1917 Galindo sent the Constituent Congress in Querétaro a memorandum demanding political rights for women. The request was rejected almost out of hand on the grounds that women were not sufficiently educated politically and that the female vote would, therefore, favor conservative forces.

In defiance of Revolutionary legislation that had denied women equal rights as citizens, in 1918 Galindo announced she was standing as a candidate in Mexico City's fifth electoral district. Knowing she would not be allowed to take up a seat in Congress, Galindo merely intended to show that a suffragette movement existed and provide a heroic example of struggle for future generations.

Venustiano Carranza did not share her enthusiasm for women's suffrage, but he trusted her politically. In mid-1916 the Constitutionalist government sent her to Cuba to explain the Carranza Doctrine, which included the principles of nonintervention in the internal affairs of sovereign nations and equality both between countries and between citizens of those countries and foreign nationals living there. In these aspects, Carranza's international policy disputed the Monroe Doctrine. Galindo's book *La doctrina Carranza y el acercamiento indolatino* (The Carranza Doctrine and Indo-Latin Rapprochement) was published in 1919 as a result of her experience in Cuba.

Despite her close relations with Venustiano Carranza, in the presidential elections of 1920 Galindo gave her support to General Pablo González instead of Ignacio Bonilla, Carranza's candidate. She explained her electoral position in 1919 in her book *Un presidenciable: El General Don Pablo González* (A Choice for President: General Pablo González).

After Venustiano Carranza's assassination on May 21, 1920, Galindo practically disappeared from political life. In 1923 she married a man from Jalisco, Miguel E. Topete, and had two daughters by him. She kept writing on political affairs but concentrated on painting.

Shortly before Hermila Galindo died on August 19, 1954, the Constitution was amended to recognize equal rights for men and women in a decree published on October 17, 1953, during Adolfo Ruiz Cortines's presidency.

Select Bibliography

Cano, Gabriela, "Revolución, feminismo y ciudadanía en México (1915–1920)." In *Historia de las mujeres en Occidente,* vol. 5, edited by Georges Duby and Michelle Perrot. Madrid: Taurus, 1991.

—GABRIELA CANO

GALVÁN, URSULO

1893–1930 • Politician and Agrarian Leader

Ursulo Galván was born on October 21, 1893, in the poor hamlet of Actopan, near the village of Tlacotepec in central Veracruz. The son of itinerant, landless *campesinos* (peasants) and a farm hand at an early age, Galván was raised by his mother, who moved the family to the port city of Veracruz when Galván was in his teens. In Veracruz he attended night school and became an apprentice in a carpentry workshop, where he met Manuel Almanza, who introduced him to anarcho-syndicalist and socialist ideas and was to be his lifelong intellectual and political mentor. Already active in radical labor circles, Galván joined the Mexican Revolution in 1915, fighting with the Constitutionalists at El Ébano; afterward he spent some seasons in the oil fields of the Huasteca mobilizing workers for the Casa del Obrero Mundial. It was at this time that he developed an interest in organizing *campesinos* and farm workers.

In late 1919, Galván returned to Veracruz. Inspired by the emancipatory ideals of the Russian Revolution, he and Almanza became founding members of the Veracruz chapter of the Mexican Communist Party, led by Manuel Díaz Ramírez. In 1921 they set out to establish *campesino* cooperatives in the outskirts of the city, but their first attempt—in Antón Lizardo—was not successful. Sobered by this experience and in tune with the legalist orientation of the Third

Communist International, Galván and Almazan then decided to promote the creation of Agrarian Committees, which under President Venustiano Carranza's Law of January 6, 1915, were entitled to petition for *ejido* (communal village) land grants. They would use the provisions of the agrarian code to build a strong rural organization. With the financial and political support of Veracruz's powerful urban tenants' union, a peasant organizing commission led by Ursulo Galván was formed in February 1923. For a few weeks, Galván traversed the coastal plains of central Veracruz, meeting with other *agraristas,* encouraging the creation of new local agrarian committees, and laying the groundwork for the establishment of a statewide *campesino* confederation. Despite harassment from landlords and federal troops, the trip was remarkably successful. It caught the attention of Governor Adalberto Tejeda, who embraced Galván's project. On March 23, the Liga de Comunidades Agrarias y Sindicatos Campesinos del Estado de Veracruz (LCAEV, or League of Agrarian Communities and Peasant Unions of the State of Veracruz)—a communist-led and state-financed organization—was founded. Ursulo Galván was its first president.

Colonel Tejeda saw the league and its *campesinos* as a potential source of strong political support, and was also a firm believer in the need for a broad agrarian reform. Galván saw Tejeda's government as an invaluable strategic ally, without whose backing widespread *campesino* organization would be exceedingly difficult to achieve. Both faced the staunch opposition not only from landlords and their irregular militias *(guardias blancas),* but also from Veracruz's military commander, General Guadalupe Sánchez. Out of this marriage of both principle and convenience emerged one of Mexico's strongest and most radical rural organizations. With Tejeda's active encouragement the pace of land redistribution quickened considerably in 1923–24, and again from 1929 to 1932, when Tejeda returned to office. In this process, Galván's political influence grew steadily. By the end of 1924, he was already one of Veracruz's most powerful public figures.

To defend the newly won lands from the aggressions of the *guardias blancas,* Tejeda began to arm the *agraristas,* initially commissioning them as state militia volunteers. In this way, he also was creating a loyal fighting force. The incipient militarization of the *campesinos* gave rise to strong opposition from many quarters, but it paid dividends in December 1923, when General Adolfo de la Huerta and General Sánchez in Veracruz rebelled against the government of Álvaro Obregón. Galván returned from a meeting of the Kresintern in Moscow and threw the league's support behind Tejeda and Obregón, who provided him with more weapons. With the backing of tens of thousands of *campesino* guerril-las, the rebels were defeated soundly. Galván was now also the leader of a mighty military force.

Beginning in 1924, Galván—and the Veracruz league—adopted a Marxist ideology, but although revolutionary socialism and the abolition of private property became their ultimate goals, the league's practical efforts continued to focus on the redistribution of land into *ejidos.* At the behest of the Communist Party and with the active support of Tejada, Galván also labored to establish a national *campesino* federation modeled after the Veracruz league. The Liga Nacional Campesina (LNC, or National Peasant League) was founded in November 1926, and Galván was elected its first president. Closely tied to the Communist Party, it became a national political force, but never a nation-wide peasant organization.

In 1928, Galván and Díaz Ramírez represented Mexico at the Sixth Comintern Congress in Moscow. Soon thereafter, Galván's decade-long association with the Communist Party would come to an end. When the party's bureaucracy decided to join the March 1929 revolt against President Pascual Ortiz Rubio and Plutarco Elías Calles, Galván refused to go along and was eventually expelled from the party. Instead he supported his old ally Adalberto Tejeda, who had remained loyal. As in 1923–24, the participation of Galván's *agrarista* guerrillas on the side of the government helped crush the rebellion of 1929. In the wake of these events, Galván forged an even stronger alliance with Tejeda, and the league became the political backbone of Tejeda's second administration. Galván was elected senator and mayor of Veracruz, and the *agraristas* came to dominate the state legislature.

In early 1930, at the height of his power, Galván fell ill, apparently of an old leg ailment produced by a childhood horse-riding accident. After an unsuccessful surgery, his condition worsened; he was taken to the Mayo Clinic in Minnesota, where he died on July 28, 1930. He was buried with full honors atop Jalapa's Macuiltépetl Hill. After his untimely death the league split, the guerrillas were disarmed, and the power of Veracruz's radical *agraristas* gradually waned. Ursulo Galván, the farm boy from Tlacotepec, was perhaps Mexico's most influential radical agrarian organizer.

Select Bibliography

Blanco, Sóstenes M., editor, *Ursulo Galván, 1893–1930: Su vida, su obra.* Jalapa: n.p., 1966.

Falcón, Romana, and Soledad García, *La semilla en el surco: Adalberto Tejada y el radicalismo en Veracruz, 1883–1960.* Mexico City: Colegio de México, 1986.

Salamini, Heather Folwer, *Agrarian Radicalism in Veracruz, 1920–1938.* Lincoln: University of Nebraska Press, 1978.

—EMILIO H. KOURÍ

GÁLVEZ, JOSÉ DE

1720–87 • *Visitador*

The main architect of the Bourbon Reforms in New Spain, José de Gálvez was born in the town of Macharaviaya in the southern Spanish province of Málaga in 1720. The son of a noble but impoverished family, Gálvez was forced to become a shepherd at a young age following the death of his father. It is reported that when Gálvez was around 12 years old, however, the Bishop of Málaga was so impressed by his abilities that he took him to the city of Málaga and took charge of his education. Under the bishop's sponsorship Gálvez obtained a scholarship to the seminary of San Sebastián, an institution open exclusively to the nobility. When the bishop died, Gálvez was able to find other patrons, and he began his law studies at the University of Salamanca. He finished his studies in Alcalá and subsequently moved to Madrid to practice law.

The public career of José de Gálvez began under the reign of the Bourbon monarch Carlos III. After the death of his first wife Gálvez married an upper-class French woman with excellent connections to French residents at the Spanish court. Through his wife Gálvez was able to make the acquaintance of much of the high nobility and eventually was appointed secretary to Carlos III's prime minister. In 1764 Gálvez was appointed mayor of house and court, enabling him to make the acquaintance of influential members of the Castilian court. Gálvez gained a reputation as a honorable, energetic, and learned man.

In 1765 Gálvez was appointed *visitador* (roughly, royal inspector general) of New Spain, after the king's first and second choices were unable to assume the post. Gálvez's mission was a delicate one, including the inspection of the viceroyalty's tribunals and assuming personal command of the Spanish fleet based in the Americas. Gálvez's most important mission, however, was to maximize tax and tribute remittances to Spain, as endemic warfare with England had forced the Spanish Crown to maintain a standing army in the viceroyalty and to use funds from New Spain to subsidize its colonies in the Caribbean, particularly Cuba.

Gálvez almost immediately clashed with the viceroy of New Spain, the Marquis of Cruillas, as the arrival of the *visitador* to a great extent signified a suspension of the viceroy's political power. Cruillas soon was replaced by the Marquis Carlos Francisco de Croix, who worked quite closely with Gálvez. Nonetheless, the royal *audiencia* (high court) viewed them both with hostility, and they consequently developed many enemies.

Gálvez implemented a number of important reforms in New Spain, most notably the establishment of a new sales tax code that increased royal tax revenues by 9 percent. He also increased support for the mining industry—improving supplies, obtaining a decrease in the price of mercury (an import from Spain needed for processing ore)—and established the Real Tribunal de Minería (Royal Mining Tribunal), which sought to increase production and the recovery of ores for the royal treasury. Perhaps his most famous measure was the establishment of the Real Estanco de Tobaco (Royal Tobacco Monopoly), which earned millions for the Spanish Crown. He also established royal gunpowder, saltpeter, and sulfur factories, and established a profitable viceroyal monopoly on the production and sale of playing cards.

Together with de Croix, Gálvez was a key figure in the expulsion of the Jesuits from New Spain in 1767, and he was responsible for putting down the various uprisings that followed in outlying areas of Mexico. Personally commanding troops sent against rebels in San Luis de la Paz, San Luis Potosí, Guanajuato, Valladolid, and other areas, Gálvez ordered the execution of many rebels and imprisoned many others in distant locations.

Gálvez also was the author of a far-reaching administrative reform in Mexico, dividing the viceroyalty into 11 large provinces called intendancies. The *alcaldes mayores* and *corregidores,* local administrators who purchased their offices and tended to use them to enhance their commercial ventures, were replace by intendants, Crown appointees whose increased salaries where thought to be a hedge against corruption. These reforms were not actually implemented, however, until Gálvez was appointed minister of the Indies; moreover, they first were established in other Spanish colonies and were not actually implemented in New Spain until 1786.

One of Gálvez's least successful ventures was his attempt to increase mining production in California and consolidate Spanish control over the so-called Provincias Internas of northwestern New Spain, which comprised the provinces of California, Sinaloa, Sonora, and Nueva Vizcaya. He also hoped to pacify the Seris and Pimas in Sonora and the Apaches of Chihuahua, who had been resisting Spanish rule. In 1768 Gálvez traveled to the Provincias Internas, taking with him a group of townspeople from San Luis Potosí and Guanajuato. He improved record keeping, established a provincial militia, lowered prices for mercury and gunpowder, and distributed land to the Indians, but his project of establishing new towns and pacifying the region was for the most part a failure. Gálvez suffered a nervous breakdown, taking several months to recover.

An important consequence of Gálvez's expedition to the northwest was the creation of a Comandancia General (General Command) for the Internal Provinces, which would govern the region independently of the viceroy. The Comandancia General would have supreme political and military authority over the region, and would defer to the

Audiencia of Guadalajara in judicial matters. The Comandancia General was not established until 1776, however, after Gálvez had been appointed minister of the Council of the Indies. De Croix's nephew was appointed the first commander of the region.

Gálvez concluded his *visita* in 1771, arriving in Cádiz in May 1772 to serve in the Council of the Indies, to which he had been appointed in 1765. In 1773 Gálvez was in charge of the Archive of the Indies and the General Archive of Simancas. Organizing the archive of Simancas, Gálvez also searched for documents that would support the beautification of the former viceroy of New Spain, Juan de Palafox. In 1774 Gálvez was named a member of the Junta General de Comercio, Moneda y Minas (General Junta of Trade, Currency, and Mines); he also served as superintendent of court regalia. In 1776 he was minister of the Indies; he later was named governor *pro tempore* of the Council of the Indies. In 1777 he was named governor of the council, and in 1780 he was named a member of the Council of State.

As a member of the Council of Indies, Gálvez promulgated a series of ordinances establishing free trade between Spain and its overseas possessions, abolishing the trade monopoly of the fleet system, and opening free traffic to 33 ports between Spain and the Americas. As a consequence Spanish customs receipts quadrupled. Prompted by the royal family, Gálvez helped reestablish the Royal Company of the Philippines, although the Philippine trade remained tightly regulated to protect Spanish producers. He also encouraged the slave trade with the Americas.

In 1785 Gálvez was named Marquis of Sonora and Viscount of Sinaloa. Although he was criticized for obtaining plum assignments for family members, most of them distinguished themselves on their own. Gálvez's brother Macías and Macías's son, Bernardo, were both viceroys of New Spain. His brother Miguel was named ambassador to Prussia and another brother, Antonio, field marshal in the royal navy.

Gálvez and his brother Miguel had a lifelong concern for their home province and were named aldermen for life. They both supported charitable causes in the episcopate of Málaga, and they also lobbied successfully for the creation of a Consulado y Junta de Comercio (Trade Council) in Málaga. A playing card factory was established in their birthplace, Macharaviaya, which under the royal monopoly produced cards for all of Spain's American possessions. Because of his distinguished service in Mexico, Gálvez was able to draw pensions from the Real Tribunal de Minería of New Spain as well as from the Royal Treasury of Mexico. He also was named Caballero Gran Cruz de la Real y Distinguido Orden de Carlos III.

Gálvez died in Aranjuez in 1787. Many whispered that he had been poisoned and that he had fallen out with the king, who had accused his nephew Bernardo, viceroy of New Spain, of favoring the cause of Mexican Independence.

Select Bibliography

Antolín Espino, María del Pópulo, "El Virrey Marqués de Cruillas (1760–1766)." In *Los virreyes de Nueva España en el reinado de Carlos III*, edited by José Antonio Calderón Quijano. Sevilla: Escuela de Estudios Hispano-Americanos, 1967.

Gálvez, José de, *Informe general que en virtud de real orden instruyó y entregó el Marqués de Sonora al Virrey Fray D. Antonio Bucareli y Ursua con fecha 31 de diciembre de 1771.* Mexico City: Santiago White, 1867.

_____, *Informe sobre las rebeliones populares de 1767 y otros documentos inéditos,* edited by Felipe Castro Gutiérrez. Mexico City: UNAM, 1990.

Hernández Sánchez-Barba, Mario, *La última expansión española en América.* Madrid: Instituto de Estudios Políticos, 1957.

México en el siglo XVIII. Mexico City: Secretaría de Relaciones Exteriores, 1983.

Navarro García, Luis, "El Virrey Marqués de Croix (1766–1771)." In *Los virreyes de Nueva España en el reinado de Carlos III,* edited by José Antonio Calderón Quijano. Sevilla: Escuela de Estudios Hispano-Americanos, 1967.

Pietschmann, Horst, "Consideraciones en torno al protoliberalismo, reformas borbónicas y revolución. La Nueva España en el último tercio del siglo XVIII." *Historia Mexicana* 41 (October–December 1991).

Priestly, Herbert Ingram, *José de Gálvez: Visitor General of New Spain (1765–1771).* Berkely: University of California Press, 1916.

—CLARA ELENA SUÁREZ ARGÜELLO

GAMIO, MANUEL

1883–1960 • Anthropologist and *Indigenista*

Manuel Gamio was an individual of creative intellect and by several accounts of great personal integrity, modesty, and idealism. He is linked with several innovative theoretical approaches and academic and governmental programs in the fields of Mesoamerican archaeology, indigenous rights, and international social and educational cooperation.

Although he is associated with the wave of nationalistic creativity in the arts and social sciences during the decades immediately following the Mexican Revolution, he belongs as well to a current of internationalism, especially of Pan-Americanism, that also flourished between the two world wars. Gamio was born in Mexico City in 1883. While his early accomplishments were realized in the field of Mexican archaeology, during the mid-1920s he turned his energies to a series of government positions related to indigenous rights and welfare, concerns that he pursued as director of the Instituto Indigenista Interamericano from 1942 until his death in 1960.

Gamio initially studied archaeology at the National Museum in Mexico City, where he also briefly taught and came to the attention of the American anthropologist Zelia Nuttall, who helped him get a scholarship at New York's Columbia University. While at Columbia, from 1909 to 1911, he became a student of Franz Boas and joined Boas in founding the International School of American Ethnology and Archaeology in Mexico City, of which both men subsequently became director. Returning to Mexico City in 1911, he carried out excavations at the site of San Miguel Amantla in Azcapotzalco (on the outskirts of Mexico City), where he employed the stratigraphic method for the first time in the Americas and determined the correct relative chronology among "Archaic" (now known as Preclassic or Formative), Teotihuacan, and Aztec pottery styles, thus establishing the basic archaeological sequence for central Mexico. During this period, he also carried out fieldwork at Chalchihuites, Zacatecas; at the Formative period site of Copilco in the Pedregal area of Mexico City; and at the Aztec Templo Mayor, in the center of the Mexican capital.

In 1917, Gamio became founding head of the Dirección de Antropología, within the Ministry of Agriculture and Development, the first such governmental office in the Americas. While in this position, until 1924, he was responsible for archaeological excavations, restoration, and site protection throughout the country. A notable achievement during this time was the agreement between the Mexican government and the Carnegie Institution of Washington for carrying out extensive fieldwork and restoration at the site of Chichen Itza, in Yucatán.

Gamio's principal theoretical contribution to the field of archaeology is known as the integral approach (integralidad), in which archaeological fieldwork is accompanied by multidisciplinary research in history, ecology, and social anthropology, so as to develop a holistic understanding of the culture of the present and past indigenous groups of a region. This concept was successfully applied in a study of the people and environment of the Valley of Teotihuacan, a northeast arm of the Valley of Mexico, published as La población del Valle de Teotihuacan in 1922, a monumental work that in many ways far outdistanced subsequent efforts at multidisciplinary research in Mesoamerican archaeology. The archaeological component of this project included the excavation and restoration of the extraordinary Temple of Quetzalcoatl in the heart of Teotihuacan.

Gamio's integral approach had a strong applied orientation, infused with a desire to improve the lot of the living indigenous inhabitants. In this respect it drew upon and contributed to the concept of indigenismo that became a major tenet of Mexican Revolutionary ideology. After 1925, Gamio increasingly turned away from archaeological research toward applied anthropological studies and programs intended to improve the conditions of Mexico's large indigenous population. That year he was appointed assistant secretary of public education, a position he soon resigned after publicly denouncing corruption in the ministry.

From temporary haven in the United States, he continued to pursue his concern for the rights and welfare of indigenous Mexican groups by undertaking pioneering studies of Mexican immigrants to the United States sponsored by the Social Science Research Council, later joined by the Mexican government. He discusses the results of his research, published as The Mexican Immigrant, His Life-Story (1930) and Mexican Immigration to the United States (1931), in characteristically self-critical, realistic terms. His methodologies are multifaceted and often original: extensive interviews with Mexican immigrants and Mexican-Americans in the principal regions of destination and origin in the United States and Mexico, analyses of quantitative demographic data collected from a variety of official sources, economic data ingeniously compiled from records of remittances and duty-free goods transferred back to Mexico by emigrants, and physical and cultural anthropological data, including extraordinary fragments of popular culture.

Returning to Mexico in 1929, he occupied a series of positions in several Mexican government ministries dealing with the economic conditions of the poor, indigenous, and rural population groups of Mexico, serving as chief of the Demographic Department of the Interior Ministry from 1938 to 1942. During this time he participated in a number of international social science organizations, joined international efforts to study and develop solutions to social problems, and published a collection of realistic short novels titled De vidas dolientes (On Sorrowful Lives; 1937).

In 1940, he served as vice president of the organizing committee of the First Inter-American Indigenous Congress, held in Pátzcuaro, Michoacán, which led to the creation of the Instituto Indigenista Interamericano. From his position as director of the institute, he promoted indigenous people's interests on a hemispheric scale, in part through two publications, América Indígena and the Boletín Indigenista.

Manuel Gamio is today a much-revered figure in Mexico, not least among indigenous groups and social scientists. His life is easily idealized, but numerous publications, monuments, and institutions provide convincing evidence of his real talents and accomplishments. He was clearly an individual of unusual integrity who struggled with issues that are equally significant in our times, including indigenous rights,

Mexican immigration to the United States, and the relevance of social science research to the solution of social problems.

Select Bibliography

Bernal, I., *A History of Mexican Archaeology: The Vanished Civilizations of Middle America.* New York: Thames and Hudson, 1980.

Gamio, Manuel, *Mexican Immigration to the United States.* New York: Arno Press and New York Times, 1969.
_____, *La población del Valle de Teotihuacan.* Facsimile edition, Mexico City: Instituto Nacional Indigenista, 1979.

—HARRY B. ICELAND

GANADERÍA

See Cattle Ranching

GANTE, PEDRO DE

c. 1486–1572 • Missionary

One of the first Franciscan missionaries to arrive in New Spain after the conquest of the Aztec Empire by Fernando (Hernán) Cortés, Pedro de Gante devoted his life to the conversion of the Indians in and around Mexico City–Tenochtitlan and Lake Texcoco. Gante's historical significance lies in his insistence on the importance of language acquisition for missionization and his other missionary methods, which included education in European arts and technologies as well as in Christian doctrine. Gante's lasting importance for modern Mexico, however, is largely symbolic: since the Revolution of 1910, the friar has frequently been portrayed as "the first of the great educators of the Americas," and his memory has been much used by Mexican intellectuals as a spur to greater governmental educational outreach to the native peoples of Mexico.

Pedro de Gante was born into privileged circumstances and was rumored to be the illegitimate son of Philip of Burgundy, father of the future Hapsburg emperor, Charles V. Educated first in the schools of the Brothers of the Common Life and later at the University of Louvain, Pedro de Gante long had been exposed to the broad currents of northern Christian humanism before entering the Franciscan monastery at Gante as a lay brother sometime after 1500. This background undoubtedly shaped his approach to pedagogy, with its attention to language study and its pragmatic conception of the Christian life as one balanced between intellectual pursuits and manual labor. After nearly two decades in the cloister, inspired perhaps by Cortés' *Cartas de Relación,* Gante requested permission from Charles V to emigrate to Mexico and assist in the "spiritual conquest." Gante received not only royal permission but also official encouragement from his provincial superior, Juan Clampion, and set out for New Spain with two other Flemish Franciscan friars from Gante, Juan Dekkers and Juan Van der Auwera, in 1522.

Arriving in Veracruz on August 13, 1523, Gante and his two companions settled first in the city of Texcoco on the lakeshore opposite Mexico City–Tenochtitlan in the Valley of Mexico. There the Flemings established the Colegio de San José, and it was there that Gante made his first efforts to study systematically the Nahuatl language. Gante's natural facility with Nahuatl quickly made him not only a popular Sunday preacher with the Indians, but also an interpreter much sought-after by both ecclesiastical and civil authorities. In 1524, when Dekkers and Auwera left to accompany Cortés on his ill-fated expedition to Honduras, Gante moved his *colegio* to a site adjacent to the Franciscan convent in Mexico City–Tenochtitlan. Here he undertook the education of large numbers of elite Indian youth. True to his Christian humanism, Gante divided San José's curriculum between reading, writing, and Christian doctrine on the one hand, and instruction in the manual arts (carpentry, sculpture, painting, etc.) on the other. Gante also embarked on an ambitious campaign of church building in the Indian towns around Lake Texcoco. By 1529, the friar wrote to Charles V that he had founded over 100 churches, most of which were built and largely staffed by Indian graduates from his *colegio.* In his own day, however, Gante was best known for building the Capilla de San José de los Naturales, a massive chapel contiguous to the *colegio,* which became a favorite feast-day destination for Indians and Spaniards alike.

Part of Gante's missionary effectiveness undoubtedly stemmed from his independence, both from the later groups of Spanish Franciscan missionaries (who came, predominantly, from a stricter branch of the Regular Observance) and from the secular hierarchy. Indeed, owing to their precedence, the Flemings had been specifically exempted from Spanish Franciscan control in New Spain by the Franciscan minister general, Francisco de los Angeles. This was fortunate for Gante, for the strident and urgent apocalypticism of the Franciscan Martín de Valencia and his "Twelve" accorded poorly with Gante's own Christian humanism and his gradualist approach to Christian conversion. Thus, while there seems to have been considerable tension between the Twelve and Pedro de Gante in the early years of the spiritual conquest, Gante's pedagogy and his missionary methods ultimately were recognized as effective and widely adopted by all of the missionary orders in New Spain. In addition, owing to his imperial connections, Pedro de Gante also was able to defy at times the secular hierarchy for the benefit of his Indian parishioners. When, for example, Archbishop Alonso de Montúfar moved to secularize two of Gante's churches in the Indian barrios of Mexico City as a cost-saving measure, Gante effectively checkmated this move through a letter-writing campaign to the Spanish Crown. An exasperated Montúfar would later write, "I am not archbishop of Mexico, that Franciscan lay brother, Pedro de Gante, is!"

Despite Gante's independence, his boundless energy, and his long life, the friar's educational enterprises among the Indians of Mexico City were, like most of the efforts during the first decades of the missionary work of Mexico, short-lived. As New Spain passed from its post-Conquest to its mature colonial phase, increasing proportions of the scarce colonial resources were diverted away from the Indians and toward projects favoring the emerging Spanish and criollo elites. Thus, while the University of Mexico, founded in 1555, quickly became and remained for centuries the intellectual center of the New World, such Indian educational institutions as the Colegio de San José and the ambitious Colegio de Santa Cruz de Tlatelolco were, by the time of Pedro de Gante's death in 1572, suffering from an acute lack of funding; they barely survived into the next century. Pedro de Gante's educational methods and enterprises would remain potent symbols for the future, but in the short term their impact on the colonial history of the indigenous peoples of Mexico was comparatively slight.

Select Bibliography

Chauvet, Fidel de J., editor, *Cartas de Fr. Pedro de Gante, O.F.M., primer educador de America.* Mexico City: n.p., 1947.
Chavez, E. A., *El primero de los grandes educadores de la América, fray Pedro de Gante.* Mexico City: Jus, 1943.
———, *El ambiente geográfico, histórico y social de fray Pedro de Gante, hasta el año 1523.* Mexico City: Jus, 1943.

—Brian Wilson

GARRIDO CANABAL, TOMÁS

1890–1943 • Governor

The anticlerical ideology of Garrido Canabal, one of the more remarkable governors of his time, had an impact on life in southeastern Mexico that would earn him both criticism and accolades throughout his life. He was born on September 20, 1890, in the "El Tinto" hacienda owned by his father Pío Garrido Lacroix and located in Playas de Catazajá, a remote Chiapan village on the frontier with Tabasco on the edge of a lake that dried up for six months of the year.

He studied a legal career at the Campeche Institute in the city of Campeche. His political career began in 1915 with his appointment as a *procurador de pueblos* (people's solicitor) for the Yucatán under Salvador Alvarado, state governor and military commander under orders from Venustiano Carranza. Shortly after Garrido took up the post of head of the legal department of Tabasco under Francisco J. Múgica, who had also been sent by Carranza to pacify the region.

He occupied other lesser jobs in local administration. In 1920 he was elected deputy but the appointment was annulled in favor of his nephew, José Domingo Ramírez Garrido, with whom he would have serious problems throughout his political life. These two were the main contenders for the governorship of Tabasco, a post that Tomás Garrido Canabal took on November 25, 1922, after some violent clashes. The following year the rebellion headed by Adolfo de la Huerta ousted him from the state, but he returned with even more power in June 1924 with the triumph of the Obregonistas.

His anticlerical bent had been clear when he put Bishop Pascual Díaz y Barreto on trial for having helped the rebels. In 1925 he passed the Law on Religious Observance, which decreed that there should only be one priest for each 100,000 inhabitants; churches were converted into schools and the Central League of Resistance was established in the cathedral. This latter organization was the brainchild of Felipe Carrillo during his governorship of Yucatán and was designed to involve workers and *campesinos* into his political project. In Tabasco there were as many leagues as there were professions and trades (stevedores, merchants, sweepers, lawyers, etc.), and all responded to the rallying cry of Garrido. In the same way, teachers organized themselves into the League of Atheist Teachers and became responsible for spreading the ideology of the Garridista movement. All the "leaguers" dressed in black trousers or skirts with red shirts.

This uniform was also used by the Bloc of Young Revolutionaries created in 1932, known as the Red Shirts. They took part in marches and meetings supporting the abolition of religion and educating youth about a materialist view of the world. These young people were the first generation to be educated in rationalist schools, following the precepts of the anarchist thinker Francisco Ferrer Guardia, who introduced the pedagogue José de la Luz Mena to Mexico. Schools in Tabasco took up rationalist basic principles, such as teaching in the open air, the absence of religious dogma, and coeducation, all of which were adaptations to a revolutionary ideology designed to create the "new men" that the country needed.

Supported by local intellectuals, Garrido undertook a cultural crusade that was remarkable for the time. Artists such as Virginia Fabregas and Bertha Singerman, important politicians including César Augusto Sandino, and journalists such as Luciano Kubli and Mariano Tovar all visited Tabasco. Local writers shared experiences with their compatriots disseminating the message of Garrido's work. His movement inspired memorable novels such as Graham Greene's *The Power and the Glory*, and *Las navajas* by Emmanuel Robles. The first was filmed by John Ford and the latter by Luis Buñuel under the title *Eso se llama la aurora*.

Garrido fought against vice, alcohol in particular, prohibiting its consumption and trying to put an end to its production. The Red Shirts denounced those who committed such offenses and many times took justice into their own hands. The graphic representation for propaganda purposes of a drunken priest was considered as the lowest state to which humankind could fall.

Some political advances took place in Tabasco thanks to Garrido's authoritarian legislation. Local parties were strongly rooted, especially the Tabasco Radical Socialist Party, prevailing even with the imposition of centralism, which was reinforced by the creation of the Partido Nacional Revolucionario (PNR, or National Revolutionary Party). Women voted in the municipal elections of 1934, prior to those in many other states, openly playing a role in politics and working professionally within the state machinery. They also established strong debates with other women's groups.

Tomás Garrido's strong links with successive revolutionary governments gave him the license to negotiate directly with the Southern Banana Corporation, which exported tropical fruit produced in Tabasco mainly to Galveston and New Orleans, over the commercialization of the Roatán banana. Under Garrido's regime, the production and export of bananas reached an all-time high, making Tabasco a strong competitor of Honduras and other Central American countries in the ambit of the United Fruit Company.

The political strength of Garrido as the recognized leader of the southeast was reflected in the rare event of his being elected twice as governor of Tabasco. The second term (1930–34) was the result of the constitutional reform that allowed for Obregón's reelection as president, a post that he was unable to take up because of his assassination.

If Garrido's relations with Plutarco Elías Calles were also excellent, this was not the case with Lázaro Cárdenas. During his visit to Tabasco in 1934 as presidential candidate of the PNR, Cárdenas paid tribute to Garrido by calling Tabasco "the laboratory of the Mexican Revolution." When he became president he nominated Garrido secretary of agriculture in his first cabinet, only to make him renounce the post in June 1935 with other Calles supporters. Clashes between his followers and enemies resulted in several assassinations and obliged Garrido to leave the country for exile in Costa Rica, only returning to Mexico a year before his death in 1943. Three years after he had left Tabasco, the churches reopened their doors, making his state the last to drop the religious embargo. Various churches had been demolished during the period of persecution, but they were of relatively minimal artistic value, the result of the limited influence of the church during the colonial period. Despite his anticlerical excesses, Garrido is considered as the founder of modern Tabasco by laying the foundations of economic development, showing the people the potential of their agricultural and livestock resources.

Select Bibliography

Caparroso, Amado Alfonso, *Tal cual fue Tomás Garrido Canabal.* Mexico City: Editorial Libros de México, 1985.

Martínez Assad, Carlos, *El laboratorio de la revolución: El Tabasco garridista.* Mexico City: Siglo XXI, 1979.

_____, *Los lunes rojos: La educación racionalista en México.* Mexico City: SEP cultura/Ediciones el caballito, 1986.

—CARLOS MARTÍNEZ ASSAD

GARRO, ELENA

1920– • Prose Writer and Dramatist

Elena Garro was born in Puebla, Mexico, on December 20, 1920. She began her writing career as a journalist; subsequently she has written novels, short stories, and plays. Her first novel *Los recuerdos del porvenir* (1963), which is also the first work she wrote, is undoubtedly her most important contribution to Spanish American letters in general, and to Mexican fiction in particular.

Garro's work explores the magical and the fantastic as they coexist with objective dimensions of reality. In her early works—*Los recuerdos del porvenir* and the short stories of *La semana de colores* (1964)—the pre-Columbian Mexican tradition, especially its conception of cyclical time, contributes to the creation of worlds that weave magic and myth with history. In her later novels—*Testimonios sobre Mariana* (1981) and *La casa junto al río* (1983)—the fantastic replaces myth, creating as in her earlier fiction, eccentric worlds characterized by the rupture of unity and the prevalence of multivalence. The ambiguity of her fictive worlds is underscored by the way in which surreal events are presented as if they were an integral part of ordinary or common experience.

Her treatment of time is one of the primary elements contributing to such diffuseness. The characters in several short stories of *La semana de colores*, for example, may simultaneously exist in two historical periods. Thus, in "La culpa es de los tlaxcaltecas," the protagonist escapes an unhappy and oppressive marriage to join her imaginary Aztec lover in a remote past. The characters of "El día que fuimos perros" live in "one day that has two days inside." *Los recuerdos del porvenir* is, however, the work that most decisively questions the linearity of time. Its characters experience multiple chronologies: the time of history corresponding to the Cristero War of the late 1920s, which submits the inhabitants of Ixtepec to the indiscriminate violence of the invading army; the time of a forever-lost Indian past that places the town "in a dimension of reality that remains still;" the timelessness of mythical time as experienced by Julia, the evasive lover of General Rosas, and Hurtado, the outsider who rescues her after introducing the Moncada siblings to poetry and the realm of the imaginary; finally, the subjective time of the Moncadas, who experience "a new and melancholic time where gestures and voices begin to move in the past."

Felipe Ángeles (1979) and *Y Matarazo no llamó* (1991), much like *Los recuerdos del porvenir*, criticize the arbitrariness and opportunism of political power. *Felipe Ángeles*, a "documentary-drama," recreates the farcical trial of one of the greatest—albeit forgotten—heroes of the Mexican Revolution. General Ángeles was a salient strategist and diplomat whose intelligence and integrity were feared by his military peers and political rivals. Forced into self-imposed exile, he returned to Mexico in 1919 only to be accused of treason by

the forces of Venustiano Carranza and shot later that year. The play exposes the violation of his rights to due process and bitterly criticizes the military leaders who sacrifice the Revolutionary ideals and the best individuals among them in their lust for power.

The main characters of her thriller *Y Matarazo no llamó,* which is probably her least successful novel, reveal the plight of two ordinary citizens who aid a group of workers on strike. Victims of their naïveté, they are used by the political forces on the left and singled out as scapegoats by security forces faced with increasing social unrest. Both characters are accused of committing crimes of which they are innocent. Appearances, however, prevent them from claiming their innocence, and they ultimately pay with their lives.

Some of her works of fiction, *La casa junto al río, Testimonios sobre Mariana, Reencuentro de personajes* (1981), and the short stories of *Andamos huyendo Lola* (1980) refer more specifically to the situation of women who despite their efforts often fail to find a space for themselves in a male-dominated society. Both Mariana, the main character of *Testimonios sobre Mariana,* and Verónica, of *Reencuentro de personajes,* are destroyed by their male counterparts. The principal objective of Mariana's husband, a brilliant young Mexican anthropologist, is to punish his wife for her silent but firm resistance to his overpowering personality. He submits her to physical, verbal, and psychological abuse, constantly humiliating and harassing her in public. Verónica, on the other hand, becomes entangled in a sadomasochistic relationship with a bisexual man who reduces her to passivity by means of constant harassment, verbal abuse, and persecution.

The female characters of *Andamos huyendo Lola* suffer the effects of political forces and exclusionary government policies. Most of them are women in exile escaping persecution in their countries of origin, but unable to find a living space abroad. Unable to return to their homelands, they become the victims of poverty, isolation, and uprootedness in foreign lands.

La casa junto al río tells the story of a Mexican woman who returns after her father's death to his hometown in Asturias, hoping to renew the family ties severed by the civil war. She encounters, however, the hostility of the locals, understanding too late that her relatives will kill her in order to lay claim to her sizable inheritance, the existence of which she ignored. As with most of her other women characters, Consuelo is unaided in her struggle against forces that will ultimately defeat her.

Garro's works are best understood and fully appreciated in a thorough consideration of their technical and stylistic sophistication. Her fiction, especially *Los recuerdos del por-*

venir, *Testimonios sobre Mariana,* and the short stories of *La semana de colores,* are central to the understanding of the development of contemporary Mexican fiction in general, and of Mexican women's writing in particular.

Select Bibliography

Anderson, Robert K., "Myth and Archetype in Recollections of Things to Come." *Studies in Twentieth Century Literature* 9:2 (1985).

Balderston, Daniel, "The New Historical Novel: History and Fantasy in *Los recuerdos del porvenir.*" *Bulletin of Hispanic Studies* 66 (1989).

Callan, Richard J., "Analytical Psychology and Garro's *Los Pilares de doña Blanca.*" *Latin American Theatre Review* 16:2 (1983).

Cypress, Sandra Messinger, "Visual and Verbal Distances in the Mexican Theatre: the Plays of Elena Garro." In *Woman as Myth and Metaphor in Latin American Literature,* edited by Naomi Lindstrom and Carmelo Virgillo. Columbia: University of Missouri Press, 1985.

Dauster, Frank N., "Elena Garro y sus 'Recuerdos del porvenir.'" *Journal of Spanish Studies: Twentieth Century* 8:1–2 (1980).

Galvín, Delia V., *La ficción reciente de Elena Garro, 1979–1983.* Querétaro: Universidad Autónoma de Querétaro, 1988.

Kaminsky, Amy, *Reading the Body Politic.* Minneapolis: University of Minnesota Press, 1993.

Meyer, Doris, "Alienation and Escape in Elena Garro's *La semana de colores.*" *Hispanic Review* 55 (1987).

Mora, Gabriela, "A Thematic Exploration of the Works of Elena Garro." In *Latin American Women Writers Yesterday and Today,* edited by Yvette Miller and Charles Tatum. Pittsburgh: Latin American Review Press, 1977.

Rubio, Patricia, "Functiones del nivel descriptivo en *Los recuerdos del porvenir.*" *Cahiers du Monde Hispanique et Luso-Brésilien* 49 (1987).

Stoll, Anita, editor, *A Different Reality: Essays on the World of Elena Garro.* Lewisburg, Pennsylvania: Bucknell University Press, 1990.

Taylor, Kathy, *The New Narrative of Mexico.* Lewisburg, Pennsylvania: Bucknell University, Press, and London: Associated University Presses, 1994.

—Patricia Rubio

GARZA, CATARINO (CATO)

1859–95 • Guerrilla

Catarino Garza, also known as Cato, was a Mexican political firebrand active on both sides of the lower Rio Grande valley who in the early 1890s declared war on the Porfirian regime that ruled his country. For more than a year he led forays into his homeland, futilely endeavoring to incite a general rebellion. While the Mexican army contained his sorties on its side of the river, American military units and a variety of law enforcement outfits pursued him in the dense chaparral and among his protective sympathizers on U.S. soil. Although his revolution finally petered out, authorities never caught up with their quarry.

Garza was a remarkable visionary. Born in 1859 into a family of some social standing in the border town of Matamoros, like most other locals he crisscrossed the Rio Grande at whim and in the early 1880s worked for a sewing machine company in Brownsville, Texas, the town where he also married a Tejana-Mexicana. He displayed an early taste for political combativeness, writing articles for newspapers that decried the discrimination perpetrated by Anglos (as well as authorities of Mexican descent) against Hispanics in the district. He soon divorced and traveled to St. Louis, where he fell in with radical liberals agitating for civil rights and human dignity among all mankind. By the mid-1880s, however, Garza was back in the Rio Grande valley as a journalist more strident than ever in his demands for equality and fairness for everyone.

Both Catarino Garza's published writings and the letters he penned to his new fiancee, the daughter of a prominent rancher from Palito Blanco, Texas, were couched in the soaring romantic rhetoric of his day. His sharp exchanges with local authorities naturally led to animosities and violence. In one dispute, Garza was shot in the jaw by an irate deputy sheriff.

As much as he disdained the boss-ridden politics on the U.S. side of the river, he detested the authoritarian dictatorship of Porfirio Díaz in Mexico. He was certain that many Mexicans felt his own contempt for the regime and would rally to overpower it. On September 15, 1891, as Mexicans commemorated their Independence from Spain, Garza crossed the Rio Grande with 38 armed followers and proclaimed revolution against Porfirian rule. Garza received underground support from powerful resources in Mexico—wealthy hacendados, disaffected generals, elements of the Roman Catholic hierarchy—as well as neighboring Hispanics (and perhaps some avaricious American capitalists) but could not induce a general rebellion.

His main antagonist on the U.S. side was the arrogant Cavalry Captain John J. Bourke, who had ridden against Geronimo and in more tranquil moments had proved himself to be an able anthropologist. His job was to prevent insurgents from mounting an attack from U.S. soil against a friendly power, Mexico. As the American public followed the chase through newspapers with an audible applause for the underdog (Garza), Bourke stewed in his frustrations, which he reported in detail to his superiors. Still the military steadily chipped away at Garza's forces and his support group, rendering the Cato's position untenable. Therefore he fled to South America to continue his crusade. Fighting for liberals who aimed to seize government control in Colombia, he was killed attacking a military post in 1895.

In overview, Garza numbered among the *revoltosos*—border rebels, often radical liberals—who yearned for a semblance of democracy in Porfirian Mexico. Their guerrilla-like endeavors culminated in the Revolution of 1910. But

Catarino Garza's vision of justice was much more ethereal than that of his fellow revolutionaries. It flamed through trodden Mexican and Mexican American communities along the U.S. side of the southern Rio Grande and then through much of Latin America to all humanity.

Select Bibliography

Garza Guajarado, Celso, *El Busca de Catarino Garza, 1859–1895.* Monterrey: Universidad Autónoma de Nuevo León, 1989.

—PAUL J. VANDERWOOD

GATT

See General Agreement on Tariffs and Trade (GATT)

GENDER

This entry includes four articles that discuss the social construction of gender and sexuality:

Gender: Mesoamerican
Gender: Colonial
Gender: 1821–1910
Gender: 1910–96

See also Eugenics; Family and Kinship; Feminism; Gender and Mexican Spanish; Homosexuality; Limpieza de Sangre; Llorona, La; Malinche and Malinchismo; Narrative and National Identity, 1910–96; Women's Status and Occupation

GENDER: MESOAMERICAN

Scholars have only recently begun to ask serious questions about Mesoamerican gender and sexuality, and the answers, so far, have been few and, often, tentative. To date, our best data pertain to two groups: (1) the Postclassic period (A.D. 900–1521) Yucatec Maya speakers of the Yucatán Peninsula in Mexico, for whom our best source is Bishop Diego de Landa's *Relación de la las cosas de Yucatán,* written around 1566, and (2) the very late Postclassic (1300–1521) Nahuatl speakers (Nahuas, or Mexica-Aztecs) of central Mexico, for whom we depend heavily on the Franciscan Bernardino de Sahagún. Sahagún left us a number of important texts written over the span of his missionizing career in New Spain, but the

richest by far on the subject of Nahua sexuality is his illustrated Nahuatl text known as the *Florentine Codex (Códice florentino),* completed during the 1570s. Most studies of Mesoamerican gender and sexuality accordingly have focused on the Yucatec Maya and the Nahua, and what follows is largely based on what we currently can say about them.

With so many Mesoamericans' notions of gender and sexual practices so poorly understood, it is dangerous to generalize extensively about the area, whether over time or across space. On the basis of colonial writings about native beliefs and behavior, however, it is probably fair to say that, throughout much of Mesoamerica, at least at the time of the

Spanish Conquest in the early sixteenth century, sex was viewed as a highly positive force when practiced in moderation. Among the Nahua, sex was a gift of the gods and one of the pleasures of life; not to use it, and not to use it wisely, was to offend the gods and evoke their displeasure. Improper sexual conduct, as well as sexual inactivity, consequently brought on disease in humans and animals and had the potential to adversely affect the rest of nature, as well. Accordingly, certain illnesses and natural calamities were attributed to sexual improprieties. The goal of successful living was therefore to attain a state of equilibrium between too much and too little sex, between sex that was morally and socially acceptable, and sex that was not.

Nahuas believed that the moral attributes of sex and affection were seated in the heart, while sexual desire and passion were rooted in the liver. Sexual transgression, however, was referred to as "filth" and appears to have been identified, both metaphorically and physiologically, with excrement. For this reason, repentant sexual offenders are occasionally depicted in Mesoamerican pictorial manuscripts eating their own excrement. The Nahua adopted a Huastec goddess of sexuality whom they called Tlazolteotl (Filth Goddess), as well as Tlaelquani (Eater of Filth); she was said to "eat" the sexual sins of those who confessed to her. Accordingly, she sometimes appears in manuscript paintings with excrement in her hand or on her nose. The Nahua associated Tlazolteotl with lust and other forms of illicit sex, as well as with conception, pregnancy, childbirth, midwifery, and the moon. As a goddess of childbirth, she rivaled another goddess named Cihuacoatl (Snake-Woman), to whom midwives and women in labor addressed their petitions. Tlazolteotl and Cihuacoatl's Yucatec Maya counterparts included the moon goddesses of childbirth, Ix-Chel and Chac-Chel, known to scholars as Goddesses I and O. Their cults, like those of the Nahua goddesses, were predominantly tended by women. Ix-Chel sometimes appeared as a young goddess; when she did, she had associations that partially paralleled those of a Nahua goddess named Xochiquetzal (Precious Flower), who presided over erotic love, prostitution, and adultery.

Among the Nahua, moral and social equilibrium was thought to be attainable through the close collaboration of men and women who, as complementary opposites, must work together if they are to have a full and productive life. This belief reflected the fact that, throughout Mesoamerica, the basic social unit was the married couple and its offspring, among whom labor was divided primarily on the basis of gender. Because the notion of sexual complementarity was so fundamental to the Nahua economy, the natural and supernatural realms also tended to be conceptualized in terms of male-female gender relations. Deities, for example, were typically defined as male-female pairs whose relationships were familial—that is, certain deities were the offspring of older deities and the spouse, parent, or sibling of others. All Nahua supernaturals were said to have descended from an apparently bisexual dual creator god called Ometeotl (God Two),

who at times took the form of a primordial couple whose names were Ometecuhtli (Two Lord), and Omecacihuatl (Two Lady).

The Mesoamerican cosmos was itself divided into a male upper half, which represented the sky, and a watery female underworld below the earth's surface. Even time and the seasons were gendered; for example, the summer rainy season, like nighttime, was typically female, while the dry winter, like daytime, was male. At the points and periods of interface of these divisions, however, gender distinctions tended to blur and destabilize. The surface of the earth, which separates the skies from the underworld, was sometimes identified as female, at other times as male, while bisexuality, asexuality, and even homosexuality often characterized periods of temporal transition and liminality. Gender categories, in other words, were not sharply divided, but rather graded and, to some degree, overlapping, and neither the male nor the female gender predominated in the areas that both joined and separated them. Thus, while it is accurate to say that Mesoamericans conceived of their world primarily in terms of two complementary genders, male and female, it is not accurate to say that they recognized only two gender categories.

The understanding that gender is capable of shifting and changing under certain conditions appears to have affected Mesoamerican patterns of childrearing. Although Nahuatl words for children do not differentiate sex prior to adolescence, the Nahua apparently quickly assigned a gender to infants, presumably on the basis of the baby's visible sexual organs. Evidence of this appears in a statement by Sahagún to the effect that an infant boy's umbilical cord was buried on the battlefield as a sign of his future military obligations to the state, while an infant girl's umbilical cord was buried at home by the family hearth. In the post-Conquest *Codex Mendoza* illustration of an elderly Nahua midwife preparing to bathe a newborn, we see, above the bath water, the darts and shield emblematic of the strictly male role of warrior, while below are quintessentially female domestic implements: a broom, a spindle, and a woven reed box to hold weaving tools. It appears from this that a (possibly miniature) set of the appropriate instruments was presented to the newborn as a sign of its gender. The same manuscript also makes it clear that children were taught to use such gender-appropriate tools by the age of four. So closely was gender identity associated with occupation that Nahua parents tried to prevent their sons from so much as touching a woman's weaving tool lest they become effeminate. The impression we get is that parents perceived the gender of young children to be somewhat ambiguous and potentially unstable, leading them to assign a gender to them at the first opportunity and then reinforce it by inculcating gender-specific behavioral norms.

The *Codex Mendoza* illustration may depict a formal baptism, since we know that the Nahua ritually bathed their children soon after birth to remove impurities. From that point until they reached adolescence, children remained the-oretically pure, apparently because they were perceived as devoid of sexual desire. At its baptismal ceremony, a Nahua infant received the first of several names to be used until puberty, when a new name was bestowed. Both girls and boys were allowed to run completely naked until that time. According to Landa, Yucatec children also went without clothes until the age of four or five, but at that time were given a cloak for sleeping and "some little strips to conceal their nakedness." Since Yucatec children, like Nahua chil-dren, were weaned at age four, this award of clothing may have marked the Maya child's first phase of independence from its mother. Young Yucatec Maya girls also began to wear a small shell over their private parts, while a small white stone was attached to the top of the heads of little boys. These gender markers were ritually removed during formal puberty rites that, in Yucatán, took place when the child was around twelve years of age. Their removal signified that the child was of marriageable age and was accompanied by assumption of sexually appropriate clothing, as well as a new, family name.

Little is said in colonial texts about menstruation, but Nahuatl terms for it suggest that it was viewed as an illness or infirmity. There is no evidence that it was perceived as a period of impurity, although menstruating women, like preg-nant and nursing women, were thought to have the power to harm children just by looking at them. Unlike the Yucatec, the Nahua do not appear to have held puberty rites per se. Sahagún tells us that very young Nahua children were taken to the ceremonial precinct to be formally dedicated to the particular temple they would later serve. The pact was sealed with small cuts made, in the case of boys, in the lower lip, where a lip jewel eventually would be placed, and, in the case of girls, on the breasts and hips. Apparently, the child did not perform this religious service until puberty, when he or she left home to attend school in the temple precinct. By this time, Nahua children were wearing the clothing appropriate to their gender and were kept strictly segregated by sex. Boys in the *telpochcalli,* or military school largely attended by commoners, were permitted sexual liberties with prostitutes during off hours, but noble youths at the *calmecac,* where boys were trained for government posts and the priesthood, were, like all unmarried girls, required to remain chaste.

Adolescent Maya boys in Yucatán kept largely to them-selves and away from married people. They marked their sta-tus by painting their bodies black. Although they may not have attended schools per se, we are told that each town had a special building where unmarried boys could congregate, amuse themselves, and sleep. Access to women was largely denied these youths, since Yucatec girls, like their Nahua counterparts, were expected to remain virgins until marriage. Maya girls, in fact, could not so much as look directly or laugh at a man, and they ate apart from men, as well. Unmarried Maya boys, like Nahua boys in the *telpochcalli,* were permitted, however, to take advantage of what Landa calls "public women."

Among the Nahua, all terms for people ranging from adolescence through advanced maturity belonged to either the male or female gender; some words for an elderly person did not specify sex. For example, although the word for great grandfather differed from that for great grandmother, the word *mintontli* signified both great-great-grandfather and great-great-grandmother. This suggests that the gender of very elderly people, like that of children, was perceived to shift somewhat toward the point where the two genders overlap, a perception that has parallels in other cultures. Indeed, although the elderly were generally respected, and elderly women, at least, were characterized as perpetually hungry for sex, very old people were seen as capable of becoming like children again. It is probably because their gender at this stage of life was ambiguous that some very elderly Nahua women went about naked from the waist up. Younger Nahua women, in contrast, never exposed their breasts in public, for to do so would have been regarded as the height of immodesty.

Thus, the last phase of the life cycle, like childhood, was perceived as relatively asexual and, in terms of gender identity, unstable. But adolescence, too, was problematic, since Nahuas feared that young people in the flush of puberty might become sexually destructive, even deviant. The Nahuatl word for young woman, like that for young man, referred directly to the physical changes that marked the beginnings of sexual maturity: *ichpochtli* means "she of the dark down," *telpochtli* "he of the dark protuberance." Thus, at puberty gender identity was directly correlated with the changed appearance of the genitalia, and social normalcy depended on genitals that were either distinctly male or dis-tinctly female. Parents must have closely watched the physio-logical and behavioral changes taking place in their adolescent children, fearing that their children might not develop along an exclusively male or female line. Like the present-day Tzutujil Maya, pre-Hispanic peoples may have associated immaturity with bisexuality that must be trans-formed into masculinity in the case of men and femininity in the case of women in order for two people to marry.

In a culture where the notion of dual but complemen-tary genders structured both thought and behavior, people whose physiology or behavior placed them outside the norm for either sex posed a social as well as conceptual problem. Indeed, among the Nahua, hermaphrodites, rather than being perceived as a third sex, were apparently perceived as les-bians, since Sahagún's informants described them as women with penises. Both lesbianism and male homosexuality were generally abhorred, and homosexuals, like prostitutes and adulterers, were classified as "dead" and "inhuman." Like sex-ual profligacy and adultery, homosexuality could bring on sickness and social mayhem. The Nahuatl word *cocoxqui,* for example, means both ill and sodomitical or effeminate. Les-bians and passive homosexuals, like transvestites of either gender, were punished with death; by one account a passive was executed by removing his intestines through his anus. On the battlefield, accusations of homosexuality served both to demean and hopefully demoralize the enemy, much as impotence was associated with military defeat. There is some artistic evidence in the form of clay and stone statues of men wearing the flayed skins of sacrificed war captives that, from early times until the Conquest, defeated enemies were castrated and thus deprived of their sexual potency and identity.

This is not to say that there were no instances of sanctioned homosexuality; indeed there are several reports of young men in the Nahua priesthood who were permanently transvested and who may have served older priests in a homosexual capacity. Moreover, the second most important official in the Nahua capital, the *cihuacoatl,* took his title and his ritual costume from a goddess, appearing "in drag" on certain state occasions. In Nahua ideology, however, as among the Maya, homosexuality in general was identified as corrupt and dangerous and was associated with darkness, disorder, unpredictability, instability, and disease. For the average person, it was to be avoided at all costs.

Women who possessed certain traits normally seen and admired in men could, on the other hand, be valorized. Such a woman was said to have a "virile heart" and was likely to be referred to as a "manly woman." Similarly, a Nahua ruler urged his daughter to behave well by pretending to be a valiant warrior, promising that "you will be esteemed as if you were in the halls of those who through their exploits in war merited honor, you will assume the shield like the good soldiers." The comparisons extended to the woman's body, as well; for example, a woman's buttocks and genital region were a metaphorical "shield" that both protected her husband and accepted his "arrows." Presumably, in pre-Hispanic times, as among many Mesoamerican groups today, breast milk was equated with semen. A woman's weaving batten, moreover, was described as her "sword," while her domestic tasks of cooking and sweeping, like the act of childbirth itself, were likened to—indeed described as—acts of war. Sahagún tells us that a woman having a difficult labor was urged to "seize well the little shield, to be a brave woman." Once the baby was delivered, the midwife shouted war cries signifying that the mother "had fought a good battle, had become a brave warrior, had taken a captive, had captured a baby."

This suggests that, among the Nahua at least, success and virtue tended to be defined in male terms, in keeping with an ideology of male dominance in which virility epitomized that which was desirable. In Yucatán, on the other hand, women apparently were perceived as unclean. With few exceptions, Yucatec women were excluded from blood letting rites and from entering temples. According to one report, the only woman present when the gods were being honored was a virgin who made the bread (tamales) used as offerings, although Landa mentions some "old women" who entered the temple to dance during certain festivals. Only water brought from woods that had never been entered by a woman could be used to purify sacred paraphernalia. Although Nahua women performed autosacrifice right along with men, similar restrictions regarding temple admittance

applied to Nahua priestesses. Whether or not any or all of these practices reflect a belief that females represented the lesser of the two genders is controversial, but it is clear that among the Nahua "manly" women enjoyed high social status within the same system that ridiculed and demoted effeminate men.

Male military values were specifically used to channel and control the reproductive powers of Nahua women. In a society where descent was traced through both the maternal and paternal lines, and where lineage was prerequisite to a man's social rank and political office, it was necessary for men to know for certain that the children their wives bore were their own. While youths of both sexes were cautioned that sex before marriage would stunt their growth and intelligence, as well as bring on serious illness, violations on the part of young women, at least those of the upper class, were severely punished. An intact hymen was metaphorically referred to as a "jewel," and a bride who did not have one on the night of her wedding was likely to be repudiated by her husband, as well as certain to live thereafter in disgrace. It is possible that masturbation was tolerated among the unmarried to help prevent premature sexual intercourse, since we are told that Moteuczoma II's concubines masturbated when he was absent. The likelihood is strengthened by the fact that retention of semen was thought to harm men. The challenge for unmarried men, then, was to find an acceptable way to balance the periodic need of sexual release with the dictates of a moral code that demanded complete chastity prior to marriage.

As mentioned earlier, some male youths in both Nahua and Yucatec Maya society solved this problem by consorting with women who made a profession of selling their bodies. Among the Maya, these women seem to have had little social status and a hard life; Landa states that they often were used by so many men at one time that they sometimes actually died. The status of Nahua "pleasure women," as Sahagún liked to refer to them, is more complicated, since there were apparently several classes of what the Spaniards unilaterally regarded as "prostitutes." The friar speaks of a group of these women who, during certain month festivals, danced publicly with high-ranking warriors and nobles and, for a fee, spent the night with them as well. He describes them as courtesans and says that they were beautifully dressed, being "the best ones, the chosen ones, those set apart." The fees for their services were paid to both them and their "matrons," who kept guard over them at the Cuicacalli, or "House of Song." Since the Cuicacalli was located near the main temple in the ceremonial precinct of the capital, where it served as a school or training ground for court singers, dancers, and musicians, it would appear that these women were professional entertainers whose services extended to the sexual realm and that they enjoyed a relatively high status in Nahua society.

The average Nahua prostitute, or *auiani,* however, lived in the streets or, as the Nahua who lived in the capital, which was laced with canals, liked to put it, "on the water." Sahagún's native informants characterized such a woman as restless, brazen, vain, merry, gum-chewing, drunk, and fond of hallucinogens, a woman with "itching buttocks" and a damaged heart. Lazy and careless as well, she was, at least theoretically, in danger of being sold into slavery and eventually sacrificed, and it is quite possible that some prostitutes met just this fate. Among the nobility, we are told, all prostitution was punishable by death. Nahua princesses were admonished to work hard and avoid vain behavior lest they be compared to, or worse yet become, prostitutes.

At least some prostitutes were managed by older women who procured customers for them. These procuresses apparently were detested, at least in colonial times, when they were said to be possessed by demons and, like their clients, were described as dead and inhuman. A special group of women called *mociuaquetzque* (valiant women) reportedly accompanied Nahua warriors into battle, where they provided them with moral support and probably tended to their sexual needs, at times actually joining in the fighting. Their relation to urban prostitutes is uncertain. In any event, they probably primarily, if not exclusively, serviced commoner men, since men of the nobility were supposed to stay away from prostitutes. The *Florentine Codex* includes a ruler's admonishment to his son not to eat or drink anything given him by a prostitute because it would cause a man "to discharge his fluid" and thus become "dried up." If he copulates with a prostitute more than several times within a short period of time, he will quickly die. The scholar Margaret Arvey has suggested that such characterizations of the *auiani* as evil, dangerous, and corrupt reflect a Spanish, rather than native, moral code, but Alfredo López Austin disagrees. According to López Austin, the earliest colonial sources are uniform on the subject of illicit sex and discuss it in strictly Nahua terms.

Since it was just as dangerous for a noble youth to have intercourse with prostitutes as to have premarital relations with someone of his own station or to refrain from sexual activity altogether (except for short periods of ritual abstinence), it followed that he should consider marriage at the earliest opportunity. The same held true for young women of all social classes since they, too, were required to remain chaste until marriage. Throughout Mesoamerica, moreover, celibacy was socially condemned. Both Nahua and Yucatec young people, however, reportedly did not marry until age 20. In Yucatán, fathers sometimes contracted a marriage for a child while it was still prepubescent, waiting until later to fulfill the vow. In the case of a son, the father carefully chose the mate by himself, but for a daughter, he hired a matchmaker. In Yucatán, as in central Mexico, these matchmakers were elderly women, and in both places children were bound by their parents' decision.

Yucatec girls brought to the marriage small dowries, but the groom was expected to move in with her and her parents and to work for his father-in-law for five or six years. In central Mexico, in contrast, in addition to their parents' consent, boys had to request permission to marry from the elder in charge of their school; apparently they could move

in with either family. Nahua couples also had to make sure to choose a wedding date that was propitious, for the purpose of which they consulted a diviner. Once married, their names were recorded in a register kept by state officials, a practice that directly reflects the state's interest in controlling human reproduction.

In central Mexico, a couple could not have the same day sign in their calendrical name, which was the official date of their birth. In Yucatán, on the other hand, one could not marry someone with the same family name on the father's side. In both cultures, people were prohibited from marrying their in-laws, stepparents, and maternal aunts (if men) or paternal uncles (if women), and incest was punishable by death. Nahua nobles often married their daughters to leading men of other polities in order to effect strategic political alliances, whereas commoners tended to marry within their own residential district and kin group. Widowers in both the Maya and Nahua areas, like those who had divorced, could remarry, with Nahua widows customarily marrying their brother-in-law. In central Mexico, divorce was frowned upon, but Landa complained that in Yucatán it was common and easy to obtain. Maya daughters tended to go with the mother, while the sons went with the father.

Landa insists that Yucatec men never had more than one wife at a time, but it is likely that leading Maya men had female slaves who served them as concubines. In central Mexico, polygyny was prohibited among commoners but was typical of men of noble birth and apparently an option for commoner men who had distinguished themselves in battle. Nahua rulers had numerous wives, but only one, typically the first, could bear him legitimate children. A ruler's sexual prowess was tied ideologically to the efficacy of his rule, the idea being that the more active he was sexually, the better off would be his people. His sexual potency was thought to directly affect—and reflect—the valor of his army and to aid him in controlling nature, specifically rainfall and the growth of crops. For this reason, Moteuczoma II reportedly was given aphrodisiacs. Conversely, illicit sexual relations could drain a Nahua ruler's energy and valor, causing his kingdom serious damage. Similar beliefs seem to have circulated in the Maya area. A Quiche Maya history, for example, tells of three Quiche chiefs who successfully avoided a trap set for them by their enemy in the form of three beautiful young women.

Married couples viewed having children as a social as well as personal responsibility, since reproduction was an obligation to the state, as well as an asset to the family. Not only was infant mortality probably high, but younger children were needed to help at home while their fathers and older brothers were away at war. Sterility, like the loss of a child, was therefore greatly lamented among the Nahua and was just cause for a man to divorce his wife, since the woman always was held responsible for childlessness. We know that both contraception and abortion were practiced, but only abortion is known to have been punished. Women who had an abortion were reportedly killed, along with the doctor who had assisted them. It is unclear if this penalty applied to unmarried women and prostitutes, the latter a group who often resorted to abortion.

As one would expect, adultery was regarded as one of the gravest of crimes among both the Nahua and the Yucatec Maya. Governments clearly bore some responsibility for such behavior, since a Yucatec Maya text, the *Chilam Balam* of Tizimin, tells of a ruler who destroyed his people by allowing them to commit adultery. Accordingly, illegitimate children had very low social status. Nahua princesses were warned against promiscuity in married life by their parents, who showed concern that such behavior would disgrace the line. The typical Nahua sentence for adultery, as for rape, was death. Adulterers were executed by dragging or stoning, whereas the Yucatec Maya tore out the offender's entrails through the navel. At one time this practice probably was more widespread than it was just prior to the Conquest, since we see deities removing the intestines of sexual offenders through the navel in several pre-Hispanic painted manuscripts from south-central Mexico. Although the miscreants in these paintings are apparently all male, we know that the Nahua punished both of the offending parties.

A married Nahua man who committed adultery with an unmarried woman, on the other hand, was not considered an adulterer and was not officially punished. Instead he, like other profligates, was subject to physical deterioration and illness. Because illness was attributed to immoral acts, ailing Nahuas, like Yucatecans who were sick or dying, were encouraged to confess their sexual transgressions. To do so, it was believed, might save them. Similarly, a woman in danger of dying in childbirth was urged to confess her adulteries, and if she died anyway, it was said that she had not revealed all of them. If she had died giving birth to her first child, she joined a group of female spirits called the Cihuateteo, or Cihuapipiltin, "The Holy Women," or "Little Princesses," who likewise had died in their first childbirth. The Cihuateteo were said to incite adulterers on earth, presumably because they themselves had been adulteresses.

Both Nahua and Yucatecan women petitioned goddesses for help in conceiving a child, and Yucatec women even placed small statues of Ix-Chel under their beds in the hope of gaining her assistance. At the time of the Conquest, Maya women desirous of children traveled in numbers to the island of Cozumel, where there was a popular shrine to Ix-Chel. Apparently she, like Nahua fertility goddesses, could help ensure conception, a healthy pregnancy, and a safe delivery. Exactly how the Maya thought a child was conceived is unknown. Among the Nahua, it was said that children were a gift from the dual creator god Ometeotl, who breathed life into them from his/her residence in the highest layer of the heavens. A depiction of Tlazolteotl giving birth in the post-Conquest Nahua painted manuscript known as *Codex Borbonicus* shows the infant twice, once emerging fully dressed from the birth canal and once, naked, above the goddess's head. Tiny footprints leading from the top of the page to this second infant indicate that the baby's "life force," if not the baby itself, had descended into the goddess's body from above.

Popular wisdom held it, however, that a child was conceived from semen that had accumulated in the womb over the course of several copulations. Although it was thought that not all of the semen need come from the same father, married couples who wanted a child felt it necessary to have sexual relations with each other on a frequent basis. They did so until the fetus was well formed and the mother-to-be had begun to "show." At that point, relations were supposed to cease, since additional semen could cause the child to adhere to the womb, causing a difficult delivery and, possibly, a breech birth.

During this period, it was important that the husband not turn to other women, since any adulteries could harm the child in his wife's womb. For this reason, we are told, a man who had sex with his pregnant wife was punished, although exactly how is not stated. Infidelities on the part of either spouse at this time also may have been linked to the birth of twins, which were unwanted—and often killed. This may explain why twins were associated with the goddess of illicit sexuality, Xochiquetzal. The ban on conjugal relations continued well past delivery, since women who had recently delivered were thought to continue to generate noxious forces capable of rendering the entire family vulnerable to harm. Moreover, nursing mothers were not supposed to conceive again until their child was weaned, since to do so was to harm it. Weaning, as we have seen, did not occur until the child was four years old. The need for sexual continence over such a prolonged period of time must have created serious problems for married couples who were in the process of having children.

Like childbirth, the sex act was conceived of as a battle, in this case between man and woman. Just as the woman's sexual organs were likened to the war shield, the man's phallus was compared to his arrows and darts; intercourse, as we have seen, involved penetrating the woman's "shield." A poem composed by the people of Chalco to celebrate that city's repudiation of a neighbor's military advances describes intercourse in terms of grasping a war shield on the battlefield. Moreover, in the same way that sexual matters could be expressed in terms of war, Nahua references to warfare could be drawn from the world of love. One of the metaphors used in both discourses is the flower. On one hand, certain flowers represented human sexuality, especially that of women, and could signify anything from lust, prostitution, and infidelity to a woman's genitalia. On the other hand, in the Chalcan poem mentioned earlier, the warrior's shield is referred to as a flower that "opens" on the battlefield, evoking an image both botanical and sexual.

The most pervasive metaphor for sexual intercourse, however, was weaving, which symbolized conception, pregnancy, and birth, as well. Among the Nahua, as among the Yucatec Maya, cloth was produced mostly by women, who sold it in the marketplace. For this reason, weaving was regarded as a quintessentially female act. Because cloth constituted one of the most important commodities in the economy, serving as a form of currency among the Nahua, women were highly valued for their labors at the loom. This helps to explain why Nahua nobles acquired as many wives as they could support and why, following the Conquest, they were so loathe to give them up. Brides within this social class were urged to weave well so that their husbands would continue to love and keep them. A woman who did not weave well was considered socially as well as domestically useless and was compared to the harlot; like the harlot, she was threatened with slavery and the prospect of being sacrificed.

So central to the gender identity and social status of women was weaving that the weaving implements of Nahua women who had died were burned along with them so that the women could continue working in the next world. Women were, in fact, themselves metaphorically textiles, an individual woman being sometimes referred to as "the blouse, the skirt." A Nahua myth tells of five goddesses sacrificed at the time of creation in order to get the sun moving, who later returned to earth in the form of *mantas,* the rectangular panels of fabric that women wrapped around their lower bodies to form a skirt. All of the major Mesoamerican goddesses affiliated with female sexuality and reproduction were archetypal weavers, and several appear in painted manuscripts with spindles and raw cotton in their hair and a weaving batten in their hand. Tlazolteotl's original Huastec name, in fact, was Ixcuina, or "Lady Cotton."

Among the present-day Huichol of Nayarit, the goddess Takutsi Nakave wears two weaving battens in her dress. The first woman to learn how to spin and weave, Takutsi's first task was to create life in the world. She did this by watching the spider spin its web and then spinning her own thread. To make thread therefore is to give life among the Huichol, and a woman's weaving reenacts Takutsi's primordial feat every time she sits down to her loom. At the same time, she metaphorically gives life to the sun, helping it along its path. When their husbands went deer hunting in former times, Huichol wives used the loom to metaphorically "snare" or "capture" the souls of the deer. Similar ideas about weaving exist among the modern Tzutujil Maya of highland Guatemala. There, too, weaving is equated with birthing, and weavings therefore are "born" just as human beings are "woven." The wood sticks that make up the loom are identified with female deities and are believed to contain their divine powers. Tzutujil midwives, who represent the moon goddess, herself a weaver, use these sticks to induce labor, cure menstrual problems, and ease the pain of childbirth.

Among the Tzutujil, the very movements of the weaver are identified with birth contractions, whereas the way in which a Huichol weaver inserts and withdraws the batten is said to simulate sexual intercourse. In the Huichol case, the batten is surely a metaphor for the phallus. Like the top and bottom beams of the loom, as well as the pickup sticks, the Huichol batten is made from the same wood that is used for staffs of office and other male power objects. At the time of the Conquest, Nahua weaving implements seem to have been similarly gendered. Battens were compared to machetes, the

large, almost sword-like knives carried and used only by men. Today, among the Mixtecs of southern Mexico, the machete is called "the scepter of male potency."

Weaving, however, was not the only female task that combined male and female elements in a grand metaphor of the reproductive process. One of Mesoamerican women's most important duties was to sweep the family home on a regular basis; for this reason, as we have seen, a broom figured among the work tools assigned to baby girls in *Codex Mendoza.* Among the Nahua, sweeping was intimately linked to female fertility. The goddess Tlazolteotl, whose name meant "Filth Goddess," and whose job was to remove the filth that accrued to a person through sexual immoderation, was closely identified with the broom, which she wielded at times like a weapon. During the month festival of Ochpaniztli, in which Tlazolteotl was honored as Toci (Our Grandmother), her impersonator used a broom to chase off men who tried to attack her. Other women also wielded brooms in mock battles enacted during Ochpaniztli. In some present-day Nahua communities, curers use brooms to remove illness from patients, and curing rituals are referred to as "sweeping" or "cleaning." It is women of childbearing age who sweep the Huichol patio as a way of welcoming the sun and praying to the goddess of childbirth for luck in conceiving and bearing healthy children.

Cooking, too, was a female task with sexual and military connotations. Maize, or corn, was said to be "tortured" and to "suffer" during preparation and cooking, and to require a periodic respite in order to revive. The *olla,* or standard cooking pot, on the other hand, was a symbolic womb, while the *metate,* or grinding stone, is today associated with female sexual organs throughout Mesoamerica. The act of grinding clearly was equated with sexual intercourse, as the hand stone used to grind the corn on the *metate*'s surface today represents testicles among some Nahuas. Pre-Hispanic Nahuas said that mankind was created out of the bones of a previous race that were ground by the goddess Cihuacoatl on a *metate.* Human flesh throughout Mesoamerica was and is identified with maize, and people's sexual parts are still equated with food. In pre-Hispanic times, for example, tamales represented human flesh, while Mixtecs today sometimes call the vagina "the folded tortilla" and refer to the sexual act as "going to eat the large tamale."

In Mesoamerica, then, ideas about gender and sexuality helped to shape a person's social identity and behavior at the same time that social norms and the division of labor affected how people thought about gender, the body, and sexual morality. This is nowhere more evident than in the case of the Nahua women who died in first childbirth, the Cihuateteo or Cihuapipiltin. These women, Sahagún tells us, went to live in Cihuatlampa (The Region of Women), which was located in the west. From there, armed as warriors, they sallied forth every morning to escort the sun from its noonday zenith in the sky to its demise at dusk at the mouth of the underworld at the western horizon. In so doing, the Cihuateteo paralleled the actions of the spirits of honored dead warriors, whose job it was to daily escort the reborn sun from the eastern horizon to zenith. The dead warriors, however, lived in a verdant place, whereas the Cihuateteo lived in the place of darkness and dying. Moreover, the former were said to return permanently to earth after four years to live forever as birds and butterflies among the flowers. The dead parturients, in contrast, returned only occasionally and for brief periods when they came searching for their lost clothing and weaving instruments—that is, their lost femininity. At these times they descended, head first, at midnight at crossroads where mothers left offerings to them at special shrines. The offerings were made in the hope that the spirits of these childless women would not take out their frustration on the living by harming other women's children. It was presumably at these times that the goddesses, themselves former adulteresses, also tried to incite women on earth to commit adultery.

Since the Cihuateteo represented individuals who had failed to meet Nahua requirements for womanhood, it follows that their gender had been compromised. Indeed, in the *Codex Borgia* and in cognate scenes in *Codex Vaticanus 3773,* both painted in south-central Mexico not long before the Conquest, the Cihuateteo are depicted with their breasts exposed. As we have seen, exposed breasts were characteristic of very elderly women who were long past their childbearing years and who were therefore regarded as essentially asexual. In colonial manuscripts, as presumably in pre-Conquest imagery, a naked torso also characterizes female adulterers, that is women who had abused their sexuality. The ambiguous gender of the Cihuateteo can best be seen in *Codex Vaticanus 3373,* where these same unhappy women wear, in addition to a short skirt or hip cloth, what is clearly a loincloth normally worn by men. The Cihuateteo's gender, in other words, is destabilized in these manuscripts to signify their sexual failures. The ways in which the Nahua related social deficiencies to the body are further illustrated by these women's illnesses and deformities. Some of the Cihuateteo have skin pustules, some are blind, and one in *Codex Borgia* has hands and feet that are turned backwards. In Nahua ideology, then, women who did not conform to the ideal of a reproductive housewife were deprived of good health and female gender, and could be saddled with signs of masculinity, as well. The Nahua exemplify, in this regard, the way in which gender categories and moral codes governing human sexuality throughout Mesoamerica served not only to reinforce social norms but, in the process, to maintain sexual, economic, and political hierarchies, as well.

Select Bibliography

Arvey, Margaret Campbell, "Women of Ill-repute in the Florentine Codex." In *The Role of Gender in Pre-Columbian Art and Architecture,* edited by Virginia E. Miller. Lanham, Maryland: University Press of America, 1988.

Berdan, Frances, and Patricia Anawalt, *The Codex Mendoza.* 4 vols., Berkeley: University of California Press, 1992.

Burkhart, Louise, "Mujeres mexicas en 'el frente' del hogar: Trabajo doméstico y religión en el México azteca." *Mesoamérica* 23 (1992).

Cline, S. L., *Colonial Culhuacan, 1580–1600: A Social History of an Aztec Town.* Albuquerque: University of New Mexico Press, 1986.

Furst, Peter T., "The Thread of Life: Some Parallels in the Symbolism of Aztec, Huichol, and Pueblo Earth-Mother Goddesses." In *Balance y perspectiva de la antropología e Mesoamérica y del norte de México.* Jalapa, Mexico: Sociedad Mexicana de Antropología, 1975.

Hunt, Eva, *The Transformation of the Hummingbird: Cultural Roots of a Zinacantan Mythical Poem.* Ithaca, New York: Cornell University Press, 1977.

Ingham, John M., *Mary, Michael, and Lucifer: Folk Catholicism in Central Mexico.* Austin: University of Texas Press, 1986.

Klein, Cecelia F., "Fighting with Femininity: Gender and War in Aztec Mexico." In *Gender Rhetorics: Postures of Dominance and Submission in Human History,* edited by Richard C. Trexler. Binghamton: Center for Medieval and Early Renaissance Study, State University of New York, 1994.

_____, "The Shieldwomen: Resolution of an Aztec Gender Paradox." In *Current Topics in Aztec Studies: Essays in Honor of Dr. H. B. Nicholson,* edited by Alana Cordy-Colins and Douglas Sharon. Balboa Park, California: San Diego Museum of Man, 1993.

_____, "Teocuitlatl, 'Divine Excrement': The Significance of 'Holy Shit' in Ancient Mexico." *Art Journal* 53:3 (1993).

López Austin, Alfredo, *The Human Body and Ideology: Concepts of the Ancient Nahuas,* translated by Thelma Ortiz de Montellano and Bernard Ortiz de Montellano. 2 vols., Salt Lake City: University of Utah Press, 1988.

McCafferty, Sharisse D., and Geoffrey G. McCafferty, "Powerful Women and the Myth of Male Dominance in Aztec Society." *Archaeological Review from Cambridge* 7:1 (1988).

_____, "Spinning and Weaving as Female Gender Identity in Post-Classic Mexico." In *Textile Traditions of Mesoamerica and the Andes: An Anthology,* edited by Margot Blum Schevill, Janet Catherine Berlo, and Edward B. Dwyer. New York: Garland, 1991.

Monaghan, John, *The Covenants with Earth and Rain: Exchange, Sacrifice, and Revelation in Mixtec Sociality.* Norman: University of Oklahoma Press, 1995.

Ortiz de Montellano, Bernard R., *Aztec Medicine, Health, and Nutrition.* New Brunswick, New Jersey: Rutgers University Press, 1990.

Prechtel, Martin, and Robert S. Carlsen, "Weaving and Cosmos: Amongst the Tzutujil Maya of Guatemala." *Res* 15 (1988).

Quezada, Noemí, *Amor y magia amorosa entre los Aztecas: Supervivencia en el México colonial.* Mexico: UNAM–Institutio de Investigaciones Antropológicas, 1975.

Restall, Matthew, and Pete Sigal, "'May They Not Be Fornicators Equal to These Priests': Post-conquest Yucatec Maya Sexual Attitudes." *Indigeneous Writing in the Spanish Indies: Special Issue of the UCLA Historical Journal* 12 (1992).

Rodríguez Valdés, María J., *La mujer azteca.* Toluca, Mexico: Universidad Autónoma del Estado de México, 1988.

Sahagún, Bernardino de, *Florentine Codex: General History of the Things of New Spain,* translated by Arthur J. O. Anderson and Charles E. Dibble. 13 vols., Santa Fe, New Mexico: The School of American Research, and Salt Lake City: University of Utah, 1953–82.

Sandstrom, Alan R., *Corn is Our Blood: Culture and Ethnic Identity in a Contemporary Aztec Indian Village.* Norman: University of Oklahoma Press, 1991.

Schaefer, Stacy B., *Becoming a Weaver: The Woman's Path in Huichol Culture.* Ph.D. diss., UCLA, 1990.

Sullivan, Thelma D., "Tlazolteotl-Ixcuina: The Great Spinner and Weaver." In *The Art and Iconography of Late Post-Classic Central Mexico,* edited by Elizabeth Hill Boone. Washington, D.C.: Dumbarton Oaks, 1982.

Tarn, Nathaniel, and Martin Prechtel, "Constant Inconstancy: The Feminine Principle in Atiteco Mythology." In *Symbol and Meaning beyond the Closed Community: Essays in Mesoamerican Ideas,* edited by Gary H. Gossen. Albany: State University of New York at Albany–Institute for Mesoamerican Studies, 1986.

Tozzer, Alfred M., *Landa's Relación de las cosas de Yucatan.* Cambridge, Massachusetts: Harvard University, 1941.

Trexler, Richard C., *Sex and Conquest: Gendered Violence, Political Order, and the European Conquest of the Americas.* Ithaca, New York: Cornell University Press, 1995.

Zorita, Alonso de, *Life and Labor in Ancient Mexico: The Brief and Summary Relation of the Lords of New Spain,* translated by Benjamin Keen. New Brunswick, New Jersey: Rutgers University Press, 1963.

—CECELIA F. KLEIN

GENDER: COLONIAL

The women of New Spain, their stations and their destinies, were as diverse as the overall population was complex. A noble Spanish lady would not have thought she had much in common with the black girl who scrubbed her patio, nor with the Indian woman slaving over hot stoves in her kitchen. She would not have identified with the mestiza who provided her fruit and vegetables, or with the mulatto nurse who rocked her children. And if all these could rub elbows in the same city, indeed in the same household, the differences become compounded if we consider the contrasts between secular and religious life, town and country, and even among the various indigenous groups, from the northern deserts to the tropical south.

It is not only geographical terrain or ethnic traits that account for these differences. Over the course of 300 years of colonial life, the position of women evolved in various directions according to social class, family situation, potential for achieving a degree of autonomy, and community recognition. In spite of all these contrasts and changes, standard religious discourse remained strictly homogeneous. It resorted to one and the same criterion to define the duties, virtues, merits and shortcomings of women whether white or black, rich or poor, noble or plebeian. In practice, however, the rhetoric of the equality of souls and the blessedness of the poor was quite flexibly applied to specific situations, depending on the designation of "quality." And the concept of quality encapsulated notions of race, wealth, dynastic prestige, and legitimacy of birth.

In the eyes of the Catholic Church, as in those of civil law, woman—whatever her condition—was formed in the image of Eve and Mary. She was both temptress and redemptress, weak by nature but able to display the highest virtue, with the proviso that any virtues allowed of the weaker sex were those appropriate to a servile condition: obedience, discretion, industriousness, chastity, piety, perseverance, resignation, humility, tenderness, and above all, temperance, queen of virtues and safeguard against unseemly fits of imprudence or outbursts.

The gulf between theory and practice was glaring, starting with the fact that identical virtues were urged upon all women regardless of their differences. As in most colonial systems gender was secondary to class, so that on the hierarchical scale, a Spanish or criolla woman (one of Spanish descent born in Mexico) would rank higher than any colored male. The multiplicity of traditions lent even further intricacy to the spectrum of customs and attitudes proper to the women of New Spain. Even within the same social group, there were clear differences between a lady hailing from Biscay—where women could own, inherit, and administer property—and another from Andalusia or Extremadura, raised for reclusive domesticity in a vestigial echo of Moslem attitudes toward their womenfolk. Likewise, the life experiences of an indigenous woman confined to her ancestral community had little in common with those of her urban sisters, while the black chambermaid and the black plantation slave had to adapt to completely different work environments.

Early Colonial Society

The plurality of feminine models began to incubate from the moment of Conquest, when some Spanish women with the expedition, such as María de Estrada, took up arms to win titles and *encomiendas* (land trusts worked by Indian inhabitants) in their own right, while others remained at camp, tending the wounded and taking a new partner each time the previous one died in combat. On the indigenous side, caciques' (chiefs') daughters were treated with more deference than common women: the first were ceremoniously delivered to Fernando (Hernán) Cortés's captains, the second raffled among the troops and branded with the iron of slavery.

On the islands of Cuba and Hispaniola (modern Dominican Republic and Haiti), with several decades of Spanish settlement, there simmered a perpetual population in transit, restless for news of fresh discoveries in hopes of being the first to exploit the opportunities open to pioneers. Seville was another meeting point for prospective travelers, as they waited for official permits or ships with available berths.

Both groups included women, either with their families or lone adventuresses who claimed to be joining relatives in the Americas, although their likelier motive was to snare a rich husband who might overlook their racy past, plain face, or empty pockets. Some of these women—be they married, widowed, maidens, or experienced spinsters—reached New Spain without hindrance and shortly found more or less suitable or trustworthy mates.

For at least 20 years after the surrender of Tenochtitlan, the scarcity of Spanish women ensured a high demand for fair-skinned wives, since these were valued far more highly than Indian companions. Another factor was the homesickness that could make strong soldiers weep at the thought of a tasty *puchero gallego* or a refreshing *ajoblanco* from Córdoba. Widows had no trouble remarrying, and deceased husbands could even be an asset if they had earned merits for which some reward might be claimed.

Settlers and conquistadors also married the daughters and widows of noble caciques, who brought a dowry of lands and vassals. A majority of mixed couples, however, were pledged temporarily or permanently without benefit of either religious blessing or civil registration. Sexual liaisons with local women were not necessarily interrupted by the arrival of some official spouse. The municipal authorities of Mexico City frequently lamented the fact that so many Spaniards, having respectable families at hand in the capital, still visited the barrios to "perpetrate wickedness" with Indian girls.

This first period of hasty marriages and tolerated cohabitations exerted a decisive influence upon the formation of family life in New Spain, with habits that soon diverged as widely from those prevalent in Castile as they did from ancient Mesoamerican custom. Any offspring of a Spanish man and an Indian woman who were recognized by the father were considered Spanish, and those who were only accepted by their mother's community were taken to be Indian. The stigma of mixed blood, or *mestizaje,* was added to that of illegitimacy in case of rejection by both parties; to be a mestizo meant originally to be abandoned, without a family. As there was no institutional abode for homeless children in Mexico City for over 250 years, almost all orphans and rejected illegitimate children had to seek for themselves a more or less comfortable haven where the lucky ones might get legally adopted, while the rest became servants, apprentices, or vagrants.

During this early period, an Indian woman married to a Spaniard or accepted as his companion wore fine clothes, attended Christian devotion, founded chaplaincies among other charitable works and, in short, was thoroughly assimilated into criollo society. Conquistadors' daughters, legitimate or otherwise, were much in demand as wives, for apart from their dowries they also brought inherited *encomiendas* or at least their fathers' list of merits that might be worth the prize of public office for their spouse.

A local aristocracy soon emerged, with titles of nobility and heraldries that perpetuated the memory of epic deeds. The gleam of coats of arms was enhanced by the presence of a rich *encomienda* or silver mine to balance the finances. Rel-atives of viceroys sought mates from among wealthy criollas, and prosperous merchants consolidated their status by means of matrimonial alliances that lent them the prestige they lacked. While Spanish ladies were making much of their refinement and the lofty purity of their origins, Indian women without land or fortune secluded themselves within their communities or worked as domestics or market vendors. Those descended from noble families usually lost their ancestral accreditation (noble status) after a couple of generations.

Year by year the number of mestizas increased, while black and mulatto women merged into the population. Slave ships always carried many more men than women, but whereas the former were mostly sent to the haciendas, the latter ended up in the cities where they were preferred to indigenous women as servants, for the possession of slaves was deemed a sign of wealth. Slave women became part of inheritable family property. They could be mortgaged (despite a law against this), form part of a dowry, accompany postulants entering some convent of less than rigid observance, or work to maintain single women who depended on the income generated by the labor of their slaves.

Baroque Society

One hundred years after the Conquest of Mexico, established society was vigorously defending its privileges, and obsessed with fixing demarcations between social groups. The criollos were ever more anxious to demonstrate their unsullied Hispanic ancestry, while cross-racial groups known as "castes" were becoming even more numerous. The logical conclusion might have been for Spaniards to avoid extramarital liaisons, and for their wives to carry out the mandates of sexual morality to the letter. How else could the purity of blood and lineage, which so preoccupied them, be guaranteed? It might also be reasonable to expect illegitimate unions to have been celebrated exclusively between members of castes or between Spanish men and women of inferior status, whose offspring would go to swell the number of mestizos and mulattos. But reality was otherwise.

From the baptism and marriage registers of a representative set of urban and rural parishes, we now know that all groups had a variable tendency to ethnic endogamy (marrying within the group); but in towns, the inclination to establish family bonds with members of one's own group did not prevent relations of concubinage, with the result that illegitimate children could appear within any group whatsoever. The situation was quite different in rural communities, with an indigenous population removed from Spanish or caste influence. Here marriage was early and almost universal, and births out of wedlock were a rarity.

In large towns, illegitimacy was so widespread that it has to be viewed as an intrinsic part of family life. This does not imply that women enjoyed their freedom or that they rejected marriage. A single woman was apt to suffer material want and was helpless in the face of harassment or abuse; moreover, it was unlikely that she could attain any social rank. A husband to provide economic security, protection, and respectability was a dream of almost all women, although many became resigned to mistresshood if a husband did not materialize for them. The younger, wealthier maidens secured the most eligible bachelors, of their own rank or higher. Affluent widows had a wide choice of second husbands, and single women might even bring illegitimate children to a marriage if their lack of virginity was compensated by other assets.

Although there are no census data prior to the eighteenth century from which to calculate the proportion of female heads of households, we may suppose that a number of those with illegitimate children were eventually forced to become the breadwinners. Over 35 percent of total births in Mexico City were illegitimate. The record of castes and Spaniards in the parish of La Santa Veracruz were very similar, and the same results obtain among the Spaniards of El Sagrario, a fashionable parish inhabited by the richer and more distinguished citizens. Such consistency reveals that there was very little difference between Spanish and other women, where concubinage and other illicit relations were concerned. The rate of illegitimacy was even higher, reaching 52 percent, among the caste population whose christenings were registered at El Sagrario. The discrepancy may be attributed to the fact that the parish was mostly inhabited by wealthy Spaniards, owning a large number of slaves and servants as well as attracting a slew of occasional employees and hangers-on, a concentration of rootless persons, with no family and no respect for the principles of social conduct. The illegitimate children of caste women also were likely to include not a few offspring of Spanish gentlemen.

The social opprobrium against single mothers could hardly be very severe, when approximately one-third of all mothers were in that situation. Most families continued lending support, by acting, for example, as godparents. But economic penury could not always be alleviated by the family in the absence of a man to take responsibility for woman and children. Widows were in a similar predicament, often obliged to support themselves through some skill such as needlework, or a partnership in small businesses. There are records of many female-owned haciendas, mines, workshops, and stores, whose administration was commonly handled by some trusted male associate. More active in economic life were the modest pulque-sellers and foodstuff vendors, who set up their stalls or stoves on the corners of streets and squares. The hardest life was reserved for female laborers, whether voluntarily contracted or forced into work by the debts of their spouses. Even in cases of comparative financial independence, the scales were weighted in favor of men, who owned the most profitable businesses, construction sites, or workshops. Families headed by women tended to be poorer and smaller.

The Bourbon Reform Era

With the arrival of a time of reformist zeal and socially regenerative projects, civil functionaries and members of the church hierarchy discovered a panorama of female life that was very different from the modest, cloistered, and chaste image evoked from the pulpit. Here were wives gossiping in the markets and avenues, young women flaunting their charms at dances, little girls playing freely in the streets, and disreputable widows calling on young ladies with messages from their suitors. Inside the convents themselves, where life was surely the very model of Christian perfection, nuns were running salons in the visiting rooms and sharing their cells with a bevy of children and servants, keeping pets in the cloisters, and spending most of their time on such unspiritual pursuits as cookery, sewing, weaving, and herbalism in order to make money, at the expense of prayer schedules and community chanting.

Among the many reforms enacted throughout the eighteenth and early nineteenth centuries, some were directed at women of all ages and walks of life. Their success was nonetheless uneven: those in line with time-honored practice were more effective than those going against the grain of local custom. Permission for women to engage in artisanal production, regardless of guild regulations, was granted at a time when many were already busy in the workshops. The nunneries reform, intended for calced orders (whose rules were generally less rigorous), occasioned dramatic scenes of protest until it was revoked. The Royal Pragmatic on Marriage only was applied among well-to-do sectors, where an unsuitable alliance somewhere in the family might lead to money trouble and even jeopardize dynastic prestige; and the establishment of the state tobacco monopoly, centralizing production in the factory, severely affected the livelihoods of many families that had been collectively employed at this task at home, where mothers did not have to leave their children for the day.

There always had been women living on the margins, and these too, in distorted fashion, embodied society's expectations of the female sex. Prostitutes played the prophylactic role that was demanded of them, and indeed explicitly assigned to them by city authorities looking to safeguard the reputations of "decent" women. As long as mestizo and mulatto women performed the jobs no one raised an eyebrow, but should a Spanish woman try her luck, then immediate action was taken by the authorities to protect the dignity of her race. Naturally, the male clientele vanished as though by magic as soon as the constables knocked at a suspect door, leaving only the women to plead ingenuous reasons for such late-night visits. Whatever the case may be, the ease in arranging for mistresses or concubines reduced the significance of sexual professionals.

At the other extreme, although equally foreign to mainstream behavior, we find the *ilusas,* or visionaries, cloaked in an odor of sanctity that the officers of the Inquisition were all too ready to dispel. Such figures testify to the importance of piety as an alternative means of winning recognition and prestige. Some feigned supernatural raptures to conceal irregular sexual adventures, but most were content with maidenhood and wished only to indulge their self-importance.

Witches and healers, usually Indian and sometimes mulattos, acted as a bridge between men and women of different ethnicity, for their clients were indiscriminately white, brown, or a mix; people from all races and classes resorted to spells and sorcery to confound an enemy or some pesky relative, or to force the attentions of a reluctant love-object. Bigamist women were also at risk from the Inquisition, for this was an offense carrying serious penalties, which did not discourage many from attempting it in their longing to be accepted by society.

Thus the official Bourbon modernization campaign was not welcomed by nuns who did not aspire to the extreme austerity of barefoot orders, nor by young women who saw it as a threat to their freedom to form a love match, nor by home workers who found themselves herded into factories. Affluent women, on the other hand, were delighted by the new opportunities for frivolous diversion brought by modern fashions and hairstyles, the codes of gallantry and courtship, the racy plays and exciting dances and music coming from Europe. As so often in women's history, the deceptive freedoms of vanity and occasional entertainment turned out to be the privilege of a tiny elite group.

See also Convents in New Spain

Select Bibliography

Arrom, Silvia Marina, *La mujer mexicana ante el divorcio eclesiástico, 1800–1857.* Mexico City: Secretaría de Educación Pública, 1976.
_____, *The Women of Mexico City, 1790–1857.* Stanford, California: Stanford University Press, 1985.
Atondo Rodríguez, Ana María, *El amor venal y la condición femenina en el México colonial.* Mexico City: Instituto Nacional de Antropología e Historia, 1992.
Gonzalbo Aizpuru, Pilar, *Las mujeres en la Nueva España: Educación y vida cotidiana.* Mexico City: Colegio de México, 1987.
_____, editor, *Familias novohispanas: Siglos XVI–XIX.* Mexico City: Colegio de México, 1991.
_____, and Cecilia Rabell, editors, *La familia en el mundo iberoamericano.* Mexico City: Universidad Nacional Autónoma de México, 1994.
Lavrin, Asunción, editor, *Latin American Women: Historical Perspectives.* Westport, Connecticut: Greenwood Press, 1978.
_____, *Sexuality and Marriage in Colonial Latin America.* Lincoln and London: University of Nebraska Press, 1989.
Muriel, Josefina, *Conventos de monjas en la Nueva España.* 2 vols., Mexico City: Santiago, 1946.
_____, *Cultura femenina novohispana.* Mexico City: Universidad Nacional Autónoma de México, 1982; 2nd edition, 1994.
Ramos-Escandon, Carmen, editor, *Presencia y transparencia: La mujer en la historia de México.* Mexico City: Colegio de México, 1987.
Seed, Patricia, *To Love, Honor and Obey in Colonial Mexico: Conflicts over Marriage Choice, 1574–1821.* Stanford, California: Stanford University Press, 1988.
Simposio de Historia de las Mentalidades, *Familia y sexualidad en Nueva España.* Mexico City: Fondo de Cultura Económica, 1982.
Seminario de Historia de las Mentalidades, *El placer de pecar y el afán de normar.* Mexico City: Mortiz, 1988.

—PILAR GONZALBO AIZPURU

GENDER: 1821–1910

From the mid–nineteenth through the first decade of the twentieth centuries, concepts of gender and sexuality changed ideologically and practically based on the social class of Mexicans and whether they lived in urban or rural areas. Although gender ideologies that subordinated women to men remained in place throughout Mexican society in this period, essential aspects of the power relationship were contested and at points altered, especially among the more highly educated, middle- and upper-class urban strata.

Rural Society

Because Mexico was an overwhelmingly rural country in this period, the relationships that existed in the countryside were the social norm. Patrilocal residence was standard after marriage: the newly married couple moved into the house of the groom's parents, where the bride worked under the supervision and authority of her mother-in-law. The parents of the bride received a small bride price in compensation for the loss of the labor of their daughter after her marriage. A woman remained in this relationship with her in-laws until her mother-in-law died, although she achieved a level of autonomy at about midlife, when the family resources allowed for her own family unit to establish a separate household. She then assumed the matriarchal role in the home, served and provided for her husband and family, and one day supervised her own daughters-in-law.

The gendered division of labor meant that rural women worked mainly within their households procuring and preparing the food and clothing for the family. In the marketplace where they occasionally sold eggs or handicrafts, women were able to engage in public activities and even at times to earn a small amount of money, which was then turned over to the household, kept for children, spent for ceremonies or rituals, and occasionally, retained for their personal use. In these few public forums, women interacted with other women and with unrelated men, but generally only in the limited milieu of the village market.

In a strictly gender-encoded ideology, women's sense of worth moved from generation to generation within the family. They began adult life as servants in the homes of their husbands' family, eventually established their own kitchens with their own utensils and control over the domestic work routines, and finally they assumed authority over their daughters-in-law. Similarly, rural men worked under the supervision of their fathers, cultivating corn on their own land or as laborers on large haciendas, and remained under the authority of their fathers until such day as they left for work or army service, usually returning to raise families and continue the generational life cycle.

In the country villages, the communal assembly served as a forum for resolving conflicts, including cases involving wife beating, adultery, and divisions within the marriage. Although an arm of the wider patriarchal relations, the legitimacy of the communal assembly rested on the maintenance of collective approval, which could in turn serve as a forum for female interests. In cases of wife abuse, for example, the interests of a woman and of her family could not be ignored, since communal cooperation and public order needed to be maintained. The communal assembly and the peer pressure of community relations served as an intervening system for mediating potential tensions between men and women despite the traditional male hierarchy.

A gendered division of authority in the community dovetailed with the gendered hierarchy of the household. Rural men aspired to the respect conferred by public office. The control of men over the community, and of communal religious, political, social, and economic matters, reinforced the ties between the family and community and the essential dominant role that men maintained in both the private and public arena. A "good patriarch," however, assiduously assured communal order, which implied a level of peace and sexual harmony in the home. The insertion of communal authority therefore cut against the kind of domestic abuse of women and children excused in many modern industrial societies under the rubric of privacy or noninterference in the private, family arena.

The social strife that accompanied Independence from Spain, and the subsequent conflicts over regional and political power that marked the nineteenth century, influenced the traditional gendered division of labor in many rural villages. Not only did men fight and die in battle, leaving women who remained behind in the villages in numerical dominance, but women also traveled with the troops, serving as cooks, nurses, and caregivers for the men. Accordingly, the conduct of war had a sexual division of labor. One estimate based on a core area of five villages of central Mexico shows that each town provided combatants in the area with a ration of about 150 to 200 tortillas. Women from each town were making between 1,800 and 2,400 tortillas every day, including husking, degraining, and soaking the corn, and making and cooking the tortillas. To meet the food demands for war, women in this area probably rose at two o'clock in the morning, toiled all day making tortillas, in addition to carrying out the other tasks required for the maintenance of children, the family, and the household. As a result, the contribution of women to the war efforts may have in only exceptional cases involved direct combat, but their participation was absolutely essential for the conduct of war and mind-boggling in the scale of arduous work.

Regional studies have pointed to the intersection between concepts of masculinity and the emergence, or lack of emergence, of revolutionary movements. In the late eighteenth and early nineteenth centuries, the state rewarded the "honorable" men of Chihuahua—those who dominated Indians—with land and an esteemed position as a member of the corporate community. According to scholar Ana María Alonso's study of Namiquipa, Chihuahua, the cultural ideal held that honorable men dominated, owned land, and bore arms in defense of family and community; dishonorable men, on the other hand, worked for someone else, were subservient, cuckolded, and without land and family. When after 1880 the Mexican state under dictator Porfirio Díaz attempted to take away the land from the peasantry, these "honorable" men saw the encroachment as an attack on their masculinity. Likewise, the scholar John Womack's depiction of the 1909 town meeting that elected Emiliano Zapata the new leader of Anenecuilco, Morelos, notes that the villagers called out to Zapata, "We just want a man with pants on, to defend us." By contrast, in Michoacán peasants lived in the shadow of the Virgin of Guadalupe, which, as a symbol of purity and submission, conditioned their cultural outlook. These peasants did not resist the Porfirian state as did those in Chihuahua or Morelos, since they lacked what Marjorie Becker calls an "ideology of entitlement." Regional studies have contrasted the masculinized concepts of ownership in some districts with emasculinized and disempowered cultures in others.

Urban Areas

Rural society underwent few changes in the patriarchal order, while in urban areas more substantial restructuring occurred. In the decades after Independence, women took up work in textile mills, especially in those manufactures located in medium-sized towns and the larger urban areas. Women outnumbered men in the mill workforce when the demands, and effects, of war resulted in a shortage of men available for the industrial workforce. Men had died in battle, many men remained in agricultural production, and the highly labor-intensive and low-paying work in textile mills attracted more female than male laborers. In Cocolapam textile mill in Orizaba, Veracruz, 73 percent of the workers were women; in Sinaloa, El Coloso, 75 percent were women; and at the Dolores mill in Chihuahua 65 percent of the workers were women.

By the late nineteenth century, the situation had reversed, as men moved from agriculture to industry in greater numbers, especially after the textile industry became more capital-intensive and wages rose. Simultaneously, the number of women in the mills declined, and the percentage of women to men dropped. If, however, in 1893 women comprised 13 percent of the total workforce in Mexico, this was an increase over women's labor force participation before Independence, and it was a benchmark number that climbed during subsequent decades. Textile mills that were the least capital-intensive, and paid the lowest wages, did continue to employ many women.

The growth of industry, fostered by foreign investment in more highly capitalized enterprises, marked the era of Porfirio Díaz (1876–1910). One characteristic of industrial development during the Porfiriato was demarcated by the separation of women workers into low-wage, lesser-skilled industries and men into more capital-intensive and better-paid jobs. Cigar making was commonly a female occupation; in fact, more women worked in cigar making during the Porfiriato than in any other job except sewing and domestic service. Not only did women work 14- to 15-hour days in cigar factories, but the owners constantly increased the daily quota of cigars. The production expectation rose from 2,185 cigars daily in 1881 to 3,200 in the early twentieth century. Most *cigarreras,* as women cigar makers were called, needed to work all day and a good part of the night to meet these quotas.

Company records reveal that at the end of the day factory guards subjected the women to body searches to make sure they did not take any cigars. The body searches at cigar factories illustrate the hypocritical stance toward the changing gender division of labor that developed during the Porfirian era. On the one hand, a powerful wing of Porfirian ideology, drawn from positivism, argued that women should be the moral educators of the population. On the other hand, the push for industrial output drew many more women into factory labor at low wages and subjected them to harsh factory discipline, including the full-body searches that contradicted any notion of women as morally superior members of modern society.

Positivist Ideology, Work, and Education

The positivist doctrine that the Porfirian regime promoted sought to promote progress and social improvement through the existing hierarchical class structure, further ensuring the political power of the bourgeoisie while justifying the poverty and degradation of the poor, Indians, and the working class as natural and unavoidable in a system based on "scientific principles." According to positivist doctrine, the education of all Mexican women would ensure greater stability and order in society. However, educational opportunity was carefully circumscribed within the existing class structure. For example, the Porfirian government proclaimed that women should be educated to raise "strong, intelligent families," that they should not enter the workforce since "out of door" labor, as Auguste Comte, positivism's ideological father, stated, created disorder in society. Women should serve as educators in the home. By contrast, the government did encourage women from the middle and even working class to obtain an education so that they could take jobs in the expanding industrial sector and as teachers.

Ideologically, the Porfirian system of education sought to prescribe class-based limits to educational opportunities, but in so doing it inadvertently opened opportunities for all women. The contradiction faced by the Porfirian emphasis on education was that it wanted an enlarged source of cheap labor while at the same time it condemned the disruption to the family unit (traditionally based on a strict gendered division of labor) caused by women's entrance into the workforce. Middle-class women attended school to train as teachers in heightened numbers in the 1870s. In 1878 Mexico City's Escuela Nacional Secundaria de Niñas rapidly grew in size; in 1910 under the name Normal de Professoras, the school enrolled 401 students. In San Luis Potosí, the Escuela de Artes y Oficios para Mujeres opened in 1881, and in 1891 women were admitted for the first time to the Escuela Normal de Jalapa in Puebla. By 1895 over one-half of all of the nation's teaching positions, and two-thirds of the elementary teaching positions, were held by women, the vast majority of whom received two pesos a day as a salary.

The Porfirian regime educated working-class women in vocational and technical schools, preparing them for jobs in Mexican industry. In 1871 the first female vocational school opened with only a few students, but by 1899 over 1,000 women attended vocational schools. Although the Porfirian government proclaimed allegiance to positivist views on women and education, it likewise condoned female participation in the workforce. Women were the most efficient and available source of cheap labor. In 1885, in the Hercules factory in Querétaro, women were paid an average of 20 to 25 centavos on a piece-work basis, while operators (men) received between 31 and 52 centavos. If a factory owner could hire a woman for 50 percent less than a man, he would choose the woman, which led to male unemployment and lower wages for the entire working class.

In contrast to lower-middle-class and working-class women who were working, Mexican women of the upper ranks of society most accurately reflected the positivist ideal. They were raised to be good wives, educators of their children, and intelligent companions to their professional and elite husbands. Motherhood became their profession and their most important responsibility. Porfirian women of the upper class rarely sought professional positions in society, nor were they educated to take positions outside the domestic sphere. Their economic position never left the home.

The contrasting educations and designated roles for women in late-nineteenth-century society most aptly demonstrate the class boundaries of gender ideology during the Porfiriato. Since economic progress translated into financial improvement for the bourgeoisie, the government justified various levels of education and work for different classes of women. The working-class women were educated to create a larger labor pool of industrial workers; middle-class women were touted as the ideals of morality but employed as teachers who were willing to work in poor conditions for less wages than male instructors. Women of the bourgeoisie actually mirrored the ideal role for women as outlined in the Comtian philosophy: their job was the domestic sphere.

Breakdown of Patriarchy

Magazines and newspapers during the late nineteenth century illustrated the contradictory nature of gender ideology. Liberal and conservative publications vied with each other to promote contradictory roles for women in Mexican society.

While conservative magazines such as *El Tiempo Ilustrado* and *La Mujer* attempted to place women in the home as moral educators, more liberal periodicals such as *Las Hijas del Anáhuac* and *El Diario de Hogar* tried to liberate women from gender-related social constraints through the promotion of educational opportunities.

If official pronouncements, magazines, political speeches, and learned writings all talked about the limits and nonlimits of education, none of the official pronouncements demarcated the real class and gender limits in Mexican society. For most women and men, life was difficult and based on long hours of work on rural haciendas and in urban workplaces—the vast majority of all Mexicans were poor, working people. Beginning in the mid–nineteenth century, however, and continuing into the twentieth, increasingly large numbers of women were forced by economic necessity to add additional labor to their ongoing, unpaid, domestic obligations for the household. They joined men as wage laborers in industrial production. As was the case with their male counterparts, most Mexican women remained uneducated or obtained the level of education necessary for the reproduction of an industrial society, no more.

For educated women, however, the door cracked open to greater participation in society. The Constitution of 1857 had not explicitly excluded women from voting, but election laws had kept suffrage in the hands of men. Most women did not contest this practice. By the eve of the 1910 Revolution, women had begun to demand a share in the political process. Francisco I. Madero, Venustiano Carranza, and a number of the post-Revolution presidents did exhibit some interest in promoting women's suffrage but never found it expedient to push the issue. Other areas such as equality in marriage, a divorce law, and civil codes to protect women's rights and property would not enter Mexican law until after the Revolution, and then quite belatedly, especially in the case of suffrage, which was not fully realized until 1953.

Traditional ideas of femininity and masculinity underwent gradual change when women of all classes joined the public arena as workers, consumers, participants in public leisure activities such as bicycle riding, spectators at sporting events, and as traders in the marketplaces. Women dressed in more casual clothing for work and sports; they voiced their opinions in their own magazines and newspapers, joined labor unions, and contested the domination of men on the public terrain. Whether as elite women who now walked, bicycled, and entertained increasingly in public, as middle-class women who took jobs as teachers and secretaries, or as working women who joined the ranks of the industrial proletariat, women's seclusion in the home began to end as the Revolution approached. The opening fissures in the traditional gendered hierarchy in society and in the strict gender division of labor separating the household from the workplace began to appear in the first decade of the twentieth century.

Prostitution

The emphasis on morality and productivity that stood at the core of Porfirian society was challenged most directly by prostitution. As a symbol of degeneracy, the prostitute (but not her male client) became the object of elite and middle-class regulatory efforts. Considering the focus on industrialization, education, and productivity, it is not unusual that prostitution was the object of considerable distress in nineteenth- and early-twentieth-century society. The concern with prostitution had two sides. On the one hand, to many observers the presence of women in workplaces outside the home was in itself a sign of moral degeneracy, even to the extent that any woman alone in a city was viewed as a prostitute. On the other hand, the appearance of prostitution as a visibly widespread practice was a product of urbanization and industrialization. As such, the sight of prostitutes, overwhelmingly females, indicated to authorities that society was slipping away from preferred standards of public morality and refinement. The same emphasis on moralizing the working class that had accompanied the emphasis on education, work, and home stability came to bear on prostitutes, women who were seen as the most degenerate objects in a world turned upside down.

The idealized working-class family was the antidote to instability and class conflict, the assumption being that stable family life would cut against worker immorality, lack of discipline, and budding political consciousness. As scholar William French remarks, the Porfirians regarded the home as the symbolic opposite of the tavern: "Along with alcoholic libations, the tavern offered crime, shame, and repugnant passions, while home offered dignity, hope, high ideals, life and the sweet nectar of domestic bliss." The breakdown of the home was tied closely to the role of women in society. If women left the domestic sphere to work, the home came into jeopardy, and by extension the very morality and civilization of the society. Thus prostitution, the unchecked and decidedly immoral "work" of women on the street, symbolized the extreme breakdown of morality. Work was bad enough, sexual work was beyond the pale. Newspaper campaigns stressing the importance of moral reform always focused on prostitution as the extreme flaunting of civilization, since it symbolized the absolute loss of the ideal mother image.

Sexuality, Homosexuality, and Lesbianism

The literature on homosexual and lesbian cultures in Mexico is scant, which limits any discussion of the main contours of these forms of sexual interaction. Documents showing a long history of homosexuality in Mexican society support the assumption that bisexuality, homosexuality, and lesbianism have been active subcultures from precolonial times to the present. Records of the Spanish conquerors indicate that they were repulsed by the acceptance of homosexuality among indigenous groups such as the Zuni and Pueblo of northern Mexico. During the colonial period, the Catholic Church recorded accusations of homosexual behavior, and punishment for it, in the records of the Inquisition.

Undoubtedly homosexuality and lesbianism continued after Independence, but one finds no notice of it in accounts of the late-nineteenth- and early-twentieth-century records. Scholar Steve Stern notes that the issue of homosexuality did not appear in the criminal records he studied for the late colonial period either. He suggests, however, that sexually stigmatized conduct in Mexican society was associated with sexual passivity among men, whether in homosexual or heterosexual acts. Thus, passive men in heterosexual culture may have been more stigmatized than aggressive men in homosexual culture. The issue of assertive sexual conduct, associated with male dominance in patriarchal society, was reflected in the general conduct of gender relations, in the colonial as well as the postcolonial periods. One can presume that there are records in need of greater scrutiny that will shed light on this aspect of gender relations in future research.

Select Bibliography

Alonso, Ana María, *Thread of Blood: Colonialism, Revolution, and Gender on Mexico's Northern Frontier.* Tucson: University of Arizona Press, 1995.

Balderston, Daniel, and Donna Guy, *Sex and Gender in Latin America: An Interdisciplinary Reader.* New York: New York University Press, 1996.

Becker, Marjorie, *Setting the Virgin on Fire: Lázaro Cárdenas, Michoacán Peasants, and the Redemption of the Mexican Revolution.* Berkeley: University of California Press, 1995.

Calderón de la Barca, Frances, *Life in Mexico.* Berkeley: University of California Press, 1962.

Foster, David William, *Gay and Lesbian Themes in Latin American Writing.* Austin: University of Texas Press, 1991.

Franco, Jean, *Plotting Women: Gender and Representation in Mexico.* New York: Columbia University Press, 1989.

French, William E., "Prostitutes and Guardian Angels: Women, Work and the Family in Porfirian Mexico." *Hispanic American Historical Review* 72 (November 1992).

Gutiérrez, Ramón A., *When Jesus Came, the Corn Mothers Went Away: Marriage, Sexuality, and Power in New Mexico, 1500–1846.* Stanford, California: Stanford University Press, 1991.

Keremitsis, Dawn, "Latin American Women Workers in Transition: Sexual Divisions of the Labor Force in Mexico and Colombia in the Textile Industry." *The Americas* 40 (1984).

Macías, Anna, *Against All Odds: The Feminist Movement in Mexico to 1940.* Westport, Connecticut: Greenwood Press, 1982.

Mallon, Florencia E., *Peasant and Nation: The Making of Postcolonial Mexico and Peru.* Berkeley: University of California Press, 1995.

Morton, Ward M., *Woman Suffrage in Mexico.* Gainesville: University of Florida Press, 1962.

Nugent, Daniel, *Spent Cartridges of Revolution: An Anthropological History of Namiquipa, Chihuahua.* Chicago: University of Chicago Press, 1993.

Stern, Steve J., *The Secret History of Gender: Women, Men, and Power in Late Colonial Mexico.* Chapel Hill: University of North Carolina Press, 1995.

Towner, Margaret, "Monopoly Capitalism and Women's Work during the Porfiriato." *Latin American Perspectives* 2 (1979).

Womack, John, Jr., *Zapata and the Mexican Revolution.* New York: Random House, 1968.

—TERESA A. MEADE

GENDER: 1910–96

Along with generational, ethnic, and class differences, gender is one of the major social divisions running throughout the twentieth century in Mexico, although, to be sure, gender identities and relations in modern Mexico emerge in remarkably varied ways. This diversity is the reason why making useful generalizations with respect to gender for all regions of Mexico in the twentieth century as a whole is difficult if not impossible, except in the sense that gender is consistently one of the key social axes around which society is understood, organized, divided, and contested. Only in the final three decades of the century in Mexico was gender in its own right established as a major field of scholarly research, beginning with systematic studies on women as wage earners and family networkers, as political activists and sexual partners, as victims of domestic violence, single mothers, and domestics. As to the study of men, masculinity, and of gender and sexuality in the most inclusive sense, this work had barely begun as the century closed.

Gender and sexuality in twentieth century Mexico is a topic with society-wide ramifications and implications, and it is a subject that must be described and explained as well at the more immediate levels of neighborhoods, *ranchos,* and households. Beginning with the participation of women in the Mexican Revolution, continuing with an expanding presence of women in the labor force, and ending the century with the spiraling immiseration of households throughout the country, the modern history of gender and sexuality in Mexico manifests profound changes in relations of power and inequality at every level of society, transformations that have been marked by a process challenging a variety of arrangements in political, economic, and cultural citizenship for Mexican society as a whole.

End of the Porfiriato, the Mexican Revolution, Cardenismo: 1900–40

With the close of the nineteenth century, various factors significantly transformed gender relations in Mexico, among them the consolidation of land holdings, migration, and the encouragement, within the context of relative political stability, of industrial development. Regional and ethnic differences in gender identities and relations were especially conspicuous in this era when Mexico was still predominantly rural in terms of the economy and population. Among Zapotecos in the Tehuantepec Isthmus, for instance, and in marked contrast to most other parts of the country, women dominated in mercantile activities—not that such activities implied, then or later, any form of matriarchal society on the isthmus. In the Sierra Nahua region it was customary early in the century for children to sleep with their fathers and not their mothers between infancy and puberty, whereas in other regions it was unusual for a father to even carry a child much less have such regular bodily contact for hours each night. As subsequent scholarship clearly has shown, distinct cultural values in different indigenous communities were an important factor in shaping diverse ideas and activities relating to gender and sexuality throughout the twentieth century in Mexico.

Industrial development during the Porfiriato (the rule of Porfirio Díaz) drew large numbers of *campesinos* (peasants) into the cities, especially Mexico City, with women constituting more than half the migrants in the years between 1895 and 1910. At the same time that women's participation in wage labor in urban areas increased dramatically between 1890 and 1910, women continued to be largely responsible not only for housework and the care of their own children but often the care of other dependent relatives as well. Nor were single women heads of households uncommon in the capital or other industrial hubs.

The first decades of the twentieth century witnessed the entry of women of all social classes into arenas of social life previously considered more exclusively male preserves, an illustration of overall changes in the meanings and activities associated with femininity. For women in the upper and middle classes, opportunities opened in education and in selected professions like book-binding and printing, although the majority of women from these strata continued to regard work outside the home as a secondary priority at this time. But controversy about women's participation in public activities, including paid work and politics, did develop into an important subject of social debate among the better-off strata in the late nineteenth century and continuing early in the twentieth. As to the working class, employment patterns were highly segregated, with women dominating in service trades like *tortillerías*, in waged domestic labor, in food packaging and processing, and in cigarette manufacture.

The Revolution of 1910 challenged gender relations at several levels. The military mobilization and uprooting of people throughout the country destabilized domestic life and redefined the domestic sphere for many households. As camp followers in the battles of the Revolution, and in the absence of an official commissary corps, women filled the crucial role of feeding the male soldiers. The soldiers and officers in combat were primarily men, although women also joined in the actual fighting, and popular perceptions about women changed as a result of this participation. The realities of the *soldaderas'* contributions to the Revolution, for example, as

reflected in many *corridos* (popular songs) and folk tales of the time, were clearly at odds with persistent representations of women as prostitutes, self-sacrificing patriots, or fierce women who were being effectively tamed by male prowess. Yet from the beginning there was disagreement within the ranks of the Revolution regarding women's contributions, and with the professionalization-masculinization of the military forces beginning in 1914, camp followers were forbidden and very little of what women had done for the cause was recognized by the Mexican government in the form of officer commissions or veterans' and widows' pensions.

After the violence of the Revolution subsided, women in areas such as Mérida and the Federal District took to heart the campaign slogans "Effective Suffrage. No Reelection," and began their long struggle for women's suffrage. Revolutionary leaders at the time complained that women were controlled by priests and conservative religious values that were antithetical to the government's liberal political project. When women fought and gained the right to vote in state and municipal elections in the 1920s and 1930s, this was done with the tacit understanding that granting such rights represented an extension of the recognition of women's important *domestic* duties rather than a redefinition of femaleness to include nondomestic and political activities. Indeed, as part of the suffrage movement of this time women were compelled to dispute the latest "scientific" findings that "revealed" irremediable biological differences between men and women that in turn were utilized to argue that, for the best of the Mexican nation, women should exploit their nurturing and emotional strengths and devote themselves to child rearing and the home.

In legislative terms, 1917 was a watershed year in which the legal rights of women were changed. Venustiano Carranza passed the *Ley sobre relaciones familiares* that year, thereby allowing couples limited rights to divorce. How these rights were held to differ for men and women is revealing with respect to distinct legal definitions of male and female conjugal responsibilities. Although adultery on the part of women, for instance, was seen as a legitimate cause for divorce, male infidelity was a justification only in certain instances, such as when male adultery caused public scandal or occurred inside the conjugal home. If a woman did not give cause for a divorce, she had the right to the provision of food and housing by the husband, providing she lived an honest life and did not enter into a new marriage. In a major campaign led by the newspaper *Excelsior* in 1922, and explicitly modeled after a holiday in the United States that served a similar purpose, women's roles as mothers and housekeepers were reinforced as well through the establishment of May 10 as El Día de la Madre, Mother's Day.

Controversy concerning women's sexuality was widespread in intellectual circles during this period, and policies were proposed to deal quite broadly in Mexican society with issues like prostitution early in the century and sex education in the 1930s and 1940s. How to control women's sexuality became the focus of sociological, criminological, medical, and hygienic studies. In part, of course, these debates regarding the Mexican female body denoted the latest chapter in a centuries-old public debate over the Virgin of Guadalupe and la Malinche. Just as the symbolic importance these icons has constantly shifted according to divergent historical exigencies in Mexico, so too in the early twentieth century the Virgin and Malinche were treated as particularly Mexican embodiments of female virtue and traitorous women, respectively.

The 1930s were a golden age of women's public political organizing in Mexico, a time when the boundaries of what was considered feminine were expanded. During the Cárdenas administration women organized in the Frente Único Pro Derechos de la Mujer, most active between 1935 and 1938, which in turn contributed to cross-class alliances among women, and, among upper- and middle-class women, an extension of their concept of womanhood to include working-class women and *campesinas*. A social backlash of sorts developed as well during this time, when various male organizations protested women's entrance into employment and public administration, testifying to the contentious nature of official gender politics, the persistence of publicly proscribed behavior for women, and the incipient conflation of Mexican nationalism and masculinity that would erupt in the mid-century years in Mexico.

"The Dead Time": 1940–70

With a growing dependence on national and international markets, and a consequent decline in independent *campesino* household economies in even the tiniest *pueblos* in Mexico, there occurred in the twentieth century an accelerated transformation of the domestic sphere as issues previously regarded as private and individual became increasingly public and social. With respect to gender and sexuality, for instance, it can be said fairly that the twentieth century has been marked by reproduction "going public." Certain activities have been defined as "women's issues," and such concerns as domestic violence, child care and other domestic work, and reproductive freedom have been socialized. The twentieth century also has seen a trend toward the "denaturalization" of sexuality altogether.

The period following the populist waves of Cardenista reform in the 1930s spelled a temporary lull in women's widespread participation in political campaigns, if not necessarily women's activities in labor outside the home, ushering in what some scholars such as Esperanza Tuñón Pablos have referred to as a "dead time" in the history of Mexican women. Therefore, when women were finally granted the right to vote in 1953—making Mexico one of the last countries in Latin America to grant women suffrage—this marked less a concession to a powerful movement for women's equality in the country at the time than an attempt by the ruling Partido Revolucionario Institucional (PRI, or Institutional Revolutionary Party) to capture and co-opt an enormous new voting bloc in an era of relative social calm. The earlier suffrage movement had significantly expanded the scope of women's activities in the public sphere; at the same time, in many respects women's public political influence remained severely circumscribed.

Beginning in the late 1930s and gathering momentum in the 1940s, Mexico's quest for its own national identity acquired an ever more profoundly gendered and sexual tone. In the cinema, newspapers, and the belles-lettres of the period, images of daring macho men and passive self-sacrificing women—*las mujeres abnegadas*—were increasingly popularized as indicative of the special qualities that made up what was "typical" about Mexican culture. Mexican male identities in the twentieth century were consistently associated with the prestige and politics of the Mexican nation, in particular with the very modern image of the Mexican macho. Beginning with the virile cinematic presence of *charro*-cowboy hero Jorge Negrete, Mexico came to be seen, both internally and internationally, as the consummate land of self-confident, independent, and oftimes violent masculinity, typified by the Negrete standard, "Yo soy mexicano":

> I am a Mexican, and this wild land is mine.
> On the word of a macho, there's no land lovelier
>   and wilder of its kind.
> I am a Mexican, and of this I am proud.
> I was born scorning life and death.
> And though I have bragged, I have never been
>   cowed.

In this period and subsequently, changes in Mexican masculinities, and in what it meant to be a man, were consistently insinuated in changes in Mexican national identity overall. No ubiquitous form of Mexican manhood existed during this or any other historical era, any more than were the women of the time uniform in their beliefs, desires, and actions. Nonetheless, widespread literary, psychological, and sociological interpretations of Mexican men and women, of potent Mexican machos and of self-sacrificing Mexican *abnegadas*, took on an authority that was to last for the remainder of the century, an official history of gender in Mexico challenged only in the closing decades by feminist scholarship that documented widespread diversity and change among women and men along the lines of class, ethnicity, generation, and region.

With industrialization in a boom period beginning in the 1940s, migration to the cities from the countryside, still home to four out of five Mexicans, spelled an increasing separation of home from work for men entering the newly built factories, and brought about a concomitant increase in child care responsibilities in the cities for women, who now more often were expected to single-handedly raise all their children, female and male. Mortality rates, especially for infants, continued to fall during this time, and women's responsibilities in the home increased as families had more children.

In the 1950s, when capitalist development in the countryside intensified and rural families became still more vulnerable to the vicissitudes of larger economic forces, the erosion of relations of reciprocity in rural areas was dramatically accelerated. Indeed, the most important factor affecting gender relations in the Mexican countryside through the 1960s was women's entry into the rural labor market. This led to severe disruptions in families throughout the *campo* (countryside), both in terms of labor patterns outside the home, as well as child-rearing practices within. For example, no longer were men nearly as able or expected to train their sons in farming techniques, nor, with the increasing separation of domicile and workplace, could they participate as actively in raising their children in general.

Migration to urban areas of Mexico and to the United States as a result of the increasingly socialized economy of the *campo* led to other new situations for men and women. When migrants from certain communities were primarily men, mothers and older women often were left alone in the *pueblos* and forced to work the fields as well as to continue their previous chores. In other communities during the years after World War II, young women, frequently those from indigenous ethnic groups, traveled to the capital and other cities to seek employment as domestic servants for the expanding middle class. As a result of rural-urban migration overall, and perhaps paradoxically, women played a key role in extending kinship and household ties in the cities as recent migrants there became increasingly dependent upon the utilization of such family and social networks to meet their daily needs such as housing and employment. The impact of migration in this period on gender relations in Mexico is thus extremely mixed, part of larger developments toward economic globalization and integration, as well as ongoing cultural contention over household divisions of labor, class and ethnic inequalities, and intellectual concerns within the Mexican nation.

The Millennium Closes: 1970–96

The last three decades of the twentieth century were marked by the emergence in Mexico, as elsewhere, of a feminist movement with broad influence, albeit often indirect, among the middle and lower strata of society. Simultaneously, paid work for women, in the countryside and especially in the cities, drew more and more mothers and sisters out of their homes and threw women onto assembly lines, into the streets as *vendedoras ambulantes,* and throughout the service sector across the country. Further, beginning in the early 1970s, a dramatic drop in fertility rates occurred, in part due to Mexican government programs designed to lower the average of almost seven babies per woman. Within 20 years this figure was cut nearly in half, suggesting not simply demographic transitions, but also dramatic changes in cultural attitudes and behavior associated with sexuality, child rearing, and family.

In addition to more demographically traceable transformations, in the late 1970s and 1980s there was an explosion of popularly based movements for social services, for instance, in squatter settlements around older urban cores, in land-rights struggles in the *campo,* among the *damnificados*

(loosely, "victims") of the 1985 earthquake in Mexico City, and in the Chiapas Zapatista uprising of 1994, whose stated aims included confronting gender inequalities in immediate ways. Within these popular struggles, women in particular played a prominent role as militants and sometimes leaders, and women's participation in such political organizing activities became part of debates regarding preexisting gender identities and relations. At the same time, this period witnessed the initiation of feminist publications, some appearing as supplements to daily newspapers, centers for battered women, and campaigns to legalize abortion.

The consequences of feminism and women's activities in social movements were mixed, and did not simply result in the extension of gender equality in Mexican society: simultaneous with these demographic and political transformations affecting women and men there occurred an increase in domestic violence, divorce, and child abuse. Though far from indicating uniform or permanent responses to these changes, in part these problems seemed connected to negative reactions on the part of husbands and fathers to women's increasing independence from them in political arenas and in the home. And the domain of official politics seemed particularly resistant to change: it was not until 1974, with the reform of Article 4 of the Constitution of 1917, that women were guaranteed equal rights under the law; as for elected officials, in 1995 women still made up less than 14 percent of the representatives and senators in Mexico's national Congress.

Women's work increasingly came to include remunerated employment during the final three decades of the century. In 1990, nationally over 20 percent of women over 12 years old worked for money, whereas the figure for women in Mexico City was over 30 percent. In addition, unlike women in the rural areas, women in Mexico City continued to labor for wages far longer: over 40 percent of women in the capital worked for money through their early 40s; only slightly more than 20 percent of women in the country as a whole did so in 1990. Certain sectors of the economy, such as the assembly plants situated largely along the Mexico-U.S. border, employed a majority of women as workers, although by the mid-1990s the number of women in these factories had dropped to 60 percent, at least partially as a result of increased mechanization of the plants and the preferential hiring of men to work the new equipment.

In spite of the fact that the figures were debated as to the precise number of women working in various sectors of the economy, in this period, as throughout the twentieth century, it was beyond dispute that women's income was crucial to the survival of most urban families and many rural ones. More controversial was the impact of women's labor activities with respect to household gender relations and gender divisions of labor, and specifically whether women's participation in the labor market and in the generation of income had given women any significantly greater share of control, power, and authority overall in society. Similarly, although girls' attendance in schools continued to increase in this period—by 1975 there was parity of boys and girls in elementary school, by 1989 parity in junior high school, and by 1989 around 42 percent of those enrolled in Mexican universities were women—the exact implications of these figures for equality of men and women in society more broadly continued to be debated hotly in official and popular circles.

One outcome of what some scholars referred to as the "privatization of the crisis" in Mexico, beginning especially in the late 1970s, was the growing number of *madres solteras* (single mothers) whose vulnerabilities owing to more acute levels of poverty may have been offset, in part, by lower levels also of violence, greater equitable distribution of income and consumption, and more attention to children's nutrition than in many households in which men were at least nominally present. Thus, creative and alternative strategies of survival among the poor in Mexico in the last quarter of the century depended in good measure on the specific nature of gender relations as they developed and were changed (or not) within specific households.

In keeping with official Catholic doctrine, and certainly revealing a closer practical relation between church and state than was required by Mexican law, abortions of any kind remained illegal throughout the twentieth century, although they certainly were readily available for women of wealth. As a partial reflection of the gendered influence of Catholicism, in most churches in Mexico in the twentieth century women made up the strong majority of parishioners. Yet it is also important to recognize that attitudes about and practices relating to sexuality changed during this period, at least as marked by the increasing utilization of birth control (few would argue that the fall in birthrates was a result of lessened sexual activity) and, to a lesser extent, to the increasing openness of homosexuality as a social phenomenon in Mexico.

With respect to birth control, from the beginning this was viewed broadly by women and men in Mexico as mainly a female responsibility. In practice this meant that the most common contraception methods employed were tubal ligations for women who would no longer bear children, and intrauterine devices for younger women. As to homosexuality, a Movimiento de Liberación Homosexual (MLH) emerged in the late 1970s in Mexico City, Guadalajara, and a few other locations, and this together with a more general *"salida del clóset"* (coming out of the closet) in Mexican society contributed to a somewhat greater permissiveness regarding sexual tolerance and interpersonal relations in the country as a whole. Although AIDS cases have not been numerically as widespread in Mexico as in many other countries since the disease first appeared in the 1980s, the epidemic nonetheless had a chilling effect on the openness of cultural practices such as homosexuality in Mexico.

Both the increased use of birth control and the MLH contributed to altered perceptions concerning sexuality on the part of many in Mexico, as captured in the growing belief that sexuality should be regarded as more of an option and a matter of individual proclivities and less as an issue of innate and natural drives. This process can be termed the "denaturalization" of sexuality in Mexico. Nonetheless, double standards regarding sexuality between men and women certainly persisted, and men far more than women were "allowed" their sexual peccadilloes, despite the fact that adultery among women, many scholars believe, was on the rise in Mexico at the end of the twentieth century.

Finally, concerning health care in general, here too gender differences were apparent throughout the twentieth century in Mexico. In terms of life expectancy, for instance, by 1993 the figures were 76 years for women and 69 years for men. More specifically, cervical cancer was the leading cause of death for women aged 30 to 44, and, of course, illegal and botched abortions were the cause of female deaths alone; incidence of alcoholism and alcohol-related deaths—directly from cirrhosis of the liver and alcoholic psychosis, and indirectly from accidents and homicides—were the leading causes of death among men in the so-called productive ages in Mexico at the end of the century.

Conclusion

In households, marketplaces, factories, and *milpas* (maize fields), in education, politics, reproduction, and play, gender and sexual relations have been at the very heart of the modern Mexican experience. Whether couched in terms of common goals or uncontrollable antagonisms, general questions relating to cultural citizenship in Mexico have received concentrated expression throughout the century in the form of the issues of gender and sexuality, in particular the conspicuous chasm between official claims to equality and the myriad realities of inequalities large and small in every corner of the society.

Reproduction is central to social life, and it is anything but stagnant. Whether in terms of the relation of men to the Mexican state, in regard to marital relations within families, or with respect to the impact of paid work on women's authority in society, factors such as education, migration, mass media, fertility rates, and the powerful participation of women in political struggles in the 1970s and 1980s are more than mere statistics. They must be seen in their convergence in order to perceive more clearly a portrait of Mexican society undergoing enormous transformations in the twentieth century, including, and in many respects especially, as concerns gender and sexuality.

See also Soldaderas and Coronelas

Select Bibliography

Basurto, Jorge, *Vivencias femininas de la revolución.* Mexico City: INEHRM, 1993.

De Barbieri, Teresita, *Mujeres y vida cotidiana.* Mexico City: Fondo de Cultura Económica, 1984.

Fowler-Salamini, Heather, and Mary K. Vaughan, editors, *Women of the Mexican Countryside, 1850–1990.* Tucson: University of Arizona Press, 1994.

González de la Rocha, Mercedes, *The Resources of Poverty: Women and Survival in a Mexican City.* Oxford and Cambridge, Massachusetts: Blackwell, 1994.

González Montes, Soledad, and Vania Salles, editors, *Relaciones de género y transformaciones agrarias: Estudios sobre el campo mexicano.* Mexico City: Colegio de México, 1995.

Gutmann, Matthew C., *The Meanings of Macho: Being a Man in Mexico City.* Berkeley: University of California Press, 1996.

Lau, Ana, and Carmen Ramos-Escandon, editors, *Mujeres y revolución, 1900–1917.* Mexico City: INEHRM, 1993.

Macías, Ana, *Against All Odds: The Feminist Movement in Mexico to 1940.* Westport, Connecticut: Greenwood, 1982.

Massolo, Alejandra, *Por amor y coraje: Mujeres en movimientos urbanos de la ciudad de México.* Mexico City: Colegio de México, 1992.

Monsiváis, Carlos, *Escenas de pudor y liviandad.* Mexico City: Grijalbo, 1981.

Oliveira, Orlandina de, editor, *Trabajo, poder y sexualidad.* Mexico City: Colegio de México, 1989.

Stephen, Lynn, *Zapotec Women.* Austin: University of Texas Press, 1991.

Tuñón Pablos, Esperanza, *Mujeres que se organizan: El frente único pro derechos de la mujer, 1935–1938.* Mexico City: Porrúa, 1992.

—MATTHEW C. GUTMANN AND SUSIE S. PORTER

GENDER AND MEXICAN SPANISH

Whether found in the sounds of language, grammar, vocabulary, or even daily conversation, gender distinctions are found in all languages worldwide. Indo-European languages such as Spanish offer a particular variation on a theme, a particular array of grammatical genders, phonemes (elementary units of sound), morphemes (elementary units of meaning), and sociocultural contexts. What most distinguishes Mexican Spanish from other versions of Spanish with regard to gender and language is the cultural and social institutions within which phonetically, grammatically, and lexically gendered discourses are spoken and interpreted by native Mexican speakers.

Spanish is composed of grammatical genders—words or parts of words that are classified or marked as feminine (f.), masculine (m.), or both feminine and masculine. Grammatical genders are a property of nouns that requires syntactical agreement on the part of other nouns, adjectives, and articles. For example, in the Spanish translation of the phrase "the red house"—*la casa roja*—both the article *(la)* and the adjective *(roja)* must agree with the feminine gender of the noun *(casa)*. Spanish words can be of two types: double-form and single-form words. Double-form words have both a masculine and a feminine form, such as *amigo* (a male friend) and *amiga* (a female friend). Single-form words only have a masculine, feminine, or androgynous form despite the sex of the referent. For example, *la persona* and *la gente* are feminine grammatically, but refer generically to person and people respectively; *el personaje* is masculine grammatically, but refers generically to a personage; *el/la juez* is androgynous grammatically, and refers generically to a judge.

Spanish words that refer to animate beings (people and animals) as opposed to inanimate things (objects and concepts) do so in three ways: by explicitly or implicitly referring to men, women, or both men and women. *Amigo* is explicitly masculine and *amiga* is explicitly feminine owing to their clearly marked syntactic properties (the suffix *o* versus the suffix *a*), and the sexes of their referents correspond directly to their grammatical genders. *Amigo* refers to a male friend, *amiga* to a female friend. In contrast to double-form words such as *amigo/amiga,* single-form words have an implicit or indirect (rather than an explicit or direct) relationship to the sex of the referent. In these cases qualifiers are required to determine the sex of the implied referent. For example, *la persona* is grammatically feminine but semantically of either or both sex; *la persona* may refer to a man, a woman, or generically to a person, depending upon the context or the qualifiers used by the speaker. In such cases, the speaker must explicitly state the referent's sex if the speaker wishes to convey this information. Ways of doing this are numerous. For example, one may state *"Él es una persona buena"* (he is a good person), emphasizing the subject as male with the pronoun *él* (he). For nouns with ambiguous syntactical endings, an article before the noun is sufficient to make the distinction explicit (e.g., *el juez* or *la juez, el artista* or *la artista, el periodista* or *la periodista*).

For centuries scholars have wondered whether grammatical genders convey any semantic message of femininity and masculinity. Despite the fact that *el hombre* refers to mankind, does its grammatically masculine form carry any intrinsic meaning of masculinity? In a study of Mexican Spanish, Toshi Konishi found that grammatical gender categories affect meaning and correlate with social and cultural ideas about femininity and masculinity. Significantly, he also found that speakers of Spanish perceive these correlates to have unequal values. Konishi discovered that words in the masculine gender were consistently perceived as higher in potency than those in the feminine. "Gender stereotypes," he writes, "played a role in the choice of he vs. she since antecedents of he tended to be strong, active, brave, wise, and clever, whereas antecedents of she tended to be weak, passive, and foolish." For example, in children's literature, the sun *(el sol)* is referred to as "he" and is thought of as more powerful than the moon *(la luna),* which is personified as "she" and thought of as less potent. Work by other scholars has shown that this phenomenon is not limited to Mexican Spanish.

There is another aspect of the gender-sex relationship worth noting. To explicitly signify men/males there is one gender, the masculine gender. In contrast, to signify women/females there are two genders: one that is feminine (*amiga*) and the other that is masculine/generic (*amigo*), which linguistically, if not psychologically, includes women/females. In other words, the masculine gender in double-form words has two possible referents; *amigo* can refer explicitly to the sex (a male friend) or implicitly to the general class of friends (male or female, friend as a category of person) just as the word *man* in English has traditionally stood for the sex (a person who is male) as well as the generic (a person/mankind, male or female). *Amiga* has only one referent, and it is explicitly female. While *amigos* is the plural for friends and includes both men and women, the plural *amigas* includes only women. Semantic asymmetry such as this, where the masculine gender dominates over the feminine in the generic as the plural form, requires Spanish speakers to make leaps in their understanding. It is also the reason many women listeners rely heavily on context to determine whether or not they are included when the masculine form of a noun is in use. Recent studies such as Konishi's demonstrate that when the generic term is chosen by a speaker—*amigo(s)*—few speakers think of anything other than male referents. To remedy this discrepancy scholars of the Spanish language such as García Meseguer have suggested that speakers employ the generic only as the generic and make use of qualifiers when referring to the specific sexes; thus, *hombre* unqualified refers only to mankind (to both men and women) but never exclusively to men/males. With qualifiers, however, *hombre* may refer specifically to males if stated specifically as *hombre macho* and to females if stated as *hombre hembra*.

Unlike grammatical genders, which show gender with grammatical markers, the lexicon, or vocabulary, creates gender distinctions with words and meanings. For example, the proper term of address for a man is *señor*, which may be used on its own or with a surname. It is a term of address applied indiscriminately to adult males. There is no equivalent term in Spanish to signify an adult woman. Instead there are two terms to address a woman, *señora* and *señorita*, each of which discriminates two categories of women, married and unmarried. A *señorita* is an unmarried woman or girl; a *señora*, a married one. *Señor* makes no such distinction. In Mexico there are numerous occasions when it is more polite to address a woman whose marital status is unknown as *señorita* than *señora*, despite her age, not so much for the youth but the virginity the former implies. The categorization of women, but not men, along such lines occurs in many other semantic domains. The term *hombre público* is a man in the public eye or sphere, but a *mujer pública* is a prostitute; an *hombre honrado* is an honest man, but a *mujer honrada* is a chaste woman. Words that describe the sexuality of men do so in celebratory tones as *viril* and *potente*. Those same traits

in a woman are considered negative. Not surprisingly, words for coitus almost always are cast in phallocentric terms, focused on *penetración* by the male; terms for the female role are passive, unless negatively described. The colloquial terms for sex in Mexico are based on metaphors of conquest: striking, causing harm, even killing; penises are sticks, clubs, and guns, which men, depending often but not always on their class, either put into (*meter*) or throw at (*echar*) a woman. While married men commonly refer to their spouses generically by their sex and in the possessive as *mi mujer*, "my woman," women have no such equivalent available to them, only words for husband (*marido* or *esposo*) or personal names. And finally, while a *señora* does not change her name to that of her husband, as is common practice in English-speaking countries, she often adds her husband's name to hers by using the possessive *de* (of), as in "Señora García de Bustos."

In Mexico and around the world, cultural codes and social conventions have an enormous impact on the shaping of language and its messages. *Padre* and *madre* are two words that provide an example of culturally encoded gender difference in Mexican Spanish. Literally, *padre* is a noun and means "father." When part of the expression *que padre*, however, *padre* is an adjective that translates as "that's terrific." It is a mundane expression, as common as its counterpart *me vale madre*, which literally translates as "it's worth a mother." While *madre* means mother, both as a noun (e.g., the mother of children) and an adjective (e.g., the mother country), idiomatically *madre* is used to describe any number of bad experiences, objects, or circumstances. *Me vale madre* stands in contrast to *que padre*. Instead of referring to greatness, it refers to uselessness. In free translation *me vale madre* renders into something like "it's worthless" or "I don't give a damn." Yet mothers are revered in Mexico, in both the religious (the Virgin Mary, the Mother of God) and secular spheres.

According to Alan Riding there are many words in Mexican Spanish filled with multiple meanings rich in "psychosexual and religious connotations." However, few are as complex in meaning and abundant in variation as *madre*. For example,

> *Nuestra madre* refers to the Virgin Mary, yet, puzzlingly, the word usually is used negatively. The insult *chinga tu madre* can be reduced to *tu madre* with little loss of intensity, while *una madre* can signify something that is unimportant, and *un desmadre* converts a situation into chaos. A *madrazo* is a heavy blow, a *madreador* is a bouncer or hired thug, and *partir la madre*—to "divide" the mother—means to shatter someone or something. . . . A son will use the diminutive form *madrecita* to address his own mother, but *mamacita* is a vulgar street comment to a passing girl or a term of endearment for a mistress.

According to A. Bryson Gerrard's handbook of everyday spoken Spanish, *madre* "should need no entry but Mexican usage makes one essential; insults connected with mothers are so common . . . and so offensive that in Mexico [that Mexicans] have steered off the word altogether when it is a matter of referring to immediate relatives." It is better to ask friends about the health of their *mamás* than it is to ask about their *madres,* the handbook warns. "In contrast," Riding notes, "the father figure—*el padre*—plays a lesser linguistic role. A *padrote,* or big father, is a pimp, while something that is excellent is *muy padre."* The list of idioms deriving from *padre* are all but exhausted by these few expressions, not one of which connotes worthlessness.

The inconsistencies that surround the cultural meaning of the term *madre* are intriguing. Along with *me vale madre* there are expressions such as *a toda madre* and *de poca madre.* The former literally translates into "a total mother," the latter into "of little mother." Yet both are as powerful in their reference to greatness as is *que padre.* The gender-blending of common Mexican names like María José for a girl and José María for a boy or Jesús for a boy and Jesusa for a girl offers some hint of the complexity of gender difference and maintenance with regard to mother-father issues. They suggest that the linguistic construction of gender difference is more than a simple black-and-white matter.

It is quite possible that gender differences may be encoded in the most elementary units of sound in Mexican Spanish. In 1954 Roman Jakobson suggested that there might be biological and psychological roots to the phonology of the terms mother and father. Based on a study by George Peter Murdock of unrelated languages from around the world, Jakobson observed a correspondence in the structure of parental terms used by infants. Words for mother *(mama)* more often than not begin with a nasalized consonant (/m/, /n/, /ng/), and those for father *(papa)* frequently begin with a bilabial or palatal stop (/p/, /b/, /t/ or /d/). Jakobson traced the sounds for mother to the nasalized murmur that children make while sucking at a mother's breast. In Spanish, sounds associated with sucking *(mamar,* to suck) also begin with a nasalized sound. Jakobson did not explore the possible biological and psychological roots to the /p/ of papa, but if he had he might have noted that the sound [p] is forceful whether aspirated as it is in English or unaspirated as in Spanish. It may be that the forcefulness of a consonantal stop such as /p/ or /t/ as opposed to a nasalized murmur such as /m/ was not an arbitrary choice by the infant to signify her/his father any more than the choice of a nasalized murmur to represent the mother was arbitrary. Approximately 30 percent of men's names in Spanish begin with a consonantal stop, but only 4 percent of women's names do. Despite these provocative general data, however, there have been no studies of the phonetic encoding of gender in Mexican Spanish.

Over the past 15 years sociolinguists have demonstrated that in addition to language itself, other nonlinguistic factors have a large impact on the perception and perpetuation of gender difference in language, particularly conversational contexts. Class, culture, ethnicity, and gender (meaning in this case the cultural construction of one's sexuality) can each influence the message conveyed by a language. Gender-specific speech styles, for example, affect the way men and women interact and interpret one another. Confusing linguistic genders (masculine and feminine words) with sexual difference (male and female) on the one hand and socioculturally constructed genders (e.g., masculinity and femininity) on the other is a common occurrence among speakers of a language filled with gender-encoded sounds, syntax, and semantics. Making this confusion conscious is a central activity of many Mexican Spanish speakers, particularly in marked situations such as joking sessions, musical lyrics, and other out-of-the-ordinary performances.

In Mexico there is a social form of discourse found primarily among men, a particular kind of joking called *albur.* Men of all classes and in almost all parts of Mexico outside the indigenous populations engage in these joking sessions. *Albures* are always about sex and sexual conquests that, while stated in male-female terms, are contests between two men, the speakers themselves. There are many circumstances that might spark an *albur:* food at the dinner table, a word, a color. But most commonly *albures* center around women: a passing woman on a street, someone's grandmother, sister, and only on rare occasions, mother. *Albures* are often but not always set pieces, which a boy learns growing up. Just as an English speaker might follow someone's "see you later" with "alligator" so a Mexican man might follow someone's *chico* or *pequeño* with *pásame el plato grande,* thereby initiating a contest that will appear competitive only to someone educated in the craft. While "see you later, alligator" is a simple rhyme without contest, an *albur* always has a winner and a loser so that the initiator in the case above must respond quickly with some sexual reference or he loses. He asks *¿cómo?,* which might on the surface translate into "what did you say?," but is quickly interpreted by his contestant to be the first person singular of the verb *comer,* to eat, thereby making it easy for the respondent to win by feminizing his contestant with the retort *Siéntate que te veo cansado* (sit down [on me], you look tired). Although the contestants in *albures* are generally men, on occasion women will participate in them. Nonetheless, women's participation in *albures* is limited.

The women's movement in Mexico has sought to change the perception and position of women in Mexican society by several means, including cultural and sociolinguistic ones. Mexican women writers, playwrights, performance artists, and songwriters such as Elena Poniatowska, Jesusa Rodríguez, Astrid Hadad, and Gloria Trevi have in their novels, plays, performances, and songs challenged the sexual biases in Mexican Spanish and society. In addition the Chicanisma movement in the United States, which includes such Mexican American women writers as Sandra Cisneros and Gloria Anzaldúa, has through its written poetry, poetry slams, short stories, and novels challenged the social construction and linguistic usage of Mexican Spanish that subordinate women. All these verbal artists have as their ancestor Sor Juana Inés de la Cruz, the seventeenth-century nun who left a legacy of poetry and letters she had written about sex discrimination. For Sor Juana it was colonial society and the Catholic Church that regulated women's behavior, including what they had to say. Much has changed since the seventeenth century, although some Mexican women argue that the continuities are more striking. What becomes of Mexican Spanish in the days ahead will depend on the work of feminist linguists and verbal artists, as well as such individuals as the young married Mexican woman who responded to the inquiry "Do you use *de* García after your name to indicate you are married?" with "No, I occasionally use *con* (with) or *contra* (against) but never *de* (of)".

Select Bibliography

Frank, Francine Harriet, and Frank Anshen, *Language and the Sexes.* Albany: SUNY Press, 1983.

García Meseguer, *¿Es sexista la lengua española? Una investigación sobre el género gramatical.* Barcelona: ediciones Paidós Ibérica, S.A., 1994.

Gerrard, A. Bryson, *Cassell's Beyond the Dictionary in Spanish: A Handbook of Everyday Usage.* 2nd edition, New York: Funk and Wagnalls, 1972.

Hill, Jane H., and Kenneth C. Hill, *Speaking Mexicano: Dynamics of Syncretic Language in Central Mexico.* Tucson: University of Arizona Press, 1986.

Jakobson, Roman, "Why Mama and Papa?" In *Perspectives in Psychological Theory.* New York: International Universities Press, 1960.

Konishi, Toshi, "The Semantics of Grammatical Gender: A Cross-Cultural Study." *Journal of Psycholinguistic Research* 22:5 (1993).

Riding, Alan, *Distant Neighbors: A Portrait of the Mexicans.* New York: Knopf, 1985.

—Elizabeth Bakewell

GENERACIÓN DEL MEDIO SIGLO

During the 1940s the foundation was laid for the consolidation of modern Mexico. The governments of Manuel Avila Camacho (1940–46) and Miguel Alemán Valdés (1946–52) not only put an end to the internecine struggle among Revolutionary factions, but also imposed relative political stability and economic growth and diversification. Mexico passed through a process of transformation from a largely agrarian to a primarily industrial economy, with strong participation both domestic businesses and foreign capital.

The repercussions of this process for Mexico's cultural life were felt immediately. If Mexican culture before the 1940s largely had been rural, by then end of the decade it had become more urban-based and cosmopolitan. If the arts had responded to the Revolutionary project in previous decades, in the 1940s their political engagement suffered a marked decline. By 1940, for example, the Mexican muralism of David Alfaro Siqueiros, Diego Rivera, and José Clemente Orozco had produced its most important works and began to lose ground to other, more emphatically avant-garde visual arts. During the Alemán administration muralism and the Mexican School of painting was reduced to a purely decorative art form, insipid ornamentation for public buildings and luxury hotels, whose Revolutionary commitment amounted to little more than empty posturing. As the artist Rufino Tamayo acidly remarked, "The peasants have triumphed in Mexico only in murals."

A new current in the visual arts gained strength in the 1940s, however, and in the 1950s would displace Mexican muralism. Its mentor was Rufino Tamayo, who insisted that the Revolutionary character of art rested not in its content but in its forms of expression. This current soon came to known as the Generación de Ruptura: first, Carlos Mérida, Juan Soriano, Pedro Coronel, and Alfonso Michel; and later younger artists such as Vicente Rojo, Manuel Felguérez, Lilia Carrillo, Fernando García Ponce, Alberto Gironella, and Arnaldo Coen. The Generación de Ruptura also spurred a revalorization of the work of such artists as Gunther Gerszo and Leonora Carrington, which had been largely forgotten during the heyday of muralism.

A similar trend occurred in music. The nationalist current of Silvestre Revueltas, Carlos Chávez, and Pablo Moncayo began to lose ground to the work of artists who followed the experiments of avant-garde composers in other countries. This current would rise to prominence during the 1950s and 1960s and included such artists as Joaquín Gutiérrez Heras, Armando Lavalle, Raúl Cosío, Manuel Henríquez, Héctor Quintanar, and Julio Estrada.

Literature was far more resistant to these changes. The 1940s continued the long-running conflict between socially engaged literature—emerging largely out of the novel of the Mexican Revolution—and avant-garde currents led by the Estridentistas (Stridentists) and the Contemporáneos Group, which already had produced its best work in the previous decades. The first group included such writers as José Rubén Romero, Gregorio López y Fuentes, Mauricio Magdaleno, Francisco Rojas González, José Mancisidor, Ermilo Abreu Gómez, Juan de la Cabada, Rubén Salazar Mallén, and José Revueltas. The second group centered on the journals *Taller* and *Tierra Nueva* and included such writers as Octavio Paz, Efraín Huerta, Neftalí Beltrán, Rafael Solana, and Alí Chumacero. The 1940s closed with the publication Agustín Yáñez's *Al filo del agua,* which synthesized to two basic currents of the 1940s. If the content of the novel puts its firmly in the tradition of socially engaged literature, it also incorporated the formal experiments of the avant-garde, particularly the innovations of John Dos Passos's *Manhattan Transfer.*

Nonetheless, in the first half of the 1940s the avant-garde currents began to eclipse the nationalist discourse of previous decades. In 1950 Octavio Paz published *El laberinto de la soledad,* which—together with the work of the Hiperión Group—culminated a series of reflections on Mexican national character initiated by Samuel Ramos in the 1930s. Nonetheless, the dichotomy between a more socially engaged literature and a more urban, cosmopolitan literature continued in Mexico letters. If the first tendency is epitomized by Juan Rulfo's *El llano en llamas* and *Pedro Páramo,* the second is represented by such works as *¿Águila o sol?* by Octavio Paz, Alfonso Reyes's *La X en la frente,* and Juan José Arreola's *Confabulario.* This last current reached its apogee in Carlos Fuentes's *La región más transparente* (1958), whose mosaic of voices, social classes, and urban scenes would be seen by critics as the great novel of Mexico City, the indisputable point of departure for the contemporary urban novel.

In 1956 a new theatrical movement appeared, Poesía en Voz Alta. This movement shortly would overturn the theatrical trends of the previous decades, which had been founded in bucolic representations of the countryside. Rather than being composed only of professionals from the theater, Poesía en Voz Alta drew on a heterodox amalgam of writers, musicians, painters, dramatists, and actors. The intention of the group was to return to the origins of theater, eliminating unnecessary artifice and making the spoken word its driving force. It sought to meld work from the golden age of Spanish literature in the sixteenth and seventeenth centuries with the European avant-garde, particularly the one-act plays of García Lorca. Presenting its works in tents and drawing on the popular traditions of circuses, pantomime, and music halls, Poesía en Voz Alta emphasized theater as spectacle. The movement was a point of departure for Mexican experimental theater.

If all of these movements helped define the cultural panorama of midcentury Mexico, the group that would be known as the Generación del Medio Siglo (Midcentury Generation) was founded on a shared conception of literature and a desire to write outside the norms established by Mexican culture. The Generación del Medio Siglo included such authors as Jorge Ibargüengoitia, Juan Garcá Ponce, Carlos Valdés, José Emilio Pacheco, Fernando del Paso, and Carlos Monsiváis. The critical work of these authors helped redefine Mexican music, painting, theater, film, poetry, narrative, and essays.

The Generación del Medio Siglo was above all a movement based on a shared intellectual agenda, but its cohesion was facilitated by a number of institutions and literary publications. One of the most important of these was the Centro Mexicano de Escritores. Founded in 1951 by the U.S. author Margaret Shedd and funded by the Rockefeller Foundation, the Centro Mexicano de Escritores funded several authors from the Generación del Medio Siglo from the mid-1950s through the 1970s. Another key institutions was the Coordi-

nación de Difusión Cultural of the Universidad Nacional Autónoma de México (UNAM), which initially was directed by Jaime García Terrés. The main function of the Coordinación was to organize conferences, round tables, poetry recitals, expositions of painting, concerts, ballets, theatrical productions, film screenings, and book publications, bringing the cultural ferment of the university to society at large. The Generación del Medio Siglo continued to play a key role in the Coordinadora. Tomás Segovia and later Juan Vicente continued the work of the Coordinadora's founder, Juan José Arreola. Juan García Ponce served as editor in chief of the *Revista de la Universidad,* José de la Colina ran the film club, and Juan José Gurrola the university theater and television. Inés Arredondo worked in the Coordinadora's publishing activities, and Huberto Batis was in charge of the university press. The UNAM had ceased to be an institution for teaching and research and had become one of the main cultural centers of Mexico, and the work of the Generación was decisive in this transformation.

Parallel to their work in the university, the members of the Generación del Medio Siglo also worked in the most important literary and artistic journals of the day: their namesake, *Medio Siglo;* the *Revista de la Universidad; Cuadernos del Viento,* directed by Huberto Batis and Carlos Valdés; *La Palabra y el Hombre,* which published the first works of many of the Generación's members; the *Revista de Bellas Artes;* and most important, the *Revista Mexicana de Literatura.* The Generación also worked in the cultural supplements of many of the newspapers and mass-circulation magazines of the day, most notably "México en la Cultura" in the newspaper *Novedades* and "La Cultura en México" in the magazine *¡Siempre!,* both of which were founded and directed by Fernando Benítez. The poetry, narrative, and essays published by the Generación helped consolidate a literature that had escaped the restrictions of nationalism and was enriched by its contact with literary currents worldwide.

If 1956 was the point of departure for the Generación de Medio Siglo, 1968 marked its end. If the Generación ceased to be a coherent group; however, its members individually continued their literary and artistic work, enriching Mexican culture with their sense of irony, acid criticism, openness, and imagination.

Select Bibliography

Agustín, José, *Tragicomedia mexicana.* Mexico City: Planeta, 1991.

Batis, Huberto, *Lo que "Cuadernos del Viento" nos dejó.* Mexico City: Editorial Diógenes, 1984.

González Levet, Sergio, *Letras y opiniones.* Mexico City: Punto y Aparte, 1980.

Pereira, Armando, "La Generación de Medio Siglo: Un momento de transición en la cultura mexicana." *Literatura Mexicana* 6:1 (1995).

—ARMANDO PEREIRA

GENERACIÓN DE 1915

The intellectual group called the Generation of 1915 had its roots in two important historical events of the early decades of the twentieth century: first, the impact that the Mexican Revolution had in the lives of those living in Mexico City, when in the darkest moments the extreme anarchy and violence of the armed conflict were felt by all; and, second, the period of post-Revolutionary national reconstruction that started in the 1920s and during which many of the ideals of the Revolution began to be fulfilled. The so-called Chaos of 1915 forced many Mexican intellectuals to rediscover the roots of their own country; later, during the 1920s, many members of this generation were given the opportunity of participating in the country's political life by occupying positions in the administrations of Presidents Adolfo de la Huerta, Álvaro Obregón, and Plutarco Elías Calles, which finally gave them the opportunity to change Mexican society by attempting to carry out many of the Revolution's promises.

In his famous work *1915,* the intellectual Manuel Gómez Morín not only baptized his generation but also gave it a feeling of a common cause based on its members' shared experiences and their desire of shaping a new nation:

> Those who were students in the year 1915 and who participatedin the Revolution's political and military events, yearning to give it an ideal, those who followed the events trying to understand them, and the youngest ones who were born during the Revolution, and all of those who lived through those difficult years, with the hope that all that pain had not been in vain, all of them are part of a new Mexican generation, the Generación de 1915.

The most prominent leaders of this generation were Vicente Lombardo Toledano, Manuel Gómez Morín, Alfonso Caso, Teófilo Olea y Leyva, Miguel Palacios Macedo, Alberto Vázquez del Mercado, Manuel Toussaint, Narciso Bassols, Antonio Castro Leal, and Daniel Cosío Villegas, young men who in 1915 were between 17 and 21 years old, some enrolled in the Escuela Nacional Preparatoria (National Preparatory School), and others already taking law courses at the Universidad Nacional (National University). Owing to the circumstances surrounding the fall of the dictator Victoriano Huerta and the taking of the capital by the Revolutionary forces, this generation faced the challenge of assuming the leadership of the new political-cultural milieu, now that the old Positivist generation of the Porfirio Díaz regime had perished and the intellectual leaders of the former movement of cultural reform known as the Ateneo de la Juventud (Youth Athenaeum) were either exiled or had joined in the fighting.

Lacking great teachers (an exception being Alfonso Caso, the only member of the Ateneo still in the profession), the members of the Generación de 1915 abandoned their exclusive literary and aesthetic interests based on the principles of the Ateneo and turned their attention to the social problems caused by a world devastated by World War I and a country in the midst of a revolution. Again, in the words of Gómez Morín's *1915,*

> The agrarian problem . . . surfaced to become the Revolution's central theme. The labor problem was formally incorporated in the Revolutionary banner. The opportunity to gain back what had been ours was born: the oil and the song, the nationality and the ruins. And in an expansive movement of vitality we recognized the substantial Spanish-American unity extending the longing to Magallanes.

The generation's earliest accomplishment was the founding of the Society of Conferences and Concerts in 1916, a group created at the request of a group of law students known by the nickname of los Siete Sabios (the Seven Wise Men), composed of Lombardo Toledano, Gómez Morín, Caso, Olea y Leyva, Vázquez del Mercado, Castro Leal, and Jesus Moreno Vaca. These students, influenced by the teachings of Antonio Caso, proposed the renewed publication of the work of the members of the Ateneo with the aim of "propagating learning among the students of the Universidad Nacional." Cycles of conferences dealing with Mexico's problems (social, educational, judicial, and those pertaining to labor movements) were organized; members of the group would tackle these same issues later in their professional careers.

The political restlessness of several members of the Generación de 1915 found an outlet through the form of college militancy. Already in 1917, los Siete Sabios started defending college autonomy, as expressed in a document they sent to the Mexican House of Deputies. For a while, Gómez Morín and Lombardo Toledano were responsible for the "college page" of a leading Mexico City newspaper, *El Universal.* On the other hand, Palacios Macedo became the president of the Mexican Student Federation in 1919, succeeded by Cosío Villegas two years later.

The pillars of their political philosophy were the concern for better education and an attempt to eradicate "improvisation" and supplant it with "technique" in the practice of public administration, especially after 1920, when many members of the generation occupied posts in the Ministry of Public Education, the Mexico City Hall, and in the Ministry of the Treasury (Hacienda).

Secretary of Education José Vasconcelos became the intellectual guide for most of the generation's members owing to his ambitious project of cultural and educational renovation. The nationalism of his cultural proposals, the antimilitarism of his politics, and his belief in the necessity of opening political space for intellectuals made him a hero, so Vasconcelos and the members of the Generación de 1915 saw themselves not only as pillars of a new social order, but also as the ones responsible for its intellectual guidance. The Revolution's programs needed theoretical foundations and "technical" expertise that would allow their application, thereby translating the people's wishes into actual works and policies. In the words of Cosío Villegas in *La Riqueza de México* (1925),

> The Revolution failed because it was only a military triumph . . . the triumphant political and military leaders of the Revolution will never be able to carry out a social movement because for its success you need a new ideology, a new point of view . . . of a new generation, and we are that new generation, we affirm that we are the Revolution.

During the interim presidency of Adolfo de la Huerta (1920), Vázquez del Mercado was appointed chief clerk of Mexico City, and he soon secured important posts for other members of the Generación de 1915: Palacios Macedo was appointed chief of security and jails of the Federal District, and Alfonso Caso became consulting attorney. A little later, Vázquez del Mercado was promoted to general secretary of the government of the Federal District, his former post being taken by Lombardo Toledano. Manuel Gómez Morín was named private secretary to General Salvador Alvarado, de la Huerta's treasury minister; Castro Leal became a diplomat, serving in Washington and Santiago, Chile; Toussaint was sent to Madrid on an official mission; Olea y Leyva was already president of the legislature of Guerrero; Cosío Villegas joined Vasconcelos's team, first at the Universidad Nacional and later at the Ministry of Education; and Narciso Bassols remained for a while in his teaching post at the Law School, eventually joining public service after 1925. From their positions of power, the members of the Generación de 1915 made a deep and lasting impact on Mexico's institutions, policies, and laws. In the realm of public revenue and finance, Gómez Morín stood out as one of the initiators of the Bank of Mexico. As the bank's adviser from 1925 to 1929, he was responsible for the writing of the Law of Agricultural Credit, which was the predecessor of the National Bank of Agricultural Credit; in the same manner, he collaborated in the creation of the National Mortgage Bank and the National Bank of Public Works. Until the early 1930s, he wrote many of the country's banking and financial laws, especially those dealing with currency, credit operations, insurance, and chambers of commerce. During the administration of Plutarco Elías Calles (1924–28), he overhauled the credit and taxation systems after years of fiscal and monetary chaos.

In another field, Lombardo Toledano joined Vasconcelos when the latter established the Ministry of Education,

becoming chief of all public libraries and, subsequently, principal of the Escuela Nacional Preparatoria. His area of concern soon became the education of the lower classes, so he gradually became involved with the unions, finally becoming their leader: he was one of the founders of the Confederación Regional Obrera Mexicana (CROM, or Regional Confederation of Mexican Workers), and its general secretary from 1936 to 1940. In the cultural and educational field, many members of the Generación de 1915 excelled: Manuel Toussaint was a pioneer of Mexican art history, founding the Laboratory of Art at the Universidad Nacional, which would later evolve into the Instituto de Investigaciones Estéticas (Institute of Aesthetic Research). Antonio Castro Leal combined literary scholarship with political and cultural posts, including the chancellorship of the Universidad Nacional in 1928–29 (a post also given to Gómez Morín in 1933–34 and Caso in 1944–45). Alfonso Caso gradually abandoned law to dedicate his life to Mexican archaeology, eventually directing the famous excavations at Monte Albán between 1931 and 1943.

Two members of this generation, Vázquez del Mercado and Olea y Leyva, centered their professional activities on the study of law, both becoming members of the Supreme Court. Bassols in 1927 wrote the Statutory Law of Article 27 of the Constitution, and two years later he was elected dean of the School of Law of the Universidad Nacional, where he introduced the program of economics, predecessor of the School of Economics. During the administrations of Presidents Pascual Ortiz Rubio (1930–32) and Abelardo Rodríguez (1932–34), Bassols served as secretary of education, and in 1934 he occupied an important post in the Ministry of the Interior (Gobernación). One year later he was appointed by President Lázaro Cárdenas to be first secretary of the Ministry of Finance. Subsequently, he joined the diplomatic corps and was sent to London, Madrid, Paris, and Oslo. While in Paris, he coordinated the effort of bringing countless Spanish Republican exiles to Mexico, helped in this task by Cosío Villegas, who later would take advantage of so many renowned Spanish scientists and intellectuals exiled in Mexico to create El Colegio de Mexico and give an added impetus to the Fondo de Cultura Económica, two of the most distinguished creations of the youngest member of the generation.

The generation's sense of a common cause did not survive beyond the 1920s. The cause of the rupture was the 1929 electoral campaign of Vasconcelos, which showed them the limits of their trust in the political institutions of the country. For example, Gómez Morín retreated from public life in order to resume private law practice, especially as a consultant to important banking and industrial groups. In the political field, his estrangement from the post-Revolutionary regimes culminated in the founding of the Partido de Acción Nacional (PAN, or National Action Party) in 1939. A similar course, although along opposite sides of the political spectrum, was followed by Lombardo Toledano. After a close collaboration with the administration of Lázaro Cárdenas, he distanced himself from the administration of

Manuel Avila Camacho (1940–46), eventually founding the opposition Partido Popular (Popular Party) in 1947 with the help of Narciso Bassols, who held the party's vice presidency until his estrangement in 1949. Another important political estrangement was Vázquez del Mercado's, who resigned from his post of magistrate to the Supreme Court in open disagreement with the administration of Pascual Ortiz Rubio in 1931.

In only a few years, the initial optimism of the Generación de 1915, which had been centered on a "mission" of guidance in restructuring national life, waned owing to the new political reality, which showed the intellectuals the limit of their power and their inability to fully influence the course of events. This was the nation's first group of post-Revolutionary intellectuals to fill government posts; in this way, according to Octavio Paz, "the intellectual became the secret or public adviser of the illiterate general, of the peasant or union leader, of the strongman in power." With their policies, the Generación de 1915 made far-reaching contributions to the creation of the modern Mexican state, but they also showed, paradoxically, the limits of collaboration between intellectuals and rulers in the national political scenario.

Select Bibliography

Calderón Vega, Luis, *Los 7 Sabios de México*. Mexico City: Jus, 1961.

Castillo Peraza, Carlos, *Estudio introductorio de Manuel Gómez Morín, constructor de instituciones*. Mexico City: FCE, 1994.

Cosío Villegas, Daniel, "La Riqueza de México." *La Antorcha* (May 1925).

_____, *Memorias*. Mexico City: Joaquín Martes, 1976.

Gómez Morín, Manuel, *1915*. Mexico City: Cultura, 1927.

González y González, Luis, "La ronda de las generaciones." In *Todo es Historia*. Mexico City: Cal y Arena, 1989.

Krauze, Enrique, *Caudillos culturales en la Revolución Mexicana*. Mexico City: Siglo XXI, 1986.

Monsivais, Carlos, "La nación de unos cuantos y las esperanzas románticas." In *En torno a la cultura nacional*, edited by H. Aguilar Camín, et al. Mexico City: SEP-INI, 1976.

—Pablo Yankelevich

GENERACIÓN DE 1968 AND GENERACIÓN FIN DEL SIGLO

In "Cuatro estaciones de la cultura mexicana," the scholar Enrique Krauze develops an inventory-schema of generations of Mexican writers, intellectuals, and academics during the twentieth century. He baptizes the first generation, made up of those born between 1891 and 1905, as the "Generación de 1915." The second he names the "Generación de 1929" (born 1906–20), the third is the "Generación del Medio Siglo" (the Generation of the Midcentury, born 1921–35), and the fourth and last is the "Generación de 1968"(born 1936–50). The schema itself is rigorous and creative, but life goes on; yet another generation has since emerged and matured: the Generación Fin del Siglo (the Generation of the End of the Century) or the Generación Postista (the Post-Generation, born 1951–65).

The Critique of the Subdued Revolt

The Generación de 1968 was above all opposed to ossified ideological posturings. "What they had in common during the 1960s," points out Krauze, "was neither risk nor challenge but rather a negativity, a culture of protest against Industrial Society." This negativity also had an element of positive action and social risk. In reality the Generación de 1968 offered a very positive critique of "negativity," that of a creative renewal of culture, bringing together rupture and suture, novelty and tradition.

There were two stages in the development of the Generación de 1968: the first from 1965 to 1968 and the second that continued until the end of the 1970s. The first wave of the Generación de 1968 (those born between 1936 and 1943) wanted to be the bad boys of "Formal Mexico," criticizing the establishment and refusing to take things seriously. In his essay "De algunas características de la literatura mexicana contemporanea," Carlos Monsiváis indicated the following characteristics of the culture of the Generación de 1968: an educated middle-class, the growth of higher education, and the development of a schematic structuralist Marxism that provided "unified concepts of the world." Other factors included the mass reproduction of works of art and the narrowing of the distance between "high" and "popular" culture. According to Monsiváis, the youth of the Generación de 1968 wanted to feel modern, in other words, contemporary with world culture (a phrase that Octavio Paz emphasized in his *Labyrinth of Solitude*). Monsiváis concludes that "until 1968 cultural modernity had concentrated in defending criticism as a corrective element to authoritarianism, in opposition—worldly, antiserious, informed, ironic—to traditional Mexico." The young members of the collective La Espiga Amotinada (1960) belonged to this first stage responsible for producing "committed" poetry. La Espiga, under the direction of Jaime Labastida and Eraclio Zepeda, attempted to create left-wing poetry that was nevertheless of great literary merit, as pointed out by Octavio Paz in *Poesía en movimiento: México 1915–1966*.

The antisolemn young men of la Onda (literally meaning "the wave," the term came to signify the burgeoning Mexican counterculture) also belong to this period, consisting of Mexican middle-class hippies such as the precocious José Agustín and the young Gustavo Sainz and Parménides García Saldaña. José Agustín achieved popular success with his novels *La tumba* (1964) and *De perfil* (1966). This writer was recognized as one of the leaders of *ondero* humor, the creator of adolescent, middle-class, and unsophisticated characters who truly attempted to represent the humor of a generation that believed itself to have a phobia about old age but in fact were only playful utterances that were presaging the events of the crucial year of 1968. José Agustín's characters enthusiastically confronted that abstraction known as boredom. They were spoiled, socially domesticated children, rebels without a cause bent on mischief and possessed of a diverting lack of inhibition, all the while attempting to mythologize their forays, believing themselves epic characters who were launching an assault on a heaven that was crashing down out of pure tedium. Gustavo Sainz, the next *ondero* of importance, is known for his novels *Gazapo* (1965) and *Obsesivos días circulares* (1969), and last but not least Parménides García Saldaña was responsible for the novel *Pasto verde* (1968) and a collection of short stories entitled *El rey criollo* (1970). Parménides was the one who best captured the 1968 flavor of la Onda and la Rebelíon Anti-Solemne. In the short story "El rey criollo," young men arrive at a cinema in the Federal District to dutifully discharge adolescent hormonal excess. There ensue kicks, yells, and the defiance of aggressive young machismo. Parménides knew how to describe with relish the total anarchy of his generation, a portent of the great demonstrations of 1968, in which the students introduced democracy into the ludic spirit of the period.

The youth of the Generación de 1968 were antinationalist, fighting against the orthodoxy of the muralists and the precepts of stuffed-shirt patriots. René Avila Fabila caricatured these generational battles in his novel *Los juegos* (1967), in which he satirized the nationalist old guard by pitting them against the bad kids of the Generación de 1968. In one unforgettable scene, the old guard take to the streets of the capital against the young "contemporaries of the world." The sham battle becomes open warfare with bottles being hurled on both sides and ends in a historic draw.

Carlos Monsiváis deserves separate mention as a cultural and literary figure. His overall project is the critical review of Mexican ideological myths (such as nationalism and *mexicanidad,* or "Mexicanness") and popular symbols (the heroes of mass culture and the cultural response of the masses to the personalities of the time). Enrique Krauze asserts that Monsiváis, in his iconoclasm and use of satire, is the paradigmatic figure of the Generación de 1968. Monsiváis is the critical conscience that also teases his generation, and he is the journalist who bequeathed a particular style to Mexican literature. This style is also a genre, that of cultural-journalism, a branch of essay writing known as the *crónica* (chronicle). According to Krauze, the Generación de 1968 "had little concern for poetry, narrative, and the visual arts, or any kind of expression, in favor of genres more pro-

pitious to politicization: the *crónica,* theoretical essays, caricature, and militant and doctrinaire journalism." The Generación de 1968 (along with Carlos Monsiváis) recovered additional marginal genres: cultural journalism, documented reviews, and academic literary criticism. *La cultura en México,* a supplement to the magazine *¡Siempre!,* assiduously promoted writers of the stature of Jorge Ayala Blanco, David Huerta, and Luis González de Alba. Indeed *La cultura en México,* under the editorship of Monsiváis from March 1972 to February 1987, was the pulse of cultural events during this period.

The playful euphoria manifested by the Generación de 1968 died the night of October 2, 1968, with the Massacre of Tlatelolco. The massacre of peaceful student protesters by government troops transformed joyous youthful rebellion into disenchantment, fury, and desperate impotence. The slaughter of the students divided the experience of this generation into two currents. Publications began to appear that blended disenchantment and sarcasm. Luis González de Alba, author of *Los días y los años* (1970), reproduced the student atmosphere of the large demonstrations prior to the massacre and the sense of disenchantment that arose afterward. Emilio Carballido published *Teatro joven de México* (1971), in which he presented dramatists such as Oscar Villegas, who staged his farce *El renacimiento* in 1968. In this work Villegas certifies the desperation of the Generación de 1968 as a generational-institutional conflict: the rationale of the students versus the unreasonableness of the universities. These literary interpretations coincided with the political responses of many young people of the time who entered the urban guerrilla group Liga Comunista 23 Septiembre (23rd of September Communist League), which was destroyed at the end of the 1970s. In *Memorias de la guerra de los justos* (1996) by Gustavo Hilares, a militant leader of the "subversive" current of the Generación de 1968 documents the passionate disenchantment of a survivor of the breakdown of Marxism after Tlatelolco.

This later period reveals an emotional state and attitude quite different from the initial creative output of the generation. In *Días de guardar* (1970), Carlos Monsiváis notes:

> After a misfortune as unjust, irreparable, and unpunished, as the massacre of Tlatelolco, things never were the same again. Certitude disappeared, security was eliminated . . . fear obliged us to dispense with intelligence, skepticism was confused with cynicism that was mixed in turn with a sense of abandonment that contaminated an indifference that was blended with lethargy.

The post-1968 spirit, concluded Monsiváis, was a "sense of shared frustration, of repression in every sense of the word." This generation ran into difficulties as the options were reduced to military resistance or giving in to the establishment. The act of making such a choice had an apocalyptic character. Enrique Krauze himself abandoned his position as an impartial historian and attacked the Generación de 1968, declaring that their capacity to deceive themselves and their inability to exercise self-criticism, pluralism, and tolerance were morally sad. The Generación de 1968 would live out a kind of moral schizophrenia and an identity split that would be reflected in the essays collected in *Días de guardar,* especially "14 de Febrero, día de la amistad y el amor: yo y mis amigos," in which Monsiváis' makes a devastating critique of his generation.

The final years of the 1970s were dominated by works infused with a sense of impotence: Elena Poniatowska's *La noche de Tlatelolco* (a journalistic testimony), González de Alba's *Los días y los años* (a novel and testimony), and Monsiváis's *Días de guardar* (which initiated the contemporary *crónica*). Poetry meanwhile took refuge in "minority" themes. In Sandro Cohen's celebrated anthology *Palabra nueva: Dos decadas de poesía en México* (1981), socially committed poetry was markedly absent.

In *Un chavo bien helado: Crónicas de los años ochenta* (1990), José Joaquín Blanco would make a Postista verdict on the 1970s. For him the "great crisis" of the 1980s did away with the "1960s' counterculture that arrived in the 1970s and proliferated and prospered in youthful artistic and intellectual circles of the period. We lived," states Blanco, "in asphyxia and agony. And those who participated in the counterculture were left hanging without knowing what happened." Mexico at the end of the 1970s and beginning of the 1980s "was as before, an enormous ranch set in prehistoric times—the time of the cave men." Marxism, the last bulwark of European romanticism, disappeared; the dream of modernity came to an end; it was good-bye to the signs of Revolution: "Nonconformity, rock music, anti-authoritarianism, feminism, gay liberation, the return of sensuality and risk, the rejection of the bourgeois approach to life, the cult of simplicity and the moment; to sum up, an end to hating Daddy and to the angry pressures of Revolution Now and Paradise Now." The generation after that of 1968 saw the mass renunciation of "anti" postures. The Generación de 1968 finished up "alone, worn out by asphyxia and fear. And in the asphyxia of asphyxia and fear of fear. What a way to go!" In the mid-1980s Mexico would become a place of

stopping smoking, keeping trim, drinking within moderation, being nice. Only the search for individual prosperity and the good conscience . . . lived in sanctified and healthy comfort. . . . [G]ood-bye to difficult books, to criticism and the wild party: [now there would be] only unadulterated masterworks—a few musty scraps—of great status and very presentable socially. The function of art returned to the one it had always possessed: beautiful objects wrapped in cellophane with a red bow.

Blanco concluded that the only escape from his asphyxiating fear was the return to the counterculture, the return to "the tradition of criticism and nonconformity." But the counter-

culture would have other names, other media, and other ends. Thus began la Generación Postista, criticizing the critical tradition along with the modernist rebellious attitudes of its elder brothers.

Postismo versus the Dream of Cynical Reason

The Postistas were born between 1951 and 1965. Heirs to the spirit of Paz of the 1960s and that of Monsiváis of the 1970s, they were more concerned with understanding the tradition they confronted than trying to make a break from it. In an article entitled "El romanticismo y la poesía contemporánea" (1987), Octavio Paz wrote the following:

Today we are witnessing the twilight of the aesthetic of change. Art and literature at the end of the century have gradually lost their powers of negation; for a long time their denials have been repetitive rituals, their rebellions mere formulas and their transgressional ceremonies. It is not the end of art but the end of the idea of modern art. In other words the end of the aesthetic based on the cult of change and rupture.

We are, says Paz, beyond an avant-garde crisis; today we are witnessing the phenomenon of the "art of convergence." Paz refers to that which today we know as the postmodern condition. Art is an ill-assorted syncretism, a kind of neobaroque that is consciously parodic. After the Massacre of 1968, Mexican intellectuals brought a halt to their modernist desire for progress and change. The aesthetic of change had become an official sign: Mexico must be modernized, declared the politicians. Meanwhile, intellectuals (those of 1968 and their younger brothers), bereft of Marx and Rousseau, reoriented their searches toward the new French poststructuralist theories. They read Roland Barthes and Michel Foucault and reeducated themselves under the sign of the times: postmodernism. In "de algunas caracteristicas," Carlos Monsiváis noted that sometime after the trauma of 1968 an atmosphere was created of a "different sensibility that expresses, above all, the possibility of choice in terms of behavior." The characteristics of this new generation are as follows:

everything can be found in their books; erotic obsession (the mystique of Bataille or Klossowski); prose rhythms that are techniques for reproducing the movement of reality; mirror games with language; spasmodic versions of personal and social deterioration; the search for marginality as a protective shield in the face of conformism that expresses nothing, and open rejection and involuntary approbation of tradition.

Mexican postmodern literature emerged between the crisis of the intellectual old guard and the official-social crisis. Many members of the Generación de 1968 contributed to this diffusion, especially from the pages of *La cultura en*

México, which between 1985 and 1986 published a variety of texts by the main theoreticians of postmodernism. The magazine *Universidad de México* also participated, publishing magnificent essays from 1987 to 1988 on the theme of postmodernity. In 1987 the magazine *Vuelta* published Octavio Paz's polemic on this "new aesthetic." Among those writers from the Generación de 1968 who have written books of postmodernist characteristics are Carlos Monsiváis, with his essays on Mexican culture. His work *Los rituals de chaos* (1995) examines the relationship between culture in crisis and its new popular symbols. The poet David Huerta continued to publish his very self-reflexive, poststructuralist, and intertextual poetry such as the *Cuaderno de noviembre* (1976–80), in which Nictálope confesses in more than 100 pages his grammatical schizophrenia. Jorge Ayala Blanco is another whose postmodernist style has transformed the marginal genre of the film review into an "art of convergence." In *La disolvencia del cine mexicano: Entre lo popular y lo exquisito* (1994) and *La eficacia del cine mexicano: Entre lo viejo y lo nuevo* (1994), Blanco provides a magnificent exercise in intercontextual criticism. Also worthy of mention is the writer Paco Ignacio Taibo II, who has published various post-Marxist crime novels that include intercontextual games (this term refers to the fact that the writer makes references to other texts and historical contexts in a kind of vertiginous game).

The young members of the postmodern generation matured in an atmosphere of crisis and decline. Whole cycles of modern thought had come to an end. In his essay "Muerte y resurreción del nacionalismo mexicano" (1987), Monsiváis baptized the 1980s and 1990s as "postnationalism in crisis," consisting of the violent democratization of social life "from beneath," the "rejection of the unifying panoramas," the "taste for fragmentation," and "the restoration of faith in localism, but no longer the small village of Azuela or López Velarde but the district, the barrio, and the group." A sardonic spirit also predominates in order to deal with Mexico's permanent crisis that admits "the massive incorporation of women to the national project via their entry into the economy, the demolition of grandiloquent ideas: Honor, immutable Respect, and Authority that does not brook argument." Other characteristics he marked as indicative of Mexican postnationalism include "the visible absence of theories, which have to do with the difficulties of putting actions for mutual benefit into operation and with the lack of confidence in politics." La Generación Postista pays attention to the periphery. It might be feminist but not traditionally so. Feminist, homosexual, and "provincial" literature has arrived to stay. The periphery has been converted into the center. This "marginality" is no longer naive and anticynical, with a literary output that goes beyond the messianic or disenchanted literature of 1968. The Postistas have learned to combat the critical cynicism of their older brothers (now well-ensconced in the establishment) in a different or more sophisticated way. The new writers are responding with their literature with its intertextual games, fragmentary labyrinths, local loyalties and textual humor, neobaroque syncretism and play with the rules of modern literary genres and frankly gay or feminist discourse. With this fin de siècle generation Mexico once again is on a contemporary basis with the world, this time a postmodern one.

The members of la Generación Postista disdain the great messianic theories (Marxism and liberalism), and their response to the cynical rationale behind capitalism in crisis is beginning to be heard. José Joaquín said that the counterculture should rise again, and that it had been doing so but under other names and styles. Jaime Moreno Villarreal, for example, published *La linea y el círculo* (1981), in which he evaluated the heritage of the Generación de 1968, integrating in his text the ideas of Michel Foucault and Carlos Monsiváis to fathom the "new attitudes" of young poets. He abandoned artificial divisions between "cultivated" writers and "good savages," eliminating the moral dilemmas and the opposition between "high" and "popular" culture and between "dominant" and "peripheral" subjects. Villarreal also participated with other writers such as Adolfo Castañón and Fabio Morábito in the creation of *Macrocefalia* (1988), an exercise in intergenres, composed of fragments submitted every two weeks in which the explicit intention was to abolish the author (in the singular): "each subject exhibits the features of his individual style, then intends to eliminate it." The work utilizes the "techniques of insertion, transposition, dialoguism, suppression, subversion, insistence, and intensity."

La Generación Postista developed most in the genre of feminist literature exemplified by writers such as Ethel Krauze in *Infinita* (1992) and *Mujeres en Nueva York* (1993) in which love triangles and problematic heterosexual and bisexual relationships appear. Even in the case of Mexican feminist literature, spokespersons and examples multiply, as in the case of the novels of Carmen Boullosa, *La Milagrosa* (1993) and *Duerme* (1994). In the former the author blends the crime story, politics, and fantasy with the techniques of the letter and the *recado* (popular means of giving thanks for the miracles of a saint). The second novel concerns a transvestite woman immersed in the dawn of Hispanic machismo of the New World. Martha Cerda has developed a cutting parody of the Latin American "boom" (the literary resurgence in the years following the Cuban Revolution, which included such authors as Gabriel García Márquez, Mario Vargas Llosa, and Carlos Fuentes). Cerda plays with the counter current to Magic Realism. Her "novel" *La Señora Rodríguez y otros mundos* (1990) is clearly a postmodernist exercise. *Karenina Express* (1995) by Margarita Mansilla is a first novel that reveals mastery in the use of the intertextual games and intergenres as well as a neobaroque play with languages. The poetry of Minerva Margarita Villarreal also belongs to this fin de siècle current. Her collection of poems, *Epigramísticos* (1995), violates previous feminist discourse; a feminist of the old school would see betrayal where in fact only ironic games exist. For example in the text "Envidia del coño," the poet states "It is correct Ligia, you are feminist/except when, arrow in flight, a phallus crosses between us."

La Generación Postista is very well represented in gay literature by Luis Zapata, José Joaquín Blanco, and Luis Montaño. Luis Zapata is the dean of Mexican homosexual literature with novels of great quality, such as *El vampiro de la Colonia Roma* (1979) and *La hermana secreta de Angélica María* (1989) to his credit. Both works are true tragicomedies about marginal beings misunderstood by society. In *El vampiro* a male prostitute recounts his misadventures; in the second novel we are treated to the story of a hermaphrodite who ends up in a lunatic asylum. José Joaquín Blanco also writes novels on homosexual themes, but his narrative power is to be found in his essays, located in two books, *Cuando todas las chamacas se pusieron medias de nylon* (1989) and *Un chavo bien helado: Crónicas del los años ochenta* (1990). Luis Montaño wrote the novel *Brenda Berenice o el diario de una loca* (1985), the "diary" of a transvestite who narrates his life as a Mexican drag queen. Despite the humor in the novel, the narrator suffers social isolation. Most notable is his use of Mexican gay drag slang terms.

There are other postmodernist categories. Armando Ramírez gives rein to his local obsessions; there is only one subject in his work: the working-class neighborhood of Tepito in Mexico City. In his *Crónica de los chorrocientos mil días del Barrio de Tepito* (1973), Ramírez challenges the reader, who has no idea whether he is reading chronicles, a novel, or a sequence of short stories. It is also necessary to mention the use of post-*ondero* marginal language. Enrique Serna is also important as the author of the novel *Uno soñaba que era rey* (1989), a tough satire against the cynical rationale of the Generación de 1968. He mocks racism and the immorality of the Mexican middle class. Serna's characters are the aging youth of la Onda that once were mythologized by José Agustín. A similar approach appears in the work of the poet Ricardo Castillo. In his poetry collection entitled *El Pobrecito señor X* (1980) appears one of the most important poems of Postismo, "La oruga." Here the postmodern laughter floats out on the darkness of the crisis: "Because your hope has remained at the margin of celestial stories/Because your love is no longer bestowed upon Utopias." He envelops us in the seductive spin of chaos: "Man took a luminous slope that led to Chaos/And Chaos breathed hard on the ruins of man."

Two more writers can be numbered among the Postistas-postmodernists: Pablo Espinosa and Oscar de la Borbolla. If Jaime Moreno Villarreal is the critic of culture in process, Pablo Espinosa is Monsiváis's successor as the new chronicler of mass cultural movements. His style is colloquial, like that of Armando Ramírez and his themes mix "high" with "low" culture (as does Monsiváis) to study the expressions of the Mexican carnival. Less critical than José Joaquín Blanco, his style is equally seductive. Oscar de la Borbolla is better defined as a "postchronicler" (in the same style as Armando

Ramírez), or as he himself would describe, as an *ucronista*. In *Ucronías* (1989) de la Borbolla emphasizes his concept of literature whereby life is a simulacrum and literature an opportunity to lie with simulated truth. Other members of la Generación Postista include the narrative writers Guillermo J. Fadanmelli, Ricardo Chávez Castañeda, Luis Humberto Crosthwaite, Alfredo Espinosa, and Herminio Martínez; the poet Jorge Humberto Chávez; and the critics Lauro Zavala and Christopher Domínguez.

Recognized authors such as Carlos Fuentes; José Emilio Pacheco; Emmanuel Carballo; and new luminaries such as Angeles Mastretta, author of *Arráncame la vida!* (1985), and Laura Esquivel with *Como agua para chocolate* (1989) are publishing work alongside the previously mentioned writers. Ana Rosa Domenella has pointed out that both writers began their careers in journalism (bearing an obvious relation with the Generación de 1968), that their novels have popular themes and a subliterary treatment, parodying the pamphlet, popular music, culinary recipes, and oral traditions, such as the rumor. These characteristics lead them to be included in the postmodern Postismo group and convert them into a sign of the times; each belongs both to modernity and postmodernity. Each coexist in the same space and time in contemporary Mexico.

Select Bibliography

Blanco, José Joaquín, *Un chavo bien helado: Crónicas de los años ochenta.* Mexico City: Era, 1990.

Burgess, Ronald D., *The New Dramatists of Mexico: 1967–1975.* Lexington: University of Kentucky Press, 1991.

Brushwood, John S., *La novela mexicana (1967–1982).* Mexico City: Grijalbo, 1985.

Carballido, Emilio, *Teatro joven de México.* Mexico City: Editores Mexicanos Unidos, 1985.

Cortés, Elodio, editor, *Dictionary of Mexican Literature.* Washington, D.C.: Library of Congress Cataloging Publication Data, 1992.

Dauster, Frank, "Poetas nacidos en las décadas de 1920, 1930 y 1940." *Revista Iberoamericana* 55 (July–December 1989).

_____, *Antología de la poesía mexicana.* Zaragoza, Mexico: Clásicos Ebro, 1970.

Diccionario de escritores mexicanos. UNAM–Instituto de Investigaciones Filológicas, 1988.

Domenella, Ana Rosa, "Escritura, historia y género en 20 años de novela mexicana escrita por mujeres." *Revista de Literatura Mexicana Contemporánea* 2 (January–April 1996).

Domínguez, Christopher M., *Antología de la narrativa mexicana del siglo XX,* vols. 1 and 2. Mexico City: Fondo de Cultura Económica, 1991.

Debicki, Andrew, editor, *Antología de la poesía mexicana moderna.* London: Tamesis, 1977.

Elizondo, Salvador, *Museo poético.* Mexico City: UNAM, 1974.

Evodio, Escalante, *Poetas de una generación, 1950–1959.* Mexico City: UNAM–Premiá, 1988.

Foster, Merlin H., "Four Contemporary Mexican Poets." In *Tradition and Renewal,* edited by Merlin H. Foster. Urbana: University of Ilinois Press, 1975.

García Nuñez, Fernando, "20th-Century Prose Fiction: Mexico." In *Handbook of Latin American Studies: No. 54*, edited by Dolores Moyano Maritin. Austin: University of Texas Press, 1995.

Kohut, Karl, *Literatura mexicana hoy: Del 68 al ocaso de la revolución*. Frankfurt am Main: Vervuert, 1991.

Krauze, Enrique, "Cuatro Estaciones de la cultura mexicana." *Vuelta* 60 (November 1981).

Monsiváis, Carlos, *Días de guardar*. Mexico City: Era, 1970.

_____, "Muerte y resurreción del nacionalismo mexicano." *Nexus* 109 (January 1987).

Moreno Villarreal, Jaime, *La línea y el círculo*. Mexico City: Universidad Autónoma Metropolitana, 1981.

Menton, Seymour, "Las cuentistas mexicanas en la época feminista 1970–1988." *Hispania* 73 (May 1990).

Paz, Octavio, et al., *Poesía en movimiento*. Mexico City: Siglo XXI, 1966.

_____, "El romanticismo y la poesía contemporánea." *Vuelta* 127 (June 1987).

Stabb, Martin S., "The New Essay of Mexico: Text and Context." *Hispania* 70 (March 1987).

Zavala, Lauro, "El nuevo cuento mexicano, 1978–1988." *Revista Iberoamericana* 55 (July–December 1989).

—JOSÉ MANUEL GARCÍA-GARCÍA

GENERAL AGREEMENT ON TARIFFS AND TRADE (GATT)

Mexico's admission to the General Agreement on Tariffs and Trade in 1986 and its participation in the Uruguay Round negotiations (finalized on April 15, 1994) represented a crucial part of the outward-oriented development strategy that the nation adopted in the mid-1980s. Mexico's participation in the multilateral forum of international trade contributes to the consolidation of the outward-oriented development strategy and the diversification of export markets. GATT/WTO (World Trade Organization) membership also reduces the power of rent-seeking protectionist groups that previously flourished because the commitments accepted by Mexico constrain the state's capacity to reverse the opening of its trade and investment policies. Accordingly, inclusion in the World Trade Organization contributes to the durability, stability, and predictability in Mexico's liberalization reforms.

In addition to solidifying domestic reform, Mexico's participation in the Uruguay Round provided it with more instruments to counteract global protectionist trends, while WTO membership grants Mexico with a clear and transparent set of rules for its export activities, reducing the likelihood of facing unilateral trade restrictions.

However, while membership in the trade forum will facilitate Mexican trade in general, GATT/WTO commitments will also constrain Mexico's ability to develop an industrial policy. The Uruguay Round diminished Mexico's ability to use economic instruments, such as subsidies or production and export requirements to promote industrialization. While Mexico has tried to integrate into the world economy to achieve growth, the result has been a two-tiered industrial structure, in which conglomerates are able to export significantly.

Mexico's participation in the multilateral trade negotiations will yield benefits in terms of market access, market diversification, and international trade rules. However, in order to take full advantage of GATT/WTO membership Mexico must find mechanisms to adjust its productive structure to make its outward-oriented model a successful one. Mexico will have to rely on external sources of financing and technology transfer to close the breach between an inefficient inward industrial sector and a small competitive outward-oriented one.

Mexico's First Attempt at Entering GATT

Since the 1940s, Mexico had followed a policy of import substitution industrialization (ISI), which sought to promote industrialization by substituting domestic manufactures for imports. ISI had allowed the country to experience annual Gross Domestic Product (GDP) growth rates of 6 percent during the so-called era of stabilizing development. Mexico had remained skeptical of the multilateral forum because GATT was considered a threat to the capacity of the state to implement development policies and generally inconsistent with ISI. Through the 1970s and under two different presidents, Mexico twice attempted to introduce trade liberalization reforms but was unsuccessful. First, there was a lack of political support for an outward-oriented model within the administration, the bureaucracy, and domestic groups that had flourished under protection. Second, other short-term solutions available at that time, such as foreign indebtedness and oil exports, were easier to implement and politically less costly. At the same time, international banks needed to lend the oversupply of OPEC "petrodollars"; Mexico's ability to borrow massive amounts of money at reasonable interest rates made liberalization unnecessary.

For these reasons, although GATT was created in 1947, Mexico first attempted to become a member in 1979, when the seventh round of multilateral trade negotiations (the Tokyo Round) was about to come to an end. Since the Luis Echeverría Álvarez administration (1970–76), it had become increasingly evident that relying on a closed domestic market would be insufficient to promote economic growth. During the José López Portillo administration (1976–82), following a trade liberalization effort (1977–79) Mexico solicited GATT membership in January 1979. Policy makers sought an export-oriented development strategy based on a gradual reduction of protection, industrial export promotion, and access to foreign markets.

As a result of GATT changes that responded to developing countries' concerns, such as special and differential treatment, Mexico became interested in joining the organization. Likewise, the failure of the 1979 negotiations for a Mexican trade agreement with the United States made Mexico realize that the alternative to secure market access for its exports was through the multilateral forum, which also provided some legal recourse against a growing trend of U.S. protectionism. The Protocol of Accession that let in Mexico was negotiated during the Tokyo Round and was ready in October 1979. A public debate immediately followed.

The terms of the Protocol were very favorable, as the country was permitted to obviate GATT rules when they threatened domestic policies such as subsidized industrial programs, thus guaranteeing Mexico's capacity to implement a targeted industrial policy. Notwithstanding the favorable conditions, on March 18, 1980, the date that commemorates Mexico's 1938 oil expropriation, President López Portillo announced his decision to decline membership. This resolution coincided with the end of Mexico's trade liberalization.

What accounts for this reversal? Mexico's decision to "postpone" its accession to GATT can be explained by a combination of domestic and international factors: a deeply entrenched inward-oriented model, the 1979 oil boom, the opposition of small- and medium-sized industrialists, and free-trade ambivalence on the part of the president and Mexico's trade policy makers.

Domestic producers that had enjoyed high rents as a result of protection adamantly opposed any attempt to liberalize the economy, even though Mexico's 1979 Protocol of Accession guaranteed these groups protection from competition for a lengthy period. In fact, during the negotiation, Mexico made concessions on only 328 products, which represented less than 10 percent of its total imports. In addition, tariff reductions were accorded for just 21 items, and the elimination of import permits would only affect 34 items. Mexico also obtained other favorable concessions, such as the capacity to use export subsidies and grant tax incentives to industry, the right to protect its industry and agriculture, and permission to utilize quantitative restrictions that were inconsistent with GATT. Such concessions could hardly be considered a radical move toward the opening of Mexico's economy.

However, business associations such as the Cámera Nacional de la Industria de la Transformación (CANACIN-TRA, or National Chamber of Transformation Industry) and

the National College of Economists, which had close ties with the ruling party (the Partido Revolucionario Institucional—PRI, or Institutional Revolutionary Party) became vociferous opponents to GATT's accession. Other associations such as the Confederación Patronal de la República Mexicana (COPARMEX, or Employer's Confederation of the Republic of Mexico), and ANIERM (National Association of Mexican Importers and Exporters) and informal business groups such as the Monterrey Group supported GATT membership but were unable to make their position prevail. Given the lack of consensus among the business community, President López Portillo ultimately decided to maintain the status quo.

Mexico's decision to postpone GATT accession also resulted from bureaucratic conflict between an "inward-oriented" group led by budget minister Carlos Tello and industrial promotion czar José Andrés de Oteyza, on one hand, and the "outward-oriented" faction headed by finance minister Julio Rodolfo Moctezuma Cid and trade minister Héctor Hernández Cervantes. López Portillo initially supported the internationalist group. However, when massive oil reserves were discovered, Mexico's supposed new economic independence tilted the balance against liberalization in general, and GATT in particular. In 1979 the international price of oil soared to record highs. Mexico sought to replace GATT with oil as a means of securing foreign market access and attracting foreign capital; for example, the 1981 Franco-Mexican trade agreement gave Mexico the equivalent of Most-Favored-Nation (MFN) status in the French market in exchange for oil. Thus, the "petrolization" of the Mexican economy seemed to obviate the need to promote exports of manufactures through free trade, because oil provided Mexico with a strong negotiation position. However, this state of affairs would prove short-lived.

Mexico's Unilateral Trade Liberalization

In 1982 the international price of oil collapsed while Mexico's foreign debt had reached almost US$100 billion, resulting in a debt crisis that threatened not only Mexico's economy but also the stability of the international financial system. Mexico had to negotiate a rescue package with the International Monetary Fund (IMF) that required a stabilization program and the introduction of deep economic reforms, among which trade policy was a fundamental component. The moderate unilateral trade liberalization that Mexico initiated in 1983 gradually eliminated official prices, quotas, licenses, and import permits and was accelerated in 1985 when oil prices collapsed again. President Miguel de la Madrid was convinced that going back to ISI would only deepen the crisis. In June 1985 Mexico instituted a set of reforms to rationalize its imports and eliminated import permits for 2,000 tariff items (around 20 percent of the import tariff schedule).

President de la Madrid openly pursued an outward-oriented strategy in which export activity was to become the backbone of Mexico's development strategy. In contrast with the 1979 process, almost no public discussion took place, although business organizations such as the elitist CCE (Business Coordinating Council) and the ANIERM were clear enthusiasts; most public and private organizations acted only as advisers. Ultimately, in the context of an enduring crisis affecting all business interests, the decision to make Mexico a GATT member came from the president.

Mexico's 1986 Protocol of Accession established a tariff ceiling of 50 percent and the elimination of official prices. Mexico was the first acceding country that agreed to bind all of its tariff schedule. As in 1979, Mexico's concessions were rather small; only 5 percent of total import categories were negotiated (373 out of 8,143 import items), which represented 15 percent of the value of imports in 1985. Agriculture and industrial integration programs (automotive, electronics, and pharmaceutical) received a waiver from GATT obligations. Mexico also became a signatory to four of the six Tokyo Round Codes of Conduct—antidumping, customs valuation, import licenses, and technical barriers to trade—which contained special provisions for developing countries.

Domestic macroeconomic reforms led Mexico to go far beyond its GATT commitments. In 1987, just one year after Mexico acquired GATT membership, a bold unilateral trade liberalization reduced the highest tariff level from 100 percent to 20 percent as part of a national stabilization pact including business and labor. By the late 1980s, Mexico had become one of the most open economies among developing countries.

The Uruguay Round

GATT's Uruguay Round, the eighth round of multilateral trade negotiations, was finalized after eight years on April 15, 1994. The Final Act establishes the WTO that comprises 28 different agreements signed by 125 countries. The Uruguay Round Agreements entered into effect on January 1, 1995, and are the result of the most ambitious and comprehensive effort of multilateral trade liberalization.

Mexico's participation in the Uruguay Round marked the country's entrance into the multilateral trade forum. For Mexico, the Uruguay Round was the first step toward the consolidation of what had been a unilateral liberalization process and an outward-oriented development strategy; GATT membership allows Mexico the possibility of using the international trade regime to guarantee export market access and to counteract any possible surge of protectionism. Mexico had a number of objectives: to guarantee the consistency between its regional trade agreements and the WTO rules, avoid manipulating environmental measures for trade protection, secure market access for its exports, and reduce the use of unilateral measures and unfair trade practices. To analyze Mexico's role in the multilateral trade negotiations as well as those benefits it received, trade issues can be divided into three main areas: market access, institutional framework and rules, and new areas.

Market Access

The most important area for developing countries in general, and Mexico in particular, was that of market access. In addition to tariff reductions, the incorporation of the textile and agricultural sectors into GATT was key for Mexico, given these sectors' weight in trade activities. Mexico and other newly industrializing countries demanded that the developed economies open these markets in return for liberalization in services, intellectual property rights, and investment.

Although liberalization in manufactures already had progressed significantly in GATT negotiations before the Uruguay Round, market access concessions were important for Mexico because industrial goods have become the most significant component of its exports. Between 1985 and 1990, Mexico's growth of manufactured exports showed an annual growth rate of 24 percent. By 1995, the trade-to-production ratio represented 17 percent of GDP, compared with 11 percent in 1980. The Uruguay Round ensured market access for manufactures by reducing tariff rates, tariff escalation, and tariff peaks. Mexico committed to a linear tariff reduction from 50 percent to 35 percent ad valorem, to grant duty-free access to 1 percent of its imports, and to apply quantitative restrictions to less than 2 percent of its import tariff items. Mexico retained the capacity to require import licenses for agricultural products, oil and oil products, weapons and ammunications, certain vehicles, and, on a temporary basis, pharmaceutical products.

Through the gradual dismantling of the protectionist Multifiber Agreement quota system, liberalization in textiles is expected to stimulate Mexico's exports. In the short term, multilateral liberalization will not translate into increased access to export markets. The benefit derives more from the principles and rules established to liberalize trade in textiles than from immediate market access.

Mexico's outward-oriented strategy has been supported through the liberalization of the domestic market because Mexican producers can buy cheaper imports. As a result of the Uruguay Round, Mexico accomplished substantive market access benefits given tariff reduction and nontariff barrier elimination. But liberalization does not automatically mean increased competitiveness in the world market for all firms or sectors. Since Mexico started its process of unilateral trade liberalization in 1985, firms in traditionally inward-oriented manufacturing sectors (e.g., toys, garment, footwear, electric appliances, and electronics) have been unable to gain a competitive position, and many already have disappeared. In contrast, a group of large multinational export-oriented firms involved in sectors such as automobiles, electronics, glass, cement, and textiles have shown their ability to take advantage of the benefits acquired under the Uruguay Round.

Although policy makers hope that export-oriented firms will make inward-oriented firms more competitive through technological and management "spillovers" as well as subcontracting opportunities, it is unclear how inefficient firms will improve if Mexico relies just on market access benefits. Indeed, access to foreign markets will be meaningless without international levels of competitiveness among Mexican industry, something that GATT membership does not guarantee.

Mexico's two-tiered industrial structure also has had political economy implications. Business organizations such as CANACINTRA, which had been very protected although silent during the accession to GATT in 1986, have become open critics of liberalizing policies. Thus, it has been necessary to build political support for economic reforms among those groups that will reap the benefits of liberalization.

With respect to agriculture, liberalization was a major feat of the Uruguay Round. Mexico initially opposed agricultural liberalization because around 40 percent of its population survives on the consumption of maize, most of which was produced by small, inefficient farmers. In addition, Mexico supports domestic production through direct payments to the producer. In fact, Mexico's Protocol of Accession had excluded the agricultural sector from its GATT commitments.

Liberalization means that trade-distorting domestic subsidies will be phased out and export subsidies regulated while quantitative restrictions will be tariffed. Mexico was not enthusiastic about the "tarrification" of all its agriculture nontariff barriers but ended up agreeing to it in all products under the general rules, even those products that were considered "sensitive" such as maize, kidney beans, and dairy products. Mexico, however, bound its tariffs for rice and coarse grains at higher levels than its previous tariff ceiling of 50 percent (to more than 100 percent in some cases). A minimum tariff reduction of 10 percent on all agriculture products and an average of 24 percent over a 10-year period was agreed.

Mexico's agriculture is not homogeneous, and policies in this sector have reflected social demands dating from the 1910 Revolution. Given the disparities in this sector, market access benefits will help those fruit and vegetable producers that have targeted the export market. Most liberalization in agriculture focused on temperate products as opposed to tropical ones, such as coffee, tea, cocoa, spices, cut flowers, and live plants, because the latter already enjoyed duty-free access or preferential treatment through the unilateral Generalized System of Preferences (GSP). Mexico expects to obtain increased access for its exports of honey, lemons, mangoes, orange juice, rum, cut flowers, unprocessed coffee, avocados, beer, and tequila. The concessions obtained in these products allowed Mexico to obtain reciprocity for its unilateral liberalization and aimed at supporting the efforts to diversify exports to the Japanese, European, and Southeast Asian markets.

Mexico sought to improve access for its key exports (i.e., tropical products, fruits, and vegetables) to generate the income required to compensate for an expected price increase on imports of agricultural commodities with the reduction or elimination of subsidies. Liberalization of trade in agriculture poses a political economy challenge for Mexico given the traditional protection granted to peasants and the subsidies transferred to consumers. Small agriculture producers are now facing open competition from imports, while consumers are having to pay international prices for agriculture products. Opening trade in agriculture implied removing protection and transforming land property rights that involved the termination of land redistribution and the development of a new legal framework that primarily affected the *ejido,* a form of communal land ownership sanctified under the Revolution. Traditional Mexican farmers in the officialist Confederación Nacional Campesina (CNC, or National Peasant Confederation) have questioned the traditional alliance with government as protection and subsidies to this sector are eliminated.

Agriculture not only has been protected but also widely subsidized among developed and developing countries, and Mexico had not been the exception. As a result of the Uruguay Round, Mexico will reduce subsidies (domestic support) from 29 billion pesos to around 25 billion pesos in the period between 1995 and 2004. Mexico, however, is not obliged to eliminate the rural income support program (PROCAMPO) introduced in 1993, which has become the only source of assistance for Mexican peasantry. This program provides farmers twice a year with fixed acreage payments. The program replaces the previous system of guaranteed prices for grain and oilseed producers. In the case of export subsidies, Mexico had already eliminated them, but it registered export subsidies for maize, beans, wheat, sorghum, and sugar to keep the flexibility to grant in the future such subsidies consistent with the provisions of the agreement. Nonetheless, Mexico has committed to eliminate subsidies, and the challenge will be to create the economic conditions that will allow displaced groups to adjust to import competition or to relocate in other areas of production.

Institutional Framework and Rules

For Mexico, the changes to international trade rules regarding such issues as safeguards, antidumping, and subsidies, as well as the strengthening of the dispute-settlement mechanism, were significant to the extent that they are expected to increase transparency and reduce the likelihood that Mexico's major trading partners will use unilateral trade rules to restrict market access. Mexico's participation in the Uruguay Round aimed at achieving access to legal instruments with which to counteract protectionist trends among industrialized countries.

Of particular importance to Mexico was the Agreement on Safeguards, which prohibits the establishment of "gray area measures" such as voluntary export restraints (VERs) and orderly marketing agreements (OMAs), which in the past have been imposed to provide relief to import-competing domestic industries. Mexican exports of iron and steel, footwear, and consumer electronics have faced U.S. VERs, while its tomato exports have been subject to U.S. OMAs.

Mexico considers these Uruguay provisions as a step forward in introducing discipline to neo-protectionist behavior.

Antidumping and countervailing duties have become very popular instruments of protection and pose a threat to the international trading system. Mexico wanted stricter discipline on antidumping actions because such measures have been widely used by its trading partners in very competitive exports such as cement. Mexico itself also has developed strong antidumping legislation. Between 1985 and 1993, Mexico initiated 131 cases of dumping against GATT members, while 25 investigations were initiated against Mexican exports.

The Agreement on Subsidies strengthens existing rules. The Uruguay Round defined subsidies for the first time and recognized three categories: prohibited, actionable, and nonactionable. Mexico has already eliminated its export subsidies, but it sought to obtain nonactionable status for certain environmental subsidies, including those for environment-related research and development. Mexico also obtained similar status for certain regional subsidies that will be used to move economic activity away from Mexico City and other industrial centers. Mexico was a proponent of granting a "credit" for those developing countries that phase out their export subsidies ahead of the scheduled time limit of eight years.

Mexico limited its own ability to pursue an industrial policy because changes to trade rules imply a prohibition against subsidies or other forms of industrial incentives and requirements. GATT/WTO has curtailed Mexico's credit and subsidy instruments and its ability to support industrial activities. In addition, the capital scarcity that Mexico has persistently suffered puts it in an extremely vulnerable position because industrial development will depend on foreign capital inflows whose levels are largely determined beyond Mexican borders. Unlike countries such as Korea or Taiwan, which successfully managed to direct foreign investment toward targeted areas and achieved technology transfer through joint ventures, Mexico will have limited policy-making discretion to influence the kind of industry that may develop.

The Uruguay Round was successful in strengthening GATT's mechanism of settling disputes; it set a six-month limit for panels' decisions, expedited panel proceedings, and unified the previously fragmented procedure. Panel decisions no longer depend upon the approval of the parties to a dispute because a party will no longer have the capacity to refuse the establishment of a panel or its obscure term composition. For Mexico such improvements were crucial given the number of trade disputes, particularly from the United States, that it has taken to GATT. It is expected that the new dispute-settlement procedures will translate into the actual implementation of panels' decisions.

In terms of institutional reforms, the creation of the WTO as a peak institution aimed at granting a permanent character to the multilateral trade organization and constraining the capacity of governments to unilaterally impose trade restrictions that are inconsistent with GATT. Mexico along with Canada and the United States was the first participant to submit a concrete proposal to establish the World Trade Organization. Thus, GATT was subsumed under the WTO as one of those agreements.

New Areas

As a result of the increasing importance of services in the international economy, the Uruguay Round incorporated new areas of negotiation such as services, trade-related investment measures, and intellectual property rights. Trade in services represents 25 percent of world trade (around US$1 trillion annually) and almost 60 percent of foreign direct investment.

The General Agreement on Trade in Services (GATS) establishes a benchmark level of market access based on existing national regulations. It is based on the principles of national treatment and reciprocity; future negotiations will address areas where agreement could not be reached, such as financial services. For Mexico, liberalization of services was not something totally new because its own process of economic reform and the North American Free Trade Agreement (NAFTA) negotiations had set the context for negotiating this sector multilaterally. Mexico agreed to allow 100 percent foreign participation in the case of certain professional services, scheduled distribution services, and certain tourism and trade-related services.

Since market access in services is closely linked to investment rules, trade-related investment measures (TRIMs) became part of the negotiation. The Uruguay Round did not go far in liberalizing investment; it only established the framework to initiate consultations toward establishing disciplines on the effects of investment measures on trade. The list of TRIMs includes instruments that Mexico has used to encourage industrialization, such as local content requirements, trade balancing requirements, foreign exchange balancing, and export limits. As part of its economic reforms, Mexico has eliminated almost all of its TRIMs, although some are still in place in the automotive sector, for example. Mexico will eliminate the remaining TRIMs within a five-year period unless an extension is granted. This type of commitment reduces Mexico's capacity to target industrial development through these instruments, which although not economically optimal, have been used worldwide to attain international competitiveness and domestic protection.

Among the new areas, the Agreement on Trade-Related Intellectual Property Rights (TRIPs) is the most comprehensive and reflects the areas of importance to industrialized countries. This agreement covers minimum standards for copyright, trademarks, geographical indications, industrial design, patents, layout designs of integrated circuits, and protection of undisclosed information. Under NAFTA, Mexico had already accepted standards of protection similar to those in the TRIPs Agreement.

For Mexico, participation in the negotiation of these new areas was significant, even though NAFTA would eventually become more important than the WTO in service trade. As an importer of services and technology, it was in Mexico's interest to define the terms of its liberalization to be able to encourage domestic as well as foreign participation in the sector. Mexico's economic growth cannot be tied only to manufacture production or agriculture exports; Mexico has the potential of becoming a strong supplier of services such as construction and tourism. Thus, trade in services may well support Mexico's economic growth.

Conclusions

With Mexico's formal accession to GATT, the likelihood of a sudden reversal of its liberalized trade regime was dramatically reduced while such reforms became more predictable and sustainable. GATT/WTO membership reflects a shift in Mexico's economic model equilibrium from protection and rent-seeking to the support of outward-oriented sectors that benefit from an open economy. Mexico's international commitments forced a distance from groups within business, agriculture, and the bureaucracy that saw their political and economic privileges fade away. The new political economy is still in the process of consolidation, and there exists the risk that this dramatic reform will provoke destabilizing opposition from those groups that refuse or are unable to adjust to the new competition conditions.

Trade liberalization and access to export markets will not automatically translate into increased industrialization, economic growth, and development. Mexico will reap the benefits of its unilateral trade liberalization process and of its deregulation policies by receiving reciprocity from other GATT members. However, Mexico faces the challenge of promoting competitiveness of all its manufacturing, agricul-

ture, and service sectors to take full advantage of the Uruguay Round Agreements. The country's dependence on foreign capital and multinational corporate strategies severely limits the extent to which GATT membership will help strengthen Mexico's outward-oriented industrialization.

Select Bibliography

GATT, *Trade Policy Review of Mexico.* Geneva: GATT, 1993.

Mares, David R., "Explaining Choice of Development Strategies: Suggestions from Mexico, 1970–1982." *International Organization* 39:4 (Autumn 1985).

Newell, Roberto G., and Luis Rubio F., *Mexico's Dilemma: The Political Origins of Economic Crisis.* Boulder, Colorado: Westview Press, 1984.

Rubio, Luis F., Cristina Rodríguez D., and Roberto Blum V., "The Making of Mexico's Trade Policy and the Uruguay Round." In *Domestic Trade Politics and the Uruguay Round,* edited by Henry Nau. New York: Columbia University Press, 1989.

Story, Dale, "Trade politics in the Third World: A case study of the Mexican GATT decision." *International Organization* 36:4 (Autumn 1982).

———, *Industry, the State and Public Policy in Mexico.* Austin: University of Texas Press, 1986.

Rajapatirana, Sarath, "Latin America and the Caribbean after the Uruguay Round: An Assessment." World Bank Internal Document (July 20, 1995).

Torres, Blanca, and Pamela S. Falk, editors, *La adhesión de México al GATT: Repercusiones internas e impacto sobre las relaciones México–Estados Unidos.* Mexico City: El Colegio de México, 1989.

World Bank, *World Development Report 1987.* Washington, D.C.: World Bank, 1987.

—LUZ MARÍA DE LA MORA

GERONIMO

c.1829–1909 • Apache Chief

A fearsome Apache Indian warrior and medicine man of mythic stature, Geronimo and his band boldly raided ranchos and trading routes on both sides of the U.S.-Mexico border from the 1850s to the 1880s, defying the military's mission to pacify the region for modern development. His surrender to the U.S. Army in 1886 ended an epoch called "The Apachería," which had characterized the area for nearly two centuries.

Born about 1829 on the upper reaches of the Gila River (near the present-day mining town of Clifton, Arizona), Geronimo belonged to the Be-don-ko-he band of the southern Chiricahua Apaches. He was known as Goyathlay or Goyaklay, meaning "one who yawns." It is not clear how

he came to be called Geronimo; the name could have been given to him by his Mexican military adversaries. Few specifics are known of his early life, but he emerged as a leader in 1858 in the wake of personal tragedy. According to Geronimo, he had gone in the company of other Apaches and their families to trade peacefully with settlers around the Mexican military post at Janos in northern Chihuahua. While Geronimo and other adult males were away, a troop of Mexican soldiers from the neighboring state of Sonora swooped down on the family encampment and slaughtered most of the Apaches there, including Geronimo's mother, wife, and three children. As a result, Geronimo swore revenge on the Mexicans. Later in old age he said, "I shall never go on the warpath again, but if I were young, and followed the warpath, it would lead to Old Mexico."

Soon after the calamity at Janos, Geronimo received a spirit's voice that told him (sounding typical millenarian strains), "No gun can ever kill you. I will take the bullets of the Mexicans so that they will have nothing but powder. And I will guide your arrows." In the ensuing forays, Geronimo was wounded many times, and as late as 1897 still advised those who would listen that no bullet could kill him. Indeed, foes and followers alike thought that Geronimo was endowed with supernatural powers. Eye-witnesses declared him clairvoyant; he could interpret signs, explain the unknowable, and predict the future.

In concert with its uncertain and fluctuating policy, the U.S. Government tried to tame the Apaches by shifting them from one reservation to another in Arizona and New Mexico. The Apaches, themselves not of one mind on how to approach their plight, might settle down as farmers for a spell but sooner or later a faction would "break out" of the reservation and hit the plunder trail, plunging the region into turmoil and bloodshed. Geronimo himself often led these militant factions. He might be captured or surrender and be returned to a reservation for a period of peace (although other Apaches might be on the warpath), but he eventually would break out again.

In May 1885 Geronimo "broke out" with 35 men, 8 boys, and 101 women. Ten months later he again surrendered to the American military in northern Sonora (a treaty between the U.S. and Mexico allowed security forces from each nation to traverse the border in pursuit of hostile Indians) only to bolt for freedom one more time. With 5,000 American soldiers and 500 Indian auxiliaries in pursuit,

Geronimo, with 16 warriors, 14 women, and 6 children surrendered for the last time on September 3, 1886, at Skeleton Canyon in southern Arizona. He was promised that after an indefinite exile in Florida, he and his followers would be allowed to return to Arizona, but that was a promise not kept. Geronimo died of pneumonia at Fort Sill on February 17, 1909, and is buried in the Indian cemetery at that post.

The end of the Apachería opened northwestern Mexico to a flood of capitalist investment, mainly in mines and ranches. Over centuries it had forged a distinctive culture that Mexicans call Norteño, characterized by people said to be more independent, openly brash, touchy, competitive, and pragmatic than in other parts of the country. Norteños are quick to remind that their ancestors fought bravely and at great loss to themselves to defend the republic against Apache peril. Now they demand their due, especially from the federal government. Meanwhile, Geronimo himself has been elevated in the public mind from barbarian scourge to honorable adversary.

Select Bibliography

Betzines, Jason, and Wilbur Sturtevant Nye, *I Fought with Geronimo.* Harrisburg, Pennsylvania: Stackpole, 1959.

Griffen, William B., *Apaches at War and Peace: The Janos Presidio, 1750–1858.* Albuquerque: University of New Mexico Press, 1988.

_____, *Utmost Good Faith: Patterns of Apache-Mexican Hostilities in Northern Chihuahua Border Warfare, 1821–1848.* Albuquerque: University of New Mexico Press, 1988.

Sweeney, Edwin R., *Cochise: Chiricahua Apache Chief.* Norman: University of Oklahoma Press, 1991.

—PAUL J. VANDERWOOD

GILLOW Y ZAVALZA, EULOGIO GREGORIO

1841–1922 • Archbishop

Eulogio Gillow, archbishop of Antequera (Oaxaca), was one of the wealthiest and most prominent clerics of the Porfirian period and a leading player of Porfirio Díaz's policy of conciliation toward the Roman Catholic Church. He was the son of Thomas Gillow, a Liverpool jeweler from a prominent family of British Catholics, and an aristocratic Spanish woman, doña María J. Zavalza y Gutiérrez, marquesa de Selva Nevada. For the sake of social appearances, Thomas Gillow abandoned his trade and settled into farming the extensive properties of his wife's family. His fortune grew to be vast, and his influence was considerable in Mexican business circles. In 1860, he founded the Agricultural Society of

San Martín Texmelucan, which provided the prototype for the Mexican Agricultural Society, a leading organization of Mexico's large-scale commercial farmers.

Eulogio Gillow was born in Puebla. In 1851, at the age of 10, he accompanied his father to the Universal Exposition in London and stayed to pursue his education, first with a private tutor and later at the Jesuit college of Stonyhurst. At the age of 15, Gillow transferred to Alost College in Belgium, where he spent six years. In 1862, he traveled to Rome for Holy Week, arriving there at a time when the Papal States were besieged by Italian nationalists under Giuseppe Garibaldi and King Victor Emmanuel II. While in

Rome, Gillow won an audience with Pope Pius IX, who encouraged the youth to study for the priesthood at the Academia Eclesiástica de Nobles in Rome and to continue his studies at the Universidad Gregoriana. Gillow was present at the ceremonies fêting Emperor Maximilian as he embarked for Mexico, and was closely associated with many opponents of Mexican liberalism. He returned to Mexico in 1865, where he was ordained in the Cathedral of Puebla. He then returned to Rome, where he became a personal secretary to Pius IX. He received his doctorate in canon law in 1869, and he attended the First Vatican Council in 1870 as theological adviser to Archbishop Márquez of Oaxaca. Prior to his return to Mexico, the pope made him an officer to the Supreme Tribunal of Grace and Justice; he was now dependent directly on the Roman Curiat rather than on any Mexican diocese.

Upon returning to Mexico, Gillow appears to have taken less interest in church matters than in managing and expanding his personal fortune. His base of operations was the magnificent hacienda of Chautla in Puebla. Gillow became intensely active in the Mexican Agricultural Society, built a hydroelectric plant, secured railroad concessions, set up telephone and telegraph lines, imported farm machinery, and participated in a variety of fairs and expositions.

It was in this last capacity that he met Porfirio Díaz, the authoritarian president of Mexico from 1876 to 1880 and from 1884 to 1911. In 1877, Gillow helped organize an agricultural exposition in Puebla, which hoped to attract U.S. investors to Mexico. Díaz, who was just beginning his first presidential term, inaugurated the exposition, and he relied on Gillow to act as interpreter and intermediary between himself and the U.S. businessmen in attendance. He was impressed greatly with the urbane churchman, who spoke five languages, was a personal friend of the pope, and could intelligently discuss the fine points of agriculture, mining, and industry. Clearly, Gillow could be quite useful to Díaz, inasmuch as the dictator was eager to move beyond the debilitating conflict between church and state. Those attending a banquet at the exposition witnessed a curious scene in which Alfredo Chavero, a "33 degree" mason, spoke rhapsodically in praise of the clergy in general and of the Puebla clergy in particular. It appeared to be the dawn of a veritable era of good feeling between church and state.

Shortly thereafter, Díaz asked Gillow to preside over his wedding to Carmen Romero. Gillow diplomatically declined the honor in favor of the archbishop of Mexico, Pelagio Antonio de Labastida y Dávalos, a notoriously intransigent monarchist who once had been a prominent member of the French Regency government. The wedding hence came to have tremendous symbolic importance, for it suggested an apparent reconciliation between a hero of Mexican liberalism and its most vociferous opponent.

Gillow was not without his critics. Some of his more conservative fellow clergymen felt that his embrace of the elements of modernity was unseemly, even while traditional anticlericals objected to his growing influence with the Díaz regime. Opponents of the Mexican latifundia (great landed estates) denounced him as a feudal land baron who monopolized land and abused his workers. A man who worked with him to organize Mexico's participation in the New Orleans Cotton Centennial Exposition in 1883 and 1884 accused him of corruption and embezzlement of the exposition's funds.

Such charges appear ultimately to have done little lasting harm to Gillow's reputation. In 1891, Gillow—perhaps with some intervention by Díaz—was named archbishop of Oaxaca. His tenure as archbishop was marked by important and expensive works of restoration, including the seminary, the Cathedral of Oaxaca, and various churches throughout the diocese. He also established several free schools as well as asylums for orphans and the elderly, and had a magnificent palace built as his own archepiscopal residence on the Avenida Independencia. In 1909, Pope Leo XIII nominated him for the position of cardinal of Mexico, but he was obliged to decline the honor because such a position in Mexico was unconstitutional.

In 1914, invading Constitutionalist forces took over Gillow's Puebla hacienda. With the increasing anticlericalism in Mexico, Gillow found himself forced to flee into exile, which he spent primarily in Los Angeles, California. He returned to Mexico shortly before his death in 1922. He achieved a measure of immortality when he was chosen by D. H. Lawrence as the model for Bishop Severn in his 1926 novel *The Plumed Serpent*.

Select Bibliography

Gillow y Zavalza, Eulogio Gregorio, *Reminiscencias del Illmo. y Rmo. Sr. Dr. D. Eulogio Gillow y Zavalza, Arzobispo de Antequera (Oaxaca)*, prologue by José Antonio Rivera G. Los Angeles: El Heraldo de México, 1920.

Santa Fé, Alberto, "Carta abierta del socialista Alberto Santa Fé." In *Documentos para la historia económica de México*, volume 10, *Orígenes del agrarismo en México*, edited by Luis Chávez Orozco. Mexico City: Secretaría de la Economía Nacional, 1936.

Parmenter, Ross, *Lawrence in Oaxaca: A Quest for the Novelist in Mexico*. Salt Lake City, Utah: G. M. Smith, 1984.

—TIMOTHY J. HENDERSON

GÓMEZ FARÍAS, VALENTÍN

1781–1858 • President

Born to a middle-class Guadalajara family, Valentín Gómez Farías studied to become a physician and practice medicine until 1820, at which time he became town councilor of Aguascalientes. Over the next 30 years, Gómez Farías immersed himself in Mexican politics and emerged as one of the most important Liberal statesmen of his generation. Although some historians characterize him as an ineffective political leader and a traitor who sold out Mexico to the United States during the U.S.-Mexican War, a more balanced assessment of Gómez Farías suggests otherwise. He held to his beliefs with uncommon tenacity and devoted his life to the idea of turning Mexico into a federal republic free from domination by the Catholic Church, the army, and the landed elite.

In 1822 Gómez Farías made his first major imprint on Mexico's domestic affairs. He was among those legislators who endorsed Agustín de Iturbide's accession to the throne, but he withdrew his support when the emperor dissolved Congress in October of that year. Gómez Farías represented his home state of Jalisco in the national legislature between 1824 and 1830, and by the end of the decade he had assumed a leadership position among the radical Liberals (known as *puros*). In the fall of 1832, as one of the directors of a civilian opposition group to the Anastasio Bustamante regime, Gómez Farías sought a partner in the regular army that would allow the *puros* to obtain the political power necessary to protect state autonomy and implement socioeconomic reforms. He struck an alliance with General Antonio López de Santa Anna, who in turn required Gómez Farías's support to gain the presidency because his earlier revolt against the government had stalled. This coalition succeeded in ousting Bustamante and inaugurated a short-lived era of reform.

Left as caretaker of the executive branch by Santa Anna following elections in the spring of 1833, Gómez Farías sponsored a series of laws designed to weaken the army and the clergy by eliminating *fueros* (which had granted the army and the clergy broad privileges and immunities within civil law), secularizing education, and controlling church wealth and patronage. Since the proposed changes alarmed both the Catholic Church and the army, in the spring of 1834 Santa Anna deemed it prudent to side with those who opposed the reformist project and launch Mexico on the path to centralism. Faced with this uprising, Gómez Farías did not muster the armed forces needed to crush Santa Anna and his allies because he believed that such an action was unconstitutional. The experience left its mark on Gómez Farías; upon returning from exile to center stage in Mexico's political arena in the late 1830s, he advocated armed rebellion as a means of obtaining the political power that would allow the *puros* to implement their agenda.

Gómez Farías participated in several attempts to overthrow the established government during the early 1840s, and by 1845 two goals stood out in his mind: restoring the 1824 Constitution as the basic law of the land and launching a military campaign to recover the former Mexican territory of Texas. Gómez Farías sincerely believed that this package of reforms best suited Mexico's needs, as they would solve the country's domestic problems and halt U.S. expansionism. At this time, as before, Gómez Farías lacked the institutional support to reach power and implement these objectives, but the specter of war with the United States provided him and Santa Anna another opportunity to renew their previous alliance. The August 1846 rebellion of the Ciudadela left the *puros* in charge of the government, and within a few months the scenario of 1833 had repeated itself. In the December elections Santa Anna won the presidency and Gómez Farías the vice presidency, after which Santa Anna left his subordinate in charge of the executive branch owing to his own position as commander in chief of the Mexican army in San Luis Potosí.

To finance the war against the United States, in January 1847 Gómez Farías issued a decree authorizing the government to raise 15 million pesos by mortgaging or selling ecclesiastical property. Although this piece of legislation was not intended to eradicate the church's power and influence, the law nonetheless fostered public animosity toward Gómez Farías. *Moderado* (moderate liberal) politicians, senior army chiefs, and high-ranking clerical leaders began to plot against him, and their intrigues culminated in the February 27, 1847, Revolt of the Polkos. This uprising, which erupted just a few days before General Winfield Scott and the U.S. expeditionary army landed in Veracruz, culminated in Gómez Farías's ouster from the executive branch and in the *puros'* demise as Mexico's dominant political bloc.

Following General Scott's occupation of Mexico City in September 1847, some *puro* politicians broke from Gómez Farías and made it known to U.S. officials that they hoped the United States would establish a protectorate over Mexico. Gómez Farías, however, spearheaded efforts to continue hostilities and invalidate the Treaty of Guadalupe Hidalgo. In the end, the *puros'* failure to achieve these goals, as well as the inability of postwar regimes to address the country's long-standing political and economic problems, frustrated Gómez Farías. Advancing age and failing health also affected him, and Gómez Farías withdrew from public life during the early 1850s.

By the time of his death in 1858, Gómez Farías's position had become reduced to that of respected *puro* elder statesman. The state of Jalisco chose him to serve in the Constitutional Congress that met in Querétaro through the summer of 1856, but Gómez Farías's health problems prevented him from participating in the deliberations. Nonetheless, as his life drew to a close, the objectives that Gómez Farías strove to implement over the course of his public life were near to bearing fruit. A few months after the enactment of the 1857 Constitution, and amid the applause of his fellow legislators, Gómez Farías was brought into the chambers to swear an oath upholding this charter. In the end, the Catholic Church may have refused to bury him in consecrated ground, but Gómez Farías probably rested in peace; he died knowing that Mexico had adopted a constitution that severely circumscribed the privileges of the church and the military and also provided for a federal republic (albeit with a strong central government).

Select Bibliography

Costeloe, Michael P., *The Central Republic of Mexico, 1835–1846: Hombres de Bien in the Age of Santa Anna.* New York: Cambridge University Press, 1993.

Fowler, Will, "Valentín Gómez Farías: Perceptions of Radicalism in Independent Mexico, 1821–1847." *Bulletin of Latin American Research* 15:1 (1996).

Hutchinson, Cecil Allan, *Valentín Gómez Farías: La vida de un republicano,* translated by Marco Antonio Silva. Guadalajara, Mexico: Unidad Editorial de la Secretaría General del Gobierno de Jalisco, 1983.

Mills, Elizabeth, *Don Valentín Gómez Farías y el desarrollo de sus ideas políticas.* Mexico City: UNAM, 1957.

Santoni, Pedro, *Mexicans at Arms: Puro Federalists and the Politics of War, 1845–1848.* Fort Worth: Texas Christian University Press, 1996.

—Pedro Santoni

GÓMEZ MARÍN, MANUEL

1761–1850 • Priest, Educator, and Writer

Manuel José Francisco Gómez Marín was born on May 22, 1761, in San Felipe el Grande, now known as Villa de San Felipe del Progreso, in the state of Mexico, and died of cholera on July 7, 1850, in Mexico City. He studied theology at the Royal Seminary of the Archbishopric of Mexico and at the Royal Pontifical University of Mexico, obtaining his bachelor's degree in 1791 and his doctorate one year later; he obtained the bachelor's and master's degrees in arts in 1801. He was ordained as a priest in 1790, and joined the Oratory of St. Philip Neri of Mexico in 1817, where he worked until his death in 1850.

Gómez Marín was a distinguished professor of theology at the seminary and the university; in the former he introduced the study of modern philosophy, giving emphasis to scholasticism and the experimental sciences of physics and chemistry. He was also *synodal* of the archbishopric, the university's librarian, and vice chancellor of the Mining School. He served as director of spiritual exercises at the oratory, and his contemporaries described him as a great orator and an expert in Latin. He befriended the literary personalities of his time and often participated in the salons organized by the printer Luis Abadiano y Valdés, which took place in his book shop. The brilliant career of Gómez Marín led him to become a consultant in important ecclesiastical matters.

Gómez Marín responded to the university's summons to compete in a literary contest in 1790, and he won with a chant and an ode written "in eulogy of Carlos IV, King of Spain and the Indies." Subsequently, during the installation of the equestrian statue of Carlos IV in Mexico City in 1803, his Latin inscription and his romance commemorating the event were widely praised. Gómez Marín's work generally is read as praising courtly life, but if, for example, we analyze his chant praising Carlos IV, we note that it is more a description of the history of the Spanish kings since the times of Carlos I (Emperor Charles V) until the Bourbons, and the current monarch is described only as an embodiment of expected virtues; there is no direct eulogy of his reign, and thus the poet avoids any kind of commitment.

In 1799, Gómez Marín published his satire *El currutaco por alambique* (The Dandy in Dribs and Drabs), a work recommended by Francisco Pimentel in his *Critical History* for "its charm, naturalness and fluency." This work saw several editions throughout the nineteenth century and it has been regarded by the critics as an amusing, but untypical satire of imperfect rhyme, which nevertheless derides the current fashion introduced by the dandies of society, whose origin is depicted as deriving from hell. Gómez Marín's text alludes to the French customs adopted by the Spanish Bourbons; using a subtle irony, he criticizes the existing contempt shown toward Spanish Americans and points out the defects of the Francophiles who have conquered the world with their irreverences.

In 1819, Gómez Marín published his *Defensa Guadalupana* (Defense of the Virgin of Guadalupe), a text that generated many discussions of the miraculous origin of the Virgin's image. Gómez Marín wrote the *Defensa* to rebut a speech given by Juan Bautista Muñoz to the Royal Academy of History in Spain, in which he denied the appearances and miraculous origin of the Virgin's image; Juan Bautista Muñoz based his argument on the fact that the Virgin is not mentioned in Fray Bernardino de Sahagún's *Historia general de las cosas de Nueva España* (General History of the Things of New Spain), a work written at the time of the appearances. Gómez Marín was the first intellectual to refute this attack, and his opinion was shared by others, including José María Guiridi y Alcocer. The *Defensa* forced many writers to define their posture, being either for or against the Virgin's appearances. Gómez Marín's participation in the debate can be found as late as 1820 in a passionate newspaper article titled "Challenge," written for the *Noticioso General.* In this text, the theologian offered an invitation to discuss the matter; the journalist José Joaquín Fernández de Lizardi accepted it not only as a means to define his posture against the miraculous origins of the Virgin's images, but also to emphasize the figure of Gómez Marín as an eminent theologian.

In collaboration with other personalities, Gómez Marín presented to President Antonio López de Santa Anna on July 19, 1834, a writing pleading for the reestablishment of the university, which had been closed by presidential decree by his predecessor Valentín Gómez Farías a year earlier. The text was published later in the newspaper *El Tiempo,* and Santa Anna acceded to the plea and reopened the university that same year.

In 1836, the printer Luis Abadiano y Valdés published Gómez Marín's famous sermon honoring the beatification of Sebastián Valfré, which he delivered at the Oratory of St. Philip Neri in the form of a panegyrical prayer. This is believed to be Gómez Marín's last work, and in it he shows a temperate style. The prayer is an example of a refined oration of the Mexican nineteenth century.

His work was much admired throughout the nineteenth century; Francisco Pimentel regarded him as an important writer and gave him space in his *Historia Critica.* Gómez Marín was included in the *Antología del centenario* (Anthology of the Centennial, 1910), but subsequently his work was rarely mentioned in historical surveys of Mexican literature. In 1981, Jesús Yhmoff Cabrera rescued and edited his remaining texts. Gómez Marín is an example of those humanists who lived during the boom of the Bourbon period in New Spain and whose presence in ecclesiastical matters was felt in the newly independent republic.

Select Bibliography

Carballo, Emmanuel, *Historia de las letras mexicanas en el siglo XIX.* Guadalajara: Universidad de Guadalajara–Xalli, 1991.
Gómez Marín, Manuel, *Obras castellanas y latinas en verso y prosa.* Toluca: FONAPAS, 1981.

—María Elena Victoria Jardón

GÓMEZ PEDRAZA, MANUEL

1789–1851 • President

The career of Manuel Gómez Pedraza epitomizes the aspirations of the *moderado* (moderate Liberal) political bloc within Mexico's upper-middle-class ruling elite of *hombres de bien.* As the foremost *moderado* statesman in early republican Mexico, Gómez Pedraza strove to implement various reforms that would ensure the country's well-being. These included the establishment of a federal republic as well as the gradual reduction of the political and economic influence of the Catholic Church and the army. His political activities also shed light on the personal animosities that made consensus between elite factions difficult to achieve. The antagonism that characterized his relationship with *puro* (radical Liberal) leader Valentín Gómez Farías over the pace of socioeconomic reform exacerbated the *puro-moderado* rift. This animosity compromised Gómez Pedraza's capacity to cooperate with the national defense effort at the time of the U.S. invasion in 1846.

Born to a prominent Querétaro family, Gómez Pedraza served as a royalist officer during the Wars of Independence,

like many of his contemporaries. He went on to represent New Spain as a deputy to the 1820 Spanish Parliament, and he received a succession of military commands during the imperial interlude of Agustín de Iturbide. Following Iturbide's abdication, Gómez Pedraza made the ideological switch to federalism and occupied several high offices between 1825 and 1828, including the governorship of the state of Puebla and minister of war. In the latter office he developed a reputation as an industrious, energetic administrator and won the plaudits of Yorkino newspapers (those that supported the radical federalist York Rite Masons) for his vigorous prosecution of the individuals involved in the 1827 Arenas conspiracy and Montaño uprising.

Gómez Pedraza's accomplishments positioned him to run for president in 1828 as the candidate of the moderate Yorkinos. Although he won the elections, a rebellion instigated by supporters of the defeated radical Yorkinos prevented Gómez Pedraza from taking the presidential chair. After a self-imposed exile in France and New Orleans,

Gómez Pedraza returned to Mexico in late 1832 following the overthrow of Anastasio Bustamante's regime. As he served out the final months of his presidential term, Gómez Pedraza endeavored to chart a moderate course and to prevent opposing political factions from open conflict.

Following the short-lived 1833–34 Gómez Farías administration, Mexico adopted a centralist republic. However, as disenchantment with the 1836 Constitution (Siete Leyes) began to mount, Gómez Pedraza worked for a gradual and peaceful transition to federalism. He accepted a ministerial post in December 1838 on condition that the government convene a new congress to reform the 1824 federal charter but resigned within a few days when President Anastasio Bustamante (then in his second term as chief executive) withdrew his support. In 1841 Gómez Pedraza reentered the national political scenario and renewed his efforts to return Mexico to some kind of a federal structure. He contributed articles to the *moderado* daily *El Siglo XIX,* served as minister of foreign relations between October and November, and was elected to the 1842 Constitutional Congress. Gómez Pedraza's efforts did not meet with success at this time, but in 1844 his political star skyrocketed. As a member of the Senate, Gómez Pedraza spearheaded legislative resistance to General Antonio López de Santa Anna's personalistic dictatorship. This opposition culminated in the December 6 movement, a coup d'état that deposed Santa Anna and installed a *moderado* national government.

Gómez Pedraza exerted considerable influence over domestic affairs between 1845 and 1848 as Mexico drifted into war with the United States. Although he did not hold an official cabinet post in the administration of José Joaquín Herrera, contemporaries believed that Gómez Pedraza held considerable sway throughout 1845 over Herrera and his ministers. Therefore, the *puros* held him personally responsible for devising and implementing what they considered to be ill-advised policies of attempting to reach an amicable accord with the United States over the Texas question and preserving the centralist, conservative Bases Orgánicas of 1843 as Mexico's constitution.

The unmerciful tirades to which *puro* newspapers subjected Gómez Pedraza surely remained vivid in his memory and influenced his conduct once the *puros* assumed power in August 1846. Over the next eight months, Gómez Pedraza, sometimes in conjunction with Santa Anna and at other times in association with conservative or *moderado* politicians, attempted to sabotage the *puros'* efforts to achieve national unity as Mexico tried to fend off the U.S. invasion. He participated in intrigues such as the February 1847 Revolt of the Polkos, which ousted Gómez Farías from the presidential chair and ended the *puros'* political ascendancy.

Gómez Pedraza shied away from any public posts that might have compromised his political reputation for the rest of the year. He refused to join the commission that entered into peace negotiations with the United States in August 1847, and after the occupation of Mexico City in mid-September he retreated to a nearby hacienda so as not to shoulder an active role in a *moderado* government whose foremost priority would be the end of the war. In the spring of 1848, however, Gómez Pedraza was elected to the national legislature, and in late May he twice addressed the Senate to argue in favor of ratifying the Treaty of Guadalupe Hidalgo. Gómez Pedraza's initial address—the most significant of the two—sought to vindicate his support of Herrera's foreign policy in 1845 and also pointed out the immense benefits that Mexico would accrue if it settled for peace. Although this discourse received little publicity at the time, the speech probably strengthened the convictions of those senators who needed further reassurance that Mexico could only begin to put its internal affairs in order by settling for peace with the United States.

Gómez Pedraza remained an active participant in Mexico's domestic affairs following the war with the United States. Like many of his counterparts, he believed that the patronage of a strong foreign country was necessary for national redemption and survival, and in January 1850 Gómez Pedraza signed an agreement with U.S. minster plenipotentiary Robert P. Letcher to build a canal through the isthmus in Tehuantepec (the Mexican Congress later nullified the deal). He also was nominated to run for president that year and served as director of the national pawnshop (Monte de Piedad) in Mexico City at the time of his death in 1851.

Select Bibliography

Costeloe, Michael P., *La primera república federal de México (1824–1835),* translated by Manuel Fernández Gasallo. Mexico City: Fondo de Cultura Económica, 1975.

——, *The Central Republic in Mexico, 1835–1846: Hombres de Bien in the Age of Santa Anna.* New York: Cambridge University Press, 1993.

Di Tella, Torcuato, *National Popular Politics in Early Independent Mexico, 1820–1847.* Albuquerque: University of New Mexico Press, 1996.

Gómez Pedraza, Manuel, *Manifesto que . . . , ciudadano de la República de México, dedica a sus compatriotas, o sea una reseña de su vida política.* Guadalajara: Brambila, 1831.

Santoni, Pedro, *Mexicans at Arms: Puro Federalists and the Politics of War, 1845–1848.* Fort Worth: Texas Christian University Press, 1996.

—PEDRO SANTONI

GÓMEZ-PEÑA, GUILLERMO

1955– • Writer and Experimental Artist

Guillermo Gómez-Peña was born in Mexico City in 1955. While studying at the Facultad de Filosofía y Letras in the mid-1970s, he began doing experimental performances, or "interdisciplinary troublemaking" as he called it, on the streets of Mexico City with the performance troupe Anarquía S.A. In 1978 he moved to California, where he founded Poyesis Genética in 1981 with Sara-Jo Berman and a fluctuating core of eight to ten other students at the California Institute of the Arts. Poyesis was a troupe dedicated to culturally pluralistic, collaborative, and interdisciplinary performances and included Isaac Artenstein and David Avalos. The troupe went through a series of artistic and theoretical regroupings, slowly fading into the Border Arts Workshop (BAW) in 1985. Gómez-Peña left the BAW in 1990 to perform solo and collaboratively in the United States, Mexico, and internationally.

Gómez-Peña's work has used the border as an elastic metaphor from which to challenge restricted notions of "national culture" and "Americanness." Gómez-Peña's main objective has been to develop intercultural performances and cross-racial collaborative models that are congruent with, reflective of, and disruptive to what he has called "the-end-of-the-century society." In this period of unprecedented changes in geopolitical conditions and transnational migration, fears of and desires for cultural others develop simultaneously with nostalgias for outdated modes of identity based upon stable, impermeable national borders. Hierarchies of difference and practices of "othering" that result from contemporary geopolitical and cultural imperialism, especially as embodied in the multifaceted relationships between the United States and Mexico, are at the center of Gómez-Peña's work. Conceptualizing these cultural conditions and relationships has meant that his work includes a variety of projects—essays, performance pieces, poetry, radio performances—performed solo as well as in collaboration with a range of artists. Gómez-Peña utilizes a variety of venues, including on-site performances ("Couple in the Cage," 1992; "The Loneliness of the Immigrant," 1979), television ("1992: The Rediscovery of America by the Warrior for Gringostrokia," 1992), newspapers ("The End of the Line," 1986), radio ("Borderless Radio"), and art institutions, in order to reach an audience of participants in end-of-the-century society, not simply those drawn to his work who are generally art, performance, and postmodernist border theory aficionados.

Gómez-Peña developed three key strategies for developing and enacting models that draw attention to the contingencies and emergencies of end-of-the-century society. The first is performance as intercultural intervention, most notable in his work on the relationships between Mexico and the United States. The second is performance diplomacy, as in his 1990 trip to the Soviet Far East as part of a binational human rights commission to exchange information with Soviet groups. The third is cross-cultural/interdisciplinary collaboration between artists of different cultural, regional, and national backgrounds, evident in his work with Coco Fusco, Robert Sanchez, and the artists of the Mexican Museum's installation, *Norte/Sur.* His work has developed within the context of the Mexican, U.S., and international performance art worlds, in which a number of artists, upon consideration of contemporary cultural conditions, have developed multiple forms and strategies for communicating their ideas and enacting cultural critique. Gómez-Peña's early work in Mexico with Anarquía S.A. engaged in disrupting everyday activities and special events alike, drawing attention to the creation of authority by posing absurd questions, and showing up in public places in disguise. His later work demonstrates continuities with these early tactics, but his cultural critique has become much more sophisticated and focused. In works such as "The End of the Line" (with the BAW), which used "border stereotypes" in a site-specific performance staged at the terminus of the U.S.-Mexican border at the Pacific Ocean, both the imagery and the content confront the viewer with the theme of binational interactions, separatisms, and their ramifications. Gómez-Peña's early dissatisfaction with aesthetic protectionism and cultural solemnity in Mexico developed into a desire to create a new continental map of the Americas.

Gómez-Peña's work is exemplary for the way it addresses both voluntary and involuntary audiences, and for its modes of performing and translating the sexual, political, and cultural relationships between the United States and Mexico. In an early U.S. performance entitled "The Loneliness of the Immigrant," which depicted the pain and despair of the immigrant, Gómez-Peña spent 24 hours wrapped in a batik cloth in a public elevator, where he remained still and silent as the elevator's occupants interacted with him. Whereas his early works with Poyesis were enriched by the fusions and collaborations enabled by the U.S.-Mexican border, in later works, especially with the BAW, the U.S.-Mexican border figures as a site itself. "Border Brujo" (1988, 1990) exemplifies Gómez-Peña's attempts to use intercultural dialogue as a means to exorcise the demons of dominant cultures. In this work, Gómez-Peña builds upon his earlier experiments with disguise and cultural confrontation, performing 15 cultural voices of U.S.-Mexican border areas, including the *pachuco,* the radio commentator, the redneck, the newscaster, the upper-class Latino, and the drunken tourist. Unlike plays, in which characters address each other in a dramatic narrative, the characters in "Border Brujo" literally and metaphorically address the audience. The voice with a thick Mexican accent points at a specific audience member and declares,

> I speak Spanish therefore you hate me
> I speak in English therefore they hate me
> . . . I speak in tongues therefore you desire me.

To challenge the audience to self-examination, the authoritative voice uses a megaphone,

> I mean to ask you some questions
> dear curator
> dear collector
> dear anthropologist
> where can we draw the line between curiosity and exploitation?
> between dialogue and entertainment?
> between democratic participation and tokenism?
> where is the borderline between my Spanish and your English?

Through monologues and staging, "Border Brujo" reenacts and critiques the visual and verbal border narratives that establish divided and divisive cultural identities.

After 1992, Gómez-Peña's portrayal of the border shifted increasingly from a site-specific border to a global border consciousness. Performed the year of the Columbus quincentenary, "1992: The Rediscovery of America by the Warrior for Gringostrokia" portrays the multiple ways the colonizing past occupies the present. "The Couple in the Cage," performed with Coco Fusco internationally in museums and at exhibitions, featured the two "recently discovered Guatinaui Indians" displayed in a cage available for certain native performances for a fee. The audiences did not know that the Guatinaui exhibition was a performance, and many of their reactions demonstrated that the model of the savage spectacle, which has for so long underwritten colonialism and imperialism, was still alive. "Temple of Confessions" (1995), a museum piece performed in the United States with Robert Sanchez, featured the performers as "saints" on display, one a pre-Colombian *vato* and the other a *pocho* Aztec. In front of them were kneelers and microphones from which the audience could confess their intercultural fears and desires. The "confessions," which included crimes against Mexican immigrants as well as fears of and sexual encounters with Latinos, were recorded and played over the public address system the next day. In these as in most of his performances, Gómez-Peña occupies the role of an artist-shaman who exorcises cultural borders by enacting them and bringing them to consciousness.

Select Bibliography

Behar, Ruth, and Bruce Mannheim, "In Dialogue: The Couple in the Cage: A Guatinaui Odyssey." *Visual Anthropoloy Review* (Spring 1995).

Fox, Claire F., "Mass Media, Site Specificity, and the U.S.-Mexico Border: Guillermo Gómez-Peña's *Border Brujo* (1988, 1990)," in *The Ethnic Eye: Latino Media Arts*. Minneapolis: University of Minnesota Press, 1996.

Fusco, Coco, "Bilingualism, Biculturalism, and Borders," in *English is Broken Here: Notes on Cultural Fusion in the Americas*. New York: New Press, 1995.

Gómez-Peña, Guillermo, *Warrior For Gringostroika: Essays, Performance Texts, and Poetry*. St. Paul, Minnesota: Graywolf Press, 1993.

—BRENDA JO BRIGHT

GÓMEZ ROBLEDO, ANTONIO

1908–94 • Jurist, Intellectual, and Diplomat

Antonio Gómez Robledo was a famous Mexican intellectual, who was outstanding as a diplomat, researcher, writer, and humanist. In the best traditions of Mexican diplomacy, Gómez represented Mexico on numerous foreign missions.

He was born in Guadalajara, Jalisco, on November 7, 1908. He read law at the University of Guadalajara and subsequently received a doctorate in philosophy at Universidad Nacional Autónoma de México (UNAM or National Autonomous University of Mexico). His academic training was enhanced by specialized courses at the Faculté de Droit de Paris, the Académie de Droit International of The Hague, Fordham University of New York, and the University of Rio de Janeiro.

He began teaching in 1939. At various points in his career, he taught at the Facultades de Derecho, Ciencias Políticas y Filosofía y Letras (Faculties of Law, Political Science, and Philosophy and Arts) of UNAM, the Escuela Libre de Derecho (Free Law School), the Instituto Tecnológico de Estudios Superiores (Institute of Higher Technological Studies) of Monterrey, the Universidad de San Marcos of Peru, and the Academia de Derecho Internacional (Academy of International Law) of Havana, Cuba.

His intellectual and professional excellence marked him as a notable member of important national and international associations and societies. He was a member of the Academia Mexicana de Legislación y Jurisprudencia (Mexican Academy of Law and Jurisprudence), the Barra Mexicana de Abogados (Mexican Bar Association), the Academia Mexicana de la Lengua (Mexican Academy of Language), the Instituto de Investigaciones Filológicas (Institute of Philological Research) of UNAM, the Colegio Nacional (National College), the Comité Jurídico Interamericano (the Inter-American Legal Committee), the Sociedad Brasileña de Filosofía (Brazilian Philosophical Society), the Instituto Hispano-Ruso-Americano de Derecho Internacional (Hispanic-Russian-American Institute of International Law), the Sociedad Europea de Cultura (European Cultural Society), and the International Law Association of the United States.

Among his awards were the Premio Nacional Ciencias y Artes (National Prize for Science and Art) 1976, the Medalla Justo Sierra (Justo Sierra Medal) for university excellence, the Premio Jalisco (Jalisco Prize), and the Premio Universidad Nacional (National University Prize) 1991.

His prolific written work includes books and essays on philosophy, diplomacy, and international law. A renowned Latinist and Hellenist, he is considered an outstanding authority in the field of classical Greek philosophical thought, and he made significant contributions to the analysis of international relations and political rights.

Gómez was a tireless researcher and prolific author. He published articles and essays in innumerable specialized journals, in particular *Jus, ábside, Cuadernos Americanos, Letras de México, Filosofía y Letras, Revista Mexicana de Política Exterior,* and *Onda.*

In 1941 he joined the Mexican Foreign Service, and by 1959 had risen to the rank of ambassador. Some of the positions he held in the Foreign Ministry were adviser to the Mexican Embassy in the United States (1951–54), head of the consultative Technical Commission of the Foreign Ministry (1954–59), permanent representative to the Disarmament Committee of United Nations (1964–66), and legal consultant to the Foreign Ministry (1971–74). He also acted as extraordinary and plenipotentiary ambassador to nations such as Brazil (1959–61), Italy (1966–71), Greece (1974–77), and Switzerland (1977–80). In recognition of his brilliant performance in the Mexican Foreign Ministry, in March 1992 a presidential resolution designated him Ambassador Emeritus, one of the greatest honors to which a member of the Mexican Foreign Service can aspire.

Gómez died in Mexico City on October 3, 1994. After his death the foreign minister and all the Foreign Ministry staff paid tribute to him. Gómez symbolized the best of the Mexican tradition of intellectuals serving their country abroad. A cultured and intelligent man, his intensely productive life had a major impact on the educational, political, and cultural development of modern Mexico.

—JOSÉ BORJÓN LÓPEZ COTERRILLA

GONZÁLEZ CASAVANTES, ABRAHAM

1864–1913 • Governor and Provisional Vice President

Abraham González Casavantes was born on June 7, 1864, in Ciudad Guerrero, Chihuahua, and died on March 7, 1913, near Estación Mápula, Chihuahua. He studied in Chihuahua's Instituto Científico y Literario, in the Escuela Nacional Preparatoria in Mexico City, and Indiana University in the United States. He returned to Chihuahua in 1887 and worked as a translator of English, a cashier in the Banco de Chihuahua, as well as a cattle raiser and a miner. In 1909 he was nominated president of Chihuahua's Anti-Reelectionist Club (opposition candidate Francisco I. Madero's party), and on the outbreak of the Revolution in 1910 he joined up with Toribio Ortega's forces in the Ojinaga region. In 1911 he reunited with Madero in El Paso, Texas, and when he returned to Mexico he did so with the nominal posts of interim governor of Chihuahua and provisional vice president of the country. His work, the organization of civil authorities

of the towns that had fallen into the hands of Revolutionary forces, was exclusively political. On the triumph of Madero, González was nominated provisional state governor by the Chihuahua legislature. His immediate task was to deal with armed socialist and anarchist movements in the northeast of the state.

As governor he showed tremendous ability in the organization of a conciliatory civilian administration as well as being extremely respectful of human rights. He tried to make political, social, and financial changes in Chihuahua by means of a far-reaching program of pacification and economic and administrative reform. A total of 1,600 Revolutionaries were demobilized, and when peace talks with armed bands collapsed as a result of the intransigence of the rebels, the Federal Army started an energetic campaign against them.

González attempted to reorganize society. He honored the Constitution of 1857, reemployed Porfirian officials, and raised all salaries in every branch of public administration. He favored the lower classes, canceling their state and municipal taxes for six months but not canceling the taxes of the great mining companies, the iron and steel industries, merchants, industrialists, and owners of ranches and landholdings valued in excess of 25,000 pesos. He lowered taxes on farming properties valued at less than 5,000 pesos and raised duties on large properties, thinking that the high prices would force landowners to divide their haciendas. Those who owned more than 8,700 hectares (21,500 acres) had to pay between one and four pesos per hectare instead of five centavos. He canceled the sale of public lands to surveying companies and changed the so-called "company towns" into municipalities.

In cases of labor conflict, González implemented obligatory arbitration, as well as dealing with strikes orchestrated by the socialist leader Lázaro Gutiérrez de Lara in Chihuahua and dictating resolutions on accidents in the workplace. He took drastic measures to put an end to gambling in Ciudad Juárez, while restricting the consumption and sale of alcoholic beverages. Moreover González organized public works projects to reduce unemployment and supported the opening of small independent businesses. A program to construct and repair schools also was initiated, reemploying headmasters from the days of Porfirio Díaz's rule at primary and secondary school level. As an advocate of democracy he established self-government for the municipalities and eliminated the previous system of local political bosses. The threat of new socialist revolts, whose participants were plundering the northeast of the state, put a brake on Chihuahua's development and made it difficult to implement his projects.

As governor, González reopened investigations into the robbery of the Banco Minero in 1908, which never had been resolved. Enrique Creel, former governor of the state and son-in-law of local strongman Luis Terrazas, asked for Madero to intervene in the investigation, however. Despite rumors that he might be assassinated by the supporters of the anarchist Flores Magón brothers because of his efforts to attract foreign investment into the state, González traveled to El Paso in October 1911 to meet with the governors of Texas, Arizona, and New Mexico.

In October 1911, after having won the first democratic elections in the history of the state with a wide majority, he took over as constitutional governor of Chihuahua, a post that he held for only one month. In November of the same year he traveled to Mexico City, where Madero appointed him minister of the interior. Meanwhile Aureliano González took over as interim governor, Pascual Orozco resigned his post as the leader of the Rurales (local revolutionary militia), and political agitation spread rapidly throughout the state. Madero, who had full confidence in Orozco's loyalty, asked the latter to stay in his post until March to delay Abraham

González's return to Chihuahua. Meanwhile the Chihuahua oligarchy, afraid of the changes that Abraham González intended to implement, declared against his government. In the middle of February a group of armed anarcho-socialists captured Casas Grandes, cut the rail links, and nominated Pascual Orozco as their leader. The latter, supported on one side by the state oligarchy and on the other by socialist and anarchist rebels, renounced his post. With the Rurales still effectively under his command, Orozco was now in charge of the counter-Revolution.

After some initial successes, Orozco was overthrown by the Federal Army under General Victoriano Huerta and the forces of Francisco Villa, who had responded to Abraham González's call. In July 1912 the latter took up the governorship of Chihuahua once more and made numerous efforts to pacify the state. In February 1913, when a coup d'état surprised the Madero government in Mexico City, the president appointed General Huerta as the head of the loyal troops but was subsequently betrayed by the general, arrested, and finally assassinated on February 22. The army controlled most of the country, and Huerta took over as president of the Republic. When González refused to recognize the new dictator, he was arrested in the Governor's Palace in Chihuahua. In March three officials of the Federal Army left with him for Mexico City. In the area of Estación Mápula they stopped the train, made González descend, and murdered him in cold blood. In 1914, when Francisco Villa was governor of the state, González's remains were rescued, and the people of Chihuahua paid them their respects in the Governor's Palace before they were buried in the Panteón de Dolores in Mexico City. In 1956 his remains were taken back to Chihuahua and interred in the Rotunda of Illustrious Men of Chihuahua.

Select Bibliography

Almada, Francisco R., *La revolución en el estado de Chihuahua*. 2 vols., Mexico City: Talleres Gráficos de la Nación, 1965.

_____, *Vida, Proceso y Muerte de Abraham González*. Mexico City: Talleres Gráficos de la Nación, 1967.

_____, *Gobernadores del estado de Chihuahua*. Chihuahua: Centro Librero La Prensa, 1980.

Beezley, William H., "Revolutionary Governor: Abraham González and the Mexican Revolution in Chihuahua, 1909–1913." Ph.D. diss., University of Nebraska, 1968.

Hart, John M., *Anarchism and the Mexican Working Class, 1869–1931*. Austin: University of Texas Press, 1978.

Katz, Friedrich, *The Secret War in Mexico*. Chicago: University of Chicago Press, 1980.

Osorio, Rubén, *La correspondencia de Francisco Villa: Cartas y telegramas de 1912 a 1923*. Mexico City: Talleres Gráficos de la Nación, 1986.

Raat, Dirk, *Revoltosos. Mexico's Rebels in the United States, 1903–1923*. Austin: Texas A & M University Press, 1981.

—RUBÉN OSORIO ZUÑIGA

GONZÁLEZ FLORES, ANACLETO

1888–1927 • Politician and Ideologue of the Cristero Rebellion

Anacleto González Flores was born in 1888 in Tepatitlán, Jalisco, part of the dry and rugged region known as Los Altos, a region rich in Hispanic traditions. Almost forgotten by Mexican historiography, he is considered one of the few true ideologues of the Cristero Rebellion of 1926 to 1929, a peasant-based religious and agrarian rebellion that found its greatest support in the home area of *"el maestro,"* as González Flores became known.

Between 1908 and 1913, González Flores studied at the seminary in San Juan de los Lagos. However, he did not continue his formal religious studies and instead obtained his law degree in 1922 from the Escuela Libre de Leyes in the capital city of Guadalajara, receiving highest honors. Nevertheless, his life would be guided by his religious upbringing, and his career can be described as a constant and uphill battle against the anticlerical laws in place in his home state, especially since the Mexican Revolutionary Constitution of 1917.

In 1913, he was an organizer of the Partido Católico Nacional, then legally recognized and vying for power at national and local elections. It was not in the realm of politics where he would make his mark, however. After a brief stint with the followers of Francisco "Pancho" Villa between 1914 and 1915—he joined the Villistas in part because the state was then controlled by forces of Villa's anticlerical rival Venustiano Carranza—he returned home, where he led and organized Catholic workers. In 1916, he joined the newly formed Mexican Association of Catholic Youth, taking with him many who by then saw him as their leader.

In the face of constraints that the governor put on the Catholic Church from 1918 to 1919, González Flores devised a tactic based on civic disobedience and an economic boycott to force the state government to relent. To the surprise of many, he effectively succeeded. It was only a temporary triumph, however, and by 1924, the anticlericalism in the state—and across the nation—was reaching its highest point under the influence of Mexico's future strongman Plutarco Elías Calles.

As a way effectively to counter the explicit laws banning many of the rights and privileges of the church and its clergy, such as the inability to claim ownership of church buildings, convents, or religious schools, he modified his stance of purely passive resistance and in 1925 created the Unión Popular, a secretive and aggressive organization with the ability to penetrate all sectors of Jalisco society. This group—made famous by songs and folklore—was absorbed by the newly formed National League for the Defense of Religious Liberty, which advocated for armed resistance in defense of the constitutionally attacked Catholic religion.

When the Cristero Rebellion started, González Flores became its chief ideologue. With a clergy unwilling or unable openly to support the armed revolt and with a league leadership intent on a winning strategy and on seeking monetary contributions, *el maestro* provided ideological support for Cristero actions. Among his major works are *El plebicito de los martires,* in which he defends the moral right of Catholics to defend their faith, and *La cuestion religiosa en Jalisco,* in which he criticizes Mexico's Revolutionary, anti–Catholic Church trajectory. Furthermore, as leader of Jalisco's Unión Popular, he outlined a set a guidelines for members. Such ideological and organizational leadership made González Flores a prime target, and he subsequently was captured on April 1, 1927, along with two of his followers. He was tortured to death the same or the following day. As soon as his death was known, however, his political ideas circulated even more widely, adding strength and legitimacy to the growing Cristero Rebellion.

Select Bibliography

Casillas, José Alberto, *Sendero de un Mártir: Anacleto González Flores.* Mexico City: n.p., 1960.
Gómez Robledo, Antonio, *Anacleto González Flores: El Maestro.* 2nd edition, Mexico City: Editorial Jus, 1947.

—LORENZO C. LOPEZ

GONZÁLEZ MARTÍNEZ, ENRIQUE

1871–1952 • Physician, Diplomat, and Writer

Some have called González Martínez the last great modernist poet; others prefer to consider him the first of the postmodernists. In the end, both opinions are partially correct. He never completely abandoned certain key features of mod-

ernism. Similarly, by avoiding its superficial aspects and focusing instead on the hidden property of things, González Martínez paved the way for a type of poetic sensibility that for the first time in Latin American literature paid attention to local concerns. González Martínez's poetic production was abundant, even though he led a very active life. He was a medical doctor, professor, and diplomat to Chile (1920–22), Argentina (1922–24), and Spain and Portugal (1924–31); and he occupied several ministerial positions in the Mexican government. At the same time, he founded various literary magazines (Argos, Arte) and translated the poetry of John Milton, Paul Verlaine, and Charles-Pierre Baudelaire, among others.

González Martínez was born in Guadalajara, Jalisco, on April 13, 1871. His poetic output spans many years. He started publishing when he was very young and in time became the leading poet of Mexico. He was especially important to the Contemporáneos, although by the early 1920s his appeal among young Mexican poets had begun to dwindle. When González Martínez began to publish at the end of the nineteenth century, Mexico was perhaps the most important center of the modernist movement. Not surprisingly, therefore, the whole gamut of symbolist elements pervade his poetry. His first two collections of poems, many of which he later discarded, were Preludios (1903) and Lirismos (1907). As John S. Brushwood correctly asserts, Preludios could be conceived as the poet's "reflection of modernismo"; "Rústica," a poem made up of 14 related sonnets, is unquestionably the best of the collection. Lirismos is characterized by an unmistakable mystical proclivity that, along with a pantheistic view of the world, is evident in all of his subsequent poetic works.

In Silénter (1909), his third book of poems and the first of real importance, the shift from an artificial to a more authentic rendering of expression is marked not only by a deeper search of self but also by a passionate penetration of every object of the universe. The poem "Irás sobre la vida de las cosas" is typical of this facet of González Martínez's poetic development. The painstaking probe of this "philosophic poet" continues in Los senderos ocultos (1911), his fourth and probably best-known collection of poems and one of the most significant in the evolution of Mexican poetry. This collection owes its reputation mainly to one poem, "Tuércele el cuello al cisne. . ." (Twist the Swan's Neck). This sonnet has been considered traditionally, but erroneously, the anti-modernist manifesto par excellence; likewise, González Martínez has been seen as the poet who gave modernism its coup de grâce. This is far from the truth. In many respects, González Martínez continued being a modernist poet the rest of his life. Aside from the symbolist elements of his verse, he never quite forsook two of the most salient aspects of modernism: perfection of form and precision of expression. Thus, "Tuércele el cuello al cisne . . ." ought to be regarded chiefly as a rejection of surface rhetorical devices and exquisite frivolity, and not as a repudiation of the entire modernist movement. By "wringing" the neck of the swan with its "deceitful plumage"—and not of all swans, let it be clear—and by replacing it with the owl as the symbol for the new poetry, the lyric voice was in essence replicating Verlaine's wringing

of the neck of the vacuous eloquence of Romanticism in "Éloquence." In his perennial exploration of inner life, González Martínez came to reject the ostentatious aspects of modernism. His poetry is above all poetry of introspection, austerity, simplicity, and intimacy; the lyric voice's goal consists ultimately of deciphering the signs of the universe and finding the soul of objects. Unlike the swan, whose domain is the outside of things, the owl's eyes can pierce the surface of reality and resolve life's manifold conundrums.

The poet's quest did not end with Los senderos ocultos, however. His following two books of poetry, La muerte del cisne (1915) and El libro de la fuerza, de la bondad y del ensueño (1917), continue to manifest a deep regard for nature as an increase in mystic symbolism provides a shield against the turmoil of the Mexican Revolution and World War I; in the poem "Meditación bajo la luna," the poet regains once again the serenity of times past. González Martínez's propensity toward mysticism is especially evident in Parábolas y otras poemas (1918), La palabra del viento (1921), and El romero alucinado (1923). Formally, from around this time forward he abandons traditional versification (eleven- and fourteen-syllable verses) and begins to experiment with new currents such as anti-poetic language. Despite these efforts, he never became an assiduous member of the Latin American avant-garde.

His last books of poetry reveal a religious orientation bordering on the metaphysical, which was accentuated by the deaths of his wife and son. Among these volumes are Poemas truncos (1935), Vilano al viento (1948), Babel (1949), and El nuevo narciso (1952). Babel is a kind of compendium of his previous poetic production. In the life of this poet who was frequently accused of elitism, this text of 14 poems focuses on the world, a world envisioned as united in a species of fraternal love. The move from the very personal to the collective at the end of his life, nonetheless, does not mean that González Martínez renounced the search. His poetry must be seen as a spiritual autobiography marked paradoxically by a perpetual ascension and a deeper understanding of reality. Enrique González Martínez died in Mexico City on February 19, 1952.

Select Bibliography
Avrett, Roberto, "Enrique González Martínez, Philosopher and Mystic." Hispania 14 (1931).
Brushwood, John S., Enrique González Martínez. New York: Twayne, 1969.
Martínez, José Luis, editor, La obra de Enrique González Martínez. Mexico City: Colegio Nacional, 1951.
Rosser, Harry L., "Enrique González Martínez: 'Matacisnes' y concepción artística." Cuadernos americanos 243 (1982).
Schulman, Ivan A., "Antonio Machado and Enrique González Martínez: A Study in Internal and External Dynamics." Journal of Spanish Studies: Twentieth Century 4 (1976).

—J. AGUSTÍN PASTÉN B.

GONZÁLEZ ORTEGA, JESÚS

1822–81 • Soldier and Politician

Jesús González Ortega was born in the state of Zacatecas in 1822. Little is known of his childhood and adolescence, except that he had to abandon his literary studies in Guadalajara and move to Teúl, Zacatecas. He spent several years there, writing passionate articles for various newspapers in support of the Liberal cause. He was persecuted during Antonio López de Santa Anna's last period of dictatorship for his reformist ideas and for having fought with President Mariano Arista against supporters of the Plan del Hospicio, which called for Santa Anna's return to power.

After the success of the Plan de Ayutla, which toppled Santa Anna, he was appointed prefect of Tlaltenango by the governor of Zacatecas and shortly afterward was elected deputy to the Constituent Assembly, a post he never occupied. In 1857, he was elected by popular vote to be a deputy in the local assembly. Not long afterward, after the exile of Ignacio Comonfort, the anti-Conservative forces suffered a series of setbacks and the governor of Zacatecas fled, leaving the governorship vacant. The post passed to González Ortega, and he took office in October 1857. He immediately recognized General Santos Degollado as chief military commander and legitimate representative of the republican government.

As state governor, González Ortega acted with energy, honesty, and patriotism, paying the Treasury's debts, organizing troops to fight Conservative guerrillas, abolishing unnecessary posts, and even signing a decree (June 16, 1859) introducing the death penalty for all those conspiring against the constitutional order. González Ortega was also known as an outstanding army recruiter, convincing volunteers to join up by the power of his rhetoric alone.

The leader from Zacatecas had numerous confrontations with the Conservatives, sometimes winning, sometimes losing, but nearly always fighting a numerically superior and better organized army. Motivated by instinct and the desire to win, he invented unusual and audacious strategic movements that disconcerted the academy-trained officers on the Conservative side.

Among González Ortega's most famous military actions are the defeats he inflicted on General Miguel Miramón in Silao, General Adrián Woll in Sombrerete, and Silverio Ramírez in Peñuelas. This stage of his career culminated in the battle of Calulalpan on December 22, 1860, in which he finally defeated the Conservative forces under Miramón and clinched victory for the republican movement.

González Ortega also was known as a political reformer. While he was governor of Zacatecas, reacting to the executions of Liberal prisoners of war in Tacubaya on April 11, 1859, he implemented the anticlerical Reform Laws in the state of Zacatecas, and this at a time when all seemed lost for the Liberals. He also kept the torch of republicanism alight by forming a united front with the different state governors and coordinating actions in all the federal states.

After the Liberal victory of December 25, 1860, he entered Mexico City. He issued a manifesto guaranteeing the safety of the inhabitants of the city and on January 1 of the following year organized the triumphant arrival of the republican army. He was subsequently appointed minister of war by the new president, Benito Juárez. Then, after the assassinations of Melchor Ocampo, Degollado, and Leandro Valle, Juárez sent him in pursuit of Conservative general Félix Zuloaga, whom he defeated in Jalatlaco on August 14, 1860. A few days earlier, on July 2, the Assembly in Mexico City had named him president of the Supreme Court, which automatically made him the country's vice president. He nearly became president on two occasions (first in 1861 and again in 1864) in place of Benito Juárez, because a sector of Liberals were not happy with the way Juárez was governing.

During the French occupation, on the death of General Ignacio Zaragoza, he was named head of the Western Army. His most notable feat during this time was the defense of Puebla, which began on March 16, 1863, and lasted 65 days. Learning of Comonfort's defeat at San Lorenzo on May 8, 1863, and running out of ammunition, González Ortega ordered that guns and artillery be destroyed, disbanded his army, and surrendered unconditionally. Shortly afterward, while he was being taken to Orizaba on his way to exile in France, he managed to escape and make his way to the United States.

Sometime later, González Ortega tried to reassume his position as president of the Supreme Court. However, President Juárez signed a decree on November 8, 1865, suspending constitutional rule until the end of the war with France. At the same time he ordered González Ortega's arrest for having left the country without the Assembly's consent and having abandoned command of his troops without permission of the president.

In 1867, González Ortega presented himself to the governor of Zacatecas, who arrested him and sent him to Monterrey. On his release he traveled to Saltillo, where he died in 1881.

—Vicente Quirarte

GOROSTIZA, JOSÉ

1901–79 • Poet

José Gorostiza was born to a middle-class family in Villahermosa, Tabasco, and is related to Manuel Eduardo de Gorostiza, who wrote popular plays for the Spanish theater and was a Mexican diplomat. Gorostiza's brother was also a playwright, as well as a critic and man of letters. As a youth before and during the Mexican Revolution, Gorostiza moved around Mexico with his family, who eventually settled in the capital. There he came under the influence of writers such as Enrique González Martínez, Antonio Caso, and José Vasconcelos; he later worked with Vasconcelos in the Education Ministry. Gorostiza also formed a lifelong friendship with the poet Carlos Pellicer and collaborated on various projects with such writers as Bernardo de Montellanos and Xavier Villaurrutia. The literary scene in the 1920s was a lively one, and Gorostiza was an important figure in it.

After publishing *Canciones para cantar en las barcas* in 1925, Gorostiza embarked on a diplomatic and cultural bureaucratic career, which took him to London, Copenhagen, Guatemala, Cuba, Greece, Holland, San Francisco, and the United Nations, where he served as the Mexican representative, and into various diplomatic and cultural agencies in the government. He wrote *Muerte sin fin,* his most important work, over a six-month period in the early morning hours at his desk in the Ministry of Foreign Relations of Lázaro Cárdenas's administration. In an interview he once stated that he started arriving early at the offices at the behest of the minister, Eduardo Hay. Hay would arrive late, and one morning Cárdenas himself phoned to see when his ministers started work. Gorostiza answered, made excuses, and eventually was asked by Hay to start arriving at 7:00 AM. At that hour he was alone in the ministry, and he put the time to good use.

The major mystery about Gorostiza's life is why he virtually stopped writing poetry after *Muerte sin fin,* which was published in 1939. There has been much discussion of the matter—whether Gorostiza, a stylistic perfectionist, felt that he could not supersede *Muerte sin fin,* whether the theme and nature of the poem represented the end of poetry for him, whether the political and cultural atmosphere after the Cárdenas period became inimical to cultural innovation (many members of the Contemporáneos group, which included Gorostiza, were removed from cultural offices), or whether he felt that the needs of society could best be addressed through more concrete activities. Nonetheless, Gorostiza continued to write insightful literary essays, if not poetry, throughout his life. He died in Mexico City on March 16, 1979.

José Gorostiza's most lasting contribution lies in his work as a poet. There have been two major collections of his work, *Poesías* (1964), which he compiled and edited himself, and a more complete posthumous anthology, *Poesía y poética*

(1988), which includes several poems not previously collected. The first part of *Poesías* consists of *Canciones para cantar en las barcas* (1925), which is reminiscent of the work of Juan Ramón Jiménez, Jorge Guillén, Rafael Alberti, and other Spanish poets of the period. It is written in a spare, "pure poetry" style, an extreme distillation of the turn-of-the-century modernist aesthetic that so influenced the course of twentieth-century poetry in the Spanish language. Gorostiza also was a member of the loose group of poets known as "Los Contemporáneos," which, along with the very different avant-garde group "Los Estridentistas," ushered contemporary Mexican poetry onto the world stage.

Del poema frustrado consists of work written between *Canciones para cantar en las barcas* and *Muerte sin fin.* It contains poems published in magazines and was assembled by the poet after writing *Muerte sin fin,* to be included in his *Poesías* of 1964. It consists of several poems in the style of *Canciones para cantar en las barcas,* and several others such as "Preludio" and "Presencia y fuga" (a sequence of four sonnets) that are clearly early attempts to deal with the concerns and styles more fully developed in *Muerte sin fin.*

Muerte sin fin is the work that has earned Gorostiza a permanent place in twentieth-century literary history, and it belongs with a handful of major long poems of the Spanish language, such as Sor Juana Inés de la Cruz's *Primero sueño* or Luis de Góngora y Argote's *Soledades.* The author had thought about writing it for several years, and although it originally was written over a six-month period, it went through an extended period of polishing before being published in 1939. *Muerte sin fin* is a long poem about the nature and place of consciousness and the self, revolving around the central image of a glass of water. The water and its glass serve as metaphors for the soul, self, mind, and such more specific concepts as eye, dream, God, art, poetry, form, content, and the sea. The "endless death" of the title refers to the consciousness of death, the fundamental fact of human life and mind. Awareness of death is life and thus is endless except in the sense that death must end when life does, a paradoxical, self-reflective idea that lies at the heart of the work.

The poem is full of lines that repeat or resonate with lines in other parts of the poem, like reflections on glass and water, and like the mind in a state of extended meditation. There are moments when the eschatological themes, the diction, the use of paradox, and the extended syntactical structure are reminiscent of the writing of Sor Juana, Góngora, or Francisco Gómez de Quevedo y Villegas, poets who also created works that contemplate the nature of the mind, awareness, knowledge, and human existence. Gorostiza's language is his own, however: finely crafted, spare, and compelling, with extend stretches of controlled passion and irony. The poem also combines elegant diction and, particularly in the poem's sardonic conclusion, the lively everyday slang of Mexico's streets. *Muerte sin fin* might be characterized as having a very elegant and clear surface that, like water, reveals a complex and turbulent life beneath. The work has been extensively studied by numerous critics and scholars, who have approached it from quite different perspectives. The greatness of the poem is reflected in the fact that none of these approaches can be seen as definitive. The work is infinitely reflective of the reader and itself and is constantly changing in significance; indeed, this very flux is one of its major themes.

Select Bibliography

Debicki, Andrew P., *La poesía de José Gorostiza*. Mexico City: Andrea, 1962.

Gelpi, Juan, *Enunciación y dependencia en José Gorostiza: Estudio de una máscara poética*. Mexico City: UNAM, 1984.

Paz, Octavio, "Muerte sin fin." In *Las Peras del Olmo*. Mexico City: Imprenta Universitaria, 1957.

Rubín, Mordecai S., *Una poética moderna: Muerte sin fin de José Gorostiza, análisis y comentario*. Mexico City: UNAM, 1966.

—JOHN M. BENNETT

GREAT DEPRESSION

The panic of October 1929 on Wall Street unleashed a series of depressive forces in the world economy that had been latent for several years. The general effect was an enormous economic contraction in the United States, which rapidly spread to many other countries. Between 1929 and 1933 the gross domestic product of the United States declined at an annual rate of 8.2 percent, diminishing demand for goods and services from other countries. These countries in turn responded by raising protectionist trade barriers to keep employment and economic activity inside the country, causing a drop in the volume of international trade.

The impact of the Great Depression, then, was keenly felt throughout Latin America, particularly in Mexico. The drop in the national income of the United States diminished demand for goods and services from Mexico, starting a three-pronged depressive process in the Mexican economy. First, the volume and value of Mexican exports to the United States declined dramatically. Between 1929 and 1932 the value of exports contracted almost 65 percent and the terms of trade dropped 20.8 percent, reducing Mexico's capacity to import by half. This enormous contraction in the external sector reduced the export activity and thus employment levels in this sector. The balance of trade suffered grave deterioration as commercial surplus declined from US$97 million in 1929 to only US$39 million in 1932.

The external economic crisis also resulted in a deterioration in Mexico's balance of trade and a consequent reduction of more than 53 percent in the Bank of Mexico's reserves between 1929 and 1931. The money supply also contracted 60 percent during this period, contributing to the economic depression in Mexico. In other words, the contraction in international trade brought with it a strong monetary restriction, hindering economic transactions and raising the cost of money. Thus, general economic activity was reduced and the crisis that had begun in the external sector spread to the rest of the economy.

The third important impact of the international economic crisis was in public finances, since taxes on the external sector had represented more than half of the government's income. As the external sector contracted, government revenues also declined, dropping from 322 million pesos in 1929 to only 179 million pesos in 1932. Moreover, during the depression taxation was the only possible source of government income, as a moratorium was imposed on external lending and as the government was unable to find a source for domestic lending. The drop in state revenues brought with it a decline in public spending, which in turn contributed to the contraction in aggregate demand in Mexico.

The only factor that dampened the impact of the depressive forces was the depreciation of the exchange rate as a result of the deterioration in the balance of payment. Although the peso officially was based on a gold standard and thus had a fixed exchange rate, the generalized use of silver currency as a means of exchange meant that the decline in the price of silver would constitute a depreciation in the value of the peso. Thus, the depreciation of almost 22 percent between 1929 and 1931 helped mitigate the drop in demand over the short term. Nonetheless, Mexico's gross domestic product contracted dramatically, falling at an average rate of 4 percent between 1929 and 1931 with an attendant decline in employment levels and the overall well-being of the population. Moreover, the Great Depression in the United States led to the deportation of approximately 300,000 workers, aggravating the already difficult situation in Mexico.

The crisis began to ease in the second trimester of 1932, more than a year before it did in the United States. Mexico's recuperation was spurred by two factors. On the one hand, the export sector began to return to life with the recovery of export prices, particularly for petroleum and silver, and the depreciation of the peso, which accelerated after 1932. On the other, from December 1931 almost through the end of the following year the Mexican government implemented a radical change in the economic policy, which permitted a rapid recovery for the economy.

Most notably, the Bank of Mexico abandoned the gold standard in July 1931 as international reserves were exhausted, and a few months later it cautiously adopted the silver standard. This permitted the Bank of Mexico to begin printing significant quantities of money, since up to that point the bank could only print bills that were backed fully by gold reserves. The Mexican public naturally was chary of these measures, since it remembered the hyperinflation that had accompanied the government's decision to print excessive amounts of paper money during the Revolution; however, as the government began to pay its employees in paper money rather than coins, paper money increasingly was accepted. The increase in the money supply began to reverse the effects of the monetary contraction of the Great Depression; indeed, the reversal was quite rapid as the number of bills in circulation climbed from approximately 100,000 in November 1931, to more than 42 million in December 1932. The Mexican treasury also was able to obtain extraordinary earnings through seigniorage, minting silver coins with less expensive metals during the initial contraction in world silver prices. This permitted the government to engage in public spending over and beyond its fiscal income.

The changes in the Mexican economic policy helped spur a rapid recovery in the export sector. First, starting in 1933 the increase in export prices increased the value of the export sector. Second, the abandonment of the gold standard allowed the peso to drop to levels the market could support; the devaluation of the peso accelerated starting in 1932. These two factors spurred exports and thus aggregate demand, also contributing to the resolution of the broader crisis that had begun in the export sector.

The consequence of these changes was the rapid recovery of the gross domestic product (GDP) starting in the second trimester of 1932, which would continue almost through the end of the decade; between 1932 and 1934 the real GDP increased 18.8 percent. Nonetheless, the reaction was not uniform in all sectors of the Mexican economy. In the agricultural sector the recovery was relatively slow. In part this slow recovery was owing to the fact that the decline in the agricultural sector had been relatively small, since the consumption of basic goods such as food had not fluctuated radically with the population's level of income. Industrial product, however, grew by a staggering 46.7 percent. Indeed, during the 1930s industry was the leading sector of the economy and grew far more rapidly than all other economic activities. Moreover, industrial development was stimulated by a vigorous process of import substitution as imports became relatively expensive. In other words, import substitution was generated by the very mechanisms of the market and not by a premeditated protectionist policy. Such a trade policy was not put into place until the very end of the 1940s.

Another important, albeit indirect, effect of the Great Depression was the maturation of diverse mechanisms of economic policy. Most notably, the scarce means of payment in 1931–32 spurred growing acceptance of paper money from the Bank of Mexico. The acceptance of paper money, together with the affiliation of most Mexican banks with the Central Bank, constituted the first instruments of monetary policy: the printing of paper money, the possibility of modifying legal reserves, and later the opening of a line of credit for the Central Bank of the Federal Government, which would be abused in subsequent decades. The introduction of an income tax in 1926 permitted the government to count on an additional instrument of fiscal policy in the 1930s. Moreover, the abandonment of the gold standard in 1931 was much more than a simple devaluation, since—at least during the 1930s—it would allow policy to become much more flexible and become a true instrument of economic policy. These new fiscal tools and increased room to maneuver gave economic policy a far more important and effective role. More important, however, was the new activist agenda of the state in determining economic policy, not only in Mexico but throughout Latin America.

Select Bibliography

Cárdenas, Enrique, *La industrialización mexicana durante la gran depresión.* Mexico City: Colegio de México, 1977.
_____, *La hacienda pública y la política económica, 1929–58.* Mexico City: Fondo de Cultura Económica–Colegio de México, 1994.
Haber, Stephen H., *Industry and Underdevelopment: The Industrialization of Mexico, 1890–1940.* Palo Alto, California: Stanford University Press, 1989.
Thorp, Rosemary, editor, *Latin America in the 1930's: The Role of the Periphery in World Crisis.* London: Macmillan, 1984.

—ENRIQUE CÁRDENAS

GUADALUPANISMO

See Virgin of Guadalupe and Guadalupanismo

GUADALUPE HIDALGO, TREATY OF

Named after the small village near Mexico City where it was signed, the Treaty of Guadalupe Hidalgo formally ended the U.S.-Mexican War on February 2, 1848. With this agreement, Mexico affirmed the U.S. possession of Texas including all areas north of the Rio Grande (Río Bravo in Mexico). The country also ceded to the United States most of the California and New Mexico territories. Following the 1853 Gadsden Purchase, that area ultimately came to comprise all of the current U.S. states of Arizona, California, New Mexico, Nevada, and Utah, as well as parts of Colorado, Oklahoma, and Wyoming. The total cession amounted to more than half of Mexico's territory; in return, the U.S. government made a cash payment of US$15,000,000 and assumed Mexican debts totaling US$3,250,000. The U.S. government also promised to respect life, liberty, and property of the Mexican residents of the new U.S. territories, and it vowed to help prevent Indian incursions against Mexico.

As Mexican and U.S. goals in the war had diverged widely, the negotiation and ratification of the treaty was a long and arduous process. The Mexican government insisted on respecting the old borders of the 1819 Adams-Onís Treaty, minus Texas northeast of the Nueces River. On the other hand, U.S. president James K. Polk sought the annexation of a wide swath of territory including Baja California, as well as the granting of transit rights across the Isthmus of Tehuantepec.

When U.S. armies penetrated into the Mexican heartland, however, the Mexican position became more difficult to maintain. In September 1847, the presence of General Winfield Scott's troops just outside Mexico City prompted Mexican negotiators to soften their stance. When the resultant armistice agreement failed due to the intransigence of both sides, the U.S. forces occupied Mexico City. With a protracted guerrilla war as the only alternative, the Mexican government agreed to terms among the harshest that the winner of an international war have ever imposed upon the losers. Apart from the Baja California cession and the demand for transit rights, U.S. negotiator Nicholas P. Trist reached all of the significant goals of what had constituted an extreme U.S. position. All the same, the U.S. Senate almost derailed ratification; the northern Whigs feared the expansion of slaveholding territory, while many southern Democrats desired the annexation of more or all of Mexico. In Mexico, ratification was even more difficult. Even though, as the late-nineteenth-century thinker Justo Sierra put it, the Mexican representatives "did as much as they could; they

accomplished as much as they should have," influential opposition figures decried the treaty. Only the potential cost of a prolonged occupation in both political and economic terms convinced the Mexican Congress to approve the agreement.

The Treaty of Guadalupe Hidalgo was one of the most traumatic events in post-Conquest Mexican history, and it brought important consequences. First of all, the alienation of a scarcely populated, yet vast part of the national territory constituted an unprecedented act of national humiliation. This humiliation helped bring about a reorientation of Mexican politics, away from caudillismo and toward the formation of true national parties. The Conservatives and Liberals both developed strategies to attempt to prevent further U.S. landgrabbing. In addition, the agreement spurred a widespread fear of further U.S. expansion, a fear that would resonate much later in Mexican foreign policies. The Treaty of Guadalupe Hidalgo came to exemplify not only national shame but also the fundamentally avaricious nature of the "gringos" to the north. In the long run, the treaty brought the United States and Mexico closer together, for better and for worse. For Mexico, the settlement and economic development of the new U.S. Southwest created new opportunities for export-led development. When it became clear during the late Porfiriato that many aspects of this close relationship were less than benign, many Mexicans blamed the "Peaceful Conquest" by U.S. economic penetration on the "Violent Conquest" exemplified by the Treaty of Guadalupe Hidalgo.

Even today, in the age of the North American Free Trade Agreement, the Treaty of Guadalupe Hidalgo remains on the minds of many Mexicans. In recent decades, many millions of Mexicans have taken up residence in the territories lost to the United States in 1848. Most of these territories today form part of *la frontera,* the bicultural border region that is neither exclusively part of the United States nor exclusively Mexican. In that sense, the borders drawn by the Treaty of Guadalupe Hidalgo have begun to lose some of their significance.

Select Bibliography

Griswold de Castillo, Richard, *The Treaty of Guadalupe Hidalgo: A Legacy of Conflict.* Norman: University of Oklahoma Press, 1990.

—Jürgen Buchenau

GÜEMES PACHECO Y PADILLA, JUAN VICENTE DE

1740–99 • Count of Revillagigedo and Viceroy of New Spain

Juan Vicente de Güemes Pacheco y Padilla was born in 1740 in Havana, the eldest son of Juan Francisco Güemes y Horcasitas, the captain general of Cuba and (eventually) first count of Revillagigedo. In 1746 his father was appointed viceroy of New Spain, and the family moved to Mexico City. Both Juan Vicente and his brother eventually were appointed captains of the palace guards. When his father's term as viceroy of New Spain ended in 1755, the family returned to Spain, where Juan Vicente continued his military career, distinguishing himself in the Portugal campaign and the siege of Gibraltar. He was a gentleman in waiting to don Luis, brother of King Carlos III, and upon his father's death in 1768 Juan Vicente became the second count of Revillagigedo. In 1789, following Carlos IV's ascension to the throne the year before, Revillagigedo was appointed viceroy of New Spain, replacing Manuel Antonio Flores.

Revillagigedo is considered to be one of New Spain's ablest viceroys, and his term of office was one of the colony's most prosperous periods. He is remembered for combating what had been rampant corruption, completely reorganizing and reforming public administration, establishing administrative districts, reintroducing the Comandancia General de Provincias Internas (with tighter viceregal oversight), ensuring that sentences passed by the Inquisition could be revised by the viceroy's office, combating crime, protecting commerce and agriculture, and stimulating industry. Revillagigedo not only initiated public works but also tried to improve the lives of ordinary people by encouraging education and combating unemployment. He was portrayed by his contemporaries as a man of many talents, strong and energetic, brave and disciplined, renowned for his stamina.

Revillagigedo perhaps is remembered best today for enhancing the beauty of Mexico City. The capital was in a dilapidated state when he arrived. The streets were not paved, and they lacked gutters, drains, and pavements. There were piles of garbage and standing pools of water everywhere. The viceroy ordered the streets paved and drains installed. He improved Alameda and Bucareli Avenues, built the San Cosme and Verónica Highways, and repaired the roads to Tacubaya, Tlalnepantla, and San Agustín de Las Cuevas. Many other streets were given formal names for the first time. Revillagigedo also ordered the cleaning of the viceregal palace. He cleared the main square, removing peddlers and setting up markets such as the Mercado del Volador and La Cruz del Factor.

The viceroy undertook the regulation of all markets, bath houses, and pulque taverns. He also introduced various public health restrictions, such as preventing cows and pigs from roaming the streets freely, prohibiting the sale of clothes belonging to people who had died of infectious diseases, forbidding burials inside churches, and encouraging the construction of cemeteries.

Revillagigedo's reforms and public works projects not only improved the look of Mexico City, they also influenced public life in the outlying provinces. Mayors were encouraged to follow the viceroy's example and provide street lighting, a police force, and road sweepers. Revillagigedo sought to improve communications within all of New Spain by repairing roads from the capital to Veracruz and Acapulco and by building new roads to Toluca and several others in Yucatán. He equipped and strengthened the coastal ports and introduced regulations for coast guard boats. Other achievements during his term of office included creating the National Archives to store all official documents relating to the Viceroyalty of New Spain; founding the Royal Mining College and the Botanical Gardens; providing new lecturers for the Academy of San Carlos; improving the quality of the Real y Pontificia Universidad; and supporting the creation of other universities in Guadalajara, Puebla, and Mérida.

The viceroy's activism earned him many enemies, however, and led to a case being brought against him in the Juicio de Residencia by members of the Mexico City Municipal Council. The viceroy was found not guilty, but the case was brought to the Council of the Indies in Spain, where it continued for four years after Revillagigedo's death in 1799. Ultimately, Revillagigedo was found not guilty, and the achievements of his administration were praised by the council. Those who had brought the case to trial at the council were made to pay the costs.

Select Bibliography

Arnold, Linda, *Bureaucracy and Bureaucrats in Mexico City, 1742–1835.* Tucson: University of Arizona Press, 1988.

Lynch, John, *Bourbon Spain, 1700–1808.* Oxford and Cambridge, Massachusetts: Blackwell, 1989.

—IRMA ISABEL FERNÁNDEZ ARIAS

GÜERA RODRÍGUEZ, LA

See Rodríguez de Velasco y Osorio Barba, María Ignacia (La Güera Rodríguez)

GUERRERO, VICENTE

1782–1831 • General and President

Vicente Guerrero was born on April 4, 1782, at Tixtla, in the province (now state) of Mexico. His parents, Juan Pedro Guerrero and María Guadalupe Saldana, were peasant farmers. Vicente Guerrero had mestizo and African bloodlines. As an adult, he was tall and robust, strong-willed, and physically powerful. His complexion was dark and reflected his mixed heritage. "El Negro," as he was called, was intelligent, insightful, shrewd, and persuasive as well as personally committed to ending racially defined caste distinctions. He was more conversant in the indigenous dialect of his region than in Spanish. He claimed to be a descendant of King Neza-hualcoyotl of Texcoco.

Until 1810 Guerrero spent his young adult life as a laborer and muleteer. Then in 1810, Miguel Hidalgo y Costilla proclaimed a revolt in Guanajuato against the colonial authority. The revolution spread quickly, and the same year José María Morelos y Pavón raised an army in the south in support of the revolution. Hidalgo and Morelos demanded sweeping social and political changes that would redress the worst grievances of the masses. Guerrero agreed with their cause and enlisted in Morelos's army on December 15, 1810.

Guerrero proved quickly to be a resourceful and brave leader. A captain by 1811, he received promotion to lieutenant colonel a year later. In 1812 he participated in the capture of Oaxaca and commanded forces raiding the western harbors of Tehuantepec, Puerto Escondido, and Santa Cruz. On February 8–9, 1813, he took part in the victory against royalist forces at Santa Cruz; Guerrero was cited for his bravery. While Morelos assaulted Acapulco, Guerrero protected the rebels' southern flank and repulsed a royalist attack at Quantepec on July 1, 1813. During the next few months, the southern insurgents consolidated their gains; the army elected Morelos as *generalísimo,* and the insurgents created a government with a congress to rule over their territory.

However, in late 1813 and early 1814, the insurgents suffered disastrous defeats and had to withdraw into the mountainous interior. During the summer of 1814, Guerrero became a colonel and insurgents concentrated on rebuilding their armies. A dispute over regional command temporarily left Guerrero with 500 men armed with only three rifles. Showing his courage and resourcefulness, Guerrero launched this force against a royalist detachment on the Tacachi River. The surprise night assault routed the enemy, and Guerrero captured 400 rifles and other military supplies.

1815 was another difficult year for the insurgents. Despite various successes, the rebels retreated, and on November 6, 1815, Morelos himself was captured; the royalists executed him in December 1815. Most of the insurgent leaders had now been captured or killed, and there was some confusion as to who should become the insurgent commander. On March 20, 1816, Guerrero achieved the rank of general. Guerrero stressed that he was doing so only to continue Morelos's cause for the underprivileged classes. Guerrero realized that standard attacks were now impossible, so instead he quickly crossed the Mescala River and began large raids and ambushes in the Acapulco area.

Despite this new strategy, the insurgency weakened. In August 1816 a new viceroy, Juan Ruíz de Apodaca, attempted to stamp out the revolution. He initiated aggressive military campaigns that shattered most of the insurgent forces and even worse, offered generous pardons that enticed many insurgents to quit the cause. In 1816 Guerrero was almost captured, and in March 1817 his fortress at Xonacatlan was besieged and then overrun. Despite numerous appeals to surrender and accept a pardon—one such appeal delivered by Guerrero's father—Guerrero continued to fight. At the battle of Calavera, Guerrero was defeated soundly and lost most of his remaining men and equipment. Until later in 1818, he was forced to avoid any large royalist forces. In September 1818, however, Guerrero defeated several viceregal units and dominated the Balsas Valley. He established his own civil government—modeled after Morelos's previous government led by a junta and a congress. Although it dispersed later in 1819 and Guerrero suffered another severe defeat at Aguazarca on November 5, 1819, he continued to mount significant attacks. By 1820 the situation was a stalemate. The insurgents could no longer threaten important areas of New Spain, but the royalists were unable to destroy the insurgent bases.

When the conservatives and church officials of New Spain finally agreed to create an autonomous government, they backed Agustín de Iturbide's compromise. Meanwhile, the viceroy appointed Iturbide as the commander of the southern royalist forces. On November 16, 1820, Iturbide left Mexico City to crush Guerrero's insurgents. Instead, Guerrero defeated the royalists at Zapotepec on January 2, 1821, and at Cueva del Diablo on January 27, 1821. On January 20, Guerrero had urged Iturbide to support Independence and offered to place himself under Iturbide's command in return for such a pledge. Iturbide realized quickly that he could not destroy the insurgents. Therefore he arranged a meeting with Guerrero and offered the rebels a place in his new, independent government. Guerrero agreed formally to Iturbide's Plan de Iguala on February 24, 1821. The plan protected the lives and property of the Catholic Church and the elites and maintained their privileges under a constitutional monarchy. It also created an Independent Mexico and offered all races civil liberties and abolished the caste system. Although Guerrero objected to some of the plan's details, he accepted it and hoped for improvements. As commander of the first division of Iturbide's army, Guerrero issued a manifesto proclaiming Iturbide's "magnanimous," heroic qualities while emphasizing his subordination to the "Father of the Nation." Insurgent and royalist forces alike joined the cause, and on September 27, 1821, Guerrero marched victoriously into Mexico City with Iturbide.

Iturbide soon alienated Guerrero and his new insurgent allies. He appointed a governing junta of 38—none of whom were insurrectionaries—and they named Iturbide president of the interim regency (which was to rule until the selection of an emperor). Iturbide organized the empire into five districts headed by military officers known as captains general. Guerrero became captain general of the south and received promotion to field marshal. But Iturbide humiliated Guerrero by ordering him to Mexico City so that "El Negro" could carry the imperial insignia in the coronation ceremony. In May 1822, Iturbide persuaded the new Congress to elect him emperor. Later Iturbide dismissed the Congress and imposed forced loans to finance his government. Insurgent leaders began a new insurrection, and on January 5, 1823, Guerrero joined the first phase of the movement that eventually toppled Iturbide. On January 25, 1823, Guerrero was shot in the lungs at the battle of Cerro de Almolonga. His severe wound forced Guerrero to spend the rest of the revolt convalescing. He never fully recovered, and the wound plagued him the rest of his life. The forces arrayed against Iturbide swelled, and on March 19, 1823, Iturbide abdicated in the face of increasing demands that Congress be reestablished. In May, Iturbide left the country.

As Guerrero recuperated from his wound, the imperial system disappeared from Mexico. An executive commission of three was created and alternates were elected. After refusing several offers of military command—due to poor health—Guerrero agreed to accept one of the executive alternate positions. As part of the *poder ejecutivo*, Guerrero proved to be a crucial harmonizer and was instrumental in uniting various factions. In June 1824, a national election was held and Guadalupe Victoria was elected president,

Nicolás Bravo was elected vice president, and Guerrero received the third-largest number of votes (thus losing). Guerrero retired from public life and tried to improve his health. Unfortunately, the Victoria administration suffered from a worsening financial situation and the increasingly bitter federalist-versus-centralist conflict. Despite his ill health, Guerrero accepted the position of supreme tribunal of war and marine on May 17, 1827. In August, he left Mexico City to restore order in Veracruz. Then in December, an antifederalist rebellion demanded the dismissal of the ruling officials. Vice President Bravo and several other generals joined the rebellion. Guerrero was sent to quell the rebellion, and on January 7, 1828 he killed or captured the entire rebel force at Tulancingo. Guerrero returned a hero, but the rebellion heightened tensions as the 1828 elections approached.

Guerrero decided to run for president and at first seemed certain to win. A symbol of resistance to Spanish colonial rule, Guerrero became the nominal leader of the federalists. However, conservative centralists and the Mexican upper class supported General Manuel Gómez Pedraza. The campaign became bitter as newspapers on both sides smeared the opposing candidates. When the elections took place in September, Gómez Pedraza won with eleven states to Guerrero's nine. Gómez Pedraza thus won the presidency and Guerrero the vice presidency. Guerrero's supporters refused to accept the results and raised accusations that the election had been fixed. Guerrero himself refused to accept the vote. The spreading sentiment in favor of rebellion then became reality as Antonio López de Santa Anna and other Guerrero supporters began to revolt. On November 30, a revolt began within Mexico City. The lame-duck Victoria government vacillated and tried to negotiate a compromise. Support for Guerrero intensified, especially after Guerrero publicly joined the revolt. Gómez Pedraza realized that his cause was becoming hopeless; he renounced his election victory and soon left Mexico. Guerrero's supporters marched in victoriously but then lost discipline and looted the Parián market—a visible symbol of Hispanic, elite culture. Although Congress validated Guerrero's subsequent election "victory," the illegality of his triumph and the looting of the Parián market convinced the conservatives and elites that Guerrero could not be trusted.

When Guerrero became president on April 1, 1829, he faced immense problems but his populist approach angered the elites. The government was bankrupt, the economy was in shambles, few sources for further revenues existed, the threat of a Spanish invasion loomed, and Guerrero now had enemies among the upper class, the government, and the army. Furthermore, the end of African slavery, which Guerrero supported and legalized in 1829, angered Anglo settlers in Texas. Guerrero's enforcement of the second Spanish expulsion law on March 20, 1829, further alienated the Hispanic community, while his leniency in issuing exemptions upset the radical nativists. Guerrero supported Secretary of the Treasury Lorenzo de Zavala's efforts to gain revenue, including a graduated income tax and property taxes. Spanish merchants particularly hated Guerrero's attempts at tariff protection when he prohibited imports of all but the most expensive cloth.

When the long-awaited Spanish invasion began in July 1829, Guerrero responded firmly. During a short-lived burst of national unity, Santa Anna gathered military forces and, despite bitter resistance, Congress granted Guerrero special war powers. This was the first of many occasions when presidents would be given such authority. Zavala came under heavy criticism when he enacted forced loans, reductions in pensions and salaries, wide-ranging new taxes, and property confiscations, all to fund the war effort. Mexican forces bottled the Spanish army up in Tampico, and Spanish ineptitude as well as yellow fever forced them to surrender in September 1829.

The Spanish invasion had temporarily breathed new life into Guerrero's regime but the added burdens of war proved to be Guerrero's undoing. In August, the Jalisco legislature called for a northern confederation. Their main grievances included accusations that de Zavala's new taxes encroached upon provincial domains and that Guerrero was misusing his emergency powers. In order to appease the opposition, de Zavala agreed to resign on October 12, 1829. But more of Guerrero's opponents forced many of his supporters out of government. Then in December, officers in charge of a reserve army—created to fight the Spanish invaders—drew up an insurrectionary plan at Jalapa. Vice President Anastasio Bustamante "consented" to lead the rebels. Guerrero resigned voluntarily his war powers and attempted to gain congressional support. When this failed, he personally led an army to quell the revolt. Within a week, the capital fell to the conspirators, who established a new regime. Guerrero's army deserted him, and on December 25, 1829, Guerrero promised to abide by the will of the new government.

The oppressive Bustamante government soon triggered a new revolt. Efforts to centralize power and fear of permanent national army garrisons in the interior but controlled by the central government created most of the unrest. By March 1830, the insurrection had spread to the south, and Guerrero decided to lead the revolt because of the persecution of his indigenous allies and because he suspected that Bustamante had sent assassins to kill him. But in January 1831, General Bravo decisively defeated the rebels near Chilpancingo, and on January 14, Guerrero's supposed friend, Francisco Picaluga, betrayed him by turning Guerrero over to Bustamante's troops. The government court-martialed and executed Guerrero in Oaxaca on February 14, 1831. It is more than likely that the upper class wanted Guerrero shot as a warning to those of mixed blood who aspired to mobilize the masses against the Hispanic social order.

Select Bibliography

Anna, Timothy E., *The Mexican Empire of Iturbide.* Lincoln: University of Nebraska Press, 1990.

Bazant, Jan, "From Independence to the Liberal Republic, 1821–67. In *Mexico Since Independence,* edited by Leslie Bethell. New York: Cambridge University Press, 1991.

Green, Stanley, *The Mexican Republic: The First Decade 1823–32.* Pittsburgh: University of Pittsburgh Press, 1987.

Sims, Harold, *The Expulsion of Mexico's Spaniards, 1821–1836.* Pittsburgh: University of Pittsburgh Press, 1990.

Sprague, William, *Vicente Guerrero, Mexican Liberator: A Study in Patriotism.* Chicago: Donnelley, 1939.

—Douglas W. Richmond

GUILLÉN Y SÁNCHEZ, PALMA

1898–1981 • Academic and Diplomat

Palma Guillén y Sánchez, born in Mexico City on March 26, 1898, the daughter of Adalberto Guillén and Macaria Sánchez, was the first woman to represent Mexico as a foreign diplomat. A professor with degrees obtained at the Escuela Normal de México (Mexican Teachers' Training College) and the Faculty of Philosophy and Arts of the Universidad Nacional de México (Mexican National University), she specialized in philosophy, psychology, and literature.

The first stage of Guillén's professional career spanned the years 1920 to 1935, during which she gained well-deserved prestige in academic and cultural circles in the following posts: professor of psychology, logic, ethics, Spanish, and literature at the Escuela Normal de México; professor of logic, psychology, and ethics at the Escuela Nacional Prepara-toria de Mexico; professor of psychology and epistemology at the Faculty of Philosophy of the Universidad Nacional de México; and head of the Department of Secondary Education of Mexico's Ministry of Education.

During those years she also carried out a number of educational assignments in Europe on behalf of the Ministry of Education and Universidad Nacional de México. She carried out special studies in Europe (France, Belgium, and Switzerland) and worked for two years in the Arts Department of the Institute of Intellectual Cooperation of Paris and two years at the Institute of Educational Cinema of Rome, both of which foundations were dependent on the League of Nations.

While Guillén was on a visit to Barcelona at the beginning of 1935, President Lázaro Cárdenas, who knew of her work in public education, offered her the task of representing Mexico as envoy extraordinaire and minister plenipotentiary in Venezuela. She accepted the offer and, although the position was changed to envoy extraordinaire and minister plenipotentiary in Colombia, she was still determined to enter the Mexican diplomatic service. She was therefore appointed and sworn in on February 1, 1935, in Mexico City, and after an interview with the president of Mexico, she left for Colombia, arriving there at the beginning of April 1935.

Guillén shared the left-wing ideology of President Lázaro Cárdenas's regime, which was most pronounced in agrarian, labor, and educational legislation. She also held a progressive view regarding what her mission should be as a representative of Mexico. On her arrival in Colombia, she made the following declaration to the Colombian newspaper *El Relator*:

> Diplomacy has had a sense of being a game of bridge, a tea party, a slow waltz. Of course all that is necessary but not indispensable. In my opinion, my country's diplomacy has begun a transformation in that it assembles the work of its agents into three categories: commercial propaganda, cultural propaganda, and ideological propaganda. The rest comes on top of all that.

Although the progressive ideas of post-Revolutionary Mexico that Guillén represented to Colombia were well-received by the government of President Alfonso López, there was a negative response in some of the more conservative sectors of Colombian public opinion. Faced with growing hostility, in the spring of 1936 the Mexican diplomat requested a transfer to a European, preferably Scandinavian, country. On September 1, 1936, Guillén was appointed Mexico's special envoy and minister plenipotentiary to Denmark.

Despite Guillén's interest in Scandinavian countries and her knowledge of their advanced social legislature, as well as of their corporate organization methods, her mission in Denmark was short-lived. In response to the needs of the Mexican Foreign Service, she was designated Mexican third delegate at the eighteenth assembly of the League of Nations, in Geneva; in January 1938 her appointment as Mexican minister in Denmark officially ceased.

Guillén was not a career member of the Mexican Foreign Service. Nevertheless, thanks to the prestige she had gained in Mexico on the educational front, she had the necessary political support to carry out a new diplomatic charge in Europe, this time as technical adviser to the Mexican permanent delegation at the League of Nations in Geneva and as first secretary from February 1, 1938.

Here, the Mexican diplomat was witness to the decline of the League of Nations on the eve of World War II. In contrast to this ominous development, she also had the opportunity, and a genuine desire, to take part in the humanitarian work that the Mexican government was carrying out through its diplomatic representatives in France to help the thousands of political refugees from the Spanish Civil War. To that end, between March and April 1940, she was assigned to the Mexican consulate in Paris, which was in the charge of the distinguished consul Gilbert Bosques.

In November 1941, in view of the situation in Europe, the Mexican delegation to the League of Nations was closed, and at the beginning of 1942 Guillén was recalled to Mexico, where she was appointed consultant to the Mexican embassy in Havana, Cuba, from June of that year.

Her stay in Cuba was a brief one. Officially, her appointment in Havana ended on January 1, 1943, although she already had been recalled to Mexico from September 1942 to take part in special work at the Foreign Ministry.

From 1943 to 1952 she was without diplomatic post, which allowed her to take up teaching again. From May 1952 she was given a temporary appointment as cultural attaché at the Mexican embassy in Rome, which was not renewed in January of the following year and meant Guillén's final departure from the Mexican Foreign Service.

From that time until her death in 1981, she dedicated herself to academic activities, concentrated to a great extent on Spanish exiles in Mexico. Guillén figures in Mexican history as the predecessor of those women who, just as she did, rose rapidly in the Mexican diplomatic service.

Select Bibliography

Bosques, Gilberto, *Historia Oral de la Diplomacia Mexicana*. Mexico City: Secretaría de Relaciones Exteriores, 1988.

—CARLOS FERNÁNDEZ DITTMANN

GUTIÉRREZ, EULALIO

1880–1939 • President

A native of the state of Coahuila, Gutiérrez joined the opposition to Mexico's longtime president, Porfirio Díaz, as early as 1900. He joined the anarchist Mexican Liberal Party under the Flores Magón brothers in 1906 but switched to Francisco

I. Madero's Anti-Reelectionist movement in 1909. Although he possessed little formal training and education, he rose through the ranks to become a military leader in the rebel army in his home state in the early stages of the Revolution.

Gutiérrez soon developed a fearsome reputation. While occupying the post of mayor of the city of Concepción del Oro, Zacatecas, he erected a guillotine in the city's main square and executed a number of the community's wealthy, upper-class residents. As a common laborer in local mines as a young man, he had developed strong feelings of resentment toward those whom he felt had exploited the working class.

After Díaz went into exile in 1911, Gutiérrez remained in the army. When army general Victoriano Huerta overthrew the Madero government and executed its leader, Gutiérrez quickly joined the movement against the usurper. He raised a force of 700 men locally to join what came to be known as the Army for the Retention of the Constitution under Venustiano Carranza, the "First Chief." Soon Gutiérrez's command reached 2,000 men, for he attracted many of the miners with whom he had formerly worked. Gutiérrez seized control of the states of Zacatecas and Coahuila. He confiscated church property, introduced minimum wage laws, and abolished company stores and debt peonage, actions all reflecting his radical convictions.

After Huerta's defeat by the combined forces of Emiliano Zapata, Francisco "Pancho" Villa, and Carranza, the victorious factions soon began to quarrel among themselves as to who would head the Revolutionary movement and assume the presidency. Representatives of all three groups met at a convention in Aguascalientes on October 10, 1914. Gutiérrez became a member of the Permanent Pacification Committee that sought to solve the leadership problems of the rebel group.

A split developed at Aguascalientes between the followers of Carranza (such as Álvaro Obregón), who came to be known as the Constitutionalists, and the combined forces of Villa and Zapata, called the Conventionalists. The latter group seized control of the convention and named Gutiérrez to be provisional president pending national elections. He assumed that position on December 13, 1914.

The high point in Gutiérrez's career occurred when he moved with the Conventionalist army to Mexico City to shoulder the responsibilities of his new office. Followers of both Zapata and Villa became virtually uncontrollable soon after they arrived at the capital, and the provisional president had no way to restrain them. Gutiérrez left the capital because of threats from Villa and moved his now powerless government back to the northern state of San Luis Potosí. Making his peace with Carranza, he resigned as provisional president in May 1915.

Gutiérrez never returned to the national political scene, although he remained active in local politics in his native state of Coahuila in the years following the Revolution. In 1929 a confused Gutiérrez joined the Escobar Rebellion, whose members sought to overthrow the government of Emilio Portes Gil. Gutiérrez believed that his comrades from Revolutionary days, Generals Juan Andreu Almazán and Saturnino Cedillo, had taken sides against the government also. Such was not the case, however, and the Escobar Rebellion quickly was crushed by the central government. Gutiérrez went into exile to the United States to avoid arrest. He died in 1939.

Select Bibliography

Knight, Alan, *The Mexican Revolution.* 2 vols., Cambridge: Cambridge University Press, 1986.

Hart, John M., *Revolutionary Mexico.* Berkeley: University of California Press, 1987.

—CARL HENRY MARCOUX

GUZMÁN, LEÓN

1821–84 • Politician and Jurist

León Guzmán was born on November 5, 1821, apparently in Joquicingo, Mexico State. Guzmán studied law at the Instituto Científico y Literario in Toluca, the precursor of the state university.

His parliamentary career began in 1849 when he was elected deputy to the Congress of the Union. He remained a member of that institution until its dissolution in 1853 by Juan Bautista Ceballos, interim president and puppet of Antonio López de Santa Anna. During this congressional term, Guzmán backed the idea of linking the Isthmus of Tehuantepec coast-to-coast by a railway. As vice president of the Congress, he responded to the labor report of the then-president, Mariano Arista, on May 21, 1852. Moreover, Guzmán initiated procedures of political accountability in the country by denouncing President Ceballos before Congress on January 21, 1853, the first time in Mexico that this type of charge was made against the head of government. Ceballos dissolved Congress three days later to prepare for Santa Anna's last bid for power.

After Santa Anna's banishment, Guzmán returned to take a seat in the Constitutional Congress of 1856–57, participating in two important commissions, one on the constitution presided over by Ponciano Arriaga, and the other, on writing style under the presidency of Melchor Ocampo. In the former commission he supported the abolition of the Senate within the Congress and the presidential veto, having affiliated himself with the majority tendency to make the legislative branch predominate over the executive. Proponents of this realignment believed that the only way of doing this was by consolidating the Chamber of Deputies and increasing its authority to control the executive. Hence the proposal of making secretaries accountable to congressional scrutiny. Guzmán also proposed the elimination of the death penalty. "Society has no right over the life of a man," he would argue in the sessions of August 21 and 26, 1856. Later, as a judge, his convictions on this matter compelled him to resign rather than impose a death sentence.

As a member of the commission on style, he later would be blamed in 1879 for having omitted trial by jury from *juicio por amparo* (legal protection). In his newspaper *La verdad desnuda,* Guzmán defended himself from the accusations of having left out the jury by declaring that it had been an accidental omission, which had been made concrete by the final approval of the corrected text.

Guzmán accompanied Benito Juárez during the War of Reform (1858–61) and the French Intervention (1862–67), coming into prominence largely for his skill as mediator among the diverse revolutionary and military groups. In the final year of the war, Juárez appointed him governor and military commander of Guanajuato State. Even though the task of these temporary or emergency governorships was to maintain public order within the state after the triumph of Juárez's Republican forces, Guzmán made important advances in the political development of the state. He supported the first law on civil procedure, the prototype of the code of civil procedure that he promulgated on May 5, 1867. He also passed a law on the administration of justice, through which he established for the first time the concept of judicial permanence in the state, and he created the official gazette with the name *La voz de la ley* in June 1867.

Nevertheless, as governor, León Guzmán clashed with Mariano Escobedo, the great general responsible in no small part for the restoration of the Republic, and later with President Benito Juárez himself. He argued with Escobedo over the government's administration of confiscated goods. His disagreement with Juárez concerned legislation that provided the means whereby Juárez not only called for elections but organized a popular referendum to reform fundamental aspects of the Constitution of 1857, such as the restoration of the Senate and the reestablishing of the presidential power of veto. Both revisions had been provoked by the internecine struggle within the Liberal group that had devastated the country. Juárez's referendum tried to reform the Constitution in order to strengthen the presidency against the all-embracing congressional powers established in the 1857 Constitution. This method of reforming the Constitution—which had been used, of course, by the Conservatives in 1835 to change the Constitution of 1824—put Guzmán firmly against Juárez and his secretary of foreign affairs, Lerdo de Tejada. Guzmán was not alone in this confrontation. The president recently had received complaints from the city halls of Puebla and Culiacán, as well as from Governor Domingo Rubí of Sinaloa, against such an initiative for constitutional reform. Finally, on September 11, 1867, Guzmán was relieved of his position by President Juárez.

Perhaps Guzmán was right to oppose the reform procedure proposed by Juárez, given that its measures were not approved by Congress; indeed, they continued to be the object of enormous debate in subsequent legislatures. The five reforms in the referendum itself were not approved by Congress until 1874, after Juárez's death.

After this political setback, Guzmán was elected *procurador general* (attorney general) to the Supreme Court of Justice, from which position he defended the procedure of right of *amparo* against state judicial decisions. As *procurador,* Guzmán was criticized for double imposition of burdens above all on real estate, as exemplified in the case of José del Cueva of May 22, 1869. He supported the idea of bringing back the Senate in a small work published in 1870 on the legislature of two chambers entitled *Cuestiones Constitucionales: El sistema de dos cámaras y sus consecuencias.*

The constitutional crisis that emerged with the presidential elections of 1876 led Guzmán to distance himself from Porfirio Díaz, the new dictator, at the start of the latter's presidential career. During this time, the last post Guzmán occupied was that of president of the High Court of Justice for the state of Puebla. In 1878 Guzmán mediated a dispute between the governor of Puebla, Juan Crisóstomo Bonilla, and a faction in the state legislature. Assuming questionable powers, a section of the state congress removed Guzmán from the high court. Guzmán sought the intervention of the federal judiciary and was reinstalled the following year. He died in Monterrey, Nuevo León, on May 3, 1884.

Select Bibliography

González Oropeza, Manuel, *Introduccion: León Guzmán.* Mexico City: Senado de la República, 1987.

—MANUEL GONZÁLEZ OROPEZA

GUZMÁN FRANCO, MARTÍN LUIS

1887–1976 • Novelist and Journalist

Martín Luis Guzmán Franco, one of the novelists whose work is most representative of twentieth-century Mexican fiction, personally experienced the development of Mexican and Spanish politics of his day.

The son of a colonel in the federal army, this native of Chihuahua was named chancellor of the Mexican consulate in Phoenix, Arizona, in 1909. On his father's death in one of the first Revolutionary skirmishes, Guzmán returned to Mexico City in 1911 and joined the Ateneo de la Juventud, where he became friends with Alfonso Reyes, José Vasconcelos, and Pedro Henríquez Ureña. He soon joined the editorial staff of *El Imparcial*.

With the start of the Decena Trágica (Tragic Ten Days) accompanying the overthrow of President Francisco I. Madero in 1913, Guzmán, together with other Maderistas, founded the newspaper *El Honor Nacional*. Soon after, he returned to the United States, intending to join the Revolutionary forces that fought against the supporters of Victoriano Huerta. However, financial problems obliged him to return to Mexico City. In February 1914 he joined the staff of General Álvaro Obregón. In March, commissioned by Venustiano Carranza, he moved to Ciudad Juárez to serve under General Francisco "Pancho" Villa. His proximity to the "Centaur of the North" was reflected sometime later in two of his most important books: *El águila y la serpiente* (1928) and *Memorias de Pancho Villa* (1951). In August 1914 he was sent by Villa to witness the entry of the Constitutional Army into Mexico City, where he was jailed on Carranza's orders. The Military Convention in Aguascalientes, which had been convened in a short-lived attempt to unite the various Revolutionary factions, later ordered his release.

By December 1914 Guzmán had decided to go abroad because of the fighting among the various Revolutionary factions. After spending a short time in Paris, he moved to Madrid, where he stayed a year carrying out scholarly research and writing articles for *España*, a weekly magazine founded by the philosopher José Ortega y Gasset. He worked closely with many of the Spanish intellectuals who later were to form part of the Second Republic. In 1915 he published *La querella de México*, his first book, a collection of reflections on the problems and limitations of the Mexican people.

At Pedro Henríquez Ureña's suggestion, Guzmán moved to the United States in 1916, representing the magazine *España* in New York and giving short courses at the University of Minnesota. In 1918 he directed *El Gráfico* and was a contributor to the *Revista Universal*, New York publications written in Spanish. The following years he returned to Mexico, where he was made head of the editorial section of *El Heraldo de México*. Once the uprising against Carranza

began, Guzmán left for San Diego, California, accompanying General Ramón F. Iturbe. After Carranza's death, Guzmán continued to represent General Iturbe in Mexico City.

In December 1920 he became private secretary to Alberto Pani, minister of foreign affairs in the government of Álvaro Obregón, helping to organize the celebration of the centenary of Mexican Independence. The following year, after being elected a deputy, he founded the newspaper *El Mundo*, which was confiscated by the Obregón government in 1924 because of its support of the presidential candidacy of Adolfo de la Huerta. A few months later, after the de la Huerta uprising failed, Guzmán went into exile again for 10 years in Spain and France.

In Madrid he became contributor, editor, and lead writer of the newspapers *El Debate, Ahora,* and *Luz.* Naturalized as a Spanish citizen, Guzmán planned a short-lived Republican newspaper trust during the government of Manuel Azaña, an initiative that led to his taking on the position of managing director of *El Sol* and *La Voz,* also Ortega y Gasset's projects. During those years he was also a contributor to *El Universal* of Mexico, *La Prensa* of San Antonio, and *La Opinión* of Los Angeles. In Spain he published the book that made him one of the most representative authors of Revolutionary fiction: *El águila y la serpiente*, a clear demonstration of the fusion Guzmán achieved between journalism and literature. Tinged with autobiographical touches, the work is a wide fresco of the Revolution, shaped by short scenes of tremendous expressive strength and of almost cinematic style. To Guzmán this book was, rather than pure history or autobiography, simply a novel. In 1929 Guzmán published a second historical novel, *La sombra del caudillo*, which also achieved wide recognition.

The books that appeared after this point were in a way obligatory exercises, owing to the political restrictions imposed by President Plutarco Elías Calles on Guzmán's publishing house. They gave Guzmán the opportunity of tackling, with the skill and intensity of Joseph Conrad or Robert Louis Stevenson, that unique moment when American and Spanish histories matched each other. Guzmán confronted the various Independence movements from the point of view of action and not through archetypal characters or conventional ideas. Works from this period, such as *Mina el mozo: Héroe de Navarra* (1932), contain some of the most poetic descriptions of his fiction and abound in passages of mystery and adventure.

In 1936, shortly before the Spanish Civil War erupted, Guzmán went to Mexico at the invitation of President Lázaro Cárdenas. Once settled there, he continued his contributions to *El Universal* and began *Memorias de Pancho Villa*. He also founded the journal *Tiempo,* several publishing houses, and the Librería de Cristal.

Memorias de Pancho Villa is among the most stylistically refined of Revolutionary novels; it is a substantial work that refers to François-Auguste-René de Chateaubriand's *Mémoires d'outre-tombe* (1849–50). Compared with this major work of Mexican literature or the portraits included in *Muertes históricas* (1958), the other books that Guzmán produced after receiving the National Literary Prize in 1958, such as *Islas Marías* (1959) or *Necesidad de cumplir las Leyes de Reforma* (1963), are minor works. Nevertheless, Guzmán regained the spirit of the great Revolutionary works in *Academia* (1959), the aforementioned *Muertes históricas, Febrero de 1913* (1963), and *Crónicas de mi destierro* (1964), one of the best compilations of this genre and unquestionably on par with the exile works of Alfonso Reyes , Luis Gonzaga Urbina, or Francisco L. Urquizo.

Guzmán last took part in Mexican public life as a senator, from 1969 to 1976, the year of his death.

Select Bibliography

Abreu Gómez, Emilio, *Martín Luis Guzmán.* Mexico City: Empresas, 1968.

Bruce-Novoa, Juan, "Martín Luis Guzmán's Necessary Overtures." *Discurso Literario* 4:1 (1986).

Gyurko, Lanin, "Martín Luis Guzmán." In *Latin American Writers,* edited by Carlos A. Solé and María Isabel Abreu. New York: Scribner, 1989.

Leal, Luis, "*La sombra del caudillo,* roman à clef." *Modern Language Journal* 36:1 (January 1952).

Portal, Marta, *Proceso narrativo de la revolución mexicana.* Madrid: Cultura Hispánica, 1977.

—HÉCTOR PEREA

H

HABSBURG, FERDINAND MAXIMILIAN VON

See Maximilian (Ferdinand Maximilian von Hapsburg)

HACIENDA

The hacienda—which can defined most broadly as a sizeable property of privately titled land—has been at the heart of the story of post-Columbian Mexico. It emerged as a key institution soon after the Conquest and provided the context for the transformation of the Mesoamerican environment with the introduction of draft animals, plow technology, and a variety of European crops. Above all, the hacienda has stood out in this history because of its resilience and survival over almost four centuries, a Hispanic imprint starting with the New Laws of the Indies in 1542 and only finally ending with the full impact of the agrarian reform of 1934 to 1940 under President Lázaro Cárdenas. It is precisely this durability, despite the punctuation of two mass rural insurrections in 1810 and 1910, that has prompted and shaped the analysis and understanding of the elusive hacienda and its complex contribution to the making of Mexico. The hacienda is elusive especially as an analytical concept because of its actual diversity—not only across a duration of 400 years, but also within a territory of dramatic differences from tropical coastland to arid plateau.

At least the estate's origins are relatively free of confusion and contention. One of the institutions that the Spaniards had developed during their Reconquest of the Iberian Peninsula and then transplanted to the Americas was the feudal *encomienda*; in the Americas this took the form of grants of Indians who henceforward had to supply unremunerated labor and goods to their lord, but without entailing any accompanying permanent concession of land or jurisdiction (the lands occupied by the Indian laborers were merely to be held in trust by the *encomendero*). Although Fernando (Hernán) Cortés secured royal approval for his own miniature state of 30,000 tributaries, the largest of the *encomiendas* established in the wake of the Conquest, the institution was soon threatened by the humanist defense of the Indians mounted by Bartolomé de Las Casas, and it also was threatened by the Spanish Crown's unease with the prospect of a strong and independent aristocracy evolving in the Americas.

The New Laws of the Indies emerged as a result of these twin pressures, thereby transforming all servile Indians into free vassals of the Crown and simultaneously depriving all Spaniards in the New World of rights of dominion over Indian labor. Despite intense opposition from the colonists, and even open rebellion in Peru, the feudal regime of the *encomienda* was thus discontinued, effectively depriving the new settler society of its economic foundations. By way of compensation for such a loss, however, and in recognition that an alternative resource was urgently required, the Crown began a program of land grants for Spanish settlers—concessions of private property that in turn opened the way for the development of the hacienda throughout Spain's colonies in America.

This radical shift in emphasis from dominion to land ownership was somewhat at odds with the culture of the Conquest, since the latter had been powered largely by a more militaristic ethos of heroic courage and prowess, to be rewarded commensurately with high status and material ease. The Crown attempted to reflect this ethos in the land grants' designation and scale: *caballería* thus denoted an area of land appropriate for a knight at some 100 acres, while a mere foot soldier was deemed worthy only of a *peonía*—one-fifth the size of the knight's *caballería*. It is also clear that the new land base of the settler economy took time to be accepted by a society shaped by conquest and crusading ideals; some 20 years after the initiation of the land grant program the viceroy felt the need to introduce a new clause forbidding resale within three years of ownership and to impose the requirement that land be improved and developed (i.e., brought into cultivation). The perils of crossing the Atlantic and conquering the New World had been transcended only by dreams of El Dorado, the city of gold; the prospect of scratching a lowly living from the soil apparently paled bitterly in comparison.

In this way the hacienda suffered an awkward and induced birth, a resented disappointment in place of an ideal entitlement. Sensitive to the dangers of such disillusion, the Crown moved to cushion the blow by at least facilitating the provision of Indian labor for Spanish enterprise, thereby saving the settlers the ultimate indignity, and perhaps final straw before rebellion, of manual labor. Therefore, hard on the heels of phasing out *encomienda* came the compensatory legislation of *repartimiento de labor* in 1550. This enactment required Indian villages to provide draft labor to work Spanish lands, an affliction administered by the Crown's apparatus and organized at the local level by village authorities; on average 2 to 4 percent of adult males were to be drafted, with a seasonal peak of 10 percent at harvest time.

The blow thus was partially cushioned; labor was at least secured. But Las Casas's pro-Indian crusade nonetheless had left a sting in the tail. Spaniards were entitled to get Indians to work involuntarily for them, but they had to pay them a wage sufficient for subsistence. In this way the settler economy on the land (at whatever scale) was inextricably linked to the Indian village—and remained so throughout the long duration of the hacienda's existence. At the same time, however, the hacienda was left with the imprint of an institutional metamorphosis from the feudal *encomienda*, carried out within the context of a relatively unchanged culture of conquest, while at the same time being associated with the ambiguity of *repartimiento*, a hybrid system of exploitation caught between dominion and free labor. The complex association with institutions of dominion left an indelible impression on the hacienda, not least in terms of the way in which the hacienda has been represented and understood.

As it turned out, the system of labor draft was doomed to operate under the least favorable circumstances. Alien diseases already had devastated the indigenous population, but the two greatest epidemics struck in just this period of hacienda consolidation—1543 to 1547 and 1576 to 1580—traumatically carrying off the bulk of Indian labor and leaving the countryside with great swathes of depopulated land. Two consequences followed: the burden of *repartimiento* fell ever more heavily on the decimated villages (even prompting some Indians to flee from their homes in search of work beyond the yoke of the involuntary levy), and the Crown was able to accommodate growing numbers of immigrants by accelerating the distribution of land under the grant program. Thus the issuing of such concessions was concentrated in two 10-year periods following these great epidemics, 1553 to 1563 and 1585 to 1595, respectively. Illegal squatting also occurred throughout this first century of the colony, a process that was regularized by way of a fee-payment in Crown *composición*, already under way between 1591 and 1616, but which peaked from 1643 to 1645.

The combination of these legal land grants, especially in the aftermath of depopulation, along with the regularization of title for territory illegally squatted, together effected an early and wholesale transformation of Mesoamerican landed society and thereby brought into being the regime of the hacienda. With the exception of remote and peripheral areas such as the northern frontier and the southern tropics, the estate economy as private property was fully formed by 1700 in terms of its defined limits vis-à-vis the Indian village and its legal title. This expansionist formation within the context of drastically declining Indian population has provided the foundations for the most pervasive characterization of "the hacienda."

To a large extent this characterization is the product of recent historiography, but it also mirrors some of the earliest reflections on rural New Spain. This early typification came from the work of the Austrian Manuel Abad y Queipo, which, in turn, contributed directly to the influential and widely read writings of the German baron, Alexander von Humboldt. Both were struck by dramatic inequalities between rich and poor and were deeply affected by the degradation of the Indian, with the former remarking that "the color, ignorance, and poverty of the Indians place them at an infinite distance from a Spaniard." Abad y Queipo's diagnosis of the ills of New Spain focused on the inequitable distribution of property, and he advocated, true to the liberal mode, individual ownership of land as the chief remedy. He also was critical of the way in which Mexican agriculture failed to compete with U.S. flour in the lucrative Cuban market, for which deficiency he held the hacienda responsible and concluded that "the indivisibility of haciendas, the difficulty in managing them, the lack of property, among the people, has produced and continues to produce deplorable effects for agriculture, for the population, and the state in general."

Humboldt's account in his highly respected *Essai politique sur le royaume de la Nouvelle-Espagne* (published at the beginning of the nineteenth century) echoed this gloomy assessment and more specifically linked Indian poverty and backwardness to their feudal subordination within the initial system of *encomienda* and thereafter in its visible legacy, the hacienda. In this way the authoritative word of a hugely reputable figure from enlightened Europe sealed the characterization of the Mexican great estate as "feudal," derivative of the *encomienda* and thus a medieval anachronism responsible for both Indian degradation and the countryside's economic stagnation. At the same time Humboldt paradoxically enthused about the prodigious fertility and underexploited potential of the Mesoamerican soil—thereby laying the foundations for another resilient national image, Mexico as a superabundant cornucopia.

The tag of anachronism never was shaken off, and the main emphasis of the hacienda's historiography thus has focused on the question of the great estate's survival, as though it amounted to an unlikely destiny, somehow wrested artificially from the jaws of time. And so its first great historian, François Chevalier, echoing Humboldt, depicted the birth and maturation of the colonial hacienda over the sixteenth and seventeenth centuries in terms of the European past, the Middle Ages, with Mexico witnessing "the survival and revival of ancient institutions—a thousand years of history gathered into one spot," at the same time appearing as "a depository for archaisms that were passing out of existence in Europe. . . ."

According to Chevalier's analytical characterization, the main features of this "feudal" world were, first, the monumental scale of the landed properties, virtual miniature states dwarfing their European predecessors and passed from generation to generation; and, second, their near absolute autonomy in terms both economic (self-sufficiency made possible by enserfed or endebted labor) and political (where the landowners "set themselves up as dispensers of justice and captains of private armies entrusted with local policing"). The inherent logic of these properties was therefore not production or profit, but dominion—commensurately reflected in the proprietors' "mentality," on the one hand "not conducive to thinking in terms of efficient production," while on the other, compulsively expansionist where the acquisition of land served "not to increase earnings, but to eliminate rivals and hold sway over an entire region."

The importance of Chevalier's work, first published in 1952, was that, despite its focus on the institution's formation and origins in the sixteenth and seventeenth centuries, it provided a model of the hacienda with implicit claims for general validity: that is, an analytical account of the hacienda's "essential characteristics" throughout its final destiny and demise in the agrarian reform of the 1930s. Chevalier's thesis also coincided with another influential book, Woodrow Borah's *New Spain's Century of Depression* (1951), which located the emergence of the hacienda, and thus its internal essence, in precisely the same sixteenth- and seventeenth-century context of the demographic and economic decline subsequent to the first great cycle of economic growth and silver production from 1530 to 1630.

Both authors thus argued the case that the great estate as a type emerged in reaction to this protracted depression, thereby taking on its essential and permanent characteristics: on the one hand autarchic introversion, made possible by the sheer scale of land ownership, while on the other, the system of endebted labor or *peonaje,* equally typical, securing survival for the estate economy in the midst of market collapse and labor scarcity. The defining quintessences of the hacienda were therefore functions of radical depopulation and severe economic contraction, but according to the Chevalier-Borah model, once in place, they remained as fundamentals long after this period of formation and into the twentieth century. Thus for Borah "latifundia [great landed estates] and debt peonage, the twin aspects of Mexican life . . . helped provoke the Revolution of 1910–17."

The trend in historiography thereafter led toward the elaboration of the hacienda as a specific agrarian type, to be categorized according to the presence of certain features. The hacienda thus has been identified as an extensive landholding, exploited under conditions of minimal capitalization for a limited and largely local market, worked with a labor force that was sustained with concessions of land and basic necessities rather than paid a wage, and finally held together by way of a regime of domination sufficient to tie the worker to the estate—not only through the monopolization of land but also via the appropriation of the judicial process such that "Mexican haciendas tended to have their own police, their own judges, and their own jails."

Conceptual emphasis thus came to bear further on the hacienda as an anachronistic brake on agrarian development, but the model's regular reiteration occurred in the absence of much in the way of case study validation. In fact empirical research tended to run against the thesis of the model by pointing up the extent to which regional cases diverged from the analytical norm. Charles Gibson's classic study (1964) on the Valley of Mexico led the way. Chevalier's general model (based on the center-north and north of Mexico) was seriously undermined by the findings for a different region: far from the uniform and underutilized *latifundia* based on autarchy and endebted labor, the Valley of Mexico's agrarian economy emerged as a varied patchwork of vibrant and commercial estates linked to the market demand of Mexico City and largely devoid of any form of debt peonage. Further damage was done to the model of the hacienda by Gibson's revelations that the Indian village existed comfortably alongside the hacienda, successfully sustaining its administrative autonomy and retaining possession of a good part of its ancestral lands until the close of the colonial period.

Additional subversion came with William B. Taylor's (1972) study of a different region, the Valley of Oaxaca. There the Indian village held control of more than sufficient land, leaving the hacienda with an independent and inaccessible labor supply; hacienda profitability was demonstrably weak, and properties were shown to have been burdened with clerical debts, leading in turn to a high turnover in ownership. The regional evidence again ran counter to the model of an omnipotent regime featuring lineal continuity, even if it corresponded to the model of undercapitalization—the Oaxacan hacienda appeared to be weak, unstable, with little in the way of family dynasties, and teetering on the edge of bankruptcy.

Other illuminating regional studies followed, each shedding light on different dimensions of the agrarian estate and thereby challenging the validity of the dominant analytical version of the Mexican hacienda. Work by Eric Van Young (1981) and Claude Morín (1979) revealed an agrarian dynamism on the colonial hacienda in western Mexico in response to recovering population and urbanization. Similar important hacienda trends of internal colonization with new lands cleared, enclosed, and brought into cultivation were also uncovered for areas to the north of Mexico City by David A. Brading (1978) and John Tutino (1986), as well as the dramatic exposure of a wide variety of existent property-scales that blurred both the definition of the hacienda and the rural polarity of great estate–Indian village with other intermediate units called *labores* and *ranchos*.

The most crucial empirical revelations for the model came over the question of labor. First of all, mounting evidence demonstrated that the system of peonage or endebtedness was not in any way comparable to European-style enserfment, which had legally tied generations of laborers to the estate, backed up by the juridical powers of the lord. The system in Mexico was shown in contrast to be quintessentially dynamic, a function of the shifting relationship between demography and market rather than a fixed refraction of dominion. Haciendas certainly tried to hold their wage bills to a minimum, especially in an economy that suffered from a shortage of hard currency, but most of the evidence available suggests that estate labor was waged and free and was very seldom secured through extralegal or coercive means during the colony—or indeed thereafter, with the exception of certain developments on the periphery during the late nineteenth and early twentieth centuries, such as the henequen estates in the Yucatán. Indeed, at times of especially tight profit margins, haciendas were even found to be in debt to their workers, rather than the other way around.

In light of the pressures on hacienda profitability, it is relatively clear that the incidence of peonage or endebtedness on the estate was an index of labor's bargaining power rather than its subordination. Advances made in cash or kind should therefore be seen not as an index of "the feudal hacienda" but rather of an employer having to resort to desperate measures and inducements in the recruitment of labor from a reluctant population already certain of its subsistence. Conversely, the occurrence of endebtedness (or access to interest-free advances) on the Mexican hacienda dwindled away from high levels in the seventeenth century to a state of relative rarity later in eighteenth and nineteenth centuries as population growth produced pressure on village lands and a surplus in the labor market.

And yet, despite this volume of regional evidence, the orthodox model of the hacienda has survived. Perhaps this is a result of the fact that, as Brading suggests, the new empirical data has been driven by an implicit critique of the old formula and has never been rephrased or extended as an alternative general theory of the great estate and agrarian development in Mexico. In any event, in the absence of such a direct conceptual challenge, the original script from Chevalier and Borah, albeit somewhat amended, continues to dominate the stage.

The survival of this orthodoxy in the teeth of piecemeal subversion from below is also partly the result of the way in which the theory accommodates the two major events of modern Mexico—the Insurgency in 1810 and the Mexican Revolution a century later. Both events have been set against the rural world in which they occurred, thereby making a central place for the role of the hacienda as a factor in political upheaval, and thus once again raising the profile of the estate as a form of domination rather than as an economic adaptation. Such an emphasis has been particularly strong within the earliest interpretations of the Revolution, which paint a picture of a mass movement overturning an ancien régime based primarily on feudal land ownership and thereby paving the way for the emergence of an agrarian bourgeoisie.

Other more recent attempts to sustain conceptual clarity while accommodating empirical complexity have paid greater attention to the detail of economic change in the countryside. Outstanding work from Alan Knight (1986) and John Tutino (1986) have thus left the impression of an agrarian economy in the midst of dynamic change preceding the outbreak of both the Insurgency and the Mexican Revolution. Too much evidence from regional revisionism has appeared on both these periods for the old orthodoxy of the "feudal hacienda" to hold unmitigated sway, and so the model has been amended to take account of the acknowledged commercial outlook or market sensitivity on the part of the hacienda regime. However, even here the orthodoxy's

resilience has been sufficient to interpret new information as support for the fundamentals of the old model—as in Enrique Florescano (1969), where such market extroversion has been depicted as a speculative device of hoarding staples until scarcity drove up prices and is thus cited as one of the main strategies for hacienda survival without having to modernize production practices. In much the same way Knight's version of the commercializing hacienda during the Porfiriato (1876–1910) is characterized (at least in the domestic sector) by this hybrid quality of market opportunism alongside archaic production methods.

According to these arguments, then, hacienda success in both periods was thus presupposed by extra-economic advantage rather than productive innovation. Dominion rather than accumulation still figures as the key in this conceptual schema of the great estate: its survival was thus secured by virtue of political advantage rather than economic efficiency, necessarily entailing a commensurate squeeze on the peasant/Indian economy in order to eliminate competition and capture subordinate or cheap labor. The logic behind the Insurgency and the Revolution in these accounts thus remains true in its essentials to the orthodoxy of the Chevalier-Borah model: a fundamental bias toward dominion within the largely unchanging makeup of the hacienda accounted for both its capacity to survive over 400 years without modernizing its productive structure (thereby retarding Mexican development) as well as an intrinsic compulsion to expand at the expense of the village economy and land base (thereby precipitating mass rural insurrections in 1810 and 1910 and others in between).

The view taken here, however, is that this orthodoxy and its emphasis on the hacienda as an institution of dominion rather than production has, for all its importance as an instrument to interpret the political development of Mexico, finally run out of steam. It leaves many major issues underresearched, such as the relatively subdued nature of popular antagonism to the hacienda at times of opportunity and the collapse of the state. But, above all else, it has left neglected the crucial question of the economic contribution made by the great estate to Mexican development.

Trapped by the pervasive imagery of dominion and its artificial survival, the analytical exploration of "the hacienda" has for too long labored under the assumption that it acted at worst as a parasitic siphon of conspicuous aristocratic consumption on capital accumulated elsewhere, or at best, as an archaic and inefficient device for sustaining elite lifestyles by way of market distortions and labor repression, while at the same time exposing the population at large to hazardous shortfalls in food supply and a damaging trading deficit with the United States. The "feudal" stereotype marketed back in 1909 by a pamphleteering Molina Enríquez, who depicted the great estate as squandering Humboldt's cornucopia with archaic consumption and market distortion while leaving the peasant/Indian village to feed the nation in normal years from a mere marginal tenth of the national lands, always has been given undue credence in the twentieth century's historiography of agrarian Mexico.

In short, research now needs to be focused on the hacienda as a source of accumulation rather than domination. The revisionist story that emerges from the regional cases already has exposed the weakness of the orthodox account, but it has failed to reach the point at which the whole is greater than the sum of its parts. Work on both the colonial period and the nineteenth century already has provided abundant evidence that the estate economy adjusted dynamically to prevailing conditions of climatic and political hazard, in tune with trends of population growth, urban demand, and market access. Accelerated trends of this dynamism with raised levels of productivity and capital investment thus particularly marked the late colonial period and the Porfiriato, as evidenced by the process of internal estate colonization in the first period and by the moves toward irrigation, mechanization, and improved stock lines in the second. Key contexts for this dynamism, as ironically pointed out by Abad y Queipo, were political stability, demographic growth, access to credit, and market integration via efficient transport—factors that finally came together only in the fleeting golden age of the Porfiriato.

Thus to move toward a new theoretical threshold we need to strike out from data already available with a fresh and challenging heresy—that is, that the hacienda's resilience over 400 years was not so much a function of its dominion but rather a measure of its economic versatility in the midst of the most adverse of circumstances, both political and environmental, and that this versatility in turn represented an optimum adaptation to these circumstances for the purpose of accumulation and the transition to capitalism.

Select Bibliography

Borah, Woodrow Wilson, *New Spain's Century of Depression.* Berkeley: University of California Press, 1951.

Brading, Douglas A., *Haciendas and Ranchos in the Mexican Bajío.* Cambridge and New York: Cambridge University Press, 1978.

Chevalier, François, *Land and Society in Colonial Mexico.* Berkeley: University of California Press, 1963.

Florescano, Enrique, "The hacienda in New Spain." In *The Cambridge History of Latin America,* vol. 4, edited by L. Bethell. Cambridge: Cambridge University Press 1984.

_____, *Precios del Maíz y crisis agrícolas en México (1708–1810).* Mexico City: Colegio de México, 1969.

Gibson, Charles, *The Aztecs under Spanish Rule.* Stanford, California: Stanford University Press, 1964.

Harris, Charles, *A Mexican Family Empire: The Latifundio of the Sánchez Navarros, 1765–1867.* Austin: University of Texas Press, 1975.

Holden, Robert H., *Mexico and the Survey of Public Lands.* DeKalb: Northern Illinois University Press, 1994.

Knight, Alan, *The Mexican Revolution.* Lincoln and London: University of Nebraska Press, 1986.

Miller, Simon, *Landlords and Haciendas in Modernizing Mexico.* Amsterdam: CEDLA, 1995.

Morín, Claude, *Michoacán en la Nueva España del Siglo XVIII: Crecimiento y disigualdad en una economía colonial.* Mexico City: Fondo de Cultura Económica, 1979.

Schryer, Frans J., *The Rancheros of Pisaflores.* Toronto: University of Toronto Press, 1978.

Taylor, William B., *Landlord and Peasant in Colonial Oaxaca.* Stanford, California: Stanford University Press, 1972.

Tutino, John, *From Insurrection to Revolution in Mexico.* Princeton, New Jersey: Princeton University Press, 1986.

Van Young, Eric, *Hacienda and Market in Eighteenth-Century Mexico.* Berkeley: University of California Press, 1981.

Wasserman, Mark, *Capitalists, Caciques, and Revolution.* Chapel Hill: University of North Carolina Press, 1984.

Wells, Allen, *Yucatán's Gilded Age.* Albuquerque: University of New Mexico Press, 1985.

—SIMON MILLER

HANDICRAFTS

When Mexico emerged from the Revolution of 1910, the new ruling elite believed that it was necessary to take various steps to legitimate and maintain its recently acquired power. The power of this new elite depended not only on its capacity to create and maintain the new relations of production needed to develop the economy, but also on a politically united country. The elite had to impose its vision of the world on all of Mexican society.

The new elite faced tremendous obstacles. The political, ethnic, and linguistic divisions in Mexico hampered communication. Even when different communities, regions, and political factions spoke the same languages, they needed to overcome years of bitter distrust. The ruling elite introduced various strategies to integrate Mexico into a single nation and nationality, including agrarian reform, nationalization of the petroleum industry and railroads, creation of a single political party, organization of state-sponsored labor unions, construction of roads, and teaching Spanish language and culture to indigenous communities. A fundamental part of this new project of nation-building was the idea of a national culture as the synthesis of symbols of identity.

The search for a Mexican nationality implied the reinvention of a mestizo national culture, a hybrid of western and indigenous cultures. The theoretical work and historical research of social scientists played a key role in this reinvention of Mexico. Intellectuals did not imagine all elements of indigenous culture were admirable; indeed, some intellectuals believed that indigenous communities were 400 years behind in their cultural development. Nonetheless, there was considerable agreement among intellectuals—and artists— that indigenous arts and crafts were the most valuable and genuine part of Mexican culture.

As early as 1921 the Mexican state publicly declared its admiration for indigenous handicrafts, which were called "traditional industries" at the time. During the presidency of Álvaro Obregón (1920–24), the centenary of Mexican Independence was celebrated with a vast exposition including ceramics, painting on wood, bone and horn carvings, embroidery, lace, and threadwork. The catalogue for the exposition—written by the painter and folklorist Gerardo Murillo (better known as Dr. Atl)—is one of the pioneer works on what is now known as "popular art."

Several other expositions were organized over the next two decades in Mexico and the United States, and Mexican intellectuals and artists wrote a veritable flood of material on artisanal production. Intellectuals of the period tended to take a romantic perspective, believing that the *pueblo* (the people) transcended class divisions and possessed a "popular soul" that would be the source of popular art and culture. This idea of the *pueblo* was the touchstone of a new "revolutionary nationalism," which helped redefine Mexican art, music, literature—and social policy and political discourse.

The promotion of indigenous handicrafts became the task of both anthropologists and economists. Initially, collecting art and other examples of indigenous culture— stories, legends, music, dance—was the preserve of the Departamento Autónomo de Asuntos Indígenas (Autonomous Department of Indigenous Affairs). In 1948 the Instituto Nacional Indigenista (INI, or National Indigenist Institute) was founded at the recommendation of the Primer Congreso Indigenista Interamericano (First Interamerican Indigenist Congress), which had met in Mexico in 1940. The INI was to resolve the "Indian problem" in an "integral" way with the cooperation of all government agencies. *Indigenismo* (valorization of Mexico's indigenous heritage and present-day indigenous communities) was understood to be a process of acculturation planned and directed by the Mexican state combined with a measure of protection for indigenous communities. In the INI's own words, this meant "giving indigenous communities cultural values considered positive, substituting them for cultural elements considered negative."

From its inception the INI sought to protect handicrafts, developing artisans' unions, organizing fairs, expositions, and contests, and protecting the sale of artisanal products. The INI also became involved in the actual production of handicrafts, however, promoting handicrafts that it considered "authentically Mexican." In 1951 the INI and the Instituto Nacional de Antropología e Historia (INAH, or National Institute of Anthropology and History) formed the

Patronato de Artes e Industrias Populares (Popular Arts and Industries Foundation). The first task of the Patronato was to create the Museum of Popular Arts and Industries, a space where indigenous handicrafts and popular arts could be exhibited and—until 1995—sold.

In the 1960s the promotion of artisanal production became a key element in government economic strategy and in official "developmentalist" discourse. Measures were taken to create employment and develop national and international markets for artisanal products. Many new government programs were created to provide technical, commercial, and marketing assistance to would-be artisans. Nonetheless, this assistance did little to improve dismal standards of living in the Mexican countryside; indeed, the new government programs (and private initiatives) tended to encourage the commercialization of handicrafts, benefiting only the business sector and a very small number of artisans who produce handicrafts for the wealthiest consumers.

These institutional changes have helped shape the dominant culture's very understanding of what handicrafts are. If the objective has been to collect artifacts for museums, the criteria for defining handicrafts have generally been aesthetic and ethnic. When public and private institutions have viewed artisanal production as a way to alleviate rural poverty, however, the term "handicrafts" encompasses all rural artisanal production. If the intention is to preserve disappearing traditions, indigenous peoples are encouraged to learn craft skills in workshops. If the aim is to recognize the inherent creative ability of popular classes, artisanal production is promoted as "popular art" in national and international galleries. If the goal is to broaden the market for handicrafts, criteria of ethnicity and tradition are combined with accessibility—size, weight, and price. If the goal is to promote tourism, the variety of regional production is stressed.

Institutional involvement in artisanal production has helped create a two-tiered market for handicrafts in Mexico. Members of the low-income working class tend to purchase basic handicrafts—furniture, baskets, pottery, *huaraches* (a type of footwear resembling sandals)—which cost less than their manufactured counterparts. They also purchase luxury goods produced at certain times of the year or for special occasions, including clothing, objects for religious rituals, and utensils used in the preparation of special foods.

The upper tier of the market for artisanal goods generally has been geared toward high-income tourists from other parts of Mexico and abroad. The aesthetic is valued over the functional. Handcrafted domestic products and work utensils generally are not considered handicrafts, while objects whose shapes, color, design, use of raw materials, and decoration are believed to reflect peasant, indigenous, and mestizo life are considered handicrafts. The tourist market has also fundamentally changed the ways in which handicrafts are used and understood. For example, masks used in regional dances or the richly embroidered clothes made by indigenous women in certain parts of Mexico are no longer symbols of ethnic identity but adornments in the homes of their new users.

The strength of the popular market for domestic and ritual artisanal goods—and the variety of conditions under which artisans work—has helped maintain the diversity of handicrafts in Mexico. With even the most basic information it is possible to identify which region or locality handicrafts come from, and sometimes even which individual craftsperson made them. Dating from pre-Hispanic times, this living tradition includes such crafts as carpentry, needlework, fireworks, waxwork, rope making, pottery, silver and gold work, basket making, wood and stone work, papier mâché, embroidery, feather work, lacquer work, broom making, harness making, glass work, tanning, iron work, tin work, dying and weaving of vegetable fibers, toy making, painting, copper work, masonry, and cabinet making.

Part of the vitality of these artisanal traditions comes from the fact that many handicrafts used in Mexican ritual life simply cannot be replaced with manufactured goods. Clay figures are used by shamans to remove *aires* (bad winds) from high places to permit the planting of crops and to drive away evil spirits. The elaborate embroidered patterns on a Maya woman's *huipil* symbolize the cosmos, and a similar garment adorns the Virgin during religious festivals. A man gives his betrothed the jewelry she will wear on their wedding day. Churches are adorned with woven flower canopies.

Handmade candles are carried in religious processions. Masks are worn by dancers in a variety of rituals. Huge jars and pots hold food and pulque (a beverage made from the fermented sap of maguey) for feast days. These handicrafts and countless others are part and parcel of Mexican cultural identity. They play a functional role, but they also represent technique, knowledge, and wisdom.

See also Artisans and Artisanal Production

Select Bibliography

Brenner, Anita, editor, *Mexico This Month* 8:1 (1962).

Bronowski, Judith, *Artesanos mexicanos.* Los Angeles: Crafts and Folk Art Museum, 1978.

Cordry, Donald, and Dorothy Cordry, *Mexican Indian Costumes.* Austin: University of Texas Press, 1968.

Enciso, Jorge, *Design Motifs of Ancient Mexico.* New York: Dover, 1953.

Rockefeller, Nelson A., "Foreword" to *The Nelson A. Rockefeller Collection of Mexican Folk Art.* New York: Museum of Primitive Art, 1969.

Toor, Frances, *A Treasury of Mexican Folkways.* New York: Crown, 1973.

—Victoria Novelo

HENEQUEN

The hard fiber henequen *(Agave fourcroydes)* dominated the landscape, the economy, and the social structure of northwestern Yucatán and neighboring portions of Campeche for approximately a hundred years (1850–1950). Commonly, but incorrectly, known as sisal hemp by U.S. fiber buyers (after the port from which it was originally exported), *henequen blanco,* or *sacci,* as it was known in Maya, was indigenous to the Yucatán Peninsula and had been cultivated there since pre-Columbian times. It was not until the late colonial era that Spanish entrepreneurs began to recognize its commercial potential. The fibrous agave was used for hammocks, mosquito nets, bagging, and rope throughout the peninsula and only began to be exported in significant quantities for low-end cordage and rigging purposes during the early nineteenth century. Fortunately, demand was assured as technological advancements throughout the late nineteenth century continued to find new industrial applications for the agave.

The new application of greatest consequence was binder twine. The invention of the mechanical twine knotter in the late 1870s substituted twine for wire, and, in the process, revolutionized grain farming in the North American heartland and the farm implement industry. As acreage under cultivation increased dramatically, sales of mechanical grain binders climbed in North America and Europe. Henequen had found its calling; it could be fashioned into a pliable, smooth single-strand cord, perfect for the binder. The U.S. market purchased more than 90 percent of the total henequen output, and by 1900, Yucatán's chief export supplied fiber for 85 percent of the binder twine manufactured by U.S. cordage factories, harvesting machine companies, and prison twine mills. Henequen exports soared to meet the growing demand, from 40,000 bales (a bale equals 350 pounds) in 1875 to more than 600,000 bales by 1910.

This demand-driven export-led model was typical of the Latin American export boom (1850–1930), as the region supplied raw materials and other consumer commodities to meet the requirements of western Europe and the United States. In Yucatán the impact dramatically transformed the regional economy as a complex organic partnership evolved that helped define the choices made by planters, local import-export agents, and peasants. From marketing arrangements to land tenure patterns, from labor relations to the willingness of local producers to introduce labor-saving processing equipment and infrastructure, henequen producers (henequeneros) had to mesh the idiosyncrasies of the monocrop with their own social, economic and political institutions *and* a market constantly in flux. In the process, the fiber boom exposed the regional economy to violent shocks brought on by volatile price fluctuations and favored the dominance of large landowners and exporters, who played an increasingly oligopolistic role in the fiber trade.

Until the export boom tethered the northwestern quadrant of the peninsula to the international economy, Yucatán was a relatively isolated region. Even though local elites and colonial administrators experimented with a number of different crops and products, native Maya peasants remained largely oriented toward subsistence agriculture. Of particular concern was the region's physical geography that strongly limited the location and nature of agricultural production. The northern and north-central part of the peninsula—what is today largely the state of Yucatán—is a massive limestone rock covered with a thin layer of soil and a dry, rugged scrub forest. The thin topsoil quickly becomes exhausted, porous surface conditions make irrigation ditches impossible, and surface water is almost entirely lacking. Until the boom, land-extensive cattle and corn haciendas dotted the arid, calcareous landscape, except for the southeast, where somewhat better soil, water, and climactic conditions are found. In these southeastern tracts, sugarcane, cotton, and tobacco were cultivated with success after Independence. The southeast's economic development, however, contributed to the midcentury Caste War, as rebellious Maya, seeking to reclaim lands lost to expansionist landlords, razed sugar mills and devastated this productive subregion. Some regional historians contend that the southeast's decimation contributed to the growth of henequen monoculture in the state's northwest quadrant, the only sector safe from rebel Maya attacks.

Ironically, *sac ci* grows best in partly decomposed limestone, in soils that are too dry and stony for the production of most crops. The northwestern quadrant affords excellent natural drainage and aeration for the plant's roots. In richer soils, henequen leaves contain too much pulp, and the fiber extracted is inferior in quality and quantity; the northwest received just enough rain for the hardy agave to survive. A henequen zone developed surrounding Mérida (roughly within a radius of 70 to 80 kilometers, or 45 to 50 miles, of the state capital), as hacendados increasingly rationalized their land and labor and turned their corn and cattle haciendas into modern fiber estates. In some ways this necessitated major adjustments, and in other ways it built on structures already present. Land tenure patterns, labor relations, technological improvements, and marketing and credit practices either were overhauled or fine-tuned in the wake of the boom.

As a result, the henequen estate was neither a true commercial plantation nor a traditional hacienda. If, on the one hand, the henequen estate was equipped with modern machinery, narrow-gauge tramways and land-intensive cultivation of a staple crop, traditional forms of management and

mentalité (roughly, "ideology" or "consciousness") continued to imbue the institution with characteristics of the pre-henequen hacienda.

Yucatecans creatively adapted new technology to enhance production capacity. Prior to the boom, time-consuming hand scrapers were the norm. With these tools, 500 leaves had to be scraped to secure one pound of raw fiber. The invention and perfection of a defibering, or rasping, machine by Yucatecans during the 1850s, however, enabled the industry to cut production costs and meet rising demand. Improvements in technology continued, and with the introduction of steam power to the machine house in 1861, henequen production increased. Motivated by the growing hard fibers trade and by state government attempts to stimulate advances in machine productivity and safety, Yucatecan inventors had defibering machines made to specifications in the United States. By 1900, automatic Prieto machines manufactured in Paterson, New Jersey, cleaned 150,000 leaves within a 10-hour period, a far cry from the first rasping machines.

The combination of powerful defibering machines and a level landscape meant that landowners could take advantage of economies of scale. Throughout the henequen zone, hacendados expanded their holdings, gobbling up adjoining tracts of land owned by smallholders and taking advantage of individual family heads of nearby villages. Sometimes violence accompanied disputes between property owners and villagers. In general, however, the emergence of the large landed estate met with little resistance during the boom, as hacendados utilized state and federal laws to their advantage; small proprietors were powerless to offer objection.

Yucatán's level topography also enabled *henequeneros* to make the most of improvements in transportation. In the 1880s hacendados began to lay a network of inexpensive, portable Decauville gauge rails, which transported the leaves from field to rasping machine and from processing house to the nearby major railhead. Four railway lines built by and for *henequeneros* fastened outlying villages and estates into a tight orbit around their Mérida hub. From the state capital, fiber was sent to Progreso on the Gulf Coast. This transportation revolution served to reduce transaction costs as it enlarged productive capacities.

The emergence of a full-fledged plantation society was inhibited by the way in which hacendados interacted with labor. Treatment of workers included a thinly veiled paternalism, fictive kinship, and the ever-present agency of human force, exemplified in floggings meted out by overseers—all carryovers from the past. Again with the assistance of an accommodating state political apparatus, three complementary mechanisms of social control—isolation, coercion, and security—allowed *henequeneros* to maintain the disciplined work rhythms of monocrop production. These mechanisms worked in unison to cement the structural relationship that not only suited the production requirements of management, but also served the subsistence needs of workers.

Institutions like the hacienda store, for instance, gave *henequeneros* a sure-fire mechanism for raising workers' debts (coercion). On another level, by providing basic foodstuffs and household needs, it also diminished the need for resident peons to leave the property to purchase goods, thereby minimizing the chances of potentially disruptive contact between indebted peons and neighboring villagers (isolation). Finally, through the sale of corn, beans, and other staples, it ensured subsistence for resident peons (security). The hacienda store was, in essence, a perfect vehicle for appropriating labor in a scarce market, since it facilitated dependency and immobility, while conveying a measure of convenience and security to landless peons. Not until the Mexican Revolution would debt peonage be outlawed, even though working conditions on henequen estates were not significantly altered until the 1930s.

Gender relations on henequen estates only reinforced these complementary mechanisms. In fact, masters and servants found common ground in their perceptions of the role Maya women should play on the estates. First and foremost, they agreed on a rigid division of labor. Male debt peons toiled in the fields, performing all the tasks related to planting, harvesting, and processing fiber on the estates. If daughters or wives occasionally worked in the fields to remove the spines from the henequen leaves after cutting (just as they had helped in the past with harvesting corn), they were accompanied by their fathers or husbands and were not paid for their labors. Not surprisingly, women on henequen estates were relegated to the domestic sphere. Indeed, it appears that the fiber boom brought little change to the *campesinas'* regimen, for this strictly observed division of labor on the estates was consistent with pre–fiber boom patterns. Even at the height of the fiber boom, when planters were desperate for workers, Maya women were not used in the fields.

Why did planters, who regularly complained about the scarcity of labor in the henequen zone and who did not shrink from employing coercive strategies when it suited their purposes, not employ *campesinas* in the fields? By permitting the male peon to earn "wages," to provide for his family through access to corn plots and hunting and to exercise power over women in his household, the hacendado was securing the loyalty and limiting the mobility of his worker. As a consequence, families rarely were separated in the henequen zone, nor does it appear that hacendados used the threat of separation to ensure loyalty.

Henequeneros applied this thin veneer of reciprocity, which formalized gender relations on the estates. When they arranged weddings for their peons, they provided grooms with a loan—their first debt—to pay for the religious and civil ceremonies and a fiesta. The result was a complicitous arrangement among males on the estate in which the master permitted the peon to preside over his own household as a subordinate patriarch. If this led to cases of domestic violence, more often than not they were handled circumspectly on the estate; rarely did grievances find their way to the local courtroom. Typically, hacendados and overseers put gross offenders in the hacienda jail.

Such *campesino* patriarchy, however, had limits. Often enough, the *henequenero* or his overseer invaded the peon's hut and violated his spouse or daughter, exercising the humiliating "privilege" of the "right of first night." While such an affront undermined the reciprocal nature of the shared sense of patriarchy, it did provide the peon with one more object lesson in where power ultimately resided on the estate. The servant would seldom take revenge on his boss; more often, we learn of unfortunate cases of misdirected rage, as peons abused their wives to reassert their dominion in the home. Planters were reluctant to tamper with the peons' patriarchal control of their families because, in the long run, it suited their economic interests. As far as the hacendado was concerned, the principal task of Maya women was to procreate and raise the next generation of henequen workers. To permit women to work in the fields would undermine that role and upset social relations on the estate—relations that reflected the acculturated Maya's evolving cultural identity, as well as the requirements of fiber production.

Marketing of fiber increasingly came under the control of a cohesive oligopoly that limited competition. Social and family connections were utilized to build economic empires and to restrict entry to the market through political connections and the control of capital. Instead of the archetypical enclave, an informal empire evolved between accommodating elites and foreign buyers. The International Harvester Company, the largest farm implement manufacturer in the world and one of the principal purchasers of raw fiber, funneled capital through local agents to regional producers. Some scholars contend that by World War I, International Harvester dominated the fiber industry and influenced price trends on the local fiber market. Other researchers respond that market forces overcame collaborative efforts to keep prices down.

To be sure, when fiber prices were high, *henequeneros* secured bountiful profits. Yet local hacendados had to borrow money in advance from import-export merchants *(casas exportadoras)*. The *casas,* in turn, were lent capital by banks and buyers in the United States. A small hacendado class, numbering between 300 and 400, promised its fiber to the *casas* in exchange for cash advances.

If most *henequeneros* found it difficult to negotiate this treacherous monocrop economy, a close-knit elite of 30 families not only survived but flourished. This group dominated the regional economy, controlling land, labor, the import-export trade, and transportation. As the monocrop economy prospered at the turn of the century, however, competition within this familial elite intensified. By 1902, a much smaller, more cohesive group constituted an oligarchical faction in the region. This faction was based on the Molinista faction, led by Governor Olegario Molina and his son-in-law, Avelino Montes. The Molina-Montes clan had homogeneous interests, a relatively closed membership, and—owing in part to its collaboration with the principal buyer of raw fiber, International Harvester Company—such control over the region's economic and political levers of power that it was able to thwart the opportunities of rival factions.

Planters, merchants, politicians, and journalists openly discussed the role of International Harvester and its collaboration with Molina and Montes. Harvester became a target in the regional press as the perception of guilt seemed proof enough for many intellectuals and planters, who were disposed to saddle the collaborators with more blame that they probably deserved for the ills of an inherently unstable economy.

Earlier attempts to withhold production, create a shortage of fiber on the market, and elevate prices had failed miserably. Many *henequeneros* were unable to participate in these cooperatives, since their product was fully or partially promised to *casas exportadoras* for advances tendered in years past. A contentious lot even under favorable market conditions, the planters were hampered from the start by a lack of solidarity. *Henequeneros* prided themselves on their individualism, and when they needed assistance to weather the bust cycles of the fluctuating regional economy, they preferred to rely on extensive kinship networks, rather than unite to do battle against the powerful *casas exportadoras*. Generally speaking, planter cooperative societies only coalesced when the price of henequen dropped so low that it cut into the planters' considerable profits. This was precisely the worst time for such a maneuver to succeed, since money was stretched so thin when the price of henequen declined.

The *casas exportadoras*, however, did not take demonstrations of incipient planter solidarity lightly. Playing on the fears of the *henequeneros,* the *casas* and henequen speculators manipulated stocks of fiber and circulated wild rumors of the imminent demise of the market. More times than not, growers, fearing a further drop in price, sold their fiber to speculators who turned a tidy profit at the expense of the edgy *henequeneros.*

Not until the Revolutionary government of Salvador Alvarado committed the resources of the state to a valorization scheme in 1915, did planter solidarity effectively confront the fiber buyers. Yet, it is instructive that many planters had to be coerced by the state to participate in the valorization campaign. Unlike past attempts to organize, the timing favored the producers. The Comisión Reguladora del Mercado de Henequén was aided by high fiber prices, as World War I stimulated demand for cordage and twine. The rise in prices was short-lived, however; valorization proved to be a temporary solution, as prices plummeted after the war.

During the 1920s, a new fiber challenged henequen's comfortable niche in the hard fibers trade. Yucatecans were well acquainted with this newcomer. *Yaxcí (Agave sisalana)* was indigenous to the peninsula and had been used by local artisans to make hammocks, bagging, and other products. This true sisal had been identified formally by the U.S. consul to Campeche in the 1830s, Henry Perrine, who after his stay in the peninsula, brought the sisal plant to southern Florida and conducted experiments there. Although sisal did not become popular in the United States, German growers carried the plant from Florida to German East Africa in 1892. By the 1920s sisal plantations were flourishing in Tanganyika and Kenya. Later the island of Java in the south Pacific would commit to *yaxcí.*

Sisal proved to be a formidable opponent; labor costs in these areas were even lower than in Yucatán. By 1927 Asian and African nations accounted for nearly half of world hard fiber production. The Great Depression and the invention of the combine, which did not use twine, also hurt the henequen industry. Production fell drastically; henequen exports reached a low in 1940, when they were less than one-fourth of their level during World War I. Although henequen would recover somewhat with the introduction of automatic baler machines, the introduction of low-cost synthetic fibers in the 1960s and 1970s would devastate the henequen economy.

Appraising the costs and benefits of the commodity for the economy of Yucatán, it is clear that the fiber boom enriched a small group of foreign investors, merchants, and local elites. And if a few profited greatly, the great majority of producers (not to mention, the tens of thousands of laborers) found themselves tied to the capricious whims of an unforgiving market.

In 1937, President Lázaro Cárdenas sought to redress this inequity by implementing a controversial land reform throughout Mexico by ordering the breakup of large haciendas and turning the land over to agrarian collectives *(ejidos)*. This recasting of land and labor arrangements, however, could not arrest henequen's inexorable decline on the world market, nor would a state-directed attempt to manufacture binder twine (Cordemex) after World War II.

Select Bibliography

Brannon, Jeffery T., "Corporate Control of a Monocrop Economy: A Comment." *Latin American Research Review* 18 (Fall 1983).

_____, and Eric M. Baklanoff, *Agrarian Reform in Mexico: The Political Economy of Yucatán's Henequen Industry.* Tuscaloosa: University of Alabama Press, 1987.

Carstensen, Fred V., and Diane Roazen-Parrillo, "International Harvester, Molina y Compañía, and the Henequen Market: A Comment." *Latin American Research Review* 18 (Fall 1983).

Gill, Christopher J., "Campesino Patriarchy in the Times of Slavery: The Henequen Plantation Society of Yucatán, 1860—1915." Master's thesis, University of Texas, Austin, 1991.

González Navarro, Moisés, *Raza y tierra: La guerra de castas y el henequén.* 2nd edition, Mexico City: Colegio de México, 1979.

Irigoyen, Renán, *¿Fué el auge del henequén producto de la guerra de castas?* Mérida: Henequeneros de Yucatán, 1947.

Joseph, Gilbert M., *Rediscovering the Past at Mexico's Periphery: Essays on the History of Modern Yucatán.* Tuscaloosa: University of Alabama Press, 1986.

_____, and Allen Wells, "Collaboration and Informal Empire in Yucatán: The Case for Political Economy." *Latin American Research Review* 18 (Fall 1983).

_____, "Corporate Control of a Monocrop Economy: International Harvester and Yucatán's Henequen Industry During the Porfiriato." *Latin American Research Review* 17 (Spring 1982).

Peniche Rivero, Piedad, "Gender, Bridewealth, and Marriage: Social Reproduction on Henequen Haciendas in Yucatán (1870—1901)." In *Women of the Mexican Countryside, 1850—1990: Creating Spaces, Shaping Transitions,* edited by Heather Fowler-Salamini and Mary Kay Vaughan. Tucson: University of Arizona Press, 1994.

Remmers, Lawrence J., "Henequen, the Caste War, and the Economy of Yucatán, 1846—1883: The Roots of Dependence in a Mexican Region." Ph.D. diss., University of California, Los Angeles, 1981.

Suárez Molina, Víctor, *La evolución económica de Yucatán a través del siglo XIX.* 2 vols., Mexico City: Ediciones de la Universidad de Yucatán, 1977.

Wells, Allen, *Yucatán's Gilded Age: Haciendas, Henequen and International Harvester, 1860–1915.* Albuquerque: University of New Mexico Press, 1985.

—ALLEN WELLS

HENRÍQUEZ GUZMÁN, MIGUEL

1898–1972 • General and Politician

Born in Piedras Negras, Coahuila, Miguel Henríquez Guzmán entered the Colegio Militar in 1913 during the presidency of Francisco I. Madero. Before finishing his engineering studies, Henríquez joined the Mexican Revolution in 1914. Under the banner of the Constitutionalists, he fought against the Conventionalists, the Villistas, and the Zapatistas in different areas of the country over the following years.

In 1922 he met Lázaro Cárdenas, then the chief of operations of the Isthmus of Tehuantepec, and began what would be a long friendship. One year later, when Adolfo de la Huerta's rebellion erupted, Henríquez Guzmán took part in the fighting that put down the uprising. After approximately three years in Mexico City, he directed his energies toward combating the Cristero Rebels in the central part of the country. In 1928 he moved to Guerrero in order to direct a countercampaign against banditry ín the state. All of these activities contributed to his receiving the rank of general in 1929.

In July 1935 Cárdenas, now president of Mexico, sent Henríquez to Tabasco as commander of the Twenty-Ninth Military Zone. Henríquez's attempts to neutralize the followers of the populist Tabascan strongman Tomás Garrido Canabal reinforced rumors that he was a tool of Cárdenas.

His job finished in the southeast, Henríquez was given another assignment of pacification, this time in the states of Nayarit and Durango. From there he went to Sonora, and in 1938 he was transferred to Torreón to take charge of the military zone made up of Coahuila and some Durango municipalities. It was here that one of the most important agrarian distributions of the Cárdenas government was carried out.

Shortly thereafter, Henríquez was designated chief of the Twelfth Military Zone in San Luis Potosí. This time, the general's operation removed any remaining doubts concerning his fidelity to and support of President Cárdenas. In May 1938, with federal forces at his command, Henríquez was put in charge of suppressing the armed rebellion attempt headed by Saturnino Cedillo. The military mission did not end until January 11, 1939, when Cedillo died in the confrontation with Cerro Ventanas in the middle of the Potosí range. Some months later, Henríquez was promoted to brigadier general.

During the period of presidential succession, Lázaro Cárdenas once more turned to the loyalty of the Coahuila military. On July 1, 1939, Henríquez was appointed chief of the Seventh Military Zone, which was comprised of Nuevo León and the frontier strip of Tamaulipas. He was a substitute for General Juan Andreu Almazán, who was launching his candidacy for the presidency of the Republic. The appointment was not a coincidence. Henríquez's presence was necessary in order to neutralize the Almazanista force in Nuevo León and above all in order to prevent a possible rebellion of the Nuevo León officer corps in favor of the opposition candidate. The dubious electoral defeat of Almazán provoked violent reactions in some zones, among them Monterrey. It was here, just days after the election, that General Manuel Zarzoza, Almazán's right-hand man , died in an encounter with government forces under Henríquez Guzmán.

On January 1, 1942, Cárdenas's successor, General Manuel Avila Camacho, appointed Henríquez chief of the Fifteenth Military Zone, with headquarters in Guadalajara. Henríquez's collaboration with former president Cárdenas was maintained during those years; World War II led Cárdenas to take command of the Military Region of the Pacific and later to be in charge of the Ministry of Defense.

On January 1, 1944, Henríquez Guzmán began to be considered seriously as a presidential candidate for the ruling

Partido de la Revolución Mexicana (PRM, or Party of the Mexican Revolution). Supporting him were groups within the military, as well as various Cardenista politicians and officials. Nevertheless, he decided in June 1945 formally to withdrawal his bid for the candidacy upon consideration that President Avila Camacho and the leadership of the party were supporting Miguel Alemán Valdés, an official of the Department of the Interior.

Five years later, in 1950, Henríquez Guzmán returned to the race for the presidency, this time to replace President Alemán. Henríquez's initial strategy consisted of politically pressuring the ruling party, now called the Partido Revolucionario Institucional (PRI, or Institutional Revolutionary Party), to obtain their candidacy, while at the same time working openly for the Henríquez Guzmán ticket. This strategy led to a direct confrontation with the PRI leadership, which tried to control and immobilize the political groups formed around the candidates. The confrontation resulted in the expulsion of Henríquez Guzmán and his followers from the rank and file of the PRI.

However, Henríquez Guzmán decided to continue in the presidential battle as the opposition candidate. In 1951, his supporters reorganized the Federación de Partidos del Pueblo Mexicano (Federation of Parties of the Mexican People), which was originally founded in 1945. On July 29, 1951, the reorganized party formally sought the candidacy of the general. Unlike in 1945, Henríquez Guzmán's presidential candidacy this time managed to articulate a strong opposition movement known as Henriquismo.

The general's supporters proposed the recuperation of the principles of the Mexican Revolution as their major party platform. They assumed the role of legitimate heirs of the armed movement of 1910, thereby revindicating their revolutionary function. They insisted upon criticizing the "traitors of revolutionary principles" and questioned the revolutionary credentials of the Alemán platform throughout the electoral campaign of 1951–52.

The electoral victory of the PRI candidate, Adolfo Ruiz Cortines, definitively marked the exclusion of General Henríquez Guzmán from the political scene. He subsequently dedicated himself to private activities. He died on August 29, 1972, in Mexico City.

Select Bibliography

Correa, Francisco Estrada, *Henriquismo: El arranque del cambio.* Mexico City: Costa-Amic, 1988.

Farell, Arsenio, *Miguel Henríquez Guzmán: Esbozobiográfico.* Mexico City: Botas, 1950.

Martínez Assad, Carlos, *El Henriquismo: Una Piedra en el Camino.* Mexico City: Martín Casillas, 1982.

—ELISA SERVÍN

HERNÁNDEZ, LUISA JOSEFINA

1928– • Writer and Educator

Luisa Josefina Hernández has written prolifically for more than 40 years. Her first play, *Aguardiente de caña* (1950), received a prize in the Concurso de la Primavera de Bellas Artes (1951) in Mexico City. Almost all the professional directors of the 1950s and 1960s directed her plays: Celestino Gorostiza, Fernando Wagner, Xavier Rojas, and later, other experimental directors such as Héctor Mendoza and Luis de Tavira. She has written approximately 40 plays and a significant number of novels, for example *El lugar donde crece la hierba* (1959), *La cólera secreta* (1964), *La primera batalla* (1965), and *El valle que elegimos* (1965). Her other works include an introduction to Shakespeare's *King Lear* (1966), a discussion of the works of *Francisco de Goya* (1979), and translations of Shakespeare, Arthur Miller, Dylan Thomas, Bertold Brecht, Jersy Kawalerowicz, and Tadeus Konwistky. As a playwright, she belongs to the same university generation as Sergio Magaña, Emilio Carballido, and Jorge Ibargüengoitia, which recognized Rodolfo Usigli as their mentor.

Hernández started writing plays for students of high schools and junior high schools with the purpose of educating them in the history of Mexico. The *Fiesta del mulato* (1971; The Mulatto's Feast) is about social oppression in Mexico shortly before the War of Independence in 1810. The workers in this play are deprived of the gold they have mined. A part-owner of the mine attempts to distribute the gold to the miners and to the poor, without realizing that there are absentee landlords in Mexico City. As a consequence, he finds himself in severe legal difficulties. The play criticizes a particular kind of social structure, but Hernández is not a programmatic reformer. When gold is found, joy sets in, and there is a fantastic festival. Suddenly, everyone has access to whatever he or she needs. In this play Hernández is writing about the ultimate removal of oppressive social structures and the possibility of a world in which all will have a *fiesta*, a festival of joy. Another representative work by Hernández is *Plaza de Puerto Santo* (1961), a clever satire on provincial society. The novel, which also was produced as a play called

Escándalo en Puerto Santo (Scandal in Puerto Santo), takes place in a small town in which, after dinner, the women retire to the kitchen to wash the dishes and the men go off for a stroll; but it turns out that their strolls have just been a pretext for window peeping. Hernández enjoys deflating the male characters in this tale and exposing the oppression of the women, while also objecting to the kind of social, political, and economic functioning that reduces people to such a level.

Many of her works have analyzed her contemporary culture, such as *El orden de los factores* (1982). The play criticizes the confused Mexican middle class, which finally was beginning to shed its sexual myths and extreme insincerity but proved unable to free itself completely from such views. The play explores this consciousness of transition, especially through the young people who try to avoid problems with violence, drugs, and suicide. *La cadena* (1983) treats the corruption that exists at every level of Mexican political and social structures and often appears as an urge that forces Mexicans to take anything that does not belong to them. In other works by Hernández, such as *Los Trovadores* (1973), *Apostasía* (1978), and *Apocalípsis cum figuris* (1982), one can discern a remarkable withdrawal from the Mexican landscape and its sociopolitical context.

Hernández is a contradictory figure who has refused to be categorized. She has been asked on several occasions whether she considers herself a feminist writer, and her answer always has been no, that she considers herself a human writer, one who writes about problems that concern all human beings. Thus, she has regarded the problems of being a woman in a much broader context. For her, women are repressed in Mexican society, but so is practically everyone else. The bulk of the population exists on the fringes of the "modern" world. It is from this perspective that Hernández is interested in the problems of women.

—GASTÓN A. ALZATE

HIDALGO REVOLT

The insurrection that Miguel Hidalgo y Costilla sparked on September 16, 1810, marks the beginning of the armed struggle for Mexican Independence. The origins of the Hidalgo Revolt can be found as much in Napoléon Bonaparte's invasion of the Iberian Peninsula as in events in the viceroyalty of New Spain. Nonetheless, one also must look for origins in the long-term processes that began in the mid–eighteenth century.

In the latter half of the eighteenth century, a series of laws were enacted that since have come to be known as the Bourbon Reforms. Although these reforms were designed to improve Spain's administration of its overseas empire, by and large they had a negative impact on New Spain. The criollos (Mexicans of Spanish descent)—or "Americans," as they now preferred to be called—felt that they had been displaced from positions of power and prestige by European Spaniards, or *peninsulares*. Moreover, the local offices of *alcalde mayor* and *corregidor* were replaced with directly appointed intendants more accountable to the viceroy and Spanish Crown but less accountable to the local criollo population. Nonetheless, criollo dissidents tended to support local or regional autonomy, not outright independence. Although many had been exposed to Enlightenment ideals of liberty and republican government, they did not question the system of government imposed in New Spain, only the amount of control the Spanish Crown exercised over it.

If many criollos were alienated by the administrative reforms of the late eighteenth century, *peninsulares* were angered by the Consolidación de Bienes Reales of December 26, 1804. An attempt by the Spanish Crown to use colonial revenues to underwrite its political and military adventures in Europe, the Consolidación ordered the sequestration of charitable funds in America and their remission to Spain. As the charitable funds were the basis of an informal system of credit in New Spain, the Consolidación had a severe effect not only on the charitable institutions themselves, but also on the entire financial infrastructure of the viceroyalty. The Consolidación also was seen as an attack on the income of the Catholic Church, and many lower-level clergy were impoverished. Protests from all sectors fell on deaf ears, reinforcing autonomist sentiments.

If the Consolidación created some degree of consensus among the peninsular and criollo elites of New Spain, however, this consensus evaporated with the French invasion of the Iberian Peninsula and the resignation of Fernando VII. In the absence of a legitimate monarch, the *ayuntamiento* (city council) of Mexico City became a mouthpiece for the criollos, promoting autonomist interests and declaring the equality of Spain and its American colonies before the law. In the name of all of New Spain, it proposed a meeting of a "junta of authorities" from Mexico's cities and towns, which would fill the vacuum left by the king's departure and defend the kingdom against the French. As the city council's proposals for all practical intents and purposes would create a legitimate, representative, and autonomist government, the *audiencia* (judicial council) of Mexico opposed the *ayuntamiento*'s proposals, becoming the mouthpiece for those interests (primarily peninsular) that felt threatened by any change from the status quo.

The viceroy of New Spain, José de Iturrigaray, sympathized with the *ayuntamiento*'s proposals, convoking a number of meetings to discuss them. Nonetheless, he was unable to patch together any sort of consensus, and the divisions among New Spain's elites continued to widen. These conflicts reached their climax in a coup d'état orchestrated by the peninsular merchant Gabriel de Yermo on September 15, 1808, with the approval of Spanish authorities. The coup and subsequent imprisonment of the viceroy and principal criollo leaders not only created serious doubts about regimes that followed, but also radicalized both the criollo and peninsular factions; indeed, following the coup the terms "peninsular" and "criollo" or "American" took on an additional political connotation: for or against the colonial regime. Moreover, the coup convinced dissident and autonomist criollos of the necessity of conspiracy—and later of armed force—to achieve their political ends.

In December 1809 Spanish authorities uncovered an autonomist conspiracy in the important urban center of Valladolid de Michoacán (present-day Morelia), in which various members of the militia and the clergy had taken part. The conspirators, who had sent envoys to other cities, proposed a junta or congress composed of delegates of the principal cities of New Spain, which would govern in the name of Fernando VII. In order to bring the junta to power they called for an uprising by key parts of the army and militia as well as by a number of Indian governor and their subjects. Various members of the conspiracy went over to the authorities, and its principal leaders were imprisoned, although they were treated leniently by the current viceroy, the archbishop Francisco Xavier de Lizana y Beaumont.

A second conspiracy grew out of the first, the so-called Conspiracy of Querétaro, which also included officers in the militia and clergy. The conspiracy met under the cover of an Academy of Literature, which was permitted to hold meetings and conferences, and with the support of the *corregidor* of the city of Querétaro, Miguel Domínguez, and his wife, Josefa Ortiz de Domínguez, *"la corregidora."* The conspiracy was able to form cells in various other cities, including Celaya, San Miguel el Grande, and Guanajuato. One of the most active conspirators, Ignacio de Allende, was captain of the Queen's Regiment in San Miguel and had been in contact with the conspirators in Valladolid. As a military man, Allende had formed part of the canton of troops established in Jalapa years before by the deposed viceroy Iturrigaray, and like many of his companions he admired Iturrigaray and was disgusted by the people who had overthrown him. The priest of the nearby village of Dolores, Miguel Hidalgo y Costilla, joined the conspiracy at the behest of Allende and became one of its principal leaders.

When the conspiracy was discovered in September 1810, it still did not have a defined plan. One of the conspirators, Manuel Iturriaga, had proposed to organized revolu-

tionary juntas in the principal cities of New Spain to propagate hatred of the *peninsulares*. The juntas would call for Independence in order to prevent New Spain from falling into the hands of the French and imprison the authorities. The *peninsulares* would be arrested and expelled from New Spain, and their goods would finance the Independence movement. The government would remain in the hands of a junta of representatives of the provinces and would govern in the name of Fernando VII.

When Epigmenio González, one of the conspirators, was arrested, a second plan was discovered. This plan called for the establishment of an empire with feudal kingdoms and elector princes. The lands of the criollos would be rented to the Indians, and the haciendas of the *peninsulares* would be seized and granted to the Indians outright. This plan called for a general insurrection not simply of the criollo militias, but of all the people of New Spain. Various conspirators reported this plan to the authorities, forcing Corregidor Miguel Domínguez to crack down. Nonetheless, his wife was able to pass word to Allende, who was able to alert Hidalgo.

On the morning of Sunday, September 16, Hidalgo issued his famous call to arms against the Spanish colonial regime, the so-called Grito de Dolores. He called the villagers of Dolores to mass and informed them of his decision to launch an insurrection to prevent the *peninsulares* from turning New Spain over to the French; the Spanish authorities and peninsular population of Dolores was thrown in prison. Hidalgo's forces included elements from the Queen's Regiment, prisoners who had been liberated from the town jail, and many inhabitants of the region around Dolores. Although the rhetoric of the leaders of the movement was basically the same as that of other criollo autonomists, Hidalgo's movement also sought to unite peasants and workers around such basic issues as land tenure and working conditions, and it sought redress for grievances dating back to the Conquest.

The insurgent movement found broad support among the inhabitants of the prosperous Bajío region of north-central Mexico, a densely populated region where the traditional separation of Indians and Spanish had begun to break down. In the early stage of Hidalgo's revolt the bulk of his troops were composed, on the one hand, of hacienda workers, who formed a cavalry unit under the direction of their foremen; on the other hand were Indians who grouped themselves into an improvised infantry with their bows and arrows, lances, and spears. Relatively few soldiers from the militia accompanied Hidalgo's insurgent army. The army was followed by a large number of women and children with very few arms and little discipline.

After sacking a few stores in Dolores, the insurgents made their way to Atotonilco, where they adopted for their flag the image of the Virgin of Guadalupe, the Indian virgin so deeply venerated by criollos. They entered San Miguel el Grande and Celaya without resistance, and there they were able to find additional support for their forces. In Celaya some degree of organization was imposed on the inchoate insurgent army, and Hidalgo was named "General of America;" Allende also was named general.

On September 28 the insurgents won their first victory over Spanish forces in Guanajuato, the center of silver production in New Spain and the richest city in the viceroyalty. Guanajuato was attacked by nearly 50,000 insurgents and taken after a prolonged and bloody battle. Commanded by the intendant Juan Antonio Riaño, the meager Spanish forces and the *peninsulares* who remained in Guanajuato took refuge with their families in the Granaditas granary, leaving the city at the mercy of the attackers. The local population felt abandoned by the local authorities; taking the side of the insurgents, they helped them sack the granary and massacre of its defenders. The insurgents and the local population then proceeded to sack the city.

The violence of the insurgent forces in the sack of Guanajuato provoked the Spanish regime and its partisans to conduct a war without quarter. Viceroy Francisco Xavier de Venegas, who had arrived from Spain only a few days before the insurrection erupted, took personal charge of counterinsurgency operations. Venegas was a skilled military commander, having participated in the Peninsular Wars against the French, but he also was a skilled politician, winning the support of the high clergy. The bishop elect of Michoacán, Manuel Abad y Queipo, excommunicated Hidalgo and his companions for sacrilege and disturbing the peace, and he prohibited under pain of excommunication that anyone help them; Abad y Queipo's decree later was ratified by the archbishop of Mexico, Francisco Xavier de Lizana y Beaumont. Throughout Mexico priests who were sympathetic to the colonial regime denounced Hidalgo's movement from the pulpit. The press of New Spain, which was completely under the control of colonial authorities, published a veritable flood of material attacking the insurrection. Venegas offered 10,000 pesos for the heads of the principal revolutionary leaders, and throughout the viceroyalty colonial authorities condemned the revolt and threatened the rebels and their supporters with the most severe punishments.

After the taking of Guanajuato the war radicalized. Not only did Europeans abandon towns threatened by the insurrection, but many autonomist criollos allied themselves with the colonial regime, as the insurgents did not always clearly distinguish between criollos and *peninsulares*. If the insurgents had lost much of their elite support, however, they also had gained important resources: men, matériel, and funds. Concerned about the violence their movement had unleashed, the insurgent leaders organized a government in Guanajuato. They also established a mint and a forge for cannon, and they managed to organize their numerous and undisciplined troops.

From Guanajuato the insurgents proceeded to Valladolid, reorganizing the government of the intendancy of Michoacán. Determined to take the capital of the viceroyalty, they proceeded first to Acámbaro, where Hidalgo, in addition to being designated commander-in-chief, named a minister of police and "good order," José María Chico. On the Monte de las Cruces, near the city of Mexico, the insurgents defeated royalist troops under Torcuato Trujillo, but at a very high cost. The rebels remained camped outside Mexico City for three days, demanding that Venegas surrender. They received no answer, however, and over Allende's protests, Hidalgo decided to withdraw to Querétaro without attacking Mexico City.

Hidalgo's decision to fall back was based on a number of factors: lack of munitions, meager support in the central part of the country, and fear of the royalist troops under Félix María Calleja del Rey and Manuel de Flon, which were already close on the insurgents' heels. On November 7 the insurgents suffered a major defeat with great loss of men and matériel. Hidalgo retreated to Valladolid, while Allende returned to Guanajuato to organize its defense.

Meanwhile the conflict had spread to other parts of the viceroyalty, carried both by Hidalgo's own envoys and local leaders, particularly members of the lower clergy. Friar Luis de Herrera launched a rebellion in San Luis Potosí, while José Antonio "El Amo" Torres took Guadalajara. Torres linked up with José María Mercado, who organized the revolutionary movement in Nayarit, taking Tepic and San Blas. Ignacio Jiménez occupied Saltillo, and Texas remained in the hands of Juan Bautista Casas. José María Morelos, who had spoken with Hidalgo in Charo and Indaparapeo, ably fulfilled his commission to launch a rebellion in the southern part of the viceroyalty and take Acapulco.

Nonetheless, the royalists began to recover the cities and towns that had been taken by the insurgents. Guanajuato fell on November 25. Hidalgo retreated to Guadalajara, where the insurgent movement had become quite strong, and united with Allende, attempting to reorganize his movement politically and militarily. Chico was named minister of "mercy and justice" and president of the *audiencia*. Ignacio López Rayón, who had been his personal secretary, was named secretary of state, and Hidalgo's brother Mariano was named treasurer. Hoping to obtain recognition and aid from the United States, Hidalgo named Pascasio Ortíz ambassador to the United States. Hidalgo also addressed many of the land and labor issues foremost on the minds of his followers, abolishing slavery and community chests (which had required ever-increasing contributions from the inhabitants of communal villages), and established that communal lands were inalienable and for the exclusive use of indigenous villagers. Hidalgo's movement also gained use of a printing press, which they used to publish proclamations and a few editions of the first insurgent newspaper in Mexico, *El despertador americano*. Finally, Hidalgo attempted to impose some degree of order and discipline on the recruits he had been able to add to his force in Guadalajara.

Hidalgo was unable to consolidate his movement, however. He continued to clash with Allende and ordered the indiscriminate massacre of numerous Europeans, in most cases without any justification whatsoever. The insurgent movement was defeated decisively at Puente de Calderón on January 17, 1811. The insurgent troops, by that time numbering more than 100,000, left Guadalajara to meet the well organized, disciplined, and supplied troops of Brigadier José de la Cruz, who had just taken Valladolid. In a bloody battle the insurgents suffered enormous losses, and the leaders of the movement fled to the north, heading first to Aguascalientes and later to Zacatecas. At the Hacienda del Pabellón, Allende replaced Hidalgo as commander-in-chief, and in a meeting in Saltillo it was decided that the principal leaders of the insurgent movement should go to the United States to seek help, leaving Ignacio Rayón as the head of the movement in New Spain. On March 21, 1811, Hidalgo, Allende, and their companions were captured in Acatita de Baján by a former insurgent leader, Ignacio Elizondo. They were taken to Monclava and then to Chihuahua, where they were tried and condemned to death. Allende, Aldama, and Jiménez were shot on July 26, and Hidalgo was defrocked on July 29 and executed the following day. Their heads were placed on the four corners of the granary of Granaditas.

The death of the first insurgent leaders marked the end of the first stage of the Wars of Independence. The armed struggle against the colonial regime would be conducted in a more systematic and organized fashion by Rayón and Morelos. The insurgent cause also would be pursued, in many cases without the least order or coordination, by innumerable smaller groups who often only were seeking redress for local grievances. The movement begun by Hidalgo never did achieve independence, and even once Independence was achieved Hidalgo's specific proposals were not accepted. Nonetheless, the Hidalgo Revolt helped make eventual Independence a certainty.

Select Bibliography

Alamán, Lucas, *Historia de México desde los primeros movimientos que prepararon su independencia en el año de 1808 hasta la época presente.* Mexico City: Jus, 1990.

Anna, Timothy, "The Independence of Mexico and Central America." In *The Independence of Latin America,* edited by Leslie Bethell. Cambridge and New York: Cambridge University Press, 1987.

Farriss, Nancy M., *Crown and Clergy in Colonial Mexico, 1759–1821: The Crisis of Ecclesiastical Privelege.* London: Athlone, 1968.

Flores Caballero, Romeo, *Counter-revolution: The Role of the Spaniards in the Independence of Mexico, 1804–38,* tranlated by Jaime E. Rodríguez O. Lincoln and London: University of Nebraska Press, 1974.

Hamill, Hugh M., Jr., *The Hidalgo Revolt: Prelude to Mexican Independence.* Westport, Connecticut: Greenwood, 1981.

Hamnett, Brian R., *Roots of Insurgency: Mexican Regions, 1750–1824.* New York and Cambridge: Cambridge University Press, 1986.

Lynch, John, *The Spanish American Revolutions, 1808–1826.* 2nd edition, New York and London: Norton, 1986

—Virginia Guedea

HIDALGO Y COSTILLA, MIGUEL

1753–1811 • Priest and Leader of the Independence Movement

Miguel Hidalgo y Costilla, the "father of his country," was descended from an old criollo family. He was born on May 8, 1753, in the hacienda of Corralejo in the jurisdiction of Pénjamo, Guanajuato, where his father worked as an administrator. He was the second of five children from the marriage of Cristóbal Hidalgo y Costilla and Ana María Gallaga Mandarte y Villaseñor. Intelligent and interested in learning, for which he could count on the support of his father, for many years Hidalgo was able to enjoy the possibility of satisfying his intellectual curiosity and the advantages of a high level of education. Together with his older brother José Joaquín, he studied Latin grammar and rhetoric in the Jesuit College of San Francisco Xavier of Valladolid, Michoacán (today the city of Morelia).

In 1767, the year the Jesuits were expelled from Spanish dominions, he moved to the College of San Nicolás Obispo in the same city, one of the most important educational centers of the viceroyalty, distinguishing himself in courses on philosophy, theology, and the liberal arts. In 1770 he gained his baccalaureate in arts and three years later a baccalaureate in theology from the Real y Pontifica Universidad de México, the most important institution of higher education in New Spain. He decided on a career in the church, receiving four minor orders in 1774; the following year he was made a subdeacon. In 1776 he was ordained as deacon and as priest in 1778.

Hidalgo taught philosophy, theology, Latin grammar, and arts in the College of San Nicolás, where he was nicknamed "the Fox" by both fellow teachers and pupils. Interested in education, he was concerned with revising teaching methods. In 1785 in his capacity as professor in scholastic theology, he won a competition organized by the dean of Valladolid Cathedral in which he showed evidence of his reformist enthusiasm. He was appointed treasurer of the College of San Nicolás Obispo in 1787, its secretary a year later, and rector in 1790. By this time he was also owner of three haciendas: Santa Rosa, San Nicolás, and Jaripeo. In 1792 the ecclesiastical authorities decided to banish him from Valladolid because of the enmity he had stirred up in the college, particularly on account of his keenness for innovative teaching practices, but also for his irregular handling of some funds, his passion for gambling, and the fact that he had two children, Agustina and Lino Mariano, with Manuela Ramos Pichardo. In 1789 another child of his, Joaquín, was born to Bibiana Lucero.

Hidalgo thus abandoned his studious way of life to take up a career as a minister of the church. His new activities allowed him to both practice and develop his sense of social justice while continuing to cultivate his intellectual interests and social activities. The bishop first sent him to serve as interim curate in Colima, where he bought a house that on his departure for San Felipe de los Herreros, or Torres Mochas, in 1793 he gifted to the city hall in order to establish a public school. Apart from attending to his new parish, Hidalgo organized some social and cultural events, including literary and gambling evenings in his house and, the result of his interest in music, dances. He translated and interpreted, among other works, Molière's *Tartuffe*. During this time Hidalgo was reading historical and theological works as well as volumes on political economy and literature; by this time his library was large and well stocked. As a result of these cultural and social activities and his enlightened attitudes, but most of all because of his way of treating everyone as his equal, Hidalgo's house became known as "Little France." By this stage he had two daughters, Micaela and Josefa, with Josefa Quintana, who acted in the theatrical works that Hidalgo directed. The royal directive on consolidation of royal promissory notes, which seriously affected the credit system in New Spain, proved problematic for Hidalgo, who already owed money on his haciendas.

In 1807 he was denounced for the first time by the Tribunal of the Inquisition for speaking against Catholic orthodoxy and the monarchical government, but no proceedings were taken against him. A year later similar charges were made against him by Manuela Herrera, a one-time lover, and in 1809 Father Diego Miguel Bringas denounced him for possessing prohibited books, but nothing came of these indictments either. In 1803 Hidalgo took over the curacy of Dolores Hidalgo on the death of his eldest brother, Joaquín, the former incumbent. There he concerned himself more with promoting agriculture and industry than the spiritual administration of his congregation. This task was relegated to the priest Francisco Iglesias. Hidalgo encouraged viticulture (which was controlled and indeed prohibited by the authorities to protect the wine trade of Spain), the cultivation of silkworms, and apiculture. He also established a ceramics factory, another for brick making, and various workshops as well as tanks to cure skins. His progressive and innovative approach, his sense of social justice, and his openhandedness with money won him the favor of a large number of his congregation. Keen on music, he started a small orchestra. The curate also held salons at home, where themes of cultural and political interest were discussed. An avid reader, Hidalgo knew Latin, Italian, French, and several indigenous languages. A man of the Enlightenment, as were many of his colleagues, he was a friend of some of the outstanding individuals of his time who shared his enlightened attitudes: men such as the bishop-elect of Michoacán, Manuel Abad y Queipo; Doctor Antonio Labarrieta; José Antonio Rojas; and the intendant of Guanajuato, Juan Antonio Riaño. He also knew the French general Octaviano D'Almivar, sent by Napoléon Bonaparte and imprisoned by the Spanish authorities in Nacogdoches, who passed through Dolores en route for Mexico City.

After a conspiracy was uncovered in December 1809 in Valladolid that attempted to establish a governing junta in New Spain in the name of Fernando VII by force of arms, some of the conspirators moved to Querétaro. There they held meetings under the cover of a literary academy, relying on the support of the *corregidor* (mayor by royal appointment) of the city, Miguel Domínguez, and his wife Josefa Ortíz de Domínguez. Although their plans never were defined clearly, the conspirators had projected a popular uprising in various areas for the purpose of arresting peninsular Spaniards (those born in Europe), whose property would help them to finance the movement. They also discussed the formation of a governing junta to rule in the name of Fernando VII. Hidalgo joined the plot through his friendship with Ignacio Allende, a captain in the regiment of Dragoons of New Spain. As well as attending some of the reunions of the conspirators in Querétaro and San Miguel el Grande, Hidalgo started to find others of the same persuasion and manufacture lances in Dolores and the hacienda of Santa Barbara. This plot also was denounced to the colonial authorities, and Corregidor Domínguez was obliged to imprison various of the conspirators. Warned by Josefa Ortiz, Allende went to Dolores to discuss with Hidalgo what decision to take.

When Juan de Aldama arrived at dawn on September 16, 1810, Hidalgo decided to enter the armed struggle against the colonial authorities. He freed the prisoners, armed them, and secured the support of part of the regiment quartered in Dolores. In his celebration of the mass held later that day, he incited those attending to join his uprising against the colonial regime. The *grito* or "shout" (the word for a call to arms) given by Hidalgo included *vivas* for America and death to bad government. He then imprisoned the subdelegate and the *peninsulares* of the town, and the insurgents sacked some European shops.

In his appeal to and securing of the support of the masses, Hidalgo brought together two very different movements that were largely contradictory. On one side were the urban criollos (those of Spanish descent born in the Americas), who sought greater participation in decision making; on the other side were the *campesino* (peasant) groups and workers, who sought to improve their work conditions. In Atonilco, Hidalgo took an image of the Virgin of Guadalupe, the most venerated in colonial Mexico, and converted it into the flag of the revolt.

Even though he was joined by some troops, such as the regiment in San Miguel el Grande, Hidalgo's forces were badly armed and even less disciplined. On September

19, having entered Celaya without resistance, Hidalgo was named General of America and Allende Lieutenant General. The insurgents went on to attack and capture the wealthy city of Guanajuato on September 28 after the bloody combat of the Alhondiga de Granaditas, the city granary where the Intendant Riaño and the *peninsulares* had taken refuge. Hidalgo managed to stop the sacking of Guanajuato and the murder of Europeans, and he organized the government of the city, appointing various authorities. He also established a mint and a cannon foundry and attempted to marshal his disorganized troops. The violence of the capture of Guanajuato provoked the colonial government to organize a equally violent counterinsurgency. Thus a war without quarter was declared, in which not only weapons of war but also sermons and the press played important roles. This brutality also prevented many who supported Independence or were discontented with the regime from backing the insurgents, fearful of the disorder and violence that accompanied the movement.

The bishop-elect of Michoacán excommunicated Hidalgo and his followers, an edict that was ratified by the archbishop of Mexico City, Francisco Xavier de Lizana y Beaumont. The Tribunal of the Inquisition reopened the case against Hidalgo, and the Council of the University asked (without success, since Hidalgo had not taken his doctorate) for his name to be removed from the list of those so honored. Viceroy Francisco Xavier Venegas offered a handsome bounty for the head of each of the leading insurgents. A number of aggressive propaganda pieces were written against the movement.

Hidalgo himself decided to move from Guanajuato to Valladolid. En route men continued to flock to his army, including some corps of militia. As they drew close to their objective, the Europeans left the city, and Valladolid was handed over to Hidalgo's army without a fight. Hidalgo took advantage of his stay in the city to regroup his troops, which were increased by some colonial troops, and organize the political control of the Intendency of Michoacán. He also responded to the edict of the Inquisition with his own manifesto. Hidalgo marched on to Mexico City. In Acámbaro he was nominated commander in chief. Here he appointed José María Chico as minister of police and public order. On the march through Michoacán two individuals joined the movement who would be key to the revolt in its second stage: Ignacio López Rayón, who would shortly become Hidalgo's personal secretary, joined in Maravatío; the curate José María Morelos y Pavón, interviewed by Hidalgo in Charo and Indaparapeo, was put in charge of inciting the south to take up arms and capturing the port of Acapulco.

On October 30 at the Monte de las Cruces, on the road between Toluca and Mexico City, the insurgents confronted the royalist militia led by Torquato Trujillo. The latter were defeated but at a great loss of life. From Cuajimalpa, in sight of the capital, Hidalgo demanded the surrender of Viceroy Venegas, but received no response. He could not decide whether or not to march on Mexico City despite the favorable response of Allende. They lacked munitions, had

little support in the region, and the royalist forces of Brigadier Félix María Calleja del Rey and the intendant of Puebla, Manuel de Flon, Conde de la Cadena, were drawing closer. The insurgents fell back to Querétaro and began to desert. They met up with Calleja's army in San Jerónimo Aculco and were soundly defeated on November 7, losing a large number of troops on the battlefield and through the taking of prisoners and desertion; equipment and military supplies also were lost. Allende marched to Guanajuato to put the city on defense alert, and Hidalgo went to Valladolid.

Despite these setbacks, the revolt began to gather more adherents and take hold in various areas of the New Spain, largely owing to the forces deployed by various of Hidalgo's agents, such as in New Galicia. As a result, he decided to move on to Guadalajara, which had been taken by José Antonio "The Master" Torres, where he was received with every honor. Here the disagreements that had for various reasons emerged between the two leaders of the movement became clear. Allende wanted Hidalgo to defend Guanajuato; the city was subsequently lost on November 25. He also showed his disgust at the maladministration and disorder, the lack of precision in formulating the objectives of the movement, and the lack of discipline among the troops.

Hidalgo tried to establish a government in Guadalajara and nominated two ministers, Rayón as secretary of state and Chico as minister of justice and president of the Audiencia. He also appointed various other functionaries, including his brother Mariano as treasurer and Pascasio Ortiz de Letona as ambassador to the United States to secure the support and recognition of that country. On the other hand, he dictated important decrees, such as the abolition of slavery, tribute, and state monopolies, and he established the communal lands of the Indians as being for their own exclusive use.

In control of a printing press, Hidalgo published various documents, including proclamations and edicts and the manifesto against the Inquisition that he had written in Valladolid. He was acting as representative of the nation that had elected him to defend its rights. He founded the newspaper *El Despertador Americano,* which published several issues at the same time that he was also marshaling and organizing troops. Nevertheless, he committed various excesses such as surrounding himself with a guard of honor and giving himself the titles of Excellency and Serene Highness. He also ordered the indiscriminate killing of numerous European prisoners. When Calleja drew close to Guadalajara, the insurgent forces, by this time numbering some 100,000 men led by Hidalgo and Allende, marched out of the city to do battle only to be defeated at the Calderón Bridge after a bloody contest on January 17, 1811.

This action marked the beginning of the end of the movement. The rebel army disbanded, and Hidalgo was obliged to retire. He traveled to Aguascalientes toward Zacatecas, and in the hacienda of Pabellón he was divested of his post of commander in chief. In a meeting held in El Saltillo, it was agreed that the main leaders would travel to the United States to seek help while Rayón stayed at the head of the movement in New Spain. Hidalgo, Allende, and his companions were taken prisoner on March 21, in Acatita de Baján by an ex-insurgent, Ignacio Elizondo. Hidalgo was taken to Monclova and from there to Chihuahua, where he instructed the administrator of the post office in Zacatecas, Angel Abella, to plead his case. The legal process was carried out by the military and the church, and Hidalgo was condemned to be executed by a firing squad. During this time Hidalgo showed evidence of repentance for some of his acts and dictated a manifesto in which he condemned the excesses of the movement. This document was later published by the colonial authorities. Defrocked on July 29, he was shot the following day. His head and those of Ignacio Allende, Juan Aldama, and José Mariano Jiménez were set up on the four corners of the Alhondiga de Granaditas.

Select Bibliography

Alamán, Lucas, *Historia de México desde los primeros movimientos que prepararon su independencia en el año de 1808 hasta la época presente.* Mexico City: Jus, 1990.

Anna, Timothy, "The Independence of Mexico and Central America." In *The Independence of Latin America,* edited by Leslie Bethell. Cambridge and New York: Cambridge University Press, 1987.

Farriss, Nancy M., *Crown and Clergy in Colonial Mexico, 1759–1821: The Crisis of Ecclesiastical Privelege.* London: Athlone, 1968.

Flores Caballero, Romeo, *Counter-revolution: The Role of the Spaniards in the Independence of Mexico, 1804–38,* tranlated by Jaime E. Rodríguez O. Lincoln and London: University of Nebraska Press, 1974.

Hamill, Hugh M., Jr., *The Hidalgo Revolt: Prelude to Mexican Independence.* Westport, Connecticut: Greenwood, 1981.

Hamnett, Brian R., *Roots of Insurgency: Mexican Regions, 1750–1824.* New York and Cambridge: Cambridge University Press, 1986.

Lynch, John, *The Spanish American Revolutions, 1808–1826.* 2nd edition, New York and London: Norton, 1986

—Virginia Guedea

HILL, BENJAMÍN GUILLERMO

1874–1920 • General and Politician

Benjamin Hill was born in the municipality of Choix in the state of Sinaloa, but both his later military and political career and his family tied him to Sonora. His grandfather, William Hill, was a doctor who fought with the Confederate Army in the U.S. Civil War. After the defeat of Southern forces, he emigrated to Álamos, Sonora, where he married doña Jesús Salido, whose sister Cenobia would later give birth to the future president of Mexico, Álvaro Obregón. Benjamin was the only son of William and Jesús's third child. Although he attended elementary school in Culiacán, Sinaloa, he later was sent to secondary school in Hermosillo, Sonora.

Benjamin's family was well enough off to send him to Europe, some say to study in a military academy, others to study singing. He traveled to Milan and Rome, where he fell in love with a countess. When her family would not allow them to marry they eloped. They settled in southern Sonora, where she died in childbirth. Hill later married the daughter of a local farmer.

Hill was active in the opposition to the dictatorship of Porfirio Díaz and to the Catholic Church, and he might have joined a Masonic lodge. Elected alderman in the town of Navojoa, he was active in the Partido Antireeleccionista (Antireelectionist Party) of Francisco I. Madero. Hill accompanied Madero during much of his presidential campaign, and he later was jailed from late 1910 until April 1911 at the orders of governor Luis Torres. As soon as he was released Hill took up arms, taking Navojoa and heading toward Álamos. Before he could reach Álamos, however, federal forces surrendered to Revolutionary forces at Ciudad Juárez.

In 1912 Hill was one of many Sonorans who volunteered to combat the counterrevolutionary forces of Pascual Orozco. He later was named prefect of Arizpe and Hermosillo. He refused to recognize Victoriano Huerta, who had overthrown Madero in a military coup, and he organized an uprising in southern Sonora. He occupied Álamos and headed toward Navojoa, linking up with the troops of Álvaro Obregón in the Yaqui region. Hill's military successes brought him a promotion to the rank of brigadier general in the division of the northeast. Following the triumph of constitutionalist forces and the split in the Revolutionary movement, Hill sided with Venustiano Carranza. Named provisional governor of Sonora, Hill promulgated such revolutionary laws as the suppression of political prefectures and the establishment of "free municipalities," which could elect their own officials rather than having them appointed by the state government. He also resisted a three-month siege in the city of Naco by the Villista forces of José María Maytorena. He later joined Obregón and took part in the defeat of Villa's army at Celaya. When Obregón was seriously wounded at Celaya, Hill took command of the Constitutionalist forces, inflicting a final defeat against the Villista forces at the Battle of Trinidad. Following the battle of Trinidad, Hill was named one of the ten division generals in the constitutionalist army.

From 1916 to 1917 Hill commanded the garrison in the plaza of Mexico, the highest military authority in Mexico City. A conflict with the press led him to arrest Félix F. Palavicini, the director of the prominent newspaper *El Universal.* During this period he helped found and was one of the main figures in the Partido Liberal Constitucionalista (PLC, or Constitutionalist Liberal Party), which united most of the victorious Revolutionary generals. His political life was linked to that of his cousin Álvaro Obregón. When Obregón resigned as secretary of war and navy in April 1917 Hill continued as head of the PLC and organized Obregón's supporters in Mexico City. When Obregón announced that he was running for president, Hill coordinated his campaign in the capital. He supported a pro-Obregón newspaper, *El monitor republicano,* directed by Basilio Vadillo, and he developed close relations with the Zapatista general Genovevo de la O. When the Plan de Agua Prieta, which called for the overthrow of Carranza, was promulgated in April 1923 the Zapatistas protected Obregón during his flight to the state of Guerrero. After the triumph of the Sonorans Hill resumed his command of the plaza garrison until Obregón's inauguration in December 1920.

Hill joined Obregón's cabinet as secretary of war and the navy, but he was able to serve only for 14 days. He died following a banquet; it is assumed that he was poisoned. There is some testimony of his disagreements with general Plutarco Elías Calles, who succeeded him as secretary of war. It also has been said that he had cancer. Following the death of Hill the remaining strongmen of Sonora—Álvaro Obregón, Plutarco Elías Calles, and Adolfo de la Huerta—formed the so-called Sonoran Triangle, which would determine the course of Mexican politics for years to come.

—Álvaro Matute

HISTORIETAS

Historieta can mean both "comic book" and "comic strip," and the term refers to stories told through a series of pictures to which text has been added, usually within word balloons. These pictures are sometimes photographs, with models who act out the stories; this type of *historieta* is called a *fotonovela. Historietas* of all kinds have been the most popular form of print media in Mexico in the twentieth century, far outselling books, magazines, and newspapers and supporting a lively secondary trade in used comic books. Their audience has cut across lines of age, gender, and class.

The first Mexican *historietas* appeared in special sections of the Sunday editions of newspapers, beginning with *El Universal* of Mexico City in 1918. These *dominicales* imitated the Sunday supplements of U.S. newspapers and reprinted translations of such syndicated features as *Tarzan.* But they also included Mexican creators, who quickly grew popular; by 1919 the Mexico City paper *El Heraldo* was running a daily strip written and drawn by two local teenagers as a front-page selling point.

In 1934 the first successful comic book, *Paquín,* was founded by Spanish immigrant Francisco "Paquín" Sayrols. *Paquín* was soon joined by three other weekly comic books: *Paquito* in 1935 and *Pepín* in 1936 (both published by José García "Pepín" Valseca, who went on to gain enormous power and wealth as owner of the Novedades chain of newspapers), and *Chamaco* in 1936 (founded by innovative editor Ignacio "Chamaco" Herrerias). Sales were so good that, by 1938, all were published three times a week, and by 1939 *Chamaco* had become the world's first daily comic book with a circulation of 750,000. Not to be outdone, *Pepín* not only also appeared daily but in 1940 began publishing a second Sunday edition, for a total of eight issues a week. It claimed a daily circulation of more than 1 million; its popularity was so great that for at least two decades, comic books were commonly called *pepines.* Probably it was the single most successful comic book in the global history of the medium.

From 1937 to 1950, the original four *pepines* were joined by dozens of less successful imitators. They never matched the popularity of the originals, but all of them followed the pattern that *Paquín* set. Each issue of the *pepines,* usually 48 or 64 small pages, offered readers a variety of stories told in serial form. The most popular serials, such as "Adelita y las guerrillas" in *Pepín* or "Los Supersabios" in *Chamaco,* went on indefinitely, resembling the U.S. comic strips that the *pepines* also contained. More frequently, however, stories ended after 3 to 12 months of daily episodes, each 6 to 12 pages long. The comic book industry soon employed hundreds of artists and writers to fill all these pages; some of these, such as Yolanda Vargas Dulché, moved between writing for *historietas,* radio dramas, cinema, and eventually *telenovelas* (soap operas). Like Vargas Dulché (who with her husband owned Editorial Vid, publishers of the best-sellers *Memin Pinguin* and *Lagrimas, risas y amor,* which Vargas Dulché also wrote), some artists and writers eventually founded their own profitable companies. The most notorious of these was José G. Cruz, author of "Adelita y las guerrillas," who grew rich publishing *El Santo,* based very loosely on the adventures of the eponymous masked wrestler.

Fotonovelas like *El Santo* were produced as quickly and cheaply as possible. For convenience, they mixed painted or drawn backgrounds with figure photography, and sometimes used stock poses of torsos onto which new head shots would be pasted as necessary; at times this gave them a startling, almost surrealist effect. But on the whole, the new comic books were not very visually innovative. Nor were they closely related to the Mexican graphic arts tradition. Their formal conventions were borrowed from United States models (which in turn relied upon models for visual story-telling imported from Germany.)

Readers were not assumed to be highly literate, so *pepines* used a limited vocabulary and simplified grammar. But comic-book narratives did not assume that their readers were stupid; plots could be tortuously complex, and sometimes required audiences to keep track of dozens of characters. *Historietas* in the period from 1934 to 1950 encouraged audience participation. Some offered prizes for the "most sincere" fan letter to an author, artist, or character; others asked readers to submit their autobiographies as potential story material; others reprinted readers' portraits. But audiences responded to more in the *pepines* than the possibility of prizes. *Historieta* stories—like radio dramas and soap operas—did not accurately represent Mexican realities, but they did speak to the concerns of their readers. Plots often turned on generational strain caused by migration away from rural areas, or on conflicts over gender roles as women began working outside their homes, or on class conflict, or on the pleasures and dangers of city life. Sometimes, as in *La Familia Burrón,* these concerns were played for laughs. More often, they underpinned melodramatic or romantic narratives. The stories often ended happily, but their power to compel readers arose from their recognition of social tensions that in reality could not be resolved so easily.

Conservatives—especially those organized by the Catholic Church—responded to the *historietas* as though they helped cause the social changes that they depicted. They especially objected to scenes in which young people were rude to their elders, plots involving divorce, and mildly sexual scenes (such as an engaged couple kissing). Protest campaigns sent thousands of letters and telegrams to the office of the President from 1942 to 1944, from 1952 to 1956, and from 1971 to 1974. Protesters also burned comic books at public rallies, published alternative "clean" comic books, and harassed newsstand operators. In 1944 the government responded to calls for comic-book censorship by setting up La Comisión Calificadora de Publicaciones y Revistas Ilustradas. This office was intended to supervise the *pepines* but soon extended its mandate to the licensing of all Mexican periodicals. Granted few enforcement powers, the censorship office did not substantially alter the content of any Mexican periodical. It did, however, make the entry of comic books from the United States onto the Mexican market somewhat more difficult, helping to preserve the local industry.

Between 1948 and 1953 all four of the original *historietas* folded. Their most important creators had begun their own publishing enterprises, taking their more important characters with them, but public taste had shifted, too. Although comics remained wildly popular, the older *pepines* had gained a racy reputation. They were often read in barbershops, at shoe-shine stands, and at other gathering places for adult men, and the censorship campaigns had tainted the older comics in the public mind.

Consumers preferred newer, smaller, better-printed comic books—usually weeklies—aimed at specific segments of the audience. Hundreds of comics were available on most cities' street corners in the period from 1950 to 1980. Newer comics covered a wide variety of topics, ranging from romances about truck drivers to "true life" adventures based roughly on the lives of movie stars (the movie star Pedro Infante alone inspired at least four weekly or monthly *fotonovelas* between 1951 and 1955.) There were *historietas* telling soccer and bullfighting stories, tales of doctors and nurses, lives of the saints, and adventures loosely modeled on Aztec myth. Most of these *historietas,* however, continued to rely on the visual and narrative conventions established in the first *pepines.* And they continued, in their sentimental and sensationalistic fashion, to concern themselves with social problems many Mexicans faced, particularly those attendant upon rapid urbanization.

In the 1960s, a few artists and writers of *historietas* moved from portraying social problems to tackling overtly political questions. Eduardo del Río, who wrote and drew under the pen name Rius, gained international fame by doing so. Less famous, but probably more influential in Mexico, was Carlos Vigil. His comic book *Torbellino,* a best-selling adventure story, also could be read as a fairly complex critique of the long-term effects of the PRI's rule. Other artists took advantage of the boom years of youth culture in the late 1960s to begin making and selling frankly pornographic, but apolitical, *fotonovelas.*

Almost from the beginning, the distribution of comic books was concentrated in the hands of *La Unión de Expendedores, Voceadores y Repartidores de la Prensa,* which was founded in 1923. Between 1960 and 1990, the production of comic books also grew increasingly concentrated. The majority of comic books—and nearly all the best-sellers—were now published by one or another subsidiary of the Televisa media empire. By the 1990s these comics were distributed throughout the Spanish-speaking world; like *telenovelas,* they spread Mexico's cultural influence. Comic books probably reached their peak circulation between 1980 and 1990, although audited circulation figures are closely held trade secrets. By then, the number of *historietas* published had declined somewhat, the profusion of subjects had been trimmed drastically, and their stories had become entirely formulaic. They do continue to reflect, in their fashion, on contemporary issues from AIDS to environmental woes. After 1990 circulation certainly declined, reflecting rising productions but, more importantly, competition from television.

Select Bibliography

Aurrecoechea, Juan Manuel, and Armando Barta, *Puros Cuentos: La historia de la historieta en Mexico, 1874–1934.* Mexico City: Grijalbo, 1988.

_____, *Puros Cuentos II: Historia de la historieta en Mexico, 1934–1950.* Mexico City: Grijalbo, 1993.

_____, *Puros Cuentos III: Historia de la historieta en Mexico, 1934–1950.* Mexico City: Grijalbo, 1994.

Herner, Irene, *Mitos y monitos*. Mexico City: Nueva Imagen, 1980.

Hinds, Harold, and Charles Tatum, *Not Only for Children: The Mexican Comic Book in the 1960s*. Westport, Connecticut: Greenwood, 1992.

Rius, *La Vida de Cuadritos: Guia incompleta de la historieta.* Mexico City: Grijalbo, 1984.

—ANNE RUBENSTEIN

HISTORIOGRAPHY

"Few countries cultivate history with as much enthusiasm as Mexico," writes one of Mexico's most respected historians, Luis González. Mexico's love affair with history encompasses historiography, which Álvaro Matute has called a privileged branch of *la Clío mexicana*. Historiography is the study of historical writing and texts, method and theory, teaching and preservation, and discourse. Historiography privileges the written word—history as literature—and until very recently has neglected other forms of representing the past, such as oral tradition, collective memory, and historical commemoration. History writing in Western nations since the nineteenth century has centered on national history ("tribal history" in the evocative phrase of novelist Conor Cruise O'Brien), and Mexican historiography has followed this path more closely than most. In the second half of the twentieth century, however, the writing of history in Mexico, although still largely directed toward the Mexican past, has become thoroughly professional and therefore much more methodologically sophisticated, politically detached, thematically varied and specialized, and voluminous.

For nearly two centuries Mexican historiography has been preoccupied by the transcendent struggle to define and construct the Mexican nation. The first national historians of the nineteenth century looked for the origins and nature of Mexico in the contrasting interpretations of the sixteenth-century conquistadors, chroniclers, and missionaries. Traditionalist Hispanophile conservatives were influenced by the original imperial school of history. Fernando (Hernán) Cortés in his letters to Emperor Charles V and the chronicles by Gonzalo Fernández de Oviedo, Francisco López de Gómara, Bernal Díaz de Castillo, and Gonzalo Jiménez de Quesada justified and glorified the military Conquest of the Mexica (Aztec) empire. The Spanish chroniclers emphasized individual heroism but displayed a messianic sense of history. They generally denigrated native culture, characterized it as brutal and savage, and particularly condemned its idolatrous and "satanic" nature. Nineteenth-century conservatives accordingly interpreted the Conquest as the birth of the Mexican nation, Cortés as its founding father, and the apparition of the Virgin Mary only 10 years following the Conquest as its christening.

Rationalist Hispanophobe liberals imagined a very different Mexico, which was derived from very different and more complicated historiographical traditions. Their condemnation and rejection of the Conquest was based on the chronicles and histories of Bartolomé de las Casas, Gerónimo de Mendieta, and Agustín Dávila Padilla. Their appreciation, even glorification, of the ancient Mexicans was based on the early Franciscan ethnologies of Toribio de Benavente (Motolinía) and Bernardino de Sahagún and the later elaborations of Carlos de Sigüenza y Góngora and Francisco Javier Clavijero. A sophisticated anti-Spanish criollo patriotism was forged in the seventeenth and eighteenth centuries, and it interpreted the Conquest as the beginning, not of the nation but of hundreds of years of colonial captivity tempered by valiant evangelization. The Mexican nation from this perspective arose from an ancient indigenous past, was brought to the Christian faith originally by the apostle St. Thomas and later by saintly missionaries, and was blessed by the Virgin of Guadalupe. This providential nation, the new Jerusalem in Anáhuac, was awakened to freedom by Father Miguel Hidalgo y Costilla in 1810 and shepherded to independence by Agustín de Iturbide in 1821.

National historical writing began with the revolution for independence, the Insurgency. José Servando Teresa de Mier (*La Historia de la Revolución de Nueva España antiguamente Anáhuac,* 1813) and Carlos María de Bustamante (*Cuadro histórico de la revolución de la América mexicana,* 1823–32) provided historical justification for the Insurgency and the rebirth of the Mexican nation. In exalting the last Mexica emperor Cuauhtemoc and the Insurgents Hidalgo and José María Morelos, they tried to give the infant country the prepackaged heritage found in criollo patriotism. Liberal ideologues and part-time historians, José María Luis Mora (*México y su revoluciones,* 1836) and Lorenzo Zavala (*Ensayo histórico de las revoluciones de México,* 1831) could not accept the fundamental premise of criollo patriotism, Mexico's providential history. Their anti-Spanish interpretation emphasized condemnation of the Catholic Church—which had itself condemned the Insurgency—as part and parcel of three centuries of Spanish colonialism. Thereafter anticlericalism would be the touchstone of liberal ideology and historiography.

During the first decades after Independence no one faction or ideology dominated politics and the state. The historical vision of Mexico advanced by an emerging liberal tradition was contested by an emerging conservative tradition as represented by Lucas Alamán (*Disertaciones sobre la historia de la República mejicana,* 1844–49, and *Historia de Méjico,* 1849–52). Alamán argued that the church was Spain's premier gift to Mexico and the core of Mexican nationality. The liberator was not Hidalgo, the excommunicated rebel priest, but former-royalist soldier Agustín de Iturbide, who achieved national independence with a guarantee to maintain the Catholic religion. The first great non-Mexican contribution to Mexican historiography, William H. Prescott's romantic epic *The History of the Conquest of Mexico* (1843), affirmed the conservative tradition even though it came from the pen of a New England Protestant. (This was no coincidence, since the Yankee historian was favored by the collegial advice and assistance of Alamán and Joaquín García Icazbalceta.) Prescott's disdain for the "barbaric" Indians concurred with the conservative vision of the nation founded by Cortés, the conquistador.

The absence of any consensus regarding the nature of the nation did not interfere with the creation of the principal institutions promoting national history. The Archivo General de la Nación (AGN), comprising the records of Mexico's colonial government, was founded in 1823 by the monarchical Iturbide government. The Conservatorio de Antigüedades, the official repository of ancient artifacts and monuments, was established in 1822 and its mission defined and name changed to the Museo Nacional in 1831 by Alamán. During the next several decades the Museo Nacional was the institutional home and patron of several noted conservative historians. In 1833 the Sociedad Mexicana de Geografía y Estadística opened its doors, and two years later the Academia Nacional de la Historia was formed by both liberal and conservative intellectuals. The Biblioteca Nacional was established by a liberal government in 1846. What could be considered Mexico's first scholarly history journal, *Anales del Museo Nacional de México,* began publication in 1877.

The two opposing, nearly contradictory visions of the Mexican past, present, and future inspired almost perpetual political conflict. The liberal revolution called la Reforma in the 1850s and the subsequent War of the Reform, and the French Intervention in the 1860s roundly defeated and thoroughly discredited the conservative cause in Mexico. Liberals officially proclaimed their cause to be the cause of Mexico, their heroes to be Mexico's heroes, and their interpretation of history to be *the* history of Mexico. This vision was reinforced in the 1860s and 1870s by the essays and orations of Ignacio Ramírez and Ignacio Manuel Altamirano, which adopted the indigenism of criollo patriotism (and the Black Legend of Las Casas, which denounced the Conquest, for good measure), but replaced its providential view of history with a quasihistoricist evolutionary one, and replaced its mystical Catholicism with radical anticlerical Hispanophobia. Naturally they glorified the Insurgency and its sequel, the Reforma. Mexico at last possessed a master narrative that found expression in official histories, school textbooks, commemorative monuments, and patriotic orations.

Conservative historians in the age of liberal ascendancy preserved historical documents and manuscripts and pub-

lished impressive documentary collections. Manuel Orozco y Berra, director of the AGN and the Museo Nacional, Joaquín García Icazbalceta, Francisco Pimentel, Francisco del Paso y Troncoso, and Carlos Pereyra published thick volumes of colonial documents and brought out new editions of classic colonial ethnologies and chronicles. José Fernando Ramírez, a liberal, spent a lifetime collecting historical documents and books and became perhaps the most respected historian of his time. These men were talented scholars, not dabblers in history. Although they contributed little directly to the master narrative, they were giants of colonial historiography as a result of their scholarly labor, upon which twentieth-century historians have come to depend.

Mexico's first official history, the five-volume *México a través de los siglos* (1887–89), was the most ambitious and successful national history of the nineteenth century. Its many reprints can be found today in most bookstores and in many homes. Vicente Riva Palacio and three prominent liberal intellectuals integrated what had been different, neglected, and often opposed pasts into one conciliatory national history. They structured national history into five epochs, one per volume: the ancient Mexican civilizations, colonial New Spain, the Insurgency, independent Mexico, and the Reforma. A little more than a decade later Justo Sierra and leading lights of the next generation of liberals produced a similar official history, *México: su evolución social* (1900–02). Sierra's history was, in comparison with its predecessor, organized thematically, politically sycophantic toward the current regime, and available in Spanish, English, and French editions. It was also supposedly more scientific in its social Darwinian conception of Mexico as an organism that had evolved from both Indian and Spanish roots to create a new mestizo people and nation. Together these bibliographic monuments created what modern scholar Edmundo O'Gorman has termed the liberal synthesis in Mexican historiography.

The rebellions, reforms, and anticlericalism of the second and third decades of the twentieth century, called the Mexican Revolution, revived the historiographical dispute Justo Sierra thought had ended with the previous century. José Vasconcelos (*Breve historia de México,* 1937), Mariano Cuevas, Alberto María Carreño, and Carlos Pereyra vigorously defended the essential Catholic and Hispanic elements of Mexican nationality despite (or perhaps because of) the defeat of the most conservative political forces in the Revolution. "We joined the ranks of civilization," Vasconcelos wrote, "under the standard of Castile." The accusation that the Spanish destroyed an indigenous civilization was false and ignorant, "since there was nothing worthy of preserving when they arrived on these shores."

Liberal historiography (which came to be called Revolutionary) prospered and multiplied, was modified at the edges, and remained *una historia de bronce,* that is, official. The so-called Revolutionary historians wanted a "new history," a Revolutionary history, one more genuinely Mexican in terms of ethnicity, a more popular and inclusive history of peasants and workers, and a more social and economic—

materialistic—history. Their critics decried partisan Revolutionary history ("I know of no history of Mexico," one proclaimed in 1927, "that is written with impartiality") and demanded objectivity.

Manuel Gamio (*Forjando patria,* 1916) and Andrés Molina Enríquez (*La Revolución agraria en México,* five volumes, 1932–36) made *mestizaje* (race mixture) the centerpiece of the new Revolutionary cultural nationalism. These founders of revolutionary indigenism—a more accurate term is mestizophilia—interpreted national history through the lens of ethnicity. They modified the rather neutral mestizophilia found in the old liberal synthesis to create what Agustín Basave Benítez has called "a quasi-indigenist Hispanophobic mestizophilia." The Conquest was now interpreted as neither a victory nor a defeat but the painful birth of the Mexican people and nation. Molina Enríquez argued that national history was essentially a struggle of Indian-mestizos sometimes allied with criollo-mestizos against Spanish and criollo dominance and oppression. Revolutionary nationalism and agrarian reform were the creative achievements of Indian-mestizos, the genuine, popular core of the nation, or what Guillermo Bonfil Batalla later called *México profundo.*

Marxist and pseudo-Marxist historians viewed Mexico's history through the lens of social justice more than social class. Alfonso Teja Zabre, Rafael Ramos Pedrueza, Luis Chávez Orozco, and Agustín Cue Cánovas pioneered a more social and economic focus in modern Mexican historiography. All Revolutionary historians maintained that Mexican history was essentially a history of popular revolution against Spanish, later oligarchical, imperialist, and reactionary tyranny and injustice. The preeminent official history of the Revolution, *Historia de la Revolución Mexicana* (1951) by Alberto Morales Jiménez, argued that the Insurgency, the Reforma, and the Revolution were three stages of an interrupted but ongoing revolution for political, spiritual, and economic emancipation and social justice. The Revolution of 1910 to 1920 was the culmination of national history and the synthesis of the different Revolutionary programs of the precursors, Francisco I. Madero, Venustiano Carranza, Emiliano Zapata, and Álvaro Obregón. The institutionalization of official history began in 1953 with the establishment by the national government of the Instituto Nacional de Estudios Históricos de la Revolución Mexicana (INEHRM). Its mission was to collect documentation and publish works "of an official character, relating to the history of the Revolution." In time the INEHRM superseded its mission statement and has published histories of all periods of national history. Its greatest contribution has been the reprinting of many of the classics of Mexican historiography in affordable editions. After 1960 official history entered every classroom when the national government distributed free textbooks "obligatory for instruction." Not surprisingly, as Josefina Zoraida Vázquez has noted, "none of the traditional conservative textbooks attained official approval."

The liberal synthesis survived well into the twentieth century. Generations of Mexican school children learned Mexican history from the multiple editions of Justo Sierra's textbooks (*Catecismo de Historia Patria,* 1894; *Veinticuatro cuadros de historia patria,* 1907; and *Elementos de Historia Patria,* 1894, 1904, 1916, and 1922, in use until 1958). Félix F. Palavicini after World War II attempted to update the liberal synthesis in the style of Vicente Riva Palacio and Justo Sierra with his multiauthor and multivolume *México, Historia de su evolución constructiva* (1945). The work of Fernando Iturribarría, Jesús Silva Herzog, and particularly Jesús Reyes Heroles (*El liberalism mexicano,* 1957–61) argued again that the liberal cause more broadly redefined was and is the cause of Mexico. "Liberalism," Iturribarría wrote, "that is, social democracy, has triumphed at last, with the program of the Mexican Revolution."

The professionalization and institutionalization of history teaching, writing, publishing, and preservation in Mexico, the United States, and Canada, and Europe in the twentieth century, and particularly since 1940, has transformed Mexican historiography. This professionalization was assisted by the arrival of Spanish historians following the Spanish Civil War, who found academic homes in the Instituto Nacional de Antropología e Historia (founded in 1939), El Colegio de México (1940), and the National University's Instituto de Investigaciones Históricas (1945). Professionalization was built on earlier accomplishments such as the formation of the first research libraries during the Porfiriato (rule of Porfirio Díaz), the establishment of the Escuela Nacional de Altos Estudios in 1910 and the organization of the first graduate degrees in history in 1927, the founding of the AGN's *Boletín* in 1930, and the initiation of the Mexican Congress of History in 1933. The establishment of the first genuine professional journal of history, *Historia Mexicana,* in 1951 was a notable turning point.

The example of an amateur was, curiously enough, of enormous importance in the intellectual professionalization of Mexican historiography. José C. Valadés practiced his craft for nearly 50 years and wrote scholarly biographies of many of Mexico's leading statesmen as well as histories of the new nation, the war with the United States, the Porfiriato, the Revolution, and of the Mexican people. Valadés was a scholar who collected and conducted research in primary and secondary sources and an author who wrote clearly and with style. His significance lay in his approach to history. To Valadés objectivity was not simply "a noble dream" but a practical challenge that he satisfied better than most. In the early 1930s he undertook to reexamine three of the most reviled personages in national historiography: Lucas Alamán, Antonio López de Santa Anna, and Porfirio Díaz. "History is not the science," he wrote, "called to extirpate epochs or individuals." His history of the Porfiriato, he stressed, was "historia aoficial." Indeed, all of his biographies and histories rose above liberal, conservative, Revolutionary, Hispanophobic, Hispanophilic, indigenist, and mestizophilic prejudices; he relished telling the truth as he saw it even if his judgments were politically incorrect at the time. While Valadés endeavored to be objective and was once unjustly accused of lacking any conviction at all, he embraced a healthy kind of subjectivity that spurned partisanship. He never disavowed his one bias, however, which was Mexico itself. What we should remember above all about *el maestro de la historiografía mexicana* (the master of Mexican historiography), writes Andrés Lira, "is the independence of his ideas and judgments in the face of the standard interpretations in our historiography."

Valadés's devotion to "historia aoficial" became the norm in academic historiography in the 1950s and 1960s. María de la Luz Parcero emphasizes "the liquidation, at least in the academic realm, of the traditional struggle between liberals and conservatives." Although some of his best work predates the age of professionalization, Silvio Zavala brought detailed research, a keen mind, and a sense of objectivity to the study of colonial institutions (*La encomienda indiana,* 1935). He contributed significantly to the professionalization of history in Mexico as a founder of institutions (most notably the Centro de Estudios Históricos at El Colegio de Mexico) and professor of history. Vito Alessio Robles (*Coahuila y Texas,* 1945–46), Wigberto Jiménez Moreno, Luis Weckman Muñoz, Carlos Bosch García, Manuel Carrera Stampa—the list is much, much longer—contributed to professionalization by example and instruction.

The philosopher José Gaos, a Spanish exile and student of José Ortega y Gasset, with his famous seminar on the Study of Ideas in Hispanic America, made possible Mexico's most important contribution to modern historiography: the Mexican school of historicism and historiography. From his seminar came such classics as Leopoldo Zea's *El positivismo en México,* 1943, and *El apogeo y decadencia del positivismo en México,* 1945; Edmundo O'Gorman's *La idea del descubrimiento de América,* 1951, and *La invención de América,* 1958; and Luis Villoro's *Los grandes momentos del indigenismo en México,* 1950. The work of Justino Fernández, Francisco López Camara, Juan Antonio Ortega y Medina, Josefina Zoraida Vázquez, and more, from the 1940s to the 1960s, reveal the obvious influence of Gaos.

The unquestioned apogee of postwar academic historiography is the 10-volume *Historia moderna de México* (1955–72) conceived, organized, and directed by Daniel Cosío Villegas. This collaborative endeavor, as Charles A. Hale has pointed out, is in fact three distinct works in one: the political history of the Restored Republic and the Porfiriato in three volumes written by Cosío Villegas, the social and economic history of the entire period in five volumes by several of the luminaries at El Colegio de Mexico (Moisés González Navarro to name but one), and the diplomatic history of the Porfiriato in two volumes by Cosío Villegas. The *Historia moderna de México* forcefully contradicted official Revolutionary history to portray the Porfiriato as a part of Mexico's heritage rather than a reactionary and obsolete aberration. Cosío Villegas also coordinated the best and most recent national synthesis, the four-volume *Historia general de México* (1976–77) and began El Colegio de México's 23-volume *Historia de la Revolución Mexicana.*

Accompanying the historiographical renaissance in Mexico was a dramatic increase in the number of non-Mexican historians conducting archival research in Mexico. Americans and Europeans had long viewed Mexico as exotic and wrote scores of travel narratives. Journalists discovered Mexico at the time of the Revolution and a few (Ernest Gruening and Carleton Beals) wrote good pro-Revolutionary history in the best progressive tradition. Scholars such as Herbert Ingram Priestly, Charles Hackett, and Frank Tannenbaum arrived in the 1920s and 1930s, and their many students in the postwar era were prolific writers and bridge-builders. Periodic international congresses of Mexican history, begun in 1949 and continued in 1958, 1969, 1973, 1977, 1981, 1985, 1990, and 1994, initiated a process of cross-fertilization of ideas and methods that has benefited the research and writing of Mexican history worldwide.

Just as the Mexican historians graciously integrated Spanish refugees into their intellectual and academic world, a decade and two later they welcomed and accommodated foreign historians and graduate students. Mexican scholars read, reviewed, debated, praised and criticized the work of foreign historians in English, French, and German as well as Spanish, hosted the international congresses in a style that non-Mexican historians certainly were not accustomed to, and translated and published more than a few historical monographs. Mexican graciousness apparently encouraged good work, as evidenced by the accomplishments of Woodrow Borah, François Chevalier, Charles Cumberland, Charles Gibson, Stanley Ross, and Leslie Simpson, to name a few.

In the glory days of institutional expansion, increasing numbers of grants and fellowships, and new journals and presses in the 1960s and 1970s, historians of Mexico launched a full-scale assault upon official history. This revisionism, often guided by Marxist theory, was aimed first and foremost at official Revolutionary history. Revisionism, however, soon engulfed nearly all periods and topics. Arnoldo Córdova, Adolfo Gilly, John Hart, Friedrich Katz, Jean Meyer, Michael C. Meyer, Robert Quirk, Ramón Eduardo Ruiz, and Arturo Warman, among others, reexamined the Revolution and helped create, as David Bailey put it in 1978, "a historiography that is almost as complex as the Revolution itself."

Revisionists were particularly interested in history from below and outside of Mexico City. This trend was best exemplified by one historian's history of his hometown, an unremarkable village in Michoacán: Luis González's *Pueblo en vilo: Microhistoria de San José de Gracia,* 1968 (English translation *San José de Gracia: Mexican Village in Transition,* 1974). This Mexican missionary of local and regional history issued his "invitation to microhistory" repeatedly at historical conferences in the 1960s and 1970s. The replies were phenomenal. Regional studies have significantly contributed to the revisionist interpretation of the Revolution as a failed popular revolution and a triumphant bourgeois movement. Héctor Aguilar Camín, Raymond Buve, Romana Falcón, Gilbert Joseph, Carlos Martínez Assad, and John Womack—the list is much longer—reconstructed the provinces of the Revolution. The regional perspective also was adopted by students of the nineteenth century and colonial history as demonstrated by Charles Berry, D. A. Brading, Brian Hamnett, William Taylor, and Eric Van Young.

Worldwide interest in Mexican history has not generated an equal and opposite reaction—Mexican interest in the history of other countries and regions. In 1967 Daniel Cosío Villegas was alarmed at the paucity of interest in and research about the history of the United States in Mexico. No one in Mexico had done more to broaden horizons: he established the publishing house Fondo de Cultura Económica in the 1940s, and thereafter it provided translations of many of the classics of European, U.S., and world history. By the 1980s and 1990s there were more academic programs offering a greater diversity of history courses and more historians specializing in non-Mexican history. Nevertheless, *historia patria* continues its magnetic hold on the large majority of historians and history students in Mexico.

The writing and publishing of Mexican history in the 1990s was an international industry. The chapters by Mexican authors and about Mexican periods in *The Cambridge History of Latin America* (1984–95) demonstrate the quality and diversity of production. There are approximately 1,000 historians writing about Mexico, according to the estimate of Luis González. About half are Mexican, *historiadores de casa,* as he refers to his Mexican colleagues. They are academic historians mostly, teaching at the 30-some institutions that grant undergraduate degrees in history and the eight that grant graduate degrees, or they can be found in the numerous public and private research institutions. Among their ranks are some of the most accomplished and imaginative historians working anywhere in the world today, scholars such as Enrique Florescano (*Precios del maíz y crisis agrícola en México, 1708–1810,* 1969; *El poder y la lucha por el poder en la historiografía mexicana,* 1980; *Memory, Myth and Time in Mexico from the Aztecs to Independence,* 1994), Héctor Aguilar Camín, Jan Bazant, Enrique Krauze, Lorenzo Meyer, and the dean of Mexicanists, Luis González.

The other 500 historians are, of course, not Mexican, again nearly all employed in colleges and universities. Most come from the United States, but Canada, Great Britain, France, Australia, and Germany are well represented. And, again, among their ranks are some of the best historians in the world, scholars such as William Beezley, John Coatsworth, Charles A. Hale, and James Lockhart of the United States; David Brading, Brian Hamnett, and Alan Knight of Great Britain; Serge Gruzinski and Francois-Xavier Guerra of France; Christon Archer of Canada; Jan de Vos of Belgium; Hans Werner Tobler of Germany; and Inga Clendinnen (now deceased) of Australia.

These scholars are the intellectual descendants of William H. Prescott, who wrote the first classic of world history on a Mexican topic. A British historian, Hugh Thomas, has at last surpassed Prescott with his impressively researched and decidedly unromantic *Conquest: Montezuma, Cortés, and the Fall of Old Mexico* (1993). Thomas uncovered more primary sources than Prescott on Cortés and the Spanish but also much more on Moteuczoma and the Aztecs. His treatment of indigenous Mexico, as a result, is respectful and balanced. Thomas also had access to 150 years of Mexican historiography denied Prescott. As a result, this "amazing book," according to Enrique Krauze, "testifies to the undeniable progress in the historical study of Mexico."

The history of Mexican history is much like Carlos Fuentes's "buried mirror": it is a reflection both of the past and the present. The past has always been the handmaid of authority in Mexico, as J. H. Plumb put it, a weapon in the battle for the future. Mexican historiography, however, is not and has never been simply and purely an ideological form. If there has been "undeniable progress" in Mexican historiography, it is owing first and foremost to the contributions of several generations of Mexican historians, then to the research of their recent colleagues from abroad, and finally to the interchange of ideas and collaboration among all historians of this fascinating land and people.

Select Bibliography

Bailey, David C., "Revisionism and the Recent Historiography of the Mexican Revolution." *Hispanic American Historical Review* 58:1 (1978).

Benjamin, Thomas, and Marcial Ocasio, "Organizing the Memory of Modern Mexico: Porfirian Historiography in Perspective, 1880s–1980s" *Hispanic American Historical Review* 64:2 (1984).

Brading, D.A., *The First America: The Spanish Monarchy, Creole Patriots, and the Liberal State, 1492–1867.* Cambridge: Cambridge University Press, 1991.

Comité Mexicana de Ciencias Históricas, *Memorias del simposio de historiografía mexicanista.* Mexico City: Instituto de Investigaciones Históricas, UNAM, 1990.

Crespo, Horacio, et al., *El historiador frente a la historia: Corrientes historiográficas actuales.* Mexico City: UNAM, 1992.

Florescano, Enrique, *Memory, Myth, and Time in Mexico from the Aztecs to Independence.* Austin: University of Texas Press, 1994.

_____, *El nuevo pasado mexicano.* Mexico City: Cal y Arena, 1991.

Galeana de Valdés, Patricia, et al., *José C. Valadés: Historiador y Político.* Mexico City: UNAM, 1992.

González, Luis, *El oficio de historiar.* Zamora: Colegio de Michoacán, 1988.

Wells, Allen, "Oaxtepec Revisited: The Politics of Mexican Historiography, 1968–1988." *Mexican Studies/Estudios Mexicanos* 7:2 (Summer 1991).

—Thomas Benjamin

HOMOSEXUALITY

Homosexuality in Mexico has a long and complex history that predates the arrival of the Spanish as a colonial ruler. Diverse cultures in the region have held varied views on homosexuality, ranging from acceptance to hostility. With the arrival of the Spanish, hostility as the response to homosexuality became the dominant theme in Mexico. The origins of this hostility can be found in an examination of pre-Columbian and Spanish-held views that have intertwined in the present dominant Mestizo culture created in the clash of these two worlds. (It must be remembered that the use of the terms homosexual or homosexuality to describe same-sex relationships or sex in pre-twentieth-century-Mexico is a matter of convenience to maintain a continuity of understanding throughout this essay. Such use is not meant to indicate that same-sex relationships or sex during these time periods had the same meaning that homosexual, homosexuality, gay, lesbian, or bisexual have in the twentieth century. The exact meaning of those same-sex relationships or sex is difficult to judge from imperfect historical records.)

Sketchy historical records indicate that when the Spanish arrived in the region, diverse indigenous societies held differing views on homosexuality. In what is the Veracruz region of Mexico, according to some Spanish chroniclers such as Fernando (Hernán) Cortés, homosexuality was widely practiced with what appears to be social acceptance. In the Yucatán, the Spaniard Bernal Díaz del Castillo reported finding homoerotic religious statuary.

While the Mexica (Aztecs) permitted conquered peoples to maintain their own cultural practices, they executed men and women engaging in homosexual acts within Mexica territory. Punishment for the passive male partner included having his intestines ripped out through his anus prior to being burned to death; women found engaging in homosexual acts were strangled to death. At the same time, within Mexica religion, homosexuality found an institutional role in worship and rite. One Mexica deity who possessed a male/female dual nature, Xochiquetzal, was known in his/her male aspect as Xochipilli and was worshipped in this aspect as the deity of male homosexuality.

In colonial Mexico, as in pre-Columbian Mexico, the historical records are sketchy at best in regards to homosexuality. The Spanish arrived in Mesoamerica with a strong homophobic attitude. Having blamed the Moors for the introduction of homosexuality into the Iberian Peninsula, the Spanish worked to eliminate any trace of it there and in their territories in the Americas. The Spanish Inquisition was the tool used to attack homosexuality. In 1658, one case presented to the Inquisition involved 15 homosexuals; 14 of these were burned to death, while the fifteenth, a boy, was whipped and sold as an indentured servant.

Information on lesbianism during the Spanish colonial period is virtually nonexistent. The notable exception is the literary work of a nun who lived in the second half of the seventeenth century, Sor Juana Inés de la Cruz. The sexuality of Sor Juana herself can, perhaps, be inferred from her literary works, but not confirmed. More important, the interpretation of some of her literary works, specifically her poetry, as a representation of what today could be described as lesbianism gives voice to a sexuality reality of her time, but one that was not discussed as a possibility. This reading of her works is not merely an academic exercise of reinterpreting literature based upon today's concepts of sexuality, but has been used by lesbians and gays of Mexico to reclaim part of their hidden history. This process of reclamation is indicated, in part, through the name of one Mexican group that calls itself El Closet de Sor Juana. The reclamation of hidden history is an important step by gay and lesbian movements in claiming a place in the society in which they live.

Following Independence from Spain, Mexico adopted the Napoleonic Code that decriminalized homosexuality between consenting adults; however, homosexuality remained socially unacceptable. The hostility toward homosexuality of the Mexica (except in a limited religious arena) and the Spanish combined in the Mestizo culture to carry that tradition into modern-day Mexico. Even as it dominates, it has not subsumed the diversity that existed in pre-Columbian Mexico. One example is the Isthmus Zapotecs. Within their culture there is wide acceptance of bisexuality, especially after an individual has had children.

Gender and the Social Construction of Homosexuality

Although there exists a long history of hostility toward homosexuality in Mexico, there also exists a dual nature of Mexican society in which male homosexuality is tolerated in a limited fashion. It is difficult to discuss lesbianism outside of the gay and lesbian movement, as much of lesbian history is erased or hidden.

Traditionally, male homosexuality has been socially constructed in an active-passive dichotomy. In this social construct, the active male partner is considered to be heterosexual. The passive male partner, on the other hand, plays the role of a social female and is stigmatized as a homosexual.

Although homosexuality may remain socially unacceptable to Mexican society, this active-passive dichotomy is tolerated as it remains within the bounds of gender and sexual roles. The active partner demonstrates his machismo in his sexual conquest of the social female, the passive male. Conditions of manliness are maintained without fear of stigmatization attached to his sexual acts. The passive partner, in the submissive role of the female, exists as a sexual outlet for the active male. He is stigmatized as the receptor of the penis, a role reserved for the female.

This dichotomy is tied in part to ancient roots of concepts of honor and shame in manliness found in the Mediterranean region. In Mexico this is described as machismo and was brought to the Americas through Spanish soldiers and adventures. According to the scholar Evelyn Stevens, the "chief characteristics of machismo, the cult of virility, are exaggerated aggressiveness and intransigence in male-to-male interpersonal relationships and arrogance and sexual aggression in male-to-female relationships. . . ." Maintaining manliness is vital, as nonmasculine behavior is ridiculed. Passive male homosexuality places one in the position of not maintaining a dominant position, giving up masculinity by engaging in nonmasculine, feminine behavior.

While male homosexuality has been constructed in an active-passive dichotomy, lesbianism has traditionally been socially constructed to be nonexistent. This in part may be related to an aspect of the traditional social construct of female identity, that a woman is either a desexualized virgin or a whore who can be sexual only in relation to a man. Sex between two women becomes unimaginable.

Traditional female identity also springs from ancient sources found in the worship of mother goddess figures. In Mexico this ancient cult of the spiritual superiority of women, called *marianismo,* comes through the Virgin Mary in the form of the Virgin of Guadalupe. Within this social construct, the ideal woman is one who lives up to the picture of femininity found in the Virgin of Guadalupe. Her destiny is to be the dutiful and submissive daughter, wife, and mother, inhibit her sexuality, and remain a virgin until marriage. Self-sacrifice toward the home and children, especially male children, is the hallmark of the good mother. Men are raised to expect a wife who is like their mother, dutiful to the image of the virgin; such an image does not include sexual fulfillment; except for a procreative role, the woman becomes desexualized.

As with male homosexuality, traditional concepts of female identity also exhibit a dual nature. The virgin represents one side, the whore the other. The whore is represented in history by la Malinche (doña Marina), an indigenous woman given to Cortés. She served as one of his interpreters and advisers and later bore him a son. By some she is considered the traitor to her people, by others the mother of the Mestizo race. La Malinche represents the untrustworthy sexual nature of women in Mexican cultural history. As the whore, women are available as a sexual outlet for men, sexual beings who are not socially acceptable for marriage.

In either the role as a virgin or the whore, a woman is sexually defined in relation to men in her life. Traditionally, female identity did not exist outside of these two roles. Lesbianism, as an identity, stands outside these concepts and so has been erased, hidden, and denied.

The Gay and Lesbian Movement

The gay and lesbian movement in Mexico addresses the hostility toward homosexuality, the male homosexual dichotomy, erasure of lesbianism, and the stigmatization of gays and lesbians. Gay men in Mexico have come out, no longer willing to be cast as a social female or a heterosexual male who has sex with a homosexual. Lesbians and gay men have come out to confront their stigmatization and place in Mexican society. In opening the social discourse on sexuality, gays and lesbians have forced the discussion of their lives and issues into the open. Their sexual, political, and social consciousness has been raised and continues to challenge the social system in which they live.

The Mexican gay and lesbian rights movement grew out of a diffusion of ideas from movements in Europe and the United States. This dispersion began early in the twentieth century and continues through the interaction between Mexican gays and lesbians and their foreign counterparts. This evolution has not been the result of an imposition of foreign movements on the Mexican society. Instead, Mexican men and women have taken the influence of foreign movements and transformed it to fit their own long history of oppression and culturally constructed concepts.

The modern Mexican gay and lesbian movement grew out of the counter-culture movement that developed in Mexico in the 1960s. The critical event that precipitated this movement was the massacre of student and worker protesters at Tlatelolco on October 2, 1968. Following the massacre, the exile of student leaders, forced as well as self-imposed, spurred contact between gay, lesbian, and bisexual movements in Europe and the United States with Mexican men and women. This contact would prove a key factor in the emergence of homosexual rights movements in Mexico.

The emergence of the gay and lesbian movement onto the Mexican social scene occurred in 1971, following the dismissal of a Sears employee in Mexico City for alleged homosexuality. According to Ian Lumsden, this event "was the catalyst that brought together the first group of gays and lesbians in Mexican history that would question their stigmatization and social oppression." This event is thus analogous to the Stonewall Riots of June 27–28, 1969, in New York City, which are identified as the event that gave rise to the modern gay, lesbian, bisexual, and transgendered/transsexual movement in the United States.

The early gay and lesbian movement in Mexico remained underground in Mexico City during most of the 1970s. By the late 1970s, the Mexico City movement had coalesced around three main groups: Frente Homosexual de Acción Revolucionaria, a largely gay male organization; Grupo Lambda de Liberación Homosexual, a lesbian and gay organization; and OIKABETH, a lesbian organization. All three of these groups advocated socialism as a political tool.

By 1982, the Mexican gay and lesbian movement had moved to the national scene with the Mexican national elections. The Partido Revolucionario de los Trabajadores (PRT) made homosexual rights part of its political plank. During this election, several gay and lesbian candidates for federal deputy ran campaigns under the PRT umbrella: Lupita García de Alba and Pedro Preciado in Guadalajara, and Claudia Hinojosa and Max Mejía in Mexico City.

Following the 1982 elections, the movement in Mexico City suffered a political and organizational decline. The relationship with the PRT dissolved as the party no longer had a politically strategic use for the relationship, in part owing to the fact that the relationship alienated many of the PRT's core supporters. In addition, the growing economic crisis in the country forced gay and lesbian activism to the background as daily survival became more important.

Floundering without a set purpose, the gay and lesbian movement in Mexico City limped forward until the 1984 Gay Pride Day march. Conflicts over leadership, which direction to take the movement, and the realization that the movement was losing its radical subversive nature as it became popular turned the parade into a verbally violent confrontation among its participants.

Even as the Mexico City movement collapsed, the gay and lesbian movement grew in other parts of the country. In Guadalajara, Grupo de Orgullo Homosexual de Liberación (GOHL), under the leadership of Pedro Preciado, flourished as it fought political repression and police harassment of homosexuals. GOHL, together with Grupo Lesbico Patlatonalli, the main lesbian group in Guadalajara, made the transition from the 1982 electoral campaign to focusing on gay and lesbian issues. They developed service programs for the gay and lesbian communities, including AIDS projects and legal and psychological counseling. Finally, GOHL helped to bring the Mexican gay and lesbian movement into the international arena. In 1991, GOHL invited the International Lesbian and Gay Association to hold its annual meeting in Mexico, the first such meeting outside of Europe or Anglo–North America.

During the early 1990s, the movement in Mexico City was reemerging, building upon the legacy of the early movement of the late 1970s and early 1980s. In the years that the Mexico City movement rebuilt itself, the gay and lesbian movement has spread beyond Mexico City and Guadalajara to many other urban centers, including Tijuana, Oaxaca, Monterrey, and Cuernavaca. Since the early 1990s, gay and lesbian organizations have proliferated to over 60 in number throughout the country. Besides social and political organizations, the religious community for gays and lesbians has opened up with the establishment of the Iglesia de la Comunidad Metropolitana (ICM) in Mexico City, Cuernavaca, and Guadalajara. The ICM is similar to the Metropolitan Community Church in the United States.

Lesbian Politics: A Case Study

Lesbian politics gleaned from available sources indicate a pattern of socialism, feminism, and separatism. Manifestos published by three groups, OIKABETH, Akratas, and Seminario Marxista Leninista Feminista de Lesbianas (SMLFL) represent this spectrum of lesbian political identity from the late 1970s through the late 1980s, but they do not necessarily represent all lesbian organizations.

OIKABETH was one of the first openly lesbian groups to coalesce in Mexico City in the late 1970s, and continued to exist at least until the mid-1980s. OIKABETH represented a lesbian organization that used an interpretation of socialism integrated with feminism. For the members of OIKABETH it was not enough to love another woman; one had to take that capacity into the social struggle to overturn the patriarchal social structure. They did not define lesbianism as a sexual activity; instead, lesbianism was a political choice that was defined outside the context of the male-dominated society. Through a lesbian, feminist, socialist interpretation of society, the members of OIKABETH felt that they could better understand the world, develop their talents, and work to overturn the social system in which they lived. As a group, OIKABETH sought to raise consciousness of social oppression, search for a new lesbian identity, recover the hidden lesbian past, and support the struggles of other marginal and exploited groups.

A second group was Akratas, probably also formed in the late 1970s and continued until the early-to-mid-1980s. Akratas consisted of lesbians and straight women in a feminist alliance. Feminism was the political base of Akratas. Through it, members could understand their oppression as women and fight the patriarchal society in which they lived. Akratas sought to build a political structure that was outside of and not based upon patriarchal social structures, thereby not replicating the oppression its members felt was inherent within that structure. Akratas was also a separatist group; its members did not want their social and political struggle to be subsumed under the gay, male homosexual movement, and like the members of OIKABETH, did not want their lesbianism defined as a sexual issue. Their struggle was based upon the oppression of women, and as lesbians a double oppression, as women and as women who loved women. Akratas was attempting to build a social and political space in which women could define themselves outside of the context of a relationship with men.

From a manifesto published in 1987, it is apparent that socialism and feminism were the underlying philosophical base to the SMLFL. The SMLFL advocated the radical overthrow of the patriarchal-capitalistic world social system and replacing it with a socialist state. According to the SMLFL, the most radical position that could be taken by women struggling against oppression was that of lesbianism combined with communism and feminism in a political struggle against the patriarchal-capitalistic world system. Only those women radical enough to take this position had the ability to be the natural leaders of a socialist revolution.

For the members of SMLFL, every aspect of life held a political meaning, including sexuality. As a political question, sexuality was a state institution and heterosexuality was the repressive tool of the state. Addressing sexuality in the socialist revolution was a necessity, or the socialist revolution could not be complete.

SMLFL held the belief that lesbianism was a biological, mental, and social capacity of women to love other women. Lesbianism was a possibility for every woman, and therefore a political choice that could create a solidarity among women that heterosexuality could not accomplish. Lesbianism was viewed as a useful political tool, but could not of and by itself overthrow the state; instead, it was only one aspect of the socialist revolution that would lead to a communist state.

Violence

Gays and lesbians in Mexico face serious problems of violence and harassment from official sources and the public. There is no concerted national campaign by the government to repress gays and lesbians, and no national law makes lesbian and gay sexual activity illegal, except in regard to minors. However, several areas of the country appear to be more repressive and violent than others.

The government of Guadalajara has used political and police repression against gays and lesbians. For example, in November 1988 police raided a bar in Guadalajara frequented by lesbians. The women were taken from the bar to a secluded area of the city and raped. Rape and physical punishment often have been used as tools to enforce social conformity, in this case that heterosexuality is the only permissible sexual norm.

Mexico City also has been the scene of official harassment. In June 1992 two prominent gay activists and AIDS prevention workers, Gerardo Ruben Ortega Zurita and José Cruz-Reyes Potenciano, were arrested, each charged with rape and sexual assault of a minor. In custody, the men were beaten by the police and by other prison inmates. After almost a year, in March 1993, both men were convicted and sentenced to 13 years, nine months imprisonment. On July 9, 1993, after an appeal, the men were cleared of all charges and released. The arrest and conviction appear to have been motivated by their work on gay issues.

Rape, beatings, and imprisonment are not the only violence that gay men and lesbians face in Mexico. Murder, the ultimate violence, also occurs. In the state of Chiapas, near Tuxtla Gutiérrez, between June 1991 and February 1993, at least 11 gay men were killed. The pattern of these murders has left the impression of a systematic targeting of gay men. Dozens of similar murders occurred throughout Mexico in the following years. The lack of serious investigation of such murders and the failure to bring those responsible to justice, at least with the Chiapas murders, suggest at a minimum state governmental tolerance and possible complicity in the murders.

Conclusion

In 1980, Carlos Monsiváis commented upon the patriarchal machismo of Mexican culture in relation to the gay and lesbian movement and feminism. He noted that patriarchal machismo was "no longer the unquestioned norm of Mexican culture. There has been a 'rupture of verbal and social taboos' and a real corrosion of traditional machismo. . ." (quoted in Lumsden, 1991). The gay and lesbian movement has helped to break social taboos against challenging traditional machismo and *marianismo*. The movement has had only a small impact upon Mexican society and its long history of hostility toward homosexuality. However, gay and lesbian Mexicans continue to challenge social norms in their search to be integral members of their society.

See also Feminism; Gender

Select Bibliography

Breaking the Silence: Human Rights Violations Based on Sexual Orientation. New York: Amnesty International, 1994.

Carrier, Joseph, *De Los Otros: Intimacy and Homosexuality among Mexican Men.* New York: Columbia University Press, 1995.

Chiñas, Beverly Newbold, *The Isthmus Zapotecs: A Matrifocal Culture of Mexico.* 2nd edition, Fort Worth, Texas: Harcourt Brace, 1992.

Lumsden, Ian, *Homosexuality, Society and the State in Mexico.* Toronto: Canadian Gay Archives, 1991.

Martínez, Elena M., *Lesbian Voices from Latin America: Breaking Ground.* New York: Garland, 1996.

Rominske, Anthony G., "Subverting Social Norms: Lesbianism in Mexico." M.A. thesis, Ohio University, Athens, 1996.

Stevens, Evelyn P., "Marianismo: The Other Face of Machismo." In *Confronting Change, Challenging Tradition: Women in Latin American History,* edited by Gertrude M. Yeager. Wilmington, Delaware: Scholarly Resources, 1994.

Taylor, Clark, "El Ambiente: Male Homosexual Social Life in Mexico City." Ph.D. diss., University of California, Berkeley, 1978.

_____, "Legends, Syncretism, and Continuing Echoes of Homosexuality from Pre-Columbian and Colonial Mexico." In *Latin American Male Homosexualities,* edited by Stephen O. Murray. Albuquerque: University of New Mexico Press, 1995.

—ANTHONY G. ROMINSKE

HUERTA, EFRAÍN

1914-1982 • Writer

Born in Silao, Guanajuato, on June 18, 1914, Efraín Huerta belongs to the same generation of poets that includes Octavio Paz. After abandoning his law studies in Mexico City,

Huerta's career began in earnest when, together with Paz, he collaborated on *Taller,* the literary journal that would replace *Contemporáneos* in the late 1930s as Mexico's preeminent forum for poetry. The *Taller* Group distinguished itself from the generation that preceded it by combining the Contemporáneos's interest in innovation and esthetics with an increased consciousness of the connection between society and poetry. If Octavio Paz represents a dedication to the esthetic possibilities of a more subjective poetry, Huerta continually emphasized social and political themes. Eschewing the estheticism of many of his peers, he came to be known as one of Mexico's most committed social poets.

Huerta won international acclaim early in his career when he was awarded the Academic Palms in 1945 by the French government, but he would have to wait 20 years before receiving similar attention in Mexico. In 1975 he was awarded the Villaurrutia Prize and one year later, the National Literature Prize. In 1968, Joaquín Mortíz published an anthology of his poetry *(Poesía 1935–1968)* that was received enthusiastically by readers who were frustrated with Mexico's conservatism and appalled by the massacre at Tlatelolco. Critical interest in his work has been rekindled by younger writers who see in him an alternative to the high art establishment represented by Paz and his colleagues.

Huerta's poetry frequently employs images of the city, celebrates the erotic, recovers colloquial speech, and denounces social injustice. His first two books, *Absoluto amor* (1933) and *Línea del alba* (1936), were published together with additional material in 1944 under the title *Los hombres del alba*. The poems in this collection and in the one that immediately preceded it, *Poemas de guerra y esperanza* (1943), demonstrate the impact effect of the Spanish Civil War and World War II on Huerta and his generation. In "Los hombres del alba" the poetic voice combines images of night and death to illustrate the brutality of violent conflict. "Declaración de odio" uses images of an impersonal and barren cityscape to evoke a sense of alienation and desperation.

The city is the refuge of "the vulgar bourgeoisie," "hypocrites," and "American films."

U.S. imperialism is also the theme of what may be Huerta's most well known poem, "Avenida Juárez" from *Estrella en alto* (1956). The poem's voice evokes images of one of Mexico City's most important avenues to convey a sense of desperate solitude and impotence in the face of U.S. cultural and corporate influence. In the final stanza of "Avenida Juárez," U.S. tourists, "neurotic millionaires one-hundred-times divorced," "gangsters," and "Miss Texas" cheapen the landscape and leave behind "crumpled post cards of Chapultepec," the Military Academy stormed by U.S. troops in 1947. Huerta also published *Los poemas de viaje, 1949–1953,* in 1956 and united in this collection poems detailing his travels in the Soviet Union and Warsaw Pact nations. The collection has been criticized for its elegies to Joseph Stalin and strong ideological bent.

Not all of Huerta's poetry is so stridently political. In *La rosa primitiva* (1950), *El Tajín* (1963), and *Los eróticos y otros poemas* (1973), Huerta combines an intensely personal perspective with the themes of eroticism, love, abandonment, and solitude to produce elaborately structured lyrical verses that are decidedly apolitical. Later in his career he also developed a poetic form that he called *poemínimos* (minipoems). These short, often humorous poems help break his stereotype as a grim ideologue.

Select Bibliography
Aguilar, Ricardo, *Efraín Huerta.* Mexico City: Tinta Negra, 1984.
Dauster, Frank, *The Double Strand.* Lexington: University of Kentucky Press, 1987.
Leiva, Raúl, *Imagen de la poesía mexicana contemporánea.* Mexico City: UNAM, 1959.

—Dan Rogers

HUERTA, VICTORIANO
1854–1916 • General and President

Despite recent attempts to portray Victoriano Huerta as a reformer, there is little question that he was a self-serving dictator. Huerta had little in common with the rebels who sought either reform or revolution during the civil war years of 1910 to 1920.

Victoriano Huerta's background soon brought him into prominence as a military figure. Born in a small Jalisco village in 1854, Huerta's mestizo father and indigenous mother provided him only a rudimentary education. When a federal general passed through his community, however, Huerta took up with the soldier and became his personal secretary; ultimately, Huerta's patron obtained his admittance into the Colegio Militar. Huerta became commissioned as an officer in 1877, upon his graduation from the corps of engineers.

Huerta soon demonstrated his skills as a military commander. Huerta participated in the Tepic and Sinaloa pacification campaigns from 1878 to 1879. Then he helped organize the general staff by supervising geographic studies in Puebla and Jalapa for nine years as part of a plan to prepare a new military map of Mexico. Huerta's cartographic work carried him to nearly every state until his recall to permanent membership on the General Staff in 1890.

It soon became clear that Huerta excelled in ruthlessly crushing domestic opposition. In October 1893, the dictator

Porfirio Díaz sent Huerta to snuff out a revolt in Guerrero. Huerta executed several rebels despite an amnesty. After more cartographic and staff work, Huerta fought Yaqui rebels in Sonora and then fought in the Yucatán campaign of 1900. During the defeat of the Maya, Huerta devised fairly successful antiguerrilla tactics. He was promoted to general in 1901.

As the Porfiriato came to a close in the early years of the new century, Huerta supported Bernardo Reyes. Huerta particularly was grateful when Reyes recommended that Huerta be appointed undersecretary of war. But the Científicos (prominent advisers to Díaz) stopped Huerta's nomination. Angry, Huerta obtained an indefinite leave of absence and worked as an engineer in Monterrey, where Reyes again had assumed the state governorship.

Despite his anger with the Científicos, Huerta had no intention of supporting the insurrection of Francisco I. Madero in 1910. The uprising led Huerta to apply for active military duty. The federal army welcomed Huerta back, issuing him orders to fight in Morelos. In April 1911, he prepared to defend Cuernavaca before being recalled to Mexico City. There, he and other officers consulted with Díaz on the president's decision to resign on May 25, 1911. Díaz feared an attack might be made on his life as he departed for Europe; therefore, Huerta commanded the railroad convoy that escorted the dictator to Veracruz.

Following Díaz's departure, Provisional President Francisco León de la Barra sent Huerta to Morelos in order to speed the demobilization of the 2,500 troops under the command of Emiliano Zapata. Huerta arrived on August 10, 1911; the following day, Zapatistas ambushed his troops. Huerta became frustrated when Zapata demanded the federal troops be withdrawn despite the government's demands that Huerta maintain order. Huerta overreacted several times and pursued Zapatista forces unsuccessfully.

After Madero's electoral victory, the new president ordered Huerta removed from the army because the general supported the ambitions of Madero's political rival, Bernardo Reyes. Huerta fought back but remained inactive as revolts erupted against Madero. When Reyes attempted to revolt, Huerta had no troops under his command and thus could offer no assistance. But when another of Madero's political rivals, Pascual Orozco, revolted in March 1912, the Madero cabinet convinced a reluctant president to allow Huerta to lead government forces against the rebels. Huerta triumphed at the Second Battle of Rellano on May 23, 1912. Orozco retreated, but Madero recalled Huerta to Mexico City, where his prestige among conservatives soared.

But Huerta also attempted to execute Francisco "Pancho" Villa—who had been fighting under his command—for the alleged theft of an expensive Arabian mare after its owner complained to Huerta after the Rellano triumph. Only the intervention of Madero's brothers prevented Villa from being shot, which helps explain Villa's long loyalty to Madero and his passionate hatred of Huerta.

It was only a matter of time before Huerta moved against Madero. Although he agreed that Madero should resign, Huerta initially refused to join the conspiracy led by Félix Díaz (nephew of Porfirio) and Bernardo Reyes; nevertheless, Huerta did not tell Madero about the fatal plot being planned against his presidency. When the revolt finally broke, Madero named Huerta interim commander of loyal troops. Huerta's sympathies lay with the Felicistas, but he wanted a commanding position in a new regime. Therefore, a military stalemate resulted from Huerta's discussions with Félix Díaz about what to do after the fall of Madero. Once the Mexican Senate and U.S. ambassador Henry Lane Wilson favored Madero's resignation, Huerta's forces arrested Madero, and Félix Díaz agreed that Huerta should be provisional president.

Initially, Félix Díaz did not approve of Huerta's appointing himself chief executive on February 18, 1913 (before Madero had had a chance to resign). But Henry Lane Wilson brokered a compromise so that Huerta became provisional president with a Felicista cabinet. It was understood that Huerta then would support Félix Díaz in upcoming elections. Madero and his vice president, José María Pino Suárez, resigned on February 19; according to the 1857 Constitution, the minister of foreign relations, Pedro Lascuráin, now was supposed to assume the presidency. Lascurain performed only one act as chief executive; he appointed Huerta as minister of the interior, next in line for the presidency, and then resigned. By this maneuver, Huerta became interim president in a technically legal sense. Fearing the presence of Huerta's troops, Congress accepted this charade as the archbishop of Mexico offered a Te Deum.

Huerta's role in the death of Madero remains controversial. At one point, Huerta intended to send Madero out of the country but learned that an attempt would be made to free him. Therefore, he jailed Madero in the National Palace and requested the advice of Henry Lane Wilson, a key supporter. Wilson simply advised Huerta to do "what was best for the peace of the country." Madero and Pino Suárez were executed on the night of February 22, 1913, the day after a Huerta cabinet meeting; circumstantial evidence strongly indicates Huerta's guilt in planning the murders.

The new president received strong backing from foreign diplomats and their governments. Wilson introduced Huerta to his colleagues as "the savior of Mexico" and ordered all U.S. consuls to do everything possible to aid the Huerta regime. Eager for Mexican oil to fuel their new petroleum-powered navy, the British extended recognition to Huerta, and other Europeans followed suit. Meanwhile, Huerta gradually began a process of dismissing Felicista cabinet members as he consolidated power.

Huerta's seizure of power convinced Venustiano Carranza, the governor of Coahuila and a former supporter of Madero, to revolt. He became the first governor to reject Huerta's February 18 circular telegram, a message declaring that the Senate had authorized Huerta to assume executive authority. Carranza disputed the legality of Huerta's status; on February 19, Carranza called upon all of Mexico to join him in armed revolt against Huerta.

Its narrow political focus limited the early phase of Carranza's movement. His followers called themselves Constitutionalists because their general concern became defeating Huerta and holding new elections. Despite his record as a proven reformer, Carranza's Plan de Guadalupe said little about social or economic reform. Initially, Carranza insisted upon unconditional victory, but the federal army soon forced him to retreat from Coahuila. After a 79-day horseback journey, a bedraggled Carranza arrived in Sonora while Pancho Villa, Álvaro Obregón, Jesús Carranza, and Pablo González battled Huerta's offensive. These leaders offered a much more reform-oriented, populist brand of Revolution, and the uprising soon drew widespread support.

Huerta's war measures were extensive. War on two fronts weakened Huerta, who had to send troops to Morelos after Zapata rejected the dictator's offer to become governor. Zapata's peasant army became a formidable opponent because the Zapatistas distributed land wherever they operated. Furthermore, revolts erupted in 13 other states as civil war coincided with increased social revolution. Huerta generally responded with military reflexes. He quickly dismissed Maderista governors and convinced Pascual Orozco to serve in the *rurales* (the rural military police force). Huerta declared that he would win at whatever cost, and his federal army campaigned ruthlessly. Huerta also tried to militarize society. Nearly everyone had to wear a uniform as thousands were drafted. Schools provided military instruction, and war production increased. Although the army numbered 200,000, many of these troops deserted at first opportunity. Defeats in Chihuahua by the fall of 1913 made Huerta's situation quite serious.

By now, U.S. president Woodrow Wilson had grown vehemently opposed to the Huerta regime and was determined to topple the dictator one way or the other. President Wilson dismissed Ambassador Henry Lane Wilson (no relation) and sent a series of emissaries to obtain Huerta's resignation. John Lind, a Minnesota governor who knew little about Mexico, became the first envoy. In August 1913, Lind demanded an armistice, free elections, and that Huerta not be a presidential candidate. Huerta became angered even more when Lind offered him a loan to stay out of the election. Once Huerta publicized the notes of the "peace" mission, Wilson temporarily backed the Catholic Party to succeed Huerta. Wilson's attempt to ally with the Constitutionalists also collapsed. By clamping an arms embargo upon the Huerta regime, Wilson sought sympathy from Carranza. But Carranza refused to accept Wilson's proposal for armed U.S. intervention on a joint basis and for northern Mexico to separate itself from the rest of the country. Although lifting the embargo in February 1914 enabled the Constitutionalists to unleash a spring offensive, Carranza decided to win with minimal foreign aid.

Meanwhile, Huerta's European foreign policy failed as well. Huerta had decided to maintain the Porfirian policy of supporting European capital to provide a check against U.S. investments. Initially, his approach appeared successful. In return for favored treatment, the Europeans quickly extended diplomatic relations. In order to improve their position in Mexican oil fields, the British opposed Woodrow

Wilson. But when the British admiralty discovered that Mexican oil was of too low a quality for their fleet, British policy began to slacken in its backing for Huerta. As World War I approached, the British needed U.S. support. The Germans initially backed Huerta as strongly as the British, but the German determination to avoid war with the United States made Berlin back off from outright alliance with Huerta as well.

In his domestic policy, Huerta was a ruthless dictator. The government shut down critical newspapers as a vast network of secret agents spied on the population. The Huerta regime is responsible for dozens of assassinations, including those of Deputy Serapio Rendón and Senator Belisario Domínguez. When legislators protested publicly, Huerta closed Congress and marched the lawmakers to jail.

To tighten his grip, Huerta sent former ally Félix Díaz out of the country. Díaz represented the only legal opposition in presidential elections. Even though Huerta did not conduct a political campaign and had promised that he would not be a candidate during the October 1913 elections, the government declared Huerta the winner. His hand-picked deputies and senators also "won."

Generally a conservative restoration, the Huerta regime lasted longer than Madero's partially because the military and landowners knew that they faced the loss of land and the end of the traditional military if the insurgents won. Nevertheless, Huerta was not as reactionary as traditionally portrayed. He tripled petroleum taxes and discussed nationalizing Mexican oil, he modestly increased educational opportunities in a few areas, and he redistributed small amounts of land. It must be noted, of course, that the latter measures took place toward the end of Huerta's tenure, by which point the end of his regime was in sight. Huerta's bloody counterinsurgency already had cost him much of his popular support, and the Constitutionalists effectively controlled most of the country.

The reasons for Huerta's fall are numerous; not the least was the dictator's personality. Although a brave and disciplined soldier, he was given to egotism, stubborn impatience, and temper tantrums. There is no question that he was an alcoholic, and he reportedly smoked marijuana as well. He also was corrupt; he apparently stole 1.5 million pesos during the Orozco campaign, and after he ousted Madero, Huerta stuffed his pockets with 500-peso notes given him by conservative Mexican supporters and U.S. businessmen.

Such a personality would not tolerate independence among subordinates. As a result, Huerta constantly shuffled his cabinet members, leading to great instability in the government. Over his 17 months in power, Huerta used 32 different ministers. To make matters worse, he often met with them in taverns and restaurants, further disrupting any sense of ministerial authority or administrative continuity.

Fiscal problems also weakened Huerta's regime. European banks that controlled Mexican finances became angered when Huerta seized customs revenue committed to previous loans. Printing an excessive supply of paper money that rapidly lost its value, the government operated with a deficit that amounted to 6 million pesos monthly. Fiscal crises resulted when foreign governments called in debts; forced loans added to Mexico's miseries. Meanwhile, the Constitutionalist rebels occupied key production centers, particularly once they defeated the federal army in the cotton-producing region at Torreón on April 2, 1914. The same month, Carrancista troops probed Tampico's defenses in the oil-producing northeast.

In states such as Coahuila, Huertista policy alienated virtually everyone. Heavy taxes upon cattle ranchers reduced the size of herds while the Huertistas seized horses and cattle in exchange for worthless promissory notes. Municipal taxes increased by as much as five time the original assessments. Huerta continually demanded more taxes and diverted these funds to Mexico City instead of local authorities. After Huerta centralized the Coahuila school system rigidly and withdrew funds, the Coahuila government closed all its schools by May 1914. An increase in vice, repression of civil liberties, and the reintroduction of the hated *jefes políticos* (local political bosses) angered many.

Nor could Huerta prevent U.S. intervention. The pretext that Woodrow Wilson used was the brief detention of a U.S. officer and six sailors by a Huertista garrison during their defense of Tampico on April 9, 1914. The U.S. Navy lodged a strong protest, and the Mexican commander apologized, ordering the arrest of the unfortunate officer. But the U.S. State Department claimed that the whaleboat from which the shore party had arrived flew a U.S. flag. Wilson demanded that the flag be hoisted on the shoreline with the Mexicans obliged to fire a 21-gun salute to it. When Huerta refused to submit to all these demands, Wilson obtained congressional approval to intervene in Mexico.

The intervention—an attack upon Veracruz—is immortalized in Mexico's national memory as one of the ugliest deeds ever inflicted upon the country by its neighbor to the north. When Wilson learned that a large cargo of U.S. armaments purchased by British and French investors would arrive in Veracruz aboard a German vessel from Hamburg, U.S. forces invaded the city on April 21. With no warning, the fleet shelled the port and inflicted many civilian casualties. The cynical Huerta withdrew federal troops, but enraged inhabitants fought U.S. sailors and marines. Young Mexican naval cadets became some of the bravest defenders until literally blown out of their fortifications by point-blank shelling from U.S. naval guns. Many women died in the streets, and U.S. troops executed those suspected of resistance.

Huerta, however, tried to use the tragedy at Veracruz to strengthen his position. Huerta claimed falsely that Spanish war vessels fought for him against the U.S. fleet in Veracruz. Huerta also attempted to induce Carranza to join him in defending the country, but Carranza refused. Despite Carranza's protests, Huerta ordered his governors to convince the public that Villa and Zapata would march on Veracruz. The saddest aspect of Huerta's opportunism is that many citizens flocked to join the federal army in burst of anti-U.S. patriotism only to be sent north to battle the Constitutionalists. Meanwhile, the German vessel that had caught Wilson's attention sailed from Veracruz with its deadly cargo and unloaded the armaments at a southern port.

As domestic opposition to this fiasco mounted in the United States, Wilson agreed to mediation but once again failed when he attempted to use the peace table to impose a government to his liking in Mexico. By this time, however, Huerta could no longer hold out. As the Constitutionalists marched toward Mexico City, they shattered federal units at Zacatecas in June 1914. Huerta resigned on July 15 and sailed to Spain on a German cruiser. There he plotted to return with German aid in conjunction with Orozco. After arriving in the United States, judicial agents arrested Huerta and jailed him in Fort Bliss, Texas. In January 1916, while under the care of a U.S. doctor in El Paso, he passed away, possibly as a result of cirrhosis of the liver.

Select Bibliography

Katz, Friedrich, *The Secret War in Mexico: Europe, the United States and the Mexican Revolution.* Chicago: University of Chicago Press, 1981.

Meyer, Michael C., *Huerta: A Political Portrait.* Lincoln: University of Nebraska Press, 1972.

Richmond, Douglas W., "Factional Political Strife in Coahuila, 1910–1920." *Hispanic American Historical Review* 60 (February 1980).

—Douglas W. Richmond

HUMAN RIGHTS

The notion of human rights in Mexico dates back to the colonial period, when a famous polemic between Bartolomé las Casas, then bishop of Chiapas, and the theologian Ginéz de Sepúlveda, over the rights of the vanquished Indians, led to legislation, the Leyes de Indias, granting Indians basic rights deserving of protection by the Spanish Crown.

During the Wars of Independence from Spain, the Constitution of Apatzingán, whose first version was drafted by the insurgent priest José María Morelos y Pavón in 1814, specified in very clear terms that such rights as popular sovereignty and representation, universality of the law, freedom from slavery and torture, and the obligation of Congress to pass laws ensuring just wages and education for the poor were among the fundamental natural rights of the *americanos,* or people of the former colony of New Spain. Upon achieving independence, individual rights were protected by the Constitution of 1824, and this protection expanded in the Constitution of 1857.

The constitutional history of Mexico is linked closely to the notion of human rights, to the point that one of the provisions established by Mexico in the Treaty of Guadalupe Hidalgo of 1848, in which possession of its northern territories was ceded to the victorious United States after the U.S.-Mexican War, was that slavery not be reinstated in those lands. The Constitution of 1917, the result of the Mexican Revolution, became the first to establish the protection of social rights, two years before the Constitution of the Weimar Republic did the same in Europe.

During the first part of the twentieth century, post-Revolutionary Mexican governments developed a foreign policy consistent with the principles of peace and nonintervention. This facilitated Mexico's adherence to the League of Nations, its endorsement of the United Nations Charter, and, in 1948, its endorsement of the Universal Declaration of Human Rights drafted by the United Nations and its regional counterpart, the American Declaration of Human Rights, by the Organization of American States (OAS). By the mid-1990s, Mexico was a party to 38 binding international human rights treaties and conventions, both of a regional and universal scope, designed to protect the full range of human rights: individual, civil, political, social, economic, and cultural, as well as the rights of minorities. These conventions were, by virtue of Article 133 of the Constitution of 1917, to be incorporated into domestic legal provisions.

However, the profusion of constitutional provisions and international treaties does not mean that human rights have been respected or systematically promoted in Mexico. In fact, there are really very few domestic legal remedies available to ordinary citizens, and rights proclaimed in international treaties rarely have been upheld by Mexican courts. On closer examination, many abuses have even been encouraged by legal practices. Thus, Supreme Court rulings establishing confession as the most valuable source of evidence in criminal proceedings had the perverse effect of endorsing the use of torture of detainees in order to force them to declare their guilt.

Protection of human rights always has been a constitutionally enshrined goal more than a fact in Mexico. The challenges posed by the complex political and economic issues facing the country made the numerous rights embodied in its succeeding constitutions more a desired objective than a reality. Even this tradition had deteriorated by the mid-1990s, however, especially after the entrance of Mexico into a free trading zone with the United States and Canada, formalized in 1993 by the North American Free Trade Agreement (NAFTA). In the process of instituting a free market economy, Mexican governments modified the Constitution and, as a result, curtailed both social and individual rights. Articles 16, 19, and 20 were reformed in 1996, restricting protection of defendants during criminal proceedings. Article 27, which established land rights, was modified in 1992 in order to allow the privatization of *ejido* (communal village) land.

The Struggle for Political Rights in an Authoritarian Regime

The political system, which emerged from the Mexican Revolution and prevailed as of the mid-1990s, has demonstrated an authoritarian and corporativist nature and has fostered a political culture that emphasizes loyalty and obedience to those in power, rather than the assertion of rights. Its political machinery has been characterized by U.S. social scientist Roderic Camp as "secretive, centralized, uninnovative, discontinuous, arbitrary, uncoordinated, and personalistic."

The Mexican political regime has existed in a class by itself for several reasons, not least among them its resilience and durability. Although by no means a democracy, it has been quite successful in adopting several policies associated with democratic governments, such as formally guaranteed civil and political rights as well as regular elections and opposition parties. However, in practice, the regime has institutionalized human rights abuse and protected its perpetrators. This abuse has been exercised through a complex mixture of co-optation and repression of members of opposition movements. The regime has exercised political domination through a high degree of institutionalization and corporativization of the political process. The political system was founded on a strong presidential figure and an official ruling party that "represents" the interests of society through its sectors: workers, peasants, business, and middle classes.

As of 1996, the country suffered from the effects of an intense but uncertain political transition as a result of the emergence of new political actors demanding a democratic political process. From the late 1960s through the mid-1990s, the political regime underwent a protracted and agonizing crisis of legitimacy, resulting in sporadic, but ever more frequent incidents of serious political violence and repression. This process began with the challenge to the regime posed by the students' movement in 1968, which ended in a massacre of demonstrators in the square of Tlatelolco, a few days before the inauguration of the Olympic Games that were held in Mexico City that year.

In 1996, the ruling Partido Revolucionario Institucional (PRI, or Institutional Revolutionary Party), in power since 1929, controlled the majority of both houses in the Federal Congress along with 28 governorships and 84 percent of municipal governments. Political rights consistently have been violated both legally and in practice until very recently and, as of 1996, still had virtually no constitutional protection. As a rule, elections have been neither free nor fair, although beginning in the 1980s, and thanks to intense citizen mobilization, more overt forms of electoral fraud were eliminated in some regions of Mexico, allowing opposition parties to control 4 governorships of a total of 32, and 325 municipalities of a total of 2,395.

Postelectoral strife always has been a major cause of political violence, and more consistently after 1988, when a belligerent opposition took to electoral politics in the hope of defeating the PRI. This strategy partly was successful, but it also resulted in the assassination of several hundred members and supporters of the center-left party, the Partido de la Revolución Democrática (PRD, or Party of the Democratic Revolution), and the harassment and detention of many members of the main opposition party, the right-of-center Partido de Acción Nacional (PAN, or National Action Party).

The tide of violence also caught the PRI when its reformist candidate for the presidential election of 1994, Luis Donaldo Colosio, was assassinated in a campaign rally by hired gunmen and members of a still obscure plot. Months later, José Francisco Ruiz Massieu, PRI general secretary, was shot in his automobile after leaving a meeting with elected members of Congress. Prominent members of the government of Carlos Salinas de Gortari, including the president's brother, Raúl Salinas, have been implicated in both crimes, although the investigations still are inconclusive.

The period between 1988 and 1994 was marked by the emergence of a vocal and highly organized civil society that took it upon itself to ensure free and fair elections, as well as the full protection of political rights. Hundreds of social and civil organizations joined in the effort to monitor local and federal elections and to report on the numerous irregularities and fraudulent practices that they registered. By the time of the presidential election in 1994, these organizations had acquired considerable expertise as well as international standing, which enabled them to observe the election closely. There is a general consensus that Ernesto Zedillo Ponce de León, who replaced PRI candidate Colosio, was elected in a relatively clean contest in August of 1994. The election was monitored closely by more than 10,000 national and international observers organized by several civic organizations. Alianza Cívica, the most important coalition of observer organizations, reported that although it was clear that Zedillo was undoubtedly the winner, the election had not been a fair competition, since the PRI candidate had a virtual monopoly of the media and many times more resources than the other candidates. Upon taking office, President Zedillo promised a definitive electoral reform that would, once and for all, put an end to conflict and uncertainty.

Social, Economic, and Cultural Rights

The struggle with issues of inequality has defined Mexican political history. This state of affairs led to a social revolution and the reiteration of social justice as the basis of legitimacy of government, proclaimed in the Constitution of 1917. However, the country never has been able to reach its goal of social justice.

For the three decades following World War II, Mexico enjoyed high economic growth and broad-based development giving rise to an extensive middle class, a new industrial working class with steadily rising wage levels, and a rural sector that also increased its income thanks to the opening of new lands, rising productivity, and government-sponsored irrigation projects.

This inward looking, state-led model of development did not mean that income was being distributed evenly, however. Tripartite negotiations under the auspices of PRI labor and peasant organizations, business, and government ensured that a portion of this expanding national wealth trickled down to the lower reaches of society. An aggressive extension of medical and educational services by the government during this period of "stabilizing development" provided the illusion that welfare and social mobility were on the increase. Nevertheless, Mexico never was able to break the pattern of highly skewed income distribution.

The facade began to crumble in the 1970s, when the development model openly began to show its flaws. In 1982, Mexico suffered a severe economic crisis caused by a spiraling foreign debt and the fall of oil prices (its main export) in the international market. The economy under the government of President José López Portillo (1976–82) had been borrowing heavily from foreign banks to finance the rapid development of the nationalized oil industry. In actual fact, very little of this money actually was used in productive investments; according to James Henry, "billions were squandered on noncompetitive steel plants, a $6 billion nuclear plant that still doesn't function, a gas pipeline to nowhere, wasteful development loans, arms and payoffs to contractors and public officials."

In August 1982, the Mexican government announced that it could not meet its debt payments for lack of foreign reserves. The international banking community and the U.S. Treasury came to the rescue with fresh money. Payments were stretched out and new loans were written with the result that Mexico became socially and economically dominated by the debt problem. In order to face the monumental payments on the debt, severe austerity measures recommended by the International Monetary Fund (IMF) and the World Bank were adopted. Thus, wages were slashed, government services and subsidies cut drastically, state-owned industry privatized, and inflation restricted at the cost of higher taxes and interest rates and less credit. The impact of this recovery program preserved the stability of the international trading and finance system, but it caused a dramatic slowing of development. Succeeding administrations continued and increased the breadth and scope of these economic policies with a net loss of economic sovereignty.

At the end of the twentieth century, Mexico seems farther than ever from reaching its desired goal of a more equitable and inclusive social structure. The economy never fully recovered after 1982 and was subjected to periodic bouts of currency devaluation, massive capital flight, and increased dependency on foreign lending. Economic restructuring under the auspices of the international financial community led to the implantation of a free market economy based on exports of a few goods, mainly to the United States and

Canada, its major trading partners. The social cost of this policy was devastating. Inequality increased, producing a highly polarized society with rampant unemployment.

Social welfare policies and their legal provisions, which provided subsidized food, health, and education for the majority of the population, were dismantled. Consumption per capita of corn, beans, and wheat dropped more than 35 percent in the 10 years following their price increase at double the rate of the minimum wage. Malnutrition, coupled with a decline of the health budget to almost half of what it had been in 1980, caused a tripling of infant deaths in 1992. Overall spending on education declined from 5.5 percent to 2.5 percent of Mexico's Gross Domestic Product.

In 1992, the Salinas government promoted a bill to reform Article 27 of the Constitution, encouraging the privatization of the *ejido* land ownership in the countryside by a series of measures that included the termination of agrarian reform and of government subsidies and credit loans to small farmers. Mexican agriculture plummeted as a result: as of 1996, almost one-third of the populace still lived in rural areas, but agriculture accounted for only 8 percent of the gross domestic product. Less than 1 percent of rural producers were competitive in the international market, and more than half of Mexican *campesinos* (peasants) and farmers were excluded totally from the formal economy.

Undoubtedly, the Indian population of Mexico was the most negatively affected by these economic policies. As of 1993, approximately one-third of all the municipalities in the country were populated by Indians, and in these, 43 percent of the population was illiterate, more than three times the national average. Six out of ten Indians were unemployed, and the average wage when they found a job was half the national average.

Mexican society had become far more unequal than ever before, with a related increase in violence and a general loss of legitimacy of the political regime. The increase of social protests was dramatic. In Mexico City alone there was an average of six public demonstrations a day in 1995, making a total of 2,522 for that year. In many regions, migration to the United States and Canada became the only hope for employment. Unable to protect the social and economic rights of its population, especially of women and children, and unwilling to concede full recognition of civil and political rights, the Mexican government also became a consistent violator of the right to life, justice, and security.

The Rights to Life, Justice, and Security

Torture, arbitrary detention and imprisonment, forced disappearances, extrajudicial executions, usually for political motives, abysmal prison conditions, repression of the labor movement, and abuse of indigenous and rural populations have been the most persistent violations of the rights to life, justice, and security in Mexico. The perpetrators overwhelmingly have been members of the security forces: police and military, or hired thugs with close connections to the former. These violations have occurred in the context of a society striving for change and democratization. Redress would entail promoting social justice and electoral reform, including truly free elections and an independent Congress and judiciary system.

In rural areas, abuses have been more widespread, especially in the southern states where there is an acute conflict over land between indigenous *campesinos* and landowners. *Guardias blancas,* or vigilantes, have murdered peasant squatters, and in some regions large landowners have maintained private militias to protect their property from invasions. Local and federal authorities have closed their eyes to these militias, which often have employed police or military personnel. Rural violence became more widespread after an armed rebellion of Maya peasants of the Ejército Zapatista de Liberación Nacional (EZLN, or Zapatista Army of National Liberation) erupted in the southernmost state of Chiapas on January 1, 1994.

In addition to the state of Chiapas, the state of Guerrero has witnessed extreme violence against peasants and indigenous populations. State police killed 17 peasants in Aguas Blancas on June 28, 1995, while they were en route to protest against failure of the local government to provide them with fertilizer and herbicides. The police alleged self-defense as the motive for the massacre, but subsequent investigations by official and unofficial bodies established that the unarmed peasants were ambushed by several hundred security personnel under orders from higher state officials. Receiving much pressure from the press and civil society groups, the local government detained and prosecuted several lower-level state officials, but the higher-level authorities were never prosecuted for ordering the killings. In the name of restoring order, various rural areas have been militarized, and human rights groups have reported much increased human rights violation.

Torture has been frequent according to estimates by such organizations as Amnesty International, the Comisión Mexicana de Defensa y Promoción de los Derechos Humanos (CMDPDH, or Mexican Commission for the Defense and Promotion of Human Rights), and the U.S. State Department. Criminal procedures in Mexico consider confessions of detainees as the primary source of evidence in convictions. This fact, when combined with an ill-trained and underpaid police force, has rendered torture and similar abuses an integral part of criminal proceedings. False accusations and undue process of law have become two of the most generalized human rights abuses in the country, affecting all sectors of the population.

Criminal activity in Mexico has reached alarming proportions. According to research by the CMDPDH, the crime rate increased by 47 percent in Mexico City for the first half of 1995, as compared to the same period in 1994. The protracted economic crisis may have been a cause for this rise in criminal activity, since there is a direct relationship between falling income levels and the rise of criminality. Ironically, the large number of police also may have played a role. Mexico has more police per capital than the United States and most European countries, but these forces historically have been riddled with corruption and home to a great number of criminals. According to a high-ranking official in the Ministry of the Interior, in 1995, 30 percent of all "highway robbers" were or had been policemen. Attorney general of the republic, Antonio Lozano García, estimated in the same year that 80 percent of all federal judicial policemen had engaged in criminal activity.

The failure of the government to protect the population from criminal assaults, especially in the urban areas, is a major human rights problem. In Mexico City, only 3.8 percent of reported crimes from 1990 to 1995 were resolved by the authorities. This fact, coupled with increased pressure from the U.S. government for the prosecution of drug-related crimes, has resulted in a dangerous tendency to rely on the military for public security.

Police impunity and that of politicians has been an established pattern in Mexico. Traditionally, few reported crimes are investigated, and when these crimes are committed by public officials—turning them into human rights abuses—prosecution and punishment are doubly difficult.

The government-sponsored Comisión Nacional de Derechos Humanos (CNDH, or National Commission on Human Rights) has recommended punishment by dismissal or censure of more than 2,000 public servants, most of them members of the security forces, but it has been unsuccessful in bringing criminal or civil charges against the more serious perpetrators of abuse, especially those in the security forces. In some cases, police officers dismissed in one state have found law enforcement employment in another. In other instances, they simply have continued to act in criminal activities.

Impunity has been absolute in the case of members of the military involved in gross and systematic human rights abuses. Aerial attacks on civilians, summary executions, illegal detentions and torture, as well as the rape of alleged EZLN women in Chiapas have gone unpunished. The army has denied any responsibility for these abuses, which have been documented carefully by both official and independent human rights groups, both national and international.

The Defense and Promotion of Human Rights

The defense and promotion of human rights has become a social movement in Mexico. Despite its novelty compared to other forms of collective action, this movement has had a considerable impact on the prevailing political culture as well as a partial institutionalization of its claims. It began in the 1970s with the quest of a group of women, under the leadership of Rosario Ibarra de Piedra, for their disappeared children and husbands held in clandestine prisons by army and security forces as a consequence of guerrilla activity. Twenty years later, in 1994, some estimates put the number of civil organizations devoted to human rights at 239, the second-largest group of nongovernmental organizations at the time.

The movement has been committed to the expansion of a culture of civility, stressing the notion that citizens have rights and that these must be defended by civil society. In addition to mobilizing thousands of election observers, the human rights movement played an essential role in peacekeeping activities, both by deflecting violence resulting from postelectoral conflicts as well as in advocating for a peaceful solution to the armed conflict in Chiapas.

Human rights organizations have flourished all over the country, despite the fact that many have been harassed and their members threatened and, in some cases, even killed by the police, as was the case with Norma Corona Sapiens, president of the Sinaloa nongovernmental human rights group in May 1990.

In 1990, in an unprecedented acknowledgment of the gravity of human rights violations, the government of Carlos Salinas de Gortari created a governmental institution to address the problem. Thus, the Comisión Nacional de Derechos Humanos came into existence. Its creation was almost simultaneous with the announcement that Mexico and the United States would begin negotiations on NAFTA. This was no coincidence; the Mexican government was already under scrutiny for serious human rights abuses that had come to light. The CNDH was vested with very little prosecutorial powers and virtually no independence. Electoral and labor rights also were excluded from its mandate, despite the fact that abuses arising from these two areas represented a substantial percentage of all reported violations.

In 1992, the Constitution was amended to establish a national system of state-sponsored human rights commissions in the 32 federal entities. These commissions were to function separately from the CNDH. Their performance has been variable, and dependent on many factors, not least of them their degree of autonomy from local governments.

Several years of severe criticism and continual prodding of these official commissions by nongovernmental organizations resulted in an increased effectiveness of their efforts, especially at the national level. They also legitimized the claim for respect of human rights and helped to open the political space for their defense. In its annual report for 1995, the CNDH claimed to have received a total of 9,488 complaints, and it dealt with 2,660, referring the rest to other government agencies. The majority of the former were handled by a process that the CNDH referred to as amicable agreement. Only when this proved impossible was greater pressure exerted in the form of public recommendations. As of July 1996, 1,053 recommendations had been issued, dealing with very serious violations, and 66 percent had been complied with fully.

The EZLN uprising in 1994, with its demands for work, land, justice, and freedom, brought the issue of human rights to the fore. In the 10 days of actual fighting that took place in Chiapas, at least 145 people were killed and hundreds wounded. More than 200 were arbitrarily detained, tortured, and forced to confess their involvement in the movement by members of the Mexican army and security forces. Several cases of aerial bombings of civilians, disappearances, and extrajudicial executions by the military were reported, and 25,000 people were displaced forcibly from their villages.

The nongovernmental human rights community in the country reacted immediately to this situation after the first news reports reached the public. An immense effort to mobilize national and international public opinion ensued. In three weeks, more than 140 nongovernmental organizations from across Mexico, accompanied by their counterparts from other countries (mainly the United States, Canada, and Spain), visited the area of conflict in Chiapas.

A few days after the EZLN had declared war on the Mexican government, more than 200,000 demonstrators marched in Mexico City, in sympathy with the cause of the rebels, demanding a negotiated settlement of the conflict. The main speaker at the peace rally was Miguel Concha, a Dominican friar and prominent human rights activist closely associated with Bishop Samuel Ruiz García of the San Cristóbal de las Casas, Chiapas diocese.

On January 12, 1994, shortly after the rally, President Salinas announced a unilateral cease-fire with the rebels and called for peace talks, which soon began under the auspices of the Congress with the mediation of Bishop Ruiz. Over the ensuing two years, more than 300 prominent intellectuals and leaders of social and civil organizations would participate as advisors to the EZLN on the issues of Indian rights, democracy, justice, social development, and women's rights, which are the agenda for the negotiation. In fact, the EZLN peace talks would produce a blueprint for a new, more inclusive social pact. In principle, the government pledged to honor the outcome of these negotiations, still ongoing in 1996.

Conclusion

The gap between constitutional proclamation of human rights and its enforcement in Mexico began to close in the mid-1990s. This does not mean that the immediate future for human rights is promising. The steady evaporation of social consent for the legitimacy of the prevailing economic and political systems predicts a period of great instability and coercion. However, the long period of crisis and the insertion of Mexico in the global economy has spawned social forces that have pushed the country toward a more open political system. Human rights undoubtedly have played an important part in the national debate, and pressure for their full recognition and protection will increase.

In July 1996, the Inter-American Human Rights Commission (IAHRC) of the Organization of American States (OAS) visited Mexico at the request of President Zedillo Ponce de León; it was the first such visit in 37 years. For a period of 10 days, the commission investigated the general situation of human rights in the country and visited Chiapas, Guerrero, and Baja California. Its members met with the president and his government; members of Congress, the Supreme Court, and the armed forces; religious officials, the EZLN, politicians, businessmen, and more than 100 nongovernmental human rights organizations. In its preliminary report, the IAHRC was impressed by the existence of a large, multifaceted, and diverse civil society, expressed in a number of nongovernmental organizations involved in multiple activities of national relevance. It also stressed the importance and need for an ongoing dialogue between them and the government in order to further human rights and democracy in Mexico.

For more than 20 years, civil society slowly constructed an agenda for justice and democracy in Mexico. Recognition for it has come from the international community. Widespread claims for the reform of the justice system, demilitarization of the police forces, an end to impunity for government and military officials, and the full observance of Indian people's and women's rights were supported by the IAHRC as valid and in accordance with Mexico's obligations under the American Convention for Human Rights adopted in 1978. This acknowledgment by the OAS legitimized society's struggle for human rights and issued a strong signal for change to the Mexican government.

Select Bibliography

Acosta, Mariclaire, "Elecciones en México: La sociedad civil y la defensa de los derechos humanos." In *Los derechos políticos como derechos humanos,* edited by Miguel Concha. Mexico City: UNAM and Jornada Ediciones, 1994.

Alba, Mario Rojas, *Las manos sucias: Los derechos humanos en México en el alba del Tratado de Libre Comercio de América del Norte (1988–1993).* Montréal: Mario Rojas Alba, 1993.

Americas Watch, *Human Rights in Mexico: A Policy of Impunity.* New York: Human Rights Watch, 1990.

Amnesty International, *Human Rights Violations in Mexico: A Challenge for the Nineties.* London: AI, 1995.

Barry, Tom, *Mexico: A Country Guide.* Albuquerque, New Mexico: Inter-Hemispheric Education Center, 1992.

Campos, Julieta, *¿Qué hacemos con los pobres? La reiterada querella por la nación.* Mexico City: Aguilar, Nuevo Siglo, 1995.

Collier, George, *Basta! Land and the Zapatista Rebellion in Chiapas.* San Francisco, California: Food First Books, 1994.

Comisión Mexicana de Defensa y Promoción de los Derechos Humanos A.C., *Informe sobre la situación de los derechos humanos en México durante la administración de Ernesto Zedillo, 1 de diciembre de 1994 a 31 de enero de 1996.* Mexico City: CMDPDH AC, 1996.

Comisión Nacional de Derechos Humanos, *Informe Anual: Mayo 1995–Mayo 1996.* 2 vols., Mexico City: CNDH, 1996.

Harrell, Rafael Ruíz, *Confesión y tortura.* Mexico City: CMDPDH AC, 1994.

Kotler, Jared, *The Clinton Administration and the Mexican Elections.* Albuquerque, New Mexico: Resource Center Press, 1994.

Olson, Eric, *The Evolving Role of Mexico's Military in Public Security and Antinarcotics Programs.* Washington, D.C.: Washington Office on Latin America, 1996.

Partido de la Revolución Democrática, Human Rights Commission, Parliamentary Group, *The Political Violence in Mexico: A Human Rights Affair.* Mexico City: Congreso de la Unión, 1992.

Rochlin, James, "Redefining Mexican Security during an Era of Post-Sovereignty." *Social Transformation and Humane Governance* 20:3 (July–September 1995).

—Mariclaire Acosta

HUMBOLDT, ALEXANDER VON

1769–1859 • Scientist, Traveler, and Writer

In March 1803 Alexander von Humboldt, hailed in his time as the "monarch of the sciences," set foot on Mexican shores at Acapulco. His visit was part of an ambitious 14-year program of scientific reconnaissance in the New World, begun in 1790 and made possible by the unusual generosity of Spain's King Carlos IV and his liberal minister of state, Manuel de Urquijo. They gave Humboldt a passport that allowed him, unlike most foreigners, to travel anywhere in Spanish America.

Humboldt had expected to remain in Mexico only four months, but his stay lengthened to almost a year (March 23, 1803, to March 7, 1804). His visit resulted in the publication of two books in 1810 that made an immense contribution to Europe's knowledge and understanding of Mexico as it moved toward Independence as well as of ancient Mexican civilization: *Essai politique sur le royaume de la Nouvelle Espagne* (Political Essay on the Kingdom of New Spain) and *Vues des cordillères et monuments des peuples indigènes de l'Amérique* (Views of the Cordilleras and Monuments of the Native Peoples of America). The impact of these works on the European mind amounted to a second discovery of Mexico.

Political Essay is an intensive study of the physical and human geography of Mexico, based on Humboldt's own investigations and on a wealth of statistical data generously furnished to him by colonial officials. For the first time, observes modern scholar José Miranda, "a great American region was viewed through the scientific and historical prisms of the Enlightenment." Here the European reader could find a clear and precise description of the geography of Mexico, its agriculture, mines, commerce, cultural achievement, and even its social classes and relations, for Humboldt was both physical scientist and sociologist.

Humboldt's panoramic vision was on the whole extremely favorable to Mexico and was optimistic—indeed, overly optimistic—about its future. He criticized the great landed estates, observing that "the property of New Spain, like that of Old Spain, is in great measure in the hands of a few powerful families, who have gradually absorbed the smaller estates." But he painted a glowing picture of the prospects of Mexican agriculture, claiming that there was not a single plant in the rest of the world that could not grow in its soil, and that it could maintain a population eight or nine times its current size. Although he found the mining technology there obsolete, Humboldt's description of Mexico's great mineral resources played a part in attracting British capital to the country after Independence, resulting in a partial revival of mining. He had little good to say, however, about Mexican manufacturing, describing the backwardness of the technical processes used in the great textile *obrajes* (workshops)

and commenting indignantly on the bad treatment of the workers, often held in debt servitude.

Humboldt paid warm tribute to Mexican scientific achievement, noting that under the enlightened Bourbon kings, the study of the physical sciences had made great progress, "not only in Mexico but in all the Spanish colonies." He claimed that no other city of the New World displayed "such great and solid scientific establishments as the capital of Mexico." He singled out for mention the School of Mines, the first founded in the New World, the Botanical Garden, and the Academy of Painting and Sculpture. Among Mexican scientists, Humboldt called special attention to José Antonio Alzate, who gained the distinction of becoming a correspondent of the Academy of Sciences of Paris; Joaquín Velázquez Cárdenas y León, "the most remarkable geometrician produced by New Spain"; and Antonio de León y Gama, "an able and well-informed astronomer."

Humboldt's other important work dealing with Mexico, *Views of the Cordilleras,* is a pictorial atlas of 60 plates and a companion volume of text that discusses, often in detail, the subjects of the plates. Mexican codices, monoliths, and other artifacts formed the largest single group of topics in the book. Humboldt incorporated both the results of his Mexican researches and of his search for codices in European museums and libraries.

Humboldt's conclusions about ancient Mexican civilization reflect two conflicting sets of guiding ideas. One stemmed from Humboldt's acceptance of the evolutionist teachings of the German philosopher Johann Gottfried von Herder, who stressed the uniqueness of every age and culture and insisted that cultures that belong to different stages of human progress must not be evaluated in terms of each other. This led Humboldt to reject the scorn that some eighteenth-century rationalist historians had shown for Aztec civilization. Humboldt argued that a society like the Aztec was no less interesting as an object of study because it differed from the classic Greek and Roman models. But Humboldt's laissez-faire liberalism, his hatred of all despotic, theocratic government, also caused him to see in ancient Mexico a striking example of "the oppressive and paralyzing effects" of such a government.

The importance of Humboldt's *Views of the Cordilleras* can hardly be overstated. It not only increased European interest in Aztec civilization but raised its study to a higher scientific level. Most important of all was his empirical, rigorously scientific yet generalizing approach. He sought to avoid the two reefs of "brilliant hypotheses founded on frail bases" and the sterile accumulation of data. His monographic studies of topics such as writing, religion, and architecture took as their point of departure a specific artifact. This approach provided a model for later scholars, such as the great German archaeologist Eduard Seler, who contributed to the making and maturing of Mexican archaeology.

Select Bibliography

de Terra, Helmut, *Humboldt: The Life and Times of Alexander von Humboldt, 1769–1859.* New York: Octagon, 1979.

Facultad de Filosofía y Letras, Seminario de Historio de la Filosofía en México, *Ensayos sobre Humboldt.* Mexico City: UNAM, 1962.

Miranda, José, *Humboldt y México.* Mexico City: UNAM, 1962.

—Benjamin Keen

I

IMPORT SUBSTITUTION INDUSTRIALIZATION (ISI)

Much of late-nineteenth-century Latin America responded to the international Industrial Revolution by means of an Export-Import Model. This model was defended primarily in terms of comparative advantage arguments. Governments of countries practicing this form of economic development focused their efforts on promoting the export of primary products to industrialized nations. They then used the foreign exchange gained from the export of primary products to buy manufactured imports from more advanced industrial nations. Export-Import produced rapid growth in many Latin American countries, including Mexico, where foreign trade increased nine-fold between 1877 and 1910.

The armed phase of the Mexican Revolution seriously disrupted this trajectory of rapid economic growth. During the 1920s, the Mexican economy was erratic but showed some signs of recovery using the Export-Import Model, especially during the years of 1925 and 1926. The collapse of international markets beginning in 1929 forced Latin American countries to shift their economies away from such heavy reliance on export-led growth to models that more actively encouraged domestic industrialization. Although Mexico was not as dependent upon foreign markets as some other Latin American countries, it nevertheless suffered from a decline in markets for its most valuable exports. Mining decreased in value by 50 percent and oil by almost 20 percent between 1929 and 1932. This translated into a decline in the Gross Domestic Product (GDP) of 10 percent. The primary reason that the fall in GDP was so much less than the loss of export earnings was that the Mexican economy and the majority of the Mexican population were still involved in traditional agriculture.

The global situation encouraged Latin American countries to develop their own industrial bases capable of meeting domestic demand, and thus the Latin American policy of Import Substitution Industrialization, or ISI, was born. Simply put, ISI refers to a set of policies implemented by an activist, interventionist state that are designed to encourage the domestic production of manufactured goods previously imported under the Export-Import models.

ISI was a complicated set of policies administered by a strong state densely involved in finance, production, and regulation. Central to ISI was the notion of "infant industries." Policy makers in Mexico and elsewhere in Latin America argued that new industrial countries could not be expected to compete with already established international firms. Central to Mexican ISI was the implementation of protectionist policies against foreign import competition and extensive restrictions against foreign investment. The rhetoric carried strong biological overtones: "infant industries" must be protected at first until they grew in strength and became able to compete in the "adult world" of international competition.

Unlike some other Latin American countries, such as Argentina and Chile, Mexico had developed neither a strong entrepreneurial class nor effective mechanisms of social mobility into the middle class. Furthermore, it was clear, especially to President Lázaro Cárdenas (1934–40), that the long-term stability of the political regime was dependent upon successfully incorporating the working class and the peasantry as allies into the political regime. This political incorporation was in turn dependent upon state-sponsored economic growth and redistributive programs. ISI provided the potential to make progress on all these fronts. It promised to serve as the primary engine of economic wealth, expand the urban working class with decent wages, offer social mobility into the middle class via the private and public sectors, and legitimize the post-Revolutionary political regime as protector and promoter of the national interest.

ISI in Action: 1940–70

The so-called Mexican Miracle of 1940 to 1970 often is referenced as dramatic testimony to the success of the ISI model. The economy grew 6.5 percent per year on average, making it one of the fastest-growing economies in the world. The peso remained relatively stable and average inflation rates were low. Although wealth became more concentrated, the majority of the population experienced increases in their standards of living (particularly urban dwellers). New Mexican industries, the so-called infant industries, were protected through a combination of tariffs and import licensing, by which the government controlled goods imported into the country. By the 1950s, import licensing, rather than tariffs, had become the preferred strategy for protecting Mexican industry. A persuasive argument can be made that whatever the economic merits of such a preference, political considerations contributed to the decided preference for licensing: it provided the Mexican state with leverage over specific industries and firms that tariffs would not allow.

Mexican public policy designed to provide advantages to Mexican firms should not be interpreted to mean that foreign investment was entirely disallowed. To the contrary, according to Hector Aguilar Camín and Lorenzo Meyer, "Of the 101 most important industrial companies in 1972, 57 had foreign capital participation." Whereas in previous periods of Mexican history the bulk of foreign investment had been directed at mining, agriculture, and transportation, by 1970 almost all of it was in the manufacturing industry. Throughout this period, the federal government had to balance the need for foreign investment and technology with the preference for domestic ownership.

The left-leaning policies of Lázaro Cárdenas had threatened the unity of the post-Revolutionary compromise. The administrations of Manuel Avila Camacho (1940–46) and Miguel Alemán Valdés (1946–52), however, finally arrived at a strategy for industrial development known as "Mexicanization," welcoming foreign investment within limits prescribed by the state. According to the scholar Judith Adler Hellman,

> Mexicanization divides all industries into four categories. The first are fields reserved exclusively for the state. These include all key public services such as railroads, telegraph, postal service, and electricity. The oil industry and primary processing of petrochemicals all fall into this category, but concessions are granted by the government to private firms. The second category includes areas reserved for Mexican investors such as broadcasting, automotive transport, and gas. The third category covers fields in which foreign ownership is limited to 49 percent. Insurance, advertising, publishing, cinema, domestic transport, food processing and canning, soft drinks, basic chemicals, insecticide, fertilizer, mining, agriculture, and livestock all belong to this category. The fourth category covers all fields in which foreign capitalists are free to invest without restraint.

Although loopholes in the law were often found by determined entrepreneurs, the fact remained that Mexicanization and import licensing combined to restrict foreign investments and foreign imports.

Central to ISI was the encouragement of rapid rural to urban migration. With the implementation of ISI, the Mexican state promoted the notion that Mexican modernity depended on an activist state that energetically prompted large numbers of the peasantry to come to the cities to become members of a prosperous urban working class.

Although ISI was directed largely at the encouragement of urban manufacturing, its ability to underwrite Mexican notions of progress and modernity was dependent upon an associated agricultural policy aggressively implemented beginning in 1940. Agricultural production would occur on three levels. Most rural producers would continue to operate small-scale farms on rain-fed land (often of poor quality) worked primarily by family labor. They were expected to provide cheap basic grains (mostly corn and beans) to Mexico's growing urban population and cheap seasonal labor to larger commercial enterprises. The second tier of Mexican agriculture was occupied by medium-sized farmers who had

less than 40 hectares (100 acres). Finally, there were the large commercial enterprises, who at the time accounted for less than 2 percent of all farmers but held 20 percent of the arable land. Mexico depended upon the second and third levels to produce food for human consumption and livestock feed for growing urban industrial centers as well as exports (primarily to the United States) capable of generating foreign exchange earnings. While critics have argued that low-income producers did not receive their share of public spending, it is also true that Mexico entered the 1970s a net exporter of food.

ISI under Attack: 1970–76

The so-called stabilizing development that had characterized Mexico's economic policy since 1940 came to an abrupt end with the inauguration of President Luis Echeverría Álvarez in 1970. Believing that Mexican industrial policy needed to be overhauled, the new president wasted no time in establishing himself as an activist president, putting forward 160 legislative initiatives during the first year of his administration.

Echeverría put industrialists on alert that ISI as previously practiced had come to an end. He made two fundamental sets of changes, one relating to domestic producers and one directed at foreign investment. On the domestic front, Echeverría attacked those protectionist measures that he determined to have been abused sorely by capitalists who cared more for their own enrichment than they did the national interest. In particular, according to Hellman,

> Import duties originally imposed to protect domestic industries from foreign competition would be reduced in order to force Mexican manufacturers to improve the quality of their goods and increase the productivity of their factories. Subsidies and tax waivers formerly given as a matter of course to expanding Mexican industries would be phased out. Only those Mexican industries producing low-priced goods for a popular market would receive help in expanding their productive capacity.

Echeverría established new state-owned enterprises and expanded others in an effort to create new forms of competition and to deliver goods at fair prices to the general public.

On the international front, he further restricted foreign investment through a 1973 law to regulate foreign investment, which had as a key provision the requirement that all firms must now have majority Mexican ownership and that ownership laws would be enforced more strictly. The National Commission on Foreign Investment was established to scrutinize carefully all requests for foreign investments in Mexico, with the expectation that many would be refused.

Domestic capitalists understandably did not react positively to what they perceived to be an assault on their interests and honor. They responded to his economic measures principally by shrinking investment, which resulted in a serious recession in 1971 followed by high rates of inflation in subsequent years. While the strength of resistance by domestic capital caused President Echeverría to back off from more ambitious social and political reforms during the second half of his administration, it is also true that ISI once changed would never again function as it had from 1940 to 1970, when it had undergirded Mexican industrialization.

Conclusions

The economic history of Latin America includes important chapters on the limitations of ISI policy. Scholars Thomas Skidmore and Peter Smith point out three major problems. First, industrialization through ISI was structurally incomplete. The production of manufactured goods required in almost all instances the continued importation of capital goods (such as machine tools) from more advanced industrial countries. Thus, ISI did not so much end dependency on these countries as it altered the form of that dependency. The argument that ISI did not end Latin America's disadvantageous relationship to the international economy is bolstered by the fact that the value of Latin America's exports continued to fall relative to the value of imports. Second, the national demand for manufactured products was inevitably limited. Efforts at regional trade associations and common markets failed to eliminate this problem. Third, Latin America's industrialization was not governed by a concern to utilize labor-intensive technologies but rather picked up the capital-intensive technology typical of the advanced industrial economies. Although the claims by individual firms that this was necessary in order to compete may be legitimate, the fact remains that this undermined the ability of Latin American urban economies to produce adequate employment opportunities, a problem that became pronounced by the 1960s.

Many historians, including Skidmore and Smith, conclude that such limitations were integral to the imposition of repressive military regimes during the 1960s and 1970s throughout much of Latin America. While the Mexican regime weathered the challenges of the 1960s and 1970s without a change in regime, the actions of Echeverría and subsequent Mexican administrations demonstrate that the ISI model of economic development could not be sustained.

Elements of ISI continued after 1976, albeit in a form different than before. While historians debate the most appropriate time to declare the official death of ISI in Mexico, one strong candidate is 1985, the year that the Miguel de la Madrid administration (1982–88) implemented significant changes in the foreign investment law. These changes were followed up the following year when de la Madrid reversed the decision of previous presidents by finally submitting Mexico to the advantages and constraints of being a member of the General Agreement on Tariffs and Trade (GATT). These changes went beyond negation of Echeverría's reforms; they laid the groundwork for related changes (such as the North American Free Trade Agreement) that would amount to a radical departure from post-Revolutionary policy regarding foreign investment, U.S-Mexican relations, and the Mexican development model.

Select Bibliography

Aguilar Camín, Héctor, and Lorenzo Meyer, *In the Shadow of the Mexican Revolution: Contemporary Mexican History, 1910–1989.* Austin: University of Texas Press, 1993.

Barry, Tom, *Zapata's Revenge: Free Trade and the Farm Crisis in Mexico.* Boston: South End Press, 1995.

Cardoso, Fernando Henrique, and Enzo Faletto, *Dependency and Development in Latin America.* Berkeley: University of California Press, 1979.

Green, Maria del Rosario, "Mexico's Economic Dependence." In *Mexico–United States Relations,* edited by Susan Kaufman Purcell. New York: Praeger, 1981.

Hellman, Judith Adler, *Mexico in Crisis.* 2nd edition, New York: Holmes and Meier, 1988.

Skidmore, Thomas, and Peter Smith, *Modern Latin America.* 4th edition, New York: Oxford University Press, 1996.

—Paul Lawrence Haber

IMSS

See Instituto Mexicana de Seguro Social (IMSS)

INDEPENDENCE WARS

See Wars of Independence

INDIGENISMO AND ETHNIC MOVEMENTS

The term *indigenismo* most often brings to mind the policies adopted by post-Revolutionary Mexican administrations to assist indigenous ethnic groups. However, *indigenismo* as a political policy is closely related to the ideological construct of the same name that seeks to analyze or define indigenous peoples. The roots of this ideology go back to the first contacts between European colonizers and the native peoples who populated the Americas. From the Conquest until the present day, the indigenous world has been conceived in different ways, but always in terms of the needs and concerns of the non-natives. *Indigenismo* has consistently viewed Indians as objects of study, never as agents of their own history. Nevertheless, *indigenismo* has profoundly affected Mexican society both as a school of thought and as a social practice, and it has played a central role in the emergence of modern mestizo and Mexican identity. In this sense, it not only has served as part of the ideology of conquistadors and various government administrations but also of many who have sought to defend native peoples.

Origins in New Spain

For the first missionaries, the redemption of Indians and their incorporation into the course of Western history took the form of evangelization. The conquistadors and Spanish military, meanwhile, wanted to exploit them as a captive workforce in such colonizing endeavors as military incursions and in mining and sugar production. Therefore, *indigenismo* during colonial times was marked by the dichotomy between the missionaries' Gospel-based "liberating" project and the aim of Spanish military to enslave the native population.

The starting point for the supposed emancipating project, largely championed by Franciscan priests, was the physical destruction of all expressions of what they perceived as idolatry and the adoration of the devil, most notably temples and other representations of native gods. Following this supposed purification through destruction, the next step consisted of reconciliation through Christian salvation, which was a precondition of the natives' rebirth and assimilation into Western civilization.

Together with this evangelical obsession, some missionaries clearly expressed a benevolent attitude toward the indigenous population, a trend that essentially died out in the eighteenth century, but always resurfaced with the emergence of each succeeding version of *indigenismo*. This benevolent attitude is closely linked to a principle present in every brand of *indigenismo* of preserving what were regarded as "good" indigenous customs insofar as they did not conflict with the chief goals of the relevant version of *indigenismo* at a given moment. During the colonial period these goals included conversion to Christianity and an introduction to the Spanish language, which were very innocuous in compar-

ison to the cultural destruction and subjugation implemented by the conquistadors.

The acknowledgment that natives had some habits worth preserving, together with the patronizing conviction that natives needed protection as well as Christian instruction, led to the formation of *pueblos de Indios* (Indian towns), which were governed by special laws. In legal terms this implied a division of Spaniards and Indians into two separate "republics," in which the natives were subject to a special system of tutelage and protection under which they were essentially treated as minors. Spaniards and other ethnic groups that increasingly populated the continent enjoyed a different regime.

The colonial period also was marked by the formalization of the communal life of the indigenous peoples in new settlements where natives who had been dispersed during the conquest were settled. One feature of these farm communities was the establishment of a *caja de comunidad* (literally a "community chest") where community property was stored. Three keys were needed to open the *caja:* one was held by the caretaker, another by the municipal president, and the third by the (usually) Spanish governor, reflecting the political hierarchy under which native communities were structured. The status of native territories (local and municipal government for Indians, and regional and provincial bodies for Spaniards) and social segregation were two of the principal consequences of colonial policy, which subsequent *indigenismos* would seek to eradicate.

The colonial period was marked by enormous physical and symbolic violence, and the indigenous peoples mounted many forms of resistance to the military and cultural conquest. Unrest, riots, and open rebellions took place, one after another, throughout the entire period of colonial rule, while everyday forms of resistance developed at both the family and community levels. Natives not only were exploited physically but were denied access to their lands, natural resources, traditional forms of social organization, and all customs that were objectionable in the eyes of Christian civilization. Rebellions and riots were the most extreme forms of resistance and reflected an outright rejection of Western society, including the "spiritual conquest" or evangelization.

As a result many rebellions were marked by strong religious overtones, with participants announcing the advent of the old gods and rulers, with a clear aim toward crushing the Spanish order, expelling the colonizers, and reinstating the precolonial regimes. Examples of such rebellions include those of the Maya of Mérida in 1533 and 1546; the Zapotecs and Mixtecs of Oaxaca and the Isthmus of Tehuantepec in 1547, 1550, and 1660; the Maya of Campeche in 1580 and 1583; the Tzeltales and Tzotziles in the Chiapas highlands in 1712; and natives in Mexico City in 1692. Northern Mexico was permanently in a state of war. Caxcanes rose in arms in 1541; Zacatecos and Guachichiles in 1541, 1550, and 1624; Tepehuanes in 1616; Tarahumaras in 1646, 1650–52, and 1684–90; and Yaquis in 1740. Of particular significance owing to their breadth and magnitude were the Yucatan Maya rebellion of 1761, headed by Jacinto Canek; the 50-year Chichimeca War, from 1550 to 1599; the Mixton War, lead by Francisco de Tenamaxtle; and the expulsion of missionaries and conquistadors from New Mexico by the Pueblo natives from 1680 to 1692. Some wars involving border disputes between ethnic groups also took place, as well as fights between Indian nobility and commoners.

From Independence to the Revolution

Near the end of the eighteenth century the egalitarian ideas of the Enlightenment began to take hold in Mexico at the same time as some Mexican intellectuals of European descent began to take up the cause of the indigenous people. This revaluation of the Indians was an integral part of the elaboration of a new national project that entailed the rejection of the colonial period and an effort to revindicate aspects of pre-Conquest life.

Criollo intellectuals, particularly Francisco Javier Clavigero, began their defense of the Indians by trying to reinsert them into world history on an equal footing with other peoples by counterpoising a certain relativism to the traditional Western view of the Indians and arguing that no continent can judge another by its own standards. Such intellectuals argued that the barbaric rituals of the Mexica (Aztecs) were a reflection of a primitive religion and that earlier European cultures were marked by similarly objectionable practices. They defended the spiritual purity of the ancient American peoples and lambasted the corruption they were subjected to at the hands of the Spanish. Some, particularly Servando Teresa de Mier, clearly dated this degradation to the destruction of the indigenous religion (which was regarded as a primitive form of Christianity), viewing the evangelical mission as alienating rather than liberating and the Conquest as an unmitigated tragedy. This is another key ingredient of contemporary *indigenismo* and Indianismo: Europe is responsible for the fall and the presumed contemporary inferiority of indigenous peoples and, as a corollary, the idea that segregating the native population and subjecting it to a tutelage system was the ultimate degradation.

The Bourbon reforms of the eighteenth century formally recognized the equality of the Indians and rejected slavery, but it was not until the next century that these egalitarian ideas were openly espoused. Official policy was aimed at reducing inequalities by extending citizenship rights to all ethnic groups, including Indians, but obstacles were added later, such as literacy requirements and the exclusion of those who worked as servants, a restriction that would remain stubbornly in place and take on added significance with the rise of the great landed estates during the era of Porfirio Díaz (1876–1910). Meanwhile, conscription remained the norm

and more extreme measures were put into place, such as a ban on the *calzón de manta,* the simple white pants traditionally worn by men in many indigenous communities.

Between the eighteenth and nineteenth centuries *indigenismo* as an official policy essentially ceased to exist; the authorities were convinced that formal schooling would prove to be the great equalizer. Liberal intellectuals believed public education was also the key to overcoming social and cultural differences and for laying the groundwork of national unity. The Conservatives, meanwhile, were convinced that a Catholic nation already existed for which the Indians represented a social problem. Thus emerged the so-called Indian problem.

This idea that education (understood, above all, as the teaching of Spanish and assimilation into the national culture) could be used to adapt the Indians is a basic tenet of official *indigenismo* that has survived until the present day. National unity demanded this assimilation, but the prevailing peonage and corporatist systems affecting the indigenous population served as an obstacle to the Indians' incorporation into the liberal egalitarian project and their ability to achieve self-perception as individuals with full rights. This underscores one of the basic problems that has survived until the present: a legal system based on the concept of individual equality that is undermined and made prejudicial by a society marked by extreme degrees of inequality. Meanwhile, the idea of two parallel societies emerges as an ideological reflection of two separate legal codes under which the "Indian laws" were designed to isolate the indigenous population. For the Liberal school of thought, the existence of this separate legal code simply encouraged the survival of "backward" practices among the indigenous population and served as an obstacle to the Indians' full integration into Mexican society.

The Liberal project implemented during the mid–eighteenth century focused not only on the expropriation of the Catholic Church's vast land holdings but also those of the indigenous communities, both with an idea toward assuring that the land would be more fully exploited by the emerging capitalist market and inducing the Indians to compete, supposedly on an even footing, with other citizens. However, the end result was the emergence of massive estates as the Indians were driven off their lands and forced into peonage. In some cases entire Indian peoples were wiped out, while others were forced to rebel or revolt, at least in part as a way of defending their access to the land.

In fact, land became the common denominator in Indian struggles following the implementation of the liberal reforms, and rebellions occurred practically throughout the country. The political fragmentation of the nineteenth century brought with it a host of popular movements and rebellions led by Indian and non-Indian caudillos (local strongmen). Uprisings during this period included those of the Nahua Indians in 1848, 1849, and 1868, the last of which was led by Julio López on the basis of a socialist project. Between 1849 and 1868 there were revolts by the

Otomí peoples in the Sierra Gorda mountain range within the states of Querétaro, Guanajuato, and San Luis Potosí. Other rebellions of note were undertaken by the Nahua and Tarasca peoples in Mazamitla in the southern part of the state of Jalisco in 1857; the Tarascans in the center of Michoacán; the Otomís in Hidalgo between 1869 and 1870 and later in 1877; the Nahuas in the state of Morelos between 1848 and 1849; the Zapotecos in the southern part of the Tehuantepec Peninsula in 1827, 1844, and 1845 along with the Mixtecas of the same region; Nahuas and Popolucas in the Acayucan region of the south of Veracruz between 1881 and 1884; Nahuas and Totonacans in the state of Puebla between 1862 and 1863; and the Nahuas in San Martín Texmelucan in 1879.

The object of most of these uprisings, which sometimes involved the participation of more than one Indian group, were the owners of the great estates who had stolen the land of the indigenous peoples. However, some continued to assume a messianic dynamic, such as the Chamula Rebellion by the Tzotzil of Chiapas in 1869, which installed a new religious cult, complete with a new group of priests and Chamula messiah before battling the army and the criollo landowners of the region.

Among the most significant indigenous uprisings was the Caste War conducted by the Maya of Yucatán between 1847 and 1853, which had as its objective the expulsion or extermination of the nonindigenous population and the creation of a new order in which communities would win full autonomy and the old chieftains would resume their position of power. Also of particular importance was the movement led by Manuel Lozada (better known as the Tiger of Alica), which covered the northern part of Jalisco as well as the present-day state of Nayarit and parts of Durango and Zacatecas. Lozada successfully mobilized Huichol and Cora communities in a rebellion that lasted from 1857 to 1881. While its central demand was for the defense of communally held lands, the movement did not hesitate to ally with the most varied interests, including French forces who had invaded Mexico. Lastly, we should make mention of the extended struggle of the Yaquis and Mayos in the state of Sonora, which was led successfully by the Indian figures Juan Banderas, Cajeme, and Tetabiate between 1825 and 1901. Like the Maya rebellion in southern Mexico, the movement had a clear separatist, antiwhite, and anti-Mexican focus. It also forced Mexican officials to recognize the right of these two Indian cultures to live according to their own laws.

The indigenous movements of the nineteenth century were quite diverse. Some were marked by a religious or messianic nature, some focused on issues of regional autonomy, and others fought to regain access to the land. Some went so far as to formulate a program of agrarian socialism. While the years of the Porfirian regime witnessed a significant intensification of repression against the indigenous communities, these communities continued to organize politically and make legal demands in defense of their lands.

It was only near the end of the nineteenth century that interest in the Indian population took on a decidedly sociological bent, always tied to the idea of developing a Mexican national project. Liberal thinkers during the Porfirian era were more interested in analyzing modern Indians and had less regard for their historic past, drawing primarily on sociology and economics but also on anthropology. It was during this period that such thinkers, strongly influenced by the ideas of Auguste Comte, adopted as a centerpiece of both the development of a national identity and *indigenismo* the nascent science of anthropology. It was believed that the only way of changing social attitudes toward indigenous peoples was by merging them into the mestizo national identity and society, arguing that the Mexican people were a blend of two cultures that demanded not the loss of the Indians' great historical past but rather its recovery. This trend toward an increased recognition of the pre-Hispanic past was reflected in the Porfirian years in the construction of a monument to the last of the Mexica emperors, Cuauhtemoc.

As a sociological problem the Indians' position is defined by the intertwined factors of race and class. The indigenous peoples were relegated to the lowest rungs of the social ladder while the landowning classes, whose ancestors tended to be exclusively of European origin, were the most privileged section of society. Therefore, for the Liberals the search for a more representative identity required both a revindication of the mestizo identity and at the same time the negating of the position of the indigenous peoples. Those of mixed race were seen as embodying the best of both worlds and provided the ideal link in the new national identity by avoiding both extremes of the social spectrum. The Indian could only be saved through assimilation.

For the Liberal and positivist elites, education was the key to converting the indigenous population to civility, a concept that was to be shared by the *indigenistas* of the post-Revolutionary era. For both schools of thought the main objective was the modernization of Mexico, and the Indian appeared to be an obstacle to that goal. As a result, beginning in the Porfirian era, educational programs were developed with an eye toward promoting Mexico's social and cultural integration in a reflection of the integrationist version of *indigenismo* that would dominate the political life of the country in the wake of the Mexican Revolution.

Mexican Revolution to the Present

The nineteenth century also was marked by major national upheavals such as the War of Independence and foreign military interventions. Indigenous peoples participated in all of these events, chiefly in an effort to shore up their communal institutions, including their governmental bodies. This motive was reflected even more clearly in the way Indians participated in the Mexican Revolution (particularly in the case of those contingents led by Emiliano Zapata), and this participation, in turn, was reflected in the establishment of several key government institutions and programs in the succeeding years, such as the Agrarian Reform Ministry, rural and specialized Indian schools, and the People's Attorney General's Office.

The post-Revolutionary variant of *indigenismo* reflected many of the same principles and dogmas as its nineteenth-century precursor, such as the desire to integrate Indians into national life, the promotion of the mestizo identity, and the development of Indian policy based on sociological criteria. However, Revolutionary *indigenismo* was basically formulated as an ethical concern for an indigenous population subsumed in misery and backwardness. Although institutionalized *indigenismo* was one of the ideological fundamentals of the Mexican state, it was manifest primarily as an activity aimed at achieving the integration of the Indians and compensating for the state's historical indebtedness to this segment of the population.

While twentieth-century *indigenismo* was conceived as a policy or practice, it drew on culturalist and nineteenth-century evolutionary theories as part of its justification. The first led to the concept of "acculturation," which claims to avoid the idea of replacing one culture for another and instead seeks to correct what is perceived as negative aspects of a particular culture; in practice, however, this meant the imparting of the Spanish language and Western cultural traditions. The latter provided the ideas of progress and modernity, understood primarily as the integration of the Indians into the capitalist economy and Western culture. As a result it was necessary not only to build schools but also roads and other means of communication with the indigenous communities. Official efforts to promote education among the Indians (both of a technical nature and in the search for indigenous promoters of Western culture) led to the creation of a succession of institutions such as the Autonomous Indigenous Department, Mexican Rural Schools, the Cultural Missions, the National Indigenist Institute (INI), the General Office of Indigenous Education, and the General Office of Popular Cultures.

Twentieth-century *indigenistas* criticized their precursors for having assumed the existence of national or ethnic indigenous identities that implied an identity beyond the community level. While rejecting the idea of a broader indigenous identity, these thinkers argued that the indigenous communities were linked on a regional basis through a central population center, generally dominated by *ladinos* (nonindigenous residents). In these zones, which scholar Gonzalo Aguirre Beltrán has referred to as regions of refuge, a caste-based system of domination prevailed. According to this school of thought, local institutions that had survived from the colonial period served both as mechanisms of resistance and social segregation. The goal of the *indigenistas* was to eliminate the existing system of domination and clear the way for a more individualized and class-conscious arrangement. The INI's coordinating centers were to operate in the *ladino* towns that were defined as the crossroads of indigenous interaction.

These centers, other official projects, and the *indigenista* bureaucracy experienced a significant expansion in the 1970s as part of the government's turn to more populist policies. Paradoxically this is the same period in which a new school of thought emerged in Mexico and Latin America in general that challenged the integrationist pretensions of *indigenismo*. "Indianismo" was formulated by a number of intellectuals and *indigenista* activists, many of whom had worked in the same official *indigenista* institutions that they now questioned. In Mexico this development coincided with a significant rise in independent *campesino* (peasant) mobilizations in which the Indians' demands were part of a larger body of general peasant demands. Indigenous demands gradually took on a greater visibility as Indian identity was championed openly by those who rejected the official goals of national unity and cultural homogeneity. By the 1980s, and under the pressure of Indian organizations and intellectuals, the state began to shed its integrationist discourse and adopt a policy of a participatory *indigenismo*, under which Indian communities would have an enhanced voice in the formulation of policies that directly affected them.

A wide array of organizational forms and demands characterize the organizations that have championed *indigenismo*, and despite significant changes in the national and international political situation, these organizations have proven surprisingly resilient. Rather than undertaking a fight for separatism or a return to a utopian past, these organizations have fought for a role in designing national development policies; in this sense, they have emerged as subjects of their own history.

See also Agrarismo; Anthropology

Select Bibliography

Aguirre Beltrán, Gonzalo, *Regiones de refugio.* Mexico City: Colección INI–SEP, 1973.

_____, *El Proceso de aculturación.* Mexico City: Ediciones de la Casa Chata, 1981.

_____, *Formas de gobierno indígena.* Mexico City: INI–Colección Clásicos de la Antropología, 1985.

_____, and Ricardo Pozas Arciniega, *La política indigenista en México*, vol. 2. Mexico City: INI-SEP, 1973.

Barre, Marie-Chantal, *Ideologías indigenistas y movimientos indios.* Mexico City: Siglo XXI, 1983.

Bonfil Batalla, Guillermo, *Utopía y revolución: El pensamiento político contemporáneo de los indios en América Latina.* Mexico City: Nueva Imagen, 1983.

Caso, Alfonso, Silvio Zavala, José Miranda, and Moisés González Navarro, *La política indigenista en México,* vol. 1. Mexico City: Colección INI–SEP, 1973.

De la Peña, Guillermo, "Gonzalo Aguirre Beltrán: Historia y mestizaje." In *Historiadores de México en el siglo XX,* edited by Enrique Florescano and Ricardo Pérez Montfort. Mexico City: Fondo de Cultura Económica, 1995.

Mejía Piñeros, María Consuelo, and Sergio Sarmiento, *La lucha indígena un reto a la ortodoxia.* Mexico City: Siglo XXI, 1987.

Huerta, María Teresa, and Patricia Palacios, *Rebeliones indígenas de la época colonial.* Mexico City: SEP-INAH, 1976.

Reina, Leticia, *Las rebeliones campesinas en México (1819–1906).* Mexico City: Siglo XXI, 1976.

Villoro, Luis, *Los grandes momentos del indigenismo en México.* Mexico City: Ediciones de la Casa Chata, 1979.

—JOSÉ EDUARDO ZÁRATE HERNÁNDEZ

INDIGENOUS PHILOLOGIES

Shortly after Spaniards conquered Mesoamerica, friars chiefly of the Franciscan and Dominican orders taught the art of alphabetic writing to the indigenous elite. The colonial period thus saw the production of an extensive body of documentation by Mesoamericans, written in their own languages but using the Roman alphabet, overwhelmingly notarial and largely legal in nature. The three languages best represented in the surviving material and in the ethnohistorical literature are the central Mexican language of Nahuatl (sometimes misleadingly called Aztec), Yucatec Maya, and Mixtec. Also extant are materials in Cakchiquel, as well as unstudied sources in Chocho, Cuicatec, Quiché, Mixe, Otomí, Tarascan, Zapotec, and possibly other Mesoamerican languages. Most likely thousands of documents in these languages will continue to surface as the field of colonial Mesoamerican philology and ethnohistory evolves and flourishes; already it has begun to revolutionize our view of indigenous communities, in the past all too often reduced to homogeneous "Indians" or rendered mute by a Hispanocentric historical perspective.

Language and Literacy: Pre-Conquest Precedents and Colonial Patterns

Indigenous literacy in the colonial period drew upon two pre-Conquest traditions—hieroglyphic and pictographic writing, and oral discourse—contributing to the readiness with which Mesoamericans took to alphabetic writing in the late sixteenth century and the extent to which colonial-era indigenous writing represented cultural continuity, despite innovations in form and genre.

More than a millennium before Spaniards brought their alphabet to the Mesoamericans, the latter had begun developing their own systems of written communication, ranging from the most sophisticatedly hieroglyphic (Mayas) to the most pictographic (Nahuas), with the Zapotec and Mixtec systems in between. Although no Mesoamericans had developed a full syllabary by the time the Spaniards arrived, their four writing systems combined the phonetic representation of syllables with pictographs (direct depiction by images) and logograms (images conveying words or ideas). In addition, the use of homophonics, puns, and a complex numerical and calendrical system provided pre-

Conquest Mesoamericans with a sophisticated medium of communication no less capable than the alphabetic system that replaced it.

Examples of such writing have survived carved, etched, inked, or painted on stone, pottery, wood, bone, deer hide, and bark-paper; they tend to be records of dates, personal and place names, and historical, mythical, and cosmological events. This tradition translated well into Spanish legal forms of documentation, with their insistence on the recording of place, date, authors, witnesses, relevant events, and often item-by-item entries. Some pre-Conquest texts—such as Copán's Hieroglyphic Stairway—approached an extended narrative form of expression, and it is generally assumed that the most important nonmundane texts written down in the colonial period were copied from pre-Conquest nonalphabetic antecedents. Traces of the logosyllabic conventions of hieroglyphic writing are reflected in alphabetic usage in colonial-era Yucatec Maya works, from the *Books of Chilam Balam* to mundane notarial documents such as wills and land sales. The tidy style of alphabetic script by indigenous notaries may also reflect the tight order of codex and hieroglyphic style.

Because most of the Mesoamerican population was probably illiterate, many pre-Conquest texts, especially the monumental ones, would have been part of an oral tradition, in which they were publicly read or performed. Likewise, other occasions of social interaction and ritual of which Spanish custom would later require written record—such as testament and land affairs—appear to have been public and entirely spoken in pre-Conquest societies. Pre-Conquest texts often featured political propaganda that was publicly displayed and perhaps periodically narrated to an audience. These oral traditions are reflected in the style and content of much of the post-Conquest documentation in Mesoamerican languages.

There are many examples of this orality in individual documents that have been published; it is also illustrated in genres such as that of "titles," ostensibly land records that often include pseudo-historical narratives promoting the political status of a dynasty or community to both indigenous and Spanish audiences. Examples of various kinds in Nahuatl, Mixtec, Yucatec Maya, Quiché, and other languages in many ways come closest to representing continuity from pre-Conquest oral and written histories. Nahuatl literature includes manuscripts featuring orations, variously described by scholars as songs, chants, and poems, and is rich in various histories representing differing balances of Spanish and Mesoamerican form and style. These range from the *Techialoyan Codices* (primarily pictorial with Nahuatl glosses written alphabetically) to the chronicles by Ixtlilxochitl and by Chimalpahin, to titles preserved by minor *altepetl* (Nahua city-states), and are complemented by a similar but less numerous variety of histories in Mixtec and in the major Maya languages. One important manuscript, the *Popol Vuh* (whose account of pre-Conquest history goes back to the creation of the earth and the Quiché Maya people), implies that its alphabetic version was written (in the 1550s) from original glyphic and oral accounts in order to preserve this literature for a dawning age when glyphic knowledge would be lost and public performance circumscribed.

Although orality is best illustrated by nonmundane materials, it also pertains to the testament genre; it seems likely that there was some form of pre-Conquest testamentary institution because so many of the conquered Mesoamerican peoples took to the Spanish juridical form without apparent resistance. Fray Diego de Landa, bishop of Yucatán shortly after the Conquest, wrote that when a Maya minor became old enough to take possession of inherited property, the transfer was made before the community lords and elders. Landa's informant stated that all pre-Conquest legal proceedings took place under oath and before witnesses. Similarly, Mesoamerican testaments, like all post-Conquest notarial records, were communal or public in nature, dictated before the governor and members of the indigenous *cabildo* (municipal council), who represented the entire community. Thus indigenous dictated testaments, in representing a continuation of oral tradition, differed from the Spanish model.

While the format of indigenous notarial records is largely Spanish, with native notaries producing variations on introduced themes such as wills and bills of sale, the style of writing is often distinctly indigenous. One aspect of that style is ordered speech, used to introduce items in a will or sections of a territorial boundary. Another is the use of formal speech, such as the admonitions found in both Nahuatl and Maya records; the most typical translates as "nobody shall take it from them." These perorations serve to set off and emphasize individual sections. A third stylistic feature is that of semantic couplets, a tradition that acquired a bilingual component as indigenous phrases or terms became coupled with loaned Spanish ones. A fourth stylistic example is the use of colloquial speech—for example, informal asides in wills that refer to specific family members and relationships, sometimes with scorn, sometimes with affection. Combined with the shift in pronominal reference that sometimes occurs within a text, and with incidences of reported speech, such stylistic features can lend indigenous documents a conversational feel. Indeed, one might view colonial Mesoamerican

literature as dialogocentric—with notarial records a dialogue between testator and heir, vendor and purchaser, petitioner and addressee.

During the first post-Conquest generations, alphabetic text in colonial Mexico went from complementing pictorial text to replacing it (with the function of pictorial representation becoming altered by the influence of European artistic conventions and the effects of Spanish sponsorship). As early as the 1520s in central Mexico, friars (while nevertheless experimenting with pictorial communication) concentrated on the alphabetic writing of Nahuatl, which became the dominant form of Nahuatl written expression by the late sixteenth century. The alphabetization process was complete in the Maya area soon after the Conquest owing to the relative weakness of the pictorial tradition and the strong syllabic component of Maya hieroglyphs. The earliest examples of Yucatec alphabetic writing, dated in the 1550s, already feature colonial-era orthography (including a reversed *c* for today's *dz,* and horizontal bars through consonants to indicate glottal constriction), suggesting that Maya must have been adapted to the Roman alphabet by Franciscans and their noble informants shortly after Mérida's founding in 1542. Mixtec pictorial practices, however, were deeply rooted; pictorial manuscripts (some with glosses in Mixtec, Nahuatl, or Chocho) are common for the first post-Conquest decades, with exclusively alphabetic Mixtec documents surviving only from the late-1560s on. Indigenous words for paper continued to be used throughout the colonial period—*amatl* (Nahuatl), *tutu* (Mixtec), and *hun* (Yucatec Maya)—as did other terms related to writing. Although the Spanish alphabet could not perfectly represent all features of Mesoamerican languages (vowel length and tone in particular were left un- or underrepresented), Yucatec and, to a lesser extent, Quiché were the only Mexican languages for which new characters were created.

The "golden age" of Nahuatl document production, the period of greatest variety, quality, and possibly quantity, was roughly 1580 to 1610; by the late-1560s every *altepetl* seems to have had its own notary. Output was strong, however, through the 1760s, after which Spanish-language records eclipsed those in Nahuatl, partly under pressure from the colonial authorities but perhaps mostly because Nahua notaries had by then acquired the necessary Spanish-language skills. By the turn of the nineteenth century, notarial records in Nahuatl had become extremely rare.

Similarly, Maya records are extant from almost every *cah* (Maya community) in the colony of Yucatán, although the temporal contrast with central Mexico is more marked; despite early examples of Maya notarial documents, the late sixteenth century is not well represented in the extant materials. This is probably a question of survival, as well as one of the gradual diffusion of literacy to newly created notaries as a result of sporadic late colonial population growth, the extension of the colonial frontier, and the acquisition of *pueblo* and *cabildo* status by increasing numbers of Maya communities. Extant Maya document numbers increase steadily after 1720, with the greatest abundance coming from the period 1770 to 1820, the very moment when Nahuatl documents go into numerical decline. The last Yucatec manuscript found thus far is dated 1850—a testimony to the tenacity of the Maya writing tradition.

Alphabetic writing was well established in all larger Mixtec communities by the turn of the seventeenth century, subsequently spreading to smaller municipalities as these won independent *pueblo* status. Until the 1810s there is a steady stream of Mixtec notarial documentation generated by some 70 *ñuu* (Mixtec communities), with production peaking from 1670 to 1720 (between the earlier Nahuatl boom and the later Yucatec one). Like Nahuatl material, sources in Mixtec decline in numbers after 1770.

The varied nature and length of indigenous-language texts and the current rapid growth in the quantity of known extant examples make it hard to evaluate with precision the total numbers involved. Collections of manuscripts in Mexico, the United States, and Europe probably amount to tens of thousands of Nahuatl examples and about 2,000 Yucatec Maya examples; almost 500 Mixtec documents have been found in local archives.

These materials are of varying quality, in terms both of physical condition and philological and ethnohistorical potential. With respect to the latter, occasionally testaments digress from formulaic utterances to make informal asides about family relations and local business affairs. The record of a criminal proceeding might include unusually detailed statements by witnesses. A case that drew the attention of Inquisition officials might likewise fascinate scholars, or a document might prove useful not for its uniqueness but, on the contrary, because it is a typical member of a corpus of like material. With respect to condition, earlier records tend to be ravaged by water and humidity stains, fungus and worm damage, and other results of poor storage conditions, and later documents are lacerated by ink acid. Still, by and large, indigenous-language documents appear to have been written and preserved by their communities with care. Until the late colonial period, many individual communities seem to have kept discrete books for different genres of notarial record—there are Nahuatl and Maya references to "the election book" and "the book of wills."

The first generation to be taught the art of alphabetic writing by Franciscans were male representatives of indigenous ruling families, initially friars' aides, but soon members of the élite in indigenous municipal communities (the Nahua *altepetl*, the Mixtec *ñuu*, the Yucatec Maya *cah*). Literacy persisted among the Mixtec high nobility throughout the colonial period and remained widespread among the Nahua elite, but in late colonial Yucatán, writing skills tended to be limited, often just to the *cabildo* notary. Because official political activity was a male preserve, so too was literacy denied to women—with Mixtec noblewomen being the occasional exception to both monopolies, although a very small number of Nahua and Maya women may have been semiliterate.

In pre-Conquest times scribes were men of status, and the written word was highly valued, a precedent of prestige that would resound across the colonial centuries, reinforced by the Spanish preoccupation with written records. Not only the primary practitioner of writing, the colonial notary was integral to the local political structure, and, unlike his Spanish counterpart, enjoyed a status close to that of his community governor, a position to which a Nahua or Maya notary (but not a Mixtec one) might aspire. If writing was a tool of the pre-Conquest state (as the scholar Joyce Marcus has argued), it was in colonial times an instrument of the indigenous *cabildo*—in other words, literacy and writing continued to serve the interests of the dominant political class.

Thus, the indigenous notary was not the sole author of all he wrote; almost by definition, indigenous notarial documents were community products, authored by the *cabildo*, whose officials held Spanish titles but practiced self-rule as administrators, judges, and representatives more or less in the pre-Conquest tradition. Although indigenous and Spanish *cabildos* alike paid salaries to notaries, most Spanish *escribanos* (scribes) hired themselves out to individual Spaniards conducting personal business. Likewise, a great deal of personal documentation was generated in the Spanish world. By contrast, indigenous notaries and the writing they did was almost entirely community related.

As community products, colonial Mesoamerican documents fulfilled a dual purpose. On the one hand they satisfied an indigenous need to continue the traditional public rituals (now recorded on paper) of settling one's estate, exchanging property, selecting community officers, and so on. They were also an expression of the indigenous concern to protect community land from outside encroachment; the increase in land-related documentation of all genres in the late eighteenth century reflects the growing competition for land between individuals (both native and Spanish) and indigenous communities. On the other hand such documents met the requirements of the Spanish authorities that occasions and transactions such as testaments and land sales be recorded in writing.

Colonial Mesoamerican documentation might be divided into two categories: official, mundane, notarial records (the vast majority of extant material); and nonmundane, often unofficial, quasi-notarial documentation. Genres of notarial documents include petitions, election records, criminal records, ratifications of Spanish records, community budget and tribute records, *cofradía* (lay brotherhood) records, and church-sponsored texts.

Testaments are the best-represented genre, as befitting their crucial role in both indigenous and Spanish worlds. Land records are the second-most abundant, consisting of a variety of subgenres reflecting the different stages of transaction and litigation, many of which were adapted or interpreted by Mesoamerican *cabildos* according to local needs and expectations; indigenous officials often ignored Spanish law's precise procedures of land exchange or used Spanish legal terms according to local, not official, definitions. Similarly, Nahuas, Mixtecs, and Mayas continued to measure, mark, and describe land largely according to pre-Conquest practice. The most common land subgenres were the bill of sale *(carta de venta)* and the *conocimiento* (meaning, variously, acknowledgment, receipt, title, or deed; often this came in the form of a boundary agreement). The testament effectively acted as one of these subgenres; indigenous wills are full of land bequests, descriptions, and even disputes. Aside from rare collections such as those from Culhuacan, central Mexico, and Ixil, Yucatán, indigenous wills have survived because they were placed in or copied into land litigation files.

Each genre of notarial literature opens up a different window onto indigenous society. Election records, for example, combined with election-related petitions, provide information on *altepetl* or *cah* self-rule—on pre-Conquest continuity, individual political careers, factionalism, the status assigned to various offices, and the relationship between *cabildo* and class. Particular insight into colonial relations is lent by petitions, ranging from requests for permission to sell land to complaints against priests. Most petitions were part of the legal weaponry wielded by native communities in the Spanish law courts in their efforts to counter colonial demands. However, some petitions involved efforts by indigenous communities or factions (or, less often, individuals) to gain Spanish assistance in land litigation against neighbors (thus using a colonial institution to continue pursuing the age-old competition for territory), or attempts by groups of indigenous individuals to gain Spanish support in factional disputes. Petitions are often rich in a reverential language that evokes pre-Conquest precedent and indigenous style. Indigenous officials employed the traditional imagery of rulership and reverence to play with skill the role of humble, impoverished "children" to their merciful Spanish "fathers"; between the lines one can see indigenous communities playing Spanish officials against each other and using such tactics as exploiting Spanish fears of tax revenue losses.

Some genres are common in one language but rare in another. With respect to church-sponsored texts, for example, Yucatán's marginalization in New Spain is a factor; Diego de Landa was not in the same ethnographic league as Bernardino de Sahagún, never sponsoring any indigenous-language publication. Furthermore, as the first area to be conquered, central Mexico became the focus of a Franciscan and Dominican philological activity not equaled either later in the colonial period or elsewhere in New Spain. Often the first indigenous-language texts to be produced were church-sponsored materials in Nahuatl, as were most, perhaps all, printed texts in native languages. Examples of dictionaries, grammars, confessional manuals, and *doctrinas* have survived in various languages; Christian songs, biblical plays, and ethnographies (aside from Landa's work on Yucatán) exist only in Nahuatl. There are some 100 surviving church-sponsored materials in Nahuatl, and perhaps 10 for each of the other major Mesoamerican languages (others are known to have been written and perished).

What sets church-sponsored texts apart from other genres of colonial-era Mesoamerican writing is the heavy involvement of Spaniards. However, it would be misleading to characterize these materials simply as Spanish-written indigenous-language documents (translations of royal edicts would be a genre that might fit such a description). Indigenous aides and bilingual, even trilingual, natives were at the very least contributing authors. Many Nahua notaries not only wrote at a friar's suggestion or dictation, but were themselves composers (Sahagún felt that the account of the Conquest in the *Florentine Codex* too strongly reflected the viewpoint of his Nahua "assistants" to the extent that he later wrote his own Hispanocentric version), while many Nahuatl and Mixtec texts were specifically written for a literate, indigenous laity.

Nonmundane indigenous literature—the second of the two broad categories—was quasi-notarial in that the author may have been a *maestro* (literally, choirmaster) or other native individual not sanctioned as a notary by the Spanish authorities. What such an author wrote was unofficial if it served no purpose in the colonial system (unlike notarial documents). Some such writings, if discovered, most likely would have been destroyed by the ecclesiastical authorities, who tended to associate unofficial writing with non-Christian religious practices (as they had done with all pre-Conquest manuscripts). Others were rejected by colonial administrative officials as fraudulent or invalid, usually because they failed to conform to Spanish legal, textual, or narrative conventions.

Examples of nonmundane literature are the poems, annals, and dialogues in what is usually classified as "Classical Nahuatl"; in the 1570s a Texcoco Nahua aide to the Franciscans composed a volume of language lessons in the form of speeches and dialogues that revealed the persistence of a complex culture of reverence, expressed in a rich and florid language of polite social intercourse. As we have seen, the Mesoamerican élite sought to use alphabetic literacy to maintain the cultural traditions of their class; also in this genre are Maya works such as the *Popol Vuh*, the *Annals of the Cakchiquels,* and the *Books of Chilam Balam*. Compilations of calendrical and medicinal information, fables and myth/history, and satirical material, *Chilam Balam* versions vary among the Yucatec communities that maintained them (indeed, some still do) in parallel to the *libros* of official, notarial produce.

As nonmundane genres become better understood, the boundaries between genres and categories tend to dissolve. This is proving to be the case with the aforementioned genre of "titles." These documents combined the features of many genres, most notably notarial land records and nonmundane community histories, while playing both official and unofficial roles. The Maya titles from Calkini, Chicxulub, and Yaxkukul claim sixteenth-century dates of origin, but their vocabulary and context point to the eighteenth century (from whence date the earliest extant copies), while they share some stylistic and textual common ground with *Chilam Balam* passages. Each title begins with an annals-style history of community or dominant dynasty, concentrating on the Conquest period, and ends with a survey of community land boundaries. The authors portray themselves as Conquest allies of the Spaniards, who in gratitude affirmed noble status and territorial boundaries upon pacification of the uncooperative Maya; illustrated here is a distinct historical consciousness based more on class than on ethnicity.

Close cousins of the Yucatec titles include the Chontal Maya title of Acalan-Tixchel, and from Guatemala, the *Popol Vuh* (in part an extended history of the Cavek dynasty of the Quiché), the *Annals of the Cakchiquels,* the *Historia de los Xpantzay* and other manuscripts featuring dynastic or community histories preceding territorial surveys. The cultural kinship of Maya titles with each other and with those in Mixtec and Nahuatl is partially colonial—a Spanish title resulted from a recorded investigation into land claims and subsequent confirmation of sale or grant—and partially Mesoamerican. Nahuatl titles also borrow from various genres, are chronologically manipulative (from a Western viewpoint, muddled), and are expressed in a language that is neither quite "classical" nor "colonial" Nahuatl. Two recently studied titles from neighboring communities in the Valley Oaxaca, one in Nahuatl and one in Mixtec, correspond closely to the Yucatec titles in that they, too, falsely claim to be of Conquest-era vintage and rewrite Conquest events to emphasize the triumph of the author-community over rival indigenous groups (with the Spaniards either defeated or allied to the victors). As with all titles, these documents are historical (and historically valuable) not in the conventional sense of recounting events, but in their illumination of indigenous ways of looking at and attempting to exploit the past.

The Cultural and Historiographical Implications of Indigenous Literacy

While the discovery, translation, and publication of indigenous-language colonial-era documentation has deep roots—among the pioneers are Ralph Roys, who collected and published Yucatec Maya material, and Arthur Anderson and Charles Dibble, who translated the *Florentine Codex*—it is only recently that the field has come into its own, particularly with respect to the publication of scholarly analyses of indigenous-language sources. This flourishing of colonial Mexican ethnohistory has been dubbed "the New Philology" by James Lockhart, its founders and contributors being not only Lockhart himself, Frances Karttunen, and Lockhart's students, but also a growing number of other scholars in Mexico and the United States. Their scholarship includes publications of Nahuatl notarial documents in transcription and translation, often with accompanying analysis (examples are Carrasco Pizana and Monjarás-Ruiz, 1976–78; Cline and

León-Portilla, 1984; Calvo et al., 1993; Cline, 1993; and various items authored or coauthored by James Lockhart); notarial documents in other Mesoamerican languages are also now being published (Restall, 1995). A growing number of doctoral dissertations based on indigenous-language source materials in Nahuatl, Mixtec, and Yucatec Maya are in various stages of writing and publication, joining the significant body of recent Nahuatl-based monographs (such as Cline, 1986; Burkhart, 1989; Haskett, 1991; Schroeder, 1991; Lockhart, 1992; and Kellogg, 1995). The topic of indigenous literacy in colonial Mexico is treated in various monographs, articles, and compilation volumes (Karttunen, 1982 and Quiñones Keber, 1995).

It is ironic that under Spanish colonial rule the process of Nahua linguistic imperialism was far more extensive than it had been under Mexica (Aztec) auspices; in recent years Nahuatl material has been surfacing from other Mesoamerican regions (from Saltillo to Guatemala), generated not only by Nahua satellite communities but also by non-Nahua notaries using Nahuatl as a lingua franca in lieu of such languages as Amuzgo, Chatino, Chocho, Cuicatec, Ixcatec, Mazatec, Mixe, Totorame, and Trique. In the Mixteca Alta, for a brief period, alphabetic writing was produced in Nahuatl before it was in Mixtec. Nahuatl documents have not been found in Yucatán, probably due to its relative isolation from central Mexico, and because it comprised a large single-language area.

In a study of the use of Nahuatl by interpreters in the Oaxaca area, it was found that at times two interpreters were employed, one fluent in Spanish and Nahuatl, the other in Mixtec and Nahuatl. The term *nahuatlato* (one who speaks Nahuatl) came to mean "interpreter" and was still used in that sense long after Nahuatl ceased to be an intermediary language. In time, legal cases became bilingual, with the investigative proceedings in Spanish and such records as the initiating petitions and subsequent testimonies in the local indigenous language; trilingual cases tend to be early or limited to the most marginal regions of New Spain, while monolingual native cases are rarer still.

Writing was one of the ways in which the indigenous Mesoamericans exercised political self-rule at the community level, and one of the ways in which the indigenous economy was documented—often with the encouragement, and to the benefit, of the Spaniards. Yet indigenous literacy also had profound nativist and, at the same time, acculturative implications. One of the key themes that emerges from the study of indigenous notarial documentation is the nature of cultural interaction between Spaniards and Mesoamericans during the colonial period. Native-language sources illuminate this process specifically through the use of language and more broadly through the transmission of cultural information, with linguistic change acting as a barometer of acculturation in general.

Nahuatl has been shown to have evolved during the colonial period as a result of contact with Spanish, moving through a series of "stages," each with accompanying and complementary cultural developments. From initial contact in central Mexico until around 1550, the linguistic impact upon Nahuatl was minimal, confined to such changes as the Nahua adoption of Spanish personal names and the creation of neologisms to describe imported objects. The second "stage" lasted about a century and was characterized by the heavy borrowing of Spanish nouns. From around 1650 Nahuatl speakers began borrowing Spanish verbs, particles, and expressions, in reflection of the broader Hispanic impact upon Nahua culture.

Mixtec and Yucatec Maya appear to have been subject to a similar process, only one that was delayed and subject to regional variation. For example, although Maya quickly entered the second "stage" of change, it did not reach the third before the end of the colonial period, failing to adopt verbs, particles, and expressions as Nahuatl did and borrowing about half as many words from Spanish; with respect to both later stages, Mixtec's evolution was a generation or two behind Nahuatl's. In both these regions of southern Mexico, there were variations between subregions and communities, primarily determined either by proximity to Spanish-dominated centers or by community individualism. The former (the direct influence of local Spaniards and mestizos) was more the case with Mixtec, while the latter (the potency of individual community traditions and adaptations) was more Yucatán's pattern. Part of the relative conservatism of Mayas' reaction to Spanish was its retention of bilingual phrases, reflecting the Mayas' recognition of Hispanic forms and their simultaneous maintenance of indigenous systems of meaning and expression.

The way in which Mesoamericans used language not only related to their perception of the colonial society of which they were a part but also the primary role played by the indigenous community in Mesoamerican self-perception. Indeed, it could be argued that the central theme brought out by the study of indigenous-language documentation is the overwhelming importance of the native municipal community to indigenous organization and identity. Each document typically featured an *altepetl*, *ñuu*, or *cah* of provenance and the "signatures" (names signed by the notary) of the municipal *cabildo* officers. Indigenous alphabetic literacy was a symbol and expression of the independence, authority, and identity of the indigenous community; it was one of the few Spanish introductions subsequently used against the Spaniards by their colonial subjects. Taking the skill originally taught them by Franciscan friars, Mesoamerican community leaders engaged Spaniards, and sometimes triumphed over them, in the colonial law courts. Ultimately, of course, the system was tilted in favor of the Spaniards and, in a colonial center such as Mexico City, the legal system seems to have acted as a powerful acculturative tool. But that does not mean that most litigation involving indigenous individuals resulted in indigenous losses, judicial or cultural, to Spaniards. In fact, in many regions the majority of indige-nous cases were between native communities or between parties within a community—a reflection of the enduring integrity of the indigenous community. The information conveyed in the text of colonial Mesoamerican notarial literature may have been largely mundane—recording as it did the items of an individual's meager estate, the details of a land boundary, the roster of *cabildo* officers, the labor and goods supplied as taxes by a community. But the context and subtext are profound, providing us, the unintended readers, with unique access to the indigenous political, economic, social, and cultural environment—the worlds of the *altepetl*, the *ñuu*, and the *cah*.

See also Codices; Mesoamerica: Writing; República de Indios

Select Bibliography

Burkhart, Louise, *The Slippery Earth: Nahua-Christian Moral Dialogue in Sixteenth-Century Mexico.* Tucson: University of Arizona Press, 1989.

Calvo, Thomas, et al., editors, *Xalisco: La voz de un pueblo en el siglo XVI.* Mexico City: Centro de Estudios Mexicanos y Centroamericanos, 1993.

Carrasco Pizana, Pedro, and Jesús Monjarás-Ruiz, editors, *Colección de documentos sobre Coyoacán.* 2 vols., Mexico City: Instituto Nacional de Antropología e Historia, 1976–78.

Cline, S. L., *Colonial Culhuacan, 1580–1600: A Social History of an Aztec Town.* Albuquerque: University of New Mexico Press, 1986.

_____, editor, *The Book of Tributes: Early Sixteenth-Century Nahuatl Censuses from Morelos.* Los Angeles: UCLA Latin American Center, 1993.

Cline, S. L., and Miguel León-Portilla, editors, *The Testaments of Culhuacan.* Los Angeles: UCLA Latin American Center, 1984.

Haskett, Robert S., *Indigenous Rulers: An Ethnohistory of Town Government in Colonial Cuernavaca.* Albuquerque: University of New Mexico Press, 1991.

Horn, Rebecca, *Postconquest Coyoacan: Nahua-Spanish Relations in Central Mexico, 1519–1650.* Stanford, California: Stanford University Press, 1997.

Karttunen, Frances, "Nahuatl Literacy." In *The Inca and Aztec States, 1400–1800*, edited by George Collier, Renato Rosaldo, and John D. Wirth. New York: Academic Press, 1982.

Karttunen, Frances, and James Lockhart, *Nahuatl in the Middle Years: Language Contact Phenomena in Texts of the Colonial Period.* Berkeley: University of California Press, 1976.

_____, editors, *The Art of Nahuatl Speech: The Bancroft Dialogues.* Los Angeles: UCLA Latin American Center, 1987.

Kellogg, Susan, *Law and the Transformation of Aztec Culture, 1500–1700.* Norman: University of Oklahoma Press, 1995.

Lockhart, James, *Nahuas and Spaniards: Postconquest Central Mexican History and Philology.* Stanford, California: Stanford University Press, and Los Angeles: UCLA Latin American Center, 1991.

_____, *The Nahuas after the Conquest: A Social and Cultural History of the Indians of Central Mexico, Sixteenth through Eighteenth Centuries.* Stanford, California: Stanford University Press, 1992.

_____, editor, *We People Here: Nahuatl Accounts of the Conquest of Mexico.* Berkeley: University of California Press, 1993.

Marcus, Joyce, *Mesoamerican Writing Systems: Propaganda, Myth, and History in Four Ancient Civilizations.* Princeton, New Jersey: Princeton University Press, 1992.

Quiñones Keber, Eloise, et al., editors, *Chipping away on Earth: Studies in Prehispanic and Colonial Mexico in Honor of Arthur J. O. Anderson and Charles E. Dibble.* Lancaster, California: Labyrinthos, 1994.

Restall, Matthew, *Life and Death in a Maya Community: The Ixil Testaments of the 1760s.* Lancaster, California: Labyrinthos, 1995.

_____, *The Maya World: Yucatec Culture and Society, 1550–1850.* Stanford, California: Stanford University Press, 1997.

Schroeder, Susan, *Chimalpahin and the Kingdoms of Chalco.* Tucson: University of Arizona Press, 1991.

Terraciano, Kevin, "Ñudzahui History: Mixtec Writing and Culture in Colonial Oaxaca." Ph.D. diss., University of California, Los Angeles, 1994.

Thompson, Philip C., "Tekanto in the Eighteenth Century." Ph.D. diss., Tulane University, 1978.

—MATTHEW RESTALL

EL INDIO MARIANO

The possibly legendary figure known variously as el Indio Mariano, the Man with a Golden Mask, and the Governor of Tlaxcalteca played a prominent role in the native Indian uprisings that took place at the turn of the nineteenth century, starting from January 1, 1801, in the mountain ranges of Nueva Galicia in eastern Mexico (today known as the state of Nayarit); yet, no one ever had seen him. The native populations thought of Indio Mariano as a god, a new king worthy of their respect. His presence had insinuated itself on them through anonymous letters, read to them by those who knew how to read. These letters gave a vague picture of a god who would come in the guise of the Indio Mariano, whose aim would be to reinstate the ancient kingdom of the Tlaxcaltecas.

The letters, without signature or any other recognizable seal, requested "his subjects" to meet in the place called the Fig Tree, near "Lamedo's house," with bows, arrows, sticks, catapults, whistles, drums, and pennants to welcome their king on the edge of the village Tepic on the twelfth day of Christmas (January 6). Religion plays a part in explaining this sudden devotion by hundreds of Indians at such short notice. Since the latter stages of the eighteenth century, there persisted among many indigenous communities the belief that a god soon would arrive to save their ancient kingdom.

The local officials of the viceroy received word of this planned uprising on January 2 and took the military and political decisions they thought the case warranted; they informed the president of the government of Nueva Galicia, who let the viceroy himself know. On learning the time and place of the gathering, the political and military authorities summoned all their forces to apprehend any Indian they might find looking suspicious, alone or in groups, on the roads or near the spots mentioned on the days leading up to the proposed gathering.

The uprising was quickly checked, with two dead and various wounded, all Indian. Hundreds more were put in jail and interrogated about Indio Mariano. Who was he? Where did he come from? What documents confirmed his royalty? But there were no definitive answers. Opinions were split among the colonial officials. On one side, there were those who were convinced that the Indians had been deceived: they did not know what they were doing and had intended no opposition to the king of Spain. Others thought that the colonial authorities should not drop their guard, since the Indians would soon hatch new plans to overthrow the government. Still others thought that it was the English manipulating the Indians against the king of Spain.

Some of the Indians who had been imprisoned were set free in the first months of 1801; others died in prison, and of a third group nothing more is known. It is presumed that only a few would have survived until the Spanish empire was overthrown.

—JOSÉ MARIO CONTRERAS VALDÉZ

INDUSTRIAL LABOR

This entry contains three articles that discuss industrial labor:

Industrial Labor: 1876–1910
Industrial Labor: 1910–40
Industrial Labor: 1940–96

See also Anarchism and Anarchist Movements; Artisans and Artisanal Production; Communism and Communist Parties; Industry and Industrialization; Migration; Politics and Government; Social Catholicism; Socialism; Women's Status and Occupation

INDUSTRIAL LABOR: 1876–1910

By holding onto power so long, Porfirio Díaz did a disservice to the scribblers of professional history as well as to his country. Adopting a much maligned but long-honored tradition, historians label the 35 years of his rule as the "Porfiriato," as if the mere presence of don Porfirio at the head of the country lent a unity to what otherwise were nearly four decades of vast and disparate changes. For example, tracking the labor movement of those years, one uncovers not one but three distinct eras within the urban labor movement. Although its roots clearly predate the 1860s, the first era was born somewhere in the decade prior to Díaz's commandeering of the presidency in 1876. If this first era certainly was affected by the ideological and financial forces accompanying Emperor Maximilian's French-backed ruler, it was more fundamentally a product of the Liberal reforms and the preindustrial economy they fostered.

After several decades of contentious activities and brave hopes, the first phase of Porfirian labor ends somewhere in the early 1880s, a victim of state hostility, its own fragmentation, and economic hard times. The second phase lasts until the middle of the first decade of the new century, characterized by major reordering of public policy and vast economic and social changes. Strongly affected by both the international recession of 1900–01 and the return of prosperity in the following years, the final phase opens in 1906 with the "year of the strikes." Although this phase of the labor movement appears to culminate in the infamous 1907 massacre of textile workers during "la huelga de Río Blanco," in fact the labor movement and the controversies it spawned continued to play a significant role in national affairs until Díaz's resignation in 1911.

Phase One: 1876–80s

As General Porfirio Díaz led his triumphant army into Mexico City in the late fall of 1876, the Mexican labor movement looked very much alive. In the previous half decade at least 32 strikes had disturbed the nation's industrial peace, encouraged in part by an aggressive mutualist movement.

Mutualist organizations (worker benevolent societies) first had appeared in Mexico in the 1850s, and by the mid-1870s the number of members in Mexico City alone is estimated at 8,000 to 10,000 workers. In 1872 prominent Mexico City artisan leaders proposed to establish a national labor confederation. Called the Gran Círculo de Obreros de México, its purpose was to further the "moral and economic" interests of the nation's "working class." By 1875 the Gran Círculo had established 28 branches in 12 states and the Federal District, including locals in several cotton textile mills. Encouraged by its successes, the Gran Círculo called a national labor congress to meet in Mexico City in the spring of 1876. Attending were 173 delegates representing 90 labor groups.

Going beyond the traditional mutualist goals of protecting the artisan and his family from the expenses of accident, sickness, and death, the Congreso Obrero issued a *manifiesto* to "the artisan associations and all the working classes of the country." It called for educational opportunities for adult workers and compulsory education for children, establishment of cooperative shops and markets, working-class representation before the authorities, categories of wages fixed by the state, and better conditions for working women. It recognized no higher authority save the laws of the Republic and the Mexican state, and took an apolitical stance, disavowing affiliation with any political party. It was a brave and farsighted proposal, but one that masked the many divisions and factions within the Congress. The *manifiesto* itself had been the product of angry contentions between moderates and the more radical anarchists. Although the more progressive elements appear to have written the *manifiesto,* the Congress was implacably divided over many issues, including national politics.

Despite its formal apolitical stance taken in the *manifiesto,* in fact the Congress was divided between the anarchists (who warned against taking sides) and the supporters of Díaz or the partisans of his two opponents, Miguel Lerdo de Tejada and José María Iglesias. Indeed, the Gran Círculo's support of Lerdo proved an unfortunate political choice. Díaz's soldiers occupied its Mexico City offices, and subsequent official hostility crippled its activities.

The Gran Círculo lingered into the early 1880s, but economic hard times and open repression by Díaz's handpicked president, General Manuel González, led to its final demise. Mutualist organizations survived throughout much of the rest of the century within the umbrella of the Congreso Obrero, which counted 73 Mexico City affiliates and 46 branches elsewhere. By then, however, the Congreso was solidly a Porfirista organization and functioned as little more than a sinecure for its leadership, including some who had been among the radicals of the 1870s.

Yet ideological differences and political preferences explain only the means of the decline, not the reason for it. The rapid demise of the once-promising labor movement of the 1870s reflected more fundamental weaknesses. For one thing, the nature of Mexico's preindustrial economy created a weak craft economy, forcing the labor movement into contradictions from which it could not emerge. Capitalist profits were made through wholesale control of urban food markets and luxury imports, by speculation in real estate mortgages or other forms of public and private paper, and through control of credit. Industrial production was limited, for the most part, to small-scale textiles and mining. The traditional craft economy's major competitor came from merchant/capitalist-operated sweatshops and various forms of cottage ("putting out") manufacturing. Moreover, the urban market was limited by the extensive poverty, favoring low-cost sweatshop production vis-à-vis artisan crafts. The labor movement, understandably, reflected those conditions.

The most obvious impact was widespread impoverishment without proletarianization, creating a journeymen class with little hope of shop ownership, yet encouraging no development of a separate social identity beyond traditional hierarchical ranks—apprentice, journeyman, master. During the revolutions of 1848, German journeymen alarmed their masters by calling themselves workers rather than artisans. In Mexico workers who by the work they did should have been called *"obreros"* (manual laborers) were more likely to refer to themselves as *"artesanos."*

It is true that some historians have professed to find the roots of modern class consciousness and conflict within nineteenth-century labor conflicts, a view most recently and cogently argued by Carlos Illades. Others have argued the contrary, however. The scholars Juan Felipe Leal and José Wolenberg point out the inherent "contradictions" within the mutualist movement between its urban artisan and industrial proletariat members, and between master shop owners and journeymen. Such contradictions in fundamental economic interests, Leal and Wolenberg maintain, led to "discrepancies with respect to strategy, tactics, and means of action."

Take the example of Francisco Bañuelos. Bañuelos was the Guadalajara correspondent for the Mexico City newspaper *El Socialista* and at the same time the president of the city's local small businessmen's organization, Las Clases Productoras. He did not consider his situation contradictory, noting that the *"la clase obrera"* and *"la clase productora"* were the same. Yet his organization was quick to condemn agitation by journeymen against shop-owning masters, labeling them as "communist." Emphasizing artisan cooperatives, the

French "utopian" socialism, which was common in Mexico at the time, facilitated acceptance of such contradictions.

More importantly, such contradictions were not always apparent because the main "class enemies" of the wage-earning journeymen artisans and shop-owning masters alike were often the merchant *agiotistas* (loan sharks) who controlled the flow of expensive credit, or the merchant-capitalist sweatshop and cottage industry owners who engaged in ruinous competition with the small producers, or the large merchant wholesalers who even before the completion of the railroads controlled the interstate movement of imports.

In other words, the nature of the preindustrial economy itself conditioned the character of the nineteenth-century labor movement. An example is the Mexico City's hatters strike in the summer of 1875. Wage-earning masters, journeymen, and apprentices struck the city's large hat-making sweatshops and could count on the support of a number of the city's small shop-owning masters. In other words, both wage earners and small shop owners saw their economic interests in the same terms. Although one can understand the logic of that arrangement, and even note its short-term benefits, by combining masters and journeymen in a single organization, mutualist societies faced unavoidable long-term contradictions between ownership and wage earner.

Mutualist societies survived well into the twentieth century, but (mirroring the historical experience of other twentieth-century Latin American labor movements) the origins of Mexico's twentieth-century labor movement spring from the more combative, militant industrial labor force after 1900, rather than its mutualist predecessors. Faced with a large pool of unskilled labor continually being augmented by rural victims of agrarian commercialization, and forced to confront an intransigent bourgeoisie stiffened by its friendly relationship with the state, labor's successes prior to 1900 were few and often short-lived.

Phase Two: 1880s–1905

Throughout much of the last three decades of the nineteenth century, the nation's economy stagnated. However, after 1895, stimulated by the building of the railroads, the commercialization of agriculture, the expansion of the urban population, and major revisions in public policy, the nation's economy grew rapidly through the end of the century. Both stagnation and prosperity created their own special problems for Mexican labor.

Strike activity peaked in the mid-1880s (with 17 strikes in 1884 alone), only to explode again after 1905. The issues during the 1880s were overwhelmingly over wages or regulations that affected wages, as owners in those often bad years sought any means possible to reduce wages or raise productivity. Although the Constitution of 1857 technically granted the workers the right to organize, and did not specifically forbid the right to strike, the wording was vague enough to permit most states to pass laws providing fines and jail sentences for those who "impede the free exercise of industry or labor." Occasionally, however, Porfirian authorities would support workers' actions, as they did in the 1884 Puebla textile strike and the 1887 Mexico City tobacco strike. More often than not, authorities refused to intervene. Given their scarce resources, workers found that without official intervention their ability to successfully carry out strikes against their employers was minimal.

Interestingly, although the number of strikes declined in the 1890s compared to the previous decade, the number of grievances per strike actually increased. Moreover, the nature of those grievances began to change. Relative to wage grievances, issues of hiring and firing, questions of discipline, changes in shop floor practices—in other words, issues of job control and working conditions—were increasing. Longer hours of work were being imposed as electricity made extension of working hours possible. Managers attempted to force changes in traditional practices, such as refusing to allow cotton mill hands to drink pulque for lunch. New regulations were introduced, including a wide-ranging system of fines for anything from misconduct to tool breakage.

In other words, the nature of work was changing, and Mexican workers were responding to those changes. In the past, both left-wing and right-wing scholars labeled such resistance to economic modernization as a "traditional" response by artisans defending their way of life against the inevitable victory of western capitalism. Beginning in the late 1960s and led by such scholars as E. P. Thompson and Eric Hobsbawm, historians have been more likely to argue that traditional cultural norms and values may be exercised in a modern way, creating new consciousness born of old social institutions. In this case, Mexico's workers may be defined as "modern" in that they sought to challenge traditional managerial authority from being exercised arbitrarily, and they did so in a way that if successful would have given them some control over their workplace, rights that workers would demand and many receive in the next century.

A different perspective, however, is offered in a recent work by Stephen H. Haber. Haber concludes that "the low productivity of Mexican workers in the [Porfirian] textile industry was largely the result of workers' resistance to running more machines than they had historically been accustomed to." Whether or not Haber is correct on this issue, his work, which investigates such issues as firm profitability, worker productivity, market share, regional market development, and firm size and source of capital, is an important source for the management side of Porfirian labor relations.

The most extensive labor organization took place on the railroads; by 1905 nearly one-half of the nation's railroad workers were unionized. Labor's strength, however, was weakened by discrimination against Mexican workers in the U.S.-controlled brotherhood that dominated the better-paying jobs. Mexican workers founded a competing brotherhood, often at odds with the former. Prior to 1906, major strikes took place among the mechanics of the Mexican Central (1894), American engineers (1901), Mexican firemen, and American and Mexican engineers on the Mexican National lines (1902). Although most brotherhoods were apolitical craft unions, James Cockcroft (1968) claims to find syndicalist ideological influences, a belief that labor organization should be directed toward a revolutionary general strike.

The largest number of individual industrial actions prior to 1906 took place in the volatile cotton textile industry, particularly in the older, generally Mexican-owned mills of the Federal District and the states of Puebla and Tlaxcala. The complaints increased after 1900, as the owners who survived the 1900–02 recession sought to maintain their competitiveness against the larger, more modern Veracruz mills through new machinery and more stringent labor discipline. Despite the hardships those policies brought to workers, the threat of unemployment in an uncertain economic climate reduced strikes to a mere handful between 1900 and 1906.

Phase Three: 1906–10

The years after 1902 saw a slow return to prosperity, although the sluggish demand for consumer goods encouraged management to dedicate considerable efforts to improve labor efficiency and reduce labor costs. Statistically, as late as 1910 manufacturing workers accounted for only 11.6 percent of the nation's labor force. Yet the figures are misleading, for the strategic location and visibility of the modern sector greatly multiplied its importance. Moreover, nearly all industries and businesses underwent transformation in workplace conditions, occupational structure, and market organization. Even the most traditional craft occupations underwent some measure of de-skilling, as small-scale production increasingly came under competition from imports and larger-scale producers. Finally, while the industrial sector's overall percentage of the nation's labor force changed little over 1900, in fact the modern industrial sector's share had increased significantly.

It was from within this modern sector, and particularly an increasingly militant cotton textile labor, that the "labor question" emerged. "The year of the strikes," as 1906 would later be called, began with the organizing of a militant textile workers union, the Gran Círculo de Obreros Libres, among the mills of the Federal District and the states of Mexico, Puebla, Tlaxcala, and Veracruz. In the large, modern mills of Orizaba, Veracruz, a revolutionary cadre tied to the exiled Partido Liberal Mexicano (PLM, or Mexican Liberal Party) was expelled, but agitation continued to grow under less politically motivated but determined leadership.

While events simmered in Orizaba, they exploded in Cananea, Sonora, in June 1906, when a spontaneous strike erupted in violence, fueled by Mexican miners' frustration over a double standard whereby U.S. miners were paid twice what Mexican miners earned for the same work. Repressing the miners with excessive force, the state administration inflamed public opinion by permitting armed U.S. marshals and private citizens to cross the border to Cananea on the pretext of protecting American lives.

Publicly the Díaz regime charged that a PLM conspiracy had incited the miners. The regime's motives were several. It hoped to distract the nationalist anger and convince Mexicans that no labor problem existed. It also hoped to provide additional evidence for the U.S. government's case against the exiled PLM leaders then on trial in the United States for violation of U.S. neutrality laws. (The PLM leaders eventually were convicted but for their role in the abortive uprisings of 1906 and 1908, rather for any presumed connection to the labor strife. The U.S. courts also refused extradition of Manuel Sarabia, the only PLM leader formally charged with conspiracy at Cananea.) Publicly and privately, PLM leader Ricardo Flores Magón maintained that the PLM had not been involved in Cananea or in the subsequent strike at Río Blanco.

Despite the furor over U.S. involvement, Díaz refused to chastise the state governor for his role in permitting what many Mexicans saw as a violation of national sovereignty. While the scholar Alan Knight is correct that Cananea did not "lay the groundwork for revolutionary movements in the mines of Sonora," he may be drawing too strong a conclusion when he asserts that Cananea and the labor events to follow were of little significance for the Revolution that would bring down the Díaz government in 1911. More likely, the administration's continual failure to resolve the noisy labor problems more than slightly weakened the Díaz regime's previous aura of supremacy, and thereby both signified and contributed to its political weakness in dealing with later political crises. Cananea specifically is an important benchmark for the Porfirian labor movement as well as the regime. It raised the social question in a dramatic fashion, and at the same time fused it with Mexican nationalism. In the Revolution that eventually replaced Díaz, these two powerful forces would play their role.

A less violent but nonetheless important strike took place that summer on the Mexican Central Railroad. Striking mechanics shut down the line for two weeks while appealing to the governor of Chihuahua (Enrique Creel) and the president himself to arbitrate the crisis. Díaz received the workers' delegation but refused to intervene.

Despite his reluctance to get involved publicly in labor matters, Díaz quietly encouraged his governors and local political chiefs to investigate workers' complaints. When certain governors counseled a hard line, Díaz demurred, suggesting instead that they establish contact with moderate labor leaders. Events, however, quickly moved beyond the government's modest efforts to defuse labor unrest.

In the late fall of 1906 a series of failed strikes in the cotton mills of central Mexico created an atmosphere of bitter frustration. In December Puebla and Tlaxcala locals of the Gran Círculo de Obreros Libres struck some 30 area mills, followed by a Christmas Eve owners' lockout of most of Mexico's remaining cotton mills. On the request of the union and responding to a national press's increasingly negative coverage of the owners' actions, Díaz agreed to act as arbitrator. His *laudo* (finding) made some concessions to the workers' grievances but instituted a blacklisting procedure and failed to deal with the divisive issue of the company store.

Most dissatisfied with the *laudo* were the Orizaba workers, who had not struck but had been locked out by the owners and then had been made even more destitute by

being refused credit at the company stores. On January 7, the day workers were supposed to return to work, violence erupted at the huge Río Blanco textile mill near Orizaba. The tragic events that followed are well known, although interpretations differ.

Díaz ordered the troops in and workers died, shot down in the streets or, as were five union leaders, executed on the burned ruins of the company stores. It was a shocking atrocity and, as with Cananea, the image of Mexican soldiers shooting down workers on behalf of foreign capitalists did not so much begin the revolutionary process that would eventually overthrow Díaz as it did undermine the regime's political legitimacy.

Surprisingly, such a show of force did not quell workers' agitation. Only as an economic recession took hold after mid-1907 did textile strikes begin to decline. Despite the decrease in strike activity, the years after 1906 were active ones for the Mexican labor movement. Labor organization increased, not only in textiles, but on the railroads, in the tobacco industry, among electricians and printers of Mexico City, and among many other craftsmen of the Mexican capital. Moreover, workers were making their grievances public in the weekly working-class "penny-press" publications such as *La Guacamaya, El Diablo Bromista, El Diablo Rojo,* and in such older oppositionist papers as *El Paladín, El Diario del Hogar,* and *El País.* They also found a voice in *México Nuevo* and other newspapers that supported the Democratic Party's Bernardo Reyes's bid for power after Díaz's declaration to U.S. journalist James Creelman that he would not seek reelection.

Many of those letters to the editor as well as private letters written to public officials exhibited the bitter sentiments that Alan Knight has called "moral outrage," the sense that while things always had been difficult for workers, the early years of the twentieth century witnessed "new, arbitrary, unjustified exploitation." There are many examples of such outrage, but one of the most eloquent was a March 1909 letter to President Díaz from striking mill hands at La Hormiga cotton mill near Mexico City: "It seems to us that in the land which saw our birth there are no longer any honorable men left who know how to enforce respect for the laws and guarantees for all the people. . . . It just seems to us that everything is becoming a farce, and all that matters is who you know, and how easy you can make it for yourself. We have come to believe that the Republic of the Mexicans is playing out its final moments and in terrifying agony."

Díaz was sufficiently concerned with the mounting uneasiness to encourage the reformist governor of the Federal District, Guillermo Landa y Escandón to set up a new mutualist organization designed to discourage more radical solutions. Indeed, by early 1909 Díaz had given the signal to state and local authorities to once again look into labor complaints, clearly responding to the increased working-class tensions amid the renewed post-Creelman political agitation.

One of the most thorny and persistent labor problems faced by the Díaz government was that of the railroads, two-thirds of which now were controlled by the Mexican government, which had acquired majority stock ownership beginning in 1906. Nonetheless, management labor policy remained essentially unchanged, clearly favoring foreign workers for the better-paying jobs, most of which required a knowledge of English. A series of strikes, conflicts, and ugly incidents involving foreign workers (coupled with editorials and letters to the editor of many newspapers) kept the issue alive. Opposition politician Francisco I. Madero thought it significantly political to offer an Anti-Reelectionist Party platform pledge (Article 6) to accelerate the "Mexicanization" of railroad personnel.

At this point several historiographic controversies warrant discussion. First, were Mexican workers radicalized by their situation, eventually disposed to overthrow Díaz and perhaps even the capitalist structure that oppressed them? If so, what role did the anarcho-syndicalist PLM play in guiding their actions and setting their ideological agenda? The question of the PLM surfaces in the Cananea copper mine strike of June 1906 and the Río Blanco strike of January 1907, as discussed above.

Although the PLM certainly had some influence on the Mexican labor movement and the era's conflicts, the central role that many historians have assigned the PLM is doubtful. Essentially, the PLM was better known in the north than in the industrial center of Mexico, and the earlier influence of the PLM in the Orizaba textile mills had waned by the time of the Río Blanco strike. Further, most industrial workers were not anti-Díaz per se prior to 1909, and certainly not intent on overthrowing the Díaz regime, but would rather see the regime use its influence and power to better their situation. Many Mexican workers became anti-Díaz only after the failed political maneuvers of 1908–09, and by then (as will be seen) they were active in the Anti-Reelectionist cause of Franciso I. Madero, not the PLM. They were not anti-PLM, whom most knew to be a sympathetic if distant group. They simply had little direct contact with the PLM. The Mexican government compiled a list of 51 PLM supporters in Monterrey, only 13 of whom were from the working class, and of those, only 4 individuals were industrial workers; the others were identified with an artisan occupation, perhaps small shop owners rather than journeymen.

Moreover, the overwhelming majority of Mexico's industrial workers were reformist not revolutionary, desiring to improve their material position, to have a voice within the emerging industrial system, and to be treated with respect. The latter is documented in the increasing significance of "dignity" grievances after 1900, and in much of their writings.

That they were reformist can be seen not only in their actions, demanding that government intervene on their behalf, but in their writing. Their political frame of reference constantly held up the "Constitution of Benito Juárez" as their goal. That the Constitution of 1857 (and Reform liberalism for that matter) was no friend of the labor movement is obvious enough to our contemporary eyes. But to workers of the Río Blanco generation, the Constitution of 1857 and the Reform era itself were social myths, seen as a quest for social justice within the framework of national independence.

Working-class reformism, however, was not simply a naive belief in nineteenth-century liberalism. Rather it fell quite squarely in the reformist stream of contemporary social democracy with which Mexican workers were quite familiar. The PLM, of course, categorically condemned working-class efforts to obtain government support, but for most Mexican workers, seeking government support seemed justified if they were to confront such powerful adversaries as foreign capitalists. That most owners (and many supervisors) were foreign added a strong dose of nationalism to most worker pronouncements, and whether this is tactical or inherent in their ideological Juarism is difficult to judge. But pervasive it certainly was.

In the end, frustrated in their efforts to reform their situation, the Mexican labor movement came to favor the removal of Porfirio Díaz by whatever means necessary and played an active role in accomplishing just that.

Mexican Workers and the Revolution of 1910

What role did the working class play in the Revolutionary events that led to the overthrow of Porfirio Díaz? Although Alan Knight considers that urban workers "contributed little to the overthrow of the old regime," it seems likely that they contributed much, certainly far beyond their small numbers. First, as Knight acknowledges, workers' involvement in the urban riots that preceded the fall of Díaz was "among the most significant expressions of urban, working-class resentment during the Revolution." Such riots often took place in the decaying industrial centers of the Bajío, where workers suffered most from factory competition or were forced into cottage industry by the merchant-turned-petty-entrepreneur. Unorganized though such violence was, its linkage to the urban working classes and their grievances is one role labor played in the Revolution.

There are other examples of direct working-class involvement in the Mexican Revolution. Even before Madero called for revolution, textile workers from Tlaxcalan mills and the huge Metepec mill in Atlixco, Puebla, attacked the Tlaxcalan village of San Bernadino Contla. Indeed, the Tlaxcala/Metepec textile workers would be active throughout the revolt against Díaz, and they proved worrisome to local officials, killing Rurales (the rural police force), attacking mills, and harassing state forces.

More worrisome still were the Orizaba textile workers who answered Madero's call to arms with an immediate attack on the federal army's Orizaba barracks on the night of November 20. Although after this incident Orizaba textile workers remained out of the fray, the issue should not come down simply to workers shooting soldiers. For one thing, Orizaba mill hands remained potentially disloyal and were a constant cause for alarm for the Orizaba authorities and for the military head of the Veracruz sector, General Joaquin Maass. Even where workers did not take up arms, their political unreliability played a role in the Revolution by forcing federal troops and Rurales to garrison industrial towns, pinning down badly needed troops.

At least as important, if the Revolution began in the regime's political failures, then we must consider labor's role in those failures. For one thing, among the most publicized political controversies during the last five years of the Díaz regime were labor-related disputes: the angry nationalist response to the Cananea "invasion" by U.S. "rangers," the shock of Mexican troops shooting and executing workers of the Río Blanco strike, and the continuing railroad disputes involving Mexican workers' efforts to obtain equal treatment on Mexican national railway enterprises.

Further, Mexican workers played a large role in the contest for the presidency and vice presidency of 1910. Although Bernardo Reyes attracted certain labor support for his brief and abortive run for the presidency and then vice presidency, the Anti-Reelectionist campaign of Francisco I. Madero drew widespread support from a wide cross section of urban and industrial workers.

In the Federal District, in the mines of Zacatecas, the textile mills of Tlaxcala, Puebla, and Veracruz, in Jalisco and Aguascalientes, at least 30 working-class organizations were actively supporting Madero's presidential candidacy. A majority were textile workers, but typographers, electricians, commercial workers, and railroad workers were also among the enthusiasts. When pro-Madero supporters were arrested, they were often identified as workers.

While numbers are difficult to compute, we know that from the militant Santa Rosa textile mill workforce, 489 workers voted in the April 1910 caucus of the Anti-Reelectionist Party, a figure that amounts to one-fourth of all the mill's employees. (The workers at Santa Rosa had been heavily involved in the events at Río Blanco on January 7, 1907, and two of their leaders had died on the ashes of the company stores, executed by the regime's soldiers.)

When pro-Madero rallies were held in the industrial cities of Puebla and Orizaba (May 1910), in Guadalajara (December 1909), in Mazatlán and Culicán (January 1910), or when 25,000 Anti-Reelectionists converged on Mexico City (May 1910), many were artisans or other urban workers, the kind of people the press called *gente popular.* In one particularly telling incident, the pro-Díaz daily, *El Imparcial,* attempted to counter working-class support for Madero's May rally in Mexico City by publishing a series of articles elaborating the advantages that the president's economic policies had provided for Mexico's workers. The ploy backfired. For nearly two weeks workers swamped friendly newspapers (especially *México Nuevo*) with letters decrying those so-called advantages. It was an awesome example of bad press for the government, forcing it to compound the error by closing down *México Nuevo* in order to prevent the continued working-class attacks on the Díaz government.

Governments do not rule only from the barrel of a gun, nor fall only because they are outshot. Mexican urban workers, their grievances, and their political choices played a role in the overthrow of Porfirio Díaz that far outweighed their numbers, that overshadowed their armed commitment to revolution, and that, while it did not defeat Díaz, made it difficult for him to survive the crisis.

See also Obraje System; Partido Liberal Mexicano (PLM)

Select Bibliography

Anderson, Rodney D., *Outcasts in Their Own Land: Mexican Industrial Workers, 1906–1911.* DeKalb: Northern Illinois University Press, 1976.
———, "'Los mexicanos que sufren': Compilacíon documental sobre la huelga de Río Blanco." *Movimientos Sociales* 3 (1992).
———, "Guadalajara's Artisans and Shopkeepers, 1842–1907: The Origins of a Mexican Petite Bourgeoisie." In *Five Centuries of Mexican History,* edited by Virginia Guedea and Jaime E. Rodriguez O. Mexico City: Instituto de Investigaciones Mora, 1992.
Cardoso, Ciro F. S., Francisco G. Hermosillo, and Salvador Hernandez, *De la dictadura porfirista a los tiempos libertarios,* vol. 3, *La clase obrera en la historia de México,* edited by Pablo González Casanova. 17 vols., Mexico City: Instituto de Investigaciones Sociales de la UNAM, 1980.
García Luna Ortega, Margarita, *El movimiento obrero e el estado de México: Primeras fábricas, obreros y huelgas, 1830–1910.* Toluca, Mexico: Universidad Autónoma del Estado de México, 1984.
Haber, Stephen H., *Industry and Underdevelopment: The Industrialization of Mexico, 1890–1940.* Stanford, California: Stanford University Press, 1989.
Hart, John M., *Anarchism and the Mexican Working Class, 1860–1931.* Austin: University of Texas Press, 1978.
Illades, Carlos, "De los gremios a las sociedades de socorros mutuos: El artesanado Mexicano, 1814–1853." *Estudios de Historia Moderna y Contemporanea de México* 8 (1990).
———, *Hacia la república del trabajo: La organización artesanal en la ciudad de México, 1853–1876.* Mexico City: El Colegio de México, Centro de Estudios Históricos, Universidad Autónoma Metropolitana-Iztapalapa, 1996.
Keesing, Donald B., "Structural Change Early in Development: Mexico's Changing Industrial and Occupational Structure from 1895 to 1950." *Journal of Economic History* 29 (December 1969).
Knight, Alan, *Porfirians, Liberals and Peasants,* vol. 1, *The Mexican Revolution.* Cambridge: Cambridge University Press, 1986.
La France, David G., *The Mexican Revolution in Puebla, 1908–1913: The Maderista Movement and the Failure of Liberal Reform.* Wilmington, Delaware: Scholarly Resources Books, 1989.
Leal, Juan Felipe, and Jose Woldenberg, *Del estado liberal a los inicios de la dictadura porfirista,* vol. 2, *La clase obrera en la historia de México,* edited by Pablo González Casanova. 17 vols., Mexico City: Instituto de Investigaciones Sociales de la UNAM, 1980.

—RODNEY D. ANDERSON

INDUSTRIAL LABOR: 1910–40

Mexico's industrial labor movement acquired many of its most characteristic features during the first three decades following the start of the Mexican Revolution. The consolidation of the Revolutionary state, the legal frameworks that issued from it (above all the 1917 Constitution and the Federal Labor Law of 1931), and the emergence of corporativist ties that bound the state to rural and urban popular movements and created the basis of mass politics, powerfully shaping the ways in which the industrial labor force intervened in Mexican political and economic life.

The historiography of the 1980s and 1990s, however, has de-emphasized the formative role played by governments and the state. Revisionist historians of the late 1960s and 1970s exaggerated the scale, strength, and farsightedness of the state in the pre–World War II period. It is no longer possible to argue that the labor movement was simply "the creation of a Leviathan state." Industrial workers themselves reshaped the projects and scripts developed by the national state. Although governments pacted with strong unions, it is important to remember that members of the same unions frequently contested the state's efforts to dominate and regulate labor.

The history of industrial labor, therefore, needs to be considered against the backdrop of the national political drama of the three decades that span the modest reforms of the Francisco I. Madero presidency (1911–13), the bolder efforts at social and political engineering associated with the governments of the Sonoran Dynasty of the 1920s, and the more explicitly radical economic and political reorganization initiated during the term of President Lázaro Cárdenas (1934–40).

Labor's capacity to maneuver was constrained by certain characteristics of the industrial labor force itself. Mexico was still predominantly an agrarian society in 1910; in that year 68 percent of the labor force worked in agriculture. Approximately 800,000 people were involved in extractive industries, manufacturing, railroad transportation, and gas and electricity production, although the vague and excessively broad occupational classifications employed by the census takers make it difficult to distinguish between "industrial" and artisan and handicraft workers, especially within the manufacturing sector.

With the exception of some important mining centers in Mexico State, Querétaro, and Jalisco, most of the 104,000 workers employed in the extractive sector were concentrated in the northern half of the country (in Chihuahua, Guanajuato, Hidalgo, Zacatecas, Coahuila, Sonora, and Tamaulipas). Manufacturing industry, however, was predominantly concentrated in central Mexico, and particularly along the Mexico City–Puebla–Veracruz axis. The textile industry employed 32,000, with most textile production centered in Orizaba, the Atlixco district of Puebla, and the state and

city of Mexico. Other industries employing significant numbers of men and women were jute manufacture, cigarette and cigar making, beer and soft drink production, paper manufacture, boot and shoe making, and a small but growing metallurgical sector. The 18,000 railroad operating and maintenance workers active in 1910 were concentrated at the major termini and junction points: Mexico City, San Luis Potosí, Orizaba, Toluca, Veracruz, and numerous settlements in northern Mexico.

Despite the labor insurgency that punctuated the last years of Porfirio Díaz's long reign (the strikes at Cananea and Río Blanco in 1906 and 1907 are the best known examples), Mexico's industrial workers played a modest role in the rebellion that brought Francisco I. Madero to power in 1911. The worker cells of the anarcho-syndicalist Partido Liberal Mexicano (PLM, or Mexican Liberal Party) participated in some actions against the ancien régime, but the ideological stance of the group's leadership encouraged a policy of isolation and overt hostility toward the modest reformism of Madero. Industrial workers in many industrial towns (Puebla and Orizaba, for example), nevertheless, were active in Maderista anti-reelectionist clubs; mine and railroad workers, especially in the northern states, joined the Maderista insurrection in 1910 and 1911.

The Madero presidency did not pay much attention to courting industrial labor; there were no signs of an embryonic *política de masas* (mass politics). The government's achievements in the labor area were limited to the establishment of a Department of Labor and the negotiation of a new labor contract for the textile industry. Nevertheless, workers were now free to organize. There was a flurry of union organization throughout the country, with skilled workers and artisans in Mexico City, Veracruz, and Puebla States taking the lead. Railroad workers and stevedores organized, and in July 1911 coal miners in the northern state of Coahuila founded one of the earliest and largest industrial unions, the Unión Minera Mexicana. The newly formed *sindicatos* launched strikes on an unprecedented scale. By the middle of January 1912, there were over 40,000 workers out on strike.

The Casa del Obrero Mundial was the first successful attempt to set up a cross-sectoral and national federation linking trade unions and labor groups. The early Casa, founded in September 1912, acted as a center for the dissemination of information and tactical advice on labor organization. Many of the unions already in existence affiliated with it and many more were formed under its auspices. A creation of the activities and genius of skilled workers and artisans, the Casa by the middle of 1914 had won the support of artisan trades (printing workers, tailors, bakers, chauffeurs, stonemasons, and carpenters) workers in the service sector, tramway workers, and intellectuals and students. Its links with industrial workers in the metropolitan area (for example, in the large textile factories of the Federal District) were much weaker. Moreover, it was not until late 1914 that the Casa made its first serious efforts to establish contact with the large working-class nuclei of Jalisco, Nuevo León, San Luis Potosí, Puebla, and Veracruz.

The predominantly anarchist and anarcho-syndicalist-influenced Casa survived the increasing hostility of the Madero government, and it managed to continue even after the reactionary coup carried out by Victoriano Huerta in February 1913, although the Casa was banned a year later. The years of the Victoriano Huerta interregnum (1913–14) and of the war of the Revolutionary factions (1914–16) transformed the operating environment for industrial workers. As part of the effort to mobilize groups to defeat Huerta and then secure dominance within the "Revolutionary" camp, the military factions competed with each other to win support of workers. The Zapatista-Villista camp (the Convention) had its sympathizers and supporters among workers, but it was Venustiano Carranza's Constitutionalist movement, and in particular its radical or Jacobin wing, that forged the closest links with labor.

The pact signed between the Casa and the Constitutionalists in February 1915 symbolized the new kind of relationship developed between labor and the embryonic Revolutionary state. Seven thousand of the 52,000 members claimed by the Casa fought on the Constitutionalist side in Red Battalions, and the relative immunity from government harassment enjoyed by the Casa between February and July 1915 enabled it to found new unions in areas under Constitutionalist control. Nevertheless, the pact also revealed the limits of this early "alliance." After the Constitutionalists' triumphant reentry into the capital, the Casa was unable to withstand the ever more frequent Carrancista attacks on it, and it was finally crushed in the general strike of July 1916.

Workers learned different lessons from this defeat. A majority tendency explored new ways of cementing a state-labor alliance. The Confederación Regional Obrera Mexicana (CROM, or Regional Confederation of Mexican Workers), founded in 1918, embraced the path of reformist trade unionism. The CROM and its national leader Luis Napoleón Morones found a warm reception from a group of northern Revolutionaries centered around the Sonoran caudillos (regional strongmen)—Álvaro Obregón, Plutarco Elías Calles, and Adolfo de la Huerta. The Obregón-Morones pact of August 1919 marked the CROM's definitive entrance into the political arena. Together with the foundation of the Labor Party in December 1919, it inaugurated a long period of close relations between labor and the Sonoran caudillo coalition during the 1920s.

The bulk of the organized working class at this period, however, still operated within the ideological framework of mutualism or libertarian ideas. Large numbers of workers were alienated by the CROM's orientation and, in particular, its embracing of the strategy of *acción multiple,"* a combination of direct industrial action with intervention in the polit-

ical arena. Independent and "Red" workers founded separate organizations, the short-lived Gran Cuerpo Central de Trabajadores (at the end of 1918) and then the Confederación General de Trabajadores (CGT, or General Confederation of Workers) in February 1921. Mostly centered in Mexico City and drawing support from skilled artisans (bakers) and communications and manufacturing workers (streetcar employees, chauffeurs, telephone company employees, and a portion of the textile labor force of Mexico City), the "Red" unions enjoyed a brief and tempestuous relationship with the young Partido Comunista Mexicano (PCM, or Mexican Communist Party) until the Communists and anarcho-syndicalists went their different ways at the end of 1921.

In the benevolent atmosphere of the Obregón government, union membership increased rapidly. The largest union federation, the CROM, claimed an increase in members from 50,000 in 1920 to 1.2 million in 1924, and an extraordinary (and almost certainly grossly inflated) figure of 2 million in 1928. During the 1920s the CROM established a veritable empire. Although the CROM failed to win cabinet appointments under Obregón, several of its leading figures occupied important political and administrative positions, including governor of the Federal District. Leading CROMianos also secured positions within the Department of Labor of the Ministry of Industry, Commerce, and Labor. This gave the CROM considerable authority in the resolution of labor conflicts, strengthening its position against both business interests and rival labor organizations. The CROM enjoyed the full support of the repressive organs of the state in its drive to eliminate rivals and establish hegemony in the labor movement.

The de la Huerta Revolt of 1923 demonstrated to President Obregón the value of a firm political and military commitment from labor in times of crisis. For the second time in 10 years Mexican workers (aided by *agraristas*) armed themselves for the defense of the government. Internationally, the CROM lobbied the U.S. government on behalf of the Obregón administration to close the border to arms shipments for the rebels. The rebellion served to cement the close relations between Calles and the CROM leadership. During the Calles presidency CROM figures headed state governments, Labor Party deputies filled the national legislature, and Luis Morones, a cabinet minister, exercised an influence rivaled by no one except the president himself.

The CROM did have an agrarian presence—during most of the 1920s over 60 percent of its membership was made up of agricultural workers and peasants. But its strength lay in its involvement in small-scale industry; well over half of Mexican workers were artisans or worked in small-scale workshops and plants and government services. The sociological profile of the CROM, therefore, influenced the organization's interest in developing a state-labor pact. The limited bargaining power of many of the CROM's unions and their dependence on state patronage made the search for reliable allies in the state apparatus a necessity.

The CROM, it must be emphasized, did not successfully penetrate many core areas of the industrial working class. Although it had some success in organizing mine workers at the national level (its first large affiliate was the Unión Minera), its efforts to hegemonize railroad, petroleum, and electrical workers failed, and it had only partial success in the textile industry, mainly in Puebla and Veracruz States. Many of these sectors—the electrical, railroad, and petroleum workers are the best examples—enjoyed a relatively strong bargaining position with private capital and could function successfully with less state support.

It is important not to reduce the history of the CROM to the history of its often corrupt national leadership and global project. It is true that during the peak of its influence (1925–28) there was a dramatic decline in strike action undertaken by CROM-affiliated unions. This development reflected the emphasis given to economic reconstruction by Calles and Luis Morones and the CROM's commitment to identify its membership with class peace, social harmony, and the "national" and "revolutionary" aspects of the Calles administration's project; "we are not the enemies of capital but its collaborators" was the proud boast of the CROM's Mexico City union federation at the end of 1927.

In practice, though, the CROM's centrality has been exaggerated. The organization was never able to achieve total dominance over the unionized labor force. In spite of the corruption and reputation for violence enjoyed by many of its labor bosses, many *cromianos* gained a reputation for honesty at the local level. In some regions (in Veracruz State, for example) CROM unions cooperated with the Communist left in spite of the strident anti-Communism practiced by the national organization, which threw in its lot with the American Federation of Labor and its ambitions to build a Pan-American federation of "business" unions.

The political crisis that followed the assassination of Álvaro Obregón in 1928 revealed how vulnerable the CROM had become as a result of its dependence on the patronage of the political class. President Emilio Portes Gil (1928–30) was a longtime opponent of the CROM and used the power of the state to undermine the CROM's privileged position. Although the CROM maintained its strength in east-central Mexico, the confederation lost much of its membership, especially when one of its leading lights, Vicente Lombardo Toledano, broke with the organization in 1933 and formed the Confederación General de Obreros y Campesinos de México (CGOCM, or General Confederation of Workers and Peasants of Mexico) in October of that year.

The establishment of the CGOCM initiated an important new phase in the history of the labor movement. In less than a year it had become the largest single labor federation in Mexico, establishing a tradition of militancy and independence that contrasted sharply with the sycophancy exhibited by the CROM's national leadership. More significantly, the new labor federation emerged at the same time as the most proletarianized segments of the labor force—in the mining, railroad, electricity, and petroleum sectors—and began to consolidate and unify its forces with the establishment of national industrial unions (NIUs) in the first half of the 1930s. The first of these to emerge was the Mexican Railroad Worker's Union (STFRM) in January 1933, an organization that finally succeeded in breaking with the tradition of craft unions that had blocked unification for two decades. The railroad workers, with the help of the Communists, quickly helped mining and metal workers to form their own national union in April 1934. In August of the following year, the petroleum workers, another group with a long history of sectoral division, often built around individual oil companies, also created a unified national industrial union.

The emergence of the national industrial unions, whose status had been legalized by the 1931 federal Labor Code, was a watershed in the history of industrial labor. For the first time the central dynamic of organized labor in Mexico began to be moved by a solid core of industrial workers, many of whom labored in strategically sensitive industries. The new national unions occupied a position to the left of the older union movement. Their radicalism was seen in several areas. The NIUs were strong advocates of Revolutionary nationalism, anticipating the direction in which the Lázaro Cárdenas administration would soon move after taking office in late 1934. More importantly, their members, recalling the painful struggles to resist the CROM's effort to gobble them up in the 1920s, were committed to maintaining a high degree of organizational autonomy vis-à-vis the national state and political parties.

The recomposition of the labor movement took place against the background of the Great Depression. Although officially recognized strikes fell sharply during the Maximato (1929–34, the period when Calles controlled events from behind the scenes after the end of his presidential term), the pace of class conflict accelerated in the industrial and agrarian sectors, a development signaled by a fourfold increase in the number of grievances filed before arbitration and conciliation boards between 1928 and 1932. More significantly, the political and industrial weight of organized workers grew rapidly with the arrival of Lázaro Cárdenas in the presidency at the end of 1934. As the pro-labor sympathies of the new president and the Federal Labor Board became clearer, labor-capital conflict sharpened, with major strikes being declared against a series of largely foreign-owned corporations, including Standard Oil's Huasteca Petroleum Company, the U.S.-owned telephone and telegraph company, and the Canadian-controlled Mexico City tramways company. Labor mobilized in support of Cárdenas's stand against the anxious capitalists (especially in the northern city of Monterrey) and the increasingly reactionary coterie surrounding former president Calles. The CGOCM led several impressive general strikes in 1934, and in the middle of 1935 it joined with other independent and left-wing unions to create a labor body to defend the beleaguered new government: the National Committee for Proletarian Defense. The scene was now set for the emergence of the Confederación de Trabajadores de México (CTM, or Confederation of Mexican Workers) in 1936, which incorporated the CGOCM, several national industrial unions, and the small but highly politicized industrial worker base of the Mexican Communist Party.

A comparison between the new national labor federation CTM and the CROM is revealing. As in the case of the CROM, a major role in the new organization was played by networks of small unions. These constituted the bulk of the unionized workforce in the Federal District and most of the 400,000 workers belonging to the regional confederations who affiliated with the CTM. But unlike the CROM, the CTM from the very beginning incorporated national organizations representing key sectors of the industrial working class. The largest contingent of industrial workers was provided by the 100,000-strong mining and metalworkers union, followed by the railroad workers (58,000 workers), sugar industry workers (45,000), and petroleum workers (30,000).

The Cárdenas years saw the consolidation of a qualitatively new relationship between labor and the state. The first attempt to nationalize a regionally fragmented political system, provide a peaceful way of resolving conflict among military and political caudillos, and secure a smooth presidential succession had been made in 1929 when Calles created the Partido Nacional Revolucionario (PNR, or National Revolutionary Party). But this national party had been unable to anchor itself within the massively fragmented labor movement. The unification drive that culminated in the founding of the CTM and the national industrial unions allowed the state to build a mass base among industrial workers. The CTM became the core of the labor sector of the new revolutionary party—the Partido de la Revolución Mexicana (PRM, or Party of the Mexican Revolution), which the Cardenistas formed out of the PNR in 1938. Together with the peasant sector, urban and industrial labor provided the social base of Mexico's version of the popular front.

The pro-labor policies of the Cárdenas government facilitated a sharp increase in the size of the unionized workforce. In the sectors under federal labor jurisdiction alone, unionized workers increased by 45 percent. However, Cárdenas also placed sharp limitations on the development of the labor-state corporativist pact. The state would tolerate and even encourage labor assault on private capital—insofar as labor cooperated with the task of smashing "feudalism" and creating a framework for the development of national capitalism. Sometimes, this even led to experiments like the introduction of worker administration—in the railroads and newly nationalized oil industry—that stretched capitalism to its limits.

But Cárdenas also limited the CTM's power. He discouraged CTM efforts to organize agricultural workers and peasants, and his efforts to block the creation of a worker-peasant organizing alliance met with success in 1938 when the Confederación Nacional Campesina (CNC, or National Peasant Confederation) became the organizational focus of agrarian workers and peasants. Cárdenas also prevented federal government employees from joining the CTM by supporting the creation of a separate Federation of Public Service Workers' Unions. In the last years of the Cárdenas presidency—especially after 1938—the administration significantly moderated its support of labor militancy when confronted with signs of military and private sector nervousness at the pace of social and economic change.

Moreover, the state-labor pact tolerated and occasionally even encouraged the development of undemocratic practices and social relations within the union movement. The first signs of labor bossism and gangsterism, a phenomenon that would later become labeled *charrismo*, began to surface, especially within the union fiefdoms controlled by Fidel Velázquez and his allies (Fernando Amilpa, Jesús Yurén, Alfonso Sánchez Madariaga, and Blas Chumacero)—who became known as the *cinco lobitos* (five little wolves). The economic base of the *lobitos* lay in the smaller enterprise unions formed in small-scale industry and in the government services rather than in the large national industrial unions. But even the powerful national unions of rail, mine, and petroleum workers, in which the Marxist and Communist left enjoyed a substantial support base, contributed to these negative trends. Both the Marxist labor leader Vicente Lombardo Toledano and the union cadres of the Mexican Communist Party put the building and preservation of trade union unity ahead of radical economic and political projects and the development of democratic processes.

This pragmatic tendency became clear in the early months of the CTM when the Lombardistas and the PCM reluctantly agreed to accept Fidel Velázquez as secretary of organization, a strategically sensitive position within the new confederation. The important national union of miners and metalworkers withdrew from the CTM in disgust. In April of the following year, the tension between the pragmatic and more collaborationist position of the *cinco lobitos* and the left flared up again. When the industrial worker core of the CTM (including the railroad and electrical workers unions) resigned from the confederation in protest over undemocratic governance, Lombardo and the Communist International secured a rapid reversal of the walkout and a humiliating return of the rebel unions to the CTM. The Mexican Communist Party justified its about-face with the Comintern-inspired policy of "Unity At All Cost."

The state-labor pact developed during the Cárdenas presidency undoubtedly delivered major benefits to the labor movement. By 1940 nearly 15 percent of the nonagricultural labor force was unionized. Conflicts between labor and capital were more often or not resolved in labor's favor, at least during the first half of Cárdenas's term. Moreover, the sectoral reorganization of the official party appeared to guarantee a permanent place for industrial labor (and the land reform peasantry) in the post-Revolutionary political organization of Mexico. Nevertheless, the costs of the corporativist pact were also substantial. Inflation in the last years of the administration had eroded a large part of the wage gains achieved by industrial workers. Strikes against "the national interest," such as the railroad strike of 1936, were declared "nonexistent" by federal courts, and a large part of the costs incurred by the experiments in worker administration of the nationalized railroads and petroleum industry were carried by the workers themselves.

A more dangerous by-product of the unification of the industrial labor movement was the way in which the state-labor pact enhanced opportunities for verticalism and co-optation. The extent of labor's subordination to the increasingly undemocratic PRM was seen in the way in which Lombardo Toledano and Fidel Velázquez marshaled the CTM's unions behind the candidacy of Manuel Avila Camacho in the presidential elections of 1940, overriding the opposition of the electricians, railroad workers, and petroleum workers. Paradoxically, the overtly conservative platform of General Juan Andreu Almazán received the support of significant nuclei of industrial workers angered by the widening gap between the anticapitalist rhetoric of the PRM's labor sector and the undemocratic and bureaucratized processes visible within the CTM and other national labor confederations.

See also Casa del Obrero Mundial; Confederación de Trabajadores de México (CTM); Confederación Regional Obrera Mexicana (CROM); Partido Liberal Mexicano (PLM); Partido Revolucionario Institucional (PRI); Partido Socialista del Sureste (PSS)

Select Bibliography

Anguiano, Arturo, *El estado y la política obrera del cardenismo.* Mexico City: Ediciones Era, 1975.

Basurto, Jorge, *El proletariado industrial en Mexico, 1850–1930.* Mexico City: UNAM, 1975.

Carr, Barry, *El movimiento obrero y la política en México 1910–1929.* Mexico City: Ediciones Era, 1979.

Collier, Ruth Berins, and David Collier, *Shaping the Political Arena: Critical Junctures, the Labor Movement, and Regime Dynamics in Latin America.* Princeton, New Jersey: Princeton University Press, 1991.

Hamilton, Nora, *The Limits of State Autonomy: Post-Revolutionary Mexico.* Princeton, New Jersey: Princeton University Press, 1982.

Middlebrook, Kevin J., *The Paradox of Revolution: Labor, the State, and Authoritarianism in Mexico.* Baltimore: Johns Hopkins University Press, 1995.

—BARRY CARR

INDUSTRIAL LABOR: 1940–96

Within the Latin American context, the relationship between labor and the Mexican state is quite exceptional. Both actors have created a complex and durable relationship that, at least since the 1940s, can be characterized as mutually beneficial. Since the beginning of the 1980s, when Mexico began to experience the economic problems that typify other Latin American countries (most notably inflation, monetary devaluation, and developmental instability), one may note that the appearance of relatively autonomous labor organizations—so-called independent unionism—has not changed the fundamental relationship between organized labor and the political system.

Historical Origins of Labor-State Relations

When the Casa del Obrero Mundial (the House of the World Worker) was created in 1912, Mexican labor acquired representation within the process of the Revolution. During the struggle against General Victoriano Huerta, the Casa became an active supporter of the Constitutionalist forces and of General Álvaro Obregón, one of its leaders. This support eventually led to the agreement signed in 1915 whereby the Casa committed its support to the Constitutionalists in exchange for economic and social benefits for workers. This instance was the first indication of an alliance that was to be pursued when the Confederación Regional Obrera Mexicana (CROM, or Regional Confederation of Mexican Workers) was created in 1918. In many ways, the CROM was the prototypical modern Mexican labor organization in that it represented an explicit commitment of labor to the objectives of the Mexican state. Two political leaders closely associated with the CROM, Luis Napoleón Morones and Vicente Lombardo Toledano, were instrumental in the passage of a series of labor laws, with the 1931 Labor Code being the most important. As a result of such political gains, the CROM saw its membership grow from less than 10,000 workers in 1918 to over 500,000 by 1927. Political ties between labor and the state strengthened as the Revolutionary regime became more and more institutionalized, culminating under President Lázaro Cárdenas (1934–40) with the creation in 1936 of the Confederación de Trabajadores de México (CTM, or Confederation of Mexican Workers). Lombardo Toledano was central in the creation of this new labor confederation, not only of its organizational structure but also of its ideology. Indeed, his position as both a labor, political, and intellectual personality contributed to the emergence of a series of CTM commitments that continue to this day to be important in shaping the relationship between organized labor and the Mexican political system.

It is important to mention here that from 1912 to 1936, Mexico's social structure did not change as rapidly as did its political sphere. The agricultural sector continued to employ more than two-thirds of the total economically active population, while jobs in the industrial and service sectors increased very little in relative terms. After 1940, however, both total employment and its distribution changed dramatically. In political terms, the 1930s marked a deepening of the Revolution. Serious agrarian reform and the constitution of the ruling Partido Nacional Revolucionario (PNR, or National Revolutionary Party) institutionalized social change at the national level. From 1936 onward, Mexico began to industrialize within the political structure that had been consolidated during the Cárdenas presidency.

During this time, the CTM was ideologically on the left, despite its explicit commitment in support of the Mexican state. The presence of Lombardo Toledano, the existence of many high-level political leaders in the Cárdenas government who adhered to a Marxist perspective, and the then-radical nature of the regime contributed to the development of a special type of relationship between the unions and the state where each coexisted and supported mutual projects. A good example of this alliance is the oil nationalization controversy of 1938, which began as a labor conflict between the foreign oil companies and the various unions representing the workers. The refusal of the companies to negotiate forced the government to intervene and, eventually, to decree the nationalization of the oil industry. At this point, Cárdenas explicitly gave his support to the petroleum unions, thus ratifying the alliance that had emerged two years before with the creation of the CTM. As was true throughout the period from 1912 to 1940, this alliance between the state and the labor movement permitted a certain ideological commitment by the unions to Revolutionary nationalism.

The turning point for this relationship came during World War II, when Mexico intensified its industrialization as a response to difficulties in importing manufactured goods from the United States. Private and public investment increased markedly, as did output in electricity, steel, cement, communications, oil, and housing. With the resulting growth of the industrial labor force, the national industrial unions consolidated their power in the area of railroads, mining and metallurgy, oil, and electricity. Labor conflict also increased, especially in 1944.

But such conflict was not allowed to continue. In 1945, the CTM signed the Pacto Obrero Industrial (Worker Industrial Pact), in which the labor movement committed itself to support the official strategy of national industrial development. At the same time, divisions began to appear within labor leadership. A new generation of leaders, headed by Fidel Velázquez, increasingly questioned the role of Lom-

bardo Toledano. Ultimately, in 1950, Velázquez succeeded in winning the elections for the head of the CTM executive committee, a post which, as of 1996, he still held.

The Velázquez election should be seen as one consequence of President Miguel Alemán Valdés's offensive against labor radicalism. This offensive resulted in the state's consolidation of control of the national industrial unions where some supporters of Lombardo Toledano still remained. The Alemán government's intervention to exclude leaders of leftist tendencies in the railroad workers (1948) and the petroleum workers unions (1951) demonstrated that the state would not allow the existence of an autonomous labor leadership. What is usually referred to as *charrismo,* or rule through corporatist labor bosses, began at this time. Although allowing the continued presence of the labor movement within the government alliance, the state sought to subordinate the unions to the interests of its bourgeois faction, a bourgeoisie increasingly in command of a clearly defined project of capital accumulation.

This structure for controlling politics within the national industrial unions, as well as the demands of rank-and-file workers, paid off with high rates of economic growth. The Mexican Gross Domestic Product (GDP) grew at a rate of 6.1 percent from 1941 to 1946, at 5.7 percent from 1947 to 1952, and at 6.4 percent from 1953 to 1958. But if per capita distribution was slower, it permitted reinvestment in productive facilities. Real salaries actually decreased: the rural minimum salary fell 46 percent from 1939 to 1950, and the average salary in 35 industries declined approximately 26 percent over the same time span. Real salaries surpassed prewar figures only after 1959, and salaries continued to rise only until 1971, when they resumed a downward trend as a result of increasing inflation.

Such income data demonstrate that the existing relationship between organized labor and the state was highly beneficial to the process of capital accumulation. For the sake of completeness, however, one ought to mention that despite the decline in real salary, worker benefits in housing, education, health, and social security experienced substantial improvements in the same period. What labor did not obtain in salaries it obtained collectively through benefits provided directly by the state rather than by entrepreneurs. Such improvements help to explain the continued alliance between labor and the state, where an intensification of labor conflict otherwise might have been expected.

The previous mechanism could be identified as a "trade-off" in which Mexican labor maintained a relationship with the state that relied not only on the satisfaction of economic demands, but also on the satisfaction of the collective needs of the country's workers. The Mexican labor movement and its bureaucratized leadership integrated itself into the larger political system in a way that guaranteed that system's efficient operation while promoting the general welfare of the working class. The high rates of growth, in part, were the result of union quiescence. The considerable decline in the intensity of strike activity and the practice of trade-offs of economic and political demands between labor and the state reinforced the process of capital accumulation.

Linkages between the State and Labor

The preceding historical overview of the period from the Revolution to the early 1959s described the process whereby the unions integrated themselves with the Mexican political system. What this overview did not provide, however, was a structural explanation of how that system functioned in regard to organized labor. This section addresses that question, focusing in particular on three basic aspects: the legal provisions governing union activity, the national union structure itself, and an analysis of strike activity.

Legal Provisions

Article 123 of the 1917 Constitution, the basic statement regarding what labor can and cannot do in the Mexican context, distinguishes two major categories of unions. Section A of Article 123 refers to unions of "industrial workers, agricultural day laborers, domestic employees, artisans, and in general . . . all [covered by private] labor contracts." Such private sector unions are, in turn, subdivided, depending on whether they fall into federal or local-level jurisdiction. Section B pertains to all public sector workers employed by the national government, the various Mexican states, and all municipalities. Each type has a separate specified type of bargaining procedure. Defining labor unions as "associations formed for the study, betterment, and defense of the interests of workers and their employers," the law recognizes five distinct types that, with the exception of the final category, must group a minimum of 20 workers: 1) *gremiales,* or those of the same profession; 2) *de empresa,* or those of a single company; 3) *industriales,* or those in two or more companies located in the same industry; 4) *nacionales de industria,* or those in one or more companies of the same industry located in two or more states; and 5) *oficios varios,* those including less than 20 workers of the same profession, but located in the same municipality. It is also necessary to distinguish between national industrial unions—the fourth category above—where the various sections share a common charter, and the more decentralized national federations where each section has its own separate charter.

The National Union Structure

Mexican labor, through the CTM, is one of the three official components of the present dominant political party, the Partido Revolucionario Institucional (PRI, or Institutional Revolutionary Party), along with the Confederación Nacional Campesina (CNC, or National Peasant Confederation) and the amorphous popular sector. The CTM is a part of the Congreso del Trabajo (CT, or Congress of Work), an umbrella organization that groups all major labor confederations, including those not affiliated with the PRI, national industrial unions not part of the CTM, and the confedera-

tion of unions representing government workers, Federación de Sindicatos de Trabajadores al Servicio del Estado (FSTSE, or Federation of Unions of Civil Servants), regulated by Section B of Article 123 of the Constitution. The CT is a kind of forum where labor organizations present common positions to the state, going beyond the bounds of what strict PRI membership might allow. The CT is the heir to a number of earlier similar groupings, many of which also reflected CTM sponsorship. Indeed, Fidel Velázquez encouraged the formation of such a broad-based grouping so as to widen the scope of his organization and, thus, to allow for some diversity of opinion within the official labor movement. In the 1960s, the Bloque de Unidad Obrera (BUO) played a similar role.

The decision-making process in organizations such as the CTM, the CT, and the national industrial unions is cloaked in secrecy. While it is not clear how election procedures for the higher posts actually function, reelection is typical. The case of the secretary general of the CTM, Fidel Velázquez, is indicative: he occupied the post continuously for more than 45 years after first being elected in 1950. If CTM internal organs such as its National Congress and National Council have clear-cut formal functions, much of their power appears to exist largely on paper. At lower organizational levels, action is taken to persuade or force those unions departing from the CTM line to conform.

In general, the CTM fulfills a fundamental role in the capital accumulation process by maintaining wages at levels acceptable to the owners of capital, by supporting the government in critical situations, and by controlling the rank-and-file members through clientelistic means and with the aid of corrupt union officials. Until now, the CTM has been successful in making it possible for the political system to rely upon it to provide a relatively quiescent labor force. This pattern was consolidated at the end of the 1940s and has been in operation ever since.

Very few unions questioned such control, and those that did have done so only quite recently. What is most significant is the high degree of integration between the labor movement and the government. For each type of worker—blue collar, white collar, and peasant—there is a specific organization said to represent that worker's interests in the larger political world. These labor organizations are incorporated into other broader entities for the purpose of reconciling conflicting group interests. Thus, the PRI interacts with business and with government officials to discuss labor demands. The active presence of many public officials at labor congresses and, reciprocally, the presence of the CTM secretary general at many government functions, illustrates the close relationship that exists among these actors. Such multigroup integration through the political system permits a high degree of flexibility in the negotiation of mutual demands. Of necessity, labor officials, political leaders, and government officeholders must maintain steady contact in their efforts to reconcile the wishes of various groups. The presence of federal deputies in parliament recruited from the labor sector and their increasing relative weight among the PRI delegation is one indication of the importance of labor representation in the governing coalition.

In any overall evaluation of how the highly centralized Mexican political system functions, it is undoubtedly necessary to emphasize the importance of the PRI's role in overseeing the interaction of the various union groups (as in the case of the Congreso del Trabajo) as well as the reality of the interplay of interests among worker, peasant, and popular sectors. One might even assume from this depiction that the political system is not so much a place where control is imposed as the source of important political benefits for those groups so incorporated.

The usefulness of the labor movement to the political system, and vice versa, is only one aspect of their mutual relationship. At other levels such as in collective bargaining negotiation, the importance of the state is critical. The collective contracts signed reflect the political wishes of the state leadership as much as the economic realities of particular businesses. Salary increases, for example, relate directly to general development strategies defined by the government rather than to the profitability of particular companies. In recent years, the so-called *tope salarial,* or maximum salary limit set by the government, fixes the absolute level that unions cannot exceed. In cases where a union has gained what is deemed an excessive concession from management, the Labor or Budget Ministry has intervened to stop its implementation. The consequence is that official salary policy has resulted in negotiations where salary increases are not the central point of contention; instead, discussions have centered on the extent of fringe benefits, or *prestaciones,* where state control is not exerted to the same degree. One important result of the government decision to fix limits on salary hikes has been the serious undermining of union capacity to bargain at the plant level; as a result, the real negotiations are transferred to the highest political level within the government itself.

Strike Activity

An important indicator of the way the state-labor relationship functions in Mexico is the overall tendency for a decrease in the average number of strikers from the 1940s to the present, something surprising given the rising share of industrial workers in the workforce and the intensification of industrialization and urbanization in that same time span. The general decline in strikers is evidence in support of the thesis of increased state control over labor demands in recent years.

During the Cárdenas presidency, but especially in its first three years, strike activity was intense. The average number of strikers in the entire period was the highest of any moment in recent Mexican history. Such labor activism took place in an economic context of little inflationary pressure; strikes seemed more a response to political mobilization than to economic problems.

During the Manuel Avila Camacho presidency (1940–46), strike activity tended to decrease. It was during this time that the CTM signed two agreements with the administration in which it committed itself to support government economic policy. As a result, labor peace tended to prevail during the war years, while import substitution industrialization (a set of policies implemented by an activist, interventionist state designed to encourage the domestic production of previously imported manufactured goods) was intensifying. So-called national unity was the ideological message that Avila Camacho directed toward all social organizations in his attempt to reverse the confrontational politics that had prevailed under Cárdenas. The central government focused on ways to stimulate private investment and to conciliate divergent interests.

At the end of the war, when Miguel Alemán Valdés took power, the more repressive stance adopted by the government toward labor resulted in an actual overall decrease in strike activity and in the specific efforts to gain control over the railroad and oil national industrial unions where dissidents had begun to appear. On the basis of the average number of strikers per strike, one can infer from the data that strikes took place more in large enterprises than in small- and medium-sized factories. Such figures statistically reflect the influence of the very large oil and railroad workers' unions. The pro-business views of Alemán's minister of labor were reflected in his hostile attitudes toward worker demands. While the basic parameters of the relationship were not broken, it was clear that the state consolidated the subordination of labor it had been seeking to attain since 1940. The process of control was represented by the election of Fidel Velázquez as CTM secretary general and the rise to prominence of such leaders as Francisco Pérez Rios and Napoleón Gómez Sada in the electrical workers and mining unions, respectively. The phenomenon of *charrismo* had become institutionalized. After 1952, labor relations would be part of a structure where labor was still strong, but where it could not challenge state decrees.

Under President Adolfo Ruiz Cortines (1952–58), strike activity increased slightly in relation to the level attained under Alemán. The frequency of conflict increased, reaching an average of 24 strikes per year, although the average number of strikers increased slightly less; as a result, the average number of strikers per strike decreased in relation to the earlier period. Such an exclusive focus on aggregate data, however, overlooks important events like the large-scale mobilization of railroad workers that occurred at the end of the Ruiz Cortines administration.

In 1957, labor-management disagreement resulted in a long and bitter rail strike. The overlapping of the strike with the PRI presidential nomination process may have been influential in the choice of Adolfo López Mateos as the PRI's candidate. As the minister of labor in the Ruiz Cortines government, López Mateos had had a lot to do with the development of the railroad conflict. Once he assumed the presidency in December 1958, he decided to resolve the strike through the temporary militarization of the railroads. The resulting government repression against the strike leadership succeeded in finally consolidating state power in a union that had sought to challenge official authority.

After its initial show of force, the López Mateos government moved away from anti-union repression. In the entire period from 1958 to 1964, the average number of strikers and strikes sharply increased to levels not seen since the Cárdenas years. One explanation for this subsequent toleration of strikes may be found in an effort by López Mateos to seek to relegitimate his government with labor after the confrontation of 1958–59. Another relates to the sharp improvement in economic conditions as inflation decreased, nominal and real salaries reversed their previous decline, and the country experienced general economic growth. The combination of greater official toleration and better material conditions, in turn, seemed to have led to a noticeable worker mobilization marked by new strikes, an increase in union membership, and a renewed union presence in the political sphere.

The events of the López Mateos years are indicative of the particular characteristics of state-labor relations in Mexico. Here one can argue that the assumption of control by the CTM over worker demands could transform such petitions in the eyes of the state, making them more acceptable for presentation at a later time when economic conditions were more opportune. The resulting strike activity that followed should be seen as a safety valve for accumulated worker pressures, the release of which is facilitated by the political linkage of organized labor and the state. The overall labor process is oriented toward containing worker demands within official structures like the CTM rather than allowing them to be spontaneously released in the economy at large. The political opening represented by reduced repression permitted an increase in demands from accepted labor leaders operating within the ruling coalition. Responding to such labor pressure, the state provided material benefits such as salary hikes and the creation of a social security system for government workers in the Instituto de Servicios Sociales y Seguridad Social de los Trabajadores al Servicio del Estado (ISSSTE, or Institute of Social Services and Social Security for Workers at the Service of the State).

Indeed, for the entire six years of Gustavo Díaz Ordaz's presidency, strike activity decreased to very low levels. Such a decline is especially apparent in terms of the number of strikers, which averaged less than 8,000, or not even one-sixth of that seen during the López Mateos presidency. If one assumes that good economic conditions facilitate strike activity given low unemployment and high employer profits, the decrease observed in strikes during the continued economic expansion of the Díaz Ordaz years is likely to be more a response to political than to strictly economic conditions. Under such a political interpretation, the labor leadership is seen as capable of mobilizing or not mobilizing the union rank and file according to the momentary needs of the political system.

Starting with the election of Luis Echeverría Álvarez in 1970, a new labor situation appeared, characterized by continued deterioration of the national economy and the appearance of the so-called independent unions in the automobile industry and elsewhere. Both factors help explain the intensification of strike activity in this recent period, as measured by the number of strikes and of strikers. Worsening inflation, the promotion of "real prices" with the elimination of government subsidies, and the establishment of salary limits led to increased pressure for salary hikes. For the first time since Cárdenas, the demands of the labor movement were now responding to economic causes as workers sought to recover losses in their standard of living.

The same kind of economic motivation clearly continued as the cause of strikes during the presidency of José López Portillo (1977–82). The number of strikes averaged 886 per year, and the number of strikers per strike rose above 50,000, both much higher figures than those experienced under Echeverría. Such militancy was the result of the kind of economic deterioration that long had been the case in many other Latin American countries. Indeed, with price increases of 98.8 percent in 1982 and 80.8 percent in 1983, the limited salary hikes permitted by the state led to consecutive drops in real salary of 4.3 percent and 2.3 percent in those years. During this period, the relationship between labor and the state experienced considerable tension owing to the unyielding stand taken by the latter. The López Portillo presidency ended with a dramatic rise in strikes and in *emplazamientos a huelga,* the official notice given by unions to employers that a strike will occur unless worker petitions are accepted.

Events from 1982 to 1995 suggest how much the special relationship between labor and the state suffered as a result of the worsening inflation and unemployment and the drop in the standard of living. The state, in turn, sought to moderate some of these effects with new food subsidies, permission to grant fringe benefits not directly affecting salaries, and policies geared to the maintenance of existing employment levels. Additional measures included low-interest loans from the social security system to ease the short-term financial needs of workers and government employees, and loans for house construction and car purchases for middle-level technicians and professionals linked to the state sector. While not fully compensating for real salary losses, such official responses permitted at least part of aggregate economic demand to continue to rise. It is worth noting that these measures were implemented through agreements between the unions and the state where the political commitment of both to Mexico's development was always publicly emphasized. These agreements took place within the political alliance between labor and the state and were perceived as such by Mexican workers.

The Labor Market

In the mid-1990s, the Mexican labor market was characterized by stable levels of unemployment and by an increase in the levels of informalization, especially in the service sector. The economically active population also had grown as a result of the increase in the number of people in households searching for remunerated work and of the higher percentage of women in the workforce (23.5 percent in 1990). Women comprised more than 40 percent of public employment in low-paying occupations, such as secretaries or primary school teachers. In the *maquiladora* (assembly plant) industry, more than 275,000 women worked in nonunionized factories with precarious working conditions. Women's employment also was related to family-based industrial activity in the garment sector, self-employment of women in food preparation or knitting and sewing activities for the national and international market, as well as domestic employment. In general, because occupations do not require formal training nor high levels of education, skill levels in the female workforce proved to be low.

Public employment stagnated at the beginning of the 1990s after having been an important buffer for unemployment for more than two decades. From intense rates of growth of this population in the 1970s and most of the 1980s (8 percent a year from 1975 to 1985), the growth rate became more modest, and public employment actually decreased from 2,097,200 persons in 1989 to 2,056,500 persons in 1991. In addition, in some of what had been or still were state-owned enterprises, employment levels decreased as a result of the process of restructuring that these companies underwent before being privatized.

Industrial employment tended to become concentrated in small- and medium-sized companies, and the composition of employment by firm size in manufacturing, retail sales, and services gave way to a highly atomized industrial structure. Industrial employment concentration decreased; indeed, the average size of manufacturing plants and the absolute decrease in manufacturing employment after 1982 resulted in an atomized industrial sector in which medium- and small-sized companies were increasing their participation in the employment of the productive structure of the country.

The spacial distribution of the working population changed, and new concentrations of industrial employment appeared in states such as Aguascalientes, México, Sonora, Coahuila, and Chihuahua; this had resulted from the relocation of production to "greenfield" sites, geared essentially to production for export. By the mid-1990s, a new economic space was being formed, with important effects in the composition of the labor force, which had become younger, with relatively higher educational levels but not necessarily higher skill levels, and was less aware of the traditions of union organization.

The number of people benefiting from social security mechanisms stagnated, especially from 1989 to 1994, when the number held steady at around 55 percent of the employed population, considering both the institutions that provide services to public employees (the ISSSTE) and for workers in private employment (Instituto Mexicano del Seguro Social—IMSS, or Mexican Institute of Social Security). One can conclude from this figure that the other 45 percent of the employed population did not benefit from social security, health services, and other facilities that

ISSSTE and IMSS provide for the Mexican working people. In absolute numbers, there were about 11.5 million people covered by social security and 9 to 10 million people not covered by any kind of benefits. Given the dynamics of the labor market, it is likely that the inserted fraction tended to stagnate after 1991 as well.

Some of these trends within the national labor market caused an intensification of migration toward the northern border and the United States. Some depressed areas of Mexico, such as the south and central areas, home to high concentrations of Indians and the poor, experienced outward migration toward the north in increasing numbers. Migrants found jobs in the *maquiladora* industry at a very high rate: thus, total *maquiladora* employment went from 369,489 persons in 1988 to 580,498 persons in 1994, a 57.1 percent increase in the six-year period; most of these jobs were located in the electrical and electronics industry.

Such trends had a blocking effect on the process of proletarization that took place between 1940 and 1970. Therefore, the rate of unionization stagnated: indeed, when there are fewer and fewer blue- and white-collar workers with formal employment, there will inevitably be less and less unionized workers, especially if the legal framework for the constitution of unions remains the same.

The Situation in Official Unions

In 1983, the CTM and the government operated in the context of a "solidarity pact," where each of them committed to sacrifices in order to limit the effects of the crisis on the workers. For its part, the state proposed the relocation of some of the unemployed, price controls, and the creation of new jobs in the public sector. It also proposed to facilitate the creation of stores selling low-priced goods and to extend lines of credit for small- and medium-sized enterprises (traditionally flexible in matters of employment). In exchange for these concessions, organized labor promised to limit its salary demands.

Nevertheless, in parts of the private sector such as automobiles, steel, and metalworking, conflict erupted. Discontent among workers in these sectors was not only economic; it also derived from rank-and-file refusal to accept proposals that the labor leadership frequently had accepted without a fight. In their desire for a union democracy that associated demands for the renovation of the leadership with those for increased worker participation in union life, reformers never really questioned the entirety of the established union structure. Conscious of the risks entailed in such an extreme position, most limited themselves to issues relating to the particularities of their individual companies. Union democracy, as an issue, was raised within the framework of official labor law, thus making it more difficult for the state to reject it out of hand. Reformers sought merely to put into practice rights that existed on paper, but which never had been implemented.

Ironically, in the public sector where relations should have been running smoothly (as in unions representing government workers, especially the FSTSE), important manifestations of unrest surfaced, linked to the particularly strong effects of the economic crisis felt there. State-sector salary increases fell far behind inflation, while many fringe benefits—worker health care, for example—deteriorated in quality, bringing strong criticism from recipients. The ISSSTE particularly experienced such worsening service. State-sector workers, accustomed to special yearly salary increases announced in the annual presidential state of the union message every September 1, found this form of favoritism discontinued; salary policy for the bureaucracy now reflected that of the rest of the working class. Another area of discontent was among school teachers belonging to the Sindicato Nacional de Trabajadores de la Educación (SNTE, or National Union of Education Workers). Unhappy with the way the national SNTE leadership was dealing with membership problems, dissident locals organized the Coordinadora Nacional de Trabajadores de la Educación, or CNTE, which became quite active in challenging the official union. Given the sheer size of the 650,000 teachers involved, such a conflict would have major national ramifications.

The Situation in the Independent Unions

Private-sector unions not part of the official labor sector account for some 420,000 workers, found principally in the automobile, aviation, and metalworking industries. Rather than seeking to promote a radical ideology seeking fundamental changes in Mexican society, these unions have restricted their activities to local-level concerns such as improved salaries or the reform of internal union affairs, both of which they have militantly pursued. In contrast to the general passivity of the official unions in relation to salary increases, the independent unions have asked for amounts exceeding the maximum limits set by the state. Within the automobile industry, Volkswagen, Nissan, and General Motors have had to deal with such demands, as well as those of more democratically run union locals. In the course of much of the 1970s, the Unidad Obrera Independiente (UOI) played a major role in channeling demands by automobile workers for higher wages and in elaborating proposals for union democracy. Having learned from the violently repressed strikes of 1947–48 and 1958–59 that the state could not be challenged frontally, the UOI concluded that independent unionism in Mexico had to act within the limits of an official labor law that the state already accepted as legitimate. The state was faced with labor mobilization not seeking radical political ends, but limiting itself to questions of worker salary and local union democracy. The independent unions almost never questioned the political system itself; when they were initially so inclined, as in issues related to worker layoffs at the factory of Diesel Nacional (DINA), they reconsidered almost immediately.

In the public sector, a new type of independent unionism similar to the UOI appeared at various institutions of higher learning such as the Universidad Nacional Autónoma de México (UNAM, or the National Autonomous University of Mexico). The salary demands made in excess of the state-imposed limits benefited from the high visibility of union members who were both columnists in newspapers as well as university instructors. Strikes were frequent. Usually headed by unofficial leaders, these unions could go beyond what those in the private sector sought, not confining themselves to economic matters but directly challenging the state ideologically. On balance, they were not particularly successful in either regard, which eventually led to a serious internal crisis in 1984 and 1985.

Independent unionism has been a new force in the Mexican labor movement, contributing to the renovation of labor-state relations by both challenging the subordinate behavior of the official union leadership and making demands for internal union democracy. The leaders of the official unions have responded to this external competition by becoming more active in the promotion of worker interests and, at times, attempting to co-opt some of their rivals with offers of positions in the mainline union hierarchy. One case of the latter was that of the telephone workers' leader, Francisco Hernández Juárez, who was at various occasions an official in the national-level Congreso del Trabajo. He and Elba Esther Gordillo (from SNTE) played an important reformist role from 1989 to 1993 (during Carlos Salinas de Gortari's presidency) by organizing a new confederation, the Federación de Sindicatos de Bienes y Servicios (FESEBES, or Federation of Unions of Goods and Services).

Conclusion

It is impossible to believe that the present situation with regard to organized industrial labor evident in the mid-1990s will continue indefinitely. Indeed, as labor advocates remain unable to limit real salary decreases and as the state progressively distances itself from group support for its policies and becomes immeshed in defining the country's problems in a strictly technical fashion, the political integration of state and labor will be increasingly challenged. In the future, it will not be as easy as it has been to maintain labor's allegiance to the political system if significant benefits are no longer forthcoming to the union rank and file. As the official unions encounter more difficulties in limiting worker demands, the independent unions will gain greater worker support; these official unions, in turn, will be under greater pressure to support more radical positions in their efforts to maintain their support. Ultimately, the official unions may be forced to seriously question their alliance with the state if they are to retain their legitimacy. Any change of this nature would fundamentally alter one of the basic conditions under which the Mexican political system has been operating for decades. Such a change would contribute to the elimination of the Mexican paradox of mobilization without conflict and conflict without mobilization.

See also Confederación de Trabajadores de México (CTM); Partido de la Revolución Democrática (PRD); Partido Revolucionario Institucional (PRI)

Select Bibliography

Basurto, Jorge, *En el régimen de Echeverría: Rebelión e independencia.* Mexico City: Siglo XXI, 1983.

Bizberg, Ilán, *La acción obrera en Las Truchas.* Mexico City: El Colegio de México, 1982.

_____, "Política laboral y acción sindical: 1977–1982." *Foro Internacional* 100 (1985).

Carr, Barry, "El movimiento obrero y la política en México: 1910–1929." *Setentas* 256 (1976).

Chassen de López, Francie R., *Lombardo Toledano y el movimiento obrero mexicano: 1917–1940.* Mexico City: Extemporáneos, 1977.

Cook, María Lorena, *Organizing Dissent: Unions, the State and the Democratic Teacher's Movement in Mexico.* University Park: Pennsylvania State University Press, 1996.

Foweraker, Joe, *Popular Mobilization in Mexico: The Teacher's Movement, 1977–1987.* Cambridge and New York: Cambridge University Press, 1993.

Gabayet, Luisa, and Silvia Lailson, "Mundo laboral, mundo doméstico: Obreras de la industria manufacturera de Guadalajara." *Estudios Sociológicos* 8:24 (September-December 1990).

Garrido, Luis Javier, *El partido de la revolución institucionalizada: La formación del nuevo estado en México, 1928–1945.* Mexico City: Siglo XXI, 1982.

Gilly, Adolfo, "50 años después: La fundación de la CTM." *El Cotidiano* 10 (1986).

Medina, Luis, *Civilismo y modernización del autoritarismo.* Mexico City: El Colegio de México, 1978.

Meyer, Lorenzo, *México y los Estados Unidos en el conflicto petrolero: 1917–1942.* Mexico City: El Colegio de México, 1972.

Miller, Richard, "The Role of Labor Organizations in a Developing Country: The Case of Mexico." Ph.D. diss., Cornell University, 1966.

Reyna, José Luis, Francisco Zapata, Marcelo Miquet Fleury, and Silvia Gómez-Tagle, editors, *Tres estudios sobre el movimiento obrero en México.* Mexico City: El Colegio de México, 1976.

Reyna, José Luis, and Raúl Trejo Delarbre, *De Adolfo Ruiz Cortines a Adolfo López Mateos: 1952–1964.* Mexico City: Siglo XXI, 1981.

Rodriguez Araujo, Octavio, *En el sexenio de Tlatelolco: 1964–1970.* Mexico City: Siglo XXI, 1983.

Roxborough, Ian, *Unions and Politics in Mexico: The Case of the Automobile Industry.* Cambridge and New York: Cambridge University Press, 1984.

Thompson, Mark, and Ian Roxborough, "Union Elections and Democracy in Mexico." *British Journal of Industrial Relations* 20:2 (1982).

Torres, Blanca, *México en la Segunda Guerra Mundial.* Mexico City: El Colegio de México, 1980.

Yañez Reyes, Sergio L., *Génesis de la burocracia sindical cetemista.* Mexico City: El Caballito, 1984.

Zapata, Francisco, *El conflicto sindical en América Latina.* Mexico City: El Colegio de México, 1986.

_____, "Social concertation in Mexico." In *Participation in Public Policy Making: The Role of Trade Unions and Employer's Associations,* edited by Tiziano Treu. Berlin: Walter De Gruyter, 1992.

Zazueta, César, *El Congreso del Trabajo: Sindicatos, federaciones, y confederaciones obreros en México.* Mexico City: Fondo de Cultura Ecomómica, 1982.

—FRANCISCO ZAPATA

INDUSTRY AND INDUSTRIALIZATION

The great majority of scholars who have studied the industrialization of Mexico agree that it started during the long administration of Porfirio Díaz (president 1876–80 and 1884–1911), better known as the Porfiriato. In fact, even though it is possible to point out an evolution that starts in the crafts shops and textile mills of colonial times (some of which employed hundreds of workers who completed the whole manufacturing process under the same roof), the political and economical instability that characterized the first decades of Mexican Independence during the nineteenth century prevented full industrial development. It should be remembered that between 1821 and 1861, Mexico changed presidents 56 times, in addition to being invaded by the United States in 1847 and by France in 1862.

The first Mexican administrations trusted more in mining, agriculture, and trade as sources of national wealth, thereby neglecting almost completely the growth of manufacturing. The initiative of a group of industrialists to create a loan bank (Banco de Avío) in 1830, which would foster the textile industry, collapsed owing to the bank's necessity to finance some of the political groups fighting for power, while imported machinery deteriorated in port, unable to reach the factories.

The Porfiriato: The First Industrialization

It was not until the administration of Porfirio Díaz that the groundwork for industrial development was laid. The contributing factors were the country's political stability, as well as a series of measures directed, on the one hand, at creating an infrastructure of energy and transportation and, on the other, at opening the borders to U.S. and European capital. Starting in 1870, this foreign capital began flowing into the country, mainly to mining and railroads, but also to trade and manufacturing. In 1910, foreign investment reached between 67 and 73 percent of the country's total capital investment.

In those years, the most significant growth was seen in the railways; the amount of rail track in the country increased from 400 miles (640 kilometers) in 1877 to more than 3,000 miles (5,000 kilometers) in 1883, finally reaching 12,000 miles (19,000 kilometers) in 1910. This growth decreased transportation costs, which fostered mining, expanded commercial agriculture, and unified the internal market. Several scholars indicate that the growth of mining and agricultural exports also facilitated the growth of the internal market, which developed manufacturing.

Industrialists multiplied during the Porfiriato. In Chihuahua, Eduardo Creel gave an impulse to the flour industry, while in Monterrey the Garza family started its business empire with the founding of the Cuauhtémoc brewery. In Puebla, Tlaxcala, and Orizaba the textile industry grew, and local businessmen fostered the creation of electrical power plants, which not only supplied their factories but also neighboring cities. By 1910 Mexico produced cotton fabric, wool, linen, jute, leather goods, sugar, pasta, canned goods, wine, liquor, beer, cigarettes, cigars, paper, some chemical products (sulfuric acid and explosives), oils, soaps, candles, matches, stoneware, glass, and cement. In 1903, the country's first iron and steel mill was built with a starting capital of 10 million pesos, contributed by the most prominent industrialists of Monterrey. The plant had Latin America's first blast furnace, which was used to supply the railway and construction industries. By 1911, the manufacturing sector produced 12.1 percent of the gross national product (GNP) and employed 11.5 percent of the workforce.

Despite this spectacular growth of manufacturing, in the early years of the twentieth century the Mexican population was still predominantly rural, and the largest share of industrial investment was made in extractive industries (e.g., mining and oil) owned primarily by U.S. and British concerns.

Industry during the First Revolutionary Administrations

The armed conflict of 1910 to 1917 did not significantly affect manufacturing production, but the nation's economic structure suffered greatly. Thus, while the manufacturing sector's production decreased only 1 percent between 1910 and 1922, mining, agriculture, and livestock diminished by 4, 5.2, and 4.6 percent, respectively. In 1917 the banking industry was nationalized, and the currency's instability discouraged investment in all industrial sectors other than oil and mining, where foreign companies took advantage of the opportunity created by World War I to increase their production and exports.

The Constitution of 1917 also caused distrust among Mexican businessmen, who opposed Articles 27 and 123. Article 27 determined that the Mexican soil and subsoil were the nation's property, which in the opinion of businessmen meant that the principle of private property had been violated; Article 123 regulated working conditions by reducing the number of hours in the working day and creating a series of demands to employers that would lead, years later, to the Federal Work Law of 1931. Lacking a clear concept of industrial development, President Venustiano Carranza chose to invite the country's leading businessmen to discuss the issue

in a national convention of industrialists and merchants, which gave rise to two large confederations: the Confederación de Cámaras Industriales de los Estados Unidos Mexicanos (CONCAMIN, or Confederation of Industrial Chambers of the United States of Mexico, established in 1917) and the Confederación de Cámaras Nacionales de Comercio (CONCANACO, or Confederation of National Chambers of Commerce, established in 1918).

The recognition of these confederations and the creation in 1925 of the Bank of Mexico, responsible for the issue of the nation's currency, allowed the gradual recovery of Mexico's credit rating and monetary stability. The Bank of Mexico, initially composed of 51 percent state capital and 49 percent private industrial capital, created the conditions for economic recovery. The interest shown by the administration of President Plutarco Elías Calles (1924–28) in creating a better road system and greater political stability than in previous years favored the recovery of the GNP, which according to some authors reached an annual growth rate of 5.8 percent between 1925 and 1928. In those years, the relative importance of the oil and mining industries decreased (owing, among other things, to the discovery of oil in South America), while the textile and electrical industries grew. More growth also was seen in the food and drink industries, and later in the manufacturing of simple consumer goods, such as cigarettes, paper, and shoes, and the processing of raw materials (sisal and cotton, which were destined for export markets). This growth was unexpectedly interrupted by the international financial crisis in 1929, which severely decreased the demand for exports of raw materials, thereby affecting the whole economy. Between 1930 and 1934, the nation's GNP not only stopped growing but even declined by 0.5 percent.

Under the administration of Lázaro Cárdenas (1934–40), the groundwork was laid to change the nation's economic model (which until then had been based on the export of raw materials) to a different model based on the state as chief promoter of economic development and on the industrial policy of import substitution (import substitution industrialization refers to a set of policies implemented by an activist, interventionist state designed to encourage the domestic production of previously imported manufactured goods). The nationalization of the railways and of the oil industry guaranteed, in the subsequent decades, the transportation of goods and a low-cost fuel supply, starting a subsidy that would last several decades and that would increase in magnitude in the coming years with the nationalization of the power and light industry and of other basic industries, such as steel. These state-owned companies provided cheap production parts to the Mexican industry and fostered its development during many decades. Likewise, the creation of the Mexican labor movement, as evidenced by the Confederación de Trabajadores de México (CTM, or Confederation of Mexican Workers), gave legal rights to the unions and at the same time provided adequate channels to the public and the industrial sectors to negotiate workers' demands in a peaceful way. Subsequently, such development neutralized potential union conflicts, thereby shaping a climate conducive to investment.

The Industrializing Project: From Import Substitution to Stabilizing Development

Starting in 1940, Mexico formally started a new economic orientation based on the need of rapid industrialization in order to become a member of the so-called developed countries. The demands created by World War II fostered industrialization in Mexico, where manufactured goods were produced for the internal market as well as for export to the United States.

In order to promote industrialization, the administrations of Manuel Avila Camacho (1940–46) and Miguel Alemán Valdés (1946–52) established a series of successive measures designed to strengthen Mexican industry during the war years and, later, to protect it at the end of hostilities when the United States once again would start full production of manufactured goods that would compete with Mexican goods. There also arose a new generation of young businessmen who, with relatively little capital, had started small businesses with growth potential that, in the coming years, would benefit from public policies.

A first step was the Law of Industries of Transformation, issued in 1941, which granted large tax breaks to those Mexican businessmen who could prove that their companies were "new" or "necessary." At the same time, the Bank of Mexico underwent restructuring, and the actions of the National Financing Institution (created in 1934 by the Lázaro Cárdenas administration to channel federal resources to different public works) were reoriented toward selective financing of industries and the creation of infrastructure for its development. Industries considered "new and necessary" received federal financing, tax breaks for up to 10 years, permits to import machinery, and other benefits. At the same time, a protectionist policy was consolidated that closed the nation's borders to those products that could be locally manufactured and that imposed restrictions on the establishment of foreign companies, all of which helped the development of a new, protected industrial base, which has been dubbed "the greenhouse industry."

Once the first industrializing effort passed, the nation's economic strategy focused on the so-called stabilizing development, which not only maintained the protectionism of the first decade of industrialization but reinforced it with the establishment of a stable exchange rate (the peso remained at US$12.50 between 1954 and 1976). The new strategy also maintained a highly favorable tax policy to private capital, and foreign investment was curtailed. This allowed the establishment of companies of mixed capital participation, which, being part Mexican, allowed foreign investors to benefit from the protection that the Mexican government granted to the national companies. Aided by U.S. president John F. Kennedy's Alliance for Progress, foreign capital flowed to Mexico and triggered manufacturing growth. It was in this period that the large multinational corporations established many subsidiaries in the country and benefited from Mexican protectionism. Some protests from nationalist businessmen who opposed foreign competition were heard, but these protests were silenced by measures such as the nationalization of the electric industry, which guaranteed the supply of low-cost energy, and by President Adolfo López Mateos's decree requiring local car manufacturers to include at least 60 percent domestically manufactured parts in all vehicles.

The policy of import substitution, based on protectionism, was preserved for four decades. This was a period of important changes: numerous companies were founded and prospered; simultaneously, aided by state protectionism, considerable capital was accumulated, while the nation's GNP started to increase until it reached a 6 percent annual rate. Between 1940 and 1960, manufacturing activity increased its participation in the GNP from 17 to 26 percent.

Mexican industrial structure underwent a relatively fast transition from simple manufacturing (as defined by its organization, technology, and distribution channels) to more complex manufacturing, which also meant the shift from perishable goods to intermediate, nonperishable, and capital goods. Thus, while in 1950 the subsector of foods, drinks, and tobacco comprised 38.5 percent of the total value created by the manufacturing sector, in 1958 it had decreased to only 29.3 percent; such was also the case of the textile subsector, which decreased from 15.6 to 10.3 percent during the same period. In contrast, the chemical industry increased its share from 9 to 13 percent, and the machinery industry went from 2.7 to 11.9 percent of the total value created by the manufacturing sector.

At the same time, the state-controlled oil and electricity sectors grew with lightning speed, maintaining low-cost energy to Mexican industry. By 1970, Mexico was almost self-sufficient in the production of food, oil and oil-derived products, steel, and many consumer goods. Not in vain, some observers called this period of growth "the Mexican Miracle."

The Crisis of Protectionism

At the start of the 1970s, a decrease in the growth rate of industrial investment and production and a declining output in the agribusiness sector forced the government to import growing quantities of raw materials. These tendencies exposed the crisis of the protectionist model, leading decision makers to look for new alternatives.

During the administrations of Luis Echeverría Álvarez (1970–76) and José López Portillo (1976–82), the slowdown of private investment led to an increase of public investment in the manufacturing and oil industries. Owing to a decrease in oil production, however, public investment gradually meant higher foreign debt. The increase of oil prices starting in 1976, on the other hand, promoted heavy government investment in the expansion of the oil industry under the assumption that hydrocarbon exports would foster general industrial development. In this period, strong investments were made in roads and other forms of transportation, and the growth of the petrochemical industry was given priority. In 1981, the state-owned Mexican oil monopoly (Petróleos Mexicanos, or PEMEX) generated almost half of the nation's total investment.

The unexpected decrease in international oil prices made evident the decay of the old economic model of import substitution. Rapid capital flight caused a severe decrease in industrial production and justified the nationalization of the private banks in 1982. The worldwide increase of interest rates worsened the nation's external debt, and the process of economic recovery also was blocked by a series of instabilities caused by protectionism, such as the concentration of industrial production centers in a few places, geared exclusively to the internal market; disorder among industrial sectors; high production costs that prevented effective international competition; and transformation of the country's export structures.

In response to this crisis, the administration of Miguel de la Madrid (1982–88) started the implementation of a new "neoliberal" development model (that is, a model adjusted to the guidelines of the International Monetary Fund, which stressed the payment of the external debt, the reduction of direct public economic activity, and the reorientation of national production toward external markets). These policies were consolidated during the presidency of Carlos Salinas de Gortari (1988–94), characterized by faster privatization of state-owned industries, the sale of the recently acquired banks, the opening of new investment areas traditionally reserved for the state (among them the petrochemical industry, as well as the management of highways, ports, and public services).

In compliance with the new economic policy oriented toward external markets, Mexico joined the General Agreement on Tariffs and Trade (GATT) in 1985, an international organization created to foster free trade among nations and accelerate the elimination of tariff barriers. In less than three years, Mexico went from being a protected country to part of a large worldwide market of diverse consumer goods, which put many Mexican manufacturers at a disadvantage. The North American Free Trade Agreement (NAFTA) among Mexico, the United States, and Canada, which went into effect on January 1, 1994, tried to reduce protectionist policies of Mexico's two most important foreign markets, apart from establishing a series of rules for trade exchange, not only concerning industrial production but also agricultural products, communications, and services. Mexico partially closed its borders to some countries (for example, by imposing higher tariffs to Chinese products) and became part of the North American trading block.

The Limitations of the Modernizing Project

The difficulties of the plan to modernize the Mexican economy became apparent with the crisis that marked the end of the presidency of Salinas and the beginning of the new administration of Ernesto Zedillo Ponce de León in 1994. Some of these difficulties had been anticipated by scholars such as Adam Przeworsky, who repeatedly warned about the risks of an economy that relied a great deal on the regulatory capacity of the market that, inevitably, would create regional imbalances or would cause the collapse of industrial sectors. Apart from the inequality of economic development among negotiating partners and the persistence of protectionism in many countries, it is important to point out that an important limitation of the export model of economic development has been the large domestic imbalance that characterizes the nation's industrial structure; this imbalance is seen, first of all, in the concentration of capital in a very small number of companies, and, second, in the large numbers of medium-sized, small, and "micro" businesses that have low quality control and low competitiveness.

Estimates based on a number of census data show that, by 1990, there were only 2,400 industries (1.95 percent of the nation's total) that employed more than 250 workers. These same industries, according to other data, dominated 66 percent of industrial production and 49.5 percent of all industrial jobs. These industries were followed by about 3,300 "medium-sized" businesses that employed between 101 and 250 workers and that comprised 2.62 percent of the total, whereas businesses with less than 100 workers formed the other 95 percent. Generally speaking, approximately 75 percent of the nation's businesses had fewer than 15 employees. Therefore, the latter belonged to the category of "microcompanies."

The leaders among the large industrial corporations (whose number in 1990 did not exceed 130) were PEMEX and the nation's five automotive companies, which were responsible for the largest increase in exports. To a lesser extent, export also grew in the following sectors: shoes, textiles, beer, paper, glass, and products for the construction industry. By the same token, in the late 1980s and early 1990s, the importance of the *maquiladora* industry grew enormously. The *maquiladoras,* established along the U.S. border, are intermediate or final assembly plants for industrial products. In many cases, the *maquiladoras* not only include large companies, but also medium or small companies that have been able to find a market niche and therefore have taken advantage of demand for certain products in the world market.

However, the new trade climate has had a negative impact on many medium, small, and "micro" companies. Their problems have included poor organization, lack of appropriate technology, and low adaptability to market forces. Often, these companies are family-owned and characterized by the owner's lack of vision and avoidance of risk. The small company is also hampered by the lack of credit, lack of personnel to comply with tax requirements, red tape, or union matters.

Throughout the late 1980s and early 1990s, several federal programs to help the micro, small, and medium companies were implemented, but these businesses complained of a lack of a broad economic policy that would allow them to overcome their problems so that they could export. In 1996 the administration of Ernesto Zedillo launched the Program of Industrial Policy and Foreign Trade, aimed at reconciling the opposition of large corporations to government controls with necessary help to small and medium companies in such forms as technological and administrative help and tax breaks so they can survive the market's unfavorable conditions. In order to achieve this, the Zedillo administration proposed, among other things, better business training, the strengthening of production chains and industrial zones all over the country, and finally, the improvement of technological infrastructure and federal help in all export activities.

See also Artisans and Artisanal Production; Automobile Industry; Banking and Finance; Cotton Textile Industry; Ecology; Employer Organizations; Import Substitution Industrialization (ISI); Industrial Labor; Maquiladoras; Mining; Monterrey Industrialists and Industrialization; Petroleum; Steel Industry; Trade and Markets; Women's Status and Occupation

Select Bibliography

Alba, Caros y Dirk Kruijt, *La utilidad de lo minúsculo.* Mexico City: Colegio de México, 1995.

Anderson, Rodney D., *Outcasts in Their Own Land: Mexican Industrial Workers, 1906–1911.* DeKalb: Northern Illinois University Press, 1976.

Cué Cánovas, Agustín, *Historia social y económica de México: 1521–1854.* Mexico City: Trillas, 1963.

Haber, Stephen H., *Industry and Underdevelopment: The Industrialization of Mexico, 1890–1940.* Stanford, California: Stanford University Press, 1989.

Martínez del Campo, Manuel, *Industrialización en México: Hacia un analisis crítico.* Mexico City: Colegio de México, 1985.

Meyer, Lorenzo, *Historia de la Revolución Mexicana: El conflicto social y los gobiernos del maximato,* vol. 13. Mexico City: Colegio de México, 1978.

Morales, Josefina, editor, *La reestructuración industrial en México: Cinco aspectos fundamentales.* Mexico City: UNAM, 1992.

Poder Ejeccutivo Federal, *Programa de política industrial y comercio exterior.* Mexico City: Secretaría de Comercio y Fomento Industrial, 1996.

Potash, Robert A., *El Banco de Avío de México: El fomento de la industria, 1821–1846.* Mexico City: FCE, 1959.

Puga, Cristina, *México: Empresarios y poder,* edited by Miguel Angel Porrúa. Mexico City: UNAM, 1993.

_____, and Ricardo Tirado, editors, *Los empresarios mexicanos ayer y hoy.* Mexico City: El Caballito, 1992.

_____, and David Torres M., *México: La modernización contradictoria.* Mexico City: Alhambra Mexicana, 1995.

Reynolds, Clark W., *La economía mexicana: Su estructura y crecimiento en el siglo XX.* Mexico City: FCE, 1973.

Rosenzweig, Fernando, "El desarrollo económico de México de 1877 a 1911." *El Trimestre Económico* (1965).

Tirado, Ricardo, editor, *Los empresarios ante la globalización.* Mexico City: UNAM, 1994.

Torres Ramírez, Blanca, *Historia de la Revolución Mexicana, Período 1940–1952: México en la Segunda Guerra Mundial,* vol. 19. Mexico City: Colegio de México, 1979.

Villarreal, René, *El desequilibrio externo en la industrialización de México (1929–1975).* Mexico City: FCE, 1976.

—CRISTINA PUGA

INFANTE, PEDRO

1917–57 • Film Actor and Singer

A 1993 popularity poll conducted by a Mexican tabloid pitted the sex appeal of contemporary pop music icon Luis Miguel against that of Pedro Infante, film and recording star of the 1940s and 1950s. Although dead for almost four decades, Infante won decisively. No matter the survey's accuracy, its conclusion reflected Infante's very real present-day popularity, both as a figure of national nostalgia for a bygone epoch and of enduring relevancy in defining *lo mexicano* and especially machismo. Infante's charisma, as the raucous good bad-boy of Mexican film, appealed to both female and male spectators. His career coincided with and deepened two overlapping and interrelated "golden ages," still central to contemporary popular culture: those of Mexican cinema and of Mexico City in the 1940s and 1950s.

Infante was born in 1917 in Mazatlán, Sinaloa, to a lower middle-class family. His father was a music teacher and performer in Guamúchil, where Pedro was reared. As a teenager, the future star began to sing informally in various town squares and later performed professionally with a small orchestra based in his native state's capital city, Culiacán. Eventually he gave up work as a carpenter to devote himself to a full-time career in entertainment. In 1939 he moved to Mexico City in search of wider fame. His migration paralleled that of hundreds of thousands of Mexicans as the capital became, during World War II, the site of the nation's industrial expansion. This economic and population growth also made the city the center of the nation's developing interrelated culture industries—radio, recording, and film production—crucial not only to national but also international development as Mexican mass media, especially movies, rose to prominence throughout Latin America. Infante was central to forging this popularity, shaping the national and international projection of Mexico through music and film.

In Mexico City he initially was turned away from XEW, the giant radio station owned by multimedia magnate Emilio Azcárraga, but he found work singing live on the air at the slightly less glamorous, but still important, XEB. (Like most Mexican music stars, he later performed for XEW.) Radio was one sign of the modernizing aspects of the country's cultural development during World War II. Another was Mexico City's glamorous nightlife, which itself soon became a major source of Mexican motion-picture imagery in the popular *cabaretera* genre. The young singer soon found work as part of a regular act at the Hotel Reforma, home of the capital's most prominent nightclub acts, as well as a main meeting place for major movie producers. Infante began to appear in films as the industry expanded during the war. His first significant supporting role was in *La feria de las flores* (1942), which starred Antonio Badú. (Soon, Infante would receive top billing in films with Badú.) In 1943, he starred in five films and established his life-long relationship with the production company Rodríguez Hermanos.

In the same year, Infante signed an exclusive recording contract with the multinational Discos Peerless. By 1943, he was a rising presence in all of Mexico's mass media—radio, records, and film—and a singular figure in Mexico's popular culture, which was redefining the nation. An increasingly urban and industrial nation produced symbols that eased that transformation even as it reflected its inherent ideological and social tensions. Infante's films demonstrated this pattern. In the 1946 hit *Los tres García,* the rising star portrayed one of three cousins, each of whom personified a Mexican male stereotype that indicated dilemmas posed by postwar socioeconomic development to traditional constructions of machismo. Infante's character was the good-natured, half-cocked, womanizing, emotionally demonstrative *charro* in contrast with his more serious relatives: a provincial dandy (played by Victor Manuel Mendoza) and an ascetic do-gooder (played by Abel Salazar). The film also underlined postwar popular ambivalence about Mexican international relations through its personification of the United States in the character of a beautiful, U.S.-reared half-American, half-Mexican (played by Marga López) who visits her Mexican homeland and becomes the source of romantic competition for *los tres* Garcías. The film was followed by a successful sequel, *Vuelven los García* (1946), which continued to deepen Infante's persona as a boisterous *charro*. In the 1948 hit *Los Huastecos*, Infante displayed his versatility, as well as the technical facility of Mexican film production, by playing three roles in one of his most legendary screen performances. Three orphaned brothers of distinct characters take different paths in serving their hometown: one is a social bandit, another a womanizing but locally respected military officer, and the third a liberal priest. The movie includes a memo-

rable scene where Infante's three archetypes sing a trio together. The film captures the artist's ability, unique among Mexican movie stars of the golden age, to capture a wide range of masculine personae projected by popular culture. In *Dos tipos de cuidado* (1952) Infante shared top-billing with the most famous singing screen *charro* of all, Jorge Negrete, who was his single most important rival for national attention. (Offscreen the two performers were reportedly friends.) The film offered a comparison of the two actors' dominant screen images, each constructed through aptly named macho stereotypes: Infante played Pedro Malo (the mischievous yet kindly rabble rouser); Negrete was Jorge Bueno (the noble, sober stoic). As with all of Infante's postwar films described above, the movie was directed by Ismael Rodríguez, Infante's most frequent behind-the-camera collaborator.

In the 1950s Infante's screen persona and his musical recordings took more urban forms, reflecting the growth and maturation of city life and, especially, Mexico City's continuing expansion. *Nosotros los pobres* (1947) and its sequels, *Ustedes los ricos* (1948) and *Pepe el toro* (1952), presented Infante as a working-class hero rooted in the capital city's barrio culture. On the lighter side, his comedic work in *A toda máquina* (1951) and its successful sequel *Que te ha dado esa mujer* (1951), in which he played a Mexico City vagabond who transforms himself into a member of the capital's elite motorcycle police corps, transformed Infante into an urban *charro;* these films also presented the state's modernizing mission to bring social order through supposedly efficient and honest police administration (a theme present in many 1950s films set in Mexico City). In these movies, as in the los García movies, the figure of a U.S. feminine love object as a personification of the United States inverted Mexico's real-life economic and political dependence on its northern neighbor; Infante and co-star Luis Aguilar compete in the movies for the attentions of a *gringa* tourist (Aurora Segura). Infante further underlines this international commentary on the growing Americanization of Mexico City culture in a nightclub scene in *A toda máquina,* in which he parodies his U.S. counterpart, Frank Sinatra, as he woos his American object of desire.

His recording career continued to develop during the 1950s, frequently drawing on his cinematic performances. His rendition in *Nosotros los pobres* of "Las mañanitas," the song traditionally sung in Mexico for birthdays, became one of the Mexican recording industry's all-time hits, still selling steadily today. In the 1950s, Infante popularized a bolero form that mixed his provincial and Mexico City film personae by integrating mariachi musical arrangements with urban love ballads. Like his films, his recordings had transnational appeal. His wildly popular singing tours throughout the southwestern United States demonstrated the performer's popularity with the Mexicans and Mexican-Americans north of the Rio Grande who also formed the major foreign audience for his movies.

His off-screen life was complicated and sometimes scandalous (he lived openly with more than one long-term mistress, fathered children out of wedlock, and made several unsuccessful attempts to divorce his first wife while he illegally married another woman), but it did not diminish his popularity. Instead the publicity fed audience interest in the star's personal life. Much like James Dean's Hollywood legend, Infante's mystique was further enhanced by his untimely and violently macho death while at the height of his popularity. In 1957 he died in a plane crash, the last of several he had endured in pursuing his passion for aviation. The timing was symbolic, since it coincided with the end of the golden age of Mexican cinema. His penultimate film, *Tizoc* (1956), a historical epic about Mayan civilization, was a huge production made in color that costarred Mexican screen diva María Félix. It won the 1958 Ariel (Mexico's motion-picture award) for best film. The movie made an international impact too; Infante posthumously won a best actor award at the 1958 Berlin film festival. The spectacle was, however, a final burst of cinematic extravagance amidst commercial, technical, and artistic decline that reached its nadir a decade after the end of World War II.

Infante's image, however, has outlived Mexican cinema's so-called golden age. His funeral, attended by every important Mexican political, cultural, and entertainment figure, laid the groundwork for the his apotheosis as arguably the leading symbol of postwar Mexican popular culture. Into the 1990s, the anniversary of the star's death was commemorated annually by officially sanctioned public ceremonies, including gigantic outdoor projections of film clips and motorcycle demonstrations by fans clad in costumes reminiscent of *A toda máquina,* at Mexico City's Monumento de la Revolución Mexicana. Such displays demonstrate how popular culture merge with official constructions of Mexican nationalism in the state's recognition of the power of golden age Mexican cinema's most enduring legend.

Select Bibliography

de los Reyes, Aurelio, Davíd Ramón, María Luisa Amador, and Rodolfo Rivera, *80 años de cine en México.* Mexico City: Dirección General de Difusión Cultural, UNAM, 1977.

García Riera, Emilio, *Historia documental del cine mexicano,* 2nd edition, 18 vols., Guadalajara and Mexico City: Universidad de Guadalajara, Gobierno de Jalisco (Secretaría de Cutlura), Consejo Nacional para la Cultura y las Artes, Instituto Mexicano de Cinematografía, 1992–95.

Mora, Carl J., *The Mexican Cinema: Reflections of a Society, 1896–1988.* Berkeley, Los Angeles, and London: University of California Press, 1989.

—Seth Fein

INQUISITION

The Inquisition was a special ecclesiastical and political institution created to combat or suppress heresy and crimes against the colonial church and the Hapsburg viceroyalty. This institution evolved in Mexico from its early European origins, developing a complex bureaucracy and system of procedures. The Inquisition served the important function of endeavoring to maintain social, religious, and political order by the use of coercive power in enforcing religious and political orthodoxy in New Spain. The Inquisition's religious and philosophical influence on various aspects of colonial Mexican life has been abundantly researched, but the very institutional structure, functioning, and jurisdictional conflicts of the Holy Office in Mexico have, to date, received little scholarly attention. Previous studies of the Inquisition were concerned with polemics over its relative cruelty or lenient nature, and the extent of atrocities committed by officials of the Holy Office. The Inquisition's cruel and coercive methods and juridical use of torture were unarguably inhumane, and the institution itself must be condemned as a sad comment on human history. Furthermore, the Inquisition's reprehensible censorship of literature and ideas through its published "Index of Prohibited Books" hindered the development of cultural and intellectual life in New Spain. Nevertheless, early Inquisition historiography focused too much attention on those horrors and spent little time analyzing the Inquisition's impact on society and its effects upon the social and ethnic groups that made up the intricate colonial milieu of New Spain.

Modern revisionist studies, however, have moved beyond the salutary or condemnatory agendas of earlier scholarship to focus on the role the Inquisition played in the formation of the society of New Spain. Recent historical work also has drawn on the rich documentation produced by the Inquisition's complex bureaucracy to reconstruct the moral, ethical, and religious life of colonial Mexico.

Origins, Functions, and Officials of the Inquisition in Mexico

Pope Gregory IX established the Inquisition in 1233 as a permanent tribunal to combat several dissident movements during the Middle Ages. Before that time the job of punishing crimes against the faith belonged to the bishops. Pope Gregory IX, seeing the bishops burdened with their pastoral duties, created tribunals throughout France, Germany, and

Italy. Spain, busy in its "reconquest of territory" from the Moors, was left without a formal Inquisition. In 1478, at the request of Fernando V and Isabel I, Pope Sixtus IV established an independent Spanish Inquisition, which served as the model for the Inquisition in the Americas.

From its founding, a unique aspect of the Spanish Inquisition was its virtual independence from papal control. The pope conceded to the Spanish Crown the privilege of royal patronage *(patronato real),* giving the Crown control over the nomination of all ecclesiastical personnel in Spain and America, including inquisitorial personnel. Although in theory the Inquisition was an ecclesiastical institution, the appointment of inquisitors and other functionaries of the Holy Office became the privilege of the secular monarch.

King Felipe II did not officially create the Tribunal of the Inquisition in New Spain until the royal decree of January 25, 1569. Another royal order dated August 16, 1570, removed the Indians from its jurisdiction and gave the Tribunal of Mexico authority over all of New Spain, including the Philippines, Guatemala, and the Bishopric of Nicaragua. The Inquisition in New Spain functioned from 1570 until its final abolition in 1820 upon Mexico's Independence from Spain, although it changed over time in its focus and primary functions.

From 1522 to 1569, before the official founding of the Tribunal of the Inquisition in New Spain, the monastic orders and the early bishops assumed apostolic powers as inquisitors in a primitive form of Inquisition. This primitive Inquisition attempted to correct the spiritual crimes of the early conquerors and reprimand "erring" Indian neophytes and pagans. From 1571 to 1700, with the removal of its jurisdiction over the Indians, the Mexican Inquisition had as its main function the prosecution and punishment of all acts contrary to the Catholic faith, including apostasy, heresy, and the continued practice of the Jewish religion by newly converted Jews (called *conversos* or "New Christians"). Similarly, the Inquisition often was occupied in the punishment of actions contrary to Christian morality, including blasphemy, bigamy, sodomy, bestiality, fornication, concubinage, and the solicitation of sex in the confessional by priests. The Inquisition further stifled intellectual development by the publication of an alphabetical index of prohibited books, which it sent to its inquisitors and commissaries in the Americas. The Inquisition's agents in New Spain, with this "Index" in hand, made routine visits to ships *(visitas de naos)* in order to search for prohibited books, and they investigated book dealers and private collectors. The final period of the Mexican Inquisition, from 1700 to 1820, saw the growing political use of the Inquisition for the punishment of all dissidents with respect to Catholic dogma and teaching (including Lutherans and other Protestant sects) as well as those who held or stated propositions contrary to the church or the king. Hundreds of residents of New Spain faced Inquisition trials during this period, including two of the most famous leaders of the Mexican Independence movement, Father Miguel Hidalgo y Costilla and José María Morelos y Pavón.

Institutional Hierarchy

Atop the hierarchy of the Holy Office of the Inquisition (also known as the Tribunal) of New Spain sat two to three superior ecclesiastical judges. These inquisitors were aided by a *promotor fiscal* (prosecutor), who brought the initial accusation of the prisoners before the Tribunal, and a *secretario* (secretary), who authorized all of the documents, edicts, and dispatches of the Holy Office. Two *notarios del secreto* (notaries) certified the declarations and testimony of witnesses before the Tribunal and cared for the archive of the Inquisition.

The inquisitors relied on the help of six *consultores* (councillors), who gave them legal advice. These councillors included two theologians and four doctors of canon law. Along with these councillors there were eight *calificadores* (qualifiers—all doctors in theology or canon and civil law), who weighed the evidence presented in each case to decide if there was sufficient cause to proceed in a formal trial. Twelve *alguaciles* (constables) saw to the apprehension of the prisoners. Officials called *alcaldes* served as guards at the various jails used by the Inquisition, including the *carcel secreta* (secret prison for incarceration during the trial until sentencing), the *carcel de penitencia* (for short prison sentences), and the *carcel perpetua* (for those condemned to life in prison). There also were several *proveedores,* entrusted with the feeding of prisoners. The other lesser officials of the Tribunal included many doormen, several surgeons and doctors required by law to be present during the interrogation and torture of prisoners, and even a barber for the prisoners.

A separate system of secular or lay persons formed an elite group of constables or policemen of the Inquisition, called *familiares.* All those nominated to these positions had their family histories investigated to ensure that they were "old Christians of good faith and customs." These *familiares* of the Inquisition held privileged positions that gave them exemption from prosecution in civil cases. They aided the officials of the Inquisition in the discovery, apprehension, and arrest of suspects. The numbers of these *familiares* varied, but by law there were 12 *familiares* in Mexico City, 4 *familiares* in the seat of each bishopric, and 1 *familiar* in each Spanish town.

A subsidiary institution controlled by the Tribunal of Mexico was the *Real Fisco* (Royal Fiscal Office of the Inquisition), entrusted with the management of the confiscated property and goods of those convicted by the Inquisition. This branch of the Holy Office had the power and duty to oversee the finances and pay for salaries and various fees that the Inquisition incurred during its proceedings. It counted on the services of a *contador* (accountant), several lawyers, and two *notarios del secuestro,* who testified to everything relative to the confiscation of goods.

Throughout the rest of the provinces there were commissaries of the Inquisition who were nominated by the inquisitors and approved by the viceroy and the Crown. Each province held one commissary *(comisario)* of the Inquisition who operated a minor tribunal of the Holy Office, investigating crimes against the faith and then conducting the initial arrest and trial of the accused. In some cases commissaries even passed preliminary sentences, but they could not pass the definitive sentences unless ordered to do so by the Tribunal in Mexico. The commissariats of the Inquisition employed at least one notary, a constable, and a jailer.

Many of the fees and salaries of the Inquisition in New Spain were paid from the fines and confiscated goods of those convicted by the Holy Office. Interpretations of the Inquisition as a corrupt institution bent on the confiscation of as much property as possible emerged from the study of the finances of the Inquisition. Although this extreme interpretation has been disproved, the payment of the officials' salaries exclusively from the sequestered goods of the accused lent itself to corruption. In order to ensure a more secure source of revenue and eliminate corruption, Pope Urban VIII in 1627 ordered that in each cathedral seat of the Inquisition, one of the prebends or canonries funded by tithe revenues was to be suppressed and its rents applied to the payment of the Inquisition salaries. Scholars such as Henry Lea nevertheless argue that the finances of the Inquisition in New Spain remained precarious as the Holy Office continued to clash with the king and treasury officials concerning salaries.

Trials and Procedures

According to civil and canon law, all Inquisition trials had to follow a standard procedure established since the founding by the publication of Tomás de Torquemada's *Instrucciones* in 1484. The procedure usually began with an *edicto de la fé,* a proclamation requiring, under pain of excommunication, the denunciation of all offenses against the faith. These edicts were periodically placed in all parish churches and often began the process of the Inquisition by urging people to denounce themselves or others of crimes committed against the faith.

Induced by the warnings of the *edicto de la fé,* many people came forward denouncing themselves or giving testimony of crimes committed against the faith by their neighbors. Those who denounced crimes against the faith were summoned before the Inquisition to give testimony to the case. During the investigation each witness declared what he or she knew about the crime and the individual was then sworn to secrecy. Several days after taking the testimony, the witnesses would be recalled to reaffirm their testimonies. Those discovered giving false testimony were tried for the crime of perjury *(téstigo falso).*

After the testimony was taken and reaffirmed, the *calificadores* examined the documents. If they deemed the evidence of the testimony or denunciations sufficient, they authorized the inquisitors to proceed in the formation of a case. The inquisitors then ordered their *alguaciles* or the *familiares* of the Holy Office to arrest the accused. The accused remained incarcerated in the secret prison throughout the trial until sentencing. Not infrequently, prisoners would spend

years in jail waiting for their trial. Many perished in jail before the completion of their trials. The Royal Fiscal Office inventoried the prisoner's estate and embargoed his or her goods for the duration of the trial. The accused paid the cost of imprisonment from the revenues of their estate, or if they were poor the Inquisition provided for their sustenance.

The Tribunal seldom informed defendants about the nature of their alleged crimes. It instead told the accused to "examine" their conscience and make a declaration of anything that they found to be "contrary to the faith." The court instructed defendants to make a list of their enemies, whose testimony and denunciations were disregarded in the case. The accused then petitioned and presented their own witnesses, who testified to the defendants' good Christian nature.

The inquisitors and their *consultores* examined the evidence in the case and either insisted on the confession of the accused or continued the examination of witnesses. If torture were inflicted upon the prisoner, the Tribunal administered it once at this point in the trial's proceedings. Torture was used in many cases, but not all of the Inquisition's prisoners were tortured. Strict guidelines were established for the administration and duration of torture, but the process itself led to abuses. The law required that torture only be applied once, but many inquisitors and their aides "suspended" the torture sessions and resumed them over a period of several days. Perhaps more horrifying is the fact that the tortures meted out by the Inquisition and its ministers were equaled or surpassed in rigor by those administered by the civil authorities of the same period in both Spain and the Americas.

After the conclusion of a case, the inquisitors decided upon an appropriate punishment, according to the gravity of the crime. Prisoners who confessed or denounced themselves, showing repentance for their crimes, often received lighter sentences. They were given sentences of reconciliation *(sentencia de reconciliación),* including the wearing of penitential garments called *san benitos* during an *auto de fé* as a mark of shame for their crime. This punishment was combined with short- or long-term imprisonment, a pecuniary fine, forced pilgrimage, or the necessity of hearing masses with other penitents, as well as the prohibition of holding any dignity or public office.

Prisoners pronounced guilty, but who did not confess or repent, were sentenced to death *(sentencia ordinaria o de muerte).* This sentence also entailed excommunication and the total confiscation of the prisoners' estate, which went to the Royal Fiscal Office of the Inquisition. Since the inquisitors could not carry out a corporal sentence themselves, they ordered the prisoner to be "relaxed" to the secular authorities *(relajado al brazo secular),* who executed the prisoner.

The Inquisition and the secular authorities publicly administered all punishments at a formal function called an *auto de fé.* These *autos de fé* were public spectacles undertaken at great cost and attended by all major functionaries of the ecclesiastical and civil governments of New Spain. They were intended to serve as a deterrent to religious heterodoxy and were a major didactic tool of the Inquisition. The public display and humiliation of those condemned served as the Inquisition's cruelest and most degrading weapon against what it considered to be immorality and heretical movements.

Inquisition Studies and the Use of Inquisition Sources: A Historiographical Review

The formal study of the Inquisition did not begin until after the middle of the nineteenth century. Before that time the institution and its documentation were jealously guarded; even its procedures were mired in secrecy. The earliest studies of the Inquisition were tainted by the controversy over the "Black Legend" of Spanish cruelty during the Conquest. Early historians of the Inquisition in New Spain either followed their own political or religious convictions in their analyses or dedicated themselves to the publication of documents and brief institutional sketches.

The Chilean historian, José Toribio Medina, was the first serious scholar to study the Inquisition in the Americas. Following in the Germanic tradition of Leopold von Ranke, Medina limited himself to the publication of primary documents with little serious analysis. Soon after, Henry Charles Lea polemicized the history of the Inquisition in his famous book on the Inquisition published in 1908. He contributed to the "Black Legend" by naively attributing the entire failure of the Spanish Empire on the Americas to the existence of the Inquisition. Lea argued that the Inquisition retarded the political and economic development of the colonies owing to its "malignant influence" on following generations. Although Lea perhaps overstated the Inquisition's negative influence on the politics and economics of nineteenth-century Latin American nations, he was not wrong in stating that the Inquisition had a negative impact on the intellectual development of the pre-Independence period.

Nevertheless, this early historiography was deficient because it focused more on the condemnation or defense of the Inquisition, rather than on a critical analysis of the institution and its impact on colonial society. Lea and other early scholars of the Inquisition continued to focus their efforts on describing the cruel and repressive nature of the institution. This trend in the literature began to change during the late 1970s, however, with the publication of important analytical and interpretive works by scholars both in the United States and Mexico. This new approach to the critical use of Inquisition sources in the study of colonial society and religion added an exciting and progressive dimension to the study of colonial history. The new historiography focused more on the people and actors in the *"procesos"* of the Inquisition than upon the institution of the Inquisition itself. Following new trends that emphasized the necessity of regional studies, these authors focused their examination upon the analysis of the Inquisition in various geographical regions. Medina's and Lea's emphasis on continental and institutional examinations of the Inquisition were left behind as modern scholars focused their attention on the impact of the Inquisition upon the people and societies of colonial America. The focus on "Black Legend" approaches and the emphasis on political objectives in the study of the Inquisition was abandoned as scholars focused more on its impact on colonial beliefs, religious practices, and philosophy.

Inquisition trial records are now used as a rich source of information on almost every facet of life in colonial Mexico, from the examination of purported mental illnesses in the colony to the study of the impact of the French Enlightenment upon eighteenth-century New Spain. Inquisition documents have enabled historians to better understand and enrich the study of the philosophical and intellectual history of Mexico, which is difficult to trace from civil documentation alone. Ethnohistorical and social histories of the role of women and minorities during the colonial period have used Inquisition sources in order to reveal the nature of these understudied groups and their significance to colonial Mexican society. Similar studies of Inquisition documents by scholars such as Noemí Quezada, Asunción Lavrin, Laura Lewis, and Ruth Behar have added interesting interpretations of colonial and pre-Conquest witchcraft, magic, sexual mores, and gender conflicts. Soriano Ramos and José Abel's study of the Inquisition's censorship of prohibited books puts to good use the Inquisition's ominous "Index" in order to reconstruct colonial attitudes towards marriage, family, and sexuality. Stanley Hordes has examined the relationship between colonial Jews and the Inquisition in New Spain, with an emphasis on revisionism and the interpretive problems caused by previous studies' moralistic approaches to the study of Judaism. Colin Palmer's work with African slave societies in New Spain similarly employed Inquisition documents in order to describe the survival of African folk religious practices.

These exciting advances in the historiography illustrate the creative use of Inquisition documentary sources in the recreation of colonial society, the nature of colonial gender relations, sexual mores, racism, and religious beliefs. Still, more work can be done in reconstructing various facets of colonial history through the use of Inquisition materials. The Inquisition's documents offer modern historians the possibility of recreating aspects of colonial society that otherwise would have been lost to history.

See also Conversos; Historiography; Limpieza de Sangre; Religious in New Spain

Select Bibliography

Alberro, Solange, "Inquisition et société: Rivalités de pouvoirs á Tepeaca, 1656–1660." *Annales: Economies, Sociétés, Civilisations* 36:5 (September–October 1981).

_____, *Inquisición y sociedad en México, 1571–1700*. Mexico City: Fondo de Cultura Económica, 1988.

_____, editor, *Seis ensayos sobre el discurso colonial relativo a la comunidad doméstica: Matrimonio, familia y sexualidad*. Mexico City: INAH, 1980.

Behar, Ruth, "Sex and Sin: Witchcraft and the Devil in Late Colonial Mexico." *American Ethnologist* 14 (1987).

_____, "The Visions of a Guachichil Witch in 1599: A Window on the Subjugation of Mexico's Hunters-Gatherers." *Ethnohistory* 34:2 (Spring 1987).

Greenleaf, Richard E., *The Mexican Inquisition of the Sixteenth Century.* Albuquerque: University of New Mexico Press, 1969.

_____, "Historiography of the Mexican Inquisition: Evolution of Interpretations and Methodologies." In *Cultural Encounters: The Impact of the Inquisition in Spain and the New World,* edited by Mary Elizabeth Perry and Anne J. Cruz. Berkeley: University of California Press, 1991.

Hordes, Stanley, "Historiographical Problems in the Study of the Inquisition and the Mexican Crypto-Jews in the Seventeenth Century." *AJA* 34:2 (November 1982).

Lavrin, Asunción, *Sexuality and Marriage in Colonial Latin America.* Lincoln: University of Nebraska Press, 1989.

_____, *Misión de la historia e historiografía de la iglesia en el periodo colonial americano.* Seville: Escuela de Estudios Hispanoamericanos, 1989.

Lea, Henry Charles, *The Inquisition in the Spanish Dependencies.* New York: Macmillan, 1908.

Lewis, Laura, "The 'Weakness' of Women and the Feminization of the Indian in Colonial Mexico." *Colonial Latin American Review* 5:1 (1996).

Liebman, Seymour, *The Jews in New Spain: Faith, Flame and the Inquisition.* Miami, Florida: University of Miami Press, 1970.

Plaidy, Jean, "The Inquisition in Mexico." In *The Spanish Inquisition.* New York: Barnes and Noble, 1994.

Quezada, Noemí, *Amor y magia amorosa entre los aztecas.* Mexico City: UNAM, 1975.

Ramos, Soriano, and José Abel, "Libros prohibidos sobre matrimonio, familia y sexualidad en los edictos promulgados por la Inquisición, 1575–1819." In *Seis ensayos sobre el discurso colonial relativo a la comunidad doméstica: Matrimonio, familia y sexualidad,* edited by Solange Alberro. Mexico City: INAH, 1980.

Schons, Dorothy, *Book Censorship in New Spain.* Austin: University of Texas Press, 1950.

—JOHN F. CHUCHIAK IV

INSTITUTO MEXICANA DE SEGURO SOCIAL (IMSS)

Social security has been a crucial component of Mexico's social welfare state in the post-Revolutionary era. While compensation for workers injured on the job and the provision of unemployment insurance had been discussed since the late nineteenth century, it was not until 1942, during the administration of President Manuel Avila Camacho, that the Congress passed a general social security law establishing the Instituto Mexicana de Seguro Social (IMSS, or Mexican Social Security Institute). In 1944 IMSS first offered its services, providing retirement benefits, death benefits, job-related accident coverage, and health care; it rapidly became a key symbol of Mexico's social safety net. By 1988 IMSS had grown to cover approximately 40 percent of the population. This growth, however, was not automatic; social security coverage was a hard-fought struggle that often was won incrementally following periods of social unrest.

Prior to the 1940s, social security coverage was extremely limited. Some benefits had been granted to certain government workers under laws passed in 1824, and there even had been periodic discussion and a few attempts to establish pensions and related social security measures for workers in the private sector. The economic boom during the rule of Porfirio Díaz (1876–1911) and the growth in the number of wage earners led to agitation by workers and social reformers to improve the working conditions of laborers. By 1910 protective legislation was advocated by moderate reformers such as Francisco I. Madero, who, upon accepting the candidacy for the presidency on April 25,

1910, promised to initiate legislation to provide pensions for workers injured or mutilated on the job, as well as for families of those killed in job-related accidents. Such sentiments were echoed throughout the decade of revolutionary upheaval (1910–20) and were included in Article 123 of the Constitution of 1917. Several sections of Article 123 placed responsibility for on-the-job accidents on the employer, and references were made to the need to alleviate the insecurity of life and work for all workers in Mexico.

Following the penning of the Constitution, momentum gained for the establishment of a social security program. President Álvaro Obregón, who curried the support of organized labor, introduced a social security law to Congress in 1921 that called for the creation of an old-age pension plan to be funded by employer contributions equivalent to 10 percent of the employee's salary. Obregón's initiative met such fierce opposition from employers that he was forced to withdraw it. Nonetheless, social security continued to surface in the political discourse for the next several administrations. In 1929 the newly founded Partido Nacional Revolucionario (PNR, or National Revolutionary Party) endorsed the creation of a social security law. On September 6, 1929, President Emilio Portes Gil amended Section 24 of Article 123 to explicitly express the prime importance of the passage of a social security law comprising unemployment benefits and disability benefits. President Lázaro Cárdenas (1934–40) repeatedly expressed the need for a comprehensive social security law and even had one drafted. But despite Portes

Gil's amendment to the Constitution and Cárdenas's draft of social security legislation, no comprehensive social security measures for the majority of workers were implemented. Instead, such benefits were extended incrementally to government workers: federal workers in 1925, the military in 1926, teachers in 1928, petroleum workers in 1935, railroad workers in 1936, and electrical workers in 1941.

The enactment of a comprehensive social security law was a major achievement of the administration of Manuel Avila Camacho (1940–46). The 1942 law created IMSS to administer old age pensions, compensate workers injured on the job, and establish and operate clinics to provide medical attention to workers and their families. Financing of the IMSS came from a tripartite arrangement of employee contributions, employer contributions, and government funds, with employers shouldering the largest share. Since the 1940s, employer and employee contributions have constituted the majority of IMSS's funds, with workers contributing an average of roughly 4 percent of their income and employers an average amount equal to approximately 12 percent of the employee's salary.

Ironically, the creation of IMSS coincided with a period of general decline for workers. Between 1939 and 1945, the average weekly real wage for industrial workers in Mexico City fell from 28.44 pesos to 16.39 pesos, and the average daily official minimum wage fell from 2.5 pesos to 1.37 pesos during the same period. Additionally, with Mexico's entrance into World War II, prominent union officials collaborated closely with business leaders and government officials and agreed upon a "no strike pledge" to quickly resolve labor disputes. With purchasing power declining and labor leaders urging against direct action, it became crucial for both government officials and labor leaders to find a way to obtain nonmonetary benefits for members without too much disruption. The social security law was a mechanism to reduce the militancy of organized labor and thereby create stable labor relations.

The 1942 social security law sparked resistance from some sectors. Business organizations expressed concerns about the scope of the program, while in the main supporting the law. Some viewed it as a small price to pay for more stable and predictable labor relations, which would ultimately yield increased worker productivity. Segments of organized labor actively combated the measure. When payroll deductions were first taken, early in 1944, workers experienced a decline in their take-home pay at a time when their purchasing power already was eroding. Although a number of key labor leaders expressed their support for the program, a dissident faction emerged and organized a series of demonstrations against social security. The final demonstration, on July 20, 1944, in Mexico City's Zócalo culminated in bloodshed, and several leaders were arrested. This event ended overt opposition to social security.

During the administrations of Manuel Avila Camacho and Miguel Alemán Valdés (1946–52), IMSS concentrated most of its resources in the Federal District and gradually expanded to other large cities. Under the leadership of Ignacio García Tellez, IMSS undertook the construction of hospitals and a network of clinics. By 1945 IMSS began operating hospitals in Puebla and Nuevo León and over the next two years added clinics and hospitals in Jalisco and Veracruz. President Alemán accelerated his predecessor's construction of hospitals and local clinics, completing the modern, well-equipped Hospital de La Raza with 700 beds in the Federal District and adding hospitals in Tlaxcala, the state of Mexico, Oaxaca, Guerrero, and Tamaulipas. While IMSS coverage remained very limited by the close of Alemán's administration (4 percent of the population and 5 percent of the labor force), the modern clinics and hospitals became very visible signs of the growing power and paternalism of the modern Mexican state.

During the presidencies of Adolfo Ruíz Cortines (1952–58) and Adolfo López Mateos (1958–64), IMSS coverage was expanded to include 17 percent of the population, and there was an attempt to include workers outside of the Federal District and in the countryside. This extension of social security came during periods of growing militancy in both the urban areas and countryside. Throughout the 1950s and 1960s, rural unrest, characterized by an increase in land invasions and by the rise of an independent peasant federation, refocused government attention on the peasantry. In response, President Ruíz Cortines extended coverage in 1954 to permanent rural wage earners, small farmers, and workers of communal landholdings (ejidos) who were members of production cooperatives or credit associations. As rural militancy continued, President López Mateos partially met the challenge by extending IMSS coverage to seasonal and temporary rural workers in 1960 and to sugar workers in 1963, thereby expanding IMSS coverage of agricultural workers tenfold.

Labor activism was a direct contributor to the creation of a new social security institute, Instituto de Seguridad y Servicios Sociales para los Trabajadores al Servicio del Estado (ISSSTE) in 1961. ISSSTE was created to service federal employees in the wake of a number of high-profile strikes by government workers, most notably teachers and railroad workers in 1958–59. After crushing the strikes, the administration extended a number of nonmonetary benefits to federal bureaucrats, and ISSSTE was a way of providing high-quality services to an underpaid bureaucracy. While ISSSTE offered many of the same benefits of the IMSS, such as basic coverage and medical services, it often has been characterized as providing higher-quality services. This is especially the case in the provision of social benefits for its members, such as day-care centers, sports and recreation facilities, stores with reduced prices, low-interest loan programs, and a housing program. Subsequently, ISSSTE remained an important service-providing institution for an expanding bureaucracy. Between 1961 and 1986, the number of workers insured by ISSSTE skyrocketed from 133,015 to nearly 1.9 million workers.

Throughout the late 1960s and early 1970s, widespread criticism of the nature of government policy emerged in Mexico. This was propelled, in part, by growing social unrest with the student movement of 1968 and the government's violent response to this mobilization. Earlier complaints of the unevenness of IMSS coverage resurfaced. In 1966, IMSS covered only 19.8 percent of *municipios* in the country, thus excluding the majority of the national territory and workers. These data reflected the lack of hospitals and medical facilities in the countryside. Social protests and the rise of a guerrilla movement during the early 1970s pressured the federal government to address these deep-rooted inequalities.

Presidents Luis Echeverría Álvarez (1970–76) and José López Portillo (1976–82) implemented programs to address the uneven distribution of government services. The Social Security Law of 1973 moved social security coverage beyond paid workers and targeted populations that have historically remained on the margins of society. IMSS aggressively constructed clinics and hospitals in many regional cities and in the countryside, and in 1979, it began collaborating with the agency that coordinated services to poor and isolated areas, Coordinación General del Plan Nacional de Zonas Deprimidas y Grupos Marginados (COPLAMAR). The result was a rapid extension of services to marginal groups and the growing presence of the Mexican government in isolated regions: by 1985, 3,246 rural clinics and 65 rural hospitals were in operation, providing services to 14.5 million inhabitants in 24 states.

The urban areas during the 1970s also witnessed an extension of social security and the development of new programs. The creation of the Instituto del Fondo Nacional de la Vivienda para los Trabajadores (INFONAVIT) in 1972 greatly expanded one of the historical roles of the IMSS—that of constructing low-cost housing for its members. While the IMSS had been constructing housing units for workers since the late 1940s, it did so sparingly owing largely to financial reasons. After 1972, INFONAVIT assumed the function of housing construction through a tripartite relationship that led to the building of many new housing units.

Mexico's social security system reached its pinnacle in the early 1980s. Whereas in 1972 28.7 percent of the country's *municipios* were covered by IMSS programs, in 1982 the amount jumped to 57.3 percent. By 1980, 53.4 percent of the total population was covered by some sort of social security program. IMSS was the largest; separate systems existed for government workers (ISSSTE), the military, and petroleum workers. Despite tremendous strides, large numbers of people remained outside the system, forcing many living in extreme poverty to seek basic health services in the higher-cost private sector, forgo medical treatment altogether, or rely upon traditional healers. Despite the advanced technology in many of Mexico's medical facilities, the lack of trained personnel and minimal equipment in many rural areas created an unequal health delivery system. Compared to other social security systems in Latin America, Mexico ranked somewhere in the middle in terms of the percentage of the population covered, with several countries covering nearly the entire population (Cuba, Costa Rica, and Argentina) and many more covering less than a third of the population.

The economic crisis of the 1980s greatly strained Mexico's social security system. The drop in the price of petroleum in the early 1980s, the subsequent debt crisis, and government efforts to cut spending significantly curtailed IMSS's budget. IMSS funding fell from 37,546 million pesos in 1977 to 23,550 million pesos in 1987 (calculated with a constant 1976 peso value). Per capita expenditures had fallen to 1940 levels. The number of beds per IMSS member declined from approximately 1.1 per thousand in 1983 to 0.7 per thousand in 1990; doctors per member declined from 1 per thousand to 0.72 per thousand.

By the late 1980s and early 1990s, there was growing concern that IMSS was both declining in quality and becoming financially untenable. Given that the majority of IMSS's funding came from employer and employee contributions, the rise of unemployment and underemployment during the 1980s and spiraling inflation overburdened the system. To deal with the declining value of pensions, the government established a compulsory supplemental pension scheme in 1992, financed by an additional employer contribution of 2 percent of the employee's salary. Nonetheless, the deteriorating financial situation of the IMSS was exacerbated further with the onset of an economic crisis at the end of 1994. Throughout 1995 contributions by employees and employers plummeted as unemployment rates soared, and the business slump caused many employers to fall behind in their quarterly payments to the IMSS. The IMSS, historically an efficient collector of such payments, became less vigorous in collecting the quotas out of fear of a general collapse of the system.

The crisis of the 1990s led to calls for system reform. A number of social security reform models were examined, some advocating the privatization of social security. At the end of 1995, the administration of President Ernesto Zedillo Ponce de León announced the reorganization of IMSS to allow for private sector participation in pension plans and to enable IMSS members to frequent private doctors. The proposed reforms caused a public stir, with many critics arguing against what they feared was imminent privatization. Opposition parties and even some within the PRI united against the reforms of IMSS. While the IMSS had been one of the few instruments of the Mexican welfare state to escape massive reorganization, change appears to be on the horizon.

Select Bibliography

García Cruz, Miguel, "La Seguridad Social." In *Mexico, Cincuenta Años de Revolución*, vol. 2. Mexico City: Fondo de Cultura Económica, 1961.

Mesa-Lago, Carmelo, *Social Security in Latin America: Pressure Groups, Stratification, and Inequality.* Pittsburgh: University of Pittsburgh Press, 1978.

_____, *Changing Social Security in Latin America: Toward Alleviating the Social Costs of Economic Reform.* Boulder, Colorado: Lynne Rienner, 1994.

Poitras, Guy, "Welfare Bureaucracy and Clientele Politics in Mexico." *Administrative Science Quarterly* 18 (March 1973).

Soberón Acevedo, Guillermo, Jesús Kumate, and José Laguna, editors, *La Salud en México: Testimonios 1988*. 4 vols., Mexico City: Secretaría de Salud, 1989.

Spaulding, Rose, "Welfare Policymaking: Theoretical Implications of a Mexican Case Study." *Comparative Politics* 12:4 (1980).

Ward, Peter, *Welfare Politics in Mexico: Papering over the Cracks*. London: Allen and Unwin, 1986.

—ENRIQUE C. OCHOA

ISI

See Import Substitution Industrialization (ISI)

ITURBIDE, AGUSTÍN DE

1783–1824 • Leader in the Wars of Independence and Emperor of Mexico

The rule of Agustín Cosme Damian de Iturbide represents a transition between the last years of the viceregal regime and the attainment of full independence. The limitations of an empty treasury, a ruined rural economy, a swollen bureaucracy, and a large military precluded any rapid merger of the diverse political entities seeking to guide Mexico at the time. Convinced that such circumstances justified the need for a strong ruler, Iturbide attempted to rule as a constitutional monarch (1822–23). Although he failed as an emperor, Iturbide does not warrant the demonization he received from his contemporary enemies as well as most historians.

Iturbide reflected the views of upper-class criollos (those of Spanish descent born in the Americas), who were determined to preserve the status quo. Iturbide came from a noble Basque family that emigrated to Michoacán in the middle of the eighteenth century. After failing at college, Iturbide began managing his father's hacienda. Like many criollos, Iturbide became an officer in a viceregal regiment at the age of 14. After his 1805 marriage to an upper-class criolla, Iturbide supported the Mexico City revolt that dumped Viceroy José de Iturrigaray in favor of the hardliner Pedro Garibay. The Iturbide family was so conservative that they sent the new Spanish junta funds. Satisfied with this new order, Iturbide purchased a hacienda worth 93,000 pesos.

The Hidalgo Revolt of 1810, as historian Brian R. Hamnett has demonstrated, responded to myriad local and regional socioeconomic tensions that broke out during a period of imperial confusion and viceregal weaknesses. The radical nature of the Hidalgo insurrection affected Iturbide quickly. Miguel Hidalgo y Costilla's followers sacked Iturbide's property as well as his father's hacienda. Not surprisingly, Iturbide fought the Hidalgo rebels that headed for Mexico City. Iturbide performed well, and the viceroyalty promoted him to the rank of colonel after Iturbide crushed guerrillas in the Bajío area. By the end of 1813, Iturbide had been named overall regional commander of this area.

But Iturbide also became dissatisfied with Spanish rule of Mexico. His frustration resulted from his personal ambitions. Obviously a gifted military leader, Iturbide grew resentful when Spanish officials blocked his promotion because he was a criollo. According to the research of scholar William S. Robertson, the Spanish received many complaints about Iturbide, who was accused of being agnostic, jailing women, torturing prisoners, and seizing haciendas as well as reselling their crops for personal profit. The last charge resulted in the Spanish commander, Félix María Calleja del Rey, removing Iturbide from his troop command.

At this point, Iturbide was still too conservative to consider joining the rebels. In fact, according to Robertson, Iturbide dreamed of knighthood and traveling to Spain. Frustrated, the vain but ambitious Iturbide sulked in Mexico City, often spending large sums on gambling and prostitutes. As his bitterness increased, Iturbide began to reconsider his loyalty to Spain.

Meanwhile, the rebellion continued. Regional insurgency often was directed at local Spanish merchants to whom the rebels owed high debts. Fighting often was fierce, and people changed sides with alarming frequency. Often, local caciques joined the conflict, setting the stage for regional caudillos who would prevail in various regions after 1821. No one controlled the regional rebels well. At the same time, the viceroy's counterinsurgency tactics could not bring about victory. The insurgency was organized through a network of priests, muleteers, and bandits that became impossible to crush. Guadalupe Victoria emerged as a prominent rebel leader in the Puebla-Veracruz region, while Vicente Guerrero directed insurgents in Oaxaca.

Iturbide's fortunes changed when Viceroy Juan Ruíz de Apodaca gave him a chance to capture Guerrero by appointing Iturbide royal commander to defeat the resistance in Oaxaca. Iturbide's main task was to persuade Guerrero to accept a pardon. By now, however, Iturbide had begun to question the durability of Spanish power, and he considered an opportunity to join in securing Mexico's independence. Iturbide soon began negotiating with Guerrero, various generals, and bishops so that he could take power by means of a brilliant compromise. The rebel leaders were desperate to break the stalemate. Although Spain was weakening, the royalist forces had gained the upper hand over insurgent activity by 1816 or 1818. Many insurrectionaries had accepted the amnesty offer made by Viceroy Juan Ruíz de Apodaca in 1817. Later, Apodaca claimed that the rebellion could be considered finished, despite stubborn resistance in some regions.

Iturbide announced his compromise measure, the Plan de Iguala, from his Cocula headquarters on February 23, 1821. It brought together liberals and conservatives, rebels and royalists, criollos and Spaniards, under broad provisions. The most important assurances of the 26 articles in the Plan de Iguala were its "Three Guarantees": first, Catholicism would be the state religion and other faiths would not be tolerated; second, Mexico would be independent as a constitutional monarchy; finally, there would be equal treatment for Spaniards and Mexicans.

The plan called for the establishment of a monarchy, for Iturbide and the criollos believed that only this form of government could preserve order. King Fernando VII of Spain was invited to come to Mexico as its emperor; if Fernando refused, other members of the Castilian royal family or another reigning dynasty in Europe would be solicited. The plan established a provisional governing body known as the Sovereign Provisional Governing Junta, headed by Iturbide himself. The junta would name a regency to exercise executive power until a monarch arrived. Meanwhile, the junta would govern until the country elected a new congress. Therefore, the junta became an interim legislature, and the regency functioned as an interim executive. Congress would designate the new monarch if Fernando VII, his brothers, and nephews refused invitations to rule as Mexican monarch. The new congress would also write a new constitution to replace the 1812 Spanish Constitution.

The Plan de Iguala was moderate, but Iturbide skillfully played to demands everywhere for peace. Although the upper class maintained its privileges, the news that caste distinctions would be abolished excited many among the masses. The Plan de Iguala was a clever settlement that satisfied criollo army officers, church leaders, and most insurgents, partially because most Mexicans assumed Fernando VII would not leave Madrid. Spain's desperate European situation contributed as much to independence for Mexico as Iturbide's arrangements.

The Plan de Iguala received virtually universal acceptance after Vicente Guerrero, the major rebel in the southern district, accepted it. Once Guerrero placed himself under Iturbide's orders, remaining groups joined quickly. Other veteran rebel leaders, such as Guadalupe Victoria and Nicolás Bravo, accepted Iturbide's leadership because the Plan de Iguala seemed to be the best way to obtain independence. The insurrectionaries themselves simply had not been able to decide upon the most suitable form of government that could appeal to the majority. Aside from negotiations with Guerrero, therefore, Iturbide needed to conduct few face-to-face discussions with the heads of other insurgent forces. The rapid speed with which the masses and the church accepted the Plan de Iguala precluded any serious disagreements with Iturbide.

With 1,800 troops and a seized silver shipment intended for export from Acapulco, Iturbide quickly rallied Mexico to his cause. He offered land and oxen to those who would volunteer to join his Trigarantine Army. The royal army began to desert to Iturbide's forces quickly as General Antonio López de Santa Anna won key victories for Iturbide's cause in Veracruz. Iturbide treated surrendering royal forces kindly, a policy that added to his momentum. By July 1821, Iturbide controlled all of Mexico except the capital, the port of Veracruz, and Perote.

Ultimately, Spain sent a veteran liberal, Juan O'Donojú, to arrange autonomy for New Spain. Iturbide accepted O'Donojú's offer to negotiate, and they met in Córdoba. In August 1821, O'Donojú quickly accepted Iturbide's conditions, known as the Treaties of Córdoba, which mirrored the provisions of the Plan de Iguala. Spain now committed itself to recognize the new Mexican Empire as an independent monarchy. O'Donojú then resigned as Spain's last viceroy as Iturbide entered Mexico City triumphantly in September 1821.

Initially, Iturbide ruled Mexico as president of the regency. To his credit, Iturbide divided the 12 members of the junta equally between conservatives and liberals. Wide support existed for Iturbide to become emperor. Because of its regional nature, the 11-year war for independence did not unify Mexico completely, but Iturbide's victory mandated him to exercise power as Mexico's first leader after Independence. Iturbide enjoyed support from the army, and no nationwide opposition rose against his authority. When it became clear that no European monarch would assume the Mexican throne, the aggressive Iturbide usurped power. Although Congress elected Iturbide emperor on a legal basis in May 1822, the voting took place under threat of army bayonets. As scholar Timothy Anna asserts, Congress preferred Iturbide over a Bourbon monarch because the legislature could dictate the terms of his oath of office.

Iturbide's rule as monarch was characterized by a string of unsettling mistakes, such as his extravagant inauguration, a court emulating those in Europe, and an expensive palace remodeling. After he began to clash with Congress, Iturbide exercised press censorship, jailed opponents arbitrarily, militarized justice, and chose personally members of the new supreme court. Amid steadily mounting debts and bad economic conditions, the government resorted to forced loans from the Catholic Church and various merchants.

Iturbide had promised a limited monarchy, but his rule turned out to be authoritarian. The emperor's power base appears to have been built on unwarranted hopes rather than real benefits. Moreover, the monarchy became too expensive during a time of fiscal and economic crisis. The belief that a republic would bring about faster economic growth by now had become pervasive.

Iturbide's response to the growing political opposition soon sealed his fate. When deputies protested his decisions, Iturbide labeled all his critics as foreign spies. Becoming testy and impatient, Iturbide finally dissolved Congress and appointed another junta to take the place of the legislature in October 1822. Many Mexicans now viewed Iturbide as a despot, and sentiment for a republic continued to increase.

Timothy Anna alleges that Iturbide stepped down magnanimously from his throne in order to avoid civil war, but a better explanation is that the caudillos simply threw Iturbide out. Meanwhile, the Spanish garrison in Veracruz revolted at about the same time that General Santa Anna rose against Iturbide. With the support of Guadalupe Victoria and other Independence forces, Santa Anna called for the establishment of a republic. By February 1823, the emperor held little more than the Mexico City area. After promising to reconvene the legislature, Iturbide found that he could no longer continue and abdicated in March 1823.

Iturbide departed Mexico for Europe in May 1823 after accepting a handsome sum of money in return for a promise never to return. Insecure after the republic did not send him his pension, Iturbide believed that his life was in danger. Because the emerging Holy Alliance on the European continent considered Iturbide a danger, Iturbide took up residence in Britain, which opposed the other European monarchies' hostility to constitutional rule. Despite the attempts of Argentine exile José de San Martín to persuade him not to return to Mexico, Iturbide claimed that the masses wanted him back and imagined that only he could stop a feared invasion of Mexico by the Holy Alliance powers.

Iturbide's decision to return proved fatal. Six days passed after he sailed from Southhampton in May 1824 before anyone noticed that Iturbide had left. On board his ship, Iturbide wrote pamphlets stating that he came not as an emperor but as a soldier who would defend and unify Mexico. What Iturbide did not know was that the Mexican Congress already had declared that should he reenter, he would be placed outside the law and condemned as a traitor. Iturbide finally landed in Tamaulipas. Despite Iturbide's disguise, a soldier recognized his style in mounting a horse and reported him to local authorities. By almost unanimous vote, the Tamaulipas state legislature condemned Iturbide to death. Iturbide was captured and shot; he died at the age of 41. Iturbide's significance quickly faded from the minds of his countrymen. Later, in 1838, the republic brought his remains to Mexico City and gave his relatives financial security.

Iturbide experienced a strange fate for a leader who brought about Mexico's Independence, ending a bloody civil war with an imaginative plan acceptable to all. But although he was a great soldier and a skilled leader in his early days, Iturbide never truly united the country; he merely persuaded the criollo upper class to expel the Spanish overlords while maintaining their own oppressive hold on the poor. The failure of his monarchy strengthened the republic and opened the door for the liberals to take power.

Select Bibliography

Anna, Timothy E., *The Mexican Empire of Iturbide.* Lincoln: University of Nebraska Press, 1990.

Hamnett, Brian R., *Roots of Insurgency: Mexican Regions, 1750–1824.* Cambridge and New York: Cambridge University Press, 1986.

Robertson, William Spence, *Iturbide of Mexico.* Durham, North Carolina: Duke University Press, 1952.

—Douglas W. Richmond

J

JARAMILLO, RUBÉN

1900–62 • Politician and Workers' Rights Advocate

Rubén Jaramillo was a tireless defender of the rights of peasants and cane workers in the state of Morelos. His life was constantly threatened by corrupt administrators of the Zacatepec mill, and he spent many years clandestinely working and organizing. During brief periods of legal activity, Jaramillo helped form rural cooperatives, labor unions, and a regional party, the Partido Agrario Obrero Morelense (PAOM).

Born in Tlaquiltenango, Morelos, in 1900, Jaramillo entered the revolutionary army of Emiliano Zapata in 1915. He distinguished himself as a respected leader and maintained his commitment to Zapata's ideals of land and liberty despite military defeat at the hands of the Constitutionalist armies. In the 1920s he led the struggle of new *ejidos* (communal landholdings) to obtain credit for rice production, winning the animosity of local moneylenders and buyers who had traditionally been able to exploit the peasants' lack of capital by obliging them to sell their produce prior to harvest time at half its value.

Jaramillo supported the presidential campaign of Lázaro Cárdenas and worked to promote the construction of the Zacatepec sugar mill and cooperative. Jaramillo fought against the corruption and ambition of new mill administrators, but, with the change in national government in 1940, he was forced to resign from the mill's administration and, in the face of numerous death threats from local bosses, operated in armed clandestinity.

Federal soldiers engaged with armed units of Jaramillistas throughout 1943 but failed to capture their leader, who was able to escape to Mexico City. In the capital, Jaramillo sought assurances from President Avila Camacho that his life would be protected and received a guarantee of safe passage that allowed him to return to Morelos in 1945. In that year Jaramillo formed a political party to unite workers and peasants to contest the 1946 gubernatorial election in Morelos.

The PAOM was defeated through fraud and intimidation, and shortly afterward its members and leaders were persecuted by the Partido Revolucionario Institucional (PRI, or Institutional Revolutionary Party) governor, with the backing of the new, president Miguel Alemán Valdés. Jaramillo was forced back into clandestinity, but his movement continued to fight against the corrupt administration of the Zacatepec sugar mill for the democratization of *ejido* authorities and for land redistribution.

In 1950 Jaramillo came out of hiding again, using the political conjuncture of the 1952 presidential campaign of a Cárdenas loyalist, General Miguel Henríquez Guzmán, and the cover provided by the PAOM in its campaign for the governorship. In an unusual move for Mexican political parties, the PAOM held primaries to select its candidate for governor, choosing Jaramillo over another Zapatista veteran, Genovevo de la O. The political platform of the PAOM reflected Jaramillo's philosophy, favoring municipal autonomy, independence of *ejido* authorities from government, land reform, unity of workers and peasants, programs of rural and urban education, and the creation of cooperatives. The PAOM was also noteworthy for the high level of women's participation. It had a women's section and included demands for sugar mills to provide adequate day-care facilities and improved working conditions for women.

As in 1946, the 1952 elections were marked by intimidation against the PAOM supporters and Jaramillo. The federal army occupied a large number of polling stations and helped the PRI carry out fraud. In the postelectoral period a new wave of attacks was directed against the Jaramillistas. Police and soldiers raided the offices of the PAOM in Cuernavaca and Jojutla, and Jaramillo was forced to flee again to Mexico City. Many PAOM activists were abducted and killed after 1952.

Working once more in clandestinity, Jaramillo helped organize armed self-defense groups among peasants in the villages of Morelos. His group also was active in supporting cane workers in their struggles against corrupt bosses. In 1956 an attempt to kidnap the administrator of the Zacatepec mill was foiled, and the army intervened to break up Jaramillo's camp.

Jaramillo remained on the run until 1958, when President Adolfo López Mateos granted him an amnesty and appointed him special delegate of the Confederación Nacional Campesina (CNC, or National Peasant Confederation) in Morelos. This post allowed Jaramillo to supervise elections of *ejido* authorities, which was important because they participated in the management of the sugar mills and, consequently, were an integral part of the corrupt administration. Under Jaramillo, 16 *ejidos* were able to change their representatives, leading to further animosity from Jaramillo's lifelong enemies at the mill.

Jaramillo also helped the formation of the Cane Growers' Defense Committee in order to press claims of corruption against the administrators. The committee held its first meeting in November 1958 despite threats from government officials and local bosses. Gunmen at the service of Eugenio Prado, the mill's principal administrator, failed to capture Jaramillo, but Prado was able to use his political connections in Mexico City to avoid an investigation into alleged corruption and pressured the authorities to break up a subsequent protest strike by the cane growers.

Jaramillo's ambiguous position as both CNC delegate and target for local bosses was demonstrated by the land struggles in Morelos in 1959–60. Peasant protests erupted when the government broke earlier promises of land distribution that would have benefited over 6,000 peasants. When Jaramillo was unable to extract a solution through legal channels, the peasants decided to invade the disputed land. Jaramillo convinced them to withdraw, believing (for the first and last time) that the president would fulfill a promise to respect their organization and carry out the planned redistribution. After a year of waiting without response, the peasants again invaded, this time with Jaramillo's leadership, and established a socialist collective, along the lines of Mao's liberated zones in revolutionary China.

New confrontations with Prado and the police were not long in coming. When Jaramillo went to Mexico City to try and meet with López Mateos, the peasants were violently evicted and their leaders arrested. The president failed to support Jaramillo in his search for legal solutions. In fact, in 1961, Jaramillo's hideout in Mexico City was raided by police, and a group of his top cadres was arrested.

Jaramillo's political options were again narrowed to uncertain legality versus clandestinity. The latter appeared to his supporters as an inevitable consequence of the repression and the reversals of López Mateos. However, Jaramillo saw several disadvantages to renewing a clandestine struggle.

The failure of earlier armed peasant uprisings and the practical limitations implied by clandestine work could not be dismissed easily. At the same time, the spaces for legal activism for peasant movements were increasing, as demonstrated by the formation of the Central Campesina Independiente (CCI) in April 1961. The CCI also had the political backing of Lázaro Cárdenas and a number of popular organizations, left-wing parties, and trade unionists opposed to the PRI regime.

Before Jaramillo could give a definitive answer to this recurrent dilemma, however, he was assassinated by the same adversaries who had threatened his life on several occasions since the 1930s. On May 23, 1962, judicial police, soldiers, and gunmen led by former administrators of the Zacatepec mill raided Jaramillo's home. He and his wife, together with his two stepdaughters and a nephew, were taken to the ruins at Xochicalco, where they were killed. Despite public denunciations, no one ever was brought to trial. Jaramillo had a strong impact on successive generations of peasant movements in Mexico and many popular songs, or *corridos,* were dedicated to his memory.

Select Bibliography

Bartra, Armando, *Los Herederos de Zapata: Movimientos campesinos posrevolucionarios en México 1920–1980.* Mexico City: Era, 1985.

Manjarrez, Froylán C., *Rubén Jaramillo, Autobiografía y Asesinato.* Mexico City: Editorial Nuestro Tiempo, 1967.

Ravelo, Renato, *Los jaramillistas.* Mexico City: Editorial Nuestro Tiempo, 1978.

—Neil Harvey

JOURNALISTIC NOVEL

The journalistic novel first emerged at the end of the nineteenth century in the works of writers belonging to the modernist or Blue generation, born between 1855 and 1870. The journalistic novel represented an attempt to remedy the paradox expressed in an observation by Oscar Wilde that "journalism is unreadable and literature is not read." In formal terms pioneering attempts in the genre were characterized by an idiosyncratic realism with more emphasis on the unpleasant, the circumstantial, the macabre, the invisible, and the plebeian. Before the end of the century such a novel had been conceived by various writers, including Ignacio Ramírez and Guillermo Prieto, who on one occasion jointly proposed to produce a novel on the underworld of Mexico City during the early decades of the nineteenth century, modeled on the

descriptions of local customs that had entered Mexican literature through the influence of the Spanish chronicler Ramón de Mesonero Romanos.

This mix of literature and events was to become more established at the end of the century when Mexican writers came to accept the new role of newspapers, which had all but supplanted many previous functions of books. It was then that writers established the formal characteristics of this new medium. *Tomóchic* by Joaquín Clausell and Heriberto Frías, for example, was published in installments between March and April 1893 in the pages of the short-lived newspaper *El Demócrata,* distributed in the capital. Clearly inspired by Émile Zola's *La Débâcle,* this work related in novelistic form a powerful story concerning the massacre of an entire village located in the Sierra Tarahumara by the Federal Army in October 1892. Frías was both witness to and participant in this event. *Tomóchic* was read as a news story and led to imprisonment and poverty for the authors. Shortly after the publication of this first novel, Frías attempted the same journalistic formula in *El último duelo* (1896), a work that recreated a fight to the death between two public figures of the day who had become enemies in a bordello in the capital.

Authors such as Manuel Gutiérrez Nájera, Federico Gamboa, José Ferrel, Alberto Leduc, Angel de Campo, and Amado Nervo can be said only to have scratched the surface of the journalistic novel, notwithstanding their inveterate attachment to the most actual and ephemeral events of daily life and their ability to authentically record their environment. In the wake of the novelists of the Blue generation, few found this genre an interesting alternative or possessed of cultural significance. The armed period of the Mexican Revolution (1910–20), however, was a seedbed for writers who worked to recreate the conflict in epic and narrative form, blending the immediacy of journalism with the ambitious stylings of *belles lettres*.

Mariano Azuela, for example, wrote *Los de abajo* (1916), which at the time of its publication was as unnoticed as surely were the plethora of news items on the development of the conflict throughout the country. Another writer of the genre was Martín Luis Guzmán, author of a book central to the development of modern literary expression in Mexico, *El águila y la serpiente* (1928). Here the author blends the essay, chronicle, and novel with uncommon felicity to produce, in the words of the writer Carlos Monsiváis, "the condemnatory version of a revolution in which every action loses touch with its origin and its probable or clear justification for existence, transforming it into abstractions that alone qualify and situate a movement, phenomena without a past or future that, in their interminable condition of time present, denounce the innate evil of the populace."

Francisco L. Urquizo wrote with an exceptional conviction works such as *México-Tlacalantongo: Mayo de 1920* (1932) and *Tropa vieja* (1943), which to a certain extent would define the peculiar bias that the novel would take in Mexico in favor of an event's historical impact through a markedly journalistic presentation. *Return Ticket* (1928), one of the first travel books by Salvador Novo, was a journalistic novel but presented with absolute deliberation as the antithesis of the immediate and fictional, almost in the terrain of the antinovel. Bearing some similarities to the journalistic novel, at least from the point of view of Novo's careful treatment of reported speech, the book appeared to profile *Cariátide* by Rubén Salazar Mallén, a work published by Jorge Cuesta in his magazine *Examen* (1930) that made the magazine the object of a civil case (the publication disappeared from circulation after the third issue).

Perhaps today the journalistic bias of the novels recounting the Cristero Rebellion (a peasant-based, pro-Catholic, anti-Revolutionary uprising) is more evident. The most outstanding exponents of this subgenre were Fernando Robles, author of *La virgen de los cristeros* (1934) and *Sucedió ayer* (1940), and José Guadalupe de Anda, author of *Los cristeros: La guerra santa en Los Altos* (1937) and *Los bragados* (1942). Mexico City, and above all the lives and personalities of its underclass and their world, attracted various authors. The field, although broad in reality, appears to narrow when formal features of the journalistic novel are taken into consideration. Thus the atmosphere of the capital would change in this first half of the century from the lyricism of a novel such as José María Benítez's *Ciudad* (1942), which evokes life in Mexico City during the Revolution.

Juan Pérez Jolote (1952), the remarkable biography of a Tzotzil Indian brilliantly compiled by the anthropologist Ricardo Pozas, had an interesting sequel in the history of the development of the journalistic novel. The experiment began in *Hasta no verte, Jesús mío* (1969), a novel in which reportage reached both heights and depths that were not only fresh but genuinely unusual in Mexico. The author, Elena Poniatowska, presented the work from the point of view of Jesusa Palancares, a village woman who narrated her experience of recent history in Mexico. Shortly after Poniatowska published a book that over the years has come to be considered the most powerful urban novel of Mexican literature, *La noche de Tlatelolco* (1971), which documents the student movement of 1968 and the Massacre of Tlatelolco in the voices of witnesses and participants. Later Luis Zapata, using a similar technique to that of Pozas, plotted out two novels of an indisputably picaresque flavor: *El vampiro de la colonia Roma* (1979), which narrates the transformations of a male prostitute, and *Los postulados del buen golpista* (1995), the story of an eccentric thug. Sometimes various writers, clearly influenced by the varied work produced under the label of New Journalism, as the genre has been baptized by the U.S. writer Tom Wolfe, and sometimes according to personal stylistic developments, tested their luck in Mexico by bringing the literary aspect of the novel closer to the daily requirements of journalism. Among these were Jorge Ibargüengoitia, who reconstructed with coolness and economy a notorious criminal case in the pages of *Las muertas* (1977). Ricardo Garibay took the *crónica* (journalistic narrative) to the very borders of fiction in *Las glorias del gran Púas* (1978), his description of one of the last fights of the already flagging boxer Rubén El Púas Olivares. Vicente Leñero left evidence of journalistic perspicacity and narrative skill in two outstanding titles: *La gota de agua* (1984) and *Asesinato* (1985). The influence of New Journalism is also due to the critical revaluation of the *crónica* in Mexico, inspired with enthusiasm and mastery by the influential essayist Carlos Monsiváis in *A ustedes les consta: Antología de la crónica en México* (1980) as well as the deliberate creation of novels in the style of journalism, immediate in their impact, although sufficiently different from the description of customs, the picturesque and merely circumstantial, and the obligatory realism of the pamphlet. Recent examples of this enthusiasm are to be found in the work of Brianda Domecq, author of *La insólita historia de la santa de Cabora* (1990); in *Charras*

(1990) by Hernán Lara Zavala, who describes the assassination of a social leader in Mérida, Yucatán; in *Guerrra en el paraíso* (1991) by Carlos Montemayor, who reconstructs the guerrilla movement of Lucio Cabañas in the state of Guerrero; and in *El féretro de cristal* (1992) by Bruno Estañol, who narrates the story of a poor wandering fakir.

See also Narrative and National Identity: 1910–96

Select Bibliography

Blanco, José Joaquín, *Un chavo bien helado: Crónicas de los años ochenta.* Mexico City: Era, 1990.

Duncan, J., *Voices, Visions, and a New Reality: Mexican Fiction since 1970.* Pittsburgh: University of Pittsburgh Press, 1986.

Foster, David William, *Mexican Literature: A History.* Austin: University of Texas Press, 1994.

—Antonio Saborit

JUÁREZ, BENITO

1806–72 • President

Benito Juárez, who held the presidential office from January 1858 until his death in July 1872, has been the object of so much mythology that it is almost impossible to uncover the actual facts of his life. Official symbolism has transformed him into the immovable stone figure that stands in countless Mexican plazas. By way of reaction to the hagiography, a counter-mythology has developed that attributes to him all manner of failings, treasons, and abuses. Perhaps the best way to approach Benito Juárez is through the five most controversial actions of his career: the negotiation of the McLane-Ocampo Treaty with the United States in 1859; the extension in November 1865 of the presidential term for the duration of the War of the French Intervention; the execution of the Interventionists' puppet emperor, Maximilian von Hapsburg, in June 1867; the proposed plebiscite for reform of the 1857 Constitution in August 1867; and his second reelection in 1871. The first stemmed from his admiration for the United States as the model of republican liberal democracy, which he wanted Mexico to follow. The second originated from a determination not to relinquish leadership of the Liberal cause during an unfinished war against foreign intervention. The third action constituted a warning to European monarchies not to interfere with Mexican sovereignty and the republican tradition. The fourth resulted from a long-held belief that the 1857 Constitution had enabled state governors and the legislative power to gain the upper hand in the political struggle between region and center, legislature and executive. The fifth may well have been a serious miscalculation born of a belief that his work, interrupted by the French Intervention (1862–67), had not been completed.

Benito Juárez was born a Zapotec Indian in the Oaxaca highland village of Guelatao (near Ixtlán) in 1806, and he rose to become a qualified, practicing lawyer in the state capital during the 1830s and 1840s. Originally destined for an ecclesiastical career, he abandoned the Oaxaca City Seminary in 1828 and matriculated at the newly founded (1827) secular Institute of Science and Arts of the State of Oaxaca, of which he became secretary in 1832. There, he came under the influence of a leading local Liberal professor of logic, mathematics, and ethics, Miguel Méndez, another Zapotec from the highlands.

Juárez's political consciousness dawned with the presidential campaign of 1828, in which he supported the candidacy of the former insurgent chieftain, Vicente Guerrero. In 1832, Juárez became a member of the city council and in the following year a deputy in the state congress. Juárez's political position in support of the Valentín Gómez Farías administration of 1833–34 clearly identified him as a prominent provincial Liberal. During the rule of the centralists (1836–46), Juárez experienced a temporary political eclipse, but he was able to reenter political life by 1838. In 1843, he married Margarita Maza. He became secretary to state governor Antonio de León in 1844.

The collapse of Centralism in 1846 and the restoration of the Federal Constitution of 1824 opened the way for Juárez's accession to the Oaxaca state governorship in 1847 and his subsequent election to that office for the term 1848 to 1852. In spite of efforts to develop primary public education, his first term as governor was marred by the ongoing crisis in the southern sector of the Isthmus of Tehuantepec, which involved disputes of land ownership and salt collecting rights between private interests and indigenous communities, rivalry between Tehuantepec and Juchitán, and the polarization of provincial capital and subregion. Local and national conflicts combined to undermine the state Liberal regime in 1853. Juárez, along with other leading Liberals, was arrested in 1853 by the dictatorship of Antonio López de Santa Anna, and he went into exile in New Orleans. Juárez's family remained in Oaxaca under the protection of his two associates, Miguel Castro and Ignacio Mejía.

The national career of Juárez began with the triumph of the Revolution of Ayutla, which ousted Santa Anna in 1855. Juárez gained his first ministerial appointment as secretary for justice and ecclesiastical affairs under the interim presidency of Juan Alvarez (October to December 1855). From this position, on November 23, 1855, Juárez issued the decree known as the Ley Juárez, which intended to restrict the application of the *fuero eclesiástico,* or clerical exemption from civil jurisdiction, and was condemned by the archbishop of Mexico. For most of the presidency of Ignacio Comonfort (December 1855 to January 1858), Juárez was absent from Mexico City as governor of Oaxaca for the second time from January 1856 to October 1857. In this second term as governor, he implemented the Ley Lerdo of June 25, 1856, which mandated the divestment of lands belonging to the Catholic Church, and the Federal Constitution of February 1857, which in addition to codifying many Liberal reforms, gave Mexico its first real bill of rights. He returned to the national capital as president of the Supreme Court, a position that gave him the constitutional right of succession to the presidency in default of the incumbent. Juárez disapproved of Comonfort's executive coup d'état of Tacubaya on December 17, 1857, against the Constitution and the radical wing of the Liberal Party. Conservative officers' removal of Comonfort on January 11, 1858, opened the Civil War of the Reform. Within the Liberal camp, the interim presidency devolved upon Juárez, sustained by the state governors of the center-north (such as Manuel Doblado, Jesús González Ortega, and Anastasio Parrodi) and the geographical peripheries. For much of the Civil War and French Intervention period (1858–67), Juárez strove to assert executive authority and make himself independent of the state governors, who were acting in advance of administration policy on church-state relations and were holding onto federal revenues. From May 1858 until January 1861, the Liberal administration remained in the port of Veracruz under the protection of state governor Manuel Gutiérrez Zamora, an intimate associate of Miguel Lerdo de Tejada, another Veracruzano, author of the Ley Lerdo, and a leading proponent of the Reform Laws of July 1859, which severely restricted the powers of the Catholic Church. During the following year, Lerdo became an increasingly vocal critic and political rival of Juárez.

The Juárez government in Veracruz defined its position in the Manifesto to the Nation of July 7, 1859, which preceded the issue of the Reform Laws. The manifesto reaffirmed the principles codified in the Constitutions of 1824 and 1857 and declared the government's intention to subordinate the Catholic clergy to civil power, to separate church and state, and to advance the secularization of society. Such a program aroused great opposition from Conservative critics; the Conservatives' position was only strengthened by Liberal attempts to secure a U.S. loan with nationalized ecclesiastical properties as collateral, and the negotiations of the McLane-Ocampo Treaty of December 1859, which ceded to the United States right of transit across the Isthmus of Tehuantepec and along the northern border from the Gulf of Mexico to the Sea of Cortés. Nevertheless, the treaty secured U.S. recognition on April 6, 1859, which Liberals regarded as a major gain for their cause. The Reform Laws became national law after Juárez returned to the capital city in January 1861.

Juárez was elected president for the first time in March 1861, with a convincing majority over rival candidates. However, his election did not end intrigues within the Liberal camp designed to remove him in favor of González Ortega (architect of the final military victory over the Conservatives in the Civil War) or Manuel Doblado (who had made and then broken Comonfort). On September 15, 1861, a group of 51 deputies called for Juárez's removal from office, but the votes of a further 52 deputies sustained him. From May 1861 until May 1863, Juárez encountered strong congressional opposition to his call for a renewed presidential style of government. Radical deputies, in particular, argued that the 1857 Constitution had opened the way for a parliamentary type of government, while state governors continued to behave as if they were sovereigns within their own territories. With Conservative guerrilla bands operating in the countryside and deteriorating external relations over the foreign debt, the Juárez government found itself seriously constrained. On July 17, 1861, Juárez unilaterally suspended external debt payments for a two-year period; in response, Great Britain, France, and Spain formed the Tripartite Convention of London in October 1861 and embarked upon an armed intervention in Mexico, designed to enforce payment. French political designs, however, ensured that the other two powers would abandon Mexican territory by the spring of 1862.

On December 11, 1861, Juárez secured from Congress the concession of extraordinary powers to defend national sovereignty in the face of foreign intervention. Further decrees in October 1862 and May 1863 ratified this earlier decree. The draconian law of January 25, 1862, which stipulated capital punishment for collaboration with Interventionist forces, expressed Juárez's determination to resist and reverse foreign designs on Mexican sovereignty. (Under this law, Emperor Maximilian was tried by court martial in 1867 and executed by firing squad.) Juárez's decrees of October 1862, May 1863, and March 1865 defined the nature of treason.

The French advance toward Mexico City in late May 1863 obliged the Juárez administration to regroup in San Luis Potosí. From there, Juárez continued directing efforts to sustain the republic. In November 1865, Juárez's presidential term was extended until the French could be expelled. Juárez's minister in Washington, D.C., Matías Romero, a fellow Oaxacan, attempted to influence public opinion in the United States in favor of the Mexican republican cause. In the meantime, Juárez sought to take advantage of divisions within the Imperial camp. Juárez had no intention of ever abandoning national territory, in spite of considerable personal hardship during his peregrination across the northern states and unbridgeable distance from his wife, Margarita Maza, in exile in New York at a time when they both were shaken by the deaths of their two young sons (five of Juárez's children died in early childhood). He remained the personification of the embattled republic, driven to the very extremity of Paso del Norte in Chihuahua on the Río Bravo border with the United States. Despite notable defections, Juárez could count upon the support of the state governors of Michoacán, Jalisco, Zacatecas, Sonora, Sinaloa, Durango, and Chihuahua. The principal Liberal commanders, Mariano Escobedo and Porfirio Díaz, finally achieved military victory over Interventionist forces in the first half of 1867.

Juárez, supported by his principal ministers, Sebastián Lerdo de Tejada and Ignacio Mejía, was determined to bring Emperor Maximilian to trial and secure punishment for the European intervention. He intended Maximilian's execution to be a powerful deterrent to the European monarchies to refrain from further involvement in the affairs of American republics. In this sense, the long resistance of Juárez to the French during the War of the Intervention acquired an international, rather than a purely Mexican, dimension, which was recognized at the time both within the Americas and by European republican opponents of the dynasties. Even so, the execution of Maximilian remained controversial within Mexico and abroad.

Victory over the Europeans led to Juárez's first reelection in October 1867, provoking the split with General Porfirio Díaz. Thereafter, Porfiristas, a diffuse array of provincial and radical deputies and army commanders, became vocal opponents of the Juárez administration, which they repeatedly accused of constitutional violations. Juárez's abortive attempt to reform the 1857 Constitution in August 1867 to allow himself a third term in office and increase the power of the executive appeared to lend credence to these claims. A series of military-led rebellions broke out in Puebla, San Luis Potosí, Zacatecas, and other states between 1868 and 1870. These rebellions reached their climax with Díaz's Rebellion of La Noria of November 1871 to March 1872, which challenged the second reelection of Juárez in October 1871. The second reelection initially provoked a split with Sebastián Lerdo, who also aspired to succeed Juárez at the expiration of his elected term of office; however, the Porfirista rebellion threw Lerdo and Juárez back into cooperation to defeat an attempt within the military to annul a presidential election by armed force. All opposition groups in Congress and the press accused the Juárez administration of managing elections and thereby rendering them imperfect expressions of the popular will. Military rebels justified the use of armed force on those grounds. Díaz himself argued in the Rebellion of La Noria that only armed intervention could restore the purity of the 1857 Constitution. Juárez countered by branding Díaz a latter-day Santa Anna. Juárez was able to survive the crisis brought about by the Rebellion of La Noria through retaining the loyalty of the majority of army commanders, such as Ramón Corona and Sóstenes Rocha. Even so, Juárez had lost considerable political support in the period after 1867, as the presidential election results of 1871 demonstrated: Juárez collected 5,837 electoral votes, Díaz 3,555, and Lerdo 2,874. In effect, the two rival opposition candidates formed the majority. Congress, acting in its constitutional capacity as an electoral college, determined the outcome of the election in Juárez's favor. With the disintegration of the Rebellion of La Noria, Juárez once again proposed reform of the Constitution, which, as in 1867, included the reestablishment of the Senate (abolished in 1853). On April 1, 1872, Juárez argued that a senate would moderate the actions of the legislative power. Congress again rejected constitutional reform, an objective that Juárez never attained in his lifetime. The presidential term begun on December 1, 1871 would have terminated on November 30, 1875, thus ensuring Juárez 17 unbroken years in office. That prospect in itself was sufficient to concentrate the minds of members of the younger generation. However, President Juárez died of angina on July 18, 1872. No doubt his death was hastened by the stress of his long political struggles; furthermore, his wife, Margarita Maza de Juárez, had died only five months earlier at the age of 43.

The period of Juárez's predominance was particularly difficult for Mexico, beset by deep-rooted internal divisions and also external pressures. In the half-century immediately following Independence from Spain, Mexico still struggled to find its national identity and assert itself as a sovereign state. Among Juárez's strengths was his ability to understand the significance and complexity of this historical moment. Juárez defined Mexico, in opposition to Catholic and Conservative thought, as a secular and federal republic with a liberal political system in which the civil power was to be supreme. For that reason, he remained opposed throughout his career to the Spanish colonial inheritance and to contemporary European monarchies. He consistently sought to align Mexico with the United States in a common defense of representative government. During the Mexican Civil War of the Reform, Juárez fought to defend the Constitution of 1857 and sought to embody republican virtues as articulated in the Reform Laws and his own Manifesto to the Nation of 1859. During the War of the Intervention, he portrayed himself as the personification of the republic, the moral embodiment of legitimacy, in opposition to the attempt by Napoléon III to reduce independent Mexico to the status of French dependency. Throughout the Civil War in the United States (1861–65), Juárez unswervingly sympathized with the federal forces, the cause of Abraham Lincoln, and the emancipation of the slaves. He resolutely opposed the Confederacy, primarily because it was sustained by the same southern interests that had promoted expansionism at Mexico's expense during the 1840s and 1850s.

Juárez was neither one of the intellectual stars of the Reform constellation nor a leading ideologist of Liberalism. Although, like so many other political figures of his generation, he was trained in law (and, by contrast with them, actually practiced it), he was preferentially a consummate and ruthless politician not averse to the exercise and retention of power. Unlike almost all of his predecessors, he would not be removed from office by a rival politician or army general. By character, Juárez was aloof and obdurate, acerbic and tenacious, of great personal courage and capable of survival in the complex society of mid-nineteenth-century Mexico. He retained a belief in the principles of liberal constitutionalism, even if political struggles prevented their literal application. He stood for the depersonalization of political life, but by the end of the War of the Intervention, he himself had become the focus of a personality cult. Certainly, his own personality became the subject of contention during the early part of the Restored Republic, from 1867 to 1872. In that period, three defining issues emerged that would dominate Mexican politics thereafter: presidentialism, centralism, and reelectionism; he stood as a strong proponent of all three.

Events and issues, combined with the personalist tradition of Mexican political life, obliged Juárez to adopt a blend of constitutionalism and authoritarianism and a balance between principle and pragmatism. Faced with intractable ideological divisions within the country and within the Liberal movement, and with entrenched local and regional bases of power, Juárez aligned temporarily with one Liberal faction or another and tacked warily between provincial Liberal cadres. His object was always to insert the authority of the national government into the provincial milieu and, where possible, assert the supremacy of the central power and the primacy of national objectives. After 1867, these tactics earned him widespread opprobrium throughout the radical and provincial wings of Liberalism.

Select Bibliography

Cadenhead, Ivie E., *Benito Juárez.* New York: Twayne, 1973.

Hamnett, Brian R., *Juárez.* London: Longman, 1994.

Perry, Laurens Ballard, *Juárez and Díaz: Machine Politics in Mexico.* DeKalb: Northern Illinois University Press, 1978.

Roeder, Ralph, *Juárez and His Mexico: A Biographical Study.* 2 vols., New York: Viking, 1947.

Weeks, Charles A., *The Juárez Myth in Mexico.* Tuscaloosa: University of Alabama Press, 1987.

—BRIAN R. HAMNETT

KAHLO, FRIDA

1907–54 • Artist

Frida Kahlo is one of Mexico's most important twentieth-century figures, well known for the life she suffered and the wrenching self-portraits she painted. Although during her short life she was a recognized figure outside Mexico, her international reputation receded to her own country after her death. In the 1980s a number of important biographies and traveling art shows catapulted her once again into the international mainstream. The large prices her canvases command today at New York and London auction houses is evidence of her growing reputation. Frida Kahlo's legacy—her paintings and life history—has inspired self-portraits, sculptures, short stories, plays, operas, movies, and even fashion shows. In academia she has entered standard art history survey courses, scholarly journals, and the covers of many books, even those having little to do with her or Mexico. During her lifetime Frida Kahlo, the person and the personage, was a symbol of human suffering and emotional strength. Today she is honored and reproduced in various guises worldwide as a patron saint of the post-1968 generation. And, like other saints in their posthumous lives, she is known and invoked by her first name, Frida. Among her followers there can be no doubt to whom they are referring.

Frida Kahlo was born to a German Jewish father of Hungarian descent and a Mexican Catholic mother of European and Indigenous background. She was the third in a family of four daughters. Two other daughters from her father's first marriage joined the family periodically when on vacation from their home in the convent to which they were sent when their parents divorced. Kahlo was raised Catholic, attending church daily as a child with her sisters and devout mother. However, she was not a typical Mexican Catholic girl. When she was not in church or school she was seen romping in the streets outside her house with the neighborhood boys, often in boys' attire. According to those who remember her childhood, she was an accomplished rascal, a cheerful tomboy, until she was six years. From that time onward Kahlo's life was to be a life of illness, operations, recovery and setbacks until her body and soul would expire 40 years later. First polio struck Kahlo, leaving her with a deformed right leg. Twelve years later she suffered from a trolley-car accident on her way home from high school. Her back was broken in three places, her collarbone and pelvis were crushed, her right leg and both feet suffered numerous fractures, and she was impaled by a metal rod through her stomach and vagina. Finally, based on contemporary readings of her x-rays, it appears that Kahlo suffered from spina bifida,

a congenital and debilitating condition in which the spine is left partially open at birth. For the rest of her life Kahlo was to have dozens of operations and eventually a leg amputated. She would suffer several miscarriages and abortions. She would spend many months in a body cast in bed, others in a wheelchair and in pain. Despite all this, Kahlo was remarkable for her ability to rise to innumerable occasions.

Kahlo's reaction to her own handicaps and the teasing she received from her cohorts was to foster her strong personality. Kahlo became an extrovert, building friendships in the most public of circles, while simultaneously becoming an introvert, retreating into herself through her writing and her painting. With two half-sisters in a convent, an older sister preparing to be a nun, and a pious mother, Kahlo could have turned to religious devotion for comfort and inner strength. However, Kahlo found herself dissatisfied with the church and turned toward her nonreligious father for a role model. Guillermo Kahlo was an accomplished photographer, which is how he made a living, as well as an amateur painter and pianist. He was well read and had a substantial library. Frida admired all of this about him. But, it may have been his epilepsy that contributed most to the bond that grew between them. Soon after her recovery from polio, it was Frida's father who encouraged her to excel in sports. She took his advice seriously. Before the age of ten and despite her withered leg Kahlo became an accomplished runner, boxer, wrestler, bicyclist and tree climber. While recuperating from the trolley-car accident her father along with her mother brought her paints, canvases, and brushes while she lay for months on her back. From this time onward Kahlo painted her world of pain, which never subsided; indeed, it only grew worse with age.

Frida Kahlo came of age when the newly formed Revolutionary government set up programs to integrate Mexican Indians into mainstream society through public education. She also came of age when the Revolutionary *políticos* and their artistic comrades presided over the Mexicanization of several bourgeois art forms. Long before her accident Kahlo had admired the famous Mexican painter Diego Rivera, who was a central figure in this effort. He had created a mural in her high school while she was a student there, and it was then that she first caught glimpses of him while he painted. After her accident, when she was back on her feet, she met him at a party; from that time onward he would figure prominently in her life. They married in 1929 shortly after their fateful meeting—she was twenty and he forty-two—and they stayed married until her death in 1954. It was not always a smooth relationship, and it included periods of separation and even a tumultuous year of divorce and remarriage to each other. Both Kahlo and Rivera had lovers, but Rivera had a reputation for his philandering; it was almost a second occupation for him that at one time even included Frida's sister Cristina. Although Rivera's philandering hurt Frida enormously, she did her best to overlook it. In the early stages of their marriage she was a devoted wife; she regularly fixed his meals; she joined his artistic circles; she embraced his revolutionary ideologies. In addition, she joined the Communist Party of which her husband was president, and she readily embraced Mexican indigenous identities, as did her husband, casting the European pre-Revolution aesthetic aside in life as much as in art.

With Kahlo's marriage to Rivera, the most vocal and celebrated of all the Mexican muralists, Kahlo placed herself quite literally in the center of the political avant-garde. Owing to Rivera's close friendship with José Vasconcelos, the secretary of public education and architect of the Mexican Mural Renaissance following the Revolution, he was considered *the* man responsible for creating the visual vocabulary of the Revolutionary government. Kahlo and other women who on occasion modeled for Rivera found themselves scripted into the master narratives of his epic paintings that festooned the walls of the Revolutionary government buildings. Through Rivera Kahlo met the Parisian surrealist André Breton, the Russian revolutionary Leon Trotsky, the Italian-American photographer Tina Modotti, and the U.S. industrialists Edsel Ford and Norman Rockefeller, among others. She traveled across the United States with him, as he painted murals commissioned by wealthy U.S. businessmen. Kahlo managed to use the international settings in which Rivera shined as platforms for her own self, earning a separate reputation in her own right, testimony to the power of her art. By 1938 Kahlo found herself in New York City with her first one-woman show, on the cover of *Vogue* magazine that same year, invited to numerous fancy parties as the guest of honor, and a year later with a one-woman show in Paris, at the invitation of Breton.

Rivera was Kahlo's greatest admirer and most active mentor. He promoted her painting career, encouraged her own style, and had much to do with the construction of her own identity as an artist and as an independent "Mexican" woman. It was Rivera who brought Kahlo her first Tehuana outfit from one of his trips to the Isthmus of Tehuantepec in southern Mexico. These non-tailored, brightly colored outfits with their embroidered shirts and long flowing skirts worn traditionally by the Tehuanas became Kahlo's hallmark both in her life and in her self-portraits. They suited her physical needs, her political agenda, and her strong personality. They made it possible for her to hide her polio-stricken leg and her ailing feet and troubled back; they underscored her allegiance to the nationalistic rhetoric of the Revolution and its ideologies of *Indigenismo* and Mexican-made aesthetic traditions; and, they associated her with the Tehuana women who were known and continue to be known in Mexico as matriarchs of

their society. Submerging her body in Tehuana fabrics, Kahlo gave to herself an aura of empowerment and other-worldliness, especially when she traveled to New York and to Paris; they were neither of her class nor of her time. On Kahlo the Tehuana outfit traveled to worlds far beyond its home—to the art worlds of Mexico City, New York, and Paris, to the political worlds of Mexico City, New York, and Los Angeles, to the social worlds of the Rockefellers and Fords and the André Bretons and the Claire Booth Luces. She appeared dressed in this garb in many of her self-portraits, in photographs taken of her, and in the fashion magazine *Vogue*. The Tehuana clothing contributed enormously to making Kahlo a symbol *of* Mexico as well as an advertisement *for* Mexico. On Kahlo the colorful fabrics did not hang quietly as they do today in her home. Instead they were always part of a grand performance.

Although Kahlo was an ardent supporter of the mural tradition and all it claimed to be and do—she promoted it at parties; she marched in political parades—in her painting she rejected it. Her narrative was personalistic, rooted not in the Italian Renaissance and the Beaux-Arts traditions of historical painting, nor in the Mexican school of Russian socialist realism, nor in the historiographic tradition of third-person narration, all of which characterized Rivera's work. Instead Kahlo's artistry drew upon the Mexican traditions of religious folk art known as ex-votos, with their first-person narration of human tragedy and upon the European traditions of portraiture as practiced in Mexico by the church. Kahlo also drew upon images of Christ and Mary for inspiration, but she did so in her own way, challenging the gender-specific conventions of ecclesiastical representation. In Kahlo's paintings women's bodies are as naked and bloody and fully embodied as those of Christ and as clothed and emotionally stoic and disembodied as those of Mary.

Kahlo's verisimilitude, particularly her bloody and fragmented bodies, led André Breton to declare her a surrealist. Surprised, Kahlo claimed that she painted because she needed to do so and painted what came into her head. Kahlo's paintings had little in common with the French surrealist imagination. There were many homespun reasons why she constructed her portraits from the pieces of her life; not one of them connected her to war-torn Europe or to the many phallocentric manifestos of the surrealist movement. Kahlo's fragments mirrored her own personal life, especially her physical life, to her crumbling spine and her ailing foot. However, the awareness of her fragmented body was exaggerated by the conflicting character of post-revolutionary Mexican identity. What was it to be Mexican?—modern, yet pre-Columbian; young, yet old; anti-Catholic, yet Catholic; Western, yet New World; developing, yet underdeveloped; independent, yet colonized; *mestizo*, yet neither Spanish nor Indian. Kahlo identified herself with the contradictions of her *mestizaje* and through the assemblage of disparate objects, through her identity with church and national icons, and through the exposure of her own fragmented materiality she constructed a subjectivity for herself. Her pictorial honesty came less from something dream-like and imaginary than real. And the bloody Christs of Mexico, the ex-votos and their tragic tales, and her father's documentary approach to photography offered important precedents.

Although Kahlo was upper-middle class and supported many ruling-class constructions of nationhood, in her painting and private life she was at odds with them and their elitist constructions of gender, race, and class differences. She demonstrated her discomfort in various ways. She decorated her house not with European and American imports but with Mexican *artesanías,* a common practice among her artist friends. Her collections of paintings were not the easels of "great" artists, rather the ex-votos of everyday people. When she married Diego Rivera, she wore not a fancy, expensive dress, but a dress belonging to her housekeeper who lent it to her for the occasion. In 1952 she had her photograph taken with all her servants, not common practice among Mexican elites. In the pictorial as well as actual construction of her own *mestizaje* (mixed-race status), Frida Kahlo mixed Indian with European, art with craft, high with low, crossing from one strata to the other with little regard for such elite constructions of difference. Kahlo not only traversed the sacred domains of gender, constructed and preserved by church and state, but she ignored the sacred domains of high and low art and high and low social status, crossing from one level to the other. Rather than mask her racial and cultural hybridism, as other members of the elite did, Kahlo openly acknowledged hers.

As an art teacher at La Esmeralda (1943–53), Kahlo not only refused the hierarchical role of *Maestra* and asked her students to address her with the familiar, second-person *tú* instead of the formal *usted.* She also rejected the tendency to take students to the country to paint the outdoors, popular among teachers then. Instead she took them to see Francisco Goitia, an artist who retreated from the Mexico City art scene to live a peasant—not bohemian—life in Xochimilco, a town south of Mexico City. She also took them to drink at local bars and to visit slums, marketplaces, convents, and churches. "*Muchachos,*" she would announce, "locked up here in school we can't do anything. Let's go into the street. Let's go and paint the life in the street." She once had her students paint a mural, but not as the other art teachers at La Esmeralda had their students do, her husband among them. Instead, she chose the wall of a *pulquería* (a type of popular bar) on which to do it. This is what she meant by "life in the street." When she and her students were not outdoors, she encouraged them to paint what was in her house: popular art, traditional Judases, clay figures, popular toys and handcrafted furniture.

It is not surprising that Frida Kahlo is at the center of contemporary identity politics in and outside Mexico. The insistence of many young painters and writers to credit Frida Kahlo with being a heroine in an otherwise male-dominated landscape and with achieving this recognition by public admission of her personal life helps to explain her popularity among young artists today—men and women—who seek ways to construct their own identities. Her followers are numerous and varied. For women artists in Mexico City, most all of whom grew up in upper-middle-class homes where the Virgin is held as the role model for young girls, Kahlo's rejection of the self-abnegating woman introduces the possibilities of a self-awareness that is profoundly rooted in the flesh and blood of female experiences. Reconstructing womanhood by women on their terms, indeed reconstructing a sexuality that runs contrary to those advocated either by church or state, has few precedents, since historically the representation of female—not to mention male—sexuality was exclusively a male prerogative. Kahlo, through the self portrait, operationalized the psychology of being a woman as she did of being a Mexican. Her imagery is unique in the history of art. As Rivera himself put it; "This is the first time in the history of art that a woman expressed herself with utter frankness."

Select Bibliography

Bakewell, Elizabeth, "Frida Kahlo: A Contemporary Feminist Reading." *Frontiers: A Journal of Women Studies* 14:3 (1993).

Bartra, Eli, *Mujer, ideología y arte: Ideología y política en Frida Kahlo y Diego Rivera.* Barcelona: La Sal, 1987.

Billiter, Erika, *The Blue House: The World of Frida Kahlo.* Seattle: University of Washington Press, and Houston: Museum of Fine Arts, 1993.

Debroise, Olivier, *Figuras en el Tropico, Plastica Mexicana 1920–1940.* Barcelona: Oceano-Éxito, S.A., 1983.

Garduño, Blanca, and José Antonio Rodríguez, *Pasión por Frida.* Mexico City: Instituto Nacional de Bellas Artes, 1992.

Herrera, Hayden, *Frida: A Biography of Frida Kahlo.* New York: Harper and Row, 1983.

Lowe, Sarah M., *The Diary of Frida Kahlo: An Intimate Self-Portrait.* New York: Abrams, and Mexico City: La Vaca Independiente S.A. de C.V., 1995.

Mulvey, Laura, and Peter Wollen, *Frida Kahlo and Tina Modotti.* London: White Chapel Art Gallery, 1982

Tibol, Raquel, *Una Vida Abierta.* Mexico City: Oasis, 1983.

Zamora, Marta, *Frida Kahlo: The Brush of Anguish,* translated by Marilyn Sode Smith. San Francisco: Chronicle Books, 1990.

—ELIZABETH BAKEWELL

KINSHIP

See Family and Kinship

L

LABASTIDA Y DÁVALOS, PELAGIO ANTONIO DE

1817–91 • Archbishop

Pelagio Antonio de Labastida y Dávalos was born in Zamora, Michoacán, in 1817. In 1831 he entered the seminary in Morelia, where he stayed as a student, teacher, and finally as rector. His intelligence and great learning brought him many important appointments, and in July 1855 he was named bishop of Puebla.

On December 19, 1855, when Ignacio Comonfort was president of Mexico, the revolt of Zacapoaxtla broke out under the banner "Religion and Fueros [military privileges]." The rebels occupied Puebla, and Comonfort himself came to the city to put the uprising down, severely punishing the leaders. Labastida was accused of having incited and financed the uprising, and the government used this as an excuse to confiscate the bishopric's property. The bishop protested these measures, and Comonfort was forced into exile.

Labastida's powers of oratory distinguished him as one of the most ardent defenders of the Conservative ancien régime and of the interests of the clergy. He came to the fore again during the French occupation of Mexico. On June 16, 1863, General Forey, commander of the French forces, decreed the creation of a Junta Superior de Gobierno, comprising 35 members, which would appoint the executive power and call a Junta de Notables (Council of Notables), which would decide on the form of government the country wished. Together with the Conservatives Juan Nepomuceno Almonte and José Mariano Salas, Labastida was asked to preside over the Junta de Notables, which was at the time acting as a regency. Labastida was in Europe at the time, however, so his position was occupied by Bishop Juan B. Ormaechea, one of the two substitutes named.

Labastida came back to Mexico on October 11. He had recently been appointed archbishop of Mexico City. Having spoken at length with Napoléon III and Pope Pius IX about the situation of the church in Mexico, he was optimistic that a speedy solution to ecclesiastical problems would be reached. However, the first thing he did on taking up his position in the Junta de Notables (the regency) was to denounce a decree stipulating that the bonds issued to confiscate church property be settled. His outspoken and courageous protest against this measure resulted in his removal from his post.

Despite this setback, Monsignor Labastida was convinced that when a Catholic emperor arrived in Mexico, he and the clergy would work hand in hand to repair the damage suffered by the church. He was again mistaken and realized that Maximilian intended to give his policies a liberal tinge. Distancing himself from the Conservatives by proposing a series of measures to the total detriment of the interests of the church, such as abolition of ecclesiastical privileges, nationalization of the clergy's property, and freedom to worship different religions, Maximilian clearly defined the course he intended to follow. Labastida protested energetically against the emperor's liberal measures and was supported in his actions by the other Mexican bishops.

A disappointed man, Monsignor Labastida decided to emigrate to Europe in 1867. He did not, however, renounce his title of head of the Mexican church, and in this capacity he attended the Vatican Council in 1869 and 1870. In 1871, President Benito Juárez allowed him to return to Mexico. He subsequently devoted himself to promoting religious peace and restoring the church. He served as intermediary between the Mexican government and the Holy See. He died in February 1891 at his estate in Oacalco.

—VICENTE QUIRARTE

LANDA, DIEGO DE

1524–79 • Bishop

"There is in this province a friar called Fray Diego de Landa who . . . enjoys broils and having a finger in every pie, and he expects to rule in both spiritual and temporal matters," wrote the *alcalde mayor* (mayor) of Yucatán to the king of Spain in 1562. A Spanish-born Franciscan who became head of the church in the province of Yucatán, Landa played an important role in the late-sixteenth-century establishment of a Spanish colony in the peninsula. His compatriots may have seen him as "a choleric man . . . inflamed against those who have governed here," but he is known today for two seemingly paradoxical contributions to indigenous Yucatec history: a violent Inquisition prosecution of indigenous "heresy" in 1562, in which thousands of Maya leaders were tortured and their codices and religious icons destroyed; and his *Relación de las cosas de Yucatán* (Account of the Things of Yucatán), a pioneering ethnographic study of the land, its people, and its history before and after the Conquest.

Born in 1524 in Cifuentes, an old Moorish town in the Alcarría resettled during the Reconquista, the Christian "reconquest" of the Iberian Peninsula, Diego de Landa entered the Franciscan monastery in Toledo when he was 16. He was about 25 when he committed himself to the missionary challenge of Spain's new Mexican colonies, arriving in Yucatán just seven years after the 1542 founding of the provincial capital of Mérida. Assigned to pastoral duties at the new monastery at Izamal, Landa soon revealed his ambitions, not only learning Maya but translating a *doctrina* and other works (none of which have survived), as well as traveling extensively in the peninsula, preaching to Maya communities and destroying their "idols."

In 1558 Landa was elected custodian of the Franciscan order in the colony and three years later became provincial, or regional head of the order. As custodian, he inherited a legal dispute that he pursued with a zeal characteristic of his obdurate dedication to the principle of just authority—the authority of the Catholic Church over both the Spanish colonists and the newly "pacified" Maya population, and Landa's own authority as custodian, provincial, and, later, bishop. The dispute involved the prosecution by the church (meaning, in sixteenth-century Yucatán, the Franciscans) of a conquistador and *encomendero*, Francisco Hernández, who had been especially vociferous in his condemnation of the friars' interference in colonial affairs. For three years, Landa harried Hernández mercilessly, using various legal means to keep him incarcerated, until at last, lying mortally ill, Hernández confessed his "crimes" against the ecclesiastical authorities.

The conquistador families would not forget Landa's role in this affair, which symbolizes well the difficult relationship between colonists and clerics that persisted throughout the colonial period in Yucatán. Yet, ironically, Landa's fall from power and exile in Spain in the 1560s was caused not by the colonists but by another Franciscan, not by his campaign against settler activities but by his persecution of the Maya.

Francisco de Torral became the province's first resident bishop in 1560 but did not arrive until August 1562, by which time Landa already had begun investigating the alleged "return to their ancient and evil customs" (including human sacrifice—by crucifixion) by dozens of Maya communities. Their leaders and others, mostly nobles, were arrested under accusation of "worshipping idols and sacrificing to

them publicly and in secret," thereby "destroying Christianity among the simple people." Some 4,500 Maya, including women, were tortured (nearly 200 to death). In July, Landa held autos-da-fé in Maní, Sotuta, and Hocaba-Homun—public assizes at which Maya "heretics" who had survived torture were whipped and chastised and over 5,000 "idols" and 27 hieroglyphic books were burned. This "great persecution" (as one Maya noble, don Francisco de Montejo Xiu, termed it) caused the Maya, in Landa's own words, "much grief." Torral immediately began to dispute the legality of Landa's use of violence and the veracity of the confessions thereby extracted. The two men's arguments are reflected in modern historical literature: Frances V. Scholes, Ralph L. Roys, and Inga Clendinnen accept most of the Maya confessions, believing, as Landa did, that the conversion process still must have been incomplete in the 1560s; Dennis Tedlock, however, persuasively argues that the confessions tell us more about European than Maya culture.

In 1563, in the wake of a condemnatory report sent by Torral, Landa returned to Spain to defend himself in court. There, he wrote his *Relación;* drawn from the friar's own observations and from his conversations with two Maya informants, Nachi Cocom and Gaspar Antonio Chi, this work is unique to Yucatán and one of the most important such manuscripts to have survived colonial Mexico. Perhaps by trying to view Landa's inquisition as conducted in the spirit of care and concern for the Maya can we begin to reconcile their suffering at his hands with the book's veritable celebration of the Yucatec people.

In exile, Landa also worked for his political rehabilitation with typical fervor and tenacity; when Torral died in 1571, Landa himself was appointed Yucatán's bishop. He returned in 1573, vindicated yet weakened; when he attempted a renewal of his campaigns against "idolatry," he found the colonists well prepared to defend their jurisdiction over their "Indians," and he found the Maya themselves quick to use the Spanish legal system as an effective defense.

Upon his death in 1579, the bishop was buried in the Franciscan monastery at Mérida. As a defender of the Franciscan order and ecclesiastical authority, Landa was no doubt "a great friar," as his colleagues wrote in 1570; as a man who compiled knowledge about the Maya and yet burned books that were sources for the same subjects, and who strove to protect indigenous people from Spanish settlers and yet campaigned for the brutal torture of their leaders, he offers a fascinating and tantalizing window onto Mexico's colonial experience.

Select Bibliography

Clendinnen, Inga, *Ambivalent Conquests: Maya and Spaniard in Yucatan, 1517–1570.* Cambridge: Cambridge University Press, 1987.

Cogolludo, Diego López de, *Los tres siglos de la dominación española en Yucatán o sea Historia de Esta Provincia.* 2 vols., Mérida: Aldana Rivas, 1867–68.

Karttunen, Frances, *Between Worlds: Interpreters, Guides, and Survivors.* New Brunswick, New Jersey: Rutgers University Press, 1994.

Landa, fray Diego de, *Relación de las cosas de Yucatán* [1566]. Mexico City: Porrua, 1959; as *Yucatan before and after the Conquest, by Friar Diego de Landa,* translated by William Gates, Baltimore: Maya Society, 1937; as *Landa's Relación de las cosas de Yucatán: A Translation,* translated by Alfred M. Tozzer, Cambridge, Massachusetts: Peabody Museum, 1941; as *The Maya: Diego de Landa's Account of the Affairs of Yucatan,* translated by Anthony R. Pagden, Chicago: O'Hara, 1975.

Scholes, France V., and Eleanor B. Adams, editors, *Don Diego Quijada, Alcalde Mayor de Yucatán, 1561–1565.* 2 vols., Mexico City: Porrúa, 1938.

_____, and Ralph L. Roys, "Fray Diego de Landa and the Problem of Idolatry in Yucatan." In *Cooperation in Research.* Washington, D.C.: Carnegie Institute, 1938.

Tedlock, Dennis, "Torture in the Archives: Mayans Meet Europeans." *American Anthropologist* 91:1 (1993).

—MATTHEW RESTALL

LARA, AGUSTÍN

1897–1970 • Musician and Composer

Agustín Lara was born on October 30, 1897, in Mexico City and died November 6, 1970. During his lifetime, he performed throughout Mexico, Central and South America, Europe, and the United States. He penned over 400 compositions, gaining him an international reputation as one of Mexico's most prolific and dearly loved musicians.

Lara's father, Joaquín Lara Aparicio, worked as a doctor. His wife, María Aguirre del Pino, was originally from Tlalnepantla in the state of Mexico. They lived at 16 Puente del Cuervo, now República de Columbia, in central Mexico City.

Later, Lara would elect to name the charming city of Tlacotalpan, on the banks of the Papolapan river just south of the port of Veracruz, as his place of birth. During his formative years, however, he lived in Mexico City.

Agustín's father, a capable piano player in his own right, introduced his son to the instrument at an early age. As a young boy, Lara began taking lessons. He soon grew impatient with his teacher's demands, preferring to make up his own tunes.

As an adolescent during the Mexican Revolution, Lara was introduced to the shadowy world of Mexico City nightlife. Through a friend, he began working as the house entertainer for a bordello. His career as a budding musician was interrupted briefly when his father insisted Agustín attend military school. Showing little interest, Lara soon returned to working as a musician. At the age of 19, he married Esther Rivas Elorriaga in February 1917. This relationship, the first of Lara's four marriages and many other romances, ended in June 1920.

While working in Mexico City establishments, Lara made friends with a number of musicians including Rodolfo Rangel. Rangel helped him expand his repertoire to include several of the musical styles, (*danzón,* fox trot, tango, bolero, waltz, blues, etc.) popular at the time. Gradually, Lara began writing his own compositions.

In the fall of 1928, singer José Rubio, accompanied by Adelaido Casteñeda's orchestra, recorded Agustín's composition "Imposible" in Mexico City. In October of that same year, a New York company hired the Ascencio Trio to sing another of Lara's compositions, "Clavelito." He soon embarked on a national tour with singers Juan Aruízu and Ana María Fernández. Between performances in the port of Veracruz, Lara visited the city's walkways, beaches, restaurants, cafes, and clubs, beginning a love affair with the port that would last a lifetime. Hearing the young entertainer for the first time, the city became equally enchanted with Lara. The years between 1925 and 1939 would prove to be some of his most creative. During this time he produced many of his classics including "Mujer," "Amor de mis amores," "Aventurera," "Noche de Ronda," "Boca Chiquita," "Perdida," "Rosa," "Volviste," "Farolito," "Granada," among many others.

In September 1929, Lara began performing for *La Hora Intima* show on Mexico City radio station XEW. These performances gradually earned him a dedicated national following. In 1931, Lara contributed a song for the film *Santa.* Soon, the Mexican film industry would prove to be another major outlet for Lara's musical and, later, acting talents. Between 1930 and 1960, the compositions and image of Agustín Lara contributed significantly to the golden age of Mexican cinema. Films such as *Revancha* (1948), *Coqueta* (1949), *Mujeres en mi vida* (1949), *Perdida* (1949), *La mujer que yo amé* (1950), and *Los tres bohemios* (1956) saw Lara perform as an actor as well as a musician. The 1944 Walt Disney production of *The Three Musketeers* saw Dora Luz sing "Solamente una vez" in English. A film entitled *La Vida de Agustín Lara,* directed by Alejandro Galindo and starring

Germán Robles as Lara, depicting the story of Lara's life, was produced in 1958. In all, Lara's work contributed to well over 100 films.

In 1932, Lara traveled to Cuba to perform. When he became sick, a Havana newspaper mistakenly reported that he had died. In need of rest, Lara quickly returned to Mexico. Landing at Veracruz, he was greeted by a cheering crowd. There, he gave a number of free concerts and also traveled for the first time to Tlacotalpan. In addition to receiving wide support in Veracruz during this time, Lara met a resident of the port who would become one of his major interpreters, the singer María Antonia Peregrino de Chazaro, better known as Toña la Negra. A few years later, Lara, inspired by the generosity and beauty of the port, wrote the bolero "Veracruz," which soon became one of his most popular compositions and the unofficial state anthem.

During the 1940s, Lara continued to perform and tour extensively. 1943 saw the debut of the Orquesta de Soloistas de Agustín Lara. By the 1950s there was no doubt that Lara was a successful international star. He hired chauffeurs, cooks, servants, and a personal assistant to help manage his affairs. In 1954, the Mexico City Casino Español, an association of Spanish businessmen, sent Lara to Spain. Lara described the adventure as "an unforgettable trip," one in which Spaniards showered him with their appreciation for his music. Once back in Mexico, the mayor of Veracruz added to Lara's prosperity by giving him a modest house (the Casita Blanca) near the beach as well as the keys to the city. There, Lara would enjoy the company of his Veracruz friends. During this time, Lara performed in several films while also playing in theaters and nightclubs, making appearances on radio and television shows, and touring.

In 1964, Lara made another journey to Spain to be welcomed by General Francisco Ranco, the mayor of Granada, and other notables. A lover of bullfights, Lara attended several while in Spain. "Granada," along with "Solamente una vez," and "Noche de ronda" would prove to be Lara's top-selling songs. During his career, a number of artists interpreted his work including Las Hermanas Aguila, Pedro Vargas, Jorge Fernándeez, Elvira Ríos, Luis G. Roldán, Carmela Rey, and Ana María González.

During the mid-1960s, the rise of the mambo, cha-cha as well as rock and roll in Mexico signaled a change in the character of popular music. Increasingly, Lara spent more time out of the public limelight, often retiring to his house in Veracruz to rest. In 1963, he married his fourth wife, singer Rocio Duran. Although he still performed occasionally, Lara's health began to deteriorate. In October 1970, while in the hospital undergoing treatment for a fractured hip, Lara suffered a respiratory failure; he survived, but his condition remained critical. With many hundreds of well-wishers outside, Agustín Lara died of a heart attack a few weeks later on November 6, at the age of 73. At his funeral, thousands who had been moved by his music over the years walked through the streets in central Mexico City. A minute of silence was observed in many places throughout the nation. Inside the Teatro Blanquita in Mexico City, Toña la Negra sang a chilling rendition of one of Lara's most powerful songs, "Noche de Ronda," in tribute to one of Mexico's most cherished citizens.

Select Bibliography

Bruschetta, Angelina, *Agustín Lara y yo, 1928–1938.* Camelias, Puebla: Robrus, 1979.
Martínez, Gabriel Albaroa, *El flaco de oro.* Mexico City: Planeta, 1993.
Taibo I, Paco Ignacio, *La musica de Agustín Lara en el cine.* Mexico City: Filmoteca UNAM, 1984.
_____, *Agustín Lara.* Mexico City: Jucar, 1985.

—ANDREW GRANT WOOD

LAS CASAS, BARTOLOMÉ DE

1484–1566 • Dominican Friar, Bishop, and Advocate for Indians' Rights

Bartolomé de Las Casas was born in 1484, in Seville. His father was a merchant with maritime inclinations, his mother or stepmother was a well-to-do peasant. A precocious student, he earned a degree in canon and Roman law. In 1502, at the age of 18, Las Casas traveled to the Antilles, settling on the Island of Hispaniola (now the countries of Haiti and the Dominican Republic), where he won recognition as a friend of the Indians. Five years later, he returned, first to Rome, where he was ordained, and then to Spain, where he continued his studies. In 1509 he returned to Hispaniola, where he studied native languages and cultures and served as an Indian catechist.

Invited to Cuba for his expertise with the Indians, he achieved an almost peaceful acceptance of Spanish rule and, with a lay partner, organized a successful *encomienda* of "contented" Indians (*encomiendas* were native settlements "commended" to the care of a Spanish trustee—an *encomendero*—who in return for receiving the Indians' labor had the duty to protect them, maintain missionaries, and contribute to the military defense of the region). But Las

Casas was increasingly sickened as he watched the cruel oppression by his fellow Spaniards and the mounting decimation of the native peoples, especially rapid in Cuba. His was not the only voice to attack the *encomienda* system. The first Dominicans had preached against the exploitation. In Cuba, Las Casas himself preached in the same vein, but to no avail. In 1514, after considerable soul-searching and reading, he resolved to return to Spain to tell the king how to correct the situation. Like a Biblical prophet, Las Casas would spend the rest of his life, more than 50 years, pleading and writing on behalf of the Indians.

Las Casas's first six years, from 1514 to 1520, spent in these endeavors, generally are described as a failure, but they actually produced a delayed success. His initial reform plan was based on his own experience. He proposed replacing Indian forced labor for Spanish *encomenderos* with free Indian communities, organized for farming, mining, and barter, as Las Casas himself had done on his own plantation. He wanted the brutal conquistadors to be replaced by peaceful farmer-colonists, and the Indian communities to be organized into peasant cooperatives.

His proposals were partially enacted, but later were totally sabotaged. After the death of the regent and the ascent of young King Carlos I (Emperor Charles V), Las Casas was able to air his views at court. With encouragement from Carlos's tutor, Adrian of Utrecht, he won a contract to found his own colony on the Pearl Coast of Venezuela. The venture was a disaster. His colonists deserted and joined in slave raids; slaving atrocities on the mainland drove those Indians to force of arms, and they wiped out his fledgling outpost.

In a state of deep depression, Las Casas joined the Dominican order in 1522. Fray Bartolomé later wrote that for the next dozen years on Hispaniola, he "seemed to sleep." In fact, during these years he honed his skills with his greatest weapon—the pen—compiling material for a history of the Conquest and sending a series of powerful exposés and pleas to Spain. By 1530 a Reform Commission had recommended his proposals and a reformed Council of the Indies had enacted them: the abolition of future Indian enslavement and the gradual introduction of an alternate institution to the *encomienda*—free Indian towns under the Spanish Crown. In 1534, however, the antislavery law was revoked, as Cardinal Loaysa returned to head the Council of the Indies; his absence in Rome had permitted the reform to be enacted initially. From Mexico the head of the *audiencia* (high court) wrote letters of protest, and in Hispaniola Bartolomé de Las Casas once again saw his work crumble.

That same year an armada arrived from Spain to end the war with Chief Enriquillo, the Indian guerrilla who had been active militarily on the island of Hispaniola for years. However, local authorities warned the captain to avoid combat. They feared that Enriquillo would seize their weapons and take over the island. Accordingly, the captain went in alone and signed a formal peace; but Enriquillo stubbornly refused to leave his mountains. At this point, Fray Bartolomé

hastily obtained permission to go with a single companion and visit Chief Enriquillo. Las Casas stayed a month in the guerrilla camp, interviewing the chief (who had been educated by the Franciscans). Subsequently, he brought Enriquillo to the capital and persuaded him to settle with his people. Through this interaction with Enriquillo, Fray Bartolomé had found his answer to the defamation of the Indians and the revocation of the laws protecting them. Two friars alone had accomplished more than 15 years of war parties.

Las Casas's first book—*The Only Way to Draw All People to a Living Faith*—is a reflection of both his early experiences and his successful negotiation with Enriquillo. The book is a description of Indian capacity for the faith; a declaration that peace and friendship and respect for other cultures was the only way prescribed and followed by Christ and the Apostles to spread the Gospel; and a denunciation of conquest and its damnable consequences as mortal sin that required restitution.

Fray Bartolomé sent this treatise to a friend at court and arranged to set out himself as a missionary to Peru. But the ship was becalmed, and he and his small contingent of friars changed vessels and landed in Central America instead. From there Las Casas traveled to Mexico City to the headquarters of a new Dominican province, to which he agreed to transfer. In the meantime, he briefly started mission work in Nicaragua (attached to his old province), but he soon encountered hostility from the Spanish conquistadors and prudently returned to the capital. His new province promptly named him vicar of Guatemala, where he did indeed start a mission according to his beliefs in peaceful conversion—the method he had used with Enriquillo and earlier in the "peaceful reduction" of Cuba. The work was interrupted, however, when he was called back to Mexico City for a Dominican chapter meeting.

On these visits to the capital, Las Casas took part in ecclesiastical conferences. The three resulting resolutions of 1536 were officially carried to Rome by the Dominican Bernardino de Minaya along with three supporting treatises. In Rome, Pope Paul III issued his three famous pro-Indian decrees based on these three resolutions. The encyclical bull *Sublimis Deus* follows the first version of Las Casas's *Only Way* point by point, proclaiming the full humanity and rationality of the Indians (i.e., their capacity to understand and accept the Catholic faith), and the correct means of converting them by preaching and good example. The implementing brief automatically excommunicated all who robbed, oppressed, or enslaved the Indians. Nonetheless, this implementing brief was revoked the following year, at the direct request of Carlos I. Paul III agreed in order to achieve a truce between Carlos I and the king of France—temporary peace in Europe, at the price of Indian freedom.

In 1542, Las Casas helped the emperor put together a Reform Commission to draft new legislation for the colonial administration, and in particular the welfare, care, and survival of the Indians. The result was the New Laws for the Indies. These laws established a regular inspection process of colonial governments to eliminate the rampant corruption. The status of Indian communities gradually was to be changed, from the *encomienda,* which essentially bound Indians to the land as indentured workers, to free Indian towns. Slavery also was abolished. The implementation of the laws produced mixed results. Several colonial administrators were removed for corruption. The status of Indians gradually improved, but the practice of debt peonage never was eliminated. And although slavery officially was abolished among Indian populations, some African slaves were imported.

There is a persistent misconception that Las Casas encouraged the importation of African slaves to ease the lot of the Indians. In his early years at court he had, indeed, transmitted a suggestion from some wealthy *encomenderos* that they would liberate 10 Indians for every black slave they could import duty-free. Dominican friars, reforming officials, and Flemish courtiers recommended the large-scale importation of African slaves, but Las Casas did not. A slave trade license was issued around that time, but it was sold and resold at such a high price that it actually halted the importation of African slaves for almost two decades. Only when the Indians had been nearly exterminated in the Caribbean, and the gold in the rivers was gone, did the large-scale importation of African slaves begin, to man the sugar mills. Writing later, Las Casas regretted that at first he had not protested the suggestion of importing African slaves, but he then believed the lie that these blacks were captives from the "just" defensive war Europe was waging against Islam. Upon learning the truth about the nefarious traffic, he condemned black slavery in the same terms as Indian slavery.

Las Casas wanted to stay at court to ensure that the New Laws would not be undermined by the Council of the Indies, which was still headed by Cardinal Loaysa, who opposed the reforms. The emperor had offered Las Casas the bishopric of Cuzco, the capital of the Inca Empire, but he refused. The next offer was to return to his own mission that he had founded with the Dominicans. Las Casas returned to Mexico in 1544 as the bishop of Chiapas and privy counselor to the emperor. During the next three years he was able to promote the implementation of the New Laws in the area under his influence. By 1547, faced with growing resistance, Las Casas returned for the last time to Spain, where he served as the general advocate of the Indians. This was the position that he had hoped for in 1542. Now the Council of the Indies was required to set aside time on a regular basis to listen to his concerns.

First, however, he needed to repair the damage that had occurred in his absence. The emperor, crushed by debts to Flemish bankers, was tempted by a donation of several thousand ducats to repeal the prime New Law, the Law of No Inheritance that would have extinguished the *encomienda.* Once again Las Casas's life work was crumbling—the antislavery laws surely would be next. Even before he reached Spain, his adversaries had recruited an erudite champion for the conquistadors. Juan Ginéz de Sepúlveda, translator of Aristotle and an accomplished syco-

phant (witness his laudatory chronicle of the *Deeds of Emperor Charles V*), was the shrillest voice opposing freedom for the Indians. To Sepúlveda, the native peoples of the Spanish colonies belonged to the Aristotelian category of *servos a natura,* or slaves/servants/serfs by nature, to be ruled by superior beings. Even before Las Casas returned to Spain in 1547, Sepúlveda was encouraged by Cardinal Loaysa, by now the grand inquisitor, to write a justification along these lines for conquering and enslaving the Indians. The resulting Latin dialogue, *Democrates alter,* claimed that the pope practically had ordered a holy war against the Indians. Las Casas responded by having publication of the work blocked. Sepúlveda then wrote a "defense" of his work, which Las Casas promptly had censored and banned. Las Casas also had the newly reformed Council of the Indies reinforce the antislavery laws with a provision that conquest could not legitimate slavery, as the Indians had been "free" people. In addition, he persuaded the emperor to convoke a special commission on conquests and slavery, which heard Sepúlveda for a few hours and Las Casas's rebuttal for five days. But the matter did not end there.

In 1552 Las Casas wrote his most famous works: eight tracts addressed to the emperor and Prince Felipe. One of these, the *Brevissima relación,* denouncing the atrocities of the Spanish Conquest, was widely circulated in Europe by critics of Spain in subsequent centuries. Other tracts criticized the practice of *encomienda* and defended the antislavery provisions of the New Laws, demanded restitution to the Indians, and castigated Sepúlveda. Enraged, Sepúlveda called the tracts "rash, scandalous, and heretical," and he denounced Las Casas to the Inquisition. But by then Loaysa was dead, and the groundless accusations were dropped.

In 1556 Carlos I abdicated. The new king, Felipe II, inherited a mountain of debt and looked to the colonies as a way to raise money. When the gold from the Indies proved insufficient, he decided to tighten the screws on the Indians of the Viceroyalty of Peru. The rights of *encomienda* to control the Mexican Indians had been granted to last for one lifetime. Now Philip proposed to sell perpetual *encomiendas,* essentially a form of slavery, for the Indians of Peru. Las Casas strongly opposed the proposal.

Part of his response involved the presentation of a counteroffer from the Peruvian Indians to buy their own freedom. In the process, he wrote his most daring works, openly warning Felipe of the mortal danger to his salvation if he "alienated" (sold) his vassals. Las Casas received powers of attorney to represent chiefs on both continents, and with a Dominican provincial from Peru he actually represented an offer from the Peruvian Indians to pay more than whatever the *encomenderos* could assemble, along with provisions for restoring the native rulers.

Drawing on the experience of blocking the sale of the Indians, Las Casas wrote his two final treatises: *Who Owns the Treasures in the Inca Tombs?* and *Twelve Doubts on the Conquest of Peru.* His culminating offer to Felipe was literally dazzling: the promise of Inca tomb treasures for the right course; or the threat of eternal damnation for the wrong decision. With mounting courage as his strength ebbed (he was nearly 80), he was defying an implacable monarch.

His greatest work, *History of the Indies,* was never finished. He had started it in 1527 as a prior in Hispaniola. The book was to tell the story of the first six decades of the Conquest, but by the time of his death he had only covered the first 30 years. This history is the only contemporaneous account of both the Indian and Spanish versions of the encounter, based on Las Casas's own experiences plus a wealth of eyewitness interviews and key legal documents. In the process of creating this epic work, Las Casas read and transcribed the abridged log of Christopher Columbus's first voyage, creating the only surviving version of this priceless work.

Las Casas died in 1566 in Madrid. What had he ultimately accomplished in 50 years of labor? Although he could never obtain true freedom for the Indians, he had corrected the worst abuses and enabled many indigenous people to survive. The blazing finale to his life struggle on behalf of the Indians is a startling contrast to the accepted picture of him as a nonagenarian without influence. But even more remarkable is the persistence of his influence in Spain and the Americas for some 60 years after his death, in spite of the Inquisition and censorship: a counteroffer by Indians in New Spain, presented by his friend, the bishop of Verapaz; the negotiations to restore the sovereignty of native lords in Peru; his influence on the writing of the Peruvian "prince and chronicler" Guaman Poma de Ayala; and the publication of a large part of one of his later works, *Defense of Indian Civilizations,* under someone else's name and with the aid of a friendly censor. The New Laws that he drafted remain a legal landmark, the most sweeping bill of rights ever issued by a conquering nation on behalf of conquered peoples.

Las Casas's influence in modern times is even more significant. His vision of humanity and respect for Latin America's Indian peoples has found a new voice in contemporary struggles. The "preferential option for the poor" articulated at the 1968 conference of Latin American bishops in Medillín, Colombia, draws heavily on many of Las Casas's most important ideas. The author of the final report of the Medillín conference, Gustavo Gutiérrez, was a lifelong student of the ideas of Las Casas and has played an instrumental role in defining the movement of Liberation Theology that has swept Latin America and revitalized the church in the process. A move underway in the 1990s for the canonization of Las Casas represented a fitting acknowledgment of his great contributions.

Select Bibliography

Gutiérrez, Gustavo, *Las Casas: The Search for the Poor of Jesus Christ.* Maryknoll, New York: Orbis, 1992.

Parish, Helen Rand, editor, *Bartolomé de Las Casas: The Only Way,* translated and restored by Francis Patrick Sullivan. Mahwah, New Jersey: Paulist Press, 1992.

Parish, Helen Rand, and Harold E. Weidman, *Las Casas en Mexico: Historia y obra desconocidas.* Mexico City: Fondo de Cultura Económica, 1992.

Sanderlin, George, editor and translator, *Witness: The Writings of Bartolomé de Las Casas.* Maryknoll, New York: Orbis, 1992.

Sullivan, Francis Patrick, editor and translator, *Indian Freedom: The Cause of Bartolomé de Las Casas, A Reader.* Kansas City, Missouri: Sheed and Ward, 1995.

Wagner, Henry Raup, and Helen Rand Parish, *The Life and Writings of Bartolomé de Las Casas.* Albuquerque: University of New Mexico Press 1967.

—HELEN RAND PARISH

LEÑERO, VICENTE

1933– • Writer and Journalist

Vicente Leñero was born in Guadalajara, Jalisco, on June 9, 1933. He completed his studies in civil engineering in 1959. During the early 1960s, he started his career as a full-time journalist. He also has written short stories, novels, dramas, soap operas, and reviews, and he became assistant director of the magazine *Proceso* in 1976.

Juan Rulfo and Juan José Arreola influenced Leñero's first book, *La polvareda y otros cuentos,* published in 1959. Two years later, he published his first novel, *La voz adolorida;* a revised version appeared later under the title *A fuerza de palabras.* This work began a novelistic career unique in Mexican literature. *La voz adolorida* is a lengthy, detailed confession of a man who wants to save himself from self-dissolution. The novel is composed of one long flashback that reconstructs a life, a world, and a social group. Leñero is very conscious of the structure of his novels. This formal preoccupation produced a masterpiece, *Los albañiles* (1964), winner of the Biblioteca Breve prize for a novel in 1963, the most prestigious recognition that existed for Spanish-language literature at that time. The novel, based on a documentary and detective plot, portrays the male fraternity of construction workers. The death of an old and ill *velador* (night watchman) of a building under construction in Mexico City triggers confessions by his former coworkers. *Los albañiles* explores different social and economical strata of Mexican society. By using counterpoint as a structure of composition, Leñero describes the workers' work and leisure, their problems and satisfactions, their love, friendship, homo-eroticism, and resentments. Leñero's experiments with structure are also evident in *Estudio Q* (1965), one of the most ambitious of all his novels. In this work, Leñero identifies the differences between reality and fiction through the life of an actor and the soap opera in which he acts. The novelist's eye becomes a camera that examines, transmits, approaches, and moves away from the life of the main character.

In 1967 and 1968, Leñero held a John S. Guggenheim Fellowship, directing his creative energies toward the theater. Leñero's literary approach led him to explore diverse subgenres while producing a critical interpretation of reality and reflecting with clarity on some of the most important moral problems of the Mexican lower and middle classes. Recent scholars support the idea that many of his plays center on male-dominated microcosms that essentially exclude women, for example the play *Compañero* (1970), based on the life of Ernesto "Che" Guevara. This play centers on another manifestation of androcentric society, the military. Women are also scarce in Leñero's later historical, political dramas, *Martirio de Morelos* (1983) and *Nadie sabe nada* (1988). Somewhat more plentiful in its presentation of women is *La carpa* (1971), an adaptation of the novel *Estudio Q,* which dramatizes a theatrical performance and includes three women in its cast of players. Similarly, *El juicio* (1971), another documentary piece based on the trial of two religious figures of the assassination of a reelected president in the 1920s, reenacts a courtroom proceeding and incorporates two female characters. *La mudanza* (1979), which won the Premio Juan Ruiz de Alarcón, contrasts the problems of marital conflicts against the larger backdrop of socioeconomic inequality in contemporary Mexico. In the plays *La visita del ángel* (1981), *Alicia, tal vez* (1980), and *Señora* (1986), settings are less gender specific, and women are afforded more recognizably prominent roles. With the exception of *Alicia, tal vez,* all these less-gender-specific plays are set in the home.

Another critical approach to Leñero's plays involves so-called documentary theater, where the author uses direct testimonials to describe contemporary Mexican history. For instance, in *Pueblo rechazado* (1977), Leñero uses books by Gregorio Lemercier, journal articles, magazines, and his personal relationship with actual participants to recreate a particular situation: the use of psychoanalysis in a Benedictine monastery in Cuernavaca in 1967. *El juicio,* mentioned above, is an adaptation of the trial of José de León Toral y Concepción de la Llata, who was accused of the assassination of Álvaro Obregón in 1928. *Compañero* is based on the actual diaries of Che Guevara. Literary critics agree that Leñero's documentary plays have invited the public to think about and reconceptualize its own contemporary history.

A growing interest in Leñero's work has led to the publication of anthologies of his writing in various genres: *Cajón de sastre* (1982), a collection of short stories and journalistic pieces; *Justos por pecadores* (1982), a collection of three film scripts; *Vivir del teatro* (1983), Leñero's memoirs of his experiences in contemporary Mexican theater; and *Talacha periodística* (1983), an anthology of Leñero's best journalistic writing and critiques of popular Mexican culture. Undoubtedly, Vicente Leñero has proven to be one of the major literary figures of his time. Perhaps his most important contribution has been the idea that cultural production is a way of consciousness and criticism of culture itself.

—Gastón A. Alzate

LEÓN CALDERÓN, NICOLÁS

1859–1929 • Physician, Scientist, Writer, and Educator

Nicolás León Calderón was born in Villa de Cucupao, now Quiroga, Michoacán, in 1859 and died 70 years later. León studied surgery at the Morelia-based Colegio de San Nicolás Hidalgo and graduated on October 10, 1883. Three years later he published his dissertation, a history of medicine in Michoacán from pre-Columbian times until 1875. He specialized in gynecology-obstetrics, taught internal pathology in the Morelia School of Medicine, and headed the Department of Women's Surgery in Morelia's Hospital Civil.

It would be unfair, nevertheless, to define León merely as a physician and a historian of medicine. Even though he never formally studied other disciplines, he also can be considered a historian, anthropologist, linguist, ethnographer, archaeologist, literary scholar, and naturalist, given his intense work in these spheres.

During the first years of his professional life, he concentrated on medicine. However, starting in January 1886 he focused on anthropology after the governor of Michoacán, General Mariano Jiménez, founded the Museo Michoacano and appointed him to head the museum. Thereafter, León studied with special attention Purépecha (Tarascan) Indians. He also published and wrote anthropological essays for a monthly journal, the *Anales del Museo Michoacano,* the first issue of which appeared March 1, 1888. In 1892 he moved to Oaxaca to establish the Museo Oaxaqueño and remained there until 1893. In 1900 he joined Mexico City's Museo Nacional and joined its physical anthropology section, created and headed by Jesús Sánchez. León worked for this museum until his death.

Nicolás León polished his skills in several disciplines while living in Mexico City. He enrolled in several scientific societies, including the Sociedad Científica Antonio Alzate, the Sociedad Mexicana de Geografía y Estadística, the Sociedad Mexicana de Historia Natural, the Société Philologique de France, and the Société de Géographie Commerciale de Paris. He also kept contact with different academic and scientific institutions, such as the Escuela Nacional de Medicina, Hospital General, Academia Nacional de Medicina, and the Instituto Bibliográfico Mexicano. León deepened his knowledge by importing books and working instruments and traveling to congresses abroad. All this gave him access to European scientific developments, especially those of France.

Owing to the influence of Positivism in León's time, the most popular topics were biology, medicine, chemistry, physics, geography, and mining. In reaction, he allocated more time to study the humanities, in particular, Mexican history. He chiefly investigated ethnic themes, worked in indigenous communities, and studied the history of native groups, sometimes going back to pre-Hispanic times. León was interested in the physiognomy, language, religion, habits, and culture of indigenous peoples. He mostly studied Tarascans.

León played an important role in the formation of physical anthropology in Mexico and, therefore, is known as the father of this discipline in the nation. He was in permanent contact with French researchers, who exerted a profound influence on the development of physical anthropology. Systematic anthropological studies were undertaken in Mexico in 1864, when a Mexican-French organization, the Commission Scientifique du Mexique, was founded. The group was the precursor of the Academia Nacional de Medicina, headed by León in 1921. His participation in this institution induced him to write again on the history of medicine.

During his association with the Colegio de San Nicolás Hidalgo Museum, he also worked as a naturalist, training to prepare natural history samples, such as animals, plants, and minerals. In this field, he produced in 1895 the *Biblioteca Botánica Mexicana,* a bibliographical, biographical, and critical catalogue of authors from the sixteenth to the nineteenth centuries dealing with Mexican vegetation and its applications. The work also describes the result of botanical investigations made in Mexico. In 1888 he commented on Francisco Hernández's large book on the plants, animals, and minerals of New Spain utilized in medicine. His comments were based on Francisco Ximénez's 1615 edition of the book.

Few people wrote as much as Nicolás León. He summarized his own literary work in *Noticia de sus escritos originales impresos e inéditos. Los de varios autores por el deditados. Traducciones de obras impresas e inéditas,* published in 1925. He mentions 525 texts. By the standards of his epoch, León's academic production is extraordinary. He was a restive man who permanently felt an urge to write. His longest production was a book on medicine printed in 1910, *La obstetricia en México,* based on 30 years of professional experience in obstetrics. The work covers the entire Mexican territory from the sixteenth century to the first decade of the twentieth century. It deals with such topics as pregnancy, birth, abortion, child care, and midwifery. León's writings show his desire to penetrate all scientific and cultural fields and to broaden the knowledge of Mexican history.

Select Bibliography

Bernal, Ignacio, editor, *Correspondencia de Nicolás León con Joaquín García Icazbalceta.* Mexico City: UNAM, 1981.

León, Nicolás, *Compendio de la historia general de México desde los tiempos prehistóricos hasta el año de 1900.* Mexico City: Herrero Hermanos, 1902.

Quintana, José Miguel, "Correspondencia del Dr. Nicolás León." *Boletín del Instituto de Investigaciones Bibliográficas* (January–June 1975).

Serrano, Carlos, and Martha E. Rodríguez, "El pensamiento y obra pionera de Nicolás León en la antropología física mexicana." *Anales de Antropología* 30 (1993).

—Martha Eugenia Rodríguez

LERDO DE TEJADA, SEBASTIÁN

1827–89 • President

According to the historian Frank Averill Knapp Jr., "No Mexican president has been more maligned, misunderstood, and misrepresented," than Sebastián Lerdo de Tejada. From

his ascension to the interim presidency in July 1872, through the four years he served after his own election to the presidency, until the insurgent forces of Porfirio Díaz drove Lerdo from Mexico City in November 1876, libelous epithets were heaped upon him. History treated the deposed president somewhat more kindly. Lerdo was largely forgotten, his career and reputation eclipsed on one side by his predecessor, Benito Juárez, and erased on the other by the image-makers of the long-serving dictator Porfirio Díaz. Yet Lerdo's doomed efforts to implement the ideals of liberal, democratic, republican government in a Mexico bloodied and impoverished by decades of war were important, preliminary steps in the creation of the modern Mexican state.

Lerdo was born in Jalapa, Veracruz, to a Spanish father and Mexican mother. He was educated in theological colleges and enjoyed a prize-studded educational career. At the National College of San Idelfonso, he studied law and rose from student to professor to, eventually, rector during the turbulent end of the dictatorship of Antonio López de Santa Anna and ensuing Wars of the Reform. Although the rectorship of that prestigious institution provided Lerdo with contacts to most of the influential Mexicans of the day, it seems Lerdo then harbored no political ambitions. His legal studies did prepare him to serve as attorney (*fiscal*) and then magistrate of the Supreme Court between 1855 and 1857, but it was his election as a congressional deputy in 1861 that thrust Lerdo into a political arena from which only force of arms eventually would expel him.

During his congressional career in Mexico City, Lerdo stood out for his unyielding defense of national sovereignty against treaties and foreign claims that would in any fashion compromise the territorial integrity of the nation. When Juárez was forced to take his government to the harsh northern frontier as French troops occupied Mexico, Lerdo accompanied him as the vice president of the permanent delegation of Congress in recess. Juárez soon called upon Lerdo to perform still additional governmental functions, and he appointed Lerdo minister of foreign relations and minister of government. Lerdo rejected French efforts to negotiate a quick end to the Republic, which at times seemed to consist only of Lerdo, another principal minister (José María Iglesias), Juárez himself, and a small group of loyal guards and soldiers unable to decisively alter the military realities of foreign occupation. But the three men and their scattered allies labored heroically to maintain the legal existence of the Republic, until the withdrawal of French troops allowed resurgent Mexican forces to topple the French-imposed emperor Maximilian and restore Juárez in Mexico City in 1867.

When Juárez was reelected to the presidency in 1867, Congress elected Lerdo president of the Supreme Court and, thereby, next in line for succession to the presidency. Lerdo also assumed the offices of minister of foreign relations and chief of Juárez's cabinet. Lerdo thus enjoyed, in addition to his pronounced influence over Juárez based upon long years of mutual labor and risk during the French Intervention, a significant measure of both judicial and executive power. Even before Juárez's reelection, Lerdo penned and circulated a program of constitutional reforms that, if adopted, would significantly strengthen the powers of the executive branch of government at the expense of the Congress. In his controversial August 1867 circular to the nation's governors, Lerdo noted that "the despotism of a convention can be as bad, or worse, than the despotism of a dictator," and that "the peace and well-being of society depend on the convenient equilibrium in the organization of public powers." That call to revise by the unusual means of plebiscite the Constitution of 1857 provoked a storm of opposition, and Juárez eventually dropped the program, although its major provision—the creation of a senate—was finally adopted during Lerdo's term as president. In the meantime the forces in opposition to Juárez already had begun to focus upon Lerdo as a principal object of their rancor.

Restoring peace and order to Mexico after so many years of revolts, invasions, and warfare was the Herculean task of the Juárez administration. It was Lerdo's view that progress toward that end could come only from the pursuit of seemingly contradictory policies: the strengthening of the central government on the one hand, and vigorous opposition to the use of force to overthrow local authorities on the other. Lerdo understood that the project of centralization required his continuance in power, and insofar as the ability of his party to remain in power depended upon the cooperation of state governors as managers of state elections and chiefs of state militias, Lerdo found himself intervening evermore in state affairs in order to build and maintain the political machine that would construct the stable, centralized, liberal government that he envisioned. It seems inevitable now that Lerdo's project would expose him to the charges subsequently levied against him: subverter of the liberal cause, enemy of states' rights, tyrant.

Lerdo resigned from the Juárez cabinet in 1871 and competed for the presidency against Juárez and Díaz in the elections of that year. Juárez won reelection, Díaz came in second, and the weakness of Lerdo's popular and political support was exposed by his third-place finish. Lerdo remained president of the Supreme Court and, hence, next in line to succeed Juárez. Once Díaz's revolt against Juárez's reelection (the Plan of La Noria) was crushed, and with the death of Juárez in July 1872, the way was clear for Lerdo legally to assume the interim presidency. The nation apparently greeted the legal transfer of power and absence of any ongoing political revolt as promising the dawn of a new era of peace and progress. Lerdo declared his intention to govern as president of the nation, not head of any party, and much to the astonishment of his contemporaries, he retained the Juárez cabinet and many other officials appointed by his predecessor, while offering few immediate spoils to self-avowed Lerdistas. He declared a general amnesty for Porfirian rebels, all of whom, Díaz included, accepted. When Lerdo was elected without opposition in October 1872, the prospects, finally, for peace and unity throughout Mexico seemed truly bright, indeed.

According to Lerdo's principal biographer (Frank Averill Knapp Jr.), peace, order, and respect for law was Lerdo's "religion of state." In that triumvirate, peace and order would take some precedence over law, it seems. Lerdo authorized brutally effective suppression of rebellious local chieftains, sought the suspension of civil liberties in rebellious states, and ushered through Congress the renewal of the highly controversial Law of Highwaymen and Bandits, which gave local authorities power, under certain circumstances, to conduct summary examinations and executions of suspects caught in the act. While for Lerdo and many others the suppression of violence justified temporary suspensions of civil liberties, in other realms Lerdo championed civil liberties and civil tolerance to degrees only dreamed of before. At Lerdo's insistence the Laws of the Reform, only laxly enforced during Juárez's reign, were enacted as constitutional provisions. Congress was moved to pass the legislation that finally would put these reforms into effect, and Lerdo enforced these reforms (many of them drafted in the first instance by his deceased brother, Miguel Lerdo de Tejada) vigorously.

The creation of a senate was key to Lerdo's plan to centralize the power of the federal government and to provide the federal government with a secure, legal basis for intervening, forcefully if necessary, in state affairs. Lerdo managed to complete that project, which had been begun but postponed under the Juárez presidency. According to the final legislation, the 50-seat Senate would function partially as a check upon a Congress that a president otherwise might find difficult to control. Furthermore, the Senate could declare that the executive and legal power of a state had ceased to exist (in the case of armed rebellions or disputed elections, for example) and empower the president to appoint a provisional governor. Finally, the Senate could resolve disputes between the executive and legislative powers of a state and, again, authorize the federal executive to intervene. These were legal powers that would prove very useful to a president like Lerdo, who highly valued legal form but who understood as well the federal executive's need at times forcefully to influence power struggles at the state level. While Lerdo had little time to take advantage of these powers (the first Senate convened for the fall term of 1875), his successor, Porfirio Díaz, would exploit them to full advantage.

Historians have noted that little of interest can be said of Lerdo's foreign policy. As foreign minister under Juárez, Lerdo had established the policy that Mexico could not recognize the official status of representatives of foreign governments that had recognized the regime of Maximilian and had adopted a hostile stance toward the government of the Republic. European nations that fell into that category and that, after the triumph of the Republic, wished to resume normal diplomatic relations would have to take the first steps toward mending the wounds of the past. Some did, but relations with Great Britain and France were not renewed during Lerdo's tenure in office, and Mexico's access to the most important European capital markets was correspondingly limited. Lerdo's relations with the United States were cordial. Lerdo concluded the work of the U.S.-Mexican Mixed Claims Commission of 1868. Although Indian and bandit depredations on both sides of the Rio Grande, as well as occasional violence against U.S. citizens in Mexico, soon added again to the roster of claims each country held against the other, both Lerdo and the U.S. administration desired commercial relations between the two countries to expand unimpeded by such irritations. The United States sought rapid expansion in commercial relations; Lerdo envisioned a more cautious growth.

Lerdo's foreign policy had consequences for his policy of domestic economic development. His vigorous defense of national sovereignty and national honor dictated that relations with England and France would not soon be renewed. Without such relations, access to European capital markets would be restricted, and Mexico would have to rely more heavily on U.S. capital. However, Lerdo understood that in the future, U.S. capital would pose the greater threat to Mexican sovereignty, and he would not allow himself to throw wide open the doors to U.S. investment in Mexican economic infrastructure. Lerdo's administration promoted the development of railroads and communication (the completion of the Mexico City–Veracruz railroad being the principal economic trophy of Lerdo's administration), but it did so only warily, earning the criticism from many quarters that his administration neglected the pressing development needs of the country. Those who came violently to oppose Lerdo did so partly in the name of material progress and economic renovation. The great expansion of U.S.-Mexican commercial relations depended on the expansion of a transportation network connecting producers and consumers in each nation, and Lerdo's successor, Díaz, pursued that task with historic abandon.

Lerdo's task of making liberalism a practical, working political system for a Mexico at peace was far from completed by the conclusion of his first elected term as president. Much had been accomplished: steps had been taken to centralize federal power, codify reforms, and chart the future direction of a cautious policy of economic development that would not endanger national sovereignty. Further, Lerdo had labored consistently to construct an alliance of state governors (with the considerable monopoly of power and resources that they enjoyed at the local level) to support him in these endeavors. It was a seemingly inevitable, although also ill-fated decision, that Lerdo took, then, when he announced that he would seek a second term of office as president in elections scheduled for the summer of 1876. A powerful tendency of liberal thought held that reelection of high officials was inimical to the growth of liberal, democratic institutions, and that only a policy of no reelection would check the time-worn impulses of high officials to concentrate power and wield it ruthlessly for the benefit of themselves and their closest allies. So when Porfirio Díaz revolted against Lerdo in January of 1876, his Plan of Tuxtepec proclaimed the cause of "No Reelection" as central to the goals of his rebellion.

Lerdo faced many obstacles in his effort to suppress the Díaz rebellion. Lerdo's reelection, although probably no more fraudulent than that of his predecessors, was not above reproach. Lerdo's passion for respecting individual liberties and the rule of law led him to refrain from restraining a press that quickly moved from libel and scandal to open advocacy of rebellion. The still-poor state of Mexican finances hindered full, timely, effective military mobilization against the guerrilla forces of Porfirio Díaz. Finally, Lerdo faced in Porfirio Díaz a master rebel whose guerrilla war in the north drew federal forces in that direction, even as Díaz and his supporters prepared to deliver the government a death blow on a different field of battle in the south. When the president of the Supreme Court, José María Iglesias, declared Lerdo's reelection to be illegal and claimed to be the legal successor, and with the decisive victory of Díaz in battle in Tecoac in November 1876, Lerdo's fate was sealed. Several days after Tecoac, Lerdo fled the capital and headed to exile in New York.

Lerdo died in exile in New York in 1889. His body was returned to Mexico and accorded state honors under President Porfirio Díaz. As Knapp relates, only one of those who spoke at the funeral reflected upon the causes of Lerdo's downfall. Lerdo's failure, that one pointed out, was that he had not understood that bread was the "inseparable companion of peace." Lerdo governed a nation long ravaged by war, whose political and economic edifice was in ruins. Lerdo had believed that the economic development and prosperity of the nation could only be constructed upon a foundation of social peace, the rule of law, a vigorous defense of national sovereignty, and a strong, centralized government. He labored powerfully to the end of creating such a foundation, and under his rule Mexico had enjoyed a then-unprecedented degree of domestic tranquillity and tolerance. Yet when the call to rebellion was sounded again, many decided that the prosperity and progress of the nation required one last resort to arms, altering profoundly the course of modern Mexican history.

Select Bibliography

Cosío Villegas, Daniel, *Historia Moderna de México: La República Restaurada: La Vida Política.* Mexico City: Hermes, 1955.
Knapp, Frank Averill, Jr., *The Life of Sebastián Lerdo de Tejada, 1823–1889: A Study of Influence and Obscurity.* Austin: University of Texas Press, 1951.
Perry, Laurens Ballard, *Juárez and Díaz: Machine Politics in Mexico.* DeKalb: Northern Illinois University Press, 1978.

—Paul Sullivan

LIBERALISM

Liberalism had a large impact on nineteenth-century Mexico, much as it influenced the United States, Great Britain, and France in the same period. A broad current of ideas that swept across western Europe and the Americas in the eighteenth and nineteenth centuries, liberalism carried various meanings in different political contexts. At the most general level, liberalism was a rejection of traditional strongholds of power for privileged groups such as merchant guilds, religious orders, and special military courts. Liberals typically called for the abolition of these organizations—often called corporations—in order to open opportunities for energetic and ambitious individuals who formed an early version of a loosely structured middle class. Beyond this overview, it is difficult to generalize about liberalism because it followed different patterns in specific countries and time periods. In Mexico, liberal leaders adjusted their ideas and methods throughout the nineteenth century, sometimes disagreeing among themselves, so that the reader is well advised to accept the notion that change was among the most prominent characteristics of liberalism in this era.

Liberalism was probably the most dynamic political movement in nineteenth-century Mexico. With its emphasis on individual freedom and its opposition to the traditional centers of power and influence such as the Catholic Church, liberalism had a controversial impact in a nation only recently separated from the Spanish Empire, in which the Catholic Church, the military, guilds, and other privileged corporate groups had held dominant positions during the colonial era (1519–1821). The advocates of liberalism wanted to break the hold of these corporate structures on property, politics and government, and the educational system in order to clear the way for individual initiative and private enterprise, which they hoped would usher in a new era of economic prosperity. The liberals, therefore, envisioned a thorough transformation of Mexico's national life that reached from propertied wealth to the school classroom. In their pursuit of these goals, however, Mexican reformers often abandoned another basic assumption of liberalism: the call for constitutional limitations on the power of the central government. Such large-scale changes usually required a very active national government led by an assertive chief executive.

The first major confrontation between liberalism and its conservative opponents took place during one of the presidential administrations of General Antonio López de Santa Anna. The general, less interested in the pressing issues of politics than the pomp and pageantry of leadership, in 1833 left the responsibilities of governance to Vice President Valentín Gómez Farías, who was a dedicated liberal reformer. Gómez Farías and most Mexican liberals of his day drew inspiration from the writings of José María Luis Mora, a gifted essayist who placed his talent for persuasion at the service of the liberal cause. In particular, Mora argued in a widely read 1831 essay that the government should require the Catholic Church to surrender all of its property not directly related to its religious functions. This assertion was like a thunderbolt in Mexico's heated political atmosphere of the 1830s because the Catholic Church had accumulated a large portion of the nation's agricultural and urban real estate through wills and donations over the three centuries of the colonial period. Mora's proposal threatened the basic underpinnings of Mexico's economic, social, and religious structure. Vice President Gómez Farías, left in charge of the national government by Santa Anna, acted quickly across a broad front. He nationalized the Franciscan missions in the northwest province of California in an apparent first step in his efforts to secularize church property. He also closed the University of Mexico, an institution dominated by the clergy, and began to reduce the size of the army and to restrict its special privileges.

The bold actions of Gómez Farías aroused the Catholic Church, the army, and their conservative allies who moved to defend the existing hierarchy. These powerful groups appealed to Santa Anna, who, as a military officer as well as politician, decided to remove Gómez Farías from the government in order to foil the liberal reform program. Santa Anna's return to the presidency in 1834 brought an end to this short-lived effort to implant liberalism in Mexico.

Liberalism moved to the periphery of Mexican politics for the remainder of the 1830s and into the 1840s while the nation underwent the excruciating pain of war and territorial dismemberment. The distant province of Texas won its independence from the government in Mexico City in 1836. The expansionist United States annexed Texas in 1845, and soon border disputes led the two nations into a war (1846–48) that proved disastrous for Mexico. The United States invaded Mexico's capital city, defeated the nation's army, and took approximately half of the national territory, including the valuable lands that stretched from Texas to the Pacific coast of California. During this difficult period, liberalism was plagued by internal divisions. The *puros*, radical liberal followers of Gómez Farías, were more stridently anticlerical than the opposing liberal faction, the *moderados*, who tended to favor gradual methods. This division reduced the impact of liberalism on national politics in these years.

A new generation, led by Benito Juárez, managed to establish a degree of unity within the liberal movement and gained control of the national government in the 1850s. Juárez, a Zapotec Indian who first rose to prominence as the governor of his home state of Oaxaca, challenged the authority of the Santa Anna regime and its conservative supporters. Forced into exile, Juárez took refuge in New Orleans, where he and other liberals began to organize against Santa Anna. Juárez established himself as one of the foremost liberals of his generation during these difficult years. Encouraged by the success of a revolt based in the state of Guerrero, Juárez and other New Orleans exiles returned to Mexico in 1854 and 1855 to take part in a large movement, the Revolution of Ayutla. This movement brought to power a Liberal government that enacted legislation soon known as the Reform Laws. Juárez himself wrote the law that stripped the military and clergy of the right to be tried for serious crimes in special courts run by their own organizations. The Ley Juárez was the first of a series of liberal actions directed against the main strongholds of the conservatives. The second law, written largely by Miguel Lerdo de Tejada, required the Catholic Church to sell or otherwise dispose of its property not directly essential for religious practices (for example, farmland as contrasted with a church sanctuary). The stated intention of the liberals was to break loose property from the control of the Catholic Church for more productive use in the free enterprise economy. Taken together, the Ley Juárez and the Ley Lerdo went beyond the Gómez Farías reforms of the 1830s to strike at the power bases of conservatism in the military and the church. The liberals, in control of the government, also organized a constituent convention that wrote the Constitution of 1857, a document that included the Ley Juárez and Ley Lerdo and extended liberal reforms into other areas.

These sweeping reforms were intended to create a modern economy that would follow the pattern of free enterprise that had brought prosperity to Great Britain and the United States. With church property moving into the market economy and religious and military leaders deprived of their special courts, the liberals were confident that economic prosperity and social change would spread their benefits throughout Mexico. These liberal leaders miscalculated, however. The Ley Lerdo not only deprived the church of its property, it also forced native American villages (legally considered to be corporate entities like the church) to sell their traditional communally held land to individual owners. These transactions did not result in the liberals' goal of a middle class made up of small-to-middle-sized farms in the hands of yeoman farmers (as they were called in the United States). Instead, most church and village properties moved into the grasp of large landowners and speculators, two groups that had the capital necessary to make the purchases. The agrarian ideals of nineteenth-century liberalism did not find fertile ground in Mexico.

Other sources of frustration for liberal reformers came from civil strife and foreign intervention. Conservatives, supported by large segments of the military, fought a bloody war (1857–60) against the liberal government. The victory of the liberals in this conflict brought only temporary respite; conservatives next made an alliance with the French emperor Napoleon III. The result was five years of monarchy under the French-imposed leadership of the ill-fated emperor Maximilian. After the withdrawal of the French army and the defeat and death of Maximilian in 1867, Juárez returned to Mexico City to begin the difficult process of rebuilding his nation.

Juárez finally had control of the national government, but, unfortunately for him and his cause, liberalism as an ideology seemed as exhausted as the nation itself. Juárez, the Mexican president during most of these years, rode out the turmoil of war and intervention to become the symbol of the liberal movement that defended the nation against the conservatives and their imperialist collaborators. Liberalism thereby became linked with Mexican patriotism. While Juárez rose to heroic status among his followers, however, liberals began to realize that their hopes for an agricultural economy made up of a new class of prosperous, independent farmers were doomed to failure. The sale of church lands had weakened Catholic institutions, but the major beneficiaries were wealthy landowners who simply added more property to their already large estates.

Faced with the challenge of trying to govern Mexico while his fellow liberals turned against each other and some even against him, Juárez resorted to autocratic methods, thereby violating the liberal ideal of restricted executive power functioning within a limited central government. The Juárez administration expended much of its energy in dealing with the revolts of dissatisfied liberal politicians, who had expected the rewards of political office, and disappointed peasants, who had seen village lands lost to aggressive hacendados.

The last five years of the Juárez presidency were a time of change for liberalism. In his search for a new approach to Mexico's persistent and burdensome problems, Juárez turned to Gabino Barreda, a Mexican intellectual who had studied with the French philosopher Auguste Comte, the founder of positivism. Barreda returned from France with a new formula for understanding the nation's troubled half-century of Independence and a prescription for progressive political and social change that soon became integral elements in late-nineteenth-century liberalism. Juárez placed Barreda in charge of reforming the nation's educational system, which was to be based in government—not church—schools. Barreda set up the National Preparatory School to train the nation's young elite for their university education. His program became the focal point for the spread of positivist ideas, which emphasized the importance of the hierarchy of knowledge and also a hierarchy in the political and economic life of the nation. Under Juárez and Barreda, liberalism, heavily influenced by positivism, acquired an elitist tone that, coupled with an increasingly autocratic government, laid the basis for the dictatorship of Porfirio Díaz. Juárez's plans for Mexico did not reach maturity because he died of heart failure in 1872 after serving only one year of his final term of office.

Porfirio Díaz dominated Mexican politics from his seizure of power in 1876 until his resignation in the face of the Mexican Revolution in 1911. His standing in history largely has been determined by his image as the tough-minded, often cruel dictator who tamed Mexico; in the first three decades of his public career, however, Díaz earned his reputation as a champion of the liberal cause, particularly his heroic contributions to the defeat of the invading French Army in the Battle of Puebla on May 5, 1862. For the next five years Díaz continued as a loyal liberal general in the struggle against Maximilian's empire. After Juárez and the liberals emerged triumphant in 1867, Díaz turned from a military career to politics, where he encountered a series of disappointing defeats. He became a political opponent of his former mentor and fellow Oaxacan, Juárez. Although his electoral campaigns (which called for no reelection to presidency as a slap at Juárez) and political revolts consistently failed from 1867 to 1872, the hero of the Battle of Puebla gained an understanding of the nation's political system at both the state and national levels. Hardly a liberal thinker like Mora, Gómez Farías, or Juárez, Díaz became skillful in the political tasks of persuasion, image-building, and intimidation.

Liberalism completed its basic transformation in the early years of the Porfirian era. Building upon the changes initiated by Juárez in his last years in the presidency, Díaz in his first term (1876–80) and President Manuel González (1880–84, the only person other than Díaz to hold the presidency during this period) abandoned anticlerical and antimilitary policies and achieved an appreciable reconciliation with the Catholic Church and the army. Díaz and González turned their attention to what became perhaps the central component of late-nineteenth-century liberalism in Mexico: the use of the national government to promote economic development. Both Díaz and González sought and obtained contracts with firms from the United States to build railroads to connect central and northern Mexico with the rapidly expanding railroad system north of the Rio Grande. The resulting improvements in the nation's transportation system connected agricultural lands to urban markets not only in Mexico City, Monterrey, and Guadalajara but also in Denver, Kansas City, St. Louis, Chicago, and other metropolitan centers in the United States. The new Mining Code of 1884 stimulated a revival of mineral extraction as foreign investors began to find value in Mexico's lead and copper reserves as well as the legendary silver and gold mines. Liberalism thus became associated with the expansion of the modern economy.

The economic arrangements reflected the ideological refinements of the Díaz period, which originated with a group of politicians, entrepreneurs, and government ministers widely known as the Científicos. Their name derived from the "scientific" study of politics and society as devised by French positivist philosopher Auguste Comte and advocated in Mexico by Gabino Barreda during the Juárez presidency. This new political/intellectual group coalesced around Manuel Romero Rubio, the minister of the interior and also Díaz's father-in-law. Younger Científicos included educator and historian Justo Sierra, finance expert and later minister of the treasury José Yves Limantour, and agribusiness magnate Enrique Creel. The Científicos transcended regional and state political groupings that had splintered

Mexico's political history in the first half-century of Independence to form a national elite of government officials and business leaders. Their national scope along with their modifications of the ideas and practices of liberalism gave them a vital role in the Porfiriato.

Justo Sierra was one of the most outspoken members of this generation to seek a new formulation of ideas and institutions to turn Mexico away from its troubled past toward a more stable and prosperous future. Sierra cited positivism's emphasis on order and hierarchy to justify the acceleration of the trend already under way in the Juárez years: the growth of the national government and the strengthening of the presidency as its primary agent. A key element in this process was the practice of "scientific politics," through which the methods of research and analysis that had yielded such impressive results in the natural sciences would be applied to the political and social realm to provide Mexico's national leaders with definitive guidelines for the achievement of stability and prosperity.

Sierra and his fellow Científicos put forth their modifications of the liberal ideology because they were convinced that Mexico had to solve the problem of its political instability before other components of progress could take hold. According to historian Charles Hale, the Científicos called for a more powerful nation-state headed by a strong chief executive in order to rectify the flaws of early-nineteenth-century liberalism that placed unrealistic limits on governmental authority. Obviously Díaz turned this executive authority into a dictatorship, but in the 1870s and 1880s, Sierra and other members of the liberal-Científico group were preoccupied with the danger of returning to the chaos of the past.

As Díaz continued in the presidency through the 1890s and into the early twentieth century, however, some liberal elements began to object to this concentration of power. Several members of the Científico elite, led by Sierra, began to propose reforms to balance the increased presidential power with a broader distribution of authority to the judiciary and legislature. In 1893 and again in 1903, they called for such changes, but in both instances the reform effort failed. Groups within the lower classes also became disillusioned with the Díaz regime. Many peasants clung to a combination of ideology and mythology—often called popular liberalism—in which Benito Juárez was the central figure, a legendary champion of patriotism and the common people. Although they did not pose an open threat to the Díaz dictatorship, these peasants created an underlying tension in their celebrations of the collective memory of Juárez through public festivals that, at least by implication, served as expressions of grassroots discontent. The reality of Díaz's official authority and his public image as the benevolent strongman of Mexico overrode these dissident tendencies within liberalism. Díaz who, as an aspiring politician had campaigned against Juárez on the slogan "no reelection" a few decades earlier, now retained an iron grasp on the presidency.

The excesses of Porfirian liberalism also extended into the economic sphere. One of the main goals of the Díaz government, the stimulation of business activity, was accomplished as the construction of railroads and the revision of the mining code enticed foreign entrepreneurs to Mexico. Both foreign and Mexican businessmen also turned their attention to rural villages and, employing the advantages of superior knowledge of the law and close connections with the nation's political leaders, stripped these communities of their best agricultural lands. In the early nineteenth century, around 40 percent of the arable land in central and southern Mexico was held by villages; by 1911 only 5 percent of this type of land remained under their control. The vast majority of Mexican peasants were landless by the last years of the Porfiriato. During this period, some of the more avaricious Científicos ignored liberal concerns about dictatorship and concentrated on their own material gains. The 74-year-old head of state selected a Científico favorite, Ramón Corral, as his vice president in 1904, thereby giving a symbolic endorsement of this grab for property and profits.

Liberalism experienced some dramatic changes in response to the excesses of Porfirian greed and corruption. Sierra's calls for reform and the public celebrations of popular liberalism remained within the parameters of traditional ideas and symbols, but in the first decade of the twentieth century, a new political party, the Partido Liberal Mexicano (PLM, or Mexican Liberal Party) developed a coherent challenge to the Porfirian power structure and the expanding free enterprise system associated with it. Led by Ricardo Flores Magón (and his brothers Jesús and Enrique), the PLM went beyond liberalism's customary emphasis on anticlericalism and individual freedom to call for legislation to end abuse of factory workers, to abolish debt peonage, and to begin a land reform program. The bold pronouncements of the PLM, heavily influenced by anarchism, marked a major break in the history of Mexican liberalism. Ricardo Flores Magón and his small group of followers rejected the Porfirian formula for national advancement based on government support for private business expansion and instead moved their wing of liberalism toward the ideological formulations that were to have an important presence in the Mexican Revolution.

While greed and material gain were primary motives for the Porfirian elite, the public image of Mexican liberalism, both at home and abroad, contained a much more appealing character. The Científicos' mixture of liberalism and positivism found expression through cleverly written speeches and carefully orchestrated demonstrations. For example, Díaz and other government officials cultivated a sense of identification with Benito Juárez as the patriotic defender of a vague, almost mythical liberalism, thereby conveniently neglecting the rivalry between the two men from 1867 to 1872. Díaz also took advantage of the sophisticated manners of diplomat and cabinet officer Matías Romero to build a favorable reputation for his policies in the United States. Díaz perfected his own abilities in public relations through personal contacts with the large American community resident in Mexico and also through personal acquaintances with the likes of U.S. mining engineer John Hays Hammond and British construction engineer Weetman Pearson (Lord Cowdray). The Mexican president made a point of sending impressive commercial exhibits to international trade fairs in Paris, Berlin, New Orleans, and Chicago and by staging his own demonstrations of Mexico's entry into the world of modernity through the annual reviews of the highly publicized *rurales* (rural mounted police who brought law and order to the nation's roads). His government encouraged and, in some cases, sponsored the publication of articles and books—often in English—that featured Mexico's potential for progress.

The nineteenth-century evolution of Mexican liberalism contains a heavy component of irony. The ideology of Mora, Gómez Farías, and the early Juárez that identified the privileges of the Catholic Church and the military as impediments to national progress by the end of the century had become a complex set of ideas that justified the privileged position of a new elite, the Científicos. The liberalism of the late nineteenth century, however, contained considerable variety and flexibility. Liberals advocated ideas that stretched across a wide range: from the acceptance of dictatorship to bring an end to political instability, to Justo Sierra's calls for a return to the ideal of a limited executive authority based on scientific politics, to the Flores Magón brothers' potent mixture of reformism and anarchism. By the last years of the Díaz period, however, most liberals accepted the calculated, propagandistic appeals of the commercially minded elite to the international business community. Mexican liberalism, like most influential ideologies, contained an internal dynamic of its own that both reflected and changed the life of the nation.

See also Anarchism; Ayutla, Revolution of; Científicos; Conservatism; Constitution of 1824; Constitution of 1857; Constitution of 1917; Nationalism; Neoliberalism; Partido Liberal Mexicano (PLM); Popular Liberalism; Porfiriato: Interpretations; Positivism; Reform Laws; Wars of Reform

Select Bibliography

Bazant, Jan, *Alienation of Church Wealth in Mexico: Social and Economic Aspects of Liberal Revolution, 1856–1875.* Cambridge: Cambridge University Press, 1971.

Berry, Charles R., *The Reform in Oaxaca, 1856–1876: A Microhistory of the Liberal Revolution.* Lincoln: University of Nebraska Press, 1981.

Coatsworth, John, *Growth against Development: The Economic Impact of Railroads in Porfirian Mexico.* DeKalb: Northern Illinois University Press, 1980.

Coerver, Donald M., *The Porfirian Interregnum: The Presidency of Manuel González of Mexico, 1880–1884.* Fort Worth: Texas Christian University Press, 1979.

Costeloe, Michael P., *Church and State in Independent Mexico: A Study of the Patronage Debate, 1821–1857.* London: Royal Historical Society, 1978.

Hale, Charles, *Mexican Liberalism in the Age of Mora, 1821–1853.* New Haven, Connecticut: Yale University Press, 1968.

_____, *The Transformation of Liberalism in Late Nineteenth Century Mexico.* Princeton, New Jersey: Princeton University Press, 1989.

Olliff, Donathan C., *Reforma Mexico and the United States: A Search for Alternatives to Annexation, 1854–1861.* University: University of Alabama Press, 1981.

Perry, Laurens B., *Juárez and Díaz: Machine Politics in Mexico.* DeKalb: Northern Illinois University Press, 1978.

Schoonover, Thomas, *Dollars over Dominion: The Triumph of Liberalism in Mexican–United States Relations, 1861–1867.* Baton Rouge: Louisiana State University Press, 1978.

Sierra, Justo, *The Political Evolution of the Mexican People.* Austin: University of Texas Press, 1969.

Sinkin, Richard, *The Mexican Reform, 1855–1876: A Study in Liberal Nation-Building.* Austin: Latin American Institute, University of Texas, 1979.

Tenenbaum, Barbara, *The Politics of Penury: Debts and Taxes in Mexico, 1821–1856.* Albuquerque: University of New Mexico Press, 1986.

Wasserman, Mark, *Capitalists, Caciques, and Revolution: The Native Elite and Foreign Enterprise in Chihuahua, Mexico, 1842–1911.* Chapel Hill: University of North Carolina Press, 1984.

Weeks, Charles, *The Juárez Myth in Mexico.* University: University of Alabama Press, 1987.

—JOHN A. BRITTON

LIBERATION THEOLOGY

The 1960s saw Roman Catholicism undergo great change. Pope John XXIII set the church on the path to change by convening Vatican II (1962–65), a council that sought to modernize the Catholic Church in an industrial age that seemed to be passing it by. The cardinals and prelates who gathered for Vatican II initiated their own significant reforms, including termination of the 15-century-old tradition of conducting masses in Latin, but they also unlatched a Pandora's box by implicitly approving of the introduction of new ideas from the bottom up. One of the movements that found space in the context of this new spirit of innovation was Liberation Theology.

For many of its proponents, Liberation Theology was anything but new. Cautiously rereading scripture—with a focus on the synoptic gospels and the life of Christ—they found ample evidence that God was deeply concerned with the plight of the poor. "Woe to you who are rich," they read in Luke, chapter 6, "for you are receiving your comfort in full." Indeed, from even before and after the recorded life of Christ, the Gospel message seems to have had elements akin to utopian communism. John the Baptist preached that "he who has two tunics shall give one to him who has none" (Luke 3:11), and the Bible records that early Christians sold their possessions and "all became common property to them" (Acts 4:32).

And if the scriptures were not enough, those seeking social justice in the context of faith also could find inspiration in the Catholic Church's own Latin American tradition. Of particular importance were the lives of early Spanish friars who denounced their compatriots' abuses of the Indians. Clerics such as Antonio de Montesinos and Bartolomé Las Casas provided clear models of conduct with regard to justice for the region's oppressed. Las Casas, in particular, who labored tirelessly for decades in the sixteenth century on behalf of Indian rights, was a powerful example because his work was approved by both Crown and church.

The Latin American struggle for justice begun by men such as Las Casas continued in the ranks of the clergy—albeit only by way of a small minority. Even before Vatican II adjourned, devout priests working with the Third World's poor were voicing doubts about the church's long silence regarding social injustice. One of these priests, who gained prominence in 1965–66, was Colombia's Father Camilo Torres, who began to preach that such silence among believers constituted a mortal sin. Torres put his prophetic message into practice by joining a band of guerrillas, only to lose his life in combat a few months later. Although his willingness to use counterviolence against oppression was rejected by much of the emerging Liberation movement, Torres's witness had at least kept clerical awareness of gross injustice alive.

Among those who opposed Torres's use of violence was a former classmate destined to play a prominent role in calling the Catholic Church home to its Liberation message: Peruvian theologian Gustavo Gutiérrez. Gutiérrez's renewed scrutiny of the Bible led him to conclude that God stands closest to the poor. "It is not a question of idealizing poverty," he explained, "but rather of taking it on as it is—an evil—to protest against it and to struggle to abolish it." Gutiérrez and other authors, such as Brazil's Leonardo Boff, soon reached the conclusion that God has a "preferential option" for the poor. Emphasizing the deliverance of the Israelites out of bondage, the writings of the Prophets, along with the synoptics, these theologians articulated a theology that emphasized God as a Liberator, not only in a spiritual sense but in a temporal sense as well.

By the early 1970s, as a direct result of Liberation Theology, the Latin American Catholic Church saw a boom in grassroots Bible study and lay participation, as peasants and workers formed small study groups known as Christian Base Communities (CBCs). Like their predecessors in the first century, Christians in the CBCs met in homes instead of churches, and sought out community rather than delegating leadership. This in turn facilitated *concientización*, or consciousness-raising, as peasants learned to read and write in order to interpret scripture for themselves and then apply it to their own reality. Although regionwide, the CBC movement gained especially keen momentum in Central America, where it politicized the poor and drew down upon them savage repression, which in turn fueled revolution. Liberation Theology also exerted influence upward in the Catholic Church itself, especially after nearly a quarter of Latin America's bishops conferred in Medellín, Colombia, in August 1968 (at CELAM I, as the conference acronym was known).

Mexico lagged behind Central America in Liberation-inspired politicalization. Only by the late 1970s did Liberation Theology begin to have any real impact, and only then in isolated areas. If a healthy majority of Latin America's bishops were not supportive of the new theology, it can be said that in Mexico a vast majority of them opposed it. Out of some 70 bishops and archbishops only a few ever embraced Liberation thinking. The most colorful of these was Sergio Méndez Arceo, the bishop of Morelos who governed the church in a region of Indian villages once inspired by agrarian revolutionary Emiliano Zapata. Openly supportive of Fidel Castro and the Cuban Revolution, unusually candid, and often dangerously outspoken, Méndez Arceo served as the de facto spokesperson for Liberation Theology in Mexico until his retirement from the bishopric in 1982, when the mantle fell to Don Samuel Ruíz García, bishop of Chiapas.

Bishop Ruíz presided over Mexico's poorest diocese from a city named, appropriately, after Las Casas. Conditions here were aggravated in the early 1980s by the state terror in nearby Guatemala and El Salvador, as hundreds of thousands of frightened and desperate peasants sought refuge in southeastern Mexico. Ruíz and his supporters mobilized what help they could for these impoverished, mostly Indian, refugees, while the bishop himself became their advocate in the Mexican media. The Mexican government, however, was not nearly as benevolent. The army built a road through the jungle along the Guatemalan border and sought to turn back the refugee flood with harsh tactics. Ruíz exposed state terror on numerous occasions, most prominently in a 1985 Pastoral Letter that documented disappearances and use of torture by the authorities. His diocese also closely monitored local land disputes, Partido Revolucionario Institucional (PRI, or Institutional Revolutionary Party) government corruption (in itself a formidable task), and the nearly 300 political assassinations in Chiapas during the mid-1980s.

The work of Ruíz and Méndez Arceo notwithstanding, Liberation Theology made few inroads in Mexico even while it challenged the oppressive structures in Central America and elsewhere. The exceptions to this relative quiet were primarily in the Indian south, where scores of priests (out of roughly 11,000 in all of Mexico) lived with the rural poor and addressed social ills. They usually found at least tacit support from their bishops, including Bartolomé Carrasco Briseño of Oaxaca and Arturo Lona Reyes of the Diocese of Tehuantepec. In spring 1992 many of these priests joined a march for human rights from the Yucatán to Mexico City.

Once in the capital, they could meet with the other noteworthy faction of Liberation Theology adherents in Mexico: the Jesuits. Priests in the Society of Jesus had been vocal in their support of liberation since the mid-1960s, when the order closed its elitist Instituto Patria preparatory school, an action that evoked a flurry of media criticism. Jesuit influence has been most acute by way of their Miguel Agustín Pro Center for Human Rights, a think tank and publications bank that has been an invaluable resource for the progressive church for three decades. Jesuit writings on behalf of the poor has aroused the indignation of Mexico's bishops, who condemned, for example, the 1989 publication of the Palabra-Vida Plan, which addressed injustice on the eve of the Columbus Quincentennial.

Whether they be the few bishops, priests in the Indian south, or Jesuits in the capital, all Mexican advocates of Liberation have faced considerable persecution, even from within the Catholic Church. The Conference of Mexican Bishops has repeatedly chastised them, as has the powerful apostolic delegate representing the Vatican. Since 1978 the conservative and influential Jerónimo Prigione has held this post, executing the orders of the Vatican even while shrewdly advising it in favor of the appointment of anti-Liberation Theology prelates. These efforts have paid off in the form of ever more conservative pronouncements from Mexico's bishops, such as their 10-million-copy 1980s pamphlet denouncing leftism and warning that "it is impossible to be both a Christian and a Marxist."

Liberation Christians frequently have faced the charge that they are "Marxists," not just by the conservative hierarchy but also by Protestants, U.S. critics (such as televangelist "Pat" G. Robertson), and rightist politicians. It is a label not completely accurate. For although Liberation Christians have found common ground with the political left in their struggle to reform oligarchic societies, their orientation is rooted in faith and the Bible. As scholar Phillip Berryman notes, Liberation theologians actually have found little inspiration in Marx and often have been critical of the traditional left. As Jesuit Ignacio Ellacuría put it shortly before his death at the hands of the U.S.-trained and -funded military in El Salvador: "I am not a Marxist. When they accuse me, I reply 'I am a Christian.' A Christian is much more radical than any communist."

Still, the assault on Liberation Christians has continued from both outside and inside the church. The ascension of conservative Polish pontiff John Paul II in 1978 set the stage

for even sharper rebuke and isolation. The pope's hand has been strengthened in Mexico by his two highly publicized visits to the country in 1979 and 1990. The first trip, coordinated for an appearance at CELAM III in Puebla, produced enormous and enthusiastic crowds in major Mexican cities. At the Latin American Bishops' Conference, the pope preached unity, even while warning Liberation adherents that "the conception of Christ as a political figure, a revolutionary, as the subversive from Nazareth, does not tally with the church's catechesis." Unwelcome visitors such as Gustavo Gutiérrez were kept outside the high walls of the seminary compound that hosted the conference. Despite even more media hype and commercialization in anticipation of his return trip, smaller crowds greeted the pontiff in 1990.

The banks and businesses that sponsored television coverage of the pope's 1990 visit had reason to appreciate the famous visitor. By the early 1990s his intolerance for Liberation thinking and appointment of conservative bishops had paid dividends: the church was once again largely compliant with the Mexican status quo. Under President Carlos Salinas de Gortari, who warmly greeted John Paul II at Mexico City's airport, the government normalized diplomatic relations with the Vatican and the Catholic Church's conservative influence in Mexico began to grow—a valuable stabilizing force in a time of increasing political unrest and looming economic hardship. Despite substantial evidence of worsening poverty and human rights abuses, collected by the Jesuits and others, the pope kept his comments regarding temporal conditions to a minimum.

The one exception to the new ecclesiastical peace of the 1990s has been in Chiapas, where Bishop Ruíz has continued at his post even though beleaguered, largely abandoned by his church superiors, and in ill health. In January 1994 impoverished Maya rose up in rebellion as new "Zapatistas," condemning the North American Free Trade Agreement, PRI electoral fraud, and government corruption. They immediately faced savage repression. Fleeing deep into the Lacandón jungle, the poorly armed rebels opened negotiations with the government through the mediation of the diocese. In February 1995, when the army launched an offensive against the guerrillas, Ruíz again found himself in the center of the storm. Angry pro-government ranchers rallied in front of his church and called for the removal of Ruíz, whom they dubbed the "Red Bishop."

In the mid-1990s, unrest in southern Indian states such as Chiapas, Tabasco, and Guerrero was fueled by Liberation Theology, and repression against the movement will likely continue and even increase, if we look to Central America and elsewhere as previous models. Jesuits in Mexico City have received innumerable death threats, some of which appear to have originated from the Federal Judicial Police. One can safely anticipate the decline of Liberation Theology in Mexico through the violent elimination of its proponents. In other parts of Latin America, such a process has yielded fertile ground for Protestant missionaries, who carry a conservative political message of heavenly hope and Pentecostal emotionalism.

Select Bibliography

Berryman, Phillip, "What Happened at Puebla." In *Churches and Politics in Latin America,* edited by Daniel H. Levine. Beverly Hills, California: Sage, 1979.

_____, *Liberation Theology: The Essential Facts about the Revolutionary Movement in Latin America and Beyond.* New York: Pantheon, 1987.

Gutiérrez, Gustavo, *A Theology of Liberation: History, Politics, and Salvation.* Maryknoll, New York: Orbis, 1973.

López, Baltazar, *Cuernavaca: fuentes para el estudio de una diocesis: Documentos y reacciones de prensa, 1959–1968.* 2 vols., Cuernavaca: Centro Intercultural de Documentación, 1968.

Smith, Christian, *The Emergence of Liberation Theology: Radical Religion and Social Movement Theory.* Chicago: University of Chicago Press, 1991.

—JOHN W. SHERMAN

LIENAS, JUAN DE

c.1620–50 • Composer

Lienas, who was possibly the chapel master at the Convento de la Encarnación in Mexico City (founded 1595), was probably also a married man who had been cuckolded by his wife, for musical copyists identified him as "galan tiessos rolizo," "del famoso cornudo," "cornudillo," "el cornudo," "el chibato Lienas," and "del cornudo Lienas." It is believed that he may have been an Indian chief (or possibly a Spaniard of noble birth) as his name is given as "don" Juan de Lienas in several manuscripts and in the Códice del Convento del Carmen (from the Convento del Carmen near Mexico City). The Newberry Choirbooks, copied by more than 20 different copyists, contain many sacred musical works by Lienas. Sixty pages out of a total of 216 in the Códice del Carmen are devoted to pieces by Lienas. That Lienas's compositions were well esteemed and frequently performed during his lifetime and afterward can be seen from the existing manuscripts; the pages in the Newberry Choirbooks containing Lienas's works have been given the hardest use of any and were repaired on several occasions. Lienas's compositions in the Códice del Convento del Carmen, given its conventual origin, were probably performed by women. The complete extent of the use of instruments with female voices in this repertory is not currently known to any degree of certainty. The lower voices in the Newberry Choirbooks generally do not carry texts, although the names of several nuns are given in these parts, indicating that the tenor and bass lines may have been performed on instruments.

In his five-part *Missa super fa re ut fa sol la,* Lienas begins each voice part with the musical motive—or main melodic theme (based on the notes f, d, c, f, g, and a; or "fa re ut fa sol la" in the solmization system) used by Spanish composers Cristóbal de Morales throughout his *Missa cortilla* and Melchor Robledo in his *Missa a 5.* In his *Salve Regina, a 5,* Lienas shows his inclination toward the use of the first tone in the modal system (Lienas's moving *Salve Regina* is one of the first examples of early Mexican sacred polyphony performed in the twentieth century. It frequently was performed by the Roger Wagner Chorale in the 1960s, in the United States and on tour overseas). In his hymn *Te lucis ante terminum* Lienas uses the same Spanish plainchant melody used by Francisco Guerrero in his hymn *Exsultet caelum;* however, unlike the Spanish composer, Lienas writes rapid melodic passages for all of the voices except the bass. He also places the plainchant model in all of the voices instead of only in one. The text of the third verse of *Te lucis ante terminum* ("Ut solita clementia"), in the fifth choirbook at the Newberry Library, has been changed by the copyist to read "Ut pro tua clementia," probably indicating that Lienas composed this hymn setting before 1632 and the approval of the new hymnal of Pope Urban VIII for use in the Mexican church.

Lienas's vespers psalm *Credidi propter quod locutus sum* sensitively expresses the spirit and meaning of the text with its frequent changes of meter and rhythm and its subtle use of the plainchant model. Lienas espouses an older compositional style in his five-voice *Lamentations.* As with the *Lamentations* of Tomás Luis de Victoria, Lienas uses imitative counterpoint at times, especially double imitation, to evoke a mood of sorrow and sadness in the ear of the listener. Lienas's *Lamentations* are modeled on non-Roman plainchant, despite the liturgical and musical requirement imposed on the Mexican church by the Council of Trent. Lienas and other colonial composers used the Spanish lamentation tone in their works, which had been included in Juan Navarro's *Liber in qvo qvatuor Passiones Christi Domini continentur* published in Mexico City in 1604. According to the musicologist Robert Stevenson, Lienas, especially in his short polychoral responsory for Holy Thursday work, *Tristis est anima mea,* shows a sensitivity to changes in the text that align him with Spanish baroque masters such as Juan Bautista Comes and Andrés Llorente.

Select Bibliography

Bal y Gay, Jesús, *Tesoro de la música polifónica en México: I. El códice del Convento del Carmen.* Mexico City: Instituto Nacional de Bellas Artes, 1952.

Cetrangolo, Anibale E., "La misa a cinco voces de Juan de Lienas en el códice mexicano del convento de Nuetra Señora del Carmen." *Ficta: Difusora de música antigua* 1:3 (1977).

Schleifer, Eliyahu A., "New Light on the Mexican Choirbooks at the Newberry Library." *Notes* 30 (December 1973).

_____, "The Mexican Choirbooks at the Newberry Library." Ph.D. diss., University of Chicago, 1979.

_____, "Lamentations and Lamentation Tones in the Mexican Choirbooks at the Newberry Library, Chicago." *Israel Studies in Musicology* 2 (1980).

Stevenson, Robert, *Renaissance and Baroque Musical Sources in the Americas.* Washington, D.C.: Organization of American States, General Secretariat, 1970.

_____, "Mexican Baroque Polyphony in Foreign Libraries." *Inter-American Music Review* 9:1 (Fall–Winter 1987).

—JOHN KOEGEL

LIMANTOUR, JOSÉ YVES

1854–1935 • Politician and Economist

Considered the very embodiment of scientific administration, José Yves Limantour was undoubtedly the most significant minister in the government of Porfirio Díaz, in which he served as secretary of Hacienda (Treasury Department) from 1893 to 1911. Some of his contemporaries even contended that if Limantour had possessed less talent, less knowledge, and less serenity, the ruin of the country would have been inevitable. Nevertheless, once he left office, Mexico's renowned financial wizard became an obscure historical figure. In fact, modern academic research has yet to produce a full-fledged biography of Limantour despite his undeniable importance in the life of Porfirian Mexico.

While the legitimacy of his birth still remains in question, many facts of Limantour's early life can be discerned despite the legends that previously clouded them. Both his parents, Adèle Marquet and Joseph Yves Limantour, were French immigrants. His father gained a fortune as a ship captain in the Pacific trade during the 1830s and 1840s, until the war between Mexico and the United States nullified California as a source of income. Subsequently, in 1858, U.S. courts denied the elder Limantour's questionable claim to extensive tracts of land in the San Francisco area.

Already one of the richest men in Mexico City by the time of the birth of José Yves, Joseph Limantour expanded his fortune during the Wars of Reform and the French occupation through money lending, arms sales, the acquisition of disentailed property, and other real estate dealings. José Yves's childhood seems to have been defined by social privilege, physical illness, and intellectual precociousness. His higher education consisted of the positivism of the Escuela Nacional Preparatoria and the Escuela Nacional de Jurisprudencia, followed by training in economics in France. In the midst of his grand tour of Europe, Limantour stopped at Mexico's diplomatic mission in Rome in order to choose Mexican, rather than French, citizenship after his 21st birthday.

From the beginning, José Yves Limantour's political career was closely tied to Porfirio Díaz, the leader he later called "the greatest statesman of our country's history." Joseph Limantour's financial support for Díaz helped José Yves obtain teaching positions upon his return from Europe in 1876. During the next few years, he gained recognition as an authority in public administration. From 1877 to 1882, he edited *El Foro,* a journal founded by Justo Sierra and Pablo Macedo to promote the scientific study of law. Limantour moved within a circle of young positivists and supporters of Díaz, many of whom would later become known as Científicos. His closeness to Manuel Romero Rubio and the Díaz political machine made him a city councilman in the capital and a federal deputy. Socially as well as politically, Limantour was firmly linked to don Porfirio. His wife, María Cañas y Buch, the daughter of a longtime Díaz ally, was a childhood friend of Díaz's second wife, Carmen Romero Rubio.

In 1892, Limantour, along with 10 others, signed the Liberal Union manifesto calling for Díaz's reelection and giving priority to orderly material progress over the civic freedoms of traditional liberalism. Limantour's writings during the previous 15 years had argued that Mexico's backwardness required a strong central government to guide the country's economic advance. He had called for a strong—even dictatorial—president who would allow a cadre of capable, scientific administrators to construct the financial, statistical, and institutional apparatus of modern government. Limantour had described the Secretariat of Hacienda as the leading ministry of the executive branch, called upon to set Mexico's economic policies and to oversee other parts of government.

After briefly serving as chief clerk of Hacienda under his longtime ally Matías Romero, Limantour ascended to the leadership of the ministry in 1893. Recent bad harvests, burdensome railroad subsidy payments, and the steady depreciation of the silver-based Mexican peso had left the treasury in dire straights. Aided by new foreign and domestic bond issues, Limantour rapidly reorganized Mexico's finances. By the 1895–96 fiscal year, he had consolidated domestic debt and brought federal income and expenditures into balance. In 1896, legislation proposed by Limantour resulted in the abolition of the *alcabalas,* or internal customs taxes, thereby removing a long-standing obstacle to the formation of a national market. By 1898, the size of the federal budgetary surplus enabled the government to devote funds to debt reduction and to special public investments.

Limantour worked to stabilize the Mexican peso domestically and internationally. Backed by an 1896 law governing credit institutions and the printing of money, Limantour oversaw the emergence of a private banking system across Mexico. By the end of the Porfiriato, the country held some 34 banks of different types. Currency in circulation tripled between 1897 and 1911, while deposits rose almost eightfold. In 1903, following inconclusive international negotiations over the declining value of silver, Limantour sponsored legislation to put the Mexican peso on the gold standard. Since his entry into Hacienda, the exchange value of the silver-based peso had fallen by more than 40 percent in New York and London. The depreciation of the peso constituted a serious burden for import-intensive enterprises such as railroads and for the government's obligation to service the foreign debt. Limantour's monetary reform fixed the worth of the peso in 1905 at 75 centigrams of gold or 50 U.S. cents.

Yet not all of his measures were unqualified successes. Despite the expansion of banking, for example, the availability of credit remained a severe and unresolved problem. During the agricultural drought and recession of 1907–08, short-term credit actually fell 0.2 percent, aggravating existing recessionary conditions. Limantour's top-down financial reforms could not eliminate many of the internal limitations and external vulnerabilities of the Porfirian political economy. The secretary of Hacienda managed to balance Mexico's national finances, but he failed to construct a domestic fiscal regime that would keep pace with economic expansion. While overall government revenues accounted for 11.2 percent of the country's gross domestic product in 1877, they totaled only 7.2 percent in 1910. The federal government's share in 1910 constituted a meager 4 percent, woefully insufficient for coping with the inflation, weakened exports, and economic slump that resulted from the monetary reform of 1905.

Limantour's economic strategy placed a higher priority on the Díaz regime's international credit worthiness than on its capacity to extract domestic revenue. In 1899, the finance minister negotiated a conversion bond issue at 5 percent that enabled the government to reduce interest payments on its gold-denominated foreign debt. In the midst of the elections of 1910, he negotiated a similar conversion issue at 4 percent (only half of this transaction was finalized before the Maderista rebellions changed foreign bankers' minds). Limantour remained convinced that a steady influx of foreign capital would create a modern, prosperous, and ultimately more autonomous Mexican economy. He reported to Congress in December 1905 that

> the day will come, as has been exemplified by the history of other modern nations, when the population, increased by the multiplication of the means of livelihood and trained in more laborious habits, will by degrees redeem itself from indebtedness, and when that happens, the bonds, shares, and other securities of our most flourishing enterprises will be held at home and will not be allowed again to leave the country.

As the unofficial leader of the Científicos, Limantour exemplified what scholar Alan Knight has called the "new economic nationalism" that emerged in Porfirian-Científico circles early in the twentieth century. He stood behind the Porfirian state's circumspect assertion of Mexican sovereignty in the face of U.S. capital. In the words of historian Friedrich Katz, Limantour and the other Científicos believed that "American predominance was inimical to the . . . concept of what Mexico's economic development should be." The finance minister played an important part in official encouragement of British oil investment as a means of avoiding U.S. control over that nascent industry. Even more prominent was his role as the architect of the Mexicanization of the country's rail system, an effort that illustrated the precariousness of Porfirian economic nationalism in the context of limited state resources and presidential succession politics.

Ever since taking charge of Hacienda, Limantour had regarded government railway subsidies as a crucial financial issue. They formed a significant share of Mexico's foreign debt. In 1898 he presented a plan for rationalizing Mexico's rail investments by limiting future subsidies to certain major routes that would connect central and northern Mexico with both the Pacific coast and the southeast. A new railroad law the following year incorporated these ideas and set the stage for more active government rail regulation.

Mexico's improved financial position constituted the foundation for Limantour's assertiveness. Although the country's debt service payments rose by more than 50 percent between the fiscal years 1895–96 and 1910–11, they declined as a share of normal government revenues from 38 to 24 percent. Events after 1900 soon provided Limantour with opportunities to execute his vision of a comprehensive national railway grid to promote development. New rate wars among Mexico's major carriers threatened to upset the stability of the transportation system. At the same time, the financial weaknesses of the Central and Nacional Railways posed the dangerous possibility of a U.S. monopoly over the principal trunk routes between central Mexico and the country's northern border. Limantour intervened quickly, transforming the Mexican government from rail regulator to rail owner.

In 1902–03, Limantour negotiated government stock control of the Interoceánico and the Nacional Railways, thus averting the threat of U.S. monopoly. Subsequent dealings after 1906 with the Central culminated in the formation of the Ferrocarriles Nacionales de México in 1908, a government-controlled partnership with foreign investors that operated over two-thirds of the country's rail system by 1910 and employed over half of all rail workers. Limantour claimed that the creation of the Ferrocarriles Nacionales eliminated undue foreign influence while simultaneously creating the means to operate a more efficient rail system that could be extended to previously untapped areas of the country. In fact, the Nacionales did operate profitably between 1909 and 1911, attaining favorable cost-revenue ratios, adding new lines, and meeting its obligations to creditors. Limantour later argued from exile that this success would have continued if "disgraceful deeds" of the Revolution had not undermined "one of the most beautiful railway systems in the world."

Contemporaries and later historians have disputed Limantour. The improved operations of the Nacionales between 1909 and 1911 owed less to the efficiencies of consolidation than to cheaper fuel costs derived through the conversion from coal to petroleum. In a remarkably durable analysis carried out in the midst of the Revolution, Fernando González Roa noted that Limantour's 1898 report had actually worked to constrict rail expansion in Mexico, particularly the growth of feeder lines needed to make the rail system more accessible to local economic forces. Few of Limantour's priority routes had reached completion by the end of the Porfiriato. At considerable cost, González Roa contended, Limantour's creation of the Nacionales had accomplished nothing in the national interest not already achieved by his earlier prevention of U.S. monopoly in 1902–03.

The creation of the Ferrocarriles Nacionales manifested dilemmas characteristic of nationalist economic policies under dependent capitalism. To maintain the country's standing among international creditors, Limantour had to assure foreign capitalists of the future profitability of their previous investments in the Central and other consolidated lines. Thus, from its foundation, the new national railway enterprise was overcapitalized and the Mexican government saddled with a precarious level of financial guarantees to external investors. In 1910, the Nacionales devoted 35.2 percent of their gross revenues to bonded debt and dividend service payments, a financial cost that impeded both cheaper local operations and heavy further investments in the system's expansion. "The chief beneficiaries of the Mexicanization," argues historian John H. Coatsworth, "were foreigners: the foreign owners of Mexican railway bonds and the mainly foreign-owned export sector of the Mexican economy," whose operations were spared the potentially disruptive impact of U.S. railroad speculators.

González Roa questioned whether Limantour would have committed such serious errors without some personal conflict of interest. Many Científico functionaries used their influence to enrich themselves during the Porfiriato. Unlike other Científicos, however, most of whom were of lower-middle-class origin, Limantour was born into wealth. Early-twentieth-century scholars remained divided over his possible role in official corruption. Some writers absolved him of illicit conduct, while others accepted his opponents' accusations of secret financial manipulations. While an accurate historical account of the actions of the Porfirian elite remains hampered by the paucity of personal papers from the leading figures of this era, it seems clear that profiteering constituted neither the essence of Limantour's bureaucratic drive nor his purpose in establishing the Ferrocarriles Nacionales de México.

Ultimately, Porfirian Mexico's most exalted *técnico* was never able to shield his accomplishments from the overriding issue of presidential succession. As a member of a narrow elite based in Mexico City with little connection to the rest of the country, Limantour, like his fellow Científicos, overestimated the ability of the Porfirian state to manage Mexican society from the top. He was ill-equipped to cope with the processes of regional consultation that the politics of succession required. Nor could he break from his dependency upon Díaz. It is possible that the president may have forced Bernardo Reyes to resign the vice presidency in 1902 as part of a scheme to establish Limantour as his successor. Nevertheless, Díaz then backed away from the idea. Limantour's public disavowal of the vice presidency in 1904 certainly stemmed more from acquiescence to don Porfirio's will than from a personal reluctance to leave the government bureaucracy that he claimed. Díaz's selection of the unpopular Científico Ramón Corral as vice president in 1904 and his retention of Corral in 1910 blocked both Reyes and Limantour, the two rival choices for an orderly succession.

Limantour spent most of 1910 abroad. Even as late as December of that year, he failed to appreciate the deteriorated position of the regime. He wrote to Díaz from France: "The relative success obtained by the malcontents is an unfathomable mystery to me." Until the end, Limantour remained a loyal instrument of don Porfirio. He helped to negotiate the exit of the aging ruler and, despite his long friendship with the Madero family, refused to continue in his post. He left Mexico, never to return, a few days following the resignation and departure of General Díaz. Although the Revolution destroyed Limantour's work, his state-building approach to government would influence the views of post-Revolutionary elites.

Select Bibliography

Aston, B. W., "The Public Career of Don José Ives Limantour." Ph.D. diss., Texas Tech University, 1972.

Bazant, Jan, *Historia de la deuda exterior de México, 1823–1946.* Mexico City: El Colegio de México, 1968.

_____, "Joseph Yves Limantour (1812–1885) y su aventura Californiana." *Historia Mexicana* 28:1 (1978) and 29:3 (1980).

Coatsworth, John H., "El estado y el sector externo, 1800–1910." In *Los orígenes del atraso: Nueve ensayos de historia económica de México en los siglos XVIII y XIX.* Mexico City: Alianza Editorial Mexicana, 1990.

Cosío Villegas, Daniel, editor, *El Porfiriato: La vida política interior,* vol. 8, *Historia moderna de México.* Mexico City: Hermes, 1972.

Crosman, Herbert A., "The Early Career of José Ives Limantour, 1854–1886." Ph.D. diss., Harvard University, 1949.

Díaz Dufoo, Carlos, *Limantour.* Mexico City: Eusebio Gómez de la Puente, 1910.

Katz, Friedrich, *The Secret War in Mexico: Europe, the United States, and the Mexican Revolution.* Chicago: University of Chicago Press, 1981.

Knight, Alan, *The Mexican Revolution.* 2 vols., Cambridge: Cambridge University Press, 1986.

Limantour, José Yves, *Apuntes sobre mi vida pública, 1892–1911.* Mexico City: Porrúa, 1965.

María y Campos, Alfonso de, "Porfirianos prominentes: Orígenes y años de juventud de ocho integrantes del grupo de los científicos, 1846–1876." *Historia Mexicana* 34:4 (1985).

Peralta Zamora, Gloria, "La hacienda pública." In *El Porfiriato: La vida económica,* vol. 7, *Historia moderna de México,* edited by Daniel Cosío Villegas. Mexico City: Hermes, 1965.

Rosenzweig, Fernando, "Moneda y bancos." In *El Porfiriato: La vida económica,* vol. 7, *Historia moderna de México,* edited by Daniel Cosío Villegas. Mexico City: Hermes, 1965.

Schell, William, "Money as Commodity: Mexico's Conversion to the Gold Standard, 1905." *Mexican Studies* 12:1 (Winter 1996).

Turlington, Edgar, *Mexico and Her Foreign Creditors.* New York: Columbia University Press, 1930.

Turner, John Kenneth, *Barbarous Mexico.* Austin: University of Texas Press, 1969.

—ARTHUR SCHMIDT

LIMPIEZA DE SANGRE

The concept of *limpieza de sangre* (purity of blood) was introduced into Mexico in the aftermath of the Spanish Conquest. A term with deep roots in Iberian religious history and which at the time of European expansion into the "New World" meant the quality or condition of having pure Christian ancestry, *limpieza* not only would prove to be central to the logic of race relations in colonial Mexico but would become the basis of a system of racial distinctions.

As developed from the fifteenth century onward, *limpieza de sangre* referred to the genealogical purity of Christians—purity from the "contamination" of the blood of Jews, Muslims, heretics, and those condemned by the Inquisition. Although the notion of *limpieza* had long-standing antecedents on the Iberian Peninsula, it gained unprecedented vigor in the second half of the fifteenth century because of a complex set of factors, not least of which was the cultural and political unification of Spain through the nationalization of Christianity that began with the Reconquista, the Christian "reconquest" of the peninsula, which was completed in 1492 with the defeat of the Muslim kingdom of Granada. The growth of "Old-Christian" nationalism gave way not only to increasing violence against Jews and Moors but also to a series of statutes that made proof of purity a requirement for candidates to secular and clerical offices as well as for entry into universities, religious and military orders, and to certain guilds. The main target of the statutes were the *conversos* (also called New Christians), converted Jews who were suspected widely of continuing to practice Judaism and therefore thought to represent a threat to the unity of the faith and, indeed, the political order itself.

Although they were not applied universally, the statutes spread rapidly after the establishment of the Spanish Inquisition in 1480. As an ecclesiastical court, the Holy Office of the Inquisition investigated charges of heresy as well as genealogies to certify purity of lineage. In theory, genealogical inquiries were to investigate "the sins of fathers only up to the second generation." In practice, however, the discovery of a single ancestor who was a Jew or Moor or who had been condemned by the Inquisition tended to constitute an indelible "stain" *(mancha)* on the blood and disqualify even orthodox Catholics from important posts. As the idea of religious faith as an inheritable trait of the blood (and therefore ineffaceable) transformed into a powerful weapon of exclusion, *limpieza de sangre* promoted a related set of values that included purity of lineage, orthodoxy of faith, and "honor."

Honor, a Mediterranean concept that during the Middle Ages had been associated largely with noble status, became closely linked in sixteenth-century Spain to the issue of religious purity; whereas a "stained" genealogy tainted the given family and its descendants with the brush of infamy, a putatively "clean" ancestry imbued Old Christians with a deep sense of individual and familial honor. Although the association between nobility and honor by no means disappeared, unsullied Christian lineage became an essential basis of honor and social prestige. The high social value that was attached to *limpieza de sangre* in turn made endogamous marriage and legitimate birth increasingly important as tools with which to safeguard purity of lineage, at the same time that it reinforced Spanish notions regarding the proper sexual behavior of women. Since it was primarily the woman who, through adultery, could introduce "unclean" blood into a lineage, "reproducing" purity of blood necessitated guarding the chastity and premarital virginity of Old Christian women. For Old Christian men, in other words, controlling the sexuality of Old Christian women before and after marriage came to be as much a matter of "purity" as it was about "honor."

After the Conquest, Spaniards transported the concept of *limpieza,* along with the values that it inspired or reinforced, to the New World. The obsession with "clean" lineage, the emphasis on legitimate birth, the importance of preserving honor and the sexual virtue of (Spanish) women—these aspects of the metropolitan culture became a part of the ideological complex of the Spanish colonial world. Old Christian ancestry was to serve as a source of great pride for Spaniards and their descendants *(criollos)* in the New World, an index with which to measure themselves against the recently converted populations of the colonies. Because of their role in reproducing purity of blood and social preeminence, Spanish women would be valued as ideal marriage partners by Spanish males, while concubinage remained the common domestic arrangement between white males and non-European women through much of the colonial period. In New Spain (colonial Mexico), *limpieza de sangre* and "honor" in effect became markers of the moral and racial superiority of the colonists, and the tendency towards endogamous marriage among those of "pure" blood served, at least during the early colonial period, to maintain colonial boundaries of rule, even as a growing population of mixed ancestry threatened to blur them.

To understand how the concept of *limpieza de sangre* first came to operate as an organizing principle in colonial Mexico, it is essential to emphasize that the Spanish Conquest was not only a political and economic enterprise, but a religious one. A papal bull issued in 1493 by Pope Alexander VI had granted the Spanish kings political jurisdiction over most of the lands that came be known as the Americas (and that Spain called the "Indies") in order to evangelize. The legitimacy of the Spanish Empire in the Western Hemisphere, in others words, was contingent on—indeed, inseparable from—its mission to Christianize. The spiritual dimension of the Conquest, however, is to be traced not only to the conditions that the Holy See established for Spanish rule in the Americas, but to the long struggle to eradicate Islam from the Iberian Peninsula, a struggle that bequeathed to early modern Spain, on the one hand, a strong legacy of Conquest and conversion and, on the other, the sense of being divinely selected as "guardian of universal Christen-

dom" (in the words of scholar Anthony Pagden). The Reconquista officially ended with the defeat of the Muslim kingdom of Granada in 1492, but the arrival of Columbus on Caribbean shores that very year provided Spain with a new stage for the drama of Christian conquest.

Because of Spain's commitment to converting the population of the New World, virtually from the beginning of colonization the Crown tried to ensure that only those Spaniards of "clean" blood migrated to the newly acquired territories. The "Catholic Monarchs" Fernando and Isabel, as well as their successors, feared that *conversos* and other New Christians would become a source of "contamination" for the native peoples, who for their part were considered *gentiles, no infectados*—their blood, that is, had not yet been tainted by that of Jews and Muslims. Forbidden from traveling to the Spanish colonies, therefore, were Jews, Muslims, crypto-Jews, *moriscos* (converted Muslims), Gypsies, heretics, and the descendants of heretics—in short, the same categories of people being ostracized and persecuted in Spain. With a few exceptions, all emigrants were to obtain licenses to travel by providing proof of purity of blood at Seville's Casa de Contratación (Royal House of Trade). In Mexico, where the Christianizing campaign initially undertaken by Franciscan friars assumed utopian dimensions, a first edict prohibiting the arrival of those lacking "purity" credentials was issued in 1523.

The 1521 defeat of the Mexica (Aztecs), an event that was interpreted within Spain's providential conception of history as the result of the worldly expansion of the faith, gave way to a massive project of conversion in central Mexico. Technically, the converted Indians were considered free subjects of the Spanish Crown and, like the Spaniards, were recognized as a *nación,* a "community of blood." The concept of two *naciones* was reflected in the royal government's project to establish a "two republics" model, a dual social system consisting of a *república de españoles* and a *república de indios.* Under this system, each "republic" was to maintain its own internal ordering and, because of their freedom from Jewish and Muslim "stains," Indians who accepted Christianity also were to be conferred the quality of purity of blood—a formal privilege that the Crown reaffirmed as late as the eighteenth century. The Spanish political system in Mexico thus was conceptualized in terms of two *naciones* or republics that, officially at least, were entitled to similar privileges and honors.

If Spanish colonialism allowed for the possibility of granting Indians and Spaniards a certain equality of status, in actuality one *nación* not only was considered inferior, but placed in a paternalistic and in some ways discriminatory juridical status vis-à-vis the other. The notion that the Indians had not yet fully developed their capacity to reason and, ergo, were unable fully to comprehend the Catholic faith without the guidance of the Spaniards, served as the rationale for making the indigenous people legal minors, wards of the state and the church. In "exchange" for their indoctrination, the Indians were to provide tribute to the Spaniards. Notwithstanding the *limpieza de sangre* that Indians theoretically were accorded, then, the sociopolitical order constructed in colonial Mexico was fundamentally premised on the idea that Spaniards, because of their longer and presumably impeccable ties to the faith, were entitled to rule over the native people and other recently converted groups. Thus, just as *limpieza de sangre* was used to exclude converted Muslims and Jews from key political, economic, and religious positions in Spain, in Mexico "the notion of purity of blood also led to a kind of nationalization of the Church and of the faith insofar as the 'Old Christians' were the Spaniards, and the converted Indians, Jews, Moslems, and Africans were supposed to be spiritually unreliable and were therefore legitimately subordinated to the Spaniards" (Lomnitz-Adler, 1992).

Basing the colonial system of exploitation on the notion that Spaniards, by virtue of their Old Christian lineage, could legitimately, if provisionally, subordinate the Indians and other recent converts was not without its share of contradictions. For one, not all Spaniards in Mexico were Old Christians. Despite the emigration legislation and the bureaucratic mechanisms set up in Seville, a good number of New Christians were able to make their way across the Atlantic. In fact, the number was significant enough to keep vice regal authorities, as well as the Mexican Inquisition (officially established in 1570 but active since 1522), on alert through at least the seventeenth century. The arrival of New Christians also led to the adoption of purity of blood statutes by various colonial institutions. As early as 1535, New Spain's first viceroy, Antonio de Mendoza, was ordered through a *real cédula* (royal law) to make sure that those people barred from practicing medicine and obtaining university degrees in Spain also were prohibited from doing so in Mexico. By the time that New Spain's Tribunal of the Holy Office of the Inquisition was set up in the 1570s, *limpieza de sangre* was not only necessary for access to the university and public office but for certain professions, convents, guilds, *cofradías* (religious brotherhoods), and, of course, for work with the Inquisition itself.

The rigidity with which purity of blood statutes were implemented in colonial Mexico seems to have varied across space and time; some scholars believe that they were a mere formality. The institutionalization of *limpieza de sangre*, however, not only points to the fact that discriminatory mechanisms against converted Jews and Muslims were transferred to the Americas by state and church officials, but that tensions between Spaniards over the issue of purity of blood in no way disappeared in the colonial context. At times, those tensions played themselves out not between Old and New Christians, but between Spaniards born on the Iberian Peninsula *(peninsulares)* and those born in the "Indies" (criollos). By the end of the sixteenth century, for example, it was not unusual for *peninsulares* to characterize criollos, whom the former tended to call *indianos*, as having impure blood,

indeed, as an inferior caste. Poor Spaniards were particularly susceptible to those charges and often were racialized through the same derogatory terms as non-Europeans. Generally speaking, however, life in New Spain did have a certain leveling or unifying effect on the category of Spaniard, at least insofar as all Spaniards and criollos, regardless of rank and ethnic origin, came to consider themselves not only the *gente de razón* (people of reason) but the *gente de casta limpia* (people of clean caste). The difficulties inherent in tracing ancestry from the Americas, not to mention the expenses that formal investigations by the Inquisition could incur, might have made it harder for colonial Spaniards to prove their purity of blood, but such difficulties also made it easier to claim it.

While distinctions between Old and New Christians became more difficult to sustain and the lot of colonial Spaniards became the *gente de casta limpia,* it was the people of mixed ancestry, collectively called the *castas,* who were marked as having "impure" blood. The association between impurity and the *castas* did not occur immediately; the first mestizos were raised either as Spaniards or Indians and, though many were born out of wedlock, a good number were recognized by their Spanish fathers. Within a few decades after the Conquest, however, the growth of a population of mestizos and "mulattoes"—the latter being mainly the product of sexual unions between Spaniards and their female African slaves—started to turn into the source of considerable anxieties for colonial authorities. The so-called mixed-bloods not only were perceived increasingly as a highly disruptive element and a threat to the stability of New Spain, but as "impure" and irredeemably "infamous"—characteristics that in Spanish legal and social tradition almost automatically were attributed to those of illegitimate birth. For Spaniards, mulattoes were an infamous and impure caste almost by definition because African ancestry not only was associated with Islam, but carried the stigma of slavery. By the 1540s, the rights of mestizos to access public office and to inherit *encomiendas* (grants of Indian labor) were being restricted on the basis of illegitimate birth. Another wave of discriminatory laws followed in the 1570s and, by the turn of the century, the purity of blood statutes of certain institutions were beginning to add mestizos and mulattoes to the categories considered impure castes.

The gradual extension of the ideology of purity of blood to mestizos and mulattoes in New Spain was accompanied by the development of an elaborate system of racial hierarchies. Although the emergence of this system has not been studied systematically (and probably varies by region), the historiography suggests that it took place in the second half of the sixteenth century, that is, when mestizos and mulattoes acquired a clear numerical presence. The rapidly expanding population of "mixed-bloods" represented a threat to the colonial order not only because the *castas* lacked a clear place within a political and economic system that was organized around the three main categories of Spaniards,

Indians, and blacks, but because they blurred racial boundaries. To secure their exclusivity, Spaniards established the *sistema de castas,* a hierarchical ordering of different groups based on their percentage of Spanish blood, which took institutionalized form around the middle of the seventeenth century. At the top of this system were those of "pure" Spanish blood, followed by a descending order of racial categories that reflected the virtually infinite possible combinations that interracial sexual unions could produce.

The *sistema de castas* was foremost a model for how racial categories were to be determined and ordered; an attempt by elite Spaniards to contain a population that straddled the categories of "colonizer" and "colonized" and that thereby threatened their social and economic privileges. Racial designations in colonial Mexico were not, however, as rigidly determined by biology as the *castas* model implies; tracing the ancestry of most individuals beyond a few generations simply was not feasible, and socioeconomic factors tended to play an important role in the way people were categorized—and in how they identified themselves. Some *mestizos,* for example, were able to "pass" as Spaniards or *criollos* and claim *limpieza de sangre* even beyond the sixteenth century. Furthermore, the Crown offered a few wealthy individuals the possibility of purchasing their way out of illegitimate status and impure blood through certificates known as *gracias al sacar.* Colonial Mexico was thus not strictly a caste society; a person's place within the social order was not exclusively established by birth or by proportion of Spanish blood. The fluidity of the race/caste system increased in the eighteenth century, when expanding economic opportunities made it possible for a higher number of individuals to climb the social and racial ladder. Within this context of relatively rapid social change, the ideology of purity of blood once again was reinforced by those who sought to safeguard their racial exclusivity.

As a concept that had played a prominent role in the religious unification of Spain and that at the time of the Conquest referred to untainted Christian lineage, *limpieza de sangre* thus underwent a significant reformulation in colonial Mexico. Initially serving to create colonial hierarchies on the basis of the Spaniards' ostensibly orthodox ties to the faith, by the seventeenth century *limpieza de sangre,* had become the main principle behind a system of racial distinctions; it had transformed from a notion that signified Old Christian lineage to one that referred to European ancestry—to racial, not religious, purity. To be sure, purity of blood continued to mean the lack of Muslim and Jewish ancestors in certain contexts, but this association waned as the notion of *limpieza de sangre* was employed to create race/caste categories. In the words of the scholar Verena Stolcke, by the eighteenth century, the concept "lost any religious connotation, and became a purely racial notion." Whether its meaning was religious or racial, however, *limpieza de sangre* remained a primary organizing principle throughout the three centuries of Spanish colonial rule in Mexico.

See also Conquest: Spanish Antecedents; Conversos; Criollos and Criollismo; Mestizaje; Migration: Migration to New Spain; República de Indios

Select Bibliography

Aguirre-Beltrán, Gonzalo, *La población negra de México: Estudio etnohistórico.* 3rd edition, Mexico City: Fondo de Cultura Económica, 1989.

Alberro, Solange, *Inquisición y sociedad en México, 1571–1700* Mexico City: Fondo de Cultura Económica, 1993.

Greenleaf, Richard E., *The Mexican Inquisition of the Sixteenth Century.* Albuquerque: University of New Mexico Press, 1969.

Kamen, Henry, *The Spanish Inquisition.* London: Weindenfeld and Nicolson, 1965.

Lanning, John Tata, "Legitimacy and *Limpieza de Sangre* in the Practice of Medicine in the Spanish Empire." *Jahrbuch Für Geschichte* 4 (1967).

Lomnitz-Adler, Claudio, *Exits from the Labyrinth: Culture and Ideology in the Mexican National Space.* Berkeley and Los Angeles: University of California Press, 1992.

Pagden, Anthony, *Spanish Imperialism and the Political Imagination.* New Haven, Connecticut: Yale University Press, 1990.

Perry, Mary Elizabeth, and Anne J. Cruz, editors, *Cultural Encounters: The Impact of the Inquisition in Spain and the New World.* Berkeley and Los Angeles: University of California Press, 1991.

Ricard, Robert, *The Spiritual Conquest of Mexico.* Berkeley and Los Angeles: University of California Press, 1966.

Sanchiz Ruiz, Javier Eusebio, "La limpieza de sangre en Nueva España: El funcionariado del tribunal del Santo Oficio de Inquisicion. Siglo XVI." Master's thesis, UNAM, 1988.

Seed, Patricia, *To Love, Honor and Obey in Colonial Mexico: Conflicts Over Marriage Chocies, 1574–1821.* Stanford, California: Stanford University Press, 1988.

_____, "'Are these not Also Men?': The Indians' Humanity and Capacity for Spanish Civilisation." *Journal of Latin American Studies* 25:3 (1993).

Sicroff, Albert A., *Los estatutos de limpieza de sangre,* translated by Mauro Armiño. Madrid: Tauros, 1985.

Stolcke, Verena, "Invaded Women: Gender, Race, and Class in the Formation of Colonial Society." In *Women, "Race" and Writing in the Early Modern Period,* edited by Margo Hendricks and Patricia Parker. New York: Routledge, 1994.

—MARÍA ELENA MARTÍNEZ

LA LLORONA

The legend of la Llorona, or "the Weeping Woman," is so closely associated with Mexico that it is frequently assumed to be typically or solely Mexican, whereas it is in fact known not only in areas contiguous to Mexico itself but in numerous other regions of Central and South America as well. The legend exists on many levels—in oral tradition, in literature, in the popular media—and encompasses an entire complex of narratives having in common the central figure of a female phantom, more often heard than seen, whose salient characteristic is an agonized weeping and wailing. Although various explanations are given for la Llorona's presence and behavior, she most frequently is said to be mourning the loss of her child or children, for whose death she is herself responsible. The motivation provided for the infanticide varies widely, and with it the degree of sympathy that narrators of the legend may seek to elicit for the figure of the murderous mother: for example, she may, Medea-like, seek vengeance for the desertion by the children's father; she may be impelled by social pressures to conceal an illegitimate birth; she may simply reject the responsibilities of motherhood in favor of a "free life"; she may desire to facilitate a new relationship to which her children are perceived to be a hindrance; widowed or abandoned and unable to provide for her children, she may choose to take their lives as well as her own rather than see them suffer extreme deprivation; and so on. In some versions of the legend, la Llorona is not a murderess but a negligent mother who inadvertently causes the deaths of her children, while in still others she is completely blameless, having lost her children through some tragic accident or as the result of the malevolent actions of others.

Whatever the details of la Llorona's experience as a mortal woman, the outcome is the same: she now wanders endlessly, weeping, in search of her children or in mourning for them. Since in most instances the children are reported to have been drowned, she is typically seen or heard near bodies of water—lakes, rivers, canals—and therefore often serves as a cautionary figure or "bogeyman" used to keep small children indoors after dark and away from such dangerous locales. However, she also may appear as an attractive woman walking alone at night on city streets or country roads and, in this form, lures men into following her, with dangerous and even fatal consequences to her pursuers. Although in this latter manifestation she seldom weeps, she is still identified by many narrators as la Llorona, who has adopted the guise of the siren in order to seek revenge on men for her victimization by the father of her children. In some regions of Mexico, however, and often in other parts of Spanish-speaking America as well, the phantom temptress is looked upon as an entirely separate being, with a different—often indigenous—name (Matlacihua, Xtabay, Siguanaba, etc.) that strongly suggests a pre-Columbian source.

The origins of the Llorona legend are a matter of some debate. It is often described as dating to colonial times or even as being based on actual events occurring soon after the Conquest of Mexico; but such identification appears to owe more to a nineteenth-century literary penchant for setting romanticized literary legends in a relatively remote national past than to any real documentation of the legend's early existence. Published reference to la Llorona by name does not appear to antedate the second half of the nineteenth century, and in what seems to be the earliest occurrence—in a sonnet by the Mexican poet Manuel Carpio—she is identified as the weeping ghost of a woman in the poet's home town, who was murdered by her husband; there is no mention in that version of the motif of infanticide, which later came to predominate in both oral and literary tradition. Some scholars have sought to link la Llorona to certain Aztec deities—notably Cihuacoatl, the "Snake-Woman"—or to the mysterious wailing female voice said to have been heard in the streets of Tenochtitlan some time before the arrival of the Spaniards; none of these pre-Columbian analogs is connected with a story of infanticide, however, and the presence of weeping female phantoms in other cultures, both European and non-European, makes it difficult to argue that the figure of la Llorona must be considered characteristically Aztec. Indeed, as the scholar Américo Paredes and others have pointed out, la Llorona's story as it usually is told embodies European rather than native values and social attitudes and has close parallels in European tradition, although none has yet been located in Peninsular Spain. The "siren" manifestation of la Llorona appears more likely to be related to indigenous belief, although the physical description of the phantom temptress quite often reflects European ideals of feminine attractiveness. Identification of la Llorona as the remorseful spirit of doña Marina, or la Malinche, the translator and mistress of Fernando (Hernán) Cortés, is not common in oral tradition, and where it does occur, it is usually in reference to her role as the mother of Cortés's son, whom she is (erroneously) said to have murdered, and not as the accused betrayer of her people. On a literary-political level, however, the association of la Llorona with the historical doña Marina and, hence, with questions of national or ethnic identity and loyalty, dates back at least to the late nineteenth century, when José Marroqui, writing in the aftermath of the French occupation of Mexico, made a repentant Llorona/Malinche the sentimentalized narrator of a *cuento histórico,* or "historical tale," ostensibly composed for the purpose of providing his young daughter with a brief summary of Mexican history.

Other literary versions of, or references to, the Llorona legend have been numerous and for the most part have revolved around the infanticide motif, often along the lines of the classical Medea plot, sometimes with a focus on racial themes or class barriers. A versified drama by Francisco Neve, first staged in 1893, is said to be one of the most frequently presented plays in the history of Mexican theater; with the passage of time, other dramatizations of the legend, both on the stage and in film and television, have joined the printed media in the further popularization of the tale. Inevitably such versions have an effect on the forms that the legend assumes in oral tradition, but it remains the province of individual narrators to modify the details of the story in the light of their own personal and social concerns. As is the case with other such narratives, the Llorona legend persists precisely because of its ability to reflect everyday reality as that reality is perceived by those who tell it, and its meanings and functions within Mexican oral tradition are as varied and complex as the body of narratives itself. Indeed, the continued vitality of the legend, together with the fact that it is transmitted largely by women, has led the scholar José Limón to propose recognition of la Llorona as the "third legend" of Greater Mexico, a "critical female legend" that offers a folkloric counterpoint to the two male-imposed "official" legends, that of the Virgin of Guadalupe on the one hand and that of la Maliniche on the other.

Select Bibliography

Limón, José, "La Llorona, the Third Legend of Greater Mexico: Cultural Symbols, Women, and the Political Unconscious." In *Between Borders: Essays on Mexicana/Chicana History,* edited by Adelaida R. del Castillo. Encino, California: Floricanto Press, 1990.

Marroqui, José, *La Llorona: Cuento histórico mexicano.* Mexico City: Imprenta de I. Cumplido, 1887.

Paredes, Américo, "Mexican Legendry and the Rise of the Mestizo: A Survey." In *American Folk Legend: A Symposium,* edited by Wayland D. Hand. Berkeley and Los Angeles: University of California Press, 1971.

Robe, Stanley L., "Hispanic Legend Material: Contrasts Between European and American Attitudes." In *American Folk Legend: A Symposium,* edited by Wayland D. Hand. Berkeley and Los Angeles: University of California Press, 1971.

—SHIRLEY L. ARORA

LOMBARDO TOLEDANO, VICENTE
1894–1968 • Labor Leader and Intellectual

The career of Vicente Lombardo Toledano is also the history of many of the central themes in the intellectual and political trajectory of twentieth-century Mexico. As dean of Mexican Marxism, Lombardo was the best-known link between Mexico and the international world of Marxism and socialism and, therefore, a protagonist in struggles that frequently challenged the legitimacy of the capitalist state consolidated by the governments of Revolutionary Mexico. But Lombardo, more than any other intellectual, also became the key left-wing ideologue of the Mexican Revolution. While aiming to subvert and transform the character of Mexican capitalism, Lombardo's theoretical prescriptions and political action served in crucial ways to strengthen the targets of his criticism. Above all, Lombardo was the chief intellectual architect of the leftist-nationalist political project initiated during the government of Lázaro Cárdenas (1934–40) and defended with varying degrees of enthusiasm by governments and important currents of opinion within and outside the ruling Partido Revolucionario Institucional (PRI, or Institutional Revolutionary Party) until well after Lombardo's death in 1968.

The vision of the Mexican Revolution as a "progressive" nationalist and anti-imperialist experience that could serve as a model for the rest of the Americas was developed with consummate skill by Lombardo. Through his writings and energetic activity in anti-imperialist and trade union organization throughout Latin America, the Maestro, as he was known, worked unceasingly to propagate the leftist credentials of the Mexican Revolution, especially in the 1940s and 1950s.

The essence of the Lombardista project was the urgent necessity of building, and then consolidating, an alliance between the state and worker organizations. This fascination with the potential of state–social movement alliances was born early in Lombardo's career. During the presidency of Plutarco Elías Calles (1924–28), the Confederación Regional Obrera Mexicana (CROM, or Regional Confederation of Mexican Workers) labor organization, in which Lombardo was an active member, enthusiastically collaborated in the government's task of national economic and political reconstruction.

Between 1933 and 1940 the leftward shift in the balance of political and class forces in Mexico encouraged Lombardo to reformulate his concept of an alliance between the popular classes and the state. This project also drew on the Communist International's (Comintern's) idea of the Popular Front (a broad antifascist alliance between communist and bourgeois democratic parties) and exploited the opportunities opened up by Cárdenas's presidency. Now the goal was to assist in modernizing capitalism by eliminating feudal social and economic forms in agriculture (via land reform), promoting industrialization (on the assumption that industrialization would guarantee economic and political independence), and establishing the leading role of the state (*rectoría económica del estado*) in setting the framework for economic development.

The qualitatively new element in this second stage of the Lombardista state project was the formal incorporation into the ruling party of organized labor and, to a lesser extent, the peasant beneficiaries of land reform. The Confederación de Trabajadores de México (CTM, or Confederation of Mexican Workers), which Lombardo had founded in 1936, became the labor hub of the new corporativist structure established by the Partido de la Revolución Mexicana (PRM, or Party of the Mexican Revolution). Lombardo expected that a strong labor and peasant anchorage would guarantee "national unity" and force capitalist development along a path that would permanently favor the urban and agrarian masses.

By the mid-1930s Lombardo had become an enthusiastic Marxist. But his commitment to "scientific" socialism had taken a long time to develop. In his youth Lombardo's intellectual profile had been shaped by the liberal-humanism, idealism, spiritualism, and antipositivism of Antonio Caso and the Generation of 1910. The Ateneo de la Juventud, not Mexico's anarchists and early socialists, attracted his admiration. Lombardo's shift to the left, it is generally argued, flowed from early contacts with the Mexico City working class. In 1917 he became secretary of the Universidad Popular, a working-class education initiative launched by members of the Ateneo. While a representative of the Universidad Popular, the young intellectual made his first contact with the organized labor movement when he attended the founding conference of Mexico's first national labor organization, the CROM, in 1918. Over the next few years he made a decisive commitment to working-class politics. By 1923 he had become secretary of education and a member of the CROM's Central Committee.

The CROM was a staunchly anticommunist organization, and it was only in 1932, after his break with the now decisively weakened organization, that Lombardo declared himself a "non-Communist Marxist." First, within the so-called Purified CROM and the Confederación General de Obreros y Campesinos de México (CGOCM, or General Confederation of Workers and Peasants of Mexico), and then in the National Committee of Proletarian Defense that he organized in 1935 to rally support behind the embattled new president Lázaro Cárdenas, Lombardo moved steadily to the left. A visit in 1935 to the Soviet Union consolidated Lombardo's Marxism and his commitment to the newly emerging concept of the Popular Front. His growing identification with the young Soviet state did not make Lombardo an automatic ally of the Partido Comunista Mexicano (PCM, or Mexican Communist Party), with which he already had clashed numerous times. Always immensely critical of the PCM, whose intellectual shallowness and political naiveté he

resented, Lombardo never accepted the communists' claim to be the authorized interpreter of Marxism in Mexico. His power base in the CTM and the prestige he enjoyed in Mexico and later in Latin America were, nevertheless, immensely attractive to the Comintern and the Soviet Union, which generally supported Lombardo in his many disputes with the Mexican and Latin American communist parties.

A classic example of how Comintern and Soviet support for Lombardo overrode the position of Mexican communists occurred in 1937. Opposition to the increasingly antidemocratic and anticommunist policies of Lombardo Toledano and his ally Fidel Velázquez led the Communist Party to support the withdrawal of its important union allies from the labor confederation during the Fourth Council of the CTM. With the help of Earl Browder, leader of the Communist Party of the United States (CPUSA) and a major figure within the Comintern, Lombardo managed to reverse the Mexican communists' decision. The CTM was reunified—around the slogan of Unity at All Cost (Unidad a Toda Costa)—but on terms dictated by the most conservative sections of the national labor confederation. The long-term consequences of the decision were substantial—the consolidation of an increasingly bureaucratized and corrupt camarilla of union leaders at the helm of the CTM and the beginnings of the marginalization of the left—a process that, ironically, would eventually cost Lombardo his position as general secretary of the CTM in 1941.

The close relations between Lombardo and the Soviet Union also vividly manifested themselves in the fierce opposition that Lombardo and the CTM mounted against the decision to grant Trotsky exile in Mexico and in Lombardo's creation and leadership of the Confederation of Latin American Workers (CTAL), founded with Mexican government financial support in 1938. During World War II and the period from 1945 to 1948, the CTAL, under Lombardo's energetic direction, extended the Cardenista project of revolutionary nationalism throughout the Caribbean and Central and South America. The promotion of antifascist national fronts in Latin America during the war years closely followed the strategy of the ailing Comintern and the Soviet Union and succeeded in building an extensive network of progressive labor organizations throughout Latin America on the basis of the Popular Front's principles. While Lombardo was increasingly marginalized within the CTM, the dean of Mexican Marxism became the most successful hemispheric labor figure in the Americas. It was only with the onset of the Cold War and the emergence of U.S. plans to create a Western Hemispheric labor organization that the prestige and grip of the CTAL and Lombardo began to disintegrate.

The waning of Lombardo's domestic influence dates from his decision to create a new, broad, united-front party in the late 1940s. This was not Lombardo's first foray into party politics. During his years as the CROM's leading intellectual he had been a member of that organization's Labor Party (Partido Laborista) and for a few months, in 1923–24, served as interim governor of his home state of Puebla after the elected incumbent joined the de la Huerta rebellion. But it was the Comintern-inspired notion of the Popular Front that captured Lombardo's political imagination. He first proposed the idea of a Popular Front party in the late 1930s, and the project reemerged with greater energy in 1947 and 1948 during discussions that Lombardo held with left intellectuals and the leaders of the left of the labor and peasant movement.

Lombardo's proposal was for the creation of a party that would support the national democratic, antifeudal, and anti-imperialist goals of the Mexican Revolution. Its platform supported rapid industrialization, economic independence, and a deepening of the agrarian reform. It saw its historic task as combating the Mexican right, which Lombardo identified with the *sinarquista* movement and the newly established Partido de Acción Nacional (PAN, or National Action Party) and to a much lesser degree, conservative forces within the PRI. The Partido Popular (PP, or Popular Party), established in 1947 by Lombardo, was careful not to confront the PRI too openly, and when this was not possible, Lombardo always was careful to distinguish between the actions of "reactionaries" within the PRI and the figure of the president himself. Thus, during the late 1940s Lombardo had few problems in expressing loyalty to both President Miguel Alemán Valdés and Joseph Stalin.

In spite of this cautious stance, the PRI and its sectoral affiliates such as the CTM did not warmly embrace Lombardo's Popular Party, seeing the new formation as a threat to the mass base of the ruling party and its affiliates. But the weakness of the Popular Party can also be attributed to the authoritarian style of Lombardo himself. He ruled the PP with an iron fist, and the first 10 years of the new party's life were punctuated by a series of intraparty quarrels that peaked between 1956 and 1958 in a major fracas in which Lombardo lost the support of key allies such as Enrique Ramírez.

Although Lombardo stood as a presidential candidate of the PP in 1952, for most of its life, the Partido Popular, which became the Partido Popular Socialista (PPS, or Popular Socialist Party) in 1960, expressed almost unqualified political and electoral support for the PRI. Lombardo, in the last stage of his life, became a bitter opponent of attempts by unionists to break down the authoritarian controls imposed by labor bosses, or *charros*. He opposed the teachers' reform movement that emerged in Mexico City during 1957 and played an equivocal role in the great railway worker mobilizations of 1958–59. During the student-popular movement of 1968, his denunciations of the subversive actions of the young protesters were shrill and unforgiving.

The students' bitter critique of the failings of the Mexican state clashed with one of the most distinctive features of Lombardismo—its glorification of the state and its progressive nationalizing and anti-imperialist pretensions long after the radical reformism of the Mexican Revolution had run its course. While the students of 1968 and their allies practiced the libertarianism and anti-authoritarianism of the new left, Lombardismo still represented the more authoritarian strains in the culture of Marxism. Of all the currents within Mexican Marxism, it was Lombardismo that was most intimately bound up with the image and practice of the caudillo, the authoritarian populist.

The legacy of Lombardismo has been very extensive. A Mexican version of British Fabianism, it owed its strength in part to the ideological and political alliance established between its practitioners and the state bureaucracy in whose ranks an extraordinarily large number of Lombardistas and ex-Lombardistas worked. In spite of the political opportunism exhibited by Lombardo and the PPS, Lombardismo also managed to develop a substantial base among Mexican intellectuals in the 1950s and 1960s, which has not been extinguished. The links between the PPS, students, teachers, and teacher trainees meant that at the local level the Lombardistas were closely in touch with popular struggles, particularly among peasants and rural workers. Consequently, the followers of Lombardo often diverged quite strongly from the cautious line articulated by the Maestro himself. Nowhere was the enduring appeal of Lombardo's ideas seen more vividly than in the impressive mobilizations organized by the neo-Cardenista opposition during the presidential election campaign of 1987–88. The electoral earthquake of 1988 and the emergence of the center-left Partido de la Revolución Democrática (PRD, or Party of the Democratic Revolution) convincingly demonstrated the enormous convocatory power of Revolutionary nationalism two decades after the death of the Maestro in 1968.

Select Bibliography

Bartra, Roger, "Lombardo o Revueltas." In *El reto de la izquierda*. Mexico City: Grijalba, 1982.

Carr, Barry, *Marxism and Communism in Twentieth Century Mexico*. Lincoln: University of Nebraska Press, 1992.

Chassen de López, Francie R., *Lombardo Toledano y el movimiento obrero mexicano 1917–1940*. Mexico City: Extemporáneos, 1977.

Krauze, Enrique, *Caudillos culturales en la revolución mexicana*. Mexico City: Siglo XXI, 1976; 6th edition, 1990.

Millon, Robert, *Mexican Marxist: Vicente Lombardo Toledano*. Chapel Hill: University of North Carolina Press, 1966.

Quintanilla Obregón, Lourdes, *Lombardismo y sindicatos en América Latina*. Mexico City: Fontamara, 1982.

—BARRY CARR

LÓPEZ CAPILLAS, FRANCISCO

c.1608–74 • Composer, Musician, and Conductor

Francisco López Capillas—born around 1608 in Mexico to Bartolomé López and María de la Trinidad—is the first American-born composer to master his art on a par with his European competitors and rise to fame and fortune within his lifetime. He was appointed chapel master at the Mexico City Cathedral in 1654, the first criollo (person of Spanish descent born in America) to hold this prestigious position.

Little is known of López Capillas's early years, but it is surmised that he was trained at the Mexico City Cathedral under the tutelage of Chapel Master Antonio Rodríguez de Mata. The University of Mexico undoubtedly played a major role in shaping the young man's talents: his name surfaces in several university documents, and he graduated with his bachelor's degree on August 20, 1626. The Puebla Cathedral engaged the young musician as organist and bassoonist on December 17, 1741, thus placing together the two greatest musicians of midcentury: López Capillas and Chapel Master Gutiérrez Padilla. López Capillas enjoyed a lifetime of learning; he received his *licenciado* from the university sometime in 1647.

The death of Mexico City's Chapel Master Fabián Ximeno in 1654 precipitated a series of events that led to López Capillas's move from Puebla to the capital, where he served the remaining years of his life. Even though the Mexico City Cathedral Chapter had sent notification of the chapel master vacancy—establishing an application deadline of 40 days—they abruptly closed the process after only 10 days when they found that the esteemed López Capillas had applied for the job. He promptly was hired as both chapel master and principal organist. To ease the chores, they provided him with two assistants, Francisco Vidales (who was the previous chapel master's nephew) and Juan Coronado. Vidales and López Capillas took turns every other week directing the choir while seated at the organ, except on very important feast days that stipulated that both gentlemen had to be in attendance. The consecration of the new Mexico City Cathedral in 1656 demanded grandiose music; López Capillas supplied a sumptuous, awe-inspiring work requiring huge polychoral resources and four different masses that, unfortunately, are now lost.

López Capillas died on January 18, 1674 (*not* 1673 as often is stated); his will and testament from a few days earlier details his personal effects and possessions; he had amassed real estate, houses, personal property, and a general portfolio that would have been the envy of the most astute business investor. The will also elucidates that he had three sisters, one of them named Leonor; the scholar Lester Brothers has suggested that this may be the "Leonor" who is mentioned as a vocalist and viol player in the *villancico* manuscripts of Gutiérrez Padilla.

López Capillas wrote many *villancicos,* although none are extant. Choirbooks VI, VII, and VIII in Mexico City preserve splendid Mass settings and a breathtaking series of Magnificat settings. Manuscript M.2428 in Madrid's Biblioteca Nacional similarly preserves important works by López Capillas, whose gorgeous music is matched by the manuscript's exquisite beauty.

No American-born composer surpassed López Capillas in his consummate mastery of counterpoint. His polyphony is full of the strictest rigors of contrapuntal development but never gives the impression of being forced or strained. His four-voice hymn for the Virgin Mary, "Cui Luna, Sol et Omnia," has canonic points of imitation—but each of the four voices moves at different rates owing to different time signatures. His five-voice hymn of the Purification of the Blessed Virgin, "Lumen ad Revelationem," maintains the unaltered *cantus firmus* in the tenor while the remaining four voices weave a tapestry of imitation based on the paraphrased chant. Even the majestic "Et incarnatus est"—which at first glance appears to be mere block chordal motion—is in fact strictly canonic in at least three voices almost from beginning to end. His glorious "Ego enim accepi" couples this impeccable counterpoint with imaginative textures; López Capillas combines and recombines the six voices into different antiphonal groupings that respond to each other and intertwine in ever-changing, multifarious sonorities. He frequently arranges four voices into two pairs: he assigns each pair its own melody that is developed in canonic imitation, all the while melding together with the other pair's canonic melody. It is the sonic equivalent of two happy couples conversing as they stroll through the park. Rarely has a polyphonist from any century combined such logical structures with such natural, intuitively beautiful sonorities and melodies.

Select Bibliography

Barwick, Steven, transcriber and commentator, *Two Mexico City Choirbooks of 1717: An Anthology of Sacred Polyphony from the Cathedral of Mexico.* Carbondale: Southern Illinois University Press, 1982.

Brothers, Lester, "Francisco López Capillas, First Great Native New-World Composer: Reflections on the Discovery of His Will." *Inter-American Music Review* 10:2 (Spring-Summer 1989).

—Craig H. Russell

LÓPEZ DE SANTA ANNA, ANTONIO

See Santa Anna, Antonio López de

LÓPEZ MATEOS, ADOLFO

1910–69 • President

Adolfo López Mateos was born in Atizapán de Zaragoza, Mexico State, on May 26, 1910. The son of Mariano Gerardo López y Sánchez, a dental surgeon, and Elena Mateos Vega, he was the youngest of a family of five. The death of his father at a young age forced the family to move to Mexico City, where López Mateos was enabled to follow his primary education at the Colegio Francés thanks to a scholarship from the Fundación Dondé. He returned to his home state for further studies and completed his secondary and high school education at the Instituto Científico y Literario of Toluca, where he worked as a librarian to finance his studies.

He began his political activities at an early age, standing out, even then, as a good orator. At age 18 he became private secretary to the governor of Mexico State, Colonel Filiberto Gómez, and shortly afterward he became an agent of the Ministerio Público. He returned to the capital to join the faculty of the law department of the National University. In 1929 he took part in the lobbying effort that culminated in the government's granting the National University autonomy. That year he also joined the presidential campaign of José Vasconcelos, who stood as an independent candidate in opposition to the official party's candidate, Pascual Ortiz Rubio. The Vasconcelos campaign failed, and López Mateos left politics for a time and practiced law in Mexico City.

In 1934 Carlos Riva Palacio, president of the Partido Nacional Revolucionario (PNR, or National Revolutionary Party), invited López Mateos to work with him as his private secretary. In the years that followed he held a number of public posts. He worked in the Banco Obrero y de Fomento, and in 1941, during General Manuel Avila Camacho's presidential term, he was appointed to the Ministry of Education as manager of extramural and aesthetic education. Two years later, Isidro Fabela, governor of Mexico State, invited him to direct the Instituto Científicos y Literario of Toluca, where he had studied years before. When López Mateos ended his term as rector in 1946, Miguel Alemán Valdés became president of the republic, and López Mateos then took a seat in the Federal Congress as senator for his home state. During this period he took part in various foreign missions; among these he led the Mexican delegation at the Economic and Social Council of the United Nations in Geneva.

In 1951 another presidential election took place, with Adolfo Ruiz Cortines as the official party's candidate. López Mateos was named secretary general of the Partido Revolucionario Institucional (PRI, or Institutional Revolutionary Party, the successor to the PNR). On becoming president of Mexico Ruiz Cortines appointed López Mateos as secretary of labor and social security. From the very beginning, Ruiz Cortines's government faced a huge economic crisis, which led to a lowering of the standard of living for the working classes. Their dissatisfaction soon showed itself in the many strikes that erupted during the presidential term. Nevertheless, López Mateos, as minister of labor, very ably managed to defuse many strikes, in most cases by means of a skillful conciliatory policy. Only the teaching and railroad movements managed to endanger the stability of the regime.

In 1957 López Mateos was nominated as a candidate to the presidency, winning the elections with 90 percent of the popular vote. When the new administration took office on December 1, 1958, one of the first problems it confronted was the railroad workers' conflict, which was broken up by force and its principal leaders jailed. The López Mateos administration also faced a difficult economic situation from the very beginning; private investment had been withdrawn in the previous few months owing to the uncertainty caused by the labor movement, and the balance of payments failed. López Mateos decided to promote greater state participation in the economy by means of an increase in its investments, the opening of new opportunities to industry, and a greater stimulus to social security works. To do so he had to seek external finance. Additionally, he tried to reduce imports and open new markets for Mexican products by means of a common Latin American market, the Asociación Latinoamericana de Libre Comercio (ALALC).

Citing the principles of nonintervention and self-determination of people, the president expressed the sympathy of the Mexican people for the Cuban Revolution. Although the U.S. government had imposed an economic blockade of the Caribbean island, Mexico always remained firm in its support of Cuban sovereignty. In spite of this stance, López Mateos's political ability was such that relations with the United States remained cordial. In 1962 U.S. president John F. Kennedy visited Mexico, and López Mateos was able to negotiate a resolution of a long-standing border dispute with the United States, recovering the contested strip of land known as El Chamizal.

During López Mateos's presidency, Mexico diversified its international relations. The president made many foreign tours, and several foreign heads of state, as well as other prominent people, visited the country. López Mateos nationalized the electricity industry. An important part of the budget was devoted to social services. The Instituto de Seguridad y Servicios Sociales de los Trabajadores al Servicio del Estado (ISSSTE, or Institute of Social Security and Social Services of State Employees) was created; this gave benefits to a wide social sector, marginalized until then. The Instituto Nacional de Proteccion a la Infancia (INPI, or National Institute for the Protection of Children) was created to provide medical services and assistance to Mexican children. Education received particular state attention. With the Plan de Once Años (Eleven-Year-Olds' Plan), a project that sought to meet educational demand at the primary school level, school enrollment was greatly increased. Free school textbooks were another important contribution of López Mateos's presidential term, in spite of the fact that the books unleashed a strong controversy among right-wing organizations who considered this measure as a violation of the freedom of education. Huge funds were invested in electrification and irrigation projects, the road network was expanded, and large housing estates and other urban developments were constructed. López Mateos ended his term of office on December 1, 1964. Five years later, on September 22, 1969, he died of an aneurysm.

Select Bibliography

Aguilar Camín, Héctor, and Lorenzo Meyer, *In the Shadow of the Mexican Revolution: Contemporary Mexican History, 1910–1989.* Austin: University of Texas Press, 1993.

—CECILIA GREAVES LAINÉ

LÓPEZ PORTILLO Y PACHECO, JOSÉ

1920– • President

José López Portillo y Pacheco (1920) was president of Mexico from 1976 to 1982. López Portillo began his political career together with his predecessor, Luis Echeverría Álvarez. The two presidents were friends when they were teenagers, and they studied law together at Universidad Nacional Autónoma de México (UNAM, National Autonomous University of Mexico). For 10 years López Portillo taught general theory of the state at the UNAM law school, and afterward published a book on the subject. He first worked as a lawyer at private law offices but later entered public service, working for the National Property Secretariat. López Portillo headed the Federal Council for Public Works one year after entering public service in the administration of President Adolfo López Mateos. In 1965 during the presidency of Gustavo Díaz Ordaz, he worked for the President's Office, in charge of legislation and legal affairs. Later, he was promoted to deputy director of the office. During his administration, Echeverría appointed López Portillo undersecretary of national property. Afterward, he headed the state-owned electric power company, Comisión Federal de Electricidad. After occupying this position he became finance secretary. This post served as López Portillo's anteroom to the presidency.

In September 1975 López Portillo accepted his nomination as presidential candidate of the ruling Partido Revolucionario Institucional (PRI, or Institutional Revolutionary Party). The following year he was sworn in as president, and he finished his term in 1982. When Echeverría handed power to him, Mexico's economic, political, and social situation was critical; the country suffered from a US$20 billion foreign debt, rising unemployment, overgrown bureaucracy. To top it all, the Mexican peso had been devaluated only three months before he had assumed office. In his inaugural speech, López vowed to face the challenge of Mexico's distress, and he called Mexicans to strive to overcome the country's chaotic situation. One of his goals was to oversee the use and evolution of the country's debt, not so much its amount. Consequently, he drew an Overall National Development Plan that divided his six-year term into three two-year stages. The plan's aim was to overcome the crisis during the first stage, strengthen the economy during the second, and achieve economic expansion during the third.

López Portillo based his economic policy on exports made by the government-owned petroleum industry. It was a time when petroleum prices peaked on the world market. Large fields were discovered in Chiapas, Tabasco, and Campeche, which ultimately led to the construction of a natural gas pipeline to the United States. Mexico drilled deep wells in sea floors. The country eventually became the world's fourth-largest petroleum producer.

With the Public Administration Organization Act, López Portillo reorganized the country's civil service sector. The regulation enacted new federal secretariats: Planning and Budget, Government Property and Industrial Development,

Agriculture and Water, Human Settlements, Public Works, and Fisheries. The act suppressed the President's Office. He replaced the mercantile revenues tax with the value added tax and fostered industrial production. Another piece of legislation, the Federal Political Organization and Elections Act, acknowledged political parties as public interest entities and granted them access to radio and television.

In foreign policy, his administration kept the country's political asylum policy active. Mexico opened its doors to protect citizens from Chile, Argentina, Uruguay, and other countries. During his presidential term many Guatemalan refugees took shelter in Mexico. The president supported the Sandinista movement in Nicaragua and the right of Panamanian people to exercise their sovereignty over the Canal Zone. Along with the government of France, López Portillo recognized the Frente Democrático (FD, or Democratic Front) and the Frente Farabundo Martí para la Liberación Nacional (FMLN, or Farabundo Martí Front for National Liberation), the guerrilla opposition movement in El Salvador.

During his administration, the media became instruments of political control rather than means to promote education. The president's sister, Margarita López Portillo, was appointed head of the General Radio, Television, and Cinema Agency. She inadequately handled the agency's budget.

In September 1982, before ending his term, José López Portillo announced two pieces of legislation, one to expropriate Mexican banks and the other to control the exchange rate of Mexican currency.

After his term in office, López Portillo retired from public service. He then reflected on his activity as a politician and wrote his memoirs, *Mis Tiempos*. This book complements other publications on his presidential actions. He also wrote literature, including the science fiction novel *Don Q* (1969), which deals with the existence and destiny of humanity. His writing also deal with Mexican history, as in the novel *Quetzalcoatl* (1976), in which he reconstructs the image of a pre-Columbian mythological figure, based on historical sources, and reconstitutes the life and habits of pre-Hispanic Mexico.

Select Bibliography

López Portillo, José, *Filosofía política de José López Portillo.* Mexico City: Secretaría de Programación y Presupuesto, Dirección General de Documentación y Análisis, 1979.
Scherer García, Julio, *Los presidentes.* 5th edition, Mexico City: Grijalbo, 1986.

—MARÍA DEL ROCÍO GONZÁLEZ SERRANO

LÓPEZ RAYÓN, IGNACIO

1773–1832 • Insurgent Leader during Wars of Independence

Ignacio López Rayón was an exceptional military and political caudillo (strongman) during New Spain's struggle for Independence. He was the first to establish an independent government on Mexican soil. Born in Tlalpujahua, Michoacán, in 1773 into a well-to-do criollo family, he attended in 1786 the Colegio de San Nicolás Obispo in Valladolid de Michoacán (modern-day Morelia), one of the most important centers for education in the New Spanish territories, and he completed his law degree in 1796 from the Colegio de San Ildefonso in Mexico City. When his father died he returned to Tlalpujahua and began mining and farming rather unsuccessfully, and he also took charge of the postmaster's office. In August 1810 he married María Ana Martínez Rulfo, a member of one of the foremost families in the area.

When he learned of the insurrection lead by Miguel Hidalgo y Costilla, López Rayón published a manifesto in October 1810, expressing his support, and he joined the insurgency movement when Hidalgo passed nearby at Maravatío. He became Hidalgo's private secretary and suggested setting up an insurgent government junta. After taking part in the battle of Monte de las Cruces, he went back to Tlalpu-

jahua and later rejoined Hidalgo in Valladolid. He was appointed secretary of state in Guadalajara, where he began publication of the first insurgent newspaper, *El Despertador Americano*. He helped organize insurgent troops and worked to establish relations with the United States. After the defeat of the insurgents at Puente de Calderón on January 17, 1811, he took charge of the army's coffers, taking approximately $300,000 to the rebel stronghold of Aguascalientes, and under the command of Ignacio Allende he joined the successful battle for Zacatecas. He followed Hidalgo on his march toward the United States, and during a meeting of insurgent forces in Saltillo he was named commander in chief of the army with instructions to carry on the war in New Spain.

In March 1811 Hidalgo and other insurgent leaders were captured by Spanish forces, effectively making López Rayón one of the main leaders of the Independence movement. López Rayón and his troops made the long and difficult march back south to Zacatecas, taking the city from royalist forces. He organized his troops and the army's finances, acquired arms and ammunition, and began to plan the establishment of an insurgent government body that would represent the rights of the Spanish king Fernando VII, who had been imprisoned by French troops under Joseph Bonaparte. He explained to Viceroy Francisco Javier de Venegas both the reasons for the insurrection and how it could be brought to an end. As the royalist troops of Félix María Calleja del Rey drew near to Zacatecas, López Rayón withdrew toward Michoacán, constantly harried by royalist forces. After putting up resistance at various places, he reached Zitácuaro, now in insurgent hands, fortified it, and established the first insurgent government body, the Suprema Junta Nacional Gubernativa (Supreme National Governing Council) on August 19, 1811. López Rayón was elected president and José María Liceaga and José Sixto Verduzco his two deputies. Governing in the name of Fernando VII, the junta began to organize the insurgent movement finances and military forces. They made contact with other insurgents in different regions and asked, usually successfully, for their recognition and support. López Rayón's government also made contact with those unhappy with colonial rule and who found themselves in areas occupied by royalists. Under López Rayón's guidance, the junta formulated the ideological bases for the insurgency and publicized them through decrees and proclamations. López Rayón's Constitutional Elements later were taken into account in the Constitutional Decree of Apatzingan.

The secret society of Los Guadalupes sent him a printing press in 1812 from Mexico City, which proved supremely useful for his propaganda. López Rayón had been in contact with the society members and had received help of various kinds from them. Later, in October of the same year, various members of this society acted as intermediaries between Viceroy Venegas and López Rayón in negotiations about allowing supplies to pass across rebel lines from Acapulco to Mexico City, and of the possibility of reaching an armistice. Nonetheless, the attempt by Los Guadalupes to arrange an armistice failed. The bishop of Puebla, Manuel Ignacio González del Campillo, tried to dissuade López Rayón from his campaign but failed. For his part, the viceroy offered 10,000 pesos for the head of each deputy in the insurgent government. Calleja besieged Zitácuaro, and in January 1812 the junta had to abandon the town after fierce resistance, taking refuge in Sultepec. Shortly thereafter the deputies separated to take their struggle to other regions.

The separation of the insurgent deputies made it difficult for the junta to function as a coherent unit, an obstacle made more severe by important differences of opinion between López Rayón and Liceaga; soon an open rift developed between them. By this time the fourth deputy of the junta, José María Morelos y Pavón, had become a leading figure in the movement, and he tried in vain to reconcile their differences. He attempted to establish a new body of insurgent government, the Supremo Congreso Nacional Americano (Supreme National American Congress), which was installed in Chilpancingo in September 1813. Meanwhile, López Rayón led an expedition to Toluca and Lerma and set up his general camp at the Campo del Gallo, near Tlalpujahua. From there he tried to establish contact with the United Sates and Haiti to ask for help. Although he was

uncomfortable with the dissolution of the junta and the establishment of the Supreme Congress, López Rayón was persuaded by Morelos to present himself to Chilpancingo and was nominated representative for the province of Nueva Galicia. In this capacity, he objected to the proclamation of the Act of Independence on November 6 of that year, even though he was one of the signatories. Congress charged him with the defense and government of the province of Oaxaca, but he was not able to raise enough troops or provisions to present any kind of real resistance when royalist forces occupied the province in 1814.

The loss of Oaxaca not only dealt a serious blow to the insurgency, but brought to the surface López Rayón's disagreements with Juan Nepomuceno Rosáins, who had been granted the governorship of Veracruz, Puebla, and northern Mexico and who had the support of Morelos. In June 1814 López Rayón accompanied Carlos María Bustamante to Zacatlán and the northern region (controlled by José Francisco Osorno) to reorganize his troops. Osorno recognized López Rayón as the leader of the insurgency in the area and handed over the command of the region. Assisted by Bustamante, López Rayon rationalized and disciplined the insurgent troops and established an arsenal. In addition, he took charge of church administration, punishing minor crimes and organizing the finances as well as keeping in contact with the heads of other zones.

López Rayón was out of step with the other insurgent chiefs who sought to promote their own interests rather than those of the movement. When a royalist expedition was sent to take Zacatlán, López Rayón had to retreat. He took refuge in the hills of Cóporo. Supplied by his brother Ramón, López Rayón maintained resistance in the Cóporo region for many months, emerging in September 1816 to go to Tancítaro and organize a new insurgent government. After passing various strategic places of Michoacán, he went to Jaujilla, where a center of insurgent government based on the old Congress had been set up. López Rayón did not recognize the new junta, however, and was apprehended for this by Nicolás Bravo in Zacapuato and taken to Patambo. The royalists discovered him there on December 11, 1817. After being tried and condemned to death in Cuernavaca, López Rayón was sent to Mexico City, where the viceroy, Juan Ruiz de Apodaca, stayed his execution. He remained a prisoner until 1820, when the newly reestablished constitutional government pardoned him. After Independence, he was made treasurer and later mayor of San Luis Potosí. In 1825 he was nominated military commander of Jalisco and soon after president of the Military Tribunal. He died in Mexico City in 1832.

Select Bibliography

Alamán, Lucas, *Historia de Méjico desde los primeros movimientos que prepararon su independencia en el año de 1808 hasta la época independiente.* Mexico City: Imprenta de José Mariano Lara, 1849.
Anna, Timothy, *The Fall of Royal Government in Mexico City.* Lincoln: University of Nebraska Press, 1978.

Bustamante, Carlos María de, *Cuadro histórico de la revolución mexicana, comenzada por el ciudadano Miguel Hidalgo y Costilla, cura del pueblo de los Dolores, en el obispado de Michoacán.* 2nd edition, Mexico City: Imprenta de José Mariano Lara, 1843–46.

Rayón, Ignacio, Jr., et al., editors, *La independencia según Ignacio Rayón,* with introduction and biographical essay by Carlos Herrejón Peredo. Mexico City: SEP, 1985.

—Virginia Guedea

LÓPEZ VELARDE, RAMÓN

1888–1921 • Writer, Journalist, and Political Activist

Ramón López Velarde will be remembered as one of the best witnesses to the historic experience that transformed Mexico at the turn of the century; he was one of the pillars of nationalistic writing, which is traditional, paternalistic, and *"machista."* Without abandoning the nostalgia with which he described the Mexican hinterland, he established a criticism based on his experiences in the capital, which granted him an almost new, ecstatic vision of rural life. His political writing combined support for the Mexican Revolution of Francisco I. Madero and a sarcastic criticism of the political bourgeoisie. He included in his poetry the metaphors of a changing nation, and he foresaw a vision of "[national] deformation . . . against the foreign avalanche with its barbaric customs." He became useful as a national myth, since after the Revolution López Velarde became a symbol of the national cultural patrimony for both the conservatives and the progressives.

López Velarde was born in 1888 in Jerez de García Salinas, Zacatecas. His participation in the struggle against dictator Porfirio Díaz was through the Catholic sector of Madero's Anti-Reelectionist Party. In his newspaper articles, for example, he continued to support Madero's cause. "This front was worth, for its manliness, more than the sexless politicians in Mexico City, which is the home to so many of these miserable individuals . . . ," he wrote in the newspaper *El Regional* of Guadalajara in 1909. He feared the radicalism of agrarian reform, which led him in 1912 to denounce the Zapatista position as "barbaric communism." For López Velarde, Madero was the ideal candidate—liberal, but not radical. After Madero's death, López Velarde lent his support to the Constitutionalist movement.

He became familiar with Mexico City through his life as a journalist and political activist, where he rubbed shoulders with such important people as Rafael Delgado, Manuel Uguarte, and Antonio Caso. This contact contributed to his conflicting perspective on the rural hinterlands: he could be critical of them without abandoning his nostalgic tone. He transformed the provinces as a metaphor not only for the whole nation, but for himself as well. For him, tradition was in danger of being transformed by the Revolution. In his poem "Zozobra" (Capsize), for example, López Velarde pro-

jected inner conflict between eroticism and religion onto the division between city and hinterlands. The images of a "shell-shocked" hinterland and "an inverted Eden" were the themes through which López Velarde informed the Revolution of the dangers of disintegration.

"Suave Patria" (Sweet Fatherland), one of the poems López Velarde dedicated to Mexico, portrays what López Velarde would later describe as a nation undergoing a yet unidentifiable process of transformation. He depicts an "epic past":

> Patria: your mutilated territory is clothed in beads and percale. . . .
> . . . Your mud rings with silver, and [with] your fist you rattle your poorbox; held prisoner, you hear the alarm of your children, the sobbing your mythologies, la Malinche. . . .
> . . . I love you not as a myth, but for the truth of your holy bread, like a young girl who approaches the grille with her blouse buttoned to her ears and her skirt around her ankles. . . .
> The image of you, the greatness of your National Palace, yet your stature of a child and of thimblefuls.
> If I drown in your Julys, the coolness of shawls and earthen jars descends to me from your dense hair. . . .
> . . . this is worth fifty times more than an *Ave María* on the rosary, and is happier than you, Patria Suave. . . .

Octavio Paz has said that in "Patria Suave" López Velarde is "aware of the nation's problems, but limited when it comes to solutions." In the face of the Revolutionary government's drive for industrialization, urbanization, and agrarian reform, López Velarde opted for a far more simple position of good government, free of corruption.

López Velarde's masculine stance implied a paternalistic and *"machista"* attitude, which led him to use women as another metaphor for his internal religious-erotic conflict, as seen in his poem "Sangre Devota" (Pious Blood). He rejected the feminist movement, preferring to keep women in the domestic sphere. In 1912 he wrote an article called "Feminism" in response to "a woman who lectured in a small theater. She moves us to write some reactions," he wrote. "She proposed to dispense new ideas as though she had arrived to conquer new territories. . . . Mexican women are still, fortunately, too sentimental and too in charge of their homes to take last night's speaker seriously." His provincial, Catholic position would keep López Velarde from conceiving of women as political and intellectual individuals. This paternalism was not unique to him; it would manifest itself in the "new" ideology of the post-Revolutionary state.

López Velarde, who died in 1921, would become a prototype to mythify after the Revolution. For his nationalist, traditionalist, paternalist and *"machista"* qualities, he will be ensconced within that part of history that proclaims the "epic" past in the face of modernity.

Select Bibliography

de la Fuente, Carmen, *Ramón López Velarde.* Mexico City: Federación Editorial Mexicana, 1971.
Franco, Jean, *La cultura moderna en América Latina.* Mexico City: Grijalbo, 1983.
López Velarde, Ramón, *El León y La Virgen.* Mexico City: Imprenta Universitaria, 1942.
_____, *Prosa política.* Mexico City: Imprenta Universitaria, 1953.
Sefchovich, Sara, *México: País de ideas, país de novelas.* Una sociología de la literatura mexicana. Mexico City: Grijalbo, 1987.

—EMMY AVILÉS BRETÓN

LOZADA, MANUEL

1828–73 • Bandit, Soldier, and Politician

Bandit, Liberal, Conservative, imperialist, neutral, republican—Manuel Lozada was all these, "The Tiger of Alica," owner and head of the seventh Canton of the state of Jalisco, today the state of Nayarit. More than a century after his death, he is still a controversial figure. Historians from Jalisco never forgave him the secession of Nayarit, and the people of Nayarit still are divided between those who call him a bandit who preached racial hatred and the class struggle and those who celebrate the precursor of agrarian revolution, defender of villages, Spartacus, Zapata of the nineteenth century.

The son of poor peasants, a mestizo (mixed-race) orphan, Lozada is the hero of many legends that turn him into a Robin Hood, a Mexican Rob Roy who appears to have begun as a young bandit. There is a legend about Manuel Lozada that tells of an impossible love between a young laborer and a respectable girl; of pointless punishments meted out by villains; the troubadour evokes his old mother, beaten and whipped by a policeman. When she dies on the roadside, Manuel can do nothing for her but avenge the injustice and return to the sierra, a righteous outlaw.

In the city of Tepic, two families opposed each other because of their commercial interests: the Castaños (a Spanish, Liberal family) and the Barrons (a conservative English family). Their quarrel divided local society to such an extent that the state governor was called from Guadalajara to reestablish public order. Being a Liberal, he favored the Castaños, provoking a serious diplomatic incident with London in 1856. Locally, the Barrons contracted the services of the "honorable bandit" Manuel Lozada, who, between 1854 and 1855, had pledged his band to support the revolution against President Antonio López de Santa Anna. So Lozada intervened at the head of an armed group in the struggle that divided the elite of Tepic, capital of a region linked to the economic boom of the port of San Blas on the Pacific coast.

Those who knew Manuel Lozada described him as a man with a regular body, tall rather than short, with dark skin, wide nose, prominent cheek bones, bristly hair, clean shaven, and blind in the right eye. He normally dressed very simply—part Indian, part Spanish, part Mexican, with a felt hat with a band. He had a lively intelligence, and although he may not have known how to write, he could sign his name. He mixed easily with famous people. The story goes that he sometimes traveled to the traditional fiestas in San Francisco and went to the bullfights and card games escorted by an elegant woman named Eligia, dressed in fashionable diaphanous clothes, whom he introduced as his wife.

In 1857, Lozada controlled many thousands of men when he allied himself with the Conservatives in the Wars of Reform (Three-Year War, 1858–61). The victory of the Liberals did not affect his power, and the repeated offensives committed by the Liberal armies between 1860 and 1862 only strengthened his reputation. During the French Intervention (1862–67), he recognized the authority of Emperor Maximilian and was acknowledged as the supreme authority in the whole region. His rapid promotion, both political and military, was owing to the fact that he knew how to be the "man of the moment." The tragedies of the moment were the Wars of Reform, the French Intervention, and the empire of Maximilian. The situation created the perfect opportunity for a man to pass from banditry and life as a mercenary into regional and national history. Why? Lozada was a man with a problem—the agrarian problem—and he was in a situation where the local elite wanted to become independent from the state of Jalisco. From this informal alliance an unspoken pact was formed; in exchange for giving the elite the autonomy they desired, he took up the defense of the villages. The problem of land has been a constant theme in Mexican history since the second half of the eighteenth century, when demographic growth set the rural communities, whether indigenous or not, into conflict with small landowners and ranchers.

As soon as Lazada had become the strongman of the region—between 1858 and 1859—he imposed an agrarian policy of "giving everybody his due," be they rancher or villager. He had come to the conclusion that the courts were "that overused and ephemeral recourse [that] would just exasperate the people." His line of action was the following: "my idea is that the people take possession of the land that justly belongs to them in accordance with the land deeds. . . . If there was violence in the past, it was not to usurp somebody else, but to reclaim the usurped property itself, and so the end justified the means." As much by such texts as in practice obstinately carried out by Lozada, we can conclude that he was an agrarian revolutionary.

Today there is a temptation to present Lozada as an Indian leader, defender of certain ethnic groups, for example, the Coras, Huicholes, the Mexicaneros, and Tepehuanes. Although this was not strictly speaking true, it was included in the anti-Lozada propaganda. The leaders of the state of Jalisco denounced Lozada as "an outlaw," "a dangerous communist who is in the process of massive expropriation," "an agent of the caste war who wants to raise the whole Indian lineage." For more than 15 years, Lozada was the greatest authority in the region of Tepic, recognized as much by whites as by mestizos and Indians, by tradesmen and ranchers, by bureaucrats and by the Catholic clergy whom he protected.

Decorated by Maximilian and refusing all contact with the French, recognized by Liberal leader Benito Juárez, protector of the fugitive Porfirio Díaz after his first unsuccessful uprising (1872), Lozada demonstrated fabulous opportunism, an expression of how well he understood interest in the cause with which he identified, that of the people. After the death of Juárez in 1872, however, Lozada was unable to reach an agreement with President Sebastián Lerdo de Tejada; times had changed, and the now consolidated Restored Republic could not tolerate the existence of strong regional caudillos (leaders).

The chief of the people of Tepic used to fish with dynamite in the rivers of the sierra, but an accident left him blind in one eye and maimed in one arm. "Now I am useless," he said in 1872, "unable to see either distances or detail well, unable to mount a horse easily. If I were sound of sight and mind, I would want for nothing, but I do need my sight and my head." In 1873, General Ramón Corona destroyed Lozada's troops when they arrived at the gates of Guadalajara.

According to the legend, everything ended through a betrayal. Lozada was sold out by one of his men, after having been abandoned by most of his fellow men-at-arms. He was taken by surprise, unarmed, while bathing in a river with his last remaining soldiers. In the words of a ballad,

Ay Lozada! you were sold out
to the men of Jalisco.
Ay Praxedis! Ay Domingo!
he wears your betrayal on his brow.
Today they are being buried
but their fame of courage lives on.

They took him to Tepic mounted on a bad horse, wearing a sock on one foot and a traditional leather sandal on the other. The whole village, packed into the street in silence, were shocked to see him. He was tried and condemned to death. He asked for a priest and passed an entire night praying devotedly after making his will. At six o'clock in the morning, he was shot in las Lomas de los Metates. He died calmly after saying to his soldiers, "My death has been ordered by the government because God wanted it so. My conscience is clear, I never did anyone any harm and I do not regret what I have done. My intention was to win good things for the people. If the unhappiness of these people is increased in the future, it will be the fault of many, not mine alone." Some women dressed him as a Franciscan and held a wake for him.

The last of Lozada's guerrillas continued fighting until 1885. In 1917, the territory of Nayarit received recognition as a state. From 1934 to 1936, his estate lands were divided and the little village of San Luis was renamed San Luis de Lozada.

Select Bibliography

Meyer, Jean, *Esperando a Lozada.* Zamora: Colegio de Michoacán, 1984.
_____, *La Tierra de Manuel Lozada.* Mexico City: CEMCA, 1990.

—JEAN MEYER

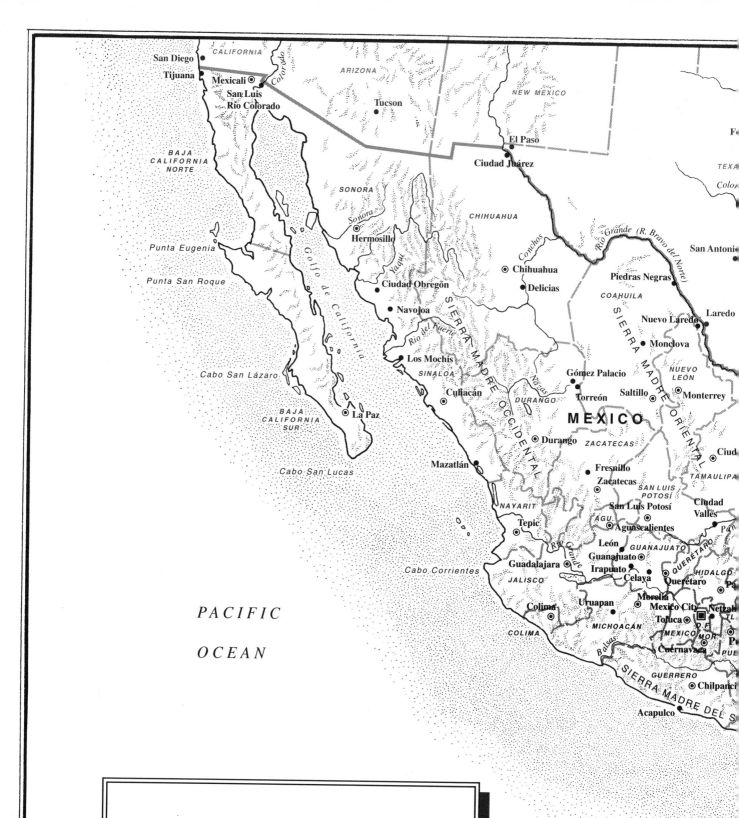

Contemporary
Mexico